WEBSTER'S CROSSWORD PUZZLE DICTIONARY

REVISED AND UPDATED

WEBSTER'S CROSSWORD PUZZLE DICTIONARY

REVISED AND UPDATED

GRAMERCY BOOKS
New York

This 1998 edition is published by Gramercy Books®, an imprint of Random House Value Publishing, Inc., by arrangement with Random House Reference and Electronic Publishing, Inc., 201 East 50th Street, New York, NY 10022.

Gramercy Books® and colophon are registered trademarks of Random House Value Publishing, Inc.

Prepared for Random House, Inc., by Sachem Publishing Associates, Inc., Stephen P. Elliott, President; Elizabeth J. Jewell, Managing Editor.

Printed in the United States of America

Random House
New York • Toronto • London • Sydney • Auckland
http://www.randomhouse.com/

Library of Congress Cataloging-in-Publication Data
Webster's crossword puzzle dictionary. — Rev. and updated.
    p.   cm.
    Rev. ed. of: The Random House crossword puzzle dictionary. c1994.
    ISBN 0-517-15008-5
    1. Crossword puzzles—Glossaries, vocabularies, etc.   I. Gramercy
Books (Firm)   II. Random House crossword puzzle dictionary.
GV1507.C7W364 1998
793.73—dc21   98-15217
                                                                   CIP

10 9 8 7 6 5 4 3

PREFACE

Although various word games and puzzles have existed almost since the beginnings of language, the modern crossword puzzle is a 20th-century innovation. The first newspaper crossword appeared on December 21, 1913, in the New York *World,* and this new type of word puzzle quickly captured the public's fancy. Within a decade, crossword puzzles were featured in most American newspapers, and they soon became the rage in England as well. Since the 1920s, crossword puzzles have been a standard feature of daily newspapers and have proved enormously popular when collected in book form.

Now found in almost every language and in variations ranging from theme puzzles to diagramless puzzles, crosswords are available for almost any age and vocabulary level. Those who solve crossword puzzles invariably relish the challenge of completing a puzzle, of "getting it right." When faced with a clue they cannot answer, they resist "cheating"—looking at the puzzle's solution. One way out of this difficulty is to consult a reference work, yet neither a dictionary nor an encyclopedia nor an almanac contains the necessary information in a useful, quick-reference format. A standard dictionary might give a few synonyms for a word, an encyclopedia would give information about countries or historical figures, and an almanac usually has information about sports figures or the Academy awards, but only a crossword puzzle dictionary combines in one handy volume the information that might be found in all three. Equally important, it does so without extraneous information and with the convenience of an arrangement by the number of letters in each word.

Webster's Crossword Puzzle Dictionary, Revised and Updated, answers the need of crossword puzzlers for one single-purpose reference work. In addition to general vocabulary and synonyms, there are entries covering history; the natural and physical sciences; literature; music, painting, and other arts; religion; mythology; sports; popular culture; and current affairs, among others. Boxed items provide easy-to-find detailed information on the continents and countries of the world, states of the United States, U.S. presidents, the months of the year, and other facts of special interest.

While *The Random House Crossword Puzzle Dictionary's* primary purpose is to meet the needs of the growing numbers of people who find crosswords both relaxing and challenging, even a cursory glance will demonstrate the book's usefulness as a reference for trivia buffs. From who won the Academy Award for best actress in 1970 (Glenda Jackson) to the name of a coffee grown in Jamaica (Blue Mountain), it's all here.

A volume of this scope is necessarily the work of many researchers, editors, and proofreaders. We would like to acknowledge the invaluable contributions made by Julianna Arbo, Suzanne Stone Burke, Francine Esposito, Gretchen Ferrante, Jan Jamilkowski, Rebecca Lyon, Julie E. Marsh, Blaine Merritt, Laurie Romanik, Christine Lindberg Stevens, and Diane Bell Surprenant; and by Patricia W. Ehresmann, Typographic Director and Production Manager, Random House, Inc., and Rita Rubin, Administrative Assistant.

HOW TO USE THIS BOOK

The main entries in *The Random House Crossword Puzzle Dictionary* are words or phrases likely to appear as crossword puzzle clues. Each entry consists of a clue word or phrase and a list of answer words, arranged first by the number of letters in each word and then alphabetically. For example, if the main entry— **banal**—is the clue for a five-letter answer, the answer—"trite"—will be found alphabetically listed under the five-letter answer words. For phrases, such as **contracted form,** the answer could be "digest," "summary," or "synopsis." Entries may also contain indented subheads and secondary subheads. If, for instance, the clue is a phrase, like **cotton fabric,** the word **cotton** will be found as a main entry in the dictionary, and **fabric** will be found as a subhead under it, with such possible answer words as "terry," "poplin," and "gingham." In some cases, the answer can be found in more than one place. For example, if the clue is **Mexican coin,** the answer could be found by looking under the main entry **Mexico** and the subhead **monetary unit,** or by looking under the main entry **coin/currency** and the subhead **of Mexico.**

Longer entries are set off in highlighted boxes so they can be found more quickly. All continents and countries of the world, states of the United States, presidents of the United States, and months of the year appear as boxed items, as do many other major entries.

There are also cross references for alternate spellings (**Epicaste** *see* **7** Jocasta) and very closely related items (**Epeans** *see* **5** Epeus—a look at **Epeus** reveals that **Epeans** are descendants of this king of the Peloponnesus).

The main entries, subheads, secondary subheads, and numbers all appear in boldface type; the answer words are in regular roman type. Most punctuation and accent marks have been omitted, since they are not used in puzzle answers; occasionally, apostrophes and other marks have been included in answers to make them more readable.

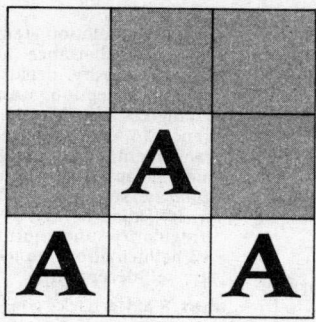

aardvark
   also: 7 ant bear **8** anteater
   family: 15 Orycteropodidae
   species: 15 Orycteropus afer
   order: 13 Tubulidentata
   native to: 6 Africa
   food: 4 ants **8** termites
   name comes from:
     9 Africaans
      meaning: **8** earth hog,
      earth pig

Aaron
   brother: 5 Moses
   father: 5 Amram
   mother: 8 Jochebed
   sister: 6 Miriam
   son: 5 Abihu, Nadab **7** Elea-
     zar, Ithamar
   wife: 8 Elisheba
   successor: 7 Eleazar
   deathplace: 3 Hor **8** Mount
     Hor
   priestly descendant of:
     8 Aaronite
   set up: 10 golden calf

Aaron, Henry (Hank)
   sport: 8 baseball
   position: 10 outfielder
   record: 8 homeruns
   team: 13 Atlanta Braves
     15 Milwaukee Braves
     16 Milwaukee Brewers

Aaron's Rod 21 miraculously
   blossomed
   yielded: 7 almonds
   herb: 21 Thermopsis
     caroliniana

Aatam *see* **4** Pima

Ab 16 fifth Hebrew month

Abaddon 4 hell **8** Appolyon

abaft 6 behind **11** to the rear
   of **12** to the stern of

Abagtha 6 eunuch
   served: 9 Ahasuerus

abandon 4 dash, drop, elan,
   jilt, junk, quit, stop **5** ardor,
   cease, forgo, gusto, leave, let
   go, scrap, verve, waive **6** desert, give up, spirit **7** discard,

forfeit, forsake, freedom **8** abdicate, evacuate, forswear, get
rid of, renounce, run out on
9 animation, cast aside, repudiate, surrender **10** depart
from, enthusiasm, exuberance,
relinquish, wantonness **11** discontinue, impetuosity, leave
behind, spontaneity, unrestraint **12** immoderation, intemperance, recklessness,
withdraw from
13 impulsiveness

abandoned 4 lewd, wild
5 loose **6** impure, jilted, sinful,
vacant, wanton, wicked **7** debased, immoral **8** cast away,
degraded, deserted, desolate,
forsaken, marooned, rejected,
unchaste **9** cast aside, debauched, discarded, dissolute,
neglected, reprobate, shameless **10** dissipated, left behind,
licentious, profligate, unoccupied **11** unrepentant **12** disreputable, incorrigible,
irreformable, relinquished, unprincipled **13** irreclaimable

abandon oneself to 7 yield
to **8** give in to, give up to
9 indulge in

Abantes
   tribe: 7 Euboean

Abaris
   origin: 5 Greek
   form: 4 sage

Abas
   mentioned in: 5 Iliad
   king of: 7 Argolis
   father: 6 Celeus **7** Lynceus
     9 Eurydamas
   mother: 8 Metanira
     12 Hypermnestra
   wife: 6 Aglaia
   son: 7 Proetus **8** Acrisius
   daughter: 7 Idomene
   changed into: 4 bird **6** lizard
   mocked: 7 Demeter
   protected by: 11 magic
     shield

   companion: 8 Diomedes
   killed by: 8 Diomedes

a bas 8 down with **11** to the
bottom

abase 4 mock **5** shame **6** debase, defame, demean, hum-
ble, malign, vilify **7** cheapen,
degrade, mortify, put down,
vitiate **8** badmouth, belittle,
besmirch, bring low, cast
down, disgrace, dishonor
9 denigrate, devaluate, discredit, downgrade, humiliate
13 bring down a peg, cut
down to size

abash 4 dash **5** daunt **6** deject,
dismay **7** depress **8** dispirit
9 discomfit, embarrass **10** discompose, disconcert, discourage, dishearten

abashed 3 shy **5** cowed, fazed
7 ashamed, bashful, crushed,
daunted, humbled, subdued
8 confused, dismayed, over-
awed **9** chagrined, mortified
10 bewildered, confounded,
humiliated, nonplussed, taken
aback **11** dumbfounded, embarrassed, intimidated **12** disconcerted, disheartened
13 self-conscious

abashment 3 awe **6** wonder
9 confusion **12** discomfiture,
discomposure **13** embarrassment **14** disconcertment

abate 3 ebb **4** cool, dull, ease,
fade, slow, wane **5** allay,
blunt, lower, quell, quiet,
slack **6** dampen, go down,
lessen, pacify, recede, reduce,
soften, soothe, temper, weak-
en **7** assuage, curtail, decline,
dwindle, fall off, lighten, mollify, relieve, slacken, subside
8 decrease, diminish, fade
away, fall away, mitigate,
moderate, palliate, restrain, restrict, slack off, slow down,
taper off **9** alleviate

abatement 3 cut, ebb **5** break

6 ebbing, waning **8** decrease, discount, soothing **9** lessening, reduction, weakening **10** concession, mitigation, moderation, slackening, subsidence **11** assuagement, curtailment **13** mollification

Abba
means: **6** father

Abbe Faria
character in: **21** The Count of Monte Cristo
author: **5** Dumas (pere)

abbey 6 cenoby, chapel, church, friary, priory **7** convent, nunnery **8** cloister, seminary **9** cathedral, hermitage, monastery

Abbey, Edwin Austin
born: **14** Philadelphia PA
artwork: **21** Quest of the Golden Grail **23** The Quest for the Holy Grail **37** Richard Duke of Gloucester and the Lady Anne

Abbott, Bud
real name: **14** William A Abbott
partner: **11** Lou Costello
born: **12** Asbury Park NJ
roles: **11** Who's on First **12** Buck Privates **13** Hold that Ghost **33** Abbott and Costello Meet Frankenstein

abbreviate 3 cut **4** clip, trim **6** reduce **7** abridge, curtail, cut down, shorten **8** boil down, compress, condense, contract, cut short, diminish, truncate **9** summarize, synopsize

abbreviated 5 brief, short **7** limited, summary **8** abridged **9** condensed, curtailed, shortened **10** compressed, summarized

abbreviation 5 brief **6** digest **7** cutting, pruning, summary **8** abstract, clipping, synopsis, trimming **9** lessening, reduction, short form **10** abridgment, diminution, shortening **11** abstraction, compression, contraction, curtailment, cutdown form, reduced form **12** condensation **13** condensed form, shortened form **14** compressed form, contracted form

Abderus
father: **6** Hermes
killed by: **5** mares **13** Diomedes mares

abdicate 4 cede, quit **5** forgo, waive, yield **6** abjure, give up, resign **7** abandon **8** abnegate, renounce **9** surrender **10** relinquish **15** vacate the throne

abdomen 3 gut, pot **5** belly, tummy **6** paunch, venter

7 stomach **8** pot belly **9** bay window **11** breadbasket, epigastrium **14** visceral cavity

Abdon 11 Hebrew judge
father: **5** Micah **6** Achbor, Jehiel **7** Shashak
city of: **5** Asher

abduct 5 seize, steal **6** kidnap **7** bear off **8** carry off, take away **10** run off with **11** make off with

Abduction from the Harem, The
also: **25** Die Entfuhrung aus dem Serail
opera by: **6** Mozart
character: **5** Osmin **6** Blonde **8** Belmonte, Pedrillo **9** Constanze **10** Pasha Selim

Abdul-Jabbar, Kareem
formerly: **11** Lew Alcindor **22** Lewis Ferdinand Alcindor
sport: **10** basketball
position: **6** center
team: **8** LA Lakers **10** UCLA Bruins **14** Milwaukee Bucks **16** Los Angeles Lakers
shot: **7** sky hook

Abednego
companion: **6** Daniel
friend: **8** Meschach, Shadrach
former name: **7** Azariah

Abel
father: **4** Adam
mother: **3** Eve
brother: **4** Cain, Seth
killer: **4** Cain

Abel, Niels Henrik
field: **11** mathematics
nationality: **9** Norwegian
theorem: **8** binomial
theory of: **19** elliptical functions

Abe Lincoln in Illinois
author: **14** Robert Sherwood
director: **12** John Cromwell
cast: **10** Alan Baxter, Mary Howard, Ruth Gordon (Mary Todd Lincoln) **11** Dorothy Tree, Minor Watson **12** Gene Lockhart **13** Howard da Silva, Raymond Massey (Abraham Lincoln)

Abelmeholah
home of: **6** Elisha

aberrance 6 oddity **7** anomaly **8** rambling, straying **9** wandering **10** aberration **11** abnormality, peculiarity **12** eccentricity, irregularity **13** nonconformity

aberrant 3 odd **7** unusual **8** abnormal, atypical, peculiar, uncommon **9** anomalous, eccentric, irregular

aberration 5 lapse, quirk **6** lunacy, oddity **7** anomaly, madness **8** delusion, illusion,

insanity, mutation, rambling, straying **9** aberrance, aberrancy, curiosity, departure, deviation, exception, wandering **10** digression, distortion, divergence **11** abnormality, derangement, incongruity, mental lapse, peculiarity, singularity, strangeness **12** eccentricity, idiosyncrasy, irregularity, unconformity **13** hallucination, nonconformity, self-deception

abet 3 aid **4** back, goad, help, spur, urge **5** egg on **6** assist, incite, lead on, second, uphold, urge on **7** advance, endorse, promote, support, sustain **8** advocate, join with, sanction **9** encourage, instigate

abettor 4 ally **6** cohort **7** partner **9** accessory, associate, colleague **10** accomplice **11** confederate **12** collaborator

ab extra 11 from outside, from without

abeyance 5 delay, on ice, pause **6** hiatus, recess **7** latency **8** deferral, dormancy, inaction **9** cessation, remission **10** quiescence, suspension **11** adjournment **12** intermission, postponement **13** in cold storage, on a back burner, waiting period **14** discontinuance

abhor 4 hate, shun **5** scorn **6** detest, eschew, loathe **7** despise, disdain, dislike **8** execrate, recoil at **9** abominate, can't stand, shudder at **10** shrink from **11** can't stomach **12** be revolted by **13** be nauseated by, find repulsive

abhorred 5 hated **8** despised, detested, disliked **10** abominated

abhorrence 4 hate **5** odium, scorn **6** hatred **7** disdain, disgust, dislike **8** aversion, contempt, distaste, loathing **9** antipathy, revulsion **10** repugnance **11** abomination

abhorrent 4 foul, vile **6** odious **7** hateful **8** accursed **9** execrable, loathsome, repellent, repugnant, repulsive, revolting **10** abominable, despicable, disgusting, nauseating

Abiathar
companion: **5** David
father: **9** Ahimelech
banished to: **7** Anatoth
conspired to overthrow: **5** David

abide 3 sit **4** bear, last, live, stay, stop **5** brook, dwell, stand, tarry, visit **6** accept, endure, linger, remain, reside, suffer 7 sojourn, stomach 8 stand for, submit to, tolerate

abide by 4 obey 6 follow 8 accede to, adhere to, submit to 9 conform to 10 comply with 11 go along with

abiding 4 fast, firm 6 steady 7 durable, eternal, lasting 8 constant, enduring, unending 9 immutable, permanent, steadfast 10 changeless, continuing, unchanging, unshakable 11 everlasting 12 indissoluble, wholehearted 13 unquestioning

Abidjan
  capital of: 10 Ivory Coast

Abigail
  husband: 5 David, Nabal
  brother: 5 David

Abihu
  father: 5 Aaron
  mother: 8 Elisheba
  brother: 5 Nadab 7 Eleazar, Ithamar
  killed with: 5 Nadab
  accompanied to Mt Sinai: 5 Moses

Abijah
  father: 8 Rehoboam
  grandfather: 7 Solomon
  grandmother: 6 Naamah

ability 4 bent, gift 5 flair, knack, power, skill 6 acumen, genius, talent 7 faculty, knowhow, mind for 8 aptitude, capacity, facility 9 adeptness, expertise, potential 10 adroitness, capability, competence 11 proficiency 12 potentiality 13 qualification

Abimelech
  king of: 5 Gerar
  means: 15 the father is king
  father: 6 Gideon 8 Abiathar
  brother: 6 Jotham
  army commander: 7 Phichol

ab initio 16 from the beginning

Abinoam
  father: 4 Saul
  son: 5 Barak

ab intra 10 from inside, from within

Abishag
  comforted: 5 David

abject 3 low 4 base, mean, vile 6 sordid 7 ignoble 8 complete, cringing, hopeless, horrible, terrible, thorough, wretched 9 groveling, miserable 10 deplorable, despicable, spiritless 11 inescapable 12 contemptible

abjuration 7 refusal 8 eschewal 9 rejection 10 abnegation,

disclaimer, retraction 11 repudiation 12 renunciation

abjure 6 desert, give up, recant, reject 7 abandon, disavow 8 disallow, disclaim, forswear, renounce 9 repudiate 10 relinquish

ablaze 5 afire, eager, fiery 6 aflame, alight, ardent, fervid, on fire, red-hot 7 blazing, burning, excited, fervent, flaming, flushed, glowing, ignited, zealous 8 feverish, hopped-up, in flames, turned-on 10 passionate, switched-on 11 conflagrant, impassioned, intoxicated

able 3 apt, fit 4 good 5 adept 6 adroit, expert, fitted 7 capable, equal to, learned 8 adequate, skillful, talented 9 competent, effective, efficient, masterful, practiced, qualified 10 proficient 11 experienced 12 accomplished

able-bodied 5 beefy, hardy, husky, lusty, thewy 6 brawny, hearty, robust, rugged, strong, sturdy 8 athletic, muscular, powerful, stalwart, vigorous 9 herculean, strapping, wellbuilt 15 broad-shouldered

ablution 4 bath, wash 7 bathing, washing, lavation 9 cleansing 12 purification 13 ritual washing 17 ceremonial washing

Abnaki (Wabanaki)
  language family: 9 Algonkian 10 Algonquian
  tribe: 6 Micmac 8 Malecite 9 Penobscot 13 Norridgewock, Passamaquoddy
  location: 5 Maine 6 Canada, Quebec 7 Old Town 9 Norumbega 10 New England 12 New Brunswick

abnegate 5 forgo, waive 6 abjure, eschew, give up, refuse 7 abstain, forbear 8 renounce 9 repudiate 10 relinquish 11 deny oneself

abnegation 7 refusal 8 eschewal, giving up 9 rejection, sacrifice, surrender 10 abstinence, continence, forbearing, self-denial, temperance 11 forbearance, resignation 12 renunciation 14 relinquishment

Abner
  commanded: 9 Saul's army
  father: 3 Ner
  cousin: 4 Saul

abnormal 3 odd 4 rare 5 queer, weird 7 bizarre, curious, deviant, strange, unusual 8 aberrant, atypical, deformed, freakish, peculiar, uncommon 9 anomalous, eccentric, gro-

tesque, irregular, monstrous, unheard of, unnatural 10 inordinate, outlandish, unexpected 11 exceptional 12 unaccustomed 13 extraordinary 14 unconventional

abnormality 6 oddity 7 anomaly 9 aberrance, curiosity, deformity, deviation 10 aberration, perversion 11 peculiarity 12 eccentricity, idiosyncrasy, irregularity, malformation, unconformity

abode 3 pad 4 home, nest 5 house 7 address, habitat, lodging 8 domicile, dwelling 9 residence 10 habitation 13 dwelling place 14 living quarters

abolish 3 end 5 annul, erase, quash 6 cancel, repeal, revoke 7 blot out, nullify, rescind, squelch, vitiate, wipe out 8 abrogate, set aside, stamp out 9 eliminate, eradicate, extirpate, repudiate, terminate 10 annihilate, do away with, extinguish, invalidate, obliterate, put an end to 11 exterminate 18 declare null and void

abolishment 7 voiding 8 recision 9 abolition, annulment 10 extinction, rescinding, revocation 11 destruction, eradication 12 cancellation 13 doing away with, nullification

abolition 6 ending, repeal 9 annulment, vitiation 10 abrogation, extinction, rescinding, retraction, revocation 11 abolishment, dissolution, elimination, eradication, recantation, repudiation, termination 12 cancellation, invalidation 13 nullification

abominable 4 base, evil, foul, vile 5 awful, lousy 6 cursed, horrid, odious 7 hateful, heinous, hellish 8 accursed, damnable, horrible, infamous, terrible, wretched 9 abhorrent, atrocious, execrable, loathsome, miserable, repellent, repugnant, repulsive, revolting 10 deplorable, despicable, detestable, disgusting, unsuitable, villainous 11 ignominious 12 contemptible, disagreeable 13 reprehensible

abominate 4 hate 5 abhor, scorn 6 detest, loathe 7 despise 8 execrate 9 can't stand 10 recoil from, shrink from 11 can't stomach 12 be revolted by 13 find repugnant, find repulsive

abomination 4 evil, hate 6 hatred, horror, plague 7 bugbear, disgust, torment

8 anathema, aversion, disgrace, loathing **9** annoyance, antipathy, bete noire, obscenity, revulsion **10** abhorrence, affliction, defilement, repugnance **11** detestation

aboriginal 5 first, prime **6** native **7** ancient, endemic, primary **8** earliest, original, primeval **9** primitive **10** indigenous, primordial **13** autochthonous

aborigine 6 native **16** indigenous person **18** original inhabitant **19** primitive inhabitant

abort 3 end **4** fail, halt, stop **7** call off **8** miscarry **9** terminate

abortion 6 ending, fiasco **7** failure, halting **8** disaster **10** calling off **11** miscarriage, termination **16** fruitless attempt **19** unsuccessful attempt

abortive 4 vain **6** futile **7** sterile, useless **8** bootless **9** fruitless, nonviable, worthless **10** profitless, unavailing, unfruitful **11** ineffective, ineffectual, unrewarding **12** unproductive, unprofitable, unsuccessful **13** inefficacious

abound 4 gush, teem **5** swarm **6** thrive **7** run wild **8** be filled, be rich in, flourish, overflow **9** be flooded, luxuriate, spill over **10** be numerous **11** be plentiful, superabound, proliferate

abounding 4 rich, rife **5** ample **6** lavish, plenty **7** profuse, replete, teeming **8** abundant, brimming, swarming **9** bounteous, bountiful **11** overflowing, running over **14** more than enough

about 2 in, of, on **4** near **5** astir, circa **6** abroad, almost, around, circum, nearby, nearly **7** close to **9** proximate, regarding **10** concerning, in regard to **13** approximately, connected with **14** associated with

about-face 5 shift **6** switch **7** reverse **8** reversal **9** disavowal, turnabout, volte-face **10** retraction, rightabout, turnaround **11** recantation **13** change of heart **14** tergiversation

above 4 atop, over **5** aloft, north, supra **6** before, beyond, dorsal, excess, heaven, higher **7** earlier **8** in heaven, overhead, superior, upstairs **9** exceeding **10** surpassing

above all 4 most **9** most of

all **10** especially **12** particularly

aboveboard 4 just, open **5** blunt, frank, moral, plain **6** candid, direct, honest, public, square **7** artless, ethical, sincere, upright **8** revealed, straight, truthful, virtuous **9** disclosed, guileless, ingenuous, righteous **10** forthright, foursquare **11** unconcealed **12** on the up and up, plain-dealing, out in the open **13** square-dealing, undissembling **15** straightforward **16** straight-shooting

ab ovo 10 from the egg **16** from the beginning

abracadabra 5 charm, magic, spell **6** voodoo **7** sorcery **8** exorcism **10** hocus-pocus, invocation, magic spell, mumbo-jumbo, open sesame, witchcraft **11** incantation

abrade 3 rub **4** file, fray, fret, rasp **5** chafe, erode, grate, grind **6** scrape **8** irritate, wear down

Abraham
former name: 5 Abram
founded: 12 Hebrew nation
father: 5 Terah
wife: 5 Sarah, Sarai **7** Keturah
brother: 5 Haran, Nahor
son: 5 Isaac **6** Midian **7** Ishmael
nephew: 3 Lot
birthplace: 15 Ur of the Chaldees
received: 17 law of circumcision
sacrificed Isaac at: 6 Moriah
burial place: 6 Hebron
tomb buried in: 9 Machpelah

Abraham Lincoln
author: 12 Carl Sandburg

Abraham's bosom 6 heaven

Abram see **7** Abraham

Abramovitz, Max
architect of: 13 ALCOA Building (Pittsburgh PA, with Wallace Harrison) **15** Avery Fisher Hall (Lincoln Center NYC)

Abrams, Creighton
served in: 4 WWII **10** Vietnam War
rank: 16 army chief of staff

abrasion 6 lesion, scrape **7** chafing, erosion, grating, rubbing, scratch **8** friction, scouring, scraping **11** excoriation, scraped spot

abrasive 5 harsh, nasty, rough, sharp **6** biting, coarse **7** caustic, chafing, cutting, galling,

grating, hurtful, rasping **8** annoying **10** irritating **11** excoriating **16** grinding material, scouring material, scraping material

abreast 6 in rank **7** aligned **10** side by side **11** in alignment

abridge 3 cut **4** trim **5** limit **6** digest, lessen, reduce **7** curtail, cut down, shorten **8** compress, condense, decrease, diminish, pare down, restrict, take away, truncate **9** scale down, telescope **10** abbreviate

abridgment 6 digest **8** decrease **9** lessening, reduction, restraint **10** diminution, limitation, truncation **11** curtailment, diminishing, restriction **12** abbreviation, condensation **13** condensed form, shortened form

abroad 3 out **4** rife **5** astir, forth **7** at large, outside **8** overseas **9** all around **10** out of doors **13** in circulation, out of the house, round and about **15** making the rounds, out in the open air, out of the country

abrogate 3 end **4** junk, undo, void **5** annul, quash **6** abjure, cancel, negate, recall, repeal, revoke **7** abolish, nullify, rescind, retract, reverse, vitiate **8** dissolve, override, renounce, set aside, throw out, withdraw **9** repudiate, terminate **10** do away with, invalidate, put an end to **11** countermand

abrogation 6 repeal **7** junking **8** recision, reneging, reversal **9** abolition, annulment **10** rescinding, retraction, revocation **11** abolishment, going back on, repudiation **12** cancellation **13** nullification

abrupt 4 curt, rude **5** blunt, brisk, crisp, gruff, hasty, quick, rapid, rough, sharp, sheer, short, steep, swift **6** sudden **7** brusque, uncivil **8** impolite **9** impulsive **10** unexpected, unforeseen, ungracious **11** precipitate, precipitous, unannounced, unlooked for **12** discourteous **13** instantaneous, unanticipated, unceremonious

Absalom
father: 5 David
mother: 6 Maacah
sister: 5 Tamar
brother: 7 Solomon **8** Adonijah
half-brother: 5 Amnon

defeated at: **6** Gilead
killed by: **4** Joab

Absalom, Absalom!
author: **15** William Faulkner
character: **5** Henry **6** Judith
10 Charles Bon **13** Rosa
Coldfield **14** Quentin Compson, Shreve McCannon
16 Goodhue Coldfield
19 Colonel Thomas Sutpen
20 Ellen Coldfield Sutpen

Absalom and Achitophel
author: **10** John Dryden

abscond 3 fly **4** flee, skip
5 split **6** escape, run off, vanish **7** make off, run away,
take off **8** steal off **9** disappear,
steal away **10** take flight

absence 3 cut **4** lack, want
6 dearth **7** truancy **8** scarcity
10 deficiency, scantiness
11 absenteeism, nonpresence
12 nonexistence **13** insufficiency, nonappearance, nonattendance **14** unavailability

Absence of Malice
director: **13** Sydney Pollack
based on story by: **11** Kurt
Luedtke
cast: **10** Bob Balaban, Paul
Newman, Sally Field
13 Melinda Dillon
setting: **5** Miami

absent 3 cut, out **4** away,
gone **5** blank, empty, vague
6 dreamy, musing, truant, vacant **7** faraway, missing, out
of it, removed, unaware
8 heedless, keep away, stay
away, tuned out **9** not appear,
not show up, oblivious
10 distracted, nonpresent, not
present, out to lunch, play
truant, unthinking **11** inattentive, preoccupied, unconscious **12** nonattendant

absentee 6 no show, truant
10 nonpresent **11** nonattendee,
nonpresence **12** nonattendant
13 nonattendance

absenteeism 5 hooky
7 truancy **11** nonpresence
13 nonappearance **19** absence
without cause

absent-minded 5 blank,
vague **6** dreamy **9** oblivious
10 abstracted, distracted
11 preoccupied **14** out in left
field **17** out of it

Absent Without Leave
author: **12** Heinrich Boll

absinthe
ingredient: **8** licorice, wormwood **9** aromatics, star anise
color: **11** yellow green
substitute: **4** Ouzo **6** Pastis,
Pernod **8** Anisette

absolute 4 full, pure, real,
sure **5** sheer, total, utter
7 certain, genuine, perfect, supreme **8** complete, decisive,
definite, outright, positive, reliable, thorough **9** confirmed,
out-and-out, unbounded, unlimited **10** conclusive, consummate, infallible, undeniable
11 unequivocal, unmitigated,
unqualified **12** unrestrained,
unrestricted **13** unadulterated,
unconditional **14** unquestionable **17** through and
through

Absolute, Sir Anthony
character in: **9** The Rivals
author: **8** Sheridan

absolutely 5 truly **6** indeed,
really, wholly **7** utterly **8** entirely **9** certainly, decidedly
10 completely, definitely, positively, thoroughly **11** indubitably, undoubtedly **13** unequivocally **14** unquestionably
15 unconditionally **17** without
limitation

absolution 5 mercy **6** pardon
7 amnesty, release **9** acquittal,
clearance, quittance, remission **10** indulgence, liberation
11 deliverance, exculpation,
exoneration, forgiveness, vindication **12** dispensation

absolve 4 free **5** clear, loose
6 acquit, exempt, pardon,
shrive **7** deliver, forgive, release, set free **9** discharge, exculpate, exonerate, vindicate
10 excuse from **13** find not
guilty, judge innocent

absolved 5 freed **6** exempt,
spared **7** cleared, excused
8 forgiven, pardoned, released,
relieved **9** acquitted **10** discharged, exonerated, vindicated **13** found innocent

absorb 3 fix **5** rivet **6** arrest,
digest, engage, enwrap, ingest,
occupy, soak up, suck up,
take up **7** consume, drink in,
engross, immerse **8** sponge
up **9** fascinate, preoccupy,
swallow up **10** assimilate
11 incorporate

absorbed 4 deep **8** immersed,
involved, soaked up, sucked
up **9** blotted up, engrossed

absorbent 6 porous, spongy
7 osmotic, thirsty **8** bibulous,
pervious **9** permeable **10** absorptive, penetrable **12** assimilative

absorbing 8 engaging, exciting **9** thrilling **10** engrossing,
intriguing **11** captivating, fascinating, interesting

abstain 5 avoid, forgo **6** desist,

eschew, refuse, resist **7** decline, forbear, refrain

abstainer 3 dry **7** ascetic
10 nondrinker, self-denier, teetotaler

abstemious 3 dry **5** sober
7 ascetic, austere, sparing,
spartan **8** teetotal **9** abstinent,
continent, temperate **10** forbearing **11** abstentious,
self-denying, straitlaced,
teetotaling **12** nonindulgent
15 self-disciplined

abstention 7 refusal **8** eschewal **9** avoidance, desisting, eschewing **10** abstaining,
refraining, resistance **11** forbearance, holding back
13 nonindulgence **14** denying
oneself **16** nonparticipation

abstinence 8 chastity, sobriety **10** abstention, continence,
discipline, self-denial, temperance **11** forbearance, selfcontrol **13** nonindulgence, selfrestraint

abstinent 3 dry **5** sober
6 chaste **8** celibate, virginal
9 continent **10** abstemious,
forbearing

abstract 4 take **5** brief **6** arcane, digest, precis, remote,
remove, resume, subtle
7 abridge, extract, general, isolate, obscure, outline, summary, take out **8** abstruse,
compress, condense, esoteric,
profound, separate, synopsis,
withdraw **9** imaginary, recondite, summarize, synopsize,
theoretic, unapplied, visionary **10** abridgment, conceptual,
dissociate, indefinite, intangible **11** generalized, impractical,
nonspecific, theoretical
12 condensation, hypothetical,
intellectual **14** recapitulation

abstruse 4 deep **6** arcane, remote, subtle **7** complex, obscure **8** abstract, esoteric,
profound, puzzling **9** enigmatic, recondite **10** perplexing **11** complicated
12 unfathomable **16** incomprehensible

absurd 4 wild **5** crazy, funny,
inane, kooky, silly **6** screwy,
stupid **7** asinine, comical, foolish, idiotic **8** farcical **9** illogical, laughable, ludicrous,
senseless **10** irrational, ridiculous **11** nonsensical **12** preposterous, unreasonable

absurdity 6 drivel, idiocy
7 fallacy, inanity **8** delusion,
nonsense **9** asininity, falsehood, silliness **10** buffoonery
11 comicalness, foolishness

13 irrationality **14** ridiculousness **15** unbelievability **16** unreasonableness

Absyrtus *see* **8** Apsyrtus

Abu Dhabi
capital of: **18** United Arab Emirates

Abuja
capital of: **7** Nigeria

abundance 4 glut, heap **5** flood **6** bounty, excess, plenty, wealth **7** surfeit, surplus **8** plethora, richness **9** plenitude, profusion, repletion **10** cornucopia **11** copiousness, full measure, sufficiency

abundant 4 rich, rife **5** ample **6** enough, galore, lavish, plenty **7** copious, profuse, replete, teeming **8** brimming, prolific **9** abounding, bounteous, bountiful, luxuriant **10** sufficient

ab urbe condita 24 from the founding of the city

abuse 4 harm, hurt, slur **5** curse, scold **6** berate, carp at, defame, deride, ill-use, injure, injury, insult, malign, misuse, rail at, revile, tirade, vilify **7** assault, bawl out, beating, carping, censure, cruelty, cursing, exploit, harming, insults, railing, slander, torment, upbraid **8** badmouth, belittle, berating, denounce, derision, diatribe, ill-treat, maltreat, mistreat, reproach, ridicule, scolding, sneering, torments **9** castigate, criticism, criticize, denigrate, disparage, excoriate, invective **10** belittling, defamation, impose upon, imposition, oppression, speak ill of, upbraiding **11** castigation **12** exploitation, maltreatment, mistreatment, vilification **13** disparagement, misemployment, tongue-lashing **14** inveigh against, misapplication **15** take advantage of

abusive 4 rude, vile **5** cruel, gross, harsh **7** harmful, hurtful, obscene **8** critical, improper, reviling, scornful **9** injurious, insulting, maligning, offensive, vilifying **10** censorious, defamatory, derogatory, scurrilous, slanderous **11** acrimonious, castigating, deprecatory, disparaging, foulmouthed **12** vituperative

abusive word 5 curse **6** insult **7** epithet **9** blasphemy, expletive, invective, obscenity

abut 4 join, meet **5** touch **6** adjoin, border

abutment 4 prop, stay **5** brace, union **7** contact, meeting, support **8** buttress, junction, shoulder, touching **9** adjacency

abutting 6 next to **7** joining, meeting **8** adjacent, touching **9** bordering **10** contiguous, juxtaposed **12** conterminous

abysmal 4 deep, vast **7** endless, extreme, immense **8** complete, enormous, profound, thorough, unending **9** boundless **10** bottomless, incredible, stupendous **12** unfathomable, unbelievable, unimaginable

abyss 4 gulf, void **5** depth, gorge, gully, nadir **7** fissure **8** crevasse **9** vast chasm **13** bottomless pit

Abyssinia *see* **8** Ethiopia

Acacallis
father: **5** Minos
mother: **8** Pasiphae
son: **11** Amphithemis

acacia
family: **6** legume **11** leguminosae
also called: **5** thorn **6** mimosa, wattle

academic 4 moot **6** remote, school **7** bookish, erudite, general, learned **8** abstract, educated, pedantic, studious **9** scholarly **10** collegiate, scholastic, university **11** conjectural, educational, liberal-arts, presumptive, speculative, theoretical **12** hypothetical, ivory-towered, nontechnical, not practical **13** nonvocational, suppositional **14** nonspecialized **18** college-preparatory

Academus
origin: **8** Arcadian
owned: **6** estate
located in: **6** Athens
served as meeting place for: **12** philosophers

Academy Award *see* box

Acanthopholis
type: **8** dinosaur **10** ornithopod

Acastus
member of: **9** Argonauts
father: **6** Pelias
mother: **10** Phylomache
sister: **8** Alcestis
wife: **8** Cretheis
daughter: **7** Sterope **8** Laodemia, Sthenele

Acawai, Akawai
language family: **7** Cariban
location: **7** Guianas **12** South America

Accad
kingdom of: **6** Nimrod

location: **13** Plain of Shinar
captured by: **6** Sargon (I)

Acca Larentia
form: **7** goddess
corresponds to: **6** Dea Dia

accede 5 admit, grant **6** accept, permit **7** abide by, agree to, approve, concede, defer to, endorse, inherit, yield to **8** assent to, submit to **9** acquiesce, conform to, consent to, succeed to **10** comply with, concur with **11** acknowledge, subscribe to, surrender to

accede to the throne 4 keep **5** claim, usurp **6** ascend **7** possess, succeed **8** take over **9** be crowned **15** ascend the throne

accelerando
music: **15** becoming quicker

accelerate 4 rush, spur **5** hurry, impel **6** hasten, step up **7** advance, augment, further, promote, quicken, speed up **8** expedite **9** intensify **10** facilitate, to go faster **11** pick up speed, precipitate

accelerator 3 gas **4** goad, prod, spur **8** gas pedal **13** encouragement

accent 4 hint, tone **5** drawl, touch, twang **6** detail, stress **7** feature **8** emphasis, ornament, tonality, trimming **9** adornment, emphasize, highlight, punctuate, spotlight, underline **10** accentuate, inflection, intonation, modulation, underscore **11** enunciation **12** articulation **13** embellishment, primary stress, pronunciation

accentuate 6 accent, stress **7** feature, point up **9** emphasize, punctuate, underline **10** underscore

accentuation 6 accent, stress **8** emphasis

accept 3 buy **4** avow, bear **5** admit **6** assume **7** agree to, fall for, swallow **8** accede to, assent to **9** consent to, undertake **11** acknowledge, go along with

acceptable 4 fair, good, so-so **6** proper, worthy **8** adequate, passable, suitable **9** agreeable, allowable, tolerable **10** admissible **12** satisfactory

acceptable person
Latin: **12** persona grata

acceptance 6 belief, taking **7** consent, receipt **8** approval, sanction **9** accepting, agreement, receiving, reception **10** concession, permission

7

Academy Award
also called: 5 Oscar

1927-28:
actor: 12 Emil Jannings
actress: 11 Janet Gaynor
director: 12 Frank Borzage 14 Lewis Milestone
picture: 5 Wings

1928-29:
actor: 12 Warner Baxter
actress: 12 Mary Pickford
director: 10 Frank Lloyd
picture: 14 Broadway Melody

1929-30:
actor: 12 George Arliss
actress: 12 Norma Shearer
director: 14 Lewis Milestone
picture: 25 All Quiet on the Western Front

1930-31:
actor: 15 Lionel Barrymore
actress: 13 Marie Dressler
director: 12 Norman Taurog
picture: 8 Cimarron

1931-32:
actor: 12 Fredric March
actress: 10 Helen Hayes
director: 12 Frank Borzage
picture: 10 Grand Hotel

1932-33:
actor: 15 Charles Laughton
actress: 16 Katharine Hepburn
director: 10 Frank Lloyd
picture: 9 Cavalcade

1934:
actor: 10 Clark Gable
actress: 16 Claudette Colbert
director: 10 Frank Capra
picture: 18 It Happened One Night

1935:
actor: 14 Victor McLaglen
actress: 10 Bette Davis
director: 8 John Ford
picture: 17 Mutiny on the Bounty

1936:
actor: 8 Paul Muni
actress: 11 Luise Rainer
director: 11 Frank Capra
picture: 16 The Great Ziegfeld

1937:
actor: 12 Spencer Tracy
actress: 11 Luise Rainer
director: 10 Leo McCarey
picture: 15 Life of Emile Zola

1938:
actor: 12 Spencer Tracy
actress: 10 Bette Davis
director: 10 Frank Capra
picture: 20 You Can't Take It with You

1939:
actor: 11 Robert Donat
actress: 11 Vivien Leigh
director: 13 Victor Fleming
picture: 15 Gone with the Wind

1940:
actor: 12 James Stewart
actress: 12 Ginger Rogers
director: 8 John Ford
picture: 7 Rebecca

1941:
actor: 10 Gary Cooper
actress: 12 Joan Fontaine
director: 8 John Ford
picture: 19 How Green Was My Valley

1942:
actor: 11 James Cagney
actress: 11 Greer Garson
director: 12 William Wyler
picture: 10 Mrs Miniver

1943:
actor: 9 Paul Lukas
actress: 13 Jennifer Jones
director: 13 Michael Curtiz
picture: 10 Casablanca

1944:
actor: 10 Bing Crosby
actress: 13 Ingrid Bergman
director: 10 Leo McCarey
picture: 10 Going My Way

1945:
actor: 10 Ray Milland
actress: 12 Joan Crawford
director: 11 Billy Wilder
picture: 14 The Lost Weekend

1946:
actor: 12 Fredric March
actress: 17 Olivia de Havilland
director: 12 William Wyler
picture: 22 The Best Years of Our Lives

1947:
actor: 12 Ronald Colman
actress: 12 Loretta Young
director: 9 Elia Kazan
picture: 19 Gentleman's Agreement

1948:
actor: 15 Laurence Olivier
actress: 9 Jane Wyman
director: 10 John Huston
picture: 6 Hamlet

1949:
actor: 17 Broderick Crawford
actress: 17 Olivia de Havilland
director: 17 Joseph L Mankiewicz
picture: 14 All the King's Men

1950:
actor: 10 Jose Ferrer
actress: 12 Judy Holliday
director: 17 Joseph L Mankiewicz
picture: 11 All About Eve

1951:
actor: 14 Humphrey Bogart
actress: 11 Vivien Leigh
director: 13 George Stevens
picture: 17 An American in Paris

1952:
actor: 10 Gary Cooper
actress: 12 Shirley Booth
director: 8 John Ford
picture: 19 Greatest Show on Earth

1953:
actor: 13 William Holden
actress: 13 Audrey Hepburn
director: 13 Fred Zinnemann
picture: 18 From Here to Eternity

1954:
actor: 12 Marlon Brando
actress: 10 Grace Kelly
director: 9 Elia Kazan
picture: 15 On the Waterfront

1955:
actor: 14 Ernest Borgnine
actress: 11 Anna Magnani
director: 11 Delbert Mann
picture: 5 Marty

1956:
actor: 10 Yul Brynner
actress: 13 Ingrid Bergman
director: 13 George Stevens
picture: 26 Around the World in Eighty Days

1957:
actor: 12 Alec Guinness
actress: 14 Joanne Woodward
director: 9 David Lean
picture: 23 The Bridge on the River Kwai

1958:
actor: 10 David Niven
actress: 12 Susan Hayward
director: 16 Vincente Minnelli
picture: 4 Gigi

1959:
actor: 14 Charlton Heston
actress: 14 Simone Signoret
director: 12 William Wyler
picture: 6 Ben-Hur

1960:
actor: 13 Burt Lancaster
actress: 15 Elizabeth Taylor
director: 11 Billy Wilder
picture: 12 The Apartment

1961:
actor: 16 Maximilian Schell
actress: 11 Sophia Loren
director: 10 Robert Wise 13 Jerome Robbins
picture: 13 West Side Story

(continued)

Academy Award (*continued*)
1962:
  actor: **11** Gregory Peck
  actress: **12** Anne Bancroft
  director: **9** David Lean
  picture: **16** Lawrence of Arabia
1963:
  actor: **13** Sidney Poitier
  actress: **12** Patricia Neal
  director: **14** Tony Richardson
  picture: **8** Tom Jones
1964:
  actor: **11** Rex Harrison
  actress: **12** Julie Andrews
  director: **11** George Cukor
  picture: **10** My Fair Lady
1965:
  actor: **9** Lee Marvin
  actress: **13** Julie Christie
  director: **10** Robert Wise
  picture: **15** The Sound of Music
1966:
  actor: **12** Paul Scofield
  actress: **15** Elizabeth Taylor
  director: **13** Fred Zinnemann
  picture: **17** A Man for All Seasons
1967:
  actor: **10** Rod Steiger
  actress: **16** Katharine Hepburn
  director: **11** Mike Nichols
  picture: **19** In the Heat of the Night
1968:
  actor: **14** Cliff Robertson
  actress: **15** Barbra Streisand **16** Katharine Hepburn
  director: **12** Sir Carol Reed
  picture: **6** Oliver!
1969:
  actor: **9** John Wayne
  actress: **11** Maggie Smith
  director: **15** John Schlesinger
  picture: **14** Midnight Cowboy
1970:
  actor: **12** George C Scott
  actress: **13** Glenda Jackson
  director: **17** Franklin Schaffner
  picture: **6** Patton
1971:
  actor: **11** Gene Hackman
  actress: **9** Jane Fonda
  director: **15** William Friedkin
  picture: **19** The French Connection
1972:
  actor: **12** Marlon Brando
  actress: **11** Liza Minnelli
  director: **8** Bob Fosse
  picture: **12** The Godfather

1973:
  actor: **10** Jack Lemmon
  actress: **13** Glenda Jackson
  director: **13** George Roy Hill
  picture: **8** The Sting
1974:
  actor: **9** Art Carney
  actress: **12** Ellen Burstyn
  director: **18** Francis Ford Coppola
  picture: **12** The Godfather (Part II)
1975:
  actor: **13** Jack Nicholson
  actress: **14** Louise Fletcher
  director: **11** Milos Forman
  picture: **25** One Flew Over the Cuckoo's Nest
1976:
  actor: **10** Peter Finch
  actress: **11** Faye Dunaway
  director: **13** John G Avildsen
  picture: **5** Rocky
1977:
  actor: **15** Richard Dreyfuss
  actress: **11** Diane Keaton
  director: **10** Woody Allen
  picture: **9** Annie Hall
1978:
  actor: **9** Jon Voight
  actress: **9** Jane Fonda
  director: **13** Michael Cimino
  picture: **13** The Deer Hunter
1979:
  actor: **13** Dustin Hoffman
  actress: **10** Sally Field
  director: **12** Robert Benton
  picture: **14** Kramer vs Kramer
1980:
  actor: **12** Robert De Niro
  actress: **11** Sissy Spacek
  director: **13** Robert Redford
  picture: **14** Ordinary People
1981:
  actor: **10** Henry Fonda
  actress: **16** Katharine Hepburn
  director: **12** Warren Beatty
  picture: **14** Chariots of Fire
1982:
  actor: **11** Ben Kingsley
  actress: **11** Meryl Streep
  director: **19** Richard Attenborough
  picture: **6** Gandhi
1983:
  actor: **12** Robert Duvall
  actress: **15** Shirley MacLaine
  director: **12** James L Brooks
  picture: **17** Terms of Endearment
1984:
  actor: **14** F Murray Abraham
  actress: **10** Sally Field
  director: **11** Milos Forman
  picture: **7** Amadeus

1985:
  actor: **11** William Hurt
  actress: **13** Geraldine Page
  director: **13** Sydney Pollack
  picture: **11** Out of Africa
1986:
  actor: **10** Paul Newman
  actress: **12** Marlee Matlin
  director: **11** Oliver Stone
  picture: **7** Platoon
1987:
  actor: **14** Michael Douglas
  actress: **4** Cher
  director: **18** Bernardo Bertolucci
  picture: **14** The Last Emperor
1988:
  actor: **13** Dustin Hoffman
  actress: **11** Jodie Foster
  director: **13** Barry Levinson
  picture: **7** Rain Man
1989:
  actor: **14** Daniel Day-Lewis
  actress: **12** Jessica Tandy
  director: **11** Oliver Stone
  picture: **16** Driving Miss Daisy
1990:
  actor: **11** Jeremy Irons
  actress: **10** Kathy Bates
  director: **12** Kevin Costner
  picture: **16** Dances With Wolves
1991:
  actor: **14** Anthony Hopkins
  actress: **11** Jodie Foster
  director: **13** Jonathan Demme
  picture: **20** The Silence of the Lambs
1992:
  actor: **8** Al Pacino
  actress: **12** Emma Thompson
  director: **13** Clint Eastwood
  picture: **10** Unforgiven
1993:
  actor: **8** Tom Hanks
  actress: **11** Holly Hunter
  director: **15** Steven Spielberg
  picture: **14** Schindler's List
1994:
  actor: **8** Tom Hanks
  actress: **12** Jessica Lange
  director: **14** Robert Zemeckis
  picture: **11** Forrest Gump
1995:
  actor: **11** Nicolas Cage
  actress: **13** Susan Sarandon
  director: **9** Mel Gibson
  picture: **10** Braveheart
1996:
  actor: **12** Geoffrey Rush
  actress: **16** Frances McDormand
  director: **16** Anthony Minghella
  picture: **17** The English Patient

accepted 5 usual **6** common, normal **7** regular **8** approved, standard **9** confirmed, customary, universal **10** acceptable, agreed upon **11** established, time-honored **12** acknowledged, conventional

access 3 way **4** path, road **5** entry **6** avenue, course, entree **7** gateway, passage **8** entrance **10** admittance, an approach, passageway

accessible 5 handy, ready **6** at hand, nearby, on hand **8** possible **9** available, reachable **10** attainable, obtainable

accession 7 seizure **9** induction **10** arrogation, assumption, investment, taking over, usurpation **11** inheritance **12** inauguration, installation

accessory 4 plus **6** accent, cohort, detail **7** adjunct, partner **8** addition **9** adornment, assistant, associate, auxiliary, colleague, component, extension **10** accomplice, attachment, complement, decoration, supplement **11** confederate, contributor **13** accompaniment

accident 4 fate, luck **5** crash, fluke, wreck **6** chance, mishap **7** smashup **8** fortuity **9** collision, mischance **10** misfortune **11** good fortune, serendipity **12** happenstance, misadventure

accidental 6 chance, random **9** haphazard, unplanned, unwitting **10** fortuitous, incidental, unexpected, unforeseen

acclaim 4 hail, laud **5** cheer, exalt, extol, honor, kudos **6** bravos, praise, salute **7** applaud, commend, ovation **8** applause, cheering, eulogize, plaudits **9** celebrate, rejoicing **10** compliment, enthusiasm **11** acclamation, endorsement

acclamation 6 cheers, homage **7** acclaim, hurrahs, ovation, tribute **8** cheering, hosannas, plaudits **9** adulation **10** salutation **11** approbation

acclimate 5 adapt, inure **6** adjust **8** accustom **9** get used to, habituate, reconcile **11** accommodate **16** become seasoned to

acclimation 9 seasoning **10** adaptation, adjustment **11** habituation

acclimatize 5 adapt **6** attune **8** accustom **9** acclimate, get used to

acclivity 4 hill, rise **6** ascent **9** elevation **11** upward slope

accolade 5 award, honor, prize **6** praise, trophy **7** acclaim, tribute **8** citation **10** admiration, compliment, decoration **11** recognition, testimonial **12** commendation

accommodate 3 aid, fit **4** help, hold **5** adapt, board, house, lodge, put up **6** adjust, assist, billet, modify, oblige, supply **7** bed down, conform, contain, furnish, provide, quarter, shelter **8** accustom **9** acclimate, entertain, get used to, harmonize, lend a hand, reconcile

accommodating 4 kind **6** polite **7** helpful **8** gracious, obliging, yielding **9** courteous **10** hospitable, neighborly **11** considerate **12** conciliatory

accommodation 5 rooms **7** concord, housing **8** lodgings, quarters **9** agreement **10** adjustment, compromise, settlement **12** arrangements **14** reconciliation

accommodative 8 friendly **9** appeasing, pacifying, placatory **10** mollifying **11** peacemaking, reconciling **12** conciliatory

accompaniment 6 escort **7** support **8** ornament **9** accessory, adornment **10** incidental

accompany 5 guard, usher **6** attend, back up, convoy, escort, follow **7** conduct, support **8** chaperon

accomplice 4 aide, ally **5** crony **6** cohort, helper, stooge **7** abettor, comrade, partner **8** henchman, sidekick **9** accessory, assistant, associate, colleague, supporter **11** confederate, participant, subordinate **12** collaborator **13** coconspirator **14** partner-in-crime

accomplish 2 do **6** attain, finish **7** achieve, execute, fulfill, get done, perform, produce, realize **8** carry out, complete, expedite, knock off **9** succeed at **10** bring about

accomplished 3 apt **4** able, deft, fine **6** adroit, expert, gifted, proved, proven **7** capable, eminent, skilled **8** accepted, effected, existing, finished, masterly, polished, realized, seasoned, skillful, talented **9** brilliant, completed, concluded, practiced, qualified **10** cultivated, proficient **11** consummated, established, experienced, well-trained

accomplishment 3 act **4** deed, feat, gift **5** skill **6** talent

7 exploit, success, triumph, victory **9** execution **10** attainment, capability **11** achievement, carrying out, culmination, fulfillment, proficiency, realization, tour de force **12** consummation

accord 4 cede, give, jibe **5** agree, allow, award, grant, match, tally **6** bestow, concur, render, square, tender, unison **7** concede, concert, conform, harmony, present, rapport **8** be in tune, bequeath, sympathy **9** agreement, harmonize, unanimity, vouchsafe **10** accordance, be in unison, comply with, conformity, consonance, correspond, uniformity

accordant 4 like **7** similar **8** parallel **10** consistent **11** homogeneous

accordingly 2 so **4** ergo, then, thus **5** hence **6** thence, whence **8** suitably **9** as a result, therefore, wherefore, whereupon **11** conformably, in due course, in which case **12** consequently **15** correspondingly

accost 3 nab **4** hail, halt, stop **5** greet **6** call to, salute, waylay **7** address, solicit **8** approach, confront **10** buttonhole **11** proposition

accouchement 10 childbirth **11** confinement

account 3 use **4** deem, hold, note, rank, rate, sake, tale **5** basis, books, cause, count, gauge, honor, judge, merit, score, story, think, value, weigh, worth **6** esteem, import, reason, reckon, record, regard, report, repute, view as **7** believe, clarify, dignity, explain, grounds, history, justify, recital, version **8** appraise, consider, estimate, megillah, standing **9** calculate, chronicle, narration, narrative, statement **10** accounting, commentary, illuminate, importance

accountable 6 guilty, liable **7** at fault, to blame **8** beholden, culpable **9** obligated **10** answerable, chargeable **11** blameworthy, responsible

accountant 3 CPA **7** actuary, auditor **10** bookkeeper **25** certified public accountant

account for 6 excuse **7** explain, justify **9** answer for

accounting 5 cause **6** answer, motive, reason **7** warrant **10** motivation **11** explanation

account rendered
   French: 11 compte rendu

accoutrements 4 gear 7 apparel 8 supplies 9 equipment, trappings 11 accessories, furnishings 13 paraphernalia

Accra, Akkra
   capital of: 5 Ghana

accredit 6 assign, credit 7 ascribe, certify, empower, endorse, license 8 sanction 9 attribute, authorize, guarantee 11 commission 19 officially recognize 22 furnish with credentials

accredited 8 ascribed, assigned, endorsed, licensed 9 authentic, certified, empowered 10 attributed, authorized, recognized, sanctioned 12 commissioned 20 officially recognized

accretion 4 rise 6 growth 7 accrual 8 addition, increase 9 expansion, extension, increment 10 supplement 11 enlargement 12 accumulation, augmentation 13 amplification

accrue 4 grow 5 add up, amass 6 pile up 7 build up, collect 8 increase 10 accumulate

accumulate 4 grow 5 amass, hoard 6 accrue, garner, gather, heap up, pile up, save up 7 collect, store up 8 assemble, cumulate 9 aggregate 10 congregate 14 gather together

accumulation 4 heap, mass, pile 5 hoard, stack, stock, store 6 pile-up, supply 7 accrual 8 amassing, hoarding 9 acquiring, gathering, stockpile 10 assemblage, collecting, collection 11 aggregation 13 agglomerating 14 conglomeration

accuracy 5 truth 6 verity 8 fidelity 9 exactness, precision 10 exactitude 11 correctness 12 accurateness, faithfulness

accurate 4 true 5 exact, right 7 careful, correct, perfect, precise 8 faithful, truthful, unerring 9 authentic, faultless 10 meticulous, scrupulous 11 punctilious 12 without error

accursed 4 base, foul, vile 6 cussed, horrid, odious 7 hellish 8 damnable, horrible, infamous 9 abhorrent, atrocious, execrable, loathsome, revolting 10 abominable, despicable, detestable, disgusting 12 contemptible

accusation 6 charge 8 citation 9 complaint 10 allegation, imputation, indictment 11 insinuation 13 incrimination

accuse 4 cite 5 blame 6 charge, indict 7 arraign, upbraid 8 reproach 10 take to task 13 call to account 22 lodge a complaint against

accuser 8 attacker 11 complainant 13 finger pointer

accustomed 3 set 5 fixed, prone, trite, usual 6 cliche, common, inured, normal, used to, wonted 7 general, given to, regular, routine 8 everyday, expected, familiar, habitual, hardened, ordinary, seasoned 9 customary, hackneyed, ingrained, prevalent, well-known 10 acclimated, habituated, prevailing 11 commonplace, established 12 conventional, familiarized

ace 2 A-1 3 top 4 star 5 crack, super 6 expert, master, tip-top, victor, winner 8 champion, medalist, terrific, top-rated 9 excellent, first-rate, headliner 10 first-class 11 crackerjack, outstanding 12 frontranking

Aceldama
   means: 12 field of blood
   purchased by: 5 Judas

Acerbas see 8 Sychaeus

acerbity 7 acidity, sarcasm 8 acridity, acrimony, pungency, sourness, tartness 9 nastiness, sharpness 10 bitterness 11 astringency, brusqueness 12 irascibility

aces 2 A-1 4 fine, tops 5 great, prime, super 6 grade-A, superb, tip-top 8 peerless, superior, terrific, top-notch 9 excellent, first-rate, marvelous, matchless, superfine, wonderful 10 first-class, tremendous 11 outstanding, superlative 13 extraordinary

Acesius
   epithet of: 6 Apollo
   means: 6 healer

Acessamenus
   origin: 8 Thracian
   mentioned in: 5 Iliad
   form: 4 king

Acetes
   origin: 6 Lydian
   duty: 8 helmsman
   protected: 8 Dionysus

Achaeus
   founder of: 6 Achaea
   father: 6 Xuthus
   mother: 6 Creusa
   brother: 3 Ion

Achan
   punishment: 13 stoned to death

Acharnians
   author: 12 Aristophanes
   character: 7 Demigod 8 Lamachus 11 Dikaiopolis

Achates
   mentioned in: 6 Aeneid
   companion of: 6 Aeneas
   position: 11 armorbearer

ache 4 hurt, need, pain, pang, want 5 covet, crave, mourn, smart, throb, yearn 6 be sore, desire, grieve, hanker, hunger, lament, sorrow, suffer, twinge 7 agonize, long for 8 soreness 10 discomfort

Achech
   origin: 8 Egyptian
   form: 8 creature
   body of: 4 lion
   wings of: 4 bird

Achelous
   form: 3 god
   habitat: 5 river
   father: 7 Oceanus
   mother: 6 Tethys
   daughter: 6 Sirens 8 Castalia 10 Callirrhoe
   defeated by: 8 Hercules
   struggled over: 8 Deianira

Acheron
   river in: 5 Hades
   ferryman: 6 Charon
   carries: 4 dead

Acheson, Dean
   author of: 20 Present at the Creation

a cheval 7 by horse 11 on horseback

achieve 2 do 3 get, win 4 earn, gain 5 reach 6 attain, effect, finish, obtain 7 acquire, fulfill, procure, realize 8 arrive at, carry out, complete, dispatch 9 succeed in 10 accomplish, bring about, effectuate 11 bring to pass

achievement 3 act 4 coup, deed, fear 5 skill 6 effort 7 command, exploit, mastery 9 expertise 10 attainment 11 acquirement, fulfillment, realization, tour de force 14 accomplishment

achieve recognition 6 arrive, make it 7 succeed 8 make good 10 be somebody 11 reach the top

Achilles
   mentioned in: 5 Iliad
   father: 6 Peleus
   mother: 6 Thetis
   foster father: 7 Phoenix
   grandfather: 6 Aeacus
   teacher: 6 Chiron

charioteer: 9 Automedon
friend: 9 Patroclus
warrior in: 9 Trojan War
vulnerability: 4 heel
killed: 6 Hector
killed by: 5 Paris

Achish
king of: 4 Gath
gave refuge to: 5 David

Achomawi
language family: 5 Hokan
location: 8 Pit River **10** California **12** Shasta County
related to: 8 Atsugewi

Achsah
father: 5 Caleb
grandfather: 9 Jephunneh
husband: 7 Othniel

acid 4 sour, tart **5** acrid, harsh, nasty, sharp **6** biting, bitter, ironic **7** acerbic, caustic, crabbed, cutting, pungent **8** scalding, scathing, stinging, vinegary **9** acidulous, irascible, sarcastic, satirical, vitriolic **10** astringent, vinegarish **11** acrimonious

acidity 8 acerbity, pungency, sourness, tartness **9** sharpness **10** bitterness **11** astringency **13** nonalkalinity

Acis
lover: 7 Galatea
killed by: 10 Polyphemus

Acis and Galatea
opera by: 6 Handel

Acis et Galatee
opera by: 5 Lully

acknowledge 3 own **5** admit, allow, grant, yield **6** accede, accept, answer, assent, concur **7** concede, confess, own up to, reply to **8** call upon, thank for **9** recognize, respond to

acknowledged 7 acceded **8** accepted, admitted, answered, called on, conceded **9** replied to **10** agreed upon, called upon, recognized, thanked for **11** established, responded to

acknowledgment 5 reply **6** answer, credit, thanks **8** response **9** admission, gratitude **10** concession, confession **11** affirmation, recognition **12** appreciation, recognizance

acme 4 apex, peak **5** crest, crown **6** apogee, climax, height, heyday, summit, zenith **8** pinnacle **9** flowering, high point **11** culmination **12** highest point
Latin: 11 ne plus ultra

Acmon
companion: 8 Diomedes
changed into: 4 bird
defied: 9 Aphrodite

acolyte 3 fan **6** helper, novice **7** admirer, devotee, groupie **8** adherent, altar boy, follower **9** assistant, attendant

Acoma
language family: 6 Pueblo
location: 3 Ako **4** Acus **8** Valencia **9** New Mexico
noted for: 7 pottery

acorn
from: 3 oak
shape: 8 balanoid

a couvert 9 sheltered **10** under cover

acquaint 4 meet, tell **6** advise, inform, notify, reveal **7** apprise **8** disclose **9** divulge to, enlighten, introduce, make aware **11** familiarize

acquaintance 8 dealings **9** awareness, knowledge **10** cognizance, friendship **11** association, conversance, familiarity **12** relationship

acquiesce 5 admit, agree, allow, bow to, grant, yield **6** accede, assent, comply, concur, give in, submit **7** concede, conform, consent **10** capitulate, fall in with **13** resign oneself **16** reconcile oneself

acquiescence 5 leave **7** consent **8** approval, giving in, sanction **10** permission, submission **11** concurrence

acquiescent 7 willing **8** amenable, yielding **9** agreeable **10** submissive

acquire 3 get, win **4** earn, gain **6** attain, obtain, pick up, secure **7** achieve, capture, procure, realize **9** cultivate

acquirement 4 gain **5** prize **7** earning **10** attainment, obtainment, possession **11** achievement, acquisition, procurement

acquisition 4 gain **5** prize **8** property, purchase **10** attainment, obtainment, possession **11** achievement, acquirement, procurement

acquisitive 6 greedy **7** selfish **8** covetous, grasping **10** avaricious, possessive **13** materialistic

acquit 3 act **5** clear **6** behave, excuse, exempt, let off, pardon **7** absolve, comport, conduct, deliver, release, relieve, set free **8** liberate, reprieve

9 discharge, exculpate, exonerate, vindicate

Acraea
epithet of: 9 Aphrodite
means: 6 height

acre
one-fourth: 4 rood
one-half: 3 erf **5** erven
two-thirds: 5 cover
ten: 6 decare **7** furlong
one hundred: 7 hectare
one hundred twenty: 4 hide

Acres, Bob
character in: 9 The Rivals
author: 8 Sheridan

acrid 4 acid **5** harsh, nasty, sharp **6** biting, bitter, ironic, smelly **7** burning, caustic, pungent **8** stinging **9** sarcastic, satirical, vitriolic **10** irritating, malodorous **11** acrimonious **12** foul-smelling

acrimonious 4 sour **5** nasty, testy **6** bitchy, biting, bitter **7** caustic, cutting, peevish **8** venomous, spiteful **9** corrosive, irascible, rancorous, sarcastic, splenetic, vitriolic **10** ill-natured

acrimony 5 anger, scorn, spite **6** animus, rancor, spleen **7** ill will **8** asperity, derision **9** animosity, hostility, malignity **10** antagonism, bitterness, malignancy **12** hard feelings, spitefulness

Acrisius
king of: 5 Argos
father: 4 Abas
mother: 6 Aglaia
twin brother: 7 Proetus
daughter: 5 Danae
grandson: 7 Perseus
killed by: 7 Perseus

acrophobia
fear of: 7 heights

acrostic 6 cipher, puzzle **7** acronym

act 2 do **3** bit, gig, law **4** bill, deed, do it, fake, feat, move, play, pose, show, skit, step, work **5** edict, enact, feign, front, order, put-on **6** action, affect, behave, decree, stance **7** execute, exploit, go about, mandate, measure, operate, perform, portray, posture, press on, routine, statute **8** carry out, function, pretense, put forth, simulate **9** enactment, ordinance, represent **10** pretension, resolution **11** achievement, affectation, counterfeit, impersonate, legislation, performance, pretend to be **14** accomplishment

Actaeon
form: **6** hunter
father: **9** Aristaeus
mother: **7** Autonoe
changed into: **4** stag
transformed by: **5** Diana
killed by: **6** hounds
killed at: **9** Gargaphia

acting 5 drama **6** deputy, ersatz, pro tem **7** interim, theater **8** the stage **9** dramatics, simulated, surrogate, temporary **10** dramaturgy, stagecraft, substitute, the theater **11** dramatic art, officiating, provisional, thespianism **12** stage playing

actinium
chemical symbol: **2** Ac

action 3 act **4** deed, feat, move, step, suit, work **5** force, power **6** battle, combat, effect, effort, motion **7** exploit, process, warfare **8** activity, conflict, endeavor, exertion, fighting, movement, progress **9** adventure, execution, influence, operation **10** enterprise, excitement, performing, production **11** achievement, functioning, performance, prosecution **14** accomplishment

Actis
father: **6** Helius
mother: **5** Rhoda
crime: **10** fratricide
taught: **9** astrology
fled to: **5** Egypt
memorial: **16** Colossus of Rhodes

activate 4 stir **5** drive, impel, start **6** prompt, propel, turn on **7** actuate **8** energize, mobilize, motivate, vitalize **9** stimulate

activated 5 drive **7** started **8** impelled, in action, in effect, turned on **9** effective, energized, mobilized, operative, vitalized **10** stimulated **11** in operation

active 4 busy, spry **5** agile, alert, alive, peppy, quick **6** acting, at work, frisky, lively, nimble **7** engaged, in force, on the go, working, zealous **8** animated, diligent, forceful, occupied, spirited, vigorous **9** ambitious, assertive, effectual, energetic, go-getting, operative, sprightly, strenuous **10** aggressive, productive **11** functioning, imaginative, industrious **12** enterprising **13** indefatigable

active person 4 doer **6** dynamo **7** hustler **8** activist, go-getter

activist 4 doer **6** zealot **7** apos-tle **8** advocate, exponent **9** proponent, supporter

activity 4 fuss, stir **6** action, bustle, flurry, hustle, tumult **7** project, pursuit, venture **8** endeavor, exercise, exertion, function, goings on, movement, vivacity **9** agitation, animation, avocation, commotion **10** assignment, enterprise, hurly-burly, liveliness, occupation **11** undertaking **13** sprightliness

act of the faith
Spanish: **8** auto da fe, auto de fe

act of war 4 raid **6** attack, strike **7** assault, offense **8** invasion **10** aggression, hostile act

actor 3 ham **4** doer, star **6** player, walk on **7** starlet, trouper **8** thespian **9** bit player, performer **11** functionary, participant, perpetrator **14** dramatic artist **15** supporting actor
type: **4** hero **7** feature, leading **9** character **10** supporting

Actor
king of: **6** Phthia
father: **8** Myrmidon
mother: **8** Pasidice
brother: **6** Augeas
son: **7** Cteatus, Eurytus

actual 4 real, sure, true **7** certain, current, factual, genuine, present **8** bona fide, concrete, existent, existing, physical, tangible **9** authentic, confirmed, corporeal **10** legitimate, prevailing, true-to-life, verifiable

actuality 4 fact, life **5** being, truth **6** effect, living, verity **7** reality **8** existing **9** existence, plain fact, substance **10** brutal fact **11** point of fact

actually 5 truly **6** indeed, in fact, really, verily **9** genuinely, literally
Latin: **7** ex facto

actually existing
Latin: **6** in esse **7** de facto

actuary 5 clerk **9** tabulator **12** statistician

actuate 4 move, stir **5** cause, drive, impel, rouse **6** arouse, excite, incite, induce, prompt **7** animate, inspire, trigger **8** activate, motivate **9** influence, instigate, stimulate **10** bring about

acumen 6 wisdom **7** insight **8** keenness, sagacity **9** acuteness, ingenuity, smartness **10** astuteness, cleverness, per-ception, shrewdness **11** discernment **12** intelligence, perspicacity **13** sound judgment **15** clearheadedness

acute 4 keen **5** sharp **6** clever, fierce, peaked, severe **7** intense, very bad **8** critical, piercing, powerful **9** agonizing, ingenious, intuitive, sensitive, very great **10** discerning, perceptive **11** distressing, penetrating **12** excruciating, needle-shaped **14** discriminating

acuteness 6 acumen **8** keenness **9** sharpness, smartness **10** astuteness, cleverness, shrewdness

acute suffering 5 agony **7** anguish, torment, torture **8** distress

adage 3 saw **4** quip, wise **5** axiom, maxim, motto **6** cliche, dictum, old saw, saying, truism **7** epigram, precept, proverb **8** aphorism **9** platitude **11** observation

adagio
music: **4** slow

Adah
also: **9** Bashemath
husband: **4** Esau **6** Lamech
son: **5** Jabal, Jubal **7** Eliphaz

Adam
wife: **3** Eve
son: **4** Abel, Cain, Seth
home: **4** Eden
grandson: **4** Enas **5** Enoch

adamant 3 set **4** firm **5** fixed, rigid, tough **7** uptight **8** obdurate, resolute, stubborn **9** immovable, insistent, unbending **10** determined, hard as rock, inexorable, inflexible, unyielding **12** intransigent **14** uncompromising

Adamas
ally of: **7** Trojans
plotted against: **10** Antilochus
thwarted by: **8** Poseidon

Adamawa-Eastern
language family: **16** Niger-Kordofanian
group: **10** Niger-Congo
includes: **5** Sango, Zande

Adam Bede
author: **11** George Eliot
character: **8** Seth Bede **11** Dinah Morris, Hetty Sorrel **12** Martin Poyser **17** Arthur Donnithorne

Adams, Henry
author of: **6** Esther **9** Democracy **14** Chapters of Erie **24** History of the United States (Under the Jefferson and Adams Administration), The Education of Henry Ad-

ams **26** Mont-Saint Michel and Chartres **34** The Degradation of the Democratic Dogma

Adams, John *see box*

Adams, John Quincy *see box, p. 14*

Adams, Parson
character in: **13** Joseph Andrews
author: **8** Fielding

Adams, Richard
author of: **4** Maia **7** Shardik **12** Girl in a Swing **13** The Plague Dogs, Watership Down

Adam's Rib
director: **11** George Cukor
script by: **10** Ruth Gordon **11** Garson Kanin
cast: **8** Tom Ewell **9** Jean Hagen **9** David Wayne **12** Judy Holliday, Spencer Tracy **16** Katharine Hepburn

Adapa
origin: **8** Akkadian
form: **4** sage
forfeits: **4** food **5** water **11** immortality
offered by: **3** Anu
patron: **2** Ea

adapt 3 fit **4** suit **5** alter,

frame, shape **6** adjust, change, modify, rework **7** conform, convert, fashion, make fit, remodel, reshape **8** attune to **9** acclimate, harmonize, recompose, reconcile, transform **10** assimilate, coordinate **11** accommodate, acculturate **12** make suitable

adaptable 6 pliant, usable **7** unrigid **8** amenable, flexible, obliging **9** alterable, compliant, easygoing, malleable, tractable **10** adjustable, applicable, changeable, open-minded **11** conformable, serviceable **13** accommodating, accommodative

adaptation 5 shift **6** change **8** revision **9** refitting, reshaping, reworking **10** adjustment, alteration, conversion, remodeling **12** modification **13** metamorphosis

Adar 18 twelfth Hebrew month

add 4 join **5** affix, sum up, total **6** append, attach, join on, reckon, tack on **7** combine, compute, count up, enlarge, include **8** figure up, increase **9** calculate, enlarge by **10** increase by, supplement

Addams, Frankie
character in: **19** A Member of the Wedding
author: **15** Carson McCullers

Addams Family, The
character: **5** Gomez, Lurch **7** Pugsley **8** Morticia **9** Grandmama, Wednesday **11** Uncle Fester
cast: **9** John Astin **10** Lisa Loring, Ted Cassidy **11** Blossom Rock **12** Carolyn Jones, Jackie Coogan **13** Ken Weatherwax

add details 6 expand **7** clarify **9** elaborate, embellish **13** particularize

added 5 extra **6** joined **7** totaled **8** appended, attached, computed, included, joined on, reckoned, summed up, tacked on **9** counted up **10** additional, enlarged by, enumerated **11** increased by **13** supplementary

addendum 7 codicil **8** addition **9** appendage **10** attachment, postscript, supplement **12** afterthought

addict 3 fan, nut **4** buff, head, hook, user **5** freak, hound **6** junkie, submit, turn on, votary **7** acolyte, devotee, druggie, habitue **8** adherent, dope fiend, indulge in, surrender

addiction 5 craze, mania, quirk **6** fetish, hangup **8** fixation **9** cocainism, obsession **10** alcoholism, compulsion, dipsomania, morphinism **11** barbiturism, enslavement **12** addictedness, enthrallment **13** preoccupation

adding machine
invented by: **6** Pascal **9** Burroughs

Addis Ababa
capital of: **8** Ethiopia

Addison, Joseph
author of: **4** Cato **9** The Tatler **12** The Spectator **13** The Freeholder
co-author: **13** Richard Steele

addition 4 wing **5** annex, extra **6** adding **7** adjunct, joining **8** addendum, additive, annexing, increase, totaling **9** adjoining, appendage, appending, attaching, embracing, expansion, extending, extension, including, increment, reckoning, summation, summing up **10** counting up, increasing **11** enlargement, enumeration **12** appurtenance, augmentation, encompassing

additional 5 added, extra, spare **7** added on **8** appended

---

Adams, John
nickname: **19** Atlas of Independence
presidential rank: **6** second
party: **10** Federalist
state represented: **2** MA
defeated: **9** Jefferson
vice president: **9** Jefferson
cabinet:
   state: **8** (John) Marshall **9** (Timothy) Pickering
   treasury: **6** (Samuel) Dexter **7** (Oliver) Wolcott
   war: **6** (Samuel) Dexter **7** (James) McHenry
   attorney general: **3** (Charles) Lee
   navy: **8** (Benjamin) Stoddert
born: **2** MA **9** Braintree
   town now called: **6** Quincy
died/buried: **6** Quincy
education: **7** Harvard
religion: **9** Unitarian
author: **18** Discourses on Davila **20** Thoughts on Government
political career: **13** vice president **24** First Continental Congress **25** Second Continental Congress
   minister: **11** Netherlands **12** Great Britain
civilian career: **6** lawyer
notable events of lifetime/term: **9** XYZ Affair
   act: **9** Judiciary **16** Alien and Sedition
father: **4** John
mother: **7** Susanna (Boylston)
siblings: **5** Elihu **13** Peter Boylston
wife: **7** Abigail (Smith)
children: **7** Charles, Susanna **10** John Quincy (6th president) **13** Abigail Amelia **14** Thomas Boylston

---

Adams, John Quincy
   nickname: 14 Old Man Eloquent
   presidential rank: 5 sixth
   party: 4 Whig **10** Federalist **20** Democratic-Republican
   state represented: 2 MA
   defeated: 4 (Henry) Clay **7** (Andrew) Jackson **8** (William H) Crawford
   vice president: 7 (John C) Calhoun
   cabinet:
      state: **4** (Henry) Clay
      treasury: **4** (Richard) Rush
      war: **6** (Peter Buell) Porter **7** (James) Barbour
      attorney general: **4** (William) Wirt
      navy: **8** (Samuel Lewis) Southard
   born: 2 MA **9** Braintree
      town now called: **6** Quincy
   died: 2 DC **10** Washington
   buried: 2 MA **6** Quincy
   education:
      studied in: **5** Paris **9** Amsterdam **11** Latin School
      University of: **6** Leyden
      College: **7** Harvard
   religion: 9 Unitarian
   author: 7 Memoirs **14** Eulogy to Monroe, The Adams Papers **17** Eulogy to Lafayette **18** Letters from Silesia
   political career: 8 US Senate **19** Massachusetts Senate **24** US House of Representatives
      secretary of: **5** state
      minister: **6** Russia **7** Prussia **8** Portugal **11** Netherlands **12** Great Britain
   civilian career: 6 lawyer
   notable events of lifetime/term: 19 Pan-American Congress **20** Tariff of Abominations
   father: 4 John
   mother: 7 Abigail (Smith)
   siblings: 7 Abigail, Charles, Susanna **14** Thomas Boylston
   wife: 6 Louisa (Catherine Johnson)
   children: 4 John **14** Charles Francis **15** Louisa Catherine **16** George Washington

---

12 over-and-above **13** supplementary

additional feature 5 extra **7** adjunct **10** attachment, complement, supplement **12** appurtenance **13** accompaniment

additive 5 extra **8** addition **10** adulterant, supplement **12** augmentation, preservative

addle 5 mix up **6** muddle **7** confuse, nonplus, stupefy **8** befuddle

addled 5 silly **7** foolish, mixed-up, muddled **8** confused **9** befuddled, nonplused **10** nonplussed

add on 5 affix **6** append, attach, tack on **7** include **10** increase by

address 4 talk **5** greet, orate **6** salute, speech, talk to **7** lecture, oration, speak to, write to **8** dwelling, locality, location **9** discourse, statement

Address to the Deil
   author: 11 Robert Burns

add to 6 expand, extend, pad out **7** amplify, augment, bolster, enlarge **8** compound, increase, lengthen **10** strengthen, stretch out, supplement

Ade, George
   author of: 13 Fables in Slang **15** The College Widow **17** The County Chairman

Aden
   capital of: 10 South Yemen

adept 3 apt **4** able, good **6** adroit, expert, gifted, master **7** skilled **8** skillful **9** dexterous, ingenious, masterful, practiced **10** proficient **12** accomplished

adequacy 7 fitness **11** sufficiency **16** satisfactoriness

adequate 3 fit **4** so-so **5** ample **6** enough **7** fitting **8** passa-ble, suitable **9** tolerable **10** sufficient **12** satisfactory

a deux 6 for two **10** two at a time

ad extremum 6 at last **7** finally **12** to the extreme

ad fin 8 at the end **12** toward the end

adhere 3 fix **4** glue, hold, keep **5** cling, paste, stick **6** be true, cement, cleave, fasten, glue on, keep to **7** abide by, be loyal, stand by **8** maintain **9** stick fast **10** be constant, be faithful

adherence 6 fealty **7** loyalty **8** adhesion, devotion, fidelity **9** constancy, keeping to, obedience **10** allegiance, attachment, observance, stickiness **12** adhesiveness, faithfulness

adherent 3 fan **4** ally **5** gummy, pupil **6** sticky, viscid **7** acolyte, devotee, viscous **8** adhering, adhesive, advocate, champion, clinging, disciple, follower, partisan, sticking, upholder **9** supporter

adhesion 9 adherence **10** attachment, sticking to

adhesive 4 glue **5** epoxy, gummy, paste **6** cement, gummed, mortar, solder, sticky **7** stickum **8** adherent, adhering, clinging, sticking **12** mucilaginous, rubber cement

ad hoc 17 with respect to this **18** for this purpose only

ad hominem 8 to the man **17** against an opponent **20** appealing to prejudice

adieu 4 by-by, ciao, ta-ta **5** adios, aloha **6** bye-bye, goodby, so long **7** a demain, cheerio, goodbye, good day **8** a bientot, au revoir, farewell, godspeed, toodle-oo **10** take it easy **11** leavetaking, see you later, valediction **14** Auf Wiedersehen

ad infinitum 9 endlessly **10** infinitely, to infinity, unendingly **11** boundlessly, ceaselessly, limitlessly, unceasingly **12** continuously, interminably, without limit

ad initium 14 at the beginning

ad interim 13 in the meantime

adios 4 by-by, ciao, ta-ta **5** adieu, aloha **6** bye-bye, goodby, so long **7** a demain, cheerio, goodbye, good day **8** a bientot, au revoir, fare-

well, godspeed, toodle-oo
10 take it easy 11 leavetaking,
see you later, valediction
14 Auf Wiedersehen

adjacency 5 union 7 contact,
meeting 8 abutment, junction,
touching 11 proximation
13 juxtaposition

adjacent 6 beside, next to
8 abutting, touching 9 bordering, proximate 10 contiguous,
juxtaposed, next door to, tan-
gential 12 conterminous

adjoining 6 joined 7 joining
8 next-door, touching 9 connected 10 contiguous 14 interconnected

adjourn 3 end 4 move 5 close
6 put off, recess, remove, repair 7 dismiss, suspend 8 break
off, dissolve, postpone, withdraw 9 depart for, interrupt
11 discontinue

adjournment 6 recess 7 removal 8 abeyance 9 dismissal
10 suspension 12 postponement

adjudge 4 rule 5 judge 6 decide, decree, ordain, rule on,
settle, umpire 7 referee 8 consider 9 arbitrate, determine,
pronounce 10 adjudicate

adjudicate 4 rule 5 judge
6 settle 7 adjudge 9 arbitrate

adjunct 9 accessory, auxiliary,
secondary 10 complement, incidental, subsidiary, supplement 12 appurtenance

adjuration 4 oath, plea, suit
6 appeal 8 advising, entreaty
12 supplication

adjure 3 beg 5 plead 6 charge,
enjoin, exhort 7 beseech, command, entreat, implore, solicit 8 appeal to, petition
9 importune 10 supplicate

adjust 3 fix, set 4 move
5 adapt, alter, order 6 attune,
change, modify 7 conform
8 accustom, regulate 9 acclimate, reconcile 11 accommodate

adjustable 7 movable 9 adaptable, alterable 11 rectifiable,
regulatable 12 controllable

adjusting 8 adapting, altering
9 modifying 10 regulating
11 acclimating, controlling

adjusting device 5 lever, tun-
er, valve 6 handle 7 adapter
8 governor 9 modulator, regulator 11 control knob

adjustment 6 fixing 7 control,
setting 8 adapting, focusing
9 adjusting, alignment, regula-

tor 10 alteration, regulating,
regulation, settlement, settling
in 11 acclimation, orientation
12 modification 13 justification, rectification, straightening 14 reconciliation

adjutant 4 aide 9 assistant,
right hand 10 aide-de-camp
12 right-hand man

ad-lib 6 make up 9 improvise
11 extemporize 13 improvisa-
tion 14 speak impromptu
15 speak off the cuff 21 speak
extemporaneously 23 extemporaneous wisecrack

ad loc, ad locum 10 at the
place, to the place

Admah
   destroyed with: 5 Sodom
   6 Zeboim 8 Gomorrah

ad majorem Dei gloriam
23 for the greater glory of
God

Admete
   father: 10 Eurystheus
   received: 12 golden girdle
      belonged to: 4 Ares
      received from: 8 Hercules
      stolen from: 9 Hippolyte

Admeto, Re di Tessaglia
   also: 21 Admetus King of
   Thessaly
   opera by: 6 Handel

Admetus
   king of: 8 Thessaly
   member of: 9 Argonauts
   father: 6 Pheres
   wife: 8 Alcestis

administer 3 run 4 boss, give
5 apply 6 direct, govern, manage, tender 7 oversee 8 dispense 9 supervise 11 preside
over, superintend 12 administrate

administering 7 bossing, running, tending 8 managing
9 directing, executing 10 dispensing, governance, overseeing 11 carrying out,
supervising, supervision
14 administration, superintending

administrate 3 run 6 direct,
govern, manage 9 supervise
10 administer 11 superintend

administration 5 brass 8 officers 9 execution, governing,
tendering 10 executives, government, leadership, management, overseeing
11 application 12 dispensation,
distribution 13 administering,
governing body 15 superintendence

administrative 9 executive
10 management, managerial

11 supervisory 14 organizational

administrative head 7 manager 8 chairman, director
9 executive, president 10 supervisor 13 administrator
14 superintendent

admirable 6 worthy 8 laudable 9 estimable, venerable
11 commendable 12 praise-
worthy

Admirable Crichton, The
   author: 12 James M Barrie

admiration 5 honor 6 esteem,
praise 7 respect 8 approval
10 high regard, veneration
11 high opinion 12 commendation

admire 5 prize, value 6 esteem,
praise 7 respect

admirer 3 fan 5 swain 6 suitor,
votary 7 acolyte, devotee
8 adherent, advocate, champion, disciple, follower, partisan 9 attendant 10 aficionado

admissible 7 allowed 8 passable 9 allowable, permitted, tolerable, tolerated 10 acceptable,
admittable, legitimate 11 permissible

admission 3 fee 5 entry 6 access, assent, charge, entree,
tariff, ticket 8 entrance 10 admittance, concession, confession, profession 11 affirmation,
declaration, entrance fee
14 acknowledgment

admit 3 let 5 allow, grant, let
in, own up 6 induct, invest,
permit 7 appoint, concede,
confess, declare, profess, receive, welcome 8 let enter
11 acknowledge

admittable 7 allowed 9 allowable, permitted, tolerable, tolerated 10 acceptable,
admissible 11 permissible

admittance 5 entry 6 access,
entree 7 ingress 8 entrance
9 admission

admixture 4 mess 5 blend
6 jumble, medley 7 amalgam,
melange, mixture 8 compound,
mishmash 9 composite, confusion, potpourri 10 commixture, hodgepodge, salmagundi
11 combination, commingling,
gallimaufry 12 amalgamation,
intermixture 13 intermingling
14 conglomeration

admonish 4 warn 5 chide,
scold 6 advise, enjoin, rebuke,
tip off 7 caution, censure,
chasten, counsel, reprove, upbraid 8 reproach 9 criticize,
reprimand 10 put on guard,

take to task **11** remonstrate **13** call to account **16** rap on the knuckles

admonition 6 advice, rebuke **7** chiding, warning **8** reproach, scolding **9** reprimand **11** mild reproof **12** remonstrance **16** rap on the knuckles

admonitor 7 advisor **9** counselor **10** admonisher

Adnah
deserted from: **4** Saul
deserted to: **5** David
fought against:
10 Amalekites
commander for:
10 Jehosaphat

ado 4 fuss, stir, to-do **5** furor **6** bother, bustle, flurry, fracas, furore, hubbub, pother, racket, tumult, uproar **7** flutter, trouble, turmoil **9** agitation, commotion, confusion **10** hurlyburly

adobe 3 mud **4** clay, silt, tile **5** brick, marly **6** earthy **7** clayish **13** sun-dried brick

adolescence 5 teens, youth **7** puberty **10** pubescence

adolescent 3 lad **4** lass, teen **5** minor, youth **6** boyish, callow, lassie **7** babyish, girlish, puerile **8** childish, immature, juvenile, teenager, young man, youthful **9** fledgling, pubescent, schoolboy, stripling, young teen **10** schoolgirl, sophomoric, young woman **11** undeveloped

Adolf Hitler 9 der Fuhrer **10** der Fuehrer

Adonai 3 God **6** my Lord

Adonia
event: **8** festival
honors: **6** Adonis

Adonijah
father: **5** David
mother: **7** Haggith
brother: **5** Amnon **7** Absalom, Chileab
executed by: **7** Solomon
conspired to overthrow:
5 David

Adonis
represents: **15** vegetation cycle
father: **7** Cinyras
mother: **6** Myrrha, Smyrna
favorite of: **9** Aphrodite
killed by: **4** boar
festival in honor of:
6 Adonia

adopt 3 use **4** take **6** accept, affect, assume, choose, employ, follow, take up **7** approve, embrace, espouse, utilize **9** con-

form to **11** acknowledge, appropriate

adorable 6 divine **7** darling, likable, lovable, winsome **8** charming, engaging, fetching, pleasing, precious **9** appealing **10** delightful **11** captivating **12** irresistible

adoration 5 honor **7** worship **8** devotion **9** adulation, reverence **10** exaltation, veneration, worshiping **11** idolization **13** glorification, magnification

adore 4 like, love **5** exalt, fancy, prize **6** admire, dote on, revere **7** cherish, glorify, idolize, worship **8** hold dear, venerate

adorer 3 fan **5** lover **7** admirer **8** follower **9** worshiper

adorn 5 array **6** bedeck **7** bejewel, deck out, furbish **8** beautify, decorate, ornament **9** embellish

adornment 6 attire, finery **7** jewelry **8** ornament **10** decoration **13** embellishment, ornamentation

ad patres 4 dead

Adrammelech 13 Sepharvite god
father: **11** Sennacherib
killed: **11** Sennacherib

Adrastea
also: **7** Nemesis
origin: **5** Greek
goddess of: **17** divine retribution
father: **9** Melisseus
reared: **4** Zeus
entrusted by: **4** Rhea

Adrastos see **8** Adrastus

Adrastus
also: **8** Adrastos
king of: **5** Argos
son: **8** Aegialus
leader of: **18** Seven against Thebes
companions: **6** Tydeus **8** Capaneus **9** Polynices **10** Amphiaraus, Hippomedon **13** Parthenopaeus
horse: **5** Arion

ad rem 9 pertinent **15** straightforward **17** without digression

Adrian, Edgar Douglas
field: **8** medicine **10** physiology
nationality: **7** British
discovered function of:
10 nerve cells
awarded: **10** Nobel Prize

Adriana
character in: **17** The Comedy of Errors
author: **11** Shakespeare

adrift 4 lost **5** at sea **6** afloat, aweigh **8** confused, drifting, unmoored, unstable **9** perplexed, uncertain, unsettled **10** bewildered, irresolute, unanchored

adroit 3 apt **4** deft **5** slick **6** artful, clever, expert, facile, nimble **7** cunning, skilled **8** skillful **9** dexterous, masterful **10** proficient

adroitness 7 aptness **8** deftness, facility **9** dexterity, handiness **10** cleverness **11** proficiency **12** skillfulness
French: **11** savoir-faire

adulation 7 fawning **8** flattery **9** adoration **11** fulsomeness **13** fulsome praise

adulatory 7 fulsome **8** admiring **10** flattering **13** complimentary

adult 3 big, man **5** elder, of age, woman **6** father, granny, mature, mother, parent, senior **7** grandma, grandpa, grownup, oldster **8** seasoned **9** developed, full-grown **11** experienced, grandfather, grandmother **13** senior citizen

adulterate 3 cut **4** thin **5** water **9** water down **10** depreciate **11** contaminate

adulterated 3 cut **6** impure, watery **7** debased, diluted, thinned, watered **8** doctored, weakened **11** watered down

adultery 9 carnality, cuckoldry **10** unchastity **11** fornication, promiscuity **14** unfaithfulness **17** marital infidelity **18** illicit intercourse **21** extramarital relations

adulthood 8 maturity, ripeness **10** full growth **11** age of reason

adumbrate 3 dim **6** darken, sketch **7** obscure, outline **8** intimate **9** prefigure **10** foreshadow, overshadow

adumbrated 3 dim **5** murky **7** shadowy **8** darkened **9** intimated **10** indistinct, prefigured **12** foreshadowed, overshadowed

advance 3 pre **4** gain, pass, step **5** add to, offer, prior **6** assign, binder, growth, move up, pay now, propel, send up **7** bring up, forward, further, improve, in front, lay down, press on, proffer, promote, upgrade, up front **8** foremost, increase, multiply, overture, previous, progress **9** go forward, promotion **10** furthering, move onward, prepayment, put up front

11 advancement, down payment, improvement, preliminary, proposition
12 breakthrough, bring forward, pay on account

advanced **7** extreme, far gone, radical **10** avant-guard **12** farther along, further along **14** industrialized

advanced in years **3** old **4** aged **5** hoary, older **7** ancient, antique, elderly **8** outmoded **9** senescent, venerable **10** antiquated, gray-haired

advancement **4** rise **5** boost **9** bettering, elevation, promotion **10** betterment, forwarding **11** improvement, progression

Advancement of Learning
author: **12** Francis Bacon

advance slowly **4** inch **5** crawl, creep

advantage **3** aid **4** boon, edge, help **5** asset, clout **6** profit **7** benefit, comfort, service, success, support **8** blessing **9** dominance, upper hand **10** precedence **11** convenience, superiority

advantageous **6** useful **7** helpful **8** enviable, superior, valuable **9** favorable, fortunate **10** auspicious, beneficial, dominating, profitable

advent **5** onset, start **6** coming **7** arrival **9** appearing, beginning, emergence, opening up **10** appearance, occurrence **12** commencement

adventitious **5** alien **6** exotic **7** foreign, strange **9** adventive, extrinsic **10** accidental

adventure **5** quest **7** emprise, venture **8** escapade **10** enterprise **11** undertaking

adventurer **4** hero **7** heroine **8** romantic, vagabond **9** buccaneer, daredevil **11** giant-killer **12** dragonslayer, swashbuckler **16** soldier of fortune

Adventures of Robin Hood, The
director: **13** Michael Curtiz **15** William Keighley
cast: **8** Alan Hale (Little John) **10** Errol Flynn (Robin Hood) **11** Claude Rains (Prince John) **13** Basil Rathbone **17** Olivia de Havilland (Lady Marion)
Oscar for: **5** score (Erich Wolfgang Korngold)

Adventures of Sherlock Holmes
author: **16** (Sir) Arthur Conan Doyle

character: **9** Mrs Hudson **10** Irene Adler **12** Dr John Watson **13** Mycroft Holmes **14** Sherlock Holmes **17** Inspector Lestrade, Professor Moriarty **21** Baker Street Irregulars

adventuresome **4** bold **6** daring **9** audacious, daredevil **11** adventurous

adventurous **4** bold **5** brave, risky **6** daring **7** valiant **8** intrepid, perilous **9** audacious, dangerous, hazardous **10** courageous **11** challenging, venturesome

adventurousness **6** daring **8** audacity, boldness **11** intrepidity

ad verbum **8** verbatim **9** to the word

adversary **3** foe **5** enemy, rival **8** opponent **10** antagonist, competitor

adverse **7** harmful, hostile **8** contrary, inimical, negative, opposing **9** difficult, injurious **10** pernicious, unfriendly **11** detrimental, unfavorable **12** antagonistic, unpropitious

adversity **3** woe **5** trial **6** mishap **7** bad luck, trouble **8** calamity, disaster, distress, hardship **9** suffering **10** affliction, ill-fortune, misfortune **11** catastrophe, tribulation

advertise **4** show, tout **5** vaunt **6** reveal **7** display **8** proclaim **9** broadcast, publicize **11** noise abroad

advertisement **5** blurb, flier, pitch, promo **6** notice, poster, want ad **7** leaflet, placard, trailer **8** circular, handbill **9** billboard, broadside, throwaway **10** commercial **12** announcement, classified ad, public notice

advice **4** news, view, word **6** report **7** account, counsel, message, opinion, tidings **8** guidance **10** advisement, suggestion **11** information **12** intelligence, notification **13** communication **14** recommendation

advisable **3** fit **4** best, wise **5** smart, sound **6** proper, seemly **7** fitting, prudent **8** a good bet, suitable **9** expedient, judicious **13** recommendable

advise **4** tell, urge, warn **6** enjoin, exhort, inform, notify, report **7** apprise, caution, commend, counsel, suggest **8** admonish **9** encourage, make known, recommend, suggest

to **10** give notice **11** communicate

advise against **8** dissuade **10** discourage, disincline

advisement **5** study **7** thought **12** deliberation **13** consideration

adviser, advisor **4** aide **5** coach, guide, tutor **6** mentor **7** monitor, teacher **8** director **9** admonitor, assistant, counselor, preceptor, surrogate **10** consultant, idea person, instructor

advisory **7** guiding, warning **10** admonitory, cautionary, counseling **11** informative, instructive **12** consultative, consultatory **13** informational

advisory board **7** cabinet, council **8** ministry

advocaat
type: **7** liqueur
origin: **7** Holland

advocacy **5** aegis **7** backing, defense, support **8** auspices, espousal **9** patronage, promotion **10** furthering, supporting **11** advancement, endorsement, pressing for, propagation, sponsorship **12** championship **14** campaigning for, recommendation

advocate **4** back, urge **5** favor **6** advise, backer, lawyer, patron **7** advance, apostle, counsel, endorse, espouse, further, pleader, promote, propose, push for, support **8** argue for, attorney, believer, champion, defender, press for, promoter, upholder **9** apologist, barrister, counselor, encourage, prescribe, propagate, proponent, recommend, solicitor, spokesman, supporter **10** mouthpiece, stand up for **11** campaign for, speak out for **12** legal adviser, propagandist, spokesperson **13** attorney-at-law

advocatus diaboli **14** devil's advocate

adz **2** ax **3** axe **5** addis **7** hatchet

Aeacides
descendants of: **6** Aeacus

Aeacus
form: **5** judge
habitat: **5** Hades
father: **4** Zeus
mother: **6** Aegina
brother: **12** Rhadamanthys
wife: **6** Endeis
son: **6** Peleus, Phocus **7** Telamon
grandson: **8** Achilles

Aechmagoras
father: 8 Hercules
mother: 6 Phialo

Aedon
father: 9 Pandareus
sister: 8 Chelidon
husband: 11 Polytechnus
transformed into:
11 nightingale
transformed by: 4 Zeus

Aeetes
king of: 7 Colchis
custodian of: 12 Golden
Fleece
father: 6 Helios
mother: 5 Perse
sister: 5 Circe 8 Pasiphae
wife: 5 Idyia 9 Asterodea
son: 8 Absyrtus, Apsyrtus
daughter: 5 Medea
9 Chalciope

Aegaeon *see* 8 Briareus

Aegean Sea
branch of: 13 Mediterranean
islands: 5 Chios, Crete, Samos 6 Euboea, Lesbos,
Rhodes 8 Cyclades 10 Dodecanese 16 Northern Sporades
rivers into: 6 Struma, Vardar 7 Maritsa 8 Menderes
surrounding countries:
6 Greece, Turkey

Aegeon
character in: 17 The Comedy
of Errors
author: 11 Shakespeare

Aegeria *see* 6 Egeria

Aegesta *see* 6 Egesta

Aegeus
king of: 6 Athens
son: 6 Medeus 7 Theseus

Aegialeus
father: 8 Adrastus
killed by: 8 Laodamas

Aegicores
father: 3 Ion

Aegimius
king of: 5 Doris 7 Dorians
father: 5 Dorus
son: 5 Dymas 9 Pamphylus

Aegina
father: 6 Asopus
mother: 6 Metope
son: 6 Aeacus
abducted by: 4 Zeus

Aeginaea
epithet of: 7 Artemis
means: 11 goat goddess

Aegiochus
epithet of: 4 Zeus
means: 11 aegis bearer

Aegipan
form: 3 god 4 goat
related to: 3 Pan

Aegir
origin: 6 Nordic
form: 5 giant
god of: 3 sea
wife: 3 Ran

aegis 4 wing 5 favor, guard
6 surety 7 backing, shelter,
support 8 advocacy, auspices,
guaranty 9 patronage 10 protection 11 sponsorship
12 championship, guardianship

Aegis
form: 6 shield
shield of: 4 Zeus 6 Athena

Aegisthus
father: 8 Thyestes
mother: 7 Pelopia
cousin: 9 Agamemnon
daughter: 7 Erigone
seduced: 12 Clytemnestra
killed by: 7 Orestes

Aegle
member of: 8 Heliades
10 Hesperides
mother of: 6 Graces

Aegyptus
king of: 5 Egypt
father: 5 Belus
twin brother: 6 Danaus
number of sons: 5 fifty

Aella
form: 6 Amazon
gift: 9 swiftness
killed by: 8 Hercules

Aello
member of: 7 Harpies

aelurophobia
fear of: 4 cats

Aemilia
character in: 17 The Comedy
of Errors
author: 11 Shakespeare

Aeneas
hero of: 4 Troy
father: 8 Anchises
mother: 5 Venus
grandfather: 5 Capys
son: 5 Iulus 7 Silvius
8 Ascanius
ancestor of: 6 Romans

Aeneas Silvius
king of: 9 Alba Longa

Aeneid
author: 6 Virgil
character: 4 Gyas 5 Amata,
Dares, Nisus 6 Arruns, Iar-
bas, Lausus, Pallas, Salius,
Turnus 7 Acestes, Allecto,
Camilla, Celaeno, Drances,
Evander, Harpies, Helenus,
Juturna, Latinus, Lavinia,
Tarchon, Trojans, Venulus,
Virbius 8 Ascanius, Entellus,
Euryalus, Messapus 9 Cloan-
thus, Mezentius, Mnestheus,
Palinurus, Sergestus 10 An-
dromache 12 Cumaean Sibyl
gods: 4 Juno 5 Diana, Ve-
nus 6 Vulcan 7 Jupiter,
Neptune
Queen of Carthage:
4 Dido
Aeneas' father: 8 Anchises
Aeneas' mother:
9 Aphrodite
Aeneas' wife: 6 Creusa
Aeneas' son: 5 Iulus
*Aeneas meets in under-
world:* 6 Charon 8 Cer-
berus 9 Palinurus
parts of the underworld:
7 Elysium 8 Tartarus 9 Ivory
Gate
river: 4 Styx 5 Lethe
Aeneas plucks: 11 Golden
Bough
Aeneas visits: 5 Crete, Delos
6 Latium, Sicily, Thrace
8 Carthage

Aenius
ally of: 4 Troy
killed by: 8 Achilles

Aeolides
descendants of: 6 Aeolus

Aeolus
ruler of: 5 winds
founder of: 8 Aeolians
father: 6 Hellen
mother: 6 Orseis
brother: 5 Dorus 6 Xuthus
wife: 7 Enarete
son: 5 Deion 6 Magnes
7 Athamas, Misenus 8 Cre-
theus, Macareus, Perieres,
Sisyphus 9 Salmoneus
daughter: 6 Calyce, Canace
7 Alcyone 8 Cleobule, Perimede, Pisidice

aerate 3 air 9 ventilate 10 mix
with air 11 expose to air

aerial 3 air 4 airy 5 by air,
lofty 6 dreamy, flying, unreal
7 antenna, elusive, soaring,
tenuous 8 airborne, ethereal,
fanciful, in the air 9 ephemeral, imaginary, visionary
10 by aircraft, from the air, of
aircraft 11 atmospheric, impractical, wind-created 13 unsubstantial 15 capable of flight

aerobatic group 10 Blue
Angels

aeronautics 6 flight, flying
8 aviation

Aerope
father: 7 Catreus, Cerheus
husband: 6 Atreus
10 Plisthenes
sister: 9 Clymene
son: 8 Menelaus
9 Agamemnon

aerophobia
fear of: 6 flying

aeroplane 5 plane 8 aircraft, airplane

Aesacus
  father: 5 Priam
  lover: 8 Hesperia

Aeschylus
  author of: 8 Oresteia 9 Agamemnon, Choephori (The Libation-bearers), Eumenides 11 The Persians 13 The Suppliants 15 Prometheus Bound 16 The House of Atreus 18 Seven Against Thebes

Aesculapius
  origin: 5 Roman
  god of: 7 healing 8 medicine
  corresponds to: 9 Asclepius

Aesepus
  mother: 9 Abarbarea
  twin brother: 7 Pedasus
  fought in: 9 Trojan War
  killed by: 8 Euryalus

Aesir
  also: 4 Asar
  origin: 12 Scandinavian
  leader: 4 Odin 5 Othin
  home: 6 Asgard
  conflicting with: 5 Vanir

aesthetic see 8 Esthetic

Aesyetes
  son: 7 Antenor

Aethalides
  member of: 9 Argonauts
  father: 6 Hermes
  trait: 6 memory

Aether
  origin: 5 Greek
  personifies: 3 air, sky

Aetheria
  member of: 8 Heliades
  father: 6 Helius
  mother: 7 Clymene

Aethra
  father: 8 Pittheus
  son: 7 Theseus

Aethylla
  brother: 5 Priam

Aetolus
  founder of: 7 Aetolia
  father: 8 Endymion
  brother: 5 Epeus, Paeon
  wife: 6 Pronoe
  son: 7 Calydon, Pleuron
  killed: 8 Laodocus

Afars and the Issas see 8 Djibouti

affability 9 geniality 10 amiability, cordiality 11 sociability 12 friendliness, pleasantness 13 compatibility

affable 4 open, warm 5 civil 6 genial 7 amiable, cordial 8 friendly, gracious, mannerly, pleasant, sociable 9 agreeable, congenial, courteous, easygoing 10 compatible 11 good-humored, good-natured

affair 5 amour, event, party 6 effort, matter 7 concern, episode, liaison, pursuit, romance, shindig 8 activity, business, function, incident, interest, intrigue, occasion 9 adventure, festivity, happening, operation 10 love affair, occurrence, proceeding 11 celebration, transaction, undertaking 12 circumstance, relationship 14 social function 15 social gathering

affaire d'honneur 4 duel 13 affair of honor

affect 4 fake, move, stir 5 act on, adopt, alter, fancy, feign, put on, touch 6 assume, change, modify, regard 7 embrace, concern, imitate, impress 8 interest, relate to, simulate 9 impinge on, influence, pertain to, pretend to 10 tend toward 11 counterfeit

affectation 4 airs, sham 5 put-on 6 facade 8 false air, pretense 10 pretension 11 insincerity 13 artificiality, false mannerism

affected 4 vain 5 moved, phony, sorry, upset 6 harmed, unreal 7 assumed, changed, grieved, injured, pompous, stirred, studied, touched 8 impaired, mannered, troubled 9 acted upon, afflicted, concerned, conceited, contrived, impressed, pertinent, sorrowful, unnatural 10 artificial, distressed, influenced, interested, not genuine 11 pretentious 12 vainglorious

affectedness 4 airs 7 hauteur, tension 9 formality 10 constraint 11 haughtiness, pretensions 12 affectations 15 pretentiousness

affection 4 love 6 liking, malady, warmth 7 ailment, disease, illness 8 disorder, fondness, sickness 10 proclivity, tenderness

affectionate 4 fond, warm 6 ardent, caring, doting, loving, tender 11 warmhearted 13 demonstrative, tenderhearted

affectionate term 7 pet name 8 nickname 9 sobriquet 10 endearment

Affery
  character in: 12 Little Dorrit
  author: 7 Dickens

affettuoso
  music: 8 tenderly

affiance 6 engage, pledge 7 betroth 13 engage to marry 15 solemnly promise

affiancing 5 troth 8 pledging 9 betrothal 10 engagement

affiche 6 poster 12 public notice

affidavit 4 oath 8 document 11 affirmation 14 sworn statement

affiliate 3 arm 4 ally, join, part 5 merge, unite 6 branch 7 chapter, connect, consort 8 division 9 associate, colleague 10 amalgamate, fraternize 11 incorporate, subdivision 12 band together

affiliated 6 allied, joined, united 9 connected 10 associated 12 incorporated

affiliation 5 union 8 alliance 10 connection 11 association 12 relationship

affinity 4 bent 5 fancy 6 liking 7 leaning, rapport 8 fondness, homology, likeness, penchant, relation, sympathy, tendency 10 connection, partiality, proclivity, propensity, similarity 11 inclination, parallelism 13 compatibility

affirm 4 aver, avow, hold 5 claim 6 allege, assert, ratify, uphold 7 approve, confirm, contend, declare, endorse, profess, support, sustain, warrant 8 maintain, proclaim, validate

affirmation 6 avowal 7 consent 8 approval 11 declaration, endorsement 12 confirmation, ratification 13 certification

affirmative 3 yes 8 emphatic, positive 9 affirming, approving, assenting, ratifying 10 conclusive, concurring, confirming 11 affirmatory, categorical 12 confirmatory 13 corroborative

affix 3 fix, tag 4 glue, seal 5 add on, paste, put on, set to, stick 6 attach, fasten, tack on

afflict 5 beset 6 plague 7 oppress, torment 8 distress

afflicted 6 cursed 7 plagued 8 affected, troubled 9 tormented 10 distressed

affliction 4 pain 5 curse, trial 6 misery, ordeal 7 anguish, torment, trouble 8 calamity, distress, hardship 9 adversity 10 misfortune, oppression 11 tribulation 12 wretchedness

affluence 5 money 6 plenty, riches, wealth 7 success 10 prosperity 14 prosperousness, successfulness

affluent 4 rich 6 loaded
7 moneyed, wealthy, well-off
8 well-to-do 9 well-fixed
10 prosperous, well-heeled

afford 4 bear, give, lend, risk
5 grant, offer, yield 6 chance,
impart, manage, supply
7 command, furnish, provide,
support, sustain

affray 4 fray 5 brawl, melee
6 fracas 7 contest, scuffle
8 conflict 9 encounter
11 altercation

affright 4 fear 5 alarm, dread,
panic, scare 6 dismay, fright,
horror, terror 8 frighten

affront 4 slur 5 abuse, wrong
6 injury, insult, offend, slight
7 offense, outrage, provoke,
put-down 8 disgrace, dishonor,
ignominy, rudeness 9 indignity, insolence 11 discourtesy,
humiliation 12 ill-treatment,
impertinence 13 mortification
16 contemptuousness

afghan 5 shawl, throw 7 blanket 8 covering, coverlet

Afghanistan *see box*

aficionado 3 fan, nut 5 freak,
pupil 7 devotee, pursuer, student 8 disciple

afield 5 amiss 6 abroad, astray
10 off the mark 11 out of the
way 16 off the right track

afire 5 fiery 6 ablaze, aflame,
alight, ardent, fervid, fuming,
on fire 7 blazing, burning, fervent, flaming, flaring, glowing,
ignited, smoking, zealous
8 aflicker, in flames, inspired
10 flickering, smoldering

afloat 5 at sea 6 adrift, wafted
7 sailing, wafting 8 drifting,
floating

afoot 5 astir 8 underway 10 in
the works

a fortiori 10 all the more

afraid 5 sorry 6 scared
7 alarmed, anxious, chicken,
fearful, panicky, unhappy
8 cowardly, timorous 9 regretful, terrified 10 apologetic,
frightened 11 lily-livered
12 apprehensive, disappointed,
fainthearted 13 anxiety-ridden,
panic-stricken 14 chicken-
hearted, chicken-livered, terror-stricken

Afreet
  also: 5 Afrit
  origin: 7 Arabian
  form: 5 demon

afresh 4 anew 5 again 11 from
scratch 16 from the beginning
  Latin: 6 de novo

Africa *see box*
Africaine, L'
  also: 14 The African Girl
  opera by: 9 Meyerbeer

African Queen, The
  director: 10 John Huston

  cast: 12 Robert Morley
  14 Humphrey Bogart
  16 Katharine Hepburn
  setting: 5 Congo
  Oscar for: 5 actor (Bogart)

Afrit *see* 6 Afreet

Afghanistan
  other name: 6 Ariana, Aryana
  capital/largest city: 5 Kabul
  others: 3 Rui 4 Jurm, Nani, Wama 5 Asmar, Balkh, Doshi,
  Farah, Herat, Kunar, Makur, Maruf, Matun, Pahra,
  Tagab, Tulak, Urgan 6 Chaman, Gardez, Ghazni, Haibak,
  Kunduz, Nauzad, Panjao, Rustak, Sangan, Sarobi, Tukzar,
  Washir 7 Andkhui, Baghlan, Bamiyan, Dilaram, Ghurian,
  Girishk 8 Charikar, Faizabad, Kandahar 9 Jalalabad
  10 Daulatabad, Pul-i-Khumri, Shibarghan 12 Mazar-i-
  Sharif
  government:
    parliament: 10 Loya-Jirgah
  leader: 4 amir, emir 5 ameer, emeer 6 sharif, sherif
  measure: 3 paw, sir 5 jerib, karoh 6 khurds 7 kharwar
  monetary unit: 3 pul 5 abaze, riyal, rupee 6 abbasi,
  amania 7 afghani
  weight: 3 pau, paw, ser, sir
  lake: 13 Hamud-i-Helmand
  mountain: 3 Koh 5 Safeo 6 Chagai, Pamirs 7 Nowshak
  8 Koh-i-Baba, Safed Koh, Sulaiman 9 Himalayas, Hindu
  Kush 11 Khwaja Amran, Paropamisus
  highest point: 9 Istoro Nal
  river: 4 Lora, Oxus 5 Cabul, Indus, Kabul, Kunar 6 Kok-
  cha, Kunduz 7 Hari Rud, Helmand, Helmund, Murghab,
  Taleqan 8 Amu Darya, Farah Rud, Harut Rud, Khash
  Rud 9 Arghandab
  sea: 5 Darya
  physical feature:
    desert: 8 Registan
    panhandle: 6 Wakhan
    pass: 6 Khyber
    wind: 9 Afghanets
  people: 5 Aimak, Aymak, Kafir, Nuris 6 Baloch, Baluch,
  Chahar, Durani, Hasara, Hazara, Kaffir, Kirgiz, Pathan,
  Tajiks, Uzbeks 7 Beluchi, Belucki, Ghilzai, Pakhton, Pakhtun, Pashtun, Pukhtun, Pushtun, Sistani, Taimani, Taimuri 8 Jamshidi, Siah Push 9 Firuzkuhi, Safed Push,
  Safid Push
    dynasty: 8 Barakzai
    leader: 5 Najib 7 Mohmand 10 Najibullah 12 Babrak
    Karmal 14 Hafizullah Amin 17 Mohammad Zahir Shah,
    Mohammed Daoud Khan 18 Burhanuddin Rabbani
    Noor Mohammed Taraki
  language: 5 Dari 5 Farsi 6 Afghan, Pashto, Pushtu 7 Balochi, Baluchi, Persian
  religion: 5 Islam
  place:
    dam: 6 Boghra 7 Kajakai 9 Arghandab
  feature:
    clothing: 7 chaderi
    coat: 6 chapan
    dance: 5 attan
    game: 8 buz-kashi
    guest room: 5 hujra
    hat: 7 karakul
    head-cloth: 7 chawdar
    house with tower: 4 qala
    medicinal plant: 9 asafetida
    wrestling: 6 ghosai
  food:
    potluck meal: 6 sohbat

Africa
  country: 4 Chad, Mali, Togo **5** Benin, Congo, Egypt, Gabon, Ghana, Kenya, Libya, Niger, Sudan, Zaire **6** Angola, Gambia, Guinea, Malawi, Rwanda, Uganda, Zambia **7** Algeria, Burundi, Comoros, Eritrea, Lesotho, Liberia, Morocco, Namibia, Nigeria, Reunion, Senegal, Somalia, Tunisia **8** Botswana, Cameroon, Djibouti, Ethiopia, Tanzania, Zimbabwe **9** Cape Verde, The Gambia, Mauritius, Swaziland **10** Ivory Coast, Madagascar, Mauritania, Mozambique, Seychelles **11** Burkina Faso, Sierra Leone, South Africa **12** Guinea-Bissau **13** Canary Islands, Western Sahara **15** South-West Africa **16** Equatorial Guinea **18** Sao Tome and Principe **22** Central African Republic
  people: 2 Ga **3** Ibo, Kru, Luo, San, Tiv, Yao **4** Arab, Beja, Bobo, Boer, Fang, Hutu, Kota, Kuba, Luba, Nuba, Nuer, Nupe, Teda, Tibu, Zulu **5** Bemba, Dinka, Galla, Hausa, Kamba, Makua, Masai, Mende, Mongo, Negro, Pygmy, Rundi, Serer, Shona, Sotho, Swazi, Temne, Tigre, Tutsi, Wolof, Xhosa **6** Bateke, Berber, Fulani, Herero, Ibibjo, Kikuyu, Mau Mau, Nubian, Ovambo, Rwanda, Senufo, Sidamo, Somali, Tswana, Tuareg, Yoruba, Watusi **7** Ashanti, Baganda, Bambara, Bushmen, Chaamba, Makonde, Mashoma, Ndebele, Nilotic, Oshogbo, Songhai, Turkana **8** Khoikhoi, Mangbetu, Matabele **9** Africaner, Hottentot
  desert: 5 Namib **6** Sahara **8** Kalahari
  island: 5 Bioko, Pemba **6** Canary **7** Comoros, Madeira, Mayotte, Reunion **8** St Helena, Zanzibar **9** Ascension, Cape Verde, Mauritius **10** Madagascar, Seychelles
  ancient people/empire: 3 Oyo **4** Kush, Mali, Toro **5** Aksum, Benin, Ghana, Kongo, Mossi, Nubia, Wadai **6** Ankole, Tekrur **7** Ashanti, Buganda, Bunyoro, Dahomey, Songhai **8** Baguirmi, Carthage **10** Kanem-Bornu, Monomotapa **11** Ife and Benin
  ancient city: 5 Kilwa, Meroe **8** Timbuktu
  language: 4 Afar, Peul, Teda **5** Bantu, Bemba, Click, Hausa, Masai, Wolof **6** Arabic, Berber, French, Kanuri, Tsonga **7** Amharic, Khoisan, Lingala, Nilotic, Songhai, Swahili, Turkana **8** Cushitic, Mandingo **9** Afrikaans
  river: 4 Juba, Nile, Sudd **5** Congo, Kasai, Niger **6** Kwango, Orange, Ubangi **7** Senegal, Zambezi **8** Blue Nile **9** White Nile
  lake: 4 Chad, Kivu, Tana **5** Assal, Nyasa **6** Albert, Edward, Kariba, Malawi, Nassar, Red Sea, Rudolf **8** Victoria **10** Tanganyika **12** Chott Melrhir
  falls: 8 Victoria
  mountain/mountain range: 3 Air **4** Bihu, Meru **5** Atlas, Elgon, Kenya **6** Hoggar **7** Ahaggar, Crystal, Tibesti, Toubkal **8** Cameroon **9** Emi Koussi, Munchinga, Ruwenzori **10** Futa Jallon **11** Drakensberg, Kilimanjaro **13** Tibesti Massif
  lowest point: 17 Qattari Depression
  mineral/natural resource: 3 oil, tin **4** gold **5** ivory **6** cloves, copper, rubber **7** diamond, palm oil, uranium
  disease: 4 AIDS **7** malaria **9** bilharzia **11** yellow fever **16** sleeping sickness
  homeland: 4 Venda **6** Ciskei **8** Transkei **14** Bophuthatswana
  game reserve: 5 Tsavo **6** Kruger **8** Amboseli **9** Serengeti
  tree: 4 cork, teak **5** cedar, ebony, olive **6** acacia, baobab, okoume, rubber **7** juniper, oil palm **8** date palm, mahogany, tamarisk **10** silk-cotton
  animal: 4 lion **5** bongo, hippo, hyena, zebra **6** jackal, monkey **7** buffalo, cheetah, giraffe, gorilla, leopard, wild pig **8** aardvark, antelope, elephant **9** crocodile **10** chimpanzee, rhinoceros **11** wildebeeste **12** hippopotamus
  bird: 5 heron, stork **6** falcon **7** bustard, ostrich, pelican **8** flamingo, hornbill **10** kingfisher
  fly: 6 tsetse
  snake: 5 cobra, mamba **6** python

after 4 next, post **5** later **6** behind **9** afterward, following **10** conclusion, subsequent, succeeding

aftereffect 6 result **11** consequence

After Hours
  director: 14 Martin Scorsese
  cast: 12 Griffin Dunne **15** Rosanna Arquette

Afterlife
  god of: 4 Gwyn

aftermath 6 payoff, result, sequel, upshot **7** outcome **8** follow-up, offshoot **9** byproduct **11** consequence

afterpart 4 back, tail **6** far end **7** back end, rear end, tail end **8** backside, hind part **9** posterior

after the fact 4 late **5** tardy **7** belated, delayed, too late **10** behindhand, behind time

After the Fall
  author: 12 Arthur Miller

after this, therefore because of it
  Latin: 21 post hoc ergo propter hoc
  describes: 14 logical fallacy

afterword 4 coda **8** addendum, epilogue **10** conclusion

Agacles
  king of: 9 Myrmidons

Agag
  king of: 10 Amalekites
  captured by: 4 Saul
  killed by: 6 Samuel

again 4 also, anew, more **7** besides **8** moreover, once more **10** in addition, repetition **11** another time, duplication, furthermore **12** additionally **Latin: 6** de novo

against 7 adverse, opposed **8** conflict, contrary, opposite **10** opposition **11** unfavorable

against an opponent
  Latin: 9 ad hominem

Against Our Will
   author: **16** Susan Brownmiller

against the property
   Latin: **5** in rem
   describes: **15** legal proceeding

against the thing
   Latin: **5** in rem

Agamede
   father: **6** Augeas
   husband: **6** Mulius
   gift: **7** healing
   healed with: **5** herbs

Agamemnon
   author: **9** Aeschylus
   mentioned in: **5** Iliad
   king of: **7** Mycenae
   leader of: **6** Greeks
   fought in: **9** Trojan War
   father: **6** Atreus
   brother: **8** Menelaus
   sister: **8** Anaxibia
   wife: **12** Clytemnestra
   daughter: **7** Electra **9** Iphigenia **12** Chrysothemis
   son: **7** Orestes
   cousin: **9** Aegisthus
   captive: **9** Cassandra
   Clytemnestra's lover: **9** Aegisthus
   killed by: **12** Clytemnestra

Aganippe 8 fountain
   location: **6** Greece **7** Helicon
   sacred to: **5** Muses

Aganus
   father: **5** Paris
   mother: **5** Helen

agape 4 agog **6** amazed, gaping **8** wide open **9** awestruck, stupefied **10** astonished, dumbstruck, spellbound **11** dumbfounded **12** wonderstruck **13** flabbergasted

Agassiz, Jean Louis Rodolphe
   field: **7** zoology
   worked on: **7** fossils **8** glaciers **14** classification

Agastrophus
   father: **5** Paeon
   killed by: **8** Diomedes

agate
   species: **6** quartz
   variety of: **10** chalcedony
   type: **3** eye **4** moss, onyx, ring **9** landscape **13** fortification
   source: **4** Ider **6** Brazil **7** Uruguay **9** Oberstein **14** Rio Grande de Sul

Agathon
   father: **5** Priam

Agathyrsus
   father: **8** Hercules

Agave
   father: **6** Cadmus
   mother: **8** Harmonia

sister: **3** Ino **6** Semele **7** Autonoe
   husband: **6** Echion
   son: **8** Pentheus

age 3 eon, era **4** date **5** epoch, phase, ripen **6** mature, mellow, period, season **7** develop, forever, make old **8** life span, lifetime **9** adulthood, a long time, grow older, seniority **10** generation, millennium **11** stage of life, stage of time
   French: **6** siecle

aged 3 old **4** ripe **6** mature, mellow **7** ancient, as old as, elderly, ripened **8** enduring, grown old **9** developed, fullgrown, long-lived

Agee, James
   author of: **10** Agee on Film **17** A Death in the Family **23** Let Us Now Praise Famous Men
   screenwriter for: **15** The African Queen **19** The Night of the Hunter

Agelaus
   mentioned in: **5** Iliad **7** Odyssey
   occupation: **8** herdsman
   father: **8** Hercules, Phradmon
   mother: **7** Omphale
   courted: **8** Penelope
   raised: **5** Paris
   employer: **5** Priam

ageless 7 classic, eternal **8** enduring, timeless

agency 5 force, means, power **6** action, bureau, charge **8** activity **9** influence, mediation, operation **10** department, instrument **12** intervention **15** instrumentality

agenda 6 docket **7** program **8** schedule **9** timetable

Agenor
   mentioned in: **5** Iliad
   king of: **9** Phoenicia
   father: **7** Antenor **8** Poseidon
   mother: **5** Libya **6** Theano
   twin brother: **5** Belus
   wife: **10** Telephassa
   son: **5** Cilix **6** Cadmus **7** Phoenix
   daughter: **6** Europa
   gift: **7** bravery

agent 4 doer **5** cause, envoy, force, means, mover, power **6** agency, author, deputy, worker **7** vehicle **8** advocate, emissary, executor, operator **9** go-between, performer **10** instrument, negotiator **11** perpetrator **12** intermediary, practitioner **14** representative

Age of Innocence, The
   author: **12** Edith Wharton
   character: **10** May Welland

12 Ellen Olenska **13** Newland Archer

age-old 4 aged **7** ancient, antique, very old **9** venerable

agglomerate 4 clot, mass **5** amass, bunch, clump, rally **6** gather, heap up, muster, pile up **7** cluster, collect **8** assemble, condense, mobilize **10** accumulate, collection **12** accumulation, conglomerate, heap together, lump together **14** conglomeration **15** gather into a mass

agglomeration 4 heap, mass, pile **5** bunch, clump **7** cluster **10** collection **12** accumulation **14** conglomeration

aggrandize 5 bloat, exalt, widen **6** beef up, blow up, dilate, expand, extend, puff up, step up **7** amplify, broaden, build up, distend, enhance, enlarge, inflate, magnify, stretch **8** escalate, increase **9** intensify **10** strengthen

aggrandizement 8 increase, widening **9** expansion, extension **10** broadening, escalation, exaltation, stepping up **11** enhancement, enlargement **13** amplification, magnification **15** intensification

aggravate 3 vex **4** rile **5** anger, annoy **6** nettle, worsen **7** affront, inflame **8** heighten, increase, irritate **9** intensify, make worse **10** exacerbate, exasperate

aggravating 7 irksome **9** inflaming, vexatious, worsening **10** irritating **11** heightening **12** exacerbating, exasperating, intensifying

aggregate 3 mix **4** mass **5** blend, union **7** mixture **8** amassing, compound **9** composite, gathering, summation **10** collection **11** combination **12** accumulation, conglomerate **14** conglomeration

aggregation 3 mob **4** army, band, bevy, crew, gang, host, mass, pack **5** crowd, horde, swarm **6** throng **7** cluster **9** multitude **10** collection

aggression 4 raid **7** assault, offense **8** act of war, invasion **9** hostility, pugnacity **11** viciousness **12** belligerence **13** combativeness

aggressive 4 bold **5** harsh, pushy **7** dynamic, hostile, intense, vicious, warlike, warring, zealous **8** forceful, militant **9** ambitious, assailant, assertive, attacking, combative, energetic **10** pugnacious

11 belligerent, competitive, contentious, quarrelsome **12** antagonistic, enterprising **13** self-assertive **15** tending to attack

aggressiveness 9 hostility, pugnacity **10** antagonism **12** belligerence **13** combativeness

aggressor 7 invader **8** attacker **9** assailant **11** belligerent **12** antagonistic

aggrieved 3 sad **4** hurt **5** stung **6** abused, pained **7** injured, put upon, tearful, wounded, wronged **8** grieving, mournful, offended, saddened, troubled **9** affronted, disturbed, sorrowful **10** distressed, ill-treated, maltreated, persecuted **11** imposed upon **13** grief-stricken

aghast 6 amazed **7** shocked, stunned **8** appalled **9** astounded, horrified, terrified **10** astonished, fear-struck, frightened **12** horror-struck **13** thunderstruck

agile 4 keen, spry **5** alert, fleet, lithe, quick, swift **6** active, clever, limber, nimble, supple **8** athletic, graceful **9** dexterous

agility 8 alacrity, spryness **9** dexterity, quickness, swiftness **10** limberness, nimbleness **12** gracefulness

agitate 3 jar, mix **4** beat, goad, rock, stir **5** alarm, churn, shake, upset **6** excite, foment, stir up, work up **7** disturb, provoke, shake up, trouble **8** disquiet

agitated 6 uneasy **7** anxious, frantic, nervous **8** confused, seething **9** disturbed, perturbed, unsettled **10** disquieted, distracted, distraught **11** discomfited, discomposed **12** disconcerted

agitation 7 anxiety **9** confusion **10** discomfort, uneasiness **11** disquietude, distraction, nervousness **12** discomfiture, discomposure, perturbation

agitato
music: **8** agitated

agitator 7 inciter **8** fomentor, inflamer, provoker **9** firebrand **10** incendiary, instigator **11** provocateur **12** rabble-rouser, troublemaker **13** mischief-maker, revolutionary **16** agent provocateur

Aglaia
member of: **6** Graces
father: **7** Jupiter
mother: **8** Eurynome

sister: **6** Thalia
 10 Euphrosyne
husband: **4** Abas
son: **7** Proteus **8** Acrisius
daughter: **7** Idomene

Aglauros see **8** Agraulos

Aglaus
father: **8** Thyestes
mother: **5** naiad
killed by: **6** Atreus

aglow 4 warm **5** fiery **6** ablaze, red-hot **7** blazing, glowing, radiant, shining

Agnes Grey
author: **10** Anne Bronte
character: **8** Mr Weston
 13 Rosalie Murray

agnostic 5 pagan **7** atheist, doubter, heathen, heretic, infidel, skeptic **10** empiricist, free spirit, secularist, unbeliever **11** disbeliever, freethinker, nonbeliever **14** doubting Thomas

ago 4 gone, over, past **5** since **6** gone by **7** earlier **8** backward **15** retrospectively

agog 5 astir **7** excited **8** thrilled, worked up **9** awestruck **10** enthralled **11** openmouthed

Agon
ballet by: **10** Stravinsky

agonize 5 labor, sweat, worry **6** strain, suffer **7** anguish, wrestle **8** struggle

agonizing 6 severe **7** painful, racking **8** grievous, worrying **9** suffering, torturous **10** tormenting, unbearable **11** distressing, intolerable, unendurable **12** excruciating, insufferable

agony 3 woe **4** pain **5** trial **6** effort, misery, sorrow, strain, throes **7** anguish, anxiety, torment, torture **8** distress, striving, struggle **9** suffering **10** affliction **11** tribulation

Agony and the Ecstasy, The
author: **11** Irving Stone

Agoraea
epithet of: **6** Athena
means: **16** of the marketplace

Agoraeus
epithet of: **4** Zeus **6** Hermes
means: **16** of the marketplace

agoraphobia
fear of: **10** open spaces

Agraeus
epithet of: **6** Apollo
means: **6** hunter

agrarian 5 rural **7** farming **8** pastoral **11** agronomical, crop-raising **12** agricultural

Agraulos
also: **8** Aglauros
father: **7** Actaeus
husband: **7** Cecropa
daughter: **9** Pandrosos

agree 4 jibe **5** admit, allow, chime, grant, match, tally **6** accede, accept, accord, assent, concur, settle, square **7** concede, conform, consent, support **8** coincide, side with **9** harmonize, subscribe **10** correspond, think alike

agreeable 7 fitting **8** amenable, in accord, pleasant, pleasing, suitable **9** approving, complying, congenial **10** acceptable, concurring, consenting, gratifying **11** appropriate
German: **9** gemutlich

agreeableness 7 amenity **9** geniality **10** amiability **11** sociability **12** pleasantness

agreed
French: **7** d'accord

agreed upon 6 common, normal **8** accepted, approved **9** confirmed, customary **10** acceptable **11** established **12** acknowledged

agreement 4 deal, pact **6** accord **7** analogy, bargain, compact, concert, concord, harmony, promise **8** affinity, alliance, contract, covenant **10** accordance, compliance, conformity, settlement, similarity **11** arrangement, concordance, conformance **13** compatibility **14** correspondence

agricultural 4 farm **5** rural **7** farming **8** agrarian **9** gardening **11** agronomical, crop-raising **13** nonindustrial

agriculture 7 farming, tillage **8** agronomy **9** geoponics, husbandry **10** agronomics **11** crop-raising, cultivation **15** market gardening

Agriculture
god of: **4** Dago **5** Dagan, Dagon, Picus **6** Saturn **12** Bonus Eventus
goddess of: **5** Ceres **6** Brigit, Dea Dia, Vacuna

Agriope see **8** Eurydice

Agrius
member of: **8** Gigantes
form: **7** centaur
mother: **5** Circe
father: **8** Odysseus
son: **9** Thersites
attacked: **8** Hercules

agronomics 7 farming, tillage **8** agronomy **9** geoponics **11** agriculture, crop-raising

agronomy 7 farming 9 gardening, husbandry 11 agriculture, cultivation

Agrotera
epithet of: 7 Artemis
means: 8 huntress

aground 5 stuck 6 ashore 7 beached 8 grounded, stranded 9 foundered

ague 5 chill, fever 7 malaria, shivers 12 sweating fits

Aguecheek, Sir Andrew
character in: 12 Twelfth Night
author: 11 Shakespeare

Agyius
epithet of: 6 Apollo
means: 15 god of the streets

Ah, But Your Land Is Beautiful
author: 9 Alan Paton

Ah! Wilderness
author: 12 Eugene O'Neill

Ahab
character in: 8 Moby Dick
author: 8 Melville

Ahab
father: 4 Omri
wife: 7 Jezebel
son: 7 Ahaziah
daughter: 8 Athaliah
opposed: 6 Elijah
killed by: 4 Aram

Ahasuerus
known as: 6 Xerxes 8 Cyaxares
wife: 6 Esther
divorced: 6 Vashti
son: 6 Darius
eunuchs: 6 Biztha, Carcas, Zethar 7 Abagtha, Harbona, Mehuman
servant: 7 Abagtha
conqueror of: 7 Nineveh

Ahaz
father: 6 Jotham

Ahaziah
father: 4 Ahab 7 Jehoram
mother: 7 Jezebel 8 Athaliah
uncle: 7 Jehoram
defeated by: 6 Hazael
killed by: 4 Jehu
died at: 7 Megiddo

ahead of time 5 early 6 before, in time, sooner 7 betimes, earlier 9 before now, in advance 10 beforehand, in good time 13 before the fact

Ahib 16 first Hebrew month

Ahiezer
father: 11 Ammishaddai

Ahimelech
father: 6 Ahitub
son: 8 Abiathar
killed by: 4 Saul
friend: 8 Ahuzzath

Ahithophel
counseled: 5 David
rebelled with: 7 Absalom
granddaughter: 9 Bathsheba

Ahuzzath
friend: 9 Abimelech
visited: 5 Isaac

Aias see 4 Ajax

aid 4 abet, alms, dole, help 5 serve 6 assist, foster, relief 7 advance, charity, further, promote, subsidy, support, sustain 8 donation, minister 9 allowance 10 assistance, contribute, facilitate 11 accommodate, helping hand 12 contribution

Aida
opera by: 5 Verdi
character: 4 Aida 6 Ramfis 7 Amneris, Radames 8 Amonasro, Rhadames

aide 5 gofer 6 deputy, helper 7 abettor, acolyte 8 adherent, adjutant, follower, retainer, sidekick 9 assistant, associate, auxiliary, man Friday 10 aide-de-camp, apprentice, girl Friday, lieutenant 11 helping hand, subordinate 12 right-hand man

aide-de-camp 4 aide 6 helper 8 adjutant 9 assistant, man Friday, right hand 12 right-hand man

aide memoire 4 memo, note 10 memorandum

aider 4 aide 6 helper 7 abettor 9 assistant 11 helping hand

Aidos
origin: 5 Greek
personifies: 10 conscience

Aiken, Conrad Potter
author of: 6 Ushant 10 Blue Voyage 12 Reviewer's ABC 14 The Charnel Rose 15 Earth Triumphant

Aiken, Howard H
field: 11 mathematics
designed: 15 digital computer

ail 4 pain 5 annoy, be ill, upset, worry 6 be sick, bother, sicken 7 afflict, make ill, trouble 8 be infirm, be unwell, distress 12 be indisposed, fail in health

ailing 3 ill 4 sick 6 infirm, sickly, unwell 8 delicate

ailment 6 malady 7 disease, illness 8 disorder, sickness, weakness 9 complaint, infection, infirmity 10 affliction, disability, discomfort 13 indisposition

ailurophobia
fear of: 4 cats

aim 3 try 4 beam, goal, mean, plan, seek, want, wish 5 essay, focus, level, point, sight, slant 6 aiming, design, desire, direct, intend, intent, object, scheme, strive, target 7 attempt, be after, purpose, take aim, train on 8 ambition, aspire to, endeavor 9 intention 10 aspiration, have in mind, have in view, work toward 11 have an eye to, line of sight 12 marksmanship

aim at 4 seek 6 pursue, target 8 aspire to, shoot for

aimless 6 chance, random 7 erratic, wayward 8 unguided 9 frivolous, haphazard, hit-or-miss, pointless, unfocus(s)ed 10 accidental, rudderless, undirected 11 purposeless, unorganized 12 inconsistent, unsystematic 13 directionless, unpredictable 14 indiscriminate

aine 5 elder 6 eldest

Ainsworth, William Harrison
author of: 8 Boscobel, Crichton, Rookwood 9 Guy Fawkes 10 Old St Paul's 12 Jack Sheppard 13 Windsor Castle 16 The Flitch of Bacon, The Tower of London 17 The Miser's Daughter, The South Sea Bubble 20 The Lancashire Witches

Ainu
language spoken in: 8 Hokkaido, Sakhalin

air, airs 3 lay, sky 4 aura, look, mood, puff, song, tell, tone, tune, vent, waft, wind 5 blast, carol, ditty, draft, ozone, style, swank, utter, voice, whiff 6 aerate, ballad, breath, breeze, expose, manner, melody, reveal, spirit, strain, zephyr 7 declare, display, divulge, exhibit, express, feeling, hauteur, quality 8 ambience, disclose, pretense, proclaim 9 arrogance, publicize, ventilate 10 appearance, atmosphere, make public 11 haughtiness, pretensions 12 affectations, affectedness, stratosphere 16 superciliousness
god of: 5 Enlil
goddess of: 6 Ninlil

airborne 5 aloft 6 aerial 8 in flight 12 off the ground

aircraft 3 jet, SST 4 bird 5 blimp, crate, plane 6 copter, glider 7 balloon, chopper, prop-jet, zepplin 8 airplane, jumbo jet 10 helicopter, whirlybird

air current 4 puff, wind

5 blast, draft, whiff 6 breeze, zephyr 11 breath of air

airdrome, aerodrome 7 airbase, airport, jet base 8 airfield 11 flying field 12 landing field

airfield 7 air base, airport, jet base 8 airstrip 11 flying field 12 landing field, landing strip

airfoil
insect: 4 wing

airless 8 stifling 10 overheated, sweltering 16 poorly ventilated

airplane *see box*

airport 5 field 7 air base, jet base 8 airdrome, airfield, airstrip 9 aerodrome 11 flying field 12 landing field, landing strip

airship 5 blimp 7 balloon 9 dirigible 19 lighter-than-air craft

airship, rigid dirigible
invented by: 8 Zeppelin

airstrip 6 runway 12 landing field, landing strip

air weapon
German: 9 Luftwaffe

airy 5 light, merry, sunny, windy 6 breezy, cheery, drafty, dreamy, jaunty, lively 8 cheerful, ethereal, fanciful, gossamer, illusory, spacious 9 idealized, imaginary, sprightly 10 frolicsome, immaterial 11 unrealistic 12 light-

hearted, light-of-heart 13 unsubstantial 14 well-ventilated

aisle 3 way 4 lane, path, walk 5 alley 6 avenue 7 passage, walkway 8 cloister, corridor 10 ambulatory, passageway

Aius Locutius
form: 5 voice
warned: 6 Romans
warned of: 14 Gallic invasion

ajar 4 open 5 agape 6 gaping 8 unclosed 10 partly open

Ajax
also: 4 Aias
called: 9 Great Ajax 10 Oilean Ajax 11 Locrian Ajax 13 Ajax the Lesser 14 Telamonian Ajax
king of: 7 Locrius
father: 6 Oileus 7 Telamon
mother: 8 Periboea
brother: 6 Teucer
author: 9 Sophocles
character: 8 Achilles, Odysseus 9 Agamemnon
son: 9 Eurysaces
slave: 8 Tecmessa
seer: 7 Calchas
rescued body of: 8 Achilles
violated shrine of: 6 Athena
killed in: 9 shipwreck

Akawai *see* 6 Acawai

Akela
character in: 14 The Jungle Books
author: 7 Kipling

Akeldama *see* 8 Aceldama

Akh
origin: 8 Egyptian
transfiguration of: 4 dead

Akihito
position: 7 emperor 11 crown prince
reign name: 6 Heisei 17 Establishing Peace
family:
father: 5 Showa 8 Hirohito
mother: 6 Nagako
wife: 7 Michiko
children: 4 Hito 8 Narahito
schools: 6 Oxford 9 Gakushuin

akin 3 kin 4 like 5 alike 6 allied 7 kindred, related, similar, uniform 8 agreeing, parallel 9 analogous, congenial, connected, identical 10 affiliated, comparable, resembling 11 correlative 13 corresponding 14 consanguineous

Akkad *see* 5 Accad

Akutagawa, Ryunosuke
author of: 5 Kappa 8 Rashomon 13 The Hell Screen

a la 9 in honor of 13 in the manner of

Alabama *see box, p. 26*

Alabama, Alibamu
language family: 9 Muskogean
location: 5 Texas 9 Louisiana 10 Polk County 12 Alabama River
related to: 7 Koasati

alacrity 4 zeal 6 fervor 7 agility, avidity 8 dispatch 9 alertness, briskness, eagerness; readiness 10 enthusiasm, liveliness, nimbleness, promptness 11 willingness 13 sprightliness

Aladdin
character in: 27 Arabian Nights' Entertainments

Al Aiun, El Aaiun
capital of: 13 Western Sahara

a la mode 12 in the fashion, in the style of 13 in the manner of

Alarcon, Pedro Antonio de
author: 10 The Scandal 12 Captain Venom 14 El Nino de la Bola 19 The Three-Cornered Hat

alarm 4 fear 5 alert, panic, scare 6 appall, dismay, fright, terror, war cry 7 agitate, disturb, terrify, trouble, unnerve, warning 8 affright, distress, frighten 9 agitation, hue and cry, misgiving 11 trepidation 12 apprehension, perturbation 13 consternation

alarmed 6 afraid, scared

airplane 3 jet 4 bird 5 crate, plane 7 airship, prop-jet 8 aircraft 9 aeroplane 11 flying jenny 19 heavier-than-air craft 20 propeller-driven plane
invented by:
automatic pilot: 6 Sperry
jet engine: 5 Ohain
with motor: 12 Wilbur Wright 13 Orville Wright 14 Wright Brothers
hydro: 7 Curtiss
first: 5 Flyer
part: 3 fin 4 flap, nose, tail, wing 5 cabin, cargo, pylon 6 rudder 7 aileron, cockpit, turbine 8 elevator, fuel tank, fuselage, throttle, turbofan, turbojet 9 empennage, propeller, turboprop 10 flight deck, power plant, stabilizer 11 landing gear 13 undercarriage
kind: 3 MIG 4 Zero 5 Eagle, Gotha, Piper, Sabre 6 Boeing, Cessna, Fokker, Mirage 7 Concorde, Piper Cub 10 Beechcraft, Dornier Do-X 11 Piper Navajo 12 Lockheed Vega, Sopwith Camel 13 Boeing Clipper, Messerschmitt, Piper Cherokee, Super Fortress 14 Cessna Citation, Flying Fortress, Grumman Hellcat, Stratofortress 15 Hawker Hurrican 16 De Havilland Comet
variation: 3 SST 4 STOL, VTOL 5 blimp, drone, VSTOL 6 bomber, glider 7 airship, fighter 8 zeppelin 10 hang glider, helicopter, supersonic
battle: 8 dog fight

Alabama
  abbreviation: 2 AL 3 Ala
  nickname: 6 Cotton 12 Heart of Dixie, Yellowhammer
  capital: 10 Montgomery
  largest city: 10 Birmingham
  others: 5 Selma 6 Athens, Dothan, Marion, Mobile 7 Decatur, Gadsden 8 Anniston 10 Huntsville, Tuscaloosa
  colleges: 5 Miles 6 Auburn 7 Alabama 8 Tuskegee 9 Talladega 10 Huntingdon
  explorer: 12 Hernan DeSoto
  feature:
    festival: 11 Azalea Trail
    statue: 6 Vulcan
  tribe: 5 Creek 6 Tohome 7 Alabamu, Alibamu, Koasati 8 Tuskegee
  people: 8 Joe Louis 9 Hank Aaron, Hugo Black 10 Willie Mays 11 Helen Keller, Nat King Cole 13 George Wallace, William C Handy, William Gorgas
  lake: 12 Guntersville
  land rank: 11 twenty-ninth
  physical feature:
    gulf: 6 Mexico
    highest point: 6 Cheaha
    highlands: 11 Appalachian
  river: 3 Pea 5 Coosa 6 Mobile 7 Alabama 9 Tombigbee, Tennessee 10 Tallapoosa 13 Chattahoochee
  state admission: 12 twenty-second
  state bird: 7 flicker 12 yellowhammer
  state fish: 6 tarpon
  state flower: 8 camellia 9 goldenrod
  state motto: 21 We Dare Defend Our Rights
  state song: 7 Alabama
  state tree: 20 southern longleaf pine

7 anxious, fearful, panicky, worried 8 dismayed 9 concerned, terrified 10 frightened 12 apprehensive 13 panic-stricken 14 terror-stricken

alarming 5 awful, dread 7 fearful 8 dreadful 10 horrifying, terrifying 11 frightening, hair-raising

alas
  expresses: 4 pity 5 grief 6 sorrow 7 concern 9 weariness 11 unhappiness 12 wretchedness

Alaska *see box*

Alaskan Adventures
  author: 8 Rex Beach

Alastor
  epithet of: 4 Zeus 5 demon 11 avenging god
  means: 7 avenger
  father: 13 Neleus of Pylos
  brother: 6 Nestor
  wife: 9 Harpalyce
  killed by: 8 Hercules

Albach-Retty, Rosemarie
  real name of: 13 Romy Schneider

Albania *see box, p. 28*

Albanian
  language family: 12 Indo-European
  spoken in: 7 Balkans

Albee, Edward
  author of: 3 Box 7 All Over 8 Seascape, Zoo Story 9 Tiny Alice 10 The Sandbox 16 A Delicate Balance, The American Dream 18 The Lady from Dubuque 21 The Ballad of the Sad Cafe, The Death of Bessie Smith 25 Who's Afraid of Virginia Woolf?
  identified with: 18 theater of the absurd

Albeniz, Isaac
  born: 5 Spain 9 Camprodon
  composer of: 6 Iberia 12 The Magic Opal 13 Henry Clifford

Alberich
  origin: 8 Teutonic
  king of: 6 dwarfs
  possessed treasure of: 8 Niblungs 9 Nibelungs
  also possessed: 9 Tarnkappe

Albert, Eddie
  real name: 21 Eddie Albert Heimberger
  wife: 5 Margo

born: 12 Rock Island IL
  roles: 8 Oklahoma 10 Brother Rat, Green Acres 11 Room Service 12 Roman Holiday 13 The Longest Day 16 The Heartbreak Kid 19 The Boys from Syracuse

Alberta
  abbreviation: 4 Alta
  capital/largest city: 8 Edmonton
  others: 7 Calgary, Reddeer 10 Lethbridge 11 Medicine Hat
  lakes: 5 Banff, Claire 6 Jasper 8 Waterton 9 Athabasca 11 Lesser Slave
  rivers: 3 Bow 4 Milk 6 Oldman, Wapiti 9 Athabasca 12 Saskatchewan
  religion: 13 Roman Catholic 20 United Church of Canada 22 Anglican Church of Canada
  people: 5 Dutch 6 French, German 7 British, English 9 Ukrainian 12 Scandinavian

Albert Herring
  opera by: 7 Britten

Alberti, Leon Battista
  architect of: 15 Palazzo Rucellai 18 Church of Sant' Andrea, Temple Malatestiano 20 Church of San Sebastian 25 Church of Santa Maria Novella

Albertosaurus
  type: 8 dinosaur, theropod
  period: 10 Cretaceous

Albertson, Jack
  born: 8 Malden MA
  roles: 14 Chico and the Man 15 The Sunshine Boys 18 Days of Wine and Roses, The Subject Was Roses

Albion *see* 7 England

album 2 LP 4 book 6 record 8 register 9 portfolio, scrapbook

Albunea
  origin: 5 Roman
  form: 5 nymph
  habitat: 8 fountain

Alcaeus
  father: 9 Androgeus
  mother: 9 Andromeda
  grandfather: 5 Minos
  brother: 9 Sthenelus

Alcaids
  descendants of: 7 Alcaeus

Alcandre
  husband: 7 Polybus
  received: 5 Helen 8 Menelaus

Alceste
  opera by: 5 Gluck

Alaska
abbreviation: 2 AK 4 Alas
nickname: 9 Great Land, Sourdough 12 Last Frontier
20 Land of the Midnight Sun
capital: 6 Juneau
largest city: 9 Anchorage
others: 4 Nome 5 Sitka 6 Barrow, Kodiak 7 Cordova,
Douglas, Skagway 9 Fairbanks, Ketchikan
feature: 5 Alcan 13 Alaska Highway
national park: 13 Mount McKinley
tribe: 3 Han 5 Aleut, Haida 6 Ahtena, Akkhas, Eskimo,
Karluk, Tetlin 7 Amerind, Ingalik, Kayukon, Khotana,
Kutchin, Tanaina, Tlingit, Tlinkit, Venetie 9 Tsimshian,
Unakalett
island: 4 Adak, Atka 5 Aleut 6 Kodiak, Unimak 7 Diomede,
Nunivak 8 Aleutian, Pribilof 9 Alexander
lake: 6 Naknek 7 Iliamna 8 Becharof 9 Teshekpuk
land rank: 5 first
mountain: 3 Ada 4 Muir 5 Coast 6 Alaska, Brooks 7 Foraker, St Elias 8 Aleutian, Wrangell 9 Blackburn
highest point: 8 McKinley
physical feature:
bay: 7 Glacier, Prudhoe
channel: 9 Gastineau
glacier: 9 Malaspina
pass: 8 Chilkoot
peninsula: 5 Kenai 6 Alaska, Seward
rapids: 10 Whitehorse
sea: 6 Arctic 8 Beaufort
strait: 6 Bering
river: 5 Kobuk, Yukon 6 Copper, Noatak, Tanana 7 Koyu-
kuk, Susitna 8 Colville 9 Kuskokwim, Matanuska,
Porcupine
state admission: 10 forty-ninth
state bird: 15 willow ptarmigan
state fish: 10 king salmon
state flower: 11 forget-me-not
state motto: 16 North to the Future
state song: 11 Alaska's Flag
state symbol: 9 bald eagle
state tree: 11 sitka spruce

Alcestis
author: 9 Euripides
character: 6 Apollo 7 Admetus 8 Heracles, Thanatos

Alcestis
father: 6 Pelias
mother: 8 Anaxibia
10 Phylomache
husband: 7 Admetus
son: 7 Eumelus 8 Hippasus
returned from: 5 Hades
returned by: 8 Hercules

Alchemist, The
author: 9 Ben Jonson
character: 4 Face 5 Surly
6 Dapper, Subtle 7 Ananias,
Drugger, Kastril, Love-wit
9 Dol Common 10 Dame
Pliant 16 Sir Epicure Mammon 20 Tribulation
Wholesome

alchemy 5 magic 7 sorcery
8 wizardry 10 conversion,
witchcraft 11 magic appeal

13 transmutation 17 medieval
chemistry
god of: 6 Hermes

Alcides *see* 8 Hercules

Alcidice
husband: 10 Salmoneaus
daughter: 4 Tyro

Alcimede
father: 8 Phylacus
mother: 7 Clymene
husband: 5 Aeson
son: 5 Jason

Alcimedon
origin: 8 Arkadian
mentioned in: 5 Iliad
father: 7 Laerces
daughter: 6 Philao
captain of: 9 Myrmidons

Alcina
opera by: 6 Handel
character: 6 Alcina
8 Ruggiero

Alcindor, Lew
former name of: 17 Kareem
Abdul-Jabbar

Alcinous
origin: 5 Greek
mentioned in: 7 Odyssey
king of: 10 Phaeacians
father: 10 Nausithous
mother: 8 Periboea
brother: 8 Rhexenor
wife: 5 Arete
son: 8 Laodamas
daughter: 8 Nausicaa
niece: 5 Arete

Alcis
father: 10 Antipoenus
sister: 9 Androclea

Alcithoe
father: 6 Minyas
mocked: 8 Dionysus

Alcmaeon
father: 10 Amphiaraus
mother: 8 Eriphyle
brother: 11 Amphilochus
wife: 10 Callirrhoe
son: 7 Acarnan
10 Amphoterus
daughter: 9 Tisiphone
commanded: 7 Thebans

Alcmaon
father: 7 Thestor
wounded by: 7 Glaucus
killed by: 8 Sarpedon

Alcmene
father: 9 Electryon
mother: 5 Anaxo
husband: 10 Amphitryon
12 Rhadamanthys
twin sons: 8 Hercules,
Iphicles

alcohol 3 ale 4 beer, wine
5 drink 6 liquor 7 whiskey
9 the bottle
Latin: 9 aqua vitae

alcoholic 3 sot 4 hard, lush,
soak 5 drunk, rummy, souse,
toper 6 barfly, boozer, strong
7 guzzler, imbiber, tippler
8 drunkard 9 distilled, fermented, inebriate 10 spirituous 11 dipsomaniac, hard
drinker, inebriating, inebria-
tive, whiskey head
12 intoxicating

alcoholism 3 DT's 9 oeno-
mania 10 dipsomania 12 intemperance 15 delirium
tremens

Alcon
form: 6 archer, Trojan
7 warrior
aided: 8 Hercules
wounded: 8 Odysseus
abducted: 13 Geryons cattle
killed by: 8 Odysseus

Alcott, Louisa May
author of: 7 Jo's Boys 9 Lit-

Albania
  other name: 8 Shqiperi 9 Shqiprija, Shqyptare
  capital/largest city: 6 Tirana, Tirane
  others: 3 Opp 4 Fier, Klos, Puka, Puke 5 Berat, Dukat, Korce, Kruje, Pecin, Peqin, Qukes, Rubic, Spash, Vlore 6 Avlona, Bitsan, Dardhe, Durres, Karaje, Preshe, Valona 7 Chimara, Coritza, Durazzo, Elbasan, Koritsa, Preyesa, Scutari, Shkoder 8 Tepeleni 11 Gjirokaster
  monetary unit: 3 lek 5 franc 6 qintar 7 quintar
  island: 6 Saseno
  lake: 4 Ulze 5 Matia, Ohrid 6 Prespa 7 Ochrida, Scutari, Shkoder 8 Ohridsko
  mountain: 5 Shala 6 Pindus 8 Koritnjk 12 Albanian Alps
  highest point: 10 Mount Korab
  river: 3 Mat 4 Arta, Drin 5 Byene, Erzen, Seman 6 Bojana, Bojane, Vijosa, Vijosa, Vijose 7 Drin-i-ci, Shkumbi
  sea: 6 Ionian 8 Adriatic
  physical feature:
    bay: 5 Vlore
    cape: 6 Glossa
    gulf: 4 Drin
    lagoon: 10 Kara Vastas
    peninsula: 6 Balkan
    promontory: 13 acroceraunium
    strait: 7 Otranto
    wind: 4 bora
  people: 3 Geg 4 Cham, Gheg, Gueg, Tosk 6 Arnaut, Arnout 8 Illyrian, Skipetar
  king: 3 Zog 9 Ahmet Zogu
  leader: 4 Alia 5 Hoxha 7 Berisha 10 Scanderbeg, Skenderbeg 13 Bishop Fan Noli
  language: 3 Geg 4 Cham, Gheg, Hish, Tosk 5 Greek 8 Albanian
  religion: 5 Islam 7 Bektash 13 Roman Catholic 15 Eastern Orthodox
  place:
    square: 10 Skenderbeg
  feature:
    lute: 6 luhata
    soldier: 7 palikar
    stone house: 4 kula
  food:
    cheese: 8 kackaval

tle Men 11 Little Women 12 Eight Cousins, Flower Fables 15 Aunt Jo's Scrap-Bag 18 An Old-Fashioned Girl

alcove 3 bay 4 nook 5 niche 6 corner, recess 7 cubicle, opening 11 compartment

Alcyone
  also: 7 Halcyon
  father: 6 Aeolus
  husband: 4 Ceyx
  son: 6 Anthas
  transformed into: 10 kingfisher

Alcyoneus
  form: 5 giant
  hurled: 5 stone
  victim: 8 Hercules
  killed by: 8 Hercules

Alda, Alan
  born: 9 New York NY
  father: 10 Robert Alda
    real name: 15 Alfonso D'Abruzzo
  roles: 4 MASH 9 Paper Lion 12 Sweet Liberty 13 Betsy's Wedding, Hawkeye Pierce 14 The Four Seasons 16 Same Time Next Year, The Mephisto Waltz

Alden, Roberta
  character in: 17 An American Tragedy
  author: 7 Dreiser

al dente 10 to the tooth

alder 5 Alnus
  varieties: 3 Red 5 Black, Hazel, White, Witch 6 Oregon, Smooth, Yellow 7 Italian, Seaside 8 Japanese, Mountain, Speckled 9 Caucasian 10 Manchurian 13 American green, European green

Aldiss, Brian W
  author of: 7 Non-Stop 9 Greybeard 13 The Saliva Tree 19 Frankenstein Unbound, The Billion Year Spree, The Eighty Minute Hour

ale 4 beer, brew 5 stout 12 malt beverage 15 English festival

Alea
  epithet of: 6 Athena
  means: 9 sanctuary

Alebion
  father: 8 Poseidon
  brother: 8 Dercynus
  killed by: 8 Hercules

Alecto
  member of: 6 Furies

alehouse 3 pub 6 saloon, tavern 7 taproom 11 public house

Aleichem, Sholom
  author of: 12 The Great Fair 14 Tevye's Daughter

Alembert, Jean le Rond d'
  field: 11 mathematics
  nationality: 6 French
  studied: 13 fluid dynamics 18 celestial mechanics 28 partial differential equations

Aleph and Other Stories
  author: 15 Jorge Luis Borges

alert 4 warn, wary 5 alarm, aware, quick, siren 6 active, inform, lively, nimble, notify, signal 7 careful, heedful, on guard, warning 8 diligent, forewarn, keen-eyed, vigilant, watchful 9 attentive, observant, sprightly, wideawake 10 perceptive 11 intelligent

alertness 8 alacrity, dispatch 9 awareness, readiness, vigilance 10 liveliness 12 watchfulness

Alethia
  origin: 5 Greek
  personifies: 5 truth

Aleus
  king of: 5 Tegea
  father: 7 Aphidas
  brother: 6 Pereus
  cousin: 6 Neaera
  wife: 6 Neaera
  son: 7 Cepheus 8 Lycurgus 10 Amphidamas
  daughter: 4 Auge

Aleut
  language family: 6 Eskimo
  tribe: 4 Atka 8 Unalaska
  location: 6 Alaska 15 Shumagin Islands 17 Aleutian Peninsula
  noted for: 7 hunting

Aleutians
  islands: 3 Fox, Rat 4 Near

9 Andreanof **25** Islands of the Four Mountains
state: **6** Alaska
people: **6** Aleuts
language: **5** Atkan **9** Unalaskan

Alexander, Jane
real name: **11** Jane Quigley
born: **8** Boston MA
roles: **9** Testament **17** The Great White Hope **18** Eleanor and Franklin **19** All the President's Men

Alexander's Feast
author: **10** John Dryden

Alexander the Great
battle: **5** Issus **9** Gaugamela
birthplace: **5** Pella
conquered: **6** Darius, Persia
father: **8** Philip II
founded: **10** Alexandria
friend: **11** Hephaestion
general: **7** Cleitus **8** Philotas **9** Parmenion
horse: **10** Bucephalus
mother: **8** Olympias
nationality: **10** Macedonian
tutor: **9** Aristotle
wife: **6** Roxana

Alexandra see **9** Cassandra

Alexandrinus 16 Greek unical codex

alexandrite
species: **11** chrysoberyl
source: **8** Sri Lanka
color: **3** red **5** green

Alexiares
father: **8** Hercules
mother: **4** Hebe

Alexicacus
epithet of: **6** Apollo
means: **13** averter of evil

Alfader see **7** Alfadir

Alfadir
also: **7** Alfader
origin: **12** Scandinavian
epithet of: **4** Odin **5** Othin

Alfheim
origin: **12** Scandinavian
dwelling place of: **5** elves
location: **11** above ground

Alfie
director: **12** Lewis Gilbert
based on play by: **12** Bill Naughton
cast: **12** Michael Caine **14** Shelley Winters

alga, algae 6 fungus **8** pond scum
contains: **4** agar **5** algin **11** carrageenan, chlorophyll
type: **3** red **5** brown, green **9** blue-green, euglenids **11** golden-brown, yellow-green **15** dinoflagellates
forms: **4** kelp **5** dulse **7** diatoms, seaweed **8** plankton,

rockweed **9** Irish moss, stonewort

Alger, Horatio
author of: **10** Ragged Dick **11** Tattered Tom **12** Luck and Pluck

Algeria see box

Algiers
Arabic: **8** al-Jazair
building: **11** Great Mosque
capital of: **7** Algeria
center of city: **6** Casbah

Algeria
other name: **7** Algerie, Numidia, Pomaria **9** al-Djazair
capital/largest city: **7** Algiers
others: **4** Bona, Bone, Oran **5** Aflou, Arzew, Batna, Blida, Medea, Saida, Setif, Tenes **6** Abadla, Annaba, Aumale, Barika, Bechar, Bejaia, Benoud, Biskra, Bougie, Dellys, Djanet, Djelfa, Dzioua, Eloued, Frenda, Guelma, Skikda **7** Boghari, Mascara, Miliana, Negrine, Nemours, Ouargla, Tebessa, Tlemcen **8** Ghardaia, Laghouat **9** Touggourt **11** Constantine **12** Sidi-bel-abbes
division: **4** Oran **6** Annaba **7** Algiers **11** Constantine
leader: **3** bey, dey **6** disawa **9** beylerbey
measure: **3** pik **5** rebis, tarri **6** termin
monetary unit: **5** dinar **7** centime
weight: **4** rotl
lake: **5** Hodna **6** Sabkha **7** Cherqui, Fedjadj, Meirhir **10** Azzel Matti, Mekerrhane
mountain: **5** Aissa, Atlas, Aures, Dahra **6** Chelia **7** Ahaggar, Kabylia, Mouydir **8** Djurjura **9** Djurdjura, Tell Atlas **12** Saharan Atlas
highest point: **5** Tahat
river: **6** Shelif **7** Cheliff **8** Medjerda **15** Cheliffmedjerda
sea: **13** Mediterranean
physical feature: **14** Tropic of Cancer
  desert: **6** Sahara
  giant sand dune: **3** erg
  grass: **4** diss **7** esparto
  hill: **4** tell
  oasis: **4** Mzab
  oil field: **7** Edjeleh, El Gassi **10** Zarzaitine **13** Hassi Messaoud (happy spring), Tiguentourine
  plain: **7** Cheliff, Mitidja
  rocky plateau: **7** hammada
  salt basin: **5** chott, shatt
  wind: **7** sirocco
people: **4** Arab **6** Berber, Kabyle, Shawia, Tuareg **7** Haratin
  author: **3** Dib **5** Camus, Fanon **6** Yacine
  leader: **9** Bendjedid **10** Abd al-Qadir, Abd-al-Kadir, Abdel-Kader **11** Boumedienne **13** Ahmed Ben Bella
  ruler: **8** Jugurtha **9** Masinissa
language: **6** Arabic, Berber, French, Zenata **7** Senhaja
religion: **5** Islam
place:
  monastery: **5** Ribat
  ruins: **7** Djemila
feature:
  camel: **6** mehari
  cavalry man: **5** spahi **6** spahee
  commune: **5** setif
  dwelling: **6** gourbi
  French settler/landowner: **5** colon **8** piednoir
  holy man: **8** marabout
  kingdom: **7** Numidia
  native quarter: **6** casbah, kasbah
  pirate: **7** corsair
  ship: **5** xebec, zebec
  slum: **10** bidonville
food:
  dish: **8** couscous
  fruit drink: **5** syrop
  seasoning: **4** mint **5** anise, cumin **6** cloves, fennel, ginger, pepper **7** parsley, pimento **8** cinnamon **9** coriander

French: 5 Alger
hills: 5 Sahel
Roman: 7 Icosium
ruled by: 5 Turks **6** French
7 Berbers **10** Free French
14 Barbary Pirates
sea: 13 Mediterranean

Algonkian-Mosan
language branches: 5 Mosan
7 Kutenai **15** Algonkian-
Ritwan

Algonkian-Ritwan
language family: 14 Algonkian-Mosan
subgroup: 3 Fox **4** Cree,
Sauk **5** Wiyot, Yurok
6 Ojibwa **7** Abenaki, Arapaho, Mohican **8** Cheyenne,
Delaware, Menomini
9 Blackfoot

Algonkin, Algonquin
language family: 9 Algonkian **10** Algonquian
tribe: 7 Abitibi **8** Algonkin
9 Nipissing **11** Temiscaming
location: 6 Canada **11** Ottawa
River
spirit of nature: 7 Manitou

Algonquian, Algonkian
tribe: 3 Fox, Sac **4** Cree,
Innu, Sauk **5** Miami **6** Abnaki, Atsina, Micmac,
Ojibwa, Ottawa, Pequot
7 Arapaho, Mahican, Mohegan, Mohican, Ojibway,
Shawnee **8** Algonkin, Cheyenne, Chippawa, Delaware,
Haaninin, Iliniwek, Illinois,
Kickapoo, Menomini, Merrimac, Powhatan, Puyallop
9 Algonquin, Blackfeet,
Blackfoot, Massasoit, Me-
nominee, Menomonie, Mes-
quakie, Pennacook,
Penobscot, Pokanoket,
Twightwee, Wampanoag
10 Leni-Lenape, Potawatomi **11** Gros Ventres
12 Narragansett **17** Montagnais-Naskapi

algophobia
fear of: 4 pain

Algum 13 red sandalwood

Ali, Muhammad
formerly: 11 Cassius Clay
sport: 6 boxing
class: 11 heavyweight
won: 8 Olympics **16** heavyweight title

alias 9 pseudonym **11** assumed
name, nom de guerre

Ali Baba
character in: 27 Arabian
Nights' Entertainments

Alibamu see **7** Alabama

alibi 3 out **6** excuse **7** pretext
11 explanation **13** justification

Alice Adams
author: 15 Booth Tarkington
character: 6 Mr Lamb
11 Virgil Adams, Walter Adams **13** Arthur Russell,
Mildred Palmer

**Alice's Adventures in
Wonderland**
author: 12 Lewis Carroll
character: 5 Alice **7** Duchess
9 Mad Hatter, March Hare
10 Mock Turtle **11** Cheshire
Cat, White Rabbit **12** King
of Hearts **13** Queen of
Hearts

Alice Sit-by-the-Fire
author: 12 James M Barrie

alien 6 exotic, remote, unlike
7 distant, foreign, opposed,
strange **8** contrary, newcomer,
outsider, stranger **9** different,
estranged, foreigner, immigrant, not native, outlander,
separated, unrelated **10** dissimilar, outlandish **11** conflicting, incongruous,
unconnected **12** incompatible,
inconsistent **13** contradictory
German: 9 Auslander

alienate 7 divorce **8** estrange,
separate, turn away

alienation 5 exile **7** divorce
9 isolation **10** separation, withdrawal **13** repulsiveness

alight 4 land **6** get off **7** deplane, descend, detrain, get
down **8** come down, dismount **9** climb down, disembark, thump down, touch
down

align 4 ally, even, join, side
6 even up, line up **9** affiliate,
associate **10** straighten

alignment 7 allying, evening
9 evening up **13** straightening

alike 4 akin, even, same
5 equal **6** evenly **7** equally,
kindred, uniform **8** of a piece,
parallel **9** analogous, identical,
similarly, uniformly **10** equivalent, synonymous **11** homogeneous, identically
13 corresponding

Alisande (Sandy)
character in: 36 A Connecticut Yankee in King Arthur's
Court
author: 5 Twain

alive 4 spry **5** alert, aware, eager, quick, vital **6** active, extant, lively, living, viable
7 animate, in force, not dead
8 animated, possible, spirited,
vigorous **9** breathing, energetic, operative, vivacious
10 subsisting, unquenched

11 above ground, in existence,
in operation
14 unextinguished

alive to 5 alert, awake, aware
7 heedful, mindful **8** watchful
9 attentive, conscious, wide-
awake

alkaline 5 salty **7** antacid
9 nonacidic

alkaloid 7 alkaline, codeine,
guinine **8** morphine, nicotine
16 colorless complex

all 4 each, full, very **5** any of,
every, fully, total, utter,
whole **6** each of, entire, to a
man, utmost, wholly **7** highest, perfect, totally, utterly
8 any one of, complete, entirely, everyone, greatest, the
sum of, the total, the whole
9 every item **10** altogether,
completely, every one of,
everything, the total of, the
whole of **11** every member,
every part of, exceedingly, the
entirety

All About Eve
director: 17 Joseph L
Mankiewicz
cast: 10 Anne Baxter, Bette
Davis **11** Celeste Holm, Gary
Merrill **12** Thelma Ritter
13 George Sanders, Marilyn
Monroe
Oscar for: 7 picture **8** direc-
tor **10** screenplay **15** sup-
porting actor (George
Sanders)

Allan-a-Dale, Alan-a-Dale
character in: 9 Robin Hood

allargando
music: 13 getting slower

all around 6 abroad **7** all over
10 everywhere, far and wide
15 making the rounds

all-around 5 broad **6** adroit,
gifted **8** flexible **9** adaptable,
many-sided, versatile **11** well-
rounded **12** ambidextrous,
multifaceted **13** comprehensive

allay 4 calm, dull, ease, hush
5 blunt, check, quell, quiet,
slake **6** lessen, pacify, quench,
reduce, smooth, soften,
soothe, subdue **7** appease, assuage, lighten, mollify, relieve,
slacken **8** diminish, mitigate,
moderate **9** alleviate, put to
rest **14** cause to subside

all but 6 almost, nearly **7** close
to **8** not quite **10** not far
from, very nearly **14** except
everyone, within an inch of
16 everything except

all by oneself 5 alone **7** unaided **9** on one's own **10** unassisted **13** unaccompanied

all-consuming 3 hot **5** fiery **6** ardent, fervid, raging, redhot **7** burning, fanatic, fervent, frantic, glowing, intense, zealous **8** frenzied **10** passionate **11** impassioned

allegation 5 claim **6** avowal, charge **9** assertion, statement **10** accusation, contention, indictment, profession **11** declaration

allege 3 say **4** aver, avow **5** claim, state **6** accuse, affirm, assert, charge, impugn, impute **7** contend, declare, profess **8** maintain

allegiance 6 fealty, homage **7** loyalty **8** devotion, fidelity **9** adherence, constancy, deference, obedience **12** faithfulness

allegory 5 fable **7** parable

allegro
    music: **4** fast

all-embracing 5 broad **6** allout **7** general, overall **8** complete, sweeping, thorough **9** expansive, extensive, universal, unlimited **10** exhaustive, widespread **11** far-reaching, wide-ranging **12** all-inclusive, encyclopedic **13** comprehensive

Allen, Arabella
    character in: **14** Pickwick Papers
    author: **7** Dickens

Allen, Ethan
    served in: **16** Revolutionary War
    commander of: **17** Green Mountain Boys
    captured: **15** Fort Ticonderoga

Allen, Fred
    real name: **20** John Florence Sullivan
    born: **11** Cambridge MA
    roles: **11** What's My Line **16** The Fred Allen Show

Allen, Steve
    real name: **12** Stephen Allen
    wife: **12** Jayne Meadows
    nickname: **10** Mr Midnight
    born: **9** New York NY
    roles: **13** I've Got a Secret **14** The Tonight Show

Allen, William Hervey
    author of: **7** Israfel **14** Anthony Adverse

Allen, Woody
    author of: **11** Getting Even, Side Effects **15** Without Feathers
    real name: **22** Allen Stewart Konigsberg

wife: **12** Louise Lasser
born: **10** Brooklyn NY
roles: **5** Zelig **7** Bananas, Sleeper **9** Annie Hall, Manhattan **16** Stardust Memories **19** Hannah and Her Sisters
director of: **5** Zelig **7** Bananas, Sleeper **9** Annie Hall (Oscar), Interiors, Manhattan **16** Stardust Memories **19** Hannah and Her Sisters **20** The Purple Rose of Cairo

alleviate 4 dull, ease, quit **5** abate, allay, blunt, check, slake **6** lessen, quench, reduce, soften, subdue, temper **7** assuage, lighten, mollify, relieve, slacken **8** diminish, mitigate, moderate

alleviation 6 easing, relief **9** lessening **10** palliation

alley 4 lane **5** byway **7** passage, pathway **10** passageway **16** narrow back street

Alley Oop
    creator: **14** Vincent T Hamlin
    character:
        girlfriend: **4** Oola
        dinosaur: **5** Dinny
        king: **6** Guzzle
        scientist: **8** Dr Wonmug
    place:
        kingdom of: **3** Moo

All for Love
    author: **10** John Dryden
    character: **6** Antony, Caesar **7** Octavia **9** Cleopatra, Dolabella, Ventidius

All God's Chillun Got Wings
    author: **12** Eugene O'Neill
    character: **6** Mickey **9** Jim Harris **10** Ella Downey

alliance 4 pact **5** union **6** league, treaty **7** compact, company **9** agreement, coalition, concordat **10** federation **11** affiliation, association, confederacy, partnership **13** confederation **15** entente cordiale

allied 4 akin, like **5** alike, joint **6** united **7** cognate, kindred, related, similar **8** combined **9** corporate, federated **10** affiliated, associated, resembling **11** amalgamated **12** incorporated

all in 4 beat **5** spent, tired, weary **6** bushed, done in, pooped **7** drained, wearied, worn out **8** dog tired, fatigued, tired out **9** bone weary, dead tired, exhausted, played out

all in all 5 in sum **10** on the whole **20** when all is said and done

all-inclusive 5 broad **6** all-out, entire **7** general, overall **8** absolute, complete, sweeping, thorough **9** expansive, extensive, universal, unlimited **10** altogether, exhaustive, widespread **11** far-reaching, wide-ranging **12** all-embracing **13** comprehensive

All in the Family
    character: **10** Joey Stivic, Mike Stivic (Meathead) **11** Edith Bunker (Dingbat) **12** Archie Bunker **18** Gloria Bunker Stivic
    cast: **9** Rob Reiner **13** Jean Stapleton **14** Carroll O'Connor, Sally Struthers
    spinoffs: **5** Maude **12** Archie's Place **13** The Jeffersons

allocate 5 allot, allow **6** assign, budget **7** earmark **8** set aside **9** apportion, designate **11** appropriate

allocation 5 quota, share **7** measure, portion **8** division **9** allotment, meting out **10** dealing out **11** consignment, designation **12** apportioning, dispensation, distribution **13** apportionment

Allosaurus see **10** Antrodemus

allot 5 allow, grant **6** assign **7** appoint, consign, dole out, earmark, give out, mete out, provide **8** allocate, dispense, divide up **9** apportion, parcel out **10** distribute, portion out

allotment 5 grant, quota, share **6** ration **7** measure, portion **9** allowance **10** allocation **11** consignment **12** dispensation **13** apportionment, appropriation

all-out 5 broad, total **7** full-out, maximum **8** complete, sweeping, thorough **9** extensive, full-scale **11** unqualified, unremitting **12** all-embracing, all-inclusive **13** comprehensive, thoroughgoing

all over 5 ended, kaput **8** finished **9** concluded **10** everywhere **11** universally

All Over
    author: **11** Edward Albee

allow 3 let **4** give **5** allot, grant **6** assign, permit **7** agree to, approve, concede, provide **8** allocate, sanction **9** authorize

allowable 7 allowed **8** accepted **9** permitted, tolerable, tolerated **10** acceptable, admissible, admittable, authorized, sanctioned **11** permissible

allowance 5 grant **6** bounty, income, ration **7** annuity, payment, pension, stipend, subsidy 8 discount 9 allotment, deduction, reduction 10 concession 11 subtraction

allow to go 4 free 5 let go 6 excuse 7 dismiss, release, set free 8 liberate 9 discharge

allow to pass
   French: 13 laissez passer

alloy 3 mix 5 admix, blend 6 commix, dilute, fusion, impair 7 amalgam, combine, mixture 8 compound, intermix 9 admixture, composite, synthesis 10 adulterate, commixture, interblend 12 conglomerate

alloyed 5 mixed 6 impure 7 debased

All Quiet on the Western Front
   author: 18 Erich Maria Remarque
   character: 6 Muller, Tjaden 10 Paul Baumer 11 Albert Kropp, Haie Westhus 20 Stanislaus Katczinsky (Kat)
   director: 14 Lewis Milestone
   cast: 8 Lew Ayres 12 Louis Wolheim 14 Russell Gleason
   setting: 3 WWI
   Oscar for: 7 picture

all right 2 OK 3 yes 4 fair, hale, safe, well 6 hearty 7 healthy 8 properly, unharmed 9 certainly, correctly, uninjured 10 absolutely, acceptably, unimpaired 14 satisfactorily
   Spanish: 5 bueno

All Said and Done
   author: 16 Simone de Beauvoir

allspice
   botanical name: 7 pimenta, p dioica 12 p officinalis
   also called: 7 pimento
   origin: 7 Jamaica 16 Caribbean Islands
   flavor: 5 clove 6 nutmeg 8 cinnamon
   use: 6 baking

Allston, Washington
   born: 10 Waccamaw SC
   artwork: 9 The Deluge 13 Uriel in the Sun 16 Belshazzar's Feast, Moonlit Landscape 20 Spanish Girl in Reverie

All's Well That Ends Well
   author: 18 William Shakespeare
   character: 5 Diana 6 Helena 7 Bertram 8 Parolles 12 King of France 14 Duke of Florence 19 Countess of Rousillon

All That Jazz
   director: 8 Bob Fosse
   cast: 9 Ben Vereen 11 Ann Reinking, Cliff Gorman, Roy Scheider 12 Jessica Lange, Leland Palmer

All the King's Men
   author: 16 Robert Penn Warren
   character: 10 Jack Burden, Judge Irwin, Sadie Burke 11 Adam Stanton, Willie Stark 12 Annie Stanton
   director: 12 Robert Rossen
   cast: 9 Joanne Dru, John Derek 11 John Ireland 17 Broderick Crawford 19 Mercedes McCambridge
   Oscar for: 5 actor (Crawford) 7 picture 17 supporting actress (McCambridge)

all the more
   Latin: 9 a fortiori

All the President's Men
   author: 11 Bob Woodward 13 Carl Bernstein
   subject: 16 Watergate scandal
   newspaper: 14 Washington Post
   director: 11 Alan J Pakula
   cast: 10 Jack Warden 11 Hal Holbrook 12 Jason Robards, Martin Balsam 13 Dustin Hoffman (Carl Bernstein), Jane Alexander, Robert Redford (Bob Woodward)
   Oscar for: 12 screenwriter 15 supporting actor (Robards)

all the same 5 alike 7 however, uniform 8 unvaried 9 identical 11 homogeneous

all together 7 en masse, in a body 8 as a group, in a group, in unison
   French: 12 tout ensemble

all told 5 in sum, total 6 in toto 7 totally 8 as a whole 10 altogether

allude 4 hint 5 refer 7 mention, speak of, suggest 8 intimate 9 touch upon

allure 4 bait, lure 5 charm, tempt 6 entice, lead on, seduce 7 attract, beguile, enchant, glamour 8 intrigue 9 captivate, fascinate 10 attraction, enticement, temptation 11 enchantment, fascination

allurement 4 draw, lure 5 charm 9 magnetism 10 attraction 11 fascination

alluring 4 sexy 8 charming, enticing, magnetic 10 attractive 11 fascinating

allusion 4 hint 7 mention 9 reference 10 suggestion

Allworthy, Squire
   character in: 8 Tom Jones
   author: 8 Fielding

ally 5 unite 6 league 7 combine, partner 8 confrere 9 accessory, affiliate, associate, colleague 10 accomplice, join forces 11 confederate 12 band together, bind together, collaborator, join together

Allyson, June
   real name: 11 Ella Geisman
   husband: 10 Dick Powell
   born: 9 New York NY
   roles: 8 Good News 9 Interlude, The Shrike 11 Little Women 12 My Man Godfrey 16 The Stratton Story 18 The Glen Miller Story

Almagest
   author: 7 Ptolemy
   title means: 11 the greatest
   subject: 9 astronomy

Al Maghrib see 7 Morocco

almandite
   species: 6 garnet
   color: 3 red

Almaviva, Count and Countess
   author: 12 Beaumarchais
   characters in: 18 The Barber of Seville 19 The Marriage of Figaro

Almayer's Folly
   author: 12 Joseph Conrad

almighty 7 supreme 8 absolute, infinite 9 sovereign, unlimited 10 invincible, omnipotent 11 all-powerful 12 transcendent

Almira
   opera by: 6 Handel

almond 12 Prunus dulcis
   varieties: 4 Wild 5 Earth, Green, Sweet 6 Bitter, Desert, Indian 8 Tropical 9 Flowering 12 Dwarf Russian
   candy: 8 marzipan
   liqueur: 6 orgeat 7 ratafia

almost 5 about 6 all but, nearly 7 close to 8 not quite, well-nigh 9 just about 10 not far from, very nearly 11 practically, on the verge of 13 approximately 14 within an inch of

almost alike 5 close 7 similar 10 resembling 11 approaching, much the same 15 nearly identical

alms 3 aid 4 dole, gift 5 mercy 6 relief 7 charity, handout, largess, present, subsidy, tribute 8 donation, gratuity, offering, pittance 9 baksheesh 10 assistance

11 benefaction, beneficence
12 contribution

almshouse 6 asylum **9** poor-house, workhouse

almsman 5 tramp **6** beggar **9** mendicant **10** panhandler

Almug 13 red sandalwood

aloft 2 up **5** above, way up **6** high up, on high **7** sky-ward **8** in the air, in the sky, overhead **10** heavenward

Aloha state
  nickname of: **6** Hawaii

Aloidae
  name: **4** Otus **9** Ephialtes
  form: **5** giant
  father: **8** Poseidon
  mother: **9** Iphimedia
  raised by: **6** Aloeus

alone 4 only, sole **6** lonely, single, singly, solely, unique **7** forlorn, unaided **8** deserted, desolate, forsaken, isolated, lonesome, peerless, singular, solitary, uniquely **9** abandoned, matchless, nonpareil, separated, unmatched, unrivaled **10** friendless, separately, singularly, solitarily, unassisted, unattended, unequalled, unescorted **11** unsurpassed, without help **12** incomparable, unchaperoned, unparalleled, without peers **13** unaccompanied, without others **14** single-handedly
  Latin: **4** sola **5** solus
  French: **4** seul

along 2 on **4** over **6** beside, during, onward **7** abreast, forward, through

alongside 2 at, by **6** beside, next to **7** abreast, close by **9** at the side **10** parallel to **12** collaterally, parallelwise **13** equidistantly

aloof 4 cold, cool **5** above, apart **6** chilly, formal, remote **7** distant, haughty, high-hat **8** detached, reserved **10** unsociable **11** at a distance, indifferent, standoffish, unconcerned **12** uninterested, unresponsive **13** unsympathetic **14** unapproachable

aloofness 7 reserve **8** coldness, coolness **9** formality **10** detachment, remoteness **11** haughtiness **12** indifference **13** unsociability **15** standoffishness

Alope
  father: **7** Cercyon
  son: **10** Hippothous
  attacked by: **8** Poseidon

Alopecus
  origin: **7** Spartan
  form: **6** prince

aloud 7 audibly

alphabet 4 ABCs **6** schema **7** grammar, letters **8** elements **9** rudiments, tablature **10** characters, principles **13** writing system

Alphesiboea
  also: **7** Arsinoe
  form: **5** nymph
  father: **4** Bias **7** Phegeus **9** Leucippus
  mother: **9** Philodice
  husband: **8** Alcmaeon
  son: **6** Adonis
  rejected: **8** Dionysus
  nurse for: **7** Orestes

Alpheus
  father: **7** Oceanus
  mother: **6** Tethys
  loved: **8** Arethusa
  changed into: **5** river

Alphonse and Gaston
  creator: **14** Frederick Opper
  saying: **22** After you my dear Alphonse, No after you my dear Gaston

alpine 5 alpen, lofty **6** aerial **8** elevated, snow-clad, towering **9** subalpine **10** alpestrine, sky-kissing, snow-capped **11** cloud-capped, mountainous **13** cloud-piercing, cloud-touching **14** heaven-touching

Alps, Alpine
  country: **5** Italy **6** France **7** Austria, Germany **10** Yugoslavia **11** Switzerland **13** Liechtenstein
  range: **6** Carnic, Graian, Julian, Otztal **7** Bernese, Cottian, Pennine **8** Bavarian, Ligurian, Maritime, Rhaetian **9** Dolomites, Lepontine **10** Hohe Tauern
  peak: **4** Rosa **5** Eiger, Monch **8** Jungfrau **10** Karawanken, Matterhorn, Piz Bernina **13** Grossglockner
  highest point: **5** Blanc
  pass: **7** Brenner, Simplon, Splugen, Stelvio **9** Semmering **10** St Gotthard **14** Great St Bernard
  lake: **4** Como **6** Alpine, Geneva **7** Lucerne **8** Maggiore **9** Constance
  resort: **7** Zermatt **8** Chamonix, Salzburg, St Moritz **9** Innsbruck **13** Berchtesgaden
  wind: **6** foehns

already 5 early, so far **6** before **8** formerly, hitherto, until now **10** heretofore, previously

already seen
  French: **6** deja vu

also 3 and, too **4** more, plus **5** extra, as well **7** besides **8** moreover **9** including **10** in addition **12** additionally

Altaic
  language branches: **6** Turkic **8** Tungusic **9** Mongolian

altar 5 bomos **6** hestia, scribis **7** eschara **8** credence **9** holy table, prothesis **10** Lord's table

Altar
  constellation of: **3** Ara

Altdorfer, Albrecht
  born: **7** Germany **10** Regensburg
  artwork: **16** Susanna at the Bath **20** St George and the Dragon, Susannah and the Elders **24** Landscape with a Footbridge **39** The Battle of Alexander and Darius on the Issus

alter 4 vary **5** amend **6** change, modify, recast, revise **7** convert, remodel **9** transform **13** make different

alterable 7 unfixed **8** variable **9** adaptable **10** adjustable, changeable, modifiable **11** convertible

alteration 6 change **10** adjustment, conversion, remodeling **12** modification **13** transmutation **14** transformation

altercation 3 row **4** spat **5** brawl, broil, fight, melee, scene **6** affray, fracas, rumpus, scrape **7** discord, dispute, quarrel, scuffle **8** argument **9** bickering, wrangling **10** falling-out **11** controversy **12** disagreement

alter ego 4 twin **5** match **6** double **9** duplicate, other self, semblable **10** complement, other image, second self, simulacrum **11** counterpart **12** Doppelganger

alternate 3 sub **4** vary **5** alter, proxy **6** backup, change, deputy, rotate, second **7** another, standby, stand-in **9** surrogate, take turns **10** every other, reciprocal, substitute, successive, understudy **11** alternating, consecutive, every second, interchange, intersperse, pinch hitter

alternative 6 choice, option, way out **8** recourse **9** selection **10** substitute **11** other choice

Altes
  origin: **5** Greek
  mentioned in: **5** Iliad
  king of: **7** Leleges
  daughter: **7** Laothoe

Althaea
father: 8 Thestius
brother: 9 Plexippus
husband: 6 Oeneus
son: 6 Toxeus, Tydeus
8 Meleager
daughter: 5 Gorge 8 Deianira

Althaemenes
father: 7 Catreus
sister: 9 Apemosyne
killed: 7 Catreus 9 Apemosyne

although 3 but, yet 4 even
5 still 7 however 11 nonetheless 12 nevertheless
15 notwithstanding

altitude 4 apex 6 height, vertex, zenith 8 eminence, tallness 9 elevation, loftiness, sublimity 10 prominence

Altman, Robert
director of: 4 MASH
9 Nashville

altogether 5 fully, in all, in sum, quite 6 in toto, wholly 7 all told, totally, utterly 8 all in all, as a whole, entirely 9 in general, out and out, perfectly 10 absolutely, completely, in sum total, on the whole, thoroughly 12 all inclusive, collectively

altruism 7 charity 10 generosity 11 benevolence 12 philanthropy, public spirit 13 unselfishness 14 bigheartedness, charitableness 15 humanitarianism

altruistic 8 generous 9 unselfish 10 benevolent, charitable 12 humanitarian, largehearted 13 philanthropic 14 publicspirited

aluminum
chemical symbol: 2 Al

alumnus 8 graduate 12 male graduate 13 former student

Alverio, Rosita Dolores
real name of: 10 Rita Moreno

always 7 forever 8 evermore 9 eternally, every time, regularly 10 for all time, invariably 11 continually, incessantly, perpetually, unceasingly 12 consistently 13 everlastingly, unremittingly 14 forever and ever

Amadan
origin: 5 Irish
form: 5 fairy

Amadeus
director: 11 Milos Forman
cast: 8 Tom Hulce (Wolfgang Amadeus Mozart) 14 F Murray Abraham (Antonio Salieri)

choreography: 10 Twyla Tharp
Oscar for: 5 actor (Abraham) 7 picture 8 director

Amadis of Gaul
author: 16 Garcia de Montalvo
character: 6 Oriana, Perion 7 Elisena 8 Garinter, Lisuarte

Amado, Jorge
author of: 14 Tent of Miracles 15 Home Is the Sailor 19 Shepherds of the Night 24 Gabriela Clove and Cinnamon 25 Dona Flor and Her Two Husbands 30 The Two Deaths of Quincas Wateryell

Amahl and the Night Visitors
opera by: 7 Menotti

Amalek
father: 7 Eliphaz
mother: 6 Timnah
grandfather: 4 Esau
descendant of: 9 Amalekite

amalgam 5 alloy, blend, combo, union 6 fusion, league, merger 7 joining, mixture 8 alliance, compound, mishmash 9 admixture, composite 10 assemblage, commixture 11 combination 12 amalgamation, intermixture

amalgamate 3 mix 4 fuse 5 blend, merge, unify, unite 7 combine 8 coalesce, federate 9 commingle, integrate 10 synthesize 11 consolidate, incorporate 12 join together

Amalthaea
form: 4 goat 5 nymph
raised: 4 Zeus

Amarcord
director: 15 Federico Fellini
cast: 10 Bruno Zanin, Magali Noel 13 Pupella Maggio

amaretto
type: 7 liqueur
origin: 5 Italy
flavor: 6 almond
with vodka: 9 Godmother

Amaryllis
character in: 9 Ecologues
author: 6 Virgil
represented: 11 shepherdess

Amarynceus
origin: 5 Greek
mentioned in: 5 Iliad
king of: 7 Messene
ruled: 4 Elis
ruled with: 6 Augeas
killed by: 6 Nestor

Amasa
father: 6 Jether
mother: 7 Abigail
uncle: 5 David

commander for: 5 David 7 Absalom
killed by: 4 Joab

amass 6 gather, heap up, pile up 7 acquire, collect, compile, round up 8 assemble 10 accumulate

amassing 7 heaping, piling 8 piling up 9 aggregate, compiling, gathering 10 assemblage, assembling, collecting 11 compilation 12 accumulating

Amata
husband: 7 Latinus
daughter: 7 Lavinia

amateur 4 tyro 6 novice 7 dabbler 8 beginner, hobbyist, inexpert, neophyte 9 greenhorn, unskilled 10 dilettante, unpolished 13 inexperienced 14 unprofessional 15 nonprofessional

amateurish 5 inept 6 clumsy 7 awkward 8 inexpert, mediocre 9 unskilled, untrained 10 unskillful 11 incompetent, ineffective, unpracticed 13 inexperienced 14 unaccomplished, unprofessional

amatory 3 hot 4 fond, sexy 6 ardent, doting, erotic, loving, sexual, steamy, tender 7 adoring, amorous, devoted, fervent, sensual, sexed-up 8 lovesick, romantic, yearning 9 libidinal, loverlike, rapturous 10 infatuated, lascivious, passionate 11 impassioned, languishing

amaxophobia
fear of: 7 driving 8 vehicles

amaze 3 awe 4 daze, stun 5 shock 7 astound, stagger, stupefy 8 astonish, surprise 9 dumbfound 11 flabbergast

amazement 3 awe 5 shock 6 wonder 8 surprise 9 disbelief 11 incredulity 12 astonishment, bewilderment, stupefaction

Amaziah
father: 5 Joash
opposed: 7 Jehoash
captured at: 11 Bethshemesh
killed at: 7 Lachish

Amazon
occupation: 7 warrior
sex: 6 female
queen: 9 Hippolyta

amazonite
species: 8 feldspar

Amazonomachia
battle between: 6 Greeks 7 Amazons

ambassador 5 agent, envoy 6 consul, deputy, legate, nuncio **7** attache, courier **8** diplomat, emissary, minister **9** go-between **11** diplomatist **12** intermediary **13** consul general **14** representative

Ambassadors, The
author: **10** Henry James
character: **8** Strether, Waymarsh **10** Mrs Newsome **11** Mamie Pocock, Sarah Pocock **12** Maria Gostrey **15** Chadwick Newsome **17** Comtesse de Vionnet

amber
formed from: **5** resin
color: **6** yellow
Greek: **8** elektron

ambiance 3 air **4** aura, mood, tone **5** tenor **6** spirit, flavor, milieu, temper **7** climate, setting **9** character **10** atmosphere **11** environment **12** surroundings

ambiguity 9 vagueness **11** uncertainty **12** abstruseness, doubtfulness, equivocation **14** indefiniteness
French: **13** double entente

ambiguous 5 vague **7** cryptic, unclear **8** doubtful, puzzling **9** enigmatic, equivocal, uncertain **10** indefinite, misleading

ambition 3 aim **4** goal, hope, plan, push, zeal **5** dream, drive **6** design, desire, intent **7** longing, purpose **8** striving, yearning **9** objective **10** aspiration

ambitious 4 avid **5** eager **6** ardent, intent **7** arduous, zealous **8** aspiring, desirous **9** difficult, energetic, grandiose, strenuous **10** determined **11** industrious **12** enterprising

ambivalent 5 mixed **7** warring **8** clashing, confused, opposing, wavering **9** equivocal, undecided, unfocused **10** wishy-washy **11** conflicting, fluctuating, vacillating **13** contradictory

amble 6 ramble, stroll **7** meander, saunter **15** wander aimlessly

Ambler, Eric
author of: **11** The Levanter **12** A Kind of Auger **13** The Care of Time **14** The Night-Comers, Uncommon Danger **15** Journey Into Fear, The Dark Frontier **16** The Light of the Day **19** A Coffin for Dimitrios **22** The Siege of the Villa Lipp

Ambling Alp, The
nickname of: **12** Primo Carnera

ambrosial 5 balmy **8** fragrant, luscious, perfumed **9** delicious **13** sweet-smelling

ambrosia of the gods
4 food **5** drink **6** nectar **7** perfume

ambulance chaser 4 beak **6** lawyer **8** attorney **9** counselor **10** mouthpiece **12** legal advisor

ambulatory 6 mobile, moving **7** walking **10** up and about **11** peripatetic

ambush 4 trap **5** blind, cover **6** attack, entrap, hiding, lay for, waylay **7** assault **8** hideaway, surprise **9** ambuscade **11** concealment, hiding place **13** stalking-horse

Ameche, Don
real name: **17** Dominic Felix Amici
born: **9** Kenosha WI
roles: **6** Cocoon (Oscar) **13** Heaven Can Wait, Moon Over Miami, Silk Stockings **14** That Night in Rio **16** Down Argentine Way **18** The Three Musketeers **29** The Story of Alexander Graham Bell

Amelia
author: **13** Henry Fielding
character: **10** Dr Harrison **11** Mrs Atkinson **12** Miss Matthews **19** Captain William Booth

ameliorate 4 heal, help, mend **5** amend, fix up **6** better, perk up, pick up, reform, remedy, revise **7** advance, correct, improve, patch up, promote, rectify **8** palliate, progress **9** come along, get better **10** grow better **11** improve upon

ameliorative 8 remedial **9** improving **10** corrective, palliative **11** therapeutic **12** compensatory

amen 5 truly **6** it is so, so be it, verily **8** hear hear **9** let it be so, yes indeed **11** so shall it be **17** would that it were so

Amen
also: **4** Amon **5** Ammon
origin: **8** Egyptian
king of: **4** gods
worshiped at: **6** Thebes
personifies: **3** air **6** breath
represented by: **3** ram **5** goose
patron of: **6** Thebes
corresponds to: **4** Jove, Zeus **6** Amen Ra, Amon Ra **7** Jupiter

amenable 4 open **7** cordial, willing **8** obliging, yielding

9 agreeable, tractable **10** open-minded, responsive, submissive **11** acquiescent, complaisant, cooperative, persuadable, sympathetic **17** favorably disposed

amend 3 fix **4** mend **5** alter, emend **6** better, change, modify, polish, reform, remedy, revise **7** correct, develop, enhance, improve, perfect, rectify

amendment 6 change, reform **7** adjunct **8** addition, revision **10** alteration, correction, emendation **11** improvement **12** modification **13** rectification

amends 7 apology, defense, payment, redress **8** requital **9** atonement, expiation **10** recompense, reparation **11** explanation, restitution, restoration, retribution, vindication **12** compensation, satisfaction **13** justification, peace offering **14** acknowledgment **15** indemnification

amenity, amenities 8 civility, mildness, niceties **9** geniality, gentility **10** affability, amiability, courtesies, gentleness, politeness, refinement **11** gallantries, good manners **12** friendliness, graciousness, pleasantness **13** agreeableness

Amen Ra
also: **6** Amon Ra
origin: **8** Egyptian
god of: **8** universe
corresponds to: **4** Amen, Amon, Jove, Zeus **5** Ammon **7** Jupiter

America
author: **19** Stephen Vincent Benet

America, North see box, p. 36

America, South see box, p. 37

American, The
author: **10** Henry James
character: **8** Mrs Bread **10** Mr Tristram **11** Mrs Tristram **12** Noemie Nioche **13** Count Valentin **14** Claire de Cintre **17** Christopher Newman **25** Marquis Urbain de Bellegarde
setting: **5** Paris

American Caesar
author: **17** William Manchester

American Claimant, The
author: **9** Mark Twain

American Dreams
author: **11** Studs Terkel

American Graffiti
director: **11** George Lucas
cast: **9** Paul Le Mat, Ron

America, North
country: 4 Cuba 5 Haiti 6 Belize, Canada, Mexico, Panama 8 Honduras 9 Costa Rica, Guatemala, Nicaragua 10 El Salvador 12 United States 17 Dominican Republic
island: 5 Banks 6 Baffin, Kodiak 7 Bahamas, Bermuda 8 Victoria 9 Alexander, Anticosti, Ellesmere, Greenland, Vancouver 10 Aleutians, Cape Breton, Long Island, West Indies 11 Southampton 12 Newfoundland, Prince Edward 13 Prince of Wales 14 Queen Charlotte
mountain: 5 Coast, Rocky 6 Brooks 7 Cascade 9 Mackenzie 10 Bitterroot 11 Appalachian 12 Sierra Nevada
highest point: 8 McKinley
lowest point: 11 Death Valley
river: 3 Red 4 Ohio 5 Yukon 6 Copper, Fraser, Hudson, Nelson 8 Arkansas, Colorado, Columbia, Delaware, Missouri 9 Mackenzie 10 Coppermine, Sacramento, San Joaquin, St Lawrence 11 Connecticut, Mississippi
lake: 4 Erie 5 Huron 6 Carson, Walker 7 Nipigon, Ontario 8 Manitoba, Michigan, Reindeer, Superior, Winnipeg 9 Athabasca, Champlain, Great Bear, Great Salt 10 Great Slave 14 Yellowstone
animal: 3 bat, rat 4 bear, lynx, puma, wolf 5 bison, moose, skunk 6 beaver, musk ox 7 bighorn, caribou 8 sewellel 9 pronghorn, white goat
bird: 4 hawk 5 eagle, snipe 8 bobwhite, woodcock, wood ibis 9 blue heron, ptarmigan
sea: 6 Bering 7 Chukchi, Lincoln 8 Beaufort 9 Caribbean
religion: 7 Judaism 10 Protestant 13 Roman Catholic 27 Eastern Orthodox Christianity
people: 6 Eskimo 8 European 12 African Negro 14 American Indian
language: 6 French 7 English, Spanish

Howard 10 Candy Clark 11 Wolfman Jack 12 Harrison Ford 13 Cindy Williams 15 Richard Dreyfuss 17 MacKenzie Phillips

American in Paris, An
director: 16 Vincente Minnelli
cast: 8 Nina Foch 9 Gene Kelly 11 Leslie Caron, Oscar Levant 14 Georges Guetary
score: 14 George Gershwin
Oscar for: 7 picture

Americanization of Emily
director: 12 Arthur Hiller
script by: 14 Paddy Chayefsky
cast: 11 James Coburn, James Garner 12 Julie Andrews 13 Melvyn Douglas

American Tragedy, An
author: 15 Theodore Dreiser
character: 12 Roberta Alden 14 Clyde Griffiths, Sondra Finchley 15 Samuel Griffiths

America's Sweetheart
nickname of: 12 Mary Pickford

amethyst
species: 6 quartz
color: 6 purple
month: 8 February

Amfortas
leader of: 7 knights
in search of: 9 holy grail

ami, amie 6 friend

amiability 10 good nature, kindliness 12 agreeability, friendliness, pleasantness

amiable 6 genial, kindly, polite 7 affable, cordial, winning 8 amicable, charming, engaging, friendly, gracious, obliging, pleasant, pleasing, sociable 9 agreeable, congenial 10 attractive 11 good-natured

amicability 5 amity 7 concord 8 good will 9 affection 10 cordiality, friendship 12 friendliness 14 neighborliness

amicable 4 kind 5 civil 6 kindly, polite 7 amiable, cordial 8 amenable, friendly, sociable 9 agreeable, courteous, peaceable 10 benevolent, harmonious, neighborly 11 kindhearted

Amici, Dominic Felix
real name of: 9 Don Ameche

amicus curiae 17 a friend of the court

amigo, amiga 6 friend

Amis, Kingsley
author of: 8 Ending Up, Lucky Jim 10 Colonel Sun, Jake's Thing 11 I Like It Here, The Green Man 16 One Fat Englishman, Take A Girl Like You 18 Russian Hide-and-Seek, The Anti-Death League 20 That Uncertain Feeling

amiss 4 awry 5 askew, false, wrong 6 astray, faulty 7 falsely, mixed-up, off base, wrongly 8 faultily, improper, mistaken, untoward 9 erroneous, incorrect, out of line 10 fallacious, improperly, mistakenly, out of order, unsuitable, unsuitably, untowardly 11 erroneously, incorrectly 12 inaccurately 13 inappropriate 15 inappropriately

Amittai
son: 5 Jonah

amity 6 accord 7 concord, harmony 8 good will, sympathy 9 agreement 10 cordiality, fellowship, fraternity, friendship 11 brotherhood, cooperation 13 understanding

Ammishaddai
son: 7 Ahiezer

Ammon
father: 3 Lot
descendants: 9 Ammonites

Ammon see 4 Amen

Ammonite god 6 Molech, Moloch

ammunition 4 ammo, arms 5 shell 6 bullet, rocket 7 missile, torpedo 9 artillery, cartridge, small arms 11 iron rations 13 powder and shot

ammunition dump 7 arsenal 8 magazine 18 military storehouse, munitions warehouse

amnesia 4 daze 5 fugue 6 stupor 7 agnosia 8 blackout 9 memory gap 11 anterograde, trance state

amnesty 6 pardon 8 immunity, reprieve 10 absolution 11 forgiveness 14 reconciliation

amoeba, ameba 4 dyad, germ, mold 5 spore, virus 6 fungus 7 ciliate, microbe 8 bacteria, reovirus 9 bacterium, echovirus 13 microorganism
part: 7 nucleus 8 membrane 9 pseudopod 10 protoplasm 11 food vacuole 18 contractile vacuole
reproduction by: 7 fission

amok see 5 amuck

Amon see 4 Amen

America, South
country: **4** Peru **5** Chile **6** Brazil, Guyana **7** Bolivia, Ecuador, Uruguay **8** Colombia, Paraguay, Suriname **9** Argentina, Venezuela
city: **4** Lima **5** Quito **6** Bogota, Recife **7** Caracas **8** Salvador, Santiago, Sao Paulo **10** Montevideo **11** Buenos Aires, Porto Alegre **12** Rio de Janeiro **13** Belo Horizonte
island: **6** Chiloe, Chonos, Marajo **9** Galapagos **10** Wellington **11** Madre de Dios **13** Juan Fernandez, Reina Adelaida **14** Tierra del Fuego
sea: **9** Caribbean
lake: **5** Patos, Poopo, Mirim **6** Viedma **8** Titicaca **9** Maracaibo, San Martin **10** Concepcion
mountain: **6** Andes **9** Pakaraima **12** Monte Fitz Roy **14** Cerro Aconcagua, Monte Sarmiento **15** Serra dos Parecis **16** Monte San Valentin, Serra do Espinhaco
highest point: **9** Aconcagua
lowest point: **15** Peninsula Valdes
river: **3** Ica **4** Beni, Iaco, Jari, Meta, Napo **5** Abuna, Cauca, Chico, Iriri, Ituxi, Jurua, Jutai, Negro, Palma, Pardo, Purus, Tiete, Tigre, Xingu **6** Amazon, Arauca, Branco, Chubut, Cumina, Curaco, Cuyuni, Grande, Gurupi, Iguacu, Japura, Javari, Mamore, Maroni, Mortes, Parana, Salado, Vaupes **7** Bermejo, Caqueta, Deseado, Guapore, Jamunda, Juruena, Madeira, Mapuera, Maranon, Orinoco, Oyapock, Ucayali, Vichada **8** Amazonas, Araguaia, Colorado, Guaviare, Jamachim, Paraguay, Parnaiba, Putumayo, Tapajoz, Urubamba, Uruguay **9** Essequibo, Jaguaribe, Paranaiba, Saladillo, Sao Manuel, Tocantins **10** Courantyne **12** Sao Francisco
animal: **3** bat **4** bear, deer **5** llama, sloth, tapir **6** alpaca, monkey, ocelot, weasel **7** opossum, peccary, raccoon **8** capybara, javelina **9** armadillo
bird: **3** owl **4** hawk, rhea **5** eagle **6** condor, falcon, jabiru **7** hoatzin **8** flamingo **11** hummingbird
people: **6** Indian **7** African, Chibcha, Mestizo, Mulatto, Spanish **10** Araucanian, Portuguese
religion: **7** Judaism **10** Protestant **13** Roman Catholic
language: **5** Dutch **7** English, Spanish **10** Portuguese

among 2 at **3** mid **4** amid, with **6** amidst **7** amongst, between, betwixt **12** in the midst of

among other persons
Latin: **10** inter alios

among others 8 attended, escorted, in a crowd, in a group, together **11** accompanied

among other things
Latin: **9** inter alia

among themselves
Latin: **7** inter se

Amon Ra see **6** Amen Ra

Amopaon
mentioned in: **5** Iliad
form: **7** warrior
army: **6** Trojan
killed by: **6** Teucer

Amor see **5** Cupid

Amore dei Tre Re, L'
opera by: **10** Montemezzi

Amoretti
author: **13** Edmund Spenser

amorous 4 fond **6** ardent, doting, loving, tender **8** enamored, lovesick **10** passionate **11** impassioned **12** affectionate

amorousness 4 love **5** ardor **6** warmth **7** passion

amor patriae 10 patriotism **13** love of country

amorphous 5 vague **8** formless, unshapen **9** anomalous, shapeless, undefined **11** nondescript **12** undelineated **13** characterless, indeterminate

Amos
father: **4** Naum

Amos 'n' Andy
character: **8** Lightnin' **9** Amos Jones, Andy Brown **13** George (the King Fish) Stevens **15** Sapphire Stevens
cast: **8** Tim Moore **13** Ernestine Wade, Horace Stewart

14 Alvin Childress **15** Spencer Williams

amount 3 sum **4** bulk, mass **5** total **6** extent, volume **7** measure **8** quantity, sum total **9** aggregate, magnitude

amour 6 affair **7** liaison, romance **8** intrigue **10** love affair

amour propre 8 self-love **10** self-esteem **11** self-respect

Ampelos
form: **5** satyr

Ampere, Andre-Marie
field: **7** physics **11** mathematics
nationality: **6** French
founded: **15** electrodynamics **16** electromagnetism

Amphiaraus
father: **6** Oicles
mother: **12** Hypermnestra
wife: **8** Eriphyle
son: **8** Alcmaeon **11** Amphilochus
daughter: **9** Demonassa
member: **18** Seven against Thebes
charioteer: **5** Baton

amphibian 8 seaplane **10** hydroplane, vertebrate **14** aerohydroplane
kind: **4** frog, newt, toad **9** caecilian **10** salamander
young: **6** larvae **7** tadpole **8** polliwog

Amphidamas
king of: **7** Cythera
father: **5** Aleus
brother: **7** Cepheus
member of: **9** Argonauts

Amphilochus
form: **4** seer
father: **10** Amphiaraus
mother: **8** Eriphyle
brother: **8** Alcmaeon

Amphimachus
origin: **5** Greek
mentioned in: **5** Iliad
chief of: **6** Epeans
father: **13** Cteatus of Elis
killed by: **6** Hector

Amphimarus
father: **8** Poseidon
son: **5** Linus
vocation: **8** musician

Amphinome
form: **6** maiden
father: **6** Pelias
sister: **6** Evadne
deceived by: **5** Medea
killed: **6** Pelias

Amphinomus
suitor of: **8** Penelope

Amphion
father: **4** Zeus

mother: 7 Antiope
twin brother: 6 Zethus
wife: 5 Niobe
daughter: 7 Chloris
built: 11 Theban walls

Amphisbaena
form: 7 serpent
number of heads: 3 two

amphitheater 4 bowl 5 arena
7 gallery, stadium 8 coliseum
10 auditorium
Roman: 9 Colosseum

Amphithemis
also: 7 Garamas
father: 6 Apollo
mother: 9 Acacaelis
son: 8 Nausamon
9 Caphaurus

Amphitrite
origin: 5 Greek
goddess of: 3 sea
father: 6 Nereus
mother: 5 Doris
husband: 8 Poseidon

Amphitruo (Amphitryon)
author: 7 Plautus
character: 4 Zeus 7 Alcmena,
Jupiter, Mercury
10 Amphitryon

Amphitryon
father: 7 Alcaeus
grandfather: 8 Perseus
uncle: 9 Electryon, Sthenelus
wife: 7 Alcmene
son: 8 Iphicles
daughter: 8 Perimede

Amphitryon 38
author: 13 Jean Giraudoux

Amphius
ally of: 7 Trojans

amphora 3 jar, jug, urn 4 vase

Amphoterus
father: 8 Alcmaeon
mother: 10 Callirrhoe
brother: 7 Acarnan

ample 3 big 4 huge, vast,
wide 5 broad, large, roomy
6 enough, plenty 7 copious,
immense, liberal, profuse
8 abundant, adequate, ex-
tended, generous, spacious
9 bountiful, capacious, expansive, extensive, outspread,
plentiful 10 commodious, sufficient, voluminous 11 substantial 12 satisfactory 14 more
than enough

amplification 7 raising 8 increase, widening 9 expansion,
extension 10 developing, filling out, increasing 11 added
detail, development, elaboration, enlargement, expatiation,
fleshing out, heightening,
lengthening, rounding out
12 augmentation 13 magnification 14 aggrandizement
15 supplementation

amplify 5 add to, raise, widen
6 deepen, expand, extend
7 augment, broaden, develop,
enlarge, fill out 8 complete,
heighten, increase, lengthen
9 elaborate (on), expatiate, intensify 10 illustrate,
strengthen, supplement

amplitude 4 bulk, mass, size
5 range, reach, scope, sweep,
width 6 extent, volume 7 bigness, breadth, compass, expanse 8 fullness, plethora,
richness, vastness 9 abundance, dimension, largeness,
magnitude, plenitude, profusion 11 copiousness 12 completeness, spaciousness
13 capaciousness

amply 5 fully 6 richly 8 lavishly 9 copiously, liberally,
profusely 10 abundantly, adequately, completely, generously, thoroughly
11 bountifully, plentifully
12 sufficiently, unstintingly
14 satisfactorily

amputate 5 sever 6 cut off, excise, lop off, remove
9 dismember

Ampycides
epithet of: 6 Mopsus
means: 12 son of Ampycus

Amram
father: 4 Bani 6 Dishon
son: 5 Aaron, Moses
daughter: 6 Miriam

Amsterdam
airport: 8 Schiphol
canal: 11 Herengracht
13 Keizersgracht,
Prinsengracht
capital of: 7 Holland
11 Netherlands
landmark: 8 Oude Kerk
10 Nieuwe Kerk
museum: 7 Van Gogh
9 Stedelijk 11 Rijksmuseum
nickname: 16 Venice of the
North
waters: 6 Amstel 7 Ij River
9 Zuiderzee 10 Ijsselmeer
13 North Sea

amuck 4 amok, nuts 6 wildly
7 berserk, bonkers 8 crackers,
insanely 9 in a frenzy
10 frenziedly, maniacally
11 ferociously, murderously
14 uncontrollably

amulet 5 charm 6 fetish 8 talisman 10 lucky piece

Amulius
father: 5 Proca
brother: 7 Numitor

amuse 5 cheer 6 absorb, divert,
occupy, please 7 beguile, engross, enliven, gladden 8 interest 9 entertain

amusement 3 fun 4 game,
play 5 hobby, revel 7 delight,
pastime 8 pleasure 9 avocation, diversion, enjoyment,
merriment 10 recreation
11 distraction
13 entertainment

amusing 5 droll, funny, witty
7 comical, waggish 8 cheering,
farcical, humorous, pleasant,
pleasing 9 absorbing, beguiling, diverting 10 delightful,
engrossing 11 interesting,
pleasurable 12 entertaining

Amy, Gilbert
composer of: 9 Alpha-Beth
10 Epigrammes, Mouve-
ments 11 Antiphonies
12 Trajectories

Amyclas
father: 7 Amphion
10 Lacedaemon
mother: 5 Niobe 6 Sparta

Amymone
father: 6 Danaus
son: 8 Nauplius
lover: 8 Poseidon

Amyntor
king of: 8 Ormenium
father: 7 Ormenus
wife: 8 Cleobule
son: 7 Phoenix
daughter: 9 Astydamia
concubine: 6 Phthia
killed by: 8 Hercules

Amythaon
father: 4 Tyro
mother: 8 Cretheus
wife: 7 Idomene
son: 4 Bias 8 Melampus

An
origin: 8 Sumerian
god of: 6 heaven
corresponds to: 3 Anu

Anadyomene *see* 9 Aphrodite

anagram 4 code 6 cipher

Anakim 11 giant people

analects 8 extracts 9 gleanings 10 miscellany, selections
11 collectanea, miscellanea

Analects of Confucius, The
author: 9 Confucius

analeptic 9 stimulant
11 restorative

analgesic 4 drug 6 opiate
7 anodyne 8 narcotic 10 anesthetic, painkiller

analogous 4 akin, like 7 similar 8 parallel 10 comparable,
equivalent 11 correlative
13 corresponding

analogy 6 simile 8 likeness,
metaphor 10 comparison, similarity, similitude 11 correla-

tion, equivalence, parallelism, resemblance **14** correspondence

analysis 4 test **5** assay, brief, study **6** digest, precis, review, search **7** breakup, inquiry, outline, summary, therapy **8** abstract, judgment, synopsis, thinking **9** appraisal, breakdown, diagnosis, partition, reasoning, reduction **10** dissection, estimation, evaluation, resolution, separation **11** examination, observation, speculation **12** dissociation **13** investigation, psychotherapy **14** interpretation, psychoanalysis

analyst 5 judge **6** shrink, tester **8** examiner, observer **9** appraiser, estimator, evaluator **12** headshrinker, investigator **13** psychoanalyst

analytic, analytical 7 logical, testing **8** rational, studious **9** inquiring, organized, searching **10** diagnostic, systematic **14** problem-solving

analyze 5 assay, judge, study **6** search **7** examine **8** appraise, consider, diagnose, evaluate, question **9** reason out **11** investigate **12** think through

Anammelech 13 Sepharvite god

Ananais
father: **8** Nebedeus
wife: **8** Sapphira
sent to: **4** Paul, Saul
lied to: **5** Peter

anarchist 5 rebel **8** mutineer, nihilist **9** insurgent, terrorist **11** syndicalist **13** revolutionary

anarchy 5 chaos **6** utopia **8** disorder **11** lawlessness **13** the millennium **19** absence of government

Anastasia
director: **13** Anatole Litvak
cast: **10** Helen Hayes, Yul Brynner **12** Akim Tamiroff **13** Ingrid Bergman
Oscar for: **7** actress (Bergman)

anathema 3 ban **5** curse, taboo **7** censure **11** abomination, malediction **12** condemnation, denunciation, proscription **13** unmentionable **15** excommunication

Anathema
author: **14** Leonid Andreyev

anathematize 4 damn **7** accurse, condemn **8** execrate, maledict **9** abominate **13** excommunicate **17** hold in abomination

Anatolia see **7** Armenia

Anatolian
language family: **12** Indo-European
spoken in: **9** Asia Minor
spoken by: **8** Hittites

anatomist 12 morphologist
American: **5** Allen, Evans **7** Herrick **8** Stockard
Arabian: **8** Avicenna
British: **4** Owen **5** Hooke **6** Harvey
Dutch: **10** Swammerdam
French: **6** Buffon, Cuvier
German: **5** Wolff **7** Schwann
Greek: **5** Galen **9** Aristotle **10** Herophilus **12** Erasistratus
Italian: **8** Malpighi
Scottish: **5** Brown

anatomize 7 analyze, dissect **18** separate into pieces

anatomy 4 body **8** analysis **9** structure **10** dissection **11** examination

Anatomy Lesson, The
author: **10** Philip Roth

Anatomy of a Murder
director: **13** Otto Preminger
cast: **8** Eve Arden **9** Lee Remick **10** Ben Gazzara **12** George C Scott, James Stewart, Kathryn Grant **14** Arthur O'Connell
score: **13** Duke Ellington

Anatomy of Melancholy, The
author: **12** Robert Burton

Anatosaurus
type: **8** dinosaur **10** ornithopod
period: **10** Cretaceous
characteristic: **10** duck-billed
location: **12** North America

Anax
member of: **8** Gigantes
son: **8** Asterius

Anaxarete
form: **8** princess

Anaxibia
father: **6** Atreus
mother: **6** Aerope
brother: **8** Menelaus **9** Agamemnon
husband: **6** Nestor **9** Strophius
son: **7** Pylades

Anaximander
field: **11** mathematics
nationality: **5** Greek
doctrine: **11** single-world
first: **22** geometric universe model

Ancaeus
father: **8** Poseidon
member: **9** Argonauts
ship: **4** Argo
vocation: **8** helmsman
gift: **8** strength

ancestor 8 begetter, forebear **9** precursor, prototype **10** antecedent, forefather, forerunner, procreator, progenitor **11** predecessor

ancestry 4 line, race **5** house, stock **6** family, origin **7** descent, lineage **8** heredity, pedigree **9** ancestors, blood line, genealogy, parentage **10** derivation, extraction, family tree **11** progenitors

Anchesmius see **4** Zeus

Anchiale
form: **5** nymph

Anchinoe
father: **5** Nilus
husband: **5** Belus
son: **6** Danaus **8** Aegyptus

Anchisaurus
type: **8** dinosaur
location: **17** Connecticut Valley

Anchises
prince of: **4** Troy
father: **5** Capys
mother: **8** Themiste
grandfather: **9** Assaracus
uncle: **8** Laomedon
brother: **7** Laocoon
son: **5** Lyrus **6** Aeneas

anchor 3 fix **4** hook, moor **5** affix, basis **6** fasten, secure **7** bulwark, defense, mooring, support **8** mainstay, security **9** safeguard **10** foundation **12** ground tackle

anchorage 3 key **4** bund, dock, pier, port, quay, slip **5** berth, haven, jetty, wharf **6** harbor, marina **7** dockage, mooring, seaport **9** harborage, roadstead

ancient 3 old **4** aged **5** early, hoary, Greek, olden, passe, Roman **6** age-old, bygone, old hat, remote **7** antique, archaic, very old **8** long past, obsolete, outmoded, primeval, timeworn **9** classical, out-of-date, primitive **10** antiquated, fossilized, Greco-Roman **11** obsolescent, prehistoric **12** old-fashioned, out-of-fashion

ancientness 8 great age **9** antiquity **11** advanced age

ancient times 9 antiquity **10** days of yore **12** the Golden Age

Ancile
origin: **5** Roman
form: **6** shield
given to: **13** Numa Pompilius
given by: **4** Mars
purpose: **10** protection
copied by: **8** Mamurius

ancillary 5 minor **7** adjunct

8 inferior **9** accessory, auxiliary, dependent, secondary
10 additional, subsidiary
11 subordinate, subservient
12 contributory
13 supplementary

Ancius
form: **7** centaur

Ancus Marcius
king of: **4** Rome

and 3 too **4** also, more, plus
10 in addition

andante
music: **4** even **14** moderately
slow

Andean
language family: **16** Andean-
Equatorial
group: **3** Ona **6** Aymara, Yahgan, Zaparo **7** Quechua
10 Araucanian

Andean-Equatorial
language branch: **6** Andean
10 Equatorial

Andersen, Hans Christian
author of: **10** Thumbelina
11 The Red Shoes **12** The
Snow Queen, The Swineherd, The Tinder Box
14 The Nightingale **15** The
Ugly Duckling **16** The Little
Mermaid **18** The Little
Match Girl **20** The Princess
and the Pea **21** The Emperor's New Clothes **22** The
Steadfast Tin Soldier **25** The
Shepherdess and the Sweep

Anderson, Frances
Margaret
real name of: **14** Judith
Anderson

Anderson, Judith
real name: **23** Frances Margaret Anderson
born: **8** Adelaide **9** Australia
roles: **5** Medea **6** Hamlet, Salome **7** Macbeth, Rebecca
8 Kings Row **16** Cat on a
Hot Tin Roof

Anderson, Maxwell
author of: **7** High Tor **8** Key
Largo **9** Winterset **11** Valley
Forge **14** Both Your Houses,
Lost in the Stars, Mary of
Scotland, What Price
Glory? **17** Elizabeth the
Queen **20** Knickerbocker
Holiday

Anderson, Sherwood
author of: **9** Poor White
12 Beyond Desire, Dark
Laughter, Horses and Men
13 Many Marriages, Winesburg Ohio **15** Death in the
Woods **18** The Triumph of
the Egg

Anderson, Sparky (George
Lee)
sport: **8** baseball
position: **7** manager
team: **9** Minnesota **14** Cincinnati Reds

Andersonville
author: **15** MacKinlay Kantor

Andersson, Bibi
born: **6** Sweden **9** Stockholm
roles: **14** The Seventh Seal
16 Wild Strawberries
19 Scenes from a Marriage
20 Smiles of a Summer
Night

Andes
Spanish: **20** Cordillera de los
Andes
peak: **6** Pissis, Sajama, Sorata **7** Illampu **8** Cotopaxi, Illimani **9** Huascaran
10 Chimborazo **14** Cristobal
Colon
highest point: **9** Aconcagua
volcano: **6** Sangay, Tolima
8 Cotopaxi **10** Tungurahua
country: **4** Peru **5** Chile
6 Panama **7** Bolivia, Ecuador **8** Colombia **9** Argentina,
Venezuela
river: **5** Cauca **6** Amazon,
Parana **7** Orinoco, Ucayali
9 Magdalena
lake: **5** Poopo **8** Titicaca
animal: **5** llama **6** alpaca, condor, huemul **10** chinchilla

And I Worked at the Writer's Trade
author: **13** Malcolm Cowley

Andorra *see box*

Andorra-la-Vella
capital of: **7** Andorra

and others 3 etc **4** et al **6** et
alii **7** and so on **8** et cetera
10 and so forth, and the rest

And Quiet Flows the Don
author: **15** Mikhail Sholokov
character: **6** Piotra **7** Bunchuk, Natalia **14** Gregor Melekhov **16** Aksinia
Astakhova

Andrea del Sarto
real name: **32** Andrea Domenico d'Agnolo di
Francesco
born: **5** Italy **8** Florence
artwork: **7** Caritas **9** A Young
Man **16** Birth of the Virgin,
Journey of the Magi
19 Madonna of the Harpies,
Portrait of a Sculptor

Andrea del Sarto
author: **14** Robert Browning

Andress, Ursula
husband: **9** John Derek
born: **5** Bern **11** Switzerland
roles: **3** She **4** Dr No **12** Casino Royale, Four for Texas

Andorra
other name: **13** Valls
d'Andorra **16** Valleys of
Andorra
capital/largest city:
14 Andorra-la-Vella
others: **3** Pal **5** Ramio
6 Ordino, Soldeu
7 Canillo, Certers **9** La
Massana **11** Les Escaldes **16** San Julian de
Loria
division: **6** Encamp, Ordino **7** Andorra, Camillo **9** La Massana, Sant
Julia
heads of state:
13 Bishop of Urgel
(Spain) **17** President of
France
head of government:
11 First Syndic
monetary unit: **5** franc
6 peseta
lake: **11** Engolasters
mountain: **6** d'Etats
8 l'Estanyo, Pyrenees
10 Cataperdis
highest point: **11** Como
Pedrosa
river: **6** Ariege, Valira
people: **7** Catalan
8 Andosian
language: **6** French
7 Catalan, Spanish
religion: **13** Roman
Catholic
place: **12** Casa de la Vall
Moorish ruin: **4** Ceca,
Meka
feature:
co-princes' representative: **7** vigueer,
viguier
fiesta: **13** Bal de
Morratxa
food payment to
bishop: **9** la quistia

Andrew 7 apostle
brother: **5** Peter, Simon

Andrews, Dana
real name: **17** Carver Dana
Andrews
brother: **12** Steve Forrest
born: **9** Collins MS
roles: **5** Laura **9** State Fair
12 Elephant Walk **13** A
Walk in the Sun, Ox-Bow
Incident **15** Two for the
Seesaw **22** The Best Years of
Our Lives

Andrews, Julie
real name: **19** Julia Elizabeth
Wells
husband: **12** Blake Edwards
born: **7** England **14** Walton-
on-Thames

roles: 10 My Fair Lady
11 Mary Poppins (Oscar)
14 Victor Victoria 15 The
Sound of Music

**Andreyev, Leonid
Nikolaevich**
author of: 3 S O S 5 Savva
7 Lazarus, Silence 8 Anathema 10 To the Stars 11 The
Red Laugh 12 The Life of
Man 16 He Who Gets
Slapped 18 Love of One's
Neighbor 19 Seven That
Were Hanged

Andria
author: 7 Terence

Androclea
father: 18 Antipoenus of
Thebes

Androcles
origin: 5 Roman
position: 5 slave

Androcles and the Lion
author: 17 George Bernard
Shaw

Androgeus
father: 5 Minos
mother: 8 Pasiphae
son: 7 Alcaeus 9 Sthenelus
battled: 6 Athens

androgenous
14 hermaphroditic

Andromache
father: 6 Eetion
husband: 6 Hector
son: 6 Pielus 8 Astyanax, Molossus, Pergamus
9 Cestrinus
author: 9 Euripides
character: 6 Peleus, Thetis
7 Orestes 8 Menelaus
mistress of:
11 Neoptolemus
rival: 8 Hermione
son: 8 Molossus
setting: 8 Thessaly

Andromaque
author: 18 Jean Baptiste
Racine
character:
son: 8 Astyanax
king: 7 Pyrrhus
setting: 6 Epirus

Andromeda
father: 7 Cepheus
mother: 10 Cassiopeia
husband: 7 Perseus
son: 6 Mestor, Perses 7 Alcaeus, Heleius 9 Electryon,
Sthenelus
daughter: 10 Gorgophone
rescued from: 10 sea
monster
rescued by: 7 Perseus

Andromeda Strain, The
author: 15 Michael Crichton

androphobia
fear of: 3 men

Androsphinx
form: 6 sphinx
head of: 3 man

and so forth 3 etc 7 and so
on 8 et cetera 9 and others
10 and the rest

and so on 3 etc 8 et cetera
9 and others 10 and so forth,
and the rest

**And Then There Were
None**
director: 9 Rene Clair
based on novel by: 14 Agatha Christie
cast: 11 Roland Young
12 Louis Hayward, Walter
Huston 15 Barry Fitzgerald
remade as: 16 Ten Little
Indians

and thou, Brutus
Latin: 9 et tu Brute
spoken by: 12 Julius Caesar

Andvari
origin: 6 Nordic
form: 5 dwarf

Andy Capp
creator: 14 Reginald Smythe
character: 5 Vicar
wife: 3 Flo
plays: 7 snooker

Andy Griffith Show, The
character: 10 Andy Taylor,
Barney Fife, Goober Pyle,
Helen Crump, Opie Taylor
11 Floyd Lawson 12 Otis
Campbell 13 Aunt Bee Taylor, Howard Sprague
cast: 8 Hal Smith 9 Don
Knotts, Ron (Ronny) Howard 10 Jack Dodson
12 Andy Griffith, Anita Corsaut, Howard McNear
13 Frances Bavier, George
Lindsey
setting: 8 Mayberry
Andy's job: 7 sheriff

anecdote 4 tale, yarn 5 story
6 sketch 12 brief account,
reminiscence

anemic, anaemic 3 wan
4 dull, pale, weak 5 quiet
6 feeble, pallid 7 subdued
9 colorless 11 thin-blooded
13 characterless

anemone 4 lily 5 plant
6 flower

Anemotis
epithet of: 6 Athena
means: 5 winds

Anesidora
epithet of: 7 Demeter
means: 15 sender up of gifts

**anesthesia, anaesthesia,
anesthesis** 6 stupor 8 numbness 11 insentience 13 loss of
feeling 15 unconsciousness

anesthetic, anaesthetic
4 drug 5 ether, local 6 caudal,
opiate, spinal 7 general 8 narcotic, procaine 9 analgesic, enflurane, halothane, lidocaine,
peridural 10 chloroform, isoflurane, painkiller, tetracaine,
thiopental 11 acupuncture,
laughing gas 12 nitrous oxide
15 sodium pentothal

anesthetize 4 dope, drug,
numb 6 deaden, sedate

anew 5 again, newly 6 afresh
8 once more 9 over again
11 from scratch
Latin: 6 de novo

**a new order of the ages is
born**
Latin: 17 novus ordo
seclorum
author: 6 Virgil
work: 8 Eclogues
motto of: 11 US great seal

angel 3 gem 4 doll 5 jewel,
power, saint 6 cherub, patron,
seraph, throne, virtue 7 sponsor 8 cherabim, seraphim,
treasure 9 archangel 10 benefactor, domination 11 underwriter 12 principality
14 celestial being, heavenly
spirit, messenger of God
15 financial backer

Angel, fallen 5 Satan 6 Azazel 7 Lucifer

angelic 4 good, pure 5 ideal
6 divine, lovely 7 saintly
8 adorable, beatific, cherubic,
ethereal, heavenly, innocent,
seraphic 9 angel-like, beautiful,
celestial, rapturous, spiritual
10 entrancing 11 enrapturing

Angelic Doctor
nickname of: 15 St Thomas
Aquinas

Angelico, Fra
real name: 13 Guido di
Pietro
born: 7 Vicchio 14 Castell
Vecchio
artwork: 12 Annunciation
15 Madonna Annalena
19 Descent from the Cross
21 Coronation of the Virgin 29 Madonna of the
Linen Drapers' Guild

Angelo
character in: 17 Measure for
Measure
author: 11 Shakespeare

Angel of Fire, The
also: 13 The Fiery Angel
opera by: 9 Prokofiev

anger 3 ire, vex 4 bile, fury,
gall, rage, rile 5 annoy, chafe,
pique, wrath 6 choler, dander,
enmity, enrage, hatred, madden, nettle, rankle, ruffle,

spleen, temper **7** incense, inflame, outrage, provoke, umbrage **8** acrimony, embitter, irritate, vexation **9** animosity, annoyance, displease, hostility, hot temper, ill temper, infuriate, petulance **10** antagonism, antagonize, exacerbate, exasperate, irritation, resentment **11** displeasure, indignation **12** exasperation, make bad blood **14** disapprobation **15** get one's dander up **16** cause ill feelings **18** ruffle one's feathers

Anger
author: **9** May Sarton

Angerboda
also: **9** Angrbodha, Angurboda
origin: **12** Scandinavian
form: **8** giantess
children: **3** Hel **6** Fenrir, Fenris **11** Iormungandr, Jormungandr **14** Midgard Serpent

Angerona
origin: **5** Roman
goddess of: **7** anguish

angle 4 bend, cusp, edge, side, turn **5** focus, slant **6** aspect, corner **7** outlook **8** position **9** viewpoint **10** divergence, standpoint **11** perspective, point of view
kind: **5** acute, right **6** obtuse **8** straight
point: **6** vertex
measure: **7** degrees

angled 4 bent **6** fished **7** crooked, slanted **8** diverged

Anglo-Frisian
language family: **12** Indo-European
branch: **8** Germanic
group: **15** Western Germanic
language: **7** English, Frisian

Angola *see box*

Angrbodha *see* **9** Angerboda

angry 3 mad **5** huffy, irate, riled, vexed **6** fuming, galled, piqued, raging **7** annoyed, boiling, burnt up, enraged, furious, hateful, hostile, nettled **8** incensed, inflamed, offended, outraged, petulant, provoked **9** affronted, indignant, irasci-

ble, irritated, resentful, splenetic, turbulent **10** displeased, embittered, infuriated **11** acrimonious, exasperated, ill-tempered **12** antagonistic

angst 5 dread **6** unease **7** anxiety **10** foreboding, uneasiness **12** apprehension

angstrom
abbreviation: **1** A

Angstrom, Anders Jon
field: **7** physics **9** astronomy
founded: **12** spectroscopy
mapped: **11** solar system
angstrom unit: **17** wavelength of light

anguish 3 woe **4** pain **5** agony, grief **6** misery, sorrow **7** anxiety, despair, remorse, torment **8** distress **9** heartache, suffering

Anguish
goddess of: **8** Angerona

anguished 6 pained **7** anxious, fearful **9** tormented **10** distressed **11** heartbroken

angular 4 bent, bony, lank, lean **5** gaunt, lanky, spare **6** jagged **7** crooked, scrawny **8** rawboned **13** sharp-cornered

Angurboda *see* **9** Angerboda

Angus Og
origin: **5** Irish
god of: **4** love **5** youth **6** beauty

Anicetus
father: **8** Hercules
mother: **4** Hebe

animadversion 4 flak **7** nagging, quibble **9** aspersion, criticism, pestering **12** faultfinding **14** censoriousness

animal 3 pet **5** beast, brute **6** mammal **8** creature, nonhuman, organism **9** quadruped
group: **4** bird, fish, worm **6** insect, mammal, sponge **7** primate, reptile, rotifer **8** ruminant **9** amphibian **10** vertebrate **12** invertebrate

Animal Crackers
director: **13** Victor Heerman
cast: **5** Chico, Harpo, Zeppo **7** Groucho **11** Lillian Roth **12** Marx Brothers **14** Margaret Dumont
song: **25** Hooray for Captain Spaulding

Animal Farm
author: **12** George Orwell
character: **5** Boxer **7** Mr Jones **8** Napoleon, Snowball

Animals in that Country, The
author: **14** Margaret Atwood

Angola
other name: **7** Bakongo **20** Portuguese West Africa
capital/largest city: **6** Luanda
others: **5** Dundo **6** Ambriz, Huambo, Lobito **7** Cabinda, Kampala, Malange, Malanje, Salazar **8** Benguela, Cassinga, Vila Luso **9** Ambrizete, Mocamedes **10** Mossamedes, Nova Lisboa, Silva Porto
division: **3** Bie **4** Uige **5** Huila, Lunda, Zaire **6** Cunene, Huambo, Luanda, Moxico **7** Cabinda, Malanje **8** Benguela, Cuanza Sul, Mocamedes **11** Cuanza Norte **13** Cuando Cubango
monetary unit: **6** escudo, macuta, macute **7** angolar, centavo
mountain: **5** Chela **6** Loviti **16** Humpata Highlands
highest point: **4** Moco
river: **4** Cuvo **5** Congo, Cuito, Longa **6** Cassai, Coanza, Cuando, Cuanza, Cunene, Kunene, Kwango, Kwanza, Luando **7** Chiumbe, Cubango, Zambezi **11** Lungue-Bungo
sea: **6** Indian **8** Atlantic
physical feature:
  basin: **8** Okavango
  desert: **9** Mocamedes
  falls: **15** Catarata Ruacana, Duque de Braganca
  plain: **8** Planalto
  plateau: **4** Rand **5** Huila **11** Benguela Bie, Lunda Divide
people: **5** Bantu, Kongo, Lundu **6** Chokwe, Herero, Mbundu, Ovambo **7** Bakongo, Kangela, Kikongo **8** Kimbundu, Kwangare **9** Ovinbundu **12** Nyaneka-Humbi
  leader: **13** Agostinho Neto **20** Jose Eduardo dos Santos
language: **5** Bantu **8** Kimbundu, Oumbundu **9** Ovinbundu **10** Portuguese
religion: **7** animism **10** Protestant **13** Roman Catholic
place:
  fortress: **9** Sao Miguel
feature:
  mahogany: **5** khaya
  weed: **6** archil

animate 4 fire, goad, move, stir, urge, warm 5 alive, impel, set on 6 arouse, excite, fire up, incite, moving, prompt, spur on, vivify, work up 7 actuate, enliven, inspire, provoke, quicken 8 activate, energize, vitalize 9 instigate, make alive, stimulate 10 invigorate, make lively 11 add spirit to 12 give energy to

animated 3 gay, hot 4 airy 5 brisk, quick, vivid 6 active, ardent, blithe, breezy, bright, elated, lively 7 buoyant, dynamic, fervent, glowing, vibrant, zealous, zestful 8 exciting, spirited, sportive, vigorous 9 ebullient, energetic, sprightly, vivacious 10 passionate 12 invigorating

animation 3 vim 4 fire, glow, life, zest 5 ardor, verve, vigor 6 action, gaiety, spirit 7 elation 8 activity, alacrity, buoyancy, vibrancy, vitality, vivacity 9 alertness, briskness, eagerness, good cheer 10 brightness, ebullience, enthusiasm, excitement, liveliness 12 exhilaration, sportiveness 13 sprightliness

animosity 4 hate 5 anger 6 enmity, hatred, malice, rancor, strife 7 dislike, ill will 8 acrimony 9 antipathy, hostility, malignity 10 antagonism, bitterness, resentment 11 malevolence 14 unfriendliness

animus 5 anger, spite, venom 6 enmity, hatred, malice, rancor 7 disdain, dislike, ill will 8 acrimony, bad blood 9 animosity, antipathy, hostility 10 antagonism, bitterness, ill feeling, resentment 12 hard feelings

anise
  botanical name: 16 Pimpinella Anisum
  origin: 5 Egypt, India 13 Mediterranean
  flavor: 8 licorice
  use: 5 cakes, fruit, rolls 7 cookies
  plant with similar flavor: 9 star anise
  legend:
    safeguards against: 7 evil eye 10 nightmares 11 indigestion
    antidote to: 12 scorpion bite

anisette
  type: 7 liqueur
  origin: 6 France
  flavor: 5 anise
  drink: 17 Suissesse cocktail
  with gin: 8 Snowball 11 Bachio Punch
  substitute for: 8 Absinthe

Ankylosaurus
  type: 8 dinosaur 10 ornithopod
  location: 12 North America
  period: 10 Cretaceous
  characteristic: 7 armored

Anna
  husband: 5 Tobit
  daughter: 4 Mary
  sister: 4 Dido
  corresponds to: 11 Anna Perenna
  died by: 8 drowning

Annabel Lee
  author: 13 Edgar Allan Poe

Anna Christie
  author: 12 Eugene O'Neill
  character: 6 Marthy 8 Mat Burke 19 Chris Christopherson
  ship: 14 Simeon Winthrop

Anna Karenina
  author: 10 Leo Tolstoy
  character: 12 Count Vronsky 13 Alexei Karenin 15 Konstantin Levin 19 Kitty Shcherbatskaya 20 Prince Stepan Oblonsky
  setting: 6 Moscow, Russia 12 St Petersburg
  director: 13 Clarence Brown
  cast: 9 May Robson 10 Greta Garbo (Anna Karenina) 13 Basil Rathbone (Karenin), Frederic March (Vronsky) 16 Maureen O'Sullivan 18 Freddie Bartholomew
  earlier film version: 4 Love

annals 7 history, minutes, records 8 archives 9 registers 10 chronicles, chronology 13 yearly records 15 historical rolls 20 chronological records

Annam *see* 7 Vietnam

Anna Marie
  character in: 16 Giants of the Earth
  author: 7 Rolvaag

Anna of the Five Towns
  author: 13 Arnold Bennett

Anna Perenna
  origin: 5 Roman
  goddess of: 9 longevity

anneal 6 harden, temper 7 toughen

Anne of Geierstein (or, The Maiden of the Mist)
  author: 14 Sir Walter Scott

annex 3 add 4 grab, join 5 affix, merge, seize 6 adjoin, append, attach, tack on 7 acquire, connect, subjoin 8 addition 9 appendage 10 attachment 11 appropriate, expropriate, incorporate

Annfwn
  also: 5 Annwn

origin: 5 Welsh
means: 8 paradise

Annie Hall
  director: 10 Woody Allen
  cast: 9 Carol Kane, Paul Simon 10 Woody Allen 11 Diane Keaton, Tony Roberts 13 Shelley Duvall 15 Colleen Dewhurst
  Oscar for: 7 actress (Keaton), picture 8 director (Allen) 10 screenplay

annihilate 3 end 5 erase, waste 7 abolish, destroy, wipe out 8 decimate, demolish, lay waste 9 eradicate, extirpate, liquidate 10 extinguish, obliterate 11 exterminate

annihilation 9 abolition, wiping out 11 destruction, extirpation, laying waste, liquidation 12 obliteration 13 extermination

anniversary 4 fete 7 holiday, name day 8 birthday, feast day 9 centenary 10 centennial 11 bicentenary, celebration 12 bicentennial 13 commemoration, golden jubilee 16 sesquicentennial

Ann-Margret
  real name: 16 Ann-Margret Olsson
  husband: 10 Roger Smith
  born: 6 Sweden 9 Valsjobyn
  roles: 5 Tommy 12 Bye-Bye Birdie 15 Carnal Knowledge

anno mundi 19 in the year of the world

anno regni 19 in the year of the reign

annotate 5 gloss 6 remark 7 comment, explain, expound 8 construe, footnote 9 elucidate, explicate, interpret 10 commentate

annotation 4 note 5 gloss 6 remark 7 comment 8 exegesis, footnote 10 commentary, marginalia 11 elucidation, explication, observation

announce 5 augur 6 herald, reveal, signal 7 betoken, declare, divulge, give out, portend, presage, publish, signify, trumpet 8 disclose, foretell, proclaim 9 advertise, broadcast, harbinger 10 promulgate 11 disseminate

announcement 9 broadcast, statement 11 declaration 12 proclamation

annoy 3 irk, nag, tax, vex 4 gall, rile 5 harry, tease, worry 6 badger, bother, harass, heckle, hector, nettle, pester, plague, ruffle 7 disturb,

provoke, torment, trouble
8 distract, irritate 10 exasperate 13 inconvenience

annoyance 6 bother 8 irritant,
nuisance, vexation 10 irritation 11 distraction, disturbance

annoyed 5 irked, upset, vexed
9 disturbed, irritated, perturbed 11 discomposed
12 disconcerted

Ann Sothern Show, The
character: 6 Johnny 10 Olive
Smith 11 James Devery,
Katy O'Connor 13 Jason
Macauley
cast: 9 Don Porter 10 Ann
Sothern, Ann Tyrrell 11 Ernest Truex 12 Jack
Mullaney

annual 4 weed 5 plant
6 flower, serial 7 gazette, journal, reports 8 bulletin, magazine, notebook, periodic
9 vegetable 10 periodical, record book

annuity 6 income 7 pension,
stipend 9 allowance

annul 4 undo, void 6 cancel,
negate, recall, repeal, revoke
7 abolish, nullify, rescind, retract, reverse 8 abrogate, dissolve 10 invalidate

annulment 6 recall, repeal
7 undoing, voiding 8 reversal
9 abolition 10 abrogation, retraction, revocation 11 dissolution, repudiation
12 cancellation, invalidation
13 nullification

annus mirabilis 13 year of
wonders

Annwn see 6 Annfwn

anodyne 4 balm 6 solace
7 comfort 9 comforter
10 palliative

anoint 3 oil 5 crown 6 ordain
8 put oil on 9 pour oil on

Anointed One 5 Jesus
7 Messiah

anomalous 3 odd 7 bizarre,
strange 8 abnormal, atypical,
peculiar 9 irregular, monstrous 11 incongruous 12 out
of keeping

anomaly 6 oddity, rarity 9 deviation 10 aberration 11 abnormality, incongruity,
peculiarity 12 eccentricity, irregularity 18 exception to the
rule

anon 4 soon, then 5 again,
later 7 by and by, shortly
8 tomorrow 9 afterward, presently 10 before long 11 immediately, in the future

anonymous 7 unnamed

8 nameless, unsigned 12 unidentified 13 bearing no
name 14 unacknowledged
19 of unknown authorship

anoplura
class: 8 hexopoda
phylum: 10 arthropoda
group: 11 sucking lice

another 4 else, more 5 extra,
other 7 further, renewed 9 accessory, otherwise 10 additional 12 supplemental
13 something else, supplementary 14 different thing

Anouilh, Jean
author of: 6 Becket 8 Antigone, Eurydice, Leocadia,
L'hermine 11 Dear Antoine
14 Time Remembered 15 Le
Bal des Voleurs, Thieves'
Carnival 16 Point of Departure, Ring Round the
Moon 19 Waltz of the Toreadors 20 L'Invitation au
Chateau 23 Traveller Without Luggage

answer 3 say 4 fill, meet, suit
5 reply, serve, solve, write
6 be like, rejoin, retort 7 conform, fulfill, react to, resolve,
respond 8 be enough, response, solution 9 be similar,
rejoinder 10 be adequate, correspond, pass muster, resolution 11 acknowledge,
explanation 12 be correlated,
be equivalent, be sufficient, do
well enough 14 acknowledgment, be satisfactory

answerable 6 liable 8 beholden 10 chargeable 11 accountable, responsible

Answer as a Man
author: 14 Taylor Caldwell

ant
caste: 4 male 5 queen
6 worker 7 soldier
kind: 3 red 4 army, fire
5 dairy, thief 6 beggar,
farmer, velvet, weaver
7 formica, janitor, pharaoh
8 honeypot, mushroom
9 Argentine, carpenter, cornfield, harvester, legionary
10 leaf cutter 11 little
black 12 fungus grower,
odorous house, southern
fire 13 mound building
14 Texas harvester
group of: 6 colony

Antaea
epithet of: 4 Rhea 6 Cybele
7 Demeter
means: 6 prayer

Antaeus
form: 5 giant
father: 8 Poseidon
mother: 2 Ge
gift: 13 invincibility

power derived from: 5 Earth
crushed by: 8 Hercules
crushed in: 3 air
home: 6 Africa

antagonism 5 spite 6 animus,
enmity, hatred, rancor, strife
7 discord, dislike, rivalry
8 aversion, clashing, conflict,
friction 9 animosity, antipathy,
hostility 10 bitterness, dissension, opposition, resentment
11 detestation

antagonist 3 foe 5 enemy, rival 7 opposer 8 attacker, opponent 9 adversary, assailant,
disputant 10 competitor,
contestant

antagonistic 7 hostile 8 contrary, inimical 9 rancorous
10 antisocial, unfriendly
11 belligerent 12 antipathetic,
disputatious

antagonize 5 repel 6 offend
8 alienate, estrange

Antagoras
occupation: 8 shepherd
home: 3 Cos
challenged: 8 Hercules

Antananarivo, Tananarive
capital of: 10 Madagascar

Antarctica see **box**

ante 3 bet, pot 5 stake, wager
12 beginning bet

anteater 5 sloth 7 echidna
8 aardvark 9 armadillo

antecede 7 precede, predate
8 go before, preexist
10 anticipate

ante Christum 12 before
Christ
abbreviation: 2 AC

antedate 7 precede, predate
8 antecede, go before 9 come
first 10 anticipate 12 happen
before

Antediluvian 14 before the
flood

antediluvian 7 antique, archaic 8 obsolete 10 antiquated

antelope 8 ruminant
family: 7 Bovidae
kind: 3 doe, gnu 4 buck,
deer, fawn, kudu, oryx,
roan 5 bongo, eland, moose,
sable 6 dik-dik, duiker, impala, lechwe, nilgai 7 gazelle, gemsbok, gerenuk
8 bluebuck, bontebok, steinbok 9 blackbuck, sitatunga,
springbok, waterbuck
10 four-horned
12 Klipspringer
habitat: 4 Asia 6 Africa

Antelope State
nickname of: 8 Nebraska

Antarctica
  division: 10 Wilkes
    Land 13 Marie Byrd
    Land, Queen Maud
    Land 14 Edith Ronne
    Land 17 Ellsworth
    Highland
  island: 4 Ross 5 Peter,
    Scott 6 Biscoe, Hearst
    7 Ballery, Charcot
    8 Adelaide, Elephant
    9 Alexander, Joinville,
    Roosevelt 10 Corona-
    tion, King George
    11 South Orkney
    13 South Shetland
  mountain: 8 Sentinel
    9 Pensacola 14 Trans-
    antarctic 23 Executive
    Committee Range
  valley: 6 Wright
  river: 4 Onyx
  natural resource/min-
    eral: 4 coal
  plant life: 4 moss 5 al-
    gae, fungi 6 lichen, pol-
    len 8 bacteria
  animal: 4 lice, mite,
    tick 5 whale 7 fur seal
    8 ross seal 9 crabeater
    11 weddell seal, wing-
    less fly
  bird: 4 skua 6 fulmar,
    petrel 7 penguin
    10 cape pigeon
  sea: 4 Ross 5 Davis
    6 Scotia 7 Weddell
    8 Amundsen
    14 Bellingshausen

antenna 6 aerial, feeler

anterior 5 front, prior 7 forward, in front 8 previous
9 precedent 10 antecedent
12 placed before

Anteros
  brother: 4 Eros
  avenger of: 14 unrequited
    love

Antevorta
  also: 6 Prorsa 7 Porrima
  form: 5 nymph
  member of: 7 Camenae
  gift: 8 prophecy

Anthas
  father: 8 Poseidon
  mother: 7 Alcyone

Anthea
  epithet of: 4 Hera
  means: 7 flowery

Antheil, George
  born: 9 Trenton NJ
  autobiography: 13 Bad Boy
    of Music
  composer of: 7 Volpone
    12 Helen Retires, Jazz Sym-

phony 13 Sonata Sauvage,
Transatlantic 14 Airplane
Sonata 15 Ballet Mecanique

anthem 4 hymn, song 5 carol,
ditty, music, paean, psalm
6 ballad, sacred 7 cantata
8 doxology 11 church music

Anthesteria
  origin: 5 Greek
  festival of: 4 wine 6 spring
    7 flowers

Antheus
  father: 7 Antenor
  killed by: 5 Paris

anthology 6 choice, digest
7 garland 8 analects, chapbook, extracts, treasury
9 gleanings, scrapbook 10 collection, compendium, miscellany, selections 11 collectanea,
compilation, florilegium, miscellanea 15 commonplace
book

Anthony Adverse
  author: 18 William Hervey
    Allen

anthophobia
  fear of: 7 flowers

anthropologist
  American: 4 Boas, Mead
    5 Lowie, Sapir 6 Geertz, Lin-
    ton, Morgan 7 Kroeber
    8 Benedict
  British: 5 Leach, Tylor
    6 Fortes, Leakey, Rivers
    14 Evans-Pritchard, Radcliffe-
    Brown
  French: 5 Mauss 8 Durkheim
    11 Levi-Strauss
  Polish: 10 Malinowski

anthropology
  term: 4 myth 6 custom, rit-
    ual 7 culture, kinship 8 arti-
    fact 9 ethnology, evolution,
    field work 11 ethnography
    16 natural selection
  type/related study: 5 legal,
    urban 6 social 7 applied,
    medical 8 cultural, eco-
    nomic, physical 9 political
    11 linguistics 12 human
    ecology 13 psychological
    19 structural-symbolist
  famous study: 3 San 4 Kung
    7 Eskimos, Samoans, Tasa-
    day 10 Aborigines 16 Pacific
    Islanders

anthropophobia
  fear of: 6 people

Antia
  husband: 7 Proetus
  daughter: 7 Lysippe
  slandered: 11 Bellerophon

antibiotic 4 drug 5 venom
6 poison 8 curative 9 antidotal,
antitoxic, pesticide 10 wonder
drug 11 insecticide, miracle
drug

kind: 8 neomycin, subtilin
9 mycomycin 10 ampicillin,
penicillin 12 erythromycin

antic, antics 5 larks, sport
6 pranks, tricks 9 escapades
10 buffoonery, skylarking,
tomfoolery 11 shenanigans
12 clownishness, monkey-
shines 14 practical jokes

anticipate 5 await 6 expect
7 count on, foresee, long for,
look for, predict 8 envision,
forecast, foretell 9 pin hope
on 10 look toward 13 look
forward to

anticipation 4 hope 10 expectancy 11 expectation,
preparation

anticlimax 7 letdown 8 comedown 14 disappointment

antidote 4 cure 6 remedy
9 antitoxin 10 antipoison, corrective 12 counteragent, coun-
tervenom 13 counterpoison
14 countermeasure

Antigone
  author: 9 Sophocles 11 Jean
    Anouilh
  character: 6 Ismene
    8 Tiresias
    father: 7 Oedipus
    mother: 7 Jocasta
    brother: 8 Eteocles
      9 Polynices
    sister: 6 Ismene
    uncle: 5 Creon
    cousin/lover: 6 Haemon
    defied: 5 Creon

Antigua and Barbuda see
box, p. 46

anti-intellectual 5 yahoo
7 lowbrow 9 ignoramus, vulgarian 10 illiterate, philistine

Antilochus
  father: 6 Nestor
  brother: 11 Thrasymedes
  friend: 8 Achilles

Antimachus
  origin: 5 Greek
  mentioned in: 5 Iliad
  chieftain of: 7 Trojans

antimony
  chemical symbol: 2 Sb

Antinous
  suitor of: 8 Penelope
  killed by: 8 Odysseus

Antiochus
  father: 8 Hercules
  mother: 4 Meda

Antiope
  form: 6 Amazon
  father: 7 Nycteus
  sister: 9 Hippolyte
  son: 6 Zethus 7 Amphion
    10 Hippolytus
  mistress of: 7 Theseus

Antigua and Barbuda
  capital/largest city: **7** St
    John's
  government:
    member of: **26** West
      Indies Associated
      States
  head of state: **14** British
    monarch **15** governor-
    general
  island: **4** Long **5** Guana
    7 Antigua, Barbuda,
    Redonda
  highest point: **9** Boggy
    Peak
  sea: **9** Caribbean
  physical feature:
    cove: **5** Royal
    harbor/harbour:
      7 English
  people: **7** African, Brit-
    ish **8** Lebanese
    10 Portuguese
  language: **7** English
  religion: **8** Anglican, Mo-
    ravian **13** Roman
    Catholic
  feature: **15** Nelson's
    Dockyard

antipathetic 6 averse **7** hostile **8** inimical **9** rancorous
11 ill-disposed

antipathy 6 enmity, rancor
7 disgust, dislike, ill will
8 aversion, distaste, loathing
9 animosity, hostility, repulsion **10** abhorrence, antagonism, repugnance
14 unfriendliness

Antiphas
  father: **7** Laocoon

Antiphates
  origin: **5** Greek
  mentioned in: **5** Iliad
    7 Odyssey
  father: **8** Melampus
  chief of: **10** Laestrygon
  occupation: **7** warrior
    9 chieftain
  killed by: **8** Leonteus

Antipholus
  character in: **17** The Comedy
    of Errors
  author: **11** Shakespeare

antiphony 6 chorus **7** refrain
8 response

Antiphus
  origin: **5** Greek
  mentioned in: **5** Iliad
    7 Odyssey
  form: **5** nymph
  father: **5** Priam
    10 Talaemenes
  half-brother: **4** Isus
  ally of: **4** Troy
  devoured by: **10** Polyphemus

antipode 8 contrary, opposite
10 antithesis

Antipoenus
  daughter: **5** Alcis **9** Androclea
  home: **6** Thebes
  descendant of: **6** Sparti

Antiquary, The
  author: **14** Sir Walter Scott

antiquated 5 dated, passe
7 antique, archaic **8** obsolete,
outdated, outmoded **9** out-of-
date **11** obsolescent **12** old-
fashioned

antique 3 old **5** curio, relic
6 rarity **7** bibelot, trinket
9 objet d'art **10** antiquated,
memorabile **11** memorabilia

antiquities 6 relics **8** artifact
9 monuments

antiquity 7 oldness **8** great
age **11** ancientness **12** ancient
times

antiseptic 7 aseptic, sterile
8 germ-free **9** germicide
10 germ killer **11** bactericide
12 disinfectant, prophylactic

antisocial 7 asocial, hostile
8 menacing, retiring, unsocial
9 alienated **10** disruptive, rebellious, unfriendly, unsociable **11** belligerent, sociopathic
12 antagonistic, misanthropic

antithesis 7 inverse, reverse
8 antipode, contrary, contrast,
converse, opposite

antithetical 8 contrary, opposing, opposite **10** discrepant, refutatory **11** conflicting,
disagreeing **13** contradictory
14 countervailing,
irreconcilable

antitoxin 5 serum **8** antidote
9 antivenom **12** counteragent
13 counterpoison

antler 4 horn, knob, rack
5 spike **6** shovel **8** deerhorn,
troching
  part: **3** bay **4** brow **5** crown,
  royal

ant lion
  also: **8** lacewing **9** doodlebug
  kind: **6** owlfly **9** dusty wing,
    mantidfly **12** spongillafly
    13 brown lacewing, giant
    lacewing, green lacewing
    14 beaded lacewing **15** ith-
    onid lacewing **16** pleasing
    lacewing

Antonello da Messina
  born: **5** Italy **7** Messina
  artwork: **8** Ecce Homo
    11 Three Angels **13** Il Con-
    dottiere (Portrait of a Man),
    Salvador Mundi **21** Saint
    Jerome in his Study

Antonio
  character in: **12** Twelfth
    Night **19** The Merchant of
    Venice
  author: **11** Shakespeare

Antonioni, Michelangelo
  director of: **6** Blowup **8** The
    Night **10** The Eclipse **12** The
    Adventure, The Passenger
    14 Zabriskie Point

Antony, Mark
  also: **14** Marcus Antonius
  member of: **11** triumvirate
  other triumvirs: **7** Lepidus
    8 Octavian (Caesar Augustus)
  lover: **9** Cleopatra
  cousin: **12** Julius Caesar
  wife: **7** Octavia
  battle: **6** Actium **8** Philippi
    9 Pharsalus
  invaded: **7** Parthia
  died by: **7** suicide

Antony and Cleopatra
  author: **18** William
    Shakespeare
  character: **7** Octavia **9** Cleo-
    patra **10** Mark Antony
    14 Octavius Caesar
  setting: **5** Egypt
  Cleopatra bitten by: **3** asp

antonym 8 opposite
10 antithesis
  abbreviation: **3** ant

Antrodemus
  type: **8** dinosaur, therapod
  also called: **10** Allosaurus
  period: **8** Jurassic
    10 Cretaceous

Anu
  origin: **8** Akkadian
  god of: **6** heaven
  corresponds to: **2** An

Anubis
  origin: **8** Egyptian
  god of: **5** tombs **9** embalming
  weigher of: **15** hearts of the
    dead
  represented by head of:
    6 jackal

Anunnaki
  origin: **8** Sumerian
  member of: **14** divine
    assembly
  assembly headed by: **2** An
    5 Enlil

anvil 5 block, incus **9** con-
verter **11** transformer

anxiety 4 fear **5** alarm, angst,
dread, worry **6** unease **7** anguish, concern, tension **8** disquiet, distress, suspense
9 misgiving **10** foreboding, solicitude, uneasiness **11** disquietude, fretfulness
12 apprehension

anxiety-ridden 7 anxious,
fearful, nervous **10** distraught

11 worried sick
12 apprehensive

anxious 4 avid, keen **5** eager, tense **6** ardent, intent, uneasy **7** alarmed, earnest, fearful, fervent, fretful, itching, uptight, wanting, worried, zealous **8** desirous, troubled, yearning **9** anguished, concerned, disturbed, expectant, impatient **10** disquieted, distressed **11** overwrought **12** apprehensive

any 3 all, one **4** each, lone, sole, some **5** every **6** single, unique **8** anything, singular, solitary **9** something **10** individual, quantifier

anybody 3 any **6** anyone **8** anything

anyhow *see* **6** anyway

anything 3 any **4** some **5** aught **6** anyone **7** anybody

anyway 6 anyhow **8** sloppily **9** at any rate, in any case **10** carelessly, in any event, regardless **11** haphazardly, just the same, nonetheless **12** nevertheless **13** indifferently **14** without concern

anywhere 8 anyplace, wherever **11** wheresoever

Aoede
muse of: **4** song

Ao-men *see* **5** Macao

A-1 3 ace **4** aces, fine, tops **5** great, prime, super **6** choice, grade-A, superb, tip-top **7** capital **8** sterling, superior, topnotch **9** excellent, first-rate, superfine **10** first-class, tremendous **11** crackerjack, outstanding, superlative

Aornis
tributary of: **4** Styx

Aornum
entrance to: **5** Hades
used by: **7** Orpheus

Aotearoa *see* **10** New Zealand

apace 4 fast **7** flat-out, hastily, quickly, rapidly, swiftly **8** speedily **9** posthaste **10** at top speed **11** double-quick, on the double **12** lickety-split **13** expeditiously, precipitately **18** hell bent for leather

Apache
language family: **10** Athabascan, Athapaskan
band: **9** Jacarilla, Mescalero, San Carlos **13** White Mountain
location: **7** Arizona **8** Oklahoma **9** New Mexico
leader: **7** Cochise **8** Geronimo
noted for: **8** basketry

apart 4 afar **5** alone, aloof, aside **6** cut off **7** asunder, distant **8** by itself, divorced, isolated, separate **9** by oneself, into parts, to one side **10** into pieces, separately

apartment 3 pad **4** flat **5** rooms, suite

Apartment, The
director: **11** Billy Wilder
cast: **10** Jack Lemmon, Ray Walston **13** Fred MacMurray **15** Shirley MacLaine
Oscar for: **7** picture

apathetic 4 cold **7** unmoved **9** impassive, unfeeling **10** disengaged, impossible, phlegmatic, spiritless **11** emotionless, indifferent, passionless, uncommitted, unconcerned, unemotional **12** uninterested, unresponsive

apathy 8 coolness, lethargy, numbness **9** lassitude, unconcern **11** impassivity, inattention, passiveness **12** indifference **13** impassibility, lack of feeling **14** lack of interest **15** emotionlessness **16** unresponsiveness

apatite
source: **5** Burma, Mogok

Apatosaurus *see* **12** Brontosaurus

ape 4 copy, echo, mock **5** mimic **6** follow, mirror, monkey, parody, parrot **7** emulate, imitate, primate **8** travesty **9** burlesque **10** caricature
family: **8** Pongidae
combining form: **8** pithecus
study of: **11** pithecology
kind: **6** gibbon **7** gorilla, siamang **9** orangutan **10** chimpanzee
famous: **8** Godzilla, King Kong

Apemius
epithet of: **4** Zeus
means: **13** averter of ills

Apemosyne
father: **7** Catreus
brother: **11** Althaemenes
ravished by: **6** Hermes
killed by: **11** Althaemenes

Apepi *see* **7** Apophis

apercu 6 glance **7** glimpse, insight, outline, summary

aperture 3 gap **4** hole, rent, rift, slit, slot **5** chink, cleft, space **6** breach **7** fissure, opening, orifice **10** interstice

apex 3 cap, tip **4** acme, peak **5** crest, crown **6** apogee, climax, height, summit, vertex, zenith **8** pinnacle **11** culmina-

tion **12** consummation, highest point **13** crowning point

Aphareus
king of: **8** Messenia
father: **8** Perieres
mother: **10** Gorgophone
grandfather: **7** Perseus
brother: **9** Leucippus
wife: **5** Arene
son: **4** Ides **7** Lynceus

aphasic 4 dumb, mute **12** inarticulate **17** incapable of speech

Aphesius
epithet of: **4** Zeus
means: **8** releaser

aphid
variety: **3** pea **4** pine, rose **5** apple, grape, peach, tulip **6** cereal, cotton, potato, spruce **7** adelgid, cabbage **8** pear root **9** elm woolly, plant lice, water lily **10** gall-making, phylloxera

Aphidas
father: **5** Arcas
son: **5** Aleus

aphorism 5 adage, axiom, maxim **6** dictum, old saw, saying, slogan, truism **7** epigram, proverb **8** apothegm

aphrodisiac 4 sexy **6** carnal, erotic **7** fleshly, philter, raunchy **8** prurient **9** cantharis **10** love potion **11** cantharides, magic potion, stimulating

Aphrodite
also: **6** Urania **7** Cyprian, Paphian **8** Cytherea **10** Anadyomene
origin: **5** Greek
goddess of: **4** love **6** beauty
husband: **10** Hephaestus
lover: **4** Ares
son: **5** Lyrus **6** Deimos, Phobus, Rhodus **7** Priapus
daughter: **8** Harmonia
corresponds to: **5** Venus
epithet: **6** Acraea, Scotia **7** Doritis, Erycina, Limenia **8** Melaenis, Nymphaea, Pandemos **9** Migonitis **11** Aphrogeneia, Apostrophia

Aphrogeneia
epithet of: **9** Aphrodite
means: **8** foam born

Apia
capital of: **12** Western Samoa

apiary 4 hive **7** beehive

apiece 4 each **9** severally **12** individually, respectively

a pied 6 on foot **7** walking

Apis
origin: **8** Egyptian
also: **3** Hap **4** Hapi
form: **4** bull
from: **7** Memphis

father: 6 Apollo **9** Phoroneus
mother: 8 Teledice
sister: 5 Niobe
nephew: 5 Argus
rid Argos of: 8 serpents
killed by: 7 Aetolus
worshipped at: 7 Memphis

aplomb 5 poise **7** balance
8 calmness, coolness **9** composure, sang-froid, stability
10 confidence, equanimity
11 intrepidity, savoir faire
13 self-assurance, self-composure **14** self-confidence, self-
possession **15** level-headedness **16** imperturbability

Apocalypse Now
director: 18 Francis Ford
Coppola
based on: 15 Heart of
Darkness
novel by: **12** Joseph
Conrad
cast: 11 Martin Sheen
12 Marlon Brando, Robert
Duvall **16** Frederick Forrest
setting: 7 Vietnam

apocalyptic 4 dire **7** ominous
8 oracular **9** far-seeing, ill-boding, ill-omened, prescient, prophetic, revealing **10** disclosing,
eye-opening, foreboding, portentous, predictive, revelatory
11 prophetical **12** inauspicious,
revelational
15 prognosticative

apocryphal 7 dubious **8** disputed, doubtful, mythical, spurious **10** fabricated, fictitious,
unofficial, unverified
11 unauthentic, uncanonical
12 questionable, unauthorized
14 probably untrue **15** unauthenticated, unsubstantiated

apogee 3 top **4** acme, apex,
peak **5** crest, crown **6** climax,
summit, vertex, zenith **8** meridian, pinnacle **9** high point
11 culmination **12** highest
point

Apollo
also: 7 Phoebus, Pythius
9 Musagetes
origin: 5 Greek, Roman
god of: 5 light, music
6 beauty, poetry **7** healing
8 prophecy
father: 4 Zeus
mother: 4 Leto
twin sister: 7 Artemis
sons: 5 Iamus **8** Laodocus
9 Aristaeus, Asclepius,
Philammon **10** Polypoetes
corresponds to: 5 Paeon
8 Hyperion
epithet: 6 Loxias **7** Acesius,
Agraeus, Agyieus, Carneus,
Phyteus, Spodius **8** Grynaeus **9** Parnopius, Smintheus **10** Alexicacus,
Archegetes, Boedromius,

Delphinius **11** Argyrotoxus,
Epibaterius **12** Platanistius

Apollyon 4 hell **7** Abaddon

apologetic 5 sorry **8** contrite,
penitent **9** defensive, regretful
10 excusatory, mitigatory, remorseful **11** exonerative, extenuatory, vindicatory
12 apological **13** justificatory,
making excuses **15** self-
reproachful

Apologia pro Vita Sua
author: 15 John Henry Newman (Cardinal)

**Apologie for Poetrie (De-
fense for Poetry)**
author: 15 Sir Philip Sidney

apologist 7 pleader **8** advocate,
defender **9** supporter

apologize 9 beg pardon
11 make apology **13** express
regret

apology 6 excuse **7** defense
11 explanation, vindication
13 begging pardon,
justification

Apomyius
epithet of: 4 Zeus
means: 14 averter of flies

Apophis
also: 5 Apepi
form: 7 serpent
habitat: 8 darkness
destroyed daily by: 4 Dawn

Apophthegms New and Old
author: 12 Francis Bacon

apostasy 7 atheism, perfidy
8 unbelief **9** defection, disbelief, recreancy **10** disloyalty,
infidelity, irreligion **11** godlessness **13** double-dealing

apostate 6 bolter **7** heretic, seceder, traitor **8** defector, deserter, recanter, recusant,
renegade, turncoat **9** dissenter,
dissident, turnabout **10** backslider **13** nonconformist,
tergiversator

apostle 5 envoy **6** zealot **7** pioneer, witness **8** activist, advocate, disciple, emissary,
exponent, preacher **9** messenger, proponent, supporter
10 evangelist, missionary,
propagator **12** propagandist,
proselytizer, spokesperson

Apostle, The
author: 10 Sholem Asch

Apostles 4 John, Jude, Levi,
Paul **5** Jacob, James, Peter, Si-
mon **6** Andrew, Philip,
Thomas **7** Matthew **8** Barna-
bas, Matthias **9** Nathanael,
Thaddaeus **11** Bartholomew
12 James the Less **13** Judas
Iscariot

apostle to the Gentiles:
4 Paul
apostle to the English:
9 Augustine
apostle to the Irish:
7 Patrick
apostle to the Goths:
7 Ulfilas
apostle to the Germans:
8 Boniface
apostle to the French:
5 Denis
**apostle to the American In-
dians: 9** John Eliot

Apostrophia
epithet of: 9 Aphrodite
means: 24 rejecter of sinful
passions

apothegm 5 adage, axiom,
maxim, motto **6** dictum **7** epigram, proverb **8** aphorism
9 catchword

apotheosis 7 epitome, essence
9 elevation **10** embodiment,
exaltation **11** deification
12 canonization, consecration,
enshrinement, idealization,
quintessence **13** dignification,
glorification, magnification
15 immortalization

Appalachian Spring
ballet by: 7 Copland

appall 4 stun **5** abash, alarm,
repel, shock **6** dismay, offend,
revolt, sicken **7** disgust, horrify, outrage, terrify, unnerve
8 frighten, nauseate
10 dishearten

appalled 6 aghast **7** alarmed,
shocked **8** dismayed, outraged,
repelled, revolted **9** disgusted,
horrified, nauseated

appalling 4 dire, grim **5** awful
6 horrid **7** fearful, ghastly
8 alarming, dreadful, horrible,
horrific, shocking, terrible
9 dismaying, frightful, repellent, repulsive, revolting, sickening **10** abominable,
disgusting, horrifying, nauseating, outrageous, terrifying
11 frightening, intolerable
12 insufferable
13 disheartening

apparatus 4 gear **5** gismo,
setup, tools **6** device, gadget,
outfit, system, tackle **7** machine **8** material, utensils
9 appliance, equipment, machinery, materials, mechanism **10** implements
11 contraption, contrivance,
instruments **12** organization
13 paraphernalia

apparatus criticus 8 exegesis
10 annotation **11** elucidation,
explication **14** interpretation

apparel 4 duds, garb, gear,
togs **5** array, dress, habit,

robes 6 attire 7 clothes, costume, raiment, threads, vesture 8 clothing, garments 9 equipment, trappings, vestments 13 accouterments

appareled 4 clad 5 robed 6 garbed, suited 7 attired, clothed, covered, dressed

apparent 4 open 5 clear, overt, plain 6 likely, marked, patent 7 blatant, evident, obvious, seeming, visible 8 clear-cut, distinct, manifest, probable 10 clear as day, ostensible, presumable 11 conspicuous, discernible, perceivable, perceptible, self-evident, unequivocal 12 unmistakable 14 understandable

apparently
Latin: 7 ex facie

apparition 5 ghost, shade, spook 6 spirit, wraith 7 phantom, specter 8 phantasm, presence, revenant 10 phenomenon 13 manifestation 15 materialization

appeal 3 beg, SOS 4 plea, pull, suit 5 apply, charm, plead, sue to, tempt 6 adjure, allure, engage, entice, excite, invite, invoke 7 attract, beseech, entreat, implore, request, solicit 8 call upon, charisma, entreaty, interest, petition 9 fascinate 10 adjuration, attraction, supplicate 11 fascination 12 solicitation, supplication

appealing 7 likable, lovable 8 adjuring, charming, engaging, enticing, fetching, inviting, pleading, pleasing, tempting 10 attractive, entreating, requesting, soliciting 11 charismatic, petitioning 12 irresistable, supplicating

appear 4 look, seem, show 5 arise 6 crop up, emerge, loom up, show up, turn up 7 be clear, be plain, come out, perform, surface 8 be patent 9 be evident, be obvious 10 be apparent, be manifest 11 be published, come to light, materialize

appearance 4 look 5 guise, image 6 advent, aspect, coming 7 arrival, pretext 8 pretense 9 appearing, emergence, showing up, turning up 10 impression 11 outward show 13 manifestation 15 materialization

appear at 6 attend, show up 8 peform at

appease 4 calm, dull, ease, lull 5 abate, allay, blunt, quell, quiet, slake, still 6 pacify,

quench, solace, soothe, temper 7 assuage, compose, mollify, placate, relieve, satisfy 8 mitigate 9 alleviate 10 conciliate, propitiate 11 accommodate

appeasement 6 easing 7 abating, dulling 8 allaying, blunting, giving in 9 abatement, assuasion, quenching 10 mitigation, submission 11 alleviation, assuagement 12 conciliation, pacification, propitiation, satisfaction 13 accommodation, gratification, mollification

appellation 3 tag 4 name 5 title 6 handle 7 epithet, moniker 8 cognomen 9 sobriquet 11 designation, nom de guerre

append 3 add 4 join 5 affix 6 attach, hang on, tack on 7 subjoin, suspend 10 supplement

appendage 3 arm, leg 4 limb, tail 6 branch, feeler, member 7 adjunct 8 addition, offshoot, tentacle 9 accessory, auxiliary, extension, extremity 10 attachment, supplement

appendix 7 codicil 8 addendum, addition 10 back matter, postscript, supplement

appertain 7 apply to, concern, refer to 8 bear upon, be part of, belong to, inhere in, relate to 9 touch upon

appetite 4 zest 5 gusto 6 desire, hunger, liking, relish, thirst 7 craving, passion, stomach 8 fondness, penchant, yearning 10 proclivity 11 inclination

appetizer 6 canape, dainty, savory, tidbit 8 aperitif, cocktail, delicacy 9 antipasto 11 bonne bouche, hors d'oeuvre

appetizing 6 savory 8 alluring, enticing, inviting, tempting 9 appealing, palatable, succulent 10 attractive 11 tantalizing 13 mouth-watering

applaud 4 clap, hail, laud 5 extol 6 praise 7 acclaim, commend 8 eulogize 10 compliment 12 congratulate

applaudable 8 laudable 9 admirable, desirable, excellent 11 commendable, meritorious, outstanding 12 praiseworthy

applause 5 kudos 6 praise 7 acclaim, ovation 8 approval, clapping, plaudits 9 accolades 11 compliments

apple 5 Malus 15 Malus Sylvestris
varieties/fruit: 4 Crab, Lodi

6 Pippin 7 Baldwin, Stayman, Winesap 8 Ben Davis, Cortland, Jonathan, McIntosh 9 Delicious 10 Rome Beauty 11 Granny Smith, Gravenstein, Northern Spy, Summer Rambo 12 Grimes Golden, York Imperial 13 Yellow Newtown 14 Stayman Winesap 15 Yellow Delicious 17 Esopus Spitzenberg, Yellow Transparent 19 Rhode Island Greening
varieties/tree: 2 Wi 3 Kai, Kau, Sea, Wax 4 Cane, Java, Jew's, Pond, Rose, Star 5 Adam's, Baked, Belle, Blade, Chess, Conch, Malay, Melon, Thorn 6 Balsam, Indian, Mammee, Possum 7 Chinese, Custard, Dead Sea, Mexican 8 Elephant, Kangaroo, Otaheite, Paradise, Peruvian 11 Soulard crab, Toringo crab 12 Siberian crab
beverage: 5 cider 8 Calvados 9 Applejack

apple brandy
drink: 8 Jack Rose 12 Jack-in-the-Box
with rum: 6 Bolero 8 Apple Pie

applejack
type: 6 brandy
origin: 6 Canada 10 New England
flavor: 10 apple cider
drink: 11 Frozen Apple 13 Harvard Cooler

Apple of discord
color: 6 golden
thrown by: 4 Eris
awarded to: 9 Aphrodite
awarded by: 5 Paris
inscription: 13 for the fairest

apple of one's eye 11 pride and joy 15 light of one's life

applesauce 3 rot 4 bull, bunk 5 hokum, hooey 6 bunkum 7 baloney, hogwash, spinach 8 tommyrot 9 poppycock 12 fiddlesticks 13 horsefeathers 16 stuff and nonsense

Apples of the Hesperides
color: 6 golden
given to: 4 Hera
kept by: 5 Ladon 10 Hesperides

appliance 4 gear 6 device 7 fixture, machine 9 apparatus, equipment, implement, mechanism 11 contraption, contrivance

applicable 3 apt, fit 6 useful 7 apropos, fitting, germane 8 relevant, suitable 9 adaptable, befitting, pertinent

applicant 7 hopeful **8** aspirant, claimant **9** candidate, job seeker, suppliant **10** petitioner

application 4 balm, form, suit, wash **5** claim, salve **6** appeal, lotion **7** request, unguent **8** dressing, entreaty, industry, ointment, petition, poultice, solution **9** assiduity, attention, diligence, emollient, putting on, relevance **10** commitment, dedication, pertinence **11** germaneness, persistence, requisition, suitability **12** appositeness, perseverance, solicitation **13** attentiveness

Appling, Luke (Lucius Benjamin)
nickname: **16** Old Aches and Pains
sport: **8** baseball
position: **9** shortstop
team: **15** Chicago White Sox

apply 3 fit, use **4** suit **5** adapt, lay on, put on, refer **6** devote, direct, employ, relate **7** address, pertain, request, utilize **8** dedicate, exercise, petition, practice, spread on **9** implement

apply oneself 6 attend **10** buckle down **13** give oneself to **15** give it all one has **16** put one's heart into

appoint 3 fix, set **4** name **5** equip **6** assign, choose, engage, fit out, select, settle, supply **7** arrange, furnish, provide **8** decide on, delegate, deputize, nominate **9** designate, determine, establish, prescribe **10** commission

appointment 3 job **4** date, post, spot **5** berth, place **6** naming, office **7** meeting, station **8** choosing, position **9** placement, selection, situation **10** assignment, engagement, nomination, rendezvous **11** designation, meeting time **13** commissioning

Appointment in Samarra
author: **9** John O'Hara
character: **8** Al Grecco, Caroline **11** Harry Reilly **13** Julian English

appointments 4 gear **6** outfit **8** equipage **9** equipment, furniture **11** furnishings **13** accouterments

apportion 5 allot, share **6** divide, ration **7** consign, deal out, dole out, mete out, prorate **8** allocate, disperse **9** parcel out, partition **10** measure out

apportioning 8 alloting, dividing **9** doling out, meting

out **10** allocating, consigning, dealing out, dispensing **12** distributing

apportionment 5 quota **6** ration **7** measure, portion **8** division **9** allotment **10** allocation **11** consignment **12** distribution, pro rata share

apposite 3 apt **7** apropos, fitting, germane **8** material, relevant, suitable **9** pertinent **10** applicable **11** appropriate

appositeness 9 relevance **10** pertinence **11** germaneness **15** appropriateness

appraisal 8 estimate, judgment **9** valuation **10** assessment, evaluation **14** estimated value

appraise 5 assay, judge, value **6** assess, review, size up **7** examine, inspect **8** evaluate

appreciable 7 evident, obvious **8** clear-cut, definite **10** detectable, noticeable, pronounced **11** discernible, perceivable, perceptible, significant, substantial **12** recognizable **13** ascertainable

appreciate 4 like **5** prize, savor, value **6** admire, esteem, relish **7** cherish, enhance, improve, inflate, realize, respect **8** perceive, treasure **9** recognize **10** comprehend, sympathize, understand **11** acknowledge

appreciation 4 rise **6** growth, liking, regard, relish, thanks **7** advance **8** sympathy **9** awareness, elevation, gratitude **10** admiration, cognizance **12** gratefulness, thankfulness **13** comprehension, understanding

apprehend 3 bag, nab, see **4** know **5** catch, grasp, seize, sense **6** arrest, collar **7** capture, discern, realize **8** perceive **9** recognize **10** comprehend, understand **12** take prisoner **15** take into custody

apprehension 5 alarm, dread, worry **6** arrest, dismay **7** anxiety, capture, concern, seizure **8** disquiet, distress, mistrust **9** misgiving, suspicion **10** foreboding, perception, uneasiness **11** premonition **12** presentiment **13** comprehension, understanding **16** apprehensiveness

apprehensive 6 afraid, scared, uneasy **7** alarmed, anxious, fearful, jittery, nervous, worried **9** concerned, misgiving **10** disquieted, distressed, suspicious **11** distrustful

apprehensiveness 5 dread, worry **6** dismay **7** anxiety **9** misgiving **10** foreboding, uneasiness **12** apprehension

apprentice 4 tyro **5** pupil **6** novice **7** learner, student **8** beginner, neophyte **19** indentured assistant

apprise 4 tell **6** advise, inform, notify **8** disclose **9** enlighten, make aware

approach 3 way **4** come, near, road **5** begin, equal, match **6** access, avenue, be like, method, system **7** advance, compare, passage, solicit **8** attitude, come near, draw near, embark on, gain upon, initiate, resemble, set about, sound out **9** come close, enter upon, procedure, technique, undertake **10** move toward, passageway **11** approximate

approachable 9 available, reachable **10** accessible

approbation 6 praise **7** acclaim, support **8** applause, approval, sanction **9** laudation **10** acceptance, compliment **11** endorsement **12** commendation, ratification **14** congratulation

appropriate 3 apt **4** take **5** allot **6** assign, proper, seemly **7** apropos, correct, earmark, fitting, germane **8** allocate, relevant, set apart, suitable **9** apportion, befitting, belonging, congruous, opportune, pertinent **10** confiscate, to the point, well-chosen, well-suited **11** expropriate **12** to the purpose **14** characteristic

appropriateness 7 aptness, fitness **9** congruity, propriety, relevance **10** pertinence **11** correctness, suitability

appropriation 6 taking **9** allotment **10** allocation, arrogation, usurpation **12** confiscation **13** expropriation, money set aside **16** misappropriation

approval 5 favor, leave **6** esteem, liking, regard **7** acclaim, consent, license, mandate, respect **8** sanction **9** agreement **10** acceptance, admiration, compliance, permission **11** approbation, concurrence, countenance, endorsement, good opinion **12** acquiescence, appreciation, confirmation **13** authorization **14** acknowledgment

approve 4 like, pass **5** allow **6** accept, affirm, defend, esteem, permit, praise, ratify, second, uphold **7** condone, confirm, endorse, respect, sustain **8** accede to, advocate, assent to, concur in, sanction **9** authorize, consent to **10** appreciate **11** countenance, go along with, rubber-stamp, subscribe to

approved 8 official **9** canonical **10** authorized, sanctioned

approving 9 endorsing, favorable **10** concurring **11** affirmative, sanctioning **12** appreciative

approximate 5 guess, rough **6** reckon **7** inexact, verge on **8** approach, border on, estimate, look like, relative, very near **9** estimated

approximately 5 circa **6** almost, around **7** close to **9** generally, just about **10** more or less, not far from, very nearly

appurtenance 4 wing **5** annex, extra **7** adjunct **8** addendum, addition **9** accessory, appendage, extension **10** attachment

Apres-midi d'un Faune, L' (The Afternoon of a Faun)
author: **16** Stephane Mallarme

April see box

April Fool's Day
French: **9** April Fish

---

a priori 6 theory **7** opinion **11** of reasoning

apron 3 bib **5** smock **8** covering **10** stagefront

apropos 3 apt **6** seemly **7** correct, fitting, germane, related **8** relevant, suitable **9** befitting, congruous, opportune, pertinent **10** applicable, to the point, well-suited **11** appropriate **12** just the thing

apry
type: **7** liqueur
origin: **6** France
flavor: **7** apricot

Apsyrtus
also: **8** Absyrtus
father: **6** Aeetes
sister: **5** Medea
killed by: **5** Medea

apt 5 prone **6** bright, clever, gifted, liable, likely, proper, seemly **7** apropos, fitting, germane, given to **8** inclined, relevant, suitable **9** befitting, congruous, opportune, pertinent **10** disposed to, well-suited **11** appropriate, intelligent, predisposed

aptitude 4 bent, gift, turn **5** flair, knack, skill **6** genius, talent **7** ability, faculty, leaning **8** capacity, facility, penchant, tendency **9** endowment, proneness, quickness **10** capability, cleverness, proclivity, propensity **11** inclination, proficiency **12** predilection **14** predisposition

aptness 4 bent, gift **5** flair, knack **6** talent **7** ability, faculty **8** aptitude, facility **11** suitability **15** appropriateness

Apuleius
author of: **12** The Golden Ass **13** Metamorphoses

aqua 4 blue **5** water **6** bluish **9** turquoise **10** aquamarine **12** greenish-blue

aquamarine 4 aqua, blue **5** beryl **9** turquoise **12** greenish-blue
color: **9** blue-green

aquaphobia
fear of: **5** water

aquarelle 10 watercolor

Aquarius
symbol: **11** water bearer **12** water-carrier
planet: **6** Saturn, Uranus
rules: **5** hopes **7** friends
born: **7** January **8** February

aquatic 6 marine **7** abyssal, fluvial, neritic, oceanic, pelagic **8** littoral **9** thalassic **10** fluviatile, lacustrine

---

aquavit
type: **6** spirit
origin: **11** Scandinavia
flavor: **4** dill **7** caraway **9** coriander
drink: **5** Glogg

aqua vitae 7 alcohol **11** water of life

aqueduct 4 duct, race **7** channel, conduit **11** watercourse **18** artificial waterway

aqueous 4 damp **5** moist **6** liquid, serous, watery **7** hydrous **8** waterish **9** lymphatic

Aqueus
epithet of: **4** Zeus
means: **6** watery

Aquilo see **6** Boreas

Aquinas, St Thomas
nickname: **13** Angelic Doctor
followers: **8** Thomists
author of: **15** Summa Theologica **21** Summa Totius Theologiae **34** Summa Catholicae Fidei contra Gentiles

Arab
clothing: **3** fez **4** veil
country: **4** Iraq, Oman **5** Egypt, Libya, Qatar, Sudan, Syria, Yemen **6** Jordan, Kuwait **7** Algeria, Bahrain, Lebanon, Morocco, Tunisia **11** Saudi Arabia **18** United Arab Emirates
habitat: **6** desert
Holy City: **5** Mecca **6** Medina
language: **6** Arabic
people: **7** Semitic
religion: **6** Muslim **7** Islamic
tribe: **4** Kurd **6** Berber, Nubian, Tuareg

Arabella
opera by: **7** (Richard) Strauss

Arabia
ancient name: **14** Jazirat al-Arab
ancient people: **6** Sabean **8** Egyptian **10** Babylonian
bounded by: **5** Syria **6** Jordan, Red Sea **10** Gulf of Aden, Gulf of Oman **11** Indian Ocean, Persian Gulf
country: **4** Oman **5** Qatar, Yemen **6** Kuwait **11** Saudi Arabia **18** United Arab Emirates
highest peak: **11** Jabal Shayib
holy book: **5** Koran
Holy City: **5** Mecca **6** Medina
island: **7** Bahrain, Socotra **9** Laccadive
language: **6** Arabic
mineral/natural resource: **3** oil **4** goat **5** sheep, wheat **6** barley, millet **7** iron ore, granite **8** porphyry **9** manganese, petroleum

nomadic tribe: 5 Maaza
6 Ababda
prophet: 8 Muhammad
religion: 6 Muslim **7** Islamic
river: 4 Nile, Oxus **5** Indus
6 Tigris **9** Euphrates
sea: 3 Red **7** Arabian **11** Persian Gulf **13** Mediterranean

Arabian Nights
director: 17 Pier Paolo
Pasolini
based on: 20 Thousand and
One Nights
cast: 11 Franco Citti **13** Ninetto Davoli **14** Ines
Pellegrina

Arabian Nights' Entertainments, The (The Thousand and One Nights)
author: 7 unknown
storyteller: 12 Scheherazade

Arabic
national language in: 4 Iraq
5 Syria **6** Jordan **7** Lebanon
11 North Africa **16** Arabian
Peninsula
also spoken in: 6 Israel
12 North America, South
America **17** Soviet Central
Asia, Sub-Saharan Africa
language of: 5 Koran

arable 6 fecund **7** fertile
8 farmable, fruitful, plowable,
tillable **10** cultivable,
productive

Arachne
origin: 6 Lydian
challenged: 6 Athena
contest: 7 weaving
changed into: 6 spider

arachnid
class: 4 mite, tick **6** spider
8 scorpion **13** daddy-longlegs
phylum: 9 Arthropod
pairs of legs: 4 four
respiratory organ: 12 pulmonary sac, tracheal tube
dwelling: 4 land **5** water
body part: 15 anterior prosoma **20** posterior
opisthosoma
way of feeding: 8 parasite,
predator **9** scavenger

arachnophobia
fear of: 7 spiders

Aram *see* **5** Syria

Aramis
character in: 18 The Three
Musketeers
author: 5 Dumas (pere)

Arapaho
language family: 9 Algonkian **10** Algonquian
tribe: 6 Atsine **11** Gros
Ventres **15** Northern Arapaho, Southern Arapaho
location: 6 Plains **8** Colorado,
Red River

related to: 8 Cheyenne
ceremony: 8 sun dance

Aras
first king of: 8 Phliasia

Arawak
language family: 8 Arawakan
tribe: 5 Taino **6** Igneri,
Lucayo
location: 4 Cuba **5** Haiti
6 Guyana **8** Antilles, Colombia **9** Venezuela **12** South
America

Arawakan
tribe: 6 Arawak **8** Boriquen
9 Borinquen

Arawn
lord of: 6 Annfwn

arbiter 5 judge **6** pundit, umpire **7** referee **9** authority
10 arbitrator **11** connoisseur

arbitrary 6 chance, random
7 summary, willful **8** absolute,
despotic, fanciful, personal
9 frivolous, imperious, unlimited, whimsical **10** autocratic,
capricious, peremptory, subjective **12** inconsistent, uncontrolled, unrestrained

arbitrate 5 judge **6** decide, settle, umpire **7** adjudge, mediate,
referee **9** reconcile **10** adjudicate **12** bring to terms **13** sit
in judgment

Arbitration, The
author: 8 Menander

arbitrator 5 judge **6** umpire
7 arbiter, referee **8** mediator
9 go-between, moderator
10 negotiator **11** adjudicator
12 intermediary

arbor 5 bower, folly, kiosk
6 gazebo, grotto **7** pergola
8 pavilion **9** belvedere
10 shaded walk
11 summerhouse

arc 3 bow **4** arch **5** curve
8 crescent, half-moon
10 semicircle

arcade 6 loggia, piazza **7** archway, areaway, gallery, skywalk **8** cloister, overpass
9 breezeway, colonnade, peristyle, underpass

Arcadia, The
author: 15 Sir Philip Sidney
character: 5 Mopsa **6** Pamela **7** Dametas, Gynecia,
Zelmane **8** Basilius, Cecropia, Pyrocles **9** Amphialus,
Musidorus, Philoclea,
Plexistus

Arcadian stag *see* **8** Cerynean

Arcanan
father: 8 Alcmaeon
mother: 10 Callirrhoe
brother: 10 Amphoterus

arcane 6 mystic, occult **7** obscure **8** abstruse, esoteric, hermetic, mystical **9** enigmatic,
recondite **10** mysterious

Arcas
father: 4 Zeus
mother: 8 Callisto
wife: 5 Erato
son: 6 Elatus
ancestor of: 9 Arcadians
set among: 5 stars
placed by: 4 Zeus

Arce
father: 7 Thaumas
sister: 4 Iris **7** Harpies
Zeus took: 5 wings
aided: 6 Titans

Arcesius
father: 4 Zeus
mother: 8 Euryodia
son: 7 Laertes
grandson: 8 Odysseus

arch 3 arc, bow, sly **4** bend,
dome, main, span, wily
5 chief, curve, major, saucy,
vault **7** cunning, primary, roguish **8** bow shape **9** curvature, designing, principal
10 curved span **11** mischievous

archaeologist
American: 7 Bingham
8 Douglass, Stephens
British: 5 Evans **6** Carter,
Childe, Layard, Leakey, Petrie, Wooley **7** Lubbock, Ventris, Wheeler **9** Rawlinson
10 Pitt-Rivers **13** Caton-Thompson
Danish: 7 Thomsen, Worsaae
French: 5 Botta **8** Cousteau
11 Champollion
German: 5 Conze **7** Curtius
8 Dorpfeld, Koldewey
9 Grotefend **10** Schliemann
11 Winckelmann
Italian: 8 Fiorelli
Swedish: 4 Geer **9** Montelius

archaic 5 passe **6** bygone **7** ancient, antique **8** obsolete
9 out-of-date **10** antiquated
11 obsolescent **12** old-fashioned

archangel 5 Satan, Uriel **7** Gabriel, Michael, Raphael

arched 4 bent **5** bowed
6 curved

Archegetes
epithet of: 6 Apollo
means: 7 founder

Archelaus
father: 7 Temenus
descendant of: 8 Hercules

Archelochus
mentioned in: 5 Iliad
father: 7 Antenor
mother: 6 Theano
killed by: 14 Telamonian
Ajax

Archemorus *see* **8** Opheltes

archenemy 3 foe 7 archfoe, bugbear, nemesis, scourge 8 opponent 9 adversary, assailant, bete noire, combatant, disputant 10 antagonist

archeology
  term: 3 dig 6 midden 9 earthwork 11 burial mound 17 aerial photography
  type: 7 salvage 8 American, medieval 9 classical, text-aided 10 Egyptology, industrial, underwater 11 Assyriology, prehistoric 12 Mesopotamian
  ages: 4 Iron 6 Bronze
    Old Stone Age:
      11 Paleolithic
    Middle Stone Age:
      10 Mesolithic
    New Stone Age:
      9 Neolithic
  dating method: 5 cross 8 absolute, carbon-14 13 geochronology 16 dendrochronology 18 thermoluminescence 28 potassium-argon varved deposits
  site/artifact: 2 Ur 4 Giza, Troy 5 Copan, Crete, Delos, Minos 6 Amarna, Carnac, Nimrud, Nippur, Tiryns 7 Alalakh, Babylon, Ephesus, Knossos, Mycenae, Nineveh, Olympia, Pompeii, Rio Azul 8 Behistun, Kuyunjik, Pergamum, pyramids 9 Arikamedu, Hissarlik, Khorsabad, New Grange, Tarquinia, Woodhenge 10 Carchemish, Persepolis, Samothrace, Stonehenge 11 Herculaneum, Machu Picchu, Mohenjodaro 12 Easter Island, Hadrian's Wall, Olduvai Gorge, Rosetta Stone 13 Avebury Circle, Zimbabwe Ruins 14 Dead Sea Scrolls, Laocoon statues 15 temple of Artemis 16 Valley of the Kings 18 Ostrava-Petrokovice, Royal Palace of Minos
  tomb: 11 Tutankhamen 15 Ch'in Shih Huang Ti

Archeptolemus
  mentioned in: 5 Iliad
  father: 7 Iphitus
  charioteer of: 6 Hector

archer 6 bowman 8 spearman
  famous: 5 Cupid 9 Robin Hood 11 William Tell

Archer
  constellation of:
    11 Sagittarius

Archer, Isabel
  character in: 18 The Portrait of a Lady
  author: 5 James

Archer, Miles
  character in: 16 The Maltese Falcon
  author: 7 Hammett

Archer, Newland
  character in: 17 The Age of Innocence
  author: 7 Wharton

Archer in Jeopardy
  author: 13 Ross MacDonald

archery
  athlete: 10 Linda Myers, Luanne Ryon 11 Darrell Pace

archetypal 5 model 7 classic 8 original 9 classical, exemplary 10 definitive, prototypal, protypical

archetype 5 model 7 classic 8 exemplar, original 9 prototype 12 prime example

Archias
  founder of: 8 Syracuse
  location: 6 Sicily
  descendant of: 8 Hercules

Archie
  creator: 10 Bob Montana 13 John Goldwater
  character: 5 Betty, Moose 6 Reggie 7 Sabrina 8 Big Ethel, Veronica 11 Mr Weatherby 12 Jughead Jones
  place: 9 Riverdale

Archimago
  character in: 15 The Faerie Queene
  author: 7 Spenser

Archipenko, Alexsandr
  born: 4 Kiev 6 Russia
  artwork: 8 Medranos 9 Gondolier, Medrano II, Pregnancy, The Bather 11 Boxing Match 12 Archipentura, Walking Woman 15 Geometric Statue 18 Wilhelm Furtwangler 19 Woman Combing Her Hair

architect 6 author, shaper 7 creator, deviser, founder, planner 8 designer, engineer 9 artificer, contriver, draftsman, innovator 10 instigator, originator, prime mover 13 master builder 16 building designer
  name 3 Pei 4 Hunt, Mead, Pope, Root, Wren 5 Hoban, Jones, Le Vau, McKim, Mills, Roche, Stone, Tange, White, Wyatt 6 Breuer, Fuller, Owings, Smirke, Wright 7 Bernini, Burnham, Gilbert, Gropius, Johnson, Latrobe, Mansart, Merrill, Renwick 8 Bramante, Harrison, Palladio, Saarinen, Skidmore, Sullivan, Yama-saki 9 Jefferson 10 Richardson 11 Le Corbusier 12 Brunelleschi, Michelangelo 14 Mies van der Rohe 15 Hardouin-Mansart
  legendary first: 8 Daedalus
    designed: 18 Minotaur's Labyrinth
  Roman: 9 Vitruvius

architecture 5 style 6 design 11 structuring 12 construction 14 architectonics 16 structural design

archives 6 annals, museum, papers 7 library, records 9 documents 10 chronicles, depository 11 memorabilia

arctic 3 icy 5 gelid, polar 6 bitter, frigid, frozen 7 glacial, ice-cold 8 freezing, icebound 9 North Pole 10 frostbound 11 far-northern, hyperborean 13 septentrional

Arden, Eve
  real name: 13 Eunice Quedens
  born: 12 Mill Valley CA
  roles: 13 Mildred Pierce, Our Miss Brooks

ardent 4 keen 5 eager, fiery, lusty 6 fierce 7 earnest, fervent, intense, zealous 8 feverish, spirited, vehement 10 passionate 11 impassioned, tempestuous 12 enthusiastic

ardor 4 love, zeal 5 gusto, verve, vigor 6 fervor, spirit 7 feeling, passion, rapture 8 devotion 9 eagerness, intensity, vehemence 10 enthusiasm, excitement, fierceness 11 amorousness 12 feverishness

Ardrey, Robert
  author of: 17 The Social Contract

arduous 4 hard 5 heavy, tough 6 severe, tiring, trying 7 onerous 8 toilsome, vigorous 9 difficult, energetic, fatiguing, Herculean, laborious, strenuous, wearisome 10 burdensome, exhausting, formidable 11 troublesome

arduousness 5 trial 8 tough job 10 difficulty, rough going, uphill work 12 hard sledding, toilsomeness 13 laboriousness, wearisomeness

area 4 turf, zone 5 arena, field, range, realm, scope, space, tract 6 domain, extent, region, sphere 7 expanse, portion, section, stretch, terrain 8 district, locality, precinct, province 9 territory

Areithous
  origin: 5 Greek
  mentioned in: 5 Iliad
  king of: 7 Arcadia

Areius
son: 10 Menesthius
nickname: 7 maceman
weapon: 8 iron mace
killed by: 8 Lycurgus

Areius see 5 Areus

arena 4 area, bowl, ring
5 field, lists, realm, scene,
stage 6 circus, domain, sector,
sphere 7 stadium, theater
8 coliseum, platform, province 9 gymnasium, territory
10 hippodrome 11 battlefield,
marketplace 12 amphitheater,
battleground, playing field

Arendt, Hannah
author of: 10 On Violence
12 On Revolution 13 Life of
the Mind 17 The Human
Condition 19 Crises of the
Republic, Eichmann in Jerusalem 27 The Origins of
Totalitarianism

Arene
son: 4 Idas 7 Lynceus

**Arensky, Anton Stepanov-
ich (Antony)**
born: 6 Russia 8 Novgorod
composer of: 7 Tempest
13 Egyptian Night 18 Variations on Legend

Areopagitica
author: 10 John Milton

Ares
also: 8 Theritas
origin: 5 Greek
god of: 3 war
father: 4 Zeus
mother: 4 Hera
sister: 4 Hebe
son: 5 Molus 6 Cycnus, Deimos, Phobos, Tereus
8 Diomedes, Eurytion, Meleager, Oenomaus, Phlegyas,
Thestius 10 Ascalaphus
daughter: 7 Alcippe 8 Harmonia 9 Melanippe
11 Penthesilea
nurse: 5 Thero
corresponds to: 4 Mars
epithet: 8 Enyalius
14 Gynaecothoenas

Arete
father: 8 Rhexenor
husband: 8 Alcinous
daughter: 8 Nausicaa
personifies: 7 courage

Arethusa
form: 5 nymph
changed into: 6 spring
saved from: 7 Alpheus

Aretus
father: 5 Priam
killed by: 9 Automedon

Areus
also: 6 Areius
father: 4 Bias
mother: 4 Pero
brother: 6 Talaus 8 Leodocus

member of: 9 Argonauts
epithet of: 4 Zeus
means: 7 warlike

**Are You There, God? It's
Me, Margaret**
author: 9 Judy Blume

Argades
father: 3 Ion

Argeiphontes
also: 11 Argiphontes
epithet of: 6 Hermes
means: 13 slayer of Argus

argent 5 white 6 silver 7 shining, silvery

Argentina see box

Arges
member of: 8 Cyclopes

Argia
also: 5 Aegia
father: 7 Oceanus
mother: 6 Tethys
husband: 7 Polybus
son: 5 Argus

Argiope
form: 5 nymph
father: 8 Teuthras
husband: 6 Agenor
8 Telephus
son: 6 Cadmus
daughter: 6 Europa

Argiphontes see
12 Argeiphontes

Argive
pertaining to: 5 Argos

Argo
ship of: 4 Argo

argon
chemical symbol: 2 Ar

Argonauts
searchers for: 12 Golden
Fleece
leader: 5 Jason
ship: 4 Argo
sailed to: 7 Colchis

argot 4 cant 5 idiom, lingo,
slang 6 jargon, patois
10 vernacular

arguable 7 at issue 9 debatable 10 disputable 12 questionable 13 controversial,
problematical

argue 4 hold, show 5 claim,
imply, plead 6 assert, bicker,
debate, denote, evince, reason 7 contend, display, dispute, exhibit, express, point
to, quarrel, quibble, wrangle
8 indicate, maintain, manifest
11 demonstrate, expostulate,
remonstrate

argument 3 row 4 case, gist,
plot, spat, tiff 5 clash, fight,
story 6 debate, reason 7 dispute, outline, quarrel, summary 8 abstract, contents,

squabble, synopsis 9 bickering,
imbroglio 10 war of words
11 altercation, central idea,
controversy, embroilment
12 disagreement

argumentation 6 debate 7 dispute 8 argument 10 discussion

argumentative 5 testy 7 peevish, scrappy 8 contrary, petulant, snappish 9 combative,
fractious, litigious, querulous
11 belligerent, contentious,
quarrelsome 12 cantankerous,
disputatious

Argus
form: 5 giant
father: 7 Phrixus
mother: 9 Chalciope
builder of: 4 Argo
number of eyes: 10 one
hundred
epithet: 8 Panoptes

Argyra
form: 5 nymph
habitat: 6 spring
loved: 8 Selemnus

Argyrotoxus
epithet of: 6 Apollo
means: 18 lord of the silver
bow

aria 3 air 4 solo, song, tune
6 melody, number 7 arietta,
excerpt, section 9 selection
10 canzonetta 13 aria
cantabile

Aria
form: 5 nymph
son: 7 Miletus
fathered by: 6 Apollo

Ariadna see 7 Ariadne

Ariadne
also: 7 Ariadna
father: 5 Minos
mother: 8 Pasiphae
husband: 8 Dionysus
son: 8 Oenopion
gave thread to: 7 Theseus
deserted by: 7 Theseus

Ariadne auf Naxos
also: 14 Ariadne on Naxos
opera by: 7 (Richard) Strauss
character: 7 Bacchus, Theseus 8 Composer
10 Zerbinetta

Ariana see 11 Afghanistan

Ariane et Barbe-Bleu
also: 19 Ariadne and
Bluebeard
opera by: 5 Dukas
character: 7 Ariadne
9 Bluebeard

Arianrhod
origin: 5 Welsh
form: 7 goddess
brother: 7 Gwydion

Argentina

name means: 6 silver
capital/largest city: 11 Buenos Aires
others: 4 Acha, Azul, Goya, Oran, Puan, Rosa 5 Jujuy, Junin, Lanus, Lujan, Metan, Monte, Salta, Tigre 6 Parana, Rufino, Zarate 7 Bolivar, Caseros, Cordoba, Dolores, Formosa, LaBanda, LaPlata, LaRioja, Mendoza, Neuquen, Posadas, Quilmes, Rafaela, Rosario, San Juan, Santa Fe, Tucuman 9 Catamarca, Rio Cuerto 10 Avellaneda, Corrientes 11 Bahai Blanca, Mar del Plata, Resistencia 17 Santiago del Estero 20 San Carlos de Bariloche
division: 5 Andes, Chaco, Pampa 9 Patagonia 11 Mesopotamia 14 Tierra del Fuego
measure: 4 sino 5 legua 6 cuadra, lastre 7 manzana
monetary unit: 4 peso 7 centavo 9 argentino
weight: 4 last 5 libra 7 quintal 8 tonelada
island: 14 Tierra del Fuego
lake: 6 Viedma 7 Cardiel, Fagnano, Musters 11 Buenos Aires, Mar Chiquita, Nahuel Huapi
mountain: 4 Toro 5 Andes, Chato, Laudo, Potro 6 Bonete, Conico, Pissis, Rincon 8 Famatina, Murallon, Olivares, Tronador, Zapaleri 9 Aconcagua, Tupungato 10 Cordillera 13 Ojos del Salado 15 Cerro Mercedario, Sierra de Cordoba
highest point: 9 Aconcagua
river: 4 Sali 5 Atuel, Chico, Coyle, Dulce, Limay, Negro, Plata, Teuco 6 Blanco, Chubut, Cuarto, Flores, Grande, Iguazu, Parana, Quinto, Salado 7 Bermejo, Deseado, Iguassu, Mendoza, Tercero, Tunuyan, Uruguay 8 Colorado, Paraguay, Picomayo, Senguerr 9 Pilcomayo
sea: 8 Atlantic
physical feature:
  falls: 6 Grande, Iguazu 7 Iguassu
  lowland: 5 chaco
  plains: 6 pampas
  plateau: 4 Puna 6 Parana
  salt flat: 14 Salinas Grandes
  volcano: 5 Lanin, Maipo 6 Domuyo 7 Peteroa
  wind: 5 Zonda 7 Pampero
people: 3 Api 4 Lule 5 Vejoz 6 Abipon, Vilela 7 Guarani, Puelche, Ranquel, Taluhet 8 Querandi, Querendy
  artist: 6 Borges
  author: 4 Wast 6 Banchs, Borges 7 Lugones 9 Guiraldes, Hernandez 10 Echeverria
  leader: 4 Roca 5 Illia, Menem, Mitre, Peron, Rosas 6 Videla 7 Urquiza 8 Aramburu, Belgrano, Eva Peron, Frondici, Galtieri 9 San Martin, Sarmiento 11 Isabel Peron
language: 7 Spanish
religion: 13 Roman Catholic
place:
  opera house: 11 Teatro Colon
  world's southernmost town: 7 Ushuaia
feature:
  bird: 6 chunga
  cowboy: 6 gaucho 7 vaquero
  dance: 5 samba, tango, zamba 6 cuando, gaucho 7 milonga 9 chacarera
  farm: 6 quinta
  knife: 5 facon
  metal straw: 8 bombilla
  ranch: 8 estancia
  school smock: 9 delantale
  shawl: 6 poncho
  trousers: 9 bombachas
  weapon: 4 bola
food:
  cocktail: 7 clarito
  dish: 4 luna 7 criollo, puchero 8 chivitos, empanada 10 parrillada

---

mistress of: 7 Gwydion
son: 14 Llew Llew Gyffes
cursed: 14 Llew Llew Gyffes

arid 3 dry 4 dull 5 vapid 6 barren, dreary, jejune 7 dried-up, parched, tedious 8 lifeless, pedantic 9 colorless, dry as dust, waterless 10 desertlike, uninspired 13 unimaginative, uninteresting 15 drought-scourged

aridity 6 dearth 7 drought, dryness 8 aridness, dullness 10 barrenness 12 lifelessness, rainlessness 17 unimaginativeness

aridness 6 dearth 7 aridity, drought, dryness 8 dullness 10 barrenness 12 lifelessness, rainlessness 17 unimaginativeness

arid region 6 desert 9 wasteland 16 barren wilderness

Ariel
author: 11 Shakespeare, Sylvia Plath
character in: 10 The Tempest

Aries
symbol: 3 ram
planet: 4 Mars
rules: 11 personality
born: 5 April, March

Arimaspians
member of: 9 Scythians
number of eyes: 3 one

Arion
form: 11 winged horse
father: 8 Poseidon
mother: 7 Demeter

Ariosto, Ludovico
author of: 14 Orlando
Furioso

Arisbe
father: 6 Teucer
husband: 5 Priam 8 Dardanus,
Hyrtacus

arise 4 dawn, go up, rise,
wake 5 awake, begin, climb,
ensue, get up, mount, occur,
set in, start 6 appear, ascend,
crop up, emerge, result, wake
up 7 emanate, stand up
8 commence, spring up, stem
from 9 originate 11 come to
light

Aristaeus
origin: 5 Greek
god of: 9 husbandry 10 beekeeping, winemaking
father: 6 Apollo
mother: 6 Cyrene
wife: 7 Autonoe
son: 7 Actaeon
caused death of: 8 Eurydice

aristocracy 5 elite 6 gentry
7 peerage, society 8 nobility
9 beau monde 10 patricians,
upper class, upper crust
11 high society

aristocrat 4 duke, earl, lady,
lord, peer 5 noble 7 Brahmin,
duchess, grandee, marquis
8 countess, marquess, nobleman 9 blue blood, gentleman,
patrician 10 noblewoman
11 gentlewoman 12 silk
stocking

aristocratic 5 noble, regal,
royal 6 lordly, titled 7 courtly,
genteel, refined 8 highborn,
highbred, wellborn 9 dignified,
patrician 10 of high rank,
upper-class 11 blue-blooded,
gentlemanly 12 silk-stocking
13 of gentle blood

Aristodemus
member of: 10 Heraclidae
father: 12 Aristomachus
son: 7 Procles 11 Eurysthenes
killed by: 9 lightning

Aristomachus
member of: 10 Heraclidae
son: 7 Temenus 11 Aristodemus, Cresphontes
granddaughter: 8 Hyrnetho
invaded: 12 Peloponnesus

Aristophanes
author of: 6 Plutus 8 The
Birds, The Frogs, The Peace,
The Wasps 9 The Clouds
10 Lysistrata, The Knights
13 Ecclesiazusae, The
Acharnians

Aristotle
author of: 7 Physics, Poetics
8 On Plants, Politics, Rhetoric, Sophisms 9 On the
Soul 10 Generation 11 Metaphysics 12 On the Heav-
ens 14 Parts of Animals,
Prior Analytics 17 Nicomachean Ethics 18 Posterior
Analytics 23 On Beginning
and Perishing

Arizona *see box*

ark 3 box 4 ship 5 barge,
chest 8 flatboat 9 houseboat
10 Noah's boat

Arkansas *see box*

Arkin, Alan
born: 9 New York NY
roles: 7 Catch-22 13 Wait
Until Dark 21 Last of the
Red-Hot Lovers 23 The
Heart Is a Lonely Hunter
40 The Russians Are Com-
ing The Russians Are
Coming

Ark of the Covenant
gold covering: 9 mercy seat
12 propitiatory

arm, arms 4 guns 5 brace,
crest, equip, prime 6 branch,
outfit, sector 7 forearm, fortify, prepare, protect, section,
weapons 8 armament, bla-
zonry, division, firearms, insignia, materiel, offshoot,
ordnance, weaponry 9 ap-
pendage, make ready, upper
limb 10 coat of arms, department, detachment, obtain
arms, projection, strengthen,
take up arms 12 anterior
limb 13 prepare for war
14 heraldic emblem 18 furnish
with weapons

armada 4 navy 5 fleet 8 flotilla,
squadron 10 escadrille

armadillo
family: 11 Dasypodidae
order: 8 Edentata
body: 5 armor 6 plates
habitat: 12 South America,
United States 14 Central
America
habit: 9 nocturnal

Armageddon 8 doomsday
11 final battle 13 great conflict
author: 8 Leon Uris

armagnac
type: 6 brandy 7 liqueur
origin: 6 France

Arizona
abbreviation: 2 AZ 4 Ariz
nickname: 11 Grand Canyon
capital/largest city: 7 Phoenix
others: 3 Ajo 4 Eloy, Mesa, Naco, Yuma 5 Globe, Leupp,
Tempe 6 Bisbee, McNary, Salome, Toltec, Tucson 7 Cor-
taro 8 Chandler, Glendale, Prescott 9 Flagstaff
10 Scottsdale
college: 11 Grand Canyon 12 Southwestern
explorer: 8 Coronado 12 Marcos de Niza
feature:
  dam: 6 Hoover 8 Coolidge 9 Roosevelt
  national park: 11 Grand Canyon 15 Petrified Forest
tribe: 4 Hano, Hopi, Pima 6 Apache, Navaho, Navajo,
Papago
people: 7 Cochise 8 Geronimo 14 Barry Goldwater
lake: 4 Mead 6 Havasu, Mohave, Mormon, Powell
9 Roosevelt
land rank: 5 sixth
mountain: 5 White 6 Lemmon 7 Hualpai 8 Mazatzal
9 Baldy Peak 13 Santa Catalina
  highest point: 13 Humphreys Peak
physical feature:
  canyon: 5 Grand
  desert: 6 Sonora 7 Painted
  forest: 9 Petrified
river: 4 Gila, Salt, Zuni 5 Verde 6 Puerco 8 Colorado
12 Bill Williams 14 Little Colorado
state admission: 11 forty-eighth
state bird: 10 cactus wren
state flower: 13 saguaro cactus
state motto: 11 God Enriches
state song: 7 Arizona
state tree: 9 palo verde

armament 4 arms, guns
7 weapons **8** ordnance, weaponry **9** equipment, munitions **10** outfitting **13** military
might **16** war-making machine

Armenia *see box*

Armenian
  language family: **12** Indo-
European
  spoken in: **4** USSR **6** Russia
7 Armenia

Armida
  opera by: **5** Gluck, Haydn,
Lully **6** Dvorak **7** Rossini
10 Eszterhazy

Armies 7 Sabaoth

Armies of the Night
  author: **12** Norman Mailer

armistice 5 peace, truce
9 cease-fire **23** suspension of
hostilities

armlet 6 bangle **8** bracelet,
ornament

arm of the sea 5 bight, firth,
fjord (fiord), inlet **6** strait
7 channel, estuary, narrows

armoire 8 cupboard, wardrobe
12 clothespress

armor 4 mail **5** chain **6** shield
7 bulwark **10** coat of mail,
protection **11** suit of armor
18 protective covering

armorial bearings 4 arms
5 crest **10** coat of arms,
escutcheon

armory 7 arsenal **9** arms depot **13** ordnance depot

Arms and the Man
  author: **17** George Bernard
Shaw

arms depot 6 armory **7** arsenal **13** ordnance depot
18 military storehouse

Armstrong, Henry
  sport: **6** boxing
  class: **11** lightweight
12 welterweight

army 3 mob **4** band, bevy,
crew, gang, host, mass, pack
5 crowd, force, horde, swarm
6 legion, throng, troops **7** legions, militia **8** military, soldiers, soldiery **9** land force,
multitude **10** land forces
11 aggregation, fighting men
12 congregation **13** military
force **15** military machine

Arnaeus
  also: **4** Irus
  origin: **5** Greek
  mentioned in: **7** Odyssey
  form: **6** beggar **9** errandboy
  errandboy for: **16** Penelopes
suitors

Arkansas
  abbreviation: **2** AR **3** Ark
  nickname: **4** Bear **9** Bowie Land **17** Land of Opportunity
  capital/largest city: **10** Little Rock
  others: **3** Coy, Cuy, Keo, Ola, Roe, Ulm **4** Alma, Bono,
Casa, Dell, Diaz, Moro **5** Enola, Perla, Rondo **6** Alicia,
Camden **8** El Dorado **9** Fort Smith, Jonesboro, Pine Bluff,
Texarkana **10** Hot Springs **11** Blytheville **12** Fayetteville
  feature:
    national park: **10** Hot Springs
  tribe: **5** Caddo, Osage **6** Quapaw **7** Choctaw, Wichita
8 Cherokee
  people: **8** Alan Ladd **10** Dick Powell **11** Bill Clinton
16 Douglas MacArthur
  lake: **6** Beaver, Chicot, Conway, Nimrod **7** Greeson, Nor-
fork **8** Maumelle, Ouachita **10** Bull Shoals **11** Greers
Ferry **12** Blue Mountain
  land rank: **13** twenty-seventh
  mountain: **4** Blue **5** Ozark **6** Boston, Gaylor **7** Fourche
8 Magazine, Ouachita
    highest point: **8** Magazine
  river: **3** Red **5** Black, White **6** Saline **7** Buffalo, Current
8 Arkansas, Cossatot, Ouachita **9** St Francis **11** Mississippi
  state admission: **11** twenty-fifth
  state bird: **11** mockingbird
  state flower: **12** apple blossom
  state motto: **13** (Let) The People Rule
  state song: **8** Arkansas
  state tree: **13** shortleaf pine

Armenia
  other name: **5** Minni **6** Urartu **8** Anatolia
  former name: **31** Armenian Soviet Socialist Republic
  capital/largest city: **6** Erivan **7** Yerevan
  ancient capital: **3** Ani **7** Artashat, Artaxata
  others: **3** Van **5** Sivas **7** Trabzon **9** Kirovakan, Leninakan,
Trabizond **13** Bitlisarzurum
  head of state: **9** President
  monetary unit: **5** ruble
  lake: **3** Van **5** Sevan, Urmia **8** Urumiyah
  mountain: **6** Ararat, Taurus **7** Aladagh **8** Karabakh
  highest peak: **12** Mount Aragats
  river: **3** Ara **4** Aras, Kura **5** Araks, Cyrus, Halys, Zanga
6 Araxes, Razdan, Tigris **9** Euphrates **10** Kizil-Irmak
  physical feature:
    volcano: **7** Aragats
  people: **5** Armen, Ermyn, Gomer, Hadji
    apostle: **7** Gregory
    gypsy: **5** bosha
    hero: **4** haik **6** vartan
    leader: **26** Levon Akopovich Ter Petrosyan
    me: **3** ara
    saint: **5** Sahak **6** Mesrop
  language: **7** Russian **8** Armenian
  religion: **16** Armenian Orthodox
  feature:
    cap: **6** calpac
    fortress: **7** erebuni
    game: **7** barbout
    kingdom: **6** Urartu, Vannic **7** Cilicia, Sophene **8** Ardsruni
  food:
    bread: **4** peda
    cucumber: **4** guta
    dish: **7** lahvosh **9** paraghatz, sou-beoreg

Arne
  author: **20** Bjornstjerne Bjornson

Arne
  son: **6** Aeolus **7** Boeotus
  foster father: **9** Desmontes

Arne, Thomas Augustine
  born: **6** London **7** England
  composer of: **6** Alfred, Judith **8** Rosamond, Tom Thumb **10** Artaxerxes **14** Love in a Village, Thomas and Sally

Arness, James
  real name: **12** James Aurness
  brother: **11** Peter Graves
  born: **13** Minneapolis MN
  roles: **8** Gunsmoke **10** Matt Dillon

Arnold, Matthew
  author of: **7** Thyrsis **10** Dover Beach **15** Sohrab and Rustum, The Scholar-Gypsy **16** Empedocles on Etna **17** Culture and Anarchy, Essays in Criticism **18** On Translating Homer

Arnold, Roseanne *see* Roseanne

aroma 4 odor **5** savor, scent, smell **7** bouquet **9** fragrance, redolence

aromatic 5 spicy **7** odorous, piquant, pungent, scented **8** fragrant, perfumed, redolent **11** odoriferous

around 4 near **5** about, circa **10** encircling, on all sides, roundabout **11** surrounding

Around the World in Eighty Days
  author: **10** Jules Verne
  director: **15** Michael Anderson
  character: **11** Phileas Fogg **12** Passepartout
  cast: **10** Cantinflas, David Niven **12** Robert Newton **15** Marlene Dietrich, Shirley MacLaine
  score: **11** Victor Young
  Oscar for: **5** score **7** picture

arouse 3 fan **4** goad, move, spur, warm, whet **5** pique, rouse, waken **6** awaken, bestir, excite, foment, foster, heat up, incite, kindle, stir up, wake up **7** provoke, quicken, sharpen **8** summon up **9** stimulate

Arowhena
  character in: **7** Erewhon
  author: **6** Butler

arpeggio 5 chord, scale **8** flourish **13** musical device

arraign 6 accuse, charge, impute, indict **7** censure **8** denounce **9** criticize

arrange 4 file, plan, plot, pose, rank, sort **5** adapt, array, fix up, group, order, range, score **6** assort, design, devise, lay out, line up, map out, set out, settle **7** agree to, marshal, prepare, provide **8** classify, contrive, organize, schedule **9** methodize **11** orchestrate, systematize

arrangement 5 order **8** arraying, disposal, grouping, ordering **10** assortment **12** distribution, organization **13** methodization **14** categorization, classification **15** systematization
  German: **9** Ausgleich

arrangements 5 plans, score, terms **7** compact **8** measures **9** agreement **10** adaptation, provisions, settlement **12** preparations **13** orchestration

arrant 4 rank **5** utter **7** extreme **8** flagrant, outright, thorough **9** confirmed, downright, egregious, notorious, out-and-out **11** undisguised, unmitigated **13** thoroughgoing

array 4 deck, garb, pose, rank, robe, show, wrap **5** adorn, align, dress, group, order, place, range **6** attire, bedeck, clothe, deploy, finery, fit out, outfit, parade, set out, supply **7** apparel, arrange, display, marshal, raiment **8** clothing, garments, organize **9** pageantry **10** assortment, collection, exhibition, marshaling **11** arrangement, disposition

arrears 5 debit **9** liability **10** balance due, obligation, unpaid debt **11** overdue debt **12** indebtedness **15** outstanding debt

arrest 3 end, fix, nab **4** bust, halt, hold, slow, stay, stop **5** block, catch, check, delay, pinch, rivet, roust, seize, stall **6** absorb, collar, detain, engage, hinder, occupy, retard, secure **7** attract, capture, engross, inhibit, seizure, slowing, staying **8** blocking, checking, hold back, restrain, stoppage, stopping, suppress **9** apprehend, interrupt, retention **10** inhibiting **11** holding back **12** apprehension, take prisoner

Arrhenius, Svante August
  field: **7** physics **9** chemistry
  nationality: **7** Swedish

theory of: **24** electrolytic dissociation

arriere pensee 12 hidden motive **17** mental reservation

arrival 5 comer **6** advent, coming **7** entrant, visitor **8** approach, arriving, entrance, newcomer, visitant **10** appearance

arrive 4 come, near **5** get to, occur, reach **6** appear, befall, happen, show up, turn up **7** succeed **8** approach, make good

arrivederci, a rivederci 7 goodbye **8** farewell **16** until we meet again

arrogance 5 scorn **6** egoism, vanity **7** bluster, conceit, disdain, swagger **8** contempt **9** assurance, insolence, loftiness, vainglory **10** lordliness, pretension **11** braggadocio, haughtiness, presumption **13** imperiousness **14** self-importance

arrogant 4 vain **6** lordly **7** haughty, pompous **8** insolent, scornful **9** conceited, imperious **10** disdainful, egoistical, swaggering **11** egotistical, overbearing, overweening, pretentious **12** contemptuous, presumptuous, self-assuming, supercilious, vainglorious **13** high-and-mighty, self-important

arrogate 5 adopt, claim, seize, usurp **6** assume **7** preempt **8** take over **10** commandeer **11** appropriate

arrogation 6 taking **7** seizure **10** assumption, usurpation **12** confiscation **13** appropriation, expropriation

arrow 3 bow **4** bolt, dart **5** shaft **7** pointer **9** direction **12** pointed shaft

Arrow
  constellation of: **7** Sagitta

Arrowsmith
  author: **13** Sinclair Lewis
  character: **10** Leora Tozer **11** Max Gottlieb **12** Terry Wickett **14** Capitola McGurk **15** Gustaf Sondelius **16** Martin Arrowsmith **18** Dr Almus Pickerbaugh

arroyo 4 wadi **5** gorge, gully **6** ravine, trench

arsenal 6 armory **7** weapons **8** magazine **9** arms depot **11** arms factory **13** ordnance depot **14** ammunition dump

arsenic
chemical symbol: **2** As

Arsenic and Old Lace
director: **10** Frank Capra
cast: **9** Cary Grant **10** Jack Carson, Peter Lorre **13** Josephine Hull, Priscilla Lane, Raymond Massey

Arsinoe *see* **11** Alphesiboea

Arsinous
son: **8** Aecamede

Arsippe
father: **6** Minyas
mocked: **8** Dionysus

ars longa, vita brevis 20 art is long life is short

Ars Poetica
author: **5** Homer

art, arts 5 craft, knack, skill **6** genius, finesse, mastery, methods **8** artistry, facility, strategy **9** dexterity, expertise, technique **10** fine points, humanities, principles, subtleties, virtuosity
goddess of: **6** Athena, Athene, Pallas, Saitis **7** Minerva **11** Tritogeneia **12** Pallas Athena **18** Alalcomenean Athena

Artacia
origin: **5** Greek
mentioned in: **7** Odyssey
means: **6** spring
in the land of: **10** Laestrygon

Artegall
character in: **15** The Faerie Queene
author: **7** Spenser

Artemis
also: **7** Cynthia **9** Astrateia
origin: **5** Greek
form: **6** virgin **7** goddess **8** huntress
habitat: **4** moon
mother: **4** Leto
twin brother: **6** Apollo
companion: **4** Opis **5** Oread
corresponds to: **5** Diana **6** Phoebe, Selene **11** Britomartis
epithet: **6** Orthia **7** Eurippa, Laphria, Limnaea, Pyronia **8** Aeginaea, Agrotera, Calliste, Caryatis, Daphnaea **9** Hemerasia, Lygodesma **10** Polymastus **11** Leucophryne

Artemision
shrine of: **7** Artemis

artery 3 way **4** path, road, vein **5** aorta **6** street **7** channel, highway **11** blood vessel

artful 3 apt, sly **4** able, deft, foxy, wily **5** adept, quick, sharp, smart **6** adroit, astute, clever, crafty, gifted, shifty, shrewd, subtle, tricky **7** cunning, knowing, politic **8** masterly, scheming, skillful, talented **9** deceitful, deceptive, designing, dexterous, ingenious, inventive, strategic, underhand **10** contriving, diplomatic, proficient **11** imaginative, machinating, maneuvering, resourceful **12** disingenuous

artfulness 5 guile **6** deceit **7** cunning, slyness **8** artifice, foxiness, scheming, subtlety, trickery, wiliness **10** craftiness **11** machination

Arthur
director: **11** Steve Gordon
cast: **11** Dudley Moore, John Gielgud **12** Liza Minnelli **19** Geraldine Fitzgerald
Oscar for: **15** supporting actor (Gielgud)

Arthur
began: **10** Round Table
father: **14** Uther Pendragon
half-sister: **11** Morgan le Fay
home: **7** Camelot
island: **6** Avalon
knights: **3** Kay **6** Gareth, Gawain **7** Geraint **8** Bedivere, Lancelot, Percival, Tristram **9** Launcelot
knights sought: **9** Holy Grail
mother: **7** Igraine, Ygaerne
nephew: **6** Modred
sword: **9** Excalibur
given by: **13** Lady of the Lake
wife: **9** Guinevere
wizard: **6** Merlin

Arthur, Chester Alan *see box, p. 60*

artichoke 14 Cynara Scolymus
varieties: **5** Globe **7** Chinese **8** Japanese **9** Jerusalem **14** White Jerusalem

article 4 item, part, term **5** count, essay, paper, piece, point, story, theme, thing **6** clause, detail, matter, object, review, sketch **7** portion, product, proviso, write-up **8** division **9** commodity, condition, paragraph, provision, substance **10** commentary, particular **11** proposition, stipulation

articulate 4 join **5** hinge, state, utter, voice **6** convey, facile, fluent, hook up **7** connect, enounce, express **8** eloquent, organize **9** enunciate, formulate, pronounce **10** enunciated, expressive, meaningful, speechlike **12** intelligible

articulation 5 hinge, joint **7** diction **8** juncture **9** elocution, utterance **10** connection **11** enunciation **13** pronunciation

artifact 4 tool **7** manmade **9** arrowhead

artifice 4 hoax, ruse, trap, wile **5** blind, dodge, feint, guile, trick **6** deceit, device, tactic **7** cunning, slyness **8** foxiness, intrigue, maneuver, scheming, trickery, wiliness **9** deception, duplicity, falsehood, imposture, ingenuity, invention, stratagem **10** artfulness, cleverness, craftiness, subterfuge **11** contrivance, machination **13** inventiveness

artificer 7 artisan, deviser **9** contriver, craftsman

artificial 4 fake, mock, sham **5** false, phony, stagy **6** ersatz, forced **7** feigned, labored, manmade, stilted **8** affected, mannered, specious, spurious **9** imitation, insincere, pretended, simulated, synthetic, unnatural **10** factitious, nonnatural, theatrical **11** counterfeit **12** manufactured

artillery 6 cannon **7** big guns **8** ordnance **11** mounted guns

artisan 6 master **9** craftsman **10** technician **14** handicraftsman

art is long life is short
Latin: **18** ars longa vita brevis

artist 6 expert, master **8** virtuoso

artistic 7 elegant, stylish **8** graceful, handsome, tasteful **9** aesthetic, exquisite **10** attractive

artistic ability 6 talent **7** mastery **8** artistry **10** virtuosity

artistry 5 taste, touch **6** talent **7** mastery **10** virtuosity **11** proficiency, sensibility **14** accomplishment

artless 4 open, pure, true **5** crude, frank, naive, plain **6** candid, honest, humble, simple **7** natural, sincere **8** innocent, trusting **9** guileless, ingenuous, primitive, unadorned **10** inartistic, lacking art, unaffected, untalented **11** open-hearted, undesigning **13** unpretentious **15** straightforward, unselfconscious, unsophisticated

artlessness 6 candor **7** honesty, naivete **8** openness **9** frankness, sincerity **10** simplicity **11** naturalness **13** guilelessness, ingenuousness **14** unaffectedness

art object
French: **9** objet d'art

Arthur, Chester Alan
nickname: **4** Chet **16** The Gentleman Boss
presidential rank: **11** twenty-first
party: **10** Republican
state represented: **2** NY
defeated: **5** no-one
succeeded upon death of: **8** Garfield
vice president: **4** none
cabinet:
state: **6** (James Gillespie) Blaine **13** (Frederick Theodore) Frelinghuysen
treasury: **6** (Charles James) Folger, (William) Windom **7** (Walter Quintin) Gresham **9** (Hugh) McCulloch
war: **7** (Robert Todd) Lincoln
attorney general: **8** (Benjamin Harris) Brewster, (Isaac Wayne) MacVeagh
navy: **4** (William Henry) Hunt **8** (William Eaton) Chandler
postmaster general: **4** (Timothy Otis) Howe **5** (Thomas Lemuel) James **6** (Frank) Hatton **7** (Walter Quinton) Gresham
interior: **6** (Henry Moore) Teller **8** (Samuel Jordan) Kirkwood
born: **2** VT (or Canada) **9** Fairfield
died: **2** NY **11** New York City
buried: **2** NY **6** Albany
education:
college: **5** Union
studied: **3** law
religion: **12** Episcopalian
interests: **8** good food (an epicure) **13** salmon fishing
political career: **13** vice president **26** customs collector for New York
civilian career: **6** lawyer **7** teacher
military service: **8** Civil War
quartermaster general of: **12** state militia (New York)
notable events of lifetime/term: **5** Panic (of 1883)
Act: **9** Pendleton **16** Chinese Exclusion **19** Edmunds Anti-Polygamy
father: **7** William
mother: **7** Malvina (Stone)
siblings: **4** Jane, Mary **6** Almeda, George, Regina **7** Malvina, William **8** Ann Eliza
wife: **5** Ellen (Lewis Herndon)
nickname: **4** Nell
children: **11** Chester Alan **12** Ellen Herndon **19** William Lewis Herndon

Art of Living, The
author: **11** John Gardner

Art of Love, The (Ars Amatoria)
author: **4** Ovid

arty 6 dainty **7** foppish **8** affected, highbrow, overnice, precious **9** dandified, overblown **10** effeminate **11** overrefined, pretentious **12** artsy-craftsy, bluestocking, high-sounding

Aruns
killer of: **7** Camilla

Arval
also: **13** Arval Brothers **14** Fratres Arvales
priests of: **6** Dea Dia
number of priests: **6** twelve

Arval Brothers *see* **5** Arval

Aryan
modern name: **13** Indo-European
origin: **10** North India **11** Central Asia
family of languages: **5** Hindi **7** Bengali, Panjabi **9** Sinhalese
religion: **8** Hinduism
originated: **11** caste system

Aryana *see* **11** Afghanistan

as 4 that, when **5** while **7** because, equally

Asa
father: **6** Abijah
grandfather: **8** Rehoboam
grandmother: **6** Maacah
deposed: **6** Maacah
defeated: **6** Baasha

as above
Latin: **7** ut supra

as a group 7 en masse, in a body **8** as a whole, together **11** all together

as a matter of form
Latin: **8** pro forma

Asar *see* **5** Aesir

as a result 2 so **5** due to **7** because **9** therefore, wherefore, whereupon **11** accordingly **12** consequently **13** in consequence

as a whole 8 all in all **10** altogether **19** all things considered
French: **6** en bloc

as below
Latin: **7** ut infra

Ascalabus
form: **5** youth
mocked: **7** Demeter
changed into: **6** lizard

Ascalaphus
occupation: **6** sentry **8** gardener
location: **10** underworld
father: **4** Ares
brother: **8** Ialmenus
member of: **9** Argonauts
killed by: **9** Deiphobus
changed into: **3** owl
changed by: **7** Demeter

Ascanius
also: **5** Iulus
father: **6** Aeneas
mother: **6** Creusa
founder of: **9** Alba Longa

ascend 4 rise **5** climb, mount, scale **7** inherit **9** succeed to

ascendancy, ascendance 4 edge, rule, sway **5** power, reign **7** command, control, mastery **8** whip hand **9** advantage, authority, dominance, influence, supremacy, upper hand **10** domination, leadership **11** preeminence, sovereignty, superiority **12** predominance

ascension 6 ascent, rising **7** scaling **8** climbing, mounting **10** ascendancy

ascent 4 rise **5** climb, grade, slope **6** rising **7** advance, incline, scaling, upgrade **8** climbing, gradient, mounting, progress **9** ascension **11** advancement, progression

ascertain 5 learn **6** detect, verify **7** certify, find out, unearth **8** discover **9** determine, establish, ferret out

ascertainable 10 detectable

11 discernible, perceivable, perceptible

ascetic 3 nun **4** monk, yogi **5** fakir, stern **6** hermit, strict **7** austere, dervish, eremite, recluse, Spartan **8** celibate, cenobite, rigorous, solitary **9** abstainer, anchorite, religious **10** abstemious, flagellant, self-denier **11** self-denying **13** self-mortifier **14** self-mortifying

Asch, Sholem
   author of: **4** Mary **5** Moses **8** A Village **10** The Apostle, The Prophet **11** The Nazarene, Three Cities **15** Song of the Valley **17** The God of Vengeance

Asclepiade
   descendants of: **9** Asclepius

Asclepius
   origin: **5** Greek
   god of: **7** healing **8** medicine
   father: **6** Apollo
   mother: **7** Coronis
   wife: **6** Epione
   son: **7** Machaon **10** Podalirius
   daughter: **4** Iaso **6** Hygeia
   nurse: **6** Trygon
   corresponds to:
      11 Aesculapius
   epithet: **8** Cotyleus

ascribe 6 assign, credit, impute, relate **7** trace to **8** accredit, charge to **9** attribute

Ascus
   form: **5** giant
   helped: **8** Lycurgus
   chained: **8** Dionysus

asea 4 lost **6** addled, adrift **7** puzzled **8** confused **10** bewildered

Asenath
   father: **10** Potipherah
   husband: **6** Joseph
   son: **7** Ephraim **8** Manasseh

Asgard
   home of: **4** Asar **5** Aesir
   origin: **12** Scandinavian
   connected to earth by:
      7 bifrost **13** rainbow bridge
   location of: **8** Valhalla

ash 4 dust **6** cinder **7** residue **12** powdered lava
   family: **5** olive
   genus: **8** Fraxinus
   climatic zone: **17** northern temperate
   varieties: **3** Pop, Red, Sea **4** Blue **5** Black, Green, Manna, Texas, Wafer, Water, White **6** Alpine, Ground, Shamel, Syrian, Velvet **7** Arizona, Modesto, Prickly **8** Carolina, Stinking **9** Evergreen, Flowering **10** Manchurian, Montebello **18** Yellow-topped mallee

   use: **4** fuel **6** timber **7** barrels **8** landscape **9** furniture **10** motor parts, sport goods
   most common species:
      8 white ash

ashamed 3 shy **7** abashed, bashful, prudish **9** chagrined, mortified, squeamish **10** chapfallen, distressed, humiliated, shamefaced **11** crestfallen, discomfited, embarrassed **12** disconcerted **13** guilt-stricken **18** conscience-stricken

Ashby, Hal
   director of: **10** Being There, Coming Home

ashen 3 wan **4** gray, pale **5** livid, pasty **6** anemic, leaden, pallid **8** blanched

Asher
   father: **5** Jacob
   mother: **6** Zilpah
   brother: **3** Dan, Gad **4** Levi **5** Judah **6** Joseph, Reuben, Simeon **7** Zebulun **8** Benjamin, Issachar, Nephtali
   sister: **5** Dinah
   city in: **8** Manasseh
   descendant of: **8** Asherite

Ashkenaz
   father: **6** Japhet
   mother: **5** Gomer

Ashley, Lady Brett
   character in: **15** The Sun Also Rises
   author: **9** Hemingway

ashore 6 on land **7** aground **9** on dry land

Ashton-Warner, Sylvia
   author of: **5** Three **6** Myself **7** Teacher **8** Spinster **10** Greenstone

Ashtoreth
   origin: **7** Semitic
   corresponds to: **6** Inanna, Ishtar **7** Astarte, Mylitta

Ash-Wednesday
   author: **7** T S Eliot

ashy 3 wan **4** pale **5** ashen, pasty, white **6** pallid, sallow **7** ghastly, ghostly **8** blanched **9** colorless

Asia see box, p. 62

aside 4 away **5** apart **6** aslant, beside **7** whisper

As I Lay Dying
   author: **15** William Faulkner
   character:
      Bundren family: **4** Anse, Cash, Darl **5** Addie, Jewel **9** Dewey Dell

Asimov, Isaac
   author of: **6** I Robot **10** Foundation (trilogy) **12** Caves of Steel, Robots of

Dawn **17** The Gods Themselves
   character: **12** Elijah Bailey **13** R Daneel Olivaw

asinine 5 silly **6** absurd, insane, stupid **7** foolish, idiotic, moronic, witless **9** brainless, imbecilic, senseless **10** halfwitted, irrational, muddlehead, ridiculous **11** lamebrained, thickheaded, thick-witted **12** dunderheaded, feebleminded, simpleminded, thickskulled

asininity 5 folly **8** dumbness **9** silliness, stupidity **10** imbecility **11** doltishness, foolishness **16** simplemindedness

as it should be
   French: **11** comme il faut

Asius
   origin: **5** Greek
   mentioned in: **5** Iliad
   king of: **7** Percote
   father: **8** Hyrtacus
   killed by: **9** Idomeneus

ask 3 beg, bid, sue **4** call, pump, quiz, seek, urge **5** apply, claim, grill, plead, press, query **6** appeal, charge, demand, desire, expect, invite, summon **7** beseech, entreat, implore, inquire, request, solicit **8** petition, question, sound out **10** supplicate **11** interrogate

Ask
   origin: **6** Nordic
   first: **3** man
   made from: **7** ash tree
   made by: **4** gods

askance 11 skeptically **12** disdainfully, suspiciously **13** distrustfully, mistrustfully **14** disapprovingly

askew 4 awry **6** aslant **7** crooked **8** cockeyed, lopsided, sleeping **9** crookedly

Askkimey *see* **6** Eskimo

aslant 4 awry **5** askew **7** crooked **8** cockeyed, lopsided **9** crookedly, obliquely, slantwise

asleep 6 dozing **7** napping **10** slumbering **13** taking a siesta **14** dead to the world

as much as this
   Latin: **8** quoad hoc

Asner, Ed
   born: **12** Kansas City KS
   roles: **5** Roots **8** Lou Grant **14** Rich Man Poor Man **18** Mary Tyler Moore Show

asocial 8 unsocial **9** nonsocial, reclusive **10** antisocial **12** misanthropic

Asia
 country: 4 Iran, Iraq, Laos, Oman 5 Burma, China, India, Japan, Macao, Nepal, Qatar, Syria, Tibet, Yemen 6 Bhutan, Brunei, Cyprus, Israel, Jordan, Russia, Sikkim, Taiwan, Turkey 7 Armenia, Bahrain, Georgia, Kashmir, Lebanon, Myanmar, Vietnam 8 Cambodia, Hong Kong, Malaysia, Maldives, Mongolia, Pakistan, Sri Lanka, Thailand 9 Indonesia, Kirghizia, Singapore 10 Azerbaijan, Bangladesh, Kazakhstan, Kyrgyzstan, North Korea, South Korea, Tajikistan, Uzbekistan 11 Afghanistan, Saudi Arabia 12 North Vietnam, South Vietnam, Turkmenistan 13 Inner Mongolia 14 Papua New Guinea 15 Sinkiang-Uighur 18 United Arab Emirates
 desert: 4 Gobi, Thar 6 Syrian 7 Arabian, Karakum 8 Kyzylkum 10 Takla Makan
 island: 5 Kuril, Japan 6 Taiwan 7 Hai-nan 8 Sri Lanka 9 Indonesia: 3 Aru 4 Java, Sulu 5 Ceram, Sumba, Timor 6 Borneo, Flores 7 Celebes, Sumatra 8 Moluccas, Tanimbar 9 Halmahera, New Guinea 11 Philippines
 ancient people/empire: 4 Elam, Thai 5 Akkad, Aryan, Indus, Khmer, Media, Shang 6 Mongol, Ohoman, Semite 7 Amorite, Assyria, Hwang Ho, Parthia, Persian 8 Sumerian 9 Babylonia, Dravidian, Sassanian 11 Hephthalite, Mesopotamia
 ancient city: 2 Ur 5 Pagan, Sumer 6 Anyang 7 Ayuthia, Harappa 8 Mandalay 12 Mohenjo-daro
 ancient leader: 5 Asoka, Kassi 6 Darius 9 Anawratha, Zoroaster 13 Cyrus the Great 17 Alexander the Great
 religion: 5 Islam 6 Muslim, Shinto, Taoism 7 Jainism, Judaism 8 Buddhism, Hinduism 12 Christianity, Confucianism 13 Protestantism 16 Roman Catholicism
 language: 5 Hindi 6 Arabic, French 7 Chinese, English, Russian, Spanish
  Chinese dialects: 2 Wu 3 Min 5 Hakka 8 Mandarin 9 Cantonese
 river: 2 Ob 3 Amu, Hsi, Syr 4 Amur, Lena 5 Indus 6 Ganges, Mekong, Tigris 7 Hwang Ho, Salween, Yangtze, Yenisei 9 Euphrates, Irrawaddy 11 Brahmaputra 16 Tigris-Euphrates
 lake: 6 Baikal 7 Aral Sea 8 Balkhash 10 Caspian Sea
 mountain/mountain range: 5 Altai, Urals 6 Kunlon, Pamirs, Taurus, Zagros 8 Caucasus, Sulaiman, Tien Shan 9 Himalayas, Hindu Kush, Karakoram 10 Arakan Yoma
 highest point: 12 Mount Everest
 lowest point: 7 Dead Sea
 mineral/natural resources: 3 oil, tin 4 coal, mica, talc, zinc 7 bauxite, iron ore, mercury 8 chromium, graphite, selenium, tungsten 9 manganese 10 natural gas
 largest city: 8 Shanghai
 vegetation: 3 fir, sal 4 moss, pine, teak 5 larch 6 bamboo, lichen, spruce 8 ironwood
 animal: 3 elk, yak 4 bear, wolf 5 camel, panda, sable, takin, tiger 6 ermine, kuland 7 markhor 8 antelope, elephant, reindeer 9 arctic fox, polar bear
 people: 4 Huis, Kurd, Thai, Turk 5 Aryan, Khmer, Malay, Tungu 6 Buryat, Chuang, Kalmyk, Mongol, Semite, Vighor 7 Baluchi, Burmese, Chinese, Chukchi, Persian, Russian, Tadzhik, Tibetan 8 Armenian, Filipino, Japanese 9 Dravidian 10 Han Chinese, Indonesian, Vietnamese

Asopus
 form: 3 god
 habitat: 5 river
 father: 7 Oceanus
 mother: 6 Tethys
 wife: 6 Metope
 son: 7 Ismenus, Pelagon

 number of daughters:
  6 twenty

asparagus
 varieties: 4 Cape 6 Common, Garden, Smilax 7 Cossack 8 Prussian, Sprenger

aspect 3 air 4 look, side 5 angle, facet, point 7 feature 10 appearance 13 consideration

aspen 7 Populus
 varieties: 7 Chinese, Quaking 8 European, Japanese 9 Trembling 12 Large-toothed

asperity 5 rigor 6 rancor 8 acrimony, hardship, severity 9 harshness, hostility, roughness 10 difficulty

Aspern Papers, The
 author: 10 Henry James

aspersion 4 slur 5 abuse, smear 7 calumny, censure, obloquy, railing, slander 8 reproach, reviling 10 defamation, detraction 11 deprecation 12 vilification 13 disparagement

Asphalius *see* 8 Poseidon

Asphodel Fields
 meadow of: 10 dead heroes

asphyxiate 5 choke 6 stifle 7 smother 9 suffocate 11 strangulate

aspirant 7 hopeful, nominee 9 applicant, candidate 10 competitor, contestant

aspiration 3 end 4 hope, mark, wish 6 design, desire, intent, object 7 craving, longing, purpose 8 ambition, daydream, endeavor, yearning 9 hankering, intention, objective

aspire 4 seek 5 aim at, covet, crave 6 desire, pursue 7 hope for, long for, pine for, wish for 8 yearn for 9 pant after 10 hunger over 11 hanker after, thirst after

ass 4 dolt, fool, jerk 5 booby, burro, dunce, idiot, moron, ninny 6 donkey, dum-dum, nitwit 7 half-wit, jackass 8 bonehead, imbecile, lunkhead, numskull 9 blockhead, lamebrain 10 dunderhead, nincompoop 11 male jackass

assail 5 fly at 6 attack 7 assault, lunge at, set upon 9 pitch into 11 descend upon

assailant 6 mugger 8 assailer, attacker, molester 9 aggressor, assaulter

assailer 8 attacker 9 aggressor, assailant, assaulter

Assamese
 language family: 12 Indo-European
 branch: 11 Indo-Iranian
 group: 5 Indic
 spoken in: 5 (northern) India

Assaracus
origin: 5 Greek
mentioned in: 5 Iliad
father: 4 Tros
son: 5 Capys
founder of: 10 royal house

assassin 6 hit man, killer,
slayer 8 murderer
11 executioner

assassinate 4 kill, slay 6 murder, rub out 7 bump off 9 do
to death, liquidate 10 put to
death 11 exterminate

assault 4 push, raid 5 drive, fly
at, foray, lunge, sally, siege,
storm 6 assail, attack, charge,
invade, strike, thrust 7 besiege,
bombard, lunge at, offense, set
upon 8 fall upon, invasion,
storming, strike at, thrust at
9 assailing, lash out at, onslaught 10 aggression
11 bombardment

assaulter 6 mugger 8 assailer,
attacker 9 aggressor, assailant

assay 3 try 4 rate, test 5 essay,
prove 6 assess 7 analyze, attempt 8 appraise, endeavor, estimate, evaluate 9 undertake

assemblage 4 body, heap,
herd, mass, pack, pile 5 batch,
bunch, clump, flock, group,
stock, store 6 throng 7 cluster,
company 8 assembly, con-
clave 9 aggregate, amassment,
gathering 10 collection 11 aggregation 12 accumulation,
congregation

assemble 4 join, meet
5 amass, flock, rally 6 gather,
heap up, muster, pile up,
summon 7 collect, compile,
connect, convene, convoke,
marshal, round up 9 construct,
fabricate 10 accumulate, congregate 11 fit together, put together 12 call together, come
together 13 bring together,
group together

assembly 4 body, herd, mass,
pack 5 crowd, flock, group,
troop 6 throng 7 cluster, company, council 8 conclave, congress 9 aggregate, gathering
10 assemblage, collection
11 aggregation, convocation,
legislature 12 congregation

assembly hall 8 auditory
10 auditorium 11 concert hall,
lecture hall, meeting hall

assent 5 agree, allow, grant,
yield 6 accept, accord, comply,
concur, permit 7 approve, concede, consent, defer to 8 approval, sanction 9 acquiesce,
admission, agreement 10 acceptance, compliance, concession, fall in with

11 affirmation, approbation,
concurrence, endorsement, recognition, subscribe to 12 acquiescence, confirmation,
ratification, verification
13 corroboration
14 acknowledgment

assent to 4 okay 5 allow
6 accept, permit 7 approve
8 sanction, say yes to 9 agree
with, authorize 11 acquiesce
to, go along with

assert 4 aver, avow 5 argue,
claim, state, swear 6 accent, affirm, avouch, insist, stress, uphold 7 advance, contend,
declare, profess 8 advocate,
maintain, propound, set forth
9 emphasize 10 put forward

assertion 5 claim 6 avowal,
dictum 8 argument, averment
9 statement, upholding 10 allegation, contention 11 declaration, maintaining
12 protestation

assertion without proof
Latin: 9 ipse dixit

assertive 5 pushy 8 cocksure,
decisive, emphatic, forceful,
positive 9 confident, insistent,
outspoken 10 aggressive
11 domineering, self-assured
12 strong-willed

assertiveness 10 insistence
11 forwardness 12 cocksureness, forcefulness, positiveness 13 agressiveness,
outspokenness 14 self-
confidence

assess 3 tax 4 levy 5 judge,
value 6 charge 8 appraise, consider, estimate, evaluate, look
over

assessment 3 fee, tax 4 dues,
fine, rate, toll 6 charge, impost, tariff 8 judgment 9 appraisal 10 estimation,
evaluation

asset 3 aid 4 boon, help, plus
7 benefit, service 9 advantage

assets 4 cash 5 goods, means,
money 6 wealth 7 capital, effects 8 property, reserves 9 resources 10 belongings
11 possessions

asseverate 4 aver, avow
5 state, swear 6 affirm, assert,
attest, avouch, insist 7 certify,
contend, declare, protect
8 maintain, proclaim 9 emphasize, pronounce

as shown below
Latin: 7 ut infra

assiduity 8 industry, tenacity
9 diligence 10 dedication,

doggedness 11 application,
persistence 13 determination

assiduous 6 dogged 7 earnest
8 constant, diligent, sedulous,
tireless, untiring 9 laborious,
steadfast, tenacious 10 determined, persistent, unflagging
11 hardworking, industrious,
persevering, unremitting
13 indefatigable

assign 3 fix, set 4 give, name
5 allot, grant 6 charge, choose,
invest 7 appoint, consign, entrust, mete out, specify 8 allocate, delegate, dispense, set
apart 9 apportion, designate,
determine, prescribe, stipulate
10 commission, distribute

assignation 4 date 5 tryst
7 meeting 10 rendezvous
11 appointment

assignment 3 job 4 duty, post,
task 5 chore 6 lesson 8 exercise, homework 9 allotment
10 allocation, commission
11 appointment, designation
12 distribution
13 apportionment

assimilate 6 absorb, digest, imbibe, ingest, take in 9 integrate 10 metabolize
11 incorporate

Assiniboine, Assiniboin
language family: 6 Siouan
location: 9 Minnesota
12 Lake Winnipeg,
Saskatchewan
related to: 7 Dakotas

assist 3 aid 4 abet, hand, help
5 boost, serve 6 back up, uphold, wait on 7 benefit, support, sustain 9 cooperate, lend
a hand, reinforce 11 accommodate, collaborate, helping
hand

assistance 3 aid 4 alms, help
6 relief 7 charity, service, stipend, subsidy, support
10 sustenance 11 cooperation,
helping hand 12 contribution
13 collaboration, reinforcement 16 financial support

assistant 3 aid 4 aide, ally
5 aider 6 helper 7 partner
8 adjutant, co-worker, sidekick 9 accessory, associate,
auxiliary, colleague, subaltern,
supporter 10 accomplice, apprentice, cooperator, lieutenant 11 confederate, helping
hand, subordinate 12 collaborator 15 second-in-command

associate 3 mix, pal, tie
4 ally, bind, chum, club, join,
link, mate, pair, peer, yoke
5 buddy, crony, merge, unite
6 allied, couple, fellow, friend,
hobnob, league, mingle, re-

late **7** combine, comrade, connect, consort, hang out, partner, related **8** confrere, coworker, identify, intimate, sidekick **9** affiliate, colleague, companion, confidant, correlate, pal around, rub elbows, run around **10** accomplice, affiliated, fraternize **11** confederate, subordinate **12** collaborator

associated 6 allied, joined, united **9** connected **10** affiliated **11** amalgamated

association 3 tie **4** body, bond, club, meld **5** blend, group, union **6** clique, league **7** combine, company, linkage, mixture, society **8** alliance, intimacy, mingling, relation **9** coalition, community, relations, syndicate **10** assemblage, connection, federation, fellowship, fraternity, friendship, membership **11** affiliation, camaraderie, combination, confederacy, corporation, correlation, familiarity, partnership **12** acquaintance, friendliness, organization, relationship **13** collaboration, companionship, confederation, participation **14** fraternization, identification

assorted 5 mixed **6** motley, sundry, varied **7** diverse, various **9** different **11** diversified **13** heterogeneous, miscellaneous

assortment 5 array, stock, store **6** medley, motley **7** melange, mixture, sorting, variety **8** grouping, quantity **9** arranging, assorting, diversity, potpourri, selection **10** collection, hodgepodge, miscellany **11** arrangement, classifying, disposition **14** classification, conglomeration

as stated below
   Latin: 7 ut infra

assuage 4 calm, ease **5** allay, quiet, still **6** lessen, pacify, soften, soothe, temper **7** appease, lighten, mollify, relieve **8** mitigate, tone down **9** alleviate **14** take the edge off

assuagement 6 easing, relief, solace **7** comfort **8** blunting, easement **9** abatement, lessening, tempering **10** mitigation **11** appeasement **13** mollification

assume 4 take **5** fancy, guess, infer, judge, seize, think, usurp **6** accept, deduce, gather, take on, take up **7** believe, imagine, presume, suppose, surmise, suspect **8** arrogate,

shoulder, take over, theorize **9** postulate, speculate, undertake **10** commandeer, conjecture, understand **11** appropriate, expropriate, hypothesize **14** take for granted

assumed 4 fake **5** bogus, false, phony **6** made-up **8** presumed, supposed **9** falsified **10** fictitious **11** make-believe, presupposed, pseudonymic **12** pseudonymous

assumed name 5 alias **7** pen name **9** pseudonym **13** false identity
   French: 10 nom de plume **11** nom de guerre

assuming 4 bold **5** nervy, pushy **6** brazen, cheeky **7** forward, haughty **8** arrogant, insolent **9** audacious, presuming **11** overbearing **12** presumptuous **13** self-assertive

assumption 6 belief, taking, theory **7** premise, seizure **8** assuming, taking on, taking up **9** accepting, postulate **10** acceptance, arrogation, hypothesis, usurpation **11** postulation, presumption, shouldering, supposition, undertaking **13** appropriating **14** presupposition

assurance 3 vow **4** oath **5** poise **6** binder, pledge **7** promise **8** averment, boldness, coolness, sureness, warranty **9** certainty, certitude, guarantee **10** confidence, profession **11** affirmation, assuredness, word of honor **12** self-reliance **14** aggressiveness, self-confidence, self-possession

assure 5 vow **6** clinch, ensure, secure **7** confirm, promise **8** pledge to **9** guarantee **11** make certain **14** give one's word to

assured 4 sure **5** fixed **6** poised, secure **7** certain, settled **8** positive **9** confident, undoubted **10** dependable, guaranteed **11** indubitable, irrefutable **12** indisputable **13** self-confident, self-possessed **14** unquestionable

Astaire, Fred
   real name: 19 Frederick Austerlitz
   partner: 12 Ginger Rogers
   born: 7 Omaha NE
   roles: 6 Top Hat **9** Funny Face, Let's Dance, Swing Time **10** Holiday Inn **12** Easter Parade, Royal Wedding, Shall We Dance **14** The Gay Divorcee

Astarte
   origin: 7 Semitic
   goddess of: 9 fertility **12** reproduction
   habitat: 4 moon
   corresponds to: 6 Inanna, Ishtar **7** Mylitta **9** Ashtoreth

aster 12 Callistephus
   varieties: 4 Tree **5** Black, China, Heath **6** Annual, Golden, Mojave, Stoke's **7** Italian **8** Blue-wood **9** Tartarian, White wood **10** New England **11** White upland

Asteria
   form: 8 Titaness
   father: 5 Coeus
   mother: 6 Phoebe
   sister: 4 Leto
   husband: 6 Perses
   son: 8 Paropeus
   daughter: 6 Hecate
   changed into: 5 Delos **6** island

Asterion
   also: 8 Asterius
   father: 7 Cometes
   member of: 9 Argonauts

Asterius
   also: 8 Asterion
   form: 5 giant **8** minotaur
   king of: 5 Crete
   father: 4 Anax **8** Tectamus **10** Cretan Bull, Hyperasius
   mother: 8 Pasiphae
   wife: 6 Europa
   adopted sons: 5 Minos **8** Sarpedon **12** Rhadamanthys
   daughter: 5 Crete
   member of: 9 Argonauts

astern 3 aft **5** abaft **6** behind **9** to the rear

Asterodia
   form: 5 nymph
   type of nymph: 9 Caucasian

asteroid 6 debris **9** meteorite, planetoid

Asteropaeus
   origin: 5 Greek
   mentioned in: 5 Iliad
   father: 7 Pelegon
   ally of: 4 Troy
   killed by: 8 Achilles

Asterope see **7** Sterope

astir 2 up **5** afoot, awake **6** active, roused **8** in motion, out of bed **10** up and about

astonish 4 daze, stun **5** amaze, shock **6** dazzle **7** astound, confuse, perplex, stagger, startle, stupefy **8** bewilder, confound, dumfound, surprise **9** electrify, overwhelm, take aback **10** strike dumb **11** flabbergast **15** make one's eyes pop **18** take one's breath away

astonishing 7 amazing **8** daz-

zling, shocking, striking
9 confusing, startling 10 astounding, impressive, perplexing, staggering, stupefying, surprising 11 bewildering, confounding 12 breathtaking, electrifying, overpowering, overwhelming

astonishment 3 awe 5 shock 6 wonder 8 surprise 9 amazement, confusion 10 perplexity, wonderment 12 bewilderment, stupefaction

Astor, Mary
real name: 28 Lucille Vasconcellos Langhanke
born: 8 Quincy IL
roles: 6 Marmee 11 Little Women, The Great Lie 15 Meet Me in St Louis 16 The Maltese Falcon 17 The Palm Beach Story 18 The Prisoner of Zenda

astound 4 daze, stun 5 amaze, shock 6 dazzle 7 stagger, startle, stupefy 8 astonish, dumfound, surprise, take back 9 electrify, overwhelm 10 strike dumb 11 flabbergast 15 make one's eyes pop 18 take one's breath away

Astrabacus
origin: 5 Greek 7 Spartan
form: 6 prince
found: 11 wooden image
hidden by: 7 Orestes
co-finder: 8 Alopecus

Astraea
also: 6 Astrea
goddess of: 7 justice
father: 4 Zeus
mother: 6 Themis

Astraeus
form: 5 Titan
consort of: 3 Eos
father of: 4 wind 5 stars

astral 6 starry 9 celestial 12 astronomical

astraphobia
fear of: 9 lightning

Astrateia see 7 Artemis

astray 3 off 5 amiss 6 afield 10 off the mark 12 off the course 16 off the right track

Astrea see 7 Astraea

astringent 4 acid, keen, sour, tart 5 brisk, sharp, stern, tonic 6 biting, severe 7 acerbic, austere, bracing, puckery, styptic 8 curative, incisive, piercing, salutary, stabbing, vinegary 10 antiseptic, salubrious 11 contracting, penetrating, restorative 12 invigorating

astrology 6 Zodiac 9 horoscopy, starcraft 10 astromancy,

astrometry, stargazing 11 genethliacs 13 mathematicals 14 astrodiagnosis
belief in: 8 siderism
term: 4 sign 5 house, trine 6 alnath, apheta, aspect 7 almuten, anareta, mansion, mundane, sextile 8 alkahest, nativity, quartile, synastry 9 planetary 10 opposition 11 conjunction

astronomer 4 Bode, Gold 5 Adams, Baade, Bayer, Bethe, Gould, Hoyle, Royer 6 Bessel, Halley, Hubble, Jansky, Kepler, Newton, Piazzi 7 Bradley, Celcius, Galileo, Huggins, Huygens, Kapteyn, Laplace, Ptolemy, Russell, Shapley, Slipher 8 Angstrom, Einstein, Herschel, Hevelius, Lacaille, Lemaitre, Mercator 9 Eddington, Leverrier 10 Copernicus, Hipparchus, Tycho Brahe 11 Aristarchus, Hertzsprung 13 Petrus Apianus

astronomy
term: 5 comet, orbit 6 apogee, meteor, nebula, parsec, quasar 7 azimuth, eclipse, equinox, perigee, transit 8 aphelion, asteroid, ecliptic, meridian, solstice 9 meteorite, satellite 10 perihelion, precession 11 declination, occultation 12 perturbation, spectroscopy 16 celestial equator
type/related study: 9 cosmogony, cosmology 10 astrometry, photometry 12 astrophysics 18 celestial mechanics
see also: 4 star

Astrophel and Stella
author: 15 Sir Philip Sidney

astute 3 sly 4 able, foxy, keen, wily 5 acute, sharp, smart 6 adroit, artful, bright, clever, crafty, shrewd, subtle 7 cunning, knowing, politic 9 designing, sagacious 10 discerning, keen-minded, perceptive 11 calculating, intelligent, penetrating 13 Machiavellian, perspicacious

astuteness 6 acumen 8 keenness 9 acuteness, smartness 10 cleverness, shrewdness 12 perspicacity

Astyanax
also: 11 Scamandrius
father: 6 Hector 9 Strophius
mother: 10 Andromache
thrown from: 11 Trojan walls
thrown by: 6 Greeks
slain by: 8 Menelaus

Astydamia
father: 7 Amyntor
husband: 7 Acastus

daughter: 8 Laodamia
abducted by: 8 Hercules

Asuncion
capital of: 8 Paraguay

asunder 4 rent 5 apart 8 in pieces, to shreds 9 torn apart 11 broken apart

asylum 4 home 5 haven 6 harbor, refuge 7 retreat, shelter 8 madhouse, preserve 9 almshouse, orphanage, poorhouse, sanctuary 10 sanatorium, sanitarium 11 institution 13 children's home, state hospital 14 mental hospital 15 place of immunity 17 mental institution 23 eleemosynary institution

Asynjur
origin: 12 Scandinavian
goddesses of: 4 Asar 5 Aesir
leader: 3 Fri 5 Frigg, Frija 6 Frigga

As You Like It
author: 18 William Shakespeare
character: 5 Celia (Aliena) 6 Audrey, Jaques, Oliver 7 Orlando 8 Rosalind (Ganymede) 9 Frederick 10 Touchstone

Atabyrian see 4 Zeus

at a distance 4 afar, away 5 above, aloof, apart 6 far off 9 separated

Atala
author: 21 Francois Chateaubriand

Atalanta
also: 8 Atalante
form: 6 virgin 8 huntress
father: 5 Iasus
mother: 7 Clymene
son: 13 Parthenopaeus
wounded: 14 Calydonian boar
lost race to: 10 Hippomenes

Atalanta in Calydon
author: 24 Algernon Charles Swinburne

Atalante see 8 Atalanta

at any rate 6 anyhow, anyway 9 in any case 10 in any event

at cross purposes 7 counter, opposed 8 contrary, converse, inimical, opposite 9 disparate 10 at variance, discordant 11 conflicting 12 antithetical, incompatible 13 contradictory

Ate
origin: 5 Greek
form: 7 goddess
personifies: 12 recklessness 16 divine punishment

at ease 4 calm, cool 6 at rest,

serene **7** content, relaxed, unmoved **8** composed **9** at leisure, confident, unruffled **10** complacent, nonchalant, unbothered, untroubled **11** comfortable, unconcerned

a tergo 9 at the back **10** from behind

at fault 6 guilty **8** culpable **10** implicated **11** blameworthy, responsible

at full length
　Latin: **9** in extenso

Athabascan, Athapascan (Slave Indians)
　language family: **10** Athabascan, Athapaskan
　location: **6** Canada **14** Great Slave Lake
　dominated by: **4** Cree
　related to: **9** Chipewyan
　tribe: **4** Dine **5** Slave **6** Apache, Navaho, Navajo **9** Mescalero **10** Athabascan

Athaliah
　father: **4** Ahab
　mother: **7** Jezebel
　husband: **7** Jehoram
　son: **7** Ahaziah

Athalie
　author: **18** Jean Baptiste Racine

Athamas
　king of: **6** Thebes
　father: **6** Aeolus
　wife: **3** Ino **7** Nephele
　son: **5** Ptous **6** Leucon **7** Phrixus **8** Learchus **10** Melicertes
　daughter: **5** Helle

at hand 4 near, nigh **5** close, handy, on tap, ready **6** nearby **7** close by **8** imminent **9** available, impending **10** accessible, convenient **11** at one's elbow, forthcoming **14** at one's disposal **15** within arm's reach

atheism 8 apostasy, unbelief **9** disbelief **10** irreligion **11** godlessness

atheist 7 infidel **10** unbeliever **11** disbeliever, nonbeliever **13** godless person

Athena
　also: **6** Athene, Pallas, Saitis **11** Tritogeneia **12** Pallas Athena **18** Alalcomenean Athena
　origin: **5** Greek
　goddess of: **4** arts **6** wisdom **7** warfare **9** fertility
　father: **4** Zeus **6** Triton
　mother: **5** Metis
　sprang from head of: **4** Zeus
　raised by: **12** Alalcomeneus
　symbol: **3** owl
　corresponds to: **7** Minerva

epithet: 4 Alea **5** Meter, Xenia **6** Ergane, Itonia, Polias **7** Agoraea, Cissaea, Paeonia, Pronaus, Pronoea **8** Anemotis, Poliates, Zosteria **9** Oxyderces, Parthenia, Poliuchus, Promachus **10** Axiopoenus, Chalinitis, Cyparissia **11** Promachorma

Athens
　capital of: **6** Greece
　Greek: **7** Athinai
　hills: **9** Acropolis **14** Hagios Georgios
　landmark: **4** Stoa **9** Areopagus, Parthenon **10** Erechtheum, Propylaeum **17** Theater of Dionysus
　marketplace: **5** Agora
　mountain: **6** Parnes **8** Aigaleos, Hymettus **10** Pentelikon
　named for: **6** Athena
　port: **7** Piraeus
　river: **7** Ilissus
　sea: **6** Aegean **11** Saronic Gulf
　square: **8** Syntagma (Constitution)

Athens Graces 4 Auxe **8** Hegemone

athirst 4 avid, keen **5** eager **6** raring **7** longing, panting **8** yearning

athlete 4 jock **8** champion **9** contender, sportsman **10** contestant, game player

athletic 5 burly, hardy, husky, manly **6** brawny, robust, strong, sturdy, virile **8** muscular, powerful, stalwart, vigorous **9** masculine, strapping **10** able-bodied

athletics 5 games **6** sports **8** exercise **9** exercises **10** gymnastics

at home 6 at ease, inside, shut in **7** indoors **8** confined **10** in the house **11** comfortable
　French: **4** chez

Athos
　character in: **18** The Three Musketeers
　author: **5** Dumas (pere)

athwart 6 across **7** astride **8** sideways, sidewise **9** crossways, crosswise **12** transversely

Atlanta
　baseball team: **6** Braves
　basketball team: **5** Hawks
　football team: **7** Falcons

Atlantean
　pertaining to: **5** Atlas

Atlantic
　pertaining to: **10** Titan Atlas

Atlantic City
　director: **10** Louis Malle

cast: 8 Kate Reid **13** Burt Lancaster, Michel Piccoli, Susan Sarandon

at large 5 astir, loose **6** abroad **8** as a whole, at length **9** at liberty, in general **10** on the loose, unconfined **11** out and about **13** in circulation **14** around and about **15** making the rounds

Atlas
　form: **5** Titan
　father: **7** Iapetus
　mother: **7** Clymene
　brother: **9** Menoetius **10** Epimetheus, Prometheus
　wife: **7** Pleione
　daughters: **6** Hyades **7** Calypso **8** Pleiades **10** Hesperides
　supported: **3** sky
　identified with: **14** Atlas Mountains

Atlas Shrugged
　author: **7** Ayn Rand
　character: **8** John Galt **11** Hank Reardon **12** Dagny Taggart, James Taggart

at last
　Latin: **10** ad extremum

at leisure 4 idle **7** off duty **8** inactive **9** at liberty **10** unemployed, unoccupied

Atli
　origin: **12** Scandinavian
　sister: **8** Brynhild
　wife: **6** Gudrun, Kudrun **7** Guthrun
　killed by: **6** Gudrun, Kudrun **7** Guthrun
　represents: **6** Atilla

atmosphere 3 air **4** aura, feel, mood, tone **5** color **6** spirit **7** feeling, quality **8** ambience **11** environment **12** surroundings

atmospheric 3 air **4** airy **8** ethereal

at odds 6 unlike **8** contrary **9** different **10** at variance, discordant, discrepant, dissimilar **11** contrasting

at odds with 9 counter to **10** contrary to **14** at variance with

atom 3 bit, dot, jot **4** iota, mite, mote, whit **5** crumb, grain, scrap, shred, speck, trace **6** morsel, tittle **7** smidgen **8** fragment, particle **9** scintilla **10** smithereen

atomic 6 cobalt **7** fission, neutron, nuclear, uranium **8** hydrogen **9** molecular, plutonium, subatomic, unseeable **10** impalpable **11** fissionable, microcosmic, microscopic, superatomic **13** imperceptible, indiscernible, infinitesimal, thermonuclear

atom part 6 proton **7** neutron **8** electron

at once
French: **11** tout de suite

atone 6 pay for, redeem, repent, shrive **7** expiate **9** make up for **10** compensate, recompense, remunerate **12** do penance for **13** make amends for **17** make reparation for

atonement 6 amends, shrift **7** penance, redress **9** expiation **10** recompense, redemption, reparation, repentance **12** compensation, satisfaction **14** penitential act

at one's disposal 5 handy **6** at hand, on hand **9** available **10** accessible, convenient **11** at one's elbow, ready for use **13** at one's service

at one's elbow 5 handy **6** at hand, nearby **9** available **10** accessible, convenient

Atrax
father: **6** Peneus

at rest 5 quiet, still **6** asleep, at ease, serene **7** at peace, content **8** in repose **9** quiescent **10** motionless

Atreus
father: **6** Pelops
mother: **10** Hippodamia
sister: **7** Nicippe
wife: **6** Aerope
son: **8** Menelaus **9** Agamemnon **10** Plisthenes
daughter: **8** Anaxibia
killed: **6** Aglaus

Atridae
descendants of: **6** Atreus
family name of: **8** Anaxibia, Menelaus **9** Agamemnon **10** Plisthenes

atrium 4 hall **6** cavity **7** auricle **8** entrance **13** Roman entrance

atrocious 3 bad, low **4** dark, evil, rude, vile **5** black, cruel **6** brutal, savage, tawdry, vulgar **7** heinous, hellish, inhuman, uncouth, vicious **8** dreadful, enormous, fiendish, flagrant, grievous, horrible, infamous, infernal, pitiless, ruthless, terrible **9** barbarous, execrable, merciless, monstrous, nefarious, tasteless **10** diabolical, outrageous, villainous

atrociousness 6 infamy **7** cruelty **8** enormity, vileness **9** barbarity, brutality, depravity **11** heinousness, vicious-

ness **13** monstrousness, offensiveness **14** outrageousness

atrocity 6 horror **7** outrage **8** enormity, savagery, villainy **9** barbarism, barbarity, brutality **10** inhumanity **11** heinousness

atrophy 7 decline **8** decaying, drying up **9** lack of use, withering **10** emaciation, shriveling **11** wasting away **12** degeneration **13** deterioration

Atropos
member of: **5** Fates
cuts thread of: **4** life

Atsina (Gros Ventres, Haaninin)
language family: **9** Algonkian **10** Algonquian
location: **6** Canada **7** Montana **9** Milk River **12** Saskatchewan **13** Missouri River
related to: **7** Arapaho

attach 3 fix **4** join **5** affix, allot, annex **6** append, assign, couple, detail, secure **7** connect, destine, earmark **8** allocate, be fond of, fasten to, make fast **9** affiliate, associate, designate

attache 4 aide **5** envoy **6** consul **8** adjutant, diplomat, emissary, minister **9** assistant **10** ambassador, vice consul **11** diplomatist, subordinate **12** ambassadress **13** consul general

attachment 4 bond, love **6** fixing, liking, regard **7** adjunct, fixture, respect **8** addendum, addition, affinity, affixing, appendix, coupling, devotion, fondness, securing **9** accessory, affection, appendage, attaching, fastening **10** connection, friendship, supplement, tenderness **12** predilection

attack 3 fit **4** damn, go at **5** abuse, blame, fault, fly at, onset, spasm, spell **6** assail, charge, impugn, strike, stroke, tackle **7** assault, censure, lunge at, offense, seizure **8** denounce, fall upon, invasion, paroxysm **9** criticism, criticize, denigrate, disparage, incursion, offensive, onslaught, pitch into, undertake **10** aggression, impugnment **11** denigration **13** disparagement

attacker 6 mugger **7** accuser **8** assailer, opponent **9** adversary, aggressor, assailant **10** antagonist **11** belligerent

attain 3 win **4** earn, gain,

reap **5** reach **6** effect, obtain, secure **7** achieve, acquire, procure, realize **10** accomplish

attainable 6 at hand **9** available, reachable **10** accessible, achievable, realizable **11** within reach

attainment 5 skill **6** talent **7** earning, gaining, getting, mastery, success, winning **8** securing **9** acquiring, attaining, obtaining, procuring **10** competence **11** achievement, acquirement, acquisition, fulfillment, procurement, proficiency, realization **14** accomplishment

attempt 3 aim, try **4** seek **5** essay **6** attack, effort, hazard, strive, tackle, work at **7** assault, venture **8** endeavor **9** have a go at, onslaught, undertake **11** undertaking **12** make an effort, take a crack at, take a whack at

Attenborough, Richard
director of: **6** Gandhi (Oscar) **12** Young Winston **13** A Bridge Too Far

attend 4 go to, heed, mark, mind, note **5** serve, usher, visit **6** convoy, escort, follow, show up, squire, tend to **7** care for, conduct, observe, oversee, service **8** appear at, consider, frequent, harken to, listen to, wait upon **9** accompany **11** superintend
French: **4** oyez
cry used by: **10** court crier
preceded: **12** proclamation

attendance 4 gate **5** crowd, house **8** audience, presence **10** appearance, assemblage, being there

attendant 3 aid **6** escort, flunky, helper, lackey, menial **7** related, servant **8** adherent, chaperon, follower **9** accessory, assistant, companion, underling **10** associated, consequent **12** accompanying

attention 4 care, heed, mind, note, suit **5** court **6** homage, notice, regard, wooing **7** concern, respect, service, thought **8** civility, courtesy, devotion, wariness **9** alertness, deference, diligence, vigilance **10** observance, politeness **11** assiduities, compliments, gallantries **12** deliberation **13** concentration, consideration, contemplation **14** thoughtfulness

attentive 5 alert, awake **6** intent, polite **7** devoted, heedful, mindful, zealous **8** diligent, obliging **9** courteous, dedicated, listening, observant,

wide awake 10 respectful, thoughtful **11** considerate, deferential, painstaking **13** accommodating

attentiveness 7 concern **8** devotion, industry **9** alertness, attention, diligence **10** commitment, dedication **11** application, devotedness, heedfulness, mindfulness **14** thoughtfulness

attenuate 6 dilute, impair, lessen, reduce, weaken **7** draw out, spin out **8** decrease, diminish, enervate, enfeeble **9** water down **10** adulterate

attest 4 show **5** prove **6** affirm, assert, assure, evince, verify **7** bear out, certify, confirm, declare, display, exhibit, support, swear to, testify, warrant **8** vouch for **11** bear witness, corroborate, demonstrate **12** substantiate

attestation 9 testimony **10** deposition **11** declaration

at the back
Latin: **6** a tergo

at the beginning
Latin: **9** ad initium

at the bottom
French: **6** au fond

At the Edge of the Body
author: **9** Erica Jong

at the end
Latin: **5** ad fin

at the place
Latin: **5** ad loc **7** ad locum

At the Sign of the Reine Pedauque
author: **13** Anatole France

attic 4 loft **6** garret **7** mansard **8** cockloft **10** clerestory
French: **7** grenier
German: **9** Dachboden
Spanish: **9** guardilla

attire 3 don **4** duds, garb, gown, robe, togs **5** array, dress **6** bedeck, clothe, finery, fit out, invest, outfit, rig out **7** apparel, clothes, costume, deck out, raiment, turn out **8** clothing, garments, glad rags, wardrobe **9** vestments **11** habiliments

Attis
also: **4** Atys
form: **5** youth
home: **7** Phrygia
loved: **6** Cybele
driven mad by: **6** Cybele

attitude 3 air **4** pose **6** manner, stance **7** outlook, posture **8** demeanor, position **11** disposition, frame of mind, perspective, point of view

attorney 4 beak **6** lawyer **7** counsel **8** advocate **9** barrister, counselor, solicitor **10** mouthpiece **12** legal adviser **14** member of the bar **15** ambulance chaser

attract 4 draw, lure, pull **5** cause, charm, evoke **6** allure, beckon, entice, induce, invite **7** bewitch, enchant, provoke **8** appeal to, interest **9** captivate, fascinate **11** precipitate

attraction 4 lure, pull **5** charm **6** allure, appeal **7** glamour **8** affinity, charisma, tendency **9** magnetism **10** enticement, inducement, temptation **11** captivation, enchantment, fascination **12** drawing power

attractive 4 chic, fair **6** lovely, pretty **7** elegant, likable, sightly, winning **8** alluring, becoming, charming, engaging, enticing, fetching, handsome, inviting, pleasant, pleasing, tasteful, tempting **9** agreeable, appealing, beautiful, seductive **10** bewitching, delightful, enchanting **11** captivating, charismatic, fascinating

attractiveness 5 charm **6** beauty **9** good looks **11** pulchritude **12** handsomeness

attribute 4 gift **5** facet, grace, lay to, trait **6** aspect, assign, credit, impute, talent, virtue **7** ability, ascribe, blame on, cause by, faculty, feature, quality, trace to **8** charge to, property **9** character, endowment, set down to **10** account for, attainment, derive from, saddle with **11** acquirement, bring home to, distinction **14** accomplishment, characteristic

attrition 4 loss **7** erosion **8** abrasion, decrease, friction, grinding, scraping **9** reduction **10** decimation **11** wearing away, wearing down **14** disintegration

attune 5 adapt **6** adjust, tailor **8** accustom **9** acclimate **11** acclimatize

attune to 3 fit **5** adapt **6** adjust **7** conform **9** harmonize **11** accommodate

at variance 7 counter, opposed **8** contrary, converse, inimical, opposite **9** disparate **10** discordant **11** conflicting **12** antithetical, incompatible **13** contradictory **15** at cross purposes

Atwood, Margaret
author of: **8** Survival **9** Surfacing **10** Bodily Harm, Lady Oracle **11** Second Words **13** Life Before Man, Power Politics, The Circle Game **23** The Animals in That Country

at work 4 busy **5** in use **6** active **7** engaged, working **8** occupied

Atymnius
mentioned in: **5** Iliad
companion of: **8** Sarpedon
killed by: **10** Antilochus

atypical 7 unusual **8** abnormal, contrary, uncommon **9** anomalous, irregular, unnatural, untypical **10** nontypical **11** uncustomary, unlooked for **12** out of keeping **16** unrepresentative

Atys see **5** Attis

Auber, Daniel Francois Esprit
born: **4** Caen **6** France
composer of: **6** Haydee **7** La Macon **10** Fra Diavolo **12** Le Domino Noir **14** The Bronze Horse **16** Le Cheval de Bronze, The Crown Diamonds **17** La Muette de Portici **19** La Bergere Chatelaine **20** The Dumb Girl of Portici **22** Le Premier Jour de Bonheur **23** Les Diamants de la Couronne

auberge 3 inn **6** tavern

auburn 5 henna, tawny **6** russet **8** cinnamon, nutbrown **11** golden-brown, rust-colored **12** reddish-brown **13** copper-colored **15** chestnut-colored

Aucassin and Nicolette
author: **7** unknown

Auchincloss, Louis
author of: **10** Watchfires **11** The Dark Lady, The Partners **12** Second Chance, The Embezzler **14** A World of Profit **16** Powers of Attorney, Tales of Manhattan, The Country Cousin **17** The Rector of Justin **19** The Winthrop Covenant **20** Portrait in Brownstone

au contraire 13 on the contrary

au courant 8 up-to-date

auction 3 sale **7** bidding **8** offering

Auction Block, The
author: **8** Rex Beach

audacious 4 bold, pert, rash, rude, wild **5** bossy, brave, fresh, gutsy, risky, saucy **6** brazen, cheeky, daring, plucky **7** defiant, forward, valiant **8** assuming, fearless, heedless, impudent, insolent, intrepid, reckless, stalwart, un-afraid, valorous **9** breakneck, daredevil, dauntless, desperate, foolhardy, hotheaded, imprudent, shameless, unabashed **10** courageous, outrageous, self-willed **11** adventurous, impertinent, injudicious, lion-hearted, venturesome **12** death-defying, devil-may-care, discourteous, enterprising, presumptuous, stouthearted **13** disrespectful

audaciousness 6 daring **8** audacity, boldness **11** forwardness **13** assertiveness **14** aggressiveness **15** adventurousness

audacity 4 gall, grit, guts **5** brass, cheek, nerve, pluck, spunk, valor **6** daring, mettle **7** bravery, courage **8** backbone, boldness, chutzpah, rashness, temerity **9** brashness, derring-do, impudence, insolence **10** brazenness, effrontery **11** forwardness, presumption **12** fearlessness, impertinence, recklessness **13** bumptiousness, foolhardiness, shamelessness **15** venturesomeness

Auden, W H
author of: 11 Another Time, Thank You Fog **12** Homage to Clio, The Dyer's Hand **13** About the House, Journey to a War **15** For the Time Being, The Age of Anxiety **16** City Without Walls, Epistle to a Godson **17** In Memory of W B Yeats, Musee des Beaux Arts **20** The Dog Beneath the Skin **22** Forewords and Afterwords

Audhumbla
also: 8 Audhumla
origin: 12 Scandinavian
form: 3 cow
owner: 4 Ymir
birth from: 3 ice
uncovered: 4 Buri

Audhumla see **9** Audhumbla

audible 5 clear, heard **8** distinct **11** discernible, perceptible

audience 4 talk **5** house **6** market, parley, public **7** hearing, meeting **8** assembly, audition **9** following, interview, listeners, onlookers, reception **10** conference, discussion, readership, spectators **12** congregation, constituency, consultation

audit 5 check **6** go over, review, verify **7** balance, examine, inspect **10** inspection, scrutinize **11** examination, investigate, take stock of

12 scrutinizing, verification **13** investigation

audition 6 tryout **7** hearing **15** test performance

auditor 8 listener **10** accountant, bookkeeper **11** comptroller **17** financial examiner

auditorium 4 hall **5** arena **7** theater **8** auditory, coliseum **11** concert hall, lecture hall, meeting hall **12** assembly hall

Audrey
character in: 11 As You Like It
author: 11 Shakespeare

Audubon
author: 16 Robert Penn Warren

Audubon, John James
born: 8 Les Cayes **12** Santo Domingo
artwork: 14 Birds of America **34** Viviparous Quadrupeds of North America

Auel, Jean M
author of: 17 The Mammoth Hunters, The Valley of Horses **20** The Clan of the Cave Bear

Auerbach, Arnold (Red)
sport: 10 basketball
position: 5 coach
team: 13 Boston Celtics

au fait 6 expert, versed **11** experienced **13** knowledgeable

Aufklarung 13 enlightenment **16** the Enlightenment

au fond 9 basically, in reality **11** at the bottom

auf Wiedersehen 7 goodbye **8** farewell **16** until we meet again

Auge
priestess of: 6 Athena
father: 9 King Aleus
mother: 6 Neaera
son: 8 Telephus
assaulted by: 8 Hercules

Augean stables
owned by: 10 King Augeas
number of oxen: 13 three thousand
cleaned by: 8 Hercules
river running through: 7 Alpheus

Augeas
king of: 6 Epeans
realm: 4 Elis
member of: 9 Argonauts
brother: 5 Actor
son: 7 Eurytus, Phyleus **10** Agasthenes
daughter: 7 Agamede
grandson: 9 Polyxenus

auger 4 bore **5** drill **6** pierce **10** boring tool

aught 3 all, zip **4** love, nada, null, zero **6** naught **7** a cipher, nothing **8** goose egg **11** horse collar

augment 5 add to, boost, raise, swell, widen **6** deepen, expand, extend **7** amplify, build up, enlarge, inflate, magnify **8** flesh out, heighten, increase, lengthen **9** intensify

augmentation 5 boost, extra, raise **8** addition, increase, swelling, widening **9** deepening, expansion, extension, inflation **10** supplement **11** elaboration, enlargement, heightening, lengthening **13** amplification, magnification **15** intensification

augur 4 bode, seer **6** herald, oracle **7** diviner, portend, predict, presage, promise, prophet, signify **8** forecast, foretell, forewarn, intimate, prophesy **9** be a sign of **10** be an omen of, foreshadow, soothsayer **13** prognosticate **14** prognosticator

augury 4 omen, sign **5** token **6** herald **7** auspice, portent, promise, warning **8** prophecy **9** harbinger, precursor, sortilege **10** divination, forerunner, indication **11** forewarning, soothsaying **14** fortunetelling **15** prognostication

august 5 grand, lofty, noble, regal **6** solemn, superb **7** eminent, exalted, stately, sublime, supreme **8** glorious, imposing, majestic **9** dignified, estimable, grandiose, venerable **10** impressive, monumental **11** high-ranking, illustrious, magnificent **12** awe-inspiring **13** distinguished

August see box, p. 70

Augustine, St (of Hippo)
author of: 10 Civitas Dei **11** Confessions, Enchiridion **12** The City of God

augustness 7 dignity, majesty **8** eminence, nobility **9** loftiness **11** distinction **13** monumentality **15** illustriousness

August 1914
author: 23 Aleksandr Solzhenitsyn Jr

au naturel 4 nude **8** uncooked **15** in a natural state

Auntie Mame
author: 13 Patrick Dennis

Aunt Jo's Scrap-Bag
author: 15 Louisa May Alcott

August
Anglo-Saxon: 10 Weod-Monath
characteristic: 7 dog days
flower: 5 poppy
French: 4 Aout
gem: 7 peridot 8 sardonyx 9 carnelian
German: 6 August
holiday:
   England/Scotland:
   11 Harvest Home (1)
Italian: 6 Agosto
number of days:
   9 thirty-one
original name: 8 Sextilis 12 Metageitnion
origin of name: 6 Augere (Latin to open) 8 Augustus (Roman emperor)
place in year:
   Roman: 5 sixth
   Gregorian: 6 eighth
Spanish: 6 Agosto
zodiac sign: 3 Leo 5 Virgo

Aunt Julia and the Scriptwriter
author: 16 Mario Vargas Llosa

au pair 4 maid 5 nanny 9 governess 13 mother's helper

aura 3 air 4 feel, mood 5 aroma 7 essence, feeling, quality 8 ambience 9 character, emanation 10 atmosphere, suggestion

Aura
companion of: 7 Artemis
bore: 5 twins
   fathered by: 9 Dionysius
changed into: 6 spring
   changed by: 4 Zeus

au revoir 7 goodbye 8 farewell 16 until we meet again

Aurness, James
real name of: 11 James Arness

Aurora
origin: 5 Roman
goddess of: 4 dawn
corresponds to: 3 Eos

Aurora Leigh
author: 24 Elizabeth Barrett Browning

Ausgleich 10 compromise 11 arrangement 12 equalization

Auslander 5 alien 9 foreigner, outlander

Aurora-borealis

auspice 4 omen, sign 6 augury 7 portent, warning 10 indication 15 prognostication

auspices 4 care 5 aegis 6 charge 7 control, support 8 advocacy, guidance 9 authority, influence, patronage 10 protection 11 countenance, sponsorship 12 championship

auspicious 4 good 5 happy, lucky 6 benign, timely 7 hopeful 9 favorable, fortunate, opportune, promising, red-letter 10 felicitous, heartening, propitious, reassuring, successful 11 encouraging

Austen, Jane
author of: 4 Emma 10 Persuasion 13 Mansfield Park 15 Northanger Abbey 17 Pride and Prejudice 19 Sense and Sensibility

austere 5 rigid, spare, stark, stern 6 chaste, severe, simple, strict 7 ascetic, Spartan 8 rigorous 10 abstemious, forbidding 11 self-denying, strait-laced

Austerlitz, Frederick
real name of: 11 Fred Astaire

Australia *see box*

Austria *see box, p. 72*

Austroasiatic
language subfamily: 5 Khasi, Munda 8 Annamite, Mon-Khmer 9 Palaung-Wa 10 Nicobarese 11 Semang-Sakai 13 Annamite-Muong
spoken in: 5 Burma, India 7 Nicobar, Vietnam 8 Cambodia, Malaysia 9 Kampuchea

authentic 4 pure, real, true 5 valid 6 actual 7 factual, genuine 8 accurate, attested, bona fide, faithful, original, reliable, verified 9 veritable 10 accredited, dependable, legitimate 11 trustworthy 12 unquestioned 13 authoritative, unadulterated

authenticate 6 attest, avouch, verify 7 certify, confirm, endorse, warrant 8 document, validate, vouch for 9 guarantee 11 corroborate 12 substantiate

authenticated 7 genuine 8 attested, verified 9 validated 10 accredited, vouched for 13 substantiated

authentication 7 voucher 10 validation 11 certificate 12 verification 13 authorization, certification

author 4 poet 5 maker 6 father, framer, writer 7 creator, founder, planner 8 essayist, inventor, novelist, producer 9 initiator, innovator, organizer 10 originator, playwright, prime mover 16 short-story writer
see author under each country

authoritarian 5 harsh 6 severe, strict, tyrant 7 austere, fascist 8 autocrat, dogmatic, martinet 9 by the book, by the rule 10 inflexible, tyrannical, unyielding 11 dictatorial, doctrinaire 12 disciplinary, rule follower 14 disciplinarian, little dictator, uncompromising

authoritative 5 sound, valid 6 lordly, ruling 7 factual, learned 8 arrogant, decisive, dogmatic, imposing, official, reliable 9 authentic, masterful, scholarly, sovereign 10 autocratic, commanding, definitive, dependable, imperative, impressive, peremptory, sanctioned, tyrannical 11 dictatorial, trustworthy 14 administrative

authoritativeness 6 belief 9 authority 10 conviction 11 credibility 14 conclusiveness

authorities 6 expert, police, pundit 7 scholar 10 mastermind, specialist 11 connoisseur, officialdom 12 powers that be

authority 4 rule, sway 5 clout, force, might, power 6 esteem, weight 7 command, control, respect 8 dominion, prestige, strength 9 influence, supremacy 10 domination, importance 12 jurisdiction 14 administration

authorization 7 license 8 approval, sanction 10 commission, imprimatur, permission 11 entitlement 12 confirmation, legalization 13 accreditation, certification

authorize 5 allow 6 enable, invest, permit 7 approve, certify, charter, confirm, empower, entitle, license, warrant 8 accredit, sanction, vouch for 9 give leave 10 commission

authorized 8 approved, official 9 canonical 10 sanctioned

Autobiography of Alice B Toklas
author: 13 Gertrude Stein

Autobiography of Miss Jane Pittman, The
author: 13 Ernest J Gaines

Australia

other name: 9 Down Under
name means: 19 unknown southern land
capital: 8 Canberra
largest city: 6 Sydney
others: 3 Ayr **4** Yass **5** Dubbo, Perth **6** Albury, Cairns, Casino, Coburg, Darwin, Hobart **7** Bendigo, Geelong, Kogarah, Mildura, Mitcham, Whyalla **8** Adelaide, Ballarat, Bathurst, Brighton, Brisbane, Essendon, Randwick, Ringwood **9** Melbourne, Newcastle, Port Pirie, Toowoomba **10** Broken Hill, Kalgoorlie, Waggawagga, Wollongong **11** Collingwood, Rockhampton **12** Alice Springs
division: 8 Tasmania, Victoria **10** Queensland **13** New South Wales **14** South Australia **16** Western Australia **17** Northern Territory **26** Australian Capital Territory
head of state: 14 British monarch **15** governor general
measure: 4 arna, naut, saum
monetary unit: 4 dump, tray, zack **5** pound **6** dollar **8** shilling
island: 4 Cato, King **5** Cocos, Green, Timor **6** Barrow, Koolan **7** Coringa, Keeling, Neptune, Norfolk **8** Flinders, Kangaroo, Lacepede, Melville, Rottnest, Tasmania, Thursday **9** Admiralty
lake: 4 Eyre **5** Carey, Cowan, Frome, Moore, Wells **6** Austin, Barlee, Bulloo, Dundas, Harris, Mackay **7** Amadeus, Blanche, Everard, Torrens **8** Carnegie, Gairdner **9** MacDonald **10** Yammayamma **14** Disappointment
mountain: 3 Ise **4** Blue, Olga, Ossa, Zeil **5** Bruce, Snowy **6** Cradle, Doreen, Garnet, Gawler, Magnet, Morgan **7** Bongong, Gregory, Herbert **8** Augustus, Brockman, Cuthbert, Jusgrave, Mulligan, Surprise **9** Murchison, Woodroffe **14** Australian Alps **15** New England Range **18** Great Dividing Range
highest point: 9 Kosciusko
river: 3 Hay **4** Avon, Daly, Swan, Yule **5** Bullo, Comet, Drava, Naomi, Paroo, Roper, Yarra **6** Barcoo, Barwon, Bulloo, Culgoa, Degrey, Hunter, Isaacs, Murray, Norman **7** Darling, Derwent, Fitzroy, Georges, Gilbert, Lachlan, Staaten, Warrego **8** Belyando, Brisbane, Burdekin, Clarence, Drysdale, Flinders, Gascoyne, Georgina, Mitchell, Thompson, Victoria, Weeribee, Wooramel **9** Ashburton, Fortescue, Hawksbury, MacKenzie, Macquarie, Murchison, Saltwater **10** Diamantina, Shoalhaven **12** Murrambidgee
sea: 5 Coral, Timor **6** Indian, Tasman **7** Arafura, Pacific
physical feature:
 bay: **5** Bight, Shark **6** Botany **7** Moreton **11** Port Phillip
 cape: **4** Howe, York **5** Byron **9** Southeast
 channel: **5** Cowal **9** Anabranch, Billabong
 desert: **6** Arunta, Gibson, Stuart, Tanami **7** Simpson **10** Great Sandy **13** Great Victoria
 gulf: **8** Spencers **9** Van Dieman **11** Carpentaria **15** Joseph Bonaparte **20** Great Australian Bight
 peninsula: **4** Eyre
 reef: **12** Great Barrier
 strait: **4** Bass
people: 3 Abo **4** Koko, Mara, Wong **5** Anzac, Binge, Dieri, Maori, Myall **6** Aranda, Arunta, Aussie, Binghi, Digger, Kipper, Papuan **7** Arawong, Ilpirra **8** Antipode, Barkinji, Billijim, Euahlayi, Warragal, Warrigal **9** Aborigine **10** Australoid, Melanesian, Sandgroper
 actor: **9** Judy Davis, Mel Gibson, Paul Hogan **10** Bryan Brown
 author: **4** West **5** White **7** Russell **10** Richardson
 explorer: **4** Bass, Cook **6** Mawson, Tasman **7** Wilkins
 leader: **4** Holt **5** Hawke **7** Keating, Menzies, Whitlam
 nurse: **11** Sister Kenny
language: 7 English
religion: 7 Judaism **8** Anglican **10** Protestant **13** Roman Catholic
place: 7 outback **9** billabong **11** back country
 aborigine area: **9** Arhemland
 beach: **5** Manly
 dam: **4** Hume
possession: 12 Cocos Islands **13** Norfolk Island **16** Christmas Islands
feature:
 animal: **5** dingo **6** kelpie **7** wallaby **8** anteater, kangaroo **9** koala bear **18** duckbilled platypus
 bird: **3** emu **10** kookaburra
 cowboy: **6** waddie **8** jackaroo
 dance: **6** dreher
 flower: **7** boronia, fuchsia, waratah **9** coachwood **12** kangaroo paws
 game: **3** sye **10** tambaroora
 tree: **3** gum **10** eucalyptus
 weapon: **5** kiley, kyley **7** wommera **9** boomerang
food: 3 kai **6** tucker
 cake: **6** damper **7** brownie
 dish: **8** coolamon
 drink: **9** arkaloola
 fruit: **5** nonda **7** kumquat **11** desert-lemon

Austria

other name: 10 Osterreich

name means: 12 eastern state

capital/largest city: 6 Vienna

others: 4 Enns, Graz, Lech, Linz, Ried, Wels 5 Krems, Steyr, Traun 6 Leoben 7 Bregenz, Modling, Spittal, Villach 8 Bad Ischl, Dornbirn, Salzburg 9 Innsbruck, Semmering 10 Kapfenberg, Klagenfurt 11 Sankt Polten 14 Wiener Neustadt

division: 5 Tirol, Tyrol 6 Istria, Styria, Triest 7 Bohemia, Galicia, Moravia, Silesia 8 Bukowina, Dalmatia, Earniola, Gradisca 9 Earinthia 10 Burgenland, Vorarlberg 12 Lower Austria, Upper Austria
  Roman province: 6 Raetia 7 Noricum 8 Pannonia

government:
  legislature: 9 Bundesrat, Reichsrat 10 Herrenhaus, Reichsrath

head of government: 10 Chancellor

other leader: 7 emperor 12 burgomeister

measure: 4 fass, fuss, joch, mass, muth, yoke 5 halbe, linie, meile, metze, pfiff, punkt 6 achtel, becher, leipoa, seidel 7 dlafter, viertel 8 dreiling 12 futtermassel

monetary unit: 4 lira 5 crown, ducat, krone 6 florin, gulden, heller, zehner 8 albertin, groschen, kreutzer 9 schilling

weight: 4 marc, unze 5 denat, karch, stein 7 centner, pfennig 8 vierling 9 quantchen

lake: 6 Almsee 7 Fertoto, Mondsee 8 Bodensee, Traunsee 9 Constance 10 Neusiedler

mountain: 4 Alps 6 Stubai, Tirols, Tyrols 8 Eisenerz, Rhatikon 9 Dolomites, Kitzbuhel 10 Hohe Tauern 14 Silvretta Group

highest point: 13 Grossglockner

river: 3 Inn, Mur 4 Drau, Elbe, Enns, Iser, Kamp, Lech, Murz, Raab 5 Donau, Drava, Drave, March, Salza, Thaya, Traun 6 Danube, Moldau

physical feature:
  basin: 7 Styrian
  canal: 6 Danube
  mountain pass: 7 Brenner
  wind: 6 Foehen
  woods: 6 Vienna

people: 5 Poles 6 Croats, Czechs 7 Germans, Gypsies 8 Slovenes 10 Hungarians
  botanist: 6 Mendel
  composer: 5 Haydn 6 Czerny, Mahler, Mozart, Webern 7 Amadeus, Strauss 8 Bruckner, Schubert 9 Beethoven 10 Schoenberg
  emperor: 7 Charles, Francis 9 Ferdinand, Habsburgs, Hapsburgs 10 Franz Josef
  philosopher: 12 Wittgenstein
  psychiatrist: 5 Adler, Freud, Reich
  statesman: 10 Metternich 12 Kurt Waldheim

language: 5 Czech 6 German, Magyar 8 Croatian 9 Slovenian

religion: 7 Judaism 10 Protestant 13 Roman Catholic

place:
  boulevard: 3 Kai 11 Ringstrasse
  cathedral: 9 St Stephen
  city hall: 7 Rathaus
  fortress: 13 Hochosterwitz, Hohensalzburg
  imperial palace: 7 Hofburg
  monastery: 4 Melk 8 Gottweig 14 Klosterneuburg
  museum: 6 Mozart 9 Johanneum
  people's garden: 11 Volksgarten
  resort: 5 Baden 7 Bregenz 8 Bad Ischl 9 Innsbruck, Semmering

feature: 8 yodelers 11 ice grottoes
  clothing: 5 loden 10 lederhosen
  dance: 5 waltz 6 dreher 7 landler 13 schuhplattler 14 grand polonaise
  festival: 8 Salzburg
  horse: 10 Lippizaner
  pastry shop: 12 konditoreien

food:
  breaded veal cutlet: 15 Wiener schnitzel
  cake: 11 linzer torte, sacher torte
  cookie: 7 kipferl
  roll: 10 golatschen

autochthonous 5 first 6 native, primal 7 ancient 8 earliest, original, primeval 10 aboriginal, indigenous, primordial

autocracy 7 czarism, tyranny 8 autarchy, monarchy 9 Caesarism, despotism, Hitlerism, kaiserism, monocracy, Stalinism 10 absolutism 11 Bonapartism 12 dictatorship 14 tyrannical rule 15 totalitarianism 16 absolute monarchy

autocrat 5 ruler 6 despot, tyrant 7 monarch 8 dictator, overlord 13 absolute ruler

autocratic 8 despotic 9 czaristic, imperious, tyrannous 10 iron-handed, oppressive, repressive, tyrannical 11 dictatorial, monarchical 13 authoritarian

auto da fe, auto de fe 13 act of the faith 17 burning of heretics
  from: 18 Spanish Inquisition

autograph 4 mark, sign 5 x-mark 9 John Henry, signature 11 endorsement, handwriting, inscription, John Hancock 16 countersignature

Autolycus
  character in: 14 The Winter's Tale
  author: 11 Shakespeare

Autolycus
  form: 5 thief
  father: 6 Hermes
  mother: 6 Chione
  half-brother: 9 Philammon
  wife: 9 Amphithea
  daughter: 8 Anticlea
  grandson: 8 Odysseus
  gift: 12 invisibility 13 shape changing

automated 9 automatic 10 mechanical, mechanized 15 machine-operated

automatic 6 reflex 7 natural, routine 8 electric, habitual, inherent, unwilled 9 automated 10 mechanical, push-button, self-acting, self-moving 11 instinctive, involuntary, spontaneous, unconscious 12 uncontrolled 13 nonvolitional, self-operating 14 self-propelling

automaton 4 pawn, tool 5 patsy, robot 6 puppet, stooge 7 android, cat's-paw, fall guy, machine 10 fantoccino, marionette

Automedon
  charioteer of: 8 Achilles

automobile
  invented by:
    differential gear: 4 Benz
    electric: 8 Morrison
    gasoline: 6 Duryea 7 Daimler
    muffler: 5 Maxim
    self-starter: 9 Kettering
  see also: car

Automobile state
  nickname of: 8 Michigan

Autonoe
  father: 6 Cadmus
  mother: 8 Harmonia
  sister: 3 Ino 5 Agave 6 Semele
  husband: 9 Aristaeus
  son: 7 Actaeon
  daughter: 6 Macris

autonomous 4 free 9 sovereign 11 independent, self-reliant 13 self-governing 14 self-determined, self-sufficient

autonomy 7 freedom 8 home rule, self-rule 10 liberation 11 sovereignty 12 independence 14 self-government 17 self-determination

auto racing
  driver: 6 A J Foyt 7 Al Unser 8 Tom Sneva 9 Niki Lauda 10 Bobby Unser, Juan Fangio 11 Jack Brabham 12 Bobby Allison, Janet Guthrie, Richard Petty 13 Jackie Stewart, Mario Andretti 14 Barney Oldfield, Cale Yarborough, Craig Breedlove 16 Johnny Rutherford

Autry, Gene
  horse: 8 Champion
  born: 7 Tioga TX
  roles: 11 Melody Ranch 16 The Singing Cowboy 19 Tumbling Tumbleweeds 22 Springtime in the Rockies

autumn 4 fall 11 harvest time 12 Indian summer 15 autumnal equinox

auxiliary 6 backup, helper 7 partner, reserve 9 accessory, ancillary, assistant, associate, companion, emergency, secondary 10 accomplice, subsidiary, supplement 11 subordinate 13 supplementary

avail 3 aid, use 4 help 5 serve 6 assist, profit 7 benefit, purpose, service, success, utilize 9 advantage 10 usefulness

available 4 free, open 5 handy, on tap 6 at hand, on hand 9 in reserve 10 accessible, convenient, obtainable

avalanche 4 heap, mass, pile 5 flood 6 deluge 7 barrage, cascade, torrent 8 blizzard 9 cataclysm, rockslide, snowslide 10 earthslide, inundation 11 bombardment

Avalon
  island of: 8 Paradise
  burial place for: 6 heroes 10 King Arthur

avant-garde 7 leaders 8 pioneers, vanguard 10 innovators 11 forerunners, originators, tastemakers 12 advance guard, trailblazers, trendsetters

avarice 5 greed 6 penury 8 rapacity, venality 9 parsimony 10 greediness, stinginess 11 miserliness 12 covetousness, graspingness 13 money-grubbing, niggardliness, penny-pinching 15 close-fistedness

Ave Maria 8 Hail Mary

avenge 5 repay 6 injure, punish 7 revenge 9 retaliate

Avengers, The
  character: 8 Emma Peel, Tara King 9 John (Jonathan) Steed
  cast: 9 Diana Rigg 12 Linda Thorson 13 Patrick Macnee

avenue 3 way 4 gate, path, road 5 means, route 6 access, chance, course, outlet 7 gateway, parkway, passage, pathway 8 approach 9 boulevard, concourse, direction, esplanade 10 passageway 11 opportunity 12 thoroughfare

aver 4 avow 5 state, swear 6 affirm, assert, avouch, insist, verify 7 certify, contend, declare, profess, protest 8 maintain, proclaim 9 emphasize, guarantee, pronounce, represent 10 asseverate

average 3 par 4 fair, mean, norm, so-so 5 ratio, usual 6 common, medial, median, medium, normal, not bad 7 the rule, typical 8 mediocre, midpoint, moderate, ordinary, passable, standard, standing, the usual 9 tolerable 10 mean amount 11 indifferent, rank and file 12 run-of-the-mill

averment 5 claim 6 avowal 8 argument 9 assertion, assurance 10 allegation, contention, profession 11 affirmation

averse 5 loath 7 opposed 8 inimical 9 reluctant, unwilling 10 indisposed, unamenable 11 disinclined, ill-disposed, unfavorable 12 antipathetic, recalcitrant

aversion 6 hatred, horror 7 disgust, dislike 8 distaste, loathing 9 animosity, antipathy, hostility, prejudice, repulsion, revulsion **10** abhorrence, opposition, reluctance, repugnance **11** detestation **13** unwillingness **14** disinclination

avert 4 turn **5** avoid, deter, shift **7** beat off, deflect, fend off, keep off, prevent, ward off **8** preclude, stave off, turn away **9** forestall, frustrate, keep at bay, sidetrack **11** nip in the bud

aviary 4 cage **9** birdhouse, enclosure

aviation 6 flight, flying **11** aeronautics **12** aerodynamics

aviator, aviatrix 4 bird **5** flyer, pilot **6** airman, flyboy **7** birdman

avid 4 keen **5** eager, rabid **6** ardent, greedy, hungry **7** anxious, devoted, fanatic, intense, zealous **8** covetous, desirous, grasping **9** rapacious, voracious **10** avaricious, insatiable **11** acquisitive **12** enthusiastic

avidity 4 zeal **5** greed **6** fervor, hunger **8** rapacity, voracity **9** eagerness **10** enthusiasm, fanaticism, greediness **12** covetousness **15** acquisitiveness

Avignon Papacy 15 Babylonian Exile **19** Babylonian Captivity

avocado 9 dark green **13** alligator pear, tropical fruit
  origin: 6 Mexico **12** South America **14** Central America
  family: 9 Lauraceae
  used to make: 9 guacamole

avocation 5 hobby **7** pastime **8** sideline **9** diversion **10** recreation **11** distraction **13** entertainment

Avogadro, Amedeo
  field: 7 physics **9** chemistry
  nationality: 7 Italian
  formulated: 19 molecular hypothesis

avoid 4 shun **5** avert, dodge, elude, evade, skirt **6** escape, eschew **7** boycott, forbear, forsake **8** sidestep **10** fight shy of **11** refrain from **12** steer clear of

avoidance 7 eluding, evasion **8** shirking, shunning, skirting

avoid the issue 4 duck **5** dodge, evade, hedge, stall **10** equivocate **17** beat around the bush

a votre sante 12 to your health

avouch 5 argue, swear **6** af-

firm **7** declare **8** advocate, maintain

avow 3 own **4** aver **5** admit, state, swear **6** affirm, assert, reveal **7** confess, declare, profess **8** announce, disclose, proclaim **11** acknowledge

avowal 4 word **8** averment **9** admission, assertion, assurance, statement **10** confession, profession **11** affirmation, declaration **12** proclamation, protestation **14** acknowledgment

avowed 5 sworn **8** admitted, declared **9** confessed, professed **12** acknowledged, self-declared **14** self-proclaimed

await 6 attend, expect **7** look for **10** anticipate

awake 5 alert, aware, spark **6** arouse, awaken, bestir, excite, incite **7** alive to, heedful, inspire, mindful, provoke **8** open-eyed, vigilant, watchful **9** attentive, conscious, stimulate

Awake and Sing!
  author: 13 Clifford Odets

awaken 3 fan **4** fire **6** arouse, excite, kindle, revive, stir up **9** stimulate

awakening 7 arising, arousal **8** sparking, stirring **11** stimulation

award 4 give **5** allot, allow, grant, honor, medal, prize **6** accord, assign, bestow, decree, trophy **7** appoint, concede, laurels, tribute **8** citation, confer on **10** decoration

aware 6 with it **7** alert to, alive to, awake to, mindful **8** apprised, informed, sensible, sentient **9** cognizant, conscious, tuned in to **10** conversant **11** enlightened **12** familiar with **13** knowledgeable

awareness 9 acuteness, alertness, appraisal, knowledge **10** cognizance, perception **11** familiarity, information, mindfulness, realization, recognition, sensibility **12** acquaintance **13** consciousness, understanding

away 3 far **4** gone **6** absent, at once, way off **8** distance **9** elsewhere

awe 3 cow **4** fear **5** abash, alarm, amaze, dread, panic, shock **6** dismay, fright, horror, terror, wonder **7** perturb, quaking, respect, terrify **8** astonish, disquiet, frighten **9** abashment, adoration, amazement, quivering, rever-

ence, solemnity, trembling **10** exaltation, intimidate, veneration **11** disquietude, trepidation **12** apprehension, astonishment, perturbation **13** consternation

awe-inspiring 5 giant, grand, great, noble **6** august, mighty **7** eminent, exalted, mammoth, sublime, supreme, titanic **8** colossal, enormous, gigantic, glorious, imposing, majestic, wondrous **9** excessive **10** impressive, incredible, monumental, prodigious, stupendous, tremendous **11** astonishing, extravagant, illustrious, magnificent, spectacular **12** breathtaking, over-whelming

awesome 6 solemn **7** amazing, fearful **8** alarming, dreadful, fearsome, majestic, wondrous **9** inspiring **10** formidable, perturbing, stupefying, terrifying **11** astonishing, disquieting, frightening, magnificent **12** breathtaking, intimidating, overwhelming

awestruck 6 humble **8** overcome **11** reverential

awful 3 bad, low **4** base, dire, mean, ugly **5** lousy **6** solemn **7** amazing, awesome, fearful, ghastly, heinous, hideous **8** alarming, dreadful, fearsome, gruesome, horrible, majestic, shocking, terrible, wondrous **9** appalling, frightful, monstrous, revolting **10** deplorable, despicable, formidable, horrendous, horrifying, stupefying, terrifying, unpleasant **11** displeasing, disquieting, distressing, redoubtable **12** awe-inspiring, contemptible, disagreeable **13** reprehensible

awfully 4 very **5** quite **8** horribly, terribly **9** extremely, immensely **10** dreadfully **11** excessively **13** exceptionally

awkward 5 inept **6** clumsy, touchy, trying **7** unhandy **8** bungling, delicate, inexpert, ticklish, ungainly, unwieldy **9** difficult, graceless, maladroit **10** blundering, cumbersome, unpleasant, unskillful **11** troublesome **12** embarrassing, inconvenient, unmanageable **13** disconcerting, uncomfortable, uncoordinated
  French: 6 gauche

Awkward Age, The
  author: 10 Henry James

awkwardness 9 gaucherie **10** clumsiness, difficulty, ineptitude **12** ungainliness, unwieldiness **13** embarrassment, inconvenience

awl 4 nail **6** gimlet **11** leather tool, sharp device

awning 4 hood **6** canopy **7** marquee **8** covering, sunshade

awry 5 amiss, askew, wrong **6** astray, uneven **7** crooked, twisted **8** unevenly **9** crookedly, obliquely **11** out of kilter

axe, ax 3 can **4** chop, fire, oust, sack **5** let go, split **6** bounce, cut out, delete, remove **7** cut down, dismiss **8** get rid of, tomahawk **9** discharge, terminate **11** send packing
   type: 4 pick **6** poleax **7** hatchet **8** tomahawk

Axe, The
   author: 12 Sigrid Undset

Axelrod, Julius
   field: 9 chemistry
   studied: 24 nerve-impulse transmission
   awarded: 10 Nobel Prize

axiom 3 law **5** basic **7** precept **9** postulate, principle **10** assumption **14** fundamental law

axiomatic 5 banal, given **6** cliche **7** assumed **8** accepted, manifest **9** apodictic **10** aphoristic **11** self-evident **12** demonstrable, epigrammatic, indisputable, unquestioned **13** incontestable, platitudinous

Axiopoenus
   epithet of: 6 Athena
   means: 12 just requital

axis 4 stem **5** pivot, shaft **7** compact, entente, spindle **8** alliance **9** alignment, coalition **10** center line **11** affiliation **12** pivotal point **13** confederation **14** line of rotation, line of symmetry

axle 3 bar, pin **5** shaft, wheel **7** spindle **8** crossbar **10** turning bar

ayah 4 maid **5** nurse

aye 3 yea, yes **11** affirmative

Aykroyd, Dan
   born: 6 Canada, Ottawa **7** Ontario
   roles: 12 Ghostbusters **13** Doctor Detroit, Trading Places **16** The Blues Brothers, Driving Miss Daisy, The Great Outdoors **17** Saturday Night Live

Aymara
   location: 4 Peru **7** Bolivia **12** South America

Ayres, Lew
   wife: 8 Lola Lane **12** Ginger Rogers
   born: 13 Minneapolis MN
   roles: 7 Holiday, The Kiss **9** Dr Kildare **25** All Quiet on the Western Front

azalea 12 Rhododendron
   varieties: 4 Cork, Mock, Snow **5** Coast, Dwarf, Early, Flame, Hiryu, Hoary, Luchu, Royal, Sims's, Swamp, Sweet, Torch **6** Alpine, Balsam, Clammy, Indian, Korean, Kurume, Kyushu, Oconee, Pontic, Smooth, Spider, Summer, Yellow **7** Alabama, Chinese, Maries's, Mt Amagi, Oldham's, Western **8** Five-leaf, Japanese, Piedmont, Rusticum, Yodogawa **9** Kirishima, Mayflower, Pink-shell, Rose-shell, Wild-thyme **10** Cumberland, Macranthum, Plum-leaved, White swamp **11** Gable hybrid, Ghent hybrid, Molle hybrid **12** Arnold hybrid, Florida flame, Sander hybrid **13** Indicum hybrid **15** Glenn Dale hybrid, Kaempferi hybrid, Knapp Hill hybrid **16** Rutherford hybrid **24** Rusticum Flore Pleno hybrid

Azan
   father: 5 Arcas
   mother: 5 Erato

Azariah
   also: 6 Uzziah
   father: 4 Jehu **5** Ethan **6** Nathan **7** Hilkiah, Jehoram, Johanan **11** Jehoshaphat
   son: 4 Joel
   known as: 8 Abednego
   companion: 6 Daniel
   friend: 7 Meshach **8** Shadrach
   succeeded: 5 Zadok

Azazel 9 scapegoat **11** fallen angel

Azerbaijan
   capital/largest city: 4 Baku
   others 9 Kirovabad
   division 24 Nagorno-Karabakh Territory **29** Nakhichevan Autonomous Republic
   head of state: 9 president
   government: 8 republic
   monetary unit: 5 manat
   mountain: 8 Caucasus
   sea: 7 Caspian
   people: 5 Azeri **11** Azerbaijani
   language: 6 Turkic
   religion: 6 Muslim

Aziz, Dr
   character in: 15 A Passage to India
   author: 7 Forster

Aztec (Nahua, Mexica)
   language family: 7 Nahuatl **10** Uto-Aztecan
   location: 6 Mexico, Puebla **8** Guerrero, Veracruz **9** Guatemala, Michoacan **11** Lake Texcoco **14** Central America
   leader: 9 Montezuma
   worshipped: 12 Quetzalcoatl
   capital: 12 Tenochtitlan

Azuela, Mariano
   author of: 8 The Flies **9** The Bosses **12** The Underdogs **26** Trials of a Respectable Family

azure 5 lapis **6** cobalt **7** sky blue **8** cerulean **9** clear blue, cloudless **11** lapis lazuli

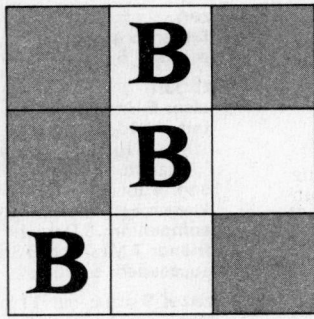

Baade, Walter
field: **9** astronomy
discovered: **15** Hidalgo
asteroid

Baal 3 god **5** deity

Baal Merodach *see* **6** Marduk

Babbage, Charles
field: **11** mathematics
nationality: **7** British, English
first: **15** actuarial tables
inventor of: **13** adding machine **18** calculating machine
invented forerunner of: **15** digital computer
planned: **10** calculator

Babbitt 9 bourgeois
10 conformist, middlebrow, philistine

Babbitt
author: **13** Sinclair Lewis
character: **11** Myra Babbitt, Seneca Deane **12** Paul Riesling **15** Mrs Tanis Judique **22** George Folansbee Babbitt

babble 3 coo, din, gab, hum **4** blab, talk **5** prate **6** burble, clamor, drivel, gabble, gibber, gurgle, hubbub, jabber, murmur **7** blabber, blather, chatter, prattle, twaddle **8** chitchat, rattle on **9** jabbering, murmuring **14** chitter-chatter

babbling 6 drivel, hubbub **7** blabber, twaddle **8** burbling, gabbling, gurgling, nonsense **9** clamoring, gibberish, jabbering, murmuring

babe 3 tot **4** baby **5** child **6** infant

babe in arms 4 baby **6** infant **7** neonate, newborn

babe in the woods 8 innocent **9** fledgling, greenhorn **10** tenderfoot

babel, Babel 3 din **6** bedlam, clamor, hubbub, tumult, uproar **7** turmoil **9** confusion

10 hullabaloo
11 pandemonium

Babel, Isaac
author of: **9** Benia Krik **11** Odessa Tales **13** The Red Cavalry

Babe Ruth
nickname of: **16** George Herman Ruth

Babe the Blue Ox
character in: **10** Paul Bunyan

baboon 6 monkey
breeding: **9** year round
characteristic: **4** mane, pads **6** muzzle
diet: **6** plants **8** scorpion **12** small animals
dwelling: **5** Egypt, Sudan **6** Africa, Arabia **7** Somalia **8** Ethiopia
family: **15** cercopithecidae
habitat: **5** hills **6** plains
largest genus: **6** Chacma
most sacred: **6** Anobis
smallest genus: **7** Western

babushka 4 baba, veil **5** scarf, stole **8** kerchief

baby 3 wee **4** babe, tiny **5** dwarf, humor, pygmy, small, spoil, young **6** bantam, coddle, coward, infant, little, midget, minute, pamper, petite **7** crybaby, indulge, neonate **8** dwarfish, sniveler **9** miniature, youngster **10** babe in arms, diminutive **11** mollycoddle, overindulge, pocket-sized

Baby
nickname of: **12** Lauren Bacall

baby carriage 4 cart, pram **6** cradle **12** perambulator

babyish 7 puerile **8** childish, immature, juvenile **9** infantile

babylike 3 wee **4** tiny **5** small **9** infantile **10** diminutive

Babylonian Captivity
13 Avignon Papacy **15** Babylonian Exile

Babylonian god 3 Bel **6** Marduk

Babylonian Mythology *see box*

Baby Roo
character in: **13** Winnie-the-Pooh
author: **5** Milne

Baby Snookums
character in: **12** The Newlyweds

Bacall, Lauren
real name: **15** Betty Joan Perske

Babylonian Mythology
chief of gods: **6** Marduk **8** Merodach **12** Baal Merodach
demon: **6** Namtar
goddess of air: **6** Ninlil
goddess of death: **10** Ereshkigal
goddess of love/war/fertility: **6** Ananna, Inanna, Ishtar **7** Astarte, Mylitta **9** Ashtoreth
god of air: **5** Enlil
god of dead: **6** Nergal
god of fire: **5** Ishum
god of heaven: **2** An **3** Anu
god of moon: **3** Sin
god of pastures/vegetation: **6** Dumuzi
god of pestilence: **4** Irra
god of shepherds: **6** Tammuz
god of sun: **3** Utu **7** Shamash
god of wisdom: **4** Enki
hero: **5** Ninib **7** Ninurta
king: **9** Gilgamesh
king of gods: **5** Enlil
mother of gods: **5** Nammu
queen of heaven: **6** Ishtar
world of dead: **3** Kur

husband: 12 Jason Robards **14** Humphrey Bogart
nickname: 4 Baby
born: 9 New York NY
roles: 8 Applause, Key Largo **11** Dark Passage, The Big Sleep **12** Cactus Flower **16** To Have and Have Not **22** How to Marry a Millionaire

Bacchae
form: 11 priestesses
attendants of: 7 Bacchus
participants in: 11 Bacchanalia

Bacchae, The
author: 9 Euripides
character: 4 Zeus **5** Agave **6** Cadmus, Semele **8** Dionysus, Pentheus, Tiresias

bacchanal 4 orgy **5** feast, revel, spree **6** frolic **7** carouse, debauch, revelry, wassail **8** carnival, carousal, festival **10** debauchery, Saturnalia **11** merrymaking

Bacchanalia
festival honoring: 7 Bacchus

Bacchant
priest who worships: 7 Bacchus

Bacchante
also: 6 Thyiad
priestess who worships: 7 Bacchus

Bacchus
also: 5 Evius **8** Dionysus
god of: 4 wine **5** drama **9** fertility
father: 4 Zeus
mother: 6 Semele
son: 6 Phlias **7** Narcaus, Priapus **8** Oenopion
epithet: 6 Lyaeus **7** Bromius, Cresius **8** Thyoneus, Triambus **9** Pyrigenes **11** Dithyrambus, Mitrephorus

Bach, Carl (Karl) Philipp Emanuel
born: 6 Weimar **7** Germany
father: 19 Johann Sebastian Bach
composer of: 14 Prussian Sonata **19** Wurtembergian Sonata

Bach, Johann Sebastian
born: 7 Germany **8** Eisenach
composer of: 8 Chaconne **10** Giant Fugue, Inventions, Magnificat, Wedge Fugue **11** Dorian Fugue, Fiddle Fugue, Little Fugue **12** Corelli Fugue, French Suites, Fuga alla Giga, German Suites, St Anne's Fugue **13** Coffee Cantata, English Suites, St John Passion **14** Alla Breve Fugue, Easter Oratorio, Peasant Cantata,
Wedding Cantata **15** Jesu Meine Freude, Musical Offering **16** St Matthew Passion, The Art of the Fugue **17** Christmas Oratorio **18** Goldberg Variations **20** Brandenburg Concertos **22** The Well-Tempered Clavier **24** The Wise and Foolish Virgins **30** The Dispute Between Phoebus and Pan

Bach, Richard
author of: 25 Jonathan Livingston Seagull

bachelor 6 single **9** single man, unmarried **12** unmarried man

Bachelor Father
character: 9 Peter Tong **10** Kelly Gregg **12** Bentley Gregg **13** Ginger Farrell
cast: 10 Sammee Tong **12** John Forsythe **14** Noreen Corcoran **17** Bernadette Withers

bachelorhood 8 celibacy **13** baccalaureate **14** unmarried state

bacillus 3 bug **4** germ **7** microbe **8** pathogen **9** bacterium **13** microorganism

Bacis
origin: 8 Boeotian
form: 7 prophet

back *see box*

back away from 7 back off **11** retreat from **12** draw back from, withdraw from

backbiter 5 scold **6** carper, critic **7** reviler **8** vilifier **9** slanderer

backbiting 5 abuse, catty **6** gossip, malice **7** abusive, calumny, gossipy, hurtful, obloquy, slander **8** libeling, reviling **9** aspersion, cattiness, censuring, contumely, injurious, invective, malicious, maligning, vilifying **10** belittling, bitchiness, calumnious, defamation, defamatory, derogating, detracting, detraction, scandalous, scurrility, slanderous, traduction **11** badmouthing, denigrating, deprecating, disparaging, traducement **12** backstabbing, calumniation, vilification, vituperation **13** disparagement, maliciousness **16** scandal-mongering

backbone 4 grit, guts, sand **5** basis, chine, nerve, pluck, spine, spunk **6** dorsum, mettle, spirit **7** bravery, courage, resolve **8** firmness, mainstay, strength, tenacity **9** character, fortitude, manliness, vertebrae **10** foundation, resolution **11** intrepidity

back 3 aid, ebb **4** abet, gone, help, hind, late, past, rear, tail **5** after, guard, minor, rural, spine, tardy **6** affirm, assist, attest, behind, bygone, caudal, dorsal, dorsum, far end, former, hinder, hold up, praise, recede, recoil, remote, retire, return, revert, second, succor, tergal, uphold, verify **7** belated, bolster, certify, confirm, delayed, distant, earlier, elapsed, endorse, expired, far side, finance, not paid, overdue, promote, protect, rear end, rebound, retract, retreat, reverse, sponsor, support, sustain, tail end, warrant **8** advocate, backbone, hind part, hindmost, maintain, move away, obsolete, previous, sanction, secluded, turn tail, validate, vouch for, withdraw **9** afterpart, encourage, in arrears, out-of-date, patronize, posterior, reinforce, subsidize **10** retrogress, testify for, underwrite, untraveled **11** bear witness, corroborate, countenance, countrified, countryside, farthermost, furthermost, reverse side, undeveloped, unimportant, unpopulated **12** beat a retreat, hindquarters, spinal column, substantiate **13** take sides with

12 resoluteness, spinal column **13** dauntlessness, steadfastness **15** vertebral column **19** strength of character

back-country 4 farm **5** rural **6** rustic **7** farming **10** provincial

back down 7 back off **8** draw back, move away **9** withdrawn

backdrop 4 flat **7** curtain, scenery **10** background

backer 4 ally **5** angel **6** patron **7** sponsor **8** adherent, advocate, champion, follower, investor, promoter **9** financier, guarantor, supporter **10** well-wisher **11** underwriter

backfire 4 flop, miss **5** crash **6** fizzle, go awry **8** backlash, lay an egg, miscarry, ricochet **9** boomerang **10** bounce back, disappoint **11** come to grief, fall through **12** come to naught **13** come to nothing

background 3 set 4 past, rear 5 flats 6 milieu 7 context, history, rearing, setting 8 backdrop, breeding, distance, heritage, training 9 education, grounding, landscape, life story 10 experience, upbringing 11 antecedents, credentials, environment, mise-en-scene, preparation 13 circumstances

backhanded 7 awkward 8 reversed 9 insincere

backing 3 aid 4 core, help 5 aegis 6 succor 7 support 8 advocacy, interior, sanction 9 patronage, prompting 10 assistance, inner layer, sustenance 11 championing, cooperation, endorsement, helping hand, sponsorship 13 encouragement

backlash 4 flop, snag 5 crash, ravel 6 fizzle, go away, recoil 7 rebound 8 backfire, kick back, miscarry, ricochet, snap back 9 animosity, boomerang, hostility, reversion 10 antagonism, bounce back, opposition, resistance 11 come to grief, fall through 12 come to naught 13 come to nothing, counteraction, recalcitrance

backlog 5 hoard, stock, store 6 assets, excess, supply 7 nest egg, reserve, savings 9 abundance, amassment, inventory, reservoir, stockpile 12 accumulation 13 reserve supply 14 superabundance

back matter 5 index 8 addendum, appendix 10 supplement 12 bibliography

back off 7 retreat 8 back down, pull back, withdraw

backpack 4 hike, load 5 pouch 6 bundle 8 knapsack

backside 3 can 4 buns, butt, duff, prat, rear, rump, seat, tail 5 fanny 6 behind, bottom, settee, setter, sitter 7 keister, rear end 8 buttocks, derriere 9 fundament, posterior

backslide 5 lapse 6 revert 7 relapse 10 recurrence, regression 11 deteriorate 14 slip from virtue

back street 5 alley, byway 8 alleyway 13 secondary road

Back Street
director:
    1941 version: 15 Robert Stevenson
    1961 version: 11 David Miller
based on story by: 11 Fannie Hurst

cast:
    1932 version: 9 John Boles 10 Irene Dunne
    1941 version: 12 Charles Boyer 16 Margaret Sullavan
    1961 version: 9 John Gavin, Vera Miles 12 Susan Hayward

back talk 3 jaw, lip 4 gall, guff, rude, sass 5 cheek 8 pertness, rudeness 9 impudence, insolence, sassiness, sauciness 12 impertinence

Back to the Future
director: 14 Robert Zemeckis
cast: 11 Lea Thompson, Michael J Fox 16 Christopher Lloyd

backup 6 second 7 reserve, standby, stand-in 9 alternate, auxiliary, emergency, secondary 10 substitute, understudy 11 pinch-hitter 13 supplementary

back up 4 abet 6 assist, uphold 9 reinforce 11 corroborate

backward, backwards 3 shy 4 dull, slow 5 dense, tardy, timid, wrong 6 behind, ebbing, remiss, toward 7 bashful, impeded, laggard, messily, reverse, the rear 8 inverted, rearward, receding, reserved, retarded, reticent, reversed, sluggish 9 in retreat, in reverse, inside out, returning, slow-paced, to the past, to the rear, withdrawn 10 disorderly, improperly, regressive, retreating, retrograde, slow-witted, topsy-turvy, upside down 11 chaotically, undeveloped, withdrawing 12 wrong side out 13 retrogressive 15 uncommunicative
French: 9 en arriere

backwash 4 burg, wake 6 result, sticks, upshot 7 boonies, outcome 8 frontier, tank town 9 aftermath, backwater, boondocks, provinces, upcountry 10 hinterland 11 aftereffect, backcountry, consequence

backwater 3 ebb 5 slack 7 retreat, reverse 8 holdback, stagnant, withdraw

backwoods 5 rural, wilds 6 rustic, simple, sticks 7 boonies, country 8 woodland 9 boondocks, rural area 10 hinterland, provincial 11 back-country, countryside, hinterlands 15 unsophisticated

bacon 3 pig 4 pork 6 gammon 8 porkslab 10 smoked pork 11 porkbellies
measure: 6 rasher

Bacon, Francis
author of: 6 Essays 11 New Atlantis 12 Novum Organum 14 Maxims of the Law 16 Instauratio Magna 17 History of Henry VII 18 De Sapientia Veterum 20 Apophthegms New and Old 21 Advancement of Learning 25 Reading on the Statute of Uses

Bacon, Francis
born: 6 Dublin 7 Ireland
artwork: 15 Henrietta Moraes 35 Three Studies at the Base of a Crucifixion 44 Studies After Velazquez' Portrait of Pope Innocent X

Bacon, Henry
architect of: 15 Lincoln Memorial

bacteria 3 bug 4 germ 5 virus 7 microbe 8 bacillus, pathogen 13 microorganism

bactericide 9 germicide 10 antiseptic, germ killer 12 disinfectant

bacteriologist
American: 4 Reed
British: 7 Fleming
German: 4 Koch 7 Behring, Ehrlich 10 Wassermann
Japanese: 7 Noguchi 8 Kitasato

bad *see* box

bad faith 7 perfidy, treason 8 betrayal 9 falseness, treachery, two timing 10 disloyalty 11 double-cross 13 breach of faith, double-dealing 14 unfaithfulness

badge 4 mark, seal, sign 5 brand, stamp, token 6 device, emblem, ensign, shield, symbol 7 earmark 8 hallmark, insignia 9 medallion

badger 3 nag, vex 4 bait, goad 5 annoy, beset, bully, chafe, harry, hound, tease 6 coerce, harass, hector, nettle, pester, plague 7 provoke, torment, trouble 8 irritate 9 persecute
group of: 4 cete

Badger State
nickname of: 9 Wisconsin

badinage 5 chaff 6 banter, joking 7 jesting, joshing, kidding, ragging, ribbing, waggery 8 chaffing, raillery, repartee, word play

bad judgment 5 folly 10 imprudence 11 foolishness 12 carelessness 13 senselessness 15 thoughtlessness 16 shortsightedness, unperceptiveness

bad 3 ill, sad, sin **4** base, dire, evil, foul, glum, grim, mean, poor, rank, sick, sour, vile **5** acrid, acute, angry, awful, cross, false, fetid, grave, harsh, lousy, moldy, nasty, risky, sorry, unfit, wrong **6** ailing, bitter, crimes, faulty, gloomy, guilty, infirm, odious, putrid, rancid, rotten, severe, sickly, sinful, touchy, tragic, turned, unwell, wicked, wrongs **7** baneful, beastly, corrupt, decayed, harmful, hurtful, immoral, joyless, lacking, naughty, not good, noxious, painful, searing, serious, spoiled, tainted, unsound, useless **8** below par, contrite, criminal, dreadful, grievous, inferior, menacing, mildewed, offenses, polluted, terrible, troubled, villainy, wretched **9** agonizing, dangerous, defective, deficient, erroneous, frightful, hazardous, imperfect, incorrect, injurious, irascible, irritable, loathsome, miserable, nefarious, obnoxious, offensive, regretful, repugnant, repulsive, revolting, sad events, sickening, troubling, unethical, unhealthy, unnerving, unwelcome, valueless **10** calamitous, decomposed, deplorable, detestable, disastrous, disgusting, distressed, disturbing, fallacious, immorality, inadequate, indisposed, melancholy, misfortune, nauseating, not correct, perfidious, putrescent, remorseful, second-rate, unpleasant, villainous, wickedness **11** detrimental, discouraged, distasteful, distractive, distressing, ineffective, inefficient, opprobrious, regrettable, substandard, troublesome, unpalatable **12** contaminated, disagreeable, discouraging, disreputable, excruciating, questionable, unprincipled, unproductive **13** below standard, disappointing, disheartening, harmful things, nonproductive, reprehensible, short-tempered **14** disappointment **15** disadvantageous, under the weather **18** conscience-stricken

---

bad luck 6 mishap **7** ill wind **8** bad break **9** adversity, mischance **10** ill fortune, misfortune

badly 5 wrong **6** basely, poorly, sorely, vilely **7** acutely, greatly, ineptly, not well, wrongly **8** faultily, horribly, severely, shoddily, sinfully, sloppily, terribly, very much, wickedly **9** corruptly, extremely, immorally, intensely, unsoundly **10** carelessly, criminally, dreadfully, improperly, wretchedly **11** defectively, deficiently, desperately, erroneously, exceedingly, frightfully, imperfectly, incorrectly, nefariously, offensively, unethically **12** disreputably, inadequately, villainously **13** incompetently, in the worst way **16** unsatisfactorily

bad manners 8 rudeness **9** surliness **10** incivility **11** boorishness, discourtesy **12** impoliteness

bad mark 4 blot **7** demerit **9** poor grade

badminton
racket: **10** battledore
racket used to hit: **4** bird **7** shuttle **11** shuttlecock
Indian version: **5** poona
stroke: **4** drop **5** clear, smash **7** service **13** backhand drive, forehand drive

badmouthing 5 barbs **7** insults, slander **9** criticism, insulting **10** slandering **11** criticizing

bad taste 9 crudeness, vulgarity **10** coarseness, garishness, tawdryness

bad tasting 4 sour **5** nasty **6** bitter **7** spoiled **9** medicinal, revolting **10** disgusting **11** unpalatable

bad-tempered 5 cross, testy **6** grumpy **7** grouchy **8** choleric, churlish **9** difficult, irascible, irritable **10** ill-natured **11** acrimonious **12** disagreeable

bad times 4 bust **5** slump **9** hard times, recession **10** depression

bad turn 4 harm, hurt **5** wrong **6** injury **7** ill turn **8** disfavor **9** injustice **10** disservice **11** discourtesy

Baekeland, Leo Hendrik
field: **9** chemistry
invented: **8** Bakelite **32** artificial light photographic paper

Baer, Max (Maximillian Adalbert)
nickname: **17** Livermore Larruper
sport: **6** boxing
class: **11** heavyweight

Baeyer, Johann Friedrich Wilhelm Adolph von
field: **9** chemistry
nationality: **6** German
synthesized: **6** indigo
discovered: **13** phthalein dyes
awarded: **10** Nobel Prize

baffle 3 bar **4** daze, dull, foil, stop **5** amaze, check, stump **6** deaden, muddle, puzzle, reduce, thwart **7** astound, confuse, inhibit, mystify, nonplus, perplex **8** astonish, befuddle, bewilder, confound, dumfound, minimize, restrain, surprise **10** disconcert

baffling 7 elusive **8** puzzling **9** confusing, enigmatic **10** mysterious, mystifying, perplexing **11** confounding **16** incomprehensible

bag 3 get, sag **4** hunt, kill, sack, take, trap **5** bulge, catch, droop, pouch, purse, shoot, snare **6** bundle, entrap, obtain, packet **7** acquire, capture, collect, ensnare **8** paper bag, protrude, suitcase **10** receptacle

bagatelle 6 trifle **7** nothing, trinket **10** knickknack, light music **11** unimportant

baggage 4 bags, gear **5** grips **6** trunks **7** bundles, effects, luggage, valises **8** movables, packages **9** apparatus, equipment, suitcases, trappings **10** belongings **11** impedimenta **13** accouterments, paraphernalia

baggy 4 limp **5** loose, slack **6** droopy, flabby, puffed **7** bloated, bulbous, flaccid, paunchy, sagging, swollen **9** unpressed, unshapely **12** loose-fitting

Baghdad
capital of: **4** Iraq
founder: **8** (Caliph) al-Mansur
landmark:
minaret: **10** Suq al-Ghazi
mosque: **8** Madrasah **14** al-Mustansiriya
means: **8** God-given
river: **6** Tigris

Bagheera
character in: **14** The Jungle Books
author: **7** Kipling

bagnio 4 bath, stew **5** house **6** bordel, prison **7** brothel **8** bordello, cathouse **10** bawdy house, fancy house, whorehouse **13** sporting house **14** house of ill fame **16** house of ill repute **19** house of prostitution

Bagnold, Enid
author of: **14** National Vel-

vet, The Chalk Garden
23 The Chinese Prime
Minister

Bagstock, Joe
character in: 12 Dombey and
Son
author: 7 Dickens

Bahamas
capital/largest city:
6 Nassau
others: 8 Freeport
9 Rock Sound
10 George Town
11 Mastic Point
12 Spanish Wells
head of state: 14 British monarch 15 governor general
island: 3 Cat 4 Long
5 Berry, Exuma 6 Andros, Bimini, Caicos,
Rum Cay 7 Crooked,
Harbour, Watling
9 Eleuthera, Mayaguana 10 Great Abaco
11 Grand Bahama,
Great Inagua, Great
Ragged, San Salvador
13 New Providence
sea: 8 Atlantic
9 Caribbean
physical feature:
strait: 7 Florida
swamp: 8 mangrove
people: 5 black 7 Haitian
language: 6 Creole
7 English
religion: 12 Christianity
place:
harbor: 9 Governors
naval base:
9 Mayaguana
feature:
key: 3 cay
native: 5 conch

Bahrain *see box*

bail 3 dip 4 bond, lade 5 ladle,
scoop, spoon 6 surety 9 guarantee 11 post bond for

bailiff 6 deputy 8 marshall,
overseer 9 assistant, constable
12 court officer

bailiwick 4 area, beat, turf
5 arena, orbit, place, realm
6 domain, sphere 7 compass
8 dominion, province 9 territory 10 department
12 neighborhood

Baird, Spencer Fullerton
field: 7 zoology
authority on: 5 birds
7 mammals
established: 30 US Commission of Fish and Fisheries

Bahrain
capital/largest city:
6 Manama
others: 5 Rifaa 7 Jidhafs 8 Muharraq
head of state/government: 4 emir
monetary unit: 4 fils
5 dinar
island: 5 Hawar, Jidda
6 Sitrah 7 Bahrain
9 Umm Nassan 10 al-Muharraq 11 An Nabi
Salih
physical feature:
gulf: 7 Bahrain,
Persian
people: 4 Arab 6 Indian
7 Persian 8 American,
European 9 Pakistani
ruling family: 9 al-Khalifa
language: 4 Urdu
5 Farsi 6 Arabic
7 English, Persian
religion: 5 Islam

laboratory at: 11 Woods
Hole MA

bait 3 vex 4 lure, ride, worm
5 annoy, bribe, harry, hound,
tease, worry 6 allure, badger,
come-on, harass, heckle, hector, magnet, needle 7 provoke,
torment 9 put bait on, tantalize 10 allurement, antagonize,
attraction, enticement, inducement, temptation

bake 3 fry 4 boil, burn, cook,
sear, stew 5 grill, roast, saute,
toast 6 braise, pan-fry, scorch,
simmer 7 parboil, swelter

Baked Bean State
nickname of:
13 Massachusetts

**Baker, Norma Jean
Mortenson**
real name of: 13 Marilyn
Monroe

Baking
goddess of: 6 Fornax

Balaam
father: 4 Beor
brother: 4 Bela
lived at: 4 Aram 6 Pethor
commanded by: 5 Balak
killed by: 6 Israel

Balak
father: 6 Zippor
commanded: 6 Balaam

Balakiref, Mily
born: 6 Russia 13 Nijni-Novgorod
member of: 7 Kutchka, The
Five

composer of: 6 Russia, Tamara, Thamar 7 Islamey
8 King Lear (overture)

balance, balances 3 pay
4 cool, mean, rest 5 poise, ratio, scale, sum up, tally, total,
tot up, weigh 6 aplomb,
equate, offset, parity, ponder,
reckon, scales, set off, square,
steady, weight 7 compare,
compute, harmony, opinion,
reflect, remnant, residue
8 cogitate, consider, contrast,
coolness, equality, estimate,
evaluate, judgment, leftover,
level off, parallel, presence,
symmetry 9 appraisal, calculate, composure, equipoise,
juxtapose, make level, remainder, stability, stabilize
10 amount owed, comparison,
counteract, deliberate, equanimity, evaluation, keep
steady, neutralize, proportion,
steadiness 11 equilibrium
12 counterpoise, equalization,
middle ground 13 compensate
for, consideration, judiciousness 14 amount credited, self-possession, unflappability
15 level-headedness
16 imperturbability
constellation of: 5 Libra

balanced 4 fair, just 9 equitable, impartial 12 unprejudiced
13 disinterested

balance out 6 cancel, offset
9 make up for 10 neutralize
13 compensate for
14 counterbalance

Balanchine, George
choreographer of: 4 Agon
6 Jewels 8 Episodes, Ivesiana, Serenade 15 Concerto
Barocco 16 Allegro
Brillante

balcony 4 deck 5 boxes, foyer,
loges 6 loggia 7 portico, terrace, veranda 9 mezzanine

bald 4 bare, flat, open 5 blunt,
naked, plain, stark, utter
6 barren, simple, smooth
7 denuded, obvious 8 flagrant,
glabrous, hairless, outright,
treeless 9 depilated, out-and-out, unadorned 11 categorical,
undisguised, unqualified, unvarnished 12 without cover
13 unembellished, unequivocable 15 straightforward

Balder
also: 5 Baldr 6 Baldur
origin: 6 Nordic
god of: 6 beauty 8 radiance
father: 4 Odin 5 Othin
mother: 3 Fri 5 Frigg, Frija
6 Frigga
twin brother: 5 Hoder, Hodur
killed by: 5 Hoder, Hodur

balderdash 3 rot 4 bosh, bull,

bunk **5** crock, trash **6** bunkum, drivel, hot air **7** twaddle **8** buncombe, claptrap, flummery, nonsense, tommyrot **9** gibberish, poppycock **10** double-talk, tomfoolery **11** obfuscation **16** stuff and nonsense

baldheaded 8 hairless **9** baldpated, depilated **10** skinheaded **11** chrome-domed

Baldr
see: **6** Balder

Baldung Grien, Hans
born: **6** Alsace **10** Weyersheim
artwork: **9** Todentanz **17** Death and the Maiden **19** Death Kissing a Maiden **21** The Bewitched Stable Boy **24** Rest on the Flight into Egypt

Baldur
see: **6** Balder

Baldwin, James
author of: **13** Giovanni's Room, The Amen Corner **14** Another Country **15** Just Above My Head, The Fire Next Time **17** Going to Meet the Man, Nobody Knows My Name, No Name in the Street **21** Blues for Mister Charlie, Go Tell It on the Mountain

bale 4 case, load, pack **6** bundle, packet, parcel **7** package **11** bound bundle

balefire 6 beacon **9** watchfire **10** signal fire

baleful 3 icy **4** cold, dire, evil **6** deadly, malign **7** baneful, furious, harmful, hurtful, ominous **8** sinister, spiteful, venomous **9** malicious, malignant **10** malevolent **11** coldhearted, threatening

Balfe, Michael William
born: **6** Dublin **7** Ireland
composer of: **15** The Bohemian Girl, The Maid of Artois **17** I rivali di se stessi **18** The Siege of Rochelle

Balfour, David
character in: **9** Kidnapped
author: **9** Stevenson

Bali
province of: **9** Indonesia
capital: **8** Denpasar
city: **10** Singaraja
island: **11** Lesser Sunda
highest peak: **6** Agoeng
climate: **3** dry **7** monsoon
tree: **8** waringin
animal: **4** deer **5** tiger
people: **7** Malayan
religion: **8** Hinduism
agriculture: **3** pig **4** corn,

rice **6** cattle, coffee **7** tobacco

Balius
horse of: **8** Achilles
gift: **11** immortality

balk 3 bar **4** foil, shun **5** block, check, demur, evade, shirk, spike, stall **6** baffle, defeat, derail, eschew, hinder, impede, recoil, refuse, resist, stymie, thwart **7** inhibit, prevent **8** draw back, hang back, hesitate, obstruct **9** forestall, frustrate **10** shrink from

Balkan 16 Forested mountain
agriculture: **5** grain **6** cotton, grapes, olives **7** tobacco
ancient people: **4** Slav **5** Greek, Roman **8** Illyrian, Thracian
language: **9** Slovenian **10** Macedonian **14** Serbo-Croatian
mountain: **6** Balkan, Massif **7** Rhodope **10** Carpathian **11** Dinaric Alps **13** Transylvanian
religion: **5** Islam **8** Orthodox **13** Roman Catholic
river: **6** Danube, Morava, Vardar
sea boundary: **5** Black **6** Aegean, Ionian **8** Adriatic **13** Mediterranean
state: **6** Greece, Turkey **7** Albania, Romania **8** Bulgaria **10** Yugoslavia

balky 6 mulish, ornery, unruly **7** restive, wayward, willful **8** contrary, perverse, stubborn **9** fractious, obstinate, pigheaded **10** rebellious, refractory **11** disobedient, intractable **12** recalcitrant, unmanageable

ball 3 hop, orb **4** prom, shot **5** dance, globe **6** pellet, soiree, sphere **7** bullets, globule **8** spheroid **9** cotillion, promenade **11** projectiles

Ball, Lucille
husband: **9** Desi Arnaz
children: **4** Desi **5** Lucie
born: **11** Jamestown NY
roles: **9** Here's Lucy, I Love Lucy **11** The Lucy Show

Balla, Giacomo
born: **5** Italy, Turin
artwork: **8** The Sewer **11** The Mad Woman **18** Speeding Automobile **20** Rhythm of the Violinist **22** Dynamism of a Dog on a Leash **26** The Street Light—Study of Light **29** Mercury Passing in Front of the Sun **40** Swifts Paths of Movement and Dynamic Sequences

ballad 3 lay **4** song **5** carol, ditty **6** chanty **8** folk song

12 rhyming story **13** narrative poem **14** narrative verse

Ballad of Reading Gaol, The
author: **10** Oscar Wilde

Ballads and Poems
author: **19** Stephen Vincent Benet

ballast 6 weight **7** balance, control **9** equipoise **10** ballasting, dead weight, makeweight, stabilizer **12** counterpoise **13** counterweight **14** counterbalance **19** stabilizing material

Ballesteros, Severiano
nickname: **4** Seve
sport: **4** golf
nationality: **7** Spanish

ballet *see box, p. 82*

Ball of Fat
author: **15** Guy de Maupassant

balloon 4 grow **5** belly, bloat **6** billow, blow up, dilate, expand **7** distend, enlarge, fill out, inflate, puff out **8** increase, swell out

ballot 4 poll, vote **5** slate **6** ticket, voting **7** polling **13** round of voting **16** list of candidates

ballyhoo 4 hype, puff, push, tout **6** herald, hoopla **7** buildup, promote, puffery, trumpet **8** proclaim **9** advertise, promotion, publicity, publicize **10** hullabaloo, propaganda **11** advertising **15** public relations

balm 5 cream, salve **6** balsam, lotion, solace **7** anodyne, comfort, unguent **8** curative, narcotic, ointment, sedative **9** comforter, emollient **10** palliative **11** restorative **12** tranquilizer

balmy 3 odd **4** calm, fair, mild, soft, warm **5** bland, kooky, weird **6** easing, gentle **7** calming, clement, summery **8** aromatic, fragrant, perfumed, pleasant, redolent, soothing **9** agreeable, ambrosial, eccentric, temperate **10** refreshing, salubrious

Balnibari
fictional land in: **16** Gulliver's Travels
author: **5** Swift

baloney 3 rot **4** bull, bunk **5** hokum, hooey, stuff **6** bunkum, hot air, humbug **7** hogwash, sausage, spinach **8** claptrap, nonsense, tommyrot **9** poppycock **10** applesauce **11** foolishness

ballet 4 Agon **5** Manon, Rodeo **6** Apollo, Parade **7** Giselle, Orpheus **8** Coppelia, Episodes, Ivesiana, Les Noces, Serenade, Swan Lake, The Doves **9** Anastasia, Fancy Free, Interplay, Petrushka, The Jewels **10** La Sylphide, Petrouchka **11** Billy the Kid, Lilac Garden, Soccer Dance, Symphony in C, The Firebird **12** Pillar of Fire, Sailor's Dance, Spring Waters, The Partisans **13** The Nutcracker **14** Romeo and Juliet **15** Concerto Barocco, Fall River Legend, The Rite of Spring **16** Allegro Brillante, La Fille Mal Gardee, Specter of the Rose **17** The Sleeping Beauty **18** Raymonda Variations **19** The Afternoon of a Faun, The Four Temperaments **24** Stravinsky Violin Concerto

ballet company: 5 Kirov, Royal **7** Bolshoi, Joffrey **9** Mariinsky, Maryinsky **11** New York City **13** Ballets Russes **20** Dance Theater of Harlem **21** American Ballet Theater **22** National Ballet of Canada

choreographer: 9 Hanya Holm, Lev Ivanov **10** John Weaver **11** Jules Perrot **12** Agnes de Mille, Igor Moiseyev, Marius Petipa, Michel Fokine **13** Jean Dauberval, Jerome Robbins, Leonid Massine **15** Arthur Saint-Leon **16** George Balanchine, Kenneth MacMillan **18** August Bournonville, Bronislava Nijinska, Jean Georges Noverre, Sir Frederick Ashton

chorus: 8 ensemble **13** corps de ballet

dancer: 9 Karen Kain **10** Anton Dolin, Marie Lieta, Serge Lifar **11** Allegra Kent, Anna Pavlova, Anthony Blum, Lucile Grahn, Lynn Seymour, Nadia Nerina **12** Fanny Cerrito, Marie Camargo, Peter Martins **13** Alicia Markova, Andre Eglevsky, Anthony Dowell, Carlotta Grisi, Frank Augustyn, Galina Ulanova, Margot Fonteyn, Marie Taglioni, Melissa Hayden, Patricia Neary, Rudolf Nureyev **14** Arthur Mitchell, Cynthia Gregory, Edward Villella, Gelsey Kirkland, Leonide Massine, Maria Tallchief, Suzanne Farrell, Vaslav Nijinsky **15** Jacques D'Amboise, Martine Van Hamel, Maya Plisetskaya, Natalia Makarova, Patricia McBride, Tamara Karsavina **16** Antoinette Sibley, Olga Spessivtseva **17** Alexandra Danilova, Marina Kondratieva **18** Mikhail Baryshnikov

fast movement: 7 allegro

first ballet: 22 Ballet Comique de la Reine

impresario: 12 Marie Rambert **15** Ninette de Valois, Sergei Diaghilev

kick: 9 battement

modern dancer/choreographer: 8 Ted Shawn **9** Eliot Feld **10** Mary Wigman, Paul Draper, Twyla Tharp **11** Anna Sokolow, Antony Tudor, Eric Hawkins, Ruth St Denis **12** Martha Graham **13** Alwin Nikolais, Doris Humphrey, Isadora Duncan **14** Charles Weidman **15** Merce Cunningham

position/step: 4 jete, plie, tour **5** saute **6** releve **7** en avant, fouette, on point, pas seul, turnout **8** batterie, cabriole, en dedans, en dehors, glissade **9** arabesque, developpe, en arriere, entrechat, pas de chat, pas-de-deux, pirouette **10** demi-pointe, port de bras, tour en l'air **11** rond de jambe, terre-a-terre **12** pas de bourree, saut de basque **17** changement de pieds

principal female dancer: 9 ballerina **14** prima ballerina

principal male dancer: 12 danseur noble

skirt: 4 tutu

slow movement: 6 adagio

term: 4 coda **5** barre **6** ballon **14** divertissement

Baloo
character in: **14** The Jungle Books
author: **7** Kipling

balsam 3 fir **4** balm **5** cream, salve **7** unguent **8** ointment **9** Impatiens

varieties: **2** He **3** Fir, She **4** Rose, Wild **6** Garden **8** Zanzibar

Balsam, Martin
born: **9** New York NY
roles: **6** Psycho **7** Catch-22

---

15 A Thousand Clowns, On the Waterfront

Baltic
language family: **12** Indo-European
group: **11** Balto-Slavic
subgroup: **7** Latvian **10** Lithuanian

Baltimore
baseball team: **7** Orioles
football team: **5** Stars

Baltimore, David
field: **12** microbiology
studied: **11** animal cells **13** viral genetics
awarded: **10** Nobel Prize

Balto-Slavic
language family: **12** Indo-European
branch: **6** Baltic, Slavic

baluster 4 post, rail **6** column, pillar **7** support, upright **8** pilaster

balustrade 7 railing **8** baluster, banister, handrail

Balzac, Honore de
author of: **7** Gobseck **10** La Vendetta **11** Cousin(e) Bette **12** Father Goriot, Le Cousin Pons, Le Pere Goriot **13** Lost Illusions **14** Eugenie Grandet, The Human Comedy **15** The Wild Ass's Skin **16** La Comedie Humaine **23** The Physiology of Marriage

Bamako
capital of: **4** Mali

Bambi
author: **11** Felix Salten
character: **6** Faline, Flower **7** Thumper

bamboo 4 Sasa **7** Bambusa **9** Shibataea **10** Pseudosasa **11** Arundinaria **13** Phyllostachys **14** Chimonobambusa **15** Semiarundinaria

varieties: **4** Moso **5** Arrow, Black, Dwarf, Giant, Hardy, Hedge, Henon, Meyer, Pygmy, Simon, Stake **6** Buddha, Common, Forage, Oldham, Sacred, Sickle, Square, Tonkin **7** Allgold, Beechey, Mexican **8** Calcutta, Feathery, Heavenly, Narihira **9** Canebrake, Castillon **10** Red-berried, Square-stem **11** Punting-pole **12** Alphonse Karr, Yellow-groove **13** Dwarf fern-leaf, Fern-leaf hedge, Oriental hedge **14** Chinese-goddess **16** Dwarf white-stripe **17** Silver-stripe hedge **18** Stripe-stem fern-leaf

bamboozle 3 con, gyp **4** coax, dupe, fool, gull, hoax, lure, rook, take 5 cheat, cozen, trick 6 delude 7 beguile, deceive, defraud, mislead, swindle 8 hoodwink 9 victimize

ban 3 bar 5 debar, taboo 6 banish, enjoin, forbid 7 barring, embargo, exclude 8 disallow, prohibit, stoppage, suppress 9 exclusion, interdict, proscribe, restraint 10 banishment, censorship 11 forbiddance, prohibition, restriction 12 interdiction, proscription

banal 4 dull 5 corny, stale, stock, tired, trite, vapid 6 jejune 7 humdrum, insipid, prosaic 8 bromidic, everyday, ordinary, shopworn 9 hackneyed 10 pedestrian, threadbare, unexciting, unoriginal 11 commonplace, stereotyped 12 cliche-ridden, conventional 13 platitudinous, unimaginative, uninteresting

banality 6 cliche 7 bromide 9 platitude, staleness, triteness 10 insipidity

banana 4 Musa
varieties: 3 Fe'i 4 Fehi, Koae 5 Dwarf 6 Edible 7 Chinese 9 Flowering 10 Abyssinian, Ladyfinger 12 Canary Island, Chinese dwarf
similar to: 8 plantain

Bananas
director: 10 Woody Allen
cast: 10 Woody Allen 12 Howard Cosell, Louise Lasser 15 Carlos Montalban

Bancroft, Anne
real name: 23 Anna Maria Louise Italiano
husband: 9 Mel Brooks
born: 7 Bronx NY
roles: 11 Mrs Robinson, The Graduate 15 The Pumpkin Eater, The Turning Point, Two for the Seesaw 16 The Miracle Worker (Oscar)

band 3 set 4 belt, body, club, crew, gang, hoop, join, pack, ring, sash 5 bunch, crowd, group, junta, party, strap, strip, swath, thong, troop, unite 6 caucus, circle, clique, collar, fillet, gather, girdle, league, ribbon, streak, stripe, throng 7 bandeau, binding, circlet, company, society 8 assembly, cincture, ensemble 9 multitude, orchestra, surcingle 10 fellowship, sisterhood 11 association, brotherhood, confederacy, consolidate 13 confederation

bandage 4 bind 5 dress 7 binding, plaster 8 compress, dressing

bandanna, bandana 5 scarf 8 kerchief 10 silk square 11 neckerchief 12 handkerchief

Bandar Seri Begawan
capital of: 6 Brunei

bandeau 3 bra 4 band 6 fillet 7 binding, circlet 9 brassiere

bandit 4 thug 5 crook, thief 6 badman, outlaw, robber 7 brigand, burglar, footpad, ladrone 8 blackleg 9 desperado, road agent 10 highwayman

bandleader 6 master 7 maestro 8 director 9 conductor
famous: 11 Glenn Miller, Tommy Dorsey 12 Lawrence Welk

Band of Merry Men
followers of: 9 Robin Hood

band together 5 unify, unite 6 league 7 combine 10 join forces 11 consolidate

bandy 4 swap 5 trade 6 barter 7 shuffle 8 exchange 9 toss about 11 interchange 16 toss back and forth

bandying 4 swap 5 trade 8 exchange 9 tit for tat 10 quid pro quo 11 give and take

bane 3 woe 4 ruin 5 curse, toxin, venom 6 blight, burden, canker, plague, poison 7 scourge, torment, tragedy 8 calamity, disaster, downfall, nuisance 9 destroyer, detriment, ruination 10 affliction 13 pain in the neck 14 thorn in the side 16 fly in the ointment

baneful 4 evil 6 deadly, malign, woeful 7 harmful, noxious 8 venomous 9 injurious, malignant, poisonous 10 malevolent 11 destructive

bang 3 box, hit, pop, rap, tap 4 beat, blow, boom, clap, cuff, kick, lick, slam, slap, sock 5 burst, clout, crash, knock, smack, thump, whack 6 buffet, charge, report, thrill, thwack, wallop 7 delight 8 good time, headlong, pleasure, suddenly 9 enjoyment, explosion 10 crashingly, excitement

Bangkok, Bankok
also: 9 Krung Thep
capital of: 8 Thailand
landmark: 5 Wat Po 11 Grand Palace 16 Wat Emerald Buddha
means: 12 City of Angels
nickname: 15 Venice of the East
port: 8 Klongtoi
river: 10 Chao Phraya

Bangladesh
other name: 10 East Bengal 12 East Pakistan
capital/largest city: 5 Dacca
others: 6 Khulna, Sylhet 7 Comilla, Jessore, Rangpur, Saidpur 8 Jamalpur, Rajshahi 9 Madaripur 10 Chittagong 11 Narayanganj 12 Brahmanbaria
monetary unit: 4 taka 5 paisa
island: 10 Sundarbans
mountain: 15 Chittagong Hills
highest point: 10 Keokradong
river: 5 Padna 6 Ganges, Meghna 10 Burhi Ganga, Karnaphuli 11 Brahmaputra
physical feature:
bay: 6 Bengal
people: 7 Bengali
guerrillas: 11 muktibahini
leader: 6 Ershad 11 Ziaur Rahman 19 Sheikh Mujibur Rahman
language: 6 Bihari 7 Bengali, English
religion: 5 Hindu, Islam
feature:
clothing: 4 sari 5 lungi

bangle 3 fob 5 chain, charm 6 armlet, bauble, gewgaw, tinsel 7 bibelot, fribble, trinket 8 bracelet, gimcrack, ornament, wristlet 10 knickknack 11 junk jewelry 14 costume jewelry

Bangui
capital of: 22 Central African Republic

banish 3 ban, bar 4 drop, oust 5 eject, erase, evict, exile, expel 6 deport, dispel, outlaw, reject, remove 7 cast out, discard, dismiss, exclude, put away, shut out, turn out 8 cast away, dislodge, drive out, get rid of, send away, shake off 9 discharge, eliminate, eradicate, extradite 13 excommunicate 14 send to Coventry

banished person 5 exile 6 emigre, pariah 7 outcast 8 deportee, expellee 10 expatriate 14 deported person 15 displaced person

banishment 3 ban 5 exile 6 ouster 7 removal 8 eviction

9 dismissal, exclusion, expulsion **11** deportation **12** expatriation **14** transportation **15** excommunication

Banjo Eyes
  nickname of: **11** Eddie Cantor

Banjul, Bathurst
  capital of: **9** The Gambia

bank 3 bar, row, tip **4** dike, dune, edge, file, flat, fund, heap, hill, keep, line, mass, pile, rank, reef, rise, save, side, tier, tilt **5** amass, array, brink, chain, knoll, mound, ridge, shelf, shoal, shore, slant, slope, stack, store, train **6** barrow, line up, margin, pile up, series, strand, string, supply **7** deposit, parapet, reserve, savings, shallow, terrace **8** keyboard, sandbank **9** exchequer, reservoir, stockpile **10** depository, embankment, repository, storehouse, succession **12** accumulation, trust company **14** savings and loan

Bank Dick, The
  director: **10** Eddie Cline
  cast: **8** W C Fields **9** Una Merkel **15** Cora Witherspoon

Bankhead, Tallulah
  father: **16** William B Bankhead
  born: **12** Huntsville AL
  roles: **8** Lifeboat **14** The Little Foxes **17** The Skin of Our Teeth

banknote 4 bill **9** greenback **11** certificate, legal tender **12** currency note, treasury note **17** silver certificate

bank of pity
  French: **11** mont-de-piete
  literal name for: **10** pawnbroker

bankrupt 5 broke **6** busted, failed, ruined **8** depleted, indigent, in the red, wiped out **9** destitute, exhausted, insolvent, penniless **12** impoverished, without funds

Bankruptcy, A
  author: **20** Bjornstjerne Bjornson

Banks, Ernie
  nickname: **5** Mr Cub
  sport: **8** baseball
  noted for: **7** hitting
  team: **11** Chicago Cubs

banner 4 flag **6** burgee, colors, ensign, record **7** leading, notable, pendant, pennant, winning **8** standard, streamer **9** red-letter **10** profitable

11 outstanding **14** most successful

Bannock
  language family: **10** Shoshonean
  location: **5** Idaho

banquet 4 dine **5** feast, revel **6** dinner, repast **9** symposium

Banquo
  character in: **7** Macbeth
  author: **11** Shakespeare

bantam 3 hen, wee **4** cock, fowl, tiny **5** dwarf, pygmy, runt, small, teeny, weeny **6** little, midget, minute, petite **7** chicken, dwarfed, rooster, stunted **9** miniature **10** diminutive, pocket-size, teeny-weeny **11** Lilliputian, pocket-sized

banter 3 kid, rib **4** dish, josh, mock, ride, twit **5** chaff, jolly, taunt, tease **6** joking, needle **7** jesting, joshing, kidding, ragging, ribbing, teasing, waggery **8** badinage, chaffing, raillery, repartee, word play

Banting, Frederick Grant
  field: **8** medicine
  nationality: **8** Canadian
  extracted: **7** insulin
  awarded: **10** Nobel Prize

Bantu
  means: **9** the people
  dwelling: **6** Africa
  tribe: **5** Xosas, Zulus **6** Swazis **7** Basutos, Kalanga

baptism 9 beginning, immersion, sacrament **10** initiation, sprinkling **11** christening **12** introduction, purification **13** rite of passage **16** spiritual rebirth

baptize 3 dub **4** name **8** christen

bar 3 ban, pub, rib, rod **4** band, bank, beam, belt, bolt, cake, curb, flat, line, lock, oust, pale, pole, rail, reef, snag, spar, spit, stay, stop **5** block, catch, check, court, debar, eject, evict, exile, expel, forum, ingot, jimmy, lever, limit, shelf, shoal, slice, sprit, stake, stick, strip, taboo **6** banish, enjoin, fasten, forbid, impede, lounge, paling, ribbon, saloon, secure, streak, stripe, stroke, tavern **7** barrier, block up, canteen, cast out, close up, crowbar, exclude, grating, lock out, measure, prevent, sandbar, shallow, shut out, taproom **8** alehouse, crossbar, disallow, judgment, obstacle, obstruct, preclude, prohibit, restrain, restrict, tribunal **9** barricade, blackball, blacklist, hindrance, long ta-

ble, lunchroom, restraint, speakeasy **10** constraint, crosspiece, impediment, injunction, limitation **11** obstruction, public house, restriction **14** cocktail lounge, serving counter, stumbling block **15** legal profession

Bara, Theda
  real name: **16** Theodosia Goodman
  nickname: **7** The Vamp
  born: **12** Cincinnati OH
  roles: **6** Carmen, Salome **7** Camille **8** The Vixen **9** Cleopatra **13** A Fool There Was, Madame Du Barry

Barabbas 6 robber **8** murderer

Barak
  father: **7** Abinoam
  summoned by: **7** Deborah
  defeated: **6** Sisera

barb 3 cut, dig, nib **4** cusp, jibe, snag, spur, tine **5** point, prong, spike **6** insult **7** affront, barbule, bristle, prickle, putdown, sarcasm, spicule **9** complaint, criticism **11** badmouthing

Barbados see box

barbarian 4 boor, hood, lout, punk **5** alien, bully, crude, rowdy, tough, yahoo **6** savage, vandal **7** boorish, hoodlum, lowbrow, peasant, ruffian, uncouth **8** hooligan **9** ignoramus, outlander, roughneck, vulgarian **10** delinquent, illiterate, philistine, provincial, troglodyte, uncultured **11** knownothing **12** uncultivated **15** unsophisticated **16** anti-intellectual

barbaric 4 rude, wild **5** crude **6** coarse, savage, vulgar **7** boorish, uncouth, untamed **9** barbarian, barbarous **10** unpolished **11** ill-mannered, uncivilized

barbarism 7 cruelty **8** savagery **9** brutality **10** inhumanity **11** viciousness

barbarity 7 cruelty **9** brutality **10** savageness **12** ruthlessness

barbarous 4 mean **5** crass, crude, cruel, harsh, rough **6** brutal, coarse, vulgar **7** inhuman, vicious **8** barbaric, impolite **10** outrageous

barber 3 cut **4** trim **5** dress, shave, style **7** arrange, stylist, tonsure **10** haircutter **11** hairdresser

Barber, Samuel
  born: **13** West Chester PA
  composer of: **7** Vanessa **10** Dover Beach **16** Adagio for Strings **17** Capricorn

Barbados
capital/largest city:
10 Bridgetown
others: 7 Oistins **8** Boscabel, Crab Hill, Hastings, Holetown, Portland, Worthing **9** Bathsheba **10** Martin's Bay **11** Belleplaine **12** Speightstown
school: 10 Codrington
head of state: 14 British monarch **15** governor general
mountain: 6 Chalky
highest point: 7 Hillaby
river: 12 Constitution
sea: 8 Atlantic **9** Caribbean
physical feature:
bay: 4 Foul, Long **8** Carlisle
beach: 5 Crane
gully: 12 Welchman Hall
hill: 10 Cherry Tree
point: 5 North, South **6** Ragged **8** Harrison, Kitridge
people: 5 Bajan **9** Barbadian
leader: 5 Adams
language: 7 English
religion: 8 Anglican
place:
airport: 7 Seawell
castle: 8 Sam Lords
church: 7 St Johns
feature:
sea crab: 7 shagger

Concerto **19** Anthony and Cleopatra, The School for Scandal

Barber of Seville, The
author: 12 Beaumarchais
opera by: 7 Rossini
character: 6 Bazile, Figaro, Rosine, Rosina **8** Almaviva, Bartholo **9** Dr Bartolo **13** Count Almaviva

barbette 5 mound **7** bastion, rampart **8** platform **9** earthwork **10** breastwork

barbiturate 8 euphoria, hypnotic, sedative **10** depressive **13** anesthesiatic **14** barbituric acid
kind: 7 seconal **10** thiopental **11** amobarbital **12** secobarbital **13** phenobarbital

barbule 4 barb **11** feather part

Barchester Towers
author: 15 Anthony Trollope
sequel to: 9 The Warden
character: 7 Mr Slope, Mrs Bold **8** Mr Arabin **9** Dr

Proudie, Mr Harding **10** Mrs Proudie **11** Mr Quiverful **13** Canon Stanhope **17** Archdeacon Grantly **18** Signora Vesey-Neroni

bard 4 poet **6** rhymer, writer **8** epic poet, minstrel, poetizer **9** poetaster, rhymester, troubador, versifier **10** poet-singer **13** narrative poet

Bardell, Mrs
character in: 14 Pickwick Papers
author: 7 Dickens

Bardot, Brigitte
husband: 10 Roger Vadim
born: 5 Paris **6** France
roles: 18 And God Created Woman

bare 4 bald, mere, nude, open, show, thin, void, worn **5** basic, blank, empty, naked, offer, plain, scant, stark, strip **6** denude, divest, expose, meager, peeled, reveal, simple, unclad, unmask, unveil, vacant **7** austere, exposed, hapless, uncover, undrape, undress, unrobed **8** disrobed, in the raw, marginal, stripped **9** endurable, essential, unadorned, unclothed, uncolored, uncovered, undressed, unsheathe **10** elementary, just enough, threadbare **11** fundamental, supportable, undecorated, undisguised, unvarnished **12** unelaborated, unornamented **13** unembellished **15** straightforward

barefaced 4 bald, bold, flip **5** brash, fresh, sassy **6** brazen, cheeky, snotty **7** forward **8** flippant, impudent, insolent, palpable **9** shameless, unabashed **11** transparent

barefoot 6 unshod **8** shoeless **9** discalced **10** unsandaled **11** discalceate

Barefoot Boy
author: 21 John Greenleaf Whittier

Barefoot in the Park
director: 8 Gene Saks
based on play by: 9 Neil Simon
cast: 9 Jane Fonda **12** Charles Boyer **13** Robert Redford

barely 4 just **6** almost, hardly **7** faintly, scantly **8** meagerly, only just, scarcely, slightly **9** almost not, just about, sparingly **10** no more than **20** by the skin of one's teeth

bareness 6 nudity **9** bleakness, emptiness, nakedness **10** barrenness

Baresark
origin: 12 Scandinavian
form: 7 warrior
trait: 7 courage

Baretta
character: 7 Rooster **11** Billy Truman, (Det) Tony Baretta, (Lt) Hal Brubaker
cast: 8 Tom Ewell **11** Robert Blake **12** Edward Grover **15** Michael D Roberts
Tony's pet: 8 cockatoo
named: 4 Fred

barfly 3 sot **4** lush, soak **5** drunk, rummy, souse, toper **7** tippler **8** drunkard **9** alcoholic **11** dipsomaniac

bargain 4 deal, pact **5** steal **6** accord, barter, dicker, haggle, higgle, pledge, treaty **7** compact, entente, good buy, promise **8** contract, covenant, good deal **9** agreement, negotiate **10** settlement **11** arrangement, transaction **13** understanding
French: 9 bon marche

bargain for 6 expect **7** foresee **8** envision, reckon on **11** contemplate

barge 4 bust, scow, ship **6** launch, vessel **7** freight, intrude

barium
chemical symbol: 2 Ba

bark 3 bay, cry, rub, yap, yip **4** flay, hide, howl, hull, husk, peel, rind, roar, skin, woof, yell, yelp **5** crust, scale, shout, strip **6** abrade, arf-arf, bellow, bow-wow, casing, cry out, holler, scrape **7** howling **8** covering, periderm **9** sheathing

Barker, Lex
real name: 25 Alexander Crichlow Barker Jr
wife: 10 Arlene Dahl, Lana Turner
born: 5 Rye NY
roles: 6 Tarzan **11** La Dolce Vita

Barkis
character in: 16 David Copperfield
author: 7 Dickens

Barkley, Catherine
character in: 15 A Farewell to Arms
author: 9 Hemingway

Barlach, Ernst
born: 5 Wedel **7** Germany **8** Holstein
artwork: 9 Expellees **10** Seated Girl, Singing Man **11** Man in a Stock **13** Mater Dolorosa **14** Crippled Beggar, The Hovering

One **16** Man Drawing a Sword **25** The Community of the Holy Ones

barn 4 mews **6** corral, stable

Barnabas
companion: **4** Paul

Barnaby Jones
character: **7** J R (Jedediah Romano) Jones **8** Lt Biddle **10** Betty Jones
cast: **9** Mark Shera **10** Buddy Ebsen, John Carter **13** Lee Meriwether

Barnaby Rudge
author: **14** Charles Dickens
character: **8** Mrs Rudge **9** Miss Miggs **10** John Willet **11** Dolly Varden **12** Emma Haredale **13** Edward Chester, Gabriel Varden **14** Reuben Haredale, Simon Tappertit, Sir John Chester **16** Dennis the Hangman, Geoffrey Haredale
subject: **11** Gordon riots

Barnard, Christiaan
field: **7** surgery **8** medicine
nationality: **12** South African
performed first: **15** heart transplant

Barnard, Edward Emerson
field: **9** astronomy
named for him: **12** red dwarf star

Barnes, Jake
character in: **15** The Sun Also Rises
author: **9** Hemingway

Barney Google
creator: **11** Billy DeBeck
character: **11** Snuffy Smith
baby: **5** Bunky
horse: **9** Spark Plug

Barney Miller
character: **8** (Det) Phil Fish **9** (Det) Ron Harris **10** (Det Wojo) Wojohowicz, (Det) Nick Yamana, (Officer) Carl Levitt **14** Inspector Luger, (Det) Arthur Dietrich
cast: **7** Jack Soo **8** Ron Carey, Ron Glass **9** Abe Vigoda, Hal Linden **11** Maxwell Gail **12** James Gregory **15** Steve Landesberg

Barnstock *see* **9** Branstock

Baroja y Nessi, Pio
author of: **15** Caesar or Nothing **23** The Struggle for Existence **26** Memorias de un Hombre de Accion

barometer
invented by: **10** Torricelli

baroque 6 florid, ornate **10** flamboyant **11** extravagant

Barrack-Room Ballads
author: **14** Rudyard Kipling

barracks 3 BOQ **4** base, camp **7** lodging **8** garrison

barrage 5 blast, burst, salvo, spray **6** ack-ack, deluge, shower, stream, volley **7** battery, torrent **8** shelling **9** cannonade, fusillade **10** outpouring **11** bombardment

barrel 3 keg, tub, tun, vat **4** butt, cask, drum, tube **8** hogshead
abbreviation: **3** bar, bbl

barren 3 dry **4** arid, dull **5** stale, waste **6** farrow, futile **7** austere, prosaic, sterile, useless **8** depleted, desolate, infecund **9** fruitless, infertile **10** lackluster, unfruitful **11** ineffectual, uninspiring, unrewarding **12** unproductive **13** uninformative, uninstructive, uninteresting

barrenness 8 bareness **9** bleakness, emptiness **10** desolation

barren wilderness 6 desert **9** wasteland

barricade 5 block, fence **7** barrier, bulwark, rampart **8** blockade, obstacle, obstruct **10** impediment **11** obstruction

Barrie, Sir James M
author of: **7** The Will **8** Mary Rose, Peter Pan **10** Dear Brutus **13** Quality Street **15** Margaret Ogilvie, The Wedding Guest **17** Alice Sit-By-the-Fire, The Little Minister **18** A Kiss for Cinderella, The Twelve-Pound Look **19** What Every Woman Knows **20** Shall We Join the Ladies?, The Admirable Crichton
character: **8** Peter Pan **10** Tinkerbell **11** Captain Hook
Darling children: **4** John **5** Wendy **7** Michael
nurse/Newfoundland dog: **4** Nana
setting: **14** Never-Never Land

barrier 3 bar **4** moat, wall **5** ditch, fence, hedge **6** hurdle, trench **7** rampart **8** blockade, handicap, obstacle **9** barricade, hindrance **10** difficulty, impediment, limitation **11** obstruction, restriction **13** fortification **14** stumbling block

Barrier, The
author: **8** Rex Beach

barring 3 but **4** save **6** except, saving **7** besides **9** excepting, excluding, other than **11** exclusive of

barrister 6 lawyer **7** counsel **8** advocate, attorney **9** counselor **10** mouthpiece **13** attorney-at-law

barroom 3 bar, pub, **6** bistro, lounge, saloon, tavern **7** taproom

barrow 4 heap, pile **5** mound **7** tumulus **8** handcart, pushcart **11** wheelbarrow

Barrow, Joe Louis
real name of: **8** Joe Louis

Barry, Gene
real name: **11** Eugene Klass
born: **9** New York NY
roles: **9** Burke's Law **11** Thunder Road **12** Bat Masterson **16** The Name of the Game **17** The War of the Worlds

Barry, John
served in: **16** Revolutionary War
commander of ship: **7** Raleigh **8** Alliance **9** Effingham, Lexington
ship captured: **6** Edward

Barry, Redmond
character in: **11** Barry Lyndon
author: **9** Thackeray

Barry, Sir Charles
architect of: **8** Cliveden **14** City Art Gallery (Manchester) **18** Houses of Parliament (London)

Barry Lyndon
author: **25** William Makepeace Thackeray
character: **12** Redmond Barry **14** Lord Bullingdon **17** Lady Honoria Lyndon (Countess of Lyndon) **19** Chevalier de Balibari
director: **14** Stanley Kubrick
cast: **9** Ryan O'Neal **11** Hardy Kruger **12** Patrick Magee **14** Marisa Berenson

Barrymore, Ethel
real name: **14** Ethel Mae Blythe
brother: **4** John **6** Lionel
born: **14** Philadelphia PA
roles: **11** A Doll's House **14** The Corn Is Green **16** Portrait of Jennie **19** Trelawney of the Wells **21** None But the Lonely Heart, Rasputin and the Empress

Barrymore, John
real name: **10** John Blythe
brother: **6** Lionel
sister: **5** Ethel
son: **17** John Drew Barrymore
daughter: **14** Diana Barrymore
nickname: **12** Great Profile

born: 14 Philadelphia PA
roles: 6 Hamlet **7** Don Juan
8 Moby Dick, Svengali
9 Richard IV **10** Grand Hotel **11** Beau Brummel
13 Dinner at Eight **17** Dr
Jekyll and Mr Hyde **21** Rasputin and the Empress

Barrymore, Lionel
real name: 12 Lionel Blythe
brother: 4 John
sister: 5 Ethel
born: 14 Philadelphia PA
roles: 7 The Jest **9** A Free
Soul (Oscar), Dr Kildare
11 Dr Gillespie **13** Peter Ibbitson, The Copperhead
21 Rasputin and the
Empress

Barsabbas see **6** Joseph

Barstad, John
character in: 16 A Tale of
Two Cities
author: 7 Dickens

Bart, Lily
character in: 15 The House
of Mirth
author: 7 Wharton

barter 4 swap **5** trade **8** exchange **11** interchange

Bartered Bride, The
opera by: 7 Smetana
character: 5 Jenik, Kecal,
Micha, Vasek **7** Marenka

Barth, John
author of: 7 Chimera
12 Giles Goat-Boy **15** The
End of the Road **16** The
Floating Opera, The Sot-
Weed Factor **17** Lost in the
Funhouse

Barthelme, Donald
author of: 7 Sadness **8** City
Life **9** Great Days, Snow
White **12** Sixty Stories
13 The Dead Father
15 Guilty Pleasures **18** Come
Back Dr Caligari **33** Unspeakable Practices Unnatural Acts

Bartholdi, Frederic-Auguste
born: 6 Alsace, Colmar
artwork: 13 Lion of Belfort
26 Liberty Enlightening the
World (Statue of Liberty)

Bartholo, Dr
character in: 18 The Barber
of Seville **19** The Marriage
of Figaro
author: 12 Beaumarchais

Bartholomew 7 apostle
also called: 9 Nathanael

Bartholomew Fair
author: 9 Ben Jonson

Bartok, Bela
born: 7 Hungary

15 Nagyszentmiklos
composer of: 9 Wrestling
11 Mikrokosmos **12** Divertimento **14** Cantata Profana
15 The Wooden Prince
20 Duke Bluebeard's Castle
21 The Miraculous
Mandarin

Bartolommeo, Fra
born: 5 Italy **8** Florence
real name: 31 Bartolommeo
di Pagolo del Fattorino
artwork: 5 Jonah **6** Isaiah
13 Salvator Mundi **15** The
Last Judgment **17** Vision of
St Bernard **24** Madonna
della Misericordia **30** The
Mystic Marriage of St
Catherine

Barton, Benjamin Smith
field: 6 botany
noted for first American:
14 botany textbook

Bartram, John
field: 6 botany
noted for first American:
12 hybrid plants

Baruch
father: 5 Judah **6** Neriah
friend and scribe of:
8 Jeremiah

basal 3 key **4** easy **5** basic, vital **6** simple **7** initial, minimal,
primary **8** cardinal **9** beginning, essential, intrinsic, necessary **10** elementary,
lower-level, simplified **11** fundamental, rudimentary **12** prerequisite **13** indispensable

bas bleu 12 bluestocking

base 3 bad, bed, key, low
4 camp, core, foul, mean,
post, root, vile **5** basis, dirty,
gross, heart, petty, place,
stand **6** abject, billet, bottom,
craven, ground, impure, locate, scurvy, sinful, sneaky,
sordid, source, vulgar, wicked
7 alloyed, corrupt, debased, essence, found on, ignoble, immoral, install, model on,
scrubby, situate, station, support **8** backbone, cowardly, degraded, depraved, garrison,
infamous, inferior, pedestal,
rudiment, shameful, spurious,
unworthy **9** dastardly, dissolute, establish, faithless, insidious, nefarious, principle
10 degenerate, derive from,
despicable, detestable, evilminded, foundation, groundwork, iniquitious, villainous
11 adulterated, disgraceful, ignominious, poor quality,
scoundrelly **12** black-hearted,
contemptible, dishonorable,
disreputable, installation, substructure, underpinning, unprincipled **13** discreditable,
reprehensible

baseball
athlete/coach: 6 Mel Ott, Ty
Cobb **7** Al Lopez, Cy Young,
Jim Rice **8** Al Kaline, Babe
Ruth, Lou Brock, Pete Rose,
Rod Carew, Vida Blue **9** Alvin Dark, Bob Feller, Bob
Gibson, Bowie Kuhn, Dizzy
Dean, Ford Frick, Gil
Hodges, Hank Aaron, Hank
Bauer, Jim Palmer, Jimmy
Foxx, Joe Morgan, Lou Gehrig, Luis Tiant, Nellie Fox,
Nolan Ryan, Ralph Houk,
Ron Guidry, Ted Turner,
Tom Seaver, Tommy John,
Yogi Berra **10** Boog Powell,
Connie Mack, Duke Snider,
Earl Weaver, Ernie Banks,
John McGraw, Lefty Grove,
Maury Wills, Ralph Kiner,
Roger Maris, Sparky Lyle,
Stan Musial, Whitey Ford,
Willie Mays **11** Billy Martin,
Carl Hubbell, Dave Kingman,
Don Drysdale, Frank
Thomas, George Brett,
George Weiss, Honus Wager,
Joe DiMaggio, Joe McCarthy,
Johnny Bench, Leo Durocher, Luke Appling, Mark Fidrych, Mike Schmidt, Pee
Wee Reese, Phil Rizzuto,
Rich Gossage, Sandy Koufax,
Ted Williams, Tris Speaker,
Warren Spahn **12** Branch
Rickey, Casey Stengel, Graig
Nettles, Dave Winfield, Dennis McLain, Dick Williams,
Eddie Mathews, Elston Howard, Gaylord Perry, George
Sisler, Ken Griffey Jr.,
Mickey Mantle, Satchel
Paige, Steve Carlton, Tommy
Lasorda **13** Catfish (Jim)
Hunter, Frank Robinson,
Reggie Jackson, Rocky Colavito, Rogers Hornsby, Roy
Campanella, Thurman Munson, Walter O'Malley, Willie
McCovey **14** Al Schoendienst,
Brooks Robinson, Jackie
Robinson, Keith Hernandez,
Peter Ueberroth, Sparky Anderson, Willie Stargell
15 Carl Yastrzemski, Charly
Gehringer, Harmon Killebrew, Rickey Henderson, Roberto Clemente **16** Christy
Mathewson, Darryl Strawberry **18** Fernando Valenzuela, George Steinbrenner
21 Kenesaw Mountain Landis
24 Grover Cleveland
Alexander

baseball leagues
National: 11 Chicago Cubs,
New York Mets **13** Atlanta
Braves, Houston Astros,
Montreal Expos **14** Cincinnati Reds, San Diego
Padres **16** St Louis Cardinals **17** Los Angeles Dodg-

ers, Pittsburgh Pirates
18 San Francisco Giants
20 Philadelphia Phillies
American: 9 Oakland A's
12 Boston Red Sox, Texas
Rangers **13** Detroit Tigers
14 Minnesota Twins, New
York Yankees **15** Chicago
White Sox, Seattle Mariners,
Toronto Blue Jays **16** Baltimore Orioles, California Angels, Cleveland Indians,
Kansas City Royals, Milwaukee Brewers

baseball team *see box*

baseless 7 unsound **9** unfactual, unfounded **10** groundless,
ungrounded **11** unjustified, unsupported **12** without basis
13 unjustifiable **14** uncorroborated **15** unsubstantiated

basement 5 below **6** bottom,
cellar **15** underground room

baseness 7 lowness **8** meanness, vileness **9** depravity
11 ignobleness **14** iniquitous-
ness **16** contemptibleness

base of operations
Greek: **6** pou sto

bash 4 blow **5** blast, clout,
crack, knock, party, whack
7 clopper **8** wingding
9 bacchanal

Bashemath *see* **4** Adah

bashful 3 shy **5** timid **6** demure, modest **8** blushing, reserved, reticent, retiring,
sheepish, skittish, timorous
9 diffident, shrinking, uncertain **10** shamefaced **11** constrained, unconfident

bashfulness 7 shyness **10** diffidence **12** sheepishness
14 self-effacement
15 unassertiveness

basic 3 key **4** base, core
5 prime, vital **7** bedrock, primary **8** rudiment **9** essential,
intrinsic **10** elementary, foundation **11** fundamental, rudimentary **12** foundational,
prerequisite, underpinning

basically
French: **6** au fond

basic ideas 6 basics **7** essence,
factors, origins **8** elements,
features **9** rudiments **10** principles **11** foundations

basic need 9 essential, necessity, requisite, vital part
10 key element, sine qua non

basic part 4 unit **7** element
9 component **10** ingredient
11 constituent **13** building
block

basic quality 6 nature **7** essence **9** principle, substance
12 quintessence

---

baseball team
Atlanta: 6 Braves
  stadium: **7** Atlanta
Baltimore: 7 Orioles
  stadium: **11** Camden
  Yards
Boston: 6 Red Sox
  stadium: **10** Fenway
  Park
California: 6 Angels
  stadium: **7** Anaheim
Chicago: 4 Cubs
  stadium: **12** Wrigley
  Field
Chicago: 8 White Sox
  stadium: **12** Comiskey
  Park
Cleveland: 7 Indians
  stadium: **11** Jacobs
  Field
Cincinnati: 4 Reds
  stadium: **10** Riverfront
Colorado: 7 Rockies
  stadium: **8** Mile High
Detroit: 6 Tigers
  stadium: **5** Tiger
Florida: 7 Marlins
  stadium: **9** Joe Robbie
Houston: 6 Astros
  stadium: **9** Astrodome
Kansas City: 6 Royals
  stadium: **8** Kauffman
Los Angeles: 7 Dodgers
  stadium: **6** Dodger
  18 Los Angeles
  Coliseum

Milwaukee: 7 Brewers
  stadium: **6** County
Minnesota: 5 Twins
  stadium: **12** Metropol-
  itan **24** Hubert H
  Humphrey
  Metrodome
Montreal: 5 Expos
  stadium: **7** Olympic
New York: 4 Mets
  stadium: **4** Shea
New York: 7 Yankees
  stadium: **6** Yankee
Oakland: 2 A's
  9 Athletics
  stadium: **7** Oakland
Philadelphia: 8 Phillies
  stadium: **8** Veterans
Pittsburgh: 7 Pirates
  stadium: **11** Three
  Rivers
St Louis: 9 Cardinals
  stadium: **13** Busch
  Memorial
San Diego: 6 Padres
  stadium: **10** Jack
  Murphy
San Francisco: 6 Giants
  stadium: **15** Candle-
  stick Park
Seattle: 8 Mariners
  stadium: **8** Kingdome
Texas: 7 Rangers
  stadium: **11** The Ball
  Park
Toronto: 8 Blue Jays
  stadium: **7** Sky Dome

---

basics 8 elements **9** rudiments
10 principles **11** nitty-gritty
12 fundamentals

basil
also called: **6** tulasi
botanical name: **6** Ocimum
  8 O minimum **10** O
  basilicum
means: **5** royal **6** kingly, lizard (basilisk)
nickname: **14** kiss-me-Nicholas
origin: **5** India
sacred to: **6** Vishnu
  7 Krishna, Lakshmi
symbol of: **4** hate, love
use: **10** vegetables

basilica 6 church **10** house of
God **14** house of worship

Basilisk
form: **6** dragon

basin 3 pan, tub, vat **4** bowl,
dale, dell, font, glen, sink
5 gulch, gully, stoup **6** crater,
hollow, lavabo, ravine, tureen,
valley **7** dishpan, washtub
8 lavatory, sinkhole, washbowl **9** porringer, washbasin,

washstand **10** depression, finger bowl

basis, bases 4 base, root
6 ground **7** bedrock **9** essential,
principle **10** foundation, touchstone **11** cornerstone, fundamental **12** underpinning
13 starting point

bask 5 revel, savor **6** relish,
wallow **7** delight **8** sunbathe
9 luxuriate **11** warm oneself
12 soak up warmth, toast
oneself

basket 5 crate **6** barrel, hamper **7** carrier, pannier **8** bassinet, canister

basketball
athlete/coach: **7** K C Jones
  8 Bob Cousy, Hal Greer, Joe
  Fulks, Pat Riley, Sam Jones
  9 Bob McAdoo, Bob Pettit,
  Jerry West, Larry Bird, Rick
  Barry, Wes Unseld **10** Bill
  Walton, Danny Ainge, Dave
  Cowens, Earl Monroe, Elvin
  Hayes, John Wooden, Paul
  Arizin, Red Holzman, Willis

Reed **11** Alex English, Bill Bradley, Bill Lambeer, Bill Russell, Bill Sharman, Elgin Baylor, George Mikan, James Worthy, Kevin McHale, Lew Alcindor, Moses Malone, Red Auerbach, Walt Frazier **12** Calvin Murphy, Dolph Schayes, George Gervin, Isaiah Thomas, John Havlicek, Julius (Dr J) Erving, Lenny Wilkens, Patrick Ewing, Robert Parish **13** Connie Hawkins, David Robinson, Earvin (Magic) Johnson, Michael Jordan, Nate Archibald, Scottie Pippen **14** Charles Barkley, Hakeem Olajuwon, Shaquille O'Neal, Oscar Robertson **15** Billy Cunningham, Dave DeBusschere, Wilt Chamberlain **17** Kareem Abdul-Jabbar

basketball team *see box*

Basque
  language spoken in: **5** Italy, Spain **6** France

bas-relief
  Italian: **12** basso-rilievo

bass **3** low **4** alto **5** basso **7** harmony **8** baritone, bass clef

basketball team
  league: **3** NBA **29** National Basketball Association
  Atlanta: **5** Hawks
  Boston: **7** Celtics
  Charlotte: **7** Hornets
  Chicago: **5** Bulls
  Cleveland: **9** Cavaliers
  Dallas: **9** Mavericks
  Denver: **7** Nuggets
  Detroit: **7** Pistons
  Golden State: **8** Warriors
  Houston: **7** Rockets
  Indiana: **6** Pacers
  Los Angeles: **6** Lakers **8** Clippers
  Miami: **4** Heat
  Milwaukee: **5** Bucks
  Minnesota: **12** Timberwolves
  New Jersey: **4** Nets
  New York: **14** Knickerbockers
  Orlando: **5** Magic
  Philadelphia: **5** 76ers **13** Seventy-sixers
  Phoenix: **4** Suns
  Portland: **12** Trail Blazers
  Sacramento: **5** Kings
  San Antonio: **5** Spurs
  Seattle: **11** Supersonics
  Toronto: **7** Raptors
  Utah: **4** Jazz
  Vancouver: **9** Grizzlies
  Washington: **7** Bullets

bass
  types: **3** sea **4** rock **5** black **6** calico **7** striped, sunfish
  characteristic: **10** forked-tail **12** spiny-finned

Bassanio
  character in: **19** The Merchant of Venice
  author: **11** Shakespeare

basso-rilievo **9** bas-relief

Bast, Jacky and Leonard
  characters in: **10** Howard's End
  author: **9** E M Forster

bastard **6** impure **8** inferior, spurious **9** imperfect, irregular, love child **12** natural child **17** illegitimate child

bastardize **6** debase, weaken **7** degrade **9** downgrade

baste **3** sew **4** drip **5** roast **6** cudgel, flavor, stitch, thrash **15** temporary stitch

bastinado **4** beat, blow, cane, drub **5** whale **7** beating **8** drubbing

bastion **4** fort **5** tower **6** pillar **7** bulwark, citadel, rampart **8** barbette, fortress **10** breastwork, stronghold

bat **3** hit, rod **4** cane, clip, club, cuff, mace, slug, sock **5** baton, billy, knock, smack, staff, stick, whack **6** buffet, cudgel, mallet, strike, thwack, wallop **7** clobber **8** bludgeon **9** blackjack, truncheon **10** shillelagh

batch **3** lot **5** bunch, crowd, group, stock **6** amount, number **8** quantity **9** aggregate **10** collection

Bates, Alan
  born: **7** England **9** Allestree **10** Derbyshire
  roles: **8** The Fixer **10** Georgy Girl **12** King of Hearts **13** Zorba the Greek **16** An Unmarried Woman **22** Far From the Madding Crowd

Bates, Miss
  character in: **4** Emma
  author: **6** Austen

Bateson, William
  field: **7** biology
  nationality: **7** British
  founded: **8** genetics

bath **3** dip, tub **4** wash **5** sauna **6** douche, shower **7** washing **8** ablution, lavement **9** cleansing, immersion, steam bath **10** irrigation
  type: **2** hip **4** sitz **5** steam **6** shower, sponge **7** Turkish bath

bathe **3** dip, tub, wet **4** lave, soak, wash **5** douse **6** douche, shower, sponge **7** cleanse **8** irrigate

bathing **3** dip, tub **6** laving, plunge **7** washing **8** swimming **9** ablutions, immersion

bathos **4** corn, mush **5** slush **8** schmaltz **9** mushiness, soppiness **10** maudlinism, slushiness **11** false pathos, mawkishness **14** sentimentalism, sentimentality

bathroom **2** W C **3** can, loo **4** head, john **5** biffy **6** toilet **7** commode, latrine **8** facility, lavatory, men's room, restroom, washroom **10** ladies' room, powder room **11** water closet **14** little boys' room **15** little girls' room

Bathsheba
  also: **8** Bathshua
  father: **5** Eliam
  husband: **5** David, Uriah
  son: **7** Solomon
  grandfather: **10** Ahithophel

Bathshua *see* **9** Bathsheba

Bathurst
  see: Banjul

Batia
  form: **5** nymph
  father: **6** Teucer
  husband: **8** Dardanus
  son: **12** Erichthonius

Batman
  character: **6** Alfred **7** Egghead, King Tut **8** Catwoman, The Joker **10** Bruce Wayne (Batman), Chief O'Hara, The Penguin, The Riddler **11** Dick Grayson (Robin) **13** Barbara Gordon (Batgirl) **17** Aunt Harriet Cooper **24** Police Commissioner Gordon
  cast: **8** Adam West, Burt Ward **9** John Astin **10** Alan Napier, Eartha Kitt, Madge Blake **11** Cesar Romero, Julie Newmar, Victor Buono, Yvonne Craig **12** Frank Gorshin, Neil Hamilton, Stafford Repp, Vincent Price **13** Lee Meriwether **15** Burgess Meredith
  city: **10** Gotham City
  nickname: **9** Boy Wonder **10** Dynamic Duo **13** Caped Crusader
  gimmick: **6** Batlab **8** Batphone **9** Batmobile, Batsignal

Bat Masterson
  cast: **9** Gene Barry

baton **3** bat, rod **4** club, mace, wand **5** billy, crook, staff, stick **6** cudgel, fasces **7** crosier, scepter, war club **8** bludgeon,

caduceus **9** billy club, truncheon **10** nightstick, shillelagh

Baton
  chariroteer of: **10** Amphiaraus

batter 4 beat, lash, maul
5 break, crush, pound, smash,
smite **6** beat up, buffet, mangle, pummel **7** clobber, shatter

battercake 6 waffle **7** biscuit,
pancake

battered 4 shot **6** beat-up, ruined, shabby **8** decrepit **11** dilapidated **12** disreputable

battery 3 set **4** army, band,
pack, team **5** block, cadre,
force, group, suite, troop
6 caning, cannon, convoy, legion, lineup, outfit, series
7 beating, brigade, company,
hitting, hurting, maiming,
phalanx, section **8** armament,
cannonry, clubbing, division,
drubbing, flogging, ordnance,
squadron, whipping, wounding **9** cudgeling, spearhead,
strapping, thrashing

battle 3 war **4** bout, duel, feud,
fray, meet **5** argue, brawl,
clash, fight, siege **6** action, affray, combat, debate, engage,
tussle **7** contend, contest, crusade, dispute, quarrel, warfare **8** campaign, conflict,
skirmish, struggle **9** agitation,
encounter, firefight **10** engagement **11** altercation, controversy **13** confrontation

Battle, final
  place: **10** Armageddon

battle cry 6 war cry **8** Geronimo, war whoop **9** Rebel yell

Battle Cry
  author: **8** Leon Uris

battlefield 5 arena, lists **8** the
front, war arena **9** front line
10 battle line, no man's land
11 battlefront **12** battleground

battleground 5 arena, lists
11 battlefield, battlefront

Battle of the Books
  author: **13** Jonathan Swift

battle-ready 5 armed **7** arrayed **8** prepared **9** fortified

battleship 4 Iowa **5** Maine
6 Oregon **7** carrier, warship
8 Missouri **9** Ironsides, New
Jersey, Wisconsin **10** bluish-
gray **11** Dreadnought
12 Constitution
  first: **7** Gloire
  largest: **6** Yamato

Battus
  ruler of: **5** Libya
  form: **7** peasant
  witness to: **11** cattle theft
  thief: **6** Hermes

turned to: **5** stone
cured of: **16** speech
impediment

batty 4 nuts **5** crazy, loony,
queer, wacko, wacky **6** cuckoo, crazed **7** bat-like, cracked

bauble 3 toy **4** bead **6** geegaw
trifle **7** trinket **8** gimcrack,
ornament

Baucis
  form: **7** peasant
  home: **7** Phrygia
  husband: **8** Philemon
  offered hospitality to:
    4 Zeus **6** Hermes

Baudelaire, Charles
  author of: **13** Flowers of
    Evil **14** Les Fleurs du Mal

Baugh, Sammy
  nickname: **13** Slinging
    Sammy
  sport: **8** football
  position: **11** quarterback
  team: **18** Washington
    Redskins

Bauhin, Gaspard
  field: **6** botany
  nationality: **5** Swiss
  devised: **14** binomial system
  described: **14** ileocecal valve

Baum, Lyman Frank
  author of: **13** The (Wonder-
    ful) Wizard of Oz **18** Father
    Goose His Book, Mother
    Goose in Prose

Baum, Vicki
  author of: **8** Shanghai
    10 Grand Hotel, Grand Op-
    era **12** Men Never Know
    13 A Tale from Bali, And
    Life Goes On

Baumer, Paul
  character in: **25** All Quiet on
    the Western Front
  author: **8** Remarque

Baumgarner, James
  real name of: **11** James
    Garner

Bauto
  nurse of: **6** Celeus

bawdy 4 blue, lewd, sexy
5 dirty, gross, lusty **6** coarse,
earthy, ribald, risque, sexual,
vulgar **7** raunchy **8** immodest,
improper, indecent, off-color
10 indecorous, indelicate, licentious, suggestive

bawdy house 7 brothel **8** bordello, cathouse **10** fancy
house, whorehouse **13** sporting house **14** house of ill
fame **16** house of ill repute
19 house of prostitution

bawl 3 cry **4** call, howl, roar,
wail, weep, yell, yowl
5 shout **6** bellow, clamor, cry
out, squall **7** blubber, call out

bawling out 6 rebuke **7** censure, chiding, reproof **8** reproach, scolding **9** reprimand
10 chewing out, upbraiding
11 castigation, reprobation
12 dressing-down, remonstrance **13** tongue-lashing

bawl out 5 scold **6** berate, rail
at, rebuke, yell at **7** censure,
chew out, reprove, upbraid
8 admonish, reproach **9** castigate, dress down, reprimand
10 take to task, tongue-lash
14 read the riot act

Bax, Arnold Edward Trevor
  born: **6** London **7** England
  composer of: **8** Tintagel
    13 November Woods
    14 Mater Ora Filium **15** The
    Garden of Fand **27** Overture
    to a Picaresque Comedy

Baxter, Anne
  grandfather: **16** Frank Lloyd
    Wright
  born: **14** Michigan City IN
  roles: **8** Applause **11** All
    About Eve **13** The Razor's
    Edge

Baxter, Jody
  character in: **11** The Yearling
  author: **8** Rawlings

Baxter, William Sylvanus
  character in: **9** Seventeen
  author: **10** Tarkington

bay 3 cry, yap **4** bank, bark,
cove, gulf, howl, nook, road,
yelp **5** basin, bayou, bight,
fiord, firth, inlet, niche,
sound **6** alcove, bellow,
clamor, lagoon, recess, strait
7 barking, estuary, howling,
narrows, yapping, yelling,
yelping **9** bellowing **11** compartment **13** natural harbor

bay (at bay) 7 trapped
8 cornered

bay leaf
  botanical name: **12** Pimenta
    acris
  expression: **16** to win one's
    laurels
  from tree: **9** bay laurel
    transformation of:
      6 Daphne
    tree sacred to: **6** Apollo
    laurel berries called:
      10 bacca lauri
    source of:
      13 baccalaureate
  gives gift of: **8** prophecy
  helps girls win back: **12** er-
    rant lovers
  origin: **5** Italy
  protects against: **5** death
    6 poison **7** sorcery **11** evil
    spirits
  symbol of: **7** victory (laurel
    wreath)
  use: **4** fish, fowl, meat, soup,
    stew

bayou 4 slew **5** creek, inlet, marsh, river, swamp **6** outlet, slough, stream **9** backwater **13** stagnant marsh

Bayou State
nickname of: **9** Louisiana **11** Mississippi

Bay Psalm Book
author: **9** John Eliot

Bay State
nickname of:
13 Massachusetts

bazaar, bazar 4 fair, mart **6** market **8** carnival, exchange **11** charity fair, charity sale, marketplace

Bazile
character in: **18** The Barber of Seville
author: **12** Beaumarchais

Bazzard, Deputy
character in: **22** The Mystery of Edwin Drood
author: **7** Dickens

B C
creator: **10** Johnny Hart
character: **3** Tor **4** Grog **5** Peter **8** anteater **10** Clumsy Carp **11** the Fat Broad
poet: **5** Wiley
era: **11** Neanderthal, prehistoric

be 4 last, live, stay **5** exist, occur **6** befall, endure, happen, remain **7** persist, subsist **8** continue **9** be present, take place **10** come to pass

be absent 4 miss **12** fail to attend

beach 5 coast, shore **6** strand **8** littoral, seashore **10** water's edge

Beach, Rex
author of: **6** The Net **7** Oh Shoot **8** Pardners **9** Going Some **10** Jungle Gold, The Barrier **11** Don Careless, The Spoilers **12** Son of the Gods **13** The Goose Woman, The Ne'er-do-well **15** The Auction Block **17** Alaskan Adventures

beached 7 aground **8** grounded, stranded **11** shipwrecked **12** washed ashore

beacon 4 beam **5** light **6** pharos, signal **7** seamark **8** bale-fire, landmark **9** watch fire **10** lighthouse, watchtower **11** lighted buoy

bead 3 dot **4** blob, drop, pill **5** speck **6** bubble, pellet **7** droplet, globule **8** particle, spherule

be adequate 2 do **6** answer **8** be enough **10** pass muster

12 be sufficient, do well enough **14** be satisfactory

be afraid of 4 fear **5** dread **7** cower at **8** cringe at **10** shrink from

beak 3 neb, tip **4** bill, nose, pike, prow **5** lorum, snout, spout **7** process, rostrum, snozzle **8** hooknose **9** headmaster, proboscis **10** magistrate

beaker 3 cup **5** glass **6** vessel **9** container

beam 3 ray **4** emit, glow, prop, spar, stud **5** brace, glare, gleam, glint, joist, shine, width **6** girder, rafter, streak, stream, timber **7** breadth, expanse, glimmer, glitter, radiate, trestle **8** transmit **9** broadcast, radiation

bean 9 Phaseolus
varieties: **3** Goa, Pea, Soy, Wax, Yam **4** Jack, Lima, Moth, Mung, Rice, Seim, Snap, Soja, Soya, Tick, Wild **5** Azuki, Black, Broad, Civet, Coral, Field, Green, Horse, Lubia, Pinto, Salad, Screw, Sewee, Sieva, Snail, Sword, Tonka **6** Butter, Castor, Common, French, Indian, Kaffir, Kidney, Lablab, Locust, Manila, Mescal, Nicker, Potato, Romano, Runner, Sacred, String, Tepary, Velvet, Winged, Wonder **7** Cluster, English, Sarawak, Windsor **8** Bovanist, Bush lima, Carolina, Cherokee, European, Egyptian, Hyacinth, Yard-long **9** Algarroba, Asparagus, Bonavista, Dwarf lima, Java glory **10** Dwarf sieva, Giant stock, Hottentot's **12** Italian queen, Scarlet flame **13** African locust, Florida velvet, Scarlet runner **14** Dutch case-knife **16** White Dutch runner

be a party to 3 aid **4** abet **7** support **9** connive in **11** cooperate in **13** be accessory to, participate in

be apparent 6 appear **7** be clear, be plain **8** be patent **9** be evident, be obvious **10** be manifest

bear 4 bend, drop, give, haul, have, lead, push, show, take, tend, tote, turn, wear **5** abide, admit, allow, apply, brace, brave, bring, brook, carry, curve, drive, force, hatch, press, refer, spawn, stand, whelp, yield **6** affect, aim for, convey, convoy, create, endure, escort, go with, harbor, invite, permit, relate, render, suffer, take on, uphold **7** bol-

ster, cherish, concern, conduct, contain, deliver, develop, deviate, display, diverge, exhibit, pertain, possess, produce, stomach, support, sustain, undergo, warrant **8** bear down, engender, generate, maintain, manifest, shoulder, submit to, tolerate, transfer, underpin **9** accompany, appertain, encourage, germinate, hold close, propagate, put up with, reproduce, touch upon, transport **10** bring forth, keep in mind **11** give birth to, hold up under

bear
combining form: **4** arct, ursi **5** arcto
constellation: **4** ursa **9** ursa major, ursa minor
family: **7** Ursidae
group of: **6** sleuth
kind: **3** sun **5** black, brown, koala, malay, panda, polar, sloth **6** kodiak, wombat **7** grizzly **9** roachback, silvertip **10** spectacled, thalarctos
male: **4** boar
mythological: **8** Callisto
order: **9** carnivora
young: **3** cub

beard 4 dare, defy, face, trap **5** brave **6** confront **7** stubble **8** bristles, confront, whiskers **10** bring to bay **16** five-o'clock shadow

bearded 5 bushy, hairy **6** shaggy **7** bristly, hirsute **8** unshaven **9** whiskered **11** bewhiskered

bear down 4 push **5** press **13** apply pressure

bear down upon 6 assail, attack, come at **7** assault **11** descend upon

Beardsley, Aubrey Vincent
born: **7** England **8** Brighton
artwork: **6** Salome **10** Lysistrata **12** Morte d'Arthur

Beard's Roman Women
author: **14** Anthony Burgess

bearer 5 Atlas **6** holder, porter **7** carrier **8** conveyer, producer **9** messenger **13** beast of burden **16** one holding a check
Spanish: **8** escudero, portador

bear fruit 4 bear **6** mature **7** develop, prosper **8** fructify

bearing 3 air **4** mien, port **5** sense **6** import, manner **7** concern, meaning **8** attitude, behavior, breeding, carriage, demeanor, presence, relation **9** producing, reference, relevance **10** conception, connection, deportment, importance, pertinence **11** application, association, comportment, germination, giving birth, procreation, propagation, reproducing **12** relationship, reproduction, significance **13** applicability

bearing no name 7 unnamed **8** unsigned **9** anonymous

bearings 3 way **6** course **8** position **9** direction **11** orientation **16** sense of direction

bearish 5 cross, gruff, surly, testy **6** crusty, sullen **7** brusque, crabbed, grouchy **8** churlish **9** crotchety, irascible **10** ill-humored, out of sorts **11** ill-tempered, pessimistic **12** cantankerous

bear off 5 seize, steal **6** abduct, convey, kidnap

bear out 5 prove **6** verify **7** confirm **11** corroborate **12** substantiate

Bear State
nickname of: **8** Arkansas

bear up under 4 bear, take **5** abide, brave, brook, stand **6** endure, suffer **7** stomach, undergo, weather **9** go through, withstand

bear witness 4 back **6** attest **7** confirm, testify **11** corroborate, demonstrate **12** give evidence, substantiate

beast 3 cad, cur, pig, rat **4** ogre **5** brute, swine **6** animal, mammal, savage **8** creature **9** barbarian, quadruped

beastly 3 bad **4** vile **5** awful, cruel, gross, lousy, nasty **6** brutal, coarse, savage **7** bestial, brutish, inhuman, swinish **8** degraded, dreadful, terrible **9** barbarous, loathsome, monstrous **10** abominable, deplorable, disgusting, unpleasant **12** contemptible, disagreeable

beat 3 bat, hit, mix, rap, tap, way **4** area, bang, best, blow, cane, club, drub, flap, flog, flop, lick, maul, path, rout, slap, time, whip, zone **5** clout, count, crush, flail, knock, meter, outdo, pound, pulse, punch, quake, quell, realm, repel, route, shake, smack, smite, strap, throb, whack **6** accent, batter, course, defeat, domain, hammer, master, pummel, quiver, rhythm, rounds, stress, strike, stroke, subdue, switch, thrash, thwack, twitch, wallop **7** cadence, circuit, clobber, conquer, destroy, eclipse, flutter,

pulsate, put down, repulse, scourge, shellac, surpass, trounce, vibrate, win over **8** overcome, vanquish **9** excel over, fluctuate, go pit-a-pat, overpower, palpitate, pulsation, territory **10** win out over **11** predominate, prevail over, triumph over **14** stir vigorously

beat a retreat 6 beat it **7** back off **8** turn tail, withdraw **10** high tail it

beat around the bush 5 dodge, evade, hedge, stall **10** equivocate, mince words

beatific 4 rapt **6** divine, serene **7** angelic, exalted, saintly, sublime **8** blissful, ecstatic, glorious, heavenly **9** rapturous **10** enraptured **14** transcendental

beat it 2 go **3** out **4** away, scat, shoo **5** be off, leave, scram **6** begone, cut out, depart, get out, go away **7** get lost, vamoose **10** hit the road, make tracks

beatitude 5 bliss **7** ecstasy, rapture **8** euphoria, felicity **10** exaltation **11** blessedness, exaltedness, saintliness **13** transcendence **15** transfiguration

be at loggerheads 5 clash **7** quarrel **8** disagree

be at odds 6 differ **7** dispute, diverge **8** conflict, disagree

beat rhythmically 3 rap, tap **4** drum **6** tattoo **7** pulsate

Beatrice
character in: **12** Divine Comedy
author: **5** Dante

Beatrice
character in: **19** Much Ado About Nothing
author: **11** Shakespeare

Beatrice et Benedict
opera by: **7** Berlioz

Beat the Clock
host: **10** Bud Collyer

Beattie, Ann
author of: **11** Distortions **14** Falling in Place **15** The Burning House **19** Secrets and Surprises **20** Chilly Scenes of Winter

Beatty, Warren
real name: **11** Warren Beaty
sister: **15** Shirley MacLaine
born: **10** Richmond VA
roles: **4** Reds **11** All Fall Down **13** Heaven Can Wait **14** Bonnie and Clyde **18** Splendor in the Grass

24 The Roman Spring of Mrs Stone
director of: **4** Reds (Oscar)

beat up 3 mug **4** lick, maul, whip **6** batter, pummel **7** assault, clobber

beat-up 4 shot **6** shabby **7** worn-out **8** battered **10** broken-down **11** dilapidated

Beaty, Shirley MacLean
real name of: **15** Shirley MacLaine

Beaty, Warren
real name of: **12** Warren Beatty

beau, beaux 3 fop, guy, nob **4** buck, dude, love, stud, toff **5** blade, dandy, flame, lover, Romeo, spark, swain, swell, wooer **6** adorer, escort, fellow, fiance, garcon, squire, steady, suitor **7** admirer, beloved, courter, coxcomb, cupidon, Don Juan, gallant, playboy **8** cavalier, courtier, gay blade, Lothario, paramour, popinjay, true love, young man **9** betrothed, boyfriend, courtesan, gentleman, inamorato, ladies' man **10** sweetheart, young blood **15** gentleman caller, gentleman friend
nickname of: **14** George Brummell

Beauchamp's Career
author: **14** George Meredith

Beau Geste
author: **6** P C Wren **15** Christopher Wren
director: **14** William Wellman
cast: **10** Gary Cooper, Ray Milland **12** Brian Donlevy, Susan Hayward **13** Robert Preston
silent version starred: **12** Ronald Colman
setting: **19** French Foreign Legion

Beaumarchais, Pierre Augustin Caron de
author of: **18** The Barber of Seville **19** The Marriage of Figaro

beau monde 5 elite **6** gentry **7** society **10** upper class, upper crust **11** aristocracy, high society **15** beautiful people

Beaumont, Ned
character in: **11** The Glass Key
author: **7** Hammett

Beauregard, P G T (Pierre Gustave Toutant)
served in: **8** Civil War
side: **11** Confederate
rank: **7** general

ordered firing on: 8 Ft Sumter
battle: 7 Bull Run

beaut 4 lulu **5** daisy, dandy **6** beauty **7** stunner **8** knockout **10** good-looker

beautification 9 adornment **10** decoration **13** embellishment, ornamentation

beautiful 4 fair, fine **5** bonny, great **6** comely, lovely, pretty, seemly, superb, worthy **7** radiant **8** alluring, gorgeous, handsome, pleasing, splendid, very good **9** admirable, beauteous, enjoyable, estimable, excellent, exquisite, first-rate, ravishing, wonderful **10** attractive, stupendous **11** captivating, commendable, fine-looking, good-looking, resplendent **15** pulchritudinous

beautify 4 do up **5** adorn, grace **7** dress up, enhance, gussy up, improve **8** ornament **9** embellish, glamorize

beauty 4 boon, doll **5** asset, beaut, belle, grace, Venus **6** eyeful, looker **7** benefit, feature, goddess, stunner **8** knockout, radiance, splendor **9** advantage, good looks, good thing **10** attraction, excellence, good-looker, loveliness **11** pulchritude **12** handsomeness, magnificence, resplendence **14** attractiveness
goddess of: 6 Graces **7** Gratiae **9** Aphrodite, Charities
god of: 5 Baldr **6** Apollo, Balder, Baldur **7** Angus Og, Phoebus, Pythias **9** Musagetes

Beauvoir, Simone de
author of: 12 The Mandarins, The Second Sex **14** A Very Easy Death, All Said and Done, The Coming of Age, The Prime of Life **17** Ethics of Ambiguity **22** The Force of Circumstance **25** Memoirs of a Dutiful Daughter **34** Brigitte Bardot and the Lolita Syndrome

beaver
young: 3 kit

Beaver State
nickname of: 6 Oregon

be blessed with 3 own **4** have **5** enjoy **7** possess **16** have the benefit of

because 2 so **3** for **4** that, then, thus **5** cause, hence, since **6** whence **7** whereas **8** inasmuch **9** therefore **10** seeing that **11** considering

Bechuanaland
now called: 8 Botswana

beck 3 bid **4** call **7** bidding, summons **9** summoning

Becket
author: 11 Jean Anouilh **18** Alfred Lord Tennyson
director: 14 Peter Glenville
cast: 11 John Gielgud, Peter O'Toole (King Henry II) **13** Richard Burton (Becket)

Beckett, Samuel
author of: 4 Not I, Play, Watt **6** Embers, Molloy **7** Endgame **8** That Time **9** Footfalls, Happy Days **10** Malone Dies **11** All that Fall, The Lost Ones **13** The Unnameable **15** Waiting for Godot **16** Mercier and Camier **20** Murphy Krapp's Last Tape **25** Stories and Texts for Nothing

Beckmann, Max
born: 7 Germany, Leipzig
artwork: 6 Kasbek **7** Perseus **8** Acrobats, The Night **9** The Actors **11** View of Genoa **12** Charnel House, The Argonauts, The Departure **13** Blindman's Buff, Family Picture **14** Double Portrait **17** David and Bathsheba **18** Odysseus and Calypso **19** Sinking of the Titanic **20** Destruction of Messina **22** The Descent from the Cross

beckon 4 call, coax, draw, lure, pull **6** allure, entice, invite, motion, signal, summon, wave at, wave on **7** attract, gesture **11** gesticulate **14** crook a finger at

be clear 6 appear **7** be plain **8** be patent **9** be evident, be obvious **10** be apparent, be manifest

becloud 3 fog **4** blur, hide, veil **5** befog, cloud **6** muddle, screen, shroud **7** confuse, cover up, eclipse, obscure **8** confound, make hazy, overcast **9** obfuscate **10** camouflage, overshadow **14** make indistinct

become 3 get **4** grow, suit, turn **6** go with **7** enhance, flatter, get to be **8** come to be **9** agree with, begin to be **10** complement **11** be reduced to, turn out to be

become apparent 4 dawn, loom **5** arise **6** appear, crop up, emerge, turn up **7** develop, surface

become bigger 4 grow

5 swell **6** expand **7** develop, enlarge, inflate **8** increase

become irrational 5 break, crack **7** crack up **9** break down, fall apart, go berserk **10** go to pieces **11** lose control **12** lose one's mind

become one 3 wed **4** fuse **5** blend, marry, merge, unite **7** combine **8** coalesce **10** amalgamate **11** consolidate

become seasoned to 5 adapt, inure **6** adjust **8** accustom **9** acclimate, get used to, habituate **15** learn to live with

become smaller 6 lessen, shrink **7** decline, dwindle, shrivel **8** decrease, diminish

become visible 4 loom, show **6** appear, crop up, emerge, show up, turn up **7** surface **11** come to light **12** come into view

becoming 3 apt, fit **4** meet **6** pretty, proper, seemly, worthy **7** fitting **8** suitable **9** befitting, congenial, congruous, enhancing, in keeping **10** attractive, compatible, consistent, flattering, harmonious **11** appropriate, good-looking

Becquerel, Antoine Henri
field: 7 physics
nationality: 6 French
discovered: 13 radioactivity
awarded: 10 Nobel Prize

bed 3 cot, hay **4** band, bank, base, belt, bunk, crib, lode, plot, sack, seam, zone **5** berth, floor, layer, patch **6** bottom, cradle, pallet **7** deposit, stratum **8** bedstead **10** foundation

bedazzle 4 daze **6** dazzle **7** astound, confuse, enchant, fluster, nonplus, stagger, stupefy **8** befuddle, bewilder, confound, dumfound **9** captivate, overpower, overwhelm **10** disconcert **11** flabbergast **19** sweep one off one's feet

bed chamber 7 bedroom, boudoir

bed down 5 sleep **7** lie down, sack out **8** doss down **10** hit the hay, settle down **11** accommodate, hit the sack

bedeck 4 deck, trim **5** adorn, array **7** garnish **8** decorate, ornament **9** embellish

be deficient in 4 fail, lack, want **7** be scant **9** be short of **10** have too few

be deprived of 4 lack, lose, want

be deserving of 4 earn, rate

5 merit 7 deserve 10 be worthy of 12 be entitled to

bedevil 3 dog 5 annoy, hound, worry 6 badger, harass, pester, plague 9 beleaguer

be devoted to 4 love 5 adore 6 dote on 7 cherish 8 be fond of

bedim 4 blur 6 darken 7 obscure

Bedivere
    character in: 16 Arthurian romance

bedizen 5 adorn, array 6 bedeck, rig out 7 bejewel, costume

bedlam 5 chaos 6 tumult, uproar 7 turmoil 8 madhouse 11 pandemonium

bed of justice
    French: 12 lit de justice

Bedouin, Beduin
    also: 4 Absi, Arab 5 nomad 7 bedawee
    Arabic: 6 badawi
        means: 13 desert dweller
    found in: 5 Egypt, Syria 6 Arabia 11 North Africa
    religion: 5 Islam

bedraggled 4 limp 5 dirty, dowdy, messy, seedy, soggy, tacky, tatty 6 blowsy, frowsy, frumpy, matted, ragtag, sloppy, soiled, untidy 7 unkempt 8 frumpish, sluttish, tattered 10 disarrayed, disordered, disheveled, slatternly, threadbare 11 disarranged 13 draggletailed 14 down-at-the-heels, out-at-the-elbows

bedridden 7 invalid 8 disabled, immobile 13 incapacitated

bedroom 7 boudoir, chamber 10 bedchamber

bedspread 5 quilt 8 bedcover, coverlet 9 comforter

bedstead 3 bed 8 bed frame 10 four poster

bee
    caste: 5 drone, queen 6 worker
    classification: 6 social 8 solitary
    communication: 13 dance language
    family: 6 Apidae 7 Apoidea 8 Bombidae 10 Andrenidae, Halictidae 11 Meliponidae, Xylocopidae 12 Megachilidae
    group of: 5 grist, swarm
    order: 11 Hymenoptera
    scent: 10 pheromones
    variety: 5 mason, miner 6 alkali, cuckoo 8 burrower, honeybee 9 bumblebee, car-

penter, plasterer 10 leafcutter 11 yellow-faced

beech 5 Fagus
    varieties: 4 Blue 5 Water 6 Copper, Purple 7 Cut-leaf, Weeping 8 American, European, Fern-leaf, Japanese

Beedle, William Franklin, Jr,
    real name of: 13 William Holden

beef 4 heft, kick, meat 5 brawn, gripe, steer 6 cattle, grouch, grouse 7 grumble 8 complain 9 bellyache, complaint, criticize, find fault

Beef State
    nickname of: 8 Nebraska

beefy 5 bulky, burly, hefty 6 brawny, robust 8 thickset 9 strapping

beehive 4 hive 6 apiary 9 busy place 10 powerhouse

Beehive State
    nickname of: 4 Utah

Beekeeping
    god of: 9 Aristaeus

Beelzebub
    character in: 12 Paradise Lost
    author: 6 Milton

be enough 2 do 6 answer 7 suffice

be entitled to 4 rate 5 merit 7 deserve 10 be worthy of 13 be deserving of

beer-bust 4 toot 5 binge, drunk, spree 6 bender 8 carousal 9 bacchanal

Beery, Noah
    brother: 7 Wallace
    son: 6 Noah Jr
    born: 12 Kansas City MO
    roles: 7 Lord Jim, The Dove 9 Beau Geste 10 The Sea Wolf 14 The Mark of Zorro

Beery, Wallace
    brother: 4 Noah
    nephew: 6 Noah Jr
    wife: 13 Gloria Swanson
    born: 12 Kansas City MO
    roles: 8 The Champ (Oscar) 9 The Bowery, Viva Villa 10 Grand Hotel 11 The Big House 13 Dinner at Eight 14 Treasure Island 15 The Mighty Barnum 16 A Message to Garcia

beet 12 Beta vulgaris
    varieties: 3 Red, Sea 4 Leaf, Wild 5 Sugar 6 Garden, Yellow 7 Spinach

Beethoven, Ludwig van
    born: 4 Bonn 7 Germany
    composer of: 5 Laube (sonata) 6 Egmont, Eroica (symphony no 3), Spring (sonata) 7 Fidelio, Leonore 8 Coriolan, Dramatic (sonata), Kreutzer (sonata), Pastoral (symphony no 6), The Storm 9 Moonlight (sonata), Pastorale (sonata), Waldstein (sonata) 10 Bagatellen, Great Fugue (no 133), Pathetique

beer 3 ale, keg, mum 4 bier, bock, brew, dark, faro, flip, gail, grog, gyle, hops, kvas, malt, mild, quas, scud, suds 5 chang, chica, draft, grout, kvass, lager, light, quass, scuds, stout, weiss 6 bitter, chicha, double, gatter, porter, spruce, stingo, swanky, swipes, wallop, zythum 7 bottled, cerveza, pangasi, pharaoh, Pilsner, tankard, taplash, tapwort 8 bock beer, cervisia, near beer, pilsener 10 malt liquor
    add to beer: 7 krausen
    bad/inferior beer: 4 tack 5 belch 6 swanky 7 taplash
    brand: 5 Beck's, Coors, Pabst, Piels 6 Miller, Molson, Stroh's 7 Schlitz 8 Bud Light, Michelob 9 Budweiser, Lowenbrau 10 Miller Lite, Molson Gold 13 Guinness Stout 15 Pabst Blue Ribbon
    cask: 4 butt
    cup: 3 mug 4 toby 5 glass, stein 6 flagon, seidel 7 tankard 8 schooner 9 blackjack
    hot beer and gin: 4 purl
    ingredient: 4 hops, malt 5 yeast 6 barley
    maker: 6 brewer 8 brewster, maltster
    mythological inventor: 9 Gambrinus
    quantity of: 3 keg 4 case 7 six-pack
    small beer: 4 tiff 5 grout
    sour beer: 4 kuas, kvas 5 quash, quass 8 beeregar
    thin beer: 6 pritch, swipes
    Tibetan beer: 5 chang
    warm beer and oatmeal: 6 storry
    with whiskey: 11 Boilermaker

(sonata), Spirit Trio
11 Grosse Fugue (no 133),
Harp Quartet (no 74), Na-
mensfeier **12** Appassionata
(sonata), Archduke Trio,
Konig Stephan **13** Ham-
merklavier (sonata), Missa
Solemnis **15** Emperor Concerto (No 5) **16** Christus am
Olberg, The Mount of Ol-
ives, The Ruins of Athens
17 Die Ruinen von Athen,
Die Weihe des Hauses
18 An die ferne Geliebte,
Rage over a Lost Penny
20 Rasoumoffsky Quartets
(no 59) **24** The Creatures of
Prometheus **25** Die Ge-
schopfe des Prometheus

beetle
variety: **3** bog, may, sap
4 bark, bean, flea, leaf,
mold, moss, pill, rove, sand,
stag **5** cedar, click, flour,
grain, marsh, penny, tiger,
water **6** beaver, diving,
flower, fungus, ground, his-
ter, lizard, spider, weevil
7 bessbug, blister, burying,
carrion, firefly, goldbug, goliath, ladybug, soldier **8** elephant, glowworm, hercules,
Japanese, ladybird, tortoise
9 ant loving, bombadier,
burrowing, checkered, fruit-
worm, goldsmith, grassroot,
scavenger, tumblebug, whirligig **10** deathwatch, false
clown, longhorned, mammal
nest, shiptimber **11** reticu-
lated, trout stream **12** ant-
like stone, lightning bug
13 feather winged, horseshoe crab

Beetle Bailey
creator/artist: **9** Dik
Browne **10** Mort Walker
12 Bob Gustafson
character: **5** Cosmo, Plato
6 Killer, Lt Flap, Lt Fuzz
10 Miss Buxley **12** Gen
Halftrack **17** Sgt Orville
Snorkel
chef: **6** Cookie
place: **10** Camp Swampy

be evident 6 appear **7** be
clear, be plain **8** be patent
9 be obvious **10** be apparent,
be manifest

befall 5 ensue, occur **6** betide,
chance, follow, happen
10 come to pass
11 materialize

befitting 3 apt, fit **5** right
6 decent, proper, seemly **8** becoming, relevant, suitable
11 appropriate

be fond of 6 dote on **11** be
devoted to **12** be in love with

before 3 ere, yet **5** afore,

ahead, prior **6** rather, sooner
7 already, earlier, vis-a-vis
8 erewhile, until now **9** in advance, in front of, in sight
of **10** face-to-face, previously

before Christ
abbreviation: **2** BC
Latin: **2** AC **12** ante Christum

beforehand 6 in time, sooner
7 earlier **9** in advance
11 ahead of time

before now 6 in time,
sooner **7** earlier **9** in advance

before the fact 6 in time
9 in advance **10** beforehand
11 ahead of time

before the public
Latin: **11** coram populo

befoul 4 soil **5** dirty, smear,
stain, sully, taint **6** defile, poison **7** blacken, corrupt, pollute, tarnish **8** besmirch
9 desecrate **11** contaminate

befriend 4 help **6** assist, defend, succor, uphold **7** comfort, embrace, help out,
protect, stand by, stick by,
support, sustain, welcome
8 side with **9** give aid to, look
after **10** minister to **11** consort
with **13** associate with
14 fraternize with, sympathize
with **17** take under one's
wing

be friends 7 consort **9** associate, pal around **10** fraternize

befringe 3 hem **4** bind, edge,
trim **6** border **7** festoon
8 decorate

befuddle 4 daze **5** addle, mix
up **6** baffle, muddle, puzzle,
rattle **7** confuse, fluster, perplex, stupefy **8** bewilder, confound, unsettle **9** disorient,
inebriate, make drunk, make
tipsy **10** intoxicate, make
groggy **11** disorganize

beg 3 bum, sue **4** pray, shun
5 avert, avoid, cadge, dodge,
evade, mooch, parry, plead,
shirk **6** escape, eschew, hustle,
sponge **7** beseech, entreat,
fend off, implore, solicit **8** appeal to, petition, sidestep
9 importune, panhandle
10 supplicate

beg, bey 4 lord **6** prince
8 governor

beget 3 get **4** sire **5** breed,
cause, spawn **6** effect, father,
lead to **7** produce **8** engender,
generate, occasion, result in
9 call forth, procreate, propagate **10** bring about, give rise
to

begetter 4 sire **6** father **7** creator **9** generator **10** progenitor

beggar 3 bum, guy **4** chap
5 devil, tramp **6** baffle, fellow
7 almsman, moocher, sponger,
surpass **8** be beyond **9** challenge, mendicant
10 panhandler

Beggar 7 Lazarus

Beggar's Opera, The
author: **7** John Gay
form: **11** ballad opera
character: **6** Lockit **10** Lucy
Lockit **12** Polly Peachum
15 Captain Macheath

begin 5 arise, found, start **6** be
born, crop up, emerge,
launch, set out **8** break out,
commence, embark on, initi-
ate **9** establish, institute, introduce, originate, undertake
10 burst forth, inaugurate
11 set in motion **16** take the
first step

beginner 4 babe, tyro **6** author, father, novice, rookie
7 creator, founder, learner,
starter, student **8** freshman,
neophyte **9** fledgling, greenhorn, initiator, organizer
10 apprentice, originator,
prime mover, tenderfoot
11 inaugurator **14** babe in the
woods

beginning 3 new **4** germ, seed
5 birth, onset, start **6** embryo,
novice, origin, outset, source,
spring **7** kickoff, student, untried **8** neophyte, zero hour
9 embryonic, inception, incipient, launching **10** foundation,
wellspring **11** preliminary,
springboard **12** commencement, fountainhead, inauguration, introduction
13 inexperienced, starting
point
Latin: **12** terminus a quo

Beginning of Wisdom, The
author: **19** Stephen Vincent
Benet

Beginnings
god of: **5** Janus

begone 3 out **4** away, scat,
shoo **5** be off, leave, scram
6 beat it, depart, get out, go
away **7** get lost, vamoose

begonia
varieties: **3** Rex, Wax **4** Fern,
King, Star, Wild **5** Hardy,
Trout **6** Bamboo, Kidney,
Shrimp, Winter, Zigzag
7 Bedding, Dewdrop, Elm-
leaf, Eyelash, Fuchsia, Leopard, Lily-pad, Swedish
8 Climbing, Fern-leaf, Fire-
king, Lorraine, Palm-leaf,
Pond-lily, Star-leaf, Trailing
9 Alder-leaf, Angel-wing,
Beefsteak, Calla-lily, Christmas, Crazy-leaf, Grape-leaf,

Grapevine, Hollyhock, Holly-leaf, Honey-bear, Iron-cross, Maple-leaf, Miniature, Pennywort, Trout-leaf, Whirlpool **10** Bronze-leaf, Castor-bean, Finger-leaf, Guinea-wing, Seersucker, Strawberry **11** Fairy-carpet, Lettuce-leaf, Painted-leaf **12** Blooming-fool, Elephant's Ear, Metallic-leaf **13** Peanut-brittle **14** Hybrid tuberous, Nasturtium-leaf, Youth-and-old-age **15** Winter-flowering **16** Manda's woolly-bear, Philodendron-leaf **17** Miniature pond-lily **18** Trailing watermelon

beg pardon 6 excuse **9** apologize **13** express regret, say one is sorry

be grateful 9 be obliged **10** appreciate, be beholden, be thankful **11** be obligated

begrime 4 soil **5** dirty, muddy, smear, stain, sully **6** smudge, soot up **7** besmear, tarnish

begrimed 5 dirty, grimy, muddy **6** filthy, grubby, soiled **7** unclean **8** unwashed **9** tarnished

begrudge 4 envy **5** covet **6** grudge, resent **11** be jealous of, hold against

beguile 4 dupe, hoax, lull, lure **5** amuse, charm, cheat, cheer, trick **6** delude, divert, occupy, please **7** bewitch, deceive, enchant, ensnare **8** distract, hoodwink **9** bamboozle, captivate, entertain **10** lead astray

beguiling 7 winning, winsome **8** charming, magnetic **9** appealing, disarming **10** bewitching, entrancing **11** captivating **12** ingratiating, irresistible

behalf 3 aid, for **4** part, side **5** favor **7** benefit, by proxy, defense, in aid of, support **8** interest

Behan, Brendan
author of: **10** Borstal Boy, The Hostage **12** The Scarperer **14** The Quare Fellow **25** Confessions of an Irish Rebel

be handed down 4 pass **7** descend **11** be inherited

behave 3 act **13** acquit oneself, deport oneself **14** comport oneself, conduct oneself, control oneself

behavior 4 acts **5** deeds **6** action, habits, manner **7** actions, bearing, conduct, control **8** activity, attitude, demeanor,

practice, reaction, response **9** operation **10** deportment **11** comportment, functioning, performance, self-control

behead 9 decollate **10** decapitate, guillotine **15** bring to the block

behest 4 fiat **5** edict, order, say-so **6** charge, decree, ruling **7** bidding, command, dictate, mandate **9** direction, ultimatum **10** injunction **11** instruction

behind 4 rump, seat, slow **5** abaft, after, fanny **8** backward, buttocks, in back of **9** fundament, in arrears **11** to the rear of **12** hindquarters

behind closed doors 7 sub rosa **8** in secret, secretly **9** in private, privately

behindhand 4 late, slow **5** tardy **7** belated **8** backward **10** unpunctual

behind the times 5 passe **7** archaic **9** out-of-date **10** antiquated **12** old-fashioned

behind time 4 late, slow **5** tardy **7** belated, delayed **12** after the fact

behold 3 see **4** heed, look, mark, note, scan, view **5** watch **6** attend, gaze at, look at, notice, regard, survey **7** discern, examine, inspect, observe, stare at, witness **8** look upon **10** scrutinize **11** contemplate **12** pay attention

beholden 5 bound **6** liable **7** obliged **8** indebted **9** obligated **10** answerable, in one's debt **11** accountable, responsible **15** under obligation

behold the man
Latin: **8** ecce homo
said by: **13** Pontius Pilate
spoken of: **6** Christ

behoove 4 suit **5** be apt, befit **6** become, be wise **7** benefit **8** be proper **9** be fitting **11** be advisable, be necessary **13** be appropriate **14** be advantageous

Behring, Emil Adolph von
field: **12** bacteriology
nationality: **6** German
developed: **19** diphtheria antitoxin
awarded: **10** Nobel Prize

beige 3 tan **4** ecru, fawn **6** greige **8** brownish

be ill 3 ail **6** be sick **8** be unwell **12** be indisposed **13** be in ill health

be in a class with 5 equal,

match **6** be up to **7** compare **8** approach **10** be as good as **11** compete with **12** be comparable, be on a par with **13** hold a candle to

being 4 core, life, soul **5** human **6** living, mortal, nature, person, psyche, spirit **7** essence, persona, reality **8** creature, existing **9** actuality, existence **10** individual, occurrence **11** subsistence

be inherited 4 pass **7** descend **12** be handed down

be in short supply 4 lack, want **8** be scanty, be scarce **9** fall short

be intemperate 7 carouse, debauch **9** dissipate **11** overindulge

be in tune 4 jibe **5** agree, match, tally **6** accord, square **7** conform **9** harmonize

Beirut, Beyrouth
capital of: **7** Lebanon
Phoenician name: **7** Berytus
sea: **13** Mediterranean
settled by: **11** Phoenicians

be jealous of 4 envy **6** resent **8** begrudge

Bekesy, Georg von
field: **7** physics
researched: **3** ear **7** cochlea, hearing
awarded: **10** Nobel Prize

Bel 3 god **5** deity

Bela
father: **4** Beor
brother: **6** Balaam

belabor 6 rehash, repeat **7** dwell on **9** reiterate **11** pound away at **12** hammer away at, recapitulate **14** beat a dead horse

Bel-Ami
author: **15** Guy de Maupassant

Belarus
other name: **10** Belorussia **11** Byelorussia, White Russia
capital/largest city: **5** Minsk
head of state: **9** president
government: **8** republic
monetary unit: **5** ruble
river: **5** Dvina **7** Dnieper
physical feature: **13** Pripet Marshes
people: **12** Byelorussian

Belasco, David
author of: **7** DuBarry **15** Madame Butterfly **21** The Return of Peter Grimm **22** The Girl of the Golden West

belated 4 late, slow **5** tardy **6** behind **7** delayed, overdue, past due **8** deferred **10** behindhand, behind time, unpunctual **12** after the fact

belch 4 burp, emit, gush, spew, vent **5** eject, eruct, erupt, expel, issue, spout, spurt, vomit **7** cough up, issuing **8** disgorge, ejection, emission, eruption

9 discharge, roar forth, send forth **10** eructation

Belch, Sir Toby
character in: **12** Twelfth Night
author: **11** Shakespeare

beleaguer 3 vex **5** annoy **6** assail, badger, bother, harass,

hector, pester, plague **7** besiege, bombard **8** blockade, surround

bel-esprit 3 wit **12** intellectual

belfry 4 dome **5** spire **7** steeple **9** bell tower, campanile

Belgian Congo see **5** Zaire

Belgium
other name: 13 Gallia Belgica **15** Cockpit of Europe **16** Koninkrijk Belgie **17** Royaume de Belgique
capital/largest city: 8 Brussels **9** Bruxelles
others: 2 As **3** Aat, Ans, Ath, Hal, Huy, Mol, Spa **4** Aath, Amay, Asse, Boom, Bree, Doel, Gaud, Geel, Genk, Gent, Hoei, Lier, Looz, Mons, Vise, Waha, Zele **5** Aalst, Alost, Arlon, Ciney, Ecklo, Essen, Eupen, Evere, Genck, Ghent, Heist, Ieper, Jette, Jumet, Liege, Namur, Ronse, Tielt, Uccle, Vorst, Wezet, Ynoir, Ypres **6** Aarlen, Anvers, Bergen, Bilzen, Bruges, Deurne, Izegem, Leuven, Lierre, Merxem, Opwijk, Ostend **7** Antwerp, Ardooie, Berchem, Brabant, Hainaut, Herstal, Hoboken, Ixelles, Leliven, Limburg, Louvain, Malmedy, Mechlin, Roulers, Seraing, Tournai **8** Bastogne, Courtrai, Doorwick, Flanders, Kortrijk, Mouscron, Turnhout, Verviers, Waterloo **9** Antwerpen, Charleroi **10** Anderlecht, Borgerhout, Luxembourg, Quatrebras, Schaerbeek
school: 7 Louvain
division: 5 Liege, Namur **7** Antwerp, Brabant, Hainaut, Limburg **8** Flanders, Wallonia
head of state: 4 king
measure: 3 vat **4** aune, pied **5** carat **6** perche **8** boisseau
monetary unit: 5 belga, franc **7** brabant, centime, crocard
weight: 4 last **5** carat, livre **6** charge **7** chariot **8** esterlin
mountain: 8 Ardennes
highest point: 16 Signal de Botrange
river: 3 Lys **4** Dyle, Leie, Maas, Mark, Yser **5** Boucq, Demer, Lesse, Meuse, Nethe, Rupel, Senne **6** Dender, Escaut, Manjel, Ourthe, Sambre, Semois, Vesdre, Warche **7** Ambleve, Schelde, Scheldt
sea: 5 North
physical feature:
  canal: **4** Yser **5** Union **6** Albert **7** Campine
  cave: **7** Furfooz **8** Grenelle
  forest: **8** Ardennes
  plateau: **8** Hohevenn
people: 4 Remi **6** Nervii **7** Belgian, Fleming, Flemish **8** Walloons **9** Bellovaci
  artist: **5** Ensor **6** Rubens **7** Delvaux, Van Dyck, Van Eyck **8** Brueghel, Magritte
  author: **6** Coster **7** Simenon **9** Verhaeren **10** Conscience, Ghelderode **11** Maeterlinck
  composer: **6** Franck
  king: **6** Albert **7** Leopold **8** Baudouin
  leader: **5** Spaak **9** Tindemans
language: 5 Dutch **6** French, German **7** Flemish
religion: 13 Roman Catholic
place:
  battleground: **5** Bulge **8** Waterloo
  breadhouse: **9** Broodhuis
  castle: **5** Steen
  cathedral: **5** Ghent **13** Saint Rombauts
  city hall: **12** Hotel de Ville
  home for elderly women: **9** Beguinage
  museum: **9** Beaux Arts
  palace: **10** Gruuthuuse
features:
  horse: **9** Brabancon
  lace: **5** fichu **6** Bruges **7** Malines, Mechlin **8** Brussels
  lawn bowling: **6** boules
  linen: **7** brabant
  musical instrument: **8** carillon
  religious procession: **9** Holy Blood
  tapestry: **9** oudenarde
food:
  cheese: **9** Limburger
  gingerbread: **12** pain d'espices
  raisin bread: **8** cramique
  soup: **9** Waterzooi

Belgrade, Beograd
capital of: 10 Yugoslavia
landmark:
fortress: 10 Kalemegdan
parliament house:
9 Skupstina
name means: 11 white forest
river: 4 Sava 6 Danube
Roman fort: 10 Singidinum
Serbian: 7 Beograd

Belial
character in: 12 Paradise
Lost
author: 6 Milton

belie 4 defy, deny, mask
5 cloak 6 betray, negate, refute 7 conceal, falsify, gainsay 8 disguise, disprove
9 repudiate 10 camouflage,
contradict, controvert, invalidate 12 misrepresent

belief 4 view 5 faith, guess,
trust 6 theory 7 feeling, opinion 8 judgment, reliance 9 assurance, certitude, deduction,
inference 10 assumption, conclusion, confidence, conviction, firm notion, hypothesis,
impression, persuasion 11 expectation, presumption,
supposition

beliefs 5 canon, creed, dogma,
faith, tenet 6 ethics, gospel,
morals 8 doctrine, morality
9 principle, teachings 10 conviction, persuasion

believable 8 credible, knowable, possible 9 plausible, thinkable 10 acceptable, convincing,
imaginable, supposable
11 conceivable, perceivable

believe 4 hold 5 guess, infer,
judge, think, trust 6 assume,
credit, deduce, rely on 7 count
on, fall for, imagine, presume,
suppose, surmise, suspect,
swallow, swear by 8 be sure
of, consider, depend on, maintain, theorize 9 speculate
10 conjecture, presuppose, put
faith in 11 hypothesize

believe in 5 trust 6 accept, esteem 7 approve, go in for, respect 11 have faith in 16 have
confidence in

Believe It or Not
author: 13 Robert L Ripley

believer 7 admirer 8 advocate,
disciple, partisan 9 supporter
16 faithful adherent

be like 5 equal, match 8 approach, resemble

Bel-Imperia
character in: 17 The Spanish
Tragedy
author: 3 Kyd

Belinda
character in: 16 The Rape of
the Lock
author: 4 Pope

belittle 5 knock, scorn 6 deride, malign 7 disdain, put
down, run down, sneer at
8 minimize, mitigate, play
down, pooh-pooh 9 deprecate,
disparage, underrate 10 depreciate, undervalue 11 make
light of 13 underestimate
16 cast aspersions on

belittling 5 snide 10 derogatory 11 deprecating, disparaging, unfavorable
12 depreciating
15 uncomplimentary

Belize
other name: 15 British
Honduras
capital: 8 Belmopan
largest city/former capital: 10 Belize City
head of state: 13 prime
minister 14 British
monarch 15 governor-general
monetary unit: 6 dollar
island: 8 Turneffe
mountain range: 4 Maya
highest point: 12 Victoria Peak
river: 3 New 4 Moho
6 Belize, Monkey
sea: 9 Caribbean
physical feature:
gulf: 8 Honduras
peninsula: 7 Yucatan
swamp: 8 mangrove
people: 5 Mayan 6 Indian, Syrian 7 African,
Chinese 15 Spanish-American
language: 7 English

bell 4 gong, peal 5 chime
6 tocsin 7 ringing 8 carillon
16 tintinnabulation

Bell, Alexander Graham
born: 8 Scotland
inventor of: 9 telephone
14 record cylinder
saying: 24 Mr Watson come
here I want you

Bellamann, Henry
author of: 8 King's Row

Bellamy, Edward
author of: 8 Equality
15 Looking Backward

Bellamy, Ralph
born: 9 Chicago IL
roles: 11 Ellery Queen, Mike

Barnett 13 The Awful
Truth 14 Detective Story
15 Man Against Crime,
State of the Union 19 Sunrise at Campobello

Bellarius
character in: 9 Cymbeline
author: 11 Shakespeare

Bellaston, Lady
character in: 8 Tom Jones
author: 8 Fielding

bell buoy 5 float 6 signal
13 channel marker

belle 4 star 5 queen 6 beauty
7 charmer 12 heart-stopper

Belle Dame Sans Merci, La
author: 9 John Keats

Bellefleur
author: 15 Joyce Carol Oates

Belle Helene, La
also: 14 Beautiful Helen
operetta by: 9 Offenbach

Bellerophon
form: 4 hero
brother: 8 Deliades
son: 11 Hippolochus
home: 7 Corinth
rode: 7 Pegasus
killed: 7 Chimera

Bell for Adano, A
author: 10 John Hersey
director: 9 Henry King
cast: 10 John Hodiak
11 Gene Tierney 13 William
Bendix

bellicose see 11 belligerent

belligerence, belligerency
9 animosity, hostility, pugnacity 10 aggression, antagonism
11 bellicosity 12 warmongering 13 combativeness 14 aggressiveness, unfriendliness

belligerent 7 fighter, hostile,
martial, warlike, warring 8 attacker, inimical 9 adversary,
aggressor, bellicose, combatant, combative, irascible, irritable, truculent 10 aggressive,
antagonist, pugnacious, unfriendly 11 bad-tempered, contentious, quarrelsome
12 antagonistic, cantankerous

belligerent state 3 foe 5 enemy 9 aggressor 13 hostile
nation

Bellini, Gentile
born: 5 Italy 6 Venice
father: 6 Jacopo
brother: 8 Giovanni
artwork: 24 The Miracle of
the True Cross 26 A Procession in St Mark's Square,
The Miracle at Ponte di
Lorenzo 27 St Mark Preaching in Alexandria 38 A
Procession of Relics in the
Piazza San Marco

Bellini, Giovanni (Giambellino)
born: 5 Italy 6 Venice
father: 6 Jacopo
brother: 7 Gentile
artwork: 8 St Jerome 16 Venus with a Mirror 18 St Francis in Ecstasy, The Madonna and Child 19 Allegory of Purgatory, The Agony in the Garden, The Barberini Madonna

Bellini, Jacopo
born: 5 Italy 6 Venice
son: 7 Gentile 8 Giovanni
artwork: 11 Crucifixion 16 Christ on the Cross 35 The Madonna and Child with Lionello d'Este

Bellini, Vincenzo
born: 5 Italy 7 Catania
composer of: 5 Norma, Zaira 8 Il Pirata 9 I Puritani 11 La Straniera 12 La Sonnambula 15 Bianca e Fernando

Bell Jar, The
author: 11 Sylvia Plath

Bellona
origin: 5 Roman
goddess of: 3 war
husband: 4 Mars
brother: 4 Mars
corresponds to: 4 Enyo

bellow 4 bawl, roar, yell 5 shout, whoop 6 holler, scream, shriek

Bellow, Saul
author of: 6 Herzog 13 Dean's December, Humboldt's Gift, Mosby's Memoirs 15 The Last Analysis 16 Mr Sammler's Planet 18 To Jerusalem and Back 25 The Adventures of Augie March

Bellows, George Wesley
born: 10 Columbus OH
artwork: 8 Lady Jean 11 Billy Sunday, Edith Cavell, Floating Ice, Up the Hudson 12 Forty-Two Kids 13 Men of the Docks 14 Rain on the River, Stag at Sharkey's 16 The Cliff Dwellers 18 Emma and her Children 21 Both Members of This Club

Bells Are Ringing
director: 16 Vincente Minnelli
cast: 9 Fred Clark 10 Dean Martin 12 Judy Holliday
song: 10 Just in Time 13 The Party's Over

Bells in Winter
author: 13 Czeslaw Milosz

Bells of St Mary's, The
director: 10 Leo McCarey
cast: 10 Bing Crosby (Father O'Malley) 12 Henry Travers 13 Ingrid Bergman
sequel to: 10 Going My Way
song: 20 Aren't You Glad You're You

bell tower 5 spire 6 belfry 7 steeple 9 campanile

Belluschi, Pietro
architect of: 21 Bank of America Building (San Francisco) 22 Juilliard School of Music (NYC) 31 Pan American World Airways Building (NYC, with Gropius)

bellwether 4 lead 5 doyen, guide, pilot 6 leader 8 director, shepherd 9 conductor, guidepost, precursor 10 forerunner, pacesetter 14 standard-bearer

belly 3 gut, yen 4 guts 5 taste, tummy 6 bowels, depths, desire, hunger, liking, paunch, vitals 7 abdomen, insides, midriff, stomach 8 appetite, interior, recesses 11 breadbasket

bellyache 4 beef, kick 5 gripe 6 grouch, grouse, squawk 7 grumble 8 complain 9 tummy ache 11 stomach ache 12 upset stomach

belong 6 go with 7 concern 8 attach to, be held by, be part of 9 be owned by, pertain to 10 be allied to 11 be a member of 12 be included in 15 be connected with, be the property of

belongings 4 gear, junk 5 goods, stuff 6 things 7 effects 8 movables 11 possessions 13 accouterments, paraphernalia 16 personal property

beloved 4 beau, dear, love, wife 5 loved, lover 6 adored, fiance, spouse, steady 7 admired, darling, dearest, fiancee, husband, revered 8 endeared, esteemed, loved one, precious 9 betrothed, boyfriend, cherished, respected, treasured 10 girlfriend, sweetheart

below 4 less 5 lower, under 6 in hell 7 beneath, on earth, short of 8 inferior, unworthy 9 at a low ebb, downwards 10 downstairs, downstream, second-rate, underneath 11 at a discount, at the foot of, indifferent, subordinate, underground

below par 3 bad 4 poor 8 inferior 9 imperfect 10 second-rate 12 below average, not up to snuff

below standard 3 bad 4 poor 5 lousy 6 faulty, shoddy 8 below par, inferior, slipshod, terrible 9 imperfect 10 second-rate 12 not up to snuff

Belshazzar
father: 9 Nabonidus 14 Nebuchadnezzar

belt 4 area, band, land, sash, zone 5 cinch, layer, strip 6 circle, girdle, region, stripe 7 country 8 district, encircle 9 waistband 10 cummerbund

Belteshazzar
Babylonian name of: 6 Daniel
friend: 7 Meshach 8 Abednego, Shadrach

Belus
king of: 7 Chemmis
father: 8 Poseidon
mother: 5 Libya
twin brother: 6 Agenor
wife: 8 Anchinoe
son: 6 Danaus 8 Aegyptus
daughter: 4 Dido

Belushi, John
born: 9 Chicago IL
roles: 9 Neighbors 11 Animal House 16 The Blues Brothers 17 Saturday Night Live

be manifest 6 appear 7 be clear, be plain 8 be patent 9 be evident, be obvious 10 be apparent

bemoan 3 rue 5 mourn 6 bewail, lament, regret 7 cry over 8 weep over 9 whine over 10 grieve over

bemused 5 dazed, fuzzy 7 muddled, stunned 8 confused 9 engrossed, stupefied 10 bewildered, dull-witted, thoughtful 11 preoccupied 12 absent-minded

be nauseated by 4 hate 5 abhor 6 detest, loathe 7 despise 8 execrate 9 abominate 11 can't stomach 13 be disgusted by, find repulsive, find revolting, find sickening

Benbow, Horace
character in: 9 Sanctuary
author: 8 Faulkner

Ben Casey
character: 12 Dr David Zorba, Dr Ted Hoffman 13 Nick Kanavaras 14 Dr Maggie Graham
cast: 8 Sam Jaffe 10 Nick Dennis 12 Harry Landers, Vince Edwards 14 Bettye Ackerman

bench 3 pew 4 seat 5 board, court, stool, table 6 settee 7 counter, take out, trestle 8 sideline, tribunal 9 judiciary, workbench, worktable 10 second team **11** judge's chair, substitutes **12** second string

Benchley, Peter
author of: **4** Jaws **7** The Deep

Benchley, Robert
author of: **14** From Bed to Worse **21** Benchley Beside Himself, My Ten Years in a Quandary

benchmark 4 norm **5** gauge, guide, model **7** example, measure **8** exemplar, paradigm, standard **9** criterion, principle, prototype, reference, yardstick **10** touchstone

bend 3 arc, bow **4** flex, hook, lean, loop, mold, sway, turn, warp, wind **5** crook, curve, defer, force, shape, stoop, twist, yield **6** accede, attend, buckle, coerce, compel, crouch, give in, relent, submit **7** bow down, contort, control, succumb **9** genuflect, influence, surrender **10** buckle down, capitulate **11** make crooked

Bend in the River, The
author: **9** V S Naipaul

Bendix, William
born: **9** New York NY
roles: **8** Hostages, Lifeboat **11** The Hairy Ape **13** A Bell for Adano **14** The Life of Riley **16** Guadalcanal Diary, The Babe Ruth Story

bend to one's own will
4 tame **5** break, train **6** master, subdue **8** overcome **10** discipline **12** show who's boss **18** have under one's thumb

beneath 5 below, lower, under **9** covered by **10** inferior to, underneath, unworthy of **11** subordinate, underground **16** below one's dignity

Benedick
character in: **19** Much Ado About Nothing
author: **11** Shakespeare

benedictine
type: **6** brandy, cognac **7** liqueur
flavor: **4** herb
with brandy: **5** B and B
with bourbon: **9** Twin Hills **13** Brighton Punch
with whiskey: **10** Frisco Sour

benediction 6 prayer **7** benison **8** blessing **10** invocation **12** consecration **13** closing prayer

benefaction 4 alms, gift **5** grant **7** charity **8** bestowal, donation, offering **9** endowment **10** almsgiving **12** contribution, dispensation, philanthropy

benefactor 5 angel, donor **6** backer, friend, helper, patron **7** sponsor **8** upholder **9** supporter **11** contributor **14** fairy godmother

beneficent 6 benign, kindly **7** liberal **8** generous, salutary **10** beneficial, benevolent, charitable **11** magnanimous **13** philanthropic

beneficial 6 useful **7** good for, healing, helpful **8** valuable **9** favorable, healthful **10** productive, profitable, propitious **12** advantageous, contributive

beneficiary 4 heir **7** grantee, heiress, legatee **8** receiver **9** inheritor, recipient

benefit 3 aid, use **4** gain, good, help **5** asset, avail, serve, value, worth **6** assist, behalf, better, profit **7** advance, be aided, service **8** be helped, be served, blessing, interest **9** advantage, do good for **10** be useful to, betterment, profit from **13** charity affair **18** charity performance

Benet, Stephen Vincent
author of: **7** America **8** Tiger Joy **11** Western Star **14** John Brown's Body, Thirteen O'Clock, Young Adventure **16** Five Men and Pompey **19** Tales Before Midnight, The Headless Horseman **20** The Beginning of Wisdom **24** The Devil and Daniel Webster

benevolence 7 charity **8** good will, kindness **9** benignity **10** compassion, generosity, kindliness, liberality **13** bountifulness **14** charitableness **15** humanitarianism, kindheartedness

benevolent 3 kin **6** benign, humane, tender **7** liberal **8** generous **9** benignant, bounteous, bountiful, unselfish **10** bighearted, charitable **11** considerate, kindhearted, warmhearted **12** humanitarian **13** compassionate, philanthropic

Bengali
language family: **12** Indo-European
branch: **11** Indo-Iranian
group: **5** Indic
spoken in: **5** (northern) India

Ben-Hur
author: **10** Lew Wallace
character: **4** Iras, Isas **5** Jesus **6** Esther **7** Messala **9** Balthasar, Simonides **11** Judah Ben-Hur
director: **12** William Wyler
cast: **11** Jack Hawkins, Ste-

phen Boyd **12** Hugh Griffith **14** Charlton Heston (Judah Ben-Hur)
setting: **9** Palestine
Oscar for: **5** actor (Heston) **7** picture **8** director **14** cinematography **15** supporting actor (Griffith)

benighted 4 dumb **5** crude, unhip **8** backward, ignorant, untaught **9** primitive, untutored **10** illiterate, uncultured, uneducated, uninformed, unlettered, unschooled **11** emptyheaded, know-nothing, uncivilized **12** uncultivated **13** unenlightened

benign 4 good, kind, mild, nice, soft **5** balmy, lucky **6** genial, gentle, humane, kindly, tender **7** affable **8** gracious, harmless, pleasant, salutary **9** favorable, healthful, innocuous, temperate **10** auspicious, benevolent, propitious **11** encouraging, kindhearted, softhearted **13** tender-hearted

benignant 4 kind **6** benign, humane, kindly, tender **9** forgiving **10** benevolent **11** kindhearted **13** compassionate, tenderhearted

benignity 8 good will, kindness **10** compassion, kindliness **11** benevolence **15** kindheartedness

Benin see box

Benito Cereno
author: **14** Herman Melville

Benjamin
father: **5** Jacob
mother: **6** Rachel
also known as: **6** Benoni
brother: **3** Dan, Gad **4** Levi **5** Asher, Judah **6** Joseph, Reuben, Simeon **7** Zebulun **8** Issachar, Naphtali
sister: **5** Dinah
descendant of: **11** Benjaminite

Bennet family
characters in: **17** Pride and Prejudice
members: **4** Jane, Mary **5** Kitty, Lydia **9** Elizabeth
author: **6** Austen

Bennett, Arnold
author of: **8** Accident **10** Clayhanger, Lord Raingo, Milestones, These Twain **11** Buried Alive **13** Hilda Lessways, Riceyman Steps **15** The Old Wives' Tale **18** Anna of the Five Towns

Benny, Jack
real name: **16** Benjamin Kubelsky
born: **10** Waukegan IL
roles: **12** Charley's Aunt

Benin
other name: 17 Republic of Dahomey
capital: 9 Porto-Novo
largest city: 7 Cotonou
others: 4 Pobe 5 Kandi, Kerou, Ketou, Porga 6 Abomey, Ouidah 7 Parakou, Savalou 8 Aplahoue
government: 30 Military Council of the Revolution
monetary unit: 5 franc 7 centime
lake: 5 Aheme 6 Nokoue
mountain: 7 Atakora
river: 4 Mono 5 Niger, Oueme 6 Couffo
sea: 8 Atlantic
physical feature:
gulf: 6 Guinea
plains: 6 Borgou
people: 3 Fon, Pla 4 Adja, Aizo, Mina, Peul 5 Pedah, Peuhl, Somba 6 Bariba, Fulani, Yoruba 8 Pilapila 9 Dahomeyan
language: 3 Fon 5 Dendi 6 Bariba, French, Fulani, Yoruba
religion: 5 Islam 6 tribal 7 animism 13 Roman Catholic
food:
tapioca: 4 gari

13 Jack Benny Show, To Be or Not To Be 16 Artists and Models

Benoni *see* 8 Benjamin

Benson
character: 5 Kraus 12 (Lt Gov) Benson DuBois 13 (Gov) Eugene Gatling
cast: 10 James Noble 11 Inga Swenson 15 Robert Guillaume

bent 4 bias, gift, mind 5 bowed, flair, knack 6 angled, arched, curved, genius, liking, talent 7 ability, aptness, crooked, faculty, hunched, leaning, stooped, twisted 8 aptitude, capacity, facility, fondness, penchant, tendency 9 contorted, endowment 10 attraction, partiality, proclivity, propensity 11 disposition, inclination 12 predilection 14 predisposition

bent into folds 6 fluted, ridged 7 creased, grooved, pleated 8 crinkled, furrowed, puckered, wrinkled 10 corrugated

Benton, Robert
director of: 14 Kramer vs Kramer (Oscar) 16 Places in the Heart

Benton, Thomas Hart
born: 8 Neosho MO
artwork: 7 Bubbles 8 Boomtown 9 Homestead 12 American Life 13 Arts of the West, Cotton Pickers 14 Threshing Wheat 19 Louisiana Rice Fields, The Lord Is My Shepherd

Benue-Congo
language family: 16 Niger-Kordofanian
group: 10 Niger-Congo
includes: 3 Tiv 4 Zulu 5 Bantu, Jukun 6 Chwana, Nyanja 7 Kikongo, Luganda, Swahili

benumb 4 daze, dull 5 blunt 6 deaden 7 stupefy 15 make insensitive

Benvolio
character in: 14 Romeo and Juliet
author: 11 Shakespeare

Benz, Karl
nationality: 6 German
inventor of: 22 electric ignition engine 26 differential gear automobile
built first practical: 10 automobile

be obvious 6 appear 7 be clear, be plain 8 be patent 9 be evident 10 be apparent, be manifest

be off 2 go 5 leave, scram 6 beat it, begone, cut out, depart, go away, set out 8 set forth, withdraw 10 make tracks

be of one mind 5 agree 6 accord, concur 10 think alike 11 see eye to eye

be of use 3 aid 4 help 5 serve 6 assist 7 benefit

be on a par with 5 equal 6 be up to 7 compare 10 be as good as 12 be comparable 14 be in a class with

be on the sick list 3 ail 5 be ill 6 be sick 8 be unwell 12 be indisposed 13 be in ill health 17 be under the weather

Beor
son: 4 Bela 6 Balaam

Beothuk (Red Indians)
location: 6 Canada 12 Newfoundland
intermixed with: 7 Naskapi

Beowulf
author: 7 unknown
character: 4 Finn 5 Breca, Hnaef, Oslaf, Scyld 6 Wig-laf 7 Guthlaf, Hengest, Higelac, Hrethel, Unferth 8 Aeschere, Heardred, Hondscio, Hrothgar 9 Hildeburh
great hall: 6 Heorot
monster: 7 Grendel 14 Grendel's mother
tribe: 5 Danes, Geats 8 Frisians
Beowulf tears from Grendel: 3 arm

bequeath 4 will 5 endow, leave 6 impart 7 consign 8 hand down

bequest 6 legacy 8 bestowal 9 endowment 10 settlement 11 inheritance

be part of 4 form 6 make up 8 belong to 9 appertain, pertain to 10 constitute

be patent 6 appear 7 be clear, be plain 9 be evident, be obvious 10 be apparent, be manifest

be pertinent to 4 bear 5 apply, refer 6 affect, relate 7 concern, pertain 9 appertain, touch upon

be plain 6 appear 7 be clear 8 be patent 9 be evident, be obvious 10 be apparent, be manifest

be pleased with 4 like 5 favor 7 approve

berate 5 scold 6 rail at, rebuke 7 bawl out, chew out, reprove, upbraid 8 reproach 9 castigate, criticize, reprimand 10 take to task, tongue-lash

Berber
language family: 11 Afroasiatic 13 Hamito-Semitic
spoken in: 6 Sahara 11 North Africa

Berchta *see* 7 Perchta

bereave 3 rob 5 strip 6 divest 7 deprive 10 dispossess

Berecyntia *see* 6 Cybele

Berenice's Hair
constellation of: 13 Coma Berenices

be resigned to 6 accept 8 tolerate

Beret
character in: 16 Giants of the Earth
author: 7 Rolvaag

be revolted by 4 hate 5 abhor 6 detest, loathe 7 despise 8 execrate 9 abominate 10 recoil from, shrink from 11 can't stomach 13 find repulsive

berg 4 floe **7** glacier, iceberg, icefloe
South African: 8 mountain
French: 4 neve **5** serac

Berg, Alban
born: 6 Vienna **7** Austria
composer of: 4 Lulu
7 Wozzeck

Bergen, Candace
father: 11 Edgar Bergen
born: 14 Beverly Hills CA
roles: 8 The Group **15** Carnal Knowledge

Berger, Thomas
author of: 7 The Feud
9 Neighbors **10** Vital Parts
11 Killing Time **12** Little Big Man, Sneaky People
15 Regiment of Women

Bergman, Ingmar
director of: 14 The Seventh Seal **16** Cries and Whispers, Wild Strawberries **17** Fanny and Alexander **19** Scenes from a Marriage **20** Smiles of a Summer Night

Bergman, Ingrid
born: 6 Sweden **9** Stockholm
roles: 8 Gaslight (Oscar)
9 Anastasia (Oscar), Joan of Arc, Notorious **10** Casablanca, Intermezzo, Spellbound **17** A Woman Called Golda, The Bells of St Mary's **19** For Whom the Bell Tolls **24** Murder on the Orient Express **25** The Inn of the Sixth Happiness

Berith, Berit, Brith, Brit
8 covenant **12** circumcision

Berle, Milton
real name: 15 Milton Berlinger
nickname: 11 Uncle Miltie
12 Mr Television
born: 9 New York NY
roles: 17 The Texaco Star Hour **18** Who's Minding the Mint **23** Always Leave Them Laughing

Berlin (East, West)
landmark: 14 Humboldt Castle **15** Gruenwald Castle
16 Berlin Opera House, Markisches Museum
21 Scharlottenburg Castle
29 Kaiser-Wilhelm-Gedachtniskirche
river: 5 Spree
square: 14 Alexander-Platz

Berlin, Elaine
real name of: 9 Elaine May

Berlinger, Milton
real name of: 11 Milton Berle

Berlioz, (Louis) Hector
born: 6 France **13** La Cote St Andre

composer of: 6 Rob Roy, Te Deum **7** Requiem, **8** Herminie, King Lear, Waverley **9** Cleopatra, Nuits d'Ete **10** Le Corsaire, Les Troyens, The Trojans **11** Sardanapale **13** Harold in Italy **14** Les Francs Juges, Romeo and Juliet **16** Benvenuto Cellini, Damnation of Faust, Le Carnaval Romain, L'Enfance du Christ **18** Beatrice et Benedict **20** Symphonie Fantastique **28** Symphonie Funebre et Triomphale

Bermuda
other name: 13 Somers Islands
capital/largest city: 8 Hamilton
others: 8 St George
head of state: 14 British monarch **15** governor general
island: 4 Boaz **5** Coney **7** Bermuda, Ireland, Watford **8** Somerset, St Davids **9** St Georges
highest point: 8 Town Hill
sea: 8 Atlantic
physical feature:
harbor: 6 Castle
hill: 5 Gibbs
people:
discoverer: 14 Juan de Bermudez
language: 7 English
religion: 8 Anglican
10 Protestant
15 Church of England
feature:
dancers: 6 Gombey

Bern
capital of: 11 Switzerland
landmark: 10 Clock Tower
12 Nydegg Church
river: 4 Aare

Bernard, Henriette-Rosine
real name of: 14 Sarah Bernhardt

Bernhardt, Sarah
real name: 22 Henriette-Rosine Bernard
nickname: 11 Divine Sarah
born: 5 Paris **6** France
roles: 6 Phedre **7** Hernani, Ruy Blas **8** King Lear **14** Queen Elizabeth **17** La Dame aux Camelias

Bernini, Gianlorenzo (Giovanni Lorenzo)
born: 5 Italy **6** Naples
father: 6 Pietro
artwork: 7 Montoya **8** Louis

XIV, Vigevano **10** Bellarmine, St Longinus **13** Cathedra Petri, Francis I d'Este, The Assumption **15** Apollo and Daphne **18** Costanza Buonarelli **19** The Rape of Proserpina **21** Saints Andrew and Thomas, The Ecstasy of St Theresa **24** Blessed Lodovica Albertoni **25** Aeneas Anchises and Ascanius
architect of: 12 Santa Bibiana **16** Piazza of St Peter's (Rome) **19** Palazzo Montecitorio **21** Sant' Andrea al Quirinale **22** Palazzo Chigi-Odescalchi **23** Fountain of the Four Rivers **24** Santa Maria dell' Assunzione

Bernoulli, Daniel
field: 11 mathematics
nationality: 5 Swiss
theory of: 5 gases **6** fluids
18 Bernoulli's Equation

Bernstein, Carl
author of: 12 The Final Days (with Bob Woodward)
19 All the President's Men (with Bob Woodward)
newspaper reporter for: 14 Washington Post

Bernstein, Leonard
born: 10 Lawrence MA
composer of: 4 Mass **7** Candide, Kaddish **8** Jeremiah **9** Facsimile, Fancy Free, On the Town **13** West Side Story, Wonderful Town **15** The Age of Anxiety, Trouble in Tahiti **16** Chichester Psalms

Beroe
father: 6 Adonis
mother: 9 Aphrodite
nurse of: 6 Semele

Berowne
character in: 16 Love's Labour's Lost
author: 11 Shakespeare

Berra, Yogi (Lawrence Peter Berra)
sport: 8 baseball
position: 5 coach **7** catcher
team: 14 New York Yankees

berry 3 egg **4** seed **5** fruit, grain, grape **6** dollar, kernel, tomato, banana **7** currant **8** allspice, bayberry, mulberry **9** blueberry, cranberry, raspberry **10** blackberry, gooseberry, peppercorn, strawberry **11** boysenberry, huckleberry, pomegranate **12** checkerberry
poisonous: 9 baneberry

Berryman, John
author of: 8 Recovery **9** Delusions **11** Love and Fame **12** 77 Dream Songs **13** The Dream Songs **16** Berryman's Sonnets **19** The Freedom of

the Poet 21 His Toy His Dream His Rest 26 Homage to Mistress Bradstreet

berserk 4 amok, wild 5 crazy 6 insane 7 frantic, violent 8 demented, deranged, frenzied, maniacal, wild-eyed 9 desperate 10 distracted, distraught 12 out of control

Berserker
origin: 6 Nordic
form: 7 warrior

berth 3 bed, job 4 bunk, dock, pier, post, quay, slip, spot 5 haven, niche, place, wharf 6 billet, employ, office 8 position 9 anchorage, situation 11 appointment 12 resting place 13 sleeping place

Berthollet, Claude Louis
field: 9 chemistry
nationality: 6 French
researched: 7 ammonia 8 chlorine

Bertram
character in: 20 All's Well That Ends Well
author: 11 Shakespeare

Bertram family
characters in: 13 Mansfield Park
members: 3 Tom 5 Julia, Maria 6 Edmund 9 Sir Thomas
author: 6 Austen

beryl
color: 5 green 6 yellow

Berzelius, Jons Jakob
field: 9 chemistry
nationality: 7 Swedish
developed: 15 chemical symbols
discovered: 6 cerium 7 silicon, thorium 8 selenium, titanium 9 zirconium
founded: 15 modern chemistry

be satisfactory 2 do 6 answer 7 suffice 8 be enough 10 be adequate, pass muster 12 be sufficient, do well enough

be scant 4 lack, want 8 be skimpy 9 fall short 14 be insufficient 15 be in short supply

beseech 3 beg 4 pray 6 adjure 7 entreat, implore 9 plead with 10 supplicate

beset 3 dog, set 4 bead, deck, stud 5 annoy, array, hem in, hound, worry 6 assail, badger, harass, pester, plague 7 bedevil, besiege, set upon 8 surround 9 beleaguer, embellish

be sick 3 ail 5 be ill 8 be unwell 12 be indisposed 13 be in ill health

beside 2 by 4 near 5 saved 6 except, nearby, unless 7 abreast, barring, without 8 let alone 9 adjoining, alongside, aside from, other than 10 on a par with, side by side 12 compared with, in addition to

beside oneself 4 wild 6 elated, joyful, joyous, raging 7 berserk, exalted, frantic, furious, ranting 8 agitated, blissful, distrait, ecstatic, frenetic, frenzied 9 delirious, in a frenzy, overjoyed, rapturous 10 distracted, distraught, distressed, enraptured 11 carried away, overwrought, transported 13 out of one's wits

besides 3 but 4 also, save 6 as well, except, saving 7 barring 8 moreover 9 excepting, excluding, other than 11 exclusive of, furthermore

besiege 3 dog 5 annoy, beset, hound 6 assail, badger, harass, pester, plague 7 assault, bedevil 9 beleaguer 10 lay siege to

besmear 4 soil 5 dirty, muddy, smear, stain, sully 6 mess up, slop up, smudge 7 begrime, tarnish 8 besmirch

besmeared 5 dirty, grimy, messy 6 grubby, smudgy 7 muddied, sullied 8 begrimed 10 besmirched

besmirch 4 soil 5 smear, stain, sully, taint 6 defame, defile 7 blacken, corrupt, debauch, degrade, slander, tarnish 8 discolor, disgrace, dishonor 9 discredit

besotted 5 drunk 6 sodden, soused, wasted, zapped, zonked 7 smashed 9 plastered 10 inebriated, infatuated 11 intoxicated 17 under the influence 20 three sheets to the wind

bespangle 3 dot 4 gild, star, stud 5 adorn, jewel 6 bedeck 7 dress up, festoon, garnish 8 decorate, ornament 9 embellish 10 illuminate

bespatter 4 blot, soil, spot 5 decry, dirty, libel, smear, stain, sully, taint 6 debase, defame, defile, smudge, splash 7 condemn, slander, smotter, tarnish 8 denounce, reproach 9 deprecate, fling dirt 10 calumniate, disapprove

Bessemer, Sir Henry
nationality: 7 English
inventor of manufacturing process for: 5 steel

best 3 top 4 most, pick

5 cream, elite 6 choice, finest, nicest, utmost 7 hardest, largest 8 foremost, greatest, superior, topnotch 9 greetings, loveliest, most fully, most of all, unequaled, unrivaled 10 unexcelled 11 compliments, unsurpassed 13 most competent, most desirable, most excellent 14 highest quality, kindest regards

Best, Charles Herbert
field: 10 physiology
nationality: 8 Canadian
discovered: 7 insulin

best group 3 top 5 cream, elite 6 choice 9 chosen few 10 select body 14 cream of the crop, creme de la creme

bestial 5 cruel 6 brutal, savage 7 beastly 8 barbaric, depraved, inhumane, ruthless 9 barbarous, merciless

bestir 4 goad, spur, stir, urge 5 rouse, speed 6 arouse, excite, hasten 7 quicken 8 activate 9 get moving

bestir oneself 5 rouse 8 be active 9 make haste 10 get up early, lose no time 11 keep moving 15 make short work of 19 seize the opportunity

bestow 3 use 4 give, mete 5 apply, award, grant, lay on, spend 6 accord, confer, devote, donate, employ, expend, impart, occupy, render 7 consign, consume, deal out, deliver, hand out, present, utilize 8 dispense, give away 9 apportion 10 settle upon, turn over to

bestowal 4 alms, gift 5 bonus, favor, grant 6 reward 7 charity, present, tribute 8 donation, gratuity, offering 9 endowment 10 conferment, recompense 11 benefaction 12 contribution, dispensation

best society
French: 10 grand monde

Best Years of Our Lives, The
director: 12 William Wyler
based on story by: 15 MacKinlay Kantor
script: 14 Robert Sherwood
cast: 8 Myrna Loy 11 Dana Andrews 12 Teresa Wright, Virginia Mayo 13 Frederic March, Harold Russell 15 Hoagy Carmichael
Oscar for: 5 actor (March) 7 picture 8 director

be sufficient 6 answer 7 suffice 8 be enough 10 be adequate, pass muster 12 do well enough 14 be satisfactory

bet 4 ante, risk 5 stake, wager 6 chance, gamble, hazard, plunge 7 venture 8 make a bet 9 speculate 11 speculation

bete noir 5 bogey 6 plague 7 bugaboo, bugbear 8 anathema, bogeyman 9 annoyance 10 black beast

be thankful 8 thank God 10 appreciate 11 thank heaven 19 thank one's lucky stars

Bethe, Hans Albrecht
field: 7 physics
developed: 8 atom bomb
awarded: 10 Nobel Prize

be the same 5 agree, equal, match 6 equate 7 balance 11 be identical

Bethuel
son: 5 Laban

betide 4 fall 5 occur 6 befall, chance, happen 10 come to pass

betimes 5 early 10 in good time

betoken 4 show 5 augur 6 attest, denote 7 portend, presage, signify 8 foretell

betray 4 dupe, fink, jilt, show, tell 5 rat on, trick 6 expose, reveal, squeal, tell on, unmask 7 abandon, deceive, divulge, lay bare, let down, let slip, sell out, two-time, uncover, violate 8 blurt out, disclose, give away 9 play Judas 10 be disloyal 11 double-cross 12 be unfaithful 13 inform against, play false with 14 break faith with

betrayal 7 perfidy, telling, treason 8 bad faith, sedition, trickery 9 chicanery, deception, duplicity, falseness, treachery, two-timing, violation 10 disclosure, disloyalty, divulgence, revelation 11 double-cross 13 breach of faith, double-dealing 14 unfaithfulness

betrayal of trust 7 falsity, perfidy 8 apostasy, cheating 9 falseness, recreancy 10 disloyalty, infidelity 11 inconstancy 13 deceitfulness, double-dealing, faithlessness 14 unfaithfulness

Betrayer 13 Judas Iscariot

betroth 6 commit, engage, pledge 7 espouse, promise 8 affiance, contract

betrothal 5 troth 8 espousal 10 affiancing, betrothing, engagement

betrothed 6 fiance 7 engaged, fiancee 8 promised 9 affianced

Bettelheim, Bruno
author of: 15 Love Is Not Enough 16 The Informed Heart 20 The Uses of Enchantment

better 3 top 4 more 5 finer, outdo, raise 6 bigger, enrich, exceed, fitter, larger, longer, refine, uplift 7 advance, elevate, enhance, farther, forward, further, greater, improve, mending, promote, surpass, upgrade 8 heighten, improved, increase, outstrip, stronger, superior 9 cultivate, healthier, improving 10 preferable, recovering, strengthen 11 more healthy, progressing

bettering 9 elevation 10 betterment 11 advancement, improvement

betterment 4 good 6 reform 7 benefit 8 revision 9 advantage, amendment, promotion 10 correction, enrichment 11 advancement, improvement 12 amelioration, regeneration 13 rectification 14 reconstruction

better than average 2 A-1 3 A-OK 4 aces, fine, good, tops 5 great, prime, super 6 choice, grade-A, superb 7 capital, special 8 peerless, sterling, superior, terrific, topnotch 9 excellent, first-rate, marvelous, matchless, wonderful 10 first-class, inimitable, preeminent, remarkable, tremendous 11 exceptional, outstanding, superlative 12 incomparable 13 extraordinary

between 4 amid 5 among, entre 6 amidst, atwixt, shared 7 betwixt, joining 9 in the midst 10 connecting

between ourselves
French: 9 entre nous
Latin: 8 inter nos

Between the Battles
author: 20 Bjornstjerne Bjornson

between themselves
Latin: 7 inter se

between us 9 entre nous, privately 14 confidentially 15 between you and me 16 between me and thee, between ourselves

betwixt and between 4 soso 7 average 8 confused 9 in between, undecided 14 halfway between 21 neither one nor the other

Beulah, Land of
place in: 16 Pilgrim's Progress
author: 6 Bunyan

be unlike 4 vary 6 differ 7 deviate, diverge 8 conflict, disagree 12 be at variance, be discordant, be dissimilar

be unwell 3 ail 5 be ill 6 be sick 12 be indisposed 13 be in ill health

be unwilling to pursue
Latin: 13 nolle prosequi

bevel 4 blow, cant, ream, tool 5 angle, bezel, miter, mitre, slant, slope, snape, splay 6 aslant 7 incline, oblique 8 slanting

beverage 3 ade, ale, cup, nog, pop, tea 4 beer, brew, dram, grog, milk, soda, soup, wine 5 broth, cider, cocoa, draft, drink, juice, julep, lager, leban, punch, toddy, water 6 bishop, coffee, cordial, eggnog, liquid, liquor, potion 7 limeade, seltzer, spirits, wassail 8 aperitif, cocktail, highball, lemonade, libation, potation 9 champagne, chocolate, orangeade

Beverley, Constance de
character in: 7 Marmion
author: 5 Scott

Beverly Hillbillies, The
character: 11 Jed Clampett 12 Jane Hathaway, Jethro Bodine 14 Granny Clampett, Milton Drysdale 16 Ellie May Clampett
cast: 9 Irene Ryan, Max Baer Jr, Nancy Kulp 10 Buddy Ebsen 12 Donna Douglas 13 Raymond Bailey

Beverly Hills Cop
director: 11 Martin Brest
cast: 11 Eddie Murphy 13 Judge Reinhold, Lisa Eilbacher

bevy 4 band, body, herd, host, pack 5 brood, covey, crowd, drove, flock, group, horde, party, shoal, swarm 6 clutch, flight, gaggle, school, throng 7 company, coterie 9 gathering, multitude 10 assemblage, collection

bewail 3 rue 5 mourn 6 bemoan, lament, regret 7 cry over, deplore 8 moan over, weep over 10 grieve over

beware 4 mind 6 be wary 7 look out 8 take care, take heed 9 be careful 11 take warning, watch out for 12 be on the alert, guard against 15 take precautions

beware of the dog
Latin: **9** cave canem

bewhiskered 5 bushy, hairy
6 shaggy **7** bearded, bristly,
hirsute **8** unshaven
11 mustachioed

bewilder 5 addle, mix up
6 baffle, bemuse, muddle, puzzle **7** confuse, fluster, mystify,
nonplus, perplex, stupefy
8 befuddle **10** disconcert

bewildered 7 at a loss, up a
tree **8** all at sea, confused
9 perplexed **10** confounded,
nonplussed **12** disconcerted

bewilderment 9 confusion
10 perplexity, puzzlement
11 frustration **13** mystification

bewitch 4 jinx **5** charm,
spook **6** turn on **7** bedevil, beguile, delight, enchant **8** entrance **9** captivate, enrapture,
fascinate **12** cast a spell on
14 put under a spell

bewitched 7 charmed, seduced **8** beguiled **9** bedeviled,
enchanted, entranced **10** captivated, enraptured, fascinated,
spellbound **11** under a spell

Bewitched
character: **6** Endora, Serena
7 Maurice **9** Aunt Clara, Es-
merelda, Larry Tate **11** Uncle Arthur **12** Abner
Kravitz **13** Gladys Kravitz
14 Darrin Stephens **15** Tabitha Stephens **16** Samantha
Stephens
cast: **8** Dick York **9** Paul
Lynde **10** David White
11 Dick Sargent, Marion
Lorne, Sandra Gould
12 George Tobias, Maurice
Evans **13** Alice Ghostley
14 Agnes Moorehead
19 Elizabeth Montgomery

bewitching 8 alluring, charming, enticing, fetching, tempting **9** appealing, beguiling,
disarming, seductive **10** enchanting, entrancing **11** captivating, fascinating
12 irresistible

be worthy of 4 earn, rate
5 merit **7** deserve

bey, beg 4 lord **6** prince
8 governor

beyond 2 by **4** over, past
5 above, later, ultra **6** abroad,
except, yonder **7** beneath, besides, farther, further, outside,
passing **8** superior **9** exceeding,
hereafter **10** out of range, out
of reach **11** at a distance, in
addition to

Beyond Desire
author: **15** Maxwell Anderson

beyond hope 8 hopeless
9 desperate **10** despairing

Beyond Human Power
author: **20** Bjornstjerne
Bjornson

beyond one's means 10 immoderate **11** extravagant
15 too high on the hog

beyond question 4 sure
6 surely **7** certain, decided, settled **9** certainly, decidedly
10 absolutely, positively
12 without doubt

Bharat (Varsha) see **5** India

Bhot see **5** Tibet

Bhutan see box

Bia
origin: **5** Greek
personifies: **5** force
father: **11** Titan Pallas
mother: **4** Styx
brother: **5** Zelos **6** Cratus
sister: **4** Nike

Biadice
husband: **8** Cretheus

Bianca
character in: **19** The Taming
of the Shrew
author: **11** Shakespeare

Bianchi, Mose
born: **5** Italy, Milan
artwork: **11** Snow in Milan
21 Return from the Festival

bias 4 bent, sway **5** angle,
slant **7** bigotry, feeling, leaning **8** tendency **9** fixed idea,
prejudice, proneness **10** narrow view, partiality, predispose, proclivity, propensity,
unfairness **11** inclination, intolerance **12** diagonal line,
one-sidedness, predilection
13 preconception **16** narrow-
mindedness, preconceived idea

Bias
father: **8** Amythaon
mother: **7** Idomene
brother: **8** Melampus
wife: **4** Pero **10** Iphianassa
son: **6** Talaus
daughter: **8** Anaxibia
secured: **6** cattle
cattle owned by:
8 Phylacus

biased 6 unfair, unjust **7** bigoted, slanted **8** inclined **9** arbitrary **10** intolerant, prejudiced
11 close-minded, opinionated
12 narrow-minded

bibelot 5 curio **7** trinket **8** ornament **9** objet d'art

bible 5 guide **6** manual
8 handbook **9** authority, guidebook **13** reference book

Bible 6 Gospel **7** the Book

Bhutan
other name: **7** Druk-Yul
15 Kingdom of Bhutan,
Land of the Dragon
capital/largest city:
6 Thimbu **7** Thimphu
others: **4** Paro
12 Phuntsholing
14 Wangdu Phedrang
government:
assembly: **7** Tsongdu
head of state/
government:
hereditary king:
10 dragon king, druk
gyalpo
other leader:
spiritual leader:
10 dharma raja
temporal ruler: **7** deb
raja
monetary unit: **5** paisa,
rupee **8** chetrums,
ngultrum
mountain: **5** Black
9 Himalayas **10** Chomo
Lhari
highest point: **10** Kula
Kangri
river: **4** Kuru, Paro
5 Machu, Manas, Pa-
chu, Torsa **6** Amochu,
Raidak, Tongsa **7** San-
kosh, Thinchu
physical feature:
plain: **5** Duars
people: **5** Monpa **6** Bhutia **7** Tibetan **8** Assamese, Nepalese
dragon people:
7 Drukpas
language: **5** Hindi,
Lhoke **7** Tibetan
8 Dzongkha, Nepalese
religion: **15** Tibetan
Buddhism
place:
fortress (dzong):
4 Paro **6** Bya Kar,
Tongsa **8** Tashi Cho
feature:
pony: **6** Tangun

8 good book, Holy Writ
10 Scriptures **11** bibliotheca,
the Good Book **13** holy scripture **14** Holy Scriptures, sacred
writings

Bible, books of
Old Testament: **3** Job
4 Amos, Ezra, Joel, Osee,
Ruth **5** Hosea, Jonah, Jonas,
Josue, Kings, Micah, Na-
hum, Tobit **6** Abdias, Ag-
geus, Baruch, Daniel, Esdras,
Esther, Exodus, Haggai, Isa-
iah, Isaias, Joshua, Judges,
Judith, Psalms, Samuel, Sir-

ach, Tobias, Wisdom
7 Ezekiel, Genesis, Habacuc,
Malachi, Micheas, Numbers,
Obadiah **8** Ezechiel, Habakkuk, Jeremiah, Jeremias,
Nehemiah, Proverbs **9** Leviticus, Maccabees, Machabees,
Malachias, Sophonias,
Zacharias, Zechariah,
Zephaniah **10** Chronicles·
11 Deuteronomy, Song of
Songs **12** Ecclesiastes, Lamentations **13** Paralipomenon,
Song of Solomon **14** Ecclesiasticus **19** Canticle of
Canticles
New Testament: 4 Acts,
John, Jude, Luke, Mark
5 James, Peter **6** Romans
7 Hebrews, Matthew, Timothy **9** Ephesians, Galatians
10 Colossians, Revelation
11 Corinthians, Philippians
13 Thessalonians, Titus
Philemon
first five books called:
3 Law **5** Torah
10 Pentateuch
first seven books called:
10 Heptateuch

Bible scholar 7 biblist
9 biblicist

Bible version 6 The Way
7 Vulgate **8** Peshitta **9** Gutenberg, Jerusalem, King James
10 New English **11** New
American, Rheims-Douay **14**
The Living Bible **15** American
revised, revised standard

Biblical animal 7 unicorn

Biblical gemstone 6 ligure
7 sardius **8** sardonyx

Biblical instrument 7 sackbut

Biblical length
reed: 9 six cubits

Biblical measure 3 cab, cor
4 epah, omet, reed, seah
5 cubit, epheh, homer
6 shekel **9** half homer

Biblical personage 9
patriarch

Biblical plant 6 hyssop
12 Rose of Sharon

Biblical precept
Hebrew: 7 mitsvah, mitzvah

Biblical tree 5 algum, almug
6 storax **7** juniper **8** sycamire
10 gopherwood **11** shittim
wood **12** opobalsammum
13 red sandalwood

Biblical weed 4 tare **6** darnel

Biblical weight 6 talent

Biblicist 12 Bible scholar

Bibliotheca 5 Bible **14** sacred
writings

Biblist 12 Bible scholar

**Bickel, Ernest Frederick
McIntyre**
real name of: 13 Frederic
March

bicker 4 spar, spat **5** argue,
fight **6** haggle **7** dispute, quarrel, wrangle **8** disagree,
squabble

bickering 4 spat **5** fight **7** arguing, dispute, quarrel **8** argument, fighting **9** wrangling
10 quarreling, squabbling
12 disagreement

Bickford, Charles
born: 11 Cambridge MA
roles: 12 Anna Christie
13 Johnny Belinda **16** Song
of Bernadette **18** The Farmer's Daughter

bicycle 4 bike, ride **5** cycle,
moped **10** two-wheeler
invented by: 7 Starley

Bicycle Thief, The
director: 14 Vittorio De Sica
cast: 14 Lianella Carell
18 Lamberto Maggiorani

bid 3 ask, say, try **4** call, tell,
wish **5** greet, offer, order
6 beckon, charge, demand, direct, effort, enjoin, insist, invite, ordain, summon, tender
7 attempt, command, proffer,
propose, request, require **8** call
upon, endeavor, instruct, offering, proposal **10** invitation

bidding 4 beck, call **5** offer, order **6** behest, charge, demand,
offers **7** command, dictate,
mandate, request, summons
8 offering, proposal **9** direction, summoning, tendering
10 injunction, invitation, proffering **11** instruction

bide 4 stay, wait **5** abide,
dwell, stand, tarry **6** endure,
linger, remain, suffer **8** tolerate **9** put up with

Bierce, Ambrose
author of: 15 Can Such
Things Be? **16** In the Midst
of Life **19** The Devil's
Dictionary

Bierstadt, Albert
born: 7 Germany **8** Solingen
artwork: 11 Laramie Park
13 Mount Corcoran **17** The
Rocky Mountains **20** Discovery of the Hudson,
Storm on the Matterhorn
21 Sunrise Yosemite Valley
22 Settlement of California
31 Thunderstorm in the
Rocky Mountains

bifocal lenses
invented by: 8 Franklin

Bifrost
origin: 12 Scandinavian
form: 6 bridge

bridge of: 4 gods
made of: 7 rainbow
from: **6** Asgard
to: **5** earth

bifurcate 4 fork **5** split
6 branch, divide **7** diverge
8 separate

big 3 top **4** head, high, huge,
just, kind, main, vast **5** adult,
ample, bulky, chief, great,
grown, heavy, husky, large,
major, noble, prime, vital
6 heroic, humane, mature
7 eminent, grown-up, haughty,
hulking, immense, leading,
liberal, mammoth, massive,
notable, pompous, sizable,
weighty **8** abundant, arrogant,
boastful, bragging, colossal,
enormous, generous, gigantic,
gracious, princely **9** conceited,
grandiose, honorable, important, momentous, prominent,
strapping **10** benevolent, chivalrous, high-minded, monumental, prodigious
11 magnanimous, pretentious,
significant, substantial **12** considerable **13** consequential

Big Apple
nickname of: 11 New York
City

Big Bend State
nickname of: 9 Tennessee

Big Chill, The
director: 14 Laurence Kasdan
cast: 10 Kevin Kline **11** William Hurt

Big Daddy
character in: 16 Cat on a
Hot Tin Roof
author: 8 Williams

Big E
nickname of: 10 Elvin Hayes

Bigfoot 4 Yeti **9** Sasquatch
17 Abominable Snowman

big guns 4 VIPs **5** brass **6** cannon **7** bigwigs, top dogs **8** big
shots, ordnance **9** artillery
14 heavy artillery, high
mucky-mucks **15** important
people

bighearted 6 lavish **7** liberal
8 generous, handsome,
princely, prodigal **9** bounteous,
bountiful, unselfish **10** beneficent, benevolent, charitable,
free-handed, open-handed, unstinting **11** magnanimous,
open-hearted **12** humanitarian

bight 3 bay **4** bend, cave,
road

Biglow Papers
author: 18 James Russell
Lowell

Big Money, The
author: 13 John Dos Passos

bigness 4 bulk **8** enormity, hugeness **9** amplitude, great size, greatness, largeness, magnitude **11** massiveness

Big O, The
nickname of: **14** Oscar Robertson

bigoted 6 biased **10** intolerant, prejudiced **12** closed-minded, narrow-minded

bigotry 4 bias **6** racism **9** prejudice **10** unfairness **11** intolerance **14** discrimination **16** closed-mindedness, narrow-mindedness

Big Parade, The
director: **9** King Vidor
cast: **11** John Gilbert, Renee Adoree **14** Hobart Bosworth

big shot 3 VIP **4** name **5** mogul, nabob, wheel **6** big gun, bigwig, fat cat, tycoon **7** big deal, magnate, notable **8** somebody **9** big cheese, dignitary, personage **13** high-muck-a-muck, wheeler-dealer

Big Six
nickname of: **16** Christy Mathewson

Big Sky, The
author: **11** A B Guthrie Jr

Big Sky State
nickname of: **7** Montana

Big Sleep, The
author: **15** Raymond Chandler
director: **11** Howard Hawks
cast: **12** Elisha Cook Jr, Lauren Bacall **13** Dorothy Malone, Martha Vickers **14** Humphrey Bogart (Philip Marlowe)
setting: **10** Los Angeles

Big Train
nickname of: **13** Walter Johnson

Big Valley, The
character: **11** Nick Barkley **12** Audra Barkley, Heath Barkley **13** Jarrod Barkley **15** Victoria Barkley
cast: **9** Lee Majors **10** Linda Evans, Peter Breck **11** Richard Long **15** Barbara Stanwyck

bigwig 3 vip **7** big shot, notable **9** dignitary, personage

bikini 8 two-piece **11** bathing suit
topless: **8** monokini
type: **6** string

Bikini 5 atoll **9** Namu islet **10** West Pacific **15** Marshall Islands

Bilah, Bilhah
concubine of: **5** Jacob

son: **3** Dan **8** Maphtali, Naphtali
served: **6** Rachel

Bildad
friend: **3** Job **5** Elihu **6** Zophar **7** Eliphaz

bile 4 gall, rage **5** anger, venom, wrath **6** choler, spleen

bilge 3 rot **4** bosh, bull, bunk, tosh **5** hooey, tripe **6** drivel, humbug, jabber, piffle **7** baloney, hogwash, rubbish, twaddle **8** malarkey, nonsense **9** gibberish **10** balderdash **11** foolishness, jabberwocky **13** horsefeathers **16** stuff and nonsense

bilious 4 sick **5** angry, cross, huffy, nasty, testy **6** crabby, cranky, grumpy, queasy, sickly, touchy **7** grouchy, peevish **8** bilelike, greenish, nauseous, petulant, snappish **9** irritable, sickening **10** ill-humored, out of sorts **11** ill-tempered **12** cantankerous **13** short-tempered **15** green at the gills

bilk 3 gyp **4** dupe, gull, rook, take **5** cheat, cozen, trick **6** fleece, rip off **7** deceive, defraud, swindle **8** hoodwink **9** bamboozle, victimize

bill 3 act, fee, law **4** card, chit, list **5** tally **6** agenda, charge, decree, docket, poster, roster, ticket **7** account, catalog, charges, invoice, leaflet, measure, placard, program, statute **8** banknote, brochure, bulletin, calendar, circular, handbill, proposal, register, schedule **9** greenback, inventory, ordinance, reckoning, statement **10** regulation **12** treasury note **13** advertisement **17** silver certificate

billet 3 job **4** base, bunk, camp, digs, note, post **5** berth, house, lodge, place, put up **6** letter, office **7** bed down, lodging, quarter, shelter **8** domicile, dwelling, lodgment, position, quarters **9** residence, situation **11** accommodate, appointment **13** accommodation

billfold see **6** wallet

billiards
player: **11** Willie Hoppe **13** Minnesota Fats, Willie Mosconi

Bill of Divorcement, A
director: **11** George Cukor
cast: **11** Billie Burke **13** John Barrymore **16** Katharine Hepburn

billow 4 roll, wave **5** belly,

cloud, crest, surge, swell **6** puff up **7** balloon, breaker

Billy Budd
author: **14** Herman Melville
character: **8** Claggart **11** Captain Vere

billyclub 3 bat **5** billy, stick **8** bludgeon **9** truncheon

bin 3 box **4** cart, crib, silo **5** crate, frame, hatch **6** barrel, basket, bunker, hamper, holder, trough, vessel **9** container, inclosure **10** receptacle

binate 4 dual **6** double **7** coupled, two fold **14** growing in pairs

bind 3 rim, tie **4** edge, gird, glue, join, lash, rope, trim, wrap **5** affix, chafe, cover, cramp, force, frame, hitch, paste, stick, strap, tie up, truss **6** attach, border, coerce, compel, encase, fasten, fringe, oblige, secure, swathe **7** bandage, confine, require **8** encumber, obligate **9** prescribe **11** necessitate

binder 4 glue, roux **5** paste **6** cement **8** notebook **9** assurance, guarantee **11** down payment **12** earnest money **17** looseleaf notebook

binding 4 band, face, tape **5** valid **6** edging, ribbon **7** styptic **8** fastener, ligative **9** stringent **10** compulsory, obligatory, peremptory **12** constricting

binge 3 jag **4** bust, orgy, tear, toot **5** blast, drunk, fling, revel, spree **6** bender **7** carouse **8** beer-bust, carousal **11** bacchanalia **12** drunken spree

Bingham, George Caleb
born: **15** Augusta County VA
artwork: **13** Stump Speaking **17** The Trapper's Return **18** Verdict of the People **19** The Jolly Flatboatman **20** Raftsmen Playing Cards **31** Fur Traders Descending the Missouri

Bingley, Mr
character in: **17** Pride and Prejudice
author: **6** Austen

biochemist 17 biological chemist
American: **4** Cori **5** Bloch, Moore, Ochoa **7** Axelrod, Lipmann **8** Kornberg
English: **5** Krebs **6** Porter, Sanger **8** Mitchell
French: **5** Monod **7** Duclaux
German: **5** Lynen

biogenesis
discoverer: **12** Louis Pasteur

biography 3 bio 4 life, vita
6 memoir 7 account, history
9 life story

biologist
American: 6 Carson, Yerkes
7 Burbank 8 Delbruck
British: 6 Darwin, Huxley
7 Bateson, Medawar
French: 5 Jacob, Monod
7 Lamarck
German: 7 Schwann
Swiss: 6 Haller

biology
branch: 6 botany 7 zoology
classification: 15 Carolus
Linnaeus

birch 6 Betula
varieties: 3 Low, Red 4 Fire,
Gray 5 Black, Canoe, Dwarf,
Paper, River, Swamp, Sweet,
Water, White 6 Cherry, Yel-
low 7 Monarch 8 Mahog-
any, Old-field 10 West
Indian 13 European white,

Japanese white, Young's
weeping 14 Japanese
cherry

Birches
author: 11 Robert Frost

bird *see box*

Bird, Larry
sport: 10 basketball
position: 7 forward
team: 13 Boston Celtics

bird
anatomy: 3 bec, neb, nib 4 beak, bill, cere, crop, lora, lore, mala, nape, rump, tail, tuft,
wing 5 alula, crest, crown, flank, larum, lorum, pilea, rosta 6 breast, gullet, pecten, pileum,
pinion, syrinx, tarsus 7 ambiens, crissum, gizzard, rostrum 8 gigerium, pectines, scapular
9 auchenium, gastraeum 10 cordylanus
aquatic/water: 3 auk, cob, ern, mew 4 cobb, coot, duck, erne, gony, gull, ibis, loon, rail,
shag, skua, snipe, swan, teal, tern 5 booby, cahow, crane, diver, goose, grebe, heron, murre,
ousel, rotch, snipe, solan, stilt, stork 6 avocet, curlew, cygnet, dipper, fulmar, gannet, godwit, hagdon, jabiru, jacana, osprey, petrel, plover, puffin, rotche, scoter, wigeon 7 anhinga,
bidcock, bittern, bustard, dovekey, dovekie, finfoot, mallard, moorhen, pelican, penguin, seriema, skimmer, widgeon 8 alcatras, baldpate, dabchick, flamingo, murrelet, umbrette 9 alba-
tross, baptornis, cormorant, gallinule, guillemot, kittiwake, phalarope, snakebird, spoonbill
10 gaviformes, kingfisher, shearwater, sheathbill, yellowlegs 13 whooping crane
bird cage/home: 4 cote, mews, nest 5 roost 6 aviary, volary, volery 7 rookery
bird of freedom: 9 bald eagle
bird of ill-omen: 5 raven
bird of Jove: 5 eagle
bird of June: 7 peacock
bird of Minerva: 3 owl
bird of peace: 4 dove
bird of prey: 3 owl 4 gled, hawk, kite 5 buteo, eagle, glead, glede, harpy, saker 6 condor, ela-
net, elenet, falcon, musket, osprey, raptor 7 buzzard, goshawk, harrier, kestrel, stooper, vulture 8 caracara 9 accipiter, gyrfalcon, peregrine 11 accipitrine, lammergeier
bird of wonder/rebirth: 7 phoenix
carrion-eater: 4 aura 5 urubu 6 condor 7 buzzard, vulture
class: 4 Aves
combining form: 3 avi 4 orni 5 ornis 6 ornith 7 ornitho 8 ornithes
crow family: 3 daw, jay, kae 4 crow, rook 5 crake, raven 6 chough, corbie, magpie 7 corvine,
jackdaw
duck family: 4 clee, coot, lory, smew, teal, wood 5 eider, goose 6 scoter 7 gadwall, mallard,
Muscovy, pintail, pochard 8 baldpate, redshank, shoveler 9 merganser 10 bufflehead,
canvasback
extinct: 3 auk, jib, moa 4 dodo, jibi, mamo 5 didus 8 Diatryma 9 aepyornis, apatornis, gastor-
nis, hespornis, solitaire 11 archaeornis
flightless: 3 emu, ihi, moa 4 dodo, gorb, kagu, kiwi, rhea, weka 5 nandu 6 callow, kakapo,
moorup, ratite, takahe 7 apteryx, horling, ostrich, peacock, penguin, roatelo 8 notornis
9 cassowary
game: 4 duck, guan, rail, sora, teal 5 brant, goose, quail, snipe 6 chukar, colima, grouse, pigeon, plover, turkey 7 bustard, chicken, flapper, gadwall, mallard, pintail, prairie, widgeon
8 baldpate, bobwhite, moorfowl, pheasant, shoveler, tragopan, wildfowl, woodcock 9 merganser, partridge, ptarmigan 10 canvasback
group of birds: 3 nye 4 bank, bevy, cast, nide, sord 5 aerie, brood, covey, drove, flock,
plump 6 covert, flight, gaggle, litter, spring
largest: 7 ostrich 11 lammergeier
legendary: 3 roc 6 simurg 7 phoenix, simurgh 9 feng-huang, feng-hwang
loss of feathers: 7 molting
smallest: 11 hummingbird
nocturnal: 3 owl 5 cahow, owlet, potoo 7 bullbat, dorhawk 8 guacharo, nightjar 9 nighthawk,
thickknee 10 goatsucker 11 nightingale
pet: 4 myna 5 mynah 6 canary, parrot, pigeon 8 cockatoo, lovebird, parakeet
plumage: 8 ptilosis
poultry: 3 hen 4 duck 5 goose 6 pigeon, turkey 7 chicken, rooster 8 pheasant 14 Cornish
game hen
talking: 4 myna 5 mynah 6 parrot

Birdman of Alcatraz
director: 17 John Frankenheimer
cast: 10 Karl Malden 12 Edmond O'Brien, Neville Brand, Thelma Ritter 13 Burt Lancaster (Robert Stroud)

Bird of Paradise
constellation of: 4 Apus

Birds, The
author: 12 Aristophanes

character: 4 Iris 5 Meton 8 Basileia, Cinesias 9 Euelpides 10 King Tereus, Prometheus 12 Peithetairos

Birds, The
director: 15 Alfred Hitchcock
based on story by: 15 Daphne du Maurier
cast: 9 Rod Taylor 11 Tippi Hedren 12 Jessica Tandy 16 Suzanne Pleshette
setting: 10 California

Birds Fall Down, The
author: 15 Dame Rebecca West

Birkin, Rupert
character in: 11 Women in Love
author: 8 Lawrence

Birmingham
football team: 9 Stallions

Birmingham, Stephen
author of: 8 Our Crowd

---

wingless: 4 kiwi, weka 7 apteryx
young: 4 eyas, gull 5 chick, piper, poult, squab 6 gorlin, pullus 7 flapper, nestler 8 birdikin, nestling 9 fledgling
of Africa: 4 coly, fink, taha, tock 5 crane, paauw 6 barbet, bulbul, cuckoo, jabiru, quelea, whidah 7 courser, finfoot, marabou, ostrich, touraco 8 hornbill, oxpecker, parakeet, umbrette 9 beefeater, broadbill, francolin, napecrest, trochilus 10 hammerhead, weaverbird
of Antarctic/Arctic: 3 auk 4 gull, knot, skua, xema 5 brant, murre, rotch 6 dunlin, falcon, fulmar, jaeger, rotche 7 dovekey, dovekie, penguin 8 grayling 9 guillemot, gyrfalcon, ptarmigan 10 sheathbill
of Asia: 4 kora, myna, ruff, smew 5 mynah, pewit, pitta 6 bulbul, chukar, drongo, dunlin, hoopoe, linnet 7 boobook, courser, hill tit, lapwing, peacock, sirgang 8 accentor, dotterel, hornbill, leaf bird, parakeet, tragopan, wheatear 9 brambling, francolin, muted swan
of Australia: 3 emu 4 kahu, kiwi, koel, koil, lory 5 arara, galah, lowan, pitta 6 drongo, leipoa 7 boobook, bustard, figbird, grinder, waybung 8 bellbird, bushlark, cockatoo, ganggang, lorikeet, lyrebird, megapode, manucode, morepork, parakeet, platypus 9 bowerbird, cassowary, coachwhip, cockatiel, frogmouth, pardalote, thornbird 10 kookaburra
of Central America: 4 guan, ibis 5 booby, macaw 6 barbet, jabiru, quezal, toucan 7 bittern, cotinga, jacamar, quetzal, tinamou 8 curassow, puffbird, troupial
of Cuba: 6 trogon 8 tocororo 14 bee hummingbird
of England: 4 kite, rook 9 cormorant 11 carrion crow
of Europe: 3 dar, mag, mew, nun 4 clee, gled, mall, merl, pope, rook, ruff, shag, smew, wren 5 amsel, crake, egret, finch, glede, merle, ousel, ouzel, pewit, pipit, stilt, stork, swift, tarin, terek, whaup 6 cuckoo, dunlin, godwit, grouse, hoopoe, linnet, martin, merlin, missel, redleg, roller, siskin, thrush 7 bittern, bustard, jackdaw, kestrel, lapwing, martlet, ortolan, redwing, ruddock, skylark, sparrow, starnel, wagtail, wryneck 8 bee eater, blackcap, brantail, daychick, dotterel, garganey, nightjar, nuthatch, peesweep, redstart, reedling, starling, throstle, wheatear, whimbrel, whinchat, whinshat, woodcock 9 brambling, chaffinch, crossbill, field fare, gallinule, sheldrake, stonechat 10 chiffchaff, goatsucker, kingfisher, lammergeir, turtledove 11 lammergeier, nightingale, wallcreeper 12 capercaillie
of Hawaii: 2 io 3 ava, ioa, iwa, poe 4 nene, iiwi, koae, mamo, moho, omao 6 parson 7 frigate
of India: 4 baya, kala, koel, koil 5 sarus, shama 6 argala, bulbul, homrai, luggar 7 peacock 8 adjutant, amadavat, pheasant, tragopan 11 red hornbill
of Jamaica: 7 vervain
of Java: 7 sparrow 8 rice bird 9 fruit dove
of Madagascar: 6 drongo 7 anhinga, kirombo, roatelo
of Mexico: 6 jacana
of New Guinea: 9 cassowary 14 bird of paradise
of New Zealand: 3 ihi, kea, moa, poe, tui 4 huia, kaka, kaki, kiwi, koko, kuku, ruru, titi, weka 6 kakapo 7 apteryx 8 morepork, notornis
of North America: 3 ani, auk, tit 4 coot, crow, dove, ibis, lark, loon, pape, rook, sora, stib, swan, tern, wamp, wren 5 booby, brant, colin, crane, egret, finch, grebe, junco, murre, quail, robin, snipe, swift, veery, vireo 6 chebec, cuckoo, curlew, darter, dunlin, fulmar, grouse, hagdon, magpie, martin, oriole, phoebe, plover, shrike, thrush, towhee, turkey, verdin, willet 7 anhinga, bittern, blue jay, catbird, flicker, goshawk, grackle, lapwing, pelican, sparrow, swallow, tanager, warbler 8 bluebird, bobolink, bobwhite, cardinal, grosbeak, killdeer, nuthatch, poorwill, starling, thrasher, titmouse, wheatear 9 blackbird, chickadee, crossbill, goldfinch, gyrfalcon, nighthawk, partridge, sandpiper, snakebird 10 bufflehead, kingfisher, meadowlark, woodpecker 11 hummingbird, mockingbird 12 whippoorwill
of South America: 3 ara, hia 4 anna, guan, jacu, loro, mitu, rhea, soco, toco, yeni 5 egret, macaw, potoo, sylph 6 barbet, chatja, chunga, cracid, jabiru, motmot, sappho, toucan 7 cariama, cotinga, hoatzin, jacamar, limpkin, manakin, seriema, tinamou, warrior 8 boatbill, caracara, curassow, guacharo, hoactzin, screamer, tapacolo, tapaculo, terutero, troupial 9 campanero, trumpeter 11 scarlet ibis
of West India: 3 ani 4 tody

11 The Grandees 14 The Right People 15 Life at the Dakota

Birnbaum, Nathan
real name of: 11 George Burns

birth 5 blood, start, stock 6 family, origin, source, strain 7 bearing, descent, genesis, lineage 8 ancestry, breeding, delivery 9 beginning, being born, emergence, genealogy, inception, parentage 10 background, beginnings, childbirth, derivation, extraction 11 confinement, parturition 12 commencement

Birth of a Nation, The
director: 10 D W Griffith
cast: 8 Mae Marsh 11 Lillian Gish 14 Henry B Walthall

Birth of Tragedy, The
author: 18 Friedrich Nietzsche

birthstones
January: 6 garnet
February: 8 amethyst
March: 6 jasper 10 aquamarine, bloodstone
April: 7 diamond 8 sapphire
May: 5 agate 7 emerald
June: 5 pearl 7 emerald 9 moonstone 11 alexandrite
July: 4 onyx, ruby 8 star ruby
August: 7 peridot 8 sardonyx 9 carnelian
September: 8 sapphire 10 chrysolite 12 star sapphire
October: 4 opal 5 beryl 10 aquamarine, tourmaline
November: 5 topaz
December: 4 ruby 6 zircon 9 turquoise

biscuit 3 bun 4 cake, roll 5 cooky, scone, wafer 6 bisque, cookie, muffin, parking, simnel 7 cracker, dogbone 8 hardtack, zwieback 9 pale-brown 10 crisp bread, quick bread 15 unglazed pottery

bisect 5 cross, split 8 cut in two 9 cut in half, intersect

bishop 4 abba, pope 5 punch 6 cleric, despot, priest 7 pontiff, prelate, primate 8 overseer 9 clergyman, patriarch 10 chesspiece, high priest
of Rome: 4 pope
Greek: 9 episkopos
means: 8 overseer
district: 7 diocese
headdress: 5 miter, mitre

Bismarck, Otto von
nickname: 14 Iron Chancellor
unified: 7 Germany

chancellor / minister for: 15 Emperor William I
policy: 12 "iron and blood"

bison 4 urus 6 wild ox, wisent 7 aurochs, buffalo
native to: 6 Europe 12 North America

Bissau
capital of: 12 Guinea-Bissau

Bisset, Jacqueline
real name: 22 Jacqueline Fraser Bisset
born: 7 England 9 Weybridge
roles: 5 Class 7 Airport, The Deep 11 Day for Night 12 Anna Karenina 16 The Mephisto Waltz 24 Murder on the Orient Express

bistro 3 bar 4 cafe 6 tavern 7 cabaret 9 nightclub 10 supper club
French: 9 estaminet

bit 3 dab 4 chip, drop, iota, mite, snip, whit 5 crumb, grain, pinch, scrap, shred, speck, spell, trace 6 dollop, moment, morsel, paring, trifle 7 droplet, granule, shaving, smidgen 8 fragment, particle 9 short time 10 short while, small piece, smithereen, sprinkling
type: 5 auger, drill 6 gimlet, wimble 7 bradawl 11 brace and bit

bitch 3 nag 5 botch, brood, cheat, fault, shrew, spoil, witch, whine 6 kvetch, virago 7 blunder, bungle, grouse 8 complain, harridan 9 complaint, female dog, termagant

bitchy 4 mean 5 catty, cruel, nasty 6 wicked 7 hateful, vicious 8 spiteful 9 heartless, malicious 10 backbiting, malevolent, vindictive

bite 3 bit, dab, dig, nip 4 gnaw, grip, snip 5 champ, crumb, gnash, prick, scrap, shred, smart, speck, sting, taste 6 morsel, nibble, pierce 7 eat into 8 mouthful, stinging, take hold 10 small piece, tooth wound 12 small portion

biting 5 harsh, sharp 6 bitter 7 caustic, cutting, mordant, nipping 8 piercing, scathing, smarting, stinging 9 sarcastic, trenchant, withering 12 sharp-tongued

Biton
father: 7 Cydippe

bit player 5 extra 6 walk on 14 minor character

bitte 6 please 12 you're welcome 14 I beg your pardon

bitter 4 acid, mean, sour, tart

5 acrid, angry, cruel, harsh, sharp 6 biting, morose, severe, sullen 7 acerbic, caustic, crabbed, painful 8 grievous, piercing, scornful, smarting, spiteful, stinging, wretched 9 rancorous, resentful 10 astringent 11 distressing

bitterness 5 anger, scorn, spite 6 animus, rancor, spleen 7 ill will 8 acerbity, acrimony, sourness 9 animosity, harshness, hostility, malignity, sharpness 10 antagonism, malignancy 11 astringency 12 hard feelings, spitefulness 14 unpleasantness

bitters
type: 6 spirit
flavor: 6 orange 7 gentian
brand: 9 Angostura

bivalve 4 clam 5 pinna 6 cockle, mussel, mollusk, scallop 8 mollusca 9 pelecypod 13 lamellibranch

bivouac 4 camp 5 tents 10 campground, encampment

bizarre 3 odd 5 kinky, kooky, queer, weird 7 strange, unusual 8 freakish 9 fantastic, grotesque 10 outlandish

Bizet, Georges
real name: 26 Alexandre Cesar Leopold Bizet
born: 5 Paris 6 France
composer of: 4 Roma (suite) 6 Carmen, Patrie 8 Djamileh 11 Don Procopio, L'Arlesienne 12 Jeux d'enfants, Pearl Fishers 14 Children's Games 15 Ivan the Terrible 16 Le Docteur Miracle 18 The Fair Maid of Perth

Biztha 6 eunuch

Bjornson, Bjornstjerne
author of: 4 Arne 7 The King 8 Magnhild 9 A Happy Boy, In God's Way, Lame Hulda, The Editor 10 King Sverre 11 A Bankruptcy, The Bankrupt 12 Sigurd Slembe 14 Arnljot Gelline, Beyond Our Power 15 The Fisher Maiden, The Newly Married 16 Beyond Human Might, Sigurd the Bastard 17 Between the Battles 20 Mary Stuart in Scotland 24 Paul Lange and Tora Parsberg 27 Flags Are Flying in Town and Port

blab 3 rat 6 babble, tattle 7 blabber, prattle 9 tell tales 13 spill the beans 20 let the cat out of the bag

blabber 3 gab, gas, yak 4 blab, bull 5 prate 6 babble, drivel, gabble, gibber, gossip, jabber 7 blather, chatter, palaver, prattle, twaddle **8** blah-blah, chitchat, idle talk **9** jabbering **10** mumbo-jumbo **12** gobbledegook **14** chitter-chatter

blabbermouth 6 gabber, gossip, prater **7** blabber **8** bigmouth, busybody, gossiper, informer, jabberer, liverlip, prattler, quidnunc **9** chatterer **10** chatterbox, talebearer, tattletale **11** rumormonger **12** gossipmonger **13** scandalmonger

black, Black 3 bad, dim, jet **4** dark, evil, grim, inky **5** angry, ebony, murky, Negro, raven, sable **6** dismal, gloomy, somber, sullen, wicked **7** colored, furious, hostile, stygian, sunless, swarthy **8** moonless **9** coal-black, lightless, nefarious, unlighted **10** calamitous **11** dark-skinned, threatening **12** Afro-American **13** unilluminated

Black Arrow, The
author: **20** Robert Louis Stevenson

blackball 3 ban, bar, cut **4** snub **5** debar **6** banish, outlaw, reject **7** boycott, exclude, keep out, shut out **8** pass over, turndown **9** blacklist, ostracize, proscribe **11** vote against **12** cold-shoulder **14** send to Coventry

black beast
French: **9** bete noire

blackberry 5 Rubus
variety: **4** Sand **5** Swamp **7** Cut-leaf, Pacific, Running, Sow-teat **9** Evergreen **13** Parsley-leaved **18** Evergreen thornless

Blackberry Winter
author: **12** Margaret Mead

blackbird 4 crow **5** raven, slave **6** thrush **7** cowbird, grackle, redwing **8** song bird **9** slave ship **11** slave trader **17** kidnapped islander, plantation laborer
kind: **9** red-winged **12** yellow-headed
family: **8** Turdidae **9** Icteridae

Blackboard Jungle, The
director: **13** Richard Brooks
based on novel by: **10** Evan Hunter
cast: **9** Glenn Ford, Vic Morrow **11** Anne Francis **12** Louis Calhern, Paul Mazursky, Richard Kiley **13** Sidney Poitier **14** Warner Anderson

Black Boy
author: **13** Richard Wright

blacken 5 libel, smear, stain,

sully **6** befoul, darken, defame, defile, revile, vilify **7** slander, tarnish **8** besmirch, disgrace, dishonor **9** denigrate, discredit **10** stigmatize

Blackfoot, Blackfeet
language family: **9** Algonkian **10** Algonquian
tribe: **6** Bloods, Kainah, Piegan, Pikuni **7** Siksika
location: **6** Canada **7** Alberta, Montana **12** Saskatchewan

blackguard 3 cad, rat, SOB **5** knave, louse, rogue, scamp **6** rascal **7** bastard, villain **9** miscreant, scoundrel

blackhearted 4 base, vile **6** sinful, wicked **7** ignoble **10** despicable, evil-minded, villainous **11** scoundrelly **12** unprincipled **13** reprehensible

blackjack
also known as: **9** twenty-one
French: **9** vingt-et-un
play against: **6** dealer
additional card: **3** hit

Black Lamb and Grey Falcon
author: **15** Dame Rebecca West

Black Land, The see **5** Egypt

blackleg 7 cheater **8** swindler **9** trickster

blacklist 3 ban, bar **4** shun **5** debar **6** reject **7** exclude, lock out, shut out **8** preclude **9** blackball, ostracize

blacklisting 7 boycott **8** spurning **9** exclusion, ostracism, rejection **12** blackballing

black magic 7 sorcery **10** witchcraft

blackmail 5 force **6** coerce, extort, payoff **7** squeeze, tribute **8** threaten **9** extortion, hush money, shakedown

black mark 4 blot **5** stain **6** bruise **7** blemish, demerit **9** contusion

Blackmore, Richard Doddridge
author of: **10** Lorna Doone **11** Springhaven **13** The Maid of Sker

black mountain see **10** Montenegro

Black Narcissus
author: **11** Rumer Godden
director: **13** Michael Powell **17** Emeric Pressburger
cast: **4** Sabu **11** David Farrar, Deborah Kerr, Jean Simmons
setting: **9** Himalayas

blackness 4 dark **5** gloom, shade **7** dimness **8** darkness

Blackpool, Stephen
character in: **9** Hard Times
author: **7** Dickens

Black Prince, The
author: **11** Iris Murdoch

Blackstone, Sir William
author of: **12** Commentaries (on the Laws of England)

Black Uhlan
nickname of: **12** Max Schmeling

Blackwater State
nickname of: **8** Nebraska

Blackwell, Elizabeth
first American: **11** woman doctor

bladder 3 bag, sac **4** cyst **5** pouch **7** blister, pustule, sacule, utricle **10** receptacle

blade 4 leaf **5** frond, knife, razor, sword **6** cutter, needle, switch **7** scalpel **10** sled runner **11** cutting edge, skate runner

blah 4 bosh, dull, flat, guff, so-so **5** bland, ho-hum, hooey, vapid **6** boring, bunkum, dreary, hot air, humbug **7** blather, eyewash, humdrum, nothing, tedious, twaddle **8** claptrap, lifeless, listless, nonsense **9** gibberish **10** balderdash, monotonous, pedestrian **11** uninspiring **13** characterless, unimaginative, uninteresting, unstimulating

Blaik, Earl H
sport: **8** football
position: **5** coach
team: **4** Army **9** Dartmouth
military rank: **7** colonel

Blair, Eric Arthur
real name of: **12** George Orwell

Blake, Robert
real name: **28** Michael James Vijencio Gubitosi
born: **8** Nutley NJ
roles: **7** Baretta, Our Gang **8** Red Ryder **11** In Cold Blood **12** Little Beaver **23** Tell Them Willie Boy Is Here **24** The Treasure of Sierra Madre

Blake, William
born: **6** London **7** England
author of: **6** Milton, Tiriel **9** Jerusalem **13** The Book of Thel **14** Prophetic Books **15** The Book of Urigen **16** Songs of Innocence **17** Songs of Experience **21** Little Lamb Who Made Thee **23** Marriage of Heaven and Hell, Tiger Tiger Burning Bright
artwork: **6** Milton **9** Book of

Job, Jerusalem **11** The Four Zoas **12** Book of Urizen, Divine Comedy **16** Songs of Innocence **17** Songs of Experience **23** Marriage of Heaven and Hell

blamable 10 censurable, deplorable, punishable, reprovable **11** blameworthy **12** reproachable **13** reprehensible

Blamauer, Karoline
real name of: **10** Lotte Lenya

blame 4 onus **5** fault, guilt **6** accuse, burden, charge, rebuke **7** censure, condemn, reproof, reprove **8** reproach **9** castigate, criticism, criticize, liability **10** accusation, disapprove **11** castigation, culpability **12** condemnation, denunciation, remonstrance **13** find fault with, recrimination **14** accountability, responsibility **15** hold responsible

blameless 5 clear **8** innocent, spotless **9** guiltless, not guilty, unspotted, unstained, unsullied, untainted **10** inculpable, not at fault, unblamable **11** unblemished, uncorrupted **13** unimpeachable **14** irreproachable, not responsible

blameless in life
Latin: **12** integer vitae

blame on 7 trace to **8** charge to **9** set down to **11** attribute to **14** lay at the door of

blameworthy 8 blamable **10** censurable, deplorable, punishable, reprovable **12** reproachable **13** reprehensible

blanch 4 fade **6** bleach, whiten **7** lighten **8** turn pale

blanched 3 wan **4** pale **5** ashen, faded **6** chalky, pallid **8** bleached **9** bloodless

bland 4 blah, calm, dull, even, flat, mild **5** balmy, quiet, vapid **6** benign, smooth **7** calming, humdrum, nothing, prosaic, tedious **8** moderate, peaceful, soothing, tiresome, tranquil **9** peaceable, temperate, unruffled **10** monotonous, unexciting, untroubled **11** uninspiring **13** nonirritating, uninteresting, unstimulating

blandish 4 coax, lure, urge **5** charm, tempt **6** cajole, entice, prompt **7** blarney, flatter, wheedle **8** inveigle, persuade

blandishment, blandishments 7 blarney, coaxing **8** cajolery, flattery **9** sweet talk, wheedling **12** ingratiation, inveiglement

Blandois, Monsieur
character in: **12** Little Dorrit
author: **7** Dickens

blank 3 gap **4** dull, idle, void **5** clean, clear, empty, inane, plain, space **6** futile, hollow, unused, vacant, vacuum, wasted **7** useless, vacancy, vacuous **8** unmarked **9** emptiness, fruitless, valueless, worthless **10** empty space, hollowness, profitless **11** meaningless, thoughtless, unrewarding **12** inexpressive **14** expressionless

blanket 4 coat, film **5** cloak, cover, quilt, throw **6** afghan, carpet, mantle, veneer **7** coating, overlay **8** covering, coverlet **9** comforter

blare 4 honk, peal, roar **5** blast **6** bellow, scream **7** resound, trumpet

blarney 4 fibs, line **5** pitch, spiel **6** hot air **7** coaxing, fawning, snow job, stories **8** cajolery, flattery **9** hyperbole, wheedling **10** inveigling, overpraise, sweet words **12** exaggeration, honeyed words **13** blandishments, overstatement

blase 4 full **5** bored, jaded **6** gorged **7** glutted **9** apathetic, satisfied, saturated, surfeited, unexcited, unmovable **10** insouciant, nonchalant, spiritless, world-weary **11** indifferent, unconcerned **12** uninterested **14** unenthusiastic

Blasko, Bela
real name of: **10** Bela Lugosi

blaspheme 5 curse, swear **6** revile **7** profane **10** take in vain

blasphemous 7 godless, impious, profane, ungodly **10** irreverent **11** irreligious **12** sacrilegious

blasphemy 7 cursing, impiety **8** swearing **9** profanity, sacrilege **11** impiousness, irreverence, profanation

blast 4 bomb, boom, bore, gale, gust, honk, peal, roar, rush, toot **5** blare, bleat, burst, level, shell, surge **6** bellow, blow up, report, scream, shriek **7** explode, resound, torpedo **8** dynamite, eruption **9** discharge, explosion, loud noise **10** detonation **11** sound loudly

blasting material 3 TNT **8** dynamite **9** explosive

blatant 4 loud **5** cheap, clear, crass, crude, gross, harsh,

noisy, overt **6** brazen, coarse, tawdry, vulgar **7** blaring, glaring, obvious, uncouth **8** flagrant, piercing, unsubtle **9** clamorous, deafening, obtrusive, offensive, prominent, tasteless, ungenteel, unrefined **10** indelicate, unpolished **11** conspicuous, ill-mannered, undignified **12** ear-splitting, unmistakable

blather 4 stir **7** chatter, prattle **8** nonsense **9** commotion

Blatty, William P
author of: **11** The Exorcist

Blaue Reiter 10 Blue Riders
group of: **13** German artists

blaze 3 ray **4** beam, burn, fire, glow, rush **5** blast, burst, flame, flare, flash, glare, gleam, shine **6** flames **7** glisten, glitter, shimmer, torrent **8** eruption, outbreak, outburst, radiance **9** explosion **10** brightness, brilliance, effulgence **12** resplendence **13** conflagration

blazer 4 coat **6** jacket **12** sports jacket

blazing 3 hot **5** fiery, afire **6** firing, on fire **7** burning, flaming, flaring, glaring, glowing, intense, shining **8** bursting, bleaming, shooting, shouting **9** brilliant

Blazing Saddles
director: **9** Mel Brooks
cast: **9** Mel Brooks **10** Alex Karras, Dom DeLuise, Gene Wilder **11** Slim Pickens **12** Harvey Korman, Madeline Kahn **13** Cleavon Little, John Hillerman **15** David Huddleston

blazon 5 blare, boast **7** trumpet **8** proclaim **10** coat of arms, make public **16** armorial bearings

blazonry 4 arms **5** crest **6** blazon **8** insignia **10** coat of arms **14** heraldic emblem **16** heraldic bearings

bleach 4 fade **6** blanch, whiten **7** lighten, wash out **8** make pale

bleak 3 icy, raw **4** bare, cold, grim **5** chill **6** barren, biting, bitter, dismal, dreary, frosty, gloomy, somber, wintry **7** nipping **8** desolate, piercing **9** cheerless, windswept **10** depressing, forbidding **11** distressing, unpromising **13** weather-beaten

Bleak House
author: **14** Charles Dickens
character: **2** Jo (the crossing

sweeper) **4** Nemo **5** Guppy, Krook **6** Bucket, Guster **7** Snagsby **8** Chadband **9** Miss Flite **10** Mrs Jellyby, Turveydrop **11** Dr Woodcourt, Lady Dedlock, Tulkinghorn **12** John Jarndyce **13** Captain Rawdon **14** Harold Skimpole **15** Esther Summerson, Richard Carstone **19** Sir Leicester Dedlock
satire of: 3 law **6** courts **8** chancery
case: 19 Jarndyce and Jarndyce

bleakness 8 bareness, grimness **10** barrenness, desolation, dreariness, gloominess **13** cheerlessness

bleat 3 baa, cry, maa **5** whine **7** whimper

bleb 6 bubble **7** blister

bleed 3 run, tap **4** leak, soak **5** drain, valve **6** fleece, suffer **7** diffuse, extract, **8** let blood **9** draw blood, sacrifice **10** hemorrhage, overcharge **12** phlebotomize

Blefuscu
fictional land in: 16 Gulliver's Travels
author: 5 Swift

blemish 3 mar, zit **4** blot, blur, flaw, mark, spot **5** spoil, stain, sully, taint **6** blotch, defect, smirch, smudge **7** tarnish **9** disfigure **12** imperfection **13** disfigurement

blend 3 mix **4** fuse **5** merge, unite **6** fusion, go well, merger, mingle **7** amalgam, combine, mixture **8** coalesce, compound, mergence, mingling **9** harmonize **10** amalgamate, complement, concoction **11** combination, incorporate, intermingle

bless 4 give **5** endow, favor, grace, guard, honor **6** anoint, bestow, hallow, oblige, ordain **7** baptize, benefit, protect, support **8** dedicate, sanctify **9** watch over **10** consecrate

blessed 4 holy **5** happy, lucky **6** adored, graced, joyful, joyous, sacred **7** endowed, favored, revered **8** blissful, hallowed **9** fortunate, venerated, wonderful **10** felicitous, sanctified **11** consecrated

Blessed Damozel, The
author: 20 Dante Gabriel Rossetti

blessedness 5 bliss **8** felicity **9** beatitude **11** saintliness

blessing 4 gain, gift, good

5 favor, grace, leave **6** bounty, profit, regard **7** backing, benefit, consent, support **8** approval, sanction **9** advantage, hallowing **10** dedication, good wishes, invocation, permission **11** benediction, concurrence, good fortune **12** consecration, thanksgiving **14** sanctification

blessings 4 joys **5** gifts **6** favors **7** success **8** benefits, delights **10** advantages **11** good fortune

Blifil, Master
character in: 8 Tom Jones
author: 8 Fielding

Bligh, Captain William
character in: 17 Mutiny on the Bounty
authors: 4 Hall **8** Nordhoff

blight 3 pox, rot **4** harm, kill, ruin, rust **5** blast, crush, curse, decay, smash, spoil, wreck **6** cancer, canker, dry rot, fungus, injure, mildew, plague, thwart, wither **7** cripple, destroy, scourge, shrivel **8** demolish **9** frustrate **10** affliction, corruption, pestilence **12** plant disease **13** contamination

Blimber, Dr
character in: 12 Dombey and Son
author: 7 Dickens

blind 4 dull, ruse **5** cover, dodge, front, shade **6** hidden, insane, obtuse, screen **7** obscure, pretext, unaware **8** disguise, heedless, ignorant, mindless, unseeing **9** concealed, deception, senseless, sightless, sun shield, unfeeling, unknowing, unmindful, unnoticed **10** camouflage, insouciant, irrational, masquerade, neglectful, subterfuge, unthinking **11** inattentive, incognizant, indifferent, insensitive, smoke screen, unconcerned, unconscious, unobservant, unobserving **12** imperceptive, uncontrolled, undiscerning, uninterested, unnoticeable, unperceptive, unreasonable **13** unenlightened **14** uncontrollable **15** uncomprehending

blind alley 7 closure, dead-end, impasse **8** blockade, cul-de-sac, dead lock, no escape **9** hindrance, stone wall **10** impassable, standstill **11** obstruction

blinder 4 hood **5** blind, shade **6** screen **7** blinker **9** blindfold

blindfold 6 darken **7** bandage, blinder, obscure **8** covering heedless, reckless **11** strike blind

blind seer 8 Tiresias

blink 4 wink **5** flash, shine, waver **6** falter, flinch, squint **7** flicker, glimmer, shimmer, sparkle, twinkle **9** nictitate, vacillate

blinker(s) 3 eye **6** peeper **7** blinder, flasher, goggles **8** black eye **13** warning signal

blintz, blintze 4 blin **5** crepe **6** blints **7** pancake

blip 3 dot, tap **4** spot **5** bleep, image **6** censor **7** replace

bliss 3 joy **4** glee **5** heaven, luxury **7** delight, ecstasy, rapture **8** gladness, paradise **9** happiness **10** exaltation, jubilation **12** exhilaration

blissful 5 happy **6** divine, joyful, joyous **7** blessed, sublime **8** beatific, ecstatic, glorious, heavenly **9** rapturous

blithe 3 gay **4** airy, glad **5** blind, happy, jolly, merry, sunny **6** casual, cheery, jaunty, jovial, joyous, lively **7** gleeful, radiant **8** carefree, careless, cheerful, debonair, exaltant, heedless, mirthful, uncaring **9** ebullient, sprightly, unfeeling, unmindful **10** blithesome, frolicking **11** indifferent, insensitive, thoughtless, unconcerned, unconscious **12** lighthearted **13** inconsiderate

Blithedale Romance, The
author: 18 Nathaniel Hawthorne

blithesome 3 gay **5** light, merry, sunny **6** breezy, jaunty, lively **7** buoyant **8** animated, carefree, cheerful **11** free and easy

Blixen-Finecke, Karen
real name of: 11 Isak Dinesen

blizzard 4 blow, gale **5** blast **6** flurry, squall **7** tempest **8** snowfall **9** snowstorm **11** winter storm

Blizzard State
nickname of: 11 South Dakota

bloat 5 swell **6** blow up, dilate, expand, puff up **7** balloon, distend, enlarge, inflate

blob 4 daub, drop, mass **7** globule, splotch

bloc 4 body, ring, wing **5** cabal, group, union **6** clique **7** combine, faction **8** alliance **9** coalition **11** combination

Bloch, Ernest
born: 6 Geneva **11** Switzerland

composer of: **7** Macbeth, Solomon **8** Baal Shem, Schelomo **13** Sacred Service **14** Avodath Hakdesh, Israel Symphony **16** American Symphony **19** Concerto Symphonique **20** Voice in the Wilderness

block 3 bar, jam **4** cube, form, halt, mold **5** brick, check, choke, shape **6** hinder, impede, re-form, square, stop up, thwart **7** barrier, prevent, reshape **8** blockade, blockage, obstacle, obstruct **9** hindrance **10** impediment **11** obstruction **12** interference

blockade 3 bar, dam **4** dike **5** block, check, levee **6** hurdle **7** barrier, parapet, rampart **8** blockage, obstacle, obstruct, stockade, stoppage **9** barricade, hindrance, roadblock **10** checkpoint, earthworks, impediment **11** obstruction, restriction **13** fortification

blockage 3 jam **8** obstacle **9** hindrance **10** impediment **11** obstruction

blockhead 3 ass **4** clod, dolt, fool, yutz **5** booby, dummy, dunce, idiot, klutz, moron, ninny **6** dum-dum, nitwit **7** fathead, half-wit, jackass **8** bonehead, dumb-dumb, dumm kopf, imbecile, lunkhead, mushhead, numskull **9** harebrain, iamebrain, simpleton **10** chowerhead, dunderhead, nincompoop, noodlehead **12** featherbrain

block out 3 hew **5** carve **6** chisel, devise, map out, sculpt, sketch **7** outline **8** indicate **9** formulate

block up 3 bar **4** clog **6** stop up **7** brick up **9** barricade

blond, blonde 4 fair, gold, pale **5** light **6** flaxen, golden, yellow **8** light tan **9** yellowish **10** fair-haired **11** fair-skinned **12** light-colored

Blonde Bombshell
nickname of: **10** Jean Harlow

Blondell, Joan
husband: **8** Mike Todd **10** Dick Powell
born: **9** New York NY
roles: **8** The Champ **11** Blonde Crazy, Gold Diggers, The Blue Veil **14** Blondie Johnson, The Public Enemy **20** A Tree Grows in Brooklyn

Blondie
creator: **9** Chic Young

character:
husband: **15** Dagwood Bumstead
children: **6** Cookie **9** Alexander **12** Baby Dumpling
boss: **6** Julius **9** Mr Dithers
boss's wife: **4** Cora
neighbor: **11** Herb Woodley **14** Tootsie Woodley
dog: **5** Daisy

blood 4 gore **5** birth, stock **6** family, source, spirit, temper **7** descent, lineage, passion **8** ancestry, heritage, vitality **9** lifeblood **10** extraction, family line, vital fluid, vital force **11** temperament **13** consanguinity **14** vital principle

Blood, field of 8 Aceldama

Blood, Sweat and Tears
author: **17** Winston S Churchill

bloodless 4 pale **5** ashen **6** anemic, pallid **7** insipid **8** blanched, lifeless, peaceful **9** colorless, deathlike, washed out

bloodline 6 family **8** ancestry, pedigree **9** genealogy **10** family tree

Bloodline
author: **13** Sidney Sheldon

bloodshed 4 gore **6** murder, pogrom **7** carnage, killing, slaying **8** butchery, massacre **9** blood bath, blood feud, slaughter **10** mass murder **12** bloodletting, manslaughter **15** spilling of blood

Bloodsmoor Romance, A
author: **15** Joyce Carol Oates

bloodstone
month: **5** March

blood system
part: **5** blood, liver **6** spleen **9** lymph node **10** bone marrow

bloodthirsty 5 cruel **6** bloody, brutal, fierce, savage **7** bestial, demonic, inhuman, vicious **8** barbaric, demoniac, fiendish, pitiless, ruthless **9** atrocious, barbarous, cutthroat, heartless, homicidal, merciless, murdering, murderous **10** demoniacal, sanguinary **11** sanguineous

blood vessel 4 vein **5** aorta **6** artery **7** carotid **9** capillary
prefix: **5** angio

Blood Wedding
author: **19** Federico Garcia Lorca

bloody 3 red **4** gory, rude, vevy **5** cruel, lurid **6** cursed, damned **7** crimson, scarlet **8** bleeding **9** merciless, murderous **10** sanguinary

Bloody Shame see **10** Virgin Mary (drink)

bloom 3 bud **4** glow, grow, zest **5** flare, flush, prime, shine, vigor **6** beauty, flower, heyday, luster, sprout, thrive **7** blossom, burgeon, develop, prosper, succeed **8** fare well, flourish, fructify, radiance, rosiness, strength **9** bear fruit, flowerage, flowering, germinate **10** blossoming **11** florescence, flourishing

Bloom, Claire
real name: **11** Claire Blume
husband: **10** Rod Steiger
born: **6** London **7** England
roles: **6** Charly **9** Limelight **10** Richard III **15** Look Back in Anger **26** The Spy Who Came in from the Cold

Bloom, Leopold and Molly
characters in: **7** Ulysses
author: **5** Joyce

bloomers 8 knickers, trousers **9** plus fours, underwear **10** underpants **15** knickerbockers

blooming 3 fit **4** pert, rosy **5** utter **6** abloom, robust, strong **7** healthy **8** vigorous **9** healthful **10** blossoming **11** flourishing **12** efflorescent, fit as a fiddle **15** picture of health

blooper 4 goof, slip **5** boner, botch, error, fluff, gaffe, lapse **6** bobble, booboo, slip-up **7** blunder, mistake, screwup

blossom 4 grow **5** bloom **6** flower, thrive **7** burgeon, develop **8** flourish, progress

Blossomed miraculously
9 Aaron's rod

blossoming 5 bloom **8** blooming, thriving **9** flowering **10** burgeoning, developing **11** florescence, flourishing

blot 3 dry **4** flaw, mark, spot **5** smear, stain, taint **6** absorb, blotch, remove, smirch, smudge, soak up, stigma, take up **7** bad mark, blemish, splotch **8** besmirch **13** discoloration

blotch 4 blot, mark, spot **7** splotch

Blot on the 'Scutcheon, The
author: **14** Robert Browning

blot out 5 erase **6** remove, rub out **7** abolish, eclipse, expunge **9** eliminate, eradicate **10** obliterate

blotting out 7 eclipse, erasing **9** expunging, wiping out **11** eradicating, eradication **12** annihilation, obliterating, obliteration **13** overshadowing

blouse 4 coat **5** drape, tunic, shirt, smock **6** camise, billow **7** blouson **8** casaquin

blow 3 box, hit, jab, pop **4** bang, bash, belt, cuff, gale, gust, honk, jolt, play, puff, sock, toot, wind **5** blast, burst, clout, crack, knock, punch, shock, smack, sound, storm, thump, upset, whack **6** exhale, rebuff, squall, wallop **7** breathe, explode, tempest, tragedy, whistle **8** calamity, disaster, expel air, reversal **9** detriment, windstorm **10** affliction, misfortune **11** catastrophe **14** disappointment

blow from the hand
French: 10 coup de main

blowhard 6 gascon **7** boaster, bragger, egotist **8** braggart **9** big talker **11** braggadocio

blow of mercy
French: 11 coup de grace

blow out 5 burst **7** rupture **10** extinguish

blowsy, blowzy 5 messy **6** frowzy, mussed, sloppy, untidy **7** unkempt **10** disarrayed, disheveled, disordered, disorderly, in disorder **11** disarranged

blow up 5 bloat, burst **6** billow, dilate, expand **7** balloon, distend, enlarge, explode, inflate, puff out **8** dynamite, swell out **12** lose one's cool **14** lose one's temper

Blowup
director: 21 Michelangelo Antonioni
cast: 8 Verushka **10** Sarah Miles **13** David Hemmings **15** Vanessa Redgrave

blowy 5 gusty, windy **6** breezy **7** squally **8** blustery

blubber 3 cry, fat, sob **4** bawl, flab, wail, weep **6** boohoo

Blubber
author: 9 Judy Blume

bludgeon 3 bat, hit **4** club **5** billy, clout, stick **6** cudgel **7** clobber **9** billyclub, truncheon

blue 3 low, sad **4** aqua, down, navy **5** azure **6** bluish, cobalt, gloomy, indigo, morose **7** doleful **8** cerulean, dejected, downcast, sapphire **9** depressed, turquoise **10** aqua-

marine, despondent, melancholy **11** downhearted, lapis lazuli, ultra-marine **12** disconsolate **14** down in the dumps, down in the mouth

Blue Angel, The
director: 17 Josef von Sternberg
based on novel by: 12 Heinrich Mann
cast: 10 Kurt Gerron **12** Emil Jannings **15** Marlene Dietrich (Lola-Lola)
song: 18 Falling in Love Again

Bluebeard
characteristic: 9 many wives

bluebell 9 Mertensia **18** Mertensia Virginica **21** Campanula rotundifolia
variety: 7 English, Spanish **8** Virginia **10** Australian, California **11** Clanwilliam

blueberry 9 Vaccinium
variety: 3 Low **4** Male **5** Swamp **7** Lowbush, Sourtop, Western **8** Creeping, Elliott's, Highbush, Low sweet **9** Late sweet, Rabbiteye **10** Velvet-leaf **13** Black highbush

blueblood 4 peer **5** noble **8** nobleman **9** patrician, socialite **10** aristocrat, noblewoman **14** peer of the realm

blue-blooded 5 noble, regal, royal **6** titled **7** courtly **8** highbred, wellborn **9** patrician **10** upper-class **12** aristocratic, of royal blood

blue bloods 5 elite **8** nobility **9** haut monde **10** patricians **11** aristocracy, high society **14** creme de la creme

bluegrass 3 Poa
varieties: 3 Big **4** Wood **5** Rough, Texas **6** Annual, Canada **7** Bulbous, English **8** Kentucky, Sandberg **10** Rough-stalk

Bluegrass State
nickname of: 8 Kentucky

Blue Hen State
nickname of: 8 Delaware

Blue Knight, The
author: 14 Joseph Wambaugh

Blue Law State
nickname of: 11 Connecticut

blue-pencil 3 cut **4** edit, trim **6** censor, cut out, delete, digest, reduce **7** abridge, shorten **8** boil down, condense, pare down **9** expurgate **10** abbreviate

blueprint 4 plan **5** chart **6** design, scheme **7** diagram **9** schematic

Blue Riders
German: 11 Blaue Reiter
group of: 7 artists

blues 5 dumps **8** doldrums **10** depression, low spirits, melancholy **11** despondency

bluestocking
French: 7 bas bleu

bluff 3 lie **4** bank, bold, crag, curt, dupe, fake, fool, hoax, liar, open, peak, sham **5** blunt, boast, cliff, faker, frank, fraud, ridge, rough **6** abrupt, candid, crusty, delude, direct, humbug **7** bluffer, boaster, brusque, deceive, fake out, mislead, pretend **8** bragging, headland, headlong, palisade, pretense **9** bamboozle, deception, idle boast, outspoken, precipice, pretender **10** escarpment, forthright, promontory, subterfuge **11** braggadocio, counterfeit, plainspoken **13** unceremonious, straightforward

bluffer 5 bluff, faker, fraud, phony **6** humbug **9** pretender

bluish 7 off-blue **12** somewhat blue

Blume, Claire
real name of: 11 Claire Bloom

Blume, Judy
author of: 5 Wifey **6** Deenie **7** Blubber, Forever **19** Then Again Maybe I Won't **22** It's Not the End of the World **26** Tales of a Fourth Grade Nothing **27** Are You There God? It's Me Margaret

Blumenbach, Johann Friedrich
field: 7 anatomy **10** physiology
nationality: 6 German
father of: 20 physical anthropology

blunder 4 goof, slip **5** boner, error, gaffe **6** booboo, bumble, bungle, slip up **7** faux pas, mistake, stagger, stumble **8** flounder **9** gaucherie **11** impropriety, make a booboo **12** indiscretion

blunt 4 curt, dull, numb, open **5** frank, rough, thick **6** abrupt, benumb, candid, deaden, dulled, soften, weaken **7** brusque, lighten, stupefy **8** edgeless, explicit, mitigate, moderate, tactless **9** outspoken, unpointed **10** to the point

11 insensitive, unsharpened
15 straightforward

bluntness 6 candor **10** directness **14** forthrightness
15 plainspokenness

blur 3 dim, fog, run **4** blot, haze, veil **5** bedim, befog, cloud, smear **6** blotch, darken, smudge, spread **7** becloud, obscure, splotch **9** confusion, obscurity

blurb 2 ad **4** rave, spot **5** brief **10** commercial
13 advertisement

blurred 3 dim **5** vague **6** blurry **7** smeared **10** ill-defined, indefinite, indistinct

blurt out 4 blab, sing **7** confess, divulge, let slip **8** give away. **9** come clean

blush 5 color, flush **6** redden **7** grow red, turn red **8** rosy tint **9** reddening

blushing 3 coy, red **4** rosy **5** fresh, timid **6** demure, modest **7** colored, bashful, flushed, glowing **8** blooming, sheepish **9** rosaceous **10** embarrassed **11** flourishing

bluster 4 brag, crow, rant **5** bluff, boast, bully, gloat, noise, storm **7** bombast, bravado, crowing, protest, ranting, swagger **8** boasting, gloating, threaten **9** noisy talk **10** swaggering
14 boisterousness

blustery 5 blowy, gusty, windy **6** breezy **7** squally

Blythe, Ethel Mae
 real name of: 14 Ethel Barrymore

Blythe, John
 real name of: 13 John Barrymore

Blythe, Lionel
 real name of: 15 Lionel Barrymore

Boadicea
 Latin name: 8 Boudicca
 queen of: 5 Iceni
 husband: 10 Prasutagus
 ruled: 7 Norfolk (England)
 fought: 6 Romans
 died: 7 suicide

Boanerges
 means: 13 sons of thunder
 name given to: 4 John **5** James

boar
 group of: 7 sounder

board 3 bed **4** deal, feed, food, slat **5** enter, get on, house, lodge, meals, panel, plank, put up **6** batten, billet, embark, go onto **7** council, quarter **8** tribunal **9** clapboard, directors **10** daily meals

board game 4 Clue, Life, ludo **5** chess **7** Othello **8** checkers, cribbage, dominoes, draughts, fanorona, Monopoly, Scrabble **9** Alquerque **10** backgammon **14** Trivial Pursuit **15** Chinese checkers
 Egyptian: 5 Senat
 Korean: 5 Nyout, Pa-tok
 Indian: 7 pachisi **8** parchesi, shatranj **9** ashtapada **10** shaturanga
 Japanese: 2 Go **3** I-go **5** Shogi
 Chinese: 6 Ma-jong, wei-ch'i **7** Ma-jongg
 Swedish: 6 tablut

boast 4 brag, crow, have **5** vaunt **6** flaunt **7** contain, exhibit, possess, show off, talk big **15** blow one's own horn

boaster 6 gascon **7** bragger, egotist **8** blowhard, braggart **9** big talker **11** braggadocio

boastful 5 cocky **7** crowing, pompous, swollen **8** bragging, cocksure, inflated, puffed up, vaunting **9** conceited **11** braggadocio, exaggerated, pretentious **12** vainglorious

boastfulness 7 conceit, egotism **8** bragging **9** cockiness, immodesty, pomposity, vainglory **10** self-praise **11** braggadocio **12** cocksureness

boastful soldier
 Latin: 14 miles gloriosus

boat 4 ship **5** craft **6** vessel

Boaz
 father: 5 Salma **6** Salmon
 wife: 4 Ruth
 son: 4 Obed
 kinsman of: 5 Naomi **9** Elimelech

bob 3 cut, hop, nod **4** clip, crop, dock, duck, leap, trim **5** dance, shear **6** bounce **7** shorten

Bobadill
 character in: 19 Every Man in His Humour
 author: 6 Jonson

bobbin 3 pin **4** coil, cord, reel **5** quill, spool **6** piping **7** ratchet, spindle, torchon **8** cylinder

bobcat 3 cat **4** lynx **7** wildcat

Bob Cummings Show, The
 later name: 11 Love That Bob
 character: 10 Bob Collins **14** Chuck MacDonald **15** Charmaine (Shultzy) Shultz **17** Margaret MacDonald
 cast: 9 Ann B Davis **11** Bob Cummings **13** Dwayne Hickman **14** Rosemary DeCamp

Bob Newhart Show, The
 character: 12 Elliot Carlin, Emily Hartley, Howard Borden **13** Jerry Robinson, Robert (Bob) Hartley **20** Carol Kester Bondurant
 cast: 9 Bill Daily, Jack Riley **11** Peter Bonerz **13** Marcia Wallace **16** Suzanne Pleshette

Boccaccio, Giovanni
 author of: 10 Filostrato, Il Filocopo **11** Life of Dante **12** The Decameron

Boccherini, Luigi
 born: 5 Italy, Lucca
 composer of: 8 La Divina **9** The Aviary **10** Clementina **11** L'Uccelliera

Boccioni, Umberto
 born: 5 Italy **13** Reggio Emilia **16** Reggio di Calabria
 artwork: 10 Elasticity **12** The City Rises **15** Charge of Lancers **18** Dynamism of a Cyclist, The Forces of a Street **21** Fusion of Head and Window **30** Unique Forms of Continuity in Space

Bock, Hier
 field: 6 botany
 nationality: 6 German
 founded: 12 modern botany
 classified: 6 plants
 author of: 15 Neu Kreutterbuch

Bocklin, Arnold
 born: 5 Basel **7** Germany
 artwork: 13 Pan in the Reeds **16** The Isle of the Dead

Bod see **5** Tibet

bode 4 omen **5** augur **6** herald **7** betoken, ominate, point to, portend, predict, presage, signify **8** forecast, foretell, precurse **9** foreshadow, prefigure

bodega 9 warehouse **12** grocery store

bodice 3 top **5** stays, waist **6** bolero, corset, girdle **7** corsage **8** camisole, corselet **9** stomacher **10** underwaist

bodily 8 corporal, physical

Bodily Harm
 author: 14 Margaret Atwood

bodkin 3 awl **4** pick, tool **5** auger, borer, drill, point, probe **6** dagger, lancet, needle, reamer **7** hair pin, piercer **8** puncheon, stiletto

body 3 mob 4 bloc, bulk, form, mass 5 being, build, force, frame, group, shape, stiff, thing, torso, trunk 6 corpse, figure, league, person, throng 7 cadaver, carcass, combine, council, faction, remains, society 8 assembly, cohesion, congress, deceased, main part, majority, physique, quantity 9 coalition, multitude, stiffness, thickness 10 federation 11 brotherhood, consistency 13 confederation

Body and Soul
director: 12 Robert Rossen
cast: 10 Anne Revere 11 Hazel Brooks, Lilli Palmer 12 John Garfield 13 William Conrad

bodybuilder 12 Charles Atlas 20 Arnold Schwarzenegger

Boedromius
epithet of: 6 Apollo
means: 7 rescuer

Boeotus
father: 8 Poseidon
mother: 4 Arne

Boer, Boor 6 farmer 9 Afrikaner
language: 9 Afrikaans
ancestry: 5 Dutch
inhabitants of: 9 Transvaal 11 South Africa 15 Orange Free State

Boethius, Anicius Manlius Severinus
also called: 5 Boece
author of: 23 Consolation of Philosophy

Boffin
character in: 15 Our Mutual Friend
author: 7 Dickens

bog 3 fen 4 mire, sink 5 marsh, swamp 6 morass 7 be stuck 8 quagmire, wetlands 9 marshland, swampland

Bogaerde, Derek Van den
real name of: 11 Dirk Bogarde

Bogarde, Dirk
real name: 19 Derek Van den Bogaerde
born: 6 London 7 England 9 Hempstead
roles: 6 Victim 7 Darling 10 The Servant 13 Death in Venice 14 Song Without End, The Night Porter 16 A Tale of Two Cities

Bogart, Humphrey
nickname: 5 Bogie
wife: 12 Lauren Bacall
born: 9 New York NY
roles: 8 Key Largo 10 Casablanca, High Sierra 11 The Big Sleep 14 The Caine Mu-

tiny 15 The African Queen (Oscar) 16 The Maltese Falcon, To Have and Have Not 18 The Petrified Forest 27 The Treasure of the Sierra Madre

Bogdanovich, Peter
director of: 4 Mask 9 Paper Moon 18 The Last Picture Show

boggle 3 shy 4 balk, muff 5 botch, demure, hover, waver 6 bungle, shrink, wobble 7 blunder, stumble 8 flounder, frighten, hesitate, hold back 9 overwhelm 11 make a mess of

boggy 3 wet 4 soft 5 foggy, mossy, soggy 6 marshy, spongy, swampy 7 squashy

Bogie
nickname of: 14 Humphrey Bogart

Bogota
capital of: 8 Colombia

bogus 4 fake, sham 5 dummy, false, phony 6 ersatz, forged, pseudo 7 feigned, pretend 8 spurious 9 imitation, simulated, synthetic 10 artificial, fraudulent 11 counterfeit, make-believe

Boheme, La
also: 12 Bohemian Life
opera by: 7 Puccini
character: 4 Mimi 7 Colline, Musetta, Rodolfo 8 Marcello 9 Schaunard

bohemian, Bohemian 6 hippie 7 beatnik 10 unorthodox 13 nonconformist 14 unconventional

Bohr, Niels
field: 7 physics
nationality: 6 Danish
developed: 8 atom bomb 13 quantum theory, uranium theory

Boiardo, Matteo Maria
author of: 17 Orlando Innamorato

boil 4 brew, burn, foam, fume, rage, rant, rave, sore, stew, toss 5 chafe, churn, froth, storm 6 bubble, fester, quiver, seethe, simmer, sizzle, well up 7 abscess, bristle, parboil, pustule, smolder 8 furuncle 9 carbuncle, fulminate

boil down 3 cut 6 reduce 7 abridge, cut down, shorten 8 condense, contract 10 abbreviate

boiler 6 copper, geyser, heater, kettle 7 alembic, caldron, furnace

Boilermaker, the
nickname of: 20 James Jackson Jeffries

boisterous 4 loud, wild 5 noisy, rowdy 6 unruly 9 clamorous, out-of-hand 10 disorderly, uproarious 12 obstreperous, uncontrolled, unrestrained

boite, boite de nuit 7 cabaret 9 nightclub

Bojer, Johan
author of: 12 Folk by the Sea, The Emigrants 14 The Great Hunger, The Power of a Lie 16 Last of the Vikings

bold 3 hot 4 loud, rude 5 brash, brave, fiery, fresh, saucy, vivid 6 brazen, cheeky, daring, flashy, heroic 7 defiant, forward, valiant 8 colorful, creative, fearless, impudent, insolent, intrepid, spirited, stalwart, striking, unafraid, valorous 9 audacious, daredevil, dauntless 10 courageous 11 eye-catching, imaginative, impertinent, indomitable, lionhearted, unshrinking 12 stouthearted 13 adventuresome

boldfaced 5 brash, saucy 6 brassy, brazen 7 forward 8 immodest, impudent, insolent 9 audacious, barefaced, shameless, unabashed

boldness 4 grit 5 nerve, pluck, spunk 6 daring, mettle 7 bravery, courage 8 audacity 9 brashness, hardihood 10 brazenness 13 audaciousness, determination, self-assurance 14 courageousness 15 adventurousness

Bolger, Ray
born: 12 Dorchester MA
roles: 9 Scarecrow 10 On Your Toes 13 The Wizard of Oz, Where's Charley

Bolivia *see box, p. 118.*
Bolivia see box, p. 118.

Bolkonsky, Andrei
character in: 11 War and Peace
author: 7 Tolstoy

Boll, Heinrich
author of: 8 The Clown 12 The Safety Net 18 Absent Without Leave 21 Group Portrait With Lady 27 The Lost Honor of Katharina Blum 28 Missing Persons and Other Essays

bolster 3 aid 4 help 5 add to, brace 6 assist, cradle, hold up, pillow, prop up, uphold 7 cushion, shore up, support, sustain 8 buttress, maintain,

Bolivia
named for: **12** Simon Bolivar
capital:
    administrative: **5** La Paz
    legal: **5** Sucre

largest city: **5** La Paz

others: **3** Ivo **4** Icla, Itau, Mojo, Saya, Yaco, Yato, Yura **5** Cliza, Llica, Oruro, Quime, Uyuni, Zongo **6** Guaqui, Potosi, Tiraja, Tupiza **8** Pulacayo **9** Santa Cruz **10** Chuquisaca, Cochabamba **11** Vallegrande, Villa Montes

school: **6** Xavier **8** St Andrew **12** San Francisco

division: **6** Valles **7** Oriente, Valleys **8** Montanas **9** Altiplano

measure: **6** league **7** celemin

monetary unit: **7** centavo **13** peso boliviano

weight: **5** libra, marco

lake: **5** Poopo **7** Allagas, Coipasa, Rogagua **8** Titicaca **10** Desaguader

mountain: **4** Jara **5** Andes, Cusco, Cuzco **6** Pupuya, Sajama, Sorata, Sunsas **7** Illampu **8** Illimani, Mururata, Sansimon, Santiago, Zapaleri **12** Eastern Range, Western Range **18** Cordillera Oriental **20** Cordillera Occidental

highest point: **8** Ancohuma

river: **4** Beni, Yata **5** Abuna, Lauca, Orton **6** Blanco, Ichilo, Itenez, Madidi, Mamore, Mizque, Yacuma **7** Guapore, Machupo **8** Inambari, Itonamas **9** Pilcomayo, Rio Grande, San Miguel **11** Desaguadero, Madre de Dios

physical features:
    lowlands: **6** Llanos
    plateau: **9** Altiplano
    swamp: **6** Izozog
    valley: **5** Yunga
    volcano: **7** Ollague

people: **6** Aymara **7** mestizo, Quechua
    author: **7** Mendoza **8** Arguedas **11** Costa du Rels
    leader: **5** Busch, Sucre **6** Candia, Ortuno, Zamora **7** Bolivar **9** Melgarejo, Paz Zamora, Santa Cruz **10** Barrientos, Estenssoro

language: **6** Aymara **7** Quechua, Spanish

religion: **13** Roman Catholic

place:
    church: **9** St Francis, St Michael **10** San Lorenzo
    monument: **11** La Coronilla
    ruins: **10** Tiahuanaco
    tower: **6** Chulpa

feature:
    animal: **5** llama **6** alpaca, vicuna
    bar/club: **7** boliche
    boat: **5** balsa
    dance/song: **5** cueca **7** huainos, pasillo **8** morenada **9** taquirari **10** palla-palla **11** cacharpayas, waka-tokonis
    devil dance: **8** Diablado
    guitar: **8** charango
    skirt: **7** pollera
    wind instrument: **4** kena, sicu **5** erque, quena, tarka **6** pututu **9** pinquillo

food:
    chicken dish: **14** picante de pollo
    corn: **4** mote
    corn drink: **3** api **14** chicha taratena
    dish: **11** plato paceno **14** sajta de gallina
    dried meat: **7** charque
    pancakes: **7** bunulos
    potato: **5** chuno

shoulder **9** reinforce **10** strengthen

bolster one's spirits 5 cheer **7** cheer up, comfort, hearten **8** inspirit **9** buoy one up, encourage

bolt 3 bar, fly, peg, pin, rod, run **4** dart, dash, flee, gulp, jump, leap, lock, roll, rush, tear, wolf **5** bound, brand, catch, dowel, flash, hurry, latch, rivet, scoot, shaft, speed **6** fasten, gobble, hasten, hurtle, length, secure, spring, sprint, stroke **8** fastener **12** swallow whole

bolt down 4 wolf **5** scarf **6** devour, gobble **8** gulp down

bomb 3 dud, egg **4** bust, fail, flop, mine **5** lemon **6** fiasco, fizzle **7** bombard, grenade, failure, washout

bombard 5 beset, hound, shell, worry **6** assail, attack, batter, harass, pepper, pester, strafe **7** assault, barrage, besiege **8** fire upon **9** cannonade

bombardment 5 blitz, siege **7** air raid, assault, barrage, bombing **10** blitzkrieg

bombast 3 pad **4** puff, rant **6** cotton **7** bluster, fustian, palaver **8** boasting, flummery, rhapsody, tall talk, verbiage **9** bavardage **10** balderdash **12** braggadocio, exaggeration **13** magniloquence, overstatement **14** grandiloquence **17** sesquipedalianism

bombastic 5 tumid, windy, wordy **6** padded, turgid **7** pompous, verbose **8** inflated **12** magniloquent **13** grandiloquent

Bombay
area: **7** Trombay **8** Salsette **12** Bombay Island
called: **14** Gateway to India
creek: **7** Bassein
landmark: **9** High Court **13** Taj Mahal Hotel **14** Gateway of India **16** Victoria Terminus **17** Rajabai Clock Tower
rock formation: **10** Deccan Trap
sea: **7** Arabian

Bona Dea
also: **5** Fauna
origin: **5** Roman
goddess of: **8** chastity **9** fertility
worshipped by: **5** women
father: **6** Faunus
brother: **6** Faunus
husband: **6** Faunus

bona fide 4 real, true **5** legal **6** actual, honest, lawful **7** genuine, sincere **9** authentic, honorable **10** legitimate **11** in good faith

bon ami 5 lover **10** good friend

bonanza 8 gold mine, windfall

Bonanza
character: **3** Ben **4** Adam, Hoss **5** Candy **7** Hop Sing **9** Little Joe
family: **10** Cartwright
cast: **10** Dan Blocker **11** David Canary, Lorne Greene **13** Michael Landon, Victor Sen Yung **14** Pernell Roberts
ranch: **9** Ponderosa

Bonanza State
nickname of: **7** Montana

bon appetit 14 hearty appetite

Bonario
character in: **7** Volpone
author: **6** Jonson

bonbon 5 candy, sweet **7** fondant **9** sweetmeat **10** confection, sugar candy **13** confectionery **14** chocolate cream

bond, bonds 3 tie **4** cord, knot, link, rope **5** irons, scrip, union **6** chains, pledge **7** compact, fetters, promise **8** affinity, bindings, manacles, security, shackles **9** agreement, guarantee, handcuffs **10** allegiance, attachment, connection, fastenings, obligation **11** certificate, stipulation

Bond, James
actor: **10** Roger Moore **11** Sean Connery **12** Peter Sellers **13** George Lazenby, Timothy Dalton
appears in: **4** Dr No **9** Moonraker, Octopussy **10** Goldfinger **11** Thunderball **12** A View To A Kill **13** Live and Let Die **15** For Your Eyes Only **16** The Spy Who Loved Me, You Only Live Twice **18** Diamonds Are Forever, From Russia with Love, Never Say Never Again, The Living Daylights **22** The Man with the Golden Gun **26** On Her Majesty's Secret Service
author: **10** Ian Fleming
drink: **12** vodka martini **16** shaken not stirred
employer: **3** MI-6 **20** British Secret Service
foe: **7** Blofeld, SPECTRE
office staff: **1** M, Q **14** Miss Moneypenny
university: **6** Oxford
wife: **5** Tracy

bondage 4 yoke **6** chains **7** fetters, serfdom, slavery

8 shackles **9** captivity, servitude, vassalage **11** enslavement

bone
comprise: **8** skeleton
contain: **6** marrow **9** cartilage **11** blood vessel
fitted together by: **5** joint
held by: **8** ligament
pulled by: **6** muscle
specific: **3** rib **4** ulna **5** femur, skull, tibia **6** carpal, fibula, pelvis, radius, sacrum, tarsal **7** humerus, patella, scapula, sternum **8** clavicle, vertebra **9** vertebrae

bone chilling 3 icy **4** cold **5** harsh, sharp **6** arctic, biting, bitter, frigid **7** cutting, glacial **8** piercing, stinging **11** penetrating **15** teeth-chattering

bonehead 3 ass **4** clod, dolt, fool **5** booby, dunce, idiot, moron, ninny **6** dimwit, nitwit **7** fathead, half-wit **8** dumb-dumb, imbecile, lunkhead **9** blockhead, lamebrain, numbskull **10** dunderhead, nincompoop **11** chowderhead

boner 4 goof, slip **5** error **6** boo-boo, slip-up **7** blooper, blunder, mistake

boneyard 4 dump **7** ossuary **8** Boot Hill, cemetery, junkyard **9** graveyard **10** churchyard **12** burial ground **13** burying ground

Bonheur, Rosa
real name: **19** Marie Rosalie Bonheur
born: **6** France **8** Bordeaux
artwork: **12** The Horse Fair **23** Ploughing in the Nivernais

bonjour 5 hello **7** good day

Bonjour Tristesse
author: **14** Francoise Sagan

bon marche 7 bargain

bon mot 4 quip **7** epigram **9** witticism

Bonn
capital of: **11** West Germany
landmark: **10** Bundeshaus **11** Munsterkerk
museum: **18** Ludwig van Beethoven
river: **5** Rhine
Roman fort: **15** Castra Bonnensia

Bonnard, Pierre
born: **6** France **16** Fontenay-aux-Roses
artwork: **8** Intimist, Luncheon **9** The Review **13** Nude in the Bath, The Open Window, Women with a Dog **14** After the Shower, Farm at Le Cannet **16** The

Breakfast Room **17** The Terrasse Family **22** Figure Before a Fireplace

bonne amie 5 lover **6** friend **10** good friend

bonne nuit 9 good night

bonnet 3 cap, hat **4** cowl, hood, sail **5** cover, toque **7** chapeau, commode **8** headgear **9** headdress

Bonnie and Clyde
director: **10** Arthur Penn
cast: **11** Faye Dunaway (Bonnie Parker), Gene Hackman **12** Warren Beatty (Clyde Barrow) **15** Michael J Pollard

bonny 4 fair **6** comely, lovely, pretty, seemly **7** winning, winsome **8** engaging, fetching, handsome, pleasing **9** beautiful, exquisite, ravishing **10** attractive

bon soir 9 good night **11** good evening

bonus 4 gift **5** prize **6** bounty, reward **7** benefit, premium **8** dividend, gratuity **10** honorarium

Bonus Eventus
also: **7** Eventus
origin: **5** Roman
god of: **4** luck **10** prosperity **11** agriculture

bon vivant 7 epicure, gourmet **8** gourmand, sybarite **10** gastronome

bony 4 lean **5** gaunt, lanky, spare **6** skinny **7** angular, scrawny **11** full of bones **12** skin-and-bones

boo 3 pan **4** hiss **5** taunt **6** deride, heckle, revile **7** catcall **8** ridicule **9** criticize, shout down **11** give the bird **16** give the raspberry

boo-boo 4 goof, slip **5** boner, error **6** slip-up **7** blunder, mistake

boobtube 2 TV **3** box **8** idiot box **13** television set

booby 4 bird, dope, fool **5** dummy, dunce, idiot, moron, ninny **6** dimwit, gannet, nitwit **7** fathead, halfwit **8** bonehead, dumb-dumb, imbecile, lunkhead, numskull **9** blockhead, lamebrain, simpleton **10** nincompoop **11** chowderhead

Booby, Lady
character in: **13** Joseph Andrews
author: **8** Fielding

boodle 4 loot, swag **5** booty, bribe, crowd, graft, group

7 plunder **10** collection
11 stolen goods

Boog
   nickname of: **10** John Powell

boohoo 3 cry, sob **4** bawl,
weep **7** blubber **9** shed tears

book 4 bill, file, list, note,
opus, post, tome **5** album, enter, index, slate **6** accuse,
charge, engage, enroll, indict,
insert, line up, record, tablet,
volume **7** catalog, procure,
program, put down, reserve
8 mark down, notebook, register, schedule, treatise **9** bound
work, write down **10** arrange
for **11** publication, written
work **16** make reservations

bookish 7 erudite, learned,
stilted **8** academic, educated,
informed, literary, pedantic,
studious, well-read **9** scholarly
11 pedagogical, impractical
12 intellectual

bookkeeper 5 clerk **7** auditor
10 accountant **11** comptroller

booklet 5 folio **7** leaflet, program **8** brochure, circular,
pamphlet

Book of Common Prayer
   author: **10** Joan Didion

Book of Lights, The
   author: **10** Chaim Potok

Book of Manuel
   author: **13** Julio Cortazar

Book of Odes
   author: **9** Confucius

Book of psalms 12 psalter

Book of Sand, The
   author: **15** Jorge Luis Borges

Book of the Duchess, The
   author: **15** Geoffrey Chaucer

boom 3 bar **4** bang, beam,
gain, grow, push, roar, spar
5 blast, boost, shaft, spurt
6 growth, rumble, thrive,
thrust, upturn **7** advance, develop, prosper, thunder, upsurge **8** flourish, increase
9 expansion, good times

Boom Boom
   nickname of: **15** Bernie
   Geoffrion

boomerang 5 kalie, kiley, ky-
lie, wango **6** atlatl, recoil
7 rebound, womerah, woom-
era **8** backfire, ricochet, trom-
bush **9** bound back, solitaire
10 projectile

Boomer State
   nickname of: **8** Oklahoma

boon 3 fun, gay **4** gift **5** favor,
jolly, merry **6** kindly **7** benefit,
bequest **8** blessing, donation,

offering, pleasant **9** advantage,
congenial, convivial, endowment **11** full of cheer, good-
natured

boon companion 3 pal
4 chum **5** buddy, crony
6 friend **7** comrade **8** confrere,
intimate **9** confidant **10** bosom
buddy

boondocks 4 bush, veld **6** Podunk, sticks **7** boonies, country, outback **8** frontier
9 backwater, backwoods, provinces **10** hinterland **11** back-
country, countryside
12 squaresville **13** nowheres-
ville **14** wide open spaces

Boone, Richard
   born: **12** Los Angeles CA
   roles: **5** Medic **6** Hombre
   7 Paladin **8** The Alamo
   11 The Shootist **12** Ten
   Wanted Men, The Desert
   Fox **17** Have Gun Will
   Travel

boonies 6 sticks **7** country
9 backwoods, boondocks, provinces **10** hinterland
11 countryside

boor 3 oaf **4** hick, lout, rube
5 brute, churl, yokel **6** rustic
7 bumpkin, hayseed, peasant
9 vulgarian **10** clodhopper,
philistine **11** guttersnipe

boorish 4 rude **5** crude
6 coarse, gauche, oafish, rustic, vulgar **7** loutish, uncouth
9 unrefined **10** unpolished
11 peasantlike

boorishness 8 rudeness **9** surliness, vulgarity **10** bad manners, coarseness, incivility,
oafishness **12** churlishness,
impoliteness

boost 4 hike, laud, lift, plug,
push, rise **5** add to, extol,
heave, hoist, pitch, raise,
shove **6** expand, foster, free
ad, growth, pickup, praise, upturn, urge on **7** acclaim, advance, develop, elevate,
enlarge, forward, further, improve, nurture, promote, root
for, support, sustain, upsurge,
upswing **8** addition, applause,
good word, increase, pro-
pound **9** expansion, increment,
promotion **10** compliment,
give a leg up, stick up for
11 development, enlargement,
improvement, speak well of

boot
   French: **9** chaussure

booth 3 pen **4** coop, nook,
tent **5** hutch, stall, stand, table **7** counter **9** cubbyhole, enclosure **11** compartment

Booth, Shirley
   real name: **15** Thelma Booth
   Ford
   born: **9** New York NY
   roles: **5** Hazel **13** The Matchmaker **19** Come Back Little
   Sheba (Oscar)

bootleg 5 hooch **7** illegal, illicit **8** unlawful **9** moonshine
12 football play

bootless 6 futile **7** useless
11 ineffective, ineffectual
12 unproductive, unprofitable

bootlick 4 fawn **5** toady
6 cringe, grovel **7** flatter,
truckle

bootmaker 7 cobbler
9 shoemaker

booty 4 gain, loot **5** prize
6 boodle, spoils **7** pillage,
plunder, takings **8** pickings,
winnings

booze 4 bout, soak **5** drink,
hooch, spree **6** guzzle, liquor,
tipple **7** alcohol, spirits, swizzle **8** cocktail **10** intoxicant
14 drink like a fish
   type: **3** gin, rum, rye **4** beer,
   wine **5** vodka **6** scotch
   7 bourbon, whiskey

boozer 3 sot **4** lush **5** drunk,
souse, toper **7** tippler **8** drunkard **9** alcoholic, inebriate
11 hard drinker

bordello, bordel 4 stew
5 house **6** bagnio **7** brothel
8 cathouse **10** bawdy house,
fancy house, whorehouse
13 sporting house **14** house of
ill fame **16** house of ill repute **19** house of prostitution

border 3 hem, rim **4** abut,
bind, brim, curb, edge, join,
line, pale, trim **5** brink, flank,
frame, limit, skirt, touch,
verge **6** adjoin, fringe, margin
8 befringe, be next to, boundary, frontier, outskirt **9** extremity, perimeter, periphery
13 circumference

borderline 4 open **5** vague
7 halfway, inexact, obscure,
unclear **8** marginal **9** ambiguous, equivocal, uncertain, undecided, unsettled
10 ambivalent, indefinite
11 indefinable, problematic
13 indeterminate

bore 4 drag, drip, sink, tire
5 drill, drive, weary **6** burrow,
pierce, tunnel **7** caliber, exhaust, fatigue, wear out
8 gouge out **9** hollow out
10 wet blanket **14** inside
diameter

Boreadae
   decendants of: **6** Boreas

Boreal
pertaining to: 6 Boreas

Boreas
origin: 5 Greek
personifies: 9 north wind
father: 8 Astraeus
mother: 3 Eos
twin sons: 5 Zetes 6 Calais
daughter: 6 Chione
9 Cleopatra

bored 5 jaded 7 wearied
12 discontented, uninterested

boredom 6 tedium 8 doldrums,
dullness, monotony 9 weariness 11 tediousness
French: 5 ennui

Borges, Jorge Luis
author of: 8 The Aleph
10 Labyrinths 11 Dreamti-
gers 13 The Book of Sand
18 A Personal Anthology, In
Praise of Darkness 19 Doctor Brodie's Report, Fervor
of Buenos Aires 25 A Uni-
versal History of Infamy

Borghild
origin: 12 Scandinavian
mentioned in: 8 Volsunga
husband: 7 Sigmund

Borgia, Alfonso de 16 Pope
Callistus III

Borgia, Rodrigo de 15 Pope
Alexander VI

Borglum, (John) Gutzon
born: 10 Bear Lake ID
artwork: 7 Lincoln 18 Mt
Rushmore Memorial, The
Mares of Diomedes

Borgnine, Ernest
real name: 18 Ermes Effron
Borgnine
wife: 11 Ethel Merman
born: 8 Hamden CT
roles: 5 Marty (Oscar) 8 Barabbas 11 McHale's Navy
12 The Wild Bunch 13 The
Dirty Dozen 17 Bad Day at
Black Rock 18 From Here
to Eternity 20 The Poseidon
Adventure

boring 4 dull, flat 5 stale 6 tiring 7 humdrum, insipid, tedious 8 tiresome 9 wearisome
10 monotonous, unexciting
11 repetitious 13 uninteresting

boring tool 3 bit 5 auger,
drill 11 brace and bit

Borinquen see 10 Puerto Rico

Boriquen, Borinquen
language family: 8 Arawakan
location: 10 Puerto Rico
related to: 5 Taino

Boris Godunov
author: 16 Alexander Pushkin
opera by: 10 Mussorgsky

12 Shostakovich 14 Rimsky-
Korsakov
character: 6 Dmitri, Feodor,
Maryna 7 Gregory, Grigory
8 Basmanov, Otrepyev

born 6 innate 7 natural 9 delivered, intuitive 12 brought
forth

Born, Max
field: 7 physics
nationality: 7 British
worked on: 13 quantum
theory
awarded: 10 Nobel Prize

borne 6 afloat, braved 7 carried, endured 9 put up with,
tolerated 11 gone through,
went through 12 given birth
to

Borneo see box

Born Yesterday
director: 11 George Cukor
cast: 12 Judy Holliday
13 William Holden 17 Broderick Crawford
Oscar for: 7 actress (Holliday)

Borodin, Alexander
born: 6 Russia 12 St
Petersburg
member of: 7 The Five
composer of: 8 Bogatyri
10 Prince Igor 25 In the
Steppes of Central Asia

boron
chemical symbol: 1 B

borough 4 burg, town 5 borgo,
shire 6 county, parish 7 village 8 district, precinct, province, township 12 municipality
of New York City: 5 Bronx
6 Queens 8 Brooklyn
9 Manhattan 12 Staten
Island

Borromini, Francesco
architect of: 10 San Carlino
17 Palazzo Falconieri
20 Sant' Ivo della Sapienza
23 Oratory of San Filippo
Neri 24 Collegio di Propaganda Fide 26 San Carlo
alle Quattro Fontane (Rome)

borrow 3 get, use 4 copy,
take 5 filch, steal, usurp 6 obtain, pilfer, pirate 7 acquire
10 commandeer, plagiarize,
take on loan 11 appropriate

Borrow, George Henry
author of: 8 Lavengro 9 Romany Rye, Wild Wales
10 The Zincali 15 The Bible
in Spain

Bors
character in: 16 Arthurian
romance

Bosch, Hieronymus
real name: 13 Jerome van

Borneo
other name: 10 Kalimantan
largest city: 12 Bandjermasin
others: 5 Kumai 6 Sambas, Sampit 7 Malinau, Pagatan,
Sanggau, Sintang, Tarakan 8 Ketapang 9 Pontianak
10 Balikpapan
division of island:
independent: 6 Brunei
Malaysian state: 5 Sabah 7 Sarawak
part of Indonesia: 10 Kalimantan
measure: 7 gantang
weight: 4 para 6 chapah
mountain: 4 Iran, Raja 5 Saran 6 Kapuas, Muller, Nijaan,
Tebang 8 Kinibalu, Schwaner
highest point: 8 Kinabalu
river: 4 Arut, Iwan 5 Bahau, Berau, Kajan, Padas, Pawan
6 Barito, Kapuas, Rajang, Sebuku 7 Kahajan, Mahakam,
Mendawi 8 Pembuang
sea: 4 Java, Sulu 7 Celebes 10 South China
physical feature:
bay: 5 Adang, Kumai 6 Sampit
cape: 3 Aru 4 Datu 5 Lojar 6 Puting, Sambar 7 Selatan
port: 4 Miri 5 Balik, Papan 6 Brunei 9 Pontianak
12 Bandjermasin
strait: 8 Macassar
people: 4 Iban 5 Bukat, Dajak, Dayak, Dusan, Malay,
Punan 6 Illano 7 Bakatan, Chinese, Illanum
language: 5 Malay 6 tribal 7 Chinese, English
religion: 5 Islam 7 animism 12 Christianity
feature:
tree: 5 kapor, kapur 7 billian

Aeken **17** Jeroen
Anthoiszoon
artwork: 7 Hay-Wain **11** Ship
of Fools **14** The Crucifixion
19 Adoration of the Kings
21 The Crowning with
Thorns **26** The Garden of
Earthly Delights

bosh 3 rot **4** bunk **6** bunkum,
drivel **7** twaddle **8** claptrap,
nonsense, tommyrot **10** balderdash, tomfoolery **11** foolishness **16** stuff and nonsense

bosky 5 bushy, drunk, shaded,
tipsy, treed **6** wooded

Bosnia-Herzegovina
capital/largest city: 8 Sarajevo
others: 4 Neum **5** Tuzlal
6 Citluk, Kupres, Lenica,
Mostar **8** Prijedor **9** Banja
Luka, Bijeljina **10** Srebre-
nica **12** Bosanski Brod, Si-
roki Brijeg
head of state: 9 president
monetary unit: 5 dinar
mountain: 11 Dinaric Alps
river: 3 Una **4** Sava **5** Bosna,
Drina, Vrbas **7** Neretva
sea: 8 Adriatic
people: 4 Serb **5** Croat
6 Muslim **8** Yugoslav
language: 13 Serbo Croatian
religion: 11 Sunni Muslim
15 Serbian Orthodox

bosom 4 bust, core, dear, soul
5 chest, close, heart, midst
6 breast, center, spirit **7** beloved, nucleus **8** intimate
9 cherished **11** inner circle

bosom buddy 4 chum
5 crony **6** cohort **7** best pal,
comrade **8** alter ego, intimate,
sidekick **9** companion, confidant **10** best friend

bosomy 5 busty, buxom **6** zaftig **11** full-figured **13** large-
breasted

boss 4 head, push **5** chief,
order **6** leader, master **7** command, foreman, kingpin, manager **8** employer **9** big cheese,
executive **10** supervisor **13** administrator **14** superintendent

bossy 3 cow **9** imperious
10 commanding, tyrannical
11 dictatorial, domineering

Boston
airport: 5 Logan
area: 7 Back Bay **10** Bunker
Hill, Fenway Park **11** Faneuil
Hall **14** Kennedy Library, Old
North Church
baseball team: 6 Red Sox
basketball team: 7 Celtics
dish: 10 baked beans
hockey team: 6 Bruins
landmark: 10 Beacon Hill
leader: 7 Brahmin
nickname: 8 Bean town
river: 7 Charles

Bostonians, The
author: 10 Henry James

Boston Strong Boy
nickname of: 13 John L
Sullivan

Boswell, James
author of: 22 The Life of
Samuel Johnson

botanist
American: 6 Barton, Torrey
7 Bartram
Austrian: 6 Mendel
Dutch: 7 DeVries
German: 4 Bock, Cohn
Scottish: 5 Brown
Swedish: 8 Linnaeus
Swiss: 6 Bauhin

botch 3 err, mar **4** blow, fail,
flop, flub, goof, hash, mess,
muff, ruin **5** spoil **6** bungle,
foul up, fumble **7** blunder,
butcher, failure, louse up
8 butchery **9** mismanage
11 make a mess of

bother 3 ado, irk, nag, tax, try,
vex **4** care, drag, fret, fuss,
load, onus, stir **5** annoy,
harry, trial, upset, worry
6 dismay, flurry, harass, pester, racket, rumpus, strain,
stress, tumult **7** attempt, disturb, problem, trouble **8** disquiet, distress, hardship,
headache, irritate, nuisance,
vexation **9** aggravate, commotion, hindrance **10** affliction,
difficulty, impediment, irritation **11** aggravation, disturbance, encumbrance **12** make
an effort **13** inconvenience,
pain in the neck
14 responsibility

bothersome 6 taxing, vexing
8 annoying **9** worrisome
10 disturbing **11** aggravating,
disquieting, distressing, troublesome **12** inconvenient

Botswana *see box*

Botticelli, Sandro
real name: 30 Alessandro di
Mariano dei Filipepi
born: 5 Italy **8** Florence
artwork: 12 Birth of Venus
14 Mystic Nativity **16** Calumny of Apelles **18** Adoration of the Magi **22** Pallas
Subduing a Centaur **25** The
Madonna of the Magnificat

bottle 3 jar **4** vial **5** flask, phial
6 carafe, flagon, vessel
7 canteen

bottleneck 3 bar, jam **4** clog,
stop **5** block **6** detour **7** barrier,
embolus **8** blockage, embolism,
gridlock, obstacle, stoppage,
thrombus **10** congestion, impediment, infarction **11** costive-
ness, obstruction

Botswana
other name:
12 Bechuanaland
capital/largest city:
8 Gaborone
9 Gaberones
others: 5 Kanye, Orapa,
Tsane **6** Serowe **7** Lob-
atse, Lobotsi, Mochudi,
Palapye, Thamaga
10 Molepolole **11** Fran-
cistown, Selebi-Pikwe
monetary unit: 4 pula,
rand
lake: 3 Dow, Xau
5 Ngami
highest point: 11 Tsodilo
Hill
river: 4 Nata, Okwa
5 Chobe, Nosob
6 Cuando, Molopo,
Shashi **7** Cubango, Limpopo **8** Botletle, Oko-
vango **9** Okovanggo
physical feature:
desert: 8 Kalahari
salt pans:
10 Makarikari
swamp: 8 Okavango
people: 5 Bantu
6 Tswana **7** Bakatla,
Bakwena, Bushman
8 Bamalete, Baralong,
Batawana, Batlokwa,
Botswana **10** Bamang-
wato **11** Bangwaketse
language: 5 Bantu,
Click **6** Tswana
7 English, Khoisan
8 Setswana
religion: 7 animism
10 Protestant
12 Christianity

bottom 3 can **4** base, core,
foot, gist, root, rump, seat,
sole **5** basis, belly, cause,
fanny, heart, lower **6** center,
deeper, depths, ground, lowest,
origin, source, spring **7** deepest, essence **8** backside, buttocks, pedestal, riverbed
9 beginning, fundament, principle, rudiments, substance,
underpart, underside **10** foundation, mainspring, well-
spring **12** quintessence

Bottom
character in: 21 A Midsummer Night's Dream
author: 11 Shakespeare

bottomless 4 deep **7** abysmal
8 profound **11** measureless
12 immeasurable,
unfathomable

Boucher, Francois
born: 5 Paris **6** France
artwork: 9 The Rising

13 Madame Boucher, Reclining Girl **16** Evening Landscape, Rinaldo and Armida, The Toilet of Venus **17** Chinese Tapestries, The Triumph of Venus **18** The Setting of the Sun

boudoir 7 bedroom **10** bedchamber **12** dressing room

bough 4 limb **6** branch

bougie 3 dip, wax **5** light, taper **6** candle, cierge, tallow

boulder, bowlder 3 nob **4** crag, knob, rock **5** block, stone **6** gibber **7** dornick **8** megalith

boulevard 6 avenue **7** parkway **9** concourse

bouleversement 7 turmoil **9** confusion, upsetting **11** overturning

bounce 3 bob, hop, pep **4** bump, life **5** bound, thump, verve, vigor **6** energy, jounce, recoil, spirit **7** rebound **8** dynamism, ricochet, vitality, vivacity **9** animation **10** liveliness

bouncing 3 big **4** full **5** jolly, large, lusty, plump **6** chubby, lively, robust, strong **7** healthy **8** animated, vigorous **12** in good health

bound 3 bob, orb, rim **4** area, edge, jump, leap, line, mark, pale, romp, sure, tied **5** dance, fated, hedge, limit, orbit, range, realm, vault **6** border, bounce, define, domain, doomed, forced, fringe, gambol, liable, prance, region, spring, tied up **7** certain, compass, confine, covered, encased, enclosed, flounce, going to, in bonds, limited, obliged, rebound, secured, trussed, wrapped **8** beholden, boundary, confined, destined, district, encircle, fastened, province, required, resolute, resolved, surround, tethered **9** bailiwick, committed, demarcate, extremity, periphery, territory **10** determined, restrained **11** demarcation **12** circumscribe

Boundaries
  god of: **8** Terminus

boundary 3 rim **4** edge, line, pale **6** border, margin **7** barrier **8** frontier, landmark **9** extremity, periphery **11** demarcation **12** dividing line

boundary line 4 edge **5** bound **6** border **8** sideline

bounder 3 cad, rat **4** heel

5 knave, louse, rogue **6** rascal, rotter **7** caitiff, dastard, villain **9** scoundrel **10** blackguard

Bounderby, Mr
  character in: **9** Hard Times
  author: **7** Dickens

boundless 4 vast **7** endless, immense **8** infinite, unending **9** limitless, perpetual, unbounded, unlimited **10** without end **11** everlasting, measureless **12** immeasurable, incalculable, unrestricted **13** inexhaustible

bounteous, bountiful 4 free, full, rich **5** ample, large **6** lavish **7** copious, liberal, profuse, teeming **8** abundant, generous, prolific **9** abounding, plenteous, plentiful, unsparing **10** beneficent, benevolent, charitable, munificent, unstinting **11** magnanimous, overflowing

Bountiful, Lady
  character in: **17** The Beaux Stratagem
  author: **8** Farquhar

bountifulness 10 liberality, generosity **11** benevolence, magnanimity, munificence **14** charitableness **15** humanitarianism

bounty 3 aid **4** gift, help **5** bonus, favor, grant **6** giving, reward **7** charity, present, tribute **8** bestowal, donation, gratuity **9** endowment **10** almsgiving, assistance, generosity, liberality, recompense **11** benefaction, benevolence, munificence **12** contribution, philanthropy **14** charitableness, openhandedness

bouquet 4 odor **5** aroma, scent, spray **7** essence, garland, nosegay, perfume **9** fragrance **11** boutonniere

bouquet garni
  ingredient: **5** basil, thyme **6** celery, savory **7** bay leaf, chervil, parsley **8** rosemary, tarragon

bourbon
  variety of: **7** whiskey
  origin: **7** America
  ingredient: **4** corn
  type: **7** blended **8** straight
  drink: **9** Mint Julep **10** Boston Sour **11** John Collins **12** Old Fashioned
  with Benedictine: **9** Twin Hills
  with brandy and Benedictine: **13** Brighton Punch
  with Cointreau: **10** Temptation
  with rum: **14** Artillery Punch
  with sloe gin: **9** Black Hawk

  with Southern Comfort: **14** Blended Comfort
  with triple sec: **10** Chapel Hill
  with vermouth: **9** Allegheny

bourgeois 6 square **7** Babbitt, burgher **8** commoner, ordinary **11** middle-class **12** conventional **13** unimaginative

Bourgeois Gentleman, The
  author: **7** Moliere
  character: **6** Lucile, Nicole **7** Cleonte, Dorante **8** Covielle, Dorimene **14** Madame Jourdain **16** Monsieur Jourdain

Bourget, Charles Joseph Paul
  author of: **11** The Disciple **12** A Cruel Enigma **14** The Night Cometh

Bourgh, Lady Catherine de
  character in: **17** Pride and Prejudice
  author: **6** Austen

Bourjaily, Vance
  author of: **11** The Violated **14** The End of My Life **18** Brill Among the Ruins **22** Now Playing at Canterbury

Bourne Identity, The
  author: **12** Robert Ludlum

bout 4 fray, term, tilt, turn **5** brush, clash, cycle, fight, match, set-to, siege, spell, spree **6** affair, battle, course, period, series **7** contest, goround, scuffle, session, tourney **8** conflict, interval, skirmish, struggle **9** encounter **10** contention, engagement **11** boxing match, embroilment

boutonniere 4 posy **7** nosegay **16** buttonhole flower

bow 3 arc **4** bend, knot, prow, stem **5** agree, curve, defer, front, stoop, yield **6** archer, comply, curtsy, give in, kowtow, relent, salaam, submit, weapon **7** concede, succumb, crescent **9** acquiesce, genuflect, surrender **10** capitulate, forward end **12** genuflection, knuckle under

Bow, Clara
  nickname: **6** It Girl
  born: **10** Brooklyn NY
  roles: **2** It **7** Mantrap **12** The Wild Party

bowdlerize 6 censor **9** expurgate **10** blue-pencil

bow down 5 yield **6** give in, submit **9** surrender **10** capitulate **12** knuckle under

bowed 4 bent **6** arched,

curved, nodded **7** hunched, stooped

bowels 3 gut, pit **4** core, guts, womb **5** abyss, belly, bosom, heart, midst **6** depths, hollow, vitals **7** innards, insides, stomach, viscera **8** entrails, interior, recesses **10** intestines **11** vital organs **13** innermost part

Bowen, Elizabeth
author of: **8** Eva Trout, The Hotel **10** To the North **11** Bowen's Court, Little Girls, The Cat Jumps **12** A World of Love **15** The Heat of the Day, The House in Paris **18** The Death of the Heart

Bowen's Court
author: **14** Elizabeth Bowen

bower 4 jack, joker, nook **5** arbor **6** alcove, anchor, pandal **7** bedroom, chamber, cottage, enclose, retreat, sanctum, shelter **8** dwelling, snuggery

Bowie, David
real name: **16** David Robert Jones
born: **6** London **7** England
roles: **9** Cat People, The Hunger **20** The Man Who Fell to Earth **24** Merry Christmas Mr Lawrence

Bowie Land, Bowie State
nickname of: **8** Arkansas

bowl 4 boat **5** arena, basin **6** cavity, hollow, tureen, valley, vessel **7** dishful, helping, portion, stadium **8** coliseum, deep dish **9** container, porringer **10** depression, receptacle **12** amphitheater

bowler 11 Earl Anthony

bowling
variation: **7** tenpins **8** duckpins, fivepins **10** candlepins
term: **4** miss **5** frame, spare, split **6** strike **10** gutterball
perfect score: **12** three hundred

bow-shape 3 arc **4** arch, bend **5** curve **9** curvature

bow to 5 yield **6** give in, give up, submit **9** acquiesce

box 3 bat, hit, rap **4** belt, cuff, slap, spar **5** booth, caddy, chest, crate, fight, punch, stall, whack **6** buffet, carton, coffer, strike, thwack **8** thumping **9** container **10** receptacle **11** compartment **13** exchange blows

boxer 7 Max Baer **8** Joe Louis **10** Barney Ross, Gene Tunney, Joe Frazier, Joe Walcott, Leon Spinks **11** Archie Moore, Jack Dempsey, Jack Johnson, Jake LaMotta, Larry Holmes, Muhammad Ali, Sonny Liston **12** Benny Leonard, James Corbett, John Sullivan, Johnny Dundee, Max Schmeling, Mickey Walker, Primo Carnera, Roberto Duran, Thomas Hearns **13** Carmen Basilio, Ezzard Charles, George Foreman, James Jeffries, Rocky Graziano, Rocky Marciano **14** Bob Fitzsimmons, Floyd Patterson, Henry Armstrong **15** Maxie Rosenbloom, Sugar Ray Leonard **16** Sugar Ray Robinson

boy 3 lad **5** youth **8** man child **9** male child, stripling, youngster
French: **6** garcon

Boy
character in: **6** Tarzan
author: **9** Burroughs

boycott 5 spurn **6** reject **7** exclude **8** spurning **9** blackball, blacklist, exclusion, ostracism, ostracize, rejection **12** blackballing, blacklisting

Boyd, James
author of: **5** Drums **8** Long Hunt **9** Roll River **10** Marching On

Boyd, William
born: **13** Hendrysburg OH
roles: **15** Hopalong Cassidy

Boyer, Charles
born: **6** Figeac, France
roles: **7** Algiers **8** Conquest, Gaslight **10** Back Street **11** Lost Horizon **16** The Garden of Allah **19** All This and Heaven Too

boyfriend 3 man **4** beau, date **5** flame, lover, swain, wooer **6** escort, fellow, old man, squire, steady, suitor **7** admirer, beloved, Don Juan **8** cavalier, Lothario, paramour, truelove, young man **9** companion, inamorato **10** sweetheart **15** gentleman caller

boyish 5 boyey, fresh **6** callow, tender **7** boylike, puerile **8** childish, immature, innocent, juvenile, youthful **9** childlike **10** sophomoric

Boylan, Blazes
character in: **7** Ulysses
author: **5** Joyce

Boyle, Robert
field: **9** chemistry
nationality: **7** British
father of: **9** chemistry
advocated: **20** experimental approach
established: **9** Boyle's Law

boylike 5 fresh, young **6** boyish, callow **7** puerile **8** childish, immature, innocent, juvenile, youthful **9** childlike

Boys Town
director: **12** Norman Taurog
cast: **9** Henry Hull **12** Mickey Rooney, Spencer Tracy (Father Flanagan)
Oscar for: **5** actor (Tracy)
sequel: **13** Men of Boys Town

Boy Wonder
nickname of: **5** Robin **6** Mel Ott

brace 3 duo **4** pair, prop, stay **5** shore, strut, truss **6** bracer, couple, hold up, prop up, steady **7** bolster, bracket, fortify, prepare, shore up, support, sustain, twosome **8** buttress **9** reinforce, stanchion **10** strengthen **13** reinforcement

bracelet 6 armlet, bangle

bracer 10 stiff drink, stimulator, wristguard **11** invigorator **12** strengthener, strong drink

Brachiosaurus
type: **8** dinosaur, sauropod
location: **10** East Africa **12** United States
period: **8** Jurassic

bracing 8 arousing, reviving **10** energizing, fortifying, refreshing **11** restorative, stimulating **12** exhilarating, invigorating **13** strengthening

Brack, Judge
character in: **11** Hedda Gabler
author: **5** Ibsen

bracken 4 fern **5** brake, brush, ferns **10** underbrush **11** undergrowth

bracket 4 prop, rank, stay **5** brace, class, group, range, shore, strut, truss **6** prop up, status **7** shore up, support **8** category, classify, division, grouping **9** designate, stanchion **10** categorize **11** designation **14** classification

brackish 4 salt **5** briny, salty **6** saline

Bracknell, Lady Augusta
character in: **27** The Importance of Being Earnest
author: **5** Wilde

bract 4 leaf

Bradbury, Ray
author of: **13** Dandelion Wine, Fahrenheit 451 **17** The Illustrated Man **20** The Martian Chronicles **27** Something Wicked This Way Comes

Bradford, Barbara Taylor
author of: **17** A Woman of Substance

Bradford, Richard
author of: **15** Red Sky at Morning

Bradley, Bill (William Warren)
nickname: **10** Dollar Bill
sport: **10** basketball
team: **13** New York Knicks
elected: **7** Senator
from: **9** New Jersey

Bradstreet, Anne
author of: **35** The Tenth Muse Lately Sprung Up in America

Brady Bunch, The
character: **3** Jan **4** Greg **5** Alice, Bobby, Cindy, Peter **6** Marcia **9** Mike Brady **10** Carol Brady
cast: **8** Eve Plumb **9** Ann B Davis **10** Robert Reed, Susan Olsen **13** Barry Williams **14** Mike Lookinland **16** Maureen McCormick **17** Christopher Knight, Florence Henderson

brag 4 crow **5** boast, vaunt **7** big talk, crowing, talk big **8** boasting, bragging **10** exaggerate, self-praise **12** boastfulness, exaggeration **15** blow one's own horn **19** pat oneself on the back

Brage *see* **5** Bragi

Bragg, William Henry and William Lawrence
field: **7** physics
nationality: **7** British
determined: **16** crystal structure
by: **15** X-ray diffraction
established: **9** Bragg's Law
awarded: **10** Nobel Prize

braggadocio 5 pride **6** egoism, vanity **7** bluster, conceit, swagger **9** cockiness, vainglory **10** pretension **14** self-importance

braggart 7 boaster, bragger **8** blowhard **9** big talker

Bragi
also: **5** Brage
origin: **6** Nordic
god of: **5** music **6** poetry
father: **4** Odin **5** Othin
wife: **4** Idun **5** Iduna, Ithun **6** Ithunn
mother: **3** Fri **5** Frigg, Frija **6** Frigga

Brahe, Tycho
field: **9** astronomy
nationality: **6** Danish
built: **11** observatory

Brahman
country: **5** India
religion: **8** Hinduism
system: **5** caste
rank: **7** highest
function: **6** leader, priest **7** teacher

Brahms, Johannes
born: **7** Germany, Hamburg
composer of: **7** Rinaldo **10** Rain Sonata **11** Triumphlied, Volkslieder **12** Thuner-Sonate **13** German Requiem, Song of Destiny, Song of Triumph **14** Schicksalslied, Song of the Fates, Tragic Overture **15** Gesang der Parzen, Hungarian Dances **19** Liebeslieder Waltzes, Meistersinger Sonata **24** Academic Festival Overture **31** Variations on the St Anthony Chorale

braid 4 knit, lace **5** plait, ravel, twine, twist, weave **7** entwine, wreathe **9** interlace **10** intertwine

brain
part: **7** medulla **8** cerebrum **9** pituitary **10** cerebellum

brainchild 8 creation **9** invention **12** original work **15** imaginative work

braininess 6 genius **9** smartness **10** brightness, brilliance, cleverness **12** intelligence

brainless 4 dumb **6** stupid **7** asinine, foolish, idiotic, moronic, witless **8** mindless **9** imbecilic **10** half-witted **11** lamebrained **12** feebleminded, simple-minded

brain power 4 mind **9** intellect **12** intelligence **14** mental capacity

Brainworm
character in: **19** Every Man in His Humour
author: **6** Jonson

brainy 5 smart **6** bright, clever **9** brilliant **11** intelligent

brake 4 curb, drag, halt, rein, slow, stay, stop **5** check **6** arrest **7** control **9** restraint **10** constraint **11** reduce speed

Bramante, Donato
architect of: **9** Tempietto **14** Belvedere Court (the Vatican), Palazzo Caprini **19** Santa Maria della Pace **21** Santa Maria della Grazie

bramble 4 bush, vine **5** rough, shrub **7** thicket **8** prickers **13** raspberry bush **14** blackberry bush

Bramble, Matthew
character in: **14** Humphry Clinker
author: **8** Smollett

Bran
origin: **5** Welsh
king of: **7** Britain
habitat: **3** sea
saint in: **12** Christianity
brother: **9** Evnissyen **10** Manawyddan
sister: **7** Branwen
head buried in: **6** London

branch 3 arm, leg **4** fork, limb, part, wing **5** bough, prong, spray **6** agency, bureau, divide, feeder, member, office, ramify **7** channel, chapter, diverge, radiate, section, segment **8** division, offshoot, separate, shoot off **9** bifurcate, component, extension, tributary **10** department **11** subdivision **12** ramification

branched 6 forked, parted **7** divided **8** extended **9** spread out

Branchus
father: **6** Apollo
power of: **6** augury
power given by: **6** Apollo

Brancusi, Constantin
born: **7** Romania **13** Pestisani Gorj
artwork: **4** Fish **7** Chimera, The Kiss, The Seal **9** Sorceress **10** Adam and Eve, Prometheus **11** Bird in Space, Prodigal Son **12** Flying Turtle, Sleeping Muse **13** Endless Column **20** Sculpture for the Blind

brand 4 blot, kind, make, mark, sear, sign, slur, sort, spot, type **5** class, grade, label, smear, stain, stamp, taint **6** burn in, emblem, smirch, stigma **7** blemish, quality, variety **8** besmirch, disgrace **9** discredit, trademark **10** imputation, stigmatize **11** manufacture

brandish 4 wave **5** shake, swing, wield **6** flaunt, waggle **7** display, exhibit, show off **8** flourish

brand new 5 fresh, young **6** unused

Brando, Marlon
born: **7** Omaha NE
roles: **8** Sayonara **10** The Wild One, Viva Zapata **12** Julius Caesar, The Godfather (Oscar refused) **13** Apocalypse Now **15** On the Waterfront (Oscar) **16** Last Tango in Paris **17** Mutiny on the Bounty **21** A Streetcar Named Desire

brandy 6 cognac, grappa, kahlua, kirsch, metaxa **8** Calvados, Tia Maria **9** applejack, Slivovitz **12** Grand Marnier, Peter

Heering 14 forbidden fruit
French: 8 eau de vie

Brangwen, Ursula and Gudrun
characters in: 11 Women in
Love
author: 8 Lawrence

Branstock
also: 9 Barnstock
origin: 12 Scandinavian
mentioned in: 8 Volsunga
form: 3 oak 4 tree
location: 7 Volsung
house of: 7 Volsung
Odin (Othin) thrusts:
4 Gram 5 sword

Brant, Captain Adam
character in: 22 Mourning
Becomes Electra
author: 6 O'Neill

Branwen
origin: 5 Welsh
brother: 4 Bran
husband: 10 Matholwych
son killed by: 9 Evnissyen

Braque, Georges
born: 6 France 18 Argenteuil
sur Seine
artwork: 7 Atelier, Grand Nu
(Great Nude), The Echo
8 The Table 13 The Portu-
guese 14 Man with a Gui-
tar 16 Violin and Palette,
Violin and Pitcher
18 Woman with a
Mandolin

brash 4 bold, rash, rude
5 fresh, hasty, sassy 6 brazen,
cheeky, madcap 7 forward
8 careless, heedless, impudent,
reckless 9 foolhardy, impetuous, imprudent, know-it-all
10 incautious 11 impertinent,
precipitous, smart-alecky
12 unconsidered
13 overconfident

brashness 4 gall 5 brass,
cheek, nerve 8 audacity, boldness, chutzpah, temerity
10 brazenness, effrontery
11 forwardness, presumption

Brasilia
capital of: 6 Brazil

brass 4 gall, sand, VIPs
5 cheek, nerve 8 audacity,
boldness, chutzpah, officers, temerity 9 impudence 10 brazenness, effrontery
11 forwardness, presumption

Brass, Sampson
character in: 19 The Old Curiosity Shop
author: 7 Dickens

brass instrument 4 tuba
5 bugle 6 cornet 7 trumpet
8 trombone 9 euphonium
10 French horn, sousaphone
ancient: 3 lur 7 Alphorn,

buisine, serpent
10 ophicleide

brass tacks 4 crux, meat
7 details 9 realities, substance
10 essentials 11 nitty-gritty
15 sum and substance

brassy 4 bold 5 brash, cocky,
sassy, saucy 6 brazen 7 forward 8 arrogant, impudent, insolent, overbold 9 barefaced,
outspoken, shameless, un-
abashed 10 unblushing
11 impertinent

brat 3 imp 4 chit 5 whelp
6 hoyden, rascal 9 rude child
12 spoiled child

Brauhaus 6 tavern 7 brewery

Brautigan, Richard
author of: 15 Sombrero Fallout 18 The Hawkline Mon-
ster 21 Trout Fishing in
America 38 The Pill Versus
the Springhill Mine
Disaster

bravado 7 big talk, blowing,
bluster, bombast, bravura,
crowing, puffery, swagger
8 boasting, bragging 9 cockiness 10 swaggering 11 braggadocio 12 boastfulness 13 show
of courage

brave 4 bear, dare, defy, face,
game, take 5 abide, brook,
gutsy, stand 6 breast, endure,
gritty, heroic, plucky, spunky,
suffer 7 doughty, stomach, sustain, undergo, valiant,
weather 8 confront, fearless,
intrepid, stalwart, tolerate, unafraid, valorous 9 challenge,
dauntless, outbrazen, put up
with, stand up to, undaunted,
withstand 10 courageous
11 lionhearted, unflinching,
unshrinking 12 stouthearted

brave deed 4 feat 7 exploit
9 heroic act 11 achievement

Brave New World
author: 12 Aldous Huxley
character: 4 John 11 Bernard
Marx 12 Lenina Crowne,
Mustapha Mond

bravery 4 grit 5 pluck, spunk,
valor 6 daring, mettle, spirit
7 courage, heroism 8 audacity,
boldness 11 intrepidity
12 fearlessness
13 dauntlessness

Bravo, The
author: 19 James Fenimore
Cooper

brawl 3 row 4 fray, tiff 5 broil,
clash, fight, melee, scrap, set-
to 6 battle, fracas, ruckus,
rumpus, uproar 7 dispute,
quarrel, scuffle, wrangle
8 squabble 9 imbroglio 11 altercation, embroilment

brawn 5 might, power 7 muscles, stamina 8 strength
9 beefiness, huskiness 10 robustness, ruggedness, sturdiness 19 muscular development

brawny 5 burly, husky
6 mighty, robust, rugged,
strong, sturdy 8 muscular,
powerful 9 strapping

Bray, Madeline
character in: 16 Nicholas
Nickleby
author: 7 Dickens

brazen 4 bold, open 5 brash,
saucy 6 brassy, cheeky 7 forward 8 arrogant, immodest,
impudent, insolent 9 audacious, barefaced, boldfaced,
shameless, unabashed

brazenness 4 gall 5 brass,
cheek, nerve 8 audacity, boldness, chutzpah 9 impudence
10 effrontery, fowardness
11 presumption

Brazil see box

Brazil
director: 12 Terry Gilliam
cast: 8 Ida Lowry 9 Kim
Greist 12 Robert De Niro
13 Jonathan Pryce

Brazilian Bombshell
nickname of: 13 Carmen
Miranda

Brazzaville
capital of: 5 Congo

breach 3 gap 4 gash, hole,
rent, rift, slit 5 break, chink,
cleft, crack, split 7 crevice,
failure, fissure, neglect, opening, rupture 8 defiance, trespass 9 disregard, violation
10 infraction 11 dereliction
12 disobedience, infringement
13 noncompliance, nonobservance, transgression

breach of faith 7 perfidy
8 bad faith, betrayal 9 falseness, treachery, two-timing
10 disloyalty 11 double-cross
13 double-dealing

breach of order 4 riot 6 fracas, mutiny, ruckus, uproar
7 turmoil 8 uprising 9 commotion, rebellion 10 dissension
11 disturbance, pandemonium
18 disturbance of peace

breach of trust 7 falsity, perfidy 9 falseness, treachery
10 disloyalty, infidelity 13 deceitfulness, double-dealing

bread 3 rye 4 food, pita
5 bucks, dough, money,
wheat 6 staple 9 sourdough
10 livelihood, sustenance
11 staff of life
12 pumpernickel

bread and butter 3 job 6 ca-

Brazil

capital: 8 Brasilia

former capital: 12 Rio de Janeiro

largest city: 8 Sao Paulo

others: 5 Bahia, Belem **6** Recife, Sabara, Santos **7** Vitoria **8** Salvador **9** Ouro Preto, Paranagua **10** Diamantina **11** Porto Alegre **13** Belo Horizonte, Cruzeiro do Sul

school:
  junior high: **7** ginasio
  senior high: **7** colegio

measure: 2 pe **4** moio, sack, vara **5** braca, legoa, milha, tonel **6** canada, cuarto, quarto, tarefa **7** garrafa **8** alqueire

monetary unit: 3 joe **4** reis **5** dobra **7** centara, halfjoe, milreis **8** cruzeiro

weight: 3 bag **4** onca **5** libra **6** arroba, oitava **7** quilate, quintal **8** tonelada

island: 6 Maraca, Marajo **7** Bananal, Cardoso, Caviana, Mexiana **8** Comprida

lake: 4 Aima, Feia **5** Mirim **13** Logo dos Platos

mountain: 3 Mar **5** Geral, Organ, Piaui **6** Acarai, Gurupi, Parima, Urucum **7** Amambai, Carajas, Gradaus, Oragaos, Roraima **8** Bandeira, Itatiaja, Roncador, Tombador **9** Pacaraima, Sugar Loaf **10** Tumuc-Humac

highest point: 7 Neblina

river: 3 Apa, Ica **4** Doce, Geio, Ivai, Jari, Para, Paru, Sono, Tefe **5** Abuna, Anaua, Apore, Capim, Claro, Corua, Icana, Iriri, Itapi, Jurua, Jutai, Manso, Negro, Pardo, Piaui, Preto, Tiete, Turvo, Urubu, Verde, Xingu **6** Ajuana, Amazon, Arinos, Balsas, Branco, Canuma, Contas, Cuiaba, Demini, Grajau, Grande, Gurupi, Ibicui, Iguacu, Japura, Javari, Mearim, Mortes, Mucuri, Parana, Purpus, Ronuro, Sangue, Tacutu, Tibagi, Uatuma, Uaupes **7** Corumba, Iguassu, Madeira, Madiera, Orinoco, Paraiba, Sucuriu, Tapajos, Taquari, Teodoro, Uruguai, Uruguay, Velhass **8** Araguaia, Padauiri, Paracatu, Paraguay, Parnaiba, Solimoes, Tarauaca **9** Tocantins **12** Sao Francisco

sea: 8 Atlantic

physical feature:
  bay: **9** All Saints
  cape: **4** Frio **6** Blanco, Buzios, Gurupy, Orange **7** Saotome **8** Saoroque
  dam: **6** Furnas **7** Peixoto
  estuary: **4** Para
  rain forest: **5** selva
  waterfall: **6** Guaira, Iguacu **7** Iguassu **11** Paulo Afonso

people: 2 Ge **4** Anta **5** Acroa, Arara, Araua, Bravo, Carib, Guana, Negro **6** Arawak, Caraja **7** Carayan, Javahai, Tariana **8** Botocudo, Chambioa **9** Caucasian, mamelucos, mulattoes **10** Portuguese **11** Tupi-Guarani
  architect: **8** Niemeyer
  artist: **6** Segall **9** Portinari **10** Cavalcenti
  author: **5** Amado, Bilac, Ramos **6** Freyre
  composer: **10** Villalobos
  discoverer: **6** Cabral
  leader: **6** Aranha, Branco, Collor, Franco, Geisel, Medici, Vargas **7** Goulart
  sculptor: **11** Aleijadinho

language: 10 Portuguese

religion: 10 Protestant **13** Roman Catholic

place:
  beach: **7** Ipanema **9** Boa Viagem **10** Copacabana

feature:
  bird: **4** mitu **5** mitua
  dance: **5** frevo, samba **6** maxixe **9** bossa nova
  fish: **7** piranha
  gourd: **4** cuia
  plantation: **7** fazenda
  slums: **7** favelas
  tree: **5** icica **6** ucuuba **7** arariba

food:
  dish: **6** vatapa **8** feijoada
  dried salted beef: **7** charque
  drink: **4** acai **9** cafezinho
  tea: **4** mate
  turtle soup: **16** cas quinho de mucua

reer, living 7 calling 8 business, vocation 9 life's work 10 livelihood 14 means of support

Bread and Wine
author: 13 Ignazio Silone

breadbasket 3 gut 5 belly, tummy 6 paunch 7 abdomen, labonza, midriff, Midwest, stomach 11 solar plexus

breadth 4 area, size, span 5 range, reach, scope, width 6 extent, spread 7 compass, expanse, measure, stretch 8 latitude, wideness 9 broadness 10 dimensions 13 extensiveness

break *see* box

breakable 5 frail, shaky 6 flimsy 7 brittle, crumbly, fragile 8 delicate

break apart 7 crumble, shatter 8 collapse 9 fall apart 12 disintegrate, fall to pieces

breakdown 6 mishap 7 crackup, decline, failure 8 analysis, collapse, disorder, division 12 detailed list 13 deterioration 14 categorization

break down 6 divide 7 dissect 8 collapse, separate 9 decompose 11 deteriorate

breaker 4 cask, wave 6 comber 7 crusher 8 boat cask 9 destroyer

break faith with 6 betray 7 do wrong 9 play false 11 double-cross 12 be unfaithful 13 be treacherous 16 sell down the river

Breakfast at Tiffany's
author: 12 Truman Capote
director: 12 Blake Edwards
cast: 10 Buddy Ebsen 12 Mickey Rooney, Patricia Neal 13 Audrey Hepburn (Holly Golightly), George Peppard
score: 12 Henry Mancini
song: 9 Moon River

Breakfast Club, The
director: 10 John Hughes
cast: 10 Ally Sheedy 13 Emilio Estevez, Molly Ringwald 18 Anthony Michael Hall

Breakfast of Champions
author: 12 Kurt Vonnegut

break free 4 bolt, flee, skip 6 escape 7 get away, make off, run away 9 cut and run 10 fly the coop 12 make a getaway

breakfront 5 hutch 7 cabinet 8 bookcase, cupboard 12 china cabinet

break in 5 train 7 intrude 8 accustom, initiate 9 acclimate, interrupt 10 burglarize 12 indoctrinate

break-in 5 theft 7 robbery 8 burglary, stealing 12 burglarizing 13 housebreaking 19 breaking and entering

Breaking Away
director: 10 Peter Yates
screenplay: 11 Steve Tesich
cast: 10 Paul Dooley 11 Daniel Stern, Dennis Quaid 13 Barbara Barrie 16 Jackie Earle Haley 17 Dennis Christopher

setting: 7 Indiana 11 Bloomington

break loose 4 bolt, flee, skip 6 escape 7 get away, make off 9 cut and run 10 fly the coop 12 make a getaway

breakneck 4 rash 5 risky 8 reckless, very fast 9 dangerous, daredevil 12 death-defying

break of day 4 dawn 5 sunup 7 dawning, sunrise 8 daybreak 11 crack of dawn

break off 3 end 4 halt 5 cease 6 recess 7 adjourn, snap off, suspend 8 conclude, shut down 11 discontinue

breakout 6 escape, flight 7 getaway 10 decampment

break out 4 bolt, skip 5 begin, erupt 6 escape 7 bust out, get away 10 burst forth, fly the coop 12 make a getaway

Break the Bank
host: 9 Bert Parks 10 Bud Collyer

break the habit 4 kick, quit, stop 6 eschew, give up 8 renounce, withdraw 14 quit cold turkey

breakthrough 7 advance 11 advancement, improvement, penetration, step forward

breakup 5 split 7 crackup 9 dispersal, splitting 10 separation 14 disintegration

break with 5 leave 8 be untrue, part from 10 be disloyal 11 divorce from 12 fall away from, separate from

breast 4 bust, core 5 bosom, chest, heart 10 very marrow Italian: 5 petto

breastwork 7 bastion, rampart 8 barbette 9 earthwork 13 fortification

breath 4 wind 6 spirit 9 animation, breathing, lifeblood, life force 10 exhalation, inhalation, vital spark 11 divine spark, respiration, vital spirit 12 vitalization

breathe 4 gasp, huff, pant, puff 5 utter 6 impart, murmur 7 respire, whisper 9 draw in air 10 draw breath 15 inhale and exhale

breathe in 6 inhale 7 inspire, respire

breathe out 4 huff, pant, puff 6 exhale, expire 7 respire

breathing 4 live 5 alive 6 living 7 animate 11 respiratory 13 drawing breath

---

break 3 cap, end, fly, gap, off, run, top 4 beat, bust, chip, dash, defy, flee, gash, halt, hole, rend, rent, rest, rift, rive, ruin, snap, stop, tame, tear, tell 5 burst, cease, cleft, crack, crush, erupt, excel, lapse, occur, outdo, pause, sever, shirk, smash, split, train 6 appear, better, breach, chance, cleave, detach, divide, escape, exceed, happen, hiatus, ignore, inform, lessen, master, powder, recess, reveal, soften, subdue, sunder, weaken 7 control, cushion, destroy, disobey, divulge, eclipse, fissure, fortune, give out, lighten, neglect, opening, pull off, respite, run away, rupture, shatter, surpass, suspend, tear off, violate, wipe out 8 announce, bankrupt, burst out, cracking, demolish, diminish, disclose, disjoint, division, fracture, fragment, go beyond, interval, outstrip, overcome, proclaim, renege on, separate, shut down, slip away, splinter 9 dismember, disregard, granulate, interlude, interrupt, make a dash, pulverize, splitting, transcend 10 discipline, disconnect, fall back on, fly the coop, fracturing, impoverish, infringe on, make public, overshadow, separation, shattering, take flight, wrench away 11 discontinue, get away from, opportunity, pay no heed to 12 be derelict in, disintegrate, intermission, interruption, make a getaway, stroke of luck 13 strap for funds 14 bend to one's will, take the force of 15 take to one's heels

Breathless
director: 14 Jean-Luc Goddard
written by: 16 Francois Truffaut
cast: 10 Jean Seberg 16 Jean-Paul Belmondo
setting: 5 Paris

breathtaking 7 amazing, awesome 8 exciting 9 startling 10 surprising 11 astonishing

Brecht, Bertolt
author of: 13 Mother Courage 15 Drums in the Night 18 The Threepenny Opera 21 St Joan of the Stockyards 23 The Caucasian Chalk Circle 27 The Resistable Rise of Arturo Ui 29 The Private Life of the Master Race

Breck, Alan
character in: 9 Kidnapped
author: 9 Stevenson

breech 4 rump, seat 6 behind 8 buttocks, haunches, hind part 9 fundament, posterior 12 hindquarters

breeches 5 pants 8 trousers

breed 4 bear, grow, kind, race, sire, sort, type 5 beget, cause, order, raise, spawn, stock 6 family, father, foster, lead to, mother, strain 7 develop, nurture, produce, promote, species, variety 8 generate, multiply, occasion 9 cultivate, give forth, procreate, propagate, reproduce 10 bring forth, give rise to 11 proliferate 16 produce offspring

breeding 4 line 5 grace 6 mating, polish 7 bearing, descent, growing, lineage, manners, raising, rearing 8 ancestry, courtesy, hatching, heredity, pedigree, spawning, training 9 begetting, bloodline, genealogy, gentility, parentage, producing 10 background, extraction, family tree, generation, politeness, production, refinement, upbringing 11 cultivation, germination, multiplying, procreation, propagation 12 reproduction

breeze 4 flit, pass, sail, waft 5 coast, float, glide, sweep 6 zephyr 9 light gust, light wind 10 gentle wind, puff of wind

breezy 3 gay 4 airy, pert, spry 5 blowy, brisk, fresh, gusty, light, merry, peppy, sunny, windy 6 bouncy, casual, frisky, jaunty, lively 7 buoyant, squally 8 animated, blustery, carefree, cheerful, debonair,

spirited 9 energetic, resilient, sprightly, vivacious, windswept 10 blithesome 11 free and easy

Brennan, Walter
born: 12 Swampscott MA
roles: 8 Kentucky 12 Come and Get It, The Westerner 13 The Real McCoys 16 To Have and Have Not

Brent, George
real name: 18 George Brendan Nolan
wife: 11 Ann Sheridan 14 Ruth Chatterton
born: 7 Ireland 14 Shannonsbridge
roles: 7 Jezebel 11 Dark Victory, The Great Lie 17 Forty-Second Street

Bres
origin: 5 Irish
king of: 7 Ireland

Breton, Andre
author of: 5 Nadja 21 Manifesto of Surrealism

Breuer, Marcel
architect of: 17 IBM Research Center (La Gaude France) 18 UNESCO headquarters (Paris) 25 St John's Abbey and University (Collegeville MN) 26 Whitney Museum of American Art (NYC)

brevity 9 briefness, pithiness, quickness, shortness, terseness 10 transience 11 conciseness 12 ephemerality, impermanence, succinctness

brew 3 ale 4 beer, boil, cook, form, make, plan, plot, soak 5 begin, drink, hatch, ripen, start, steep, stout 6 cook up, devise, foment, gather, porter, scheme, seethe 7 arrange, concoct, ferment, mixture, prepare, produce, think up 8 beverage, contrive, initiate 9 formulate, germinate, originate 10 concoction, malt liquor

brewery
German: 8 Brauhaus

Brian de Bois, Sir
character in: 7 Ivanhoe
author: 5 Scott

Briareus
also: 7 Aegaeon
member of: 13 Hecatonchires

bribe 5 graft 6 buy off, grease, pay off, payola, suborn 9 hush money 10 inducement 11 illegal gift 15 grease the hand of, grease the palm of
French: 7 douceur

bric-a-brac 7 baubles,

gewgaws 8 bibelots, trinkets 9 gimcracks, kickshaws, ornaments 11 knickknacks

Brick
character in: 16 Cat on a Hot Tin Roof
author: 8 Williams

Bricks
god of: 5 Kulla

bridal 7 nuptial, wedding 8 marriage 11 matrimonial

Bridehead, Sue
character in: 14 Jude the Obscure
author: 5 Hardy

Bride of Lammermoor, The
author: 14 Sir Walter Scott
character: 10 Lady Ashton, Lucy Ashton, Ravenswood 14 Laird of Bucklaw 16 Sir William Ashton

Brideshead Revisited
author: 11 Evelyn Waugh
character: 5 Celia, Julia 8 Cordelia 9 Sebastian 10 Brideshead (Bridey), Rex Mottram 12 Boy Mulcaster, Charles Ryder 13 Lady Marchmain, Lord Marchmain 14 Anthony Blanche

bridge 3 tie 4 band, bind, bond, link, span 5 cross, unify, union 6 go over 7 catwalk, connect, liaison, viaduct 8 alliance, overpass, traverse 9 cross over 10 connection, passageway 11 association, reach across 12 extend across

bridge
derived from: 5 whist
variation: 14 contract bridge
partnership: 9 East/West 11 North/South
cards/hand: 8 thirteen
no cards of a suit: 4 void
one card of a suit: 9 singleton
two cards of a suit: 9 doubleton
rule book by: 5 Goren

Bridge of San Luis Rey, The
author: 14 Thornton Wilder
character: 5 Clara, Jaime 6 Manuel, Pepita 7 Esteban, Viceroy 8 Uncle Pio 11 La Perichole 14 Brother Juniper 20 Marquesa de Montemayor

Bridge on the River Kwai, The
director: 9 David Lean
based on story by: 12 Pierre Boulle
cast: 11 Jack Hawkins 12 Alec Guinness 13 Wil-

liam Holden **14** Sessue
Hayakawa
Oscar for: **5** actor (Guin-
ness) **7** picture

Bridges, Beau
real name: **21** Lloyd Vernet
Bridges III
father: **5** Lloyd
brother: **4** Jeff
born: **12** Los Angeles CA
roles: **5** Space **8** Norma Rae
11 The Landlord **25** The
Other Side of the Mountain

Bridges, Jeff
father: **5** Lloyd
brother: **4** Beau
born: **12** Los Angeles CA
roles: **4** Tron **7** Starman
8 King Kong **10** Jagged
Edge **13** Kiss Me Goodbye
14 Against All Odds **18** The
Last Picture Show

Bridges, Lloyd
son: **4** Beau, Jeff
born: **12** San Leandro CA
roles: **7** Sea Hunt **8** Airplane,
High Noon

Bridges at Toko-ri, The
author: **13** James Michener

Bridget
character in: **19** Every Man
in His Humour
author: **6** Jonson

Bridge Too Far, A
author: **13** Cornelius Ryan

Bridgetown
capital of: **8** Barbados

bridle **3** gag **4** curb, rule
5 check **6** arrest, direct, draw
up, flinch, hinder, manage,
master, muzzle, rear up, recoil **7** control, harness, inhibit,
repress **8** draw back, restrain,
restrict, suppress **9** constrain,
restraint **11** bit and brace,
head harness

brief **4** case **5** hasty, pithy,
quick, short, swift, terse **6** advise, inform, precis, resume
7 capsule, compact, concise,
defense, limited, prepare, summary **8** abridged, abstract, argument, fill in on, fleeting,
instruct, succinct **9** condensed,
curtailed, momentary, shortened, temporary, thumbnail,
transient **10** abridgment, compressed, contention, describe
to, short-lived, summarized,
transitory **11** abbreviated
12 legal summary

brief account **6** precis, sketch
7 outline, summary **8** anecdote

brier, briar **4** Rosa **5** Rubus,
thorn **6** Smilax **7** bramble
varieties: **3** Cat, Dog, Hag,
Saw **4** Bull **5** Green, Horse,
Sweet **7** Jackson **8** Austrian

9 Sensitive **14** Austrian
copper

brigade **4** crew, team, unit
5 corps, force, group, squad
6 legion, outfit **7** company
9 regiments, squadrons
10 army groups, battalions,
contingent, detachment

Brigadoon
director: **16** Vincente
Minnelli
based on Broadway hit by:
14 Lerner and Loewe
cast: **9** Gene Kelly **10** Van
Johnson **11** Cyd Charisse

brigand **5** thief **6** bandit, gunman, looter, outlaw, pirate,
robber, vandal **7** corsair, hoodlum, ruffian, rustler, spoiler
8 marauder, pilferer, pillager
9 buccaneer, cutthroat, desperado, despoiler, plunderer, privateer **10** highwayman

bright **3** gay **4** glad, good,
keen, rosy, sage, warm,
wise **5** acute, alert, aware,
grand, great, happy, jolly,
merry, quick, sharp, smart,
sunny, vivid **6** astute,
blithe, brainy, clever,
gifted, joyful, joyous,
lively, shrewd **7** beaming,
blazing, capable, glowing,
healthy, hopeful, intense,
lambent, radiant, shining
8 cheerful, dazzling, exciting, gleaming, luminous,
lustrous, profound, splendid, talented **9** brilliant,
competent, effulgent, excellent, favorable, ingenious,
inventive, masterful, promising, sagacious, sparkling,
wide-awake **10** auspicious,
discerning, glittering, optimistic, perceptive, proficient, propitious,
prosperous, remarkable,
shimmering, successful
11 clearheaded, illuminated, illustrious, intelligent, light-filled,
magnificent, outstanding,
quick-witted, resourceful,
resplendent **12** exhilarating

brighten **4** lift **5** boost, cheer,
light **6** buoy up, lift up, perk
up **7** animate, enliven, gladden, lighten **9** make happy,
stimulate **10** illuminate

bright-eyed **5** alert, awake
9 wide-awake **12** on the qui
vive

Bright Flows the River
author: **14** Taylor Caldwell

brightness **4** glow **5** glare,
gleam, shine **6** dazzle, luster
7 glitter, sparkle **8** radiance
9 lightness **10** brilliance, luminosity **12** intelligence

bright spot **3** joy **6** solace
7 comfort **8** pleasure
13 consolation

Brigit
origin: **5** Welsh
goddess of: **4** fire **6** wisdom
9 fertility, household
11 agriculture

**Brigitte Bardot & the Lolita
Syndrome**
author: **16** Simone de
Beauvoir

Brill Among the Ruins
author: **14** Vance Bourjaily

brilliance, brilliancy **4** gift,
glow **5** blaze, gleam, sheen,
shine **6** acuity, dazzle, genius,
luster, talent, wisdom **7** glitter,
shimmer, sparkle **8** grandeur,
keenness, radiance, sagacity,
splendor **9** alertness, awareness, greatness, ingenuity, intensity, quickness, sharpness,
smartness, vividness **10** braininess, brightness, capability,
cleverness, competence, effulgence, excellence, luminosity,
perception, profundity,
shrewdness **11** discernment,
distinction, proficiency **12** intelligence, magnificence, resplendence **13** inventiveness,
masterfulness **15** clearheadedness, illustriousness,
resourcefulness

brilliant *see* **6** bright

brim **3** fill, lip, rim **5** brink,
flood, ledge, verge **6** border,
fill up, margin, well up
8 overflow

brimless hat **3** cap **5** beret
6 beanie **11** stocking cap, tam
o'shanter

brimming **4** full **7** flooded,
teeming **8** overfull, swarming
11 overflowing

Brimo
origin: **5** Greek
form: **7** goddess
corresponds to: **6** Hecate
7 Demeter **10** Persephone

brine **6** the sea **8** sea water
9 salt water **12** salt solution
14 saline solution **16** pickling
solution

bring **4** bear, make, take, tote
5 begin, carry, cause, fetch,
force, start **6** compel, convey,
create, effect, induce **7** deliver,
produce, sell for, usher in

8 convince, engender, generate, initiate, persuade, result in **9** accompany, institute, originate, transport **10** bring about

bring about 2 do **4** form, open **5** begin, cause, found, set up, start **8** attain, create, effect, lead to **7** achieve, execute, produce **8** carry out, generate, initiate, organize **9** establish, institute, succeed at **10** accomplish, effectuate, inaugurate **11** bring to pass, precipitate **18** bring into existence

bring back 6 return **7** restore **8** recreate **9** surrender **10** return with

bring down a peg 5 abase **6** humble **7** mortify **9** humiliate **13** cut down to size

bring down to earth 10 disenchant **11** disenthrall, disillusion, open the eyes **13** break the spell **14** burst the bubble **20** shatter one's illusions

bring forth 4 bear **5** breed, elicit, evoke, hatch, spawn, whelp **7** deliver, produce **9** reproduce **10** make appear **11** give birth to

bring home to 7 blame on, clarify **11** attribute to **15** place emphasis on

bringing together 7 joining, wedding **8** amassing **9** combining, gathering, including **10** assembling, collecting **12** accumulating **13** incorporating

Bringing Up Baby
director: **11** Howard Hawks
cast: **9** Cary Grant **14** Charlie Ruggles **16** Katharine Hepburn

Bringing Up Father
creator: **13** George McManus
character: **5** Jiggs **6** Maggie
daughter: **5** Rosie
brother-in-law: **5** Bimmy
place: **11** Dinty Moore's
favorite dish: **20** corned beef and cabbage

bring into being 4 bear, form, make **5** erect, hatch, spawn, whelp **6** create, design, devise, invent, render **7** concoct, deliver, develop, fashion, produce **8** contrive, generate **9** construct, fabricate, formulate, originate **10** bring forth **11** give birth to

bring into existence 4 form **5** begin, set up, start **6** create **8** organize **9** establish, institute **10** bring about, inaugurate

bring into line 5 adapt **6** adjust **7** conform, shape up **9** harmonize, reconcile **10** discipline **11** accommodate **13** whip into shape

bring into question 11 cast doubt on **18** throw suspicion upon

bring into relief 6 accent, stress **7** dwell on, feature, point up **9** emphasize, press home, underline **10** accentuate, underscore

bring low 5 abase, shame **6** humble **8** cast down **9** denigrate, humiliate

bring off 4 gain **6** attain, effect, secure **7** achieve **10** accomplish

bring to an end 5 cease **6** finish **8** break off, conclude **9** call a halt, terminate **11** discontinue

bring to a standstill 3 end **4** halt, stay, stop **5** block, check **6** arrest **12** bring to a halt

bring to bay 4 trap, tree **6** corner **8** confront, hunt down

bring to bear 5 apply **6** employ **7** utilize **9** implement

bring together 5 amass **6** gather, muster **7** collect, marshal, round up **8** assemble **10** accumulate

bring to light 6 expose, reveal, unveil **7** clarify, divulge, explain, uncover **8** disclose **9** explicate, make known, make plain **10** illuminate, make public

bring to one's senses 3 jar **5** alarm, alert, shock **9** make aware

bring to pass 5 cause **6** create, effect **8** carry out **10** bring about, effectuate

bring to terms 6 settle **7** mediate **9** arbitrate, reconcile

bring to view 5 dig up **6** reveal **7** exhibit, uncover, unearth **8** disclose, retrieve **10** come up with

bring word 4 tell **6** advise, convey, inform, notify, relate, reveal **7** divulge, publish **8** announce, disclose, proclaim **9** apprise of, broadcast, make known, publicize **11** communicate

brink 3 rim **4** bank, brim, edge **5** point, shore, skirt, verge **6** border, margin **9** threshold

briny 4 salt **5** salty **6** saline

brio, con
music: **9** with vigor **10** with spirit

Briseis
origin: **5** Greek
mentioned in: **5** Iliad
father: **18** Briseus of Lyrnessus
husband: **5** Mynes
captured by: **8** Achilles
caused: **7** quarrel
between: **8** Achilles **9** Agamemnon

Briseus
origin: **5** Greek
mentioned in: **5** Iliad
daughter: **7** Briseis
death by: **7** suicide

Brisingamen 8 necklace
origin: **12** Scandinavian
trait: **5** magic
owned by: **5** Freia, Freya

brisk 4 busy, spry **5** alert, fresh, peppy, quick, swift **6** active, breezy, lively, snappy **7** bracing, chipper, dynamic, rousing **8** animated, bustling, spirited, stirring, vigorous **9** energetic, sprightly, vivacious, vivifying **10** refreshing **11** stimulating **12** exhilarating, invigorating

briskness 3 pep **5** vigor **6** energy **8** alacrity, spryness **9** quickness, swiftness **13** sprightliness

bristle 4 hair **5** quill **7** stiffen, whisker

bristles 5 barbs **6** quills **7** stubble **8** prickles, whiskers

bristletail
variety: **7** jumping **8** firebrat **9** primitive **10** nicoletiid, silverfish

bristly 5 rough **6** barbed, coarse **7** prickly, stubbly **8** unshaven **9** whiskered **11** bewhiskered

Britannia *see* **7** England

British 6 Breton, Briton **7** English **8** Brittany

British Columbia
bordered by: **5** Idaho, Yukon **6** Alaska **7** Montana **10** Washington **12** Pacific Ocean, United States **20** Northwest Territories
country: **6** Canada
Indian: **5** Haida **6** Nootka, Salish **8** Kwakiutl **9** Tsimshian **10** Bella Coola
island: **9** Vancouver **14** Queen Charlotte
mountain: **5** Coast, Rocky **7** Cascade **8** Columbia

11 Cordilleran 14 Cassiar
Omineca
nickname: 2 BC
park: 7 Glacier
rank in size: 5 sixth
river: 6 Fraser
section: 8 province

British Guiana see 6 Guyana

British Honduras see 6 Belize

British Mythology
god of rebirth/afterlife:
4 Gwyn
chief of gods: 5 Woden
island of paradise: 6 Avalon

Britomart
character in: 15 The Faerie
Queene
author: 7 Spenser

Britomartis
origin: 6 Cretan
goddess of: 7 hunters, sailors 9 fishermen
father: 4 Zeus
mother: 5 Carme
corresponds to: 7 Artemis
8 Dictynna

Briton 4 Celt 6 Celtic 7 British

Brittany
coast: 5 Armor
country: 6 France
inhabitant: 5 Celts 6 French,
Romans
interior: 6 Argoat
land form: 9 peninsula
language: 6 Breton
other name: 5 Breiz 6 Breton 8 Bretagne

Britten, (Edward) Benjamin
born: 7 England 9 Lowestoft
composer of: 8 Gloriana
9 Billy Budd 10 Paul Bun-
yan, War Requiem 11 Cur-
lew River, Peter Grimes,
Winter Words 12 Owen
Wingrave, The Poet's Echo
13 Albert Herring, Death in
Venice 14 The Prodigal Son,
Turn of the Screw 15 Phan-
tasy Quartet 17 A Ceremony
of Carols, A Charm of Lul-
labies, Sinfonia da Requiem,
The Rape of Lucretia
18 Holderlin Fragments
20 Cantata Misericordium
21 A Midsummer Night's
Dream, Sonnets of Michel-
angelo 22 The Burning
Fiery Furnace

brittle 7 crumbly, fragile, friable 9 breakable, frangible

Brize
form: 6 gadfly
sent by: 4 Hera
sent to annoy: 2 Io

Brizo
origin: 5 Greek
goddess of: 7 sailors

prophesied through:
6 dreams

broach 4 pose 6 launch, open
up, submit 7 advance, bring
up, mention, propose, suggest,
touch on 9 institute, introduce

broad 4 full, open, wide 5 ample, clear, large, plain, rangy,
roomy, thick 7 general, immense, obvious, sizable 8 extended, spacious, sweeping
9 capacious, expansive, extensive, inclusive, outspread, universal, unlimited
10 undetailed 11 far-reaching,
nonspecific, wide-ranging
12 all-embracing, ency-
clopedic 13 comprehensive

broadcast 4 beam, show, talk
5 cable, radio, relay 7 program, send out 8 televise,
transmit 9 statement 10 distribute 11 disseminate, put on
the air 12 announcement

broaden 5 boost, raise, swell,
widen 6 dilate, expand, extend 7 advance, amplify, augment, build up, develop,
distend, enlarge, improve,
stretch 8 increase 9 intensify,
reinforce, spread out
10 strengthen, supplement

broadened 7 dilated, swelled,
swollen, widened 8 enlarged,
expanded, extended 9 dis-
tended, spread out

broad-minded 7 liberal
8 amenable, catholic, flexible,
tolerant, unbiased 9 receptive,
unbigoted 10 charitable, open-
minded, undogmatic 11 magnanimous 12 unprejudiced,
unprovincial

Broadway Joe
nickname of: 9 Joe Namath

Brobdingnag
fictional land in: 16 Gulliver's
Travels
author: 5 Swift

Brobdingnagian 4 huge
5 giant 7 immense, mammoth
8 colossal, enormous, gigantic
10 gargantuan, tremendous
11 elephantine

broccoli 9 vegetable 12 Brassica rapa 16 Brassica oleracea
(Botyris Group) 17 Brassica
septiceps
variety: 6 Turnip 7 Italian
9 Asparagus, Sprouting

brochure 5 flier 6 folder
7 booklet, leaflet 8 circular,
handbill, pamphlet
9 throwaway

Brockton Blockbuster
nickname of: 13 Rocky
Marciano

Broglie, Louis Victor de
field: 7 physics
nationality: 6 French
developed: 13 wave
mechanics
awarded: 10 Nobel Prize

broil 3 fry 4 bake, burn, cook,
sear 5 parch, roast, toast
6 scorch 7 blister

broiler 3 hot, pan 4 rack
5 grill 6 cooker 8 scorcher
12 young chicken

broke 8 bankrupt, strapped,
wiped out 9 insolvent, penniless 10 down and out 12 impoverished, on one's uppers,
without funds 16 strapped for
funds

broken 4 torn 5 rough, split,
tamed 6 ruined, uneven
7 crushed, damaged 8 bankrupt, in pieces, ruptured
9 fractured, separated, shattered 10 incomplete 11 fragmentary, interrupted

Broken Commandment, The
author: 14 Toson Shimazaki

broken-down 6 beat-up, ruined 7 rickety, worn-out
8 battered, decrepit 10 ramshackle 11 dilapidated
12 deteriorated

broken-hearted 3 sad
6 gloomy, woeful 7 crushed,
doleful, forlorn, unhappy
8 dejected, desolate, downcast,
mournful, wretched 9 de-
pressed, long-faced, miserable,
sorrowful, woebegone 10 despairing, despondent, melancholy 11 heartbroken
12 disconsolate, inconsolable

Brom Bones
also: 12 Brom Van Brunt
character in: 23 The Legend
of Sleepy Hollow
author: 6 Irving

Brome
form: 5 nymph
cared for: 8 Dionysus

Bromfield, Louis
author of: 11 Early Autumn,
Malabar Farm 12 The Rains
Came 13 Mrs Parkington,
Night in Bombay 14 Wild Is
the River 15 The Green Bay
Tree 31 The Strange Case of
Miss Annie Spragg

bromide 6 cliche 8 banality
9 platitude 10 stereotype
11 trite phrase 19 hackneyed
expression

bromidic 4 dull 5 banal, corny,
stale, tired, trite, vapid 6 jejune 7 humdrum, insipid
8 ordinary 9 hackneyed
10 pedestrian, unexciting, uno-

riginal **13** platitudinous, unimaginative

bromine
chemical symbol: **2** Br

Bromius
epithet of: **8** Dionysus
means: **7** thunder

Bronson, Charles
real name: **16** Charles Buchinsky
wife: **11** Jill Ireland
born: **11** Ehrenfeld PA
roles: **9** Death Wish **13** The Dirty Dozen **14** The Great Escape **16** Battle of the Bulge, The Valachi Papers **19** The Magnificent Seven

Bronte, Anne
author of: **9** Agnes Grey **23** The Tenant of Wildfell Hall

Bronte, Charlotte
author of: **7** Shirley **8** Jane Eyre, Villette **12** The Professor

Bronte, Emily
author of: **16** Wuthering Heights

Brontes
member of: **8** Cyclopes

brontophobia
fear of: **7** thunder

Brontosaurus
also: **11** Apatosaurus
type: **8** dinosaur, sauropod
period: **8** Jurassic

Bronx Bull
nickname of: **11** Jake La Motta

bronze 3 tan **5** metal **8** brownish, chestnut **10** reddish-tan **12** reddish-brown **13** copper-colored

brooch 3 pin **5** clasp

brood 4 chew, fret, mope, mull, sulk **5** cover, dwell, hatch, spawn, worry, young **6** chicks, family, litter **7** agonize, sit upon **8** children, incubate **9** offspring **10** hatchlings

brook 3 run **4** bear, rill, take **5** abide, allow, creek, stand **6** accept, endure, stream, suffer **7** rivulet, stomach **8** tolerate **9** put up with, streamlet

Brooks, Gwendolyn
author of: **4** Riot **10** Annie Allen **14** Family Pictures

Brooks, James L
director of: **17** Terms of Endearment (Oscar)

Brooks, Mel
real name: **14** Melvin Kaminsky

wife: **12** Anne Bancroft
born: **10** Brooklyn NY
director of/roles: **11** High Anxiety, Silent Movie **12** The Producers **14** Blazing Saddles **17** Young Frankenstein **20** The History of the World

Brooks, Richard
director of: **11** Elmer Gantry, In Cold Blood **16** Cat on a Hot Tin Roof, Sweet Bird of Youth **19** The Blackboard Jungle

broom 4 bush **5** besom, brush, whisk **7** sweeper

Broteas
father: **8** Tantalus
devotee of: **6** Cybele
denied divinity of: **7** Artemis

broth 5 stock **8** bouillon, consomme **9** clear soup

brothel 4 stew **5** house **6** bagnio, bordel **8** bordello, cathouse **10** bawdy house, fancy house, whorehouse **11** maison close **13** maison de passe, sporting house **14** house of ill fame **16** house of ill repute **19** house of prostitution

brother 3 pal **4** chum, monk, peer **5** buddy, friar **6** cleric **7** comrade, kinsman, partner, sibling **8** confrere, landsman, monastic, relative, relation **9** associate, colleague, companion, fellowman **10** countryman **11** male sibling **12** fellow member **13** fellow citizen
French: **5** frere

brotherhood 4 club **5** amity, lodge **10** fellowship, fraternity, friendship **11** association

Brother Juniper
character in: **21** The Bridge of San Luis Rey
author: **6** Wilder

Brothers Karamazov, The
author: **10** Dostoevsky **17** Fyodor Dostoyevsky
character: **4** Ivan **6** Dmitri **7** Alyosha (Alexey), Zossima **8** Katerina **9** Grushenka **10** Smerdyakov **15** Fyodor Karamazov

brougham 3 car **8** carriage **10** automobile

brought 6 caused **7** carried, fetched, sold for **8** conveyed **9** conducted, convinced, persuaded

brow 3 rim **4** brim, edge, side **5** brink, verge **6** border, margin **8** boundary, forehead **9** periphery

browbeat 3 cow **5** abash, bully, cower **6** badger, harass,

hector **7** henpeck **8** bulldoze, domineer, frighten, threaten **9** terrorize, tyrannize **10** intimidate

browbeater 5 bully **6** despot **7** coercer **9** oppressor, tormenter, tormentor **11** intimidator, petty tyrant

browbeating 8 bullying **11** threatening, tyrannizing **12** intimidation

brown 3 bay, dun, fry, tan **4** buff, cook, drab, fawn, puce, roan, rust **5** beige, camel, cocoa, hazel, khaki, saute, tawny, toast, umber **6** auburn, bronze, brunet, coffee, copper, ginger, russet, sorrel, walnut **8** brunette, chestnut, cinnamon, mahogany **9** chocolate, olive drab **10** terra-cotta **11** dirt-colored, sand-colored **12** liver-colored

Brown, Angeline
real name of: **14** Angie Dickinson

Brown, Berenice Sadie
character in: **19** A Member of the Wedding
author: **9** McCullers

Brown, Charles Brockden
author of: **6** Ormond **7** Wieland **11** Edgar Huntly **12** Arthur Mervyn

Brown, Claude
author of: **16** The Children of Ham **25** Manchild in the Promised Land

Brown, Dee
author of: **15** Creek Mary's Blood **24** Bury My Heart at Wounded Knee

Brown, Helen Gurley
author of: **19** Sex and the Single Girl
editor of: **12** Cosmopolitan

Brown, Helen Hayes
real name of: **10** Helen Hayes

Brown, Jim (Jimmy)
sport: **8** football
position: **8** fullback
team: **15** Cleveland Browns
actor in: **10** Dirty Dozen

Brown, Robert
field: **6** botany
nationality: **8** Scottish
established: **16** Brownian movement

Brown Bomber
nickname of: **8** Joe Louis

Browne, Dik
creator/artist of: **9** Hi and Lois **12** Beetle Bailey **16** Hagar the Horrible

Browne, Sir Thomas
author of: 9 Urn Burial
12 Hydriotaphia 13 Religio
Medici 16 The Garden of
Cyrus

brownie 3 elf 4 cake, puck
5 fairy, pixie 6 sprite
10 leprechaun

Browning, Elizabeth Barrett
author of: 11 Aurora Leigh
14 How Do I Love Thee
16 Casa Guidi Windows
24 Sonnets from the
Portuguese

Browning, Robert
author of: 8 Sordello 10 Par-
acelsus 11 Pippa Passes
13 Fra Lippo Lippi, My Last
Duchess 14 Andrea del
Sarto 17 The Ring and the
Book 20 The Pied Piper of
Hamlin 29 Soliloquy of the
Spanish Cloister 30 Childe
Roland to the Dark Tower
Came

brownish 3 tan 5 taupe
6 bronze 8 chestnut 13 copper-
colored

Brownlow, Mr
character in: 11 Oliver Twist
author: 7 Dickens

Brownmiller, Susan
author of: 14 Against Our
Will

Brown's Descent
author: 11 Robert Frost

browse 3 eat 4 feed, scan,
skim 5 graze 6 nibble, peruse,
survey 7 dip into, pasture
8 look over 9 check over
11 look through 13 glance
through

Bruckner, Anton
born: 7 Austria 9 Ansfelden
composer of: 6 Te Deum
7 Psalm CL 11 Grosse
Messe 16 Romantic Sym-
phony 26 Intermezzo for
String Quartet

Brueghel, Pieter (the Elder)
born: 5 Breda 8 Flanders
nickname: 14 Peasant Bruegel
son: 11 Jan Brueghel
artwork: 9 Blue Cloak, The
Months 10 Dulle Griet (Mad
Meg) 12 Fall of Icarus,
Peasant Dance, Tower of
Babel 14 Children's Games,
The Misanthrope 15 Return
of the Herd 16 Hunters in
the Snow 17 The Triumph
of Death 19 Peasant Wed-
ding Dance 21 Peasant Wedding Banquet, The Magpie
on the Gallows 22 Massacre
of the Innocents 23 The
Blind Leading the Blind,
The Fall of the Rebel
Angels

Brueghel, Jan
born: 8 Brussels, Flanders
nickname: 6 Velvet
father: 13 Pieter Bruegel
artwork: 12 Four Elements
13 Village Street 15 The
Garden of Eden (with Rub-
ens) 17 The Battle of
Arbela

**Brueghel, Pieter (the
Younger)**
born: 8 Brussels, Flanders
nickname: 12 Hell Brueghel
19 The Infernal Brueghel
father: 13 Pieter Bruegel (the
Elder)
artwork: 11 Village Fair
14 The Crucifixion 16 The
Burning of Troy

Brugh, Spangler Arlington
real name of: 12 Robert
Taylor

bruise 3 mar 4 hurt, mark
5 abuse, wound 6 damage, injure, injury, offend 7 blacken,
blemish 8 discolor 9 black
mark, contusion
13 discoloration

bruit 3 din 5 noise, rumor
6 clamor, hubbub, racket, report, uproar 7 clangor 10 clattering, noise about 11 voice
abroad

Brunei
capital/largest city:
17 Bandar Seri
Begawan
others: 4 Labi 5 Badas,
Danau, Muara, Seria
6 Bangar, Tutong
7 Kampong 10 Kuala
Abang, Kuala Balai
11 Kuala Belait
head of state/govern-
ment: 6 sultan
island: 6 Borneo
8 Sipitang
mountain: 6 Teraja 9 Ulu
Tutong
highest point: 10 Pagon
Priok
river: 6 Belait, Brunei,
Tutong 9 Temburong
sea: 10 South China
physical feature:
bay: 6 Brunei
people: 4 Iban 5 Dayak,
Malay 7 Chinese,
Kadazan
language: 4 Iban 5 Ma-
lay 7 Chinese, English
religion: 5 Islam
6 Taoism 7 animism
8 Buddhism
12 Christianity
feature: 3 oil

Brunelleschi, Filippo
architect of: 10 San Lorenzo 11 Pazzi Chapel (Santa
Croce), Pitti Palace 12 Santo
Spirito 14 Badia Fiesolana
15 Duomo of Florence
16 Palazzo Quaratesi
21 Santa Maria degli An-
geli 22 Ospedale degli Innocenti 23 Dome of Florence
Cathedral

brunet, brunette 4 dark
5 black 9 brown-eyed, dark
brown 10 dark-haired
11 brown-haired, dark-
skinned 12 olive-skinned
16 dark-complexioned

Brunhild
origin: 8 Germanic
Scandinavian: 8 Brynhild
character in:
14 Nibelungenlied
queen of: 8 Isenland
husband: 7 Gunther
won by: 9 Siegfried

brunt 5 force 6 impact, stress,
thrust 8 violence 9 full force,
main shock

brush 4 bush, dust, fern, wash
5 clean, copse, flick, graze,
groom, paint, run-in, scrub,
sedge, set-to, shine, sweep,
touch, whisk 6 battle, bushes,
caress, duster, forest, fracas,
polish, shrubs, stroke
7 bracken, cleanse, dusting,
grazing, meeting, scuffle,
thicket, varnish 8 skirmish,
woodland 9 encounter, shrubbery, woodlands 10 engagement, underbrush,
whiskbroom 11 bush country,
undergrowth 12 bristled tool
13 confrontation
type: 4 hair, nail, shoe,
wash 5 paint, scrub, tooth
7 clothes

brush aside 6 slight 7 neglect
8 pass over 9 disregard

brush-off 3 cut 4 snub
5 brush 6 rebuff, slight 7 put-
down, squelch 9 disregard, rejection 11 repudiation 12 cold
shoulder

brusque 4 curt, rude, tart
5 bluff, blunt, gruff, harsh,
rough, short 6 abrupt, crusty
7 bearish 8 impolite, ungentle
10 ungracious 12 discourteous
13 unceremonious

Brussels
canal: 9 Charleroi
10 Willebroek
capital of: 7 Belgium
cathedral: 26 Saint Michel
and Sainte Gudule
early name: 10 Bruoc-sella
means: 16 marshy
settlement
Flemish: 7 Brussel

French: 9 Bruxelles
headquarters of: 3 EEC
4 NATO **12** Common Market **25** European Economic
Community
landmark: 11 Royal Palace
15 Palace of Justice **17** Palace of the Nation
province: 7 Brabant
river: 5 Senne, Zenne
square: 11 Grande Place

brutal 5 crude, cruel, harsh
6 bloody, coarse, fierce, savage **7** brutish, hellish, inhuman, vicious **8** barbaric,
pitiless, ruthless **9** atrocious,
barbarous, heartless, merciless,
unfeeling **10** demoniacal
11 hardhearted, remorseless
12 bloodthirsty

brutality 7 cruelty **8** ferocity,
savagery **9** barbarity, harshness **10** inhumanity, savageness **11** brutishness,
viciousness **12** ruthlessness

brute 5 beast, demon, devil,
fiend, swine **6** animal, savage
7 monster **9** barbarian **10** wild
animal **11** cruel person
12 dumb creature

brutish 5 cruel, feral **6** bloody,
brutal, fierce, savage **7** inhuman **8** barbaric **9** barbarous,
ferocious, unfeeling
11 remorseless

brutishness 8 ferocity, savagery **9** barbarity, brutality
10 bestiality, coarseness, inhumanity, savageness **11** viciousness **15** remorselessness

Brutus
also: 12 Marcus Brutus
character in: 12 Julius
Caesar
author: 11 Shakespeare

Bruxelles *see* **8** Brussels

Bryan, C D B
author of: 12 Friendly Fire
24 Ugly Scenes Beautiful
Women

Bryant, Bear (Paul)
sport: 8 football
position: 5 coach
team: 7 Alabama **11** Crimson
Tide

Brynhild
origin: 12 Scandinavian
Germanic: 8 Brunhild
husband: 6 Gunnar
won by: 6 Sigurd
position: 8 Valkyrie

Brynhildr Sigrdrifa *see*
9 Sigrdrifa

Brynner, Yul
real name: 10 Taidje Khan
born: 14 Sakhalin Island
roles: 9 Anastasia, West
World **11** The King and I

(Oscar) 18 The Ten Commandments **19** The Magnificent Seven **20** The Brothers
Karamazov **23** Invitation to
a Gunfighter

Brythonic
language family: 12 Indo-European
group: 5 Welsh **6** Breton
7 Cornish, Pictish

**Bschliessmayer, Oskar
Josef**
real name of: 11 Oskar Werner

Bubba Smith
nickname of: 17 Charles
Aaron Smith

bubble, bubbles 4 bleb, boil,
fizz, foam **5** froth **6** burble, fizzle, gurgle, seethe **7** air ball,
blister, droplet, globule, sparkle **9** percolate **10** effervesce
13 effervescence

bubbliness 9 fizziness, foaminess **10** ebullience, enthusiasm, frothiness, liveliness
11 high spirits
13 effervescence

bubbling 5 fizzy, foamy
6 frothy **7** fizzing, foaming
9 sparkling **12** effervescent

bubbly 5 fizzy, foamy **6** frothy,
lively **7** fizzing, foaming
9 champagne, sparkling **12** effervescent, high-spirited

Bubona
origin: 5 Roman
protectress of: 4 cows, oxen

buccaneer 6 pirate **7** corsair
9 privateer **10** freebooter

**Buchan, John (Baron
Tweedsmuir)**
author of: 10 John Macnab
11 Greenmantle, Pilgrim's
Way **17** John Burnet of
Barns **18** The Thirty-Nine
Steps

Buchanan, Daisy
character in: 14 The Great
Gatsby
author: 10 Fitzgerald

Buchanan, Edgar
born: 13 Humansville MO
roles: 5 Shane, Texas **7** Arizona **8** Cimarron **9** McLintock **13** Penny Serenade
17 Petticoat Junction
18 Ride the High Country

Buchanan, James *see box,*
p. 136

Bucharest
capital of: 7 Romania,
Rumania
founder: 5 Bucur
landmark: 8 Scinteia **13** Village Museum
river: 9 Dimbovita
Rumanian: 9 Bucuresti

Buchinsky, Charles
real name of: 14 Charles
Bronson

buck 3 man **4** beau, deer,
dude, kick, male **5** dandy
6 dollar, oppose **7** coxcomb
8 cavalier, gay blade **9** go
against **10** young blood

Buck
character in: 16 The Call of
the Wild
author: 6 London

Buck, Pearl S
author of: 8 The Exile
9 Other Gods **10** Dragon
Seed **12** The Good Earth
13 A House Divided

bucket 3 can, hod, tub **4** cask,
pail **5** scoop **6** vessel **7** pailful,
pitcher, scuttle **9** container
10 receptacle

Buckeye State
nickname of: 4 Ohio

buckle 3 sag **4** bend, clip, curl,
hasp, hook, warp **5** bulge,
catch, clasp **6** cave in, couple,
fasten, secure **7** contort, crinkle, crumple, distort, wrinkle
8 belly out, collapse, fastener

buckle down 6 attend **12** apply oneself

Buckley, William F Jr
author of: 11 Who's on
First? **15** God and Man at
Yale, God Save the Queen

Buck Rogers
creator: 14 Richard Calkins
character: 5 Alura, Buddy,
Dercu, Kayla, Wilma **6** Ardala **10** Killer Kane

bucolic 4 idyl, poem **5** idyll,
rural **6** poetic, rustic **7** eclogue,
idyllic, peasant **8** pastoral,
shepherd

Bucolion
father: 8 Laomedon
son: 7 Aesepus
wife: 9 Abarbarea

bud 4 open **5** shoot **6** flower,
sprout **7** blossom, burgeon,
develop

Bud, Rosa
character in: 22 The Mystery
of Edwin Drood
author: 7 Dickens

Budapest
area: 4 Buda, Pest **5** Obuda
capital of: 7 Hungary
cathedral: 13 Saint Matthias
hill: 10 Castle Hill
island: 6 Csepel
river: 6 Danube
Roman town: 8 Aquincum

Buddenbrooks
author: 10 Thomas Mann

Buchanan, James
  nickname: **7** Old Buck
  presidential rank: **9** fifteenth
  party: **8** Democrat
  state represented: **2** PA
  defeated: **7** (John Charles) Fremont **8** (Millard) Fillmore
  vice president: **12** (John Cabell) Breckinridge
  cabinet:
    state: **4** (Lewis) Cass **5** (Jeremiah Sullivan) Black
    treasury: **3** (John Adams) Dix **4** (Howell) Cobb **6** (Philip Francis) Thomas
    war: **4** (Joseph) Holt **5** (John Buchanan) Floyd
    attorney general: **5** (Jeremiah Sullivan) Black **7** (Edwin McMasters) Stanton
    navy: **6** (Isaac) Toucey
    postmaster general: **4** (Horatio) King, (Joseph) Holt **5** (Aaron Venable) Brown
    interior: **8** (Jacob) Thompson
  born: **11** Cove Gap PA (near Mercersburg)
  died/buried: **11** Lancaster PA
  education:
    Academy: **8** Old Stone
    College: **9** Dickinson
    studied: **3** law
  religion: **12** Presbyterian
  political career: **13** state assembly **24** US House of Representatives
    secretary of: **5** State
    minister: **6** Russia **12** Great Britain
  civilian career: **6** lawyer
  notable events of lifetime/term: **5** Panic (of 1857) **11** English Bill, Pony Express
    raid by: **9** John Brown
    raid on: **12** Harper's Ferry
    Supreme Court case: **9** Dred Scott
  father: **5** James
  mother: **9** Elizabeth (Speer)
  siblings: **4** Jane, John, Mary **5** Maria, Sarah **7** Harriet **9** Elizabeth **11** Edward Young **12** William Speer **16** George Washington
  wife: **4** none
  children: **4** none

Buddha
  also called: **5** Butsu
  born: **11** Kapilavastu
  father: **11** Suddhodhana
  founded: **8** Buddhism
  means: **15** enlightened one
  message: **6** dharma
  name for: **17** Siddhartha Gautama
  son: **6** Rahula
  tree: **2** bo **5** bodhi
  wife: **9** Yasodhara

Buddhism
  action: **5** karma
  branch: **8** Mahayana **9** Theravada **12** Great Vehicle **14** way of the elders
  doctrine: **6** duhkha **7** nirvana **9** suffering **13** eightfold path **15** four noble truths **17** pratityasamutpada
  founded by: **6** Buddha **17** Siddhartha Gautama
  monk: **7** bhikshu
  nun: **9** bhikshuni
  rebirth: **7** samsara
  religious community: **6** sangha

buddy **3** pal **4** chum, mate **5** amigo, crony **6** cohort, fellow, friend **7** brother, comrade, partner **8** confrere, intimate, playmate, sidekick **9** associate, colleague, companion, confidant **10** playfellow **11** confederate

buddy-buddy **5** close, palsy **6** chummy **8** friendly, intimate **10** palsy-walsy

budge **4** move, push, roll, stir, sway **5** shift, slide **6** change **8** convince, dislodge, persuade **9** dislocate, influence

budget **4** cost, plan **5** funds, means **6** moneys, ration **7** arrange **8** allocate, schedule **9** allotment, allowance, apportion, resources **10** allocation, portion out **12** spending plan **13** financial plan

budgetary **6** fiscal **8** economic, monetary **9** financial, pecuniary

buenas noches **9** good night

bueno **4** good

Buenos Aires
  capital of: **9** Argentina
  landmark: **11** Teatro Colon **16** Saavedra Monument, San Martin Theater **17** Wildestein Gallery, Witcomb Art Gallery **18** Church of El Salvador **27** Christopher Columbus Monument
  park: **7** Palermo
  people: **8** portenos
    means: **15** people of the port
  river: **12** Rio de la Plata

buff **3** bug, fan, nut, rub, tan **4** swab **5** freak, hound, mavin, sandy, straw, tawny **6** addict, dauber, polish, smooth, the raw **7** admirer, burnish, devotee, leather **8** bare skin, follower, polisher **9** nakedness, yellowish **10** aficionado, enthusiast **11** buffalo hide, connoisseur **14** yellowish-brown

buffalo **5** bison **6** puzzle **7** mystify **10** intimidate
  kind: **7** African **10** Asian water
  African: **14** syncerus caffer
  Asian water: **14** bubalus bubalis

Buffalo
  football team: **5** Bills
  hockey team: **6** Sabres

buffer **6** bumper, fender, shield **7** cushion **9** protector

buffet **3** box, hit, jab, rap **4** bang, beat, bump, cuff, meal, push, slap **5** baste, knock, pound, shove, thump **6** pummel, strike, supper, thrash, thwack, wallop **7** cabinet, counter **8** credenza **9** cafeteria, sideboard **11** smorgasbord

Buffone, Carlo
  character in: **22** Every Man out of His Humour
  author: **6** Jonson

buffoon **3** wag **4** fool, zany **5** clown, comic, joker, mimic, Punch **6** jester, madcap **7** Pierrot **8** comedian, funnyman **9** harlequin, pantaloon, prankster, trickster **10** Scaramouch, silly-billy **11** merry-andrew, punchinello, Scaramouche

buffoonery **6** antics, comedy **7** foolery, inanity **8** zaniness **9** asininity, horseplay, silliness, slapstick **10** tomfoolery **11** foolishness, loutishness

12 clownishness, monkey-shines, prankishness **14** clowning around, playing the fool

bug 3 nag **4** flaw, germ **5** annoy, fault, virus **6** badger, bother, defect, insect, pester **7** wiretap **8** drawback, listen in, weakness **9** eavesdrop, Hemiptera **11** Heteroptera **variety: 3** bat, bed, red **4** gnat, lace, leaf, seed, toad **5** negro, plant, shore, stilt, stink, water **6** ambush, damsel, fungus, pirate, ripple **7** boatman, stainer **8** assassin, burrower, creeping **9** royal palm **10** leaf footed **11** ashgray leaf, backswimmer, broadheaded, jumping tree, velvet water **12** velvety shore, water strider, water treader **13** jumping ground, water measurer, water scorpion **14** scentless plant **17** terrestrial turtle

bugaboo 5 scare **6** fright **7** anxiety

bugbear 4 ogre **5** bogey **6** goblin **7** bugaboo **8** bogeyman **9** bete noire

buggy 4 cart **5** wagon **7** vehicle **8** carriage **10** conveyance

bugle 4 horn **10** instrument

Bugs Bunny
creator: 15 Leon Schlesinger
character: 9 Elmer Fudd
voice of: 8 Mel Blanc
saying: 10 what's up doc

build 4 body, form, make, mold, open **5** begin, brace, erect, forge, found, put up, raise, renew, set up, shape, start, steel **6** create, extend, figure, harden, launch **7** amplify, augment, develop, enhance, enlarge, fashion, greaten, improve, produce **8** embark on, increase, initiate, multiply, physique **9** construct, establish, fabricate, institute, intensify, originate, reinforce, structure, undertake **10** inaugurate, strengthen, supplement **11** manufacture, put together **12** construction

building 7 edifice **9** structure **12** construction

building front 6 facade **8** frontage

build up 5 amass **7** develop, promote **8** increase **10** accumulate

Bujold, Genevieve
born: 6 Canada **8** Montreal
roles: 4 Coma **9** Monsignor, Obsession **12** King of

Hearts **21** Anne of the Thousand Days

Bujumbura
capital of: 7 Burundi

Bul 17 eighth Hebrew month

bulb 3 bud **4** corm, seed **5** plant, tuber **8** swelling

Bulfinch, Charles
architect of: 7 Capitol (Washington DC) **16** Hartford City Hall (CT) **23** Massachusetts State House (Boston)
style: 7 Federal

Bulgakov, Mikhail
author of: 9 Black Snow **13** The White Guard **14** The Heart of a Dog **19** The Days of the Turbins **21** The Master and Margarita

Bulgaria *see box*

bulge 3 bag, sag **4** bump,

lump **5** curve, swell **6** excess **7** distend, project, puff out, sagging **8** protrude, stand out, stick out, swelling, swell out **9** bagginess **10** projection, prominence, protrusion **12** protuberance

bulk 4 body, mass, most, size **6** extent, volume, weight **7** bigness, measure **8** enormity, hugeness, main part, majority, quantity **9** amplitude, greatness, largeness, magnitude, major part, plurality, substance **10** better part, dimensions, lion's share **11** greater part, massiveness, proportions **13** preponderance

bulky 3 big **4** huge **5** large **6** clumsy **7** awkward, hulking, immense, lumpish, massive, sizable, unhandy **8** enormous, ungainly, unwieldy **9** capacious, extensive **10** cumber-

---

Bulgaria
capital/largest city: 5 Sofia
others: 3 Lom **4** Rila, Ruse **5** Aytos, Butan, Byclu, Elena, Iskra, Stara, Varna **6** Bleven, Burgas, Devnia, Dulovo, Levsky, Pernik, Pleuna, Pleven, Plevna, Shumen, Shumla, Sliven, Slivno, Widden, Yambol, Zagora **7** Gabrovo, Karlovo, Plovdiv, Sistova, Tirnova **8** Khaskovo, Rustchuk, Svishtov **9** Ruse Vidin, Silistria **11** Kolorovgrad **12** Dimitrovgrad
school: 5 Sofia **7** Plovdiv **13** Veliko Turnovo
measure: 3 oka, oke **5** krine, lekhe, likhe
monetary unit: 3 lev **8** stotinki
weight: 3 oka, oke **5** tovar
mountain: 3 Kom **5** Botev, Pirin, Sapka **6** Balkan, Sredna **7** Vikhren **11** Rila-Rhodope
highest point: 6 Musala **8** Musallah
river: 3 Lom, Vit **4** Arda, Osma **5** Isker, Iskur, Mesta **6** Danube, Marica, Ogosta, Struma, Yantra **7** Maritsa, Stryama, Tundzha
sea: 5 Black
physical feature:
  cape: **5** Emine, Sabla **7** Kuratan
  gulf: **5** Burga
  plateau: **6** Danube
  resort: **9** Pyassatzi **13** Slunchev Bryay
  valley: **7** Maritsa
people: 4 Slav, Turk **5** Gypsy, Pomak, Tatar **6** Bulgar, Slavic **7** Chuvash **9** Cheremiss **10** Macedonian
language: 9 Bulgarian
religion: 5 Islam **24** Bulgarian Eastern Orthodox
place:
  church: **9** St Nedelja
  monastery: **4** Rila **6** Rilski
  monument: **7** Red Army
  mosque: **10** Banya Bashi
  museum: **21** Revolutionary Movement
  square: **5** Lenin
  valley of roses: **8** Kazanluk
feature:
  dance: **4** horo
  holiday: **12** St Georges Day
  newspaper: **17** Rabot Nichesko Delo
food:
  stew: **8** giuvetch

some, voluminous
12 unmanageable

bull 2 ox **4** male
male of the: 3 elk **4** seal
5 moose, whale **6** bovine
8 elephant
constellation of: 6 Taurus
Spanish: 4 toro

bulldoze 3 cow **4** bump, fell,
push, rage, raze **5** abash,
bully, drive, force, level, press,
shove **6** coerce, hector, jostle,
propel, subdue, thrust **7** buffalo, dragoon, flatten **8** bludgeon, browbeat, domineer,
shoulder **9** push about, tyrannize **10** intimidate

Bullen, Frank T
author of: 19 Told in the
Dry Watches **22** The Cruise
of the Cachalot

bullet 4 ball, lead, shot, slug
7 missile **8** buckshot

bulletin 4 note **6** report **7** account, message, release **8** dispatch **9** statement
10 communique, news report
12 notification
13 communication

Bullet Park
author: 11 John Cheever

bull fighter 6 torero **7** mata-
dor, picador **8** toreador **10** El
Cordobes **15** Miguel
Dominguin

Bullion State
nickname of: 8 Missouri

Bullitt
director: 10 Peter Yates
cast: 9 Don Gordon **12** Robert Duvall, Robert Vaughn,
Steve McQueen **16** Jacqueline Bisset
setting: 12 San Francisco

bullock 2 ox **4** beef, bull
5 steer

bullocks 4 kine, oxen **5** beefs,
bulls **6** beeves, cattle, steers

bull session 3 rap **4** talk
7 gabfest, palaver **8** dialogue
9 discourse **10** discussion
12 conversation
13 confabulation

bull's-eye 5 black **6** center
7 exactly **8** on target **9** dead
center, precisely

bully 3 cow **4** good **5** annoy,
swell, tough **6** cheers, coerce,
despot, harass, hurrah, hurray **7** coercer, right on, ruffian, tread on **8** browbeat,
bulldoze, domineer, frighten,
ride over, well done **9** oppressor, terrorize, tormentor, tyrannize **10** browbeater,
intimidate **11** intimidator

bullying 7 torment **8** coercion
9 despotism **10** harassment,
tormenting **11** browbeating,
domineering, tyrannizing
12 intimidation

bulrush 5 plant, sedge **7** cattail,
papyrus

bulwark 5 guard **7** barrier, parapet, rampart, support, de-
fense **8** mainstay **9** earthwork
10 embankment

Bulwer-Lytton, Edward
author of: 6 Harold, Pelham,
Rienzi **9** Richelieu **13** The
Coming Race **16** Kenelm
Chillingly **18** The Last of
the Barons **20** The Last
Days of Pompeii

bum 3 beg **4** grub, hobo
5 cadge, idler, mooch, tramp
6 borrow, loafer, sponge
7 drifter, vagrant **8** derelict,
vagabond

bumble 6 bungle **7** blunder,
stagger, stumble **8** flounder

Bumble
character in: 11 Oliver Twist
author: 7 Dickens

bumcombe, bunkum 3 rot
4 bosh, bunk **6** drivel **7** twaddle **8** nonsense, tommyrot
10 balderdash **16** stuff-and-
nonsense

bump 3 hit, jar, rap **4** bang,
blow, butt, hump, jolt, knob,
knot, lump, node, poke, slam,
slap, sock **5** bulge, clash,
crack, crash, gnarl, knock,
punch, shake, smack, smash,
thump, whack **6** bounce, buffet, impact, jostle, jounce,
nodule, rattle, strike, wallop
7 collide, run into **8** swelling
9 collision, crash into, smash
into **11** excrescence
12 protuberance

bump into 4 meet **7** collide,
run into **9** encounter

bumpkin 3 oaf **4** boor, lout
5 churl, yokel **8** ship beam
10 clodhopper

bump off 4 do in, kill, slay
6 murder, rub out **7** execute,
gun down **8** dispatch **11** assassinate **12** take for a ride

bumptious 4 bold **5** cocky,
pushy **6** brazen **7** forward,
haughty **8** arrogant, boastful,
cocksure, impudent, insolent
9 bodacious, conceited, obtrusive **10** aggressive, swaggering **11** impertinent,
overbearing **12** presumptuous
13 overconfident, self-assertive

bumptiousness 4 gall
5 cheek **8** audacity, boldness

9 impudence **11** forwardness,
presumption **12** impertinence
13 obtrusiveness **17** self-
assertiveness

bumpy 5 lumpy, rocky, rough
6 uneven **10** undulating

bun 4 coil, knot, roll **8** soft
roll **9** sweet roll

Bunaea
epithet of: 4 Hera
refers to: 6 temple

bunch 3 lot, mob **4** band, bevy,
gang, heap, herd, host, knot,
mass, pack, pile, team **5** array,
batch, clump, crowd, flock,
group, shock, stack, tribe,
troop **6** amount, bundle,
gather, huddle, number,
string **7** cluster, collect, company **8** assemble, assembly,
quantity **9** gathering, multitude **10** assortment, collection,
congregate **12** accumulation

bundle 3 lot **4** bale, bind, heap,
mass, pack, pile, wrap **5** array,
batch, bunch, group, sheaf,
stack, truss **6** amount, packet,
parcel **7** package **8** quantity
9 multitude **10** assortment, collection **11** tie together
12 accumulation

Bundren family
characters in: 11 As I Lay
Dying
member: 4 Anse, Cash, Darl
5 Addie, Jewel **9** Dewey Dell
author: 8 Faulkner

bungalow 5 cabin, house,
lodge **7** cottage

bungle 3 mar **4** flub, goof,
miff, ruin **5** botch, spoil **6** foul
up, mess up, muddle **7** blunder, butcher, do badly, louse
up, screw up **8** misjudge
9 mismanage, misreckon
10 miscompute **11** make a
mess of, misestimate
12 miscalculate

Bunin, Ivan Alekseyevich
author of: 10 The Village
15 The Elagin Affair **17** The
Life of Arseniev **28** The
Gentleman from San
Francisco

bunk 3 bed, cot, rot **4** bull
5 berth, hokum, hooey, stuff
6 bunkum, hot air, humbug,
pallet **7** baloney, blather, bombast, hogwash, inanity, malarky, spinach **8** claptrap,
nonsense, tommyrot **9** poppycock **10** applesauce, balderdash **11** foolishness **16** stuff
and nonsense

Bunsen, Robert Wilhelm
nationality: 6 German
inventor of: 9 gas burner

10 photo meter 12 Bunsen burner, spectroscope 24 electromechanical battery

Bunshaft, Gordon
architect of: 10 Lever House (NY) 23 Beinecke Rare Book Library (Yale) 33 Hirshhorn Museum and Sculpture Garden (Washington DC) 34 Lyndon Baines Johnson Memorial Library (Austin TX)

Bunus
father: 6 Hermes
mother: 9 Aleidamea
raised temple honoring: 4 Hera
location of temple: 7 Corinth

Bunyan, John
author of: 10 The Holy War 16 Pilgrim's Progress 25 The Life and Death of Mr Badman 33 Grace Abounding to the Chief of Sinners

buona notte 9 good night

buona sera 11 good evening

buon giorno 7 good day 11 good morning

Buono, Victor
born: 10 San Diego CA
roles: 11 The Stranger 12 Four for Texas 22 Hush Hush Sweet Charlotte 26 Whatever Happened to Baby Jane

buoy 4 bell, lift 5 boost, cheer, float, raise 6 beacon, uplift 7 cheer up, elevate, gladden, lighten 8 brighten 10 keep afloat 14 floating marker

buoyancy, buoyance 4 glee 6 gaiety 7 jollity 8 gladness, vivacity 9 animation, good humor, joviality, lightness, sunniness 10 brightness, cheeriness, enthusiasm, floatiness, joyousness 11 good spirits 12 cheerfulness, exhilaration, floatability 14 weightlessness 16 lightheartedness

buoyant 3 gay 4 glad 5 happy, jolly, light, merry, peppy, sunny 6 afloat, breezy, bright, elated, joyful, joyous, lively 7 hopeful 8 animated, carefree, cheerful, floating, sportive 9 energetic, floatable, sprightly, vivacious 10 blithesome, optimistic, weightless 11 exhilarated, free and easy 12 enthusiastic, lighthearted

buoyed 6 elated 7 exalted, pleased 8 elevated 9 confident, heartened, reassured 10 inspirited

buoy up 4 warm 6 assure,

uplift 7 comfort, hearten, inspire 8 inspirit, reassure 9 encourage

Buphagus
father: 7 Iapetus
slain by: 7 Artemis
epithet of: 8 Hercules
means: 7 ox-eater

Burbank, Luther
field: 7 biology
developed: 13 plant breeding

burble 6 babble, bubble, gurgle, murmur 8 babbling

Burce, Suzanne
real name of: 10 Jane Powell

Burchill, Mr
character in: 19 The Vicar of Wakefield
author: 9 Goldsmith

burden 3 tax, try, vex 4 care, load, onus, pack 5 cargo 6 hamper, hinder, strain, stress, weight 7 afflict, anxiety, freight, oppress, trouble 8 encumber, handicap, hardship, load with, obligate, overload 9 press down, weigh down 10 saddle with 11 encumbrance 14 responsibility

Burden, Jack
character in: 14 All the King's Men
author: 6 Warren

burden of proof
Latin: 12 onus probandi

burdensome 4 hard 5 heavy 6 tiring 7 arduous, onerous 8 wearying 9 Herculean, laborious 10 exhausting

bureau 6 agency, branch, office 7 cabinet, commode, dresser, service, station 8 division 10 chiffonier, department 14 administration, chest of drawers

bureaucrat 8 mandarin, official, politico 9 penpusher 10 politician 11 apparatchik, functionary, rubber stamp 12 civil servant, officeholder 13 public servant

burgee 4 flag 6 banner, colors, ensign 7 pennant

burgeon 3 wax 4 blow, grow, open 5 bloom 6 expand, flower, spread, thrive 7 augment, blossom, develop, enlarge, prosper, shoot up, succeed 8 escalate, flourish, fructify, increase, mushroom, spring up 9 bear fruit 10 effloresce 11 proliferate

Burgess, Anthony
author of: 2 MF 13 Man of Nazareth, Time for a Tiger

14 Enderby Outside, The Wanting Seed 16 A Clockwork Orange, Beard's Roman Women 17 Nothing Like the Sun 20 The End of the World News

burgher 7 citizen 9 bourgeois 11 townsperson

burglar 3 cat 4 yegg 5 thief 6 robber 7 prowler 8 pilferer 9 cracksman, purloiner 12 housebreaker 14 second-story man

burglary 5 theft 6 felony 7 break-in, larceny, robbery 8 filching, stealing 9 pilfering 10 purloining 13 housebreaking 19 breaking and entering

burgundy 3 red 4 wine 5 color 13 reddish-purple

Burgundy
ancient city: 5 Autun
city: 5 Dijon
district: 5 Youne 6 Nievre 7 Cote d' Or 12 Saone-et-Loire
French: 9 Bourgogne
location: 6 France
river: 5 Rhone, Saone
tribe: 9 Burgundii

Buri
origin: 12 Scandinavian
first: 3 god
revealed by: 8 Audhumla 9 Audhumbla

burial 5 rites 7 funeral 9 interment, obsequies 10 entombment, inhumation

burial ground 7 ossuary 8 boneyard, Boot Hill, catacomb, cemetery 9 graveyard 10 churchyard, necropolis 12 potter's field

buried 4 laid, sunk 6 hidden 7 covered, inhumed, immured 9 concealed, deep sixed 10 laid to rest 11 underground

Burke, Francis
character in: 21 The Master of Ballantrae
author: 9 Stevenson

Burkina Faso *see* Upper Volta

burlap 3 bag 4 hemp, jute 5 cloth 6 fabric 8 material

burlesque 5 farce, spoof 6 comedy, parody, satire 7 mockery, takeoff 8 ridicule, travesty 10 buffoonery, caricature 15 slapstick comedy

burly 3 big 5 beefy, bulky, hefty, large 6 brawny, stocky, strong, sturdy 7 hulking, sizable 8 thickset 9 ponderous, strapping

Burma *see* 7 Myanmar

burn 3 nip, tan 4 bite, char, fire, glow, hurt, pain, sear, skin 5 be hot, blaze, brown, chafe, flame, flare, flash, parch, prick, scald, singe, smart, smoke, sting 6 abrade, bronze, flames, ignite, kindle, nettle, scorch, scrape, suntan, tingle, wither 7 blister, consume, cremate, flicker, oxidize, prickle, shrivel, smolder, sunburn, swelter 8 abrasion, be ablaze, be on fire, charring, irritate, kindling 9 be flushed, reddening, set fire to, set on fire, use as fuel 10 be feverish, be in flames, blistering, incandesce, incinerate, irritation, smoldering 12 incineration 13 reduce to ashes

burnable 9 flammable, ignitable 10 combustive 11 combustible, inflammable 13 conflagrative

Burne-Jones, Sir Edward Coley
born: 7 England 10 Birmingham
artwork: 11 Laus Veneris 15 The Golden Stairs 16 The Mirror of Venus 18 The Star of Bethlehem 28 King Cophetua and the Beggar Maid

burner, gas
invented by: 6 Bunsen

Burnett, Carol
born: 12 San Antonio TX
roles: 14 The Four Seasons 19 The Carol Burnett Show

Burnett, Frances H
author of: 20 Little Lord Fauntleroy

Burney, Fanny
author of: 7 Camilla, Diaries, Evelina

Burnham, Daniel Hudson
partner: 16 John Wellborn Root

architect of: 7 Rookery 12 Union Station (Washington DC) 15 Calumet Building 16 Flatiron Building (NYC), Reliance Building 17 Monadnock Building 25 World's Columbian Exposition

burning 3 hot 5 acrid, afire, aglow, eager, fiery, sharp 6 aflame, ardent, biting, fervid, heated, raging, red-hot 7 blazing, boiling, caustic, earnest, fanatic, fervent, flaming, flaring, frantic, glowing, ignited, intense, kindled, painful, pungent, sincere, smoking, zea-

lous 8 flashing, frenzied, piercing, resolute, sizzling, smarting, stinging, tingling 9 corroding, prickling 10 astringent, compelling, flickering, irritating, passionate, smoldering 11 impassioned 12 all-consuming

burnish 3 wax 4 buff 5 rub up, shine 6 polish, smooth

burnished 5 shiny 6 bright, buffed, shined 8 lustrous, polished, smoothed

burnoose 4 cape, robe 5 cloak 6 mantle 7 pelisse

burn out 3 pop 4 blow 7 exhaust 10 exhaustion, extinguish

Burns, George
real name: 14 Nathan Birnbaum
wife: 11 Gracie Allen
born: 9 New York NY
roles: 5 Oh God 12 Going in Style 15 The Sunshine Boys 17 Burns and Allen Show

Burns, Robert
author of: 8 To a Louse, To a Mouse 11 A Red Red Rose, Tam O'Shanter 12 Auld Lang Syne 16 Address to the Deil, Coming Thro the Rye 17 Holy Willie's Prayer 20 Flow Gently Sweet Afton 22 My Heart's in the Highlands 23 The Cotter's Saturday Night 32 Poems Chiefly in the Scottish Dialect

Burnt Norton
author: 7 T S Eliot

burp 5 belch, eruct 10 eructation

burr 4 buhr, rock 5 notch, stone 9 whetstone 13 pronunciation

Burr
author: 9 Gore Vidal

Burr, Raymond
born: 6 Canada 14 New Westminster 15 British Columbia
roles: 8 Ironside 10 Perry Mason, Rear Window

burro 3 ass 4 mule 6 donkey, onager 7 jackass

Burroughs, Edgar Rice
author of: 15 Tarzan of the Apes

Burroughs, William S
author of: 5 Queer 6 Junkie 13 The Naked Lunch

Burroughs, William Seward
nationality: 8 American
inventor of: 13 adding machine
grandson: 17 William S Burroughs (author)

burrow 3 den, dig 4 cave, hole, lair 6 covert, dugout, furrow, tunnel 8 excavate, scoop out 9 hollow out

Burrows, Abe
author of: 41 How to Succeed in Business without Really Trying

bursa 3 bag, sac 5 pouch, purse 6 cavity

bursar 6 purser 7 cashier 9 paymaster, treasurer 10 cashkeeper

burst 3 fly, pop, run 4 bang, bust, rend, rush 5 barge, blast, break, crack, erupt, split, spout 6 blow up, detach, divide, sunder 7 disjoin, explode, rupture, shatter, torrent 8 breaking, break out, cracking, crashing, detonate, eruption, fly apart, fracture, fragment, outbreak, separate, splinter 9 break open, discharge, explosion, gush forth, pull apart, splitting, tear apart 10 detonation, disconnect, outpouring, shattering 11 spring forth 12 disintegrate

burst forth 5 arise, begin, erupt, start 6 arrive, emerge 8 break out, commence

Burstyn, Ellen
real name: 14 Edna Rae Gillooly
born: 9 Detroit MI
roles: 11 The Exorcist 16 Same Time Next Year 18 The Last Picture Show 26 Alice Doesn't Live Here Anymore (Oscar)

Burton, Richard
real name: 22 Richard Walter Jenkins Jr
wife: 15 Elizabeth Taylor
born: 5 Wales 11 Pontrhydfen Wales
roles: 6 Becket, Hamlet 7 Camelot, The Robe 9 Cleopatra 14 My Cousin Rachel 19 The Night of the Iguana, The Taming of the Shrew 21 Anne of the Thousand Days 25 Who's Afraid of Virginia Woolf 26 The Spy Who Came in from the Cold

Burton, Robert
author of: 22 The Anatomy of Melancholy

Burundi
  capital/largest city:
  9 Bujumbura
  others: 5 Ngozi **6** Bururi,
  Gitega, Kitega, Rutana,
  Ruyigi **7** Kibumbu,
  Muyinga
  monetary unit: 5 franc
  7 centime
  lake: 7 Rugwero **8** Tshohoha **10** Tanganyika
  mountain: 9 Nyamisana
  highest point:
  8 Nyarwana
  river: 6 Akanya, Ruvuvu,
  Ruzizi **8** Rukagera
  10 Malagarasi
  people: 3 Twa **4** Hutu
  5 Bantu, Batwa, Pygmy,
  Tutsi **6** Bahutu, Watusi
  7 Barundi
  language: 6 French
  7 Kirundi, Swahili
  religion: 5 Islam **7** animism **10** Protestant
  13 Roman Catholic
  feature:
      king: **4** mwam
  food:
      coffee: **7** Arabica

Burushaski
  language spoken in: 7 Kashmir

bury 4 hide **5** cache, cover, inter **6** encase, engulf, entomb,
inhume **7** conceal, cover up,
enclose, immerse, secrete
8 submerge, submerse **13** lay in
the grave **17** consign to the
grave

**Bury My Heart at
Wounded Knee**
  author: 8 Dee Brown

bush 4 veld **5** brush, hedge,
plant, shrub, woods **6** forest,
jungle **7** barrens **9** shrubbery,
woodlands

bush country 5 scrub, wilds
7 outback **10** wilderness

bushed 4 beat **5** all in, spent,
tired, weary **6** done it,
pooped **7** drained, wearied,
worn out **8** dog tired, fatigued,
tired out **9** dead tired, exhausted, played out

bushel
  abbreviation: 2 bu **4** bush

bushes 5 brush **6** shrubs
9 brushwood, shrubbery
10 underbrush **11** undergrowth

bushy 5 hairy **6** fluffy, shaggy
7 hirsute **9** overgrown

business 3 job **4** case, duty,
firm, line, shop, task, work

**Bush, George Herbert
Walker**
  presidential rank:
  10 forty-first
  party: 10 Republican
  state represented:
  2 TX **5** Texas
  defeated: 7 (Michael)
  Dukakis
  defeated by: 7 (Bill)
  Clinton
  vice president: 6 (James
  Danforth) Quayle
  born: 8 Milton MA
  education: 4 Yale
  7 Andover
  religion: 12 Episcopalian
  vacation spot: 5 Maine
  13 Kennebunkport
  political career: 13 vice
  president **14** representative **21** Ways and
  Means Committee
      ambassador to: **2** UN
      13 United Nations
      chairman of: **27** Re-
      publican National
      Committee
      head of: **3** CIA
      liaison with: **5** China
  civilian career: 3 oil
  14 Zapata Offshore
  military career: 5 pilot
  6 US Navy
  vice president under:
  12 Ronald Reagan
  **notable events of life-
  time/term: 7** Gulf War
  14 Persian Gulf War
  20 Operation Desert
  Storm
      *Supreme Court ap-
      pointments:* **11** David
      Souter **14** Clarence
      Thomas
      invasion of: **6** Panama
  father: 15 Prescott
  Sheldon
  mother: 13 Dorothy
  Walker
  wife: 13 Barbara Pierce
  children: 4 John, Neil
  5 Robin (died 1953)
  6 George, Marvin
  7 Dorothy

5 chore, field, place, point,
store, topic, trade **6** affair, career, living, matter, office,
racket **7** affairs, calling, company, concern, dealing, factory,
mission, problem, pursuit, subject, venture **8** activity, commerce, function, industry,
position, province, question,
vocation **9** procedure, situation,
specialty **10** assignment, bargaining, employment, enterprise, livelihood, occupation,
profession, walk of life **11** cor-

poration, negotiation, partnership, transaction, undertaking
13 establishment, manufacturing, merchandising **14** bread
and butter, responsibility

businesslike 7 careful, correct,
orderly, regular, serious **8** diligent, sedulous, thorough **9** assiduous, efficient, organized,
practical **10** methodical, systematic **11** industrious, painstaking **12** professional

Busiris
  king of: 5 Egypt
  father: 8 Poseidon
  mother: 10 Lysianassa

Busoni, Ferruccio
  born: 5 Italy **6** Empoli
  composer of: 8 Turandot
  10 Arlecchino **11** Doctor
  Faust, Doktor Faust **12** Die
  Brautwahl **14** Comedy Overture **25** Fantasia
  Contrappuntistica

bus station 5 depot **8** terminal,
terminus

Bus Stop
  director: 11 Joshua Logan
  cast: 9 Don Murray **10** Betty
  Field **13** Eileen Heckart, Marilyn Monroe **14** Arthur
  O'Connell

bust 3 nab **4** head, raid **5** bosom, chest, seize **6** arrest,
breast, collar **7** capture **9** apprehend, sculpture **12** take prisoner **15** take into custody

Buster Brown
  creator: 10 RF Outcault
  bulldog: 4 Tige
  trademark: 9 sailor hat
  10 wide collar

bustle 3 ado, fly **4** dash, flit,
fuss, rush, stir, tear, to-do
5 hurry **6** bestir, flurry, hustle,
pother, scurry, tumult **7** be
quick, fluster, flutter, press on,
scamper, scuttle **8** activity, be
active, scramble **9** agitation,
commotion, make haste **10** excitement, hurly-burly

busy 4 full **6** active, employ,
engage, intent, occupy, on
duty, work at **7** engaged, labor
at, slaving, toiling, working
8 absorbed, bustling, employed,
laboring, occupied **9** engrossed,
in harness, strenuous **10** hard
at work **11** industrious **12** be
absorbed in, keep occupied
13 be engrossed in

busybody 3 pry **5** snoop **6** gossip **7** blabber, meddler, Paul
Pry **8** telltale **10** chatterbox,
newsmonger, talebearer, tattletale **12** blabbermouth **13** scandalmonger

busy place 4 hive **6** warren **7** anthill, beehive

but 3 yet **4** save, than that **5** if not, still **6** except, saving, unless **7** however, outside, that not **9** excepting, other than, otherwise **10** except that **14** on the other hand

Butch Cassidy and the Sundance Kid
director: **13** George Roy Hill
cast: **10** Paul Newman (Butch) **13** Katharine Ross (Etta Place), Robert Redford (The Kid)
score: **13** Burt Bacharach
Oscar for: **5** score
song: **27** Raindrops Keep Fallin' on My Head

butcher 4 goof, kill, muff, ruin, slay **5** botch, purge, spoil **6** boggle, bungle, fumble, hack up, hit man, killer, mess up, murder **7** louse up, screw up **8** assassin, decimate, homicide, massacre, murderer **9** liquidate, manhandle, mishandle, slaughter **10** annihilate, hatchet man, liquidator **11** assassinate, exterminate, make a mess of, slaughterer **12** exterminator, mass-murderer **15** homicidal maniac

butchery 4 flop, mess **5** botch **8** massacre **9** slaughter

Butes
father: **6** Boreas **7** Pandion
mother: **8** Zeuxippe
brother: **8** Lycurgus **10** Erechtheus
sister: **6** Procne **9** Philomela
son: **4** Eryx
priest of: **6** Athena **8** Poseidon
member of: **9** Argonauts
stricken with: **8** insanity
enticed by: **6** Sirens
leaped into: **3** sea
rescued by: **9** Aphrodite

Butkus, Dick (Richard Marvin)
sport: **8** football
position: **10** linebacker
team: **12** Chicago Bears

Butler, Rhett
character in: **15** Gone With the Wind
author: **8** Mitchell

Butler, Samuel
author of: **7** Erewhon **8** Hudibras **16** The Way of All Flesh **20** The Elephant in the Moon

butt 3 end, hit, jab, ram, rap **4** buck, bump, bunt, dupe, goat, mark, push, slap, stub **5** knock, shank, shove, smack, stump, thump **6** bottom, buffet, jostle, object, strike, target, thrust, thwack, victim **8** blunt end **13** laughingstock

buttercup 10 Ranunculus
variety: **4** Tall **5** Early **6** Common **7** Bermuda, Bulbous, Persian **8** Colombia, Creeping **11** Yellow water

butterfingered 6 inept **6** clumsy **7** awkward **8** bungling **9** maladroit **10** ungraceful

butterfly
pupa: **9** chrysalis **10** chrysalids **11** chrysalides
variety: **4** blue **5** giant, nymph, satyr, snout, tiger, zebra **6** alpine, apollo, arctic, kalima **7** alfalfa, budwing, dogface, monarch, peacock, viceroy **9** Baltimore, bathwhite, brimstone, christmas, metalmark, orange tip, wood nymph **10** Parnassian **11** painted lady, spring azure **12** blue mountain, cabbage white, clouded white, silver stripe, white admiral **13** chalkhill blue, mourning cloak, pearl crescent **14** American copper, gulf fritillary, tailed birdwing **15** longtail skipper, regal fritillary **16** black swallowtail, black veined white, camberwell beauty, green veined white, Leonardus skipper, red-spotted purple **18** orchard swallowtail **19** European swallowtail **20** spicebush swallowtail, variegated fritillary **21** great purple hairstreak, questionmark anglewing, white admiral wood nymph

butter up 4 coax **6** cajole **7** flatter, wheedle **8** soft-soap

buttocks 4 buns, butt, rear, rump, seat **5** fanny, nates **6** behind, bottom **7** keister, rear end **8** backside, derriere, haunches **9** fundament, posterior **12** hindquarters

buttonhole 4 halt, slit, stop **6** accost, waylay **7** solicit **8** approach, confront

button one's lip 7 keep mum **10** keep silent **16** keep one's trap shut **18** keep one's lips sealed

Buttons, Red
real name: **11** Aaron Chwatt
born: **9** New York NY
roles: **8** Sayonara **13** The Longest Day **20** The Poseidon Adventure **23** They Shoot Horses Don't They

buttress 4 arch, prop, stay **5** boost, brace, shore, steel **6** prop up **7** bolster, shore up, support **8** abutment, shoulder **9** reinforce, stanchion **10** strengthen

buxom 5 plump **6** bosomy, chesty, robust, zaftig **9** strapping **10** voluptuous **13** large-breasted, well-developed

buy 3 get **4** deal, gain **5** bribe **6** buy off, obtain, pay for, suborn **7** acquire, bargain, corrupt, procure **8** invest in, purchase **9** influence

buy and sell 4 deal **5** trade **6** market

buy off 5 bribe **6** pay off **13** grease the palm

Buzi
son: **7** Ezekiel

Buz Sawyer
creator: **8** Roy Crane
sidekick: **7** Sweeney

Buzuhov, Pierre
character in: **11** War and Peace
author: **7** Tolstoy

buzz 3 hum **4** whir **5** drone **6** murmur **7** whisper

by 4 near, over, past **5** along **6** beside, beyond, during, toward **7** through **9** alongside **10** concerning, on or before **11** according to, no later than

by air
French: **8** par avion

Byam, Roger
character in: **17** Mutiny on the Bounty
authors: **4** Hall **8** Nordhoff

Byblis
father: **7** Miletus
mother: **6** Cyanea
twin brother: **6** Caunus
loved: **6** Caunus
changed into: **8** fountain

by few words
Latin: **12** paucis verbis

bygone 4 past **5** olden **6** former, gone by, of yore **7** ancient, earlier **8** departed, obsolete, previous **10** antiquated

by horse
French: **7** a cheval

Byington, Spring
born: **17** Colorado Springs CO

roles: 7 Jezebel **11** Little Women **13** December Bride, Heaven Can Wait **17** Mutiny on the Bounty **20** The Devil and Miss Jones, You Can't Take It with You **26** The Charge of the Light Brigade

by itself 4 solo **5** alone, aloof, apart **8** isolated **13** unaccompanied

Byng, Admiral
character in: 7 Candide
author: 8 Voltaire

by oneself 4 solo **5** alone, aloof **8** isolated **10** solitarily **13** unaccompanied
Latin: 4 sola **5** solus

by operation of law
Latin: 8 ipso jure

bypass 4 go by **5** avert, avoid, dodge **8** go around **10** circumvent **12** detour around

bypath 3 way **4** lane **5** alley, byway, track, trail **6** bypass **7** footway, pathway, towpath, walkway **8** back road, dirt road, footpath, shortcut, side road **10** beaten path, bridle path, garden path

by-product 8 offshoot **9** aftermath **16** incidental result

by right
Latin: 6 de jure

Byron, Lord (George Gordon)
author of: 7 Don Juan, Manfred **10** The Corsair **19** The Vision of Judgment **20** The Prisoner of Chillon **23** Childe Harold's Pilgrimage

byrrh
type: 8 aperitif
origin: 6 France
flavor: 6 orange **7** quinine

bystander 6 viewer **7** watcher, witness **8** attender, beholder, looker-on, observer, onlooker, passerby **9** spectator

by the book 9 by the rule **13** authoritarian **16** according to Hoyle

by the fact itself
Latin: 9 ipso facto

by the grace of God
Latin: 9 Dei gratia

by the law itself
Latin: 8 ipso jure

by the month
Latin: 9 per mensem

by the rule 9 by the book **11** as specified **13** authoritarian

by the skin of one's teeth 6 barely, hardly **8** only just, scarcely **11** by an eyelash

by the very nature of the deed
Latin: 9 ipso facto

by the way
French: 9 en passant

by virtue and arms
Latin: 13 virtute et armis
motto of: 11 Mississippi

byway 4 lane **5** alley **6** detour, street **8** shunpike

by what right?
Latin: 7 quo jure

byword 3 law, saw **4** rule **5** adage, axiom, maxim, motto, truth **6** dictum, saying, slogan **7** precept, proverb **8** aphorism, apothegm **9** catchword, pet phrase, principle, watchword **10** shibboleth

Byzantine 6 complex **8** scheming **9** expedient, intricate **13** Machiavellian

Byzas
founder of: 9 Byzantium
father: 8 Poseidon

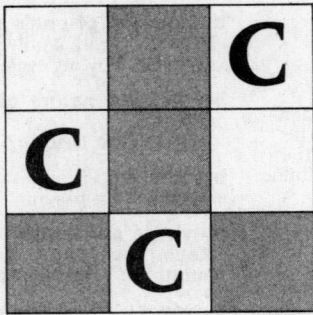

Caan, James
 born: 9 New York NY
 roles: 9 Funny Lady
  10 Brian's Song, Rollerball
  12 Brian Piccolo, The Godfather 13 Sonny Corleone
  17 Cinderella Liberty

Caanthus
 father: 7 Oceanus
 sister: 5 Melia
 killed by: 6 Apollo

cab 4 hack, taxi 7 taxi cab

Cab 15 Biblical measure

cabal 4 band, plan, plot, ring
 5 junta 6 design, league,
 scheme 7 faction 8 intrigue
 10 connivance, conspiracy
 11 combination, machination

cabalistic 6 arcane, mystic, occult, secret 7 cryptic, obscure,
 strange 8 abstruse, esoteric,
 mystical 10 mysterious, unknowable 11 inscrutable
 12 impenetrable, supernatural,
 unfathomable
 16 incomprehensible

cabaret 4 cafe, club 6 bistro
 9 nightclub 10 supper club
 French: 5 boite 11 boite de
 nuit

Cabaret
 director: 8 Bob Fosse
 based on stories by:
  20 Christopher Isherwood
 cast: 8 Joel Grey 11 Fritz
  Wepper, Helmut Griem, Michael York 12 Liza Minnelli
  (Sally Bowles) 14 Marisa
  Berenson
 Oscar for: 7 actress (Minnelli) 8 director 15 supporting actor (Grey)
 song: 12 The Money Song

cabbage 16 Brassica oleracea
 (Capitata Group)
 varieties: 3 Cow 4 Deer,
  Head, Wild 5 John's, Savoy,
  Skunk 6 Celery 7 Chinese
  9 Flowering, Tronchuda

10 Portuguese 11 Yellow
skunk 12 Western skunk

Cabecar
 language family:
  10 Talamancan
 location: 9 Costa Rica 12 Sixaola River 14 Central America, Talamanca Plain
 intermixed with: 6 Bribri

Cabell, James Branch
 author of: 6 Jurgen 12 The
  High Place 14 Figures of
  Earth 17 The Cream of the
  Jest

cabin 3 hut 4 room 5 hutch,
 lodge, shack 6 shanty 7 cottage 8 bungalow, log cabin,
 quarters 9 stateroom
 11 compartment

cabinet 3 box 4 case, file
 5 chest 6 bureau 7 council
 8 advisors, cupboard, ministry
 10 breakfront, counselors, receptacle 11 china closet
 13 advisory board 14 chest of
 drawers

cable 4 cord, line, rope, wire
 5 chain, wires 6 hawser
 7 mooring 8 wire line, wire
 rope 12 electric wire 16 overseas telegram

Cable, George W
 author of: 8 Dr Sevier 13 Old
  Creole Days 15 The
  Grandissimes

cablegram 4 wire 5 cable
 7 message 8 wireless 16 overseas telegram

Cabot, Ephraim
 character in: 18 Desire Under
  the Elms
 author: 6 O'Neill

Caca
 origin: 5 Roman
 goddess of: 6 hearth
 corresponds to: 5 Vesta

Cacambo
 character in: 7 Candide
 author: 8 Voltaire

cache 4 heap 5 hoard, stock,
 store 8 hideaway 9 stockpile
 11 hiding place, secret place

cachet 4 mark, seal 5 stamp,
 wafer 6 design, slogan
 7 capsule

cackle 7 chatter 10 harsh
 laugh 11 shrill laugh
 sound made by: 3 hen
  4 chicken

cacophonous 5 harsh 6 off-
 key 7 grating, jarring, raucous 8 off-pitch, screechy, strident 9 dissonant, out of tune,
 unmusical 10 discordant
 11 unmelodious 12 inharmonious, nonmelodious
 13 disharmonious

cacophony 7 discord 9 harshness 10 disharmony,
 dissonance

cactus *see box*

Cacus
 form: 5 giant
 father: 6 Vulcan
 eats: 3 men
 killed by: 8 Hercules

cad 3 cur, rat 4 heel, lout
 5 churl, knave, louse, rogue
 6 rascal, rotter 7 bounder, caitiff, dastard, villain 9 scoundrel

cadaver 4 body 5 stiff
 6 corpse 7 remains 8 dead
 body, deceased

cadaverous 4 pale 5 ashen,
 gaunt 6 chalky, pallid
 7 deathly, ghastly 8 blanched
 9 bloodless, deathlike
 10 corpselike

caddisfly
 variety: 5 micro 8 northern
  9 fingernet, primitive, snail-
  case 10 longhorned, trum-
  petnet, tubemaking
  11 netspinning

Caddoan
 tribe: 6 Pawnee
  14 Chahiksichhiks

144

cactus
varieties: **3** Cob, Sun **4** Ball, Cane, Chin, Claw, Club, Comb, Crab, Hook, Lace, Leaf, Moon, Rose, Star, Toad, Vine, Yoke **5** Agave, Apple, Brain, Chain, Coral, Crown, Devil, False, Giant, Leafy, Melon, Paper, Plain, Prism, Snake, Spice, Torch **6** Barrel, Button, Cholla, Dagger, Dollar, Easter, Hatpin, Hot-dog, Myrtle, Nipple, Old-man, Orchid, Peanut, Pencil, Ribbon, Spider **7** Cushion, Eve's pin, Feather, Hatchet, Hat-rack, Jumping, Old-lady, Popcorn, Rainbow, Rattail, Redbird, Serpent, Thimble, Whisker **8** Cinnamon, Dumpling, Fishbone, Fishhook, Flapjack, Gold lace, Golf-ball, Hedgehog, Old-woman, Polka-dot, Pond-lily, Snowball, Snowdrop, Starfish, Tortoise, Turk's-cap **9** Bird's nest, Chain-link, Christmas, Cow-tongue, Electrode, Fire-crown, Hairbrush, Lamb's-tail, Mistletoe, New old-man, Organ-pipe, Porcupine, Red orchid, Sea-urchin, Spineless, Teddy-bear, Toothpick, Totem-pole, Turk's-head, White chin **10** Bluebarrel, Candelabra, Cotton-pole, Easter-lily, Golden ball, Golden-star, Living-rock, Powder-puff, Silver ball, Strawberry, Unguentine, White torch, Wickerware **11** Frilled lace, Grizzly-bear, Joseph's coat, Large barrel, Scarlet ball, Woolly torch **12** Dancing-bones, Golden barrel, Mule-crippler, Scarlet crown, Thanksgiving **13** Colombian ball, Creeping-devil, Dutchman's pipe, Peruvian apple, Peruvian torch, Silver cluster **15** Golden bird's nest **16** Mexican dwarf tree **17** Burbank's spineless **18** Fishhook pincushion

---

caddy 3 box, can, tin **5** chest **6** coffer

cadence 4 beat, lilt **5** meter, pulse, swing, tempo, throb **6** accent, rhythm **7** measure

Caderousse
character in: **21** The Count of Monte Cristo
author: **5** Dumas (pere)

cadet 5 plebe **7** recruit, student **11** youngest son **14** military student

cadge 3 beg, bum **5** mooch **6** hustle, peddle, sponge **7** solicit, scrounge **9** panhandle

cadmium
chemical symbol: **2** Cd

Cadmus
form: **6** prince
realm: **9** Phoenicia
father: **6** Agenor
mother: **10** Telephassa
brother: **5** Cilix **7** Phoenix
sister: **6** Europa
wife: **8** Harmonia
son: **8** Illyrius **9** Polydorus
daughter: **3** Ino **5** Agave **6** Semele **7** Autonoe
introduced to the Greeks: **7** writing
founded: **6** Thebes
planted: **12** dragons teeth

Caduceus
staff of: **7** Mercury

Caeneus
also: **6** Caenis
member of: **9** Argonauts

---

gift: **15** invulnerability
former identity: **6** Caenis

Caenis
also: **7** Caeneus
father: **6** Elatus
violated by: **8** Poseidon
changed into: **3** man
subsequent identity: **7** Caeneus

caesar, Caesar 5 ruler **6** despot, tyrant **7** emperor **8** autocrat, dictator

Caesar, Julius *see box*

Caesar, Sid
partner: **11** Imogene Coca
born: **9** Yonkers NY
roles: **15** Your Show of Shows

Caesar and Cleopatra
author: **17** George Bernard Shaw

Caesar or Nothing
author: **9** Pio Baroja

caesura 5 break, pause **6** hiatus **12** interruption

cafe 3 bar, inn **5** diner **6** bistro, eatery, nitery, tavern **7** automat, beanery, cabaret **9** cafeteria, chophouse, hash house, lunchroom, nightclub **10** restaurant, supper club **11** bar and grill, coffeehouse, discotheque **12** luncheonette
French: **9** estaminet

cafe au lait 10 light brown **14** coffee with milk

cafe noir 11 black coffee

---

cage 3 pen **4** coop **5** pen in **6** coop up, encage, lock up, shut in **7** confine, impound **8** imprison, restrain, restrict **9** enclosure

cagey 3 sly **4** foxy, keen, wary, wily **5** alert, chary, leery, sharp **6** artful, crafty, shifty, shrewd **7** careful, cunning, heedful, prudent **8** cautious, discreet, watchful

Cagliari
capital of: **8** Sardinia

Cagney, James
nickname: **5** Jimmy
born: **9** New York NY
roles: **7** Ragtime **14** The Public Enemy **17** Yankee Doodle Dandy (Oscar) **19** Man of a Thousand Faces

Cagney and Lacey
cast: **8** Tyne Daly **11** Sharon Gless

Cahita
tribe: **5** Yaqui

Cain
father: **4** Adam
mother: **3** Eve
brother: **4** Abel, Seth
home: **4** Eden
son: **5** Enoch
killed: **4** Abel
traveled to: **3** Nod

Caesar, Julius
adopted son: **8** Octavian **14** Caesar Augustus
author of: **13** On the Civil War **14** On the Gallic War
battle: **4** Zela **5** Munda **7** Durazzo, Thapsus **8** Mytilene **9** Pharsalus **11** Dyrrhachium
conquered: **4** Gaul
crossed: **7** Rubicon (river)
defeated: **6** Pompey
lover: **9** Cleopatra
member of: **16** First Triumvirate
murdered by: **5** Casca **6** Brutus **7** Cassius
murdered on: **11** Ides of March
other triumvirs: **6** Pompey **7** Crassus
saying: **9** Et tu Brute? (Even you Brutus?) **12** Veni vidi vici (I came I saw I conquered)
wife: **7** Pompeia **8** Cornelia **9** Calpurnia

Caine, Michael
   real name: 24 Maurice Joseph Micklewhite
   born: 6 London 7 England
   roles: 4 Zulu 5 Alfie
   6 Sleuth 9 Deathtrap 13 Ed-
   ucating Rita 14 The Ipcress
   File

Caine Mutiny, The
   author: 10 Herman Wouk
   director: 13 Edward Dmytryk
   cast: 7 May Wynn 9 Lee
   Marvin 10 E G Marshall,
   Jose Ferrer, Van Johnson
   13 Fred MacMurray, Robert
   Francis 14 Humphrey Bogart
   (Captain Queeg)

Caingua see 7 Guarani

Cairo
   Arab camp: 8 al-Fustat
   Arabic: 9 al-Qahirah
   capital of: 5 Egypt
   island: 5 Rodah
   7 Zamalik
   landmark:
     mosque: 7 al-Azhar
     11 Muhammed Ali
     statue: 8 Ramses II
   museum: 8 Egyptian
   river: 4 Nile
   Roman fortress:
   7 Babylon
   rulers: 5 Turks 7 British,
   Saladin 8 Fatimids
   9 Mamelukes 11 Ismail
   Pasha, Muhammed Ali
   12 Ottoman Turks
   university: 7 Al-Azhar
   8 Ain Shams, American

Cairo, Joel
   character in: 16 The Maltese
   Falcon
   author: 7 Hammett

caitiff 3 cad, cur, rat 4 heel
   5 churl, knave, louse, rogue
   6 rascal, rotter 7 bounder, dastard, villain 9 scoundrel
   10 blackguard

cajole 4 coax 7 beguile, deceive, flatter, wheedle 8 blandish, inveigle, persuade

cajolery 7 blarney, coaxing,
   fawning 8 flattery, promises,
   soft soap 9 adulation, sweet
   talk, wheedling 10 enticement,
   inveigling, persuasion 11 be-
   guilement 12 blandishment

cake 3 bar, bun, dry 4 lump,
   mass 5 block, crust, tort
   6 cookie, eclair, gateau,
   harden, pastry, 7 congeal, cup-
   cake, thicken 8 compress, solidify 9 coagulate, sweet roll
   11 consolidate

Cakes and Ale
   author: 16 W Somerset
   Maugham

cakewalk 5 cinch, dance
   9 promenade 12 dance contest

calaboose 3 pen 4 jail, stir
   6 prison 7 slammer
   8 hoosegow

Calah
   founder: 6 Nimrod

Calais
   origin: 5 Greek
   member of: 9 Argonauts
   father: 6 Boreas
   mother: 8 Orithyia
   twin brother: 5 Zetes

calamitous 5 fatal 6 tragic,
   woeful 7 adverse, baleful,
   harmful, ruinous, unlucky
   8 dreadful 9 blighting 10 disastrous, pernicious 11 cataclysmic, deleterious,
   destructive, detrimental, distressful, unfortunate
   12 catastrophic

calamity 3 ill, woe 4 blow,
   ruin 5 trial 6 misery, mishap
   7 bad luck, failure, ill wind,
   reverse, scourge, tragedy, trouble, undoing 8 disaster, distress, downfall, hardship
   9 adversity, cataclysm, mischance 10 affliction, ill fortune, misfortune
   11 catastrophe, tribulation
   13 sea of troubles 15 stroke of
   ill luck

calando
   music: 22 getting weaker and
   slower

Calchas
   vocation: 10 soothsayer
   father: 7 Thestor
   burial place: 6 Notium

calcium
   chemical symbol: 2 Ca

calculate 4 mean, plan 5 add
   up, aim at, count, judge, sum
   up 6 design, devise, figure, intend, reckon 7 compute, measure, predict, project, surmise,
   work out 8 estimate 9 ascertain, determine 10 conjecture

calculated 7 planned 10 deliberate, purposeful, thought out
   11 intentional, prearranged
   12 premeditated

calculating 3 sly 4 foxy, wily
   6 artful, crafty, shrewd, tricky
   7 cunning, devious 8 plotting,
   scheming 9 designing 10 contriving, intriguing 12 manipu-
   lative 13 Machiavellian

calculating machine
   invented by: 7 Babbage

calculation 6 answer, result
   8 figuring, judgment 9 reckon-

ing 10 estimation
11 computation

calculator 6 abacus 7 counter,
   thinker 8 computer, reckoner

Calcutta
   captured by: 5 Clive
   founded by: 23 British East
   India Company
   landmark: 10 Jain Temple
   12 Howrah Bridge, Indian
   Museum 16 Botanical Gardens, Victoria Memorial
   17 Zoological Gardens
   18 Dakshineswar Temple
   opposite city: 6 Howrah
   river: 7 Hooghly
   state: 10 West Bengal

Calder, Alexander
   born: 14 Philadelphia PA
   sculptures also called:
   7 mobiles
   artwork: 3 Man 5 Whale
   6 Spiral 10 Teodelapio
   12 Ticket Window 13 La
   Grande Voile 14 The Brass
   Family 23 Lobster Traps and
   Fish Tail

**Calderon de la Barca,
Pedro**
   author of: 12 Life Is a
   Dream

caldron, cauldron 3 pot
   6 boiler, kettle

Caldwell, Erskine
   author of: 10 Georgia Boy
   11 Tobacco Road 14 God's
   Little Acre

Caldwell, Taylor
   author of: 12 Answer as a
   Man 13 A Pillar of Iron
   14 Great Lion of God
   17 Testimony of Two Men,
   The Devil's Advocate
   19 Bright Flows the River
   20 Glory and the Lightning
   22 The Captains and the
   Kings 24 Dear and Glorious
   Physician

Caleb
   father: 8 Jepunneh
   brother: 5 Kenaz
   daughter: 6 Achash
   nephew: 7 Othniel
   descendant: 8 Calebite

Caleb Williams
   author: 13 William Godwin

Caledonia see 8 Scotland

calendar 4 list 5 chart, diary,
   table 6 agenda, docket 7 day
   book, program 8 register,
   schedule

Caletor
   origin: 5 Greek
   mentioned in: 5 Iliad
   cousin: 6 Hector
   killed by: 14 Telamonian
   Ajax

calf 4 veal **5** dogie **6** weaner **7** leg part
    young of: 3 cow **4** bull, seal **5** whale **8** elephant

Calgary
    hockey team: 6 Flames

Calhern, Louis
    real name: 13 Carl Henry Vogt
    born: 10 Brooklyn NY
    roles: 8 King Lear **12** Julius Caesar **15** Annie Get Your Gun **16** The Asphalt Jungle **20** The Magnificent Yankee

Calhoun, Rory
    real name: 20 Francis Timothy Durgin
    born: 12 Los Angeles CA
    roles: 8 The Texan **21** Treasure of Pancho Villa **22** How to Marry a Millionaire, Requiem for a Heavyweight

Caliban
    character in: 10 The Tempest
    author: 11 Shakespeare

caliber 4 bore, rank **5** gifts, merit, place, power, scope, skill, worth **6** repute, talent **7** ability, quality, stature **8** capacity, diameter, eminence, position, prestige **10** capability, competence, estimation, excellence, importance, prominence, reputation **11** achievement, distinction

California *see box*

Calinieff, Martin
    real name of: 13 Michael Callan

Calinky State
    nickname of: 13 South Carolina

calisay
    type: 7 liqueur
    origin: 5 Spain **9** Catalonia
    flavor: 5 herbs **7** quinine

Calkins, Richard
    creator/artist of: 10 Buck Rogers

call 3 ask, bid, cry, dub, tag **4** bawl, buzz, hail, name, need, plea, ring, roar, stop, term, yell **5** cause, claim, label, order, phone, rally, right, shout, style, title, visit **6** appeal, ask for, bellow, charge, clamor, cry out, decree, demand, direct, drop in, excuse, gather, halloo, holler, invite, invoke, know as, muster, notice, outcry, pray to, reason, scream, stop by, summon **7** collect, command, contact, convene, convoke, declare, entitle, entreat, grounds, refer to, request, require, specify, stop off, summons, warrant

---

California
    abbreviation: 2 CA **3** Cal **5** Calif
    nickname: 6 Golden **8** Eldorado **12** Promised Land
    capital: 10 Sacramento
    largest city: 10 Los Angeles
    others: 4 Lodi **5** Azusa, Chico, Chino, Indio **6** Blythe, Carmel, Covina, Eureka, Fresno, Lompoc, Merced, Oxnard, Pomona, Sonoma, Tulare **7** Alameda, Anaheim, Burbank, Gardena, Needles, Oakland, Salinas, Vallejo, Visalia **8** Altadena, Berkeley, Palo Alto, Pasadena, Redlands, San Diego, Stockton **9** Cucamonga, Long Beach **11** Palm Springs, Santa Monica **12** Beverly Hills, San Francisco, Santa Barbara
    college: 3 USC **4** UCLA **5** Mills **6** Pitzer, Pomona **7** Caltech, Chapman, Scripps **8** Stanford, Whittier **10** Occidental, Pepperdine
    explorer: 6 Cortez
    feature:
        amusement park: **10** Disneyland **15** Knotts Berry Farm
        area: **9** Hollywood **15** Fishermans Wharf
        dam: **6** Hoover, Shasta **7** Boulder
        island prison: **8** Alcatraz
        mill: **7** Sutters
        national park: **7** Redwood, Sequoia **8** Yosemite **11** Kings Canyon **14** Channel Islands, Lassen Volcanic
        parade: **4** Rose
        prison: **6** Folsom **10** San Quentin
    tribe: 4 Hupa, Pomo, Yana, Yuki **5** Karok, Maidu, Miwok, Wappo, Wiyot, Yurok **6** Patwin, Shasta, Tolowa, Yokuts **7** Chumash, Luiseno, Salinan, Serrano **8** Diegueno
    people: 6 Sutter **10** Earl Warren **11** Robert Frost **13** George S Patton, John Steinbeck **14** William Saroyan
    island: 4 Goat, Mare **7** Anacapo, Channel **8** Alcatraz, Catalina, Coronado **9** Farallone
    lake: 4 Mono, Soda **5** Clear, Eagle, Owens, Tahoe **6** Salton, Tulare **7** Almanor **8** Elsinore **9** Berryessa
    land rank: 5 third
    mountain: 4 Muir **5** Coast **6** Lassen, Shasta, Wilson **7** Cascade, Klamath, Palomar, Whitney **10** Peninsular, Transverse **12** Sierra Nevada
    highest point: **7** Whitney
    physical feature:
        bay: **8** Monterey, San Diego **12** San Francisco
        cape: **9** Mendocino
        desert: **6** Mohave, Mojave **8** Colorado
        fault: **10** San Andreas
        glacier: **8** Palisade
        sea: **6** Cortez **7** Pacific
        tree: **7** redwood
        valley: **5** Death
        volcano: **6** Lassen
        wind: **7** Collada **8** Santa Ana
    president: 13 Richard M Nixon, Ronald W Reagan
    river: 3 Eel, Mad, Pit **4** Kern **5** Kings, Owens, Putah, Smith, Stony **6** Little, Merced, Salmon **7** Feather, Klamath, Rubicon, Russian, Salinas, Trinity, Truckee **10** Sacramento, San Jacinto, San Joaquin, Stanislaus
    state admission: 11 thirty-first
    state bird: 21 California Valley quail
    state fish: 21 California golden trout
    state flower: 11 golden poppy
    state motto: 6 Eureka (I have found it)
    state song: 18 I Love You California
    state symbol: 11 grizzly bear
    state tree: 17 California redwood
    baseball team: 6 Angels, Padres **7** Dodgers
    basketball team: 6 Lakers **8** Clippers **19** Golden State Warriors
    football team: 4 Rams **7** Raiders **8** Chargers **11** Forty-Niners

8 announce, appeal to, assemble, christen, entreaty, identify, instruct, look in on, occasion, petition, proclaim 9 crying out, designate, direction, pay a visit, telephone 10 describe as, invitation, supplicate 11 declaration, instruction 12 announcement, call together, characterize, proclamation, supplication 13 justification

Callan, Michael
real name: 15 Martin Calinieff
born: 14 Philadelphia PA
roles: 9 Cat Ballou 10 The Interns 18 Gidget Goes Hawaiian, The Flying Fontaines 23 The Magnificent Seven Ride

call for 4 need 6 demand, pick up 7 request, require

call forth 4 spur 5 evoke, raise 6 arouse, awaken, excite, incite, invoke, kindle, stir up 7 command, conjure, provoke 8 summon up 9 make aware, stimulate 10 make appear

Callidice
form: 5 queen
realm: 10 Thesprotia
husband: 8 Odysseus
son: 10 Polypoetes

calling 3 job 4 line, work 5 craft, field, forte, trade 6 career, crying, living, metier, outcry 7 hailing, mission, passion, yelling 8 activity, business, devotion, function, province, shouting, vocation 9 bellowing, crying out, first love, hallooing, life's work, screaming, specialty 10 assignment, attachment, dedication, employment, enthusiasm, livelihood, occupation, profession, walk of life 14 bread and butter, means of support, specialization

calling off 6 ending 7 halting 8 giving up 11 termination 12 backing out of, cancellation

calling oneself thus
French: 9 soi-disant

Calliope
member of: 5 Muses
presided over: 10 epic poetry
father: 4 Zeus
mother: 9 Mnemosyne
son: 7 Orpheus

Callipolis
father: 9 Alcathous

Callirrhoe, Callirhoe
father: 6 Oeneus 8 Achelous
husband: 4 Tros 8 Alcmaeon
son: 4 Ilus 8 Ganymede 10 Amphoterus

---

ended plague in: 7 Calydon
death by: 9 sacrifice

Calliste
epithet of: 7 Artemis
means: 7 fairest

Callisto
form: 5 nymph
attended: 7 Artemis
loved: 4 Zeus
changed into: 4 bear
killed by: 7 Artemis

call off 3 end 4 halt 5 abort 6 cancel, give up 8 postpone 9 back out of, terminate 10 summon away 12 dispense with

Call of the Wild, The
author: 10 Jack London
dog: 4 Buck
master: 12 John Thornton

callous 4 cold, hard 5 cruel, horny, tough 6 inured 8 hardened, uncaring 9 apathetic, heartless, unfeeling 11 hardhearted, indifferent, insensitive 12 thick-skinned, unresponsive 13 dispassionate, unsympathetic 14 pachydermatous

call out 3 cry 4 bawl, hail, yell 5 shout 6 bellow, cry out, holler, summon 9 challenge

callow 3 raw 5 crude, green, naive 7 artless, awkward, puerile, shallow, untried 8 childish, ignorant, immature, juvenile 9 infantile 10 sophomoric, uninformed, unschooled, unseasoned 11 uninitiated 13 inexperienced 15 unsophisticated

call to 4 hail 5 greet 6 accost, salute 7 address, shout at

call to account 5 chide, scold 6 accuse, charge, rebuke 7 arraign, bawl out, censure, chasten, reprove, upbraid 8 admonish, denounce, reproach 9 criticize, dress down, reprimand 10 take to task 11 remonstrate

call to arms 6 war cry 9 battle cry 11 rallying cry

call to order 4 open 6 muster 7 convene, convoke

call upon 3 ask, bid 4 urge 5 visit 6 charge, enjoin, exhort, invite, invoke 7 beseech, entreat, request, require 8 appeal to, petition, summon up 9 encourage 11 acknowledge

callused 4 hard 5 horny, tough 8 hardened 12 thick-skinned 14 pachydermatous

calm 4 cool, ease, mild 5 allay, balmy, bland, quell, quiet, still 6 becalm, gentle, lessen,

---

pacify, placid, reduce, repose, sedate, serene, smooth, soothe, subdue 7 assuage, collect, compose, cool off, halcyon, mollify, pacific, placate, relaxed, relieve 8 composed, coolness, diminish, mitigate, moderate, peaceful, serenity, tranquil, unshaken 9 alleviate, collected, composure, impassive, placidity, quietness, stillness, unexcited, unruffled 10 cool-headed, motionless, simmer down, smoothness, unagitated, untroubled 11 impassivity, passionless, restfulness, self-control, tranquility, tranquilize, undisturbed, unflappable, unperturbed 12 peacefulness, tranquillity, windlessness 13 imperturbable, self-possessed, stormlessness 14 self-possession 16 imperturbability

calmness 5 poise 6 aplomb 8 coolness, serenity 9 composure, placidity, sangfroid, stillness 10 equanimity, steadiness 11 self-control, tranquility 12 peacefulness, tranquillity 14 presence of mind, self-possession 16 imperturbability

Calpurnia
character in: 12 Julius Caesar
author: 11 Shakespeare

calumnious 8 libelous 9 maligning, vilifying 10 defamatory, derogatory, slanderous 11 disparaging

calumny 4 barb, slur 5 libel, smear 6 malice 7 slander 8 innuendo 9 aspersion 10 backbiting, defamation, derogation, revilement 11 denigration, deprecation, insinuation 12 backstabbing, calumniation, depreciation, vilification 13 animadversion, disparagement, malicious lies

calvados
type: 6 brandy
origin: 6 France 8 Normandy
flavor: 5 apple
aged in: 3 oak

Calvary 8 Golgotha
means: 10 skull place

Calyce
father: 6 Aeolus
mother: 7 Enarete
son: 8 Endymion

Calydonian boar
sent by: 5 Diana
killed by: 8 Meleager

Calydonian hunt
pursuit of: 4 boar

Calypso
form: 5 nymph

home: 6 Ogygia
father: 10 Titan Atlas
detained: 8 Odysseus
   for: 10 seven years

calyx 4 husk 5 sepal

cam 3 cog 4 disk 8 cylinder
10 projection
located on: 5 shaft, wheel
motion: 7 rocking 8 circular
12 back and forth

Cambodia
other name: 7 Camboja
  8 Cambodge
  9 Kampuchea
capital/largest city:
  8 Pnom-Penh
others: 3 Som 4 Ream
  5 Takeo 6 Kampot, Kra-
  tie, Pursat 7 Kohnieh,
  Kompong, Kracheh,
  Rovieng, Samrong
  8 Siem Reap, Sisophon
  10 Battambang, Stung
  Treng 11 Kompong
  Cham 12 Krungkoh
  Kong 13 Sihanoukville
head of state: 4 King
monetary unit: 3 sen
  4 quan, riel 6 puttan
  7 piaster
weight: 4 mace, tael
island: 4 Kong, Rong
lake: 8 Tonle Sap
mountain: 3 Pan 7 Dangrek, Dong Rek 8 Car-
  damom, Elephant
highest point: 10 Phnom
  Aoral, Phnom Aural
river: 3 San, Sen
  5 Sreng 6 Bassac,
  Chinit, Mekong, Po-
  rong, Pursat, Srepok
  7 Kamlong, Sekhong
  8 Tonle Sap
physical feature:
  bay: 10 Kompongsom
  cape: 5 Samit
  gulf: 4 Siam
    8 Thailand
people: 4 Cham, Thai
  5 Khmer 7 Chinese
  10 Vietnamese
  leader: 6 Pol Pot
    8 Sihanouk
language: 5 Khmer
  6 French 9 Cambodian
  10 Vietnamese
religion: 7 animism
  8 Buddhism
  12 Christianity
places:
  ruins/temple: 6 Ang-
  kor 9 Angkor Wat
feature:
  Communist group:
  10 Khmer Rouge

---

camaraderie 7 jollity 8 bon-
homie, good will 10 affability,
clubbiness, fellowship, friendship 11 brotherhood, comradeship, sociability 12 con-
geniality, conviviality,
friendliness 13 companionship,
esprit de corps 14 good-
fellowship

Camarasaurus
type: 8 dinosaur, sauropod
location: 12 United States
period: 8 Jurassic

Cambodia *see box*

Cambria *see* 5 Wales

cambric 5 cloth, linen 6 cotton, fabric 8 material

camel
called: 13 beast of burden
  15 ship of the desert
chews: 3 cud
group: 4 herd
habitat: 4 Asia 6 Africa,
  desert
kind: 7 Arabian 8 Bactrian
  9 dromedary
number of humps: 3 one,
  two
species: 6 mammal
type of: 8 ruminant
young: 4 calf

camellia
varieties: 5 Silky 6 Common
  8 Mountain, Sasanqua

Camenae
means: 11 foretellers
form: 6 nymphs 7 deities
gift: 8 prophecy
names: 6 Egeria 8 Carmenta
  9 Antevorta, Postvorta
habitat: 8 fountain
correspond to: 5 Muses

camera
invented by:
  Kodak: 6 Walker
    7 Eastman
  Polaroid: 4 Land
  photography: 6 Niepce,
  Talbot 8 Daguerre
  film, celluloid: 6 Edison
  11 Reichenbach
  film, transparent: 7 Eastman, Goodwin
  color photo: 4 Ives

Cameroon *see box*

Camilla
form: 5 woman
occupation: 7 warrior
father: 7 Metabus
mother: 7 Casmila
fought with: 6 Turnus
fought against: 6 Aeneas

Camille
also: 17 La Dame aux
  camelias
author: 14 Alexander Dumas
  (fils)
character: 6 Nanine 11 Ar-

Cameroon
capital: 7 Yaounde
largest city: 6 Douala
others: 3 Wum 4 Bali,
  Buea, Edea, Tiko
  5 Kumba, Lomie,
  Mamfe 6 Garona, Mar-
  oua 7 Batouri, Dschang,
  Ebolowa, Foumban
  8 Victoria 10 N'Gaoun-
  dere, N'Kongsamba
monetary unit: 5 franc
  7 centime
island: 5 Nanny
  8 Fernando
lake: 4 Chad
mountain: 5 Mbabo
  7 Bambuto, Kapsiki,
  Mandara 8 Batandji
  9 Atlantika
highest point:
  8 Cameroon
river: 3 Dja, Lom 4 Faro,
  Mbam, Vina 5 Benue,
  Campo, Cross, Kadei,
  Mbere, Nyong, N'Goko,
  Sanga, Shari 6 Djerem,
  Ivindo, Logone, Sanaga
sea: 8 Atlantic
physical feature:
  cape: 10 Debundscha
  gulf: 6 Guinea
  plateau: 7 Adamawa
  8 Mambilla
people: 3 Abo, Edo, Ibo
  4 Beti, Bulu, Ekoi, Ijaw,
  Sara 5 Bantu, Bassa,
  Kirdi, Pygmy, Tikar
  6 Bamoun, Donala,
  Ewondo, Fulani, Ibibio
  7 Bakweri 8 Bamileke
  Fulani chief:
  7 Lamidos
language: 4 Bulu
  5 Bantu, Bassa, Hausa
  6 Douala, Ewondo,
  French, Fulani
  7 English 8 Bamileke,
  Fulfulde
religion: 5 Islam 7 animism 12 Christianity
places:
  *home of prime minis-
  ter:* 7 Schloss

---

mand Duval 17 Marguerite
Gautier (Camille)
director: 11 George Cukor
cast: 10 Greta Garbo (Camille) 12 Henry Daniell, Robert Taylor (Armand)
14 Elizabeth Allan, Laura
Hope Crews 15 Lionel
Barrymore

Camillo
character in: 14 The Winter's
  Tale
author: 11 Shakespeare

Camirus
origin: **5** Greek
grandfather: **6** Helios, Helius

camisole 3 top **4** slip **6** jacket
10 underwaist

camouflage 4 hide, mask,
veil **5** blind, cloak, cover,

front **6** screen, shroud **7** conceal, cover up **8** disguise
10 masquerade, subterfuge
11 concealment

camouflaged 6 hidden,
masked **7** cloaked **8** shrouded
9 concealed, disguised

camp 4 tent **5** tents **7** bivouac,
lodging, rough it **8** army base,
barracks, quarters **10** pitch a
tent

campaign 3 run **4** push
5 drive, stump **6** action, effort
7 crusade **8** endeavor, move-

Canada
capital: **6** Ottawa
largest city: **8** Montreal
others: **4** Hull **5** Banff, Laval **6** Dawson, Guelph, London, Oshawa, Quebec, Regina, Sarnia,
Val d'or **7** Calgary, Halifax, Moncton, Nanaimo, Sudbury, Toronto, Welland, Windsor **8** Edmonton, Hamilton, Kingston, Moose Jaw, Victoria, Winnipeg **9** Saskatoon, Vancouver
10 Port Arthur, Sherbrooke **11** Fredericton **12** Niagara Falls, Peterborough, Prince Albert,
Prince George **13** Charlottetown **21** St Catherines Stratford
school: **3** UBC **5** Laval **6** McGill, Queens **7** Toronto **8** McMaster, Montreal **9** Concordia, Dal-
housie **11** Simon Fraser
division: **5** Yukon **6** Quebec **7** Alberta, Ontario **8** Manitoba **10** Nova Scotia **12** Newfoundland,
New Brunswick, Saskatchewan **15** British Columbia **18** Prince Edward Island **20** Northwest
Territories
New division: **7** Nunavut
head of state: **14** British monarch **15** governor general
measure: **3** ton **5** minot, perch, point **6** arpent **7** chainon
island: **4** Read **5** Banks, Bylot, Coats, Devon, Grand, Manan, Parry, Sable **6** Baffin, Breton,
Mansel, Middle **7** Belcher **8** Bathurst, Magdalen, Victoria **9** Anticosti, Ellesmere, Vancouver
10 Campobello, Manitoulin **11** Southampton **14** Queen Charlotte
lake: **4** Cree, Erie, Gras, Seul **5** Garry, Huron, Rainy **6** Louise, St John **7** Abitibi, Dubawnt,
Nipigon, Ontario, Testlin **8** Kootenay, Manitoba, Okanagan, Reindeer, Superior, Winnipeg
9 Athabaska, Great Bear, Nipissing **10** Great Slave, Mistassini **12** Winnipegosis
mountain: **5** Coast, Royal **6** Robson, Skeena **7** Cariboo, Cascade, Purcell, Rockies, Selkirk, St
Elias **8** Columbia, Hazelton, Monashee **9** Mackenzie, Notre Dame, Tremblant **10** Laurentian,
Richardson, Shickshock **14** Jacques Cartier
highest point: **5** Logan
river: **3** Hay, Red **4** Peel **5** Liard, Peace, Slave, Yukon **6** Albany, Fraser, Nelson, Nicola, Ottawa, Skeena, St John, Thames, Thelon **7** St Marys **8** Columbia, Gatineau, Kootenay, Peta-
wawa, Saguenay **9** Athabasca, Athapaska, Churchill, Mackenzie, Richelieu **10** Coppermine, St
Lawrence **11** Assiniboine, **12** Saskatchewan
sea: **6** Arctic **7** Pacific **8** Atlantic, Labrador
physical features:
  bay: **5** Basin, Fundy, Hecla, James, Minas **6** Baffin, Griper, Hudson, Ungava **8** Georgian
  canal: **3** Soo **7** Welland **10** Wellington
  cape: **5** Canso
  falls: **7** Niagara **9** Horseshoe
  gulf: **10** St Lawrence
  pass: **8** Chilkoot
  peninsula: **5** Gaspe **7** Boothia **8** Labrador, Melville
  plain: **11** Barren lands
  port: **6** Quebec **7** St Johns **8** Hamilton, Victoria **9** Churchill
  strait: **5** Cabot, Davis, Dease **6** Hecate, Hudson **7** Georgia **9** Belle Isle **10** Juan de Fuca
people: **5** Inuit **6** Canuck, Eskimo, French **7** English
  explorer: **5** Cabot **6** Fraser, Joliet **7** Cartier, LaSalle, Selkirk **8** Thompson **9** Champlain,
  MacKenzie, Marquette
  leader: **4** King, Riel **5** Clark **6** Borden **7** Laurier, Trudeau **8** Campbell, Chretien, Mulroney
  9 Macdonald, St Laurent **11** Diefenbaker
language: **6** Eskimo, French **7** English
religion: **8** Anglican **13** Roman Catholic **20** United Church of Canada
places:
  battlefield: **15** Plains of Abraham
  national park: **4** Yoho **5** Banff **6** Jasper **7** Glacier **8** Kootenay **9** Elk Island **10** La Mauricie,
  Revelstoke **11** Wood Buffalo **12** Prince Albert **13** Waterton Lakes
  resort: **5** Banff **10** Lake Louise
feature:
  airport: **6** Gander
  emblem: **9** maple leaf
  fish: **5** charr, trout
  flower: **10** Juneflower
  police: **8** Mounties **12** Royal Mounted
food:
  soup: **7** rubaboo

ment **9** offensive, operation **11** electioneer, whistle-stop **12** battle series, beat the drums, solicit votes

campanile 6 belfry **9** bell tower

campari
type: **7** bitters **8** aperitif
origin: **5** Italy

Campe
form: **8** old woman
occupation: **6** jailer
place: **8** Tartarus

campground 7 bivouac **8** tent city **16** temporary shelter

Campin, Robert
born: **8** Flanders
also known as/identified with: **14** Master of Merode **16** Master of Flemalle
artwork: **10** St Veronica, The Trinity **13** The Entombment **16** Merode Altarpiece (Merode Triptych) **17** The Virgin and Child **18** The Thief on the Cross

Camptosaurus
type: **8** dinosaur **10** ornithopod
location: **12** North America
period: **8** Jurassic
characteristic: **10** duck-billed

Camus, Albert
author of: **4** L'ete **6** Summer **7** The Fall **8** Caligula, The Rebel **9** The Plague **11** A Happy Death, The Stranger **12** Cross Purpose **17** The Myth of Sisyphus

can 3 tin **4** buns, fire, rump, seat **5** fanny, put up **6** bottom **8** backside, buttocks, preserve **9** container, fundament, give the ax

Canaan
father: **3** Ham
brother: **4** Cush
grandfather: **4** Noah
known as: **12** promised land
see also **6** Israel

Canace
father: **6** Aeolus
brother: **8** Macareus
death by: **7** suicide

Canada see box

canaille 6 proles, rabble **8** riffraff **9** commoners, hoi polloi **11** proletariat **13** great unwashed

canal 4 duct, tube **7** channel, conduit, passage **8** aqueduct

Canaletto
real name: **20** Giovanni Antonio Canal
born: **5** Italy **6** Venice
artwork: **18** The Stonemason's Yard

canard 4 hoax **5** rumor **7** slander **9** falsehood **12** exaggeration

---

Canary Islands
other name: **14** Fortunate Isles **15** Isles of the Blest
named for: **3** dog **5** canis **6** canine
capital: **9** Las Palmas **19** Santa Cruz de Tenerife
largest city: **9** Las Palmas
others: **4** Icod **6** Laguna **7** Orotava **8** Arrecife, Valverde **12** San Sebastian
government: **16** overseas province
of: **5** Spain
measure: **8** fanegada
monetary unit: **6** peseta
island: **4** Roca **5** Clara, Perro, Lobos, Rocca **6** Gomera, Hierro **7** Inferno, La Palma **8** Graciosa, Tenerife **9** Lanzarote **10** Lanzarotte **11** Gran Canaria **13** Fuerteventura
mountain: **6** La Cruz **8** El Cumbre, Tenerife
highest point: **5** Teide, Teyde
sea: **8** Atlantic
people: **7** Spanish
language: **7** Spanish
religion: **13** Roman Catholic

---

canasta
number of players: **4** four
cards/hand: **6** eleven
meld: **12** three of a kind
wild card: **5** deuce, joker

Canberra
capital of: **9** Australia
territory: **13** New South Wales **26** Australian Capital Territory
lake: **13** Burley Griffin

cancel 4 void **5** annul, erase, quash **6** delete, offset, recall, recant, repeal, revoke **7** abolish, call off, nullify, rescind, retract, vitiate **8** abrogate, call back, set aside **9** repudiate **10** balance out, blue-pencil, do away with, invalidate, neutralize **11** countermand **12** dispense with **13** compensate for **14** counterbalance **18** declare null and void

cancellation 6 repeal **9** abolition **10** abrogation, efface-

---

ment, rescinding, revocation **11** abolishment, eradication, repudiation, termination

cancer 3 rot **6** plague **7** sarcoma, scourge **8** neoplasm, sickness **9** carcinoma **10** malignancy **14** malignant tumor **15** malignant growth

Cancer
symbol: **4** crab
planet: **4** Moon
rules: **4** home **6** family
born: **4** July, June

Cancer Ward, The
author: **21** Aleksandr Solzhenitsyn

candelabrum 7 menorah **8** dikerion **9** girandole, trikerion **11** candlestick **12** candleholder

Candia see **5** Crete

candid 4 fair, free, just, open **5** blunt, frank, plain **6** direct, honest **7** genuine, natural, relaxed, sincere, unposed **8** informal, outright, truthful **9** downright, impromptu, outspoken **10** forthright **11** plain spoken, spontaneous, unvarnished **14** extemporaneous **15** straightforward

Candida
author: **17** George Bernard Shaw

candidate 7 hopeful, nominee **8** aspirant, eligible **9** applicant, contender, job seeker **10** competitor, contestant **11** possibility **12** office seeker

Candid Camera
host: **9** Allen Funt
co-host: **11** Bess Myerson **12** Durward Kirby **13** Arthur Godfrey

Candide
author: **8** Voltaire
character: **6** Martin **7** Cacambo **8** Pangloss **9** Cunegonde **11** Admiral Byng **17** Thunder-ten-Tronckh

candidness 6 candor **7** honesty, openess **9** frankness, sincerity **10** directness **12** truthfulness **13** guilelessness

candle 3 dip, wax **5** light, taper **6** bougie, cierge, tallow **9** rush light

candleholder, candlestick 6 sconce **7** menorah **8** dikerion **9** girandole, trikerion **10** chandelier **11** candelabrum

candor 7 honesty **8** fairness, justness, openness **9** bluntness, frankness, sincerity **10** directness **11** artlessness **12** impartiality, truthfulness **14** forthrightness **15** plainspokenness **19** straightforwardness

candy 3 bar 4 kiss 5 cream, fudge, jelly, sweet, taffy 6 bonbon, comfit, dainty, nougat, sweets, toffee 7 brittle, caramel, fondant, gumdrop, praline 8 lollipop 9 chocolate, jellybean, sweetmeat 10 confection 12 all-day sucker 13 confectionery, peanut brittle

cane 3 hit, rap, rod, tan 4 beat, drub, flog, lash, whip 5 baste, flail, smite, staff, stick, whack 6 strike, switch, thrash, wallop 7 trounce 12 walking stick

cane 11 Arundinaria
varieties: 4 Dumb, Wild 5 Arrow, Sugar 6 Rattan, Switch, Tobago, Tonkin 7 Tsingli 8 Southern 11 Spotted dumb 12 Chinese sweet 14 Yellow-leaf dumb

Canea
capital of: 5 Crete

Canens
father: 5 Janus
mother: 7 Venilia
betrothed to: 5 Picus
cried over: 5 Picus
death by: 6 crying

Canephora
form: 7 maidens
carried: 7 baskets

Canetti, Elias
author of: 8 Auto da Fe 12 Tower of Babel 14 Crowds and Power 15 The Torch in My Ear 16 Kafka's Other Trial, The Tongue Set Free

Caniff, Milton
creator/artist of: 10 Dickie Dare 11 Steve Canyon 14 The Gay Thirties 18 Terry and the Pirates

canine 3 cur, dog, fox, pup 4 mutt, wolf 5 hound, hyena, puppy 6 coyote, cuspid, jackal 7 mongrel 8 eyetooth

canker 4 sore 5 ulcer 6 blight, cancer, lesion 9 mouth sore 12 inflammation

Cannibal Galaxy, The
author: 12 Cynthia Ozick

cannon 3 bit, gun 4 bone 5 carom 6 mortar 7 battery 8 field gun, howitzer, ordnance 9 artillery 10 field piece, mounted gun, pickpocket

Cannon
character: 11 Frank Cannon
cast: 13 William Conrad

Cannon, Dyan
real name: 19 Samille Diane Friesen

husband: 9 Cary Grant
born: 8 Tacoma WA
roles: 6 Shamus 9 Deathtrap 13 Heaven Can Wait 15 Such Good Friends 19 Bob & Carol & Ted & Alice 23 Revenge of the Pink Panther

cannonade 5 burst, salvo 6 volley 7 barrage, battery 8 shelling 9 fusillade 11 bombardment

canny 4 foxy, wary, wily, wise 5 cagey, sharp 6 artful, astute, clever, crafty, shrewd, subtle 7 careful, cunning, knowing 8 skillful 9 judicious, sagacious 10 convincing 11 circumspect, intelligent 13 perspicacious

Cano, Alonso
born: 5 Spain 7 Granada
artwork: 16 Granada Cathedral (facade) 18 Madonna of the Rosary 20 Immaculate Conception 23 The Seven Joys of the Virgin

canoe 4 boat 5 bungo, kayak 6 dugout 7 pirogue

canoeing
athlete: 11 Marcia Smoke

canon 3 law 4 code, rule 5 dogma, edict, model, order 6 decree 7 pattern, precept, statute 8 doctrine, standard 9 bench mark, criterion, ordinance, principle, yardstick 10 regulation, touchstone

canonical 6 proper 8 accepted, approved, official orthodox 9 authentic, customary 10 authorized, legitimate, recognized, sanctioned 12 conventional 13 authoritative

Canonization, The
author: 9 John Donne

canopy 4 hood 5 cover 6 awning, tester 8 covering

Canova, Antonio
born: 5 Italy 8 Possagno
artwork: 7 Perseus 12 Venus Victrix (Pauline Bonaparte Borghese) 14 Cupid and Psyche 16 Letizia Bonaparte 17 Daedalus and Icarus

Cansino, Margarita Carmen
real name of: 12 Rita Hayworth

cant 4 sham, talk 5 argot, lingo, slang 6 humbug, jargon 8 parlance, pretense 9 hypocrisy 10 lip service, vernacular 11 insincerity 15 pretentiousness 17 sanctimoniousness

cantabile
music: 7 flowing, singing 8 songlike

cantaloupe 5 fruit, melon 9 muskmelon

cantankerous 4 mean 5 cross, huffy, short, sulky, surly, testy 6 cranky, crusty, grumpy, morose, sullen, touchy 7 bearish, crabbed, fretful, grouchy, peevish, waspish 8 choleric, churlish, contrary, snappish 9 irascible, irritable, splenetic 10 ill-humored, ill-natured 11 contentious, ill-tempered, quarrelsome 12 disagreeable 13 argumentative

cantatrice 6 singer 9 chanteuse 10 songstress 18 professional singer

canteen 2 PX 4 club 5 flask 6 bottle 10 commissary 11 pocket flask 12 post exchange

canter 4 gait, lope, trot 6 gallop, singer, whiner

Canterbury Tales, The
author: 15 Geoffrey Chaucer
starting point: 9 Southwark, Tabard Inn
goal:
tomb of: 6 Becket
character/tale: 3 Nun 4 Cook, Dyer, Monk 5 Canon, Friar, Reeve, Webbe 6 Knight, Miller, Parson, Squire, Yeoman 7 Shipman, Tapicer 8 Franklin, Manciple, Merchant, Pardoner, Prioress, Summoner 9 Carpenter, Ploughman 10 Wife of Bath 11 Haberdasher 13 Clerk of Oxford, Sergeant of Law 14 Doctor of Physic

Canthus
member of: 9 Argonauts

Cantor, Eddie
real name: 21 B Edward Israel Iskowitz
nickname: 9 Banjo Eyes
wife: 9 Ida Tobias
born: 9 New York NY
roles: 7 Whoopee 8 Kid Boots 9 Banjo Eyes

cantor of a synagogue
Hebrew: 5 hazan

Cantos
author: 9 Ezra Pound

can't stand 4 hate 5 abhor 6 detest, eschew, loathe 7 despise 8 execrate 9 abominate, can't abide 11 can't stomach 14 hate the sight of

can't stomach 4 hate 5 abhor 6 detest, loathe 7 despise 8 execrate 9 abominate, can't abide, can't stand

10 shrink from **13** find repulsive

canvas 4 duck **7** painting **8** painting **9** sailcloth, tarpaulin, tent cloth

canvass 4 poll, scan, sift **5** study, tally **6** survey **7** analyze, discuss, examine, explore, inquiry, inquire, inspect, solicit **8** analysis, campaign, scrutiny **10** evaluation, scrutinize **11** enumeration, exploration, inquire into, investigate, take stock of **13** give thought to, investigation

canyon 3 col, cut, gap **4** draw, pass, wadi, wash **5** break, chasm, cleft, crack, gorge, gulch, gully, notch **6** arroyo, coulee, defile, divide, ravine, valley **7** fissure, opening **8** corridor, crevasse, water gap

cap 3 lid, top **4** seal **5** cover, outdo **6** better, exceed, top off **7** surpass **8** headgear, outstrip **9** headdress **10** visored hat ~~Beanie, Tam~~

capability 3 art **4** gift **5** flair, knack, power, skill **6** talent **7** ability, faculty, know-how **8** capacity, efficacy, facility **9** potential **10** attainment, competence, competency **11** proficiency **12** potentiality **13** qualification

capable 3 apt **4** able, deft **5** adept **6** adroit, artful, clever, expert, gifted **7** skilled **8** masterly, skillful, talented **9** competent, effective, ingenious **10** proficient **11** efficacious, intelligent **12** accomplished

capable of assuming legal responsibility
Latin: **8** sui juris

Capable of Honor
author: **10** Allan Drury

capable of managing one's own affairs
Latin: **8** sui juris

capacious 3 big **4** huge, vast, wide **5** ample, broad, large, roomy **7** mammoth, massive **8** gigantic, spacious **9** expansive, extensive **10** commodious, expandable, tremendous, voluminous **13** amplitudinous

capaciousness 9 amplitude, roominess **12** spaciousness **14** commodiousness

capacitate 5 allow **6** enable, permit **7** empower, qualify **8** make able

capacity 4 mind, role, room, size **5** gifts, limit, might, power, range, scope, space **6** extent, talent, volume

7 ability, faculty **8** aptitude, facility, function, judgment, position, sagacity, strength **9** amplitude, endowment, intellect, potential **10** brain power, capability **11** discernment **12** intelligence, perspicacity **15** maximum contents

Capaneus
member of: **18** Seven against Thebes
father: **9** Hipponous
mother: **8** Astynome
wife: **6** Evadne
son: **9** Sthenelus
crime: **9** blasphemy
destroyed by: **4** Zeus

caparison 5 adorn, equip **6** bedeck **9** equipment, trappings

cape 4 spit **5** cloak, manta, point, shawl **6** mantle, poncho, serape, tabard, tongue **7** pelisse **8** headland **9** peninsula **10** promontory

Capek, Karel
author of: **3** R U R **8** Hordubal, Krakatit **9** The Mother **13** Power and Glory **18** The War with the Newts

caper 3 hop **4** jape, jump, lark, leap, romp, skip **5** antic, bound, fling, frisk, prank, spree, stunt, trick **6** bounce, cavort, frolic, gambol, prance **7** caprice **8** escapade **9** adventure, high jinks **10** carrying on **11** shenanigans **14** monkey business

Cape Verde *see box*

capital 4 cash, fine **5** great, money, super **6** center, riches, superb, wealth **7** supreme **9** excellent, financing, first-rate, majuscule, matchless, principal, resources **10** cash on hand, first-class **11** large letter, wherewithal **12** headquarters **13** working assets **14** available means **15** investment funds, upper-case letter

capital city (of countries) *see box, p. 154*

capital city (of states) *see* **13** state capitals

capitalism 14 free enterprise

capitalist 5 mogul **6** tycoon **8** investor **9** financier, plutocrat **14** businessperson

capitalize 4 back, fund **5** stake **7** exploit, finance, support, trade on, utilize **8** bankroll, cash in on, profit by **9** subsidize **11** foot the bill **13** make the most of **17** turn an honest penny **23** strike while the iron is hot **24** make hay while the sun shines

Cape Verde
capital: **5** Praia
largest city: **7** Mindelo
others: **6** Sal Rei **7** Espargo **8** Assomada, Palmeira, Tarrafal **9** Pedra Lume, Sao Filipe **10** Nova Sintra, Santa Maria **11** Porto Ingles **13** Ribeira Grande **16** Vila de Nova Sintra **18** Vila de Ribeira Brave
division: **9** Solavento **10** Barlavento **14** Leeward Islands **15** Windward Islands
monetary unit: **6** escudo **7** centavo
island: **3** Sal **4** Fogo, Maio, Razo **5** Brava, Secos **6** Branco **8** Boa Vista, Sao Tiago **10** Santa Luzia, Santo Antao, Sao Nicolau, Sao Vicente
mountain: **4** Fogo
highest point: **4** Cano **10** Pico de Cano
sea: **8** Atlantic
physical feature:
volcano: **4** Cano
people: **6** Creole **7** mulatto **8** Africans **9** Europeans **10** Portuguese
language: **7** Crioulo **10** Portuguese **13** Verdean Creole
religion: **13** Roman Catholic

capitalize on 7 exploit, utilize **8** profit by **13** turn to account **14** use to advantage

capitol 10 statehouse **11** legislature **15** government house

capitulate 5 yield **6** accede, give in, give up, relent, submit **7** succumb **8** cry quits **9** acquiesce, surrender **11** come to terms, sue for peace **15** lay down one's arms **17** acknowledge defeat, hoist the white flag

capitulation 8 giving in, giving up, quitting, yielding **9** surrender **10** submission

Capote, Truman
author of: **11** In Cold Blood **12** A Tree of Night **19** Breakfast at Tiffany's
character: **14** Holly Golightly

Capp, Al
real name: **18** Alfred George Caplin
creator/artist of: **8** Li'l Abner

Capra, Frank

director of: 11 Lady for a
Day, Lost Horizon **15** State
of the Union **17** Arsenic
and Old Lace, It's a Won-
derful Life, Mr Deeds Goes
to Town (Oscar) **18** It Happened One Night (Oscar)
20 You Can't Take It with
You (Oscar) **23** Mr Smith
Goes to Washington

caprice 3 fad **4** lark, whim
5 antic, caper, craze, fancy,
fling, prank, quirk, spree,
stunt **6** notion, oddity, vagary
7 impulse **8** crotchet, escapade **10** erraticism **11** peculiarity **12** eccentricity,
idiosyncrasy

capricious 6 fickle, fitful,
quirky, uneven **7** erratic, fad-

dish, flighty **8** fanciful, skittish, unstable, unsteady,
variable, wavering **9** eccentric,
impulsive, mercurial, uncertain, undecided **10** changeable,
indecisive, irresolute **11** vacillating **12** inconsistent **13** irresponsible **15** shilly-shallying

capriciousness 7 caprice
10 fickleness **11** instability
12 irresolution **13** impulsiveness, inconsistency

Capricorn

symbol: 4 goat
planet: 6 Saturn
rules: 6 career
born: 7 January **8** December

capsicum peppers

origin: 15 tropical America
variety: 7 cayenne, paprika
9 red pepper **11** chili pepper,

chili powder, curry powder,
sweet pepper
use: 5 chili, curry, pizza **8** barbecue **9** paprikash

capsize 5 upset **6** invert **7** tip
over **8** flip over, keel over,
overturn, turn over **10** turn
turtle

capsule 4 case, pill **6** ampule
7 cockpit **8** covering **9** spore
case **12** condensation

captain 4 boss, head **5** chief,
pilot **6** leader, master, old
man **7** headman, skipper
9 chieftain, commander
10 commandant **12** chief officer **16** company commander
17 commanding officer

Captain Blood

director: 13 Michael Curtiz

---

capital city (of countries)
- **of Afghanistan: 5** Kabul
- **of Albania: 6** Tirana, Tirane
- **of Algeria: 7** Algiers
- **of Andorra: 14** Andorra-la-
  Vella
- **of Angola: 6** Luanda
- **of Antigua and Barbuda:
  7** St John's
- **of Argentina: 11** Buenos
  Aires
- **of Armenia: 6** Erivan
  7 Yerevan
- **of Australia: 8** Canberra
- **of Austria: 6** Vienna
- **of Azerbaijan: 4** Baku
- **of the Bahamas: 6** Nassau
- **of Bahrain: 6** Manama
- **of Bangladesh: 5** Dacca
- **of Barbados: 10** Bridgetown
- **of Belarus: 5** Minsk
- **of Belgium: 8** Brussels
  9 Bruxelles
- **of Belize: 8** Belmopan
- **of Benin: 9** Porto-Novo
- **of Bermuda: 8** Hamilton
- **of Bhutan: 6** Thimbu
  7 Thimphu
- **of Bolivia: 5** Sucre
- **of Bosnia-Herzegovina:
  8** Sarajevo
- **of Botswana: 8** Gaborone
  9 Gaberones
- **of Brazil: 8** Brasilia **12** Rio de
  Janeiro
- **of Brunei: 17** Bandar Seri
  Begawan
- **of Bulgaria: 5** Sofia
- **of Burkina Faso:
  11** Ouagadougou
- **of Burundi: 9** Bujumbura
- **of Cambodia: 8** Pnom-Penh
- **of Cameroon: 7** Yaounde
- **of Canada: 6** Ottawa
- **of the Canary Islands: 9** Las
  Palmas **19** Santa Cruz de
  Tenerife

- **of Cape Verde: 5** Praia
- **of the Central African Republic: 6** Bangui
- **of Chad: 8** Fort-Lamy,
  N'Djamena
- **of Chile: 8** Santiago
- **of China: 6** Peking
- **of Colombia: 6** Bogota
- **of Comoros: 6** Moroni
- **of the Congo: 11** Brazzaville
- **of Costa Rica: 7** San Jose
- **of Crete: 5** Canea **8** Iraklion
- **of Croatia: 6** Zagreb
- **of Cuba: 6** Havana **8** Le
  Habana
- **of Cyprus: 7** Nicosia
- **of Czechoslovakia/Czech Republic: 6** Prague
- **of Denmark: 10** Copenhagen
- **of Djibouti: 8** Djibouti
- **of the Dominican Republic:
  12** Santo Domingo **14** Ciudad Trujillo
- **of Ecuador: 5** Quito
- **of Egypt: 5** Cairo
- **of El Salvador: 11** San
  Salvador
- **of England: 6** London
- **of Equatorial Guinea:
  6** Malabo
- **of Eritrea: 6** Asmara
- **of Estonia: 7** Tallinn
- **of Ethiopia: 10** Addis Ababa
- **of Fiji: 4** Suva
- **of Finland: 8** Helsinki
  11 Helsingfors
- **of France: 5** Paris
- **of the Gabon Republic:
  10** Libreville
- **of The Gambia: 6** Banjul
  8 Bathurst
- **of Georgia: 7** Tbilisi
- **of Germany (East): 10** East
  Berlin
- **of Germany (West): 4** Bonn
- **of Ghana: 5** Accra, Akkra
- **of Greece: 6** Athens

- **of Greenland: 3** Nuk **8** Godthaab, The Point
- **of Grenada: 9** St Georges
- **of Guatemala: 13** Guatemala
  City
- **of Guinea: 7** Conakry
- **of Guinea-Bissau: 6** Bissau
- **of Guyana: 10** Georgetown
- **of Haiti: 12** Port-au-Prince
- **of Honduras: 11** Tegucigalpa
- **of Hong Kong: 8** Victoria
- **of Hungary: 8** Budapest
- **of Iceland: 9** Reykjavik
- **of India: 8** New Delhi
- **of Indonesia: 7** Jakarta
  8 Djakarta
- **of Iran: 6** Tehran **7** Teheran
- **of Iraq: 7** Baghdad
- **of Ireland: 6** Dublin
- **of Israel: 9** Jerusalem
- **of Italy: 4** Roma, Rome
- **of the Ivory Coast: 7** Abidjan
- **of Jamaica: 8** Kingston
- **of Japan: 3** Edo **5** Tokyo
- **of Java: 7** Jakarta **8** Djakarta
- **of Jordan: 5** Amman
- **of Kazakhstan: 7** Alma-Ata
- **of Kenya: 7** Nairobi
- **of Kiribati: 6** Tarawa
- **of Korea (North):
  9** Pyongyang
- **of Korea (South): 5** Seoul
- **of Kuwait: 10** Kuwait City
- **of Kyrgyzstan: 7** Bishkek
  (Frunze)
- **of Laos: 9** Viengchan,
  Vientiane
- **of Latvia: 4** Riga
- **of Lebanon: 6** Beirut
  8 Beyrouth
- **of Lesotho: 6** Maseru
- **of Liberia: 8** Monrovia
- **of Libya: 7** Tripoli

of **Liechtenstein: 5** Vaduz
of **Lithuania: 5** Vilna **6** Kausas **7** Vilnius
of **Luxembourg:**
10 Luxembourg
of **Macedonia: 6** Skopje
of **Madagascar:**
10 Tananarive
12 Antananarivo
of **Malawi: 8** Lilongwe
of **Malaysia: 11** Kuala Lumpur
of **Maldives: 4** Male
of **Mali: 6** Bamako
of **Malta: 8** Valletta
of **Mauritania: 10** Nouakchott
of **Mauritius: 9** Port Louis
of **Mexico: 10** Mexico City
of **Moldova: 8** Chisinau, Kishinev
of **Monaco: 11** Monaco-Ville
of **Mongolia: 9** Ulan Bator
of **Montenegro: 7** Cetinje
8 Titograd **9** Podgorica
of **Morocco: 5** Rabat
6 Rabbat
of **Mozambique: 6** Maputo
15 Lourenco Marques
of **Myanmar: 6** Yangon
7 Rangoon
of **Namibia: 8** Windhoek
of **Nauru: 13** Yaren District
of **Nepal: 8** Katmandu
9 Kathmandu
of **Netherlands: 8** The Hague
9 Amsterdam
of **New Guinea: 11** Port Moresby
of **New Zealand:**
10 Wellington
of **Nicaragua: 7** Managua
of **Niger: 6** Niamey
of **Nigeria: 5** Abuja, Lagos
of **Norway: 4** Oslo
11 Christiania
of **Oman: 6** Masqat, Muscat

of **Pakistan: 9** Islamabad
of **Panama: 10** Panama City
of **Paraguay: 8** Asuncion
of **Peru: 4** Lima
of **the Philippines: 6** Manila
of **Poland: 6** Warsaw
of **Portugal: 6** Lisbon
of **Puerto Rico: 7** San Juan
of **Qatar: 4** Doha **7** al-Dawha
of **Romania: 9** Bucharest
of **Russia: 6** Moscow
of **Rwanda: 6** Kigali
of **Samoa (American): 8** Pago Pago
of **Samoa (Western): 4** Apia
of **San Marino: 9** San Marino
of **Sao Tome and Principe:**
7 Sao Tome
of **Sardinia: 8** Cagliari
of **Saudi Arabia: 6** Riyadh
of **Scotland: 9** Edinburgh
of **Senegal: 5** Dakar
of **Seychelles: 8** Victoria
of **Sicily: 7** Palermo
of **Sierra Leone: 8** Freetown
of **Sikkim: 7** Gangtok
of **Singapore: 9** Singapore
of **Slovakia: 10** Bratislava
of **Slovenia: 9** Ljubljana
of **the Solomon Islands:**
7 Honiara
of **Somalia: 9** Mogadishu
10 Mogadiscio
of **South Africa: 8** Cape Town, Pretoria
12 Bloemfontein
of **Spain: 6** Madrid
of **Sri Lanka: 7** Colombo
of **the Sudan: 8** Khartoum
of **Suriname: 10** Paramaribo
of **Swaziland: 7** Mbabane
of **Sweden: 9** Stockholm
of **Switzerland: 4** Bern
of **Syria: 8** Damascus
of **Taiwan: 6** Taipei

of **Tajikistan: 8** Dushanbe
of **Tanzania: 11** Dar es Salaam
of **Thailand: 6** Bankok
7 Bangkok **8** Thonburi
9 Ayutthaya
of **Tibet: 5** Lassa, Lhasa
of **Togo: 4** Lome
of **Tonga: 9** Nukualofa
of **Trinidad and Tobago:**
11 Port of Spain
of **Tunisia: 5** Tunis
of **Turkey: 6** Ankara
of **Turkmenistan:**
9 Ashkhabad
of **Tuvalu: 8** Funafuti
of **Uganda: 7** Kampala
of **Ukraine: 4** Kiev
of **United Arab Emirates:**
8 Abu Dhabi
of **United States: 12** Washington DC
of **Upper Volta:**
11 Ouagadougou
of **Uruguay: 10** Montevideo
of **Uzbekistan: 8** Tashkent
of **Vanuatu: 4** Vila
of **Venezuela: 7** Caracas
of **Vietnam: 5** Hanoi
6 Saigon
of **Wales: 7** Cardiff
of **Western Sahara: 6** Al Aiun **7** El Aaiun
of **Western Samoa: 4** Apia
of **Yemen (North): 4** Sana
5 Sanaa
of **Yemen (South): 4** Aden
14 Madinat al-Shaab
of **Yugoslavia: 7** Beograd
8 Belgrade
of **Zaire: 8** Kinshasa
of **Zambia: 6** Lusaka
of **Zimbabwe: 6** Harare
9 Salisbury

cast: 10 Errol Flynn **12** Lionel Atwill **13** Basil Rathbone **17** Olivia de Havilland

Captain Hook
character in: 8 Peter Pan
author: 6 Barrie

Captain Horatio Hornblower
author: 10 C S Forester

Captains Courageous
author: 14 Rudyard Kipling
director: 13 Victor Fleming
cast: 12 Mickey Rooney, Spencer Tracy **13** John Carradine, Melvyn Douglas **15** Lionel Barrymore **18** Freddie Bartholomew
Oscar for: 5 actor (Tracy)

Captain's Daughter, The
author: 16 Alexander Pushkin

Captain Video and His Video Rangers
character: 7 Dr Pauli **9** The Ranger **12** Captain Video
cast: 7 Al Hodge **10** Hal Conklin **11** Don Hastings **13** Richard Coogan
slogan: 29 Guardian of the Safety of the World
villain: 4 Atar **7** Nargola **8** Dahoumie, Kul of Eos **9** Dr Clysmok **12** Heng Foo Seeng **14** Mook the Moon Man
gimmick: 5 Tobor **9** Discatron **11** Atomic Rifle **16** Barrier of Silence, Radio Scillograph **17** Cosmic Ray Vibrator **18** Opticon Scillometer **19** Cloak of Invisibility, Trisonic Compensator
spaceship: 6 Galaxy

caption 5 title **6** legend **7** heading, subhead **8** headline, subtitle **11** explanation

captious 4 mean **5** picky, testy **6** ornery **7** carping, cutting, peevish **8** caviling, contrary, niggling, perverse, petulant, picayune, snappish **9** fractious, querulous **10** belittling, censorious, nitpicking **11** deprecating **12** cantankerous, faultfinding **13** hypercritical

captivate 4 lure **5** charm **6** dazzle, enamor, seduce **7** attract, bewitch, delight, enchant, win over **8** enthrall **9** carry away, enrapture, fascinate, hypnotize, infatuate, mesmerize, transport **13** turn the head of **14** take the fancy of

captivated 7 charmed, pleased 9 delighted, enchanted 10 enraptured, enthralled, spellbound

captivating 7 winning, winsome 8 adorable, charming, dazzling, engaging, fetching, magnetic 9 appealing, beguiling, disarming 10 attractive, bewitching, delightful, enchanting, entrancing 11 enthralling, fascinating, mesmerizing 12 ingratiating, irresistible

captive 5 caged 6 penned 7 hostage 8 confined, enslaved, interned, locked up, prisoner 9 oppressed 10 imprisoned, subjugated 12 incarcerated

captivity 7 bondage, holding, slavery 9 servitude 10 detainment 12 imprisonment

capture 3 bag, nab 4 bust, grab, snag, take, trap 5 catch, grasp, pinch, seize, snare 6 arrest, collar, taking 7 bagging, ensnare, procure, seizure, snaring 8 catching, trapping 9 apprehend, collaring, ensnaring, lay hold of 12 apprehension, laying hold of, take prisoner 14 taking prisoner 15 take into custody

Capulet family
  characters in: 14 Romeo and Juliet
  author: 11 Shakespeare

Capys
  father: 9 Assaracus
  son: 7 Laocoon 8 Anchises
  grandson: 6 Aeneas
  founded: 5 Capua
  warned against: 11 Trojan horse

car 4 auto, heap 5 buggy, coach, diner, motor 6 boxcar, hot rod, jalopy, wheels 7 flivver, machine, sleeper, vehicle 8 carriage 9 tin lizzie 10 automobile 12 motor vehicle
  kind: 4 coal 5 cable, horse, motor 6 cattle, dining, parlor, street 7 baggage, freight, Pullman, railway 8 sleeping

Car
  father: 9 Phoroneus
  mother: 5 Cerdo
  founder of: 6 Megara

carabiniere 9 policeman

Caracas
  birthplace of: 12 Simon Bolivar
  capital of: 9 Venezuela
  founder: 13 Diego de Losada
  museum: 7 Bolivar 8 Criolan 11 Colonial Art, Raul Santana
  river: 6 Guaire

carafe 5 flask 6 bottle, vessel 9 container

carapace 4 case 5 shell 6 lorica, shield 7 carapax 8 calipash, covering 11 turtle shell

Caravaggio, Michelangelo Merisi da
  born: 5 Italy 10 Caravaggio
  artwork: 12 Young Bacchus 14 Burial of St Lucy 16 Raising of Lazarus 17 The Supper at Emmaus 18 Calling of St Matthew, The Life of St Matthew 20 St Matthew and the Angel 21 The Conversion of St Paul 23 The Crucifixion of St Peter 30 The Beheading of St John the Baptist

caravan 4 band, file, line 5 queue, train, troop 6 coffle, column, convoy, parade, string 7 company, cortege, retinue 9 cavalcade, chain gang, entourage, motorcade 10 procession, wagon train

caravansary 3 inn 5 hotel 8 hostelry

caraway
  botanical name: 10 Carum carvi
  origin: 6 Europe 9 Asia Minor 14 the Netherlands
  liqueur: 6 Kummel
  candy-covered caraway seeds: 6 comfit 12 whisky-killer
  use: 4 pork, soup, stew 8 rye bread

carbohydrate
  consists of: 5 water 6 carbon, oxygen 8 hydrogen 13 carbon dioxide
  kinds: 5 sugar 6 simple, starch, xylose 7 complex, glucose, lactose, maltose, sucrose 8 dextrose, fructose 9 cellulose

carbon 4 coal, coke, copy 8 charcoal 9 lampblack
  chemical symbol: 1 C

carbon copy 5 clone 7 replica 9 duplicate, facsimile 12 reproduction

carbonize 4 burn, char, sear 5 singe 6 scorch 10 incinerate

carbuncle 4 boil, sore 11 excrescence 12 inflammation

carcass 4 body, bouk, husk, wall 5 shell, stiff, trunk 6 corpse 7 cadaver, carrion, remains 8 dead body, fireball, skeleton 9 framework

carcinoma 5 tumor 6 cancer 8 neoplasm 10 malignancy 15 malignant growth

card 4 bill 6 ticket 7 program 8 postcard
  kind: 7 calling, get-well, playing 8 birthday, business, greeting 9 Christmas, Valentine

cardamon
  botanical name: 19 Elettaria cardamomum
  origin: 4 Asia 5 India 13 southeast Asia
  related to: 6 ginger
  color: 5 black
  use: 5 curry 7 dessert 12 Danish pastry

Cardea
  origin: 5 Roman
  goddess of: 6 family 10 door hinges

Cardew, Cecily
  character in: 27 The Importance of Being Earnest
  author: 5 Wilde

card game *see* box

Cardiff
  capital of: 5 Wales

cardigan 5 corgi 6 jacket, wampus 7 sweater 10 Welsh corgi

cardinal 3 key, top 4 head, main 5 basic, chief, first, prime, vital 6 cherry, claret 7 carmine, central, deep-red, highest, leading, primary, scarlet 8 blood-red, dominant, foremost, greatest 9 essential, intrinsic, necessary, paramount, principal, uppermost 10 elementary, preeminent, underlying 11 fundamental, outstanding, predominant, wine-colored 13 indispensable, most important

care 4 heed, load, mind, want, wish 5 grief, pains, worry 6 bother, charge, desire, effort, misery, regard, sorrow, strain, stress 7 anguish, anxiety, caution, concern, control, custody, keeping, sadness, thought, trouble 8 distress, hardship, nuisance, pressure, vexation 9 annoyance, attention, be worried, diligence, exactness, heartache, vigilance 10 affliction, management, precaution, protection, solicitude 11 application, be concerned, bother about, carefulness, supervision, tribulation, unhappiness 12 ministration, trouble about, watchfulness 13 attentiveness, consideration 14 be interested in, circumspection, discrimination, fastidiousness, meticulousness, responsibility, scrupulousness 17 conscientiousness

card game 3 loo, war **4** brag, fish, skat, vint **5** ombre, poker, rummy, whist **6** boston, bridge, casino, chemmy, ecarte, euchre, go fish, hearts, memory, piquet, pocher **7** bezique, canasta, coon-can, Old Maid, plafond, primero **8** baccarat, conquian, cribbage, gin rummy, napoleon, patience, pinochle, slapjack **9** blackjack, pelmanism, solitaire, spoil five, twenty-one **11** chemin de fer, crazy eights **13** concentration **14** contract bridge **16** beggar-my-neighbor, trente et quarante

  card names: 4 ace **4** fool, jack, king, trey **5** joker, queen

  combination of cards: 4 meld

  one hand or round: 5 trick

  rulebook by: 5 Hoyle

  suits: 4 club **5** heart, spade **7** diamond

   French: 5 coeur, pique **6** trefle **7** carreau

   German: 4 grun, herz, piks **5** karos, treff **6** eichel **7** schelle

   Italian: 5 coppa, cuori, fiori, spada **6** denaro, picchi, quadri **7** bastone

   Spanish: 3 oro **4** copa **5** basto **6** espada

Careas 6 eunuch

careen 3 tip, yaw **4** lean, list, sway, tilt, veer **5** heave, slant, slope **7** capsize **8** lean over, overturn

career 3 job **4** line, work **7** calling, pursuit **8** activity, business, lifework, vocation **10** employment, livelihood, occupation, profession, walk of life

care for 4 like, mind, tend **5** fancy **7** oversee **8** attend to, wait upon **9** look after, watch over **10** minister to, provide for

carefree 3 gay **4** glad **5** happy, jolly, sunny **6** breezy, elated, jaunty, joyous **7** buoyant, gleeful, radiant, relaxed, smiling **8** cheerless, cheerful, jubilant, laughing **9** easygoing **10** full of life, optimistic, untroubled **11** free-and-easy **12** happy-go-lucky, light-hearted, without

worry **13** in high spirits **23** without a worry in the world

  French: 9 sans souci

careful 4 fine, nice, wary **5** alert, chary, exact, fussy **7** correct, guarded, heedful, mindful, on guard, precise, prudent, tactful **8** accurate, cautious, diligent, discreet, vigilant, watchful **9** attentive, concerned, judicious, observant, regardful **10** fastidious, meticulous, particular, scrupulous, solicitous, thoughtful **11** circumspect, painstaking, punctilious **13** conscientious

carefulness 7 caution **10** steadiness **12** deliberation **14** circumspection

careless 3 lax **4** rash **5** messy, slack **6** casual, sloppy, untidy **7** inexact, offhand **8** heedless, mindless, slapdash, slipshod, slovenly **9** forgetful, imprecise, incorrect, negligent, unmindful **10** disorderly, inaccurate, neglectful, nonchalant, unthinking, untroubled **11** indifferent, thoughtless, unconcerned **12** absent-minded, devil-may-care **13** inconsiderate, lackadaisical

carelessness 6 laxity **7** neglect **9** messiness, slackness **10** inaccuracy, negligence, sloppiness, untidiness **11** imprecision, inexactness **12** heedlessness, indiscretion, slovenliness **13** unmindfulness **14** disorderliness **15** thoughtlessness **16** absentmindedness, irresponsibility

Care of Time, The
  author: 10 Eric Ambler

caress 3 hug, pat, pet **5** clasp, touch **6** cuddle, fondle, stroke **7** embrace, petting, toy with **8** fondling, stroking **11** gentle touch

caretaker 6 keeper, porter, warden **7** curator, janitor, steward **8** overseer, watchman **9** concierge, custodian **10** gatekeeper **14** superintendent

careworn 7 haggard, worried **8** fatigued, troubled **11** pessimistic

cargo 4 load **5** goods **6** burden, lading **7** freight **8** shipment **11** consignment, merchandise

Carib
  language family: 7 Cariban
  location: 7 Guianas **9** Caribbean, Venezuela **12** South America
  custom: 11 cannibalism

Cariban
  tribe: 5 Carib **6** Acawai, Akawai

Caribbean 3 sea
  channel: 7 Yucatan
  city: 6 Havana **7** San Juan **8** Santiago **10** Guantanamo **12** Port au Prince **13** Santo Domingo **15** Charlotte Amalie
  Indian: 5 Carib **6** Arawak
  island: 4 Cuba **5** Aruba, Haiti, Nevis **6** Cayman, Nassau, Tobago, Virgin **7** Antigua, Bahamas, Barbuda, Curacao, Grenada, Jamaica, Leeward **8** Anguilla, Dominica, Trinidad, Windward **9** Saint John **10** Guadeloupe, Hispaniola, Martinique, Montserrat, Puerto Rico, Saint Kitts, Saint Lucia **11** Saint Thomas **12** Saint Vincent **14** Lesser Antilles **15** Greater Antilles **19** Dominican Republic, Netherlands Antilles
  language: 6 gullah **10** papiamento
  product: 3 rum **5** fruit, spice, sugar **6** coffee

caricature 4 mock **6** parody, satire **7** lampoon, mockery, takeoff **8** satirize, travesty **9** absurdity, burlesque **10** distortion **12** exaggeration

Carker
  character in: 12 Dombey and Son
  author: 7 Dickens

Carlisle, Kitty
  real name: 13 Katherine Conn
  husband: 8 Moss Hart
  born: 12 New Orleans LA
  roles: 13 She Loves Me Not **14** To Tell the Truth **16** A Night at the Opera **19** Murder at the Vanities

Carlton, Steve (Steven Norman)
  nickname: 5 Lefty
  sport: 8 baseball
  position: 7 pitcher
  team: 20 Philadelphia Phillies

Carlyle, Thomas
  author of: 8 Cromwell **14** Sartor Resartus **17** Frederick the Great **19** The French Revolution **20** Heroes and Hero-Worship

Carmanor
  king of: 5 Crete
  purified: 6 Apollo **7** Artemis

Carme
  daughter: 11 Britomartis

Carmen
  author: 14 Prosper Merimee
  opera by: 5 Bizet
  setting: 7 Seville

character: 7 Don Jose **9** Escamillo, Frasquita

Carmen Jones
director: 13 Otto Preminger
based on opera by: 5 Bizet (Carmen)
   adaptation by: **18** Oscar Hammerstein II
cast: 11 Pearl Bailey **14** Harry Belafonte **16** Dorothy Dandridge

Carmenta
origin: 5 Roman
member of: 7 Camanae
protectress of: 10 childbirth
husband: 7 Evander
son: 7 Evander

carmine 3 red **6** cherry **7** crimson, deep red, scarlet **8** blood red **9** bright red

carnage 8 butchery, massacre **9** blood bath, slaughter

carnal 4 lewd **6** erotic, impure, sexual, sinful, wanton **7** fleshly, immoral, lustful, sensual **8** prurient, sensuous, unchaste, venereal **9** lecherous, salacious **10** lascivious, libidinous, voluptuous

Carnegie, Dale
author of: 33 How To Win Friends and Influence People

carnelian
species: 6 quartz

Carnera, Primo
nickname: 13 the Ambling Alp
sport: 6 boxing
class: 11 heavyweight

Carneus
epithet of: 6 Apollo
alludes to: 11 cornel trees

Carney, Art
real name: 26 Arthur William Matthew Carney
partner: 13 Jackie Gleason
born: 13 Mount Vernon NY
roles: 8 Ed Norton **13** Harry and Tonto (Oscar) **15** The Honeymooners

carnival 4 fair, fete, gala **6** circus **7** holiday, jubilee **8** festival, jamboree, sideshow **9** Mardi Gras **11** celebration

carnivore 3 cat, dog, fox **4** bear, lion, lynx, mink, puma, wolf **5** civet, dingo, fossa, hyena, otter, panda, skunk, tayra, tiger **6** badger, bobcat, coyote, ferret, grison, hyaena, jackal, jaguar, marten, olingo, weasel **7** polecat, raccoon, suricat **8** aardwolf, kinkajou, mongoose **9** meat eater, wolverine **10** cacomistle, coatimundi, flesh eater

carnivorous 9 predatory **10** meat-eating, predaceous **11** flesh-eating

Carnus
occupation: 4 seer
seer of: 6 Apollo
killed by: 10 Heraclidae

carol 4 hymn, noel, sing **5** paean **6** warble **8** canticle **9** song of joy **12** song of praise

Caroline Islands
district: 3 Yap **4** Truk **5** Palau **6** Ponape
inhabitant: 10 Polynesian **11** Micronesian
island: 3 Yap **6** Ponape, Ulithi **8** Nukuroro **10** Babelthuap **14** Kapinamarangi
language: 7 English **10** Polynesian **11** Micronesian
ocean: 7 Pacific

carom 6 bounce, strike **7** collide, rebound, **8** billiard, ricochet **9** bounce off

Caron, Leslie
born: 6 France **19** Boulogne-Billancourt
roles: 4 Gaby, Gigi, Lili **5** Fanny **11** Father Goose **13** Daddy Longlegs **14** The L-Shaped Room **17** An American in Paris

Carothers, Wallace Hume
field: 9 chemistry
discovered: 5 nylon

carousal 4 orgy **5** binge, drunk, spree **7** debauch **9** bacchanal **10** debauchery, saturnalia

carouse 5 drink, party, quaff, revel **6** guzzle, imbibe, tipple **7** roister, wassail **8** live it up **9** make merry **10** go on a binge **11** make whoopee

Carousel
director: 9 Henry King
based on: 6 Liliom
   adaptation by: **21** Rodgers and Hammerstein
cast: 12 Gordon MacRae (Billy Bigelow), Shirley Jones **15** Cameron Mitchell
song: 9 Soliloquy **11** If I Loved You **19** You'll Never Walk Alone

carp 3 nag **5** cavil, chide, decry, knock **6** deride, impugn, jibe at, pick on **7** censure, condemn **8** belittle, complain, reproach **9** criticize, deprecate, disparage, fault-find, find fault **10** disapprove

Carpaccio, Vittore
born: 5 Italy **6** Venice
artwork: 13 Two Courtesans

18 The Dream of St Ursula **19** The Legend of St Ursula **21** St Augustine in his Study **24** St George Killing the Dragon **28** St Augustine's Vision of St Jerome **29** The Arrival of St Ursula at Cologne

carpal
bone of: 5 wrist

carpe diem 11 seize the day **15** enjoy the present

carpenter 6 fitter, joiner **7** builder **8** repairer **10** woodworker **12** cabinetmaker
ant: 10 camponotus
bee: 8 xylocopa
bird: 10 woodpecker
fish: 10 hammerhead
moth: 10 prinoxysus

Carpenter, Harlean
real name of: 10 Jean Harlow

carper 6 critic **7** caviler **9** nitpicker **11** fault-finder

carpet 3 mat, rug **5** cover, layer, sheet **7** blanket, matting **8** covering

Carpetbaggers, The
author: 13 Harold Robbins

Carpo
origin: 5 Greek
member of: 5 Horae
goddess of: 11 summer fruit

Carpophorus
epithet of: 7 Demeter **10** Persephone
means: 11 fruit bearer

Carr, Emily
born: 6 Canada **8** Victoria **15** British Columbia
artwork: 3 Sky **8** Big Raven **14** Blunden Harbour, Kispiax Village **15** Woods and Blue Sky **17** Forest Landscape II **36** Cape Mudge An Indian Family with Totem Pole

Carra, Carlo
born: 5 Italy **9** Quargneto
artwork: 13 Lot's Daughters **16** Metaphysical Muse **20** Patriotic Celebration **29** The Funeral of the Anarchist Galli

Carradine, David
father: 4 John
half-brothers: 5 Keith **6** Robert
born: 11 Hollywood CA
roles: 6 Kung Fu **13** Bound for Glory **14** The Serpent's Egg

Carradine, John
real name: 21 Richmond Reed Carradine
son: 5 David, Keith **6** Robert

born: 18 Greenwich Village NY
roles: 9 Cleopatra, Kidnapped 10 Stagecoach 12 Count Dracula 15 The Invisible Man 18 Captains Courageous, The Three Musketeers

Carradine, Keith
father: 4 John
brother: 6 Robert
half-brother: 5 David
born: 10 San Mateo CA
roles: 9 Nashville 10 Pretty Baby

Carraway, Nick
character in: 14 The Great Gatsby
author: 10 Fitzgerald

Carrere, John Merven
partner: 14 Thomas Hastings
architect of: 19 House Office Building (Washington DC) 20 New York Public Library, Senate Office Building (Washington DC) 21 Henry Clay Frick mansion (now Frick Collection NYC)
style: 18 French neo-classical, Spanish Renaissance

carriage 3 air, rig 4 mien 5 buggy, coach, poise, wagon 6 aspect, manner 7 bearing, posture, vehicle 8 attitude, behavior, demeanor, presence 10 appearance, conveyance, deportment 11 comportment

Carrie
author: 11 Stephen King

carried away 7 excited, frantic, seduced 8 ecstatic, frenzied, overcome 9 delirious 10 fascinated, infatuated 11 transported

carrier 3 bus, car 4 rack, wave 5 agent, barge, plane, coach, drain, ferry, train, truck, wagon 6 bearer, boxcar, pigeon, porter 7 airline, channel, mailman, postman, trucker, vehicle 8 airplane, aircraft, carriage, catalyst, railroad 9 messenger 11 transmitter, wheelbarrow

carrion 5 bones, offal, waste 6 corpse, refuse 7 cadaver, carcass, garbage, remains, wastage 8 crowbait, dead body, leavings

Carroll, Leo G
born: 6 Weedon 7 England
roles: 6 Topper 7 Rebecca 9 Suspicion 10 Spellbound 11 Cosmo Topper 15 A Christmas Carol, The Man from UNCLE, The Paradine Case 16 Father of the Bride, North by Northwest

Carroll, Lewis
real name: 22 Charles Lutwidge Dodgson
author of: 11 Jabberwocky 22 Through the Looking Glass 28 Alice's Adventures in Wonderland

carrousel 4 ride, tray 8 conveyor 9 quadrille, whirligig 10 tournament 12 merry-go-round

carry 3 lug, run 4 bear, cart, haul, lift, move, prop, ship, take, tote 5 brace, bring, fetch, offer, print, shift, stock 6 convey, hold up, supply, uphold 7 conduct, deliver, display, publish, release, support, sustain 8 displace, maintain, shoulder, transfer, transmit 9 broadcast, transport 10 keep on hand 11 communicate, disseminate

carry away 4 lure 6 abduct, kidnap, seduce 7 attract 9 captivate, fascinate, infatuate, transport

carry off 5 seize, steal 6 abduct, kidnap 7 bear off 9 succeed at 11 get away with

carry out 2 do 6 effect, wind up 7 achieve, execute, fulfill, perform, realize 8 complete, conclude, dispatch 9 discharge, dispose of, succeed at 10 accomplish, bring about 11 bring to pass

carry through 6 effect, finish 7 achieve, develop, execute, fulfill, perform, realize 8 complete, conclude 9 discharge 10 accomplish, consummate, effectuate, perpetuate 13 put into effect

Carson, Rachel Louise
field: 7 biology
studied: 9 pollution
author of: 12 Silent Spring 14 The Sea Around Us 15 The Edge of the Sea

Carstone, Richard
character in: 10 Bleak House
author: 7 Dickens

cart 3 gig, lug 4 bear, dray, haul, move, take, tote, trap 5 bring, carry, fetch, truck, wagon 6 barrow, convey 7 schlepp, tumbrel 8 curricle, transfer, transmit 9 transport 10 handbarrow, transplant, two-wheeler 11 wheelbarrow
kind: 2 go 3 dog, tip 4 dump, hand, push

carte blanche 7 license 9 a free hand, free reign 10 blank check 12 open sanction 13 full authority 18 unconditional power

cartel 4 pool 5 chain, trust 7 combine 8 monopoly 9 syndicate 10 consortium, federation 11 corporation

Carter, Charles
real name of: 14 Charlton Heston

Carter, James Earl, Jr *see box, p. 160*

Carthage *see* 7 Tunisia

carton 3 box 4 case 5 crate 9 container 11 packing case 12 cardboard box, packing crate 18 cardboard container

Carton, Sydney
character in: 16 A Tale of Two Cities
author: 7 Dickens

cartoon 5 comic 6 design, satire, sketch 7 drawing, funnies, picture 8 animated 10 caricature, comicstrip

cartoonist 6 artist, drawer 7 gagster 12 caricaturist
famous: 6 Al Capp, C C Beck, Ted Key 8 Herblock (Herbert L. Block), Jim Davis, Roy Crane 9 Bud Fisher, Chic Young, Dik Browne, Frank King, Hal Foster, Ham Fisher, Walt Kelly 10 Bob Montana, Harold Gray, Johnny Hart, Mort Walker, Paul Conrad, Thomas Nast, Walt Disney 11 Alex Raymond, Bill Mauldin, Dale Messick, David Levine, Ding Darling, Elzie C. Segar, Hank Ketcham, Max Beerbohm, Rollin Kirby 12 Brad Anderson, Chester Gould, Garry Trudeau, James Thurber, Jeff MacNelly, Jules Feiffer, Milton Caniff, Rube Goldberg, Rudolph Dirks, Virgil Partch 13 Charles Addams, Charles Schulz, George McManus, Honore Daumier, Joseph Keppler, Saul Steinberg 14 Homer Davenport, William Hogarth 15 Ernie Bushmiller, Patrick Oliphant, Richard Outcault 16 Benjamin Franklin, George Cruikshank

cartridge 3 dud 4 case, tape 5 blank, shell 6 holder 7 capsule, package 8 cassette, cylinder 9 container

Cartwright, Edmund
nationality: 7 English
inventor of: 9 power loom 18 wool-combing machine

carve 3 hew, saw 4 etch, form, hack, mold, rend, turn, work 5 allot, cleve, cut up, model, shape, slash, slice, split 6 chisel, divide, incise, sculpt

Carter, James Earl, Jr
nickname: **3** Hot **5** Jimmy **7** Hotshot
presidential rank: **11** thirty-ninth
party: **10** Democratic
state represented: **2** GA **7** Georgia
defeated: **4** (Gerald R) Ford **8** (Eugene) McCarthy
vice president: **7** (Walter Frederick "Fritz") Mondale
cabinet:*state:* **5** (Cyrus R) Vance **6** (Edmund S) Muskie-
 treasury: **6** (G William) Miller **10** (W Michael) Blumen-
 thal*defense:* **5** (Harold) Brown*attorney general:*
 4 (Griffin B) Bell **9** (Benjamin R) Civiletti*interior:*
 6 (Cecil D) Andrus*agriculture:* **8** (Robert S) Bergland-
 commerce: **5** (Juanita Morris) Kreps **9** (Philip M)
 Klutznick*labor:* **8** (F Ray) Marshall*HEW:* **6** (Patricia
 Roberts) Harris **8** (Joseph A) Califano (Jr)*HUD:* **6** (Patricia Roberts) Harris **8** (Moon) Landrieu*transportation:*
 5 (Brockman) Adams **11** (Neil E) Goldschmidt*education:*
 10 (Shirley) Hufstedler
born: **2** GA **6** Plains
education: **14** US Naval Academy **26** Georgia Southwestern
 College **28** Georgia Institute of Technology
religion: **15** Southern Baptist
interests: **5** track **6** tennis **7** fishing, hunting **8** football, soft-
 ball **10** basketball **12** cross country **13** square dancing
 17 collecting bottles*music:* **8** folk rock **9** classical
author: **13** Why Not the Best?
political career: **12** state senator*governor of:* **7** Georgia
civilian career: **12** peanut farmer
military service: **6** US Navy
notable events of lifetime/term: **6** SALT II **9** Love Canal,
 recession **18** Habitat for Humanity*deaths at:* **9** Jonestow-
 n*eruption of:* **13** Mount St Helens*first baby from:*
 8 test tube*hostages taken in:* **4** Iran*nuclear accident:*
 15 Three Mile Island*pipeline:* **5** Alcan*scandal/investiga-
 tion:* **6** Abscam **9** Bert Lance, Koreagate **11** Billy
 Carter*Supreme Court case:* **5** Bakke*treaty:* **11** Panama
 Canal **16** Camp David Accords
father: **11** James Earl Sr
mother: **7** Lillian (Gordy)*nickname:* **11** Miss Lillian
siblings: **6** Gloria **17** William "Billy" Alton **19** Ruth Carter
 Stapleton
wife: **8** Rosalynn (Smith)
children: **7** Amy Lynn **11** John William (Jack) **12** James
 Earl III (Chip) **13** Donnel Jeffrey (Jeff)
first lady: **36** Presidential Commission on Mental Health*author:* **19** First Lady from Plains

7 engrave, fashion, pattern,
quarter **8** block out, dissever
9 apportion, sculpture

Carver, George Washington
field: **9** chemistry
worked in: **11** agriculture
studied: **6** peanut **7** soybean
 11 sweet potato

carving 5 cameo **8** intaglio,
triptych **9** sculpture

Carya
origin: **8** Laconian
form: **6** maiden
home: **7** Laconia
changed into: **10** walnut tree
changed by: **8** Dionysus

Caryatis
epithet of: **7** Artemis
means: **15** of the walnut tree

Casablanca
director: **13** Michael Curtiz
cast: **10** Peter Lorre **11** Claude
 Rains (Louis), Conrad Veidt,
 Paul Henreid (Victor Laslo)
 12 Dooley Wilson (Sam),
 13 Ingrid Bergman (Ilsa
 Lund) **14** Humphrey Bogart
 (Rick) **17** Sydney Greenstreet
Oscar for: **7** picture
song: **12** As Time Goes By

Casanova 3 cad, rip **4** beau,
lech, roue, wolf **5** lover, Romeo, swain, wooer **6** chaser,
lecher, suitor **7** admirer, bounder, Don Juan, gallant, rounder
8 cavalier, Lothario, lover boy,
paramour **9** ladies' man, libertine, womanizer **10** lady-killer,
profligate **11** philanderer

Casby
character in: **12** Little Dorrit
author: **7** Dickens

cascade 4 fall, gush, pour, rush
5 chute, falls, surge **6** plunge,
rapids, tumble **7** Niagara **8** cataract **9** waterfall

case 3 bin, box **4** plea, suit,
tray **5** cause, chest, cover,
crate, event **6** action, affair,
appeal, carton, debate, injury,
jacket, matter, sheath, victim
7 cabinet, concern, disease, dispute, episode, example, hearing, housing, inquiry, invalid,
lawsuit, overlay, patient, wrapper **8** argument, business, covering, envelope, incident,
instance, sufferer **9** condition,
container, happening, incidence, sheathing, situation
10 litigation, occurrence, proceeding, protection, receptacle,
sick person **11** controversy
12 circumstance, illustration

case in point 7 example **8** instance **12** illustration

**Case of Sergeant Grischa,
The**
author: **11** Arnold Zweig

Casey
nickname of: **20** Charles Dillon Stengel

cash 5 bills, bread, coins,
dough, money **6** change, redeem **8** currency, exchange
9 bank notes **10** paper money
11 legal tender **13** turn into
money **14** coin of the realm

cashier 6 banker, bursar,
purser, teller **9** treasurer
10 bank teller

cash register
invented by: 5 Ritty

casing 4 skin 5 frame
9 sheathing

Casino Royale
author: 10 Ian Fleming

cask 3 keg, tub, tun, vat
4 butt, pipe 6 barrel
8 hogshead

casket 4 case, pall 5 chest
6 coffer, coffin 8 jewel box
11 sarcophagus

Cask of Amontillado, The
author: 13 Edgar Allan Poe
character: 9 Fortunato,
Montresor

Cassandra
also: 9 Alexandra
father: 5 Priam
mother: 6 Hecuba
brother: 5 Paris
concubine of: 9 Agamemnon
son: 6 Pelops 9 Teledamus
cursed by: 6 Apollo
violated by: 4 Ajax
killed by: 12 Clytemnestra

Cassatt, Mary
born: 15 Allegheny City PA
artwork: 6 La Loge 7 The
Bath 11 The Cup of Tea
12 After the Bath, Woman
Bathing 14 Gathering Fruit
15 Reading Le Figaro
20 Girl Arranging Her Hair,
Woman and Child Drawing

Cassavetes, John
wife: 12 Gena Rowlands
born: 9 New York NY
roles/films: 8 Husbands
10 The Tempest 13 Rose-
mary's Baby, The Dirty
Dozen 23 A Woman Under
the Influence

casserole 4 dish, food, mold
6 tureen, vessel 8 saucepan

Cassio
character in: 7 Othello
author: 11 Shakespeare

Cassiopeia
husband: 7 Cepheus
daughter: 9 Andromeda
offended: 7 Nereids

Cassius
also: 12 Caius Cassius
character in: 12 Julius
Caesar
author: 11 Shakespeare

Cass Timberlane
author: 13 Sinclair Lewis
character: 11 Bradd Criley
24 Jinny Marshland
Timberlane

cast 3 set, sow 4 fire, form,
hurl, look, mien, mint, mold,
pick, shed, toss 5 fling, heave,
model, pitch, shape, shoot,

sling, stamp, throw 6 actors,
assign, casing, choose, direct,
launch, let fly, propel, sculpt,
spread, troupe 7 appoint, company, deposit, diffuse, pattern,
players, project, scatter 8 catapult, disperse 9 broadcast, circulate, discharge, launching,
semblance 10 appearance, distribute, impression, performers, propulsion 11 disseminate,
give parts to 16 dramatis
personae

Castalia
origin: 5 Greek
sacred: 6 spring
location: 14 Mount Parnassus
sacred to: 5 Muses 6 Apollo
source of: 11 inspiration

Castalides see 5 Muses

cast aside 4 junk, shed 6 desert, reject 7 abandon, discard,
forsake, neglect 8 get rid of,
renounce, throw out 9 repudiate, throw away
11 discontinue

cast a spell on 5 charm
7 bewitch, conjure, enchant
8 entrance 11 work magic on

cast aspersions on 5 knock,
scorn 6 deride, malign 7 disdain, put down, run down,
sneer at 8 belittle, pooh-pooh
9 criticize, disparage 13 find
fault with

castaway 3 bum 4 hobo, waif
5 exile, leper, nomad, rover,
stray 6 outlaw, pariah 7 Ishmael, outcast, vagrant 8 deportee, derelict, renegade,
unperson, vagabond, wan-
derer 9 foundling, nonperson
10 expatriate 11 beachcomber,
offscouring, untouchable
12 down-and-outer 15 knight-
of-the-road

cast away 4 junk 6 launch,
propel, reject 7 abandon, discard, toss out 8 get rid of,
pitch out, throw out 9 throw
away

cast down 5 abase, droop,
lower 6 abased, deject, droopy,
humble, sadden 7 depress,
humbled, lowered 8 bring low,
dejected, disgrace, saddened
9 depressed, disgraced, humiliate 10 brought low, dis-
hearten, humiliated
11 crestfallen 12 disheartened

caste 4 rank 6 status 7 lineage,
station 8 position 9 condition
Hindu: 5 sudra, varna
6 vaisya 7 brahman
9 kshatriya

castigate 5 chide, scold 6 berate, punish, rebuke 7 bawl
out, censure, chasten, chew

out, correct, reprove, upbraid
8 admonish, chastise, penalize,
reproach 9 criticize, dress
down, reprimand 10 discipline,
take to task 15 call on the
carpet 16 haul over the coals

castigation 9 reprimand
10 chastening, correction, discipline, penalizing, punishment 12 chastisement

Castiglione, Baldassare
author of: 20 The Book of
the Courtier

castle 4 hall, keep 5 manor,
tower, villa 6 palace 7 chateau, citadel, mansion 8 fortress 10 stronghold

Castle, The
author: 10 Franz Kafka
character: 1 K

Castle of Otranto, The
author: 13 Horace Walpole
character: 6 Conrad 7 Al-
fonso, Manfred, Matilda
8 Isabella, Theodore 12 Father Jerome

Castle Rackrent
author: 14 Maria Edgeworth

cast off 4 shed 6 reject 7 discard, set sail, toss out 8 throw
off, throw out 9 repudiate,
throw away 11 weigh anchor

Castor and Pollux
also: 8 Dioscuri 10 Poly-
deuces, Tyndaridae
form: 8 twin sons
mother: 4 Leda
father: 4 Zeus
sister: 5 Helen
12 Clytemnestra
members of: 9 Argonauts
protectors of: 6 seamen

cast out 4 oust 5 eject, evict,
exile, expel 6 banish, reject
7 discard, dismiss, turn out
8 drive out, send away, throw
out

cast up 4 spew 5 eject, expel,
vomit 6 spew up 7 cough up,
throw up 8 disgorge

casual 4 cool, so-so 5 blase,
vague 6 chance, random,
sporty 7 offhand, passing, relaxed 8 informal 9 easygoing,
haphazard, non-dressy, unplanned 10 accidental, fortuitous, incidental, nonchalant,
unarranged, undesigned, undirected, unexpected, unforeseen 11 half-hearted,
indifferent, unlooked for
13 lackadaisical, serendipitous,
unintentional 14 indiscriminate, unpremeditated

Casuals of the Sea
author: 12 William McFee

casualty 6 injury, victim 7 injured 8 fatality

casuistry 5 guile 6 deceit 7 fallacy, sophism 8 subtlety 9 Jesuitism, quibbling, sophistry 10 nitpicking 12 equivocation, pettifoggery, speciousness 13 deceptiveness, hair-splitting 14 sophistication

casus belli 10 cause of war

Casy, Jim
character in: 16 The Grapes of Wrath
author: 9 Steinbeck

cat see **box**

cataclysm 4 blow 7 debacle 8 calamity, disaster, upheaval 11 catastrophe, devastation

cataclysmic 4 dire 6 tragic 7 ruinous 10 calamitous, disastrous 12 catastrophic, earth-shaking

catacomb 4 tomb 7 ossuary 8 cemetery 10 passageway 12 burial ground

Cataebates
epithet of: 4 Zeus
means: 9 descender

catafalque 3 box 4 pall 6 casket, coffin

catalog, catalogue 4 file, list, post, roll 5 index 6 record, roster 7 listing 8 classify, register, syllabus, tabulate 9 directory, enumerate, inventory

Catamitus see 8 Ganymede

Cat and Mouse
author: 11 Gunter Grass

catapult 4 cast, hurl, toss 5 fling, heave, pitch, shoot, sling, throw 6 hurtle, propel 9 slingshot 13 hurling engine

cataract 5 falls, flood 6 deluge, rapids 7 cascade, torrent 8 downpour 9 waterfall 10 inundation

catastrophe 4 blow 5 havoc 6 mishap, ravage 7 debacle, scourge, tragedy 8 calamity, disaster 9 cataclysm 10 affliction, misfortune 11 devastation

catastrophic 6 tragic 7 ruinous 10 calamitous, disastrous 11 cataclysmic

catcall 3 boo 4 gibe, hiss, hoot, jeer 7 whistle 8 heckling 9 raspberry 10 Bronx cheer

catch 3 bag, bat, get, hit, nab 4 bait, bang, belt, bump, bust, dupe, feel, find, fool, grab, hasp, haul, hoax, hook, lock, lure, make, snag, snap, spot, take, trap 5 booty, break, charm, clasp, crack, get to,

---

cat 3 pet 4 puss, whip 5 kitty, pussy, tabby 6 feline, kitten, mouser, tomcat
anatomy: 3 paw 4 loin, nape, rump, tail 5 break, flank, shank 6 feeler 7 dewclaw, leather, whisker 8 vibrissa 10 metatarsus
breed/kind: 3 tom 4 coon, Eyra, lion, lynx, Manx, puma 5 alley, civet, hyena, kitty, Korat, tabby, tiger 6 Angola, angora, bobcat, cougar, jaguar, ocelot, serval 7 Burmese, caracal, cheetah, leopard, linsang, Maltese, panther, Persian, polecat, Siamese, Turkish, wildcat 8 Balinese, Cheshire, Egyptian, ringtail 9 Himalayan, shorthair 10 Abyssinian, chinchilla 11 Russian blue 13 tortoise-shell
combining form: 5 aelur, ailur, felin 6 aeluro, ailuro, felino
Egyptian goddess of: 4 Bast
extinct: 10 saber-tooth
family: 7 Felidae
famous: 6 Morris 8 Cheshire, Garfield, Kilkenny 9 Mehitabel 10 Heathcliff
fastest: 7 cheetah
fear of: 12 aelurophobia, ailurophobia
female: 5 queen 7 lioness, tigress 8 wheencat 9 grimalkin
genus: 5 Felis
grinning: 8 Cheshire
group: 7 clowder, clutter
group of kittens: 6 kendle, kindle
lover: 11 aelurophile, ailurophile
male: 3 gib, tom 6 tomcat
ring-tailed: 6 serval 10 cacomistle
tailless: 4 Manx
young: 6 kitten

---

grasp, hitch, latch, prize, reach, seize, sense, smack, smite, snare, trick, whack, yield 6 allure, arrest, betray, buffet, collar, corner, corral, dazzle, deceit, delude, descry, detect, expose, fasten, fathom, kicker, snatch, strike, take in, turn on, unmask 7 attract, bewitch, capture, closure, deceive, delight, discern,

---

enchant, ensnare, find out, gimmick, mislead, rasping, seizure 8 catching, come upon, contract, coupling, discover, drawback, enthrall, hoodwink, overtake, perceive, pickings, surprise 9 apprehend, bamboozle, captivate, carry away, enrapture, fastening, intercept, lay hold of, play false, recognize, transport 10 comprehend, understand 11 take captive 12 break out with, come down with, disadvantage, seize and hold, take off guard 14 stumbling block 15 take into custody 18 become infected with

catch-as-catch-can 7 cursory 9 haphazard, hit-or-miss, unplanned 10 disorderly, incomplete 11 superficial, unorganized 12 disorganized, unsystematic

Catcher in the Rye, The
author: 10 J D Salinger
character: 15 Holden Caulfield

catching 10 contagious, infectious 12 communicable 13 transmittable

catch on to 3 get 5 grasp, savvy 6 absorb, digest, fathom, pick up 10 assimilate, comprehend, get the idea, understand

catch sight of 3 see 4 espy 6 behold, descry, detect, notice 7 discern, make out, observe, pick out 8 perceive

Catch-22
author: 12 Joseph Heller
character: 9 Yossarian

catchword 5 motto 6 byword, cliche, slogan, war cry 8 password 9 battle cry, guide word, pet phrase, watchword 10 shibboleth

categorical 4 flat, sure 7 certain, express 8 absolute, definite, emphatic, explicit 10 pronounced, unreserved 11 unequivocal, unqualified 12 unmistakable 13 unconditional

categorically 10 absolutely, definitely, positively 12 conclusively

categorization 5 order 11 arrangement 14 classification

category 5 class, group 8 division, grouping 14 classification

cater 5 humor 6 pamper, pander, please 7 gratify, indulge, satisfy

caterpillar 4 moth, worm 5 larva 7 cutworm, tractor, webworm 8 hangworm, silkworm, wortworm **9** butterfly, woolybear **10** astragalus

caterwaul 3 cry **4** bawl, howl, wail, yelp **5** whine **6** clamor, scream, shriek, squawk, squeal **7** screech **10** rend the air

catfish 4 barb **5** banjo **6** dorado, madtom, mudcat, sucker **7** ariidae, bluecat **8** bagridae, bullhead, claridae, electric, flathead **9** siluridae **10** channel cat, cuttlefish, mochocidae, plotosidae, spotted cat **11** ictaluridae, pimelodidae, schilbeidae **12** aspredinidae, ostariophysi **14** malapteruridae **16** trichomycteridae

Catfish
nickname of: **9** Jim Hunter

catharsis 7 purging, release, venting **9** cleansing **12** purification

Catharsius
epithet of: **4** Zeus
means: **8** purifier

cathartic 5 purge **6** physic **8** aperient, evacuant, laxative **9** castor oil, purgative, purifying

cathedral 3 see **6** church, temple **7** lateran **8** basilica, official **9** authority **10** pontifical
Italian: **5** duomo

Cather, Willa
author of: **9** A Lost Lady, My Antonia, One of Ours, O Pioneers! **13** My Mortal Enemy **16** Shadows on the Rock, The Song of the Lark **18** The Professor's House **23** Sapphira and the Slave Girl **26** Death Comes for the Archbishop

cathode ray tube
abbreviation: **3** CRT
invented by: **7** Crookes

catholic, Catholic 5 broad **7** liberal **9** universal, worldwide **12** all-embracing, all-inclusive **13** comprehensive

cathouse 4 stew **5** house **6** bagnio, bordel **7** brothel **8** bordello **10** bawdy house, fancy house, whorehouse **13** sporting house **14** house of ill fame **16** house of ill repute **19** house of prostitution

Cat Jumps, The
author: **14** Elizabeth Bowen

catlike 5 catty, lithe **7** sinuous **8** stealthy **14** light on the feet

Catlin, George
born: **13** Wilkes-Barre PA
artwork: **16** Gallery of Indians

catnap 3 nap **4** doze **6** siesta, snooze **10** forty winks, light sleep

Cato
author: **13** Joseph Addison

Cat on a Hot Tin Roof
author: **17** Tennessee Williams
director: **13** Richard Brooks
cast: **8** Burl Ives (Big Daddy) **10** Jack Carson, Paul Newman (Brick) **14** Judith Anderson **15** Elizabeth Taylor (Maggie)

Catreus
king of: **5** Crete
father: **5** Minos
mother: **8** Pasiphae
son: **11** Althaemenes
daughter: **6** Aerope **7** Clymene **9** Apemosyne
grandson: **8** Menelaus

cats-eye
species: **11** chrysoberyl
source: **8** Sri Lanka

cat's paw 4 dupe, pawn, tool **5** patsy **7** fall guy

cattle 4 cows, kine, oxen **5** beefs, bulls, stock **6** beeves, calves, dogies, steers **8** bullocks, milk cows **9** livestock
family: **7** Bovidae
group of: **5** drove
kind: **2** ox **3** yak **4** Zebu **5** Angus **6** Ankole, Jersey **7** Brahman **8** Ayrshire, Guernsey, Hereford, Highland, Holstein **9** Charolais **12** water buffalo **13** Texas Longhorn **16** English Shorthorn, Holstein-Friesian
young: **4** calf **6** heifer **8** yearling

Catton, Bruce
author of: **22** A Stillness at Appomattox

catty 4 mean **7** catlike **8** spiteful **9** malicious, malignant **10** malevolent

catwalk 6 bridge **7** walkway **10** passageway

Caucasian
language branch: **5** Ubykh **9** Daghestan **10** Circassian **11** Khartvelian

Caucon
brought mysteries to: **8** Messenia

caucus 6 parley, powwow **7** council, meeting, session **8** assembly, conclave **10** conference

caudal 4 back, tail **7** tail-end

cauldron see **7** caldron

Caulfield, Holden
character in: **18** The Catcher in the Rye
author: **8** Salinger

Caulfield, Joan
real name: **21** Beatrice Joan Caulfield
born: **8** Orange NJ
roles: **8** Dear Ruth **17** My Favorite Husband

Caunus
brother: **6** Byblis

causation 4 root **5** cause **6** author, origin, reason, source **7** creator, genesis **8** etiology, inventor, stimulus **9** generator, invention **10** antecedent, conception, mainspring, originator **11** determinant, inspiration, origination

cause 4 goal, make, root, side **5** ideal, impel, tenet **6** belief, create, effect, incite, lead to, motive, object, origin, reason, source, spring, stir up **7** genesis, grounds, incline, inspire, produce, provoke, purpose **8** etiology, generate, motivate, occasion, stimulus **9** incentive, principle, stimulate **10** aspiration, bring about, conviction, foundation, give rise to, inducement, initiation, mainspring, motivation, persuasion, prime mover **11** bring to pass, inspiration, instigation, precipitate, provocation

cause of war
Latin: **10** casus belli

cause to appear 6 expose, reveal **7** uncover **8** disclose **12** bring to light **13** bring into view

caustic 4 tart **5** acrid, harsh, sharp **6** biting, bitter **7** burning, cutting, erosive, gnawing **8** scathing, stinging **9** corroding, corrosive, sarcastic **10** astringent, **11** acrimonious

caution 4 care, heed, warn **5** alarm, alert **6** advise, caveat, exhort, notify, regard, tip-off **7** concern, thought, warning **8** admonish, forewarn, prudence, wariness **9** alertness, restraint, vigilance **10** admonition, discretion, precaution **11** carefulness, forewarning, guardedness, heedfulness, mindfulness **12** deliberation, watchfulness **14** circumspection, put on one's guard

cautionary 7 warning **8** advisory **10** admonitory **11** admonishing

cautious 4 wary **5** alert, cagey **7** careful, guarded, prudent **8** discreet, vigilant, watchful

9 attentive, judicious **11** circumspect

cavalcade 5 troop **6** column, parade **7** caravan, retinue **10** procession

Cavalcade
director: **10** Frank Lloyd
based on play by: **10** Noel Coward
cast: **10** Clive Brook **11** Ursula Jeans **12** Diana Wynyard **13** Herbert Mundin **15** Margaret Lindsay
Oscar for: **7** picture

cavalier 3 fop **4** beau **5** blade, cocky, dandy, swell **6** hussar, lancer **7** cursory, dragoon, gallant, haughty, offhand, playboy **8** arrogant, courtier, gay blade, horseman, uncaring **9** easygoing **10** cavalryman, disdainful, nonchalant **11** indifferent, thoughtless

cavalry 7 hussars, lancers **8** dragoons **10** mounted men **11** horse troops **13** horse soldiers, mounted troops

cavalryman 6 hussar, lancer **7** dragoon **8** cavalier, horseman **12** horse soldier, horse trooper **14** mounted soldier

cave 3 den **4** lair, sink **6** burrow, cavern, cavity, dugout, grotto, hollow
growth: **10** stalactite, stalagmite
explorer: **9** spelunker

caveat 5 alarm, alert, aviso **6** tip-off **7** caution, red flag, warning **8** high sign, red light **10** admonition, danger sign, yellow jack **11** forewarning **12** admonishment, flea in the ear **13** word to the wise **20** handwriting on the wall

caveat emptor 17 let the buyer beware

cave canem 14 beware of the dog

cave in 6 buckle, fall in, give up, submit **7** crumple, give way, implode **8** collapse **10** capitulate **12** fall to pieces

Cavendish, Henry
field: **7** physics **9** chemistry
nationality: **7** British
discovered: **8** hydrogen
determined composition of: **3** air **5** water **10** nitric acid
method: **19** Cavendish experiment

cavernous 4 huge, vast **5** roomy **6** gaping **7** chasmal, immense, yawning **8** cavelike, enormous, spacious **10** tremendous

cavil 6 deride **7** nitpick, quib-

ble **8** belittle, complain **9** criticize, deprecate, discredit, disparage, faultfind, find fault **12** pick to pieces

cavity 3 dip, pit **4** bore, dent, hole, sink **5** basin, niche **6** burrow, crater, hollow, pocket, tunnel **7** opening, orifice, vacuity **8** aperture **9** concavity **10** depression, excavation

cavort 4 play, romp **5** bound, caper, frisk **6** frolic, gambol, prance

Cawdor
author: **15** Robinson Jeffers

Caxtons, The
author: **12** Bulwer Lytton

Cayster
river in: **5** Lydia

Cayuga
language family: **9** Iroquoian
location: **4** Ohio **6** Canada **7** New York **8** Oklahoma **9** Wisconsin
branch of: **10** Six Nations **19** Iroquois Confederacy, League of the Iroquois

cease 3 end **4** halt, pass, quit, stop **5** abate, pause **6** desist, finish **7** adjourn, die away, forbear, suspend **8** break off, conclude, leave off **9** terminate **11** abstain from, discontinue, refrain from **12** bring to an end

cease-fire 5 truce **9** armistice

ceaseless 7 endless, eternal **8** constant, enduring, unending **9** continual, incessant, permanent, perpetual, unceasing **10** continuous, protracted **11** everlasting, never-ending, unremitting **12** interminable **13** uninterrupted

cease to be 3 die, end **6** die out, expire, vanish **9** disappear, evaporate **13** become extinct

Cebriones
father: **5** Priam
brother: **6** Hector
charioteer for: **6** Hector

Cecilia (Memoirs of an Heiress)
author: **11** Fanny Burney

Cecrops
also: **8** Cecropia
form: **3** man **3** dragon
founder of: **6** Attica
king of: **6** Attica
father: **14** King Erechtheus
brother: **6** Metion, Orneus
wife: **8** Aglaurus
son: **11** Erysichthon
daughter: **5** Herse **8** Aglaurus **9** Pandrasos
renamed Attica: **8** Cecropia

Cedalion
occupation: **5** smith
forge owner: **10** Hephaestus
served as guide for: **5** Orion

cedar 6 Cedrus
varieties: **3** red **4** pink, salt **5** Atlas, giant, white **6** Alaska, Cyprus, ground, Mlanje **7** Bermuda, incense, Russian, Spanish **8** Barbados, cigar-box, creeping, Japanese, stinking **10** Ozark white, Port Orford, swamp white, western red, West Indian, Willowmore **11** Clanwilliam, Colorado red, southern red **13** Atlantic white, southern white **14** Chilean incense, Formosa incense **17** California incense

cede 4 give **5** grant, leave, yield **6** tender **7** abandon, deliver, release **8** hand over, transfer **9** deliver up, surrender **10** relinquish

cedez
music: **8** slow down

Cedreatis
epithet of: **7** Artemis
means: **14** of the cedar tree

Cedric the Saxon
character in: **7** Ivanhoe
author: **5** Scott

ceiling 3 top **4** roof **5** cover, limit **6** canopy, cupola, lining **7** maximum **8** altitude **10** upperlimit

Celaeno
member of: **7** Harpies **8** Pleiades

Celebes
also: **8** Sulawesi
bordered by: **6** Borneo **8** Moluccas **10** Celebes Sea, Kalimantan **12** Flores Strait **14** Makassar Strait
city: **4** Poso **6** Manado **7** Kendari, Madjene **8** Bonthain, Donggala, Makassar **9** Gorontalo
location: **9** Indonesia
people: **4** Bugi, Laki, Mori, Muna, Napu, Palu, Peso, Seko, Wana **5** Besoa, Buton, Toala **6** Bungku, Butung, Parigi, Sadang, Sangir, Toland **7** Banggai, Bolaang, Kabaena, Loinang, Toradja **8** Balantak, Buginese, Mongondu, Rongkong, Sanghike **9** Gorontalo **11** Makassarese
province: **13** North Sulawesi, South Sulawesi **15** Central Sulawesi **17** Southeast Sulawesi

celebrate 4 laud **5** bless, cheer, exalt, extol, honor **6** hallow, praise, revere **7** acclaim, applaud, commend, glorify, observe **8** proclaim, sanctify, venerate **9** broadcast, ritualize, solemnize **10** consecrate **11** commemorate **13** ceremonialize

celebrated 5 famed, noted **6** famous, prized **7** eminent, honored, notable, revered **8** lionized, renowned **9** acclaimed, important, prominent, respected, treasured, venerable, well-known **11** illustrious, outstanding **13** distinguished

Celebrated Jumping Frog of Calaveras County, The
author: **9** Mark Twain

celebration 4 fete, gala **5** feast, party **6** ritual **7** jubilee, revelry **8** carnival, ceremony, festival **9** festivity, hallowing **10** ceremonial, observance **13** commemoration, solemnization **14** sanctification **15** memorialization

celebrity 3 VIP **4** fame, name, note, star **5** glory, wheel **6** bigwig, renown **7** big shot, notable, stardom **8** eminence, luminary **9** dignitary, notoriety, personage **10** notability, popularity, prominence **11** distinction, personality **12** famous person, person of note

celerity 5 haste, hurry, speed **6** hustle **8** alacrity, dispatch, fast clip, fastness, legerity, rapidity **9** briskness, quickness, swiftness **10** expedition, snappiness, speediness **12** precipitance **14** lightning speed **15** expeditiousness

celery seed
also called: **8** smallage
origin: **13** Mediterranean
use: **4** soup **5** salad, sauce **6** pickle **10** vegetables

celestial 3 sky **5** solar **6** astral, divine **7** angelic, elysian, stellar, sublime **8** beatific, blissful, empyrean, ethereal, hallowed, heavenly, seraphic **9** planetary, unearthly **12** astronomical, otherworldly, paradisiacal

celestial being 3 god **5** angel, deity **7** goddess **8** divinity **11** divine being

Celestial City
place in: **16** Pilgrim's Progress
author: **6** Bunyan

Celia (Aliena)
character in: **11** As You Like It
author: **11** Shakespeare

celibacy 8 chastity **9** virginity **10** abstinence, continence **12** bachelorhood, spinsterhood

celibate 4 pure **5** unwed **6** chaste, single **8** bachelor, spinster, virginal **9** abstinent, continent, unmarried

Celine, Louis-Ferdinand
author of: **12** Guignol's Band **25** Death on the Installment Plan, Journey to the End of the Night

cell
part: **7** nucleus **8** membrane **9** cytoplasm
made of: **3** fat **4** salt **5** water **7** protein **9** compounds **12** carbohydrate
theory of: **7** (Rudolf) Virchow, (Theodor) Schwann

cellar 3 den **4** cave **6** dugout **8** basement **10** downstairs

Cellini, Benvenuto
born: **5** Italy **8** Florence
artwork: **7** Cosimo I, Perseus **13** Bindo Altoviti **18** The Crucified Christ **20** Nymph of Fontainebleau
autobiography: **22** Life of Benvenuto Cellini

Celsius
abbreviation of: **1** C

Celt 4 Gaul, Kelt, Manx, Scot **5** Irish, Welsh **6** Breton, Briton, chisel **8** Scottish **10** Highlander

Celtic
language group: **6** Gaelic **9** Brythonic
family: **12** Indo-European
language of: **5** Gauls

cement 3 fix, set **4** bind, fuse, glue, join, seal, weld **5** paste, stick, unite **6** mortar, secure **8** concrete

cemetery 7 ossuary **8** boneyard, Boot Hill, catacomb **9** graveyard **10** churchyard, necropolis **12** burial ground, memorial park, potter's field **13** burying ground

Cenaean see **4** Zeus

Cenchrias
father: **8** Poseidon
mother: **6** Pirene
killed by: **7** Artemis

Cenci, The
author: **18** Percy Bysshe Shelley

cenobite 4 monk **7** ascetic **8** celibate **9** religious

censor 4 blip, edit **5** amend, judge, purge **6** critic, delete, excise **7** amender, clean up **8** black out, examiner, reviewer, suppress **9** expurgate, inspector **10** blue-pencil, bowdlerize, expurgator, suppressor **11** bowdlerizer, faultfinder, scrutinizer

12 investigator **17** custodian of morals **25** guardian of the public morals

censorious 5 picky **7** abusive, carping **8** critical **10** defamatory **12** faultfinding

censurable 8 blamable **10** deplorable, punishable, reprovable **11** blameworthy **12** reproachable **13** reprehensible

censure 3 pan, rap **5** chide, scold **6** berate, rebuke **7** bawl out, chew out, chiding, condemn, reproof, reprove, upbraid **8** admonish, denounce, reproach, scolding **9** castigate, complaint, criticism, criticize, reprehend, reprimand **10** admonition, bawling-out, chewing-out, disapprove, upbraiding **11** castigation, disapproval, reprobation **12** condemnation, dressingdown, remonstrance **13** tongue-lashing **14** disapprobation **16** rap on the knuckles, take over the coals
god of: **5** Momos, Momus

census 3 tax **4** data, list, poll **5** count **6** amount, number **11** enumeration **12** registration

Centaur
form: **3** man **5** horse **7** monster **16** half-man half-horse
constellation of: **9** Centaurus
famous: **6** Chiron
represents: **11** Sagittarius

Centaurus
father: **5** Ixion
mother: **7** Nephele
father of: **8** Centaurs

Centennial
author: **13** James Michener

Centennial State
nickname of: **8** Colorado

center, centre 3 fix, hub, mid **4** axis, core, crux **5** focus, heart, pivot, point **6** direct, gather, middle **7** address, essence, nucleus **8** converge, interior **9** middle **10** focal point **11** concentrate

centered 4 even, true **5** right **7** focused **8** straight **10** pinpointed **12** concentrated

centigrade 5 scale **6** degree **7** celcius **11** thermometer

centigram
abbreviation of: **2** cg

centiliter
abbreviation of: **2** cl

Centimani see
13 Hecatonchires

centimeter
abbreviation of: **2** cm

centipede 4 boat 5 shrub
6 earwig, insect 8 chilopod,
multiped 9 arthropod
13 muehlenbeckia

central 3 key 4 main 5 basic,
chief, focal, inner, major,
prime 6 inmost, middle
7 leading, midmost, pivotal,
primary 8 dominant, foremost,
interior 9 essential, paramount, principal 10 middlemost 11 fundamental,
predominant 13 most
important

**Central African
Republic**
  other name: 11 Ubangi-
  Chari 20 Central Afri-
  can Empire
  capital/largest city:
  6 Bangui
  others: 3 Obo 4 Bria,
  Ippy 5 Birao, Bouar,
  Kembe, Ndele, Ngoto,
  Paoua, Rafai, Zemio
  6 Baboua, Bakala, Bo-
  zoum, Mbaiki 7 Bam-
  bari, Grimari,
  Zemongo 9 Bangassou,
  Berberati, Bossangoa,
  Fort-Sibut
  monetary unit: 5 franc
  7 centime
  lake: 4 Chad
  mountain: 5 Karre,
  Tinga 6 Mongos 9 Dar
  Challa
  highest point:
  11 Kayagangiri
  river: 4 Bomu, Nana
  5 Chari, Kotto, Mbari,
  Mpoko, Ouaka
  6 Chinko, Lobaye,
  Mbomou, Ubangi
  11 Upper Sangha
  people: 4 Baya, Sara
  5 Banda, Bwaka,
  Sango 6 Azande, Yak-
  oma 7 Banziri, Mandjia,
  Nzakara
  language: 5 Sango,
  Zande 6 French
  religion: 5 Islam 7 animism 12 Christianity
  13 Roman Catholic
  place:
    plaza: 13 Edouard
    Renard
  food:
    tapioca: 6 manioc
    7 cassava

Central America *see box*
Central Amerind
  language branch: 9 Oto-Man-
  gue 10 Uto-Aztecan
  11 Kiowa-Tanoan

Central America
  land form: 7 isthmus
  countries: 6 Belize, Panama 8 Honduras 9 Costa Rica, Guatemala, Nicaragua 10 El Salvador
  bordered by: 6 Mexico, 8 Colombia 12 Caribbean Sea,
  North America, Pacific Ocean, South America
  capital city: 7 Managua. San Jose 8 Belmopan 10 Panama
  City 11 San Salvador, Tegucigalpa 13 Guatemala City
  river: 3 New 4 Axul, Coco, Sico, Tuma, Ulua, Wawa
  5 Aguan, Chepo, Hondo, Lempa, Wauks 6 Chixoy,
  Grande, Pasion, Patuca, Sulaco, Waspuk 7 Motagua, Paulaya, San Juan, Sarstun, Segovia 8 Kukalaya 9 Choluteca,
  Escondido 10 Chucunague 11 Prinzapolca
  lake: 5 Gatun, Guija, Yojoa 7 Atitlan, Managua 9 Nicaragua, Peten Itza
  mountain: 4 Maya, Pija 5 Colon, Huapi, Minas, Pando
  6 Blanco 7 Dipilto, Gongora, San Blas 8 Brewster, Dar-
  iense, Isabelia, San Pablo, Santa Ana 9 Esperanza
  14 Chirripo Grande
  people: 3 Mam 5 Zambo 6 Indian, Ladino, Quiche 7 mestizo 8 Miskitas 10 Black Carib, Cakchiquel
  animal: 5 tapir 6 agouti 7 opossum, peccary 8 anteater,
  kinkajou, marmoset 9 armadillo, porcupine, tree sloth
  12 howler monkey, spider monkey 14 capuchin monkey

---

central city 8 core city, downtown 9 inner city, urban area
10 metropolis 16 business district, metropolitan area

central idea 3 nut 4 core,
crux, gist, meat 5 heart,
theme 6 kernel 7 essence
9 main point

centralization 5 focus 11 convergence 13 concentration,
consolidation

centralize 5 focus, unify
6 center, gather 7 collect, compact 8 center on, coalesce,
converge, pinpoint 9 integrate
10 congregate 11 concentrate,
consolidate

central part 4 core, crux, gist,
pith 5 heart 6 center, kernel
7 nucleus

century
  abbreviation of: 4 cent
  French: 6 siecle

cephalopod 5 squid 7 mollusk,
octopus 8 nautilus 10 cuttlefish

Cephalus
  father: 6 Hermes
  mother: 5 Herse
  brother: 5 Ceryx
  wife: 7 Clymene, Procris

Cephas *see* 5 Peter

Cepheus
  king of: 8 Ethiopia
  wife: 10 Cassiopeia
  daughter: 9 Andromeda

Cerambus
  form: 6 beetle

ceramic ware 5 china, glass
7 pottery 8 crockery 9 chinaware, glassware, porcelain,

stoneware 10 enamelware
11 earthenware

ceratopsid
  type of: 8 dinosaur
  member: 10 Torosaurus
  11 Monoclonius, Triceratops 13 Protoceratops, Styracosaurus 14 Psittacosaurus

Ceratosaurus
  type: 8 dinosaur
  period: 8 Jurassic

Cerberus
  form: 3 dog
  father: 6 Typhon
  mother: 7 Echidna
  sibling: 5 Hydra 7 Orthrus
  8 Chimaera 10 Nemean
  lion 12 Theban Sphinx
  number of heads: 5 three
  guarded: 10 Underworld

Cercopes
  race of: 6 Gnomes

Cercyon
  king of: 7 Arcadia
  daughter: 5 Alope

cereal 4 corn, oats, rice, seed
5 grain, grass, gruel, plant,
wheat 6 barley, pablum 7 oatmeal, pabulum 8 porridge

cerebellum
  part of: 5 brain
  controls: 7 balance
  8 movement

cerebrum
  part of: 5 brain
  controls: 6 seeing 7 hearing,
  tasting 8 deciding, feelings,
  learning, smelling, thinking,
  touching 9 awareness
  11 remembering

ceremonial 4 rite 6 formal, ritual **7** liturgy, service **8** ceremony **9** formality, sacrament **10** liturgical, observance **11** celebration, ritualistic

ceremonialize 7 observe **9** celebrate, ritualize **11** commemorate

ceremonious 5 exact, fussy, rigid, stiff **6** formal, proper, solemn **7** careful, correct, pompous, precise **8** starched **9** dignified **10** methodical, meticulous **11** punctilious

ceremony 4 rite **6** custom, nicety, ritual **7** amenity, decorum, pageant, service **8** function, protocol **9** etiquette, formality, propriety **10** observance, politeness **11** celebration, formalities **13** commemoration

Cerenkov, Pavel Alekseevich
 field: **7** physics
 nationality: **7** Russian
 discovered: **12** cause of light **14** Cerenkov effect

Ceres
 origin: **5** Roman
 goddess of: **11** agriculture
 corresponds to: **7** Demeter

certain 4 sure **5** valid **6** secure **7** assured, express, settled, special **8** absolute, cocksure, definite, positive, reliable, specific **9** confident, convinced, satisfied **10** conclusive, individual, inevitable, particular, undeniable, undisputed, undoubtful, undoubting, unshakable **11** indubitable, inescapable, irrefutable, unalterable, unequivocal, unqualified **12** indisputable, unchangeable, unmistakable, well-grounded **13** bound to happen, incontestable **14** unquestionable **16** incontrovertible

certainly 5 truly **6** indeed, surely **7** for sure **8** of course **9** decidedly **10** absolutely, definitely, positively **11** indubitably, undoubtedly **13** unequivocally, without a doubt **14** unquestionably **21** beyond a shadow of a doubt

Certain Smile, A
 author: **14** Francoise Sagan

certainty 4 fact **5** faith, trust **6** belief, surety **7** reality, sure bet **8** sureness **9** actuality, assurance, certitude, sure thing **10** confidence, conviction **11** presumption **12** positiveness **13** inevitability **14** conclusiveness, inescapability **17** authoritativeness

certificate 4 deed **6** permit **7** diploma, license, voucher **8** document, warranty **9** affida-

vit **10** credential **11** testimonial **13** authorization **14** authentication

certification 7 voucher **8** approval **10** validation **11** endorsement **12** confirmation, ratification, verification **13** authorization, corroboration **14** authentication, substantiation

certify 4 aver **5** swear, vouch **6** assure, attest, ratify, second, verify **7** confirm, declare, endorse, support, warrant, witness **8** notarize, sanction, validate **9** authorize, guarantee, testify to **10** underwrite **11** corroborate **12** authenticate, give one's word, substantiate

certitude 5 faith, trust **6** belief, surety **7** reliance, sureness **9** assurance, certainty **10** confidence **12** positiveness **14** conclusiveness

cerulean 4 blue **5** azure **6** cobalt **7** sky blue **9** clear blue

Cervantes Saavedra, Miguel de
 author of: **20** Don Quixote de la Mancha

Cerynean stag
 also: **12** Arcadian stag
 home: **7** Arcadia
 captured by: **8** Hercules

Ceryx
 herald of: **4** gods
 father: **6** Hermes
 mother: **5** Herse
 brother: **8** Cephalus

Cesar Birotteau
 author: **14** Honore de Balzac

cessation 3 end **4** halt, stay, stop **5** pause **6** ending, recess **7** ceasing, halting, respite **8** quitting, stopping, surcease **9** desisting **10** concluding, leaving off, suspension **11** adjournment, breaking off, termination **12** interruption **13** coming to a halt, discontinuing **14** discontinuance

c'est la vie 9 that's life **10** such is life

Cestrinus
 father: **7** Helenus
 mother: **10** Andromache

Cestus
 girdle of: **5** Venus

cetacean 4 apod **5** whale **6** beluga, mammal **7** cetacea, dolphin, dowfish, grampus, narwhal **8** porpoise, sturgeon **9** blue whale **11** baleen whale, killer whale

Cetinje
 capital of: **10** Montenegro

Ceto
 father: **6** Pontus
 mother: **4** Gaea
 brother: **7** Phorcys
 husband: **7** Phorcys
 mother of: **6** Graeae **7** Gorgons
 children called: **8** Phorcids

Ceylon *see* **8** Sri Lanka

Ceyx
 father: **9** Eosphorus
 wife: **7** Alcyone

Cezanne, Paul
 born: **6** France **13** Aix-en-Provence
 artwork: **7** Bathers **11** Card Players **13** The Black Clock, The Railway Out **14** Uncle Dominique **15** La Maison du Pendu **16** The Suicide's House **17** Grandes Baigneuses **19** Woman with a Coffee Pot **36** Mont-Sainte-Victoire with Large Pine Trees

Chabrier, (Alexis) Emmanuel
 born: **6** Ambert, France
 composer of: **6** Espana **7** L'Etoile **10** Gwendoline **13** Marche Joyeuse **14** Le Roi Malgre Lui **18** King Despite Himself **19** Une Education Manquee

Chad
 other name: **5** Tchad
 capital/largest city: **8** Fort-Lamy, N'Djamena
 others: **3** Ati, Bol, Lai, Mao **4** Fada, Faya, Sarh **5** Mongo **6** Abeche, Bongor **7** Largeau, Moundou **8** Moussoro
 monetary unit: **5** franc **7** centime
 lake: **4** Chad
 mountain: **7** Tibesti, Touside
 highest point: **9** Emi Koussi
 river: **5** Chari **6** Logone **8** Bahraouk
 physical feature:
  plateau: **6** Ennedi
 people: **4** Arab, Daza, Maba, Sara, Teda, Tubu **5** Barma, Hakka, Kreda, Massa **6** Fulani, Kotoko, Toubou, Wadaii **7** Kamadja, Kanembu, Moundan
 language: **4** Sara **5** Turku **6** Arabic, French
 religion: **5** Islam **7** animism **12** Christianity

Chadband
  character in: **10** Bleak House
  author: **7** Dickens

Chadic
  language family: **11** Afroasiatic **13** Hamito-Semitic
  includes: **5** Hausa
  spoken in: **6** Africa **8** Lake Chad

Chadwick, James
  field: **7** physics
  nationality: **7** British
  discovered: **7** neutron
  awarded: **10** Nobel Prize

chafe 3 rub **4** boil, burn, foam, fume, rage, rasp **6** abrade, rankle, scrape, seethe **7** scratch **9** be annoyed **11** be irritated

chaff 3 bug, kid, rag, rib **4** josh, junk, pods, razz, ride, slag, twit **5** dross, hulls, husks, jolly, trash, waste **6** banter, debris, litter, refuse, rubble, shells, shoddy, shucks **7** kidding, ragging, remnant, residue, ribbing, rubbish, waggery **8** badinage, chaffing, leavings, raillery, ridicule **9** sweepings **9** give and take

chaffing 6 banter **7** jesting, joshing, kidding, ragging, ribbing, waggery **8** badinage, raillery

chafing 5 harsh **6** fuming **7** rasping, rubbing **8** abrading, abrasive **10** irritating

Chagall, Marc
  born: **6** Liosno, Liozno, Russia
  artwork: **8** Birthday, Cockcrow **9** The Circus, The Red Sun **10** The Juggler **11** Over Vitebsk **12** The Violinist **14** Double Portrait, I and the Village **16** The Jewish Wedding **17** Lovers with Rooster **20** Paris Through My Window

chagrin 5 shame **6** dismay **8** distress **11** humiliation **13** embarrassment, mortification

chagrined 7 abashed, ashamed **9** mortified **10** humiliated **11** embarrassed

Chahiksichhiks see **6** Pawnee

chain 3 fob **5** cable, links **7** shackle **8** necklace **10** metal links **11** linked cable
  abbreviation: **2** ch

Chain, Ernst Boris
  field: **12** biochemistry
  nationality: **7** British
  discovered: **10** penicillin
  worked with: **6** Florey **7** Fleming
  awarded: **10** Nobel Prize

Chained Lady
  constellation of: **9** Andromeda

chains 3 tie **4** bind, lash, moor **5** bonds, irons, tie up, train **6** fasten, fetter, secure, series, string, tether **7** bondage, fetters, manacle, serfdom, shackle, slavery **8** leg irons, manacles, sequence, shackles **9** handcuffs, servitude, thralldom **10** put in irons, succession **11** enslavement, subjugation

chair 4 seat **5** bench, couch, sedan stool **6** chaise, lounge, rocker, settee, throne **7** conduct, ottoman **11** preside over **16** presiding officer

chairman 4 head **5** chair, emcee **6** leader **7** manager, speaker **8** director **9** chairlady, executive, moderator **10** chairwoman, supervisor **11** chairperson, toastmaster **13** administrator **16** presiding officer **18** master of ceremonies

Chair of Forgetfulness
  form: **4** seat
  made of: **5** stone
  location: **10** Underworld

chaise 3 gig **4** shay **5** chair **6** daybed, lounge **7** calesin **8** carriage, duchesse

chalcedony 3 gem **4** onyx, opal, sard **5** agate, prase **6** jasper, plasma, quartz, silica **7** catseye, mineral, opaline, sardius **8** hematite, sardonyx **9** carnelian **10** bloodstone, heliotrope **11** chrysoprase **12** semiprecious **14** silicon dioxide

Chalcis
  father: **6** Asopus
  mother: **6** Metope

Chaldean 4 seer **5** magic **6** Syriac **7** Aramaic, semitic **8** magician **9** astrology, enchanter, Nabonidus **10** astrologer, Babylonian, soothsayer **12** Nabopolassar **14** Nebuchadnezzar

chalice 3 cup **5** grail **6** goblet, vessel

Chalinitis
  epithet of: **6** Athena
  means: **7** bridler

chalk 4 draw **6** crayon, pastel, sketch **9** limestone

chalk up 4 earn **5** score **6** attain, charge, credit **7** achieve, ascribe

chalky 3 wan **4** pale **5** ashen, white **6** pallid **7** powdery **8** blanched **9** bloodless

challenge 3 bid, tax, try **4** dare, defy, gage, test **5** doubt, trial **6** demand, impute, summon **7** defiant, dispute, summons **8** question **15** take exception to **20** fling down the gauntlet

chamber 4 diet, hall, room **5** board, court, house, salon **6** office, parlor **7** bedroom, boudoir, council **8** assembly, congress **9** apartment

Chamberlain, Owen
  field: **7** physics
  developed: **8** atom bomb
  awarded: **10** Nobel Prize

Chamberlain, Richard
  real name: **24** George Richard Chamberlain
  born: **12** Los Angeles CA
  roles: **6** Shogun **9** Dr Kildare **10** Wallenberg **13** The Thorn Birds **17** The Bourne Identity **21** The Count of Monte Cristo

Chamberlain, Wilt (Wilton Norman)
  nickname: **6** Dipper **12** Wilt the Stilt
  sport: **10** basketball
  position: **5** coach **6** center
  team: **16** Los Angeles Lakers **17** Philadelphia 76ers **20** Philadelphia Warriors, San Francisco Warriors **21** San Diego Conquistadors

chambermaid
  French: **14** femme de chambre

chambord
  type: **7** liqueur
  origin: **6** France
  flavor: **9** raspberry

chameleon 4 newt **6** lizard **8** renegade, turncoat **10** fickleness **14** changeableness

champ 4 bite, chew, gnaw **5** chomp, crush, grind, munch **6** crunch **8** champion

champagne
  type: **4** wine
  drink: **7** the Pope
  with white wine: **8** Cold Duck
  with orange juice: **6** Mimosa
  measure: **6** magnum **8** jeroboam, rehoboam **9** balthazar **10** methuselah, salmanazar **14** Nebuchadnezzar

Champaigne, Philippe de
  born: **7** Belgium **8** Brussels
  artwork: **6** Ex Voto **17** Cardinal Richelieu **26** The Adoration of the Shepherds

champion 3 aid **4** abet, back **6** backer, defend, master, uphold, victor, winner **7** espouse,

paragon, promote, support
8 advocate, defender, fight for,
laureate, promoter, speak for,
upholder **9** battle for, conqueror, protector, supporter
10 stand up for, vanquisher
11 protagonist, title holder

Champion
  constellation of: **7** Perseus

championship 3 cup **5** crown,
title **7** backing, defense, support, winning **8** advocacy,
espousal

Chamyne
  epithet of: **7** Demeter

chance 3 try **4** fall, fate, luck,
risk **5** lucky, occur **6** befall,
danger, gamble, happen, hazard, random **7** attempt, destiny, fortune, turn out,
venture **8** accident, jeopardy,
occasion **9** come about, fortunate, unplanned **10** accidental,
fortuitous, likelihood, likeli-
ness, providence, undesigned,
unexpected, unforeseen **11** opportunity, possibility, probability, speculation, unlooked for
12 happenstance **13** unintentional **14** unpremeditated

chance upon 4 find, meet
7 learn of, run into **8** come
upon, discover **9** encounter,
light upon **10** happen upon
11 stumble upon

chancy 4 iffy **5** dicey, risky
6 touchy, tricky **7** dubious, erratic, unsound **8** doubtful
9 hazardous, uncertain, whimsical **10** capricious, precarious
11 speculative, venturesome
13 problematical, unpredictable

chandelier 11 hanging lamp
12 candleholder **15** lighting
fixture

Chandler, Jeff
  real name: **10** Ira Grossel
  born: **10** Brooklyn NY
  roles: **7** Cochise **11** Broken
  Arrow **17** Merrill's
  Marauders

Chandler, Raymond
  author of: **11** The Big Sleep
  14 The Long Goodbye
  16 Farewell My Lovely
  character: **13** Philip Marlowe
  screenplay: **13** The Blue Dahlia **15** Double Indemnity
  17 Strangers on a Train

Chaney, Lon
  real name: **12** Alonso Chaney
  son: **9** Creighton (Lon Chaney Jr)
  nickname: **19** Man of a
  Thousand Faces
  born: **17** Colorado Springs CO
  roles: **14** The Unholy Three
  18 Tell It to the Marines
  20 Hunchback of Notre

Dame, The Phantom of the
Opera

Chaney, Lon Jr
  real name: **9** Creighton
  father: **3** Lon
  born: **14** Oklahoma City OK
  roles: **6** Lennie **8** The
  Mummy **10** The Wolf Man
  12 Of Mice and Men, Son
  of Dracula **20** Frankenstein's
  Monster

change 4 swap, turn, vary
5 alter, coins, shift, trade
6 modify, mutate, recast, reform, silver, switch **7** convert,
novelty, remodel, replace, re-
style, shuffle, variety, veering
8 pin money, swapping, transfer **9** deviation, diversion, exception, restyling, transform,
transmute, turn about, variation **10** alteration, conversion,
difference, remodeling, reorganize, revolution, small coins,
substitute **11** fluctuation,
pocket money, reformation
12 metamorphose, modification, substitution **13** make different, metamorphosis,
revolutionize, transmutation,
transposition **14** reorganization, transformation
15 transfiguration

changeable 6 fickle, fitful
7 erratic, flighty, mutable,
varying **8** unstable, unsteady,
variable, volatile **9** deviating,
irregular, mercurial, uncertain
10 capricious, inconstant,
modifiable, reversible **11** alternating, convertible, fluctuating, vacillating
13 transformable

change in plan
  French: **8** demarche

changeless 4 fast **5** fixed
6 stable **7** abiding, certain,
durable, eternal, lasting
8 constant, enduring **9** immutable, steadfast, unvarying
10 unshakable **11** everlasting,
unalterable **12** indissoluble

changelessness 9 certainty,
constancy, stability **10** durability, permanence **12** immutability **13** steadfastness

change of heart 10 conversion **16** change of attitude

changeover 10 conversion

channel 3 cut **4** gash, lead,
send **5** guide, route, steer
6 convey, course, direct, furrow, groove, gutter, strait,
trough **7** narrows, passage
11 watercourse **21** avenue of
communication

Channing, Carol
  born: **9** Seattle WA
  roles: **10** Hello Dolly

22 Gentlemen Prefer
Blondes, Thoroughly Mod-
ern Millie

chanson 4 song

Chanson de Roland
  also: **12** Song of Roland
  author: **7** unknown
  character: **4** Aude **6** Turpin
  7 Ganelon, Marsile, Olivier
  11 Charlemagne, Twelve
  Peers
  foe: **8** Saracens

chant 3 ode **4** hymn, lied, sing,
song **5** carol, croon, dirge, elegy, psalm, theme, trill, troll
6 chorus, intone, melody,
monody, strain **7** chanson,
chorale, descant **8** canticle,
doxology, threnody, vocalize
9 homophony, monophony, offertory, plainsong **11** Gloria
Patri **14** Gregorian chant

chanteuse 6 singer (female)

Chants de Maldoror, Les
  author: **18** Comte de
  Lautreamont

Chaon
  father: **5** Priam
  mother: **6** Hecuba
  brother: **5** Paris **6** Hector
  7 Helenus
  sister: **8** Polyxena
  9 Cassandra

chaos 4 mess **5** furor **6** bedlam,
jumble, muddle, tumult, up-
roar **7** turmoil **8** disarray, disorder, upheaval **9** agitation,
commotion, confusion **10** turbulence **11** pandemonium
12 discomposure **14** disarrangement **15** disorganization

Chaos
  origin: **5** Greek
  personifies: **9** confusion

chaotic 7 jumbled, mixed-up,
muddled, tangled **8** confused
9 confusing, illogical, turbulent **10** disjointed, incoherent,
in disarray **11** unorganized
12 disorganized
13 disharmonious

chap 3 boy, dry, guy, jaw, lad,
man, rap **4** chop, gent
5 bloke, buyer, crack, knock,
split **6** fellow, redden, split,
stroke **7** fissure, roughen
8 customer **9** purchaser

chapbook 7 garland **8** treasury **9** anthology **10** collection **11** florilegium

chapeau 3 hat

chapel 6 church, shrine **7** oratory **9** sanctuary **10** house of
God, tabernacle **14** place of
worship

chaperon, chaperone
5 guard, watch **6** duenna, es-

cort **7** oversee **8** guardian, shepherd **9** accompany, attendant, custodian, protector, safeguard **11** keep an eye on

chaperoned 7 oversaw **8** attended, escorted **10** supervised **11** accompanied

chapfallen 6 droopy **8** cast down, dejected **9** depressed

chaplain 4 abbe **5** padre, rabbi, vicar **6** cleric, curate, father, parson, pastor, priest, rector **7** Holy Joe **8** minister, preacher, reverend, sky pilot **9** churchman, clergyman **12** ecclesiastic

chaplet 4 band **6** fillet, wreath **7** circlet, coronet

Chaplin, Charlie
real name: **24** Sir Charles Spencer Chaplin
nickname: **14** the Little Tramp
wife: **10** Oona O'Neill **15** Paulette Goddard
daughter: **9** Geraldine
born: **6** London **7** England
director of/roles: **6** The Kid **8** The Tramp **9** Limelight **10** City Lights **11** Modern Times, The Gold Rush **15** Monsieur Verdoux **16** The Great Dictator

Chaplin, Geraldine
father: **14** Charlie Chaplin
mother: **17** Oona O'Neill Chaplin
born: **13** Santa Monica CA
roles: **12** The Hawaiians **13** Doctor Zhivago

chapter 3 era **4** body, part, span, unit **5** group, phase **6** branch, clause, period **7** episode, portion, section **8** division **9** affiliate **11** subdivision

Chapters of Erie
author: **10** Henry Adams

char 4 burn, sear **5** singe **6** scorch **9** carbonize **10** incinerate

character 4 part, role, self **5** being, honor **6** makeup, nature, person, traits, weirdo **7** honesty, oddball, persona **8** goodness, morality, original, specimen **9** eccentric, integrity, odd person, qualities, rectitude **10** attributes, individual, one-of-a-kind **11** personality, uprightness **13** individuality, moral strength **15** distinctiveness **16** dramatis personae

characteristic 4 mark **5** trait **6** aspect **7** earmark, feature, quality, typical **8** property, symbolic **9** attribute, mannerism, specialty, trademark **10** emblematic, indicative

11 distinctive, peculiarity **14** distinguishing, representative

characterization 8 portrait **9** depiction, picturing, portrayal **11** delineation, description **12** representing **14** representation

characterize 4 mark **5** class **6** define, depict, typify **7** earmark, portray **8** classify, describe, indicate **9** designate, represent **11** distinguish

characterless 4 weak **5** vague **6** anemic **11** nondescript **13** indeterminate **14** expressionless

Characters of Shakespeare's Plays, The
author: **14** William Hazlitt

Charcot, Jean Martin
nationality: **6** French
father of: **9** neurology

Chardin, Jean Baptiste Simeon
born: **5** Paris **6** France
artwork: **7** The Kiss **8** The Grace **14** Young Governess **16** The Copper Cistern **17** Attributes of Music **19** Attributes of the Arts **28** Rayfish Cat and Kitchen Utensils

charge 3 ask, bid, fee **4** care, cost, duty, fill, heap, lade, levy, load, pack, pile, rate, rush, toll **5** beset, blame, debit, exact, onset, order, price, stack, storm, stuff **6** accuse, advice, amount, assail, assess, assign, attack, come at, demand, direct, enjoin, impute, indict, sortie, summon **7** ascribe, assault, bidding, command, control, custody, dictate, expense, keeping, payment, require **8** call upon, instruct, storming **9** attribute, complaint, direction, enjoining, onslaught **10** accusation, allegation, assessment, indictment, injunction, management, protection **11** arraignment, incriminate, instruction, safekeeping, supervision **12** delay payment, guardianship, jurisdiction **14** administration, lay the blame for, request payment **15** superintendence **16** put on one's account

chargeable 6 liable **10** answerable **11** responsible

charged 5 taxed, tense **6** blamed, filled, levied, loaded, priced **7** accused, ordered, uptight **8** assessed, attacked, exhorted, mandated, prepared **9** commanded, entrusted

10 accusation, allegation, indictment

Charge of the Light Brigade, The
author: **18** Alfred Lord Tennyson
director: **13** Michael Curtiz
cast: **10** David Niven, Errol Flynn, Nigel Bruce **11** Donald Crisp **13** Patric Knowles **15** Henry Stephenson **17** Olivia de Havilland
setting: **6** Russia

charger 5 horse, mount, steed **6** vessel **7** accuser, platter **8** warhorse

charge with 5 trust **6** assign, commit **7** consign, entrust **8** delegate, hand over, turn over **9** authorize

Chariclo
husband: **6** Chiron
son: **8** Tiresias
companion of: **6** Athena

chariot 3 car **5** buggy **7** phaeton, vehicle **8** carriage

Charioteer
constellation of: **6** Auriga

Chariots of Fire
director: **10** Hugh Hudson
cast: **7** Ian Holm **8** Ben Cross (Harold Abrahams) **11** John Gielgud, Nigel Havers **12** Ian Charleson (Eric Liddell)
Oscar for: **5** score (Vangelis) **6** script **7** picture

Charis
member of: **6** Graces
husband: **10** Hephaestus

charisma 5 charm **6** allure, appeal **7** glamour **8** presence, witchery **9** magnetism, sex appeal **10** bewitchery **11** enchantment, fascination **14** attractiveness

charitable 4 kind **6** giving, kindly **7** lenient, liberal **8** generous, gracious, tolerant **9** bounteous, bountiful, forgiving, indulgent **10** almsgiving, benevolent, munificent, openhanded **11** considerate, kindhearted, magnanimous, sympathetic, warmhearted **12** eleemosynary, sympathizing **13** philanthropic, understanding

charitableness 10 liberality **11** benevolence, generousity **12** philanthropy **13** bountifulness **14** openhandedness **15** humanitarianism

Charites see **6** Graces

charity 3 aid **4** alms, fund, gift, help, love **6** bounty, giving **7** handout **8** altruism, donating, good will, goodness, humanity, kindness, offering, sympathy 9 benignity, donations, endowment, tolerance 10 alms-giving, assistance, compassion, generosity 11 benefaction, benevolence, fundraising, munificence 12 graciousness, philanthropy 13 contributions, financial help, love of mankind 14 open-handedness

charlatan 4 fake 5 cheat, fraud, quack 7 cozener 8 deceiver, imposter, impostor, swindler 9 trickster 10 mountebank 16 confidence artist

Charles, Nick and Nora
characters in: 10 The Thin Man
author: 7 Hammett

Charles O'Malley
author: 12 Charles Lever

Charleston 5 dance 13 ballroom dance
capital of: 9 W Virginia

Charlie's Angels
character: 10 Jill Monroe, John Bosley, Kris Munroe 12 Kelly Garrett 13 Sabrina Duncan 15 Charlie Townsend
cast: 10 Cheryl Ladd, David Doyle 11 Jaclyn Smith, Kate Jackson 18 Farah Fawcett-Majors
voice of Charlie: 12 John Forsythe

Charlotte's Web
author: 7 E B White

Charly
director: 11 Ralph Nelson
based on story by: 11 Daniel Keyes (Flowers for Algernon)
cast: 10 Leon Janney, Lilia Skala 11 Claire Bloom 13 Dick van Patten 14 Cliff Robertson
Oscar for: 5 actor (Robertson)

charm 4 draw, grip, lure, take 5 magic, spell 6 allure, amulet, bauble, cajole, engage, please, seduce, turn on 7 attract, beguile, bewitch, conjure, delight, enchant, gratify, sorcery, trinket, win over 8 charisma, enthrall, entrance, ornament, talisman 9 captivate, enrapture, fascinate, magnetism 10 allurement, attraction, cast a spell, lucky piece 11 conjuration, enchantment, fascination, incantation, work magic on

charmer 4 vamp 5 belle, siren 9 enchanter, temptress 11 en-

chantress, femme fatale, spellbinder

charming 6 lovely 7 likable, winning, winsome 8 alluring, engaging, enticing, fetching, graceful, magnetic, pleasing 9 agreeable 10 attractive, bewitching, delightful, enchanting, entrancing 11 captivating, charismatic, enthralling, fascinating 12 irresistible

charmless 4 dull 5 blunt 6 dreary 9 repulsive, unlikable, unlovable 10 unpleasant 12 disagreeable, unattractive

Charon
father: 6 Erebus
mother: 3 Nyx
occupation: 8 ferryman
river: 4 Styx

Charops
epithet of: 8 Hercules
means: 14 with bright eyes

Charpentier, Gustave
born: 6 Dieuze, France
composer of: 6 Julien, Louise 18 Impressions of Italy

chart 3 map 4 plan, plot 5 draft, graph, table 6 design, draw up, lay out, map out, scheme, sketch 7 diagram, outline 8 tabulate 9 blueprint, delineate 10 tabulation

charter 3 let 4 deed, hire, rent 5 grant, lease 6 employ, engage, permit 7 compact, license 8 contract, covenant, sanction 9 agreement, authority, authorize, franchise 10 commission, concession

Charterhouse of Parma, The
author: 23 Marie Henri Beyle Stendhal
character: 8 Marietta 10 Count Mosca 11 Clelia Conti 14 Gina Pietranera 16 Fabrizio del Dongo

chartreuse
type: 7 liqueur
origin: 6 France 15 Carthusian monks
flavor: 4 herb
color: 5 green 6 yellow
with apricot brandy: 13 Golden Slipper
with gin: 5 Bijou 9 Green Lady

chary 3 shy 4 wary 5 alert, cagey, leery 7 careful, guarded, heedful, prudent, sparing 8 cautious, hesitant, vigilant, watchful 10 economical, suspicious 11 circumspect, distrustful

Charybdis
form: 7 monster

father: 8 Poseidon
mother: 4 Gaea
identified with: 9 whirlpool

chase 3 dog 4 hunt, oust, rout, shoo, tail 5 drive, evict, hound, quest, stalk, track, trail 6 dispel, follow, pursue, shadow 7 cast out, go after, hunting, pursuit, repulse, scatter 8 pursuing, run after, send away, stalking, tracking 9 drive away, following 11 put to flight, send packing

Chase, Chevy
real name: 19 Cornelius Crane Chase
born: 9 New York NY
roles: 8 Foul Play, Vacation 10 Caddyshack 17 Saturday Night Live

chasm 3 gap, pit 4 gulf, hold, rift 5 abyss, break, cleft, crack, gorge, gulch, split 6 breach, cavity, crater, divide, ravine 7 fissure 8 crevasse

chasseur 6 hunter

chaste 4 pure 5 clean 6 decent, modest, severe, strict 7 austere, classic, precise, sinless 8 virginal, virtuous 9 continent, righteous, unadorned, unsullied, untainted, wholesome 10 immaculate, restrained 11 clean-living, uncorrupted 12 unornamented 13 unembellished

chasten 5 chide, scold 6 berate, punish, rebuke 7 censure, reprove, upbraid 8 admonish, chastise, reproach 9 reprimand 10 discipline, take to task

chastened 7 humbled 8 contrite, penitent 9 repentant 10 remorseful 18 conscience-stricken

chastise 4 beat, flog, whip 5 chide, roast, scold, spank, strap 6 berate, punish, rebuke, thrash 7 censure, chasten, correct, reprove, scourge, upbraid 8 admonish, call down, penalize, reproach 9 castigate, criticize, reprimand 10 discipline, take to task, tongue-lash 15 call on the carpet 16 fulminate against, haul over the coals

chastisement 10 correction, discipline, punishment 11 castigation 12 reprimanding

chastity 6 purity 8 celibacy 9 innocence, virginity 10 abstinence, continence, singleness 12 bachelorhood, spinsterhood 14 abstemiousness
goddess of: 5 Diana, Fauna 7 Artemis, Bona Dea

chasuble 6 casual 7 garment 8 vestment

Chasuble, Reverend Canon character in: 27 The Importance of Being Earnest author: 5 Wilde

chat 3 gab, rap 4 talk 5 prate 7 chatter, palaver, prattle 8 chitchat, converse 10 chew the fat, chew the rag, rap session 11 talk session 12 conversation 13 confabulation 16 heart-to-heart talk

chateau 4 wine 6 castle, estate 7 mansion 8 chatelet 12 country house

Chateaubriand, Francois Rene author of: 4 Rene 5 Atala 10 Los Natchez, The Martyrs 19 Memoires d'Outretombe 24 Memoirs from Beyond the Tomb

Chateau d'If prison in: 21 The Count of Monte Cristo author: 5 Dumas (pere)

Chateaupers, Phoebus de character in: 23 The Hunchback of Notre Dame author: 4 Hugo

chattel 4 gear 6 things 7 effects 8 movables 9 trappings 10 belongings 13 accouterments, paraphernalia 15 personal effects 19 personal possessions

chatter 3 gas 4 blab, talk 5 clank, click, prate 6 babble, gabble, gibber, gossip, jabber, patter 7 blabber, blather, clatter, palaver, prattle, talking, twaddle 8 blabbing, chitchat, idle talk, talk idly 11 confabulate 14 chitterchatter

chatterbox 6 gabber, gasbag, gossip, talker 7 babbler, tattler, windbag 8 jabberer, prattler, tell tale 9 chatterer 10 talebearer, tattle tale 12 blabbermouth, blatherskite, hot-air artist 13 chatterbasket

chatty 5 gabby, gassy, gushy, talky, windy 7 gossipy, gushing, prating, verbose, voluble 8 babbling, chatting, effusive 9 garrulous, jabbering, talkative 10 blabbering, longwinded, loquacious 11 looselipped 12 loose-tongued 13 tongue-wagging

Chaucer, Geoffrey author of: 18 The Canterbury Tales, Troilus and Criseyde 19 The Book of the Duchess 20 The Legend of Good Women, The Parlement of Fowles

Chauchoin, Claudette Lily real name of: 16 Claudette Colbert

chauffeur 6 driver

chaussure 4 boot, shoe 8 footwear

chauvinism 8 jingoism 10 flagwaving, militarism, patriotism 11 nationalism 15 ethnocentricity, superpatriotism

cheap 4 base, easy, mean, poor 5 close, gaudy, petty, tacky, tight 6 common, flashy, meager, paltry, shabby, shoddy, sordid, stingy, tawdry, trashy, two-bit, vulgar 7 ignoble, immoral, miserly 8 costless, gimcrack, indecent, inferior, wretched 9 inelegant, low-priced, penurious, worthless 10 despicable, economical, effortless, in bad taste, reasonable, second-rate 11 inexpensive, tightfisted 12 contemptible

Cheaper by the Dozen author: 14 Frank B Gilbreth (with Ernestine Gilbreth Carey)

cheat 3 con, gyp 4 bilk, dupe, fake, foil, fool, gull, hoax, rook, take 5 cozen, crook, fraud, quack, shark, trick 6 baffle, betray, defeat, delude, dodger, escape, fleece, humbug, outwit, thwart 7 deceive, defraud, mislead, swindle 8 chiseler, deceiver, hoodwink, imposter, impostor, swindler 9 bamboozle, charlatan, con artist, frustrate, trickster, victimize 10 circumvent, mountebank 11 short-change 13 break the rules, double-crosser

check 3 bar, end, fit, gag 4 curb, halt, hold, jibe, mesh, rein, slow, stay, stop, test 5 agree, block, brake, chime, choke, limit, probe, stall, study, tally 6 arrest, bridle, impede, look at, muzzle, peruse, rein in, retard, review, search, survey, thwart 7 barrier, conform, control, examine, explore, harness, inhibit, inspect, explore, prevent, smother 8 hold back, look into, look over, obstacle, obstruct, restrain, scrutiny, stoppage, suppress 9 cessation, constrain, frustrate, harmonize, hindrance, restraint 10 circumvent, constraint, correspond, impediment, inspection, limitation, prevention, repression, scrutinize 11 examination, exploration, investigate, obstruction, prohibition, restriction, take stock of

13 investigation 18 bring to a standstill

checkered 4 pied 6 fitful, motley, seesaw, uneven, varied 7 checked, dappled, mottled, piebald 9 irregular, up-and-down 10 inconstant, variegated 11 fluctuating, vacillating 12 parti-colored

checkmate 4 rout, stop 6 corner, defeat, outwit, stymie, thwart 8 deadlock 9 frustrate, overthrow 11 countermove

cheder, heder 12 Jewish school

cheek 4 jowl 5 brass, nerve 8 audacity, boldness, temerity 9 arrogance, brashness, impudence, insolence 10 brazenness, effrontery 11 forwardness 12 impertinence

cheep 4 peep 5 chirp, tweet 7 chirrup, chitter, twitter

cheer 3 cry, fun, joy 4 glee, hail, hope, root, warm, yell 5 bravo, shout 6 assure, buoy up, gaiety, hooray, hurrah, huzzah, shriek, uplift 7 acclaim, animate, comfort, delight, enliven, fortify, gladden, hearten, inspire, revelry 8 brighten, buoyance, buoyancy, gladness, optimism, pleasure, reassure, vivacity 9 animation, assurance, encourage, festivity, geniality, joviality, merriment, rejoicing 10 joyfulness, jubilation, liveliness 11 acclamation, high spirits, hopefulness, merrymaking, reassurance 13 encouragement

cheerful 3 gay 4 airy, glad 5 happy, jolly, merry, sunny 6 blithe, breezy, bright, cheery, elated, jaunty, jovial, joyful, joyous, lively 7 buoyant, gleeful 8 gladsome, pleasant 9 agreeable, sparkling, sprightly 10 optimistic 11 in high humor 12 high-spirited, lighthearted

cheerfulness 5 gaity 7 jollity 8 buoyancy, optimism 9 joviality, merriment 10 brightness, cheeriness 11 high spirits 16 lightheartedness

cheerless 3 sad 4 dull, glum, gray, grim 5 bleak 6 dismal, dreary, gloomy, morose, rueful, solemn, somber, sullen, woeful 7 austere, doleful, forlorn, joyless, sunless, unhappy 8 dejected, desolate, dolorous, downcast, funereal, mournful 9 miserable, saturnine, woebegone 10 depressing, despondent, dispirited, lugubrious, melancholy, spiritless, uninviting **11** comfortless, downhearted **12** disconsolate, heavy-hearted

Cheers
location: **3** bar **6** Boston
character: **4** Norm **5** Cliff, Coach, Woody **5** Lilith **7** Rebecca **9** Sam Malone **13** Carla Tortelli, Diane Chambers
cast: **9** Ted Danson **11** George Wendt, Rhea Perlman, Shelley Long **12** Kirstie Alley **13** Kelsey Grammer **14** Woody Harrelson **16** John Ratzenberger

cheer up 5 pep up **6** buoy up **7** comfort, enliven, hearten **8** brighten, inspirit **9** bolster up, encourage **18** bolster one's spirits

cheery 3 gay **5** happy, jolly, merry, sunny **6** bright, joyful **9** sprightly **12** lighthearted

Cheeryble Brothers
nephew: **5** Frank
characters in: **16** Nicholas Nickleby
author: **7** Dickens

cheese
French: **7** fromage
kind: **4** bleu, blue, brie, edam, feta, jack **5** brick, colby, cream, gouda, Swiss **6** romano, samsoe **7** cheddar, cottage, fontina, gjetost, gruyere, limburg, munster, ricotta, sapsago, stilton **8** American, bel paese, cheshire, emmental, muenster, parmesan, port wine, raclette **9** camembert, jarlsberg, limburger, port salut, provolone, roquefort **10** caerphilly, Danish blue, Gloucester, gorgonzola, mozzarella, neufchatel **11** emmenthaler, liederkranz, petit suisse, port du salut, wensleydale **12** monterey jack

Cheever, John
author of: **8** Falconer **10** Bullet Park **16** The Enormous Radio, The World of Apples **17** The Wapshot Scandal **19** The Wapshot Chronicle **20** The Way Some People Live **22** Oh What a Paradise It Seems

Chekhov, Anton
author of: **6** Ivanov **10** The Sea Gull, Uncle Vanya **15** The Three Sisters **16** The Cherry Orchard

Chelciope
father: **6** Aeetes
mother: **5** Idyia
sister: **5** Medea
husband: **7** Phrixus

son: **5** Argus, Melas **8** Phrontis **9** Thessalus **10** Cytissorus

Chelidon
sister: **5** Aedon
brother-in-law: **11** Polytechnus
changed into: **7** swallow
changed by: **7** Artemis

---

chemical symbols
actinium: **2** Ac
aluminum: **2** Al
antimony: **2** Sb
argon: **2** Ar
arsenic: **2** As
barium: **2** Ba
boron: **1** B
bromine: **2** Br
cadmium: **2** Cd
calcium: **2** Ca
carbon: **1** C
chlorine: **2** Cl
chromium: **2** Cr
cobalt: **2** Co
columbium: **2** Cb
copper: **2** Cu
fluorine: **1** F
gold: **2** Au
hafnium: **2** Hf
helium: **2** He
hydrogen: **1** H
iodine: **1** I
iron: **2** Fe
krypton: **2** Kr
lead: **2** Pb
lithium: **2** Li
magnesium: **2** Mg
manganese: **2** Mn
mercury: **2** Hg
molybdenum: **2** Mo
neon: **2** Ne
nickel: **2** Ni
nitrogen: **1** N
oxygen: **1** O
phosphorus: **1** P
platinum: **2** Pt
plutonium: **2** Pu
potassium: **1** K
radium: **2** Ra
radon: **2** Rn
rhodium: **2** Rh
rubidium: **2** Rb
silicon: **2** Si
silver: **2** Ag
sodium: **2** Na
sulfur: **1** S
thorium: **2** Th
tin: **2** Sn
titanium: **2** Ti
tungsten: **1** W
uranium: **1** U
xenon: **2** Xe
zinc: **2** Zn
zirconium: **2** Zr

---

chemise 4 slip **5** dress, shift, shirt, smock **6** blouse **7** garment **8** camisole, lingerie, unbelted **12** undergarment

chemist
American: **4** Urey **5** Tatum **6** Carver **7** Axelrod, Lipmann, Pauling **8** Kornberg, Langmuir, McMillan **9** Carothers **10** Baeklel and
British: **4** Davy **5** Boyle, Chain, Soddy **6** Dalton, Ramsay **7** Faraday **8** Smithson **9** Cavendish, Priestley, Wollaston
Dutch: **4** Hoff
French: **5** Curie, Le Bel **6** Cuvier, Dulong **7** Pasteur **9** Gay-Lussac, Lavoisier **10** Berthollet **11** Joliot-Curie
German: **4** Hahn **5** Krebs **6** Baeyer, Wohler **7** Glauber, Ostwald
Italian: **8** Avogadro
Russian: **9** Mendeleev **10** Mendeleyev
Scottish: **5** Dewar
Swedish: **7** Scheele **9** Arrhenius, Berzelius
Swiss: **6** Muller

Chemosh 10 Moabite god

Chennault, Claire L
served in: **4** WWII **15** Sino-Japanese War
commander of: **12** Flying Tigers
general in: **12** Army Air Force
air advisor to: **13** Chiang Kai-shek

cherchez la femme 15 look for the woman

cherie 4 dear **10** sweetheart

cherish 4 love **5** honor, nurse, prize, value **6** dote on, esteem, revere, succor **7** care for, idolize, nourish, nurture, shelter, sustain **8** hold dear, treasure, venerate **10** appreciate, take care of

cherished 4 dear **5** loved **7** beloved, darling, dearest **8** favorite, held dear, precious **9** treasured

Cherokee
language family: **9** Iroquoian
location: **7** Alabama, Georgia **8** Oklahoma, Virginia **9** Tennessee **13** North Carolina, South Carolina
associated with: **12** Trail of Tears
scholar: **7** Sequoya

cherry
varieties: **3** pie, pin, rum **4** bing, bird, duke, fire, sand, sour, wild **5** black, brush, choke, dwarf, Higan, Naden, sweet **6** bitter, Brazil, ground, Indian, Madden, Oregon, Taiwan, winter **7** bastard, Cayenne, Morello, Nanking, Potomac, prairie, rosebud, sargent, Spanish, St

Lucie, wild red, Windsor, Yoshino **8** Barbados, Catalina, oriental, perfumed, Suriname **9** christmas, cornelian, evergreen, Jerusalem, wild black **10** west indian **11** downy ground, Hansen's bush, holly-leaved, western sand **12** clammy ground, European bird, Japanese bush, purple ground **13** European dwarf **14** European ground, false Jerusalem, purple-leaf sand **15** Australian brush **17** Japanese cornelian, Japanese flowering, north Japanese hill
drink: **6** kirsch

cherry brandy 6 kirsch
12 Peter Heering

Cherry Orchard, The
author: **12** Anton Chekhov
character: **4** Anya, Gaev
5 Fiers, Varya, Yasha **7** Pischin **8** Dunyasha, Lopakhin, Trofimov **9** Charlotta
16 Madame Ranevskaya

cherub 4 amor **5** angel, child, cupid, youth **6** moppet **8** cherubim **13** heavenly being

cherubic 7 angelic **8** innocent
9 spiritual

Cherubin
character in: **19** The Marriage of Figaro
author: **12** Beaumarchais

chervil
botanical name: **20** Anthriscus cerefolium
origin: **6** Europe, Russia
use: **4** soup **5** salad **11** fines herbes, potato salad

Chesapeake
author: **13** James Michener

Cheshire Cat
character in: **28** Alice's Adventures in Wonderland
author: **7** Carroll

chess *see* box

chest
Italian: **5** petto

Chester, Edward
character in: **12** Barnaby Rudge
author: **7** Dickens

chesterfield 4 coat, sofa
5 couch **8** overcoat
9 davenport

Chesterton, G K (Gilbert Keith)
author of: **20** The Man Who Was Thursday **24** The Napoleon of Notting Hill **25** The Innocence of Father Brown

chess
also called: **9** Royal Game
chess champion:
4 Euwe, Fine, Tahl
6 Karpov, Lasker
7 Fischer, Kashdan, Smyslov, Spassky
8 Alekhine, Kasparov, Philador, Steinitz **9** Anderssen, Botvinnik, Petrosian, Reshevsky
10 Capablanca
French: **6** echecs
German: **11** schachspiel
horizontal rows: **4** rank
international chess federation: **4** FIDE
patron goddess/muse:
6 Caissa
piece: **4** king, pawn, rook **5** queen **6** bishop, castle, knight **8** chessman, material
Russian: **8** shakhmat
Spanish: **7** Ajedrez
term: **3** pin **4** fork, hole **5** check, tempo **6** center **7** isolani, outpost **8** castling, majority, open file, queening, zugzwang **9** checkmate, en passant, promotion **10** fianchetto **11** zwischenzug
tied game: **4** draw
9 stalemate
vertical rows: **4** file

chestnut 8 Castanea
varieties: **4** Cape, Wild **5** Horse, Water **6** Guiana, Marron **7** Chinese, Spanish **8** American, Eurasian, European, Japanese, Red horse **10** Dwarf horse, Moreton Bay **11** Common horse **12** Chinese water **13** European horse, Japanese horse **15** California horse

chestnut-colored 6 auburn, russet, sienna **8** cinnamon, nut-brown **11** golden-brown, rust-colored **12** reddish-brown

chest of drawers 5 chest **6** bureau, lowboy **7** cabinet, commode, dresser, highboy, tallboy **10** chiffonier

cheval 5 horse

chevalier 4 lord **5** cadet, noble **6** knight **7** gallant **8** cavalier

Chevalier, Maurice
born: **5** Paris **6** France
roles: **4** Gigi **5** Fanny **6** Can-Can **13** The Love Parade,

The Merry Widow **18** Love in the Afternoon

chew 4 gnaw **5** champ, crush, grind, munch **6** crunch, nibble **8** ruminate **9** masticate

Chew
character in: **21** The Master of Ballantrae
author: **9** Stevenson

chewing-out 6 rebuke **7** censure, chiding, reproof **8** reproach, scolding **9** reprimand **10** bawling-out, upbraiding **11** castigation, reprobation **12** dressing-down, remonstrance **13** tongue-lashing

chew noisily 4 gnaw **5** chomp, gnash, grind, munch **6** crunch

chew out 5 scold **6** berate, rail at, rebuke **7** bawl out, reprove, upbraid **8** reproach **9** castigate, reprimand **10** take to task, tongue-lash **14** read the riot act

chew the fat 3 gab, gas **4** blab, chat, talk **5** prate **6** gossip, patter **7** blather, chatter, palaver, prattle, twaddle **8** chitchat, converse, talk idly **10** chew the rag **11** confabulate **14** chitterchatter

chew the rag 3 gab, gas, jaw, rap **4** chat, chin, talk **5** prate **7** chatter, palaver, prattle **8** chitchat, converse **10** chew the fat **11** confabulate

Cheyenne
language family: **9** Algonkian **10** Algonquian
location: **6** Platte **7** Montana, Wyoming **8** Oklahoma, Red River **9** Minnesota **11** South Dakota
allied with: **7** Arapaho

Cheyenne
character: **6** Smitty **13** Cheyenne Bodie
cast: **7** L Q Jones **11** Clint Walker

chez 4 with **6** at home

Chiang Kai-shek
leader of: **5** China **6** Taiwan
ally: **9** Sun Yat-sen
party: **10** Kuomintang **11** Nationalist
defeated by: **10** Communists
wife: **12** Soong Mei-ling

Chibcha (Muisca)
location: **6** Bogota, Panama **8** Colombia **12** South America
associated with: **8** El Dorado

Chibchan
language family: **13** Macro-Chibchan
group: **4** Cuna, Paya, Rama **5** Lenca, Xinca **7** Chibcha

chic 5 natty, ritzy, smart, swank **6** classy, modish, snazzy, swanky **7** elegant, stylish, voguish **11** fashionable

Chicago
author: **12** Carl Sandburg

Chicago see box

chicanery 4 ruse, wile **5** craft, fraud, guile **6** deceit, duping **7** cunning, gulling, knavery, roguery **8** artifice, cozenage, trickery, villainy **9** deception, duplicity, rascality, sophistry **10** craftiness, hocus-pocus, humbuggery, subterfuge **11** hoodwinking **12** pettifoggery **13** double-dealing

chichi 4 arty **5** fussy, showy **6** flashy, frilly, garish, prissy, vulgar **7** finical, pompous, splashy **8** affected, gimcrack, overnice, precious, sissyish **9** arty-tarty, grandiose, nastynice **10** flamboyant **11** overrefined, pretentious **12** artsycraftsy, ostentatious

chick
group of: **5** brood **6** clutch

Chickasaw
language family: **10** Muskhogean
location: **8** Oklahoma **9** Tennessee **11** Mississippi
related to: **7** Choctaw
member of: **19** Five Civilized Tribes

chicken, chickenhearted 3 hen **4** cock, fowl **5** layer, timid **6** afraid, coward, craven, pullet, scared, yellow **7** caitiff, dastard, fearful, gutless, rooster **8** cowardly, poltroon, timorous **9** flinching, fraidy-cat, shrinking **11** lily-livered, yellow-belly **12** fainthearted **13** pusillanimous, yellow-bellied **22** showing the white feather

chickenheartedness 8 timidity **9** cowardice **10** yellowness **11** fearfulness, poltroonery **12** timorousness **13** pusillanimity **16** faintheartedness

chide 5 scold **6** berate, rebuke **7** censure, chasten, reprove, upbraid **8** admonish, denounce, reproach **9** criticize, find fault, reprimand **10** take to task

chief 3 key **4** boss, head, lord, main **5** first, major, prime, ruler **6** leader, master, ruling **7** captain, highest, leading, monarch, primary, supreme **8** cardinal, chairman, crowning, director, dominant, foremost, greatest, overlord, overseer **9** chieftain, com-

mander, governing, number-one, paramount, potentate, principal, sovereign, uppermost **10** prevailing, ringleader, supervisor **11** outstanding, predominant **12** preponderant **13** administrator

chief good
Latin: **11** summum bonum

chiefly 5 first **6** mainly, mostly **8** above all **9** expressly, in the main, most of all, primarily **10** especially **11** principally **12** particularly **13** predominantly

chieftan 4 boss, head **6** leader **7** captain, head man

chiffonier 6 bureau **7** dresser **8** cupboard **14** chest of drawers

chignon 3 bun **4** knot, roll **6** hairdo **9** hairpiece, hairstyle

child 3 boy, kid, lad, son, tad, tot **4** baby, girl, lass, tyke **5** youth **6** infant, moppet **7** toddler **8** daughter, juvenile **9** little one, offspring, youngster

childbearing 5 birth **11** parturition

childbirth 8 delivery **11** confinement, parturition
French: **12** accouchement
goddess of: **4** Upis **5** Parca **6** Lucina, Matuta **7** Artemis **8** Ilithyia **10** Eileithyia

Childe Harold's Pilgrimage
author: **21** George Gordon Lord Byron

Childe Roland to the Dark Tower Came
author: **14** Robert Browning

childhood 5 youth **7** boyhood **8** girlhood **10** school days **11** adolescence, nursery days

childish 5 naive, silly **6** callow, simple **7** asinine, babyish, foolish, puerile **8** immature, juvenile **9** infantile **10** adolescent

childlike 8 childish, immature, innocent **9** ingenuous

child prodigy
German: **10** Wunderkind

children 4 boys, kids, sons, tads, tots **5** girls, issue, young **6** babies, result, youth **7** infants, product, progeny **9** daughters, juveniles **11** descendants

Children of God
author: **12** Vardis Fisher

Children of Paradise
director: **11** Marcel Carne
cast: **7** Arletty **11** Albert Remay **14** Pierre Brasseur **17** Jean-Louis Barrault

Child's Garden of Verses, A
author: **20** Robert Louis Stevenson

Chile see box, p. 176

chill, chilly 3 icy, nip, raw **4** bite, cold, cool, keen **5** aloof, brisk, crisp, fever, harsh, nippy, sharp, stiff, stony **6** arctic, biting, bitter, frigid, frosty, frozen, wintry

---

Chicago
airport: **5** O'Hare **6** Midway
baseball team: **4** Cubs **8** White Sox
basketball team: **5** Bulls
downtown area: **4** Loop
football team: **5** Bears
fort: **8** Dearborn
hockey team: **10** Black Hawks
lake: **4** Wolf **7** Calumet **8** Michigan
landmark: **10** Meigs Field, Sears Tower **12** Board of Trade, Comiskey Park, Humboldt Park, Soldier Field, Wrigley Field **13** Shedd Aquarium **15** Lincoln Monument, Merchandise Mart, Newberry Library, Wrigley Building **16** Adler Planetarium **17** Holy Name Cathedral, John Hancock Center **18** Mercantile Exchange, Prudential Building **20** Midwest Stock Exchange **21** Art Institute of Chicago **23** Museum of Contemporary Art **26** Museum of Science and Industry **27** Field Museum of Natural History
mayor: **5** Byrne, Daley **10** Washington
nickname: **9** Windy City
river: **7** Chicago **10** Des Plaines
street: **11** Wacker Drive **13** Chicago Skyway **14** Lake Shore Drive
university: **6** DePaul, Loyola **9** Roosevelt **12** Northwestern **29** Illinois Institute of Technology

Chile

other name: 6 Tchile

name means: 21 deepest part of the Earth

capital/largest city: 8 Santiago

others: 4 Boco, Cuya, Lebu, Lota, Ocoa, Tome 5 Angol, Arica, Cobya, Talca 6 Arauco, Calama, Curico, Gatico, Osorno, Ovalle, Serena, Temuco, Vicuna, Yumbel, Yungay 7 Caldera, Chillan, Copiapo, Iquique, Valdiva 8 Coquimbo, Rancagua, Santiago, Vallenar 9 Cauquenes 10 Concepcion, Coquembana, Valparaiso, Vina del Mar 11 Antofagasta, Puerto Montt, Punta Arenas, San Bernardo

measure: 4 vara 5 legua, linea 6 cuadra, fanega

monetary unit: 4 peso 5 libra 6 condor, escudo

weight: 5 grano, libra 7 quintal

island: 3 Luz 4 Prat 5 Byron, Guafo, Hoste, Mocha, Nueva, Nunez, Vidal 6 Chiloe, Chonos, Dawson, Easter, Lennox, Piazzi, Picton, Quilan, Riesco, Stosch, Talcan 7 Angamos, Campana, Hanover, Hermite, Pajaros, Refugio, Tranqui 8 Chauques, Clarence, Huamblin, Nalcayec, Navarino, Traiguen 13 Juan Fernandez 14 Tierra del Fuego

lake: 5 Ranco 6 Yelcho 7 Puyehue, Rupanco 8 Cochrane 10 General Paz, Llanquihue 11 Buenos Aires

mountain: 4 Maca, Toro 5 Chato, Maipo, Maipu, Paine, Potro, Pular, Torre, Yogan 6 Apiwan, Burney, Conico, Jervis, Poquis, Rincon 7 Chaltel, Copiapo, Fitzroy, Palpana, Velluda 8 Cochrane, Tronador, Yanteles 9 Tupungato

highest point: 13 Ojos del Salado

river: 3 Loa 4 Laja, Yali 5 Alhue, Azapa, Bravo, Bueno, Elqui, Lauca, Lluta, Maipo, Maule, Puelo, Rahue, Rapel, Stata, Vitor 6 Biobio, Camina, Choapa, Choros, Cisnes, Colina, Huasco, Limari, Morado, Palena, Poscua, Tolten 7 Copiapo 8 Valdivia

sea: 7 Pacific

physical features:
  bay: 4 Cook, Eyre, Nena, Tarn 5 Lomas, Otway, Sarco 6 Darwin, Inutil, Moreno, Stokes, Tongoy 7 Dyneley, Inglesa, Skyring 8 Desolate
  cape: 4 Dyer, Horn 6 Choros, Falsos, Hornos, Quilan, Tablas 7 Deseado 10 Tres Montes
  channel: 5 Ancho, Cheap 6 Beagle 8 Cockburn, Moraleda
  desert: 7 Atacama
  gulf: 5 Ancud, Guafo, Penas 6 Arauco
  isthmus: 5 Ofqui
  peninsula: 5 Hardy, Lacuy 6 Taitao, Tumbes
  point: 4 Toro 5 Gallo, Liles, Lobos, Loros, Morro, Talca, Tetas, Vieja 6 Cachos, Galera, Molles 7 Angamos, Lavapie
  strait: 6 Nelson 8 Magellan
  volcano: 5 Lanin, Maipo 6 Antuco, Llaima, Oyahue, Tacora 7 Peteroa, Socomap

people: 3 Ona 4 Auca, Inca, Onan 6 Arauca, Chango, Yahgan 7 Mapuche, mestizo, Moluche, Pampean, Patagon, Puegian, Ranquel 8 Alikuluf, Picunche, Tsonecan
  author: 5 Bello 6 Donoso, Neruda 7 Mistral
  conqueror: 7 Valdiva
  explorer: 8 Magellan
  leader: 7 Allende 8 O'Higgins, Pinochet 9 San Martin 10 Alessandri

language: 7 Spanish

religion: 13 Roman Catholic

places:
  copper mine: 12 Chuquicamata
  resort: 8 Portillo 10 Vina del Mar

possession: 12 Easter Island 20 Juan Fernandez Islands

feature:
  cowboy: 5 huaso
  dance: 5 cueca 6 pequen 9 resbalosa
  shrub: 5 litre
  slum: 9 callempas
  tree: 5 rauli
  wind instrument: 4 sicu

food:
  drink: 5 pisco 6 chicha
  hot red pepper: 3 aji
  meat pie: 8 empanada
  soup: 7 cazuela 8 caldillo

7 callous, coolish, cutting, glacial, hostile, iciness, rawness, shivery **8** coolness, uncaring **9** crispness, frigidity, sharpness, unfeeling **10** forbidding, frostiness, unfriendly **11** indifferent, passionless, penetrating **12** unresponsive

chilled 4 cold, iced **6** cooled, frozen **7** frosted **8** hardened **10** dispirited **11** discouraged **12** refrigerated

chilling 3 icy, raw **5** nippy, on ice **6** frigid **7** bracing, cooling **10** unfriendly

Chillingworth, Roger
character in: **16** The Scarlet Letter
author: **9** Hawthorne

chime 4 gong, peal, ring, toll **5** knell, sound **6** jingle, tinkle **7** pealing, ringing **8** carillon, ding-dong, tinkling, tollings **10** set of bells **14** tintinnabulate **16** tintinnabulation

Chimene
character in: **6** The Cid
author: **9** Corneille

chimera 5 dream, fancy **6** bubble, mirage **7** fantasy, monster, phantom **8** daydream, delusion, idle whim, illusion **9** pipe dream **10** self-deceit, she-monster **12** will-o'-the-wisp **13** castle in Spain, fool's paradise, hallucination, self-deception **14** castle in the air **24** figment of one's imagination

Chimera
form: **7** monster
father: **6** Typhon
mother: **7** Echidna
breathes: **4** fire

Chimera
author: **9** John Barth

chimerical 6 absurd, unreal **7** utopian **8** delusive, ethereal, fabulous, fanciful, illusory, mythical quixotic **9** fantastic, imaginary, visionary **10** impossible, phantasmal, **11** nonexistent

chimney 4 flue, tube, vent **5** cleft, gully, spout, stack **6** funnel, hearth **7** opening **9** stovepipe **10** smokestack

chimpanzee 3 ape **6** animal, baboon, monkey

chin 3 gab, jaw, rap **4** chat, talk **7** chatter, palaver **8** chitchat, converse **10** chew the fat, chew the rag **11** confabulate

china 6 dishes, plates **7** pottery **8** crockery **9** chinaware, porcelain, stoneware, table-

ware **11** ceramic ware, earthenware **14** cups and saucers

China *see box, p. 178*

China Syndrome, The
director: **12** James Bridges
cast: **9** Jane Fonda **10** Jack Lemmon, Scott Brady **14** Michael Douglas
setting: **17** nuclear power plant

Chinatown
director: **13** Roman Polanski
cast: **10** John Huston **11** Faye Dunaway **13** Jack Nicholson
Oscar for: **5** story **10** screenplay

chinaware 6 dishes, plates **7** pottery **8** crockery **9** porcelain, stoneware, tableware **11** ceramic ware, earthenware **14** cups and saucers

chine 5 spine **6** dorsum **8** backbone

Chinese book of divination
6 I Ching

Chingachgook
character in: **13** The Pathfinder **20** The Last of the Mohicans
author: **6** Cooper

chink 3 cut, gap **4** gash, hole, rent, rift, ring, slit **5** break, clank, cleft, clink, crack, fault, split **6** breach, jangle, jingle, rattle, tinkle **7** crevice, fissure, opening **8** aperture

Chinook (Flathead)
language family: **9** Chinookan
location: **7** Pacific **10** Washington
ritual: **15** head deformation

Chinookan
tribe: **7** Chinook **8** Flathead

chintzy 5 cheap, close, dowdy, tacky, tatty, tight **6** frowzy, frumpy, shabby, sleazy, stingy **7** miserly **8** grudging, schlocky, stinting **9** niggardly, penurious **11** closefisted **12** parsimonious **13** penny-pinching

Chione
father: **6** Boreas **9** Daedalion
mother: **8** Orithyia
son: **9** Autolycus, Philammon

chip 3 bit, cut, hew **4** chop, gash, hack, nick **5** chunk, crumb, flake, scrap, shred, slice, split, wafer **6** chisel, morsel, paring, sliver **7** cutting, shaving, whittle **8** fragment, splinter

chipmunk 6 chippy, gopher, rodent **8** chipmuck, squirrel **14** ground squirrel **16** chipping squirrel

chipper 3 gay **4** pert, spry **5** alive, brisk, peppy **6** frisky, jaunty, lively **8** animated, carefree, cheerful, spirited **9** easygoing, energetic, sprightly, vivacious **12** high-spirited, light-hearted

Chippewa (Ojibwa, Ojibway)
language family: **9** Algonkian **10** Algonquian
tribe: **4** Cree **6** Ottawa **8** Chippewa **10** Missisauga
location: **6** Canada **9** Lake Huron **11** North Dakota **12** Lake Superior, Niagara Falls
leader: **7** Pontiac

CHiPS
character: **8** (Officer) Jon Baker **10** (Sgt) Joe Getraer **16** (Officer) Frank (Ponch) Poncherello
cast: **10** Robert Pine **11** Erik Estrada, Larry Wilcox

Chirico, Giorgio de
born: **5** Volos **6** Greece
artwork: **15** Enigma of the Hour **19** Enigma of an Afternoon **21** Enigma of an Autumn Night **22** Nostalgia of the Infinite **32** The Melancholy and Mystery of a Street

Chiron
also: **7** Cheiron
form: **7** centaur
father: **6** Cronos, Cronus, Kronos
mother: **7** Philyra
wife: **8** Chariclo
daughter: **6** Endeis
grandson: **6** Peleus
occupation: **7** teacher

chirp 4 peep, sing **5** cheep, chirr, tweet **7** chirrup, chitter, peeping, twitter **8** cheeping

chirrup 4 peep **5** cheep, chirp, tweet **7** chitter, twitter

chisel 3 cut, gyp **4** gull, hoax, rook, tool **5** blade, cheat, slice **6** incise
type: **4** cape, cold, wood **7** v-shaped

Chisel
constellation of: **6** Caelum

chiseler 4 fake **5** cheat, fraud, quack **7** cheater **8** swindler

Chislev 16 ninth Hebrew month

chit 3 IOU, tab **4** note **5** check **7** voucher

chitchat 3 gab **4** chat **5** prate **6** drivel, gossip **7** chatter, palaver, prattle **8** converse **9** small talk **10** chew the fat, chew the rag **11** confabulate **13** confabulation

China

other name: 3 PRC 13 Middle Kingdom 14 Flowery Kingdom 22 People's Republic of China

capital: 6 Peking 7 Beijing

largest city: 8 Shanghai

others: 3 Bai, Noh 4 Ahpa, Amoy, Fuyu, Guma, Hami, Huma, Ipin, Kian, Kisi, Lini, Loho, Luta, Moho, Moyu, Niya, Noho, Omin, Rima, Saka, Sian, Taku, Tali, Tayu, Wuhu, Yaan 5 Chiai, Fusin, Kirin, Koklu, Linyu, Macao, Penki, Shasi, Soche, Taian, Talai, Tihwa, Tuyun, Wuhan, Wusih, Yenan, Yenki, Yulin, Yumen 6 Anshan, Antung, Canton, Dairen, Fuchau, Fuchow, Fushun, Hankow, Harbin, Ilhasa, Kalgan, Loyang, Lushun, Mukden, Nanhai, Ningpo, Singan, Sining, Taipei, Tsinan, Yangku, Yunnan 7 Fuskhih, Hanyang, Kunming, Lanchow, Lioyang, Mengtze, Nanking, Nanning, Paoshan, Peiping, Soochow, Taiyuan, Tatshan, Urumchi, Urumsti, Waichow, Wuchang, Yenping 8 Chinchow, Fengkiek, Fengtien, Hangchow, Kingchow, Nanchang, Shanghai, Shenyang, Siangtan, Tientsin, Tungchow, Wanchuan, Wanhsien 9 Chungking, Kiangling, Tsingyuan 10 Chiangling, Port Arthur

school: 5 Futan 6 Peking 7 Nanking 8 Hangchow 9 Sun Yat-sen 16 Cheng-tu Technical

division:
  province: 5 Honan, Hunan, Hupei, Kansu 6 Anhwei, Fukien, Shansi, Shensi, Yunnan 7 Kiangsi, Kiangsu 8 Chekiang, Kweichow, Shantung, Szechwan, Tientsin, Tsinghai 9 Kwangtung, Manchuria

measure: 3 cho, fan, fen, pau, tou, tun, yan, yin 4 chek, chih, fang, kish, papa, quei, shih, teke, tsan, tsun 5 catty, chang, ching, sheng, shing 6 chupak, gungli, kungho, kungmu, tching 7 kungfen, kungyin 8 kungchih, kungshih, 9 kungching

monetary unit: 4 cash, cent, fyng, mace, tael, tiao, yuan 5 sycee 12 jen nin piao pu

weight: 3 fan, fen, hao, kin, ssu, tan, yin 4 chee, chin, dong, shih, tael, tsin 5 catty, chien, picul, tchin, tsien 6 kungli 7 haikwan, kungfen, kungssu, kungtun 8 kungchin 9 candareen 10 kupingtael

island: 4 Amoy 5 Macao, Matsu, Namki, Taipa 6 Chusan, Hainan, Pratas, Quemoy, Taiwan, Tinian, Yuhwan 7 Coloane, Formosa, Hungtow, Tungsha 8 Ching Hai, Chouchan, Kulangsu

lake: 3 Tai 4 Chao, Na-mu 5 Kaoyu, Oling, Telli 6 Bamtso, Bornor, Ebinor, Erhhai, Khanka, Lopnor, Namtso, Poyang 7 Chaling, Hungtse, Karanor, Kokonor 8 Hulunnor, Montcalm, Taroktso, Tellinor, Tienchih, Tsinghai, Tungting

sea: 6 Yellow 9 East China 10 South China

physical features:
  bay: 7 Laichow 8 Hangchow
  cape: 7 Olwanpi
  channel: 5 Bashi
  desert: 4 Gobi 5 Ordos, Shamo 7 Alashan 10 Takla Makan
  dry lake: 6 Lopnor
  gulf: 5 Pohai 6 Chihli, Tonkin 7 Pechili 8 Liaotung
  peninsula: 6 Leichu 7 Luichow 8 Liaotung
  plateau: 5 Loess 7 Tibetan
  port: 4 Amoy, Wuhu 5 Aigun, Shasi 6 Antung, Canton, Chefoo, Dairen, Ichang, Ningpo, Pakhoi, Swatow, Wuchow 7 Foochow, Hunchun, Luichow, Nanking, Samshui, Santuao, Soochow, Wenchow, Yinkkow, Yungkia 8 Changsha, Hangchow, Kiukiang, Kongmoon, Shanghai, Tengyueh, Tientsin, Tsingtao, Wanhsien 9 Kwangchow, Weihaiwei 10 Tsingkiang
  strait: 6 Hainan, Taiwan 7 Formosa

people: 3 Han, Yis 4 Huis, Lolo, Miao, Pu-is 5 Hakka, Hoklo, Seres, Sinic 6 Cataia, Chuang, Johnny, Korean, Manchu, Mongol, Serian, Uighun 7 Sinaean, Tibetan
  leader: 9 Sun Yat-sen, Zhou Enlai 10 Kublai Khan, Mao Tse-tung 11 Genghis Khan 12 Deng Xiaoping 13 Chiang Kai-shek
  philosopher: 6 Lao-tzu 9 Confucius

language: 7 Chinese 8 Mandarin, Shanghai 9 Cantonese

religion: 5 Islam 6 Taoism 8 Buddhism 12 Christianity, Confucianism

place:
  palace: 6 Summer 8 Imperial 13 Forbidden City
  ruins: 9 Ming Tombs
  square: 9 Tiananmen
  wonder: 9 Great Wall

feature:
  boat: 4 junk
  conspirators: 10 Gang of Four
  dynasty: 3 Han, Sui 4 Chou, Ch'in, Ming, Sung, T'ang 5 Ch'ing, Shang 6 Manchu
  military academy: 7 whompoa
  watercolor: 8 shan shiu

Chitimacha
language family: 6 Tunica
location: 9 Louisiana
noted for: 8 basketry

chitter 4 peep 5 cheep, chirp,
tweet 7 chatter, chirrup,
twitter

chitter-chatter 3 gab 4 blab
6 babble, drivel, gabble, jabber 7 blabber, prattle, twaddle 8 chitchat 9 jabbering
16 idle conversation

chivalrous 6 polite 7 courtly,
gallant 8 mannerly

chivalry 8 courtesy 9 gallantry
10 knighthood, politeness
11 courtliness

Chivery, Young John
character in: 12 Little Dorrit
author: 7 Dickens

chivy 3 nag 4 hunt, race 5 annoy, chase, chevy, hound,
trail, worry 6 badger, bother,
harass, pursue 7 scamper,
torment

Chlidanope
form: 5 Naiad

Chloe
epithet of: 7 Demeter
means: 5 green

chloride 7 muriate 8 chemical,
compound

chlorine
chemical symbol: 2 Cl

Chloris
father: 7 Amphion
mother: 5 Niobe
daughter: 4 Pero

chocolate 5 brown, candy, cacao, cocoa, drink 6 bon bon
10 confection

Choctaw
language family:
10 Muskhogean
location: 7 Alabama
11 Mississippi
related to: 9 Chickasaw

Choephoroe
author: 9 Aeschylus
character: 6 Furies 7 Electra,
Orestes, Pylades 9 Aegis-
thus 12 Clytemnestra

choice 3 say 4 A-one, best,
fine, pick, vote 5 array, elite,
prime, prize, stock, store,
voice 6 better, opting, option,
select, supply, tip-top 7 display, special, variety 8 choosing, deciding, decision,
superior 9 excellent, exclusive,
first-rate, preferred, selection,
top drawer 10 assemblage, assortment, collection, consummate, discretion, first-class,
preferable, preference, well-
chosen 11 alternative, appoint-

ment, exceptional, superlative
13 determination,
extraordinary

choice food 5 treat 8 delicacy

choicest part
French: 14 creme de la
creme

choir 4 band 5 quire 6 angels,
chorus 7 chorale, singers
10 choristers

Choirboys, The
author: 14 Joseph Wambaugh

choke 3 dam, gag 4 clog, plug
5 block, check, dam up, stuff
6 arrest, bridle, hamper,
hinder, impede, plug up, retard, stifle, stop up 7 congest,
garrote, inhibit, repress,
smother 8 blockade, hold
back, obstruct, restrain, strangle, suppress, throttle 9 constrain, constrict, suffocate
10 asphyxiate

choler 3 ire 4 fury, rage 5 anger, wrath 6 spleen, temper

choleric 3 mad 5 angry, irate,
testy, vexed 6 cranky, grumpy,
shirty, touchy 7 enraged, furious, grouchy, peevish, waspish 8 snappish, wrathful
9 dyspeptic, indignant, irritable, irascible, splenetic 10 infuriated, short-fused
11 contentious, hot-tempered,
ill-tempered, thin-skinned
12 cantankerous, sour-
tempered 13 quick-tempered,
short-tempered

choose 4 opt 4 like, pick, take,
wish 5 adopt, elect 6 decide,
desire, intend, opt for, prefer,
see fit, select 7 call out, embrace, espouse, extract, fix
upon, pick out, resolve 8 decide on, settle on 9 determine,
single out 10 be inclined
13 commit oneself 14 make
up one's mind

choosy 5 fussy, picky 7 finicky 9 selective 10 fastidious,
particular 14 discriminating

chop 3 cut, hew, hit, lop
4 blow, chip, crop, cube, dice,
fell, gash, hack 5 cut up,
mince, slash, slice, split,
swipe, whack 6 cleave, cutlet,
stroke, sunder 8 fragment, rib
slice 9 cotelette, pulverize

Chopin, Frederic Francois
born: 6 Poland
12 Zelazowawola
companion: 10 George Sand
composer of: 5 Etude 7 Ballade 8 Berceuse, Cat Valse,
Dog Valse, Fantasie 9 Ecossaise 10 Barcarolle 11 Minute Valse 15 Andante
Spianato, Heroic Polonaise

(No 6), Raindrop Prelude,
Winter Wind Etude
16 Shepherd Boy Etude
17 Impromptu Fantasie,
Rondo a la Krakowiak
18 Revolutionary Etude
20 Butterfly's Wings Etude

choral ode
Greek: 7 parodos 8 stasimon

chord 4 cord, line, note, tone
5 music, triad 6 accord, string,
tendon 7 cadence, emotion,
feeling, harmony 9 harmonize

chore 3 job 4 duty, task, work
5 stint 6 burden, errand,
strain 8 farm task, small job
10 assignment 13 household
task 14 responsibility

choreography 5 dance
12 stage dancing 16 dance
composition

chorister 6 singer 7 changer
8 choirboy

chortle 5 laugh 7 chuckle

chorus 5 choir, unity 6 accord,
unison 7 concert, concord, refrain 8 glee club, one voice,
response 9 antiphony, consensus, unanimity 11 concor-
dance 12 singing group

chosen 5 elite 6 picked, sorted
7 elected 8 selected 9 picked
out

Chosen, The
author: 10 Chaim Potok

Choson see 5 Korea

Chouans, The
author: 14 Honore de Balzac

chough
group of: 10 chattering

Chowbok
character in: 7 Erewhon
author: 6 Butler

Christ, the see 5 Jesus

christen 3 dip, dub 4 name
6 launch 7 baptize, immerse
8 dedicate, sprinkle 9 designate

Christian
character in: 16 Pilgrim's
Progress
author: 6 Bunyan

Christian, Fletcher
character in: 17 Mutiny on
the Bounty
authors: 4 Hall 8 Nordhoff

Christian, Linda
real name: 16 Blanca Rosa
Welter
husband: 11 Tyrone Power
12 Edmund Purdom
born: 6 Mexico 7 Tampico
roles: 6 Athena 15 Slaves of
Babylon 18 Green Dolphin
Street

Christiania
capital of: **6** Norway

Christie, (Dame) Agatha
author of: **7** Curtain **12** The
Mousetrap **14** Death on the
Nile **15** The Mirror Crack'd
16 Ten Little Indians
19 Murder at the Vicarage
20 And Then There Were
None **22** What Mrs Mc-
Gillicuddy Saw! **23** The
Murder of Roger Ackroyd
24 Murder on the Orient
Express, Witness for the
Prosecution **27** The Mysterious Affair at Styles
character: **10** Jane Marple
13 Hercule Poirot

Christie, Julie
born: **5** Assam, India
6 Chukua
roles: **7** Darling (Oscar),
Shampoo **9** Billy Liar
11 Heat and Dust **13** Doctor
Zhivago, Fahrenheit 451,
Heaven Can Wait **18** Mc-
Cabe and Mrs Miller **22** Far
From the Madding Crowd

Christine
author: **11** Stephen King

Christmas
also: **4** Noel, Yule **8** Yuletide
feature/symbol: **4** bell, star,
tree **5** angel, gifts, holly
6 candle, carols, creche,
manger, sleigh, wreath
7 Yule log **8** presents **9** evergreen, mistletoe, snow-
flake, stockings **10** Santa
Claus

Christmas, Joe
character in: **13** Light in
August
author: **8** Faulkner

Christmas Carol, A
author: **14** Charles Dickens
character: **7** Tiny Tim **8** Fezziwig **11** Bob Cratchit
12 Marley's Ghost **15** Ebenezer Scrooge
ghosts of: **13** Christmas
Past **15** Christmas Future
16 Christmas Present
director: **17** Brian Desmond
Hurst
cast: **10** Jack Warner
11 Alastair Sim (Ebenezer
Scrooge), Mervyn Johns
14 Michael Hordern
16 Kathleen Harrison

Chrome Yellow
author: **12** Aldous Huxley

chromium
chemical symbol: **2** Cr

chronic 7 abiding, lasting
8 constant, enduring, habitual,
periodic **9** confirmed, continual, ingrained, perennial, recurrent, recurring

10 continuous, deep-rooted,
deep-seated, inveterate, persistent, persisting **12** intermittent, longstanding

chronicle 3 log **4** epic, list,
note, post, saga **5** diary, enter,
story **6** annals, docket, record,
relate, report **7** account, history, journal, narrate, recount,
set down **8** archives **9** narrative **10** chronology

**Chronicles of England,
Scotland, and Ireland**
author: **16** Raphael
Holinshed

chronological 5 dated **6** serial
7 ordered, sequent **10** sequential, succeeding, successive
11 consecutive, progressive,
time-ordered **12** chronometric,
chronoscopic **13** chronographic

chronology 6 annals, record
7 history **9** chronicle **13** order
of events

chronometer 5 clock **8** horologe **9** timepiece

chrysanthemum
varieties: **3** Max **4** Corn
5 Daisy, Tansy **6** Nippon
7 Garland **8** Florist's, Tricol-
or **10** Portuguese

Chrysaor
father: **8** Poseidon
mother: **6** Medusa
brother: **7** Pegasus

Chryseis
father: **7** Chryses
concubine of: **9** Agamemnon

Chryses
priest of: **6** Apollo
daughter: **8** Chryseis

Chrysippus
father: **6** Pelops
abducted by: **5** Laius
half-brother: **6** Atreus
8 Thyestes

chrysoberyl
variety: **7** cat's-eye
11 alexandrite

chrysolite 4 iron, lava **5** beryl,
green, stone **6** yellow **7** mineral, olivine, peridot **8** silicate
9 magnesium **10** aquamarine

chrysoprase
species: **6** quartz
color: **5** green

Chrysothemis
father: **9** Agamemnon
mother: **12** Clytemnestra
brother: **7** Orestes
sister: **7** Electra **9** Iphigenia
daughter: **5** Rhoeo

Chthonian
form: **5** deity **6** spirit
habitat: **10** underworld

Chthonius
member of: **6** Sparti
epithet of: **4** Zeus
means: **15** of the underworld

Chuang-tzu, Chwang-tse
author: **9** Chuang-tzu

chubby 3 fat **5** buxom, plump,
podgy, pudgy, stout, tubby
6 chunky, flabby, fleshy,
portly, rotund, stocky, zaftig
7 paunchy **8** heavyset, roly-
poly, thickset **9** corpulent
10 overweight **15** pleasingly
plump

chuck 3 pat, pet, tap **4** cast,
toss **5** fling, heave, pitch,
sling, throw **6** tickle

chuckle 5 cluck, laugh
6 clumsy **7** cackle, chortle,
snicker

chum 3 pal **5** buddy, crony
6 cohort, friend **7** comrade
8 intimate, playmate, sidekick
9 companion, confidant
10 bosom buddy, playfellow
11 close friend

chummy 5 close, palsy **7** devoted **8** familiar, friendly, intimate **9** congenial **10** buddy-
buddy, palsy-walsy
12 affectionate

chump 4 dolt, dupe, fool, goof,
goon, head **5** champ, munch
6 sucker **9** blockhead

chunk 3 gob, wad **4** clod,
hunk, lump, mass **5** batch,
block, piece **6** nugget, square

chunky 5 beefy, dumpy,
lumpy, pudgy, squat, stout,
thick **6** chubby, portly, stocky,
stodgy, stubby **7** squabby
8 heavyset, thickset **11** thick-
bodied

church 4 cult, sect **5** faith
6 belief, chapel, mosque, temple **7** service **8** basilica, religion **9** cathedral, devotions,
synagogue **10** house of God,
Lord's house, persuasion, tabernacle **11** affiliation **12** denomination **13** divine
worship **14** house of worship

Church, Frederick Edwin
born: **10** Hartford CT
artwork: **14** Andes of Ecuador, Falls of Niagara (Niagara Falls) **18** The Heart of
the Andes **19** Morning in
the Tropics

Churchill, Frank
character in: **4** Emma
author: **6** Austen

Churchill, Sarah
father: **19** Sir Winston
Churchill
born: **6** London **7** England
roles: **12** Royal Wedding

Churchill, Winston Spencer
born: **7** England **14** Blenheim Palace
father: **8** Randolph
mother: **12** Jennie Jerome
wife: **16** Clementine Hosier
daughter: **5** Sarah
school: **6** Harrow **9** Sandhurst
captured by: **5** Boers
position: **13** prime minister
author of: **11** Marlborough, My Early Life **14** The World Crisis **17** The Second World War **35** A History of the English-Speaking Peoples

churchly 8 clerical, pastoral, priestly **9** parochial **11** ministerial **14** ecclesiastical

churchman 5 vicar **6** bishop, cleric, curate, deacon, parson, pastor, priest, rector **7** prelate **8** chaplain, minister, preacher **9** clergyman **12** ecclesiastic

church official 5 elder **6** beadle, deacon **9** presbyter

churchyard 8 cemetery **9** graveyard **12** burial ground **13** burying ground

churl 3 cad, oaf **4** boor, lout **7** bounder

churlish 4 rude, sour, tart **5** crude, surly, testy **6** crusty, sullen **7** bearish, bilious, boorish, brusque, crabbed, grouchy, ill-bred, uncivil, uncouth, waspish **8** arrogant, captious, choleric, impolite, impudent, insolent, petulant **9** dastardly, insulting, irascible, irritable, obnoxious, rancorous, splenetic **10** unmannerly **11** ill-mannered, ill-tempered, quarrelsome **12** contemptible, discourteous

churn 4 beat, foam, rage, roil, roll, toss, whip **5** heave, shake, swirl, whisk **6** stir up **7** agitate, disturb, pulsate, shake up, vibrate **8** convulse **9** palpitate

chute 5 rapid, slide, slope **7** incline, passage **9** parachute

chutzpa, chutzpah 4 gall **5** brass, cheek, nerve **8** audacity, boldness, temerity **9** brashness, impudence **10** brazenness, effrontery **11** forwardness, presumption

Chwatt, Aaron
real name of: **10** Red Buttons

ciao 2 hi **5** hello **6** so long **7** goodbye **11** see you later

Cicero, Marcus Tullius
lived in: **11** ancient Rome
noted as: **6** author, lawyer, orator **9** statesman **11** philosopher **12** letter writer

position: **6** aedile, consul **7** praetor
author of: **9** De finibus, De oratore **10** De amicitia, De officiis **11** De re publica, De senectute, In Catilinam **14** De natura deorum, Pro lege Manilia **23** Tusculanae Disputationes

cicerone 5 guide, pilot **8** conductor **9** explainer

cicisbeo 5 lover

Cid, The
also: **11** Poema del Cid
author: **7** unknown **15** Pierre Corneille
character: **7** Chimene **8** Rodrigue
Cid also called: **14** el Cid Campeador **18** Rodrigo Diaz de Bivar
horse: **7** Babieca

ci-devant 6 former **7** retired **10** heretofore

cierge 3 dip, wax **5** light, taper **6** bougie, candle, tallow

cigar 4 toby **5** claro **6** corona, havana, maduro, stogie **7** cheroot **8** panatela, panetela, perfecto **9** cigarillo, panatella
ingredient: **11** tobacco leaf
part: **6** binder, filler **7** wrapper
made in: **4** Cuba **6** Havana
kept in: **7** humidor

cigarette, cigaret 3 cig, fag **4** biri **5** smoke **6** gasper, reefer **10** coffin nail
ingredient: **3** tar **7** menthol, tobacco **8** nicotine

Cilissa
nurse of: **7** Orestes

Cilix
father: **6** Agenor
sister: **6** Europa
searched for: **6** Europa

Cilla
brother: **5** Priam
killed by: **5** Priam

Cillus
charioteer of: **6** Pelops

Cimabue
real name: **11** Cenni di Pepi
born: **5** Italy **8** Florence
artwork attributed: **18** The S Trinita Madonna **29** Madonna Enthroned with St Francis **45** Madonna and Child Enthroned with Angels and Prophets .

Cimarron
author: **10** Edna Ferber
director: **13** Wesley Ruggles
cast: **10** Irene Dunne, Richard Dix **13** Estelle Taylor
Oscar for: **7** picture **10** screenplay

Cimarron Strip
character: **8** (US Marshal) Jim Crown **9** Mac Gregor **12** Francis Wilde **17** Dulcey Coopersmith
cast: **10** Randy Boone **12** Jill Townsend, Percy Herbert **13** Stuart Whitman

Cimino, Michael
director of: **11** Heaven's Gate **13** The Deer Hunter (Oscar)

Cimmerian
mentioned by: **5** Homer
form: **10** Westerners
live in: **8** darkness

cinch 4 band, snap **5** girth **6** clinch, ensure, girdle, shoo-in **8** lead-pipe **9** pull tight, sure thing **11** piece of cake

Cincinnati
baseball team: **4** Reds
football team: **7** Bengals

cincture 4 band, belt, cord, sash **6** girdle

cinder 3 ash **4** slag **5** ashes, dross, ember **6** embers, scoria **8** clinkers, iron slag **10** burned coal, burned wood

Cinderella
author: **7** unknown
source: **8** Perrault
character: **14** Fairy Godmother, Handsome Prince **15** Ugly Stepsisters **16** Wicked Stepmother
coach: **7** pumpkin
horses: **9** white mice
footman: **4** frog
loses: **12** glass slipper

cinema 5 films **6** flicks, movies **7** theater **14** motion pictures, moving pictures

cinnamon 5 spice
botanical name: **20** Cinnamomum zeylanicum
variety: **6** cassia, Ceylon **10** zeylanicum
color: **4** buff **5** tawny **6** auburn **8** nut-brown **11** golden-brown, yellow-brown **12** reddish-brown **13** chestnut-brown **14** yellowish-brown
origin: **5** China **7** Vietnam **9** Indonesia **10** East Indies

Cinyras
king of: **6** Cyprus
son: **5** Melus
daughter: **6** Myrrha
introduced worship of: **9** Aphrodite
crime: **6** incest
death by: **7** suicide

cipher 3 nil, zip **4** code, zero **5** aught **6** naught, nobody **7** anagram, nothing, nullity **8** acrostic, goose egg **9** nonen-

tity, obscurity **10** cryptogram
11 cryptograph

Cipus
  origin: 5 Roman
  occupation: 7 praetor

Circe
  form: 11 enchantress
  father: 6 Helios
  mother: 5 Perse
  brother: 6 Aeetes
  son: 6 Agrius **7** Latinus
    9 Telegonus
  home: 5 Aeaea
  turned men into: 4 pigs
    5 swine

circle 3 orb, set **4** belt, curl,
gird, girt, halo, hoop, knot,
loop, reel, ring, turn **5** arena,
bound, cabal, crowd, curve,
cycle, field, girth, group, hem
in, orbit, pivot, range, reach,
realm, round, sweep, swing
6 border, bounds, clique, cordon, corona, course, domain,
girdle, region, sphere **7** circlet,
circuit, company, compass, coterie, enclose, envelop, hedge
in, revolve, ringlet, society,
theater **8** dominion, encircle,
province, sequence, surround
9 bailiwick, encompass, territory, wind about **10** move
around, revolution, ring
around **11** curve around, progression **12** circumrotate, circumscribe **13** revolve around
14 circumnavigate

Circle 6 gilgal

circlet 4 band, halo, ring
5 tiara **6** diadem, fillet,
wreath **7** chaplet, coronet,
ringlet

circuit 3 lap, run **4** area, beat,
edge, tour, trek, walk **5** jaunt,
limit, round, route **6** border,
bounds, course, margin,
sphere **7** compass, confine,
journey **8** circling, frontier, or-
biting, pivoting **9** excursion,
extremity, perimeter, revolving, territory **10** revolution
13 circumference **14** distance
around

circuitous 7 devious, turning,
winding **8** circular, indirect,
rambling, tortuous, twisting
10 meandering, roundabout,
serpentine **12** labyrinthine
14 circumlocutory

circular 4 bill **5** flier, round
6 curved, notice, rotary **7** coiling, curling, leaflet, rocking,
rolling, rounded, turning,
winding **8** bulletin, gyrating,
handbill, pivoting, spinning,
twirling **9** revolving, spiraling,
swiveling, throwaway **10** circuitous, ring-shaped **12** announcement **13** advertisement

circulate 4 flow **5** issue, strew
6 circle, course, spread, travel
7 give out, go forth, journey,
publish, radiate, scatter **8** announce, disperse, go around,
put about **9** broadcast, get
abroad, make known, move
about, publicize **10** distribute,
make public, move around,
pass around, put forward
11 disseminate, pass through,
visit around **13** make the
rounds

circulation 4 flow **6** motion
7 flowing **8** circling, rotation
9 diffusion, radiation **10** dispersion **11** propagation **12** distribution, promulgation,
transmission **13** dissemination

circulatory system
  part: 4 vein **5** heart **6** artery
    9 capillary **15** lymphatic
    vessel
  carries: 6 plasma **9** platelets
    13 red blood cells **15** white
    blood cells

circumcision
  Hebrew: 4 Brit **5** Berit, Brith
    6 Berith

circumference 3 rim **4** edge
5 girth **6** border, bounds,
fringe, girdle, limits, margin
7 circuit, compass, outline
8 boundary **9** extremity, perimeter, periphery **14** distance
around

circumlocution 8 rambling,
verbiage **9** garrulity, verbosity,
wordiness **10** digression,
meandering **14** discursiveness,
long-windedness,
roundaboutness

circumlocutory 5 wordy **7** diffuse, verbose **8** rambling
9 wandering **10** digressive, discursive, maundering,
roundabout

circumnavigate 5 skirt **6** bypass, circle **8** encircle, go
around **10** circumvent

circumnavigation 8 circling,
skirting **9** bypassing **11** going
around **12** encirclement
13 circumvention

circumscribe 3 fix **4** curb
5 check, hem in, limit **6** bridle, circle, corset, define,
impede **7** confine, enclose,
outline **8** encircle, restrain, restrict, surround **9** constrain,
delineate, encompass, proscribe

circumscribed 6 narrow
7 limited **10** restricted

circumscription 5 limit **7** outline **9** hemming in, restraint
10 constraint **11** confinement
12 encirclement
14 restrictedness

circumspect 4 sage, wary
5 alert **7** careful, guarded, prudent **8** cautious, discreet, vigilant, watchful **9** judicious,
sagacious, wide-awake **10** deliberate, discerning, particular,
thoughtful **13** contemplative,
perspicacious **14** discriminating

circumspection 4 care, heed
7 caution **8** prudence **10** discretion, precaution, steadiness
11 carefulness, heedfulness,
mindfulness **12** deliberation

circumstance 4 fact, item
5 event, point, thing **6** detail,
factor, matter, ritual **7** element **8** ceremony, incident,
splendor **9** condition, formality, happening, pageantry
10 brilliance, occurrence, particular, phenomenon **11** vicissitude **12** happenstance,
magnificence, resplendence
14 state of affairs

circumstances 5 state **9** situation **11** environment **16** living
conditions

circumstantial 4 full **6** minute **7** deduced, hearsay, implied, precise **8** accurate,
complete, detailed, explicit, inferred, presumed, thorough
9 secondary **10** blow-by-blow,
evidential, exhaustive, extraneous, incidental, particular,
unabridged **11** conjectural, inferential, provisional
12 nonessential

circumvent 4 miss, shun
5 avoid, dodge, elude, evade,
skirt **6** bypass, circle, escape,
outwit, thwart **8** go around
9 frustrate **12** keep away
from **14** circumnavigate

circumvention 7 dodging,
ducking, eluding, evasion
9 avoidance, bypassing
11 frustration **12** sidestepping

circus 4 ring **5** arena **6** big top,
circle, uproar **8** carnival, coliseum **9** spectacle **10** exhibition, hippodrome
11 ampitheater **12** intersection
  act: 5 clown, flyer **7** acrobat,
    juggler, trapeze **8** side show
    9 lion tamer, menagerie
    10 equestrian **13** flying
    trapeze
  famous: 6 Astley **12** Cirque
    d'Hiver **15** Barnum and Bai-
    ley **16** Ringling Brothers

Cissaea
  epithet of: 6 Athena
  means: 10 ivy goddess

Cist
  form: 9 sacred box
  used for: 8 utensils

cistern 3 box, tub, vat **4** tank,

well **6** cavity, vessel **8** aqueduct **9** reservoir

citadel 4 fort **7** bastion, rampart **8** fortress **10** stronghold **13** fortification

citation 4 cite **5** award, honor, kudos, medal, quote **7** example, excerpt, extract, passage **8** instance **9** quotation **12** commendation, illustration **14** official praise

cite 4 name, note **5** honor, quote **6** praise **7** advance, commend, mention, present, refer to, specify **8** allude to, document, indicate **9** enumerate, exemplify **12** bring forward **13** give as example

Cithaeron
  brother: **7** Helicon
  crime: **6** murder
  changed into: **8** mountain

Cithaeronian *see* **4** Zeus

citified 5 urban **6** urbane **12** cosmopolitan **13** sophisticated

citizen 6 native **7** denizen, subject **8** national, resident **10** inhabitant
  French: **7** citoyen

Citizen Kane
  director: **11** Orson Welles
  script: **11** Orson Welles **17** Herman J Mankiewicz
  cast: **11** Orson Welles **12** Joseph Cotten **13** Everett Sloane **14** Agnes Moorehead
  score: **15** Bernard Herrmann
  sled: **7** Rosebud

citizenry 4 folk **6** people, public **7** society **8** populace **9** community **10** population

citoyen 7 citizen

citrine
  species: **6** quartz
  color: **6** yellow

citron 3 rue **4** lime, rind **5** lemon **6** cedrat, orange, yellow **8** Rutaceae **9** tangerine **10** watermelon **12** citrus medica
  Jewish: **6** ethrog

city 4 burg, town **7** big town **8** denizens, township **9** residents **10** metropolis **11** inhabitants, megalopolis, townspeople **12** municipality **16** incorporated town, metropolitan area

city hall
  French: **12** hotel de ville

City Life
  author: **15** Donald Barthelme

City Lights
  director: **14** Charles Chaplin
  cast: **8** Hank Mann **10** Harry Myers **14** Charlie Chaplin **16** Virginia Cherrill

City of God, The (De Civitate Dei)
  author: **11** St Augustine

City of the Lion *see* **9** Singapore

city slicker 4 dude **8** urbanite **11** cosmopolite **12** sophisticate

City Without Walls and Other Poems
  author: **7** W H Auden

Ciudad Trujillo
  capital of: **17** Dominican Republic

Civ 17 second Hebrew month

civic 5 local **6** public **8** citizen's, communal **9** community

civil 3 lay **4** city **5** civic, state **6** genial, polite, public **7** affable, amiable, citizen, cordial, secular **8** citizen's, communal, decorous, gracious, mannerly, obliging **9** civilized, community, courteous, municipal **10** individual, neighborly, respectful **11** gentlemanly, nonmilitary **12** conciliatory, well-mannered

Civil Disobedience
  author: **17** Henry David Thoreau

civilian 9 lay person **14** private citizen **17** nonmilitary person **18** nonuniformed person

civility 4 tact **7** manners, respect **8** courtesy **10** affability, amiability, cordiality, good temper, politeness **11** good manners **12** graciousness, pleasantness **13** agreeableness, courteousness **14** respectfulness

civilization 7 culture, society **10** refinement **11** cultivation, worldliness **13** enlightenment **14** sophistication

civilize 5 edify, teach, train **6** inform, polish, refine **7** culture, develop, educate, elevate **8** humanize, instruct **9** cultivate, enlighten **11** acculturate **12** sophisticate

civil law
  Latin: **9** jus civile

clad 6 garbed **7** arrayed, attired, clothed, dressed **9** outfitted

Claggart
  character in: **9** Billy Budd
  author: **8** Melville

claim 3 ask **4** avow, call, plea, take **5** exact, right, title **6** access, affirm, allege, assert, avowal, charge, demand, pick up **7** call for, collect, command, declare, profess, request **8** exaction, insist on, maintain, proclaim **9** assertion, ownership, seek as due, statement **10** allegation, lay claim to, pretension, profession **11** affirmation, declaration, postulation, requirement **12** proclamation, protestation

claimant 6 suitor **9** applicant, pretender **10** petitioner

clairvoyant 7 psychic **8** divining, oracular **9** prescient, prophetic **10** telepathic **11** foreknowing, telekinetic **12** extrasensory, precognitive, psychometric **13** psychokinetic, second-sighted

clam 4 vise **5** clamp, clasp **6** dollar, marine **7** bivalve, mollusk
  kind: **5** pismo, razor **6** butter, quahog **7** geoduck, steamer **10** little neck **11** cherrystone
  part: **4** foot, palp **5** gills, shell, valve **6** mantle, siphon **7** sinuses **8** ligament
  habitat: **3** mud **4** sand
  relative: **6** mussel, oyster

clamber up 5 climb, mount, scale **10** scramble up, struggle up

clamminess 4 damp **7** wetness **8** dampness, dankness **10** stickiness, sweatiness

clammy 3 wet **4** damp **5** pasty, slimy **6** sticky, sweaty **10** perspiring **11** cold and damp

clamor 3 cry, din **4** call, howl, yell **5** blast, chaos, noise, shout, storm **6** bedlam, bellow, cry out, hubbub, jangle, outcry, racket, rumpus, tumult, uproar **7** bluster, call out, clangor, thunder **8** brouhaha, shouting **9** commotion, hue and cry **10** hullabaloo, vociferate, wild chorus

clamorous 4 loud **5** noisy **10** boisterous, uproarious

clamp 4 clip, grip, vise **5** brace, clasp **6** clench, clinch, fasten, secure **7** bracket **8** fastener

clan 4 gang, knot, line, ring **5** breed, cabal, crowd, group, guild, house, party, stock **6** circle, league, strain **7** company, dynasty, lineage, society **8** alliance, pedigree **10** fraternity **11** affiliation, association, brotherhood, family group, lineal group **12** tribal family

clandestine 6 covert, hidden, masked, secret, veiled **7** cloaked, furtive, private **8** secluded, sneaking, stealthy **9** concealed, secretive, underhand **10** undercover, unrevealed 11 underground, underhanded, undisclosed 12 confidential 13 surreptitious

clang 3 din 4 bong, gong, peal, toll 5 chime, clank, clash, knell 6 jangle 7 clangor, resound, ringing, tolling 8 clashing 10 resounding, ring loudly

clangor 3 din 5 noise 6 clamor, hubbub, jangle, racket, uproar

clank 5 chink, clang, clash, clink 6 jangle, rattle 7 clangor, clatter 8 clashing

clannish 4 cold 5 aloof 6 narrow 7 distant, insular 8 cliquish, snobbish 9 exclusive, parochial, sectarian 10 provincial, restricted, unfriendly 11 unreceptive

Clan of the Cave Bear, The
author: 9 Jean M Auel

clap 3 bat, hit, rap, tap 4 bang, bump, cast, cuff, dash, hurl, peal, push, roar, rush, slam, slap, swat, toss 5 burst, clack, crack, drive, fling, force, pitch, shove, smack, smite, thump, whack 6 buffet, plunge, propel, strike, thrust, thwack, wallop 7 applaud, clatter 9 explosion 11 set suddenly

claptrap 3 rot 4 bosh, bull, bunk, sham, 5 bilge, hokum, hooey, stuff, trash, tripe 6 bunkum, drivel, hot air, humbug, tinsel 7 baloney, blarney, fustian, hogwash, spinach, twaddle 8 buncombe, nonsense, quackery, tommyrot 9 gaudiness, poppycock, staginess 10 applesauce, flapdoodle, tawdriness, tomfoolery 12 foolishness 15 pretentiousness 16 stuff and nonsense

claque 10 sycophants 15 cheering section

Clare, Ada
character in: 10 Bleak House
author: 7 Dickens

claret 3 red 7 carmine, deep red, red wine 8 blood-red, Bordeaux, cardinal 11 purplish red, wine-colored

clarification 10 commentary 11 elucidation, explanation, explication 14 further comment
French: 15 eclaircissement

clarify 5 clear, purge, solve 6 purify, refine 7 clear up, explain, lay open, resolve 9 elucidate, explicate, make clear, make plain 10 illuminate 11 disentangle, shed light on

12 bring to light 18 make understandable

clarinet 4 wind 8 woodwind 11 transposing
mouthpiece: 4 reed
ancestor: 9 chalumeau
musician: 12 Benny Goodman

clarion 5 acute, clear, sharp 6 shrill 7 blaring, ringing 8 distinct, piercing, resonant, sonorous, stirring 10 commanding, compelling, imperative 11 high-pitched

Clarissa Harlowe
author: 16 Samuel Richardson
character: 8 Miss Howe 11 John Belford 14 Robert Lovelace 20 Colonel William Morden

clarity 6 purity 8 lucidity, radiance 9 clearness, exactness, plainness, precision 10 brightness, brilliance, directness, effulgence, glassiness, luminosity, simplicity 12 explicitness, translucence, transparency 15 intelligibility 17 comprehensibility

Clark, Mark W
served in: 3 WWI 4 WWII 9 Korean War
rank: 22 allied commander in Italy 24 commander of forces in Korea 30 chief of staff of army ground forces 42 commander of Allied occupation forces in Austria
president of: 7 Citadel

Clark, Walter Van Tilburg
author of: 16 The Ox-Bow Incident

Clarke, Arthur C
author of: 10 (2010) Odyssey Two 13 (2001) A Space Odyssey, Childhood's End

clash 4 bang, boil, feud, fray, tiff 5 argue, clang, clank, crash, fight, set-to 6 battle, combat, fracas, jangle, rattle, tussle 7 clangor, clatter, contend, contest, discord, dispute, grapple, jarring, quarrel, wrangle 8 conflict, crashing, friction, skirmish, squabble, struggle 9 altercate, encounter, lock horns 10 antagonism, difference, disharmony, dissidence, opposition 11 cross swords 12 disagreement 13 exchange blows

clash of arms 5 fight 6 battle, combat 8 conflict, skirmish, struggle 9 encounter 10 engagement

clash with 9 fight with 12 do battle with 14 contend against 15 cross swords with

clasp 3 hug 4 bolt, clip, grip, hasp, hold, hook, link, lock, snap 5 catch, clamp, grasp, latch, press 6 buckle, clinch, clutch, couple, fasten, secure 7 coupler, embrace, grapple, squeeze 8 fastener 9 fastening

clasp in the arms 3 hug 4 hold 6 enfold 7 embrace

class 3 set 4 form, kind, rank, rate, size, sort, type 5 brand, breed, caste, genre, genus, grade, group, index, label, order, state 6 circle, clique, codify, course, lesson, number, sphere, status 7 arrange, catalog, section, session, species, station, variety 8 category, classify, division, pedigree, position 9 condition, designate 10 categorize, pigeonhole, social rank 11 set of pupils 13 social stratum 14 classification 15 departmentalize, graduating group

classic, classical 4 epic 5 model 6 heroic 7 ageless, paragon 8 absolute, accepted, enduring, masterly 9 archetype, excellent, exemplary, first-rate, prototype 10 archetypal, consummate, definitive, first-class, Greco-Roman, prototypal 11 masterpiece, outstanding, traditional 12 ancient Greek, ancient Roman, standard work 13 authoritative, distinguished 14 distinguishing 17 first-class example

classification 4 kind, rank, sort, type 5 class, genus, group, order 6 family, series 7 section, species 8 category, classing, division, grouping, labeling, ordering, taxonomy 9 arranging, gradation 10 assortment, organizing 11 arrangement, designation, disposition 12 categorizing, codification, organization 14 categorization 15 systematization

classified 5 secret 6 sorted 7 classed 8 assorted 10 restricted 11 categorized 12 confidential

classify 3 tag 4 list, rank, rate, size, type 5 brand, class, grade, group, index, label, order, range 6 assort, codify, number, ticket 7 arrange, catalog 8 organize 9 segregate 10 categorize, pigeonhole 11 distinguish

classy 4 chic, posh, tony 5 nifty, nobby, ritzy, smart, swank, swell 6 dressy, modish, spiffy, swanky 7 elegant, genteel, opulent, refined, stylish 8 cultured, polished, tasteful

9 high-class **10** ultrasmart **11** fashionable, in good taste **12** aristocratic, well-mannered

clatter 4 bang **5** clack, clang, clank, clash, clink, clump, crash **6** clamor, jangle, racket, rattle **7** chatter **8** crashing, rattling

clattering 3 din **6** clamor, hubbub, racket, uproar **7** clangor

Claude
real name: **12** Claude Gellee
also called: **14** Claude Lorraine
born: **6** France **8** Chamagne
artwork: **7** The Mill **16** Hagar and the Angel **18** Ascanius and the Stag, The Enchanted Castle **27** The Rest on the Flight into Egypt **31** The Embarkation of the Queen of Sheba

Claudel, Paul
author of: **6** L'Otage **10** The Hostage **13** Partage de Midi **15** The Satin Slipper **20** Tidings Brought to Mary

Claudia Quinta
freed: **12** grounded ship
feat proved: **8** chastity

Claudio
character in: **17** Measure for Measure **19** Much Ado About Nothing
author: **11** Shakespeare

Claudius
character in: **6** Hamlet
author: **11** Shakespeare

Claudius the God
author: **12** Robert Graves

clause 4 term **7** article, proviso **8** covenant **9** condition, provision **11** proposition, stipulation **13** specification **14** simple sentence

claustrophobia
fear of: **12** closed spaces **14** confined spaces

Clavell, James
author of: **6** Shogun, Tai-Pan **7** King Rat **9** Whirlwind **10** Noble House

clavicle
bone of: **10** collarbone

claw 3 paw **4** foot, grip, maul, tear **5** seize, slash, talon **6** clutch, pincer, scrape **7** scratch **8** lacerate **10** animal nail

Clay, Cassius
former name of: **11** Muhammad Ali

Clayburgh, Jill
born: **9** New York NY
roles: **9** Semi-Tough **12** Starting Over **16** An Unmarried Woman, North Dallas Forty **21** I'm Dancing as Fast as I Can

Clayhanger Trilogy, The
author: **13** Arnold Bennett

clean 3 mop **4** dust, fine, neat, pure, tidy, trim, wash **5** bathe, clear, fresh, moral, order, scour, scrub, sweep **6** bathed, chaste, decent, neaten, tidy up, vacuum, washed **7** cleaned, cleanse, healthy, launder, orderly, perfect, scoured, shampoo, upright **8** cleansed, decorous, flawless, innocent, sanitary, scrubbed, spotless, unsoiled, virtuous, well-made **9** exemplary, faultless, honorable, laundered, stainless, undefiled, unspotted, unstained, unsullied, untainted, wholesome **10** immaculate, uninfected, unpolluted **11** unblemished **13** unadulterated **14** uncontaminated

cleaner, cleanser 4 soap **5** borax **6** washer **7** ammonia, janitor **8** purifier, scrubber **9** detergent **14** scouring powder

cleaning 7 bathing, washing **8** scouring **9** cleansing, going-over, scrubbing, tidying up **10** laundering

cleanse 3 rid **4** free, wash **5** bathe, clean, clear, erase, flush, scour, scrub **7** absolve, deliver, expunge, launder, release, shampoo **8** sweep out, unburden **9** expurgate

clean-shaven 6 smooth **9** unbearded **11** unwhiskered **12** smooth-shaven

cleansing 7 bathing, healing, purging, washing **8** flushing, scouring **9** expunging, purifying, scrubbing **10** absolution

cleanup 4 gain **6** profit **8** windfall
baseball: **12** fourth batter

clear *see box*

clearance 4 room, sale **6** margin, permit **7** removal **8** clearing **10** offsetting **11** elimination **13** authorization, certification

clear as day 5 plain **7** obvious **8** apparent, clear-cut, manifest **11** self-evident

clear-cut 4 open **5** exact, lucid, plain **6** patent **7** evident, express, obvious, precise **8** definite, detailed, distinct, explicit, manifest **10** clear as day, unconfused, undeniable **11** appreciable, conspicuous, self-evident, substantial,

clear 3 rid **4** fair, free, keen, make, open **5** alert, clean, empty, gauzy, lucid, plain, sharp, sunny **6** acquit, bright, patent, remove, serene, unstop, wholly **7** absolve, audible, audibly, certain, clearly, evident, express, fly over, glowing, halcyon, hop over, lighten, obvious, plainly, radiant, unblock **8** apparent, brighten, clearcut, dazzling, definite, distinct, entirely, explicit, gleaming, leap over, luminous, manifest, pass over, pellucid, positive, skip over, unhidden **9** all the way, bound over, brilliant, cloudless, exculpate, exonerate, sparkling, unblocked, unclouded, unimpeded, unmuddled, vindicate, wideawake **10** articulate, become fair, completely, diaphanous, discerning, distinctly, glistening, pronounced, unconfused, undeniable, unobscured **11** crystalline, inescapable, self-evident, translucent, transparent, unambiguous, unconcealed, undisguised, unequivocal, unqualified **12** articulately, intelligible, recognizable, unencumbered, unmistakable, unobstructed **14** comprehensible **15** distinguishable, straightforward

unambiguous, undisguised, unequivocal, well-defined **12** crystal-clear, unmistakable **14** comprehensible, understandable **15** straightforward

clearheaded 5 acute, alert, awake, aware, sharp **6** astute **8** rational, sensible **9** on the ball, practical, realistic, wideawake **10** discerning, insightful, on one's toes, on the stick, perceptive **13** perspicacious

clearheadedness 7 insight **8** sagacity **9** alertness, sharpness **10** perception **11** discernment **12** perspicacity

clearing 5 glade

clearly 6 surely **7** plainly **8** markedly, palpably, patently **9** assuredly, certainly, decidedly, evidently, obviously **10** distinctly, manifestly, noticeably, observably, undeniably **11** beyond doubt, indubitably, perceptibly, undoubtedly **12** recognizably, unmistakably **13** unequivocally **14** beyond question, unquestionably

clearly expressed 8 coherent **10** articulate **11** unambiguous **12** intelligible

clearness 7 clarity **10** brightness, brilliance **12** explicitness **15** unmistakability

clear-sighted 4 sage, wise **5** acute, sharp **6** astute, shrewd **8** piercing **9** judicious, sagacious, sensitive **10** discerning, perceptive **11** intelligent, keen-sighted, penetrating **12** sharp-sighted **13** perspicacious

clear up 6 settle **7** clarify, unsnarl **8** untangle **11** disentangle **12** uncomplicate **13** straighten out

Cleary, Beverly
author of: **6** Ramona **7** Fifteen **12** Henry Huggins **13** Jean and Johnny **15** Beezus and Ramona **16** Sister of the Bride

cleat 5 block, chock, spike, wedge **6** batten **7** bollard

cleavage 3 gap **4** rent, rift, slit **5** cleft, crack, notch, split **6** furrow, trench, trough **7** crevice, fissure, opening **8** crevasse

cleave 3 cut, hew **4** chop, fuse, hack, hold, open, part, plow, rend, rive, slit, tear **5** cling, crack, halve, sever, slash, slice, split, stick, unite **6** adhere, be true, bisect, cut off, detach, divide, furrow, sunder, uphold **7** abide by, chop off, disjoin, lay open, stand by **8** be joined, break off, hold fast, separate **9** disengage, dismember

cleaver 3 axe **4** tool **5** knife ridge

cleft 3 gap **4** rent, rift, slit **5** break, crack, notch, split **6** breach, cloven, cranny, divide, forked, furrow, trench, trough **7** crevice, divided, fissure, notched, opening, slotted **8** aperture, bisected, branched, cleavage, crevasse, division **10** separation **11** indentation

clemency 5 mercy **7** charity **8** humanity, kindness, leniency, mildness, softness, sympathy **9** tolerance **10** compassion, indulgence, moderation, temperance **11** benevolence, forbearance, magnanimity **12** mercifulness, pleasantness **13** forgivingness

clement 4 kind, mild, warm **5** balmy **6** benign, gentle, humane **7** lenient **8** merciful, tolerant **9** not severe, not strict **10** benevolent **13** compassionate

clench 3 set **4** grip **5** clasp, tense **6** clinch, clutch **7** stiffen, tighten **8** fasten on, hold fast **11** grasp firmly, strain tight **12** close tightly

Clennam, Arthur
character in: **12** Little Dorrit
author: **7** Dickens

Cleobis
mother: **7** Cydippe
brother: **5** Biton

Cleodaeus
father: **6** Hyllus
mother: **4** Iole
grandfather: **8** Hercules

Cleone
father: **6** Asopus

Cleopas *see* **4** Mary

Cleopatra
queen of: **5** Egypt
father: **7** Ptolemy
brother/husband: **7** Ptolemy
lover: **10** Mark Antony **12** Julius Caesar
son: **9** Caesarion **15** Alexander Helios **19** Ptolemy Philadelphos
daughter: **15** Cleopatra Selene
death by: **3** asp **7** suicide

Cleopatra
director:
1934 version: **13** Cecil B DeMille
1963 version: **17** Joseph L Mankiewicz
cast:
1934 version: **13** Henry Wilcoxon, Warren William **16** Claudette Colbert
1963 version: **11** Rex Harrison **13** Richard Burton, Roddy McDowall **15** Elizabeth Taylor

Cleothera
father: **9** Pandareus

clergy 6 rabbis **7** clerics, pastors, priests **8** ministry, prelates, the cloth **9** churchmen, clergymen, clericals, ministers, pastorate, preachers, rabbinate, the church, the pulpit **10** priesthood **14** the first estate

clergyman 5 padre, rabbi **6** cleric, father, parson, pastor, priest **7** prelate **8** chaplain, minister, preacher, reverend, sky pilot **9** churchman **13** man of the cloth

cleric 6 parson, pastor **8** chaplain, preacher **9** churchman,

clergyman 13 man of the cloth

clerical 6 cleric, filing, office, typing **7** clerkly **8** churchly, of clerks, pastoral, priestly **10** accounting, rabbinical **11** bookkeeping, ministerial **13** recordkeeping **14** ecclesiastical

clerical worker 5 clerk **6** typist **9** file clerk **10** bookkeeper, keypuncher **12** office worker **13** data processor

clerk 6 typist **8** salesman **9** file clerk **10** bookkeeper, salesclerk, saleswoman **11** salesperson **12** office worker

Cleta
member of: **6** Graces
worshipped at: **6** Sparta

Cleveland
baseball team: **7** Indians
basketball team: **9** Cavaliers
football team: **6** Browns

Cleveland, Grover *see box*

clever 4 able, cute, deft, keen **5** acute, quick, sharp, smart, witty **6** adroit, artful, astute, bright, crafty, expert, shrewd **8** creative, humorous, original **9** ingenious, inventive **11** imaginative, intelligent, quick-witted, resourceful

cleverly 6 deftly **7** sharply, smartly, wittily **8** adroitly, artfully, craftily, expertly **10** creatively, humorously **11** ingeniously, inventively **13** imaginatively, intelligently

cleverness 3 wit **6** acumen **8** ableness, deftness, keenness **9** expertise, ingenuity, quickness, sharpness, smartness **10** adroitness, artfulness, astuteness, brightness, craftiness **12** intelligence, skillfulness **13** inventiveness **15** imaginativeness, quick-wittedness

clew *see* **4** clue

Clew
thread in: **9** Labyrinth
showed way to: **7** Theseus
given by: **7** Ariadne

cliche 3 saw **6** old saw **7** bromide **8** banality, old story **9** platitude **10** stereotype **11** trite phrase

cliche-ridden 5 corny, stale, tired, trite, vapid **6** jejune **8** bromidic **9** hackneyed **10** unoriginal **13** platitudinous, unimaginative

click 3 tap **4** clap, snap **5** clack, clink, crack **6** rattle **7** crackle

Clide
form: **5** nymph
habitat: **5** Naxos

Cleveland, Grover
name at birth: 22 Stephen Grover Cleveland
nickname: 5 Grove
presidential rank: 12 twenty-fourth, twenty-second
party: 8 Democrat
state represented: 2 NY
defeated: 4 (Simon) Wing 6 (Benjamin Franklin) Butler, (James Baird) Weaver, (James Gillespie) Blaine, (John Pierce) St John 7 (John) Bidwell 8 (Belva Ann Bennett) Lockwood, (Benjamin) Harrison
vice president: 9 (Adlai Ewing) Stevenson, (Thomas Andrews) Hendricks
cabinet:
 state: 5 (Richard) Olney 6 (Thomas Francis) Bayard 7 (Walter Quinton) Gresham
 treasury: 7 (Daniel) Manning 8 (John Griffin) Carlisle 9 (Charles Stebbins) Fairchild
 war: 6 (David Scott) Lamont 8 (William Crowninshield) Endicott
 attorney general: 5 (Richard) Olney 6 (Judson) Harmon 7 (Augustus Hill) Garland
 interior: 5 (Hoke) Smith, (Lucius Quintus Cincinnatus) Lamar, (William Freeman) Vilas 7 (David Rowland) Francis
born: 2 NJ 8 Caldwell
died/buried: 2 NJ 9 Princeton
education:
 high school: 16 Liberal Institute
religion: 12 Presbyterian
interests: 7 fishing 8 shooting 13 gun collecting
political career:
 mayor of: 7 Buffalo
 governor of: 7 New York
civilian career: 6 lawyer
notable events of lifetime/term: 5 Panic (of 1893) 10 gold crisis (of 1895)
 Act: 6 Tariff 14 Dawes Severalty 18 Interstate Commerce
 strike: 7 Pullman
father: 13 Richard Falley
mother: 4 Anne (Neal)
siblings: 7 Ann Neal 9 Mary Allen 11 Susan Sophia, William Neal 12 Richard Cecil 13 Rose Elizabeth 14 Lewis Frederick 20 Margaret Louise Falley
wife: 7 Frances (Folsom)
children: 4 Ruth 6 Esther, Marion 13 Francis Grover, Richard Folsom

client 5 buyer 6 patron 7 advisee, shopper 8 customer 9 purchaser 17 person represented

cliff 3 tor 4 crag 5 bluff, ledge 8 palisade 9 precipice 10 promontory

Cliff Dwellers *see* 6 Pueblo

Clift, Montgomery
real name: 21 Edward Montgomery Clift
nickname: 5 Monty
born: 7 Omaha NE
roles: 9 The Search 10 The Heiress, The Misfits 14 A Place in the Sun 18 From Here to Eternity, Suddenly Last Summer

climactic 7 crucial 8 critical, dramatic 11 sensational, suspenseful

climate 3 air 4 mood, tone 5 pulse 6 spirit, temper 7 quality, weather 8 ambience, attitude 9 character, condition 10 atmosphere 11 disposition, frame of mind, weather zone 12 usual weather 13 weather region 14 general feeling, weather pattern

climax 4 acme, apex, peak 5 crown 6 crisis, height, summit 8 best part, pinnacle 9 high point 10 denouement 11 culmination 12 highest point, turning point 13 critical point, crowning point, decisive point, supreme moment 18 moment of revelation

climb 4 go up, rise 5 mount, scale 6 ascend, ascent, come up 8 climbing 9 clamber up 10 scramble up

climb down 6 go down 7 descend 8 back down, come down

clinch 3 cap, fix, win 4 bind, bolt, grip, nail 5 cinch, clamp, clasp, close, crown, grasp, screw 6 assure, clutch, couple, decide, fasten, obtain, secure, settle, verify, wind up 7 confirm, grapple 8 complete, conclude, make fast, make sure 9 culminate, establish, finish off 10 grab hold of, hold firmly 12 seize and hold 13 ensure victory

cling 3 hug 4 fuse, grip, hold 5 clasp, grasp, stick 6 adhere, be true, cleave, clutch 7 stand by 8 hang on to, hold fast, hold on to, maintain 9 stay close 10 be constant, be faithful, grab hold of

clinging 6 sticky 7 holding 8 adherent, adhering, adhesive, clasping, cleaving, grasping, gripping, sticking 9 hanging on, holding on 11 holding fast 12 grabbing hold

clinic 9 infirmary 10 polyclinic 13 medical center 15 outpatients' ward

Clinis
form: 3 man
home: 11 Mesopotamia
loved by: 6 Apollo 7 Artemis

clink 4 ting 5 clack, clank, click 6 jangle, jingle, rattle, tinkle 11 ring sharply

clinkers 4 duds, slag 5 dross, flops 6 cinder, scoria 8 failures

Clinton, William Jefferson
see box p. 188

Clio
muse of: 7 history

clip 3 bob, cut, fix 4 crop, grip, hook, snip, trim 5 clamp, clasp, shear 6 attach, buckle, clinch, couple, cut off, cut out, fasten, paring, secure, staple 7 cutting, shorten 8 clipping, cropping, cut short, fastener, shearing, snipping

clipper 4 boat, ship 6 cutter, shears 8 aircraft, airplane, sailboat, scissors 9 racehorse

clipping 7 cutting, pruning, snippet 8 trimming

clique 3 set 4 clan, gang 5 crowd, group 6 circle 7 coterie, faction

cliquish 4 cold 5 aloof 7 distant 8 clannish, snobbish 9 exclusive 10 unfriendly 11 unreceptive

Clite
father: 6 Merops

Clinton, William Jefferson
original last name: **6** Blythe
nickname: **4** Bill
presidential rank: **11** forty-second
party: **10** Democratic
state represented: **2** AR **8** Arkansas
defeated: **4** (George) Bush **4** (Robert) Dole
vice president: **4** (Albert) Gore
cabinet:
  state: **8** (Madeleine) Albright **11** (Warren) Christopher
  treasury: **5** (Robert) Rubin **7** (Lloyd) Bentsen
  attorney general: **4** (Janet) Reno
  defense: **5** (William) Cohen
  interior: **7** (Bruce) Babbitt
  labor: **5** (Robert) Reich
  HUD: **8** (Henry) Cisneros
born: **2** AR **4** Hope
education: **6** Oxford **7** Yale Law **10** Georgetown
honor: **13** Rhodes scholar
political career:
  governor of: **8** Arkansas
  attorney general of: **8** Arkansas
notable events of lifetime/ term: **5** NAFTA **6** Bosnia **10** Whitewater **13** Anti-crime Bill, **15** Branch Davidians
  Supreme Court appointments: **13** Stephen Breyer **17** Ruth Bader Ginsburg
father: **13** William Blythe
mother: **21** Virginia Cassidy Blythe
stepfather: **12** Roger Clinton
sibling: **12** Roger Clinton
wife: **13** Hillary Rodham
children: **7** Chelsea

husband: **7** Cyzicus
killed by: **7** hanging, suicide

cloak 4 cape, hide, mask, robe, veil, wrap **5** cover, tunic **6** mantle, screen, shield, shroud **7** conceal, curtain, pelisse, secrete **8** burnoose, disguise **10** camouflage **11** concealment

cloaked 7 covered, muffled, wrapped **9** disguised

cloaking 7 masking, veiling **8** covering **9** obscuring **10** disguising

cloakroom 8 anteroom, coatroom

clobber 3 hit **4** beat, belt, drub, lick, maul, rout, slug, sock, trim, whip **5** clout, pound, punch, smash, smear, whack **6** batter, beat up, strike, subdue, thrash, wallop **7** conquer, shellac, trounce **8** beat up on, lambaste

clock 5 watch **8** horologe **9** timepiece **11** chronometer

Clockwork Orange, A
  author: **14** Anthony Burgess
  director: **14** Stanley Kubrick
  cast: **12** Patrick Magee **13** Adrienne Corri **15** Malcolm McDowell

clod 3 oaf, wad **4** boor, dolt, dope, glob, hunk, lout, lump, rube **5** chunk, clown, clump, dummy, dunce, moron, yokel **7** bumpkin, fathead **8** imbecile, numskull **9** blockhead, ignoramus, simpleton

clodhopper 3 oaf **4** boot, clod, hick, lout, rube, slob **5** hobby, clown, yokel **6** galoot, lubber, lummox, rustic **7** bumpkin, hayseed, peasant, plowboy, redneck **8** clodpole, lunkhead **9** heavy shoe, hillbilly **10** provincial

clog 4 stop **5** block, check, choke, close, dam up **6** stop up

7 barrier, congest **8** blockage, obstacle, obstruct, stoppage **9** restraint **10** impediment **11** obstruction

clogged 6 choked, halted, jammed **7** clotted, impeded **8** choked up, filled up, hampered, hindered, restrained **10** encumbered, obstructed, overloaded

cloister 4 stoa, walk **5** abbey, aisle **6** arcade, closet, coop up, friary, hole up, immure, shut up, wall up **7** conceal, confine, convent, embower, gallery, nunnery, passage, portico, seclude, walkway **8** shut away **9** colonnade, courtyard, monastery, promenade, sequester **10** ambulatory, passageway

cloistered 5 alone, aloof, apart **6** hidden **7** immured, recluse **8** closeted, confined, detached, isolated, secluded, secreted, separate, solitary **9** concealed, insulated, sheltered, withdrawn **11** dissociated, sequestered

clone 4 copy **5** robot **6** double **7** android, replica **9** automaton, duplicate, replicate **10** carbon copy **12** doppelganger **13** identical copy

close *see box*

closed 6 secret **7** private **9** exclusive

closed-minded 5 rigid **7** adamant, uptight **8** obdurate, stubborn **9** hidebound, obstinate, pig-headed, unbending **10** inflexible, unyielding **12** intransigent **14** uncompromising

close 3 end, hot, pen **4** akin, clog, fast, fill, firm, fuse, halt, join, keen, link, near, neat, nigh, plug, shut, stop, trim, warm **5** alert, block, cease, dense, fixed, humid, muggy, pen in, sharp, short, solid, stuff, tight, unite **6** allied, at hand, clog up, coop up, couple, ending, fill in, fill up, finale, finish, hard by, intent, jammed, loving, narrow, nearby, next to, plug up, recess, secure, shut in, shut up, smooth, stingy, stop up, stuffy, windup **7** adjourn, careful, close up, closing, compact, confine, connect, cramped, crowded, devoted, dismiss, enclose, intense, miserly, pinched, seal off, shut off, similar, stuffed, suspend, teeming **8** attached, blockade, break off, conclude, confined, familiar, friendly, grudging, imminent, intimate, leave off, obstruct, populous, shut down, squeezed, stagnant, stifling, stinting, swarming, thorough, vigilant, watchful **9** attentive, congested, impending, niggardly, penurious, scrimping, terminate **10** almost like, completion, compressed, conclusion, nearly even, nip-and-tuck, resembling, restricted, sweltering, ungenerous **11** almost alike, approaching, approximate, close-fisted, discontinue, forthcoming, impermeable, in proximity, inseparable, nearly equal, neighboring, suffocating, termination, tight-fisted, well-matched **12** bring to an end, impenetrable, parsimonious, unventilated **13** bring together, near to the skin, penny-pinching, uncomfortable **14** thick as thieves

Close Encounters of the Third Kind
director: 15 Steven Spielberg
cast: 8 Teri Garr 13 Melinda Dillon 15 Richard Dreyfuss 16 Francois Truffaut
score: 12 John Williams

closefisted 4 mean 5 cheap, close, mingy, tight 6 stingy 7 miserly 8 grudging 9 niggardly, penurious 10 economical, ungenerous 11 close-handed, tightfisted 12 parsimonious 13 penny-pinching

close-fitting 4 snug 5 tight 9 skintight 11 constricted, form-fitting 12 constricting, tight-fitting 15 like a second skin

close friend 3 pal 4 chum, mate 5 buddy, crony 6 cohort 7 best pal 8 alter ego, intimate 9 companion, confidant 10 bosom buddy 17 intimate confidant

close loudly 4 bang, clap, slam

closely 6 keenly 7 alertly, sharply 8 intently 9 carefully, heedfully, intensely 10 diligently, vigilantly, vigorously, watchfully 11 attentively

close-mouthed 3 shy 4 cool 5 terse 7 bashful, distant 8 reserved, reticent, retiring, taciturn 9 diffident, secretive, withdrawn 11 tight-lipped 15 uncommunicative

closeness 8 meanness, nearness 10 stinginess 11 familiarity, miserliness 15 tightfistedness

close of day 3 eve 4 dusk, even 5 sunset 7 evening, sundown 8 eventide, gloaming, twilight 9 nightfall

closet 2 WC 4 eury, safe 5 ambry, cuddy 6 covert, hidden, locker pantry, secret, toilet 7 cabinet, private 8 coatroom, cupboard, imprison, secluded 9 cloakroom, storeroom, visionary 11 speculative, theoretical, unpractical, water closet

close tightly 3 set 4 seal, slam 5 latch 6 clench, secure 13 press together

close to 4 near 6 almost, around 9 just about 12 on the point of 13 approximately

closure 3 lid, tap 4 bung, cork, plug, stop 5 cover 6 ending, faucet, finish, spigot 7 barring, bolting, closing, cloture, locking, sealing, stopper 8 securing, shutting, stoppage 9 cessation 10 conclusion, stoppering 11 termination 14 discontinuance 15 discontinuation

clot 3 gob 4 lump, mass 7 congeal, thicken 8 embolism, solidify, thrombus 9 coagulate, occlusion 11 coagulation

Cloten
character in: 9 Cymbeline
author: 11 Shakespeare

cloth 5 goods 6 fabric 7 textile 8 dry goods, material 9 yard goods 10 piece goods

clothe 3 don 4 case, coat, deck, garb, robe, veil, wrap 5 array, cloak, cloud, cover, drape, dress 6 attire, bedeck, encase, enwrap, outfit, rig out, screen, shroud 7 bedizen, costume, deck out, envelop, sheathe, swaddle 8 accouter

clothed 4 clad 5 robed 6 draped 7 cloaked, couched, covered, dressed, mantled, wearing 8 equipped, provided 9 expressed, furnished

clothes 4 duds, garb, rags, togs, wear 5 dress 6 attire, finery 7 apparel, costume, raiment, regalia 8 clothing, ensemble, garments, wardrobe 11 habiliments

clotheshorse 3 fop 5 dandy, model 12 Beau Brummell, fashion plate, man of fashion, sharp dresser 14 woman of fashion

clothing see 7 clothes

Clotho
member of: 5 Fates
spinner of: 12 thread of life

cloud 3 dim, mar 4 blur, hide, veil 5 blind, cloak, cover, muddy, shade, sully, upset 6 darken, impair, muddle, screen, shadow, shroud 7 conceal, confuse, curtain, distort, disturb, eclipse, obscure, tarnish 8 overcast 9 discredit, make vague 10 overshadow 11 cast doubt on 14 call to question 19 place under suspicion

cloudburst 6 deluge 8 downpour, rainfall 9 rainstorm

clouded 3 dim 5 dusky, murky 7 blurred, obscure, sullied, tainted, unclear 8 confused, darkened, obscured 10 ill-defined, indistinct

cloudless 4 fair 5 clear, sunny 6 bright 7 halcyon 8 sunshiny 9 unclouded 10 unobscured

Clouds
goddess of: 3 Fri 5 Frigg, Frija 6 Frigga

Clouds, The (Nephelai)
author: 12 Aristophanes
character: 8 Just Plea, Socrates 10 Unjust Plea 11 Strepsiades 12 Pheidippides

cloudy 4 dark, gray, hazy 5 murky, vague 6 dreary, gloomy, leaden, veiled 7 clouded, obscure, sunless, unclear 8 confused, nebulous, overcast 9 confusing, undefined 10 indefinite, mysterious 11 overclouded

Clouet, Jean
born: 8 Flanders
artwork attributed: 13 Guillaume Bude 16 Madame de Canaples, Man with Gold Coins 17 The Count of Brissac, The Dauphin Francis 22 Man with a Book by Petrarch

clout 3 box, hit, jab 4 bash, belt, blow, pull, sock 5 crack, knock, punch, smack, thump, whack 6 wallop 9 influence 10 importance

clove
botanical name: 16 Eugenia aromatica 18 Syzygium aromaticum
origin: 5 Pemba 7 Far East 8 Moluccas, Zanzibar 9 Mauritius 10 Madagascar
use: 3 ham 8 pickling, pomander 16 yellow vegetables

cloven 5 cleft, split 7 divided, notched, slotted 8 bisected

clover 9 Trifolium
varieties: 3 bur, elk, hop, low, pin, red 4 bush, holy, Kura, musk, owl's, tick 5 Alyce, Hubam, lucky, sweet, water, white 6 Alsike, cow hop, indoor, Korean, Ladino, yellow 7 Bukhara, crimson, Italian, mammoth, Mexican, Persian, prairie 8 Japanese, large hop, reversed, small hop, stinking 9 Hungarian 10 strawberry, toothed bur, white Dutch, white sweet 11 yellow sweet 12 silky prairie, subterranean, white prairie 13 European water 16 strawberry-headed

clown 3 wag, wit 4 card, fool, jest, joke, mime, zany 5 comic, cut up, joker 6 jester, madcap 7 buffoon 8 comedian, humorist 9 harlequin, kid around 10 comedienne, fool around 11 funny person, merry-andrew

clownishness 6 antics 10 buffoonery, tomfoolery 12 monkeyshines 14 playing the fool

cloy 3 gag 4 bore, glut, pall, sate, tire 5 choke, weary 6 benumb, overdo 7 exhaust, satiate, surfeit 8 nauseate, saturate

cloying 5 sweet 6 sugary 9 excessive, satiating 10 saccharine

club 3 bat, hit 4 bash, beat, flog, slug 5 billy, flail, group, guild, lay on, lodge, stick, union 6 batter, buffet, cudgel, league, pommel, pummel, strike 7 society 8 alliance, bludgeon, sorority 9 billyclub, clubhouse, truncheon 10 fraternity, shillelagh, sisterhood 11 affiliation, association, brotherhood, country club

clubhouse 4 club, hall 5 lodge 11 locker rooms 12 meeting house

clue 3 cue, key 4 clew, hint, mark, sign 5 guide, scent, trace 7 glimmer, inkling, pointer 8 evidence 9 indicator, inference 10 indication, intimation, suggestion 11 insinuation

clump 4 bulb, bump, knob, knot, lump, mass, plod, thud 5 batch, bunch, clomp, clunk, copse, group, grove, plunk, shock, stamp, stomp, thump, tramp 6 lumber 7 cluster, thicket 9 aggregate 10 assemblage, collection

clumsiness 9 gawkiness 10 ineptitude 11 awkwardness 12 carelessness, ungainliness 13 gracelessness, maladroitness

clumsy 5 bulky, crude, gawky, inept, rough 6 klutzy 7 awkward, unhandy 8 bungling, careless, ungainly, unwieldy 9 graceless, makeshift, maladroit, unskilled 10 blundering, cumbersome, ungraceful 11 heavy-handed 12 ill-contrived, unmanageable 14 butterfingered 21 like a bull in a china shop

cluster 4 band, bevy, heap, herd, knot, mass, pack, pile 5 amass, batch, bunch, bunch, clump, crowd, flock, group, sheaf, shock, swarm 6 gather, muster, throng 7 collect, company 8 assemble, converge 9 aggregate 10 accumulate, assemblage, collection, congregate 12 accumulation, congregation 13 agglomeration 14 conglomeration

cluster around 6 gather 7 collect 10 congregate 12 herd together 13 flock together

clutch 3 hug 4 grip, hold 5 clasp, grasp 6 clench 7 cling to, embrace, squeeze 8 hang on to

clutter 4 fill, heap, mess, pile 5 chaos, strew 6 jumble, litter, tangle 7 scatter 8 disarray, disorder 9 confusion 10 hodgepodge

cluttered 5 messy 7 chaotic, crowded, jumbled, muddled 8 confused, littered 9 scattered 10 disordered, disorderly

Clymene
origin: 5 Greek
mentioned in: 5 Iliad
form: 5 nymph
habitat: 5 ocean
father: 6 Mimyas, Minyas 7 Catreus, Oceanus
mother: 6 Tethys
husband: 7 Iapetus 8 Cephalus, Phaethon, Phylacus
son: 4 Oeax 5 Atlas 8 Iphiclus, Phaethon 9 Palamedes 10 Epimetheus, Nausimedon, Prometheus
daughter: 8 Alcimede
attended: 11 Helen of Troy
sold to: 8 Nauplius
beloved of: 3 Sun

Clymenus
king of: 10 Orchomenus
grandfather: 7 Phrixus
son: 7 Erginus
daughter: 9 Harpalyce
violated: 9 Harpalyce
home: 7 Arcadia

Clytemnestra
father: 9 Tyndareus
mother: 4 Leda
brother: 6 Castor, Pollux
sister: 5 Helen 8 Timandra
cousin: 8 Perilaus
husband: 9 Agamemnon
son: 7 Orestes
daughter: 7 Electra, Erigone 9 Iphigenia 12 Chrysothemis
lover: 9 Aegisthus
killed: 9 Agamemnon
killed by: 7 Orestes

Clytie
form: 5 nymph
habitat: 5 water
loved: 6 Apollo
changed into: 10 heliotrope

Clytius
member of: 8 Gigantes
father: 8 Laomedon
brother: 5 Priam
companion of: 5 Jason
killed by: 8 Hercules

coach 3 bus 5 drill, guide, sedan, stage, teach, train, tutor 6 advise, direct, mentor 7 omnibus, trainer 8 carriage, instruct 9 limousine, preceptor 10 automobile, four-in-hand, motor coach, stagecoach 11 four-wheeler, second class 12 economy class 14 private teacher 16 athletic director

coachman 3 fly 4 jehu, whip 5 pilot 6 driver 10 charioteer

Coactrice 14 poisonous snake

coagulate 3 gel, set 4 clot,

jell 6 curdle, harden 7 congeal, jellify, thicken 8 solidify

coagulation 3 gob 4 clot, mass 8 clotting, curdling, thrombus 10 thickening

coal 4 ash, bass, char, coke, coom, culm, dust, fuel, slag, smut, swad 5 ember 6 cannel, cinder 7 lignite, clinker 8 charcoal 10 fossil fuel 11 charred wood
box: 3 hod 7 scuttle
made from: 6 carbon
type: 4 hard, soft 7 lignite 10 anthracite, bituminous
mining method: 4 deep 8 opencast 10 strip auger 11 underground
mine: 5 drift, shaft, slope, strip
size: 3 egg, nut, pea 5 stove

coal-black 3 jet 4 dark, inky 5 black, ebony, raven, sable 9 pitch-dark

coalesce 3 mix 4 ally, form, fuse, join, meld 5 blend, merge, unify, unite 6 cohere 7 combine 9 become one, integrate 10 amalgamate, join forces 11 agglutinate, consolidate 12 band together, come together 14 form an alliance

coalition 5 union 6 fusion, league 7 society 8 alliance 9 syndicate 10 federation 11 affiliation, association, combination, confederacy, partnership 12 amalgamation 13 agglomeration, consolidation 14 conglomeration

Coal Miner's Daughter
director: 12 Michael Apted
cast: 9 Levon Helm 11 Sissy Spacek (Loretta Lynn) 13 Tommy Lee Jones 14 Beverly D'Angelo
Oscar for: 7 actress (Spacek)
screenplay: 10 Tom Rickman

Coaluitecan
tribe: 6 Payaya

coarse 4 lewd, rude, vile 5 crass, crude, dirty, gross, harsh, rough 6 common, nubly, odious, ribald, shaggy, sordid, vulgar 7 boorish, bristly, brutish, ill-bred, loutish, obscene, prickly, uncouth 8 impolite, improper, indecent, scratchy 9 bristling, inelegant, offensive, repulsive, revolting, sandpaper, unrefined 10 disgusting, indecorous, indelicate, lascivious, licentious, scurrilous, unladylike, unpolished 11 foul-mouthed, ill-mannered 12 lacking taste 13 rough-textured, ungentlemanly

coarse-grained 5 crude, harsh,

nubby, rough **6** coarse, grainy, shaggy **7** bristly **8** scratchy **9** unrefined **13** rough-textured

coarseness 9 crudeness, grossness, roughness, vulgarity **10** indelicacy, inelegance **11** boorishness **16** lack of refinement

coast 4 skim, slip, waft **5** drift, float, glide, shore, slide, sweep **6** strand **7** seaside **8** glissade, littoral, seaboard, seacoast, seashore **9** shoreline

coaster 3 mat **4** ship, sled, tray **5** wagon **6** cradle, glider, slider **8** toboggan **9** tray stand **13** decanter stand, roller coaster

coat 3 fur **4** hair, hide, pelt, wrap **5** cover, glaze, layer, paint, smear **6** blazer, enamel, encase, jacket, spread **7** coating, encrust, envelop, lacquer, overlay, plaster, slicker, topcoat **8** covering, laminate, mackinaw, overcoat, raincoat **9** whitewash **10** mackintosh, sports coat

coating 4 coat, film, skin **5** layer, sheet **6** veneer **7** overlay **8** covering, envelope

coat of arms 4 arms **5** crest **6** creast **8** insignia **9** blaconwry **10** escutcheon **14** heraldic emblem **16** armorial bearings

coat of mail 4 mail **5** armor **9** chain mail **11** suit of armor

Coat of Varnish, A
author: **6** C P Snow

coax 6 cajole **7** wheedle **8** butter up, inveigle, soft-soap, talk into **9** sweet-talk

cobalt 4 blue **5** azure **7** element, sky blue **10** bright blue **12** greenish blue
chemical symbol: **2** Co

Cobb, Lee J
born: **9** New York NY
roles: **10** Willy Loman **12** The Virginian **14** Twelve Angry Men **16** On the Waterfront **16** Death of a Salesman

Cobb, Ty (Tyrus Raymond)
nickname: **12** Georgia Peach
sport: **8** baseball
position: **8** outfield
team: **13** Detroit Tigers

cobbler 3 pie **9** bootmaker, shoemaker **12** shoe repairer **16** deepdish fruit pie

cobra
also: **3** asp **5** mamba **11** hooded snake
native to: **4** Asia **6** Africa

kind: 4 king **6** hooded, Indian **8** Egyptian
enemy: **8** mongoose

Coburn, Charles
born: **10** Savannah GA
roles: **9** Boss Tweed **17** The More the Merrier

Coburn, James
born: **8** Laurel NE
roles: **11** In Like Flint, Our Man Flint **14** The Great Escape **19** The Magnificent Seven

Coca, Imogene
partner: **9** Sid Caesar
born: **14** Philadelphia PA
roles: **15** Your Show of Shows

Cocalus
king of: **6** Sicily

Coccygius
epithet of: **4** Zeus
means: **6** cuckoo

cock 3 tip **4** knob **5** raise, valve **6** faucet, handle, perk up **7** rooster, stand up **8** cockerel, male bird, set erect **9** bristle up **11** chanticleer **13** turn to one side **16** raise the hammer of **17** draw back the hammer

cockade 4 knot **5** badge **6** ribbon **7** rosette **8** ornament **10** party badge

Cockade State
nickname of: **8** Maryland

cock-and-bull story 3 fib, lie **4** myth, yarn **5** fable **7** fiction, untruth, whopper **9** fairy tale, falsehood, fish story, invention, tall story **11** fabrication **13** prevarication

Cockcroft, John Douglas
field: **7** physics
nationality: **7** British
developed: **24** Cockcroft-Walton generator
worked with: **6** Walton
awarded: **10** Nobel Prize

cockeyed 3 mad **4** awry, wild **5** askew, crazy, goofy, inane, nutty, weird **6** absurd, aslant, insane, tilted **7** crooked, foolish, twisted **8** lopsided, sideways **9** irregular, off-center, senseless **10** cockamamie, out of whack, ridiculous, unbalanced **11** nonsensical **12** asymmetrical, preposterous

Cockpit of Europe *see* **7** Belgium

cockscomb 4 comb **5** crest **7** celosia, coxcomb **8** amaranth, caruncle

cocksure 4 pert, smug, vain

5 brash, cocky, pushy **6** cheeky, snooty **8** arrogant, positive **9** assertive, audacious, bumptious, conceited **10** aggressive, swaggering **11** overbearing, self-assured, swellheaded **13** overconfident, self-confident

cocktail 5 drink, fruit, horse **6** shrimp **10** docked tail, semiformal
type: **4** grog **6** brandy, gibson, gimlet, mai tai, rob roy, zombie **7** gin fizz, martini, sidecar, stinger **8** daiquiri, highball, hot toddy, pink lady **9** cuba libre, hurricane, gin rickey, manhattan, margarita, mint julep, rusty nail **10** bloody mary, tom collins **11** boilermaker, gin and tonic, grasshopper, screwdriver, sloe gin fizz **12** black russian, old-fashioned, tom and jerry, whiskey sour **13** planter's punch **15** brandy alexander
mixer: **4** soda **5** tonic, water **7** bitters, seltzer **9** ginger ale
garnish: **4** lime **5** lemon, olive, orange, twist **16** maraschino cherry

cocktail lounge 3 bar **6** saloon, tavern **7** gin mill, taproom

cocky 5 brash, saucy **6** jaunty **8** arrogant, cocksure, impudent **9** conceited, egotistic **10** swaggering

Cocles *see* **8** Horatius

Coco, James
born: **9** New York NY
roles: **11** Sancho Panza **13** Man of La Mancha **21** Last of the Red Hot Lovers

cocoa 5 brown, cacao **9** chocolate **12** hot chocolate

cocoon
covering for: **5** larva
stage: **5** pupal
made of: **4** silk

Cocteau, Jean
author of: **7** Orpheus **8** Antigone **12** Blood of a Poet **18** The Infernal Machine **19** Les Enfants Terribles, Les Parents Terribles **20** The Beauty and the Beast

Cocytus
river in: **5** Hades

coddle 3 pat, pet **4** baby **5** humor, spoil **6** caress, cuddle, dote on, fondle, pamper **7** indulge **11** mollycoddle

code 4 laws **5** rules **6** cipher **7** statute **8** precepts **9** ordinance, standards **10** crypto-

gram, guidelines, principles
11 cryptograph, proprieties,
regulations **13** secret writing
14 secret language

codger 5 crank, miser **6** oddity,
old man **9** eccentric, odd
person

codicil 5 rider **8** addendum, addition, appendix **9** extension,
subscript **10** postscript, supplement **11** added clause

codify 4 rank, rate **5** grade,
group, index, order **7** arrange,
catalog **8** classify, organize,
tabulate **9** methodize **10** categorize, coordinate, regularize
11 systematize

coelenterate 5 coral, hydra,
polyp **6** Medusa **7** acaleph, radiate **8** acalephe **9** jellyfish
10 sea anemone
  habitat: 5 ocean **9** salt water

Coelophysis
  type: 8 dinosaur, therapod
  location: 7 Arizona
  period: 8 Triassic

coequal 5 equal **10** coordinate
16 equally important

coequality 6 parity **8** equality,
evenness, sameness **10** uniformity **11** equivalency
14 correspondence

coerce 3 cow **4** make **5** bully,
drive, force **6** compel, oblige
7 dragoon **8** browbeat, bulldoze, pressure, threaten
9 constrain, strong-arm
10 intimidate

coercer 5 bully **9** oppressor,
tormenter, tormentor
10 browbeater **11** intimidator,
petty tyrant

coercion 5 force **6** duress
7 threats **8** bullying, pressure
10 compulsion, constraint
11 browbeating
12 intimidation

coercive 8 enforced, forcible
10 compulsory, obligatory
11 threatening

Coeus
  form: 5 Titan
  father: 6 Uranus
  mother: 4 Gaea
  daughter: 4 Leto **7** Asteria

coexist with 12 go hand in
hand, go side by side, live together **13** go hand in glove

coffee 6 Coffea **13** Coffea
arabica
  varieties: 4 Java, Kona,
  Wild **5** Irish, Mocha **6** Almond, Common **7** Arabian,
  Arabica, Robusta, Vanilla
  8 Liberian, Zanzibar **9** Colombian **11** French
  Roast, Wild robusta **13** De-

caffeinated **20** Jamaican
Blue Mountain
  beverage: 6 kahlua **8** espresso **10** cafe au lait,
  cappuccino
  small cup: 9 demitasse

coffee (black)
  French: 8 cafe noir **10** cafe
  nature

coffee brandy 6 Kahlua **8** Tia
Maria

coffee with milk
  French: 10 cafe au lait

coffer 3 box **4** case **5** chest
9 strongbox **10** depository, repository **13** treasure chest

coffers 5 safes **6** vaults **8** treasury **9** cash boxes **11** money
supply

coffin 3 box **4** pall **6** casket
10 catafalque **11** sarcophagus

cog 3 cam, lie **4** gear **5** cheat,
cozen, tenon, tooth, wedge,
wheel **8** small boat
10 projection

cogent 5 sound, valid **6** potent **7** weighty **8** forceful,
powerful **9** effective, trenchant **10** compelling, convincing,
persuasive, undeniable
11 meritorious, well-founded
12 well-grounded
16 incontrovertible

cogitate 5 study, think, weigh
6 ponder **7** reflect **8** meditate,
mull over, ruminate **9** think
over **10** deliberate, think
about **11** contemplate, reflect
upon **18** consider thoroughly

cogito ergo sum 18 I think
therefore I am
  said by: 9 Descartes

cognac
  type: 6 brandy **7** liqueur
  origin: 6 France
  brand: 7 Bisquit, Martell
  8 Hennessy **10** Remy Martin **11** Courvoisier
  label: 2 VO (very old), VS
  (very special), XO (extra
  old) **3** XXO (extra extra
  old) **4** VSOP (very superior
  old pale) **8** Napoleon (5 year
  premium)
  drink: 9 Andalusia
  with Cointreau: 10 Rolls
  Royce
  with Triple Sec: 7 Chicago
  10 Rolls Royce
  with vodka: 7 Cossack

cognate 4 akin, like **5** alike,
close **7** kindred, related, similar **8** familial, parallel, relative **9** affiliate **10** derivative
11 consanguine

cognition 7 knowing **9** awareness, knowledge **11** familiar-

ity **13** comprehension,
understanding

cognizance 4 heed, note
5 grasp **6** notice, regard
8 scrutiny **9** attention, awareness, cognition, knowledge
10 perception **11** familiarity,
observation, recognition, sensibility **12** apprehension
13 comprehension, consciousness, understanding

cognizant 5 aware **6** posted
7 knowing, mindful **8** familiar,
informed, versed in **9** conscious **10** acquainted, conversant, instructed
11 enlightened **13** knowledgeable, understanding

cognomen 4 name **6** handle
7 epithet, moniker, surname
11 appellation, designation

cognoscenti 6 judges **7** experts **8** insiders **11** authorities
12 connoisseurs **14** those in
the know

cohere 3 fit, set **4** bind, fuse,
glue, hold, jibe, join **5** agree,
cling, match, stick, tally,
unite **6** cement, concur,
square **7** combine, conform,
congeal **8** coalesce, coincide,
dovetail, solidify **9** coagulate,
harmonize **10** correspond
11 consolidate, synchronize
12 hold together **13** stick
together

coherence 5 logic, unity
7 clarity, concord, harmony
8 cohesion **9** congruity **10** accordance, conformity, consonance **11** consistency,
rationality **12** organization

coherent 5 clear, lucid **7** logical, orderly **8** cohesive, rational **9** congruous, connected, in
keeping, organized **10** articulate, consistent, harmonious,
meaningful, systematic **11** in
agreement **12** intelligible
13 corresponding **14** comprehensible, understandable

cohesion 4 bond **5** union, unity **7** bonding **8** adhesion
10 attraction, solidarity

cohesive 3 set **5** solid **6** sticky
7 viscous **8** cemented, coherent, cohering, sticking **9** connected **11** indivisible,
inseparable **12** consolidated
13 agglutinative

Cohn, Ferdinand Julius
  field: 6 botany
  nationality: 6 German
  founded: 12 bacteriology

Cohn, Robert
  character in: 15 The Sun
  Also Rises
  author: 9 Hemingway

cohort 3 pal 4 chum 5 buddy, crony 6 fellow, friend 7 comrade 8 follower, myrmidon 9 associate, companion 10 accomplice

coif 3 cap 4 hood, veil 6 beggin, burlet, hairdo 8 biggonet, coiffure, skull cap 9 head-dress

coiffed 6 capped, styled 7 dressed 8 arranged

coiffeur 7 stylist 11 hairdresser 15 male hairdresser

coiffure 2 DA, GI 3 bob, bun 4 Afro, coif, perm, shag, trim, wave 6 hairdo 7 beehive, blow-cut, comb-out, flattop, haircut, pageboy, upsweep 8 cold wave, cornrows, ducktail 9 hairstyle, permanent, pompadour

coil 4 curl, loop, ring, roll, wind 5 braid, twine, twist 6 circle, spiral, writhe 7 entwine 8 encircle

coin 4 mint 5 hatch, money, piece 6 change, create, devise, invent, make up, silver, strike 7 concoct, dream up, think up 8 conceive 9 fabricate, originate

coin/currency *see box*

coincide 3 fit 4 jibe, meet 5 agree, cross, match, tally 6 accord, concur, square 7 conform 8 converge, dovetail 9 harmonize 10 correspond 11 synchronize 12 be concurrent, come together 19 occur simultaneously

coincidence 4 fate, luck 6 chance 8 accident 11 concurrence, synchronism 12 happenstance 22 simultaneous occurrence

coincident 10 coexistent, concurrent 12 contemporary, simultaneous 15 contemporaneous

---

coin/currency

of Afghanistan: 3 pul 5 abaze, riyal, rupee 6 abbasi, amania 7 afghani
of Albania: 3 lek 5 franc 6 qintar 7 quintar
of Algeria: 5 dinar 7 centime
of Andorra: 5 franc 6 peseta
of Angola: 6 escudo, kwanza, macuta, macute 7 angolar, centavo
of Argentina: 4 peso 7 centavo 9 argentino
of Armenia: 5 ruble
of Australia: 4 dump, tray, zack 5 pound 6 dollar 8 shilling
of Austria: 4 lira 5 crown, ducat, krone 6 florin, gulden, heller, zehner 8 albertin, groschen, kreutzer 9 schilling
of Azerbaijan: 5 manat
of Bahrain: 5 dinar
of Bangladesh: 4 taka 5 paisa
of Belarus: 5 ruble
of Belgium: 5 belga, franc 7 brabant, centime, crocard
of Benin: 5 franc 7 centime
of Bhutan: 5 paisa, rupee 7 chetrum 8 ngultrum
of Bolivia: 4 peso 7 centavo 9 boliviano
of Bosnia-Herzegovina: 5 dinar
of Botswana: 4 pula, rand
of Brazil: 3 joe 4 reis 5 dobra 7 centara, halfjoe, milreis 8 cruzeiro
of Bulgaria: 3 lev 8 stotinki
of Burkina Faso: 5 franc 7 centime
of Burundi: 5 franc 7 centime

of Cambodia: 3 sen 4 quan, riel 6 puttan 7 piaster
of Cameroon: 5 franc 7 centime
of Canary Islands: 6 peseta
of Cape Verde: 6 escudo 7 centavo
of Central African Republic: 5 franc 7 centime
of Chad: 5 franc 7 centime
of Chile: 4 peso 5 libra 6 condor, escudo
of China: 4 cash, cent, fyng, mace, tael, tiao, yuan 5 sycee 12 jen nin piao pu
of Colombia: 4 peso, real 6 condor, peseta 7 centavo
of Comoros: 5 franc 7 centime
of Congo: 5 franc 7 centime
of Costa Rica: 5 colon 6 colone 7 centimo
of Crete: 7 drachma
of Croatia: 5 dinar
of Cuba: 4 peso 7 centavo 8 cuarenta
of Cyprus 4 para 5 pound
of Czechoslovakia/Czech Republic: 5 crown, ducat 6 heller, koruna
of Denmark: 3 one, ora, ore 4 fyrk 5 krone 8 frederik, skilling 9 rigsdaler
of Djibouti: 5 franc 7 centime
of Dominican Republic: 3 oro 4 peso 6 franco
of Ecuador: 5 sucre 7 centavo
of Egypt: 4 fils, kees, para 5 asper, dinar, fodda, gersh, girsh, medin, pound, riyal 6 ahmadi, dirham, foddah, guinea, junayh, maidin,

medine, medino 7 piaster, piastre, tallard 8 bedidlik, millieme
of El Salvador: 4 peso 5 colon 7 centavo
of England: 3 ora 4 rial 5 achey, crown, groat, noble, pence, penny, pound 6 bawbee, florin, guinea 7 angelet, hapenny 8 farthing, shilling, sixpence, tuppence, tuppenny 13 pound sterling
of Equatorial Guinea: 6 ekuele, peseta 7 centimo
of Estonia: 3 lat 4 sent 5 kroon 7 estmark
of Ethiopia: 4 besa, birr, harf 5 amole, girsh 6 dollar, kharaf, levant, pataca, talari 7 ashrafi, menelik, plaster, tallero 12 maria theresa
of Fiji: 6 dollar
of Finland: 4 mark 5 penni 6 markka 7 markkaa
of France: 5 franc 7 centime 8 napoleon
of Gabon Republic: 5 franc 7 centime
of the Gambia: 5 pound 6 butbut, dalasi
of Georgia: 5 ruble
of Germany: 4 mark 7 Ostmark, pfennig 12 Deutsche mark
of Ghana: 4 cedi, cidi 5 ackey
of Greece: 5 lepta 7 drachma
of Greenland: 3 ore 5 krone
of Guatemala: 4 peso 7 centavo, quetzal

(continued)

coin/currency (*continued*)

of Guinea: 4 iliy, syli 5 franc 6 cauris

of Guinea-Bissau: 4 peso 6 escudo 7 centavo

of Haiti: 6 gourde 7 centime

of Honduras: 4 peso 7 centavo, lempira

of Hungary: 4 gara 5 balas, krone, pengo 6 filler, forint, gulden, korona, ongara, ungara

of Iceland: 5 aurar, eyrir, krona 6 kronur

of India: 3 lac, pie 4 anna, fels, lakh, pice, tara 5 abidi, crore, paisa, rupee

of Indonesia: 3 sen 6 rupiah

of Iran: 3 pul 4 asar, gran, lari, rial 5 bisti, daric, dinar, larin, shahi, toman 6 stater 7 ashrafi, kasbeke, pahlavi

of Iraq: 4 fils 5 dinar

of Ireland: 3 rap 4 real 5 pence, pound 6 turney 8 shilling

of Israel: 3 mil 5 agora, agura, pound, pruta 6 agorot, shekel

of Italy: 4 lira, lire, tara 5 grano, paoli, paolo, scudo, soldo 6 danaro, denaro, ducato, sequin 7 testone 8 zecchino 9 centesini

of Ivory Coast: 5 franc 7 centime

of Jamaica: 7 quattie

of Japan: 2 bu 3 mon, rin, rio, sen, shu, yen 4 cash, mibu, oban 5 koban, obang, tempo 6 cobang, ichebu, ichibu, itzebu, kogang 7 itzeboo, itziboo

of Jordan: 4 fils 5 dinar

of Kazakhstan: 5 ruble

of Kenya: 4 cent 5 pound 8 shilling

of Kiribati: 4 cent 6 dollar

of Korea: 3 woh, won 4 chun, hwan, kwan

of Kuwait: 4 fils 5 dinar

of Kyrgyzstan: 3 som

of Laos: 2 at 3 att, kip

of Latvia: 3 lat 4 latu 6 rublis, santim 7 kapeika, santima

of Lebanon: 5 livre, pound 7 piastre

of Lesotho: 4 cent, rand 6 maloti

of Liberia: 4 cent 6 dollar

of Libya: 5 dinar

of Liechtenstein: 5 franc 6 rappen 7 franken

of Lithuania: 3 lit 5 litas, marka 6 centas, fennig

of Luxembourg: 5 franc 7 centime

of Macao: 3 avo 6 pataca, pataco

of Macedonia: 5 denar

of Madagascar: 5 franc 7 centime

of Malawi: 6 kwacha 7 tambala

of Malaysia: 3 sen, tra 4 taro, trah 7 ringgit, tampang

of Maldives: 5 laree, rupee 7 rufiyaa

of Mali: 5 franc 7 centime

of Malta: 4 cent 5 grain, grano, pound

of Mauritania: 5 khoum 7 ouguiya

of Mauritius: 4 cent 5 rupee

of Mexico: 4 onza, peso 5 adobe, claco, tlaco 6 azteca, cuarto, dinero 7 centavo, piaster

of Moldova: 5 ruble

of Monaco: 5 franc 7 centime

of Mongolia: 5 mongo, mungo 6 tugrik 7 tughrik

of Montenegro: 4 para 6 florin 7 perpera

of Morocco: 4 flue, okia, rial 5 floos, franc, okieh, ounce 6 dirham, miskal 8 mouzouna

of Mozambique: 6 escudo 7 centavo, metical

of Myanmar: 3 pya 4 kyat

of Namibia: 4 cent, rand

of Nauru: 4 cent 6 dollar

of Nepal: 4 anna, pice 5 mohar, rupee

of the Netherlands: 4 doit, oord, raps 5 crown, daler, rider, ryder 6 florin, gulden, stiver, suskin 7 daalder, ducaton, escalan, escalin, guilder, stooter, stuiver 8 albertin, ducatoon 9 dubbeltje 12 rijksdaalder 13 albertustaler

of New Guinea: 4 kina, toea

of New Zealand: 4 cent 6 dollar

of Nicaragua: 4 peso 7 centavo, cordoba

of Niger: 5 franc 7 centime

of Nigeria: 4 kobo 5 naira

of Norway: 3 ore 5 krone 6 kroner

7 ostmark, skatiku 8 auksinas, skatikas

of Oman: 3 gaj, gaz 4 rial 5 baiza, ghazi 7 mahmudi

of Pakistan: 4 anna, pice 5 paisa, rupee

of Panama: 4 cent 6 balboa 9 centesimo

of Paraguay: 4 peso 7 centimo, guarani

of Peru: 3 sol 5 libra 6 dinero, reseta 7 centavo

of the Philippines: 4 peso 6 conant, peseta 7 centavo

of Poland: 4 abia 5 dalar, ducat, grosz, marka, zloty 6 fening, groszy, gulden, halerz, korona 8 groschen

of Portugal: 3 avo, joe 4 peca, real 5 conto, crown, dobra, indio, justo, rupia 6 escudo, macuta, octave, pataca, testad, tostao, vintem 7 angalar, centavo, crusado, miereis, moidore, testone 8 equipaga, johannes

of Qatar: 5 riyal 6 dirham

of Rumania: 3 ban, lei, leu, lev, ley 4 bani 5 uncia 6 triens

of Russia: 5 altin, bisti, copec, genga, grosh, kopek, ruble, shaur 6 abassi, copeck, grivna, kopeck, piatak, rouble 7 poltina, valiuta 8 auksinas, deneshka, imperial, polushka 9 poltinnik 10 altininink, chervonets

of Rwanda: 5 franc 7 centime

of San Marino: 4 lira, lire 9 centesimi

of Samoa: 4 tala

of Sao Tome and Principe: 5 dobra 6 escudo 7 centavo

of Sardinia: 7 carline

of Saudi Arabia: 5 girsh, gursh, pound, riyal

of Scotland: 3 ecu 4 demy, doit, lion, mark, rial, ryal 5 bodle, broad, groat, plack, rider, turne 6 bawbee, folles 7 unicorn 8 atchison, hardhead 9 halfpenny 11 bonnetpiece

of Senegal: 5 franc 7 centime

of Sicily: 5 litra, oncia, uncia 6 carlin 7 carline, oncetta

of Sierra Leone: 4 cent **5** leone
of Singapore: 4 cent **6** dollar
of Slovakia: 6 koruna
of Slovenia: 5 tolar
of Solomon Islands: 4 cent **6** dollar
of Somalia: 4 besa **6** somalo **8** shilling **9** centesimi
of South Africa: 4 cent, pond, rand **5** pound **6** florin **7** daalder **9** krugerand
of Spain: 3 cob **4** duro, peso, real **5** dobla **6** cuarto, dinero, doblon, escudo, peseta **7** alfonso, centimo, pistole, realdor **8** doubloon
of Sri Lanka: 4 cent **5** rupee
of Sudan: 5 dinar, pound **7** piastre
of Suriname: 4 cent **7** guilder
of Swaziland: 4 rand **9** lilangeni
of Sweden: 3 ore **5** krona, krone **7** carolin **8** skilling **9** rigsdaler
of Switzerland: 5 franc,

rappe **6** hallar, rappen **7** angster, centime, duplone **8** baetzner, blaffert
of Syria: 4 lira **5** pound **6** talent **7** piaster
of Taiwan: 4 yuan **6** dollar
of Tajikistan: 5 ruble
of Tanzania: 4 cent **8** shilling
of Thailand: 2 at **3** att **4** baht **5** cutty, fuang, tical **6** pynung, salung, satang **11** bullet money
of Tibet: 5 tanga
of Togo: 5 franc **7** centime
of Tonga: 6 paanga, seniti
of Trinidad and Tobago: 4 cent **6** dollar
of Tunisia: 5 dinar **6** dollar **7** millime
of Turkey: 4 lira, para **5** akcha, asper, attun, kurus, pound, rebia **6** akcheh, sequin, zequin **7** aetilik, beshlik, pataque, piaster **8** medjidie, zecchino
of Turkmenistan: 5 ruble

of Tuvalu: 4 cent **6** dollar
of Uganda: 4 cent **8** shilling
of Ukraine: 6 grivna **10** karbovanet
of United Arab Emirates: 3 fil **6** dirham
of Uruguay: 4 peso **9** centesimo, centisimo
of Uzbekistan: 5 ruble
of Vanuatu: 5 franc **6** dollar
of Venezuela: 4 peso, real **5** medio **6** fuerte **7** bolivar, centimo **8** morocota **10** venezolano
of Vietnam: 2 xu **4** dong **7** piaster
of Western Samoa: 4 sene, tala
of Yemen: 4 fils, rial **5** dinar, riyal
of Yugoslavia: 4 para **5** dinar
of Zaire: 5 zaire **6** makuta
of Zambia: 5 ngwee **6** kwacha **of Zimbabwe: 4** cent **6** dollar

---

coincidental 6 chance **9** unplanned **10** accidental, contiguous, synchronal **11** concomitant, synchronous **12** happenstance, simultaneous

cointreau
type: 7 liqueur
variety: 7 curacao **9** triple sec
origin: 6 France
flavor: 8 orange
drink: 8 Applecar
with bourbon: 10 Temptation
with brandy: 7 Sidecar
with cognac: 10 Rolls Royce
with gin: 7 Florida **9** White Lady **13** Sweet Patootie **14** Flying Dutchman
with rum: 8 Acapulco **10** Casa Blanca **11** Beachcomber **12** Blue Hawaiian
with rye: 10 Temptation
with tequila: 9 Margarita
with whiskey: 16 Canadian Cocktail

Colavito, Rocky (Rocco Domenico)
sport: 8 baseball
team: 16 Cleveland Indians

Colbert, Claudette
real name: 22 Claudette Lily Chauchoin
born: 5 Paris **6** France
roles: 8 Tovarich **9** Cleopatra **14** Palm Beach Story **18** It Happened One Night (Oscar)

cold *see box*

cold-blooded 4 evil, hard **5** cruel, harsh, stiff, stony **6** brutal, flinty, formal, frigid, inured, savage, steely **7** callous, demonic, inhuman, passive, satanic, unmoved **8** detached, fiendish, hardened, inhumane, pitiless, reserved, ruthless, uncaring **9** barbarous, heartless, impassive, merciless, unfeeling, unpitying, unstirred **10** deliberate, diabolical, disdainful, impervious, implacable, unfriendly, unmerciful, villainous **11** calculating, hardhearted, indifferent, insensitive, passionless, unconcerned, unemotional, unexcitable **12** bloodthirsty, contemptuous, uninterested, unresponsive **13** disinterested, unimpassioned, unimpressible, unsympathetic **16** unimpressionable

cold-hearted 5 cruel **9** heartless, unfeeling **11** hard-hearted **13** unsympathetic

cold 3 icy, old **4** cool, dead, flat, hard **5** aloof, brisk, chill, crisp, cruel, faded, faint, gelid, harsh, nippy, polar, sharp, stale, stiff, stony **6** arctic, biting, bitter, chilly, cooled, frigid, frosty, frozen, inured, numbed, remote, severe, snappy, steely, wintry **7** callous, chilled, cutting, distant, frosted, glacial, haughty, nipping, passive, unmoved **8** chilling, coolness, detached, freezing, hardened, piercing, reserved, reticent, stinging, uncaring, unheated, unloving, unwarmed **9** apathetic, heartless, impassive, insensate, unfeeling, unstirred **10** disdainful, forbidding, impervious, insensible, phlegmatic, unfriendly **11** frozen stiff, indifferent, passionless, penetrating, unconcerned, unconscious, unemotional, unexcitable **12** antipathetic, bone-chilling, inaccessible, supercilious, uninterested, unresponsive **13** uninteresting, unsympathetic **14** marrow-chilling, unapproachable **15** teeth-chattering, uncommunicative, undemonstrative **16** chilled to the bone, unimpressionable **18** chilled to the marrow

coldness 5 chill 7 iciness
9 aloofness 10 chilliness, frostiness 12 indifference 13 unfeelingness 14 unfriendliness
15 hardheartedness

Cole, Thomas
 born: 7 England 13 Bolton-le-
 Moors
 artwork: 8 The Ox-Bow
 15 The Voyage of Life 17 The
 Course of Empire

coleoptera
 class: 8 hexopoda
 phylum: 10 arthropoda
 group: 6 beetle, weevil

Coleridge, Samuel
 author of: 9 Kubla Khan
 10 Christabel 14 Dejection An
 Ode, Lyrical Ballads (with
 Wordsworth) 19 Biographia
 Literaria 26 The Rime of the
 Ancient Mariner

Colette (Sidonie)
 author of: 4 Gigi, Sido 5 Cheri
 8 Claudine 11 La Vagabonde
 14 The Evening Star

coliseum 4 bowl 5 arena 6 circus 7 stadium, theater 10 hippodrome 12 amphitheater
14 exhibition hall

collaborate 4 join 5 unite 6 assist, team up 7 collude 9 cooperate 10 join forces 12 work
together 14 work side by side

collaborationist 6 puppet
7 traitor 8 quisling

collaborator 4 ally 6 puppet
7 traitor 8 co-worker, quisling,
teammate 9 associate, colleague, co-partner
11 confederate

collapse 4 coma, fail, fall, flop,
fold 5 faint, swoon 6 attack,
buckle, cave-in, fizzle 7 break
up, crack-up, crumple, failure,
give way, seizure 8 be in vain,
buckling, downfall, flounder,
keel over, take sick 9 become
ill, break down 10 be stricken,
break apart, run aground
11 fall through 12 disintegrate,
falling apart, fall helpless, fall
to pieces 13 come to nothing,
sudden illness 14 disintegration
17 become unconscious

collapsed 4 limp 7 caved in,
compact 8 deflated, fallen in,
folded up 13 disintegrated

**Collapse of the Third Re-
public, The**
 author: 14 William L Shirer

collapsible 7 folding 8 foldable
10 deflatable

collar 3 nab 4 eton, grab
5 catch, fichu, pinch, seize
6 arrest, bertha 7 capture 9 apprehend, neckpiece 12 take
prisoner 15 take into custody

collate 5 order 6 bestow, verify
7 compare 8 assemble, organize
9 integrate 11 put together

collateral 4 bond 5 extra
6 pledge, surety 7 warrant
8 parallel, security, warranty
9 accessory, ancillary, auxiliary,
guarantee, insurance,
secondary 10 additional,
incidental, supporting, supportive 11 endorsement, subordinate 12 contributory
13 supplementary

collation 3 tea 4 meal 5 lunch
6 brunch, repast, sermon 7 address, reading 8 hotchpot, luncheon, treatise 10 comparison
11 description

colleague 4 mate 6 fellow
7 partner 8 confrere, co-
worker, teammate 9 associate,
co-partner 11 confederate
12 collaborator, fellow worker

collect 3 get 4 calm, meet
5 amass, raise, rally 6 gather,
heap up, muster, obtain, pick
up, pile up, summon 7 call for,
compile, compose, control,
convene, marshal, prepare, receive, solicit 8 assemble, gather
up, scrape up 9 aggregate, get
hold of 10 accumulate, congregate 11 concentrate, get
together

collectanea 8 analects, treasury 9 anthology, gleanings
10 collection, miscellany, selections 11 miscellanea

collected 4 calm, cool 5 quiet
6 placid, poised, serene, steady
8 composed, peaceful, tranquil
9 confident, unruffled 10 cool-
headed, restrained 11 levelheaded, self-assured,
undisturbed, unemotional, unflappable, unperturbed
12 even-tempered 13 self-
possessed 14 self-controlled

collection 3 mob 4 bevy, body,
gift, heap, mass, pack, pile
5 array, bunch, clump, crowd,
drove, flock, group, hoard,
store, swarm 6 corpus, jumble,
muster, throng 7 cluster, clutter, variety 8 amassing, assembly, oblation, treasury
9 anthology, gathering, offertory, receiving 10 assemblage,
assortment, hodgepodge, mis-

cellany, soliciting 11 aggregation, compilation
12 accumulating, accumulation

collective 5 joint 6 common,
mutual, united 7 unified
8 combined, gathered 9 aggregate, composite 10 cumulative,
integrated 11 accumulated,
cooperative

collector 6 grouper 7 dustman
8 antiquer, compiler, composer,
gatherer, zamindar 9 assembler
10 garbageman 11 anthologist

Collector, The
 author: 10 John Fowles

college 7 academy 8 seminary
9 institute 10 university
11 institution

college-preparatory 4 prep
8 academic 11 liberal-arts
12 nontechnical

collegiate 8 academic 10 scholastic, university 11 educational

collembola
 class: 8 hexopoda
 phylum: 10 arthropoda
 group: 10 springtail

collide 3 hit 4 meet 5 clash,
crash, smash 7 crack up, diverge, run into 8 bump into,
conflict, disagree 9 knock into
10 meet head on 11 beat
against 13 hurtle against, strike
against

Collins, Mr
 character in: 17 Pride and
 Prejudice
 author: 6 Austen

Collins, Wilkie
 author of: 6 No Name 12 The
 Moonstone 15 The Woman
 in White

collision 4 bump 5 clash, crash,
fight, smash 6 battle, combat,
impact 7 smash-up 8 accident,
conflict, skirmish, struggle
9 encounter 10 engagement
11 clash of arms

colloquial 5 homey, plain 6 casual, chatty, common, folksy
8 everyday, familiar, homespun, informal, ordinary,
workaday 9 idiomatic 10 vernacular 14 conversational

colloquy 4 chat, talk 6 caucus,
parley 7 council, palaver, seminar 8 commerce, congress,
converse, dialogue 9 commun-

ion, discourse **10** conference, discussion, rap session **11** interchange, intercourse **12** conversation **13** confabulation

collude 4 plot **7** connive **8** conspire, intrigue **9** cooperate **11** collaborate

collusion 5 fraud **7** treason **8** intrigue **10** complicity, connivance, conspiracy **13** collaboration **15** secret agreement **17** guilty association

Colman, Ronald
born: **7** England **8** Richmond
roles: **9** Beau Geste **10** Arrowsmith **11** A Double Life (Oscar), Lost Horizon **16** A Tale of Two Cities

cologne 5 scent **7** essence, perfume **9** fragrance **11** toilet water

Colomba
author: **14** Prosper Merimee

Colombia *see box*

Colombo
capital of: **8** Sri Lanka

colon 4 coin **6** farmer, vitals **7** pioneer, planter, settler, viscera **9** hemistich, intestine **15** plantation owner, punctuation mark

colonize 5 found, plant **6** gather, settle **7** migrate **8** establish **10** infiltrate

colonnade 3 row **4** stoa **5** porch **6** arcade, piazza **7** portico, terrace **8** cloister **9** peristyle

colony 3 set **4** band, body **5** flock, group, swarm **7** mandate **8** dominion, province **9** community, territory **10** dependency, possession, settlement **12** protectorate **14** satellite state

colophon 6 design, device, emblem **7** insigne **8** insignia **11** inscription

color 3 dye, hue **4** bias, burn, cast, glow, mood, tint, tone, warp, wash **5** bloom, blush, chalk, drift, flame, flush, force, paint, sense, shade, slant, stain, taint, tinge, twist **6** affect, aspect, crayon, effect, import, intent, redden, spirit, stress **7** distort, feeling, meaning, pervert, pigment, redness, skin hue **8** dyestuff, rosiness **9** go crimson, influence, intention, prejudice **10** intimation **11** connotation, implication, insinuation **12** become florid, pigmentation, significance **17** natural complexion

Colorado *see box, p. 198*

Colombia
other name: **6** Darien **10** New Granada
capital/largest city: **6** Bogota
others: **3** Ten **4** Amza, Buga, Cali, Mitu, Muzo, Paez, Sipi, Tado, Tolu, Yari **5** Bello, Chinu, Guapi, Neiva, Pasto, Tulua, Tunja **6** Cucuta, Ibaque, Lorica, Quibdo, Sangil, Tumaco **7** Cartago, Ipiates, Leticia, Palmira, Pereira, Popayan **8** Girardot, Maganque, Medellin, Monteria **9** Cartagena, Manizales **10** Santa Marta **11** Bucaramanga **12** Barranquilla, Buenaventura
school: **5** Andes, Valle **20** Instituto Caro y Cuervo **21** Industrial de Santander
measure: **4** vara **7** azumbre, celemin
monetary unit: **4** peso, real **6** condor, peseta **7** centavo
weight: **3** bag **4** saco **5** libra **7** quintal
island: **4** Baru **5** Naipo **6** Fuerte **7** Gorgona, Malpelo **8** Cusachon **9** San Andres **11** Providencia
lake: **4** Tota
mountain: **5** Abibe, Andes, Baudo, Chita, Cocuy, Huila, Pasto **6** Ayapel, Perija, Purace, Tolima, Tunahi **7** Chamusa, del Ruiz **8** Oriengal **10** Santa Marta **17** Central Cordillera, Eastern Cordillera, Western Cordillera
highest point: **14** Cristobal Colon
river: **3** Uva **4** Bita, Meta, Muco, Sinu, Tomo, Yari **5** Cauca, Cesar, Isana, Mesai, Nechi, Pauto, Sucio **6** Amazon, Arauca, Ariari, Atrato, Atroto, Caguan, Pattia, Yapura **7** Apapois, Caqueta, Guainia, Inirida, Truando, Vichada **8** Casanare, Guaviara, Putumayo **9** Magdalena
sea: **7** Pacific **9** Caribbean
physical feature:
cape: **4** Vela **5** Aguja, Marzo, Punta **7** Augusta **8** Gallinas
falls: **10** Tequendama
gulf: **5** Uraba **6** Cupica, Darien, Tibuga **8** Tortugas
inlet: **6** Tumaco
plains: **6** Ilanos
point: **6** Cruces, Lacruz, Solano **8** Caribana, Gallinas
people: **4** Boro, Cuna, Duit, Hoka, Macu, Muso, Muzo, Paez, Tama, Tapa **5** Carib, Catio, Choco, Cofan, Cogui, Cubeo, Guane, Haida, Mocoa, Paeze, Pijao, Seona, Yagua **6** Arawak, Betoya, Calima, Colima, Ingano, Mirana, Saliva, Tahami, Ticuna, Tucano, Tunebo, Witoto, Yahuna **7** Achagua, Andaqui, Chibcha, Chimila, Churoya, Guahibo, Guajiro, Panches, Puinave, Puitoto, Quechua, Shuswap, Tairona, Telembi **8** Coconuco, Guarauno, mestizos, Motilone, Puinavis, Quimbaya, Sinsigas **9** Cocanucos, Coconucan, mulattoes, Panaquita **10** Bellacoola
leader: **7** Bolivar
language: **7** Spanish
religion: **13** Roman Catholic
place:
museum: **4** Gold **8** Colonial
palace: **11** Inquisition
feature:
dance: **7** bambuco **8** merengue
game: **4** tejo
guitar: **5** tiple
poncho: **5** ruana
shoes: **10** alpargatas
shoulder bag: **7** carriel
tree: **8** arboloco
woven hat: **5** jipas

colored 4 dyed, hued **5** dusky **6** biased, shaded, tinged, tinted **7** blushed, excused, flushed, glossed, labeled, painted, stained **8** affected, labelled, reddened **9** chromatic, distorted, pigmented **10** influenced, prejudiced **12** complex-ioned **13** characterized **14** misrepresented

colorful 3 gay **4** loud **5** showy, vivid **6** bright, florid, unique **7** dynamic, graphic, unusual, vibrant, zestful **8** animated, forceful, spirited, vigorous

Colorado
- **abbreviation:** 2 CO 4 Colo
- **nickname:** 10 Centennial
- **capital/largest city:** 6 Denver
- **others:** 4 Vail 5 Aspen, Delta, Lamar, Ouray 6 Arvada, Aurora, Denver, Golden, Pueblo, Salida 7 Alamosa, Boulder, Durango, Greeley, Manassa, Manitou 8 Gunnison, Loveland, Trinidad 9 Purgatory, Silverton, Telluride 11 Central City 12 Cripple Creek 13 Grand Junction 15 Colorado Springs
- **college:** 5 Regis 6 Denver 7 Boulder 17 US Air Force Academy
- **feature:** 11 Four Corners 15 Garden of the Gods 17 Continental Divide
  - *national monument:* 8 Dinosaur 14 Great Sand Dunes
  - *national park:* 5 Estes 9 Mesa Verde 13 Rocky Mountain
- **tribe:** 3 Ute 7 Arapaho 8 Cheyenne
- **people:** 11 Jack Dempsey 12 Ralph Edwards 14 Scott Carpenter 18 Douglas Fairbanks Sr
- **lake:** 6 Frozen
- **land rank:** 6 eighth
- **mountains:** 5 Longs, Rocky 7 San Juan 9 Pikes Peak 14 Sangre de Cristo
  - *highest point:* 6 Elbert
- **physical feature:**
  - *canyon:* 5 Black
  - *gorge:* 5 Royal
  - *plains:* 5 Great
  - *wind:* 7 Chinook
- **river:** 4 Gila 5 Yampa 6 Platte 7 Dolores 8 Apishapa, Arikaree, Arkansas, Gunnison 9 Rio Grande 10 Purgatoire
- **state admission:** 12 thirty-eighth
- **state bird:** 11 lark bunting
- **state flower:** 22 Rocky Mountain columbine
- **state motto:** 24 Nothing Without Providence
- **state song:** 22 Where the Columbines Grow
- **state tree:** 18 Colorado blue spruce

9 brilliant, full-toned, vivacious 10 compelling, variegated 11 distinctive, interesting, many-colored, picturesque 12 multicolored, particolored

coloring 3 dye 4 tint 5 color, shade, stain 10 coloration, complexion

colorless 3 wan 4 ashy, drab, dull, flat, pale 5 ashen, dingy, faded, pasty, vapid, white 6 anemic, boring, dreary, grayed, pallid, sallow, sickly, undyed 7 ghastly, ghostly, insipid, natural, neutral, prosaic 8 blanched, bleached, lifeless, ordinary, whitened 9 bloodless, washed out 10 cadaverous, lackluster, monotonous, spiritless, unanimated, unexciting, uninspired 11 commonplace 13 uninteresting

Color Purple, The
- **author:** 11 Alice Walker
- **director:** 15 Steven Spielberg
- **cast:** 11 Danny Glover 12 Adolph Caesar, Oprah Winfrey 13 Margaret Avery 14 Whoopi Goldberg

colors 4 flag, jack 6 banner, ensign, pennon 7 pennant 8 standard

colossal 4 huge, vast 5 giant, grand, great 6 mighty 7 extreme, immense, mammoth, massive, titanic 8 enormous, gigantic, imposing 9 exceeding, excessive 10 incredible, inordinate, monumental, prodigious, tremendous 11 extravagant, spectacular 12 awe-inspiring, overwhelming

Colossus of Rhodes
- **statue of:** 6 Apollo

colt 4 foal 5 horse 6 novice 8 equuleus, yearling 9 fledgling, youngster
- **constellation of:** 8 Equuleus

columbium
- **chemical symbol:** 2 Cb

Columbo
- **character:** 9 Lt Columbo
- **cast:** 9 Peter Falk

column 3 row 4 file, line, post 5 pylon, queue, shaft, train 6 parade, pillar, string 7 caravan, phalanx, support, upright 8 pilaster 9 cavalcade, formation 10 procession 11 vertical row 12 vertical list

columnist 6 writer 7 analyst
- **famous:** 7 Heloise 8 Dear Abby, Herb Caen 9 HL Mencken, Jack Smith 10 Ann Landers 11 Miss Manners 15 Abigail van Buren

coma 6 stupor, torpor 8 collapse 15 unconsciousness

Comaetho
- **form:** 9 priestess
- **father:** 9 Pterelaus
- **loved:** 10 Amphitryon
- **lover:** 10 Melanippus
- **killed by:** 10 Amphitryon

Comanche
- **language family:** 10 Shoshonean
- **location:** 5 Texas 6 Kansas, Mexico 8 Oklahoma
- **noted as:** 8 horsemen

comatose 3 lax 4 dull, idle, lazy 5 inert 6 leaden, torpid 7 drugged, languid, passive 8 inactive, indolent, lifeless, listless, slothful, sluggish 9 apathetic, catatonic, lethargic, stuporous 10 cataleptic, insensible, narcotized, phlegmatic, spiritless 11 indifferent, unconcerned, unconscious 12 unresponsive

comb 4 card, tuft 5 curry, dress, groom, plume, scour, style 6 search 7 arrange, explore, panache, ransack, topknot 8 head tuft, hunt over, untangle 9 cast about, cockscomb, currycomb 11 look through 14 rummage through

combat 5 clash, fight 6 action, attack, battle, oppose, resist 7 contest, go to war, wage war 8 conflict, fighting, skirmish, struggle 9 encounter 10 contention, engagement, war against 11 come to blows, grapple with, make warfare, work against 12 do battle with, march against 13 confrontation 14 military action

Combat
- **character:** 4 Caje (Caddy Cadron) 5 Kirby 8 (Pvt) Braddock 9 Doc Walton, (Lt) Gil Hanley 12 (Sgt) Chip Saunders
- **cast:** 9 Jack Hogan, Rick Jason, Vic Morrow 12 Shecky Greene, Steven Rogers 13 Pierre Jalbert

combatant 7 fighter, soldier, warrior 9 man-at-arms 10 serviceman 11 fighting man

combating 8 battling, clashing, fighting, opposing 9 waging war 10 contention, contesting, opposition, struggling **11** doing battle **13** grappling with **17** coming to blows with

combative 6 bantam **8** militant **9** agonistic, bellicose **10** aggressive, pugnacious **11** belligerent, contentious **12** antagonistic

combativeness 9 hostility, pugnacity **10** antagonism **12** belligerence **14** aggressiveness **15** contentiousness

combination 3 mix **5** alloy, blend, union **6** fusion, league, medley, merger, mixing **7** amalgam, joining, mixture, pooling, variety **8** alliance, blending, compound **9** coalition, composite, synthesis **10** assortment, coalescing, federation **11** association, composition, confederacy **12** amalgamation **13** confederation

combine 3 mix **4** fuse, join, pool **5** blend, merge, unify, unite **6** couple, league, mingle **8** compound **9** commingle **10** amalgamate, synthesize **11** consolidate, incorporate

combo 4 band **5** group **11** aggregation, combination

comb out 4 curl **5** dress **7** arrange, unsnarl **8** untangle

combustible 8 burnable **9** flammable, ignitable **10** combustive, incendiary **11** inflammable **13** conflagrative

combustion 6 firing **7** burning, flaming **8** ignition, kindling **12** incineration **13** conflagration

combustive 8 burnable **9** flammable, ignitable **11** combustible, inflammable **13** conflagrative

come 2 be, go **3** bud **4** fall, loom, rise **5** arise, issue, occur, range, reach **6** appear, arrive, be made, drop in, emerge, extend, follow, happen, impend, show up, spread, spring, turn up **7** advance, descend, emanate, stretch **8** approach, draw near, go toward, grow to be **9** be a native, germinate, take place **10** be imminent, move toward **11** be a resident, be in the wind, materialize, originate in, spring forth

come about 5 occur **6** chance, happen **7** turn out **10** come to pass

come afterward 5 ensue **6** derive, follow, result **7** succeed

come apart 6 detach **7** disjoin, unstick **8** separate

come back 5 rally **6** answer, retort, return **7** rebound **8** recovery

Come Back Little Sheba
   director: 10 Daniel Mann
   based on play by: 11 William Inge
   cast: 10 Terry Moore **12** Shirley Booth **13** Burt Lancaster
   Oscar for: 7 actress (Booth)

come clean 4 sing **5** own up **7** confess **14** unbosom oneself **18** make a clean breast of

come close to 7 verge on **8** approach, border on **11** approximate, nearly equal

comedian 3 wag **4** fool, zany **5** clown, comic, cutup, joker **6** jester, madcap **7** buffoon **8** humorist, jokester **9** prankster **10** comedienne, comic actor **14** practical joker

comedown 4 drop **8** lowering **10** anticlimax

come down 4 dive, drop, fall, sink **6** plunge, tumble **7** descend, plummet **8** decrease

come down a peg 5 deign, stoop **6** unbend **7** descend **10** condescend **12** lower oneself **13** humble oneself

comedy 3 fun, wit **5** farce, humor **6** banter, joking, pranks, satire **7** foolery, jesting **8** drollery, raillery, travesty **9** burlesque, cutting up, horseplay, silliness **10** buffoonery, pleasantry, tomfoolery **13** fooling around

Comedy of Errors, The
   author: 18 William Shakespeare
   character: 6 Aegeon, Dromio **7** Adriana, Aemilia, Luciana, Solinus **10** Antipholus

come face to face with 4 meet **8** confront **9** encounter

come first 7 precede, predate **8** antecede, antedate, go before **10** anticipate

come into being 4 dawn, show **5** arise, begin, occur, set in, start **6** appear, be born, crop up, emerge, sprout **8** commence, spring up **9** germinate, originate **11** come to light

come into port 4 dock **5** berth

come into view 4 show **6** appear, come up, emerge, show

up **7** surface **11** come to light **13** become visible

come loose 5 let go **6** detach, loosen **7** slip off **8** break off, separate, unfasten **9** break away **10** come undone, come untied, disconnect **11** come unglued, come unstuck

comely 4 fair, nice **5** bonny **6** pretty, proper, seemly, simple **7** correct, fitting, natural, sightly, winning, winsome **8** becoming, blooming, charming, decorous, engaging, fetching, pleasant, pleasing, suitable, tasteful **9** agreeable, appealing, wholesome **10** attractive, unaffected **11** well-favored

come near 4 loom, near **6** appear **8** approach **9** draw close **10** move toward

come-on 4 bait, hook, lure, trap **5** decoy, snare **6** magnet **9** seduction **10** allurement, attraction, bewitchery, enticement, inducement, seducement, temptation **12** inveiglement

comestibles 5 foods **7** edibles **8** victuals **10** foodstuffs, provisions

Cometes
   lover of: 8 Aegialia

come to a decision 6 decide, settle **7** resolve **8** conclude **9** determine

come to an understanding 5 agree **6** settle **11** come to terms **12** agree to marry **16** reach an agreement

come to a standstill 4 halt, quit, stop **5** abate, cease **7** die away **8** quit cold

come to blows 5 fight **7** contest **8** do battle **9** square off **12** start to fight

come together 4 meet **5** flock, group, rally **6** gather **7** collect, convene **8** assemble **10** congregate **11** get together

come to light 4 dawn **5** arise **6** appear, crop up, emerge, evolve, show up, turn up, unfold **7** develop, surface, turn out

come to nothing 4 fail, flop, fold **6** fizzle **8** be in vain, collapse **9** break down **11** fall through **12** come to naught **17** fail to materialize

come to pass 5 ensue, occur **6** arrive, befall, follow, happen **9** take place

come to terms 5 agree, yield **6** give up, settle **7** suc-

cumb 8 contract, cry quits
9 make a deal, negotiate, surrender 10 capitulate, compromise 11 come to grips, meet
halfway, sue for peace 13 resign oneself 14 strike a bargain 15 lay down one's arms
16 reach an agreement 17 acknowledge defeat, hoist the
white flag 18 split the
difference

come unglued 6 detach,
loosen 8 separate 9 fall apart
11 come unstuck

come unstuck 4 lift 6 detach,
loosen 8 break off, unfasten
9 break away, come apart,
come loose, fall apart 11 come
unglued

come up 4 rise 5 arise
7 quicken, sharpen 8 heighten,
increase 9 intensify 10 accelerate, strengthen 12 be re-
ferred to

come upon 4 find, meet
7 learn of, run into 8 discover 9 encounter

comfit 5 candy, sweet 9 sweetmeat 10 confection, sugar
candy 13 confectionery

comfort 4 calm, ease, help
5 cheer, peace, quiet 6 luxury,
relief, solace, soothe, succor,
warmth 7 cheer up, compose,
console, hearten 8 coziness,
opulence, pleasure, reassure,
serenity, snugness 9 bolster
up, comforter, composure,
encourage, well-being
10 cheering up, relaxation
11 consolation, contentment,
reassurance 12 satisfaction
13 encouragement, gratification 14 quiet one's fears
16 source of serenity
17 lighten one's burden
18 bolster one's spirits

Comfort, Alex
author of: 11 The Joy of
Sex 12 More Joy of Sex

comfortable 4 cozy, easy 6 at
ease, at home, serene 7 relaxed 8 adequate, pleasant,
suitable 9 agreeable, congenial,
contented 10 giving ease, gratifying, untroubled 11 pleasurable, undisturbed
12 satisfactory 16 free from
distress

comforter 4 balm, puff 5 quilt,
scarf 6 afghan, solace 7 anodyne, blanket, comfort,
soother 8 coverlet 10 palliative

comic, comical 4 rich 5 droll,
funny, merry, silly, witty
6 absurd, jocose, jovial
7 amusing, jocular, risible
8 farcical, humorous, mirthful
9 facetious, laughable, ludi-

crous, whimsical 10 ridiculous 11 nonsensical 12 nimble-
witted

coming 4 next 6 advent, future, in view, to come 7 arrival, nearing 8 approach,
arriving, imminent, on the
way 9 advancing, emergence,
imminence, impending, in the
wind, proximity 10 appearance, occurrence, subsequent
11 approaching, forthcoming,
prospective 12 on the horizon 13 materializing

Coming Home
director: 8 Hal Ashby
cast: 9 Bruce Dern, Jane
Fonda, Jon Voight 15 Rob-
ert Carradine
Oscar for: 5 actor (Voight)
7 actress (Fonda)
10 screenplay

Coming into the Country
author: 10 John McPhee

Coming of Age, The
author: 16 Simone de
Beauvoir

Coming of Age in Samoa
author: 12 Margaret Mead

Coming Race, The
author: 18 Edward Bulwer-
Lytton

command 3 bid, get 4 boss,
call, draw, fiat, grip, head,
hold, lead, rule 5 edict, evoke,
grasp, guide, order, power
6 adjure, behest, charge, compel, decree, demand, direct,
elicit, enjoin, govern, incite,
induce, kindle, manage, ordain, prompt, summon 7 call
for, conduct, control, deserve,
extract, inspire, mastery, provoke, receive, require, summons 8 call upon, instruct,
motivate 9 authority, call
forth, direction, directive, governing, knowledge, ordinance,
supervise, ultimatum 10 administer, be master of, domination, injunction, leadership,
management 11 familiarity,
instruction, superintend, supervision 12 have charge of
13 comprehension, understanding 14 administration 17 have
authority over

commandant 7 captain 9 commander 12 chief officer

commandeer 4 take 5 seize,
usurp 8 shanghai 11 appropriate, expropriate

commander 4 boss, head
5 chief, ruler 6 leader 7 manager 8 director 9 conductor

commanding 4 head 5 chief,
grand, lofty 6 ruling, senior,
strong 7 dynamic, leading,

ranking, stately 8 forceful,
gripping, imposing, powerful,
striking, towering 9 arresting,
directing, governing, important, prominent 10 compelling,
dominating, impressive
11 controlling, significant
13 authoritative, distinguished,
overshadowing

commandment
Hebrew: 7 mitsvah, mitzvah

comme il faut 6 proper 7 fitting 12 as it should be

commemorate 4 hail, mark
5 extol, honor 6 hallow, revere, salute 7 acclaim, glorify,
observe 8 venerate 9 celebrate,
solemnize 11 acknowledge,
memorialize, pay homage to
12 pay tribute to

commence 5 begin, start 8 get
going, initiate 10 get started,
inaugurate, originated

commencement 4 dawn
5 birth, onset, start 6 outset
7 genesis, morning 9 beginning, first step, inception
10 graduation, initiation
11 origination 12 inauguration 13 graduation day
20 graduation ceremonies

commend 2 OK 4 back, give,
laud 5 extol 6 commit, confer,
convey, praise 7 acclaim, approve, consign, endorse, entrust, stand by, support
8 delegate, give over, hand
over, pass over, relegate,
transfer 13 speak highly of

commendable 6 worthy
7 notable 8 laudable 9 admirable, deserving, estimable, exemplary, honorable
10 creditable 11 meritorious
12 praiseworthy

commendation 5 honor
6 praise 7 support 8 approval
10 acceptance 11 acclamation,
approbation

commendatory 8 admiring,
praising 9 laudatory, praiseful
10 plauditory 13 complimentary 14 congratulatory

**commensurate, commensur-
able** 4 even, meet 5 equal
6 square 7 fitting 8 balanced,
in accord, parallel, relative,
suitable 10 comparable, compatible, consistent, equivalent
11 appropriate, in agreement
13 corresponding, proportionate 14 on a proper scale

comment 4 note, word 6 remark 7 clarify, discuss, explain, expound 8 expand on
9 assertion, criticism, elucidate,
shed light, statement, talk
about, touch upon, utterance

10 annotation, expression, reflection 11 elucidation, explanation, explication, observation 13 clarification 15 exemplification

commentary 6 review 8 critique, scholium, treatise 9 criticism 10 exposition 11 explanation, explication 12 dissertation 14 interpretation 16 explanatory essay

commentator 6 critic, writer 7 speaker 8 panelist, reporter, reviewer 9 columnist, explainer 10 newscaster 11 interpreter, news analyst

comment upon 7 clarify, clear up, explain 8 spell out 9 delineate, elucidate, explicate, interpret, make plain 10 illuminate, illustrate 14 throw light upon

commerce 5 trade 6 barter 7 trading, traffic 8 business, exchange, industry 12 mercantilism 16 buying and selling
  god of: 6 Hermes 7 Mercury

commercial 2 ad 5 sales, trade 8 business 10 mercantile, sales pitch 12 profit-making 13 advertisement 16 buying-and-selling

commingle 3 mix 4 fuse 5 blend, merge, unify 7 combine 10 amalgamate

commiserate 7 feel for 8 show pity 10 grieve with, lament with 13 express sorrow 14 sympathize with 15 share one's sorrow 17 have compassion for

commiseration 4 pity 8 sympathy 10 compassion, tenderness 13 fellow feeling

commission *see box*

commissioner 5 envoy, trier 7 officer, pristaw 8 delegate, official 9 authority, commissar

commissioning 10 assignment, delegation 11 appointment, designation, entrustment 13 authorization

commit 2 do 3 act, put 4 bind, pull 5 enact, place 6 assign, decide, effect, engage, intern, pursue 7 confine, consign, deliver, deposit, entrust, execute, perform, pull off, resolve 8 carry out, give over, obligate, practice, transact, transfer 9 determine 10 make liable, perpetrate 13 participate in 16 institutionalize

commitment 3 vow 4 bond, word 5 stand 6 pledge 7 promise 8 decision, delivery,

---

commission 3 act, bid, cut, fee 4 duty, hire, name, rank, role, task 5 board, doing, order, piece, power, proxy, trust 6 agency, assign, charge, direct, employ, engage, office 7 appoint, certify, charter, conduct, council, empower, license, mandate, mission, portion, rake-off, stipend, warrant 8 capacity, contract, delegate, dividend, document, exercise, function, position 9 acting out, allotment, allowance, authority, authorize, committal, committee 10 assignment, commitment, committing, delegation, deputation, entrusting, percentage, performing 11 appointment, carrying out, certificate, performance, transacting 12 officer's rank, perpetration 13 authorization, written orders 14 give the go-ahead 15 representatives 16 piece of the action 17 appointment papers, grant officer's rank

---

transfer, warranty 9 assurance, detention, guarantee, liability, restraint 10 assignment, giving over, internment, obligation, resolution 11 confinement, consignment, dispatching 12 imprisonment 13 determination, incarceration 14 responsibility 18 institutionalizing

commit oneself 3 act 7 resolve 8 dedicate, obligate 9 determine

---

committed 6 active, liable 8 confined, detained, interned 9 concerned, delivered, entrusted, obligated 10 interested, responsive 11 responsible 17 institutionalized

committee 4 body, jury 5 bench, board, group, junta, table 6 bureau, soviet 7 cabinet, council 9 gathering, syndicate 10 assemblage 12 organization

commode 6 bureau 7 cabinet, dresser 9 washstand 14 chest of drawers

commodious 5 ample, large, roomy 8 spacious 9 capacious, uncramped 11 unconfining

commodity 4 ware 5 asset, goods, stock 6 staple 7 chattel, holding, product 8 property 9 advantage, belonging 10 possession 11 convenience, merchandise 14 article of trade 17 article of commerce

common *see box*

commoners 5 plebs 6 masses 8 plebians

common law
  Latin: 13 lex non scripta

commonly 5 often 6 widely 7 as a rule, usually 8 normally, of course 9 generally, in general, most often, popularly, regularly, routinely 10 by and large, familiarly, frequently, habitually, informally, ordinarily, repeatedly 11 customarily 13 traditionally 14 by force of habit, conventionally, for the most part 15 in most instances 17 generally speaking

common people 5 demos, plebs 6 masses 8 populace

---

common 3 bad, low 4 base, lewd, mean, rude, vile 5 brash, cheap, crass, crude, gross, joint, lowly, minor, plain, stock 6 brazen, brutal, coarse, lesser, normal, old-hat, public, ribald, shared, simple, smutty, tawdry, vulgar 7 average, boorish, callous, general, ignoble, ill-bred, loutish, low-bred, obscene, obscure, popular, prosaic, regular, routine, settled, uncouth, unknown, worn-out 8 communal, everyday, familiar, frequent, homespun, impolite, informal, mediocre, middling, nameless, ordinary, plebeian, shameful, standard, workaday, worn thin 9 bourgeois, customary, deficient, household, low-minded, moth-eaten, obnoxious, offensive, pervasive, shameless, tasteless, unexalted, universal, unnoticed, unrefined, well-known 10 collective, colloquial, despicable, dime-a-dozen, inglorious, threadbare, unblushing, uncultured, unpolished, widespread 11 disgraceful, established, ill-mannered, insensitive, middle-class, oft-repeated, subordinate, traditional, unimportant, widely known, without rank 12 contemptible, conventional, disagreeable 13 garden-variety, insignificant 15 undistinguished

9 hoi polloi, plebeians
11 bourgeoisie

commonplace 3 old **4** dull
5 adage, banal, stale, trite,
usual **6** cliche, old-hat, truism
7 bromide, general, humdrum,
regular, routine, worn-out
8 banality, everyday, familiar,
ordinary, standard, worn thin
9 customary, hackneyed,
moth-eaten, platitude **10** pedestrian, threadbare, un-
original, widespread
11 oft-repeated, stereotyped,
traditional **12** received idea,
run-of-the-mill **13** unimaginative, uninteresting

commonplace book 9 anthology, gleanings, scrapbook

Common Sense
   author: **11** Thomas Paine

common-sense 5 sound
8 everyday, sensible **9** mother
wit, practical, pragmatic, realistic **10** no-nonsense **11** down-
to-earth, levelheaded,
serviceable, utilitarian
12 matter-of-fact

commonwealth 5 state **6** nation **8** republic
   Latin: **10** res publica

commotion 3 ado **4** fuss, stir,
to-do **5** furor **6** bustle, racket,
ruckus, tumult, uproar **7** clatter, turmoil **9** agitation **10** excitement, hullabaloo
11 disturbance **12** perturbation

communal 5 joint **6** common,
mutual, public, shared **9** community **10** collective

commune 3 gab, rap, yak
4 chat, chin, talk **5** visit
6 babble, confer, gossip, parley, powwow **7** chatter, palaver, prattle **8** converse,
schmooze **9** discourse **10** chew
the fat, chew the rag **11** communicate, confabulate
14 shoot the breeze

communicable 8 catching
10 contagious, infectious
12 transferable **13** transmissible, transmittable

communicate 3 say **4** give,
show, talk, tell **5** state, write
6 advise, convey, impart, notify, pass on, relate, reveal
7 declare, divulge, exhibit,
mention, publish, signify
8 announce, converse, disclose,
inform of, proclaim, transmit
9 apprise of, bring word,
broadcast, make known, publicize **10** correspond

communication 4 news, note,
wire **5** cable **6** letter, missal,
report **7** liaison, message, missive, notices, rapport, writing
8 bulletin, dispatch, document,
speaking, telegram **9** broadcast,
cablegram, directive, statement **10** communique **11** declaration, information
12 conversation, intelligence,
proclamation, radio message
13 telephone call
14 correspondence

communicative 4 open
5 frank **6** candid, chatty **7** voluble **8** friendly, outgoing, sociable **9** revealing, talkative
10 expressive, forthright, free-
spoken, loquacious, revelatory,
unreserved **11** informative

communion, Communion
6 accord **7** concord, harmony,
rapport, sharing **8** affinity,
sympathy **9** agreement **12** the
Eucharist **13** communication,
contemplation

communique 4 note, wire
5 aviso, cable, flash **6** report,
letter, notice **7** epistle, message, missive, release, telegram **8** bulletin, dispatch
9 directive, statement
10 memorandum **12** announcement, intelligence, notification **13** communication

Communist 3 red **6** soviet
7 comrade, marxist **8** Leninist
9 bolshevik, socialist **10** bol-
shevist **12** totalitarian

Communist Manifesto
   author: **8** Karl Marx
   15 Friedrich Engels

community 4 area, folk, town
5 arena, field, group, range,
realm, scope **6** locale, people,
public, sphere, suburb **7** quarter, society **8** affinity, district,
environs, likeness, populace,
province, sameness, vicinity
9 agreement, citizenry **10** population, similarity **11** environment, social group
12 commonwealth, neighborhood, surroundings

commute 4 ride, trip **5** alter
6 adjust, change, redeem,
soften, switch, travel **7** convert, journey, replace, reverse
8 diminish, exchange, mitigate **9** alleviate, supersede,
transform, transmute, trans-
pose **10** substitute **11** transfigure **12** metamorphose,
transmogrify

comodo
   music: **9** leisurely

Comoros *see box*

compact 4 bond, cram, deal,
pack, pact, snug, tidy **5** close,
dense, press, small, stuff **6** little, treaty **7** bargain, crammed,
pressed, squeeze, stuffed **8** alliance, compress, contract, cove-

Comoros
   other name: **26** lost
      pearls of the Indian
      Ocean
   capital/largest city:
      6 Moroni
   others: **6** Bambao
      7 Fomboni **8** Dzaoudzi
      9 Mutsamudu
      11 Mitsamiouli
   monetary unit: **5** franc
      7 centime
   island: **6** Moheli **7** An-
      jouan, Mayotte
      12 Grande Comoro
   highest point: **7** Kartala
      8 Karthala
   sea: **6** Indian
   physical feature:
      channel:
         10 Mozambique
   people: **4** Arab **5** Bantu,
      Malay **7** African
      8 Malagasy
   language: **6** Arabic,
      French **7** Swahili
      8 Malagasy
   religion: **5** Islam **13** Ro-
      man Catholic

nant **9** agreement, clustered,
concordat **10** compressed
11 arrangement, pack closely
12 concentrated **13** tightly
packed, understanding

compactness 7 density
8 snugness **9** smallness **10** lit-
tleness **11** compression
13 concentration

companion 3 pal **4** chum,
mate **5** buddy, crony **6** escort,
friend, helper **7** comrade **9** assistant, associate, attendant

companionable 6 social
7 amiable, cordial **8** friendly,
sociable **9** agreeable, congenial, convivial

companionate 4 warm **6** genial **7** cordial **8** amicable,
friendly, platonic, suitable
9 accordant, agreeable, consonant, easygoing, nonsexual,
spiritual, unfleshly **10** compatible, concordant, harmonious
11 nonphysical, passionless,
warm-hearted **12** affectionate
13 companionable

companionship 4 pals
5 chums **7** buddies, company,
friends **8** comrades **10** associates, companions, fellowship,
friendship **11** camaraderie,
comradeship, familiarity, sociability **17** close acquaintance,
friendly relations

company 3 mob **4** band, firm,

gang 5 bunch, group, guest, party 6 guests, outfit, people, throng 7 callers, concern, friends, society, visitor 8 assembly, comrades, presence, visitors 9 gathering, multitude, syndicate 10 assemblage, companions, fellowship, friendship 11 camaraderie, comradeship, corporation, sociability 12 conglomerate, congregation 13 companionship, establishment 15 business concern

comparable 4 like, up to 5 close, equal 6 akin to 7 similar 8 as good as, parallel 9 a match for, analogous 10 equivalent, on a par with, tantamount 11 approaching, approximate 12 commensurate, in a class with 13 commensurable

comparative 4 near 8 relative 11 approximate

compare 5 equal, liken, match 6 be up to, equate, relate 7 vie with 8 approach, contrast 9 correlate 11 compete with 12 be on a par with 13 hold a candle to 14 be in a class with 20 draw a parallel between

compare notes 6 confer 7 consult 8 talk over 13 exchange views

comparison 7 analogy, kinship 8 contrast, equality, likeness, parallel, relation 10 connection, similarity 11 correlation, resemblance 13 comparability

compartment 3 box, pew 4 brig, cell, crib, hold, hole, nook, room 5 berth, booth, cabin, crypt, niche, stall, vault 6 alcove, bunker, closet 7 chamber, cubicle, section 8 anteroom, roomette 9 cubbyhole 10 pigeonhole 11 antechamber

compass 5 bound, range, reach, scope, sweep 6 domain, extent 8 boundary, province 13 circumference

Compass, Mariner's Compass
constellation of: 5 Pyxis

Compasses, Pair
constellation of: 8 Circinus

compassion 4 pity 5 heart 7 empathy, feeling 8 humanity, sympathy 10 tenderness 13 commiseration, fellow feeling 17 tender-heartedness
Latin: 12 misericordia

compassionate 4 kind 6 humane 7 pitying 8 merciful

10 benevolent, charitable 11 kindhearted, sympathetic 13 tender-hearted

compatibility 6 accord 7 concord, harmony, rapport 8 affinity 9 agreement, unanimity 12 congeniality 14 likemindedness

compatible 3 apt, fit 6 seemly 7 fitting 8 in accord, suitable 9 congenial, in harmony, in keeping 10 like-minded 11 appropriate

compel 4 make 5 drive, force 6 oblige 7 require 11 necessitate

compelled 4 must 5 bound, urged 6 driven, forced 7 coerced, obliged, pressed 8 commanded, dragooned, enforced, impelled, obsessed, pressured, required 11 constrained, overpowered

compelling 7 driving, dynamic 8 forceful 10 commanding 12 overwhelming

compel obedience to
5 force 6 coerce 7 enforce 8 carry out, insist on 10 administer

compendium 4 list 5 brief 6 apercu, digest, precis, survey 7 abstract, capsule, catalog, epitome, summary 8 syllabus, synopsis 9 catalogue 11 abridgement, compilation 12 condensation

compensate 3 pay 5 cover, repay 6 make up, offset, redeem, square 7 balance, pay back, redress 9 indemnify, reimburse 10 make amends, recompense, remunerate 14 counterbalance 15 make restitution

compensation 3 fee, pay 4 gain 5 wages 6 income, profit, return, reward, salary 7 payment, redress 8 benefits, earnings, gratuity 9 indemnity, repayment 10 recompense, settlement 11 restitution 12 remuneration, satisfaction 13 consideration, reimbursement

compete 3 vie 5 fight 6 battle, combat, oppose 7 contend, contest 8 be rivals 9 lock horns, match wits

competence 5 skill 7 ability, know-how, mastery 8 ableness 9 expertise 10 capability, competency, expertness 11 proficiency

competent 3 fit 6 expert, versed 7 skilled, trained 8 skillful 9 efficient, practiced, qualified 10 dependable, profi-

cient 11 experienced, responsible, trustworthy

competition 4 game 5 event, match, rival 7 contest, rivalry, tourney 8 conflict, opponent, struggle 9 contender 10 contention, opposition, tournament

competitive 8 fighting, opposing, striving 9 combative 10 aggressive, contending

competitor 5 rival 7 fighter 8 opponent 9 adversary, contender 10 contestant, opposition

compilation 4 body 5 group 9 collating, garnering, gathering, mustering 10 assemblage, assembling, assortment, collecting, collection, compendium, marshaling 11 aggregating, aggregation, marshalling 12 accumulating, accumulation

compile 5 amass 6 garner, gather, heap up, muster 7 collate, collect, marshal 8 assemble 10 accumulate

complacent 4 smug 6 at ease 7 content 9 contented 10 self-secure, unbothered, untroubled 13 self-satisfied

complain 3 nag 4 beef, carp, kick, moan, pick 5 cavil, gripe, whine 6 grouch, grouse, squawk 7 grumble 9 bellyache, criticize, find fault 15 state a grievance

complaint 4 beef, kick 5 gripe 6 malady, squawk, tirade 7 ailment, illness, protest 8 debility, disorder, sickness 9 criticism, grievance, infirmity, objection 10 impairment 12 faultfinding 15 dissatisfaction

complaisance 7 pliancy 8 docility 10 affability, amiability, compliance 12 acquiescence

complaisant 4 warm 7 affable, amiable, cordial 8 friendly, gracious, obliging, pleasant, pleasing 9 agreeable, compliant, congenial, easygoing 10 solicitous 11 good-humored, good-natured

Compleat Angler, The
author: 11 Izaak Walton

complement 3 cap 5 crown, match, total, whole 7 balance, perfect 8 ensemble, entirety, parallel, round out 9 aggregate, companion 10 completion, consummate, full amount, full number, supplement 11 counterpart, rounding-out 12 consummation 14 required number

complementary 7 matched
8 integral, opposite 9 companion 10 additional, compatible,
completing 11 correlative
12 interrelated, supplemental
13 correspondent,
corresponding

complete 3 cap, end 4 full
5 crown, total, utter, whole
6 entire, finish, intact, settle,
wrap up 7 achieve, execute,
fulfill, perfect, perform, plenary, settled 8 absolute,
achieved, carry out, conclude,
executed, round out, thorough, unbroken 9 discharge,
make whole, performed, polish off, terminate, undivided
10 accomplish, carried out,
complement, conclusive, consummate, unabridged 11 consummated 12 accomplished

completed 4 done 5 ended,
whole 6 closed, entire, filled
7 matured, through
8 achieved, finished, realized
9 concluded, executed, fulfilled, perfected 10 terminated,
wrapped up 11 consummated
12 accomplished

completeness 8 fullness, richness 9 wholeness 10 perfection 12 thoroughness

completion 3 end 5 close
6 ending, finish, windup
7 closing 9 finishing 10 concluding, conclusion, expiration 11 fulfillment,
terminating, termination
12 consummation

complex 4 maze 5 mixed
6 knotty, system 7 network,
tangled 8 compound, involved,
manifold, multiple, puzzling
9 aggregate, composite, difficult, enigmatic, fixed idea, intricate, obsession
10 perplexing, variegated
11 bewildering, complicated
12 conglomerate, labyrinthian,
labyrinthine, multifarious
13 preoccupation

complexion 3 hue 4 look,
tone 5 color, guise, image,
slant 6 aspect 7 outlook 8 coloring 9 character 10 appearance, coloration, impression
11 countenance, skin texture
12 pigmentation, skin coloring

complexity 6 puzzle 9 intricacy, obscurity 10 bafflement,
involution, perplexity
11 crabbedness, elaboration,
involvement 12 complication,
entanglement 15 inextricability 17 unintelligibility
19 incomprehensibility

compliance 6 assent 7 pliancy
8 docility, giving in, meekness,
yielding 9 deference, obedi-

ence, passivity 10 conforming,
conformity, submission 12 acquiescence, complaisance
13 nonresistance

compliant 8 flexible, yielding
9 agreeable 10 submissive

complicate 4 knot 5 ravel,
snarl 6 muddle, tangle 7 confuse, involve 8 confound, entangle 11 make complex
13 make difficult, make
intricate

complicated 7 complex 8 involved 9 elaborate, intricate

complication 4 snag 5 hitch
7 dilemma, problem 8 drawback, handicap, obstacle,
quandary 9 hindrance 10 difficulty, impediment, perplexity
11 aggravation, obstruction,
predicament 12 disadvantage
14 stumbling block

complicity 8 abetment, intrigue, plotting, schemery,
scheming 9 collusion, finagling 10 connivance, conspiracy 11 confederacy,
contrivance, implication, involvement 12 entanglement

compliment 5 honor, kudos
6 homage, praise 7 tribute
8 flattery 9 adulation, laudation 11 acclamation 12 commendation 14 congratulation

complimentary 4 free 6 gratis
8 admiring, praising 9 adulatory, extolling, laudatory, panegyric, praiseful 10 flattering,
gratuitous, plauditory 12 appreciative, commendatory
13 without charge
14 congratulatory

compliments 4 best, laud
5 exalt, extol, toast 6 homage,
praise, salute 7 applaud, commend, regards 8 respects
9 greetings 10 best wishes,
good wishes 11 salutations
13 felicitations
15 congratulations

comply 3 bow 4 bend, meet,
mind, obey 5 defer, yield
6 accede, adhere, follow, give
in, submit 7 abide by, conform, consent, fulfill, observe,
satisfy 9 acquiesce, surrender

component 4 item, part
5 piece 6 detail, member, module 7 element, modular, segment 8 material 9 composing,
elemental, essential, intrinsic
10 elementary, ingredient, particular 11 constituent, fundamental 13 component part

component part 4 item, part
5 piece 6 detail, member
7 element 10 ingredient, par-

ticular 11 constituent,
fundamental

comport 3 act 4 bear 5 carry
6 acquit, behave, deport
7 conduct

comportment 7 bearing, conduct 8 attitude, behavior, carriage, demeanor, presence
9 acquittal 10 appearance,
deportment

comport oneself 3 act 6 behave 13 acquit oneself
14 conduct oneself

compose 4 calm, form, lull,
make 5 frame, quell, quiet, relax, shape, write 6 create, devise, make up, pacify, settle,
soothe 7 collect, fashion, placate 8 be part of, belong to,
comprise, conceive, modulate
9 formulate 10 constitute

composed 4 calm, cool
5 quiet 6 at ease, placid,
poised, sedate, serene, steady
8 peaceful, tranquil 9 collected,
quiescent, unexcited, unruffled 10 controlled, coolheaded, restrained, unagitated,
untroubled 11 level-headed,
undisturbed, unemotional, unflappable, unperturbed
12 even-tempered 13 dispassionate, imperturbable
15 undemonstrative

composer 4 bard, poet 6 author, writer 7 creator 8 musician, producer 10 compositor,
typesetter

composite 6 mosaic 7 blended
8 combined, compound
10 compounded

composition 4 form, opus,
work 5 essay, etude, piece
6 design, layout, make-up,
making 7 forming, framing,
product, shaping 8 creating,
creation, devising, exercise
9 framework, structure
10 concoction, fashioning, organizing, production 11 arrangement, combination,
compilation, formulation,
preparation 12 constitution,
organization 13 configuration

compos mentis 4 sane
13 mentally sound

composure 4 calm, cool, ease
5 poise 6 aplomb 7 control,
dignity 8 calmness, coolness,
patience, serenity 9 sangfroid 10 equanimity
11 self-control 13 selfassurance, self-restraint
14 cool-headedness, selfpossession, unexcitability,
unflappability 15 levelheadedness 16 even-temperedness,
imperturbability

compound 3 mix 4 fuse, make 5 add to, alloy, blend, boost, mixed, union, unite 6 devise, fusion, mingle 7 amalgam, amplify, augment, blended, combine, complex, concoct, enlarge, magnify, mixture, prepare 8 combined, heighten, increase 9 composite, fabricate, formulate, reinforce 10 synthesize 11 combination, complicated, composition, incorporate, put together 12 conglomerate 14 conglomeration

comprehend 3 dig, get 5 catch, grasp, savvy 6 absorb, digest, fathom 7 make out 8 conceive, perceive 9 penetrate 10 appreciate, assimilate, understand

comprehensible 5 clear, plain 7 evident 8 apparent 11 unambiguous 12 intelligible

comprehension 5 grasp 7 insight 9 awareness 10 conception, perception 11 realization 12 acquaintance, appreciation, apprehension 13 consciousness, understanding

comprehensive 4 full 5 broad 7 copious, general, overall 8 complete, sweeping, thorough 9 expansive, extensive, universal 10 exhaustive, widespread 11 compendious 12 all-embracing, all-inclusive

compress 4 cram, pack 5 press 6 reduce, shrink 7 abridge, bandage, compact, curtail, plaster, shorten, squeeze 8 condense, dressing 10 abbreviate

compressed 5 dense 6 jammed, packed 7 crowded 8 squashed, squeezed 9 compacted 12 concentrated

compressed form 5 digest 7 summary 8 cake form, synopsis 10 shortening 11 abridgement, contraction, curtailment 12 abbreviation, condensation

compression 9 narrowing, squeezing, stricture, tightness 10 compaction, constraint 12 constriction

compressor 4 pump 7 presser, reducer 8 squeezer 9 compactor, condenser

comprise 4 form 6 make up 7 compose, contain, include 8 be made of 9 consist of 10 constitute 12 be composed of

compromise 4 risk 5 agree, truce 6 settle 7 balance, compact, imperil 8 endanger, undercut 9 agreement, discredit, embarrass, implicate, make a deal, prejudice 10 adjustment, jeopardize, settlement 11 arrangement, come to terms, happy medium, make suspect, meet halfway 12 conciliation 13 accommodation, rapprochement 14 make vulnerable, strike a bargain 16 mutual concession 18 split the difference 21 come to an understanding
German: 9 Ausgleich

compromising 7 risking 8 settling 9 adjusting 10 bargaining 11 give and take, making a deal 12 embarrassing, jeopardizing 13 accommodating, coming to terms 14 meeting halfway

Compsognathus
type: 8 dinosaur, theropod
characteristic: 8 smallest
location: 6 Europe 7 Bavaria
period: 8 Jurassic

Compson, Quentin
character in: 14 Absalom Absalom 18 The Sound and the Fury
author: 8 Faulkner

Compson family
characters in: 18 The Sound and the Fury
member: 5 Benjy, Caddy, Jason 7 Candace, Quentin 8 Benjamin
author: 8 Faulkner

compte rendu 6 record, report, review 7 account 15 account rendered

comptroller 7 auditor 9 treasurer 10 accountant, bookkeeper, controller

compulsion 5 force 6 demand, duress, urging 8 coercion, pressure 9 necessity 10 obligation 11 domineering, requirement

compulsive 6 driven, hooked 7 driving, fanatic 8 addicted, habitual 9 compelled, obsessive 10 compelling 14 unable to resist, uncontrollable

compulsory 7 binding 8 coercive, demanded, enforced, forcible, required 9 mandatory, requisite 10 compulsive, imperative, obligatory 11 unavoidable 12 prescriptive

compunction 5 demur, qualm, shame 6 regret, unease 7 anxiety, concern, remorse, scruple 9 misgiving 10 contrition 16 pang of conscience

computation 5 tally, total 8 figuring 9 numbering, reckoning 10 numeration 11 calculation, enumeration

compute 3 add 5 add up, sum up, tally, total 6 figure, reckon 7 count up, work out 9 ascertain, calculate, figure out

computer 5 adder 9 processor 10 calculator
language: 3 ADA 4 LOGO 5 ALGOL, BASIC, COBOL 6 PASCAL 7 FORTRAN
term: 2 PC 3 bit, CAD, CAM, CPU, RAM, ROM 4 boot, byte, chip, hack 5 drive, input, modem, pixel, queue 6 analog, glitch, hacker, memory, online, output 7 digital, network, offline, program 8 database, hardware, lightpen, printout, software, terminal 9 interface, mainframe 10 binary code, floppy disk 12 minicomputer 13 microcomputer, word processor 14 microprocessor

comrade 3 pal 4 ally, chum 5 buddy, crony 6 friend 7 partner 8 confrere, coworker, helpmate, intimate 9 associate, colleague, companion, confidant 10 bosom buddy 11 confederate 12 collaborator 13 boon companion
Russian: 8 tovarich

comradeship 8 alliance 10 fellowship, friendship 11 association, camaraderie 13 companionship

comte 5 count

Comte Ory, Le
also: 8 Count Ory
opera by: 7 Rossini
character: 13 Countess Adele

Comus
author: 10 John Milton

Comus
origin: 5 Roman
god of: 7 revelry 8 drinking

con 3 gyp 4 anti, bilk, coax, fool, gull, hoax, lure, rook 5 cheat, cozen, felon, trick 6 delude 7 against, beguile, convict, defraud, mislead, swindle 8 hoodwink, jailbird, prisoner, yardbird 9 bamboozle

Conakry
capital of: 6 Guinea

concatenation 4 link 5 union 6 hookup 7 joining, linking, reunion 8 coupling, junction 10 bracketing, confluence, connection 11 conjunction 12 interlinking 15 interconnection 16 interassociation 18 intercommunication

concave 6 hollow, sunken 8 indented 9 depressed 13 curving inward

conceal 4 hide, mask 5 cloak, còver 6 screen, shield 7 cover up, obscure, secrete 8 disguise 10 camouflage, keep secret

concealed 5 blind, doggo 6 covert, hidden, latent, masked, perdue, secret, veiled 7 cloaked, covered, obscure, unknown, wrapped 8 abstruse, shrouded, ulterior 9 disguised, incognito 11 clandestine

concealment 5 cover 6 hiding 7 hideout, masking 8 covering, hideaway 9 screening, secreting, secretion 10 covering up, under cover

concede 3 own 4 cede 5 admit, agree, allow, grant, yield 6 accept, give up, resign, tender 7 abandon, confess, deliver 8 hand over 9 acquiesce, recognize, surrender, vouchsafe 10 relinquish 11 acknowledge, be persuaded

conceit 5 pride 6 vanity 7 ego trip, egotism 8 bragging, self-love 9 vainglory 10 self-esteem 12 boastfulness 14 self-importance

conceited 4 smug, vain 7 stuck-up 8 arrogant, boasting, bragging, puffed up 9 bombastic, overproud, strutting 11 egotistical, swell-headed 12 vainglorious 13 self-important

conceivable 8 credible, knowable, possible 9 thinkable 10 believable, imaginable, supposable 11 perceivable

conceive 4 form 5 frame, hatch, start 6 create, invent 7 concoct, dream up, imagine, produce, think of, think up 8 consider, contrive, envisage, envision, initiate 9 originate 10 comprehend, understand

concentrate 4 mass 5 amass, bunch, focus, hem in 6 center, gather, heap up, reduce 7 close in, cluster, pay heed, thicken 8 assemble, attend to, condense, converge, fasten on 10 accumulate, congregate 11 bring to bear 12 direct toward

concentrated 5 dense 7 crowded, focused, thought 8 centered 10 compressed

concentration 4 mass 5 focus 7 cluster 9 diligence, gathering, reduction 10 absorption, assemblage, collection, intentness, thickening 11 aggrega-tion, boiling down, convergence, deep thought, engrossment 12 accumulation 13 concentrating, consolidation 14 centralization

concept 4 idea, view 5 image 6 belief, notion, theory 7 opinion, surmise, thought 9 postulate 10 conviction, hypothesis, impression 11 supposition

conception 4 idea 5 birth, image, start 6 notion 7 forming, genesis, inkling, picture 8 creating, devising, hatching 9 beginning, formation, imagining, inception, invention, launching 10 conceiving, concocting, initiation, perception 11 envisioning, formulation, originating 12 apprehension 13 fertilization, understanding 16 becoming pregnant

conceptual 8 abstract 9 visionary 11 conjectural, ideological, speculative, theoretical 12 experimental, hypothetical 15 impressionistic

concern 3 job 4 care, duty, firm, heed 5 chore, house, store, touch, worry 6 affair, affect, charge, matter, occupy, regard 7 anxiety, apply to, company, disturb, involve, mission, trouble 8 bear upon, business, distress, interest, relate to 9 attention, pertain to 10 disconcert, enterprise, solicitude 11 appertain to, corporation, disturbance, involvement, undertaking 12 apprehension 13 consideration, establishment 14 thoughtfulness

concerned 5 upset 6 active, caring, uneasy 7 alarmed, anxious, engaged, fearful, worried 8 involved, troubled 9 attentive, committed, disturbed 10 disquieted, distressed, interested, solicitous 12 apprehensive 13 participating

concerning 2 of, on, re 3 for 4 as to, over, upon 5 about, anent 7 apropos 8 engaging, touching, worrying 9 affecting, involving, mattering, regarding 10 relating to, respecting

concert 5 union, unity 6 accord, settle 7 concord, harmony 8 teamwork 9 agreement, congruity, unanimity 10 accordance, complicity 11 association, cooperation 13 collaboration 14 correspondence 18 musical performance

concerted 5 joint 6 united 7 planned 8 by assent 10 agreed upon 11 coopera-tive, prearranged 12 premeditated 13 predetermined

concert hall 9 music hall 10 auditorium 12 symphony hall

concession 5 lease 6 assent 8 giving in, yielding 9 admission, franchise, privilege 10 adjustment, compromise, indulgence 12 acquiescence, modification 14 acknowledgment

Conch
form: 7 trumpet
made of: 5 shell
owned by: 7 Tritons

Conchobar
origin: 5 Irish
king of: 6 Ulster
nephew: 10 Cuchulainn

concierge 7 janitor 9 custodian 10 doorkeeper

conciliate 6 pacify 7 appease, placate 9 make peace, reconcile 11 accommodate

conciliation 11 appeasement, peacemaking 12 propitiation 13 accommodation 14 reconciliation

conciliatory 8 friendly 9 appeasing, pacifying, placatory 10 mollifying, reassuring 11 peacemaking, reconciling 13 accommodative

concise 5 brief, pithy, short, terse 7 compact 8 succinct 9 condensed 10 to the point 11 abbreviated

conciseness 7 brevity 9 terseness 11 compactness 12 condensation, succinctness

conclave 6 parley, powwow 7 council, meeting, session 8 assembly 10 conference, convention 11 convocation 13 secret council

conclude 3 end 4 halt, stop 5 close, infer, judge 6 decide, deduce, effect, finish, gather, reason, settle 7 arrange, resolve, surmise 8 break off, carry out, complete 9 determine, terminate 10 accomplish 11 bring to pass, discontinue 12 draw to a close

concluded 5 bound, ended, guess 6 closed, judged 7 decided, deduced, expired, settled, wound up 9 completed 10 culminated, determined, restrained, terminated

conclusion 3 end 5 close 6 finale, finish, result, upshot, windup 7 finding, outcome 8 decision, judgment 9 agreement, deduction, final part, inference, summation

10 completion, denouement, resolution, settlement, working out **11** arrangement, presumption, termination **13** determination

conclusive 5 clear **6** patent **7** certain, obvious **8** absolute, decisive, definite, manifest, palpable **9** clinching **10** compelling, convincing, undeniable **11** categorical, determining, inescapable, irrefutable **12** demonstrable, unanswerable **13** incontestable, unimpeachable **14** unquestionable **16** incontrovertible

concoct 3 mix **4** brew **5** frame, hatch **6** cook up, create, devise, invent, make up **7** think up **8** compound, contrive **9** fabricate, formulate

concoction 4 brew **5** blend **6** jumble, medley **7** mixture **8** compound, creation **9** invention, potpourri **11** contrivance, fabrication **14** conglomeration

concomitant 7 related **9** accessory, attendant, connected, corollary, secondary **10** additional **12** accompanying, contributing, supplemental **13** complementary

concord 5 amity, peace **6** accord **7** harmony **8** goodwill **9** agreement **10** friendship **11** amicability, cooperation **16** cordial relations **19** mutual understanding

concordance 5 index **6** accord **7** concord **9** agreement, consensus, unanimity **17** meeting of the minds

concordant 6 unison **7** calming **8** agreeing, unifying **9** assenting, consonant **10** concurrent, harmonious

concordat 4 pact **8** covenant **9** agreement

Concordia
  origin: 5 Roman
  goddess of: 5 peace
    7 harmony

concourse 7 conflux, joining, linkage, meeting **8** junction **9** amassment **10** assembling, concursion, confluence **11** aggregation, association, convergence **12** congregation, focalization **13** concentration **14** conglomeration **15** flowing together **16** flocking together

concrete 4 real **5** solid **6** cement **7** express, factual, precise **8** definite, distinct, explicit, material, specific, tangible **10** particular **11** fused stones, substantial **12** alloyed rocks

concupiscence 4 itch, lust **6** desire **7** craving, lechery, longing, passion **8** appetite, hot pants, lewdness, satyrism **9** horniness, lubricity, prurience, randiness **10** wantonness **11** goatishness, libertinism, lustfulness **12** sexual desire **13** lecherousness **14** lasciviousness, libidinousness

concur 5 agree, match, tally **6** square **7** conform **8** coincide, hold with **9** be uniform **10** be in accord, correspond **11** go along with **12** go hand in hand

concur in 7 approve **9** agree with **11** go along with

concurrence, concurrency 6 accord **7** concord, consent, harmony **8** approval **9** agreement, consensus, unanimity **10** acceptance, conformity **11** affirmation, coexistence, coincidence, conjuncture, cooperation, synchronism **12** acquiescence **13** collaboration, mutual consent **14** correspondence **15** working together **17** meeting of the minds **22** simultaneous occurrence

concurrent 5 at one **6** allied **7** aligned **8** agreeing, matching **9** congenial, congruous, consonant **10** coexisting, coincident, coinciding, compatible, harmonious **11** in agreement, sympathetic, synchronous **12** commensurate, contemporary, in accordance, simultaneous **13** correspondent, of the same mind **15** contemporaneous

concurring 8 agreeing **10** consenting **11** affirmative, in agreement, synchronous **12** coincidental, simultaneous **13** corresponding

concussion 3 jar **4** blow, bump **5** clash, shock **6** buffet, impact **7** shaking **8** pounding **9** agitation, collision **11** brain injury

condemn 4 damn, doom **5** decry **6** rebuke **7** censure **8** denounce, sentence **9** criticize, proscribe, reprehend **10** disapprove

condemnation 6 rebuke **7** censure, reproof **8** judgment, reproach, sentence **9** criticism **10** conviction, punishment **11** disapproval **12** denunciation, reprehension **14** disapprobation **20** pronouncement of guilt

condensation 6 digest **9** reduction **10** abridgment **13** shortened form **16** condensed version

condense 3 cut **4** trim **6** digest, reduce **7** abridge, compact, liquefy, shorten, thicken **8** boil down, compress, contract, pare down **10** abbreviate, blue-pencil **11** concentrate, consolidate, precipitate

condensed form 6 digest **7** summary **8** synopsis **10** shortening **11** abridgement, compression, contraction, curtailment **12** abbreviation

condescend 5 deign, stoop **6** submit, unbend **7** descend, disdain **9** patronize **10** look down on, talk down to **12** come down a peg, lower oneself **13** humble oneself

condescending 7 high-hat **8** superior **10** disdainful **11** overbearing, patronizing

condescension 4 airs **7** disdain, hauteur, modesty **8** humility **9** deference, loftiness **10** humbleness **11** haughtiness **12** graciousness **13** self-abasement **14** self-effacement **19** patronizing attitude **20** assumption of equality **21** high-and-mighty attitude

condign 3 due **4** fair, just, meet **5** right **6** earned, proper, worthy **7** fitting, merited **8** deserved, suitable **9** warranted **11** appropriate

condiment 4 herb **5** sauce, spice **8** dressing, flavorer, seasoner **9** seasoning
  kind: 3 bay **4** dill, mace, mint, sage, salt **5** caper, clove, curry, onion, thyme **6** catsup, garlic, ginger, nutmeg, pepper, pickle, relish **7** caraway, chutney, ketchup, mustard, parsley, oregano, paprika, pimento, tabasco, vinegar **8** cardamon, marjoram, turmeric **9** pimpernel **10** bell pepper, mayonnaise

condition 3 fit **4** term **5** adapt, equip, ready, shape, state, train **6** demand, fettle, malady, status, tone up **7** ailment, prepare, problem, proviso **8** accustom, position, standing **9** agreement, complaint, provision, requisite, situation **10** limitation, make used to, put in shape **11** arrangement, contingency, malfunction, reservation, restriction, stipulation **12** prerequisite **13** circumstances, qualification, state of health **14** state of affairs **15** physical fitness

conditional 7 limited 9 dependent, qualified, tentative
10 contingent, restricted
11 provisional, stipulative
16 with reservations

condolence 4 pity 6 solace
7 comfort 8 sympathy
10 compassion 11 consolation
13 commiseration

Condon, Richard
author of: 11 Winter Kills
18 Death of a Politician
22 The Manchurian
Candidate

condonation 11 forgiveness,
overlooking 12 disregarding
13 putting up with

condone 6 excuse, forget, ignore, pardon, wink at 7 absolve, forgive, justify, let pass
8 overlook 9 disregard, put up with

conduce 3 aid 4 help, lead,
tend 5 bring, favor, guide 6 effect 7 advance, forward, further, promote 10 contribute

conducive 7 helpful 8 salutary
9 favorable, promotive
10 beneficial 11 expeditious
12 contributive, contributory,
instrumental 19 calculated to
produce 22 helpful in bringing
about

conduct 3 act 4 bear, lead,
rule, ways 5 carry, chair,
deeds, enact, guide, pilot,
steer, usher 6 action, attend,
behave, convey, convoy, direct, escort, govern, manage,
manner 7 carry on, comport,
control, execute, marshal, operate, perform 8 behavior,
carry out, dispatch, guidance,
regulate, transact 9 accompany, direction, discharge,
look after, supervise 10 administer, deportment, government, leadership,
management 11 comportment,
generalship, preside over, superintend, supervision
14 administration

conduct oneself 3 act 6 behave 13 acquit oneself
14 comport oneself

conductor 3 cad 5 guide
6 carman, escort, leader
7 cathode, channel, maestro,
manager 8 aqueduct, batonist,
cicerone, conveyor, director,
operator, stickman, trainman
9 collector, drum major
10 impresario, supervisor
11 choirmaster, transmitter
13 concert master

conduit 4 duct, main, pipe,
tube 5 canal, drain, flume,
sewer 6 gutter, trough 7 channel, passage 8 aqueduct
11 watercourse

cone 5 bevel, shape, spire
6 bobbin, conoid, funnel
7 pyramid, volcano 8 pyramid
kind: 3 fir 4 pine 5 larch
7 conifer, retinal 8 ice
cream

confabulate 4 chat, talk
6 confer, patter 7 chatter, discuss 8 chitchat, converse, talk
idly

confabulation 4 chat, talk
8 chitchat 10 conference, discussion 12 conversation

confection 3 jam 5 candy
6 pastry 7 dessert 8 conserve,
delicacy 9 preserves, sweetmeat 10 sugar candy

confectionery 5 candy
6 sweets 7 goodies, pasties
10 sugar candy, sweetmeats

confederacy, Confederacy
3 CSA 4 band, bloc 5 guild,
union 6 fusion, league 7 combine, society 8 alliance, the
South 9 coalition, syndicate
10 federation 11 association
13 confederation 14 Southern
states 18 secessionist states
26 Confederate States of
America

confederate 4 ally 5 merge,
unite 6 cohort, helper 7 abettor, comrade, partner 8 coalesce, coworker 9 accessory,
affiliate, associate, colleague,
companion 10 accomplice, cooperator, join forces 11 consolidate, helping hand 12 band
together, collaborator, right
hand man 17 fellow
conspirator

Confederates
author: 14 Thomas Keneally

confederation 4 band 5 guild,
union 6 fusion, league 7 combine, society 8 alliance 9 coalition, syndicate
10 federation 11 association,
confederacy

confer 4 give 5 award 6 accord, parley 7 consult, discuss,
palaver 8 converse 9 present
to 10 bestow upon 12 compare notes, talk together
15 hold a conference 18 deliberate together

conference 4 talk 6 parley
7 council, meeting, seminar
8 conclave 9 symposium
10 convention, discussion
12 consultation, deliberation

conferment 4 gift 5 award
8 bestowal 12 presentation

confess 4 avow, sing 5 admit,
own up 6 expose, reveal 7 declare, divulge, lay bare 8 blurt
out, disclose 9 come clean,
make known 11 acknowledge
12 bring to light 14 unbosom
oneself 18 make a clean
breast of

confessed 6 avowed 8 admitted 9 professed 12 self-declared 14 self-proclaimed

confession 6 avowal, shrift
9 admission 10 disclosure, divulgence, revelation 11 declaration 12 confessional
14 acknowledgment

**Confessions of an English
Opium Eater**
author: 15 Thomas
DeQuincey

**Confessions of Nat Turner,
The**
author: 13 William Styron

confidant, confidante
5 crony 6 friend 8 intimate
10 bosom buddy 15 trusty
companion

confide 6 impart, reveal 7 confess, divulge, lay bare, let in
on, let know 8 disclose
9 make known 12 tell secretly 13 tell privately 14 unbosom oneself

confidence 4 grit, guts 5 faith,
nerve, pluck, spunk, trust
6 belief, daring, mettle, secret,
spirit 7 courage 8 audacity,
boldness, credence, intimacy,
reliance 9 certainty, certitude
10 conviction 11 intrepidity
12 self-reliance 13 private matter, self-assurance 14 faith in
oneself 17 inside information

confidence man 5 cheat 6 con
man 8 swindler 9 charlatan,
trickster 10 mountebank

confident 4 bold, sure
5 cocky 6 daring, secure 7 assured, certain 8 cocksure, intrepid, positive 9 convinced,
dauntless, expectant 10 optimistic 11 self-assured, self-reliant 13 sure of oneself

confidential 5 privy 6 secret
7 private 8 hush-hush 9 top-secret 10 classified 11 undisclosed 12 off-the-record 16 not
to be disclosed

confidentially 7 sub rosa 8 in
secret, secretly 9 privately
16 between ourselves 17 behind closed doors
French: 9 entre nous

confiding 6 trusty 7 reliant
8 trustful, trusting 9 confident
11 trustworthy

configuration 4 form 6 design,
makeup 11 arrangement,
composition

confine 3 pen, tie **4** bind, cage, hold, jail, keep **5** limit **6** coop up, govern, keep in, lock up, shut in, shut up **7** fence in, impound **8** imprison, regulate, restrain, restrict **9** sequester **11** incarcerate **13** hold in custody

confined 5 close, tight **6** jailed, narrow **7** cramped **8** locked up **10** imprisoned, restricted

confinement 7 custody, lying in **9** cooping up, detention, restraint **10** childbirth, constraint, limitation, shutting in **11** parturition, restriction **12** accouchement, imprisonment **13** incarceration **15** circumscription

confines 4 edge **6** border, bounds, limits **7** margins **8** precinct **10** boundaries **13** circumference

confirm 5 prove **6** accept, clinch, ratify, uphold, verify **7** agree to, approve, bear out, certify, sustain **8** make firm, validate **9** authorize, establish **11** acknowledge, corroborate, make binding, make certain **12** authenticate, substantiate

confirmation 5 proof **6** assent **8** approval, sanction **9** agreement **10** acceptance, validation **11** affirmation, endorsement **12** ratification, verification **13** corroboration **14** authentication, substantiation

confirmed 3 set **5** fixed **7** chronic **8** hardened, verified **9** ingrained, validated **10** deep-rooted, deep-seated, inveterate, proven true **11** established **12** corroborated **13** authenticated, dyed-in-the-wool, substantiated

confiscate 4 take **5** seize **7** impound, possess, preempt **8** take over **9** sequester **10** commandeer **11** appropriate, expropriate

confiscation 7 seizure **10** impounding, preemption **13** appropriation, commandeering, expropriation

conflagration 4 fire **5** blaze **7** bonfire, inferno **8** conflict, fighting, wildfire **9** brush fire, firestorm, holocaust **10** forest fire, raging fire, wall of fire **11** sea of flames **12** sheet of flame

conflagrative 8 burnable **9** flammable, ignitable **10** combustive, incendiary **11** combustible, inflammable

conflict 4 fray **5** clash, fight, melee, set-to **6** action, battle, combat, fracas, oppose, strife, tussle **7** collide, discord, dissent, scuffle, warfare **8** disagree, division, friction, skirmish, struggle, variance **9** encounter, hostility **10** antagonism, be contrary, difference, dissension, engagement **12** disagreement **13** confrontation **14** be inharmonious **15** be contradictory
Spanish: 9 mano a mano

conflicting 7 warring **8** clashing, opposing **10** ambivalent **13** contradictory

confluence 5 union **7** conflux, joining, linkage, meeting **8** junction, juncture **9** concourse, gathering **10** assembling, concursion **11** association, convergence **13** concentration **14** coming together **15** flowing together

conform 3 fit **4** obey **5** adapt **6** adjust, follow **8** adhere to, jibe with, submit to **9** agree with, reconcile, tally with **10** be guided by, comply with, fall in with, square with **11** acquiesce in **12** correspond to

conformable 8 amenable **9** agreeable, malleable **10** submissive **12** in compliance

conformance 7 harmony **9** agreement **10** accordance, compliance, conformity **13** compatibility

conformation 4 form **5** build, shape **6** figure **7** anatomy **9** formation, framework, structure **11** arrangement **13** configuration

conformist 12 well-adjusted **13** unadventurous

conformity 6 accord, assent **7** harmony **8** likeness **9** agreement, obedience **10** compliance, observance, similarity, submission, uniformity **11** resemblance **12** acquiescence **14** correspondence **15** conventionality

confound 5 amaze, mix up **6** baffle, puzzle, rattle **7** astound, confuse, fluster, mystify, nonplus, perplex, startle **8** astonish, bewilder, dumfound, surprise, unsettle **10** disconcert **11** flabbergast **16** strike with wonder, throw off the scent

confounded 8 confused **10** bewildered, nonplussed **11** dumbfounded **12** disconcerted

confraternity 4 body **5** guild, union **7** society **8** sodality **9** confrairy **11** association, brotherhood

confrere 3 pal **4** ally, chum **5** buddy **6** friend **7** brother, comrade, partner **9** associate, colleague

confront 4 dare, defy, face, meet **5** brave **8** cope with, face up to **9** challenge, encounter, withstand

confrontation 5 clash, run-in, set-to **6** battle, combat, debate **7** contest, dispute, face-off **8** conflict, showdown, skirmish **9** encounter **10** engagement, opposition **11** controversy **17** face-to-face meeting
Spanish: 9 mano a mano

Confucius
author of: 10 Book of Odes **11** The Analects

confuse 5 addle, befog, mix up, stump **6** baffle, muddle, puzzle, rattle **7** fluster, mistake, mystify, nonplus, perplex **8** befuddle, bewilder, confound, unsettle **10** discompose, disconcert **11** make unclear **12** make baffling **14** make perplexing **17** throw into disorder

confused 5 fazed **6** addled **7** abashed, baffled, chaotic, jumbled, mixed-up, muddled, tangled **8** rambling **9** befuddled, illogical, perplexed, unsettled **10** bewildered, disjointed, distracted, incoherent, nonplussed **11** dumbfounded **12** disconcerted, disorganized **13** disharmonious, heterogeneous

confusing 7 addling **8** baffling, blinding, blurring, dizzying, jumbling, mixing up, muddling **9** deranging, mistaking **10** befuddling, disorderly, flustering, mystifying, perplexing, stupefying **11** bewildering, confounding **13** disconcerting, unintelligible

confusion 4 mess, riot **5** chaos, snarl **6** bedlam, hubbub, jumble, muddle, tangle, tumult, uproar **7** clutter, ferment, turmoil **8** disarray, disorder, madhouse, shambles, upheaval **9** abashment, commotion **10** bafflement, hodgepodge, hullabaloo, perplexity, puzzlement, untidiness **11** disturbance, pandemonium **12** bewilderment, discomposure, stupefaction **13** mystification **14** disarrangement, disconcertment **15** disorganization
French: 14 bouleversement

confutation 6 denial
7 counter 8 negation, rebuttal
10 refutation 13 contradiction

confute 4 deny 5 rebut 6 impugn, oppose, refute
7 counter, gainsay 10 contradict, controvert 12 be contrary to

congeal 3 set 4 clot, jell 6 curdle, freeze, harden 7 stiffen, thicken 8 solidify 9 coagulate
10 gelatinize

congenial 4 like 6 genial, social 7 affable, cordial, kindred, related, similar 8 agreeing, amenable, gracious, pleasant, pleasing, sociable 9 agreeable, convivial 10 compatible, consistent, harmonious, wellsuited 11 sympathetic 13 companionable, corresponding
French: 9 en rapport
German: 9 gemutlich

congeniality 7 harmony, rapport 8 affinity 11 sociability
12 conviviality, friendliness, pleasantness 13 compatibility
14 like-mindedness

congenital 6 inborn, inbred, innate, native 7 natural 8 inherent 9 ingrained, inherited, intrinsic 10 hereditary

congested 6 filled, gorged, jammed, packed 7 crowded
9 saturated 11 overcrowded

congestion 3 jam, mob
4 mass 5 snarl 6 pile-up
8 crowding 10 bottleneck
11 obstruction
12 overcrowding

conglomerate 4 heap, mass, pile 5 amass, blend, stack
7 mixture 8 assemble 9 aggregate 10 accumulate, assemblage 12 accumulation
16 large corporation

conglomeration 6 jumble, medley 7 mixture 8 mishmash 9 aggregate, potpourri
10 assortment, collection, hodgepodge 11 aggregation, combination 13 agglomeration

Congo *see box*

congratulate 4 hail 6 salute
10 compliment, felicitate, wish

one joy 11 rejoice with
18 give one's best wishes
28 wish many happy returns of the day

congratulations 6 salute
9 blessings, greetings 10 best wishes, good wishes 11 wellwishing 13 felicitations
24 many happy returns of the day

congregate 4 mass 5 amass, flock, swarm 6 gather, throng
7 cluster, collect 8 assemble
12 come together 13 crowd together

congregation 5 crowd, flock, group, horde, laity 6 parish, throng 8 assembly, audience, brethren 9 gathering, multitude 12 parishioners
16 church membership 17 religious assembly

congress, Congress 4 diet
6 caucus 7 council 8 assembly
9 delegates, gathering 10 conference, convention, parliament 11 legislature 14 federal council 15 discussion group, legislative body, national council, representatives
17 chamber of deputies

Congreve, William
author of: 11 Love for Love
15 The Double-Dealer
16 The Mourning Bride, The Way of the World

congruity 7 harmony 9 agreement, coherence 10 consonance 11 consistency
12 congeniality 13 compatibility 14 correspondence
15 appropriateness

congruous 4 meet 6 seemly
7 apropos 8 becoming, relevant, suitable 9 congenial, consonant, in keeping 10 harmonious 11 appropriate, in agreement 13 corresponding

conifer
means: 11 cone bearing
order: 11 coniferales
class: 10 gymnosperm
kind: 3 fir, yew 4 pine 5 cedar, larch, pinal 6 ginkgo, pinale, spruce, torrey 7 cypress, hemlock, juniper, redwood, sequoia 8 softwood
9 evergreen

Coningsby
author: 16 Benjamin Disraeli

conjectural 7 reputed 8 abstract, academic, doubtful, putative, supposed, surmised
11 inferential, speculative, theoretical 12 hypothetical
13 suppositional
14 supposititious

conjecture 4 idea, view

Congo
other name: 10 Moyen Congo 11 Middle Congo
capital/largest city: 11 Brazzaville
others: 3 Ewo 4 Boko 5 Epena, Kayes, Kelle, Okoyo, Sembe 6 Dongou, Komono, Makoua, Matadi, M'Binda, M'Vouti, Ouesso, Sibiti, Zanaga 7 Cabinda, Dolisie, Etoumbi, Gamboma, Kinkala, Loubomo, Loudima, Madingo, Mossaka, Souanke 8 Djambala, Impfondo, Kibangou, Madingou, Mindouli 9 Mossendjo 11 Fort-Rousset, Pointe-Noire 17 Mayombe Escarpment
school: 13 Marien Ngoubai
monetary unit: 5 franc 7 centime
lake: 5 Mweru, Tumba 6 Albert, Nyanza, Upemba 7 Leopold 11 Stanley Pool
highest point: 6 Leketi
river: 3 Dja 4 Uele 5 Alima, Congo, Kasal, Kwilu, Lulua, Ngoko, Niari, Sanga, Swilu, Wamba, Zahir, Zaire 6 Kwango, Kwenge, Loange, Lobaye, Lomami, Ogooue, Ubangi 7 Aruwima, Kouilou, Lualaba, Luapula, N'Gounie 8 Itimbiri, Likouala, Lubilash
sea: 8 Atlantic
physical feature:
  plateau: 6 Bateke
people: 3 Rua 4 Akka, Susa, Teke, Vili 5 Amadi, Bantu, Figot, Kongo, Mantu, Pygmy, Sanga, Warua, Zambi 6 Ababua, Bafyot, Bateke, Mbochi, Nzambi, Wabuma 7 Bacongo, Bakongo, Bangala, Batetla, Manyema 10 Binga Pygmy
  discoverer: 3 Cam
language: 4 Susu 5 Bantu, Fiote 6 French, Kituba 7 Bangala, Lingala
religion: 5 Islam 7 animism 10 Protestant 13 Roman Catholic
place:
  church: 9 Saint Anne
  stadium: 5 Eboue
feature:
  tree: 5 limba

5 fancy, guess, infer, judge, think **6** augury, notion, reckon, theory **7** imagine, opinion, presume, suppose, surmise **8** estimate, forecast, judgment, theorize **9** calculate, deduction, guesswork, inference, speculate, suspicion **10** assumption, guestimate, hypothesis, presuppose **11** guess-timate, hypothesize, speculation, supposition **13** shot in the dark

conjoin 4 join, knit, link **5** touch, unite **7** combine, connect, overlap **8** together **9** associate

conjoined 6 joined, linked, united **7** knitted, meeting **8** combined, touching **9** connected **10** associated **11** overlapping **14** joined together

conjugal 6 wedded **7** marital, married, nuptial, spousal **9** connubial **11** matrimonial

conjugate 4 join, pair, yoke **5** mated, unite, yoked **6** couple, joined, paired, united **7** connect, coupled, related **9** connected **10** paronymous

conjunction 5 union **7** joining, meeting **11** association, coincidence, combination, concurrence

conjuration 5 charm, spell, trick **11** incantation

conjure 5 allay, charm, raise **6** invoke, summon **7** bewitch, command, enchant **8** call away, call upon **9** call forth **10** cast a spell, make appear **13** make disappear **15** practice sorcery

conjurer 6 wizard **8** magician

conk 3 die, hit **4** bean, blow, fail, head **5** decay, faint, sleep, stall **6** fungus, strike **7** bracket **8** knock out **9** break down **10** straighten

Conn, Katherine
   real name of: **13** Kitty Carlisle

connect 3 tie **4** join **5** hinge, merge, unite **6** attach, couple, relate **7** combine, compare **9** associate, correlate **14** fasten together

connected 4 tied **6** joined, merged, united **7** coupled **8** abutting, adjacent, attached, combined, touching **9** bordering, proximate **10** connecting, contiguous, juxtaposed **12** conterminous **16** fastened together

connected group 5 cycle **6** series **8** sequence **11** progression

Connecticut
   abbreviation: **2** CT **4** Conn
   nickname: **6** Nutmeg **7** Blue Law **9** Freestone **12** Constitution **18** Land of Steady Habits
   capital/largest city: **8** Hartford
   others: **4** Avon **6** Bethel, Canaan, Cos Cob, Darien, Hamden, Mystic, Sharon, Storrs **7** Ansonia, Bristol, Danbury, Enfield, Madison, Meriden, Milford, Niantic, Norwalk, Norwich, Shelton, Tolland, Windsor **8** Guilford, New Haven, Simsbury, Stamford, Westport **9** Greenwich, Naugatuck, New London, Stratford, Waterbury **10** Bridgeport, Manchester, New Britain, Torrington **11** Wallingford
   college: **4** Yale **7** Trinity **8** Hartford, St Joseph, Wesleyan **9** Fairfield **10** Bridgeport, Quinnipiac **11** Sacred Heart **12** U S Coast Guard
   feature: **10** Charter Oak
      museum: **8** PT Barnum
      seaport: **6** Mystic
      theater: **27** American Shakespeare Festival
   tribe: **6** Pequot **7** Mohegan, Niantic **10** Quinnipiac
   people: **8** PT Barnum **9** John Brown **10** Nathan Hale **11** Noah Webster **12** Thomas Hooker **19** Harriet Beecher Stowe
   lake: **10** Candlewood
   land rank: **11** forty-eighth
   mountain: **4** Bear **7** Taconic
      hills: **10** Berkshires
      highest point: **8** Frissell
   physical feature: **15** Long Island Sound
   river: **6** Thames **9** Naugatuck **10** Housatonic **11** Connecticut
   state admission: **5** fifth
   state bird: **5** robin
   state flower: **14** mountain laurel
   state motto: **30** He Who Transplanted Still Sustains
   state song: **12** Yankee Doodle
   state tree: **8** white oak

Connecticut Yankee in King Arthur's Court, A
   author: **9** Mark Twain
   character: **5** Sandy **6** Merlin **8** Alisande, Clarence **11** Morgan le Fay **12** Hello-Central **18** Sir Kay the Seneschal

connection 3 kin, tie **4** bond, link **5** nexus **6** family, friend **7** contact, coupler, kinfolk, kinsman, linkage **8** affinity, alliance, coupling, junction, kinsfolk, relation, relative **9** associate, connector, fastening **10** attachment, kith and kin **11** association, correlation **12** acquaintance, relationship **13** flesh and blood, interrelation

Connelly, Marc
   author of: **16** The Green Pastures
      with Frank Elser: **19** The Farmer Takes a Wife
      with George S Kaufman: **5** Dulcy **11** To the Ladies **17** Beggar on Horseback, Merton of the Movies

Connery, Sean
   real name: **13** Thomas Connery
   born: **8** Scotland **9** Edinburgh
   roles: **6** Marnie **14** Robin and Marian **15** The Untouchables **16** The Molly Maguires **20** The Man Who Would Be King **28** Darby O'Gill and the Little People
      James Bond: **4** Dr No **10** Goldfinger **11** Thunderball **16** You Only Live Twice **18** Diamonds Are Forever, From Russia with Love, Never Say Never Again

connivance 4 plot **5** cabal **6** design, scheme **8** intrigue **9** collusion **10** complicity, conspiracy **11** machination

connive 3 aid **4** abet, plan, plot **5** allow **6** wink at **7** collude **8** conspire **10** be a party to **13** be accessory to, lend oneself to **14** shut one's eyes to **17** be in collusion with, cooperate secretly

conniving 4 wily **6** artful,

crafty **7** cunning **8** plotting, scheming **9** designing **10** intriguing **11** calculating

connoisseur 5 judge, maven, mavin **6** expert **7** epicure, gourmet **9** authority **11** cognoscente **17** person of good taste

Connolly, Maureen
  nickname: **8** Little Mo
  sport: **6** tennis

Connor, Dale
  creator/artist of: **9** Mary Worth

connotation 5 drift **6** import, spirit **8** coloring **9** evocation, undertone **10** intimation, suggestion **11** implication, insinuation **12** significance

connote 5 imply **6** hint at **7** suggest **8** intimate **9** insinuate **11** bring to mind

connubial 6 wedded **7** marital, married, nuptial **8** conjugal **11** matrimonial

conquer 4 beat, best, drub, lick, rout, rule, trim, whip **5** floor, quell **6** defeat, humble, master, occupy, subdue, thrash **7** possess, win over **8** overcome, surmount, vanquish **9** overpower, rise above, subjugate **11** prevail over, triumph over **14** get the better of

conqueror 6 victor, winner **7** subduer **8** champion **10** subjugator, vanquisher **12** conquistador

conquest 3 fan **4** sway **5** lover **6** adorer, defeat **7** captive, mastery, triumph, victory, winning **8** adherent, follower, whip hand **9** upper hand **10** ascendancy, conquering, domination, overcoming **11** acquisition, subjugation **12** vanquishment **17** captured territory

Conrad, Joseph
  real name: **29** Josef Teodor Konrad Korzeniowski
  author of: **6** Chance **7** Lord Jim, Typhoon, Victory **8** Nostromo **13** Almayer's Folly **14** The Secret Agent **15** Heart of Darkness **16** Under Western Eyes **21** An Outcast of the Islands **23** The Nigger of the Narcissus

consanguine 4 akin **7** cognate, kindred, related **8** relative

consanguineous 3 kin **4** akin **7** kindred, related **9** connected **21** having a common ancestor

conscience 8 scruples **10** moral sense, principles **15** ethical feelings **20** sense of right and wrong

conscience-stricken 6 guilty **7** ashamed **8** contrite, penitent **9** chastened, regretful, repentant **10** remorseful **13** guilt-stricken

conscientious 5 exact **6** honest **7** careful, dutiful, ethical, upright **10** fastidious, meticulous, particular, scrupulous **11** painstaking, responsible, trustworthy **12** conscionable **14** high-principled

conscious 5 aware **7** alert to, alive to, awake to, studied **8** noticing, sensible, sentient **9** cognizant, in the know, observing **10** calculated, deliberate, discerning, perceiving **12** apperceptive, premeditated **13** knowledgeable

consciousness 4 mind **6** senses **8** feelings, thoughts **9** awareness **10** cognizance, perception **11** discernment, sensibility

conscript 3 PFC **4** boot, hire, levy **5** draft **6** call up, employ, engage, enlist, enroll, induct, muster, rookie, seaman, select, take on **7** draftee, impress, private, recruit **8** enlistee, inductee, mobilize, register, selectee, shanghai **9** conscribe **11** buck private

consecrate 5 bless **6** hallow **7** glorify **8** sanctify **10** make sacred **11** immortalize **13** declare sacred

consecrated 4 holy **7** blessed **8** hallowed **10** sanctified

consecutive 6 in turn, serial **8** unbroken **10** continuous, sequential, successive **11** progressive **13** uninterrupted **19** following one another

consensus 6 accord **7** concord **9** unanimity **11** concurrence **13** common consent **14** general opinion **15** majority opinion **16** general agreement

consent 5 agree, allow, yield **6** accede, accept, accord, assent, concur, permit, ratify, submit **7** approve, concede, concord, confirm, endorse **8** approval, sanction **9** acquiesce, agreement **10** acceptance, fall in with, permission **11** concurrence, endorsement, willingness **12** acquiescence, confirmation, ratification

Consenting Adults
  author: **12** Peter DeVries

consent to 2 OK **4** okay

6 permit **7** approve **8** accede to **10** concur with **11** acquiesce to, go along with **14** give the go-ahead

consequence 3 end **4** note **5** avail, fruit, issue, value, worth **6** import, moment, result, sequel, upshot **7** account, gravity, outcome **9** aftermath, influence, magnitude, outgrowth **10** importance, notability, prominence, usefulness **11** development, distinction, seriousness **12** significance

consequent 7 ensuing **8** eventual **9** following, resulting

consequential 7 crucial, epochal **8** historic **9** important, momentous **10** meaningful **11** significant

consequently 2 so **4** ergo, then **5** and so, hence, later **9** as a result, therefore **11** accordingly **12** subsequently

conservation 4 care **6** upkeep **9** husbandry **10** careful use, protection **11** maintenance, safekeeping **12** preservation

conservative 5 quiet **6** square **7** old-line **8** cautious, moderate, undaring **9** right-wing **10** nonliberal, unchanging **11** reactionary, right-winger, traditional **13** unprogressive **15** middle-of-the-road **16** opponent of change **17** middle-of-the-roader **22** champion of the status quo

conservatoire 11 music school **12** conservatory, music academy

conservatory 7 nursery **8** hothouse **9** arboretum **10** glasshouse, greenhouse **11** music school **12** music academy **13** conservatoire

conserve 4 save **5** guard **7** care for, cut back, husband, use less **8** maintain, not waste, preserve **9** safeguard **12** use sparingly

consider 4 deem, hold, note **5** gauge, honor, judge, opine, study, think, weigh **6** ponder, regard, review **7** believe, examine, pay heed, respect **8** appraise, envision, hold to be, mull over **9** be aware of, reflect on **10** bear in mind, cogitate on, think about **11** contemplate **12** deliberate on **17** make allowances for **18** turn over in one's mind

considerable 4 tidy **5** ample, great, large **6** goodly **7** notable, sizable **8** not small **9** estimable, important **10** impressive, noteworthy, noticeable, of some size, remarkable **11** a good deal of, significant, substantial

considerably 5 amply **7** greatly, largely, notably, sizably **9** estimably **10** abundantly, noticeably, remarkably **13** significantly, substantially

considerate 4 kind **6** kindly **7** mindful **8** obliging **9** attentive, concerned **10** solicitous, thoughtful

consideration 4 heed, tact **5** cause, honor, point, study **6** factor, ground, motive, notice, reason, regard, review **7** concern, respect, thought **8** interest, judgment **9** attention **10** advisement, cogitation, inducement, kindliness, meditation, reflection, solicitude **11** examination **12** deliberation **13** contemplation **14** thoughtfulness **15** considerateness

consider closely 7 pay heed **11** concentrate **12** pay attention **13** put one's mind to **21** give one's full attention

considered 5 mused **6** deemed, heeded, judged, mulled **7** advised, express, honored, noticed, studied, thought, weighed, willful **8** believed, esteemed, looked on, pondered, regarded, supposed **9** reflected, respected, ruminated **10** considered, deliberate, looked upon, thought out **11** deliberated, entertained, intentional **12** contemplated, premeditated, thought about

consign 5 remit **6** assign, commit, convey, remand **7** deliver, entrust **8** delegate, hand over, relegate, transfer **9** commend to **11** deposit with

consignment 8 delivery, shipment, transfer **10** assignment, committing, consigning, delegation, depositing, entrusting, relegation **11** handing over **12** goods for sale, goods shipped **19** goods sent on approval

consist 3 lie **6** reside **7** contain, include **10** be made up of **11** to be found in **13** be comprised of **14** to be composed of

consistency, consistence 4 body **5** unity **6** makeup **7** density, harmony, texture **8** firmness **9** agreement, coherence, congruity, stiffness, structure, thickness, viscosity **10** accordance, conformity, connection, uniformity **11** compactness, composition, persistence **12** construction, faithfulness, steady effort **13** compatibility, steadfastness **14** correspondence **16** uniform standards **19** constant performance, undeviating behavior

consistent 4 meet **6** steady **7** regular, unified **8** agreeing, constant, of a piece, suitable **9** congenial, congruous, consonant **10** compatible, harmonious, persistent, unchanging **11** in agreement, undeviating **13** correspondent **16** conforming to type

consolation 4 help **5** cheer **6** relief, solace, succor **7** comfort, support **8** easement, soothing, sympathy **10** condolence **11** alleviation, assuagement **13** encouragement

Consolation of Philosophy (De Consolatione Philosophiae) author: 31 Anicius Manlius Severinus Boethius

console 4 calm, ease **5** cheer **6** soothe, succor **7** comfort, support, sustain **10** lament with, sympathize **11** condole with **13** express sorrow **15** commiserate with **18** express sympathy for

consolidate 4 fuse, join **5** merge, unify, unite **6** league **7** combine, fortify **8** coalesce, compress, condense, federate, make firm, make sure, solidify **9** integrate, make solid **10** amalgamate, centralize, strengthen **11** concentrate, incorporate **12** band together **13** bring together

consolidation 5 union **6** fusion, merger **8** alliance **9** coalition **11** unification **12** amalgamation **13** agglomeration **14** conglomeration

consomme 4 soup **5** broth **9** madrilene

consonance 5 amity, unity **6** accord, unison **7** concord, harmony, oneness **9** agreement, coherence, congruity, unanimity **10** accordance, conformity, congruence, consonancy **11** concordance, consistency, homogeneity **13** compatibility **14** correspondence, like-mindedness

consonant 8 in accord **9** agreeable, congruous, in harmony **10** concordant, consistent **11** in agreement

consort 3 mix **4** club, mate, wife **6** mingle, spouse **7** hang out, husband, pair off, partner **8** go around, sidekick

9 accompany, associate, companion, other half, pal around, rub elbows **10** fraternize **11** keep company

conspicuous 5 clear, great, plain **6** famous, patent **7** eminent, evident, glaring, notable, obvious **8** distinct, flagrant, glorious, manifest, renowned, splendid, striking **9** arresting, brilliant, memorable, notorious, prominent, well-known **10** celebrated, easily seen, remarkable **11** illustrious, outstanding, standing out **13** distinguished, easily noticed, highly visible

conspicuousness 9 celebrity, flagrance, notoriety **10** prominence, visibility **11** obviousness **13** noticeability

conspiracy 4 plot **7** treason **8** intrigue, sedition **9** collusion, treachery **10** connivance, secret plan **11** machination **12** criminal plan **14** treasonous plan

conspirator 7 plotter, schemer, traitor **8** conniver **9** intriguer **10** subversive

conspire 5 unite **6** concur, scheme **7** collude, combine, connive **8** intrigue **9** cooperate, machinate **11** plot treason **12** work together

Constable, John born: 7 England **12** East Bergholt **artwork: 10** The Haywain **12** Cloud Studies **14** Hadleigh Castle **39** Salisbury Cathedral from the Bishop's Grounds

constancy 6 fealty **7** loyalty **8** devotion **9** fixedness, stability **10** allegiance, permanence **12** faithfulness, immutability **13** dependability, invariability, steadfastness **15** trustworthiness **16** unchangeableness

constant 4 even, true **5** fixed, loyal **6** stable, steady, trusty **7** abiding, devoted, endless, eternal, regular, staunch, uniform **8** diligent, enduring, faithful, resolute, stalwart, unbroken, unvaried **9** ceaseless, continual, immutable, incessant, permanent, perpetual, steadfast, sustained, unceasing, unfailing **10** dependable, invariable, persistent, unchanging, unflagging, unswerving, unwavering **11** everlasting, never-ending, trustworthy, unalterable, undeviating, unrelenting **12** interminable, tried-and-true **13** uninterrupted

Constant Nymph, The
director: **14** Edmund
Goulding
cast: **11** Alexis Smith
12 Charles Boyer, Joan Fontaine **14** Brenda Marshall

constellation *see box*

consternation 5 alarm, panic,
shock **6** dismay, fright, horror,
terror **11** trepidation
12 apprehension

constituent 4 atom, part
5 piece, voter **6** factor, member **7** elective, element, essence **8** electing, integral,
making up **9** component, formative, principal, supporter
10 appointing, ingredient

constitute 4 form, make,
name **5** found, set up **6** create,
invest, make up **7** appoint,
compose, empower, produce
8 compound, delegate **9** authorize, establish, institute
10 commission

constitution 6 figure, health,
make-up, mettle **7** charter,
stamina, texture **8** physique,
strength, vitality **9** basic laws,
formation, structure **10** figuration **11** composition **12** construction **13** configuration
16 governing charter **17** physical condition **21** fundamental
principles

constitutional 4 turn, walk
5 basic **6** inborn, ramble,
stroll, vested **7** natural, organic **8** inherent, internal,
physical **9** chartered, intrinsic
10 congenital **11** fundamental

Constitution State
nickname of: **11** Connecticut

constrain 4 curb, urge **5** check,
crush, drive, force, quash

6 coerce, compel, oblige, subdue **7** confine, enforce, put
down, repress, squelch **8** hold
back, pressure, restrain, restrict, suppress **9** fight down,
necessity, strong-arm **14** put
the screws on

constrained 3 shy **5** timid
6 forced **7** bashful **8** reserved,
reticent **9** compelled, diffident
10 restricted **11** embarrassed

constraint 5 force **6** duress
7 reserve **8** coercion, pressure
9 restraint **10** compulsion, diffidence, inhibition, obligation
11 enforcement
13 necessitation

constrict 4 bind **5** choke,
cramp, pinch **6** shrink
7 squeeze **8** compress, contract,
strangle **11** strangulate

constriction 7 binding, choking **8** cramping, pinching
9 narrowing, shrinking,
squeezing, stricture, tightness
10 constraint, strangling
11 compression, contraction

construct 4 form, make
5 build, erect, frame, set up,
shape **6** create, design, devise
7 arrange, fashion **8** organize
9 fabricate, formulate

construction 4 form, make
5 build, style **6** format **7** edifice, raising, reading, rearing,
version **8** building, creation,
erecting **9** rendition, structure
10 fashioning, production
11 composition, elucidation,
explanation, explication, fabrication, manufacture **12** conformation, constructing
13 configuration **14** interpretation **15** putting together

constructive 5 handy **6** useful

7 helpful **8** valuable **9** practical **10** beneficial, productive
12 advantageous

construe 4 read, take **7** explain, make out **8** decipher
9 elucidate, figure out, interpret, translate **10** comprehend,
understand

Consuelo
author: **10** George Sand

consul 5 envoy **8** emissary,
minister **14** foreign officer,
representative **15** diplomatic
agent

Consul, The
opera by: **7** Menotti
character: **10** Magda Sorel

consult 6 confer, parley, regard **7** refer to **8** consider, talk
over **9** inquire of **11** ask advice of, have an eye to
12 compare notes **13** exchange
views **15** discuss together, seek
counsel from, take into account **16** seek the opinion of
18 deliberate together

consultant 6 expert **7** adviser,
advisor, counsel **9** discusser

consultation 7 council, hearing, meeting, palaver **9** interview **10** conference,
discussion **12** deliberation

consumable 6 edible **7** eatable **10** comestible

consume 3 eat **4** gulp **5** drain,
eat up, spend, use up, waste
6 absorb, devour, expend, guzzle, ravage **7** deplete, destroy,
drink up, engross, exhaust
8 demolish, lay waste, squander **9** devastate, dissipate,
swallow up **10** annihilate

consumed 4 used **5** burnt,
drank, drunk, eaten, spent
6 used up, wasted **7** drained,
outworn **8** absorbed, burned
up, expended, perished **9** destroyed, engrossed, exhausted,
swallowed **10** squandered
11 annihilated

consume greedily 6 devour
7 stuff in **8** bolt down, gobble
up, gulp down, wolf down
12 swallow whole **13** eat ravenously **14** eat voraciously

consumer 4 user **5** buyer,
drain **6** client, patron, waster
7 spender **8** customer **9** purchaser **10** dissipater,
squanderer

consummate 2 do **5** sheer, total, utter **6** effect, finish
7 achieve, execute, fulfill, perfect, perform, realize, supreme **8** absolute, carry out,
complete, finished, thorough
9 faultless **10** accomplish,

---

constellation 4 host **5** group, rally **6** circle, galaxy, nebula,
spiral, throng **7** cluster, company, pattern **9** gathering **10** assemblage, collection **12** spiral nebula **13** configuration **14** island universe
name: **3** Ara, Leo **4** Apus, Crux, Grus, Lynx, Lyra, Pavo,
Vela **5** Aries, Cetus, Draco, Hydra, Indus, Lepus, Libra,
Lupus, Mensa, Musca, Norma, Orion, Pyxis, Virgo **6** Antlia, Aquila, Auriga, Bootes, Caelum, Cancer, Carina, Corvus, Crater, Cygnus, Dorado, Fornax, Gemini, Hydrus,
Octans, Pictor, Pisces, Puppis, Scutum, Taurus, Tucana,
Volans **7** Cepheus, Columba, Lacerta, Pegasus, Perseus,
Phoenix, Sagitta, Serpens, Sextans **8** Aquarius, Circinus,
Equuleus, Eridanus, Hercules, Leo Minor, Scorpius, Sculptor **9** Andromeda, Centaurus, Delphinus, Monoceros,
Ophiuchus, Reticulum, Ursa Major, Ursa Minor, Vulpecula **10** Canis Major, Canis Minor, Cassiopeia, Chamaeleon,
Horologium, Triangulum **11** Capricornus, Sagittarius, Telescopium **12** Microscopium **13** Canes Venatici, Coma
Berenices **14** Camelopardalis, Corona Borealis **15** Corona
Australis, Piscis Austrinus **18** Triangulum Australe

bring about, undisputed
11 unmitigated 12 accomplished, unquestioned 13 unconditional 17 through-and-through

consummation 3 end 5 close
6 finish 9 execution 10 attainment, completion, conclusion
11 achievement, culmination,
fulfillment, realization
14 accomplishment

consumption 2 TB 3 use 7 using up 9 consuming, depletion 10 exhaustion
11 expenditure, utilization
12 exploitation, tuberculosis

Consus
origin: 5 Roman
god of: 11 good counsel,
horse racing
protector of: 5 grain
corresponds to: 3 Ops

contact 4 join, meet 5 reach,
touch, union 7 connect, meeting 8 abutment, junction,
touching 9 adjacency, get hold
of 10 connection 11 association 13 communication 14 get
in touch with 15 communicate with

contagion 7 disease 8 epidemic, outbreak 9 infection,
spreading 13 contamination

contagious 8 catching
9 spreading 10 infectious,
spreadable 12 communicable
13 transmittable

contain 4 curb, hold 5 check
6 embody, hold in 7 control,
embrace, enclose, include, inhibit, involve, repress 8 hold
back, keep back, restrain, suppress 11 accommodate, incorporate 12 keep the lid on
16 keep within bounds

container 3 bag, box, can, jar,
vat 4 pail 6 barrel, bottle,
bucket, carton, holder, vessel
10 receptacle

containment 7 control 9 restraint, retention

contaminate 4 foul, soil
5 dirty, spoil, taint 6 befoul,
blight, debase, defile, infect,
poison 7 corrupt, pollute
8 besmirch 10 adulterate,
make impure

contamination 5 filth 7 fouling, soiling 8 dirtying, foulness, impurity, spoiling
9 dirtiness, poisoning, polluting, pollution, putridity 10 defilement 11 uncleanness
12 adulteration

Conte, Richard
real name: 18 Nicholas Peter
Conte
born: 12 Jersey City NJ

roles: 8 Barabbas 13 A Bell
for Adano 24 The Greatest
Story Ever Told

contemplate 4 note, plan,
scan 5 weigh 6 expect, gaze
at, intend, ponder, regard, survey 7 examine, imagine, inspect, observe, project, stare
at, think of 8 aspire to, envision, mull over, ruminate
9 muse about 10 anticipate,
cogitate on, have in view,
meditate on, think about
11 reflect upon 12 deliberate
on 13 consider fully, look at
fixedly, look forward to
14 speculate about 15 view
attentively

contemplation 5 study 6 gazing, musing, seeing, survey
7 looking, reverie, thought,
viewing 8 scanning, thinking
9 pondering 10 cogitation,
inspection, meditation,
reflection, rumination
11 examination, observation
12 deliberation
13 consideration

contemplative 6 musing
7 pensive 8 studious 9 engrossed 10 cogitative, meditative, reflective, ruminating,
thoughtful 11 speculative
13 introspective, lost in
thought

contemporaneous 6 coeval
10 coexistent, coincident, concurrent 11 synchronous
12 contemporary, simultaneous

contemporary 3 new 4 late
6 modern, recent, with-it
7 current 8 advanced, brand-new, up-to-date 10 coexistent,
coincident, concurrent, new-fangled, present-day 11 ultra-modern 12 simultaneous 13 of
the same time, up-to-the-minute 15 contemporaneous

contempt 4 hate 5 scorn,
shame 6 hatred 7 disdain, disgust 8 aversion, derision, disfavor, disgrace, dishonor,
distaste, ignominy, loathing,
ridicule 9 antipathy, disregard,
disrepute, revulsion 10 abhorrence, repugnance 11 detestation, humiliation

contemptible 3 low 4 base,
mean, vile 5 cheap 6 abject,
paltry, shabby 8 shameful, unworthy, wretched 9 miserable,
repugnant, revolting 10 despicable, detestable, disgusting
11 ignominious

contemptuous 6 lordly
7 haughty, pompous 8 arrogant, derisive, insolent, scornful, snobbish 10 disdainful
12 supercilious 13 condescending, disrespectful

contemptuousness 5 scorn
7 disdain 8 contempt, rudeness 9 arrogance, insolence

contend 3 vie, war 4 aver,
avow, hold, spar 5 argue,
claim, clash, fight 6 allege, assert, battle, combat, debate,
insist, jostle, strive, tussle
7 compete, contest, declare,
dispute, grapple, quarrel, wrestle 8 be a rival, maintain, propound, skirmish, struggle
10 put forward

content 4 area, core, gist,
load, size, text 5 cheer, happy,
heart, ideas, peace 6 at ease,
at rest, matter, please, serene,
thesis, volume 7 appease, comfort, essence, gratify, insides,
meaning, pleased, satisfy, suffice, unmoved 8 capacity,
make easy, pleasure, serenity,
thoughts 9 contented, gratified,
happiness, satisfied, set at
ease, substance 10 complacent,
untroubled 11 comfortable,
contentment, peace of mind,
unconcerned 12 satisfaction
13 gratification

contented 5 happy 6 at ease,
serene 7 at peace, content,
pleased 9 gratified, satisfied
11 comfortable

contentedness 4 ease
5 peace 7 comfort, content
8 pleasure, serenity 9 happiness 11 contentment 12 satisfaction 13 gratification

contention 5 clash, fight
6 battle, combat, strife 7 contest, discord, dispute, rivalry
8 argument, conflict, disunity,
fighting, friction, skirmish,
struggle, variance 9 assertion,
encounter, wrangling 10 dissension, quarreling 11 competition, discordance
12 disagreement
13 confrontation

contentious 5 angry, cross
7 bateful, scrappy 8 captious
9 bellicose 10 pugnacious
11 belligerent, competitive,
quarrelsome 12 cantankerous,
disputatious 13 argumentative,
controversial

contentment 4 ease 5 peace
7 comfort, content 8 pleasure,
serenity 9 happiness 12 satisfaction 13 contentedness,
gratification

conterminous 8 abutting, adjacent, touching 9 bordering
11 right beside 14 contiguous
with

contest 3 war 4 bout, game
5 fight, match 6 battle, combat, debate, oppose, vie for
7 dispute, rivalry, tourney

8 conflict, fight for, object to, struggle **9** battle for, challenge, combat for, encounter **10** compete for, contend for, controvert, engagement, tournament **11** competition, struggle for **12** argue against **14** call in question

contestant 5 rival **6** player **7** entrant, fighter **8** competer, prospect **9** combatant, contender **10** challenger, competitor

context 6 milieu **7** climate, meaning, setting **8** ambience **9** framework, precincts, situation **10** atmosphere, background, conditions, connection **11** environment **12** relationship, surroundings **13** circumstances **16** frame of reference

contiguous 5 close, handy **6** nearby **7** close-by, tangent **8** abutting, adjacent, next-door, touching **9** adjoining, bordering, in contact **10** juxtaposed **11** neighboring **12** conterminous

continence 6 purity **8** chastity, sobriety **10** abstinence, moderation, temperance **11** forbearance **13** self-restraint

continent 4 Asia, pure **6** Africa, chaste, Europe **8** celibate, land mass, mainland, virginal **9** abstinent, Australia, temperate **10** abstemious, Antarctica **12** North America, South America

contingency 7 urgency **8** accident **9** emergency, extremity **10** likelihood **11** possibility, predicament **15** unforeseen event

contingent 9 dependent, subject to **11** conditioned **12** controlled by

continual 7 endless, eternal **8** constant, frequent, habitual, unbroken, unending **9** ceaseless, incessant, perennial, perpetual, recurring, unceasing **10** continuous, persistent **11** everlasting, never-ending, oft-repeated, unremitting **12** interminable **13** uninterrupted

continually 3 aye **4** ever **6** always, steady **7** endless, eternal, forever, on and on **8** steadily **9** recurring **10** constantly, frequently, repeatedly

continuance 4 stay, term **6** extent, period **7** lasting **8** duration **9** extension **10** continuing, permanence **11** adjournment, persistence,

protraction **12** continuation, perseverance, prolongation

continuation 6 sequel **8** addition, sequence **9** extension **10** continuing, supplement **11** continuance, protraction **12** prolongation

continue 4 go on, last, stay **5** abide **6** drag on, endure, extend, keep on, keep up, remain, resume, stay on **7** carry on, persist, proceed **9** persevere

continued 6 kept on, kept up, lasted, went on **7** endured **8** extended **9** carried on, persisted, proceeded, prolonged **10** persevered, protracted

continuing 6 steady **7** abiding, eternal, ongoing **8** constant, enduring, extended, unbroken, unending **9** ceaseless, incessant, perpetual, prolonged **10** dragged out, persistent, protracted **11** persevering, unremitting **12** interminable **13** uninterrupted

continuity 4 flow **5** chain **9** continuum **10** succession **11** continuance, progression **12** continuation

continuous 6 linked, steady **7** endless, eternal, lasting **8** constant, enduring, unbroken **9** ceaseless, connected, continual, extensive, incessant, perpetual, prolonged, unceasing **10** continuing, persistent, protracted, successive **11** consecutive, everlasting, persevering, progressive, unremitting **12** interminable **13** uninterrupted

continuum 4 flow **5** chain **8** sequence **10** continuity, succession **11** continuance, progression **12** continuation

contort 4 bend, warp **5** twist **6** deform **7** distort **11** be misshapen

contorted 4 bent **7** crooked, twisted **8** deformed **9** distorted

contortion 7 bending **8** twisting **10** distortion **11** crookedness

contour 4 form **5** lines, shape **6** figure **7** outline, profile **10** silhouette **11** physiognomy

contraband 11 bootlegging **13** smuggled goods **14** illegal exports, illegal imports **15** unlicensed goods **17** black-marketeering **18** prohibited articles **19** unlawful trafficking

contract 3 get **4** pact, take **5** agree, incur **6** absorb, assume, narrow, pledge, reduce,

shrink, treaty **7** acquire, compact, develop, dwindle, promise, shorten, tighten **8** compress, condense, covenant, engender **9** constrict, enter into, negotiate, undertake **11** arrangement, come to terms **12** draw together, make a bargain **13** become smaller, legal document **15** sign an agreement **16** written agreement

contracted form 6 digest **7** summary **8** synopsis **9** short form **11** abridgement, compression **12** abbreviation, condensation

contraction 8 decrease **9** drawing in, lessening, narrowing, reduction, shrinkage **10** shortening, shriveling, tightening **11** compression **12** abbreviation, condensation, constriction

contradict 4 deny **5** belie, rebut **6** impugn, oppose, refute **7** confute, counter, dispute, gainsay **8** disprove **10** controvert **12** be contrary to, disagree with

contradiction 6 denial **7** counter **8** negation, rebuttal **10** refutation **11** confutation **12** disagreement

contradictory 8 contrary, opposing **10** discrepant, dissenting, refutatory **11** conflicting, disagreeing **12** antithetical, inconsistent **14** countervailing, irreconcilable

contradistinction 8 contrast **10** difference **13** dissimilarity

contraption 6 device, gadget **9** apparatus, invention **11** contrivance

contrariety 9 deviation **10** difference, divergence **13** contradiction

contrary 5 balky **7** adverse, counter, froward, hostile, opposed, wayward, willful **8** converse, inimical, opposite, stubborn, untoward **9** disparate, obstinate, unfitting **10** at variance, discordant, headstrong, refractory, unsuitable **11** conflicting, disagreeing, intractable, unfavorable **12** antagonistic, antithetical, disagreeable, inauspicious, incompatible, recalcitrant, unpropitious **13** contradictory **15** at cross purposes, unaccommodating

contrast 6 depart, differ **7** deviate, diverge **8** variance **9** disparity **10** comparison, difference, divergence, unlikeness **11** distinction **12** disagree with **13** differentiate, dissimilarity **15** differentiation, set in opposition

contrasting 8 clashing, dividing, opposing **9** comparing, differing **10** discordant, juxtaposed **14** distinguishing **15** differentiating

contravene 4 deny **5** annul, fight, spurn **6** abjure, breach, combat, disown, negate, offend, oppose, reject, resist **7** disobey, exclude, gainsay, infract, nullify, violate **8** abrogate, disclaim, overstep **9** overreach, repudiate **10** act against, contradict, infringe on, transgress **12** encroach upon **15** trespass against

contretemps 4 spat **5** clash, set-to **7** dispute, quarrel **8** argument, squabble **10** difference, falling out **12** disagreement **18** embarrassing mishap

contribute 4 give **5** endow, grant **6** bestow, confer, donate, lead to **7** advance, forward, hand out, present **9** bear a part, influence **11** have a hand in **13** be conducive to **14** help bring about

contribution 4 alms, gift **5** grant **6** charity, subsidy **8** bestowal, donation, offering **9** endowment **11** benefaction **12** dispensation

contributive 8 valuable **9** favorable **10** beneficial

contributory 9 accessory, ancillary, auxiliary **13** supplementary

contrite 6 rueful **7** humbled **8** penitent **9** chastened, regretful, repentant, sorrowful **10** apologetic, remorseful **18** conscience-stricken

contrition 6 regret **7** penance, remorse **9** atonement, penitence **10** repentance **11** compunction **12** self-reproach **18** qualms of conscience

contrivance 4 plan, plot, tool **5** gizmo, trick **6** design, device, doodad, gadget **7** machine, measure **8** artifice, intrigue **9** apparatus, implement, invention, mechanism, stratagem **10** instrument **11** contraption, machination, thingamajig

contrive 4 plan, plot **6** create, design, devise, invent, manage, scheme **7** concoct **8** maneuver **9** improvise **11** devise a plan **17** effect by stratagem

contrived 7 labored, studied **8** mannered **9** unnatural **10** artificial

contriver 7 creator, deviser **8** designer, inventor **9** architect

control 4 curb, rule, sway **5** brake, steer **6** bridle, charge, govern, manage, master, subdue **7** command, contain, mastery, repress **8** dominate, dominion, regulate, restrain, restrict **9** authority, direction, reign over, restraint, supervise **10** domination, management, manipulate, regulation **11** superintend, supervision, suppressant **12** have charge of, jurisdiction

controlled 5 ruled **6** curbed, steady, swayed **7** checked, managed, powered, servile, subdued **8** directed, governed, held back, kept down, reserved, verified **9** commanded, contained, dominated, moderated, regulated, repressed **10** authorized, regimented, restrained, supervised **11** manipulated

controlling 6 ruling **8** dominant **9** governing **10** commanding **11** influencing, predominant **13** predominating

controversial 7 at issue **8** arguable **9** debatable, polemical **10** disputable **12** questionable **13** causing debate **15** widely discussed **16** open to discussion

controversy 6 debate **7** dispute, quarrel, wrangle **8** argument, squabble **10** contention, discussion, dissension **11** altercation **12** disagreement

controvert 4 deny **5** belie, rebut **6** negate, oppose, refute **7** confute, dispute, gainsay, protest **8** confound, disprove, question **9** challenge, disaffirm **10** contradict, contravene, invalidate **12** give the lie to

contumacious 6 unruly **7** froward **8** contrary, factious, insolent, mutinous, perverse **9** fractious, seditious **10** headstrong, rebellious, refractory **11** disobedient, intractable **12** ungovernable, unmanageable **13** disrespectful, insubordinate

contumely 5 abuse, insult, scorn **7** disdain, obloquy **8** contempt, diatribe, reproach, rudeness **9** arrogance, insolence, invective, pomposity **10** opprobrium, scurrility **11** brusqueness, haughtiness **12** billingsgate, vituperation **15** overbearingness

contusion 4 hurt, mark, sore **5** mouse **6** bruise, injury, shiner **7** blemish **8** abrasion,

black eye **9** black mark **13** discoloration **16** black-and-blue mark

conundrum 5 poser, rebus **6** enigma, puzzle, riddle **7** arcanum, mystery, paradox, problem, puzzler, stopper, stumper **11** brain-teaser **13** Chinese puzzle

convalesce 4 mend **5** rally **6** revive **7** improve, recover, restore **8** progress **9** get better **10** recuperate

convalescence 7 recruit **8** recovery **11** restoration **12** recuperation **14** return to health

convene 6 gather, muster, summon **7** collect, convoke, round up **8** assemble **12** call together, come together, hold a session **13** bring together

convenience 3 use **4** ease **6** chance **7** benefit, comfort, service, utility **8** facility, pleasure **9** appliance, enjoyment, handiness, work saver **10** usefulness **11** opportunity **12** availability, satisfaction, suitable time **13** accessibility, accommodation

convenient 5 handy **6** at hand, nearby, suited, useful **7** adapted, helpful **8** suitable **9** easy to use **10** beneficial **11** serviceable **12** advantageous **16** easily accessible

convent 7 nunnery **8** cloister **13** society of nuns

convention 4 code **6** caucus, custom **7** meeting, precept **8** assembly, conclave, congress, practice, propriety, protocol, standard **9** formality, gathering **10** conference, social rule **11** convocation

conventional 5 usual **6** common, normal, proper **7** regular, routine **8** accepted, orthodox, standard **9** customary **11** traditional

converge 4 meet **5** focus **8** approach **11** concentrate **12** come together **13** bring together

convergence 6 accord **8** junction **9** congruity **10** confluence **12** meeting place **14** correspondence

conversant 4 up on **5** aware **6** au fait **7** erudite, privy to, skilled, tutored **8** familiar, informed, sensible, sentient **9** au courant, cognizant, practiced **10** acquainted, proficient **12** well-informed **13** knowledgeable

conversation 3 rap **4** chat,

talk **7** gabfest, palaver **8** chit-chat, dialogue **9** discourse, tete-a-tete **11** bull session **13** confabulation
Italian: 13 conversazione

Conversation, The
director: 18 Francis Ford Coppola
cast: 10 John Cazale **11** Gene Hackman **13** Allen Garfield

conversational 6 casual, chatty **8** everyday, informal **9** idiomatic **10** colloquial, vernacular

conversazione 12 conversation

converse 3 gab, jaw, rap **4** chat, chin, talk **7** palaver, reverse **8** chitchat, contrary, opposite **10** antithesis, chew the fat, chew the rag **11** confabulate **13** speak together **14** shoot the breeze

conversely 12 contrariwise **14** antithetically, on the other hand

conversion 6 change **10** changeover **12** modification **13** change of heart, metamorphosis, transmutation **14** transformation **15** change in beliefs, transfiguration **16** change of religion

convert 4 turn **6** change, modify, novice **8** neophyte **9** proselyte, transform **11** proselytize

convex 7 bulging, rounded **11** protuberant **13** curved outward

convey 4 bear, cede, deed, give, move, tell, will **5** bring, carry, grant, leave **6** impart, relate, reveal **7** conduct, consign, deliver, divulge **8** bequeath, disclose, dispatch, transfer, transmit **9** confide to, make known, transport **11** communicate

conveyance 3 bus, car, rig, van **4** cart **5** buggy, truck, wagon **7** vehicle **8** carriage, carrying, movement, transfer **9** conveying, transport **12** transmission **14** transportation

convict 3 con **4** doom **5** felon **7** condemn **8** jailbird, prisoner, yardbird **10** find guilty **11** prove guilty **13** declare guilty

conviction 4 view, zeal **5** ardor, creed, dogma, faith, fever, tenet **6** belief, fervor **7** opinion **8** doctrine, judgment, position **9** assurance, certainty, certitude, intensity, principle, viewpoint **10** per-

suasion **11** earnestness **13** steadfastness

convince 4 sway **6** assure **7** satisfy, win over **8** persuade **9** influence **11** bring around, prevail upon

convincing 5 sound, valid **6** cogent, potent **7** evident **8** assuring, forceful, powerful **9** plausible **10** persuading, persuasive, satisfying

convivial 5 merry **6** genial, jovial **7** affable, festive **8** friendly, sociable **9** agreeable, fun-loving **10** gregarious **13** companionable

convocation 6 caucus, muster, roster **7** council, meeting, roundup **8** assembly, conclave, congress **9** gathering **10** conference, convention **11** ingathering

convoke 4 meet, open **6** gather, muster **8** assemble, converse **11** call to order **12** call together

convolute 4 coil, wave, wavy, wind **5** twirl, twist **6** coiled, rolled, spiral, tangle **7** contort, sinuous, twisted **8** involved, spiraled **9** intricate **11** complicated **12** turn and twist

convolution 4 coil, maze **5** twist **7** coiling, winding **8** twisting **9** labyrinth, sinuosity **10** contortion, undulation **11** sinuousness **12** tortuousness

convoy 5 fleet, usher **6** column, escort **7** conduct **9** accompany, formation, safeguard **10** armed guard, protection

convulse 4 rock, stir **5** laugh, shake, spasm, wring **6** excite **7** agitate, disturb, perturb, trouble **8** double up

convulsion 3 fit **5** spasm **6** tumult **7** seizure **8** outburst, paroxysm **9** agitation, commotion **10** contortion **11** disturbance

convulsive 6 fitful **7** hurtful, rending, shaking **8** exciting, stirring **9** agitating, epileptic, spasmodic, troubling **10** disturbing

Conway, Tim
real name: 18 Thomas Daniel Conway
born: 12 Willoughby OH
roles: 11 McHale's Navy **16** Carol Burnett Show **17** The Steve Allen Show

coo 6 babble, gurgle, murmur **20** whisper sweet nothings

Coogan, Jackie
real name: 16 Jack Leslie Coogan
wife: 11 Betty Grable
born: 12 Los Angeles CA
roles: 6 The Kid **9** Tom Sawyer **11** Oliver Twist, Peck's Bad Boy **15** Huckleberry Finn

cook 3 fix **4** chef, fire, heat, make **5** occur **6** cookie, doctor, happen, seethe **7** concoct, falsify, prepare, process **8** work well **9** improvise
method: 3 fry **4** bake, boil, brew, sear, stew **5** baste, broil, grill, poach, roast, saute, scald, shirr, steam **6** braise, coddle, simmer **7** parboil **8** barbecue **9** fricassee

Cooke, Alistair
author of: 14 One Man's America **18** A Generation on Trial **26** Around the World in Fifty Years
TV host of: 18 Masterpiece Theatre

cooked sufficiently 4 done **5** ready **7** al dente **11** done to a turn

cookie 3 bar, gal, gul **4** cake, cook **5** wafer **6** person **7** biscuit, brownie **10** shortbread
type: 4 oreo **5** sugar **7** oatmeal **8** macaroon, molasses **9** girl scout, tollhouse **10** gingersnap, lorna doone **12** peanut butter **13** chocolate chip

cooking, fine / gourmet
French: 12 haute cuisine

cooking term 3 a la, cut, dot, fry **4** bake, beat, boil, chop, coat, cube, dice, dust, flan, fold, lard, roux, sear, snip, stew, toss, whip **5** aspic, au jus, baste, blend, bread, broil, brush, candy, cream, crepe, devil, dough, flake, glace, glaze, grate, grill, knead, plank, puree, roast, saute, scald, score, shirr, steep, stock, torte **6** au lait, blanch, braise, coddle, devein, dredge, fillet, flambe, fondue, render, simmer, skewer, sliver **7** a la mode, compote, crouton, garnish, goulash, liquefy, parboil, precook, preheat, rissole, scallop, stir-fry **8** aperitif, au gratin, barbecue, conserve, consomme, julienne, marinate, pot roast **9** brochette, demitasse, drippings, forcemeat, fricassee, lyonnaise, macedoine **10** caramelize, cracklings
boneless strips of meat / fish: 6 fillet
clear soup: 8 bouillon, consomme

cubed toasted bread:
7 crouton
food cooked and served in foil or paper: 11 en papillote
fruit preserve with nuts/raisins: 8 conserve
fruits in syrup: 7 compote
in the fashion: 7 a la mode
remove veins: 6 devein
skewered meat: 5 kebab **9** brochette
small cup of black coffee: 9 demitasse
thin strips: 6 sliver **8** julienne
with cheese: 8 au gratin
with ice cream: 7 a la mode
with juice/with its own juices: 5 au jus
with milk: 6 au lait

cook up 3 mix **4** brew **5** hatch **6** create, devise, invent, make up **7** concoct, think up **8** compound, contrive **9** fabricate, formulate

cool 3 icy **4** calm, cold **5** aloof, chill **6** chilly, frosty, offish, serene **7** distant, not warm **8** composed, lose heat, make cool, reserved **9** collected, impassive, uncordial, unexcited **10** become cool, cool-headed, deliberate, nonchalant, unfriendly, unsociable, untroubled **11** indifferent, standoffish, undisturbed, unemotional, unflappable **12** slightly cold, somewhat cold, unresponsive **13** dispassionate, imperturbable, self-possessed

cooler 3 ade, can, fan, jug **4** coop, icer, jail **5** drink, icier **6** calmer, icebox, lockup, prison **11** refrigerant **12** refrigerator **14** air conditioner

Cool Hand Luke
director: 15 Stuart Rosenberg
cast: 8 J D Cannon **10** Jo Van Fleet, Lou Antonio, Paul Newman **12** Anthony Zerbe, Dennis Hopper **13** George Kennedy **14** Strother Martin
Oscar for: 15 supporting actor (Kennedy)

Coolidge, Calvin *see box*

coolness 5 chill **7** dislike **8** distance **9** aloofness, composure, sangfroid **10** chilliness, detachment, frostiness **11** impassivity **12** indifference **13** lack of emotion, lack of feeling **14** unfriendliness **15** emotionlessness, standoffishness **16** imperturbability, unresponsiveness

coop 3 car, mew, pen, sty **4** auto, cage, cote **5** cramp, hutch **6** encase, prison **7** confine **8** imprison **9** enclosure **11** cooperation, cooperative

Cooper, Gary
real name: 16 Frank James Cooper
born: 8 Helena MT

Coolidge, Calvin
name at birth: 18 John Calvin Coolidge
nickname: 9 Silent Cal
presidential rank: 9 thirtieth
party: 10 Republican
state represented: 2 MA
succeeded: 7 Harding
defeated: 5 (Frank Thomas) Johns, (Herman P) Faris, (John William) Davis **6** (William Zebulon) Foster **7** (Gilbert O) Nations, (William James) Wallace **10** (Robert Marion) La Follette
vice president: 4 none (first term) **5** (Charles Gates) Dawes
cabinet:
  state: **6** (Charles Evans) Hughes **7** (Frank Billings) Kellogg
  treasury: **6** (Andrew William) Mellon
  war: **5** (Dwight Filley) Davis, (John Wingate) Weeks
  attorney general: **5** (Harlan Fiske) Stone **6** (Charles B) Warren **7** (John Garibaldi) Sargent **9** (Harry Micajah) Daugherty
  navy: **5** (Edwin) Denby **6** (Curtis Dwight) Wilbur
  postmaster general: **3** (Harry Stewart) New
  interior: **4** (Hubert) Work, (Roy Owen) West
  agriculture: **4** (Howard Mason) Gore **7** (Henry Cantwell) Wallace, (William Marion) Jardine
  commerce: **6** (Herbert Clark) Hoover **7** (William Fairfield) Whiting
  labor: **5** (James John) Davis
born: 2 VT **13** Plymouth Notch
died: 2 MA **11** Northampton
buried: 2 VT **8** Plymouth
education:
  College: **7** Amherst
  later studied: **3** law
religion: 17 Congregationalist
vacation spot: 10 Black Hills
author: 32 The Autobiography of Calvin Coolidge
political career: 13 vice president
  state senator/lieutenant governor/governor of: **2** Ma **13** Massachusetts
civilian career: 6 lawyer **17** bank vice president **18** newspaper columnist
notable events of lifetime/term: 22 Pennsylvania coal strike
  Act: **8** Volstead **10** Boulder Dam **11** Immigration **17** Japanese Exclusion
  bribery case: **8** Elks Hill
  conference: **11** Geneva Naval
  flight by: **16** Charles Lindbergh
  Lindbergh's plane: **15** Spirit of St Louis
  Pact: **13** Kellogg-Briand
  trial: **6** Scopes **12** Scopes monkey
quote: 35 (After all) the chief business of America is business **43** Spend less than you make and make more than you spend
father: 10 John Calvin
mother: 8 Victoria (Josephine Moor)
  stepmother: **8** Caroline (Brown)
sibling: 13 Abigail Gratia
wife: 5 Grace (Anna Goodhue)
children: 4 John **6** Calvin

---

roles: 8 High Noon (Oscar) **9** Beau Geste **12** Sergeant York (Oscar), The Virginian **15** A Farewell to Arms **17** Mr Deeds Goes to Town **19** For Whom the Bell Tolls, The Cowboy and the

Lady **20** The Pride of the Yankees **22** North West Mounted Police

Cooper, James Fenimore
author of: **6** The Spy **8** The Bravo, The Pilot **9** Wyandotte **10** The Prairie **11** The Pioneers, The Red Rover **13** The Deerslayer, The Pathfinder, The Water-Witch **20** Leatherstocking Tales, The Last of the Mohicans
character: **4** Cora **5** Alice, Magua, Uncas **7** Hawkeye **11** Natty Bumppo **12** Chingachgook

cooperate 4 join **5** unite **7** go along, pitch in, share in **8** take part **9** join hands **10** act jointly, bear part in, join forces **11** collaborate, participate **12** pull together, work together **14** work side by side

cooperation 7 concert, detente **8** teamwork **9** agreement **10** accordance **11** concurrence, cooperating, give and take, joint action **13** collaboration, participation **15** pulling together, working together

coop up 3 pen **4** cage **5** pen in **6** closet, encage, shut in **7** confine, impound **8** restrain, restrict

coordinate 4 mesh **5** equal, match, order **6** relate **7** arrange, coequal **8** organize, parallel **9** correlate, harmonize **11** correlative, systematize **16** equally important

coordination 4 bond **5** skill **6** accord **7** harmony, liaison **10** adaptation, adjustment **12** equalization, organization **15** synchronization

cop 3 bag, nab, rob, win **4** bull, grab, take **5** bobby, catch, filch, pinch, snare, steal, swipe **6** peeler, pilfer, snatch **7** capture **8** gendarme, purchase **9** policeman **11** acquisition, policewoman **13** police officer

cope 4 face, spar **6** hurdle, manage, strive, tussle **7** contend, wrestle **8** struggle **11** hold one's own

copious 4 full **5** ample **6** lavish **7** liberal, profuse **8** abundant, generous **9** bountiful, extensive, plenteous, plentiful

copiousness 6 bounty, plenty, wealth **7** surfeit **8** fullness, plethora **9** abundance, ampleness, plenitude, profusion **10** lavishness, oversupply

Copland, Aaron
born: **10** Brooklyn NY
composer of: **5** Rodeo **9** Quiet City **10** Statements **11** Billy the Kid **12** Connotations **13** Dance Symphony, El Salon Mexico, The Tender Land **15** Outdoor Overture **17** Appalachian Spring **18** Music for a Great City, Music for the Theater

Copley, John Singleton
born: **8** Boston MA
artwork: **11** Samuel Adams **19** The Siege of Gibraltar **21** The Boy with the Squirrel **22** Brook Watson and the Shark, The Death of Major Pierson **26** The Death of the Earl of Chatham

copper
chemical symbol: **2** Cu

copper-colored 5 henna **6** auburn, russet **11** golden-brown, rust-colored **12** reddish-brown

coppice 4 bosk, wood **5** bluff, copse, firth, grove **6** forest, growth **7** boscage, thicket

Coppola, Francis Ford
director of: **12** The Godfather (Part I) (Part II, Oscar) **13** Apocalypse Now, The Cotton Club **15** The Conversation

Copreus
father: **6** Pelops
son: **10** Periphetes
herald of: **14** King Eurystheus

copse 5 brush, clump, grove **6** forest **7** coppice, thicket **8** woodland

copy 3 ape **4** fake, sham, text **5** clone, mimic, story, Xerox **6** follow, mirror, parody, repeat **7** emulate, forgery, imitate, replica **8** likeness **9** duplicate, facsimile, imitation, photostat, reportage, reproduce **10** carbon copy, manuscript **11** counterfeit, make a copy of **12** reproduction **14** representation **15** written material

coquette 4 vamp **5** flirt, tease **12** heart-breaker

coquettish 3 coy **9** kittenish **11** flirtatious

Cor 15 Biblical measure

Cora see **10** Persephone

coral 3 red **4** fire, pink, rose **5** horny, polyp, snake **6** orange, sea fan **8** acropora, hydrozoa, staghorn **9** gorgonian **10** sea feather **12** coelenterata

coram populo 8 publicly **15** before the public

corban 8 offering

Corbett, James (John)
nickname: **12** Gentleman Jim
sport: **6** boxing
class: **11** heavyweight

cord 5 braid, twine **8** thin rope **11** heavy string
abbreviation: **2** cd

Cordelia
character in: **8** King Lear
author: **11** Shakespeare

cordial 4 warm **6** genial, hearty **7** affable, amiable, sincere **8** friendly, gracious **9** heartfelt **11** good-natured **12** affectionate, wholehearted

cordiality 6 warmth **8** goodwill **9** affection, geniality, sincerity **10** affability, amiability, heartiness **11** amicability, earnestness **12** friendliness, graciousness, pleasantness **13** agreeableness

cordial relations 5 amity **6** accord **7** concord, harmony **8** goodwill **9** agreement **10** friendship **11** amicability **15** entente cordiale

cordon 4 cord, ring, rope **6** circle **8** encircle

cordon bleu 4 bird **5** finch **7** waxbill **10** red cheeked **11** estrildidae
school for: **5** chefs **7** cooking
where: **5** Paris **6** France
founded by: **13** Marthe Distell
means: **10** blue ribbon

core 3 nub **4** crux, gist, guts, meat, pith **5** heart **6** center, kernel **7** essence, nucleus **9** substance **10** brass tacks **11** central part, nitty-gritty **13** essential part, innermost part **15** sum and substance

Corelli, Arcangelo
born: **5** Imola, Italy
composer of: **7** La Folia (sonata No 12) **14** Concerti Grossi

Coresus
form: **6** priest
father: **6** Asopus
loved: **10** Callirrhoe
rejected by: **10** Callirrhoe

coriander
botanical name: **17** Coriandrum sativum
origin: **13** Mediterranean
color: **5** brown, white **6** yellow
flavor: **4** sage **5** cumin **7** caraway **9** lemon peel
candy: **6** comfit

Corinth, Lovis
born: **6** Tapiau **7** Prussia
artwork: **6** Salome **8** Ecce

Homo **10** Apocalypse **29** The Walchensee with a Yellow Field

Corinthus
founder of: 7 Corinth
possible father: 4 Zeus
8 Marathon

Coriolanus
author: 18 William Shakespeare
character: 8 Cominius, Virgilia, Volumnia **9** Junius Brutus, Titus Lartius **14** Tullus Aufidius **15** Menenius Agrippa, Sicinius Velutus **22** Caius Marcius Coriolanus

cork 3 bob, oak **4** bark, bung, plug, seal, stop **5** check, close, float **7** confine, filling stopper, stopple **8** restrain, suppress **10** insulation

corker 3 ace **4** whiz **7** stopper **8** clencher, striking, top notch **9** excellent, humdinger **10** remarkable **11** astonishing

corkscrew 4 coil, curl **5** twist **6** spiral **7** winding **10** serpentine **12** bottle opener

Corleone family
characters in: 12 The Godfather
author: 4 Puzo
member: 5 Sonny **7** Don Vito, Freddie, Michael

corn 4 cure **5** grain **6** callus **7** Zea Mays **8** preserve, schmaltz **9** vegetable
varieties: 3 Pod **4** Crow, Dent, Rice, Sand **5** Broom, Flint, Kafir, maize, Sugar, Sweet **6** Indian, Turkey **8** Egyptian, Squirrel
bread/cake: 4 pone **7** hoecake **8** tortilla **9** hushpuppy **10** johnnycake
beverage: 7 bourbon, whiskey

Corncracker State
nickname of: 8 Kentucky

Corneille, Pierre
author of: 5 Cinna, Le Cid, Medea, Medee **6** Horace, The Cid **8** Nicomede **9** Polyeucte

Cornelius, Peter von (van)
born: 7 Germany **10** Dusseldorf
artwork: 12 Last Judgment **24** The Wise and Foolish Virgins **30** The Four Horsemen of the Apocalypse

Cornell, Katharine
nickname: 21 first lady of the theater
born: 6 Berlin **7** Germany
roles: 8 Dear Liar **9** Saint Joan **18** Antony and Cleopatra **26** The Barretts of Wimpole Street

corner 3 fix, jam, nab **4** bend, grab, hole, nail, nook, spot, trap **5** angle, seize **6** collar, pickle, plight, scrape **7** dead end, dilemma, impasse **10** blind alley, pigeonhole **11** predicament

cornerstone 4 base **5** basis **9** principle **10** foundation **11** fundamental

cornet 4 cone, horn **7** trumpet **9** cornopean

Cornhuskers, The
author: 12 Carl Sandburg

Cornhusker State
nickname of: 8 Nebraska

cornice 4 drip **5** ancon, crown **7** molding, valance **8** astragal

Cornopian see **8** Hercules

Cornwallis, Charles
also: 10 second Earl **13** first Marquess
nationality: 7 British
served in: 5 India **7** Ireland **18** American Revolution
battle: 8 Yorktown **10** Brandywine
captured: 10 Charleston **12** Philadelphia
surrendered at: 8 Yorktown

Cornwell, David
real name of: 11 John Le Carre

corny 5 banal, hokey, inane, stale, tired, trite, vapid **6** jejune, square **7** fatuous, insipid **8** bromidic, ordinary, shopworn **9** hackneyed **10** threadbare, unoriginal **11** commonplace, stereotyped **12** cliche-ridden, old-fashioned **13** platitudinous, unimaginative **15** unsophisticated

Coroebus
form: 4 hero
home: 5 Argos
father: 6 Mygdon
built: 6 temple
  temple honored: **6** Apollo
killed: 5 Poena
killed by: 8 Diomedes

corona 4 halo, ring **5** cigar **6** circle, nimbus

coronet 5 tiara **6** diadem **7** chaplet, circlet **10** small crown

Coronis
form: 5 nymph **8** princess
father: 9 Phylegyas
husband: 6 Ischys
son: 9 Asclepius
cared for: 8 Dionysus
killed by: 6 Apollo

Coronus
king of: 7 Lapiths
father: 7 Caeneus
son: 8 Leonteus
daughter: 10 Anaxirrhoe
companion: 5 Jason

Corot, Jean-Baptiste-Camille
born: 5 Paris **6** France
artwork: 9 Pastorale **11** Ville d'Avray, Woman in Blue **15** Woman with a Pearl **16** The Farnese Garden, Woman in the Studio **21** Memory of Mortefontaine **23** Souvenir de Mortefontaine

corporal 6 bodily **8** physical **9** corporeal

corporation 7 combine, company **9** syndicate **11** association **14** conglomeration

corporeal 6 bodily, mortal **7** worldly **8** material, physical **11** perceptible **12** nonspiritual

corps 4 band, crew, team **5** force, party, squad, troop **6** outfit

corpse 4 body **5** stiff **7** cadaver, remains **8** dead body

corpselike 4 pale **5** ashen **6** pallid **9** bloodless, deathlike **10** cadaverous

corpulent 3 fat **5** dumpy, hefty, obese, plump, pudgy, stout **6** chubby, chunky, fleshy, portly, rotund **7** lumpish, well-fed **8** roly-poly **10** overweight, well-padded

corral 4 herd **5** pen in **6** shut in **7** enclose, fence in, round up

correct 3 fit, fix **4** true **5** alter, amend, chide, exact, right, scold **6** adjust, berate, change, modify, proper, punish, rebuke, remedy, repair, revamp, revise, rework, seemly **7** censure, chasten, factual, fitting, improve, lecture, perfect, precise, rectify, reprove **8** accurate, admonish, becoming, chastise, flawless, regulate, suitable, unerring **9** castigate, dress down, faultless, make right, reprimand **10** acceptable, discipline, take to task **11** appropriate **12** conventional **16** haul over the coals, read the riot act to

correction 6 change **8** revision **10** adjustment, alteration, discipline, emendation, punishment **11** castigation, improvement, reformation **12** chastisement, modification **13** rectification

corrective 7 counter **8** remedial 9 improving 10 palliative, rectifying 11 reformatory, restorative, therapeutic 12 ameliorative, compensatory 13 counteractive 16 counterbalancing

correctness 8 accuracy 9 exactness, precision, propriety, rightness 10 exactitude, seemliness 11 suitability 12 becomingness, flawlessness 13 acceptability

Correggio
real name: 14 Antonio Allegri
born: 5 Italy 6 Emilia 9 Correggio
artwork: 5 Danae 12 Jupiter and Io 14 Leda and the Swan 17 The Rape of Ganymede 21 The Madonna of St Francis 23 Adoration of the Shepherds 28 Mystic Marriages of St Catherine

correlate 7 compare, connect 8 parallel 10 correspond

correlation 8 parallel 10 comparison, connection 14 correspondence

correlative 4 akin 7 related 8 agreeing, parallel 9 analogous 10 comparable, connecting, equivalent 13 corresponding

correspond 3 fit 4 jibe, suit 5 agree, match, tally 6 accord, be like, concur, equate, square 7 conform 8 coincide, dovetail, parallel 9 harmonize 11 communicate, drop a line to, keep in touch

correspondence 4 mail 7 analogy, letters 8 epistles, missives, relation 9 bulletins 10 dispatches, similarity 11 association, communiques, resemblance

corresponding 4 akin 5 alike, equal 7 similar 8 agreeing, matching, tallying 9 according 10 equivalent 11 correlative 12 proportional

corridor 3 way 4 hall, road 5 aisle 6 artery 7 hallway, passage 8 approach 10 passageway

Corridors of Power
author: 6 C P Snow

corroborate 4 back 5 prove 6 affirm, back up, uphold, verify 7 bear out, certify, confirm, endorse, support, sustain 8 validate 9 vindicate 12 authenticate, substantiate

corroborated 6 backed, proved, proven, upheld 7 factual 8 affirmed, backed up,

borne out, verified 9 certified, confirmed, supported, sustained, validated 10 vindicated 11 well-founded 12 well-grounded 13 authenticated, substantiated

corroboration 5 proof 7 support 8 evidence 10 validation 11 affirmation, endorsement, vindication 12 confirmation, verification 13 certification, documentation 14 authentication, substantiation

corroborative 7 proving 9 affirming, backing up, upholding, verifying 10 bearing out, concurring, confirming, supporting, validating 11 affirmative 12 confirmative 14 substantiating

corrode 4 rust 7 oxidize 12 disintegrate

corrosive 4 acid 7 burning, caustic, erosive, mordant 8 abrasive 9 corroding 11 destructive

corrugated 6 fluted, ridged 7 creased, grooved, pleated 8 crinkled, furrowed, puckered, wrinkled 10 crenulated

corrupt 3 low 4 base, evil, mean 5 shady 6 debase, poison, seduce, sinful, wicked 7 crooked, debased, debauch, deprave, immoral, pervert, subvert 8 depraved 9 dishonest, unethical 10 fraudulent, iniquitous 11 contaminate 12 dishonorable, unprincipled, unscrupulous

corruption 4 vice 5 fraud, graft 7 bribery 8 iniquity 9 decadence, depravity, looseness, turpitude 10 debauchery, degeneracy, dishonesty, immorality, perversion, sinfulness, wickedness, wrongdoing 11 malfeasance

corsair 6 pirate, sea dog, Viking 7 brigand, sea wolf 8 marauder, picaroon, sea rover 9 buccaneer, plunderer, privateer, sea looter, sea robber 10 Blackbeard, freebooter 11 Captain Kidd 14 Long John Silver

corset 5 laces 6 girdle 8 corselet 17 foundation garment

Corsica 6 island
located in: 16 Mediterranean Sea
capital: 7 Ajaccio
colony of: 4 Rome
purchased by: 6 France
birthplace of: 8 Napoleon
industry: 7 tourism 10 wine making 12 sheep raising, cheese making

Corsican Brothers, The
author: 14 Alexandre Dumas (pere)

Cortazar, Julio
author of: 7 Rayuela 9 A Model Kit, Bestiario, Hopscotch 10 The Winners 12 Book of Manuel, End of the Game 15 All Fires the Fire 18 We Love Glenda So Much

cortege 4 line 5 court, staff, suite, train 6 column, escort, parade, string 7 caravan, company, retinue 9 cavalcade, entourage, following, motorcade 10 attendants, procession 17 funeral procession

corundum
variety: 4 ruby 8 sapphire, star ruby 12 star sapphire

coruscate 4 beam 5 flash, gleam 7 glimmer, glitter, shimmer, sparkle

Corybant
attendant of: 6 Cybele

Corycia
form: 5 nymph
bore son to: 6 Apollo

Corynetes
also: 8 Pelasgus
epithet of: 10 Periphetes
means: 12 cudgel bearer

Coryphaeus
epithet of: 4 Zeus
means: 7 highest

Corythosaurus
type: 8 dinosaur 10 ornithopod
period: 10 Cretaceous
characteristic: 10 duck-billed

Corythus
father: 5 Priam
mother: 6 Oenone
adopted son: 8 Telephus
loved: 5 Helen
killed by: 5 Priam
birthplace of: 8 Dardanus

Cosby, Bill
born: 14 Philadelphia PA
roles: 4 I Spy 12 The Cosby Show 19 Mother Juggs and Speed, Uptown Saturday Night

Cosby Show, The
character: 4 Rudy, Theo 6 Denise, Sondra 7 Vanessa 13 Clair Huxtable, (Dr) Cliff (Heathcliff) Huxtable
cast: 9 Bill Cosby, Lisa Bonet 14 Sabrina LeBeauf 15 Tempestt Bledsoe 18 Malcolm Jamal-Warner 19 Keshia Knight Pulliam, Phylicia Ayers-Rashad

Cosi fan tutte
  also: 11 So Do They All
    16 Women Are Like That
  opera by: 6 Mozart
  character: 7 Despina 8 Ferrando 9 Dorabella, Guglielmo 10 Don Alfonso, Fiordiligi

Cosmetas
  epithet of: 4 Zeus
  means: 7 orderer

cosmetic 5 paint, rouge
  6 powder 7 mascara, surface
  8 artifice, eyeliner, lipstick
  9 cold cream, eye shadow
  10 foundation, nail polish
  11 beautifying 13 eyebrow
  pencil

cosmic 4 vast 7 immense 8 colossal, enormous, infinite
  9 grandiose, universal 10 stupendous, widespread 12 interstellar 14 interplanetary
  16 extraterrestrial

cosmopolitan 6 urbane
  7 worldly 8 traveler 11 broadminded, worldly-wise
  12 globetrotter, sophisticate
  13 international, sophisticated

cosmos 5 stars 8 universe
  9 macrocosm 10 starry host
  13 vault of heaven

Cossack 7 czarist, Russian,
  trooper 8 horseman 10 cavalryman

cosset 3 pet 6 caress, coddle,
  fondle, pamper

cost 3 fee, run, tab 4 bill,
  harm, hurt, loss, pain, take,
  toll 5 fetch, go for, price,
  value, worth 6 amount, burden, charge, come to, damage,
  injure, injury, outlay 7 bring
  in, expense, penalty, sell for,
  set back 8 amount to, distress
  9 face value, sacrifice, suffering, valuation, weigh down
  11 expenditure, market price

Costa-Gavras, Constantine
  director of: 7 Missing

Costard
  character in: 16 Love's Labour's Lost
  author: 11 Shakespeare

Costa Rica *see box*

Costello, Lou
  real name: 21 Louis Francis
    Cristillo
  partner: 9 Bud Abbott
  born: 10 Paterson NJ
  roles: 11 Who's on First

costly 4 dear 5 steep, stiff
  7 harmful 8 damaging, precious 9 expensive 10 disastrous, exorbitant, high-priced
  11 deleterious, extravagant
  12 catastrophic

Costa Rica
  name means: 9 rich coast
  other name: 19 Land of Eternal Spring
  capital/largest city: 7 San Jose
  others: 5 Canas, Limon, Vesta 6 Boruca, Nicoya 7 Cartago, Golfito, Heredia, Liberia, Negrita 8 Alajuela, Colorado, Guapiles 9 Turrialba 10 Puntarenas
  measure: 4 vara 5 cafiz, cahiz 6 fanega, tercia 7 cajuela, cantaro, manzana 10 caballeria
  monetary unit: 5 colon 7 centimo
  weight: 3 bag 4 caja 5 libra
  island: 4 Cano, Coco
  lake: 6 Arenal
  mountain: 4 Poas 5 Barba, Irazu 6 Blanco 7 Central, Gongora 9 Talamanca, Turrialba 10 Guanacaste
  highest point: 14 Chirripo Grande
  river: 4 Poas 5 Irazu 6 Matina 7 San Juan, Sixaola, Tenoria 8 Tarcoles
  sea: 7 Pacific 9 Caribbean
  physical feature:
    bay: 7 Salinas 8 Coronada
    cape: 5 Velas 6 Blanco 8 Matapalo 10 Santa Elena
    crater: 4 Poas
    gulf: 5 Dulce 6 Nicoya 8 Papagayo
    hot springs spa: 12 Agua Caliente
    peninsula: 3 Osa 6 Nicoya
    point: 5 Judas 6 Blanca, Burica, Quepos 7 Cahuito, Galonos, Guionos, Llerena
    valley: 8 Tarcoles 10 Reventazon
  people: 4 Voto 6 Boruca, Bribri, Guaymi 7 Guatuso, mestizo, Spanish
  explorer: 8 Columbus, Coronado
  language: 7 Spanish
  religion: 13 Roman Catholic
  place:
    shrine: 18 Our Lady of the Angels
    theater: 14 Teatro Nacional
  feature:
    barbecue: 5 asado
    dance: 6 torito 9 botijuela, zapateado 11 baile suelto 17 punto guanacasteco
    drum: 8 quijonga
    gourd: 4 caro
    outdoor concerts: 7 retreta
    plantation: 5 finca
    wind instrument: 8 chirimia
  food:
    hearts of palm salad: 7 palmito
    pudding: 10 tamal asado

Costner, Kevin
  born: 2 CA 10 Los Angeles
  films: 3 JFK 9 Silverado
    10 Bull Durham 12 The
    Bodyguard 13 Field of
    Dreams, A Perfect World
    15 The Untouchables
    16 Dances With Wolves
    24 Robin Hood: Prince of
    Thieves

costume 4 garb 5 dress 6 attire, livery, outfit 7 apparel,
  clothes, raiment, uniform
  8 clothing, garments

costuming 8 disguise
  10 masquerade

cot 3 bed, hut, pen 4 coop,
  crib 5 cover, stall 7 cottage

cotelette 3 cut 4 chop 5 slice
  6 cutlet

coterie 3 set 4 band, camp,
  clan, club, crew, gang
  5 crowd, group 6 circle,
  clique 7 faction

cottage 3 cot, hut 5 lodge,
  shack 6 chalet 8 bungalow

Cotten, Joseph
  born: 12 Petersburg VA
  roles: 8 Gaslight 11 Citizen
    Kane, The Third Man
    12 Duel in the Sun
    14 Shadow of a Doubt
    15 Journey into Fear
    16 Portrait of Jennie 23 The
    Magnificent Ambersons

cotton 9 Gossypium
varieties: 3 bog **4** tree, wild **6** kidney, levant, upland **8** lavender **9** sea island **11** Arizona wild
fabric: 4 duck, jean, lawn, pima **5** baize, chino, denim, drill, khaki, lisle, pique, scrim, terry, twill **6** burlap, calico, canvas, chintz, dimity, madras, muslin, nankin, oxford, poplin, sateen **7** batiste, buckram, cambric, flannel, fustian, gingham, holland, jaconet, oilskin, organdy, percale, ticking **8** chambray, cretonne, sheeting **9** crinoline, sailcloth **10** broadcloth, hopsacking, printcloth, seersucker, terrycloth **11** cheesecloth, dotted Swiss

Cotton Club, The
director: **18** Francis Ford Coppola
cast: **9** Diane Lane **11** Richard Gere **12** Gregory Hines

cotton gin
invented by: **7** Whitney

Cotton State
nickname of: **7** Alabama

cottonwood 7 Populus **16** Populus deltoides
varieties: **5** black, Jack's, swamp **7** Fremont **9** Rio Grande **10** Wislizenus **11** Great Plains

Cottus
member of: **13** Hecatonchires

Cotyleus
epithet of: **9** Asclepius
means: **13** of the hip joint

Cotys, Cotytto
origin: **8** Thracian
form: **7** goddess
corresponds to: **6** Cybele **11** Great Mother

couch 3 put **4** sofa, word **5** divan, draft, frame, state, utter, voice **6** daybed, draw up, lounge, phrase, settee **7** express **8** love seat, set forth **9** davenport **12** chesterfield

cougar 3 cat **4** lion, puma **7** panther **9** catamount **12** mountain lion

cough 4 hack **6** tussis **9** pertussis

cough up 3 pay **5** eject, expel **7** deliver **8** disgorge, hand over **9** surrender **11** regurgitate

Coulomb, Charles Augustin de
field: **7** physics
nationality: **6** French
invented: **14** torsion balance
discovered: **16** inverse square law

council 5 board, panel, synod **7** cabinet, chamber **8** assembly, colloquy, conclave, congress, ministry **9** committee, gathering, sanhedrin **10** conference, convention **11** convocation **12** congregation **15** representatives

counsel 4 urge, warn **6** advice, advise, charge, lawyer, prompt **7** call for, caution, opinion, suggest **8** admonish, advocate, attorney, guidance, instruct **9** barrister, counselor, recommend, solicitor **10** advisement, suggestion **12** consultation **14** recommendation

counsel house
German: **7** Rathaus

Counsellor-at-Law
director: **12** William Wyler
based on play by: **9** Elmer Rice
cast: **11** Bebe Daniels, Doris Kenyon **12** Isabel Jewell **13** John Barrymore, Melvyn Douglas, Onslow Stevens

counselor, counsellor 5 tutor **6** lawyer, mentor **7** adviser **8** advocate, attorney, minister **9** barrister, solicitor **10** instructor

counselor-at-law 6 lawyer **8** advocate, attorney **9** barrister, solicitor **10** mouthpiece

count 4 deem, hold, lord, rate, tell **5** add up, judge, noble, tally, total **6** impute, look on, matter, number, reckon, regard **7** ascribe, include, tick off **8** consider, estimate, look upon, numerate **9** attribute, enumerate, numbering, reckoning **10** numeration **11** calculation, computation, enumeration
German: **4** Graf
French: **5** comte
Italian: **5** conte

countenance 3 aid, air **4** back, face, help, look, mien **5** build, favor **6** aspect, permit, traits, uphold, visage **7** advance, approve, condone, endorse, forward, further, profile, promote, support, work for **8** advocacy, advocate, approval, auspices, champion, contours, features, presence,

sanction **9** promotion **10** appearance, assistance, expression, silhouette **11** approbation, physiognomy **12** championship, moral support **13** encouragement

counter 3 bar, man **4** defy, disk **5** piece, stand, table **6** buffet, contra, offset, oppose, resist **7** against, get even, hit back, opposed, pay back, reverse **8** contrary, fountain, opposite **9** fight back, retaliate **11** conflicting **13** contradictory

counteract 4 curb, undo **5** check, fight **6** defeat, hinder, negate, offset, oppose, resist, thwart **7** assuage, nullify, repress **8** overcome, restrain **9** alleviate, frustrate, overpower **10** annihilate, contravene, neutralize

counteraction 8 negation **10** offsetting, opposition **13** contravention, nullification **14** neutralization

counteractive 7 adverse **8** inimical **10** corrective **11** unfavorable **12** antagonistic, neutralizing

counteractor 7 negator **9** nullifier, offsetter **11** neutralizer

counteragent 8 antidote **9** antitoxin **10** antipoison **11** double agent

counterbalance 5 amend, check **6** cancel, offset, redeem, set off **7** correct, rectify **8** atone for, equalize, make good, outweigh **9** make up for **10** balance out, neutralize, outbalance, recompense **12** compensation

counterfeit 4 copy, fake, sham **5** bogus, fraud, phony **6** ersatz, forged **7** feigned, forgery **8** spurious **9** facsimile, imitation, simulated **10** artificial, fraudulent, substitute **11** make-believe

Counterfeiters, The
author: **9** Andre Gide

countermand 4 void **5** annul, quash **6** cancel, recall, repeal, revoke **7** abolish, nullify, rescind, retract, reverse **8** abrogate, call back, disenact, override, overrule, set aside, withdraw, write off **12** disestablish

counterpart 4 copy, mate, twin **5** equal, match **6** double, fellow **8** parallel **9** duplicate **11** correlative **12** doppelganger **13** correspondent, spitting image

counterpoise 7 balance **9** stability **11** equilibrium

countersign 4 sign **7** certify, confirm, endorse **8** validate **9** authorize **11** corroborate **12** authenticate

countess
French: **8** comtesse
Italian: **8** contessa

countless 6 myriad, untold **7** endless **8** infinite **9** limitless, unlimited **10** numberless, unnumbered **11** innumerable, measureless **12** immeasurable, incalculable **13** multitudinous

Count of Monte Cristo, The
author: **14** Alexandre Dumas (pere)
character: **6** Albert, Haydee, Morrel **7** Fernand (Comte de Morcerf) **8** Danglars, Mercedes **9** Abbe Faria, Valentine, Villefort **10** Caderousse, Maximilian **12** Edmond Dantes
prison: **10** Chateau d'If

count on 6 expect **7** hope for **10** anticipate

countrified 5 rural **6** rustic **9** backwoods **15** unsophisticated

country 4 area, farm, land **5** realm, rural, state **6** nation, people, public, region, rustic, simple, sticks **7** boonies, farming, kingdom, natives, scenery, terrain **8** citizens, district, homeland, populace **9** backwoods, boondocks, community, landscape, territory **10** fatherland, native land, native soil, population, provincial, rural areas **11** farming area, hinterlands, inhabitants, nationality **12** commonwealth **15** unsophisticated

Country Cousin
author: **16** Louis Auchincloss

Country Girl, The
director: **12** George Seaton
based on play by: **13** Clifford Odets
cast: **10** Bing Crosby, Grace Kelly **11** Anthony Ross **13** William Holden
Oscar for: **7** actress (Kelly)

countryman 4 hick, rube **5** yokel **6** farmer, rustic **7** bumpkin, hayseed, peasant **8** landsman **10** clodhopper, compatriot, provincial

Country of the Pointed Firs, The
author: **15** Sarah Orne Jewett

country place 4 farm **5** manor **6** estate

countryside 6 sticks **7** boonies **9** backwater, backwoods, boondocks, rural area **10** hinterland

count up 3 add **5** tally, total **6** reckon **7** compute **9** calculate

count upon 6 expect **7** foresee **10** anticipate

coup 3 act **4** blow, deed, feat **6** stroke **12** master stroke

coup de grace 9 deathblow **11** mercy stroke **12** decisive blow **15** finishing stroke
literally: **11** blow of mercy

coup de main 14 surprise attack **17** sudden development
literally: **15** blow from the hand

coup d'etat 6 mutiny **8** uprising **9** overthrow, rebellion **10** revolution, subversion

coup de theatre 15 theatrical trick

coup d'oeil 11 quick glance
literally: **14** stroke of the eye

Couperin, Francois (Le Grand)
born: **5** Paris **6** France
composer of: **9** La Sultane, Les Fastes (de la grande et ancienne) **13** Concert Royaux **16** Apotheose de Lulli, Pieces de Clavecin **17** Lecons des Tenebres **20** Les Follies Francoises **31** Le Parnasse on l'Apotheose de Corelli

couple 3 duo, tie **4** bind, join, link, pair, yoke **5** hitch **6** fasten **7** connect, doublet, twosome **10** man and wife **11** man and woman **14** husband and wife

coupler 4 link, lock **5** clasp, hitch **6** buckle **8** fastener **9** fastening

Couples
author: **10** John Updike

coupling 5 clasp, hatch **6** hookup, yoking **7** joining, pairing **8** hitching **9** attaching, fastening **10** attachment, connecting, connection

courage 4 grit, guts, sand **5** nerve, pluck, spunk, valor **6** daring, mettle **7** bravery **8** boldness **9** derring-do, fortitude **11** intrepidity **12** fearlessness **13** dauntlessness **16** stoutheartedness

courageous 4 bold **5** brave, manly **6** dogged, heroic **7** dashing, doughty, gallant, valiant **8** fearless, intrepid, resolute, stalwart, unafraid, valorous **9** dauntless **10** chivalrous **11** indomitable **12** boldspirited **13** stronghearted

Courbet, Jean Desire Gustave
born: **6** France, Ornans
artwork: **16** The Artist's Studio, The Stonebreakers **17** The Burial at Ornans **19** The Peasants of Flagey **25** Self-Portrait with a Black Dog

courier 4 mule **5** envoy **6** herald, legate, runner **7** Gabriel, mailman, Mercury, postman **8** emissary **9** go-between, harbinger, messenger, postrider **11** herald angel, internuncio

course 3 run, way **4** flow, gush, mode, path, pour, race, road **5** march, orbit, round, route, surge, track **6** action, circle, method, policy, stream **7** channel, circuit, classes, conduct, lessons, passage, subject **8** behavior, lectures, sequence **9** direction, procedure, unfolding **10** curriculum, racecourse, trajectory **11** development, progression

court 3 bar, woo **4** hall, quad, seek, suit, yard **5** bench, manor, plaza, staff, train **6** atrium, castle, homage, induce, invite, palace, pursue, wooing **7** address, attract, chateau, cortege, council, flatter, hearing, meeting, provoke, retinue, session **8** advisers, assembly, audience, blandish, fawn upon, pander to, respects, run after **9** entourage, following **10** attendants, quadrangle **13** solicitations

Courtenay, Tom
born: **4** Hull **7** England
roles: **9** Billy Liar **10** The Dresser **36** The Loneliness of the Long Distance Runner

courteous 4 kind, mild **5** civil **6** polite **7** refined, tactful **8** gracious, mannerly, wellbred **10** diplomatic, respectful, soft-spoken **11** considerate, well-behaved **12** wellmannered

courtesy 5 favor **7** manners, regards, respect **8** civility, kindness, respects **9** deference, gallantry, gentility **10** indulgence, politeness, refinement **11** cultivation **12** graciousness **13** consideration

courtier 4 beau **7** gallant **8** cavalier **9** attendant **18** gentleman-in-waiting

Courtier, The
author: **21** Baldassare Castiglione

Court Jester
director: **11** Melvin Frank **12** Norman Panama

cast: 9 Danny Kaye
11 Glynis Johns **13** Basil
Rathbone **14** Angela
Lansbury

courtly 5 suave **6** polite **7** elegant, gallant, genteel, refined,
stately **8** debonair, decorous,
highbred, ladylike, mannerly,
polished **9** civilized, courteous,
dignified **10** chivalrous
11 blue-blooded, gentlemanly
12 aristocratic **14** silk-
stockinged

courtship 4 suit **6** wooing
14 keeping company

Courtship of Eddie's Father, The
character: 4 Tina **10** Tom
Corbett **12** Eddie Corbett,
Norman Tinker **13** Mrs
Livingston
cast: 9 Bill Bixby **11** Brandon
Cruz, James Komack
12 Miyoshi Umeki **15** Kristina Holland

Courtship of Miles Standish, The
author: 24 Henry Wadsworth
Longfellow
character: 9 John Alden,
Priscilla

courtyard 4 area, quad **9** curtilage, enclosure **10** quadrangle

cousin 7 kinsman **8** relation,
relative **9** kinswoman

Cousin Bette
author: 14 Honore de Balzac
character: 6 Crevel **7** Adeline **10** Baron Hulot
11 Mme Marneffe **13** Hortense Hulot, Marechal Hulot **14** Lisbeth Fischer
23 Count Wenceslas
Steinbock

Cousin Pons
author: 14 Honore de Balzac

Cousy, Bob
nickname: 12 Mr Basketball
sport: 10 basketball
position: 5 guard
team: 13 Boston Celtics

couturier, couturiere 8 designer **9** midinette **10** dressmaker, seamstress

cove 3 bay **5** inlet **6** lagoon
7 estuary

covenant 3 vow **4** bond, oath,
pact **6** pledge, treaty **7** bargain,
promise **8** contract **9** agreement **15** solemn agreement
Hebrew: 4 Brit **5** Berit, Brith
6 Berith

Covenant, The
author: 13 James Michener

cover *see* **box**

coverage 7 payment **8** analy-

cover 3 cap, lid, top
4 case, hide, hood, mask,
veil, wrap **5** cloak, cross,
guard, lay on, put on,
quilt **6** asylum, clothe, defend, embody, enwrap,
jacket, refuge, report,
screen, sheath, shield,
shroud, take in, tell of
7 binding, blanket, conceal,
contain, defense, embrace,
envelop, include, involve,
obscure, overlay, protect,
put over, secrete, sheathe,
shelter, wrapper, write up
8 comprise, deal with, describe, disguise, envelope,
pass over, traverse
9 chronicle, comforter, eiderdown, encompass, sanctuary **10** camouflage,
comprehend, encasement,
protection **11** concealment,
hiding place

sis **9** indemnity, reporting
10 protection, publishing
11 description **12** broadcasting **13** reimbursement

covered 4 clad **6** hidden
7 aimed at, cloaked, guarded,
insured **8** included, overlaid,
screened **9** blanketed, concealed, protected, sheltered,
traversed **10** overspread

covering 6 casing, sheath
7 wrapper **8** envelope, wrapping **11** descriptive, explanatory **12** introductory

coverlet 5 quilt, throw **6** afghan, spread **7** blanket **9** bedspread, comforter

Coverly, Sir Roger de
character in: 12 The
Spectator
authors: 6 Steele **7** Addison

covert 6 hidden, secret, veiled
7 sub rosa, unknown **9** concealed, disguised **11** clandestine **13** surreptitious

cover up 4 hide, mask, veil
6 hush up **7** conceal **8** disguise, keep back, suppress,
withhold **9** gloss over,
whitewash

cover-up 4 mask **5** blind
6 screen **8** disguise **9** whitewash **11** concealment

covet 4 want **5** crave, fancy
6 desire **7** long for

covetous 6 greedy **7** craving,
envious, jealous, lustful, selfish **8** desirous, grasping, yearning **9** mercenary, rapacious
10 avaricious

covetousness 4 envy **5** greed
7 avarice **8** jealousy, rapacity
10 greediness **12** graspingness
13 mercenariness

covey 4 bevy **5** flock, group
6 family

cow 4 beef **5** abash, bossy,
bully, deter, scare **6** bovine,
cattle, dismay **7** terrify
8 browbeat, bulldoze, frighten,
threaten **9** terrorize **10** discourage, dishearten, intimidate, make cringe
young: 4 calf **6** heifer

coward 3 cad **5** sissy **6** craven
7 caitiff, chicken, dastard,
milksop **8** poltroon **11** Milquetoast, mollycoddle, yellowbelly

Coward, Sir Noel
author of: 8 Hay Fever
9 Cavalcade **10** Sigh No
More **12** Blithe Spirit, Private Lives **14** In Which We
Serve, Nude with Violin
15 Design for Living

cowardliness 8 timidity
10 yellowness **12** irresolution
13 pusillanimity, spinelessness
18 chicken-heartedness

cowardly 5 shaky, timid
6 afraid, craven, yellow **7** anxious, fearful, gutless, nervous
8 timorous **9** dastardly, tremulous **10** frightened **11** lily-
livered **12** apprehensive,
fainthearted, uncourageous
13 pusillanimous, yellow-
bellied **14** chicken-hearted

Cowardly Lion
character in: 13 The Wizard
of Oz
author: 4 Baum

cowboy 6 drover, gaucho
7 vaquero **8** buckaroo
10 roughrider **12** broncobuster,
cattle-herder

cowed 5 fazed **7** abashed,
crushed, subdued **8** dismayed
11 intimidated **12** disconcerted **14** under one's thumb

cower 5 crawl, quail, toady
6 cringe, flinch, grovel, recoil,
shrink **7** tremble, truckle
8 bootlick, draw back

cowl 4 cope, hood **5** cloak

Cowley, Malcolm
author of: 12 Exile's Return
16 A Second Flowering
27 And I Worked at the
Writer's Trade **28** The
Dream of the Golden
Mountains

coworker 7 partner **8** teammate **9** associate, colleague
10 accomplice **11** confederate
12 collaborator

Cowper, William
author of: 7 The Task 11 The Cast-Away

Cowperwood, Frank
character in: 8 The Titan 12 The Financier
author: 7 Dreiser

coxcomb 3 fop 4 beau 5 dandy 8 popinjay

coy 3 shy 5 timid 6 demure, modest 7 bashful, prudish 8 blushing, sheepish, skittish, timorous 9 diffident, kittenish, shrinking 10 coquettish, overmodest

Coyote State
nickname of: 11 South Dakota

cozen 3 con, gyp 4 bilk, coax, dupe, gull, rook 5 cheat, trick 6 fleece 7 deceive, defraud, swindle, wheedle 9 bamboozle, victimize

cozener 4 fake 5 cheat, fraud, quack 6 con man 8 deceiver, swindler 9 charlatan, trickster 10 mountebank 13 confidence man

coziness 6 warmth 7 comfort 8 intimacy, snugness 11 contentment

cozy 4 easy, snug 5 comfy, homey 7 restful 8 homelike, relaxing 9 gemutlich, simpatico 11 comfortable 16 snug as a bug in a rug
French: 6 intime

Cozzens, James Gould
author of: 12 Guard of Honor 15 By Love Possessed

CPA 7 auditor 10 accountant, bookkeeper 25 certified public accountant

crab 4 carp 5 crank, gripe, grump 6 grouch, grouse 8 complain, sourball 9 shellfish 10 crustacean, curmudgeon
constellation of: 6 Cancer

Crabbe, Buster
real name: 20 Clarence Linden Crabbe
nickname: 16 King of the Serials
born: 9 Oakland CA
roles: 6 Tarzan 10 Buck Rogers 11 Flash Gordon 15 King of the Jungle

crabbed 4 mean, sour 6 cranky, morose 7 grouchy, peevish, pinched 8 churlish, spiteful 9 irascible, irritable, rancorous

crabby 5 cross, testy 6 cranky, touchy 7 grouchy, peevish 8 petulant, snappish 9 irritable 10 ill-humored, out of

sorts 11 ill-tempered 12 cantankerous

crack 3 gag, jab, pop 4 chip, clap, gash, gibe, jest, joke, quip, rent, rift, slit, snap 5 break, burst, cleft, split, taunt 6 cleave, insult, report 7 crackle, crevice, fissure, give way, rupture, thunder 8 fracture, splinter 9 break down, wisecrack, witticism 10 go to pieces

cracked 3 mad 4 daft, nuts 5 crazy, nutty 6 crazed, insane 8 demented, deranged, unhinged 10 unbalanced 12 mad as a hatter 13 off one's rocker, out of one's head 14 off one's trolley 15 mad as a March hare

cracker 5 snack, wafer 7 biscuit, redneck 10 party favor 11 backsetter 12 backwoodsman

crackerjack 2 A-1 3 ace 4 a-one, fine 5 super 6 superb, tip-top 8 splendid, terrific 9 excellent, fantastic, first-rate, wonderful 10 first-class

Cracker State
nickname of: 7 Georgia

crackle 4 snap 5 craze, crink 9 crepitate

crackpot 3 nut, odd 4 fool, kook 5 balmy, crank, flake, freak, kinky, kooky, loony, nutty, wacko 6 freaky, insane, looney, madman, maniac, weirdo 7 dingbat, foolish, lunatic, oddball 9 character, eccentric, screwball 11 impractical

cracksman 4 yegg 7 burglar 10 cat burglar 14 second-story man

crackup 5 crash, smash, split, wreck 6 mishap, pileup 7 breakup, debacle, smashup 8 accident, calamity, collapse, disaster 9 breakdown, collision, splitting 10 exhaustion, shellshock 11 catastrophe, prostration 14 disintegration

cradle 3 hug 4 crib, font, rock 6 cuddle, enfold, origin, source, spring 7 nursery, snuggle 8 bassinet, fountain 10 birthplace, wellspring 12 fountainhead

craft 3 art 4 boat, ruse, ship, wile 5 guile, knack, plane, skill, trade 6 deceit, vessel 7 ability, calling, cunning, know-how, mastery, perfidy, pursuit 8 airplane, artifice, business, commerce, deftness, fineness, industry, intrigue, trickery, vocation 9 adeptness,

chicanery, deception, duplicity, expertise, technique 10 adroitness, artfulness, competency, craftiness, employment, expertness, handicraft, occupation 11 proficiency

craftiness 4 ruse, wile 5 guile 7 cunning, slyness 8 artifice, foxiness, scheming, trickery, wiliness 9 chicanery 10 artfulness 11 machination

craftsman 4 hand 5 smith 6 worker, wright 7 artisan 8 mechanic

crafty 3 sly 4 foxy, wily 5 canny, sharp 6 artful, astute, shifty, shrewd, tricky 7 cunning, devious 8 guileful, plotting, scheming 9 deceitful, deceptive, designing, dishonest, underhand, unethical 10 intriguing, perfidious, suspicious 11 calculating

crag 3 tor 4 rock 5 bluff, cliff 9 precipice

craggy 5 rocky, rough, sheer, steep, stony 6 abrupt, jagged, ragged, rugged, snaggy 7 scraggy 8 bouldery 9 rockbound 10 rock-ribbed 11 precipitous

Crain, Jeanne
born: 9 Barstow CA
roles: 5 Pinky 6 Margie 9 State Fair 17 Cheaper by the Dozen 19 A Letter to Three Wives

cram 3 jam 4 fill, pack 5 crowd, force, grind, press, stuff 7 congest, squeeze 8 compress 9 overcrowd, study hard

Cram, Ralph
architect of: 17 US Military Academy (West Point) 29 Cathedral of Saint John the Divine (NYC)
style: 13 Gothic Revival

crammed 4 full 6 filled, packed 7 studied, stuffed 9 jam-packed 11 overflowing, well-stocked

cramp 4 pang 5 block, check, crick, limit, spasm 6 hamper, hinder, stitch, stymie, thwart 7 prevent, seizure 8 handicap, obstruct, restrain, restrict 9 frustrate 12 charley horse

cramped 5 close, tight 6 narrow 7 compact, pinched 8 confined 10 compressed, restrained, restricted

Cranach, Lucas (Lukas) (the Elder)
born: 7 Kronach, Germany
artwork: 6 Luther 10 Adam and Eve 11 Crucifixion 14 Apollo and Diana

15 Rest on the Flight
18 The Judgment of Paris
22 Duke and Duchess of
Saxony

Cranaus
king of: 6 Athens, Attica
wife: 6 Pedias
daughter: 6 Atthis, Cranae
renamed Athens: 6 Attica

cranberry 9 Vaccinium
19 Vaccinium vitis-idaea
20 Vaccinium macrocarpon
varieties: 3 bog 4 rock, tree
5 large, small 8 American,
European, highbush, moun-
tain 10 Australian

crane 4 bird, boom 5 davit,
heron 7 derrick 10 wading
bird
group of: 5 sedge, siege
constellation of: 4 Grus

Crane, Bob
born: 11 Waterbury CT
roles: 12 Colonel Hogan, Hogan's Heroes

Crane, Hart
author of: 9 The Bridge
14 White Buildings

Crane, Ichabod
character in: 23 The Legend
of Sleepy Hollow
author: 6 Irving

Crane, Roy
creator/artist of: 9 Buz Sawyer, Wash Tubbs 11 Captain
Easy

Crane, Stephen
author of: 11 The Open
Boat 20 The Red Badge of
Courage 23 Maggie: A Girl
of the Streets 24 The Bride
Comes to Yellow Sky

Cranford
author: 10 Mrs Gaskell

cranium 4 head 5 skull 6 noggin 8 brain box, brainpan
9 brain case

crank 4 turn, whim 5 brace,
winch 6 grouch, handle 7 fanatic 8 crotchet 9 eccentric

cranky 5 cross, testy 6 crabby,
touchy 7 bearish, grouchy,
peevish, waspish 8 captious,
petulant 9 crotchety, irascible,
splenetic 10 ill-humored, out
of sorts 11 ill-tempered
12 cantankerous

cranny 3 gap 4 nook, slit
5 break, chink, cleft, crack,
notch, split 7 crevice, fissure
8 cleavage

crash 3 din 4 bang, boom,
bump, dash, ruin 5 crack,
slump, smash, wreck 6 hurtle,
invade, pileup, plunge, racket,
slip in, topple, tumble
7 bumping, clangor, clatter,

collide, crackup, decline, failure, hitting, intrude, setback,
shatter, smashup, sneak in
8 accident, smashing, toppling,
tumbling 9 collision, recession 10 bankruptcy, depression, shattering

crass 5 crude, cruel, gross
6 coarse, oafish, vulgar
7 boorish 8 uncaring 9 inelegant, unfeeling, unrefined
10 unpolished 11 hardhearted,
insensitive 13 unsympathetic

crassness 9 crudeness, grossness, vulgarity 10 coarseness,
inelegance, oafishness
11 boorishness 13 insensitivity

Crataeis
daughter: 6 Scylia

Cratchit, Bob
character in: 15 A Christmas
Carol
author: 7 Dickens

crate 3 box, car 4 auto, case,
pack 5 plane 6 jalopy, pallet
8 airplane 9 container

crater 3 pit 4 hole 6 cavity
10 depression

Cratus
origin: 5 Greek
personifies: 8 strength

cravat 3 tie 5 ascot, scarf,
stock 7 necktie 11 neckerchief

crave 4 need, want 5 covet
6 desire 7 hope for, long for,
pine for, require, sigh for,
wish for 8 yearn for 9 hunger
for, lust after, thirst for
11 hanker after, have a yen
for 13 have a fancy for

craven 3 low 4 base 5 timid
6 scared, yellow 7 fearful, low-
down 8 cowardly, timorous
9 dastardly 10 frightened
11 lily-livered 12 mean-
spirited 13 pusillanimous
14 chicken-hearted

craving 3 yen 4 need 6 desire,
hunger, thirst 7 longing
9 hankering

Crawford, Broderick
real name: 24 William Broderick Crawford
wife: 11 Jan Sterling
born: 14 Philadelphia PA
roles: 6 The Mob 10 The Interns 12 Of Mice and Men
13 Born Yesterday, Highway
Patrol 14 All the King's
Men (Oscar)

Crawford, Henry
character in: 13 Mansfield
Park
author: 6 Austen

Crawford, Joan
real name: 17 Lucille Fay Le
Sueur

husband: 12 Franchot Tone
18 Douglas Fairbanks Jr
daughter: 6 Cheryl
9 Christina
born: 12 San Antonio TX
biography: 13 Mommie
Dearest
roles: 8 The Women
10 Grand Hotel 13 Mildred
Pierce (Oscar) 26 What Ever
Happened to Baby Jane

crawl 4 drag, inch, poke,
worm 5 creep, mosey
6 squirm, wiggle, writhe
7 slither, wriggle

Crawley, Rawdon
character in: 10 Vanity Fair
author: 9 Thackeray

crayon 5 chalk, draft 6 pastel,
pencil, sketch 7 drawing
8 charcoal

craze 3 fad 4 rage 5 furor,
mania 6 dement 7 derange,
passion, unhinge
11 infatuation

crazed 3 mad 6 insane
7 cracked, lunatic 8 demented,
deranged

crazy 3 mad, odd 4 avid, daft,
gaga, keen, nuts, wild 5 nutty,
rabid, silly, weird 6 absurd,
far-out, insane, stupid, unwise 7 berserk, bizarre,
cracked, excited, foolish, frantic, idiotic, strange, touched,
unusual, zealous 8 demented,
deranged, maniacal, peculiar,
uncommon, unhinged 9 fanatical, foolhardy, imprudent,
laughable, senseless 10 hysterical, infatuated, outrageous,
passionate, ridiculous, unbalanced 11 smitten with 12 enthusiastic, mad as a hatter
13 out of one's head 15 mad
as a March hare

creak 4 rasp 5 grate, grind
6 scrape, screak, squeak
7 screech

Creakle
character in: 16 David
Copperfield
author: 7 Dickens

cream 3 top 4 beat, best, drub
5 elite 6 choice, flower 7 the
pick, trounce 8 greatest, off-
white 14 creme de la creme

Cream, Arnold Raymond
real name of: 10 Joe Walcott

cream of the cream
French: 14 creme de la
creme

Cream of the Jest, The
author: 17 James Branch
Cabell

creamy 5 thick, foamy
6 smooth, yellow 8 emulsive

crease 4 fold **5** crimp, pleat, ridge **6** furrow, pucker, ruffle, rumple **7** crimple, crinkle, wrinkle **9** corrugate **11** corrugation

create 4 form, make, mold **5** cause, erect, found, set up **6** design, devise, invent **7** appoint, concoct, develop, fashion **8** conceive, contrive, organize **9** construct, establish, fabricate, formulate, institute, originate

creation 5 world **6** making, nature **8** building, devising, erection, founding **9** all things, formation, handiwork, invention **10** brainchild, conception, concoction, fashioning, production **11** development, fabrication, institution, origination **12** construction **13** establishment

Creation
  author: 9 Gore Vidal

creative 8 fanciful, original **9** ingenious, inventive **11** imaginative, resourceful

creator 5 maker **6** author, father, framer **7** founder **8** begetter, designer, inventor, producer **9** architect, generator, initiator **10** originator

creature 3 man **4** bird, fish **5** beast, human **6** animal, insect, mammal, mortal, person **7** critter, reptile **9** earthling, quadruped **10** individual, vertebrate **12** invertebrate

credence 5 faith, trust **6** belief, credit **8** reliance **9** certainty, certitude **10** confidence **11** reliability **13** believability **14** acceptableness, dependableness **15** trustworthiness

credentials 6 permit **7** diploma, license, voucher **9** reference **11** certificate, testimonial **13** authorization

credenza 5 shelf, table **6** buffet **8** bookcase **9** sideboard

credible 6 likely **7** tenable **8** possible, probable, reliable **9** plausible, thinkable **10** believable, dependable, imaginable, reasonable **11** conceivable, trustworthy

credit 3 buy **4** time **5** glory, honor, trust **6** accept, assign, esteem, rely on **7** acclaim, ascribe, believe, fall for, swallow **9** allowance, attribute, recognize **10** prepayment **11** acknowledge, recognition **12** commendation **14** acknowledgment

creditable 6 worthy **8** laudable **9** admirable, estimable,

reputable **11** commendable, meritorious, respectable **12** praiseworthy

credo 4 code, rule **5** maxim, motto, tenet **8** doctrine **10** philosophy

credulous 5 naive **8** gullible, trusting **9** believing **12** overtrustful, unsuspecting, unsuspicious **13** unquestioning **15** unsophisticated

Cree
  language family: 9 Algonkian **10** Algonquian
  tribe: 10 Plains Cree **13** Woodlands Cree
  location: 6 Canada **8** Manitoba
  related to: 8 Chippewa

creed 5 dogma **6** belief, canons, gospel **8** doctrine

creek 3 run **4** rill **5** brook **6** branch, spring, stream **7** freshet, rivulet **10** millstream, small river

Creek
  language family: 10 Muskhogean
  location: 7 Alabama, Florida, Georgia **11** Mississippi
  leader: 8 Red Eagle **15** William McIntosh **20** Alexander McGillivray

Creek Mary's Blood
  author: 8 Dee Brown

creep 4 inch, worm **5** crawl, sneak, steal **6** dawdle, squirm, writhe **7** slither, wriggle

creeper 3 ivy **4** bird, iron, vine, worm **5** snake **7** climber, crawler, grapnel, trailer

creepy 4 eery **5** eerie, scary **6** crawly, spooky, uneasy **12** apprehensive

cremate 4 burn, char, fire, sear **5** roast **6** ignite, kindle, scorch **8** enkindle **10** incinerate **11** conflagrate **17** consume with flames

creme de banane
  type: 7 liqueur
  flavor: 6 banana
  color: 6 yellow

creme de cacao
  type: 6 brandy **7** liqueur
  origin: 6 France
  flavor: 9 chocolate
  color: 5 brown, white
  drink: 11 Fifth Avenue
  with rum: 6 Panama
  with tequila: 8 Toreador
  with vodka: 9 Ninotchka **11** Russian Bear **12** Velvet Hammer, White Russian

creme de cassis
  type: 7 liqueur
  origin: 6 France **8** Burgundy

  flavor: 12 black currant
  with gin: 8 Parisian

creme de fraise
  type: 7 liqueur
  flavor: 10 strawberry

creme de framboise
  type: 7 liqueur
  flavor: 9 raspberry

creme de la creme 3 top **4** best **5** cream, elite **6** choice, flower **8** choicest, very best **12** choicest part **15** cream of the cream

creme de menthe
  type: 7 liqueur
  flavor: 4 mint
  color: 5 green, white
  with brandy: 7 Stinger
  with cream: 11 Grasshopper
  with gin: 6 Caruso, Virgin

creme de noyau
  type: 7 liqueur
  flavor: 6 almond

creme de violette
  type: 7 liqueur
  flavor: 7 violets
  color: 8 lavender

creme Yvette
  type: 7 liqueur
  origin: 12 United States
  flavor: 7 violets
  with gin: 9 Union Jack

Crenna, Richard
  born: 12 Los Angeles CA
  roles: 9 Death Ship **13** Our Miss Brooks, The Real McCoys

Creole 6 patois **7** criollo, dialect, Haitian **10** West Indian

Creole State
  nickname of: 9 Louisiana

Creon
  king of: 6 Thebes **7** Corinth
  father: 9 Lycaethus, Menoeceus
  sister: 7 Jocasta
  daughter: 6 Creusa, Glauce
  nephew: 7 Oedipus **8** Eteocles **9** Polynices
  niece: 6 Ismene **8** Antigone
  defeated: 18 Seven against Thebes

crescendo
  music: 22 gradually getting louder
    abbreviation: 5 cresc

crescent 3 arc, bow **4** arch **5** curve **8** half-moon

crescit eundo 15 it grows as it goes
  motto of: 9 New Mexico

Cresius
  epithet of: 8 Dionysus
  means: 6 Cretan

Cresphontes
  member of: 8 Heraclid

Cressida
father: **12** Aristomachus
brother: **7** Temenus
11 Polyphontes
wife: **6** Merope
father-in-law: **8** Cypselus
son: **7** Aepytus
controlled: **8** Messenia
invaded: **12** Peloponnesus

Cressida
also: **8** Criseyde **9** Crisseyde
based on characters of:
7 Bryseis **8** Chryseis
setting: **9** Trojan War
loved: **7** Troilus
deserted Troilus for:
8 Diomedes

crest 3 tip, top **4** apex, arms,
comb, peak, tuft **5** crown,
plume **6** emblem, height, summit **7** topknot **8** pinnacle
10 coat of arms, escutcheon

crestfallen 8 dejected, downcast **9** depressed, woebegone
10 despondent, dispirited
11 discouraged, downhearted,
low-spirited **12** disappointed,
disheartened

Creta
daughter: **8** Pasiphae

Cretaceous period
dinosaur from: **9** Euhelopus,
Iguanodon **10** Allosaurus,
Antrodemus **11** Anatosaurus,
Ankylsaurus, Deinonychus,
Gorgosaurus, Triceratops
12 Lambeosaurus, Ornithomimus **13** Albertosaurus, Corythosaurus, Hypselosaurus,
Hypsilophodon, Palaeoscincus, Protoceratops, Stru-
thiomimus, Styracosaurus,
Tyrannosaurus **14** Psittacosaurus, Thescelosaurus
15 Parasaurolophus,
Procheneosaurus

Cretan bull
also: **15** Marathonian bull
form: **4** bull
son: **8** Minotaur
captured on: **5** Crete
captured by: **8** Hercules
roamed: **8** Marathon
recaptured by: **7** Theseus

Cretan Mythology
goddess of fishermen/hunt-
ers/sailors: **11** Britomartis
corresponds to Greek:
7 Artemis
goddess of the sea:
8 Dictynna
maze: **9** labyrinth
monster: **8** Minotaur

Crete *see box*

Cretheis
husband: **7** Acastus
killed by: **6** Peleus

Cretheus
founder of: **6** Iolcus
father: **6** Aeolus
mother: **7** Enarete
brother: **9** Salmoneus
wife: **4** Tyro
son: **5** Aeson **6** Pheres
8 Amythaon
companion: **6** Aeneas

Creusa
also: **6** Glauce
father: **5** Creon, Priam **8** Cychreus **10** Erechtheus
mother: **6** Hecuba
husband: **6** Aeneas **7** Telamon
son: **3** Ion **8** Ascanius
bride of: **5** Jason
killed by: **5** magic, Medea

crevasse 3 gap **4** rift **5** abyss,
break, chasm, cleft, gorge,
gulch, gully, split **6** breach, divide **7** fissure

crevice 4 rent, rift, slit
5 chasm, cleft, crack, split
6 breach **7** fissure **8** crevasse,
fracture

crew 3 mob **4** band, body,
herd, mass, pack, team
5 corps, force, group, hands,
horde, party, squad, troop
6 seamen, throng **7** company,
sailors **8** mariners **9** multitude,
seafarers **10** assemblage,
complement

crib 3 bed, bin, cot, hut, key
4 pony **5** cheat, shack, stall,
steal **6** creche, manger **7** purloin **8** bassinet **10** plagiarize

cribbage
score kept on: **5** board
points/game: **8** sixty-one
third hand: **4** crib

Crich, Gerald
character in: **11** Women in
Love
author: **8** Lawrence

Crichton, Michael
author of: **5** Congo **6** Sphere
9 Rising Sun **12** Jurassic
Park **14** The Terminal Man
18 The Andromeda Strain
20 The Great Train
Robbery

cricket *see box*

cricket
variety: **4** bush, cave, sand,
tree **5** camel, field, house
6 ground **9** Jerusalem,
pygmy mole

Cries and Whispers
director: **12** Ingmar Bergman
cast: **10** Liv Ullmann **12** Ingrid Thulin **16** Harriet
Andersson

crime 3 sin **4** tort **5** wrong
6 felony **7** misdeed, offense,
outrage **8** foul play, iniquity,
villainy **10** misconduct, wrongdoing **11** abomination, lawbreaking, malfeasance,
misdemeanor **13** transgression

Crime and Punishment
author: **16** Fyodor Dostoevsky
character: **5** Sonya **6** Dounia
7 Porfiry **9** Razumihin
11 Raskolnikov

Crete
other name: **5** Kriti **6** Candia
capital/largest city: **5** Canea **8** Iraklion
others: **3** Hag **4** Lato **5** Khora, Sitia, Zakro **6** Anoyia, Candia, Khania, Lisamo, Mallia, Meleme, Retimo **7** Malerni
8 Kastelli, Nikolaos, Sphakion **9** Heraclion, Heraklion, Re-
thymnon, Tympakion **11** Palaiophora
government: division of: **6** Greece
monetary unit: **7** drachma
mountain: **3** Ida **5** Dikte, Phino **6** Juktas **7** Lasithi, Madaras **8** Leuka Ori, Theodore, Thriphte **9** Psiloriti
highest point: **3** Ida
sea: **5** Crete **6** Aegean **13** Mediterranean
physical feature:
bay: **4** Suda **5** Kanca **6** Kisamo, Mesara
cape: **4** Buza **5** Liano **6** Salome, Sidero, Spatha **7** Stavros **8** Lithinon, Sidheros
gulf: **6** Khania **9** Merabello
people: **7** Candiot, Cretans, Minoans **9** Caphtorim, Sphak-
iots **11** Philistines
artist: **7** El Greco
author: **11** Kazantzakis
conqueror: **8** Metellus
king: **5** Minos
language: **5** Greek **6** Minoan **7** Linear A, Linear B
religion: **14** Greek Orthodoxy
place:
ruins: **15** Palace at Knossos

cricket
  players/team: 6 eleven
  equipment: 3 bat **4** bail,
  ball **5** stump **6** wicket
  position: 5 gully, mid on,
  slops **6** bowler, long on,
  mid off **7** batsman, fine
  leg, long off **8** third man
  9 mid wicket, square leg
  10 cover point, extra
  cover, silly mid on
  11 silly mid off **12** wicket
  keeper **13** deep mid
  wicket **16** backward
  short leg
  lines: 7 creases
  period of play: 4 over
  7 innings
  championship game:
  9 test match
  England/Australia match:
  8 the Ashes

criminal 4 hood **5** crook, felon,
wrong **6** guilty, outlaw
7 crooked, culprit, illegal, illicit,
lawless **8** culpable, offender,
unlawful, wasteful **9** felonious,
senseless, wrongdoer **10** abominable, delinquent, indictable,
lawbreaker, malefactor, outrageous, villainous **11** blameworthy, disgraceful,
lawbreaking **12** transgressor

crimp 4 curl, fold, kink, wave
5 clamp, flute, frill, frizz **7** crinkle, frizzle, wrinkle **8** obstacle

crimple 4 curl **6** pucker **7** crinkle, crumple, wrinkle
9 corrugate

crimson 3 red **5** blush, flush
6 redden **7** carmine, scarlet

cringe 4 duck **5** cower, dodge,
quail, toady **6** blench, flinch,
grovel, recoil, shrink **7** truckle

cringing 6 abject **7** fawning, ignoble, servile, wincing **8** cowering, toadying **9** flinching,
groveling, shrinking, sniveling

crinkle 5 crush **6** rumple, rustle
7 crumple, wrinkle

crinkly 4 wavy **5** curly, kinky
6 crimpy, frizzy **7** cockled,
crimped, crimply, puckery, ruffled, rumpled, twisted, wrinkly
8 crimpled, frizzled, puckered,
wrinkled **9** shriveled

crinoline 4 hoop **5** skirt **9** hoopskirt, petticoat **10** underskirt

Criophorus
  epithet of: 6 Hermes
  means: 9 ram bearer

cripple 4 gimp, halt, harm,
maim, stop **6** damage, impair
7 disable **8** make lame, paralyze **9** hamstring **10** debilitate,
inactivate **12** incapacitate

crisis 6 climax **9** emergency

crisp 5 brisk, fresh, nippy,
sharp, terse, witty **6** candid,
chilly, crispy, lively, snappy
7 bracing, brittle, crunchy,
pointed **8** incisive **9** energetic,
sparkling, vivacious **10** refreshing **12** invigorating

crisscross 4 awry **5** cross **8** confused, traverse

Crisseyde see **8** Cressida

Cristillo, Louis Francis
  real name of: 11 Lou Costello

criterion 3 law **4** norm, rule
5 gauge, model **7** example,
measure **8** standard **9** guidepost, precedent, principle,
yardstick **10** touchstone

critic 5 judge, mavin, scold
6 carper, censor, expert, rapper
7 analyst, arbiter, knocker, reviler **8** attacker, vilifier, virtuoso **9** authority, backbiter,
detractor, evaluator **10** antagonist, criticizer **11** cognoscente,
commentator, connoisseur,
faultfinder

critical 5 fussy, grave, hairy,
picky, risky, vital **6** urgent
7 carping, crucial, finicky,
judging, nagging, serious **8** caviling, decisive, perilous, pressing **9** dangerous, harrowing,
hazardous, judicious, momentous, sensitive **10** analytical,
censorious, derogatory, diagnostic, nitpicking, precarious
11 disparaging **12** disapproving,
faultfinding

critical situation 3 jam **4** mess
6 crisis, pickle **7** straits, trouble
8 hot water **9** deep water
10 difficulty **11** predicament

critical stage 6 climax, crisis
9 emergency

critical success
  French: 13 succes d'estime

criticism 4 fire, flak, slam
5 blame, knock **7** review **7** censure, comment **8** analysis, critique, judgment **9** aspersion,
stricture **10** commentary, evaluation **12** faultfinding

criticize 4 carp, fuss, pick
5 cavil, nag at **7** censure, nitpick, reprove **8** denounce, reproach **9** disparage

critique 6 review **8** analysis

Crna Gora see **10** Montenegro

croak 3 caw, die **4** kill, moan,
roup **7** grumble, kick off
8 complain, harsh cry **13** kick
the bucket

Croatia
  capital/largest city: 5 Zagreb
  others: 4 Knin **5** Split, Zadar
  6 Osijek, Rijeka (Fiume)
  7 Vukovar, Sibenik **8** Karlo-
  vac, Varazdin, Vinkovci
  9 Dubrovnik **10** Kostajnica
  head of state: 9 president
  government: 9 democracy
  monetary unit: 5 dinar
  mountain: 10 Julian Alps
  11 Styrian Alps
  sea: 8 Adriatic
  people: 5 Serbs **6** Croats
  7 Muslims **9** Yugoslavs
  language: 8 Croatian **10** Serbo
  Croat
  religion: 17 Catholic Christian,
  Orthodox Christian

Crocetti, Dino Paul
  real name of: 10 Dean Martin

crocodile 4 croc **6** cayman, ga-
vial, lizard **7** reptile, asurian

crock 3 jar, pot **9** container

crockery 5 china **6** dishes,
plates **7** pottery **8** clayware
9 chinaware, tableware **11** ceramic ware, earthenware
14 cups and saucers

Crock of Gold
  author: 13 James Stephens

crocus
  varieties: 4 fall, wild **5** dutch
  6 autumn, scotch **7** Chilean,
  saffron **8** tropical **9** celandine
  12 iris-flowered

Crocus
  form: 5 youth
  changed into: 12 saffron plant

Crome Yellow
  author: 12 Aldous Huxley

Crommyonian sow
  also: 5 Phaea
  killed by: 7 Theseus

Cromwell, Oliver
  also: 13 Lord Protector
  served in: 15 English Civil
  War
  fought against: 8 Charles I
  9 Cavaliers
  fought for: 10 Parliament,
  Roundheads
  regiment: 9 Ironsides
  battle: 6 Naseby, Oxford
  7 Preston **11** Marston Moor

crone 3 hag **5** witch **6** beldam
7 beldame, old wife

Cronia
  festival in: 6 Athens

Cronus
  also: 6 Cronos, Kronos
  form: 5 Titan
  father: 6 Uranus
  mother: 4 Gaea
  sister: 4 Rhea
  wife: 4 Rhea
  son: 4 Zeus 5 Hades
    8 Poseidon
  daughter: 4 Hera 6 Hestia
    7 Demeter
  corresponds to: 6 Saturn

crony 3 pal 4 ally, chum,
  mate 5 buddy 6 bunkie, cohort, friend 7 comrade
  8 bunkmate, intimate, ship-
  mate, sidekick 9 accessory, associate, companion, old
  friend 10 accomplice, bosom
  buddy 11 confederate 12 acquaintance, collaborator
  13 coconspirator

Cronyn, Hume
  wife: 12 Jessica Tandy
  born: 6 London 7 Canada,
    Ontario
  roles: 13 The Fourposter
    17 Phantom of the Opera
    19 Sunrise at Campobello

crook 3 arc, bow 4 bend, hook,
  thug, turn 5 angle, cheat,
  curve, knave, thief, twist
  6 bandit, outlaw, robber
  7 burglar 8 criminal, swindler
  9 curvature, embezzler

crooked 4 awry, bent, wily
  5 askew, bowed, shady
  6 crafty, curved, hooked,
  shifty, sneaky, spiral, warped,
  zigzag 7 corrupt, sinuous,
  twisted, winding 8 criminal,
  deformed, tortuous, twisting,
  unlawful 9 deceitful, deceptive,
  dishonest, distorted, nefarious,
  unethical 10 fraudulent, meandering, perfidious, serpentine
  11 underhanded 12 dishonorable, unscrupulous

crookedness 10 dishonesty
  11 deviousness 13 deceitfulness, double-dealing

Crookes, William
  nationality: 7 British
  invented: 8 thallium 10 radi-
    ometer 11 Crookes tube

croon 3 hum 4 sing 6 murmur,
  warble

crop 3 bob, cut, lop 4 clip,
  snip, trim 5 prune, shear,
  yield 6 growth 7 harvest, reaping 8 cut short, gleaning
  9 gathering 10 production

crop-raising 7 farming, tillage
  11 agriculture 12 agribusiness,
  truck farming 15 market
  gardening

crop up 5 arise, ensue, occur
  6 appear 7 develop, surface
  11 come to light

croquet
  equipment: 4 hoop 6 mallet,
    wicket
  variation: 5 roque
  term: 5 rover

Crosby, Bing
  real name: 17 Harry Lillis
    Crosby
  partner: 7 Bob Hope 10 Hedy
    Lamarr 13 Dorothy Lamour
  nickname: 8 Der Bingle
  wife: 8 Dixie Lee 12 Kathryn
    Grant
  born: 8 Tacoma WA
  roles: 10 Going My Way (Os-
    car), Holiday Inn 11 High
    Society 14 The Country Girl,
    White Christmas 17 The
    Bells of St Mary's
    22 Christmas in Connecticut
    Road to: 3 Rio 4 Bali
    7 Morocco 8 Hong Kong,
    Zanzibar 9 Singapore

cross 3 mad, mix 4 crux,
  ford, meet, rood 5 angry,
  blend, erase, gruff, surly,
  testy, trial 6 burden, cancel, cranky, delete, go
  over, hybrid, ordeal, shirty,
  touchy 7 amalgam, an-
  noyed, athwart, grouchy,
  oblique, peevish, trouble,
  waspish 8 captious, choleric, churlish, contrary,
  crucifix, distress, intermix,
  pass over, petulant, snappish, traverse 9 adversity,
  crotchety, half-breed, hybridize, intersect, irascible,
  irritable, querulous, splenetic, strike out, suffering
  10 affliction, difficulty, ill-
  humored, interbreed, misfortune, obliterate, out of
  sorts, transverse 11 combination, ill-tempered, intractable, tribulation
  12 cantankerous, disagreeable, intersecting

crossbar 3 bar 4 spar 5 sprit
  6 stripe

crossbreed 3 mix 8 intermix
  9 hybridize 10 interbreed

cross-fertilize 9 hybridize

crossing 4 pass 7 mixture, passage 8 blocking, opposing, traverse 9 thwarting
  10 traversing 11 hybridizing,
  intersection 13 hybridization

cross over 4 span 5 cross
  6 bridge 8 traverse

crosspiece 3 bar 4 spar 5 sprit

cross-pollinate 9 hybridize

crossroad 12 intersection,
  turning point

cross swords 5 clash, fight
  6 battle, combat, tussle 7 contend, contest 8 skirmish

crossways 7 athwart
  12 transversely

crosswise 6 across 7 athwart
  8 sideways, traverse
  10 transverse

crotchet 4 bent, whim 5 habit,
  quirk, trait 6 foible, hang-up,
  oddity, vagary, whimsy 7 caprice 8 quiddity 9 mannerism
  10 erraticism 11 peculiarity
  12 eccentricity, idiosyncrasy,
  irregularity 14 characteristic

crotchety 3 odd 5 fussy
  6 cranky 7 erratic, grouchy
  8 contrary, peculiar 9 eccentric

Crotopus
  king of: 5 Argos
  daughter: 8 Psamathe
  killed: 8 Psamathe

Crotus
  father: 3 Pan
  skilled in: 7 archery
  companion of: 5 Muses

crouch 4 bend, duck 5 cower,
  squat, stoop 6 cringe, recoil,
  shrink 9 hunch over
  10 hunker down 11 scrooch
  down, scrunch down

crow 3 daw, jay, kae 4 blow,
  brag, rook 5 boast, crake, exult, gloat, raven, strut, vaunt
  6 cackle, chough, corbie, magpie 7 corvine, jackdaw, rejoice,
  swagger, triumph, trumpet
  8 jubilate 14 cock-a-doodle-doo
  group of: 6 murder

Crow
  constellation of: 6 Corvus

Crow
  language family: 6 Siouan
  tribe: 9 River Crow
    12 Mountain Crow
  location: 7 Montana,
    Wyoming
  related to: 7 Hidatsa

crowbar 3 bar, pry 5 jimmy,
  lever

crowd 3 jam, mob, set 4 cram,
  gang, herd, host, mass, push
  5 crush, flock, group, horde,
  press, shove, surge, swarm
  6 circle, claque, clique, gather,
  huddle, legion, throng 7 cluster, coterie, elbow in,
  squeeze 8 assemble 9 gathering, multitude 10 assemblage,
  congregate 11 concentrate
  12 congregation

Crowd, The
  director: 9 King Vidor
  cast: 9 Bert Roach 11 James

Murray **15** Eleanor
Boardman

crowded 4 full **6** filled,
jammed, mobbed, packed
7 crammed, teeming **8** swarming, thronged **9** congested,
jampacked **11** overflowing

crowd out 8 displace
9 overwhelm

crown 3 cap, top **4** acme, apex,
head, pate, peak **5** crest, tiara
6 climax, diadem, noggin,
noodle, summit, top off,
wreath, zenith **7** chaplet, circlet, coronet, fulfill, garland,
perfect, royalty **8** complete,
monarchy, pinnacle, round
out **11** sovereignty

Crowne, Lenina
character in: **13** Brave New
World
author: **6** Huxley

crowning point 3 cap, tip
4 apex, peak **6** summit, vertex,
zenith **8** pinnacle

crown of thorns 4 bane
5 cross **6** burden, ordeal **7** torment **8** vexation **10** affliction
11 tribulation

crow over 5 gloat **9** brag
about **10** boast about

crucial 3 grave **6** knotty, urgent **7** serious, weighty **8** critical, decisive, pressing
9 essential, important, momentous **11** determining,
significant

Crucible, The
author: **12** Arthur Miller

crude 3 raw **5** crass, gross,
rough **6** coarse, vulgar **7** obscene, sketchy, uncouth **9** imperfect, tasteless, unrefined
10 incomplete, unfinished, unpolished, unprepared **11** uncompleted, undeveloped,
unprocessed

crudeness 7 rawness **8** bad
taste **9** crassness, grossness,
obscenity, vulgarity **10** coarseness, indelicacy
13 tastelessness

cruel 6 brutal, savage **7** inhuman, vicious **8** inhumane, pitiless, ruthless, sadistic
9 heartless, merciless, unfeeling **10** unmerciful **11** cold-
blooded, hardhearted, remorseless **15** uncompassionate

cruelty 6 sadism **8** ferocity,
savagery **9** barbarity, brutality
10 bestiality, inhumanity
11 viciousness **12** ruthlessness
13 heartlessness

cruet 3 jar, jug **6** bottle **7** ur-
ceole **9** dispenser

cruise 4 sail, scud, skim
5 coast, drift, float, glide,
sweep **6** stream, voyage **7** sea-
fare **8** navigate

Cruise, Tom
original name: **21** Thomas
Cruise Mapother
born: **2** NY **8** Syracuse
wife: **10** Mimi Rogers **12** Nicole Kidman
films: **4** Taps **6** Top Gun
7 The Firm, Rain Man
8 Cocktail **10** Far and
Away **11** Endless Love, A
Few Good Men **12** The Outsiders **13** Risky Business
15 The Color of Money
16 All the Right Moves
21 Born on the Fourth of
July

crumb 3 bit **5** grain, scrap,
shred, speck **6** morsel, sliver
8 fragment, particle

crumble 5 crush, decay, grate,
grind **6** powder **8** fragment,
splinter **9** decompose, pulverize **12** disintegrate

crumbly 7 brittle, friable
9 breakable

Crummles, Vincent
character in: **16** Nicholas
Nickleby
author: **7** Dickens

crummy 5 awful, lousy **6** rotten **8** terrible

crumple 4 fall **5** crush **6** cave
in, crease, pucker, rumple
7 crimple, crinkle, wrinkle
8 collapse **9** corrugate

crunch 4 chew, gnaw **5** chomp,
gnash, grind, munch
9 masticate

Cruncher, Jerry
character in: **16** A Tale of
Two Cities
author: **7** Dickens

crunchy 3 dry **5** crisp **6** crispy
7 crackly

crusade, Crusade 5 drive,
rally **8** movement

crusader, Crusader 6 knight,
zealot **7** pilgrim, Templar
8 champion **11** Hospitaller

crush 4 mash **5** break, press,
quash, quell, smash **6** enfold,
quench, squash, subdue
7 crumble, crumple, embrace,
put down, shatter, squeeze,
squelch **8** compress, overcome,
suppress **9** granulate, overpower, overwhelm, pulverize
10 extinguish

crushed 3 sad **5** cowed **6** broken, mashed, woeful
7 abashed, doleful, forlorn,
pressed, put down, quashed,
quelled, smashed, subdued

8 crumbled, crumpled, dejected, desolate, overcame,
overcome, quenched, squashed,
squeezed, wretched **9** flattened,
miserable, squelched, woebegone **10** compressed, despondent, pulverized, suppressed
11 overpowered, over-
whelmed **12** disconsolate, extinguished, inconsolable
13 broken-hearted

crushing 7 mashing **8** decisive,
quelling, smashing **10** shattering **11** humiliating, putting
down, stamping out, suppression **12** obliterating, overwhelming **13** pulverization

crust 4 coat, gall, hull, rind,
scab **5** brass, nerve, shell
6 harden **7** coating **8** chutzpah,
covering, pie shell **9** impudence **11** pastry shell

crustacean 4 crab, flea
5 louse, prawn **6** isopod,
shrimp **7** lobster **8** barnacle,
crawfish, crayfish **9** shellfish,
water flea

crusty 4 curt **5** blunt, gruff,
rough, short, stern, surly,
testy **6** abrupt, crabby, cranky,
shirty, snippy, sullen
7 brusque, peevish, waspish
8 choleric, snappish, snippety
9 irascible, splenetic **10** ill-
natured **11** ill-tempered
13 short-tempered

crux 3 nub **4** core, gist **5** basis,
heart **7** essence **9** essential
10 brass tacks **11** nitty-gritty

cry 3 beg, sob, sue **4** bawl, call,
hawk, howl, keen, moan,
plea, roar, wail, weep, yell,
yelp **5** blare, cheer, groan,
mourn, plead, shout, utter,
whoop **6** appeal, bellow, blazon, boohoo, clamor, hurrah,
huzzah, lament, outcry,
prayer, scream, shriek, snivel
7 blubber, call out, exclaim,
implore, request, screech,
trumpet, whimper **8** entreaty,
petition, proclaim **9** advertise,
importune **10** adjuration, promulgate **11** exclamation
12 solicitation, supplication

Cry, the Beloved Country
author: **9** Alan Paton
locale: **11** South Africa

cry out 4 bark, bawl, call,
howl, roar, yell **5** shout **6** bellow, clamor, holler **7** exclaim
8 proclaim **9** ejaculate

cry over 5 mourn **6** bemoan,
bewail, lament

crypt 4 tomb **5** vault **8** catacomb **9** mausoleum, sepulcher

cryptic 4 dark **5** vague **6** arcane, hidden, occult, secret
7 obscure, strange **8** esoteric,

mystical, puzzling **9** ambiguous **10** cabalistic, mysterious, perplexing **11** enigmatical

cryptogram 4 code **6** cipher

cryptograph 4 code **6** cipher, encode

crystal 3 ice **5** clear, flake, glass, lucid **6** quartz **7** diamond **8** stemware **9** glassware, snowflake, watch part **10** rhinestone **11** transparent

crystallize 3 fix, gel **4** firm, jell **5** candy **6** harden **8** solidify **9** granulate

Csonka, Larry (Lawrence Richard)
 nickname: 9 Lawnmower

sport: 8 football
position: 8 fullback
team: 13 Miami Dolphins, New York Giants

Cteatus
 origin: 5 Greek
 mentioned in: 5 Iliad
 father: 5 Actor
 mother: 7 Molione

Ctesippus
 father: 8 Hercules
 suitor of: 8 Penelope

Ctesius
 epithet of: 4 Zeus
 means: 9 god of gain

cub 3 boy, pup **4** bear, lion **5** scout, whelp **6** novice **8** re-

porter **9** youngling, youngster **10** apprentice

Cuba *see box*

cubbyhole 4 nook **5** niche **6** cranny **10** pigeonhole **11** compartment

cube of deep-fried pork
 American Spanish:
  10 cuchifrito

cubic centimeter
 abbreviation: 4 cu cm

cubic dekameter
 abbreviation: 5 cu dkm

cubic foot
 abbreviation: 4 cu ft

Cuba
 other name: 18 pearl of the Antilles
 capital/largest city: 6 Havana **8** Le Habana
 others: 5 Bauta, Colon, Duabi, Guane, Manes **6** Baines, Bayamo, Gibara, Guines, Mayari **7** Antilla, Baracoa, Fomento, Holguin, Holquin, Jiguani, Niquero, Palmira, Sanhuis **8** Artemisa, Camaguey, Cardenas, Guaimaro, Guayabal, Marianao, Matanzas, Nuevitas, Varadero, Yaguajay **9** Cabaiguan, Camajuani, Cienfuego **10** Cienfuegos, Guanabacoa, Guantanamo, Manzanillo, Santa Clara **11** Campechuela, Pinar del Rio, Puerto Padre **12** Ciego de Avila **13** Sagua de Tanamo **14** Sancti Spiritus, Santiago de Cuba **17** Aguada de Pasajeros, Consolacion del Sur
 measure: 4 vara **5** bocoy, cocoy, tarea **6** cordel, fanega **10** caballeria
 monetary unit: 4 peso **7** centavo **8** cuarenta
 weight: 5 libra **6** tercio
 island: 5 Pines, Pinos **6** Sabana **8** Camaguey, Juventud **9** Canarreos **17** Jardines de la Reina
  cay: **4** Coco **5** Largo **6** Romano **7** Guajaba, Rosareo, Sabinal **8** Cantiles **9** San Felipe **10** Santa Maria
 mountain: 6 Copper **7** Cristal, Maestra, Organos **8** Camaguey, Trinidad **9** Las Villas **11** Pinar del rio **12** Guaniguanico **14** Sancti-Spiritus
 highest point: 8 Turquino
 river: 4 Zaza **5** Cauto **8** San Pedro
 sea: 8 Atlantic **9** Caribbean
 physical feature:
  bay: **4** Nipe, Pigs **6** Jiguey **8** Cochinos **10** Buena Vista, Guantznamo
  cape: **4** Cruz **5** Maisi **8** Lucrecia **10** Corrientes, San Antonio
  channel: **8** Nicholas **9** Old Bahama
  falls: **3** Toa **7** Agabama, Caburni
  gulf: **6** Mexico **7** Cazones **8** Anamaria, Batabano **12** Guancanayabo
  inlet: **4** Broa **10** Corrientes
  peninsula: **6** Zapata
  point: **7** Guarico
  swamp: **6** Zapata
 people: 5 Carib, Negro, Taino, white **6** Arawak **7** Ciboney, mestizo **8** Ciboneye
  conqueror: **9** Velazquez
  explorer: **8** Columbus
  leader: **6** Castro **7** Batista **10** Che Guevara
 language: 7 Spanish
 religion: 13 Roman Catholic
  cult: **6** Chango, Yemaya
 places:
  castle: **5** Morro
  cathedral: **8** Santiago
 feature:
  dance: **5** conga, rumba **6** danzon, rhumba **8** guaracha, pachanga
  harvest: **5** zafra
  peasant: **7** guajiro
  tree: **5** jique, jiqui
  witch doctor: **7** nanigos
 food:
  dish: **6** paella
  drink: **4** pina

mia-Culpa (handwritten)

cubic inch
abbreviation: 4 cu in

cubicle 3 bay 4 cell, nook
5 booth, niche 6 alcove, recess

cubic meter
abbreviation: 3 cu m

cubic millimeter
abbreviation: 4 cu mm

cubic yard
abbreviation: 4 cu yd

cubit 15 Biblical measure

cuchifrito 19 cube of deep-
fried pork

Cuchulainn
origin: 5 Irish
hero of: 6 Ulster
uncle: 9 Conchobar
guarded house of: 10 Smith
Culan
killed by: 6 Lugaid

cuckoo 3 ani 4 bats, bird, fool,
gaga, nuts 5 balmy, batty,
crazy, daffy, dotty, goofy,
loony, nutty, silly, wacky
6 screwy 7 idiotic 9 screwball
12 crackbrained 13 off one's
rocker 14 off one's trolley

cucumber 14 Cucumis sativus
varieties: 3 bur 4 mock, star,
wild 6 bitter 7 prickly, serpent 9 squirting 13 African
horned

cuddle 3 pet 5 clasp 6 caress,
curl up, fondle, huddle, nestle,
nuzzle 7 cling to, embrace, lie
snug, snuggle

Cuddly Dudley
nickname of: 11 Dudley
Moore

cudgel 4 club 5 baton, staff,
stick 8 bludgeon 9 billy club,
blackjack, truncheon 10 shillelagh 12 quarterstaff

cue 3 key, tip 4 clue, hint,
sign 6 signal 7 inkling 10 intimation, suggestion
11 insinuation

cuff 3 box, hit, rap 4 blow
5 clout, smack, thump,
whack 6 thwack, wallop

cui bono 10 for what use, of
what good 15 for whose
benefit

cuisine 4 fare, food, menu
5 table 6 viands 7 cookery,
cooking, edibles 8 victuals, vittles 11 comestibles

Cukor, George
director of: 7 Camille 8 Adam's Rib, Gaslight, The
Women 10 My Fair Lady
(Oscar) 11 A Double Life, A
Star Is Born, Little Women
13 Born Yesterday, Dinner
at Eight 14 Romeo and Ju-

liet 16 David Copperfield
18 A Bill of Divorcement
20 The Philadelphia Story

cul-de-sac 6 pocket 7 dead-
end, impasse 10 blind alley

cull 4 junk, pick, sift, take
5 dross, glean, scrap, trash,
waste 6 choose, divide, garner,
gather, jetsam, reject, second,
select, winnow 7 castoff, collect, discard, excerpt, extract,
leaving 8 abstract, scouring,
separate 9 segregate

culminate 3 cap, end, top
5 crown, end up 6 climax, finish, result, top off, wind up
8 complete, conclude 9 terminate 10 consummate

culmination 4 acme, apex,
peak 6 apogee, climax, height,
zenith 7 epitome 8 pinnacle
10 conclusion 11 fulfillment,
realization 12 consummation

Culp, Robert
born: 10 Berkeley CA
roles: 4 I Spy 20 Greatest
American Hero

culpability 4 onus 5 blame,
fault, guilt 9 liability 14 accountability, responsibility

culpable 6 guilty, liable 7 at
fault, to blame 8 blamable
10 censurable 11 blameworthy

culprit 5 felon 6 sinner 8 criminal, evildoer, offender 9 miscreant, wrongdoer
10 lawbreaker, malefactor
12 transgressor

cult 4 sect 7 faction, zealots
8 admirers, devotees, devotion 9 disciples, followers
10 admiration

cultivable 6 arable 7 fertile, friable 8 farmable, plowable,
tillable

cultivate 3 dig, hoe, sow
4 farm, grow, plow, seek, till,
weed 5 court, plant, spade
6 enrich, garden 7 acquire, advance, develop, elevate, enhance, improve

cultivated 3 dug 4 fine, grew,
hoed 6 farmed, forked, sought,
spaded, tilled, weeded
7 courted, planted 8 advanced,
cultured, elevated, enhanced,
enriched, finished, improved,
polished 9 developed

cultivation 5 grace 6 polish,
sowing 7 farming, manners,
tilling 8 agronomy, planting
9 elevation, gardening, gentility, good taste, husbandry
10 refinement 11 agriculture

culture 3 art 5 music 7 the
arts 8 learning 9 erudition,
knowledge 10 enrichment, lit-

erature, refinement 12 civilization 13 enlightenment
15 accomplishments

Culture and Anarchy
author: 13 Matthew Arnold

cultured 7 elegant, erudite,
genteel, learned, refined
8 polished, well-bred, well-
read 11 enlightened 12 accomplished, well-educated
13 sophisticated

culvert 5 ditch, drain, sewer
6 trench 7 channel, conduit,
fox-hole

Cumaean sibyl
prophetess of: 5 Cumae
guided: 6 Aeneas

cumbersome 5 bulky, hefty
6 clumsy 7 awkward 8 cum-
brous, ungainly, unwieldy
9 ponderous 12 unmanageable

cum grano salis 15 not too
seriously 16 with a grain of
salt

cumin
botanical name: 14 Cuminum
cyminum
other name: 6 comino, jir-
aka, kummel
origin: 5 Egypt
family: 7 parsley
symbol of: 5 greed
guards against straying:
7 pigeons 8 chickens,
husbands
use: 4 fish, meat, rice, soup,
stew 5 bread, curry
6 cheese 7 pickles, sausage
8 potatoes 11 chili powder

cum laude 10 with praise

**cummings, e e (Edward
Estlin)**
author of: 12 in just spring
15 The Enormous Room
17 Tulips and Chimneys
18 Chansons Innocentes

Cummings, Robert
real name: 29 Clarence Robert Orville Cummings
born: 8 Joplin MO
roles: 8 King's Row 14 Dial
M for Murder 18 The Bob
Cummings Show

cumulate 5 amass 6 gather,
heap up, pile up
10 accumulate

cumulative 7 amassed, piled
up 8 additive, heaped up
9 aggregate 10 collective
12 accumulative, conglomerate

Cunegonde
character in: 7 Candide
author: 8 Voltaire

Cunina
origin: 5 Roman
goddess of: 15 sleeping
infants

cunning 3 art, sly 4 foxy, wily 5 canny, craft, guile, knack, skill 6 artful, crafty, deceit, genius, shifty, shrewd, talent, tricky 7 ability, devious, finesse, slyness 8 aptitude, artifice, deftness, foxiness, guileful, subtlety, trickery, wiliness 9 chicanery, deceitful, deception, deceptive, dexterity, duplicity, ingenious, underhand 10 adroitness, artfulness, cleverness, craftiness, expertness, shrewdness 11 deviousness 13 Machiavellian
god of: 6 Hermes

Cunning Little Vixen, The
opera by: 7 Janacek

cup 3 cup 5 glass, grail, stein 6 beaker, goblet, vessel 7 chalice, tankard 8 schooner
abbreviation: 1 c

Cup
constellation of: 6 Crater

Cupava
companion of: 6 Aeneas

cupbearer of gods
8 Ganymede

cupboard 6 buffet, bureau, closet 7 armoire, cabinet 9 sideboard, storeroom 10 chiffonier 11 china closet 12 clothespress

Cupid
also: 4 Amor
origin: 5 Roman
god of: 4 love
mother: 5 Venus
corresponds to: 4 Eros

cupidity 5 greed 7 avarice, avidity 8 rapacity 10 greediness 11 selfishness 12 covetousness, graspingness 13 concupiscence, insatiability, rapaciousness 14 avariciousness 15 acquisitiveness

cupola 4 dome, roof 5 tower, vault 6 belfry, turret 7 ceiling

cur 3 cad 4 mutt 5 rogue 6 rascal, varlet, wretch 7 mongrel, varmint, villain 9 scoundrel 10 blackguard

curacao
type: 7 liqueur
origin: 19 Netherlands Antilles
flavor: 6 orange
with gin: 8 Blue Moon, Napoleon 9 Blue Devil 14 Flying Dutchman
with rum: 6 Mai-Tai 8 Blue Lady 12 Blue Hawaiian
with vodka: 8 Aqueduct

curate 5 vicar 6 cleric, deacon, parson, pastor, priest, rector 8 minister, preacher 9 churchman, clergyman 12 ecclesiastic

curative 4 balm 7 healing 11 restorative

curator 5 doyen 6 keeper 8 director, overseer 9 caretaker, custodian

curb 3 rim 4 edge, rein 5 brink, check, ledge, limit 6 border, bridle, halter, retard, slow up 7 control, harness, inhibit, repress, slacken 8 hold back, moderate, restrain, restrict, slow down, suppress 9 curbstone, hindrance, restraint 10 decelerate, limitation 11 restriction, retardation

curdle 3 rot 4 clot, curd, sour, turn 5 decay, go bad, go off, spoil 7 clabber, congeal, ferment, putrefy, thicken 8 putresce, solidify 9 coagulate 11 deteriorate

cure 3 dry 4 heal, salt 5 smoke 6 remedy 8 antidote, make well, preserve 10 corrective

cure-all 4 balm 6 elixir, remedy 7 panacea 10 catholicon

cured 5 dried 6 healed, mended, smoked 8 made well, remedied 9 preserved, recovered

Curetes
form: 8 demigods
attendants of: 4 Zeus

Curiatii see 7 Horatii

Curie, Marie Sklodowska and Pierre
field: 7 physics 9 chemistry
discovered: 6 radium 8 polonium 13 radioactivity
awarded: 10 Nobel Prize

curio 7 bibelot, trinket 9 bric-a-brac, objet d'art

curiosity 5 freak, sight 6 marvel, oddity, prying, rarity, wonder 7 novelty 8 interest, nosiness 10 phenomenon, rare object 11 questioning 15 inquisitiveness

curious 3 odd 4 nosy, rare 5 funny, novel, queer, weird 6 prying, quaint, unique 7 bizarre, strange, unusual 8 peculiar, singular, snooping, uncommon 9 inquiring, searching 11 inquisitive, questioning

Curitis
epithet of: 4 Juno
means: 10 of the spear

curl 4 coil, lock, wave, wind 5 crimp, frizz, swirl, twirl, twist 6 spiral 7 frizzle, ringlet, scallop 8 curlicue 9 corkscrew

curled 3 set 5 kinky, waved, wound 6 coiled, frizzy spiral

7 crimped, frizzed, twisted 8 crinkled, scrolled 9 curlicued

curlicue 4 coil 5 twist 6 spiral 8 flourish

curly 4 wavy 5 kinky 6 frizzy 7 rippled 8 crinkled 9 ringleted

curmudgeon 4 crab 5 crank, grump 6 grouch 8 grumbler, sourball

currant 5 Ribes
varieties: 3 red 5 black, fetid, skunk, squaw, stink 6 alpine, cherry, common, garden, Indian, Sierra 7 Buffalo 8 Missouri, mountain, swamp red 9 chaparral, wild black 11 northern red 12 bristly black 13 American black, European black, northern black, white-flowered 15 California black

currency 4 cash, coin 5 bills, money, vogue 7 coinage 9 bank notes 10 acceptance, popularity, prevalence 12 predominance, universality

current 3 now 4 flow, flux, mood, tide 5 draft, drift, trend 6 modern, spirit, stream, with-it 7 feeling, in style, in vogue, popular, present 8 existing, tendency, up-to-date 9 prevalent, zeitgeist 10 atmosphere, present-day, prevailing 11 inclination 12 contemporary, undercurrent

current of air 4 wind 5 draft 6 breeze, zephyr

curricle 3 gig 4 cart, trap 6 chaise 8 carriage

curry powder
origin: 5 India
ingredient: 5 cumin 6 cloves 8 capsicum, turmeric 9 coriander, fenugreek, red pepper 13 cayenne pepper
use: 5 kebab, kebob, kofta, malai 6 kormas 7 curries, pea soup 8 meat loaf, vindaloo, zucchini 11 potato salad

curse 3 vex 4 bane, cuss, damn, oath 5 blast, cross, swear, trial 6 burden, ordeal, plague, whammy 7 afflict, condemn, evil eye, scourge, swear at, torment, trouble 8 anathema, denounce, execrate, swearing, vexation 9 annoyance, blasphemy, damnation, evil spell, expletive, obscenity, profanity 10 affliction, execration, misfortune 11 imprecation, malediction, tribulation 12 anathematize, denunciation

cursory 5 brief, hasty, quick, swift 6 casual, random 7 hurried, offhand, passing 8 careless 9 desultory, haphazard

11 inattentive, perfunctory, superficial

curt 4 rude **5** bluff, blunt, gruff, short, terse **6** abrupt, crusty, snappy **7** brusque, summary **8** petulant **10** peremptory

curtail 3 cut **4** clip, trim **6** reduce **7** abridge, shorten **8** condense, contract, cut short, decrease, diminish, pare down **10** abbreviate

curtailed 3 cut **7** checked, concise, cut back, reduced, slashed **8** abridged, cut short **9** shortened **10** retrenched

curtailment 7 cutback, cutting, halting, pruning **8** clipping, decrease, trimming **9** lessening, reduction, restraint **10** limitation, shortening **11** abridgement, contraction **12** abbreviation, condensation

curtain 3 end **4** mask, veil **5** blind, cover, drape, shade, sheet **6** screen, shroud **7** conceal, drapery, hanging **8** portiere

Curtis, Tony
   real name: 15 Bernard Schwartz
   wife: 10 Janet Leigh
   daughter: 8 Jamie Lee
   born: 9 New York NY
   roles: 7 Houdini, Trapeze **12** The Great Race **13** Some Like It Hot **14** The Defiant Ones **16** The Great Imposter **18** The Boston Strangler **22** The Sweet Smell of Success

Curtius
   also: 6 Marcus
   volunteered as: 17 sacrificial victim

Curtiz, Michael
   director of: 10 Casablanca (Oscar), The Sea Hawk **12** Captain Blood **13** Mildred Pierce **14** Life with Father **17** Yankee Doodle Dandy **24** The Adventures of Robin Hood (with William Keighley) **26** The Charge of the Light Brigade **34** The Private Lives of Elizabeth and Essex

curtsy, curtsey 3 bob, bow, dip **5** honor **6** homage **9** obeisance, reverence **11** bend the knee

curvature 3 arc **4** arch, bend **5** crook **6** bowing

curve 3 arc, bow **4** arch, bend, coil, hook, loop, turn, wind **5** crook, twist **6** spiral, swerve

curved 4 bent **5** bowed **6** arched, looped, turned

curved span 3 bow **4** arch, dome **5** vault **6** bridge

Curve of Binding Energy, The
   author: 10 John McPhee

curving 4 bent **5** bowed **6** arched **7** bending, looping, turning, winding **8** twisting

curving inward 6 hollow, sunken **7** concave **8** hollowed **9** depressed

curving outward 5 bowed **6** convex **7** bulging, rounded **8** bellying **11** protuberant

Cuscatlan see **10** El Salvador

Cush
   father: 3 Ham
   grandfather: 4 Noah
   brother: 6 Canaan
   son: 6 Nimrod
   Hebrew for: 8 Ethiopia

cushion 3 mat, pad **4** damp **5** quiet **6** dampen, deaden, muffle, pillow, soften, stifle **7** bolster **8** suppress

Cushitic
   language family: 11 AfroAsiatic **13** Hamito-Semitic
   branch: 6 Somali **8** Gallinya
   spoken in: 7 Somalia **8** Ethiopia, Tanzania

cusp 4 apex, barb, horn, peak **5** angle, point, tooth **6** corner

custard 4 flan, fool **5** creme **6** junket **7** dessert, pudding **8** flummery **10** blanc-mange, zabaglione

Custer, George A
   served in: 8 Civil War **10** Indian Wars
   side: 5 Union
   battle: 13 Little Big Horn
   defeated: 11 Black Kettle
   defeated by: 10 Crazy Horse

custodian 6 duenna, keeper, warden **7** janitor **8** chaperon, guardian, watchman **9** attendant, caretaker, chaperone, concierge **14** superintendent

custody 4 care **5** watch **6** charge **9** detention **10** possession, protection **11** confinement, safekeeping, trusteeship **12** conservation, guardianship, preservation

custom 4 form, mode **5** habit, usage **7** fashion **10** convention

customarily 7 as a rule, usually **8** commonly, normally **9** generally, regularly **10** frequently, habitually, ordinarily **13** traditionally

customary 5 usual **6** common, normal, wonted **7** general, regular, routine, typical **8** everyday, habitual, ordinary

10 accustomed **11** traditional **12** conventional

customer 5 buyer **6** client, patron **7** habitue, shopper **9** purchaser

customs 4 duty, levy, toll **6** excise, tariff **9** import tax **10** assessment

cut 3 mow, saw **4** chop, clip, crop, cube, dice, fall, gash, hack, move, nick, pare, part, rent, rive, slit, snip, snub, trim **5** carve, cross, lance, mince, piece, prune, sever, share, shave, shear, slash, slice, split, wound **6** bisect, course, delete, divide, furrow, hollow, ignore, incise, pierce, reduce, sunder, trench **7** abridge, channel, curtail, decline, dissect, opening, passage, portion, section, segment **8** condense, contract, decrease, diminish, incision, lacerate **9** abatement, intersect, lessening, reduction, shrinkage **10** abbreviate, diminution, excavation, shortening **11** contraction, curtailment, indentation

cut and run 4 bolt, flee, skip **6** escape **7** abscond, get away, make off, run away **8** slip away **9** break free **10** break loose, fly the coop **12** make a getaway

cut apart 7 dissect **9** anatomize

cutback 8 decrease, trimming **9** reduction **11** abridgement, curtailment

cut back 4 trim **5** prune **6** reduce **7** abridge, curtail **8** decrease

cut costs 4 save **5** skimp, stint **6** scrimp **7** husband **8** conserve **9** economize **15** tighten one's belt

cut down 4 kill, trim **5** limit **6** lessen, reduce **7** abridge, curtail, destroy, disable, remodel, shorten **8** condense, decrease, diminish, restrict **10** abbreviate

cut-down form 6 digest, precis **7** summary **8** synopsis, trimming **10** shortening **11** abridgement, contraction, curtailment **12** abbreviation, condensation

cut down to size 5 abase
6 humble **7** mortify **8** belittle,
bring low, disgrace **9** humiliate **13** bring down a peg

cute 5 sweet **6** dainty, pretty
7 darling, lovable **8** adorable,
handsome, precious **9** beautiful **10** attractive

cut expenses 4 save **5** skimp,
stint **6** scrimp **8** conserve
9 economize **12** pinch pennies **15** tighten one's belt

cut in half 5 halve **6** bisect

cut in two 5 halve, sever
6 bisect

cutlet 3 cut **4** chop **5** slice
9 cotelette, croquette

cut off 4 dock, trim **5** apart,
sever **6** detach, remove **7** chop
off, divorce, isolate **8** amputate, divorced, isolated, separate **10** disconnect

cut out 2 go **4** blow, exit **5** be
off, erase, leave, scram, split
6 beat it, delete, depart, escape, excise, go away, remove,
set out **7** abolish **8** designed,
get rid of, set forth **9** eliminate **10** do away with, hit the
road, make tracks **11** exterminate, take a powder

cut short 4 clip, crop, dock,
trim **7** abridge, shorten
8 truncate **10** abbreviate

cutter 4 boat **5** blade, hewer,
knife **6** sledge, sleigh, tailor
11 cutting edge

cutthroat 5 cruel **6** outlaw
7 brigand, hoodlum, ruffian
8 ruthless **9** merciless

cutting 3 raw **4** acid, cold
5 harsh, nasty, sharp **6** biting,
bitter **7** acerbic, caustic, nipping, pruning, searing **8** clipping, derisive, piercing,
scathing, smarting, snubbing,
stinging, trimming **9** reduction,
sarcastic, stringent **11** abridgement, acrimonious, compression, contraction, curtailment,
disparaging, penetrating
12 abbreviation, condensation

cutting edge 5 blade **8** vanguard **9** forefront

cutting off 8 severing **9** severance **10** detachment, separation **13** disconnection,
disengagement

cutting remark 3 dig **4** gibe,
jeer **5** taunt

Cuttle
character in: **12** Dombey and
Son
author: **7** Dickens

cut up 4 chop, hack, maim,
rend **5** caper, carve, halve,
mince, slash, slice, split
6 cleave, deface, deform, divide **7** portion, quarter **8** dissever, mutilate **9** apportion,
kid around **10** fool around
11 clown around, play the
fool

Cuvier, Georges
field: **7** geology, zoology
nationality: **6** French
founded: **12** paleontology
18 comparative anatomy

Cyane
form: **5** nymph **8** princess
violated by: **6** father
unsuccessful rescuer of:
10 Persephone

Cyaxares *see* **9** Ahasuerus

Cybele
also: **9** Dindymene **10** Berecyntia, Magna Mater
11 Great Mother **12** Mater
Turrita **17** Great Idaean
Mother
origin: **8** Phrygian **9** Asia
Minor
goddess of: **6** nature
priest: **5** Galli **10** Corybantes
corresponds to: **3** Ops
4 Rhea
epithet: **6** Antaea

Cychreus
king of: **7** Salamis
father: **8** Poseidon
mother: **7** Salamis
daughter: **6** Glauce

Cyclades 3 Dos, Zea **4** Keos,
Nios, Sira, Syra **5** Delos, Melos, Naxos, Paros, Siros, Syros,
Tenos, Tinos **6** Andros
7 Amorgos, islands, Kythnos
13 Aegean islands

cycle 3 run **6** series **8** sequence **10** succession **11** progression **14** connected group

cyclone 4 gale, gust, wind
5 storm **7** tornado, twister, typhoon **9** whirlwind, windstorm
Australian: **10** willy-nilly

Cyclone (Cy)
nickname of: **15** Denton True
Young

Cyclops, Cyclopes
form: **5** giant
number of eyes: **3** one
father: **6** Uranus
mother: **2** Ge
blinded by: **8** Odysseus

Cycnus
father: **4** Ares
killed in: **4** duel
killed by: **8** Hercules
changed into: **4** swan

Cydippe
priestess of: **4** Hera
location: **5** Argos
father: **7** Ochimus
son: **5** Biton **7** Cleobis

cylinder 3 can, tin **4** drum,
pipe, roll, tube **5** spool **6** barrel, column, pillar, piston,
platen, roller **13** piston
chamber

cylindrical 5 round **6** tarete
7 tubular **8** columnar

Cyllene
form: **5** nymph
nursed: **6** Hermes

Cyllenian
pertains to: **6** Hermes
12 Mount Cellene

Cymbeline
author: **18** William
Shakespeare
character: **6** Cloten, Imogen
7 Iachimo, Pisanio **9** Bellarius **17** Leonatus Posthumus

Cymodoce
mentioned in: **6** Aeneid
form: **4** ship
fleet of: **6** Aeneas
changed by: **6** Cybele
changed into: **8** sea nymph

Cymru *see* **5** Wales

cynic 7 scoffer, skeptic **9** pessimist **10** misogynist **11** faultfinder, misanthrope

cynical 8 derisive, sardonic,
scoffing, scornful, sneering
9 misogynic, sarcastic, skeptical **12** misanthropic

Cynortes
father: **7** Amyclas
mother: **7** Diomede

Cynosura
nurse of: **4** Zeus

Cynthia *see* **7** Artemis

Cynurus
father: **7** Perseus

Cyparissia
epithet of: **6** Athena
means: **14** cypress goddess

Cyparissus
killed: **4** stag
changed into: **11** cypress tree

cypress 8 Taxodium
9 Cupressus
varieties: **3** toy **4** bald, berg,
pond **5** false, Gowen, Modoc, Piute **6** Bhutan, Hinoki,
Lawson, MacNab, Nootka,
Sawara, summer, Tecate
7 African, Arizona, Italian,
Mexican, Sargent **8** Cuyamaca, golf-ball, Monterey,
mourning, Siskiyou, standing **9** Guadalupe, Mendocino, Montezuma, red
summer, Santa Cruz **10** Portuguese, tennis-ball
12 Chinese swamp
18 rough-barked Arizona
19 smooth-barked Arizona

Cyprian *see* **9** Aphrodite

Cyprus
biblical name: 6 Kittim
capital/largest city:
7 Nicosia
city: 6 Paphos 7 Kyrenia,
Larnaca 8 Limassol
9 Famagusta
monetary unit: 4 para
5 pound
mountain: 7 Kyrenia,
Troodos
highest point: 7 Olympus
river: 6 Pedias
sea: 13 Mediterranean
physical feature:
   bay: 8 Episkopi
   cape: 4 Gata 5 Greco
   7 Andreas, Arnauti
   9 Kormakiti
   peninsula: 6 Karpas
   plain: 8 Mesaoria
   9 Messaoria
people: 5 Greek, Turks
   9 Cypriotes
   ruler: 5 Turks 6 Greeks,
   Romans 7 British
   9 Egyptians, Lusignans,
   Venetians 10 Byzan-
   tines 11 Phoenicians
language: 5 Greek
   7 Turkish
religion: 5 Islam 6 Muslim
13 Greek Orthodoxy
16 Eastern Orthodoxy

Cypselus
king of: 7 Arcadia
father: 7 Aepytus
daughter: 6 Merope
son-in-law: 11 Cresphontes
grandson: 7 Aepytus

Cyrano de Bergerac
director: 13 Michael Gordon
author: 13 Edmond Rostand
cast: 10 Jose Ferrer (Cyrano),
Mala Powers 13 William
Powers
character: 6 Roxane 22 Christian de Neuvillette
setting: 5 Paris
Oscar for: 9 best actor (Ferrer)

Cyrano de Bergerac, Savinien
author of: 25 Voyages to the
Moon and the Sun
play based on his life by:
13 Edmond Rostand

Cyrene
father: 7 Hypseus
mother: 6 Creusa
lover: 6 Apollo
son: 5 Idmon 9 Aristaeus

Cytherea *see* 9 Aphrodite

Cytissorus
father: 7 Phrixus
mother: 9 Chalciope
brother: 5 Argus, Melas
8 Phrontis

cytology
study of: 5 cells

czar, tsar 4 king 5 ruler 6 caesar, despot, tyrant 7 emperor,
monarch 8 dictator, overlord
9 potentate, sovereign

czarina 7 empress

czaristic 10 autocratic 11 all-
powerful, dictatorial,
monarchical

Czechoslovakia *see box*

Czechoslovakia/Czech Republic see Slovakia
capital/largest city: 5 Praha 6 Prague
others: 2 As 4 Asch, Brno, Cheb, Most 5 Brunn, Nitra,
Opava, Plzen, Tabor, 6 Aussig, Bilina, Kladno, Kosice, Pilsen, Presov, Sadowa, Trnava, Vsetin 7 Budweis, Jihlava,
Liberec, Olomouc, Ostrava, Teplitz 8 Carlsbad, Jachymov,
Karlsbad 9 Pressburg 10 Austerlitz, Bratislava, Koniggratz
11 Reichenberg
university: 7 Charles
division: 7 Bohemia, Moravia, Silesia 8 Ruthenia, Slovakia
measure: 3 Lan 4 Mira 5 Korec, Liket, Stopa 6 Merice,
Strych
monetary unit: 5 crown, ducat 6 heller, Koruna
mountain: 3 Erz, Ore 5 Giant, Tatra 6 Sumava 7 Sudeten,
Sudetes 8 Krkonose 10 Carpathian
highest point: 7 Gerlach 11 Gerlachovka
river: 2 Uh, 3 Mze, Vag, Vah 4 Dyje, Eger, Elbe, Gran,
Hron, Ipel, Iser, Labe, Nisa, Oder, Odra, Ohre, Olse,
Waag 5 Becva, Dunaj, March, Nitra, Slana, Tisza 6 Danube, Moldau, Morava, Ondava, Sazava, Torysa, Vltava
7 Laborec, Luznice 8 Berounka
physical feature:
   plateau: 8 Bohemian 11 Sudetenland
people: 4 Slav 5 Czech 6 Slovak 8 Bohemian, Moravian
   author: 5 Capek, Hasek, Havel 7 Kundera, Seifert
   composer: 6 Dvorak 7 Janacek, Martinu, Smetana
   director: 11 Milos Forman
   philosopher/reformer: 8 Comenius, John Huss
language: 5 Czech 6 German, Magyar, Slovak 7 Russian
9 Hungarian
religion: 6 Uniate 8 Lutheran 9 Orthodoxy 13 Roman
Catholic
place:
   castle: 8 Hradcany
   cathedral: 7 St Vitus 10 St Nicholas
   resort/spa: 8 Carlsbad, Piestany 9 Marienbad 10 Luha-
   covice 11 Karlovy Vary 14 Marianske Lazne
   square: 9 Wenceslas
feature:
   dance: 5 polka 6 redowa, talian 7 furiant
   gymnastics festival: 11 spartakiada
   song: 7 Ma Vlast
food:
   beer: 6 pilsen
   sausage: 5 parky 6 vursty

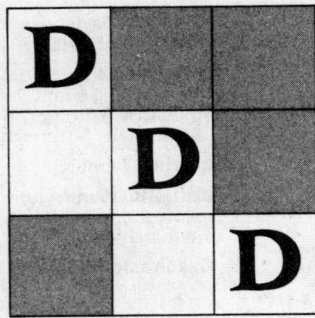

dab 3 bit, pat, tap 6 stroke 7 smidgen, soupcon

dabble 5 slosh 6 fiddle, putter, splash 7 spatter, toy with 8 sprinkle

dabbler 7 amateur, trifler 10 dilettante 12 experimenter 15 nonprofessional

da capo
 music: 22 repeat from the beginning
 abbreviation: 2 D C

Dacca
 capital of: 10 Bangladesh

d'accord 2 OK 6 agreed 7 granted

Dactyls
 also: 7 Daktyls
 dwellers of: 8 Mount Ida

dad 2 da, pa 3 pop 4 papa, pops, sire 5 daddy, pappy, pater 6 father, parent 11 the old man

Daedala
 festival in: 7 Boeotia

Daedalion
 father: 9 Eosphorus
 mother: 10 Phosphorus
 daughter: 6 Chione
 leaped off: 9 Parnassus
 changed into: 4 hawk

Daedalus
 occupation: 9 architect
 father: 6 Metion
 son: 5 Iapyx 6 Icarus
 nephew: 5 Talos 6 Perdix
 killed: 5 Talos
 built: 9 labyrinth
  for: 5 Minos
 made: 5 wings

daffodil 9 Narcissus 24 Narcissus pseudonarcissus
 varieties: 3 sea 6 winter 8 Peruvian 9 petticoat 13 hoop-petticoat

daft 3 mad 4 loco 5 balmy, batty, crazy, daffy, dizzy, goofy, loony, nutty, silly, wacky 6 cuckoo, insane, screwy 7 foolish, lunatic, witless

Dagan
 origin: 12 Mesopotamian
 god of: 5 earth 11 agriculture
 corresponds to: 5 Dagon

dagger 4 dirk, snee 5 blade, knife 6 weapon 7 poniard 8 stiletto

Dagon
 origin: 10 Philistine, Phoenician
 god of: 5 earth 11 agriculture
 corresponds to: 5 Dagan

Daguerre, Louis J M
 nationality: 6 French
 inventor of: 11 photography 13 daguerreotype

dahlia
 varieties: 3 sea 4 tree 6 common, garden 7 bedding 8 bell tree 10 candelabra

Dahomey, Republic of *see* 5 Benin

daily 7 diurnal, per diem 9 circadian, quotidian

Daimler, Gottlieb
 nationality: 6 German
 inventor of: 10 carburetor, motorcycle 14 gasoline engine 18 gasoline automobile 25 compression ignition engine

daimyo 4 lord 10 feudal lord

dainty 4 fine 5 fussy, tasty 6 choice, choosy, lovely, pretty, savory 7 choosey, elegant, refined 8 delicate, pleasing 9 beautiful, delicious, exquisite 10 attractive, fastidious, particular

Daira
 father: 7 Oceanus

dais 5 stage 6 podium 7 rostrum 8 platform

daisy 6 Bellis 23 Chrysanthemum frutescens 25 Chrysanthemum leucanthemum
 varieties: 4 blue, cape, high, lazy 5 crown, giant, globe, oxeye, Paris, veldt, white 6 butter, Easter, Nippon, shasta, sleepy, Tahoka 7 African, English, painted, seaside, turfing 8 Dahlberg, mountain, panamint 9 Barberton, Englemann, Swan River, Transvaal 10 Kingfisher, Michaelmas, Portuguese 11 Clanwilliam, Livingstone, Namaqualand 12 Boston yellow, double orange 15 blue-eyed African

Daisy Miller
 author: 10 Henry James
 character: 10 Giovanelli 12 Winterbourne

Dakar
 capital of: 7 Senegal

Dakota (Sioux)
 language family: 6 Siouan
 tribe: 5 Teton 6 Lakota, Nakota, Santee 7 Yankton 8 Sisseton, Wahpeton, Wiciyela 9 Wahpekute, Yanktonai 11 Mdewakanton
 location: 7 Montana 9 Minnesota 11 North Dakota, South Dakota
 leader: 4 Gall 10 Crazy Horse 11 Sitting Bull 13 Jashunca-Uiteo
 noted for: 15 military prowess
 deity: 10 Wakan Tanka

Daktyls *see* 7 Dactyls

dale 4 dell, dene, glen, vale 6 dingle, hollow, valley

D'Alembert
 author of: 12 Encyclopedia

Dali, Salvador
 born: 5 Spain 7 Figuras
 artwork: 10 Last Supper 17 Atomic Leda and Swan 19 Persistence of Memory 22 Accommodations of De-

sire **24** Christ of St John of the Cross

Dalibor
 opera by: **7** Smetana
 character: **6** Milada

Dallas
 airport: **23** Dallas-Fort Worth Regional
 basketball team: **4** Mavs **9** Mavericks
 football team: **7** Cowboys
 landmark: **15** Turtle Creek Park **16** Museum of Fine Arts **19** Dallas Theater Center **25** Margo Jones Memorial Theater
 river: **7** Trinity
 stadium: **10** Cotton Bowl
 university: **3** SMU **13** Bishop College **17** Southern Methodist

Dallas
 character: **7** JR Ewing **9** Jack Ewing, Jenna Wade, Jock Ewing, Miss Ellie, Ray Krebbs **10** Bobby Ewing **11** Christopher, Cliff Barnes, Mandy Winger, Mark Graison **12** Digger Barnes **13** Clayton Farlow, John Ross Ewing, Sue Ellen Ewing **16** Donna Culver Krebs **17** Pamela Barnes Ewing **22** Eleanor Southworth Ewing
 cast: **8** John Beck **9** Dack Rambo, Linda Gray **10** Howard Keel **11** Larry Hagman, Steve Kanaly, Susan Howard **12** Ken Kercheval, Patrick Duffy **16** Barbara Bel Geddes, Priscilla Presley **17** Victoria Principal
 ranch: **9** Southfork
 business: **3** oil **8** Ewing Oil

dalliance 6 affair, toying **7** romance **8** fiddling, trifling **10** flirtation, lovemaking

dally 3 toy **4** play **5** flirt **6** dawdle, loiter, trifle

Dalmatia *see* **10** Yugoslavia

Dalton, John
 field: **7** physics **9** chemistry
 nationality: **7** British
 formulated: **12** atomic theory
 first: **18** atomic weights table
 described: **14** color blindness

dam 3 bar, cow **4** clog, mare, plug, stop, wall **5** bitch, block, check **6** bridle, hinder, hold

in, impede, plug up, stanch, stop up **7** barrier, block up, confine, congest, inhibit, repress, stopper, stuff up **8** blockade, hold back, obstruct, restrain **9** barricade, hindrance **11** obstruction

damage, damages 3 mar **4** cost, harm, hurt, loss **6** impair, injure, injury, ravage **10** impairment, reparation, settlement **11** destruction **12** compensation, despoliation

damaging 7 harmful, hurtful, ruinous **9** injurious **11** destructive, detrimental

Damascus
 ancient kingdom: **8** Aramaean
 Arabic: **7** Dimashq
 capital of: **5** Syria
 monastery: **22** Suleiman the Magnificent
 mosque: **5** Great **7** Umayyad
 mount: **6** Qasyun
 museum: **8** National **9** Qasr al-Azm
 river: **4** Awaj **6** Barada
 rulers: **5** Arabs, Timur **6** Romans **7** Mongols, Saladin **8** Assyrian **9** Caliphate, Seleucids **12** Ottoman Turks **15** Byzantine Empire **17** Alexander the Great
 tomb: **7** Saladin

Damastes *see* **10** Procrustes

Dame Pliant
 character in: **12** The Alchemist
 author: **6** Jonson

Damia
 spirit of: **9** fertility

damn 4 doom **5** blast **6** rail at **7** censure, condemn **8** denounce **9** criticize, disparage

damned 4 lost **6** cursed, darned, doomed, fallen **7** doggone, dratted, godless **8** accursed, doggoned **9** condemned, execrated, reprobate **12** unregenerate

Damocles
 offended: **9** Dionysius
 seated under: **14** suspended sword

Damon
 friend: **7** Pythias

damp 3 wet **4** curb, dank, dash, dewy, dull, mist **5** check, foggy, humid, misty,

moist, muggy, rainy, soggy, spoil **6** clammy, deaden, hamper, hinder, reduce, soaked, sodden **7** depress, drizzly, inhibit, sopping, wettish **8** dankness, diminish, dripping, humidity, moisture, restrain **9** mugginess, restraint **10** clamminess, discourage **14** discouragement

dampen 3 wet **7** moisten, wet down

dampen one's spirits 5 daunt, unman **6** deject **7** depress **10** discourage, dishearten

damper 4 curb **8** obstacle **9** hindrance, restraint **10** constraint, impediment, wet blanket **14** discouragement

damsel 4 girl, lass **6** maiden **9** young lady

damselfly
 varieties: **8** forktail **10** civilbluet **11** black-winged, broad-winged **12** narrowwinged, spread-winged, violet dancer

dam up 4 clog, plug **5** block, choke **6** plug up, stop up **7** congest **8** obstruct

Damysus
 member of: **8** Gigantes

Dan
 means: **5** judge
 father: **5** Jacob
 mother: **6** Bilhah
 brother: **3** Gad **4** Levi **5** Asher, Judah **6** Joseph, Reuben, Simeon **7** Zebulun **8** Benjamin, Issachar, Naphtali
 sister: **5** Dinah
 descendant of: **6** Danite

Dana *see* **4** Danu

Dana, Richard Henry
 author of: **21** Two Years Before the Mast

Danae
 form: **6** maiden
 father: **8** Acrisius
 mother: **8** Eurydice
 imprisoned by: **8** Acrisius
 lover: **4** Zeus
 son: **7** Perseus

Danai
 members of: **6** Greeks **7** Argives

Danaides
 daughters of: **6** Danaus
 number of daughters: **5** fifty

Dan August
 character: **9** (Sgt) Joe Rivera **14** (Sgt) Charles Wilentz **16** (Chief) George Untermeyer
 cast: **9** Ned Romero **10** Nor-

man Fell **12** Burt Reynolds
15 Richard Anderson

Danaus
ruler of: **5** Argos
father: **5** Belus
twin brother: **8** Aegyptus
daughters called: **8** Danaides
number of daughters: **5** fifty

dance *see box*

dance of death
French: **12** danse macabre

Dandelion Wine
author: **11** Ray Bradbury

dander 5 anger, Irish **6** temper

Dandie Dinmont terrier
24 soft-coated wheaten terrier,
Staffordshire bull terrier, West
Highland white terrier

dandy 3 fop **4** beau, dude,
fine **5** beaut, great, super,
swell **6** beauty, superb **7** coxcomb, peacock **8** terrific **9** excellent **12** clotheshorse

danger 4 risk **5** peril **6** hazard,
menace, threat **8** jeopardy
12 endangerment

dangerous 5 hairy, risky
6 chancy, unsafe **8** menacing,
perilous **9** hazardous **10** pre-

carious **11** threatening,
treacherous

danger signal 5 alarm, alert
7 red flag, warning

dangle 3 sag **4** drag, hang,
sway **5** droop, swing, trail
6 depend **7** draggle, hang out,
suspend **8** hang down, hang
over **9** oscillate

Daniel
Babylonian name:
12 Belteshazzar
companion: **7** Meshach
8 Abednego, Shadrach

Daniel Boone
character: **5** Mingo **6** Yadkin
11 Cincinnatus, Israel
Boone, Jemima Boone
12 Rebecca Boone
cast: **6** Ed Ames **10** Fess Parker **11** Albert Salmi, Dal
McKennon, Darby Hinton
13 Patricia Blair **18** Veronica
Cartwright

Danielovitch, Issur
real name of: **11** Kirk
Douglas

dank 3 wet **4** cold, damp **5** humid, moist, muggy, soggy
6 chilly, clammy, sodden,
sticky

danke 8 thank you

danke schon 16 thank you
very much

dankness 4 damp **7** wetness
8 dampness, humidity **9** humidness, moistness, mugginess **10** clamminess

Danner, Blythe
born: **14** Philadelphia PA
roles: **8** Betrayal **15** The
Great Santini **16** Man
Woman and Child

Danny Deever
story in: **18** Barrack-Room
Ballads
author: **14** Rudyard Kipling

Danny Thomas Show, The
character: **6** Clancy **12** Uncle
Tonoose **13** Danny Williams,
Linda Williams, Rusty Williams, Terry Williams
16 Mrs Kathy Williams
18 Uncle Charley Halper
cast: **9** Sid Melton **10** Rusty
Hamer **11** Hans Conried
12 Marjorie Lord, Penney
Parker **13** Sherry Jackson
16 Angela Cartwright

danse macabre 12 dance of
death

Dante (Alighieri)
author of: **9** Vita Nuova
15 The Divine Comedy
Divine Comedy Part I:
10 The Inferno

---

dance 3 hop **4** ball, jump, leap, prom, reel, skip **5** lindy,
party, polka, twist **6** bounce, cavort, frolic, gambol, prance,
square **7** fox-trot, perform **8** cakewalk **9** jitterbug **10** Charleston **11** Boston waltz **12** choreography, Virginia reel **15** hesitation waltz
Renaissance/17th century: **3** jig **5** galop, gigue **6** branle,
pavane, redowa **7** bourree, gavotte, lancers, lavolta, mazurka **8** canaries, chaconne, courante, galliard, rigadoon,
rigaudon, tourdion **9** allemande, passepied, polonaise, sar-
abande **10** danse basse, danse haute
18th century: **6** minuet **9** cotillion **11** contre danse
12 country dance
19th century: **5** waltz **9** quadrille
early 1900's: **7** foxtrot, one-step, two-step **8** bunny hug
10 turkey trot **11** grizzly bear
1920's: **5** tango **6** shimmy, toddle **10** Charleston **11** black
bottom
1930's: **4** shag **5** conga, rumba, samba, Suzy-Q **7** pecking
8 big apple, lindy hop, trucking **9** jitterbug
1940's: **5** mambo **6** cha-cha
1950's and 1960's: **4** frug, go-go **5** twist **6** monkey
9 rock-'n'-roll
1970's: **5** disco
Argentine: **5** tango
Austrian: **13** schuhplattler
Balinese: **6** legong
Brazilian: **5** samba **6** maxixe
Cuban: **5** conga, rumba **6** cha-cha
Czech: **5** polka
Dominican: **8** marengue, merengue
folk: **6** Morris **7** maypole
French: **6** can-can **8** galliard **9** ecossaise
German: **11** schottische
Indian: **6** kathak **8** manipuri **9** kathakali **13** bharata nat
yam
Japanese: **6** bugaku **7** dengaku **8** sarugaku
dance/theater: **2** no **3** noh **6** kabuki
Mexican: **3** hat
Polish: **7** mazurka **9** krakoviak, polonaise **11** varsovienne
Scottish: **5** sword
Siamese: **10** wayang wong
Spanish: **4** jota **6** bolero **8** flamenco **9** sevillana
10 seguidilla
modern dancer/choreographer: **4** Juba **8** Ted Shawn
9 Eliot Feld, Gene Kelly, Ray Bolger **10** Mary Wigman,
Paul Draper, Twyla Tharp **11** Anna Sokolow, Antony Tu-
dor, Eric Hawkins, Fred Astaire, Irene Castle, Ruth St
Denis **12** Bill Robinson, Ginger Rogers, Martha Graham,
Vernon Castle **13** Alwin Nikolais, Doris Humphrey, Isadora Duncan **14** Charles Weidman **15** Merce Cunningham
see also: **6** ballet

Divine Comedy Part II:
9 Purgatory
Divine Comedy Part III:
8 Paradise
heroine: 8 Beatrice

Dantes, Edmond
character in: 21 The Count
of Monte Cristo
author: 5 Dumas (pere)

Danton, Ray
born: 9 New York NY
roles: 14 I'll Cry Tomorrow
18 The George Raft Story
27 The Rise and Fall of
Legs Diamond

Danu
also: 4 Dana
origin: 5 Irish
mother of: 14 Tuatha De
Danann

Danvers, Mrs
character in: 7 Rebecca
author: 9 Du Maurier

Daphnaea
epithet of: 7 Artemis
means: 11 of the laurel

Daphne
form: 5 nymph
father: 5 Ladon 6 Peneus
pursued by: 6 Apollo
9 Leucippus
changed into: 7 bay tree

Daphnephoria
festival of: 6 Apollo

Daphnis
occupation: 7 cowherd
8 shepherd
father: 6 Hermes
originated: 14 pastoral poetry
blinded by: 5 Nomia

Daphnis and Chloe
characters in: 12 Greek
romance
author: 6 Longus

Daphnis et Chloe
ballet by: 5 Ravel
choreographer: 12 Michel
Fokine

dapper 4 neat, trim 5 natty,
smart 6 jaunty, modish, spiffy,
sporty, spruce 7 stylish

dapple 3 dab, dot 4 spot
6 mottle

dappled 7 flecked, mottled,
spotted 10 variegated

Darcy, Fitzwilliam
character in: 17 Pride and
Prejudice
author: 6 Austen

Dardanus
father: 4 Zeus
mother: 7 Electra
twin brother: 6 Iasion
wife: 6 Myrina
son: 12 Erechthonius
ancestor of: 7 Trojans

dare 3 bet 4 defy 5 taunt
7 venture 9 challenge
11 provocation

daredevil 4 bold, rash 5 risky
8 heedless, reckless 9 audacious, breakneck, risk-taker
11 adventurous 12 death-
defying, devil-may-care
13 adventuresome

daredevilry 6 daring 8 rashness 9 derring-do 10 imprudence 12 carelessness,
heedlessness, recklessness
13 foolhardiness

Dares
companion of: 6 Aeneas
noted for: 6 boxing

Dares Phrygius
priest of: 10 Hephaestus

Dar es Salaam
former capital of: 8 Tanzania

Darien *see* 8 Colombia

daring 4 bold, game 5 brave
6 plucky 7 bravery, courage,
gallant, valiant 8 audacity,
boldness, intrepid 9 audacious,
dauntless, undaunted 10 courageous 11 adventurous, venturesome 13 audaciousness
15 adventurousness

daring deed 4 feat 7 exploit
11 achievement

dark 3 dim 4 deep, evil, inky
5 angry, black, bleak, dingy,
dusky, murky, night, shady
6 dismal, dreary, gloomy, hidden, opaque, secret, somber,
sullen, wicked 7 evening, joyless, obscure, ominous, shadowy, sunless 8 eventide,
frowning, hopeless, overcast,
sinister, twilight 9 concealed,
nightfall, nighttime, sorrowful 10 forbidding 11 threatening 12 discouraging
13 disheartening

darken 3 dim, dye 4 tint
5 cloud, color 6 sadden
7 blacken, obscure 8 dispirit

darkened 3 dim 5 dusky, unlit 6 cloudy, gloomy
7 clouded 8 blackened, tenebrous, unlighted 10 blacked
out 13 unilluminated

darkening 7 eclipse, shading
8 clouding, lowering 9 obscuring, shadowing 10 blackening
12 clouding over

Dark Frontier, The
author: 10 Eric Ambler

dark-hued 5 black, dusky,
ebony, raven 6 somber
7 swarthy

Dark Is Light Enough, The
author: 14 Christopher Fry

Dark Lady, The
author: 16 Louis Auchincloss

Dark Laughter
author: 16 Sherwood
Anderson

darkness 4 dusk 5 night,
shade 7 dimness, evening
8 eventide, twilight 9 blackness, nightfall, nighttime

Darkness at Noon
author: 14 Arthur Koestler

Darkness Visible
author: 14 William Golding

Dark Victory
director: 14 Edmund
Goulding
cast: 10 Bette Davis
11 George Brent 12 Ronald
Reagan 14 Humphrey Bo-
gart 19 Geraldine Fitzgerald
remade as: 11 Stolen Hours

darling 4 cute, dear, love
5 loved, sweet 6 adored,
lovely 7 beloved, dearest, lovable 8 adorable, charming, precious 9 cherished 10 attractive,
enchanting, sweetheart
11 captivating

Darling
director: 15 John Schlesinger
cast: 11 Dirk Bogarde 13 Julie Christie 14 Laurence
Harvey
Oscar for: 6 script 7 actress
(Christie)

Darling, Wendy
character in: 8 Peter Pan
author: 6 Barrie

darn 4 damn, dang, dash, drat,
mend 5 blast, patch, sew up
6 hang it, stitch 7 consarn,
doggone, goldang 8 confound
10 confound it

Darnay, Charles
character in: 16 A Tale of
Two Cities
author: 7 Dickens

darnel 12 Biblical weed

Darnell, Linda
real name: 20 Monetta
Eloyse Darnell
born: 8 Dallas TX
roles: 12 Blood and Sand,
Forever Amber 14 The Mark
of Zorro 17 Unfaithfully
Yours

Darren, James
real name: 13 James Ercolani
born: 14 Philadelphia PA
roles: 6 Gidget 13 The Time
Tunnel

dart 3 run 4 bolt, dash, flit,
jump, leap, race, rush, tear
5 bound, fling, hurry, spear,
spurt 6 hasten, spring, sprint
7 javelin, missile 10 projectile

D'Artagnan
character in: 18 The Three Musketeers
author: 5 Dumas (pere)

Dartle, Rosa
character in: 16 David Copperfield
author: 7 Dickens

Darwin, Charles
author of: 15 The Descent of Man 18 The Origin of Species 20 The Voyage of the Beagle
studied: 16 Galapagos Islands
field: 6 nature 7 biology
nationality: 7 British
theory of: 9 evolution 16 natural selection
ship: 6 Beagle

Dascylus
member of: 9 Argonauts
father: 5 Lycus

dash 3 bit, run, zip 4 bolt, dart, drop, elan, foil, hurl, race, ruin, rush, slam, tear, zeal 5 bound, crash, flair, fling, hurry, oomph, pinch, smash, speed, spoil, throw, touch, verve, vigor 6 dampen, energy, hasten, pizazz, spirit, splash, sprint, thrust, thwart 7 a little, panache, shatter, soupcon, spatter 8 splatter, splinter, vivacity 9 animation, frustrate 10 disappoint, discourage

dashing 4 bold 5 brave 6 daring, plucky 7 gallant 8 fearless, spirited, unafraid 9 audacious, impetuous 10 courageous 13 swashbuckling

dash one's hopes 5 daunt, unman 6 deject 7 depress 8 dispirit 10 discourage, dishearten

Dashwood, Elinor and Marianne
characters in: 19 Sense and Sensibility
author: 6 Austen

DaSilva, Howard
real name: 17 Harold Silverblatt
born: 11 Cleveland OH
roles: 8 Oklahoma 12 Sergeant York 14 The Great Gatsby 20 Abe Lincoln in Illinois

Dass, Secundra
character in: 21 The Master of Ballantrae
author: 9 Stevenson

dastard 3 cad 6 coward, craven 7 bounder, caitiff, chicken 8 poltroon 11 yellow-belly

dastardly 3 low 4 base, mean, vile 6 sneaky 8 cowardly, shameful 9 atrocious 10 despicable

data 4 dope, info 5 facts 7 dossier, figures 8 evidence 9 documents 11 information

Datchery, Mr
character in: 22 The Mystery of Edwin Drood
author: 7 Dickens

date 3 age, era 5 court, epoch, stage 6 escort, period 7 partner, take out 9 companion, originate 10 engagement, rendezvous 11 appointment

date 18 Phoenix dactylifera
varieties: 5 cliff 6 Ceylon 7 Chinese 9 Jerusalem 12 Canary Island

dated 5 passe 6 old hat 8 obsolete, outmoded 9 out-of-date 10 antiquated 12 old-fashioned 13 unfashionable

daub 4 blot, coat, soil, spot 5 cover, dirty, paint, smear, stain 6 blotch, smirch, smudge 7 splotch

Daudet, Alphonse
author of: 6 Sappho 15 The Woman of Arles 17 Letters from My Mill 18 Tartarin of Tarascon

Daughter of the Regiment, The
opera by: 9 Donizetti

Daumier, Honore
born: 6 France 10 Marseilles
artwork: 7 Bathers 9 Gargantua 12 Men of Justice 13 Bluestockings 14 The Washerwoman 16 The Good Bourgeois 18 The Legislative Body 19 Professors and Pupils 20 Stories from Antiquity 21 The Third-Class Carriage

daunt 3 cow 4 dash, faze 5 abash, alarm, scare 6 deject, dismay, menace, subdue 7 depress, unnerve 8 affright, browbeat, frighten, threaten 10 discourage, dishearten, intimidate

dauntless 4 bold 5 brave, gutsy 6 daring, heroic 7 gallant, valiant 8 fearless, resolute, unafraid, valorous 10 courageous 12 stouthearted

dauntlessness 4 grit, guts, sand 5 nerve, pluck, spunk, valor 6 daring, mettle 7 bravery, courage, resolve 8 boldness 9 fortitude 10 resolution 12 fearlessness, resoluteness 16 stout-heartedness

Davers, Lady
character in: 6 Pamela
author: 10 Richardson

David
king of: 6 Israel
father: 5 Jesse
wife: 6 Maacah, Michal 7 Abigail, Ahinoam, Haggith 9 Bathsheba
son: 5 Amnon 7 Absalom, Chileab, Solomon 8 Adonijah
daughter: 5 Tamar
brother: 5 Eliab 7 Shammah 8 Abinadab
sister: 7 Abigail
friend: 5 Abner 8 Jonathan
nephew: 5 Amasa
city of: 9 Bethlehem, Jerusalem
anointed by: 6 Samuel
killed: 7 Goliath
wrote: 6 Psalms
comforter: 7 Abishag
conspirators against: 4 Joab 8 Abiathar, Adonijah
pertaining to: 7 Davidic

David, Jacques-Louis
born: 5 Paris 6 France
artwork: 13 Mme de Verninac 15 The Death of Marat 19 The Oath of the Horatii 23 The Coronation of Napoleon 26 View of the Luxembourg Gardens 31 The Intervention of the Sabine Women

David Copperfield
author: 14 Charles Dickens
character: 3 Ham 6 Barkis, Mr Dick 7 Creakle 8 Traddles 9 Mr Spenlow, Uriah Heep 10 Aunt Betsey, Little Em'ly, Mr Micawber, Rosa Dartle, Steerforth 11 Dora Spenlow, Little Emily, Mr Murdstone, Mr Wickfield, Mrs Gummidge 13 Clara Peggotty 14 Agnes Wickfield, Betsey Trotwood
director: 11 George Cukor
cast: 8 W C Fields 10 Madge Evans 11 Frank Lawton, Roland Young 13 Basil Rathbone, Edna May Oliver 15 Lionel Barrymore 16 Maureen O'Sullivan 18 Freddie Bartholomew

David Harum
author: 19 Edward Noyes Westcott

Davies, Arthur Bowen
born: 7 Utica NY

artwork: 5 Dream **8** Unicorns **9** Crescendo **13** Every Saturday **15** Dancing Children, Sacramental Tree **17** Along the Erie Canal **18** Leda and the Dioscuri

Davies, Marion
real name: 19 Marion Cecilia Douras
lover: 21 William Randolph Hearst
born: 10 Brooklyn NY
roles: 12 Cain and Mable **13** Runaway Romany **15** Tillie the Toiler

Davis, Bette
real name: 18 Ruth Elizabeth Davis
husband: 11 Gary Merrill
born: 8 Lowell MA
roles: 7 Jezebel (Oscar) **9** Dangerous (Oscar), The Letter **10** Now Voyager, The Old Maid **11** All About Eve, Dark Victory **14** Of Human Bondage, The Little Foxes **18** The Petrified Forest **22** Hush Hush Sweet Charlotte **26** What Ever Happened to Baby Jane?

Davis, H L
author of: 14 Honey in the Horn

Davis, Ossie
wife: 7 Ruby Dee
born: 9 Cogdell GA
author: 16 Purlie Victorious
roles/films: 7 Jamaica **15** A Raisin in the Sun **18** No Time for Sergeants **19** Cotton Comes to Harlem

Davis, Sammy Jr
wife: 8 May Britt
group: 14 Will Master Trio
born: 9 New York NY
autobiography: 7 Yes I Can
roles: 11 Mr Wonderful **12** Porgy and Bess **20** The Benny Goodman Story

Davis, Stuart
born: 14 Philadelphia PA
artwork: 4 Visa **9** Eggbeater **11** Lucky Strike, Ready to Wear **11** Owh! In Sao Pao **12** The Mellow Pad **14** Colonial Cubism **15** Cigarette Papers

Davy, Humphrey
field: 9 chemistry
nationality: 7 British
isolated: 5 boron **6** barium, sodium **7** calcium **8** chlorine **9** magnesium, potassium, strontium
invented: 8 Davy lamp **10** miner's lamp

dawdle 4 idle, loaf **5** dally, delay **6** loiter **10** dillydally **12** putter around **13** procrastinate

dawdler
French: 7 flaneur

dawdling
French: 8 flanerie

dawn 4 rise **5** begin, birth, occur, start, sunup **6** advent, appear, Aurora, emerge, origin, strike, unfold **7** develop, sunrise **8** commence, daybreak, daylight **9** beginning, emergence, inception, unfolding **12** commencement
god of: 8 Heimdall
goddess of: 3 Eos **6** Aurore, Matuta

dawning 5 sunup **7** morning, sunrise **8** daybreak, daylight

Dawn Patrol, The
director: 14 Edmund Goulding
cast: 10 David Niven, Errol Flynn **11** Donald Crisp **13** Basil Rathbone **14** Melville Cooper **15** Barry Fitzgerald

day 3 age **4** date, time **5** epoch **6** period

Day, Clarence (Jr)
author of: 14 God and My Father, Life with Father, Life with Mother

Day, Doris
real name: 18 Doris von Kappelhoff
born: 12 Cincinnati OH
autobiography: 19 Doris Day Her Own Story
roles: 10 Pillow Talk **12** Calamity Jane **13** The Pajama Game **15** Move Over Darling, The Doris Day Show **23** Please Don't Eat the Daisies

daybed 5 couch **6** lounge **12** chaise longue

day book 5 diary **6** agenda **7** journal **8** calendar, schedule

daybreak 4 dawn **5** sunup **7** sunrise

daydream 4 muse **5** fancy **7** fantasy, imagine, reverie **9** fantasize **10** wool-gather **14** castle in the air

Day for Night
director: 16 Francois Truffaut
cast: 15 Jean-Pierre Leaud **16** Francois Truffaut, Jacqueline Bisset, Jean-Pierre Aumont
Oscar for: 11 foreign film

daylight 4 dawn **5** sunup **7** morning, sunrise **8** full view, openness, sunlight, sunshine

Days and Nights
author: 17 Konstantin Simonov

day's end 3 eve **4** dusk, even **6** sunset **7** evening, sundown **8** gleaming, twilight **9** nightfall

Days of Heaven
director: 14 Terrence Malick
cast: 9 Linda Manz **10** Sam Shepard **11** Brooke Adams, Richard Gere
Oscar for: 14 cinematography

Days of Wine and Roses
director: 12 Blake Edwards
cast: 9 Lee Remick **10** Jack Lemmon **11** Jack Klugman **15** Charles Bickford
score: 12 Henry Mancini

daze 4 numb, stun **5** amaze, shock **6** benumb, dazzle, excite, muddle, stupor **7** astound, confuse, stagger, startle, stupefy **8** astonish, bewilder, surprise **9** disorient, electrify **11** flabbergast **12** astonishment, bewilderment, blow one's mind **14** discombobulate

dazed 5 woozy **6** groggy **7** confused, dazzled, stunned **9** befuddled, stupefied **10** bewildered, punch-drunk

dazzle 3 awe **4** blur, daze **5** blind **6** excite **7** confuse, overawe **9** electrify, overpower, overwhelm

dazzling 7 radiant **8** blinding **9** sparkling **10** impressive, staggering **11** coruscating **12** breathtaking, electrifying, overwhelming **14** flabbergasting

deacon 6 cleric **9** churchman, clergyman **12** ecclesiastic

deactivate 6 defuse **9** switch off **10** neutralize

dead, the dead 4 beat, cold, dull, flat **5** depth, exact, midst, quiet, spent, tired, total, utter, vapid **6** entire, middle, unused **7** defunct, expired, extinct, insipid, precise, useless, utterly, worn-out **8** abruptly, absolute, complete, deceased, entirely, inactive, lifeless, obsolete, perished, stagnant, suddenly, thorough, unerring **9** exhausted, inanimate, inorganic **10** absolutely, completely, lackluster, unemployed, unexciting **11** ineffectual, inoperative **12** unproductive, unprofitable
Latin: 8 ad patres
god of: 6 Osiris **7** Veiovis

dead body 5 stiff **6** corpse **7** cadaver, remains

deaden 4 dope, drug, dull, mute, numb **5** abate, blunt **6** lessen, muffle, soothe, subdue, weaken **7** assuage, smother **8** diminish, mitigate, moderate **9** alleviate **11** anesthetize

deadened 5 muted **6** dulled, numbed **7** muffled, subdued

Dead Father, The
author: **15** Donald Barthelme

Dea Dia
origin: **5** Roman
goddess of: **11** agriculture
corresponds to: **13** Acca Laurentia

deadlock 7 impasse **8** standoff **9** stalemate **10** standstill

deadly 3 wan **4** dull **5** ashen, awful, fatal, fully, undue **6** boring, lethal, mortal, pallid **7** awfully, baneful, destroy, extreme, ghostly, tedious, totally **8** dreadful, entirely, horribly, terrible, terribly, tiresome **9** excessive, malignant, wearisome **10** cadaverous, completely, implacable, inordinate, relentless, thoroughly **11** destructive, unrelenting

deadpan 5 sober **8** detached **9** impassive **11** unemotional **13** straight-faced

dead ringer 4 copy, mate, twin **6** double **9** duplicate **11** counterpart **13** spitting image

Dead Souls
author: **12** Nikolai Gogol

dead to the world 6 asleep **7** out cold **9** konked out **10** fast asleep, slumbering **11** sound asleep

dead weight 7 ballast **9** inert mass

Dead Zone, The
author: **11** Stephen King

deal 3 act **4** give, hand **5** round, see to, trade, treat **6** behave, handle, market **7** bargain, concern, deliver, dole out, give out, mete out, oversee **8** consider, dispense **9** agreement, apportion **10** administer, distribute, **11** arrangement **12** distribution **13** apportionment

dealer 5 agent **6** monger, trader, vendor **8** merchant **10** trafficker **11** distributor

dealing, dealings 5 trade **7** traffic **8** business, practice **9** relations, treatment **12** transactions

dealing out 8 dividing **9** allotting, bestowing **10** conferring, consigning, dispensing **12** apportioning, distributing

Dea Marica *see* **6** Marica

Dean, Dizzy (Jay Hanna)
sport: **8** baseball
position: **7** pitcher
team: **16** St Louis Cardinals
part of: **12** Gashouse Gang
brother: **4** Paul

Dean, James (Jimmy)
real name: **14** James Byron Dean
born: **8** Marion IN
roles: **5** Giant **10** East of Eden **18** Rebel Without a Cause

Deane, Seneca
character in: **7** Babbitt
author: **5** Lewis

Dean's December
author: **10** Saul Bellow

dear 4 love **5** angel, loved **6** costly **7** beloved, darling **8** esteemed, favorite, precious **9** cherished, expensive, respected **10** sweetheart
French: **5** cheri **6** cherie

Dear Antoine
author: **11** Jean Anouilh

Dear Brutus
author: **12** James M Barrie

dearest 7 beloved, darling

dearth 4 lack **7** paucity **8** scarcity, shortage **10** deficiency

death, Death 5 dying **6** demise **7** decease, passing **9** departure **10** expiration, grim reaper
goddess of: **3** Hel **7** Berchta, Perchta **10** Ereshkigal

Death Be Not Proud
author: **9** John Donne

death blow
French: **11** coup de grace

Death Comes for the Archbishop
author: **11** Willa Cather
character: **7** Jacinto **9** Kit Carson **16** Bishop Jean Latour **20** Father Joseph Vaillant

death-dealing 5 fatal **6** lethal, mortal **7** killing **11** destructive

death-defying 4 bold, rash **5** risky **6** daring **8** reckless **9** audacious, breakneck, daredevil

Death in the Family, A
author: **9** James Agee

Death in Venice
director: **15** Luchino Visconti
author: **10** Thomas Mann
cast: **9** Mark Burns **11** Dirk Bogarde **14** Marisa Berenson

deathless 7 eternal **8** immortal **9** perpetual **11** everlasting

deathlike 3 wan **4** pale **5** ashen **6** pallid **7** ghastly

9 bloodless **10** cadaverous, corpselike

deathly 4 very **7** extreme, intense **8** terrible **9** extremely **12** overwhelming **15** resembling death

Death of a Salesman
director: **12** Laslo Benedek
author: **12** Arthur Miller
character: **4** Biff **5** Happy, Linda **7** Bernard, Charley **8** Uncle Ben **10** Willy Loman
cast: **13** Frederic March, Kevin McCarthy **14** Mildred Dunnock **15** Cameron Mitchell

Death of Ivan Ilyich, The
author: **10** Leo Tolstoy

Death of the Gods, The
author: **17** Dmitri Merejkowski

Death of the Heart
author: **14** Elizabeth Bowen

Death on the Nile
author: **14** Agatha Christie

Death Takes a Holiday
director: **14** Mitchell Leisen
cast: **11** Guy Standing **13** Evelyn Venable, Frederic March (Death)

Death Valley Days
host: **12** Robert Taylor, Ronald Reagan **13** Dale Robertson **14** Stanley Andrews

debacle 4 rout, ruin **5** havoc, wreck **8** collapse, disaster, downfall **9** breakdown, cataclysm, overthrow, ruination **10** bankruptcy **11** catastrophe, devastation, dissolution **12** vanquishment **14** disintegration

debar 3 ban **6** reject **7** exclude, keep out **8** preclude, prohibit **9** blackball, blacklist

debark 4 land

debarment 7 removal **8** omission **9** exception, exclusion, exemption, rejection **11** elimination, prohibition **12** nonadmission

debase 5 lower **6** befoul, defile **7** corrupt, degrade **8** disgrace, dishonor **9** desecrate **10** adulterate **11** deteriorate **16** impair the worth of **18** reduce the quality of

debased 4 vile **6** impure **7** corrupt, defiled, lowered **8** degraded, depraved **9** debauched, disgraced, dissolute, perverted **10** degenerate, dissipated **11** adulterated

debasement 9 decadence, depravity **10** corruption, debauchery, degeneracy, immorality, perversion 13 dissoluteness

debatable 4 iffy 6 unsure 7 dubious 8 arguable, doubtful 9 uncertain, undecided 10 disputable 12 questionable 13 problematical

debate 5 argue 6 ponder 7 discuss, dispute, reflect 8 argument, cogitate, consider, hash over 10 cogitation, deliberate, discussion, meditation, reflection, think about 12 deliberation, meditate upon 13 consideration

debauch 4 orgy 5 revel, spree 6 debase 7 carouse, corrupt, deprave, revelry, subvert 8 carousal 9 bacchanal 10 lead astray, saturnalia

debauched 4 lewd 6 wanton 7 corrupt, debased, immoral 8 degraded, depraved, perverse, vitiated 9 abandoned, corrupted, dissolute, lecherous, led astray, perverted, reprobate, shameless 10 degenerate, dissipated, lascivious, libidinous, licentious, profligate 12 disreputable

debauchery 6 excess 11 dissipation 12 immoderation, intemperance 14 self-indulgence

DeBeck, Billy creator/artist of: 12 Barney Google 20 Parlor Bedroom and Sink

debilitate 6 weaken 7 wear out 8 enervate 10 devitalize, make feeble 17 deprive of strength

debilitated 5 frail 6 feeble, infirm 7 worn out 8 delicate, weakened 9 enervated 11 devitalized

debilitation 8 handicap, weakness 9 infirmity 10 affliction, disability, impairment, inadequacy 11 disablement

debility 7 fatigue, frailty 8 asthenia, handicap, senility, weakness 9 infirmity, lassitude, weakening 10 affliction, enervation, exhaustion, feebleness, impairment, invalidism, sickliness 11 decrepitude, prostration

Debir conqueror: 7 Othniel

debit 4 debt 6 red ink 7 account, payable 9 liability 10 balance due, obligation 11 ledger entry, shortcoming

debonair 5 suave 6 dapper, jaunty, urbane 7 buoyant, elegant, genteel, refined 8 care-

free, charming, gracious, well-bred 9 sprightly 11 free and easy 12 lighthearted 13 sophisticated

Deborah 11 Hebrew judge companion: 7 Rebekah summoned: 5 Barak

debouch 5 drain 6 emerge, let out 7 flow out 9 discharge

debris 4 crap, junk 5 dreck, dregs, dross, ruins, scrap, trash, waste 6 litter, rubble, shards 7 clutter, garbage, rubbish 8 detritus, wreckage 9 fragments

debt 4 bill 5 debit 7 arrears 9 liability 10 obligation 15 deferred payment, that which is owed

debunk 4 bare 5 strip 6 expose, send up, show up, unmask 7 deflate, lampoon, take off, uncloak, uncover 8 ridicule, satirize 9 burlesque, demystify, disparage 13 demythologize

Debussy, Claude Achille born: 6 France 15 St Germain-en-Laye composer of: 5 La Mer 6 Gigues, Iberia, Images 8 Estampes 9 Nocturnes, Printemps 11 Clair de Lune 13 En Blanc et Noir 15 Children's Corner, L'Enfant prodigue 16 La Demoiselle Elue, Suite Bergamasque 17 Rondes de Printemps, The Blessed Damozel 18 Pelleas et Melisande 24 The Girl with the Flaxen Hair 26 Prelude a l'apres-midi d'un faune 28 Prelude to the Afternoon of a Faun

debut 9 coming out 12 presentation

decadence 5 decay 7 decline 10 corruption, debasement, degeneracy, immorality 12 degeneration 13 deterioration

decadent 7 corrupt, debased, immoral 8 decaying, depraved, perverse 9 debauched, dissolute, perverted 10 degenerate French: 11 fin de siecle

Decalogue 15 Ten Commandments

Decameron, The author: 17 Giovanni Boccaccio

decamp 7 move off, run away, take off 8 march off, sneak off

decampment 6 escape, flight 7 getaway

decant 4 pour 7 draw off, pour out

decanter 6 bottle, carafe, vessel

decathlon winner 11 Bruce Jenner

Decatur, Stephen served in: 11 Algerine War, Barbary Wars 13 Tripolitan War 19 War of Eighteen Twelve commander of ship: 12 United States defeated ship: 10 Macedonian (British) saying: 22 "Our country right or wrong"

decay 3 rot 5 spoil 7 corrode, putrefy, rotting 8 spoiling 9 decompose 12 disintegrate, putrefaction 13 decomposition goddess of: 4 Hour 5 Horae

decayed 3 bad 6 putrid, rotted, rotten, ruined 7 corrupt, gone bad, spoiled 10 decomposed 12 deteriorated 13 disintegrated

deceased see 4 dead

deceit 5 fraud 8 cheating, trickery 9 duplicity 10 dishonesty, trickiness 11 fraudulence 13 double-dealing 15 underhandedness 17 misrepresentation

deceitful 5 false 6 crafty, sneaky, tricky 7 cunning 9 dishonest, insincere 11 duplicitous, treacherous, underhanded 12 hypocritical 13 double-dealing, untrustworthy

deceitfulness 5 fraud 7 cunning, slyness 9 falseness, hypocrisy, treachery 10 craftiness, dishonesty, sneakiness, trickiness 11 insincerity 15 underhandedness 17 untrustworthiness

deceive 3 con 4 fool 5 cheat, put on, trick 6 delude 7 defraud, mislead, swindle

deceiver 4 fake 5 cheat, fraud, quack 6 con man 7 cozener 8 impostor, swindler 9 charlatan, trickster 10 mountebank 13 confidence man

decelerate 5 brake 8 slow down

deceleration 7 braking, slowing

December *see box, p. 248*

decency 7 decorum, modesty 9 propriety 14 respectability 15 appropriateness

decent 4 fair, nice 5 ample 6 proper, seemly 7 correct, fitting 8 adequate, gracious, obliging, passable, suitable

December
  event: **11** Pearl Harbor
    (7), Winter solstice (21,
    22)
  flower: **5** holly
    9 narcissus
  French: **8** Decembre
  gem: **4** ruby **6** zircon
    9 turquoise
  German: **8** Dezember
  holiday: **8** Hanukkah
    9 Boxing Day (26),
    Christmas (25) **16** Saint
    Nicholas Day (6)
  Italian: **8** Dicembre
  number of days:
    9 thirty-one
  origin of name: **5** decem
    (Latin meaning ten)
  place in year:
    Gregorian: **7** twelfth
    Roman: **5** tenth
    Julian: **7** twelfth
  Spanish: **9** Diciembre
  Zodiac sign: **9** Capri-
    corn **11** Sagittarius

9 courteous **10** acceptable, sufficient **11** appropriate **12** satisfactory **13** accommodating

deception 5 fraud, trick
7 cunning **8** artifice, illusion,
trickery **9** duplicity, treachery
10 trickiness **11** fraudulence,
insincerity **13** double-dealing

deceptive 5 phony **9** dishonest **10** fraudulent, misleading

deceptiveness 5 fraud
11 fraudulence

decibel
  abbreviation: **2** dB

decide 4 rule **5** elect, judge
6 choose, decree, select, settle
7 resolve **9** determine

decided 4 firm **7** certain
8 clear-cut, definite, emphatic,
resolute **9** assertive **10** deliberate, determined, unwavering
12 indisputable, strong-willed,
unhesitating, unmistakable
14 unquestionable

decidedly 9 certainly **10** absolutely **11** indubitably, undoubtedly **12** indisputably,
unmistakably **13** unequivocally **14** unquestionably

decidedness 7 purpose, resolve **10** resolution **12** resoluteness **13** determination
14 purposefulness

decide on 5 adopt, elect
6 choose, opt for, select, settle **7** appoint, arrange, embrace, espouse, pick out

8 settle on **9** determine, establish, single out

decigram
  abbreviation: **2** dg

deciliter
  abbreviation: **2** dL

decimate 6 reduce **7** destroy
8 massacre **9** slaughter
13 greatly reduce

decimeter
  abbreviation: **2** dm

decipher 5 solve **6** decode, deduce, render **7** decrypt, dope
out, explain, make out, unravel **8** construe, untangle
9 interpret, translate
12 cryptanalyze

decision 6 decree, ruling
7 finding, outcome, purpose,
resolve, verdict **8** judgment
10 conclusion, resolution
12 resoluteness **13** determination **14** purposefulness

decisive 4 firm **5** final **8** absolute, definite, positive, reso-
lute **10** conclusive, convincing,
definitive, determined, unden-
able **12** indisputable

decisive blow 9 deathblow
11 coup de grace

decisiveness 7 purpose, resolve **10** resolution **12** resoluteness **14** purposefulness

decisive point 3 nut **4** core,
crux, gist **5** basis, heart **6** kernel **7** essence **9** essential

deck 4 garb, trim **5** adorn, array, dress, prank **6** clothe, doll
up, enrich, outfit, tog out
7 apparel, bedizen, festoon,
furbish, garnish, gussy up
8 accouter, beautify, ornament,
spruce up **9** embellish

Decker, Mary
  sport: **7** running
  married name: **6** Slaney

deck out 5 adorn, array,
dress **6** attire, clothe, fit out,
outfit, rig out **7** costume

declaim 4 rail **5** orate **6** recite
7 inveigh **9** sermonize
11 pontificate

declaration 6 avowal, notice
8 document **9** assertion, statement, testimony **10** deposition **11** affirmation, attestation,
publication **12** announcement,
notification, proclamation
14 acknowledgment

declare 4 show **6** affirm, reveal **7** express **8** announce,
proclaim **9** pronounce

declare null and void 6 cancel, repeal, revoke **7** abolish,
rescind, retract **8** abrogate, set

aside **9** repudiate **10** invalidate **11** countermand

declare untrue 4 deny **9** repudiate **10** contradict

decline 3 ebb **4** drop, fail, flag,
sink, wane **5** decay, slump,
spurn **6** balk at, eschew,
lessen, refuse, reject, weaken,
worsen **7** dwindle **8** decrease,
diminish, downfall **9** downgrade, downswing **11** deteriorate **13** deterioration

Decline and Fall
  author: **11** Evelyn Waugh

**Decline and Fall of the Ro-
man Empire, The**
  author: **12** Edward Gibbon

declivity 4 drop **5** slant, slope
6 plunge **7** descent

decompose 3 rot **5** decay,
spoil **7** putrefy **8** separate
10 go to pieces **12** disintegrate

decomposed 6 putrid, rotted,
rotten **7** decayed, spoiled
9 putrefied **13** disintegrated

decontaminate 6 purify **9** disinfect, sterilize

decor 13 ornamentation

decorate 4 trim **5** adorn, array, honor **7** festoon, garnish
8 beautify, ornament
9 embellish

decorated 5 fancy **6** decked,
ornate **7** adorned, trimmed
8 bedecked **9** bemedaled, bedizened, garnished **10** ornamented **11** embellished

decoration 4 trim **5** award,
badge, medal **6** emblem, ribbon **7** garnish **8** ornament,
trimming **9** adornment **13** embellishment, ornamentation
14 beautification

decorous 3 fit **6** decent, polite,
proper, seemly **7** correct **8** becoming, mannerly, suitable
9 dignified **10** respectful
11 appropriate

decorum 4 tact **5** taste **7** dignity **8** good form **9** gentility,
propriety **10** politeness
14 respectability

decoy 4 bait, lure **5** plant,
snare **6** allure, come-on, entice **10** enticement, inducement **11** smoke screen

decrease 4 drop, ease, loss
5 abate, taper **6** lessen, reduce **7** cutback, decline, dwindle, fall-off, slacken, subside
8 diminish **9** abatement, dwindling, lessening, reduction
10 de-escalate, diminution
12 de-escalation

decree 3 law **5** edict, order

6 dictum, ruling **7** command, mandate, statute **8** proclaim **9** authorize **12** proclamation

decrepit 7 rickety **8** battered **10** broken-down **11** dilapidated

decrescendo
music: **22** gradually getting softer
abbreviation: **4** decr

decry 7 censure, condemn **8** denounce **9** criticize, deprecate, disparage

Dedalus, Stephen
character in: **7** Ulysses **30** Portrait of the Artist as a Young Man
author: **5** Joyce

dedicate 6 commit, devote, launch, pledge **7** address, present **8** inscribe

dedication 8 devotion **10** commitment **11** devotedness **16** prefatory address **20** prefatory inscription

Dedlock, Sir Leicester and Lady
characters in: **10** Bleak House
author: **7** Dickens

deduce 5 infer **6** gather, reason **8** conclude **10** comprehend, understand

deduct 4 take **6** remove **8** subtract, take from, withdraw **10** decrease by

deduction 5 guess **6** belief, credit, rebate **7** removal **8** analysis, decrease, discount, judgment, markdown, rollback **9** abatement, allowance, exemption, gathering, inference, lessening, reasoning, reduction **10** assumption, concession, conclusion, diminution, hypothesis, reflection, taking away, withdrawal **11** calculation, presumption, speculation, subtraction, supposition **13** comprehension, consideration, understanding **14** interpretation

Dee, Ruby
real name: **14** Ruby Ann Wallace
husband: **10** Ossie Davis
born: **11** Cleveland OH
roles: **15** A Raisin in the Sun **16** Purlie Victorious

Dee, Sandra
real name: **13** Alexandra Zuck
husband: **10** Bobby Darin
born: **9** Bayonne NJ
roles: **6** Gidget **12** A Summer Place **15** Tammy Tell Me True

deed 3 act **4** feat **5** title **6** action, effort **11** achievement **14** accomplishment

deeds are manly, words are womanish
Italian: **24** fatti maschii parole femine
motto of: **8** Maryland

deem 4 hold, view **5** judge, think **6** regard **7** believe **8** consider

de-emphasize 8 play down **9** underplay

deep 3 far, sea **4** dark, late, lost, rich, wise **5** far in, midst, ocean, vivid **6** astute, strong **7** extreme, intense, learned **8** absorbed, immersed, involved, profound, resonant, sonorous **9** engrossed, sagacious **10** discerning **11** intelligent **13** philosophical

Deep, The
author: **13** Peter Benchley

deeply 6 richly **7** acutely, gravely, greatly, vividly **8** entirely **9** intensely, seriously **10** completely, profoundly, resonantly, sonorously, thoroughly **12** passionately

deeply felt 6 ardent, fervid **7** earnest, fervent, intense, sincere, zealous **9** heartfelt **10** passionate **11** impassioned **12** wholehearted

deepness 10 profundity

deep-rooted 7 abiding, lasting **8** enduring **9** confirmed, ingrained

deep-seated 7 abiding, lasting **8** enduring **9** confirmed, ingrained

deep thought 10 absorption, brown study, intentness **11** engrossment **13** concentration

deep water 3 jam **4** mess **5** ocean **6** pickle **7** trouble **8** distress **10** difficulty **11** dire straits, predicament **12** over one's head

deer
young: **4** fawn
female: **3** doe

Deer Hunter, The
director: **13** Michael Cimino
cast: **10** John Cazale, John Savage **11** Meryl Streep **12** Robert De Niro **17** Christopher Walken
Oscar for: **7** picture **8** director **15** supporting actor (Walken)

Deerslayer, The
author: **19** James Fenimore Cooper
first of: **20** Leatherstocking Tales
character: **4** Hist **5** Hetty **6** Judith **10** Hurry Harry **11** Natty Bumppo (Deerslayer) **12** Chingachgook, Thomas Hutter

de-escalate 5 limit **6** lessen, narrow **8** contract, minimize

deface 3 mar **4** mark, scar **5** spoil **6** bruise, damage, impair, injure **9** disfigure

de facto 4 real **6** actual, really **8** actually

defalcate 8 embezzle **14** misappropriate

defamation 5 libel **7** calumny, slander **8** vilification **13** disparagement

defamatory 8 libelous **9** vilifying **10** calumnious, derogatory, slanderous **11** disparaging

defame 5 libel **6** malign, vilify **7** degrade, slander **8** derogate **9** denigrate, discredit, disparage **10** calumniate

Defarge, Madame
character in: **16** A Tale of Two Cities
author: **7** Dickens

default 10 nonpayment

defeat 4 foil, loss, rout **5** cream, crush, elude, quell **6** baffle, thwart **7** conquer, setback, shellac, trounce **8** confound, overcome, vanquish **9** frustrate, overpower, overthrow, overwhelm, thwarting **11** frustration **14** disappointment

defeated 4 beat **5** upset **6** beaten, bested, licked, routed **7** outdone, whipped, worsted **8** overcame **9** conquered, overthrew, put to rout **10** frustrated, overthrown **11** overpowered, overwhelmed **12** hors de combat

defect 4 flaw, scar, spot **5** break, crack, fault, stain **6** blotch, foible **7** blemish, default, failing, frailty **8** omission, weakness **10** deficiency **11** shortcoming **12** imperfection **14** incompleteness

defective 6 broken, faulty, flawed **7** lacking, wanting **8** abnormal, impaired **9** deficient, imperfect, subnormal **10** inadequate, out of order **11** inoperative **12** insufficient

Defence of Poetry
author: **18** Percy Bysshe Shelley

defend 5 guard **6** secure, shield, uphold **7** endorse, protect, shelter, stand by, support, sustain **8** advocate, champion, maintain, preserve **9** safeguard

defender 8 advocate, champion, guardian, upholder **9** protector, supporter

Defender of the Faith
Latin: **13** Fidei Defensor
title of: **17** English sovereigns

Defenders, The
character: **10** Joan Miller **14** Helen Donaldson, Kenneth Preston **15** Lawrence Preston
cast: **10** E G Marshall, Robert Reed **11** Joan Hackett, Polly Rowles

defense 4 care **5** guard **7** custody, support **8** advocacy, security **9** barricade, safeguard, upholding **10** protection, stronghold **11** maintenance, safekeeping **12** preservation **13** fortification, justification

defenseless 7 unarmed **8** helpless **10** on one's back, vulnerable, weaponless **11** unprotected, unresisting

defensible 3 fit **5** valid **6** proper **7** tenable **8** sensible, suitable **9** allowable, excusable **10** admissible, condonable, forgivable, pardonable, vindicable **11** justifiable, permissible, supportable, warrantable

defer 4 obey **5** delay, table, yield **6** accede, give in, put off, shelve, submit **7** respect, suspend **8** postpone **10** capitulate

deference 5 honor **6** esteem, regard **7** respect **9** obedience, reverence **12** capitulation **13** consideration

deferential 5 civil **6** polite **7** dutiful **8** obedient, reverent **9** courteous, regardful **10** respectful, submissive **11** acquiescent, considerate, reverential

deferment 4 stay **5** delay **9** extension **12** postponement

deferral 5 pause **6** hiatus, recess **8** abeyance **10** suspension **12** postponement **14** discontinuance

defiance 9 hostility, obstinacy, rebellion **12** disobedience **14** rebelliousness

defiant 4 bold **9** truculent **10** aggressive, rebellious **11** disobedient, provocative

Defiant Ones, The
director: **13** Stanley Kramer
cast: **10** Tony Curtis **11** Lon Chaney Jr **12** Cara Williams **13** Charles McGraw,

Sidney Poitier, Theodore Bikel
Oscar for: **10** screenplay

deficiency 4 flaw **6** defect **7** failing, frailty **8** shortage, weakness **10** inadequacy **11** shortcoming **12** imperfection **13** insufficiency

deficient 4 weak **6** flawed **7** lacking, short on **8** inferior **9** defective **10** inadequate **11** substandard **12** insufficient **14** unsatisfactory

deficit 8 shortage **9** shortfall **10** deficiency

de fide 10 of the faith

defile 4 soil **5** smear, spoil, stain, taint **6** befoul, debase **7** degrade, profane, tarnish **8** besmirch, disgrace, dishonor **9** desecrate

defiled 5 dirty **6** fouled, impure, soiled **7** debased, dirtied, stained, sullied, tainted, unclean **8** befouled, polluted, ravished, smirched, violated **9** blackened, corrupted, tarnished **10** besmirched **12** contaminated

define 5 state **7** clarify, explain, specify **8** describe, spell out **9** delineate, designate

definite 3 set **4** sure **5** exact, fixed **7** certain, precise **8** clearcut, positive

definitely 5 truly **6** indeed, surely **7** for sure, no doubt **9** assuredly, certainly, decidedly, doubtless, expressly **10** absolutely, decisively, explicitly, positively, undeniably **11** indubitably, inescapably, unavoidably, undoubtedly **12** unmistakably **13** categorically, unequivocally **14** unequivocally, unquestionably **16** incontrovertibly

definiteness 8 sureness **9** certainty, precision **10** exactitude **11** unambiguity

definition 6 limits **7** clarity, purpose **11** description **15** distinctiveness

definitive 5 exact **7** decided, perfect **8** complete, decisive, reliable **10** conclusive, consummate

deflate 6 reduce **7** flatten **8** contract **9** devaluate

deflect 6 divert, swerve

Defoe, Daniel
author of: **6** Roxana **11** Colonel Jack **12** Moll Flanders **14** Robinson Crusoe **23** A Journal of the Plague Year

DeForest, Lee
invented/worked on: **10** audion tube, television **13** sound pictures

deform 3 mar **4** maim **5** twist **6** mangle **7** contort, distort **9** disfigure

deformation 9 deformity **10** distortion **12** malformation **13** disfigurement

deformed 6 marred, warped **7** defaced, mangled, spoiled, twisted **8** crippled **9** misshapen, monstrous **10** disfigured

deformity 12 malformation

defraud 3 con **4** bilk, rook **5** cheat **6** fleece, rip off **7** swindle

defray 3 pay **5** cover **11** foot the bill

deft 3 apt **4** able, sure **5** quick **6** adroit, expert **8** skillful **9** dexterous

deftness 5 knack, skill **7** ability **8** facility **9** adeptness, dexterity, handiness **10** adroitness, competency **11** proficiency **12** skillfulness

defunct 4 dead **7** extinct

defy 5 spurn **6** oppose, resist **7** disdain **8** confront **9** challenge, disregard, withstand

degage 4 easy **8** detached **10** disengaged **13** unconstrained

Degas, (Hilaire Germain) Edgar
born: **5** Paris **6** France
artwork: **14** The Ballet Class, The Morning Bath **15** Ballet Rehearsal **16** The Millinery Shop **17** The Glass of Absinth **23** Woman with Chrysanthemums **30** The Little Fourteen-Year-Old Dancer

degeneracy 9 decadence, depravity **10** debasement, debauchery, immorality, perversion **11** dissolution

degenerate 3 rot **4** base, sink, vile **5** decay **6** revert, wanton, wicked, worsen **7** corrupt, debased, decline, go to pot, immoral, pervert, vicious **8** decadent, degraded, depraved **9** abandoned, backslide, debauched, dissolute, perverted **10** dissipated, go downhill, profligate, retrograde, retrogress **11** deteriorate, hit the skids **12** disintegrate

degeneration 7 decline **9** depravity **10** corruption, debasement, immorality, perversion **11** degradation, dissolution, viciousness **13** deterioration

degradation 8 disgrace **11** humiliation

Degradation of the Democratic Dogma, The
author: **10** Henry Adams

degrade 5 lower, shame **6** debase, demote **7** corrupt **8** disgrace, dishonor

degraded 4 vile **6** wicked **7** corrupt, debased, lowered **8** depraved, shameful, unworthy **9** debauched, perverted, reprobate **10** degenerate **11** undignified **12** unregenerate

degrading 3 low **6** menial **8** shameful **11** humiliating

degree 4 mark, step, unit **5** grade, level, order, phase, point, stage **8** division, interval
abbreviation: **3** deg

De Guiche, Lillian
real name of: **11** Lillian Gish

de gustibus non est disputandum 29 there is no disputing about tastes

De Havilland, Joan de Beauvoir
real name of: **12** Joan Fontaine

De Havilland, Olivia
sister: **12** Joan Fontaine
born: **5** Japan, Tokyo
roles: **7** Melanie (Oscar) **10** The Heiress (Oscar) **11** The Snake Pit **12** Captain Blood, To Each His Own (Oscar) **14** Anthony Adverse, My Cousin Rachel **15** Gone With the Wind, Hold Back the Dawn **16** Light in the Piazza **22** Hush Hush Sweet Charlotte **24** The Adventures of Robin Hood

dehydrate 3 dry **5** parch **6** dry out

dehydrated 3 dry **7** parched, thirsty **8** dried-out **9** shriveled **10** desiccated

Deianira
father: **6** Oeneus
mother: **7** Althaea
brother: **8** Meleager
husband: **8** Heracles
killed: **8** Heracles

Deicoon
father: **8** Hercules
mother: **6** Megara
killed by: **8** Hercules

Deidamia
father: **9** Lycomedes
lover: **8** Achilles
son: **11** Neoptolemus

deification 7 worship **8** idolatry **10** exaltation **13** glorification

deify 5 exalt **7** glorify, idolize, worship

Deighton, Len
author of: **4** SS-GB **14** The Ipcress File **15** Funeral in Berlin **16** Catch a Falling Spy

deign 4 deem **5** stoop **6** see fit **7** consent **8** think fit **10** condescend

Dei gratia 15 by the grace of God

Deimos
origin: **5** Greek
father: **4** Ares
mother: **9** Aphrodite
brother: **6** Phobus
personifies: **4** fear

Deino
member of: **6** Graeae, Graiae

Deinonychus
type: **8** dinosaur
period: **10** Cretaceous

Deiope
father: **11** Triptolemus

Deiphobe
form: **5** sibyl
father: **7** Glaucus

Deiphobus
father: **5** Priam
mother: **6** Hecuba
brother: **6** Hector
wife: **5** Helen
killed by: **8** Menelaus

Deipyle
father: **8** Adrastus
husband: **6** Tydeus
son: **8** Diomedes

Deipylus
grandfather: **5** Priam

Deirdre
origin: **5** Irish
husband: **6** Naoise
father-in-law: **8** Usnach
uncle: **9** Conchobar

Deirdre of the Sorrows
author: **19** John Millington Synge

deity, the Deity 3 god **4** idol **7** goddess, godhead, Jehovah **8** Almighty, divinity, immortal, Olympian

deja vu 11 already seen

dejected 3 low, sad **4** blue, down **7** doleful, unhappy **8** desolate **9** depressed, sorrowful **10** despondent, dispirited, spiritless **11** discouraged, downhearted, low-spirited **12** disconsolate, disheartened

dejection 5 gloom **7** sadness **10** depression, low spirits, melancholy **11** despondency **15** dispiritedness, downheartedness

dejeuner 5 lunch

de jure 7 by right **14** according to law

dekagram
abbreviation: **3** dkg

dekaliter
abbreviation: **3** dkL

dekameter, decameter
abbreviation: **3** dkm

Dekker, Thomas
author of: **11** Westward Ho! (with John Webster) **20** The Shoemaker's Holiday

de Kooning, Willem
born: **9** Rotterdam **14** The Netherlands
artwork: **5** Woman **8** Painting **15** Woman and Bicycle

Delacroix, Eugene
born: **6** France **18** Charenton-St Maurice
artwork: **8** Paganini **14** Women of Algiers **15** Massacre at Chios **16** The Barque of Dante **19** Chopin and George Sand **20** Dante and Virgil in Hell **22** Liberty at the Barricades, The Death of Sardanapalus

Delaroche, Paul
born: **5** Paris **6** France
artwork: **24** The Death of Queen Elizabeth, The Death of the Duke of Guise, **26** The Execution of Lady Jane Grey **36** Children of Edward Imprisoned in the Tower

Delaunay, Robert
born: **5** Paris **6** France
artwork: **5** Disks **6** Cities, Rhythm **7** Runners, Windows **10** Cathedrals **11** City of Paris, Eiffel Tower **14** The Cardiff Team **19** Cosmic Circular Forms **28** Simultaneous Prismatic Windows

Delaware *see box, p. 252*

Delaware (Lenni-Lenape)
language family: **9** Algonkian **10** Algonquian
tribe: **5** Munsi, Unami **6** Munsee **11** Unalachtigo
location: **7** New York **8** Delaware **9** Manhattan, New Jersey **10** Long Island **12** Pennsylvania, Staten Island
leader: **7** Tamanen, Tammany
deity: **11** Kitanitowet

delay 4 slow, stay **5** check, table, tarry **6** dawdle, detain, hamper, hinder, hold up, impede, linger, put off, retard, shelve **7** inhibit, slowing, sus-

Delaware
abbreviation: **2** DE **3** Del
nickname: **5** First **7** Blue Hen, Diamond
capital: **5** Dover
largest city: **10** Wilmington
others: **5** Acoma, Lewes **6** Easton, Newark, Smyrna **7** Briston, Elsmere, Milford **8** Claymont **9** New Castle **10** Georgetown
college: **6** Wesley **10** Brandywine, Wilmington **12** Goldey Beacom
feature: **10** Winterthur **15** Old Swedes Church **17** E I du Pont de Nemours
tribe: **4** Leni **5** Lenni **6** Lenape, Munsee
people: **10** Howard Pyle
island: **7** Fenwick
land rank: **10** forty-ninth
physical feature:
　bay: **8** Delaware, Rehoboth
　sea: **8** Atlantic
river: **8** Delaware **9** Christina, Nanticoke **10** Brandywine
state admission: **5** first
state bird: **14** blue hen chicken
state flower: **12** peach blossom
state motto: **22** Liberty and Independence
state song: **11** Our Delaware
state tree: **13** American holly

pend **8** dawdling, obstruct, postpone, reprieve, stoppage, tarrying **9** deferment, lingering, loitering **10** suspension **12** postponement, prolongation **13** procrastinate

delayed 4 late **6** put off, slowed **7** held up, stalled, tarried **8** arrested, deferred, detained, retarded **9** postponed, slackened **12** dillydallied **14** procrastinated **15** dragged one's feet

Delbruck, Max
field: **7** biology **17** molecular genetics
researched: **20** genetic recombination
awarded: **10** Nobel Prize

delectable 8 pleasant **9** agreeable, delicious, enjoyable **10** delightful, gratifying **11** pleasurable

delegate 4 give, name **5** agent, envoy, proxy **6** assign, charge, deputy **7** entrust **8** give over, transfer **9** authorize, designate **10** commission **14** representative

delegation 11 designation, entrustment **13** authorization, commissioning

delete 3 cut **4** omit **5** erase **6** cancel, remove

deleterious 7 harmful, hurtful, ruinous **9** dangerous, injurious **11** destructive, detrimental

Delia
festival of: **6** Apollo

deliberate 4 easy, slow, wary **5** weigh **6** confer, debate **7** careful, discuss, examine, express, planned, prudent, willful **8** cautious, cogitate, consider, measured, meditate, mull over **9** leisurely, unhurried **10** calculated, considered, purposeful, thoughtful **11** circumspect, contemplate, intentional, prearranged **12** premeditated

deliberate together 6 confer **7** consult, discuss

deliberation 4 care **6** debate **10** conference, discussion, steadiness **11** calculation, carefulness, forethought **13** premeditation **14** circumspection

Delibes, C P (Clement Philibert) Leo
born: **6** France **14** St Germain-du-Val
composer of: **5** Lakme **6** Sylvia **8** Coppelia **10** Le Roi l'a dit

delicacy 4 tact **5** taste **7** frailty **8** accuracy, elegance, fineness, softness, weakness **9** fragility, frailness, lightness, precision **10** perfection, smoothness **11** savoir-faire, sensibility, sensitivity, unsoundness **13** consideration, exquisiteness, sensitiveness **14** discrimination

delicate 4 fine, soft **5** frail, muted **6** ailing, dainty, feeble,

flimsy, infirm, minute, savory, sickly, touchy, unwell **7** careful, elegant, fragile, refined, subdued, tactful **8** detailed, luscious, tasteful, ticklish, weakened **9** breakable, delicious, difficult, exquisite, palatable, sensitive, toothsome **10** appetizing, diplomatic, fastidious, perishable, precarious, scrupulous **11** debilitated

Delicate Balance, A
author: **11** Edward Albee

delicious 5 tasty **6** joyful, savory **8** charming, luscious, pleasant **9** palatable **10** appetizing, delectable, delightful **11** pleasurable **13** mouthwatering

delight 3 joy **5** amuse, charm, cheer, revel **6** please **7** enchant, gratify, rapture **8** pleasure **9** enjoyment, fascinate, happiness **13** gratification

delighted 6 elated **7** pleased **8** ecstatic **9** enchanted **10** captivated, enraptured, enthralled

delightful 6 peachy **7** amiable, amusing **8** charming, engaging, pleasing **9** agreeable, congenial, enjoyable **10** enchanting **11** pleasurable **12** entertaining

delight in 4 love **5** adore, eat up, enjoy, fancy, savor **6** dote on, relish **7** cherish **8** treasure **10** appreciate

Delilah
lover: **6** Samson
betrayed: **6** Samson

delineate 4 draw **5** draft **6** define, depict, design, lay out, sketch **7** outline, portray **8** describe **9** represent **12** characterize

delineation 9 depiction, portrayal **11** description **12** illustration **14** representation **16** characterization

delineavit 6 he drew (this) **7** she drew (this)

delinquency 7 misdeed **10** misconduct, negligence **11** dereliction, misbehavior **19** neglect of obligation

delinquent 3 due **4** late **6** remiss **7** hoodlum, misdoer, overdue **8** derelict **9** in arrears, miscreant, negligent, wrongdoer **10** neglectful

delirious 6 raving **7** excited, frantic **8** ecstatic, frenzied **10** incoherent **11** carried away **13** hallucinating

delirium 5 fever **6** frenzy, raving **7** madness, ranting **8** insanity **10** brain fever

Deliro
character in: 22 Every Man Out of His Humour
author: 6 Jonson

Delisle, Guillaume
field: 9 geography
nationality: 6 French
founder of: 15 modern geography

Delius, Frederick
born: 7 England 8 Bradford
composer of: 5 Paris 6 Koanga 7 Eventyr, Irmelin 8 Sea-Drift 9 Brigg Fair 10 Appalachia 11 A Mass of Life, Sur les Cimes 17 Fennimore and Gerda 20 North Country Sketches 22 A Village Romeo and Juliet, Over the Hills and Far Away

deliver 3 aim, say 4 bear, deal, free, give, save 5 bring, carry, throw, utter 6 convey, direct, launch, rescue, strike 7 release, set free 8 give over, hand over, liberate, proclaim, turn over 9 surrender 10 emancipate

deliverance 6 rescue 7 release 9 salvation 10 liberation 12 emancipation

Deliverance
director: 11 John Boorman
author: 11 James Dickey
cast: 8 Ronny Cox 9 Jon Voight, Ned Beatty 12 Burt Reynolds
song: 13 Dueling Banjos

deliver up 4 cede, give 5 grant, yield 8 fork over, hand over, transfer 9 surrender 10 relinquish

delivery 8 transfer 11 transferral, transmittal 12 transmission

dell 4 dale, dene, glen, vale 5 glade 6 dingle, hollow, valley

Della Robbia, Luca
born: 5 Italy 8 Florence
artwork: 8 Cantoria (Singing Gallery) 12 The Ascension 13 Altman Madonna 15 Madonna and Child, The Resurrection

Dello Joio, Norman
born: 9 New York NY
composer of: 7 The Ruby 12 Psalm of David 15 New York Profiles, The Trial at Rouen, Triumph of St Joan 20 Proud Music of the Storm, The Lamentation of Saul

Delon, Alain
born: 6 France, Sceaux
roles: 10 Purple Noon, The Leopard 13 The Black Tulip

14 Is Paris Burning?
19 Rocco and His Brothers

Delphic
pertains to: 6 Apollo, Delphi

Delphic oracle
oracle of: 6 Apollo
located at: 6 Delphi
priestess: 6 Pythia

Delphinia
festival of: 6 Apollo

Delphinius
epithet of: 6 Apollo
means: 7 dolphin

Delphinus
function: 12 intermediary
persuaded Amphitrite to marry: 8 Poseidon

Delphus
father: 8 Poseidon
mother: 8 Melantho

Delphyne
also: 6 Python
form: 7 monster
guarded: 4 Zeus 5 chasm
location: 6 Delphi
killed by: 6 Apollo

Del Rio, Dolores
real name: 21 Lolita Dolores Negrette
born: 6 Mexico 7 Durango
roles: 11 The Fugitive 13 Madame duBarry 15 Flying Down to Rio, Journey into Fear, Maria Candelaria

Delta Wedding
author: 11 Eudora Welty

delude 3 con 4 dupe, fool 5 put on, trick 7 deceive, mislead

deluge 4 bury, glut 5 drown, flood, spate, swamp 6 engulf 7 barrage, torrent 8 inundate, overflow, submerge 10 inundation

DeLuise, Dom
born: 10 Brooklyn NY
roles: 5 Fatso 6 The End 11 Silent Movie 14 Blazing Saddles

delusion 8 illusion 9 misbelief 10 aberration 11 derangement 13 hallucination, irrationality, misconception, self-deception

Delusions, Etc. of John Berryman
author: 12 John Berryman

deluxe 4 fine, posh 5 grand 6 choice, classy 7 elegant 8 splendid 9 luxurious

delve 5 probe 6 search 7 examine, explore 8 look into

demagogue 6 ranter 7 hothead, spouter 8 agitator, fomenter, inflamer 9 firebrand,

haranguer 10 incendiary, malcontent, tub-thumper 12 rabble-rouser, troublemaker

demand 4 call, need, want 5 exact, order 7 command, require 11 requirement

demanding 4 hard 5 harsh, rigid 6 strict 8 exacting 9 difficult

demantoid
species: 6 garnet

demarche 4 gait, plan

demean 5 lower, shame 6 debase, humble 7 degrade 8 disgrace 9 humiliate

demeanor 6 manner 7 bearing, conduct 8 behavior, presence 10 appearance, deportment 11 comportment

demented 3 mad 4 nuts 5 crazed 6 crazy, cuckoo, insane 7 lunatic 8 deranged

dementia praecox 13 schizophrenia

dementophobia
fear of: 8 insanity

demesne 4 land 5 realm 6 domain, estate 8 property

Demeter
origin: 5 Greek
goddess of: 5 earth 9 fertility
protectress of: 8 marriage 11 social order
father: 6 Cronus
mother: 4 Rhea
daughter: 10 Persephone
corresponds to: 5 Brimo, Ceres 8 Despoena
epithet: 5 Chloe, Lusia, Mysia 6 Antaea, Erinys, Stiria 7 Chamyne, Thesmia 8 Stiritis 9 Anesidora, Thermasia 11 Carpophorus 13 Thesimophorus

Demetrius
character in: 21 A Midsummer Night's Dream
author: 11 Shakespeare

DeMille, Cecil B
director of: 9 Cleopatra 18 The Ten Commandments 22 The Greatest Show on Earth

Demiphon
form: 4 king
sacrificed: 7 maidens
to prevent: 6 plague

demise 3 end 4 fall, ruin 5 death 7 decease, passing 8 collapse 10 expiration

demobilization 7 release 9 discharge 10 disbanding

demobilize 7 disband, release 9 discharge

Democoon
father: 5 Priam
birth: 12 illegitimate
killed by: 8 Odysseus

democracy 8 equality, fairness

Democracy
author: 10 Henry Adams

Democracy in America
author: 19 Alexis de
Tocqueville

Democratic Party
symbol: 6 donkey
president belonging to:
4 Polk 6 Carter, Pierce, Truman, Wilson 7 (Lyndon
Baines) Johnson, Jackson,
Kennedy 8 Buchanan, Van
Buren 9 Cleveland, (Franklin
D) Roosevelt

**Democratic Republican
Party**
president belonging to:
5 (John Quincy) Adams
6 Monroe 7 Madison
9 Jefferson

demode 8 outmoded
13 unfashionable

Demodocus
minstrel of: 8 Alcinous

Demogorgon
object of: 3 awe 4 fear

demoiselle 4 girl

demolish 4 raze, ruin 5 level,
total, wreck 7 destroy
9 devastate

demolition 6 razing 8 leveling,
wrecking 11 destruction

demon 5 devil, fiend 7 monster 8 go-getter

Demonassa
father: 10 Amphiaraus
mother: 8 Eriphyle
husband: 10 Thersander
son: 9 Tisamenus

demonic, demoniacal 6 hectic 7 frantic, hellish 8 devilish,
fiendish, frenzied

demonstrable 7 evident 8 apparent, manifest, palpable
11 supportable

demonstrate 4 show 5 march,
prove, teach 6 parade, picket,
reveal 7 display, exhibit, explain 8 describe, manifest
9 establish 10 illustrate

demonstration 5 march, rally
6 parade 7 display 9 picketing
10 exhibition, exposition,
expression 12 illustration, presentation 13 manifestation

demonstrative 7 gushing 8 effusive 12 affectionate

demonstrativeness 9 gushi-

ness 12 effusiveness,
emotionalism

Demophon
father: 7 Theseus
mother: 7 Phaedra
brother: 6 Acamas
wife: 7 Phyllis

Demophoon
father: 6 Celeus
mother: 8 Metanira
nursed by: 7 Demeter

demoralize 8 dispirit 9 undermine 10 disconcert, discourage, dishearten 11 disorganize

de mortuis nil nisi bonum
26 of the dead say nothing
but good

demos 5 plebs 6 masses
7 commons 8 populace
9 commoners

demote 4 bust 7 degrade

**Dempsey, Jack (William
Harrison)**
nickname: 13 Manassa
Mauler
sport: 6 boxing
class: 11 heavyweight

demur 5 qualm 6 object 7 protest, scruple 8 disagree 9 misgiving, objection
10 hesitation 11 compunction

demure 3 shy 4 prim 6 modest 7 bashful 8 reserved

demurrer 5 doubt, qualm
7 dissent, protest, scruple
8 objector, question, rebuttal
9 challenge, exception, misgiving, objection, protester,
protestor, stricture 11 compunction 12 remonstrance

den 4 lair 5 haunt, study
6 hotbed 7 hangout, library,
retreat, shelter 9 sanctuary

denial 7 refusal 9 disavowal,
disowning, rejection
10 disclaimer

denigrate 4 soil 5 abuse,
smear, sully 6 defame, dump
on, malign, revile, vilify 7 asperse, blacken, degrade, run
down, slander, traduce
8 backbite, badmouth, belittle,
besmirch, tear down 9 call
names, discredit, disparage,
downgrade 10 calumniate,
stigmatize

De Niro, Robert
born: 9 New York NY
roles: 10 Raging Bull (Oscar),
Taxi Driver 11 Mean
Streets 13 The Deer Hunter
14 New York New York,
The Godfather II 15 The
King of Comedy, True
Confessions 17 Bang the
Drum Slowly

denizen 7 dweller 8 resident
10 inhabitant

Denmark *see box*

Dennis, Patrick
author of: 10 Auntie Mame

Dennis, Sandy
real name: 16 Sandra Dale
Dennis
born: 10 Hastings NE
roles: 12 Any Wednesday
15 A Thousand Clowns
18 Up the Down Staircase
25 Who's Afraid of Virginia
Woolf?

Dennis the Hangman
character in: 12 Barnaby
Rudge
author: 7 Dickens

Dennis the Menace
creator: 11 Hank Ketcham
character: 9 Mrs Elkins
10 John Wilson 12 Eloise
Wilson, George Wilson,
Joey McDonald, Martha
Wilson 13 Alice Mitchell,
Henry Mitchell, Tommy An-
derson 14 Dennis Mitchell
dog: 4 Ruff
cast: 8 Gil Smith, Jay North
10 Billy Booth, Gale Gor-
don, Sara Seeger 11 Gloria
Henry, Irene Tedrow, Sylvia
Field 12 Joseph Kearns
15 Herbert Anderson

denomination 4 name, sect,
size 5 class, value 8 category,
grouping 10 persuasion
11 designation

denotation 4 mark, name,
sign 6 symbol 7 meaning
10 indication

denote 4 mark, mean, name
6 signal 7 signify 8 indicate

denouement 3 end 6 finale,
upshot 7 outcome 8 solution
10 conclusion 11 termination

denounce 6 accuse, vilify
7 censure, condemn 9 criticize

denouncement 7 censure
12 condemnation,
denunciation

de novo 4 anew 5 again
6 afresh 16 from the
beginning

dense 4 dull, dumb, slow
5 close, heavy, thick 6 stupid
7 compact, crowded, intense
8 ignorant 9 dimwitted
10 compressed 11 thick-
headed 12 concentrated,
impenetrable

Densher, Merton
character in: 17 The Wings
of the Dove
author: 5 James

density 4 mass 6 weight

Denmark

other name: 17 Kongeriget Danmark

capital/largest city: 9 Kobenhavn 10 Copenhagen

others: 3 Hov 4 Hals, Koge, Nibe, Ribe, Soro 5 Arhus, Kosor, Vejle 6 Aarhus, Abenra, Alborg, Dorsor, Dragor, Nyberg, Odense, Skagen, Struer, Viborg 7 Aalborg, Esbjerg, Horsens, Kolding, Morsens, Randers 8 Ballerup, Elsinore, Gentofte, Glostrup, Hillerod, Naestred, Roskilde, Slagelse 9 Haderslev, Helsingor, Svendborg 10 Fredericia 13 Frederikshavn

school:
   university institute of: 18 Theoretical Physics
   folk high school: 14 folkehojskoler
   continuation school: 11 efterskoler

division: 3 Fyn 7 Jutland, Lolland 9 Schleswig, Sjaelland

measure: 3 ell, fod, mil, pot 4 alen, favn, last, rode 5 album, anker, kande, linje, paegl, tomme 6 achtel, paegel, skeppe 7 landmil, oltonde, ortonde, skieppe, viertel 8 fjerding 9 ottingkar 10 korntonmde

monetary unit: 3 one, ora, ore 4 fyrk 5 krone 8 frederik, skilling 9 rigsdaler

weight: 2 es 3 lod, ort, vog 4 last, mark, pund, unze 5 carat, kvint, pound, quint, tonde 6 toende 7 centner, lispund, quintin 8 lispound, skippund 9 skibslast, skippound 10 bismerpund

island: 2 Oe 3 Als, Fyn, Mon, Rum, Thy 4 Aaro, Aero, Fano, Fohr, Moen, Mors, Romo 5 Baago, Faero, Faroe, Funen, Laeso, Samso, Sando 6 Amager, Sandoy, Sejero, Sudero 7 Faeroes, Falster, Hesselo, Laaland, Lolland, Seeland, Zealand 8 Bornholm, Eysturoy, Sudhuroy 9 Greenland, Langeland, Sjaelland 10 Vendsyssel

lake: 6 Arreso

hill: 12 Ejer Bavnehoj 14 Himmelbjaerget

highest point: 12 Yding Skovhoj

river: 3 Asa 4 Holm, Omme, Stor 5 Skive, Susaa, Varde 6 Gelsaa, Gudena, Vorgod 7 Gudenaa, Lilleaa, Lonborg

sea: 5 North 6 Baltic 7 Oresund 8 Atlantic, Kattegat 9 Skagerrak

physical feature:
   fjord: 3 Ise 4 Isse 5 Lamme
   inlet: 3 Ise 5 Fjord, Vejle 6 Nissum, Odense 7 Horsens, Logstor 8 Limfjord, Mariager
   peninsula: 7 Jutland
   strait: 7 Otesund 8 Kattegat 9 Skagerrak

people: 4 Dane, Jute 5 Angle 6 Cimbri, Eskimo, German, Ostmen, Teuton, Viking 12 Scandinavian
   astronomer: 10 Tycho Brahe
   author: 11 Isak Dinesen 21 Hans Christian Andersen
   founder: 4 Axel 7 Absalon
   king: 4 Hans, Knud 6 Canute 8 Frederik 9 Christian 10 Gorm the Old 15 Harold Bluetooth
   philosopher: 11 Kierkegaard
   physicist: 9 Niels Bohr
   queen: 9 Margrethe 12 Thyra Danebod
   sculptor: 11 Thorvaldsen
   teacher: 4 Kold

language: 4 Odan 6 Danish, German 8 Faeroese 11 Greenlander

religion: 19 Evangelical Lutheran

place:
   airport: 7 Kastrup
   castle: 7 Egeskov 8 Kronborg 13 Frederiksborg
   museum: 6 Rebild 9 Glyptotek 11 Thorvaldsen 15 Rosenborg Castle
   park: 10 Langelinie 13 Tivoli Gardens
   royal palace: 11 Amalienborg
   statue: 13 Little Mermaid
   stock exchange: 5 Borse 6 Borsen

feature:
   dance: 6 sextur
   drink: 5 glogg 7 aquavit

food:
   beer: 6 Tuborg 9 Carlsberg
   cheese: 3 Ost 4 Blue, Tybo 5 Esrom, Samso 6 Samsoe 7 Havarti, Mycella
   meat patty: 11 frikadeller
   pudding: 15 rodgrod med flode

7 opacity 8 dullness, solidity
9 stupidity, thickness 10 obtuseness, opaqueness
11 compactness

dent 3 pit 4 nick 6 hollow
10 depression 11 indentation

denude 4 bare 5 strip 6 divest
7 lay bare 8 unclothe

denuded 4 bare 5 naked 6 barren 8 stripped 9 unclothed,
uncovered

denunciation 7 censure
12 condemnation, denouncement 13 attack against

Denver
    basketball team: 7 Nuggets
    football team: 4 Gold
        7 Broncos

deny 6 refuse, refute 7 disavow 8 disallow, disclaim
9 disaffirm 10 contradict

deny oneself 5 avoid, forgo
6 eschew, give up, refuse
7 abstain, forbear 8 renounce
9 sacrifice

deny responsibility 7 disavow

Deo gratias 13 thanks be to
God

Deo volente 10 God willing

DePalma, Brian
    director of: 6 Carrie
        13 Dressed to Kill

depart 2 go 4 exit 5 leave
7 deviate, digress

departed 4 dead, gone, late,
left, past, went 6 at rest, bygone 7 gone off 8 gone away
10 passed away 11 gone to
glory 12 late-lamented
20 gone the way of all flesh

depart for 8 leave for 9 adjourn to, set off for, set out
for 10 head toward, move
toward

depart hastily 3 fly 4 flee
6 decamp, escape 7 abscond
9 skedaddle

department 4 unit 6 branch,
bureau, sector 7 section 8 district, division, province

departure 4 exit 5 going 6 exodus 7 leaving 9 deviation
10 digression, divergence

depend 4 rely, rest 5 count,
hinge 6 hang on

dependable 4 sure, true
5 loyal 6 steady, trusty
7 trusted 8 faithful, reliable
9 steadfast, unfailing
11 trustworthy

dependence 5 trust 8 reliance
10 confidence, dependency

dependency 10 dependence

dependent 7 reliant

depict 4 draw, limn 5 carve,
chart, draft, paint 6 define, detail, map out, recite, record,
relate, sculpt, sketch 7 diagram, narrate, picture, portray,
recount 8 describe 9 chronicle,
delineate, dramatize, represent,
verbalize 10 illustrate
12 characterize

depiction 6 sketch 7 drawing,
picture 8 portrait 9 picturing,
portrayal 11 delineation 12 illustration 14 representation
16 characterization

deplete 5 drain, use up
6 lessen, reduce 7 consume,
exhaust 8 decrease
10 impoverish

depleted 5 empty, spent,
waste 6 barren, used up
7 drained, emptied, reduced,
worn out 8 bankrupt, con-
sumed, expended, lessened
9 exhausted, infertile
10 unfruitful

depletion 5 drain 7 using up
8 decrease 9 lessening, reduction 10 exhaustion
11 consumption

deplorable 5 awful
8 wretched 9 miserable
11 blameworthy 13 reprehensible 17 deserving reproach

deplore 5 mourn 6 bemoan,
bewail, lament 7 censure, condemn 9 grieve for 12 disapprove of

deport 3 act 4 oust 5 carry, exile, expel 6 banish, behave
7 cast out 10 expatriate
14 conduct oneself

deported person 2 DP 5 exile 8 deportee 10 expatriate
14 banished person

deportment 7 conduct 8 behavior, demeanor
11 comportment

depose 4 oust 6 unseat 8 dethrone 16 remove from office

deposit 3 put 4 pile 5 place
7 put down, set down 8 sediment 10 accumulate 11 down
payment, give in trust, installment 12 accumulation 14 partial payment

deposition 7 deposit 9 statement, testimony 11 declaration 12 accumulation

depository 4 bank, safe
5 vault 6 museum 7 library
8 archives 10 storehouse

depot 4 dump 8 terminal, terminus 10 bus station 15 railroad station 20 military
storage place

depraved 4 vile 6 wicked
7 corrupt, debased 8 degraded
9 debauched, perverted
10 degenerate

depravity 8 vileness 9 decadence 10 corruption, debasement, debauchery, degeneracy,
immorality, perversion,
wickedness 11 degradation,
dissolution

deprecate 7 condemn, protest
8 belittle, object to, play
down 10 depreciate 15 take
exception to

deprecated 7 defamed, put
down 8 despised 9 belittled,
derogated, disdained

deprecation 4 slur 5 abuse
7 protest, put-down 9 aspersion 10 aspersions, belittling,
defamation, derogation 11 disapproval 12 condemnation
13 disparagement

deprecatory 8 critical 9 maligning, vilifying 10 belittling,
defamatory, derogatory, slanderous 11 disparaging
12 disapproving

depreciate 5 scorn 7 run
down 8 belittle, diminish
9 denigrate, disparage, downgrade, lose value 13 reduce in
value, lower the value

depreciation 5 scorn 7 disdain 8 contempt 9 criticism,
deflation 10 belittling, disrespect 11 devaluation
13 disparagement

depredation 4 sack 6 rapine,
ravage 7 looting, pillage, plunder, robbery, sacking 8 spoiling 9 marauding
10 brigandage, ravishment,
spoliation 11 desecration, devastation, freebooting, laying
waste

depress 5 lower 6 deject,
lessen, reduce, sadden,
weaken 7 cut back 8 diminish,
dispirit 9 press down 10 dishearten 14 lower in spirits

depressed 3 sad 4 blue 7 unhappy 8 dejected, downcast
10 despondent, dispirited, melancholy 11 low-spirited
12 disconsolate, inconsolable

depressing 3 sad 6 gloomy
8 lowering 9 dejecting, saddening 10 oppressing 11 casting
down, dispiriting, melancholic,
pushing down 12 discouraging, pressing down, weighing
down 14 causing sadness

depression 5 gloom 6 dimple,
hollow 7 sadness 9 dejection,
recession 10 desolation, melancholy 11 despondency, indentation, melancholia

14 discouragement **15** downheartedness, economic decline

deprive 5 strip **6** divest **8** take from **10** confiscate, dispossess

deprived 8 divested, stripped **11** handicapped **12** dispossessed, impoverished **13** disadvantaged **15** underprivileged

deprive of honor 5 abase, shame, sully **6** defame **7** blacken, tarnish **8** disgrace, dishonor **9** discredit **10** stigmatize

deprive of strength 6 hinder, weaken **7** disable, wear out **8** enervate, enfeeble, handicap **10** debilitate, devitalize

de profundis 13 from the depths

depth 6 timbre **8** deepness **10** profundity **19** downward measurement **24** perpendicular measurement

depths 4 deep **6** bowels **8** interior, recesses

deputation 9 committee **10** commission, delegation **15** representatives

deputize 6 assign **7** appoint **8** delegate **10** commission

deputy 4 aide **5** agent, envoy, proxy **6** second **8** delegate, emissary, minister **9** alternate, assistant, go-between, messenger, middleman, surrogate **10** ambassador, substitute **11** pinch hitter **12** spokesperson **14** representative **15** second-in-command

DeQuincey, Thomas
author of: **19** The English Mail-Coach **31** On the Knocking at the Gate in Macbeth **32** Confessions of an English Opium-Eater

derail 3 bar **4** balk, foil **5** block, check, spike **6** hinder, impede, thwart **7** inhibit, prevent **8** obstruct **14** throw off course

deranged 5 crazy **6** insane **8** demented **10** irrational, unbalanced

derangement 6 lunacy **7** madness **8** insanity **9** craziness **11** peculiarity **13** irrationality, mental illness **14** mental disorder

Der Bingle
nickname of: **10** Bing Crosby

Derek, Bo
husband: **4** John
roles: **3** Ten (10) **6** Bolero, Tarzan

derelict 3 bum **4** hobo

5 tramp **6** remiss **7** outcast, vagrant **8** careless, deserted **9** abandoned, negligent **10** delinquent, neglectful

dereliction 7 failure, neglect **9** disregard **10** negligence **11** delinquency **13** noncompliance, nonobservance

De rerum natura
author: **9** Lucretius

deride 4 mock **5** scoff, scorn **7** sneer at **8** ridicule

de rigueur 11 fashionable **16** strictly required

derision 5 scorn **7** disdain, mockery **8** ridicule, sneering

derivation 5 stock **6** origin, source **7** descent, getting, lineage **8** ancestry, deriving, heritage **9** acquiring, etymology, parentage **10** background, beginnings, extraction **21** historical development

derive 4 gain **5** arise, enjoy, glean **6** obtain **7** descend **8** stem from **9** originate

dermaptera
class: **8** hexapoda
phylum: **10** arthropoda
group: **6** earwig

dermatitis 4 rash **6** eczema **9** psoriasis **12** inflammation

Dern, Bruce
born: **9** Chicago IL
roles: **6** Marnie, Tattoo **10** Coming Home, Family Plot **11** Black Sunday **13** The Wild Angels **14** The Great Gatsby **22** The King of Marvin Gardens

dernier 4 last **5** final **8** ultimate

dernier cri 9 latest cry **10** latest word **13** latest fashion

derogate 4 blot **5** taint **6** smirch **8** disgrace **9** disparage

derogation 4 blot **5** odium, stain **7** blemish **8** contempt, disfavor, disgrace, ignominy **9** disesteem, disrepute **10** disrespect **11** humiliation **13** disparagement

derogatory 9 injurious **10** belittling **11** disparaging, unfavorable **12** unflattering **15** uncomplimentary

derrick 3 rig **5** crane, hoist, tower **9** framework
kind: **3** oil **6** sheers **7** gin-pole
part: **3** gin, leg **4** boom, mast **6** pulley **7** guy line

derring-do 6 daring **8** audacity, boldness **11** daredevilry **12** daredeviltry, recklessness **15** venturesomeness

dervish 5 fakir **6** Muslim **7** ascetic

De Sapientia Veterum
author: **12** Francis Bacon

Descartes, Rene
author of: **17** Discourse on Method
field: **11** mathemathics
nationality: **6** French
developed: **18** analytical geometry
quote: **13** Cogito ergo sum **18** I think therefore I am

descend 3 dip **4** drop, pass **5** slant, slope, swoop **6** go down, invade **7** incline **8** come down, inherited **11** come in force **12** be handed down, move downward

descendant 5 issue **7** progeny **9** offspring

descend upon 6 assail, attack, charge **7** assault, set upon **12** bear down upon

descent 4 drop, fall, raid **5** slant, slope **6** origin **7** assault, decline, lineage **8** ancestry **9** declivity, incursion **10** coming down **11** sneak attack, sudden visit

describe 4 draw **5** trace **6** depict, detail, recite, relate **7** explain, mark out, narrate, outline, portray, recount, speak of **9** delineate **10** illustrate **12** characterize

description 3 ilk **4** kind, sort, type **5** brand, class, genus **6** manner, nature **7** account, species, variety **9** depiction, narration, portrayal **12** illustration **16** characterization

descry 3 see **4** spot **6** behold, notice **7** discern, observe, pick out **8** discover **12** catch sight of

Desdemona
character in: **7** Othello
author: **11** Shakespeare

desecrate 6 defile **7** profane, violate **8** dishonor

desecration 8 dishonor **9** violation **10** defilement **11** profanation

desert 3 dry **4** arid, wild **5** leave, waste **6** barren **7** abandon, forsake **8** desolate, untilled **9** infertile, wasteland **10** arid region **11** run away from, uninhabited **13** uncultivated **16** barren wilderness

deserted 4 AWOL, left **5** empty **6** lonely, vacant **7** cast off, forlorn, reneged **8** defected, desolate, forsaken, marooned **9** abandoned, ab-

sconded **12** quit one's post
14 left in the lurch

desertedness 9 emptiness
10 desolation
13 uncrowdedness

Deserted Village, The
author: **15** Oliver Goldsmith

desertion 8 quitting **9** forsaking **11** abandonment
14 relinquishment

desertlike 3 dry **4** arid
5 sandy **6** barren **7** dried up,
parched **9** waterless

deserts 3 due **5** worth **6** reward **7** payment

deserve 4 rate **5** merit **7** warrant **9** earn as due **10** be worthy of, qualify for **12** be
entitled to **13** be deserving
of

deserving 6 worthy **9** qualified

deserving reproach 8 blamable **10** deplorable, punishable,
reprovable **11** blameworthy
12 reproachable
13 reprehensible

De Sica, Vittorio
director of: **15** The Bicycle
Thief **27** The Garden of the
Finzi-Continis

desiccate 5 dry up, parch
6 wither **7** shrivel **9** dehydrate

design 3 aim, end **4** draw,
form, goal, plan, plot **5** draft,
motif, set up **6** devise, intend,
scheme, sketch, target **7** destine, diagram, drawing, fashion, outline, pattern, project,
purpose **8** conceive, intrigue
9 blueprint, intention, objective **11** arrangement **14** draw
up plans for

designate 4 call, name, term
5 elect, label **6** assign, choose,
select **7** appoint, signify, specify **8** identify, indicate, nominate, pinpoint

designation 5 label **6** naming
10 delegation **11** appointment
13 specification
14 identification

designer 7 creator, deviser,
planner **9** contriver
10 originator

designing 4 wily **6** artful,
crafty **7** cunning **8** plotting,
scheming **9** conniving

desirable 4 fine **8** in demand,
pleasing **9** advisable **10** beneficial **11** worth having
12 advantageous

desire 4 need, urge, want,
wish **5** crave **6** ask for, hunger, thirst **7** craving, longing,
long for, request **8** yearning,

yearn for **9** hunger for, thirst
for

Desire Under the Elms
author: **12** Eugene O'Neill
character: **4** Eben **5** Peter
6 Simeon **11** Abbie Putnam
12 Ephraim Cabot

desirous 4 avid, keen **5** eager
7 hopeful, longing, wishful
8 yearning

desist 4 stop **5** cease **6** lay off
7 suspend **8** leave off **11** discontinue, refrain from

Desk Set
director: **10** Walter Lang
cast: **8** Gig Young **11** Dina
Merrill **12** Joan Blondell,
Spencer Tracy **16** Katharine
Hepburn

Desmontes
foster son: **4** Arne

desolate 3 sad **4** bare, ruin
5 bleak, empty **6** barren,
grieve, ravage, sadden **7** depress, destroy, forlorn **8** dejected, demolish, deserted,
distress, downcast, forsaken,
lay waste, wretched **9** abandoned, depressed, devastate,
miserable, sorrowful **10** despondent, discourage, dishearten, melancholy
11 downhearted,
uninhabited

desolating 6 tragic **7** ruinous
8 dreadful, grievous, terrible
10 calamitous, horrendous
11 devastating **12** catastrophic

desolation 4 ruin **6** misery,
sorrow **7** sadness **8** bareness,
distress, solitude **9** bleakness,
dejection, emptiness, seclusion **10** barrenness, depression,
dreariness, loneliness, melancholy, wilderness **11** destruction, devastation, unhappiness
12 solitariness

despair 5 gloom, trial **6** burden, ordeal **9** lose heart
10 depression, have no hope
11 despondency, lose faith in
12 hopelessness
14 discouragement

despair of 5 doubt **8** give up
on **10** have no hope

desperado 4 thug **5** rowdy
6 bandit, gunman, outlaw
7 brigand, convict, hoodlum,
ruffian **8** criminal, fugitive,
hooligan **9** terrorist
10 lawbreaker

desperate 4 dire, rash, wild
5 grave, great **6** daring, urgent **7** extreme, frantic, serious **8** critical, hopeless,
reckless, wretched **9** dangerous, incurable **10** beyond
hope, despairing, despondent

Desperate Hours, The
director: **12** William Wyler
cast: **8** Gig Young **11** Dewey
Martin, Martha Scott **13** Arthur Kennedy, Frederic
March **14** Humphrey Bogart

Desperately Seeking Susan
director: **14** Susan Seidelman
cast: **7** Madonna **15** Rosanna
Arquette

desperation 7 despair
12 hopelessness, recklessness

despicable 4 base, mean, vile
10 detestable, outrageous
11 disgraceful **12** contemptible **13** reprehensible

despise 5 abhor, scorn **6** detest, loathe **7** contemn, disdain, dislike **10** look down on

Despoena
origin: **5** Greek
father: **8** Poseidon
mother: **7** Demeter
corresponds to:
10 Persephone

despoil 3 rob **4** loot **6** ravage
7 pillage, plunder

despoiler 6 looter, robber, vandal **7** brigand **8** pillager
9 plunderer

despondency 5 gloom **6** dismay **7** despair, sadness **9** dejection, pessimism
10 depression, desolation, low
spirits, melancholy **11** melancholia **12** hopelessness **14** discouragement
15 downheartedness

despondent 3 low **4** blue,
down **8** dejected, downcast,
hopeless **9** depressed **11** discouraged, downhearted **12** disconsolate, disheartened

despot 6 tyrant **8** autocrat, dictator **9** oppressor

despotic 9 imperious **10** autocratic, tyrannical **11** dictatorial **13** authoritarian

despotism 7 tyranny **9** autocracy **10** absolutism

dessert 3 pie **4** cake, nuts,
tart **5** fruit, sweet **8** ice cream
11 final course

destination 3 aim, end **4** goal,
plan **6** object, target **7** purpose **8** ambition **9** objective
11 journey's end

destiny 3 lot **4** fate **5** karma,
moira **6** future, kismet **7** fortune **9** necessity
goddess of: **5** Fates, Morae,
Parca **6** Moerae, Moirai,
Parcae

destitute 4 poor **5** broke,
needy **6** busted **8** indigent
9 penniless **15** poverty-stricken

destitution 4 lack, want
6 penury 7 beggary, poverty
9 indigence, privation 11 extreme want 13 pennilessness
14 impoverishment

destroy 4 ruin 5 waste, wreck
6 ravage 8 demolish
9 devastate

destroy completely 3 end
7 abolish, wipe out 8 lay
waste 9 eradicate, extirpate,
liquidate 10 annihilate, obliterate 11 exterminate

destroyer 4 bane 6 blight,
killer 7 gunboat, warship
10 affliction 11 annihilator

destruct 3 gut 4 raze, ruin
5 wreck 7 despoil, destroy,
wipe out 8 decimate, demolish, desolate, pull down, tear
down 9 devastate 10 lay in
ruins

destruction 4 ruin 5 havoc
8 wreckage, wrecking 10 demolition 11 devastation

destructive 7 harmful, hurtful,
ruinous 8 damaging 9 injurious 11 detrimental, devastating 15 not constructive

Destry Rides Again
   director: 14 George Marshall
   based on a story by: 8 Max
   Brand
   cast: 12 Brian Donlevy,
   James Stewart 15 Marlene
   Dietrich 16 Charles
   Winninger
   song: 35 See What the Boys
   in the Back Room Will
   Have

desultory 6 casual, chance, fitful, random 7 aimless, cursory 9 haphazard 10 without
aim 11 unconnected

detach 5 sever 6 loosen 7 unhitch 8 separate, unfasten
9 disengage 10 disconnect
11 disentangle

detached 4 fair 5 aloof 7 distant, neutral, severed 8 reserved, unbiased 9 impartial,
objective, separated, uncoupled, unhitched 10 disengaged,
fair-minded, unfastened 11 indifferent, unconnected 12 disconnected, unprejudiced
13 disinterested, dispassionate
   French: 6 degage

detachment 4 unit 5 force
8 coolness, fairness, severing
9 aloofness, isolation, severance 10 cutting off, neutrality,
separation 11 objectivity
12 impartiality, indifference
13 disconnection, disengagement, preoccupation 16 special
task force

detail 4 fact, iota, item 6 as-

pect, relate 7 appoint, feature,
itemize, recount, respect, specify 9 component, delineate,
designate, enumerate 10 detachment, particular 11 special
duty 13 assign to a task, particularize 14 special service
20 particular assignment

detailed 6 minute 8 itemized,
thorough 10 item by item
12 point by point

detailed list 9 breakdown
11 itemization
14 categorization

detain 4 hold, slow, stop 5 delay 6 arrest, hinder, retard,
slow up 7 confine 8 slow
down 13 keep in custody

detainment 7 custody, holding 9 detention 11 confinement 12 imprisonment
13 incarceration

detect 3 see 4 espy, note,
spot 5 catch 6 notice 7 observe, uncover 8 discover,
perceive

detectable 10 noticeable
11 appreciable, discernible,
perceivable, perceptible
13 ascertainable

detective 2 PI 6 shamus,
sleuth 7 gumshoe 10 private
eye 12 investigator 19 special
investigator

detention 7 custody, holding
9 keeping in 10 detainment
11 confinement, holding back
12 imprisonment
13 incarceration

deter 4 stop 5 daunt 6 divert,
hinder, impede 7 prevent
8 dissuade 10 discourage

deteriorate 3 ebb 4 fade,
wane 5 decay, lapse 6 worsen
7 crumble, decline, fall off
10 degenerate 12 disintegrate

deteriorated 6 shabby 7 rickety 8 decaying, worsened
9 crumbling 10 broken-down,
tumble-down 11 dilapidated, in
disrepair 13 disintegrated

deterioration 5 decay, lapse
6 fading, waning 7 decline
9 crumbling, decadence, worsening 12 degeneration, dilapidation 14 disintegration

determination 4 grit 5 pluck,
power, spunk 6 fixing 7 finding, resolve, verdict 8 boldness, decision, judgment,
settling, solution, tenacity
9 reasoning, resolving 10 conclusion, resolution 11 determining, persistence
12 perseverance, resoluteness
13 act of deciding, steadfastness 16 stick-to-it-iveness

determine 5 learn 6 affect, decide, detect, settle 7 control,
find out, resolve 8 conclude,
discover, regulate 9 ascertain,
establish, figure out, influence 15 come to a decision,
give direction to

determined 7 dead set, decided, settled 8 found out, obdurate, resolute, stubborn
9 obstinate, tenacious 10 figured out 11 ascertained, established 15 come to a
decision

deterrent 4 curb 5 check
9 hindrance, restraint
14 discouragement

detest 4 hate 5 abhor
6 loathe 7 despise 10 recoil
from 16 dislike intensely

detestable 4 vile 6 odious
7 hateful 9 abhorrent, loathsome, obnoxious, offensive, repulsive, revolting
10 disgusting, unpleasant
12 disagreeable

detestation 4 hate 6 hatred
7 disgust, dislike 8 aversion,
distaste, loathing 9 antipathy,
repulsion, revulsion 10 abhorrence, repugnance

dethrone 4 oust 6 depose,
unseat

detonate 4 fire 5 blast, burst,
erupt, go off, shoot 6 blow
up, ignite, report, set off
7 explode 8 touch off 9 discharge, fulminate

detonation 5 blast, burst 6 report 9 discharge, explosion

detour 5 skirt 6 bypass, byroad,
divert 7 digress 9 deviation, diversion 10 digression

detract 5 lower 6 lessen, reduce 8 diminish 12 subtract
from, take away from

detraction 4 flaw 11 shortcoming 12 disadvantage

detractor 5 enemy 6 critic
8 opponent 9 adversary, belittler, slanderer 10 antagonist,
bad mouther, disparager

detriment 4 harm, loss 6 damage, injury 10 impairment
12 disadvantage

detrimental 7 adverse, harmful 8 damaging 9 injurious
10 pernicious 11 deleterious,
destructive, unfavorable
15 disadvantageous

Detroit
   baseball team: 6 Tigers
   basketball team: 7 Pistons
   football team: 5 Lions
   hockey team: 8 Redwings

de trop 7 too many, too

much **8** in the way **9** not
wanted

Deucalion
father: **10** Prometheus
mother: **7** Pronoia
wife: **6** Pyrrha
son: **6** Hellen
founded: **9** human race
after: **6** deluge

deus ex machina 15 god
from a machine **18** improbable solution

Deus vobiscum 12 God be
with you

Deus vult 8 God wills (it)
cry of: **9** Crusaders

devaluate 6 lessen, reduce
7 deflate, degrade
10 depreciate

devaluation 4 drop **7** decline
12 depreciation

devalue 5 lower, taint **6** debase, defile, infect **7** cheapen,
corrupt, degrade, pervert, pollute, revalue **8** mark down
9 devaluate, underrate, write
down **10** adulterate, degenerate, demonetize, depreciate,
remonetize **11** contaminate

devastate 4 ruin **5** level, spoil,
waste, wreck **6** ravage **7** despoil, destroy **8** demolish, desolate, lay waste

devastating 7 ruinous **8** damaging **9** injurious **11** calamitous, disastrous **11** cataclysmic,
destructive, detrimental
12 catastrophic

devastation 4 ruin **9** ruination **10** demolition
11 destruction

develop 4 grow **5** print, ripen
6 evolve, expand, finish,
flower, mature, pick up, unfold **7** acquire, advance, amplify, augment, broaden, build
up, convert, enlarge, improve,
process, turn out **8** contract,
energize **9** cultivate **10** come
to have **11** come to light,
elaborate on

development 5 event
6 growth, result **7** advance,
history **8** progress **9** evolution

deviant 4 warp **5** shift **7** deviate, pervert **8** aberrant, abnormal **9** deflected, divergent

deviate 4 part, vary, veer
5 stray **6** depart, swerve, wander **8** go astray **9** sidetrack,
turn aside

deviation 6 change **7** veering
8 rambling, straying **9** wandering **10** aberration, digression, divergence
11 abnormality, fluctuation

device 4 plan, plot, ploy, ruse,
wile **5** angle, trick **6** design,
gadget, scheme **7** gimmick
8 artifice, strategy **9** apparatus,
invention, mechanism, stratagem **11** contraption,
contrivance

devil, the Devil 3 guy
5 rogue, Satan, thing **6** Azazel,
fellow, wretch **7** hellion, Lucifer, ruffian, serpent, villain
8 creature **9** Archfiend, Beelzebub, scoundrel **11** unfortunate **12** spirit of evil
13 mischief-maker **16** prince
of darkness

**Devil and Daniel Webster,
The**
author: **19** Stephen Vincent
Benet
director: **15** William Dieterle
character: **5** Devil **7** Webster
9 Mr Scratch
cast: **10** James Craig
11 Anne Shirley **12** Edward
Arnold, Walter Huston
score: **15** Bernard Herrmann
Oscar for: **5** score
also titled: **18** All That
Money Can Buy

devilish 4 evil **6** wicked **7** demonic, heinous, impious, satanic, vicious **8** demoniac,
fiendish **9** nefarious **10** demoniacal, diabolical, villainous

devil-may-care 4 bold, rash,
wild **5** risky **6** daring, rakish
8 heedless, reckless **9** audacious, daredevil

devil's advocate
Latin: **16** advocatus diaboli

Devil's Advocate
author: **14** Taylor Caldwell

Devil's Disciple, The
author: **17** George Bernard
Shaw

Devine, Andy
real name: **16** Jeremiah
Schwartz
born: **11** Flagstaff AZ
roles: **7** Jingles **9** Andy's
Gang **14** Wild Bill Hickok

devious 3 sly **4** wily **6** sneaky,
tricky **7** crooked **9** deceitful,
dishonest **11** treacherous
12 dishonorable **13** doubledealing

devise 4 plot **5** forge, frame
6 design, invent, map out
7 concoct, prepare, think up
8 block out, conceive, contrive **9** construct, formulate

deviser 6 author, framer **7** creator, planner **8** inventor **9** architect, contriver **10** originator

devitalize 4 kill **6** deaden,
weaken **8** enervate
10 debilitate

devoid 5 empty **6** barren
7 lacking, wanting, without
8 bereft of **9** destitute **11** unblest with

devote 5 apply **6** direct **7** address, utilize **8** dedicate
10 consecrate, give over to
11 concentrate **15** give oneself
up to **22** center one's attentions on

devoted 4 fond, true **5** loyal
6 ardent, loving **7** earnest,
staunch, zealous **8** adhering,
faithful **9** dedicated, steadfast
10 passionate, unwavering
17 strongly committed

devotedness 8 devotion
10 commitment, dedication
13 attentiveness **17** earnest
attachment

devoted to luxury 9 sybaritic **10** hedonistic, voluptuous

devotee 3 fan **6** rooter
7 booster **8** adherent, advocate,
champion, disciple, follower
10 aficionado, enthusiast
11 afficionado

devotion, devotions 4 love,
zeal **5** ardor, piety **6** fealty, regard **7** loyalty **8** fondness, holiness **9** adherence, godliness,
reverence **10** allegiance, commitment, concern for, dedication, devoutness, meditation
11 religiosity **12** faithfulness,
spirituality **13** attentiveness,
prayer service **15** religious fervor **17** earnest attachment
19 religious observance

De Voto, Bernard A
author of: **21** Across the
Wide Missouri

devour 7 stuff in **8** bolt down,
gobble up, gulp down, knock
off, wolf down **9** go through
10 read widely **14** eat voraciously **15** absorb oneself in,
consume greedily **16** read
compulsively, take in ravenously **17** become engrossed in

devout 5 pious **6** ardent **7** earnest, fervent, intense, serious,
zealous **8** orthodox, reverent
9 religious **10** passionate,
worshipful

devoutness 5 piety **8** devotion,
holiness **9** godliness, reverence **12** spirituality **15** religious fervor

DeVries, Hugo
field: **6** botany
nationality: **5** Dutch
researched: **8** heredity,
mutation

DeVries, Peter
author of: **16** Consenting
Adults **24** Slouching Toward
Kalamazoo

dew 8 moisture 12 condensation 18 droplets of moisture

Dewar, James
field: 7 physics 9 chemistry
nationality: 8 Scottish
liquified: 8 hydrogen
solidified: 8 hydrogen
developed: 7 cordite
10 Dewar flask 12 liquid oxygen

Dewey, George
served in: 18 Spanish-American War
battle: 9 Manila Bay
destroyed: 12 Spanish fleet

Dewhurst, Colleen
husband: 12 George C Scott
born: 6 Canada 8 Montreal
roles: 12 The Nun's Story
18 Desire Under the Elms
22 A Moon for the Misbegotten

De Wilde, Brandon
born: 10 Brooklyn NY
roles: 3 Hud 5 Shane 11 All Fall Down

dewy 4 damp 5 moist
7 bedewed

Dexamenus
form: 7 centaur
king of: 6 Olenus

dexterity 8 deftness, facility
9 handiness 10 adroitness, nimbleness 11 manual skill, proficiency

dexterous 4 able, deft 5 agile, quick 6 active, adroit, gifted, nimble 8 skillful 9 efficient, ingenious 11 resourceful

Dhegiha
tribe: 5 Omaha

Dia
father: 7 Eioneus
husband: 5 Ixion
son: 9 Pirithous

diabolic, diabolical 4 evil, foul 6 wicked 7 baleful, demonic, heinous, impious, satanic, vicious 8 devilish, fiendish 9 monstrous, nefarious 10 malevolent, villainous

diadem 4 halo 5 crown 7 circlet, coronet 8 headband

diagnosis 5 study 8 analysis, scrutiny 11 examination 13 investigation, medical report 16 scientific report 22 conclusion from symptoms, specification of illness

diagonal line 4 bias 5 angle, slant

diagram 3 map 4 plan 5 chart 6 sketch 7 drawing, outline 9 breakdown 11 line drawing 12 illustration 14 representation 15 rough projection

dialect 5 argot, idiom, lingo 6 jargon, patois 8 localism 10 vernacular 11 regionalism 13 colloquialism, provincialism 15 language variety

Dial M for Murder
director: 15 Alfred Hitchcock
based on play by: 14 Frederick Knott
cast: 10 Grace Kelly, Ray Milland 14 Robert Cummings

dialogue, dialog 4 talk 5 lines 6 parley, speech 8 conclave 10 conference 12 conversation 14 verbal exchange 15 personal meeting 16 formal discussion

diamond
characteristic: 7 hardest
color: 4 blue, pink 9 blue-white 12 canary yellow
element: 6 carbon
famous: 4 Hope 6 Jonker 8 Cullinan, Idol's Eye, Kohi-Noor 9 Excelsior 12 Star of Africa 13 Star of the East 17 Star of Sierra Leone
quality: 3 cut 4 fire 5 color 7 clarity 10 brilliance
source: 5 Congo, India 6 Africa, Borneo, Brazil, Guyana 8 Tanzania 9 Australia, Venezuela 11 South Africa, Soviet Union 12 South America 15 South West Africa
weight: 5 carat, point

Diamond State
nickname of: 8 Delaware

Diana
origin: 5 Roman
goddess of: 4 moon 6 slaves 7 hunting
protectress of: 5 women
corresponds to: 6 Phoebe 7 Artemis
epithet: 10 Nemorensis
  means: 10 of the grove

Diana of the Crossways
author: 14 George Meredith
character: 9 Mr Warwick 11 Diana Merion, Percy Dacier 12 Lady Dunstane 14 Thomas Redworth 15 Lord Dannisburgh

diaphanous 4 filmy, gauzy, lucid, sheer 6 flimsy, limpid 8 gossamer, pellucid 11 translucent, transparent

diary 3 log 7 daybook, journal 9 chronicle 12 daily journal 14 day-to-day record

Diary of Anne Frank, The
author: 9 Anne Frank
director: 13 George Stevens
cast: 6 Ed Wynn 9 Lou Jacobi 10 Diane Baker 13 Millie Perkins, Richard Beymer 14 Shelley Winters (Mrs Van Daan) 17 Joseph Schildkraut (Father Frank)
Oscar for: 17 supporting actress (Winters)

Diasia
festival of: 4 Zeus

diatribe 6 tirade 9 contumely, invective 11 castigation 12 vituperation 13 stream of abuse 14 bitter harangue 18 accusatory language 19 violent denunciation

dice 4 chop, cube 5 bones, cubes, cut up, mince
singular: 3 die

Dice
also: 4 Dike
origin: 5 Greek
member of: 5 Horae
goddess of: 7 justice
father: 4 Zeus
mother: 6 Themis

Dick, Mr
character in: 16 David Copperfield
author: 7 Dickens

Dickens, Charles
author of: 9 Hard Times 10 Bleak House 11 Oliver Twist 12 Barnaby Rudge, Dombey and Son, Little Dorrit 14 Pickwick Papers 15 A Christmas Carol, Our Mutual Friend 16 A Tale of Two Cities, David Copperfield, Martin Chuzzlewit, Nicholas Nickleby 17 Great Expectations 19 The Old Curiosity Shop 22 The Mystery of Edwin Drood

dicker 4 deal 6 haggle, higgle, outbid 7 bargain, chaffer, quibble, wrangle 8 beat down, talk down, underbid 9 negotiate 17 drive a hard bargain

Dickey, James
author of: 9 The Zodiac 11 Deliverance 16 Strength of Fields 17 Buckdancer's Choice

Dickinson, Angie
real name: 13 Angeline Brown
husband: 13 Burt Bacharach
born: 6 Kulm ND
roles: 8 Rio Bravo 11 Police Woman 13 Dressed to Kill 19 The Sins of Rachel Cade

Dick Tracy
creator: 12 Chester Gould
character: 8 BO Plenty, Moonmaid 12 Gravel Gertie 13 Sparkle Plenty 16 Jeremiah Truehart
wife: 12 Tess Truehart
daughter: 11 Bonny Braids
assistant: 9 Pat Patton

protege: 6 Junior
villain: 5 Itchy 6 B-B Eyes 7 Flattop, Flyface, Measles, Mumbles, The Brow, The Mole 8 The Blank 9 Pruneface, The Midget, The Rodent
equipment: 16 two-way wristradio

Dick Van Dyke Show, The
character: 9 Alan Brady, Rob Petrie 11 Jerry Helper, Laura Petrie, Sally Rogers 12 Buddy Sorrell, Melvin Cooley, Millie Helper 13 Ritchie Petrie
cast: 9 Rose Marie 10 Carl Reiner, Jerry Paris 13 Larry Matthews, Richard Deacon 14 Mary Tyler Moore, Morey Amsterdam 17 Ann Morgan Guilbert

dictate 4 rule 5 edict, order 6 decree, dictum, direct, enjoin, impose, ordain, ruling, urging 7 bidding, counsel, lay down, mandate 8 set forth 9 determine, ordinance, prescribe, prompting, pronounce, stricture 11 exhortation, inclination, requirement

dictator 4 czar, duce 6 caesar, despot, fuhrer, kaiser, tyrant 7 emperor 8 autocrat 13 absolute ruler
Argentinian: 5 Peron
German: 6 Hitler
Italian: 9 Mussolini
Russian: 5 Lenin 6 Stalin
Spanish: 6 Franco

dictatorial 6 lordly 7 haughty, willful 8 absolute, arrogant, despotic 9 arbitrary, imperious, unlimited 10 autocratic, peremptory, tyrannical 11 categorical, domineering, magisterial, overbearing 12 supercilious, unrestricted 13 authoritative 17 inclined to command

diction 7 wording 8 delivery, rhetoric, verbiage 9 elocution 10 intonation, use of idiom, vocabulary 11 enunciation, phraseology, verbal style 12 articulation 13 choice of words, pronunciation 16 turn of expression 17 command of language 18 manner of expression

dictum 3 saw 4 fiat 5 adage, axiom, edict, maxim, order 6 decree, saying, truism 7 dictate, precept, proverb 11 commandment 13 pronouncement 15 dogmatic bidding 22 authoritative statement

Dictynna
origin: 6 Cretan
goddess of: 3 sea

corresponds to: 11 Britomartis

Dictys
occupation: 9 fisherman
found: 5 chest
  containing: 5 Danae 7 Perseus

didactic 7 donnish, preachy 8 academic, edifying, pedantic, tutorial 9 doctrinal, homiletic, pedagogic 10 expository, moralizing 11 educational, instructive, lecturelike, overbearing 12 prescriptive 17 inclined to lecture

didactics 8 teaching 9 education, teachings 10 pedagogics 11 instruction

Diderot, Denis
author of: 12 Encyclopedia 13 Rameau's Nephew

Didion, Joan
author of: 8 Salvador 10 White Album 14 Play It as It Lays 19 A Book of Common Prayer 24 Slouching Toward Bethlehem

Dido
queen of: 8 Carthage
father: 5 Mutto
brother: 9 Pygmalion
sister: 4 Anna
husband: 8 Sychaeus
lover: 6 Aeneas
corresponds to: 6 Elissa

Dido and Aeneas
opera by: 7 Purcell
character: 4 Dido (Queen of Carthage) 6 Aeneas

Didymaea
festival of: 4 Zeus 6 Apollo

Didymus see 6 Thomas

die 3 ebb, rot 4 ache, fade, fail, long, pass, stop, wane 5 croak, yearn 6 depart, expire, go flat, pass on, perish, recede, run out, wither 7 be eager, decline, die away, go stale, run down, subside 8 fade away, melt away, pass away, pass over, wear away 9 be anxious, break down, lose force, lose power, meet death 10 degenerate, want keenly 11 come to an end, suffer death 12 wish ardently 13 come to one's end, desire greatly, go to one's glory, kick the bucket 14 leave this world, pine with desire, become inactive 15 slowly disappear 17 become inoperative
plural: 4 dice

die away 4 fade 5 abate, cease 8 diminish

die down 5 abate 7 subside 8 diminish, slack off

die out 6 vanish 9 cease to be, disappear 13 become extinct

Diesel, Rudolf
field: 11 engineering
invented: 12 Diesel engine

diet 5 board, synod 7 edibles, nurture 8 congress, victuals 9 nutriment, nutrition 10 assemblage, convention, parliament, provisions, sustenance 11 comestibles, convocation, legislature, nourishment, subsistence 12 eating habits, eat sparingly 13 eating regimen, lawmaking body 14 eat judiciously 15 eat abstemiously, eat restrictedly, general assembly 16 limitation of fare, regulate one's food 17 bicameral assembly 18 nutritional regimen, representative body, restrict one's intake

Dietrich, Marlene
real name: 22 Maria Magdalene Dietrich
born: 7 Germany
roles: 8 Lola Lola 11 Blonde Venus 12 The Blue Angel 15 Rancho Notorious 16 Destry Rides Again, The Garden of Allah 17 The Scarlet Empress 24 Witness for the Prosecution

Dietrich von Bern
origin: 8 Germanic
king of: 10 Ostrogoths
Latin name: 9 Theodoric

Diety 3 Bel, God 4 Baal 6 Marduk, Molech, Moloch, Yahweh 7 Chemosh, Jehovah 10 Anammelech 11 Adrammelech

Dieu et mon droit 13 God and my right
motto of: 18 royal arms of England

differ 5 demur 7 dispute, dissent 8 be unlike, contrast, disagree 9 take issue 10 be distinct, depart from, stand apart 11 be disparate, deviate from, diverge from 12 be at variance, be dissimilar, stand opposed

difference 4 spat 5 clash, set-to 7 dispute, quarrel 8 argument, contrast, squabble 9 deviation, disparity, variation 10 divergence, falling out, unlikeness 11 contrariety, contretemps, discrepancy, distinction 12 disagreement 13 contradiction, dissimilarity, dissimilitude 17 contradistinction, lack of resemblance

different 4 rare 6 divers, sundry, unique, unlike 7 bizarre, diverse, foreign, several, strange, unusual, various

8 aberrant, atypical, distinct, manifold, not alike, peculiar, separate, singular, uncommon **9** anomalous, disparate, divergent, other than, unrelated **10** dissimilar, individual, variegated **11** contrasting, distinctive, diversified, not ordinary **12** not identical **13** miscellaneous **14** unconventional

differential 8 contrast **11** distinction

differentiate 6 set off **8** contrast, separate, set apart **11** distinguish, draw the line **12** discriminate **13** make different

differentiation 8 contrast **10** comparison, separation **11** discernment, distinction

differing 6 unlike **7** variant **8** distinct, opposing **9** deviating, disparate, dissident, divergent **10** dissenting, dissimilar **11** contrasting, disagreeing

difficult 4 grim, hard **5** hairy, rough, tough **6** knotty, thorny, trying, unruly, uphill **7** arduous, complex, forward, not easy, onerous, tedious, willful **8** critical, exacting, perverse, stubborn, ticklish, toilsome **9** demanding, enigmatic, fractious, Herculean, intricate, laborious, obstinate, Sisyphean, strenuous, wearisome **10** burdensome, exhausting, fastidious, formidable, inflexible, perplexing, unyielding **11** bewildering, complicated, hard to solve, intractable, troublesome **12** hard to manage, hard to please, obstreperous, rambunctious, recalcitrant, unmanageable **13** hard to satisfy, problematical, unpredictable **14** hard to deal with **15** unaccommodating

difficulty 3 jam **4** mess, snag **5** trial **6** crisis, muddle, pickle, puzzle **7** barrier, dilemma, problem, straits, trouble **8** hot water, obstacle, quandary, tough job **9** deep water, hindrance, intricacy **10** impediment, perplexity, rough going, uphill work **11** arduousness, obstruction, predicament **12** hard sledding **13** laboriousness **14** stumbling block **15** troublesomeness **17** critical situation

diffidence 7 reserve, shyness **8** meekness, timidity **9** hesitancy, timidness **10** constraint, humbleness, insecurity, reluctance **11** bashfulness **12** introversion, sheepishness, timorousness **14** extreme modesty **15** unassertiveness **19** lack

of self-assurance, retiring disposition

diffident 3 shy **6** modest **7** anxious, bashful **8** doubtful, hesitant, reserved, reticent, retiring **11** distrustful, unassertive **12** apprehensive

diffuse 5 wordy **7** verbose **8** rambling **9** desultory, dispersed, scattered, spread out, wandering **10** digressive, discursive, disjointed, long-winded, maundering, meandering, roundabout **14** circumlocutory, extended widely, unconcentrated, vaguely defined **15** not concentrated **18** lacking conciseness

diffuseness 8 rambling **9** prolixity, verbosity, wandering, wordiness **10** dispersion **11** indirection **14** circumlocution, long-windedness

diffusion 6 spread **8** rambling, verbiage **9** dispersal, prolixity, verbosity, wordiness **10** maundering, scattering **11** indirection, profuseness **14** circumlocution, discursiveness, disjointedness, roundaboutness

dig 3 jab **4** gibe, jeer, poke, prod, slur **5** aside, drive, gouge, punch, taunt **6** exhume, thrust **7** put-down, salvage, unearth **8** disinter, excavate, pinpoint, retrieve, scoop out **9** extricate, find among, hollow out **10** come up with, excavation, wry comment **11** bring to view **12** verbal thrust **13** cutting remark, search and find

digest 3 dig **5** grasp **6** absorb, fathom, precis, resume **7** realize, summary **8** abstract, dissolve, synopsis **10** abridgment, appreciate, assimilate, comprehend, understand **12** condensation, take in wholly **14** take in mentally

digestive system component: 5 liver, mouth, teeth **6** tongue **7** stomach **8** appendix, pancreas **9** esophagus, intestine **11** gall bladder **13** salivary gland

dig in 4 root **5** embed, imbed, plant **6** anchor **7** pitch in **8** entrench, go to work **10** begin to eat **12** apply oneself

digit 3 one, six, two, toe **4** five, four, nine, unit, zero **5** light, seven, three **6** cipher, figure, finger, number **7** integer, numeral

dignified 5 proud **6** august, proper **7** upright **8** decorous, reserved **9** honorable **10** upstanding **11** circumspect **13** distinguished **14** self-respecting

dignify 5 raise **6** uplift **7** elevate, inflate, promote

dignitary 3 VIP **7** notable **8** luminary **9** personage **12** person of note

dignity 5 honor **7** decorum, majesty, station **9** loftiness, solemnity **10** augustness, importance **11** comportment, stateliness **12** high position, lofty bearing **13** proud demeanor **14** self-possession

digress 5 stray **6** back up, wander **7** deviate **8** divagate **9** turn aside **15** go off on a tangent **17** depart from subject

digression 6 detour **8** straying **9** departure, deviation, diversion, wandering **10** divagation, divergence, side remark **12** obiter dictum

digressive 7 diffuse **9** wandering **10** disjointed, maundering, roundabout **11** off the point **14** circumlocutory

dig up 6 locate **7** find out, root out, uncover, unearth **8** discover **9** ferret out **12** bring to light

dike 4 bank **5** levee, ridge **10** embankment

Dike *see* **4** Dice

dikerion 11 candelabrum, candlestick **12** candleholder

dilapidated 4 shot **6** beat-up, ruined, shabby **7** rickety, rundown, worn-out **8** battered, decaying, decrepit **10** broken-down, ramshackle, tumble-down **11** in disrepair **12** deteriorated, falling apart **15** falling to pieces

dilate 5 swell, widen **6** expand, extend **7** broaden, distend, enlarge, inflate, puff out **9** make wider

dilation 8 swelling, widening **9** expansion **10** broadening, distension, distention

dilatory 4 lazy, slow **5** tardy **6** remiss **8** dawdling, indolent, slothful, sluggish **9** negligent, reluctant **10** phlegmatic **13** lackadaisical **15** inclined to delay, procrastinating

dilemma 4 bind **6** crunch, plight **7** impasse, problem **8** deadlock, quandary **9** stalemate **11** predicament **13** Hobson's choice **15** difficult choice

dilettante 7 amateur, dabbler, trifler 12 experimenter 16 cultured hobbyist

diligence 4 zeal 8 industry 10 commitment, dedication 11 persistence 12 perseverance

diligent 6 active 7 careful, earnest, patient, zealous 8 plodding, sedulous, studious, thorough, untiring 9 assiduous, concerted 10 persistent 11 hardworking, industrious, painstaking, persevering 12 pertinacious 15 well-intentioned

dill
botanical name: 17 Anethum graveolens
origin: 9 Asia Minor 13 Mediterranean
family: 7 parsley
guards against: 7 Evil Eye 10 witchcraft
use: 6 sauces 7 pickles 10 vegetables

Dillon, Matt
roles: 3 Tex 10 Rumblefish 12 The Outsiders

dillydally 3 lag 4 idle, loaf 5 dally, delay 6 dawdle, loiter 8 kill time 9 waste time 10 fool around 13 procrastinate

Dilsey
character in: 18 The Sound and the Fury
author: 8 Faulkner

dilute 4 thin, weak 6 reduce, temper, watery 7 weaken 7 diffuse, diluted, thin out 8 decrease, diminish, make weak, mitigate, liquidify, water down 10 add water to, adulterate, thinned out 11 adulterated, make thinner, watered down

diluted 4 weak 6 dilute, watery 8 weakened 10 thinned out 11 adulterated, watered down

dilution 8 thinning 9 weakening 12 watering down

dim 3 low 4 hazy, soft, weak 5 dusky, faint, foggy, murky, muted, vague 6 blurry, feeble, gloomy, remote 7 blurred, clouded, muffled, shadowy 8 darkened, nebulous, obscured 9 not bright, tenebrous 10 adumbrated, ill-defined, indefinite, indistinct, intangible 13 unilluminated

DiMaggio, Joe
nickname: 9 Joltin Joe
sport: 8 baseball
position: 8 outfield
team: 14 New York Yankees
wife: 13 Marilyn Monroe

dime-a-dozen 6 common 7 humdrum 8 ordinary, workaday 9 plentiful 10 ubiquitous 11 commonplace 12 easy to come by 13 garden-variety 15 undistinguished

dimension, dimensions 4 bulk, mass, size 5 range, scope, width 6 extent, height, length, volume, weight 7 measure 9 amplitude, greatness, magnitude, thickness 10 importance, proportion 11 massiveness 12 measurements 14 physical extent

diminish 3 ebb 4 wane 5 abate, lower 6 lessen, narrow, reduce, shrink 7 decline, dwindle, fall off, shorten, shrivel, subside 8 decrease, peter out 9 be reduced 11 make smaller 13 become smaller

diminuendo
music: 22 gradually getting softer
abbreviation: 3 dim

diminution 6 ebbing, waning 7 decline 8 decrease, lowering 9 dwindling, lessening, reduction, shrinkage 10 falling off, shortening, shriveling, subsidence 11 petering out, slacking off

diminutive 3 wee 4 tiny 5 elfin, short, small, teeny 6 little, minute, petite, slight 7 pet name, stunted 8 dwarfish, half-pint, nickname 9 miniature, short form 10 pocket-size, undersized, vest-pocket 11 lilliputian, small-scale, unimportant 13 insignificant 14 inconsiderable

Dimmesdale, Arthur
character in: 16 The Scarlet Letter
author: 9 Hawthorne

dimness 4 dusk 5 gloom, shade 8 darkness 14 indistinctness

dimwit 4 fool 5 dummy, dunce, idiot, moron 6 cretin, nitwit 7 dingbat, dullard, dumbell, pinhead 8 dumbbell, dummkopf, imbecile, meathead, numskull 9 birdbrain, blockhead, ding-a-ling, lamebrain, numbskull, simpleton 11 chowderhead, knucklehead

dim-witted 4 dull, dumb 5 dense 6 stupid 7 foolish, idiotic, moronic, witless 8 retarded 9 cretinous, imbecilic

din 4 stir, to-do 5 bruit 6 babble, clamor, hubbub, racket, ruckus, tumult, uproar 7 clangor 9 commotion 10 clattering, hullabaloo

Dinah
father: 5 Jacob
mother: 4 Leah
brother: 3 Dan, Gad 4 Levi 5 Asher, Judah 6 Joseph, Reuben, Simeon 7 Zebulun 8 Benjamin, Issachar, Naphtali
violated by: 7 Shechem

Dindymene see 6 Cybele

dine 3 eat, sup 4 feed 5 feast, lunch 6 fall to, supper 7 banquet, partake 9 breakfast, eat dinner 10 break bread, gluttonize, have dinner 11 gourmandize 14 take sustenance

Dine see 6 Navajo

Dinesen, Isak
real name: 18 Karen Blixen-Finecke
author of: 9 Last Tales 11 Out of Africa 12 Winter's Tales 16 Seven Gothic Tales

dinghy 5 skiff 7 rowboat 8 sailboat 9 small boat

dingy 4 dull 5 dusty, grimy, murky, tacky 6 dismal, dreary, gloomy, shabby 12 dirty and drab

dining room
French: 12 salle a manger

dinner 4 food, meal 5 beano, feast, repast, supper 7 banquet
French: 8 dejeuner 10 table d'hote

Dinner at Eight
director: 11 George Cukor
author: 10 Edna Ferber 14 George S Kaufman
cast: 8 Lee Tracy 10 Jean Harlow 11 Billie Burke 12 Wallace Beery 13 John Barrymore, Marie Dressler 15 Lionel Barrymore

dinosaur see box

dint 4 push, will 5 drive, force, labor, might, power 6 charge, effort, energy, strain, stress 8 endeavor, exertion, strength, struggle 10 insistence 12 forcefulness 13 determination 14 relentlessness

diocese 3 see 7 eparchy 9 bishopric 14 church district
jurisdiction of: 6 bishop

Diomedes
king of: 6 Thrace
father: 4 Ares 6 Tydeus
mother: 6 Cyrene 7 Deipyle
member of: 7 Epigoni
kept: 9 wild mares
fed mares on: 10 human flesh
death planned by: 8 Hercules

dinosaur
  means: 14 fearfully great, terrible lizard
  subclass: 11 Archosauria
  characteristic: 7 diapsid 14 teeth in sockets, two-arched skull 18 three-element pelvis
  group: 11 Saurischian 13 Ornithischian
    flesh-eating biped: 8 therapod
    plant-eating quadruped: 8 sauropod
    plant-eating biped: 10 ornithopod
    armored: 10 ceratopsid
  of Africa: 9 Iguanodon 13 Brachiosaurus 17 Heterodontosaurus
  of Asia: 13 Hypselosaurus, Protoceratops
  of Europe: 9 Iguanodon 12 Plateosaurus 13 Compsognathus, Hypselosaurus, Hypsilophodon
  of North America: 10 Diplodocus, Edmontonia, Nodosaurus 11 Anatosaurus, Anchisaurus, Gorgosaurus, Monoclonius, Saurolophus, Scolosaurus, Stegosaurus, Triceratops 12 Ankylosaurus, Camarasaurus, Camptosaurus, Coelophysics, Lambeosaurus, Paleoscincus 13 Brachiosaurus, Styracosaurus, Tyrannosaurus 14 Thescelosaurus 15 Parasaurolophus, Procheneosaurus
  of South America: 12 Pisanosaurus
  fictional: 6 Barney 12 Jurassic Park

Dione
  consort of: 4 Zeus

Dionysia
  festival of: 8 Dionysus

Dionysus *see* 7 Bacchus

Diores
  father: 10 Amarynceus
  fought against: 7 Trojans

Dioscuri *see* 15 Castor and Pollux

dip 4 bail, dish, dunk, sink, skim, soak 5 droop, ladle, scoop, slope, spoon 6 dabble, dish up, peruse, shovel 7 decline, descend, dish out, run over 8 drop down, glance at, submerge, turn down 13 study slightly 14 immerse briefly, lift by scooping, try tentatively 15 incline downward

dip into 4 scan, skim 5 ladle 6 browse, peruse 7 deplete 8 look over 13 glance through, make inroads in

Diplodocus
  type: 8 dinosaur, sauropod
  period: 8 Jurassic
  location: 8 North America

diplomacy 4 tact 5 craft, skill 7 finesse 8 delicacy, prudence, subtlety 10 artfulness, discretion 11 maneuvering, savoir-faire 13 statesmanship 14 foreign affairs 16 artful management 18 foreign negotiation 21 international politics

diplomat 5 envoy 6 consul 7 attache 8 emissary, minister 9 statesman 10 ambassador, negotiator 12 interlocutor 13 tactful person

  acceptable: 12 persona grata
  unacceptable: 15 persona non grata

diplomatic 5 adept, suave 6 artful, urbane 7 attuned, politic, prudent, tactful 8 discreet 9 sensitive, strategic 13 ambassadorial 14 foreign-service 15 state-department

Dipolia
  festival of: 4 Zeus
  location: 6 Athens
  slaughter of: 2 ox

Dipper
  nickname of: 15 Wilt Chamberlain

Dipsas
  form: 7 serpent

dipsomaniac 3 sot 4 lush, soak, wino 5 drunk, rummy, souse, toper 6 barfly, boozer 7 tippler 8 drunkard 9 alcoholic, inebriate

diptera
  class: 8 hexapoda
  phylum: 10 arthropoda
  group: 7 true fly

Dirae *see* 6 Furies

dire 4 grim 5 awful, grave 6 dismal, urgent, woeful 7 crucial, extreme, fearful, ominous, ruinous 8 critical, dreadful, horrible, terrible 9 appalling, desperate, harrowing, ill-boding, ill-omened 10 calamitous, disastrous, portentous 11 apocalyptic, cataclysmic 12 catastrophic, inauspicious

direct 3 aim 4 head, lead, urge 5 blunt, clear, focus, frank, guide, order, pilot, usher 6 advise, candid, charge, enjoin, handle, head-on, honest, manage 7 address, command, conduct, control, earmark, forward, level at, oversee, pointed, sincere, train at 8 explicit, indicate, instruct, navigate, personal 9 conduct to, designate, firsthand, intend for, supervise 10 administer, face-to-face, forthright, point-blank, show the way, unmediated 11 plain-spoken, point the way, point toward, preside over, superintend 15 straightforward

direction 3 aim, way 4 bent, care, path 5 drift, order, route, track, trend 6 charge, course, recipe 7 bearing, command, control, current 8 guidance, headship, tendency 9 alignment 10 guidelines, leadership, management, regulation 11 inclination, instruction, line of march, supervision 12 line of action, prescription, surveillance 13 line of thought 14 administration, point of compass 15 superintendence

directive 5 ukase 8 bulletin 9 statement 10 communique 11 declaration 12 instructions, proclamation 13 communication

directly 4 soon 6 at once, openly 7 exactly, frankly 8 candidly, honestly, in person, promptly, straight 9 forthwith, precisely, presently, right away 10 face-to-face, in a beeline, personally 11 immediately, momentarily 12 in plain terms, not obliquely, unswervingly 13 unambiguously, unequivocally 14 as the crow flies 15 in a straight line 16 as soon as possible 17 on a straight course, straightforwardly

directness 6 candor 9 bluntness, frankness 10 candidness 14 forthrightness 19 straightforwardness

direct opposite 7 reverse 8 converse 10 antithesis

director 4 boss, head 5 chief 6 leader, master 7 curator, foreman, manager 8 chairman, governor, overseer 9 commander, conductor, organizer 10 controller, supervisor 13 administrator 14 superintendent

dirge 6 lament 7 requiem 8 threnody 9 death song 10 burial hymn, death march 11 funeral song 13 mournful sound **19** mournful composition

dirigo 7 I direct
motto of: **5** Maine

dirk 3 sny **4** snee, stab **5** knife, skean **6** dagger, skiver **7** poniard
origin: **8** Scotland

Dirks, Rudolph
creator/artist of: **12** Hans and Fritz **17** Captain and the Kids **19** The Katzenjammer Kids

dirt 3 mud **4** dust, loam, mire, muck, scum, slop, smut, soil, soot **5** dross, earth, filth, grime, humus, offal, rumor, slime, trash **6** gossip, ground, refuse, sludge, smudge **7** garbage, rubbish, scandal, slander **8** impurity, leavings, vileness **9** excrement, indecency, obscenity, profanity, sweepings **10** foul matter, moral filth, scurrility **11** pornography, scuttlebutt, squalidness **12** scabrousness **13** salaciousness **14** defamatory talk **15** filthy substance, unclean language **17** sensational expose

dirt-cheap 6 a steal **7** bargain **11** inexpensive **14** very reasonable **15** bargain-basement

dirty 4 base, foul, hard, lewd, mean, soil, spot, vile **5** grimy, messy, muddy, nasty, smear, stain, sully **6** coarse, filthy, grubby, mess up, muck up, risque, rotten, shabby, slop up, smudge, smudgy, smutty, soiled, sordid, untidy, vulgar **7** begrime, besmear, blacken, corrupt, crooked, devious, illegal, illicit, immoral, low-down, muddied, obscene, pollute, squalid, sullied, tarnish, unclean **8** befouled, begrimed, indecent, off-color, polluted, prurient, scabrous, unwashed **9** besmeared, deceitful, difficult, dishonest, tarnished, unsterile **10** despicable, fraudulent, licentious, perfidious, unpleasant, villainous **11** distasteful, treacherous **12** contemptible, disagreeable, dishonorable, pornographic, unscrupulous **14** morally unclean

Dirty Dozen, The
director: **13** Robert Aldrich
cast: **8** Jim Brown **9** Lee Marvin **10** Robert Ryan, Trini Lopez **11** Clint Walker **13** George Kennedy **14** Charles Bronson, Ernest Borgnine, John Cassavetes, Richard Jaeckel **16** Donald Sutherland

Dis
also: **8** Dis Pater
means: **5** Hades
god of: **10** underworld
corresponds to: **5** Orcus, Pluto

disability 5 minus **6** defect **8** handicap, weakness **9** infirmity, unfitness **10** affliction, impairment, impediment, inadequacy **11** shortcoming **12** debilitation, disadvantage **16** disqualification

disable 6 damage, hinder, impair, weaken **7** cripple **8** handicap **12** incapacitate

disabled
French: **12** hors de combat

disabuse 8 set right **9** relieve of **10** disenchant **11** disillusion, set straight

disaccord 7 discord **10** disharmony **12** disagreement **15** incompatibility

disacknowledge 4 deny **6** disown **7** disavow **8** disallow, disclaim **9** repudiate

disadvantage 4 flaw **6** burden **7** trouble **8** drawback, handicap, hardship, nuisance, weakness **9** detriment, hindrance, in arrears, weak point **10** impediment **12** weak position **13** inconvenience **16** fly in the ointment

disadvantaged 8 deprived, emergent, emerging, troubled **10** struggling **11** handicapped **12** impoverished **14** underdeveloped **15** underprivileged

disadvantageous 7 harmful **9** injurious **11** detrimental, inadvisable, inexpedient, undesirable, unfavorable, unfortunate

disaffect 4 wean **8** alienate, estrange **10** drive apart

disaffected 5 upset **7** hostile **8** agitated, inimical **9** alienated, disturbed, estranged, withdrawn **10** unfriendly **11** belligerent, discomposed, disgruntled, quarrelsome **12** antipathetic, discontented, dissatisfied **14** irreconcilable

disaffection 7 dislike **8** aversion, distaste **9** antipathy **10** alienation, discontent, disloyalty **12** estrangement

disaffirm 4 deny **5** annul **6** disown **7** decline, disavow **8** abnegate, disclaim, forswear, renounce **9** repudiate **15** wash one's hands of

disaffirmation 6 denial **9** annulment, disavowal **10** abnegation, disclaimer

11 repudiation **12** renunciation **13** contradiction

disagree 4 vary **5** clash, upset **6** depart, differ **7** deviate, diverge, make ill **8** be unlike, conflict, distress **9** discomfit **10** disconcert, stand apart **11** be injurious, fail to agree, not coincide **12** be at variance, be discordant, be dissimilar **13** cause problems **14** be unreconciled **15** be at loggerheads, differ in opinion **16** oppose one another, think differently

disagreeable 5 cross, harsh, nasty, surly, testy **7** grating, grouchy, peevish **8** churlish, petulant **9** difficult, irascible, irritable, obnoxious, offensive, repellent, repugnant, repulsive, unamiable, unwelcome **10** disgusting, ill-natured, uninviting, unpleasant **11** acrimonious, bad-tempered, displeasing, distasteful, ill-tempered, uncongenial, unpalatable **13** uncomfortable

disagreeing 6 at odds **7** deviant, varying **8** clashing **9** deviating, differing, disputing **10** quarreling **11** conflicting **13** at loggerheads

disagreement 5 clash, fight **7** discord, dispute, quarrel **8** argument, squabble, variance **9** deviation, disaccord, disparity, diversity **10** difference, divergence, falling-out, unlikeness **11** discrepancy, incongruity **13** dissimilarity, dissimilitude, lack of harmony **15** incompatibility **16** misunderstanding

disallow 4 deny, veto **6** abjure, forbid, refuse, reject **8** prohibit **9** repudiate

disallowance 4 veto **6** denial **7** refusal **9** rejection **11** prohibition, repudiation

disallowed 6 vetoed **7** abjured, refused **8** rejected **9** forbidden **10** repudiated **12** inadmissible, unacceptable

disappear 2 go **3** end **4** exit, fade, flee **5** leave **6** be gone, depart, die out, retire, vanish **8** be no more, fade away, melt away, withdraw **9** evaporate **12** be lost to view, cease to exist, leave no trace **13** cease to appear, cease to be seen **14** become obscured, cease to be known, pass out of sight **15** vanish from sight

disappearance 9 vanishing **11** evanescence **16** passing from sight

disappoint 4 foil **6** hinder, sadden, thwart **7** chagrin, let down, mislead **9** frustrate **10** dishearten **11** disillusion

disappointing 11 frustrating **12** unfulfilling **13** dissatisfying **14** unsatisfactory

disappointment 3 dud **4** bomb, loss **6** defeat, fiasco, fizzle **7** failure, letdown, setback, washout **8** disaster **9** the knocks **11** frustration **13** unfulfillment, unrealization **15** disillusionment, dissatisfaction

disapprobation 7 censure **8** disfavor **9** criticism, disesteem, objection **11** disapproval, displeasure **12** condemnation **15** dissatisfaction

disapprove 4 veto **5** decry **6** refuse, reject **7** censure, condemn, deplore, dislike **8** denounce, disallow, object to, turn down **9** criticize, deprecate, disparage, frown upon **10** think ill of **13** look askance at, regard as wrong **14** discountenance, refuse assent to **15** take exception to **16** find unacceptable, view with disfavor

disapprove of 7 censure, condemn, deplore **8** object to

disarm 4 move, sway **5** charm **6** entice **7** attract, bewitch, enchant, win over **8** convince, persuade **9** captivate, fascinate, influence, prevail on

disarming 7 melting, winning, winsome **8** charming, magnetic **9** appealing, beguiling, ingenuous, seductive **10** bewitching, entrancing **11** captivating **12** ingratiating, irresistible

disarrange 5 mix up, upset **6** jumble, mess up, muddle, ruffle, rumple **7** confuse, scatter **8** disarray, dishevel, disorder, displace, put askew, scramble **11** disorganize **13** put out of order **14** turn topsy-turvy

disarranged 5 messy **6** mussed, sloppy, untidy **7** jumbled, ruffled, rumpled, tousled, unkempt **8** uncombed **9** cluttered **10** disarrayed, disheveled, disordered, disorderly, in disorder **11** in a shambles

disarrangement 4 mess **5** chaos, mix-up, upset **6** jumble, mixing, muddle **7** clutter **8** disarray, disorder, scramble, shambles **9** confusion, messiness, messing up **10** disharmony, disruption, sloppiness, untidiness **12** dishevelment

14 disorderliness **15** disorganization, heaping together

disarray 5 chaos, mix-up, upset **6** jumble **7** clutter **8** disorder, scramble, shambles **9** confusion, messiness **10** disharmony, sloppiness, untidiness **12** dishevelment **14** disarrangement **15** disorganization

disarrayed 5 messy **6** mussed, sloppy, untidy **7** chaotic, jumbled, mixed up **10** disheveled, disordered, disorderly, in disorder **11** disarranged

disarticulate 6 detach **7** unhinge **8** disjoint, disunite, separate **9** disengage, dislocate **10** disconnect **13** put out of joint

disarticulated 5 apart **7** divided **8** unhinged **9** disunited, separated **10** disengaged, disjointed, dislocated, unattached **11** unconnected **12** disconnected **13** helter-skelter

disassemble 7 disband, scatter **8** disperse **9** knock down, take apart

disassociate 7 divorce **8** separate **10** disconnect **12** disaffiliate

disassociation 5 break, split **6** schism **7** divorce **8** division **10** separation

disaster 4 harm **5** wreck **6** blight, fiasco **7** scourge, tragedy, trouble **8** accident, calamity **9** adversity, cataclysm, ruination **10** misfortune **11** catastrophe, great mishap **12** misadventure

disastrous 4 dire **5** fatal **6** tragic **7** adverse, hapless, harmful, ruinous **8** dreadful, grievous, ill-fated, terrible **9** harrowing **10** calamitous, desolating, horrendous, ill-starred **11** destructive, devastating, unfortunate **12** catastrophic, inauspicious

disavow 4 deny **6** abjure, disown, recant, reject **7** gainsay, retract **8** denounce **9** repudiate **10** contradict

disavowal 6 denial **8** demurrer **9** rejection **10** abjuration, disclaimer, refutation **11** repudiation **13** contradiction

disband 7 adjourn, dismiss, scatter **8** disperse, dissolve **11** disassemble

disbelief 5 doubt **7** dubiety **8** distrust, mistrust, unbelief **10** skepticism **11** incredulity **12** doubtfulness **14** lack of credence

disbelieve 5 doubt **6** refuse, reject **7** suspect **8** discount, distrust **9** discredit, unbelieve **10** misbelieve

disbeliever 7 atheist, skeptic **8** apostate

disbursable 7 payable **9** available, spendable **10** expendable

disburse 6 lay out, pay out **7** fork out **8** allocate, shell out **10** distribute

disbursement 6 outlay **7** payment **8** spending **9** paying out **10** dispensing **11** expenditure **12** dispensation, distribution

discard 4 drop, dump, junk, shed **5** scrap **6** remove, shelve **7** abandon, weed out **8** get rid of, jettison, throw out **9** cast aside, dispose of, eliminate, throw away **10** relinquish **11** thrust aside **12** dispense with, have done with **14** throw overboard

discarded 6 dumped, junked **7** cast off, dropped **8** deserted, forsaken, rejected, scrapped **9** abandoned, cast aside, tossed out **10** jettisoned, left behind, thrown away

discern 3 see **4** espy **6** behold, descry, detect, notice **7** make out, observe, pick out **8** perceive **9** ascertain **12** catch sight of

discernible 7 visible **8** apparent **10** detectable, noticeable **11** perceivable, perceptible

discerning 4 sage, wise **5** acute, sharp **6** astute, shrewd **8** piercing **9** judicious, sagacious, sensitive **10** perceptive **11** intelligent, keen-sighted, penetrating **12** clear-sighted, sharp-sighted **13** perspicacious **14** discriminating

discernment 6 acumen, senses **7** insight **8** feelings, sagacity, thoughts **10** cognizance, discretion, perception **11** distinction **13** consciousness, judiciousness **14** discrimination **15** differentiation

discharge 3 axe, can **4** emit, fire, flow, free, gush, ooze, oust, sack, shot **5** blast, burst, eject, expel, exude, issue, let go, shoot **6** bounce, firing, launch, lay off, let fly, propel, report, set off **7** cashier, dismiss, explode, fire off, project, release, seepage, set free, trigger **8** activate, detonate, drainage, emission, get rid of, liberate, throw off, touch off **9** allow to go, exploding, explosion, firing off, fusillade, give forth, pour forth, secretion, send forth, terminate 10 activating, detonating, detonation, triggering 11 send packing, suppuration 13 give the gate to, walking papers 14 demobilization 15 release document 16 remove from office

disciple 3 nut 5 freak, pupil 7 admirer, convert, devotee, pursuer, student 8 adherent, believer, follower, neophyte, partisan 9 proselyte, supporter 10 aficionado 11 afficionado

Disciple, The
author: 11 Paul Bourget

disciplinarian 8 martinet 13 authoritarian 16 stickler for rules, strict taskmaster

disciplinary 8 punitive 9 punishing 10 corrective 13 authoritarian

discipline 5 drill, prime, rigor, train 6 method, punish 7 break in, chasten, regimen 8 chastise, drilling, instruct, practice, training 9 schooling 11 preparation 14 indoctrination 15 prescribed habit, teach by exercise 16 course of exercise

disclaim 4 deny 6 disown 7 decline, disavow 8 abnegate, forswear, renounce 9 disaffirm, repudiate

disclaimer 6 denial 8 demurrer 9 disavowal 10 abnegation 11 repudiation 12 renunciation

disclose 4 bare, leak, show, tell 6 expose, impart, reveal, unveil 7 divulge, lay bare, publish, uncover 9 broadcast, make known 10 make public 11 communicate 12 bring to light 13 allow to be seen, bring into view, cause to appear

discolor 4 spot 5 stain, tinge 6 bleach, streak 7 tarnish

discoloration 4 blot, mark, spot 5 smear, stain 6 blotch, bruise, smudge 7 blemish 9 contusion

discolored 4 doty 5 dingy, dirty, faded, livid 6 soiled, tinged 7 bruised, stained 9 tarnished

discomfit 5 upset 6 thwart 7 chagrin 8 confound, distress 9 embarrass, frustrate 10 disconcert

discomfited 5 upset 6 uneasy 7 ashamed 8 thwarted 9 chagrined, ill at ease 10 dis-

tressed 11 embarrassed 12 disconcerted

discomfiture 7 anxiety 9 agitation, confusion 10 uneasiness 11 disquietude, distraction, nervousness 12 discomposure, perturbation 13 embarrassment

discomfort 3 try 4 ache, hurt, pain 5 trial 6 misery 7 malaise, trouble 8 disquiet, distress, hardship, nuisance, soreness, vexation 9 annoyance, discomfit, embarrass 10 affliction, discompose, irritation, make uneasy 11 disquietude

discompose 5 abash, upset 6 rattle 7 agitate, confuse, disturb, fluster, nonplus, perturb, trouble, unnerve 8 disquiet, distract, distress, unsettle 9 discomfit, embarrass 10 disconcert

discomposed 5 upset 6 jolted, rocked. shaken, uneasy 7 anxious, nervous, worried 8 agitated, confused, troubled 9 disturbed, flustered, perturbed 10 disquieted, distracted 11 discomfited, uncollected

discomposure 6 flurry 7 anxiety 8 disquiet 9 agitation, confusion 10 discomfort, uneasiness 11 awkwardness, disquietude, distraction, nervousness 12 discomfiture, perturbation 13 embarrassment 17 self-consciousness

disconcert 5 abash, annoy, upset 6 raffle, ruffle 7 agitate, confuse, disturb, nonplus, perturb, trouble 8 unsettle 10 discompose

disconcerted 5 fazed, upset 7 annoyed, rattled, ruffled 8 agitated, confused, troubled 9 disturbed, perturbed, thrown off, unsettled 10 distracted, nonplussed

disconcertment 8 rattling 9 abashment, agitation, confusion 11 disturbance 12 discomposure

disconnect 6 detach 8 separate, uncouple 9 disengage

disconnected 5 split 6 cut off 7 jumbled, mixed-up, severed 8 confused, detached, rambling 9 illogical, separated, uncoupled 10 disengaged, disjointed, incoherent, irrational, unattached, unfastened 12 disorganized

disconnection 8 severing 9 severance 10 cutting off,

detachment, separation 13 disengagement

disconsolate 3 sad 4 blue, down 6 woeful 7 crushed, doleful, forlorn, unhappy 8 dejected, desolate, downcast, wretched 9 depressed, miserable, sorrowful, woebegone 10 despondent, dispirited, melancholy 11 discouraged, lowspirited, pessimistic 12 heavyhearted, inconsolable 13 brokenhearted 14 down in the dumps, down in the mouth

discontent 9 displease 10 discomfort, disgruntle 11 displeasure, unhappiness 15 dissatisfaction

discontented 5 bored 7 fretful, unhappy 9 miserable, regretful 10 displeased, malcontent 11 disgruntled 12 dissatisfied

discontinuance 3 end 4 halt, stop 6 ending, recess 7 ceasing, halting 8 abeyance, giving up, quitting, stoppage, stopping, surcease 9 cessation, desisting 10 concluding, leaving off, suspension 11 abandonment, breaking off, termination

discontinue 3 end 4 drop, quit, stop 5 cease 6 desist, give up 7 abandon, abstain, suspend 8 break off, leave off 9 interrupt, terminate 10 put an end to

discontinuous 8 discrete, episodic, sporadic 9 segmented, spasmodic 10 occasional 11 interrupted 12 disconnected, intermittent

discord 6 strife 7 dispute 8 clashing, conflict, disunity, division, friction 9 cacophony, harshness, wrangling 10 contention, disharmony, dissension, dissonance, quarreling 11 being at odds, differences, discordance 12 disagreement, grating noise 13 lack of concord 15 incompatibility 16 unpleasant sounds
goddess of: 4 Eris 9 Discordia

discordance 6 strife 7 discord, dispute 8 clashing, conflict, disunity, division, friction 9 wrangling 10 contention, disharmony, dissension, quarreling 12 disagreement 15 incompatibility

discordant 6 at odds 9 disparate, dissonant 10 at variance, discrepant 11 conflicting, disagreeing 12 unharmonious

Discordia
origin: 5 Roman

goddess of: 7 discord
corresponds to: 4 Eris

discount 3 cut 5 break 6 rebate 7 cut rate 9 abatement, allowance, deduction, exemption, reduction 10 concession 11 subtraction

discountenance 7 condemn, despise, disdain, dislike 8 object to 9 frown upon 10 disapprove, think ill of 12 look down upon 13 look askance at, regard as wrong 14 hold in contempt 15 take exception to

discourage 4 do in 5 daunt, deter, unman 6 deject, dismay 7 depress, unnerve 8 decimate, dispirit, dissuade, keep back, restrain 9 disparage, prostrate 10 dishearten, disincline, divert from 13 advise against, dash one's hopes 17 dampen one's spirits

discouraged 3 low 7 daunted 8 dejected, downcast, hopeless 9 depressed 10 despondent, dispirited 11 downhearted, pessimistic 12 disconsolate, disheartened

discouragement 4 curb 5 gloom, worry 6 damper, dismay 7 despair 8 obstacle 9 dejection, hindrance, pessimism, restraint 10 constraint, depression, impediment, low spirits, melancholy, moroseness 11 despondency 12 hopelessness, lack of spirit 13 consternation 15 downheartedness

discourse 3 gab 4 chat, talk 5 essay 6 confer, sermon, speech 7 address, discuss, lecture, oration 8 colloquy, converse, dialogue, diatribe, harangue, treatise 10 discussion 11 intercourse 12 conversation, dissertation, talk together 16 formal discussion

Discourse on Method
   author: 13 Rene Descartes

discourteous 4 rude 5 fresh, surly 6 cheeky 7 boorish, illbred, uncivil, uncouth 8 impolite, impudent, insolent 9 uncourtly, ungallant 10 ill-behaved, ungracious, unladylike, unmannerly 11 illmannered, impertinent 13 disrespectful, ungentlemanly

discourtesy 8 rudeness 9 impudence, insolence 10 incivility 11 boorishness 12 impoliteness

discover 3 see 4 find, spot 5 dig up 6 detect, locate, notice 7 discern, find out, learn of, realize, root out, uncover, unearth 8 come upon, per-

ceive 9 ascertain, determine, ferret out, light upon, recognize 10 chance upon 11 gain sight of, stumble upon 12 bring to light

discredit 4 deny, slur 5 abuse, smear, sully, taint 6 debase, defame, demean, reject, smirch, vilify 7 degrade, dispute, tarnish, vitiate 8 disallow, disgrace, dishonor, disprove, question 9 challenge, disparage, undermine 10 prove false, stigmatize 16 shake one's faith in 17 drag through the mud

discreditable 8 shameful, shocking 9 appalling 10 outrageous, scandalous 11 disgraceful, ignominious 12 dishonorable, disreputable

discreet 6 polite 7 careful, politic, prudent, tactful 8 cautious 9 judicious, sensitive 10 diplomatic, thoughtful 11 circumspect

Discreet Charm of the Bourgeoisie, The
   director: 10 Luis Bunuel
   cast: 11 Fernando Rey 14 Delphine Seyrig, Stephane Audran
   Oscar for: 11 foreign film

discrepancy 3 gap 8 variance 9 disparity 10 difference, divergence 11 discordance, incongruity 12 disagreement 13 dissimilarity, inconsistency

discrepant 6 at odds 8 contrary, opposing 9 disparate 10 at variance, discordant, dissimilar, refutatory 11 conflicting, contrasting, disagreeing 12 antithetical, inconsistent 13 contradictory 14 countervailing, irreconcilable

discrete 7 several, various 8 detached, distinct, separate 9 different 10 unattached 11 disjunctive, independent 12 disconnected, unassociated 13 discontinuous

discretion 4 tact 6 acumen, option 8 judgment, prudence, sagacity, volition 9 good sense 10 preference 11 discernment, inclination 12 good judgment, predilection 13 judiciousness, sound judgment 14 discrimination 15 power of choosing 16 individual choice

discretionary 8 optional 9 voluntary 10 nonbinding 11 nonrequired, unnecessary 12 nonrequisite, unimperative 13 nonobligatory

discriminate 7 disdain 8 separate 11 distinguish 12 disfranchise 13 differentiate

discriminating 5 acute 6 astute, biased, shrewd 7 bigoted, refined 9 judicious, sensitive 10 cultivated, discerning, fastidious 11 intelligent, prejudicial 13 perspicacious 15 differentiating

discrimination 4 bias 5 taste 6 acumen 7 bigotry 8 inequity, judgment, keenness, sagacity 9 prejudice 10 astuteness, discretion, favoritism, refinement, shrewdness 11 discernment, distinction 12 perspicacity 21 differential treatment

discursive 7 diffuse 8 rambling 9 wandering 10 circuitous, digressive, long-winded, meandering, roundabout

discursiveness 8 rambling 10 digression, meandering 14 circumlocution

discuss 6 debate, parley, review 7 dissect, examine, speak of 8 consider, talk over 9 talk about 13 converse about, exchange views 14 discourse about

discussion 3 rap 4 talk 6 debate, parley, powwow, review 7 inquiry 8 analysis, argument, colloquy, dialogue, scrutiny 9 discourse 10 hashing-out 11 disputation 12 deliberation 13 consideration, investigation

disdain 4 snub 5 abhor, scorn, spurn 6 deride, detest, loathe 7 despise, dislike 8 contempt, distaste 9 frown upon 10 abhorrence, brush aside, disrespect 11 intolerance 12 icy aloofness, look down upon 14 deem unbecoming, discountenance

disdained 7 derided, scorned, spurned 8 abhorred, despised 10 deprecated, disparaged 14 held in contempt

disdainful 4 cold 5 aloof 7 haughty, high-hat 8 derisive, scornful, superior 11 overbearing, patronizing 12 contemptuous, supercilious 13 condescending

disease 6 malady 7 ailment, illness 8 sickness 9 ill health, infirmity 10 affliction 15 morbid condition 16 physical disorder

disembark 4 land 7 deplane, detrain, pile out 10 leave a ship 11 get off a ship

disenchant 6 put off 7 turn off 8 alienate, disabuse, turn away 9 undeceive 11 disenthrall, disillusion 12 open one's eyes 13 break the spell

15 burst one's bubble **16** bring down to earth

disencumber 8 unburden **9** disburden, extricate **11** disentangle

disengage 5 sever **6** detach **7** disjoin **8** separate **9** extricate **10** disconnect

disengaged 7 unmoved **8** detached **9** apathetic, disjoined, separated **11** indifferent, uncommitted, unconcerned **12** disconnected, unresponsive French: **6** degage

disengagement 6 apathy **8** severing **9** severance, unconcern **10** detachment, separation **12** indifference **13** disconnection **16** unresponsiveness

disentangle 4 free **6** detach, loosen, remove **7** unravel **9** extricate

disenthrall 9 undeceive **10** disenchant **11** disillusion **12** open one's eyes **13** break the spell **15** burst one's bubble **16** bring down to earth

disesteem 7 dislike **8** disfavor **9** disrepute **11** disapproval, displeasure **14** disapprobation

disfavor 5 odium **7** dislike, ill turn **8** disgrace, ignominy **9** disesteem, disregard **10** disrespect, disservice, harmful act **11** disapproval, discourtesy, displeasure **14** disapprobation **15** dissatisfaction **16** unacceptableness

disfigure 3 mar **4** maim, scar **5** cut up **6** damage, deface, deform, impair **7** blemish, scarify **8** make ugly, mutilate

disfigurement 4 blot, flaw, mark, scar, spot **6** blotch, defect **7** blemish **12** imperfection

disfranchise, disenfranchise 15 deprive of a right **19** discriminate against

disgorge 4 spew **5** eject, expel, spout, vomit **6** cast up, spew up **7** cough up, throw up **8** dislodge **9** discharge **10** vomit forth **11** regurgitate

disgrace 4 blot **5** abase, shame, stain, taint **6** debase, smirch **7** blemish, degrade, eyesore, scandal, tarnish **8** contempt, derogate, disfavor, dishonor, ill favor, reproach **9** discredit, disparage, disrepute, embarrass, humiliate **13** embarrassment, in the doghouse **14** bring shame upon

disgraceful 3 low **4** base, mean, vile **6** odious **8** infamous, shameful, shocking, un-

seemly, unworthy **9** appalling, degrading, obnoxious **10** despicable, detestable, inglorious, outrageous, scandalous, unbecoming **11** ignominious, opprobrious **12** dishonorable, disreputable **13** discreditable, reprehensible

disgruntled 5 sulky, testy, vexed **6** grumpy, shirty, sullen **7** grouchy, peevish **8** petulant **9** irritated **10** displeased, malcontent **12** discontented, dissatisfied

disguise 4 garb, hide, mask, pose, sham, veil **5** blind, cloak, cover, feign, getup, guise **6** facade, muffle, screen, shroud, veneer **7** conceal, cover-up, dress up, falsify **8** pretense, simulate **9** costuming, dissemble, gloss over **10** camouflage, false front, masquerade **11** concealment, counterfeit **12** misrepresent **13** false identity **15** false appearance

disguised 6 masked, veiled **7** cloaked **9** dressed up, incognito **10** undercover **11** camouflaged **14** unrecognizable

disgust 5 repel **6** appall, hatred, offend, put off, revolt, sicken **7** dislike **8** aversion, contempt, distaste, loathing, nauseate **9** antipathy, disrelish, repulsion, revulsion **10** abhorrence, repugnance **11** detestation, displeasure **12** disaffection **13** be repulsive to, cause aversion **15** turn one's stomach

disgusting 4 vile **5** hasty **6** horrid, odious **7** hateful **9** abhorrent, appalling, loathsome, offensive, repellent, repugnant, repulsive, revolting, sickening **10** abominable, despicable, nauseating **13** reprehensible

dish 4 dole, fare, food **5** ladle, place, plate, scoop, serve, spoon **6** recipe, saucer, vessel **7** bowlful, dishful, edibles, helping, platter, portion, serving **8** dispense, plateful, transfer, victuals **10** comestible **11** shallow bowl

dishabille 7 undress **8** bathrobe, disarray, disorder, informal, negligee **9** housecoat

disharmonious 7 chaotic **8** clashing, confused **9** dissonant, illogical **10** discordant, incoherent **11** conflicting, contentious **12** incompatible **13** heterogeneous

disharmony 5 chaos **6** strife **7** discord **8** clashing, conflict,

disarray, disunity, division, friction **9** cacophony, confusion, disaccord, harshness **10** contention, dissension, dissonance **11** discordance **12** disagreement, grating noise **15** disorganization, incompatibility

dishearten 4 dash, faze **5** abash, crush, daunt **6** deject, dismay, sadden **7** depress **8** dispirit **10** discourage

disheartened 3 low **6** dismal **8** dejected, desolate, downcast **9** depressed **10** despondent, dispirited **11** discouraged **12** disconsolate

disheartening 4 dark **7** adverse **8** hopeless **11** dispiriting **12** discouraging, inauspicious

disheveled 5 messy **6** blowsy, frowzy, mussed, sloppy, untidy **7** ruffled, rumpled, tousled, unkempt **8** uncombed **10** bedraggled, disarrayed, disorderly, in disorder **11** disarranged

dishevelment 5 chaos, mix-up, upset **6** jumble **7** clutter **8** disarray, disorder, scramble, shambles **9** messiness **10** sloppiness, untidiness **14** disarrangement **15** disorganization

dishonest 5 false **7** corrupt, crooked **8** cheating, specious, spurious, two-faced **9** deceitful, deceptive, faithless, insincere, not honest **10** fraudulent, mendacious, misleading, perfidious, untruthful **11** underhanded **12** disingenuous, falsehearted, unprincipled, unscrupulous **13** untrustworthy

dishonesty 8 cheating **9** duplicity, falseness, mendacity **10** corruption **11** crookedness **12** speciousness **14** untruthfulness

dishonor 4 blot **5** abase, odium, shame, stain, sully **6** debase, defame, infamy, insult, slight, stigma **7** affront, blacken, blemish, degrade, offense, scandal, tarnish **8** disfavor, disgrace, ignominy **9** discredit, disparage, disrepute, humiliate, ill repute **10** derogation, stigmatize **11** discourtesy, humiliation **12** bring shame on **14** public disgrace

dishonorable 4 base **7** debased, ignoble **8** shameful **10** despicable **12** contemptible, disreputable **13** reprehensible

dishonorableness 4 blot **5** odium, shame, stain **6** stigma **7** blemish **8** disfavor, disgrace, ignominy **9** discredit,

disrepute, ill repute **10** derogation **11** humiliation

dishonoring 8 disgrace **10** debasement **11** degradation, humiliation

dish up 3 dip **5** ladle, serve, spoon **7** dish out, serve up

disillusion 6 clue in **8** disabuse **9** undeceive **10** disenchant **11** disenthrall **13** break the spell, open the eyes of **14** burst the bubble **16** bring down to earth

disinclination 8 aversion **9** hesitancy **10** reluctance **13** indisposition, unwillingness

disincline 5 deter **8** dissuade, keep back, restrain **10** discourage, divert from **13** advise against **16** attempt to prevent

disinclined 5 loath **6** averse **8** hesitant **9** reluctant, unwilling **10** indisposed

disinfect 6 purify **7** cleanse **8** sanitize **9** kill germs, sterilize **13** decontaminate **15** destroy bacteria

disinfectant 9 germicide **10** antiseptic, germ killer **11** bactericide

disinherit 6 cut off, disown **15** deprive of rights

disintegrate 7 break up, crumble, shatter **8** splinter **9** fall apart **10** break apart, go to pieces

disintegration 4 ruin **5** decay **7** breakup, erosion **8** biolysis **9** crumbling **10** dispersion, dissolving, separation **11** decomposing **12** falling apart **13** decomposition, deterioration, pulverization

disinter 5 dig up **6** exhume **7** unearth

disinterest 6 apathy **9** disregard, unconcern **12** indifference

disinterested 7 neutral, outside **8** unbiased **9** impartial **10** impersonal, uninvolved **12** free from bias, unprejudiced **13** dispassionate

disinterment 9 digging up **10** exhumation, unearthing

disjecta membra 15 disjointed parts **16** scattered members

disjoin 4 part, undo **5** break, sever **6** detach, divide **8** disunite, separate **9** disengage

disjoint 6 detach **7** unhinge **8** disunite, separate **9** dislocate **10** disconnect **13** disarticulate

disjointed 5 apart, split **7** chaotic, divided, jumbled, mixed-up, tangled **8** confused, detached, rambling **9** illogical, spasmodic **10** incoherent, irrational, unattached **11** unconnected **12** disconnected, disorganized **13** discontinuous, disharmonious, helter-skelter, heterogeneous **14** disarticulated

disjointedness 8 rambling **11** indirection **14** discursiveness **16** disconnectedness

disjointed parts
  Latin: **14** disjecta membra

disk, disc 3 cam **4** aten, coin, dial, face, plow, puck **5** plate, wafer, wheel **6** harrow, record, sequin **7** discuss **8** diskette **9** cultivate, videodisc **11** discotheque
  type: 4 hard **5** fixed **6** floppy **8** magnetic **10** Winchester

dislike 4 hate **5** abhor, scorn **6** animus, detest, enmity, hatred, loathe, malice, rancor **7** despise, disdain, disgust, not like **8** aversion, distaste, loathing, object to **9** abominate, animosity, antipathy, hostility, repulsion, revulsion **10** abhorrence, antagonism, repugnance **11** abomination, detestation **12** disaffection

disliked 5 hated **7** loathed, unloved **8** abhorred, despised, detested **10** abominated

dislike intensely 4 hate **5** abhor **6** detest, loathe **7** despise **9** abominate **10** recoil from

dislocate 6 uproot **7** unhinge **8** disjoint, disunite, separate **9** disengage **10** disconnect **13** disarticulate, put out of joint

dislodge 4 oust **5** eject, expel **6** dig out, dispel, remove, uproot **7** disturb **8** displace, force out **9** extricate **11** disentangle

disloyal 6 untrue **8** recreant **9** faithless, seditious, undutiful **10** inconstant, perfidious, subversive, traitorous, unfaithful **11** treacherous, treasonable **12** dishonorable

disloyalty 7 falsity, perfidy, treason **8** apostasy, betrayal, sedition **9** falseness, rebellion, recreancy, treachery **10** infidelity, subversion **11** inconstancy **12** insurrection **13** breach of trust, deceitfulness, double-dealing, faithlessness **14** lack of fidelity, perfidiousness, unfaithfulness **15** betrayal of trust, breaking of faith **18** subversive activity

dismal 3 sad **4** drab, grim, poor **5** awful, bleak **6** dreary, gloomy, morbid, rueful, somber, woeful **7** abysmal, doleful, forlorn, joyless, unhappy, very bad, visaged **8** dejected, desolate, dolorous, downcast, dreadful, hopeless, horrible, mournful, terrible **9** cheerless, depressed, long-faced, sorrowful, woebegone **10** abominable, despondent, in the dumps, lugubrious, melancholy **11** pessimistic **12** disconsolate, disheartened, heavy-hearted **13** unmentionable **14** down-in-the-mouth

dismantle 5 strip **6** denude, divest **9** take apart

dismay 3 cow **5** abash, alarm, daunt, dread, panic, scare **6** appall, fright, horror, put off, terror **7** anxiety, concern, horrify, unnerve **8** affright, distress, frighten **10** disappoint, discourage, dishearten, intimidate **11** disillusion, trepidation **12** apprehension, exasperation, intimidation, perturbation **13** consternation **14** disappointment, discouragement **15** disillusionment

dismayed 7 abashed, daunted **8** appalled **10** confounded, nonplussed **12** disconcerted

dismember 4 limb **6** hack up **8** disjoint **16** tear limb from limb

dismiss 3 can **4** fire, free, oust, sack **5** let go **6** bounce, excuse, reject **7** adjourn, cashier, disband, discard, release **8** disclaim, disperse, dissolve, lay aside, liberate, pink-slip, set aside **9** disregard, eliminate, repudiate, send forth, terminate **10** permit to go **11** send packing **12** allow to leave, put out of a job, put out of mind **14** give the heave-ho **17** remove from service, give walking papers **19** discharge from office

dismissal 6 firing **7** release **9** discharge, dispersal, disregard **10** disclaimer **11** adjournment, repudiation

Disney, Walt
  creator/artist of: 10 Donald Duck **11** Mickey Mouse

disobedience 8 defiance **9** rebellion **10** resistance **13** noncompliance, nonconformity **14** rebelliousness

disobedient 6 unruly **7** defiant, froward, haughty, wayward **8** contrary, mutinous, perverse, stubborn **9** fractious, insurgent, obstinate, seditious, undutiful

10 disorderly, rebellious, refractory, unyielding **11** intractable **12** noncompliant, recalcitrant, ungovernable, unmanageable, unsubmissive **13** insubordinate

disobey 4 defy **5** break **6** ignore, resist **7** violate **8** overstep **9** disregard **10** infringe on, transgress **11** go counter to **12** rebel against

disoblige 5 annoy **6** bother **7** trouble **13** inconvenience

disobliging 4 rude **8** churlish **9** unhelpful **13** inconsiderate

disorder 4 mess, riot **5** chaos **6** fracas, jumble, malady, muddle, ruckus, uproar **7** ailment, clutter, disease, illness, turmoil **8** disarray, sickness **9** commotion, complaint, confusion **10** affliction, disruption, dissension **11** disturbance **13** indisposition, minor uprising **14** disarrangement **15** disorganization

disordered 7 jumbled **8** confused, messed up **9** haphazard **11** disarranged **12** disorganized

disorderliness 4 mess **5** chaos **6** muddle **8** disarray **9** confusion **10** disruption **14** disarrangement **15** disorganization

disorderly 3 bad **4** wild **5** messy, noisy, rowdy **6** sloppy, unruly, untidy **7** chaotic, jumbled, lawless, riotous, unkempt, wayward **8** careless, confused, improper, pell-mell, rowdyish, slipshod, slovenly, unlawful, unsorted **10** boisterous, disheveled, disordered, disruptive, rebellious, straggling, topsy-turvy **11** disarranged **12** disorganized, disreputable, obstreperous, unrestrained, unsystematic **13** helter-skelter, undisciplined **14** rough-and-tumble, unsystematized

disorganization 4 mess **5** chaos, upset **6** jumble, muddle **7** clutter **8** disarray, disorder, shambles **9** confusion, messiness **10** disharmony, disruption, sloppiness, untidiness **12** dishevelment **14** disarrangement, disorderliness

disorganize 5 mix up, upset **6** jumble, mess up, muddle **7** confuse, scatter **8** disarray, disorder, put askew, scramble **10** disarrange **13** put out of order **14** turn topsy-turvy

disorganized 5 messy, upset **7** chaotic, jumbled, mixed-up, muddled **8** confused, rambling **9** haphazard, illogical **10** disordered, disorderly, incoherent,

in disarray, irrational **12** unsystematic **16** at sixes and sevens

disoriented 7 mixed-up **8** confused, unstable **10** distracted, out of joint, out of touch **11** not adjusted

disown 6 reject **7** cast off, disavow, forsake **8** denounce, disclaim, renounce **9** repudiate **10** disinherit **17** refuse to recognize **19** refuse to acknowledge

disparage 4 mock **6** demean, slight **7** put down, run down **8** belittle, derogate, ridicule **9** denigrate, discredit, underrate **10** depreciate, undervalue **11** detract from

disparaged 7 ran down **9** belittled, ridiculed **10** denigrated, deprecated **11** depreciated

disparagement 5 abuse, libel **7** slander **8** ridicule **9** criticism **10** belittling, defamation, derogation, detraction **11** denigration, putting down **12** vilification **17** defamatory remarks

disparaging 5 snide **10** belittling, derogatory **11** unfavorable **15** uncomplimentary

disparate 6 at odds, unlike **9** different **10** at variance, discordant, discrepant, dissimilar **11** contrasting

disparity 3 gap **8** contrast, imparity, variance **10** difference, divergence, inequality, unlikeness **11** discrepancy, incongruity **12** disagreement, dissemblance **13** contradiction, disproportion, dissimilarity, dissimilitude, inconsistency

dispassion 6 apathy **8** coolness **10** detachment **12** indifference

dispassionate 4 calm, cool, fair **6** serene **7** neutral, unmoved **8** composed, detached, unbiased **9** collected, impartial, unexcited, unruffled **10** impersonal, uninvolved **11** levelheaded, undisturbed, unemotional **12** unprejudiced **13** disinterested, imperturbable

dispatch 4 item, kill, post, slay **5** flash, haste, piece, speed, story **6** finish, letter, murder, report, settle, wind up **7** bump off, execute, forward, message, missive, send off **8** alacrity, bulletin, carry out, celerity, complete, conclude, expedite, massacre, rapidity **9** finish off, quickness, slaughter, swiftness **10** communique, expedition, prompt-

ness, put an end to, put to death **11** assassinate, news account **12** send on the way **14** execute quickly, summarily shoot, swift execution **15** make short work of, transmit rapidly **16** carry out speedily, dispose of rapidly **18** telegraphic message **21** official communication

Dis Pater see **3** Dis

dispel 4 rout **5** allay, expel, repel **6** banish, remove **7** diffuse, dismiss, resolve, scatter **8** drive off **9** dissipate, drive away, eliminate **10** put an end to **11** disseminate **13** make disappear

dispensable 8 nonvital **9** accessory, extrinsic, secondary **10** disposable, expendable, extraneous **11** superfluous, unessential, unimportant, unnecessary **12** nonessential

dispensation 6 decree **8** approval, bestowal, division **9** allotment, diffusion, exemption, meting out **10** allocation, conferment, credential, dealing out, dispensing, permission, reparation **11** consignment, designation **12** apportioning, distribution, remuneration **13** authorization, dissemination

dispense 6 confer **7** dole out, mete out **8** allocate **9** apportion **10** administer, distribute

dispense with 4 drop, dump, junk, shed **5** scrap **6** shelve **7** abandon, discard **9** dispose of

dispensing 9 bestowing, doling out, meting out **10** allocating, conferring **12** distributing

dispersal 7 breakup, parting **9** dismissal **10** breaking up, scattering **12** distributing, distribution

disperse 4 rout **6** dispel **7** diffuse, disband, scatter, send off **8** drive off **9** dissipate **10** disseminate **11** disseminate **13** send scurrying **16** spread throughout

dispersed 7 diffuse **9** scattered, spread out **10** dissipated **11** distributed **14** extended widely, unconcentrated

dispersion 9 dispersal **10** disbanding, scattering **11** dissipation **12** distribution

dispirit 5 cloud **6** darken, deject, sadden **7** depress **10** demoralize, dishearten

dispirited 3 sad **4** blue, down, glum **5** moody **6** morose

7 forlorn, unhappy **8** dejected, downcast, listless **9** cheerless, depressed **10** melancholy **11** crestfallen, demoralized, discouraged, downhearted, pessimistic **12** disconsolate, disheartened **14** down in the dumps, down in the mouth, unenthusiastic

dispiriting 4 cold, dark **6** chilly, dismal, gloomy **9** dampening **10** depressing **12** discouraging **13** disheartening

displace 4 bump, move, oust **5** shift **6** unseat **7** replace **8** crowd out, dislodge, force out, supplant **9** dislocate, supersede

displaced person 2 DP **5** exile **6** emigre **7** refugee **8** expellee **10** expatriate

display 4 show **6** reveal **7** exhibit **8** manifest **10** exhibition **11** demonstrate, make visible **12** presentation **13** bring into view, demonstration, manifestation **15** put in plain sight

display case 7 cabinet, vitrine **8** showcase

displease 3 irk **5** annoy, pique **6** offend **7** disturb, incense, provoke **8** irritate

displeasing 8 annoying **9** loathsome, offensive, repellent, repugnant **10** irritating **11** distasteful, distressing **12** disagreeable

displeasure 5 wrath **7** dislike **8** vexation **9** annoyance **10** irritation **11** disapproval, indignation **15** dissatisfaction

disport 3 act **4** play, romp **5** amuse, caper, sport **6** divert, frolic, gambol **7** display, pastime **9** amusement, entertain **10** recreation **13** entertainment

disposal 5 array, order, power **7** command, control, dumping, junking, pattern, ridding **8** grouping, riddance **9** authority, clearance, direction, placement **10** discarding, government, management, regulation, settlement **11** arrangement, destruction, disposition, supervision **12** distribution, organization, throwing away **13** authorization, configuration, juxtaposition **14** administration

dispose 4 rank **5** array, order, place **7** arrange, deal out, incline **8** classify, get rid of, motivate, organize **9** be willing **10** distribute

dispose of 4 dump **5** scrap **6** unload **7** discard **8** get rid

of, throw out **9** cast aside, throw away

disposition 6 nature, spirit **7** control **8** bestowal, grouping, tendency **9** placement **11** arrangement, inclination, temperament **12** distribution, organization **14** predisposition **15** final settlement

dispossess 4 oust **5** evict, expel **8** take away, take back **9** deprive of

disproportionate 7 unequal **9** disparate **10** dissimilar, unbalanced

disprove 6 refute **9** discredit **10** controvert

disputable 7 dubious **8** doubtful **9** debatable, uncertain **12** questionable **14** controvertible

disputant 5 rival **7** opposer **8** opponent **9** adversary **10** antagonist, competitor, contestant

disputation 6 debate, review **8** argument, dialogue **10** discussion

dispute 4 feud **5** argue, clash, doubt **6** debate, impugn **7** quarrel, wrangle **8** argument, question, squabble **9** bickering, challenge **10** contradict **11** altercation, controversy **12** disagreement

disputed 6 argued **8** wrangled **9** debatable, in dispute, quarreled **10** in question, unverified **12** questionable **13** controversial **15** unsubstantiated

disqualification 5 minus **8** handicap **10** disability **11** shortcoming **13** ineligibility

disqualify 7 disable **9** make unfit **17** declare ineligible, deny participation

disquiet, disquietude 3 awe **6** unease **7** anxiety **8** distress **9** agitation **10** uneasiness **11** fretfulness, trepidation **12** apprehension, discomposure, perturbation **13** consternation

disquieted 6 uneasy **7** anxious, worried **9** concerned **10** distressed **12** apprehensive

disquieting 6 vexing **8** annoying **9** troubling, upsetting **10** bothersome, disturbing, irritating, perturbing, unsettling **11** distressing **13** disconcerting

disquisition 8 tractate, treatise **9** discourse, monograph **12** dissertation

disregard 6 ignore **8** overlook **11** pay no heed to **13** lack of respect **14** take no notice of **15** lack of attention **16** willful oversight

disregardful 8 careless, heedless **9** unmindful **11** insensitive, thoughtless **13** inconsiderate

disreputable 5 shady **8** infamous, shameful, shocking **9** notorious **10** scandalous **11** disgraceful **12** dishonorable, unprincipled **14** not respectable, of bad character

disrespect 8 contempt, dishonor, rudeness **9** disregard **11** discourtesy, irreverence **12** impoliteness

disrespectful 4 rude **8** impolite **11** impertinent **12** contemptuous, discourteous

disrobe 5 strip **7** undress **16** divest of clothing

disrupt 5 upset **9** interrupt **13** interfere with **17** throw into disorder

disruption 5 upset **8** disorder **9** confusion **11** disturbance **12** interference, interruption **14** disarrangement **15** disorganization

dissatisfaction 4 veto **7** protest **9** rejection **10** discontent **11** disapproval, displeasure, unhappiness

dissatisfied 7 unhappy **10** displeased **12** discontented

dissect 5 study **7** analyze, lay open **8** cut apart, separate **9** anatomize, break down

dissemble 4 hide, mask **5** feign **7** conceal **8** disguise **10** camouflage **11** dissimulate

disseminate 6 spread **7** diffuse, scatter **8** disperse **9** broadcast, circulate

dissemination 9 diffusion, dispersal, spreading **10** scattering **12** broadcasting, distribution

dissension 7 discord, dispute **8** conflict, disunity, division **9** rebellion **10** contention, disharmony, quarreling **11** discordance **12** disagreement **14** rebelliousness

dissent 6 object, oppose **7** discord, protest **8** disagree **10** difference, dissension, opposition **12** disagreement **14** withhold assent **16** withhold approval

dissenter 5 rebel **9** dissident, protester **13** nonconformist

dissenting 9 differing, dissident 11 disagreeing

dissertation 6 memoir, thesis 8 tractate, treatise 9 discourse, monograph 12 disquisition

disservice 4 harm, hurt 5 wrong 6 injury 7 bad turn 9 injustice

dissever 3 saw 4 hack, rend 5 carve, sever, slash, slice, split 6 cleave, divide 8 disunite, separate

dissident 5 rebel 8 agitator, opposing 9 differing, dissenter 10 dissenting 11 disagreeing

dissimilar 6 unlike 8 distinct 9 different, disparate

dissimilarity 8 contrast, variance 9 disparity 10 difference, dissonance, divergence, inequality, unlikeness 11 discrepancy 12 disagreement 13 inconsistency 17 lack of resemblance

dissimilitude 8 variance 9 disparity 10 difference, unlikeness 11 incongruity 12 disagreement 17 lack of resemblance

dissimulate 4 hide, mask 7 conceal 8 disguise 9 dissemble 10 camouflage

dissipate 5 waste 6 dispel 7 carouse, deplete, scatter 8 disperse, misspend, squander 11 fritter away, overindulge 13 be intemperate 14 spend foolishly

dissipated 6 wasted 8 misspent 9 abandoned, debauched, dispelled, dispersed, dissolute, scattered 10 squandered 11 intemperate 12 disreputable 13 frittered away

dissipater 5 waste 7 wastrel 8 prodigal 10 profligate, squanderer 11 spendthrift

dissipation 6 excess 7 wasting 9 dispersal 10 debauchery, dispelling, scattering 11 dissolution, loose living 12 immoderation, intemperance 14 disintegration, frittering away, self-indulgence

dissociate 8 separate 10 disconnect 12 break off with

dissociation 7 breakup 10 separation

dissolute 5 loose 7 corrupt, immoral 9 abandoned, debauched 10 dissipated 12 unrestrained

dissolution 9 annulment 10 separation 11 termination 14 disintegration

dissolve 3 end, run 4 fade, melt, thaw, void 5 annul, sever 6 finish, render, soften, vanish 7 break up, disband, liquefy, thaw out 8 abrogate, conclude, evanesce 9 disappear, dissipate, terminate 10 deliquesce 12 disintegrate 13 dematerialize

dissonance 5 clash 7 discord 9 cacophony, harshness 10 difference, disharmony 11 discordance 12 disagreement 13 dissimilarity

dissonant 5 harsh 7 grating, hostile, jarring, raucous, warring 8 clashing, jangling 10 discordant, discrepant 11 cacophonous, disagreeing, incongruent, incongruous, unmelodious 12 incompatible, inconsistent, inharmonious 13 contradictory 14 irreconcilable

dissuade 9 urge not to 10 discourage 13 advise against, persuade not to

distance 3 gap 4 span 7 reserve, stretch 8 coldness, coolness, interval 9 aloofness, formality, restraint, stiffness 11 reservation 16 intervening space

distant 3 far 4 cold, cool 5 aloof 6 far-off, remote 7 faraway 8 detached, reserved 10 far-removed, restrained, unfriendly 11 standoffish 17 not closely related

Distant Mirror, A
author: 15 Barbara W Tuchman

distaste 7 disgust, dislike 8 aversion 9 antipathy 10 repugnance 11 displeasure

distasteful 9 loathsome, repugnant 10 disgusting, unpleasant 11 displeasing 12 disagreeable

distastefulness 13 offensiveness 14 unpleasantness 16 disagreeableness

distasteful work 8 drudgery 11 menial labor

distend 5 bloat, bulge, swell 6 billow, expand 7 inflate, puff out 8 swell out

distended 4 full, taut 5 puffy, tumid 7 blown up, bloated, dilated, swelled, swollen 8 enlarged, expanded, extended, inflated, patulous 9 edematous, stretched

distill 7 draw out, extract 8 condense, vaporize 9 draw forth, evaporate

distillate 7 essence, extract

distilled 9 condensed, extracted, vaporized 10 evaporated

distinct 5 clear, lucid, plain 7 diverse, supreme 8 clear-cut, definite, explicit, separate 9 different 10 dissimilar, individual 11 unmitigated, well-defined 12 not identical, unmistakable 13 extraordinary 14 unquestionable

distinction 6 renown 8 contrast, eminence 9 greatness 10 difference, excellence, importance, notability, prominence, separation 11 discernment, preeminence, superiority 12 differential 14 discrimination 15 differentiation

distinctive 6 unique 7 special 8 atypical, original, singular, uncommon 9 different 10 individual 13 extraordinary 14 characteristic

distinctiveness 7 clarity 9 character 10 definition, uniqueness 11 personality 13 individuality

distingue 13 distinguished

distinguish 6 decide, define 7 discern 8 set apart 9 single out 10 make famous 12 characterize, discriminate 13 differentiate, make prominent, make well known 14 make celebrated 15 make distinctive, note differences

distinguished 5 grand, great 6 famous, superb 7 elegant, eminent, notable, refined 8 renowned, splendid 9 acclaimed, dignified, distingue, prominent 10 celebrated 11 illustrious, magnificent
French: 9 distingue

distort 6 deform 7 contort 8 misshape 9 disfigure 11 misconstrue 12 misrepresent 15 twist out of shape, twist the meaning

distorted 4 awry 5 askew 6 belied, loaded, warped 7 altered, colored, crooked, twisted 8 cockeyed, deformed, wrenched 9 contorted, falsified, grotesque, irregular, misshapen, misstated, perverted 13 unsymmetrical 14 misrepresented 15 misproportioned

distortion 7 skewing 8 twisting 10 aberration, caricature 11 crookedness, deformation 12 malformation 17 misrepresentation

distract 5 amuse, craze,

worry 6 divert, madden 7 agitate, confuse, disturb, perplex, torment, trouble 8 bewilder, disorder 9 entertain

distracted 3 mad 4 wild 6 amused, crazed, insane, raving 7 frantic, pleased, puzzled 8 agitated, confused, deranged, diverted, frenzied, harassed, heedless, occupied 9 disturbed, stirred up 10 bewildered, distraught, irrational 11 entertained, turned aside

distraction 5 fazed, upset 6 frenzy 7 frantic, madness, pastime, rattled, ruffled 8 agitated, confused 9 amusement, diversion, unsettled 10 distraught, distressed, nonplussed, recreation 11 desperation 12 disconcerted 13 entertainment 14 mental distress

distractive 9 confusing 10 disturbing, unsettling 11 distressing, troublesome

distraught 3 mad 7 anxious, frantic 8 agitated, frenzied, seething 10 distracted, distressed 13 beside oneself

distress 4 need, pain, want 5 agony, upset 6 danger, grieve 7 anguish, disturb, torment, torture, trouble 14 acute suffering

distressed 5 upset 7 anxious, fearful, frantic, grieved, unhappy, worried 8 agitated, troubled 9 anguished, concerned, disturbed, tormented 10 distracted, distraught

distressing 5 acute 7 nagging, painful 8 grievous 9 agonizing, upsetting 10 disturbing, tormenting, unpleasant 11 displeasing, troublesome, unfortunate 13 uncomfortable

distribute 5 allot, class 6 divide, parcel 7 arrange, catalog, deliver, dole out, give out, scatter 8 classify, dispense, disperse, separate, tabulate 9 apportion, circulate, methodize, spread out 11 disseminate, systematize

distribution 7 sorting 8 division, grouping 9 allotment, spreading 10 allocation, dispersion, scattering 11 arrangement, circulation, disposition 12 organization 13 apportionment, dissemination

distribution center French: 8 entrepot

district 4 area, ward 6 parish, region 8 precinct 12 neighborhood

distrust 5 doubt 7 suspect

8 question 9 misgiving, suspicion 11 lack of faith

distrustful 3 shy 4 wary 5 leery 7 dubious, jealous 8 cautious, doubtful, doubting 9 diffident 10 suspicious, untrusting 11 incredulous, mistrustful 12 disbelieving

disturb 5 annoy, upset, worry 6 bother 7 disrupt, perturb, trouble 8 distress, unsettle 9 dislocate, interrupt, intrude on 10 disarrange 11 disorganize

disturbance 5 upset, worry 6 bother, hubbub, ruckus, tumult, uproar 7 rioting, turmoil 8 disorder, distress, outbreak 9 annoyance 11 distraction 12 interruption, perturbation

disturbance of peace 4 riot 6 fracas, ruckus, uproar 7 turmoil 8 disorder 9 commotion 13 breach of order

disturbed 5 upset 6 uneasy 7 annoyed, anxious, nervous, rattled 8 agitated, confused, troubled 9 perturbed 10 disquieted 11 discomfited 12 disconcerted

disunion 7 divorce 8 division 9 secession 10 separation 14 disintegration

disunite 4 part 6 divide 7 divorce 8 separate 9 disengage 10 disconnect 12 disintegrate 13 disarticulate

disunited 6 parted 8 diverged, divorced, unallied 9 came apart, dispersed, separated 10 uncombined 13 disassociated

disunity 6 strife 7 discord 8 clashing, conflict, division, friction 9 wrangling 10 contention, dissension, separation 11 being at odds, discordance 12 disagreement 15 incompatibility

ditat Deus 11 God enriches motto of: 7 Arizona

ditch 3 pit 4 junk 5 scrap 6 hollow, trench 7 abandon, discard 8 get rid of 10 excavation

dither 4 flap, fuss 5 tizzy, waver, whirl 6 bother, flurry, lather, quiver, shiver, thrill 7 fluster, tremble, twitter 8 hesitate 9 agitation, commotion, confusion, vacillate, vibration 10 excitement

Dithyrambus epithet of: 8 Dionysus means: 20 child of the double door

ditty 3 lay 4 song, tune 6 ballad 7 refrain

Dius Fidius origin: 5 Roman god of: 5 oaths 11 hospitality 20 international affairs corresponds to: 6 Sancus 10 Semo Sancus

divagation 8 straying 9 wandering 10 digression, divergence

divan 4 book, hall, poem, room, salon, seat, sofa 5 couch, court 6 canape, daybed, leewan, lounge, settee 7 chamber, council, ottoman, davenport

dive 4 dash, fall, jump, leap 5 lunge 6 plunge 7 gin mill 9 honky-tonk, shabby bar 15 sleazy nightclub

Diver, Dick and Nicole characters in: 16 Tender Is the Night author: 10 Fitzgerald

diverge 6 differ, swerve 7 deflect, deviate 8 be at odds, conflict, disagree, separate, split off

divergence 7 parting 8 conflict, rambling, straying, variance 9 deviation, disparity, wandering 10 difference, separation 11 discrepancy, incongruity 13 dissimilarity, inconsistency

divergent 8 separate 9 different 11 conflicting, disagreeing 12 drawing apart, splitting off

diverse 6 sundry, varied 8 eclectic, far-flung, opposite 9 different, differing, disparate 10 dissimilar 11 conflicting; of many kinds 13 contradictory

diversified 6 divers 7 various 8 manifold 9 different, unrelated 13 miscellaneous

diversify 4 vary 7 diffuse 8 divide up 9 spread out, variegate

diversion 5 hobby 7 pastime 9 amusement, avocation 10 deflection 11 distraction, drawing away 12 turning aside French: 14 divertissement

diversity 7 variety 8 variance 10 assortment, difference 13 heterogeneity

divert 5 amuse 7 deflect 8 distract 9 entertain, sidetrack, turn aside

diverting 7 amusing 10 deflecting 11 distracting 12 entertaining, sidetracking

divertissement 9 diversion 13 entertainment

divest 3 rid 4 free 5 strip 7 deprive, disrobe, peel off, take off 8 get out of 10 dispossess 14 remove clothing

divest oneself of 6 give up 7 take off 8 get rid of, give over, hand over, put aside, strip off 9 surrender 10 relinquish

divide 4 part, sort 5 share, split 7 arrange, deal out, divvy up 8 allocate, classify, disunite, separate 9 apportion, partition 10 distribute, put in order

divide and rule
Latin: 14 divide et impera
maxim of: 11 Machiavelli

divided 5 apart, split 6 parted 8 meted out 9 disunited, separated 10 unattached 11 apportioned 12 disconnected, portioned out

divide et impera 13 divide and rule
maxim of: 11 Machiavelli

divide in two 5 halve, split 6 bisect 8 cut in two, separate 9 cut in half 10 break in two 11 split in half 18 split down the middle

dividing line 4 edge 5 brink, verge 6 border, margin 8 boundary 9 threshold

divination 5 guess 6 augury 8 prophecy 10 conjecture, foreboding, prediction, prescience 11 premonition, soothsaying 15 prognostication

divine 4 holy 5 guess 6 fathom, sacred 7 predict, surmise, suspect 8 forecast, foretell, heavenly, prophesy 9 admirable, celestial, excellent, marvelous, wonderful

divine being 3 god 5 deity 7 goddess 8 divinity 14 celestial being

Divine Comedy
author: 14 Dante Alighieri
part: 7 Inferno 8 Paradiso 10 Purgatorio
guide: 6 Virgil 8 Beatrice

diviner 4 seer 5 augur 10 soothsayer 14 prognosticator

Divine retribution
goddess of: 7 Nemesis 8 Adrastea

Divine Sarah
nickname of: 14 Sarah Bernhardt

divinity 3 god 5 deity 7 goddess 8 holiness, religion, theology 9 theosophy 12 science of God 14 celestial being

division 4 part, unit, wing 5 split 6 branch 7 discord, divider, section 8 disunion, variance 9 partition 10 department, difference, divergence, separation 11 splitting up 12 disagreement

divorce 4 rift 5 split 6 breach, divide 7 rupture 8 disunite, separate 9 segregate 10 dissociate, separation

divulge 4 tell 6 impart, relate, reveal 8 disclose 9 make known 11 communicate

divulgence 7 telling 8 exposure 9 imparting 10 disclosure, giving away, laying open, revelation 13 communication 15 bringing to light 17 bring out in the open

divulge to 4 tell 6 advise, inform, notify, reveal 7 apprise 8 acquaint, disclose 9 enlighten, make aware 11 familiarize 13 spill the beans 20 let the cat out of the bag

Dix, Otto
born: 7 Germany 11 Unterhausen
artwork: 6 The War 7 The City 12 The Procuress 15 Sylvia von Harden 18 Parents of the Artist 39 Prague Street—Dedicated to My Contemporaries

Dixie Dugan
creator: 8 J P McEvoy 13 John H Striebel

dizzy 5 fleet, giddy, quick, rapid, shaky, swift 6 whirly 7 confuse, reeling 8 bewilder, unsteady 9 make giddy 11 lightheaded, vertiginous 12 make unsteady

Djawa see 4 Java

Djebel al-Tarik see 9 Gibraltar

Djibouti see box

do 3 act 4 fare 5 clean, cover, get on, serve, visit 6 behave, finish, look at, stop in 7 achieve, arrange, carry on, conduct, execute, fulfill, make out, perform, prepare, proceed, suffice 8 be enough, carry out, complete, conclude, organize 10 accomplish, administer, bring about, put in order 13 travel through 14 be satisfactory, comport oneself, conduct oneself

do a favor 4 help 6 assist, oblige 7 help out 11 accommodate, do a kindness

do away with 3 end 4 junk, kill, void 5 erase, quash 6 banish, cancel, cut out, give

---

Djibouti
other name: 16 French Somaliland 39 The French Territory of the Afars and the Issas
capital/largest city: 8 Djibouti
others: 5 Obock 6 Dikhil 8 Tadjoura 9 Ali-Sabieh
monetary unit: 5 franc 7 centime
lake: 4 Abbe 5 Assal
mountain: 5 Gouda
highest point: 9 Moussa Ali
sea: 3 Red
physical feature:
gulf: 4 Aden 8 Tadjoura
strait: 11 Bab el-Mandeb
people: 4 Afar, Arab 5 Issas 6 French 8 European
language: 4 Afar 6 Arabic, French, Somali
religion: 5 Islam

---

up, remove, repeal, revoke, rub out 7 abolish, blot out, nullify, rescind, weed out, wipe out 8 abrogate, stamp out, throw out 9 eliminate, eradicate, terminate 10 annihilate, put an end to 11 exterminate

Dobbin, Captain William
character in: 10 Vanity Fair
author: 9 Thackeray

Dobie Gillis, The Many Loves of
character: 11 Zelda Gilroy 13 Maynard G Krebs 14 Herbert T Gillis, Milton Armitage, Winifred (Winnie) Gillis 15 Thalia Menninger 19 Chatsworth Osborne Jr
cast: 9 Bob Denver 11 Frank Faylen, Sheila James, Tuesday Weld 12 Warren Beatty 13 Dwayne Hickman 14 Florida Friebus, Stephen Franken
Dobie imitated pose of: 7 Thinker

do business 4 deal 5 trade 10 buy and sell

docile 4 tame 7 willing 8 obedient, obliging 9 agreeable, compliant, tractable 10 manageable 11 complaisant

docility 7 pliancy 8 meekness 9 passivity 10 placidness 12 acquiescence, complaisance 13 nonresistance

277

dock 4 crop, join, pier, quay 5 berth, wharf 6 couple, cut off, deduct, hook up, link up 7 landing 8 cut short 10 waterfront 12 come into port 13 subject to loss 14 fasten together

dock 5 Rumux
varieties: 3 Bur 4 Sour 5 Green 6 Golden 7 Prairie, Spinach, Tanner's, Western 8 Patience 9 Purple-wen 10 Giant water

docket 4 bill, card, list 5 slate 6 agenda, lineup, roster 7 program 8 calendar, schedule 9 timetable 14 things to be done 15 order of business

doctor 2 GP, MD 3 PhD 5 alter, treat 6 change 7 dentist, falsify, surgeon 9 internist, osteopath, physician 10 podiatrist, tamper with 11 pathologist 12 gynecologist, obstetrician, pediatrician, psychiatrist, veterinarian 15 ophthalmologist 17 apply medication to 19 general practitioner, medical practitioner

Doctor Brodie's Report
author: 15 Jorge Luis Borges

Doctor Faustus
author: 10 Thomas Mann 18 Christopher Marlowe

Doctor Grimshaw's Secret
author: 18 Nathaniel Hawthorne

Doctor J
nickname of: 12 Julius Erving

Doctorow, E L
author of: 7 Ragtime 15 The Book of Daniel

Doctor's Dilemma, The
author: 17 George Bernard Shaw

Doctor Zhivago
director: 9 David Lean
author: 14 Boris Pasternak
cast: 10 Omar Sharif (Zhivago), Rod Steiger 12 Alec Guinness, Tom Courtenay 13 Julie Christie (Lara) 14 Rita Tushingham 15 Ralph Richardson 16 Geraldine Chaplin

doctrinaire 5 rigid 6 mulish 8 absolute, dogmatic, stubborn 9 arbitrary, imperious, pigheaded 10 bullheaded, inflexible, pontifical 11 dictatorial, opinionated, overbearing, stiff-necked 12 narrowminded 13 authoritarian 14 disciplinarian

doctrinal 8 didactic, dogmatic, edifying, tutorial 11 educational, instructive 12 prescriptive

doctrine 5 dogma, tenet 6 belief, gospel 7 precept 8 teaching 9 principle 10 conviction, philosophy

document 6 back up, record, verify 7 certify, support 9 legal form 10 instrument 12 give weight to, substantiate 13 official paper

documentation 5 proof 7 support 8 evidence 12 verification 13 corroboration 14 substantiation

doddering 4 weak 6 feeble, senile 7 shaking 8 decrepit 9 tottering, trembling

dodge 4 duck, wile 5 avoid, elude, evade, hedge, trick 6 device, swerve 7 fend off 8 sidestep 9 jump aside, stratagem, turn aside 10 equivocate 11 machination

dodging 7 ducking, eluding, evading 8 shunning 12 sidestepping 13 circumventing

Dodgson, Charles Lutwidge
real name of: 12 Lewis Carroll

Dodoma
capital of: 8 Tanzania

Dodonian
epithet of: 4 Zeus

Dodsworth
director: 12 William Wyler
author: 13 Sinclair Lewis
character: 4 Fran 12 Arnold Israel 14 Edith Cortright, Renee de Penable 15 Samuel Dodsworth 16 Kurt von Obersdorf 17 Major Clyde Lockert
cast: 9 Mary Astor, Paul Lukas 10 David Niven 12 Walter Huston 14 Ruth Chatterton

doer 6 dynamo 7 hustler 8 activist, go-getter 12 active person

doff 4 bare, drop, junk, shed 5 scrap, strip 6 put off, remove 7 abandon, cast off, discard, disrobe, take off, toss off, undress 8 throw off, throw out 9 eliminate, step out of 10 do away with

dog see box, p. 278

Dogberry
character in: 19 Much Ado About Nothing
author: 11 Shakespeare

Dog Day Afternoon
director: 11 Sidney Lumet
cast: 8 Al Pacino 10 John Cazale 14 Charles Durning

dogged 8 stubborn 9 tenacious 10 determined, persistent 11 unremitting

dogie 4 calf 14 motherless calf

dogies 6 calves, cattle 16 motherless calves

dogma 5 credo, tenet 7 beliefs 8 doctrine 9 teachings 10 philosophy, principles 11 convictions

dogmatic 6 biased 8 stubborn 9 arbitrary, doctrinal, imperious, obstinate 10 prejudiced 11 dictatorial, domineering, opinionated

Dog Star
constellation of:
Hunting Dogs: 13 Canes Venatici
Larger Dog: 10 Canis Major
Smaller Dog: 10 Canis Minor

dogwood 6 Cornus
varieties: 5 Brown, Creek, False, Giant, Silky, Stiff 6 Pagoda, Poison 7 Chinese 8 American, Jamaican, Mountain, Panicled, Redosier, Siberian, Tatarian 9 Blood-twig, Flowering, Tartarian 10 Golden-twig, West Indian 11 Roundleaved 13 White Mountain

Doha, al-Dawha
capital of: 5 Qatar

do in 4 kill 6 murder 7 destroy, exhaust, tire out

Doktor Faust
opera by: 6 Busoni
character: 5 Faust 14 Duchess of Parma 14 Mephistopheles

dolce
music: 7 sweetly

dolce far niente 18 pleasing inactivity 20 it is sweet to do nothing

dolce vita 9 sweet life

Dol Common
character in: 12 The Alchemist
author: 6 Jonson

doldrums 5 blues, dumps, gloom 10 depression, melancholy

dole 4 deal, give 5 share 6 parcel 7 charity, handout, welfare 9 allotment 10 allocation 13 apportionment

doleful 3 sad 6 dismal, dreary, gloomy, woeful 7 joyless, unhappy 9 sorrowful

dolente
music: 9 sorrowful

dog 3 cur, pup **4** heel, mutt **5** beast, puppy **6** canine **7** mongrel, villain **9** scoundrel **10** blackguard

Alaskan: 5 husky **8** malamute, malemute

anatomy: 3 hip, lip, pad, paw, toe **4** arch, back, hock, loin, rump, stop **5** cheek, crest, croup, flews, skull **6** carpus, dewlap, muzzle, stifle, tarsus **7** brisket, cushion, knuckle, occiput, pastern, withers **8** heelknob, shoulder **10** metacarpus, metatarsus

Australian: 5 dingo **8** warragal

barkless: 7 basenji

breed:

   herding group: **5** pulik **6** briard, collie **13** bearded collie **14** German Shepherd **15** Belgian malinois, Belgian sheepdog, Belgian tervuren **16** Shetland sheepdog **18** Cardigan Welsh corgi, Old English sheepdog, Pembroke Welsh corgi **19** Australian cattle dog, Bouviers des Flandres

   hound group: **6** beagle, borzoi, saluki **7** basenji, harrier, whippet **9** dachshund, greyhound **10** bloodhound, otter hound **11** Afghan hound, basset hound, Ibizan hound **12** pharaoh hound **14** Irish wolfhound **15** English foxhound **16** American foxhound **17** Norwegian elkhound, Scottish deerhound **18** Rhodesian ridgeback **20** black and tan coonhound

   nonsporting group: **6** poodle **7** bulldog **8** chow chow, keeshond **9** dalmatian, lhasa apso **10** keeshonden, schipperke **11** Bichon frise **13** Boston terrier, French bulldog **14** Tibetan spaniel, Tibetan terrier

   sporting group: **6** vizsla **7** pointer **8** Brittany **10** weimaraner **11** Irish setter **12** field spaniel, Gordon setter **13** cocker spaniel, English setter, Sussex spaniel **14** Clumber spaniel **15** golden retriever **17** Irish water spaniel, Labrador retriever **19** flat-coated retriever **20** American water spaniel, curly-coated retriever, English cocker spaniel, Welsh springer spaniel **22** Chesapeake Bay retriever, English springer spaniel **23** German wirehaired pointer **24** German shorthaired pointer **25** wirehaired pointing griffon

   terrier group: **10** fox terrier **11** bull terrier, Skye terrier **12** Cairn terrier, Irish terrier, Welsh terrier **13** border terrier **14** Norfolk terrier, Norwich terrier, wire fox terrier **15** Airedale terrier, Lakeland terrier, Scottish terrier, Sealyham terrier **16** Kerry blue terrier, smooth fox terrier **17** Australian terrier, Bedlington terrier, Manchester terrier **18** miniature schnauzer **20** Dandie Dinmont terrier **24** soft-coated wheaten terrier, Staffordshire bull terrier, West Highland white terrier **28** American Staffordshire terrier

   toy group: **3** pug **7** Maltese, shih tzu **8** papillon **9** chihuahua, pekingese, toy poodle **10** pomeranian **12** Japanese chin, silky terrier **13** affenpinscher **15** Brussels griffon **16** Italian greyhound, Yorkshire terrier **17** English toy spaniel, Manchester terrier, miniature pinscher

   working group: **5** akita, boxer **7** mastiff, samoyed **8** kuvaszok **9** great Dane, St Bernard **10** komondorok, rottweiler **11** bullmastiff **12** Newfoundland **13** great Pyrenees, Siberian husky **14** giant schnauzer **15** Alaskan malamute **16** doberman pinscher **17** standard schnauzer **18** Bernese mountain dog, Portuguese water dog

Buster Brown's: 4 Tige

Chinese: 7 shih tzu

coach: 9 dalmatian

combining form: 3 cyn **4** cani, cyno

constellation: 12 Canis Majoris

Dorothy's: 4 Toto

family: 7 Canidae

FDR's: 4 Fala **5** Falla

female: 3 dam, gip, gyp **4** slut **5** bitch, brach **7** brachet

genus: 5 Canis

group: 4 pack **5** leash **6** kennel

"His Master's Voice": 6 Nipper

Hungarian: 4 puli **6** kuvasz, vizsla

Indian: 5 dhole

Japanese: 5 akita

Little Orphan Annie's: 5 Sandy

male: 3 dog

movie/TV: 4 Asta, Lady **5** Benji, Tramp **6** Lassie **9** Old Yeller, Rin Tin Tin

mythical: 8 Cerberus

Nixon's: 8 Checkers

Punch and Judy's: 4 Toby

Russian: 6 borzoi **7** samoyed

star: 6 Sirius **8** Canicula

Welsh: 5 corgi

wild: 5 adjag, dhole, dingo, guara, rabid **6** jackal **7** agouara **8** cimarron

young: 3 pup **5** puppy, whelp

dole out 4 give, mete **5** allot **6** parcel **7** portion **8** allocate, dispense **9** apportion **10** distribute

doling out 7 dealing **9** allotment, parceling **10** allocation, assignment **12** distribution **13** apportionment

Dolius
epithet of: **6** Hermes
means: **6** crafty
form: **5** slave
given to: **8** Penelope

doll 5 dolly, dummy, honey **6** beauty, puppet **7** darling, rag doll **8** baby doll, figurine, golliwog **9** teddy bear **10** marionette, sweetheart **11** pretty child

dollar 3 one **4** bean, bill, buck, coin, note, skin, yuan **5** money, tater, token **6** single **7** ironman, smacker **8** cartwheel, simolean

Dollar A Second
host: **9** Jan Murray

Dollar Bill
nickname of: **11** Bill Bradley

dollop 3 dab **4** blob, dash, lump **11** small amount

Doll's House, A
author: **11** Henrik Ibsen
character: **8** Krogstad **10** Nora Helmer **13** Torvald Helmer

dolly 3 toy **4** cart, doll **9** plaything **15** wheeled platform

Dolon
mentioned in: **5** Iliad
father: **7** Eumedes
killed by: **8** Diomedes, Odysseus

dolor 5 grief **6** sorrow **7** anguish, sadness

dolorous 3 sad **6** rueful, woeful **7** doleful, tearful, unhappy **8** dejected, downcast, grievous, mournful, pathetic, pitiable, wretched **9** anguished, cheerless, harrowing, miserable, sorrowful, woebegone **10** calamitous, despondent, lamentable, melancholy **11** distressing **12** disconsolate, heavy-hearted **13** grief-stricken

Dolphin
constellation of: **9** Delphinus

Dolphin, The
author: **12** Robert Lowell

dolt 4 clod, fool, jerk **5** idiot, moron **6** nitwit **7** half-wit, jackass **8** bonehead, imbecile, numskull **9** blockhead

doltish 4 dumb, slow **5** thick **6** simple, stupid **7** asinine, foolish, idiotic, moronic, witless **8** ignorant, retarded **9** brainless, imbecilic **10** halfwitted, slow-witted **12** dunderheaded, muddleheaded, simpleminded **13** rattlebrained **14** featherbrained

domain 4 area, fief, land **5** field **6** empire, estate, region, sphere **7** kingdom **8** dominion, property, province **9** bailiwick, territory

Dombey and Son
author: **14** Charles Dickens
character: **4** Paul **5** Toots **6** Carker, Cuttle **8** Florence, Mr Dombey **9** Dr Blimber, Walter Gay **11** Joe Bagstock, Susan Nipper **12** Cousin Feenix, Edith Granger, Solomon Gills

dome
Italian: **5** duomo

Domenichino
real name: **16** Domenico Zampieri
born: **5** Italy **7** Bologna
artwork: **11** Hunt of Diana **16** Monsignor Agucchi **18** The Four Evangelists, The Life of St Cecilia **23** Last Communion of St Jerome **30** Landscape with Tobias and the Angel

domestic 4 cook, maid, tame **6** butler, native **7** endemic, servant **8** homemade, houseboy **9** attendant, home-grown **10** indigenous, not foreign **11** housebroken, native-grown, not imported **12** domesticated, hearth-loving **13** household help

domesticated 4 tame **11** housebroken

domicile 4 home **5** house **8** dwelling **9** residence **14** legal residence

dominance 4 edge **8** hegemony **9** advantage, authority, upper hand **10** precedence **11** preeminence, superiority

dominant 5 chief, major **6** ruling **8** superior **9** principal **10** commanding **11** controlling, outstanding **13** authoritative, most important, most prominent

dominate 4 rule **5** dwarf **6** direct, govern **7** command, control **8** domineer **9** tower over **11** preside over

dominating 6 lordly, ruling **7** topmost **8** dominant **9** directing, governing, principal, prominent **10** commanding **11** controlling, domineering, outstanding **12** advantageous

13 authoritative, most important **15** most outstanding

domination 4 rule **5** power **7** command, control, mastery **9** authority **11** superiority

domineer 7 control **8** dominate, lord over **9** dictate to, tyrannize

domineering 8 arrogant, despotic, dogmatic **9** imperious **10** commanding, oppressive, tyrannical **11** dictatorial, overbearing **13** authoritative

Dominican Republic *see box, p. 280*

dominion 4 land, rule **5** realm **6** domain, empire, region **7** command, mastery **9** authority, supremacy, territory **11** sovereignty **12** jurisdiction
Hindu: **3** raj

Dominus 3 God **4** Lord

Dominus vobiscum 16 the Lord be with you

don 4 wear **5** put on **6** pull on **7** dress in, get into

Don
origin: **5** Welsh
form: **7** goddess
son: **7** Gwydion
daughter: **8** Arianrod

dona 4 lady **5** madam

Dona Flor and Her Two Husbands
author: **10** Jorge Amado

Donalbain
father: **6** Duncan
brother: **7** Malcom

Donald Duck
creator: **10** Walt Disney
character:
girlfriend: **5** Daisy
nephew: **4** Huey **5** Dewey, Louie
uncle: **7** Scrooge

Donar
origin: **8** Germanic
god of: **7** thunder

donate 4 give **6** bestow **7** present **8** bequeath **10** contribute **11** make a gift of

Donatello
real name: **15** Donato di Niccolo
born: **5** Italy **9** Florence
artwork: **5** David **6** St Mark **7** Zuccone **8** Jeremiah, St George **11** Gattamelata **12** Mary Magdalen **19** Judith and Holofernes, St John the Evangelist **22** Cavalcanti Annunciation

donation 4 gift **7** present **12** contribution

Dominican Republic
capital/largest city: **12** Santo Domingo **14** Ciudad Trujillo
others: **4** Azua, Bani, Moca, Pena, Polo **5** Bonao, Cotui, Nagua, Neiba, Nizao, Sosua **6** Higuey, La Vega, Oviedo **7** Sanchez **8** Barahona, Santiago **11** Puerto Plata **17** San Pedro de Macoris **21** San Francisco de Macoris
measure: **3** ona **5** tarea **6** fanega
monetary unit: **3** oro **4** peso **6** franco
island: **5** Beata, Saona **8** Altovelo, Catalina **10** Hispaniola
lake: **10** Enriquillo
mountain: **4** Tina **5** Gallo, Neiba **7** Baoruco, Central **8** Bahoruco, Oriental **13** Sententrional
highest point: **6** Duarte
river: **4** Yuna **5** Ozama **11** Yaque del Sur **13** Yaque del Norte
sea: **8** Atlantic **9** Caribbean
physical feature:
  bay: **4** Ocoa, Yuma **5** Neiba **6** Rincon, Samana **7** Isabela **8** Calderas, Escocesa
  cape: **5** Beata, Falso **6** Cabron, Engano **7** Caucedo, Isabela, Macoris
  valley: **4** Real **5** Neyba
people: **5** Negro, Taino **6** Indian **7** mulatto, Spanish **9** Caucasian
  discoverer: **8** Columbus
language: **6** French **7** English, Spanish
religion: **13** Roman Catholic
feature:
  dance: **8** merengue
  religious pilgrimage: **8** romerias
food:
  dessert: **8** pinonate
  fish/meat pastry: **10** pastelitos
  stew: **8** sancocho

Don Careless
author: **8** Rex Beach

Don Carlos
author: **14** Johann Schiller
opera by: **5** Verdi
character: **7** Rodrigo **8** Philip II **9** Don Carlos **13** Princess Eboli **15** Grand Inquisitor **17** Elizabeth de Valois

Dondi
creator: **8** Gus Edson **10** Irwin Hasen
dog: **7** Queenie

done **5** ready **8** finished, prepared **9** completed **12** cooked enough **18** cooked sufficiently

done for **4** dead, gone, over, sunk **5** all up, ended, kaput, spent **6** beaten, doomed, ruined **7** all over, damaged, through **8** finished **9** exhausted

done in **4** beat **5** all in, slain, spent, tired, weary **6** bushed, killed, pooped **7** drained, wearied, worn out **8** dog tired, fatigued, murdered, tired out **9** bone weary, dead tired, played out **10** knocked off

Don Giovanni
also: **7** Don Juan **15** The Rake Punished
opera by: **6** Mozart
setting: **7** Seville
character: **7** Masetto, Zerlina **9** Donna Anna, Leporello **10** Don Ottavio **11** Donna Elvira **15** The Commendatore

Donizetti, Gaetano
born: **5** Italy **7** Bergamo
composer of: **10** Anna Bolena, La Favorita **11** Don Pasquale **12** Elixir of Love, Maria Stuarda **13** L'elisir d'amore, Marino Faliero, Torquato Tasso **14** Lucrezia Borgia **15** Roberto Devereux **16** Linda di Chamounix **17** Lucia di Lammermoor **21** Daughter of the Regiment

Don Juan **3** man **4** beau, wolf **5** Romeo, swain, wooer **6** fellow, squire, steady, suitor **7** admirer, courter, gallant, pursuer **8** Casanova, lothario, lover boy, paramour, young man **9** boyfriend, Lochinvar **10** lady-killer **15** gentleman caller

Don Juan
author: **21** George Gordon Lord Byron
character: **6** Haidee **9** Donna Inez **10** Donna Julia

donkey **3** ass **4** fool, mule **5** burro, idiot **7** jackass

Donlevy, Brian
wife: **12** Marjorie Lane
born: **7** Ireland **9** Portadown
roles: **9** Beau Geste **15** The Great McGinty **21** Two Years Before the Mast

Donn, Arabella
character in: **14** Jude the Obscure
author: **5** Hardy

donna **4** lady **5** madam

Donna Reed Show, The
character: **9** Jeff Stone, Mary Stone **10** Donna Stone **11** Dr Alex Stone, Midge Kelsey, Trisha Stone **12** Dr Dave Kelsey
cast: **8** Bob Crane, Carl Betz **9** Ann McCrea, Donna Reed **12** Paul Peterson **13** Patty Peterson **14** Shelley Fabares

Donne, John
author of: **7** Sermons **10** The Ecstasy, The Extasie **11** Holy Sonnets **15** Death Be Not Proud, Songs and Sonnets, The Canonization **20** Paradoxes and Problems **30** A Valediction Forbidding Mourning

donnish **7** preachy **8** academic, didactic, pedantic **9** pedagogic

Donnithorne, Arthur
character in: **8** Adam Bede
author: **5** Eliot

donnybrook **3** row **4** fray **5** brawl, fight, melee, set-to **6** affray, dustup, fracas, ruckus, rumpus **7** ruction, scuffle **8** skirmish **10** free-for-all **19** knock-down-and-drag-out

donor **5** giver **10** benefactor **11** contributor **12** humanitarian **14** philanthropist

do-nothing **5** idler **6** loafer **14** good-for-nothing

do not prosecute
Latin: **13** nolle prosequi

do not repeat
Latin: **12** non repetatur

Don Pasquale
opera by: **9** Donizetti
character: **6** Norina **7** Ernesto **11** Dr Malatesta

Don Quixote de la Mancha
also: **38** El ingenioso hidalgo Don Quijote de la Mancha
author: **17** Miguel de Cervantes (Saavedra)
character: **10** Pedro Perez

11 Sancho Panza 17 Dulcinea del Toboso
horse: 9 Rosinante
musical: 13 Man of La Mancha

doodad 5 gizmo 6 device, gadget 8 ornament 9 doohickey 10 decoration 11 contraption, contrivance, thingamabob, thingamajig 15 whatchamacallit

doohickey 5 gizmo, thing 6 device, dingus, gadget, object, widget 7 dojiggy, whatsis 8 dojigger 9 thingummy 11 thingamabob, thingamajig 14 thingamadoodle 15 whatchamacallit

Dooley, Thomas Anthony
founded: 6 MEDICO 31 Medical International Corporation
worked in: 13 Southeast Asia

Doolittle, Eliza
character in: 9 Pygmalion 10 My Fair Lady
author: 4 Shaw

doom 3 end, lot 4 fate, ruin 5 death, judge 7 condemn, convict, destiny, portion, verdict 8 judgment 10 Armageddon 11 destruction, Judgment Day 13 consign to ruin, end of the world, pronouncement 15 resurrection day, the Last Judgment 17 mark for demolition

doomed 5 fated 6 damned, ruined 8 ill-fated 9 condemned

doomsday 11 Judgment Day 13 Day of Judgment, end of the world 15 the Last Judgment

do one's best 3 try 6 strive 7 attempt 8 endeavor, go all out 9 take pains 12 make an effort 13 give all one has 15 knock oneself out

Doonesbury
creator: 12 Garry Trudeau
character: 2 B D 5 Honey, Rufus 6 Calvin 7 Boopsie 9 Uncle Duke 12 Joanie Caucus 14 Mark Slackmeyer 18 Michael J Doonesbury

door 4 exit 5 entry 6 egress, portal 7 hallway, ingress 8 entrance 11 entranceway

Door hinges
goddess of: 6 Cardea

doorway 5 entry 7 ingress, opening 8 entrance

Doorways
god of: 5 Janus

dope 3 tip 4 drip, drug, fool, jerk, nerd, news 5 creep,

drugs, dummy, klutz, scoop 6 sedate, uppers 7 downers, opiates 8 additive 9 narcotics, narcotize, substance 10 antiseptic, astringent, medication 11 anesthetize, preparation 12 disinfectant 17 inside information

dope fiend 4 head, user 5 doper, freak 6 addict, junkie 7 hophead 8 cokehead 10 dope addict, drug abuser, drug addict

do penance 5 atone 7 expiate 10 make amends

dopey 4 dumb 6 leaden, stupid, torpid 7 asinine, idiotic, witless 8 comatose, mindless, sluggish 9 brainless, lethargic 10 dull-witted, slow-witted, slumberous 11 block-headed, thickheaded 12 simple-minded

Doppelganger 6 double 13 ghostly double
literally: 12 double-walker

Doppler, Christian Johann
field: 7 physics
nationality: 8 Austrian
discovered: 13 Doppler Effect

Dorcas
also called: 7 Tabitha
revived by: 5 Peter
hometown: 5 Joppa

Doris
father: 7 Oceanus
mother: 6 Tethys
husband: 6 Nereus
mother of: 7 Nereids

Doritis
epithet of: 9 Aphrodite
means: 9 bountiful

dormancy 7 latency 8 inaction 10 inactivity, quiescence, somnolence 11 hibernation

dormant 4 idle 8 inactive, sleeping 9 quiescent, somnolent 11 hibernating

Dorothy
character in: 13 The Wizard of Oz
author: 4 Baum

Dorset, Bertha and George
characters in: 15 The House of Mirth
author: 7 Wharton

dorsum 5 chine, spine 8 backbone

Dorus
father: 6 Apollo, Hellen
mother: 6 Orseis, Phthia
killed by: 7 Aetolus

dose 2 OD 3 cut, nip 4 dram, pill, shot, slug 5 quota, share, slice 6 amount, needle, ration, tablet 7 capsule, measure, portion, section, segment 8 divi-

sion, overdose, quantity 9 allotment, allowance, daily dose, injection 10 percentage

Dos Passos, John
author: 3 U S A 11 The Big Money 13 Three Soldiers 16 Nineteen Nineteen 17 Manhattan Transfer 22 The Forty-Second Parallel

dossier 4 file 5 brief 6 record 9 portfolio 14 detailed report

Dostoevsky, Fyodor Mikhailovich
author: 8 The Idiot 9 The Double 10 The Gambler 12 The Possessed 18 Crime and Punishment 20 The Brothers Karamazov 23 Notes from the Underground

dot 3 dab 4 mark, spot 5 fleck, point, speck 6 dapple, period 9 small spot

dotage 8 senility 15 second childhood 16 feeblemindedness

dote 8 be senile, fuss over

dote on 5 adore, prize, spoil, value 6 pamper 7 cherish, indulge 8 fuss over, treasure 15 lavish affection

doting 4 fond 6 loving 9 indulgent, pampering 12 affectionate

double 4 dual, twin 5 clone 6 paired 7 replica, two-part 8 two-sided 9 ambiguous, duplicate 10 dead ringer 11 again as much, counterpart, meant for two, twice as much 12 twice as great 13 multiply by two, spitting image 15 increase twofold
German: 12 Doppelganger

Double, The
author: 16 Fyodor Dostoevsky

double-cross 5 rat on 6 betray, do dirt, tell on, turn in 7 abandon, deceive, let down, sell out, two-time 8 denounce, inform on, run out on, snitch on 9 play Judas 10 be disloyal 13 be treacherous, inform against, play false with 14 break faith with 16 blow the whistle on, sell down the river

double-crosser 5 cheat 7 traitor 8 betrayer, deceiver, informer

Double-Dealer, The
author: 15 William Congreve

double-dealing 5 false 6 deceit, sneaky, tricky 7 crooked, devious, perfidy 8 bad faith, betrayal, disloyal 9 deceitful, duplicity, falseness, treachery,

two-timing 10 disloyalty, per-fidious, sneakiness **11** crook-edness, double-cross, duplicitous, treacherous **12** dishonorable **13** breach of faith, faithlessness

double entendre 12 off-color joke, risque remark **18** ambig-uous statement

double entente 9 ambiguity

Double Indemnity
director: **11** Billy Wilder
cast: **13** Fred MacMurray **15** Barbara Stanwyck, Ed-ward G Robinson
script: **9** James Cain **15** Ray-mond Chandler

Double Life, A
director: **11** George Cukor
cast: **10** Signe Hasso **12** Ed-mond O'Brien, Ronald Col-man **14** Shelley Winters
Oscar for: **5** actor (Colman)
script: **10** Ruth Gordon **11** Garson Kanin

double meaning 9 ambiguity
French: **13** double entente **14** double entendre

doublet 4 pair **5** tunic **6** cou-ple, jacket **10** two of a kind

double-talk 4 bunk, jazz **5** hokum **6** bunkum, drivel, gabble, jabber **7** baloney, blather, palaver, prattle, twad-dle **8** flimflam, flummery, non-sense **9** gibberish **10** balderdash, hocus-pocus, mumbo jumbo **11** obfuscation **12** gobbledygook

double-walker
German: **12** Doppelganger

Double X
nickname of: **9** Jimmy Foxx

doubt 5 qualm **6** wonder **7** sus-pect **8** distrust, mistrust, ques-tion **9** misgiving, skeptical, suspicion **10** be doubtful, inde-cision **11** uncertainty **12** ap-prehension **13** feel uncertain **14** waver in opinion **15** have doubts about **16** lack confi-dence in, lack of conviction

Doubter *see* **6** Thomas

doubtful 5 vague **7** dubious, obscure, suspect, unclear **9** tentative, uncertain, unde-cided, unsettled **10** hesitating, irresolute, suspicious **11** un-convinced **12** inconclusive, questionable

doubtfulness 5 doubt **7** du-biety **8** distrust, mistrust, unbelief **9** disbelief, suspicion **10** skepticism **11** incredulity **14** lack of credence

Doubting *see* **6** Thomas

doucement
music: **6** gently

douceur 3 tip **5** bribe **8** gratu-ity **9** sweetness

dough 4 cash, duff, spud **5** bread, crust, money, paster **6** batter, change, leaven, noo-dle **8** doughboy **11** infantryman

doughnut 4 cake, tire **5** bagel, torus **6** cymbal, dunker, sinker **7** beignet, cruller, twister

doughty 4 bold **5** brave **6** strong **8** fearless, intrepid, unafraid **9** confident, daunt-less **10** courageous, deter-mined **12** stout-hearted

Douglas, Archibald
character in: **7** Marmion
author: **5** Scott

Douglas, Kirk
real name: **17** Issur Danielovitch
son: **7** Michael
born: **11** Amsterdam NY
roles: **8** Champion **9** Sparta-cus **10** The Vikings **11** Lust for Life **14** Detective Story, Seven Days in May **17** The Glass Menagerie, Young Man with a Horn **18** Letter to Three Wives **22** Mourn-ing Becomes Electra

Douglas, Lloyd C
author of: **7** The Robe **23** The Magnificent Obsession

Douglas, Melvyn
real name: **23** Melvyn Edouard Hesselberg
wife: **12** Helen Gahagan
born: **7** Macon GA
roles: **3** Hud **9** Ninotchka **10** Being There

Douglas, Michael
father: **4** Kirk
roles: **4** Coma **10** Wall Street **11** Star Chamber **14** Jewel of the Nile **15** Fa-tal Attraction (Oscar) **16** The China Syndrome **17** Ro-mancing the Stone

dour 4 sour **6** gloomy, morose, solemn, sullen **9** cheerless **10** forbidding, unfriendly

Douras, Marion Cecilia
real name of: **12** Marion Davies

douse 4 soak **5** souse **6** drench **7** immerse **8** saturate, submerge **15** plunge into water

Dove, Noah's
constellation of: **7** Columba

Dover Beach
author: **13** Matthew Arnold

dovetail 4 jibe, join **5** match, tally, unite **8** coincide **9** har-monize **11** fit together **12** interlocking

dowager 5 widow **6** relict **7** elderly

dowdy 4 drab **5** tacky **6** frumpy, shabby, sloppy **8** slovenly **12** unattractive

dowel 3 peg, pin, rod **4** pole **5** stick **7** spindle

down 3 ill **4** blue, deck, drop, fell, gulp, sick **5** drink, floor **6** ailing **7** put away, swallow **8** dejected, downcast, feathers **9** depressed **10** dispirited **12** disheartened

down-and-out 4 sick **5** broke **9** penniless **12** impoverished, on one's uppers **13** incapaci-tated **15** under the weather

downcast 3 low, sad **4** blue **7** unhappy **8** dejected **9** cheer-less, depressed **11** discouraged **12** disconsolate, disheartened

downfall 4 fall, ruin **6** shower **8** collapse, downpour **9** rain-storm, ruination **10** rain shower **11** destruction

downgrade 4 drop **5** lower **6** debase **7** decline, descent, way down **8** belittle, mini-mize **9** declivity, denigrate, de-valuate **10** depreciate

downhearted 3 sad **7** un-happy **8** dejected, downcast **9** depressed, sorrowful **10** dispirited **11** discouraged **12** disheartened

downheartedness 5 gloom **6** dismay **7** despair, sadness **9** dejection, pessimism **10** depression, low spirits, melancholy **11** despondency **12** hopelessness **14** discouragement

down in the dumps 4 blue, glum **6** gloomy **7** in a funk **9** depressed **10** despondent **13** in the doldrums

down in the mouth 3 sad **6** dismal, woeful **7** joyless, un-happy **8** dejected, downcast **9** depressed, sorrowful, woebe-gone **10** lugubrious **12** disconsolate

downpayment 6 binder **7** ad-vance, deposit **9** money down

downpour 6 shower **9** rain-storm **10** cloudburst, rain shower

downright 4 open **5** blunt, frank, total, utter **6** candid, di-rect, honest, really **7** in truth, plainly, sincere, utterly **8** ab-solute, actually, complete

9 out-and-out **10** aboveboard, completely, thoroughly **12** unmistakably **13** thoroughgoing, unequivocally **15** straightforward

Downright
  character in: **19** Every Man in His Humour
  author: **6** Jonson

downstairs 5 below **6** cellar **8** basement **10** first floor **11** ground floor

down the drain 4 gone, lost **9** up in smoke **12** out the window

down-to-earth 5 crass, plain, sober, solid **6** casual, coarse, earthy, simple **7** relaxed **8** informal, sensible **9** practical, pragmatic, realistic **10** hardheaded, hard-boiled, nononsense **11** plain-spoken, substantial **12** matter-of-fact, unidealistic **13** unsentimental

downtown 9 inner city, urban area **10** center city, metropolis **16** business district, metropolitan area

downtrodden 9 exploited, oppressed **10** tyrannized **11** subservient **12** harshly ruled

downturn 3 dip, sag **4** drop, fall, skid, slip **5** slide, slump **6** plunge, waning **7** decline, reverse, setback **8** decrease **9** downslide, downswing, downtrend, dwindling, recession **10** depression, diminution **12** degeneration **13** deterioration

Down Under see **9** Australia

down with
  French: **4** a bas

downy 4 soft **5** fuzzy, nappy, plumy, quiet **6** fleecy, fluffy **7** cunning, knowing **8** feathery **9** featherbed

do wrong 3 err, sin **8** go astray **9** misbehave **10** transgress

Doyle, Sir Arthur Conan
  author of: **13** The Sign of Four **15** A Study in Scarlet, The White Company **25** The Hound of the Baskervilles **26** Adventures of Sherlock Holmes
  character: **12** Dr John Watson **13** Mycroft Holmes **14** Sherlock Holmes **17** Inspector Lestrade, Professor Moriarty

doze 3 nap **6** catnap, siesta, snooze **10** forty winks, light sleep **12** sleep lightly

dozy 4 lazy **6** drowsy, sleepy

7 languid **9** lethargic, somnolent

D P 5 exile **6** emigre **7** outcast, refugee **8** deportee **10** expatriate **14** banished person, deported person **15** displaced person **16** political refugee

drab 4 dull, gray **5** dingy **6** dismal, dreary, gloomy, somber **9** cheerless, dull brown **10** lackluster

drabness 8 dullness **9** dinginess **10** dreariness, gloominess **13** colorlessness

Dracula
  author: **10** Bram Stoker
  character: **8** Dr Seward **10** Mina Murray **12** Count Dracula, Dr Van Hesling, Lucy Westenra **14** Arthur Holmwood, Jonathan Harker

draft 4 drag, gulp, haul, pull, wind **5** drink **6** breeze, induct, sketch **7** diagram, outline, swallow **9** conscript, induction **10** money order **11** postal order, rough sketch **12** conscription, current of air **15** military service **16** drawing from a cask **18** preliminary version **22** call for military service

drafty 6 breezy, chilly

drag 3 lug **4** bore, haul, pull **5** bring, crawl, trail **6** dredge **7** be drawn **9** inch along **10** creep along, move slowly, spoilsport, wet blanket **11** party-pooper

Dragnet
  character: **8** (Sgt) Ed Jacobs **9** (Sgt) Ben Romero, (Sgt) Joe Friday **10** (Officer) Bill Gannon, (Officer) Frank Smith
  cast: **8** Jack Webb **9** Herb Ellis **11** Harry Morgan **12** Ben Alexander **14** Barney Phillips **16** Barton Yarborough
  setting: **10** Los Angeles

Dragon 14 Leviathan
  constellation of: **5** Draco

drag on 4 last **6** endure, keep on, keep up **7** persist **8** continue **9** persevere

drag one's feet 5 crawl, creep **6** dawdle **9** waste time **10** move slowly **13** procrastinate

dragonfly
  varieties: **5** biddy **6** darner **7** skimmer **8** clubtail, grayback **9** amberwing **12** elisa skimmer

Dragon Seed
  author: **10** Pearl S Buck

Dragon's teeth
  sown by: **6** Cadmus
  location: **6** Thebes
  grew into: **8** warriors

dragoon 5 bully, force **6** coerce, compel **7** trooper **8** browbeat, bulldoze, cavalier, horseman, pressure **9** strongarm **10** cavalryman **12** horse soldier, horse trooper **14** mounted soldier

drag through the mud 5 smear, sully, taint **6** debase, defame, smirch, vilify **7** degrade, tarnish, vitiate **8** disgrace, dishonor **9** discredit, disparage **10** stigmatize

drain 3 sap **4** drag, pipe, tube **5** empty, sewer, use up **6** outlet, strain **7** channel, conduit, debouch, deplete, flow out, pump off **8** empty out **9** depletion, discharge, dissipate **10** impoverish

drainage 4 flow **9** discharge

drained 4 beat **5** all in, empty, spent, tired, weary **6** bushed, done in, pooped, used up **7** emptied, wearied, worn out **8** consumed, depleted, dog tired, expended, fatigued, finished, tired out **9** dead tired, enervated, exhausted, played out

Drake, Stan
  creator/artist of: **21** The Heart of Juliet Jones

Drake, Temple
  character in: **9** Sanctuary
  author: **8** Faulkner

dram
  abbreviation: **2** dr

drama 4 play **6** acting **8** the stage **9** direction, vividness **10** excitement, the theater **11** mise-en-scene **15** dramatic quality, intense interest, theatrical piece
  god of: **7** Bacchus

dramatic 8 striking **9** climactic, emotional **10** theatrical **11** sensational, suspenseful **12** melodramatic **13** for the theater

dramatics 6 acting **7** emoting **9** theatrics **10** dramaturgy, stagecraft **11** hamming it up, histrionics, thespianism

dramatis personae 4 cast **6** actors **7** players **10** performers **16** cast of characters, list of performers

dramaturgy 5 drama **7** theater **10** stagecraft **11** dramatic art

Drambuie
  type: **7** liqueur

origin: 8 Scotland
flavor: 5 herbs, honey
with scotch: 9 Rusty Nail

Drances
enemy of: 6 Turnus

drape 4 deck, garb, veil, wrap
5 adorn, array, cloak, cover,
dress 6 attire, bedeck, enrobe,
enwrap, shroud, swathe, wrap
up 7 apparel, bedight, envelop,
festoon, sheathe, swaddle
8 enshroud, enswathe

drastic 4 dire, rash 7 bizarre,
extreme, radical 8 dreadful
9 dangerous 10 outlandish
11 deleterious

Dravidian
language group: 3 Kui
5 Ghond, Tamil 6 Teluga
8 Kanarese 9 Malayalam
spoken in: 5 India 6 Ceylon
8 Sri Lanka

draw 3 get, tie, tow 4 drag,
etch, haul, limn, lure, pick,
pull, take 5 charm, draft,
drain, evoke, infer, write 6 allure, come-on, deduce, elicit,
entice, extend, make up, siphon, sketch 7 attract, distort,
draw out, extract, make out,
pick out, pull out, pump out,
stretch, suck dry, take out,
wrinkle 8 contract, deadlock,
elongate, protract 9 attenuate,
pull along, stalemate 10 attraction, bring forth, enticement, inducement, make
appear 14 make a picture of

draw away 2 go 5 leave 6 go
back, shrink 7 retreat
8 withdraw

drawback 8 handicap, obstacle 9 detriment, hindrance
10 impediment 12 disadvantage 14 stumbling block

draw back 6 flinch, recoil
7 back off, retreat 8 move
away, withdraw

draw close 3 hug 4 come,
near 6 arrive, enfold 7 embrace 8 approach, come nigh,
gain upon 10 move toward

drawers 5 pants 6 shorts
7 panties 8 bloomers, calzoons,
trousers 9 pantalets, underwear 10 underpants

draw forth 5 evoke 6 elicit
7 distill, extract

drawing 5 study 6 sketch
7 lottery, picture 9 depiction,
selection 11 delineation
12 illustration

drawing apart 8 dividing
9 diverging 10 separating
12 splitting off

drawing out 9 expansion, ex-

tension 10 elongation, stretching 11 attenuation,
lengthening, protraction
12 prolongation

drawing power 4 pull 6 allure, appeal 9 magnetism
10 attraction, enticement
11 fascination

drawing room 5 salon 6 parlor 10 living room 11 sitting
room 13 reception room

drawn out 4 long 7 lengthy
8 extended 9 elongated, prolonged 10 lengthened,
protracted

draw out 5 educe, evoke
6 elicit, expand, extend, extort 7 distill, enlarge, extract,
prolong, spin out, stretch
8 elongate, lengthen, protract
9 attenuate, call forth
10 stretch out

draw the line 5 limit 8 contrast, separate 12 fix a boundary 13 differentiate

draw to a close 3 end 6 finish 8 conclude 11 come to an
end

draw together 4 herd, mass,
pack 5 bunch, crowd, flock,
group 6 gather, huddle 7 cluster, collect, tighten 8 assemble,
compress, contract 9 constrict
10 congregate

draw up 3 map 5 draft 6 make
up, map out 7 charter, diagram, outline 9 blueprint

draw up plans 5 draft 6 design, sketch 7 outline

dray 4 cart 5 wagon 7 tipcart,
tumbrel 8 dumpcart

dread 4 fear 5 awful 6 fright,
terror 7 anguish, anxiety,
cower at, fearful 8 alarming,
cringe at 10 be afraid of, horrifying, shrink from, terrifying 11 fearfulness, frightening,
trepidation 12 apprehension
20 anticipate with horror

dreaded object
French: 9 bete noire

dreadful 5 awful 6 tragic
7 fearful 8 alarming, horrible,
shocking, terrible 9 frightful
11 distressing

dream 3 joy 4 goal, hope,
muse, wish 5 think 6 desire,
vision 7 delight, fantasy, hope
for, incubus, reverie, think
up 8 consider, pleasure, prospect 9 nightmare 11 expectation, have as a goal 13 look
forward to, lost in thought

Dream Merchants, The
author: 13 Harold Robbins

**Dream of the Golden
Mountains, The**
author: 13 Malcolm Cowley

Dreams
god of: 6 Icelus, Oniros
7 Oneiros 8 Morpheus
9 Phantasus

Dream Songs, The
author: 12 John Berryman

dream up 5 frame, hatch
6 create, invent 7 concoct
8 conceive, contrive

dreamy 4 airy 5 blank, empty,
vague 6 absent, musing, unreal 8 ethereal, fanciful, illusory, soothing 9 fantastic,
wonderful 10 delightful
11 preoccupied, unrealistic
13 unsubstantial 14 out of this
world

dreariness 9 bleakness 10 desolation, dismalness, gloominess, melancholy
13 cheerlessness

dreary 3 sad 4 drab 5 bleak
6 dismal, gloomy 7 forlorn
8 mournful 9 cheerless 10 depressing, melancholy

dregs 6 rabble 7 deposit,
grounds, residue 8 canaille,
riffraff, sediment 9 settlings,
worst part 11 lower depths

**Dreiser,
Theodore**
author of: 8 The Titan
12 Sister Carrie, The Financier 17 An American
Tragedy

drench 3 wet 4 soak 5 douse
8 saturate

dress 4 curl, deck, do up,
garb, gown, robe, trim
5 adorn, frock, groom, treat
6 attire 7 apparel, arrange,
bandage, cleanse, clothes,
comb out, costume, garnish
8 clothing, decorate, ornament 9 disinfect, embellish
12 put on clothes 13 clothe
oneself

Dressed to Kill
director: 12 Brian De Palma
cast: 10 Nancy Allen
11 Keith Gordon 12 Michael
Caine 14 Angie Dickinson

dressed up 7 adorned, duded
up 8 costumed, dolled up,
tarted up 9 decorated, disguised, in costume 10 ornamented 11 embellished

dresser 6 bureau 7 cabinet,
commode 8 cupboard 10 chiffonier 14 chest of drawers

dressing-down 6 rebuke
7 censure, chiding, reproof
8 reproach, scolding 9 reprimand 10 bawling-out,

chewing-out, upbraiding
11 castigation, reprobation
12 remonstrance **13** tongue-lashing

dressing-gown
French: **13** robe-de-chambre

dressmaker 9 couturier, midinette **10** couturiere, seamstress

dress up 5 adorn **6** doll up
7 enhance, improve **8** beautify, ornament, spruce up **9** embellish, embroider, smarten up
10 exaggerate

Dreyfuss, Richard
born: **10** Brooklyn NY
roles: **4** Jaws **6** Tin Men
8 Stakeout **14** The Goodbye Girl (Oscar) **15** Moon Over Parador **16** American Graffiti **24** Down and Out in Beverly Hills **29** Close Encounters of the Third Kind **31** The Apprenticeship of Duddy Kravitz

dribble 4 drip, kick **6** bounce
7 drizzle, trickle **11** fall in drops, run bit by bit

driblet 4 drip, drop, tear
7 droplet, globule

dried up 4 arid **7** drained, parched **9** prunelike, shriveled **10** dehydrated, desiccated

drift 3 aim **4** flow, gist, heap, mass, pile **5** amass, amble, sense **6** course, gather, object, pile up, ramble, stream, wander **7** current, meander, meaning, purpose, scatter
8 movement **9** direction, intention, objective **10** accumulate **11** implication, peregrinate **12** accumulation, be borne along

drifter 3 bum **4** hobo **5** idler, tramp **6** loafer **8** derelict, vagabond **16** ne'er-do-well

drill 4 bore **5** punch, train
6 pierce **8** exercise, practice, puncture, training, work with **10** boring tool, repetition **11** instruction **17** repeated exercises
type: **4** hand **5** twist **8** electric

drilling 4 rote **6** boring **8** practice, training **9** schooling
10 discipline **11** preparation

drink 3 sip **4** gulp, swig
5 booze, taste, toast **6** absorb, imbibe, ingest, salute, take in **7** alcohol, swallow **8** beverage, libation **9** partake of, the bottle **10** alcoholism **11** drunkenness **15** alcoholic liquor
17 liquid refreshment
type of: **3** cup, fix **4** fizz, flip, mull, puff, sour **5** daisy, julep, punch, shrub, sling,

smash **6** cooler, frappe, rickey **7** cobbler, stinger
8 highball

drinker 3 sot **4** lush, wino
5 dipso, drunk, rummy, souse **6** bibber, boozer, sponge
7 guzzler, imbiber, tippler, waterer **8** drunkard **9** alcoholic, inebriate

drink in 6 absorb, digest, soak up, take in **10** assimilate
14 immerse oneself

Drinking
god of: **5** Comus

drinking spree 4 orgy, toot
5 binge, drunk **6** bender
8 beer-bust, carousal
9 bacchanal

drink up 4 gulp **5** quaff **6** absorb, guzzle, soak up **7** consume, swallow

drip 3 ass **4** bore, jerk, nerd
5 creep, dummy, klutz
6 splash **7** dribble, drizzle, trickle **8** sprinkle

dripping 3 wet **4** damp
5 soggy **6** soaked, sodden
10 soaking wet

drive 4 goad, lead, mean, move, prod, push, ride, rush, spur, urge **5** force, guide, impel, motor, press, steer, surge **6** coerce, compel, incite, intend, outing **7** advance, conduct, go by car, impulse, operate, suggest **8** ambition, campaign, motivate **9** excursion, insinuate, trip by car, urge along **10** motivation

drive apart 8 alienate, estrange **9** disaffect

drive away 4 rout, shoo
5 chase, deter, repel **6** rebuff **7** repulse **8** alienate **11** put to flight, send packing

drive home 7 impress **8** hammer at

drivel 5 drool **6** babble, ramble, slaver **7** dribble, slobber
8 babbling, nonsense, rambling **9** gibberish **12** talk nonsense **13** senseless talk, talk foolishly

drive out 4 fire **5** chase, depel, eject, evict, exile, expel, force, roust **6** compel, remove **7** dismiss, repulse **8** discharge, exorcise

driver 6 cowboy, drover
8 herdsman **9** chauffeur

drizzle 3 fog **4** mist, rain
7 dribble **8** sprinkle

drizzly 3 wet **4** damp **5** foggy, misty, rainy

Dr Jekyll and Mr Hyde
author: **20** Robert Louis Stevenson
character: **5** Poole **10** Mr Utterson **13** Dr Henry Jekyll
14 Dr Hastie Lanyon

Dr Kildare
character: **14** Dr James Kildare **18** Dr Leonard Gillespie
cast: **13** Raymond Massey
18 Richard Chamberlain
hospital: **12** Blair General

Dr No
author: **10** Ian Fleming

Dr Strangelove or How I Learned to Stop Worrying and Love the Bomb
director: **14** Stanley Kubrick
cast: **9** Peter Bull **10** Keenan Wynn **11** Slim Pickens
12 George C Scott, Peter Sellers **14** James Earl Jones, Sterling Hayden

Dr Zhivago
author: **14** Boris Pasternak
character: **4** Lara
setting: **17** Russian Revolution

droll 5 funny **7** offbeat, strange **8** humorous **9** eccentric, laughable, whimsical **12** oddly amusing

drollery 3 wit **5** humor **6** banter, comedy, whimsy **7** jesting

Dromio
character in: **17** The Comedy of Errors
author: **11** Shakespeare

drone 3 hum **4** buzz, whir
5 idler **6** loafer **7** vibrate
8 parasite **9** murmuring, vibration **10** lazy person

drool 6 drivel, slaver **7** dribble, slobber **8** salivate **15** water at the mouth

droop 3 dim, sag **4** flag, sink
5 lower **6** weaken, wither
8 diminish, hang down **9** lose vigor **14** hang listlessly **15** incline downward

droopy 4 bent, blue, down, limp **5** baggy, bowed, slack
6 dashed, pining **7** doleful, sagging, subdued **8** cast down, dangling, dejected, downcast
9 depressed **10** despairing, despondent, dispirited, spiritless, world-weary **11** downhearted, hanging down, languishing
14 down in the mouth

drop 3 can, dab **4** bead, dash, deck, dive, drip, fall, fell, fire, omit, sack, sink, tear **5** abyss, floor, leave, lower, pinch, slide, slope, smack, trace
6 give up, lessen, plunge
7 abandon, decline, descend,

descent, dismiss, dribble, driblet, dwindle, forsake, globule, plummet, slacken, smidgen, soupcon, trickle **8** decrease, diminish, leave out, lowering **9** declivity, discharge, knock down, precipice, terminate **10** sprinkling **12** bring to an end **13** fail to include **15** cease to consider, fail to pronounce

drop anchor 4 dock, moor **5** tie up

drop in 4 call, come **5** visit **6** appear, come by, look in, show up, stop by, turn up **7** stop off **9** pay a visit

droplet 4 bead, drip, tear **7** driblet, globule **8** spherule

droplets of moisture 3 dew, fog **4** mist **5** sweat **12** condensation

drop out 4 quit **5** leave **6** resign, retire

dross 4 scum, slag **5** waste **6** cinder, scoria **8** clinkers, impurity

drought, drouth 4 lack, need, want **6** dearth **7** aridity, paucity **8** scarcity, shortage **10** deficiency, dry weather, lack of rain **13** insufficiency

drover 6 cowboy, driver **7** cowpoke **8** herdsman, shepherd **10** cowpuncher

drown 4 soak **5** flood **6** deluge, drench, engulf **7** immerse **8** inundate, overcome, submerge **9** overpower, overwhelm, suffocate, swallow up **10** asphyxiate

drowse 3 nap, nod **4** doze, laze **5** dover, drone, sleep **6** snooze **7** slumber **8** languish **10** sleepiness

drowsy 4 dozy, lazy, slow **5** tired **6** sleepy **7** languid **8** hypnotic, listless, sluggish, soothing **9** lethargic, somnolent, soporific

drub 3 hit **4** beat, cane, flog, whip **5** whale **6** thrash **9** bastinado

drubbing 6 caning **7** beating, licking, tanning **9** trouncing **11** shellacking

drudge 4 grub, hack, plod, toil **5** labor, slave **6** lackey, menial, toiler **7** grubber **8** inferior, struggle **9** underling **11** subordinate

drudgery 4 toil **5** grind **7** travail **8** hack work **11** menial labor **15** distasteful work

Druk-Yul *see* **6** Bhutan

drum 3 din, keg, rap, tap, tub **4** beat, cask, roar, roll **5** expel, force **6** barrel, harp on, rumble, tattoo **7** dismiss, pulsate **8** drive out, hammer at **9** discharge, drive home, reiterate **11** beat a tattoo, din in the ear, reverberate

Drums
author: **9** James Boyd

Drums Along the Mohawk
author: **14** Walter D Edmonds
character: **4** Lana **9** Blue Black, John Wolff **11** Joseph Brant, Mark Demooth **12** Mrs McKlennan **13** Gilbert Martin **20** Magdelena Borst Martin

drunk 3 sot **4** bust, lush, soak **5** binge, rummy, souse, tipsy, toper **6** barfly, bender, looped, sodden, soused, stewed, zapped, zonked **7** smashed **8** beer-bust, besotted, carousal **9** alcoholic, plastered **10** inebriated **11** dipsomaniac, intoxicated **13** drinking spree, under the influence

drunkard 3 sot **4** lush, soak, wino **5** rummy, souse, toper **6** barfly **9** alcoholic **11** dipsomaniac

drunkenness 10 alcoholism **11** inebriation **12** intoxication

Drury, Allen
author of: **14** Capable of Honor, Return to Thebes **15** The Promise of Joy **16** Advise and Consent **19** Come Nineveh Come Tyre

dry 4 arid, blot, dull, wipe **5** droll **6** boring, low-key **7** deadpan, parched, tedious, thirsty **8** rainless **9** dehydrate, desiccate, shrivel up, wearisome **10** dehydrated, monotonous **13** uninteresting

Dryad
form: **5** deity, nymph
location: **5** woods

Dryas
father: **8** Lycurgus
killed by: **8** Lycurgus

dry as dust 4 arid, dull, sere **7** parched **8** pedantic, withered **9** shriveled **13** unimaginative

Dryden, John
author of: **10** All for Love **11** Mac Flecknoe **14** Annus Mirabilis **15** Alexander's Feast, Marriage-a-la-Mode **20** Absalom and Achitophel, Essay on Dramatic Poesy, The Hind and the Panther

22 Fables Ancient and Modern

dry goods 5 cloth, goods **6** fabric **8** material **9** yard goods **10** piece goods

dryness 7 aridity, drought **8** aridness **11** dehydration

Dryope
form: **5** nymph
changed into: **6** poplar

Dry Salvages
author: **7** T S Eliot

dry up 6 wither **7** shrivel **9** dehydrate, desiccate, evaporate

dual 6 double **7** twofold, two-part

dub 4 call, name **5** label **6** knight **7** baptize **8** christen, nickname **9** designate

dubiety 5 doubt **8** unbelief **9** disbelief **10** skepticism **11** incredulity **12** doubtfulness **14** lack of credence

Dubin's Lives
author: **14** Bernard Malamud

dubious 5 shady **6** unsure **7** suspect **8** doubtful **9** skeptical, uncertain **10** suspicious, unreliable **11** unconvinced **12** questionable, undependable **13** untrustworthy

Dublin
brewery: **8** Guinness
capital of: **7** Ireland
Irish: **8** Dubh Linn (black pool) **15** Baile Atha Cliath (town of the Hurdle Ford)
landmark: **10** Four Courts **11** Custom House **12** Abbey Theater, Christ Church, Dublin Castle **13** Leinster House **18** Kilmainham **19** St Patrick's Cathedral
mountain: **7** Wicklow
museum: **8** National **10** James Joyce
park: **7** Phoenix
river: **6** Liffey
rulers: **7** English, Vikings
scene of: **12** Easter Rising (1916)
university: **14** Trinity College

Dubliners
author: **10** James Joyce

DuBois, Blanche
character in: **21** A Streetcar Named Desire
author: **8** Williams

Du Bois, W E B
founded: **5** NAACP
author of: **19** The Souls of Black Folk

Dubonnet
type: **8** aperitif
origin: **6** France

ingredient: 7 quinine, red wine
with gin: 3 BVD 8 Napoleon
with rum: 10 Bushranger

duc 4 duke

Duccio di Buoninsegna
born: 5 Italy 6 Sienna
artwork: 6 Maesta 18 The Rucellai Madonna (attributed)

duce, il duce 6 despot, tyrant 8 dictator 9 Mussolini

Duchamp, Marcel
born: 6 France 8 Normandy 10 Blainville
artwork: 5 LHOOQ 9 Given That 11 Etant Donnes 12 Bicycle Wheel 13 The Large Glass (The Bride Stripped Bare by Her Bachelors Even) 24 Nude Descending a Staircase 37 The King and Queen Surrounded by Swift Nudes

Duchess of Malfi, The
author: 11 John Webster
character: 6 Bosola 7 Antonio 8 Giovanna 9 Ferdinand 11 The Cardinal

duck 4 clee, coot, lory, smew, teal, veer 5 avoid, dodge, drake, eider, elude, evade, goose, ruddy, shirk, stoop 6 canard, canvas, crouch, gannet, Peking, scoter, swerve 7 gadwall, mallard, Muscovy, pintail, pochard 8 baldpate, freckled, redshank, shelduck, shoveler, sidestep, submerge 9 merganser, whistling 10 bufflehead, canvasback 11 wood steamer 13 give the slip to
male: 5 drake
group of: 5 brace

Duck Soup
director: 10 Leo McCarey
cast: 5 Chico, Harpo, Zeppo 7 Groucho (Rufus T Firefly) 12 Louis Calhern, Raquel Torres 14 Margaret Dumont
setting: 9 Freedonia

duct 4 pipe, tube 6 vessel 7 channel, conduit

ductile 6 docile, pliant, supple 7 elastic, plastic, pliable, tensile 8 amenable, bendable, flexible, formable, moldable, shapable, swayable 9 adaptable, compliant, malleable, tractable 10 extensible, manageable, submissive 11 complaisant, manipulable, stretchable, susceptible

dud 3 dog 4 bomb, bust, flop, hash 5 botch, lemon, loser 6 bummer, fiasco, fizzle 7 clinker, debacle, failure,

washout 11 lead balloon, miscarriage 14 disappointment

dude 3 fop 4 beau 5 dandy 7 peacock 11 city dweller, city slicker 12 Beau Brummell

Dudevant, Aurore
real name of: 10 George Sand

duds 4 togs 5 flops 6 attire 7 apparel, clothes, fizzles, threads 8 clothing, failures, garments

due 4 owed 5 ample, owing 6 enough, proper, unpaid 7 fitting, merited 8 adequate, becoming, deserved, expected, plenty of, rightful, suitable 9 in arrears, scheduled 10 sufficient 11 appropriate, outstanding

duel
French: 15 affaire d'honneur

Duel, The
author: 15 Alexander Kuprin

duenna 8 guardian 9 attendant, chaperone, custodian, protector

dues 4 fees 7 charges 10 assessment

Duessa
character in: 15 The Faerie Queene
author: 7 Spenser

duet 3 duo, two 4 pair 6 couple 7 twosome

Dufy, Raoul
born: 6 France 7 Le Havre
artwork: 7 The Palm 15 Riders in the Wood 16 Chateau and Horses 18 Deauville Racetrack, Posters at Trouville

dugout 3 den 4 cave 5 canoe 6 cavity, hollow 7 shelter

Duino Elegies
author: 16 Rainer Maria Rilke

Dukas, Paul
born: 5 Paris 6 France
composer of: 6 La Peri 18 Ariane et Barbe-Bleue 19 Ariadne and Bluebeard 22 The Sorcerer's Apprentice

duke
French: 3 duc

Duke
nickname of: 9 John Wayne

Duke, Patty (Patty Duke Astin)
real name: 13 Anna Marie Duke
husband: 9 John Astin
born: 10 Elmhurst NY
roles: 11 Helen Keller 16 The

Miracle Worker, The Patty Duke Show, Valley of the Dolls

Dukenfield, William Claude
real name of: 8 W C Fields

Duke Snider
nickname of: 11 Edwin Snider

dulcet 7 lyrical, musical, tuneful 8 pleasing, sonorous 9 melodious 11 mellifluous

Dulcinea del Toboso
character in: 10 Don Quixote
author: 9 Cervantes

dull 4 slow 5 blunt, dense, muted, quiet, thick, trite, vapid 6 boring, obtuse, stupid 7 muffled, not keen, prosaic, subdued, vacuous 8 deadened, inactive, not brisk, not sharp 9 dimwitted 10 indistinct, lackluster, uneventful 13 unimaginative, uninteresting

Dull
character in: 16 Love's Labour's Lost
author: 11 Shakespeare

dullard 4 dolt 5 dummy, dunce 6 nitwit 7 halfwit 8 dumbbell, imbecile

Dullea, Keir
born: 11 Cleveland OH
roles: 12 David and Lisa 18 Butterflies Are Free 27 Two Thousand One: A Space Odyssey

dullness 6 idiocy, tedium 8 dumbness, lethargy, monotony, slowness 9 bluntness, ignorance, stupidity, vapidness 10 boringness, imbecility, obtuseness 11 tediousness 13 dim-wittedness 15 thickheadedness

dull-witted 5 dazed, fuzzy 7 bemused, muddled, stunned 8 confused 9 stupefied

Dulong, Pierre-Louis
field: 7 physics 9 chemistry
nationality: 6 French
discovered: 19 nitrogen trichloride
studied: 4 heat 13 atomic weights

duly 6 on time 8 properly, suitably 9 correctly 10 deservedly, punctually, rightfully 13 appropriately 15 at the proper time

Dumaine
character in: 16 Love's Labour's Lost
author: 11 Shakespeare

Dumas, Alexandre (fils)
author of: 7 Camille 11 Le Demi-Monde 17 La Dame

aux Camelias **21** The Lady of the Camellias
Camille inspired: 10 La Traviata
opera by: **5** Verdi

Dumas, Alexandre (pere)
author of: 17 The Queen's Necklace **18** The Three Musketeers **19** The Man in the Iron Mask **21** The Count of Monte Cristo **22** The Vicomte de Bragelonne

Du Maurier, Daphne
author of: 7 Rebecca **10** Jamaica Inn **11** Don't Look Now **14** My Cousin Rachel **15** Frenchman's Creek **19** The House on the Strand

Du Maurier, George
author of: 6 Trilby **10** The Martian **13** Peter Ibbetson

dumb 3 mum **4** dull, mute **5** dense, dopey **6** silent, stupid **7** foolish, aphasic **8** aphasiac **9** dim-witted **13** unintelligent **17** incapable of speech

dumbbell 3 oaf **4** clod, dolt, dope, fool **5** booby, clown, dummy, dunce, idiot, moron **6** dimwit, nitwit **7** dullard, halfwit **8** dumb-dumb, dummkopf, imbecile, lunkhead, meathead, numskull **9** birdbrain, blockhead, ignoramus, lamebrain, numbskull, simpleton **10** noodlehead

dumb-dumb 3 ass **4** dope, fool **5** booby, dunce, idiot, moron, ninny **6** dimwit, nitwit **7** halfwit **8** bonehead, imbecile, lunkhead, numskull **9** blockhead, lamebrain, numbskull **10** nincompoop

dumbfound, dumfound
4 stun **5** amaze **7** startle **8** astonish **11** flabbergast

dumbfounded 5 agape **6** amazed **7** stunned **9** astounded, stupefied **10** astonished, speechless **11** openmouthed **13** flabbergasted

dumbness 6 idiocy **8** dullness **9** asininity, stupidity, thickness **10** imbecility **11** witlessness **12** wordlessness **14** speechlessness **15** thickheadedness

dumbstruck 5 agape **6** amazed, gaping **7** riveted **9** awestruck, stupefied **10** speechless **11** electrified, open-mouthed **13** flabbergasted

dummy 3 oaf **4** dolt, form **5** clown, idiot, klutz, model **6** figure **9** blockhead, mannequin, simpleton **10** dunderhead **11** chowderhead, knucklehead

dump 3 hut **4** hole, toss **5** empty, hovel, shack **6** shanty, unload **8** get rid of, junkyard **9** dispose of **10** refuse pile **11** rubbish heap

dumpy 5 squat **7** lumpish **13** short and stout

Dumuzi
origin: 8 Sumerian
god of: 8 pastures **10** vegetation
consort of: 6 Inanna

Dunaway, Faye
real name: 18 Dorothy Faye Dunaway
born: 8 Bascom FL
roles: 6 Barfly, Milady **7** Network (Oscar) **8** The Champ **9** Chinatown **13** Mommie Dearest **14** Bonnie and Clyde **15** Towering Inferno **17** The Four Musketeers **18** The Three Musketeers

Duncan
character in: 7 Macbeth
author: 11 Shakespeare

Duncan, Sandy
born: 11 Henderson TX
roles: 8 Peter Pan **9** Funny Face **12** The Boyfriend

dunce 4 fool **5** dummy, idiot, moron **6** dimwit, nitwit **8** imbecile, numskull **9** blockhead, numbskull, simpleton

Dunciad, The
author: 13 Alexander Pope

dunderhead 3 ass **4** dolt, fool **5** booby, dunce, idiot, moron, ninny **6** dimwit, nitwit **7** dullard, fathead, halfwit **8** bonehead, dumb-dumb, imbecile, lunkhead, numskull **9** blockhead, dumb bunny, lamebrain, numbskull **10** nincompoop **11** chowderhead

dune 4 bank **5** mound **8** sandbank, sandpile

dunk 3 dip, sop **4** duck, soak **5** bathe, douse, drown, slosh, souse, steep **6** deluge, drench, engulf, plunge **7** baptize, immerse **8** inundate, saturate, submerge

Dunne, John Gregory
author of: 11 Dutch Shea Jr **18** Quintana and Friends

Dunnock, Mildred
born: 11 Baltimore MD
roles: 8 Baby Doll **12** The Nun's Story **14** The Corn Is Green **16** Butterfield Eight, Cat on a Hot Tin Roof, Death of a Salesman

duo 4 pair **5** combo **6** couple **7** twosome **11** combination

duomo 4 dome **9** cathedral

dupe 4 fool, pawn **5** patsy, trick **6** humbug, sucker **7** cat's paw, deceive, fall guy, mislead **8** hoodwink **9** bamboozle

duplicate 4 copy **5** clone, match **6** repeat **7** replica **8** parallel **9** facsimile, imitation, make again, photocopy, photostat **10** carbon copy **12** reproduction

duplicity 5 fraud, guile **6** deceit **7** cunning **9** deception, falseness **10** dishonesty **13** deceitfulness

Du Pont Labs
founder: 17 E I du Pont de Nemours
inventor of: 5 nylon

Duquesnoy, Francois
born: 8 Brussels, Flanders
nickname: 11 Il Fiammingo
artwork: 8 St Andrew **9** St Susanna

dur
musical term: 5 major **8** major key

durability 7 stamina **8** strength **9** endurance, toughness **10** sturdiness

durable 5 sound, tough **6** strong, sturdy **7** lasting **8** enduring **11** long-wearing, substantial

Durand, Asher Brown
born: 18 Jefferson Village NJ
artwork: 14 Kindred Spirits

Durant, Will and Ariel
authors of: 20 The Story of Philosophy **21** Rousseau and Revolution **22** The Story of Civilization

Durante, Jimmy
real name: 19 James Francis Durante
nickname: 10 Schnozzola **15** Inka Dinka Doo Man
born: 9 New York NY
roles: 5 Jumbo **21** It's a Mad Mad Mad Mad World

duration 4 term **6** extent, period **11** continuance **12** continuation

Durdles
character in: 22 The Mystery of Edwin Drood
author: 7 Dickens

Durer, Albrecht
born: 7 Germany **9** Nuremberg
artwork: 10 Adam and Eve, Apocalypse, The Triumph **11** Wehlsch Pirg **12** Four Apostles, Large Passion, Melancholia I **13** Castle of Trent **15** Life of the Virgin **18** St Jerome in his Study **19** Virgin with the Siskin

21 Christ Among the Doctors **22** Knight Death and the Devil **24** Crowned Death on a Thin Horse **25** The Feast of the Rose Garlands **28** The Festival of the Rose Garlands

duress 5 force **6** threat **8** coercion, pressure **10** compulsion, constraint

Durgin, Francis Timothy
real name of: **11** Rory Calhoun

during litigation
Latin: **12** pendente lite

Durocher, Leo
nickname: **9** Leo the Lip
sport: **8** baseball
position: **7** manager
team: **11** Chicago Cubs **13** New York Giants **15** Brooklyn Dodgers
saying: **18** Nice guys finish last

Durrenmatt, Friedrich
author of: **5** Traps **8** The Visit **9** The Pledge, The Quarry **13** The Physicists **21** The Judge and His Hangman **27** The Marriage of the Mississippi

Durrie, James and Henry
character in: **21** The Master of Ballantrae
author: **9** Stevenson

dusk 6 sunset **7** sundown **8** twilight **9** nightfall

dusky 3 dim **4** dark **5** murky **6** cloudy, gloomy, veiled **7** swarthy **8** dark-hued

dust 4 dirt, lint **5** brush, motes **8** sprinkle

duster 3 rag **4** coat, robe **5** brush, cloth, whisk **9** housecoat **10** whisk broom

Dutch Guiana *see* **8** Suriname

Dutch Shea, Jr
author: **16** John Gregory Dunne

dutiful 5 loyal **8** diligent, faithful, obedient **9** compliant **13** conscientious

duty 3 tax **4** levy, onus, task **6** charge, excise, tariff **7** customs **8** business, function, province **10** assignment, obligation **14** responsibility

Duval, Armand
character in: **7** Camille
author: **5** Dumas (fils)

Duvall, Robert
born: **10** San Diego CA
roles: **4** MASH **11** Godfather II **12** The Godfather **13** Apocalypse Now, Tender Mercies (Oscar) **15** The Great Santini, True Confessions **18** To Kill a Mockingbird

Duvall, Shelley
born: **9** Houston TX
roles: **6** Popeye **9** Nashville **10** The Shining, Three Women **15** Brewster McCloud

Dvorak, Antonin
born: **11** Nelahozeves **14** Czechoslovakia
composer of: **5** Dumky **6** Hymnus, Te Deum **8** Carnival (overture) **8** St Ludmilla **11** Stabat Mater **15** American Quartet, From the New World (Symphony in E Minor) **16** The Specter's Bride **17** The Bells of Zlonice

dwarf 3 dim, elf, imp **4** baby, tiny **5** fairy, gnome, pixie, pygmy, small, troll **6** bantam, goblin, petite, sprite **8** diminish **9** miniature **10** diminutive, leprechaun, overshadow

dwarfish 3 wee **4** tiny **5** pygmy, short, small **6** bantam, little, midget **7** compact, squatty **10** diminutive, undersized **13** foreshortened

dwell 4 live **5** abide **6** harp on, reside **7** inhabit **10** linger over

dwelling 4 home **5** abode, house **8** domicile **9** residence **10** habitation

dwelling place 4 home **5** abode, house **7** habitat, lodging **8** domicile **9** residence **10** habitation **14** living quarters

dwell on 6 accent, stress **7** feature, iterate **9** emphasize, press home

dwindle 4 fade, wane **6** lessen, shrink **7** decline **8** decrease, diminish **13** become smaller

dye 4 tint **5** color, shade, stain **8** coloring **10** coloration

dyed-in-the-wool 9 confirmed, ingrained **10** deep-rooted, inveterate **11** established

dyestuff 14 coloring matter

Dymas
home: **4** Troy
fought with: **6** Aeneas
fought against: **6** Greeks

dynamic 5 vital **6** active **7** driving **8** forceful, powerful, vigorous **9** energetic

dynamism 3 pep **4** life **5** verve, vigor **6** energy, spirit **8** vitality, vivacity **9** animation **10** liveliness

dynamite 4 raze, ruin **5** blast, trash, wreck **6** blow up, charge **7** destroy, shatter, wipe out **8** decimate, demolish **9** devastate, dismantle, eradicate, explosive **10** annihilate, extinguish, obliterate **11** exterminate

dynamo 4 doer **7** hustler **8** activist, go-getter **9** generator **12** active person **14** bundle of energy, mover and shaker

Dynasts, The
author: **11** Thomas Hardy
subject: **17** Napoleon Bonaparte

dynasty 4 line **5** crown, reign **6** regime **7** lineage, regency **8** dominion, hegemony, kingship, monarchy, regnancy **9** authority **10** government, suzerainty **11** ruling house **12** jurisdiction **14** administration

Dynasty
character: **9** Dex Dexter, Jeff Colby **12** Alexis (Morel Carrington Colby) Dexter **14** Adam Carrington **15** Blake Carrington **16** Amanda Carrington, Steven Carrington **17** Krystle Carrington **18** Dominique Devereaux, Krystina Carrington **21** Fallon Carrington Colby
cast: **9** John James **10** Linda Evans **11** Joan Collins **12** John Forsythe
setting: **6** Denver **8** Colorado
hotel: **8** La Mirage

dyspeptic 4 mean **6** crabby, grumpy, ornery, shirty, touchy **7** grouchy, waspish **8** choleric **9** crotchety, fractious, irascible, irritable **10** ill-humored, ill-natured **11** bad-tempered, contentious, hot-tempered **12** cantankerous, sour-tempered **13** short-tempered

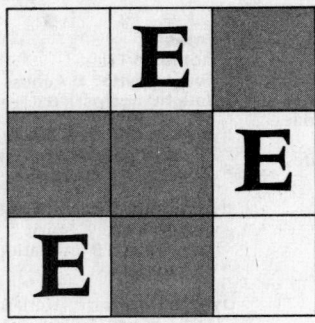

Ea
origin: **8** Akkadian
god of: **6** wisdom
father: **4** Apsu
son: **6** Marduk **8** Merodach
12 Baal Merodach
corresponds to: **4** Enki

each 5 every **6** apiece **7** that
one, this one **8** everyone, separate **12** respectively

Eagels, Jeanne
born: **12** Kansas City MO
roles: **4** Rain **8** Jealousy
9 The Letter **13** Sadie
Thompson **14** Man Woman
and Sin

eager 4 agog, avid, keen **6** ardent, fervid, intent, raring
7 athirst, earnest, excited, fervent, intense, longing, zealous **8** desirous, diligent,
resolute, spirited, yearning
9 ambitious, hungering, impatient, thirsting **10** aggressive,
passionate **11** hardworking,
impassioned, industrious, persevering **12** enterprising,
enthusiastic

eagerly 6 avidly, keenly **8** ardently, desiring, fervidly, intently **9** anxiously, earnestly,
fervently, zealously
16 enthusiastically

eagerness 4 zeal, zest **5** ardor
6 fervor **7** avidity **9** readiness
10 enthusiasm **11** willingness

eagle
young: **6** eaglet

Eagle
constellation of: **6** Aquila

Eakins, Thomas
born: **14** Philadelphia PA
artwork: **11** Agnew Clinic
13 Mrs Edith Mahon **14** The
Gross Clinic **24** Max Schmitt
in a Single Scull

ear
section: **5** inner, outer
6 middle

part: 4 drum **5** anvil, canal
6 hammer **7** cochlea, stir-
rup **8** hair cell **14** eustachian
tube

earl 4 lord, peer **5** noble
8 nobleman
wife: **8** countess

earlier 6 before, in time,
sooner **9** before now, in advance **10** beforehand **11** ahead
of time **13** before the fact

earliest 5 first **6** oldest, primal
7 ancient, initial, primary,
soonest **8** original, primeval
9 beginning, primitive **10** aboriginal, indigenous
11 fundamental

Earl of Baltimore
nickname of: **10** Earl Weaver

Earl the Pearl
nickname of: **10** Earl Monroe

early 5 first **6** primal **7** ancient,
archaic, betimes, initial, too
soon, very old **8** primeval **9** in
advance, premature, primitive
10 beforehand, in good time,
primordial **11** ahead of time,
prehistoric, prematurely

Early Autumn
author: **14** Louis Bromfield

early man 6 Peking **9** Cro-
Magnon, Steinheim **11** Neanderthal **18** Trobriand
Islanders **24** Australopithecus
robustus **25** Australopithecus
africanus

earmark 3 tag **4** band, hold,
sign **5** allot, label, stamp, token, trait **6** aspect, assign
7 feature, put away, quality,
reserve **8** allocate, property,
set aside **9** attribute, designate **11** peculiarity, singularity **14** characteristic

earn 3 get, net **4** draw, gain,
make, rate, reap **5** clear,
merit **6** attain, pick up, secure **7** achieve, collect, deserve, realize, receive,

warrant **9** bring home **12** be
entitled to

earn as due 4 rate **5** merit
7 deserve **10** be worthy of
12 be entitled to **13** be deserving of

earnest 4 firm **5** eager, fixed,
grave, sober, staid **6** ardent,
fervid, honest, intent, sedate,
solemn, stable, steady, urgent
7 devoted, fervent, intense, serious, sincere, zealous **8** constant, diligent, resolute,
spirited, vehement **9** ambitious, assiduous, heartfelt, insistent **10** deeply felt,
determined, passionate, purposeful, thoughtful **11** hardworking, impassioned,
industrious, persevering
12 enthusiastic, wholehearted

earnest attachment 4 love
6 regard **7** concern **8** devotion,
fondness **9** reverence **10** commitment, dedication **11** devotedness **13** attentiveness

earnest request 4 plea **6** appeal **8** entreaty, petition
11 importunity **12** supplication

earnings 3 pay **5** wages **6** income, salary **7** payment, profits **8** proceeds, receipts
12 compensation

Earnshaw, Catherine
character in: **16** Wuthering
Heights
author: **6** Bronte

ear-splitting 7 blaring **8** piercing **9** clamorous, deafening
10 thunderous

earth 3 sod **4** clay, dirt, dust,
land, loam, soil, turf
6 ground **7** topsoil
god of: **3** Geb, Keb **5** Dagan,
Dagon **10** Trophonius
goddess of: **2** Ge **4** Gaea,
Gaia **6** Hecate, Hekate,
Tellus

earthen pot
Spanish: 4 olla

earthenware 5 china 7 pottery 8 clayware, crockery
11 ceramic ware

earthly 6 bodily 7 mundane, secular, ungodly, worldly
8 feasible, material, physical, possible, temporal 9 corporeal, practical 10 imaginable
11 conceivable, terrestrial
12 nonspiritual 13 materialistic

earthquake 5 quake, seism, shock 6 tremor 8 tremblor, upheaval 11 earth tremor

earth tremor 5 quake, seism, shock 6 tremor 8 tremblor, upheaval 10 earthquake

earthy 5 bawdy, crude, dirty, funky, gross, lusty, rough
6 coarse, filthy, ribald, robust, smutty, vulgar 7 obscene, peasant, raunchy 8 indecent
9 primitive, unrefined 10 unblushing, uncultured
12 uncultivated

Earwicker family
characters in: 13 Finnegans Wake
author: 5 Joyce

earwig
variety: 5 black 6 little
10 long horned

ease 4 calm, rest, slip 5 abate, allay, poise, quiet, slide, still
6 aplomb, lessen, luxury, pacify, plenty, relief, repose, solace, soothe 7 assuage, comfort, console, leisure, lighten, mollify, relieve 8 diminish, easement, easiness, facility, maneuver, mitigate, palliate, security, serenity 9 abundance, affluence, alleviate, composure, disburden, readiness 10 confidence, prosperity, relaxation
11 assuagement, naturalness, peace of mind, restfulness
12 tranquillity, unconstraint
13 luxuriousness, move carefully, relaxed manner 14 effortlessness, handle with care, unaffectedness

easement 4 ease 6 relief, solace, succor 7 comfort 8 soothing 10 right of way
11 assuagement

easily 5 by far 6 freely, surely
7 clearly, handily, lightly, plainly, readily 8 facilely, smoothly, with ease 9 certainly 10 far and away, undeniably 11 beyond doubt, undoubtedly 12 effortlessly, with facility 13 without a hitch 14 beyond question, without trouble 17 without difficulty 23 beyond the shadow of a doubt

easily embarrassed 3 shy
5 timid 7 bashful 8 blushing, skittish, timorous 9 diffident, shrinking 11 constrained, unconfident

easily noticed 5 clear, plain
6 patent 7 evident, glaring, obvious, visible 8 flagrant, striking 9 arresting, prominent
10 noticeable 11 conspicuous, outstanding

easily ruffled 9 emotional, excitable 11 hot-tempered
13 quick-tempered

easiness 4 ease 10 equanimity, simplicity 11 naturalness
12 indifference
13 impassiveness

East, the 4 Asia 9 the Orient
10 the Far East 11 the Near East 17 Eastern Hemisphere

East Bengal see
10 Bangladesh

East Berlin
capital of: 11 East Germany

East Coker
author: 7 T S Eliot

Eastern Slavic
language family: 12 Indo-European
group: 11 Balto-Slavic
branch: 6 Slavic
language: 7 Russian
9 Ukrainian 12 White Russian

Easter Parade
director: 14 Charles Walters
based on musical by: 12 Irving Berlin
cast: 9 Ann Miller 11 Fred Astaire, Judy Garland
12 Peter Lawford

East Germany see Germany, East

Eastman, George
nationality: 8 American
founder of: 14 Eastman Kodak Co
inventor of: 9 Kodak film
11 Kodak camera 20 transparent photo film

East of Eden
author: 13 John Steinbeck
director: 9 Elia Kazan
cast: 8 Burl Ives 9 James Dean 10 Jo Van Fleet
11 Julie Harris 13 Raymond Massey
Oscar for: 17 supporting actress (Van Fleet)

East wind
associated with: 5 Eurus
9 Volturnus

Eastwood, Clint
born: 14 San Francisco CA
roles: 7 Firefox, Rawhide
10 Dirty Harry, Hang Em

High, Unforgiven 11 Magnum Force, The Dead Pool
12 Coogan's Bluff, Kelly's Heroes, Sudden Impact 13 A Perfect World 14 Play Misty for Me 15 In The Line of Fire, Where Eagles Dare
17 A Fistful of Dollars, Any Which Way You Can, High Plains Drifter 18 Escape from Alcatraz, For a Few Dollars More 21 Two Mules for Sister Sara 23 The Good the Bad and the Ugly
mayor of: 6 Carmel

easy 4 calm, mild, open, soft
5 cushy, frank, light, naive
6 benign, calmly, candid, docile, easily, gentle, secure, serene, simple 7 lenient, natural, not hard, relaxed, restful, wealthy 8 affluent, carefree, composed, friendly, gracious, gullible, informal, outgoing, painless, peaceful, pleasant, scarcely, serenely, tranquil, unforced, well-to-do, yielding
9 compliant, indulgent, leisurely, luxurious, tractable, unworried 10 effortless, peacefully, permissive, unaffected, untroubled 11 comfortable, comfortably 12 not difficult, unsuspicious 13 accommodating, unconstrained

easygoing 4 calm 6 casual
7 offhand, patient, relaxed
8 carefree 9 unruffled, unworried 10 insouciant, nonchalant 11 unconcerned, unexcitable 12 even-tempered, happy-go-lucky, mild-tempered

Easy Rider
director: 12 Dennis Hopper
cast: 10 Karen Black, Peter Fonda 11 Luana Anders
12 Dennis Hopper, Robert Walker 13 Jack Nicholson

easy to use 7 adapted, helpful 9 adaptable 10 convenient
11 serviceable 12 advantageous

eat 3 sup 4 bolt, dine, feed, gulp, rust, take 5 feast, lunch
6 devour, gobble, ingest, nibble 7 consume, corrode 8 dispatch, dissolve, wear away, wolf down 9 breakfast, take a meal, waste away 10 break bread, gormandize 14 take sustenance 15 take nourishment

eatable 4 food 6 edible 8 fit to eat 10 comestible, consumable

eat away 4 rust 5 erode
7 corrode, oxidize

eating habits 4 diet 13 eating regimen

eating regimen 4 diet 12 eating habits

eat into 4 bite 5 erode 6 nibble 7 consume, corrode 8 wear away 9 swallow up

eat one's fill 5 feast, gorge 6 pig out 7 banquet 12 stuff oneself

eat rapidly 4 bolt, gulp, wolf 5 scarf 6 gobble 12 swallow whole

eat up 5 enjoy, savor 6 devour, relish 7 consume, swallow 9 delight in, rejoice in 13 be pleased with, get a kick out of 14 take pleasure in

eat voraciously 6 cram in, devour, gobble 7 stuff in 8 bolt down, gulp down, wolf down 10 gormandize 12 swallow whole

eau, eaux 5 water

eau de vie 6 brandy 11 water of life

eavesdrop 3 bug, pry, spy, tap 5 snoop 6 attend, harken 7 monitor, wiretap 8 listen in, overhear 9 bend an ear 11 cock one's ear 14 strain one's ears 15 prick up one's ears

ebb 5 abate, go out 6 go down, lessen, recede, shrink, weaken 7 decline, dwindle, retreat, slacken, subside 8 decrease, diminish, fade away, fall away, flow away, flow back, move back, withdraw 9 waste away 10 degenerate 11 deteriorate

ebony 3 jet 4 dark, inky 5 black, raven, sable 8 hardwood 9 coal-black 15 Diospyros Ebenum
varieties: 5 Green, Texas 8 Macassar, Mountain 10 East Indian, Queensland

Ebsen, Buddy
real name: 23 Christian Rudolph Ebsen Jr
born: 12 Belleville IL
roles: 12 Barnaby Jones, Davy Crockett 21 The Beverly Hillbillies

ebullience 3 zip 7 elation 8 buoyancy 9 animation 10 enthusiasm, exuberance, joyousness, liveliness 11 high spirits 12 exhilaration 13 effervescence

ebullient 6 elated, joyful, joyous 9 exuberant 11 exhilarated 12 effervescent, enthusiastic, high-spirited

ecce homo 12 behold the man
said by: 13 Pontius Pilate
spoken of: 6 Christ

eccentric 3 nut, odd 4 kook, rash, sick 5 curio, flake, funny, kooky, nutty, queer, weird 6 freaky, insane, quaint, unique, weirdo 7 bizarre, curious, erratic, oddball, offbeat, strange, unusual, weirdie 8 aberrant, abnormal, crackpot, freakish, peculiar, quixotic, singular, uncommon 9 character, irregular, odd person, off center, parabolic, psychotic, screwball, unnatural, whimsical 10 capricious, elliptical, outlandish, unorthodox 13 extraordinary 14 unconventional

eccentricity 6 oddity, whimsy 7 caprice 9 deviation, queerness 10 aberration 11 abnormality, peculiarity, strangeness 12 idiosyncrasy, irregularity

ecclesiastic, ecclesiastical 5 rabbi, vicar 6 cleric, curate, deacon, parson, pastor, priest, rector 7 prelate 8 chaplain, churchly, clerical, minister, pastoral, preacher 9 churchman, clergyman, episcopal, parochial, religious

Echecles
father: 5 Actor
wife: 8 Polymela
raised child of Polymela and: 6 Hermes

echelon 4 file, line, rank, rung, tier 5 grade, level 6 office 8 position 9 authority, hierarchy

Echemus
king of: 7 Arcadia
father: 7 Cepheus
wife: 8 Timandra
son: 8 Laodocus
delayed: 18 Heraclidan invasion
killed: 6 Hyllus

Echetus
king of: 6 Epirus
daughter: 8 Amphissa
blinded: 8 Amphissa

Echidna
form: 7 monster
mother of: 5 Hydra 6 Sphinx 7 Chimera 8 Cerberus
slain by: 5 Argus

echinoderm 9 sea animal
characteristic: 10 spiny shell
form: 6 radial
kind: 6 cystid 7 crinoid 8 starfish 9 sea urchin 10 basket star 11 sea cucumber

Echion
member: 6 Sparti
wife: 5 Agave
son: 8 Pentheus

echo 3 ape 4 copy, ring 5 match 6 follow, mirror, parrot, repeat 7 imitate, reflect, resound 8 parallel, simulate 9 duplicate, reproduce, take after 11 reverberate 13 reverberation

Echo
form: 5 nymph
location: 8 mountain
loved: 9 Narcissus
loved by: 3 Pan
changed into: 4 echo

eclair 6 pastry 7 dessert 9 creampuff

eclaircissement 11 explanation 13 clarification, (the) Enlightenment

eclipse 3 dim 4 hide, loss, mask 5 cloak, cover, excel, outdo 6 darken, exceed 7 blot out, conceal, erasing, masking, obscure, surpass, veiling, wipe out 8 cloaking, clouding, covering, outrival, outshine 9 darkening, shadowing, transcend 10 obliterate, overshadow, tower above 11 blotting out, diminishing, eradicating, obscuration 12 annihilation, obliteration 13 overshadowing

eclogue 4 idyl, poem 5 idyll 7 bucolic 8 dialogue, pastoral

Eclogues
author: 6 Vergil, Virgil

ecole 6 school

economic 6 fiscal 8 material, monetary 9 budgetary, financial, pecuniary 10 productive 12 distributive

economical 5 chary, cheap 6 frugal, modest, saving 7 careful, prudent, sparing, spartan, thrifty 8 economic 9 low-priced, niggardly, penurious, scrimping 10 reasonable 11 closefisted, tightfisted 12 parsimonious

economic decline 8 downturn 9 recession 10 depression

economics
term: 3 GNP 5 labor 7 capital, Marxism, surplus 8 property 9 commodity, Communism, inflation, Keynesian, recession 10 capitalism, monetarist, supply-side 11 bourgeoisie, central bank, competition, consumption, marketplace, proletariat, stagflation 12 distribution, econometrics, fiscal policy, interest rate, laissez-faire, mercantilism 14 federal deficit, macroeconomics, microeconomics, monetary policy 17 trickle-down the-

ory **20** gross national product

economist

American: 6 George, Hansen, Sumner, Veblen **7** Commons **8** Friedman, Laughlin **10** Schumpeter
British: 4 Mill **5** Smith **6** Keynes **7** Malthus, Ricardo **8** Marshall
French: 3 Say **7** Quesnay
German: 4 Marx **7** Schacht
Italian: 6 Pareto
Scottish: 5 Smith

economize

4 save **5** pinch, skimp, stint **6** scrimp **7** husband **8** be frugal, conserve, cut costs **9** be prudent **10** avoid waste **11** cut expenses **12** be economical, use sparingly **14** be parsimonious **15** practice economy, tighten one's belt

economizing

10 conserving **11** cutting down **13** penny-pinching **14** belt-tightening **15** pinching pennies **18** tightening one's belt

economy

6 thrift **8** prudence **9** frugality **10** providence **11** thriftiness **15** financial status, productive power

ecstasy

3 joy **5** bliss **6** frenzy, thrill, trance **7** delight, emotion, madness, rapture **8** delirium, gladness, pleasure **9** happiness, transport **10** enthusiasm, exultation

ecstatic

4 glad, rapt **5** happy **6** elated, joyful, joyous **7** exalted, excited **8** blissful **9** delighted, delirious, ebullient, entranced, overjoyed, rapturous **10** enraptured **11** transported **12** enthusiastic **13** beside oneself

Ecuador *see box*

ecumenical

6 global **7** general **8** catholic **9** communist, planetary, universal, worldwide **10** heavenwide **11** communalist **12** all-embracing, all-including, all-inclusive, all-pervading, collectivist, cosmopolitan **13** communitarian, comprehensive, international

eczema

4 rash **8** eruption **10** dermatitis **12** inflammation

eddy

6 vortex **9** maelstrom, whirlpool **14** countercurrent

Eddy, Nelson

partner: 17 Jeanette MacDonald
born: 12 Providence RI
roles: 9 Rose Marie **15** Naughty Marietta **16** Northwest Outpost

---

Ecuador

name means: 7 equator
other name: 5 Quito
capital: 5 Quito
largest city: 9 Guayaquil
others: 4 Jama, Loja, Napo, Puyo, Tena **5** Guano, Manta, Pajan, Pinas, Piura, Pojan, Yaupi **6** Ambato, Cuenca, Ibarra, Tulcan, Zaruma **7** Azogues, Cayambe, Guamote, Guapulo, Machala, Pelileo, Pillaro, Salinas **8** Riobamba **10** Esmeraldas, Portoviejo
division: 5 Costa **6** Sierra **7** Oriente
measure: 5 libra **6** cuadra, fanega
monetary unit: 5 sucre **7** centavo
weight: 5 libra
island: 4 Puna, Wolf **5** Colon, Mocha, Pinta **6** Baltra, Chaves, Darwin, Pinzon, Rabida, Wenman **7** Isabela, La Plata, Sante Fe, Tortuga **8** Espanola, Floreana, Genovesa, Marchena, Santiago **9** Culpepper, Galapagos, Santa Cruz **10** Fernandina, Santa Maria **11** San Salvador **12** San Cristobal
mountain: 5 Andes **6** Condor, Sangay **7** Cayambe **8** Antisana, Cotopaxi **9** Cotacachi, Pichincha
highest point: 10 Chimborazo
river: 4 Coca, Mira, Napo **5** Cocoa, Daule, Paute, Pindo, Tigre **6** Blanco, Guayas, Tumbes, Zamora **7** Conambo, Curaray, Jubones, Pastaza, Puyango **8** Aguarico, Bobonaza, Cononaco, Naranjal, Putumayo **9** San Miguel **10** Esmeraldas, Nangaritza **12** Guaillabamba
sea: 7 Pacific
physical feature:
  bay: **5** Manta **7** Isabela **9** Elizabeth **11** Santa Elenas **15** Ancon de Sardinas
  cape: **4** Rosa **6** Pasado **8** Marshall, Puntilla **10** San Lorenzo
  channel: **7** Jambeli
  gulf: **9** Guayaquil, Pichincha
  peninsula: **10** Santa Elena
  point: **4** Jama **5** Essex **6** Galera **9** Albemarle **10** Christobal
people: 4 Cara, Cixo, Inca **5** Ardan, Aucas, Macoa, Maina, Palta, Quitu, Yumbo **6** Canelo, Jibaro, Jivaro, Puruha **7** Cayapas, Jivaros, mestizo, mulatto **8** Barbacoa, Colorado, Montuvio, Serranos **9** Montubios
  artist: **4** Egas **8** Santiago **9** Caspicara **10** Guayasamin
  author: **6** Espejo **14** Carrera Andrade
  conqueror: **7** Pizarro **10** Benalcazar **11** Huayna-Capac
  god: **5** umina
  leader: **6** Alfaro, Flores **10** Plaza Lasso, Rocafuerte **12** Garcia Moreno **13** Velasco Ibarra
language: 6 Jibaro **7** Quechua, Spanish
religion: 13 Roman Catholic
feature:
  animal: **6** vicuna
  dictator: **8** caudillo
  estate: **8** hacienda
  festival: **5** Yamor
  hat: **6** Panama **8** jipijapa, toquilla
  tree: **5** balsa
food:
  baked guinea pig: **3** cuy
  corn tamale: **6** humita
  drink: **6** chicha
  marinated raw shrimp/fish: **7** ceviche, seviche
  potato/cheese patty: **11** llapingacho
  potato soup: **5** locro

Eden 8 Paradise
see also: 4 Adam

edentate 5 manis, sloth 7 ant-bear 8 aardvark, anteater 9 armadillo, toothless

Edgar Huntly
author: 20 Charles Brockden Brown

edge 3 hem, rim 4 bind, inch, line, side, trim 5 bound, brink, creep, limit, sidle, slink, sneak, steal, verge 6 border, fringe, margin 7 contour, outline 9 extremity, periphery, threshold 12 boundary line, dividing line, move sideways

Edgeworth, Maria
author of: 7 Belinda 11 The Absentee 14 Castle Rackrent

edging 3 hem 4 trim 5 limit 6 border, fringe, margin, ruffle 7 binding, curbing, salvage 8 boundary, fringing, trimming

edgy 5 sharp, testy 7 anxious, nervous 8 snappish 9 excitable, impatient, irascible, irritable 10 highstrung

edible 7 eatable 10 comestible, consumable, digestible 12 fit to be eaten, nonpoisonous 13 safe for eating

edict 3 law 4 bull, fiat 5 order, ukase 6 decree, dictum, ruling 7 command, dictate, mandate, statute 9 enactment, manifesto, ordinance, prescript 10 injunction, regulation 12 proclamation, public notice 13 pronouncement 14 pronunciamento

edification 8 guidance, teaching 9 direction, education, elevation, uplifting 11 advancement, information, instruction 13 enlightenment 14 indoctrination

edifice 8 building 9 structure 12 construction

edify 5 teach 6 inform 7 educate, improve 8 instruct 9 enlighten

edifying 8 didactic, tutorial 11 educational, instructive 12 enlightening

Edinburgh
bay: 12 Firth of Forth
capital of: 8 Scotland
Celtic: 11 Dune-eideann (Eidin's Fort)
church: 7 St Giles
landmark: 14 Holyrood Palace 15 Edinburgh Castle
port: 5 Leith
rocks: 10 Castle Rock 11 Arthur's Seat

Edison, Thomas Alva
nickname: 17 Wizard of Menlo Park
inventor of: 6 (wax cylinder) record 9 light bulb, (quadruplex) telegraph 10 phonograph 11 kinetoscope, stock ticker 14 movie projector 16 incandescent lamp 18 automatic telegraph (transmitter and receiver) 21 flexible celluloid film 22 alkaline storage battery

edit 5 adapt, emend 6 censor, polish, redact, revise 7 abridge, clean up, correct, expunge, rewrite, touch up 8 annotate, condense, copy-edit, rephrase 9 expurgate 10 blue-pencil, bowdlerize

edition 4 book, copy, kind 5 issue 6 number 7 imprint, version 8 printing 9 redaction

editor 2 ed 6 writer 7 newsman, reviser 8 compiler, redactor 10 journalist

Edmonds, Walter D
author of: 8 Rome Haul 19 Drums Along the Mohawk

Edmonton
hockey team: 6 Oilers

Edmontonia
type: 8 dinosaur 10 ornithopod
location: 12 North America

Edmund Campion
author: 11 Evelyn Waugh

Edom
name given: 4 Esau
descendants: 8 Edomites

Edson, Gus
creator/artist of: 5 Dondi 8 The Gumps

Ed Sullivan Show, The
regular cast: 17 June Taylor Dancers 23 Ray Bloch and His Orchestra
noted appearances: 7 Beatles, Bob Hope 10 Walt Disney 12 Elvis Presley 14 Martin and Lewis

educate 5 coach, edify, teach, train, tutor 6 inform, school 7 develop 8 civilize, instruct 9 enlighten

education 5 study 7 culture 8 learning, pedagogy, teaching, training, tutelage 9 didactics, erudition, knowledge, schooling 10 pedagogics 11 cultivation, edification, information, instruction, scholarship 13 enlightenment

Education of Henry Adams, The
author: 10 Henry Adams

educe 5 evoke 6 elicit, extort 7 draw out, extract 8 bring out 9 draw forth 12 bring to light

Edward II
author: 18 Christopher Marlowe

Edwards, Blake
director of: 3 SOB, Ten 14 The Pink Panther, Victor Victoria 18 Days of Wine and Roses 19 Breakfast at Tiffany's

Edwards, Vince
real name: 18 Vincent Edward Zoimo
roles: 8 Ben Casey 13 Devil's Brigade 14 The Desperadoes 15 Three Faces of Eve

Edwin Drood, The Mystery of
author: 14 Charles Dickens
character: 7 Durdles, Mr Tatar, Rosa Bud 8 Mr Sapsea 10 John Jasper, Mr Datchery 11 Mr Grewgious 12 Mr Crisparkle 13 Deputy Bazzard 14 Helena Landless, Miss Twinkleton, Mr Honeythunder 15 Neville Landless

eel
young: 5 elver

eerie 3 odd 5 queer, weird 6 creepy, spooky, uneasy 7 bizarre, fearful, ghostly, ominous, strange, uncanny 10 mysterious, portentous 11 frightening 12 apprehensive

Eetion
king of: 6 Thebes 7 Cilicia
daughter: 10 Andromache

Eeyore
character in: 13 Winnie-the-Pooh
author: 5 Milne

efface 4 raze 5 erase 6 cancel, delete, excise, rub out 7 blot out, destroy, expunge, wipe out 9 eradicate, extirpate 10 annihilate, obliterate

effect, effects 4 fact, gist, make 5 cause, drift, force, goods, power, tenor, truth 6 action, assets, attain, create, impact, import, intent, result, sequel, things, upshot, weight 7 achieve, essence, execute, meaning, outcome, perform, produce, purport, reality, realize 8 carry out, chattels, efficacy, function, holdings, movables, validity 9 actuality, aftermath, execution, furniture, influence, intention, operation, outgrowth, trappings 10 accomplish, bring about, impression 11 commodities, consequence, development, enforcement, general idea, impli-

cation, possessions
12 significance
14 accomplishment

effective 4 real **6** active, actual, cogent, moving, potent, strong, useful **7** capable, current, dynamic, telling **8** a reality, eloquent, forceful, forcible, incisive, powerful, striking **9** activated, competent, effectual, efficient, operative **10** compelling, convincing, impressive, persuasive, productive, successful **11** efficacious, influential, in operation, serviceable

effectiveness 5 power **6** effect, impact **7** potency **8** efficacy, strength **9** influence **10** efficiency, usefulness **14** serviceability

effectual 6 acting, active, useful **7** working **8** adequate **9** effective, efficient, operative **11** efficacious, functioning

effectuate 6 effect **7** achieve, execute, realize **8** carry out, complete **9** discharge **10** accomplish, consummate, perpetrate **12** carry through **13** put into effect

effeminate 7 unmanly **8** sissyish, womanish **9** sissified

effervesce 4 fizz, foam **5** froth **6** bubble, fizzle **7** sparkle

effervescence 3 zip **4** dash, fizz, life **5** froth, vigor **6** fizzle, gaiety, spirit **7** foaming **8** bubbling, buoyancy, vitality, vivacity **9** animation, fizziness **10** bubbliness, bubbling up, ebullience, enthusiasm, liveliness

effervescent 3 gay **5** fizzy, merry **6** bubbly, lively **7** fizzing, foaming **8** animated, bubbling **9** ebullient, exuberant, sparkling, vivacious **13** irrepressible

effete 5 spent **6** barren, wasted **7** sterile, worn-out **8** decadent, depraved **9** enervated, exhausted **10** degenerate, unprolific **12** unproductive

efficacious 9 effective, effectual, efficient

efficacy 6 impact **10** efficiency **13** effectiveness

efficiency 5 skill **6** energy **8** efficacy, facility **9** apartment **10** competence **11** proficiency **13** effectiveness

efficient 3 apt **7** capable **8** skillful **9** competent, effective, effectual **10** productive, proficient, timesaving, un-

wasteful, work-saving **11** crackerjack, efficacious, workmanlike **12** businesslike

effigy 4 doll **5** dummy, image **6** puppet, statue **8** likeness, straw man **9** mannequin, scarecrow **10** marionette **14** representation

effluence 6 efflux **7** outflow, outpour **8** effluent **9** discharge

effluent 5 waste **6** efflux, sewage **7** outflow **9** effluence

effluvium 4 aura, odor, ooze, reek **5** vapor **6** efflux, flatus **8** outgoing

efflux 7 outflow **8** effluent, emission **9** discharge, effluence

effort 3 try **4** toil, work **5** force, labor, pains, power **6** energy, strain, stress **7** attempt, travail, trouble **8** endeavor, exertion, industry, struggle **11** elbow grease

effortless 4 easy **6** facile, simple, smooth **8** graceful, painless **12** not difficult **13** uncomplicated

effortlessness 4 ease **8** easiness, facility **9** readiness **12** painlessness

effrontery 4 gall **5** brass, cheek, nerve **8** audacity, temerity **9** arrogance, brashness, impudence, insolence **10** brazenness **11** presumption **12** impertinence **13** shamelessness
  Yiddish: **7** chutzpa **8** chutzpah

effulgence 6 dazzle **8** radiance, splendor **10** brilliance **12** resplendence

effulgent 6 bright **7** radiant **8** dazzling, splendid **9** brilliant **11** resplendent

effusive 5 gushy **6** lavish **7** copious, gushing, profuse **9** ebullient, expansive, exuberant **10** unreserved **11** extravagant, free-flowing, overflowing **12** unrestrained

eft 4 newt **5** again **6** lizard **9** afterward

egalitarian 10 democratic **11** equal-rights **14** constitutional

egalite 8 equality

Egeria
  also: **7** Aegeria
  member of: **7** Camenae
  husband: **13** Numa Pompilius
  instructed: **13** Numa Pompilius

Egesta
  also: **7** Aegesta
  home: **4** Troy

position: **5** slave
sold by: **8** Laomedon
rescued by: **9** Aphrodite

egg 3 ova, roe **4** bomb, goad, mine, oval, ovum, seed, spur **6** embryo, fellow, incite, person **7** albumen **9** instigate, stimulate

Eggar, Samantha
  born: **6** London **7** England
  roles: **12** The Collector, Walking Stick **15** Doctor Doolittle, The Lady in the Car **16** The Molly Maguires

egghead 8 highbrow **13** intellectual

Eggleston, Edward
  author of: **15** The Circuit Rider **19** The Hoosier Schoolboy **22** The Hoosier Schoolmaster

egg on 4 abet, back, goad, spur **6** exhort, incite **8** talk into **9** encourage

egg-shaped 4 oval **5** ovoid **7** oviform **10** elliptical

Egmont
  author: **12** Johann Goethe

egocentric 8 egoistic **11** egomaniacal, egotistical, on an ego trip, self-seeking, self-serving **12** narcissistic, self-absorbed, self-centered, self-involved, self-obsessed **13** self-concerned **14** megalomaniacal, stuck on oneself **18** wrapped up in oneself

egoism 6 vanity **8** self-love **10** narcissism **14** self-absorption, self-importance **16** overweening pride, self-centeredness

egoist 10 narcissist, selfish one **13** selfish person **18** self-centered person

Egoist, The
  author: **14** George Meredith

egoistic 7 selfish **12** narcissistic, self-centered

egotism 6 vanity **7** conceit **8** bragging, smugness **9** arrogance, immodesty, vainglory **10** self-praise **11** braggadocio **12** boastfulness

egotist 6 gascon **7** boaster, peacock **8** blowhard, braggart **9** swaggerer **11** braggadocio

egotistic 4 vain **10** egocentric **12** self-centered **13** self-important

egregious 5 gross **7** extreme, glaring, heinous **8** flagrant, grievous, shocking **9** monstrous, notorious **10** outrageous **11** intolerable **12** insufferable

Egypt

other name: 3 UAR 5 Kemet 6 To-meri 11 The Two Lands 12 The Black Land

capital/largest city: 5 Cairo

others: 3 Tor 4 Edfu, Gaza, Giza, Idfu, Said, Suez 5 Altur, Aswan, Tanta 6 Boolak, Dumyat, Faiyum, Quseir, Safaga, Sallum 7 Alemein, Memphis, Raschid, Rosetta, Zagazig 8 Damietta, Hurghada, Ismailia, Mansurah 10 Alexandria

school: 5 Cairo 7 Al-Azhar 8 American

division: 5 Lower, Nubia, Upper

measure: 3 apt, dra, hen, rob 4 arab, dira, draa, khet, nief, ocha, roub, theb, wudu 5 abdat, ardab, cubit, farde, fedan, keleh, kerat, kilah, sahme 6 artaba, aurure, baladi, kantar, keddah, robhah, schene 7 choryos, daribah, malouah, roubouh, toumnah 8 kassabah, kharouba 10 diramimari, diribaladi

monetary unit: 4 fils, kees, para 5 asper, dinar, fodda, gersh, girsh, medin, pound, riyal 6 ahmadi, dirham, foddah, guinea, junayh, maidin, medine, medino 7 piaster, piastre, tallard 8 bedidlik, millieme

weight: 3 kat, ket, oka, oke 4 dera, heml, khar, okia, rotl 5 artal, artel, deben, kerat, minae, minas, okieh, pound, ratel, uckia 6 hamlah, kantar 7 drachma, quintal

island: 4 Roda 6 Philae 7 Shadwan 11 Elephantine

lake: 4 Edku, Idku 5 Qarun 6 Maryut, Moeris, Nasser 7 Manzala 8 Burullus, Mareotis

mountain: 5 Sinai, Uekia 6 Gharib 13 Shayib al-Banat

highest point: 8 Katerina 9 Katherina

river: 4 Bahr, Nile
Nile branch: 7 Rosetta 8 Damietta

sea: 3 Red 13 Mediterranean

physical feature:
cape: 4 Sudr 5 Banas 8 Rasbanas
desert: 3 Tih 5 Dakla, Scete, Sinai, Skete 6 Libyan, Nubian, Sahara 7 Arabian
gulf: 4 Suez 5 Aqaba
isthmus: 4 Suez
oasis: 4 Siwa 6 Dakhel, Dakhla, Kharga 7 Farafra, Khargeh 8 Bahariya 9 Bahariyeh 12 Wahel-Khargeh
peninsula: 5 Sinai 6 Pharos
plain: 7 Asaseff
plateau: 3 Tih

people: 3 Kem 4 Arab, Copt, Misr, Wafd 5 Gippy, Gyppy, Gypsy, Nilot 6 Ababda, Berber, Hyksos, Nubian, Tasian 7 Mizraim, Pharian 8 Badarian, Bisharin, Memphian
leader: 5 Jawar, Sadat 6 Nasser 7 Mubarak, Saladin 10 King Farouk 11 Ismail Pasha, Mohammed Ali, Tawfiq Pasha
pharaoh: 5 Khufu, Menes, Zoser 6 Khafre, Ptulol, Ramses 8 Horemheb, Menkaure 9 Akhenaten, Amenemhet, Amenhotep 10 Mentuhotep 11 Tutankhamen
queen: 9 Cleopatra, Nefertari, Nefertiti 10 Hatshepsut, Hetepheres

language: 6 Arabic, French 7 English
for liturgy: 6 Coptic

religion: 5 Islam 18 Coptic Christianity
ancient god: 2 Ra 3 Geb, Nut, Shu 4 Aton, Atum, Isis, Ptah, Seth 5 Horus, Thoth 6 Anubis, Hathor, Osiris, Tefnut 8 Nephthys

place:
dam: 4 Sadd, Sudd 5 Aswan 6 Assuan
mosque: 5 Rifai 9 Alabaster 11 Sultan Hasan
palace: 6 Kubbeh
pyramids: 4 Giza 5 Khufu 6 Cheops 7 Saqqara
ruins: 5 Miroe 6 Abydos, Sphinx, Thebes 7 Memphis 8 Berenice 9 Abu Simbel 13 Valley of Kings, Valley of Tombs
temple: 4 Idfu 5 Edoon, Luxor, Thoth 6 Abydos, Karnak, Osiris 7 Dendera

feature:
dynasty: 5 Saite 7 Ayyubid, Fatimid 8 Mameluke 9 Ptolemaic
long robe: 10 gallabiyea
peasant: 6 fellah 8 fellahin 9 fellaheen
sacred bird: 4 benu, ibis 5 bennu
sailboat: 7 felucca
statue: 6 Sphinx 15 Colossi of Memnon

food:
bean: 5 lotus
beer: 6 zythum
bread: 6 herisa
dish: 3 ful
drink: 4 bosa, boza 5 bozah

elastic

egress 4 exit, vent **5** issue
6 escape, outlet, way out
7 leakage, outflow, seepage
8 aperture **9** departure, discharge **10** passage out,
withdrawal

Egypt *see box*

Egyptian
language family: **11** Afro-Asiatic **13** Hamito-Semitic
later form: **6** Coptic

Egyptian cross 4 ankh

Egyptian Mythology *see
box*

Ehrlich, Paul
field: **12** bacteriology
nationality: **6** German
studied: **6** toxins **8** immunity
10 antitoxins
discovered: **9** salvarsan
coined term:
12 chemotherapy
awarded: **10** Nobel Prize

Ehud 11 Hebrew judge

Eichenor
mentioned in: **5** Iliad
father: **8** Polyidus
fought with: **6** Greeks
slain by: **5** Paris

Eichmann in Jerusalem
author: **12** Hannah Arendt

eiderdown 4 puff **5** cover,

quilt **8** coverlet **9** comforter
10 featherbed

Eight and a half, 8 1/2
director: **15** Federico Fellini
cast: **10** Anouk Aimee
16 Claudia Cardinale
19 Marcello Mastroianni

Eighteen Seventy-Six, 1876
author: **9** Gore Vidal

Eijkman, Christiaan
nationality: **5** Dutch
discovered: **19** antineuritic
vitamin
researched: **8** beriberi
awarded: **10** Nobel Prize

Eileithyia
also: **8** Ilithyia
origin: **5** Greek
goddess of: **10** childbirth
father: **4** Zeus
mother: **4** Hera
corresponds to: **6** Lucina

Einstein, Albert
field: **7** physics
theory of: **10** relativity
14 uranium fission
awarded: **10** Nobel Prize

Eioneus
son: **6** Rhesus
daughter: **3** Dia

Eire *see* **7** Ireland

Eisenhower, Dwight David
see box, p. 298

ejaculate 4 howl, yell, yelp
5 shout **6** bellow, cry out
7 exclaim **10** vociferate

ejaculation 3 cry **4** howl, yell,
yelp **5** shout **6** bellow, outcry,
shriek, squeal **7** screech
11 exclamation **12** vociferation

eject 4 emit, oust, spew
5 evict, exile, expel, exude,
spout **6** banish, bounce, deport, remove **7** cast out, kick
out, spit out, turn out **8** disgorge, drive out, force out,
throw out **9** discharge
10 dispossess

ejection 4 gush **5** spurt
6 ouster **7** issuing, removal
8 emission, eruption, eviction
9 dismissal, expelling, expulsion **10** banishment **11** throwing out

Ekdal, Hjalmar
character in: **11** The Wild
Duck
author: **5** Ibsen

eke 3 add **4** also **7** augment,
enlarge, stretch **8** increase,
lengthen, likewise, moreover
10 in addition, supplement

elaborate 5 fancy, gaudy,
showy **6** expand, flashy, garish, ornate **7** clarify, complex,
elegant, labored, specify **8** involved, overdone **9** embellish,
intricate **10** add details
11 complicated, painstaking
12 ostentatious **13** particularize

elaborate on 6 expand **7** amplify, develop **9** embellish
10 supplement **11** expatiate on

elaboration 11 added detail,
rounding out **12** augmentation **13** amplification,
embellishment

Elaine
character in: **16** Arthurian
romance

Elais
father: **5** Anius
mother: **7** Dorippe
changed things into: **3** oil

elan 4 dash, zeal **5** flair, verve,
vigor **6** energy, spirit **8** vivacity **9** animation **10** enthusiasm

eland 3 elk **8** antelope
11 taurotragus

elapse 4 go by, pass **5** lapse
6 pass by, roll by, slip by
7 glide by, slide by **8** slip
away **9** intervene

Elara
mother of: **6** Tityus

elastic 6 pliant, supple **7** pliable, rubbery, springy **8** flexible, tolerant, yielding
9 adaptable, recoiling, resil-

Egyptian Mythology
deities: **6** Ennead
eight gods: **3** Heh **6** Ogdoad
goddess of evil: **7** Sekhmet
goddess of fertility: **2** Io **4** Isis
goddess of law/righteousness: **4** Maat
goddess of love/joy/music/dance: **6** Hathor
goddess of sky: **3** Nut
goddess personifying sky: **6** Hathor
god of bricks: **5** Kulla
god of creation: **4** Ptah
god of dead/Nile: **6** Osiris
god of earth: **3** Geb, Keb
god of ocean: **3** Nun **4** Nunu
god of sun: **2** Ra, Re **5** Horus
corresponds to Greek: **10** Harcorates
god of tombs/embalming: **6** Anubis
god of wisdom/magic/learning: **5** Thoth
corresponds to Greek: **6** Hermes
immortal spirit: **2** Ka
judge of dead: **6** Osiris
king of dead: **6** Osiris
king of gods: **4** Amen, Amon **5** Ammon **6** Amen Ra,
Amon Ra
corresponds to Greek: **4** Zeus
corresponds to Roman: **4** Jove **7** Jupiter
personification of femininity: **5** Neith
corresponds to Greek: **6** Athena
ram god: **5** Khnum
vulture: **7** Nekhbet

Eisenhower, Dwight David

nickname: 3 Ike
  changed name from: 21 David Dwight Eisenhower

presidential rank: 12 thirty-fourth

party: 10 Republican

state represented: 2 NY

defeated: 4 (Eric) Hass, (Harry Flood) Byrd 5 (Farrell) Dobbs 6 (Darlington) Hoopes, (William Ezra) Jenner 7 (Stuart) Hamblen, (Thomas Coleman) Andrews 8 (Enoch Arden) Holtwick, (Vincent William) Hallinan 9 (Adlai Ewing) Stevenson

vice president: 5 (Richard Milhous) Nixon

cabinet:
  state: 6 (Christian Archibald) Herter, (John Foster) Dulles
  treasury: 8 (George Magoffin) Humphrey, (Robert Bernard) Anderson
  defense: 5 (Thomas Sovereign) Gates (Jr) 6 (Charles Erwin) Wilson 7 (Neil Hesler) McElroy
  attorney general: 6 (William Pierce) Rogers 8 (Herbert) Brownell (Jr)
  postmaster general: 11 (Arthur Ellsworth) Summerfield
  interior: 5 (Douglas) McKay 6 (Frederick Andrew) Seaton
  agriculture: 6 (Ezra Taft) Benson
  commerce: 5 (Sinclair) Weeks 7 (Frederick Henry) Mueller, (Lewis Lichtenstein) Strauss
  labor: 6 (Martin Patrick) Durkin 8 (James Paul) Mitchell
  HEW: 5 (Oveta Culp) Hobby 6 (Marion Bayard) Folsom 8 (Arthur Sherwood) Flemming

born: 9 Denison TX

died: 12 Washington DC

buried: 9 Abilene KS

education: 9 West Point 17 US Military Academy

religion: 12 Presbyterian

interest: 4 golf 6 flying 7 fishing, hunting 8 football, painting

vacation spot: 2 CA 11 Palm Springs

author: 11 Waging Peace 15 Crusade in Europe 16 Mandate for Change 27 At Ease: Stories I Tell to Friends

political career: 4 none (prior to presidency)

civilian career:
  president of: 18 Columbia University

military service: 7 general 9 World War I 10 World War II 16 Army Chief of Staff
  supreme commander of: 6 Allies 15 European Defense (NATO) 18 US occupation forces (Europe)
  head of: 18 Joint Chiefs of Staff

notable events of lifetime/term: 4 D-Day, NATO
  Acts: 11 Civil Rights
  battle of the: 5 Bulge
  conference: 7 Big Four 10 NATO Summit 11 Paris Summit
  Cuba taken over by: 11 Fidel Castro
  invasion: 8 Normandy
  trial/execution of: 14 Ethel Rosenberg 15 Julius Rosenberg
  USSR shot down: 9 U-Two plane

father: 10 David Jacob

mother: 3 Ida (Elizabeth Stover)

siblings: 3 Roy 4 Earl, Paul 5 Edgar 6 Arthur, Milton

wife: 5 Marie (Geneva Doud)
  nickname: 5 Mamie

children: 10 Doud Dwight 15 John Sheldon Doud

ient 10 rebounding, responsive 11 complaisant, stretchable 12 recuperative 13 accommodating

elate 5 cheer, exalt 6 excite, lift up, please 7 animate, delight, elevate, enliven, gladden, gratify, inspire 10 exhilarate

elated 4 glad 5 happy, proud 6 joyful, joyous 7 exalted, excited, gleeful, pleased 8 animated, blissful, ecstatic, jubilant 9 overjoyed, rejoicing 10 delightful 11 exhilarated 13 in high spirits 18 flushed with success

elation 3 joy 4 glee 5 pride 7 triumph 8 gladness 9 happiness 10 excitement, exultation, jubilation 12 cheerfulness

Elatus
  father: 5 Arcas
  son: 6 Pereus 10 Polyphemus

elbow grease 4 work 5 force, labor 6 effort, energy, muscle 8 exertion, hard work 11 application

elbow in 4 push 5 force, press, shove 6 horn in 7 crowd in

El Cordobes (Manuel Benitez Perez)
  sport: 12 bullfighting

elder 4 head 5 older 6 senior 8 old-timer 9 firstborn, patriarch, presbyter 14 church official 15 church dignitary
  French: 4 aine

elder, elderberry 8 Sambucus
  varieties: 3 Box 4 Blue 5 Dwarf, Sweet 6 Ground, Poison, Yellow 8 American, European, Stinking 10 Redberried 11 American red, European red 15 Pacific Coast red

elderly 3 old 4 aged 9 venerable 11 over the hill 13 past one's prime

Eldorado
  nickname of: 10 California

Eleanor and Franklin
  author: 11 Joseph P Lash

Eleazar
  father: 4 Dodo 5 Aaron, Elind, Mahli 6 Parosh 7 Phineas 8 Abinadab
  mother: 8 Elisheba
  brother: 5 Abihu, Nadab 7 Ithamar
  succeeded: 5 Aaron

elect 4 pick 5 adopt 6 choose, opt for, select, take up 7 embrace, espouse, fix upon, pick out 8 decide on, settle on 9 single out

election 4 poll, vote 6 choice, option, voting 7 resolve 8 decision 9 balloting, selection 10 resolution 11 alternative 13 determination

electioneer 3 run 5 stump 8 campaign 11 whistle-stop 12 beat the drums, solicit votes

elective 8 optional 9 selective, voluntary 11 not required 12 open to choice, passed by vote 13 discretionary, not obligatory

Electra
author: 9 Euripides, Sophocles
character: 7 Orestes, Pylades 8 Dioscuri 9 Aegisthus 12 Clytemnestra
father: 9 Agamemnon
mother: 12 Clytemnestra
brother: 7 Orestes
sister: 9 Iphigenia 12 Chrysothemis
husband: 7 Pylades
son: 5 Medon 9 Strophius

electric 7 dynamic, rousing 8 exalting, exciting, spirited, stirring 9 inspiring, thrilling 10 full of fire 11 galvanizing, power-driven, stimulating 12 electrifying, soul-stirring

electric battery
invented by: 5 Volta

electricity measure 3 ohm 4 volt, watt 5 joule 6 ampere 10 horsepower

Electric Kool-Aid Acid Test, The
author: 8 Tom Wolfe

Electrides
form: 7 islands
color: 5 amber

electrify 4 daze, stir, stun 5 amaze, rouse 6 dazzle, excite, fire up, thrill 7 animate, astound, quicken, startle 8 astonish, surprise 9 fascinate, galvanize, stimulate 18 take one's breath away

electrifying 8 dazzling, shocking, stunning 10 astounding, stupefying 11 astonishing

electromagnet
invented by: 8 Sturgeon

Electryon
king of: 7 Mycenae
father: 7 Perseus
mother: 9 Andromeda
brother: 6 Mestor 9 Sthenelus
wife: 5 Anaxo
son: 9 Licymnius
daughter: 7 Alcmene
grandson: 8 Hercules

eleemosynary 10 altruistic, beneficent, benevolent, charitable 13 philanthropic 15 non-profitmaking

elegance 5 class, grace, taste 6 purity 7 balance 8 delicacy, grandeur, richness, symmetry 10 refinement 12 gracefulness 13 exquisiteness, luxuriousness, sumptuousness

elegant 4 fine, rich 5 grand 6 classy, dapper, lovely, ornate, polite, urbane 7 classic, courtly, genteel, refined, stylish 8 artistic, charming, debonair, delicate, graceful, gracious, handsome, polished, tasteful, well-bred 9 beautiful, dignified, exquisite, luxurious, sumptuous 10 attractive, cultivated 11 fashionable, symmetrical 16 well-proportioned

elegiac 3 sad 8 funereal, mournful 10 melancholy

elegy 7 requiem, sad poem 11 funeral song 14 melancholy poem 16 lament for the dead 17 poem of lamentation, song of lamentation 22 melancholy piece of music

Elegy Written in a Country Churchyard
author: 10 Thomas Gray

Elektra see 7 Electra

element, elements 3 air 4 fire 5 earth, water 6 basics, member, milieu 7 essence, factors, origins 8 original 9 basic part, basic unit, component, rudiments 10 basic ideas, ingredient, principles, simple body 11 constituent, environment, foundations, native state, subdivision 13 building block, component part, natural medium 14 natural habitat

elemental 5 basal, basic 10 elementary 11 fundamental, rudimentary

elementary 4 easy 5 basal, basic, crude, first, plain 6 simple 7 primary 8 original 9 elemental, primitive 11 fundamental, rudimentary, undeveloped 13 uncomplicated

elephant
group of: 4 herd

elephantine 4 huge 7 immense, mammoth, titanic 8 colossal, enormous, gigantic 9 ponderous 10 gargantuan, tremendous 14 Brobdingnagian

Elephant Man, The
director: 10 David Lynch
cast: 8 John Hurt 11 John Gielgud, Wendy Hiller 12 Anne Bancroft 14 Anthony Hopkins

Eleusinia
origin: 5 Greek
form: 8 festival

Eleusinian mysteries
in memory of: 10 Persephone
in honor of: 7 Bacchus, Demeter
celebrated at: 6 Athens 7 Eleusis
founded by: 8 Eumolpus
god of: 7 Bacchus

Eleutherius
epithet of: 4 Zeus
means: 12 god of freedom

elevate 4 lift 5 boost, cheer, elate, heave, hoist, raise 6 better, excite, lift up, move up, perk up, refine, uplift 7 advance, animate, dignify, enhance, ennoble, improve, inspire, promote, upraise 8 heighten 9 place high 10 exhilarate, raise aloft

elevated 4 high 5 lofty 6 raised 7 exalted 8 improved, uplifted 9 prominent 10 heightened

elevation 4 hill, lift, rise 5 boost 6 ascent, height 8 altitude, mountain 9 acclivity, bettering, high place, promotion 10 prominence, refinement 11 advancement, cultivation, improvement

elevator 4 cage, lift, silo, wing 5 hoist 7 granary 10 dumbwaiter

elevator brake
invented by: 4 Otis

elf 4 puck 5 fairy, gnome, pixie, troll 6 goblin, sprite 7 brownie, gremlin 9 hobgoblin 10 leprechaun

elfin 3 wee 4 tiny 7 pixyish 9 fairylike 10 diminutive

Elgar, Sir Edward William
born: 7 England 10 Broadheath
composer of: 8 Falstaff 9 Cockaigne, Froissart 10 Caractacus, The Kingdom 11 The Apostles 14 The Black Knight, The Light of Life 16 Enigma Variations 19 Pomp and Circumstance, The Banner of St George, The Dream of Gerontius 30 Scenes from the Bavarian Highlands

Eli
son: 6 Hophni 7 Phineas
home: 6 Shiloh

Eli, Eli, Lama sabachthani
means: 31 My God My God why hast thou forsaken me?

elicit 5 cause, educe, evoke, exact, fetch, wrest 6 derive, extort **7** draw out, extract **9** call forth, draw forth **10** bring forth **12** bring to light

Elicius
origin: **5** Roman
epithet of: **7** Jupiter

elide 4 omit, slur **5** annul **6** delete **7** neglect **8** slur over, suppress **9** eliminate, strikeout **10** abbreviate

Eliezar
father: **5** Moses
mother: **8** Zipporah
brother: **7** Gershom

eligible 6 proper **7** fitting **8** suitable **9** desirable, qualified **10** acceptable, applicable, authorized, worthwhile **11** appropriate

Elihu
brother: **5** David
friend: **3** Job **6** Bildad, Zophar **7** Eliphaz

Elijah
opposed: **4** Ahab, Baal **7** Jezebel
successor: **6** Elisha

Elimelech
wife: **5** Naomi

eliminate 4 drop, omit, oust **5** eject, erase, exile, expel **6** banish, cut out, delete, except, reject, remove, rub out **7** abolish, cast out, dismiss, exclude, weed out **8** get rid of, leave out, stamp out, throw out **9** eradicate **10** annihilate, do away with **11** exterminate

Eliot, George
real name: **13** Mary Anne Evans
author of: **6** Romola **8** Adam Bede **11** Middlemarch, Silas Marner **17** The Mill on the Floss

Eliot, John
author of: **12** Bay Psalm Book

Eliot, T S
author of: **9** East Coker, Gerontion, Hollow Men **11** Burnt Norton, Dry Salvages **12** Ash Wednesday, Four Quartets, The Waste Land **13** Little Gidding, The Sacred Wood **16** The Family Reunion **20** Murder in the Cathedral **27** Sweeney Among the Nightingales **28** The Love Song of J Alfred Prufrock

Eliphaz
father: **4** Adah, Esau
friend: **3** Job **5** Elihu **6** Bildad, Zophar

Elisabeth *see* **9** Elizabeth

Elisha
home: **11** Abelmeholah
succeeded: **6** Elijah

Elissa
origin: **10** Phoenician
corresponds to: **4** Dido

elite 3 top **4** best **5** cream **6** choice, flower **7** bigwigs, society, the pick, wealthy **8** big shots, notables **9** haut monde **10** blue bloods, personages, select body, upper class **11** aristocracy, celebrities, high society **14** creme-de-la-creme

elixir 7 essence, extract, spirits **8** tincture **11** concentrate **17** alcoholic solution

Eliza
character in: **14** Uncle Tom's Cabin
author: **5** Stowe

Elizabeth
husband: **9** Zacharias, Zechariah
son: **14** John the Baptist

Elizabeth I
queen of: **7** England
father: **10** Henry Tudor **14** Henry the Eighth
mother: **10** Anne Boleyn
sister: **4** Mary **10** Bloody Mary
brother: **14** Edward the Sixth
advisor: **5** Cecil **8** Burghley **10** Walsingham
suitor: **5** Essex **6** Dudley **9** Leicester
victory over: **13** Spanish Armada

Elizabeth II
father: **14** George the Sixth
mother: **9** Elizabeth
husband: **17** Philip Mountbatten
son: **6** Andrew, Edward **7** Charles
daughter: **4** Anne

Elizabeth the Queen
author: **15** Maxwell Anderson

elk
group of: **4** gang

Ellas *see* **6** Greece

Elli
origin: **12** Scandinavian
personifies: **5** aging
defeated: **4** Thor
sport: **9** wrestling

Ellice Islands *see* **6** Tuvalu

Ellington, Duke
real name: **22** Edward Kennedy Ellington
born: **12** Washington DC
composer of: **10** Mood Indigo **14** Creole Love Call, Creole Rhapsody, Hot and Bothered **17** Concerto for Cootie **18** Black and Tan Fantasy

Elliot family
characters in: **10** Persuasion
member: **4** Anne **7** William **9** Elizabeth, Sir Walter
author: **6** Austen

Ellison, Harlan
author of: **7** Paingod **10** Spider Kiss **13** A Boy and His Dog **16** Deathbird Stories **19** Approaching Oblivion **20** Alone Against Tomorrow

Ellison, Ralph
author of: **12** Invisible Man

elm 5 Ulmus
varieties: **3** red **4** bush, cork, rock, vase, wych **5** cedar, Dutch, dwarf, globe, wahoo, water, white **6** Exeter, horned, Jersey, moline, Scotch, willow, winged **7** Belgian, Chinese, Cornish, English, Holland **8** American, fern-leaf, Guernsey, Japanese, Siberian, slippery, tabletop, wheatley **9** September **10** camperdown, Chichester, Huntingdon, smooth-leaf **11** small-leaved **13** European white

Elmer Gantry
author: **13** Sinclair Lewis
director: **13** Richard Brooks
cast: **10** Dean Jagger **11** Jean Simmons **12** Shirley Jones **13** Arthur Kennedy, Burt Lancaster
Oscar for: **5** actor (Lancaster) **17** supporting actress (Jones)

elocution 6 speech **7** diction, oratory **10** intonation **11** enunciation **12** articulation **13** pronunciation **14** public speaking

Elohim 3 God

Eloisa to Abelard
author: **13** Alexander Pope

Elon 11 Hebrew judge

elongate 6 extend **7** draw out, prolong **8** lengthen, protract **10** stretch out

elongated 4 long **8** drawn out, extended **9** prolonged **10** attenuated, lengthened, protracted **12** stretched out

eloquence 5 force, grace **7** fluency, oratory **8** rhetoric **9** elocution, speakwell, vividness **10** expression **12** silver tongue
god of: **4** Ogma **6** Ogmios **7** Mercury

eloquent 5 vivid **6** moving, poetic **8** emphatic, forceful, spir-

ited, stirring, striking
10 articulate, passionate, persuasive **11** impassioned

Elpenor
companion of: **7** Ulysses
8 Odysseus

El Salvador *see box*

Elscheimer, Adam
born: **7** Germany **15** Frankfurt am Main
artwork: **17** Tobias and the
Angel **21** The Stoning of St
Stephen **24** Rest on the
Flight into Egypt

else 3 and, too **4** also, more
5 if not, other **7** besides, instead **9** different, otherwise
10 additional, contrarily, in
addition

elsewhere 4 away **6** except
7 absence, not here

Elsinore
castle in: **6** Hamlet
author: **11** Shakespeare

Elton, Mr
character in: **4** Emma
author: **6** Austen

elucidate 6 detail **7** clarify,
clear up, explain, expound
8 describe, spell out **9** delineate, explicate, interpret, make
plain **10** illuminate, illustrate
11 comment upon **14** throw
light upon

elucidation 7 account **10** commentary **11** description,
explanation, explication
13 clarification **14** interpretation **15** exemplification

elude 4 shun **5** avoid, dodge,
evade **6** escape, slip by **10** cir-

cumvent, fight shy of **11** get
away from, keep clear of

eluding 7 dodging, ducking,
evading, evasion **8** avoiding
9 avoidance **12** escaping from,
sidestepping **13** circumventing
15 getting away from

Elul 16 sixth Hebrew month

elusive 4 foxy, wily **6** crafty,
shifty, tricky **7** evasive **8** baffling, puzzling, slippery
11 hard to catch, hard to
grasp

elusory 4 wily **6** shifty **7** devious, dodging, elusive, eva-
sive, hedging **8** slippery
9 ambiguous, deceitful, deceptive, equivocal **10** misleading
12 equivocating

Elvsted, Thea
character in: **11** Hedda
Gabler
author: **5** Ibsen

elysian 7 sublime **8** blissful,
empyreal, empyrean, ethereal,
heavenly **9** celestial,
unearthly **12** otherworldly,
paradisiacal

Elysium
also: **17** islands of the blest
afterworld of the: **7** blessed

Elytis, Odysseus
real name: **19** Odysseus
Alepoudelis
author of: **10** Seemly It Is
20 Heroic and Elegiac Song

emaciated 4 lank, lean, thin
5 gaunt **6** sickly, skinny,
wasted **7** haggard, scrawny,
wizened **8** skeletal, starving,
underfed **10** cadaverous
14 undernourished

emanate 4 flow, rise, stem,
well **5** exude, issue **6** spring
7 give off, proceed **8** come
from **9** come forth, originate,
send forth

emanation 6 coming **7** arising,
flowing, issuing **8** effusion
9 effluence, radiation, springing **10** exhalation **11** coming
forth

emancipate 4 free **7** manumit,
release, set free, unchain
8 liberate, unfetter **9** unshackle **12** set at liberty

emancipation 7 freedom, liberty **10** liberation **11** manumission **12** independence

emasculate 4 geld **5** alter
6 soften, weaken **8** castrate
9 undermine **10** devitalize

Emathion
father: **8** Tithonus
mother: **3** Eos
brother: **6** Memnon

El Salvador
other name: **9** Cuscatlan
capital/largest city: **11** San Salvador
others: **6** Cutuco, Izalco **7** Corinto, Metapan **8** Acajutla,
Libertad, Santa Ana, Usulutan **9** San Miguel, Sonsonate
10 San Vicente, Santa Tecla **11** Union-Cutuco
12 Chalatenango
school: **15** Jose Simeon Canas **16** Alberto Masferrer
measure: **4** vara **5** cafiz, cahiz **6** fanega **7** batella, botella,
cantara, manzana
monetary unit: **4** peso **5** colon **7** centavo
weight: **3** bag **4** caja **5** libra
lake: **5** Guiha, Guija **8** Ilopango **10** Coatepeque
mountain: **6** Izalco
highest point: **8** Santa Ana
river: **5** Jiboa, Lempa, Lopaz **6** Torola **7** de la Paz **9** Goa-
soaran **17** Grande de San Miguel
sea: **7** Pacific
physical feature:
bay: **10** Jiquilisco
coast: **6** Balsam
gulf: **7** Fonseca
point: **7** Amapala **8** Remedios
valley: **7** Hamacas
people: **5** Lenca, Pipil **6** Indian, Mangue **7** mestizo, Spanish **9** Matagalpa
artist: **8** Salarrue **10** Mejia Vides
author: **8** Salarrue **14** Antonio Gavidia
conqueror: **8** Alvarado
leader: **6** Osorio **8** Jose Arce **13** Matias Delgado
15 Manuel Rodriguez **17** Hernandez Martinez
philosopher/journalist: **9** Masferrer
language: **7** Spanish
religion: **13** Roman Catholic
place:
ruins: **7** Tazumal
feature:
blouse: **9** volcanena
dance: **7** pasillo **15** los historiantes
drum: **8** huehuetl
estate: **5** finca
musical instrument: **7** caramba
food:
bread: **10** quesadilla
cheese pancake: **6** pupusa

Emaux et Camees
  author: **16** Theophile Gautier

Embalming
  god of: **6** Anubis

embankment 4 bank, dike,
wall **5** levee

embargo 3 ban **8** shutdown,
stoppage **10** impediment, inhibition, injunction, quarantine, standstill **11** prohibition,
restriction **12** interdiction, proscription **16** restraint of trade

embark 5 begin, board, start
6 launch, set out **7** enplane,
entrain **8** commence, go
aboard **9** board ship, enter
upon

embark on 5 begin, start
8 approach, commence, initiate, set about **9** enter upon,
undertake

embarras de richesses
13 overabundance **21** embarrassment of riches

embarrass 4 faze **5** abash,
shame, upset **6** rattle **7** agitate,
chagrin, confuse, fluster, mortify, nonplus **8** distress **9** discomfit **10** discompose,
disconcert **13** make ill at
ease **14** discountenance
17 make self-conscious

embarrassed 7 abashed **8** red-
faced **9** chagrined, mortified
10 nonplussed **11** discomfited
13 self-conscious

embarrassing 7 awkward
8 confused, crushing **9** bother-
ing **10** disturbing, mortifying,
unpleasant **12** demoralizing,
discomfiting **13** discomforting,
disconcerting, uncomfortable

embarrassment 4 blot
5 stain **6** smirch **7** blemish,
scandal, tarnish **8** disgrace
9 discredit **19** financial
difficulty

embarrassment of riches
  French: **19** embarras de
  richesses

embattled 8 fighting **9** embroiled, fortified **11** battle-
ready, hard-pressed

embed 3 fix, set **4** bond
5 plant **6** fasten **8** ensconce
9 establish

embedded 3 set **5** fixed
6 bonded **7** engaged, planted
8 immersed, inserted **9** ensconced **11** established

embellish 4 gild **5** adorn,
color **6** set off **7** dress up, enhance, fancy up, garnish,
gussy up **8** beautify, decorate,
ornament **9** elaborate, embroider **10** exaggerate

embellished 6 ornate
7 adorned, flowery **8** bro-
caded **9** decorated **10** beauti-
fied, elaborated, ornamented,
rhetorical **11** embroidered

embellishment 5 frill **6** accent **7** garnish **8** furbelow, ornament, trimming
9 adornment **10** decoration,
embroidery **11** elaboration
14 beautification **15** fuss and
feathers

ember 3 ash **4** slag **6** cinder
7 clinker **8** live coal

embezzle 4 bilk, rook **5** cheat,
filch **6** fleece **7** defraud, swindle **9** defalcate
14 misappropriate

embezzler 5 cheat, crook,
thief **8** swindler

Embezzler, The
  author: **16** Louis Auchincloss

embitter 4 sour **6** rankle **7** envenom **10** make bitter
11 make cynical **13** make rancorous, make resentful
15 make pessimistic

embittered 6 soured **7** cynical
9 rancorous, resentful
11 acrimonious

Embla
  origin: **12** Scandinavian
  first: **5** woman
  made by: **4** gods
  made from: **4** tree

emblem 4 sign **5** badge **6** design, device, symbol **7** insigna
8 colophon, hallmark

emblematic 7 typical **8** symbolic **10** indicative **11** distinctive **14** characteristic,
representative

embodiment 7 epitome, essence **14** representation **15** exemplification, personification

embody 4 fuse **5** blend, merge
6 typify **7** collect, contain, embrace, express, include, realize **8** manifest, organize
9 exemplify, personify, represent, symbolize **10** assimilate
11 consolidate, incorporate
12 substantiate

embolden 7 fortify, hearten,
inspire **8** inspirit **9** encourage

emboldened 6 poised **7** assured, unfazed **9** confident,
heartened, unabashed **10** courageous, encouraged, inspirited

embonpoint 9 plumpness,
stoutness **15** in good condition

emboss 4 knob, knot, stud
5 adorn, chase **6** indent **7** engrave, exhaust **8** decorate

embossed 4 bold **6** raised

7 adorned, antique, knotted
8 engraved, indented **9** decorated, exhausted

embrace 3 hug **5** adopt, clasp,
cover, grasp **6** accept, embody
7 contain, espouse, include, involve **8** comprise **9** encompass
10 comprehend **11** consolidate,
incorporate

embroider 5 color **7** dress up
9 elaborate, embellish, fabricate **10** exaggerate
11 romanticize

embroidery 8 tapestry
9 adornment, gros point
10 crewelwork, decoration,
needlework, petit point
11 imagination **12** exaggeration **13** ornamentation

embroil 4 trap **6** enmesh **7** ensnare, involve **8** entangle
10 complicate

embroiled 8 enmeshed **9** embattled, entangled **11** hard-
pressed

embroilment 3 row **4** fray,
tilt **5** brawl, brush, clash, melee **6** fracas, ruckus, rumpus,
uproar **7** scuffle **8** conflict, disorder, struggle **9** confusion,
imbroglio **10** contention
11 altercation **12** entanglement

embryo 3 bud, egg **4** germ
5 fetus, larva, ovule **6** budding,
source **8** immature, rudiment
9 beginning **11** rudimentary,
undeveloped

embryonic 5 rough **6** unborn
7 nascent **8** immature, inchoate **9** beginning, imperfect,
incipient **10** incomplete, unfinished **11** rudimentary,
undeveloped

emend 6 change, revise **7** correct, improve, rectify

emendation 8 revision **10** alteration, correction
11 improvement

emerald
  species: **5** beryl
  source: **4** Muzo **5** Egypt, India **6** Chivor **8** Colombia,
  Rhodesia, Zimbabwe
  11 South Africa, Soviet Union **13** Ural Mountains
  color: **5** green

Emerald City
  setting in: **13** The Wizard of
  Oz
  author: **4** Baum

Emerald Isle see **7** Ireland

emerge 3 run **4** dawn, emit,
flow, gush, loom, pour, rise
5 arise, issue **6** appear, come
up, crop up, escape, stream,
turn up **7** develop, surface
9 come forth, discharge

11 come to light **12** come into view **13** become visible **14** become apparent, become manifest

emergence 4 dawn **7** dawning **10** appearance **11** development **13** coming to light, manifestation **15** materialization

emergency 5 pinch **6** crisis **7** urgency **8** exigency **11** contingency, predicament **16** unforeseen danger

Emergency
character: **8** (Dr) Joe Early, (Paramedic) John Gage **9** (Paramedic) Roy DeSoto **11** (Nurse) Dixie McCall **13** (Dr) Kelly Brackett
cast: **10** Bobby Troup, Kevin Tighe **11** Julie London **12** Robert Fuller **16** Randolph Mantooth

Emerson, Ralph Waldo
nickname: **13** Sage of Concord
author of: **4** Fate **6** Brahma, Nature **10** Friendship, The Rhodora **12** Compensation, Self-Reliance **14** The Concord Hymn **18** The American Scholar
philosophy: **17** Transcendentalism

emeute 4 riot

emigrant 6 emigre **8** wanderer, wayfarer **10** expatriate

Emigrants, The
author: **10** Johan Bojer

emigrate 4 move, quit **5** leave **6** depart, remove **7** migrate

emigration 5 exile **6** exodus **12** expatriation

emigre 2 DP **5** alien, exile **7** evacuee, expellee **8** defector, emigrant, expellee, fugitive **9** immigrant **10** expatriate **15** displaced person **16** political refugee

Emile
author: **19** Jean Jacques Rousseau
treatise on: **9** education

Emilia
character in: **7** Othello
author: **11** Shakespeare

eminence 4 fame, hill, note, peak, rise **5** bluff, cliff, glory, knoll, ridge **6** height, repute, summit, upland **7** hillock, hummock **8** mountain, standing **9** celebrity, elevation, greatness, high place, high point **10** excellence, importance, notability, prominence, promontory, reputation **11** distinction, preeminence

12 elevated rank, high position, public esteem **15** conspicuousness

eminence grise 15 unofficial power
literally: **12** gray eminence

eminent 3 top **5** grand, great, noted **6** famous, signal, utmost **7** exalted, notable, unusual **8** elevated, esteemed, glorious, imposing, laureate, renowned **9** important, memorable, paramount, prominent, well-known **10** celebrated, noteworthy, preeminent, remarkable **11** high-ranking, illustrious, outstanding **13** distinguished, extraordinary

emir 4 amir, Arab, Turk **5** chief, emeer, ruler **6** leader, prince **9** chieftain, commander, dignitary

emissary 5 agent, envoy **6** deputy, herald, legate **7** courier **8** delegate **9** go-between, messenger **10** ambassador **14** representative

emission 5 fumes, smoke, waste **8** ejection, emitting, impurity, issuance, voidance **9** discharge, emanation, excretion, expulsion, extrusion, pollutant **10** sending out **11** throwing out **12** transmission

emit 4 beam, give, shed, vent **5** expel, issue **7** cast out, excrete, secrete, send out **8** dispatch, throw out, transmit **9** discharge, give forth, pour forth

Emma
author: **10** Jane Austen
character: **7** Mr Elton **9** Miss Bates, Mrs Weston **11** Jane Fairfax **12** Harriet Smith, Robert Martin **13** Emma Woodhouse **14** Frank Churchill **15** George Knightley

Emmanuel 7 Messiah **11** Jesus Christ
means: **9** God with us

emollient 3 oil **4** balm **5** balmy, cream, salve **6** lotion **7** calming, easeful, healing, unguent **8** allaying, lenitive, ointment, relaxing, soothing **9** assuasive, lubricant, relieving **10** palliative **11** alleviative, restorative

emolument 3 fee, pay **4** gain, wage **6** income, profit, salary **7** benefit, stipend **9** advantage **10** honorarium **12** compensation, remuneration

emotion 4 fear, hate, heat, love, zeal **5** anger, ardor,

pride **6** fervor, sorrow, warmth **7** concern, despair, passion, sadness **8** jealousy **9** agitation, happiness, sentiment, vehemence **10** excitement **12** satisfaction

emotional 4 warm **5** fiery **6** ardent, moving **7** fervent, zealous **8** stirring, touching **9** excitable, impetuous, thrilling, wrought-up **10** highstrung, hysterical, passionate, responsive, vulnerable **11** impassioned, sentimental, tearjerking **12** enthusiastic, heartwarming, heart-rending, soul-stirring **13** demonstrative, temperamental **14** hypersensitive

emotionalism 8 hysteria **9** gushiness, hysterics, melodrama, theatrics **11** mawkishness **13** melodramatics, show of emotion **14** sentimentality **17** demonstrativeness

emotionless 6 stolid **7** unmoved **9** apathetic, impassive, unfeeling **11** passionless, unemotional

emperor, empress 4 czar, king, shah **5** queen, ruler **6** caesar, kaiser, mikado, sultan **7** czarina, monarch, sultana **9** sovereign **14** dowager empress

Emperor Jones, The
author: **12** Eugene O'Neill
character: **4** Jeff **8** Smithers **11** Brutus Jones

Emperor's New Clothes, The
author: **21** Hans Christian Andersen

emphasis 6 accent, stress, weight **7** feature **10** focal point **12** accentuation, underscoring

emphasize 6 accent, stress **7** dwell on, feature, iterate, point up **9** press home, punctuate, underline **10** accentuate, underscore

emphatic 4 flat **6** marked, strong **7** certain, decided, express, telling **8** absolute, decisive, definite, distinct, forceful, striking, vigorous **9** assertive, insistent, momentous **10** pronounced, undeniable, unwavering, unyielding **11** categorical, conspicuous, significant, unequivocal, unqualified **12** unmistakable

empire 4 rule **5** realm **6** domain **8** dominion, imperium **11** sovereignty **12** commonwealth

Empire State
nickname of: **7** New York

Empire State of the South
nickname of: **7** Georgia

Empire Strikes Back, The
director: **13** Irvin Kershner
cast: **10** Kenny Baker, Mark
Hamill (Luke Skywalker)
11 David Prowse, Peter
Mayhew **12** Alec Guinness,
Carrie Fisher (Princess Leia),
Harrison Ford (Han Solo)
14 Anthony Daniels (C3P0)
16 Billy Dee Williams
(Lando Calrissian)
sequel to: **8** Star Wars
sequel: **15** Return of the Jedi

empirical 9 firsthand, practical,
pragmatic **12** experiential,
experimental

employ 3 use **4** hire **5** apply
6 devote, engage, occupy, retain, take on **7** service, utilize
8 exercise, keep busy, put to
use **9** make use of **10** commission, employment
12 retainership

employee 6 member, worker
8 hireling **9** job holder, underling **10** wage earner

employer 4 boss, firm **6** outfit
7 company **8** business **10** proprietor **12** organization
13 establishment

employment 3 job, use **4** line,
task, work **5** chore, field,
trade, using **6** employ **7** calling, pursuit, service **8** business, exercise, exertion,
vocation **9** employing **10** engagement, occupation, profession **11** application,
utilization **13** preoccupation

emporium 5 store **6** bazaar,
market **9** warehouse **10** large
store **12** general store **15** department store

empower 4 vest **5** allow, endow **6** enable, invest, permit
7 license **8** delegate, sanction
9 authorize **10** commission

empress 5 queen, ruler **7** czarina, monarch, sultana
9 sovereign

emprise 7 venture **9** adventure **10** enterprise
11 undertaking

emptied 6 used up **7** drained,
vacated **8** consumed, depleted,
finished **9** evacuated,
exhausted

emptiness 4 void **6** vacuum
7 vacancy **8** bareness **10** barrenness, desolation, hollowness

empty 4 bare, dump, flow,
idle, void **5** banal, drain, inane **6** futile, hollow, vacant
7 aimless, debouch, insipid,
pour out, shallow, trivial, vacuous **8** evacuate **9** discharge,
frivolous, worthless **10** unoccupied **11** meaningless, purposeless, unfulfilled,
uninhabited **13** insignificant

empty space 3 gap **4** void
5 blank **6** cavity, lacuna, vacuum **7** vacancy

Empusae
form: **7** monster
eats: **3** man

empyrean 7 elysian, sublime
8 blissful, heavenly **9** celestial
12 paradisiacal

emu
also: **4** emeu
form: **4** bird
characteristic: **9** nonflying,
three toed

emulate 3 ape **4** copy **5** mimic,
rival **6** follow **7** imitate

emulative 5 model
9 exemplary

enable 3 aid **5** allow **6** assist,
permit **7** benefit, empower,
qualify, support **8** make able
10 capacitate, facilitate
15 make possible for

enact 4 pass **6** decree, ratify
7 approve **8** proclaim, sanction **9** authorize, institute, legislate **11** pass into law **12** vote
to accept

enactment 3 law **4** bill **5** canon, edict, ukase **6** decree
7 statute **9** ordinance, prescript **11** legislation **12** proclamation, ratification

Enalus
loved: **7** Phineis
saved by: **7** dolphin

enamel 4 coat **5** paint **7** coating **12** glossy finish, tooth
coating

enamor 5 charm **6** allure, attach, draw to, excite **7** bewitch, enchant **8** enthrall,
entrance **9** captivate, enrapture, fascinate, infatuate
12 take a fancy to

enamored 6 in love **7** amorous **8** lovesick **10** infatuated

en arriere 8 backward

en avant 6 onward **7** forward

en bloc 8 as a whole

encage 3 pen **4** cage **5** pen in
6 coop up, lock up, shut in
7 confine **8** restrain
11 incarcerate

encamp 4 camp **7** bivouac
9 set up camp **10** pitch a tent

encampment 4 camp **5** tents
7 bivouac **8** tent city

encase 4 wrap **5** cover **6** enfold, enwrap **7** enclose, envelop, sheathe

enceinte 8 pregnant

Enceladus
form: **5** giant
hit by: **5** stone
stone flung by: **6** Athena
location: **6** Sicily
buried under: **9** Mount Etna

enchain 7 enslave, shackle
8 enthrall **11** put in chains
13 hold in bondage

enchant 5 charm **7** bewitch,
delight **8** enthrall, entrance
9 captivate, enrapture, fascinate, hypnotize, mesmerize,
transport **14** cast a spell over
16 place under a spell

enchanted 7 charmed,
pleased **9** bewitched, delighted,
entranced **10** captivated, enraptured, enthralled, spellbound **11** under a spell

enchanting 8 charming, pleasant **9** agreeable, wonderful
10 bewitching, delightful, entrancing **11** captivating, enthralling, fascinating,
hypnotizing **12** spellbinding
15 casting a spell on **17** casting a spell over

enchantment 5 spell **6** allure,
appeal **9** magnetism **10** attraction **11** captivation, fascination

enchantress 4 vamp **5** siren,
witch **7** charmer, vampire
9 sorceress, temptress **10** seductress **11** femme fatale

Enchiridion
author: **11** St Augustine

encircle 4 gird, ring, wall
5 fence, hem in **6** circle, girdle **7** enclose, wreathe **8** surround **9** encompass
12 circumscribe

enclose, inclose 4 ring **6** circle, girdle, insert, wall in
7 close in, fence in, include
8 encircle, surround **9** encompass, send along
12 circumscribe

enclosed area 4 quad **5** court,
patio **6** atrium **9** courtyard
10 quadrangle

enclosure 3 sty **4** cage, coop,
jail, wall **5** fence, hedge, stall
6 corral, kennel, pigsty **7** pad-
dock, wrapper **8** envelope,
stockade **9** cartridge, inclosure
10 receptacle

encomium 5 paean **6** eulogy
7 plaudit, tribute **8** citation

9 laudation, panegyric
11 acclamation

encompass 4 hold, ring
5 cover, hem in **6** circle, embody, girdle, take in, wall in
7 contain, embrace, enclose, fence in, include, involve, touch on **8** comprise, encircle, surround **11** incorporate
12 circumscribe

encounter 4 bout, face, meet
5 brush, clash, fight **6** affray, battle, combat, endure, fracas, suffer **7** run into, sustain, undergo **8** come upon, confront, meet with, skirmish **9** clash with **10** chance upon, engagement, experience **11** grapple with **12** do battle with, meet and fight, skirmish with
13 confrontation **14** contend against, engage in combat, hostile meeting **18** come face to face with

Encounters with the Archdruid
author: **10** John McPhee

encourage 3 aid **4** help, spur, sway **5** boost, cheer, egg on, favor, impel, rally **6** assist, exhort, foster, induce, prompt
7 advance, forward, further, hearten, inspire, promote
8 embolden, inspirit, reassure
10 give hope to

encouragement 4 lift **5** boost
6 praise **7** backing, support
11 approbation, encouraging, reassurance **12** shot in the arm **13** reinforcement

encroach 6 invade **7** impinge, intrude, overrun, violate **8** infringe, overstep, trespass
9 break into, interfere
10 transgress **11** make inroads

encumber 3 tax **4** lade, load
6 burden, hinder, impede, saddle **8** handicap, load down, obstruct, slow down **9** weigh down **13** inconvenience

encumbrance 4 load, onus
6 burden **9** hindrance **10** impediment **11** obstruction
13 inconvenience

Encyclopedia
author: **9** D'Alembert
12 Denis Diderot

encyclopedic 5 broad **7** erudite **9** scholarly, universal
10 exhaustive **11** wideranging **13** comprehensive
15 all-encompassing

end 3 aim **4** edge, goal, halt, kill, ruin, stop **5** cease, close, death, issue, limit, scrap
6 border, demise, design, effect, ending, finale, finish, object, result, run out, upshot,

windup **7** destroy, outcome, purpose, remnant **8** boundary, conclude, fragment, leave off, leftover, terminus **9** cessation, eradicate, extremity, finish off, intention, objective, terminate
10 annihilate, completion, conclusion, denouement, expiration, extinction, extinguish, put an end to, settlement
11 consequence, culmination, destruction, exterminate, fulfillment, termination **12** annihilation, consummation, draw to a close **13** extermination
. 19 bring down the curtain

endanger 4 risk **6** expose, hazard **7** imperil **8** threaten
10 compromise, jeopardize
11 put in danger

endear 8 make dear **10** ingratiate **11** make beloved

endearment 7 pet name
9 sweet talk **10** loving word
12 sweet nothing **13** fond utterance

endeavor 3 aim, job, try
4 seek, work **5** essay, labor
6 aspire, career, effort, strive, work at **7** attempt **8** exertion, interest, striving, struggle, vocation **9** take pains, undertake **10** do one's best, enterprise, occupation **11** undertaking **12** make an effort
13 preoccupation

ended 4 done, over **6** ceased, closed, halted, runout **7** expired, stopped, wound up
8 finished, over with, resulted
9 completed, concluded, destroyed **10** terminated **11** annihilated **12** discontinued, exterminated

Endeis
father: **6** Sciron
husband: **6** Aeacus
son: **6** Peleus **7** Telamon
stepson: **6** Phocus

Enderby
author: **14** Anthony Burgess

end from which
Latin: **12** terminus a quo

ending 3 end **5** close **6** finale, finish, windup **9** cessation
10 completion, conclusion, expiration **11** culmination, termination **12** consummation

ending point
Latin: **14** terminus ad quem

Ending Up
author: **12** Kingsley Amis

endless 7 eternal **8** constant, infinite, unbroken, unending
9 boundless, continual, perpetual, unlimited **10** continuous, persistent, without end **11** everlasting, measureless, never-

ending **12** interminable
13 uninterrupted

endlessly 7 forever **10** constantly **11** ceaselessly, continually, perpetually
12 continuously
Latin: **11** ad infinitum

endocrine system
component: **5** ovary **6** testes, thymus **7** adrenal, thyroid
9 pituitary **11** parathyroid

endocuticle
consists of: **6** chitin

end of the century
French: **11** fin de siecle

End of the Road, The
author: **9** John Barth

end of the world 8 doomsday **10** Armageddon **11** Judgment Day **13** Day of Judgment **15** the Last Judgment

End of the World News, The
author: **14** Anthony Burgess

endorse, indorse 2 OK
4 back, sign **6** affirm, ratify, second **7** approve, certify, support **8** advocate, champion, sanction, validate, vouch for
9 authorize, recommend
11 countersign, stand behind, subscribe to **14** lend one's name to

endorsement 2 OK **7** support
8 approval **9** signature **10** acceptance **12** commendation, ratification **14** seal of approval **16** official sanction

endow 4 will **5** award, bless, equip, favor, grace, grant, leave **6** accord, bestow, confer, invest, supply **7** furnish, provide **8** bequeath, settle on

endowed 6 graced **7** blessed, favored **8** bestowed, enriched, provided **10** bequeathed

endowment 4 gift **5** award, flair, grant **6** legacy, talent
7 ability, bequest, faculty
8 aptitude, donation **9** attribute **10** capability **11** benefaction, natural gift

end to which
Latin: **14** terminus ad quem

endue 5 dress, endow, equip, indue, put on **6** bestow, clothe, outfit, supply **7** furnish

endurable 8 bearable **9** tolerable **11** sustainable

endurance 7 stamina
8 strength, tenacity **9** fortitude, hardihood, stability **10** durability, permanence, resolution
11 durableness, persistence
12 immutability, perseverance,

staying power **13** tenaciousness **14** changelessness **16** stick-to-itiveness

endure 4 bear, last, live **5** brave, brook, stand **6** live on, remain, suffer **7** persist, prevail, sustain, undergo, weather **8** continue, cope with, tolerate **9** go through, withstand **10** experience **11** bear up under, countenance

enduring 7 abiding, durable, eternal, lasting **8** constant, unending **9** immutable, permanent, steadfast **10** changeless, continuing, unchanging **11** everlasting, long-lasting **12** indissoluble

Endymion
author: **9** John Keats
form: **5** youth
father: **8** Aethlios
mother: **6** Calyce
loved by: **4** Moon **6** Selene
son: **5** Epeus, Paeon **7** Aetolus
number of daughters: **5** fifty
granddaughter: **7** Hyrmina

enemy 3 foe **5** rival **7** nemesis **8** armed foe, attacker, opponent **9** adversary, assailant, detractor **10** antagonist, competitor

Enemy of the People, An
author: **11** Henrik Ibsen

energetic 5 alert, brisk, peppy, zippy **6** active, lively, robust **7** dynamic **8** animated, forceful, restless, spirited, vigorous **9** go-getting **11** hard-working, high-powered, industrious, quick-witted **12** enthusiastic

energize 7 animate, enliven, quicken **8** vitalize **9** galvanize, stimulate **10** invigorate, strengthen

energy 2 go **3** pep, vim, zip **4** elan, zeal, zest **5** drive, force, power, verve, vigor **6** hustle **8** dynamism, vitality, vivacity **9** animation **10** enterprise, liveliness

enervate 3 fag. **4** bush, tire **5** weary **6** tucker, weaken **7** deplete, disable, exhaust, fatigue, wash out **8** enfeeble **9** prostrate **10** debilitate, devitalize **13** sap one's energy

enervated 5 spent **6** effete, wasted **7** languid, worn-out **8** fatigued, listless, sluggish, unmanned, unnerved, weakened **9** enfeebled, exhausted, lethargic, washed out **11** debilitated, devitalized, emasculated

enervation 7 fatigue **9** tiredness, weariness **10** exhaustion

en famille 11 in the family

Enfants Terribles, Les
author: **11** Jean Cocteau

enfant terrible 16 indiscreet person **17** incorrigible child **19** irresponsible person

enfeeble 3 sap **6** impair, weaken **8** enervate **10** debilitate

enfin 7 finally **8** in the end **12** in conclusion

enfold 4 veil, wrap **5** cloak, cover **6** encase, enwrap, shroud **7** blanket, contain, embrace, enclose, envelop, sheathe **8** surround

enforce 5 apply, exact **6** defend, impose **7** execute, support **8** carry out, insist on **9** implement **10** administer

enforcement 5 force **6** duress **7** defense, support **8** coercion, pressure **9** execution **10** compulsion, constraint, imposition, obligation **11** carrying out **13** necessitation, strengthening **14** implementation

engage 4 hire **6** absorb, combat, employ, occupy, pledge, retain, secure, take on **7** betroth, engross, involve, partake, promise, war with **8** affiance, embark on, set about, takepart **9** enter into, fight with, undertake **10** commission **11** busy oneself, participate **12** give battle to **15** take into service

engaged 5 hired, in use **6** active, took on **7** partook, pledged, secured **8** absorbed, employed, involved, occupied, promised, retained, took part **9** affianced, betrothed, engrossed, undertook **10** embarked on **11** entered into, particpated **15** took into service

engagement 3 gig, job **4** bout, date, duty, fray, post **5** banns, berth, brush, fight, troth **6** action, battle, billet, combat **7** contest, meeting, scuffle **8** conflict, position, skirmish **9** betrothal, encounter, situation **10** affiancing, commitment, employment, obligation **11** appointment, arrangement

engage pleasantly 5 amuse, charm **6** divert, please **7** beguile, delight **8** enthrall, interest **9** entertain

engaging 7 likable, lovable, winning, winsome **8** charming, fetching, pleasing **9** agreeable, appealing, disarming **10** attractive, enchanting **11** captivating **12** ingratiating

Engels, Friedrich
author of: **18** Communist Manifesto (with Karl Marx)

engender 5 beget, breed, cause **7** produce **8** generate, occasion **10** bring about, give rise to **11** precipitate

engine
inventor:
 of compression ignition: **7** Daimler
 of electric ignition: **4** Benz
 of gas (compound): **10** Eickemeyer
 of gasoline: **7** Brayton, Daimler
 of piston steam: **4** Watt **8** Newcomen

engineer 5 pilot **6** driver, hogger **7** builder, hoghead, planner **8** maneuver, motorman, operator **10** accomplish

England *see box*

Engles, Friedrich
author of: **18** Communist Manifesto (with Karl Marx)

English, Julian
character in: **20** Appointment in Samarra
author: **5** O'Hara

English Mail-Coach, The
author: **15** Thomas DeQuincey

engrave 3 cut **4** etch **5** carve, stamp **6** chisel **7** decorate, stipple

engraving 3 cut, die **5** print, stamp **7** etching, gravure **9** woodblock **11** copperplate, lithography **12** photogravure

engross 4 hold **6** absorb, arrest, engage, occupy, take up **7** immerse, involve **9** preoccupy

engrossed 4 busy, deep **6** intent **7** engaged **8** absorbed, immersed, involved, occupied **11** preoccupied

engrossing 8 engaging, exciting **9** absorbing, arresting, thrilling **10** intriguing **11** captivating, fascinating, interesting

engrossment 9 immersion **10** absorption, intentness **11** involvement **13** concentration, preoccupation

engulf 4 bury **5** swamp **6** deluge **7** envelop, immerse, overrun **8** inundate, submerge **9** swallow up

enhance 4 lift **5** add to, boost, raise **7** augment, elevate, magnify **8** heighten, redouble **9** embellish, intensify **10** complement

England
other name: 6 Albion **7** Britain **9** Britannia **12** Great Britain
capital/largest city: 6 London
others: 3 Ely **4** Bath, Deal, Hull, Ryde, Ware, York **5** Blyth, Brent, Derby, Dover, Erith, Flint, Leeds, Ripon, Truro, Wigan **6** Barnet, Bolton, Bootle, Camden, Durham, Ealing, Exeter, Henley, Jarrow, Leyton, Oldham, Oxford, Yeovil **7** Bristol, Bromley, Burnley, Chelsea, Croydon, Enfield, Grimsby, Halifax, Hornsey, Ipswich, Lambeth, Newport, Norwich, Preston, Salford, **8** Bradford, Brighton, Cornwall, Coventry, Dewsbury, Hastings, Plymouth **9** Greenwich, Liverpool, Newcastle, Sheffield **10** Birmingham, Manchester **15** Stratford-on-Avon
school: 4 Eton **5** Leeds, Rugby **6** Harrow, London, Oxford **9** Cambridge, Sandhurst **23** London School of Economics
division: 4 Avon, Kent **5** Devon, Essex, **6** Dorset, Durham, Surrey, Sussex **7** Norfolk, Suffolk **8** Cheshire, Cornwall, Somerset **9** Hampshire, Wiltshire, Yorkshire **10** Derbyshire, East Sussex, Humberside, Lancashire, Merseyside, Shropshire, West Sussex **11** Oxfordshire, Tyne and Wear **12** Bedfordshire, Lincolnshire, Warwickshire, West Midlands **13** Hertfordshire, Staffordshire, West Yorkshire **14** Cambridgeshire, Leicestershire, Northumberland, North Yorkshire, South Yorkshire **15** Buckinghamshire, Gloucestershire, Nottinghamshire **16** Northamptonshire **20** Hereford and Worcester
head of state: 4 king **5** queen **7** monarch
measure: 3 cut, lea, pin, rod, ton, tun, vat **4** acre, bind, butt, comb, coom, foot, gill, goad, hand, hank, heer, hide, inch, last, line, mile, nail, pace, palm, peck, pint, pipe, pole, pool, rood, rope, sack, seam, span, trug, typp, wist, yard, yoke **5** bodge, chain, coomb, cubit, digit, float, floor, fluid, hutch, jugum, minim, ounce, perch, point, prime, quart, skein, stack, truss **6** barrel, bovate, bushel, cranne, fathom, firkin, gallon, hobbet, hobbit, league, manent, oxgang, pottle, runlet, square, strike, sulung, thread, tierce **7** auchlet, furlong, kenning, quarter, rundlet, seamile, spindle, tertian, virgate **8** carucate, chaldron, hogshead, landyard, puncheon, quadrant, standard
monetary unit: 3 ora **4** rial **5** ackey, crown, groat, noble, pence, penny, pound, sprat, unite **6** bawbee, florin, guinea, seskin **7** angelet, hapenny **8** farthing, shilling, sixpence, tuppence
weight: 3 bag, kip, tod, ton **4** keel, last, mast, maun **5** barge, fagot, grain, pound, score, stone, truss **6** bushel, cental, fangot, fother, fotmal, pocket **7** quarter, sarpler
island: 3 Man **4** Holy **5** Farne, Lundy, Wight **6** Coquet, Mersea, Scilly, Thanet, Tresco, Walney **7** Bardsey, Channel, Hayling, Ireland, Sheppey **8** Anglesea, Anglesey, Foulness, Holyhead
lake: 8 Grasmere **9** Ennerdale, Ullswater, Wastwater **10** Buttermere, Windermere **12** Derwentwater **13** Coniston Water
mountain: 5 Black **7** Pennine, Snowdon **8** Cambrian, Cumbrian
hill: **6** Formby, Lizard, Mendip **7** Brendon, Cemmaes, Trevose
highest point: 11 Scafell Pike
river: 3 Cam, Dee, Don, Esk, Exe, Lea, Nen, Ure, Wye **4** Aire, Avon, Eden, Lune, Nene, Nidd, Ouse, Penk, Tame, Tees, Till, Tyne, Wear, Yare **5** Anker, Colne, Deben, Stour, Swale, Tamar, Tawar, Trent, Tweed **6** Humber, Kennet, Mersey, Rother, Severn, Thames, Wharfe, Witham **7** Derwent, Parrett, Waveney, Welland **8** Torridge **9** Yorkshire **12** Wensum Ribble
sea: 5 Irish, North **6** Celtic **8** Atlantic
physical feature:
bay: **3** Tor **4** Lyme, Wash **5** Start **6** Mounts **7** Bigbury **8** Bideford, Cardigan, Falmouth, Tremadoc, Weymouth
chalk cliffs: **5** Dover
channel: **6** Solent **7** Bristol, English **8** Spithead
firth: **6** Solway
forest: **5** Arden **6** Exmoor **8** Dartmoor, Sherwood
point: **4** Naze **5** Lynas, Morte, Sales **6** Dodman, Lizard, Prawle **8** Hartland, Landsend
region: **5** Weald **8** Midlands **10** West Riding **11** North Riding **12** Lake District
valley: **4** Coom, Eden, Tees, Tyne **5** Combe, Coomb **6** Coquet
people: 4 Celt, Pict **5** Jutes, Norse, Saxon **6** Angles, Briton, Norman, Viking
artist: **6** Romney, Turner **7** Hogarth **8** Reynolds, Rossetti **9** Constable **12** Gainsborough
author: **3** Kyd **4** Bede, Hume, Pope, Shaw **5** Auden, Bacon, Blake, Burke, Byron, Defoe, Donne, Eliot, Hardy, Joyce, Keats, Scott, Swift, Waugh, Wilde, Woolf **6** Austen, Bronte, Bunyan, Conrad, Dryden, Gibbon, Jonson, Milton, Newton, Ruskin, Sterne, Thomas **7** Boswell, Chaucer, Dickens, Kipling, Marlowe, Shelley, Spenser, Walpole **8** Browning, Fielding, Lawrence, Sheridan, Smollett, Tennyson, Trollope **9** Churchill, Coleridge, Stevenson, Thackeray **10** Galsworthy, Richardson, Thomas More, Wordsworth **11** Shakespeare
king: **3** Hal **4** Cnut, John, Lear **5** Henry, James **6** Alfred, Arthur, Canute, Edmund, Edward, Egbert, George, Harold **7** Charles, Richard, Stephen, William **9** Cymbeline **18** Richard Coeur de Lion **19** Richard the Lionheart
leader: **4** Eden, Grey, Lamb, Peel, Pitt **5** Heath **6** Attlee, Wilson **7** Baldwin, Balfour, Canning, Fitzroy, Spencer, Stanley, Walpole **8** Disraeli, Stanhope, Thatcher **9** Cavendish, Churchill, Gladstone, Grenville, MacDonald, Macmillan **10** Palmerston, Wellington **11** Chamberlain, Douglas-Home, Lloyd George
queen: **3** Mab **4** Anne, Bess, Jane, Mary **7** Eleanor **8** Boadicea, Victoria **9** Catherine, Charlotte, Elizabeth, Guinivere **10** Bloody Mary **11** Jane Seymour

(continued)

England (*continued*)
language: 7 English
religion: 6 Jewish **8** Anglican **9** Methodist, Unitarian **13** Roman Catholic **15** Church of England
place:
  bridge: **5** Tower **6** London **11** Westminster
  cathedral: **4** York **6** Exeter **7** St Pauls **8** St Albans **9** Salisbury **10** Canterbury, Winchester **16** Westminster Abbey
  clock: **6** Big Ben
  fortification: **12** Hadrian's Wall
  museum: **4** Tate **7** British **9** Ashmolean **17** Madame Tussauds Wax
  palace: **7** St James, Windsor **10** Buckingham **12** Hampton Court
  racetrack: **5** Ascot
  ruins: **10** Stonehenge
  street: **5** Fleet **12** Threadneedle **16** Piccadilly Circus
  tower: **6** London
feature:
  dance: **6** morris
food:
  bacon: **6** gammon, rasher **7** streaky
  beer: **5** grout, stout
  cookie: **7** biscuit
  dessert: **6** trifle **11** plum pudding
  dish: **12** fish and chips **14** Cornish pasties **15** bubble and squeak **16** Yorkshire pudding
  drink: **3** ale, tea **6** squash

enhancement 11 heightening, improvement **15** intensification

Enid
  character in: 12 The Mabinogion **15** Idylls of the King **16** Arthurian romance
  author: 8 Tennyson

enigma 6 puzzle, riddle, secret **7** mystery **8** question **9** conundrum **10** perplexity

enigmatic, enigmatical
7 cryptic, elusive **8** baffling, puzzling **9** ambiguous, equivocal, secretive **10** mysterious, perplexing **11** inscrutable, paradoxical **12** unfathomable **14** indecipherable

Eniopeus
  mentioned in: 5 Iliad
  charioteer of: 6 Hector
  slain by: 8 Diomedes

enjoin 3 ask, ban, bar, beg, bid **4** urge, warn **6** advise, charge, direct, forbid **7** command, counsel, entreat **8** admonish, call upon, instruct, prohibit, restrain, restrict **9** interdict, proscribe

enjoy 3 own **4** have, like **5** eat up, fancy, savor **6** admire, relish **7** possess **9** delight in, rejoice in **10** appreciate **11** think well of **13** be blessed with, be pleased with, get a kick out of **14** take pleasure in **16** have the benefit of

enjoyable 8 pleasant, pleasing **9** agreeable, fun-filled, rewarding **10** delightful, gratifying, satisfying **11** pleasurable

enjoyment 3 fun, joy **4** zest **5** gusto, right **6** relish **7** benefit, delight **8** blessing, exercise, good time, pleasure **9** advantage, amusement, diversion, happiness, privilege **10** possession, recreation **11** prerogative **12** satisfaction **13** entertainment, gratification

Enki
  origin: 8 Sumerian
  god of: 6 wisdom
  habitat: 5 water
  corresponds to: 2 Ea

Enkidu
  origin: 8 Sumerian
  servant of: 9 Gilgamesh
  friend of: 9 Gilgamesh

enlarge 4 grow **5** add to, swell, widen **6** expand, extend **7** amplify, augment, broaden, develop, expound, inflate, magnify **8** elongate, increase, lengthen, multiply **9** discourse, elaborate, expatiate

enlarged 7 swollen, widened **8** expanded, extended, inflated **9** amplified, broadened, distended, elongated, magnified

enlargement 6 growth **8** addition, increase, swelling, widening **9** expansion, extension, inflation **10** broadening, elongation **11** development, elaboration, expatiation, lengthening **12** augmentation **13** amplification, magnification **14** multiplication

enlighten 5 edify **6** advise, inform, wise up **7** apprise, clarify, educate **8** civilize, instruct **9** make aware **10** illuminate **12** sophisticate

enlightenment 8 learning **9** erudition, knowledge **11** edification, instruction
  French: 15 Eclaircissement
  German: 10 Aufklarung

Enlil
  origin: 8 Sumerian
  king of: 4 gods
  god of: 3 air
  son: 5 Ninib **7** Ninurta

enlist 4 join **6** engage, enroll, join up, obtain, secure, sign up **7** procure, recruit **8** register **9** volunteer **19** gain the assistance of

enlistment 9 signing up **10** admittance, enrollment, recruiting

enliven 4 fire **5** pep up, renew **6** excite, vivify, wake up **7** animate, cheer up, quicken **8** brighten, vitalize **10** make lively, rejuvenate

enlivened 7 revived **8** animated, vivified **9** refreshed **11** invigorated

en masse 7 in a body **8** as a group, as a whole, in a group, together **11** all together

enmesh 4 trap **5** catch, snare, snarl **6** tangle **7** embroil, ensnare, entwine, involve **8** entangle

enmity 6 animus, hatred, malice, rancor, strife **7** ill will

8 acrimony, bad blood **9** animosity, antipathy, hostility **10** bitterness

Ennead 7 dieties
origin: **8** Egyptian
number: **4** nine

ennoble 5 raise **6** refine **7** dignify, elevate

Ennomus
vocation: **6** angler
joined: **7** Trojans

Ennosigaeus
epithet of: **8** Poseidon
means: **11** earth shaker

ennui 6 apathy, tedium **7** boredom, languor **9** lassitude, weariness **12** indifference, listlessness
Latin: **12** taedium vitae

Enoch
father: **4** Cain **5** Jared
son: **10** Methuselah
grandfather: **4** Adam

Enoch Arden
author: **18** Alfred Lord Tennyson
character: **8** Annie Lee **9** Philip Ray **10** Miriam Lane

enormity 8 baseness, evilness, hugeness, vastness, vileness, villainy **9** depravity, immensity, largeness, malignity **10** wickedness **11** heinousness, viciousness **12** enormousness **13** atrociousness, monstrousness, offensiveness **14** outrageousness

enormous 4 huge, vast **7** immense, mammoth, massive, titanic **8** colossal, gigantic **10** gargantuan, prodigious, tremendous **11** elephantine **14** Brobdingnagian

enormousness 8 enormity, hugeness, vastness **9** amplitude, immensity, largeness **11** massiveness

Enormous Room, The
author: **10** e e cummings

Enos
father: **4** Seth
grandfather: **4** Adam

enough 5 ample, amply **6** plenty **7** copious **8** abundant, adequate, passably **9** tolerably **10** abundantly, adequately, competence, plentitude, reasonably, sufficient **11** ample supply, full measure, sufficiency **12** sufficiently **14** satisfactorily

enounce 8 set forth **9** enunciate **10** articulate

en passant 8 by the way **9** in passing

enrage 5 anger **6** madden **7** incense, inflame **9** aggravate, infuriate **11** make furious **13** make one see red **14** throw into a rage **17** make one's blood boil

enraged 3 mad **5** angry, irate **7** angered, furious, violent **8** incensed, inflamed, maddened, provoked **9** irritated **10** aggravated, infuriated **11** exasperated

en rapport 8 in accord **9** congenial **10** in sympathy **11** in agreement

enrapture 5 charm **6** thrill **7** beguile, bewitch, delight, enchant **8** enthrall, entrance, hold rapt **9** captivate, transport

enraptured 4 rapt **8** beatific, blissful, ecstatic **9** delighted, enchanted **10** enthralled **11** transported

enravel 5 snare, snarl, twist **6** enmesh, tangle **7** ensnare, ensnarl, entwine **8** entangle **10** intertwine

enrich 5 adorn, endow **6** refine **7** elevate, enhance, fortify, improve, upgrade **8** make rich **9** embellish **10** ameliorate **11** make wealthy **15** feather one's nest

enroll 4 join **5** admit, enter **6** accept, engage, enlist, join up, sign up, take on **7** recruit **8** register

enrollment 6 roster **9** enrolling, signing up **10** admittance, enlistment, recruiting **12** registration **13** matriculation

en route 8 on the way **9** in transit, on the road

ensconce 4 bury, hide, seat **5** lodge **6** settle **7** conceal, secrete, shelter **9** establish

ensemble 5 getup **6** attire, outfit, troupe **7** company, costume **8** assembly, entirety, grouping, totality **9** aggregate

ensign 4 flag, jack, mark, sign **5** badge **6** banner, colors, emblem, pennon, symbol **7** pennant **8** insignia, standard

enslave 6 addict, subdue **7** capture, control, enchain, shackle **8** dominate, enthrall **9** indenture, subjugate **13** hold in bondage, put in shackles

enslavement 4 yoke **6** chains, thrall **7** bondage, serfdom, slavery **9** captivity, servitude, thralldom, vassalage **11** subjugation

ensnare 4 trap **5** catch **6** en-

mesh, entrap, tangle **7** enravel **8** entangle

Ensor, James
born: **6** Ostend **7** Belgium
artwork: **8** Intrigue **19** Bourgeois Living Room **25** Entry of Christ into Brussels **26** The Tribulations of St Anthony **29** Self-Portrait Surrounded by Masks

enstatite
source: **5** Burma, Mogok

ensue 6 derive, follow, result **7** succeed **10** come to pass **13** come afterward

ensuing 8 eventual **9** following, resulting **10** consequent, succeeding

en suite 6 in a set **9** in a series **12** in succession

ensure, insure 5 guard **6** assure, clinch, secure **7** protect, warrant **8** be sure of, make safe, make sure **9** guarantee, safeguard **13** make certain of

entail 6 demand **7** call for, include, involve, require **8** occasion **11** incorporate, necessitate

entangle 4 trap **5** catch, mix up, snare, snarl **6** enmesh, foul up, muddle, tangle **7** confuse, embroil, enravel, ensnare, involve **8** encumber **9** embarrass, implicate **10** complicate, compromise, intertwine

entanglement 5 mixup, snarl **6** foul-up, muddle **7** problem **9** confusion, imbroglio **10** difficulty, entrapment **11** embroilment **12** complication

Entellus
vocation: **5** boxer
home: **6** Sicily
defeated: **5** Dares

entente 4 pact **6** accord, treaty **7** compact **8** alliance, covenant **9** agreement, consensus, unanimity **10** consortium **12** conciliation **13** rapprochement, understanding **14** likemindedness

entente cordiale 21 friendly understanding

enter 4 go in, join, list, post **6** arrive, come in, record **8** enlist in, enroll in, inscribe, pass into, set out on, trespass **9** penetrate, sign up for **10** embark upon, take part in

enterprise 4 push, task, zeal **5** drive, vigor **6** daring, effort, energy, spirit **7** attempt, program, project, venture **8** ambition, boldness, campaign, endeavor, industry **9** alertness, eagerness, ingenuity, operation 10 enthusiasm, initiative 11 undertaking, willingness 14 aggressiveness 15 adventurousness

enterprising 4 bold, keen 5 alert, eager 6 active 7 earnest, zealous 8 intrepid 9 ambitious, energetic, inventive, wide-awake 10 aggressive 11 hardworking, industrious, self-reliant, up-and-coming, venturesome 12 enthusiastic

entertain 4 heed 5 admit, amuse, charm 6 absorb, divert, foster, harbor, please, ponder, regale 7 beguile, delight, dwell on, engross, imagine, nurture, support 8 consider, enthrall, interest, muse over, play host 10 cogitate on, give a party, have guests, keep in mind, think about 11 contemplate 13 keep open house

entertainer 4 host 5 actor 6 amuser, artist, dancer, singer 7 hostess 8 magician, musician 9 performer

entertaining 3 fun 7 amusing, hosting 8 charming, pleasing 9 beguiling, diverting, enjoyable 10 delightful, hostessing 11 playing host 12 having guests 14 having people in

entertainment 3 fun 4 play 7 novelty, pastime 8 good time, pleasure 9 amusement, diversion, enjoyment 10 recreation 11 distraction 12 satisfaction French: 14 divertissement

enter upon 5 begin 6 assume 9 undertake

enthrall, enthral 5 charm, rivet 6 seduce, thrill 7 beguile, bewitch, enchant, enslave 8 entrance, intrigue, transfix 9 captivate, enrapture, fascinate, hypnotize, overpower, spellbind, subjugate, transport 13 keep in bondage 14 put into slavery

enthralled 4 rapt 8 beguiled, enslaved 9 bewitched, enchanted, entranced, in bondage, intrigued 10 captivated, enraptured, fascinated, hypnotized, spellbound, subjugated

enthusiasm 4 love, rage, zeal, zest 5 ardor, craze, hobby, mania 6 fervor, relish 7 elation, passion 8 devotion, interest, keenness 9 diversion, eagerness 10 excitement, exuberance, hobbyhorse 11 distraction, pet activity 12 anticipation

enthusiast 3 bug, fan, nut

4 buff 5 freak 6 addict 7 devotee, fanatic 10 aficionado

enthusiastic 5 eager 6 ardent, fervid 7 fervent, zealous 8 spirited 9 exuberant 10 passionate, unstinting 11 unqualified 12 wholehearted

entice 4 coax, lure 5 tempt 6 allure, incite, induce, seduce 7 attract, beguile, wheedle 8 inveigle, persuade

enticement 4 bait, draw, lure 6 allure 9 seduction, siren song 10 attraction, temptation

entire 4 full 5 gross, total, whole 6 in toto, intact 8 absolute, complete, thorough, unbroken 9 undamaged 10 unimpaired 12 all-inclusive

entirely 5 fully 6 wholly 7 totally, utterly 10 absolutely, altogether, completely, thoroughly 12 unreservedly 13 unqualifiedly French: 9 tout a fait

entitle 3 dub, tag 4 call, name 5 allow, label, style, title 6 enable, permit 7 qualify 9 authorize, designate 12 make eligible

entity 4 body 5 being, thing 6 matter, object 7 article 8 creature, presence, quantity 9 real thing, structure, substance 10 individual

entomb 4 bury 5 inter 7 confine

entombment 6 burial 9 interment 10 inhumation

Entommeures, Frere Jean des
　　character in: 22 Gargantua and Pantagruel
　　author: 8 Rabelais

entourage 5 court, staff, suite, train 6 convoy, escort 7 cortege, retinue 9 followers, following 10 associates, attendants, companions

entrails 4 guts 5 offal 6 bowels 7 innards, insides, viscera 10 intestines

entrance 4 door, gate 5 charm, entry, way in 6 access, entree, portal 7 beguile, bewitch, delight, doorway, gateway, gladden, ingress, opening 8 approach, coming in, enthrall 9 captivate, enrapture, fascinate, hypnotize, mesmerize, spellbind, transport 10 admittance, appearance, passageway 12 introduction

entranced 4 rapt 7 charmed 8 beguiled 9 enthralled, rapturous 10 enraptured, fascinated,

spellbound 11 carried away, transported

entranceway 5 entry, foyer, way in 7 doorway, ingress 8 entryway 9 front hall, vestibule

entrancing 6 lovely 8 adorable, charming 9 appealing, beautiful, beguiling, disarming 10 bewitching, delightful 11 captivating, fascinating 12 irresistible

entrap 3 bag, nab 4 hook, land, nail 5 catch, snare, tempt 6 allure, collar, drag in, draw in, entice, rope in, seduce, suck in 7 beguile, capture, ensnare 8 inveigle

entreat 3 beg 6 adjure, enjoin, exhort 7 beseech, implore, request 8 appeal to, petition 9 importune, plead with 10 supplicate

entreaty 4 plea 6 appeal, prayer 8 petition 11 importunity 12 supplication

entree 4 pull 5 entry 6 access 7 ingress 8 entrance, main dish 9 admission 10 acceptance, admittance, main course

entremets 8 side dish

entrench, intrench 3 fix, set 4 root 5 dig in, embed, plant 6 anchor 7 implant, ingrain, install, solidly 8 ensconce 12 establish

entrenched leaders 11 ruling class 12 powers that be 13 Establishment 14 power structure

entre nous 9 between us, privately 14 confidentially 15 between you and me 16 between me and thee, between ourselves 18 in strict confidence

entrepot 5 depot 9 warehouse 18 distribution center

entrepreneur 7 manager 8 director 9 organizer 10 impresario 11 coordinator

entrust, intrust 5 trust 6 assign, commit 7 consign 8 delegate, hand over, turn over 9 authorize 10 charge with

entrustment 10 delegation 13 authorization, commissioning

entry 3 way 4 door, gate, item, memo, note 5 foyer, way in 6 access, entree, minute, portal, record 7 account, doorway, gateway, ingress, jotting 8 approach, entrance 9 admission, vestibule 10 admittance, appearance, competitor, contestant, memorandum, passageway **11** entranceway **12** entrance hall, introduction, registration

entwine, intwine 4 fold, lace, wind **5** braid, plait, twine, twist, weave **9** interlace **10** interweave

enumerable 6 finite **7** limited **11** denumerable

enumerate 3 add **4** cite, list **5** add up, count, sum up, tally, total **6** detail, number, relate **7** count up, recount, specify, tick off **8** numerate, spell out, tabulate

enumeration 4 list **5** tally **7** account, listing **8** adding up, addition, citation, tallying, totaling **9** checklist, detailing, numbering, reckoning, summing up **10** counting up, recounting, tabulation, ticking off **11** spelling out

enunciate 5 sound, speak, voice **8** vocalize **10** articulate **15** utter distinctly **16** pronounce clearly

enunciation 6 accent, speech **7** diction **9** utterance **12** articulation **13** pronunciation

envelop 4 hide, veil, wrap **5** cloak, cover **6** encase, enfold, engulf, enwrap, shroud, swathe **7** blanket, conceal, contain, enclose, obscure, sheathe, swaddle **8** encircle, surround **9** encompass

envelope 5 cover **6** jacket **8** covering, wrapping

envenom 4 sour **6** rankle **8** embitter **13** make poisonous

enviable 5 lucky **8** salutary **9** agreeable, covetable, desirable, excellent, fortunate **10** beneficial **12** advantageous

envious 5 green **7** jealous **8** covetous, grudging, spiteful **9** jaundiced, resentful

enviousness 4 envy **8** jealousy **10** resentment **12** covetousness **13** resentfulness **19** the green-eyed monster

environment 5 scene **6** locale, medium, milieu **7** climate, element, habitat, setting **8** ambience **9** situation **10** atmosphere, background **12** surroundings **13** circumstances
French: 11 mise en scene

environs 6 exurbs **7** suburbs **8** vicinity **9** outskirts, precincts **11** outer limits **12** outlying area **15** surrounding area

envisage 5 fancy **7** dream of, dream up, imagine, picture **8** conceive, envision **9** conjure up, visualize **11** contemplate **13** conceptualize **14** have a picture of **16** picture to oneself

envoy 5 agent **6** deputy, legate **7** attache, courier **8** delegate, emissary, minister **9** messenger, middleman **10** ambassador **12** intermediary **14** representative

envy 5 greed, spite **6** resent **8** begrudge, grudging, jealousy **10** resentment **11** be jealous of, enviousness, malevolence **12** covetousness **13** resentfulness **16** be spiteful toward **19** the green-eyed monster

enwrap 6 absorb, engage, enrobe **7** engross, envelop **9** preoccupy

Enyalius
epithet of: **4** Ares
means: **14** slayer of heroes

Enyeus
king of: **6** Scyrus

Enyo
origin: **5** Greek
goddess of: **3** war
companion of: **4** Ares
member of: **6** Graeae, Graiae
corresponds to: **7** Bellona

enzyme 7 protein **8** molecule **13** macromolecule
function: **8** catalyst
acts on: **9** substrate
kind: **5** amino, malic **6** lactic, lipase, pepsin, rennin, urease **7** amylase, glucose, trypsin **8** aldehyde, glutamic, glycolic, lipozyme, thrombin, xanthine **9** cellulase **12** ribonuclease

eon 3 age, era **8** eternity, long time **9** many years **15** one billion years

Eos
origin: **5** Greek
goddess of: **4** dawn
father: **8** Hyperion
mother: **5** Theia
brother: **6** Helios
sister: **6** Selene
husband: **8** Astraeus, Tithonus **9** Eosophorus
son: **6** Memnon **8** Phaethon, Zephyrus **10** Eosophorus
horse: **6** Lampos **8** Phaethon
mother of: **5** stars, winds
corresponds to: **6** Aurore **7** Hermera

Epaphus
king of: **5** Egypt
father: **4** Zeus
mother: **2** Io
wife: **7** Memphis

daughter: **5** Lybia **10** Lysianassa

Epeans see **5** Epeus

Epeus
king of: **12** Peloponnesus
father: **8** Endymion, Panopeus
brother: **5** Paeon **7** Aetolus
wife: **10** Anaxirrhoe
noted for: **9** cowardice
built: **11** Trojan horse
helped by: **6** Athena
descendants: **6** Epeans

Epheh 15 Biblical measure

ephemeral 5 brief **7** passing **8** fleeting, flitting, fugitive, temporal **9** fugacious, momentary, temporary, transient **10** evanescent, fly-by-night, inconstant, nondurable, short-lived, transitory, unenduring **11** impermanent **21** here today gone tomorrow

ephemeroptera
class: **8** hexapoda
phylum: **6** arthropoda
group: **6** mayfly

Ephialtes
form: **5** giant
member of: **7** Aloidae
father: **8** Poseidon
mother: **9** Iphimedia
brother: **5** Oteus

Ephraim
father: **6** Joseph
mother: **7** Asenath
brother: **8** Manasseh
blessed by: **5** Jacob
descendant of: **10** Ephraimite

Ephraimi 16 Greek unical codex

Epibaterius
epithet of: **6** Apollo
means: **9** seafaring

epic 4 saga **5** drama, great, noble **6** fabled, heroic **7** exalted, storied **8** fabulous, imposing, majestic **9** legendary **10** heroic poem, superhuman

Epicaste see **7** Jocasta

epicure 7 glutton, gourmet **8** gourmand, hedonist, sybarite **9** bon vivant **10** gastronome

epicurean 4 rich **6** lavish **7** gourmet, sensual **8** hedonist, Lucullan, sybarite **9** libertine, luxurious, sybaritic **10** hedonistic, sensualist, voluptuary, voluptuous **11** intemperate **13** self-indulgent

epidemic 4 rife **6** plague **7** rampant, scourge **8** catching, outbreak, pandemic **9** contagion, infection, pervasive, prevalent **10** infectious, pesti-

lence, prevailing, widespread
11 far-reaching

Epigoni
sons of: 18 Seven against
Thebes

epigram 4 quip 5 adage,
maxim 6 bon mot 8 aphorism,
apothegm 9 witticism

epilogue 4 coda 5 rider 7 codicil 8 addendum 9 afterword
10 supplement 12 final
section

Epimetheus
father: 7 Iapetus
brother: 5 Atals 9 Menoetius
10 Prometheus
wife: 7 Pandora
daughter: 6 Pyrrha

Epione
husband: 9 Asclepius

episcopal 8 churchly, diocesan,
pastoral 12 ecclesiastic(al)

episode 4 part 5 event, scene
6 affair, period 7 chapter, passage, section 8 incident 9 adventure, happening,
milestone 10 experience, occurrence 11 installment

Episode of Sparrows, An
author: 11 Rumer Godden

episodic 7 halting 8 rambling
9 segmented, wandering
10 digressive, discursive,
meandering 13 discontinuous

epistle 6 letter 7 message, missive 10 encyclical

**Epistle to a Godson and
Other Poems**
author: 7 W H Auden

Epistle to Dr Arbuthnot
author: 13 Alexander Pope

Epithalamion
author: 13 Edmund Spenser

epithet 5 curse 6 insult 8 nickname 9 blasphemy, expletive,
obscenity, sobriquet 10 ascription 11 appellation,
designation

Epithet *see* box

epitome 4 peak 5 ideal,
model 6 height 7 essence,
summary 9 summation
10 embodiment 12 typification 14 representation 15 exemplification, sum and
substance

e pluribus unum 12 out of
many one
motto of: 12 United States

epoch 3 age, era 4 time 6 period 8 interval

epochal 7 weighty 8 historic
9 important, momentous
11 significant 13 consequential

Eppie
character in: 11 Silas Marner
author: 5 Eliot

Epstein, Sir Jacob
born: 9 New York NY
artwork: 4 Adam 7 Genesis
8 Ecce Homo, Einstein
9 Rock Drill 10 Visitation
11 Night and Day, Paul
Robeson 12 Behold the
Man, Joseph Conrad
13 Haile Selassie 14 Consummatum Est 19 Social
Consciousness 20 Monument
to Oscar Wilde, St Michael
and his (the) Devil

equable 4 calm, even 5 sunny
6 placid, serene, stable,
steady 7 regular, uniform

8 constant, pleasant, tranquil,
unvaried 9 agreeable, easygoing, unruffled 10 consistent,
dependable, unchanging
11 good-natured, predictable,
unexcitable, unflappable
12 even-tempered
13 imperturbable

equably
Latin: 9 pari passu

equal 4 even, like, peer
5 match 7 matched, the same,
uniform 8 balanced, be even
to, equalize, jibe with, of a
piece, parallel 9 agree with,
identical, tally with 10 accord
with, comparable, equate with,
equivalent, square with, tantamount 11 balance with, be

Epithet
of **Aphrodite:** 6 Acraea, Scotia 7 Doritis, Erycina, Limenia
8 Melaenis, Nymphaea, Pandemos 9 Migonitis 11 Aphrogeneia, Apostrophia
of **Apollo:** 6 Loxias 7 Acesius, Agraeus, Agyieus, Carneus,
Phyteus, Spodius 8 Grynaeus 9 Parnopius, Smintheus
10 Alexicacus, Archegetes, Boedromius, Delphinius
11 Argyrotoxus, Epibaterius 12 Platanistius
of **Ares:** 8 Enyalius 14 Gynaecothoenas
of **Argus:** 8 Panoptes
of **Artemis:** 6 Orthia 7 Eurippa, Laphria, Limnaea, Pyronia 8 Aeginaea, Agrotera, Calliste, Caryatis, Daphnaea
9 Hemerasia, Lygodesma 10 Polymastus 11 Leucophryne
of **Asclepius:** 8 Cotyleus
of **Athena:** 4 Alea 5 Meter, Xenia 6 Ergane, Itonia, Polias
7 Agoraea, Cissaea, Paeonia, Pronaus, Pronoea 8 Anemotis, Poliates, Zosteria 9 Oxyderces, Parthenia, Poliuchus,
Promachus 10 Axiopoenus, Chalinitis, Cyparissia
11 Promachorma
of **Cybele:** 6 Antaea
of **Demeter:** 5 Chloe, Lusia, Mysia 6 Antaea, Erinys, Stiria 7 Chamyne, Thesmia 8 Stiritis 9 Anesidora, Thermasia 11 Carpophorus 12 Thesmophorus
of **Dionysus:** 6 Lyaeus 7 Bromius, Cresius 8 Thyoneus,
Triambus 9 Pyrigenes 11 Dithyrambus, Mitrephorus
of **Hera:** 6 Anthea, Bunaea 8 Henioche 9 Prodromia
of **Hercules:** 7 Charops 8 Buphagus 9 Ipoctonus
of **Hermes:** 6 Dolius 8 Agoraeus 9 Spelaites 10 Criophorus
11 Argiphontes 12 Argeiphontes, Psychopompus
of **Icelus:** 8 Phobetor
of **Juno:** 6 Moneta 7 Curitis, Pronuba, Sospita
of **Jupiter:** 5 Ultor 7 Elicius, Pluvius
of **Mopsus:** 9 Ampycides
of **Nestor:** 7 Nelides
of **Odin:** 7 Alfader, Alfadir
of **Odysseus:** 10 Laertiades
of **Persephone:** 11 Carpophorus
of **Pheriphetes:** 9 Corynetes
of **Poseidon:** 11 Ennosigaeus, Hippocurius 12 Prosclystius
of **Rhea:** 6 Antaea
of **Sinis:** 12 Pityocamptes
of **Vulcan:** 8 Mulciber
of **Zeus:** 5 Areus, Soter 6 Aqueus, Areius, Nemean, Philus
7 Alastor, Apemius, Ctesius, Lycaeus, Polieus, Stenius
8 Agoraeus, Aphesius, Apomyius, Cappotas, Cosmetas, Dodonian, Herceius, Leucaeus, Tropaean 9 Aegiochus,
Chthonius, Coccygius, Hecaleius, Lecheates, Mechaneus
10 Cataebates, Catharsius, Coryphaeus, Homagyrius, Laphystius, Meilichius 11 Eleutherius 12 Panhellenius

the same as, correlative, counterpart, symmetrical **12** commensurate, correspond to, proportional **13** be identical to, corresponding, evenly matched, one and the same

equality 6 parity **7** balance, justice **8** evenness, fair play, fairness, sameness **10** similarity, uniformity **11** equivalency **12** impartiality **13** fair treatment **14** correspondence
  French: 7 egalite

Equality
  author: 13 Edward Bellamy

Equality State
  nickname of: 7 Wyoming

equalization 7 balance **9** stability **11** equilibrium
14 counterbalance
  German: 9 Ausgleich

equalize 7 balance **9** make equal **11** make uniform
13 compensate for

equal to 3 fit **4** able, up to **5** adept **7** capable **8** adequate, master of **9** competent, qualified

equanimity 4 cool **5** poise **6** aplomb **8** calmness, coolness **9** composure, sangfroid **10** steadiness **11** self-control, tranquility **12** tranquillity **14** presence of mind, self-possession **16** imperturbability

equate 5 liken, match **7** average, balance, compare, even out **8** equalize, equal out **9** think of as **10** consider as **14** be commensurate, be equivalent to **17** be proportionate to

Equatorial
  language family: 16 Andean-Equatorial
  group: 8 Arawakan **11** Tupi-Guarani

Equatorial Guinea *see box*

equilibrium 7 balance **8** symmetry **9** equipoise, stability **14** sense of balance

equip 3 rig **5** stock **6** fit out, outfit, supply **7** appoint, furnish, prepare, provide **8** accoutre **9** caparison, provision

equipage 4 gear **6** outfit **8** carriage **9** equipment
13 accoutrements

equipment 4 gear **5** stuff **6** tackle **8** equipage, material, materiel, supplies **9** apparatus **11** furnishings, outfittings **13** accoutrements, paraphernalia

equipoise 7 balance **9** stability **11** equilibrium

equitable 3 due **4** fair, just **6** proper **8** unbiased **9** impartial **10** evenhanded, reasonable **12** unprejudiced

equity 4 cash **5** value **6** assets, profit **7** justice **8** fairness, justness **9** cash value **10** investment **12** fair dealings, impartiality **14** evenhandedness, fairmindedness, reasonableness

equivalency 6 parity **7** balance **8** equality **10** coequality, uniformity **14** correspondence

equivalent 4 even, peer **5** equal, match **8** of a piece, parallel **9** the same as **10** comparable, tantamount **11** correlative, counterpart, equal amount

equivocal 4 hazy **5** vague **7** dubious **8** doubtful **9** ambiguous, enigmatic, imprecise, qualified, uncertain, undecided **10** ambivalent, indefinite, suspicious
11 nonspecific **12** undetermined **13** indeterminate

equivocate 5 dodge, evade, fudge, hedge, stall **9** pussyfoot **10** mince words **11** be ambiguous, prevaricate **13** avoid the issue **16** straddle

---

Equatorial Guinea
  other name: 13 Spanish Guinea
  capital/largest city:
    6 Malabo
  others: 4 Bata **9** Rio Benito
  division: 5 Bioko **7** Rio Muni
  monetary unit: 6 ekuele, peseta **7** centimo
  island: 5 Bioko **6** Pagalu **7** Corisco **11** Chico Elobey **12** Grande Elobey
  mountain: 5 Mitra
  highest point: 11 Santa Isabel
  river: 5 Mbini
  physical feature:
    gulf: **6** Guinea
  people: 4 Bubi, Fang **5** Benge, Combe **6** Bujeba **10** Fernandino
    explorer: **2** Po
    leader: **12** Nguema Biyogo
  language: 4 Bubi, Fang **7** Spanish **13** pidgin English
  religion: 7 animism **10** Protestant **13** Roman Catholic

---

the fence **17** beat around the bush

equivocating 6 shifty **7** devious, dodging, elusive, elusory, evasive, hedging **8** stalling **9** ambiguous, deceptive, equivocal **10** misleading **11** dissembling

era 3 age **4** time **5** epoch **6** period **8** interval

eradicate 5 erase **6** remove **7** abolish, blot out, destroy, expunge, wipe out **8** get rid of **9** eliminate, extirpate, liquidate **10** annihilate, do away with, extinguish, obliterate **11** exterminate

eradication 7 erasure, removal **9** abolition **11** blotting out, destruction, elimination **12** obliteration

erase 6 delete, remove, rub out **7** expunge, scratch **8** wipe away **9** eliminate, eradicate, strike out

Erasistratus
  field: 10 physiology
  nationality: 5 Greek
  described: 5 brain, heart

Erasmus, Desiderius
  author: 14 Encomium Moriae **16** The Praise of Folly

Erato
  muse of: 10 love poetry

Ercolani, James
  real name of: 11 James Darren

Erebus
  location: 10 underworld
  means: 8 darkness

Erechtheus
  king of: 6 Athens
  father: 7 Pandion
  wife: 9 Praxithea
  son: 6 Metion, Orneus, Sicyon **7** Cecrops **8** Pandorus, Thespius **9** Eupalamus
  daughter: 6 Creusa **7** Otionia, Procris **8** Chthonia, Orithyir **10** Protogonia

erect 5 build, put up, raise, rigid, stiff **6** unbent **7** stand up, upright **8** straight, vertical **9** construct, unstooped **12** place upright

erection 7 raising **8** building **9** putting up **11** fabrication **12** construction

eremite 4 monk **6** hermit **7** ascetic, recluse **9** anchorite, religious

Ereshkigal
  origin: 8 Akkadian, Sumerian
  goddess of: 5 death
  consort of: 6 Nergal

Ereuthalion
  mentioned in: **5** Iliad
  vocation: **7** warrior
  home: **7** Arcadia
  dueled with: **6** Nestor

Erewhon
  author: **12** Samuel Butler
  title anagram of: **7** nowhere
  character: **5** Higgs **6** Strong
    7 Chowbok **8** Arowhena

Ergane
  epithet of: **6** Athena
  means: **6** worker

ergo 4 work **6** hence **7** because **9** therefore
  11 accordingly

Eriboea
  husband: **6** Aloeus

Erigone
  father: **7** Icarius **9** Aegisthus
  mother: **12** Clytemnestra
  brother: **6** Aletes
  death by: **7** suicide

Eriking
  origin: **8** Germanic
    12 Scandinavian
  form: **6** spirit
  personifies: **6** nature
  works: **8** mischief

Erin *see* **7** Ireland

Erin go bragh 14 Ireland
  forever

Erinys
  also: **6** Furies
  epithet of: **7** Demeter
  means: **4** fury

Eris
  origin: **5** Greek
  goddess of: **7** discord
  brother: **4** Ares
  threw: **14** apple of discord
  corresponds to: **9** Discordia

Eritrea
  capital/largest city:
    6 Asmara
  others: **5** Assab, Keren
    6 Ghinda **7** Massawa
  formerly division of:
    8 Ethiopia
  river: **5** Mareb
  highest point: **5** Soira
  strait: **11** Bab el Mandeb
  sea: **3** Red
  language: **7** Amharic
  religion: **5** Islam **6** Coptic,
    Muslim

ermine 3 fur **4** duty, rank
  6 weasel **7** ermalin **8** position

Ernani
  opera by: **5** Verdi
  setting: **6** Aragon
  character: **6** Ernani
    11 Donna Elvira

Ernst, Max
  born: **5** Bruhl **7** Germany
  co-founder of: **7** Dadaism
    10 Surrealism

artwork: **7** Moon Man
  8 Lady Bird **11** A Little
  Calm, Femme Oiseau
  12 The Whole City **13** The
  Table Is Set, Totem and Taboo **14** Lunar Asparagus

erode 5 spoil, waste **6** ravage
  7 corrode, despoil, eat away
  8 wear away **12** disintegrate

Eros
  origin: **5** Greek
  god of: **4** love
  mother: **9** Aphrodite
  corresponds to: **4** Amor
    5 Cupid

erosion 8 abrasion, ravaging
  9 corrosion **10** eating away
  11 wearing away, wearing
  down

erosive 7 burning, caustic
  9 corrosive

erotic 3 hot **4** lewd, sexy
  5 bawdy, lusty **6** ardent, carnal, impure, ribald, risque,
  sexual, wanton **7** amatory,
  amorous, obscene, raunchy
  8 immodest, indecent, unchaste **9** salacious **10** lascivious, passionate, suggestive

err 3 sin **6** mess up, slip up
  7 blunder, do wrong **8** go
  astray **9** be in error, misbehave **10** transgress **12** make a
  mistake, miscalculate **13** slip
  from grace

errand 4 duty, task **6** office
  7 mission **10** assignment

errant 5 wrong **6** arrant,
  astray, erring, roving **7** erratic,
  wayward **8** mistaken, straying
  9 incorrect, wandering, wayfaring **11** adventurous

errare humanum est 12 to
  err is human

erratic 3 odd **5** queer **6** fitful
  7 strange, unusual, wayward
  8 aberrant, abnormal, peculiar,
  shifting, unstable, variable
  9 eccentric, unnatural **10** capricious, changeable **11** vacillating **12** inconsistent
  13 unpredictable

erroneous 5 false, wrong **6** all
  wet, faulty, untrue **7** off base,
  unsound **8** mistaken, spurious
  9 incorrect, unfounded **10** fallacious, inaccurate **12** full of
  hot air **13** unsupportable

error 4 flaw **5** boner, botch,
  fault **6** boo-boo, bungle, howler **7** blooper, fallacy, mistake
  9 oversight **10** inaccuracy
  13 misconception **14** miscalculation **15** misapprehension
  16 misunderstanding
  17 misinterpretation

ersatz 4 fake, sham **5** bogus,

phony **9** imitation, pretended,
  synthetic **10** artificial, not genuine **11** counterfeit

Erse 4 Celt, Gael, Scot **5** Irish
  6 Celtic, Gaelic **7** Ireland
  8 Scottish **10** Highlander

erstwhile 2 ex **4** past **6** bygone, former **8** previous

eruct 4 burp **5** belch

eructation 4 burp **5** belch

erudite 4 wise **7** learned, sapient **8** cultured, literate, wellread **9** scholarly **10** cultivated,
  thoughtful, well-versed **11** intelligent **12** well-educated,
  well-informed, well-reasoned

erudition 5 skill **7** culture
  8 learning, literacy **9** education, expertise, knowledge,
  schooling **10** refinement
  11 cultivation, learnedness,
  scholarship **12** book learning
  13 enlightenment

Erulus
  king of: **5** Italy
  mother: **7** Feronia
  gift: **10** three lives

erupt 4 emit, gush, vent
  5 eruct **6** blow up **7** explode
  8 break out, throw off **9** be
  ejected, discharge, flow forth,
  pour forth **10** belch forth,
  burst forth

eruption 4 rash **6** eczema
  7 flare-up, gushing, venting
  8 ejection, emission, outbreak,
  outburst **9** blowing up, discharge, explosion, festering
  10 dermatitis, outpouring
  11 breaking out **12** flowing
  forth, inflammation, pouring
  forth **13** belching forth, bursting forth

Erving, Julius
  nickname: **7** Doctor J
  sport: **10** basketball
  position: **7** forward
  team: **11** New York Nets
    15 Virginia Squires **25** Philadelphia Seventy Sixers

Erycina
  epithet of: **9** Aphrodite

Erymanthian boar
  form: **4** boar
  plagued: **7** Arcadia
  captured by: **8** Hercules

Erysichthon
  cut sacred tree of:
    7 Demeter

Erytheis
  member: **10** Hesperides
  changed into: **3** elm

erythrophobia
  fear of: **8** blushing

Eryx
  vocation: **5** boxer

challenged: 8 Hercules
killed by: 8 Hercules

Esau
also called: 4 Edom
father: 5 Isaac
mother: 7 Rebekah
twin brother: 5 Jacob
wife: 6 Judith **8** Makalath
son: 7 Eliphaz
birthright sold to: 5 Jacob

escadrille 6 armada **8** flotilla,
squadron

escalate 4 rise **5** boost, mount,
swell **6** ascend, expand, extend, step up **7** advance, amplify, broaden, elevate,
enlarge, magnify **8** increase
9 intensify **10** accelerate,
aggrandize

Escalus
character in: 17 Measure for
Measure
author: 11 Shakespeare

escapade 4 lark **5** antic, caper,
fling, prank, revel, spree,
trick **7** caprice **8** mischief
9 adventure **11** high old time

escape 4 bolt, exit, flee, flow,
gush, leak, seep, shun, skip
5 avert, avoid, dodge, elude,
issue, skirt **6** efflux, egress,
emerge, eschew, exodus,
flight, stream **7** abscond, emanate, getaway, leakage, make
off, outflow, outpour, run
away, seepage **8** breakout,
emission, outburst, slip away,
steal off **9** be emitted, break
free, cut and run, discharge,
diversion, effluence, pour
forth **10** break loose, decampment, fly the coop **11** avoid
danger, deliverance, distraction, extrication, safe getaway **12** make a getaway

escargot 5 snail

escarpment 4 bank, crag
5 bluff, cliff, ridge, slope
8 headland, palisade **9** precipice **10** promontory

eschew 4 shun **5** avoid, forgo
6 give up **7** forbear **9** keep shy
of **11** abstain from **12** steer
clear of

eschewal 7 refusal **8** forgoing,
shunning **9** avoidance **10** abnegation, abstention, self-
denial **11** forbearance **13** nonindulgence **16** nonparticipation

escort 4 date, take **5** guard,
guide, train, usher **6** squire
7 company, conduct, cortege,
retinue **8** chaperon **9** companion, conductor, entourage
10 attendants, lead the way

escritoire 4 desk **5** table **9** secretary **10** secretaire **11** writing
desk

escutcheon 4 arms **5** crest
6 shield **10** coat of arms
16 armorial bearings

**Eskimo (Eskimantsic, Askki-
mey, Inuit, Yuit)**
tribe: 5 Aleut
location: 6 Alaska, Arctic,
Canada **9** Greenland
noted for: 7 fishing
9 mechanics

Eskimo-Aleut
language branch: 5 Aleut,
Yupik
spoken in: 6 Alaska **7** Siberia **15** Aleutian Islands

Esmeralda
character in: 23 The Hunchback of Notre Dame
author: 4 Hugo

esoteric 6 arcane, covert, hidden, occult, secret, veiled
7 cloaked, cryptic, obscure,
private **8** abstruse, mystical
9 concealed, enigmatic, recondite **10** inviolable, mysterious
11 inscrutable, undisclosed
12 confidential
16 incomprehensible

espanol 7 Spanish **13** Spanish
person **15** Spanish language

especial *see* **7** special

especially 6 really **7** notably
9 expressly, intensely, primarily, unusually **10** singularly,
uncommonly **11** exclusively,
principally **12** particularly, specifically **13** exceptionally, outstandingly **15** extraordinarily

espiegle 7 playful, roguish

espieglerie 12 playful trick

esplanade 4 mall, path, walk
5 drive **9** boardwalk
10 quadrangle

espousal 7 backing, support,
wedding **8** adoption, advocacy,
marriage, taking up **9** betrothal, promotion **10** supporting **12** championship

espouse 3 wed **4** back, tout
5 adopt, boost, marry **6** take
up **7** embrace, further, promote, support **8** advocate,
champion, side with **10** stand
up for

espressivo
music: 12 expressively
abbreviation: 4 espr

esprit de corps 10 fellowship,
group pride, group unity, high
morale, solidarity, team spirit
11 camaraderie

espy 3 see, spy **4** spot, view
6 behold, descry, detect, locate, notice **7** discern

essay 3 try **5** paper, theme,
tract **6** effort, take on **7** article,

attempt, venture **8** critique,
endeavor, treatise **9** editorial,
undertake **10** commentary, experiment **11** make a stab at,
undertaking **12** dissertation,
take a crack at, take a fling
at **14** make an effort at
16 short composition

Essay on Criticism, An
author: 13 Alexander Pope

Essay on Man, An
author: 13 Alexander Pope

Essays
author: 12 Francis Bacon

Essays in Criticism
author: 13 Matthew Arnold

esse 5 being **9** existence

essence 4 core, germ, gist,
pith, soul **5** heart, point,
scent **6** elixir, nature, spirit
7 cologne, extract, meaning,
perfume, spirits **8** tincture
9 fragrance, lifeblood, principle, substance **11** concentrate,
toilet water **12** basic quality,
quintessence, significance
15 sum and substance

essential, essentials 3 key
4 main **5** basic, vital **6** basics,
needed **7** crucial, leading
8 cardinal, inherent **9** basic
need, important, ingrained, intrinsic, necessary, necessity,
principal, requisite, rudiments,
vital part **10** key element,
principles **11** fundamental,
nitty-gritty **12** fundamentals
13 indispensable

essential ingredient 9 necessity **10** sine qua non **22** indispensable component

establish 3 fix **4** form, open,
show **5** begin, found, prove,
set up, start **6** create, settle,
uphold, verify **7** confirm, implant, install, justify, situate,
sustain, warrant **8** initiate, organize, validate **9** institute
10 bring about, inaugurate,
make secure **11** corroborate,
demonstrate **12** authenticate
16 win acceptance for
18 bring into existence

established 6 common **7** regular **8** accepted, familiar **9** customary **10** recognized

**establishment, Establish-
ment 4** firm **5** plant **6** office,
outfit, system **7** company, concern, factory **8** building, business, creation, founding
9 formation, setting up
10 foundation **11** corporation,
development, instituting, institution, ruling class **12** organization, powers that be
13 bringing about

estaminet 4 cafe **6** bistro

estate 4 rank, will 5 class, grade, manor, money, order, state 6 assets, legacy, status, wealth 7 bequest, fortune, station 8 compound, holdings, property 9 condition, situation 10 belongings, plantation 11 inheritance 12 country place

esteem 4 deem, hold 5 honor, judge, prize, think, value 6 admire, reckon, regard, revere 7 believe, cherish, respect 8 approval, consider, estimate, look up to, treasure, venerate 9 calculate, reverence 10 admiration, set store by, veneration 12 appreciation 13 think highly of 16 favorable opinion, hold in high regard 18 attach importance to

esteemed 5 great, noted 6 prized, valued, worthy 7 admired, eminent, honored, notable, revered 8 admirable, important, respected 10 looked up to, preeminent 11 illustrious 13 distinguished, well thought of 14 highly regarded

Estella
character in: 17 Great Expectations
author: 7 Dickens

Estevez, Ramon
real name of: 11 Martin Sheen

Esther
author: 10 Henry Adams

Esther
Persian name of: 8 Hadassah
father: 7 Abihail
grandfather: 6 Shimei
cousin: 8 Mordecai
husband: 9 Ahasuerus
displaced: 6 Vashti
enemy: 5 Haman

Esther Waters
author: 11 George Moore

esthetic 7 refined 8 artistic 9 sensitive 10 cultivated, fastidious 12 aesthetic 14 discriminating

estimable 4 good 6 prized 7 admired, revered 8 laudable 9 admirable, honorable, important, reputable, respected, treasured 10 worthwhile 11 commendable 12 praiseworthy 14 highly regarded

estimate 4 view 5 assay, guess, judge, opine, think, value 6 assess, belief, figure, reckon 7 believe, opinion, surmise 8 appraise, conclude, consider, evaluate, judgment, thinking 9 appraisal, calculate, reckoning 10 assessment, conjecture, evaluation 11 calculation

estimation 4 view 6 belief, esteem, regard 7 opinion, respect 8 approval, judgment 9 appraisal, reckoning 10 admiration, evaluation 13 consideration

estimator 7 analyst 8 assessor 9 appraiser, evaluator 10 calculator

Estonia *see box*

estop 3 bar 4 fill, plug, stop 7 prevent 8 obstruct

esto perpetua 17 may she live forever
motto of: 5 Idaho

Estragon
character in: 15 Waiting for Godot
author: 7 Beckett

estrange 4 part 8 alienate 9 disaffect 10 antagonize, dissociate, drive apart

estranged 5 aloof 6 cut off 7 distant 8 detached, divorced

Estonia
capital/largest city:
7 Tallinn
others: 5 Narva, Paide, Parnu, Tartu, Valga
6 Dorpat 7 Petseri
8 Paldiski 11 Kohtla-Jarve
government: 8 republic
measure: 3 tun 4 elle, liin, sund, toll, toop
5 verst 6 sagene, versta
7 kulimet 8 tonnland
monetary unit: 3 lat
4 sent 5 kroon
7 estmark
weight: 4 lood, nael, puud
island: 4 Dago, Muhu
5 Kihnu, Oesel, Saare
6 Sarema, Vormsi
7 Hiiumaa 8 Saaremaa
lake: 5 Pskov 6 Peipus
9 Vortsjarv
highest point:
8 Munamagi
river: 3 Ema 5 Narva, Parnu
sea: 6 Baltic
physical feature:
gulf: 4 Riga 5 Parnu
7 Finland
strait: 4 Irbe
people: 4 Esth, Finn
5 Aesti 6 Jewish 8 Estonian 9 Ukrainian
11 Belorussian
language: 5 Tartu
10 Finno-Ugric
religion: 8 Lutheran

---

9 alienated, separated 10 unfriendly

estrangement 8 coolness 10 alienation 12 disaffection

estuary 5 firth, inlet 10 river mouth, tidal basin

etagere 7 whatnot 11 open shelves

etc (&c) 4 et al 7 and so on, whatnot 8 et cetera, whatever 9 and others 10 and so forth, and the rest

etch 3 cut, fix 5 carve, stamp 7 corrode, engrave, impress, scratch

Eteocles
father: 7 Oedipus
mother: 7 Jocasta
10 Euryganeia
uncle: 5 Creon
brother: 9 Polynices
sister: 6 Ismene 8 Antigone
son: 8 Laodamas
slain by: 9 Polynices

eternal 7 abiding, endless 8 constant, immortal, infinite, timeless, unending 9 ceaseless, continual, perpetual 10 persistent, relentless, without end 11 everlasting, never-ending 12 interminable 13 uninterrupted

eternity 4 Zion 6 Heaven 7 forever, nirvana 8 infinity, paradise 11 ages and ages, endlessness, eons and eons, immortality 12 New Jerusalem, the hereafter, the next world 13 the afterworld 14 the world to come, time without end 15 everlasting life

Ethan Frome
author: 12 Edith Wharton
character: 5 Zeena 7 Zenobia 12 Mattie Silver

Ethanim 18 seventh Hebrew month

ether 5 ester, ethyl, ozone, vapor 7 diethyl, solvent 10 anesthetic 11 refrigerant

ethereal 4 airy, rare 6 aerial 7 elusive, refined, sublime 8 delicate, rarefied 9 celestial, exquisite, unearthly, unworldly

ethical 4 fair, just 5 moral, right 6 decent, kosher, proper 7 correct, fitting, upright 8 virtuous 9 honorable 10 aboveboard, scrupulous 15 straightforward 17 open and aboveboard

ethical feelings 9 integrity 10 conscience, moral sense 16 incorruptibility

ethics, ethic 8 morality 9 integrity, moral code 10 con-

science, principles **11** moral
values, sense of duty **14** moral
standards, rules of conduct

Ethics of Ambiguity
   author: **16** Simone de
   Beauvoir

Ethiopia *see box*

ethnic 6 native, racial, unique
8 cultural, national, original
10 indigenous

ethnic group *see box, p.
318*

etiquette 5 usage **7** decorum,
manners **8** behavior, courtesy,
good form, protocol **9** amenities, gentility, good taste
10 civilities, politeness
11 conventions, proprieties
15 rules of behavior

etoile 4 star

Ettarre
   character in: **16** Arthurian
   romance

ET The Extra-Terrestrial
   director: **15** Steven Spielberg
   cast: **10** Dee Wallace
   11 Henry Thomas, Peter
   Coyote **13** Drew Barrymore
   17 Robert MacNaughton

et tu, Brute 13 and thou
Brutus
   spoken by: **12** Julius Caesar

etymology 7 history
10 derivation

Etzel
   origin: **8** Germanic
   mentioned in:
      14 Nibelungenlied
   represents: **6** Attila
   wife: **9** Kriemhild

Euaechme
   parent: **8** Megareus
   husband: **9** Alcathous

Euboean *see* **7** Abantes

Eubuleus
   father: **9** Trochilus
   helped: **7** Demeter

Eucharist 8 viaticum **9** Communion, sacrament **13** Holy
Communion

euchre
   number of players: **3** two
   4 four **5** three
   derived from: **8** triomphe
   five tricks won: **5** march
   jack of trump: **10** right
   bower
   second highest trump: **9** left
   bower

Euclid
   field: **11** mathematics
   nationality: **5** Greek
   founder of: **8** geometry
   author of: **8** Elements

Eugene Onegin
   author: **16** Alexander Pushkin

Ethiopia
   Biblical name: 4 Cush
   other name: 9 Abyssinia
   capital/largest city: 10 Addis Ababa
   others: 3 Edd **4** Axum, Bako, Dori, Goba, Gore, Thio
   5 Adola, Adowa, Aduwa, Aksum, Assab, Awash, Dimtu,
   Elfud, Harar, Jidda, Jimma, Kecha, Meroe, Mojjo **6** An-
   talo, Asmara, Dessye, Dunkur, Gondar, Harrar, Makale,
   Napata **7** Ankober, Gambela, Gardula, Magdala, Massawa,
   Nakamti **8** Dire Dawa, Lalibala, Mustahil
   school: 13 Haile Selassie
   division: 5 Tigre **6** Amhara, Ogaden
   former division: 7 Eritrea
   measure: 3 tat **4** cubi, kuba **5** derah, messe **6** cabaho, sin-
   jer, sinzer, tanica **7** entelam, farsakh, farsang, ghebeta
   monetary unit: 4 besa, birr, harf **5** amole, girsh **6** dollar,
   kharaf, levant, pataca, talari **7** ashrafi, menelik, plaster,
   tallero **12** maria theresa
   weight: 3 pek **4** kasm, natr, oket, rotl **5** alada, artal, mocha, neter, ratel, wakea **6** wogiet **8** farasula **9** mutagalla
   island: 6 Dahlak
   lake: 3 Abe **4** Tana **5** Abaya, Shola, Tanna, Tsana, Tzana,
   Zeway **6** Dambea, Dembea **7** Rudolph **8** Stefanie **11** The
   Blue Nile
   mountain: 4 Amba, Batu, Guge, Guna, Talo **5** Ahmar,
   Choke **9** Rasdashan
   highest point: 9 Ras Deshen
   river: 3 Omo **4** Baro, Dawa, Gibe, Gila, Juba **5** Abbai,
   Akoho, Albai, Awash, Fafan, Mareb, Mofer, Rahad,
   Webbe **6** Tekeze **7** Tacazze, Takkaze **8** Gashgash, She-
   bante **11** The Blue Nile
   sea: 3 Red
   physical feature:
      desert: **17** Danakil Depression
      falls: **7** Tisisat **8** Blue Nile
      valley: **4** Rift
   people: 4 Afar, Agau, Beja, Doko, Kafa, Kala, Saho, Shoa
   5 Afara, Agows, Galas, Galla, Negro, Tigre **6** Abigar, Amhara, Annuak, Gondar, Hamite, Harari, Sidama, Sidamo,
   Somali, Tigrai, Wolamo **7** Cushite, Danakil, Donakus, Falasha, Somalis **8** Assamite, Blemmyes **10** Abyssinian,
   Troglodyte
   leader: 7 Menelik **8** Mengistu **13** Haile Selassie
   language: 3 Giz **4** Afar, Agow, Geez, Saho **5** Geeze, Ghese,
   Smali, Tigre **6** Arabic, Harari **7** Amharic, English, Italian,
   Russian **8** Gallinya, Irob-Saho, Tigrinya
   religion: 5 Islam **7** Falasha, Judaism **18** Ethiopian
   Orthodoxy
   place:
      cathedral: **8** St George
      hall: **6** Africa
      palace: **7** Jubilee **9** Menelik II
      park: **4** Lion
   feature:
      flower: **7** brayera
      game: **5** dulla **8** shum-shir
      garment: **4** toga **5** kamis **6** barnos, chamma, netela,
      shamma
      tree: **4** koho, koso **5** cusso
   food:
      banana: **4** musa **6** ensete
      beer: **5** talla
      bread dish: **6** injera
      cereal: **4** teff
      honey liquor: **3** tej
      spicy sauce: **3** wat

ethnic group

of Afghanistan: 5 Aimak, Aymak, Kafir, Nuris 6 Baloch, Baluch, Chahar, Durani, Hasara, Hazara, Kaffir, Kirgiz, Pathan, Tajiks, Uzbeks 7 Beluchi, Belucki, Ghilzai, Pakhton, Pakhtun, Pashtun, Pukhtun, Pushtun, Sistani, Taimani, Taimuri 8 Jamshidi, Siah Push 9 Firuzkuhi, Safed Push, Safid Push

of Albania: 3 Geg 4 Cham, Gheg, Gueg, Tost 6 Arnaut, Arnout 8 Illyrian, Skipetar

of Algeria: 4 Arab 6 Berber, Kabyle, Shawai, Tuareg 7 Haratin

of Andorra: 7 Catalan

of Angola: 5 Bantu, Kongo, Lundu 6 Chokwe, Herero, Mbundi, Ovambo 7 Bakongo, Kangela, Kikongo 8 Kimbundu, Kwangare 9 Ovinbundu 12 Nyaneka-Humbi

of Antigua and Barbuda: 7 African, British 8 Lebanese 10 Portuguese

of Argentina: 3 Api 4 Lule 5 Vejoz 6 Abipon, Vilela 7 Guarani, Puelche, Ranquel, Taluhet 8 Querandi, Querendy

of Armenia: 5 Armen, Ermyn, Gomer, Hadji

of Australia: 3 Abo 4 Koko, Mara, Wong 5 Anzac, Bieri, Binge, Maori, Myall 6 Aranda, Arunta, Aussie, Binghi, Digger, Kipper, Papuan 7 Arawong, Billjim, Ilpirra 8 Antipode, Barkinji, Euahlayi, Warragal, Warrigal 9 Aborigine 10 Austroloid, Melanesian, Sandgroper 12 Jindyworobak

of Austria: 4 Pole 5 Croat, Czech, Gypsy 6 German 7 Slovene 9 Hungarian

of Azerbaijan: 5 Azeri 11 Azerbaijani

of the Bahamas: 5 black 7 Haitian

of Bahrain: 4 Arab 6 Indian 7 Persian 8 European 9 Pakistani

of Bangladesh: 7 Bengali

of Barbados: 5 Bajan 9 Barbadian

of Belarus: 12 Byelorussian

of Belgium: 4 Remi 6 Nervii 7 Belgian, Fleming, Flemish, Walloon 9 Bellovaci

of Benin: 3 Fon, Pla 4 Adja, Aizo, Mina, Peul 5 Pedah, Peuhl, Somba 6 Bariba, Fulani, Yoruba 8 Pilapila 9 Dahomeyan

of Bhutan: 5 Monpa 6 Bhutia 7 Tibetan 8 Assamese, Nepalese

of Bolivia: 6 Aymara 7 mestizo, Quechua

of Borneo: 4 Iban 5 Bukat, Dajak, Dayak, Dusan, Malay, Punan 6 Illano 7 Bakatan, Chinese, Illanum

of Bosnia-Herzegovina: 4 Serb 5 Croat 8 Yugoslav

of Botswana: 5 Bantu 6 Tswana 7 Bakatla, Bakwena, Bushman 8 Bamalete, Baralong, Batawana, Batlokwa, Botswana 10 Bamangwato 11 Bangwaketse

of Brazil: 2 Ge 4 Anta 5 Acroa, Arara, Araua, Bravo, Carib, Guana, Negro 6 Arawak, Caraja 7 Carayan, Javahai, mulatto, Tariana 8 Botocudo, Chambioa, mameluco 9 Caucasian 10 Portuguese 11 Tupi-Guarani

of Brunei: 4 Iban 5 Dayak, Malay 7 Chinese, Kadazan

of Bulgaria: 4 Slav, Turk 5 Gypsy, Pomak, Tatar 6 Bulgar, Slavic 7 Chuvash 9 Cheremiss 10 Macedonian

of Burkina Faso: 4 Bobo, Lobi, Samo 5 Bella, Bissa, Dyula, Fulbe, Hausa, Mande, Marka, Mossi, Puchl 6 Fulani, Senufo, Tuareg 7 Grunshi, Voltaic, Yatenga 8 Mandingo 9 Gourounsi 15 Bunsansi Gambaga

of Burundi: 3 Twa 4 Hutu 5 Bantu, Batwa, Pygmy, Tutsi 6 Bahutu, Watusi 7 Barundi

of Cambodia: 4 Cham, Thai 5 Khmer 7 Chinese 10 Vietnamese

of Cameroon: 3 Abo, Edo, Ibo 4 Beti, Bulu, Ekoi, Ijaw, Sara 5 Bantu, Bassa, Kirdi, Pygmy, Tikar 6 Bamoun, Donala, Ewondo, Fulani, Ibibio 7 Bakweri 8 Bamileke

of Canada: 6 Canuck, Eskimo, French, Innuit 7 English

of the Canary Islands: 7 Spanish

of Cape Verde: 6 Creole 7 African, mulatto 8 European 10 Portuguese

of Central African Republic: 4 Baya, Sara 5 Banda, Bwaki, Sango 6 Azande, Yakoma 7 Banziri, Mandjia, Nzakara

of Chad: 4 Arab, Daza, Maba, Sara, Teda, Tubu 5 Barma, Hakka, Kroda, Massa 6 Fulani, Kotoko, Toubou, Wadaii 7 Kamadja, Kanembu 8 Moundang

of Chile: 3 Ona 4 Auca, Inca, Onan 6 Arauca, Chango, Yahgan 7 Mapuche, mestizo, Moluche, Pampean, Patagon, Puegian, Ranquel 8 Alikuluf, Picunche, Tsonecan

of China: 3 Han, Yis 4 Huis, Lolo, Miao, Pu-is 5 Hakka, Hoklo, Seres, Sinic 6 Cataia, Chuang, Johnny, Korean, Manchu, Mongol, Serian, Uighun 7 Sinaean, Tibetan

of Colombia: 4 Boro, Cuna, Duit, Hoka, Macu, Muzo, Muzo, Paez, Tama, Tapa 5 Carib, Catio, Choco, Cofan, Cogui, Cubeo, Guane, Haida, Mocoa, Paeze, Pijao, Seona, Yagua 6 Arawak, Betoya, Calima, Colima, Ingano, Mirana, Saliva, Tahami, Ticunu, Tucano, Tunebo, Witoto, Yahuna 7 Achagua, Andaqui, Chibcha, Chimila, Churoya, Guahibo, Guajiro, mestizo, mulatto, Panches, Puinave, Puitoto, Quechua, Shuswap, Tairona, Telembi 8 Coconuco, Guarauno, Motilone, Puinavis, Quimbaya, Sinsigas 9 Cocanucos, Coconucan, Panaquita 10 Bellacoola

of Comoros: 4 Arab 5 Bantu, Malay 7 African 8 Malagasy

of the Congo: 3 Rua 4 Akka, Susa, Teke, Vili 5 Amadi, Bantu, Figot, Kongo, Mantu, Pygmy, Sanga, Warua, Zambi 6 Ababua, Bafyot, Bateke, Mbochi, Nzambi, Wabuma 7 Bacongo, Bakongo, Bangala, Batetla, Manyema 10 Binga Pygmy

of Costa Rica: 4 Voto 6 Boruca, Bribri, Guaymi 7 Guatuso, mestizo, Spanish

of Crete: 6 Cretan, Minoan 7 Candiot 8 Sphakiot 9 Caphtorim 10 Philistine

of Croatia: 4 Serb 5 Croat 8 Yugoslav

of Cuba: 5 Carib, Negro, Taino 6 Arawak 7 Ciboney, mestizo 8 Ciboneye 9 Caucasian

of Czechoslovakia/Czech Republic: 4 Slav 5 Czech 6 Slovak 8 Bohemian, Moravian

of Denmark: 4 Dane, Jute 5 Angle 6 Cimbri, Eskimo, German, Ostmen, Teuton, Viking 12 Scandinavian

(continued)

ethnic group (*continued*)
  of Djibouti: 4 Afar, Arab 5 Issas 6 French 8 European
  of Dominican Republic: 5 Negro, Taino 6 Indian 7 mulatto, Spanish 9 Caucasian
  of Ecuador: 4 Cara, Cixo, Inca 5 Ardan, Aucas, Macoa, Maina, Palta, Quitu, Yumbo 6 Canelo,
    Jibaro, Jivaro, Puruha 7 Cayapas, Jivaros, mestizo, mulatto 8 Barbacoa, Colorado, Montuvio,
    Serranos 10 Montubious
  of Egypt: 3 Kem 4 Arab, Copt, Misr, Wafd 5 Gippy, Gyppy, Gypsy, Nilot 6 Ababda, Berber,
    Hyksos, Nubian, Tasian 7 Mizraim, Pharian 8 Badarian, Bisharin, Memphian
  of El Salvador: 5 Lenca, Pipil 6 Indian, Mangue 7 mestizo, Spanish 9 Matagalpa
  of England: 4 Celt, Jute, Pict 5 Norse, Saxon 6 Angles, Briton, Norman, Viking
  of Equatorial Guinea: 4 Bubi, Fang 5 Benge, Combe 6 Bujeba 10 Fernandino
  of Estonia: 4 Esth, Finn 5 Aesti 6 Jewish 8 Estonian 9 Ukrainian 11 Belorussian
  of Ethiopia: 4 Afar, Agau, Beja, Doko, Kafa, Kala, Saho, Shoa 5 Afara, Agows, Galas, Galla,
    Negro, Tigre 6 Abigar, Amhara, Annuak, Gondar, Hamite, Harari, Sidama, Sidamo, Somali,
    Tigrai, Wolamo 7 Cushite, Danakil, Donakus, Falasha 8 Assamite, Blemmyes 10 Abyssinian,
    Troglodyte
  of Fiji: 6 Fijian, Indian 7 Chinese 10 Melanesian, Polynesian 11 Micronesian
  of Finland: 3 Jew, Vod, Vot, Yak 4 Avar, Finn, Hame, Lapp, Turk, Veps 5 Fioun, Gypsy, Ijore,
    Inger, Suomi, Vepse, Zyrin 6 Magyar, Ostiak, Ostyak, Tarast, Tavast, Ugrian 7 Lappish, Mord-
    vin, Permiak, Samoyed, Uralian 8 Cheremis, Estonian, Karelian, Livonian, Swekoman 9 Tavas-
    tian 11 Karjalaiset, Suomalaiset
  of France: 5 Frank
  of the Gabon Republic: 4 Fang 6 Adouma, Bakota, Bateke, Echira, Okande, Omyene 7 Eshiras
    8 Bandjabi, Bapounou
  of the Gambia: 4 Fula, Jola 5 Foula, Wolof 6 Fulani 8 Mandingo, Serahuli 9 Seranuleh
  of Georgia: 5 Azeri 7 Russian 8 Armenian, Georgian, Ossetian
  of Germany: 3 Hun 4 Slav, Sorb, Wend 5 Saxon
  of Ghana: 2 Ga 3 Ewe 4 Akan, Akim, Akra, Aksa 5 Ahafo, Brong, Inkra 7 Akwapim, Ashanti,
    Dagomba, Maprusi 11 Mole-Dagbani
  of Gibraltar: 6 Jewish 7 British, Italian, Maltese, Spanish 10 Portuguese
  of Greece: 5 Greek 6 Achean, Dorian, Ionian 7 Aeolian, Hellene
  of Greenland: 3 Ita 6 Eskimo 8 European
  of Grenada: 5 Negro 6 Indian
  of Guatemala: 3 Mam 4 Chol, Itza, Ixil, Maya 5 Xinca 6 Caribe, Quiche 7 ladinos, mestizo, Po-
    comam 13 Guatemaltecos
  of Guinea: 4 Koma, Loma, Nalu, Susu, Toma 5 Kissi, Manon 6 Fulani, Guerzi 7 Landoma, Ma-
    linke 8 Kouranke, Landuman 11 Kissi-Sherbo 12 Guerze-Kpelle
  of Guinea-Bissau: 6 Fulani 7 Balanta, Balante, mulatto 8 Mandingo, Mandyako
  of Guyana: 6 Akawai, Arawak, Creole, Taruma 7 African, Chinese, mulatto 10 Portuguese
  of Haiti: 5 Taino 7 African, mulatto
  of Honduras: 4 Maya, Paya, Sumo, Ulva 5 Carib, Lenoa, Pipil 6 Tauira 7 Jicaque, mestizo, Mis-
    kito 8 Mosquito
  of Hong Kong: 5 Hakka, Haklo, Punti, Tanka 7 British, Chinese 8 American, Japanese 9 Can-
    tonese 10 Portuguese
  of Hungary: 3 Hun 4 Serb 5 Croat, Gypsy 6 Cigany, Magyar, Slovak, Ugrian
  of Iceland: 6 Celtic, Viking 8 Norseman 9 Norwegian
  of India: 2 Ao 3 Gor 4 Bhil 5 Aryan 6 Badaga, Pathan 7 Sherani 9 Dravidian 10 Andamanese
  of Indonesia: 4 Dyak 5 Batak, Dayak, Malay 6 Battak, Papuan, Toraja 7 Chinese, Igorots
    8 Acehnese, Achinese, Balinese, Javanese, Madurese, Sudanese 11 Minang Kabau
  of Iran: 3 Lur, Tat 4 Arab, Kurd, Turk 5 Medes 6 Galcha, Gilani, Jewish, Shugni 7 Baluchi, Per-
    sian 8 Armenian, Bactrian, Bartangi, Parthian, Scythian 9 Bakhtiari 11 Azerbaijani,
    Mazandarani
  of Iraq: 4 Arab, Kurd 7 Bedouin
  of Ireland: 4 Celt, Erse, Gael 5 Irish 6 Celtic 9 Hibernian
  of Israel: 3 Jew 4 Arab 5 Druze 10 Circassian
  of Italy: 5 Latin 6 Sabine 7 Italian, Lombard 8 Etruscan
  of Ivory Coast: 3 Abe, Dan, Kru, Kwa 4 Akan, Bete, Dida, Guro, Koua, Lobi, Wobe 5 Abron,
    Abure, Attie, Baule, Guere, Mande, Mossi 6 Baoule, Lagoon, Senufo, Senufu 7 Kroumen,
    Malinke, Voltaic 8 Dan-Gouro 10 Anyi-Baoule 11 Lobi-Kulango 12 Agnis-Ashanti
  of Jamaica: 7 African, Chinese 10 East Indian
  of Japan: 3 Eta 6 Korean 8 Japanese, Okinawan 10 Buramkumin
  of Java: 5 Krama, Kromo 6 Kalang 8 Javanese, Madurese, Sudanese
  of Jordan: 4 Arab, Kurd 7 Bedouin, Checher 8 Armenian, Assyrian 10 Circassian 11 Palestinian
  of Kazakhstan: 6 Kazakh
  of Kenya: 3 Luo 4 Arab, Meru 5 Bantu, Elgey, Galla, Kamba, Kisii, Luhya, Masai, Nandi,
    Tugen 6 Kikuyu, Ogaden, Somali 7 Baluyha, Hamitic, Hilotic, Kipsigi, Swahili, Turkana 8 Ka-
    lenjin, Marakwet
  of Kiribati: 8 Banabans 10 Polynesian 11 Micronesian
  of Korea: 6 Korean
  of Kuwait: 4 Arab 5 Iraqi, Saudi 6 Indian 7 Bedouin 8 Egyptian 9 Pakistani 11 Palestinian
  of Kyrgyzstan: 5 Uzbek 6 Kyrgyz 7 Kirghiz
  of Laos: 2 Lu 3 Kha, Lao, Man, Meo, Tai, Yao, Yun 4 Miao, Thai 5 Hmong 8 Lao Teung
    10 Phoutheung
  of Latvia: 3 Kur, Liv 4 Balt, Cour, Lett 7 Latgale, Latvian, Russian, Zemgale

(*continued*)

ethnic group (*continued*)
  of Lebanon: **4** Arab **9** Canaanite **10** Phoenician **11** Palestinian
  of Lesotho: **4** Zulu **5** Bantu, Tembu **6** Basuto **7** Basotho
  of Liberia: **2** Gi **3** Gio, Kra, Kru, Kwa, Vai, Vei **4** Gola, Kroo, Krou, Loma, Mano, Toma
    5 Bassa, Gibbi, Gissi, Grebo **6** Gbande, Kpelle, Kpuesi, Krooby, Kruman **7** Krooboy, Krooman
    8 Mandingo **15** Americo-Liberian
  of Libya: **4** Arab, Tebu **6** Berber, Tuareg **7** Gaetuli **8** Getulans, Harratin
  of Liechtenstein: **8** Alamanni, Alemanni
  of Lithuania: **4** Balt, Lett, Pole **5** Zhmud **6** Jewish, Litvak **7** Aistian, Russian, Yatvyag **10** Lithua-
    nian, Samogitian **11** Belorussian
  of Luxembourg: **6** French, German **12** Luxembourger
  of Macao: **6** Macaon **7** Chinese **10** Portuguese
  of Macedonia: **4** Turk **8** Albanian **10** Macedonian
  of Madagascar: **4** Arab, Bara, Hova **5** Malay **6** Merina, Tanala **7** African **8** Betsileo, Mahafaly,
    Malagasy, Sakalava **9** Antaimoro, Antaisaka, Antandroy, Tsimihety **10** Indonesian, Polynesian
    13 Betsimisaraka
  of Malawi: **3** Yao **4** Sena **5** Bantu, Lomwe, Ngoni **6** Cheiva, Maravi, Ngonde, Nyanja
    7 Tumbuka
  of Malaysia: **4** Iban **5** Dayak, Malay **6** Indian **7** Chinese, Kadazan **9** Pakistani, Sri Lankan
    10 Bangladesh, Indonesian
  of Maldives: **4** Arab **6** Indian **9** Sinhalese **10** Singhalese
  of Mali: **3** Bwa **4** Fula, Kyan, Moor, Peul **5** Dogon, Dyula, Fulbe, Marka **6** Berber, Dognon, Fu-
    lani, Senufo, Tuareg **7** Bembara, Fellata, Malinke, Miniaka, Songhai, Soninke **8** Khasonke,
    Mandingo, Senoulfo
  of Malta: **7** Maltese
  of Mauritania: **4** Arab, Fula, Moor **5** Black, Fulbe, Wolof **6** Bafour, Berber, Fulani **7** African,
    Soninke, Tukulor **8** Sarakole **9** Toucouleur **12** Halphoolaren
  of Mauritius: **6** Creole, French, Indian **7** African, Chinese **8** European **13** Indo-Mauritian
  of Mexico: **3** Ixe, Mam, Mie, Ser **4** Chol, Cora, Jova, Meco, Mixe, Pame, Pima, Roto, Seri,
    Teca, Teco, Texo, Xova **5** Aztec, Chizo, Chora, Mayan, Nahua, Opata, Otomi, Zoque **6** Eu-
    deve, Indian, Mixtec, Pueblo, Toltec, Zotzil **7** Chincha, mestizo, Nahuatl, Nayarit, Spanish, Te-
    hueco, Tepanec, Totonac, Zacatec, Zapotec **8** Lagunero, Mazateca, Tezcucan, Totonaco,
    Tzapotec, Yucateco, Zacateco, Zapoteca **9** Tlascalan **10** Coahuiltec, Cuitlateco, Tarahumara
  of Moldova: **7** Gagauzi **8** Moldovan **9** Moldovian
  of Monaco: **6** French **7** Italian **10** Monegasque
  of Mongolia: **5** Oirat, Tungu **6** Buryat, Darbet, Khoton, Mongol **7** Kazakhs, Khalkha **8** Tuvinian
    9 Dariganga
  of Montenegro: **4** Serb, Slav **11** Montenegrin
  of Morocco: **4** Arab, Moor **6** Berber, French **7** Spanish
  of Mozambique: **3** Yao **5** Bantu, Chopi, Lomue, Lomwe, Macua, Makua, Ngoni, Nguni, Shona
    6 Maravi, Thouga **7** Maconde, Makonde **10** Portuguese
  of Myanmar: **4** Shan **7** Burmese, Siamese
  of Namibia: **4** Nama **5** Bantu **6** Damara, Herero, Ovambo, Tswara **7** Bushman, Colored **8** Oka-
    vango **9** Hottentot
  of Nauru: **7** Chinese **10** Melanesian, Polynesian **11** Micronesian
  of Nepal: **3** Rai **4** Aoul **5** Limbu, Magar, Murmi, Newar, Tharu **6** Gurkha, Gurung, Nepali,
    Sherpa, Tamang **7** Bhutias, Kiranti **8** Gorkhali, Nepalese
  of the Netherlands: **5** Dutch **7** Frisian **9** Hollander **10** Surinamese **12** Netherlander **13** South
    Moluccan
  of New Guinea: **5** Pygmy **6** Papuan **7** Negrito **10** Melanesian
  of New Zealand: **3** Ati **5** Arawa, Dutch, Maori **7** British, Ringatu **10** Polynesian
  of Nicaragua: **4** Mico, Mixe, Rama, Smoo, Ulva **5** Cukra, Diria, Lenca, Sambo, Toaca **6** Mangue
    7 mestizo, Miskito **8** Mosquito **9** Matagalpa
  of Niger: **4** Daza, Idjo, Idyo, Idzo, Peul, Teda **5** Hausa, Warri **6** Djerma, Fulani, Kanuri, Songha,
    Toubou, Tuareg **13** Djerma-Songhai
  of Nigeria: **3** Abo, Aro, Djo, Ebo, Edo, Ibo, Ijo, Tiv, Vai **4** Beni, Bini, Eboe, Efik, Egba, Ejam,
    Ekoi, Idyo, Igbo, Ijaw, Nupe **5** Angas, Benin, Gwari, Hausa **6** Chamba, Fulani, Ibibio, Kanuri,
    Yoruba **11** Hausa-Fulani
  of Norway: **4** Lapp **5** Samme **6** Nordic, Viking
  of Oman: **4** Arab
  of Pakistan: **5** Sindi, Wazir **6** Afridi, Bengal, Mahsud, Pathan, Puktun, Sindhi **7** Baluchi, Bra-
    huis, Punjabi, Pushtun, Sherani **8** Khattack, Shinwari, Yusefazi **11** Mohammedzai
  of Panama: **4** Cuna **5** Choco **6** Guaymi **7** mestizo
  of Qatar: **4** Arab **6** Pushtu, Yemeni **7** Baluchi, Iranian **9** Pakistani
  of Rumania: **6** Dacian **8** Romanian, Rumanian
  of Russia: **4** Slav **5** Kulak **6** Jewish, Soviet, Velika **7** Chukchi, Cossack, Latvian, Russian, Turk-
    men **8** Armenian, Estonian, Georgian, Siberian, Ukrainian **10** Lithuanian **11** Belorussian
  of Rwanda: **3** Twa **4** Hutu **5** Batwa, Pygmy, Tutsi **6** Bahutu, Watusi **7** Batutsi
  of Samoa: **6** Samoan **10** Polynesian
  of San Marino: **7** Italian **11** San Marinese
  of Sao Tome and Principe: **7** African **10** Portuguese **11** Cape Verdean
  of Saudi Arabia: **4** Arab **7** Bedouin
  of Scotland: **4** Gael, Pict, Scot **5** Norse

(*continued*)

ethnic group (*continued*)

of Senegal: **4** Lebu, Peul, Soce **5** Diola, Dyola, Foula, Laobe, Peulh, Serer, Wolof **6** Fulani, Serere **7** Bambara, Malinke, Tukuler, Tukulor **8** Mandingo

of Seychelles: **5** Asian **6** Creole, French, Indian **7** African, Chinese

of Sicily: **5** Elymi, Sican, Sicel **6** Sicani, Siculi

of Sierra Leone: **3** Vai **4** Kono, Loko, Susu **5** Bulom, Kissi, Limba, Mande, Mendi, Temne **6** Creole, Fulani, Syrian **7** Gallina, Koranko, Kuranko, Sherbro, Yalunka **8** Lebanese, Mandingo

of Sikkim: **4** Rong **5** Bhote **6** Bhotia, Bhutia, Indian, Lepcha **7** Tibetan **8** Nepalese **9** Mongoloid

of Singapore: **5** Malay **6** Indian **7** Chinese **9** Malaysian, Pakistani, Sri Lankan

of Slovakia: **5** Czech **6** Slavik, Slovak **9** Hungarian

of Slovenia: **7** Slovene

of the Solomon Islands: **7** Chinese **8** European **10** Melanesian, Polynesian

of Somalia: **3** Sab **4** Asha **5** Galla **6** Hawiya, Isbaak, Somali **7** Danakil, Hamitic, Marehan, Samaale, Shuhali **8** Rahanwin

of South Africa: **4** Boer, Yosa, Zulu **5** Asian, Bantu, Namas, Nguni, Pondo, Sotho, Swazi, Tembu, Venda **6** Damara, Kaffir **7** African, British, Bushmen, English, Swahili **8** Bechuana, Coloured, Khoikhoi, San Xhosa **9** Afrikaner, Hottentot

of Spain: **4** Pict **5** Diego, Gente, Latin **6** Basque, Espana **7** Catalan, Espanol, Iberian **8** Galician, Gallegos, Maragato

of Sri Lanka: **5** Malay, Tamil, Vedda **6** Veddah, Weddah **7** Burgher, Mahinda, Malabar **8** Eurasian **9** Cingalese, Dravidian, Sinhalese **10** Ginghalese **12** Bandaranaike

of the Sudan: **3** Bor, Dor, Fur **4** Arab, Bari, Beri, Bobo, Daza, Egba, Fula, Golo, Nuba, Nuer, Poul, Sere **5** Anuak, Bongo, Dinka, Fulah, Hausa, Joluo, Junje, Mosgu, Mossi, Negro, Tibbu, Volta **6** Acholi, Azande, Gurusi, Hamite, Lotuho, Makari, Nilote, Nubian, Senufo, Surhai, Taureg **7** Balante, Baqqara, Gubayna, Jaaliin, Nilotes, Shilluk, Songhai, Songhay, Songhoi, Sourhai **8** Kababish, Mandingo, Menkiera **9** Sarakille **10** Gurmantshi, Shaiquiyya

of Suriname: **4** Boni, Bush, Trio **5** Djuka, Dutch **6** Creole, Wayana **7** African, Chinese **10** Amerindian, Boschneger, West Indian **11** Asian Indian

of Swaziland: **5** Asian, Bantu, Swazi **10** Eurafrican

of Sweden: **4** Lapp **5** Norse, Swede **6** Viking

of Switzerland: **5** Swiss, **6** Franks **8** Alamanni, Alemanni, Italians **12** Rhaeto-Romans

of Syria: **4** Arab, Kurd, Turk **5** Alawi, Aptal, Druse, Druze **6** Afshar, Aissor, Aushar, Avshar, Awshar **7** Amorite, Ansarie, Bedouin, Nosaris, Saracen, Shemite **8** Ansarieh, Armenian **9** Ansariyah **10** Circassian **12** Khachaturian

of Taiwan: **4** Yami **5** Hakka, Hoklo **7** Chinese, Malayan **9** Fukienese, Taiwanese **10** Indonesian, Polynesian **12** Kwangtungese

of Tajikistan: **5** Tajik, Uzbek **7** Tadzhik

of Tanzania: **2** Ha **4** Arab, Gogo, Goma, Haya, Hehe **5** Asian, Bantu, Masai **6** Arusha, Chagga, Sukuma, Wagogo, Wagoma **7** African, Makonde, Sambara, Sandawe, Shirazi, Swahili, Wabunga, Zongora **8** Nyakyusa, Nyamwezi

of Thailand: **3** Lao, Mon **4** Lawa, Shan, Thai **5** Malay **6** Indian, Khymer **7** Chinese, Siamese **9** Cambodian **10** Vietnamese

of Tibet: **5** Asian, Balti, Bodpa, Drupa **6** Bhotia, Champa, Drokpa, Khamba, Khambu, Mongol, Panaka, Sherpa, Tangut **7** Bhotiya, Bhutani, Gyarung, Taghlik, Tibetan

of Togo: **3** Ana, Ewe, Twi **4** Mina **5** Hausa **6** Akposa, Kabrai **7** Bassari, Cabrais, Kabrais, Ouatchi **8** Konkomba, Kotokoli, Lotokoli

of Tonga: **10** Polynesian

of Trinidad and Tobago: **5** Irish **6** French, Syrian **7** African, Chinese, English, Spanish **8** European, Lebanese **10** East Indian, Portuguese, Venezuelan **11** Asian Indian **13** Latin American

of Tunisia: **4** Arab **6** Berber, Jewish

of Turkey: **4** Arab, Kurd, Turk **6** Seljuk

of Turkmenistan: **7** Turkmen **10** Turkmenian

of Tuvalu: **6** Samoan **10** Polynesian

of Uganda: **4** Alur, Gisu, Soga, Teso **5** Ateso, Bantu, Chiga, Ganda, Langi, Lango, Nkole, Pygmy **6** Acholi, Ankole, Bagisu, Bakega, Basoga, Batoro **7** Baganda, Banyoro, Bunyoro, Hamitic, Lugbara, Nilotic, Sudanic **9** Nyoro-Tøro **10** Banyankole, Karamojong

of Ukraine: **7** Russian **9** Ukrainian

of United Arab Emirates: **4** Arab **6** Indian **7** African, Iranian **9** Pakistani **10** South Asian

of Uruguay: **4** Yaro **5** Swiss **6** Indian **7** Italian, mestizo, Russian, Spanish **8** Charruas

of Uzbekistan: **5** Uzbek

of Vanuatu: **8** European **10** Melanesian, Polynesian **11** Micronesian

of Venezuela: **4** Bare, Pume **5** Bello, Carib, pardo, zambo **6** Arawak, Creole, Timote **7** Charoya, Guahibo, Kaliana, mestizo, mulatto, Otomaca, Timotex **8** Caquetio, Guarauno, Matilone **11** Maquiritare

of **Vietnam:** **3** Hoa, Man, Meo, Tai, Tay **4** Cham, Kinh, Nung, Thai **5** Khmer, Malay, Muong **7** Chinese **8** Annamese, Annamite **9** Cambodian **10** montagnard, Vietnamese

of Wales: **4** Celt, Kelt **5** Cymry, Kymry, Welsh **7** Brython, Silures, Taffies **8** Awabokal, Cambrian **9** Siluridan

of Western Sahara: **4** Arab **6** Berber

of Western Samoa: **6** Samoan **10** Melanesian, Polynesian

of Yemen: **4** Arab **5** Zaidi **6** Shafai, Yemeni **8** Yemenite

of Yugoslavia: **4** Serb, Slav **5** Croat **7** Bosnian, Slovene **8** Albanian, Croatian **9** Hungarian **10** Macedonian **11** Montenegrin **13** Herzegovinian

(*continued*)

opera by: 11 Tchaikovsky
character: 4 Olga **6** Lensky, Onegin **7** Tatyana **12** Prince Gremin, Tatyana Larin **14** Vladimir Lensky

Eugenie Grandet
author: 14 Honore de Balzac
character: 5 Nanon **7** Charles, Eugenie **11** Mme d'Aubrion

Euhelopus
type: 8 dinosaur, sauropod
period: 10 Cretaceous

Euhemerism
theory of: 9 Euhemerus
reduced deification of: 4 gods

Euippe
origin: 5 Roman
form: 6 maiden
parent: 6 Daunus
husband: 8 Diomedes
changed into: 5 horse

eulogize 4 hail, laud, tout **5** boost, exalt, extol **7** acclaim, commend, glorify, magnify **9** celebrate **10** compliment, panegyrize **12** pay tribute to, praise highly

eulogy 5 paean **6** homage **7** hosanna, plaudit, tribute **8** citation, encomium **9** laudation, panegyric **10** high praise **11** acclamation

Eumedes
father: 5 Dolon
companion of: 6 Aeneas
vocation: 6 herald

Eumelus
member of: 7 Trojans
commander of:
13 Thessalonians
lost race to: 8 Diomedes
wife: 8 Iphthime
companion: 6 Aeneas

Eumenides
author: 9 Aeschylus
character: 6 Apollo, Athene, Furies **7** Orestes *see* **6** Furies

Eumolpus
king of: 6 Thrace
father: 8 Poseidon
mother: 6 Chione
son: 7 Ismarus
founded: 19 Eleusinian mysteries
supported accusations of: 9 Phylonome

Euneus
father: 5 Jason
mother: 9 Hypsipyle

Eunice
son: 7 Timothy

Eunomia
member of: 5 Horae
personifies: 5 order

Eunomus
father: 10 Architeles
cup bearer of: 6 Oeneus
slain by: 8 Hercules

Eunuch 6 Biztha, Careas, Zethar **7** Abagtha, Harbona, Mehuman

euphemism 11 prudishness, refined term **12** delicate term, overdelicacy **13** prudish phrase **14** mild expression, overrefinement

Euphemus
father: 8 Poseidon
mother: 6 Europa
aided: 9 Argonauts

Euphorbus
father: 8 Panthous
brother: 9 Hyperenor, Polydemas
fought with: 7 Trojans

euphoria 7 ecstasy, elation, rapture **9** well-being

Euphorion
father: 8 Achilles
mother: 5 Helen

Euphrosyne
member of: 6 Graces

Euphues
character in: 20 Euphues and His England **22** Euphues The Anatomy of Wit
author: 4 Lyly

Euripides
author of: 3 Ion **5** Medea **6** Hecuba **7** Electra, Orestes **8** Alcestis, Heracles **10** Andromache, Heraclidae, Hippolytus, Phoenissae, The Bacchae **13** The Suppliants **14** The Trojan Women **16** Iphigenia in Aulis **17** Iphigenia in Tauris **21** The Children of Heracles

Eurippa
epithet of: 7 Artemis
means: 18 delighting in horses

Europa
also: 6 Europe
father: 6 Agenor
mother: 10 Telephassa
brother: 5 Cilix **6** Cadmus **7** Phoenix
son: 5 Minos **8** Sarpedon **12** Rhadamanthus
daughter: 5 Crete
abducted by: 4 Zeus

Europe *see* **6** Europa

Europe *see box*

Eurotes
father: 5 Myles

Eurus
origin: 5 Greek
personifies: 8 east wind **13** southeast wind

Euryale
member of: 7 Gorgons

Eurybates
companion of: 8 Odysseus

Eurybia
father: 6 Pontus
mother: 4 Gaea
mated with: 5 Crius

Eurydice
also: 7 Agriope
form: 5 dryad
husband: 7 Orpheus
daughter: 8 Themiste
pursued by: 9 Aristaeus

Euryganeia
son: 8 Eteocles **9** Polynices

Eurylochus
companion of: 8 Odysseus

Eurynome
father: 7 Oceanus
mother: 6 Tethys
sister: 6 Thetis
daughters: 6 Graces

Eurypylus
origin: 5 Greek
occupation: 7 warrior
father: 8 Poseidon, Telephus
mother: 8 Astyoche
uncle: 5 Priam
killed by: 8 Hercules **11** Neoptolemus

Eurysaces
father: 14 Telamonian Ajax
mother: 8 Tecmessa
inherited: 6 shield

Eurysthenes
origin: 7 Spartan
father: 11 Aristodemus
twin brother: 7 Procles
shared: 6 throne
shared throne with: 7 Procles

Eurystheus
king of: 6 Tiryns **7** Mycenae
father: 9 Sthenelus
mother: 7 Nicippe
cousin: 8 Hercules
son: 9 Perimedes
imposed: 6 labors
number of labors:
6 twelve
imposed on: 8 Hercules

Europe
  country: **5** Italy, Malta, Spain, Wales **6** France, Greece, Latvia, Monaco, Norway, Poland, Russia, Sweden **7** Albania, Andorra, Armenia, Austria, Belarus, Belgium, Croatia, Denmark, England, Estonia, Georgia, Germany, Hungary, Iceland, Ireland, Romania, Ukraine **8** Bulgaria, Portugal, Scotland, Slovakia, Slovenia **9** Lithuania, Macedonia, San Marino **10** Azerbaijan, Luxembourg, Yugoslavia **11** Byelorussia, Netherlands, Switzerland, Vatican City **13** Czech Republic, Liechtenstein **14** Czechoslovakia **17** Bosnia-Herzegovina
  city: **4** Bern, Bonn, Oslo, Rome **5** Paris, Sofia, Vaduz **6** Athens, Dublin, Lisbon, London, Madrid, Monaco, Moscow, Prague, Tirana, Vienna, Warsaw **7** Cardiff **8** Belgrade, Brussels, Budapest, Helsinki, Valletta **9** Amsterdam, Bucharest, Edinburgh, Reykjavik, San Marino, Stockholm **10** Bratislava, Copenhagen, Luxembourg **14** Andorra la Vella
  river: **3** Don **4** Ebro, Elbe, Oder **5** Loire, Neman, Rhine, Rhone, Seine, Tagus, Volga **6** Danube, Thames **7** Dnieper, Pechora, Vistula **8** Dniester
  island: **3** Man **4** Skye **5** Crete, Malta **6** Faeroe, Sicily **7** Corsica, Iceland, Ireland **8** Balearic, Sardinia **12** British Isles
  mountain/mountain range: **4** Alps **7** Balkans **8** Caucasus, Pyrenees **9** Apennines **11** Carpathians **12** Sierra Nevada
  highest point: **11** Mount Elbrus
  lowest point: **10** Caspian Sea
  sea: **4** Aral, Azov, Kara **5** Black, North, White **6** Aegean, Baltic **7** Caspian, Marmara **8** Adriatic **13** Mediterranean
  people: **3** Hun **4** Gael, Pict, Serb **5** Celts, Croat, Danes, Dutch, Jutes, Kymry, Marur, Poles, Scots, Slavs, Tatar, Welsh **6** Czechs, Franks **7** Basques, Britons, Gypsies, Iberian, Magyars, Slovaks, Slovene **8** Alamanni, Cossacks, Tyrolean, Walloons
  language: **5** Czech **6** Danish, German, French, Polish, Slovak **7** English, Italian, Romance, Russian, Spanish, Swedish **8** Germanic **9** Bulgarian, Portugese **11** Balto-slavic
  religion: **5** Islam **6** Jewish, Muslim **8** Anglican, Lutheran **9** Methodist **10** Protestant **12** Presbyterian **13** Dutch Reformed, Greek Orthodox, Roman Catholic **15** Church of England, Eastern Orthodox
  holiday: **11** Bastille Day, National Day **12** Guy Fawkes Day **13** Liberation Day, St Patricks Day **14** Queens Birthday **15** Independence Day **19** Heroes of the Republic

Eurytion
  form: **7** centaur
  father: **4** Ares **5** Actor
  companion of: **6** Aeneus
  guarded cattle of: **6** Geryon
  killed by: **6** Peleus **8** Hercules

Eurytus
  form: **5** giant
  father: **5** Actor **7** Auglaus **8** Melaneus
  twin brother: **7** Cteatus
  noted for: **7** archery
  slain by: **8** Hercules

Euterpe
  member of: **5** Muses
  muse of: **5** music **11** lyric poetry

evacuate 4 quit **5** leave **6** desert, remove, vacate **7** abandon, forsake, move out, take out **8** order out **12** withdraw from

evade 4 duck, shun **5** avoid, dodge, elude, hedge, parry **6** escape, eschew **7** fend off **8** sidestep **10** circumvent, equivocate **12** steer clear of

Evadne
  father: **6** Pelias **8** Poseidon
  mother: **6** Pitana
  sister: **9** Amphinome
  husband: **8** Capaneus

evaluate 4 rate **5** assay, gauge, judge, value, weigh **6** assess, size up **8** appraise, estimate

evaluation 4 test **8** analysis, judgment **9** appraisal **10** assessment, estimation

evaluator 5 judge **6** critic, tester **7** analyst, arbiter **8** assessor, reviewer **9** appraiser, estimator

Evander
  father: **6** Hermes **9** Carmentis
  mother: **6** Themis
  daughter: **4** Roma
  allied with: **6** Aeneas

evanesce 6 vanish **8** fade away, pass away **9** disappear, dissipate, evaporate

evanescence 9 vanishing **10** fading away **12** ephemerality **13** disappearance **14** transitoriness

evanescent 8 fleeting **9** ephemeral, transient **10** short-lived, transitory

Evangeline
  author: **24** Henry Wadsworth Longfellow
  character: **17** Gabriel Lajeunesse **23** Evangeline Bellefontaine

evangelist 4 John, Luke, Mark **7** apostle, Matthew **8** disciple, minister, preacher, reformer **9** apostolic, missioner, soulsaver **10** missionary, revivalist **12** Bible Thumper, propagandist, proselytizer **17** religious crusader

Evan Harrington
  author: **14** George Meredith
  character: **6** Louisa **10** Jack Raikes **11** Rose Jocelyn **12** Tom Cogglesby **13** Count de Saldar, Juliana Bonner **14** Caroline Strike **15** Andrew Cogglesby, Ferdinand Laxley, Melville Jocelyn **16** Countess de Saldar, Harriet Cogglesby **21** Melchisedek Harrington

Evans, Dame Edith
  born: **6** London **7** England
  roles: **8** Tom Jones **11** A Doll's House **13** The Whisperers **14** The Chalk Garden **27** The Importance of Being Earnest

Evans, Mary Anne
  real name of: **11** George Eliot

Evans, Maurice
  born: **6** Dorset **7** England **10** Dorchester
  roles: **9** Saint Joan **13** Rosemary's Baby **14** Man and Superman, Romeo and Juliet **15** Heartbreak House, Planet of the Apes **17** The Devil's Disciple **18** Gilbert and Sullivan **19** Androcles and the Lion

evaporate 5 dry up 6 dispel, vanish 7 scatter 8 dissolve, evanesce, fade away, melt away, vaporize 9 dehydrate, desiccate, disappear, dissipate

evasion 7 dodging, ducking, eluding 8 shunning 9 avoidance 12 sidestepping 13 circumventing, shrinking from 15 attempt to escape

evasive 6 shifty 7 devious, dodging, elusive, elusory, hedging 9 ambiguous, deceitful, deceptive, equivocal 10 misleading 11 dissembling 12 equivocating

Eva Trout
author: 14 Elizabeth Bowen

eve 4 dusk 6 female, sunset 7 evening, sunset 8 eventide 9 day before

Eve
husband: 4 Adam
son: 4 Abel, Cain, Seth
home: 4 Eden

Evelina
author: 11 Fanny Burney

even 4 calm, fair, flat, just, true 5 equal, flush, level, plane, plumb 6 placid, smooth, square, steady 7 balance, equable, flatten, regular, the same, uniform 8 balanced, constant, equalize, matching, parallel, straight, unbiased 9 equitable, identical, impartial, make flush, unruffled, unvarying 10 straighten, unwavering 11 make uniform, unexcitable 12 even-tempered, make parallel 13 dispassionate

evening 3 eve 4 dusk, even 6 sunset 7 day's end, sundown 8 eventide, gloaming, twilight 9 nightfall 10 close of day

evenly matched 5 equal 8 of a piece 9 identical 10 well suited 13 one and the same

evenness 7 balance 8 calmness, equality, fairness, flatness, sameness 9 placidity 10 regularity, smoothness, steadiness, uniformity 11 equivalency

event 4 bout, game 7 contest, episode 8 incident, occasion 9 happening, milestone 10 experience, occurrence, tournament 11 competition

even-tempered 4 calm 6 serene 7 equable, patient 11 good-natured, unflappable 12 mild-tempered, well-adjusted

eventful 7 crucial, epochal, fateful, notable, weighty

8 critical, exciting, historic 9 important, memorable, momentous, thrilling 10 noteworthy 11 significant 13 consequential, unforgettable

eventide 4 dusk 6 sunset 7 evening, sundown 8 gloaming, twilight 9 nightfall

eventual 5 final, later 6 coming, future 7 ensuing 8 imminent, ultimate, upcoming 9 following, impending, resulting 10 consequent, subsequent 11 prospective

eventually 6 one day 7 finally 8 in the end, sometime 10 ultimately 12 in the long run 13 sooner or later 17 in the course of time 20 when all is said and done

Eventus see 12 Bonus Eventus

even up 3 tie 5 align 8 make even 10 straighten

Evenus
father: 4 Ares
mother: 8 Demonice
daughter: 8 Marpessa

Eve of St Agnes, The
author: 9 John Keats

ever 5 at all 6 always 7 forever 9 at any time, eternally, in any case 10 at all times, constantly 11 incessantly, perpetually 12 continuously

Everdene, Bathsheba
character in: 22 Far From the Madding Crowd
author: 5 Hardy

Everes
son: 8 Tiresias

Everglade State
nickname of: 7 Florida

evergreen 3 fir, yew 4 pine 5 heath, holly 6 jujube, laurel, myrtle, needle, privet 7 arbutus, casiope, conifer, jasmine, juniper 8 camellia, hawthorn, oleander, rosemary 9 mistletoe, sugarbush 11 conebearing 12 rhododendrum

Evergreen State
nickname of: 10 Washington

everlasting 7 durable, endless, eternal, lasting, tedious, undying 8 constant, immortal, infinite, timeless, tiresome 9 ceaseless, continual, incessant, perpetual, unceasing, wearisome 10 continuous, ever-living 11 long-lasting, never-ending 12 imperishable, interminable 14 indestructible

evermore 6 always 7 forever 9 eternally 10 for all time 13 everlastingly

ever upward
Latin: 9 excelsior
motto of: 7 New York (state)

everybody
French: 11 tout le monde

everyday 4 dull 5 daily, stock, trite, usual 6 common, square 7 mundane, regular, routine 8 familiar, ordinary, workaday 9 customary, hackneyed, quotidian 11 commonplace, day after day, established, stereotyped 12 conventional, run-of-the-mill 13 unimaginative

Everyman
author: 7 unknown
character: 3 God 5 Death, Goods 6 Beauty 7 Kindred 8 Strength 9 Good Deeds, Knowledge, Messenger 10 Fellowship

every man for himself
French: 12 sauve qui peut

Every Man in His Humour
author: 9 Ben Jonson
character: 6 Kitely 7 Bridget 8 Bobadill, Wellbred 9 Brainworm, Downright 13 Edward Knowell 14 Justice Clement

Every Man out of His Humour
author: 9 Ben Jonson
character: 6 Deliro 7 Fungoso, Sordido 9 Macilente, Sogliardo 10 Puntarvolo 12 Carlo Buffone 15 Fastidious Brisk

everyone
French: 11 tout le monde

everywhere 7 all over 10 every place, far and near, far and wide, throughout 11 extensively, in all places, universally 12 the world over, ubiquitously 14 to the four winds

evict 4 oust 5 eject, expel 6 remove 7 kick out, turn out 8 dislodge, get rid of, throw out 10 dispossess

evidence 4 fact, sign 5 proof, token 7 exhibit, grounds 9 testimony 10 indication 11 affirmation 12 confirmation, illustration 13 corroboration, documentation, material proof 14 authentication, substantiation 15 exemplification

evident 5 clear, plain 6 patent 7 certain, obvious, visible 8 apparent, manifest, tangible 10 noticeable, undeniable 11 conspicuous, perceptible 12 demonstrable, unmistakable 14 unquestionable 24 plain as the nose on your face

evidently 7 clearly, plainly
9 assumedly, certainly, doubtless, obviously **10** apparently, undeniably **11** doubtlessly
12 unmistakably **14** unquestionably **16** to all appearances

evil 3 bad, sin **4** base, vice, vile **5** venal **6** sinful, wicked **7** heinous, immoral, vicious **8** baseness, iniquity, sinister **9** depravity, malicious, malignant, nefarious, turpitude **10** corruption, immorality, iniquitous, malevolent, pernicious, villainous, wickedness, wrongdoing **12** black-hearted, unprincipled, unscrupulous
goddess of: 7 Sekhmet

evildoer 6 sinner **7** culprit, villain **9** miscreant, wrongdoer **10** malefactor **12** transgressor

evil-minded 4 base **5** nasty **6** wicked **7** ignoble, immoral **8** depraved **10** despicable, iniquitous, villainous **12** dishonorable, unprincipled

evilness 6 malice **7** cruelty **8** villainy **9** barbarity, malignity **10** sinfulness, wickedness

evince 4 show **6** convey, reveal **7** display, exhibit, express **11** communicate, demonstrate **12** give evidence

Evius see **7** Bacchus

Evnissyen
origin: 5 Welsh
brother: 4 Bran
10 Manawyddan
sister: 7 Branwen
caused: 3 war
between: 5 Irish **7** British
killed: 6 nephew

evoke 4 stir **5** rouse, waken **6** arouse, awaken, call up, elicit, excite, induce, invite, invoke, summon **7** produce, provoke, suggest **9** call forth, conjure up, stimulate **10** bring forth

evolution 4 rise **6** change, growth **8** fruition, increase **9** expansion, unfolding **10** maturation **11** development, enlargement, progression **13** metamorphosis
founder of theory:
13 Charles Darwin
forerunner of theory:
12 Charles Lyell **18** Chevalier de Lamarck

evolve 4 grow **5** ripen **6** expand, mature, unfold, unroll **7** develop, enlarge **8** increase

Ewell, Tom
real name: 14 Yewell Tompkins
born: 11 Owensboro KY
roles: 8 Adam's Rib **9** State

Fair **14** The Great Gatsby **16** Tender Is the Night, The Seven Year Itch

ewer 3 jug, urn **5** basin **6** vessel **7** pitcher

Ewing, Patrick
sport: 10 basketball
team: 13 New York Knicks
15 Georgetown Hoyas

exacerbate 3 irk **5** anger **6** deepen, worsen **7** inflame, magnify, provoke, sharpen **8** heighten, increase, irritate **9** aggravate, intensify **10** exaggerate **12** fan the flames **16** pour oil on the fire **17** add insult to injury **18** add fuel to the flames **19** rub salt into the wound

exact 4 take, true **5** claim, force, mulct, right, wrest **6** compel, demand, extort, strict **7** careful, correct, extract, literal, precise, require, squeeze **8** accurate, clear-cut, exacting, explicit, specific **9** on the head, on the nose **10** methodical, meticulous, scrupulous, systematic
11 painstaking, punctilious, to the letter, unequivocal

exacting 4 hard **5** harsh, rigid, stern, tough **6** severe, strict, trying **7** arduous **8** critical **9** demanding, difficult, hardnosed, strenuous, unbending, unsparing **10** hard-headed, meticulous, no-nonsense

exactly 4 just **5** fully, quite, truly **6** indeed, just so, wholly **7** quite so **8** entirely, of course, strictly **9** assuredly, certainly, correctly, literally, precisely **10** absolutely, accurately, definitely, explicitly, that's right **12** specifically

exactness 8 accuracy **9** precision **10** exactitude **12** accurateness

exact satisfaction 6 avenge, punish **7** get back, get even, revenge **9** retaliate **14** get one's own back

exaggerate 5 boast **6** overdo **7** amplify, lay it on, magnify, stretch **9** embellish, embroider, enlarge on, overstate **11** hyperbolize

exaggerated 7 extreme, intense **10** inordinate, overstated **14** overemphasized

exalt 4 laud **5** cheer, elate, extol, honor **6** praise, uplift **7** acclaim, applaud, commend, elevate, ennoble, glorify, inspire, magnify, worship **8** venerate **9** celebrate, stimulate

10 exhilarate, make much of **12** pay tribute to

exaltation 4 high **5** bliss, glory, honor **6** praise **7** dignity, ecstasy, elation, rapture, tribute, worship **8** grandeur, nobility, praising **9** happiness, panegyric, transport **10** eulogizing, exultation, veneration **11** celebration, deification **12** exhilaration

exalted 2 up **5** grand, happy, lofty, noble **6** august, elated, lordly **7** excited, notable **8** blissful, ecstatic, elevated, glorious, inspired, uplifted **9** dignified, honorable, rapturous, venerable **10** heightened **11** high-ranking, illustrious, magnificent

exaltedness 5 bliss **6** height **7** ecstasy, elation, heights, rapture **8** highness, nobility **9** elevation, loftiness, transport

examination 4 exam, quiz, test **5** assay, audit, final, orals, probe, study **6** review, survey **7** midterm, perusal **8** analysis, scrutiny **10** inspection **11** looking over **13** investigation **15** physical checkup

examine 4 pump, quiz, scan, test, view **5** audit, grill, probe, query, study **6** peruse, ponder, review, survey **7** explore, inspect, observe **8** consider, look into, look over, question **10** scrutinize **11** inquire into, interrogate, investigate, take stock of

examiner 6 tester **8** inquirer, reviewer, surveyor **12** interrogator, investigator

example 5 ideal, model **6** sample **7** paragon, pattern **8** exemplar, specimen, standard **9** archetype, prototype **11** case in point **12** illustration **14** representation **15** exemplification

exasperate 3 bug, irk, vex **4** rile **5** anger, annoy, chafe, pique **6** bother, enrage, harass, madden, offend, rankle, ruffle **7** incense, provoke, turn off **8** irritate **9** aggravate, infuriate **15** try one's patience

exasperating 7 irksome **8** annoying **9** vexatious **10** irritating **11** infuriating

ex cathedra 12 from the chair **13** with authority **22** from the seat of authority

excavate 3 dig **4** mine **5** dig up, gouge **6** burrow, cut out, dig out, furrow, groove, quarry, tunnel **7** uncover, unearth **8** scoop out **9** hollow out **11** make a hole in

excavation 3 dig, pit **4** hole, mine, sump **5** ditch, grave, shaft, space **6** cavity, dugout, trench, trough **7** digging, opening

exceed 4 pass **5** excel **6** go over, outrun, overdo **7** outpace, outrank, surpass **8** go beyond, outreach, outrival, outstrip, surmount **9** come first, overshoot, transcend **10** be superior **11** predominate

exceedingly 4 very **6** vastly **7** greatly, notably **9** amazingly, eminently, extremely, supremely, unusually **10** enormously, especially, unwontedly, very highly **11** excessively **12** immeasurably, impressively, inordinately, preeminently, surpassingly **13** astonishingly, outstandingly, superlatively **15** extraordinarily

excel 5 outdo **6** exceed **7** prevail, surpass **8** outrival, outstrip **9** rank first **10** tower above **11** predominate, take the cake **20** walk off with the honors

excellence 5 merit **7** quality **8** eminence **9** greatness **10** perfection **11** distinction, high quality, preeminence, superiority **13** transcendence

excellent 4 aces, A-one, fine, tops **5** great, nifty, prime, super, swell **6** bang-up, choice, grade A, superb **7** capital, classic, notable **8** peerless, sterling, superior, terrific, top-notch **9** admirable, exemplary, first-rate, matchless, superfine, wonderful **10** first-class, preeminent, tremendous **11** exceptional, outstanding, superlative

excelsior 10 ever upward motto of: **7** New York (state)

Excelsior State nickname of: **7** New York

except 3 ban, bar, but **4** omit, save **6** enjoin, excuse, exempt, reject, remove, saving **7** barring, besides, exclude, shut out **8** count out, disallow, pass over **9** eliminate, excepting, excluding, other than **11** exclusive of

excepted 6 exempt **7** excused **8** excluded **11** not included

exception 6 oddity, rarity **7** anomaly, removal **8** omission **9** debarment, deviation, exclusion, exemption, isolation, rejection, seclusion

10 difference, leaving out, separation **11** elimination, peculiarity, repudiation, segregation, shutting out, special case **12** disallowment, irregularity, renunciation **13** inconsistency

exceptional 3 odd **4** rare **5** great, queer **6** unique **7** special, strange, unusual **8** aberrant, abnormal, atypical, freakish, peculiar, singular, superior, terrific, uncommon, unwonted **9** anomalous, excellent, irregular, marvelous, unheard of, unnatural, wonderful **10** first-class, inimitable, noteworthy, out-of-sight, phenomenal, remarkable **11** outstanding **12** incomparable **13** extraordinary, unprecedented **17** better than average

exception to the rule 7 anomaly **11** abnormality **12** irregularity

excerpt 4 part **5** piece **7** extract, portion, section **8** abstract, fragment **9** quotation, selection **13** quoted passage

excess 4 glut **5** extra, flood, spare **7** residue, surfeit, surplus, too much **8** fullness, overflow, plethora **9** avalanche, excessive, profusion, remainder, repletion **10** inundation, lavishness, oversupply **11** undue amount **13** overabundance **14** superabundance

excessive 5 undue **6** excess **7** extreme, profuse, too much **8** needless **9** senseless **10** immoderate, inordinate **11** exaggerated, extravagant, superfluous, unnecessary **12** overabundant, unreasonable **16** disproportionate

excessively 5 enorm **7** greatly **9** extremely, intensely **11** exceedingly, fanatically **12** boisterously, exorbitantly, inordinately **14** overabundantly

exchange 4 swap **5** trade **6** barter, switch **8** bandying, trade off **9** tit for tat **10** quid pro quo **11** convert into, give-and-take, interchange, reciprocate, reciprocity

exchange blows 3 box **5** clash, fight **6** battle, combat, tussle **7** contend, contest, grapple **8** skirmish **11** cross swords

exchange of viewpoints 6 debate, parley **8** dialogue **10** conference, discussion

exchange views 6 confer, debate **7** consult, discuss **8** consider, talk over **12** compare notes

excise 3 tax **4** duty **6** cut off, cut out, impost, remove **7** extract **8** pluck out **9** eradicate, surcharge

excitable 4 edgy **5** jumpy **7** jittery, nervous **8** feverish, frenzied, skittish **9** flappable, hotheaded **10** highstrung, passionate **11** combustible, inflammable

excite 4 fire, move, whet **5** evoke, pique, rouse, waken **6** arouse, awaken, elicit, foment, incite, kindle, spur on, stir up, thrill **7** agitate, animate, inflame, provoke **8** energize **9** electrify, galvanize, instigate, stimulate, titillate **13** get a kick out of

excited 4 daft **5** afire, astir **6** ablaze **7** aroused **8** agitated, ecstatic, frenzied, inflamed, turned on **9** disturbed, stirred up **10** magnetized **11** electrified

excitement 3 ado **4** flap, stir, to-do **5** furor, kicks **6** action, flurry, frenzy, hoopla, thrill, tumult **7** elation, ferment, flutter, turmoil **8** activity, brouhaha, interest **9** adventure, agitation, animation, commotion, fireworks **10** enthusiasm **11** stimulation

exciting 5 spicy **6** moving, risque **7** rousing, zestful **8** dazzling, stirring **9** affecting, impelling, inspiring, thrilling **11** hair-raising, provocative, sensational, stimulating, titillating **12** breathtaking, electrifying **13** spine-tingling

exclaim 4 howl, yell **5** shout **6** bellow, cry out **7** call out **8** proclaim **9** ejaculate **10** vociferate

exclamation 3 cry **4** howl, yell, yelp **5** shout **6** bellow, outcry, shriek, squeal **7** screech **9** expletive **11** ejaculation **12** interjection, vociferation

exclude 3 ban, bar **4** omit, oust **5** eject, evict, expel **6** banish, except, forbid, refuse, reject, remove **7** boycott, keep out, rule out, shut out **8** disallow, leave out, prohibit, set aside, throw out **9** blackball, repudiate **13** shut the door on

excluding 3 but **4** save **6** except, saving **7** banning, barring, besides **9** excepting, other than **10** keeping out

exclusion 6 ouster **7** barring, refusal, removal **8** ejection, eviction **9** debarment, dismissal, expelling, expulsion, rejection, restraint **10** banishment, keeping out, preclusion, prevention **11** prohibition, throwing out **12** nonadmission

exclusive 4 full, posh, sole **5** aloof, total **6** closed, entire, single **7** private **8** absolute, clannish, cliquish, complete, snobbish, unshared **9** undivided, selective **10** restricted **11** restrictive

exclusive of .3 but **4** save **6** except, saving **7** barring, besides **9** excepting, excluding, other than

excommunicate 3 ban **4** oust **5** eject, expel **6** banish, remove **8** unchurch **12** anathematize

excommunication 3 ban **6** ouster **8** anathema **10** banishment **12** proscription

excoriate 4 flay **5** curse **6** berate, revile **7** censure **8** denounce, execrate **9** skin alive

excrescence 4 bump, hump, knob, knot, lump **5** bulge, gnarl **6** nodule **8** swelling **10** protrusion **12** protuberance

excrete 4 void **5** expel **8** evacuate **9** discharge, eliminate

excruciating 5 acute **6** fierce, severe **7** cutting, extreme, intense, racking, violent **9** agonizing, exquisite, torturous **10** lacerating, tormenting, unbearable **11** unendurable **12** insufferable

exculpate 5 clear **6** acquit, excuse, pardon **7** absolve **9** exonerate, let one off, vindicate

excursion 4 hike, ride, tour, trek, trip, walk **5** drive, jaunt, sally, tramp **6** cruise, flight, junket, outing, ramble, sortie, stroll, voyage **10** expedition **12** pleasure trip

excusatory 9 defensive **10** apologetic **11** extenuatory, vindicatory **13** justificatory

excuse 4 free **5** alibi, clear, spare **6** acquit, defend, exempt, let off, pardon, reason **7** absolve, condone, defense, explain, forgive, indulge, justify, release **8** argument, bear with, mitigate, overlook, palliate, pass over **9** disregard, exculpate, exemption, exonerate, extenuate, gloss over, let one off, relieve of, vindicate, whitewash **10** absolution **11** exoneration, vindication **12** apologize for **13** justification **16** make allowance for **17** accept one's apology

execrable 4 vile **5** awful

8 dreadful, terrible **9** atrocious, revolting **10** abominable

execrate 4 hate **5** abhor **6** detest, loathe **7** despise **9** abominate, can't stand, excoriate **10** shrink from **11** can't stomach **12** be revolted by **13** be nauseated by, find repulsive **15** be disgusted with **20** regard with repugnance

execration 4 hate **6** hating **7** disgust **8** loathing **9** despising, repulsion, revulsion **10** repugnance **11** abomination, detestation

execute 2 do **3** act **4** kill, play, slay **5** enact **6** effect, murder, render **7** achieve, enforce, fulfill, perform, realize, sustain **8** carry out, complete, massacre **9** discharge **10** accomplish, administer, consummate, effectuate, perpetrate, put to death **11** assassinate **12** carry through **13** put into effect

execution 5 doing **7** killing, slaying **9** discharge, effecting, rendition **10** completion **11** achievement, carrying out, fulfillment, performance, realization, transaction **14** accomplishment, administration, implementation, interpretation, putting to death

executioner 6 hit man, killer, slayer **7** butcher, hangman **8** assassin, murderer

Executioner's Song, The
author: **12** Norman Mailer

executive 7 manager **8** chairman, director, overseer **9** president **10** leadership, managerial, supervisor **11** directorial, supervisory **13** administrator **14** administrative, superintendent

executives 7 leaders **8** managers, officers **9** directors **13** governing body **14** administration

executor 4 doer **5** agent **9** performer **13** administrator

exegesis 10 exposition **11** explanation **14** interpretation **18** explication de texte

exemplar 5 ideal, model **7** example, pattern **8** original, standard **9** archetype, prototype

exemplary 5 ideal, model **6** sample **7** typical **8** laudable, sterling **9** admirable, emulative, estimable, nonpareil **10** noteworthy **11** commendable, meritorious **12** illustrative, praiseworthy **14** characteristic, representative

exemplification 7 epitome, es-

sence, example **8** citation, evidence **10** embodiment **11** case in point **12** illustration **13** documentation **14** representation **15** personification

exemplify 6 depict, embody, typify **8** instance **9** epitomize, personify, represent **10** illustrate **11** demonstrate **12** characterize

exempli gratia 6 such as **10** for example **19** for the sake of example
  abbreviation: **2** eg

exempt 4 free **5** clear, freed, spare **6** except, excuse, immune, pardon, spared **7** absolve, cleared, excused, release, relieve **8** absolved, excepted, relieved **9** not liable, privilege **10** privileged

exemption 6 excuse **7** expense, freedom, release **8** immunity **9** allowance, deduction, exception **10** absolution **12** dispensation

exercise 3 use **4** show **5** apply, drill, exert, teach, train, tutor, wield **6** employ, school, warm-up **7** break in, develop, display, execute, exhibit, perform, prepare, program, utilize, workout **8** accustom, aerobics, carry out, ceremony, movement, practice, training **9** discharge, inculcate, schooling **10** daily dozen, discipline, employment, gymnastics, isometrics **11** application, demonstrate, give lessons, performance, utilization **12** calisthenics **14** do calisthenics

exert 3 use **5** apply, wield **6** employ, expend **7** utilize **8** exercise, put forth, resort to **9** discharge, make use of **11** put in action, set in motion

exertion 4 toil, work **5** labor, pains **6** effort, energy **7** travail, trouble **8** activity, endeavor, industry, strength, struggle **11** application, elbow grease

ex facie 9 on the face **10** apparently **11** from the face

ex facto 8 actually **15** according to fact

exhalation 4 puff **6** breath, wheeze, whoosh **10** expiration **12** breathing out

exhale 4 huff, pant, puff **6** expire **7** breathe, respire **10** breathe out

exhaust 3 fag, tax **4** bush, poop, tire **5** drain, empty, spend, use up **6** expend, finish, strain, weaken **7** consume, deplete, disable, draw off, draw out, fatigue, wear out 8 enervate, overtire 9 dissipate 10 debilitate, devitalize, run through 13 sap one's energy

exhausted 4 beat, gone 5 all in, spent 6 bushed, done in, pooped, used up 7 drained, emptied, wearied, worn out 8 bankrupt, consumed, depleted, expended, fatigued, finished, tired out 9 dead tired, enervated, played out 11 devitalized 12 impoverished

exhausting 5 tough 6 tiring, uphill 7 arduous 8 toilsome 9 difficult, fatiguing, Herculean, laborious, Sisyphean, wearisome 10 burdensome

exhaustion 7 fatigue, using up 8 draining, spending 9 depletion, tiredness, weariness 10 enervation 11 consumption

exhaustive 6 all-out 7 in-depth 8 complete, profound, sweeping, thorough 9 intensive 12 all-embracing, all-inclusive 13 comprehensive

exhibit 3 air 4 show 6 flaunt, parade, reveal, unveil 7 display 8 brandish 9 put on view 10 exhibition, exposition, make public 11 demonstrate 12 bring to light 13 public showing

exhibition 4 show 5 array 7 display, exhibit, showing 9 unveiling 10 exposition 13 demonstration, public showing

exhibitionist 7 flasher, show-off 15 attention-seeker

exhilarate 4 lift 5 cheer, elate 6 excite, perk up 7 animate, delight, enliven, gladden, hearten, quicken 9 stimulate 10 invigorate

exhilaration 6 gaiety 7 delight, elation 8 gladness, vivacity 9 animation 10 exaltation, excitement, joyousness, liveliness 11 high spirits 16 lightheartedness

exhort 3 bid 4 goad, prod, spur, urge 5 egg on, press 6 advise, enjoin 7 beseech, implore 8 admonish, advocate, appeal to, persuade 9 encourage, plead with, recommend 14 give a pep talk to

exhortation 6 sermon, urging 7 bidding, lecture, pep talk 8 dictates, harangue, prodding 9 prompting

exhumation 9 digging up 12 disinterment 13 disentombment

exhume 5 dig up 8 disinter

exigency 3 fix, jam 5 needs, pinch 6 crisis, pickle, plight, scrape, strait 7 demands 8 hardship, quandary 9 emergency, extremity, urgencies 10 difficulty 11 constraints, contingency, necessities, predicament 12 circumstance, requirements

exigent 5 vital 6 urgent 8 critical, exacting, pressing 9 demanding, difficult, necessary

exile 2 DP 4 oust 5 eject, expel 6 banish, deport, emigre, pariah 7 outcast, refugee 8 drive out, expellee 9 expulsion 10 banishment, expatriate

Exile, The
author: 9 Pearl Buck

exiled person 5 exile 6 emigre 7 outcast 8 expellee 10 expatriate

Exile's Return
author: 13 Malcolm Cowley

exist 4 last, live, stay 5 abide, ensue, occur 6 endure, happen, obtain, remain 7 breathe, prevail, survive

existence 4 life 5 being 7 reality 8 presence, survival 9 actuality, animation, endurance 11 continuance, materiality, subsistence, tangibility

existent 4 real 5 alive 6 actual, extant, living 7 present 8 existing, tangible 9 surviving, to be found 11 in existence

existing 4 real 5 being 6 actual, extant, living 7 ongoing, present 9 existence, surviving, to be found 10 continuing, prevailing 11 established, in existence 12 accomplished

exit 4 blow 5 go out, leave, split 6 cut out, depart, egress, escape, exodus, way out 7 retreat 8 withdraw 9 departure 10 withdrawal 11 take a powder

ex libris 15 out of the books of 16 from the library of

ex nihilo nihil fit 25 out of nothing nothing is made 27 nothing is created from nothing

exocuticle
consists of: 9 sclerotin

exodus 4 exit 5 exile 6 flight, hegira 9 departure, migration 10 emigration, going forth

Exodus
author: 8 Leon Uris
story of founding of: 6 Israel

exonerate 4 free 5 clear 6 ac-

quit 7 absolve, forgive 9 exculpate, vindicate 12 find innocent

exoneration 8 clearing 10 absolution 11 exculpation, vindication

exorbitant 4 dear 5 undue 6 costly 7 extreme 8 enormous 9 egregious, excessive, expensive, out-of-line 10 high-priced, inordinate, oppressive, outrageous, overpriced 11 extravagant 12 extortionate, preposterous, unreasonable

exorcise 5 expel 7 cast out 8 get rid of

Exorcist, The
author: 18 William Peter Blatty
director: 15 William Friedkin
cast: 8 Lee J Cobb 10 Linda Blair 11 Jason Miller, Max von Sydow 12 Ellen Burstyn
Oscar for: 10 screenplay

exoskeleton
of insect: 5 shell 8 body wall
part: 10 epicuticle, exocuticle 11 endocuticle

exoteric 4 open 6 public, simple 7 popular 8 exterior, external, outsider

exotic 5 alien 6 quaint, unique 7 foreign, strange, unusual 8 colorful, peculiar, striking 9 different, not native 10 from abroad, intriguing, outlandish, unfamiliar 11 exceptional 13 not indigenous

expand 4 grow, open 5 swell, widen 6 dilate, evolve, extend, fatten, spread, unfold, unfurl, unroll 7 amplify, augment, develop, distend, enlarge, inflate, magnify, stretch, unravel 8 heighten, increase, multiply 9 outspread, spread out 10 aggrandize

expanded 4 grew 5 grown 7 dilated, swelled, swollen, widened 8 enlarged, extended, unfolded, unfurled, unrolled 9 augmented, broadened, increased, outspread, spread out, stretched 10 heightened 11 aggrandized

expanse 4 area 5 field, range, reach, space, sweep 6 extent 7 breadth, compass, stretch 9 magnitude

expansion 6 growth 8 dilation, increase, swelling, widening 9 enlarging, extension, spreading 10 amplifying, distention, magnifying, stretching 11 development, enlargement, lengthening, multiplying

12 augmentation
13 amplification

expansive 4 free, open, vast, wide **5** broad **6** genial **7** affable, amiable, general, liberal **8** effusive, generous, outgoing **9** bounteous, bountiful, capacious, extensive, exuberant **10** voluminous **11** extroverted, far-reaching, uninhibited, unrepressed, wide-ranging **12** unrestrained **13** comprehensive

expatiate 6 expand **7** amplify, enlarge, expound **9** discourse, elaborate

expatriate 2 DP **5** exile **6** emigre, pariah **7** outcast, refugee **15** displaced person

expatriation 5 exile **9** expulsion **10** banishment

expect 5 guess, trust **6** assume, demand, plan on, reckon **7** believe, count on, foresee, hope for, imagine, look for, presume, require, suppose, surmise **8** envision, reckon on, rely upon **9** calculate **10** anticipate, bargain for, conjecture, reckon upon **11** contemplate **13** look forward to

expectancy 11 expectation **12** anticipation

expectant 4 agog **5** eager, ready **7** anxious, hopeful, waiting **9** expecting **10** looking for, optimistic **12** anticipating, apprehensive

expectation 4 hope **5** trust **6** belief, chance **8** prospect, reliance **9** assurance **10** confidence, expectancy, likelihood **11** presumption **12** anticipation **13** contemplation

expedient 4 help, wise **5** means **6** resort, tactic, useful **7** benefit, helpful, measure, politic, selfish, stopgap **9** advantage, advisable, conniving, desirable, effective, judicious, makeshift, opportune, practical, strategem **10** beneficial, instrument, profitable, worthwhile **11** calculating, selfseeking, self-serving **12** advantageous **14** self-interested

expedite 4 rush **5** hurry **6** hasten **7** advance, forward, further, promote, quicken, speed up **8** dispatch **10** accelerate, facilitate **11** precipitate, push through

expedition 4 trek **6** voyage **7** journey, mission **8** campaign, voyagers **9** explorers, travelers, wayfarers **10** enterprise **11** adventurers, exploration

expeditious 4 fast **5** alert, awake, hasty, quick, rapid, ready, swift **6** prompt, snappy, speedy **7** instant **8** punctual **9** effective, immediate **10** bright-eyed **11** efficacious

expel 4 fire, oust, sack, spew, void **5** eject, evict, exile **6** banish, bounce, remove **7** cashier, cast out, dismiss, drum out, excrete **8** dislodge, drive out, evacuate, force out, throw out **9** discharge, eliminate

expellee 2 DP **5** exile **14** banished person **15** displaced person

expend 3 pay **4** give **5** drain, empty, spend, use up **6** donate, lay out, pay out **7** consume, exhaust, fork out, wear out **8** disburse, dispense, shell out, squander **9** dissipate, go through **10** contribute

expendable 7 payable **9** available, forgoable, spendable **10** consumable, extraneous **11** disbursable, dispensable, replaceable, superfluous **12** nonessential **14** relinquishable

expended 5 spent **6** used up **7** drained, emptied, paid out **8** consumed **9** disbursed, exhausted **10** dissipated

expenditure 3 use **4** cost **5** price **6** charge, outlay, output **7** payment **8** exertion, expenses, spending **9** expending, paying out **10** employment, money spent **11** application, consumption **12** disbursement

expense 4 cost, rate **5** drain, price **6** amount, charge, figure, outlay **9** depletion, quotation

expensive 4 dear **6** costly **9** excessive **10** exorbitant, high-priced, immoderate, overpriced **11** extravagant **12** uneconomical, unreasonable **15** beyond one's means

experience 3 see **4** bear, feel, know, meet, view **5** doing, event, sense **6** affair, behold, endure, suffer **7** episode, observe, sustain, undergo **8** exposure, incident, perceive, practice, training **9** adventure, encounter, go through, happening, seasoning, withstand **10** occurrence **11** familiarity, live through, observation **17** personal knowledge **18** firsthand knowledge

experienced 4 able, wise **6** expert, master **7** capable, knowing, skilled, trained, veteran **8** seasoned **9** competent, efficient, practical, qualified **10** well-versed **11** worldly-

wise **12** accomplished **13** sophisticated

experiential 9 empirical, firsthand, practical

experiment 4 test **5** assay, flier, trial **6** feeler, try out **7** analyze, examine, explore, venture **8** analysis, research **11** examination, investigate **12** seek proof for, verification **13** investigation **14** mess around with

experimental 3 new **4** test **5** fresh, rough, trial **7** radical **9** tentative **10** conceptual, firstdraft **11** conjectural, speculative **13** developmental, trial-and-error

experimentation 7 testing **8** analysis, research **10** experiment **11** examination, exploration **13** investigation, trial and error

experimenter 6 tester **10** researcher **15** experimentalist

expert 3 ace, apt, pro, wiz **4** able, deft, whiz **5** adept, crack, doyen, maven, mavin, shark **6** adroit, artist, facile, master, wizard **7** artiste, capable, perfect, skilled, trained, veteran **8** masterly, skillful, virtuoso **9** authority, competent, masterful, practiced, qualified **10** first-class, pastmaster, proficient, specialist **11** connoisseur, crackerjack, experienced **12** accomplished, professional **13** knowledgeable **French: 6** au fait

expertise 5 savvy, skill **7** know-how **10** expertness **12** special skill **14** specialization **15** professionalism

expertness 5 savvy, skill **7** ability, know how **8** training **9** expertise **10** capability, competence, experience **11** proficiency **12** special skill **13** qualification **14** accomplishment, specialization **15** professionalism

expiate 7 appease **8** atone for **13** make amends for **16** pay the penalty for

expiation 6 amends, shrift **7** penance **9** atonement **11** appeasement **16** paying the penalty

expiration 3 end **5** death, dying **6** demise, ending, finish **7** passing, closing **8** decrease, exhaling **10** conclusion **11** termination **12** breathing out

expire 3 die, end **5** cease, lapse **6** finish, perish, run out **7** decease, kick off, succumb

8 conclude, pass away **9** terminate **11** come to an end, discontinue **13** kick the bucket **14** give up the ghost

expired 4 dead, died **6** lapsed, ran out, run out **7** defunct, laspsed **8** deceased, lifeless, perished **10** passed away **11** came to an end, come to an end **14** gave up the ghost

explain 6 fathom **7** clarify, clear up, justify, resolve **8** describe, spell out **9** elucidate, explicate, interpret, make clear, make plain **10** account for, illuminate, illustrate **11** demonstrate, rationalize **14** give a reason for **20** give an explanation for

explainer 6 critic **7** analyst **8** reviewer **10** translator **11** commentator, interpreter

explanation
French: **15** eclaircissement

explicate 7 analyze, clarify, develop, explain **8** annotate **9** elucidate, interpret **10** elucidated, illuminate, illustrate

explication 8 analysis **10** commentary **11** elucidation, explanation **12** illumination **13** clarification **14** interpretation

explication de texte 8 exegesis **11** explanation **14** interpretation **17** literary criticism

explicit 5 blunt, clear, exact, frank, plain **6** candid, direct **7** certain, express, pointed, precise **8** absolute, definite, distinct, specific **9** outspoken **10** unreserved **11** categorical, unequivocal, unqualified **15** straightforward **16** clearly expressed

explicitness 7 clarity **9** clearness, precision **11** unambiguity

explode 5 belie, blast, burst, erupt, go off **6** blow up, expose, refute, set off **7** destroy **8** detonate, disprove **9** discredit, repudiate **10** invalidate, prove false, prove wrong **11** burst loudly **12** utter noisily **14** burst violently, express noisily **18** discharge violently **19** burst out emotionally

exploit 4 feat **5** abuse **6** misuse **7** utilize **8** profit by, put to use **9** adventure, brave deed, heroic act, make use of **10** daring deed **11** achievement **12** capitalize on **14** accomplishment, use to advantage **15** take advantage of **16** make selfish use of **21** take unfair advantage of **22** turn to practical account

exploited 6 abused **7** ill used, misused **11** downtrodden **15** took advantage of **16** taken advantage of

exploration 5 probe **7** inquiry **8** scrutiny **9** discovery **10** expedition, experiment **11** examination **12** scouting trip **13** investigation

explore 3 try **5** plumb, probe, scout **6** survey, try out **7** analyze, examine, feel out, pry into **8** look into, research, traverse **9** delve into, penetrate, range over **10** scrutinize, search into, travel over **11** inquire into, investigate, reconnoiter **14** experiment with

explorer *see box*

explosion 3 fit **4** clap **5** blast, burst, crack **6** report **7** tantrum **8** eruption, outbreak, outburst, paroxysm **9** blowing up, discharge **10** detonation **11** fulmination

explosive 5 shaky, tense **6** touchy **7** keyed up **8** critical, perilous, strained, ticklish, unstable, volatile **9** dangerous, emotional **10** ammunition, precarious **12** pyrotechnics

exponent 6 backer **8** advocate, champion, defender, promoter **9** expounder, proponent, spokesman, supporter **12** propagandist

export 7 send out **8** dispatch **10** sell abroad **11** foreign sale **12** ship overseas

expose 4 bare, risk, show **5** brand, offer, strip **6** betray, denude, divest, hazard, let out, reveal, submit **7** display, divulge, exhibit, imperil, let slip, subject, uncover, unearth **8** denounce, disclose, endanger **10** jeopardize, reveal to be **12** acquaint with, bring to light **16** leave unprotected

expose 6 baring **8** exposure **10** divulgence, revelation

exposed 4 open **5** bared **8** divulged, laid open, revealed, unmasked **9** denounced, disclosed, displayed, uncovered, unearthed **11** unprotected, unsheltered

exposition 4 expo, fair, mart, show **6** bazaar, market **7** account, display, exhibit, picture **8** exegesis **9** trade fair, trade show **10** commentary, exhibition, world's fair **11** description, elucidation, explanation, explication **12** illustration, presentation **13** clarification, demonstration **14** interpretation

expostulate 5 argue **6** enjoin, exhort, object, reason **7** caution, counsel, protest **8** forewarn **9** plead with **11** remonstrate **13** cry out against, reason against **14** inveigh against

exposure 4 view **5** vista **6** expose **7** outlook **8** frontage, prospect **9** divulging, unmasking **10** disclosure, divulgence, laying bare, laying open, reve-

---

explorer
American: 4 Byrd, Pike **5** Boone, Clark, Lewis, Peary, Perry
Australian: 4 Hume **5** Sturt **6** Stuart **8** Mitchell
British: 4 Bell, Cook, Park **5** Baker, Bligh, Bruce, Cabot, Davis, Drake, Grant, Puget, Scott, Smith, Speke **6** Baffin, Burton, Hudson, Lander **7** Raleigh, Stanley **8** Franklin **9** Frobisher, MacKenzie, Vancouver **11** Livingstone
Danish: 6 Bering **7** Niebuhr
Dutch: 6 Tasman **7** Barents, Le Maire **8** Schouten **10** Linschoten
French: 6 Joliet **7** Cartier, Jolliet, La Salle **9** Champlain, Marquette **12** Bougainville
Italian: 8 Columbus **9** Marco Polo, Verrazano **15** Amerigo Vespucci
Moslem: 10 Ibn Battuta
Norwegian: 8 Amundsen
Portuguese: 3 Cam, Cao **4** Dias, Diaz **6** Cabral, Da Gama **7** Almeida **8** Covilhao, Magellan **11** Albuquerque **23** Prince Henry the Navigator
Russian: 10 Middendorf **11** Przhevalsky
Spanish: 6 Balboa, Cortes, De Soto **7** Pizarro **8** Coronado, Orellana, Valdivia **11** Ponce de Leon
Swedish: 12 Nordenskjold
Viking: 10 Eric the Red **11** Leif Ericson

lation, subjection, submission, uncovering **11** perspective **12** public notice **15** bringing to light

expound 6 defend, uphold **7** explain **8** describe **9** elucidate, explicate, hold forth, make clear

express 3 say **4** fast, show, word **5** clear, couch, exact, lucid, plain, quick, rapid, speak, state, swift, utter, vivid, voice **6** convey, direct, evince, phrase, relate, reveal **7** certain, declare, divulge, exhibit, nonstop, precise **8** definite, describe, disclose, evidence, explicit, forceful, specific, vocalize **9** high-speed, make known, verbalize **10** articulate, particular **11** categorical, communicate, unequivocal **12** put into words

expression 4 look, mien, term, tone, word **5** idiom, style **6** airing, aspect, phrase, saying **7** emotion, meaning, stating, telling, venting, voicing, wording **8** language, locution, phrasing, relating, speaking, uttering **9** assertion, eloquence **10** appearance, modulation **11** countenance, declaration, enunciation, phraseology **12** articulation, setting forth, turn of phrase **13** communication

expressionless 5 blank, empty **6** vacant **7** deadpan **12** inexpressive

expressive 5 vivid **6** moving **7** telling **8** eloquent, forceful, poignant, powerful, striking **9** effective **10** compelling, indicative, meaningful, thoughtful **11** significant **14** characteristic

expressly 7 clearly, plainly **9** decidedly, pointedly, precisely, specially **10** definitely, distinctly, explicitly **12** particularly, specifically **13** categorically, unequivocally **18** in no uncertain terms

express sorrow 3 cry **4** weep **6** grieve, lament **7** condole, console **10** sympathize **11** commiserate

expropriate 4 take **5** seize **8** take over **10** commandeer, confiscate **11** appropriate

expropriation 7 seizure **10** arrogation, taking over **12** confiscation **13** commandeering

expulsion 5 exile **6** ouster **7** ousting, removal **8** ejection, eviction **9** debarment, discharge, dismissal, exclusion, expelling **10** banishment

11 elimination, prohibition, throwing out **12** proscription

expunge 5 erase **6** delete, efface, rub out **7** blot out, destroy, wipe out **9** eradicate, strike out **10** obliterate

expurgate 3 cut **4** blip, edit **5** purge **6** censor, cut out, delete, excise, remove **8** bleep out **10** blue-pencil, bowdlerize

exquisite 4 fine **5** dainty **6** choice, lovely, superb **7** elegant, perfect **8** delicate, flawless, peerless, precious, splendid **9** admirable, excellent, faultless, matchless **10** consummate, fastidious, impeccable, meticulous **11** superlative **12** incomparable **14** discriminating

exquisiteness 6 beauty **8** delicacy, elegance, fineness **10** loveliness, perfection **12** flawlessness

extant 6 living **7** present **8** existent, existing **9** surviving, to be found **11** in existence

Extasie, The
   author: 9 John Donne

extemporaneous 5 ad-lib **7** offhand **9** extempore, impromptu **10** improvised, off the cuff, unprepared **11** extemporary, spontaneous, unrehearsed **12** without notes **13** without notice **14** unpremeditated **15** spur-of-the-moment **19** off the top of one's head

extemporary 5 ad-lib **9** extempore, impromptu **10** improvised, off the cuff, unprepared **14** extemporaneous **19** off the top of one's head

extempore 5 ad-lib **7** offhand **9** impromptu **10** improvised, off the cuff, unprepared **11** extemporary, unrehearsed **12** without notes **14** extemporaneous, unpremeditated **15** spur-of-the-moment **19** off the top of one's head

extemporize 5 ad-lib **6** make up **9** improvise **14** speak impromptu **15** speak off the cuff

extend 4 give **5** grant, offer, widen **6** bestow, expand, impart, put out, spread, submit **7** advance, amplify, augment, broaden, draw out, enlarge, hold out, proffer, prolong, stretch **8** continue, elongate, increase, lengthen, protract, reach out **10** make longer, stretch out **12** stretch forth

extended 4 long **7** widened **8** drawn out, enlarged, ex-

panded, thorough, unfolded, unfurled **9** broadened, continued, extensive, prolonged, spread out **10** lengthened, protracted, widespread **12** stretched out **13** comprehensive

extending 8 full form **9** expansion **10** drawing out, elongation, proffering, stretching **11** enlargement, lengthening **12** putting forth

extension 3 arm **4** wing **5** annex, delay **6** branch, length, outlay **7** adjunct **8** addition, appendix, increase **9** appendage, expansion, outgrowth **10** drawing out, proffering **11** enlargement, lengthening **12** continuation, postponement, prolongation

extensive 4 huge, long, vast, wide **5** broad, great, large **7** lengthy **8** enormous, extended, far-flung, thorough **9** capacious, universal **10** protracted, voluminous **12** all-inclusive, considerable **13** comprehensive

extensiveness 4 span **5** range, reach, scope **6** extent, spread **7** breadth, compass, expanse, stretch

extent 4 area, size, time **5** range, reach, scope, sweep **6** amount, degree, length **7** breadth, compass, expanse, stretch **8** duration **9** amplitude, magnitude **10** dimensions

extenuate 6 excuse, temper **7** explain, justify, qualify **8** mitigate, moderate

extenuating 9 lessening, tempering **10** mitigating, moderating, qualifying **11** attenuating, diminishing, explanatory, justifiable

exterior 4 face, skin **5** alien, outer, shell **6** exotic, facade, finish, manner **7** bearing, coating, foreign, outside, outward, surface **8** covering, demeanor, external **9** extrinsic, outer side, outermost **10** extraneous **11** superficial

exterminate 3 zap **4** kill **5** erase, waste **7** abolish, destroy, expunge, root out, wipe out **8** demolish, massacre **9** eliminate, eradicate, slaughter **10** annihilate, extinguish

external 5 alien, outer **7** foreign, outside, outward, surface **8** exterior **9** extrinsic, outermost **10** extraneous **11** superficial

extinct 4 dead, gone, lost **6** put out **7** defunct, died out, gone out **8** quenched, vanished **12** extinguished

extinction 5 death **7** eclipse **9** wiping out **11** destruction, eradication **13** disappearance

extinguish 3 end, zap **4** dash, do in, kill **5** crush, douse, quash **6** cancel, dispel, put out, quench, stifle **7** abolish, blow out, destroy, smother, wipe out **8** demolish, snuff out **9** eliminate, eradicate, suffocate

extinguished 6 put out **7** gone out **8** quenched **15** no longer burning

extirpate 5 erase **7** abolish, destroy, extract, pull out, root out, wipe out **8** demolish **9** eradicate **10** annihilate, extinguish, obliterate **11** exterminate

extol 4 laud **6** praise **7** acclaim, applaud, commend, glorify **8** eulogize **9** celebrate **10** compliment **16** sing the praises of

extort 5 educe, exact **6** coerce, elicit **7** extract **9** shake down

extortion 5 force, graft **6** payola, ransom **7** threats, tribute **8** coercion **9** blackmail, hush money, shakedown **14** forced payments

extortionate 5 undue **7** extreme **9** excessive, out-of-line **10** exorbitant, inordinate **12** unreasonable

extra 4 more **5** spare **7** adjunct, further, surplus **9** accessory, auxiliary, redundant, unusually **10** additional, attachment, complement, especially, remarkably, uncommonly **11** superfluous, unnecessary **12** additionally, appurtenance, particularly, supplemental **13** exceptionally **15** extraordinarily

extract 3 get **4** cite, cull **5** educe, evoke, exact, gleen, juice, quote, wrest **6** choose, deduce, derive, elicit, obtain, pry out, remove, select **7** copy out, distill, draw out, essence, excerpt, passage, pull out, root out, take out **8** abstract, bring out, citation, pluck out, press out, separate **9** extirpate, extricate, quotation, selection **10** distillate, squeeze out **11** concentrate

extraction 5 stock **7** descent, removal **8** ancestry **10** derivation, drawing out, pulling out

extraneous 5 alien **6** exotic **7** foreign, strange **9** extrinsic, unrelated **10** immaterial, incidental, irrelevant, not ger-

mane **11** superfluous **12** adventitious, inadmissible, nonessential, not pertinent **13** inappropriate

extraordinary 3 odd **4** rare **5** queer **6** unique **7** amazing, notable, strange, unusual **8** uncommon **9** fantastic, monstrous, unheard of **10** incredible, phenomenal, remarkable **11** exceptional **12** unbelievable **13** inconceivable

extraterrestrial 6 cosmic **10** outer-space **12** interstellar, otherworldly **14** interplanetary

extravagance 5 folly, waste **6** excess **7** caprice **9** absurdity **10** profligacy **11** prodigality, squandering, unrestraint **12** immoderation, improvidence, overspending, recklessness, wastefulness **13** excessiveness **14** capriciousness **16** inordinate outlay, unreasonableness

extravagant 4 wild **6** absurd, costly, unreal **7** foolish **8** fabulous, lavishly, prodigal, spending, wasteful **9** excessive, expensive, fantastic, highflown, imprudent **10** exorbitant, high-priced, immoderate, inordinate, openhanded, outlandish, outrageous, overpriced, profligate **11** improvident, spendthrift, squandering **12** overspending, preposterous, unreasonable, unrestrained

extravaganza 4 fair **5** opera **6** ballet **7** pageant **8** carnival, operetta **9** spectacle, stage show **10** exposition, vaudeville **11** opera bouffe, spectacular **12** Broadway show, opera comique, son et lumiere, wild west show **14** phantasmagoria **17** sound and light show

extreme 3 end **5** depth **6** excess, height, severe **7** intense, radical, unusual **8** advanced, boundary, farthest, uncommon **9** excessive, extremity, nth degree, outermost, very great **10** avant-garde, immoderate, inordinate, outrageous **11** exaggerated, extravagant, most distant **13** extraordinary

extremely 4 very **5** quite **7** awfully **8** terribly **9** curiously, intensely, unusually **10** abnormally, especially, freakishly, peculiarly, remarkably, singularly, uncommonly **11** exceedingly, excessively, unnaturally **12** immoderately, surprisingly **13** exceptionally **15** extraordinarily

extremely painful 7 racking **9** agonizing, torturous **10** tor-

menting, unbearable **11** intolerable, unendurable **12** excruciating, insufferable

extremity 3 arm, end, leg, tip, toe **4** edge, foot, hand, limb **5** bound, brink, limit, reach **6** border, finger, margin **7** confine, extreme **8** boundary, terminus **9** outer edge, periphery

extricate 4 free **5** loose **6** get out, rescue **7** deliver, release **8** liberate, untangle **9** disengage **11** disencumber, disentangle **12** wriggle out of

extrication 6 escape **7** loosing, release **10** liberation **11** deliverance **13** disengagement **15** disentanglement

extrinsic 5 alien **7** foreign **9** accessory **10** accidental, extraneous, incidental **11** dispensable **12** nonessential

extrovert 7 show-off **13** exhibitionist **14** life of the party **17** hail-fellow-well-met

extroverted 8 outgoing, sociable **9** expansive **10** gregarious **12** unrestrained

extrude 4 spew **5** eject, expel **7** project, push out **8** force out, protrude, stickout **9** thrust out

exuberance 3 zip **4** elan, life, zeal **5** vigor **6** energy, spirit **8** buoyancy, vitality, vivacity **9** animation, eagerness **10** enthusiasm, excitement, liveliness **13** effervescence, sprightliness

exuberant 4 lush, rich **5** eager **6** lavish, lively **7** copious, excited, profuse, zealous **8** abundant, animated, spirited, vigorous **9** bounteous, energetic, luxuriant, plenteous, plentiful, sprightly **12** enthusiastic **13** superabundant

exudation 3 sap, tar **4** ooze **5** pitch, sweat **7** leakage, seepage **8** bleeding, drainage **9** discharge, excretion

exude 4 drip, emit, ooze **5** sweat **7** secrete **9** discharge

exult 4 crow **5** gloat, glory **7** rejoice **8** be elated **10** be jubilant, jump for joy **11** be delighted **13** be exhilarated **15** be in high spirits

exultant 5 happy **6** elated, joyful **7** crowing **8** boasting, ecstatic, euphoric, gloating, jubilant **9** rapturous, rejoicing **10** triumphant

exultation 3 joy **7** elation, ovation, rapture, triumph **9** rejoicing **10** jubilation

Eyck, Jan van
  born: **8** Flanders, Maaseyck
    10 Maastricht
  artwork: **9** Timotheos
    15 Ghent Altarpiece **18** Adoration of the Lamb, The Man in a Red Turban, The Virgin in a Church **20** The Arnolfini Marriage **24** Arnolfini Wedding Portrait **29** The Madonna with Chancellor Rolin **30** The Madonna with Canon van der Paele

eye 3 orb **4** scan, view **5** sight, study, taste, watch **6** behold, gaze at, look at, peeper, regard, survey, take in, vision

7 inspect, observe, stare at **8** eyesight, glance at **10** perception, scrutinize **14** discrimination
  part: **4** iris, lens, rods
    5 cones, nerve, pupil **6** cornea, muscle, retina **11** blood vessel

eyeful 4 doll **5** beaut, peach, Venus **6** beauty **7** stunner **8** knockout **10** good-looker **13** beautiful girl **14** beautiful woman

eyeglass, eyeglasses 4 lens **5** specs **6** eyecup, lenses **7** goggles, monocle **8** cheaters, contacts, pincenez **9** lorgnette **10** spectacles

Eye of the Needle
  author: **10** Ken Follett

eyesight 4 eyes **5** sight **6** vision

eyewitness 5 gaper, gazer **6** gawker, viewer **7** witness **8** attester, attestor, beholder, informer, looker-on, observer, onlooker, passerby **9** bystander, spectator, testifier **10** rubberneck

Ezekiel
  father: **4** Buzi

Ezra
  father: **7** Seraiah

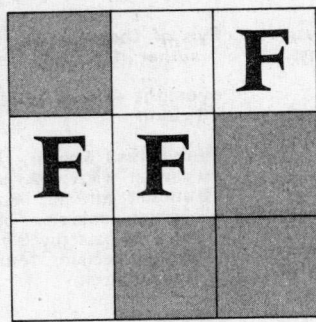

Fabares, Ruby Bernadette Nanette
 real name of: 13 Nanette Fabray

fable 3 fib, lie 4 hoax, myth, tale, yarn 6 legend 7 fiction, leg-pull, parable, romance, untruth, whopper 8 allegory 9 fairy tale, falsehood, invention, tall story 11 fabrication

fabled 6 unreal 7 storied 8 fabulous, fanciful, mythical 9 imaginary, legendary 10 fictitious 12 mythological

Fables
 author: 16 Jean de La Fontaine

Fabray, Nanette
 real name: 28 Ruby Bernadette Nanette Fabares
 partner: 9 Sid Caesar
 born: 10 San Diego CA
 roles: 7 Baby Nan 12 The Band Wagon 13 Sid Caesar Hour 15 High Button Shoes, Our Gang comedies

fabric *see box*

fabricate 4 fake, form 5 build, erect, feign, forge, frame, hatch, shape 6 design, devise, invent, make up 7 compose, concoct, falsify, fashion, produce, trump up 8 assemble, contrive, simulate 9 construct, embroider, formulate 11 counterfeit, manufacture

fabrication 3 fib, lie 4 myth, yarn 5 fable 6 makeup 7 fiction, forgery, untruth 8 building, creation, erection 9 fairy tale, falsehood, invention 10 assemblage, concoction, fashioning, production 11 composition, manufacture 12 constructing, construction 13 prevarication 16 cock-and-bull story

Fabritius, Carel
 real name: 13 Carel Pietersz
 born: 14 Midden-Beemster, The Netherlands
 artwork: 11 View of Delft 12 The Goldfinch 19 The Raising of Lazarus

fabulous 5 great 6 fabled, superb 7 amazing, storied 8 fanciful, invented, mythical, smashing 9 fantastic, imaginary, legendary, marvelous, wonderful 10 apocryphal, astounding, fictitious, incredible, stupendous 11 astonishing, spectacular 12 mythological, unbelievable 13 extraordinary

facade 4 face, mask 6 veneer 8 frontage, pretense 9 front view 10 false front 13 building front

face 3 air, mug, pan 4 coat, gall, grit, look, pout, puss, sand 5 brass, cheek, cover, front, image, nerve, pluck, spunk 6 aspect, daring, facade, kisser, mettle, repute, visage 7 bravado, dignity, front on, grimace, obverse, overlay, surface 8 boldness, confront, features, forepart, frontage, good name, overlook, prestige 9 encounter, hardihood, impudence, semblance 10 appearance, confidence, effrontery, expression, give toward, look toward, reputation,

---

fabric 5 cloth, frame, stuff 6 makeup 7 textile, texture 8 dry goods, material 9 framework, structure, substance, yard goods 10 foundation 12 organization, substructure 14 infrastructure, superstructure
 cotton: 4 duck 5 denim, drill, scrim, terry 6 burlap, calico, canvas, chintz, dimity, madras, muslin, oxford, poplin 7 batiste, buckram, flannel, gingham, organdy, percale, ticking 8 chambray 9 crinoline, sailcloth 10 broadcloth, printcloth, seersucker 11 cheesecloth, dotted Swiss
 linen: 6 canvas, damask 7 butcher, cambric 8 birds-eye 9 huckaback
 natural: 4 jute, silk, wool 5 linen 6 cotton 8 asbestos
 silk: 3 raw 4 tram 7 organza 8 organzie 9 organzine
 synthetic: 5 nylon, orlon, rayon 6 olefin 7 acetate, acrylic 9 polyester
 type: 4 felt, lace, lame 5 crepe, gauze, moire, serge, voile 6 damask, faille, jersey, melton, velour, velvet 7 brocade, chiffon, flannel, foulard, gingham, taffeta 8 chenille, corduroy, tapestry 9 gabardine, velveteen
 wool: 4 felt 5 crepe, serge, tweed, twill 6 boucle, covert, faille, melton, woolen 7 challis, doeskin, Donegal, worsted 8 homespun, Shetland 9 Astrakhan, gabardine, sharkskin 10 hopsacking 11 Harris tweed, herringbone
  from goats: 8 cashmere
  sheep: 5 Iraqi 6 Hirrik, merino, Romney, Somali 7 Lincoln 8 Cotswold, Tatarian 9 Hampshire, Southdown 10 Corriedale, Dorset Down, Dorset Horn, Shropshire, Sikkim Bera 13 Hampshire Down
  other wool-bearing animals: 5 camel, llama 6 alpaca, vicuna

turn toward **11** countenance, physiognomy, self-respect

Face
character in: **12** The Alchemist
author: **6** Jonson

facet 3 cut **4** part, side **5** angle, phase, plane **6** aspect **7** surface

facetious 5 comic, droll, funny, witty **6** clever, jocose, joking, jovial **7** amusing, comical, jesting, jocular, playful **8** humorous **12** wisecracking

face-to-face 6 direct **8** personal **9** firsthand

facile 3 apt **4** glib **5** adept, handy, quick, slick **6** adroit, artful, casual, clever, fluent, smooth **7** cursory, shallow **8** careless, skillful **10** effortless, proficient **11** superficial

facilitate 3 aid **4** ease **6** foster, help in, smooth **7** advance, forward, further, lighten, promote, speed up **8** expedite, simplify **10** accelerate, make easier

facility 3 aid **4** bent, ease **5** knack, means, skill **7** aptness, fluency **8** deftness, easiness, resource **9** advantage, appliance, dexterity, readiness **10** adroitness, capability, competence, efficiency, expertness, smoothness **11** convenience, proficiency **14** effortlessness, practicability

facsimile 4 copy **5** clone **7** replica, reprint **8** likeness **9** duplicate, imitation, photostat **10** transcript **12** reproduction

fact 3 act **4** deed **5** event, truth **6** verity **7** reality **8** incident, specific **9** actuality, certainty, happening, thing done **10** occurrence, particular **12** circumstance

faction 3 set **4** bloc, gang, ring, sect, side, unit **5** cabal, clash, group, split **6** breach, circle, clique, schism, strife **7** combine, coterie, discord, rupture, section **8** conflict, division, minority, sedition **9** rebellion **10** contention, disruption, dissension, dissidence, insurgency, quarreling **11** subdivision **12** disagreement **13** splinter group **15** incompatibility

factious 7 warring **8** divisive, fighting, mutinous **9** alienated, bickering, combative, estranged **10** contending, rebellious **11** belligerent, contentious, disaffected, disagreeing, dissentious, quarrelsome **12** disputatious **13** at loggerheads, insubordinate **15** insurrectionary **16** at sixes and sevens

factitious 4 sham **5** phony **9** pretended, synthetic, unnatural **10** artificial **12** manufactured

factor 4 part **5** cause **6** reason **7** element **9** component, influence **11** constituent **12** circumstance **13** consideration

factory 4 mill, shop **5** plant, works **8** workshop **11** manufactory

factotum 8 handyman **9** gal Friday, guy Friday, man Friday **10** girl Friday **12** right-hand man **15** jack-of-all-trades

factual 4 real, true **5** exact, plain **6** actual **7** certain, correct, genuine, literal **8** accurate, concrete, definite, faithful **9** authentic, unadorned **10** scrupulous, verifiable

faculty, faculties 4 bent, gift, wits **5** flair, knack, power, skill **6** genius, reason, talent **7** quality **8** aptitude, capacity, function, penchant, teachers **9** adeptness, endowment **10** capability, professors **12** mental powers, skillfulness **13** teaching staff

fad 4 mode, rage, whim **5** craze, fancy, mania, vogue **6** whimsy **7** fashion **10** dernier cri, latest word **11** latest thing

faddish 2 in **6** trendy **10** innovative **11** fashionable

fade 3 die, dim, ebb **4** blur, dull, fail, flag, pale, wane **5** droop, taper **6** bleach, lessen, recede, whiten, wither **7** crumble, decline, dwindle, fall off, grow dim, shrivel **8** diminish, dissolve, evanesce, languish, make pale, melt away, pass away **9** disappear dissipate, evaporate, lose color

fade away 3 die, ebb **6** recede **7** subside **8** diminish

faded 4 drab, dull, pale **5** dingy **6** grayed **7** died out **8** bleached, dwindled, whitened, withered **9** colorless, shriveled, washed out

Faerie Queene, The
author: **13** Edmund Spenser
character: **3** Una **5** Guyon **6** Duessa **8** Artegall, Gloriana (the Faerie Queen) **9** Archimago, Britomart **12** Prince Arthur **14** Red Cross Knight

Fafnir
origin: **12** Scandinavian

form: **6** dragon
father: **8** Hreidmar
brother: **5** Otter, Regin
killed: **8** Hreidmar
killed by: **6** Sigurd

fag 4 bush, butt, poop, tire, weed **5** weary **6** tucker **7** exhaust **9** cigarette

Fagin
character in: **11** Oliver Twist
author: **7** Dickens

Fahrenheit
abbreviation: **1** F

Fahrenheit 451
author: **11** Ray Bradbury

Fahrenheit, Gabriel Daniel
field: **7** physics
nationality: **6** German
invented: **16** thermometer scale **18** alcohol thermometer, mercury thermometer

fail 3 die, ebb **4** bomb, flag, flop, fold, wane **5** abort, crash, droop, flunk **6** desert, slip up **7** decline, dwindle, forsake, founder, give out, go under, let down, misfire **8** be in vain, collapse, fade away, languish, lay an egg, miscarry **9** disappear, fall short, fizzle out **10** end in smoke, go bankrupt, not succeed, run aground **11** be stillborn, come to grief, deteriorate, fall through, go up in smoke, miss the mark **12** come to naught, turn out badly **13** come to nothing **15** go out of business **16** meet one's Waterloo, meet with disaster

fail at 11 fall short of **12** be defeated in, not succeed at **16** be unsuccessful at

failed
French: **6** manque

failing 4 weak **5** shaky **6** defect, ebbing, waning **7** folding, frailty **8** drooping, flagging, giving up, slipping, weakness **9** deficient, dwindling, giving out, weakening, weak point **10** deficiency, going under **11** shortcoming **12** unsuccessful **13** insufficiency

fail to include 4 drop, omit **8** leave out

failure 3 dud **4** bomb, flop, mess, ruin **5** botch, crash, loser **6** fizzle, mishap, muddle **7** decline, default, failing, folding, misfire, washout **8** collapse, downfall **9** breakdown, ruination **10** bankruptcy, ne'er-do-well

Fainall, Mrs
character in: **16** The Way of the World
author: **8** Congreve

faint 3 dim, low **4** pale, soft, thin, weak **5** dizzy, faded, frail, giddy, muted, small, swoon, timid **6** dulcet, feeble, little, meager, remote, slight, subtle, torpid **7** fearful, fragile, languid, muffled, obscure, pass out, worn out **8** black out, collapse, cowardly, delicate, drooping, fatigued, timorous **9** exhausted, inaudible, lethargic, whispered **10** indistinct **11** lightheaded, lily-livered, vertiginous **13** inconspicuous **17** lose consciousness

fainthearted 4 weak **5** timid **6** feeble **8** cowardly **10** irresolute **11** halfhearted, indifferent, lily-livered

faintheartedness 9 cowardice **12** cowardliness, yellow streak **13** pusillanimity, yellow feather **17** pusillanimousness **18** chickenheartedness

fair 4 fine, just, pale, so-so **5** blond, bonny, sunny **6** bright, comely, creamy, decent, honest, justly, kosher, lovely, medium, pretty, proper, square **7** average, legally, not dark, upright **8** adequate, candidly, carnival, honestly, mediocre, middling, moderate, ordinary, passable, pleasant, rainless, squarely, sunshiny, unbiased **9** beautiful, cloudless, equitable, ethically, honorable, honorably, impartial, justified, objective, tolerable, unclouded **10** aboveboard, attractive, evenhanded, exhibition, legitimate, pretty good, reasonable, truthfully **11** indifferent, respectable **12** forthrightly, light-colored, light-skinned, on the up-and-up, run-of-the-mill, satisfactory, unprejudiced **13** disinterested, dispassionate **19** according to the rules

Fair, A A
  pseudonym of: **18** Erle Stanley Gardner

Fairbanks, Douglas
  real name: **17** Douglas Elton Ulman
  wife: **12** Mary Pickford
  son: **18** Douglas Fairbanks Jr
  born: **8** Denver CO
  roles: **9** Robin Hood **11** The Iron Mask **14** The Black Pirate, The Mark of Zorro **16** The Thief of Bagdad **18** The Three Musketeers **23** The Private Life of Don Juan

Fairbanks, Douglas Jr
  father: **16** Douglas Fairbanks
  wife: **12** Joan Crawford
  born: **9** New York NY
  roles: **8** Gunga Din **12** Little

Caesar **15** Sinbad the Sailor **16** That Lady in Ermine **17** Catherine the Great **18** The Prisoner of Zenda **19** The Corsican Brothers

fair dealing 7 honesty **8** fairness **15** trustworthiness

Fairfax, Gwendolen
  character in: **27** The Importance of Being Earnest
  author: **5** Wilde

Fairfax, Jane
  character in: **4** Emma
  author: **6** Austen

Fairfax, Mrs
  character in: **8** Jane Eyre
  author: **6** Bronte

Fair Land, Fair Land
  author: **11** A B Guthrie Jr

fairly 5 fully **6** justly, rather, really **7** rightly **8** actually, honestly, passably, properly, somewhat, squarely **9** equitably, honorably, so to speak, tolerably **10** absolutely, completely, moderately, positively, reasonably **11** impartially, objectively **12** evenhandedly, legitimately **15** dispassionately **19** in a manner of speaking
  Latin: 9 pari passu

fairness 7 balance, honesty, justice **8** equality, fair play **11** objectivity **12** impartiality **14** even-handedness **16** equal opportunity

fair play 7 justice **8** equality, fairness **12** impartiality **16** equal opportunity

fair-skinned 4 pale **5** blond, light **6** blonde **17** light-complexioned

fairy 3 elf **5** pixie **6** sprite **10** leprechaun

fairy tale 3 fib **4** myth **5** fable **6** legend **7** fantasy, fiction **8** tall tale **9** invention **11** fabrication **16** cock-and-bull story
  German: 7 Marchen

fait accompli 16 accomplished fact, thing already done

faith 4 sect **5** creed, trust **6** belief, church, fealty **7** loyalty, promise **8** credence, fidelity, reliance, religion, security **9** assurance, certainty, certitude, constancy **10** confidence, conviction, obligation, persuasion

faithful 4 true **5** close, exact, loyal, tried **6** honest, strict, trusty **7** devoted, factual, precise, similar, staunch, upright **8** accurate, constant, lifelike, reliable, resolute, truthful **9** steadfast **10** dependable,

scrupulous, true-to-life, unswerving, unwavering, verifiable **11** trustworthy **13** conscientious, incorruptible

faithfulness 6 fealty **7** loyalty **8** devotion, fidelity **9** constancy **10** allegiance **11** reliability **13** steadfastness

faithless 5 false **6** fickle **8** disloyal **10** inconstant, perfidious, unreliable **11** treacherous **13** untrustworthy

faithlessness 5 doubt **7** perfidy **9** disbelief, falseness, treachery **10** disloyalty, fickleness, infidelity, skepticism **11** inconstancy **13** unreliability **14** perfidiousness, unfaithfulness

fake 4 hoax, ruse, sham **5** bogus, dodge, dummy, faker, false, feign, forge, fraud, phony, put-on, quack, trick **6** deceit, forged, humbug, poseur, pseudo **7** falsify, forgery, not real, pretend, trump up **8** artifice, contrive, deceiver, delusion, imposter, invented, simulate, specious, spurious **9** charlatan, concocted, contrived, deception, dissemble, fabricate, imitation, imposture, pretender, simulated **10** artificial, fabricated, fictitious **11** contrivance, counterfeit, dissimulate, fabrication, make-believe

faker 5 fraud, phony **6** humbug **8** imposter **9** charlatan, pretender

fakir 5 Hindu **6** Muslim **7** ascetic, dervish

falcon 5 hobby, saker **6** desert, lanner, merlin **7** goshawk, kestrel, prairie, shaheen, tiercel **8** caracara, falconet **9** gyrfalcon, peregrine

Falcon and the Snowman, The
  author: **13** Robert Lindsey
  director: **15** John Schlesinger
  cast: **8** Sean Penn (Andrew Daulton Lee, the Snowman) **13** Timothy Hutton (Christopher John Boyce, the Falcon)

Falconer
  author: **11** John Cheever

Falconet, Etienne-Maurice
  born: **5** Paris **6** France
  artwork: **9** The Bather **12** Bathing Nymph **13** Milo of Crotona, Peter the Great **19** Pygmalion and Galatea

falconry 7 hawking
  equipment: **4** lure **5** cadge **6** jesses **7** creance

Falk, Lee
creator/artist of: **10** The Phantom **19** Mandrake the Magician

Falk, Peter
born: **9** New York NY
roles: **7** Columbo **9** Murder Inc **12** The Great Race **13** Murder by Death **17** The Cheap Detective **19** Pocketful of Miracles **21** It's a Mad Mad Mad Mad World, Robin and the Seven Hoods

fall, falls 3 die, ebb, err, sin **4** drop, plop, ruin, slip, wane **5** droop, lapse, occur, slope, slump, spill **6** autumn, crop up, defeat, happen, perish, plunge, topple, tumble **7** be slain, be taken, capture, cascade, cheapen, come off, crumple, decline, descend, descent, falling, plummet, sinking, succumb **8** cataract, collapse, come down, decrease, diminish, disgrace, downfall, drop down, dropping, go astray, hang down, lowering **9** crash down, overthrow, reduction, surrender, take place, waterfall **10** capitulate, come to pass, corruption, debasement, depreciate, diminution, subsidence, subversion, transgress **11** be destroyed, harvest time **12** capitulation, depreciation, Indian summer **15** loss of innocence

Fall, The
author: **11** Albert Camus

Falla, Manuel de
born: **5** Cadiz, Spain
composer of: **11** El Amor Brujo, La Atlantida, La Vida Breve, Life Is Short **14** Fantasia Betica **15** Love the Magician **19** The Three-Cornered Hat **21** El sombrero de tres picos **25** Nights in the Gardens of Spain

fallacious 5 false, wrong **6** faulty, flawed, untrue **8** delusive, mistaken **9** deceptive, erroneous, illogical, incorrect **10** inaccurate, misleading, untruthful

fallacy 4 flaw **5** catch, error, fault **7** mistake, pitfall **8** delusion, illusion **9** misbelief **10** faultiness **11** false belief, false notion **13** inconsistency, misconception **15** misapprehension

fall apart 5 decay **7** break up, crumble, shatter **8** fragment, splinter **10** go to pieces **11** fragmentize **12** disintegrate

fall away 4 fade, wane **5** abate **7** drop off, slacken, subside **8** mitigate, taper off

fall back 6 recede **7** back off, retreat

fallen 4 dead **5** loose, slain **6** ousted, ruined, sinful **7** debased, deposed, dropped, immoral, spilled, toppled, tumbled **8** sprawled **9** butchered, disgraced, massacred, turned out **10** discharged, overthrown **11** slaughtered

fallen short
French: **6** manque

fall for 7 believe, swallow

fall guy 4 dupe, pawn, tool **5** patsy **7** cat's-paw

fallible 5 frail, human **6** faulty, mortal, unsure **9** imperfect **10** unreliable

fall in drops 4 drip, rain **7** dribble, drizzle **8** sprinkle

falling apart 6 ruined, shabby **7** rickety, run-down **8** decaying, decrepit **9** crumbling **10** broken-down, collapsing, ramshackle, tumbledown **11** dilapidated **13** deteriorating

Falling in Place
author: **10** Ann Beattie

falling into decay 6 ruined, shabby **7** rotting, run-down **8** decrepit **9** crumbling, moldering **10** broken-down, tumbledown **11** dilapidated, in disrepair **13** deteriorating

falling off 3 ebb **4** fall, wane **7** decline **8** decrease **9** dwindling, lessening, reduction **10** diminution **13** deterioration

falling out 4 spat **7** dispute, quarrel **8** argument, squabble **10** difference **12** disagreement

fall in with 6 concur **7** conform **8** accede to **9** acquiesce **11** go along with

fall off 4 drop, wane **6** lessen, plunge, reduce, topple **7** decline, drop off, plummet, slacken, subside **8** decrease, diminish, moderate, peter out

Fall of the House of Usher, The
author: **13** Edgar Allan Poe
character: **8** Narrator **13** Madeline Usher, Roderick Usher

fallow 4 arid, idle **5** inert **6** barren, unused **7** dormant, unsowed, worn out **8** depleted, inactive, untilled **9** exhausted, unplanted **10** unfruitful **12** uncultivated, unproductive

fall short 6 be less, fail at, give up **9** be lacking, lag behind **10** have too few **11** fail to reach, miss the mark **12** be inadequate **14** be insufficient

fall to one's lot 4 fall **5** occur **6** befall, chance, happen **7** turn out **9** come about **10** come to pass

fall upon 5 fly at **6** assail, attack, dive at **7** embrace, lunge at, set upon **8** thrust at, tuck into

false 4 fake, sham **5** bogus, phony, wrong **6** ersatz, faulty, forged, pseudo, tricky, unreal, untrue **7** devious, feigned, inexact, invalid, unsound **8** delusive, disloyal, mistaken, spurious, two-faced **9** deceitful, deceiving, deceptive, dishonest, erroneous, faithless, imitation, incorrect, unfounded **10** apocryphal, artificial, factitious, fallacious, inaccurate, inconstant, misleading, not correct, perfidious, traitorous, unfaithful, untruthful **11** counterfeit, make-believe, treacherous **12** hypocritical **13** double-dealing

false front 4 mask, sham, show **6** facade, screen, veneer **8** pretense

false-hearted 8 two-faced **9** deceitful, deceiving, faithless **10** perfidious **13** double-dealing, untrustworthy

falsehood 3 fib, lie **5** lying, story **6** canard, deceit **7** fiction, figment, perfidy, perjury, untruth, whopper **8** bad faith, white lie **9** deception, duplicity, hypocrisy, invention, mendacity **10** dishonesty, distortion, inaccuracy **11** dissembling, fabrication, insincerity **12** misstatement, two-facedness **13** deceptiveness, dissimulation, double-dealing, falsification **17** misrepresentation

falseness 5 fraud **6** deceit **7** perfidy **9** duplicity, treachery **10** dishonesty **12** spuriousness **13** deceitfulness, double-dealing, faithlessness **14** untruthfulness

falsified 5 false, phony **6** forged, made-up **7** assumed **10** fictitious

falsify 4 fake **5** belie, rebut **6** doctor, misuse, refute **7** confute, distort, pervert **8** disprove **10** tamper with **12** misrepresent

Falstaff
opera by: **5** Verdi
character: **4** Anne **6** Fenton, Pistol **7** Dr Caius **8** Bardolph **11** Dame Quickly **12** Mistress Ford, Mistress Page **15** Mistress Quickly, Sir John Falstaff

Falstaff, Sir John
character in: 22 The Merry
Wives of Windsor
author: 11 Shakespeare

falter 3 lag 4 halt, reel 5 demur, waver 6 dodder, mumble,
shrink, teeter, totter 7 shamble, shuffle, stagger, stammer,
stumble, stutter 8 hesitate
9 fluctuate, vacillate 10 dillydally 11 be undecided 12 be
irresolute, show weakness
14 blow hot and cold

fame 4 note 5 glory 6 renown,
repute 7 laurels 8 eminence,
prestige 9 celebrity, notoriety
10 notability, popularity,
prominence, reputation
11 distinction, preeminence
15 illustriousness

famed 5 noted 6 famous 7 notable 8 renowned 9 prominent,
well-known 10 celebrated

familiar 3 pal 4 bold, chum,
cozy, free, snug 5 buddy,
close, crony, known, stock,
usual 6 chummy, common,
friend 7 forward, general
8 accepted, amicable, at home
in, everyday, frequent,
friendly, habitual, informal,
intimate, ordinary, seasoned,
versed in 9 abreast of, brotherly, confidant, customary, fraternal, gemutlich, intrusive,
simpatico, skilled in, well-
known 10 accessible, accustomed, acquainted, apprised
of, conversant, proverbial, unreserved 11 cognizant of, commonplace, impertinent,
traditional 12 confidential,
conventional, hand and glove,
no stranger to, proficient at
13 boon companion, companionable, disrespectful 15 taking
liberties

familiarity 4 ease 5 amity,
skill 7 know-how, mastery
8 coziness, intimacy 9 closeness, impudence, indecorum,
knowledge, unreserve 10 cas-
ualness, chumminess, cognizance, disrespect, experience,
fellowship, fraternity, friendship 11 association, brotherhood, conversance,
forwardness, impropriety, informality, naturalness, presumption, proficiency
12 acquaintance, impertinence,
unconstraint, undue liberty,
unseemliness 13 brotherliness,
comprehension, intrusiveness,
understanding, undue intimacy 16 acquaintanceship

familiarize 5 edify, teach, tutor 6 inform, school, season
7 educate 8 accustom, ac-
quaint, instruct 9 enlighten,

habituate, inculcate
11 acclimatize

family 3 kin, set 4 clan, kind,
line, race 5 blood, breed,
brood, class, group, house, issue, order, stock, tribe 7 dynasty, kinfolk, kinsmen,
lineage, progeny 8 ancestry,
category, division, kinsfolk
9 forebears, genealogy, offspring, parentage, relations,
relatives 10 extraction, kith
and kin 11 forefathers
14 classification
goddess of: 6 Cardea

Family Affair
character: 4 Jody 5 Buffy,
Cissy 8 Mr (Giles) French
9 Bill Davis
cast: 10 Brian Keith
11 Anissa Jones, Kathy
Garver 14 Sebastian Cabot
15 Johnnie Whitaker

family line 7 lineage 8 ancestry 9 blood line, genealogy,
parentage

Family Moskat, The
author: 19 Isaac Bashevis
Singer

Family Reunion, The
author: 7 T S Eliot

Family Ties
character: 4 Nick 5 Ellen
6 Skippy 10 Alex Keaton
11 Elyse Keaton 12 Andrew
Keaton, Steven Keaton
13 Mallory Keaton 14 Jen-
nifer Keaton
cast: 9 Marc Price 11 Mi-
chael J Fox, Tina Yothers
12 Michael Gross 14 Justine
Bateman 20 Meredith Bax-
ter-Birney

family tree 7 lineage 8 ancestry, pedigree 9 blood line,
genealogy

famine 4 lack, want 6 dearth
7 paucity, poverty 8 scarcity
9 depletion 10 deficiency, exhaustion, famishment, meagerness, scantiness, starvation
11 destitution, half rations,
short supply 13 acute shortage, extreme hunger,
insufficiency

famish 6 hunger, starve

famous 5 noted 7 eminent,
notable 8 far-famed, re-
nowned, well-known 9 notorious, prominent
10 celebrated 11 conspicuous,
illustrious 13 distinguished

famous person 4 name, star
7 notable 8 luminary, somebody 9 celebrity, personage,
superstar 11 personality

fan 3 bug, nut 4 buff 5 fiend,
freak 6 addict, rooter, zealot

7 booster, fanatic 8 follower,
partisan

fanatic 5 crazy 6 maniac,
zealot 7 hothead, radical 8 activist, militant 9 extremist
10 enthusiast 24 member of
the lunatic fringe

fanaticism 6 fervor 8 activism,
zealotry 9 dogmatism, extre-
mism, monomania, obsession
10 enthusiasm, radicalism
11 extreme zeal, militantism
12 intemperance 13 ruling
passion 15 opinionatedness

fancied 5 liked 6 dreamt, took
to, unreal 7 assumed, desired,
dreamed, thought 8 imagined,
supposed 9 conceived, imaginary, preferred

fanciful 3 odd 6 unreal 7 bizarre, curious, flighty, unusual 8 fabulous, humorous,
illusory, mythical, quixotic, romantic 9 eccentric, fantastic,
imaginary, invective, legendary, visionary, whimsical
10 apocryphal, capricious, chimerical, fictitious
11 imaginative

fanciful talk 7 blarney 9 hyperbole, tall tales 11 fish stories 12 exaggeration

fancy 3 yen 4 fine, idea, like,
want 5 crave, dream, enjoy,
favor, opine, showy, taste,
think 6 assume, custom, deluxe, desire, florid, liking, notion, ornate, relish, rococo,
take it, take to, vagary, vision, whimsy 7 baroque, caprice, conceit, dream of,
elegant, fantasy, figment,
gourmet, imagine, leaning,
longing, long for, picture, presume, reverie, special, suppose, surmise, suspect,
unusual 8 be fond of,
crotchet, daydream, fondness,
illusion, not plain, penchant,
superior, weakness, yearn for
9 elaborate, epicurean, expensive, hankering, superfine
10 be bent upon, conceive of,
conjecture, decorative, high-
priced, ornamental, partiality
11 distinctive, exceptional, extravagant, gingerbread, hanker
after, have a mind to, imagination, inclination 12 have an
eye for, predilection 13 be
pleased with, take a liking to

fancy house 4 stew 5 house
6 bagnio 7 brothel 8 bordello,
cathouse 10 bawdy house,
whorehouse 13 sporting
house 14 house of ill fame
16 house of ill repute
19 house of prostitution

fang 4 claw, nail, root, take,
tang, tusk 5 prong, seize,

tooth **6** obtain **7** capture, procure **8** eyetooth **9** chelicera

fanny 4 buns, rump, seat **6** behind, bottom **8** backside, buttocks **9** fundament

Fanny
 author: **9** Erica Jong

Fanny
 character in: **13** Joseph Andrews
 author: **8** Fielding

fan out 7 scatter **8** disperse **9** spread out

fantasize 5 dream, fancy **7** imagine **8** daydream

fantastic 3 mad, odd **4** huge, wild **5** antic, crazy, great, queer, weird **6** absurd, superb **7** amazing, bizarre, extreme, strange **8** enormous, fabulous, fanciful, freakish, illusory, quixotic, romantic, terrific **9** grotesque, imaginary, marvelous, visionary, wonderful **10** chimerical, far-fetched, incredible, irrational, outlandish, ridiculous, tremendous **11** extravagant, implausible, sensational **12** preposterous, unbelievable

fantasy 4 mind **5** dream, fancy **6** mirage, notion, vision, whimsy **7** caprice, chimera, fiction, figment, phantom, reverie **8** daydream, illusion, phantasm **9** imagining, invention, nightmare, unreality **10** apparition **11** fabrication, imagination, make-believe, supposition **13** hallucination, realm of dreams, visionary idea

Fantasy Island
 character: **6** Tattoo **8** Mr Roarke
 cast: **16** Herve Villechaize, Ricardo Montalban

far 4 afar, much **6** deeply, remote, way-off, yonder **7** distant, greatly **11** beyond range, out-of-the-way **12** considerably, immeasurably, incomparably

Faraday, Michael
 field: **7** physics **9** chemistry
 worked in: **11** electricity
 developed: **9** generator **12** electrolysis
 liquified: **8** chlorine
 discovered: **6** carbon **7** benzene **24** electromagnetic induction
 named for him: **5** farad

far and near 10 every place, everywhere, far and wide **11** in all places

far and wide 10 every place, everywhere, far and near **11** in all places

Far Away and Long Ago
 author: **8** W H Hudson

farce 4 sham **6** parody **7** mockery **8** drollery, nonsense, pretense, travesty **9** absurdity, burlesque, horseplay, low comedy **10** buffoonery, tomfoolery **11** broad comedy, make-believe **12** harlequinade **14** ridiculousness

farceur 3 wag **5** joker

farcical 5 droll, funny, silly **6** absurd, stupid **7** asinine, comical, foolish **8** humorous **9** laughable, ludicrous, senseless **10** irrational, ridiculous

fare 2 do **3** fee **4** diet, food, menu **5** board, get on, rider, table **6** charge, client, manage **7** make out, perform, regimen, turn out **8** customer, get along, victuals **10** provisions **11** comestibles, ticket price **12** food and drink, passage money **15** paying passenger **20** cost of transportation

farewell 6 so long **7** good-bye, parting **8** Godspeed **9** departing, departure **11** leave-taking, parting wish, valediction **17** parting compliment
 French: **5** adieu **8** au revoir
 German: **14** auf Wiedersehen
 Hawaiian: **5** aloha
 Italian: **4** ciao **5** addio **11** arrivederci
 Japanese: **8** sayonara
 Latin: **4** vale
 Spanish: **5** adios

Farewell to Arms, A
 author: **15** Ernest Hemingway
 character: **13** Frederic Henry **16** Catherine Barkley

far-fetched 7 dubious **8** doubtful, strained, unlikely **10** cockamamie, improbable **11** implausible **12** preposterous, unconvincing

Far From the Madding Crowd
 author: **11** Thomas Hardy
 character: **10** Fanny Robin, Gabriel Oak **12** Sergeant Troy **14** Farmer Boldwood **17** Bathsheba Everdene
 setting: **6** Wessex

farina 4 meal, mush **5** flour **6** cereal, pollen, starch **8** semolina

farm 3 sow **4** plow, reap **5** plant, ranch, tract **6** grange, spread **7** harvest **9** cultivate **10** plantation **11** till the soil **12** country place

farmable 6 arable **7** friable **8** plowable, tillable **10** cultivable

farm animal 2 ox **3** cow, ewe,

hen, hog, pig, ram, sow **4** bull, goat **5** beast, brute, horse, sheep **7** chicken, rooster

farm boundaries
 god of: **8** Silvanus, Sylvanus

farmer 6 grower, raiser, reaper **7** granger, planter, rancher **8** agrarian **9** harvester **10** agronomist, husbandman **12** sharecropper **13** agriculturist, truck gardener **15** tiller of the soil

farming
 god of: **4** Thor

far-off 6 remote **7** distant, faraway **11** unreachable **12** inaccessible **13** unforeseeable

farouche 4 shy **6** fierce, sullen **10** unsociable

far-out 3 mad **4** wild **5** crazy, weird **7** bizarre, strange **10** outlandish **14** fantastic

Far Pavilions, The
 author: **6** M M Kaye

Farragut, David
 served in: **8** Civil War **10** Mexican War **19** War of Eighteen Twelve
 captured: **9** Mobile Bay **10** New Orleans
 saying: **30** Damn the torpedoes full speed ahead

far-reaching 4 wide **5** broad **8** sweeping **9** expansive, extensive, universal, unlimited **11** wide-ranging

Farrell, James T
 author of: **11** Judgment Day **12** Studs Lonigan, Young Lonigan **29** The Young Manhood of Studs Lonigan

far-removed 6 far-off, remote **7** distant, faraway

farrow 6 barren **7** piglets, sterile **9** infertile **10** unpregnant

Farrow, Mia
 real name: **27** Maria de Lourdes Villier Farrow
 father: **10** John Farrow
 mother: **16** Maureen O'Sullivan
 husband: **11** Andre Previn **12** Frank Sinatra
 born: **12** Los Angeles CA
 roles: **5** Zelig **11** John and Mary, Peyton Place **12** The Hurricane **13** Rosemary's Baby **14** The Great Gatsby **16** Allison MacKenzie **19** Hannah and Her Sisters **20** The Purple Rose of Cairo

far side 4 back **7** reverse **8** back side

Far Side, The
 creator/artist: **10** Gary Larson

farsighted 4 wise 5 acute
6 shrewd 7 prudent 9 farseeing, hyperopic, judicious, prescient, provident
10 forehanded, foreseeing
11 clairvoyant, levelheaded

farther 6 beyond, deeper,
longer 7 further, remoter
9 lengthier 10 more remote
11 more distant, more
removed

farthermost 7 extreme 8 farthest, furthest 11 furthermost,
most distant

farthest 3 end 4 most 7 extreme, longest 8 furthest, re-
motest, ultimate 9 uttermost
11 farthermost, furthermost

fascia 4 band, sash 5 board,
strip 6 fillet, girdle, ribbon, tissue 7 bandage 8 membrane
9 dashboard

fascinate 5 charm, rivet 6 absorb, allure 7 beguile, bewitch,
delight, enchant, engross
8 enravish, enthrall, entrance,
transfix 9 captivate, enrapture,
overpower, spellbind 14 hold
spellbound

fascinating 8 alluring, charming, gripping, riveting 9 absorbing, beguiling
10 bewitching, delightful, enchanting, engrossing, entrancing 11 captivating, enthralling,
interesting 12 overpowering,
spellbinding

fascination 4 draw, lure
5 charm 6 allure 9 magnetism
10 attraction 11 captivation

fascism 6 Nazism 9 autocracy,
oligarchy 10 plutocracy
11 corporatism, police state
13 corporativism 14 corporate
state 15 totalitarianism 17 national socialism 21 right-wing
dictatorship

fascist 9 right-wing 10 repressive, tyrannical 11 dictatorial,
doctrinaire

fashion 3 air, fad, hew, way
4 form, make, mode, mold,
rage 5 carve, craze, forge,
frame, habit, shape, style,
tenor, trend, usage, vogue
6 create, custom, design, devise, manner 7 compose, pattern, produce 8 attitude,
behavior, contrive, demeanor
9 construct, fabricate 10 convention 11 manufacture

fashionable 2 in 3 hip 4 chic
5 smart 6 modish, with-it
7 current, in style, in vogue,
popular, stylish, voguish 9 in
fashion 10 all the rage,
prevailing
French: 9 de rigueur

fashionable world
French: 10 grand monde

fashion designer 4 (Christian)
Dior 5 Kenzo, (Jean) Patou
6 Adolfo, Lanvin, Poiret,
(Coco) Chanel 7 Galanos, Hal-
ston, Missoni, (Pierre) Bal-
main 8 Givenchy 9 Courreges,
Mary Quant, Valentino
10 Balenciaga, Mainbocher,
Perry Ellis 11 Calvin Klein,
Emilio Pucci, Ralph Lauren
12 Liz Claiborne, Lucien Le-
long, Norman Norell, Pierre
Cardin, Schiaparelli 13 Karl
Lagerfeld, Rudi Gernreich
14 Pauline Trigere 15 Claire
McCardell 16 Gloria Vander-
bilt, Yves Saint-Laurent
Empress Eugenie's:
5 (Charles Frederick) Worth
Marie Antoinette's: 10 Rose
Bertin
Empress Josephine's:
19 Louis Hippolyte Leroy

fashioned 4 made 5 built
6 formed, framed, molded,
shaped, styled 7 adapted,
crafted, created, devised, managed, modeled 9 contrived,
patterned 11 constructed
12 accommodated

fashion plate 4 dude 5 dandy
12 Beau Brummell, clotheshorse, man of fashion, sharp
dresser 14 woman of fashion

fast 4 firm, taut, true, wild
5 ahead, brisk, fleet, fully,
hasty, loose, loyal, quick,
rapid, rigid, swift, tight
6 famish, firmly, flying, rakish,
secure, speedy, stable, starve,
steady, wanton, winged
7 abiding, devoted, durable,
fasting, fast day, fixedly, hastily, hurried, immoral, lasting,
lustful, quickly, rapidly, solidly, soundly, staunch, swiftly,
tightly 8 constant, enduring,
faithful, fastened, go hungry,
immodest, reckless, resolute,
securely, speedily, unfading
9 debauched, dissolute, hurriedly, immovable, immovably,
in advance, permanent, resistant, steadfast 10 completely,
dissipated, firmly tied, lascivious, licentious, profligate, starvation, stationary, unswerving,
unwavering 11 accelerated, expeditious, extravagant, intemperate, pleasure-mad,
tenaciously 12 hunger strike,
ineradicable, lickety-split

Fast, Howard
author of: 9 Spartacus
11 Freedom Road 13 The
Immigrants 15 Citizen Tom
Paine

fasten 3 bar, fix, pin, tie, wed
4 bind, bolt, clip, fuse, hold,
hook, join, lash, link, lock,
moor, snap, weld, yoke 5 affix, clamp, clasp, dowel, focus,
hitch, close, latch, rivet,
screw, stick, truss, unite 6 adhere, anchor, attach, button,
cement, couple, direct, pinion,
secure, solder, tether 7 connect 8 dovetail 11 put together

fastener 3 peg, pin, tie 4 clip,
glue, grip, hook, line, nail,
snap, tack 5 catch, clamp,
clasp, cleat, latch, screw, strap,
truss 6 buckle, button, cement,
staple, thread, zipper
7 bracket 8 barrette 9 fastening, safety pin, thumbtack
10 clothespin, connection,
hook and eye

fastening 4 snap 5 clasp
8 coupling 9 attaching 10 attachment, connection

fasten together 3 tie 4 dock,
join 6 couple, hook up, link
up

fastidious 5 fussy, picky
6 choosy, dainty, proper,
queasy 7 finicky 8 exacting,
precious 9 difficult, squeamish
10 meticulous, particular
11 overprecise, overrefined,
persnickety 12 hard to please,
overdelicate 13 hypercritical

Fastidious Brisk
character in: 22 Every Man
out of His Humour
author: 6 Jonson

fastidious connoisseur 7 epicure, gourmet 9 bon vivant
10 gastronome

fastidiousness 4 care 12 ex-
actingness 14 discrimination
15 persnicketiness

fat 4 full, oily 5 beefy, fatty,
flush, heavy, obese, palmy,
plump, pudgy, stout, suety
6 chubby, fleshy, grease,
greasy, portly, rotund 7 copious, fertile, lumpish, paunchy,
replete, stuffed 8 abundant,
blubbery, chockful, fruitful,
thickset, unctuous 9 animal
fat, corpulent, fortunate, lucrative, plenteous, plentiful, rewarding 10 overweight,
potbellied, productive 11 well-
stocked 12 remunerative

fatal 6 deadly, lethal, mortal
7 ruinous 8 terminal, virulent
10 calamitous, disastrous
11 destructive 12 catastrophic,
causing death

fatalism 8 stoicism 11 resignation 12 acquiescence, helplessness 13 powerlessness
14 predestination

fatality 5 death 8 casualty 9 le-
thality, mortality 10 deadli-

ness, malignancy
11 banefulness

fatal woman
French: 11 femme fatale

fate 3 lot 4 doom 5 karma,
moira 6 effect, future, kismet,
upshot 7 chances, destiny, fortune, outcome, portion
8 prospect 10 providence
11 consequence 12 will of
heaven 14 predestination

fated 4 sure 5 bound, meant
6 doomed 7 certain 8 destined

fateful 5 fatal 7 crucial, ominous 8 critical, decisive 9 momentous 10 disastrous,
portentous 11 significant

Fates
also: 5 Morae 6 Moerae,
Moirai, Parcae
named: 6 Clotho 7 Atropos
8 Lachesis
goddesses of: 7 destiny
number of goddesses:
5 three
called: 12 weird sisters
parents: 4 Zeus 5 Night
6 Themis

father 3 dad, pop 4 abbe, cure,
papa, sire 5 beget, begin,
daddy, found, hatch, maker,
padre, pater 6 author, create,
design, old man, parson, pastor, priest 7 creator, founder
8 ancestor, begetter, designer,
engender, forebear, inventor,
preacher 9 architect, confessor,
originate, procreate 10 forefather, male parent, originator,
progenitor
French: 4 pere

Father 4 Abba

Father, The
author: 16 August Strindberg

Father Knows Best
character: 11 Jim Anderson
13 Betty Anderson (Prin-
cess), Kathy Anderson (Kitten) 15 James Anderson Jr
(Bud) 16 Margaret Anderson
cast: 9 Billy Gray, Jane
Wyatt 11 Robert Young
12 Lauren Chapin 13 Elinor
Donahue

fatherland 6 Heimat, patria,
patrie 8 homeland 10 birthplace, motherland, native land,
native soil 13 mother country,
native country

fatherly 6 benign, kindly,
tender 8 parental, paternal
9 indulgent 10 beneficent,
benevolent

father of his country
Latin: 12 Pater Patriae

father of stars/wind
8 Astraeus

Father of the Bride
director: 16 Vincente
Minnelli
cast: 11 Billie Burke, Joan
Bennett, Leo G Carroll
12 Spencer Tracy 15 Elizabeth Taylor
sequel: 21 Father's Little
Dividend

father of the family
Latin: 13 paterfamilias

Father of the Rivers *see*
4 Nile

Fathers and Sons
author: 12 Ivan Turgenev
character: 5 Katya, Pavel
6 Arkady, Vasily 8 Bazaroff,
Fenichka 9 Kirsanoff
15 Madame Odintzoff

fathom 5 probe 6 divine, follow 7 hunt out, root out, uncover, unravel 8 discover
9 ferret out, figure out, penetrate 10 comprehend, understand 16 get to the bottom of

fathom
abbreviation: 4 fath

fatigue 3 fag 4 bush, tire
5 drain, weary 6 tedium,
tucker, weaken 7 exhaust, languor, wear out 8 enervate,
overtire 9 heaviness, lassitude,
tiredness, weariness 10 debilitate, drowsiness, enervation,
exhaustion 12 debilitation, listlessness 13 overtiredness

fatigued 4 beat 5 all in, jaded,
spent, tired, weary 6 bushed,
done in, fagged, pooped
7 worn out 8 dog-tired, weakened 9 dead tired, enervated,
exhausted, overtaxed 10 overworked 11 debilitated, tuckered out

fatiguing 6 tiring 7 arduous,
tedious 8 tiresome 9 wearisome 10 exhausting

Fatima
character in: 9 Bluebeard

**fatti maschii, parole fem-
ine** 29 deeds are manly words
are womanish
motto of: 8 Maryland

fatty 4 oily 5 lardy, suety
6 greasy 7 buttery 8 blubbery
9 shortened

fatuous 5 inane, silly, vapid
6 obtuse, simple, stupid 7 asinine, foolish, idiotic, moronic,
puerile, vacuous, witless 8 besotted, imbecile 9 brainless,
senseless 10 ridiculous

faucet 3 tap 4 cock 5 spout,
valve 6 nozzle, outlet, spigot
7 bibcock

Faulkland
character in: 9 The Rivals
author: 8 Sheridan

Faulkner, William
author of: 7 The Bear 8 Sar-
toris 9 Sanctuary, The Hamlet 10 The Reivers 11 As I
Lay Dying 13 Light in Au-
gust 15 Absalom Absalom!
17 Intruder in the Dust
18 The Sound and the Fury
fictional county:
13 Yoknapatawpha

fault 3 bug, sin 4 flaw, slip,
snag 5 blame, crime, error,
guilt, stain, taint, wrong 6 defect, foible, glitch, impugn
7 blemish, blunder, censure,
failing, frailty, misdeed, mistake, offense, reprove 8 drawback, weakness 9 criticize,
infirmity, oversight, weak
point 10 deficiency, impediment, negligence, peccadillo,
wrongdoing 11 culpability,
dereliction, misdemeanor,
shortcoming 12 imperfection,
indiscretion 13 answerability,
transgression 14 accountability,
responsibility

faultfind 3 nag 4 beef, carp,
kick 5 cavil, gripe, knock
6 deride, squawk 7 nitpick
8 complain 9 criticize

faultfinder 3 nag 4 bear, crab
5 crank 6 carper, censor, critic,
grouch 7 caviler, grouser
8 quibbler, sorehead 9 deroga-
tor, detractor, Mrs Grundy,
nitpicker 10 bellyacher, complainer, curmudgeon, fuddy-
duddy, fussbudget

faultfinding 4 beef, kick
5 gripe 6 squawk 7 beefing,
carping, griping, kicking, nagging 9 complaint, criticism,
squawking 10 nitpicking
11 complaining, criticizing

faultless 5 ideal 7 correct, perfect 8 accurate, flawless 9 exemplary 10 immaculate,
impeccable 11 unblemished
13 unimpeachable 14 irre-
proachable, without blemish

faulty 3 bad 4 awry 5 amiss,
false, wrong 7 injured, unsound 8 impaired, inferior,
mistaken 9 defective, deficient,
erroneous, imperfect, incorrect 10 inadequate, out of order, unreliable
14 unsatisfactory

faun
form: 5 deity
location: 5 rural

Fauna *see* 7 Bona Dea

Faunus
origin: 5 Roman
form: 5 deity

Faure, Gabriel Urbain
location: 5 woods
also called: 5 Inuus 6 Fatuus
king of: 6 Latium
father: 5 Picus
son: 7 Latinus
corresponds to: 3 Pan

Faure, Gabriel Urbain
born: 6 France 7 Pamiers
composer of: 5 Dolly 6 Pavane 7 Ballade, Mirages, Requiem, Shylock 8 Penelope 9 Fantaisie, Promethee 12 Le Jardin Clos 13 La Chanson d'Eve 14 La Bonne Chanson 18 L'Horizon Chimerique, Pelleas et Melisande 21 Masques et Bergamasques

Faust
author: 12 Johann Goethe
character: 6 Wagner 8 Gretchen 10 Homunculus 11 Helen of Troy 14 Mephistopheles

Faust
opera by: 6 Gounod
character: 9 Valentine 10 Marguerite 14 Mephistopheles

Faustulus
vocation: 8 herdsman, shepherd
raised: 5 Remus 7 Romulus

faute de mieux 24 for lack of something better

faux pas 4 goof 5 boner, error, gaffe, lapse 6 boo-boo, howler, slip-up 7 blooper, blunder, mistake 9 false step 11 impropriety 12 indiscretion

favela 4 slum 10 shanty town

Favell, Jack
character in: 7 Rebecca
author: 9 Du Maurier

Favonius
origin: 5 Roman
personifies: 8 west wind

favor 3 aid 4 abet, back, gift, help, like 5 be for, fancy, humor 6 assist, esteem, foster, oblige, pamper, prefer, succor, uphold 7 approve, commend, endorse, go in for, indulge, kind act, memento, present, service, support 8 advocacy, approval, courtesy, espousal, good deed, good turn, goodwill, largesse, look like, resemble, sanction, side with, souvenir 9 encourage, patronage, patronize, smile upon, take after, use gently 10 act of grace, use lightly 11 accommodate, approbation, be partial to, benefaction, countenance, good opinion 12 be the image of, championship, commendation, dispensation,

kindly regard 13 accommodation, goodwill token

favorable 4 fair, good, kind 6 benign, timely 7 helpful, hopeful 8 amicable, friendly, salutary 9 approving, conducive, opportune, promising 10 auspicious, beneficial, convenient, propitious 11 predisposed, serviceable, sympathetic 12 advantageous, commendatory, well-disposed

favorable opinion 6 esteem, regard 7 respect 8 approval 10 admiration 12 appreciation

favorably disposed 7 willing 8 amenable, inclined, obliging 9 agreeable 11 sympathetic

favorite 3 pet 5 fancy, jewel 6 choice 7 darling, special 9 best-liked, preferred 11 front-runner, most popular 13 fair-haired one 14 apple of one's eye

favoritism 4 bias 10 partiality 12 one-sidedness, partisanship

Fawley, Jude and Drusilla
characters in: 14 Jude the Obscure
author: 5 Hardy

fawn 5 toady 6 pander 7 flatter, truckle 8 pay court 9 be servile, seek favor 12 be obsequious, bow and scrape

fawning 7 servile 8 flattery, toadying 9 adulating, adulation, truckling 10 flattering, obsequious 11 sycophantic 12 ingratiating 14 obsequiousness

faze 4 fret 5 abash, daunt, upset, worry 6 bother, flurry, rattle 7 disturb, fluster, perturb 8 confound 9 discomfit, embarrass 10 discompose, disconcert

fazed 5 upset 7 abashed, ruffled 8 agitated, bothered, confused 9 chagrined, unsettled 10 confounded, distracted, nonplussed 11 embarrassed 12 disconcerted

FBI, The
character: 10 Arthur Ward 21 Inspector Lewis Erskine
cast: 12 Philip Abbott 16 Efrem Zimbalist Jr

fealty 7 loyalty 8 devotion, fidelity 9 adherence, constancy 10 allegiance, attachment 12 faithfulness

fear 3 awe 4 care 5 alarm, bogey, dread, panic, qualm, worry 6 dismay, esteem, fright, horror, phobia, revere, terror, threat, wonder 7 anxiety, bugaboo, bugbear, con-

cern, quaking, specter 8 affright, venerate 9 cowardice, nightmare, reverence, shudder at, tremble at 10 be afraid of, be scared of, feel awe for, foreboding, take fright, veneration 11 trepidation 12 apprehension, perturbation 13 consternation 14 be frightened of

fearful 4 dire 5 awful, dread, eerie, lurid, timid 6 afraid, aghast, horrid, scared, uneasy 7 alarmed, anxious, ghastly, macabre, nervous, ominous, panicky, worried 8 alarming, dreadful, horrible, shocking, sinister, skittish, terrible, timorous 9 appalling, concerned, diffident, frightful, tremulous 10 formidable, frightened, portentous, terrifying 11 distressing, frightening, intimidated 12 apprehensive, fainthearted 13 panic-stricken 14 chickenhearted

fearfulness fear 5 alarm, dread, panic 6 fright, terror 7 anguish, anxiety 8 timidity 11 trepidation 12 apprehension

fearless 4 bold 5 brave 6 daring, gritty, heroic, plucky 7 doughty, gallant, valiant 8 intrepid, unafraid, valorous 9 audacious, confident, dauntless, unabashed, undaunted 10 courageous, undismayed 11 adventurous, indomitable, lionhearted, unflinching, unshrinking, venturesome, without fear 12 stout-hearted

fearlessness 4 grit 5 pluck, valor 7 bravery, courage 8 boldness 10 confidence 13 dauntlessness

Fear of Flying
author: 9 Erica Jong

feasible 6 viable 7 fitting, politic 8 possible, suitable, workable 9 advisable, desirable 10 achievable, attainable, reasonable 11 appropriate, conceivable, practicable

feast 4 dine, fete 5 festa, gorge 6 bounty 7 banquet, holiday, jubilee, surplus 8 feast day, festival 9 bacchanal, saint's day 10 gluttonize, gormandize, have a feast, rich supply 11 celebration, eat one's fill, elegant meal, wine and dine

feat 3 act 4 deed, task 6 action, stroke 7 exploit, triumph 8 maneuver 9 adventure 10 attainment, enterprise 11 achievement, performance, tour de force 14 accomplishment

feather 4 down, kind, sort
5 adorn, eider, plume, quill
7 bristle, plumage, variety
9 character, turn an oar

featherbrained 4 dumb
5 silly **6** simple, stupid **7** foolish, witless **9** brainless
12 muddleheaded, simpleminded **13** rattle-brained
14 scatterbrained

feather in one's cap
5 honor **6** credit **11** distinction

feather one's nest 6 enrich
15 fill one's pockets

feature, features 3 see
4 mark, star **5** fancy, trait
6 aspect, play up, visage
7 display, earmark, imagine, picture, present, quality **8** envision, hallmark, headline, main item, property **9** attribute, character, highlight, specialty, spotlight **10** conceive of, lineaments **14** characteristic

February *see box*

Fechner, Gustav Theodore
nationality: **6** German
founder of: **22** experimental psychology

fecit 6 he made (it) **7** she made (it)

feckless 3 lax **5** slack **6** re-

February
event: **4** Lent **5** Purim
8 Leap year **9** Mardi
Gras **12** Ash Wednesday, Groundhog Day
(2)
flower: **6** violet
8 primrose
French: **7** Fevrier
gem: **8** amethyst
German: **7** Februar
holiday: **9** Candlemas
(2) **13** Valentine's Day
(14) **14** Chinese New
Year **16** Lincoln's Birthday (12) **19** Washington's Birthday (22)
Italian: **8** Febbraio
Latin: **6** Februa
number of days:
10 twenty-nine (every 4
years) **11** twenty-eight
origin of name:
7 Februus
Roman god of:
12 purification
place in year:
Gregorian: **6** second
Roman: **7** twelfth
Spanish: **7** Febrero
Zodiac signs: **6** Pisces
8 Aquarius

---

miss **8** careless, heedless
9 negligent, worthless **10** neglectful **11** thoughtless
13 irresponsible

Fecundity
goddess of: **5** Freia, Freya

Federalist Party
president belonging to:
5 Adams **10** Washington

federate 5 unite **7** combine
12 join together

federation 5 union **6** league
7 combine **8** alliance **9** coalition, syndicate **10** sisterhood
11 association, brotherhood, confederacy **12** amalgamation
13 confederation

fee 4 fare, hire, toll, wage
5 price **6** charge, salary, tariff
7 payment, stipend **9** emolument **10** commission, honorarium **12** compensation, remuneration **13** consideration

feeble 4 flat, lame, poor, puny, tame, thin, weak **5** faint, frail, vapid **6** ailing, flabby, flimsy, infirm, meager, paltry, senile, sickly, slight **7** fragile, insipid
8 decrepit, delicate, disabled, impotent, weakened **9** colorless, declining, doddering, enervated, enfeebled, forceless, not strong, powerless **10** inadequate, spiritless, wishy-washy **11** debilitated, ineffective, ineffectual

feeble-minded 4 dull **6** senile, stupid **7** moronic **8** backward, childish, retarded **9** imbecilic, senseless, subnormal **10** half-witted, weak-minded **12** mentally slow

feeble-mindedness 6 dotage, idiocy **8** dullness, senility, slowness **9** denseness, stupidity **11** retardation

feed 3 eat **4** fare, fuel, mash
5 cater, feast, graze **6** devour, fodder, forage, foster, viands
7 augment, bolster, consume, gratify, nourish, nurture, pasture, satisfy, support, sustain
8 maintain, take food, victuals **9** encourage, foodstuff, provender **10** minister to, provisions, strengthen **11** comestibles, nourishment, wine and dine

feeder 6 branch **7** channel
9 tributary

feel 3 paw, see **4** know
5 grope, press, probe, reach, sense, think, touch **6** finger, fumble, handle, makeup, notice **7** believe, discern, feeling, observe, palpate, texture
8 perceive **9** be aware of, be moved by, character, sensa-

tion **10** comprehend, experience, manipulate, suffer from, understand **11** be convinced, be stirred by, be touched by, composition

feel aversion toward 4 hate
5 abhor **6** detest **7** despise
9 abominate, can't abide, can't stand **11** can't stomach **12** be revolted by **13** find repugnant, find repulsive **14** view with horror

feeler 7 antenna **8** proposal, tentacle **10** experiment **12** trial balloon

feel indebted 10 appreciate, be beholden, be grateful
13 feel obligated

feeling 4 aura, pity, view, zeal
5 ardor, gusto, sense, verve
6 fervor, spirit, thrill, warmth
7 concern, emotion, opinion, passion **8** attitude, instinct, reaction, response, sympathy
9 affection, awareness, intuition, sensation, sentiment, vehemence **10** atmosphere, compassion, enthusiasm, impression **11** earnestness, inclination, point of view, sensibility, sensitivity

feeling life is wearisome
Latin: **12** taedium vitae

feelings 3 ego **5** pride **8** emotions, passions **10** self-esteem
13 sensibilities, sensitivities
16 susceptibilities

feel pain 4 ache, hurt **5** smart
6 suffer **7** agonize **9** be in agony **11** be tormented **12** be in distress

Feenix, Cousin
character in: **12** Dombey and Son
author: **7** Dickens

feet 4 dogs, pads, paws
5 hoofs **6** hooves **8** gunboats, tootsies

feign 4 fake, sham **5** forge, put on **6** affect, assume, cook up, invent, make up **7** concoct, pretend **8** simulate **9** fabricate
11 counterfeit, make a show of, make believe

feigned 4 fake, sham **5** bogus, phony **6** ersatz **8** spurious
9 imitation, insincere, pretended, simulated **10** artificial
11 counterfeit, make-believe

feint 4 hoax, mask, move, pass, ploy, ruse, wile **5** blind, bluff, dodge, trick **6** gambit **7** pretext **8** artifice, maneuver, pretense **9** stratagem
10 subterfuge **13** feigned attack

Feldman, Marty
born: 6 London 7 England
roles: 11 Silent Movie
17 Young Frankenstein
24 The Last Remake of
Beau Geste

feldspar
varieties: 8 sunstone 9 amazonite, moonstone

felicitate 4 hail 6 salute
10 wish one joy 11 rejoice
with 12 congratulate 18 give
one's best wishes 28 wish
many happy returns of the
day

felicitations 3 joy 6 cheers
9 blessings, greetings 10 best
wishes, good wishes 11 compliments, salutations 12 pat on
the back 15 congratulations
24 many happy returns of the
day

felicitous 3 apt 5 happy 6 joyful, joyous 7 fitting, germane,
well-put 8 inspired, pleasing,
relevant, suitable, well-said
9 effective, fortunate, pertinent 10 propitious, well-
chosen 11 appropriate

felicity 5 bliss, charm, grace,
knack, skill 6 heaven, nicety
7 aptness, delight, ecstasy, fitness 8 paradise 9 beatitude,
happiness 12 blissfulness 13 effectiveness 15 appropriateness

Felix the Cat
creator: 11 Pat Sullivan

fell 4 raze 5 level 7 cut down,
destroy, hew down 8 demolish 9 knock down, prostrate

Feller, Bob (Robert)
nickname: 11 Rapid Robert
sport: 8 baseball
position: 7 pitcher
team: 16 Cleveland Indians

Fellini, Federico
director of: 8 Amarcord, Casanova, La Strada 11 La
Dolce Vita 15 Nights of Cabiria 18 Juliet of the Spirits

fellow 3 boy, guy, man, pal
4 chap, chum, dude, mate,
peer 6 equal 6 friend 7 comrade, consort 8 coworker 9 associate, colleague, companion
10 compatriot

fellow-conspirator 4 ally
6 cohort 7 abettor 8 henchman 9 accessory 11 confederate 12 collaborator

fellow creature 6 mortal, person 10 individual

fellow feeling 6 regard 7 kinship 8 affinity, fondness 10 attraction, partiality

fellowship 5 amity 7 society

8 intimacy 10 affability, cordiality, fraternity, friendship
11 amicability, association,
brotherhood, comradeship, familiarity, sociability 12 friendliness 13 companionship

felon 5 crook, cruel, thief
6 fierce, outlaw, wicked
7 convict, illegal, villain,
whitlow 8 criminal, gangster,
jailbird, murderer 10 lawbreaker, malefactor 11 public
enemy 12 inflammation

felony 5 arson, crime 6 murder 7 assault, misdeed, offense,
robbery 8 burglary 9 blackmail 10 kidnapping, wrongdoing 12 capital offense

female 3 cow, dam, hen, sow
4 girl, mare 5 bitch, tabby,
woman 6 heifer 7 distaff,
womanly 8 feminine, ladylike
9 womanlike

feminine 4 soft 5 woman
6 dainty, female, gentle 7 distaff, girlish, womanly 8 delicate, ladylike 10 femalelike,
like a woman 14 of the female sex

femininity 8 softness 10 femaleness, gentleness 11 girl-
ishness, womanliness
12 feminineness 13 female
quality

femme 4 wife 5 woman

femme de chambre 9 lady's
maid 11 chambermaid

femme fatale 4 vamp 5 siren
7 charmer 10 fatal woman, seductress 11 enchantress

femur
bone of: 5 thigh 8 upper leg

fen 3 bog 4 moor, sump
5 marsh, swale, swamp 6 bottom, morass, slough 7 lowland, wetland 8 quagmire

fence 3 pen 4 coop, duel, gird,
rail 5 hedge, hem in 6 corral,
secure, wall in 7 barrier, confine, palings 8 encircle, palisade, stockade, surround
9 barricade, encompass
11 cross swords

fencing
equipment: 4 epee, foil,
mask 5 saber, sword
8 plastron
part of weapon: 5 blade,
forte, guard 6 foible, handle,
medium, pommel
term: 3 hit 5 prime, sixte,
touch 6 octave, quarte,
quinte, tierce 7 on guard,
seconde, septime
deceptive move: 5 feint
movement: 4 beat 5 lunge,
parry 6 double, fleche,

thrust 7 advance, cutover,
recover, retreat, riposte
9 disengage 11 froissement

fend 2 do 5 avert, avoid, parry,
repel, shift 6 manage 7 keep
off, make out, provide, repulse, support, survive, ward
off 8 push away

fender 3 pad 4 curb 5 guard
6 buffer, bumper, shield,
sluice 7 cushion, railing
9 fireguard, protector 10 cow-
catcher, fire screen, protection,
wheel guard

fend off 5 avert, dodge, evade,
parry, repel 6 escape 7 ward
off 8 sidestep, stave off

fennel
botanical name: 17 Foenicu-
lum vulgare
family: 7 parsley
varieties: 3 dog 4 wild
5 giant 8 Florence 9 com-
mon dog 11 common
giant
mythical aid to: 9 fortifier
11 aphrodisiac, slenderizer
12 rejuvenation, stops hiccups 16 restores eyesight
use: 4 duck, fish 5 bread,
rolls 7 chicken 8 apple pie
16 seafood casserole

Fenrir
also: 6 Fenris
origin: 12 Scandinavian
form: 4 wolf 7 monster
father: 4 Loki
mother: 9 Angerboda, An-
grbodha, Angurboda
sister: 3 Hel
brother: 11 Iormungandr,
Jormungandr 14 Midgard
Serpent
ate: 4 Odin 5 Othin
killed by: 5 Vidar

Fenris see 6 Fenrir

Fenton
character in: 22 The Merry
Wives of Windsor
author: 11 Shakespeare

feral 4 wild 6 brutal, deadly,
ferine, fierce, savage 7 bestial,
untamed, vicious 9 ferocious
12 uncultivated
14 undomesticated

Ferber, Edna
author of: 5 Giant, So Big
8 Cimarron, Show Boat
9 Ice Palace, Stage Door
(with George S Kaufman)
13 Dinner at Eight (with
George S Kaufman), Sara-
toga Trunk 14 The Royal
Family (with George S
Kaufman)

Ferdinand
character in: 10 The Tempest
author: 11 Shakespeare

Ferdinand
character in: 16 Love's Labour's Lost
author: 11 Shakespeare

Ferd'nand
creator: 3 Mik 13 Dahl
Mikkelsen

Feria
origin: 5 Roman
form: 7 holiday

Fermat, Pierre de
field: 11 mathematics
nationality: 6 French
discovered: 16 analytic
geometry

ferment 4 foam, mold, sour,
turn 5 froth, yeast 6 enzyme,
fester, leaven, seethe, tumult,
unrest, uproar 7 agitate, inflame, smolder, turmoil 8 bubble up, disquiet 9 agitation,
commotion, leavening 10 disruption, effervesce, turbulence
11 be turbulent, fomentation

fermented 6 soured, worked
7 seethed 8 agitated

Fermi, Enrico
field: 7 physics
nationality: 7 Italian
developed: 10 atomic bomb
20 uranium fission theory
awarded: 10 Nobel Prize

fern *see box*

fernet-branca
type: 8 aperitif
origin: 5 Italy
flavor: 4 herb

Fern Hill
author: 11 Dylan Thomas

ferocious 6 brutal, deadly,
fierce, savage 7 bestial, brutish, enraged, violent 8 fiendish, maddened, ravening,
ruthless 9 atrocious, barbarous,
merciless, murderous, predatory, rapacious 10 relentless
11 cold-blooded
12 bloodthirsty

ferocity 7 cruelty 8 savagery
9 barbarity, brutality, harshness 10 fierceness, inhumanity, savageness 11 brutishness,
viciousness 12 ruthlessness

Ferrer, Jose
real name: 33 Jose Vincente
Ferrer de Otero y Cintron
wife: 8 Uta Hagen 15 Rosemary Clooney
born: 8 Santurce 10 Puerto
Rico
roles: 7 I Accuse 9 Joan of
Arc 11 Moulin Rouge, Ship
of Fools 14 The Caine Mu-
tiny 16 Cyrano de Bergerac
(Oscar), Lawrence of Ara-
bia 24 The Greatest Story
Ever Told

fern
varieties: 3 air, cup, lip, man, oak, saw 4 ball, blue, claw,
deer, dish, felt, fire, gold, hand, iron, king, lace, lady,
male, moss, nest, pine, sago, tara, tree, wall, wart,
wood 5 beard, beech, chain, cloak, fancy, glade, glory,
grape, grass, hedge, holly, marsh, plume, royal, strap,
swamp, sweet, sword, table, water, whisk 6 adder's, bamboo, basket, Boston, button, carrot, coffee, cotton, cuplet,
dagger, ladder, meadow, mother, ribbon, shield, silver,
tongue, turnip, winter 7 bladder, boulder, brittle, bulblet,
crested, emerald, feather, Fee's lip, fragile, Goldie's, hack-
saw, Halberd, hammock, leather, New York, ostrich, parsley, peacock, rainbow, walking 8 bear-foot, bear's-paw,
cinnamon, climbing, elk's-horn, fishtail, floating, florist's,
fragrant, hairy lip, Hartford, licorice, mosquito, Nebraska,
Savannah, snuffbox, soft tree, staghorn 9 asparagus,
bird's-nest, black tree, blond tree, Christmas, common
cup, deer's-foot, downy wood, flowering, glossy cup,
hare's foot, long beech, sensitive, vegetable, Venus hair,
viscid lip, wavy cloak, woolly lip 10 Alabama lip, Boott's
wood, broad beech, deer-tongue, Duff's sword, erect
sword, five-finger, hay-scented, lady ground, maidenhair,
scented oak, shoestring, silver tree, silver-back, silver-lace,
silver-leaf, slender lip, strawberry, upside-down, woolly
tree 11 Braun's holly, coastal wood, Coville's lip, crested
felt, crested wood, dwarf Boston, elephant-ear, Fendler's
lip, hart's-tongue, interrupted, Jamaica gold, leatherleaf,
leatherwood, narrow beech, netted chain, Northern oak,
Parry's cloak, Pursh's holly, rabbit's-foot, rattlesnake,
Sierra water, walking leaf 12 Adder's-tongue, American
wall, berry bladder, Clinton's wood, Dudley's holly, Eaton's shield, English hedge, Hawaiian tree, Java staghorn,
limestone oak, mountain wood, Northern lady, resurrection, Southern lady, squirrel-foot, toothed sword, Western
holly, Western sword 13 California lip, Cleveland's lip,
Dudley's shield, European chain, fan maidenhair, Fendler's cloak, Florida ribbon, leathery grape, Malay climbing, mountain holly, Northern holly, prickly shield,
Prince-of-Wales, spinulose wood, Tasmanian tree, triangle
water, Virginia chain, wild bird's nest 14 Anderson's
holly, Australian tree, bulblet bladder, California gold,
common staghorn, dissected grape, dwarf asparagus, hen-
and-chickens, imbricate sword, silver-king tree, West Indian tree 15 American parsley, California cloak, California holly, Delta maidenhair, East Indian holly, European
parsley, mountain bladder, mountain parsley 16 black-
stemmed tree, daisy-leaved grape, Farley maidenhair, Tassel maidenhair, Tracy's maidenhair 17 Bermuda maidenhair, brittle maidenhair, climbing bird's nest, walking
maidenhair 18 Aleutian maidenhair, American maidenhair, Barbados maidenhair, Northern maidenhair, Trailing
maidenhair, Triangular staghorn 20 Australian maidenhair, California maidenhair

ferret out 5 dig up 6 detect
7 find out, root out, uncover,
unearth 8 discover
9 ascertain

fertile 4 rich 5 loamy 6 fecund 8 creative, fruitful, original, prolific 9 fructuous,
ingenious, inventive, luxuriant, plenteous 10 fecundated,
fertilized, fructified, generative,
productive, vegetative
11 imaginative, resourceful
12 reproductive

Fertility
god of: 7 Bacchus, Mutinus
8 Lupercus, Picumnus
goddess of: 4 Isis 5 Fauna
6 Athena, Athene, Brigit,
Libera, Pallas, Saitis, Tellus
7 Astarte, Berchta, Bona
Dea, Demeter, Perchta
11 Tritogeneia 12 Pallas
Athena 16 Alalcomean
Athena

fertilize 6 enrich, manure
8 fructify 9 fecundate, polli-

nate **10** impregnate, inseminate

fertilizer 4 dung, muck **5** guano **6** manure, potash **7** compost **8** bonemeal, dressing **10** enrichener **14** superphosphate

fervent 4 keen **5** eager, fiery **6** ardent, devout, fervid, fierce, hearty, heated **7** burning, earnest, intense, zealous **8** spirited, vehement **9** heartfelt **10** passionate **11** impassioned, warmhearted **12** enthusiastic, wholehearted

fervid 5 eager **6** ardent, raging **7** burning, earnest, fanatic, fervent, intense, zealous **8** spirited **10** passionate **11** impassioned **12** all-consuming

fervor 4 fire, zeal, zest **5** ardor, gusto, piety, verve **6** warmth **7** passion **9** animation, eagerness, intensity, vehemence **10** devoutness, enthusiasm, heartiness **11** earnestness, seriousness **14** purposefulness

Feste
  character in: **12** Twelfth Night
  author: **11** Shakespeare

fester 3 rot, vex **4** fret, gall, grow, rile **5** chafe, pique **6** nettle, plague, rankle **7** blister, form pus, inflame, putrefy, smolder, torment **8** irritate, ulcerate **9** intensify, suppurate

festering 6 putrid **7** rotting **8** infected, inflamed, rankling **10** putrefying **11** suppurating

festina lente 15 make haste slowly

festival 4 fete, gala **5** feast **6** fiesta **7** gala day, holiday, jubilee **8** carnival, jamboree **11** celebration, festivities

festival of *see box*

festive 3 gay **4** gala **5** jolly, merry **6** festal, joyous **7** larkish, playful **8** sportive **9** convivial **10** frolicsome **11** celebratory **12** lighthearted

festivity 3 joy **4** fete, gala **5** feast, mirth **6** fiesta, gaiety, levity **7** fanfare, jollity, jubilee, revelry **8** festival, jamboree **9** merriment, rejoicing **11** celebration, merrymaking

festoon 3 lei **4** swag **5** chain, curve **6** wreath **7** garland, hanging **8** decorate

fetch 3 get **4** cost **5** bring, go for, yield **6** afford, obtain **7** procure, realize, sell for **8** amount to, retrieve

fetching 6 divine, lovely **8** adorable, becoming, charming, engaging, pleasing **9** appealing **10** attractive, delightful **11** captivating

fete 4 gala **5** feast, party, treat **6** regale **7** banquet, holiday **8** carnival, festival **9** bal masque **11** celebration, garden party, wine and dine **13** fete champetre

fete champetre 11 garden party **15** outdoor festival

fetid 4 foul, gamy, rank **5** fusty, moldy, musty, nasty **6** putrid, rancid, rotten **7** noisome, stenchy, tainted **8** mephitic, stifling, stinking **9** stenchful **10** malodorous **11** ill-smelling, suffocating

fetish 4 idol, joss **5** charm, craze, image, mania, totem **6** amulet, scarab **7** passion **8** idee fixe, talisman **9** obsession **10** golden calf, phylactery **11** magic object **12** superstition **13** preoccupation

fetter 4 bind, bond, cage, curb, yoke **5** chain, tie up **6** duress, hamper, hinder, hobble, impede, shut in, tether **7** confine, durance, manacle, pin down, shackle, tie down, trammel, truss up **8** bracelet,

encumber, handcuff, hold back, restrain **9** hindrance, restraint **13** put into bilbos **15** bind hand and foot

feud 3 row **4** fuss, spat, tiff **5** argue, brawl, clash, set-to **6** affray, bicker, breach, enmity, fracas, schism, strife **7** discord, dispute, faction, ill will, quarrel, rupture, wrangle **8** argument, bad blood, be at odds, clashing, conflict, disagree, squabble, vendetta **9** animosity, bickering, hostility **10** falling out **11** altercation, controversy **12** disagreement, hard feelings

Feud, The
  author: **12** Thomas Berger

feudal lord
  Japanese: **6** daimyo

Feuerbach, Anselm
  born: **6** Speyer **7** Germany
  artwork: **9** Iphigenia **15** Judgment of Paris, Plato's Symposium **18** The Fall of the Titans

fever 4 fire, heat **5** ardor, craze, flush, furor **6** desire, frenzy, warmth **7** ferment, illness, pyrexia **8** delirium, sickness **9** agitation **10** enthusiasm, excitement **11** temperature **12** restlessness

feverish 3 hot **5** fiery **6** ardent, red-hot **7** burning, excited, fanatic, febrile, fervent, fevered, flushed, parched, pyretic, zealous **8** frenzied, inflamed, restless **9** impatient, overeager, wrought-up **10** high-strung, passionate **11** impassioned

few 4 rare, some, thin **5** scant **6** meager, paltry, scanty, scarce, skimpy, sparse, unique **7** handful, limited, not many, several, unusual **8** exiguous, piddling, sporadic, uncommon **9** hardly any **10** infrequent, occasional **11** scarcely any, small number **13** infinitesimal, insignificant **14** inconsiderable

Fezziwig
  character in: **15** A Christmas Carol
  author: **7** Dickens

fiance, fiancee 6 future **7** engaged, pledge **8** intended, promised **9** affianced, betrothed, bride-to-be, groom-to-be **10** bride-elect, groom-elect

fiasco 4 bomb, flop **5** botch **6** fizzle **7** debacle, washout **8** disaster **10** nonsuccess

fiat 3 act, law **4** rule **5** edict, order, ukase **6** decree, dictum,

---

Festival of
  Adonis: 6 Adonia
  Apollo: 5 Delia **8** Didymaea **9** Delphinia **12** Daphnephoria
  Athena: 6 Lenaea **8** Diipolia **9** Pyanepsia **11** Oschophoria
  Attica: 13 Rural Dionysia **14** Lesser Dionysia
  Bacchus: 11 Bacchanalia
  Boeotians: 7 Daedala **13** Little Doedala
  Demeter: 5 Haloa
  Dionysus: 5 Haloa **8** Dionysia
  flowers: 11 Anthesteria
  Greeks: 6 Heraea **9** Pyanepsia **11** Scirophoria, Skirophoria **13** Thesmorphoria
  Persephone: 5 Haloa
  Roman: 8 Floralia, Matralia **9** Lemuralia, Liberalia **10** Larentalia, Lupercalia, Matronalia, Parentalia, Saturnalia
  spring: 11 Anthesteria
  wine: 11 Anthesteria
  Zeus: 6 Diasia **8** Didymaea

ruling 7 command, mandate 11 commandment

fiat lux 15 let there be light

fib 3 lie 5 hedge 7 fiction, untruth 8 white lie 9 half-truth, invention 10 equivocate 11 fabrication, harmless lie, prevaricate 13 falsification, prevarication, tell a white lie 15 stretch the truth 17 misrepresentation

fiber 4 hemp, jute, silk 5 fibre, linen, nylon, rayon, shred, sinew, sisal 6 cotton, dacron, manila, nature, strand, thread 7 quality, texture 8 filament 9 character, polyester, structure

fibrolite
   source: 5 Burma, Mogok

fibula
   bone of: 8 lower leg

fickle 5 giddy 6 fitful 7 erratic, flighty 8 shifting, unstable, unsteady, variable, volatile, wavering 9 frivolous, mercurial, spasmodic, whimsical 10 capricious, changeable, inconstant, irresolute, unreliable 11 fluctuating, light-headed, vacillating 12 inconsistent 13 feather-headed, unpredictable, untrustworthy 14 feather-brained

fiction 3 fib, lie 4 play, tale, yarn 5 fable, novel 7 fantasy, forgery, novella, romance, whopper 8 tall tale 9 falsehood, invention, narrative 10 concoction, short novel, short story 11 fabrication, imagination, made-up story 12 storytelling 13 prevarication 16 cock-and-bull story

fictional 6 made-up 8 invented, literary, mythical 9 storybook 10 fictitious 11 theoretical 12 hypothetical

fictitious 4 fake, sham 5 bogus, false, phony 6 forged, made-up, unreal, untrue 7 assumed, feigned 8 fanciful, invented, mythical, spurious 9 imaginary, legendary, simulated, trumped-up, unfounded 10 apocryphal, artificial, fabricated, fraudulent, not genuine 11 counterfeit 14 supposititious

fiddle 3 bow, saw, toy 4 fool 5 cheat, dally, fraud 6 dawdle, monkey, potter, putter, tamper, trifle, violin 7 falsify, finagle, fritter, swindle 9 deception 10 fool around, mess around 12 monkey around

Fidei Defensor 18 Defender of the Faith
   title of: 17 English sovereigns

Fidelio
   opera by: 9 Beethoven
   character: 5 Rocco 7 Leonora (Fidelio), Pizarro 8 Fernando 9 Florestan

fidelity 5 honor 6 fealty 7 honesty, loyalty, probity 8 accuracy, devotion 9 adherence, closeness, constancy, exactness, good faith, integrity, precision, sincerity 10 allegiance, exactitude 11 earnestness, reliability, staunchness 12 faithfulness, truthfulness 14 correspondency 15 trueheartedness, trustworthiness

Fides
   origin: 5 Roman
   personifies: 9 good faith

fidget 4 fret, fuss, jerk, stew, toss 5 chafe, worry 6 jiggle, squirm, twitch, wiggle, writhe 7 twiddle, wriggle

fidgety 5 antsy, fussy, jerky, jumpy 6 uneasy 7 jittery, nervous, restive, squirmy, twitchy, unquiet 8 restless 9 impatient, irritable, tremulous 12 apprehensive

fief 4 land 6 domain, estate 9 territory

field 3 lea 4 area, grab, lawn, line, mead, turf, yard 5 arena, catch, court, front, glove, green, heath, lists, orbit, range, reach, realm, scope, sward, sweep 6 circle, common, course, domain, extent, meadow, pick up, region, sphere 7 acreage, calling, diamond, expanse, pasture, run down, stretch 8 clearing, province, retrieve, spectrum 9 bailiwick, grassland, territory 10 department, occupation, profession 12 battleground

Field, Sally
   born: 10 Pasadena CA
   roles: 5 Sybil 6 Gidget 8 Norma Rae (Oscar) 9 Punchline, Surrender 12 The Flying Nun 14 Murphy's Romance 15 Absence of Malice 16 Places in the Heart (Oscar) 18 Smokey and the Bandit

Fielding, Cecil
   character in: 15 A Passage to India
   author: 7 Forster

Fielding, Henry
   author of: 6 Amelia 7 Shamela 8 Tom Jones, Tom Thumb 12 Jonathan Wild 13 Joseph Andrews

Field of Blood 8 Aceldama

Fields, W C
   real name: 23 William Claude Dukenfield
   born: 14 Philadelphia PA
   roles: 5 Poppy 8 Micawber 11 The Bank Dick 16 David Copperfield 17 My Little Chickadee 27 Never Give a Sucker an Even Break

Fields of Mourning
   location: 10 underworld
   inhabited by: 14 shades of lovers
      lovers who died by:
      7 suicide

Fields of Visions, The
   author: 12 Wright Morris

fiend 5 beast, brute, demon, devil, Satan 6 dybbuk 7 incubus, monster, villain 8 succubus 9 barbarian, hellhound, scoundrel 10 evil spirit 12 wicked person 14 devil incarnate 16 prince of darkness

fiendish 4 evil, foul 5 cruel 6 wicked 7 demonic, heinous, impious, satanic, vicious 8 barbaric, demoniac, devilish 9 monstrous, nefarious 10 demoniacal, diabolical, villainous

fierce 4 fell, wild 5 cruel, feral, fiery 6 brutal, fervid, raging, savage, strong 7 enraged, extreme, fearful, fervent, furious, intense, leonine, untamed, violent 8 horrible, menacing, powerful, ravening, ravenous, terrible, tigerish, uncurbed, vehement 9 barbarous, bellicose, ferocious, impetuous, merciless, truculent, unbridled, voracious 10 immoderate, inordinate, passionate 11 threatening 12 bloodthirsty, overpowering, overwhelming, unrestrained
   French: 8 farouche

fierceness 4 zeal 7 passion 8 ferocity, wildness 9 pugnacity, vehemence 10 savageness

fiery 5 afire, angry, irate 6 ablaze, alight, ardent, fervid, fierce, red-hot, torrid 7 blazing, burning, febrile, fervent, fevered, flaming, glaring, glowing, peppery, pyretic, violent, zealous 8 choleric, feverish, flashing, headlong, inflamed, spirited, vehement, wrathful 9 excitable, hotheaded, impetuous, impulsive, irascible, irritable 10 full of fire, high-strung, mettlesome, passionate, sweltering 11 hot-tempered, impassioned, precipitate 12 enthusiastic

fiesta 4 fete, gala 5 feast, party 6 picnic 7 funfair 8 carnival, feast day, festival, jamboree 9 saint's day 10 block

fig 348

party, observance, street fair
11 celebration **13** commemoration **15** festive
occasion

fig 5 Ficus
varieties: 3 keg, sea **4** bush,
cape, Java, Zulu **5** cedar,
clown, Congo, rusty **6** common, Devil's, exotic, golden,
Indian, Kaffir, Mysore, sacred **7** Barbary, cluster, oakleaf, spotted, weeping
8 climbing, creeping, Dracaena, mulberry, sycamore
9 Hottentot, mistletoe, strangler **10** East Indian, fiddleleaf, glossy-leaf, little-leaf,
Moreton Bay, Philippine
11 Port Jackson **16** West Indian laurel

Figaro
character in: 18 The Barber
of Seville **19** The Marriage
of Figaro
author: 12 Beaumarchais

fight 3 box, row, war **4** bout,
duel, feud, fray, grit, spar,
spat, tiff, tilt, wage **5** argue,
brawl, brush, clash, event,
joust, match, melee, pluck,
round, scrap, set-to **6** battle,
bicker, combat, engage, fracas,
mettle, oppose, resist, spirit,
strife, tussle **7** carry on, conduct, contend, contest, discord,
dispute, go to war, quarrel, repulse, scuffle, tourney, wage
war, wrangle **8** confront, dogfight, gameness, skirmish,
squabble, struggle **9** bickering,
encounter, pugnacity, scrimmage, toughness, wrangling
10 contention, difference, dissension, prizefight, strive with,
tournament **11** altercation,
armed action, battle royal, bellicosity, clash of arms, controversy **12** belligerency, do
battle with, rise up in arms,
struggle with **13** armed conflict, combativeness, confrontation, exchange blows, pitched
battle

fight back 7 counter, get even,
hit back, pay back **9** retaliate
10 strike back
13 counterattack

fighter 5 boxer **7** soldier, sparrer, warrior **8** pugilist, scrapper **9** combatant **10** militarist
11 belligerent

fighting 3 war **4** fray **5** brawl,
melee **6** action, battle, bicker,
combat, rumpus, tumult, tussle **7** contest, dispute, quarrel,
warfare **8** battling, brawling,
conflict, skirmish, squabble
9 bickering, disputing **10** engagement, quarreling, squabbling **11** clash of arms,
controversy, hostilities

Fighting Marine
nickname of: 10 Gene
Tunney

fighting men 4 army **6** legion,
troops **7** legions, militia **8** military, soldiers, soldiery **13** military force **15** military
machine

fighting spirit 9 animosity,
hostility, pugnacity **10** antagonism **11** bellicosity **12** belligerence **14** aggressiveness

fight shy of 5 avoid, dodge,
elude, evade, skirt **6** escape
8 sidestep

figment 5 fable, fancy, story
6 canard **7** fantasy, fiction,
product **8** creation **9** falsehood,
invention **10** concoction
11 fabrication

figuration 4 form **7** outline
9 formation, structure
12 constitution

figurative 6 florid, ironic, ornate **7** flowery **8** humorous,
symbolic **9** satirical **10** not literal **11** allegorical **12** hyperbolical, metaphorical

figure, figures 3 cut, man,
sum **4** body, cast, cost, foot,
form, mark, plan, rate, sign,
sums **5** add up, adorn, build,
count, digit, force, frame,
guess, judge, motif, price,
shape, think, total, tot up,
value, woman **6** amount, appear, assess, cipher, design,
device, emblem, factor, leader,
number, person, reckon,
schema, symbol **7** anatomy,
believe, compute, contour,
count up, diagram, drawing,
imagine, notable, numeral,
outline, pattern, presume, suppose **8** appraise, be placed,
eminence, estimate, ornament,
physique, presence **9** calculate,
character, diversify, embellish,
have a part, personage, play a
part, quotation, variegate
10 arithmetic, conjecture,
shine forth, silhouette **11** be
mentioned, be prominent
12 calculations, computations,
illustration

figurehead 4 tool **5** dummy,
front, token **6** cipher, puppet
8 ornament **9** nonentity

figure out 6 reckon **7** compute, find out, work out
8 discover **9** ascertain, calculate, determine

figure roughly 5 guess
6 reckon **8** estimate **11** approximate, make a stab at

figure up 3 add **5** add up, total, tot up **6** reckon **7** compute, count up **9** calculate

figurine 7 bibelot **8** ornament
9 statuette

Fiji *see box*

filament 4 hair, line, wire **5** fiber, fibre **6** cilium, ribbon,
strand, string, thread

filbert 7 Corylus
varieties: 3 red **4** cork,
Momi, plum **5** azure, China,
giant, Greek, joint, Nikko,
noble, white **6** alpine, balsam, Fraser, Korean, needle,
Scotch, silver, summer
7 cascade, Douglas, lowland,
Spanish **8** Algerian, Japanese, Sakhalin, Southern
9 Himalayan, Shasta Red
10 dwarf Nikko, Santa Lucia **11** bristle-cone **13** Pacific
silver **14** Southern
balsam

filch 3 cop, rob **4** copy, crib,
hook, lift **5** boost, heist, steal,
swipe **6** pilfer, pirate **7** purloin **8** arrogate **10** plagiarize
11 appropriate,
expropriate

file 3 row **4** data, line, list,
rank, tier **5** apply, chain, index, put in, queue, store

6 drawer, folder, record, stacks, string **7** catalog, dossier, put away, records, request **8** archives, classify, petition **9** catalogue, chronicle
type: 4 mill, nail, rasp, wood **5** round **9** half-round **13** three-cornered

filial 7 dutiful, sonlike **10** daughterly, respectful

fill 3 act **4** cram, glut, lade, load, meet, pack, puff, sate **5** crowd, gorge, lay by, lay in, serve, stock, store **6** answer, assign, blow up, charge, dilate, do duty, expand, infuse, make up, occupy, outfit, supply, take up **7** distend, execute, furnish, inflate, pervade, preside, provide, satiate, satisfy, suffuse, surfeit **8** carry out, function, permeate, saturate **9** discharge, provision, replenish **10** full amount, impregnate, overspread

filled in 7 stood in **9** completed, **11** substituted

filled out 6 marked **7** matured **9** completed

fillet 4 band **5** slice, strip **6** ribbon **7** bandeau, circlet

fillip 3 tap **4** flip, snap, toss **5** flick, tonic **6** buffet **8** stimulus

Fillmore, Millard *see box*

fill with air 5 bloat **6** billow, blow up, expand **7** balloon, distend, inflate, puff out **8** swell out

fill with dread 5 alarm, panic **6** dismay **7** perturb, terrify, unnerve **8** disquiet, frighten

fill with gloom 6 darken, sadden **8** dispirit

fill with wonder 3 awe **5** amaze **7** astound **8** astonish **9** fascinate

film, films 4 coat, haze, mist, skin, veil **5** cloud, flick, movie, sheet, shoot **6** cinema, flicks, movies, screen **7** coating **8** membrane

filmy 3 dim **4** fine, hazy, thin **5** gauzy, misty, sheer, wispy **8** cobwebby, finespun, gossamer **10** diaphanous

fils 3 son

filter 4 leak, ooze, seep **5** drain, exude, sieve **6** effuse, purify, refine, screen, strain **7** clarify, cleanse, dribble, trickle, well out **8** filtrate, strainer

filth 3 mud **4** dirt, dung, mire, muck, slop, smut **5** feces, offal, slime, slush, trash **6** ma-

nure, ordure, refuse, sewage, sludge **7** carrion, excreta, garbage, squalor **8** impurity, lewdness, ribaldry, vileness **9** excrement, grossness, indecency, nastiness, obscenity, pollution **10** corruption, defilement, immorality, indelicacy, putridness **11** pornography, squalidness **13** contamination **14** suggestiveness

filthy 4 foul, vile **5** black, dirty, grimy, gross, messy, nasty **6** grubby, impure, odious, soiled **7** defiled, dirtied, obscene, smirchy, squalid, unclean **8** befouled, slovenly, unwashed **9** repulsive **10** besmirched, disgusting **12** contaminated

finagle 3 con, gyp **4** plot, rook **5** cheat, mulct, trick **6** chisel, fleece, scheme, wangle **7** defraud, swindle **8** engineer, intrigue, maneuver

final 4 last, rear **6** ending, latest **7** closing, extreme **8** complete, decisive, finished, hindmost, rearmost, terminal, thorough, ultimate **10** concluding, conclusive, definitive, exhaustive, hindermost **11** irrevocable, terminating **12** unappealable, unchangeable **13** determinative
French: 7 dernier

finale 3 end **5** close, finis **6** finish, windup **7** curtain **8** epilogue, last part, swan song **10** conclusion **11** culmination, termination

final limit
Latin: 14 terminus ad quem

finally 6 lastly **10** eventually, inexorably, ultimately **11** inescapably **12** conclusively, definitively, in conclusion **16** incontrovertibly
French: 5 enfin
Latin: 10 ad extremum

Fillmore, Millard
presidential rank: 10 thirteenth
party: 4 Whig
state represented: 2 NY
defeated: 5 no one
succeeded upon death of: **6** Taylor
vice president: 4 none
cabinet:
State: **7** (Daniel) Webster, (Edward) Everett
Treasury: **6** (Thomas) Corwin
War: **6** (Charles Magill) Conrad
Attorney General: **10** (John Jordan) Crittenden
Navy: **6** (William Alexander) Graham **7** (John Pendleton) Kennedy
Postmaster General: **4** (Nathan Kelsey) Hall **7** (Samuel Dickinson) Hubbard
Interior: **6** (Alexander Hugh Holmes) Stuart
born: 7 Locke NY
died/buried: 9 Buffalo NY
education:
college: **4** none
studied: **3** law
religion: 9 Unitarian
interests: 5 civic
first chancellor of University of: **7** Buffalo
founder: **22** Buffalo General Hospital **24** Buffalo Historical Society
author: 21 Millard Fillmore Papers
political career: 13 state assembly, Vice President **24** US House of Representatives
civilian career: 6 lawyer (New York Supreme Court) **7** teacher **10** wool carder **12** cloth dresser
notable events of lifetime/term: 25 Compromise of Eighteen-Fifty
act: **13** Fugitive Slave
father: 9 Nathaniel
mother: 6 Phoebe (Millard)
siblings: 5 Cyrus, Julia **11** Phoebe Maria **12** Almon Hopkins, Calvin Turner **13** Charles DeWitt **14** Darius Ingraham, Olive Armstrong
wife: 7 Abigail (Powers) **8** Caroline (Carmichael McIntosh)
children: 11 Mary Abigail **13** Millard Powers

final section 4 coda **5** rider **6** ending **7** last act **8** addendum, epilogue **9** afterword **10** conclusion

final settlement 8 solution **11** disposition

finance 6 pay for **7** banking **8** accounts **9** economics **10** underwrite

financial backer 5 angel **6** patron **7** sponsor **9** supporter **10** benefactor

financial support 7 backing, subsidy **10** assistance **12** contribution

financier 5 angel **6** backer, banker, broker **7** rich man **10** capitalist **11** millionaire, underwriter

Financier, The
  author: 15 Theodore Dreiser
  character: 12 Aileen Butler, Edward Butler **15** Henry Cowperwood **16** Frank A Cowperwood **23** Lillian Semple Cowperwood

Finch, Peter
  real name: 15 Peter Ingle-Finch
  born: 6 London **7** England
  roles: 7 Network (Oscar) **11** Lost Horizon **12** The Nun's Story **15** The Pumpkin Eater **18** Sunday Bloody Sunday

Finchley, Sondra
  character in: 17 An American Tragedy
  author: 7 Dreiser

find 3 get, see, win **4** earn, espy, gain, meet, rule, spot **5** award, catch, dig up, judge, learn **6** attain, come by, decide, decree, detect, expose, locate, regain **7** achieve, acquire, adjudge, bargain, bonanza, discern, get back, godsend, good buy, hit upon, procure, recover, uncover, unearth **8** bump into, come upon, discover, disinter, lucky hit, meet with, retrieve, windfall **9** ascertain, determine, discovery, encounter, pronounce, repossess **10** adjudicate **11** acquisition

fin de siecle 8 decadent **15** end of the century

find fault 3 nag **4** beef, carp **5** blame, cavil, gribe **6** grouse, squawk **7** nitpick **8** complain **9** bellyache, criticize, disparage **10** disapprove

find guilty 5 blame **6** indict **7** condemn, convict **8** sentence **9** implicate

finding 6 decree, ruling **7** verdict **8** decision

find innocent 5 clear **6** acquit **9** exonerate

find out 5 learn **6** detect, locate **7** uncover, unearth **8** discover **9** ascertain, determine, establish

find repulsive 4 hate **5** abhor **6** detest, loathe **7** despise **8** execrate, recoil at **9** abominate

fine 4 airy, chic, fair, keen, neat, nice, rare, thin **5** bonny, clear, dandy, gauzy, mulct, nifty, sharp, sheer, silky, small, smart, sunny, swell **6** assess, bonnie, bright, charge, choice, comely, dainty, flimsy, ground, lovely, minute, modish, pretty, silken, slight, spiffy, subtle, superb **7** damages, elegant, forfeit, fragile, penalty, perfect, powdery, precise, refined, slender, stylish, tenuous **8** cobwebby, delicate, ethereal, flawless, gossamer, handsome, penalize, pleasant, polished, powdered, rainless, skillful, splendid, superior, tasteful **9** admirable, beautiful, brilliant, cloudless, excellent, exquisite **10** assessment, attractive, consummate, diaphanous, fastidious, pulverized, swimmingly **11** excellently, exceptional, lightweight, magnificent, transparent, well-favored **12** accomplished **13** hairsplitting, unsubstantial
    music: 3 end

fine clothes 8 glad rags **10** Sunday best **16** best bib and tucker

fine-looking 4 fair **5** bonny **6** bonnie, comely, lovely, pretty, seemly **8** gorgeous, handsome **9** beauteous, beautiful, exquisite, ravishing **10** attractive **11** resplendent **15** pulchritudinous

fineness 6 beauty **8** delicacy, elegance, thinness **10** perfection, smoothness **12** flawlessness **13** exquisiteness

fine points 3 art **7** finesse, nuances **8** niceties **10** subtleties **11** refinements **12** distinctions

finer 6 better **8** superior

finery 6 frills, tinsel **7** baubles, gaudery, gewgaws **8** frippery, spangles, trinkets **9** trappings, trimmings **13** paraphernalia

finesse 4 ruse, tact, wile **5** craft, dodge, guile, savvy **7** cunning **8** artifice, delicacy, intrigue, trickery **9** deception, stratagem **10** artfulness, discretion, subterfuge
  French: 11 savoir-faire

fine workmanship 8 delicacy **9** precision **13** craftsmanship

finger 3 paw **4** feel, poke **5** digit, punch, thumb, touch **6** caress, feeler, handle **7** pointer, squeeze, toy with, twiddle **8** play with **10** manipulate

finicky 5 fussy, picky **6** choosy **8** niggling **10** fastidious, meticulous, nitpicking, overprecise, particular, pernickety **11** persnickety **14** discriminating, overparticular

finish 3 end **4** coat, face, gild, goal, kill, last, seal, stop **5** cease, close, glaze, use up **6** clinch, defeat, devour, ending, finale, settle, veneer, wind up **7** achieve, coating, consume, curtain, destroy, fulfill, get done, lacquer, realize, surface, varnish **8** carry out, complete, conclude, dispatch, epilogue, exterior, get rid of, knock off, make good **9** discharge, eradicate, objective, polishing, terminate **10** accomplish, completion, conclusion, consummate, denouement **11** discontinue, exterminate, termination

finished 4 full **5** ended, final, ideal, whole **6** entire, urbane **7** classic, elegant, perfect, refined, shapely, skilled, trained, well-set **8** complete, flawless, polished, well-bred **9** beautiful, completed, concluded, exquisite, faultless **10** consummate, cultivated, impeccable **11** consummated **12** accomplished

finishing stroke 9 death blow
  French: 11 coup de grace

finish off 4 kill, slay **7** destroy, execute, wipe out **8** complete, dispatch **9** eradicate, polish off **10** annihilate **11** exterminate

finite **7** bounded, limited **8** confined, temporal **9** countable **10** measurable, restricted, short-lived, terminable **13** circumscribed

Finland *see box*

Finn
also: **5** Fionn **13** Fionn MacCumal
origin: **5** Irish
king of: **4** gods **14** Tuatha De Danann
son: **6** Ossian
father: **5** Cumal **6** Comhal

Finnegan's Wake
author: **10** James Joyce
family: **9** Earwicker

Finney, Albert
wife: **10** Anouk Aimee
born: **7** England, Salford
roles: **5** Annie **7** Scrooge **8** Tom Jones **10** The Dresser **12** Shoot the Moon **13** Two for the Road **17** Under the Volcano **29** Saturday Night and Sunday Morning

Finnish Mythology *see* **21** Scandinavian Mythology

Finno-Ugric
language family: **6** Uralic
Finnic group: **4** Lapp **6** Votyak, Zyryan **7** Finnish, Mordvin, Permian **8** Estonian **9** Cheremiss
Ugric group: **5** Vogul **6** Ostyak **7** Ob-Ugric **9** Hungarian

Fionn, Fionn MacCumal *see* **4** Finn

fiord, fjord **5** firth, inlet **7** estuary

fir **4** pine **5** cedar, larch **6** alpine, balsam, linden, spruce **7** conifer, cypress, douglas **9** evergreen

Firbolg
origin: **5** Greek, Irish
defeated by: **9** Fomorians
ousted by: **4** gods **14** Tuatha De Danann

fire *see box*

Fire and Ice
author: **11** Robert Frost

firearm **3** gun, rod **5** piece, rifle **6** pistol **7** shotgun **8** revolver **10** machine gun **12** shooting iron **13** submachine gun **20** Saturday-night special

---

Finland
other name: **5** Suomi **15** Suomen Tasavalta
capital/largest city: **8** Helsinki **11** Helsingfors
others: **3** Aba, Abo, Kem **4** Kemi, Ouli, Oulu, Ouou, Pori, Vasa **5** Enare, Espoo, Kotka, Lahti, Rauma, Turku, Vaasa **6** Imatra, Kuopio **7** Joensuu, Kajaani, Kokkola, Mikkeli, Tampere, Tapiola **9** Jyvaskyla, Mariehamn, Rovaniemi **12** Lappeenranta
measure: **5** kannu, verst **6** fathom, kannor **8** otlinger, skalpund, tunnland
monetary unit: **4** mark **5** penni **6** markka
island: **5** Aland, Karlo **6** Aaland **7** Hailuto **9** Vallgrund **10** Ahvenanmaa
lake: **3** Juo, Muo **4** Kemi, Kiui, Nasi, Oulu, Puru, Pyha, Simo **5** Enara, Enare, Hauki, Inari, Kalla, Lappa, Lesti, Puula, Saima **6** Ladoya, Lentua, Saimaa, Sounne, Syvari **7** Koitere, Nilakka, Pielien **9** Kallavesi, Pielavesi
mountain: **7** Laltiva **10** Saari Selka
highest point: **6** Haltia **11** Haldetsokka
river: **4** Kala, Kemi, Kymi, Oulu, Pats, Simo, Teno **5** Ivalo, Lotta, Ounas, Siika, Torne **6** Iijoki, Lapuan, Muonio, Pasvik, Tornoi, Vuoski **7** Kitinen **8** Kokemaki
sea: **6** Baltic **8** Atlantic
physical feature:
  gulf: **7** Bothnia, Finland
  isthmus: **7** Karelia
  peninsula: **13** Fennoscandian
people: **3** Jew, Vod, Vot, Yak **4** Avar, Finn, Hame, Lapp, Turk, Veps **5** Fioun, Gypsy, Ijore, Inger, Suomi, Vepse **6** Magyar, Ostiak, Ostyak, Tarast, Tavast, Ugrian, Zyrian **7** Lappish, Mordvin, Permiak, Samoyed, Uralian **8** Cheremis, Estonian, Karelian, Livonian, Swekoman **9** Tavastian **11** Karjalaiset, Suomalaiset
  athlete: **10** Paavo Nurmi
  composer: **8** Sibelius
  designer: **9** Marimekko
language: **4** Avar, Lapp **5** Karel, Ugric, Vogul **6** Magyar, Ostyak, Tarast **7** Finnish, Olonets, Samoyed, Swedish **8** Estonian **10** Olonetsian
religion: **19** Evangelical Lutheran
place:
  canal: **6** Saimaa
  castle: **10** Saint Olaf's **11** Olavinlinna
  fortress: **8** Sveaborg **11** Suomenlinna
  memorial: **8** Sibelius
  pine ridge: **10** Punkaharju
feature:
  game: **9** pesapallo
food:
  dish: **11** Karelian pie
  fruit: **16** yellow cloudberry
  liqueur: **9** Mesimarja

---

fire **3** can, vim **4** bake, boot, burn, cook, dash, dump, elan, hurl, oust, sack, stir **5** ardor, blaze, eject, flame, flare, flash, force, gusto, let go, light, power, punch, rouse, salvo, shell, shoot, spark, verve, vigor **6** arouse, bounce, depose, excite, fervor, foment, genius, ignite, incite, kindle, luster, spirit, stir up, vivify, volley **7** animate, bombard, bonfire, cashier, dismiss, inferno, inflame, inspire, project, quicken, sniping, trigger **8** enfilade, fervency, inspirit, radiance, splendor, vivacity **9** broadside, cannonade, discharge, eagerness, fusillade, galvanize, holocaust, instigate, intensity, stimulate, vehemence **10** brilliance, effulgence, enthusiasm **11** bombardment, earnestness, inspiration **13** conflagration, sharpshooting **15** imaginativeness
god of: **4** Loki **5** Ishum **6** Vulcan **10** Hephaestus, Hephaistos
goddess of: **6** Brigit

firefight 5 clash 6 battle, combat 8 skirmish

firefly 8 glowworm, lampyrid 9 candlefly 12 lightning bug

Fire Next Time, The
author: 12 James Baldwin

fire off 5 eject, shoot 6 launch 8 detonate 9 discharge

Fireside Theatre
host: 9 Jane Wyman 11 Frank Wisbar, Gene Raymond

Firestarter
author: 11 Stephen King

fire up 4 fuel, rile 5 anger, light, rouse 6 arouse, excite, ignite, incite, kindle 7 animate, enthuse, inspire 8 activate, energize, irritate, vitalize 9 galvanize, stimulate

firm 4 bent, fast, grim, hard, taut 5 close, dense, fixed, house, rigid, rocky, solid, stiff, stony, tight, tough 6 dogged, flinty, intent, moored, rooted, secure, stable, steady, steely 7 compact, company, dead set, decided, earnest, serious, settled, staunch 8 anchored, business, constant, definite, fearless, obdurate, resolute, resolved, unshaken 9 confirmed, hardnosed, immovable, obstinate, steadfast, tenacious, unbending 10 adamantine, compressed, determined, inexorable, inflexible, invincible, persistent, unwavering, unyielding 11 corporation, established, partnership, unalterable, unfaltering, unflinching 12 conglomerate, indissoluble, organization 13 establishment

firmament 3 air, sky 5 ether, space, vault 6 canopy, welkin 7 heavens, the blue, the void 10 outer space

firmness 8 tenacity 9 obstinacy 10 resolution 11 persistence, staunchness 12 resoluteness 13 determination, inflexibility, steadfastness

first 4 head, main 5 basic, prime, start, vital 6 before, eldest, maiden, outset, primal, rather, sooner 7 highest, leading, premier, primary, ranking, supreme 8 earliest, foremost, original, primeval, superior 9 beginning, essential, inception, initially, paramount, primitive, principal 10 aboriginal, elementary, preeminent, preferably, primordial 11 fundamental, rudimentary 12 commencement, introduction, introductory

first among equals
Latin: 16 primus inter pares

first appearance 4 dawn 5 debut 9 beginning 12 introduction

firstborn 5 elder, older 6 eldest, oldest

Firstborn, The
author: 14 Christopher Fry

First Circle
author: 23 Aleksandr Solzhenitsyn Jr

first god see 8 god, first

firsthand 6 direct 8 personal 9 empirical 10 unmediated 12 experimental

First Lady of the Theater
nickname of: 10 Helen Hayes 16 Katharine Cornell

first-line 4 main 5 chief 7 primary 8 foremost

first moving thing
Latin: 12 primum mobile

first-rate 3 ace 4 A-one, best, fine, tops 5 crack, elite, great, prime 6 choice, finest, select 7 top-hole 8 splendid, superior, top-notch, very good 9 admirable, estimable, excellent, exclusive, nonpareil, top drawer, topflight, wonderful 10 noteworthy, stupendous 11 commendable, outstanding 12 above-average, incomparable 13 distinguished

First State
nickname of: 8 Delaware

first step 5 start 9 beginning 12 commencement

firth 5 fjord, inlet 7 estuary

fiscal 8 economic, monetary 9 budgetary, financial, pecuniary

fish 3 net 4 cast, hook, hunt 5 angle, grope, seine, trawl, troll 6 ferret, search 7 rummage

fish see box

Fisher, Bud
creator/artist of: 11 Mutt and Jeff

Fisher, Carrie
father: 11 Eddie Fisher
mother: 13 Debbie Reynolds
role: 12 Princess Leia
films: 7 Shampoo 8 Star Wars 12 This Is My Life 16 The Blues Brothers 17 When Harry Met Sally 18 The Return of the Jedi 19 The Empire Strikes Back, Hannah and Her Sisters
author: 20 Postcards from the Edge

Fisher, Ham
creator/artist of: 10 Joe Palooka

fish
class: 7 Agnatha 12 Osteichthyes 14 Chondrichthyes
fin: 4 anal, tail 6 caudal, dorsal, median, paired, pelvic 7 adipose, ventral 8 pectoral
kind: 3 cod, eel, gar, ray 4 bass, carp, hake, opah, pike, tuna 5 brill, perch, shark, skate, sword, trout 6 bichir, blenny, marlin, minnow, mullet, salmon, tarpon 7 anchovy, catfish, dogfish, dolphin, hagfish, herring, lamprey, piranha, sunfish 8 bluefish, cavefish, crayfish, flounder, goldfish, lungfish, mackerel, menhaden, moray eel, pilchard, sea horse, squirrel, sturgeon 9 killifish, pygmy goby, swordfish 10 coelacanth, flying fish, paddlefish, rabbit fish, rocksucker, whale shark 11 anemonefish, electric eel, electric ray, lanternfish, long-nose gar 13 butterflyfish 14 largemouth bass
part: 3 fin 4 gill 5 scale 6 cirrhi 10 gas bladder 11 swim bladder 12 rete mirabile
shellfish:
  crustacean: 4 crab 6 shrimp 7 lobster 8 blue crab, king crab, snow crab 9 langouste 11 langoustine 13 Dungeness crab, horseshoe crab
  mollusk: 4 clam 6 mussel, oyster, quahog 8 surf clam 9 horse clam, razor clam 11 geoduck clam
young: 3 fry 10 fingerling

Fisher, Vardis
author of: **10** The Mothers **13** Children of God **17** The Testament of Man

fisherman 5 eeler **6** angler, caster, jacker, netter, seiner **7** trawler, troller **8** piscator **9** flycaster, Waltonian **17** the compleat angler

Fishermen
goddess of: **11** Britomartis

Fishes
constellation of: **6** Pisces

fish story 3 fib, lie **7** fiction, whopper **9** falsehood, tall story **16** cock-and-bull story

fishy 3 odd **4** dull **5** blank, queer, shady, weird **6** vacant **7** dubious, strange, suspect **8** doubtful, peculiar, slippery **9** dishonest **10** farfetched, glassy-eyed, improbable, suspicious, unreliable **11** exaggerated, extravagant **12** questionable, unscrupulous **14** expressionless

fission 7 atomize **8** breaking, cleavage, scission **9** severance, splitting **10** breaking up, sunderance **12** disseverance, reproduction

fissure 3 gap **4** rift, slit **5** chink, cleft, crack, gully, split **6** breach, cranny, groove, hiatus **8** aperture, cleavage

fit *see* **box**

fitful 4 weak **6** broken, random, uneven **7** erratic **8** listless, off-and-on, periodic, sporadic, unsteady, variable **9** irregular, spasmodic **10** capricious, changeable, convulsive **11** fluctuating **12** disconnected, intermittent

fitness
Hebrew: **7** kashrut **8** kashruth

fit out 4 robe **5** array, dress, equip **6** attire, clothe, supply **7** appoint, prepare

fitting 3 apt **4** meet **6** proper, seemly **8** decorous, suitable **9** congruous **11** appropriate
French: **11** comme il faut

fit to be eaten 6 edible **9** palatable **10** comestible, consumable, digestible

fit together 4 join **5** hinge, unite **6** hook up **7** connect **8** dovetail **9** interlock **10** articulate

Fitzgerald, Barry
real name: **20** William Joseph Shields
born: **6** Dublin **7** Ireland
roles: **10** Going My Way

11 The Quiet Man **19** How Green Was My Valley

FitzGerald, Edward
author of: **24** The Rubaiyat of Omar Khayyam (translation)

Fitzgerald, F Scott
wife: **10** Zelda Sayre
author of: **10** The Crack-Up **13** The Last Tycoon **14** The Great Gatsby **16** Tender Is the Night **18** This Side of Paradise **24** The Beautiful and the Damned

Fitzgerald, George Francis
field: **7** physics
nationality: **5** Irish
theory of: **24** electromagnetic radiation

Fitzgerald, Geraldine
born: **6** Dublin **7** Ireland
roles: **11** Dark Victory **12** Ah Wilderness, Rachel Rachel **15** Watch on the Rhine **16** Wuthering Heights **24** Long Day's Journey into Night

Fitzsimmons, Bob (Robert Prometheus)
sport: **6** boxing

FitzSimons, Maureen
real name of: **12** Maureen O'Hara

fit 4 able, good, hale, meet, ripe, suit, well, whim **5** adapt, agree, alter, burst, equal, equip, hardy, match, ready, right, shape, sound, spasm, spell, train **6** access, accord, adjust, become, concur, enable, in trim, mature, primed, proper, robust, seemly, strong, timely, worthy **7** adapted, apropos, capable, caprice, conform, correct, empower, fashion, healthy, prepare, qualify, rectify, seizure, toned up, trained **8** apposite, becoming, coincide, crotchet, decorous, eligible, graduate, grand mal, outbreak, outburst, paroxysm, petit mal, prepared, relevant, suitable **9** calibrate, competent, consonant, deserving, efficient, explosion, harmonize, initiated, opportune, pertinent, qualified **10** acceptable, applicable, capacitate, convenient, convulsion, correspond, seasonable **11** appropriate, capacitated

Five, The
group of: **16** Russian composers
member: **3** Cui **7** Borodin **9** Balakirev **10** Mussorgsky **14** Rimsky-Korsakov

Five Easy Pieces
director: **11** Bob Rafelson
cast: **10** Karen Black **11** Fannie Flagg **12** Susan Anspach **13** Jack Nicholson **14** Billy Breen Bush, Sally Struthers

Five Men and Pompey
author: **19** Stephen Vincent Benet

five-o'clock shadow 5 beard **7** stubble **8** bristles, whiskers

fix 3 jam, put, set **4** bind, make, mend, mess, moor, spot **5** place, rivet **6** adjust, anchor, attach, decide, fasten, harden, impose, muddle, pickle, plight, repair, scrape, secure, settle **7** congeal, connect, correct, dilemma, impasse, implant, patch up, prepare, rebuild **8** assemble, hot water, make fast, make firm, quandary, regulate, renovate, set right, solidify **9** establish, prescribe, retaliate, stabilize **10** difficulty **11** consolidate, involvement, predicament **12** entanglement

fixation 5 quirk **6** fetish **7** complex **8** crotchet, delusion **9** monomania, obsession **13** preoccupation

fixed 3 set **4** fast, firm **5** rigid, still **6** intent, rooted, stable, steady **8** constant, fastened, resolute, unpliant **9** immovable, unbending **10** determined, inflexible, motionless, persistent, stationary, unwavering

fixed idea 4 bias **5** slant **9** obsession **13** preconception
French: **8** idee fixe

fixedness 8 firmness **9** constancy, stability **10** immobility **12** immutability **16** unchangeableness

fixed regard 7 staring **9** diligence **10** absorption, intentness **11** engrossment **13** concentration

Fixer, The
author: **14** Bernard Malamud

fixing 6 repair **7** mending, mooring, placing, putting, setting **8** deciding, imposing, righting, riveting, settling, trimming **9** adjusting, anchoring, attaching, fastening, hardening, preparing, repairing **10** adjustment, assembling, congealing, connecting, correcting, implanting, rectifying, regulating, regulation **11** determining, prescribing, solidifying, stabilizing **12** establishing **13** consolidating

fixture 6 addict **7** devotee, habitue, regular **8** equipage **9** apparatus, appendage, appliance, equipment **10** attachment **11** appointment **12** appurtenance **13** paraphernalia

fix up 4 plan **6** design, devise **7** arrange, prepare **8** renovate, schedule

fix upon 4 pick **6** choose, opt for, select **7** call out, extract, pick out

fizz 4 foam **5** froth **7** bubbles **11** carbonation **13** effervescence

fizziness 9 foaminess **10** bubbliness, frothiness **13** effervescence

fizzing 6 bubbly **7** foaming **8** bubbling **9** sparkling **12** effervescent, effervescing

fizzle 3 dog, dud **4** bomb, fail, flop, hiss, mess **5** abort, botch **6** bubble, fiasco, gurgle, muddle, turkey **7** failure, founder, misfire, sputter, washout **8** collapse, disaster, miscarry

fizzy 6 bubbly **8** bubbling **9** sparkling **12** effervescent

flabbergast 4 stun **5** amaze, shock **6** puzzle **7** astound, stagger, stupefy **8** astonish, bewilder, bowl over, confound, overcome **9** dumbfound

flabbergasted 5 agape **6** amazed, gaping **9** awestruck, stupefied **10** astonished, dumbstruck, spellbound **11** dumbfounded **12** hornswoggled **13** thunderstruck

flabby 4 lame, limp, soft, weak **5** baggy, slack **6** doughy, effete, feeble, flimsy, floppy, spongy **7** flaccid **8** impotent, listless, yielding **9** enervated, inelastic **10** spiritless **11** adulterated, emasculated

flag 3 ebb, sag **4** fade, fail, pall, sink, tire, wane, warn, wave, wilt **5** abate, faint, slump **6** banner, colors, dodder, emblem, ensign, signal, totter **7** decline, give way, pennant, subside, succumb **8** grow weak, languish, Old Glory, standard, streamer **9** grow weary, Union Jack **12** Stars and Bars **15** Stars and Stripes

flagellant 7 ascetic **8** penitent **13** self-mortifier

flagon 3 gun, jug, mug **4** ewer **5** flask, stein **6** bottle, carafe, vessel **7** canteen **8** schooner

flagrant 5 gross, sheer **6** arrant, brazen, crying **7** blatant, glaring, heinous, obvious **8** immodest **9** audacious, barefaced, flaunting, monstrous, notorious, shameless **10** outrageous, scandalous **11** conspicuous

Flaherty, Margaret (Pegeen)
character in: 24 Playboy of the Western World
author: 5 Synge

flail 4 beat, lash, whip **5** swing **6** thresh **7** scourge

flair 4 bent, dash, feel, gift **5** knack, style, taste, touch, verve **6** genius, talent **7** faculty, feeling, panache **8** aptitude, capacity **9** ingenuity **11** discernment

flake 3 bit **4** chip, peel **5** fleck, layer, patch, scale, sheet, strip **7** chip off, crumble, peel off, shaving **8** scale off

flaky 4 bats, gaga, nuts **5** balmy, batty, crisp, daffy, dotty, goofy, loony, nutty, scaly, short, wacky **6** scabby, screwy, scurfy **8** scabious, squamous **9** eccentric **10** flocculent

flamboyant 4 wild **5** gaudy, jazzy, showy **6** flashy, florid, garish, ornate, rococo **7** baroque, dashing **8** colorful, exciting **10** theatrical **11** sensational **12** ostentatious

flame 4 beau, fire, glow **5** ardor, blaze, blush, flare, flash, flush, glare, gleam, light, lover, spark, swain **6** fervor, ignite, kindle, redden, warmth **7** passion **8** fervency **9** affection, boyfriend, intensity **10** enthusiasm, excitement, girlfriend, sweetheart **13** conflagration

flaming 5 afire, fiery **6** ablaze, alight, ardent, bright, fervid, stormy **7** blazing, burning, fervent, glaring, glowing, igneous, intense, shining, violent **8** flagrant, vehement **9** brilliant, egregious **10** passionate, smoldering **11** conspicuous, inflammable

flammable 7 igneous **10** combustive, incendiary **11** combustible, inflammable

flan 3 pie **4** gust, puff, tart

6 expand, pastry **7** custard, dessert **12** creme caramel

flanerie 8 dawdling, idleness

flaneur 5 idler **6** loafer **7** dawdler

flank 3 hip **4** edge, line, loin, side, wing **5** cover, skirt **6** border, fringe, haunch, screen, shield

Flannagan, John Bernard
born: 7 Fargo ND
artwork: 6 New One, Not Yet **9** Beginning **11** Dragon Motif **15** Triumph of the Egg **16** Jonah and the Whale

flap 3 bat, fly, tab **4** bang, beat, flop **5** apron, shake, skirt **6** lappet **7** agitate, banging, flutter, vibrate **9** oscillate

flare 4 burn, glow **5** blaze, erupt, flame, flash, glare, gleam, taper, torch, widen **6** blow up, dilate, expand, ignite, signal, spread **7** bell out, broaden, distend, explode, stretch **8** boil over, break out **9** coruscate **10** incandesce

flash 4 glow, wink **5** blaze, blink, burst, flame, flare, glare, gleam, jiffy, shake, shine, spark, touch, trice **6** minute, moment, second, streak **7** flicker, glimmer, glisten, glitter, instant, sparkle **8** instance, outburst, radiance **9** coruscate **10** occurrence **11** coruscation, fulmination, scintillate **13** incandescence

Flash Gordon
creator: 8 Dan Berry **11** Alex Raymond **12** Austin Briggs
character:
companion: 4 Dale

flashy 4 loud **5** gaudy, jazzy, showy, smart **6** garish, sporty, tawdry, tinsel, vulgar **7** raffish **8** dazzling **9** bedizened **10** flamboyant, tricked out **11** pretentious **12** ostentatious

flask 6 bottle **7** canteen **9** container

flat, flats 3 low **4** dead, dull **5** clear, equal, flush, level, marsh, plain, plane, prone, shoal, shoes, stale, total, vapid **6** direct, planar, smooth, supine **7** blowout, exactly, insipid, laid low, leveled, levelly, loafers, prairie, regular, shallow **8** absolute, complete, definite, lowlands, positive, puncture, thorough, unbroken **9** apartment, downright, precisely, prostrate, reclining, recumbent, tasteless **10** flavorless, horizontal, peremptory

11 unequivocal, unpalatable, unqualified 12 deflated tire, horizontally, unmistakable

flatfish 3 ray 4 sole 5 brill, fluke 6 turbot 7 halibut, sand dab, sunfish, teleost 8 flounder

Flathead see 5 Salis 7 Chinook

flatness 8 dullness 9 levelness, staleness 10 insipidity 13 tastelessness 14 flavorlessness

flatten 4 deck, even, fell 5 crush, floor, level, plane 6 defeat, ground, smooth 7 deflate 8 compress, overcome 9 overwhelm, prostrate

flatter 4 fool, laud 5 court, extol, honor, toady 6 become, cajole, delude 7 adulate, beguile, deceive, mislead, wheedle 8 blandish, bootlick, butter up, eulogize, soft-soap 9 brown-nose, sweet-talk, truckle to 10 compliment, overpraise, panegyrize

flatterer 5 toady 6 fawner, yes man 8 eulogist, truckler, wheedler 9 sycophant 10 bootlicker 11 lickspittle 13 apple-polisher

flattering 7 lauding 8 praising 9 extolling, favorable, laudatory 10 gratifying 13 complimentary

flattering attention 5 court 7 fawning

flattery 6 eulogy 7 blarney, fawning, snow job 8 cajolery, encomium, jollying, soft soap, toadying, toadyism 9 adulation, panegyric, servility, truckling, wheedling 10 sycophancy 12 blandishment 14 obsequiousness

Flaubert, Gustave
author of: 8 Salammbo 12 Madame Bovary 21 A Sentimental Education 24 The Temptation of St Anthony

flaunt 3 air 4 brag, wave 5 boast, sport, strut, vaunt 6 blazon, dangle, parade 7 exhibit, show off 8 brandish, flourish 9 advertise, broadcast

flavor 4 aura, lace, soul, tang, tone 5 gusto, imbue, savor, spice, style, tenor 6 aspect, infuse, lacing, relish, season, spirit 7 essence, instill 8 ambience, piquancy 9 attribute, seasoning

flavorful 4 rich 5 nutty, sapid, spicy, tangy, tasty, zesty 6 savory 7 peppery, piquant 8 aro-

matic 9 palatable, toothsome 10 appetizing

flavoring 4 herb, salt 5 spice 6 pepper 7 essence, extract, vanilla 8 additive, seasoner 9 chocolate, condiment, seasoning

flavorless 4 dull, flat, thin, weak 5 bland, stale, vapid 6 watery 7 insipid 9 tasteless

flaw 3 mar 4 blot, harm, spot, vice 5 error, fault, speck, stain 6 blotch, deface, defect, foible, impair, injure, injury, smudge, weaken 7 blemish, failing, fallacy, frailty, mistake 8 weak spot, weakness 9 deformity, disfigure 10 compromise, defacement 11 shortcoming 12 imperfection 13 disfigurement

flawed 6 faulty 8 impaired 9 defective, imperfect

flawless 5 sound 7 perfect 9 errorless, faultless 10 immaculate, impeccable

flawlessness 8 accuracy 10 perfection 11 correctness 14 immaculateness

flay 4 bark, pare, peel, skin 5 scalp, scold, strip 6 assail, fleece, punish, rebuke 7 plunder, upbraid 9 castigate, excoriate 11 decorticate

flea
varieties: 3 bat, dog, rat 5 mouse 6 rodent 9 carnivore 10 sticktight

fleck 3 dot, jot 4 drop, mark, mole, spot 5 flake, speck 6 bespot, dapple, mottle, streak, tittle 7 blemish, freckle, spatter, speckle, stipple 8 particle, small bit 9 bespeckle 10 besprinkle

Fledermaus, Die
also: 6 The Bat
operetta by: 7 (Johann) Strauss
character: 5 Adele, Falke, Frank 6 Alfred 9 Rosalinda 14 Prince Orlofsky 18 Baron von Eisenstein

fledgling 4 tyro 6 novice 8 beginner, freshman 9 greenhorn 10 apprentice, tenderfoot

flee 4 shun, skip 5 avoid, dodge, elude, evade, split 6 decamp, desert, vanish 7 abscond, fly away, make off 8 speed off 9 cut and run, disappear 10 fly the coop

fleece 3 gyp 4 bilk, dupe, gull, rook, wool 5 cheat, cozen, trick 7 deceive, defraud, swindle 9 bamboozle, victimize

fleet 3 run 4 band, fade, fast, flow, navy, skim, spry, swim, unit 5 agile, array, brief, creek, drift, float, hasty, inlet, light, quick, rapid, shift, ships, short, swift 6 abound, active, armada, nimble, number, speedy, sudden, vanish 7 caravan, cursory, hurried 8 flotilla, squadron 9 disappear, momentary, transient 10 evanescent, transitory 11 expeditious 13 instantaneous

fleeting 5 brief, quick 7 passing 8 flitting, fugitive, temporal 9 ephemeral, fugacious, momentary, temporary, transient 10 evanescent, perishable, transitory 11 impermanent, precarious, unenduring

Fleming, Alexander
field: 12 bacteriology
nationality: 7 British
discovered: 10 penicillin
awarded: 10 Nobel Prize

Fleming, Henry
character in: 20 The Red Badge of Courage
author: 5 Crane

Fleming, Ian
author of: 4 Dr No 9 Moonraker 10 Goldfinger 11 Thunderball 12 Casino Royale 13 Live and Let Die 15 For Your Eyes Only 16 The Spy Who Loved Me, You Only Live Twice 18 From Russia with Love
character: 1 M, Q 6 Oddjob 7 SPECTRE (organization) 9 James Bond 14 Miss Moneypenny 15 Auric Goldfinger

Fleming, Victor
director of: 13 The Wizard of Oz 14 Treasure Island 15 Gone With the Wind (Oscar) 18 Captains Courageous

flesh 3 fat, man 4 body, meat, pulp 5 brawn, power, vigor 6 embody, fatten, people 7 fatness, fill out, mankind, realize 8 humanity, physique, strength 9 carnality, substance 10 sensuality 11 materiality 13 individualize, particularize

flesh and blood 3 kin 4 real 5 a body, child 6 family 7 kindred 8 children 9 corporeal, offspring, relations, relatives 10 kith and kin 11 substantial

flesh-eating 9 predatory 10 predaceous 11 carnivorous

fleshy 3 fat 5 beefy, obese,

plump, stout, tubby **6** chubby, portly, rotund, stocky **7** paunchy **8** roly-poly, thick-set **9** corpulent, succulent **10** overweight, potbellied

Fletcher, Louise
 born: **12** Birmingham AL
 roles: **17** The Cheap Detective **25** One Flew Over the Cuckoo's Nest (Oscar)

Fletcher, Susannah Yolande
 real name of: **12** Susannah York

flex 4 bend **5** curve

flexible 4 mild, soft **5** lithe **6** docile, genial, gentle, limber, pliant, supple **7** amiable, ductile, elastic, plastic, pliable, springy **8** bendable, yielding **9** adaptable, compliant, malleable, resilient, tractable **10** changeable, extensible, manageable, responsive, submissive **11** complaisant

Flibbertigibbet
 character in: **10** Kenilworth
 author: **5** Scott

flick 4 film **5** brush, graze, movie, sweep, whisk

flicker 4 flit, glow, sway **5** blaze, flame, flare, flash, gleam, glint, shake, spark, throb, trace, waver **6** quaver, quiver, waggle **7** flutter, glimmer, glisten, glitter, modicum, pulsate, shimmer, sparkle, tremble, vestige, vibrate, wriggle **8** undulate **9** coruscate, fluctuate, oscillate, scintilla, vacillate

Flickertail State
 nickname of: **11** North Dakota

flicks 5 films **6** cinema, grazes, movies, sweeps, whisks **7** brushes

flier 4 bill **5** pilot **6** notice **7** aviator, leaflet, venture **8** brochure, bulletin, circular, handbill **10** experiment **12** announcement **13** advertisement

flight 4 rout, rush, wing **5** flock **6** escape, exodus, flying, hegira **7** fleeing, retreat, soaring, winging **8** squadron **10** withdrawal **11** aeronautics

flighty 5 dizzy, giddy **6** fickle **8** quixotic, reckless, unstable, volatile **9** frivolous, mercurial, whimsical **10** capricious, changeable, inconstant, indecisive, irresolute **11** harebrained, impractical, light-headed, thoughtless **13** irresponsible **14** scatterbrained

flimsy 4 poor, thin, weak **5** cheap, filmy, frail, gauzy, petty, sheer **6** feeble, shabby, shoddy, sleazy, slight, trashy **7** foolish, fragile, ill-made, shallow, trivial **8** cobwebby, delicate, gossamer, trifling **9** frivolous, worthless **10** diaphanous, inadequate, jerry-built, ramshackle **11** dilapidated, superficial **13** unsubstantial

flinch 3 fly, shy **4** jerk **5** cower, quail, quake, start, wince **6** blench, cringe, falter, quaver, quiver, recoil', shiver, shrink **7** contort, grimace, retreat, shudder

fling 2 go **3** try **4** ball, bash, cast, dash, emit, hurl, lark, toss **5** eject, expel, heave, pitch, sling, spree, trial **6** let fly, propel **7** attempt **8** bit of fun **11** precipitate

Flintstones, The
 character: **7** Pebbles **8** Bamm Bamm **11** Betty Rubble **12** Barney Rubble **14** Fred Flintstone **15** Dino the Dinosaur, Wilma Flintstone
 voice: **8** Alan Reed, Mel Blanc **10** Don Messick **12** Bea Benaderet, Gerry Johnson **13** Jean Vander Pyl
 city: **7** Bedrock
 creator: **12** Hanna-Barbera

Flintwinch
 character in: **12** Little Dorrit
 author: **7** Dickens

flinty 4 cold, hard **5** cruel, harsh, stern, stony **6** inured, steely **7** callous **8** hardened **10** unyielding **11** hardhearted, insensitive

flip 3 tap **4** bold, pert, spin, toss, turn **5** brash, flick, fresh, throw, thumb **6** cheeky, fillip **8** impudent, insolent, turn over **9** unabashed

flippant 4 glib, pert, rude **5** brash, lippy, saucy **6** cheeky, nimble **7** voluble **8** impudent, insolent, trifling **9** bumptious, frivolous, talkative **11** impertinent **12** presumptuous **13** disrespectful

Flipper
 character: **8** Bud Ricks **10** Sandy Ricks **11** Porter Ricks
 cast: **10** Brian Kelly, Luke Halpin **11** Tommy Norden
 Flipper played by: **4** Suzy

flirt 3 toy **4** play, vamp **5** dally, tease **6** trifle **8** coquette **12** heartbreaker

flit 4 dart, scud, skim, wing

5 speed **6** hasten, scurry **7** flicker, flutter

Flitch of Bacon, The
 author: **16** William Ainsworth

Flite, Miss
 character in: **10** Bleak House
 author: **7** Dickens

flivver 3 car **4** auto, heap **5** motor **6** jalopy, wheels **7** machine, vehicle **8** motorcar **9** tin lizzie **10** automobile

float 3 bob **4** waft **5** drift, hover, slide **6** bear up, buoy up, hold up, launch **8** levitate

floating 4 free **5** awash, loose **6** adrift, afloat, errant **7** buoyant, wafting **8** drifting **9** fluctuant, wandering **10** unattached

flock 2 go **3** mob, run **4** band, bevy, gang, herd, mass, pack, rush **5** bunch, crowd, crush, drove, group, surge, troop **6** clique, gather, huddle, muster, stream, throng **7** cluster, company, coterie **8** converge **9** gathering; multitude **10** assemblage, collection, congregate **11** aggregation **12** congregation
 of fish: **6** school
 of game birds: **5** covey
 of geese: **6** gaggle
 of insects: **5** swarm
 of lions: **5** pride
 of seals or whales: **3** pod
 of young birds: **5** brood

flocks
 god of: **3** Pan

flock together 6 gather, mingle **7** convene **8** assemble **9** associate **10** congregate

flog 4 beat, cane, club, cuff, drub, hide, lash, maul, whip **5** birch, flail, smite, strap **6** cudgel, paddle, strike, switch, thrash **7** scourge **8** lambaste **9** horsewhip **10** flagellate

flood 4 flow, glut, gush, tide **6** deluge, drench, shower, stream **7** cascade, current, torrent **8** downpour, flow over, inundate, overflow, saturate, submerge, wash over **9** overwhelm **10** cloudburst, inundation, outpouring, oversupply
 period before: **12** antediluvian

Flood
 author: **16** Robert Penn Warren

flooded 6 flowed, surged **7** deluged, glutted, overran, swamped **8** drenched, engulfed **9** inundated, outpoured, washed out **10** downpoured, overflowed

floor 4 base, deck, fell, tier **5** level, stage, story **6** bottom, ground **7** minimum, parquet **8** base rate, flooring, pavement **9** prostrate

flop 4 bomb, bust, drop, fail, fold, plop **5** close **6** fiasco, fizzle, topple, tumble, turkey **7** failure, go under, shutter, washout **8** disaster, lay an egg **14** disappointment

Flora
origin: **5** Roman
goddess of: **7** flowers

floral 6 bloomy **7** verdant **8** blossomy **9** botanical **10** herbaceous

Floralia
origin: **5** Roman
form: **8** festival

Florence *see box*

florescence 5 bloom **9** flowerage **10** blossoming

florid 4 rosy **5** gaudy, ruddy, showy **6** blowsy, hectic, ornate, rococo **7** baroque, flowery, flushed, reddish **8** inflamed, red-faced, rubicund, sanguine **9** elaborate **10** flamboyant, ornamented **12** ostentatious **13** grandiloquent

Florida *see box*

florilegium 7 garland **8** chapbook, treasury **9** anthology

Florizel
character in: **14** The Winter's Tale
author: **11** Shakespeare

floruit 12 he flourished **13** she flourished

flotilla 5 fleet **6** armada

Flotow, Friedrich von
born: **7** Germany **11** Mecklenburg
composer of: **6** Martha **11** Die Matrosen **19** Alessandro Stradella

flotsam 4 junk **6** debris, refuse **7** garbage **8** castoffs

flounce 3 hem **4** edge, leap, skip, trim, trip **5** bound, caper, frill, stamp, stomp, storm, strut **6** bounce, edging, fringe, gambol, prance, ruffle, sashay, spring **7** valance **8** furbelow, ornament, skirting, trimming

flounder 4 fish, flop, halt, limp **5** lurch, waver **6** falter, hobble, muddle, totter, tumble, wallow, welter **7** blunder,

Florence
artist: **6** Giotto **7** Cimabue **8** Ghiberti **9** Donatello **10** Michelozzi **11** della Robbia **12** Brunelleschi, Michelangelo
capital of: **7** Tuscany **15** Firenze province
cathedral/church: **10** San Lorenzo, San Miniato, Santa Croce **18** Santa Maria del Fiore
Italian: **7** Firenze
landmark: **5** Pieta **6** Uffizi **8** Bargello **11** Pitti Palace **12** Ponte Vecchio **13** Boboli Gardens **14** Loggia dei Lanzi, Palazzo Vecchio **19** Piazza della Signoria **22** Baptistry of San Giovanni, Ospedale degli Innocenti
mountain: **9** Apennines
religious reformer: **10** Savonarola
river: **4** Arno
ruler: **5** Goths **6** Medici, Romans **8** Lombards **9** Etruscans **15** Byzantine Empire
tomb of: **7** Galileo, Rossini **11** Machiavelli **12** Michelangelo **15** Lorenzo de Medici

Florida
abbreviation: **2** FL **3** Fla
nickname: **6** Flower **8** Sunshine **10** Peninsular
capital: **11** Tallahassee
largest city: **12** Jacksonville
others: **4** Tice **5** Cocoa, Miami, Ocala, Tampa **7** Hialeah, Orlando, Palatka, Sebring **8** Sarasota **9** Bradenton, Palm Beach, Pensacola **10** Clearwater **11** Brooksville, Coral Gables, Gainesville, St Augustine **12** Daytona Beach, Ft Lauderdale, St Petersburg
college: **4** Nova **5** Barry, Miami, Tampa **6** Eckerd **7** Rollins, Stetson
explorer: **11** Ponce de Leon
feature:
  amusement park: **5** Epcot **10** Marineland **11** Disney World
  canal: **5** Miami **7** Tamiami
  museum: **8** Ringling
  national park: **10** Everglades
tribe: **3** Ais **5** Ocale, Utina **6** Calusa, Chatot, Potano **7** Timucua **8** Seminole
people: **5** conch **7** cracker, Osceola
island: **7** Bahamas, Sanibel **8** Biscayne
  key: **4** Long, Vaca, West **5** Largo **7** Big Pine **8** Biscayne **9** Sugarloaf
lake: **4** Dora **6** Apopka, Harney, Jessup, Newnan **7** Ledwith **8** Arbuckle **9** Kissimmee **10** Okeechobee
land rank: **12** twenty-second
physical feature:
  bay: **8** Biscayne **9** Apalachee **10** Waccasassa
  cape: **5** Sable **7** Kennedy **9** Canaveral
  gulf: **6** Mexico
  sea: **8** Atlantic
  springs: **6** Silver **7** Rainbow
  swamp: **10** Everglades, Okefenokee
river: **6** Banana, Indian **7** Aucilla, Manatee, Scambia, St Johns, Suwanee **9** Ochlawaha **12** Apalachicola
state admission: **13** twenty-seventh
state bird: **11** mockingbird
state fish: **16** Atlantic sailfish
state mammal: **7** dolphin
state flower: **13** orange blossom
state motto: **12** In God We Trust
state song: **11** Swanee River **14** Old Folks at Home
state tree: **13** sabal palmetto **15** cabbage palmetto

shamble, stagger, stumble
8 flatfish, hesitate, struggle

Flounder, The
author: **11** Gunter Grass

flourish 4 curl, dash, grow, pomp, rant, show, turn **5** bloom, bluff, get on, shake, strut, sweep, swing, swish, twirl, twist, wield **6** flaunt, flower, hot air, parade, splash, thrive, waving **7** blossom, bravado, burgeon, cadenza, fanfare, fustian, glitter, prosper, shaking, succeed, swagger **8** boasting, brandish, curlicue, fare well, get ahead, swinging, vaunting, wielding **9** agitation, grace note, thrashing **10** decoration **11** braggadocio, brandishing, fanfaronade, ostentation **12** appoggiatura **13** embellishment, magniloquence, swashbuckling **14** grandiloquence

flourishing 8 swinging, swishing, thriving, wielding **9** flaunting **10** prospering, successful **11** brandishing

flout 3 rag **4** defy, mock, twit **5** chaff, scorn, spurn, taunt **6** gibe at, insult

flow 3 jet, run **4** flux, gush, pass, pour, rush, seep, tide **5** drain, drift, float, flood, glide, issue, spout, spurt, surge, sweep, swirl, train **6** abound, course, deluge, efflux, effuse, filter, plenty, rapids, stream **7** cascade, current, debouch, torrent, well out **8** effusion, millrace, plethora, sequence **9** abundance, discharge, effluence, emanation **10** outpouring, succession **11** debouchment, progression

flower 3 bud **4** best, blow, open, pick, posy **5** bloom, cream, elite, ripen **6** mature **7** blossom, bouquet, burgeon, develop, nosegay, prosper **8** flourish **11** aristocracy

flower arranging, art of
Japanese: **7** ikebana

Flower Fables
author: **15** Louisa May Alcott

flowering 4 peak **5** bloom **6** height, heyday **8** blooming, maturing **10** blossoming, developing, prospering **11** flourishing

Flowering Judas
author: **19** Katherine Anne Porter

flowers
goddess of: **5** Flora

Flowers of Evil
author: **17** Charles Baudelaire

Flower State
nickname of: **7** Florida

flowery 5 fancy **6** floral, florid, ornate **8** blooming **10** blossoming, burgeoning, euphuistic, figurative, florescent, ornamental, rhetorical **11** embellished **12** efflorescent, magniloquent **13** grandiloquent

Flowery Kingdom see
5 China

flowing 4 flux **5** fluid **6** ebbing, fluent, smooth **7** current, copious, gliding, running **8** abundant **9** liquefied, plentiful **10** continuity, pouring out, proceeding

fluctuate 4 sway, vary, veer **5** shift, swing, waver **6** dawdle, falter, wobble **8** hesitate, undulate **9** alternate, oscillate, vacillate **10** dillydally

fluctuation 5 shift **6** change **7** veering **8** shifting, swinging **9** deviation, variation **11** alternation, oscillation, vacillation

flue 3 net **4** barb, down, pipe, tube, vent **5** fluff, fluke, shaft **6** funnel **7** channel, chimney, passage **9** smokejack

fluent 4 glib **5** vocal **6** facile **7** voluble **8** effusive, eloquent **9** garrulous, talkative **10** articulate, effortless

fluff 3 err, nap **4** down, flub, fuzz, lint, miss, puff, slip, soft **5** botch, floss, froth, primp **6** forget **7** blunder **8** feathers

fluffy 5 downy, fuzzy, nappy, wooly **6** fleecy, woolly **8** feathery

fluid 6 liquid, watery **7** unfixed **8** flexible, floating, shifting, solution, unstable **9** adaptable, liquefied, unsettled **10** adjustable, changeable, indefinite

fluid ounce
abbreviation: **4** fl oz

fluke 3 hap **5** freak **6** chance **7** miracle **8** accident, windfall **9** mischance **11** vicissitude **12** stroke of luck

flummery 7 dessert, pudding **9** gibberish **10** doubletalk, mumbo jumbo **11** obfuscation

flunky 6 lackey, menial, minion **7** servant **9** attendant, underling

fluorine
chemical symbol: **1** F

flurry 3 ado **4** fuss, gust, heat, puff, stir **5** alarm, fever, flush, haste, panic **6** breeze, bustle, pother, rattle, shower, squall,

tumult **7** agitate, confuse, disturb, fidgets, fluster, flutter, perturb **8** confound, disquiet **9** agitation, commotion, confusion **10** discompose, disconcert, turbulence **11** disturbance, hurry-scurry, trepidation **12** discomposure, perturbation, restlessness

flush 4 even, glow, swab, tint, wash **5** bloom, blush, color, elate, flood, level, rinse, scour, scrub, shock, spray **6** access, dampen, deluge, douche, drench, excite, puff up, quiver, redden, sponge, thrill, tremor **7** animate, flutter, glowing, impulse, moisten, redness, wash out **8** rosiness, rosy glow, squarely, strength **9** freshness, make proud, ruddiness **10** exultation, jubilation

flushed 3 hot, red **4** rosy, ruby **5** aglow, **6** florid, torrid **7** crimson, excited, scarlet **8** blushing, feverish **10** prosperous

flushed with success
5 proud **6** elated

fluster 4 daze **5** shake, upset **6** dither, flurry, hubbub, muddle, ruffle **7** agitate, confuse, disturb, flutter, perplex, perturb, startle, turmoil **8** befuddle, bewilder **9** agitation, commotion, confusion, discomfit **10** discompose, disconcert **12** bewilderment, discomfiture, discomposure **14** discombobulate

flute 4 fife, fold, pipe, roll, tube, wind **5** crimp **6** furrow, groove **7** piccolo, whistle **8** recorder **9** wine glass **14** champagne glass

flutter 3 bob **4** flap, flit, soar, stir, wave, wing **5** hurry, shake, throb **6** flurry, quiver, ripple, thrill, tremor, wobble **7** beating, flitter, fluster, pulsate, tremble, twitter **8** flapping, tingling **9** agitation, commotion, confusion, palpitate, sensation, vibration **12** perturbation

fluvial 7 aquatic

fluviatile 7 aquatic

flux 4 flow, tide **5** flood **6** course, motion, stream, unrest **7** current **8** mutation, shifting **10** alteration, transition **11** fluctuation **12** modification **14** transformation

fly 4 flap, flee, sail, skip, soar, wave, wing **5** coast, float, glide, hover, hurry, split, swoop **6** hasten, hustle **7** flutter, run away, take off, vibrate **8** take wing, undulate

fly
varieties: 3 bat, bot **4** blow, deer, dung, gnat, horn, moth, rust, sand **5** beach, black, crane, dance, drone, flesh, fruit, horse, house, march, marsh, midge, mydas, punky **6** bee fly, cactus, maggot, pomace, robber, stable, tsetse, warble, window **7** chalcid, seaweed, skipper, soldier, tachima **8** lousefly, mosquito, stiletto **9** leaf miner **10** flatfooted, fungus gnat, humpbacked **11** thickheaded **14** black scavenger

fly apart 5 burst **6** blow up **7** explode, shatter **8** detonate, fragment

fly at 6 assail, attack

fly-by-night 5 shady **6** shifty **7** crooked **8** unstable, untrusty **9** dishonest **10** unreliable **12** disreputable, undependable **13** irresponsible, untrustworthy

Flying Dutchman, The
opera by: 6 Wagner
character: 4 Erik **5** Senta **6** Daland **11** The Dutchman

Flying Fish
constellation of: 6 Volans

Flying Nun, The
character: 9 Sister Ana **11** Sister Sixto **13** Carlos Ramirez **14** Mother Superior **15** Sister Bertrille **16** Sister Jacqueline
cast: 10 Sally Field **12** Alejandro Rey, Linda Dangcil, Marge Redmond **14** Shelly Morrison **17** Madeleine Sherwood

fly in the ointment 5 hitch **7** problem, trouble **8** drawback, nuisance **9** hindrance **10** impediment **12** disadvantage

Flynn, Errol
real name: 17 Leslie Thomas Flynn
born: 6 Hobart **8** Tasmania
roles: 10 The Sea Hawk **12** Captain Blood **14** Too Much Too Soon **15** The Sun Also Rises **24** The Adventures of Robin Hood **26** The Charge of the Light Brigade

fly off the handle 6 see red

fly the coop 4 bolt, flee **6** escape, run off **7** abscond, get away, make off, run away, skip out, take off

foal 4 cade, colt **5** filly, young **9** fledgling

foam 4 fizz, head, scum, suds **5** froth, spume **6** lather **7** sparkle **8** bubbling **13** effervescence

foaming 5 sudsy **6** bubbly, frothy **7** lathery **8** bubbling, frothing

foamy 5 fizzy **6** frothy **7** lathery **8** bubbling **9** sparkling **12** effervescent

fob 5 chain, medal, strap **6** ribbon **8** ornament **9** medallion

focal 3 key **4** main **5** chief **7** central, pivotal **8** foremost **9** principal

Foch, Ferdinand
served in: 3 WWI
nationality: 6 French
rank: 7 marshal **16** commander-in-chief
battle: 5 Marne, Somme

Foch, Nina
real name: 20 Nina Consuelo Maud Fock
born: 6 Leyden **11** Netherlands
roles: 9 Spartacus **14** Executive Suite, Song to Remember **17** An American in Paris, My Name Is Julia Ross **18** The Ten Commandments

Fock, Nina Consuelo Maud
real name of: 8 Nina Foch

focus 3 aim, fix, hub **4** core **5** haunt, heart **6** adjust, center, direct, middle, resort **7** nucleus, retreat **8** converge **9** limelight, spotlight **10** rendezvous **11** concentrate **12** headquarters

focusing 6 aiming **9** adjusting, centering, directing **10** adjustment, converging **11** pinpointing **13** concentrating

fodder 4 feed, food **6** forage, silage **7** rations **9** provender

foe 5 enemy, rival **8** attacker, opponent **9** adversary, assailant, combatant, contender, disputant **10** antagonist, competitor

fog 3 dim **4** daze, haze, smog, soup **5** brume, cloud **6** darken, muddle, stupor, trance **7** confuse, obscure, pea soup, perplex **8** bewilder **9** murkiness **10** cloudiness **12** bewilderment

Fogg, Phileas
character in: 26 Around the World in Eighty Days
author: 10 Jules Verne

foggy 3 dim **4** dark, hazy **5** dusky, filmy, fuzzy, misty, murky, musty, soupy, vague **6** cloudy, smoggy, spacey

7 brumous, clouded, obscure, shadowy, unclear **8** confused, nebulous, overcast, vaporous **9** beclouded **10** indistinct

foible 4 kink **5** quirk **6** defect, whimsy **7** failing, frailty **8** crotchet, weak side, weakness **9** infirmity **10** deficiency **11** shortcoming **12** imperfection

Foible
character in: 16 The Way of the World
author: 8 Congreve

foil 3 nip **4** balk, film, leaf **5** check, flake, match, sheet, wafer **6** hinder, lamina, set off, thwart **7** enhance, prevent **8** backdrop, contrast **9** frustrate **10** antithesis, complement, supplement **11** correlative, counterpart

foist 6 impose, unload **7** palm off, pass off

fold 3 hug, lap, pen, sty **4** bend, curl, sect, tuck, wrap, yard **5** clasp, close, crimp, flock, group, layer, pleat **6** corral, crease, dog-ear, double, encase, enfold, furrow, gather, parish, pucker, ruffle, rumple, wrap up **7** crinkle, crumple, embosom, embrace, entwine, envelop, flounce, overlap, wrinkle **8** barnyard, compound, doubling, stockade **9** community, corrugate, enclosure **12** congregation

folder 7 booklet, leaflet **8** brochure, circular, pamphlet **9** portfolio

foliage 6 leaves **7** leafage, verdure

folklore 5 myths **6** fables **7** legends **10** traditions

folks 3 kin **6** family, people **7** kinsmen, parents **8** everyone **9** relatives **10** kith and kin

folksy 6 casual, chatty **8** familiar, friendly, homespun, informal, sociable **10** neighborly **14** conversational **15** unsophisticated

folk tale
German: 7 Marchen

Follett, Ken
author of: 14 Eye of the Needle **15** On Wings of Eagles, The Key to Rebecca **22** The Man from St Petersburg

follow 3 dog **4** copy, heed, hunt, mind, note, obey, tail **5** aim at, chase, grasp, hound, stalk, trace, track, trail,

watch 6 attend, notice, pursue, regard, shadow, take up **7** cherish, emulate, imitate, observe, replace, succeed **8** practice, supplant **9** accompany, cultivate, prosecute **10** comprehend, understand

follower 3 fan **4** tail **5** pupil, toady **6** chaser, hunter, shadow, stooge **7** admirer, apostle, convert, devotee, protege, pursuer, servant, stalker **8** adherent, advocate, disciple, hanger-on, henchman, parasite, partisan, retainer, servitor **9** accessory, attendant, dependent, proselyte, satellite, supporter, sycophant

following 4 next **5** below, suite, train **6** public **7** ensuing, retinue **8** audience **9** adherents, clientele, entourage, partisans, patronage **10** attendance, consequent, sequential, subsequent, succeeding, successive **11** consecutive

Follow the Fleet
    director: 12 Mark Sandrich
    cast: 11 Fred Astaire **12** Ginger Rogers **13** Randolph Scott **21** Harriet Hilliard Nelson
    song: 11 We Saw the Sea **13** Let Yourself Go **24** Let's Face the Music and Dance

follow-up 7 ensuing **8** sequence **9** aftermath **10** subsequent

folly 6 idiocy, levity **7** inanity, mistake **8** nonsense, trifling **9** absurdity, asininity, frivolity, giddiness, silliness **10** imbecility, imprudence, tomfoolery **11** doltishness, fatuousness, foolishness **12** indiscretion **13** brainlessness, irrationality, senselessness

foment 4 goad, spur, urge **5** rouse **6** arouse, excite, foster, incite, kindle, stir up **7** agitate, inflame, promote, provoke, quicken **8** irritate **9** aggravate, galvanize, instigate, stimulate **10** exacerbate

Fomorian
    origin: 5 Irish
    form: 5 demon **6** pirate
    habitat: 3 sea
    raided: 7 Ireland
    personifies: 13 hostile nature

fond 5 naive **6** ardent, doting, loving, tender **7** amorous, devoted **8** desirous, enamored, harbored, held dear **9** cherished, indulgent, preserved, sustained **10** infatuated, passionate **11** impassioned, sentimental **12** affectionate

16 overaffectionate

Fonda, Henry
    wife: 16 Margaret Sullavan
    son: 5 Peter
    daughter: 4 Jane
    born: 13 Grand Island NE
    roles: 7 Jezebel, Warlock **8** Fail Safe **10** Fort Apache, In Harm's Way, The Best Man, The Lady Eve **12** On Golden Pond (Oscar) **13** Mister Roberts, Ox-Bow Incident, The Longest Day **14** Twelve Angry Men, Young Mr Lincoln **16** Advise and Consent, Battle of the Bulge, How the West Was Won, The Grapes of Wrath **18** The Boston Strangler **19** My Darling Clementine, The Immortal Sergeant **21** Sometimes a Great Notion

Fonda, Jane
    father: 5 Henry
    brother: 5 Peter
    husband: 9 Ted Turner, Tom Hayden **10** Roger Vadim
    born: 9 New York NY
    roles: 5 Julia, Klute (Oscar) **10** Barbarella, Coming Home (Oscar) **11** A Doll's House **12** Any Wednesday, On Golden Pond **13** China Syndrome **17** Barefoot in the Park **23** They Shoot Horses Don't They?

Fonda, Peter
    father: 5 Henry
    sister: 4 Jane
    born: 9 New York NY
    roles: 7 The Trip **9** Easy Rider **13** The Wild Angels

fondle 3 hug, pet **5** spoon **6** caress, cuddle, nestle, nuzzle, smooch, stroke **7** embrace, make out **10** bill and coo

fondness 4 bent, care, love **5** ardor, fancy **6** desire, liking **7** passion **8** devotion, penchant, weakness **9** affection **10** attachment, partiality, preference, propensity, tenderness **11** amorousness, inclination **12** predilection **14** susceptibility

fond utterance 9 sweet talk **10** endearment **12** sweet nothing

Fons
    origin: 5 Roman
    god of: 7 springs

fons et origo 15 source and origin

Fontaine, Joan
    real name: 25 Joan de Beauvoir de Havilland
    sister: 17 Olivia de Havilland
    husband: 11 Brian Aherne
    born: 5 Japan, Tokyo
    roles: 3 Ivy **7** Ivanhoe, Re-

becca **8** Casanova, Gunga Din, Jane Eyre, The Women **9** Suspicion (Oscar) **12** The Devil's Own **15** Frenchman's Creek, September Affair **16** Tender Is the Night, The Constant Nymph

Fontanne, Lynn
    husband: 10 Alfred Lunt
    born: 6 London **7** England
    roles: 8 The Visit **9** Quadrille, The Pirate **10** The Sea Gull **13** O Mistress Mine **15** Design for Living **18** The Great Sebastians **19** The Taming of the Shrew

food 4 chow, feed, grub **5** board **6** fodder, forage, silage, viands **7** edibles, nurture, pasture, rations **8** eatables, victuals **9** nutrition, pasturage, provender **10** provisions, sustenance **11** comestibles, nourishment, subsistence

food, miraculous 5 manna

fool 3 ass, con, oaf **4** bilk, clod, dolt, dupe, gull, hoax, jest, joke **5** cheat, chump, clown, cozen, cut up, dummy, dunce, feign, goose, idiot, klutz, moron, ninny, tease, trick **6** diddle, fleece, frolic, humbug, jester, nitwit, rip off, stooge **7** beguile, buffoon, deceive, defraud, half-wit, Pierrot, pretend **8** bonehead, dummkopf, flimflam, hoodwink, imbecile, lunkhead, meathead, numskull **9** bamboozle, blockhead, harlequin, ignoramus, numbskull, simpleton **10** dunderhead, nincompoop, scaramouch **11** Punchinello

fool around 3 toy **4** idle **5** clown, dally **6** dawdle, loiter, trifle

foolhardy 4 rash **5** brash, hasty **6** madcap **8** careless, heedless, reckless **9** daredevil, hotheaded, impetuous, imprudent, impulsive **10** headstrong, incautious **11** harebrained, thoughtless

foolish 5 inane, silly **6** absurd, stupid, unwise **7** asinine, fatuous, idiotic, moronic, witless **9** brainless, imbecilic, imprudent, ludicrous, senseless **10** boneheaded, incautious, indiscreet, ridiculous **12** preposterous **13** irresponsible, unintelligent

foolishness 5 folly **6** idiocy, lunacy **8** unwisdom **9** absurdity, asininity, puerility, silliness, stupidity **10** imbecility, imprudence **11** fatuousness, witlessness **12** childishness, extravagance, indiscretion brainlessness, senselessness **14** ridiculousness **15** injudiciousness 16 irresponsibility, preposterousness

Fool of Quality, The
    author: 11 Henry Brooke

foot 3 dog, pad, paw 4 base, hoof 6 bottom, tootsy 7 trotter 8 infantry 10 foundation
    abbreviation: 2 ft

football
    athlete/coach: 8 Don Shula, Jim Brown, Kyle Rote, Lou Groza, Y A Tittle 9 Amos Stagg, Bart Starr, Bob Griese, Chuck Noll, Dan Marino, Don Hutson, Earl Blaik, Jerry Rice, Joe Namath, Len Dawson, Lou Little, O J Simpson, Red Grange, Tom Landry 10 Bear Bryant, Bruce Smith, Bubba Smith, Dick Butkus, Joe Montana, Joe Paterno, Ken Stabler, Larry Brown, Otto Graham, Sammy Baugh, Troy Aikman, Walter Camp, Weeb Ewbank 11 Ahmad Rashad, Craig Morton, Deacon Jones, Deion Sanders, Earl Morrall, Ernie Nevers, Floyd Little, Gayle Sayers, George Halas, Jan Stenerud, Jim Plunkett, John Riggins, Knute Rockne, Larry Csonka, Merlin Olsen, Paul Hornung, Pete Rozelle, Reggie White, Richard Todd, Tony Dorsett 12 Bud Wilkinson, Earl Campbell, Franco Harris, Frank Gifford, George Blanda, Joe Thiesmann, Johnny Unitas, Lance Alworth, Ozzie Newsome, Raymond Berry, Roman Gabriel, Walter Payton, William Perry 13 Ara Parseghian, Eric Dickerson, Fran Tarkenton, Roger Staubach, Terry Bradshaw, Vince Lombardi 14 Bronco Nagurski, Lawrence Taylor, Lydell Mitchell, Sonny Jurgensen 15 Norm Van Brocklin

football bowl games 3 Sun 4 Rose 5 Aloha, Gator, Peach, Sugar, Super 6 Citrus, Copper, Cotton, Fiesta, Orange 7 Holiday, Liberty 10 Bluebonnet, California 12 Independence

football leagues
    National Football League (NFL): 11 New York Jets 12 Buffalo Bills, Chicago Bears, Detroit Lions 13 Dallas Cowboys, Denver Broncos, Houston Oilers, Miami Dolphins, New York Giants 14 Atlanta Falcons, Los Angeles Rams 15 Cleveland Browns, Green Bay Packers, Seattle Seahawks 16 Kansas City Chiefs, Minnesota Vi-

kings, New Orleans Saints, Phoenix Cardinals (formerly St Louis), San Diego Chargers 17 Cincinnati Bengals, Indianapolis Colts (formerly Baltimore), Los Angeles Raiders (formerly Oakland) 18 New England Patriots, Philadelphia Eagles, Pittsburgh Steelers, Tampa Bay Buccaneers, Washington Redskins 23 San Francisco Forty-niners
    United States Football League (USFL): 10 Denver Gold 12 Chicago Blitz 14 Baltimore Stars, Boston Breakers 15 Houston Gamblers, Oakland Invaders, Oklahoma Outlaws, Tampa Bay Bandits 16 Arizona Wranglers, Memphis Showboats, Michigan Panthers, Orlando Renegades, Portland Breakers

17 Jacksonville Bulls, Los Angeles Express, New Jersey Generals, Philadelphia Stars 18 Washington Federals 19 Birmingham Stallions 21 San Antonio Gunslingers

football team *see box*

footfall 3 pad 4 pace, step 5 tread 8 footstep

foothold 4 grip, hold 7 support 8 purchase

footloose 4 free 8 carefree 9 fancy-free 10 unattached 11 uncommitted 12 unencumbered

footnote 5 gloss 9 reference 10 annotation 11 explanation 12 afterthought

footpad 5 thief 6 bandit, mugger, outlaw, robber 10 highwayman

---

football team (NFC)
Arizona: 9 Cardinals
    stadium: 8 Sun Devil
    formerly in: 7 St. Louis
Atlanta: 7 Falcons
    stadium: 11 Georgia Dome
Carolina: 8 Panthers
    stadium: 8 Carolina
Chicago: 5 Bears
    stadium: 12 Soldier Field
Dallas: 7 Cowboys
    stadium: 5 Texas
Detroit: 5 Lions
    stadium: 17 Pontiac Silverdome
Green Bay: 7 Packers
    stadium: 9 Milwaukee 12 Lambeau Field
Minnesota: 7 Vikings
    stadium: 9 Metrodome
New Orleans: 6 Saints
    stadium: 18 Louisiana Superdome
New York: 6 Giants
    stadium: 6 Giants
Philadelphia: 6 Eagles
    stadium: 8 Veterans
Saint Louis: 4 Rams
    stadium: 7 TWA Dome
    formerly in: 10 Los Angeles
San Francisco: 11 Forty-Niners
    stadium: 15 Candlestick Park
Tampa Bay: 10 Buccaneers
    stadium: 5 Tampa

Washington: 8 Redskins
    stadium: 14 Robert F Kennedy

football team (AFC)
Buffalo: 5 Bills
    stadium: 4 Rich
Cincinnati: 7 Bengals
    stadium: 10 Riverfront
Cleveland: 6 Browns
    stadium: 9 Municipal
Denver: 7 Broncos
    stadium: 8 Mile High
Houston: 6 Oilers
    stadium: 9 Astrodome
Indianapolis: 5 Colts
    stadium: 11 Hoosier Dome
    formerly in: 9 Baltimore
Jacksonville: 7 Jaguars
    stadium: 9 Municipal
Kansas City: 6 Chiefs
    stadium: 9 Arrowhead
Miami: 8 Dolphins
    stadium: 9 Joe Robbie
New England: 8 Patriots
    stadium: 7 Foxboro
New York: 4 Jets
    stadium: 6 Giants
Oakland: 7 Raiders
    stadium: 8 Coliseum
    formerly in: 10 Los Angeles
Pittsburgh: 8 Steelers
    stadium: 11 Three Rivers
San Diego: 8 Chargers
    stadium: 10 Jack Murphy
Seattle: 8 Seahawks
    stadium: 8 Kingdome

footpath 4 lane, ramp 5 jetty, trail 8 sidewalk

foot soldiers 8 infantry 10 fusilliers, musketeers

footstool 6 buffet 7 hassock, ottoman 8 footrest

footwear
French: 9 chaussure

fop 4 beau, dude 5 dandy, swell 7 coxcomb 8 popinjay 9 prettyboy 11 Beau Brummel

foppish 4 vain 5 gaudy, showy 6 ornate 7 finical 8 affected, dandyish 9 dandified 12 ostentatious 13 overelaborate

forage 4 feed, food, hunt, raid, seek 6 fodder, ravage, search, silage 7 despoil, explore, pasture, plunder, rummage 8 scavenge, scrounge 9 pasturage, provender 10 provisions

foray 4 raid 5 sally 6 attack, inroad, invade, ravage, thrust 7 pillage, plunder, venture 8 invasion 9 incursion 10 expedition 11 depredation

forbear 4 quit, stop 5 cease, forgo 6 desist, endure, eschew, forego, give up, suffer 7 abstain, refrain 8 abnegate, renounce, tolerate

forbearance 4 pity 5 mercy 6 pardon 8 clemency, eschewal, leniency, meekness, mildness, patience 9 endurance, tolerance 10 abstention, abstinence, continence, indulgence, moderation, submission, temperance 11 longanimity, resignation 12 mercifulness

forbearing 6 denial 7 lenient, refusal 8 eschewal, tolerant 9 indulgent 10 abnegation, abstention, abstinence, permissive, refraining 13 nonindulgence 16 nonparticipation

forbid 3 ban, bar 4 veto 5 taboo 6 enjoin, hinder, impede, oppose, refuse, reject 7 exclude, gainsay, inhibit, obviate, prevent 8 disallow, obstruct, preclude, prohibit, restrain 9 interdict, proscribe

forbiddance 3 ban 5 taboo 7 barring, embargo 9 exclusion, interdict 11 prohibition 12 interdiction, proscription

forbidden 5 taboo 6 banned 8 debarred 10 prohibited, proscribed
German: 8 verboten

forbidden fruit
type: 6 brandy 7 liqueur
origin: 7 America

flavor: 5 honey 6 orange 10 grapefruit

forbidden marriage
goddess of: 4 Lofn

forbidding 4 dour, grim, ugly 6 odious 7 hideous, ominous 8 horrible, sinister 9 abhorrent, offensive, repellent, repulsive 10 unfriendly, unpleasant 11 prohibitive, prohibitory, threatening 12 disagreeable, inhospitable 14 unapproachable

force 3 pry, vim 4 army, body, coax, crew, drag, gang, make, pull, push, team, unit, urge 5 break, clout, corps, drive, group, impel, might, power, press, squad, value, vigor, wrest 6 coerce, compel, duress, effect, elicit, energy, enjoin, extort, impact, import, impose, induce, oblige, propel, stress, thrust, weight, wrench 7 cogency, intrude, meaning, obtrude, potency, require, squeeze, stamina 8 charisma, coercion, division, efficacy, emphasis, momentum, persuade, pressure, squadron, strength, validity, violence, vitality 9 animation, battalion, constrain, magnetism, overpower, puissance 10 attraction, compulsion, constraint, detachment 11 necessitate, weightiness 12 significance 13 effectiveness
Latin: 3 vis

forced 5 slave 7 binding, coerced, labored, obliged 8 affected, enslaved, grudging, mannered, required, strained 9 compelled, impressed, insincere, mandatory, unwilling 10 artificial, compulsory, obligatory 11 constrained, involuntary

forceful 5 pithy, valid, vivid 6 cogent, potent, robust, strong, virile 7 dynamic, intense 8 emphatic, powerful, puissant, vigorous 9 effective, energetic 10 impressive

forceless 4 weak 8 impotent

force measurement 4 dyne 6 newton 7 poundal

Force of Circumstance
author: 16 Simone de Beauvoir

Force of Destiny, The
also: 17 La Forza del Destino
opera by: 5 Verdi
character: 7 Leonora 8 Don Carlo 9 Don Alvaro

forcible 8 coercive 10 compulsory

ford 3 car 4 span, wade 5 cross, edsel, shoal 6 bridge, model T, stream 7 passage 8 crossing, tin lizzy

Ford, Gerald Rudolph *see box*

Ford, Glenn
real name: 11 Gwyllyn Ford
wife: 13 Eleanor Powell
born: 6 Canada, Quebec
roles: 4 Rage 5 Gilda, Jubal 6 Santee 8 Cimarron 11 The Rounders 14 Is Paris Burning? 17 Interrupted Melody 18 Don't Go Near the Water 19 The Blackboard Jungle 23 Teahouse of the August Moon

Ford, Harrison
born: 9 Chicago IL
roles: 7 Frantic, Witness 8 Star Wars 11 Blade Runner 15 Return of the Jedi 16 American Graffiti 19 Raiders of the Lost Ark 20 The Empire Strikes Back 30 Indiana Jones and the Temple of Doom

Ford, John
author of: 13 Perkin Warbeck 17 'Tis Pity She's a Whore 19 The Lover's Melancholy

Ford, John
director of: 10 Stagecoach 11 The Informer (Oscar), The Quiet Man (Oscar) 12 The Hurricane, The Searchers 13 Grapes of Wrath (Oscar), Mister Roberts (with Mervyn LeRoy), The Lost Patrol 17 The Long Voyage Home 19 How Green Was My Valley (Oscar), My Darling Clementine 27 The Man Who Shot Liberty Valence

Ford, Thelma Booth
real name of: 12 Shirley Booth

Ford and Mistress Ford
characters in: 22 The Merry Wives of Windsor
author: 11 Shakespeare

fore 5 front 7 frontal 8 anterior, headmost

forearm 4 ulna 5 prime, ready 7 prepare

forebear 8 ancestor, begetter 10 antecedent, procreator, progenitor

foreboding 4 omen 5 dread 6 augury, boding 7 portent 9 intuition, misgiving 10 prescience, prognostic 11 premonition 12 apprehension, presentiment

Ford, Gerald Rudolph
born: 17 Leslie Lynch King Jr
adopted by/named after: 10 stepfather
nickname: 5 Jerry 7 Mr Clean
presidential rank: 12 thirty-eighth
party: 10 Republican
state represented: 2 MI
defeated: 5 no one
elected to neither: 10 presidency 14 vice presidency
vice president: 11 (Nelson A) Rockefeller
cabinet:
  state: 9 (Henry A) Kissinger
  treasury: 5 (William E) Simon
  defense: 8 (Donald H) Rumsfeld 11 (James) Schlesinger
  attorney general: 4 (Edward H) Levi 5 (William B)
  Saxbe
  interior: 6 (Rogers Clark Ballard) Morton, (Thomas S)
  Kleppe 8 (Stanley K) Hathaway
  agriculture: 4 (Earl Lauer) Butz 6 (John A) Knebel
  commerce: 4 (Frederick B) Dent 6 (Rogers Clark Ballard)
  Morton 10 (Elliot L) Richardson
  labor: 5 (W J) Usery (Jr) 6 (John T) Dunlop 7 (Peter J)
  Brennan
  HEW: 7 (F David) Mathews 10 (Caspar W) Weinberger
  HUD: 4 (James T) Lynn 5 (Carla Anderson) Hills
  transportation: 7 (William T) Coleman (Jr) 8 (Claude S)
  Brinegar
born: 7 Omaha NE
education:
  University: 8 Michigan
  Law School: 4 Yale
religion: 12 Episcopalian
interests: 4 golf 6 boxing, skiing 8 football, swimming
vacation spot: 2 CO 4 Vail
author: 21 Portrait of the Assassin (with John R Stiles)
  27 A Time To Heal: An Autobiography
political career: 13 vice president 19 House minority
  leader 24 US House of Representatives
civilian career: 6 lawyer
  assistant football coach at: 4 Yale
military service: 6 US Navy 10 lieutenant, World War II
notable events of lifetime/term: 9 recession
  12 Bicentennial
  assassination attempts on: 4 Ford
  clemency for: 12 draft dodgers, draft evaders
  kidnapping/trial/conviction of: 11 Patty Hearst
  scandal: 8 Lockheed 10 Hays Affair
  talks: 4 SALT
quotes: 19 I am a Ford not a Lincoln 41 Indebted to no
  man—the president of all the people 50 Our long national nightmare is over Our constitution works
father:
  natural: 15 Leslie Lynch King
  adoptive: 17 Gerald Rudolph Ford
mother: 7 Dorothy (Gardner King Ford)
siblings:
  half-brothers: 12 James Francis 13 Thomas Gardner
  14 Richard Addison
wife: 9 Elizabeth (Bloomer Warren)
  nickname: 5 Betty
children: 4 John 5 Susan 6 Steven 7 Michael

forecast 5 augur 6 augury, divine, expect 7 outlook, portend, predict, presage, project
8 envisage, envision, prophesy 9 calculate, prevision,
prognosis 10 anticipate, conjecture, prediction, prescience,
projection 11 extrapolate
12 anticipation, precognition,
presentiment 13 prognosticate
15 prognostication

forefather 6 author 8 ancestor,
begetter 9 patriarch, precursor

10 antecedent, originator, procreator, progenitor
12 primogenitor

forefront 4 fame, head, lead
8 vanguard 9 celebrity

foreign 5 alien 6 exotic, remote 7 distant, strange, unknown, unusual 8 imported
9 barbarous, extrinsic, irregular, unrelated 10 extraneous,
heathenish, introduced, irrelevant, outlandish, unfamiliar
11 incongruous, inconsonant,
unconnected 12 antipathetic,
inadmissible, inapplicable, incompatible, inconsistent
13 inappropriate
16 uncharacteristic

Foreign Correspondent
director: 15 Alfred Hitchcock
cast: 10 Joel McCrea, Laraine
Day 13 George Sanders
14 Robert Benchley 15 Al-
bert Basserman, Herbert
Marshall

foreigner 5 alien, pagan
6 emigre 8 newcomer, out-
sider, stranger 9 barbarian, immigrant, nonnative, outlander
German: 9 Auslander

foreign officer 6 consul 8 diplomat, minister 10 ambassador 14 representative
15 charge d'affaires

foreknowledge 9 intuition,
prevision 10 prescience
11 premonition 12 anticipation, apprehension, clairvoyance, precognition,
presentiment

foreman 4 boss 7 manager
8 chairman, overseer 9 president, spokesman 10 supervisor 11 coordinator
14 superintendent

foremost 4 head, main 5 chief,
vital 7 capital, leading, supreme 8 cardinal 9 essential,
paramount, principal
10 preeminent

forerunner 4 omen, sign 5 token 6 augury, herald 7 portent, presage 8 ancestor
9 harbinger, precursor, prototype 10 progenitor, prognostic 11 predecessor,
premonition

foresee 5 augur 6 divine, expect 7 predict, presage 8 envision, prophesy 10 anticipate
13 prognosticate

foreshadow 5 augur 7 presage,
promise 9 prefigure

foresight 6 wisdom 8 planning,
prudence, sagacity 9 prevision
10 discretion, precaution, prescience, providence, shrewdness 12 anticipation,

clairvoyance, perspicacity, precognition, preparedness **13** premeditation **14** farsightedness

forest 4 bush, wood **5** copse, grove, stand, woods **6** jungle **7** thicket **8** wildwood, woodland **10** timberland, wilderness

forestall 5 avert, avoid, block, deter **6** thwart **7** head off, obviate, prevent, ward off **8** preclude **10** anticipate, circumvent, counteract

Forester, C S (Cecil Scott) author of: **6** The Gun **14** A Ship of the Line **15** Payment Deferred, The African Queen **24** Captain Horatio Hornblower

forests god of: **3** Pan **7** Silenus, Virbius

foretell 5 augur **6** divine **7** portend, predict, presage **8** prophesy, soothsay **9** apprehend **13** prognosticate

forethought 4 heed **7** caution **8** prudence, sagacity, wariness **10** discretion, precaution, providence, shrewdness **11** carefulness **12** anticipation, deliberation **13** consideration, premeditation **14** circumspection, farsightedness

forever 6 always **9** eternally, undyingly **10** constantly **11** ceaselessly, continually, incessantly, perpetually, unceasingly **12** interminably **13** everlastingly, unremittingly Latin: **11** in perpetuum

forewarn 4 bode **5** alert **6** advise, notify, signal, tip off **7** caution, portend, presage, prewarn **8** cry havoc

foreword 7 preface, prelude **8** preamble, prologue **12** introduction

Forewords and Afterwords author: **7** W H Auden

for example Latin: **2** eg **13** exempli gratia

forfeit 4 fine, miss **5** waive, waste, yield **6** waiver **7** damages, default, let slip, penalty **8** squander **9** surrender **10** assessment

Forfeit author: **11** Dick Francis

forge 4 copy, form, make **5** clone, shape **6** devise, hearth, smithy **7** falsify, fashion, furnace, imitate, produce, turn out **8** contrive, simulate **9** fabricate, ironworks **11** counterfeit, manufacture

forgery 4 copy, fake, hoax, sham **5** clone, fraud **7** cloning **9** deception, imitation **11** counterfeit, fraudulence **13** falsification **14** counterfeiting **17** misrepresentation

forget 6 slight **7** neglect **8** overlook, pass over **9** disregard

forgetful 6 remiss **7** out of it **8** amnesiac, careless, heedless, mindless **9** negligent, oblivious, unmindful **10** neglectful **11** inattentive

forget-me-not 8 Myosotis varieties: **5** white **6** alpine, garden **7** Chinese **8** creeping

forgive 5 clear **6** acquit, excuse, pardon **7** absolve, condone, release, set free **8** overlook, reprieve **9** discharge, exculpate, exonerate

forgiveness 6 pardon **7** amnesty **9** remission **10** absolution

forgiving 6 benign, kindly **8** excusing **9** benignant, pardoning **11** kindhearted

forgo, forego 4 skip **5** waive, yield **6** eschew, give up **8** abnegate, renounce **9** sacrifice, surrender **10** relinquish

fork 4 bend, stab **5** angle, elbow, split **6** branch, crotch, divide, impale, pierce, ramify, skewer **7** diverge, trident **8** division **9** bifurcate, pitchfork **10** divergence, separation **11** bifurcation **12** intersection

forked 5 cleft **6** horned, zigzag **7** angular, divided, pronged **8** branched **9** ambiguous, deceitful, equivocal **10** bifurcated

For Kicks author: **11** Dick Francis

fork out 5 spend **6** expend **8** disburse, dispense

for lack of something better French: **12** faute de mieux

forlorn 4 lone **6** abject, bereft, dismal, dreary, lonely **7** unhappy **8** bereaved, dejected, deserted, desolate, forsaken, helpless, hopeless, lonesome, pathetic, pitiable, solitary, wretched **9** abandoned, depressed, desperate, destitute, forgotten, miserable, woebegone **10** despairing, despondent, dispirited, friendless **11** comfortless **12** disconsolate, inconsolable **13** brokenhearted

form *see box*

formal 4 cool, prim **5** aloof,

fancy, fixed, grand, legal, rigid, smart, stiff **6** dressy, lawful, proper, solemn, strict **7** distant, outward, pompous, prudish, regular, settled, stilted, stylish **8** decorous, definite, explicit, external, official, positive, reserved, starched **9** customary **10** ceremonial, inflexible, prescribed **11** ceremonious, highfalutin, perfunctory, punctilious, ritualistic, standoffish, straitlaced **12** conventional **13** authoritative **14** uncompromising

formal discussion 6 debate, parley **8** dialogue **10** conference

formality 4 rite **6** custom, motion, ritual **7** decorum, reserve **8** ceremony, coolness **9** etiquette, propriety, punctilio **10** ceremonial, convention **15** conventionality

Forman, Milos director of: **7** Amadeus (Oscar), Ragtime **25** One Flew

---

form 3 cut, hew, way **4** body, cast, kind, make, mode, mold, plan, rite, rule, sort, trim, type **5** being, brand, build, carve, class, forge, found, frame, genre, genus, guise, habit, image, model, order, phase, set up, shape, stamp, style, usage **6** aspect, chisel, create, custom, design, devise, fettle, figure, manner, matrix, person, ritual, sculpt, system **7** acquire, anatomy, compose, conduct, contour, decorum, develop, fashion, fitness, harmony, liturgy, manners, outline, pattern, produce, species, variety **8** ceremony, comprise, contract, likeness, physique, practice, presence, roughhew, symmetry **9** character, construct, establish, etiquette, fabricate, framework, propriety, sculpture, semblance, structure **10** appearance, constitute, deportment, figuration, proceeding, proportion, regularity **11** arrangement, description, incarnation, manufacture, orderliness, shapeliness **12** denomination **13** configuration, manifestation **15** conventionality

Over the Cuckoo's Nest (Oscar)

formation 3 set 6 makeup 7 genesis 8 building, creation 9 structure 10 generation, production 11 arrangement, composition, development, fabrication, manufacture 12 organization 13 configuration, constellation, establishment

formative 7 plastic, shaping 9 sensitive 10 accessible 11 susceptible 13 determinative 14 impressionable

former 2 ex 4 gone, past 5 olden, prior 6 bygone, gone by, lapsed, of yore, whilom 7 ancient, earlier, elapsed, old-time, quondam 8 anterior, previous 9 aforesaid, erstwhile, preceding 10 antecedent, first-named 14 aforementioned **French:** 8 ci-devant

formerly 4 once 5 of old 6 ere now, lately, of yore, whilom 7 long ago 8 hitherto 9 anciently 10 originally, previously

former student 6 alumna 7 alumnus, dropout 8 graduate

formidable 6 taxing 7 awesome, fearful, mammoth, onerous 8 alarming, dreadful, imposing, menacing, terrific 9 dangerous, demanding, difficult 10 forbidding, impressive, portentous, terrifying 11 threatening 12 overpowering, overwhelming

formless 5 vague 9 amorphous, shapeless

Formosa see 6 Taiwan

formula 4 cant, plan, rule 5 chant 6 cliche, recipe, saying, slogan 7 precept 9 blueprint, guideline, platitude, principle, rigmarole 10 pleasantry 11 incantation 12 prescription

formulate 5 draft, frame, state 6 define, devise, invent 7 compose, itemize, specify 11 systematize 13 particularize

Fornax
  origin: 5 Roman
  goddess of: 6 baking

fornication 8 adultery

for one's country
  Latin: 9 pro patria

Forrest, Nathan Bedford
  served in: 8 Civil War
  side: 11 Confederate
  known for: 12 cavalry raids

forsake 4 deny, drop, flee, quit 5 leave, spurn, waive,

yield 6 abjure, depart, desert, give up, reject, resign, vacate 7 abandon, cast off, disavow, discard, lay down 8 abdicate, disclaim, go back on, jettison, part with, renounce 9 repudiate, surrender 10 relinquish

forsaken 4 bare 5 empty 8 deserted, desolate, rejected 9 abandoned, discarded, neglected 11 uninhabited

Forsete see 7 Forseti

Forseti
  also: 7 Forsete
  origin: 12 Scandinavian
  god of: 7 justice
  father: 5 Baldr 6 Balder, Baldur
  mother: 5 Nanna
  dwelling place: 7 Glitnir

Forster, E M (Edward Morgan)
  author of: 7 Maurice 10 Howard's End 14 A Room with a View 15 A Passage to India 17 The Longest Journey 22 Where Angels Fear to Tread
  member of: 15 Bloomsbury Group

forswear, foreswear 4 deny 5 spurn 6 abjure, disown, eschew, give up, recant, reject, revoke 7 disavow, gainsay, retract 8 abdicate, disclaim, renounce, take back 9 disaffirm, repudiate 10 contravene

Forsyte Saga, The
  author: 14 John Galsworthy
  trilogy including: 5 To Let 10 In Chancery 16 The Man of Property
  character: 3 Jon 4 June 5 Fleur 6 Dartie 7 Annette 8 Winifred 9 Old Jolyon 11 Young Jolyon 12 Irene Forsyte 13 Soames Forsyte 14 Philip Bosinney

Forsythe, John
  real name: 17 John Lincoln Freund
  born: 12 Penn's Grove NJ
  roles: 7 Topaz 7 Dynasty, Madame X 11 In Cold Blood 14 Bachelor Father, Charlie's Angels 15 Blake Carrington 16 And Justice for All 19 The Trouble with Harry 23 Teahouse of the August Moon

fort 4 base, camp 6 castle 7 bastion, bulwark, citadel, station 8 fastness, garrison 10 stronghold

forte 4 bent 5 knack, skill 8 strength 9 specialty 11 proficiency
  music: 4 loud
  abbreviation: 1 f

forth 5 ahead 6 onward 7 outward

forthcoming 5 handy, on tap 6 at hand 7 helpful 8 imminent 9 available, impending 10 accessible, obtainable, openhanded 11 approaching, cooperative, prospective

for the greater glory of God
  Latin: 19 ad majorem Dei gloriam

for the public good
  Latin: 14 pro bono publico

for the time being
  Latin: 10 pro tempore

For the Time Being
  author: 7 W H Auden

for this purpose only
  Latin: 5 ad hoc

forthright 4 open 5 blunt, frank 6 candid, direct, openly 7 bluntly, frankly, up-front 8 candidly, directly, straight 9 outspoken 10 truthfully 11 outspokenly, plain-spoken 15 straightforward 17 straightforwardly

forthrightness 6 candor 7 honesty 8 openness 9 frankness, sincerity 19 straightforwardness

forthwith 6 at once, pronto 7 quickly 8 directly, in a jiffy, promptly, right off 9 instantly 11 immediately 12 straightaway

fortification 5 tower 7 bastion, bulwark, citadel, rampart 8 fortress, garrison 9 earthwork 10 breastwork, stronghold

fortify 4 lace 5 boost, brace, cheer 6 buoy up, enrich, harden, secure, shield, urge on 7 build up, bulwark, hearten, protect, shore up, stiffen, support, sustain 8 buttress, embolden, garrison, reassure 9 encourage, reinforce, stimulate 10 invigorate, strengthen

fortissimo
  music: 8 very loud
  abbreviation: 2 ff

fortitude 4 dash, grit, guts, sand 5 nerve, pluck, spunk, valor 6 daring, mettle, spirit 7 bravery, courage, heroism, prowess 8 backbone, boldness, firmness, tenacity 9 endurance, hardihood 10 resolution 11 intrepidity 12 fearlessness, resoluteness 13 dauntlessness, determination

Fortitude
  author: 11 Hugh Walpole

Fort-Lamy
capital of: **4** Chad

fortress 7 bastion, bulwark,
citadel, rampart **8** buttress
9 acropolis **10** stronghold

Fortress, The
author: **11** Hugh Walpole

fortuitous 5 happy, lucky,
stray **6** casual, chance, random **9** haphazard, hit-or-miss
10 accidental, incidental, undesigned, unexpected, unin-
tended, unpurposed
11 inadvertent **12** adventitious **13** serendipitous, unintentional **14** unpremeditated

fortuity 6 chance **8** accident
12 happenstance

Fortuna
origin: **5** Roman
goddess of: **7** fortune
corresponds to: **5** Tyche

fortunate 4 fair, rich, rosy
5 happy, lucky, palmy **6** benign, bright, timely **7** blessed,
booming, favored, halcyon,
well-off **8** well-to-do **9** favorable, opportune, promising
10 auspicious, convenient, felicitous, profitable, propitious,
prosperous, successful **11** encouraging, flourishing **12** advantageous, providential

Fortunate Isles *see* **13** Canary
Islands

Fortunato
character in: **20** The Cask of
Amontillado
author: **3** Poe

fortune, fortunes 3 lot
4 doom, fate, luck, mint, pile,
star **5** means **6** chance, estate,
income, kismet, riches,
wealth **7** bonanza, capital, destiny, godsend, portion, revenue **8** accident, fatality, gold
mine, good luck, lady luck,
opulence, property, treasure,
windfall **9** affluence, haphazard, substance **10** prosperity,
providence **12** circumstance
13 circumstances
goddess of: **5** Tyche
7 Fortuna

Fortunes of Nigel, The
author: **14** Sir Walter Scott

fortuneteller 4 seer **5** augur,
Gypsy, sibyl **6** medium, oracle **7** palmist, prophet **8** magician **10** soothsayer
11 chiromancer, clairvoyant
12 crystal gazer

for two
French: **5** a deux

**Forty Days of Musa Dagh,
The**
author: **11** Franz Werfel

42nd Parallel, The
author: **13** John Dos Passos

Forty-Second Street
director: **10** Lloyd Bacon
cast: **9** Guy Kibbee, Una
Merkel **10** Dick Powell,
Ruby Keeler **11** Bebe Daniels, George Brent **12** Ginger
Rogers, Warner Baxter
choreographer: **13** Busby
Berkeley
song: **15** Young and Healthy
17 Forty-second Street
19 Shuffle Off to Buffalo
28 You're Getting to Be a
Habit with Me

Forty Thieves, The
author: **7** unknown
character: **7** Ali Baba
code word: **10** Open Sesame

forty winks 3 nap **4** doze
6 catnap, snooze

forum 6 medium, outlet **7** rostrum, seminar **8** platform
9 symposium **10** colloquium

forward, forwards 3 out
4 back, bold **5** ahead, brash,
fresh, relay, sassy **6** assist, brazen, cheeky, hasten, onward,
pass on, send on, spread
7 advance, frontal, further, go-
ahead, promote, quicken, reroute **8** anterior, champion,
immodest, impudent, insolent,
up-to-date **9** advancing, barefaced, intrusive, offensive, presuming, readdress, shameless
10 accelerate, unmannerly
11 impertinent, progressive
12 enterprising, presumptuous
13 overconfident
French: **7** en avant

forwardness 4 gall **5** brass,
cheek **8** audacity, boldness
10 brazenness, effrontery
11 presumption **13** bumptiousness, obtrusiveness

for what use
Latin: **7** cui bono

For Whom the Bell Tolls
author: **15** Ernest Hemingway
director: **7** Sam Wood
character: **5** Maria, Pablo, Pilar **6** Andres, Rafael **7** An-
selmo, El Sordo **8** Augustin,
Fernando **12** Robert
Jordan
cast: **10** Gary Cooper
12 Akim Tamiroff **13** Ingrid
Bergman, Joseph Calleia,
Katina Paxinou **15** Arturo
de Cordova
score: **11** Victor Young
Oscar for: **17** supporting actress (Paxinou)

for whose benefit
Latin: **7** cui bono

For Your Eyes Only
author: **10** Ian Fleming

Fosse, Bob
director of: **5** Lenny **7** Cabaret (Oscar) **11** All That Jazz

fossil 4 fogy, rock **5** fogey, old-
ie, relic, stone **7** imprint, antique **9** remainder
13 petrification

foster 3 aid **4** back, feed, rear,
tend **5** favor, nurse, raise
6 foment, harbor, mother, rear
up, take in **7** advance, bring
up, care for, cherish, forward,
further, nourish, nurture, promote, protect, support, sustain **8** advocate, befriend, hold
dear, sanction, side with, treasure **9** encourage, patronize,
stimulate **11** accommodate,
countenance

Foster, Alicia Christian
real name of: **11** Jodie
Foster

Foster, Harold
creator/artist of: **6** Tarzan
13 Prince Valiant

Foster, Jodie
real name: **21** Alicia Christian Foster
born: **7** Bronx NY
roles: **9** Tom Sawyer **10** Taxi
Driver **11** Bugsy Malone

Foster, Stephen Collins
born: **15** Lawrenceville PA
composer of: **11** Swanee
River **13** Camptown Races
16 Beautiful Dreamer **17** My
Old Kentucky Home, The
Old Folks at Home
27 Jeanie with the Light
Brown Hair

**Foucault, Jean Bernard
Leon**
field: **7** physics
nationality: **6** French
proved: **19** Earth spins on its
axis
measured: **15** velocity of
light
named for him: **16** Foucault
currents

foul *see box*

foul-mouthed 4 lewd, rude,
vile **5** dirty, gross **6** coarse,
filthy, vulgar **7** abusive, obscene, profane **9** offensive
10 indelicate

foul play 5 crime **6** murder
8 violence **9** treachery

foul-smelling 4 rank **5** acrid,
fetid, musty **6** putrid, smelly
7 noisome, reeking **8** stinking
10 malodorous

foul up 3 mar **4** goof, muff,
ruin **5** botch, mix up, spoil
6 bungle, mess up, muddle
7 blunder, butcher, confuse,
louse up, screw up
9 mismanage

foul 3 wet **4** base, clog, evil, lewd, soil, vile **5** dirty, foggy, grimy, gross, gusty, misty, muddy, murky, nasty, rainy, sully, taint **6** choked, cloudy, coarse, defile, filthy, grubby, odious, putrid, risque, scurvy, smelly, smutty, soiled, sordid, stormy, tangle, turbid, vulgar, wicked **7** abusive, begrime, drizzly, ensnare, hateful, heinous, impeded, obscene, pollute, profane, smeared, squalid, squally, stained, sullied, tangled, unclean **8** begrimed, besmirch, blustery, ensnared, entangle, immodest, indecent, infamous, stinking, unseemly **9** atrocious, besmeared, entangled, insulting, loathsome, monstrous, nefarious, notorious, obnoxious, repulsive, revolting **10** abominable, bedraggled, detestable, disgusting, encumbered, flagitious, indelicate, malodorous, putrescent, scurrilous, villainous **11** blasphemous, disgraceful **12** contemptible

found 4 base, rear, rest **5** build, erect, raise, set up, start **6** create, ground, locate, settle **7** develop, sustain **8** colonize, organize **9** construct, establish, institute, originate

foundation 3 bed **4** base, foot, fund, rock, root **5** basis, cause **6** bottom, cellar, ground, motive, origin, reason, source **7** charity, premise, purpose, support **8** basement, creation, pedestal **9** endowment, rationale **10** assumption, groundwork, settlement **11** benefaction, institution **12** commencement, installation, philanthropy, substructure, underpinning **13** establishment, justification **14** infrastructure, understructure

foundational 3 key **4** base, core **5** basic, prime **7** primary **9** essential **10** elementary

foundation garment 6 corset, girdle **8** corselet

founder 4 fall, limp, reel, sink, trip **5** abort, drown, lurch, swamp **6** author, father, go down, go lame, hobble, per-

ish, plunge, sprawl, topple, tumble **7** break up, builder, capsize, creator, go under, planner, stagger, stumble, succumb **8** collapse, miscarry **9** architect, organizer, shipwreck **10** originator, strategist **12** disintegrate

foundered 4 sank **6** failed **7** beached, swamped **8** capsized, went down **9** collapsed

founding 5 birth **8** creation, settling **9** beginning **11** institution, origination **12** introduction, organization **13** establishment

found on 6 base on **7** model on **8** stem from **10** derive from **11** establish on

fountain 3 jet **4** flow, gush, well **5** birth, cause, spout **6** cradle, feeder, origin, reason, source, spring **7** genesis **8** purveyor, supplier **9** beginning, reservoir, upswelling **10** derivation, wellspring

fountainhead 4 font **6** origin, source, spring **9** beginning **10** wellspring

Fountainhead, The
  author: **7** Ayn Rand

fourgon 3 van **7** tumbril

Four Horsemen of the Apocalypse, The
  author: **19** Vicente Blasco Ibanez
  based on: **10** Revelation

400 Blows, The
  director: **16** Francois Truffaut
  cast: **10** Albert Remy
    13 Claire Maurier **14** Patrick Auffray **15** Jean-Pierre Leaud

Four Quartets
  author: **7** T S Eliot

Four-Season Recreation State
  nickname of: **7** Vermont

fowl 3 hen **4** cock, duck, game **5** banty, capon, chick, goose, quail **6** bantam, grouse, pigeon, turkey **7** chicken, cornish, leghorn, poultry **8** duckling

Fowles, John
  author of: **8** Mantissa, The Magus **10** The Aristos **12** Daniel Martin, The Collector **13** The Ebony Tower **25** The French Lieutenant's Woman

fox 9 scavenger
  young: **3** kit, pup
  group of: **5** leash, skulk

Fox (Mesquakie, Red Earth People)
  language family: **9** Algonkian **10** Algonquian
  location: **4** Iowa **9** Wisconsin
  allied with: **4** Sauk **8** Kickapoo

Fox, Fontaine
  creator/artist of: **16** Toonerville Folks **18** Toonerville Trolley

foxglove 9 digitalis
  varieties: **5** false, rusty **6** common, yellow **7** Grecian, Mexican **10** downy false **12** willow-leaved

foxiness 5 guile **7** cunning, slyness **8** artifice, trickery, wiliness **10** craftiness, shrewdness

fox-trot 5 dance **13** ballroom dance

Foxx, Jimmy (James Emory)
  nickname: **7** Double X
  sport: **8** baseball
  team: **12** Boston Red Sox **21** Philadelphia Athletics

Foxx, Redd
  real name: **16** John Elroy Sanford
  born: **9** St Louis MO
  roles: **13** Sanford and Son **19** Cotton Comes to Harlem

foxy 3 sly **4** wily **5** canny, sharp, slick **6** artful, astute, clever, crafty, shifty, shrewd, sneaky, tricky **7** cunning, devious, oblique **8** guileful, scheming, stealthy **9** conniving, deceitful, deceptive, designing, insidious, underhand **10** intriguing

foyer 4 hall **5** lobby **6** loggia **8** anteroom **9** vestibule **11** antechamber

fracas 3 row **4** fray, to-do **5** brawl, broil, clash, fight, melee, scrap **6** battle, ruckus, rumpus, strife, uproar **7** scuffle **9** imbroglio **10** donnybrook, free-for-all **11** altercation, embroilment

fraction 3 bit, few **4** chip **5** crumb, piece, ratio, scrap **6** morsel, trifle **7** cutting, portion, section, segment, shaving **8** fragment, particle, quotient **10** proportion **11** subdivision

fractious 5 cross, huffy **6** shirty, touchy, unruly **7** fretful, grouchy, peevish, pettish, waspish, wayward, willful **8** contrary, perverse, petulant, shrewish, snappish **9** irascible, irritable, querulous **10** rebellious, refractory

11 quarrelsome 12 disputatious, recalcitrant, unmanageable

fracture 4 rend, rift 5 break, crack, fault, sever, split 6 breach, cleave 7 disrupt, rupture, shatter 8 cleavage, division 9 severance 10 separation

Fra Diavolo, ou L'Hotellerie de Terracine
also: 31 Brother Devil or The Inn at Terracina
comic opera by: 5 Auber
character: 7 Lorenzo, Zerlina 11 Lady Allcash, Lord Allcash 17 Marquis di San Marco

fragile 4 soft, weak 5 crisp, frail 6 dainty, feeble, flimsy, infirm, sleazy, slight, tender

7 brittle, crumbly, friable, rickety, shivery 8 decrepit, delicate 9 breakable, ephemeral, frangible, splintery 10 evanescent, tumbledown 11 dilapidated 13 unsubstantial

fragility 7 frailty 8 delicacy, weakness 9 frailness 10 feebleness 11 brittleness 12 frangibility

fragment 3 bit 4 chip, snip 5 crumb, cut up, piece, scrap, shard, shred, trace 6 chop up, divide, morsel 7 break up, crumble, portion, remnant, section, segment, shatter, vestige 8 disunite, fraction, separate, splinter, survival 12 disintegrate

fragmentary 6 broken, choppy 7 scrappy 8 detached

9 piecemeal, scattered, segmented 10 disjointed, fractional, incomplete, unfinished 12 disconnected

Fragonard, Jean-Honore
born: 6 France, Grasse
artwork: 8 The Swing 10 Stolen Kiss, The Bathers, The Warrior 12 Le Billet Doux 14 Progress of Love 16 La Chemise Enlevee 18 Storming the Citadel 40 Coresus Sacrificing Himself to Save Callirhoe

fragrance 4 aura, balm 5 aroma, scent 7 bouquet, incense, perfume 9 redolence, sweetness

fragrant 5 balmy, spicy 7 odorous 8 aromatic, perfumed, redolent 11 odoriferous

---

France
other name: 4 Gaul
anthem: 14 La Marseillaise
capital/largest city: 5 Paris
others: 4 Nice 5 Brest, Lille, Lyons, Rouen, Vichy 6 Amiens, Calais, Cannes, Carnac, Cognac, Dieppe, Grasse, Nantes, Prades, Rheims 7 Antibes, Avignon, Bayonne, Dunkirk, Le Havre, Les Baux 8 Bordeaux, Boulogne, Chartres, Grenoble, Poitiers, Toulouse 9 Cherbourg, Roquefort 10 La Rochelle, Marseilles, Saint-Denis, Strasbourg 12 Saint-Nazaire 13 Aix-en-Provence, Fontainebleau
school: 8 Grenoble, Saint Cyr, Sorbonne 10 Montpelier
division: 5 Anjou, Bearn, Berry, Maine, Savoy 6 Alsace, Artois, Marche, Poitou 7 Gascony, Guienne, Picardy 8 Auvergne, Bordeaux, Brittany, Burgundy, Dauphine, Flanders, Lorraine, Lyonnais, Normandy, Provence, Touraine 9 Aquitaine, Champagne, Languedoc 11 Ile de France 12 Bourbonnaise, Franche-Comte
measure: 3 pot, sac 4 aune, mine, muid, pied, velt 5 arpen, carat, ligne, minot, pinte, point, pouce, velte 6 arpent, hemine, league, quarte, setier
monetary unit: 5 franc 7 centime
weight: 3 sol 4 gros, kilo, once 5 carat, livre, pound, tonne 6 gramme 7 tonneau 8 esterlin 9 esterling
island: 2 Re 3 Yeu 4 Cite 5 Groix, Hyere 6 Comoro, Oleron, Tahiti, Ushant 7 Corsica, Leeward, Reunion 8 Windward 10 Guadeloupe, Martinique 12 New Caledonia
lake: 6 Annecy, Cazaux, Geneva
mountain: 4 Jura 5 Pelat 6 Vosges 8 Ardennes, Pyrenees 10 French Alps 11 Pic Montcalm
highest point: 5 Blanc 9 Mont Blanc
river: 3 Lys 4 Yser 5 Aisne, Eiser, Isere, Loire, Meuse, Rhine, Rhone, Saone, Seine 7 Garonne, Gironde
sea: 5 North 8 Atlantic 13 Mediterranean
physical feature:
  bay: 6 Biscay 7 Arachon
  beach: 5 Omaha
  cape: 5 Hague, Talma
  channel: 7 English 8 La Manche
  gulf: 4 Lion
people: 6 Franks
  artist: 5 Corot, David, Degas, Manet, Monet 6 Braque, Ingres, Millet, Renoir, Seurat 7 Cezanne, Daumier, Gauguin, Matisse, Utrillo 8 Pissarro 9 Delacroix, Fragonard, Gericault
  author: 4 Gide, Hugo, Zola 5 Camus, Dumas 6 France, Proust, Racine, Sartre, Villon 7 Moliere 8 Rabelais, Rousseau, Voltaire 9 Corneille, Descartes, Giraudoux, Montaigne 10 Baudelaire
  composer: 5 Bizet, Ravel, Satie 6 Franck, Gounod 7 Berlioz, Debussy, Poulenc
  king: 5 Henri, Louis 6 Clovis, Philip 7 Charles 9 Hugh Capet 11 Charlemagne 13 Louis Philippe 14 Henry of Navarre
  leader: 6 Danton, Petain 7 Colbert, Mazarin 8 de Gaulle, D'Estaing, Pompidou 9 Joan of Arc, Richelieu 10 Mitterrand 11 Robespierre 17 Napoleon Bonaparte

Fragrant Harbor *see* 8 Hong Kong

frail 4 puny, weak 6 feeble, flimsy, infirm, sleazy, slight, weakly 7 brittle, crumbly, fragile, rickety, shivery 8 decrepit, delicate, fallible 9 breakable, frangible, splintery 10 perishable, vulnerable 11 dilapidated 13 unsubstantial

frailness 8 delicacy, weakness 9 fragility 11 unsoundness

frailty 3 sin 4 flaw, vice 5 fault 6 defect, foible 7 blemish, failing 11 fallibility 12 imperfection 14 susceptibility

Fra Lippo Lippi author: 14 Robert Browning

frame 3 rim, set 4 body, case, cast, form, make, mold, mood, plan 5 build, draft, hatch, humor, set up, shape, state 6 border, casing, design, devise, edging, figure, indite, invent, map out, nature, scheme, sketch, system, temper 7 anatomy, backing, chassis, concoct, contour, housing, outline, setting 8 attitude, conceive, contrive, mounting, organize, physique, skeleton 9 formulate, structure 11 disposition, scaffolding, systematize, temperament 12 constitution, construction

frame of mind 4 mood 7 climate 8 attitude 10 atmosphere 11 disposition

framer 6 author, shaper 7 creator, planner 10 formulator

framework 5 shell, truss 7 carcass 8 skeleton, template 9 structure 10 foundation 11 scaffolding 14 infrastructure

Framley Parsonage author: 15 Anthony Trollope

France *see box*

France, Anatole real name: 30 Jacques Anatole Francois Thibault author of: 5 Thais 12 Golden Verses 13 My Friend's Book, Penguin Island 17 The Gods Are Athirst 20 The Revolt of the Angels 25 Le Crime de Sylvestre Bonnard 27 At the Sign of the Reine Pedauque

franchise 5 grant, right 6 ballot 7 charter, freedom, license

---

queen: 7 Eugenie 9 Josephine 13 Marie de Medici 15 Marie Antoinette
language: 6 French
religion: 5 Islam 7 Judaism 8 Huguenot 10 Protestant 13 Roman Catholic
place:
  cathedral: 6 Rheims 8 Chartres 9 Madeleine, Notre Dame 10 Sacre-Coeur 14 Sainte-Chapelle 15 Mont-Saint-Michel
  chapel: 8 Ronchamp
  gardens: 9 Tuileries
  hall of mirrors: 16 Galerie des Glaces
  museum: 6 Louvre
  palace: 6 Elysee 10 Luxembourg, Versailles 12 Grand Trianon, Petit Trianon, 13 Fontainebleau
  prison: 8 Bastille
  racetrack: 6 Le Mans 7 Auteuil 10 Longchamps
  resort: 3 Pau 5 Vichy 6 Cannes, Menton 7 Antibes, Mentone, Riviera 8 Biarritz, Chamonix, Grenoble 9 Cote d'Azur 11 Aix-les-Bains
  section of Paris: 8 Left Bank 9 Right Bank 10 Montmartre, Rive Droite, Rive Gauche 12 Latin Quarter
  street: 13 Champs-Elysees 17 Place de la Concorde
  woods: 14 Bois de Boulogne 15 Bois de Vincennes
possession: 12 French Guiana
  island: 6 Futuna, Hoorne, Wallis 7 Reunion 8 Miquelon 10 Guadeloupe, Martinique 11 Saint Pierre 12 New Caledonia 15 French Polynesia
feature:
  airport: 4 Orly 9 Le Bourget 15 Charles de Gaulle
  bicycle race: 12 Tour de France
  dance: 5 gavot 6 branle, canary, cancan 7 boutade, gavotte
  fortification: 11 Maginot Line
  holiday: 11 Bastille Day
  monument: 13 Arc de Triomphe 14 Tomb of Napoleon
  national theater: 16 Comedie Francaise
  sightseeing boat: 12 bateau mouche
  tower: 6 Eiffel
food:
  cheese: 4 bleu, Brie 6 bonbel 7 boursin 8 Muenster 9 camembert, marcillat, port-salut, Roquefort 11 coulommiers
  dessert: 6 mousse
  dish: 4 pate 5 crepe 6 canape, quiche 7 souffle 8 escargot, piperade, pot au feu 9 cassoulet, tournedos 14 pate de foie gras
  drink: 6 cognac 8 bordeaux, burgundy 9 champagne
  french fries: 12 pommes frites
  pastry: 7 brioche 8 napoleon 9 croissant
  soup: 8 a l'oignon 13 bouillabaisse
  steak: 7 bifteck

8 immunity, suffrage **9** privilege **10** permission **11** prerogative **13** authorization

Franciosa, Anthony
real name: **14** Anthony Papales
born: **9** New York NY
wife: **14** Shelley Winters
roles: **12** The Naked Maja **13** A Hatful of Rain, Long Hot Summer, Name of the Game, Wild Is the Wind **15** Assault on a Queen

Francis, Dick
author of: **4** Bolt, Risk **5** Nerve, Proof **6** Banker, Reflex **7** Break In, Enquiry, Forfeit, Rat Race **8** Dead Cert, For Kicks, Slayride, Trial Run, Twice Shy, Whip Hand **9** Bonecrack, The Danger, Knockdown **10** Blood Sport, High Stakes, In the Frame **11** Smokescreen **12** Flying Finish

Franck, Cesar
born: **5** Liege **7** Belgium
composer of: **4** Ruth **5** Hulda **6** Psyche **7** Rebecca **8** Ghiselle **9** Les Djinns **10** Les Eolides, Redemption **13** La Tour de Babel, Les Beatitudes, The Beatitudes **16** Le Chasseur Maudit **17** The Accursed Hunter

Franglais 13 French-English **14** French-American

frank 4 bold, free, open **5** clear, plain, round **6** candid, direct, honest, patent **7** artless, evident, genuine, natural, sincere, up-front **8** apparent, distinct, explicit, manifest **9** downright, ingenuous, outspoken **10** aboveboard, forthright, unreserved **11** plainspoken, transparent, unambiguous, undisguised, unequivocal **12** unmistakable **15** straightforward

Frank, Anne
author of: **19** The Diary of Anne Frank

Frankenstein
author: **17** Mary Godwin Shelley
character: **7** Clerval, Justine, William **9** Elizabeth **10** The Monster **12** Robert Walton **18** Victor Frankenstein

Franklin, Benjamin
author of: **20** Poor Richard's Almanack
inventor of: **12** lightning rod **13** bifocal lenses, Franklin stove

frankness 6 candor **7** honesty **8** openness **9** bluntness, sincer-

ity **10** directness **11** artlessness **13** guilelessness **14** forthrightness **19** straightforwardness

frantic 3 mad **4** wild **5** crazy, rabid **6** hectic, insane, raging, raving **7** berserk, excited, furious, nervous, violent **8** agitated, deranged, frenetic, frenzied **9** delirious **10** distracted, distraught, infuriated **11** impassioned, overwrought **12** ungovernable

fraternal 6 hearty, loving, social **7** devoted, kindred, related **8** amicable, friendly **9** brotherly **11** warmhearted **12** affectionate **14** consanguineous

fraternity 4 clan, club **5** union **6** circle, clique, league **7** company, coterie, kinship, society **8** alliance **9** coalition **10** federation **11** association, brotherhood, confederacy, propinquity **13** brotherliness, consanguinity, interrelation

Fraternity
author: **14** John Galsworthy

fraternize 3 mix **5** unite **6** concur, hobnob, mingle **7** combine, consort **8** coalesce **9** associate, cooperate, harmonize, pal around, socialize **10** sympathize **11** confederate

Fratres Arvales *see* **5** Arval

frau 4 lady, wife **12** married woman

fraud 4 fake, hoax, hype, ruse, sham **5** cheat, craft, guile, knave, quack, rogue, trick **6** deceit, humbug, rascal **7** swindle **8** artifice, cheating, cozenage, impostor, swindler, trickery **9** charlatan, chicanery, con artist, deception, duplicity, imposture, pretender, stratagem, swindling, treachery **10** dishonesty, mountebank, subterfuge **11** counterfeit, fourflusher, machination **13** dissimulation

fraudulence 6 deceit **8** trickery **9** deception **13** deceitfulness, deceptiveness **17** misrepresentation

fraudulent 4 sham, wily **5** bogus, false **6** crafty, tricky **7** crooked, cunning, knavish **8** cheating, guileful, spurious **9** deceitful, deceptive, dishonest **11** counterfeit, treacherous, underhanded **12** dishonorable, unprincipled

fraught 4 full **5** heavy, laden **6** filled, loaded **7** charged, replete, teeming **8** attended,

pregnant **9** abounding **11** accompanied

fraulein 9 young lady **14** unmarried woman

Fraunhofer, Joseph von
field: **7** physics
nationality: **6** German
established: **12** spectroscopy

fray 3 rub **4** fret, fuss, riot, spat, tiff **5** brawl, chafe, fight, melee, ravel, set-to **6** battle, combat, fracas, rumble, rumpus, strain, tatter, tumult, tussle **7** contest, dispute, frazzle, quarrel, scuffle, warfare, wear out, wrangle **8** conflict, skirmish, squabble **9** bickering, commotion **10** contention, dissension, engagement **11** altercation, controversy **12** disagreement

Frazer, Sir James G
author of: **14** The Golden Bough

freak 3 fad, odd **4** kink, turn, whim **5** craze, fancy, humor, queer, quirk, sport, twist **6** marvel, oddity, vagary, whimsy, wonder **7** anomaly, bizarre, caprice, erratic, monster, strange, unusual **8** crotchet, mutation, peculiar **9** curiosity, deviation **10** aberration **11** abnormality, monstrosity **12** irregularity

freakish 3 odd **5** queer, weird **7** bizarre, strange, unusual **8** peculiar, singular, uncommon **9** eccentric, fantastic **10** outlandish **13** extraordinary

Frederick
character in: **11** As You Like It
author: **11** Shakespeare

Frederick I
nickname: **10** Barbarossa
position: **16** Holy Roman Emperor
dynasty: **12** Hohenstaufen
wife: **7** Beatrix
battle: **7** Legnano

Frederick II
position: **12** king of Sicily **13** king of Germany **16** Holy Roman Emperor
battle: **8** Bouvines

Frederick the Great
nickname: **8** Old Fritz
position: **13** King of Prussia
invaded: **7** Silesia
war: **13** Seven Years' War **18** Austrian Succession

free *see* **box**

free-and-easy 6 breezy, casual, jaunty **7** buoyant, relaxed **8** debonair, informal

free 3 big, lax **4** able, bold, easy, idle, idly, open, save **5** clear, extra, let go, loose, rid of, spare **6** daring, devoid, exempt, giving, gratis, lavish, parole, ransom, redeem, unbond, uncage, wanton **7** allowed, assured, forward, liberal, loosely, manumit, release, unchain, unleash **8** at no cost, careless, costless, devoid of, familiar, fearless, generous, handsome, immune to, informal, let loose, liberate, prodigal, released, unfasten **9** abandoned, audacious, available, boundless, bounteous, bountiful, confident, delivered, discharge, disengage, dissolute, expansive, extricate, footloose, lacking in, leisurely, liberated, permitted, unblocked, unbridled, unchained, unclogged, unimpeded, unmuzzled, unshackle **10** autonomous, bighearted, carelessly, chargeless, emancipate, gratuitous, licentious, manumitted, munificent, openhanded, unattached, unconfined, unfettered, unhampered, unoccupied, unreserved, unshackled **11** emancipated, enfranchise, independent, uncluttered, uncommitted, uninhibited, unrepressed **12** enfranchised, overfamiliar, uncontrolled, unencumbered, unobstructed, unrestrained **13** complimentary, unceremonious, unconstrained

12 lighthearted, presumptuous, unrestrained **13** unconstrained

freed 6 exempt, loosed, spared **7** cleared, excused **8** absolved, let loose, released, relieved **11** emancipated

freedom 4 play **5** range, scope, sweep, swing **6** candor, margin **7** abandon, license, release **8** autonomy, boldness, latitude, openness, rudeness **9** bluntness, frankness, impudence, indecorum **10** directness, disrespect, liberation **11** abandonment, forwardness, impropriety, informality, manumission, naturalness, sovereignty, unrestraint **12** emancipation, impertinence, unconstraint **13** downrightness **14** unreservedness **15** enfranchisement

Freedom of the Poet, The
 author: **12** John Berryman

free-flowing 7 copious, gushing, profuse **8** effusive

free-for-all 3 row **4** fray **5** brawl, fight, melee, scrap **6** affray, fracas, ruckus, tussle **7** rhubarb, ruction, wrangle **9** brannigan **10** donnybrook

free from bias 7 neutral **9** impartial, unbigoted **12** unprejudiced **13** disinterested

free from moisture 3 dry **4** arid, sere **5** parch **6** dry out **7** parched **8** dried out, rainless **9** dehydrate **10** dehydrated, desertlike, desiccated

free hand 12 carte blanche, open sanction **13** full authority

free rein 12 carte blanche, open sanction **13** full authority

free-spoken 6 chatty **7** voluble **9** talkative **10** loquacious, unreserved **13** communicative

Free State
 nickname of: **8** Maryland

Freestone State
 nickname of: **11** Connecticut

Free to Choose
 author: **14** Milton Friedman (with Rose Friedman)

Freetown
 capital of: **11** Sierra Leone

freeze 3 nip **4** bite, cool, halt, stop **5** chill, frost, sting **6** arrest, benumb, harden, pierce **7** ceiling, congeal, terrify **8** glaciate, solidify **11** anesthetize, refrigerate, restriction

freezing 3 icy **6** arctic, frigid **7** glacial

Frege, Gottlieb
 field: **11** mathematics
 nationality: **6** German
 founded: **13** symbolic logic

Freia see **5** Freya

freight 4 haul, lade, load, ship **5** cargo, carry, goods **6** burden, charge, convey, lading **7** baggage, cartage, luggage, portage **8** transmit, truckage **9** transport **10** conveyance **13** transshipment

Freischutz, Der
 also: **11** The Marksman
 opera by: **5** Weber
 character: **3** Max **6** Agathe, Caspar, Samiel

Freki
 origin: **12** Scandinavian
 form: **4** wolf
 owner: **4** Odin **5** Othin
 received: **4** food
 exception: **4** meat
 fellow wolf: **4** Geri

French, Daniel Chester
 born: **8** Exeter NH
 artwork: **7** (seated) Lincoln (at Lincoln Memorial) **21** The Minute Man of Concord

French-American
 French: **9** Franglais

French civil code 12 Code Napoleon

French Connection, The
 director: **15** William Friedkin
 cast: **11** Fernando Rey, Gene Hackman (Popeye Doyle), Roy Scheider
 Oscar for: **5** actor (Hackman) **7** editing, picture **8** director **10** screenplay
 sequel: **21** The French Connection II

French-English
 French: **9** Franglais

French Guinea see **6** Guinea

French Indonesia see **7** Vietnam

French is spoken here
 French: **18** ici on parle francais

French Lieutenant's Woman, The
 director: **10** Karel Reisz
 author: **10** John Fowles
 cast: **9** Leo McKern **11** Hilton McRae, Jeremy Irons, Meryl Streep
 script: **12** Harold Pinter

French national anthem 12 Marseillaise

French national theater 16 Comedie Francaise

French parliament
 formal sessions: **12** lit de justice

French Somaliland see **8** Djibouti

French Sudan, Soudan see **4** Mali

French Togoland see **4** Togo

frenzied 3 mad **4** wild **7** excited, frantic, furious **8** agitated, ecstatic **9** delirious

frenzy 3 fit **4** fury **5** craze, furor, mania, state **6** access **7** mad rush, madness, seizure, turmoil **8** delirium, hysteria, outburst **9** obsession, transport **11** distraction

Frenzy
director: **15** Alfred Hitchcock
cast: **8** Jon Finch **10** Anna
Massey **11** Barry Foster
16 Barbara Leigh-Hunt

frequency 9 iteration **10** recurrence, regularity, repetition **11** persistence, reiteration

frequent 5 daily, haunt, usual
6 common, wonted **7** regular
8 constant, everyday, familiar,
habitual, numerous, ordinary,
resort to **9** continual, customary, incessant, perpetual, recurrent **10** accustomed
11 reiterative

frequently 5 often **7** usually
8 ofttimes **9** generally **10** constantly, habitually, ordinarily,
repeatedly **11** continually, customarily, incessantly, perpetually, recurrently

frere 4 monk **5** friar **7** brother

Frescobaldi, Girolamo
born: **5** Italy **7** Ferrara
composer of: **13** Fiori Musi-
cali **14** Musical Flowers

fresh *see box*

freshen 4 wash **5** brace, calve,
clean, groom, renew **6** air out,

breeze, desalt, revive **7** cool
off, sweeten **8** renovate, spruce
up **9** deodorize

freshet 5 crest, flood
11 overflowing

Freshman, The
director: **9** Sam Taylor
12 Fred Newmeyer
cast: **11** Harold Lloyd **13** Jo-
byna Ralston **14** Brooks
Benedict

Fresnel, Augustin Jean
field: **7** physics
nationality: **6** French
worked in: **6** optics

fret 3 eat, rub, vex **4** fray,
fume, gall, gnaw, mope, pine,
pout, stew, sulk **5** brood,
chafe, erode, sulks, worry
6 abrade, lament, ruffle, tatter
7 agonize, corrode, fidgets
8 disquiet, distress, irritate,
vexation, wear away **9** annoyance, excoriate **10** irritation
11 displeasure, peevishness
12 discomposure

fretful 5 cross, huffy, sulky,
tense **6** cranky, shirty, touchy
7 grouchy, nervous, peevish,
pettish, waspish **8** contrary,
petulant, snappish **9** crotchety,
irritable, querulous **11** complaining **12** cantankerous

fretfulness 5 worry **6** unease
7 anxiety **10** crankiness
11 peevishness **12** irritability

Freud, Sigmund
lived in: **6** Vienna
collaborator: **6** Breuer
disciple: **4** Jung **5** Adler
daughter: **4** Anna
method: **15** free association
19 dream interpretation
coined: **2** id **8** superego
14 psychoanalysis
author of: **13** Totem and Taboo **22** Interpretation of
Dreams **37** Group Psychology and the Analysis of the
Ego, Jokes and Their Relation to the
Unconscious

Freund, John Lincoln
real name of: **12** John
Forsythe

Frey
also: **5** Freyr
origin: **12** Scandinavian
god of: **5** peace **8** marriage
10 prosperity
race: **5** Vanir
father: **5** Niord, Njord
home: **7** Alfheim

Freya
also: **5** Freia
origin: **8** Teutonic
goddess of: **4** love **6** beauty
9 fecundity
race: **5** Vanir

leader of: **9** Valkyries
father: **5** Niord, Njord

Fri *see* **5** Frigg

friable 7 crumbly **9** breakable,
frangible

friar
French: **5** frere

Friar Lawrence
character in: **14** Romeo and
Juliet
author: **11** Shakespeare

Friar Tuck
character in: **9** Robin Hood

friary 5 abbey **6** priory **8** cloister **9** hermitage, monastery

friction 6 strife **7** chafing, discord, grating, quarrel, rub-
bing **8** abrasion, bad blood,
conflict, fretting **9** animosity,
attrition, hostility **10** antagonism, contention, dissension,
dissidence, opposition, resentment, resistance **12** disagreement **13** counteraction

Friday
character in: **14** Robinson
Crusoe
author: **5** Defoe

Friday
from: **5** Freya, Frigg
heavenly body: **5** Venus
French: **8** vendredi
Italian: **7** venerdi
Spanish: **7** viernes
German: **7** freitag

Friedan, Betty
author of: **19** The Feminine
Mystique
co-founder of: **3** NOW
28 National Organization for
Women

Friedkin, William
director of: **11** The Exorcist
19 The French Connection
(Oscar)

Friedman, Milton
author of: **12** Free to Choose
(with Rose Friedman)
20 Capitalism and Freedom

Friedrich, Caspar David
born: **7** Germany
10 Greifswald
artwork: **22** The Cross on
the Mountains **26** Man and
Woman Gazing at the
Moon, The Ruined Monas-
tery of Eldena, Two Men
Contemplating the Moon

friend *see box*

friendliness 5 amity **8** bon-
homie, good will **9** geniality
10 affability, amiability, cordiality, fraternity **11** amicability, camaraderie, sociability
14 neighborliness
16 companionability

fresh 3 fit, hot, new
4 bold, cool, fair, keen,
late, pert, pure, rare, rosy,
rude **5** alert, brisk, chill,
clear, green, nervy, novel,
ready, ruddy, sassy, saucy,
stiff, sweet **6** active, biting,
brassy, brazen, bright,
cheeky, lively, modern, recent, rested, snotty,
unique, unused, unworn
7 bracing, cutting, forward,
glowing, just out, nipping,
strange, uncured, undried,
unfaded, untried, unusual
8 assuming, blooming,
brand-new, creative, flippant, gleaming, impudent,
insolent, original, stinging,
unabated, undimmed, un-
salted, unsmoked, unwilted,
up-to-date **9** energetic, inventive, obtrusive, re-
freshed, sparkling,
undecayed, unpickled, un-
spoiled, unwearied, wholesome **10** meddlesome, new-
fangled, refreshing,
unfamiliar, unimpaired,
unwithered **11** flourishing,
invigorated, modernistic,
smart-alecky, untarnished
12 presumptuous,
unaccustomed

friend 3 pal **4** ally, beau, chum, date, mate **5** amigo, buddy, crony, lover **6** backer, cohort, escort, fellow, intime, minion, patron **7** brother, comrade, consort, partner **8** adherent, advocate, confrere, co-worker, defender, favorite, follower, henchman, intimate, mistress, myrmidon, paramour, partisan, playmate, retainer, sidekick, soul mate **9** associate, bedfellow, colleague, companion, confidant, copartner, supporter **10** benefactor, encourager, playfellow, well-wisher **12** acquaintance
   French: **3** ami **4** amie **9** bonne amie
   Spanish: **5** amiga, amigo

friendly 4 kind **6** allied, ardent, benign, chummy, clubby, genial, kindly, loving, social **7** affable, amiable, cordial, devoted, helpful **8** amicable, familiar, generous, gracious, intimate, salutary **9** brotherly, convivial, favorable, fortunate, fraternal, opportune **10** accessible, auspicious, beneficial, hospitable, neighborly, not hostile, propitious **11** kindhearted, sympathetic, warmhearted **12** advantageous, affectionate **13** companionable

Friendly Fire
   author: **8** C D B Bryan

Friendly Islands see **5** Tongo

Friendly Persuasion
   director: **12** William Wyler
   author: **12** Jessamyn West
   cast: **10** Gary Cooper **11** Richard Eyer **12** Marjorie Main **14** Anthony Perkins, Dorothy McGuire
   score: **14** Dimitri Tiomkin

friendly understanding
   French: **15** entente cordiale

friend of the court
   Latin: **12** amicus curiae

friendship 5 amity **6** accord, comity **7** concord, harmony **8** close tie, goodwill, intimacy, sympathy **9** consonance, cordiality, fellowship, fraternity **11** brotherhood, comradeship, familiarity **12** amicableness **13** companionship, understanding **14** neighborliness **16** acquaintanceship

Friesen, Samille Diane
   real name of: **10** Dyan Cannon

Frigg
   also: **3** Fri **5** Frija **6** Frigga
   origin: **8** Teutonic
   goddess of: **3** sky **6** clouds **8** marriage
   husband: **4** Odin **5** Othin
   race: **4** Asar **5** Aesir

Frigga see **5** Frigg

fright 4 fear, funk **5** alarm, dread, panic, scare **6** dismay, horror, terror, tremor **7** anxiety, concern, flutter, quaking **8** cold feet **9** misgiving, quivering, the creeps **10** the jitters, the willies **11** disquietude, palpitation, trepidation **12** apprehension, intimidation, perturbation **13** consternation

frighten 5 alarm, daunt, scare, shock **6** affray, excite **7** agitate, horrify, petrify, startle, terrify **8** disquiet **9** terrorize **10** intimidate

frightened 6 afraid, scared **7** alarmed, panicky **9** horrified, petrified, terrified **10** terrorized

frightening 5 awful, dread **7** fearful **8** alarming, dreadful **10** horrifying, terrifying **11** hair-raising

frightful 4 awful, lurid, nasty **6** grisly, horrid **7** baleful, extreme, fearful, ghastly, hideous, macabre, ogreish **8** alarming, dreadful, fearsome, freakish, gruesome, horrible, horrific, shocking, sinister, terrible, terrific **9** appalling, loathsome, monstrous, offensive, repellent, repulsive, revolting **10** abominable, detestable, disgusting, horrendous **12** insufferable

frigid 3 icy, raw **4** cold, cool, prim **5** aloof, bleak, gelid, stiff **6** biting, bitter, chilly, formal, frosty **7** austere, cutting, distant, glacial, nipping **8** freezing, piercing **10** forbidding **11** straitlaced **12** unresponsive

frigidity 7 iciness **8** coldness **9** aloofness **10** frostiness **16** unresponsiveness

Frija see **5** Frigg

frill 3 air **6** edging, fringe, ruffle **7** flounce **8** falderal, frippery, furbelow, ornament **9** gathering, mannerism **10** decoration **11** affectation, superfluity **13** embellishment

fringe 3 hem, rim **4** edge, mane **5** limit, skirt **6** border, edging, margin, tassel **7** enclose, outline, selvage **8** deco-

rate, frontier, skirting, surround, trimming **9** embellish, periphery

frisk 3 hop **4** jump, lark, leap, romp, skip, trip **5** bound, caper, cut up, dance, sport **6** bounce, cavort, frolic, gambol, prance, search, spring **7** disport, examine, inspect, ransack **8** look over

frisky 4 spry **5** agile, peppy **6** active, lively, nimble **7** jocular, playful, waggish **8** animated, mirthful, prankish, spirited, sportive **9** vivacious **10** frolicsome, rollicking

fritter 4 blow **5** use up, waste **7** deplete **8** fool away, idle away, squander **9** dissipate

fritter away 4 blow **5** waste **6** misuse **8** misspend, squander **9** dissipate

fritter away time 4 idle **6** dawdle **10** dillydally

Fritzi Ritz
   also named: **5** Nancy
   creator: **15** Ernie Bushmiller **16** Larry Whittington
   character: **4** Phil **5** Nancy **6** Sluggo

frivolity 3 fun **4** jest, play **5** folly, sport **6** levity, whimsy **7** abandon **8** airiness, dallying, frippery **9** emptiness, flippancy, giddiness, lightness **10** fickleness, triviality, wantonness **11** flightiness **15** thoughtlessness

frivolous 4 airy, vain **5** barmy, dizzy, empty, inane, light, minor, petty, silly **6** flimsy, frothy, paltry, slight, stupid **7** fatuous, flighty, foolish, trivial, witless **8** careless, flippant, heedless, niggling, piddling, trifling **9** brainless, imprudent, pointless, senseless, unserious, worthless **10** insouciant **11** extravagant, harebrained, impractical, improvident, nonsensical, superficial, unimportant **13** insignificant, rattlebrained **14** shallowbrained

frizzle 4 curl **5** crimp

frock 4 coat, gown, robe, suit **5** cloak, dress, smock **6** blouse **7** cassock, soutane **8** chasuble, surplice, vestment **9** clericals **10** canonicals

frog 3 pad, pod **4** knot, wood **5** frosh, hitch, track **6** holder, peeper, toggle **7** crawler, croaker, cushion, leopard, tadpole **8** bullfrog, fastener, pickerel, pollywog **9** amphibian, plow frame **12** flower holder

Frogs, The
   author: **12** Aristophanes

character: 5 Pluto **6** Charon
7 Bacchus **8** Dionysus, Hercules, Xanthias **9** Aeschylus, Euripides

Froissart, Jean
author of: 8 Meliador
10 Chronicles

frolic 3 fun **4** lark, play, romp, skip **5** act up, antic, caper, frisk, mirth, prank, sport, spree **6** cavort, gaiety, gambol **7** disport, jollity, make hay **8** escapade **9** amusement, festivity, joviality, merriment **10** buffoonery, pleasantry, recreation, skylarking, tomfoolery **11** merrymaking **13** entertainment

frolicsome 5 antic, jolly, merry **6** cheery, jaunty, lively **7** playful **8** cheerful, mirthful, prankish **9** sprightly **12** lighthearted

Frollo, Claude
character in: 23 The Hunchback of Notre Dame
author: 4 Hugo

from 2 de, ex, of **3** for, fro **5** off of, out of **7** against **8** starting **9** beginning

from abroad 5 alien **6** exotic **7** foreign **8** imported

fromage 6 cheese

from behind
Latin: 6 a tergo

From Here to Eternity
director: 13 Fred Zinnemann
author: 10 James Jones
cast: 9 Donna Reed **11** Deborah Kerr **12** Frank Sinatra, George Reeves **13** Burt Lancaster **14** Ernest Borgnine **15** Montgomery Clift
setting: 11 Pearl Harbor
Oscar for: 7 picture **8** director **12** screenwriter **15** supporting actor (Sinatra) **17** supporting actress (Reed)

from inside
Latin: 7 ab intra

from outside
Latin: 7 ab extra

From Russia With Love
author: 10 Ian Fleming

from scratch 4 anew **14** from ground zero **16** from the beginning **20** from fresh ingredients

from side to side 4 over, sway **5** cross **7** athwart, swaying, zigzag **12** back and forth

from the beginning
Latin: 5 ab ovo **6** de novo **8** ab initio

from the chair
Latin: 10 ex cathedra

from the depths
Latin: 11 de profundis

from the face
Latin: 7 ex facie

from the fact
Latin: 7 de facto

from the founding of the city
Latin: 13 ab urbe condita

from the library of
Latin: 8 ex libris

from the seat of authority
Latin: 10 ex cathedra

front 3 air, top **4** face, fore, head, lead, mask, mien **5** first **6** facade, give on, regard **7** bearing, initial, look out **8** anterior, carriage, demeanor, presence, pretense, trenches, vanguard **9** beginning, semblance

Front, The
director: 10 Martin Ritt
cast: 10 Lloyd Gough, Woody Allen, Zero Mostel **13** Joshua Shelley, Michael Murphy **16** Herschel Bernardi

frontage 7 outlook **8** exposure, prospect

frontier 4 edge **5** march, verge **6** border, limits **7** extreme, marches **8** boundary, confines, outposts **9** backlands, backwoods, outskirts, perimeter **10** hinterland **11** territories

front matter 8 foreword **9** title page **12** introduction **15** table of contents **20** introductory material

Front Page, The
author: 8 Ben Hecht **16** Charles MacArthur
director: 11 Billy Wilder **14** Lewis Milestone
actor: 9 Mae Clarke, Mary Brian, Pat O'Brien **10** Jack Lemmon, David Wayne **12** George E Stone, Carol Burnett **13** Adolphe Menjou, Allen Garfield, Susan Sarandon, Walter Catlett, Walter Matthau **14** Charles Durning **15** Andrew Pendleton, Vincent Gardenia **19** Edward Everett Horton
character: 4 Earl **5** Burns, Grant, Hildy, Peggy **6** Walter **7** Hartman, Johnson **8** Williams

frost 4 rime **5** chill **7** iciness **8** coolness, distance **9** aloofness, cold spell, frigidity **10** chilliness, glaciality **13** inhospitality **14** unfriendliness

Frost, Robert
author of: 7 Birches **10** Fire

and Ice, Home Burial **11** Mending Wall **13** Brown's Descent **15** The Road Not Taken **17** After Apple-Picking **21** The Death of the Hired Man **30** Stopping by Woods on a Snowy Evening

frostiness 3 nip **4** bite **5** chill **7** iciness **8** coldness, coolness **9** crispness, frigidity, hoariness, sharpness **10** chilliness, wintriness

frosting 3 mat **4** trim **5** glass, icing **7** cooling, topping **8** chilling, divinity, freezing, trimming **13** embellishment, ornamentation

frosty 3 icy **4** cold, cool **5** bleak, chill, hoary **6** frigid, wintry **8** freezing

froth 4 bosh, fizz, foam, fume, head, scum, suds, surf **5** spume, trash, yeast **6** lather, trivia **7** bubbles, rubbish **8** flummery, frippery, nonsense, trumpery, whitecap **9** frivolity **10** balderdash, triviality **12** fiddle-faddle

frothy 5 fizzy, foamy, light **6** bubbly **7** trivial **9** frivolous **15** inconsequential

froward 5 balky **6** unruly **7** wayward, willful **8** contrary, perverse, stubborn **9** difficult, fractious, obstinate **10** headstrong, refractory **11** disagreeing, intractable **12** recalcitrant **13** contradictory **15** unaccommodating

frown 4 fret, mope, muse, pout, sulk **5** glare, scowl **6** glower, ponder **14** discountenance

frowning 4 dark **5** angry **6** gloomy, somber, sullen **8** scowling **9** glowering

frown upon 7 condemn, dislike **8** object to **14** discountenance

frowsy, frowzy 5 fusty, musty, stale **6** sloppy, untidy **7** tousled, unkempt **8** slovenly

frozen 3 icy **4** cold, iced, numb **5** chill, gelid, polar **6** arctic, chilly, cooled, wintry **7** chilled, clogged, glacial, stymied **8** benumbed, hibernal, icebound **10** obstructed, stalemated **11** frostbitten, immobilized **12** refrigerated

fructify 5 bloom **6** sprout, thrive **7** blossom, prosper, succeed **8** flourish

frugal 4 slim **5** scant, tight **6** skimpy, stingy **7** ascetic, sparing, thrifty **9** niggardly, penny-wise **10** abstemious, economical, unwasteful **12** parsimonious

frugality 6 thrift **7** economy **8** prudence, stinting **9** parsimony **10** scantiness, stinginess **11** thriftiness **12** cheeseparing **13** niggardliness, penny-pinching **16** parsimoniousness

fruit 4 crop **5** award, issue, yield, young **6** effect, profit, result, return, reward, upshot **7** benefit, harvest, outcome, produce, product, progeny, revenue **8** earnings **9** advantage, emolument, offspring, outgrowth **10** production **11** consequence **12** remuneration

fruitful 6 fecund **7** fertile **8** blooming, prolific, yielding **9** effective **10** productive, profitable, successful **11** efficacious **12** advantageous, fructiferous

fruition 8 maturity, ripeness **10** attainment **11** achievement, fulfillment, realization **12** consummation, satisfaction **13** actualization, gratification **15** materialization

fruitless 4 arid, vain **5** empty, inept **6** barren, futile, hollow **7** sterile, useless **8** abortive, bootless, nugatory **9** infertile, pointless, worthless **10** profitless, unavailing, unprolific **11** incompetent, ineffective, ineffectual, inoperative, purposeless, unrewarding **12** unproductive, unprofitable, unsuccessful **13** inefficacious

fruit trees
goddess of: 6 Pomona

frumpy 4 drab **5** dowdy **8** slovenly **10** slatternly **12** unattractive

frustrate 3 bar **4** balk, foil **5** block, check, upset **6** baffle, cancel, defeat, hinder, impede, thwart **7** counter, cripple, fluster, inhibit, nullify, prevent **8** dispirit, obstruct, prohibit, suppress **9** forestall, hamstring, undermine **10** circumvent, disappoint, disconcert, discourage, dishearten

frustration 6 defeat **7** balking, chagrin, failure, foiling, letdown **8** futility **9** hindrance, thwarting **10** bafflement, inhibition, nonsuccess **11** obstruction **12** discomfiture, interference **13** contravention, counteraction **14** disappointment, nonfulfillment **15** dissatisfaction

fry 4 cook **5** brown, grill, saute **7** frizzle **9** fricassee

Fry, Christopher
author of: 9 Yard of Sun **12** The Firstborn **13** Venus Observed **20** The Dark Is Light Enough **21** The Lady's Not for Burning

frying pan 3 wok **6** frypan **7** browner, griddle, skillet

fuchsia
varieties: 4 cape, tree **5** hardy **10** California **11** honeysuckle

fuddled 5 bosky, dopey, drunk, tipsy **6** boozed, groggy **7** maudlin, muddled, sozzled, tippled **8** confused **9** stupefied **10** inebriated **11** intoxicated

fudge 3 lie **4** bosh, fake **5** candy, cheat, evade, hedge, hunch, patch, welch **7** falsify, penuche **8** divinity

fuel 3 fan, gas, oil **4** coal, feed, fire, wood **5** light, means, stoke **6** charge, fill up, fodder, ignite, incite, kindle **7** impetus, inflame, sustain **8** activate, energize, gasoline, material, recharge, stimulus **9** petroleum, stimulate **10** ammunition, motivation, sustenance **11** inspiration, wherewithal

fugitive 4 hobo **5** brief, exile, hasty, nomad, rover, short, tramp **6** errant, fading, flying, loafer, outlaw **7** cursory, elusive, erratic, escaped, escapee, fleeing, hurried, passing, refugee, runaway, summary, vagrant **8** apostate, deserter, escaping, fleeting, flitting, renegade, shifting, unstable, vagabond, volatile, wanderer **9** ephemeral, fugacious, itinerant, momentary, straggler, temporary, transient, uncertain **10** evanescent, expatriate, short-lived, transitory **11** impermanent

Fugitive, The
character: 9 Donna Taft **11** Fred Johnson (one-armed man) **12** (Lt) Philip Gerard **13** (Dr) Richard Kimble
cast: 10 Barry Morse, Bill Raisch **12** David Janssen **15** Jacqueline Scott

fuhrer, Fuhrer, der fuhrer 4 Nazi **6** Hitler, leader, tyrant **8** dictator **11** Adolf Hitler

fulfill 2 do **4** heed, keep, meet, obey, suit **6** answer, effect, follow, redeem **7** achieve, execute, observe, perfect, perform, realize, satisfy **9** discharge, establish, implement **10** accomplish, consummate, effectuate

fulfillment, fulfilment 7 delight **8** crowning, pinnacle, pleasure **9** execution, happiness **10** attainment, completion **11** achievement, contentment, culmination, realization **12** effectuation, satisfaction **13** contentedness, establishment, gratification **14** accomplishment, implementation

Fulks, Sarah Jane
real name of: 9 Jane Wyman

full 3 big **4** rich, very, wide **5** ample, broad, flush, laden, large, plump, quite, round, sated, total, whole **6** entire, gorged, intact, loaded, mature, packed, rotund **7** brimful, crammed, exactly, fraught, glutted, heaping, maximum, perfect, plenary, replete, shapely, stuffed, teeming **8** brimming, bursting, complete, resonant, swarming, thorough **9** abounding, capacious, perfectly, precisely, saturated, surfeited **10** unabridged, voluminous

full amount 3 all, sum **5** total, whole **8** entirety, totality **9** aggregate **10** complement

full-bodied 3 fat **4** rich **5** ample, lofty **6** hearty, mature, robust **9** flavorful **10** meaningful

Fuller, R Buckminster
architect of: 10 US Pavilion (Expo '67 Montreal) **13** Dymaxion House
form: 12 geodesic dome

full-fledged 5 adept **6** expert, mature **7** skilled, trained **8** complete, masterly, schooled **9** qualified, topflight **10** proficient **11** experienced **13** authoritative

full form 9 extension **10** elongation **11** enlargement **12** augmentation **13** amplification

full-grown 4 ripe **5** adult, manly, of age, matured, womanly **9** developed

full measure 6 enough, plenty **9** abundance, plenitude **10** competence **11** sufficiency

Full Moon
author: 11 P G Wodehouse

fullness 7 satiety **8** richness **9** amplitude, roundness, satiation **12** completeness **14** voluminousness

full of fire 7 rousing **8** electric, exciting, spirited **9** thrilling **11** galvanizing, stimulating **12** electrifying, soul-stirring

full of life 5 vital 8 animated, spirited, vigorous 9 ebullient, energetic, exuberant, vivacious

full of pep 5 vital 6 lively 8 animated

full of vim and vigor 5 peppy 6 lively 11 invigorated

full view 7 the open 8 daylight, openness

fully 5 amply, quite 6 richly, wholly 7 totally, utterly 8 entirely 9 copiously, perfectly 10 abundantly, altogether, completely, positively, throughout 11 plentifully 12 sufficiently 13 substantially

fully realized 7 perfect 8 achieved, complete, executed, finished 9 completed, perfected, performed 11 consummated 12 accomplished

fulminate 4 boil, rage, rant 7 explode 8 denounce

fulminate against 5 roast 6 berate 7 scourge 8 call down, chastise 9 castigate

fulmination 7 violent 8 bursting, eruption 9 discharge, explosion

fulsome 3 fat 4 foul 5 suave 6 lavish, odious 7 cloying, lustful, noisome, obscene 8 overdone, unctuous 9 excessive, obnoxious, offensive, repulsive, tasteless 10 disgusting, obsequious

Fulton, Robert
nationality: 8 American
inventor of: 9 steamboat (Clermont), submarine 13 marine torpedo

fumble 3 err, mar 4 blow, muff 5 grope, spoil 6 bobble, boggle, bollix, bungle, goof up, mess up, muddle 7 butcher, louse up, screw up 9 mishandle

fume 3 gas 4 boil, burn, emit, foam, haze, puff, rage, rant, rave, reek, waft 5 exude, scent, smell, smoke, stink, vapor 6 billow, exhale, miasma, seethe, stench 7 carry on, explode, flame up, flare up, smolder 10 exhalation

fun 3 gas 4 ball, game, jest, lark, play, romp, trip 5 antic, blast, cheer, mirth, prank, sport, spree 6 frolic, gaiety, joking 7 jollity, revelry, whoopee 8 escapade, good time, pleasure 9 amusement, diversion, enjoyment, horseplay, joviality, merriment 10 buffoonery, recreation, relaxation, skylarking, tomfool-

ery 11 distraction, playfulness, waggishness 13 entertainment

Funafuti
capital of: 6 Tuvalu

function 3 act, job 4 duty, fete, gala, help, role, task, work 5 feast, field, niche, party, place, power, range, scope, serve 6 affair, behave, do duty, office, soiree, sphere 7 banquet, benefit, concern, faculty, operate, perform, purpose 8 activity, business, capacity, ceremony, occasion, province 9 festivity, objective, operation, reception 13 entertainment

functional 6 useful 7 working 8 operable 9 operative, practical 11 serviceable, utilitarian

functionary 8 employee, official 10 bureaucrat 13 administrator

functioning 5 in use 6 active, at work, usable 7 working 9 effectual, operating, operative

fund 3 pot 4 bank, foot, lode, mine, pool, vein, well 5 endow, float, fount, hoard, kitty, stock, store 6 pay for, spring, supply 7 finance, nest egg, reserve, savings, support 8 treasure 9 endowment, patronize, reservoir 10 foundation, investment, repository, storehouse, underwrite 12 accumulation

fundament 3 can 4 buns, rump, seat 5 fanny 6 behind, bottom 8 backside, buttocks, haunches 9 posterior 12 hindquarters

fundamental 3 key 4 ABC's, base, main 5 axiom, basic, basis, chief, first, major, vital 7 central, crucial, element, primary 8 cardinal, integral 9 component, essential, necessary, principal, principle, requisite 10 elementary, foundation, groundwork, underlying 11 cornerstone 13 indispensable

funds 4 cash, jack, pelf 5 bread, dough, lucre, means, money, moola 6 assets, income, wampum, wealth 7 capital, scratch 8 finances, property 9 resources 11 wherewithal

funeral 4 wake 5 rites 6 burial 7 requiem 9 cremation, interment, obsequies 10 entombment, inhumation

funeral song 5 dirge, elegy

6 lament 7 requiem 8 threnody 11 lamentation

funereal 3 sad 4 grim 5 weepy 6 dismal, dreary, gloomy, solemn, somber, woeful 7 doleful 8 desolate, dirgeful, grieving, mournful 9 cheerless, woebegone 10 depressing, lachrymose, lugubrious 13 brokenhearted

fun-filled 5 happy 6 joyful, joyous 8 pleasant, pleasing 9 enjoyable 10 delightful 11 pleasurable

Fungoso
character in: 22 Every Man Out of His Humour
author: 6 Jonson

fungus, fungi 4 mold, myco, rust, smut 5 ergot, yeast 6 mildew 7 truffle 8 mushroom 9 toadstool 11 thallophyte

fun-loving 5 jolly, merry 6 genial, jovial 7 affable 8 sociable 9 convivial 10 gregarious

funnel 4 cone, duct, flue, pipe, pour 5 focus, shaft 6 direct, filter, siphon 7 channel, chimney, conduit 9 stovepipe 10 smokestack, ventilator 11 concentrate

funny 3 odd 5 antic, comic, droll, merry, queer, weird, witty 6 absurd, jocose 7 amusing, bizarre, comical, curious, jesting, jocular, offbeat, strange, unusual, waggish 8 farcical, humorous, mirthful, peculiar, sporting, uncommon 9 diverting, facetious, hilarious, laughable, ludicrous 10 outlandish, ridiculous

Funny Girl
director: 12 William Wyler
cast: 8 Lee Allen 10 Kay Medford, Omar Sharif 11 Anne Francis 13 Walter Pidgeon 15 Barbra Streisand (Fanny Brice)
score: 9 Jule Styne 10 Bob Merrill
sequel: 9 Funny Lady
song: 6 People 18 Don't Rain on My Parade

funnyman 3 wag, wit 4 card, fool, mime, zany 5 clown, comic, joker 6 jester, madcap 7 buffoon 8 comedian, humorist, jokester 9 harlequin

fuoco, con
music: 8 with fire

fur 3 fox 4 down, hair, lamb, mink, pelt, seal 5 coney, lapin, otter, sable 6 beaver, fleece, jaguar, kit fox, nutria, rabbit, red fox 7 blue fox, cheetah, leopard, muskrat, o-possum, raccoon **8** black fox, cross fox, squirrel, white fox **9** silver fox **10** animal skin, chinchilla **11** karakul lamb, Persian lamb **13** broadtail lamb **14** mouton-dyed lamb

furbelow 5 frill **6** fringe **7** falbala, flounce **8** trimming

furbish 4 buff **5** renew, shine **6** polish **7** burnish **8** renovate

Furiae see **6** Furies

Furies
also: **5** Dirae **6** Erinys, Furiae, Semnai **7** Allecto, Erinyes, Megaera **9** Eumenides, Tisiphone
corresponds to: **3** Ker

furious 3 mad **4** wild **5** angry, fiery, irate, rabid **6** enrage, fierce, fuming, raging, savage, stormy **7** intense, rampant, violent **8** frenetic, frenzied, heedless, maddened, provoked, reckless, up in arms, vehement, wrathful **9** fanatical, irascible, turbulent **10** infuriated, passionate, tumultuous, unbalanced **11** tempestuous **12** ungovernable, unrestrained

furl 4 coil, curl, fold, roll, wrap **5** truss **6** curl up, fold up, furdle, roll up, spiral

furlong
abbreviation: **3** fur

furnace 4 kiln, oven **5** forge, stove **6** boiler, heater **11** incinerator

Furnace
constellation of: **6** Fornax

furnish 3 arm, rig **4** gird, give, vest **5** array, dress, endow, equip, favor, fit up, grant, stock **6** fit out, outfit, purvey, render, supply **7** appoint, indulge, prepare, provide **8** accoutre, bestow on **9** provision **11** accommodate

furnishings 9 equipment **11** accessories **12** haberdashery

furnish room for 5 lodge, put up **6** billet **7** shelter **11** accommodate

furniture 7 effects **8** chattels, movables, property **11** possessions **12** appointments

furor 3 fad **4** flap, rage, to-do, word **5** craze, mania, noise, thing, vogue **6** fervor, frenzy, hoopla, lunacy, raving, uproar **7** fashion, madness, passion **8** brouhaha, insanity, reaction **9** agitation, commotion, obsession, transport **10** dernier cri, enthusiasm, excitement, fanaticism

furrow 3 cut, dig, rut **4** knit, line, plow, rift, seam **5** cleft, crack, ditch, ridge, track **6** crease, groove, pucker, trench, trough **7** channel, crevice, fissure, wrinkle **10** depression **11** corrugation

furry 4 soft **5** downy, hairy, scary **6** cuddly, fleecy, pelted, shaggy **8** fearsome, horrible **11** hair-raising

further 3 aid, new, too, yet **4** also, back, help, more **5** again, extra, favor, fresh, other, spare, speed **6** abroad, assist, back up, beyond, foster, hasten, oblige, to boot, yonder **7** advance, afar off, besides, farther, forward, promote, quicken, stand by, work for **8** champion, expedite, likewise, moreover **9** accessory, ancillary, auxiliary, encourage, propagate **10** accelerate, additional, strengthen **11** accommodate **12** additionally, contributory, supplemental **13** supplementary

furtherance 3 aid **4** help, lift **5** favor **6** succor **7** advance, defense, support **8** advocacy, interest **9** patronage, promotion **10** assistance **11** advancement, cooperation, countenance **12** championship

furthering 3 aid **6** aiding, growth **8** abetting, advocacy, espousal **9** assisting, fostering, promoting, promotion **10** assistance, supporting **11** advancement, encouraging, propagating, propagation **12** accelerating, acceleration, encouragement **13** strengthening

furthermore 3 too **4** also **6** as well, to boot **7** besides **8** likewise, moreover **10** in addition **12** additionally

furthermost 7 extreme **8** farthest **11** farthermost

furtive 3 sly **4** wily **5** shady **6** covert, crafty, hidden, masked, secret, shifty, sneaky, unseen, veiled **7** cloaked, elusive, evasive, private **8** secluded, shrouded, skulking, sneaking, stealthy **9** collusive, secretive, underhand **10** mysterious, undercover, unrevealed **11** clandestine **12** confidential **13** surreptitious **14** conspiratorial

fury 3 fit, hag, ire, pet **4** gall, huff, rage, snit **5** force, might, shrew, vixen, wrath **6** attack, choler, frenzy, spleen, virago

7 assault, bluster, dudgeon, hellcat, tantrum **8** acerbity, acrimony, ferocity, outburst, severity, she-devil, spitfire, violence **9** intensity, termagant, vehemence, virulence **10** excitement, fierceness, turbulence **11** impetuosity

Fury
form: **8** divinity
sex: **6** female
mother: **4** Gaea
father: **6** Uranus
born of the blood of:
  6 Uranus
Greek name: **6** Erinys
  7 Erinyes **9** Eumenides
Roman name: **5** Dirae
  6 Furiae

fuse 4 join, link, meld, melt, weld, wick **5** blend, merge, smelt, torch **6** league, mingle, solder **7** combine **8** coalesce, federate, ignition, solidify **9** associate, detonator **10** amalgamate, assimilate **11** confederate, consolidate, incorporate, intermingler

fusillade 4 hail, rain **5** salvo, spray **6** volley **7** barrage, battery **8** drumfire, enfilade **9** broadside, cannonade **11** bombardment

fusion 5 blend, union **6** league **7** combine, melding, melting, merging **8** alliance, blending, compound, smelting **9** coalition, synthesis **10** commixture, dissolving, federation **11** association, coalescence, combination, commingling, confederacy, unification **12** amalgamation, intermixture, liquefaction **13** agglomeration, confederation

fuss 3 ado, nag **4** carp, fool, fret, fume, pomp, spat, stew, stir, tiff, to-do **5** annoy, cavil, labor, set-to, worry **6** bother, bustle, excite, fidget, flurry, hubbub, hustle, niggle, pester, pother, potter, putter, rattle, scurry, tinker **7** agitate, confuse, dispute, fluster, flutter, nitpick, quarrel, quibble, perturb, trouble, turmoil **8** ceremony **9** agitation, commotion, confusion **10** disconcert, hurlyburly, turbulence **11** disturbance, superfluity **12** perturbation **15** ceremoniousness
Yiddish: **7** tzimmes

fuss over 6 dote on

fussy 4 busy 6 ornate 7 finical, finicky, nervous 8 bustling, critical, exacting 9 assiduous, cluttered, crotchety, demanding, squeamish 10 compulsive, fastidious, meticulous, nitpicking, old-maidish, particular, scrupulous 11 painstaking, persnickety

fusty 5 moldy, musty, stale 6 foisty, rancid, stuffy 8 obsolete 9 out of date 10 malodorous 12 old fashioned

Futabatei, Shimei
author of: 16 The Drifting (Floating) Cloud

futile 4 idle, vain 5 empty, petty 7 trivial, useless 8 abortive, bootless, nugatory, trifling 9 frivolous, fruitless, valueless, worthless 10 profitless, unavailing 11 ineffective, ineffectual, unimportant 12 unprofitable, unsuccessful 13 insignificant

future 4 hope 5 after, later 6 coming, latter, morrow, offing, to come 7 by-and-by, ensuing, outlook 8 eventual, prospect, tomorrow, ultimate 9 following, hereafter, impending, projected 10 in prospect, subsequent, succeeding 11 anticipated, expectation, opportunity, prospective 12 anticipation
Spanish: 6 manana

Future Shock
author: 12 Alvin Toffler

fuzz 4 down, lint 5 fluff

fuzzy 3 dim 4 hazy 5 downy, foggy, linty, misty, murky, vague, wooly 6 fluffy, frizzy, woolly 7 blurred, obscure, shadowy, unclear 8 confused 9 pubescent 10 indefinite, indistinct

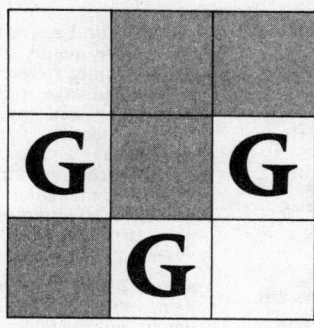

gab 3 jaw, rap 4 blab, chat
5 prate 6 babble, gibber, gossip, jabber, patter 7 baloney, blarney, blather, chatter, prattle 8 chitchat, idle talk, talk idly 10 balderdash
12 conversation

gabble 3 rap 4 blab 5 prate
6 babble, drivel, gossip, jabber 7 blather, chatter, prattle twaddle 8 babbling, chitchat, idle talk 9 gibbering, jabbering 10 blathering, chattering
14 chitterchatter

gabfest 3 rap 4 chat, talk
7 palaver 8 chitchat 10 discussion 12 conversation
13 confabulation

gable 4 edge, peak, roof, wall
6 detail, dormer, pinion 7 aileron 8 pediment, triangle

Gable, Clark
real name: 17 William Clark Gable
wife: 13 Carole Lombard
nickname: 7 The King
born: 7 Cadiz OH
roles: 7 Red Dust 8 Saratoga
10 The Misfits 11 Rhett Butler 15 Gone With the Wind 18 It Happened One Night (Oscar)

Gabo, Naum
real name: 17 Naum Neemia Pevsner
born: 6 Russia 7 Brainsk
founder: 14 Constructivism
artwork: 6 Column 11 Spiral Theme 16 Sculptural Models 19 Kinetic Construction 24 Variations of Spheric Theme

Gabon Republic *see box*

Gabor, Eva
mother: 5 Jolie
sister: 5 Magda 6 Zsa Zsa
born: 7 Hungary 8 Budapest
roles: 4 Gigi 10 Green Acres
12 My Man Godfrey 13 A Royal Scandal, Forced Land-

ing 15 Youngblood Hawke
18 The Truth About Women 20 The Last Time I Saw Paris

Gabor, Sari
real name of: 11 Zsa Zsa Gabor

Gabon Republic
capital/largest city:
10 Libreville
others: 4 Oyem 5 Bongo, Kango 6 Mitzic, Moanda, Mouila, Omvane 7 Makokou, Mounana 9 Lambarene 10 Port-Gentil 11 Franceville
monetary unit: 5 franc
7 centime
lake: 7 Anengue, Azinguo
mountain: 5 Mpele 7 Chaillu, Cristal, Mikongo 8 Balaquri, Birougou
highest point: 8 Iboundji
river: 4 Como 6 Abanga, Ivindo, Ogooue 7 Ngounie
sea: 8 Atlantic
physical feature:
cape: 5 Lopez
people: 4 Fang 6 Adouma, Bakota, Bateke, Echira, Okande, Omyene 7 Eshiras 8 Bandjabi, Bapounou
leader: 3 Mba 5 Bongo
philanthropist: 16 Albert Schweitzer
language: 6 French
religion: 5 Islam 7 animism 10 Protestant 13 Roman Catholic
feature:
tree: 6 okoume
food: 6 manioc 9 Dika bread

Gabor, Zsa Zsa
real name: 9 Sari Gabor
mother: 5 Jolie
sister: 3 Eva 5 Magda
husband: 10 Nick Hilton 13 George Sanders
born: 7 Hungary 8 Budapest
roles: 4 Lili 11 Moulin Rouge 14 Lovely To Look At 20 The Story of Three Loves

Gaboriau, Emile
author of: 9 File No 113

Gaborone, Gaberones
capital of: 8 Botswana

Gabriel 9 archangel
means: 8 man of God 11 God is strong
spoke to: 4 Mary 9 Zacharias, Zechariah

Gad
father: 5 Jacob
mother: 6 Zilpah
brother: 3 Dan 4 Levi 5 Asher, Judah 6 Joseph, Reuben, Simeon 7 Zebulun 8 Benjamin, Issachar, Naphtali
sister: 5 Dinah
descendant of: 6 Gadite

gadget 4 tool 6 device, doodad, jigger 7 gimmick, novelty 9 accessory, doohickey 10 attachment 11 contraption, contrivance, thingamabob, thingamajig

Gaea
also: 2 Ge 4 Gaia
origin: 5 Greek
goddess of: 5 earth
husband: 6 Uranus
children: 6 Pontus, Titans, Uranus 7 Cyclops, Erinyes 9 mountains 13 Hecatonchires
son: 6 Nereus 7 Iapetus, Oceanus
daughter: 4 Rhea 5 Theia 6 Phoebe, Tethys, Themis 9 Mnemosyne
corresponds to: 6 Tellus

Gaelic
  language family: 12 Indo-
    European
  branch: 6 Celtic
  subgroup: 4 Manx **5** Irish
    8 Scottish

gaffe 4 goof **5** boner **6** boo-
  boo **7** blunder **11** impropriety
  12 indiscretion
  French: 7 faux pas
    9 gaucherie

gag 4 hoax, hush, jest, joke,
  stop **5** block, choke, heave,
  retch **6** muffle, muzzle, stifle
  7 cloture, foolery, silence,
  smother **8** stoppage, suppress
  9 horseplay, restraint
  13 facetiousness

Gaia *see* **4** Gaea

gaiety, gayety 3 fun **4** show
  5 mirth **6** frolic, tinsel **7** elation, glitter, jollity, spirits
  8 airiness, frippery, trumpery,
  vivacity **9** amusement, animation, brummagem, gaudiness,
  merriment, showiness
  10 brightness, brilliance, garishness, jauntiness, joyousness,
  liveliness **11** celebration, merrymaking **12** cheerfulness, col-
  orfulness, exhilaration,
  sportiveness **13** effervescence,
  sprightliness

gain, gains 3 add, bag, get,
  hit, net, win **4** jump, leap,
  plus, reap **5** bloom, bonus,
  fetch, glean, put on, reach,
  wages, yield **6** attain, come to,
  gather, income, obtain, pick
  up, profit, return, salary, secure, thrive **7** achieve, acquire,
  blossom, capture, collect, improve, procure, produce, prosper, recover, revenue
  8 addition, arrive at, black
  ink, dividend, earnings, flourish, increase, overtake, proceeds, winnings **9** accretion,
  advantage, increment **10** attainment **11** improvement
  12 accumulation, compensation, remuneration

Gaines, Ernest J
  author of: 33 The Autobiog-
    raphy of Miss Jane Pittman

gainful 4 rich **6** paying **9** lucrative **10** productive, profitable
  12 remunerative

gainfully 8 usefully **10** profita-
  bly **11** lucratively **12** produc-
  tively **14** remuneratively

gain recognition 9 establish

gainsay 4 deny **6** abjure, oppose, refute **7** disavow, dispute **9** repudiate **10** contradict,
  controvert

Gainsborough, Thomas
  born: 7 England, Sudbury

artwork: 10 The Blue Boy
  14 The Morning Walk
  15 Mr and Mrs Andrews,
  The Hon Mrs Graham
  16 Viscount Ligonier
  26 Peasant Girl Gathering
  Sticks

gait 4 pace, step, walk **5** tread
  6 stride **7** bearing **8** carriage
  10 deportment *strut*
  French: 8 demarche

gaiter 4 boot, shoe, spat,
  vamp **5** chaps, strad **6** gaskin,
  hugger, puttee **7** legging
  8 cuttikin, overshoe

gala 3 gay **5** grand, party
  7 benefit, festive, opulent
  8 festival, majestic, splendid
  9 festivity, glamorous, sumptuous **10** ceremonial, fancy-
  dress, glittering **11** celebration,
  celebratory, magnificent, spectacular, star-studded
  French: 4 fete

Galahad
  character in: 16 Arthurian
    romance

Galatea
  form: 6 maiden, statue **8** sea
    nymph
  father: 6 Nereus
  mother: 5 Doris
  courted by: 10 Polyphemus
  lover: 4 Acis
  killed: 4 Acis
  statue carved by:
    9 Pygmalion
  brought to life by:
    9 Aphrodite
  son: 6 Paphos

gale 3 fit **4** blow, gust, stir
  6 flurry, squall, tumult, uproar **7** cyclone, tempest
  8 eruption, outbreak, outburst
  9 agitation, commotion,
  windstorm

Galeus
  form: 6 lizard
  father: 6 Apollo

Galileo Galilei
  nationality: 7 Italian
  inventor of: 6 sector
    11 thermometer
  studied: 6 motion
    8 pendulum
  discovered: 18 Jupiter's
    satellites
  constructed: 9 telescope
  formulated: 18 law of falling
    bodies
  author of: 8 Dialogue **10** Dis-
    courses **18** The Starry
    Messenger

Galinthias
  handmaiden of: 7 Alcmene

gall 3 bug, irk, vex **4** bile, flay,
  fret, miff, rile **5** anger, annoy,
  brass, chafe, cheek, gripe,
  nerve, score, sting, venom

6 abrade, bruise, enrage, harass, injure, nettle, offend,
  rancor, ruffle, spleen **7** affront,
  incense, provoke, rub sore
  8 acrimony, audacity, boldness,
  irritate, rudeness, temerity
  9 animosity, assurance, displease, excoriate, impudence,
  insolence, malignity, sauciness,
  virulence **10** bitterness, brazenness, effrontery, exacerbate,
  exasperate **11** presumption

gallant 3 fop **4** bold, dude,
  game, stud **5** blood, brave,
  dandy, gutsy, noble, suave,
  swell **6** daring, heroic, kindly,
  plucky, polite, urbane
  7 courtly, dashing, valiant
  8 cavalier, fearless, gay blade,
  intrepid, mannerly, obliging,
  resolute, stalwart, valorous,
  well-bred **9** attentive, courteous, dauntless **10** chivalrous,
  courageous, thoughtful
  11 considerate, gentlemanly,
  lionhearted **12** stouthearted

gallantries 10 attentions
  11 compliments **12** pleasantries

gallantry 4 grit, sand **5** nerve,
  pluck, valor **6** daring, mettle,
  spirit **7** bravery, courage, dashing, heroism, prowess, suavity **8** chivalry, courtesy,
  urbanity **9** derring-do, fortitude, gentility **10** politeness
  11 courtliness, intrepidity
  12 fearlessness, resoluteness
  13 attentiveness, dauntlessness,
  determination
  14 courageousness

gallery 4 stoa **5** salon **6** arcade,
  loggia, piazza **7** balcony, passage, portico **8** cloister, corridor **9** bleachers, colonnade,
  mezzanine, triforium **10** ambulatory, grandstand,
  passageway

Gallia Belgica *see* **7** Belgium

galliano
  type: 7 liqueur
  origin: 5 Italy
  flavor: 5 herbs, spice
  color: 6 yellow
  with creme de cacao:
    14 Golden Cadillac
  with rum: 9 Bossa Nova
  with vodka: 16 Harvey
    Wallbanger

gallinule 3 hen **4** coot, fowl,
  rail, sora **7** moorhen **8** dabchick, hyacinth, rallidae, rice-
  bird, swamphen

Gallipoli
  director: 9 Peter Weir
  cast: 7 Mark Lee **8** Bill Kerr
    9 Mel Gibson **11** Robert
    Grubb

gallivant, galavant 3 gad
  4 kite, roam, rove **5** jaunt,

range, stray 6 ramble, travel, wander 7 gallant, meander, traipse, 8 gad about 9 philander

gallon
abbreviation: 3 gal

gallop 3 fly, hie, jog, run 4 bolt, dart, dash, flit, race, rush, scud, skim, trot, whiz 5 bound, hurry, scoot, shoot, speed, whisk 6 hasten, scurry, spring, sprint 7 mad dash, scamper, scuttle, tear off 8 fast clip, fast gait 9 skedaddle

Galloping Ghost
nickname of: 9 Red Grange

gallows 4 rope 5 noose 6 gibbet, halter 8 scaffold

galore 7 aplenty, to spare

galosh, galoche 4 boot, clog, shoe 6 arctic, patten, rubber 8 overshoe

Galsworthy, John
author of: 5 To Let 6 Strife 7 Justice 9 Loyalties 10 In Chancery 11 The Skin Game 13 A Modern Comedy 14 The Forsyte Saga 15 End of the Chapter 16 The Man of Property 22 Indian Summer of a Forsyte

Galt, John
character in: 13 Atlas Shrugged
author: 4 Rand

galvanize 4 fire, move, stir, wake 5 rally, rouse, treat 6 arouse, awaken, charge, excite, foment, spur on, thrill 7 inspire, provoke, quicken 8 activate, energize, vitalize 9 electrify, stimulate

galvanizing 7 rousing 8 electric, exciting, spirited 9 inspiring, thrilling 11 stimulating 12 electrifying, soul-stirring

Galveston Giant
nickname of: 11 Jack Johnson

Gamaliel
father: 6 Simeon 8 Pedahzur grandfather: 6 Hillel taught: 4 Paul

Gambia, The see box

gambit 4 ploy, ruse 5 feint, trick 6 scheme 8 artifice, maneuver 9 stratagem

gamble 3 bet 4 back, risk 5 flyer, wager 6 chance, hazard, toss-up 7 trust in, venture 9 speculate 11 speculation, uncertainty

gambler 5 dicer, shark, sharp, sport 6 banker, bettor, bookie, dealer, player 7 hustler

8 gamester, hazarder 10 speculator

Gambler, The
author: 16 Fyodor Dostoevsky character: 6 Astley, Polina 10 The General 11 Mlle Blanche 15 Marquis de Grieux 16 Alexey Ivanovitch 22 Antonida Tarasyevitchev

gambol 3 hop 4 leap 5 bound, caper, frisk, sport, vault 6 bounce, cavort, frolic, prance, spring 7 disport, rollick

game see box, p. 382

gamete 3 egg 4 ovum 5 sperm 6 oocyte, zygote 8 germ cell, oosphere 12 spermatozoan, spermatozoon

Gamow, George
field: 7 physics 9 cosmology proponent of: 13 big bang theory deciphered: 11 genetic code proposed: 13 quantum theory established: 17 Gamow-Teller theory

Gamp, Sarah
character in: 16 Martin Chuzzlewit author: 7 Dickens

gamut 3 ken 5 reach, scope, sweep 6 extent 7 compass, purview *RANGE*

Gandhi
director: 19 Richard Attenborough

Gambia, The
capital/largest city: 6 Banjul 8 Bathurst
others: 5 Bakau, Basse, Mansa 7 Bintang, Brikama, Kuntaur 10 Georgetown
monetary unit: 5 butut, pound 6 dalasi
island: 7 Ft James, St Mary's 8 Elephant
river: 3 Bao 6 Gambia 7 Bintang, Nianija 9 Sandougou
sea: 8 Atlantic
people: 4 Fula, Jola 5 Foula, Wolof 6 Fulani 8 Mandingo, Serahuli 9 Seranuleh
language: 4 Fula 5 Wolof 6 Fulani 7 English, Malinke 8 Mandingo
religion: 5 Islam 10 Protestant 13 Roman Catholic

---

cast: 11 Ben Kingsley 13 Candice Bergen Oscar for: 5 actor (Kingsley) 7 picture

gang 3 mob 4 band, body, crew, pack, pals, ring, team 5 chums, crowd, flock, group, party, relay, shift, squad, troop 6 clique, outfit 7 buddies, company, coterie, cronies, friends, phalanx 8 comrades 9 coworkers, neighbors 10 associates, classmates, companions, contingent, detachment 11 schoolmates

gangster 4 goon, hood, thug 5 crook, felon, tough 6 bandit, gunman 7 hoodlum, mafioso, mobster, ruffian 8 criminal, hooligan 9 racketeer

Gant, Eugene
character in: 17 Look Homeward Angel, Of Time and the River
author: 5 Wolfe

Ganymede
also: 9 Catamitus cupbearer of: 4 gods

gap 3 cut 4 gash, hole, rent, rift, slit, slot, void 5 abyss, break, chasm, chink, cleft, crack, gulch, gully, notch, pause 6 breach, canyon, cavity, divide, hiatus, lacuna, ravine, recess, vacuum, valley 7 crevice, fissure, interim, opening 8 aperture, crevasse, fracture, interval, puncture 9 disparity, interlude 10 difference, divergence 12 intermission, interruption

gape 4 gasp, gawk, gaze, ogle, part, peer, yawn 5 split, stare 6 cleave, expand 7 fly open 8 wide open, separate 10 rubberneck

gaping 6 astare 7 gawking, staring, yawning 13 rubbernecking

Garamas see 11 Amphithemis

garb 3 rig 4 gear, gown, robe, suit, togs 5 dress, getup, habit 6 attire, finery, livery, outfit 7 apparel, clothes, costume, raiment, uniform, vesture 8 clothing, garments, vestment, wardrobe 9 trappings 11 habiliments

garbage 4 dirt, junk 5 offal, swill, trash, waste 6 debris, litter, refuse 7 carrion, rubbish 9 sweepings

garble 5 mix up 6 jumble 7 confuse, distort 8 fragment

Garbo, Greta
real name: 21 Greta Louisa Gustaffson

game 3 bad, fun **4** golf, halt, lame, lark, play, polo, pool, prey, romp **5** antic, brave, cocky, darts, gimpy, jacks, match, rugby, sport, spree **6** boccie, boxing, daring, frolic, gaiety, gambol, heroic, plucky, quarry, soccer, spunky, squash, tennis **7** archery, bowling, contest, crooked, croquet, curling, fencing, frisbee, gallant, hawking, hunting, hurling, jai alai, limping, pastime, tourney, valiant, willing **8** baseball, crippled, deformed, disabled, fearless, football, handball, hobbling, intrepid, lacrosse, ping pong, resolute, skittles, spirited, valorous, wild fowl **9** amusement, badminton, billiards, dauntless, diversion, festivity, merriment, wrestling **10** basketball, courageous, determined, horseshoes, ice-skating, lawn tennis, recreation, tournament, volleyball **11** competition, distraction, merrymaking, racquetball, table tennis, unflinching **12** shuffleboard **13** entertainment, incapacitated, roller-skating
  board game: 4 Clue, Life, ludo **5** chess **7** Othello **8** checkers, cribbage, dominoes, draughts, fanorona, Monopoly, Scrabble **10** backgammon **14** Trivial Pursuit
    Chinese: **6** Ma-jong, wei-ch'i **7** mahjong **8** Mah-jongg
    Egyptian: **5** Senat
    Indian: **7** pachisi **8** parchesi, shatranj **9** ashtapada, parcheesi **10** shaturanga
    Japanese: **2** Go **3** I-go **5** Sho-gi
    Korean: **5** Nyout, Pa-tok
    Swedish: **6** tablut
  card game: 3 loo, war **4** brag, fish, skat, vint **5** ombre, poker, rummy, tarot, whist **6** boston, bridge, casino, chemmy, ecarte, euchre, go fish, hearts, memory, piquet, pocher **7** bezique, canasta, cooncan, old maid, plafond, primero **8** baccarat, conquian, cribbage, gin rummy, napoleon, patience, pinochle, slapjack **9** blackjack, pelmanism, solitaire, spoil five, twenty-one **11** chemin de fer, crazy eights **13** concentration **14** contract bridge **16** beggar-my-neighbor, trente et quarante

born: 6 Sweden **9** Stockholm
roles: 4 Love **7** Camille **8** Conquest, Mata Hari **9** Ninotchka **10** Grand Hotel **12** Anna Christie, Anna Karenina **13** Queen Cristina, Two-Faced Woman **14** The Painted Veil **16** Flesh and the Devil

Garcia Lorca, Federico
  author of: 5 Yerma **12** Blood Wedding, Gypsy Ballads **19** House of Bernarda Alba

Garcia Marquez, Gabriel
  author of: 9 Leaf Storm **23** The Autumn of the Patriarch **25** One Hundred Years of Solitude

garcon 3 boy **6** waiter **7** servant

garden 4 Eden, lawn, plot, yard **7** Arcadia **8** paradise **10** Gethsemane
  type: 4 herb, rock, rose **5** truck **6** flower, formal **7** kitchen **9** botanical, vegetable

gardenia
  varieties: 5 crape **9** butterfly

Garden of Cypress, The
  author: 15 Sir Thomas Browne

Garden of the Finzi-Continis, The
  director: 14 Vittorio De Sica
  author: 11 Rumer Godden
  cast: 10 Fabio Testi **11** Romolo Valli **12** Helmut Berger **14** Dominique Sanda **15** Lino Capolicchio
  Oscar: 11 foreign film

Garden of the West
  nickname of: 6 Kansas

garden party
  French: 13 fete champetre

gardens
  god of: 9 Vertumnus
  goddess of: 5 Venus

Garden State
  nickname of: 9 New Jersey

garden variety 5 plain **6** common, simple **7** regular **8** everyday, familiar, ordinary **11** commonplace

Gardner, Ava
  husband: 9 Artie Shaw **12** Frank Sinatra, Mickey Rooney
  born: 12 Smithfield NC

  roles: 7 Mogambo **8** Show Boat **9** Mayerling, Naked Maja **10** On the Beach **15** The Sun Also Rises **18** Snows of Kilimanjaro **19** The Barefoot Contessa, The Night of the Iguana

Gardner, Erle Stanley
  character: 9 Paul Drake **10** Perry Mason **11** Della Street **14** Hamilton Burger
  also wrote as: 6 A A Fair

Gardner, John
  author of: 7 Grendel **12** October Light **14** Nickel Mountain, The Art of Living, The King's Indian **17** Michelson's Ghosts **20** The Sunlight Dialogues, The Wreckage of Agathon

Gareth
  character in: 16 Arthurian romance

Garfield, James Abram *see box*

Garfield, John
  real name: 15 Julius Garfinkle
  born: 9 New York NY
  roles: 6 Juarez **10** Humoresque **11** Body and Soul **26** The Postman Always Rings Twice

Garfinkle, Julius
  real name of: 12 John Garfield

Gargamelle
  character in: 22 Gargantua and Pantagruel
  author: 8 Rabelais

Gargantua and Pantagruel
  author: 16 Francois Rabelais
  character: 7 Panurge **10** Gargamelle, Grangosier, Picrochole **23** Frere Jean des Entommeures

gargantuan 4 huge, vast **5** great **7** hulking, immense, mammoth, massive, titanic **8** colossal, enormous, gigantic, lubberly, towering **9** herculean, monstrous, overgrown **10** prodigious, stupendous, tremendous **11** elephantine **13** amplitudinous

Gargaphia
  death place of: 7 Actaeon

Gargery, Joe
  character in: 17 Great Expectations
  author: 7 Dickens

garish 4 loud **5** cheap, gaudy, showy **6** brassy, bright, flashy, tawdry, tinsel, vulgar **7** blatant, glaring **9** flaunting, obtrusive **11** pretentious **12** ostentatious **13** overelaborate

Garfield, James Abram
presidential rank: **9** twentieth
party: **10** Republican
state represented: **2** OH
defeated: **3** (Neal) Dow **6** (James Baird) Weaver, (John Wolcott) Phelps **7** (Winfield Scott) Hancock
vice president: **6** (Chester Alan) Arthur
cabinet:
  state: **6** (James Gillespie) Blaine
  treasury: **6** (William) Windom
  war: **7** (Robert Todd) Lincoln
  attorney general: **8** (Isaac Wayne) MacVeagh
  navy: **4** (William Henry) Hunt
  postmaster general: **5** (Thomas Lemuel) James
  interior: **8** (Samuel Jordan) Kirkwood
born: **2** OH **6** Orange **8** log cabin
died: **9** Elberon NJ
  died by: **13** assassination
buried: **11** Cleveland OH
education:
  seminary: **6** Geauga
  college: **5** Hiram (Eclectic Institute) **8** Williams
  studied: **3** law
religion: **17** Disciples of Christ
political career: **8** US Senate (declined seat) **11** state Senate **24** US House of Representatives
civilian career: **6** lawyer **7** teacher **11** lay preacher
military service: **6** US Army **8** Civil War **12** major general
notable events of lifetime/term:
  exposure of: **15** Star Route frauds
father: **7** Abraham
mother: **5** Eliza (Ballou)
siblings: **4** Mary **5** James **6** Thomas **9** Mehitabel
wife: **8** Lucretia (Rudolph)
  nickname: **5** Crete
children: **4** Mary **5** Abram, Eliza **6** Edward **12** James Rudolph **13** Harry Augustus, Irvin McDowell

garland 3 bay, lei **4** halo **5** crown **6** corona, diadem, fillet, laurel, wreath **7** chaplet, circlet, coronet, festoon **8** chapbook, headband, treasury **9** anthology **10** collection **11** florilegium

Garland, Hamlin
author of: **18** Main-Travelled Roads **20** Rose of Dutcher's Coolly

Garland, Judy
real name: **11** Frances Gumm
husband: **7** Sid Luft **16** Vincente Minnelli
daughter: **9** Lorna Luft **12** Liza Minnelli
costar: **12** Mickey Rooney
born: **13** Grand Rapids MN
roles: **7** Dorothy **11** A Star Is Born, Babes in Arms **12** Easter Parade **13** The Wizard of Oz **14** The Harvey Girls **15** A Child Is Waiting, Meet Me in St Louis

garlic
botanical name: **13** Allium sativum

origin: 4 Asia **13** Mediterranean
charm against: **7** poverty, witches **13** whooping cough
use: **4** fish, fowl, meat **5** salad **10** vegetables **13** Italian dishes, salad dressing
varieties: **4** crow, hog's, wild **5** bear's, false, field, giant, grace, mouse, stag's, sweet **6** levant **7** serpent, society, Spanish, striped **8** daffodil, oriental **11** greatheaded, round-headed **16** fragrant-flowered

Garm
origin: **12** Scandinavian
form: **8** watchdog
watches over: **3** Hel
location: **8** Niflheim

garment, garments 4 garb, gear, togs **5** dress, habit **6** attire, outfit **7** apparel, clothes, costume, raiment **8** clothing, vestment **10** habiliment

garner 4 reap **5** amass, hoard **6** gather, heap up **7** acquire,

collect **8** assemble **10** accumulate

Garner, James
real name: **15** James Baumgarner
born: **8** Norman OK
roles: **8** Maverick, Sayonara **11** Jim Rockford **12** Bret Maverick, Hour of the Gun **13** Darby's Rangers, Rockford Files **14** Murphy's Romance, Victor Victoria **23** Support Your Local Sheriff **25** The Americanization of Emily

garnet
varieties: **6** syrope **9** almandite, demantoid, hessonite, rhodolite **12** grossularite
month: **7** January

Garnett, David
author of: **11** Lady into Fox

garnish 4 deck, gild, trim **5** adorn, array **6** bedeck, doll up, set off **7** festoon, furbish, smarten **8** beautify, decorate, emblazon, ornament, spruce up, trimming **9** adornment, embellish, embroider **10** decoration **13** embellishment

garret 4 loft **5** attic

garrison 4 fort **5** guard **6** patrol, secure **7** battery, bivouac, brigade, platoon, station **8** division, regiment, squadron **10** detachment, escadrille **13** fortification

garrulity 8 verbiage **9** loquacity, prosiness, verbosity, wordiness **13** talkativeness

garrulous 5 gabby, windy, wordy **6** chatty **7** gossipy, prating, verbose, voluble **8** babbling, chattery, effusive **9** prattling, talkative **10** loquacious

Garry Moore Show, The
cast: **9** Allen Funt, Denise Lor, John Byner, Ken Carson **11** Chuck McCann, Marion Lorne **12** Carol Burnett, Durward Kirby, Jackie Vernon, Pete Barbutti **13** Dorothy Loudon

Garson, Greer
born: **7** Ireland **10** County Down
roles: **10** Mrs Miniver (Oscar) **11** Madame Curie **12** Her Twelve Men **13** Mrs Parkington, Random Harvest **14** Goodbye Mr Chips **16** That Forsyte Woman **17** Pride and Prejudice **19** Sunrise at Campobello

gas 4 fuel, fume **5** vapor **6** petrol **7** essence

gascon 7 boaster, bragger, ego-

tist **8** blowhard, braggart
9 swaggerer **11** braggadocio

gasconade 4 brag, crow
5 boast **7** bravado **8** boasting
11 braggadocio

gash 4 hack, rend, rent, slit,
tear **5** carve, cleft, crack,
lance, slash, slice, split,
wound **6** cleave, incise, pierce
7 dissect, fissure, quarter **8** incision, lacerate

Gaskell, Elizabeth
author of: **4** Ruth **8** Cranford **10** Mary Barton
13 North and South **24** The
Life of Charlotte Bronte

Gaslight
director: **11** George Cukor
cast: **10** Terry Moore
12 Charles Boyer **13** Dame
May Whitty, Ingrid Berg-
man **14** Angela Lansbury
15 Halliwell Hobbes

Gasoline Alley
creator: **9** Bill Perry, Frank
King **10** Dick Moores
character: **3** Eve **4** Adam,
Hope **6** Clovia, Gideon, Nubbin **7** Chipper, Gabriel
10 Walt Wallet
wife: **14** Phyllis Blossom
children: **4** Judy **5** Corky
7 Skeezix
daughter-in-law: **9** Nina
Clock
dog: **5** Punky

gasp 4 gulp, pant, puff **5** blurt
6 suck in, wheeze
10 vociferate

Gasterocheires
companions of: **7** Proteus

gastronome 7 epicure, gourmet **9** bon vivant

gastronomy 9 epicurism

gastropod, gasteropod
4 slug **5** cowry, snail, whelk
6 cowrie, limpet, nerite **7** abalone, mollusk **8** univalve

gate 3 tap **5** crowd, house,
valve **6** portal, sluice, spigot
7 doorway **8** audience, hatch-
way **9** turnstile **10** attendance

gateau 4 cake **7** dessert

gatekeeper 5 guard **6** porter
8 watchman

Gates, Horatio
served in: **16** Revolutionary
War **18** French and Indian
War
battle: **6** Camden **8** Saratoga
defeated: **8** Burgoyne
defeated by: **10** Cornwallis

gateway 4 adit **5** entry **6** access, portal **7** doorway, opening **8** entrance, entryway
10 passageway

Gath 14 Philistine city

gather 4 fold, mass **5** amass,
group, infer, learn, pleat,
shirr, stack **6** assume, deduce,
heap up, muster, pile up,
pucker, ruffle **7** cluster, collect,
convene, marshal, observe
8 assemble, conclude **9** stockpile **10** accumulate, congregate, understand
11 concentrate

gathering 3 mob **4** gang, pack
5 bunch, crowd, crush, drove,
flock, horde, party, press
6 throng **7** company, meeting,
roundup, turnout **8** assembly,
conclave **9** concourse, multitude **10** assemblage, collection,
conference, convention **11** aggregation, convergence, convocation **12** accumulation,
congregation **13** concentration

gather together 4 herd
5 amass, hoard, rally **6** muster **7** collate, collect, compile,
marshal, round up, sweep up
8 assemble, shepherd **9** aggregate, stockpile **10** accumulate,
congregate

Gatling, Richard Jordan
nationality: **8** American
inventor of: **10** machine
gun **16** steam-powered plow

gatophobia
fear of: **4** cats

gauche 5 inept **6** clumsy, oafish **7** awkward, boorish, ill-
bred, uncouth **8** bungling, plebeian, tactless **9** inelegant,
maladroit, tasteless, unrefined
10 blundering, uncultured, ungraceful, unmannerly, unpolished **11** proletarian
13 ungentlemanly

gaucherie 5 gaffe **7** blunder,
faux pas **11** impropriety
12 indiscretion

Gaudeamus igitur 22 Let us
therefore be joyful

gaudy 4 loud, sham **5** cheap,
showy, vivid **6** flashy, flimsy,
garish, tawdry, tinsel, vulgar
7 glaring, intense **8** colorful,
dazzling, lustrous, striking
9 brilliant, sparkling, tasteless,
worthless **10** bespangled, glittering **11** pretentious
12 ostentatious

gauge, gage 4 rate, size
5 guess, judge, meter **6** assess
7 adjudge, measure **8** appraise,
estimate, evaluate, standard
9 ascertain, calculate, criterion,
yardstick **11** measurement
type: **4** ring **5** bevel

Gauguin, Paul Eugene Henri
born: **5** Paris **6** France
artwork: **9** Nevermore **12** The

Tahitians **13** The White
Horse **15** The Yellow Christ
18 Horsemen on the Beach
23 The Vision after the Sermon (Jacob Wrestling with
the Angel) **25** Be in Love
and You Will Be Happy
26 The Spirit of the Dead
Watching **36** Where Do We
Come From? Who Are We?
Where Do We Go?
book: **6** Noa Noa

Gaul see **6** France

gaunt 4 bony, grim, lank, lean,
slim, thin **5** bleak, lanky,
spare **6** barren, meager,
skinny, wasted **7** haggard,
pinched, scraggy, scrawny,
slender, spindly, starved **8** deserted, desolate, forsaken, rawboned, skeletal, withered
9 emaciated, shriveled **10** cadaverous, forbidding **14** spindle-shanked

Gauss, Carl Friedrich
field: **7** physics **9** astronomy
11 mathematics
nationality: **6** German
worked in: **9** magnetism
11 electricity **12** number
theory
named for him: **9** Gauss's
Law

Gautier, Marguerite
character in: **7** Camille
author: **5** Dumas (fils)

Gautier, Theophile
author of: **6** La Peri **7** Giselle **8** Albertus **11** Young
France **13** Emaux et Camees **16** Enamels and Cam-
eos **20** Mademoiselle de
Maupin, The Romance of
the Mummy
doctrine: **14** Art for art's
sake

gauzy 5 filmy, sheer **6** flimsy,
sleazy **10** diaphanous
11 translucent, transparent

gave up 4 quit **5** ceded
7 dropped, forsook, yielded
8 forswore, resigned **9** abandoned, abdicated, forfeited, renounced **11** surrendered
12 discontinued,
relinquished

Gawain
character in: **16** Arthurian
romance

gawk 4 gape, gaze, peer
10 rubberneck

gawky 6 clumsy, klutzy **7** awkward, lumpish **8** bungling,
fumbling, lubberly, ungainly,
unwieldy **9** all thumbs, graceless, ham-fisted, ham-handed,
maladroit **10** blundering,
ungraceful

gay 3 fun **4** airy, glad **5** happy, jolly, merry, showy, sunny, vivid **6** blithe, bright, cheery, elated, frisky, genial, jaunty, jocose, jovial, joyful, joyous, lively, social **7** buoyant, chipper, coltish, dashing, festive, gleeful, glowing, intense, jocular, playful, smiling, waggish **8** animated, cheerful, colorful, exultant, gladsome, humorous, jubilant, lustrous, skittish, spirited, splendid, sportive, volatile **9** brilliant, convivial, frivolous, hilarious, rejoicing, sparkling, sprightly, sumptuous, vivacious **10** flamboyant, frolicsome, glittering, insouciant, theatrical, variegated **12** effervescent, lighthearted, multicolored

Gay, John
author of dialogue/lyrics
for: **15** The Beggar's Opera

Gay, Walter
character in: **12** Dombey and Son
author: **7** Dickens

gay blade 3 fop **4** beau **5** blade, dandy **7** playboy **8** cavalier **9** ladies' man **12** boulevardier, man-about-town

Gay Divorcee, The
director: **12** Mark Sandrich
cast: **10** Alice Brady, Erik Rhodes **11** Betty Grable, Fred Astaire **12** Ginger Rogers **19** Edward Everett Horton
song: **11** Continental, Night and Day

Gay-Lussac, Joseph
field: **7** physics **9** chemistry
nationality: **6** French
discovered: **24** law of combining gas volumes
invented: **10** hydrometer

Gaynor, Mitzi
real name: **20** Franceska Mitzi Gerber
husband: **8** Jack Bean
born: **9** Chicago IL
roles: **8** Les Girls **10** Golden Girl **12** Anything Goes, South Pacific **14** The Joker Is Wild **32** There's No Business Like Show Business

gaze 3 eye **4** gape, ogle, peek, peer, scan **5** glare, lower, stare, study, watch **6** behold, glance, glower, peruse, regard, survey **7** examine, inspect, observe, witness **8** look long, pore over, scrutiny **10** rubberneck, scrutinize **11** contemplate

gaze at 4 view **5** watch **6** behold, look at **7** stare at **8** look upon **11** contemplate

Gazza Ladra, La
also: **17** The Thieving Magpie
opera by: **7** Rossini

Ge see **4** Gaea

gear 3 cam, rig **4** duds, garb, togs **5** dress, tools **6** attire, outfit, tackle, things **7** apparel, clothes, rigging **8** clothing, cogwheel, flywheel, garments, material, property **9** apparatus, equipment, trappings **10** belongings, implements **11** accessories, instruments **12** contrivances **13** accoutrements, paraphernalia

Geb
also: **3** Keb
origin: **8** Egyptian
god of: **5** earth
daughter: **4** Isis
son: **6** Osiris
sister: **3** Nut

Gedaliah
means: **14** Jehovah is great
father: **6** Ahikam, Pashur **8** Jeduthun
descendant: **9** Zephaniah

Geer, Will
born: **11** Frankfort IN
roles: **7** Grandpa **10** The Waltons **11** In Cold Blood

Gehenna 4 hell

Gehrig, Lou (Henry Louis)
nickname: **9** Iron Horse
sport: **8** baseball
position: **9** first base
team: **14** New York Yankees

Geisman, Ella
real name of: **11** June Allyson

Geist 4 mind **6** spirit

gelatin 4 agar, glue **5** aspic, gelee, jelly **6** glutin, pectin **7** protein, sericin

gelatinize 3 set **4** jell **7** congeal, stiffen, thicken **9** coagulate

gelatinous 7 colloid, viscous **8** muculent **9** jelly-like

geld 5 alter **8** castrate **10** emasculate

gelid 3 icy **6** frigid, frozen **8** freezing

Gelonus
father: **8** Hercules

gem see **box**

Gemini
symbol: **5** twins
planet: **7** Mercury
rules: **14** communications
born: **3** May **4** June

Gemini Contenders, The
author: **12** Robert Ludlum

Gem State
nickname of: **5** Idaho

gemutlich 4 easy **9** agreeable, congenial, simpatico **11** comfortable

gendarme 9 policeman

gender 3 sex **4** kind, male, sort, type **5** class **6** female, neuter **8** feminine **9** masculine

Gendre, Louis
real name of: **12** Louis Jourdan

genealogy 4 line **5** birth, house, stock **7** lineage **8** ancestry, pedigree **9** parentage **10** derivation, extraction

Gene Autry Show, The
cast: **10** Pat Buttram
horse: **8** Champion
theme song: **20** Back in the Saddle Again

general 5 basic, broad, usual, vague **6** common, normal,

gem 4 dear, doll, rock **5** beaut, bijou, jewel, peach, prize **6** marvel, wonder **8** treasure
type: **4** jade, opal, ruby, sard **5** agate, amber, beryl, coral, pearl, topaz **6** garnet, pyrope, quartz, spinel, zircon **7** apatite, cat's-eye, citrine, diamond, emerald, jadeite, kunzite, olivine, peridot **8** amethyst, corundum, feldspar, hematite, lazurite, nephrite, sapphire, steatite, sunstone **9** almandite, amazonite, carnelian, demantoid, enstatite, fibrolite, malachite, moonstone, morganite, rhodolite, scapolite, spodumene, tiger's-eye, turquoise **10** aquamarine, bloodstone, chalcedony, hessionite, rose quartz, tourmaline **11** alexandrite, chrysoberyl, chrysocolla, chrysoprase, lapis lazuli, rock crystal, topaz quartz **12** grossularite

public, wonted **7** blanket, current, generic, inexact, natural, overall, popular, regular, typical **8** everyday, frequent, habitual, ordinary, pandemic, sweeping **9** customary, extensive, imprecise, panoramic, prevalent, universal, worldwide **10** accustomed, collective, ecumenical, prevailing, widespread **11** unspecified **12** conventional, nonexclusive, nontechnical **13** comprehensive, miscellaneous

General Electric Theater
host: **12** Ronald Reagan

general idea 4 gist **5** drift, tenor **6** effect, import **7** purport **10** impression **11** implication

generality 6 cliche, truism **9** platitude **12** universality

14 collectiveness **17** miscellaneousness **18** indiscriminateness

generalization 3 law **5** axion **7** bromide **9** inference, statement

generalize 5 infer, judge **8** conclude

generally 5 often **6** always, mainly, mostly **7** as a rule, chiefly, largely, usually **9** currently, typically **10** frequently, habitually, ordinarily, repeatedly **11** extensively, principally, universally

general/military leader *see box*

generate 4 bear, coin, form, make, sire **5** beget, breed, cause, frame, spawn, yield **6** create, evolve, father, induce, invent **7** develop, fash-

ion, produce **8** contrive, engender, fructify, occasion **9** construct, fabricate, fecundate, fertilize, institute, originate, procreate, propagate, reproduce **10** effectuate, impregnate **11** proliferate

generation 3 kin **4** clan, line, race **5** breed, house, issue, stock, tribe **6** family, growth, strain **7** genesis, lineage, progeny **8** breeding, creation **9** begetting, causation, evolution, formation, offspring **10** production **11** development, engendering, origination, procreation, propagation **12** impregnation, reproduction **13** fertilization, proliferation

generic 6 common **7** general **8** sweeping **9** universal **10** collective **11** generalized, unspecified **12** nonexclusive **13** comprehensive **14** nonrestrictive

generosity 6 bounty **7** charity **8** altruism, courtesy, kindness, largesse **9** abundance, nobleness **10** liberality **11** benevolence, hospitality, magnanimity

generous 5 ample, large, lofty, noble **6** humane, lavish **7** copious, liberal **8** abundant, effusive, obliging, princely, prodigal **9** bounteous, bountiful, honorable, plenteous, plentiful, plethoric, unselfish, unstinted **10** altruistic, beneficent, benevolent, bighearted, charitable, freehanded, freegiving, high-minded, hospitable, munificent, openhanded, ungrudging, unstinting **11** considerate, extravagant, magnanimous, overflowing **12** humanitarian, largehearted, unrestricted **13** accommodating, philanthropic

genesis 4 rise, root **5** birth **6** origin **8** creation **9** begetting, beginning, inception **10** generation **11** engendering **12** commencement

geneticist
American: **5** Temin **6** Morgan, Muller

genetics
science of: **8** heredity
researcher: **6** Mendel

Genetyllis
origin: **5** Greek
protectress of: **6** births

Genghis Khan
also: **11** Jenghiz Khan
name means: **14** universal ruler
position: **13** Mongol emperor

---

general/military leader
American:
Revolutionary War: **3** (Light Horse Harry) Lee **5** Allen, Barry, Gates, Jones, Wayne **6** Arnold, Greene, Marion, Morgan **10** Washington
War of 1812: **4** Hull **5** Perry, Scott **7** Decatur
Mexican War: **5** Scott **6** Kearny
Civil War: **3** Lee **5** Early, Grant, Meade **6** Thomas, (JEB) Stuart **7** Forrest, Pickett, Sherman, (Stonewall) Jackson **8** Farragut, Sheridan **9** McClellan **10** Beauregard, Longstreet
Indian Wars: **6** Custer **7** Houston **10** Crazy Horse
WWI: **4** Sims **8** Mitchell, Pershing
WWII: **4** King **5** Clark **6** Arnold, Halsey, Nimitz, Patton **7** Bradley, Merrill **8** Marshall, Stilwell **9** Chennault, Doolittle, MacArthur **10** Eisenhower, Wainwright
Korean War: **5** Clark **9** MacArthur
Vietnam War: **6** Abrams **12** Westmoreland
Gulf War: **11** Schwarzkopf
British: 4 Byng, Haig, Howe, Slim **5** Wolfe **6** French, Gordon, Harris, Nelson, Wavell **7** Allenby, Clinton, Dowding, Wingate **8** Braddock, Burgoyne, Cromwell, Jellicoe, Lawrence **9** Alexander, Kitchener **10** Cornwallis, Montgomery, Wellington **11** Marlborough, Mountbatten
Carthagenian: 8 Hannibal **13** Hamilcar Barca
French: 3 Ney **4** Foch **5** Murat **6** Giraud, Joffre, Petain, Roland **7** Nivelle **8** De Gaulle, Montcalm, Napoleon **9** Lafayette **10** Bernadotte
German: 5 Kluck **6** Moltke, Paulus, Rommel, Scheer **7** Blucher, Goering, Tirpitz **8** Bismarck, Goebbels, Guderian **10** Falkenhayn, Hindenburg, Kesselring, Ludendorff, Schlieffen **17** Frederick the Great
Israeli: 5 Dayan
Japanese: 10 Tojo Hideki **15** Yamamoto Isoroku
Macedonian: 7 Ptolemy **8** Philip II **9** Alexander (the Great)
Norman: 7 William (the Conqueror)
Roman: 5 Sulla **6** Brutus, Pompey, Seneca, Trajan **7** Crassus, Hadrian, Lepidus **8** Gracchus, Octavian (Caesar Augustus), Tiberius **9** Vespasian **10** Flamininus, Mark Antony **11** Gaius Marius **12** Julius Caesar **15** Cassius Longinus, Scipio Africanus **18** Tarquinius Superbus
Russian: 6 Zhukov **7** Kutuzov, Voronov **8** Brusilov, Kerensky, Kornilov, Samsonov **9** Bagration **10** Timoshenko, Vasilevsky

defeated: 6 Russia 10 Chin empire
occupied: 6 Peking

genial 3 gay 4 glad, kind, warm 5 civil, happy, jolly, merry, sunny 6 bright, cheery, hearty, jaunty, jocund, jovial, joyful, joyous, kindly, lively, social 7 affable, amiable, chipper, cordial, festive 8 cheerful, friendly, gracious, mirthful, pleasant, sociable 9 agreeable, congenial, convivial, courteous, expansive, sparkling, vivacious 10 neighborly 12 lighthearted 13 companionable

geniality 10 affability, cordiality 11 sociability 12 conviviality, friendliness 13 expansiveness

genius 3 ace, wit 4 bent, gift, mind, whiz 5 brain, flair, knack 6 expert, master, wisdom 7 faculty, insight, prodigy 8 aptitude, judgment, penchant, sagacity, wizardry 9 ingenuity, intuition, invention 10 mastermind, perception, proclivity, propensity 11 imagination, percipience 12 intelligence, predilection 13 understanding

Genius, The
author: 15 Theodore Dreiser

genius loci 16 guardian of a place

genre 4 kind, sort, type 5 breed, class, genus, group, order, style 6 school 7 fashion, species, variety 8 category, division 11 description 14 classification

genteel 4 tony 5 civil, elite, ritzy, swank, swell 6 modish, poised, polite, urbane 7 courtly, elegant, high-hat, refined, stylish 8 cultured, decorous, ladylike, mannerly, polished, well-bred 9 courteous, high-class, high-toned, patrician 10 cultivated, well-spoken 11 fashionable, gentlemanly, highfalutin, overrefined, pretentious 12 aristocratic, silk-stocking, thoroughbred

gentian 8 Gentiana
varieties: 5 blind, green, horse 6 alpine, bottle, closed, Sierra, yellow 7 crested, fringed, prairie, spurred 8 Catesby's, soapwort, stemless 9 Mendocino 10 pine barren

gentil 4 kind 5 noble 6 gentle

gentile
Yiddish: 3 goy

man: 7 shegetz
woman: 6 shiksa

gentility 6 polish 7 decorum, suavity 8 breeding, chivalry, civility, courtesy, urbanity 9 gallantry, propriety, punctilio 10 refinement 11 cultivation, savoir-faire 12 mannerliness

gentle 3 low 4 calm, easy, kind, meek, mild, soft, tame 5 balmy, bland, light, quiet 6 benign, broken, docile, kindly, placid, serene, slight, smooth, tender 7 lenient, pacific, subdued 8 harmless, merciful, moderate, peaceful, tolerant, tranquil 9 indulgent, temperate, tractable 10 manageable, thoughtful, untroubled 11 considerate, sympathetic 12 domesticated 13 compassionate, tenderhearted
French: 6 gentil

gentleman 3 don, guy, man, one 4 chap, gent 5 swell 6 fellow, person, squire 7 esquire, hidalgo 8 cavalier 9 caballero, chevalier, patrician 10 aristocrat, individual

Gentleman Jim
nickname of: 12 James Corbett

gentlemanly 6 polite 7 courtly, gallant, refined 8 cultured, decorous, mannerly, polished, well-bred 9 courteous, dignified 10 cultivated

Gentleman's Agreement
director: 9 Elia Kazan
based on novel by: 12 Laura Z Hobson
cast: 10 Anne Revere 11 Celeste Holm, Gregory Peck 12 John Garfield 14 Dorothy McGuire
Oscar for: 7 picture 17 supporting actress (Holm)

Gentlemen Prefer Blondes
author: 9 Anita Loos

gentleness 8 calmness, docility, mildness, serenity, tameness 10 compassion, tenderness 12 mercifulness, peacefulness, tractability

gentle wind 4 waft 6 breath, breeze, zephyr

gently 6 easily, kindly, meekly, mildly, softly, tamely 7 amiably, lightly 8 benignly, placidly, smoothly, tenderly 9 gradually 10 delicately, moderately, pleasantly, soothingly 15 compassionately, sympathetically

gentry 5 elite 7 society 8 nobility 10 blue bloods, gentlefolk 11 aristocracy, aristocrats

genuflect 4 bend 6 kowtow

genuine 4 open, pure, real, true 5 frank, naive, plain, solid 6 actual, candid, honest, proven, simple 7 artless, earnest, natural, sincere 8 bona fide, sterling, true-blue 9 authentic, guileless, heartfelt, ingenuous, simon-pure, unalloyed, veritable 10 legitimate, unaffected 13 unadulterated 15 straightforward, unsophisticated

genuineness 7 honesty 9 frankness, sincerity 10 candidness, simplicity 11 artlessness 13 guilelessness 14 unaffectedness 19 straightforwardness

genus 4 kind, sort, type 5 class, group 7 variety 8 category, division 14 classification

geologist
British: 4 Hall
German: 6 Werner
Scottish: 6 Hutton

geoponics 7 tillage 8 agronomy 9 husbandry 10 agronomics 11 agriculture, cultivation

George Burns and Gracie Allen Show, The
character: 9 Mr Beasley (Mailman) 11 Harry Morton 13 Blanche Morton
theme song: 8 Love Nest

Georgetown
capital of: 6 Guyana

Georgia see box, p. 388

Georgia Peach
nickname of: 6 Ty Cobb

Georgics, The
author: 6 Vergil, Virgil
called: 17 agricultural poems

Georgia
capital/largest city: 7 Tbilisi
others: 6 Batumi 7 Kutaisi, Rustavi, Sukhumi
division: 7 Ossetia 8 Abkhazia, Adzharia
head of state: 9 president
government: 8 republic
monetary unit: 5 ruble
mountain: 8 Caucasus
river: 4 Kura 5 Rioni
sea: 5 Black
people: 5 Azeri 7 Russian 8 Armenian, Georgian, Ossetian 9 Abkhazian
language: 8 Georgian
religion 14 Georgian Church 15 Russian Orthodox

Georgia

abbreviation: 2 GA
nickname: 5 Peach **7** Cracker **21** Empire State of the South
capital/largest city: 7 Atlanta
others: 4 Rome **5** Jesup, Macon **6** Albany, Athens, Dalton, Plains, Sparta **7** Augusta, Conyers, Cordele, Decatur, Griffen, Vidalia **8** Columbus, LaGrange, Marietta, Moultrie, Savannah, Valdosta, Waycross **9** Brunswick **11** College Park, Gainesville, Thomasville **13** Andersonville
college: 4 Tift **5** Clark, Emory, Paine **6** Mercer **7** Atlanta, Spelman **8** Wesleyan **9** Morehouse **10** Agnes Scott **11** Georgia Tech
explorer: 15 James Oglethorpe
feature: 16 Little White House
   amusement park: **19** Six Flags Over Georgia
   national cemetery: **13** Andersonville
   national monument: **8** Ocmulgee **11** Fort Pulaski **13** Fort Frederica
tribe: 5 Creek, Guale, Yuchi **6** Chiaha, Oconee, Uchean **7** Yamasee **8** Hitchiti
people: 6 Ty Cobb **7** cracker **10** Bobby Jones **11** Juliette Low **15** Erskine Caldwell **16** Margaret Mitchell **18** Joel Chandler Harris
island: 3 Sea **6** Jekyll, Sapelo **7** Ossabaw **10** Cumberland
lake: 6 Lanier, Martin **7** Harding, Nottely **8** Bankhead, Hartwell, Sinclair
land rank: 11 twenty-first
mountain: 5 Stone **7** Lookout **8** Kennesaw **9** Blue Ridge **11** Alleghenies **13** High Point Peak
   highest point: **17** Brasstown Bald Peak
physical feature:
   sea: **8** Atlantic
   springs: **4** Warm
   swamp: **10** Okefenokee
president: 11 Jimmy Carter
river: 3 Pea **5** Flint **6** Etowah, Oconee, Pigeon **7** Conecuh, Satilla, St Mary's, Tugaloo **8** Altamaha, Ocmulgee, Ogeechee, Savannah, Suwannee **9** Chattooga **13** Chattahoochie
state admission: 6 fourth
state bird: 13 brown thrasher
state fish: 14 largemouth bass
state flower: 12 Cherokee rose
state motto: 6 Wisdom **20** Justice and Moderation
state song: 7 Georgia
state tree: 7 live oak

Ge-Pano-Carib
language branch: 7 Macro-Ge **10** Macro-Carib **11** Macro-Panoan

gephyrophobia
fear of: 7 bridges

Geraint
character in: 16 Arthurian romance

geranium 11** Pelargonium
varieties: 3 ivy **4** fish, lime, mint, pine, rock, rose, show, wild **5** apple, fancy, house, lemon, regal, zonal **6** almond, alpine, cactus, jungle, nutmeg, orange **7** apricot, bedding, coconut, feather, hanging, knotted, polecat **8** crowfoot, fern-leaf, horsehoe **9** beefsteak, oak-leaved **10** California, gooseberry, peppermint, strawberry, sweetheart, village-oak **11** grape-leaved, herb-scented, maple-leaved, rose-scented **12** silver-leaved, southernwood, sweet-scented **13** black-flowered, pansy-flowered, pheasant's-foot **14** Lady Washington, little-leaf rose **15** mint-scented rose **16** Martha Washington **17** English finger-bowl

Gerber, Franceska Mitzi
real name of: 11 Mitzi Gaynor

Gerd, Gerda
origin: 12 Scandinavian
husband: 4 Frey **5** Freyr

Gere, Richard
roles: 5 Yanks **10** Breathless, Cotton Club **12** Days of Heaven **14** American Gigolo **19** Looking for Mr Goodbar **22** An Officer and a Gentleman

Geri
origin: 12 Scandinavian
form: 4 wolf
owner: 4 Odin **5** Othin
received: 4 food
exception: 4 meat
fellow wolf: 5 Freki

germ 3 bud, bug, egg **4** ovum, root, seed **5** ovule, spark, spore, virus **6** embryo, origin, source, sprout **7** microbe, nucleus, seed bud **8** bacillus, offshoot, rudiment **9** bacterium, beginning **12** fountainhead **13** microorganism

German 3** Hun **4** balt, Goth **5** boche, heine, jerry, kraut, Saxon **6** Teuton **7** tedesco **8** Prussian, Teutonic **9** deutscher
article: 3 das, dem, den, der, des, die, ein **4** eine
empire: 5 reich
man: 4 herr
storm and stress: 13 sturm und drang
thank you: 5 danke **10** danke schon
toast: 6 prosit
woman: 4 frau **8** fraulein

German-Dutch
language family: 12 Indo-European
branch: 8 Germanic
group: 15 Western Germanic
language: 9 Low German **10** High German

germane 3 apt, fit **6** native, proper **7** apropos, fitting, related **8** material, relative, relevant, suitable **9** connected, intrinsic, pertinent **10** applicable **11** appropriate **12** appertaining

germaneness 9 relevance **10** pertinence **13** applicability **15** appropriateness

Germanic
language family: 12 Indo-European
group: 6 Gothic **15** Western Germanic

Germanic Mythology *see box*

German is spoken here
German: 25 hier wird Deutsch gesprochen

German literary movement (18th cent) 13** sturm und drang

Germanic Mythology

chief of gods: 5 Wotan
corresponds to Scandinavian: 4 Odin
dwarf:
15 Rumpelstiltskin
dwarves: 8 Niblungs
9 Nibelungs
emperor: 15 Dietrich
von Bern
epic: 14 Nibelungenlied
goddess of clouds/sky/marriage: 3 Fri 5 Frigg,
Frija 6 Frigga
goddess of death/fertility: 7 Berchta, Perchta
goddess of love/beauty/fecundity:
5 Freya
goddess of moon/witch: 5 Holle
god of thunder: 5 Donar
god of winter sports:
4 Ullr 5 Uller
hero: 6 Sigurd
9 Siegfried
heroine: 6 Gudrun, Kudrun 7 Guthrun 8 Brunhild 9 Kriemhild
king: 7 Siggeir
king of dwarves:
8 Alberich
knight of the holy grail: 9 Lohengrin
magic cloak:
9 Tarnkappe
maidens: 9 Valkyries
nature spirit: 7 Eriking
nymph: 7 Lorelei, Lurelei
water spirit: 3 Nix

Germany

capital: 6 Berlin
government leader: 10 chancellor, Helmut Kohl
monetary unit: 12 Deutsche mark
people: 3 Hun 4 Slav, Sorb, Wend 5 Saxon
artist: 4 Marc 5 Durer 7 Barlach, Cranach, Gropius, Holbein 9 Grunewald 14 Mies van der Rohe
author: 4 Mann, Marx 5 Grass 6 Brecht, Elsner, Goethe 7 Johnson, Lessing 8 Hochhuth
composer: 4 Bach 5 Weill 6 Brahms, Handel, Wagner 7 Strauss 8 Schumann 9 Beethoven, Hindemith 11 Mendelssohn
conductor: 5 Henze 6 Walter 9 Klemperer 11 Furtwangler, Stockhausen
historical leader: 6 Hitler, Kaiser 8 Bismarck 10 Barbarossa
Prussian noble: 6 Junker
religious leader: 6 Luther
language: 6 German 10 High German 11 Hochdeutsch
religion: 8 Lutheran 10 Protestant 13 Roman Catholic 17 Evangelical Church
food:
bread: 12 pumpernickel
dish: 9 lebkuchen 15 wiener schnitzel
dumpling: 6 knodel
frankfurter: 15 wiener wurstchen
fruit bread: 7 stollen
ham: 11 Westphalian
potato salad: 14 kartoffelsalat
pot roast: 11 sauerbraten
sausage: 5 wurst 9 blutwurst, bratwurst 10 brockwurst, knackwurst, leberwurst
sole: 8 seezunge

Germany, East

capital/largest city: 10 East Berlin
others: 4 Jena 5 Halle, Waren 6 Erfurt, Weimar 7 Cottbus, Dresden, Leipzig, Meissen, Potsdam, Rostock, Schwedt, Wannsee, Zwickau 9 Frankfurt, Magdeburg 10 Angermunde, Warnemunde, Wittenberg 11 Neustrelitz 13 Karl-Marx-Stadt (Chemnitz)
school: 8 Humboldt
division: 6 Saxony 9 Thuringia 11 Brandenburg, Mecklenburg 12 Saxony-Anhalt
government: 11 Volkskammer (Peoples' Chamber)
monetary unit: 4 mark 7 Ostmark, pfennig
lake: 6 Muritz
mountain: 3 Ore 4 Harz 10 Erzgebirge
highest point: 11 Fichtelberg
river: 4 Elbe, Oder 5 Havel, Saale, Spree 6 Neisse, Warnow
sea: 6 Baltic
physical feature:
forest: 10 Thuringian
place: 10 Berlin Wall 17 Checkpoint Charlie
castle: 9 Sans Souci
church: 8 St Thomas 12 Thomaskirche
city center: 13 Karl Marx Platz 14 Alexanderplatz, Neubrandenberg
comic opera: 12 Komische Oper
gate: 11 Brandenburg
museum: 7 Zwinger 8 Pergamon 10 Goethe Haus
opera house: 18 Deutsche Staatsoper
feature:
china: 7 Dresden
fair: 7 Leipzig
theater company: 16 Berliner Ensemble

Germany *see box*

Germany, East *see box*

Germany, West *see box, p. 390*

germicide 11 bactericide 12 disinfectant

Germinal
author: 9 Emile Zola

germinate 3 bud 4 blow, open 5 bloom, shoot 6 flower, push up, sprout 7 blossom, burgeon, develop 8 generate, spring up, vegetate

germination 9 sprouting 11 propagation

Gershom
means: 13 stranger there
father: 5 Moses
mother: 8 Zipporah
brother: 12 Eliezar

Gershwin, George
born: 10 Brooklyn NY

Germany, West

capital: 4 Bonn

largest city: 10 West Berlin

others: 4 Kiel 5 Essen, Mainz, Trier 6 Aachen, Bochum, Bremen, Kassel, Lubeck, Minden, Munden, Munich 7 Cologne, Hamburg, Hanover, Krefeld, Munster 8 Augsburg, Biberach, Dortmund, Duisberg, Duisburg, Freiburg, Mannheim, Solingen 9 Darmstadt, Karlsruhe, Nuremberg, Oldenburg, Stuttgart, Wiesbaden, Wuppertal 10 Dusseldorf, Heidelberg, Steingaden 11 Saarbrucken 12 Oberammergau 13 Gelsenkirchen 15 Frankfurt am Main 16 Mulheim an der Ruhr

school: 4 Bonn 7 Hamburg 10 Heidelberg 16 Ludwig-Maximilian

division: 4 Saar 5 Baden, Hesse 6 Bremen 7 Bavaria 9 Rhineland 10 Palatinate, Westphalia 11 Lower Saxony, Wurttemberg 17 Schleswig-Holstein

head of government: 10 chancellor

monetary unit: 4 mark 7 pfennig 12 Deutsche mark

island: 11 East Frisian 12 North Frisian

lake: 9 Constance 11 Inner Alster, Outer Alster

mountain: 4 Harz 8 Feldberg 11 Black Forest 12 Bavarian Alps

highest point: 9 Zugspitze

river: 3 Ems 4 Elbe, Main, Nahe, Ruhr, Saar, Wese 5 Rhine, Weser 6 Danube, Neckar 7 Moselle, Pegnitz

sea: 5 North 6 Baltic

physical feature:
  canal: 4 Kiel 10 Mittelland
  forest: 5 Black 7 Bohemia 9 Teu Toburg

place: 17 Checkpoint Charlie
  botanical garden: 18 Pflantzen und Blumen
  boulevard: 14 Kurfurstendamm
  church: 12 Frauenkirche (Cathedral of Our Lady) 13 Kaiser Wilhelm 16 Gadachtniskirche
  city center: 11 Marienplatz
  fortress: 9 Marksburg
  fountain: 14 Schoner Brunnen
  garden: 10 Englischer
  hall: 9 Beethoven
  museum: 8 Residenz 9 Durer Haus 12 Schatzkammer 14 Alte Pinakothek
  opera house: 18 Deutsches Opern Haus
  park/zoo: 18 Hagenbecks Tierpark
  residential district: 11 Hansa Vierte 12 Hanse Viertel
  resort (on Baltic): 10 Travemunde
  theater: 9 Cuvillies

feature:
  beer cellar: 11 bierkellern
  beer garden: 10 biergarten
  beer hall: 10 bierhallen
  beer room: 10 bierstuben
  cars: 3 BMW 7 Porsche 10 Volkswagen 12 Mercedes-Benz
  children: 6 kinder
  city hall: 5 Romer 7 Rathaus
  festival: 11 Oktoberfest
  folk songs: 11 volkslieder
  kitchen: 5 kuche
  old city: 8 Altstadt
  pre-Lent carnival: 8 Fasching
  secondary school: 9 gymnasium
  states: 6 lander
  wine street: 11 Weinstrasse

partner/lyricist: 11 Ira Gershwin
composer of: 9 Funny Face 11 Of Thee I Sing 12 Porgy and Bess 13 Cuban Overture 14 Rhapsody in Blue 15 Strike Up the Band 17 An American in Paris

Gertrude
  character in: 6 Hamlet
  author: 11 Shakespeare

Gervin, George
  nickname: 6 Iceman
  sport: 10 basketball
  team: 15 San Antonio Spurs

Geryon
  form: 7 monster
  father: 8 Chrysaor
  mother: 10 Callirrhoe
  home: 7 Erythea
  possessed: 6 cattle
  color of cattle: 3 red
  herdsman: 8 Eurytion
  dog: 7 Orthrus
  killed by: 8 Heracles
  cattle stolen by: 8 Heracles

Gesta Romanorum
  author: 7 unknown

gestation 9 evolution, pregnancy 10 epigenesis, generation, incubation, maturation 11 development, propagation

gesticulate 3 nod 4 wink 5 nudge, shrug 6 beckon, motion, signal 8 indicate 9 pantomime

gesture 3 nod 4 sign, wave, wink 5 nudge, shrug, touch 6 beckon, motion, signal 8 courtesy, dumb show, flourish, high sign 9 formality, pantomime 13 demonstration

get 3 bag, fix, net, wax, win 4 beat, coax, earn, gain, grab, grip, grow, have, hear, move, reap, sway, take, turn 5 annoy, catch, fetch, glean, grasp, learn, reach, seize, sense, upset 6 arrive, attain, baffle, become, collar, come by, come to, enlist, entrap, fathom, follow, induce, obtain, pick up, pocket, prompt, puzzle, secure, snatch, suborn, take in, turn to 7 achieve, acquire, capture, confuse, contact, dispose, ensnare, go after, incline, inherit, mystify, perplex, prepare, procure, realize, receive, wheedle, win over 8 bewilder, confound, contract, irritate, perceive, persuade 9 influence, transport 10 comprehend, disconcert, predispose, understand

get a kick out of 4 like 5 eat

up, enjoy, fancy, savor **6** relish **10** appreciate

getaway 6 escape, exodus, flight **10** decampment

get done 2 do **6** finish **8** complete **10** accomplish

get even 6 avenge **7** counter, hit back, pay back, revenge **9** retaliate

Gethsemane 6 garden

get into 3 don **5** enter, put on

get in touch with 5 reach **7** contact

get lost 4 scat, shoo **5** be off, leave, scram **6** beat it, begone, depart, go away **7** vamoose

get one's dander up 4 gall, rile **5** anger **6** enrage, madden, nettle, ruffle **7** incense, inflame, outrage **9** infuriate

get out of bed 4 rise **5** arise **12** rise and shine

get rid of 4 drop, dump, junk, shed **5** ditch, scrap **6** banish, cut out, delete, remove, unload **7** abolish, discard, weed out **8** jettison, stamp out, throw out **9** eliminate, eradicate **10** annihilate **11** exterminate

Get Smart
　character: 5 Hymie (CONTROL robot) **7** Agent 99, Carlson, Starker **8** Larrabee, The Chief (Thaddeus) **12** Maxwell Smart (Agent 86) **15** Conrad Siegfried
　cast: 8 Don Adams **9** King Moody **10** Stacy Keach **11** Dave Ketchum, Dick Gautier, Edward Platt **12** Bernie Kopell **13** Barbara Feldon **14** Robert Karvelas
　Max worked for:
　7 CONTROL
　foe: 4 KAOS

get the better of 4 foil, rout **5** crush, quell **6** baffle, defeat, thwart **7** conquer **8** confound, overcome **9** frustrate, overthrow

get the upper hand of 5 quell **6** master **7** conquer **8** dominate, overcome, surmount

get the worst of 4 fail, fall, lose

Getting Even
　author: 10 Woody Allen

get to 5 reach **8** approach

get-together 2 do **3** bee **4** meet **5** agree, party, visit **6** affair, gather, hobnob **7** meeting **8** assemble, assembly **9** gathering

getup 3 rig **6** attire, outfit **7** costume **8** disguise, ensemble

get up 4 find, rise **5** arise, rouse, stand **8** assemble

get used to 5 adapt, inure **6** adjust **8** accustom **9** acclimate, habituate

gewgaws 7 baubles, doodads, trifles **8** trinkets **9** bric-a-brac, gimcracks, kickshaws, ornaments **11** knickknacks

Ghana *see box*

ghastly 3 wan **4** grim, ugly **5** ashen, pasty, weird **6** dismal, glassy, grisly, horrid, odious, pallid **7** fearful, ghostly, haggard, hideous, uncanny **8** blanched, dreadful, gruesome, horrible, shocking, spectral, terrible **9** appalling, colorless, deathlike, frightful, ghostlike, loathsome, repellent, repulsive, revolting **10** cadaverous, corpselike, forbidding, horrendous, lackluster, terrifying

Ghiberti, Lorenzo
　born: 5 Italy **8** Florence
　artwork: 9 St Matthew, St Stephen **15** Gates of Paradise (baptistry doors) **16** St John the Baptist **19** The Sacrifice of Isaac

ghost 4 hint **5** demon, shade, spook, trace **6** goblin, shadow,

sprite, wraith **7** banshee, chimera, phantom, specter **8** phantasm **9** hobgoblin, phantasma, semblance **10** apparition, suggestion **12** Doppelganger **13** manifestation **15** materialization

Ghost and Mrs Muir, The
　character: 11 Candice Muir, Martha Grant **12** Jonathan Muir **13** Claymore Gregg **14** Mrs Carolyn Muir **18** Captain Daniel Gregg
　TV cast: 8 Reta Shaw **9** Hope Lange **13** Edward Mulhare **14** Harlen Carraher, Kellie Flanagan **19** Charles Nelson Reilly
　setting: 11 Gull Cottage
　director: 17 Joseph L Mankiewicz
　movie cast: 8 Edna Best **11** Gene Tierney, Rex Harrison **13** George Sanders

Ghostbusters
　director: 11 Ivan Reitman
　screenplay: 10 Dan Ackroyd **11** Harold Ramis
　cast: 10 Bill Murray, Dan Ackroyd **11** Harold Ramis **15** Sigourney Weaver

ghostly 4 pale **5** eerie, weird **6** spooky, unreal **7** ghastly, phantom, shadowy, uncanny **8** illusive, spectral **9** unearthly **10** phantasmal, wraithlike

---

Ghana
　other name: 9 Gold Coast
　capital/largest city: 5 Accra, Akkra
　others: 3 Oda **4** Axim, Fian, Keta, Tala, Tema **5** Bawku, Enchi, Lawra, Legon, Sampa, Yapei **6** Dunkwa, Karaga, Kpandu, Kumasi, Nsawam, Obuasi, Swedru, Tamale, Tarkwa, Wasipe **7** Antubia, Damongo, Mampong, Prestea, Sekondi, Sunyani, Winneba **8** Akosombo, Kintampo, Takoradi **9** Cape Coast **15** Sekondi-Takoradi
　school: 6 Kumasi **9** Cape Coast
　monetary unit: 4 cedi **5** ackey
　lake: 5 Volta **8** Bosumtwi
　mountain: 12 Akwapim Hills
　highest point: 8 Afadjato
　river: 3 Oti, Pra **4** Daka, Tano **5** Afram, Volta **7** Ankobra, Kulpawn **10** Black Volta, White Volta
　sea: 8 Atlantic
　physical feature:
　　gulf: **6** Guinea
　people: 2 Ga **3** Ewe **4** Akan, Akim, Akra, Aksa **5** Ahafo, Brong, Inkra **7** Akwapim, Ashanti, Dagomba **8** Mamprusi **11** Mole-Dagbani
　language: 2 Ga **3** Ewe, Gur, Kwa, Twi **5** Fanti, Hausa **7** Dagomba, English
　religion: 5 Islam **7** animism **13** Roman Catholic
　feature:
　　castle: **14** Christiansborg
　　dam: **8** Akosombo
　　national dress: **5** kente

11 phantomlike **12** supernatural

ghostly double
German: **12** Doppelganger

Ghosts
author: **11** Henrik Ibsen
character: **7** Manders **12** Oswald Alving **14** Jacob Engstrand, Mrs Helen Alving **15** Regina Engstrand

ghoulish 5 eerie, scary, weird **7** demonic, hellish, macabre, ogreish, satanic **8** diabolic, fiendish, gruesome, infernal, sinister **9** monstrous **10** horrifying, zombielike **11** hair-raising, necrophilic

Giacometti, Alberto
born: **11** Switzerland **12** Stampa-Tessin
artwork: **3** Dog **7** The Cage **8** Caroline **10** City Square **11** Head of Diego, Man Pointing **14** Reclining Woman **17** The Palace at Four Am **19** Hands Holding the Void

Gianni Schicchi
opera by: **7** Puccini
character: **11** Buoso Donati

giant 3 big **4** huge **5** titan **7** Goliath, spanker, thumper, whopper **8** behemoth, colossus, strapper **9** Gargantua **14** Brobdingnagian

Giant
director: **13** George Stevens
author: **10** Edna Ferber
cast: **9** James Dean **10** Chill Wills, Rock Hudson **11** Jane Withers **12** Carroll Baker **15** Elizabeth Taylor
setting: **5** Texas
Oscar for: **8** director

Giant *see* **8** Gigantes

giant people 6 Anakim

Giants in the Earth
author: **9** O E Rolvaag
character: **3** Ole **5** Beret **8** Per Hanea **9** Anna Marie **12** Hans Kristian **15** Peder Victorious

gibber 3 gab **4** blab **5** prate **6** babble, gabble, jabber **7** blabber, blather, chatter, prattle **8** chitchat

gibberish 4 blab, bosh **6** babble, drivel, gabble **7** blather, twaddle **8** nonsense **10** balderdash, double-talk, flapdoodle, hocus-pocus, mumbo-jumbo **12** gobbledegook

Gibbon, Edward
author of: **33** The (History of the) Decline and Fall of the Roman Empire

gibbous 6 convex, curved,

humped **7** bulging, rounded, swollen **8** swelling **10** humpbacked, protuberant

Gibbs family
characters in: **7** Our Town
member: **6** George **7** Rebecca
author: **6** Wilder

gibe, jibe 3 rag **4** jeer, mock, quip, razz, twit **5** chaff, flout, knock, toast, scoff, sneer, taunt **6** deride, needle, rail at **7** mockery, poke fun, sarcasm **8** brickbat, derision, ridicule, taunting **9** criticism, wisecrack

Gibraltar
other name: **11** rock of Tarik **13** Djebel al-Tarik **15** rock of Gibraltar
largest city: **9** Gibraltar
government: **18** British crown colony
head of government: **15** governor general
mountain: **6** Misery
sea: **13** Mediterranean
physical feature:
bay: **5** Ceuta, Rosia, Sandy **6** Catlan **9** Algeciras
cliffs: **17** Pillars of Hercules
people: **6** Jewish **7** British, Maltese, Spanish **8** Italians **10** Portuguese
language: **7** English, Spanish
feature: **12** King's Bastion
gardens: **7** Alameda

Gibson, Mel
roles: **6** Mad Max **9** Gallipoli, The Bounty **12** Lethal Weapon **14** The Road Warrior **26** The Year of Living Dangerously

Giddens, Regina
character in: **14** The Little Foxes
author: **7** Hellman

giddy 5 dizzy, faint, silly **6** fickle, fitful **7** awesome, erratic, flighty, muddled, reeling **8** careless, dizzying, fainting, fanciful, reckless, swimming, unsteady, volatile, whirling **9** befuddled, frivolous, impulsive, mercurial, whimsical **10** capricious, changeable, inconstant **11** hare-brained, harum-scarum, lightheaded, thoughtless, vacillating, vertiginous

12 inconsistent, overpowering **13** irresponsible, rattlebrained

Gide, Andre
author of: **13** The Immoralist **15** Strait Is the Gate **17** The Counterfeiters **18** Lafcadio's Adventure (The Vatican Swindle) **19** The Pastoral Symphony

Gideon 11 Hebrew judge
father: **5** Joash, Ophra
son: **9** Abimelech
also called: **9** Jerubbaal

Gidget
character: **5** Larue **10** Anne Cooper, John Cooper **16** Francine (Gidget) Lawrence **21** Professor Russ Lawrence
cast: **9** Don Porter **10** Peter Deuel, Sally Field **11** Betty Conner **13** Lynette Winter

Gielgud, Sir John
born: **6** London **7** England
roles: **6** Arthur, Becket, Hamlet **7** Macbeth **9** Saint Joan **26** The Barretts of Wimpole Street **27** The Importance of Being Earnest

gift 3 aid, dot, fee, sop, tip **4** alms, bent, boon, dole, help, turn **5** award, bonus, bribe, craft, dower, dowry, favor, flair, forte, graft, grant, knack, power, prize, skill **6** genius, legacy, talent, virtue **7** aptness, bequest, faculty, handout, largess, premium, present, quality, tribute **8** aptitude, capacity, donation, facility, gratuity, offering, property **9** attribute, endowment, expertise, ingenuity **10** adroitness, capability, competency **11** benefaction, proficiency **12** contribution **13** consideration, qualification

gifted 4 able, deft **5** adept, crack, handy, quick, slick **6** adroit, bright, clever, expert, facile, master, wizard **7** capable, skilled **8** finished, masterly, polished, superior, talented **9** brilliant, ingenious, inventive, practiced, qualified **10** proficient **11** crackerjack, experienced, resourceful **12** accomplished

Gift From the Sea, The
author: **19** Anne Morrow Lindbergh

gig 3 job **4** trap **5** stint **6** chaise **7** dogcart **8** carriage, curricle **10** engagement

Gigantes
single member: **5** giant
father: **6** Uranus
mother: **4** Gaea

heads of: **3** men
bodies of: **8** serpents
attacked: **4** gods

gigantic 4 huge, vast **5** bulky,
jumbo **6** mighty **7** hulking, immense, lumpish, mammoth,
massive, titanic **8** colossal,
enormous, lubberly, towering,
unwieldy **9** herculean, monstrous, ponderous, strapping
10 gargantuan, prodigious, stupendous, tremendous, voluminous **11** elephantine

Gigantomachia
war of: **6** giants

giggle 6 cackle, hee-hee, simper, tee-hee, titter **7** chuckle,
snicker, snigger, twitter

Gigi
director: **16** Vincente
Minnelli
based on story by: **7** Colette
cast: **8** Eva Gabor **11** Leslie
Caron **12** Louis Jourdan
15 Hermione Gingold,
Jacques Bergerac **16** Maurice
Chevalier
score: **14** Lerner and Loewe
Oscar for: **7** picture
8 director
song: **4** Gigi **15** I Remember
It Well **25** Thank Heaven
for Little Girls **29** The Night
They Invented Champagne

Gilbert, Cass
architect of: **14** US Customs
House (NYC) **17** Woolworth
Building (NYC) **20** Supreme
Court Building (Washington
DC) **21** Minnesota State
Capitol (St Paul) **22** George
Washington Bridge

Gilbert, John
real name: **11** John Pringle
wife: **9** Ina Claire **11** Leatrice
Joy **13** Virginia Bruce
born: **7** Logan UT
roles: **4** Love **12** The Big Parade **13** The Merry Widow
15 A Woman of Affairs
16 Flesh and the Devil

Gilbert, William
field: **7** physics
nationality: **7** British
father of: **11** electricity
named for him: **27** CGS unit
of magnetomotive force

**Gilbert, W S, and Sullivan,
Arthur Seymour**
composers of: **7** Ivanhoe
8 Iolanthe, Patience **9** Rud-
digore, The Mikado
11 H M S Pinafore, Princess
Ida, The Sorcerer, Trial by
Jury **12** The Grand Duke
13 The Gondoliers, Utopia
Limited **19** The Yeoman of
the Guard **20** The Pirates of
Penzance **24** Thespis or The
Gods Grown Old

Gilbert Islands *see* **8** Kiribati

Gil Blas (of Santillane)
author: **11** Alain LeSage
character: **6** Scipio **11** Don
Alphonso

Gilbreth, Frank B, Jr
author of: **17** Cheaper by the
Dozen (with Ernestine Gilbreth Carey)

gild 4 bend **5** slant, twist
7 cover up, stretch, touch up
10 exaggerate

Gilded Age, The
authors: **9** Mark Twain
19 Charles Dudley Warner

gilded youth
French: **13** jeunesse doree

Gileadite password
10 Shibboleth

Giles Goat-Boy
author: **9** John Barth

Gilgal 5 wheel **6** circle

Gilgamesh
origin: **8** Sumerian
king of: **4** Uruk **5** Erech
servant: **6** Enkidu

gill
abbreviation: **2** gi

Gilligan's Island
character: **7** Skipper (Jonas
Grumby) **8** Gilligan **9** Mrs
Howell (Lovey), Professor
(Roy Hinkley) **11** Ginger
Grant **14** Mary Ann Sum-
mers **17** Thurston
Howell III
cast: **9** Bob Denver, Dawn
Wells, Jim Backus **10** Alan
Hale Jr, Tina Louise **14** Na-
talie Schafer, Russell
Johnson
ship: **6** Minnow

Gillooly, Edna Rae
real name of: **12** Ellen
Burstyn

Gills, Solomon
character in: **12** Dombey and
Son
author: **7** Dickens

Gilyak
language spoken in: **4** Amur
8 Sakhalin

gimcrack 5 bijou, curio **6** bauble, gewgaw, trifle **7** trinket,
whatnot **8** kickshaw, ornament **9** bagatelle, plaything
10 knickknack **11** contrivance,
thingamabob,
thingamajig

gimmick 4 plan, ploy, ruse,
wile **5** angle, dodge, stunt
6 design, device, gadget,
scheme **7** wrinkle **9** stratagem
10 subterfuge **11** contrivance

gin *see box, p. 394*

ginger 3 pep, tan **5** brown,
spice **6** energy
varieties: **3** red **4** wild
5 crape, crepe, shell, torch,
white **6** canton, common,
Kahili, orchid, spiral, yellow **9** butterfly **10** small
shell, variegated
botanical name: **8** Zingiber
12 Z officinales
Sanskrit: **9** singabera
origin: **4** Asia **5** China, India
7 Jamaica
use: **6** tongue **7** vinegar
9 beef stock **11** baked
dishes, gingerbread
12 chicken stock

gingerly 6 warily **7** charily,
timidly **8** daintily **9** carefully,
finically, guardedly, heedfully,
mincingly, prudently **10** cau-
tiously, delicately, discreetly,
hesitantly, vigilantly, watchfully **11** squeamishly **12** fastidiously, suspiciously
13 circumspectly

gingham 5 cloth **6** cotton, fabric, striped **8** chambray
9 checkered

gin mill 4 dive **9** honky-tonk,
roadhouse

Ginnungagap
origin: **12** Scandinavian
void filled with: **4** mist
between: **9** Nifelheim
10 Muspelheim

Ginsberg, Allen
author of: **4** Howl **7** Kaddish
10 Planet News **11** Mind
Breaths **16** The Fall of
America **20** Reality and
Sandwiches

Giono, Jean
author of: **6** Regain **7** Colline,
Harvest **13** Hill of Destiny
18 The Hussar on the Roof

Giordano, Umberto
born: **5** Italy **6** Foggia
composer of: **6** Fedora
8 Mala Vita **13** Andrea
Chenier **14** Madame Sans-
Gene

Giorgione da Castelfranco
born: **5** Italy **12** Castelfranco
artwork: **10** The Tempest
13 Ordeal of Moses, Sleeping Venus **17** Judgment of
Solomon **19** The Concert
Champetre (disputed) **20** The
Three Philosophers **23** Adoration of the Shepherds

Giotto di Bondone
born: **5** Italy **8** (near)
Florence
artwork attributed: **17** O-
gnissanti Madonna **31** Presentation of Christ in the
Temple **32** St Francis Surrounded by his Brothers

gin
  origin: **11** Netherlands
  ingredient: **6** grains **12** juniper berry
  type: **6** Geneva **8** Plymouth **9** London dry
  drink: **5** Allen **6** Gibson, gimlet **7** Belmont, Bennett, gin Fizz, swizzle **8** Pink Lady **9** Gin Rickey **10** Tom Collins **11** Alabama Fizz, gin and tonic **12** Grand Passion **14** Casino Cocktail
  with anisette: **8** Snowball **11** Bachio Punch
  with apricot brandy: **14** Boston Cocktail
  with brandy: **15** Bermuda Highball
  with Chartreuse: **5** Bijou **9** Green Lady
  with cherry brandy: **14** Singapore Sling
  with Cointreau: **7** Florida **9** White Lady **13** Sweet Patootie **14** Flying Dutchman
  with creme de cacao: **9** Alexander
  with creme de cassis: **8** Parisian
  with creme de menthe: **6** Caruso, Virgin
  with creme Yvette: **9** Union Jack
  with Curacao: **8** Blue Moon, Napoleon **9** Blue Devil **14** Flying Dutchman
  with Dubonnet: **3** BVD **8** Napoleon
  with Grand Marnier: **7** Red Lion
  with grapefruit juice: **8** Salty Dog
  with kirsch, kirschwasser: **7** Florida **10** Lady Finger
  with onions: **6** Gibson
  with orange juice: **5** Abbey **13** Orange Blossom
  with Pernod: **7** Dubarry
  with rum: **3** BVD
  with scotch: **12** Barbary Coast
  with sherry: **11** Renaissance
  with strawberries: **10** Bloodhound
  with Swedish Punch: **5** Biffy
  with vermouth: **5** Bijou, Bronx, Tango **6** Caruso **7** Bermuda, Cabaret, Martini **10** Bloodhound
  with vodka: **15** Russian Cocktail

Giovanelli
  character in: **11** Daisy Miller
  author: **5** James

Giovanni's Room
  author: **12** James Baldwin

Giraffe
  constellation of: **14** Camelopardalis

girandole 11 candelabrum, candlestick **12** candleholder

Girardon, Francois
  born: **6** France, Troyes
  artwork: **13** Bathing Nymphs **14** Galley of Apollo, Virgin of Troyes **16** Rape of Persephone **17** (tomb for) Cardinal Richelieu **23** Apollo Tended by the Nymphs

Giraudoux, Jean
  author of: **5** Bella **6** Judith, Ondine, Racine **7** Electra **12** Amphitryon 38 **15** Tiger at the Gates **18** Madwoman of Chaillot **20** My Friend from Limousin

gird 3 pen, tie **4** belt, girt, loop, ring **5** brace, hem in, hitch, steel, strap, truss **6** circle, fasten, girdle, harden, secure, wall in **7** besiege, confine, enclose, fortify, hedge in, prepare, stiffen, sustain, tighten **8** blockade, buttress, encircle, lay siege, surround **9** encompass **10** strengthen **12** circumscribe

girder 4 beam **5** brace, truss **6** binder, rafter **7** support, tie-beam

girdle 3 hem **4** band, belt, ring, sash **5** girth, hedge, stays **6** bodice, circle, corset **7** baldric, circlet, contour **8** boundary, cincture, corselet **9** surcingle, waistband **10** cummerbund **12** waist cincher **17** foundation garment

girl 4 bird, cook, help, lass, maid, minx, miss **5** angel, chick, nymph, wench **6** damsel, kitten, lassie, maiden, pigeon, virgin **7** baggage, colleen, darling, fiancee, ingenue, nymphet **8** daughter, domestic, handmaid, lady love, mistress, scullion **9** affianced, betrothed, inamorata, lady's maid, soubrette **10** sweetheart **11** maidservant
  French: **10** demoiselle, jeune fille

girl Friday 4 aide **6** helper **9** assistant, secretary **10** amanuensis **12** office worker **23** administrative assistant

girlfriend 6 steady **7** beloved, sweetie **8** best girl **10** one and only, sweetheart

Girl in a Swing
  author: **12** Richard Adams

girlish 8 girl-like, maidenly, youthful **10** maidenlike

Girl of the Golden West, The
  opera by: **7** Puccini
  setting: **8** Gold Rush **10** California
  character: **6** Minnie **7** Johnson, Sheriff

girt 4 belt, bind, gird, ring **5** bound, girth **6** belted, circle, girdle, ringed **7** circled, girdled **9** encircled

girth 5 cinch **9** perimeter **10** saddle band **13** circumference

Giselle
  ballet by: **4** (Adolphe Charles) Adam

Gish, Lillian
  real name: **12** Lillian Gishi **15** Lillian de Guiche
  born: **13** Springfield OH
  roles: **8** La Boheme **10** Enoch Arden **11** Annie Laurie, Intolerance, Way Down East **12** Duel in the Sun **13** Scarlet Letter **14** Broken Blossoms **16** Portrait of Jennie **17** Orphans of the Storm, The Birth of a Nation

Gissing, George
  author of: **5** Demos **13** New Grub Street **14** The Nether World

gist 4 core, crux, meat, pith **5** drift, force, heart, sense, tenor, theme **6** burden, center, effect, import, kernel, marrow, spirit **7** essence, purport **8** main idea **9** main point, substance **11** implication **12** significance

Giuki
  also: **5** Gjuki
  origin: **12** Scandinavian
  mentioned in: **8** Volsunga
  form: **4** king
  wife: **8** Grimhild
  daughter: **6** Gudrun, Kudrun **7** Guthrun
  son: **6** Gunnar

Giukung
  also: **7** Gjukung

origin: **12** Scandinavian
family member of: 5 Giuki,
Gjuki

Giulio Romano
architect of: **12** Palazzo del
Te
style: **9** Mannerist

give *see box*

give aid to 4 help **6** assist,
succor **7** help out **8** befriend
9 look after **10** minister to

give a leg up 3 aid **4** help,
lift **5** boost, hoist, raise **6** assist **7** elevate

give and take 8 exchange
10 compromise **11** interchange, reciprocity

give a pep talk to 4 goad,
prod, spur **5** press **6** exhort
9 encourage

give a reason for 7 clarify,
clear up, explain, justify
9 elucidate **10** account for

give as security 4 pawn
6 pledge **7** deposit, pay down,
put down

give away 6 bestow, betray,
donate, reveal **7** hand out

give birth 4 bear **5** hatch
6 create, invent **7** deliver, develop **9** originate **10** bring
forth

give confidence to 7 inspire
8 embolden, inspirit
9 encourage

give courage 5 brace **6** buck
up **7** hearten **8** inspirit,
motivate

give energy to 7 animate, enliven **8** activate, energize, vitalize **9** stimulate **10** invigorate

give enjoyment 5 amuse,
charm **6** divert, please **7** be-

guile, delight **8** enthrall
9 entertain

give forth 4 emit, gush **5** exude, issue **7** send out **8** throw
off, transmit **9** discharge

give full attention 7 pay
heed **8** fasten on
11 concentrate

give in 5 defer, yield **6** accede,
cave in, submit **7** succumb
9 surrender **10** capitulate
12 knuckle under

give in to 7 yield to **9** indulge
in, partake of **16** abandon
oneself to

give leave 3 let **5** allow **6** permit **8** sanction **9** authorize
14 give permission

give moral support to 3 aid
4 abet, back, help **6** assist, uphold **7** support, sustain **8** sanction **9** encourage

given 3 apt **4** wont **5** prone
6 likely, wonted **7** awarded,
donated, granted, offered **8** ac-
corded, bestowed **9** committed,
conferred, entrusted, presented **10** accustomed, handed
over, in the habit **11** contributed **13** furnished with, made
a donation, presented with
17 made a contribution

give new life to 3 fan **4** fire
6 awaken, revive **8** revivify
10 rejuvenate **11** reincarnate

give oneself to 8 dedicate
10 buckle down, consecrate

give one's word 3 vow
5 swear **6** assure, pledge **7** certify, promise, warrant
9 guarantee

give one walking papers
3 axe, can **4** fire, oust, sack
5 let go **6** bounce, lay off
7 cashier, dismiss, release

8 get rid of **9** discharge, terminate **11** give the gate, send
packing

give out 4 quit, tell, tire **6** assign, inform, reveal, run out
7 divulge, dole out, mete out
8 allocate, announce, disclose,
dispense, proclaim **9** apportion,
broadcast, parcel out **10** distribute, make public, portion
out **11** disseminate

give over 4 cede **5** yield **9** surrender **10** relinquish

give permission 3 let **5** allow
6 accede, permit **7** approve
8 sanction **9** acquiesce, authorize, give leave

give rise to 4 sire **5** breed,
cause **6** lead to **7** produce
8 engender, generate, occasion **9** call forth **10** bring
about

give support to 3 aid **4** abet
5 serve **6** defend, prop up, second **7** bolster, comfort, sustain **8** buttress, champion
10 contribute, minister to,
provide for, stick up for

give the go-ahead 4 okay
5 order **6** direct **7** appoint,
charter, empower **8** contract
9 authorize **10** commission

give the lie to 5 belie **8** disprove **9** repudiate **10** contradict, controvert

give the raspberry 3 boo,
pan **4** razz **6** deride, hoot at
8 ridicule **11** give the bird
17 give the Bronx cheer

give the right to 5 allow
6 permit **7** entitle, qualify
9 authorize

give the slip 4 duck **5** avoid,
dodge, elude, evade

give up 4 cede, drop, lose,
quit, skip **5** forgo, let go,
waive, yield **6** eschew, resign
7 abandon, forfeit, forsake
8 abdicate, forswear, renounce **9** sacrifice, surrender
10 relinquish **11** discontinue

give up the ghost 3 die
6 expire, pass on, perish **7** decease **8** pass away **15** breathe
one's last

give vent 4 free **5** let go **7** release **8** let loose, liberate
12 give free rein

give way 4 fall **6** buckle, cave
in **7** crumple **8** collapse
10 break apart

giving birth 7 bearing **8** creating, creation, delivery, hatching **9** inventing, invention
10 childbirth, delivering

---

give 3 buy, pay, tip **4** bend, ease, emit, hire, lend, show,
sink **5** admit, allot, allow, apply, award, bribe, deign, endow,
grant, issue, leave, offer, relax, utter, voice, yield **6** accord,
addict, afford, assign, attach, bestow, bounce, commit, confer, convey, devote, donate, enable, enrich, hand to, impart,
loosen, notify, open on, permit, recede, relent, render,
shrink, supply, tender, unbend, vest in **7** concede, consign,
deliver, entrust, fork out, furnish, hand out, let know, present, proffer, provide, require, requite, retreat, slacken **8** announce,
bequeath, collapse, dispense, exchange, fork over, hand over,
lead on to, make over, move back, put forth, shell out
9 apportion, break down, dispose of, equip with, favor with,
look out on, present to, pronounce, subscribe, surrender,
vouchsafe **10** articulate, become soft, compensate, contribute,
deliquesce, distribute, recompense, remunerate, resilience,
supply with **11** communicate, flexibility, provide with,
springiness

11 originating, origination, parturition

giving up 7 refusal **8** dropping, quitting, yielding **9** resigning **10** abandoning, abdicating, abdication, abstinence, continence, forbearing, forfeiting, forfeiture, self-denial **11** abandonment, forswearing, resignation **12** renunciation, surrendering **14** relinquishment

gizmo 4 tool **6** device, doodad, gadget **9** apparatus, implement, invention, mechanism **10** instrument **11** contraption, contrivance, thingamabob, thingamajig

Gjuki *see* **5** Giuki

Gjukung *see* **7** Giukung

glacial 3 icy, raw **4** cold **5** chill, gelid, polar **6** arctic, biting, bitter, frigid, frosty, frozen, wintry **7** hostile **8** freezing, inimical, piercing **9** congealed **10** disdainful, unfriendly **12** antagonistic, bone-chilling, contemptuous

Glackens, William James
   born: 14 Philadelphia PA
   artwork: 9 Promenade **11** Chez Mouquin **15** Nude with an Apple **16** Washington Square (A Holiday in the Park) **17** Luxembourg Gardens

glad 5 happy **6** elated, joyful, joyous **7** elating, gleeful, pleased, tickled **8** blissful, cheerful, cheering, pleasing, rejoiced **9** contented, delighted, joy-giving **10** delightful, entrancing, gratifying **11** exhilarated, tickled pink **12** exhilarating

gladden 5 cheer, elate **6** please **7** animate, cheer up, delight, enliven, gratify, hearten, rejoice **8** inspirit, pleasure **9** make happy **10** exhilarate

gladdened 5 happy **6** joyful, joyous **8** cheerful

glade 4 dell, glen, lawn, vale, wood **5** grove, marsh, vista **6** canada, hollow, valley **7** opening **8** clearing

gladness 3 joy **4** glee **5** bliss, cheer, mirth **7** delight, gaiety, jollity **8** pleasure **9** happiness **10** joyfulness **11** contentment **12** cheerfulness

glad rags 5 array **6** attire, finery **10** Sunday best

Gladsheim
   origin: 12 Scandinavian

palace of: 4 Odin **5** Othin
location: 8 Valhalla

gladsome 3 gay **5** happy, merry **6** cheery, joyful, joyous **8** cheerful **12** lighthearted

glamor, glamour 5 charm, magic **6** allure **7** glitter, romance **8** illusion **9** adventure, challenge, magnetism **10** excitement **11** enchantment, fascination **14** attractiveness

glamorous, glamourous 8 alluring, charming, dazzling, exciting, magnetic **10** attractive, bewitching, enchanting **11** captivating, charismatic, fascinating

glance 4 kiss, peek, peep, scan, skim, slip **5** brush, graze, shave, touch **6** bounce, careen, squint **7** glimpse, rebound **8** ricochet **9** brief look, quick look, quick view
French: 6 apercu

glance through 4 scan, skim **6** browse, peruse **7** dip into **8** look over **9** check over

gland
   part of: 15 endocrine system
   type: 4 duct **8** ductless
   kind: 3 oil **5** sweat **7** adrenal, thyroid **8** pancreas **9** pituitary **11** parathyroid
   ductless gland secretes: 8 hormones

glare 4 glow **5** blaze, flame, flare, flash, gleam, glint, gloss, lower, scowl, sheen **6** dazzle, glower **7** flicker, glimmer, glisten, glitter, radiate, shimmer, sparkle, twinkle **8** radiance **9** angry look, black look, dirty look **10** brightness, harsh light, luminosity **12** resplendence

glaring 4 rank **5** gross, harsh, vivid **6** arrant, bright, strong **7** blatant, flaring, intense, obvious **8** blinding, dazzling, flagrant, piercing **9** audacious, brilliant, egregious **10** glittering, outrageous, shimmering **11** conspicuous, penetrating, resplendent, unconcealed, undisguised **12** unmistakable

Glasgow, Ellen
   author of: 10 Vein of Iron **12** Barren Ground **13** In this Our Life, Sheltered Life **18** They Stooped to Folly **20** The Romantic Comedians

glass 6 beaker, goblet **7** chalice, tumbler **10** tumblerful
   type of: 4 fizz, sour **5** flute, tulip **6** jigger, sherry **7** balloon, collins, cordial, red wine, snifter **8** cocktail, highball **9** champagne, white

wine **10** hollow-stem, pousse cafe **12** old-fashioned

glasshouse 7 nursery **8** hothouse **10** greenhouse **12** conservatory

glassiness 7 clarity **8** dullness, flatness **9** shininess **10** brilliance, luminosity **12** lifelessness, transparency

Glass Key, The
   author: 15 Dashiell Hammett
   character: 9 Shad O'Rory **10** Janet Henry, Opal Madvig, Paul Madvig **11** Ned Beaumont **12** Senator Henry **13** Bernie Despain

Glass Menagerie, The
   director: 12 Irving Rapper
   author: 17 Tennessee Williams
   character: 5 Laura **6** Amanda **12** Tom Wingfield
   cast: 9 Jane Wyman **11** Kirk Douglas **13** Arthur Kennedy **16** Gertrude Lawrence

glassware 5 agata **6** aurene **7** crystal, favrile, steuben, vitrics **8** amerina, stemware
   worker: 7 glazier

glassy 4 dull **5** clear, shiny **6** glazed, smooth **8** lifeless **10** glittering **11** transparent

Glauber, Johann Rudolf
   field: 9 chemistry
   nationality: 6 German
   prepared: 12 tartar emetic **13** sodium sulfate (Glauber's salt) **16** hydrochloric acid

Glauce *see* **6** Creusa

Glaucus
   god of: 3 sea
   father: 5 Minos
   ally of: 7 Trojans
   loved by: 5 Circe **6** Scylla **10** Amphitrite

glaze 4 blur **5** gloss **6** enamel, finish **7** grow dim, varnish **8** film over **9** glass over

glazed 4 iced **5** filmy **6** coated, glassy, shined, smooth **7** glossed, sugared **8** enameled, lustrous, polished **9** burnished, varnished

Glazunoff, Alex K (Glazunov, Alexander Konstantinovich)
   born: 6 Russia **12** St Petersburg
   composer of: 10 Chopiniana, The Seasons **11** Stenka Razin **13** Hymn to Pushkin **15** Memorial Cantata

gleam 3 bit, jot, ray **4** beam, drop, glow, hint, iota **5** blink, flare, flash, glare, glint, gloss, grain, sheen, shine, spark, speck, trace **6** luster, streak

7 flicker, glimmer, glimpse, glisten, glitter, inkling, shimmer, sparkle, tiny bit, twinkle **8** least bit, radiance **9** coruscate **10** brightness, brilliance, effulgence **11** coruscation, scintillate

gleaming 5 clear, shiny **6** bright, flashy, glossy **7** shining, radiant **8** dazzling, glinting, luminous, lustrous, polished, splendid **9** brilliant, burnished, sparkling **10** glistening

glean 4 cull **5** amass **6** gather, pick up **7** harvest **10** accumulate **13** piece together **14** scrape together

gleanings 8 analects, extracts **10** miscellany, selections **11** collectanea, miscellanea **15** commonplace book

Gleason, Jackie
real name: **18** Herbert John Gleason
nickname: **15** Mr Saturday Night
born: **10** Brooklyn NY
roles: **5** Gigot **6** The Toy **10** The Hustler **11** Life of Riley, The Poor Soul **12** Ralph Kramden **15** Joe the Bartender, The Honeymooners **17** Don't Drink the Water, Jackie Gleason Show, The Time of Your Life **22** Requiem for a Heavyweight **24** Reggie Van Gleason the Third

glebe 3 sod **4** clod, land, plot, soil **5** earth, field **6** termon **8** kirktown **10** church land

glee 3 joy **5** mirth, verve **6** gaiety **7** delight, ecstasy, jollity, rapture **8** gladness, hilarity, laughter **9** joviality, merriment **10** exultation, jocularity, joyfulness, joyousness, liveliness **11** playfulness **12** cheerfulness, exhilaration, sportiveness **13** jollification, sprightliness

glee club 6 chorus **12** singing group **13** choral society

gleeful 3 gay **4** glad **5** happy, jolly, merry **6** elated, jocund, jovial, joyful, joyous, lively **7** festive **8** blissful, cheerful, exultant, mirthful **9** delighted **11** exhilarated **12** lighthearted

Gleipnir
origin: **12** Scandinavian
chain that bound: **6** Fenrir, Fenris

glen 4 dale, dell, vale **6** bottom, hollow

Glencaire Cycle
author: **12** Eugene O'Neill

glib 4 oily **5** gabby, quick, ready, suave **6** facile, fluent, smooth **7** devious, voluble **8** flippant, slippery, unctuous **9** insincere, talkative

glide 3 run **4** flow, roll, sail, skim, slip, soar **5** coast, drift, float, issue, skate, slide, steal **6** elapse, stream **7** proceed **8** glissade

glider 5 swing **7** aviator **9** sailplane **10** hydroplane

glimmer 3 bit, ray **4** beam, drop, glow, hint **5** blink, flare, flash, glare, gleam, grain, shine, speck, trace **7** flicker, glimpse, glisten, glitter, shimmer, sparkle, twinkle **9** coruscate, scintilla **10** flickering, intimation **11** scintillate

glimpse 3 see, spy **4** espy, peek, peep, spot **6** glance, peek at, peep at, squint **9** brief look, quick look, quick view **12** catch sight of, fleeting look
French: **6** apercu

Glinka, Mikhail Ivanovich
born: **6** Russia **8** Smolensk
composer of: **12** Ivan Sussanin, Karaminskaya **13** Jota Aragonesa **18** Russlan and Ludmilla

glint 4 gaze, look, peep **5** flash, gleam, sheen, shine, stare **6** glance **7** appear, glimmer, glimpse, glisten, glitter, shimmer, sparkle, twinkle **9** coruscate **11** scintillate

glissade 5 coast, glide, slide

glissando
music: **7** sliding

glisten 4 glow **5** flash, gleam, glint, shine **7** flicker, glimmer, glister, glitter, radiate, shimmer, sparkle, twinkle **9** coruscate **11** scintillate

glitter 4 fire, glow, pomp, show **5** flare, flash, gleam, glint, sheen, shine **6** luster, thrill, tinsel **7** beaming, display, glamour, glimmer, glisten, radiate, sparkle, twinkle **8** grandeur, radiance, splendor **9** pageantry, showiness **10** brilliance, excitement, refulgence **11** electricity

glittering 6 bright **7** radiant, shining **8** luminous, lustrous **9** brilliant, sparkling **11** coruscating

gloaming 4 dusk **7** evening **8** twilight

gloat 4 bask, brag **5** exult, strut, vaunt **7** revel in, swagger, triumph **8** crow over **9** glory over

global 5 world **6** all-out **7** general **9** planetary, unbounded, universal, unlimited, worldwide **10** widespread **13** comprehensive, international **16** intercontinental

globe 3 orb **4** ball **5** Earth, world **6** planet, sphere **7** globule **8** spheroid, spherule **9** biosphere

globule 4 ball, bead, bleb, blob, drop **5** globe **6** bubble, pellet, sphere **7** blister, droplet **8** particle, spheroid

glogg
type: **5** punch
origin: **6** Sweden

gloom 3 woe **4** dark, dusk, murk **5** blues, dolor, grief, shade **6** misery, sorrow **7** despair, dimness, sadness, shadows **8** darkness, distress, doldrums **9** blackness, dejection, dinginess, duskiness, murkiness, obscurity **10** cloudiness, depression, gloominess, low spirits, melancholy, mopishness, moroseness, oppression **11** despondency, forlornness, unhappiness **12** hopelessness **13** cheerlessness **16** disconsolateness, heavy-heartedness

gloomy 3 dim, sad **4** dark, dour, down, dull, glum, grim, mopy, sour **5** dusky, moody, mopey, murky, shady **6** cloudy, dismal, dreary, morbid, morose, shaded, somber **7** doleful, forlorn, shadowy, sunless, unhappy **8** dejected, desolate, downcast, frowning, funereal, overcast **9** cheerless, depressed, heartsick, miserable, sorrowful, woebegone **10** chapfallen, despondent, dispirited, ill-humored, melancholy **11** comfortless, crestfallen, discouraged, downhearted, low-spirited, pessimistic **12** disconsolate, disheartened, heavy-hearted **13** in the doldrums **14** down in the dumps, down in the mouth

Gloria in Excelsis Deo 22 Glory in the highest to God

Gloriana
character in: **15** The Faerie Queene
author: **7** Spenser

Gloriana
opera by: **7** Britten
character: **10** Elizabeth I **11** Earl of Essex

glorification 7 worship **8** devotion **9** adoration, adulation

10 exaltation, veneration
13 magnification

glorify 4 laud **5** adore, deify, exalt, extol, honor **6** praise, revere **7** beatify, dignify, elevate, ennoble, idolize, worship **8** canonize, enshrine, sanctify, venerate **9** celebrate, glamorize **10** consecrate **11** apotheosize, immortalize, romanticize

glorious 4 fine **5** grand, great, noble, noted **6** august, divine, famous, superb **7** eminent, glowing, honored, notable, radiant, shining, stately, sublime, supreme **8** dazzling, gorgeous, imposing, lustrous, majestic, renowned, splendid **9** beautiful, brilliant, dignified, excellent, marvelous, sparkling, wonderful **10** celebrated, delightful, impressive, preeminent **11** illustrious, magnificent, resplendent **12** praiseworthy **13** distinguished

glory 4 fame, mark, name **5** boast, honor, revel, vaunt **6** esteem, homage, praise, renown, repute **7** dignity, majesty, worship **8** blessing, eminence, grandeur, nobility, prestige, splendor **9** adoration, celebrity, gratitude, solemnity, sublimity **10** admiration, excellence, notability, veneration **11** benediction, distinction, preeminence, stateliness **12** magnificence, resplendence, thanksgiving **14** impressiveness **15** illustriousness

Glory in the highest to God
Latin: 19 Gloria in Excelsis Deo

gloss 4 glow, mask, veil **5** cloak, color, glaze, gleam, japan, sheen, shine **6** enamel, excuse, luster, polish, veneer **7** cover up, lacquer, shimmer, varnish **8** annotate, disguise, mitigate, radiance **9** whitewash **10** annotation, brightness, brilliance, commentary, smooth over **11** explain away, explanation, rationalize **12** luminousness, treat lightly **14** interpretation

gloss over 4 hide, mask, veil **7** conceal, cover up **9** dissemble, whitewash **12** misrepresent

glossy 5 photo, shiny, showy, silky, sleek, slick **6** bright, satiny, smooth **7** picture, shining **8** gleaming, lustrous, magazine, polished **9** burnished

glove 3 kid **4** cuff, mitt, mitt **5** catch,

thumb **6** gusset, mitten, muffle **7** chevron **8** gauntlet

glow 4 fill, heat **5** ardor, bloom, blush, color, flush, gleam, gusto, shine **6** fervor, thrill, tingle, warmth **7** flicker, glimmer, glisten, glitter, radiate, shimmer, smolder, twinkle **8** radiance **9** eagerness, intensity, radiation, reddening, vividness **10** brightness, enthusiasm **11** earnestness

glower 4 pout, sulk **5** frown, glare, lower, scowl, stare

glowing 3 hot, red **4** rave **5** ruddy, vivid **6** ardent, bright, florid, raving **7** fervent, flaming, flushed **8** ecstatic, exciting **9** rhapsodic, thrilling **10** passionate **11** luminescent, sensational, stimulating **12** enthusiastic

Glubbdubdrib
fictional land in: 16 Gulliver's Travels
author: 5 Swift

Gluck, Christoph Willibald (von)
born: 7 Bavaria **8** Neumarkt
composer of: 5 Orfeo **6** Armide **7** Alceste **13** Paride ed Elena **14** Echo et Narcisse **17** Iphigenie en Aulide **18** Iphigenie en Tauride

glue 3 fix, gum **5** affix, epoxy, paste, putty, stick **6** adhere, cement, fasten, mortar **7** plaster, stickum **8** adherent, adhesive, concrete, fixative, mucilage **11** agglutinate

gluey 5 gooey, gummy, mucid, ropey, slimy, tacky, thick, **6** sticky, viscid **7** stringy, viscous **8** adhesive **12** mucilaginous

glum 6 gloomy, morose **8** dejected **9** cheerless **10** melancholy **14** down in the mouth

glut 4 bolt, clog, cram, drug, fill, gulp, jade, load, sate **5** choke, flood, gorge, stuff **6** burden, deluge, devour, excess, gobble **7** congest, overeat, satiate, surfeit, surplus **8** gobble up, obstruct, overdose, overfeed, overload, plethora, saturate **10** gormandize, oversupply, saturation **11** obstruction, superfluity **13** overabundance, supersaturate **14** superabundance

glutinous 5 gluey, bummy, mucid, ropey, slimy, tacky, thick **6** sticky, viscid **7** viscous **8** adhesive **10** gelatinous **12** musilaginous

glutton 3 hog, pig **6** gorger

7 stuffer **8** gourmand **9** chowhound, overeater **10** bellyslave **11** gormandizer, trencherman

gluttonous 6 greedy **7** hoggish, piggish, swinish **8** edacious, grasping, ravening, ravenous **9** excessive, voracious **10** insatiable, omnivorous **11** intemperate

gluttony 8 rapacity, voracity **10** overeating **11** gourmandism, hoggishness, piggishness **12** gormandizing, intemperance, ravenousness **13** voraciousness

gnarled 6 knotty, rugged, snaggy **7** crooked, knotted, nodular, twisted **8** leathery, wrinkled **9** contorted, distorted **11** full of knots **13** weather-beaten

gnash 4 gnaw **5** chomp

gnat 7 no-see-um
group of: **5** cloud, horde

gnaw 4 bite, chew, fret, gall **5** chafe, chomp, eat at, grate, graze, munch, worry **6** browse, crunch, harrow, nibble, rankle **7** torment, trouble **8** distress, nibble at, ruminate **9** eat away at, masticate

gnome 3 elf **4** pixy **5** dwarf, troll **6** goblin, sprite **10** leprechaun

gnostic 4 sage, wise **6** clever, shrewd **7** knowing **8** mandaean, simonian **10** insightful

gnothi seauton 11 know thyself

gnu 7 brindle **8** antelope **10** wildebeest
type: **5** C gnou **9** C taurinus **12** Connochaetes

go see box

goad 4 move, prod, push, spur, urge, whet **5** drive, egg on, impel, press, prick, set on **6** arouse, exhort, fillip, incite, motive, propel, stir up **8** pressure, stimulus **9** constrain, incentive, stimulant, stimulate **10** cattle prod, inducement, motivation **11** instigation

goal 3 aim, end **4** home, mark, wire **5** point, score, tally **6** design, intent, object, target **7** end line, purpose **8** ambition, goal line, terminus **9** intention, objective **10** finish line

go along with 5 usher **6** assent, convoy, escort **8** accede to, shepherd **9** accompany, agree with, chaperone, consent to **10** comply with

go 3 act, end, fit, fly, pep, run, try, vim **4** blow, dash, elan, fare, flee, flow, jibe, lead, life, pass, quit, stir, turn, wend, work **5** agree, begin, be off, blend, drive, force, get on, lapse, leave, reach, scram, slide, split, steam, tally, trial, verve, vigor, whirl **6** accord, beat it, be used, belong, chance, decamp, depart, effort, elapse, energy, expire, extend, mettle, pass by, repair, result, retire, spirit **7** advance, attempt, be given, be known, comport, fall out, glide by, move out, operate, perform, proceed, slip off, take off, turn out, vamoose, work out **8** ambition, endeavor, function, move away, progress, slip away, sneak off, spread to, start for, steal off, vitality, vivacity, withdraw **9** animation, harmonize, terminate, transpire **10** enterprise, experiment, initiative

go ashore 4 land **6** debark **9** disembark

go astray 3 err, sin **6** wander **7** deviate, do wrong **9** misbehave **10** transgress **13** fall from grace

goat *see box*

Goat, Horned Goat
constellation of:
11 Capricornus

goat god 3 Pan **5** satyr

go away 3 ebb **4** fade, scat, wane **5** abate, leave, scram **6** depart, lessen, retire **8** withdraw **9** disappear

gob 3 dab, tar **4** clot, glob, lump, mass **6** sailor **7** Jack Tar

go back 6 return **7** retreat

gobble 3 caw **4** bolt, gulp, wolf **5** raven, stuff **6** cackle, devour, gabble, gaggle **8** bolt down, cram down, gulp down

gobbledygook 4 bosh, bunk, cant, tosh **6** jargon **7** rubbish, twaddle **8** buncombe, nonsense, tommyrot **9** gibberish, moonshine **10** balderdash, double-talk, hocus-pocus, mumbo jumbo **11** foolishness **12** fiddle-faddle

gobble up 6 devour **8** bolt down, gulp down, wolf down

go before 7 precede, predate **8** antecede, antedate **9** come first, go ahead of **10** anticipate

go-between 5 agent, envoy, fixer, proxy **6** deputy, second **7** arbiter **8** delegate, emissary, mediator **9** messenger, middleman, moderator **10** arbitrator, interceder, negotiator **12** intermediary **13** intermediator **14** representative

goblet 3 cup **5** glass **6** vessel **7** chalice

goblin 4 ogre **5** bogey, demon, troll **7** gremlin **8** bogeyman

Gobseck
author: 14 Honore de Balzac

go by 4 pass **6** elapse, pass by, roll by, rush by, slip by **7** glide by, slide by **8** slip away

go by car 4 ride **5** drive, motor

go-cart 4 cart **5** buggy **6** barrow **8** carriage, handcart, pushcart, stroller **11** wheelbarrow

go crimson 4 burn, glow **5** blush, color, flame, flush **6** redden

goat 3 kid **4** buck, butt **5** billy, nanny **6** victim **7** fall guy **9** scapegoat **11** whipping boy **13** laughingstock
breed: 6 Angora, Chamal, Nubian, Saanen **7** Granada **8** La Mancha **10** Toggenburg **11** Anglo-Nubian **12** French Alpine **13** British Alpine
combining form: 4 aego **5** capri
family: 7 Bovidae
female: 3 doe **5** capra, nanny **7** doeling
genus: 5 Capra
goat-boy: 5 Giles
goat-milk cheese: 7 chevret
goat-man: 5 satyr
god: 3 Pan **5** satyr **7** Aegipan
group of: 4 herd **5** tribe
hair: 5 kasha, tibet
hair of Angora goat: 6 mohair
male: 4 buck **5** billy
meat: 7 cabrito
star: 7 capella
young: 3 kid

God, god 4 Lord **5** Allah, deity, Jeveh **6** Elohim, Yahweh **7** Holy One, Jehovah, Skaddai **8** divinity, the Deity **9** Our Father **10** the Creator, the Godhead **11** divine being, God Almighty, the Almighty **13** the Omnipotent, the Omniscient **14** the All-Merciful, the Man Upstairs **15** the Supreme Being
Hebrew: 6 Adonai
Latin: 7 Dominus

god, first
origin: 12 Scandinavian
known as: 7 Forsete, Forseti

God and Man at Yale
author: 17 William F Buckley Jr

God and my right
French: 14 Dieu et mon droit
motto of: 18 royal arms of England

God be with us
German: 10 Gott mit uns

God be with you
Latin: 12 Deus vobiscum

Godbole, Professor
character in: 15 A Passage to India
author: 7 Forster

Goddard, Jean-Luc
director of: 10 Breathless

Goddard, Paulette
real name: 10 Marion Levy
husband: 14 Charlie Chaplin **15** Burgess Meredith **18** Erich Maria Remarque
born: 11 Great Neck NY
roles: 11 Modern Times, Unconquered **15** So Proudly We Hail **16** Standing Room Only, The Great Dictator **19** Diary of a Chambermaid

Goddard, Robert Hutchings
nationality: 8 American
inventor of: 12 rocket engine **22** liquid propellant rocket

Godden, Rumer
author of: 8 The River **14** Black Narcissus, Kitchen Madonna **16** The Peacock Spring **18** In This House of Brede, The Greengage Summer **19** An Episode of Sparrows **23** The Battle of Villa Fiorita

God enriches
Latin: 9 ditat Deus
motto of: 7 Arizona

Godfather, The
author: 9 Mario Puzo
family: 8 Corleone
director: 18 Francis Ford Coppola
cast: 8 Al Pacino (Michael) **9** James Caan (Sonny)

10 John Marley **11** Diane Keaton **12** Marlon Brando (Don Vito Corleone), Richard Conte, Robert Duvall **14** Sterling Hayden **17** Richard Castellano
Oscar for: 5 actor (Brando) **7** picture **10** screenplay
sequel: 18 The Godfather Part II

Godfather, The, Part II
director: **18** Francis Ford Coppola
cast: **8** Al Pacino **10** John Cazale, Talia Shire **11** Diane Keaton **12** Lee Strasberg, Robert DeNiro, Robert Duvall
Oscar for: **7** picture **10** screenplay **15** supporting actor (DeNiro)
sequel to: **12** The Godfather

godforsaken 5 bleak **6** lonely, remote **8** deserted, desolate, wretched **9** abandoned, neglected

god from a machine
Latin: **13** deux ex machina

God is with us
German: **10** Gott mit uns

godless 4 evil **6** wicked **7** heathen, impious, profane, ungodly **8** agnostic, depraved **9** atheistic **10** unhallowed **11** blasphemous, irreligious, unrepentant, unrighteous **12** sacrilegious, unsanctified

godlessness 7 atheism **8** apostasy, unbelief **9** disbelief **10** irreligion

godlike 4 holy **5** godly, pious **6** deific, divine, sacred **8** immortal, olympian

godliness 5 piety **8** devotion, holiness **9** reverence **10** devoutness **12** spirituality

godly 4 good, holy **5** moral, pious **6** devout, divine, sacred **7** devoted, saintly **8** faithful, hallowed, reverent **9** believing, God-loving, pietistic, religious, righteous, spiritual **10** Godfearing, sanctified **11** consecrated, pure in heart, reverential

God of Vengeance, The
author: **10** Sholem Asch

go down 3 ebb **4** drop, fade, wane **5** abate, lower, slide **6** lessen, plunge, reduce, weaken **7** descend, plummet, slacken, subside **8** decrease, diminish, moderate

God Save the Queen
author: **17** William F Buckley Jr

God's Grace
author: **14** Bernard Malamud

God's Little Acre
author: **15** Erskine Caldwell

Godthaab
capital of: **9** Greenland

God willing
Latin: **10** Deo volente

God wills it
Latin: **8** Deus vult
cry of: **9** Crusaders

Godwin, William
author of: **13** Caleb Williams **35** An Enquiry Concerning Political Justice

Goes, Hugo van der
born: **5** Ghent **8** Flanders
artwork: **7** The Fall **14** The Lamentation **19** The Death of the Virgin **21** The Adoration of the Magi **22** The Adoration of the Child **26** The Adoration of the Shepherds

Goethe, Johann
author of: **5** Faust **6** Egmont **24** The Sorrows of Young Werther **29** Wilhelm Meister's Apprenticeship

go-getter 4 doer **7** hustler **8** achiever, live wire

go-getting 7 driving, dynamic **8** forceful, hustling **9** ambitious, assertive, energetic **10** aggressive **11** hard-driving, hard-working, industrious

Gogol, Nikolai
author of: **7** The Nose **9** Dead Souls **10** Taras Bulba **11** The Overcoat **19** The Inspector-General

go hand in hand 5 match, tally **6** concur, square **7** coexist **9** accompany

go hungry 4 fast **6** famish, starve **7** abstain

Going My Way
director: **10** Leo McCarey
cast: **10** Bing Crosby (Father O'Malley) **12** Gene Lockhart **15** Barry Fitzgerald
Oscar for: **4** song **5** actor (Crosby) **7** picture **8** director **15** supporting actor (Fitzgerald)
song: **15** Swinging on a Star

gold 3 bar **4** gilt **5** aurum, ingot **6** beauty, nugget, purity, yellow **7** bullion **8** goodness, goodwill, humanity, kindness **11** beneficence
chemical symbol: **2** Au

gold and silver
Spanish: **9** oro y plata
motto of: **7** Montana

Gold Bug, The
author: **13** Edgar Allan Poe

Gold Coast see **5** Ghana **11** Sierra Leone

golden 4 best, gilt, rosy **5** blest, blond, great, happy, palmy **6** bright, gilded, joyous, timely **7** aureate, halcyon, richest, shining **8** beatific, glorious, happiest, splendid **9** favorable, opportune, priceless, promising **10** auspicious, delightful, propitious, seasonable **11** exceptional, flourishing, resplendent **12** advantageous, bright-yellow **13** extraordinary

Golden Age
first age of: **3** man
world ruled by: **6** Cronus, Saturn

Golden Ass, The
author: **14** Lucius Apuleius
character: **4** Milo **5** Fotis **6** Lucius **8** Charites, Pamphile **9** Lepolemus **10** Thrasillus

Goldenberg, Emmanuel
real name of: **15** Edward G Robinson

Golden Bough, The
branch of: **9** mistletoe
sacred to: **10** Proserpina
used by: **6** Aeneas
at shrine of: **5** Diana **7** Virbius
author: **15** Sir James G Frazer

Golden Bowl, The
author: **10** Henry James
character: **8** Mr Verver **12** Maggie Verver, Mrs Assingham **13** Prince Amerigo **14** Charlotte Stant

Golden Boy
nickname of: **11** Paul Hornung

golden brown 3 tan **5** tawny, toast **6** sienna **7** tobacco **8** chestnut

Golden Cockerel, The
also: **8** Le Coq d'Or **15** Zolotoy Petushok
opera by: **14** Rimsky-Korsakov
character: **9** King Dodon **14** Queen of Shemaka

golden egg-layer
form: **5** goose
made of: **4** gold

Golden Fleece
made of: **4** gold
kept at: **7** Colchis
kept by: **10** King Aeetes
stolen by: **5** Jason **9** Argonauts
accomplice: **5** Medea

Golden Legend
author: **13** William Caxton

goldenrod 8 Solidago
varieties: **5** sweet, white
6 Wreath **7** seaside **8** blue-stem, European
10 California

Golden State
nickname of: **10** California

golden youth
French: **13** jeunesse doree

goldfinch
group of: **5** charm

Goldfinger
director: **11** Guy Hamilton
author: **10** Ian Fleming
cast: **9** Gert Frobe (Auric Goldfinger) **10** Bernard Lee (M) **11** Lois Maxwell (Miss Moneypenny) **12** Harold Sakata (Oddjob), Shirley Eaton **13** Honor Blackman (Pussy Galore), Sean Connery (James Bond, 007)

Golding, William
author of: **8** Free Fall **13** A Moving Target **14** Lord of the Flies, Rites of Passage **15** Darkness Visible

gold mine 7 bonanza
10 mother lode

Gold Rush, The
director: **14** Charlie Chaplin
cast: **9** Mack Swain, Tom Murray **11** Georgia Hale **14** Charlie Chaplin (Little Tramp)
setting: **5** Yukon

Goldsmith, Oliver
author of: **18** She Stoops to Conquer, The Deserted Village **19** The Vicar of Wakefield

Goldstein, Elliott
real name of: **12** Elliott Gould

goldwasser
form: **7** liquor
origin: **6** France **7** Germany
flavor: **4** herb **5** spice **7** caraway
flecked with: **8** gold leaf

golf *see box*

golfer 8 Ben Hogan, Lee Elder, Sam Snead **9** Carol Mann, Hale Irwin, Patty Berg, Tom Watson **10** Betsy Rawls, Bobby Jones, Deane Beman, Gary Player, Hubie Green, Jim Demaret, Judy Rankin, Lee Trevino, Nancy Lopez **11** Ben Crenshaw, Billy Casper, Byron Nelson, Calvin Peete, Donna Caponi, Gene Sarazen, Julius Boros, Tom Weiskopf, Walter Hagen **12** Arnold Palmer, Jack Nicklaus, Joanne Carner, Johnny Miller, Mickey Wright, Sandra Haynie **14** Cary Middlecoff, Kathy Whitworth **16** Roberto DeVicenzo **19** Susie Maxwell Berning **20** Severiano Ballesteros **21** Babe Didrikson Zaharias

Golgotha 7 Calvary
means: **10** skull place

Goliath
killed by: **5** David

golliwogg 3 toy **4** doll **9** plaything

---

golf
average number strokes to reach a hole: **3** par
ball in another's path: **6** stymie
championship: **6** US Open **9** Grand Slam **11** British Open **17** Masters' Tournament
club: **4** iron, wood **6** driver, putter **7** brassie **8** long iron **9** sand wedge, short iron **10** middle iron **13** pitching wedge
club carrier: **6** caddie
course also called: **5** links
golf ball formerly called: **6** guttie **8** feathery
hole scored in one stroke: **3** ace **9** hole-in-one
one stroke less than par: **6** birdie
one stroke more than par: **5** bogey
part of the course: **3** cup, tee **4** hole **5** apron, green, rough **6** bunker, hazard **7** fairway **8** sand trap
position: **3** lie
stance: **4** open **6** closed, square **7** address
two strokes less than par: **5** eagle
type of competition: **5** match **6** stroke
uprooted turf: **5** divot
warning cry: **4** fore

Gomer
father: **7** Diblaim
husband: **5** Hosea

Gomer Pyle USMC
character: **5** Bunny **7** Frankie **9** Corp Boyle **11** Duke Slayter, (Sgt) Vince Carter
cast: **9** Jim Nabors, Roy Stuart **10** Ted Bessell **11** Frank Sutton **12** Ronnie Schell **13** Barbara Stuart

Gomorrah
destroyed with: **5** Sodom **6** Zeboim **10** Admah

Gondoliers, The
operetta by: **18** Gilbert and Sullivan
character: **4** Luiz **5** Tessa **7** Casilda **8** Gianetta **13** Marco Palmieri **15** Duke of Plaza-Toro **16** Giuseppe Palmieri

gone 3 ago, out **4** away, dead, left, lost, past **6** absent, ruined, used up **7** defunct, died out, extinct, missing **8** departed, finished, hopeless, vanished **11** disappeared

Goneril
character in: **8** King Lear
author: **11** Shakespeare

Gone With the Wind
author: **16** Margaret Mitchell
character: **5** Mammy **6** Big Sam, Prissy **7** Dr Meade **10** Ellen (Robillard) O'Hara **11** Gerald O'Hara, Honey Wilkes, India Wilkes **12** Ashley Wilkes, Aunt Pittypat, Belle Watling **13** Scarlett O'Hara, Tarleton twins **15** Mrs Merriweather **21** Melanie Hamilton Wilkes
Scarlett's husband: **11** Rhett Butler **12** Frank Kennedy **15** Charles Hamilton
Scarlett's children: **4** Emma, Wade **6** Bonnie
Scarlett's sister: **7** Carreen, Suellen
director: **13** Victor Fleming
cast: **9** Ona Munson **10** Clark Gable (Rhett Butler) **11** Evelyn Keyes, Vivien Leigh (Scarlett O'Hara) **12** Leslie Howard (Ashley Wilkes) **13** Ann Rutherford **14** Hattie McDaniel (Mammy), Thomas Mitchell (Gerald O'Hara) **16** Butterfly McQueen (Prissy) **17** Olivia de Havilland (Melanie Hamilton Wilkes)
score: **10** Max Steiner
Oscar for: **7** actress (Leigh), picture **8** director **12** screenwriter **17** supporting actress (McDaniel)
producer: **14** David O Selznick

good 3 ace, fit, new **4** best, boon, fine, full, gain, kind, pure, real **5** ample, crack, favor, great, large, merit, moral, pious, prize, right, solid, sound, sunny, valid, value, worth **6** adroit, choice, devout, entire, genial, honest, humane, kindly, lively, newest, profit, proper, seemly, select, tiptop, useful, virtue, wealth, worthy **7** adapted, benefit, capable, capital, dutiful, fitting, genuine, godsend, healthy, orderly, service, sizable, skilled, success, upright, welfare **8** adequate, becoming, blessing, bonafide, cheerful, complete, decorous, gracious, innocent, interest, kindness, obedient, obliging, pleasant, precious, reliable, salutary, skillful, smartest, sociable, splendid, suitable, thorough, topnotch, valuable, virtuous, windfall **9** admirable, advantage, agreeable, authentic, convivial, deserving, efficient, enjoyable, enjoyment, excellent, exemplary, expensive, favorable, first-rate, happiness, healthful, honorable, priceless, qualified, religious, righteous, unsullied, untainted, wholesome, wonderful **10** altruistic, beneficent, beneficial, benevolent, excellence, first-class, legitimate, proficient, prosperity, sufficient, worthwhile **11** appropriate, commendable, considerate, improvement, kindhearted, substantial, sympathetic, well-behaved **12** advantageous, considerable, praiseworthy, satisfactory **13** companionable, conscientious, righteousness
French: 3 bon **4** bien
Spanish: 5 bueno
German: 3 gut

Good as Gold
author: **12** Joseph Heller

Good Book 5 Bible

good breeding 5 grace **6** polish **7** manners **9** gentility **10** refinement **11** cultivation

good buy 4 deal **5** steal **7** bargain

good-by, good-bye 3 bye **6** bye-bye, bye now, so long **7** parting, send-off **8** farewell, Godspeed **9** departure **10** separation **11** be seeing you, leave-taking, see you later **12** God be with you **15** till we meet again
French: **5** adieu **8** au revoir
German: **14** auf Wiedersehen
Hawaiian: **5** aloha
Italian: **4** ciao **5** addio **11** arrivederci
Japanese: **8** sayonara
Latin: **4** vale
Spanish: **5** adios **12** hasta la vista

Goodbye, Darkness
author: **17** William Manchester

Goodbye, Mr Chips
director: **7** Sam Wood
author: **11** James Hilton
cast: **11** Greer Garson, Paul Henreid (von Henreid), Robert Donat
Oscar for: **5** actor (Donat)
character: **7** Mr Chips

10 Mrs Wickett **12** Kathy Bridges
school: **10** Brookfield

Goodbye Girl, The
director: **11** Herbert Ross
based on play by: **9** Neil Simon
cast: **11** Marsha Mason **13** Quinn Cummings **15** Richard Dreyfuss
Oscar for: **5** actor (Dreyfuss)

Good Companions, The
author: **11** J B Priestley

good counsel
god of: **6** Consus

good day
French: **7** bonjour
German: **8** guten tag
Spanish: **10** buenos dias
Italian: **10** buon giorno

good deal 3 buy **5** steal **7** bargain

good deed 8 kindness **11** benefaction **12** philanthropy
Hebrew: **7** mitsvah, mitzvah

Good Earth, The
author: **10** Pearl S Buck
character: **4** O-Lan **6** Nung En **7** Nung Wen, The Fool **8** Wang Lung **11** Pear Blossom **12** Lotus Blossom
director: **14** Sidney Franklin
cast: **8** Keye Luke, Paul Muni **10** Tilly Losch **11** Jessie Ralph, Luise Rainer

14 Walter Connolly
15 Charley Grapewin
Oscar for: **7** actress (Rainer)

good feelings 8 good will **11** benevolence **12** friendliness

good form 9 etiquette, good taste **10** politeness **11** good manners

good-for-nothing 5 idler **6** loafer **7** useless **9** no-account, shiftless, worthless

good fortune 4 luck **7** bonanza **8** fortuity, lady luck, windfall **9** blessings **10** lucky break

good friend
French: **6** bon ami **9** bonne amie

good health 5 vigor **7** fitness **8** vitality **10** robustness

Goodhue, Bertram Grosvenor
architect of: **13** St Bartholomew (NYC) **14** St Thomas Church (NYC) **25** Chapel at US Military Academy (West Point), National Academy of Sciences (Washington DC) **28** Nebraska State Capitol Building (Lincoln)
style: **13** Gothic Revival **15** Spanish Colonial

good humor 10 affability, amiability, cheeriness, kindliness, mellowness **12** cheerfulness, complaisance, pleasantness **15** kindheartedness

good-humored 4 mild, warm **6** cheery, genial, gentle, kindly, mellow **7** affable, amiable **8** cheerful, pleasant **9** congenial, easygoing **11** complaisant

good-looker 3 fox **4** doll, hunk **5** beaut, Venus **6** Adonis, beauty, eyeful **7** stunner **8** knockout **11** handsome Dan

good-looking 4 fair, foxy, sexy **5** bonny **6** comely, lovely, pretty **8** alluring, clean-cut, gorgeous, handsome, stunning **9** beauteous, beautiful, exquisite, ravishing **10** attractive, bewitching, enchanting **11** captivating, eye-catching, well-favored **15** pulchritudinous

good looks 6 beauty **10** comeliness, loveliness **11** pulchritude **12** handsomeness **14** attractiveness

good luck
Yiddish: **8** mazel tov

goodly 4 tidy **5** ample, large **7** sizable **11** substantial **12** considerable

Goodman, Theodosia
real name of: 9 Theda Bara

good manners 8 courtesy
9 amenities, etiquette, gentility 10 politeness, refinement

good name 4 face 5 image
10 reputation 11 self-respect

good nature 6 warmth 9 geniality, good humor 10 affability, amiability, cordiality, likability 12 complaisance, pleasantness 13 agreeableness

good-natured 4 warm
5 sunny 6 genial, kindly 7 affable, amiable 8 cheerful, friendly, obliging, pleasant 9 agreeable, congenial, easygoing 11 complaisant, good-humored, warm-hearted 13 accommodating

goodness 3 boy, gee, hey, say, wow 5 favor, honor, mercy, merit, piety, value, worth, wowee 6 profit, purity, virtue 7 benefit, decorum, gee whiz, heavens, honesty, probity, service 8 boy-oh-boy, devotion, gracious, kindness, morality 9 advantage, innocence, integrity, land alive, landsakes, nutrition, propriety, rectitude 10 generosity, kindliness, sakes alive, usefulness 11 benevolence, nourishment 12 virtuousness 13 righteousness, wholesomeness 14 heavens to Betsy

good night
French: 7 bon soir 9 bonne nuit
German: 9 gute nacht
Spanish: 12 buenas noches
Italian: 10 buona notte

good opinion 6 esteem, regard 7 respect 8 approval 10 admiration

good person 4 dear, love
5 angel 7 darling
10 sweetheart

goods 4 gear 5 cloth, stock, wares 6 fabric, things 7 effects, fabrics 8 chattels, material, movables, property, textiles 9 inventory, trappings 11 commodities, furnishings, merchandise, possessions 13 appurtenances, paraphernalia

good sense 6 brains, wisdom
8 judgment 12 intelligence

good taste 10 refinement
11 cultivation, discernment 14 discrimination

good-tempered 5 sunny
7 amiable, smiling 8 cheerful 12 sweet-natured

good time 3 fun 9 amusement, diversion, enjoyment 13 entertainment

good times 4 boom 8 fat years

good turn 5 favor 7 service
8 good deed

goodwill 5 amity 8 kindness
9 benignity 10 cordiality, kindliness 11 amicability, benevolence 12 friendliness 15 kindheartedness

good wishes 4 best 5 favor
6 regard 7 consent, regards 8 approval, blessing, respects, sanction 11 compliments

Goodwood, Caspar
character in: 18 The Portrait of a Lady
author: 5 James

good word 6 praise 10 compliment 11 approbation 12 commendation 14 congratulation

Goodyear, Charles
nationality: 8 American
developed: 16 vulcanized rubber

goof 3 err 4 boob, flub, fool, mess 5 botch, error, gum up 6 bollix, boo-boo, bungle, fumble, slip up 7 blunder, mistake 9 oversight

Goolagong Cawley, Evonne
sport: 6 tennis
heritage: 19 Australian Aborigine

go on all fours 5 crawl, creep

goose
young: 7 gosling
group of: 5 flock, skein 6 gaggle

goose egg 3 nil, zip 4 zero
5 aught 6 cipher, naught 7 nothing 11 horse collar

go over 5 audit, check 6 review 7 examine, inspect 10 scrutinize 11 investigate

Gopher State
nickname of: 9 Minnesota

Gorbachev, Mikhail Sergeyevich
party: 9 Communist
country: 4 USSR 6 Russia 31 Union of Soviet Socialist Republics
born: 9 Stavropol 10 Privolnoye 16 Krasnogvardeisky
education: 21 Moscow State University
political career: 9 Politburo 16 General Secretary 20 Agriculture Secretary 23 Stavropol Communist Party 35 Deputy Supreme Soviet Central Committee

policy: 8 glasnost
11 perestroika
distinguishing characteristic: 19 strawberry birthmark (head)
wife: 15 Raisa Maksimovna
occupation: 7 teacher
daughter: 5 Irisa
occupation: 6 doctor 9 physician

Gorcey, Leo
born: 9 New York NY
roles: 4 Spit 10 Bowery Boys 11 Dead End Kids

Gordimer, Nadine
author of: 11 July's People 12 The Lying Days 13 A Guest of Honor 15 Burger's Daughter 16 A Soldier's Embrace 21 The Late Bourgeois World
award: 10 Nobel Prize

Gordon, Ruth
real name: 15 Ruth Gordon Jones
husband: 11 Garson Kanin
born: 11 Wollaston MA
roles: 11 Where's Poppa? 13 Rosemary's Baby 14 Harold and Maude 17 Inside Daisy Clover 20 Abe Lincoln in Illinois

gore 5 blood 7 carnage
8 butchery 9 bloodshed, slaughter

Gore, Albert
born: 10 Washington (DC)
wife: 6 Tipper 13 Mary Elizabeth
children: 5 Sarah 6 Albert 7 Karenna, Kristin
education: 7 Harvard 10 Vanderbilt
profession: 10 journalist
author of: 17 Earth in the Balance
political career: 6 Senate 13 vice president 22 House of Representatives

Gorgas, William Crawford
field: 8 medicine
position: 18 army surgeon general
conquered: 7 malaria 11 yellow fever
location: 11 Panama Canal

gorge 3 gap, ire 4 bolt, cram, craw, dale, dell, fill, glen, glut, gulp, pass, sate, vale 5 abyss, anger, blood, chasm, cleft, gulch, gully, mouth, stuff, wrath 6 canyon, defile, devour, gobble, gullet, hatred, hollow, muzzle, nausea, ravine, throat 7 disgust, indulge, overeat, satiate 8 crevasse 9 animosity, esophagus, repulsion, revulsion 10 gluttonize, gormandize, repugnance 11 overindulge

gormandize, repugnance
11 overindulge

gorgeous 4 fine, rich **5** grand
6 bright, costly, lovely **7** elegant, opulent, shining **8** dazzling, glorious, imposing,
splendid, stunning **9** beautiful,
brilliant, exquisite, luxurious,
ravishing, sumptuous **10** attractive, glittering, impressive
11 good-looking, magnificent,
resplendent, splendorous
13 splendiferous

Gorgons
form: 7 maidens **8** monsters
names: 6 Medusa, Stheno
7 Euryale, Sthenno
father: 7 Phorcys
mother: 4 Ceto
protectress: 6 Graeae, Graiae
hair of: 6 snakes
hands of: 5 brass
turned viewers to: 5 stone

Gorgophone
father: 7 Perseus
mother: 9 Andromeda
husband: 7 Oebalus **8** Perieres
son: 9 Leucippus

Gorgosaurus
type: 8 dinosaur, theropod
location: 7 Alberta **12** North
America
period: 10 Cretaceous

Gorgythion
mentioned in: 5 Iliad
father: 5 Priam
killed by: 6 Teucer

gorilla
group of: 4 band

Gorky, Arshile
real name: 21 Vosdanig Manoog Adokian
born: 7 Armenia
11 Khorkomvari
artwork: 5 Agony **15** Diary
of a Seducer **17** Making the
Calendar **21** The Artist and
his Mother, Water of the
Flowery Hill **22** The Liver is
the Cock's Comb

Gorky, Maxim (Maksim)
real name: 25 Alekseimaksimovich Peshkov
author of: 7 V I Lenin
11 My Childhood **14** The
Lower Depths **18** The Small
Town Okurov **20** City of the
Yellow Devil, Twenty-six
Men and a Girl **27** The Life
of Matthew Kozhemyakin

gormandize 5 feast, raven
6 devour

Gortys
father: 10 Stymphalus
12 Rhadamanthys

gory 5 scary **6** bloody, creepy

9 murderous **10** horrifying,
sanguinary, terrifying
11 bloodsoaked, ensanguined,
frightening **12** bloodstained,
bloodthirsty **13** bloodcurdling

gospel, Gospel 5 credo,
creed **8** doctrine **11** the good
news, the last word **12** the final word **13** the whole truth,
ultimate truth
**the first four books of the
New Testament: 4** Luke,
John, Mark **7** Matthew

Gospel writers 4 John, Luke,
Mark **7** Matthew **9** synoptist

gospodin 2 Mr **6** Mister

gossamer 5 filmy, gauzy,
sheer **8** cobwebby **10** diaphanous **13** insubstantial

gossip 4 news **6** babble, report,
tattle **7** comment, hearsay,
prattle, scandal, twaddle **8** idle
talk **10** backbiting **12** tittle-
tattle **13** newsmongering

gossiper 3 pry **4** blab **5** prate,
snoop, yenta **6** gabble, magpie,
meddle, tattle **7** babbler, meddler, prattle, snooper, tattler
8 busybody **9** chatterer
10 chatterbox, newsmonger,
talebearer, tattletale **11** rumor-
monger **12** blabbermouth, gossipmonger **13** scandalmonger

go stale 3 die

Go Tell It on the Mountain
author: 12 James Baldwin

Gothic
language family: 12 Indo-
European

go through 4 bear **6** endure,
suffer **7** sustain, undergo **9** encounter, withstand
10 experience

go to 3 see **5** visit **6** attend
8 appear at, frequent

go to bed 6 retire, turn in
7 lie down, sack out **8** flake
out **9** hit the hay **10** call it a
day, hit the sack **11** catch
some z's

go to pieces 5 break, crack
7 break up, crack up, crumble,
give way, shatter **8** splinter
9 break down, fall apart
11 lose control **12** disintegrate

go to work on 6 attack,
tackle **8** set about **9** undertake

go to wrack and ruin 5 decay **7** crumble **9** fall apart
12 disintegrate

Gotterdammerung 17 Twilight of the Gods
see: 8 Ragnarok

Gott mit uns 11 God be with
us, God is with us

gouge 5 carve, drill, scoop
6 chisel, extort **10** overcharge

gouge out 5 drill **6** hollow
8 carve out, scoop out **9** chisel
out, hollow out **10** whittle out

Gould, Chester
creator / artist of: 9 Dick
Tracy

Gould, Elliott
real name: 16 Elliott
Goldstein
wife: 15 Barbra Streisand
born: 10 Brooklyn NY
roles: 4 MASH **13** Little Murders **14** The Long Goodbye
15 California Split, Getting
Straight **19** Bob & Carol &
Ted & Alice

Goulding, Edmund
director of: 10 Grand Hotel
11 Dark Victory **13** The
Dawn Patrol

go under 4 fail, fall, sink **9** go
belly up **10** go bankrupt

Gounod, Charles Francois
born: 5 Paris **6** France
composer of: 5 Faust **6** Gallia, Sappho, Te Deum
8 Cinq-Mars, Mireille **9** La
Colombe, Polyeucte **10** Mors
et Vita **11** Marie Stuart, Stabat Mater **13** La Reine de
Saba **14** Romeo and Juliet
16 La Nonne Sanglante, Philemon et Baucis **17** La Tribute de Zamora **18** Le
Medecin Malgre Lui

gourd 9 Cucurbita **13** Cucurbita
pepo
varieties: 3 ash, ivy, rag,
wax **4** club **5** snake, white
6 bitter, bottle, dipper,
sponge, teasel, viper's **7** fig-
leaf, Malabar, serpent, trumpet **8** calabash, hedgehog,
Missouri **9** dishcloth
10 goareberry, gooseberry,
knob-kerrie, silver-seed
11 sugar-trough **12** Hercules'-club **14** scarlet-fruited

gourmand 7 glutton **8** big
eater **9** bon vivant, chowhound **11** gormandizer,
trencherman

gourmet 7 epicure **9** bon vivant **10** gastronome **11** connoisseur, gastronomer
12 gastronomist

gourmet cooking
French: 12 haute cuisine

Gourmont, Remy de
author of: 18 A Night in
Luxembourg

gout 5 style, taste
10 preference

govern 3 run 4 boss, curb,
form, head, lead, rule, sway,
tame 5 check, guide, pilot,
steer 6 bridle, direct, manage
7 command, control, incline,
inhibit, oversee 8 dominate,
restrain 9 influence, supervise
10 administer, discipline, hold
in hand 11 hold in check, superintend 13 be at the helm
of 14 pull the strings 16 keep
under control 17 exercise authority 18 be in the driver's
seat

governed 3 led 5 ruled
6 guided 7 steered, subject
8 directed 9 dependent
10 controlled, supervised
12 administered
13 superintended

governing 6 ruling 7 curbing,
guiding, heading, leading,
swaying 8 bridling, checking,
managing, piloting, reigning,
steering 9 directing, inclining
10 inhibiting, management,
overseeing 11 controlling, influencing, restraining, supervision 13 administering
14 administrating, administration, superintending

governing body 10 government, management, parlia-
ment 12 powers that be
14 administration 16 board of
directors, board of governors
18 executive committee

government 3 law 4 rule
5 state 6 regime 7 command,
control 8 dominion, guidance
9 authority, direction 10 domination, management, regulation 11 supervision
13 governing body, statesmanship 14 administration

governor
Turkish: 3 beg, bey

Gowan
character in: 12 Little Dorrit
author: 7 Dickens

go with 6 convey, convoy, escort 7 conduct 9 accompany

gown 4 robe 5 dress, frock
10 nightdress

goy 6 non-Jew 7 Gentile

**Goya (y Lucientes, Fran-
cisco Jose de)**
born: 5 Spain 13 Fuente de
todos
artwork: 8 Proverbs 10 Dis-
parates 11 Tauromaquia
12 Los Caprichos, The Na-
ked Maja 15 Majas on a
Balcony 17 The Disasters of
War 21 Charles IV and his
Family

grab 3 bag, nab 4 grip, hold,
pass 5 catch, clasp, grasp,
lunge, pluck, seize 6 clutch,
collar, snatch 7 capture

grace 4 deck, love, tact, trim
5 adorn, charm, endow, exalt,
favor, honor, mercy, merit,
piety, skill, taste 6 beauty, bedeck, enrich, pardon, polish,
set off, virtue 7 charity, culture, decorum, dignify, dress
up, elevate, enhance, garnish,
glorify, manners, smarten,
suavity 8 beautify, clemency,
decorate, elegance, felicity, flu-
idity, God's love, holiness, lenience, ornament, reprieve,
sanctity, spruce up, urbanity
9 embellish, endowment, etiquette, exemption, extra time,
God's favor, good looks, propriety 10 aggrandize, comeliness, devoutness, excellence,
indulgence, refinement 11 cultivation, forgiveness, lissomeness, pulchritude, saintliness,
willowiness 12 dispensation,
gracefulness, mannerliness,
mercifulness 14 accomplishment, divine goodness
French: 11 savoir faire

graceful 5 lithe 6 comely, limber, lovely 7 elegant, lissome,
shapely, sinuous, willowy
8 delicate 9 beautiful, lithesome, sylphlike 10 attractive
11 light-footed

gracefulness 8 delicacy, fluid-
ity 10 suppleness
11 lissomeness

graceless 5 gawky, inept
6 clumsy 7 awkward 10 un-
graceful 11 heavy-handed

Graces
also: 7 Gratiae 9 Charities
goddesses of: 6 beauty
father: 4 Zeus
mother: 8 Eurynome
names: 4 Auxo 5 Cleta
6 Aglaia, Thalia 7 Phaenna
8 Hegemone 10 Euphrosyne

gracious 2 my 3 boy, gee,
wow 4 kind 5 civil, mercy, oh
boy 6 benign, humane, kindly,
polite, tender, ye gods 7 affable, amiable, clement, cordial,
courtly, gee whiz, lenient, my
stars 8 friendly, goodness,
merciful, obliging, pleasant
9 benignant, courteous, landsakes 10 benevolent, charitable, chivalrous, hospitable
11 good heavens, good na-
tured, kindhearted 13 compassionate 14 heavens to Betsy

gradation 4 step 5 stage 6 degree 7 shading 8 grouping, ordering 9 arranging
11 arrangement 12 organization 14 classification

grade 4 bank, even, hill, mark,
ramp, rank, rate, sort, step
5 brand, caste, class, level, order, pitch, place, slope, stage,
value 6 degree, estate, rating,
smooth, sphere, status 7 flatten, incline, quality, station
8 classify, gradient, position,
standing 9 acclivity, condition,
declivity, intensity

grade-A 2 A-1 4 aces, a-one,
fine, tops 5 grade, great,
prime, super 6 choice, superb,
tip-top 7 capital 8 peerless,
sterling, superior, top-notch
9 excellent, first-rate, matchless, superfine 10 first-class,
preeminent, tremendous
11 outstanding, superlative

**Gradgrind, Thomas and
Louisa**
characters in: 9 Hard Times
author: 7 Dickens

gradient 4 ramp, tilt 5 pitch,
slant, slope 6 ascent 7 incline,
leaning 9 steepness
11 inclination

gradual 4 slow 6 gentle,
steady 7 regular 8 measured
9 graduated, piecemeal
10 continuous, deliberate,
drop-by-drop, inch-by-inch,
step-by-step, successive 11 incremental, progressive 13 imperceptible, slow-but-steady
14 little-by-little

graduate 5 grade 6 alumna
7 alumnus, mark off 9 calibrate 10 measure out 14 grant
a degree to, receive a
degree

Graduate, The
director: 11 Mike Nichols
cast: 12 Anne Bancroft (Mrs
Robinson) 13 Dustin Hoff-
man, Katharine Ross
14 Murray Hamilton, Wil-
liam Daniels
score: 17 Simon and
Garfunkel
Oscar for: 8 director

Graeae
also: 6 Graiae
goddesses of: 3 sea
number: 5 three
names: 4 Enyo 5 Deino
9 Pemphredo
father: 7 Phorcys
mother: 4 Ceto
sisters: 7 Gorgons
protectresses of: 7 Gorgons
personified: 6 old age
three shared: 6 one eye
8 one tooth
eye stolen by: 7 Perseus
corresponds to: 4 Enyo

Graeme, Alison
character in: 21 The Master
of Ballantrae
author: 9 Stevenson

Graf 5 count

graft 3 bud 4 join, last, slip, swag 5 booty, infix, inset, plant, scion 6 bribes, payola, splice, spoils, sprout 7 bribery, implant, ingraft, payoffs, plunder, rake-off 8 kickback 9 hush money 10 corruption, transplant 12 implantation 13 inserted shoot

Graham, Bruce
architect of: 17 John Hancock Center (Chicago)

Grahame, Kenneth
author of: 19 The Wind in the Willows

Graiae see 6 Graeae

grain 3 bit, dot, jot, rye 4 atom, corn, dash, iota, mite, oats, seed, whit 5 crumb, grist, maize, ovule, pinch, spark, speck, touch, trace, wheat 6 barley, cereal, kernel, millet, morsel, pellet, tittle, trifle 7 granule, modicum 8 fragment, molecule, particle 9 scintilla
abbreviation: 2 gr
god of: 7 Robigus
goddess of: 6 Ribigo

Grain Coast see 11 Sierra Leone

Grainger, Percy Aldridge
born: 9 Australia, Melbourne
composer of: 14 Country Gardens 17 Handel in the Strand 19 Rosenkavalier Ramble

gram
abbreviation of: 1 g

Gram
origin: 12 Scandinavian
mentioned in: 8 Volsunga
form: 5 sword
owned by: 7 Sigmund
used by: 6 Sigurd
killed by: 6 Fafnir

grand 2 A-1 3 big 4 fine, full, good, head, huge, keen, main 5 chief, fancy, great, large, lofty, noble, regal, royal, showy, super, swell 6 august, choice, groovy, kingly, lordly, superb 7 dashing, elegant, exalted, haughty, mammoth, opulent, pompous, queenly, stately, sublime, supreme 8 arrogant, complete, elevated, fabulous, glorious, imperial, imposing, majestic, palatial, princely, real cool, real gone, smashing, splendid, striking, terrific 9 admirable, dignified, excellent, first-rate, grandiose, luxurious, marvelous, principal, sumptuous, wonderful 10 impressive, monumental, out-of-sight 11 highfalutin, magnificent,

pretentious, sensational 12 ostentatious 13 comprehensive, distinguished

Grand Canyon State
nickname of: 7 Arizona

grande dame 9 great lady

grandee 5 noble 8 nobleman 9 blue blood 10 aristocrat

Grandees
author: 17 Stephen Birmingham

grandeur 4 fame, pomp 5 glory, state 6 luster 7 dignity, majesty 8 eminence, nobility, splendor 9 celebrity, loftiness, solemnity, sublimity 10 augustness, excellence, importance 11 distinction, stateliness 12 magnificence, resplendence 14 impressiveness

Grand Hotel
author: 9 Vicki Baum
character: 9 Miss Flamm 12 Baron Gaigern 14 Dr Otternschlag, Otto Kringelein 27 Herr Generaldirektor Preysing 32 Elisaveta Alexandrovna Grusinskaya
director: 14 Edmund Goulding
cast: 10 Greta Garbo 12 Joan Crawford, Wallace Beery 13 John Barrymore 15 Lionel Barrymore
setting: 6 Berlin

Grand Illusion
director: 10 Jean Renoir
cast: 5 Dalio 7 Carette 9 Dita Parlo, Jean Gabin 13 Pierre Fresnay 16 Erich von Stroheim

grandiloquent 5 lofty 6 florid, turgid 7 flowery, pompous, stilted, swollen 8 inflated 9 bombastic, grandiose, high-flown 10 rhetorical 11 highfalutin, pretentious 12 highsounding, magniloquent

grandiose 5 grand 7 pompous, splashy 8 affected 9 high-flown 10 flamboyant, theatrical 11 extravagant, highfalutin, pretentious

Grand Marnier
type: 6 brandy, cognac 7 liqueur
origin: 6 France
flavor: 6 orange
with gin: 7 Red Lion

grand monde 10 great world 11 best society 16 fashionable world

grand prix 10 grand prize

grand prize
French: 9 grand prix

Grange, Red (Harold)
nickname: 14 Galloping Ghost
sport: 8 football
team: 11 U of Illinois 12 Chicago Bears

Granger, Edith
character in: 12 Dombey and Son
author: 7 Dickens

Grangosier
character in: 22 Gargantua and Pantagruel
author: 8 Rabelais

Granite State
nickname of: 12 New Hampshire

grant 4 boon, cede, gift, give 5 admit, allot, allow, award, endow, favor, yield 6 accord, assign, bestow, confer, donate, permit 7 agree to, bequest, concede, consent, deal out, largess, present, subsidy, tribute 8 accede to, allocate, bestowal, dispense, donation, gratuity, offering 9 allotment, allowance, apportion, consent to, endowment, vouchsafe 10 assignment, concession, indulgence 11 benefaction 12 contribution, presentation 13 appropriation

Grant, Cary
real name: 23 Archibald Alexander Leach
wife: 10 Dyan Cannon 13 Barbara Hutton
born: 7 England 8 Bristol
roles: 6 Topper 9 Dream Wife, Houseboat 10 Indiscreet 11 Blonde Venus, Father Goose 13 To Catch a Thief 14 Bringing Up Baby, Monkey Business, The Bishop's Wife 15 She Done Him Wrong 16 North by Northwest 17 Arsenic and Old Lace, I Was a Male War Bride 18 Operation Petticoat 20 The Philadelphia Story 21 None But the Lonely Heart

Grant, Lee
real name: 21 Lyova Haskell Rosenthal
born: 9 New York NY
roles: 7 Shampoo 10 Plaza Suite 11 Peyton Place, The Landlord 14 Detective Story 19 In the Heat of the Night 20 Divorce American Style

Grant, Ulysses Simpson
see box

granted
French: 7 d'accord

grantee 8 receiver 9 recipient 11 beneficiary

Grant, Ulysses Simpson
real name: 17 Hiram Ulysses Grant
nickname: 3 Sam 4 Lyss 27 Unconditional Surrender Grant
presidential rank: 10 eighteenth
party: 10 Republican
state represented: 2 IL
defeated: 5 (David) Davis, (James) Black 6 (Charles) O'Conor 7 (Horace) Greeley, (Horatio) Seymour 9 (William Slocomb) Groesbeck
vice president: 5 (Thomas W) Ferry (acting) 6 (Henry) Wilson (died in office 1875), (Schuyler) Colfax
cabinet:
  state: 4 (Hamilton) Fish 9 (Elihu Benjamin) Washburne
  treasury: 7 (Alexander Turney) Stewart, (Benjamin Helm) Bristow, (Lot Myrick) Morrill 8 (George Sewall) Boutwell 10 (William Adams) Richardson
  war: 4 (Alphonso) Taft 7 (James Donald) Cameron, (John Aaron) Rawlins, (William Worth) Belknap
  attorney general: 4 (Alphonso) Taft, (Ebenezer Rockwood) Hoar 7 (Amos Tappan) Akerman 8 (George Henry) Williams 10 (Edwards) Pierrepont
  navy: 5 (Adolph Edward) Borie 7 (George Maxwell) Robeson
  postmaster general: 5 (James Noble) Tyner 6 (Marshall) Jewell 8 (James William) Marshall, (John Angel James) Creswell
  interior: 3 (Jacob Dolson) Cox 6 (Columbus) Delano 8 (Zachariah) Chandler
born: 15 Point Pleasant OH
died: 15 Mount McGregor NY
buried: 9 New York NY
education: 9 West Point 17 US Military Academy
religion: 9 Methodist
author: 24 Personal Memoirs of US Grant 30 Around the World with General Grant
political career:
  secretary of: 3 War (interim appointment)
civilian career: 6 farmer
military service: 6 US Army 8 Civil War 10 Mexican War 18 Illinois Volunteers 20 Commander of Union Army
notable events of lifetime/career: 5 Panic (of 1873) 11 Black Friday (gold panic) 16 Custer's Last Stand
  Act: 10 Salary Grab
  conspiracy: 11 Whiskey Ring
  scandal: 14 Credit Mobilier
quote: 60 "No terms except unconditional and immediate surrender can be accepted"
father: 9 Jesse Root
mother: 6 Hannah (Simpson)
siblings: 5 Clare 10 Orvil Lynch 11 Mary Frances 13 Samuel Simpson, Virginia Paine
wife: 5 Julia (Boggs Dent)
children: 5 Ellen 9 Jesse Root 13 Frederick Dent 14 Ulysses Simpson

grant immunity to 4 free 5 clear, spare 6 except, excuse, exempt 7 absolve, release, relieve 9 privilege

grantor 5 giver 8 bestower 10 benefactor

granulate 5 crush 6 powder 9 pulverize 11 crystallize

granulated 6 ground 7 crushed 8 powdered 10 pulverized 12 crystallized

granule 5 grain 7 crystal 8 particle

grape *see box*

Grapes of Wrath, The
author: 13 John Steinbeck
character: 4 Noah 6 Connie, Ma Joad, Pa Joad 7 Jim Casy, Tom Joad 12 Rose of Sharon
director: 8 John Ford
cast: 10 Henry Fonda 11 Jane Darwell 12 Dorris
Bowden 13 John Carradine 15 Charley Grapewin
Oscar for: 17 supporting actress (Darwell)

graphic 4 seen 5 clear, drawn, lucid, vivid 6 visual 7 painted, printed, visible, written 8 distinct, explicit, forcible, lifelike, pictured, striking 9 pictorial, realistic, trenchant 10 expressive 11 descriptive, picturesque 12 illustrative

grappa
type: 6 brandy 7 liqueur
origin: 5 Italy
made from: 9 grape pulp

grapple 4 face, grip, hold, meet 5 catch, clasp, fight, grasp, seize 6 breast, clutch, combat, engage, fasten, tackle, take on 7 contend, grapnel, wrestle 8 confront, deal with, do battle, make fast, struggle 9 encounter, large hook, lay hold of 11 hold tightly

grape 5 Vitis 13 Vitis vinifera
varieties: 3 cat, red, sea 4 amur, blue, bush, cape, rock, sand, tail 5 bear's, bunch, frost, Javan, sugar, veldt 6 canyon, Damson, Miller, Oregon, pigeon, possum, summer, winter 7 African, Bullace, catbird, chicken, Concord, Spanish 8 European, mountain 9 evergreen, panhandle, river-bank 10 silverleaf 11 southern fox 13 sweet mountain
wine: 5 Gamay 6 Cayuga, Duriff, Merlot, Muscat, Shiraz 7 Barbera, Catawba 8 Baco Noir, Dolcetto, Labrusca, Nebbiolo, Verduzzo 9 Aglianico, Fume Blanc, Huxelrebe, Pinot Noir, Primitivo, Trebbiano, Zinfandel 10 Chardonnay, Sangiovese 11 Chenin Blanc, Petite Sirah, Pinot Bianco, Seyval Blanc 13 Cabernet Franc, Montepulciano 14 Sauvignon Blanc 15 Gewurtztraminer 17 Cabernet Sauvignon 20 Johannisberg Riesling

grasp 3 get, ken 4 grab, grip, hold, sway, take 5 catch, clasp, infer, power, range, reach, savvy, scope, seize, sense, skill, sweep 6 clinch, clutch, deduce, fathom, follow, master, snatch, take in, talent 7 catch at, compass, control, embrace, grapple, mastery, seizing, seizure 8 clutches, gripping, perceive 9 handclasp, knowledge, seize upon 10 comprehend, perception, understand 13 comprehension, understanding

grasping 5 venal 6 greedy 7 hoggish, miserly, selfish, wolfish 8 covetous 9 mercenary, predatory, rapacious 10 avaricious 11 acquisitive

graspingness 5 greed 7 avarice 8 rapacity, venality 10 greediness 12 covetousness

grass *see box*

Grass, Gunter
author of: 6 Floods 8 Dog Years 10 The Tin Drum 11 Cat and Mouse, The Flounder 16 Local Anaesthetic 18 The Meeting at Telgte 20 From the Diary of a Snail 33 Headbirths or The Germans Are Dying Out

grasshopper
variety: 5 pygmy 6 meadow, monkey 7 katydid 10 band winged, cone headed, long-horned, slant-faced 11 bush katydid, leaf-rolling, short-

---

grass
varieties: 3 cup, cut, dog, eel, elk, mat, nut, oat, oil, pin, rib, rye, Uva 4 barn, bear, bent, blue, chee, cord, crab, deer, fish, hair, lace, love, Lyme, moor, Nard, palm, Para, rice, rush, silk, star, tape, worm, yard 5 arrow, Bahia, beach, beard, Brome, Carib, China, cloud, curly, Ditch, fever, goose, lemon, Means, Melic, Mondo, natal, quack, sedge, shave, shore, Smilo, spike, squaw, Sudan, sword, Vasey, wheat, white, witch, zebra 6 Aleppo, alkali, basket, Bengal, Buffel, Canary, carpet, Dallis, Dudder, finger, gallow, Guinea, Indian, Korean, Manila, Napier, orange, orchid, Pampas, Rescue, Rhodes, ribbon, ripple, scurvy, signal, starry, switch, Tobosa, velvet, vernal, viper's, Zoysia 7 Bermuda, Brahman, Bristle, Buffalo, Esparto, Harding, Johnson, Kleberg, Pangola, poverty, pudding, quaking, Ravenna, sea lyme, serpent, tall oat, Wallaby, Widgeon 8 Angleton, blue-eyed, blue love, Boer love, elephant, fountain, hairy cup, lazy-man's, molasses, Ree wheat, sand love, scorpion, tuber oat 9 blue conch, centipede, common rye, hairy crab, hare's-tail, Hungarian, Malojilla, Mascarene, Oregon rye, rancheria, tall wheat, water star, yellow nut 10 Amur silver, beavertail, big quaking, blue finger, citronella, English rye, false wheat, golden-eyed, Indian rice, Italian rye, Korean lawn, Kuma bamboo, purple-eyed, rabbit-foot, rabbit-tail, reed canary, tufted hair, Washington, western rye, yellow-eyed 11 annual beard, branched cup, desert wheat, domestic rye, dwarf meadow, feather love, giant finger, green needle, Lehmann love, Nepal silver, Pentz finger, prairie cord, ringed beard, St Augustine, sweet vernal, Texas needle, Texas winter, weeping love 12 Common carpet, crested wheat, crinkled hair, European dune, Indian basket, Japanese lawn, Japanese love, Korean velvet, perennial rye, slender wheat, squirreltail, western wheat 13 American beach, Australian rye, billion-dollar, European beach, Himalaya fairy, Japanese sedge, little quaking, Paraguay Bahia, plains bristle, Siberian wheat 14 African Bermuda, bluebunch wheat, Japanese carpet, Pensacola Bahia, perennial veldt, pubescent wheat, Saint Augustine, stiff-hair wheat 15 European feather, Wilmington Bahia 16 creeping windmill, Pacey's English rye 17 Australian feather, intermediate wheat, Mediterranean salt, Transvaal dog-tooth 18 Australian windmill, California blue-eyed, Mexican everlasting 19 Fairway crested wheat 20 standard crested wheat

---

horned 12 shield-backed, spur-throated

grassland 3 lea 4 farm, vale, veld 5 field, pampa, plain, range, veldt 6 meadow 7 pasture, prairie, savanna 8 farmland, flatland, savannah 10 plantation

grate 3 irk, jar, rub, vex 4 bars, burr, buzz, gall, rasp 5 annoy, chafe, clack, grill, grind, mince, shred 6 abrade, gnaw at, hearth, jangle, rankle, scrape, scream, screen 7 firebed, firebox, grating, lattice, scratch, screech 8 irritate 9 fireplace, pulverize 10 exasperate, firebasket 11 latticework

grateful 7 obliged 8 beholden, indebted, thankful 9 gratified, obligated 12 appreciative

gratefulness 6 thanks 9 gratitude 12 appreciation, thankfulness

Gratiae *see* 6 Graces

Gratiano
character in: 19 The Merchant of Venice
author: 11 Shakespeare

gratification 3 joy 4 glee, kick 5 bliss 6 relish, solace, thrill 7 comfort, delight, ecstasy, elation, rapture 8 gladness, humoring, pleasing, pleasure, soothing 9 enjoyment, happiness, transport 10 indulgence, jubilation, satisfying 11 contentment, enchantment 12 exhilaration, satisfaction

gratified 5 happy 7 content, pleased 9 satisfied 11 comfortable

gratify 4 suit 5 amuse, favor, humor 6 coddle, divert, pamper, please, regale, soothe, thrill, tickle 7 appease, delight, enchant, flatter, gladden, indulge, refresh, satisfy 8 enthrall, entrance, interest, recreate 9 enrapture, entertain, transport 10 compliment, exhilarate

gratifying 8 humoring, pleasant, pleasing, soothing 9 agreeable, enjoyable, indulging, pampering, rewarding 10 delightful, satisfying 11 pleasurable

grating 4 bars, fret, grid 5 grate, harsh, raspy 6 creaky, grille, shrill 7 jarring, lattice, rasping, raucous, squeaky, tracery, trellis 8 abrasive, annoying, filigree, fretwork, gridiron, jangling, piercing, scraping, strident **9** offensive, vexatious **10** discordant, gate of bard, irritating, unpleasant **11** cacophonous, displeasing, high-pitched **12** disagreeable, exacerbating, exasperating

grating noise 7 discord, rasping **8** grinding **9** cacophony, harshness **10** disharmony, dissonance

gratis 4 free **10** gratuitous, on the house **13** complimentary, without charge

gratitude 6 thanks **10** obligation **11** recognition **12** appreciation, beholdenness, gratefulness, thankfulness, thanksgiving **14** acknowledgment

gratuitous 4 free **6** gratis, wanton **7** donated, willing **8** baseless, unproven **9** unfounded, voluntary **10** free of cost, groundless, irrelevant, unasked for, unprovoked **11** conjectural, impertinent, presumptive, spontaneous, uncalled for, unjustified, unwarranted **13** complimentary, unrecompensed

gratuity 3 tip **4** gift **8** donation **French: 7** douceur **9** pourboire

Graustark **author: 20** George Barr McCutcheon

grave 4 dour, sage, tomb **5** acute, crypt, mound, quiet, sober, staid, vault, vital **6** gloomy, sedate, solemn, somber, urgent **7** crucial, earnest, ossuary, serious, subdued, weighty **8** catacomb, cenotaph, critical, frowning, pressing **9** dignified, important, long-faced, mausoleum, momentous, sepulcher **10** thoughtful **11** burial ground, grim visaged, significant **13** consequential, philosophical **16** last resting place, place of interment **music: 6** solemn **7** serious

Graves, Robert **author of: 9** I Claudius, King Jesus **14** Claudius the God **15** The White Goddess **16** Goodbye to All That

graveyard 7 charnel, ossuary **8** boneyard, boot hill, cemetery **10** churchyard, necropolis **12** memorial park, potter's field **13** burying ground

gravitate 4 fall, head, move, sink, tend **6** settle **7** be drawn, descend, incline **8** converge, zero in on **9** be prone to **10** lean toward

gravity 4 pull **6** danger, import, moment **7** concern, dignity, urgency **8** calmness, enormity, grimness, serenity, sobriety **9** emergency, magnitude, solemnity, staidness **10** attraction, gloominess, importance, sedateness, solemnness, somberness **11** consequence, earnestness, gravitation, seriousness **12** significance, tranquillity **13** consideration, crucial nature **14** critical nature, pull of the earth, thoughtfulness **16** mutual attraction

gray, grey 3 dun **4** ashy, dark, drab, pale **5** ashen, foggy, hoary, misty, murky, slate **6** cloudy, dismal, gloomy, silver, somber **7** clouded, grayish, grizzly, neutral, silvery, sunless **8** overcast **9** cheerless, pearl-gray **10** depressing, gray-haired, gray-headed **11** dove-colored, hoary-headed **12** mouse-colored, silver-haired **13** salt and pepper

Gray, Harold **creator/artist of: 17** Little Orphan Annie

Gray, Thomas **author of: 32** Elegy Written in a Country Churchyard

grayness 4 murk **6** pallor **8** drabness **9** bleakness **10** somberness

Grayson, Kathryn **real name: 19** Zelma Kathryn Hedrick **born: 14** Winston-Salem NC **roles: 8** Show Boat **10** Kiss Me Kate **13** Anchors Aweigh, The Desert Song **15** The Vagabond King

graze 3 rub **4** crop, rasp, skim, skin **5** brush, grind, swipe **6** abrade, browse, bruise, glance, scrape **7** pasture, scratch **8** abrasion, eat grass **16** turn out to pasture

grease 3 fat, oil **4** balm, lard **5** salve **6** anoint, tallow **7** unguent **8** ointment **9** drippings, lubricant, lubricate

grease the palm 3 tip **5** bribe **6** buy off, pay off

greasy 3 fat **4** oily, waxy **5** fatty, lardy, slick **7** buttery **8** slippery, slithery **10** lardaceous, oleaginous

great *see box*

Great Ajax **origin: 5** Greek **hero of: 9** Trojan War

greater 4 more **5** finer **6** better, bigger, larger **8** superior

Great Escape, The **director: 11** John Sturges **cast: 11** James Coburn, James Garner **12** Steve McQueen **13** David McCallum **14** Charles Bronson **15** Donald Pleasance **19** Richard Attenborough **setting: 7** Germany, POW camp

greatest 4 best, most **5** ultra **6** picked, select, utmost **7** extreme, highest, maximal, maximum, noblest, supreme **8** champion **9** first-rate **11** superlative, unsurpassed

Greatest Show on Earth, The **director: 13** Cecil B DeMille **cast: 11** Betty Hutton, Cornel Wilde **12** James Stewart

---

great 3 apt, big **4** able, a-one, fine, good, high, huge, kind, many, vast, well **5** chief, crack, grand, grave, gross, heavy, large, noble, noted, super, swell **6** adroit, choice, expert, famous, groovy, humane, loving, strong, superb **7** crucial, decided, eminent, extreme, grandly, immense, leading, mammoth, notable, serious, titanic, weighty **8** abundant, colossal, critical, enormous, esteemed, fabulous, generous, gigantic, glorious, gracious, manifold, renowned, skillful, smashing, splendid, superbly, superior, terrific, very well **9** boundless, countless, cyclopean, excellent, fantastic, first-rate, important, marvelous, momentous, monstrous, prominent, unlimited, wonderful **10** altruistic, celebrated, gargantuan, high-minded, inordinate, out-of-sight, prodigious, proficient, pronounced, remarkable, splendidly, stupendous, tremendous, voluminous **11** crackerjack, excellently, extravagant, illustrious, magnanimous, magnificent, outstanding, sensational, significant, superlative, wonderfully **12** considerable **13** consequential, distinguished, inexhaustible, magnificently, multitudinous **14** out of this world

Greece

other name: 5 Ellas 16 Hellenic Republic

capital/largest city: 6 Athens

others: 4 Enor 5 Canea, Corfu, Pylos, Volos 6 Delphi, Patras, Sparta 7 Chalcis, Corinth, Olympia, Piraeus 8 Salonika, Thessaly 9 Epidaurus, Gallipoli 10 Herakleion 11 Hermoupolis

school: 5 Crete 6 Athens, Patras, Thrace 8 Ioannina, Salonika

division: 6 Attica, Epirus, Thrace 7 Boeotia 8 Thessaly 9 Macedonia

measure: 3 pik 4 bema, piki, pous 5 baril, chous, cubit, diote, doron, maris, pekhe, podos, pygon, xylon 6 acaena, bacile, barile, cotula, dichas, gramme, hemina, koilon, lichas, milion, orgyia, palame, pechys, schene, xestes 7 amphora, bacvhel, chenica, choenix, cyathos, diaulos, metreta, stadium, stremma 8 condylos, daktylos, dekapode, dolichos, medimnos, medimnus, metretes, palaiste, plethron, plethrum, stathmos 9 hemiekton, oxybaphon

monetary unit: 5 lepta 7 drachma

weight: 3 mna, oke 4 mina, obol 5 livre, pound 6 diobol, kantar, obolos, obolus, talent 7 chalcon, drachma 8 diobolon

island: 3 Ios 5 Chios, Corfu, Crete, Delos, Melos, Naxos, Paros, Samos, Syros, Tenos, Thera, Zante 6 Andros, Euboea, Ionian, Ithaca, Lemnos, Lesbos, Patmos, Rhodes, Skyros, Thasos 7 Mykonos 8 Cyclades, Mytilene, Skiathos, Skopelos 9 Alonnisos 10 Cephalonia, Dodecanese, Samothrace 16 Northern Sporades

lake: 5 Karla, Volve 6 Copais, Kopais, Prespa, Voweis 8 Ioannina, Koroneia, Vistonis 9 Trichonis, Vegoritis

mountain: 3 Ida 4 Idhi, Oeta, Oite, Ossa 5 Athos 6 Ithome, Peleon, Pelion, Pindus 7 Grammos, Helicon, Rhodope 8 Hymettos, Smolikas, Taygetos, Taygetus 9 Parnassus 10 Hagion Oros, Lycabettus, Pentelicus

highest point: 7 Olympus

river: 4 Arta 6 Peneus, Struma, Vardar 7 Hellada, Maritsa 8 Achelous, Aliakmon

sea: 5 Crete 6 Aegean, Ionian 7 Mirtoon 13 Mediterranean

physical feature:
  gulf: 7 Corinth, Saronic
  peninsula: 6 Balkan 10 Chalcidice 12 Peloponnesus
  plain: 7 Boeotia 8 Thessaly
  plateau: 7 Arcadia
  valley: 5 Nemea

people: 5 Greek 6 Achean, Dorian, Ionian 7 Aeolian, Hellene
  artist: 7 El Greco
  author: 5 Homer 6 Hesiod, Pindar 8 Menander 9 Aeschylus, Euripides, Sophocles 11 Kazantzakis 12 Aristophanes
  god: 4 Ares, Hera, Leto, Zeus 5 Cupid 6 Apollo, Cronus, Hermes, Hestia 7 Artemis, Demeter 8 Dionysus, Poseidon 9 Aphrodite 10 Hephaestus, Persephone 12 Pallas Athena 13 Phoebus Apollo
  historian: 9 Herodotus 10 Thucydides
  king: 11 Constantine
  lawmaker: 5 Draco, Solon 8 Lycurgus, Pericles
  leader: 10 Papandreou
  mathematician: 6 Euclid 10 Archimedes, Pythagoras
  mythological: 5 Atlas, Helen, Jason, Medea, Paris 6 Hector, Medusa 7 Ariadne, Chimera, Pandora, Pegasus, Perseus, Theseus 8 Achilles, Heracles, Minotaur, Odysseus 9 Agamemnon, Andromeda, Iphigenia, King Minos 10 Prometheus 11 Bellerophon
  orator: 11 Demosthenes
  philosopher: 5 Plato 8 Socrates 9 Aristotle
  physician: 11 Hippocrates
  sculptor: 5 Myron 7 Phidias 10 Praxiteles
  tycoon: 7 Onassis

language: 5 Greek

religion: 14 Greek Orthodoxy

place:
  ruins: 5 Delos, Pella, Pylos, Samos 6 Delphi, Sparta, Thebes, Tiryns 7 Corinth, Eleusis, Elevsis, Knossos, Mycenae, Olympia 9 Acropolis, Epidaurus, Parthenon 13 Palace of Minos

feature:
  coffeeshop: 7 kaphene
  marketplace: 5 agora
  port: 7 Piraeus
  presidential guard: 7 Evzones
  village square: 7 plateia

food:
  dish: 7 mousaka 8 moussaka, souvlaka, dolmades, souvlakia 10 shish kabob
  liquor: 4 ouzo
  wine: 7 retsina

13 Dorothy Lamour, Gloria Grahame **14** Charlton Heston
Oscar for: 7 picture

Great Expectations
author: 14 Charles Dickens
character: 3 Pip **7** Estella **9** Compeyson, Mr Jaggers **10** Joe Gargery **12** Abel Magwitch, Miss Havisham **13** Herbert Pocket
director: 9 David Lean
cast: 9 John Mills **11** Martita Hunt **12** Alec Guinness, Bernard Mills **13** Valerie Hobson **16** Francis L Sullivan

Great Gatsby, The
author: 16 F Scott Fitzgerald
character: 9 Jay Gatsby **11** Tom Buchanan **12** Myrtle Wilson, Nick Carraway **13** Daisy Buchanan

Great God Brown, The
author: 12 Eugene O'Neill

Great Idean Mother *see* **6** Cybele

great lady
French: 10 grande dame

Great Lake 4 Erie **5** Huron **7** Ontario **8** Michigan, Superior

Great Land
nickname of: 6 Alaska

greatly 6 vastly **7** largely, notably **8** markedly, mightily, very much **9** immensely **10** abundantly, enormously, infinitely, powerfully, remarkably **12** considerably, immeasurably, tremendously

great mishap 5 wreck **6** blight, fiasco **7** tragedy **8** calamity, disaster **9** cataclysm, ruination **11** catastrophe

greatness 8 eminence, nobility **9** loftiness **10** excellence, importance, notability, prominence **11** preeminence, superiority **12** magnificence **15** illustriousness

Great Profile
nickname of: 13 John Barrymore

Great Railway Bazaar, The
author: 11 Paul Theroux

great world
French: 10 grand monde

Great Ziegfeld, The
director: 14 Robert Z Leonard
cast: 8 Myrna Loy **10** Fanny Brice **11** Frank Morgan, Luise Rainer (Anna Held) **13** Virginia Bruce, William Powell
Oscar for: 7 actress (Rainer), picture

grebe 4 bird, fowl, loon **5** diver **6** dipper **7** henbill **8** dabchick **9** hell-diver **10** water witch

Grecco, Al
character in: 20 Appointment in Samarra
author: 5 O'Hara

Greco, El Greco
real name: 23 Domenikos Theotokopoulos
born: 5 Crete **6** Candia
artwork: 7 Espolio (Disrobing of Christ), Laocoon **12** View of Toledo **19** Cleaning of the Temple **20** Healing of the Blind Man **21** Burial of the Count Orgaz **27** Christ Stripped of his Garments **28** San Ildefonso at his Writing Desk **29** Cardinal Fernando Nino de Guevara **42** Christ Driving the Money-Changers from the Temple

Greece *see box*

greed 7 avarice, avidity, craving **8** cupidity, rapacity **11** itching palm, money-hunger, piggishness, selfishness **12** covetousness **13** rapaciousness **14** avariciousness

greediness 7 avarice **8** gluttony, rapacity, voracity **12** covetousness, graspingness **15** acquisitiveness

greedy 4 avid **5** eager **6** ardent, hungry **7** anxious, burning, craving, fervent, hoggish, piggish, selfish, swinish, wolfish **8** covetous, famished, grasping, ravenous **9** devouring, impatient, mercenary, predatory, rapacious, thirsting, voracious **10** avaricious, gluttonous, insatiable **11** acquisitive, money-hungry **12** gormandizing

Greek
language family: 12 Indo-European
ancient branch: 5 Doric, Ionic **6** Aeolic

Greek alphabet *see box*

Greek Anthology, The
author: 8 Cephalas, Meleager

Greek measure 4 mina **5** cubit **6** obolos, talent **7** drachma, stadion

Greek Mythology *see box, p. 412*

Greek uncial codex 4 Syri **6** Regius **8** Ephraemi **9** Laudianus, Vaticanus **10** Sinaiticus **11** Basiliensis **12** Alexandrinus, Sangallensis **13** Koridethianus

green 3 raw **4** jade, lawn, lime, turf **5** crude, heath, ol-

ive, rough, sward, young **6** callow, campus, common, tender, unripe **7** awkward, emerald, verdant, verdure **8** greenish, gullible, ignorant, immature, inexpert, not cured, not dried, pea-green, sea-green, unsmoked, untanned, unversed **9** blue-green, credulous, grassplot, lime-green, unfledged, unskilled, untrained **10** aquamarine, chartreuse, golf course, grass-green, greensward, kelly-green, olive green, uninformed, unmellowed, unpolished, unseasoned **11** cobalt green, forest green, undeveloped, yellow-green **12** easily fooled, green-colored, not fully aged, putting green, village green **13** inexperienced, undisciplined **14** underdeveloped **15** unsophisticated

Green Acres
character: 7 Mr Haney **8** Eb Dawson **10** Fred Ziffel, Sam Drucker **11** Doris Ziffel, Hank Kimball, Lisa Douglas **20** Oliver Wendell Douglas
cast: 8 Eva Gabor, Fran Ryan **9** Alvy Moore, Frank Cady, Tom Lester **10** Pat Buttram **11** Eddie Albert **13** Barbara Pepper, Hank Patterson
pig: 6 Arnold
town: 11 Hooterville

green at the gills 6 queasy, sickly **7** bilious **8** nauseous **9** nauseated, sickening

greenback 4 bill **8** banknote **12** treasury note **15** legal-

---

Greek alphabet
a: **5** alpha
b: **4** beta
ch/kh: **3** chi
d: **5** delta
e: **3** eta **7** epsilon
g: **5** gamma
i: **4** iota
k: **5** kappa
l: **6** lambda
m: **2** mu
n: **2** nu
o: **5** omega **7** omicron
p: **2** pi
ph: **3** phi
ps: **3** psi
r: **3** rho
s: **5** sigma
t: **3** tau
th: **5** theta
x: **2** xi
y: **7** upsilon
z: **4** zeta

tender note **17** silver certificate

Green Bay
  football team: **7** Packers

Green Bay Tree, The
  author: **14** Louis Bromfield

Greene, Graham
  author of: **11** The Third Man **12** Brighton Rock, Ways of Escape **14** The Human Factor **16** Monsignor Quixote, **17** The End of the Affair, The Ministry of Fear, Travels with My Aunt **19** The Heart of the Matter, The Power and the Glory

Greene, Joe
  nickname: **7** Mean Joe
  sport: **8** football
  position: **7** lineman
  team: **18** Pittsburgh Steelers

Greene, Lorne
  born: **6** Canada, Ottawa **7** Ontario
  roles: **5** Adama **7** Bonanza **11** Peyton Place **12** Autumn Leaves, The Buccaneer **13** Ben Cartwright **16** The Silver Chalice **19** Battlestar Galactica

Greene, Nathanael
  served in: **16** Revolutionary War
  rank: **16** brigadier general **20** quartermaster general
  battle: **7** Cowpens, Trenton **12** Eutaw Springs, Hobkirk's Hill **18** Guilford Court House

green-eyed monster 4 envy **8** jealousy **12** covetousness

Green for Danger
  director: **13** Sidney Gilliat
  cast: **7** Leo Genn **9** Sally Gray **11** Alastair Sim **12** Rosamund John, Trevor Howard

greenhorn 4 rube, tyro **6** novice, rookie **7** learner **8** beginner, neophyte, newcomer **9** fledgling **10** apprentice, tenderfoot **14** babe in the woods

Green Hornet, The
  character: **4** Kato **9** Britt Reid (The Green Hornet)
  cast: **8** Bruce Lee **11** Van Williams
  car: **11** Black Beauty
  creator: **11** Bert Whitman
  sidekick: **4** Kato

Green House, The
  author: **16** Mario Vargas Llosa

Greening of America, The
  author: **12** Charles Reich

greenish 6 sickly **7** bilious

Greek Mythology
  afterworld of the blessed: **7** Elysium
  amber islands: **10** Electrides
  architect of labyrinth: **8** Daedalus
  blood-sucking monster: **5** Lamia
  cupbearer to the gods: **8** Ganymede **9** Catamitus
  dragon: **8** basilisk
  drink of the gods: **6** nectar
  eagle/lion monster: **7** griffin, griffon, gryphon
  enchantress: **5** Circe
  female warrior: **6** Amazon
  fire-breathing monster: **7** Chimera
  first man: **12** Alalcomeneus
  food/drink/perfume of the gods: **8** ambrosia
  the Furies: **5** Dirae **6** Erinys, Furiae, Semnai **7** Erinyes **9** Eumenides
    names: **7** Allecto, Megaera **9** Tisiphone
  goat god: **7** Aegipan
  goddess of beauty: **6** Graces **7** Gratiae **9** Charities
    names: **4** Auxo **5** Cleta **6** Aglaia, Thalia **7** Phaenna **8** Hegemone **10** Euphrosyne
  goddess of childbirth: **8** Ilithyia **10** Eileithyia
    corresponds to Roman: **6** Lucina
  goddess of the dawn: **3** Eos
    corresponds to Roman: **6** Aurora
  goddesses of destiny: **5** Fates, Morae **6** Moerae, Moirai
    names: **5** Moira **6** Clotho **8** Lachesis
    corresponds to Roman: **6** Parcae
  goddess of discord: **4** Eris
    corresponds to Roman: **9** Discordia
  goddess of divine punishment/recklessness: **3** Ate
  goddess of divine retribution: **8** Adrastea
  goddess of the earth: **2** Ge **4** Gaea, Gaia
    corresponds to Roman: **6** Tellus
  goddess of earth/fertility: **7** Demeter
    corresponds to Roman: **5** Ceres
  goddess of earth/Hades: **5** Brimo **6** Hecate, Hekate
  goddess of fortune: **5** Tyche
    corresponds to Roman: **7** Fortuna
  goddess of healing: **4** Iaso
  goddess of health: **6** Hygeia
    corresponds to Roman: **5** Salus
  goddess of the hearth: **6** Hestia
    corresponds to Roman: **5** Vesta
  goddess of justice: **4** Dice, Dike **6** Astrea **7** Astraea
  goddesses of literature/the arts: **5** Muses **7** the Nine **8** Pierides **10** Castalides
    names: **4** Clio **5** Aoede, Erato, Mneme **6** Melete, Thalia, Urania **7** Euterpe **8** Calliope **9** Melpomene **10** Polyhymnia **11** Terpsichore
    corresponds to Roman: **7** Camenae
    muse of astronomy: **6** Urania
    muse of dancing/choral song: **11** Terpsichore
    muse of history: **4** Clio
    muse of idyllic poetry/comedy: **6** Thalia
    muse of love poetry: **5** Erato
    muse of meditation: **6** Melete
    muse of memory: **5** Mneme
    muse of music/lyric poetry: **7** Euterpe
    muse of poetry/epic: **8** Calliope
    muse of sacred music/dance: **10** Polyhymnia
    muse of song: **5** Aoede
    muse of tragedy: **9** Melpomene
  goddess of love/beauty: **6** Urania **7** Cyprian, Paphian **8** Cytherea **9** Aphrodite **10** Anadyomene
    corresponds to Roman: **5** Venus
  goddess of memory: **9** Mnemosyne
  goddess of the night: **3** Nox, Nyx
  goddess of peace: **5** Irene
    corresponds to Roman: **3** Pax
  goddess of the rainbow: **4** Iris

goddess of sailors: 5 Brizo
goddess of the sea: 10 Amphitrite
goddesses of the sea: 6 Graeae, Graiae
  names: 4 Enyo 5 Deino 9 Pemphredo
goddesses of seasons/growth/decay/social order:
  4 Hour 5 Horae
  names: 4 Dice, Dike 5 Carpo, Irene 6 Thallo 7 Eunomia
goddess of spring flowers: 6 Thallo
goddess of summer fruit: 5 Carpo
goddess of victory: 4 Nike
  corresponds to Roman: 6 Athena 8 Victoria
goddess of war: 4 Enyo
  corresponds to Roman: 7 Bellona
goddess of wisdom/fertility/arts/warfare: 6 Athena,
  Athene, Pallas, Saitis 11 Tritogeneia 12 Pallas Athena
  18 Alalcomenean Athena
  corresponds to Roman: 7 Minerva
goddess of youth/spring: 4 Hebe
god of beekeeping/winemaking/husbandry: 9 Aristaeus
god of censure/ridicule: 5 Momos, Momus
god of dreams: 6 Icelus, Oniros 7 Oneiros 8 Morpheus
god of earth: 10 Trophonius
god of Eleusinian mysteries: 7 Bacchus
god of erotic desire: 7 Himeros
god of fire/metalworking/handicrafts: 10 Hephaestus,
  Hephaistos
  corresponds to Roman: 6 Vulcan
god of the heavens: 4 Zeus
  corresponds to Roman: 4 Jove 7 Jupiter
  corresponds to Egyptian: 4 Amen, Amon 5 Ammon
  6 Amen Ra, Amon Ra
god of light/healing/music/poetry/prophecy/beauty:
  6 Apollo
god of love: 4 Eros
  corresponds to Roman: 4 Amor 5 Cupid
god of male power/procreation: 7 Priapus
  corresponds to Roman: 7 Mutinus
god of marriage: 5 Hymen 9 Hymenaeus
  corresponds to Roman: 8 Talassio
god of medicine/healing: 9 Asclepius
  corresponds to Roman: 11 Aesculapius
god of oaths: 6 Horcus
god of recovery from illness: 11 Telesphorus
god of sea/caused earthquakes: 8 Poseidon
  corresponds to Roman: 7 Neptune
god of shepherds/flocks/pastures/forests: 3 Pan
  7 Sinoeis
god of sleep: 6 Hypnos, Hypnus
  corresponds to Roman: 6 Somnus
god of the sun: 6 Helios 8 Hyperion
  corresponds to Roman: 3 Sol
god of the underworld: 6 Infiri
god of war: 4 Ares 8 Theritas
  corresponds to Roman: 4 Mars
god of wine/fertility/drama: 5 Evius 7 Bacchus
  8 Dionysus
Gorgon monster: 6 Medusa
hundred-headed monster: 5 Ladon 8 Typhoeus
islands of the blessed: 10 Hesperides
man/horse monster: 7 centaur
messenger of gods/god of roads/commerce/invention/
  cunning/thieves: 6 Hermes
  corresponds to Roman: 7 Mercury
monster that asked riddles: 6 Sphinx
monsters that turn people to stone: 7 Gorgons
moon goddess/huntress/virgin: 6 Phoebe, Selene
  7 Artemis
  corresponds to Roman: 5 Diana
  corresponds to Cretan: 11 Britomartis
nine-headed water serpent: 5 Hydra
nymph: 7 Calypso

(continued)

Greenland *see box, p. 415*

Green Mansions
  author: 8 W H Hudson
  character: 4 Rima 5 Nu-
  flo 6 Mr Abel

Greenmantle
  author: 10 John Buchan

Green Mountain State
  nickname of: 7 Vermont

Greenough, Horatio
  born: 8 Boston MA
  artwork: 16 George
  Washington 18 The
  Chanting Cherubs

Green Pastures, The
  author: 12 Marc
  Connelly

Greenstreet, Sydney
  born: 7 England
  8 Sandwich
  roles: 9 The Fat Man
  10 Casablanca 16 The
  Maltese Falcon 19 Pas-
  sage to Marseilles

green with envy 7 envious,
jealous 8 covetous

greet 4 hail, meet 5 admit
6 accept, accost, salute 7 receive, speak to, welcome 9 ,
smile upon, recognize 10 bid
welcome

greeting 6 salute 7 welcome
8 saluting 9 reception, welcoming 10 salutation 12 introduction, presentation

greetings 4 best 5 hello 7 regards 8 respects 10 best
wishes, good wishes, salutation 11 compliments, remembrance, well-wishing
13 felicitations
  Latin: 5 salve

gregarious 6 genial, lively, social 7 affable 8 friendly, outgoing, sociable 9 convivial,
talkative, vivacious 11 extroverted 13 companionable

gremlin 3 imp 5 demon,
gnome 6 goblin

Grenada *see box, p. 415*

grenade 7 missile 9 pineapple

Grendel
  character in: 7 Beowulf
  author: 7 unknown

Grewgious, Mr
  character in: 22 The Mystery
  of Edwin Drood
  author: 7 Dickens

Grey, Joel
  real name: 8 Joel Katz
  born: 13 Cleveland Ohio
  roles: 7 Cabaret, George M
  13 Come September 23 The
  Seven Percent Solution

Greek Mythology (*continued*)
- **one-eyed giant:** 7 Cyclops
- **oracle of Apollo:** 13 Delphic oracle
- **personification of death:** 4 Mors 8 Thanatos
- **personification of punishment/revenge:** 5 Poena, Poine
- **personification of soul:** 6 Psyche
- **physician to gods of Olympia:** 5 Paeon
- **prophetess:** 9 Alexandra, Cassandra
- **queen of heaven:** 4 Hera, Here
  - *corresponds to Roman:* 4 Juno
- **race of gods:** 6 Titans
  - *names:* 4 Rhea, Thia 5 Coeus, Crius 6 Cronus, Phoebe, Tethys, Themis 7 Iapetus, Oceanus 8 Hyperion 9 Mnemosyne
- **river god:** 6 Asopus, Peneus, Simois 7 Inachus, Pelegon 8 Achelous
- **river in Hades:** 4 Styx 5 Lethe 7 Acheron, Cocytus
  - *ferryman:* 6 Charon
  - *river of forgetfulness:* 5 Lethe
- **ruler of the winds:** 6 Aeolus
- **satyr/god of the forest:** 7 Silenus
- **sea god:** 6 Nereus, Triton 7 Glaucus, Phorcys, Proteus
- **sea monster:** 6 Scylla
- **seer:** 6 Mopsus 8 Tiresias
- **serpent:** 6 dipsas
- **serpent of darkness:** 5 Apepi 7 Apophis
- **seven against Thebes:** 6 Tydeus 8 Adrastus, Capaneus 9 Polynices 10 Amphiaraus, Hippomedon 13 Parthenopaeus
- **seven sisters:** 8 Pleiades
  - *names:* 4 Maia 6 Merope 7 Alcyone, Celaeno, Electra, Sterope, Taygete
- **sorceress:** 5 Medea
- **spirits of disease/evil/old age/death:** 5 Keres
- **three-headed dog that guards underworld:** 8 Cerberus
- **twins:** 8 Dioscuri 15 Castor and Pollux
- **two-headed serpent:** 11 Amphisbaena
- **underworld:** 5 Hades, Pluto
  - *corresponds to Roman:* 3 Dis 5 Orcus 8 Dis Pater
- **underworld darkness:** 6 Erebus
- **underworld spirit:** 9 Chthonian
- **virgin huntress:** 8 Atalanta, Atalante
- **whirlpool:** 9 Charybdis
- **winged horse:** 5 Arion 7 Pegasus
- **woman/beast monster:** 6 Python 8 Delphyne
- **woman/bird monster:** 5 Harpy
- **woman/serpent monster:** 7 Echidna
- **wood nymph:** 5 dryad

Grey, Zane
- **author of:** 18 Valley of Wild Horses 20 The Spirit of the Border 21 Riders of the Purple Sage, The Last of the Plainsmen

greyhound
- **group of:** 5 leash

Greystoke, Lord
- **real identity of:** 6 Tarzan

griddle cake 6 blintz, waffle 7 crumpet, hot cake, pancake 8 corncake, flapcake, flapjack 10 battercake 11 flannel cake 13 buckwheat cake
- **French:** 5 crepe 12 crepe suzette
- **German:** 11 pfannkuchen

Hungarian: 10 palacsinta
Indian: 8 chapatty

Gride, Arthur
- **character in:** 16 Nicholas Nickleby
- **author:** 7 Dickens

grief 3 woe 4 care 5 agony, worry 6 burden, misery, ordeal, sorrow 7 anguish, anxiety, concern, despair, remorse, sadness, trouble 8 distress, grieving, hardship, nuisance, vexation 9 grievance, heartache, suffering 10 affliction, desolation, discomfort, heartbreak 11 despondency, tribulation 12 wretchedness 13 inconvenience

griefstricken 7 joyless, unhappy 8 saddened, wretched 9 sorrowful 13 brokenhearted

Grieg, Edvard Hagerup
- **born:** 6 Bergen, Norway
- **composer of:** 5 I Host 8 Bergljot, In Autumn, Peer Gynt 11 Lyric Pieces 12 Landjaenning 14 Fra Holbergs Tid, Lyriske Stykker 15 Sigurd Jorsalfar 16 From Holberg's Time 17 Recognition of Land 18 Foran Sydens Kloster 22 At a Southern Convent Gate

grievance 4 beef, hurt 5 wrong 6 injury 7 outrage 8 hardship, iniquity 9 complaint, injustice 10 affliction, bone to pick, disservice

grieve 3 cry, rue, sob 4 moan, pain, wail, weep 5 be sad, mourn 6 bemoan, deject, harass, lament, sadden, sorrow 7 afflict, agonize, depress, oppress, torture 8 disquiet, distress 10 discomfort 11 be anguished

grieve over 5 mourn 6 bemoan, bewail, lament 7 cry over 8 moan over, weep over

grievous 3 sad 5 acute, grave, harsh, heavy 6 severe, tragic, woeful 7 crucial, glaring, harmful, heinous, painful, serious, very bad 8 critical, shameful, shocking 9 agonizing, appalling, atrocious, monstrous, nefarious, sorrowful 10 burdensome, calamitous, deplorable, iniquitous, lamentable, outrageous, unbearable 11 destructive, distressing, intolerable, significant 12 insufferable 13 heartbreaking

griffin
- **also:** 7 griffon, gryphon
- **form:** 7 monster
- **head of:** 5 eagle
- **wings of:** 5 eagle
- **body of:** 4 lion
- **guards of:** 4 gold
- **location:** 7 Scythia

Griffith, Andy
- **real name:** 20 Andrew Samuel Griffith
- **born:** 8 Mt Airy NC
- **roles:** 7 Matlock 13 Will Stockdale 15 A Face in the Crowd, Angel in My Pocket 18 No Time for Sergeants 19 The Andy Griffith Show

Griffith, D W
- **director of:** 11 Intolerance

Greenland
alternate name: 14 Kalaalit Nunaat
capital/largest city: 3 Nuk **8** Godthaab, The Point
others: 4 Etah, Nord **5** Thule **6** Ivigut, Umanak **7** Godhavn,
Ivigtut **10** Nanortalik **11** Julianehaab **12** Angmagssalik,
Sukkertoppen **14** Christianshaab
government: 20 home rule under Denmark
monetary unit: 3 ore **5** krone
island: 5 Disko
mountain: 5 Forel, Payer **7** Khardyu **8** Peterman
15 Petermannsbjerg
highest point: 9 Gunnbjorn **16** Gunnbjornsfjaeld
sea: 6 Arctic **9** Greenland
physical feature: 9 Inland Ice
  bay: **5** Disko **6** Baffin **8** Melville
  cape: **4** Jaal **6** Grivel, Walker **8** Bismarck, Brewster, Farewell, Lowenorn **11** Morris Jesup
  glacier: **10** Jacobshavn
  strait: **5** Davis **7** Denmark
people: 3 Ita **6** Eskimo **8** European
  explorer: **10** Eric the Red
language: 6 Danish, Eskimo **11** Greenlandic
religion: 19 Evangelical Lutheran
feature:
  airbase: **4** Etah **5** Thule
  animal: **7** caribou

---

14 Broken Blossoms **17** Orphans of the Storm, The Birth of a Nation

Griffith, Hugh
born: 5 Wales **8** Anglesey **10** Marian Glas
roles: 6 Ben-Hur **8** Lucky Jim, Tom Jones

griffon *see* **7** griffin

grill 3 fry **4** cook, grid, pump, quiz, sear **5** broil, query **7** broiler, grating, griddle **8** gridiron, question **9** crossbars **11** interrogate **12** cross-examine

grim 4 foul, hard, ugly **5** cruel, harsh, lurid, stern, sulky **6** brutal, fierce, gloomy, grisly, grumpy, horrid, morose, odious, severe, somber, sullen **7** austere, ghastly, hideous, inhuman, macabre, squalid, vicious **8** dreadful, fiendish, gruesome, horrible, resolute, scowling, shocking, sinister **9** appalling, ferocious, frightful, heartless, loathsome, merciless, obstinate, repellent, repugnant, repulsive, revolting **10** determined, forbidding, implacable, inexorable, relentless, unyielding

grimace 4 face **5** scowl, smirk, sneer **6** glower **7** wry face
French: 4 moue

grime 4 dirt, dust, smut, soil, soot **5** filth **6** smudge

Grimhild
origin: 12 Scandinavian

---

mentioned in: 8 Volsunga
form: 9 sorceress
husband: 5 Giuki, Gjuki
daughter: 6 Gudrun, Kudrun **7** Guthrun
son: 6 Gunnar
tricked Sigurd to marry: **6** Gudrun, Kudrun **7** Guthrun

Grimm Brothers (Jakob and Wilhelm)
editors of: 15 Hansel and Gretel **16** Grimm's Fairy Tales

grim reaper 5 death **12** angel of death

grim-visaged 8 frowning, scowling **9** long-faced **10** sternfaced

grin 4 beam **5** smile, smirk **6** rictus, simper **11** crack a smile

grind 4 file, grit, mill, rasp, whet **5** chore, crush, gnash, grate **6** abrade, drudge, polish, powder, scrape **7** crammer, hard job, plodder, sharpen, slavery **8** bookworm, drudgery **9** granulate, pulverize, triturate

Gringoire
character in: 23 The Hunchback of Notre Dame
author: 4 Hugo

grip 3 bag **4** grab, hilt, hold **5** clasp, grasp, rivet, seize **6** clench, clutch, handle, retain, snatch, valise **7** attract, control, impress, mastery, satchel **8** clutches, hold fast, suitcase **9** gladstone, handclasp, handshake, retention, spellbind **10** domination, perception

gripe, gripes 4 beef, carp, fret, kick, pain, pang, rail **5** cavil, colic, spasm, whine **6** cramps, grouch, grouse, kvetch, mutter, squawk, twinge, twitch **7** grumble, protest, whining **8** complain, distress, grousing, bellyache, complaint, find fault, grievance, grumbling **10** affliction

Grisham, John
author of: 7 The Firm **9** The Client **10** The Chamber **11** A Time to Kill **15** The Pelican Brief
movie:
  7 The Firm
    actors: **9** Tom Cruise **11** Gene Hackman
  15 The Pelican Brief
    actors: **12** Julia Roberts **16** Denzel Washington
  9 The Client
    actors **13** Tommy Lee Jones, Susan Sarandon

grisly 4 foul, gory, grim **5** lurid **6** horrid, odious **7** ghastly, hideous, macabre **8** dreadful, gruesome, horrible, shocking, sinister **9** abhorrent, appalling, frightful, loathsome, repellent, repugnant, repulsive, revolting **10** abominable, forbidding, horrendous

Grenada
other name: 11 Isle of Spice
capital/largest city: 9 St Georges
others: 8 Sauteurs
head of state: 14 British monarch **15** governor general
island: 8 Windward **9** Carriacon **10** Grenadines
lake: 10 Grand Etang
highest point: 11 St Catherine
sea: 9 Caribbean
physical feature:
  bay: **9** St Georges'
people: 5 Black, Negro **6** Indian
  discoverer: **8** Columbus
language: 7 English
religion: 8 Anglican **10** Protestant **13** Roman Catholic
food:
  spice: **4** mace **6** nutmeg

grit 3 rub 4 dirt, dust, guts, muck, rasp, sand, soot 5 filth, gnash, grate, nerve, pluck, spunk 6 crunch, mettle, scrape 7 courage, stamina 8 backbone, tenacity 9 fortitude 10 doggedness, resolution 12 perseverance 13 determination, grind together

Grizzly Bear State 10 California

groan 4 howl, moan, roar, wail 5 bleat, crack, creak, whine 6 bellow, bemoan, lament, murmur, squeak 7 grumble, screech, whimper 8 complain

grocery store Spanish: 6 bodega

groggy 5 dazed, dizzy, dopey, shaky, woozy 6 addled, punchy 7 muddled, reeling, stunned 8 confused, sluggish, unsteady 9 befuddled, lethargic, perplexed, stupefied 10 bewildered, punch-drunk, staggering

groom 4 comb, wash 5 boots, brush, curry, dress, drill, preen, prime, primp, train, valet 6 flunky, lackey, spouse 7 clean up, consort, develop, educate, footman, freshen, hostler, husband, prepare, refresh, rub down, servant 8 exercise, initiate, make neat, make tidy, practice, spruce up 9 currycomb, make ready, stableboy 10 bridegroom, manservant 12 indoctrinate 13 livery servant

groove 3 cut, rut, use 4 rule 5 flute, habit, score, usage 6 custom, furrow, gutter, hollow, trench 7 channel, cutting, scoring 8 practice 9 procedure 10 beaten path, convention 11 corrugation 12 fixed routine, second nature

grope 3 paw 5 probe 6 finger, fumble 7 fish for, venture 9 feel about 11 feel one's way, move blindly, try one's luck 13 search blindly

Gropius, Walter architect of: 5 Fagus (factory) 7 Bauhaus (Dessau) 13 Pan Am Building (NYC) 31 Harvard University Graduate Center

gross 3 bag, big, fat 4 bulk, earn, huge, lewd, mass, rank, reap, vast 5 bulky, crude, great, heavy, large, obese, plain, sheer, total, utter, whole 6 carnal, coarse, earthy, entire, pick up, ribald, smutty, sordid, take in, vulgar 7 glaring, heinous, immense, lump sum, massive, obscene, obvious, titanic, uncouth 8 colossal, complete, enormous, flagrant, gigantic, improper, indecent, manifest, unseemly, unwieldy 9 aggregate, downright, egregious, lecherous, monstrous, offensive, unrefined 10 gargantuan, indelicate, lascivious, licentious, outrageous, overweight, prodigious, stupendous 11 unequivocal, unmitigated, unqualified

Grossel, Ira real name of: 12 Jeff Chandler

grossness 7 obesity 8 hugeness, lewdness, ribaldry 9 crudeness, heaviness, indecency, obscenity, roughness, vulgarity 10 coarseness, indelicacy, inelegance 14 lasciviousness

grossularite species: 6 garnet

Gros Ventre see 7 Hidatsa

grotesque 3 odd 4 wild 5 antic, weird 6 absurd, exotic, far-out, rococo, way-out 7 baroque, bizarre, strange 8 deformed, fanciful, peculiar 9 contorted, distorted, eccentric, fantastic, misshapen, odd-shaped, unnatural 10 outlandish 11 extravagant, incongruous 12 preposterous

grotto 4 cave 6 burrow, cavern, hollow, recess, tunnel 8 catacomb

grouch 3 cry 4 beef, carp, crab, fret, kick, mope, pout, rail, sulk 5 cavil, crank, gripe, growl, moper, whine 6 grouse, mutter, pouter 7 grumble, killjoy, protest 8 complain, grumbler 9 bellyache, find fault 10 complainer, curmudgeon, spoilsport, wet blanket

grouchy 5 cross, testy 6 crabby, cranky, grumpy, touchy 8 snappish 10 ill-humored, out of sorts 11 ill-tempered 12 cantankerous 13 short-tempered

ground, grounds 3 set, sod 4 area, base, call, dirt, farm, land, loam, soil, turf, yard 5 acres, basis, beach, cause, dregs, drill, earth, field, found, lawns, realm, teach, train 6 campus, domain, estate, excuse, inform, motive, object, reason, region, secure, settle, sphere, strand 7 account, confirm, deposit, dry land, educate, founder, gardens, habitat, prepare, purpose, support, terrain 8 district, exercise, firm land, initiate, instruct, occasion, organize, practice, premises, property, province, sediment, the earth 9 arguments, bailiwick, establish, fix firmly, institute, principle, rationale, settlings, territory 10 discipline, inducement, real estate, terra firma 11 pros and cons 12 indoctrinate 14 considerations

grounded 5 based 6 kept in, taught 7 aground, beached, bounded, drilled, founded, secured, trained 8 informed, prepared, stranded 9 foundered, initiated 10 kept at home, instructed, restricted 11 disciplined, established 12 washed ashore 13 indoctrinated

grounding 8 training 9 education 10 background, experience 11 preparation 14 indoctrination 15 familiarization

groundless 4 idle 5 empty, false 6 faulty, flimsy, unreal, untrue 8 baseless, needless, unproved 9 erroneous, illogical, imaginary, unfounded 10 chimerical, fallacious, gratuitous 11 uncalled for, unjustified, unsupported, unwarranted 13 unjustifiable, without reason

groundwork 4 base, root 5 basis 6 cradle, ground, origin, source, spring 7 bedrock, footing, grounds, taproot 8 keystone, learning, planning, practice, training 9 spadework 10 foundation 11 cornerstone, fundamental, preparation 12 fundamentals, underpinning 14 apprenticeship, indoctrination

group 3 set 4 band, clan, file, gang, herd, pack, sift, size, sort 5 align, bunch, class, crowd, flock, grade, hoard, index, party, place, range, swarm, tribe, troop 6 assign, branch, circle, clique, family, hobnob, league, line up, mingle, throng 7 arrange, catalog, cluster, combine, company, consort, coterie, faction, marshal, section, species, variety 8 classify, division, graduate, organize, register 9 associate, gathering 10 assemblage, collection, coordinate, detachment, fraternity, fraternize 11 aggregation, alphabetize, association, brotherhood, subdivision 12 congregation 14 classification, representation

Group, The author: 12 Mary McCarthy

grouping 7 sorting **8** arraying, ordering **10** assemblage, assortment **11** arrangement, disposition **12** distribution, organization

group of performers
6 troupe **7** company **8** ensemble

Group Portrait of a Lady
author: **12** Heinrich Boll

grouse 4 beef, crab, fret, fume, fuss, kick **5** gripe **6** grouch, mutter, squawk, take on **7** carry on, grumble **8** complain, gamebird **9** bellyache

grove 4 bosk **5** brake, copse **6** forest, pinery, timber **7** coppice, orchard, thicket, wood lot **8** wildwood, woodland **9** shrubbery **10** plantation

grovel 4 fawn **5** cower, crawl, stoop, toady **6** cringe, kowtow, snivel **7** flatter, truckle **12** bow and scrape **13** demean oneself, humble oneself **14** lick the boots of

groveling 6 abject **7** fawning, servile **8** cowering, crawling, cringing, toadying **9** kowtowing, truckling **11** bootlicking **17** bowing and scraping

grow 3 bud, sow, wax **4** boom, farm, rise, till **5** bloom, breed, plant, raise, ripen, surge, swell, widen **6** become, expand, extend, flower, garden, mature, spread, sprout, thrive **7** advance, amplify, blossom, develop, enlarge, fill out, get to be, improve, magnify, produce, prosper, shoot up, stretch, succeed **8** come to be, flourish, fructify, increase, mushroom, progress, spring up, vegetate **9** cultivate, germinate, propagate, skyrocket **10** aggrandize

Growing Up in New Guinea
author: **12** Margaret Mead

growl 4 fret, snap **5** croak, grind, gripe, groan, grunt, snarl, whine **6** grouse, murmur, mutter, rumble **7** grumble **8** complain, talk back

grown-up 3 big, man **4** lady, ripe **5** adult, of age, woman **6** mature, senior **7** worldly **9** full-blown, full-grown, gentleman **11** full-fledged **13** sophisticated

growth 4 crop, hump, lump, rise **5** gnarl, prime, surge, swell, tumor **6** sowing, spread **7** advance, harvest, produce, success **8** increase, maturity, planting, progress **9** expansion, extension, flowering, increment **10** burgeoning, mature-

ness, production, prospering **11** advancement, cultivation, development, enlargement, excrescence, flourishing, improvement, propagation **12** augmentation, mass of tissue **13** amplification
goddess of: **4** Hour **5** Horae

Groza, Lou
nickname: **6** The Toe
sport: **8** football
team: **15** Cleveland Browns

grub 3 bum, dig **4** food, toil, worm **5** cadge, dig up, larva, mooch, slave **6** drudge, sponge **7** rummage

grubber 5 slave **6** drudge, toiler **7** laborer

grubby 4 foul **5** dirty, grimy, messy, muddy, nasty, seedy, tacky **6** beat-up, filthy, frowzy, frumpy, shabby, shoddy, sloppy, smudgy, soiled, sordid **7** squalid, unclean, unkempt **8** begrimed, slovenly, unwashed **9** besmeared **10** bedraggled

grudge 4 envy **5** pique, spite **6** animus, hatred, malice, rancor, resent **7** dislike, ill will **8** aversion, begrudge **9** animosity **10** resentment **11** malevolence **12** hard-feelings

grudging 7 envious **8** hesitant, spiteful **9** reluctant, resentful, unwilling **10** ungenerous **13** penny-pinching

grueling 4 hard **6** brutal, tiring **7** racking **9** fatiguing, punishing, torturous **10** exhausting

gruesome 4 gory, grim **5** awful **6** grisly, horrid **7** fearful, ghastly, hideous, macabre **8** horrible, shocking, terrible **9** frightful, loathsome, repellent, repulsive, revolting **10** forbidding, horrendous, horrifying **13** bloodcurdling, spine-chilling

gruff 4 curt, rude, sour, tart **5** bluff, blunt, harsh, husky, raspy, rough, sharp, short, stern, sulky, surly **6** abrupt, croaky, crusty, grumpy, hoarse, ragged, sullen **7** bearish, brusque, caustic, crabbed, cracked, grouchy, peevish, throaty, uncivil, waspish **8** churlish, guttural, impolite, snarling, strident **9** bristling, insulting **10** ill-humored, ill-natured, ungracious **11** ill-tempered **12** discourteous

grumble 4 fret **5** chafe, gripe, growl **6** grouch, grouse, mutter **8** complain **9** find-fault

grump 4 crab **5** crank

6 grouch **8** grumbler, sourball **10** curmudgeon

grumpy 4 sour **5** moody, sulky, surly, testy **6** crabby, cranky, crusty, sullen **7** grouchy, peevish, pettish **8** churlish **9** irritable, splenetic **10** ill-humored, out of humor, out of sorts **11** disgruntled, ill-disposed, ill-tempered **12** cantankerous

grunt 3 cry **4** bark, call, gasp, howl **5** burro, croak, groan, snort, utter **6** bellow, grouch, mumble, murmur, mutter, shriek **7** howling, whisper **8** complain **9** ululation **11** foot soldier, infantryman

Grunwald, Matthais (Grunewald, Mathis)
real name: **23** Mathis Gothardt Neithardt
born: **7** Germany **8** Wurzburg
artwork: **14** The Crucifixion **15** The Resurrection **20** Altarpiece at Isenheim

Grushenka
character in: **20** The Brothers Karamazov
author: **11** Dostoyevsky

Gryce, Percy
character in: **15** The House of Mirth
author: **7** Wharton

Grynaeus
epithet of: **6** Apollo

gryphon *see* **7** griffin

Guam *see box, p. 418*

Guarani (Caingua)
language family: **7** Guarani
location: **6** Brazil **8** Paraguay **9** Argentina **12** South America
allied to: **4** Tupi

guarantee, guaranty 4 avow, bail, bond, pawn, word **5** swear **6** affirm, allege, assure, attest, avowal, insure, pledge, surety **7** deposit, endorse, promise, sponsor, testify, voucher, warrant **8** contract, covenant, security, vouch for, warranty **9** agreement, answer for, assurance, insurance **10** collateral, underwrite **11** affirmation, endorsement, word of honor **12** give one's word

guard 4 mind, save, tend **5** watch **6** attend, convoy, defend, escort, patrol, picket, screen, secure, sentry, shield, warder **7** conduct, defense, protect, shelter **8** defender, garrison, guardian, keep safe, preserve, security, sentinel, watchdog, watchman **9** bodyguard, concierge, custodian, guardsman, protector, safe-

Guam
  capital: 5 Agana
  largest city: 8 Tamuning
  others: 4 Agat, Apra,
    Toto, Yigo 5 Magua
    6 Dededo, Merizo 8 In-
    arajan, Mangilao,
    Mongmong, Sinajana,
    Talofofo, Tamuning
    9 Barrigada, Finegayan,
    Santa Rita
  member of: 7 Mariana
    (islands)
  mountain: 5 Tenjo
  highest point: 6 Lamlam
  sea: 7 Pacific
    10 Philippine
  people: 7 Spanish
    8 American, Chamorro,
    Filipino 11 Micronesian
    explorer: 8 Magellan
    ruler: 5 Japan, Spain
    12 United States
  language: 7 English
    8 Chamorro
  religion: 16 Roman
    Catholicism
  feature: 7 typhoon
    9 coral reef
  Air Force base:
    8 Andersen
  product: 5 copra 6 ba-
    nana, papaya

tion 11 safekeeping, supervision, trusteeship

Guatemala *see box*

guava 7 Psidium 16 Psidium
guineense
  varieties: 5 apple 6 common,
    purple, yellow 7 Cattley,
    Chilean 9 pineapple
    10 Costa Rican, strawberry
    13 yellow cattley 16 purple
    strawberry, yellow
    strawberry

**Gubitosi, Michael James
Vijencio**
  real name of: 11 Robert
    Blake

Gudrun
  also: 6 Kudrun 7 Guthrun
  origin: 12 Scandinavian
  mentioned in: 8 Volsunga
  father: 5 Giuki, Gjuki
    6 Hertel
  mother: 8 Grimhild

brother: 6 Gunnar
husband: 4 Atli 6 Herwig,
  Sigurd
killed: 4 Atli
corresponds to: 9 Kriemhild

Guerrillas
  author: 9 V S Naipaul

guess 4 deem, view 5 fancy,
  judge, opine, think 6 assume,
  belief, deduce, divine, gather,
  reckon, regard, theory 7 believe, daresay, feeling, imagine, opinion, predict, suppose,
  surmise, suspect, venture
  8 conclude, estimate, theorize
  9 postulate, speculate, suspicion 10 assumption, conjecture, divination, hypothesis,
  prediction 11 hypothesize,
  make a stab at, postulation,
  presumption, speculation,
  supposition

guesswork 7 surmise 10 con-

---

guard, watch over 10 doorkeeper, gatekeeper, protection
12 preservation 13 keep watch
over

guard against 6 beware
10 look out for 11 take warning, watch out for

guarded 4 wary 5 cagey,
chary, leery 7 careful, heedful,
mindful, prudent 8 cautious,
discreet, hesitant 9 in custody,
protected, tentative 10 restrained, suspicious, under
guard 11 circumspect, on
one's guard

guardian 5 guard 6 convoy, escort, keeper, patrol, patron,
picket, sentry, warden, warder 7 curator, trustee 8 advocate, champion, defender,
sentinel, shepherd, wardsman,
watchdog 9 attendant, bodyguard, caretaker, conductor,
custodian, preserver, protector,
safeguard, vigilante 10 benefactor 11 conservator 13 friend
at court, guardian angel
14 legal custodian

guardian of a place
Latin: 10 genius loci

guardianship 4 care 6 charge
7 custody, keeping 10 protec-

Guatemala
  capital/largest city: 13 Guatemala City
  others: 4 Ocos 5 Coban, Vieja 6 Chahal, Chisec, Cuilco,
    Flores, Iztapa, Jalapa, Salama, Solola, Tacana, Tecpan,
    Yaloch, Zacapa 7 Antigua, Cuilapa, Jutiapa, San Jose
    8 Progreso 9 Escuintla, Tiquisate 10 Livingston 11 Totoni-
    capan 13 Puerto Barrios, Quezaltenango 14 San Pedro
    Carcha 16 Chichicastenango
  school: 9 San Carlos
  measure: 4 vara 6 cuarta, tercia 7 cajuela, manzana
    10 caballeria
  monetary unit: 4 peso 7 centavo, quetzal
  weight: 4 caja 5 libra
  lake: 5 Dulce, Guija, Peten 6 Izabal 7 Atitlan 9 Amatitlan,
    Peten Itza
  mountain: 4 Agua, Mico 5 Fuego, Madre 6 Pacaya, Ta-
    cana 7 Atitlan, Toliman 8 La Candon, Las Minas 10 Aca-
    tenango, Santa Maria 12 Cuchumatanes
  highest point: 8 Tajumuko 9 Tajamulco
  river: 4 Azul 5 Bravo, Dulce, Lapaz 6 Belize, Chixoy, Ne-
    gino, Pasion, Samala 7 Chiapas, Motagua, Sarstun, Sas-
    toon 8 Polochic, Rio Dulce, Sarstoon 10 Usumacinta
  sea: 7 Pacific 8 Atlantic 9 Caribbean
  physical feature:
    bay: 8 Amatique
    gulf: 8 Honduras
  people: 3 Mam 4 Chol, Itza, Ixil, Maya 5 Xinca 6 Caribe,
    Quiche 7 ladinos, mestizo, Pocomam 13 Guatemaltecos
  language: 6 Quiche 7 Spanish
  religion: 13 Roman Catholic
  place:
    church: 10 Santo Tomas
    ruins: 5 Mayan, Tikal 8 Uaxactun
  feature:
    bird: 7 quetzal
    clarinet: 8 chirimta
    dance: 5 elson 8 guarimba
    flute: 3 xul
    military dictator: 8 Caudillo
  food:
    dish: 6 pepian 10 enchiladas 13 gallo en chicha
    fruit: 4 anay

jecture, hypothesis 11 supposition 13 shot in the dark

guest 5 diner 6 caller, client, friend, inmate, lodger, patron, roomer 7 boarder, company, habitue, invitee, patient, visitor 8 customer 9 sojourner 10 frequenter 14 paying customer

Guest, Edgar A
   author of: 12 A Heap of Livin'

Guest, Judith
   author of: 14 Ordinary People

guffaw 4 howl 6 scream 10 belly laugh, horse laugh

Guglielmi, Rodolfo
   real name of: 16 Rudolph Valentino

Guicciardini, Francesco
   author of: 13 Storia d'Italia

guidance 3 tip 4 clue, help, hint, lead 6 advice, escort 7 conduct, counsel, pointer 8 auspices 9 direction 10 leadership, management, protection, suggestion 11 information, instruction, supervision 12 intelligence 13 enlightenment

guide 4 lead, rule 5 model, pilot, steer, usher 6 beacon, convoy, direct, escort, govern, handle, leader, manage, marker, master, mentor 7 adviser, command, conduct, control, example, marshal, monitor, oversee, pattern, steerer, teacher 8 chaperon, cicerone, director, engineer, helmsman, landmark, lodestar, maneuver, polestar, regulate, shepherd, signpost 9 accompany, attendant, conductor, counselor 10 manipulate

guidebook 5 bible 6 manual 8 Baedeker, handbook 13 reference book

Guidry, Ron (Ronald Ames)
   nickname: 18 Louisiana Lightning
   sport: 8 baseball
   position: 7 pitcher
   team: 14 New York Yankees

guild 5 order, union 6 league 7 company, society 8 alliance 9 coalition 10 craft union, federation, fraternity, labor union, sisterhood, trade union 11 association, brotherhood, confederacy, corporation

Guildenstern
   character in: 6 Hamlet
   author: 11 Shakespeare

guile 5 craft, fraud 6 deceit, tricks 7 cunning, slyness 8 ar-

tifice, strategy, trickery, wiliness 9 chicanery, deception, duplicity, treachery 10 artfulness, craftiness, dishonesty, hanky-panky, stratagems, trickiness 11 fraudulence 13 sharp practice

guileless 4 open 5 frank, naive 6 candid, honest, simple 7 artless, natural, sincere 8 harmless, innocent, truthful 9 ingenuous, innocuous 10 aboveboard, unaffected 11 undesigning, unoffending 15 straightforward, unselfconscious, unsophisticated

guilelessness 6 candor 9 innocence, sincerity 10 candidness, directness 11 artlessness 13 ingenuousness

guilt 3 sin 4 blot, vice 5 shame, wrong 6 infamy, stigma 7 misdeed 8 disgrace, dishonor, misdoing, trespass 9 black mark, turpitude 10 guiltiness, misconduct, sinfulness, wrongdoing 11 criminality, culpability, degradation, delinquency, dereliction, humiliation, misbehavior, self-disgust 13 transgression

guiltless 4 good, pure 5 clean 6 chaste 7 angelic, sinless 8 innocent, unfallen, virtuous 9 blameless, childlike, fault-

less 10 immaculate, inculpable, unblamable 11 uncorrupted
   French: 12 sans reproche

guilt-stricken 7 ashamed

guilty 5 sorry, wrong 6 erring, sinful 7 ashamed, corrupt, hangdog, immoral 8 blamable, contrite, criminal, culpable, penitent, sheepish 9 offensive, regretful, repentant 11 blameworthy 18 conscience-stricken

Guilty Pleasures
   author: 15 Donald Barthelme

Guinea *see box*

Guinea-Bissau *see box,*
   p. 420

Guinevere
   character in: 16 Arthurian romance
   husband: 6 Arthur
   lover: 8 Lancelot

Guinness, Sir Alec
   born: 6 London 7 England
   roles: 8 Star Wars 11 Oliver Twist 13 Doctor Zhivago 14 Our Man in Havana, The Ladykillers 15 A Passage to India, Ben Obi Wan Kenobi, Lavender Hill Mob 16 Lawrence of Arabia 17 Great Expectations 21 Kind Hearts and Coronets 22 Tinker Tailor Soldier Spy 23 The

Guinea
   other name: 12 French Guinea 13 Rivieres du Sud
   capital/largest city: 7 Conakry
   others: 4 Boke, Fria, Labe 5 Beyla 6 Dabola, Kankan, Kindia 7 Dubreka, Siguiri 8 Kerouane 9 Kouroussa, Nzerekore
   measure: 7 jacktan
   monetary unit: 4 iliy, syli 5 franc 6 cauris
   weight: 4 akey, piso, uzan 5 benda, seron 6 quinto 8 aguirage
   island: 3 Los 5 Tombo 7 Tristao
   mountain: 4 Loma 6 Tamgue 11 Fouta Djalon
   highest point: 5 Nimba
   river: 4 Milo 5 Kogon, Niger 6 Bafing, Faleme, Gambia 7 Kolente, Senegal 8 Konkoure, Tinkisso 13 Great Scarcies
   sea: 8 Atlantic
   physical feature:
      cape: 5 Verga
   people: 4 Koma, Loma, Nalu, Susu, Toma 5 Kissi, Manon 6 Fulani, Guerzi 7 Landoma, Malinke 8 Kouranke, Landuman 11 Kissi-Sherbo 12 Guerze-Kpelle
   language: 5 Fulbe, Mande 6 Arabic, French, Fulani 7 English
   religion: 5 Islam 7 animism
   feature:
      plant: 11 globeflower
      tree: 4 akee 5 dalli

Guinea-Bissau
other name: 16 Portuguese Guinea
capital/largest city: 6 Bissau
others: 4 Buba 5 Catio, Farim 6 Bafata, Bolama, Cacheu, Cacine, Dandum, Mansoa 7 Bissora, Bubaque, San Joav 9 Fulacunda 10 Nova Lamego 11 Madina do Boe, Madine do Boe, Sao Domingos
monetary unit: 4 peso 6 escudo 8 centavos
island: 4 Roxa 6 Orango 7 Bijagos, Formosa
river: 4 Geba 6 Cacheu, Mansoa 7 Corubal
sea: 8 Atlantic
people: 6 Fulani 7 Balanta, Balante, mulatto 8 Mandingo, Mandyako
language: 5 Fulah 7 Balante, Crioulo 8 Mandingo 10 Portuguese 21 Cape Verde-Guinea Creole
religion: 5 Islam 7 animism 12 Christianity

Bridge on the River Kwai (Oscar)

guise 4 garb, mode 5 dress, habit 6 attire 7 apparel, clothes, costume, fashion 8 clothing, disguise, pretense 10 masquerade

Gujarati
language family: 12 Indo-European
branch: 11 Indo-Iranian
group: 5 Indic
spoken in: 5 (northern) India

Gulag Archipelago, The
author: 23 Aleksandr Solzhenitsyn Jr

gulch 3 gap 4 rift 5 abyss, chasm, cleft, crack, gorge, gully, split 6 arroyo, breach, divide, ravine 8 crevasse

gulf 4 cove, rent, rift 5 abyss, chasm, cleft, firth, fjord, gully, inlet, split 6 canyon, lagoon 7 estuary, opening 8 crevasse 10 separation

gull 3 gyp 4 dupe, rook 5 cozen, trick 7 deceive, defraud, sea gull, sea bird, swindle 9 bamboozle, victimize

gullet 3 maw 4 craw, crop 5 belly, gorge, tummy 6 dewlap, throat 7 abdomen, chan-

nel, stomach, weasand 9 beer belly, esophagus

gullible 5 green, naive 6 simple 8 innocent, trustful, trusting 9 credulous 11 easily duped 12 easily fooled, overtrusting, unsuspicious 13 easily cheated, inexperienced 14 easily deceived 15 unsophisticated

Gulliver's Travels
author: 13 Jonathan Swift
character: 14 Lemuel Gulliver
visited: 6 Laputa, Yahoos 8 Blefuscu, Lilliput, Luggnagg 9 Balnibari 10 Houyhnhnms 11 Brobdingnag 12 Glubbdubdrib

gully 3 gap 5 ditch, gorge, gulch 6 defile, furrow, gutter, ravine, trench 7 channel 11 small canyon, small valley, watercourse 13 drainage ditch

gulp 4 bolt, swig, wolf 5 quaff, swill 6 devour, guzzle 7 swallow, toss off 8 mouthful

gulp down 4 bolt 6 devour, gobble 7 swallow 8 gobble up, wolf down

gum 3 wax 5 latex, resin 6 chicle 8 mucilage 10 Eucalyptus
varieties: 3 cup, red 4 blue, cape, gray, rose, snow, sour 5 apple, black, cider, coral, giant, gully, Karri, Manna, sugar, swamp, sweet 6 cotton, Deane's, desert, gimlet, salmon, snappy, Tupelo 7 Barbary, cabbage, Fuchsia, maiden's, Morocco, scarlet, spotted 8 Formosan, Lehmann's, mountain, scribbly, spinning 9 forest red, Murray red, steedman's 10 Australian, candle-bark, red-spotted, Sydney blue, Timor white, tumble-down, urn-fruited 11 Blakely's red, blue weeping, salmon white, small-leaved, strickland's 12 lemon-scented, red-flowering, silver-dollar 13 American sweet, Oriental sweet, Tasmanian blue, Tasmanian snow 14 yellow-flowered 15 Omeo round-leaved, round-leaved snow 16 rough-barked manna, scarlet-flowering 17 heart-leaved silver 20 silver-leaved mountain

Gumm, Frances
real name of: 11 Judy Garland

gummed 5 glued, gummy, stuck 6 sticky 8 adhering, adhesive

Gummidge, Mrs
character in: 16 David Copperfield
author: 7 Dickens

gummy 5 gluey, gooey, gunky 6 gloppy, sticky, viscid 7 rubbery, viscous 8 adhesive 10 gelatinous 12 mucilaginous

gumption 3 zip 4 dash, push 5 drive, spunk, verve 6 energy, hustle, pizazz, spirit 7 courage 10 enterprise, get-up-and-go, initiative 12 forcefulness 14 aggressiveness 15 resourcefulness

gumshoe 4 dick 6 shamus 9 detective 10 private eye 12 investigator

gun 3 aim, gat, rod, try 4 Colt, hunt, iron 5 piece, rifle, shoot 6 cannon, Magnum, mortar, musket, pistol 7 attempt, carbine, firearm, Gatling, go after, Long Tom, shotgun 8 howitzer, ordnance, revolver 9 automatic, Big Bertha, derringer, equalizer, flintlock, forty-five, twenty-two, Remington 10 fieldpiece, machine gun, six-shooter, three-fifty, Walther PPK, Winchester 11 blunderbuss, thirty-eight, trusty-rusty 12 fowling piece, muzzle loader, shooting iron 13 Kentucky rifle 14 artillery piece, Smith and Wesson
invented by:
   breechloader: 8 Thornton
   magazine: 9 Hotchkiss
   silencer: 5 Maxim

Gunga Din
story in: 18 Barrack-Room Ballads
author: 14 Rudyard Kipling
director: 13 George Stevens
cast: 8 Sam Jaffe 9 Cary Grant 12 Joan Fontaine 14 Victor McLaglen 18 Douglas Fairbanks Jr
setting: 5 India
remade as: 13 Soldiers Three 14 Sergeants Three

gunman 6 bandit, outlaw, robber, sniper 7 hoodlum 9 assailant, desperado, holdup man

Gunn, Ben
character in: 14 Treasure Island
author: 9 Stevenson

Gunnar
origin: 12 Scandinavian
father: 5 Giuki, Gjuki
mother: 8 Grimhild
sister: 6 Gudrun, Kudrun 7 Guthrun
wife: 8 Brynhild
Brynhild won by: 6 Sigurd

Gunsmoke
character: **3** Sam (the bartender) **8** Doc (Dr Galen)
Adams **10** Quint Asper
11 Newly O'Brien **12** Chester
Goode, Festus Haggen, Kitty
Russell (Miss Kitty) **18** Marshall Matt Dillon **24** Clayton
Thaddeus (Thad) Greenwood
cast: **9** Ken Curtis **10** Buck
Taylor, Roger Ewing
11 Amanda Blake, James Arness **12** Burt Reynolds, Dennis Weaver, Glenn Strange,
Milburn Stone
setting: **9** Dodge City
saloon: **10** Longbranch

Guns of August, The
author: **15** Barbara W
Tuchman

Guns of Navarone, The
director: **12** J Lee Thompson
based on novel by: **15** Alistair
MacLean
cast: **10** David Niven **11** Gregory Peck, James Darren
12 Anthony Quinn, Stanley
Baker **13** Anthony Quayle

Gunther
origin: **8** Germanic
mentioned in:
14 Nibelungenlied
king of: **8** Burgundy
wife: **8** Brunhild
sister: **9** Kriemhild
killed by: **9** Kriemhild

Guppy
character in: **10** Bleak House
author: **7** Dickens

Gurdin, Natasha
real name of: **11** Natalie
Wood

gurgle 5 plash **6** babble, bubble,
burble, murmur, ripple **7** sputter **8** bubbling, gurgling

guru 5 guide **6** leader, master
7 teacher **9** preceptor
10 instructor

gush 3 gab, gas, jet, run **4** blab,
bull, rush, well **5** issue, prate,
spout, spurt **6** babble, burble,
drivel, hot air, splash, squirt,
stream **7** baloney, blabber,
blather, chatter, pour out,
prattle, rubbish, torrent, twaddle **8** nonsense, outburst, rattle
on **10** outpouring **11** mawkishness **14** emotionalism **14** sentimentalism, talk effusively
16 run off at the mouth

gushiness 12 effusiveness,
emotionalism
17 demonstrativeness

gushing 6 lavish **7** pouring,
profuse **8** effusive, spurting

10 flattering **11** free-flowing
12 demonstrative, unrestrained
16 overenthusiastic

gushy 8 effusive **12** unrestrained **13** demonstrative
16 overenthusiastic

gussy up 5 adorn **7** dress up,
enhance **8** beautify, decorate,
ornament **9** embellish

gust 3 fit **4** blow, puff, wind
5 blast, burst, draft **6** breeze,
flurry, squall, zephyr **8** outbreak, outburst, paroxysm
9 explosion

Gustaffson, Greta Louisa
real name of: **10** Greta Garbo

Guster
character in: **10** Bleak House
author: **7** Dickens

gusto 3 joy **4** zeal, zest **5** savor
6 fervor, relish **7** delight **8** appetite, pleasure **10** enthusiasm
12 appreciation, exhilaration,
satisfaction

gusto, con
music: **9** with style, with taste

gusty 5 blowy, windy **6** breezy
7 squally **8** blustery

gut 4 raze **5** belly, clean, level,
tummy **6** bowels, paunch, ravage **7** abdomen, consume, midriff, stomach, viscera **8** entrails,
lay waste **9** bay window, beer
belly, spare tire **10** disembowel,
eviscerate, intestines, midsection **11** breadbasket

guten abend 11 good evening

Gutenberg
nationality: **6** German
inventor of: **11** movable type
printer of: **14** Gutenberg Bible

guten morgen 11 good
morning

guten tag 7 good day

Guthrie, A B Jr
author of: **6** Arfive **9** The Big
Sky **10** The Way West
13 The Last Valley **16** Fair
Land Fair Land, The Blue
Hen's Chick, The Thousand
Hills

Guthrun see **6** Gudrun

Gutman, Casper
character in: **16** The Maltese
Falcon
author: **7** Hammett

guts 4 dash, grit **5** nerve, pluck,
spunk **6** bowels, daring, mettle,

spirit, vitals **7** bravado, bravery,
courage, gizzard, innards, insides, viscera **8** audacity, backbone, boldness **9** fortitude
10 intestines **11** intrepidity

gutsy 4 game **5** brave **6** heroic,
plucky **7** doughty, valiant
8 fearless, intrepid, stalwart,
unafraid, valorous **9** dauntless,
undaunted **10** courageous **11** lionhearted, unflinching
12 stouthearted

guttural 3 low **4** deep **5** gruff,
harsh, husky, raspy, thick
6 hoarse **7** throaty **8** croaking
12 inarticulate

guy 3 boy, joe, kid, man
4 body, chap, dude, gent, rope
5 bloke, human,
joker **6** fellow, hombre,
person **8** blighter, upholder **9** supporter
10 individual

Guyana
name means: **12** land of
waters
other name: **13** British
Guiana
capital/largest city:
10 Georgetown
others: **7** Charity **8** Hyde
Park, Rosignol **9** Jones-
town, Mackenzie
island: **6** Leguan
8 Wakenaam
mountain: **5** Amuku, Ariwa, Kamoa **6** Akarai,
Kanuku **7** Caburai
9 Pacaraima
highest point: **7** Roraima
river: **5** Waini **6** Barama
7 Amakura, Baruima,
Berbice **8** Demerara, Ma-
zaruni, Rupununi **9** Essequibo **10** Burro-Burro
ocean: **8** Atlantic
physical feature:
  falls: **5** Great, Tiger
  7 Kamaria **8** Kaieteur
  9 Serikoeng **10** Sur-
  wakwima **15** Fredrik
  Willem IV
people: **6** Akawai, Arawak, Creole, Taruma
7 African, Chinese, mulatto **10** Portuguese
language: **5** Hindi
7 English
religion: **5** Hindu, Islam
8 Anglican **13** Roman
Catholic

Guy Fawkes
   author: **16** William
   Ainsworth

Guy Mannering
   author: **14** Sir Walter Scott

Guyon
   character in: **15** The Faerie
   Queene
   author: **7** Spenser

Guys and Dolls
   director: **17** Joseph L
   Mankiewicz
   based on story by: **11** Damon Runyon
   cast: **10** Stubby Kaye
   11 Jean Simmons **12** Frank
   Sinatra, Marlon Brando, Vivian Blaine
   setting: **11** New York City
   score: **12** Frank Loesser
   song: **11** Luck Be a Lady
   12 Guys and Dolls **26** Sit
   Down You're Rocking the
   Boat

guzzle 4 bolt, swig **5** quaff,
swill **6** devour, imbibe, tipple
7 toss off **8** gulp down

guzzler 5 drunk **6** boozer **7** imbiber, tippler **8** devourer,
drunkard **9** alcoholic

Gwawl
   origin: **5** Welsh
   mentioned in: **10** Mabinogion
   rival of: **5** Pwyll
   sought hand of: **8** Rhiannon

Gwydion
   origin: **5** Welsh
   son: **14** Llew Llaw Gyffes
   sister: **9** Arianhrod
   lover: **9** Arianhrod

Gwyn
   origin: **7** British
   god of: **7** rebirth **9** afterlife

Gyas
   companion of: **6** Aeneas

Gyes *see* **5** Gyges

Gygaea, Gyge
   form: **5** nymph
   location: **4** lake

Gyges
   also: **4** Gyes
   member of: **13** Hecatonchires

gymnasium 5 arena **6** circus
7 stadium **10** hippodrome

gymnast 10 Olga Korbut
13 Mary Lou Retton, Nadia
Comaneci

gymnastics 9 exercises **10** ac-
robatics **11** contortions
16 physical training

Gynaecothoenas
   epithet of: **4** Ares
   means: **17** feasted by the
   women

gynophobia
   fear of: **5** women

gyp 3 con **4** bilk, burn, fake,
hoax, rook, scam, soak
5 cheat, cozen, fraud, phony,
trick **6** diddle, fleece, humbug,
ripoff **7** con game, defraud,
swindle **8** flimflam, hoodwink
9 bamboozle, deception

gypsy
   Italian: **7** zingara, zingaro

gyrate 5 swirl, twirl, wheel,
whirl **6** circle, rotate, spiral
7 revolve **9** pirouette **10** spin
around

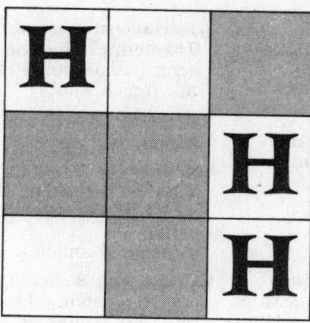

habeas corpus 11 have the body **23** produce the person in court
legal writ guards against: 19 illegal imprisonment

habiliments 4 garb, wear **5** dress **6** attire, outfit **7** clothes, costume, raiment, regalia **8** clothing, wardrobe **9** vestments

habit 3 rut, way **4** garb, gear, robe, rule, wont **5** dress, trait **6** attire, custom, groove, livery, manner, outfit **7** apparel, clothes, costume, garment, leaning, raiment, routine, uniform, vesture **8** clothing, fondness, habitude, practice **9** mannerism, trappings **10** beaten path, convention, observance, partiality, proclivity, propensity **11** habiliments, inclination, peculiarity **12** predilection, second nature **13** accoutrements, fixed practice **14** matter of course, predisposition **15** behavior pattern

habitat 3 pad **4** digs, home, spot, zone **5** abode, haunt, place, range, realm, roost **6** domain, locale, milieu, region **7** housing, lodging, setting, terrain **8** domicile, dwelling, home base, lodgment, precinct, quarters **9** territory **10** habitation **11** environment, natural home **12** place of abode **13** dwelling place **14** stamping ground **15** natural locality **17** native environment

habitation 3 pad **4** digs, home **5** abode, haunt, house, roost **6** colony **7** habitat, housing, lodging, shelter, tenancy **8** domicile, dwelling, lodgment, quarters **9** community, occupancy, residence **10** occupation, settlement **12** place of abode **13** dwelling place, temporary stay **16** place of residence

Habit of Being, The
author: 15 Flannery O'Connor

habitual 5 fixed, usual **6** common, normal, wonted **7** chronic, natural, regular, routine, typical **8** addicted, constant, expected, familiar, frequent, periodic, repeated **9** confirmed, continual, customary, incessant, ingrained, perpetual, recurrent **10** accustomed, deep-rooted, deepseated, inveterate, methodical, systematic **11** established, traditional **12** conventional, second nature **14** by force of habit

habitual practice 4 wont **5** habit **6** custom

habituate 5 adapt, drill, imbue, inure, train **6** harden, school, season **7** break in, instill **8** accustom, initiate **9** inculcate **10** discipline, make used to **12** indoctrinate

habitue 7 regular **10** frequenter **13** regular patron **15** frequent visitor **16** constant customer

hack 3 cab, cut, hew, nag **4** bark, chip, chop, gash, plug, rasp, slit, taxi **5** coach, cut up, notch, slash, slice, whack **6** cleave, mangle **7** hackney, taxicab **8** lacerate, mutilate **9** cart horse, dray horse, scribbler, workhorse **10** cough drily, cut roughly, draft horse, hired horse, shaft horse **11** common horse, penny-aliner **12** hackney coach, worn-out horse **13** carriage horse **16** grubstreet writer **18** horse-drawn carriage

hackle 3 peg **4** card, comb, hack, hook, ruff **5** curry, plume, quill **6** heckle, mangle **7** bristle, feather, plumage

Hackman, Gene
born: 15 San Bernardino CA
roles: 8 Superman **11** Popeye Doyle **14** Bonnie and Clyde **15** The Conversation **19** The French Connection (Oscar) **20** The Poseidon Adventure

hackneyed 4 dull, worn **5** banal, inane, stale, stock, trite, vapid **6** common, jejune **7** cliched, humdrum, insipid, routine, worn-out **8** bromidic, ordinary, shopworn, wellworn **9** moth-eaten **10** pedestrian, threadbare, uninspired **11** commonplace, stereotyped **12** conventional **13** platitudinous, unimaginative

Hadassah 6 Esther

Hades 4 hell
also: 5 Pluto **10** lower world, Underworld
corresponds to: 5 Orcus
god of: 5 Orcus, Pluto
goddess of: 6 Hecate, Hekate

Haemon
father: 5 Creon
loved: 8 Antigone
died at tomb of: 8 Antigone
death by: 7 suicide

Haenigsen, Harry
creator/artist of: 5 Penny **7** Our Bill

hafnium
chemical symbol: 2 Hf

hag 3 bat, nag **4** drab, fury **5** biddy, crone, frump, harpy, shrew, vixen, witch **6** beldam, gorgon, ogress, virago **7** hellcat **8** battle-ax, harridan **9** termagant

Hagar
servant of: 5 Sarah
husband: 7 Abraham
son: 7 Ishmael

Hagar the Horrible
creator: 9 Dik Browne

Hagen
origin: 8 Germanic

mentioned in:
14 Nibelungenlied
killed by: 9 Kriemhild
killed: 9 Siegfried

haggard 4 beat, wild, worn
5 gaunt, spent, tired, upset,
weary **6** bushed, fagged,
pooped, raging, wasted **7** ranting **8** careworn, drooping, fatigued, flagging, frenzied,
harassed, harrowed, overcome,
toilworn, wild-eyed **9** exhausted, woebegone **10** hol-
low-eyed **11** debilitated,
overwearied, overwrought,
tuckered out, wild-looking
12 tired-looking

Haggard, H Rider
author of: 3 She **17** King Solomon's Mines

haggle 6 barter, bicker, dicker,
higgle **7** bargain, dispute,
quarrel, quibble, wrangle
8 beat down, squabble

Hagiographa
Hebrew: 7 Ketubim

hagiographer 19 writer of
saints' lives

Hagman, Larry
mother: 10 Mary Martin
born: 13 Weatherford TX
roles: 6 Dallas **7** J R Ewing
15 I Dream of Jeannie

Hagno
origin: 8 Arcadian
form: 5 nymph
location: 6 spring

Hahn, Otto
field: 9 chemistry
nationality: 6 German
discovered: 13 protoactin-
ium **14** nuclear isomers
awarded: 10 Nobel Prize

Haida
language family: 6 Masset,
Na-Dene **10** Skidegatta
tribe: 7 Kaigani
location: 6 Alaska **15** British
Columbia **21** Queen Charlotte Islands
related to: 7 Tlingit
9 Tsimshian
associated with: 9 totem
pole **13** wood sculpture

hail 4 call **5** cheer, exalt, extol,
greet, hello, honor, shout
6 accost, call to, esteem, salute **7** acclaim, address, applaud, commend, glorify,
receive, shout at, usher in,
welcome **8** cry out to, eulogize, greeting **9** accosting
10 calling out, compliment,
panegyrize, salutation **11** make
welcome
German: 4 heil
Latin: 5 salve

Hailey, Arthur
author of: 5 Hotel **6** Wheels
7 Airport **12** In High Places
14 Final Diagnosis **16** The
Moneychangers

hail-fellow-well-met 8 familiar, friendly, intimate, outgoing, sociable **9** extrovert
10 gregarious

Hail Mary
Latin: 8 Ave Maria

Hail the Conquering Hero
director: 14 Preston Sturges
cast: 10 Ella Raines **12** Eddie
Bracken **14** Raymond Wal-
burn **15** William Demarest
16 Franklin Pangborn

hail to victory
German: 8 Sieg Heil

hair 3 fur, mop **4** coat, down,
iota, mane, pelt, wool
5 bangs, curls, locks **6** fleece
7 tresses **8** ringlets **12** narrow
margin

haircut, hairdo 3 bob, bun,
cut **4** Afro, clip, crop, perm,
shag, trim **5** bangs, braid,
butch, swirl **6** boogie, mohawk **7** beehive, chignon,
cornrow, crewcut, flattop, fuzz
cut, natural, pachuco, page
boy, pigtail, shingle, tonsure
8 bouffant, brushcut, coiffure,

ducktail, ponytail, razorcut
9 barbering, hairstyle, permanent, pompadour **10** feather-
cut, french knot

haircutter 6 barber **11** hairdresser, hair stylist

hairdresser 8 coiffeur **9** coif-
feuse **10** beautician, haircutter **11** beauty salon **12** beauty
parlor
French: 8 coiffeur

hair-raising 8 exciting **9** thrilling **10** terrifying **11** astonishing **12** breathtaking,
electrifying

hairsplitting 4 fine **6** minute,
subtle **7** carping **8** caviling,
delicate, hairline, niggling
9 minuscule, quibbling **10** nitpicking, unapparent **12** faultfinding, overcritical
13 imperceptible, inappreciable, infinitesimal
15 inconsequential

hairy 5 bushy, furry, wooly
6 fleecy, pilose, shaggy,
woolly **7** hirsute

Hairy Ape, The
author: 12 Eugene O'Neill

Haiti *see box*

Hakenkreuz 11 hooked cross
12 Nazi swastika

Haiti
name means: 15 mountainous land
other name: 12 Santo Domingo
capital/largest city: 12 Port-au-Prince
others: 5 Aquin, Furcy, Limbe **6** Hinche, Jacmel, St Marc
7 Jeremie, Leogane, Saltrou **8** Gonaives, Kenscoff, Les
Cayes **10** Cap-Haitien
monetary unit: 6 gourde **8** centimes
island: 5 Vache **6** Gonave, Tortue **7** Navassa, Tortuga
8 Caymites **10** Hispaniola **14** Grande Cayemite **15** Greater
Antilles
lake: 8 Saumatre
mountain: 4 Nord **5** Cahos **6** Macaya, Noires **7** Lahotte
8 Troudeau
highest point: 7 La Selle, Laselle
river: 9 Guayamoul **10** Artibonite
sea: 8 Atlantic **9** Caribbean
physical feature:
  gulf: **6** Gonave
  passage: **8** Windward
people: 5 Taino **7** African, mulatto
  discoverer: **8** Columbus
  liberator: **19** Toussaint Louverture
  ruler: **8** Duvalier
language: 6 Creole, French, patois
religion: 6 voodoo **13** Roman Catholic
feature:
  dance: **5** mambo
  festival: **9** Mardi Gras
  fortress: **10** La Ferriere **24** Citadelle du Roi Christophe
  security force: **8** bogeymen **15** Tontons Macoutes
food:
  sweet potato: **6** batata

Hakluyt, Richard
author of: 7 Voyages
15 Hakluyt's Voyages

HAL
character in: 14 Two Thousand One (2001)
author: 6 Clarke

Halas, George
nickname: 8 Papa Bear
sport: 8 football
position: 5 coach
team: 12 Chicago Bears

halcyon 4 calm, fair 5 happy, quiet, sunny 6 blithe, golden, hushed, joyous, placid, serene 7 pacific 8 carefree, cheerful, peaceful, tranquil 9 cloudless, contented, reposeful, unclouded, unruffled 10 unagitated, untroubled

Halcyon see 7 Alcyone

hale 3 fit 4 well 5 hardy, sound 6 hearty, robust, rugged, sturdy 7 healthy, in shape 8 vigorous 9 energetic, in the pink, strapping 10 ablebodied, robustious 12 in fine fettle

Hale, Edward Everett
author of: 21 The Man Without a Country

Hale, George Ellery
field: 9 astronomy
initiated: 20 Mt Palomar Observatory
invented:
17 spectroheliograph

Halevy, Ludovic
author of: 17 The Abbe Constantin

Haley, Alex
author of: 5 Roots

Haley, Jack
born: 8 Boston MA
roles: 6 Tin Man 13 The Wizard of Oz

half 4 part, some 6 all but, barely, fairly, feebly, halved, in part, meager, partly, rather, scanty, skimpy, slight, weakly 7 divided, faintly, limited, partial, portion, section 8 fraction, middling, moderate, passable, passably, slightly 9 deficient, imperfect, partially, tolerable, tolerably 10 fractional, inadequate, incomplete, moderately, relatively 12 fifty percent, inadequately, insufficient, pretty nearly 13 after a fashion, comparatively 14 insufficiently

half-asleep 6 drowsy, groggy, unwary 7 out-of-it, unaware 8 sluggish 9 not-with-it, oblivious

half-hearted 4 cold, cool,

tame 5 blase, faint 7 languid, passive 8 listless, lukewarm 9 apathetic, lethargic 10 ambivalent, irresolute, lackluster, phlegmatic, spiritless, unaspiring 11 indifferent, perfunctory 13 lackadaisical 14 unenthusiastic

half homer 15 Biblical measure

half-moon 3 arc, bow 4 arch 5 curve 8 crescent

halfway 6 almost, in part, medial, medium, middle, midway, nearly, partly, rather 7 midmost 8 somewhat 9 partially, to a degree 10 middlemost, moderately 11 equidistant, in the middle 12 intermediate, pretty nearly, to some extent 13 in some measure 18 between two extremes

half-wit 4 dolt, dope, fool 5 dummy, dunce, idiot, moron, ninny 6 dimwit, nitwit 7 dullard 8 dumb-dumb, imbecile, numskull 9 blockhead, numbskull, simpleton 10 nincompoop 15 mental defective, mental deficient

half-witted 4 dumb 5 silly 6 stupid 7 asinine, foolish, idiotic, moronic 9 dimwitted, imbecilic, senseless 11 lamebrained 12 feebleminded, simple-minded

Halirrhothius
father: 8 Poseidon
mother: 6 Euryte
raped: 7 Alcippe
killed by: 4 Ares

Halitherses
origin: 6 Ithaca
form: 4 seer

hall 5 entry, foyer, lobby 6 arcade 7 chamber, gallery, hallway, passage 8 anteroom, club room, corridor, entrance 9 vestibule 10 auditorium, dining hall, passageway 11 antechamber, banquet hall, concert hall, waiting room 12 amphitheater, assembly room, meeting place 13 reception room

Hall, Diane
real name of: 11 Diane Keaton

Hall, James
field: 7 geology 9 chemistry
nationality: 7 British
founded: 12 geochemistry
19 experimental geology

Hall, James Norman
author of: 17 Mutiny on the Bounty
co-author: 15 Charles Nordhoff

Hallel 6 praise 16 liturgical prayer

Haller, Albrecht von
field: 7 biology
nationality: 5 Swiss
founded: 15 modern neurology

Haller, Harry
character in: 11 Steppenwolf
author: 5 Hesse

Halley, Edmund
field: 9 astronomy
nationality: 7 British
discovered: 12 Halley's Comet

hallmark 4 sign 5 badge, stamp 6 device, emblem, symbol 14 characteristic

Hall of Fame see box, p. 426

halloo 3 cry 4 call, hail, yell 5 shout 6 cry out, holler

hallow 5 bless 7 respect 8 dedicate, sanctify, venerate 10 consecrate

hallowed 4 holy 6 sacred 7 blessed, honored 9 beatified, dedicated 10 sacrosanct, sanctified 11 consecrated

hallucination 5 dream 6 mirage, vision 7 chimera, fantasy, figment 8 delusion, illusion 9 nightmare 10 aberration, apparition 14 phantasmagoria

hallway 4 hall 7 passage 8 corridor, entryway 10 passageway

halo 6 aurora, corona, luster, nimbus 7 aureole, dignity, majesty 8 grandeur, holiness, radiance, sanctity, splendor 9 solemnity, sublimity 11 ring of light 12 chromosphere, luminousness, magnificence, resplendence 13 spiritual aura 15 illustriousness

Haloa
event: 8 festival
origin: 5 Greek
honoring: 7 Demeter 8 Dionysus 10 Persephone

Hals, Franz
born: 7 Antwerp, Holland
artwork: 9 Gypsy Girl 10 Hille Bobbe (The Witch of Haarlem) 13 The Jolly Toper 14 Jacobus Zaffius 15 The Merry Company 19 The Laughing Cavalier 22 Portrait of a Standing Man 24 The Regents of the Almshouse 26 Yonker Ramp and his Sweetheart 28 The Regentesses of the Almshouse 33 The Banquet of the St George Civic Guard

Halsey, William F
served in: 3 WWI 4 WWII

Hall of Fame
  author: 3 Poe **5** Paine, Stowe **6** Bryant, Cooper, Holmes, Irving, Lanier, Lowell, Motley **7** Clemens, Emerson, Parkman, Thoreau, Whitman **8** Bancroft, Whittier **9** Hawthorne
  aviation: 3 Six **4** Bell, Byrd, Lear, Luke, Post, Ryan **5** Beech, Eaker, Glenn, LeMay, Piper, Reeve **6** Arnold, Boeing, Cessna, Fokker, Hughes, Levier, Rogers, Spaatz, Sperry, Towers, Trippe, Wright, Yeager **7** Chanute, Earhart, Goddard, Langley, Shepherd, Twining **8** Mitchell, Northrup, Sikorsky **9** Armstrong, Chennault, Lindberg, Mcdonnell **12** Rickenbacker
  baseball: 3 Ott **4** Bell, Cobb, Dean, Ford, Foxx, Hoyt, Kell, Mack, Mays, Mize, Rice, Ruth, Ward, Wynn **5** Aaron, Anson, Baker, Banks, Berra, Carey, Duffy, Faber, Gomez, Grove, Hafey, Irvin, Kelly, Lemon, Lloyd, Paige, Reese, Rusie, Terry, Vance, Wheat, Young **6** Alston, Barrow, Bender, Cuyler, Dickey, Feller, Frisch, Galvin, Gehrig, Gibson, Goslin, Grimes, Haines, Herman, Hooper, Hunter, Kaline, Keeler, Kelley, Koufax, Lajoie, Mantle, Musial, Schalk, Sewell, Sisler, Snider, Tinker, Wagner, Wilson, Youngs **7** Averill, Appling, Beckley, Hubbell, Jackson, Leonard, McCovey, Nichols, O'Rourke, Pennock, Roberts, Stengel, Traynor, Vaughan, Waddell, Wallace, Wilhelm **8** Bancroft, Boudreau, Clemente, Comiskey, DiMaggio, Drysdale, Jennings, McCarthy, Radbourn, Robinson, Thompson, Williams **9** Alexander, Delahanty, Greenberg, Mathewson **10** Campanella, Maranville
  basketball: 4 Gola, Page, Reed, West **5** Cousy, Fulks, Greer, Hyatt, Lucas, Mikan **6** Barlow, Baylor, Cooper, Foster, Hanson, Holman, Pettit, Philip, Ramsey, Roosma, Sedran, Wooden **7** Beckman, Bradley, Johnson, Kurland, Pollard, Russell, Schmidt, Sharman **8** Borgmann, Endacott, Lapchick, Schommer **9** Robertson, Steinmetz, Vandivier **11** Chamberlain, Debusschere
  business: 4 Ford, Kroc, Land, Luce, Vail **5** Beech, Deere, Heinz **6** Batten, Carrier, Cooper, Disney, du Pont, Edison, Hilton, Lowell, Mellon, Morgan, Penney, Schwab **7** Bechtel, Merrill, Peabody, Proctor, Whitney **8** Carnegie, Eastman, Franklin **9** Baekeland, Kettering, McCormick **10** Vanderbilt **11** Rockefeller **12** Westinghouse
  football: 3 Mix, Ray **4** Bell, Carr, Ford, Hein, Huff, Hunt, Lane, Lary, Mara, Otto, Owen **5** Baugh, Berry, Brown, Clark, Davis, Fears, Green, Gregg, Groza, Guyon, Halas, Henry, Jones, Layne, Lilly, Lyman, Moore, Musso, Neale, Olsen, Perry, Pihos, Ringo, Starr **6** Atkins, Badgro, Blanda, Butkus, Connor, Dudley, Ewbank, Gatski, George, Graham, Grange, Healey, Herver, Hewitt, Hinkle, Hirsch, Hutson, Kinard, Langer, Lanier, Matson, McAfee, Motley, Namath, Nevers, Parker, Reeves, Rooney, Sayers, Strong, Taylor, Thorpe, Tittle, Trippi, Turner, Unitas, Upshaw, Walker, Willis, Wilson **7** Alworth, Battles, Bidwell, Canadeo, Donovan, Edwards, Gillman, Gifford, Hubbard, Lambeau, Lavelli, Leemans, Luckman, McNally, Millner, Schmidt, Trafton, Tunnell **8** Adderley, Bednarik, Driscoll, Fortmann, Kiesling, Lombardi, Marshall, Mitchell, Nagurski, Nitschke, Stautner, Stydahar, Van Buren, Warfield **9** Conzelman, Jurgensen, Marchetti, McElhenny, Michalske, Nomellini, Tarkenton **10** Robustelle, Waterfield **11** Chamberlain, Van Brocklin **12** Christiansen **13** Wohciechowicz
  golf: 4 Berg, Ford, Hope, Wood **5** Boros, Brady, Burke, Dutra, Evans, Hagen, Hogan, Jones, Shute, Smith, Snead **6** Armour, Barnes, Casper, Cooper, Diegel, Dudley, Ghezzi, Harper, Little, McLeod, Nelson, Ouimet, Palmer, Picard, Runyan, Travis **7** Demaret, Guldahl, Harbert, Littler, Mangrum, Revolta, Sarazen, Travers **8** Anderson, Harrison, Zaharias **9** De Vicenzo, Hutchinson, McDermott **10** Middlecoff **11** Cruickshank
  scientist: 4 Gray **5** Gibbs, Henry, Maury **6** Carver **7** Agassiz, Audubon, Burbank, Newcomb **8** Mitchell **9** Michelson
  theater: 4 Drew, Kerr **5** Brook, Hecht, Kelly, Simon **6** Prince **7** Dunnock, Youmans **8** Kingsley, Lansbury, Meredith, Sondheim **9** MacArthur **11** Bloomgarden

rank: 12 fleet admiral
  battle: 9 Leyte Gulf **11** Philippines **14** Solomon Islands

halt 3 end **4** balk, curb, foil, quit, rest, rout, stay, stem, stop, wait **5** abate, block, brake, break, cease, check, close, crush, delay, pause, quash, quell, stall, tarry **6** bridle, cut off, defeat, draw up, hamper, hinder, impede, linger, pull up, recess, rein in, scotch, subdue, thwart, wind up **7** heave to, inhibit, prevent, put down, repress, respite, squelch, suspend, time out **8** break off, breather, choke off, don't move, hang fire, interval, knock off, leave off, overturn, prohibit, restrain, restrict, shut down, suppress, vanquish **9** cessation, frustrate, interlude, interrupt, overthrow, terminate **10** call it a day, extinguish, shut up shop, standstill, suspension **11** come to a halt, come to a stop, discontinue, hold in check, termination **12** intermission, interruption, throttle down **13** spike one's guns **14** breathing spell, discontinuance

halting 6 ending **7** curbing **8** episodic, hesitant, stopping **9** faltering, stumbling **10** calling off, discursive, suspending **11** restraining, terminating **13** discontinuous **14** calling a halt to, putting a stop to

halting place
  Spanish: 6 posada

halutz 7 pioneer **26** person who emigrates to Israel

halve 6 bisect **9** cut in half **10** split in two **13** divide equally

Ham
  character in: 16 David Copperfield
  author: 7 Dickens

Ham
  father: 4 Noah
  brother: 4 Shem **7** Japheth
  son: 3 Put **4** Cush **6** Canaan **7** Misraim
  descendant of: 6 Hamite

Hamadryad
  form: 5 dryad
  spirit of: 4 tree

Haman
  served: 9 Ahasuerus

Hamill, Mark
  born: 9 Oakland CA

roles: 8 Star Wars **13** Luke Skywalker **15** Return of the Jedi **20** The Empire Strikes Back

Hamilton
capital of: **7** Bermuda

Hamilton, Charles
character in: **15** Gone With the Wind
author: **8** Mitchell

Hamilton, Iain
composer of: **6** Aurora **7** Alastor **8** Sinfonia **9** Pharsalia **11** The Bermudas **18** Threnos In Time of War **20** The Royal Hunt of the Sun **21** The Catiline Conspiracy

Hamilton, Margaret
real name: **23** Margaret Hamilton Meserve
born: **11** Cleveland OH
roles: **4** Cora **13** The Wizard of Oz **23** The Wicked Witch of the West

Hamito-Semitic
language also known as: **11** Afro-Asiatic
branch: **6** Berber, Chadic **7** Semitic **8** Cushitic, Egyptian

hamlet 4 burg **7** village **8** hick town, tank town **10** crossroads **11** whistle stop **12** one-horse town, small village **13** jerkwater town

Hamlet
author: **18** William Shakespeare
character: **7** Horatio, Laertes, Ophelia **8** Claudius, Gertrude, Polonius, The Ghost **11** Rosencrantz **12** Guildenstern
skull: **6** Yorick
castle: **8** Elsinore
setting: **7** Denmark
director: **15** Laurence Olivier
cast: **11** Basil Sydney, Felix Aylmer, Jean Simmons **12** Eileen Herlie **15** Laurence Olivier
Oscar for: **5** actor (Olivier) **7** picture

Hamlet, The
author: **15** William Faulkner
character: **4** Eula, Jody **6** Labove **8** Ab Snopes **9** V K Ratliff **10** Flem Snopes, Mink Snopes, Will Varner **11** Isaac Snopes **12** Henry Armstid

Hamlin, Vincent T
creator/artist of: **8** Alley Oop

hammer 3 hit, tap **4** bang, form, make, nail **5** drive, forge, knock, pound, punch, shape, whack **6** pummel, rammer, strike **7** beat out, fashion
type: **4** claw, jack, tack **5** gavel, steam **6** mallet, sledge **8** ballpeen **10** pile driver **12** upholsterers

Hammer, Mike
detective created by: **14** Mickey Spillane

hammered 6 banged, beaten, shaped **7** knocked, pounded, whipped, wrought **8** battered, repeated **10** terrorized

Hammett, Dashiell
author of: **10** Red Harvest, The Thin Man **11** The Glass Key **12** The Dain Curse **16** The Maltese Falcon
character: **8** Sam Spade **11** Miles Archer, Nick Charles, Nora Charles **13** Continental Op

hamper 3 gag **4** balk, curb, stem **5** block, check, stall **6** fetter, hinder, hog-tie, hold up, impede, muzzle, retard, thwart **7** inhibit, prevent, shackle **8** encumber, handicap, obstruct, restrain, restrict **9** frustrate **13** interfere with

Hampton, Hope
nickname: **22** The Duchess of Park Avenue
born: **14** Philadelphia PA
roles: **8** Star Dust **13** Lawful Larceny, The Road to Reno **16** The Price of a Party

hamstring 6 impair, muscle, tendon **7** cripple, disable **8** handicap **10** debilitate

Hamsun, Knut
author of: **3** Pan **6** August, Hunger **8** Victoria **9** Mysteries, Vagabonds **16** Children of the Age **18** The Growth of the Soil

Hananiah see **8** Shadrach

hand, hands 3 aid, man, paw **4** care, fist, give, help, hold, lift, mitt, palm, pass **5** guide, power, reach **6** assist, charge, convey, helper, menial, script, worker **7** command, control, custody, deliver, keeping, laborer, ovation, present, support, workman **8** auspices, dominion, employee, guidance, handyman, hired man, long-hand, meat-hook **9** assistant, associate, authority, hired hand **10** assistance, domination, management, minister to, penmanship, possession, turn over to, workingman **11** calligraphy, furnish with, handwriting, supervision **12** jurisdiction **13** member of a crew **15** burst of applause,
manual extremity, round of applause

handbag 3 bag **4** grip **5** purse **6** clutch, valise **7** satchel **8** moneybag, reticule **10** pocketbook, portmanteau

handbill 5 flier **6** notice **7** leaflet **8** bulletin, circular **12** announcement **13** advertisement

handbook 5 bible **6** manual **9** guidebook **13** reference book

hand by hand
Spanish: **9** mano a mano

handcart 4 cart **6** barrow **8** pushcart **10** handbarrow **11** wheelbarrow

handcuffs 5 cuffs, irons **6** chains **7** fetters **8** manacles, shackles **9** bracelets

hand down 4 will **5** leave **6** hand on, pass on **8** bequeath

Handel, George Frederick (Georg Friedrich)
born: **5** Halle **7** Germany
composer of: **4** Nero, Saul **5** Serse, Silla, Siroe, Teseo **6** Admeto, Alcina, Almira, Esther, Flavio, Jeptha, Joseph, Ottone, Samson, Semele, Xerxes **7** Amadigi, Athalia, Deborah, Lotario, Messiah, Rinaldo, Rodrigo, Solomon, Tolomeo **8** Atalanta, Berenice, Hercules, Scipione, Theodora **9** Agrippina, Radamisto, Rodelinda, Tamerlano **10** Alessandro, Belshazzar, Floridante, Water Music **12** Giulio Cesare, Il Pastor Fido, Muzio Scevola **13** Israel in Egypt, Riccardo Primo **14** Acis and Galatea, Fireworks Music **15** Alexander's Feast, Judas Maccabaeus **16** Hornpipe Concerto **19** Julius Caesar in Egypt, Ode for St Cecilia's Day **22** The Royal Fireworks Music **23** Hallelujah Organ Concerto, The Harmonious Blacksmith **24** The Triumph of Time and Truth

handful 7 minimum, modicum **10** scattering, smattering, sprinkling, thimbleful, tiny amount **11** scant amount, small number **13** small quantity

Handful of Dust, A
author: **11** Evelyn Waugh

handgun 3 rod **5** piece, rifle **6** pistol, weapon **7** firearm, shotgun **8** revolver **9** automatic, twenty-two **12** shooting iron **20** Saturday night special

handicap 4 curb **5** limit **6** burden, defect, hamper, hinder, impede, retard, thwart **7** barrier, inhibit, repress, shackle **8** deafness, drawback, encumber, hold back, lameness, obstacle, restrain, restrict, suppress **9** blindness, detriment **10** difficulty, impediment, inhibition, limitation **11** encumbrance, restriction, shortcoming **12** disadvantage **13** inconvenience **14** stumbling block

handicapped 7 limited **8** burdened, disabled, held back, hindered, impaired, retarded **10** encumbered, restrained, restricted **13** disadvantaged

handicrafts
god of: **10** Hephaestus, Hephaistos

handicraftsman 7 artisan **10** handworker **12** handicrafter

handiness 7 utility **8** deftness **9** dexterity **10** adroitness, usefulness **11** convenience **12** availability **13** accessibility

hand in glove 5 as one **10** side by side **13** close together

handle 3 paw, ply, run, tag, use **4** feel, grip, hilt, hold, knob, name, poke, pull, sell, work **5** carry, grasp, guide, knead, pilot, pinch, shaft, shank, steer, swing, touch, treat **6** caress, deal in, employ, finger, fondle, manage, market, pick up, stroke **7** care for, command, conduct, control, massage, moniker, operate, paw over, trade in, utilize **8** cognomen, deal with, maneuver **9** traffic in **10** manipulate, take care of **11** appellation, merchandise **12** offer for sale **13** bring into play

Handley Cross
author: **18** Robert Smith Surtees

handout 4 alms, dole **7** freebie **19** something for nothing

hand out 4 give **5** grant **6** bestow, confer, donate **7** dole out, mete out, present **8** dispense **9** apportion **10** contribute, distribute

hand over 4 cede **5** grant, yield **6** give up, tender **7** abandon, release **8** transfer **9** deliver up, surrender **10** relinquish

handsome 4 fair **5** ample, bonny, noble **6** benign, comely, lovely, pretty **7** elegant, liberal, sightly, sizable, stately **8** abundant, generous, gracious, imposing, merciful, princely, splendid, stunning,

tasteful **9** beauteous, beautiful, bountiful, exquisite, unselfish **10** attractive, benevolent, bighearted, impressive, sufficient, well-formed **11** fine-looking, good-looking, magnanimous **12** considerable, easy to look at, humanitarian **13** compassionate, easy on the eyes **16** well-proportioned

handy 4 deft, near, nigh **5** adept, on tap **6** adroit, at hand, clever, expert, on call, on hand, useful, wieldy **7** capable, helpful, skilled **8** skillful **9** available, competent, dexterous, easy to use, efficient, practical **10** accessible, convenient, manageable, obtainable, proficient **11** at one's elbow, close at hand, in readiness, ready to hand, serviceable **12** accomplished **14** nimble-fingered **15** within easy reach **16** easily accessible **17** at one's beck and call

hang 3 bow, sag **4** drop, gist, rest **5** affix, hinge, knack, lie in, lower, lynch, point, trail **6** append, attach, dangle, depend **7** incline, meaning, suspend, thought **8** lean over, let droop, repose in, string up, turn upon **9** be pendant, be pendent **11** be dependent, be subject to, bend forward, swing freely **12** be contingent, bend downward **13** revolve around **15** die on the gallows, fasten from above **16** execute by hanging, send to the gallows

hangdog 6 abject **7** ashamed **8** defeated, degraded, hopeless, resigned, wretched **9** miserable **10** browbeaten, chapfallen, humiliated, shamefaced **11** crestfallen, embarrassed, intimidated **13** guilty-looking

hang down 3 sag **5** droop

hanger-on 7 admirer, groupie **8** follower **9** sycophant

hanging object
Japanese: **8** kakemono

hang loosely 3 bag, sag **5** droop

hangout 3 den **5** haunt

hang out 3 mix **4** live **5** dwell **6** hobnob, loiter, mingle, reside **7** consort **9** associate, be friends, pal around, run around **10** fraternize, hang around **11** keep company

hanker after 4 want **5** covet, crave, fancy **6** desire **7** long for, pine for **8** aspire to, yearn for **9** lust after **11** have a yen for, have an eye on, hunger after, thirst after

hankering 3 yen **4** itch, urge **6** aching, desire, hunger, pining, thirst **7** craving, longing **8** yearning

Hanna-Barbera
creators of: **8** Yogi Bear **14** The Flintstones

Hannah
husband: **7** Elkanah
son: **6** Samuel

Hanoi
capital of: **7** Vietnam **12** North Vietnam
river: **3** Red **4** Yuan **7** Song Koi
delta: **6** Tonkin
airport: **6** Gia Lam

Hans Brinker
author: **5** (Mary Elizabeth Mapes) Dodge
character: **4** Raff **5** Gleck, Hilda **6** Gretel **7** Boekman, Mevrouw

Hansel and Gretel
author: **13** Grimm Brothers (Jakob and Wilhelm)
opera by: **11** Humperdinck
character: **5** Witch

Hans Kristian
character in: **16** Giants of the Earth
author: **7** Rolvaag

Hanson, Howard
born: **7** Wahoo NE
composer of: **5** Sacra (symphony No 5) **6** Nordic (symphony No 1) **7** Requiem (symphony No 4) **8** Romantic (symphony No 2) **10** Merry-Mount

Hap *see* **4** Apis

haphazard 6 casual, chance, fitful, random **7** aimless, chaotic **8** careless, on-and-off, slapdash, sporadic **9** arbitrary, hit-or-miss **10** accidental, disordered, disorderly, fortuitous, undesigned, undirected, unthinking **11** purposeless, unorganized **12** disorganized, unmethodical, unsystematic **14** indiscriminate, unpremeditated **15** catch-as-catch-can

Hapi *see* **4** Apis, Nile

hapless 5 lousy **6** cursed, jinxed, no-good, rotten, woeful **7** forlorn, unhappy, unlucky **8** accursed, hopeless, ill-fated, luckless, wretched **9** miserable **10** ill-starred **11** star-crossed, unfortunate

happen 5 arise, ensue, occur **6** appear, befall, betide, crop up, result **7** turn out **8** become of, spring up **9** be borne by, be the case, come about, eventuate, take place, transpire **10** be one's fate, come to pass **11** be endured by **12** be suffered by **13** be one's fortune, fall to one's lot, present itself

happening 4 case **5** event **6** advent, affair, matter **7** episode **8** accident, incident, occasion **9** adventure, incidence **10** experience, occurrence, proceeding **11** vicissitude **12** circumstance, happenstance **20** just one of those things

happenstance 4 luck **6** chance **8** accident, fortuity

happiness 3 joy **4** glee **5** bliss, cheer, mirth **6** gaiety **7** comfort, content, delight, ecstasy, elation, jollity, rapture **8** blessing, felicity, gladness, pleasure **9** beatitude, enjoyment, merriment, rejoicing, transport **10** cheeriness, exuberance, exultation, jubilation **11** blessedness, contentment, high spirits **12** cheerfulness, satisfaction **13** gratification **16** lightheartedness, sense of well-being

happy 3 fit, gay **4** glad, meet **5** lucky **6** elated, joyful, joyous, timely **7** content, fitting, gleeful, pleased, tickled **8** blissful, cheerful, cheering, ecstatic, exultant, jubilant, pleasant, pleasing **9** agreeable, contented, delighted, exuberant, favorable, fortunate, gratified, opportune, overjoyed, rapturous, rhapsodic **10** auspicious, convenient, delightful, felicitous, gratifying, propitious, seasonable **11** exhilarated, tickled pink, transported **12** advantageous **13** in high spirits **15** in seventh heaven

Happy Days
   character: 6 Arnold, Fonzie **10** Ralph Malph **11** Potsie Weber **12** Chachi Arcola **14** Pinky Tuscadero **15** Chuck Cunningham **16** Alfred Delvecchio, Arthur Fonzarelli, Howard Cunningham, Joanie Cunningham, Leather Tuscadero, Marion Cunningham, Richie Cunningham
   cast: 8 Roz Kelly **9** Donny Most, Erin Moran, Pat Morita, Ron Howard, Scott Baio, Tom Bosley **10** Al Molinaro, Marion Ross, Suzi Quatro **12** Henry Winkler **13** Anson Williams, Gavan O'Herlihy **15** Randolph Roberts

happy-go-lucky 6 blithe **7** buoyant, flighty, relaxed **8** carefree, careless, feckless, heedless, skittish **9** easygoing,

unworried **10** insouciant, nonchalant, optimistic, untroubled **11** free-and-easy, unconcerned **12** devil-may-care, light-hearted **13** irresponsible **14** scatterbrained **23** without a worry in the world

harangue 6 speech, tirade **7** lecture, oration **8** diatribe, scolding **9** contumely, sermonize **12** denunciation, vituperation

Harare
   capital of: 8 Zimbabwe

harass 3 cow, irk, vex **4** bait, ride **5** annoy, beset, bully, harry, hound, tease, worry **6** attack, badger, bother, heckle, hector, pester, plague **7** assault, bedevil, besiege, disturb, torment **8** browbeat, distress, irritate **9** persecute **10** discommode, exasperate, intimidate **14** raid frequently

harbinger 4 clue, omen **5** token **6** herald, symbol **7** portent **8** signaler **9** announcer, first sign, precursor **10** forerunner, indication, proclaimer

Harbonna 6 eunuch

harbor 3 bay **4** cove, dock, feel, goal, hide, hold, keep, pier, port, quay **5** basin, ha-

ven, house, inlet, lodge, wharf **6** asylum, billet, foster, lagoon, refuge, retain, shield, take in **7** care for, cling to, conceal, nurture, protect, quarter, retreat, shelter **8** hideaway, keep safe, maintain, muse over, terminus **9** brood over, sanctuary **11** concealment, destination, hiding place **12** give refuge to **13** bear in the mind, terminal point **18** protected anchorage

harbors
   god of: 8 Portunus
   goddess of: 6 Matutu

Harcorates *see* **5** Horus

hard *see* **box**

hard-and-fast 3 set **6** strict **7** binding **8** exacting, rigorous **9** mandatory, unbending **10** compelling, compulsory, inflexible, obligatory, undeniable, unyielding **11** irrevocable, unalterable, unremitting **12** indisputable **13** incontestable **14** uncompromising

Hardcastle family
   characters in: 18 She Stoops to Conquer
   author: 9 Goldsmith

hard drinker 3 sot **4** lush, soak, wino **5** drunk, rummy,

hard 3 sad **4** cold, firm, mean, ugly **5** cruel, eager, harsh, heavy, rigid, rough, solid, stern, stiff, stony, tight, tough **6** bitter, brutal, fierce, firmly, keenly, knotty, severe, steely, strict, strong, sullen, thorny, unkind **7** angrily, arduous, callous, closely, complex, cryptic, eagerly, earnest, harmful, heavily, hostile, hurtful, inhuman, intense, onerous, sharply, solidly, tightly, to heart, vicious, violent, willing, zealous **8** animated, baffling, critical, diligent, exacting, fiercely, forceful, forcibly, hardened, intently, involved, pitiless, powerful, puzzling, rocklike, ruthless, severely, spirited, spiteful, steadily, strongly, stubborn, untiring, venomous, vigorous **9** arduously, assiduous, bellicose, confusing, difficult, earnestly, energetic, furiously, Herculean, insulting, intensely, intricate, laborious, malicious, merciless, painfully, rancorous, seriously, strenuous, stringent, unbending, unpliable, unsparing, violently, wearisome **10** burdensome, diligently, forcefully, formidable, impervious, implacable, inexorable, inflexible, lamentable, melancholy, oppressive, perplexing, persistent, powerfully, relentless, rigorously, tormenting, unbearable, unflagging, unfriendly, unpleasant, untiringly, unyielding, vigorously, vindictive **11** acrimonious, agonizingly, assiduously, belligerent, bewildering, complicated, distressing, emotionally, hardhearted, industrious, insensitive, intolerable, laboriously, persevering, troublesome, unceasingly, unmalleable, unrelenting, unremitting, unsparingly **12** antagonistic, cantankerous, determinedly, disagreeable, enterprising, impenetrable, persistently, relentlessly, thick-skinned, unfathomable, unflaggingly **13** conscientious, disheartening, distressfully, energetically, indefatigable, industriously, with much anger **14** uncompromising, with much sorrow **15** conscientiously **16** with all one's might **18** with strong feelings

souse, toper **6** barfly, boozer **7** guzzler, imbiber, tippler **8** drunkard **9** alcoholic **11** dipsomaniac **14** problem drinker **16** two-fisted drinker

harden 3 dry, gel, set **4** cake, fire, firm **5** adapt, adjust, blunt, enure, inure, steel **6** anneal, freeze, season, temper **7** calcify, callous, congeal, fortify, petrify, stiffen, thicken, toughen **8** accustom, solidify **9** fossilize, make tough, reinforce **10** discipline, invigorate, strengthen **11** crystallize, turn to stone **12** restrengthen **13** make unfeeling

hard feelings 5 anger **6** grudge, hatred, rancor **7** ill

will **8** acrimony **9** animosity, hostility **10** antagonism, bitterness **12** spitefulness

hardheaded 4 cool **5** balky **6** astute, mulish, poised, shrewd **7** willful **8** contrary, sensible, stubborn **9** immovable, objective, obstinate, pigheaded, practical, pragmatic, realistic, unbending, unfeeling **10** coolheaded, impersonal, inflexible, refractory, self-willed, unyielding **11** down-to-earth, intractable, tough-minded, unemotional, unflappable **14** self-controlled

hardhearted 4 cold, hard, mean **5** cruel, stony **6** brutal **7** callous, inhuman **8** pitiless,

ruthless, uncaring **9** heartless, merciless, unfeeling, unpitying, unsparing **11** coldblooded, indifferent, insensitive, remorseless, unforgiving **12** cruelhearted, thick-skinned **13** unsympathetic

hardihood 4 grit **5** pluck, spunk **6** mettle **7** courage **8** strength **9** endurance, fortitude **10** resolution **12** resoluteness

Harding, Warren Gamaliel *see box*

hardly 4 just, only **6** barely, rarely **7** faintly, in no way **8** not often, not quite, scarcely **9** almost not, by no means **10** in no manner, uncommonly **12** certainly not, infrequently **13** not by any means **15** not by a great deal

hardnosed 4 hard **5** harsh, rigid, stern, tough **6** severe, shrewd, strict **8** critical, hardline, exacting, stubborn **9** demanding, unbending, unsparing **10** hardheaded, inflexible, no-nonsense, unyielding **11** calculating, intractable **12** unsentimental **14** uncompromising

Hardouin-Mansart, Jules architect of: **8** Orangery (Versailles) **12** Chateau du Val (St Germain-en-Laye), Grand Trianon (Versailles), Place Vendome (Paris) **15** Chateau de Clagny (Versailles) **16** Galerie des Glaces (Hall of Mirrors at Versailles), Les Invalides (Church of the Dome, Paris)

hard-pressed 7 harried, putupon **9** embattled **10** overworked

hardship 3 woe **4** load **5** agony, grief **6** burden, misery, ordeal, sorrow **7** problem, travail, trouble **8** handicap **9** adversity, privation, suffering **10** affliction, difficulty, misfortune **11** cross to bear, encumbrance, tribulation, unhappiness **12** wretchedness

hard sledding 8 tough job **10** difficulty, tough going, uphill work **11** arduousness **13** laboriousness

hard times 4 bust **5** slump **8** bad times **9** recession **10** depression

Hard Times author: **11** Studs Terkel

Hard Times author: **14** Charles Dickens character: **9** Sissy Jupe **10** Mrs Sparsit **11** Mr Boun-

---

Harding, Warren Gamaliel
presidential rank: **11** twenty-ninth
party: **10** Republican
state represented: **2** OH
defeated: **3** (James Middleton) Cox, (William Wesley) Cox **4** (Eugene Victor) Debs **7** (Aaron Sherman) Watkins **8** (Robert Charles) Macauley **11** (Parley Parker) Christensen
vice president: **8** (Calvin) Coolidge
cabinet:
  state: **6** (Charles Evans) Hughes
  treasury: **6** (Andrew William) Mellon
  war: **5** (John Wingate) Weeks
  attorney general: **9** (Harry Micajah) Daugherty
  navy: **5** (Edwin) Denby
  postmaster general: **3** (Harry Stewart) New **4** (Hubert) Work, (William Harrison) Hays
  interior: **4** (Albert Bacon) Fall, (Hubert) Work
  agriculture: **7** (Henry Cantwell) Wallace
  commerce: **6** (Herbert Clark) Hoover
  labor: **5** (James John) Davis
born: **9** Corsica OH (now Blooming Grove)
died: **2** CA (while in office) **12** San Francisco
buried: **8** Marion OH
education:
  College: **11** Ohio Central
religion: **7** Baptist
interests: **5** poker
  played musical instrument: **6** cornet **7** helicon
political career: **8** US Senate **15** Ohio State Senate
  lieutenant governor of: **4** Ohio
civilian career: **9** publisher **13** schoolteacher **15** newspaper editor **17** insurance salesman
notable events of lifetime/term:
  Act: **21** Fordney-McCumber Tariff
  peace treaty with: **7** Austria, Germany, Hungary
  scandal: **10** Teapot Dome (oil)
  Treaty: **9** Five-Power, Nine-Power **16** Four-Power Pacific
father: **9** George Tryon
mother: **6** Phoebe (Elizabeth Dickerson)
  stepmother: **4** Mary (Alice Severns) **6** Eudora (Kelley Luvisi)
siblings: **11** George Tryon **12** Mary Clarissa **14** Charity Malvina, Phoebe Caroline **15** Abigail Victoria **16** Charles Alexander, Eleanor Priscilla
wife: **8** Florence (Kling DeWolfe)
children:
  illegitimate daughter: **21** Elizabeth Ann Christian (by mistress Nan Britton)

derby **12** Tom Gradgrind
14 James Harthouse
15 Louisa Gradgrind,
Thomas Gradgrind **16** Stephen Blackpool

hard to catch 4 foxy, wily
6 crafty, shifty, tricky **7** elusive, evasive **8** slippery

hard to grasp 7 elusive **8** baffling, puzzling, slippery **9** difficult **10** perplexing
16 incomprehensible

hard to manage 6 unruly
7 froward, willful **8** perverse,
stubborn **9** difficult, fractious,
obstinate **10** inflexible, refractory, unyielding **11** intractable **12** obstreperous,
unmanageable

hard to please 5 fussy, picky
7 exigent, finicky **8** critical
10 fastidious, meticulous,
particular

hard to understand 7 complex **9** difficult, intricate
10 perplexing **11** bewildering,
complicated

Hardwick, Elizabeth
author of: **11** Simple Truth
12 A View of My Own
15 Sleepless Nights **20** Seduction and Betrayal

Hardwicke, Sir Cedric
born: **3** Lye **7** England
roles: **14** On Borrowed Time
21 Livingstone and Stanley
36 A Connecticut Yankee in
King Arthur's Court

hardwood 4 wood **8** leadwood
kind: **3** ash, elm, oak **4** teak
5 beech, birch, maple
6 cherry, linden, walnut
7 hickory **8** mahogany, rosewood, sycamore

hardworking 8 diligent, sedulous **9** assiduous **11** industrious, persevering
12 enterprising
13 conscientious

hardy 3 fit **4** hale **5** tough
6 hearty, mighty, robust, rugged, strong, sturdy **7** healthy
8 stalwart, vigorous **9** strapping **10** able-bodied **12** in fine
fettle **13** physically fit **15** in
good condition

Hardy, Oliver
partner: **10** Stan Laurel
born: **8** Harlem GA
roles: **8** Pardon Us **9** Saps at
Sea **10** Way Out West

Hardy, Thomas
author of: **10** The Dynasts
14 Jude the Obscure **20** The
Return of the Native
21 Tess of the D'Urbervilles
22 Far from the Madding

Crowd, The Mayor of
Casterbridge
mythical county: **6** Wessex

hare
constellation of: **5** Lepus
group of: **4** down, husk

harebrained 5 silly, wacko,
wacky **7** asinine, flighty, foolish **8** skittish **9** dimwitted,
senseless **10** half-witted
11 empty-headed **12** simpleminded **13** rattlebrained
14 featherbrained,
scatterbrained

Haredale, Reuben
character in: **12** Barnaby
Rudge
author: **7** Dickens

harem 5 serai **6** purdah, serail,
senana, zenana **8** love nest,
seraglio

Hargreaves, James
nationality: **7** English
inventor of: **13** spinning
jenny

Harker, Jonathan
character in: **7** Dracula
author: **6** Stoker

harlot 3 pro **4** bawd, doxy,
jade, pros, slut, tart **5** whore
6 chippy, wanton **7** jezebel,
trollop **8** call girl, mistress,
strumpet **9** courtesan, kept
woman **10** prostitute **11** fallen
woman **12** painted woman,
scarlet woman, streetwalker

Harlow, Jean
real name: **16** Harlean
Carpenter
nickname: **15** Blonde
Bombshell
born: **12** Kansas City MO
roles: **7** Red Dust **8** Riffraff,
Saratoga **9** Bombshell, China
Seas **11** Hell's Angels, Libeled Lady **13** Dinner at
Eight

harm 3 ill, mar, sin **4** evil,
hurt, maim, pain, ruin, vice
5 abuse, agony, havoc, spoil,
wound, wrong **6** damage, debase, deface, ill-use, impair,
injure, injury, malice, misuse,
trauma **7** blemish, cripple, degrade, scourge **8** aggrieve, calamity, hardship, iniquity,
maltreat, mischief, villainy
9 adversity, detriment, disfigure, suffering, undermine
10 defacement, immorality,
impairment, misfortune, sinfulness, wickedness **11** destruction, devastation, malevolence
12 do violence to **13** deterioration, maliciousness

harmful 3 bad **7** adverse, baneful, hurtful, ruinous **8** damaging **9** dangerous, injurious,
unhealthy **10** pernicious,

11 deleterious, destructive, detrimental, unhealthful, unwholesome
17 counterproductive

harmless 4 mild, safe **6** benign, gentle **7** sinless **8** innocent, nontoxic **9** blameless,
guiltless, incorrupt, innocuous,
peaceable **10** not hurtful
11 inoffensive **12** not dangerous **15** unobjectionable

harmlessness 6 safety **9** innocence **10** gentleness **11** nontoxicity **12** nonvirulence
13 innocuousness
15 inoffensiveness

Harmon, Young John
character in: **15** Our Mutual
Friend
author: **7** Dickens

Harmonia
father: **4** Ares
mother: **9** Aphrodite
husband: **6** Cadmus
daughter: **3** Ino

Harmonides see **9** Phereclus

harmonious 5 sweet **6** dulcet
7 amiable, cordial, unified
8 amicable, friendly, in accord,
matching **9** agreeable, congenial, in harmony, melodious
10 compatible, consistent, euphonious, likeminded **11** coordinated, harmonizing, in
agreement, mellifluous, sympathetic **12** synchronized
13 sweet-sounding **17** agreeably combined

harmonize 3 fit **4** jibe, mesh
5 agree, blend, chime, tally
6 accord, adjust, attune **7** conform **8** be in tune **9** reconcile
10 complement, correspond,
go together **13** sing in
harmony

harmony 5 amity, order, peace,
unity **6** accord **7** balance, concord **8** matching, symmetry,
sympathy **9** agreement, unanimity **10** conformity, fellowship, friendship, proportion
11 amicability, cooperation,
correlation, parallelism
12 congeniality, coordination,
mutual regard **13** compatibility, mutual fitness **14** likemindedness **15** organic totality **17** good understanding
19 harmonious relations,
pleasing consistency **21** concurrence in opinions

Harmony
goddess of: **9** Concordia

harness 4 curb, rein, tugs,
yoke **5** lines, reins, rig up
6 bridle, collar, employ, halter,
muzzle, straps, tackle, traces
7 exploit, hitch up, utilize
8 restrain **9** caparison, trap-

pings **12** put in harness, render useful **13** control and use, turn to account **14** make productive **22** direct to a useful purpose

Harold
author: **18** Edward Bulwer-Lytton

Harper, Joe
character in: **9** Tom Sawyer
author: **5** Twain

Harphlyce
father: **8** Clymenus
husband: **7** Alastor
vocation: **8** huntress
violated by: **8** Clymenus
killed by: **8** Clymenus
9 shepherds

Harpina
father: **6** Asopus
son: **8** Oenomaus

harp on 7 dwell on **9** reiterate **18** repeat persistently

Harpy
form: **7** monster
head of: **5** woman
body of: **4** bird
father: **7** Thaumas
mother: **7** Electra
names: **5** Aello **7** Celaeno, Ocypete, Podarge

harridan 3 hag **5** crone, shrew, witch **6** virago **8** battle-ax, old crone **12** mean old woman

harried 5 upset **7** worried **8** harassed, troubled **10** distraught

Harris, Joel Chandler
author of: **10** Uncle Remus (His Songs and Sayings)

Harris, Julie
real name: **14** Julia Ann Harris
born: **18** Grosse Pointe Park MI
roles: **6** Harper **10** East of Eden, I Am a Camera **11** The Haunting **14** A Shot in the Dark, The Hiding Place **19** The Last of Mrs Lincoln **21** The Member of the Wedding **22** Requiem for a Heavyweight **27** And Miss Reardon Drinks a Little

Harris, Richard
born: **7** Ireland **8** Limerick
roles: **7** Camelot **8** Cromwell **15** A Man Called Horse **16** The Molly Maguires, This Sporting Life **17** Mutiny on the Bounty, The Guns of Navarone **20** The Cassandra Crossing **26** The Return of a Man Called Horse

Harris, Roy
composer of: **16** Folksong Symphony **17** American Por-

traits **27** When Johnny Comes Marching Home (overture)

Harrison, Benjamin *see box*

Harrison, Lou
born: **10** Portland OR
composer of: **8** Rapunzel, Solstice **13** Changing World **15** Four Strict Songs, Johnny Appleseed **17** The Perilous Chapel **19** Almanac of the Seasons **22** At the Tomb of Charles Ives

Harrison, Peter
architect of: **11** Brick Market (Newport RI), King's Chapel (Boston) **14** Redwood Library (Newport RI), Touro Synagogue (Newport RI)

Harrison, Rex
real name: **21** Reginald Carey Harrison
nickname: **8** Sexy Rexy
wife: **10** Kay Kendall **11** Lilli Palmer **13** Rachel Roberts
born: **6** Huyton **7** England
roles: **9** Cleopatra **10** My Fair Lady (Oscar) **12** Blithe Spirit **14** Doctor Dolittle **16** The Foxes of Harrow **17** Unfaithfully Yours **18** The Ghost and Mrs Muir **20** Anna and the King of Siam

Harrison, Wallace K
architect of: **13** Lincoln Center (NYC) **14** Socony Building (NYC) **17** Rockefeller Center (NYC) **22** Metropoli-

---

Harrison, Benjamin
nickname: **3** Ben **9** Little Ben
presidential rank: **11** twenty-third
party: **10** Republican
state represented: **2** IN
defeated: **4** (Clinton Bowen) Fisk **6** (James Langdon) Curtis **7** (Robert Hall) Cowdrey **8** (Albert) Redstone, (Alson Jenness) Streeter, (Belva Ann Bennett) Lockwood **9** (Grover) Cleveland
vice president: **6** (Levi Parsons) Morton
cabinet:
  state: **6** (James Gillespie) Blaine, (John Watson) Foster
  treasury: **6** (Charles) Foster, (William) Windom
  war: **6** (Stephen Benton) Elkins **7** (Redfield) Proctor
  attorney general: **6** (William Henry Harrison) Miller
  navy: **5** (Benjamin Franklin) Tracy
  postmaster general: **9** (John) Wanamaker
  interior: **5** (John Willock) Noble
  agriculture: **4** (Jeremiah McLain) Rusk
born: **11** North Bend OH
died/buried: **14** Indianapolis IN
education:
  prep school: **14** Farmer's College
  University: **21** Miami University of Ohio
  later studied: **3** law
religion: **12** Presbyterian
interests: **7** fishing, hunting **8** swimming
author: **17** This Country of Ours **20** Views of An Ex-President
political career: **8** US Senate
  city attorney: **12** Indianapolis
  reporter of: **19** Indiana supreme court
  secretary of: **31** Republican state central committee
civilian career: **6** lawyer **12** law professor
military service: **8** Civil War **16** brigadier general
notable events of lifetime/term:
  Act: **16** Dependent Pension, Sherman Anti-Trust **21** Sherman Silver Purchase
  Tariff: **8** McKinley
father: **9** John Scott
mother: **9** Elizabeth (Ramsey Irwin)
siblings: **8** Mary Jane **9** John Irwin, John Scott **10** Anna Symmes, James Irwin **12** James Findlay **13** Carter Bassett **14** Archibald Irwin
  half sisters: **9** Elizabeth **13** Sarah Lucretia
wife: **4** Mary (Scott Lord Dimmick) **8** Caroline (Lavinia Scott)
children: **9** Elizabeth, Mary Scott **15** Russell Benjamin

tan Opera House (NYC) **25** United Nations Headquarters (NYC) **34** Nelson A Rockefeller Empire State Plaza (Albany NY), ALCOA Building (Pittsburgh, with Max Abramovitz)

Harrison, William Henry
see box

harrowing 7 fearful, painful **8** alarming, chilling **9** traumatic, upsetting **10** disturbing, terrifying, tormenting **11** distressing, frightening **13** bloodcurdling

harry 3 irk, vex **4** bait, gall, raid, ride, sack **5** annoy, beset, bully, haunt, hound, tease, worry **6** badger, bother, harass, heckle, hector, pester, plague **7** disturb, pillage, plunder, torment, trouble **8** distract, distress, irritate **9** terrorize **10** exasperate, intimidate **16** attack repeatedly

harsh 4 hard, mean **5** cruel, raspy, rough, sharp, stern **6** bitter, brutal, hoarse, severe, shrill, unkind **7** abusive, caustic, glaring, grating, jarring, rasping, raucous, squawky **8** piercing, pitiless, ruthless, scratchy, strident, ungentle **9** Draconian, heartless, merciless, too bright, unmusical, unsparing **10** discordant, overbright, unpleasant, vindictive **11** cacophonous, hardhearted **12** uncharitable, unharmonious

harshness 5 rigor **7** cruelty, discord **9** brutality, cacophony, raspiness, roughness, sternness, stridency **10** dissonance, shrillness, unkindness **12** ungentleness **13** heartlessness **14** unpleasantness **15** hardheartedness

Hart, Johnny
creator/artist of: **2** B C **13** The Wizard of Id

Hart, Moss
author of: **15** Once in a Lifetime **20** You Can't Take It with You (with George S Kaufman) **21** The Man Who Came to Dinner (with George S Kaufman)

Harte, Bret
author of: **20** The Luck of Roaring Camp **22** The Outcasts of Poker Flat

Hartford
hockey team: **7** Whalers

Harthouse, James
character in: **9** Hard Times *author:* **7** Dickens

Hartley, Vivian Mary
real name of: **11** Vivien Leigh

harum-scarum 5 giddy **6** wildly **7** erratic, flighty, foolish **8** careless, confused **9** aimlessly, haphazard, impetuous, impulsive, unplanned, unsettled **10** bewildered, recklessly, unreliable **11** haphazardly, harebrained, impulsively **12** absent-minded, capriciously, disorganized, inconsistent, undependable **13** rattlebrained **14** featherbrained, scatterbrained

harvest 3 cut, mow **4** crop, gain, pick, reap **5** amass, fruit, pluck, yield **6** gather, haying, mowing, output, result, return, reward **7** benefit, collect, cutting, picking, produce, product, reaping **8** fruition, gleaning, proceeds **9** aftermath, amassment, gathering, outgrowth **10** accumulate, collection, harvesting **12** accumulation **13** season's growth

harvest time 4 fall **6** autumn **8** maturity **12** Indian summer

Harvey
director: **11** Henry Koster *based on play by:* **9** Mary Chase *cast:* **8** Peggy Dow **12** James Stewart (Elwood P Dowd) **13** Cecil Kellaway, Josephine Hull *Oscar for:* **17** supporting actress (Hull)

Harvey, Laurence
real name: **19** Larushka Misch Skikne *wife:* **16** Margaret Leighton *born:* **9** Lithuania, Yomishkis *roles:* **7** Darling **12** Life at the Top, Room at the Top **14** Of Human Bondage, Summer and Smoke **16** Butterfield Eight **17** Walk on the Wild Side

Harvey, William
field: **7** anatomy

Harrison, William Henry
nickname: **6** Old Tip **22** The Washington of the West
presidential rank: **5** ninth
party: **4** Whig
state represented: **2** OH
defeated: **6** (James G) Birney **8** (Martin) Van Buren
vice president: **5** (John) Tyler
cabinet:
  state: **7** (Daniel) Webster
  treasury: **5** (Thomas) Ewing
  war: **4** (John) Bell
  attorney general: **10** (John Jordan) Crittenden
  navy: **6** (George Edmund) Badger
  postmaster general: **7** (Francis) Granger
born: **2** VA **17** Charles City County **18** Berkeley plantation
died: **12** Washington DC
buried: **11** North Bend OH
education: **16** privately tutored (at home)
  College: **13** Hampden-Sydney (did not graduate)
  later studied: **8** medicine
religion: **12** Episcopalian
political career: **8** US Senate **11** state Senate **24** US House of Representatives
  governor of: **16** Indiana Territory
  minister: **8** Columbia
civilian career: **6** farmer **7** soldier
military service: **6** US Army **12** major general **19** War of Eighteen Twelve
  battle: **6** (the) Thames **8** Lake Erie **10** Tippecanoe
notable events of lifetime/term: **24** Land Act of Eighteen Hundred
  campaign slogan: **21** Tippecanoe and Tyler too
  treaty of: **10** Greenville
father: **8** Benjamin
mother: **9** Elizabeth (Bassett)
siblings: **3** Ann **4** Lucy **5** Sarah **8** Benjamin **9** Elizabeth **13** Carter Bassett
wife: **4** Anna (Tuthill Symmes)
children: **8** Benjamin **9** John Scott **10** Mary Symmes **11** Anna Tuthill **12** James Findlay, William Henry **13** Carter Bassett, Lucy Singleton **16** Elizabeth Bassett, John Cleves Symmes

nationality: **7** British
discovered: **18** circulation of blood

Hasen, Irwin
creator/artist of: **5** Dondi
9 Goldbergs **11** Wonder
Woman **12** Green Lantern

hash out 6 review **7** discuss
8 consider, talk over

hasp 4 lock **5** catch, clasp,
latch **7** closure **8** fastener

Hassam, (Frederick) Childe
born: **12** Dorchester MA
artwork: **13** Southwest Wind
14 Summer Sunlight, Washington Arch **15** Against the
Light **23** Boston Commons
at Twilight

hassle 3 bug, row, vex **5** annoy, fight, harry, hound,
scrap, set-to **6** badger, battle,
bother, harass, tussle **7** contest, dispute, quarrel **8** argument, conflict, squabble,
struggle **9** persecute

hassock 4 boss, pess, seat, tuft,
weed **5** bunch, chair, group,
trush **6** buffet, plants, tuffet
7 ottoman, tussock **9** footstool,
vegetable

hasta la vista 6 good-by, so
long **7** goodbye **12** until I see
you **16** until we meet again

hasta manana 13 until tomorrow **14** see you tomorrow

haste 4 rush **5** hurry, speed
8 celerity, dispatch, rapidity,
rashness **9** fleetness, quickness,
swiftness **10** expedition, speediness, undue speed **11** hur-
riedness **12** recklessness
13 careless hurry, impetuous-
ness, impulsiveness,
precipitation

hasten 3 fly, run **4** bolt, dart,
dash, flit, jump, race, rush
5 egg on, hurry, impel, speed,
whisk **6** hustle, incite, scurry,
sprint, urge on **7** advance,
drive on, hurry on, hurry up,
promote, quicken, scamper,
scuttle, speed up **8** expedite,
make time **10** accelerate, lose
no time **11** go full blast, precipitate, push forward **12** step
on the gas **13** go on the double **14** step right along **15** go
like lightning, make short
work of, work against time
20 go hell-bent for leather

hastily 4 fast **5** apace **6** pronto,
rashly **7** quickly **8** promptly,
speedily **9** hurriedly, like a
shot, posthaste, summarily
10 carelessly, heedlessly, recklessly, too quickly **11** impetuously, impulsively, on the
double **12** lickety-split,

straightaway **13** precipitately,
thoughtlessly **18** hell-bent for
leather **20** like greased lightning, on the spur of the
moment

Hastings, Thomas *see*
17 Carrere, John Merven

hasty 4 fast, rash **5** brief, fleet,
quick, rapid, swift **6** abrupt,
prompt, rushed, speedy **7** cursory, hurried, passing **8** fleeting, headlong, heedless,
reckless **9** impetuous, impulsive, momentary **10** breathless **11** precipitate, superficial,
unduly quick **12** quick as a
wink **19** without
deliberation

hat
French: **7** chapeau

hatch 4 plan, plot **5** frame
6 cook up, create, design, devise, evolve, invent, make up
7 concoct, dream up, fashion,
produce, think up **8** conceive,
contrive **9** construct, fabricate,
formulate, improvise, originate **10** bring forth **11** give
birth to, manufacture

hatchlings 5 brood, young
6 chicks **9** offspring

hate 5 abhor, dread, venom
6 animus, detest, enmity,
hatred, loathe, malice, rancor
7 be sorry, despise, dislike,
wince at **8** acrimony, aversion,
be sick of, distaste, execrate,
loathing **9** abominate, animosity, antipathy, be tired of, dis-
liking, hostility, not care to
10 abhorrence, be averse to,
feel sick at, recoil from, repugnance, resentment, shrink
from **11** abomination, be hostile to, be reluctant, be unwilling, detestation,
malevolence, wish to avoid
12 be repelled by **14** have no
taste for, hold in contempt,
revengefulness, vindictiveness
16 bear malice toward, have
no stomach for **17** feel disinclined to, not have the heart
to **19** regard as distasteful

hateful 4 evil, foul, mean,
ugly, vile **5** nasty **6** odious,
sinful, wicked **7** heinous **8** infamous, scornful **9** abhorrent,
atrocious, loathsome, monstrous, obnoxious, offensive,
repellent, repugnant, revolting,
sickening **10** abominable, deplorable, despicable, detestable,
disdainful, disgusting, forbidding, full of hate, irritating,
unbearable, unpleasant, villainous **11** distasteful, intolerable,
unendurable **12** contemptible,
contemptuous, insufferable
13 objectionable

Hathor
origin: **8** Egyptian
goddess of: **3** joy **4** love
symbol: **4** ears, head **5** horns
patron of: **5** dance, music
personifies: **3** sky

Hat on the Bed, The
author: **9** John O'Hara

hatred 4 hate **5** venom **6** animus, enmity, malice, rancor
7 disgust, dislike, ill will **8** acrimony, aversion, bad blood,
distaste, loathing **9** animosity,
antipathy, hostility, revulsion
10 abhorrence, antagonism,
bitterness, repugnance, resentment **11** abomination, detestation, malevolence
14 revengefulness,
vindictiveness

haughtiness 4 airs **5** pride
7 conceit, hauteur **8** snobbery
9 arrogance **10** snootiness
13 condescension **14** disdainfulness, high-handedness
16 superciliousness

haughty 5 aloof **6** lordly,
snooty, uppish, uppity **7** high-
hat, stuck-up **8** arrogant,
scornful, snobbish **9** conceited,
officious **10** disdainful, high-
handed, hoity-toity **11** highfalutin, overbearing, overly
proud, patronizing, swell-
headed **12** contemptuous
13 condescending, high and
mighty

haul 3 bag, lug, tow, tug
4 cart, drag, draw, gain, jerk,
move, pull, swag, take, tote,
yank **5** booty, bring, carry,
catch, fetch, heave, truck,
yield **6** convey, profit, remove,
reward, spoils, wrench **7** capture, takings **9** transport

haunches 4 buns, rear, rump,
seat **5** nates **7** rear end **8** buttocks **9** fundament, posterior
12 hindquarters

haunt 3 vex **5** beset, worry
6 live in, obsess, plague, prey
on **7** disturb, terrify, torment,
trouble, weigh on **8** distress,
frequent, frighten **9** hang out
at, preoccupy, terrorize
10 hang around, hover about,
loiter near, visit often **11** beat
a path to **12** linger around

haunts 3 den **4** cave, hole, lair,
nest **6** burrow **7** hangout
8 hideaway **9** waterhole
10 rendezvous **12** meeting
place **14** gathering place
15 stamping grounds

Hauptmann, Gerhart
author of: **10** Before Dawn,
The Weavers

haute couture 11 high
fashion

haute cuisine 11 fine cooking **14** gourmet cooking

hauteur 5 swank **7** conceit, disdain **8** snobbery **9** arrogance, loftiness **10** snootiness **11** haughtiness **12** affectedness, snobbishness **13** condescension **14** disdainfulness, high-handedness **16** superciliousness **19** patronizing attitude

haut monde 5 elite **10** blue bloods, upper class, upper crust **11** aristocracy, high society **14** creme de la creme

Havana
capital of: 4 Cuba
gulf: 6 Mexico
landmark: 15 Cabaret Parisien **16** Castillo del Morro **17** Castillode la Punta, Jose Marti Monument **18** Castillo de la Atares, Castillo de la Fuerza, Garcia Lorca Theater **19** Maximo Gomez Monument **21** Latinamericano Stadium **22** Academy of Science of Cuba
river: 10 (Rio) Almendares
Spanish: 8 La Habana

Havasupai, Supai
location: 7 Arizona **11** Grand Canyon
related to: 7 Yavapai **8** Hualapai

have 3 buy, eat, get, own, use **4** bear, fool, gain, gull, hold, host, keep, make, must **5** beget, carry, cheat, drink, enjoy, force, grasp, ought, smoke, trick **6** accept, affirm, compel, harbor, obtain, outwit, permit, retain, suffer **7** achieve, acquire, defraud, exhibit, possess, realize, receive, swindle **8** comprise, maintain, manifest, outsmart, perceive, tolerate **9** encompass, encounter, partake of, recognize, victimize **10** comprehend, experience, understand

have a fancy for 4 want **5** covet, crave **6** desire **7** long for, wish for **8** yearn for **11** hanker after, have a yen for

have a go at 3 try **6** hazard, tackle **7** attempt **8** give a try **9** undertake **10** give a whirl **12** take a crack at, take a whack at

have a good opinion of 5 favor **6** admire, revere **7** approve, respect **9** believe in **10** appreciate

have a hand in 7 advance, forward **9** influence **10** take part in **12** contribute to **13** be conducive to, participate in **14** help bring about

have an eye on 4 want **5** covet, crave, fancy **6** desire **7** long for, pine for **8** aspire to, yearn for **9** lust after **11** have a yen for

have a yen for 4 want **5** covet, crave **6** desire **7** long for, wish for **8** yearn for **9** lust after **11** hanker after **13** have a fancy for

have bearing on 5 apply, refer **6** relate **7** concern, pertain **9** appertain, touch upon **13** be pertinent to, have respect to

have done with 4 drop, junk, shed **7** abandon, discard **9** dispose of **10** relinquish **12** dispense with

have faith in 5 trust **6** rely on **9** believe in **16** have confidence in

have guests 8 play host **9** entertain **10** give a party **13** keep open house **16** offer hospitality

Have Gun Will Travel
character: 6 Hey Boy **7** Hey Girl, Paladin
cast: 6 Lisa Lu **7** Kam Tong **12** Richard Boone
setting: 12 San Francisco **13** Hotel Carleton

have in mind 4 mean, want, wish **6** desire, intend **10** think about

haven 4 port **5** cover **6** asylum,

Hawaii
abbreviation: 2 HI
nickname: 5 Aloha **15** Sandwich Islands **20** Paradise of the Pacific
capital/largest city: 8 Honolulu
others: 3 Ewa **4** Aiea, Hana, Hilo, Laie, Paia **5** Kapaa, Kapaa, Lihue, Maili **6** Kailua, Kekaha **7** Kahului, Kaneohe, Lanikae, Wahiawa, Waianae, Wailuku
college: 9 Chaminade, Hawaii Loa **12** Brigham Young **13** Hawaii Pacific
explorer: 4 Cook **7** Gaetano
feature:
  district: **7** Lahaina
  national park: **9** Haleakala **15** Hawaii Volcanoes
people: 9 Hiram Fong **10** Polynesian **11** Sanford Dole **12** Daniel Inouye
island name: 4 Kure **9** Kahoolawe
  big isle: **6** Hawaii
  friendly isle: **7** Molokai
  garden isle: **5** Kauai
  gathering place: **4** Oahu
  house of the sun: **9** Haleakala
  mystery isle: **6** Niihau
  pineapple isle: **5** Lanai
  valley isle: **4** Maui
lake: 5 Waiau
land rank: 12 forty-seventh
mountain: 3 Kea, Loa **5** Kaala **6** Kohala, Kohala, Koolau **7** Kamakou, Waianae **8** Maunaloa **9** Lanaihale
  highest point: **8** Maunakea
physical feature:
  bay: **5** Pohue **6** Halawa, Kiholo, Mamala **7** Kamohio, Kaneohe, Waiagua **8** Kawaihae, Maunalua
  beach: **7** Waikiki
  canyon: **6** Waimea
  channel: **3** Aua **5** Kaiwi **6** Kalohi **7** Pailolo
  crater: **7** Kilauea **9** Punchbowl
  desert: **3** Kau
  harbor: **5** Pearl
  promontory: **11** Diamond Head
  valley: **3** Iao **5** Manoa
  volcano: **7** Kilauea **8** Maunakea, Maunaloa **9** Haleakala
state admission: 8 Fiftieth
state bird: 4 nene **13** Hawaiian goose
state flower: 5 lehua **11** red hibiscus **15** scarlet hibiscus
state motto: 44 The Life of the Land is Perpetuated in Righteousness
state song: 11 Hawaii Ponoi **12** Our Own Hawaii
state tree: 5 kukui **9** candlenut

harbor, refuge **7** hideout, retreat, shelter **8** hideaway **9** sanctuary

have no hope 6 give up **7** despair **11** be desperate

have plenty 6 abound, be rich **8** flourish, overflow **10** be numerous, have enough **11** be plentiful **14** be well supplied **18** have more than enough

have the body
Latin: **12** habeas corpus
legal writ guards against: **19** illegal imprisonment

have too few 4 lack, want **7** be scant **9** fall short **13** be deficient in, have a dearth of **14** have a paucity of **15** be in short supply, have a scarcity of, not have enough of

having life 5 alive, vital **6** living, viable **7** animate

having the means 3 fit **4** able **6** fitted **7** capable, equal to **8** adequate **9** qualified **12** being solvent **20** having the wherewithal

Havisham, Miss
character in: **17** Great Expectations
author: **7** Dickens

havoc 4 ruin **5** chaos **8** calamity, disaster, disorder, upheaval **9** cataclysm, ruination **11** catastrophe, destruction, devastation **12** wrack and ruin **16** widespread damage

Hawaii see box, p. 435

Hawaii
author: **13** James Michener

Hawaiian swimmer 14 Duke Kahanamoku

Hawaii Five-O
character: **4** Kono **5** Wo Fat **8** Ben Kokua **11** Chin Ho Kelly **13** Danny Williams **14** Steve McGarrett
cast: **4** Zulu **7** Kam Fong **8** Jack Lord **11** Khigh Dhiegh **12** Al Harrington **14** James MacArthur

hawk 4 bird, sell, vend **6** falcon, peddle **8** militant **9** accipiter, warmonger
young: **4** eyas
group of: **4** cast

Hawk, Sir Mulberry
character in: **16** Nicholas Nickleby
author: **7** Dickens

Hawkes, John
author of: **10** Second Skin **11** The Cannibal, The Lime Twig **12** The Beetle Leg **15** The Blood Oranges

Hawkeye State
nickname of: **4** Iowa

Hawkins, Jim
character in: **14** Treasure Island
author: **9** Stevenson

Hawkline Monster, The
author: **16** Richard Brautigan

Hawks, Howard
director of: **8** Red River, Rio Bravo, Scarface **11** The Big Sleep **12** Sergeant York **13** His Girl Friday **14** Bringing Up Baby **16** To Have and Have Not, Twentieth Century

Hawn, Goldie
husband: **12** Gus Trinkonis
born: **12** Washington DC
roles: **7** Laugh-In, Shampoo **8** Foul Play **12** Cactus Flower **15** Private Benjamin **18** Butterflies Are Free

hawser 4 line, rope **5** cable **7** mooring

hawthorn 9 Crataegus
varieties: **5** water, yeddo **6** Indian **7** English

Hawthorne, Nathaniel
author of: **13** The Marble Faun **14** Twice-told Tales **16** The Scarlet Letter **20** Mosses from an Old Manse **24** The House of the Seven Gables

Haydee
character in: **21** The Count of Monte Cristo
author: **5** Dumas (pere)

Haydn, Franz Joseph see box

Hayes, Elvin
nickname: **4** Big E
sport: **10** basketball
team: **8** San Diego **14** Houston Rockets

Hayes, Helen
real name: **15** Helen Hayes Brown
nickname: **29** First Lady of the American Theater
son: **14** James MacArthur
roles: **7** Airport **9** Anastasia **22** The Sin of Madelon Claudet (Oscar)

Hayes, Rutherford B (Birchard) see box

hayseed 4 hick, rube **5** yokel **6** rustic **7** bumpkin, peasant **10** clodhopper

Hayward, Susan
real name: **14** Edythe Marrener
husband: **10** Jess Barker
born: **10** Brooklyn NY
roles: **11** I Want to Live (Oscar) **14** I'll Cry Tomorrow, My Foolish Heart **18** With a Song in My Heart **23** Smash Up The Story of a Woman

Hayworth, Rita
real name: **22** Margarita Carmen Cansino
husband: **7** Aly Khan **10** Dick Haymes **11** Orson Welles
born: **10** Brooklyn NY
roles: **5** Gilda **9** Cover Girl **14** Separate Tables **17** Miss Sadie Thompson, You'll Never Get Rich

hazan 18 cantor of a synagogue

Haydn, Franz Joseph
born: **6** Rohrau **7** Austria
composer of: **7** The Bird, The Joke **10** Gypsy Rondo, The Seasons **11** The Creation **12** Emperor's Hymn, Wild Band Mass **13** The Apothecary **14** Lord Nelson Mass, Theresienmesse **15** Mass in Time of War **16** Il Mondo della Luna, Mariazellermesse **17** The World of the Moon **38** The Seven Last Words of Our Savior on the Cross
quartet: **3** Sun **4** Bird, Frog, Lark, Tost **5** Dream, Razor, Witch **6** Fifths, Maiden **7** Emperor, Erdoedy, Russian, Sunrise, The Bell, The Hunt **8** Farmyard, Horseman, The Jokes **9** The Donkey **14** The House on Fire, The Row in Vienna
symphony: **4** Fire **5** Paris **6** Le Midi, Le Soir, Loudon, Merkur, Oxford, The Hen **7** Evening, Le Matin, Mercury, Morning, Salomon, The Bear, The Hunt **8** Abschied, Alleluia, Drum Roll, Farewell, Military, Mourning, Surprise, The Clock, The Queen, The Storm **9** Children's, Christmas **10** La Passione, La Tempesta, The Miracle, The Passion **11** The Imperial **12** Der Philosoph, Maria Theresa, The Afternoon **13** Auf dem Anstand **14** The Philosopher **15** The Schoolmaster, Trauersymphonie, With the Horn Call **17** At the Hunting Place **18** Mit dem Hornersignal

Hayes, Rutherford B (Birchard)
  nickname: **8** Rud Hayes
  presidential rank: **10** nineteenth
  party: **10** Republican
  state represented: **2** OH
  defeated: **5** (Green Clay) Smith **6** (James B) Walker, (Peter) Cooper, (Samuel Jones) Tilden
  vice president: **7** (William Almon) Wheeler
  cabinet:
    state: **6** (William Maxwell) Evarts
    treasury: **7** (John) Sherman
    war: **6** (Alexander) Ramsey **7** (George Washington) McCrary
    attorney general: **6** (Charles) Devens
    navy: **4** (Nathan) Goff (Jr) **8** (Richard Wigginton) Thompson
    postmaster general: **3** (David McKendree) Key **7** (Horace) Maynard
    interior: **6** (Carl) Schurz
  born: **10** Delaware OH
  died/buried: **9** Fremont OH
  education:
    preparatory school: **4** Webb
    College: **6** Kenyon
    Law School: **7** Harvard
  religion: **9** Methodist
  political career: **24** US House of Representatives
  city solicitor of: **10** Cincinnati
  governor of: **4** Ohio
  civilian career: **6** farmer, lawyer
  military service: **6** US Army **8** Civil War **12** Ohio infantry **18** brevet major general
  notable events of lifetime/term: **10** Depression (of 1873) **15** railroad strikes (of 1877) **18** civil service reform **24** specie payments resumption
    Act: **26** Bland-Allison Silver Purchase
  father: **10** Rutherford
  mother: **6** Sophia (Birchard)
  siblings: **7** Lorenzo **11** Sarah Sophia **13** Fanny Arabella
  wife: **4** Lucy (Ware Webb)
  children: **5** Fanny **9** James Webb (renamed Webb Cook) **11** George Crook **12** Manning Force, Scott Russell **14** Joseph Thompson, Sardis Birchard (renamed Birchard Austin) **15** Rutherford Platt

hazard 3 bet **4** dare, luck, risk **5** fluke, guess, offer, peril, stake, wager **6** chance, danger, expose, gamble, menace, mishap, submit, threat **7** advance, daresay, imperil, pitfall, presume, proffer, suppose, venture **8** accident, chance it, endanger, jeopardy, theorize, threaten, throw out **9** mischance, speculate, tempt fate, volunteer **10** conjecture, jeopardize, misfortune **11** coincidence, hypothesize, imperilment, take a chance, trust to luck **12** endangerment, happenstance, stroke of luck

Hazard of New Fortunes, A
  author: **18** William Dean Howells

hazardous 4 iffy **5** risky, shaky **6** chancy, unsafe, unsure **7** dubious, unsound

8 doubtful, insecure, perilous, unstable **9** dangerous, uncertain **10** precarious, unreliable **11** speculative, threatening **13** untrustworthy

haze 3 fog **4** daze, film, mist, pall, veil **5** cloak, cloud, smoke, vapor **6** mantle, muddle, screen **9** fogginess **12** befuddlement, bewilderment **16** state of confusion

hazel 3 nut **4** tree **5** brown, shrub, tawny **8** brownish **14** yellowish-brown
  varieties: **4** tree **5** Chile, witch **6** winter **7** Chinese, Turkish **8** American, European, Japanese **11** spike winter **12** Chinese witch **13** Japanese witch **15** buttercup winter

Hazel
  character: **12** George Baxter,

Harold Baxter **13** Dorothy Baxter
  cast: **9** Don DeFore **12** Shirley Booth, Whitney Blake **13** Bobby Buntrock
  creator: **6** Ted Key

hazelnut 7 Corylus
  varieties: **6** beaked **7** Chinese, Turkish **8** American, European, Japanese

Hazlitt, William
  author of: **17** The Spirit of the Age **32** The Characters of Shakespeare's Plays

hazy 3 dim **5** dusky, faint, filmy, foggy, misty, murky, smoky, vague **6** bleary, blurry, cloudy, smoggy, veiled **7** bleared, general, muddled, obscure, unclear **8** confused, nebulous, overcast **9** ambiguous, uncertain **10** ill-defined, indefinite

head *see box, p. 438*

head
  contains: **4** eyes **5** brain, mouth, skull **9** braincase **10** optic nerve **12** ocular muscle **13** cranial cavity, lacrimal organ, orbital cavity **14** buccaval cavity

headache 5 trial **6** strain, stress **7** problem, trouble **8** migraine, nuisance **10** affliction, difficulty **13** inconvenience, pain in the neck

headdress 3 cap, hat **6** bonnet **7** chapeau **12** headcovering

headland 4 bank, crag **5** bluff, cliff **8** palisade **9** precipice **10** promontory

headlong 6 abrupt **8** abruptly, heedless, pell-mell, reckless **9** headfirst, impetuous **10** heedlessly, recklessly **11** impetuously, precipitate, precipitous **13** head over heels, precipitously

Headlong Hall
  author: **17** Thomas Love Peacock

headman 5 chief **6** leader **7** foreman **8** alderman, princeps **9** commander **10** councilman, supervisor **14** public official, superintendent

head-on 6 direct **7** frontal **10** face-to-face

headshrinker 6 shrink **7** analyst **12** psychiatrist **13** psychoanalyst

headstrong 4 rash **6** dogged, mulish, unruly **7** defiant, froward, willful **8** contrary, obdurate, reckless, stubborn **9** hotheaded, imprudent, impulsive, obstinate, pigheaded

head 2 go, IQ **3** aim, CEO, end, hie, tip, top **4** acme, apex, bent, boss, czar, font, fore, gift, king, lead, main, mind, peak, rise, rule, turn, well **5** begin, brain, chief, crest, crown, drive, first, front, guide, pilot, prime, queen, ruler, start, steer **6** climax, crisis, direct, genius, govern, launch, leader, manage, origin, ruling, source, spring, summit, talent, vertex, zenith **7** ability, admiral, captain, command, conduct, control, foreman, general, go first, highest, leading, make for, manager, marshal, monarch, precede, premier, primary, proceed, ranking, supreme, topmost **8** aptitude, be head of, big wheel, capacity, chairman, dictator, director, dominant, foremost, fountain, fruition, headmost, initiate, judgment, managing, pinnacle, start off, superior, suzerain, upper end **9** acuteness, beginning, commander, commodore, extremity, forefront, front rank, governing, intellect, introduce, mentality, paramount, potentate, president, principal, sovereign, supervise, uppermost **10** administer, be master of, birthplace, cleverness, commandant, commanding, conclusion, first place, gray matter, inaugurate, lead the way, move toward, perception, preeminent, supervisor, wellspring **11** be at the helm, controlling, culmination, discernment, forward part, highest rank, officiate at, preside over, superintend, take the lead, termination **12** apprehension, field marshal, fountainhead, guiding light, place of honor, take charge of, take the reins, turning point, utmost extent **13** administrator, go at the head of, most prominent, prime minister, understanding **14** chief executive, highest ranking, superintendent **15** be in the vanguard, make a beeline for, quickness of mind **16** commander-in-chief, direct one's course, inevitable result **17** commanding general, have authority over **18** be in the driver's seat, chairman of the board, go in the direction of **21** chief executive officer

10 bullheaded, incautious, refractory **11** intractable **12** incorrigible, recalcitrant, ungovernable, unmanageable **14** uncontrollable **22** bent on having one's own way

heady 4 hard **6** potent, strong **8** alluring, exciting, inviting, stirring, tempting **9** seductive, thrilling **10** high-octane **11** high-voltage, tantalizing **12** exhilarating, intoxicating

heal 4 cure, knit, mend **5** right, salve, treat **6** heal up, remedy, settle, soothe **7** compose, get well, improve, recover, rectify, relieve **8** heal over, make well **9** alleviate, make whole, reconcile **10** conciliate, convalesce, recuperate **11** set to rights **14** make harmonious, return to health **20** restore good relations

healed 4 knit **5** cured **6** mended **7** got well **8** relieved

healing 6 curing **7** mending **8** knitting, soothing **9** emollient, improving, restoring **10** making well **11** restorative **13** strengthening
  god of: **6** Apollo **7** Phoebus, Pythius **9** Asclepius, Musagetes **11** Aesculapius
  goddess of: **4** Iaso

health 5 vigor **7** fitness, stamina **8** strength, vitality **9** hardihood, hardiness, well-being **10** robustness **16** general condition **17** physical condition
  goddess of: **6** Hygeia

healthful 7 healthy **8** hygienic, salutary **9** wholesome **10** beneficial, nourishing, nutritious, salubrious **12** healthgiving, invigorating

healthiness 6 health **9** good shape, soundness **10** good health, robustness **12** salutariness **13** good condition, healthfulness, wholesomeness **14** salubriousness

healthy 3 fit **4** hale **5** hardy, sound **6** hearty, robust, strong, sturdy **8** vigorous **9** in the pink **10** able-bodied **12** in fine fettle **18** sound of mind and limb

heap 3 gob, lot **4** fill, gobs, hunk, load, lots, lump, mass, mess, pack, pile, slew **5** amass, award, batch, bunch, flood, group, mound, ocean, slews, stack, store, world **6** accord, assign, bundle, deluge, engulf, gather, jumble, load up, oceans, oodles, pile up, plenty, worlds **7** barrels, cluster, collect, mete out, present **8** good deal, inundate, pour upon **9** abundance, gathering, great deal, multitude, profusion **10** assemblage, collection, shower upon **11** aggregation, concentrate **12** accumulation **13** agglomeration

heap up 5 amass **6** pile up **7** stack up **10** accumulate

hear 4 heed **5** admit, favor, grant, judge, learn **6** attend, be told, gather, look on **7** approve, concede, examine, find out, receive, witness **8** accede to, appear at, discover, hear tell, hold with, listen to **9** acquiesce, ascertain, hearken to **10** understand **11** acknowledge

hear!
  French: **4** oyez
  cry used by: **10** court crier
  preceded: **12** proclamation

hearing 5 probe, sound **6** review **7** council, earshot, inquiry **8** audience **9** interview **10** conference **11** examination, questioning **12** consultation **13** interrogation, investigation

hearken to 4 heed, mark, mind **6** attend **8** listen to **11** take to heart **14** pay attention to

Hearns, Thomas
  nickname: **6** Hitman
  sport: **6** boxing
  class: **12** middleweight, welterweight

hearsay 4 talk **5** rumor **6** gossip, report **8** idle talk **9** grapevine **11** scuttlebutt

heart 3 hub, nub **4** base, core, crux, guts, love, meat, mood, pith, root, soul **5** humor, pluck, spunk, valor **6** center, daring, desire, kernel, middle, nature, source, spirit **7** bravery, charity, courage, emotion, essence, nucleus, stomach **8** audacity, backbone, boldness, clemency, feelings, firmness, fondness, gameness, interior, main part, sympathy **9** affection, fortitude, gallantry, inner part, rudiments **10** sentiment, tolerance **10** brass tacks, compassion, enthusiasm, essentials, foundation, gentleness, indulgence, manfulness, principles, resolution, tenderness, true nature **11** busiest part, central part, disposition, forgiveness, nitty-gritty, temperament **12** fearlessness, fundamentals, quintessence, resoluteness **13** audaciousness
  part: **5** aorta, valve **6** atrium **7** chamber **9** ventricle
  pumps: **5** blood

heartache 3 woe **4** pain

5 grief **6** misery, sorrow **7** anguish, sadness, torment, trouble **8** distress **9** suffering **11** tribulation, unhappiness

heartbreaker 4 vamp **5** flirt, tease **8** coquette

Heartbreak House
author: **17** George Bernard Shaw

hearten 4 abet **5** cheer **6** assure, solace **7** animate, cheer up, comfort, console, enliven, gladden **8** brighten, embolden, energize, inspirit, reassure **9** encourage **10** invigorate

heartening 7 hopeful **9** favorable **10** auspicious, reassuring **11** encouraging

heartfelt 4 deep, full **5** total **6** ardent, devout, entire, honest **7** earnest, fervent, genuine, intense, sincere **8** complete, profound, thorough **10** keenly felt **12** all-inclusive, wholehearted

hearth 4 home **5** abode, house **8** fireside **9** fireplace, household **10** family life **12** family circle **13** chimney corner
goddess of: **4** Caca **5** Salus, Vesta **6** Hestia

Heart Is a Lonely Hunter, The
author: **15** Carson McCullers
character: **8** Mr Singer **9** Mick Kelly **10** Dr Copeland, Jake Blount **11** Biff Brannon

heartless 4 cold, mean **5** cruel **6** brutal, savage, unkind **7** callous, inhuman, unmoved **8** pitiless, ruthless, uncaring **9** unfeeling, unpitying, unstirred **10** unmerciful **11** coldhearted, cold-blooded, hardhearted, insensitive **12** cruelhearted, unresponsive **13** unsympathetic

Heart of Darkness
author: **12** Joseph Conrad
character: **5** Kurtz **7** Marlowe

Heart of Dixie
nickname of: **7** Alabama

Heart of Juliet Jones, The
creator: **9** Stan Drake
character: **3** Eve

Heart of Midlothian, The
author: **14** Sir Walter Scott

Heart of the Matter, The
author: **12** Graham Greene
character: **5** Yusef **6** Wilson **7** Mrs Rolt **9** Mrs Scobie **11** Major Scobie

heart-stopper 5 belle **6** beauty **7** charmer, stunner **8** knockout **10** good-looker

13 beautiful girl **14** beautiful woman

hearty 4 hale, warm, well **5** ample, hardy, sound **6** lively, robust, strong **7** cordial, genuine, healthy, profuse, sincere, zestful **8** complete, effusive, generous, thorough, vigorous **9** heartfelt, unbounded **10** unreserved **12** enthusiastic, unrestrained, wholehearted **13** physically fit

hearty appetite
French: **10** bon appetit

Heaslop, Ronald
character in: **15** A Passage to India
author: **7** Forster

heat 3 fry **4** bake, boil, cook, sear, stew, warm, zeal **5** ardor, broil, roast, steam **6** braise, climax, fervor, height, simmer, stress, thrill, warmth, warm up **7** hotness, make hot, passion, rapture, swelter **8** fervency, hot spell, warmness **9** eagerness, intensity, transport **10** enthusiasm, excitement **12** bring to a boil

heated 3 hot **5** angry, fiery, irate **6** bitter, fierce, raging, stormy **7** excited, fervent, furious, intense, violent **8** frenzied, inflamed, vehement **9** emotional **10** infuriated, passionate **11** impassioned, tempestuous

heated discussion 7 dispute **8** argument **10** war of words **11** controversy **12** disagreement

heath 5 Erica
varieties: **4** Tree **5** Berry, Besom, Irish, Otago, Spike **6** Dorset, Scotch, Spring **7** Cornish, Fringed, Spanish, Twisted **9** Cranberry **11** Cross-leaved

Heathcliff
character in: **16** Wuthering Heights
author: **6** Bronte

heathen 3 goy **4** boor **5** pagan **6** savage **7** atheist, gentile, infidel **8** agnostic, idolator **9** barbarian, ignoramus **10** polytheist, troglodyte, unbeliever **11** non-believer **17** uncivilized native

heather 7 Calluna
varieties: **3** Bog, Red **4** Bell, Snow **5** Beach, False, White **6** French, Golden, Scotch **8** Corsican, Mountain **9** Christmas **11** White winter **13** Mediterranean **18** Everblooming French

Heat of the Day, The
author: **14** Elizabeth Bowen

heat up 3 fan **4** goad, warm, whet **6** arouse **7** enhance, sharpen **8** increase **9** aggravate, intensify **10** strengthen

heave 3 peg, pry, sob **4** arch, blow, cast, emit, fire, hurl, lift, moan, pant, puff, puke, toss **5** boost, bulge, chuck, eject, fling, groan, hoist, lever, pitch, raise, retch, sling, surge, swell, throw, vomit **6** dilate, drag up, draw up, exhale, expand, haul up, launch, let fly, propel, pull up, tilt up, yank up **7** elevate **8** thrust up **9** discharge, palpitate **11** regurgitate

heaven, Heaven, the Heavens 3 wow **4** Zion **5** bliss, glory, mercy, space **6** my oh my, utopia **7** delight, ecstasy, Elysium, my stars, nirvana, Olympus, rapture **8** boy oh boy, goodness, land sake, paradise, Valhalla **9** afterlife, dreamland, next world, Shangri-la **10** afterworld, Beulah Land, life beyond, outer space, perfection, sheer bliss **11** enchantment, the Holy City, world beyond, world to come **12** eternal bliss, good gracious, New Jerusalem, the City of God, the firmament **13** Abraham's bosom, Elysian fields, seventh heaven **14** heavens to Betsy, our eternal home **15** life everlasting, our Father's house, the heavenly city **16** goodness gracious, Isle of the Blessed, supreme happiness, the abode of saints, the Celestial City, the vault of heaven **17** complete happiness, the wild blue yonder **18** Island of the Blessed, the celestial sphere, the heavenly kingdom, the kingdom of Heaven **19** the celestial expanse **21** the happy hunting ground
god of: **2** An **3** Anu **4** Jove, Zeus **7** Jupiter

Heaven Can Wait (1943)
director: **13** Ernst Lubitsch
cast: **9** Don Ameche **11** Gene Tierney **12** Marjorie Main **13** Charles Coburn

Heaven Can Wait (1978)
director: **9** Buck Henry **12** Warren Beatty
cast: **10** Dyan Cannon, Jack Warden **12** Warren Beatty **13** Julie Christie
remake of: **17** Here Comes Mr Jordan

heavenly 6 divine **7** angelic, blessed, saintly, sublime **8** beatific, blissful

Heavens and Earth
 author: 19 Stephen Vincent Benet

Heaven's My Destination
 author: 14 Thornton Wilder

heavy *see box*

heavy-handed 5 harsh
 6 clumsy 7 awkward 8 bungling 9 graceless, maladroit
 10 blundering, oppressive, ungraceful

heavyhearted 3 sad 4 glum
 6 dismal, gloomy, morose
 7 doleful, forlorn, joyless, unhappy 8 dejected, downcast
 9 cheerless, depressed, sorrowful 10 despondent, melancholy 11 downhearted
 14 down in the dumps, down in the mouth

Hebe
 goddess of: 5 youth 6 spring
 father: 4 Zeus
 mother: 4 Hera
 brother: 4 Ares
 husband: 8 Hercules
 handmaiden to: 4 gods
 corresponds to: 8 Juventas

Heber
 wife: 4 Jael

Hebrew alphabet
 or: 5 aleph
 b/v: 4 beth
 g: 5 gimel
 d: 6 daleth
 h: 2 he 5 cheth
 v/w: 3 vav
 z: 5 zayin
 y/j/i: 3 yod
 k/kh: 4 kaph

l: 5 lamed
m: 3 men
n: 3 nun
`: 4 ayin
p/f: 2 pe
k: 4 koph
r: 4 resh
sh/s: 4 shin
s: 3 sin 4 sadi 6 samekh
t: 3 tav 4 teth

Hebrew Judge 4 Ehud, Elon, Jair, Tola 5 Abdon, Ibzan
 6 Gideon, Samson, Samuel
 7 Deborah, Othniel, Shamgar
 8 Jephthah

Hebrew months
 first: 4 Ahib, Nisn 6 Ehanim, Tishri
 second: 3 Bul, Civ 4 Iyar
 7 Heshvan
 third: 5 Sivan 6 Kislev
 fourth: 5 Tebet 6 Tammuz, Tebeth
 fifth: 2 Ab 7 Shelbat
 sixth: 4 Adar, Elul 6 Veadar
 seventh: 4 Abib 5 Nisan
 6 Tishri 7 Ethanim
 eighth: 3 Zif 4 Iyer
 11 Marcheshvan
 ninth: 5 Sivan 7 Chislev
 tenth: 6 Tabeth, Tammuz
 eleventh: 2 Ab 6 Shebat
 twelfth: 4 Adar, Elul

Hecabe *see* 6 Hecuba

Hecaleius
 epithet of: 4 Zeus

he carved it
 Latin: 8 sculpsit

Hecate
 also: 6 Hekate
 goddess of: 5 earth, Hades

associated with: 6 hounds
 7 sorcery 10 crossroads
 corresponds to: 5 Brimo

Hecatonchires
 also: 9 Centimani
 form: 5 giant
 names: 5 Gyges 6 Cottus
 8 Briareus
 father: 6 Uranus
 mother: 4 Gaea
 number of heads: 5 fifty
 number of arms: 10 one hundred

heckle 3 boo 4 bait, hiss, hoot, mock, ride, twit 5 annoy, bully, chivy, harry, hound, taunt 6 badger, harass, harrow, hector, jeer at, molest, needle 7 provoke 9 shout down

hectare
 abbreviation of: 2 ha

hectic 3 mad 4 wild 6 stormy
 7 chaotic, frantic, furious 8 feverish, frenetic, frenzied, headlong 9 breakneck, turbulent
 10 tumultuous

hectoliter
 abbreviation of: 2 hl

hectometer
 abbreviation of: 2 hm

hector 4 bait, ride 5 bully, harry, hound, tease, worry
 6 badger, harass, needle, plague 7 torment

Hector
 father: 5 Priam
 mother: 6 Hecuba
 brother: 5 Paris
 sister: 9 Cassandra
 wife: 10 Andromache
 son: 8 Astyanax
 hero of: 9 Trojan War
 killed by: 8 Achilles

Hecuba
 also: 5 Maera 6 Hecabe
 father: 5 Atlas
 husband: 5 Priam 8 Tegeates
 son: 5 Paris 6 Hector 7 Helenus, Polites, Troilus 9 Deiphobus, Polydorus
 daughter: 6 Creusa 7 Laodice 8 Polyxena 9 Cassandra
 changed into: 3 dog 5 bitch
 hound of: 7 Icarius

Hecuba
 author: 9 Euripides
 character: 8 Odysseus, Polyxena 9 Agamemnon, Polydorus 10 Polymestor

Hedda Gabler
 author: 11 Henrik Ibsen
 character: 10 Judge Brack
 11 Hedda Tesman, Thea Elvsted 12 George Tesman
 13 Eilert Lovberg 17 Miss Juliana Tesman

heder 12 Jewish school

heavy 3 big, fat, sad 4 deep, dull, full, hard, lazy, slow
 5 broad, bulky, dense, grave, gross, harsh, hefty, large, obese, plump, rough, stout, thick 6 clumsy, coarse, deadly, dreary, fierce, gloomy, leaden, pained, portly, raging, rugged, savage, solemn, strong, sturdy, torpid, woeful 7 awesome, complex, copious, doleful, forlorn, furious, intense, joyless, languid, lumpish, massive, notable, onerous, profuse, roaring, ruinous, serious, tearful, tedious, violent, weighty 8 abundant, agonized, burdened, crushing, cumbrous, damaging, dejected, desolate, downcast, forceful, grieving, grievous, imposing, lifeless, listless, mournful, pedantic, profound, seething, sluggish, stricken, tiresome, unwieldy 9 apathetic, cheerless, corpulent, depressed, difficult, excessive, extensive, harrowing, important, injurious, laborious, lethargic, lumbering, miserable, momentous, ponderous, rampaging, sorrowful, turbulent, wearisome 10 burdensome, calamitous, cumbersome, distressed, full of care, immoderate, impressive, inordinate, melancholy, monotonous, noteworthy, oppressive, overweight, pernicious, phlegmatic, unbearable, unstinting 11 crestfallen, deleterious, destructive, detrimental, distressing, extravagant, intemperate, intolerable, significant, tempestuous, unendurable, unrelenting, unremitting 12 considerable, disconsolate, hard to endure, overwhelming, unrestrained 13 consequential, grief-stricken, of great import 16 laden with sorrows 18 of great consequence

hedge 3 hem 4 duck, edge, ring, wall 5 bound, dodge, evade, fence, guard, hem in, limit 6 border, margin, shut in, waffle 7 barrier, enclose, mark off, outline 8 encircle, hedgerow, surround 9 be evasive, delineate, demarcate, insurance, pussyfoot, temporize 10 equivocate, protection 11 delineation, row of bushes 12 compensation 13 circumference, fence of shrubs 14 beg the question, counterbalance 17 beat around the bush

he died
Latin: 5 obiit

he does not pursue
Latin: 14 non prosequitur

hedonist 8 Sybarite 9 debauchee, libertine 10 dissipater, profligate, sensualist, voluptuary 14 pleasure seeker

hedonistic 7 sensual 9 epicurean, libertine, sybaritic 10 voluptuous 11 intemperate 13 self-indulgent 15 pleasure-seeking

he drew this
Latin: 10 delineavit

Hedrick, Zelma Kathryn
real name of: 14 Kathryn Grayson

heed 4 care, mind, obey 5 bow to, pains, study 6 concur, follow, hold to, notice, regard 7 defer to, observe, perusal, respect, yield to 8 accede to, consider, listen to, prudence, scrutiny, submit to 9 attention, be ruled by, give ear to 10 bear in mind comply with, precaution, take note of 11 carefulness, examination, heedfulness, mindfulness, observation, take to heart 12 take notice of 13 attentiveness 14 fastidiousness, meticulousness, pay attention to, scrupulousness 17 conscientiousness

heedful 4 wary 5 alert, aware, cagey, chary 7 alive to, careful, mindful, prudent 8 cautious, discreet, vigilant, watchful 9 attentive, concerned, conscious

heedless 3 lax 4 rash 5 slack 6 remiss, unwary 7 foolish, unaware, witless 8 careless, mindless, reckless, uncaring 9 foolhardy, frivolous, impetuous, imprudent, negligent, oblivious, unheeding, unmindful 10 incautious, neglectful, unthinking, unwatchful 11 harebrained, improvident, inattentive, thoughtless, un-

concerned, unobservant, unobserving 12 happy-go-lucky 14 scatterbrained

heedlessly 5 blind 6 rashly 8 headlong 9 foolishly, witlessly 10 carelessly, mindlessly, recklessly 11 frivolously, impetuously, impulsively, negligently, unmindfully 12 neglectfully, unthinkingly 13 inattentively, thoughtlessly, unconcernedly 15 inconsiderately, uncooperatively

heedlessness 8 rashness 9 unconcern 10 negligence 11 inattention, unawareness 12 carelessness, indiscretion, mindlessness, recklessness 13 unmindfulness 15 thoughtlessness 16 irresponsibility

heel 3 cad, cur, end, rat 4 list, rind, tilt 5 churl, crust, louse 6 rotter 7 bounder, caitiff, dastard

he engraved it
Latin: 8 sculpsit

Heep, Uriah
character in: 16 David Copperfield
author of: 7 Dickens

he flourished
Latin: 7 floruit

hefty 3 big 5 beefy, bulky, burly, heavy, husky, large, stout 6 brawny, hearty, mighty, robust, rugged, strong, sturdy 7 hulking, massive, sizable, weighty, well-fed 8 muscular, powerful, stalwart, thickset 9 corpulent, strapping 11 substantial

Hegeleos
father: 8 Tyrsenus

Hegemone
origin: 8 Athenian
member of: 6 Graces

hegemony 7 control 9 authority, dominance, influence, supremacy

Heggen, Thomas
author of: 9 Mr Roberts

hegira 6 exodus, flight 7 journey

Heh see 6 Ogdoad

he himself said it
Latin: 9 ipse dixit

Heidrun
origin: 12 Scandinavian
form: 4 goat
yields: 4 mead
feeds warriors in: 8 Valhalla

height 4 acme, apex, hill, peak, rise 5 bluff, cliff, crest, knoll, limit, mound, tower 6 apogee, heyday, summit, zenith 7 hilltop, maximum, pla-

teau 8 altitude, eminence, highland, highness, mountain, palisade, pinnacle, tallness, ultimate 9 elevation, extremity, flowering, high point, loftiness, supremacy 10 perfection, promontory 11 culmination 12 consummation, upward extent, utmost degree, vantage point

heighten 5 raise 7 elevate 8 increase 9 aggravate, intensify

heil 4 hail

Heimberger, Eddie Albert
real name of: 11 Eddie Albert

Heimdall
origin: 12 Scandinavian
god of: 4 dawn 5 light
number of mothers: 4 nine
guards: 7 bifrost 13 rainbow bridge
killed by: 4 Loki
noted for: 7 hearing 8 eyesight

Heine, Heinrich
author of: 9 Atta Troll 11 Book of Songs 19 Germany A Winter's Tale

Heinlein, Robert
author of: 10 Double Star 16 Starship Troopers 20 The Green Hills of Earth 22 Stranger in a Strange Land 23 The Moon Is a Harsh Mistress

heinous 4 evil, foul, vile 5 gross, nasty 6 grisly, horrid, odious, sinful, wicked 7 beastly, ghastly, hideous, inhuman, vicious 8 infamous, shocking, terrible 9 abhorrent, atrocious, loathsome, monstrous, nefarious, offensive, repugnant, repulsive, revolting, sickening 10 abominable, deplorable, despicable, detestable, disgusting, iniquitous, outrageous, scandalous, villainous 11 disgraceful, distasteful 12 contemptible 13 objectionable, reprehensible

heinousness 4 evil 7 outrage 8 atrocity, baseness, enormity, foulness, savagery, vileness, villainy 9 barbarity, depravity, malignity 10 inhumanity 13 loathsomeness, monstrousness 14 outrageousness

heir, heiress 7 legatee 9 inheritor 10 inheritrix 11 beneficiary, inheritress 12 heir apparent 15 heir presumptive

Heiress, The
director: 12 William Wyler
based on novel by: 10 Henry James

entitled: 16 Washington Square
cast: 13 Miriam Hopkins 15 Montgomery Clift, Ralph Richardson 17 Olivia de Havilland
score: 12 Aaron Copland
Oscar for: 7 actress (de Havilland)

Hekate *see* 6 Hecate

Hel
origin: 12 Scandinavian
goddess of: 5 death
rules: 8 Niflheim
father: 4 Loki
mother: 9 Angerboda, Angrbodha, Angurboda
brother: 6 Fenrir, Fenris 11 Iormungandr, Jormungandr 14 Midgard Serpent
color of body: 4 blue 5 flesh
home of: 4 dead

Helen
father: 4 Zeus
mother: 4 Leda
brother: 6 Castor, Pollux
sister: 8 Timandra 12 Clytemnestra
husband: 8 Menelaus
abducted by: 5 Paris
carried off to: 4 Troy
abduction caused: 9 Trojan War

Helena
character in: 20 All's Well That Ends Well 21 A Midsummer Night's Dream
author: 11 Shakespeare

Helenor
mentioned in: 6 Aeneid
position: 6 prince
home: 5 Lydia
accompanied: 6 Aeneas

Heliadae
sons of: 6 Helius, Rhodes

helicopter
invented by: 8 Sikorsky

Heliopolis
city of: 2 On

Helios
origin: 5 Greek
god of: 3 sun
father: 8 Hyperion
mother: 4 Thia
children: 5 Circe 6 Aeetes 8 Phaethon
corresponds to: 3 Sol

heliotrope 12 Heliotropium
varieties: 6 garden, winter, yellow 7 seaside

helium
chemical symbol: 2 He

hell, Hell 5 agony, grief, Hades 6 misery, the pit 7 Abaddon, anguish, despair, Gehenna, inferno, remorse, torment 8 Appolyons, hell fire, the abyss 9 martyrdom, perdi-

tion, suffering 10 lake of fire 12 hopelessness, wretchedness 13 bottomless pit, Satan's kingdom, the lower world, the underworld 14 place of the lost, the Devil's house, the nether world, the shades below 15 everlasting fire, home of lost souls, infernal regions 16 abode of the damned

Helle
father: 7 Athamas
mother: 7 Nephele
stepmother: 3 Ino
brother: 7 Phrixus
death by: 8 drowning

Hellen
king of: 8 Thessaly
father: 9 Deucalion
mother: 6 Pyrrha
wife: 6 Orseis
son: 5 Dorus 6 Aeolus, Xuthus
ancestor of: 8 Hellenes

Hellenic Republic *see* 6 Greece

Heller, Joseph
author of: 10 Good as Gold 14 Catch-Twenty-Two 17 Something Happened

hellion 5 devil, rogue, scamp 9 scoundrel 13 mischief-maker

hellish 4 foul, vile 5 awful 6 brutal 7 hateful 8 accursed, damnable, dreadful, horrible, infernal 9 atrocious, revolting 10 abominable, disgusting

Hellman, Lillian
author of: 5 Maybe 10 Pentimento 13 Scoundrel Time 14 The Little Foxes, Toys in the Attic 15 Watch on the Rhine 16 The Children's Hour 17 An Unfinished Woman 22 Another Part of the Forest

hello
French: 7 bonjour
German: 8 guten tag
Spanish: 10 buenos dias
Italian: 4 ciao 10 buon giorno
Latin: 5 salve

Hello-Central
character in: 36 A Connecticut Yankee in King Arthur's Court
author: 5 Twain

help *see* box

helper 3 aid 4 aide 5 angel 6 backer, deputy, patron, second 7 adjunct, partner, servant 8 adjutant, advocate, champion, confrere, coworker, employee, retainer 9 assistant, associate, auxiliary, colleague, man Friday, right hand, supporter 10 accomplice, aide-de-camp, apprentice, benefactor, girl Friday 11 confederate, helping hand, subordinate 12 collaborator, righthand man 13 good samaritan 14 fairy godmother

helpful 4 fine, good, kind, nice 6 usable, useful 8 obliging, splendid, valuable 9 excellent, favorable, practical 10 beneficial, profitable, supportive 11 considerate, cooperative, serviceable 12 advantageous, constructive 13 accommodating

helping hand 3 aid 4 aide, hand 5 boost 6 assist, hand up, helper, succor 7 abettor, support 9 assistant 10 assistance

helplessness 8 weakness 9 impotence, inability, infirmity 10 dependence, feebleness, ineptitude 12 incapability, incompetence, inefficiency 13 powerlessness, vulnerability

help 3 aid 4 back, balm, calm, care, crew, cure, ease, gift, lift, save 5 allay, emend, force, guide, hands, salve, serve, staff 6 advice, advise, assist, give to, menial, relief, remedy, rescue, soothe, succor, uphold 7 advance, backing, console, correct, endorse, further, helpers, improve, nurture, promote, rectify, relieve, servant, service, stand by, support, welfare, workers, workmen 8 advocate, befriend, champion, domestic, factotum, farmhand, guidance, laborers, maintain, mitigate, retainer, retrieve, side with 9 alleviate, chip in for, employees, encourage, extricate, lend a hand, make whole, promotion, put at ease, underling, workhands, work force 10 ameliorate, apprentice, assistance, assistants, bring round, corrective, friendship, go to bat for, hired hands, kind regard, minister to, preventive, protection, stick up for 11 advancement, benevolence, cooperation, endorsement, furtherance, good offices, helping hand, make healthy, restorative 12 bring through, contribute to, contribution, hired helpers, intercede for 13 collaboration, cooperate with, encouragement, take the part of

Helsinki
  capital of: 7 Finland

hem 3 box, rim 4 bind, brim, edge, welt 5 bound, brink, skirt, verge 6 border, edging, fringe, impede, margin, turn up 7 confine, enclose, stammer, stutter, turning 8 compress, encircle, restrain, surround

he made it
  Latin: 5 fecit

Hemera
  father: 6 Erebus
  mother: 3 Nyx
  corresponds to: 3 Eos

Hemerasia
  epithet of: 7 Artemis
  means: 13 she who soothes

hem in 4 best 5 fence 7 besiege, confine, enclose 8 encircle, surround

Hemingway, Ernest
  author of: 9 In Our Time 14 A Moveable Feast 15 A Farewell to Arms, The Sun Also Rises 16 To Have and Have Not 18 Islands in the Stream, The Old Man and the Sea 19 For Whom the Bell Tolls 21 The Snows of Kilimanjaro 34 The Short Happy Life of Francis Macomber

hemiptera
  class: 8 hexapoda
  phylum: 10 arthropoda
  group: 3 bug

Hemithea
  father: 6 Cycnus
  mother: 7 Proclea
  sister: 5 Tenes
  pursued by: 8 Achilles
  swallowed up by: 5 earth

hemlock 5 Tsuga 15 Conium maculatum
  varieties: 5 Dwarf, Water 6 Canada, Ground, Poison 7 Siebold, Spotted, Western 8 Carolina, Japanese, Mountain

hemp 14 Cannabis sativa
  varieties: 3 Bog 5 Cuban, Sisal 6 Deccan, Indian, Manila 7 African 8 Deckaner 9 Bowstring, Mauritius 10 New Zealand 13 Colorado River 15 Ceylon bowstring, Indian bowstring 16 African bowstring

hen
  young: 6 pullet

Henchard, Michael
  character in: 22 The Mayor of Casterbridge
  author: 5 Hardy

henchman 4 goon, thug

6 flunky, lackey, minion, stooge, yes-man 7 gorilla 8 hanger-on, hireling, retainer 9 attendant, bodyguard 10 hatchet man, lieutenant 12 right-hand man, strong-arm man

Henderson, Marge
  creator/artist of: 10 Little Lulu

Henioche
  epithet of: 4 Hera
  means: 10 charioteer

henna 3 dye 5 rinse 6 auburn, russet 8 cinnamon 11 rust-colored 12 reddish-brown 13 copper-colored

henpecked 4 meek 5 timid 6 docile 8 obedient 10 browbeaten, submissive, wife-ridden 11 unassertive

Henry, Frederic
  character in: 15 A Farewell to Arms
  author: 9 Hemingway

Henry Esmond
  author: 16 William Thackeray
  character: 5 Frank 7 Beatrix 9 Lord Mohun 10 Father Holt 11 James Stuart 12 Rachel Esmond 13 Francis Esmond

Henry IV
  author: 18 William Shakespeare
  character: 7 Hotspur 11 Prince Henry, Thomas Percy 14 Edmund Mortimer, Sir Walter Blunt 15 John of Lancaster, Mistress Quickly, Sir John Falstaff 18 Earl of Westmoreland, King Henry the Fourth

Henry V
  author: 18 William Shakespeare
  character: 7 Dauphin, Montjoy 15 Charles the Sixth (King of France) 17 Princess Katharine
  director: 15 Laurence Olivier
  cast: 11 Leslie Banks 12 Robert Newton 13 Renee Asherson 15 Laurence Olivier

Henry VI
  author: 18 William Shakespeare
  character: 6 Edward (Prince of Wales) 7 Charles (Dauphin of France), Eleanor, Louis XI (King of France) 8 Lady Bona, Lady Grey 9 Joan of Arc 10 Lord Talbot 11 Bolingbroke 12 John Beaufort, Lord Clifford, Lord Hastings 13 Henry Beaufort, Joan La Pucelle 15 Margaret of Anjou, Margery Jour-

dain 16 Bastard of Orleans, Cardinal Beaufort
  duke: 4 York (Richard Plantagenet) 7 Bedford, Suffolk 8 Somerset 10 Gloucester
  earl: 7 Suffolk, Warwick 9 Salisbury
  Richard Plantagenet's son: 6 Edmund, Edward, George 7 Richard

Henry VIII
  author: 18 William Shakespeare
  character: 7 Cranmer 8 Gardiner 10 Anne Boleyn 12 Thomas Wolsey 14 Queen Katharine, Thomas Cromwell 16 Cardinal Campeius
  duke: 7 Norfolk, Suffolk 10 Buckingham

Henze, Hans Werner
  born: 7 Germany 10 Westphalia
  composer of: 6 Ariosi, Ondine 8 King Stag 10 El Cimarron 11 Konig Hirsch 12 The Bassarids, The Young Lord 14 Being Beauteous 15 The Runaway Slave 17 Boulevard Solitude 18 Der Prinz von Homburg, The Raft of the Medusa 19 Elegy for Young Lovers 48 The Long and Weary Journey to the Flat of Natasha Ungeheur

Heorot
  great hall in: 7 Beowulf
  author: 7 unknown

he painted it
  Latin: 6 pinxit

Hepburn, Audrey
  real name: 19 Audrey Hepburn-Ruston
  husband: 9 Mel Ferrer
  born: 7 Belgium 8 Brussels
  roles: 6 Ondine 7 Charade, Sabrina 9 Bloodline, Funny Face 10 My Fair Lady 11 War and Peace 12 Roman Holiday (Oscar), The Nun's Story 13 Green Mansions, Wait Until Dark 18 Love in the Afternoon 19 Breakfast at Tiffany's

Hepburn, Katharine
  co-star: 12 Spencer Tracy
  born: 10 Hartford CT
  roles: 7 Desk Set, Holiday 8 Adam's Rib 10 Alice Adams, Pat and Mike, Summertime 12 Morning Glory (Oscar), On Golden Pond (Oscar), The Rainmaker 14 Woman of the Year 15 The African Queen, The Lion in Winter (Oscar) 18 Suddenly Last Summer 20 The Philadelphia Story

23 Guess Who's Coming to Dinner (Oscar) 24 Long Day's Journey into Night

Hephaestus
also: 10 Hephaistos
father: 4 Zeus
mother: 4 Hera
god of: 4 fire 11 handicrafts 12 metalworking
vocation: 5 smith
wife: 9 Aphrodite
corresponds to: 6 Vulcan

Hephaistos *see* 10 Hephaestus

Hephzibah
husband: 8 Hezekiah
son: 8 Manasseh

Hepzibah *see* 9 Hephzibah

Hera
also: 4 Here
origin: 5 Greek
queen of: 6 Heaven
father: 5 Cronos, Cronus, Kronos
mother: 4 Rhea
brother: 4 Zeus
husband: 4 Zeus
son: 4 Ares
daughter: 9 Eilithyia 10 Hephaestus
birthplace: 5 Samos
festival: 7 Daedala
counterfeit: 7 Nephele
corresponds to: 4 Juno
epithet: 6 Anthea, Bunaea 8 Henioche 9 Prodromia

Heracles *see* 8 Hercules

Heracles, Children of
author: 9 Euripides
character: 6 Hyllus, Iolaus 7 Alcmene, Macaria 8 Demophon 10 Eurystheus

Heracles, Madness of
author: 9 Euripides
character: 4 Hera 5 Lycus 6 Megara 7 Theseus 8 Heracles 10 Amphitryon

Heraclid
descendant of: 8 Hercules

Heraclidae
children of: 8 Hercules

Heraea
origin: 5 Greek
form: 8 festival

Herakles *see* 8 Hercules

herald 4 clue, omen, sign 5 crier, envoy, token, usher 6 augury, inform, report, reveal, symbol 7 courier, divulge, portent, presage, publish, usher in, warning 8 announce, forecast, foregoer, foretell, proclaim 9 advertise, harbinger, indicator, make known, messenger, precursor, prefigure, publicize 10 forerunner, indication, proclaimer 11 bruit abroad, communicate, give voice to, predecessor 13 give tidings of

heraldic emblem 4 arms 5 crest 8 blazonry, insignia 10 coat of arms

heraldry *see box*

herb 4 drug 5 plant, spice 6 annual, physic 7 herbage, perfume 8 aromatic, biennial, medicine 9 flavoring, perennial, seasoning, succulent
kind: 3 bay, rue 4 corn, dill, hemp, mint, rose, sage 5 anise, basil, curry, chili, grass, onion, peony, thyme, wheat 6 catnip, celery, chives, clover, fennel, garlic, pepper, sesame 7 boneset, caraway, ginseng, lavender, mustard, oregano, parsley 8 camomile, licorice, rosemary, tarragon 9 buttercup, marijuana, spearmint 10 peppermint 11 wintergreen

Herbert, George
author of: 9 The Temple

Herbert, Victor
born: 6 Dublin 7 Ireland
composer of: 14 Babes in Toyland, Hero and Leander 15 Naughty Marietta

herbivorous 10 vegetarian 11 plant-eating 14 noncarnivorous

Herceius
epithet of: 4 Zeus
means: 14 of the courtyard

herculean, Herculean 4 hard 5 burly, hefty, tough 6 brawny, mighty, robust, rugged, strong, sturdy 7 arduous, onerous 8 muscular, powerful, toilsome, wearying 9 difficult, fatiguing, laborious, strapping, strenuous 10 burdensome, exhausting, formidable, prodigious 12 backbreaking

Hercules
also: 7 Alcides 8 Heracles, Herakles 9 Carnopian
father: 4 Zeus
mother: 7 Alcmene
cousin: 10 Eurystheus
wife: 5 Hebe 6 Megara 8 Deianira
son: 5 Lamus 6 Hyllus 8 Telephus 11 Therimachus
daughter: 7 Macaria
teacher: 6 Chiron
gift: 8 strength
performed: 6 labors
number of labors: 6 twelve
epithet: 7 Charops 8 Buphagus 9 Ipoctonus
corresponds to: 6 Sancus 10 Semo Sancus

Hercyna
form: 5 nymph

heraldry
also called: 4 arms 10 coat of arms
black: 5 sable
blue: 5 azure
bottom: 4 base
center: 5 fesse
coat of arms of cities/countries/colleges: 14 impersonal arms
coat of arms on shield/crest/helmet/motto: 19 armorial achievement
colors: 8 tincture
concerns family's: 8 heritage 9 genealogy
described as: 9 blazoning
divided diagonally: 7 per bend
divided vertically and horizontally: 9 quartered
for holding shield: 10 supporters
fur: 4 vair 6 ermine
gold/yellow: 2 or
green: 4 vert
helmet top: 5 crest
horizontal band: 4 fess
intrafamily distinctions: 12 differencing
daughter: 7 lozenge
eldest son: 5 label
younger son: 7 cadency
left part: 8 sinister
main figure: 6 charge 8 ordinary 14 heraldic device
metal: 2 or 6 argent
motto in: 6 scroll
orange: 5 tenne
placed on lord's: 6 banner, shield 8 garments 14 horse trappings
portrayed as: 6 emblem, symbol
purple: 7 purpure
red: 5 gules
red-purple: 8 sanguine
right part: 6 dexter
shield: 10 escutcheon
sunshade: 8 mantling
held by: 6 wreath
made of: 4 silk
surface/background: 5 field
top: 5 chief
two or more colors: 16 lines of partition
vertical band: 4 pale
when worn by followers: 5 badge 6 livery
white/silver: 6 argent

location: 8 fountain
playmate: 10 Persephone

herd 3 lot, mob **4** army, band, body, gang, goad, host, lead, mass, pack, spur **5** array, bunch, crowd, drive, drove, flock, force, group, guide, horde, party, press, rally, swarm, tribe, troop **6** gather, huddle, legion, muster, number, throng **7** cluster, collect, company, convene, round up **8** assemble, assembly, conclave **9** gathering, multitude **10** assemblage, collection **11** convocation **12** congregation

Herds
god of: 8 Silvanus, Sylvanus

herdsman 6 cowboy, driver, drover **7** cowpoke **8** shepherd

Herdsman
constellation of: 6 Bootes

herd together 5 flock, group **6** gather **7** cluster, collect **10** congregate **12** band together

Here see **4** Hera

hereafter 5 limbo **6** heaven **8** paradise **9** afterlife, from now on, next world, Purgatory **10** afterworld, future life, henceforth, life beyond, ultimately **11** in the future, world to come **12** at a later date, at a later time, henceforward, subsequently **14** life after death **15** heavenly kingdom

here and there 6 around **11** at intervals **18** in this place and that
Latin: 6 passim

Here Comes Mr Jordan
director: 13 Alexander Hall
cast: 11 Claude Rains, Evelyn Keyes, Rita Johnson **16** Robert Montgomery
remade as: 13 Heaven Can Wait

hereditary 6 inborn, inbred **7** genetic **9** ancestral, heritable, inherited **10** congenital, handed-down **11** established, inheritable, traditional

here lies
Latin: 8 hic jacet

heresy 7 dissent, fallacy **8** apostasy **10** dissension, heterodoxy, iconoclasm, irreligion **11** unorthodoxy **13** nonconformity **15** unsound doctrine

heretic 7 skeptic **8** apostate, recreant, recusant, renegade **9** dissenter **10** backslider **11** freethinker, misbeliever

12 deviationist
13 nonconformist

heretical 7 radical **9** dissident **10** unorthodox **12** iconoclastic **13** nonconforming, nonconformist **14** unconventional

heretofore
French: 8 ci-devant

Hereward the Wake
author: 15 Charles Kingsley

Hergesheimer, Joseph
author of: 8 Java Head **19** The Three Black Pennys

heritage 6 estate, legacy **7** portion **9** patrimony, tradition **10** birthright **11** inheritance **16** family possession

Hermaphroditus
father: 6 Hermes
mother: 9 Aphrodite
loved by: 8 Salmacis
joined with: 8 Salmacis
became: 8 bisexual

Hermes
origin: 5 Greek
occupation: 6 herald
messenger of: 4 gods
father: 4 Zeus
mother: 4 Maia
son: 3 Pan **6** Prylis **7** Daphnis **14** Hermaphroditus
birthplace: 7 Arcadia
god of: 4 luck **5** roads, sleep **6** dreams, wealth **7** cunning, thieves **8** commerce **9** fertility, invention, merchants
invented: 4 lyre
sandals had: 5 wings
epithet: 6 Dolius **8** Agoraeus **9** Spelaites **10** Criophorus **11** Argiphontes **12** Argeiphontes, Psychopompus
corresponds to: 5 Thoth **7** Mercury

hermetic 6 mystic, occult **7** obscure **8** abstruse, airtight, esoteric, mystical **9** recondite

Hermia
character in: 21 A Midsummer Night's Dream
author: 11 Shakespeare

hermine, L'
author: 11 Jean Anouilh

Hermione
character in: 14 The Winter's Tale
author: 11 Shakespeare

Hermione
father: 8 Menelaus
mother: 5 Helen
husband: 7 Orestes
son: 9 Tisamenus

hermit 7 eremite, recluse **8** cenobite, monastic, solitary **9** anchorite **11** desert saint

14 solitudinarian **16** religious recluse

hermitage 5 abbey **6** friary, priory **7** convent, retreat **8** cloister **9** monastery

Hermod
origin: 12 Scandinavian
father: 4 Odin **5** Othin
race: 4 Asar **5** Aesir
negotiates return of: 5 Baldr **6** Balder, Baldur

hero, heroine 4 idol, star **7** gallant **8** brave man, champion, great man, male lead, male star, noble man **9** daredevil, daring man, main actor **10** adventurer, leading man **11** protagonist, valorous man **12** man of courage, man of the hour **13** chivalrous man, popular figure **15** fearless fighter, idealized person, intrepid warrior, legendary person

Hero
character in: 19 Much Ado About Nothing
author: 11 Shakespeare

Hero
vocation: 9 priestess
priestess of: 9 Aphrodite
lover: 7 Leander
death by: 7 suicide **8** drowning

Herod Antipas
father: 13 Herod the great
mother: 8 Malthace
grandfather: 9 Antipater
wife: 8 Herodias
half brother: 6 Philip
beheaded: 14 John the Baptist

Herodias
husband: 6 Philip **12** Herod Antipas
daughter: 6 Salome

Herodotus
called: 15 Father of History
wrote history of: 11 Persian Wars

Herod Philip
daughter: 6 Salome

heroic 4 bold, epic **5** brave, grand, noble **6** daring **7** classic, exalted, gallant, Homeric, valiant **8** elevated, fearless, highbrow, inflated, intrepid, mythical, resolute, valorous **9** bombastic, dauntless, dignified, grandiose, high-flown, legendary, undaunted **10** chivalrous, courageous **11** exaggerated, extravagant, lionhearted, pretentious, unflinching **12** mythological, ostentatious, stouthearted

heroic act 4 feat **7** exploit **9** brave deed

heroism 5 valor 6 daring
7 bravery, courage, prowess
8 boldness, chivalry, nobility
9 fortitude, gallantry 11 intrepidity 12 fearlessness
13 dauntlessness 14 courageousness 15 lionheartedness

Herophilus
field: 7 anatomy
nationality: 5 Greek
experimented with: 15 postmortem exams

Heros
author: 8 Menander

herpetophobia
fear of: 8 reptiles

Herrenvolk 10 master race

Herrick, Robert
author of: 10 Hesperides
20 Corinna's Going A Maying 26 Gather ye rosebuds
while ye may

Herriman, George
creator/artist of: 8 Krazy
Kat

Herschel, William
field: 9 astronomy
nationality: 7 British
discovered: 6 Uranus

Herse
father: 7 Cecrops
sister: 8 Aglauros, Aglaurus,
Agraulos
lover: 6 Hermes
son: 5 Ceryx 8 Cephalus

Hersey, John
author of: 7 The Wall 9 Hiroshima 13 A Bell for
Adano, The Conspiracy
22 My Petition for More
Space

Hertz, Heinrich
field: 7 physics
nationality: 6 German
discovered: 13 electric
waves 18 wireless telegraphy
named for him: 13 hertzian
waves

Herzog
author: 10 Saul Bellow

he sculptured it
Latin: 8 sculpsit

Hesiod
author of: 8 Theogony
12 Works and Days

Hesione
father: 8 Laomedon
husband: 7 Telamon
son: 6 Teucer
rescued by: 8 Hercules

hesitancy 10 indecision, reluctance, unsureness 11 uncertainty, vacillation
12 irresolution

hesitant 5 loath 6 unsure
7 halting 8 doubtful, waver-

ing 9 diffident, faltering, reluctant, tentative, uncertain,
undecided 10 hesitating,
indecisive, irresolute 11 halfhearted, hanging back, vacillating 15 shilly-shallying
17 lacking confidence, sitting
on the fence

hesitate 4 balk, halt 5 delay,
pause, shy at, waver 6 falter
7 scruple, stick at 8 be unsure,
hang back 9 stickle at, vacillate 10 dillydally, shrink from,
think twice 11 be reluctant,
be uncertain, be undecided, be
unwilling, stop briefly 12 be
irresolute, shilly-shally
16 straddle the fence

hesitating 8 doubtful, hesitant
10 indecisive, irresolute, on
the fence

he speaks
Latin: 8 loquitur

Hesperia
also: 5 Italy 16 Iberian
Peninsula

Hesperides
author: 13 Robert Herrick

Hesperides
form: 6 nymphs
guarded: 12 golden apples
guarded with: 5 Ladon
6 dragon
names: 5 Aegle 6 Hestia
7 Erythea, Hespera 8 Arethusa 9 Hespereia, Hesperusa
islands of the: 7 blessed
form of: 6 heaven

Hesperis
mother: 8 Hesperus
mother of: 10 Hesperides

Hess, Victor Francis
field: 7 physics
discovered: 10 cosmic rays
awarded: 10 Nobel Prize

Hesse, Hermann
author of: 6 Demian 9 Rosshalde 10 Siddhartha
11 Steppenwolf 12 Magister
Ludi 14 Peter Camenzind
15 Beneath the Wheel
16 Death and the Lover,
Journey to the East, The
Glass Bead Game

**Hesselberg, Melvyn
Edouard**
real name of: 13 Melvyn
Douglas

hessionite
species: 6 garnet

Hestia
origin: 5 Greek
goddess of the: 6 hearth
father: 6 Cronos, Cronus,
Kronos
mother: 4 Rhea
corresponds to: 5 Vesta

Heston, Charlton
real name: 13 Charles Carter
born: 10 Evanston IL
roles: 5 El Cid, Moses 6 Ben-Hur (Oscar) 15 Planet of the
Apes 18 The Ten Commandments 21 The Agony and
the Ecstasy 22 The Greatest
Show on Earth

Heterodontosaurus
type: 8 dinosaur
10 ornithopod
location: 6 Africa
period: 8 Triassic

heterogeneous 5 mixed
6 motley, unlike, varied 7 diverse, jumbled 8 assorted
9 composite, disparate, divergent, unrelated 10 dissimilar,
variegated 11 diversified
13 miscellaneous

hew 2 ax 3 cut, lop 4 chop,
form, hack, mold 5 carve,
model, prune, sever, shape
6 chisel, cut out, devise 7 cut
down, fashion, whittle 8 chop
down 9 sculpture

He Who Gets Slapped
author: 14 Leonid Andreyev

he wrote it
Latin: 8 scripsit

hex 4 harm, jinx, sign 5 curse,
spell, witch 6 hoodoo, voodoo,
whammy 7 bewitch, evil eye,
ill wind, possess 8 sorcerer
9 sorceress 11 malediction

Hexateuch 27 first six books
of Old Testament
see also: 7 Books of 12 Old
Testament

heyday 4 acme 5 bloom, crest,
flush, prime, vigor 6 zenith
9 flowering, salad days

Heyerdahl, Thor
author of: 7 Kon-Tiki 16 The
Ra Expeditions

Hezekiah
father: 4 Ahaz
wife: 9 Hephzibah
means: 18 Jehovah
strengthens

Hi and Lois
creator: 9 Dik Browne
10 Mort Walker
character:
brother: 12 Beetle Bailey
children: 3 Dot 4 Chip
5 Ditto 6 Trixie
dog: 4 Dawg
friend: 7 Thirsty

hiatus 3 gap 4 void 5 blank,
break, lapse, space 6 lacuna,
vacuum 7 interim 8 interval
10 disruption 12 interruption

Hiawatha, The Song of
author: 24 Henry Wadsworth
Longfellow

character: 5 Nahma **7** Kwasind, Nokomis, Wenonah **8** Mondamin **9** Chibiabos, Minnehaha **11** Mudjekeewis **12** Pau-Puk-Keewis, Pearl-Feather

hibernate 5 sleep **6** retire **8** withdraw **13** become dormant

hibernating 6 asleep **7** dormant **8** inactive, sleeping **9** quiescent

Hibernia see **7** Ireland

hibiscus
varieties: 7 Chinese **8** Hawaiian, Japanese

Hicetaon
father: 8 Laomedon
brother: 5 Priam

hic jacet 8 here lies

hickory 5 Carya
varieties: 4 Pale, Sand **5** Broom, Swamp, Water **6** Pignut **7** Chinese **8** Mountain, Shagbark **9** Mockernut, Shellbark **10** White-heart **12** Small-fruited

Hicks, Edward
born: 11 Attleboro PA
artwork: 19 The Peaceable Kingdom

Hidatsa (Minitari, Gros Ventre)
language family: 6 Siouan
location: 7 Montana **11** North Dakota
related to: 6 Mandan **7** Arikara

hidden away 6 buried, cached **7** stashed **8** closeted, pocketed, secluded, secreted **9** concealed **10** out of sight **11** stashed away **12** inaccessible, undiscovered

hidden meaning 6 enigma, puzzle, riddle, secret **7** mystery

hidden motive
French: 13 arriere pensee

hide 4 mask, pelt, skin, veil **5** cache, cloak, cloud, cover **6** lie low, screen, shroud **7** conceal, curtain, leather, obscure, repress, seclude, secrete **8** disguise, suppress

hideaway 7 hideout, retreat **11** hiding place, secret place

hideous 4 grim, ugly, vile **5** awful **6** horrid, odious **7** ghastly, macabre **8** dreadful, gruesome, horrible, shocking **9** abhorrent, appalling, frightful, grotesque, loathsome, monstrous, repellent, repugnant, repulsive, revolting, sickening **10** abominable,

detestable, disgusting, horrendous

hiding place 5 cache **8** hideaway **9** hidey hole **10** repository **11** secret place

Hieronimo
character in: 17 The Spanish Tragedy
author: 3 Kyd

hier wird Deutsch gesprochen 18 German is spoken here

Higgins, Henry
character in: 9 Pygmalion **10** My Fair Lady
author: 4 Shaw

Higgs
character in: 7 Erewhon
author: 6 Butler

high 3 gay, top **4** main, tall **5** aloft, chief, far up, grand, great, jolly, lofty, merry, noble, prime, sharp, undue, way up **6** alpine, august, elated, jovial, joyful, joyous, shrill **7** capital, eminent, exalted, excited, extreme, gleeful, leading, notable, playful, primary, serious, soaring, soprano **8** cheerful, elevated, exultant, foremost, imposing, jubilant, mirthful, peerless, piercing, strident, superior, towering, uncurbed **9** ascendant, excellent, excessive, exuberant, important, overjoyed, principal, prominent, unbridled, uppermost **10** exorbitant, immoderate, inordinate, preeminent **11** cloud-capped, exaggerated, exhilarated, extravagant, high-pitched, illustrious, intemperate, predominant, significant, sky-scraping **12** earsplitting, high-reaching, lighthearted, unreasonable, unrestrained **13** consequential, distinguished

high-and-mighty 5 lofty **6** lordly **7** haughty **8** arrogant **9** imperious **11** overbearing

highborn 5 noble **8** highbred, wellborn **9** patrician **10** of high rank, upper-class **12** aristocratic, of high degree, silk-stocking **13** of gentle blood

highbred 5 noble, regal **6** lordly **7** refined **8** highborn, wellborn **9** patrician **11** aristocracy, blue-blooded

highbrow 4 snob **5** brain **7** bookish, Brahmin, egghead, elitist, erudite, scholar, thinker **8** cultured, mandarin, snobbish **9** scholarly **10** cultivated, double-dome, mastermind **12** intellectual **13** knowledgeable

highest good
Latin: 11 summum bonum

highest point
Latin: 11 ne plus ultra

high fashion
French: 12 haute couture

high-flown 4 wild **5** lofty, proud **6** absurd, florid, lordly, turgid, unreal **7** flowery, orotund, pompous **8** elevated, fabulous, inflated **9** bombastic, excessive, fantastic, grandiose **10** flamboyant, immoderate, inordinate, outrageous **11** exaggerated, extravagant, highfalutin, pretentious, sententious **12** magniloquent, preposterous, presumptuous, unreasonable, unrestrained **13** grandiloquent, self-important

High-German
language family: 12 Indo-European
branch: 8 Germanic
group: 15 Western Germanic
subgroup: 11 German-Dutch
division: 6 German **7** Yiddish

high-hat 5 aloof **6** formal, ladi-da, snooty **7** haughty **8** snobbish **12** supercilious

highjinks, hijinks 6 antics, capers, pranks, stunts **11** shenanigans **12** monkeyshines

highland, Highlands 4 rise **7** heights, plateau, uplands **8** headland **9** tableland **10** promontory **11** hill country **17** mountainous region
refers especially to:
8 Scotland

highlight 4 peak **6** accent, climax, stress **7** feature, point up **9** emphasize, high point, underline **10** accentuate, focal point, make bright

highly qualified 3 fit **4** able **7** trained **8** eligible, prepared, skillful **9** practiced **10** proficient **11** experienced **12** accomplished

highly regarded 6 prized **7** admired, revered **8** esteemed **9** respected, treasured **13** well thought of

highly valued 4 dear **5** loved **6** adored **7** beloved, revered **8** esteemed, precious **9** cherished, treasured

highly visible 7 glaring, obvious **8** distinct **9** prominent **11** conspicuous, outstanding

high-minded 4 fair, just **5** lofty, moral, noble **6** honest, worthy **7** ethical, sincere, upright **8** truthful, virtuous **9** exemplary, honorable, reputable, righteous, uncorrupt **10** chivalrous, idealistic, principled, scrupulous **13** conscientious, square-dealing

High Noon
director: 13 Fred Zinnemann **cast: 10** Gary Cooper (Will Kane), Grace Kelly **12** Lloyd Bridges **14** Thomas Mitchell **score: 14** Dimitri Tiomkin **Oscar for: 5** actor (Cooper)

high old time 4 ball, lark **5** fling, revel, spree **8** escapade

high-pitched 5 acute, sharp **6** shrill **7** clarion, squeaky **8** piercing

high place 4 hill, peak, rise **5** bluff, cliff, knoll, ridge **6** height, summit, upland **7** hillock, hummock, plateau **8** eminence, mountain **9** elevation **10** prominence, promontory

high point, highest point **3** cap, top **4** acme, apex, peak **5** crest, crown **6** apogee, climax, height, heyday, summit, tiptop, vertex, zenith **8** eminence, pinnacle **9** flowering **10** prominence **11** culmination

high position 4 note **8** eminence, high rank, standing **9** supremacy **10** ascendancy, importance, notability, prominence **11** distinction, preeminence

high-powered 7 driving, dynamic **8** forceful **9** ambitious, assertive, energetic, go-getting **10** aggressive **11** hard-driving

high praise 5 kudos, paean **6** eulogy **7** hosanna, plaudit **8** encomium **9** laudation, panegyric **11** acclamation

high-priced 4 dear, high **6** costly, pricey **9** expensive **10** exorbitant, overpriced **11** extravagant

high-principled 5 moral, noble **6** chaste, honest, worthy **7** ethical, upright **9** honorable, reputable **10** idealistic **11** responsible, trustworthy **13** conscientious

high quality 5 merit **7** quality **9** greatness **10** excellence, perfection **11** distinction, superiority

high-ranking 3 top **5** grand, great, lofty, regal, royal **6** august **7** eminent, exalted, supreme **8** elevated, esteemed, imposing **9** important, paramount, venerable **10** preeminent **11** illustrious **13** distinguished

High Sierra
director: 10 Raoul Walsh **cast: 9** Ida Lupino **10** Alan Curtis, Joan Leslie **13** Arthur Kennedy **14** Humphrey Bogart (Mad Dog Earle) **remade as: 17** Colorado Territory **19** I Died a Thousand Times

high society 5 elite **9** haut monde, top drawer **11** aristocracy **14** creme de la creme **French: 9** haut monde

High Society
director: 14 Charles Walters **cast: 10** Bing Crosby, Grace Kelly **11** Celeste Holm **12** Frank Sinatra, Louis Calhern **14** Louis Armstrong **score: 10** Cole Porter **remake of: 20** The Philadelphia Story **song: 8** True Love **10** Did You Evah? **16** You're Sensational

high-speed 4 fast **5** quick, rapid, swift **6** speedy **7** express

high-spirited 5 vital **6** lively **8** animated **9** exuberant, vivacious **12** effervescent, enthusiastic

high spirits 5 vigor **6** gaiety **7** delight, elation **8** gladness, vitality, vivacity **9** animation **10** enthusiasm, exaltation, excitement, joyousness, liveliness **12** exhilaration **16** lightheartedness

high-strung 4 edgy **5** jumpy, moody, tense **6** uneasy **7** jittery, nervous, uptight **8** neurotic, restless, skittish **9** emotional, excitable, impatient, wrought-up **10** hysterical **13** oversensitive, temperamental **14** easily agitated, hypersensitive

High Tor
author: 15 Maxwell Anderson

highway 7 freeway, parkway, thruway **8** hard road, highroad, main road, speedway, turnpike **9** paved road **10** expressway, interstate, main artery **12** four-lane road, thoroughfare **British: 9** coach road, royal road **12** King's highway **13** Queen's highway

highwayman 5 crook, thief **6** bandit, outlaw, robber **7** brigand, footpad

hike 4 rise, roam, rove, trek, walk **5** leg it, march, raise, tramp **6** draw up, hoof it, jerk up, pull up, ramble, trudge, wander **7** hitch up, raise up **8** addition, increase **9** expansion **10** escalation **12** augmen-

tation **13** journey on foot **14** go by shank's mare

Hilaira
vocation: 9 priestess **priestess of: 7** Artemis **father: 9** Leucippus **abducted by: 6** Castor

hilarious 3 gay **5** jolly, merry, noisy **6** jocund, jovial, joyful, joyous, lively **7** comical, gleeful, riotous **8** jubilant, mirthful **9** exuberant, laughable, very funny **10** boisterous, hysterical, rollicking, uproarious, vociferous **11** exhilarated **12** high-spirited **13** highly amusing **14** laugh-provoking

hilarity 3 fun, gig, joy **4** glee, riot **5** laugh, mirth, noisy **6** comedy, gaiety, giggle, levity **7** chortle, chuckle, jollity **8** hysteria, laughter **9** amusement, funniness, joviality, jubilance, merriment **10** exuberance **12** exhilaration, humorousness **14** uproariousness

Hilbert, David
field: 8 geometry **11** mathematics **nationality: 6** German **formulated: 12** modern axioms

Hilda Lessways
author: 13 Arnold Bennett

hill 4 bank, dune, heap, pile, ramp, rise **5** bluff, butte, cliff, climb, grade, knoll, mound, mount, slope **6** height **7** hillock, hilltop, hummock, incline, upgrade **8** eminence, foothill, highland, hillside **9** acclivity, declivity, downgrade, elevation **10** prominence, promontory

Hill, Arthur
born: 6 Canada **7** Melfort **12** Saskatchewan **roles: 13** All the Way Home **15** The Ugly American **17** Look Homeward Angel **25** Who's Afraid of Virginia Woolf?

Hill, George Roy
director of: 8 The Sting (Oscar) **23** The World According to Garp **29** Butch Cassidy and the Sundance Kid

Hiller, Arthur
director of: 25 The Americanization of Emily

hillock 4 hill, rise **5** knoll, mound **7** hummock **8** eminence

Hill Street Blues
character: 5 LaRue, Renko **9** Bobby Hill, Jablonski, Joe

Coffey, Lucy Bates **10** Fay Furillo, Mick Belker, Washington **11** (Lt) Norman Buntz **12** Howard Hunter, (Captain) Frank Furillo **13** Henry Goldblum **14** Joyce Davenport
cast: **8** Joe Spano **10** Bruce Weitz, Ed Marinaro, Kiel Martin **11** Betty Thomas, Charles Haid, Dennis Franz **12** Robert Prosky **13** James B Sikking, Michael Warren, Veronica Hamel **14** Taurean Blacque **15** Daniel J Travanti

Hilton, James
author of: **11** Lost Horizon **14** Good-Bye Mr Chips

Himeros
origin: **5** Greek
god of: **12** erotic desire
associated with: **4** Eros

Hind see **5** India

Hind and the Panther, The
author: **10** John Dryden

Hindarfjall see **8** Hindfell

Hindemith, Paul
born: **5** Hanau **7** Germany
composer of: **8** The Demon **9** Cardillac **10** Heriodiade **12** Ludus Tonalis, Neues vom Tage, News of the Day **13** Sancta Susanna **14** Cupid and Psyche, Mathis Der Maler **15** In Praise of Music **17** Murder Hope of Women **18** Die Harmonie der Welt, Nobilissima Visione **19** The Four Temperaments **23** Morder Hoffnung der Frauen

hinder 3 bar **4** curb, foil, stay, stop **5** block, check, delay, deter, spike, stall **6** arrest, detain, fetter, hamper, hobble, hog-tie, hold up, impede, retard, stifle, stymie, thwart **7** inhibit **8** encumber, handicap, hold back, obstruct, restrain, slow down **9** frustrate, hamstring **13** interfere with

Hindfell
also: **11** Hindarfjall
origin: **12** Scandinavian
mountain slept on by: **8** Brynhild

Hindi
language family: **12** Indo-European
branch: **11** Indo-Iranian
group: **5** Indic
official language of: **5** India

hindmost 4 last, rear **7** tail end **12** farthest back

hindpart 4 tail **6** far end **7** rear end **8** backside, buttocks, haunches **9** afterpart, posterior

hindquarters 4 rear, rump **7** rear end, tail end **8** back legs, backside, buttocks, haunches **9** posterior

hindrance 3 bar **4** clog, curb, snag **5** catch **6** fetter **7** barrier, shackle **8** blockade, blockage, handicap, obstacle **9** barricade, restraint, retardant **10** constraint, difficulty, impediment, limitation **11** encumbrance, obstruction, restriction **12** interference **14** stumbling block

hinge 4 hang, rest, turn **5** pivot, swing **6** depend **7** be due to **9** arise from **10** result from **11** be subject to, emanate from **13** revolve around

hint 3 bit, jot, tip **4** clue, idea, iota **5** grain, imply, pinch, tinge, touch, trace, whiff **6** little, notion, tip off **7** inkling, pointer, signify, soupcon, suggest, whisper **8** allusion, indicate, innuendo, intimate **9** insinuate, suspicion **10** impression, indication, intimation, smattering, suggestion **11** implication, indirection, insinuation **12** flea in the ear, slight amount **13** word to the wise

hinted 7 implied, oblique **8** implicit, indirect **9** suggested

hinterland 6 sticks **7** boonies, country **8** interior, midlands **9** backwater, backwoods, boondocks, rural area **11** countryside

Hiordis
also: **7** Hjordis
origin: **12** Scandinavian
mentioned in: **8** Volsunga
husband: **7** Sigmund
son: **6** Sigurd

Hippalectryon
form: **7** monster
head and forelegs of: **5** horse
legs, tail and body of: **4** cock

Hippocampus
form: **7** monster
body of: **5** horse
tail of: **4** fish

Hippocrene
form: **6** spring
location: **12** Mount Helicon

Hippocurius
epithet of: **8** Poseidon
means: **12** horse tending

Hippodamas
daugher: **8** Perimele
drowned: **8** Perimele

hippodrome 5 arena **6** circus **7** stadium **8** coliseum

Hippogriff
form: **7** monster
combined: **5** horse **7** griffin

Hippolochus
father: **11** Bellerophon
son: **7** Glaucus

Hippolyta see **9** Hippolyte

Hippolyte
also: **7** Antiope **9** Hippolyta
queen of: **7** Amazons
husband: **7** Theseus
son: **10** Hippolytus
Hercules stole her: **6** girdle

Hippolytus
author: **9** Euripides
character: **7** Artemis, Phaedra, Theseus **9** Aphrodite

Hippolytus
father: **7** Theseus
mother: **9** Hippolyta
stepmother: **7** Phaedra
loved by: **7** Phaedra
killed by: **8** Poseidon

Hippomedon
member of: **18** Seven against Thebes

Hippomenes
suitor of: **8** Atalanta
son: **13** Parthenopaeus

Hipponous
vocation: **7** warrior
home: **4** Troy
daughter: **8** Periboea
killed by: **8** Achilles

Hippothous
king of: **7** Arcadia
father: **8** Poseidon
mother: **5** Alope

hire 3 fee, get, let, pay **4** cost, gain, rent **5** lease, wages **6** charge, employ, engage, income, obtain, profit, retain, reward, salary, secure, take on **7** appoint, charter, payment, procure, stipend **8** earnings, receipts **9** emolument **10** recompense **12** compensation, remuneration

hireling 4 goon, thug **6** flunky, lackey, menial, minion, stooge **7** gorilla **8** henchman, retainer **9** strong-arm **10** hatchet man

Hiroshima
author: **10** John Hersey

hirsute 5 bushy, downy, hairy, nappy, wooly **6** shaggy, woolly **7** bearded, bristly, prickly, unshorn **8** bristled, unshaven **9** whiskered **11** bewhiskered

His Girl Friday
director: **11** Howard Hawks
cast: **9** Cary Grant **12** Gene Lockhart, Ralph Bellamy **15** Rosalind Russell

remake of: 12 The Front Page

Hispania *see* **5** Spain

hiss 3 boo **4** mock, razz **6** deride, heckle, hoot at, jeer at, revile **7** catcall, scoff at, sneer at **9** shout down **10** Bronx cheer **16** give the raspberry

histology
study of: **6** tissue

---

historian
American: **4** Webb **5** Adams **6** Brooks, De Voto, Durant, Fisher, Miller, Nevins, Sparks, Turner **7** Morison, Parkman, Taussig **8** Bancroft, Channing, Prescott, Robinson **10** Hofstadter
British: **4** Bede (the Venerable) **6** Gibbon, Turner **7** Toynbee **8** Macaulay **9** Trevelyan
Chinese: **10** Ssu-ma Ch'ien, Ssu-Ma Kuang
French: **5** Bayle, Blanc, Bloch, Taine **7** Braudel **8** Mabillon, Michelet, Voltaire **11** Tocqueville
German: **5** Ranke **7** Mommsen **8** Spengler **10** Burckhardt, Treitschke
Greek: **8** Polybius **9** Herodotus **10** Thucydides
Islamic: **8** al Tabari **10** Ibn Khaldun
Italian: **4** Polo, Vico **5** Croce **11** Machiavelli **12** Guicciardini
Latin: **4** Livy **7** Sallust, Tacitus
Scottish: **7** Carlyle

---

historic 5 famed **7** notable **8** renowned **9** memorable, well-known **10** celebrated **11** outstanding

historical 4 past, real, true **6** actual, bygone, former **7** ancient, factual **8** attested, recorded **9** authentic **10** chronicled, documented

historical period 3 age, era **4** date, time **5** epoch, stage

history 4 epic, saga, tale **5** story **6** annals, change, growth, record, resume, review **7** account, the past **8** old times **9** chronicle, days of old, narration, narrative, portrayal, tradition, yesterday **10** bygone days, days of yore, olden

times, the old days, yesteryear **11** bygone times, development, former times, local events, major events, world events **12** actual events **13** an unusual past, human progress **14** military action, national events, recapitulation **15** political change

History of Colonel Jacque, The
author: **11** Daniel Defoe

History of Henry VII
author: **12** Francis Bacon

History of Mr Polly, The
author: **7** H G Wells
character: **6** Miriam **8** Uncle Jim **13** The Plump Woman

History of the English-Speaking Peoples, A
author: **17** Winston S Churchill

His Toy, His Dream, His Rest
author: **12** John Berryman

histrionics 4 fuss **6** acting, tirade **7** bluster, bombast **8** outburst **9** dramatics, hamminess, staginess, theatrics **10** dramaturgy, playacting **11** performance, rodomontade **13** melodramatics, temper tantrum, theatricality **16** ranting and raving

hit *see box*

hit back 7 counter, get even, pay back **9** fight back, retaliate **10** strike back

hitch 3 tie, tug **4** curb, draw, halt, haul, hike, jerk, knot, loop, pull, snag, stop, yank, yoke **5** catch, check, clamp, delay, raise, tying **6** attach, couple, fasten, mishap, secure, tether **7** bracket, connect, harness, joining, mistake, problem, trouble **8** coupling, handicap, make fast, obstacle **9** attaching, fastening, hindrance, mischance, restraint **10** connection, difficulty, impediment, limitation **11** restriction **12** complication, interruption, loop together, put in harness **14** stumbling block

Hitchcock, Alfred
director of: **6** Frenzy, Marnie, Psycho **7** Rebecca, Vertigo **8** Lifeboat, The Birds **9** Notorious, Suspicion **10** Family Plot, Rear Window, Spellbound **13** To Catch a Thief **14** Dial M for Murder, Shadow of a Doubt **15** The Lady Vanishes **16** North by Northwest **17** Strangers on a Train **18** The Thirty-Nine

---

hit 3 bat, jab, lob, rap, tap **4** bang, bash, beat, belt, blow, boon, bump, butt, clip, club, coup, cuff, damn, drub, find, flog, hurt, move, pelt, poke, slam, slap, slug, sock, stir, swat **5** abash, baste, clout, crack, crush, flail, knock, paste, pound, punch, reach, rouse, smack, smash, smite, thump, touch, upset, whack **6** affect, arouse, assail, attack, attain, batter, cudgel, effect, impact, incite, pommel, revile, strike, thrash, thwack, wallop, winner **7** achieve, assault, censure, clobber, condemn, execute, godsend, impress, inflame, provoke, quicken, realize, shatter, success, triumph, trounce, victory **8** arrive at, bang into, blessing, bring off, denounce, lambaste, overcome, reproach **9** criticize, deal a blow, devastate, lash out at, overwhelm, sensation, smash into **11** collide with, connect with, deal a stroke, strike out at **12** go straight to **13** make a bull's-eye, send to the mark **14** popular success, strike together **16** mount an offensive

---

Steps **19** The Trouble with Harry **20** Foreign Correspondent

hither 2 on **4** here, near **5** close **6** closer, nearby, nearer, onward **7** close by, forward **8** over here **11** to this place **12** to the speaker

hitherto 6 ere now, hereto **7** thus far, till now, up to now **8** until now **10** before this, heretofore

Hitler, Adolf
author of: **9** Mein Kampf

hit man 6 killer, slayer **8** assassin, hired gun, murderer **11** executioner **12** exterminator

Hitman
nickname of: **12** Thomas Hearns

hit-or-miss 3 lax **6** casual, fitful **7** aimless, cursory **8** slapdash **9** haphazard **10** incomplete **11** purposeless, superficial, unorganized **12** unsystematic **15** catch-as-catch-can

hive 3 hub 5 heart 6 center, colony 7 cluster 9 busy place 11 swarm of bees

Hjordis *see* 7 Hiordis

Hliod *see* 4 Liod

H M S Pinafore
subtitle: 23 The Lass That Loved a Sailor
operetta by: 18 Gilbert and Sullivan
character: 11 Dick Deadeye 14 Ralph Rackstraw 15 Captain Corcoran, Little Buttercup, Sir Joseph Porter 17 Josephine Corcoran

Hoagland, Edward
author of: 15 African Calliope 17 The Tugman's Passage

hoar 3 old 4 aged, rime 5 frost, moldy, mushy, passe, stale, white 6 old hat 7 ancient, antique, elderly, grayish 8 grizzled 9 out of date

hoard 4 fund, heap, mass, pile 5 amass, buy up, cache, lay up, store 6 save up, supply 7 acquire, collect, lay away, reserve 8 quantity 9 amassment, gathering, stockpile, store away 10 accumulate, collection 12 accumulation

hoarse 5 gruff, harsh, husky, raspy, rough 6 croaky 7 cracked, rasping, raucous, throaty 8 gravelly, guttural, scratchy

hoary 3 old 4 aged, gray, hoar 5 dated, passe, white 6 grayed, old hat 7 ancient, antique, grizzly 8 grizzled, whitened 9 out-of-date 11 gray with age 12 white with age

hoax 3 gyp 4 bilk, dupe, fake, fool, gull, yarn 5 bluff, cheat, cozen, fraud, prank, spoof, trick 6 canard, delude, humbug, take in 7 deceive, defraud, fiction, mislead, swindle 8 hoodwink 9 bamboozle, chicanery, deception, fish story, victimize 10 hocus-pocus

Hoban, James
architect of: 13 The White House, Great Hotel (Washington, DC)

Hobbes, Thomas
author of: 9 Leviathan

Hobbit, The
part of: 14 Lord of the Rings
author: 10 J R R Tolkien

hobble 4 bind, gimp, halt, limp 5 block, check, cramp 6 fetter, hamper, hinder, hog-tie, impede, lumber, stymie, thwart, toddle 7 inhibit, manacle,

shackle, shamble, shuffle, stagger, stumble 8 encumber, handicap, hold back, lame gait, obstruct, restrain, restrict 9 constrain, frustrate, hamstring 10 uneven gait, walk lamely 13 interfere with

hobby 7 pastime, pursuit 8 sideline 9 amusement, avocation, diversion 10 relaxation 13 entertainment 14 divertissement

hobbyhorse 5 hobby 7 pastime 8 interest, toy horse 9 diversion 10 enthusiasm 11 distraction 12 rocking horse

hobgoblin 3 imp 5 bogey 6 goblin 7 bugaboo

hobnob 3 mix 4 club 6 mingle 7 consort, hang out 9 associate, rub elbows 10 fraternize

hobo 3 beg, bum 5 stiff, tramp 6 beggar, cadger, loafer 7 drifter, migrant, moocher, vagrant 8 derelict, vagabond, wanderer 9 scrounger 11 beachcomber

hoc est 6 this is

Ho Chi Minh City
formerly: 6 Saigon
river: 6 Saigon
delta: 6 Mekong
former capital of: 9 Indochina 11 Cochin China 12 South Vietnam

hockey
athlete: 8 Bobby Orr, Brad Park 9 Bobby Hull, Ken Dryden, Mike Bossy 10 Doug Harvey, Eddie Shore, Ed Giacomin, Gordie Howe, Guy Lafleur, Ray Bearque, Rod Gilbert, Stan Mikita 11 Bobby Clarke, Brian Leetch, Denis Potvin, Eric Lindros, Jean Ratelle, Mark Messier 12 Emile Francis, Jean Beliveau, Marcel Dionne, Mario Lemieux, Phil Esposito, Wayne Gretzky 13 Bernard Parent, Jacques Plante, Larry Robinson, Pat La Fontaine 14 Alex Delvecchio, Maurice Richard 15 Bernie Geoffrion

hockey team *see box*

hocus-pocus 4 bosh, bull, hoax, sham 5 chant, charm, cheat, magic, spell 6 bunkum, deceit, fakery, humbug 7 con game, hogwash, rubbish, swindle 8 delusion, flimflam, tommyrot, trickery 9 deception, moonshine, poppycock 10 dishonesty, flapdoodle, hankypanky, magic spell, magic words, mumbo jumbo, subterfuge 11 bewitchment, incantation, legerdemain, magic tricks

hockey team
Anaheim: 11 Mighty Ducks
Boston: 6 Bruins
Buffalo: 6 Sabres
Calgary: 6 Flames
Chicago: 10 Black Hawks
Colorado: 9 Avalanche
formerly: 15 Quebec Nordiques
Dallas: 5 Stars
Detroit: 8 Red Wings
Edmonton: 6 Oilers
Florida: 8 Panthers
Hartford: 7 Whalers
Los Angeles: 5 Kings
Montreal: 9 Canadiens
New Jersey: 6 Devils
New York: 7 Rangers 9 Islanders
Ottawa: 8 Senators
Philadelphia: 6 Flyers
Pittsburgh: 8 Penguins
St Louis: 5 Blues
San Jose: 6 Sharks
Tampa Bay: 9 Lightning
Toronto: 10 Maple Leafs
Vancouver: 7 Canucks
Washington: 8 Capitals
Winnipeg: 4 Jets

12 fiddle-faddle, magic formula 13 sleight of hand

Hoder
also: 5 Hodur
origin: 12 Scandinavian
brother: 5 Baldr 6 Balder, Baldur
father: 4 Odin 5 Othin
killed: 5 Baldr 6 Balder, Baldur

hodgepodge, hotchpotch 3 mix 4 hash, mess 6 jumble, medley, muddle 7 melange, mixture 8 mishmash 9 composite, confusion, patchwork, potpourri 10 miscellany

Hodur *see* 5 Hoder

Hoenir
origin: 12 Scandinavian
race: 5 Vanir
created: 3 Ask 5 Embla

Hoff, Jacobus Hendricus van't
field: 9 chemistry
nationality: 5 Dutch
researched: 7 gas laws 10 carbon atom 14 thermodynamics
awarded: 10 Nobel Prize

Hoffman, Dustin
born: 12 Los Angeles CA
roles: 5 Lenny 6 Ishtar 7 Tootsie 8 Papillon 9 Ratso Rizzo 11 The Graduate 12 Little Big Man 14 Kramer vs Kramer (Oscar), Midnight Cowboy 19 All the President's Men

Hofmann, Hans
born: 7 Germany
11 Weissenberg
artwork: 6 Spring 7 The
Gate 13 Effervescence
14 Fantasia in Blue, Ma-
genta and Blue 16 Sanctum
Sanctorum

Hofstadter, Richard
author of: 14 The Age of
Reform

hog 3 pig, sow 4 arch, boar,
trim 5 broom, sheep, swine
6 gorger, porker 7 baconer,
glutton, take all 9 razorback
10 locomotive

Hogan, Paul
country: 9 Australia
roles: 10 Mick Dundee
15 Crocodile Dundee

Hogan's Heroes
character: 7 (Peter) Newkirk
8 Lt Carter 10 Sgt (Hans)
Schultz 11 Louis LeBeau
14 Col Robert Hogan 15 Col
Wilhelm Klink
cast: 8 Bob Crane 10 John
Banner, Larry Hovis
11 Robert Clary 13 Richard
Dawson 15 Werner
Klemperer

Hogarth, William
born: 6 London 7 England
artwork: 12 Captain Coram
14 A Rake's Progress
15 Marriage a la Mode, The
Beggar's Opera 16 A Har-
lot's Progress 19 Garrick as
Richard III

hogshead 3 keg, tun, vat
4 butt, cask, drum 6 barrel

hogwash 3 rot 4 bull, bunk
5 hokum, hooey, stuff
6 bunkum, drivel, hot air,
humbug 7 baloney, blather,
spinach, twaddle 8 claptrap,
nonsense, tommyrot 9 poppycock 10 applesauce 11 foolishness 13 horsefeathers 16 stuff
and nonsense

hoi polloi 6 rabble, the mob
7 the herd 8 canaille, populace, riffraff, the crowd, the
plebs 9 the masses, the proles,
the vulgar 12 commonalty
12 the multitude 14 the lower
orders, the proletariat, the
rank and file 15 the common
people, the lower classes, the
working class

hoist 4 lift 5 heave, raise, run
up 6 bear up, pull up, take
up, uplift 7 elevate, raise up,
upraise 9 bear aloft

Hokan
language family: 17 Hokan-
Coahuiltecan
subgroup: 4 Pomo, Seri,
Yana 5 Karok, Washo, Yu-

man 7 Chontal, Chumash,
Esselen, Jicaque 8 Subtiaba
9 Chimariko 14 Shasta-
Achomawi
tribe: 8 Achomawi

Hokan-Coahuiltecan
language branch: 5 Hokan
12 Coahuiltecan 17 Sub-
tiaba-Tlappanec

Hokusai, Katsushika
born: 3 Edo 5 Japan, Tokyo
artwork: 5 Crabs, Manga
10 Waterfalls 11 Chushin-
gura 25 Thirty-six Views of
Mount Fuji

Holabird, William
partner: 11 Martin Roche
architect of: 12 Gage Building 13 Cable Building,
Crerar Library (City Hall,
Chicago) 14 Tacoma Build-
ing 15 McClurg Building
17 Marquette Building

Holbein, Hans (the Elder)
born: 7 Germany 8 Augsburg
son: 11 Hans Holbein (the
Younger)
artwork: 11 St Sebastian
14 Fountain of Life
18 Kaisheim Altarpiece
31 Presentation of Christ in
the Temple

**Holbein, Hans (the
Younger)**
born: 7 Germany 8 Augsburg
father: 11 Hans Holbein (the
Elder)
artwork: 7 Erasmus 9 Henry
VIII 11 Jane Seymour
12 Dance of Death 13 The
Dead Christ

hold *see box*

hold a candle to 5 equal,
match 6 be up to 7 compare

8 approach 10 be as good as
11 come close to, compete
with 12 be comparable
14 bear comparison

hold against 6 resent
8 begrudge

hold back 3 lag 4 curb, deny,
keep, slow 5 check, dally,
limit, stall 6 arrest, bridle, falter, refuse 7 contain, inhibit,
keep out, reserve, retrain
8 hesitate, keep back, maintain, restrain, withhold
9 constrain

hold close 3 hug 5 clasp
6 cuddle, harbor 7 cherish,
embrace, snuggle

Holden, William
real name: 23 William
Franklin Beedle Jr
nickname: 4 Bill
born: 9 O'Fallon IL
roles: 6 Picnic 7 Network, Sabrina 9 Golden Boy 13 Born
Yesterday 14 The Country
Girl 15 Stalag Seventeen
(Oscar), Sunset Boulevard
23 The Bridge on the River
Kwai

hold fast 4 fuse, hold 5 cling,
stick 6 adhere

hold firmly 4 grip 5 clasp,
grasp 6 clench, clinch, clutch
10 grab hold of

hold forth 7 expound 9 discourse, expatiate

hold in abeyance 5 table
6 recess, shelve 7 suspend
8 lay aside, postpone

hold in bondage 7 control,
enchain, enslave, entrall
8 dominate 9 subjugate
12 make a slave of

hold 4 bear, bind, bond, curb, deem, grip, halt, have, hilt,
keep, knob, lock, prop, rule, stay, sway, take, urge 5 block,
brace, carry, check, clasp, cling, count, defer, grasp, guard,
limit, offer, power, shaft, shore, stall, stand, stick, strap,
think, unite, watch 6 adhere, affirm, assert, assume, cleave,
clinch, clutch, deduct, detain, direct, enfold, handle, hinder,
hold up, join in, manage, occupy, reckon, regard, retain,
submit, take in, tender, thwart, uphold 7 advance, believe,
carry on, command, conduct, confine, contain, control, declare, embrace, enclose, enforce, execute, hold off, include,
inhibit, mastery, possess, present, presume, prevent, profess,
propose, protect, repress, reserve, support, suppose, surmise,
suspend, toehold, venture 8 advocate, conceive, conclude,
consider, engage in, foothold, handhold, hold back, hold
down, leverage, maintain, obligate, postpone, purchase, put
forth, restrain, restrict, set aside, suppress, withhold 9 advantage, anchorage, authority, be in force, dominance, forestall,
frustrate, influence, keep valid, ownership, stay fixed, stick
fast 10 ascendancy, attachment, desist from, domination, possession, put forward, understand 11 accommodate, preside
over

holdings 6 assets 8 property 10 securities 11 commodities

hold in high regard 5 honor, prize, value 6 admire, esteem, revere 7 cherish, respect 8 look up to, treasure, venerate 10 rate highly, set store by 13 think highly of 18 attach importance to

hold one's own 4 cope 6 manage 7 contend 11 be a match for 20 maintain one's position 22 keep one's head above water

hold rapt 5 charm 7 beguile, bewitch, enchant 8 enthrall, entrance 9 captivate, enrapture, fascinate, spellbind, transport

hold to 4 bind 8 obligate

hold together 4 bind, fuse, glue, hold, join 5 cling, stick, unite 6 cement, cohere 7 combine 11 consolidate

holdup 3 rob 4 bear, halt, stay, stop 5 delay, heist, steal, theft 6 hijack, retain, uphold 7 robbery, stickup, support, sustain 8 stoppage 9 hindrance 12 interruption

hold up 4 prop, slow 5 block, brace, check, delay 6 bear up, detain, endure, hinder, impede, manage 7 bolster, present, stand up, support, sustain 8 keep back, obstruct 13 rob at gunpoint

hold up under 4 bear 6 endure, manage 8 tolerate

hold warmly 3 hug 5 clasp 6 cuddle 7 embrace, snuggle

hole 3 den, gap, pit 4 brig, cage, cave, flaw, keep, lair, rent, slit, slot 5 break, crack, fault, shaft 6 breach, burrow, cavern, cavity, crater, defect, dugout, lockup, pocket, prison, tunnel 7 dungeon, fallacy, opening, orifice, slammer 8 aperture, dark cell, puncture 9 concavity, open space 10 depression, excavation 11 discrepancy, hollow place, indentation, perforation 13 inconsistency

Holgrave, Mr
character in: 24 The House of the Seven Gables
author: 9 Hawthorne

holiday *see box*

holiness 8 sanctity 9 godliness 10 sacredness 11 blessedness, saintliness

Holland *see* 11 Netherlands

Holle
origin: 8 Germanic

holiday 3 gay 4 fete, gala 6 cheery, fiesta, joyful, joyous, junket, outing 7 festive, holy day, jubilee 8 cheerful, feast day, festival, vacation 11 celebrating, celebration, merrymaking
American: 6 Easter 8 Arbor Day, Labor Day 9 Christmas (Dec 25), Halloween (Oct 31) 10 Father's Day, Good Friday, Mother's Day 11 Columbus Day, Election Day, Memorial Day, New Year's Day (Jan 1), Veterans' Day (Nov 11) 12 Children's Day, Thanksgiving 15 Independence Day (July 4), St Valentine's Day (Feb 14) 23 National Grandparents' Day
   birthday: 8 Lincoln's 11 Robert E Lee's (Jan 19), Washington's 17 Martin Luther King's (Jan 15)
   Hawaiian: 13 Kamehameha Day (June 11)
British: 8 Hogmanay (Dec 31) 9 Boxing Day (Dec 26) 11 Harvest Home 12 Guy Fawkes Day (Nov 5), Twelfth Night (Jan 5) 14 Queen's Birthday (June) 15 Commonwealth Day (May 24), Mothering Sunday 19 Feast of Saint Swithin (July 15)
Canadian: 11 Victoria Day 14 Queen's Birthday, Remembrance Day
Chinese: 7 New Year 15 Lantern Festival 17 Confucius' Birthday (Sept 28) 18 Dragon Boat Festival
French: 11 Bastille Day (May 14)
German: 11 Oktoberfest
Greek: 7 Genesia 11 Feast of Pots
Indian: 4 Holi 6 Basant, Diwali (New Year) 17 Hindu fire festival 22 Mahatma Gandhi's Birthday (Oct 2)
Irish: 16 Saint Patrick's Day (March 17)
Italian: 13 Liberation Day (April 25)
Japanese: 11 Hina-Matsuri 12 Children's Day (May 5), Feast of Dolls (March 3) 15 Constitution Day (May 3) 17 Girls' Doll Festival
Jewish: 5 Purim 6 Sukkot 7 Shavuot, Sukkoth 8 Hanukkah, Passover 9 Yom Kippur 12 Rosh Hashanah 20 Hamishah Assar B'Shevat, The New Year of the Trees 21 Feast of the Tabernacles
Korean: 6 Ch'usok
Latin American: 12 Day of the Race
Moslem: 7 Mouloud 8 Id-al-Adha, Id-al-Fitr 12 Maulid-an-Nabi 14 month of Ramadan
religious: 6 Advent 7 Lady Day (Mar 25) 8 Epiphany, Shabuoth 9 Candlemas, Mardi Gras, Martinmas (Nov 11), Pentecost 10 Whitsunday 11 All Souls' Day (Nov 2) 12 Ascension Day, Ash Wednesday, Feast of Weeks 13 Shrove Tuesday, Trinity Sunday 15 Annunciation Day (Mar 25) 16 Feast of All Saints 20 Feast of Corpus Christi 23 Day of Our Lady of Guadalupe (Dec 12) 27 Purification of the Virgin Mary 30 Feast of the Immaculate Conception (Dec 8)
Roman: 7 Feralia 10 Saturnalia
Scottish: 8 Hogmanay 12 Candlemas Day 19 Festival of the Virgin
South American: 21 Simon Bolivar's Birthday (July 24)
Sri Lankan: 5 Wesak
Soviet Union: 6 May Day (May 1) 14 Lenin's Birthday (April 22) 39 Day of the Great October Socialist Revolution (Nov 7)
Swedish: 13 Santa Lucia Day (Dec 13)
Thailand: 11 Visakha Puja

goddess of: 4 moon
corresponds to: 7 Berchta, Perchta
form: 5 witch

holler 4 bark, roar, yell 5 gripe, shout 6 bellow, cry out, grouse 8 complain 9 hue and cry

Holliday, Judy
real name: 11 Judith Tuvim
born: 9 New York NY
roles: 8 Adam's Rib 13 Born Yesterday (Oscar) 15 Bells Are Ringing

Hollinshed, Raphael
author of: 37 Chronicles of

England Scotland and Ireland

hollow 3 dip, low, rut **4** cave, dale, deep, dell, dent, dull, glen, hole, sink, vain, vale, void **5** ditch, empty, false, muted **6** cavern, cavity, crater, dig out, dimple, furrow, futile, groove, pocket, sunken, vacant, vacuum, valley **7** channel, concave, useless **8** crevasse, empty out, excavate, gouge out, indented, not solid, nugatory, rumbling, scoop out, specious, unfilled **9** cavernous, concavity, deceptive, depressed, fruitless, pointless, valueless, worthless **10** depression, profitless, sepulchral, unavailing, unresonant **11** indentation, meaningless, nonresonant **12** unprofitable **13** curving inward, disappointing, reverberating **14** expressionless, unsatisfactory **15** inconsequential

Holloway, Stanley
    born: 6 London **7** England
    roles: 10 My Fair Lady **15** Alfred Doolittle **18** The Lavender Hill Mob

Hollow Men
    author: 7 T S Eliot

hollowness 4 void **6** vacuum **7** vacancy **9** emptiness

hollow out 4 bore **5** drill **6** dig out **8** carve out, gouge out, scoop out **9** chisel out **13** tunnel through

holly 4 Ilex
    varieties: 3 box, sea **4** dune **5** Cuban, Dutch, dwarf, false, Furin, Kashi, swamp, Tsuru **6** desert, horned, Oregon, Sarvis, Soyogo, summer **7** African, Chinese, English, Georgia, Madeira **8** American, European, hedgehog, Japanese, Kurogane, mountain **9** box-leaved, Highclere, miniature, moonlight, porcupine, Singapore **10** Costa Rican, luster-leaf, West Indian **11** large-leaved, Puerto Rican, screw-leaved **12** Canary Island, gold hedgehog, myrtle-leaved, smooth-leaved **14** silver hedgehog

hollyhock 6 mallow **7** Antwerp, figleaf **8** biennial **9** ficifolia, Malvaceae **10** alcea rosea

Hollywood's Mermaid
    nickname of: 14 Esther Williams

Hollywood Squares
    host: 12 John Davidson **13** Peter Marshall
    regular: 8 Wally Cox **10** Joan

Rivers **13** Charley Weaver, Shadoe Stevens

Holmes, Oliver Wendell
    author of: 12 Old Ironsides **30** The Autocrat of the Breakfast Table

Holmes, Sherlock
    address: 11 (221B) Baker Street
    appears in: 13 The Sign of Four **14** The Naval Treaty **15** A Study in Scarlet, The Speckled Band **16** Scandal in Bohemia, The Blue Carbuncle, The Copper Beeches **18** The Red-Headed League, The Solitary Cyclist **22** Hound of the Baskervilles
    assistants: 21 Baker Street Irregulars
    author: 16 (Sir) Arthur Conan Doyle
    brother: 7 Mycroft
    foe: 17 Professor Moriarty
    hat: 11 deerstalker
    hobby: 6 violin
    housekeeper/landlady: 9 Mrs Hudson
    keeps tobacco in: 7 slipper **14** Turkish slipper
    police: 17 Inspector Lestrade
    sidekick: 12 Dr John Watson
    vice: 7 cocaine **17** hypodermic syringe **20** seven-per-cent solution

Holmwood, Arthur
    character in: 7 Dracula
    author: 6 Stoker

holocaust 4 ruin **5** havoc **6** ravage **7** bonfire, carnage, inferno, killing **8** butchery, genocide, massacre **10** deadly fire, mass murder **11** devastation **12** annihilation **13** conflagration

Holofernes
    character in: 16 Love's Labour's Lost
    author: 11 Shakespeare

Holofernes
    general of: 14 Nebuchadnezzar
    killed by: 6 Judith

Holst, Gustav Theodore
    born: 7 England **10** Cheltenham

composer of: 7 Savitri **10** Egdon Heath, Ode to Death, The Planets **11** Hammersmith **12** St Paul's Suite **13** Fugal Concerto **14** The Hymn of Jesus, The Perfect Fool **16** Somerset Rhapsody **17** The Cloud Messenger **19** Hymns from the Rig-Veda

holy 4 pure **5** godly, moral, pious **6** adored, devout, divine, sacred, solemn **7** angelic, blessed, from God, revered, saintly, sinless **8** faithful, hallowed, heavenly, reverent, virtuous **9** from above, guileless, religious, righteous, spiritual, undefiled, unspotted, unstained, unworldly, venerated, worshiped **10** heaven-sent, immaculate, inviolable, sacrosanct, sanctified, worshipped **11** consecrated, pure in heart, uncorrupted
    Latin: 7 sanctus

Holy Ark
    Hebrew: 10 Aron Kodesh

holy of holies
    Latin: 16 sanctum sanctorum

Holy one see **5** Jesus

Holy Spirit, Holy Ghost
    9 Paraclete **13** presence of God **23** third person of the Trinity
    Latin: 15 Spiritus Sanctus
    Greek: 12 Hagion Pneuma

holy war
    Arabic: 5 jehad, jihad

Holy Willie's Prayer
    author: 11 Robert Burns

Homadus
    form: 7 centaur
    killed by: 8 Hercules

homage 5 honor **6** esteem, praise, regard **7** respect, tribute, worship **8** devotion **9** adoration, adulation, deference, obeisance, reverence **10** exaltation, veneration **13** glorification

Homagyrius
    epithet of: 4 Zeus
    means: 9 assembler

hombre 3 man

home 5 abode, haunt, haven, house **6** asylum, cradle, refuge **7** habitat, hangout **8** domicile, dwelling, hospital **9** orphanage, poorhouse, residence **10** habitation, native land, sanatorium **11** institution **12** fountainhead **13** dwelling place, home sweet home **14** stamping ground **16** place of residence **18** natural environment **25** place where one hangs one's hat

Home Burial
author: 11 Robert Frost

homegrown 5 local 6 native 8 domestic 10 indigenous

Home Is the Sailor
author: 10 Jorge Amado

homelike 4 cozy 5 comfy, homey 6 simple 8 cheerful, domestic, familiar, informal, inviting 11 comfortable

homely 4 cozy, drab, snug 5 comfy, homey, plain 6 modest, rustic, simple 7 artless, natural 8 everyday, familiar, homelike, homespun, ordinary, uncomely 9 graceless 10 ill-favored, provincial, unaffected, unassuming, ungraceful, unhandsome 11 comfortable 12 plain-looking, unattractive 13 unpretentious

homer 15 Biblical measure

Homer
author of: 5 Iliad 7 Odyssey

Homer, Winslow
born: 8 Boston MA
artwork: 9 High Cliff 10 Breezing Up, Eight Bells 11 Marine Coast, Northeaster, The Life Line 13 The Fog Warning, The Gulf Stream 21 Inside the Bar Tynemouth, Prisoners from the Front

home rule 8 autonomy 11 sovereignty 12 independence 14 self-government

homespun 5 plain 6 folksy, homely, modest, native, simple 7 artless, natural 8 downhome, homemade 9 handwoven 10 hand-loomed, unaffected 11 hand-crafted, hand-wrought 13 unpretentious

homey 4 cozy 6 casual, folksy 8 down-home, homelike, homespun, informal 15 unsophisticated

homicide 6 killer, murder, slayer 7 slaying 8 foul play, murderer, regicide, vaticide 9 bloodshed, man killer, manslayer, matricide, parricide, patricide, uxoricide 10 fratricide 11 infanticide 12 manslaughter

homiletic 7 preachy 8 didactic 10 moralizing

homily 6 sermon 7 lecture 10 preachment 11 exhortation

homogeneous 4 akin, pure 7 kindred, similar, uniform, unmixed 8 all alike, constant, of a piece 9 identical, unvarying 10 consistent 13 of the same kind, unadulterated

homology 7 analogy 8 likeness, relation 10 similarity 12 relationship 14 correspondence

Honduras *see box*

hone 4 long, moan, pine, tool, whet 5 stroke, strope, whine, yearn 6 hanker, grumble, mutter, sharpen 9 whetstone

Honegger, Arthur
born: 5 Havre 6 France
nationality: 5 Swiss
member of: 6 Les Six, The Six
composer of: 5 Rugby 6 Judith 7 L'Aiglon 8 Antigone 9 The Eaglet 10 Le Roi David 13 Pastorale d'ete 18 Jeanne d'Arc au Bucher, Liturgical Symphony 19 Pacific Two-Thirty-One

honest 4 fair, just, open, real, true 5 blunt, frank, legal, plain, solid, valid 6 candid, decent, lawful, proper, square 7 artless, ethical, genuine, sincere, upright 8 bona fide, clear-cut, faithful, innocent, reliable, straight, true-blue, truthful, virtuous 9 authentic, blameless, guileless, honorable, ingenuous, reputable, righteous 10 aboveboard, dependable, forthright, law-abiding, legitimate, on the level, principled, reasonable, scrupulous, unaffected, unreserved 11 plainspoken, trustworthy, undisguised 12 on the up-and-up, tried and true 13 conscientious, fair and square 15 straightforward, unsophisticated 16 as good as one's word, straight-shooting 17 open and aboveboard

honesty 4 word 5 honor 7 probity 8 fairness, good name, morality, scruples, veracity 9 innocence, integrity, rectitude, sincerity 10 principles 11 just dealing, uprightness 12 faithfulness,

Honduras
name means: 6 depths
capital/largest city: 11 Tegucigalpa
others: 4 Tela, Yoro 5 Copan, Danli, Lapaz 6 Roatan 7 Gracias, La Ceiba 8 Trujillo, Yuscaran 9 Choluteca, Juticalpa 10 El Progreso 11 Comayaguela 12 Puerto Cortes, San Pedro Sula
measure: 4 vara 5 milla 6 mecate 7 cajuela
monetary unit: 4 peso 7 centavo, lempira
island: 3 Bay 5 Bahia, Utila 6 Roatan 7 Bonacca, Guanaja
lake: 5 Criba, Yojoa 6 Brewer
mountain: 4 Pija 6 Agalta 7 Celaque 9 Esperanza
highest point: 8 Las Minas
river: 4 Coco, Sico, Ulua 5 Aguan, Lempa, Negro, Tinto, Wanks 6 Patuca, Sulaco 7 Olancho, Paulaya, Segovia 8 Guiavope, Santiago 9 Choluteca 10 Chamelecon
sea: 7 Pacific 8 Atlantic 9 Caribbean
physical feature:
  coast: 5 North 8 Mosquito 10 Costa Norte
  gulf: 7 Fonseca 8 Honduras
  port: 7 Laceiba 8 Trujillo
people: 4 Maya, Paya, Sumo, Ulva 5 Carib, Lenca, Pipil 6 Tauira 7 Jicaque, mestizo, Miskito 8 Mosquito
  discoverer: 8 Columbus
  farmer: 9 campesino
language: 7 English, Spanish
religion: 13 Roman Catholic
place:
  ruins: 5 Copan 8 Tenampua
feature:
  bird: 9 zenzontle
  dance: 5 sique 7 mascaro
  estate: 10 latifundia
  farm: 6 milpas 10 minifundia
  musical instrument: 7 caramba, marimba
  tree: 8 cockspur
food:
  beans: 8 frijoles
  beef dish: 6 tapado
  corn: 5 maize
  stuffed corn cake: 10 naca tamale
  tripe stew: 8 mondongo

reputability, truthfulness
13 guiltlessness, square dealing **15** trustworthiness **16** incorruptibility, straight shooting

honeybee
classification: 6 social
live in: 4 hive **6** colony
headed by: 5 queen
male: 5 drone
laborer: 6 worker
food-gatherer: 7 forager
gather: 6 nectar, pollen
produce: 5 honey
queen's food: 10 royal jelly

honeyed 4 kind **5** sweet **6** sugary **7** cloying, fawning **10** flattering, saccharine
12 ingratiating
13 complimentary

honeyed words 4 line **7** blarney **8** cajolery, flattery, soft
soap **9** sweet talk

Honey in the Horn
author: 7 H L Davis

Honeymooners, The
character: 8 Ed Norton
12 Alice Kramden, Ralph
Kramden, Trixie Norton
cast: 8 Jane Kean **9** Art Carney **12** Sheila MacRae
13 Audrey Meadows, Jackie
Gleason, Joyce Randolph
Ralph's job: 9 bus driver
Ed's job: 5 sewer
lodge: 8 Raccoons

---

honor 3 pay **4** cash, fame, laud, note, take **5** adore, exalt,
extol, favor, glory, grant, leave, power, right, truth, value
6 accept, admire, credit, esteem, homage, praise, redeem, regard, renown, repute, revere, virtue **7** acclaim, commend, decency, dignify, glorify, honesty, liberty, probity, respect,
tribute, worship **8** eminence, fairness, good name, goodness,
justness, look up to, make good, pleasure, prestige, sanction,
venerate, veracity **9** adoration, celebrity, constancy, deference, greatness, integrity, principle, privilege, rectitude, reverence, sincerity **10** admiration, compliment, exaltation, good
report, importance, notability, permission, prominence, veneration **11** acknowledge, approbation, distinction, pay homage to, recognition, think much of, uprightness
12 commendation, faithfulness, high standing, pay tribute to,
truthfulness **13** authorization, bow down before, glorification,
have regard for, honorableness, make payment on **14** high-
mindedness, scrupulousness **15** illustriousness, trustworthiness **17** a feather in one's cap, conscientiousness

---

honeysuckle 8 Lonicera
19 Aquilegia canadensis, Justi-
cia californica **24** Rhododendron prinophyllum
varieties: 3 fly **4** bush, cape
5 coral, giant, grape, hairy,
swamp **6** desert, French,
purple, yellow **7** Arizona,
Jamaica, trumpet **8** Himalaya, Japanese, swamp fly,
Tatarian **9** chaparral, Tartarian **10** yellow cape **11** European fly **12** giant
Burmese, long-flowered,

Hong Kong
name means: 13 incense harbor **14** fragrant harbor
capital: 8 Victoria
largest city:
section: 7 Kowloon **8** Hong Kong, Victoria
others: 4 Tai O **5** Tai Po **8** Aberdeen, Pingshan, Yuenlong
9 Shataukok **10** Sheungshui
division: 7 Kowloon **8** Hong Kong **14** New Territories
government: 18 British crown colony
head of state: 14 British monarch **15** governor general
island: 5 Lamma **6** Lan Tao, Lantau, Middle, Poi Toi
8 Hong Kong **9** Ap Lei Chau **11** Stonecutter
mountain: 6 Castle **8** Victoria
highest point: 9 Tai Mo Shan
river: 5 Pearl **6** Canton **8** Sham Chun
sea: 10 South China
physical feature:
bay: 4 Mirs **6** Quarry **7** Kowloon, Repulse **9** Deep Water
harbor: 4 Tolo **8** Aberdeen, Hong Kong, Victoria
peak: 8 Victoria
peninsula: 7 Kowloon
people: 5 Hakka, Haklo, Punti, Tanka **7** British, Chinese
8 American, Japanese **9** Cantonese **10** Portuguese
language: 7 Chinese, English **9** Cantonese
religion: 5 Hindu, Islam **6** Taoism **8** Buddhism
12 Christianity
feature:
airport: 6 Kai Tak
clothing: 6 samfoo **9** cheongsam
houseboat: 6 sampan
rock: 5 Amahs **6** Sha Tin
temple: 18 Ten Thousand Buddhas

South African **13** Hall's
Japanese

Honeythunder, Mr
character in: 22 The Mystery
of Edwin Drood
author: 7 Dickens

Hong Kong *see box*

Honiara
capital of: 14 Solomon
Islands

honi soit qui mal y pense
31 shamed be the one who
thinks evil of it
motto of: 16 Order of the
Garter

honk 4 toot **5** blare, blast
7 trumpet

honky-tonk 4 dive **7** gin mill
9 roadhouse, nightclub

honor *see box*

honorable 4 good **5** noble, title **6** decent, honest, lordly,
square **7** upright **9** elevated,
reputable, respected **10** creditable **11** distinctive, illustrious,
respectable, trustworthy
12 considerable
13 distinguished

hood 4 cowl, lout, punk
5 bully, rowdy, scarf, tough
6 vandal **7** hoodlum, ruffian
8 hooligan **9** barbarian, roughneck **10** delinquent
12 headcovering

Hood, Raymond
architect of: 11 RCA Building (Rockefeller Center)
17 Daily News Building
(NYC) **18** McGraw-Hill Building (NYC) **22** Chicago Tribune Building **24** American
Radiator Building
style: 13 International

hoodlum 4 hood, punk, thug
5 crook, rowdy, tough **6** gun-

man **7** bruiser, gorilla, mobster, ruffian **8** criminal,
gangster, hooligan, plug-ugly
9 desperado, strong arm
10 delinquent

hoodwink 3 gyp **4** dupe, fool,
gull, hoax, rook **5** cheat,
cozen, trick **7** deceive, defraud,
mislead, swindle **8** inveigle
9 bamboozle, victimize

hook 3 arc, bag, bow, nab,
net **4** arch, bend, bill, curl,
gaff, grab, loop, take, trap,
wind **5** angle, catch, crook,
curve, elbow, fluke, hitch,
latch, seize, snare **6** buckle,
collar, fasten, peavey, secure
7 capture, crampon, ensnare,
grapnel, grapple, pothook
8 crescent, make fast
9 horseshoe

Hooke, Robert
field: **7** physics **9** astronomy
nationality: **7** British
discovered: **9** Orion star
    15 Jupiter rotation
    20 moon's center of gravity
    21 earth's center of gravity
invented: **10** microscope
named for him: **15** law of
    elasticity

hooked 8 addicted **9** compelled,
obsessive **10** compulsive, habituated **14** uncontrollable

hooked cross
German: **10** Hakenkreuz

hook up 4 ally, dock, join
5 hinge **6** couple, link up
7 connect **8** assemble **10** articulate **11** fit together **14** fasten
together

hooligan 4 hood, lout, punk
5 bully, rowdy, tough **6** vandal **7** hoodlum, ruffian **9** barbarian, roughneck
10 delinquent

hoopla 4 hype **8** ballyhoo
9 promotion, publicity **10** hullabaloo, propaganda **11** advertising **15** public relations

Hoosier Schoolmaster, The
author: **15** Edward Eggleston

Hoosier State
nickname of: **7** Indiana

hoot 3 boo, din **4** bawl, blow,
hiss, honk, howl, jeer, moan,
mock, razz, roar, wail, yelp,
yowl **5** shout, sneer, taunt,
whoop **6** bellow, chorus, cry
out, deride, outcry, racket,
scream, shriek, shrill, tumult,
uproar **7** catcall, cry down,
scoff at, screech, sing out,
sneer at, snicker, ululate, wailing, whistle **8** proclaim, shouting **9** caterwaul, commotion,
raspberry, screaming, snicker
at **10** Bronx cheer, screeching

Hoover, Herbert Clark
nickname: **13** Great Engineer **14** Great Secretary **17** Great
    Humanitarian **18** Great Public Servant
presidential rank: **11** thirty-first
party: **10** Republican
state represented: **2** CA
defeated: **5** (Alfred Emanuel) Smith **6** (George William)
    Norris, (Norman) Thomas, (William Frederick) Varney,
    (William Zebulon) Foster **8** (Verne L) Reynolds
vice president: **6** (Charles) Curtis
cabinet:
    state: **7** (Henry Lewis) Stimson
    treasury: **5** (Ogden Livingston) Mills **6** (Andrew William)
        Mellon
    war: **4** (James William) Good **6** (Patrick Jay) Hurley
    attorney general: **8** (William DeWitt) Mitchell
    navy: **5** (Charles Francis) Adams
    postmaster general: **5** (Walter Folger) Brown
    interior: **6** (Ray Lyman) Wilbur
    agriculture: **4** (Arthur Mastick) Hyde
    commerce: **6** (Robert Patterson) Lamont, (Roy Dikeman)
        Chapin
    labor: **4** (William Nuckles) Doak **5** (James John) Davis
born: **12** West Branch IA
died: **13** New York City NY
buried: **12** West Branch IA
education:
    University: **8** Stanford
religion: **5** Quaker **16** Society of Friends
interests: **7** fishing
vacation spot: **10** Camp Hoover **11** Rapidan Camp
    22 Shenandoah National Park
author: **7** Memoirs **11** On Growing Up **14** An American
    Epic **16** Years of Adventure **18** Principles of Mining, The
    Great Depression **20** America's First Crusade **21** American
    Individualism, The Challenge to Liberty **24** The Ordeal of
    Woodrow Wilson **25** The Problems of Lasting Peace
    26 The Cabinet and the Presidency **28** Addresses Upon
    the American Road **51** The State Papers and Other Public
    Writings of Herbert Hoover
political career: **19** US Food Administrator
    head of: **23** American Relief Committee **28** Commission
        for Relief in Belgium
    director: **38** General Relief and Reconstruction of
        Europe
    member/chairman: **22** Supreme Economic Council
    secretary of: **8** Commerce
    chairman of: **17** Hoover Commissions
civilian career: **6** author **14** mining engineer **18** consulting
    engineer
notable events of lifetime/term: **15** Great Depression
    conference: **11** London Naval
    crash of: **11** stock market
    independence for: **11** Philippines
    Tariff: **11** Hawley-Smoot
father: **10** Jesse Clark
mother: **6** Huldah (Randall Minthorn)
siblings: **3** May **13** Theodore Jesse
wife: **3** Lou (Henry)
children: **10** Allan Henry **12** Herbert Clark
first lady:
    vice president of: **10** Girl Scouts

hop 3 bob **4** ball, jump, leap,
prom, romp, skip, step, trip
5 bound, caper, dance, frisk,
mixer, vault **6** bounce, gambol, prance, soiree, spring
7 Humulus
 varieties: **4** Wild **5** False

6 Common **8** European,
Japanese

hope 3 yen **4** help, wish
5 crave, dream, faith, fancy,
trust **6** aspire, belief, chance,
desire, expect, hunger, rescue,

yen for **7** believe, count on, craving, dream of, longing, long for **8** ambition, daydream, feel sure, optimism, prospect, reckon on, reliance, yearn for, yearning **9** assurance, hankering, have faith, hunger for, salvation, take heart **10** anticipate, aspiration, assumption, be bent upon, confidence, conviction, expectancy **11** be confident, contemplate, expectation, have an eye to, possibility, presumption, reassurance, saving grace **12** anticipation, be optimistic, heart's desire **13** encouragement, have a fancy for, look forward to **14** have a hankering **17** great expectations **18** have one's heart set on **19** look on the bright side

Hope, Anthony
  real name: 21 Sir Anthony Hope Hawkins
  author of: 15 Rupert of Hentzau **18** The Prisoner of Zenda

Hope, Bob
  real name: 16 Leslie Townes Hope
  co-star: 10 Bing Crosby **13** Dorothy Lamour
  born: 6 Eltham **7** England
  roles:
    Road to: 3 Rio **4** Bali **6** Utopia **7** Morocco **8** Hong Kong, Zanzibar **9** Singapore

hopeful 7 assured, in hopes **8** cheering, sanguine, trusting **9** confident, expectant, favorable, fortunate, promising **10** auspicious, heartening, of good omen, optimistic, propitious, reassuring **11** encouraging **12** anticipative

hopeless 3 sad **4** lost, vain **6** abject, futile **7** forlorn, useless **8** dejected, downcast **9** depressed, incurable, pointless **10** beyond help, despairing, despondent, impossible, melancholy, past remedy **11** downhearted, heartbroken, irreparable, irrevocable, pessimistic, sick at heart **12** beyond recall, disconsolate, heavyhearted, irredeemable, irreversible **13** grief-stricken, irretrievable **14** down in the mouth, sorrow-stricken

hopelessness 7 despair **8** futility **9** pessimism **11** uselessness

Hopi (Hopitu, Moki)
  language family:
    10 Shoshonean
  location: 7 Arizona
  adapted culture of: 6 Pueblo
  ceremony: 10 snake dance

Hopkins, Anthony
  born: 5 Wales **10** Port Talbot
  roles: 10 Audrey Rose **11** A Doll's House **12** Young Winston **14** The Elephant Man **15** The Lion in Winter

Hoples
  father: 3 Ion

Hopper, Edward
  born: 7 Nyack NY
  artwork: 10 Nighthawks **18** Early Sunday Morning, House by the Railroad **19** Second Story Sunlight **20** Sunlight in a Cafeteria **21** Lighthouse at Two Lights

Horae
  also: 4 Hour
  goddesses of: 5 decay **6** growth **7** seasons **11** social order
  names: 4 Dice, Dike **5** Irene **7** Eunomia

Horatii
  form: 7 triplets **8** brothers
  sister: 7 Horatia
  champions of: 4 Rome
  fought: 8 Curiatii

Horatio
  character in: 6 Hamlet
  author: 11 Shakespeare

Horatio
  character in: 17 The Spanish Tragedy
  author: 3 Kyd

Horatius
  origin: 5 Roman
  defended: 6 bridge
    over: 5 Tiber
    against: 9 Etruscans

Horcus
  origin: 5 Greek
  god of: 5 oaths

horde 3 mob **4** band, gang, host, pack **5** bunch, crowd, crush, drove, party, swarm, tribe, troop **6** legion, throng **7** company **8** assembly **9** gathering, multitude **10** assemblage **12** congregation

Horgan, Paul
  author of: 10 Whitewater **13** Lamy of Santa Fe **18** The Thin Mountain Air

horizon 4 area **5** field, range, realm, scope, vista, world **6** bounds, domain, sphere **7** compass, expanse, outlook, purview, stretch **8** frontier, prospect **11** perspective

horizontal 4 even, flat **5** flush, level, plane, plumb, prone **6** supine **8** parallel (to something) **9** lying down, prostrate, reclining, recumbent **14** flat on one's back

horizontal support 3 tie

4 beam **5** brace, joist **6** girder, header, lintel **8** crossbar

hormone 5 auxin **6** cortin **7** estrone, insulin, steroid **8** endocrin, estrogen, galactin, lactogen, secretin **9** adrenalin, cortisone **12** progesterone, testosterone

horn 4 tusk **5** cornu, point, spike **6** antler **11** excrescence
  brass instrument: 4 oboe, tuba **5** bugle **6** cornet **7** bassoon, trumpet **8** alto horn, baritone, clarinet, trombone **9** euphonium, saxophone **10** French horn, mellophone, sousaphone **11** English horn

Horn of Africa *see* **7** Somalia

Hornung, Paul
  nickname: 9 Golden Boy
  sport: 8 football
  position: 6 runner **11** placekicker
  team: 15 Green Bay Packers

horny 4 hard **5** tough **7** callous **8** callused, hardened **12** thick-skinned **14** pachydermatous

horologe 5 clock **9** timepiece **11** chronometer

horrendous 4 gory **5** awful **6** horrid **7** ghastly, hideous **8** dreadful, horrible, shocking, terrible **9** appalling, frightful, repellent, repulsive, revolting **10** horrifying

horrible 3 bad **4** foul, rank, vile **5** awful, nasty **6** grisly, horrid, odious **7** ghastly, hideous **8** dreadful, gruesome, shocking, terrible, unsavory **9** abhorrent, appalling, atrocious, frightful, harrowing, loathsome, monstrous, obnoxious, repellent, repulsive, revolting, sickening **10** abominable, despicable, detestable, disgusting, forbidding, nauseating, unbearable, unpleasant **11** disquieting, distasteful, unspeakable **12** disagreeable, insufferable

horrid 3 bad **4** foul, grim, ugly **5** awful, nasty, rough **6** bratty, horror, shaggy, wicked **7** fearful, hideous **8** dreadful, gruesome, horrible, shocking, terrible **9** bristling, frightful, offensive, revolting, vexatious **10** abominable, detestable, unpleasant **11** troublesome **12** disagreeable

horrific 4 dire **5** awful **7** fearful, ghastly **8** dreadful, horrible, shocking, terrible **9** appalling

horrified 6 aghast **8** appalled

9 petrified, terrified **10** frightened **13** thunderstruck **14** terror-stricken

horrify 5 daunt, repel, shock **6** appall, dismay, revolt, sicken **7** disgust, petrify, terrify **8** affright, disquiet, frighten, nauseate **10** disconcert, dishearten **11** make one sick **15** make one turn pale **18** make one's flesh creep **22** make one's hair stand on end

horrifying 5 awful, dread **8** alarming, dreadful **10** terrifying **11** frightening, hairraising

horror 3 woe **4** fear **5** alarm, crime, dread, panic **6** dismay, hatred, misery, terror **7** anguish, cruelty, disgust, dislike, outrage, torment **8** atrocity, aversion, distaste, distress, hardship, loathing **9** antipathy, awfulness, privation, repulsion, revulsion, suffering **10** abhorrence, affliction, discomfort, inhumanity, repugnance **11** abomination, detestation, hideousness, trepidation **12** apprehension, terribleness, wretchedness

horror-struck 6 aghast **7** fearful **8** appalled **9** horrified, terrified **10** frightened **13** scared to death

hors de combat 8 disabled **13** out of the fight

hors d'oeuvre 3 dip **6** canape, relish, tidbit **9** antipasto, appetizer **10** finger food

horse see box, p. 460

horseback riding
    athlete: **11** Frank Chapot **17** William Steinkraus

horse collar 3 zip **4** zero **5** aught, zilch **6** cipher, naught **8** goose egg

Horse Knows the Way, The
    author: **9** John O'Hara

horseman 5 groom, rider **6** hussar, jockey, lancer, ostler **7** cossack, dragoon, hostler, trainer, trooper **9** postilion, stableboy, stableman **10** cavalryman, equestrian, roughrider **11** horse marine, stable owner **12** equestrienne, horse breeder, horse soldier, stable keeper **14** cavalry soldier, horseback rider, mounted trooper

horseplay 6 pranks **7** foolery **9** cutting up **10** buffoonery, tomfoolery **13** fooling around, horsing around

horse racing
    jockey: **8** Del Insko **11** Bill Hartack, Eddie Arcaro **12** Angel Cordero, Bill Haughton, Laffit Pincay, Steve Cauthen **13** Johnny Longden, Stanley Dancer **15** Willie Shoemaker
    god of: **6** Consus

Horseshoe Robinson
    author: **12** John P Kennedy

horse soldier 6 hussar, lancer **7** dragoon, trooper **8** cavalier, horseman **10** cavalryman

horse trooper 6 hussar, lancer **7** dragoon, Mountie **8** cavalier, horseman **10** cavalryman **12** horse soldier **14** mounted soldier **16** mounted policeman

Horton, Edward Everett
    sidekick of: **11** Fred Astaire
    born: **10** Brooklyn NY
    roles: **15** Cinderella Jones, Her Primitive Man **18** Springtime for Henry

Horus
    origin: **8** Egyptian
    god of: **3** sun
    Greek name: **10** Harcorates
    symbol: **6** falcon
    mother: **4** Isis
    father: **6** Osiris
    enemy: **3** Set **4** Seth

hosannas 4 yeas **5** kudos **6** bravos, cheers, paeans **7** acclaim, hurrahs, huzzahs, yippees **8** applause **10** hallelujas **11** halleluiahs

hose 5 socks **7** hosiery **9** stockings

Hosea
    father: **5** Beeri

hosiery 3 sox **4** hose **5** socks **6** nylons, tights **7** leotard **9** stockings

hospitable 4 open, warm **6** genial **7** cordial **8** amenable, amicable, friendly, gracious, sociable, tolerant **9** agreeable, convivial, receptive, welcoming **10** accessible, gregarious, neighborly, openhanded, openminded, responsive **12** approachable

hospital 4 home **6** asylum, clinic **7** sick bay **8** pavilion, rest home **9** infirmary **10** polyclinic, sanatorium **11** nursing home **13** medical center
    French: **9** hotel Dieu

hospital, private
    French: **13** maison de sante

hospitality 5 cheer **6** warmth **7** welcome **8** openness **9** geniality **10** cordiality, heartiness, kindliness **11** amicability,

sociability **12** congeniality, conviviality, friendliness **13** Gemutlichkeit **14** hospitableness, neighborliness **15** warmheartedness
    god of: **6** Sancus **10** Dius Fidius, Semo Sancus

host, hostess 3 lot, mob **4** army, band, body, crew, gang, mess **5** array, crowd, drove, group, horde, party, swarm, troop **6** legion, throng **7** company, maitre d', meeting **8** conclave, congress, hosteler, hotelier, landlord, welcomer **9** gathering, innkeeper, multitude **10** confluence, convention, headwaiter, party giver, proprietor **11** convocation, hotel keeper **12** congregation, head waitress, hotel manager, proprietress, receptionist **17** restaurant manager **18** master of ceremonies **20** mistress of ceremonies

hostage 7 captive **8** prisoner

Hostage, The
    author: **12** Brendan Behan

hostel 3 inn **4** hall **5** hotel, lodge **7** hospice, lodging, shelter **8** hospital, hostelry

hostile 3 icy **4** cold, mean, ugly **5** angry, at war, enemy, testy **6** at odds, at outs, bitter, chilly, cranky, malign, touchy, unkind **7** opposed, vicious, warring **8** battling, clashing, contrary, fighting, opposing, snappish, spiteful, venomous **9** bellicose, bristling, dissident, malicious, malignant, truculent **10** contending, ill-natured, malevolent, on bad terms, unfriendly **11** belligerent, contentious, disagreeing, ill-disposed, quarrelsome **12** antagonistic, cantankerous, disagreeable, disputatious, incompatible **13** argumentative, at loggerheads, unsympathetic

hostile act 4 raid **6** strike, threat **7** assault, offense **8** act of war, invasion **9** hostility, incursion **10** aggression

hostile nation 5 enemy **7** invader

hostility 3 war **4** duel, feud, fray, hate **5** anger, clash, fight, venom **6** battle, combat, enmity, fracas, hatred, malice, rancor, spleen **7** contest, dispute, ill will, scuffle, warfare, warring **8** act of war, argument, battling, conflict, fighting **9** animosity, antipathy, bickering **10** antagonism, bitterness, contention, dissidence, opposition, state of war **11** altercation, malevolence, vi-

horse 4 colt, foal, hack, jade, mare, plug, pony, sire, stud **5** bronc, filly, mount, pacer, pinto, steed **6** bronco, dobbin, equine **7** cavalry, charger, cow pony, gelding, hackney, hussars, lancers, mustang, palfrey, trotter **8** cossacks, dragoons, galloper, stallion, troopers, yearling **9** broodmare, racehorse **10** cavalrymen, draft horse **12** horse cavalry, horse marines, quarter horse, thoroughbred **13** horse soldiers, mounted troops **15** mounted troopers, mounted warriors

Achilles': 7 Xanthus
Alexander the Great's: 10 Bucephalus
anatomy: 4 hock, hoof, loin, mane, tail **5** croup, flank, shank **6** cannon, gaskin, haunch, stifle **7** coronet, crupper, fetlock, gambrel, nostril, pastern, withers **11** throatlatch
Australian: 5 dingo, myall **8** warragal, warrigal, yarraman
breed: 6 Morgan, Nubian, Tarpan **7** Arabian, Belgian, mustang **8** Galloway, Shetland **9** Appaloosa, Percheron **10** Clydesdale, Lippizaner **12** Narragansett, Standardbred, Thoroughbred **15** Tennessee-Walker
Caligula's: 9 Incitatus (made a senator)
castrated: 7 gelding
color: 3 bay, dun **4** gray, pied, roan, zain **5** morel, pinto **6** calico, dapple, sorrel **7** piebald **8** chestnut, palomino, schimmel (gray)
combining form: 4 eque, equi **5** hippo
Dick Turpin's: 9 Black Bess
Don Quixote's: 9 Rosinante
family: 7 Equidae **9** Miohippus, Orohippus
female: 3 dam **4** mare **5** filly
French: 6 cheval
gear: 3 bit **4** rein, tack **6** saddle **7** blinder, harness, snaffle **9** surcingle **11** saddlecloth
Gen Custer's: 8 Comanche
Gen Grant's: 10 Cincinnati
Gen Robert E Lee's: 9 Traveller
Gen Sherman's: 6 Rienzi
genus: 5 equus
Gulliver's Travels: 9 Houyhnhnm
kind: 3 cob **4** race **6** bronco, hunter, jumper **7** charger, mustang, palfrey, quarter, trotter **8** destrier
legendary: 6 Trojan
Lone Ranger's: 6 Silver
male: 4 colt **8** stallion
measure: 4 hand
Mohammed's: 7 Alborak
movie/story: 6 Flicka **8** Champion **11** Black Beauty **14** National Velvet **16** The Black Stallion
Napoleon's: 7 Morengo
Orlando's: 11 Vegliantino
pace: 4 lope, trot **5** amble **6** canter, gallop
pair of: 4 span, team **6** tandem
race: 5 derby, plate **6** exacta **7** pick six **8** claiming, handicap **9** allowance **11** daily double, sweepstakes **12** steeplechase, weight-for-age
  Triple Crown: **7** Belmont **9** Preakness **13** Kentucky Derby
riding show: 8 gymkhana
Rinaldo's: 6 Bayard
Roy Rogers': 7 Trigger
Sigurd's: 5 Grani
small: 4 pony
Stonewall Jackson's: 12 Little Sorrel
Tom Mix's: 4 Tony
three: 6 random, troika **7** unicorn
Wellington's (at Waterloo): 10 Copenhagen
wild: 5 fuzzy **6** bramby, kumrah, outlaw, tarpan **7** jughead **8** bangtail, fuzztail, warragal, warrigal
Will Rogers': 8 Soapsuds **10** Bootlegger
winged: 7 Pegasus
young: 4 colt, foal **5** filly **8** yearling

---

ciousness **12** belligerence, contrariness, disagreement **14** unfriendliness, vindictiveness

hot 3 new, top **4** good, late, live, near, warm **5** fiery, fresh, nippy, sharp **6** ardent, baking, biting, fervid, fierce, heated, hectic, latest, molten, raging, recent, red-hot, stormy, sultry, torrid **7** boiling, burning, earnest, excited, furious, intense, melting, peppery, piquant, popular, pungent, searing, violent **8** agitated, animated, broiling, feverish, frenzied, roasting, scalding, sizzling, steaming, vehement, very warm **9** emotional, excellent, scorching, simmering, very close, wrought-up **10** attractive, blistering, passionate, smoldering, successful, sweltering **11** electrified, fast-selling, most popular, radioactive, sought after, tempestuous **12** incandescent **14** fast and furious, highly seasoned, in close pursuit

hot air 7 bombast **8** rhetoric **9** hyperbole **12** exaggeration **13** overstatement

hotel 3 inn **5** lodge, motel **6** hostel **7** hospice, lodging **8** hostelry, motor inn

Hotel, The
author: **14** Elizabeth Bowen

hotel de ville 9 a city hall
literally: **16** mansion of the city

hotel Dieu 9 a hospital **12** mansion of God

Hotel New Hampshire, The
author: **10** John Irving

hothouse 6 tender **7** fragile, nursery **8** delicate **10** glasshouse, greenhouse **12** conservatory **13** over-protected

hot temper 4 fire **5** anger **6** pepper **8** acrimony **9** short fuse

hot-tempered 7 peppery **9** emotional, excitable **13** easily ruffled, quick-tempered

hot water 3 jam **4** mess **6** pickle **7** trouble **10** difficulty **11** predicament

Houghston, Walter
real name of: **12** Walter Huston

hound 3 dog, fan, nag, nut, pup **4** bait, buff, hunt, mutt, tail **5** annoy, chase, doggy, freak, harry, lover, pooch, puppy, stalk, track, trail, whelp, worry **6** addict, badger, canine, follow, harass, hector, keep at, needle, pester, pursue **7** bedevil, poochie **9** keep after **10** aficionado, hunting dog **11** afficionado
dog breed: **6** beagle, borzoi, saluki **7** basenji, harrier, whippet **9** dachshund, greyhound **10** bloodhound, otter hound **11** Afghan hound, basset hound, Ibizan hound **12** pharaoh hound **14** Irish wolfhound **15** English foxhound **16** American foxhound **17** Norwegian elkhound, Scottish deerhound **18** Rhodesian ridgeback **20** black and tan coonhound
group of: **3** cry **4** mute, pack

Hound of the Baskervilles, The
author: **19** Sir Arthur Conan Doyle
character: **8** Dr Watson **14** Sherlock Holmes **19** Sir Henry Baskerville

hour 3 day **4** span, time **5** space **6** period **8** interval
abbreviation: **2** hr

Hour see **5** Horae

house, House 4 clan, firm, hall, home, keep, line, shop **5** abode, board, lodge, put up, store **6** billet, church, family, garage, harbor, strain, temple **7** Commons, company, concern, contain, council, descent, dynasty, lineage, quarter, shelter, theater **8** ancestry, assembly, audience, building, business, congress, domicile, dwelling **9** ancestors, household, residence **10** auditorium, family tree, habitation, hippodrome, opera house, spectators **11** accommodate, concert hall, corporation, legislature, noble family, partnership, royal family **12** business firm, lower chamber, meeting place, organization **13** dwelling place, establishment
god of: **8** Silvanus, Sylvanus

housebreaker 5 thief **6** robber **7** burglar **8** pilferer **9** purloiner **10** cat burglar **14** second-story man

housebreaking 5 theft **7** break-in, robbery **8** burglary, stealing **12** burglarizing **19** breaking and entering

House Divided, A
author: **9** Pearl Buck

House for Mr Biswas, A
author: **9** V S Naipaul

household 4 home **5** house **6** family, hearth **8** of a house **9** for a house **10** for a family, for home use **12** family circle
goddess of: **6** Brigit

household help 4 cook, maid **7** footman, steward **8** domestic, gardener, handyman, houseboy **9** charwoman, chauffeur, domestics, majordomo, nursemaid **11** housekeeper

household of three
French: **12** menage a trois

House in Paris, The
author: **14** Elizabeth Bowen

House Made of Dawn
author: **13** N Scott Momaday

House of Atreus, The
author: **9** Aeschylus
character: **7** Electra, Orestes **9** Aegisthus, Agamemnon, Cassandra **12** Clytemnestra

house of health
French: **13** maison de sante

House of Mirth, The
author: **12** Edith Wharton
character: **8** Lily Bart, Mr Selden **9** Gus Trenor **10** Judy Trenor, Mr Rosedale, Percy Gryce **12** Bertha Dorset, George Dorset

House of the Seven Gables, The
author: **18** Nathaniel Hawthorne
character: **10** Mr Holgrave **14** Phoebe Pyncheon **16** Clifford Pyncheon **20** Judge Jaffrey Pyncheon, Miss Hepzibah Pyncheon

house of worship 6 chapel, church, mosque, temple **8** basilica **9** cathedral, synagogue **10** house of God, Lord's house, tabernacle

housewife 4 wife **9** homemaker **11** housekeeper

housing 4 case, home **5** abode, house **6** casing, jacket, sheath, shield **7** lodging, shelter **8** covering, domicile, dwelling, envelope, lodgment, quarters **9** enclosure, residence **10** habitation **14** accommodations

Housman, A E
author of: **14** A Shropshire Lad

Houston
baseball team: **6** Astros
basketball team: **7** Rockets
canal: **11** Houston Ship
channel: **12** Buffalo Bayou
football team: **6** Oilers **8** Gamblers
landmark: **4** NASA **12** Alley Theater **14** Jesse James Hall **22** Manned Spacecraft Center **29** San Jacinto Battlefield Monument
battleship: **5** Texas
named after: **10** Sam Houston
planned by: **7** A C Allen, J K Allen
stadium: **9** Astrodome
street: **15** Old Spanish Trail
university: **4** Rice **12** Texas Medical **13** Texas Southern

Houston, Sam
position: **9** US Senator
governor of: **5** Texas **9** Tennessee
president of: **15** Republic of Texas
served in: **9** Creek Wars **15** Texas Revolution
battle: **10** San Jacinto
defeated: **9** Santa Anna

Houyhnhnms
fictional people in: **16** Gulliver's Travels
author: **5** Swift

hovel 3 hut **4** dump, hole **5** cabin, shack **6** shanty

hover 4 flit, hang **5** float, haunt, pause, poise, waver **6** attend, falter, seesaw **7** flitter, flutter **9** fluctuate, hang about, vacillate

Hovhaness, Alan
born: 12 Somerville MA
composer of: 10 Magnificat

how
Latin: 7 quo modo

Howard, Ron
born: 2 OK 6 Duncan
roles: 4 Opie 9 Happy Days
16 American Graffiti, Richie
Cunningham 19 The Andy
Griffith Show
director of: 6 Cocoon, Gung
Ho, Splash, Willow

Howard, Sidney
author of: 13 The Silver
Cord 22 They Knew What
They Wanted

Howard, Trevor
born: 7 England
12 Cliftonville
roles: 6 The Key 13 Ryan's
Daughter, Sons and Lovers
14 Brief Encounter 23 The
Invincible Mr Disraeli

Howard's End
author: 9 E M Forster
character: 9 Jacky Bast
10 Paul Wilcox, Ruth Wil-
cox 11 Henry Wilcox, Leonard Bast 13 Charles Wilcox,
Helen Schlegel 16 Margaret
Schlegel, Theobald Schlegel

how are you
German: 8 wie geht's 9 wie
geht es

Howe, Elias
nationality: 8 American
invented: 13 sewing machine

Howells, William Dean
author of: 12 Indian Sum-
mer 15 A Modern Instance
20 A Hazard of New For-
tunes, The Rise of Silas
Lapham

How Green Was My Valley
author: 16 Richard Llewellyn
director: 8 John Ford
character: 6 Marged 7 Bron-
wen 10 Beth Morgan
11 Iestyn Evans 12 Gwilym
Morgan
    Morgan children: 4 Davy,
    Huur, Ivor, Owen
    5 Ianto 6 Gwilym
    8 Angharad
cast: 7 Anna Lee 9 John
Loder 11 Donald Crisp
12 Maureen O'Hara
13 Roddy McDowall, Walter
Pidgeon
Oscar for: 7 picture 8 director 15 supporting actor
(Crisp)

howl 3 bay, cry 4 bark, hoot,
roar, wail, yell, yelp, yowl
5 groan, shout, whine 6 bellow, clamor, cry out, outcry,
scream, shriek, uproar
7 ululate

howler 4 goof 5 error 6 boo-
boo 7 blooper, blunder,
mistake

**How To Win Friends and
Influence People**
author: 12 Dale Carnegie

hoyden 3 imp 4 brat, chit
6 tomboy

Hoyle, Fred
field: 9 astronomy
nationality: 7 British
developed: 17 steady-state
theory

Hoyt, Rosemary
character in: 16 Tender Is
the Night
author: 10 Fitzgerald

Hreidmar
origin: 12 Scandinavian
mentioned in: 8 Volsunga
son: 5 Otter, Regin 6 Fafnir
killed by: 6 Fafnir

Hsitsang *see* 5 Tibet

Hualapai
language family: 5 Yuman
location: 7 Arizona
related to: 7 Yavapai
9 Havasupai

hub 3 nub 4 axis, core 5 focus,
heart, pivot 6 center, middle
10 focal point

Hubble, Edwin Powell
field: 9 astronomy
studied: 15 galactic nebulae
named for him: 14 Hubble
constant

hubbub 3 din 4 fuss, stir, to-
do 5 noise 6 babble, bedlam,
bustle, clamor, pother, racket,
ruckus, tumult, uproar 7 ferment, turmoil 8 disorder 9 agitation, commotion, confusion,
hue and cry 10 hullabaloo,
hurly-burly 11 disturbance,
pandemonium 12 perturbation

Hubert
creator: 11 Dick Wingert

huckleberry 9 Vaccinium
11 Gaylussacia
varieties: 2 He 3 Box, Red
4 Blue, Shot 5 Black, Dwarf,
Hairy, Squaw, Sugar 6 Garden 8 Thin-leaf 9 Evergreen
10 California, Little-leaf

**Huckleberry Finn (The Ad-
ventures of)**
author: 9 Mark Twain
character: 3 Jim 9 Tom Sawyer 12 Widow Douglas
13 Judge Thatcher

huckster 5 adman 6 badger,
hawker, kidder, seller, vendor
7 haggler, peddler

Hud
director: 10 Martin Ritt
cast: 10 John Ashley, Paul

Newman 12 Patricia Neal
13 Melvyn Douglas
14 Brandon de Wilde
Oscar for: 7 actress (Neal)
15 supporting actor
(Douglas)

huddle 4 heap, herd, mass,
mess 5 bunch, crowd, group
6 cuddle, curl up, jumble,
medley, muddle, nestle,
throng 7 cluster, collect, meeting, snuggle 8 converge, disarray, disorder 9 confusion,
gathering 10 conference, discussion, hodge-podge 12 think
session

Hudibras
author: 12 Samuel Butler
character: 6 Ralpho 8 Crow-
ders 9 Sidrophel

Hudson, Rock
real name: 12 Roy Scherer Jr
co-star: 8 Doris Day
born: 10 Winnetka IL
roles: 5 Giant 10 Pillow
Talk 15 A Farewell to Arms,
McMillan and Wife
20 Magnificent Obsession

Hudson, W H
author of: 13 Green Man-
sions, The Purple Land
17 Far Away and Long Ago

hue 4 cast, tint, tone 5 color,
shade, tinge 8 tincture
10 coloration

hue and cry 4 call, howl,
roar, yell, yowl 5 alarm, alert,
shout, storm 6 bellow, clamor,
hubbub, outcry, shriek, uproar 7 thunder 10 cry of
alarm, hullabaloo

huff 3 pet 4 fury, rage, snit
7 bad mood, dudgeon, out-
rage 8 ill humor, vexation
9 annoyance, petulance 10 fit
of anger, fit of pique,
resentment

huffy 4 curt, hurt 5 angry,
cross, irate, moody, sulky,
surly, testy 6 cranky, grumpy,
moping, morose, shirty, sullen,
touchy 7 in a snit, peevish,
waspish, wounded 8 churlish,
offended, petulant, snappish
9 glowering, in a lather, in a
pucker, irritable, querulous,
rancorous, resentful, sensitive
10 ill-humored, out of sorts
11 disgruntled, quarrelsome,
thin-skinned 12 discontented
14 easily offended, hard to
live with, hypersensitive

hug 4 hold 5 clasp 6 clutch,
cuddle, nestle 7 cling to, embrace, snuggle, squeeze 9 hold
close, hover near 11 keep
close to 13 cling together, follow closely 15 parallel closely,
press to the bosom

huge 4 vast **5** giant, great, jumbo **6** mighty **7** immense, mammoth, massive, titanic **8** colossal, enormous, gigantic, imposing **9** cyclopean, extensive, herculean, leviathan, monstrous **10** gargantuan, monumental, prodigious, staggering, stupendous **11** elephantine, extravagant, spectacular **12** overwhelming **14** Brobdingnagian

hugeness 4 bulk **8** enormity, vastness **9** great size, immensity, largeness, magnitude **11** massiveness

Huggins, Charles Brenton
field: 10 physiology
researched: 6 cancer
12 chemotherapy
awarded: 10 Nobel Prize

Hughes, Langston
author of: 9 The Big Sea
12 One-Way Ticket **13** The Weary Blues **19** Shakespeare in Harlem **20** The Panther and the Lash

Hughes, Richard
author of: 18 A High Wind in Jamaica

Hughes, Thomas
author of: 19 Tom Brown's Schooldays

Hugh the Drover
opera by: 15 Vaughan Williams
character: 4 Mary **12** The Constable **14** John the Butcher

Hugin
origin: 12 Scandinavian
form: 5 raven
owned by: 4 Odin **5** Othin
personifies: 7 thought
duty: 10 newsbearer
other raven: 5 Munin

Hugo, Victor
author of: 13 Les Miserables **16** Notre Dame de Paris **23** The Hunchback of Notre Dame
character: 9 Esmeralda, Quasimodo

hulk 4 ship **5** giant, wreck **8** behemoth

hulking 3 big **5** bulky, heavy, husky **7** massive **8** powerful, unwieldy **9** oversized, ponderous **10** cumbersome

hull 3 pod **4** case, husk, peel, rind, skin **5** shell, shuck **7** coating **8** carapace **9** epidermis, tegmentum **10** integument

Hull, Isaac
served in: 19 War of Eighteen-Twelve

sunk ship: 9 Guerriere (British)
commander of ship: 12 Constitution

hullabaloo 3 din **4** stir **5** babel **6** bedlam, clamor, hubbub, ruckus, tumult, uproar **9** confusion **11** pandemonium
Yiddish: 7 tzimmes

hum 4 buzz, purr, whir **5** croon, drone, thrum **6** be busy, bustle, intone, murmur, thrive **7** buzzing, droning, purring, vibrate **8** be active, whirring **9** vibration **10** faint sound **13** be in full swing

human 3 man **5** of men, of men **6** gentle, humane, kindly, mortal, person **7** hominid, like man, manlike **8** merciful, personal **10** anthropoid, individual **11** Homo sapiens, sympathetic

Human Comedy, The
author: 14 Honore de Balzac, William Saroyan

Human Condition, The
author: 12 Hannah Arendt

humane 4 kind **5** human **6** kindly, tender **7** pitying **8** merciful **9** unselfish **10** benevolent, bighearted, charitable, goodwilled **11** magnanimous, sympathetic, warmhearted **12** humanitarian **13** compassionate, philanthropic

humaneness 8 kindness, sympathy **10** compassion, gentleness, kindliness **11** benevolence **12** mercifulness **15** warmheartedness

Human Factor, The
author: 12 Graham Greene

humanitarian 4 kind **6** humane **8** generous **10** altruistic, benevolent, charitable **11** kindhearted **12** large-hearted **13** compassionate, philanthropic **14** philanthropist

humanity 3 man **4** love **5** mercy **6** people **7** charity, mankind, mortals **8** goodwill, kindness, sympathy **9** humankind, humanness, mortality **10** compassion, gentleness, humaneness, kindliness, tenderness **11** benevolence, Homo sapiens, human beings, human nature, magnanimity **12** the human race **13** brotherly love, fellow feeling **15** warmheartedness **16** fraternal feeling

humanum est errare 12 to err is human

Humbert Humbert
character in: 6 Lolita
author: 7 Nabokov

humble 3 low **4** meek, poor **5** abase, abash, crush, lower, lowly, plain, shame **6** common, debase, demean, demure, gentle, modest, shabby, simple, subdue **7** chasten, conquer, degrade, mortify, obscure, put down **8** bring low, derogate, disgrace, dishonor, inferior, ordinary, plebeian, pull down, wretched **9** bring down, embarrass, humiliate, make lowly, miserable **10** inglorious, low-ranking, make humble, obsequious, put to shame, respectful, unassuming **11** deferential, subservient, unimportant, unpresuming **12** self-effacing, take down a peg **13** insignificant, unpretentious **14** unostentatious **15** inconsequential, undistinguished

humbled 5 cowed **7** abashed, debased, subdued **9** conquered, disgraced **10** brought low, humiliated

Humboldt, Alexander von
nationality: 6 German
originator of: 7 ecology
10 geophysics

Humboldt's Gift
author: 10 Saul Bellow

humbug 3 fib, gyp, lie **4** bull, bunk, dupe, fake, fool, gull, hoax, liar, lies, sham **5** cheat, cozen, dodge, faker, fraud, hokum, lying, quack, spoof, trick **6** bunkum, con man, deceit, fibber, phooey, take in **7** beguile, blather, cheater, deceive, falsify, fiction, forgery, mislead, rubbish, sharper, swindle **8** artifice, claptrap, flimflam, flummery, hoodwink, impostor, nonsense, perjurer, pretense, swindler, trickery **9** bamboozle, charlatan, deception, fabricate, falsehood, hypocrisy, hypocrite, imposture, mendacity, poppycock, trickster **10** balderdash, hocus-pocus, mountebank, pretension **11** counterfeit, make-believe **12** equivocation, misrepresent **13** confidence man, double-dealing, falsification **15** pretentiousness

humdinger 4 lulu **5** dandy, doozy **6** beauty, hummer, marvel **8** Jim dandy, superior **10** ripsnorter **12** lollapalooza **13** extraordinary

humdrum 4 blah, dull, dumb, flat **5** banal, trite **6** boring, common, dreary **7** insipid, mundane, routine, tedious, trivial **8** everyday, lifeless, mediocre, ordinary, tiresome, wearying **9** hackneyed, unvarying, wearisome **10** monotonous, pedestrian, uneventful, unexciting, uninspired **11** commonplace, indifferent, uninspiring **12** conventional, run-of-the-mill **13** unexceptional, uninteresting

humerus
bone of: **8** upper arm

humid 4 damp, dank **5** moist, muggy, soppy **6** clammy, steamy, sticky, sultry

humidity 4 smog **8** dampness, moisture **9** mugginess **10** stickiness

humiliate 5 abash, crush, shame **6** debase, humble, subdue **7** chagrin, chasten, degrade, mortify, put down **8** belittle, bring low, disgrace, dishonor **9** discomfit, embarrass **11** make ashamed **13** bring down a peg

humiliated 7 abashed, crushed, debased, humbled **8** degraded **9** chagrined, disgraced, mortified

humiliation 5 shame **7** chagrin **8** disgrace, dishonor **9** abasement **10** debasement **11** degradation **12** discomfiture **13** embarrassment, mortification

humility 7 modesty, shyness **8** meekness, timidity **9** lowliness **10** demureness, diffidence, humbleness **11** bashfulness **13** self-abasement **17** unpretentiousness

hummock 4 hill, rise **5** knoll, mound **7** hillock, tussock

Humologumena 17 New Testament books

humor 3 wit **4** baby, gags, mood, puns **5** farce, jests, jokes, spoil **6** cajole, comedy, joking, pamper, parody, satire, soothe, suffer, temper, whimsy **7** appease, flatter, foolery, fooling, indulge, jesting, mollify, placate, spirits, waggery **8** drollery, give in to, jocosity, low humor, nonsense, raillery, ridicule, tolerate, travesty, wordplay **9** burlesque, funniness, low comedy, put up with, slapstick, wittiness **10** buffoonery, caricature, comicality, comply with, high comedy, jocoseness, jocularity, tomfoolery, wisecracks, witticisms **11** broad comedy, disposition, foolishness, frame of mind, go along with **12** monkeyshines **13** ludicrousness **14** ridiculousness

humorist 3 wag, wit **4** card **5** comic **8** comedian

humorous 5 comic, droll,

funny, witty **6** jocose **7** amusing, comical, jocular, waggish **8** farcical, mirthful, sportive **9** facetious, laughable, ludicrous, satirical, whimsical **10** ridiculous **11** nonsensical, rib-tickling **13** sidesplitting

hump 4 arch, bend, bump, knob, lift, lump, rise **5** bulge, hunch, knurl, mound, put up, tense **8** swelling **9** convexity **10** projection, prominence **11** excrescence

Humperdinck, Engelbert
born: **4** Bonn **7** Germany
composer of: **10** The Miracle **15** Hansel and Gretel

Humphry Clinker
author: **19** Tobias George Smollet
character: **10** Mr Dennison **12** Jerry Melford, Lydia Melford **14** George Dennison, Matthew Bramble **15** Winifred Jenkins **18** Miss Tabitha Bramble **26** Lieutenant Obadiah Lismahago

Humpty Dumpty
character in: **22** Through the Looking Glass
author: **7** Carroll

hunch 4 arch, bend, clue, hump, idea **5** tense **7** feeling, glimmer, inkling **8** good idea **9** intuition, suspicion **10** foreboding **11** premonition **12** presentiment

Hunchback of Notre Dame, The
author: **10** Victor Hugo
character: **9** Esmeralda, Gringoire, Quasimodo **12** Claude Frollo **20** Phoebus de Chateaupers

hunched 4 bent **7** crooked, slumped, stooped **9** contorted

hundredweight
abbreviation: **3** cwt

Hungary *see box*

hunger 3 yen **4** itch, love, lust, want, wish **5** crave, greed **6** desire, famine, hanker, liking, relish, thirst **7** burn for, craving, itch for, long for, pant for **8** appetite, fondness, voracity, yearn for, yearning **9** hankering, lust after **10** greediness, starvation **11** have a yen for, thirst after **12** malnutrition, ravenousness

hungry 5 eager **6** greedy **7** starved **8** ravenous, starving **9** voracious

hunk 3 gob, wad **4** clod, glob, lump, mass **5** block, chunk, piece **6** gobbet **7** portion **8** quantity

hunt 4 seek **5** chase, probe, shoot, stalk, trace, track, trail **6** course, follow, pursue **7** explore, go after, look for **8** coursing, drive out **9** ferret out, search for, try to find **11** go in quest of, inquire into **14** riding to hounds **20** leave no stone unturned

Hunt, Richard Morris
architect of: **8** Biltmore (Asheville NC) **11** Marble House (Newport RI), The Breakers (Newport RI) **12** Lenox Library (NYC) **14** Studio Building (NYC) **19** National Observatory (Washington DC) **22** William Vanderbilt House (NYC) **23** Metropolitan Museum of Art (NYC)

hunter
constellation of: **5** Orion
French: **8** chasseur

Hunter, Jim
nickname: **7** Catfish
sport: **8** baseball
position: **7** pitcher
team: **14** New York Yankees **16** Oakland Athletics

Hunter, Kim
real name: **8** Jane Cole
born: **9** Detroit MI
roles: **16** Stairway to Heaven, The Seventh Victim **21** A Streetcar Named Desire

Hunters
goddess of: **11** Britomartis

Hunting
god of: **7** Verbius
goddess of: **5** Diana **7** Artemis

Hunting Dogs
constellation of: **13** Canes Venatici

hurdle 4 jump, leap, snag, wall **5** bound, clear, fence, hedge, vault **6** hazard **7** barrier **8** obstacle, surmount **9** hindrance, roadblock **10** difficulty, impediment, spring over **11** obstruction **12** interference **14** stumbling block

hurl 4 cast, toss **5** chuck, fling, heave, pitch, sling, throw **6** launch, let fly, propel **7** fire off, project **9** discharge

hurly-burly 4 stir **5** furor **6** action, bustle, hubbub, hustle, uproar **8** activity **9** commotion **10** hullabaloo

hurrah, hurray 4 fine, good **5** bravo, cheer, great, huzza **6** huzzah, salute **7** acclaim, hosanna **9** excellent, halleluia, wonderful **10** exaltation, hallelujah

Hungary
  capital/largest city: 8 Budapest
  others: 4 Gyor, Pecs 5 Harta 6 Mohacs, Sopron, Szeged 7 Komarom, Miskolc, Szentes 8 Dubrecen, Kaposuar, Szegedin 9 Kecskemet 10 Albertirsa 11 Nagykanizsa, Szombathely
  measure: 3 ako 4 hold, yoke 5 itcze, marok, metze 7 huvelyk
  monetary unit: 4 gara 5 balas, krone, pengo 6 filler, forint, gulden, korona, ongara, ungara
  weight: 7 vamfont 8 vammazsa
  island: 8 Margaret
  lake: 5 Ferto 7 Balaton, Velence 9 Blatensee 10 Neusiedler, Plattensee
  mountain: 4 Alps, Bukk 5 Matra, Tatra 6 Bakony, Mecsek, Vertes 7 Cserhat, Gerecse 8 Borzsony, Zempleni 9 Korishegy 10 Carpathian
  highest point: 5 Kekes
  river: 3 Mur, Sio 4 Duna, Raab, Raba, Sajo, Zala 5 Bodva, Drava, Drave, Ipoly, Kapos, Koros, Maros, Tarna, Tisza 6 Danube, Henrad, Poprad, Szamos, Theiss, Zagyva 7 Vistula 8 Berretyo
  physical feature:
    canal: 3 Sio 6 Sarviz
    forest: 6 Bakony
    plain: 6 Puszta
    port: 5 Fiume
  people: 3 Hun 4 Serb 5 Croat, Gypsy 6 Cigany, Magyar, Slovak, Ugrian
    composer: 5 Lehar, Liszt 6 Bartok, Kodaly
    national hero: 5 Arpad
    playwright: 6 Molnar
  language: 6 German, Magyar, Slovak 8 Croatian 9 Hungarian 10 Finno-Ugric
  religion: 8 Lutheran 9 Calvinism 13 Roman Catholic 16 Eastern Orthodoxy
  place:
    church: 32 Gothic Coronation Church of Matthias
    ruins: 8 Aquincum
    square: 6 Heroes
    tomb: 14 Turbe of Gul Baba 16 Father of the Roses
  feature:
    dance: 3 kos 7 czardas 10 varsoviana
    dog: 4 puli
    musical instrument: 8 taragata 9 czimbalom
  food:
    dish: 6 gulyas 7 goulash 15 chicken paprikas
    pastry: 4 rete 5 torte
    wine: 5 Tokay 10 Bulls Blood

hurricane 7 cyclone, monsoon, tempest, typhoon 9 windstorm

Hurricane, The
  director: 8 John Ford
  cast: 7 Jon Hall 9 Mary Astor 12 C Aubrey Smith 13 Dorothy Lamour, Raymond Massey
  setting: 9 Manikoora

hurried 4 fast 5 hasty 6 hectic, rushed, speedy 7 cursory, frantic 8 careless, feverish, frenetic, headlong, slapdash, slipshod 9 breakneck, haphazard, impulsive 11 precipitate, superficial

hurry 3 ado, zip 4 bolt, dart, dash, fuss, goad, prod, rush, stew, whiz 5 egg on, haste, speed 6 flurry, hasten, hustle, push on, scurry, tumult, urge on 7 drive on, flutter, press on, scuttle, speed up, turmoil 8 make time, move fast, pressure, scramble, step on it 9 commotion, go quickly, make haste, step along 10 accelerate, get a move on, get hopping, lose no time, make tracks 11 come quickly, get cracking, go like a shot, go like sixty 12 step on the gas 13 go like the wind 14 cover the ground 15 hustle and bustle

hurt see box, p. 466

Hurt, John
  born: 7 England 22 Chesterfield Derbyshire
  roles: 5 Alien 8 Partners 14 The Elephant Man 15 Midnight Express

Hurt, William
  roles: 8 Body Heat 9 Gorky Park 10 Eyewitness 11 The Big Chill 13 Broadcast News 20 Kiss of the Spider Woman, Children of a Lesser God

hurtful 5 cruel 6 deadly 7 abusive, baleful, harmful 8 crushing, improper, stinging, wounding 9 injurious

hurtle 3 fly, hie, run, zip 4 bolt, dart, dash, race, rush, tear, whiz 5 bound, lunge, scoot, shoot, speed, spurt, whisk 6 charge, gallop, plunge, scurry 7 scamper, scuttle 11 go like a shot 13 go like the wind 14 go lickety-split

husband 3 man 4 keep, mate, save 5 amass, groom, hoard, hubby, store 6 old man, retain, save up, spouse 7 consort 8 conserve, maintain, preserve, set aside 10 accumulate, bridegroom, married man

husbandry 7 farming 9 geoponics 11 agriculture, cropraising 12 conservation
  god of: 9 Aristaeus

hush 4 calm 5 quell, quiet, shush, still 6 shut up, soothe 7 be quiet, be still, keep mum, mollify, silence 8 be silent, pipe down, quietude 9 quiet down, quietness, stillness 10 knock it off 11 tranquility 12 peacefulness, tranquillity

hushed 4 calm 5 quiet, still 6 calmed, gentle, lulled, silent 7 allayed, quieted, soothed, stifled 8 pacified, silenced, tranquil 12 tranquilized 13 tranquillized

hush money 5 bribe 6 payoff, payola 7 tribute 9 blackmail, extortion

huskiness 5 brawn 9 beefiness 10 hoarseness, robustness, ruggedness, sturdiness 11 muscularity

husky 3 big 5 beefy, burly, gruff, harsh, hefty, plump, rough, solid, stout, thick 6 brawny, coarse, hoarse, robust, stocky, strong, sturdy 7 cracked, grating, rasping, raucous, throaty 8 athletic, croaking, guttural, muscular, powerful, thickset 9 strapping 10 overweight 12 strong as an ox 15 broad-shouldered

> **hurt** 3 cut, mar 4 ache, balk, burn, foil, harm, lame, maim, mark, maul, pain, pang, scar 5 agony, block, check, grief, limit, lower, pique, smart, spike, sting, stung 6 aching, bruise, damage, deface, dismay, grieve, hamper, hinder, impair, impede, injure, lessen, mangle, marked, miffed, misery, morose, narrow, offend, oppose, pained, piqued, reduce, retard, thwart, weaken 7 agonize, bruised, chagrin, cripple, crushed, damaged, disable, exclude, inhibit, injured, mangled, painful, scarred, scratch, torment, torture, trouble, wounded 8 aggrieve, crippled, decrease, dejected, diminish, disabled, dismayed, distress, encumber, hold back, minimize, mutilate, obstruct, offended, preclude, restrain, smarting, soreness, wretched 9 aggrieved, annoyance, chagrined, dejection, disfigure, forestall, frustrate, heartsick, indignant, miserable, mortified, mutilated, resentful, scratched, suffering 10 discomfort, distressed, heartbreak, melancholy, resentment 11 aggravation, crestfallen, heartbroken 12 disheartened, wretchedness 13 cut to the quick, embarrassment, mortification

hussar 8 cavalier, horseman 10 cavalryman 12 horse soldier, horse trooper 14 mounted soldier

hussy 4 bawd, jade, minx, tart 5 wench, whore 6 harlot, wanton 7 baggage, trollop 8 strumpet 9 brash girl, lewd woman, saucy miss 10 adulteress, loose woman, prostitute 11 brazen woman, fallen woman 12 scarlet woman 17 woman of easy virtue

hustle 3 ado, fly 4 bolt, dart, dash, fuss, prod, push, rush, stir, toss 5 elbow, hurry, nudge, scoot, shove, throw 6 bounce, bustle, flurry, hasten, hubbub, jostle, scurry, tumult 7 flutter, scuttle, speed up, turmoil 8 make time, scramble, shoulder, step on it 9 commotion, make haste, step along 10 lose no time 11 hurry-scurry, move quickly 12 be aggressive

hustler 4 doer 6 con man, dynamo, hooker 8 go-getter, livewire, swindler 10 prostitute 12 streetwalker

Hustler, The
director: 12 Robert Rossen
cast: 10 Paul Newman 11 Piper Laurie 12 George C Scott 13 Jackie Gleason (Minnesota Fats)

Huston, John
director of: 8 Key Largo 10 The Misfits 11 Moulin Rouge 12 Prizzi's Honor 13 Asphalt Jungle 15 The African Queen 16 The Maltese Falcon 19 The Night of the Iguana 27 The Treasure of the Sierra Madre (Oscar)
father: 12 Walter Huston
wife: 11 Evelyn Keyes

born: 8 Nevada MO
roles: 9 Chinatown 11 Winter Kills

Huston, Walter
real name: 15 Walter Houghston
son: 10 John Huston
born: 6 Canada 7 Toronto
roles: 9 Dodsworth 18 All That Money Can Buy 27 The Treasure of the Sierra Madre

hut 4 shed 5 cabin, hutch, shack 6 lean-to, shanty 7 cottage, shelter

hutch 3 pen, sty 4 cage, coop, cote, crib, shed 5 stall 9 enclosure

Hutchinson, A S M
author of: 13 If Winter Comes

Hutton, Betty
real name: 18 Betty June Thornburg
born: 13 Battle Creek MI
roles: 15 Annie Get Your Gun 19 Greatest Show on Earth

Hutton, James
field: 7 geology
nationality: 8 Scottish
founder of: 7 geology

Hutton, Timothy
father: 9 Jim Hutton
roles: 4 Taps 6 Daniel 14 Ordinary People 22 The Falcon and the Snowman

Huxley, Aldous
author of: 11 Crome Yellow 13 Brave New World 17 Point Counter Point

Huxley, Julian
field: 7 biology
nationality: 7 British
promoted theory of: 9 evolution

Huygens, Christiaan
nationality: 5 Dutch
invented: 13 pendulum clock
discovered: 12 Saturn's rings
formulated: 17 wave theory of light

hyacinth 10 Hyacinthus 20 Hyacinthus orientalis
varieties: 4 musk, pine, star, wild, wood 5 Dutch, grape, Roman, water 6 common, garden, meadow, nutmeg, starry, summer, Tassel 7 feather, peacock 11 common grape

Hyacinthus
father: 7 Amyclas
daughter: 7 Orthaea
loved by: 6 Apollo 8 Zephyrus
killed by: 5 quoit 6 discus
from his blood sprang: 6 flower
petals marked: 4 AI-AI
means: 4 alas

Hyades
also: 5 Hyads 10 Palilicium
form: 6 nymphs
father: 5 Atlas 7 Oceanus
mother: 6 Tethys 7 Pleione
sisters: 8 Pleiades
nurtured: 8 Dionysus
placed among: 5 stars

Hyads see 6 Hyades

hybrid 5 cross 7 amalgam, mixture 9 composite, half-breed 10 crossbreed

hybridize 5 cross 14 cross-fertilize, cross-pollinate

Hydra
form: 12 water serpent
number of heads: 4 nine
killed by: 8 Hercules

hydrangea
varieties: 4 Wild 6 French, Peegee 8 Climbing

hydrogen
chemical symbol: 1 H

hydrophobia 6 rabies
fear of: 5 water

Hygeia
father: 9 Asclepius
goddess of: 6 health
corresponds to: 5 Salus

hygienic 4 pure 5 clean 7 aseptic, healthy, sterile 8 germ-free, harmless, salutary, sanitary 9 healthful, wholesome 10 salubrious, unpolluted 11 disease-free, disinfected, uninjurious 12 prophylactic 14 uncontaminated

Hylaeus
form: 7 centaur
born on: 5 cloud

Hylas
father: 9 Thiodamas
mother: 8 Menodice
companion of: 8 Hercules

Hyllus
father: 8 Hercules
mother: 6 Melite 8 Deianira
wife: 4 Iole
son: 9 Cleodaeus
grandson: 7 Temenus
built: 11 funeral pyre
for: 8 Hercules

Hymen
also: 9 Hymenaeus
god of: 8 marriage
holds: 5 torch
corresponds to: 8 Talassio

Hymenaeus *see* 5 Hymen

hymenoptera
class: 8 hexapoda
phylum: 10 arthropoda
group: 3 ant, bee 4 wasp
6 chacid, sawfly 12 ichneu-
mon fly

hymn 5 paean, psalm 6 anthem 12 song of praise 14 devotional song 17 song in
praise of God

Hymn to Proserpine
author: 24 Algernon Charles
Swinburne

Hypatia
author: 15 Charles Kingsley

hyperbole 8 metaphor 11 enlargement 12 exaggeration
13 magnification, overstatement 14 figure of speech

hyperbolize 6 overdo 7 amplify, magnify, stretch 9 embroider, overstate
10 exaggerate

hyperborean 6 arctic 8 freezing, northern 13 septentrional

Hyperborean
inhabitant of: 8 Paradise

Hyperenor
mentioned in: 5 Iliad
brother: 9 Euphorbus,
Polydamas
member of: 6 Sparti
killed by: 8 Menelaus

Hyperion
also: 6 Helios
form: 5 Titan
father: 6 Uranus
mother: 4 Gaea
sister: 5 Theia
son: 6 Helios

daughter: 3 Eos 6 Selene
corresponds to: 6 Apollo

Hyperion
author: 9 John Keats
24 Henry Wadsworth
Longfellow

Hypermnestra
member of: 8 Danaides
husband: 7 Lynceus
son: 4 Abas

hypersensitive 6 touchy
9 emotional 13 temperamental

Hypnos
also: 6 Hypnus
god of: 5 sleep
father: 6 Erebus
mother: 3 Nyx
brother: 8 Thanatos
corresponds to: 6 Somnus

hypnotic 9 soporific 11 mesmerizing 12 spellbinding

hypnotize 7 control 9 mesmerize, spellbind

Hypnus *see* 6 Hypnos

hypocrisy 6 deceit, fakery
7 falsity 9 duplicity, mendacity, phoniness 10 dishonesty
11 dissembling, insincerity
12 two-facedness

hypocrite 5 phony 8 deceiver
9 pretender 10 dissembler

Hypocrite 15 whited sepulcher

hypocritical 5 false, phony
7 feigned 8 feigning, two-
faced 9 deceitful, deceptive,
dishonest, insincere, truthless
11 counterfeit

hyporchema
form: 9 choral ode
origin: 5 Greek
honored: 6 Apollo 8 Dionysus

hypothalamus
regulates: 15 body
temperature
located in: 5 brain

hypothesis 6 theory, thesis
7 premise, theorem 8 pro-
posal 9 assertion, postulate
10 assumption, conclusion,
conjecture 11 explanation,
guesstimate, presumption,
proposition, speculation,
supposition

hypothesize 5 infer 6 assume
7 imagine, presume, suppose
8 theorize 9 postulate, speculate 10 conjecture

hypothetical 7 assumed, dubious 8 possible, supposed
9 imaginary, uncertain
10 contingent, postulated
11 conditional, conjectural,
presumptive, speculative, theoretical 12 questionable
13 suppositional

Hypselosaurus
type: 8 dinosaur, sauropod
location: 6 France 8 Mongolia
period: 10 Cretaceous

Hypseus
king of: 7 Lapiths
father: 6 Peneus
mother: 6 Creusa
daughter: 6 Cyrene 8 The-
misto 9 Astyagyia

Hypsilophodon
type: 8 dinosaur
10 ornithopod
location: 7 England
period: 10 Cretaceous

Hyrie
transformed into: 4 swan

Hyrmina
grandfather: 8 Endymion
son: 5 Actor

Hyrnetho
father: 7 Temenus
grandfather: 12 Aristomachus
husband: 10 Deiphontes

Hyrtius
allied with: 7 Trojans

hyssop 8 Hyssopus 18 Hyssopus officialis
varieties: 5 anise, giant, water 9 blue giant 10 nettle-
leaf 11 fennel giant, purple
giant, yellow giant 12 Mexican giant 13 fragrant giant,
wrinkled giant

Hyssop 13 Biblical plant

hysteria 3 fit 5 panic 6 frenzy
8 delirium

hysterical 5 crazy, droll 6 absurd, crazed, raving 7 amusing, comical 8 farcical,
frenzied, worked-up 9 laughable, ludicrous, wrought-up
10 distracted, distraught, ridiculous, uproarious 11 carried
away, overwrought, wildly
funny 13 beside oneself, out
of one's wits
14 uncontrollable

hysterics 3 fit 12 emotionalism

I, Claudius
　　author: **12** Robert Graves
　　story of: **36** Tiberius Claudius
　　　Drusus Nero Germanicus
　　　(Emperor of Rome)

I, the Jury
　　author: **14** Mickey Spillane

Iache
　　form: **5** nymph
　　companion of: **10** Persephone

I Am a Fugitive from a Chain Gang
　　director: **11** Mervyn LeRoy
　　cast: **8** Paul Muni **11** Helen
　　　Vinson **13** Glenda Farrell,
　　　Preston Foster

Iambe
　　occupation: **11** storyteller
　　storyteller for: **7** Demeter

I am unwilling to contend
　　Latin: **14** nolo contendere

Iamus
　　father: **6** Apollo
　　mother: **6** Evadne
　　became: **7** prophet

Ianthe
　　husband: **5** Iphis

Iapetus
　　member of: **6** Titans
　　father: **6** Uranus
　　mother: **4** Gaea
　　wife: **6** Themis
　　son: **5** Atlas **9** Menoetius
　　　10 Epimetheus, Prometheus

Iapyx
　　father: **8** Daedalus

Iardanus
　　king of: **5** Lydia
　　daughter: **7** Omphale

Iasion
　　founder of: **7** Trojans
　　twin brother: **8** Dardanus

Iaso
　　goddess of: **7** healing
　　father: **9** Asclepius

Iasus
　　father: **8** Lycurgus

daughter: **8** Atalanta
abandoned: **8** Atalanta

Ibanez, Vicente Blasco
　　author of: **30** The Four
　　　Horsemen of the Apocalypse

Iberian Peninsula
　　also: **8** Hesperia

Ibsen, Henrik
　　author of: **6** Ghosts **8** Peer
　　　Gynt **11** A Doll's House,
　　　Hedda Gabler, Rosmersholm,
　　　The Wild Duck **16** The Master
　　　Builder **18** An Enemy of
　　　the People, John Gabriel
　　　Borkman

Iceland
　　other name: **15** Lydveldid Island
　　capital/largest city: **9** Reykjavik
　　others: **3** Hof **6** Geysir **7** Akranes, Husavik **8** Akureyri,
　　　Keflavik, Kopasker **9** Kopavogur **10** Hveragerdi, Isafjordur **12** Siglufjordur **13** Hafnarfjordur, Neskaupstadur,
　　　Seydisfjordur
　　government:
　　　general assembly: **7** Althing
　　measure: **3** set **4** alin **5** almud **6** almenn, ferfet, pattur
　　　7 fathmur, fermila, oltunna
　　monetary unit: **5** aurar, eyrir, krona
　　weight: **4** pund **5** pound, tunna **6** smjors
　　island: **7** Heimaey, Surtsey, Westman
　　lake: **6** Myvatn **10** Thorisvatn **14** Thingvallavatn
　　mountain: **5** Jokul **10** Orafajokul
　　　volcano: **4** Laki **5** Askja, Hekla, Katla **7** Surtsey
　　highest point: **17** Hvannadalshnjukur
　　river: **5** Hvita **7** Fnjoska, Thjorsa **15** Jokulsa a Fjollum
　　sea: **9** Greenland **13** North Atlantic
　　physical feature:
　　　fjord: **4** Eyja
　　　geyser: **5** gryla **6** geysir **11** Great Gusher
　　　glacier: **6** Jokull **11** Orafajokull, Vatnajokull
　　　plain: **15** Skeidharasandur
　　　waterfall: **8** Godafoss, Gullfoss **9** Dettifoss
　　people: **6** Celtic, Viking **8** Norseman **9** Norwegian
　　　first settler: **8** Arnarson
　　　hero: **4** Bele, Eric, Leif **10** Sigurdsson
　　language: **5** Norse **9** Icelandic
　　religion: **19** Evangelical Lutheran
　　place:
　　　national shrine: **11** Thingvellir
　　feature:
　　　airport: **9** Kopavogur
　　　bird: **4** gull **6** falcon **9** gyrfalcon
　　　literary genre: **4** saga
　　　wrestling: **5** glima
　　food:
　　　dish: **4** skyr, svio **7** bloomor **8** harofisk

Ibzan 11 Hebrew judge

I came, I saw, I conquered
Latin: 12 veni vidi vici
author: 12 Julius Caesar

Icarius
son: 8 Perilaus
daughter: 7 Erigone
8 Penelope
hospitable to: 8 Dionysus
hound dog: 5 Maera

Icarus
father: 8 Daedalus
built: 5 wings
flew too near: 3 sun
death by: 8 drowning

ice 3 gem 4 berg, floe, gems,
rime 5 chill, frost, glace
6 freeze, icicle, jewels 7 crystal, dessert, glacier, jewelry,
sherbet 8 diamonds 11 refrigerant, refrigerate

ice-cold 3 icy 4 cold 5 gelid,
polar 6 arctic, bitter, frigid,
frosty, wintry 7 chilled,
frosted, glacial, subzero
8 chilling, freezing, Siberian,
unheated, unwarmed 9 stone-
cold, supercold 11 hyperborean, supercooled 12 bone-
chilling

ice cream 7 dessert, sherbet

Iceland *see box*

Icelus
origin: 5 Greek
god of: 6 dreams
assumed shapes of:
7 animals
epithet: 8 Phobetor
corresponds to: 8 Morpheus

Iceman
nickname of: 12 George
Gervin

Iceman Cometh, The
author: 12 Eugene O'Neill

Ice Palace
author: 10 Edna Ferber

ice skating
athlete: 9 Janet Lynn, John
Curry 10 Carol Heiss, Dick
Button, Eric Heiden, Sonja
Henie 11 Sheila Young
12 Peggy Fleming 13 Doro-
thy Hamill, Scott Hamilton
14 Linda Fratianne

ich dien 6 I serve
motto of: 13 Prince of Wales

I Ching 30 ancient Chinese
book of divination

ichor
form: 5 fluid
in veins of: 4 gods

Ichthyocentaur
form: 8 creature
location: 3 sea
head/torso: 5 human

legs: 5 horse
tail: 4 fish

iciness 4 cold 5 chill 9 frigidity 10 chilliness, frostiness,
wintriness 12 slipperiness

ici on parle francais
18 French is spoken here
19 here one speaks French

icky 5 gluey, gooey, gross,
gucky, gummy, mushy, nasty,
tacky, weepy 6 sticky, syrupy,
viscid 7 maudlin, viscous
8 bathetic 9 glutinous, offensive, repulsive, revolting
10 disgusting 12 mucilaginous

icon, ikon 4 idol 5 image 6 effigy, figure, statue 7 picture
8 likeness 11 sacred image

iconoclast 5 rebel 7 radical,
upstart 9 dissenter 13 nonconformist, revolutionary

icy 3 raw 4 cold, cool 5 aloof,
gelid 6 arctic, chilly, frigid,
frosty, frozen, glazed, sleety,
wintry 7 distant, glacial,
haughty, hostile 8 chilling,
freezing, slippery 9 impassive
10 forbidding, unfriendly
11 coldhearted, unemotional

Ida
form: 5 nymph
watched over: 4 Zeus

Idaea
form: 5 nymph
domain: 8 Mount Ida
husband: 7 Phineus
9 Scamander
son: 6 Teucer

Idaho *see box*

Idas
father: 8 Aphareus
mother: 5 Arene
brother: 7 Lynceus
wife: 8 Marpessa
daughter: 9 Cleopatra

idea 4 clue, hint, view 6 belief,
notion 7 concept, feeling, inkling, insight, opinion, outlook,
thought 8 approach, proposal,
solution 9 sentiment 10 conception, conclusion, conviction, impression, indication,
intimation, suggestion 12 apperception, appreciation
13 approximation, mental picture, understanding 14 interpretation, recommendation

ideal 3 aim 4 hero, idol

Idaho
abbreviation: 2 ID 3 Ida
nickname: 3 Gem
capital/largest city: 5 Boise
others: 4 Buhl 5 Malad, Nampa 6 Moscow 7 Orofino, Rex-
burg 8 Caldwell, Lewiston 9 Pocatello, Twin Falls
10 Idaho Falls 11 Coeur d'Alene
college: 17 Northwest Nazarene
explorer: 13 Lewis and Clark
feature: 9 Sun Valley 17 Continental Divide
  dam: 5 Oxbow 8 Brownlee
  national monument: 16 Craters of the Moon
tribe: 5 Banak, Shake 6 Cayuse, Paiute, Spokan 7 Bannock,
Kutenai, Spokane 8 Kalispel, Nez Perce, Sahaptin, Shoshone, Shoshoni 9 Shoshonee 11 Coeur d'Alene
people: 9 Ezra Pound, Sacagawea 11 Chief Joseph 17 William Edgar Borah
lake: 4 Bear 5 Grey's 6 Priest 11 Coeur d'Alene, Pend Oreille 22 American Falls Reservoir
land rank: 10 thirteenth
mountain: 4 Ryan 5 Rocky 6 Rhodes, Taylor, Tetons
7 Cabinet 8 Bannocks, Big Baldy, Bluenose, Sawtooth
9 Wasatches 10 Clearwater 11 Beaverheads, Bitterroots
13 Selkirk Ranges
  highest point: 5 Borah
physical feature:
  falls: 5 Moyie 8 Shoshone 9 Upper Mesa
  springs: 4 Soda 6 Hooper 7 Lavahot
river: 4 Bear 5 Boise, Snake, St Joe 6 Locksa, Salmon
7 Payette, Spokane 8 Kootenai 11 Coeur d'Alene, Pend
Oreille
state admission: 10 forty-third
state bird: 16 mountain bluebird
state flower: 7 syringa
state motto: 13 It Is Perpetual 16 Let It Be Perpetual
state song: 15 Here We Have Idaho
state tree: 16 western white pine

5 dream, model **7** epitome, optimal, pattern, perfect **8** exemplar, last word, paradigm, standard, ultimate **9** archetype, criterion, excellent, exemplary, faultless, matchless, objective **10** impeccable **11** inspiration

idealism 8 optimism **9** meliorism **10** utopianism **11** romanticism

idealist 7 dreamer, utopian **8** romantic **9** Pollyanna, stargazer, visionary **11** romanticist **13** perfectionist

idealized 6 dreamy **7** utopian, wishful **8** fanciful, illusory, romantic **10** optimistic **11** pie-in-the-sky, unrealistic **13** insubstantial

idea man 7 advisor **8** inventor **9** innovator **10** consultant **12** entrepreneur

idee fixe 9 fixed idea
  music: 14 recurring motif

idem 24 the same as previously given **28** the same as previously mentioned

identical 4 twin **7** uniform **8** self-same, very same **9** duplicate **15** interchangeable **17** indistinguishable

identification 5 badge, label **8** passport **9** detection **10** connection, revelation **11** affiliation, association, credentials, pinpointing, recognition **12** confirmation, verification **13** ascertainment

identify 4 know **5** place **6** verify **7** combine, pick out, specify **9** associate, designate, determine, recognize, single out **11** distinguish

identifying device 4 logo, mark, sign **5** badge **6** emblem, ensign, symbol **8** insignia, logotype

identity 4 name, self **6** accord **7** harmony, oneness, rapport **9** unanimity **11** delineation, duplication, personality **13** individuality **15** differentiation, distinctiveness

ideology 5 dogma, ethos **6** ideals, theory **7** program **8** doctrine **9** rationale **10** principles

Ides of March, The
  author: 14 Thornton Wilder

id est 6 that is
  abbreviation: 2 ie

idiocy 5 folly **6** lunacy **7** fatuity, inanity, madness, suicide **8** insanity **9** absurdity, asininity, cretinism, mongolism, stupidity **11** foolishness **13** foolhardiness, senselessness

idiom 5 argot, lingo, slang **6** brogue, jargon, patois, phrase, speech **7** dialect **8** language, localism, parlance **10** vernacular **13** colloquialism

idiomatic 6 common **8** informal, ordinary **10** vernacular **14** conversational

idiosyncrasy 5 quirk **6** oddity **7** anomaly **9** mannerism **11** distinction, peculiarity **12** eccentricity

idiot 3 ass **4** boob, dolt, dope, fool, jerk **5** cluck, dummy, dunce, moron, ninny **6** cretin, dimwit, nitwit **7** halfwit **8** dumbbell, numskull **9** blockhead, numbskull, simpleton **10** nincompoop

Idiot, The
  author: 16 Fyodor Dostoevsky
  character: 7 Myshkin **11** Mme Epanchin **14** Aglaya Epanchin, Parfen Rogozhin **16** Natasha Filipovna **19** Ganya Ardalionovitch **22** Prince Lef Nicolaievitch

idiotic 5 crazy, dopey, nutty **6** absurd, addled, stupid **7** asinine, doltish, foolish, moronic **9** foolhardy, imbecilic, senseless **10** half-witted, irrational, ridiculous **12** feebleminded **13** rattlebrained

I direct
  Latin: 6 dirigo
  motto of: 5 Maine

idle 4 laze, lazy, loaf, vain **5** empty, inert, petty, vapid, waste, while **6** drowsy, fallow, futile, otiose, putter, torpid, unused **7** aimless, fritter, jobless, languid, trivial, useless, wait out **8** baseless, bootless, fool away, inactive, indolent, listless, slothful, sluggish, trifling **9** at leisure, enervated, fruitless, lethargic, out of work, pointless, somnolent, valueless, worthless **10** not working, unemployed, unoccupied **11** unimportant **12** unproductive **15** unsubstantiated

idleness 5 sloth **7** inertia **8** laziness, lethargy **9** indolence **10** inactivity **11** joblessness, languidness **12** sluggishness, unemployment
  French: 8 flanerie

idler 3 bum **6** loafer **7** drifter, vagrant **10** ne'er-do-well
  French: 7 flaneur

idol 4 hero, icon **5** relic **6** effigy, statue **7** darling **8** artifact **10** simulacrum, golden calf **11** graven image, inspiration

idolatry 5 mania **7** madness, passion, worship **8** devotion **9** adoration, obsession **10** veneration **11** idolization, infatuation **12** image worship **13** preoccupation

idolization 7 worship **9** adulation, reverence **10** exaltation, veneration

idolize 5 adore, deify, honor, prize **6** admire, revere **7** worship **8** treasure, venerate **9** reverence **11** apotheosize

Idomeneo, re di Creta
  also: 20 Idomeneus King of Crete
  opera by: 6 Mozart
  character: 4 Ilia **7** Electra **8** Idamante, Poseidon

Idomeneus
  king of: 5 Crete
  father: 9 Deucalion

I don't know what
  French: 12 je ne sais quoi

Idothea
  form: 5 nymph
  father: 7 Proteus

I Dream of Jeannie
  character: 7 Jeannie **9** Dr Bellows **10** (Captain) Tony Nelson **11** Gen Peterson, (Captain) Roger Healey **13** Amanda Bellows
  cast: 9 Bill Daily **11** Barbara Eden, Hayden Rorke, Larry Hagman **13** Barton MacLane, Emmaline Henry
  Tony's job: 9 astronaut

Idun, Iduna
  also: 5 Ithun **6** Ithunn
  origin: 12 Scandinavian
  goddess of: 6 spring
  husband: 5 Brage, Bragi
  kept: 11 youth apples

idyllic 6 rustic, sylvan **7** bucolic **8** arcadian, pastoral, peaceful, romantic **9** unspoiled

Idylls of the King, The
  author: 18 Alfred Lord Tennyson
  based on story of: 10 King Arthur

Ierne *see* **7** Ireland

if 2 an **6** though **7** whether **8** although, provided **9** condition, supposing **10** even though **11** stipulation, supposition

iffy 4 moot **5** risky **6** chancy, unsure **7** dubious, erratic **8** arguable, doubtful **9** debatable, uncertain, undecided, unsettled, whimsical **10** capricious, disputable, unresolved **11** conjectural, speculative **12** questionable **13** problematical, unpredictable

Ifriqiyah *see* 7 Tunisia

If Winter Comes
author: 13 A S M Hutchinson

if you please
French: 12 s'il vous plait

Iggdrasil *see* 9 Yggdrasil

ignitable 8 burnable 9 flammable 10 combustive, incendiary 11 combustible, inflammable 13 conflagrative

ignite 4 burn, fire 5 blaze, flame, light 6 blow up, kindle 7 explode, inflame 8 take fire, touch off 9 catch fire, set fire to, set on fire 11 catch on fire

ignoble 3 low 4 base, foul, mean, vile 6 craven 7 debased, heinous 8 cowardly, degraded, depraved, indecent, infamous, inferior, shameful, unworthy 9 dastardly, nefarious 10 degenerate, despicable 11 disgraceful 12 contemptible, dishonorable 13 discreditable, pusillanimous 14 unconscionable

ignominious 3 low 5 sorry 6 abject 8 grievous, shameful, wretched 9 degrading 10 despicable, inglorious, unbearable 11 disgraceful, humiliating 12 dishonorable, disreputable 13 discreditable

ignominy 5 shame 6 infamy 8 contempt, disgrace, dishonor 11 degradation, humiliation

ignoramus 4 fool 5 dunce 6 nitwit 7 low-brow 8 numskull 9 numbskull, simpleton 10 illiterate 11 know-nothing

ignorance 9 confusion 10 illiteracy 11 unawareness 12 backwardness 13 obliviousness, unfamiliarity 15 unenlightenment

ignorant 4 dumb 5 naive 6 stupid 7 asinine, blind to, fatuous, shallow, unaware 8 innocent, untaught 9 in the dark, unknowing, unlearned, untrained, untutored, unworldly 10 illiterate, uneducated, uninformed, unlettered, unschooled 11 insensitive, uncognizant 12 unperceptive 13 irresponsible, unenlightened, unintelligent 15 unknowledgeable

ignore 4 omit, skip, snub 5 scorn 6 eschew, slight 7 neglect 8 overlook, pass over 9 disregard

Igraine
character in: 16 Arthurian romance
son: 6 Arthur

Iguanodon
type: 8 dinosaur 10 ornithopod
means: 11 iguana tooth
found by: 13 Gideon Mantell
location: 6 Africa, Europe, Sussex 7 Belgium, England
period: 10 Cretaceous
characteristic: 10 duck-billed

ikebana
Japanese: 21 art of arranging flowers

Ile de France *see* 9 Mauritius

Ilha Formosa *see* 6 Taiwan

Iliad, The
author: 5 Homer
character: 5 Paris, Priam 6 Hector 8 Achilles, Menelaus 9 Agamemnon, Patroclus 11 Helen of Troy
subject: 9 Trojan War

Iliniwek *see* 8 Illinois

Ilion
Greek name for: 11 ancient Troy

Ilione
father: 5 Priam
mother: 6 Hecuba
husband: 11 Polymnestor
son: 8 Deipylus
raised: 9 Polydorus

Ilioneus
mentioned in: 6 Aeneid
home: 4 Troy
vocation: 7 warrior
fled: 4 Troy
fled with: 6 Aeneas
killed by: 8 Peneleus

Ilithyia *see* 10 Eileithyia

Ilium
Latin name for: 11 ancient Troy

ill, ills 3 woe 4 evil, foul, harm, sick, vile 5 abuse, cross, no way, surly, trial 6 ailing, damage, hardly, injury, laid up, malady, malice, nowise, plague, poorly, sickly, sorrow, unkind, unwell, wicked 7 ailment, cruelty, disease, failing, harmful, invalid, not well, ominous, outrage, peevish, trouble, unlucky, unsound 8 diseased, mischief, scarcely, sinister, vengeful 9 afflicted, complaint, infirmity, malicious, unhealthy 10 affliction, disturbing, foreboding, indisposed, misfortune, wickedness 11 abomination, acrimonious, malefaction, threatening, unfavorable 12 inauspicious, unpropitious 15 under the weather

ill-advised 4 dumb, rash 5 hasty, silly 6 myopic, stupid, unwise 7 foolish 9 foolhardy, ill-judged, impolitic, imprudent, misguided, senseless 10 indiscreet, unthinking 11 injudicious 12 shortsighted 13 ill-considered, irresponsible

ill-at-ease 3 shy 4 edgy 6 on edge, uneasy 7 abashed, fidgety, nervous 8 bothered, troubled 9 disturbed, nonplused, perturbed 10 disquieted, nonplussed 11 discomfited, discomposed, embarrassed 12 disconcerted 13 self-conscious, uncomfortable 15 discountenanced

ill-boding 4 dire 7 ominous 9 ill-omened 11 apocalyptic 12 inauspicious

ill-bred 4 rude 5 crude 7 boorish, uncivil, uncouth 8 churlish, impolite 10 unmannerly 11 ill-mannered 12 discourteous

ill-defined 3 dim 4 hazy 5 faint, murky 6 blurry 7 blurred, clouded, shadowy 8 nebulous, obscured 10 indistinct

illegal 5 wrong 6 banned 7 illicit 8 criminal, not legal, outlawed, unlawful 9 felonious, forbidden 10 actionable, prohibited, proscribed 12 illegitimate, unauthorized, unsanctioned 13 against the law

illegible 7 unclear 8 obscured 9 scribbled 10 unreadable 14 indecipherable, undecipherable, unintelligible

illegitimate 7 bastard, illegal, illicit, lawless, natural 8 baseborn, improper, unlawful 10 prohibited 11 misbegotten, unwarranted 12 unauthorized, unsanctioned

ill-fated 6 doomed, jinxed 7 hapless, unlucky 8 blighted, luckless 9 ill-omened 10 ill-starred

ill-favored 4 ugly 5 plain 6 homely 8 unlovely 9 repulsive, unsightly 12 disagreeable, unattractive

ill-fortune 6 mishap 7 bad luck 8 calamity, disaster, hardship 9 adversity 10 misfortune 11 catastrophe

ill health 6 malady 7 ailment, disease, illness 8 sickness 9 infirmity

ill-humored 5 sulky, testy 6 crabby, grumpy, sullen 7 grouchy 10 in a bad mood, unfriendly, unsociable

illiberal 5 petty, small **6** biased, narrow **7** bigoted **9** hidebound **10** brassbound, intolerant, prejudiced, ungenerous **11** opinionated, small-minded **12** narrow-minded, shortsighted

illicit 7 illegal, lawless **8** criminal, improper, not legal, unlawful **9** felonious **10** prohibited **11** black-market, clandestine **12** illegitimate, not permitted, unauthorized **13** against the law, impermissible **15** under-the-counter

Illinois *see box*

Illinois (Iliniwek)
  language family: 9 Algonkian **10** Algonquian
  tribe: 6 Peoria **7** Cahokia, Tamaroa **9** Kaskaskia, Moingwena **10** Michigamea
  location: 4 Iowa, Ohio **7** Indiana **8** Illinois, Michigan, Missouri **9** Wisconsin
  built: 12 Cahokia Mound
  murdered: 7 Pontiac

related to: 5 Miami **6** Ojibwa **7** Ojibway

illiterate 7 witless **8** childish, ignorant, unversed **9** unlearned, untutored **10** amateurish, incoherent, uneducated, uninformed, unlettered, unreliable, unschooled **11** not educated, uninitiated, unscholarly **12** uninstructed **13** unenlightened, ungrammatical **15** unknowledgeable

ill-made 6 shoddy **7** awkward **8** deformed, inferior **9** makeshift, malformed **10** jerry-built, jury-rigged **15** misproportioned

ill-mannered 4 rude **5** crude **6** coarse **7** boorish, ill-bred, loutish, uncivil **8** impolite **9** offensive, ungallant **10** ill-behaved, ungracious **12** discourteous **13** disrespectful

ill-natured 4 sour **5** cross, nasty, surly **6** bitter, cranky, malign **7** caustic, grouchy,

peevish **8** captious, churlish, spiteful, venomous **9** crotchety, irascible, irritable, malignant, rancorous, splenetic **10** ill-humored, unfriendly **11** acrimonious, contentious, quarrelsome **12** antagonistic, cantankerous

illness 6 malady **7** ailment, disease **8** disorder, sickness **9** complaint, ill health, infirmity **10** affliction, disability, poor health **11** malfunction **13** indisposition

illness recovery
  god of: 11 Telesphorus

illogical 4 wild **5** crazy, dopey, nutty, silly, wacky **6** absurd, far-out, screwy **7** asinine, offbeat, unsound **9** erroneous, senseless **10** fallacious, irrational, off-the-wall, .ridiculous **11** incongruent, incongruous, nonsensical, unreasoning **12** inconsistent, preposterous, unreasonable **13** contradictory

ill-omened 4 dire **7** adverse, ominous **9** ill-boding **11** apocalyptic, unfavorable **12** inauspicious, unpropitious

ill-smelling 4 foul, high, olid, rank **5** fetid, fusty **6** putrid, rancid, smelly, stinky, strong **7** reeking **8** stinking **10** malodorous

ill-starred 4 dire **5** fatal **6** tragic **7** adverse **8** ill-fated **10** calamitous, disastrous **11** unfortunate **12** catastrophic, inauspicious

ill-suited 5 inapt **8** mismated, unsuited **9** misjoined, unfitting **10** ill-adapted, ill-matched, malapropos, mismatched, unbecoming, unsuitable **11** incongruous, unbefitting, uncongenial **12** incompatible, inconsistent **13** inappropriate

ill-tempered 4 mean, rude, sour **5** angry, cross, harsh, nasty, testy **6** bitter, cranky, shirty **7** acerbic, furious, grouchy, peevish, waspish **8** choleric, churlish, petulant **9** crotchety, irascible, irritable **10** bad-natured, ill-humored, ill-natured, in a bad mood, unpleasant **11** acrimonious **12** cantankerous

ill-treatment 4 harm **5** abuse **6** ill-use, injury, misuse **7** cruelty **13** mortification

illuminate 5 edify, light **7** clarify, enhance, explain, light up **8** brighten, illumine, instruct, spell out **9** elucidate, enlighten, exemplify, irradiate, make clear **12** throw light on **13** cast light upon

---

Illinois
  abbreviation: 2 IL **3** Ill
  nickname: 4 Tall **6** Sucker **7** Prairie **13** Land of Lincoln
  capital: 11 Springfield
  largest city: 7 Chicago
  others: 4 Pana **5** Alton, Cairo, Elgin, Flora, Olney, Pekin **6** Albion, Berwyn, Canton, Herrin, Joliet, Peoria, Skokie **7** Batavia, Decatur, Genesco, Mendota, Nokomis **8** Evanston, Rockford, Waukegan **9** Centralia **10** Barrington **11** Bloomington
  college: 4 Knox **5** Barat **6** Aurora, DePaul, Eureka, Loyola, Olivet, Quincy, ‹nimer **7** Bradley, Chicago, Wheaton **8** Millikin **9** Augustana **12** Northwestern **16** Illinois Wesleyan **23** Illinois Institute of Tech
  explorer: 6 Joliet **7** Jolliet **9** Marquette
  feature: 10 stockyards
    airport: **5** O'Hare
    museum: **18** Science and Industry
    seaway: **10** St Lawrence
    trail: **7** Lincoln
  tribe: 3 Fox **4** Sauk **9** Kaskaskia
  people: 9 Black Hawk, Jack Benny **10** Jane Addams, Walt Disney **12** Carl Sandburg **15** Ernest Hemingway **18** Engineer Casey Jones **20** William Jennings Bryan
  lake: 3 Fox **5** Grass **7** Calumet **8** Michigan, Pistakee
  land rank: 12 twenty-fourth
  mountain: 6 Ozarks
    highest point: **12** Charles Mound
  physical feature:
    hills: **7** Shawnee
  president: 14 Abraham Lincoln
  river: 4 Ohio, Rock **5** Spoon **6** Wabash **7** Chicago, Elkhorn **8** Big Muddy, Illinois, Mackinaw, Sangamon **9** Kaskaskia **10** Des Plaines **11** Mississippi
  state admission: 11 twenty-first
  state bird: 8 cardinal
  state flower: 6 violet
  state motto: 29 State Sovereignty—National Union
  state song: 8 Illinois
  state tree: 7 burl oak **8** white oak

illuminated 3 lit **5** lit up
6 bright **7** lighted **9** clarified, decorated, illumined
10 brightened, elucidated, irradiated

illumination 6 lights, wisdom
7 insight **8** lighting **9** education, knowledge **10** illumining, lighting up, perception, revelation **11** edification, information, instruction, irradiation
13 comprehension, enlightenment

Illuminations, Les
author: **13** Arthur Rimbaud

illumined 3 lit **7** lighted **8** luminous **11** illuminated

ill-use 4 harm, hurt **5** abuse
6 injure, misuse **7** assault, cruelty, harming **8** maltreat, mistreat **10** bodily harm
12 maltreatment, mistreatment

illusion 5 error, fancy **6** mirage, vagary, vision **7** caprice, chimera, fallacy **8** delusion, phantasm **9** deception, false idea, misbelief, semblance, unreality **10** apparition, false image, hocus-pocus, humbuggery, impression **11** false belief
13 hallucination, misconception, misimpression
15 misapprehension

illusive 5 false **6** unreal
7 phantom, seeming **8** apparent, chimeric, fanciful, fantastic, illusory **9** deceptive
10 ostensible **11** illusionary

illusory 4 sham **5** false **6** unreal **7** seeming **8** apparent, delusive, fanciful, illusive, spurious **9** deceptive, erroneous, imaginary **10** fallacious, misleading, ostensible
11 counterfeit, unrealistic
13 hallucinatory

illustrate 4 show **6** define
7 clarify, explain, picture, point up, portray **8** decorate, ornament **9** bring home, delineate, elucidate, emphasize, make clear, represent **10** illuminate **11** demonstrate **12** pictorialize, throw light on
16 make intelligible

illustration 5 image, plate
6 figure **7** drawing, example, picture **8** instance, specimen
9 portrayal **10** photograph
14 representation
15 exemplification

illustrious 5 famed, great **6** famous **7** eminent, honored
8 glorious, lustrous, peerless, renowned, splendid **9** acclaimed, brilliant, exemplary, matchless, prominent **10** celebrated **11** magnificent
13 distinguished

illustriousness 8 grandeur
9 greatness **11** distinction
12 magnificence

ill will 4 gall **5** anger, spite
6 animus, enmity, hatred, malice, rancor, spleen **7** dislike
8 acrimony, aversion, bad blood, loathing **9** animosity, antipathy, hostility **10** abhorrence, antagonism, bitterness, contention **11** malevolence
12 hard feelings, spitefulness

ill wind 7 bad luck **8** bad break, hard luck **9** adversity, mischance **10** misfortune

Illyrius
father: **6** Cadmus

Ilmarinen
origin: **7** Finnish
form: **10** blacksmith
hero in: **8** Kalevala
forged: **5** Sampo
Sampo's owner: **5** Louhi

I Love Lucy
character: **9** Fred Mertz
10 Ethel Mertz **11** Little Ricky, Lucy Ricardo
12 Ricky Ricardo
cast: **9** Desi Arnaz **11** Lucille Ball, Vivian Vance **14** William Frawley
Ricky's club: **7** Babaloo
9 Tropicana

Il Penseroso
author: **10** John Milton
companion piece: **8** L'Allegro

image 4 copy, icon, idea, idol
6 double, effigy, fetish, figure, memory, simile, statue, symbol, visage **7** concept, picture, replica **8** likeness, metaphor, portrait **9** depiction, duplicate, facsimile, mirroring, semblance **10** photograph, reflection, simulacrum
11 countenance, delineation, incarnation **12** recollection, reproduction **13** mental picture
14 figure of speech, representation

imaginable 8 feasible **9** thinkable **11** conceivable

imaginary 4 sham **5** fancy, phony **6** made-up, unreal
7 fancied, fiction, figment
8 delusion, fabulous, fanciful, illusion, illusory, invented, mythical, romantic **9** fantastic, figmental, legendary **10** factitious, fictitious **11** counterfeit, make-believe

imagination 5 fancy **7** cunning, thought **9** ingenuity, invention **10** astuteness, creativity, enterprise **12** creativeness
13 inventiveness **14** thoughtfulness **15** creative thought, resourcefulness

imaginative 6 clever **7** unusual **8** creative, inspired, original **9** ingenious, inventive
10 innovative **11** resourceful
12 enterprising **16** off the beaten path, out of the ordinary

imagine 5 fancy, guess, infer, judge **6** assume, gather **7** believe, dream up, picture, presume, pretend, project, suppose, surmise, suspect
8 conceive, envisage, envision
9 fantasize, visualize
10 conjecture

imbecile 3 ass **4** dolt, dope, fool, jerk **5** dummy, dunce, idiot, moron, ninny **6** nitwit
7 dingbat **8** dumbbell **9** blockhead, simpleton
10 nincompoop

imbecilic 4 dumb **5** inane, silly **6** absurd, stupid **7** asinine, foolish **8** careless, mindless
11 thoughtless

imbecility 6 idiocy **8** dullness, dumbness **9** asininity, stupidity, thickness
16 simplemindedness

imbibe 4 swig, tope **5** drink, quaff **6** guzzle, ingest, tipple
7 consume, partake, swallow
8 chugalug, toss down, wash down

imbiber 4 wino **5** drunk, toper
7 drinker, tippler **8** consumer, drunkard, ingester

Imbrius
mentioned in: **5** Iliad
father: **6** Mentor
killed by: **6** Teucer

imbroglio 3 row **4** fray
5 brawl, broil, clash, fight, melee, scrap **6** fracas, ruckus, rumpus, uproar **7** scuffle **8** argument **9** confusion **11** altercation, embroilment
12 entanglement
13 embarrassment

imbue 4 fill, fire, tint **5** bathe, color, endow, steep, tinge
6 arouse, infuse **7** animate, impress, ingrain, inspire, instill, pervade, suffuse **8** permeate, tincture **9** inculcate

Imhotep
father: **4** Ptah
mother: **7** Sekhmet
position: **6** scribe, vizier, writer **9** architect, physician
architect of pyramid:
8 Sakkarah

imitate 3 ape **4** copy, mime
5 mimic **6** mirror, parody, parrot **7** emulate, pass for **8** look like, simulate **9** duplicate, represent **10** caricature **11** counterfeit, impersonate

imitation 4 fake, mock, sham
5 aping, phony **6** ersatz, parody **7** man-made, mimicry, takeoff **8** travesty **9** burlesque, facsimile, semblance, simulated, synthetic **10** adaptation, artificial, caricature, impression, similarity, simulation **11** counterfeit, duplication, make-believe **12** reproduction **13** impersonation **14** representation

Imitation of Christ, The
author: **13** Thomas a Kempis

immaculate 4 pure **5** clean, ideal **6** chaste, intact, virgin **7** perfect, saintly, sinless **8** flawless, innocent, spotless, unsoiled, virginal, virtuous **9** faultless, guiltless, shipshape, stainless, unstained, unsullied **11** spic and span, untarnished **13** above reproach, unimpeachable **14** irreproachable **15** unexceptionable

immanent 6 inborn, inbred, innate **7** natural **8** inherent **9** ingrained, intrinsic **10** congenital, deep-rooted, deep-seated, indigenous, indwelling **11** instinctive, instinctual

Immanuel 7 Messiah **11** Jesus Christ
means: **9** God with us

immaterial 7 ghostly, shadowy, trivial **8** bodiless, ethereal, mystical, noumenal, spectral, trifling, unbodied **9** spiritual, unearthly **10** evanescent, extraneous, impalpable, intangible, irrelevant, of no moment **11** disembodied, incorporeal, not relevant, unimportant **12** extramundane, extrasensory **13** insignificant, insubstantial, unsubstantial **14** of no importance **15** inconsequential, of little account

immature 5 green, young **6** callow, unripe **7** babyish, kiddish, puerile **8** childish, juvenile, unformed, youthful **9** embryonic, half-grown, infantile, not mature, pubescent **10** unfinished, unmellowed **11** out of season, rudimentary, undeveloped **16** wet behind the ears

immeasurable 7 endless, immense **8** infinite **9** boundless, limitless, unbounded, unlimited **10** fathomless **11** illimitable, inestimable, measureless, never-ending **12** incalculable, interminable, unfathomable **13** inexhaustible

immediate 4 near, next, nigh **5** close, hasty, local, swift **6** abrupt, nearby, prompt, recent, speedy, sudden **7** express,

instant, nearest **8** adjacent, punctual **9** proximate, undelayed **10** contiguous **13** instantaneous

immediately 3 now **9** instantly, right away **10** this minute **12** without delay
French: **11** tout de suite

immemorial 5 olden **7** ageless, ancient **8** dateless, hallowed, timeless **9** ancestral, legendary, venerable **11** time-honored **12** long-standing, mythological **15** long-established

immense 4 huge, vast **5** great **7** mammoth, massive **8** colossal, enormous, gigantic **9** extensive, monstrous **10** prodigious, stupendous, tremendous **11** measureless **14** Brobdingnagian

immensity 8 enormity, hugeness, vastness **9** largeness **12** enormousness

immerse 3 dip **4** duck, dunk, sink, soak **5** bathe, douse, lower, steep **6** absorb, drench, engage, occupy, plunge **7** engross **8** submerge

immerse briefly 3 dip **4** dunk

immersion 7 bathing, dunking **8** drowning **10** absorption, submersion **11** engrossment, involvement, submergence **13** concentration, preoccupation

immigrant 5 alien **7** migrant, settler **8** colonist, newcomer **9** foreigner, nonnative

immigrate 6 move to, settle **7** migrate **8** colonize

imminent 4 near **7** looming **8** menacing, perilous **9** immediate, impending **10** near at hand **11** approaching, close at hand, threatening

immobile 4 fast **5** fixed, quiet, rigid, stiff, still **6** at rest, laid up, rooted, secure, stable, static **7** riveted **9** immovable, not moving, quiescent, steadfast **10** motionless, stationary, stock-still **11** unbudgeable **13** incapacitated

immobilize 3 fix, set **4** stud **6** disarm, freeze, splint **7** disable **8** paralyze, transfix **12** incapacitate

immoderate 5 undue **7** extreme **8** whopping **9** excessive, unbridled **10** exorbitant, gargantuan, inordinate, prodigious **11** extravagant, intemperate, uncalled-for **12** unreasonable, unrestrained **14** unconscionable

immoderation 6 excess **10** de-

bauchery **11** dissipation, prodigality, unrestraint **12** extravagance, intemperance, recklessness **13** excessiveness **14** prodigiousness

immodest 4 lewd, vain **5** gross, loose **6** brazen, coarse, risque, wanton **7** pompous **8** boastful, braggart, indecent, inflated, unchaste **9** bombastic, conceited, shameless **10** indecorous, indelicate, peacockish, suggestive **11** exaggerated, pretentious **12** self-centered

immoral 4 evil, lewd **5** dirty, wrong **6** sinful, wicked **7** corrupt, heinous, obscene, raunchy, vicious **8** depraved, indecent, infamous, prurient **9** debauched, dissolute, nefarious, salacious, unethical **10** dissipated, iniquitous, licentious, profligate **12** pornographic, unprincipled

Immoralist, The
author: **9** Andre Gide

immorality 3 sin **4** evil **9** decadence, depravity, indecency, obscenity, prurience **10** corruption, debasement, degeneracy, sinfulness **13** salaciousness

immortal 3 god **6** divine **7** abiding, eternal, undying **8** enduring **9** deathless **11** everlasting **12** imperishable

Immortals 6 giants, greats, titans **7** the gods **8** demigods **13** all-time greats
Greek/Roman: **8** pantheon

immovable 3 icy, set **4** cold, fast **5** fixed **6** dogged, secure, steely, stolid **7** adamant, settled **8** detached, fastened, immobile, obdurate, resolute, stubborn **9** heartless, impassive, unfeeling **10** inexorable, inflexible, stationary, unbendable **11** coldhearted, unbudgeable **12** unchangeable **13** unimpressible, unsympathetic **16** unimpressionable

immune 4 free, safe **5** clear **6** exempt **9** protected, resistant **12** invulnerable **13** unsusceptible

immunity 7 freedom **9** exemption **10** resistance **16** unsusceptibility

immure 3 hem, pen **4** cage, coop, jail, wall **6** entomb, intern, wall in, wall up **7** confine, enclose, seclude **8** cloister, imprison **11** incarcerate

immutability 9 endurance, stability **14** changelessness

immutable 4 firm **5** fixed,

solid **6** stable **7** lasting **8** constant, enduring **9** permanent, unaltered, unvarying **10** changeless, inflexible, unchanging **11** unalterable **12** unchangeable, unmodifiable **14** intransmutable **16** incontrovertible

Imogen
character in: **9** Cymbeline
author: **11** Shakespeare

imp 3 elf **4** brat **5** demon, devil, gnome, pixie, scamp **6** goblin, hoyden, rascal, sprite, urchin **7** upstart **9** hobgoblin **10** evil spirit, leprechaun

impact 4 jolt **5** brunt, crash, force, shock, smash **6** burden, effect, thrust **7** contact **9** collision, influence **10** concussion **11** implication **12** repercussion

impair 3 mar **4** harm, hurt **6** damage, hinder, injure, lessen, reduce, weaken, worsen **7** cripple, subvert, vitiate **8** decrease, enervate, enfeeble, undercut **10** debilitate **11** detract from

impaired 6 broken, faulty, flawed **7** damaged **9** defective, deficient, imperfect

impairment 4 flaw, harm **5** fault **6** damage, defect, injury, malady **7** ailment, illness **8** debility, disorder, handicap, sickness, weakness **9** detriment, hindrance, infirmity **10** disability, impediment, inadequacy **12** debilitation

impale 3 fix, pin **4** tack **5** affix, stick **8** transfix **10** run through

impart 4 give, lend, tell **5** grant, offer, share **6** accord, afford, pass on, relate, render, report, reveal **7** confide, consign, deliver, divulge, mention **8** bestow on, confer on, disclose, dispense **9** make known **10** contribute **11** communicate

impartial 4 fair, just **7** neutral **8** detached, unbiased **9** equitable, objective **10** evenhanded, fair-minded, open-minded **11** nonpartisan **12** unprejudiced **13** disinterested, dispassionate

impartiality 7 justice **8** equality, fair play, fairness **10** detachment, neutrality **11** objectivity

impasse 4 snag **7** dead end, dilemma **8** cul-de-sac, deadlock, quandary, standoff **9** stalemate **10** blind alley, bottleneck, standstill **11** predicament

impassioned 5 eager, fiery **6** ardent, heated **7** earnest, excited, fervent, intense, rousing, zealous **8** animated, forceful, inspired, stirring

impassive 4 calm, cool **5** aloof, stony **6** sedate, stolid **7** stoical, unmoved **8** reserved **9** apathetic, untouched **10** impervious, insensible, phlegmatic **11** emotionless, indifferent, inscrutable, unemotional, unperturbed **13** dispassionate, imperturbable, unimpressible **16** unimpressionable

impassiveness 8 coldness **9** aloofness, stolidity **12** indifference **15** emotionlessness

impassivity 6 apathy **8** coolness, stoicism **9** aloofness, stolidity **10** dispassion **15** emotionlessness **16** imperturbability

impatient 4 edgy **5** fussy, hasty, itchy, rabid, tense, testy **6** ardent, touchy **7** annoyed, anxious, brusque, hurried, nervous, peevish, restive **8** agitated, feverish, restless **9** excitable, irascible, irritable, irritated **10** high-strung, intolerant, passionate **12** enthusiastic

impeach 4 slur **6** accuse, assail, attack, charge, impugn, indict **7** arraign, slander **8** badmouth, belittle, question **9** challenge, discredit, disparage, inculpate **11** incriminate **16** call into question

impeccable 7 perfect **8** flawless **9** blameless, excellent, faultless **10** immaculate **11** unblemished **12** irreprovable, unassailable **13** unimpeachable **14** irreproachable **15** unexceptionable

impecunious 4 poor **5** broke, needy **6** hard-up **7** pinched **8** bankrupt, indigent **9** destitute, insolvent, penniless **10** down-and-out, straitened **12** impoverished **15** poverty-stricken

impede 5 block, check, delay, deter, stall **6** arrest, halter, hamper, hinder, retard, stymie, thwart **7** disrupt, inhibit **8** hold back, obstruct, slow down **9** frustrate, interrupt, sidetrack **13** interfere with

impediment 4 flaw **5** block, delay **6** defect **7** barrier **8** blockage, drawback, handicap, obstacle **9** deformity, hindrance **10** detraction **11** obstruction **12** interference **14** stumbling block

impedimenta 4 gear **7** bag-

gage **9** equipment **13** accoutrements, paraphernalia

impel 4 goad, prod, push, spur, urge **5** drive, force **6** compel, incite, induce, prompt **7** require **8** motivate **9** constrain, stimulate **11** necessitate

impend 4 brew, hang, loom **5** hover, lower **6** menace **8** approach, draw near, overhang, threaten

impending 4 near **6** coming **7** brewing, looming **8** imminent, menacing, oncoming **9** immediate **11** approaching, forthcoming, threatening

impenetrable 5 dense, solid, thick **6** sealed **7** elusive, obscure **8** puzzling **9** insoluble **10** impassable, impervious, insensible, intangible, inviolable, mysterious, unpalpable **11** inscrutable, unenterable **12** inaccessible, inexplicable, invulnerable, unfathomable **16** incomprehensible

impenitent 4 lost **6** inured **7** callous, defiant **8** hardened, obdurate **9** unashamed **10** uncontrite **11** remorseless, unrepentant, unrepenting **12** incorrigible, unapologetic **13** irreclaimable

imperative 6 urgent **7** crucial, needful **8** critical, pressing **9** essential, mandatory, necessary, requisite **10** compulsory, obligatory **11** unavoidable

imperceptible 5 minor, scant, small **6** hidden, minute, slight, subtle **7** minimal **8** academic **10** indistinct **12** undetectable, unnoticeable **13** infinitesimal, insignificant, unappreciable, unperceivable **14** inconsiderable

imperceptive 5 blind **9** unfeeling **11** insensitive, unobservant **12** inpercipient, unperceptive **13** unsympathetic

imperfect 6 faulty, flawed **8** deformed, fallible, impaired **9** blemished, defective

imperfection 4 flaw **5** fault **6** defect **7** blemish **8** weakness **9** deformity **10** faultiness, impairment, inadequacy **11** fallibility, shortcoming **13** insufficiency **14** incompleteness

imperial 5 bossy **6** feudal, lordly **8** despotic **9** arbitrary, imperious **10** autocratic, highhanded, peremptory, repressive, tyrannical **11** dictatorial, domineering, magisterial, overbearing **13** authoritarian

Imperial Presidency, The
author: 20 Arthur M Schlesinger Jr

imperil 4 risk 6 chance, expose, gamble, hazard 8 endanger 10 compromise, jeopardize 13 put in jeopardy

imperious 5 bossy, lofty 6 lordly 7 haughty 8 arrogant, despotic, imperial 10 autocratic, commanding, peremptory, tyrannical 11 dictatorial, domineering, overbearing 13 high-and-mighty

imperiousness 9 arrogance, loftiness 11 haughtiness

imperishable 6 stable 7 durable, lasting 14 indestructible

imperium 4 rule 5 realm 6 domain, empire 8 dominion 11 sovereignty

impermanent 7 passing 8 fleeting, fugitive, not fixed, unstable 9 ephemeral, temporary, transient 10 evanescent, transitory, unenduring

impermeable 5 dense, solid, tight 6 opaque 9 nonporous 10 impervious, waterproof

impersonal 4 dead 6 remote 7 general, inhuman, neutral 8 detached, lifeless, soulless 9 impartial, impassive, inanimate, inorganic, objective 10 spiritless 11 perfunctory 13 disinterested, dispassionate

impersonate 3 ape 4 copy, mime 5 mimic 6 pose as 7 imitate, portray 9 personify, represent 11 pretend to be 12 masquerade as

impertinence 4 sass 5 cheek, sauce 7 affront 8 audacity, boldness, rudeness 9 freshness, impudence, insolence, sauciness 10 cheekiness, disrespect, effrontery, incivility 11 irrelevance 17 disrespectfulness, inappropriateness

impertinent 4 rude 5 fresh, surly 6 brassy, brazen, smarty 7 uncivil 8 arrogant, impudent, insolent 9 extrinsic, insulting, unrelated 10 extraneous, immaterial, irrelevant, not germane, peremptory, unmannerly 11 unimportant 12 discourteous, presumptuous 13 disrespectful, inappropriate 14 beside the point

imperturbability 5 poise 6 aplomb 8 calmness, coolness 9 composure, sangfroid 10 equanimity, steadiness 11 self-control, tranquility 12 tranquillity 14 presence of mind, self-possession

imperturbable 4 calm, cool 6 sedate, serene 8 composed 9 collected, impassive, unanxious, unfazable, unruffled 10 impervious 11 levelheaded, undisturbed, unexcitable, unflappable, unflustered 13 dispassionate, unsusceptible

impervious 6 closed 8 immune to 11 impermeable 12 impenetrable, inaccessible, invulnerable 14 unapproachable

impetuosity 8 rashness 11 spontaneity, unrestraint 12 recklessness 13 impulsiveness 14 capriciousness

impetuous 4 rash 5 hasty 6 abrupt, stormy 7 rampant, violent 8 forcible, headlong, vehement 9 impulsive 10 capricious, inexorable, relentless, unexpected 11 precipitate 14 unpremeditated

impetus 4 prod, push, spur 5 boost, drive, force, start 6 motive 7 impulse 8 momentum, stimulus 9 impulsion, incentive 10 motivation, propulsion 11 moving force, stimulation

impiety 9 blasphemy, sacrilege 10 disrespect, irreligion 11 irreverence, ungodliness

impinge 7 intrude, obtrude, violate 8 encroach, infringe, trespass 10 transgress

impious 7 godless, immoral, profane, ungodly 8 apostate, renegade 9 perverted 10 iniquitous, irreverent 11 blasphemous, irreligious 12 iconoclastic, sacrilegious 13 disrespectful

impiousness 7 impiety 9 blasphemy, sacrilege 10 disrespect 11 irreverence, ungodliness

impish 5 elfin 7 implike, puckish, roguish 8 prankish, rascally, sportive 11 mischievous

implacable 10 inexorable, inflexible, relentless, unamenable 11 intractable, unrelenting 12 unappeasable, unpacifiable 14 irreconcilable, uncompromising

implant 3 fix, set, sow 4 root 5 embed, graft, imbed, inlay, teach 6 infuse, insert 7 impress, instill 8 entrench 9 establish, inculcate 10 impregnate

implausible 8 doubtful, unlikely 9 illogical, senseless 10 far-fetched, improbable, incredible, outrageous, ridiculous 12 preposterous, unbelievable, unreasonable 13 inconceivable

implement 4 tool 5 begin, enact, piece, start 6 device 7 achieve, article, fulfill, realize, utensil 8 activate, carry out 9 apparatus, appliance, equipment, materials 10 accomplish, bring about, instrument 11 set in motion 13 put into effect

implicate 7 connect, embroil, ensnare, involve 8 entangle 9 associate, inculpate 11 incriminate

implication 6 effect 7 outcome 8 innuendo, overtone 9 inference 10 connection, intimation, suggestion 11 association, connotation, consequence, insinuation, involvement 12 entanglement, ramification, significance

implicit 5 total 6 hinted, innate 7 certain, implied, staunch 8 absolute, complete, inferred, inherent, profound, resolute 9 deducible, steadfast, suggested 10 understood, unreserved, unshakable 13 unquestioning

implied 5 tacit 7 oblique 8 indirect 9 implicity, indicated

implode 11 burst inward 17 compress violently

implore 3 beg 4 urge 6 obtest 7 beseech, entreat 9 importune, plead with 10 supplicate

imply 4 hint, mean 6 denote 7 bespeak, betoken, connote, presume, signify, suggest 8 evidence, indicate, intimate 9 insinuate 10 presuppose

impolite 4 rude 7 ill-bred, uncivil 9 impolitic, unfitting, ungenteel, unrefined 10 undecorous, unmannerly 12 discourteous 13 disrespectful, inconsiderate

impoliteness 8 rudeness 10 bad manners, incivility 11 boorishness, discourtesy

import 6 burden, moment, thrust 7 meaning 9 overtones 10 importance 11 connotation, implication 12 ramification, significance

importance 4 rank 5 value, worth 6 esteem, import, moment, repute, weight 7 stature 8 eminence, position 9 influence, relevance 11 consequence, seriousness, weightiness 12 significance 13 essentialness, momentousness

Importance of Being Earnest, The
author: 10 Oscar Wilde
character: 12 Cecily Cardew,

Jack Worthing, Letitia Prism **16** Gwendolen Fairfax **17** Algernon Moncrieff (Algy) **20** Lady Augusta Bracknell **21** Reverend Canon Chasuble

important 5 great, major **7** leading, notable, seminal, serious, weighty **8** creative, esteemed, foremost, original **9** momentous, prominent **10** imperative, meaningful, preeminent, remarkable **11** distinctive, influential, significant **13** consequential

imported 5 alien **6** exotic **7** foreign **9** not native

importunate 7 begging **8** pleading **9** imploring **10** entreating, persistent **11** troublesome **12** supplicating

importune 3 beg, sue **4** pray **5** plead **6** adjure, exhort **7** beseech, entreat, implore **8** appeal to, petition **10** supplicate

importunity 4 plea **6** appeal **7** request **8** entreaty, petition **12** supplication

impose 3 set **4** levy **5** apply, enact, foist, force, lay on **6** peddle, slap on **7** command, dictate, inflict, palm off, place on **9** establish, institute, introduce, prescribe **10** thrust upon

impose upon 5 annoy **6** bother, ill-use **8** ill-treat, maltreat, mistreat **15** take advantage of

imposing 5 grand, lofty **7** massive, stately **8** majestic, striking, towering **10** commanding, impressive, monumental **11** outstanding **12** awe-inspiring

imposition 5 abuse **6** burden, ill use **8** foisting **10** obligation **15** taking advantage

impossible 8 stubborn **9** insoluble **10** unbearable, unsolvable, unyielding **11** intolerable, intractable, not possible **12** insufferable, intransigent, unachievable, unanswerable, unattainable, unimaginable, unmanageable **13** inconceivable **16** out of the question

impost 3 fee, tax **4** duty, fine, toll **6** charge, excise, tariff **10** assessment

impostor 4 sham **5** cheat, duper, fraud, phony, quack **6** con man **7** bluffer, shammer **8** deceiver **9** charlatan, defrauder, pretender, trickster **10** dissembler, mountebank **11** counterfeit, flimflam man, masquerader, pettifogger **12** impersonator

imposture 4 fake, hoax, play, ruse, sham **5** cheat, fraud, trick **6** deceit, humbug **7** forgery, swindle **8** artifice, delusion, pretense, quackery **9** deception, falsehood, imitation **10** pretension **11** charlatanry, counterfeit, fraudulence **12** charlatanism **13** impersonation, mountebankery

impotence 8 weakness **9** paralysis **10** disability, incapacity, inefficacy **12** helplessness **13** powerlessness **14** ineffectuality **15** ineffectiveness

impotent 4 weak **5** frail **6** feeble **7** hapless **8** disabled, feckless, helpless **9** paralyzed, powerless **11** ineffective

impound 3 pen **4** cage **5** pen in, seize **6** coop up, encage, lock up, shut in **7** confine **13** hold in custody

impoverish 4 bust, ruin **5** break, drain **6** beggar, pauper, reduce **7** deplete, exhaust **8** bankrupt, make poor **9** pauperize **18** send to the poorhouse

impoverished 4 poor **6** abject, barren, bereft, effete, used up **7** drained, sterile, wanting, worn out **8** depleted, indigent, wiped out **9** destitute, exhausted **10** down-and-out, pauperized **11** impecunious **12** unproductive, without means

impractical 6 sloppy, unwise **8** careless, quixotic, romantic **10** loose-ended, starry-eyed **11** unrealistic **12** disorganized **13** helter-skelter, unintelligent

imprecation 5 curse **8** anathema **11** malediction

impregnable 6 mighty, potent, strong, sturdy **8** powerful **10** invincible **12** invulnerable, unassailable, unattackable **13** unconquerable

impregnate 3 wet **4** soak **5** steep **6** dampen, drench, imbrue, infuse **7** moisten, suffuse **8** fructify, inundate, permeate, saturate **9** fecundate, fertilize **10** inseminate

impresario 7 manager, sponsor **8** director **9** conductor, organizer **12** entrepreneur

impress 4 grab, move, stir, sway **5** reach, touch **6** affect, excite, sink in, strike **8** bedazzle **9** electrify, influence, overpower, overwhelm

impression 4 idea, mark, mold, view **5** hunch, stamp, trace, track **6** belief, effect, impact, notion **7** contour, feeling, impress, imprint, opinion, outline, surmise **9** influence, reception, sensation **10** conviction **11** indentation **13** understanding

impressionable 8 gullible, passible, sentient **9** affective, receptive **10** vulnerable **11** suggestible

impressive 5 grand **6** august, moving **8** exciting, imposing, majestic, striking **9** memorable, thrilling **11** magnificent, outstanding **12** awe-inspiring, overpowering, soul-stirring **13** unforgettable

imprimis 15 in the first place

imprint 3 fix **4** etch, mark, sign **5** infix, press, stamp, title **6** indent **7** engrave, impress **8** inscribe **9** engraving **10** depression, impression **11** indentation

imprison 3 pen **4** jail **6** coop up, engage, entomb, immure, lock up **7** confine, fence in, impound, shackle **8** restrain **9** constrain **11** hold captive, incarcerate

improbable 8 doubtful, unlikely **9** illogical **11** implausible **12** unreasonable **13** unforeseeable

improbable solution in a play's plot
Latin: **13** deus ex machina

impromptu 6 sudden **7** offhand **9** impulsive, makeshift, on the spot **10** improvised, off the cuff, unexpected, unprepared **11** spontaneous, unrehearsed **14** extemporaneous, unpremeditated, without warning **15** spur-of-the-moment **16** extemporaneously, on a moment's notice **19** off the top of one's head

improper 4 lewd **5** inapt, unfit **8** indecent, off-color, unseemly **9** ill-suited, irregular **10** indecorous, malapropos, out of place, suggestive, unbecoming, unsuitable **12** inharmonious **13** inappropriate, unconformable
French: **5** outre

impropriety 5 gaffe **7** blunder, faux pas **9** gaucherie, indecorum, vulgarity **10** bad manners **11** boorishness **12** impoliteness, indiscretion

improve 4 help **5** rally **6** better, enrich, repair **7** correct, develop, enhance **9** cultivate **10** ameliorate, recuperate

improvement 4 gain **6** reform, repair **7** advance, upswing

8 additive, progress 9 amendment 10 betterment, emendation, refinement
11 advancement, enhancement, reclamation 12 amelioration 14 reconstruction

improvidence 10 imprudence
11 prodigality 12 extravagance, wastefulness 13 shiftlessness
16 shortsightedness

improvident 6 lavish 8 prodigal, reckless, wasteful 9 imprudent, negligent, unthrifty
10 thriftless 11 extravagant, spendthrift 12 shortsighted
14 unparsimonious

improvise 5 ad-lib 6 make up, wing it 11 extemporize

improvised 5 ad-lib 7 devised, offhand 8 invented 9 concocted, contrived, dreamed-up, extempore, hatched-up, impromptu, makeshift 10 off-the-cuff, originated, unprepared
11 extemporary, spontaneous, unrehearsed 12 extemporized
14 extemporaneous, unpremeditated 15 improvisational, spur-of-the-moment

imprudent 4 rash 5 crazy, dopey 6 unwise 7 foolish
8 heedless, mindless, untoward 9 foolhardy 10 illadvised, incautious, indiscreet, unthinking 11 inadvisable, injudicious, thoughtless 13 illconsidered

impudence
Yiddish: 7 chutzpa 8 chutzpah

impudent 4 bold, rude 5 brash, fresh, nervy, saucy 6 brazen, cheeky 7 forward, upstart
8 impolite, insolent 9 bumptious, shameless 11 impertinent, smart-alecky, wiseacreish 12 discourteous
13 disrespectful

impugn 4 deny 5 knock, libel
6 assail, attack, berate, negate, oppose 7 asperse, slander
8 denounce, question 9 challenge, criticize 10 contradict
14 call in question, cast aspersions 16 call into question

impugnment 7 slander
10 aspersions

impulse 4 bent, goad, push, spur, urge, whim 5 drive, fancy, force 6 desire, motive, notion, thrust, whimsy 7 caprice, impetus, whimsey 8 instinct, momentum, movement, stimulus, stirring 9 incentive
10 incitement, motivation
11 inclination, inspiration, instigation

impulsive 4 rash 7 driving, offhand 8 forceful, forcible, no-

tional 9 impelling, impetuous, impromptu, unplanned, whimsical 10 capricious, incautious, propellant, propelling 11 involuntary, spontaneous
12 devil-may-care 13 unpredictable 14 extemporaneous, unpremeditated 15 spur-of-the-moment

impulsiveness 8 rashness
11 impetuosity, spontaneity, unrestraint 12 recklessness, whimsicality 14 capriciousness

impunity 8 immunity 9 clearance, exemption, privilege
10 absolution 11 prerogative
12 dispensation

impure 4 foul, lewd 5 dirty
6 coarse, filthy, smutty 7 debased, defiled, immoral, lustful, noisome, noxious, obscene, sullied, tainted, unclean 8 degraded, devalued, immodest, improper, indecent, polluted, prurient, unchaste, vitiated 9 lecherous, salacious, unrefined 10 indecorous, indelicate, libidinous, licentious
11 adulterated, depreciated, unwholesome 12 contaminated

impurity 5 alloy, dross, filth, taint 6 foulness 9 dirtiness, pollutant, pollution 10 adulterant, corruption, defilement
11 contaminant, taintedness, uncleanness 12 adulteration
13 contamination, foreign matter 15 unwholesomeness

imputation 6 charge 10 accusation, allegation, ascription
11 attribution

impute 5 refer 6 assign, charge, credit, relate 7 ascribe
9 attribute

inability 10 inaptitude, incapacity, ineptitude 12 helplessness, incapability, incompetence
13 maladroitness, powerlessness

in absence
Latin: 10 in absentia

in absentia 9 in absence

inaccessible 9 not at hand
11 unreachable 12 unattainable, unobtainable
14 unapproachable

in accord 9 agreeable, approving, in harmony, of one mind 10 concurring, consenting 11 in agreement
French: 9 en rapport

inaccuracy 4 goof, slip 5 error, fault, wrong 6 boo-boo
7 blunder, erratum, fallacy, mistake 9 unclarity 10 faultiness 11 imprecision, inexactness 13 incorrectness, unreliability 14 fallaciousness

inaccurate 3 off 5 false, wrong 6 faulty 7 inexact
8 mistaken 9 erroneous, imprecise, incorrect, off target
10 fallacious, unreliable 11 not on target, off the track
13 wide of the mark

Inachus
god of: 6 rivers
king of: 5 Argos
father: 7 Oceanus
mother: 6 Tethys
wife: 5 Melia
son: 9 Aegialeus, Phoroneus
daughter: 2 Io

inaction 8 abeyance, deferral, dormancy, dullness, idleness
9 cessation, indolence 10 inactivity, quiescence, somnolence, suspension 11 complacency

inactive 4 dull, idle, lazy 5 inert, quiet, still 6 low-key, otiose, static, torpid, unused
7 dormant, languid 8 indolent, slothful, sluggish 9 do-nothing, easygoing, leisurely, sedentary, somnolent 10 on the shelf
11 inoperative 12 out of service

inactivity 4 rest 5 quiet 6 disuse 7 inertia 8 dormancy, idleness, inaction 9 stillness
10 quiescence

in actuality
Latin: 6 in esse

in addition 3 and, too 4 also, more, plus, then 5 above, added, again, extra 6 as well, beyond 7 besides, further
8 moreover 10 additional
12 additionally, supplemental

inadequacy 4 lack 7 failing
10 deficiency, impairment
11 shortcoming
13 insufficiency

inadequate 5 inept, short, unfit 6 meager, scanty, too raw
7 lacking, not up to, wanting
8 below par, unfitted 9 deficient, imperfect, incapable
11 incompetent, unqualified
12 insufficient

inadmissible 10 disallowed, extraneous 11 intolerable 12 not permitted, unacceptable
14 nonpermissible

in advance 6 before, in time, sooner 7 earlier 9 before now
10 beforehand 11 ahead of time 13 before the fact

inadvertent 7 unmeant 10 accidental, fortuitous, unintended, unthinking
11 involuntary 13 unintentional 14 unpremeditated

inadvisable 5 risky 6 chancy, unwise 9 impolitic, imprudent

10 ill-advised 11 inexpedient, injudicious, inopportune

in aeternum 7 forever

in agreement
French: 9 en rapport

inalienable 6 sacred 8 absolute, defended, inherent 9 protected 10 inviolable, sacrosanct 12 unassailable 13 unforfeitable, unimpeachable

in all
Latin: 6 in toto

in all places 10 every place, everywhere, far and near, far and wide

in a low voice
Latin: 9 sotto voce

inamorata 4 lady, love 5 lover 7 beloved, darling 8 ladylove, mistress, paramour, truelove 10 sweetheart

inane 4 dumb 5 dopey, empty, silly, vapid 6 absurd, jejune, stupid 7 asinine, fatuous, foolish, idiotic, insipid, shallow, vacuous 9 pointless, senseless 10 ridiculous, unthinking 11 meaningless, nonsensical 13 unintelligent

inanimate 4 cold, dead, dull 5 inert 6 asleep, stolid 8 lifeless, soulless 9 inorganic, insensate, nonliving, senseless, unfeeling 10 insensible, insentient 11 unconscious

inanity 6 drivel 7 hogwash, vacuity 8 nonsense, vapidity 9 absurdity, asininity, silliness 11 foolishness 13 pointlessness, senselessness 14 ridiculousness

Inanna
origin: 8 Sumerian
goddess of: 3 war 4 love
sister: 10 Ereshkigal
realm: 6 heaven
corresponds to: 6 Ishtar 7 Astarte, Mylitta 9 Ashtoreth

in any case 6 anyhow, anyway 9 at any rate 10 in any event

in any event 6 anyhow, anyway 9 at any rate, in any case

inapplicable 5 unfit 6 not apt 8 unsuited 10 inapposite, irrelevant, not germane, unsuitable 12 incompatible, not pertinent 13 inappropriate

inappropriate 5 inapt 8 illtimed, improper, unsuited 9 unfitting 10 indecorous, in bad taste, out of place, unbecoming, unsuitable 11 incon-

gruous 12 incompatible, infelicitous
French: 10 mal a propos

inapt 8 improper, unseemly, unsuited 9 ill-suited, incorrect, unfitting 11 incongruous 13 inappropriate

inaptness 9 inability, ineptness 10 clumsiness, inaptitude, ineptitude 12 incompetence 13 maladroitness 14 unskillfulness

in arrears 4 late 7 overdue 10 delinquent

inarticulate 4 dumb, mute 7 babbled, blurred, garbled, mumbled 8 confused, wordless 9 paralyzed 10 incoherent, indistinct, speechless, tonguetied 12 inexpressive 14 unintelligible 15 uncommunicative

inartistic 9 graceless, inelegant, tasteless 10 ungraceful 11 unaesthetic 12 unattractive

in a series
French: 7 en suite

in a set
French: 7 en suite

in attendance 4 here 7 present, serving 9 appearing, caring for, on the spot, waiting on 12 accompanying, looking after, taking care of

inattention 6 apathy 10 negligence 12 carelessness 14 lack of interest 16 absentmindedness, unresponsiveness

inattentive 7 unaware 8 careless, heedless 9 forgetful, negligent, unmindful 10 distracted 11 daydreaming, thoughtless, unobservant 12 absentminded

inaugurate 5 set up, start 6 induct, launch 7 instate, kick off, usher in 8 initiate 9 institute, undertake 10 embark upon 11 set in action

inauguration 5 start 9 beginning, induction 10 dedication 11 origination 12 commencement

inaugurator 6 author, father 7 creator, founder, starter 9 initiator, organizer 10 originator, prime mover

inauspicious 7 unlucky 9 illchosen, ill-omened 10 badly timed, disastrous 11 unfavorable, unfortunate, unpromising 12 infelicitous, unpropitious

in a vacuum
Latin: 7 in vacuo

in bad faith
Latin: 8 mala fide

in being
Latin: 6 in esse

in blazing crime
Latin: 18 in flagrante delicto

inborn 5 basic 6 inbred, innate, native 7 natural 8 inherent 9 inherited, intrinsic, intuitive 10 congenital 11 fundamental, instinctive 14 constitutional

inbred 6 inborn, innate, primal 7 natural 8 inherent 9 ingrained, inherited, intrinsic, intuitive 10 congenital, deep-rooted, deep-seated, hereditary, indwelling 11 instinctive, instinctual 12 deeply rooted 14 constitutional

Inca
language family: 7 Quechua
location: 4 Peru 5 Chili 7 Bolivia, Ecuador 9 Argentina 12 South America
leader: 7 Huascar 8 Topa Inca 9 Atahualpa, Pachacuti 10 Manco Capac 11 Huayna Capac
conquered by: 7 Pizarro
ruins: 11 Machu Picchu, Sacsahuaman, Tambo Machay

incalculable 7 dubious 8 infinite 9 countless, uncertain 11 inestimable, innumerable, measureless, uncountable 12 immeasurable, incomputable 13 unforeseeable, unpredictable

incandesce 4 burn, glow 5 flare, flash

incandescent 7 dynamic, glowing, radiant 8 electric, galvanic, magnetic, white-hot 9 brilliant 11 high-powered 12 electrifying 13 scintillating

incantation 3 hex 4 jinx 5 chant, charm, magic, spell 6 voodoo 7 sorcery 8 wizardry 10 black magic, hocus-pocus, invocation, mumbo-jumbo, necromancy, witchcraft 11 abracadabra, conjuration

incapable 5 inept, unfit 6 unable 8 helpless, impotent, inferior 9 powerless, unskilled, untrained 10 inadequate 11 incompetent, ineffective, inefficient, unqualified

incapacitate 4 maim, undo 5 lay up 7 cripple, disable 8 enfeeble, handicap, paralyze, sideline 9 make unfit 10 disqualify 13 make powerless 14 put out of action 15 render incapable

incapacitated 6 laid up 8 crippled, disabled, disarmed, helpless, stricken 9 hamstrung, paralyzed, sidelined 10 on the shelf, prostrated 11 immobilized, out of action **12** hors de combat **14** flat on one's back

incapacity 7 illness **8** sickness **9** crippling **10** deficiency, disability **12** incapability

incarcerate 3 pen **4** jail **6** commit, coop up, immure, intern, lock up **7** confine, impound **8** imprison, restrain

incarceration 9 detention **10** commitment, internment **11** confinement, durance vile **12** imprisonment **18** institutionalizing

incarnate 8 embodied, manifest **9** personify **10** actualized, in the flesh **11** objectified, personified

Incarnations
  author: **16** Robert Penn Warren

incautious 4 rash **5** brash **6** unwary **8** careless, heedless, reckless **9** hotheaded, impetuous, imprudent, impulsive, overhasty **10** headstrong, indiscreet, unthinking **11** injudicious, thoughtless

incendiary 8 agitator, arsonist **12** inflammatory

incense 5 anger **6** burn up, enrage, madden **7** inflame, provoke **9** infuriate, make angry **13** make indignant
  spice: **6** stacte

incensed 3 mad **5** angry, irate **6** fuming, raging **7** enraged, furious **8** burned up, inflamed, outraged, provoked **9** affronted, indignant **10** infuriated

incentive 4 lure, spur **6** come-on, motive **8** stimulus **10** enticement, inducement, motivation **11** inspiration **13** encouragement

inception 5 birth, debut, onset, start **6** origin, outset **7** arrival **9** beginning **12** commencement, inauguration

incessant 8 constant, unbroken, unending **9** ceaseless, continual, perpetual, unceasing **10** continuous, persistent **11** everlasting, unrelenting, unremitting **12** interminable **13** uninterrupted

inch
  abbreviation: **2** in

In Chancery
  author: **14** John Galsworthy
  part of trilogy: **11** Forsyte Saga

inchoate 7 budding, nascent **8** formless, unformed, unshaped **9** amorphous, begin-

ning, embryonic, incipient, shapeless **10** commencing, disjointed, uncohesive **11** unorganized **12** disconnected

incidence 4 rate **5** range, scope **6** extent **8** occasion **9** frequency, happening **10** commonness, occurrence, phenomenon **11** routineness

incident 5 clash, event, scene **6** affair **7** episode, related **8** occasion **9** happening **10** incidental, occurrence **11** contretemps, disturbance

incidental 5 minor **9** accessory, secondary **10** extraneous, unexpected **11** subordinate, unlooked-for

incidentally 7 apropos, by the by **8** by the way **9** in passing **14** speaking of that **15** parenthetically **21** while we're on the subject

incidentals 6 extras **8** minutiae **10** minor items **11** accessories, odds and ends **13** appurtenances

incinerate 4 burn **7** consume, cremate **9** carbonize **13** reduce to ashes

incineration 6 firing **7** burning, flaming **8** ignition, kindling **9** cremation **10** combustion **13** carbonization

incinerator 4 oven **6** burner **7** furnace

incipient 7 budding, nascent **8** inchoate **9** beginning, embryonic, fledgling, promising **10** developing, half-formed **11** rudimentary

in circulation 4 rife **6** abroad, around **7** at large **9** all around **11** going around **12** spread around **14** around and about **15** making the rounds

incise 4 etch **5** carve **7** cut into, engrave

incision 3 cut **4** scar, gash, nick, slit **5** cleft, notch, score, slash, slice, wound **6** furrow

incisive 4 curt, keen **5** acute, brisk, crisp, sharp **6** biting, shrewd **7** cutting, express, mordant, precise, probing, summary **8** analytic, piercing **9** trenchant, well-aimed **10** perceptive **11** intelligent, penetrating

incite 4 goad, prod, stir **5** drive, egg on, impel, rouse **6** arouse, excite, fire up, foment, induce, prompt, stir up, urge on **7** actuate, agitate, inflame, provoke **8** activate **9** instigate, stimulate

incitement 6 urging **7** arousal, driving, goading **8** egging on, exciting, firing up, stirring **9** agitating, fomenting, inflaming, prompting, provoking **10** activation, stirring up **11** provocation, stimulation

incivility 8 rudeness **9** barbarism, impudence, indecorum, surliness, vulgarity **10** bad manners, coarseness, disrespect **11** boorishness, discourtesy, misbehavior, uncouthness **12** impoliteness, tactlessness **14** unpleasantness

inclement 3 raw **4** foul **5** harsh, nasty, rough **6** bitter, severe, stormy **7** violent **11** tempestuous

inclination 3 bow, dip, nod **4** bend, bent, hill, rake, rise **5** grade, pitch, slant, slope **6** liking, bending, leaning, sloping **8** fondness, lowering, penchant, tendency **9** acclivity, inclining, proneness **10** preference, proclivity, propensity **11** disposition **12** predilection **14** predisposition

incline 3 bow **4** bend, cant, hill, lean, like, rake, seem, tend, tilt, wont **5** be apt, enjoy, pitch, slant, slope **6** prefer **7** decline **8** be likely, gradient **9** acclivity **10** lean toward **11** bend forward, have a mind to

inclined 3 apt **5** prove **6** liable, likely **7** given to **10** disposed to **11** predisposed

incline downward 3 dip, sag **4** sink **5** droop, slant, slope

inclined to delay 4 slow **5** tardy **6** remiss **8** dawdling, dilatory, sluggish **9** reluctant **12** foot-dragging **13** dillydallying **15** procrastinating

include 5 cover **6** enfold, entail, take in **7** contain, embrace, involve, subsume **8** comprise **9** encompass **10** comprehend **11** incorporate

inclusive 7 general, overall **8** sweeping, taking in **9** embracing, including **10** comprising, encircling **11** surrounding **12** encyclopedic **13** comprehending, comprehensive, incorporating **15** all-encompassing

incognito 7 unknown, unnamed **8** nameless **9** concealed, disguised, protected **10** in disguise, uncredited, undercover, unrevealed **11** undisclosed **12** unidentified **14** unacknowledged, unrecognizable

incognizant 6 obtuse **7** unaware **8** ignorant, unseeing **9** unknowing **13** unconscious of **15** uncomprehending

incoherent 7 muddled, unclear **8** confused, rambling **9** illogical **10** disjointed, irrational **11** bewildering, nonsensical **12** inconsistent **14** unintelligible

In Cold Blood
author: 12 Truman Capote
director: 13 Richard Brooks
cast: 11 Paul Stewart, Robert Blake, Scott Wilson **12** John Forsythe

income 5 means, wages **6** salary **7** revenue **8** earnings **9** emolument **10** livelihood

income, annual
French: 5 rente

incomparable 8 peerless **9** matchless, unequaled, unrivaled **10** inimitable **11** superlative **12** transcendent **13** beyond compare **14** unapproachable

incompatible 6 at odds **7** jarring **8** clashing, contrary, unsuited **10** at variance, discordant, mismatched **11** disagreeing, incongruous, uncongenial **12** antagonistic, inconsistent, inharmonious **13** contradictory, inappropriate

incompatibility 6 strife **7** discord **8** friction, variance **9** disaccord, wrangling **10** antagonism **11** being at odds, discordance **13** lack of harmony

incompetency 9 inability, unfitness **10** ineptitude **11** lack of skill **12** inefficiency **15** ineffectiveness

incompetent 5 inept, unfit **8** inexpert **9** incapable, unskilled, untrained **11** ineffective, ineffectual, inefficient, unqualified **14** lacking ability

incomplete 6 broken **7** partial, wanting **9** defective, deficient **10** unfinished **11** fragmentary

incompleteness 8 omission **10** deficiency **11** shortcoming **15** unfinished state

incomprehensible 7 obscure **8** abstruse, baffling **9** confusing **10** befuddling **11** bewildering, inscrutable, ungraspable **12** impenetrable, unfathomable **14** unintelligible **19** beyond comprehension, beyond understanding

incomprehension 10 bafflement, puzzlement **12** bewil-

derment **19** failure to understand

inconceivable 7 strange **8** unlikely **10** improbable, incredible **11** unthinkable **12** beyond belief, unbelievable, unimaginable **14** highly unlikely

in conclusion
French: 5 enfin

inconclusive 4 open **9** unsettled **10** indecisive, indefinite, unresolved, up in the air **11** not definite **12** unconvincing, undetermined **13** indeterminate

incongruity 8 variance **9** disparity **10** aberration, disharmony, divergence **11** abnormality, discrepancy **13** dissimilarity, inconsistency, unsuitability **17** inappropriateness

incongruous 3 odd **6** far-out **8** contrary **10** at variance, discrepant, out of place, outlandish, unsuitable **11** conflicting, disagreeing **12** incompatible, inconsistent, out of keeping **13** contradictory, inappropriate **14** irreconcilable

inconsequential 5 petty **6** slight **7** trivial **8** nugatory, picayune, piddling, trifling **9** valueless **10** negligible, of no moment **11** meaningless, unimportant **13** insignificant **15** of no consequence

inconsiderable 5 light, minor, petty, small **6** little, modest, paltry, slight **7** minimal, trivial **8** picayune, trifling **9** no big deal **10** negligible **11** unimportant **13** insignificant, no great shakes **15** inconsequential

inconsiderate 4 rash, rude **6** remiss, unkind **7** uncivil **8** careless, impolite, tactless, uncaring **9** negligent **10** ungracious, unthinking **11** insensitive, thoughtless **12** disregardful, uncharitable

inconsistency 8 variance **9** disparity **10** difference, divergence **11** discrepancy, incongruity **12** disagreement **13** dissimilarity

inconsistent 6 fickle **7** erratic, wayward **8** contrary, notional, unstable, variable **9** changeful, dissonant **10** changeable, discrepant, inconstant, irresolute **11** inaccordant, incongruous, inconsonant, vacillating **12** incompatible, inharmonious **13** contradictory, unpredictable **14** irreconcilable

inconsolable 7 crushed **8** de-

jected, desolate, wretched **9** miserable **10** despondent **12** disconsolate **13** brokenhearted

inconsonant 10 discordant **12** out of keeping, unharmonious

inconspicuous 3 dim **5** faint, muted **6** modest **9** unnoticed **10** unapparent, unassuming **11** unobtrusive **12** not egregious, unnoticeable **14** unostentatious

inconstancy 10 fickleness, infidelity **11** instability **14** capriciousness, changeableness, unfaithfulness

inconstant 6 fickle, untrue **7** erratic **8** cavalier, disloyal, unstable **9** mercurial **10** capricious, changeable, unfaithful **11** interrupted, uncommitted, undedicated, unsteadfast

incontinence 8 rashness **12** recklessness **13** lack of control **16** irresponsibility

incontinent 8 unchaste **12** unrestrained

incontrovertibility 8 sureness **9** certainty **12** absoluteness, definiteness **13** undeniability **14** irrefutability, conclusiveness **15** indisputability **16** incontestability **17** unquestionability

incontrovertible 9 apodictic **10** unarguable, undeniable **11** established, irrefutable **12** indisputable **14** beyond question, unquestionable

inconvenience 6 bother, put out **7** trouble **8** hardship, headache, nuisance **9** annoyance, disoblige, put one out **10** discomfort **13** be a nuisance to, pain in the neck

inconvenient 7 awkward, unhandy **8** annoying, tiresome, untimely **10** bothersome, burdensome **11** distressing, inopportune, troublesome

Incoronazione di Poppea, L'
also: 22 The Coronation of Poppaea
opera by: 10 Monteverdi
character: 4 Nero **6** Ottone **7** Ottavia

incorporate 4 fuse **6** embody, work in **7** include **10** amalgamate, assimilate **11** consolidate

incorporated 6 united **8** embodied, included **11** amalgamated, assimilated **12** consolidated

incorporeal 6 occult, unreal **7** ghostly, phantom **8** bodiless **9** spiritual, unearthly, un-

fleshly, unworldly **10** immaterial, intangible
11 disembodied **12** supernatural **13** insubstantial

incorrect 5 false, wrong **6** untrue **7** inexact **8** mistaken
9 erroneous **10** fallacious, inaccurate

incorrectness 5 error
9 wrongness **10** inaccuracy
12 carelessness, slovenliness

incorrigible 6 unruly **8** hardened, hard-core, hopeless
10 beyond help, delinquent
11 intractable **12** beyond saving, past changing, unmanageable **14** uncontrollable

incorrigible child
French: **14** enfant terrible

incorruptible 4 pure **6** honest
7 upright **8** reliable **9** faultless, righteous **10** unbribable
11 trustworthy
14 irreproachable

increase 3 wax **4** grow **5** add
to, swell **6** enrich, expand
7 advance, augment, burgeon, enhance, enlarge **8** multiply
12 become larger

increasing 7 growing **9** enlarging, expansion, extending, extension **10** drawing out
11 enlargement
12 augmentation

incredible 6 absurd **7** amazing, awesome **10** astounding, far-fetched, remarkable **11** astonishing **12** preposterous, unbelievable, unimaginable
13 extraordinary, inconceivable

Incredible Hulk, The
character: 9 Jack McGee
11 David Banner
cast: 9 Bill Bixby **10** Jack
Colvin **11** Lou Ferrigno

incredulous 7 dubious
8 doubtful **9** skeptical **10** suspicious **11** distrustful
12 disbelieving

increment 4 gain, rise **5** raise
6 growth, profit **7** benefit
8 addition, increase **9** accretion **10** supplement **11** enlargement **12** accumulation, appreciation, augmentation
13 proliferation

incriminate 5 blame **6** accuse, charge, indict

incrimination 5 blame
7 charges **10** accusation, indictment

incubate 3 set, sit **4** plot
5 breed, brood, clock, cover, hatch **6** scheme **7** develop, gestate, sit upon **8** generate

incubus 5 demon **8** bad dream
9 nightmare

inculcate 5 drill, imbue, infix, teach, train **6** impart, infuse
7 implant, impress, instill
8 instruct **9** brainwash, condition, enlighten
12 indoctrinate

inculpable 5 clear **8** innocent
9 blameless, guiltless, not
guilty **10** not at fault, unblamable **14** not responsible

incur 6 arouse, assume, incite, stir up **7** acquire, bring on, involve, provoke **8** bring out, contract, fall into

incurable 8 cureless, hopeless
9 ceaseless **10** beyond cure, inveterate, relentless, unflagging **12** incorrigible, irremediable **13** dyed-in-the-wool, uncorrectable

incursion 4 push, raid **5** foray
6 attack, inroad, sortie **7** assault **8** invasion **11** advance
into, impingement **12** encroachment, infiltration

indebted 5 bound **7** bounden
8 beholden, grateful, thankful
9 obligated **10** chargeable
11 accountable **15** under
obligation

indebtedness 4 debt **5** debit
7 arrears **9** liability **10** balance
due, obligation **11** liabilities

indecency 10 immorality
12 unseemliness **13** offensiveness, salaciousness
14 indecorousness

indecent 4 blue, lewd, rude
5 bawdy, dirty **6** filthy, smutty, vulgar **7** ignoble, ill-bred, immoral, obscene, uncivil **8** immodest, improper, prurient, unseemly **9** offensive, salacious **10** in bad taste, indecorous, indiscreet, licentious, unbecoming **11** unwholesome
12 pornographic

Indecent Obsession, An
author: 17 Colleen
McCullough

indecipherable 7 cryptic
9 enigmatic, illegible **10** unreadable **11** inscrutable

indecision 5 doubt **6** acrisy
7 dilemma, swither **8** wavering **10** hesitation **11** fluctuation, vacillating, vacillation, uncertainty **12** irresolution

indecisive 4 weak **7** dubious, unclear **8** doubtful, hesitant, wavering **9** confusing, debatable, mercurial, uncertain, unsettled **10** disputable, hesitating, irresolute, wishy-washy **11** halfhearted, vacillat-

ing **12** inconclusive **13** indeterminate **17** blowing hot and
cold

indecorous 5 gross **6** sinful, wicked **7** ill-bred **8** immodest, improper, low-class, unseemly
9 unfitting **10** unbecoming, unsuitable **11** blameworthy
13 inappropriate, reprehensible

indecorum 8 bad taste **9** immodesty, indecency, vulgarity
11 impropriety **12** impoliteness, unseemliness

indeed 5 truly **6** in fact, really
7 for sure, in truth **8** actually, to be sure **9** certainly, in reality, veritably **10** positively, to be honest, undeniably **11** joking apart **13** in point of fact, with certainty **14** to tell the truth **15** as a matter of fact, without question **16** strictly speaking

indefatigable 6 dogged
7 staunch **8** diligent, sedulous, tireless, untiring **9** energetic
10 persistent, unflagging, unwearying **11** persevering, unfaltering **13** inexhaustible

indefensible 8 improper, vincible **9** pregnable, untenable
10 vulnerable **11** defenseless, inexcusable, unprotected, unspeakable **12** open to attack, unpardonable **13** unjustifiable

indefinite 3 dim **5** vague **6** unsure **7** inexact, obscure, unknown **8** doubtful
9 ambiguous, amorphous, limitless, tentative, uncertain, unsettled **10** ill-defined, indecisive, indistinct, inexplicit **11** illimitable, measureless, unspecified **12** undetermined
13 indeterminate

indefiniteness 6 vagary **9** ambiguity, vagueness **10** indecision **11** uncertainty
12 equivocation

indelible 4 fast **5** fixed, vivid
7 lasting **8** deep-dyed **9** ingrained, memorable, permanent **10** unerasable
11 unremovable **12** ineradicable **13** unforgettable

indelicate 4 lewd, rude
5 broad, crude, gross **6** clumsy, coarse, risque, vulgar **7** awkward, obscene **8** immodest, improper, indecent, off-color, unseemly **9** offensive, unrefined **10** indecorous, indiscreet, suggestive, unbecoming

in demand 7 popular **9** desirable **11** sought after

indemnification 7 payment
10 recompense, reparation
12 compensation

indemnify 3 pay **5** atone, cover, repay **6** insure, secure **7** pay back, protect, rectify, requite, satisfy **8** make good **9** make right, make up for, reimburse **10** compensate, make amends, recompense, remunerate **15** make restitution

indemnity 7 redress **8** coverage, security **9** insurance, repayment **10** protection **11** restitution **12** compensation **15** indemnification

indent 5 notch, set in **6** recess **7** set back

indentation 3 bay, cut, pit **4** dent, nick **5** gouge, inset, niche, notch, score **6** cavity, furrow, pocket, recess **8** incision **9** concavity **10** depression

indented 6 hollow, sunken, zigzag **7** concave, notched **9** depressed

indenture 4 bind **8** contract **10** apprentice

indentured 5 bound **10** contracted **11** apprenticed

independence 7 freedom, liberty **8** autonomy **10** liberation **11** sovereignty **12** emancipation, self-reliance **14** self-government **17** self-determination

independent 4 free **7** solvent, well-off **8** affluent, separate, unallied, well-to-do **9** apart from, exclusive, on one's own, sovereign, uncoerced, well-fixed **10** autonomous, well-heeled **11** self-reliant, unconnected **12** unassociated, uncontrolled **13** self-directing, self-governing, unconstrained **15** individualistic, self-determining

indescribable 9 ineffable **11** beyond words, indefinable, unutterable **12** overwhelming **13** inexpressible **17** beyond description **20** beggaring description

indestructible 8 enduring **9** permanent **11** everlasting, infrangible, unbreakable **12** imperishable

indeterminate 5 vague **7** obscure, unclear **8** not clear **9** ambiguous, uncertain, undefined **10** indefinite, perplexing, unresolved **11** problematic, unspecified **12** undetermined, unstipulated

index 4 clue, mark, sign **5** proof, token **7** catalog, symptom **8** evidence, glossary, register **9** catalogue, indicator **10** indication **13** manifestation **16** alphabetical list

Index Librorum Prohibitorum 22 index of prohibited books

index of prohibited books Latin: **25** Index Librorum Prohibitorum

India *see box, p. 484*

Indian constellation: **5** Indus

Indiana *see box, p. 485*

Indiana basketball team: **6** Pacers

Indiana author: **10** George Sand character: **4** Noun **7** Delmare **13** Rodolphe Brown **15** Raymon de Ramiere

Indianapolis football team: **5** Colts

Indic language family: **12** Indo-European branch: **11** Indo-Iranian subgroup: **5** Hindi, Oriya **6** Nepali, Sindhi **7** Bengali, Marathi, Pakrits, Panjabi **8** Assamese, Gujarati, Kashmiri **9** Sinhalese

indicate 4 mean, show, tell **5** imply **6** denote, evince, record, reveal **7** bespeak, point to, signify, specify, suggest **8** point out, register, stand for **9** be a sign of, designate, establish, make known, represent, symbolize

indication 4 clue, hint, mark, omen, sign **5** token **6** augury, boding, signal **7** gesture, mention, portent, presage, showing, symptom, telling, warning **8** evidence, pointing **9** foretoken **10** foreboding, indicating, intimation, signifying, suggestion **11** designation, premonition **13** demonstration, manifestation

indicative 8 symbolic **10** denotative, emblematic, evidential, expressive, indicatory, suggestive **11** connotative, designative, significant, symptomatic **13** symptomatical **14** characteristic, representative

indicator 4 clue **5** guide **7** pointer **10** indication

indict 4 cite **6** accuse, charge, have up, impute, pull up **7** arraign, bring up, impeach **9** criminate, inculpate, prosecute **11** incriminate **13** prefer charges

indifference 6 apathy **7** disdain, neglect **8** coldness, no import **9** aloofness, unconcern **10** negligence, paltriness, triviality **11** disinterest, impassivity, inattention, insouciance, nonchalance **12** carelessness, unimportance **13** impassiveness, insensibility, insensitivity **14** insignificance, lack of interest

indifferent 4 cool, fair, rote, so-so **5** aloof **6** medium, modest **7** average, unmoved **8** detached, mediocre, middling, moderate, ordinary, passable **9** apathetic, impassive, not caring, unmindful **10** impervious, insensible, insouciant, nonchalant, second-rate, uninspired **11** commonplace, perfunctory, unconcerned **12** uninterested **13** insusceptible **15** undistinguished **17** betwixt and between, neither good nor bad

indigence 4 need, want **6** penury **7** begarry, poverty **9** pauperism, privation **11** destitution, dire straits **13** pennilessness

indigenous 6 native **7** endemic **8** domestic, homebred **9** home-grown **10** aboriginal **13** autochthonous, originating in

indigent 4 poor **5** needy **6** hard-up, in need, in want **7** pinched **8** badly off **9** destitute, moneyless, penniless **12** impoverished **15** poverty-stricken

indiges title in: **4** Rome suggests: **11** deification *for service to:* **7** country

indigestible 4 rich **13** unassimilable

indignant 3 mad **4** sore **5** angry, huffy, irate, riled **6** fuming, miffed, peeved, piqued, put off, put out **8** incensed, offended, provoked, steaming, worked up, wrathful **9** resentful, wrought up **10** displeased, infuriated **15** on one's high horse

indignation 3 ire **4** fury, huff, rage **5** pique, wrath **6** animus, choler, dismay, uproar **7** umbrage **8** vexation **9** annoyance **10** irritation, resentment **11** displeasure

indignity 4 slur **5** abuse **6** insult, slight **7** affront, offense, outrage **8** dishonor, rudeness **9** injustice **11** discourtesy, humiliation **12** mistreatment **13** slap in the face

indigo 3 dye **4** blue **8** dark blue, deep blue, navy blue **10** Indigofera varieties: **4** wild **5** false

India

other name: 4 Hind 6 Bharat 12 Bharat Varsha
capital: 8 New Delhi
largest city: 8 Calcutta
others: 4 Agra, Gaya, Pune 5 Dacca, Poona, Surat 6 Bombay, Jaipur, Kanpur, Lahore, Madras, Madura, Mysore, Nagpur 7 Banaras 8 Kolhapur, Mandalay, Mirzapur, Shahpura, Srinagar 9 Ahmedabad, Bangalore, Hyderabad 10 Darjeeling
division: 3 Goa 5 Assam, Bihar, Jammu 6 Kerala, Orissa, Punjab, Sikkim 7 Gujarat, Haryana, Kashmir, Manipur, Tripura 8 Nagaland 9 Karnataka, Meghalaya, Rajasthan, Tamil Nadu 10 West Bengal 11 Daman and Diu, Maharashtra, Pondicherry 12 Uttar Pradesh 13 Andhra Pradesh, Madhya Pradesh 15 Himachal Pradesh
measure: 3 ady, gaz, gez, jow, lan 4 byee, coss, depa, doph, hath, koss, kunk, raik, rati, seit, taun, tola 5 bigha, covid, crosa, denda, depoh, drona, erosa, garce, hasta, krosa, parah, ratti, salay, yojan 6 adhaka, amunam, covido, cudava, dumbha, geerah, moolum, mushti, ouroub, palgat, parran, prasha, ropani, tipree, unglee, yojana 7 dhanush, gavyuti, khahoon, niranga, prastha 8 okthabah
monetary unit: 3 lac, pie 4 lakh, pice 5 abidi, rupee
weight: 3 mod, pai, vis 4 drum, hoen, kona, pala, pank, pice, ruay, tael, tali, tola, wang, yava 5 adpad, candy, hubba, maund, tical 6 karsha 8 mangelin
island: 6 Agatti, Chilka 7 Andaman, Minicoy, Nicobar 8 Amindivi 9 Laccadive 11 Lakshadweep
lake: 5 Jheel, Lonar, Wular 6 Chilka, Colair, Dhebar, Kolair 7 Kolleru, Pulicat, Pushkar, Sambahr
mountain: 8 Aravalli 9 Broad Peak, Distaghil, Himalayas, Karakoram, Nanda Devi, Rakaposhi 10 Gasherbrum, Masherbrum 11 Nanga Parbat 12 Eastern Ghats, Kanchenjunga, Western Ghats
  hills: 4 Chin, Naga 5 Khasi 6 Lushai 7 Nilgiri
highest point: 12 Godwin Austen
river: 3 Son 4 Beas, Kosi, Tapi 5 Gogra, Indus, Jumna, Tapti 6 Gandak, Ganges, Jhelum, Kaveri, Kistna, Sutlej, Yamuna 7 Cauveri, Cauvery, Chambal, Damodar, Hooghly, Krishna, Narbada, Narmada 8 Godavari, Mahanadi 10 Bhagirathi 11 Brahmaputra
sea: 6 Indian 7 Arabian
physical feature:
  bay: 6 Bengal
  cape: 7 Comorin
  desert: 4 Thar 9 Rajasthan
  forest: 3 Gir
  gulf: 5 Kutch 6 Cambay, Mannar
  pass: 9 Karakoram
  plain: 12 Indo-Gangetic
  plateau: 6 Deccan 7 Shillon 11 Chota Nagpur
  rains: 7 monsoon
  strait: 4 Palk
  swamp: 9 Sundarban 11 Rann of Kutch
  valley: 13 Vale of Kashmir
people: 2 Ao 3 Gor 4 Bhil 5 Aryan 6 Badaga, Pathan 7 Sherani 9 Dravidian 10 Andamanese
  caste: 3 Jat 5 Sudra 6 Rajput, Shudra 7 Brahman, Brahmin, Harijan, Maratha, Vaishya 9 Kshatriya 11 Untouchable
  dynasty: 5 Gupta, Mogul 6 Maurya, Rajput 8 Marathas 14 Delhi Sultanate
  god: 4 Kali, Rama, Siva 5 Durga, Laxmi, Shiva 6 Brahma, Kumara, Vishnu 7 Ganesha, Hanuman, Krishna, Lakshmi 9 Kartikeya 10 Subramanya
  ruler: 5 Akbar, Asoka, Babur, Timur 7 Humayun 8 Hyder Ali, Jahangir 9 Aurangzeb, Shah Jahan 11 Rajiv Gandhi, Tippu Sultan 12 Indira Gandhi 13 Queen Victoria 15 Jawaharlal Nehru, Mohandas K (Mahatma) Gandhi 18 Chandragupta Maurya
language: 4 Urdu 5 Hindi, Oriya, Tamil 6 Sindhi, Telugu 7 Bengali, English, Kannada, Malayam, Marathi, Punjabi 8 Assamese, Gujarati, Kashmiri, Sanskrit 9 Malayalam
religion: 4 Sikh 5 Hindu, Islam, Parsi 7 Jainist, Judaism 8 Buddhism 11 Zoroastrian 12 Christianity
place:
  cathedral: 10 Saint Thome
  fortress: 3 Red 11 Saint George
  mausoleum: 8 Taj Mahal
  minaret: 9 Qutb Minar
  mosque: 10 Jama Masjid
  park: 6 Maidan
  president's residence: 17 Rashtrapati Bhavan
  railway station: 8 Victoria
  shrine: 7 Raj Ghat
  street: 7 Raj Path 11 Chowringhee, Marine Drive 12 Chandni Chauk 14 Connaught Place
  temple: 5 Birla 6 Ellora, Golden 7 Kailasa 10 Ajanta Cave
feature:
  dance: 6 nautch 7 cantico
  religious text: 7 Rig Veda
  shrine: 5 stupa
food:
  beer: 5 apong
  bread: 7 chapati
  liquor: 4 soma, sura 5 shrab
  tea: 5 assam

Indiana

abbreviation: 2 IN 3 Ind
nickname: 7 Hoosier
capital/largest city: 12 Indianapolis
others: 4 Gary, Peru 6 Brazil, Goshen, Hobart, Jasper, Kokomo, Marion, Muncie, Wabash 7 Elkhart, Ft Wayne, Hammond, LaPorte, Whiting 8 Columbus, Richmond 9 Lafayette, Mishawaka, South Bend, Vincennes 10 Evansville, Huntington, Logansport, Terre Haute 11 Bloomington, East Chicago 12 Connorsville, Michigan City
college: 4 Ball 6 Bethel, Butler, DePauw, Goshen, Marion, Purdue, Wabash 9 Notre Dame 10 Evansville, Valparaiso
explorer: 7 La Salle
feature: 10 New Harmony 12 Indian mounds
 national memorial: 14 Lincoln boyhood
tribe: 3 Wea 5 Miami 7 Shawnee
people: 7 Hoosier 10 Cole Porter, Eugene Debs, Gus Grissom, Red Skelton 12 Wilbur Wright 15 Booth Tarkington, Theodore Dreiser 18 James Whitcomb Riley
lake: 5 Clear, James 6 Monroe 7 Manitou, Wawasee 8 Michigan 9 Mansfield 11 Maxinkuckee
land rank: 12 thirty-eighth
mountain: 13 Greensfort Top
physical feature:
 cave: 9 Wyandotte
river: 4 Ohio 5 White 6 Maumee, Wabash 8 Kankakee 10 Tippecanoe, Whitewater
state admission: 10 nineteenth
state bird: 8 cardinal
state flower: 5 peony 6 zinnia
state motto: 19 Crossroads of America
state song: 28 On the Banks of the Wabash Far Away
state tree: 5 tulip 11 tulip poplar

7 bastard 8 wild blue 9 blue false 10 plains wild, white false 12 prairie false 13 fragrant false

indirect 5 vague 6 remote, zigzag 7 crooked, devious, distant, evasive, hedging, oblique, winding 8 rambling, tortuous 9 ancillary, secondary 10 circuitous, derivative, digressive, discursive, incidental, meandering, roundabout, unintended 13 unintentional

indirection 8 rambling 10 digression, meandering, zigzagging 14 circuitousness, circumlocution, roundaboutness

indiscernible 6 hidden 9 invisible 10 indistinct 12 undetectable, unnoticeable 13 imperceptible

indiscreet 6 unwise 7 foolish 8 careless, tactless, unseemly 9 foolhardy, ill-judged, impolitic, imprudent, tasteless, untactful 10 incautious 11 improvident, injudicious, thoughtless, unbefitting, uncalled-for 12 undiplomatic 13 inconsiderate, uncircumspect

indiscretion 8 rashness 10 imprudence 12 carelessness, heedlessness, recklessness, tactlessness 13 foolhardiness, insensitivity 15 thoughtlessness 16 irresponsibility

indiscriminate 6 motley, random 7 aimless, chaotic, jumbled, mongrel 8 confused, slapdash, unchoosy 9 haphazard, hit-or-miss 10 hodgepodge 11 promiscuous, unselective 12 disorganized, unsystematic 16 higgledy-piggledy, undistinguishing

in disorder 5 messy 6 blowsy, frowsy, mussed, sloppy, untidy 7 ruffled, rumpled, tousled, unkempt 8 uncombed 10 disarrayed, disheveled, disordered, disorderly 11 disarranged

indispensable 5 basic, vital 6 needed 7 crucial, needful 8 required 9 essential, mandatory, necessary, requisite 10 compulsory, imperative, obligatory 11 fundamental

indispensable condition
 Latin: 10 sine qua non

indispensable element 9 basic need, essential, necessity, requisite 10 sine qua non 11 requirement

indisposed 3 ill 5 loath 6 ailing, averse, laid up, sickly, unwell 7 opposed 8 hesitant, taken ill 9 bedridden, reluctant, unwilling 10 not oneself 11 disinclined 15 under the weather

indisposition 5 upset 6 malady 7 ailment, illness 8 sickness 9 complaint, ill health

indisputable 4 sure 7 assured, certain, decided, evident, obvious 8 absolute, apparent, clear-cut, definite, positive 10 conclusive, unarguable, undeniable 11 indubitable, irrefutable 12 unassailable, unmistakable 13 incontestable 14 unquestionable 16 incontrovertible 20 beyond a shadow of doubt

indissoluble 5 fixed 7 abiding, lasting 8 constant, enduring 9 immutable, indelible, permanent, perpetual 11 everlasting 12 imperishable, ineradicable

indistinct 3 dim 4 weak 5 faint, muddy, murky, vague 6 cloudy, hidden 7 blurred, clouded, muffled, obscure, shadowy, unclear 8 confused, nebulous, puzzling 9 ambiguous, enigmatic, illegible, inaudible, uncertain 10 ill-defined, incoherent, indefinite, mysterious, out of focus 11 not distinct 13 indeterminate 14 indecipherable, unintelligible 16 incomprehensible

indistinguishable 7 obscure, unclear 9 invisible 10 indistinct, unapparent 12 unnoticeable, unobservable 13 a carbon copy of, identical with, imperceptible, inconspicuous, indiscernible

individual 6 person, unique 7 one's own, private, special, unusual 8 distinct, especial, original, personal, separate, singular, somebody, specific, uncommon 9 different, exclusive 10 particular 11 distinctive, independent 12 personalized 14 characteristic, unconventional

individuality 6 cachet 10 uniqueness 11 distinction, singularity, specialness 13 particularity 15 distinctiveness

individually 4 each 5 apart 6 apiece, singly 8 a la carte, uniquely 10 one at a time, peculiarly, personally, separately 12 respectively 13 distinctively 18 characteristically

indoctrinate 5 brief, drill, teach, train, tutor 6 infuse, school 7 educate, implant, instill **8** initiate **9** brainwash, inculcate **12** propagandize

indoctrination 5 drill **8** drilling, teaching, training **9** education, schooling **10** initiation, instilling **11** inculcation, instruction

Indo-European
language branch: **5** Greek **6** Celtic, Italic **7** Romance **8** Albanian, Armenian, Germanic **9** Anatolian, Tocharian **11** Balto-Slavic, Indo-Iranian

Indo-Iranian
language family: **12** Indo-European
ancient: **7** Avestan **8** Sanskrit **10** Old Persian
modern Iranian: **5** Indic, Tajik **6** Pashto **7** Baluchi, Kurdish, Persian
modern Indic: **4** Pali **5** Hindi, Oriya **6** Nepali, Sindhi **7** Bengali, Marathi, Panjabi **8** Assamese, Gujarati, Kashmiri **9** Sinhalese

indolence 5 sloth **7** inertia, languor, laxness **8** idleness, laziness **10** inactivity

indolent 4 lazy **5** inert, slack **7** lumpish **8** dawdling, dilatory, inactive, listless, slothful, sluggish **9** do-nothing, easygoing, lethargic, shiftless **13** lackadaisical

indomitable 6 dogged **7** doughty, staunch, valiant **8** cast-iron, fearless, intrepid, resolute, stalwart, stubborn **9** dauntless, steadfast, undaunted **10** courageous, formidable, invincible, unwavering, unyielding **11** insuperable, persevering, unflinching, unshrinking **12** invulnerable, unassailable **13** indefatigable, irrepressible, unconquerable

Indonesia *see box*

indoors 6 at home, inside, shut in, shut up, within **10** in the house **11** sequestered

Indo-Pacific
language subgroup: **4** Kate **5** Kiwai **7** Andaman, Merauke **8** Highland, Tasmania **9** Ekari-Moni, Hollandia, Timor-Alor **10** New Britain **12** Astrolabe Bay, Bougainville **14** Vogelkop-Kamoro **16** Eastern New Guinea, Northern Salomons **17** Northern Halmahera

indorse *see* **7** endorse

In Dubious Battle
author: **13** John Steinbeck

indubitable 4 sure **7** certain **9** undoubted **10** conclusive **11** irrefutable, unequivocal **12** indisputable, unmistakable **14** unquestionable **16** incontrovertible

indubitably 6 surely **7** for sure **8** of course **9** certainly, doubtless **10** for certain **11** undoubtedly **12** without doubt **14** unquestionably, with no question

induce 3 get **4** coax, spur, sway **5** cause, impel **6** arouse, effect, incite, lead to, prompt **7** actuate, bring on, dispose, incline, inspire, produce, provoke, win over **8** activate, motivate, occasion, persuade **9** encourage, influence, instigate, prevail on **10** bring about, bring round, give rise to **11** prevail upon, set in motion

inducement 4 bait, goad, spur **5** cause **6** ground, motive, reason **8** stimulus **9** incentive **10** allurement, attraction, en-

---

Indonesia
other name: **9** Nusantara **12** Tanah Airkita **21** Netherlands East Indies
capital/largest city: **7** Jakarta **8** Djakarta
others: **5** Bogor, Medan **6** Malang, Manado **7** Bandung **8** Macassar, Semarang, Surabaya **9** Hollandia, Palembang, Surakarta **10** Jogjakarta, Yogyakarta **11** Banjarmasin
measure: **5** depah, depoh
monetary unit: **3** sen **6** rupiah
weight: **5** catty, ounce, thail **6** soekoe
island: **3** Aru **4** Bali, Buru, Java **5** Ambon, Ceram, Seram, Spice, Sumba, Timor **6** Bangka, Borneo, Flores, Lombok, Madura, Tidore **7** Belawan, Celebes, Morotai, Sumatra, Sumbawa, Ternate **8** Belitung, Moluccas, Sulawesi **9** Halmahera, New Guinea **10** Kalimantan **11** Lesser Sunda **12** Greater Sunda
lake: **4** Toba **5** Ranau **6** Towuti
river: **4** Hari, Musi, Solo **5** Rokan **6** Asahan, Barito, Kampar **7** Brantas, Kaptuas **9** Indrogiri, Mamberamo, Martapura
sea: **4** Java, Savu **5** Banda, Ceram, Timor **6** Flores, Indian **7** Arafura, Celebes, Molucca, Pacific **10** Philippine, South China
physical feature:
  strait: **5** Sunda **7** Makasar, Malacca **8** Makassar
  volcano: **6** Slamet **8** Krakatoa
people: **5** Batak, Dayak, Dyaks, Malay **6** Papuan, Toraja **7** Battaks, Chinese, Igorots **8** Acehnese, Achinese, Balinese, Javanese, Madurese, Sudanese **11** Minang Kabau
  leader: **7** Suharto, Sukarno
language: **5** Tetum **6** Bahasa, Igorot **7** English, Gyarung, Malayan **8** Balinese, Chamorro, Javanese, Madurese, Sudanese **10** Indonesian, Polynesian
religion: **5** Hindu, Islam **7** animism **8** Buddhism **12** Christianity, Confucianism
place:
  palace: **6** Kraton
  pyramid: **5** Stupa **9** Borobudur
  shrine: **6** Dagoba, Kraton
feature:
  cap: **5** pitji
  cloth: **5** batik
  jacket: **6** kebaja
  lizard: **12** Komodo dragon
  scarf: **9** selendang
  shadow play: **6** wajang, wayang
  skirt: **4** kain **6** sarong
  tree: **4** supa
food:
  ceremonial dinner: **9** selamatan

ticement, incitement, persuasion, temptation
11 inspiration, instigation, provocation

induct 5 crown, draft, frock **6** enlist, invest, lead in, ordain, sign up **7** bring in, install, instate, usher in **8** enthrone, initiate, register **9** conscript, establish, introduce **10** consecrate, inaugurate

in due course 4 then **6** thence **10** eventually **11** accordingly **15** at the proper time **19** in the fullness of time

indulge 4 baby **5** favor, humor, serve, spoil, treat **6** coddle, cosset, oblige **7** appease, cater to, gratify, yield to **8** pander to **9** give way to **11** accommodate, go along with, mollycoddle

indulgence 6 excess, luxury **8** kindness, lenience, patience **9** allowance, benignity, tolerance **10** compassion, debauchery, profligacy, sufferance **11** dissipation, forbearance, forgiveness **12** extravagance, graciousness, immoderation, intemperance **13** understanding **14** permissiveness

indulgent 4 kind **6** benign, tender **7** clement, lenient, patient, sparing **8** humoring, obliging, tolerant, yielding **9** easygoing, forgiving, pampering **10** forbearing, permissive **11** complaisant, forebearing **12** conciliatory **13** understanding

industrious 4 busy **6** active **7** zealous **8** diligent, occupied, sedulous, tireless **9** assiduous, energetic **10** productive, purposeful, unflagging **11** hardworking, painstaking, persevering, unremitting **12** businesslike, enterprising **13** indefatigable

industry 2 go **4** toil, zeal **5** field, labor, trade **6** bustle, energy, hustle **8** activity, business, commerce, hard work **9** assiduity, diligence **10** enterprise **11** application, manufacture **12** perseverance, sedulousness **13** assiduousness **15** industriousness **16** indefatigability

inebriate 3 sot **4** lush, soak, wino **5** drunk, rummy, souse, toper **6** barfly, boozer **7** tippler **8** drunkard **9** alcoholic **11** dipsomaniac

inebriated 4 high **5** drunk, oiled, tight, tipsy **6** bombed, loaded, potted, stoned, tanked, zonked **7** drunken, smashed, sozzled, wrecked **8** besotted **9** befuddled, plastered **10** in one's cups **11** intoxicated **12** drunk as a lord **17** under the influence **20** three sheets to the wind

ineffable 5 ideal **6** divine, sacred **9** spiritual **10** indefinite, untellable **11** indefinable, unspeakable, unutterable **12** transcendent **13** indescribable, inexpressible **14** incommunicable, transcendental

in effect 6 active **8** a reality **9** activated, effective, operative **11** in operation

ineffective 4 vain, weak **6** futile **7** useless **8** impotent **9** fruitless, incapable, powerless, worthless **10** inadequate **11** inefficient, inoperative, not much good, of little use **12** unproductive

ineffectual 4 lame, vain, weak **5** inept **6** feeble, futile **7** hapless, useless **8** impotent **10** inadequate, not up to par, profitless, unavailing **11** incompetent, ineffective, inefficient **12** unproductive, unprofitable, unsuccessful **13** inefficacious **14** unsatisfactory

inefficient 5 inept, slack **6** futile **8** slipshod **9** pointless, unskilled **10** inadequate **11** incompetent, indifferent, ineffective, ineffectual **12** not efficient, unproductive **13** inefficacious **14** good-for-nothing

inelegance 9 crudeness, grossness, roughness, vulgarity **10** coarseness **13** tastelessness

inelegant 4 ugly **6** coarse, common **8** inferior **9** tasteless, unrefined **10** ungraceful

ineligible 5 unfit **10** unentitled, unsuitable **11** not eligible, unqualified **12** disqualified, unacceptable

ineluctable 4 sure **5** fated **7** certain **10** ineludible, inevasible, inevitable, inexorable, sure as fate, unevadable **11** inescapable, irrevocable, unavoidable, unstoppable **13** unpreventable

inept 5 empty, inane, silly, unapt **6** clumsy **7** asinine, awk-

ward, fatuous, foolish **8** bungling **9** maladroit, pointless, senseless, unfitting, unskilled, untrained **10** out of place, unsuitable **11** incompetent, ineffective, ineffectual, inefficient, nonsensical, unqualified **13** inappropriate, inefficacious

ineptitude 9 inability **10** clumsiness, inadequacy **11** awkwardness **12** incompetence **14** ineffectuality **15** ineffectiveness

inequality 8 imparity, inequity **9** disparity, diversity, prejudice **10** difference, divergence, favoritism, unfairness, unlikeness **11** inconstancy, unequalness **12** irregularity, variableness **13** disproportion, dissimilarity, dissimilitude

inequity 4 bias **9** injustice, prejudice **10** favoritism, inequality, unfairness **14** discrimination

ineradicable 7 lasting **9** indelible, permanent **10** inerasable **12** ineffaceable **14** indestructible

inert 4 dull, numb **5** slack, still **6** leaden, static, supine, torpid **7** languid, passive **8** immobile, inactive, listless, sluggish **9** impassive, inanimate, quiescent **10** motionless, phlegmatic, stationary

inertia 6 apathy, stupor, torpor **7** languor **8** dullness, inaction, laziness, lethargy **9** indolence, inertness, lassitude, passivity, torpidity, weariness **10** inactivity, supineness **11** passiveness **12** listlessness, sluggishness

inertness 6 apathy **8** lethargy **9** passivity **10** quiescence **12** sluggishness **14** motionlessness

inescapable 4 sure **7** certain, evident **8** manifest, positive **10** inevitable **11** ineluctable, predestined, unavoidable

in esse 7 in being **11** in actuality **16** actually existing

inestimable 7 sumless **8** precious **9** priceless **10** invaluable **11** beyond price, measureless **12** immeasurable, incalculable, unmeasurable

inevitable 4 sure **5** fated **7** certain **8** destined **10** ineludible **11** ineluctable, inescapable, predestined, unavoidable **13** predetermined, unpreventable

inexact 3 off 6 faulty, sloppy 8 careless, slovenly 9 defective, imperfect, imprecise 10 inaccurate, unspecific 11 approximate

in exactly the same words
Latin: 19 verbatim et literatim

inexcusable 10 unbearable 11 intolerable, unallowable 12 indefensible, unforgivable, unpardonable 13 unjustifiable

inexhaustible 7 endless 8 infinite, tireless, unending 9 boundless 13 indefatigable 15 measurelessness

in existence 5 alive 6 extant, living 8 existent, existing 9 surviving, to be found

inexorable 4 firm 5 cruel, stiff 6 dogged 7 adamant 8 obdurate, pitiless, ruthless 9 immovable, merciless, unbending 10 adamantive, determined, inflexible, relentless, unyielding 11 inescapable, intractable 12 irresistible 14 uncompromising

inexpedient 6 futile, unwise 7 useless 11 detrimental, impractical, inadvisable, injudicious, undesirable 13 not worthwhile 15 disadvantageous

inexpensive 5 cheap 8 moderate 9 low-priced 10 economical, reasonable 13 nominal-priced, popular-priced

inexpensive table wine
French: 12 vin ordinaire

inexperienced 5 fresh, green, naive 6 callow 7 untried 8 inexpert, unversed 9 unfledged, unskilled, untrained, untutored 10 unfamiliar, unschooled, unseasoned 11 uninitiated, unpracticed 12 unaccustomed, unacquainted, unconversant 15 unsophisticated

inexpert 5 inept 6 clumsy, gauche 7 awkward 8 bungling 9 incapable, maladroit 10 amateurish, unpolished, unskillful 11 incompetent, ineffective, inefficient, unqualified 14 unaccomplished

inexplicable 8 abstruse, baffling, puzzling 9 insoluble 10 insolvable, mysterious, mystifying, perplexing 11 enigmatical, inscrutable 12 unfathomable 13 unaccountable, unexplainable 14 undecipherable 16 incomprehensible

inexpressive 5 blank, empty 6 vacant 14 expressionless

in extenso 12 at full length

in extremis 9 near death 11 in extremity 15 on the outer edges 19 at the uttermost limit

in extremity
Latin: 10 in extremis

in fact
Latin: 7 de facto

infallible 4 sure 7 assured, certain, perfect 8 flawless, inerrant, positive, reliable, surefire, unerring 9 apodictic, faultless, foolproof, unfailing 10 dependable, impeccable 11 irrefutable 13 unimpeachable 16 incontrovertible

infamous 3 low 4 base, evil, foul, vile 6 odious, sinful, sordid, wicked 7 corrupt, heinous, ignoble, immoral, knavish 8 damnable, recreant, shameful 9 abhorrent, monstrous, nefarious, notorious 10 abominable, detestable, iniquitous, of evil fame, outrageous, perfidious, profligate, scandalous, scurrilous, villainous 11 disgraceful, of ill repute, opprobrious, treacherous 12 dishonorable, disreputable

infamy 4 evil 5 odium, shame 7 scandal 8 contempt, disgrace, dishonor, ignominy, villainy 9 discredit, disesteem, disrepute, notoriety 10 corruption, opprobrium, wickedness 11 abomination 13 despicability, notoriousness

infancy 6 cradle, nonage 8 babyhood, minority 9 beginning, childhood, inception 10 immaturity

infant 3 kid 4 babe, baby 5 child 7 neonate, newborn, toddler 8 nursling, suckling

infantile 7 babyish 8 childish, juvenile 9 childlike, infantine 10 infantlike, sophomoric

infantryman 6 Zouave 7 dogface, dragoon 8 chasseur, doughboy, sorefoot 11 foot soldier

infatuated 7 charmed, smitten 8 beguiled, enamored, inflamed, obsessed 9 bewitched, enchanted, entranced 10 captivated, enraptured, enthralled, spellbound 11 carried away, intoxicated 12 having a crush

infatuation 4 rave 5 craze, crush, folly, mania 6 desire 7 passion 9 obsession, puppy love 10 enthusiasm 11 fascination, foolishness 12 passing fancy

infect 4 ruin 5 spoil, taint, touch 6 blight, damage, poison 7 afflict, corrupt 9 indispose, influence 11 contaminate

infected 6 impure, morbid, septic 7 corrupt, tainted 8 cankered, diseased, poisoned 12 contaminated

infection 6 blight 7 disease 9 contagion, virulence 11 suppuration

infectious 8 catching, epidemic, virulent 9 catchable, infective, spreading 10 compelling, contagious, inoculable 11 captivating 12 communicable, irresistible

infecund 6 barren, farrow 7 sterile 9 infertile 12 unproductive

infer 4 deem 5 glean, guess, judge, opine 6 deduce, gather, reason, reckon 7 presume, suppose, surmise 8 conclude 9 speculate 10 conjecture

inference 4 clue 10 intimation, suggestion 11 insinuation

inferior 4 poor 6 junior 8 lowgrade, mediocre 9 secondary 10 low-quality, second-rate, subsidiary 11 indifferent, subordinate, subservient, substandard 12 not up to snuff

infernal 4 vile 5 awful, black, lower 6 cursed, Hadean, nether 7 heinous, hellish, Stygian, vicious 8 accursed, damnable, devilish, fiendish, horrible, terrible 9 atrocious, execrable, malicious, monstrous, nefarious, Plutonian 10 abominable, demoniacal, diabolical, flagitious, horrendous, iniquitous
also: 9 Tartarean
refers to: 10 underworld

inferno 4 hell, oven 5 abyss, Hades 6 hotbox, the pit, Tophet 7 furnace, roaster, sizzler 8 hellfire, hellhole, scorcher 9 perdition 10 lower world, underworld 11 netherworld 12 fiery furnace 13 nether regions 15 infernal regions 16 fire and brimstone, the bottomless pit

Inferno
part I of: 12 Divine Comedy
author: 14 Dante Alighieri

infertile 4 arid, bare 6 barren, effete, fallow 7 drained, sterile 8 depleted, desolate, impotent, infecund **9** exhausted, fruitless **10** unfruitful, unprolific **12** unproductive **13** nonproductive

infest 4 team **5** beset, crawl, creep, swarm **6** abound, infect, plague, ravage **7** overrun, torment **9** crawl with, swarm with

infestation 6 plague, ravage **9** lousiness, pervasion **11** overrunning **12** overswarming

in few words
Latin: **12** paucis verbis

infidel 5 pagan **6** savage **7** atheist, heathen, heretic, skeptic **8** agnostic, apostate, idolater **9** barbarian **10** unbeliever **11** nonbeliever

infidelity 6 breach **7** falsity, perfidy **8** adultery, betrayal **9** disregard, violation **10** disloyalty, infraction **12** nonadherence **13** nonobservance, transgression **14** unfaithfulness

infiltrate 4 leak, seep **5** imbue, steep **6** absorb, seep in **7** pervade **8** colonize, permeate **9** insinuate, penetrate

infinite 4 vast **5** great **7** endless, immense **8** enormous **9** boundless, limitless, unbounded, unlimited **10** tremendous, without end **11** illimitable, measureless **12** immeasurable, incalculable, interminable **13** inexhaustible **15** uncircumscribed

infinitesimal 3 wee **4** puny, tiny **6** minute **10** diminutive, negligible **11** microscopic **13** imperceptible, inappreciable, insignificant, undiscernible **14** extremely small, inconsiderable

infinity 7 forever **8** eternity **10** infinitude, perpetuity **11** endlessness, eternal time **12** sempiternity **13** boundlessness, limitlessness **14** illimitability **15** everlastingness, immeasurability, incalculability, measurelessness **16** inexhaustibility **19** incomprehensibility

Infiri
gods of: **10** underworld

infirm 3 ill **4** weak, worn **5** anile, frail, shaky **6** ailing, feeble, poorly, sickly **7** failing, fragile, unsound **8** decrepit, disabled, helpless, unstable, weakened **9** doddering, emaciated, enervated, enfeebled,

powerless **11** debilitated **12** strengthless

infirmary 6 clinic **7** sick bay **8** hospital

infirmity 4 flaw **5** fault **6** defect, malady **7** ailment, failing, frailty, illness **8** debility, disorder, handicap, sickness **9** fragility, frailness **10** deficiency, disability, infirmness **11** instability **12** debilitation, imperfection, unstableness **13** indisposition, vulnerability

in flagrante delicto 14 in blazing crime **22** in the heat of the evil deed

inflame 4 fire, rile **5** craze, rouse **6** arouse, enrage, excite, heat up, ignite, incite, kindle, madden, stir up, work up **7** agitate, incense, provoke **8** enkindle **9** electrify, stimulate **10** intoxicate

inflamed 3 mad **5** angry, irate, riled **6** crazed, fuming, roused **7** aroused, enraged, excited, fired up, furious, incited **8** agitated, incensed, provoked, reddened **9** steamed up, stirred up **10** infuriated **11** intensified

inflame with love 6 enamor **9** enrapture, impassion, infatuate

inflammable 5 fiery **8** choleric, volatile **9** excitable, flammable, ignitable, impetuous, overhasty, sensitive **10** high-strung, incendiary **11** combustible, precipitate **12** inflammatory

inflammation 4 acne, fire, gout, sore **6** canker, firing **7** arousal, chafing **8** bursitis, ignition, kindling, soreness, sore spot, swelling **9** agitation **10** incitement, irritation **13** conflagration, rabblerousing
suffix: **4** itis

inflammatory 5 fiery, rabid **8** arousing, enraging, inciting, mutinous, volcanic **9** demagogic, explosive, insurgent **10** incendiary, rebellious **11** combustible, fulminating, inflammable, intemperate, provocative **13** rabble-rousing, revolutionary

inflate 5 bloat, swell **6** blow up, dilate, expand, fill up, pump up **7** distend, improve, puff out **10** appreciate **11** rise in value

inflated 5 blown, gassy, tumid, wordy **6** blew up, turgid **7** bloated, blown up, dilated, flowery, pompous, swollen,

verbose **8** boastful, enlarged, expanded **9** bombastic, distended, overblown, swelled up **10** rhetorical, swelled out **11** exaggerated, pretentious

inflection 4 tone **5** tenor **6** accent **10** modulation **11** enunciation, tone of voice **12** articulation **13** pronunciation

inflexible 4 firm, hard, taut **5** fixed, rigid, solid, stiff **6** dogged, mulish **7** adamant **8** obdurate, resolute, stubborn **9** hidebound, immovable, immutable, ironbound, obstinate, pigheaded, stringent, tenacious, unbending, unplastic **10** adamantine, determined, headstrong, impervious, implacable, inexorable, unwavering, unyielding **11** hard and fast, intractable, not flexible, unmalleable **12** unchangeable **14** uncompromising

inflict 4 dump **5** lay on, wreak **6** impose, unload **7** put upon **9** visit upon **10** administer, perpetrate **11** bring to bear

inflorescence 5 bloom **6** flower **7** blossom, cluster **8** blooming **9** flowering **10** blossoming
type: **4** cyme **5** spike, umbel **6** corymb, raceme, spadix **7** panicle **9** capitulum **14** verticillaster

influence 4 hold, move, pull, stir, sway **5** clout, guide, impel, power **6** arouse, effect, incite, induce, prompt, weight **7** act upon, actuate, control, dispose, incline, inspire, mastery, potency, provoke **8** dominion, leverage, persuade, pressure, prestige **9** advantage, authority **10** ascendancy, domination, predispose

influential 6 moving, potent, strong **7** leading, weighty **8** forceful, powerful, puissant **9** effective, effectual, important, inspiring, momentous **10** activating **11** efficacious, significant **12** instrumental **13** consequential

influx 5 entry **6** inflow **7** arrival, indraft, ingress **9** flowing in, incursion, inpouring **10** converging, inundation **12** infiltration

in force 6 extant **7** en masse **8** in effect **9** effective, operative **11** in existence, in operation, operational **14** in large numbers

inform 3 rat **4** fink, tell
5 edify **6** advise, clue in, notify, snitch, squeal, tattle, tell
on, tip off **7** apprise, let
know **8** acquaint, denounce,
forewarn, report to **9** declare
to, enlighten **11** communicate,
familiarize, serve notice
14 blow the whistle

inform against 5 rat on **6** betray, fink on, tell on **7** sell
out **8** denounce, squeal on
11 double-cross **16** blow the
whistle on

informal 4 easy **6** casual, simple **7** natural, offhand **8** familiar **9** easygoing, not formal
10 unofficial **11** spontaneous
12 come-as-you-are **13** unceremonious, unconstrained
14 unconventional

**informal preliminary
conference**
   French: **10** pourparler

informant 6 source **7** adviser,
tipster **8** appriser, informer,
notifier, reporter **9** announcer,
spokesman **10** respondent
11 enlightener, horse's mouth,
spokeswoman

information 4 data, news
5 facts, notes **6** notice, papers,
report **7** account, tidings
8 briefing, bulletin, evidence,
material **9** documents, knowledge, materials **10** communique **11** fact-finding
12 announcement, intelligence,
notification **13** enlightenment

informed 4 told, up on, wise
5 aware, posted, talked,
taught, warned **7** abreast, advised, knowing, learned, tat-
tled **8** apprised, betrayed,
educated, notified, reported,
snitched, up to date **9** au
courant, permeated **10** acquainted, instructed **11** enlightened, intelligent
13 knowledgeable

informer 3 rat **4** fink **5** Judas
6 canary **7** blabber, stoolie, tattler, traitor **8** betrayer, mou-
chard, snitcher, squealer
11 stool pigeon

Informer, The
   author: **13** Liam O'Flaherty
   director: **8** John Ford
   cast: **10** Una O'Connor
   11 Wallace Ford **12** Heather
   Angel **13** Margot Grahame,
   Preston Foster **14** Victor
   McLaglen
   score: **10** Max Steiner
   remade as: **7** Up Tight

infraction 6 breach **8** trespass
9 violation **10** peccadillo
11 lawbreaking **12** disobedience, encroachment, infringe-

ment, unobservance
13 nonobservance,
transgression

infrastructure 4 base, root
5 basis **6** bottom, fabric,
ground **7** bedrock, footing,
support **9** framework, substrate **10** foundation, groundwork, substratum
12 substructure, underpinning
14 understructure

infrequent 3 few **4** rare **6** fitful, seldom, unique **7** unusual
8 sporadic, uncommon **9** spasmodic **10** occasional **16** few
and far between

infringe 5 break **6** butt in, invade **7** disobey, impinge, infract, intrude, violate
8 encroach, overstep, trespass
10 contravene, transgress

in front 5 ahead, first **6** before **7** forward

**in full possession of one's
faculties**
   Latin: **12** compos mentis

infuriate 3 vex **4** gall, rile
5 anger, chafe **6** enrage, madden, offend **7** incense, inflame,
outrage, provoke **8** irritate
9 aggravate, burn one up,
make angry **10** exasperate
15 raise one's dander

infuriating 7 irksome **8** annoying, enraging **9** maddening,
provoking **10** irritating **11** aggravating **12** exasperating,
inflammatory

infuse 5 imbue **7** fortify, implant, inspire, instill **8** impart
to, pour into **9** inculcate, insinuate, introject

in futuro 11 in the future

Inge, William
   author of: **6** Picnic **7** Bus
   Stop **19** Come Back Little
   Sheba **26** The Dark at the
   Top of the Stairs

in general 7 as a rule, usually **10** by and large, on the
whole

ingenious 4 deft **6** adroit, artful, clever, crafty, expert,
shrewd **7** cunning **8** masterly,
original, skillful, stunning
9 brilliant, dexterous, inventive, masterful **11** resourceful

ingenuity 5 flair, skill **7** cunning, know-how, mastery
8 aptitude, deftness, facility
9 adeptness, dexterity, expertise, sharpness **10** adroitness,
astuteness, brilliance, cleverness, shrewdness **11** imagination **12** good thinking,
skillfulness **13** ingeniousness,
inventiveness **15** imaginative-

ness, quick-wittedness,
resourcefulness

ingenuous 4 open **5** frank, naive **6** direct, honest **7** artless,
genuine, natural, up front
8 trusting **9** guileless **10** unaffected **11** openhearted **13** sim-
plehearted **15** straightforward,
unsophisticated **16** straight-
shooting

ingenuousness 7 naivete
8 openness **9** frankness
11 artlessness

ingest 3 eat **4** gulp, take
5 drink **6** absorb, devour, imbibe, take in **7** consume, swallow **8** gulp down

inglorious 3 low **4** base, evil,
mean, vile **6** odious **7** corrupt,
heinous, ignoble **8** depraved,
flagrant, infamous, shameful,
shocking **9** atrocious, degrading, nefarious **10** despicable,
detestable, outrageous, scandalous **11** disgraceful, ignominious, opprobrious
12 contemptible,
dishonorable

in good condition
   French: **10** embonpoint

in good health 2 OK **4** fine,
hale, well **6** hearty, robust,
tiptop **7** healthy **8** all right,
blooming, vigorous **9** full of
pep, in the pink **17** full of
vim and vigor

in good time 5 early **7** betimes **11** ahead of time

ingot 3 bar **5** block

ingrained 4 deep, firm **5** fixed
6 inborn, inbred, innate,
rooted **8** inherent, thorough
9 confirmed, implanted, indelible, intrinsic **10** deep-rooted,
deep-seated, inveterate
14 constitutional

Ingram, Blanche
   character in: **8** Jane Eyre
   author: **6** Bronte

ingratiating 4 oily **5** sweet
6 genial, smarmy **7** affable,
amiable, cordial, fulsome,
gushing, likable, lovable, winning, winsome **8** charming,
engaging, friendly, gracious,
magnetic, pleasing, unctuous
9 appealing, congenial **10** attractive, enchanting, obsequious, oleaginous, personable,
persuasive **11** captivating,
good-humored, self-serving
12 presumptuous

ingratiation 7 blarney **8** flattery **9** sweet talk **12** inveiglement **13** blandishments

ingratitude 14 ungratefulness
18 lack of appreciation

ingredient 4 part **6** aspect, factor **7** element, feature **9** component, essential, principle **11** constituent, contributor **12** integral part

Ingres, Jean-Auguste-Dominique
  born: 6 France **9** Montauban
  artwork: 9 Odalisque, The Source **13** Mme Moitessier **14** The Turkish Bath **15** Valpincon Bather **16** Roger and Angelica **17** The Vow of Louis XIII **21** Comtesse d'Haussonville **25** The Ambassadors of Agamemnon **26** The Vow of Louis the Thirteenth

ingress 5 entry, way in **6** access **8** entrance

inhabit 5 lodge **6** live in, occupy, people, settle, tenant **7** dwell in **8** populate, reside in

inhabitant 6 inmate, lessee, lodger, native, renter, tenant **7** boarder, citizen, denizen, dweller, settler **8** occupant, occupier, resident, villager **9** inhabiter

inhalation 4 gasp **5** sniff **6** breath **11** breathing in

inhale 5 sniff, snuff **6** suck in **7** inspire, respire **9** breathe in, inbreathe

inherent 6 inborn, inbred, innate, native **7** natural **9** essential, ingrained, intrinsic **10** deep-rooted, hereditary, inveterate **11** inalienable, inseparable **14** constitutional

inherit 3 get **6** be left, come by **7** acquire **8** come into **9** come in for **10** fall heir to

inheritance 6 devise, estate, legacy **7** bequest **8** bestowal, heritage **9** endowment, patrimony **10** bequeathal, birthright

inherited 8 came into, heirloom, unearned **10** handed down

inheritor 4 heir **7** legatee **11** beneficiary

Inherit the Wind
  director: 13 Stanley Kramer
  based on play by: 10 Robert E Lee **14** Jerome Lawrence
  cast: 8 Dick York **9** Gene Kelly **10** Elliot Reid **11** Harry Morgan **12** Spencer Tracy (Clarence Darrow) **13** Frederic March (William Jennings Bryan) **16** Florence Eldridge

inhibit 3 bar, gag **4** curb, stop **5** block, check **6** arrest, enjoin, forbid, hinder, impede, muzzle **7** control, harness, prevent, repress, smother **8** hold back, obstruct, prohibit, restrain, restrict, suppress **9** constrain **11** hold in leash

inhibited 4 cold **6** barred, curbed, frigid **7** bridled, checked, guarded **8** hindered, reserved **9** repressed **10** controlled, obstructed, restrained **11** constrained, discouraged, held in check **12** unresponsive **14** under restraint

inhibition, inhibitions 5 check **7** reserve **8** blockage **9** misgiving, restraint, stricture **10** constraint, impediment **11** guardedness, mental block, obstruction, restriction **12** constriction **17** self-consciousness

in high spirits 2 up **3** gay **5** happy, merry **6** elated, jaunty, joyful, joyous **7** buoyant **8** carefree, ecstatic, exultant, jubilant **9** overjoyed **11** exhilarated, on cloud nine **13** up in the clouds **15** on top of the world

in hoc signo vinces 26 in this sign shalt thou conquer
  motto of: 19 Constantine the Great
    from vision of: 5 cross

inhospitable 4 cold, cool, rude **5** aloof **6** unkind **7** distant, hostile **8** impolite **10** unfriendly, ungracious, unobliging, unsociable **11** standoffish, uncongenial, unreceptive, unwelcoming **12** discourteous, unneighborly **13** inconsiderate **14** unapproachable **15** unaccommodating

inhuman 5 cruel **6** brutal, savage **7** brutish, satanic, vicious **8** barbaric, demoniac, fiendish, pitiless, ruthless, venomous **9** barbarous, heartless, malignant, merciless, monstrous, unfeeling **10** diabolical, malevolent **11** coldhearted, cold-blooded, hardhearted

inhumane 6 brutal, savage **7** inhuman **8** fiendish, pitiless, ruthless **9** barbarous, heartless, merciless, unfeeling, unpitying **10** unmerciful **11** coldblooded, hardhearted **12** bloodthirsty **13** unsympathetic

inhumanity 6 sadism **7** cruelty **8** atrocity, savagery **9** barbarism, barbarity, brutality **11** brutishness, heinousness, malevolence, viciousness **12** fiendishness, ruthlessness **13** heartlessness, mercilessness **15** cold-bloodedness **16** bloodthirstiness

inhumation 6 burial **9** interment **10** entombment

inimical 5 toxic **6** at odds **7** harmful, hateful, hostile, hurtful, ruinous **8** venomous, virulent **9** dangerous, ill-willed, injurious, on the outs, poisonous, rancorous **10** unfriendly **11** acrimonious, deleterious, destructive, detrimental, ill-disposed **12** antagonistic, antipathetic, disputatious **13** at loggerheads, at sword's point

inimitable 4 rare **6** unique **7** supreme **8** peerless **9** matchless, nonpareil, unequaled, unmatched, unrivaled **10** consummate, preeminent, unexcelled **11** superlative, unsurpassed **12** incomparable, unparalleled **13** beyond compare

iniquitous 4 base, evil, vile **6** sinful, wicked **7** corrupt, debased, immoral, vicious **8** depraved, infamous **9** nefarious **10** evil-minded **12** blackhearted **13** reprehensible

iniquity 3 sin **4** evil, vice **5** wrong **6** infamy **7** knavery, outrage, roguery **8** inequity, villainy **9** depravity, evildoing, flagrancy, turpitude **10** corruption, dishonesty, immorality, miscreancy, profligacy, sinfulness, unfairness, unjustness, wickedness, wrongdoing **11** abomination **13** transgression **14** gross injustice **15** unrighteousness

in isolation
  Latin: 7 in vacuo

initial 5 first **6** maiden, primal **7** opening, primary **8** germinal, original, starting **9** beginning, inaugural, incipient **10** commencing, initiatory **12** introductory

initiate 4 haze, open **5** begin, found, set up, start **6** induct, invest, launch, take in **7** bring in, install, kick off, receive, usher in **8** be opened, commence, get going, set afoot, set going **9** enter upon, establish, institute, introduce, originate **10** inaugurate, lead the way **11** break ground, get under way, take the lead **12** acquaint with **13** blaze the trail **15** familiarize with **16** lay the first stone, lay the foundation **19** start the ball rolling

initiation 5 onset, start **6** outset **7** genesis, opening **8** entrance, guidance, outbreak, starting **9** beginning, inception, induction **10** admittance, initiating, ushering in **11** inculcation **12** commencement, inauguration, introduction **14** indoctrination **15** formal admission

initiative 4 lead **8** dynamism **9** first move, first step **10** creativity, enterprise, get-up-and-go, leadership **11** originality **12** forcefulness **14** aggressiveness

in its original place
   Latin: **6** in situ

inject 3 put **4** pump **5** force, imbue, infix **6** infuse, insert **7** instill, throw in **8** intromit **9** interject, introduce **11** interpolate

injection 4 hypo, shot **7** booster, vaccine **9** antitoxin, insertion **10** hypodermic **11** inoculation, vaccination **12** shot in the arm

injudicious 4 dumb, wild **5** crazy **6** stupid, unwise **7** foolish, unsound **8** heedless, reckless **9** audacious, foolhardy, hotheaded, imprudent, senseless **10** self-willed, unsuitable **11** inadvisable

injunction 4 writ **5** edict, order **7** command **10** admonition, court order

Injun Joe
   character in: **9** Tom Sawyer
   author: **9** Mark Twain

injure 3 mar **4** harm, hurt, lame, maim **5** abuse, spoil, stain, sting, sully, wound, wrong **6** bruise, damage, debase, deface, deform, impair, malign, mangle, misuse, offend, scathe **7** afflict, affront, blemish, violate, vitiate **8** do harm to, ill-treat, lacerate, maltreat, mutilate **9** disfigure

injured 4 hurt, lame **6** abused, harmed, maimed, marred, piqued **7** bruised, damaged, defaced, grieved, scathed, wounded, wronged **8** crippled, deformed, impaired, insulted, offended **9** afflicted, affronted, aggrieved **10** disfigured

injurious 7 abusive, adverse, harmful, hurtful, noxious, ruinous **8** damaging, inimical **9** corrosive **10** calamitous, disastrous, pernicious **11** deleterious, destructive, detrimental

injury 3 cut **4** blow, gash, harm, hurt, stab **5** abuse, wound **6** bruise, damage, lesion **7** affront, outrage, scratch **9** aspersion, contusion, indignity, injustice **10** afflic-

tion, defamation, detraction, disservice, impairment, laceration, mutilation **12** vilification

injustice 3 sin **4** bias, evil **5** wrong **6** injury **7** bigotry, offense, tyranny **8** foul play, inequity, iniquity **9** prejudice, unjust act **10** disservice, favoritism, inequality, infraction, partiality, unfairness, unjustness, wrongdoing **11** malpractice, persecution **12** encroachment, infringement, partisanship **13** transgression

in keeping 6 normal **7** natural **8** becoming **9** congruous, consonant **10** consistent **11** appropriate, in agreement **12** in compliance, in conformity

inkling 3 cue, tip **4** clue, hint, idea **6** notion **7** glimmer, whisper **8** innuendo **9** suspicion, vague idea **10** conception, glimmering, indication, intimation, suggestion **11** insinuation, supposition

inky 3 jet **4** dark **5** black, raven, sable **7** stygian **9** coalblack

inlet 3 bay **4** cove, gulf **5** bight, fiord, firth, fjord **6** harbor, strait **7** estuary, narrows **8** waterway

in line 4 even **6** in a row **7** aligned, in order **8** queued up, straight **12** under control

in loco 7 in place **16** in the proper place

in loco parentis 16 replacing a parent **19** in the place of a parent

inmate 3 con **5** felon **6** lodger, tenant **7** convict, denizen **8** prisoner, resident **10** inhabitant

in medias res 19 in the middle of things **21** in the middle of the story

in memoriam 10 in memory of **13** as a memorial to, to the memory of

In Memoriam A H H
   author: **18** Alfred Lord Tennyson

in memory of
   Latin: **10** in memoriam

In Memory of W B Yeats
   author: **7** W H Auden

inmost 5 inner **6** inside **7** central **8** interior **9** innermost

in motion 5 afoot, astir **6** active, moving **7** on the go, working **8** under way **9** on the

move, operating, operative **10** responsive

In My Father's Court
   author: **19** Isaac Bashevis Singer

inn 5 hotel, lodge, motel **6** hostel, tavern **7** hospice, pension **8** hostelry **9** roadhouse **11** caravansary, public house
   French: **7** auberge
   Spanish: **6** posada

innards 4 guts **6** bowels, vitals **7** gizzard, insides, viscera **10** intestines **14** liver and lights

innate 6 inborn, inbred, native **7** natural **8** inherent **9** essential, ingrained, inherited, intrinsic, intuitive **10** congenital, hereditary, indigenous **11** instinctive **14** constitutional

inner 6 hidden, inside, inward, mental, middle **7** central, private, psychic **8** esoteric, interior, internal **9** concealed, emotional, spiritual, unobvious **10** more secret **12** more intimate **13** psychological

inner circle 4 core **5** bosom, heart **6** center **7** nucleus

inner city 8 core city, downtown **9** urban area **10** city limits, metropolis **11** central city **16** metropolitan area

Inner Mongolia
   other name: **9** Neimenggu, Neimengku
   capital: **6** Hohhot **7** Huhehot
   desert: **4** Gobi
   tent: **4** yurt

innermost 6 inmost, secret **7** deepest **10** deep-rooted, deep-seated **11** most private **12** most intimate, most personal

innermost part 4 core, crux, pith, soul **6** center, kernel **7** essence, nucleus

Inness, George
   born: **10** Newburgh NY
   artwork: **7** The Monk **14** Home of the Heron, Peace and Plenty **15** Delaware Water Gap **17** The Delaware Valley **19** The Lackawanna Valley

Innisfail *see* **7** Ireland

innkeeper 4 host **6** tapper, venter **7** padrone **8** boniface, hosteler, hotelier, landlord, publican **10** proprietor **12** maitre d'hotel, restaurateur

innocence 6 purity **7** naivete **8** chastity **9** freshness **10** clean hands, simplicity **11** artlessness, sinlessness **12** incorrup-

tion, spotlessness
13 blamelessness, guilelessness, guiltlessness, impeccability, inculpability, ingenuousness, stainlessness
14 immaculateness

innocent 3 tot **4** baby, naif, open, pure, tyro **5** clean, naive **6** chaste, honest, novice, simple **7** artless, ingenue, sinless, upright **8** harmless, pristine, spotless, virginal, virtuous **9** blameless, childlike, faultless, greenhorn, guileless, guiltless, ingenuous, innocuous, little one, stainless, uncorrupt, undefiled, unstained, unsullied, unworldly, well-meant **10** artless one, immaculate, impeccable, inculpable, tenderfoot, young child **11** inoffensive, unblemished, uncorrupted, unmalicious, unoffending **12** unsuspicious **13** meaning no harm, unimpeachable **14** above suspicion, irreproachable
15 unsophisticated
Latin: 12 integer vitae

Innocents, The
director: 11 Jack Clayton
based on story by: 10 Henry James (The Turn of the Screw)
cast: 11 Deborah Kerr, Megs Jenkins **13** Peter Wyngarde **15** Michael Redgrave
script: 12 Truman Capote **16** William Archibald

Innocents Abroad, The
author: 9 Mark Twain (Samuel Clemens)

innocuous 4 dull, mild **5** banal, empty, trite, vapid **6** barren **7** insipid **8** harmless, innocent, painless **9** pointless **11** commonplace, inoffensive, meaningless

innocuousness 6 safety **9** blandness, innocence **12** harmlessness **15** inoffensiveness

in no uncertain terms 7 clearly, plainly **9** expressly **10** definitely, distinctly **13** categorically, unequivocally

innovation 5 shift **7** novelty **8** updating **10** alteration, dernier cri, new measure, remodeling, renovation **11** institution, latest thing **12** commencement, inauguration, introduction, streamlining **13** modernization

innovator 7 deviser, planner **9** contriver **10** instigator, originator **11** inaugurator

Innu see **17** Montagnais-Naskapi

innuendo 4 hint **7** whisper **8** overtone **9** inference **10** imputation, intimation **11** implication, insinuation

innumerable 6 myriad **8** numerous **9** countless **10** numberless, unnumbered **12** incalculable **13** multitudinous

Ino
also: 9 Leucothea
goddess of: 3 sea
father: 6 Cadmus
mother: 8 Harmonia
sister: 5 Hgave **6** Semele **7** Autonoe
husband: 7 Athamas
son: 8 Learchus **10** Melicertes
stepson: 7 Phrixus
stepdaughter: 5 Helle
saved: 8 Odysseus
cared for infant: 8 Dionysus
changed into: 10 sea goddess

inoculate 5 imbue, shoot **6** infuse, inject, insert **7** implant, instill **8** immunize **9** inculcate, vaccinate

inoculation 4 shot **6** needle **7** booster **9** injection **10** hypodermic **11** vaccination **12** immunization

inoffensive 4 mild, safe **5** bland **7** neutral **8** harmless, innocent **9** endurable, innocuous, tolerable **10** sufferable **11** unoffending **15** unobjectionable

inoffensiveness 6 safety **9** innocence **10** neutrality **12** harmlessness **13** innocuousness

in one's debt 7 obliged **8** beholden, indebted **9** obligated **15** under obligation

in one's own person
Latin: 16 in propria persona

in one's own place
Latin: 7 suo loco

in one's own right
Latin: 7 suo jure

in one's rightful place
Latin: 7 suo loco

inoperable 6 broken **10** broken down, unworkable **11** ineffective

in operation 5 in use **7** in force, working **8** in effect **9** operating, operative

inoperative 4 dead, down **8** inactive **10** not working, out of order

inopportune 7 awkward **8** ill-timed, untimely **10** badly timed, ill-advised, unsuitable **11** troublesome, undesirable, unfavorable, unfortunate **12** inauspicious, incommodious, inconvenient, unpropitious, unseasonable **13** inappropriate **15** disadvantageous

in order 2 OK **4** neat, tidy **6** proper **7** correct, perfect **8** all right

inordinate 5 undue **6** lavish, wanton **7** extreme, profuse, surplus **8** needless, overmuch, shocking **9** excessive **10** deplorable, exorbitant, immoderate, irrational, outrageous, scandalous **11** disgraceful, extravagant, intemperate, overflowing, superfluous, uncalled-for, unnecessary **12** unreasonable, unrestrained **13** superabundant **14** supersaturated, unconscionable **16** disproportionate

inordinately 6 overly, unduly **9** extremely **11** excessively **12** immoderately, outrageously, prodigiously **13** extravagantly, intemperately, superfluously, unnecessarily

inorganic 4 dead **7** mineral **8** lifeless **9** inanimate, nonliving **10** artificial

in passing
French: 9 en passant

in perpetuum 7 forever

in petto 11 in the breast **12** not disclosed

in pieces 6 broken **7** asunder, smashed **8** in shreds, sundered **9** torn apart **13** in smithereens

in place
Latin: 6 in loco, in situ

in plain sight 7 exposed, obvious **10** in full view, noticeable **12** out in the open **17** in front of one's nose

in posse 11 potentially **13** in possibility

in possibility
Latin: 7 in posse

In Praise of Darkness
author: 15 Jorge Luis Borges

in propria persona 15 in one's own person

inquest 5 probe **7** autopsy, delving, hearing, inquiry, probing **8** necropsy **10** postmortem **11** inquisition **13** investigation

inquire 3 ask **5** probe, query, study **6** search **7** examine, explore, inspect **8** check out, look into, look over, question **9** track down **10** look deeper, scrutinize **11** investigate

inquirer 5 asker, snoop
6 seeker **7** auditor, querier,
quizzer, student **8** pollster,
searcher **9** catechist **10** inquisitor, questioner **12** interlocutor, interrogator, investigator

inquiry, enquiry 4 hunt, quiz
5 probe, query, quest, study
6 search, survey **7** inquest
8 analysis, question, research,
scrutiny **9** interview **10** inspection **11** examination, exploration, inquisition,
questioning **13** interrogation,
investigation

inquisitive 4 nosy **6** prying,
snoopy **8** meddling, snooping
9 inquiring, intrusive, searching **10** meddlesome, too curious **11** interfering,
overcurious, questioning

in re 13 in the matter of

in reality
Latin: **7** de facto

in rem 15 against the thing
of a legal proceeding:
18 against the property

in rerum natura 19 in the
nature of things

in retreat 10 backing off, retreating **11** withdrawing, backing away

in reverse 8 backward **9** backing up **22** in the opposite
direction

insalubrious 7 harmful, noisome, noxious **8** inimical, virulent **9** injurious, unhealthy
10 pernicious **11** deleterious,
detrimental, unhealthful,
unwholesome

insane 3 mad **4** bats, daft,
dumb, loco, nuts, wild, zany
5 balmy, batty, crazy, loony,
manic, nutty, potty **6** absurd,
crazed, raving **7** berserk, bizarre, bonkers, cracked, foolish, idiotic, lunatic, tetched,
touched, unsound **8** demented,
frenzied, maniacal, unhinged
9 eccentric, imbecilic, imprudent, insensate, paranoiac,
psychotic, senseless **10** ridiculous, unbalanced **11** injudicious **12** mad as a hatter, off
one's chump, round the bend,
unreasonable **13** off one's
rocker, out of one's head, out
of one's mind, out of one's
wits, schizophrenic **15** bats in
the belfry, mad as a March
hare, stark staring mad
17 nutty as a fruitcake

insanity 5 folly, mania **6** idiocy, lunacy, raving **7** madness **8** dementia, paranoia
9 aberrance, absurdity, craziness, monomania, psychosis,

stupidity **10** aberration **11** derangement, foolishness, unsoundness **12** loss of reason
13 hallucination, mental illness, schizophrenia,
senselessness

insatiable 8 ravenous **9** insatiate, limitless, voracious
10 bottomless, gluttonous, implacable, omnivorous **12** unappeasable, unquenchable

inscribe 3 pen **4** etch, mark,
seal, sign **5** blaze, brand,
carve, write **6** chisel, incise,
letter, scrawl **7** engrave, impress, imprint **8** scribble
9 autograph

inscription 5 motto, title
6 legend, rubric **7** address, caption, epigram, epitaph, heading, titulus, writing
8 colophon, epigraph, graffiti
9 engraving, lettering
10 dedication

inscrutable 6 arcane, hidden,
masked, veiled **7** deadpan, elusive **8** baffling, puzzling **9** concealed, enigmatic
10 mysterious, mystifying, perplexing, poker-faced, unknowable, unreadable, unrevealed
12 inexplicable, unfathomable,
unsearchable **14** indecipherable, unintelligible
16 incomprehensible

In Search of Identity
author: **12** Anwar el-Sadat

insect 3 ant, bee, bug, fly
4 flea, gnat, moth, pest, wasp
5 aphid, imago **6** bedbug, beetle, cicada, earwig, hornet,
mantis, mayfly, vermin
7 chigger, cricket, firefly, katydid, ladybug, termite **8** horsefly, housefly, lacewing,
mosquito **9** arthropod, butterfly, cockroach, dragonfly
10 silverfish **11** grasshopper
study of: 10 entomology
young: 4 grub, pupa **5** larva,
nymph **6** larvae, maggot
9 chrysalis **11** caterpillar
anatomy: 4 palp **5** cerci, notum **6** cercus, feeler, labium,
labrum, ocelli, thorax **7** antenna, maxilla, ocellus
8 antennae, mandible, maxillae **9** proboscis, spiracles
10 ovipositor **11** exoskeleton

insectivore 4 mole **5** shrew
6 desman, tenrec **7** moon rat
8 alamiqui, anteater, hedgehog **9** solenodon

insecure 4 weak **5** frail, risky,
shaky **6** infirm, unsafe, unsure, wobbly **7** dubious, exposed, not firm, not sure,
rickety, unsound **8** critical,
doubtful, in danger, perilous,

unstable, unsteady **9** dangerous, diffident, hazardous, in a
bad way, tottering, unassured,
uncertain, under fire **10** endangered, precarious, ramshackle, unreliable, unshielded,
vulnerable **11** defenseless, dilapidated, unprotected,
unsheltered

insecurities 4 risk **5** peril
6 danger, hazard **7** pitfall
8 jeopardy **11** contingency

insecurity 5 doubt **9** self-doubt,
shakiness **10** diffidence, unsafeness **11** dubiousness, incertitude, instability, uncertainty
12 doubtfulness, endangerment, insecureness, unsteadiness **13** vulnerability
14 precariousness **15** defenselessness, lack of assurance
16 apprehensiveness

insensate 4 cold **5** cruel
6 brutal **8** inhumane **9** heartless, unfeeling **11** unconscious

insensibility 4 coma **5** swoon
6 apathy, torpor, trance
8 blackout, dullness, lethargy,
numbness, obduracy, oblivion,
stoicism **9** analgesia, catalepsy
10 anesthesia, obtuseness
12 incognizance, indifference,
mindlessness **13** insensitivity,
unfeelingness
15 unconsciousness

insensible 4 cold **9** insensate,
senseless **11** unconscious

insensitive 4 cold, dead,
numb **5** blase **7** callous
8 hardened **9** apathetic, impassive, insensate, unaware of,
unfeeling **10** impervious, insensible **11** indifferent, unconcerned **12** thick-skinned
15 uncompassionate

insensitiveness 8 rudeness
10 coarseness, indelicacy
12 tactlessness **13** insensibility,
insensitivity
17 inconsiderateness

inseparable 8 attached **11** indivisible, unseverable
12 indissoluble

insert 3 add **5** embed, enter,
imbed, infix, inlay, inset, pop
in, put in, set in **6** infuse, inject, push in, tuck in **7** drive
in, implant, intrude, place in,
press in, slide in, stick in,
stuff in, wedge in **8** thrust in
9 interject, interlard, interpose,
introduce **10** put between
11 interpolate, intersperse

insertion 2 ad **5** entry, graft,
inlay, inset **7** implant **11** insinuation, parenthesis **12** interjection **13** advertisement

inset 4 gore **5** embed, godet,

imbed, inlay, panel **6** insert
9 insertion

in seventh heaven 6 elated,
joyful, joyous **8** ecstatic, euphoric **9** exuberant, rapturous
11 on cloud nine **13** up in the
clouds

inside 2 in **5** inner **6** inmost,
inward, secret **7** private **8** cliquish, esoteric, interior, internal, intimate **9** inner part,
inner side, innermost
12 confidential

inside information 3 tip
10 inside dope

inside out 9 backwards **10** in
disorder, topsy turvy **11** wrong
side to

insides 4 guts **6** bowels, vitals
7 gizzard, innards, viscera
10 intestines

insidious 3 sly **4** foxy, wily
5 shady **6** artful, covert, crafty,
sneaky, subtle, tricky
7 crooked, cunning, devious,
furtive **8** guileful, slippery,
sneaking, stealthy **9** concealed,
deceitful, designing, disguised,
secretive, underhand **10** contriving, perfidious, pernicious,
undercover, undetected
11 clandestine, deleterious,
treacherous, underhanded
12 disingenuous, falsehearted
13 Machiavellian, surreptitious

insight 6 acumen **9** intuition
10 perception **11** discernment,
penetration **12** apprehension,
perceptivity, perspicacity
13 comprehension, intuitive-
ness **14** perceptiveness
French: 6 apercu

insignia 3 bar **4** mark, sign,
star **5** badge, medal, patch
6 emblem, stripe, symbol
7 chevron, epaulet, oak leaf
10 decoration **13** badge of
office

insignificance 8 puniness
9 pettiness, smallness **10** meagerness, triviality **11** irrelevance **12** unimportance

insignificant 4 puny **5** petty,
small **6** flimsy, meager, minute, paltry **7** trivial **8** niggling, not vital, nugatory,
picayune, piddling, trifling
9 minuscule, worthless **10** immaterial, irrelevant, negligible,
of no moment, second-rate
11 indifferent, meaningless,
unimportant **12** nonessential
13 small potatoes **14** inconsiderable **15** inconsequential, of
little account, of no consequence **18** not worth
mentioning

insincere 5 false, lying **6** un-

true **7** devious, evasive
8 guileful, two-faced, uncan-
did **9** deceitful, dishonest,
equivocal **10** fraudulent, perfidious, untruthful **11** dissembling **12** disingenuous,
hypocritical, mealymouthed
13 dissimulating, double-
dealing

insincerity 4 sham **6** deceit
8 pretense, uncandor **9** deception, falseness, hypocrisy,
mendacity **11** affectation, shallowness, unfrankness **12** un-
candidness **13** artificiality
16 disingenuousness

insinuate 5 imply **6** inject, insert **7** asperse, let fall, suggest,
wheedle, whisper **8** intimate
10 ingratiate **11** worm one's
way

insinuation 4 hint **8** allusion,
infusion, innuendo **9** aspersion, insertion, intrusion
10 allegation, imputation, intimation, suggestion **11** implication, penetration
12 ingratiation, interjection

insipid 4 arid, blah, drab, dull,
flat, lean **5** banal, bland,
empty, inane, stale, trite,
vapid **6** barren, boring, jejune,
stupid **7** prosaic **8** lifeless, zest-
less **9** pointless, savorless,
tasteless, wearisome **10** monotonous, namby-pamby,
wishy-washy **11** commonplace **12** unappetizing
13 characterless,
uninteresting

insist 4 aver, hold, urge, warn
5 claim, vouch **6** assert, demand, exhort, repeat, stress
7 caution, command, contend,
persist, protest, require **8** admonish, maintain **9** reiterate
10 asseverate **13** lay down the
law **14** take a firm stand
15 stand one's ground

insistence 6 demand, urging
7 urgency **8** exigency, pressure **9** clamoring **11** persistence **12** perseverance
14 imperativeness

insistent 4 firm **7** adamant
8 emphatic, repeated, stubborn **9** assertive, demanding
10 determined, unyielding
11 unrelenting

in situ 7 in place **18** in its
original place

insolence 4 gall **7** disdain, hauteur **8** audacity **9** arrogance,
impudence **10** brazenness, disrespect, effrontery, incivility,
lordliness **11** haughtiness, presumption **12** disobedience, impertinence, impoliteness
13 bumptiousness, imperious-

ness **14** unmannerliness
16 superciliousness

insolent 4 rude **5** fresh, nervy
6 brazen, cheeky **7** defiant,
galling, haughty **8** arrogant,
impolite, impudent **9** audacious, bumptious, insulting
10 disdainful, outrageous, unmannerly **11** impertinent,
overbearing **12** contemptuous,
discourteous, presumptuous,
supercilious **13** disrespectful

insoluble 12 inexplicable, unanswerable **13** undissolvable,
unexplainable **14** undecipherable **16** incomprehensible

insolvent 5 broke **6** ruined
8 bankrupt, wiped out **9** destitute, moneyless, penniless
10 down-and-out, out of
money **11** impecunious
12 impoverished, overextended

insomnia 11 nuit blanche, per-
vigilium, wakefulness **12** in-
somnolence **13** sleeplessness

insouciant 4 airy **5** perky
6 breezy, casual, jaunty
7 buoyant, offhand **8** carefree,
debonair, flippant **9** easygoing,
mercurial, unruffled, sans
souci, whimsical **10** capricious,
nonchalant, untroubled **11** free
and easy, indifferent, unconcerned **12** devil-may-care,
happy-go-lucky, lighthearted

inspect 3 eye **4** scan **5** probe,
study **6** peer at, peruse, review, survey **7** examine, explore, observe **8** pore over
10 scrutinize **11** contemplate,
investigate, reconnoiter

inspection 4 scan **5** audit,
check, probe, study **6** review,
survey **7** perusal **8** checking,
scrutiny **9** appraisal, oversight
11 examination

inspector 7 analyst, auditor
8 analyzer, examiner, overseer,
reviewer **9** appraiser, detective **11** scrutinizer
12 investigator

**Inspector-General, The
author: 12** Nikolai Gogol
character: 4 Anna, Osip
5 Maria **26** Ivan Alexandro-
vich Hlestakov **35** Anton
Antonovich Skvoznik-
Dmukhanovsky

inspiration 4 idea, spur
5 fancy, flash **6** motive **7** impulse **8** afflatus, stimulus **9** incentive, influence, prompting
10 compulsion, incitement,
motivation, revelation
13 encouragement

inspire 4 fire, stir **5** cause, exalt, impel, rouse **6** arouse, excite, induce, prompt, vivify

7 animate, enliven, hearten, produce, promote, provoke, quicken 8 embolden, engender, enkindle, illumine, inspirit, motivate, occasion 9 encourage, galvanize, influence, stimulate 10 give rise to, illuminate

inspired 3 apt 5 fired, moved 6 elated 7 elegant, exalted, excited, incited, touched, well-put 8 creative, original, prompted 9 impressed, ingenious, inventive, motivated 10 encouraged, felicitous, influenced, stimulated, well-chosen 11 exhilarated, imaginative 13 well-expressed

inspiring 5 grand 6 moving 7 awesome 8 eloquent, stirring 9 affecting, brilliant 10 impressive 11 encouraging, magnificent, stimulating

inspirit 5 boost, cheer, rouse 6 buoy up, uplift 7 animate, comfort, enliven, hearten, inspire 9 encourage, give a lift

in spite of himself
French: 9 malgre lui

instability 8 wavering, weakness 9 hesitancy 10 fitfulness, hesitation, indecision, insecurity 11 flightiness, fluctuation, inconstancy, vacillation 12 irresolution, unstableness, unsteadiness 13 changeability, inconsistency, mercurialness, vulnerability 14 capriciousness, changeableness

install, instal 3 lay 4 seat 5 crown, embed, imbed, lodge, plant 6 induct, invest, locate, move in, ordain 7 arrange, emplace, instate, receive, situate, station, usher in 8 coronate, initiate, position 9 establish 10 inaugurate, set in place

installation 5 plant 6 agency 8 facility 9 formation, induction 10 foundation, initiation, ordination 11 appointment, institution, investiture 12 inauguration, military base, organization 13 establishment

installment 4 part, unit 5 issue 6 laying 7 chapter, payment, section, segment 8 division, fragment, locating

instance 4 case, time 6 sample 7 example 8 occasion, specimen 9 precedent, prototype 10 antecedent 11 case in point 12 circumstance, illustration

instant 5 flash, jiffy, quick, trice 6 abrupt, minute, moment, prompt, second, sudden 8 premixed 9 immediate,

on the spot, precooked, twinkling 10 ready-to-use 11 split second 12 unhesitating

instantaneous 5 rapid, swift 6 abrupt, direct, prompt, speedy, sudden 9 immediate 13 quick as a flash

instantaneously 6 at once 7 quickly, rapidly 8 in a flash, in no time, instanter, right now 9 on the spot, right away 11 immediately 21 in the twinkling of an eye

instantly 6 at once 7 quickly 8 directly, in a flash, promptly, right now 9 instanter, on the spot 10 here and now 11 immediately 12 quick as a wink, without delay 15 instantaneously 17 without hesitation

instar
insect period between:
5 molts 7 molting

in statu quo 17 in the state in which (something is or was)

Instauratio Magna
author: 12 Francis Bacon

instead 6 in lieu, rather 10 in its place

instigate 4 goad, spur, urge 5 begin, rouse, start 6 foment, incite, kindle, prompt, stir up 7 provoke 8 initiate 9 stimulate 10 bring about 11 set in motion

instigator 6 shaper 7 inciter 9 architect, innovator 10 prime mover, ringleader

instill, instil 4 pour 5 mix in, teach 6 impart, induce 7 implant, inspire 8 engender 9 inculcate

instinct 4 gift 5 knack 6 genius, nature 7 faculty 8 aptitude, capacity, tendency 9 intuition, mother wit 10 proclivity

instinctive 6 inborn, inbred, innate, native 7 natural 8 inherent, inspired 9 automatic, impulsive, intuitive, unlearned 10 deep-seated, unacquired 11 instinctual, involuntary, spontaneous

institute 4 pass 5 begin, enact, found, set up, start 6 ordain, school 7 academy, college, society 8 commence, get going, initiate, organize 9 establish, introduce, originate, prescribe, undertake 10 constitute, foundation, inaugurate 11 association, get under way 13 put into effect 14 bring into being

institution 4 rite 5 habit,

usage 6 custom, prison, ritual, school 7 academy, college, company, fixture 8 bughouse, madhouse, nuthouse, seminary 9 institute 10 convention, crazy house, foundation, university 11 association 12 organization 13 establishment

institutionalize 6 commit, detain 7 confine, put away 8 imprison 11 incarcerate

in strict confidence 7 sub rosa 9 between us, entre nous, privately 14 confidentially 15 between you and me 16 between me and thee, between ourselves

instruct 3 bid 5 brief, coach, drill, guide, order, teach, train, tutor 6 advise, direct, inform, notify, school 7 apprise, command, educate 8 acquaint 9 catechize, enlighten 12 indoctrinate

instruction 8 coaching, guidance, pedagogy, teaching, training, tutelage, tutoring 9 education 11 instructing 14 indoctrination

instructions 4 rule 5 maxim, moral, motto 6 advice, homily, lesson 7 precept 9 direction, guideline 11 explanation, information 12 prescription 13 specification 14 recommendation

instructive 8 didactic, edifying 11 educational 12 enlightening

instructor 3 don 4 guru 5 coach, guide, tutor 6 mentor 7 counsel, maestro, teacher, trainer 8 educator, lecturer 9 governess, pedagogue, preceptor, professor 10 schoolmarm 12 schoolmaster 13 schoolteacher 14 schoolmistress

instrument 4 deed, tool 5 agent, grant, means, paper 6 agency, device, gadget, medium 7 charter, machine, utensil, vehicle 8 contract 9 apparatus, appliance, equipment, expedient, implement, mechanism 11 contrivance

Instrument, The
author: 9 John O'Hara

instrumental 5 vital 6 active, useful 7 crucial, helpful 8 a means to, decisive, valuable 9 assisting, conducive, effective, effectual, essential 10 functional 12 contributory

instrumentality 5 force, means 6 agency, charge 9 in-

fluence, mediation
12 intervention

insubordinate 6 unruly **7** defiant **8** insolent, mutinous
9 fractious **10** disorderly, rebellious, refractory **11** disobedient, intractable, uncompliant
12 recalcitrant, ungovernable, unsubmissive

insubordination 6 mutiny, revolt **7** anarchy **8** sedition **9** rebellion **10** dissention, insurgence, unruliness **12** disobedience, insurrection
13 noncompliance
14 refractoriness

insubstantial 4 airy, weak
5 frail, shaky, small **6** flimsy, modest, paltry, slight, unreal
7 fragile, trivial, unsound
8 baseless, bodiless, delicate, ethereal, gossamer, piddling, trifling, unstable **9** imaginary, visionary **10** groundless, immaterial, impalpable, intangible **12** apparitional
14 inconsiderable

in succession
   French: **7** en suite

insufferable 7 hateful **8** dreadful **10** abominable, detestable, disgusting, outrageous, unbearable **11** intolerable, unendurable, unspeakable
13 insupportable

insufficiency 4 lack, need, want **6** dearth **7** drought, paucity **8** scarcity, shortage
10 deficiency, inadequacy, meagerness, scantiness
11 undersupply

insufficient 6 scanty, skimpy, sparse **7** lacking, wanting
8 impotent **9** deficient, not enough **10** inadequate **11** incompetent **14** unsatisfactory

insular 5 petty **6** biased, narrow **7** bigoted, limited **8** isolated **9** illiberal, insulated, parochial **10** intolerant, prejudiced, provincial **12** narrowminded

insulate 5 cover **6** cut off, detach, enisle, shield **7** cushion, isolate, protect, seclude **8** separate **9** segregate, sequester
10 disconnect

insult 3 cut **4** slap **5** abuse, cheek, scorn **6** deride, offend, slight **7** affront, offense, outrage **8** be rude to, belittle, rudeness **9** disparage, impudence, indignity **11** discourtesy, lese majesty

insulting 4 rude **5** nasty **7** abusive, uncivil, vicious **8** impolite, insolent **9** invidious, offensive **10** defamatory, de-

rogatory **11** disparaging
12 discourteous
13 disrespectful

insuperable 8 crushing **9** defeating **10** impassable, impossible, invincible, unbeatable, unyielding **12** inexpugnable, overpowering, overwhelming
13 overmastering, unconquerable **14** insurmountable

insurance 6 policy **8** coverage, security, warranty **9** assurance, guarantee, indemnity

insure 6 secure **10** underwrite

insurgent 5 rebel **7** lawless
8 mutineer, mutinous, partisan, renegade, resister, revolter **9** breakaway, dissident, guerrilla **10** disorderly, rebellious **11** disobedient **13** insubordinate, revolutionary, revolutionist **15** insurrectionist

insurmountable 8 hopeless, too great **10** unbeatable
11 beyond reach, insuperable
13 unconquerable

insurrection 4 riot **6** mutiny, revolt, rising **8** outbreak, uprising **9** rebellion **10** insurgence, revolution

intact 4 safe **5** sound, whole
6 unhurt **7** perfect **8** complete, integral, unbroken, unharmed
9 undamaged, uninjured, untouched **10** in one piece, unimpaired **11** in good shape
15 without a scratch

intangible 5 vague **7** elusive, shadowy **8** abstract, ethereal, fleeting, fugitive **9** transient
10 accidental, evanescent, immaterial, impalpable **11** abstraction, untouchable
12 imponderable **13** imperceptible, insubstantial

integer 5 digit, whole **6** entity, figure, number **7** numeral
11 whole number

integer vitae 8 innocent
15 blameless in life

integral 4 full **5** basic, total, whole **6** entire, intact **7** perfect, rounded **8** complete, finished, inherent **9** component, essential, fulfilled, necessary, requisite **10** fulfilling **11** constituent, well-rounded
13 indispensable

integrate 3 mix **4** fuse **5** blend, merge, unify, unite **6** mingle
7 combine **8** intermix
10 amalgamate **11** desegregate **13** bring together

integrated 6 entire, joined, linked, united **7** blended, merged, unified, unitary
8 combined **9** composite, undi-

vided **10** harmonized, reconciled **11** coordinated, synthesized **12** desegregated, unsegregated

integration 5 union **6** fusion, mixing **8** blending **9** combining, synthesis **11** combination
12 assimilation
13 desegregation

integrity 5 unity **6** purity, virtue **7** decency, honesty, probity **8** cohesion, morality, strength **9** character, coherence, principle, rectitude, wholeness **11** reliability, self-respect, uprightness
12 completeness

integument 4 coat, hide, husk, rind, skin **5** shell, **7** coating, cuticle, epiderm, exoderm
8 covering, envelope, membrane

integumentary system
   component: **4** hair, skin
   5 nails

intellect 3 wit **4** mind **5** brain, sense **6** brains, wisdom
7 thinker **9** cognition, mentality **10** perception **11** mental power, rationality **12** intellectual, intelligence **13** consciousness, understanding

intellectual 4 sage **5** brain
6 brainy, mental, pundit, savant **7** bookish, egghead, scholar, thinker **8** abstract, academic, cerebral, highbrow, longhair, mandarin, rational, studious **9** intellect, of the mind, reasoning, scholarly
10 thoughtful **11** intelligent
   French: **9** bel-esprit

intelligence 4 dope, news
6 acumen, advice, brains, notice, report, wisdom **7** tidings
8 sagacity **9** intellect, knowledge **10** advisement, shrewdness **11** information
12 notification, perspicacity
13 comprehension, understanding

intelligent 4 keen, sage, wise
5 alert, canny, quick, sharp, smart **6** astute, brainy, bright, clever, shrewd **7** knowing, prudent **8** informed, sensible, thinking **9** brilliant, sagacious
10 perceptive, thoughtful
11 clearheaded, quick-witted, sharp-witted **12** well-informed
13 perspicacious

intelligentsia 7 academe
8 thinkers **10** ivory tower
13 intellectuals

intelligible 5 clear, lucid **7** evident, obvious **8** apparent, clear-cut, coherent, definite, distinct **11** unambiguous, well-defined **12** unmistakable

14 comprehensible, understandable

intemperance 10 alcoholism, insobriety **11** dissipation, drunkenness, inebriation **12** immoderation, recklessness **13** excessiveness **16** irresponsibility

intemperate 5 harsh **6** brutal, rugged, severe **7** extreme, violent **8** bibulous, uncurbed **9** dissolute, excessive, inclement **10** dissipated, gluttonous, immoderate, inordinate **11** extravagant, inabstinent, incontinent **12** unrestrained **13** overindulgent

intend 3 aim **4** mean, plan, wish **6** aspire, design, expect **7** project, propose, resolve **9** calculate, determine **10** have in mind **11** contemplate

intended 5 meant **6** fiance, future **7** engaged, fiancee, implied, willful **8** proposed, purposed **9** affianced, betrothed, bride-to-be, groom-to-be, voluntary **10** calculated, deliberate **11** intentional

intense 4 deep, keen **5** acute, sharp **6** ardent, potent, strong **7** burning, earnest, extreme, fervent, violent **8** emphatic, forceful, forcible, powerful, vehement **10** passionate **12** concentrated, considerable

intensely 4 very **5** hotly **6** deeply, keenly **7** acutely, eagerly, vividly **8** ardently, heatedly, terribly **9** extremely, fervently, seriously, violently, zealously **10** forcefully, powerfully, profoundly, vehemently, vigorously **11** excessively, exquisitely, strenuously **12** considerably, passionately **13** energetically

intensify 5 boost **6** deepen, worsen **7** magnify, quicken, sharpen **8** escalate, heighten, increase, redouble **9** aggravate, reinforce **10** accelerate, strengthen

intensifying 9 worsening **10** increasing, magnifying, redoubling, sharpening **11** aggravating, heightening, reinforcing **12** exacerbating **13** strengthening

intensity 4 zeal **5** ardor, depth, force, power, vigor **6** energy, fervor **7** emotion, passion, potency **8** severity, strength **9** magnitude, vehemence **11** earnestness **12** forcefulness

intensive 6 all-out **7** growing, radical **8** complete, sweeping, thorough **10** exhaustive, increasing **11** comprehensive

12 concentrated **13** thoroughgoing

intent 3 aim, end, set **4** bent, gist, plan **5** drift, fixed **6** burden, design, import, steady **7** earnest, intense, meaning, purport, purpose **8** absorbed, piercing, resolved **9** engrossed, insistent, intention, steadfast, substance, tenacious, unbending **10** determined, unwavering **11** preoccupied **12** concentrated, significance, undistracted **13** determination, premeditation

intention 3 aim, end **4** goal, plan **6** design, intent, object, target **7** purpose, resolve **9** objective **10** resolution **13** determination

intentional 6 willed **7** planned **8** designed, intended **9** voluntary **10** calculated, deliberate, purposeful **12** contemplated, premeditated **13** done on purpose

intently 6 deeply, raptly **9** fervently, zealously **10** absorbedly **11** attentively **12** passionately **18** without distraction **22** with undivided attention

intentness 10 absorption **11** engrossment **13** concentration

inter 4 bury **5** inurn **6** entomb, inhume **7** inearth, lay away **9** lay to rest **11** ensepulcher

interact 4 join, mesh **5** coact, unite **6** engage **7** combine, conjoin **8** dovetail **9** cooperate, interlace, intermesh, interplay, interwork **10** coordinate, interreact

inter alia 16 among other things

inter alios 17 among other persons

interbreed 3 mix **5** cross **8** intermix **10** crossbreed

intercede 5 plead **6** step in **7** mediate, speak up **9** arbitrate, interpose, intervene, offer help **12** offer support **14** put in a good word **16** lend a helping hand

intercept 3 nab **4** grab, stay, stop, take **5** catch, seize **6** ambush, arrest, cut off, detain **7** deflect, reroute

intercessor 5 agent **6** bishop, broker **8** advocate, mediator **9** go-between, middleman **12** intermediary, spokesperson

interchange 5 shift **6** switch **7** trading **8** exchange, junction, swapping, transfer **9** alternate,

crossover **10** substitute **11** give and take, reciprocity

interchangeable 8 parallel, tradable **9** analogous **10** equivalent, switchable, synonymous **12** exchangeable, transposable **13** corresponding

interconnected 8 adjacent **10** contiguous, juxtaposed **12** conterminous, labyrinthine

intercourse 4 talk **5** trade **6** coitus, parley **7** pairing, traffic **8** colloquy, commerce, congress, coupling, dealings, exchange **9** communion, discourse, relations **10** connection, copulation **12** conversation **14** communications, correspondence

interdict 3 ban, bar **5** taboo **6** enjoin, forbid **7** barring, censure **8** prohibit, restrain, restrict **9** proscribe **11** forbiddance, prohibition **12** proscription

interdiction 3 ban **7** barring **11** forbiddance, prohibition **12** proscription

interest, interests 4 gain, good, part, weal **5** bonus, hobby, share, stake, touch, yield **6** absorb, affect, behalf, divert, engage, notice, profit, regard **7** attract, benefit, concern, holding, involve, pastime, portion, pursuit, service **8** dividend **9** advantage, attention, avocation, curiosity, preoccupy, suspicion **10** absorption, investment **11** engrossment **13** preoccupation

interested 6 active **7** engaged **8** diverted **9** committed, concerned **10** fascinated, responsive

interesting 7 curious **8** engaging, magnetic, pleasing, riveting, striking **9** absorbing, appealing, arresting **10** attractive, suspicious **11** fascinating, stimulating **12** entertaining

interfere 3 jar, mix **6** butt in, horn in, meddle, rush in, step in **7** counter, intrude **8** conflict **9** frustrate, intercede, interpose, intervene **11** get in the way **14** be a hindrance to, be an obstacle to, be inconsistent, stick in one's oar

interference 3 bar **6** static **8** clashing, conflict, friction, invasion, meddling **9** collision, hindrance, intrusion **12** interception, interruption, intervention

interfere with 6 hinder, impede, thwart **7** disrupt **9** interrupt

interim 7 stopgap **8** interval, meantime, temporal **9** interlude, temporary, tentative **10** pro tempore **11** provisional

interior 4 bush **5** inner **6** inmost, inside, inward **8** internal **9** backwoods, heartland, innermost, upcountry **10** hinterland

Interiors
director: **10** Woody Allen
cast: **10** E G Marshall **11** Diane Keaton **12** Marybeth Hurt **13** Geraldine Page **15** Kristin Griffith **16** Maureen Stapleton
screenplay: **10** Woody Allen

interject 5 put in **6** inject, insert, slip in **7** force in, sneak in, throw in **9** interpose, introduce **11** interpolate

interjection 2 ah, er, lo, oh, ow, um **3** aha, cry, fie, hey, huh, ugh, wow **4** ahem, alas, darn, dear, drat, egad, gosh, heck, jeez, oops, ouch, phew, rats **5** aside, golly, zowie **6** eureka, hooray, hurrah, hurray **7** gee-whiz, jeepers **9** insertion **11** ejaculation, exclamation **13** interpolation, interposition

interlace 3 mix **4** knit, link **5** braid, plait, twine, twist, weave **7** wreathe **9** alternate **10** intertwine, interweave **11** intersperse

interlaced 5 woven **6** linked, twined **7** braided, knitted, plaited, twisted **8** entwined, latticed, wreathed **9** interknit **10** interwoven **11** intertwined **12** interspersed

interlocutor 8 minstrel **9** converser, dialogist **12** interrogator **14** man in the middle

interlope 6 invade, meddle **7** intrude, obtrude **8** encroach, infringe, trespass **9** interfere

interloper 7 invader, meddler **8** intruder, outsider **10** interferer, trespasser **11** gatecrasher **15** persona non grata

interlude 5 break, event, letup, pause **6** recess **7** episode, respite **8** incident, interval **12** intermission **14** breathing spell

intermediary 6 midway, umpire **7** referee **8** bridging, mediator **9** go-between, inbetween, mediating, middleman **10** arbitrator **11** adjudicator, arbitrating

intermediate 3 mid **4** fair, mean, so-so **6** median, medium, middle, midway **7** average, halfway, mediate,

---

midmost **8** mediocre, middling, moderate **11** intervening

interment 6 burial **7** funeral **10** entombment, inhumation

Intermezzo
director: **13** Gregory Ratoff
cast: **8** Edna Best **12** Leslie Howard **13** Cecil Kellaway, Ingrid Bergman

interminable 6 prolix **7** endless **8** infinite, unending **9** boundless, ceaseless, incessant, limitless, perpetual, unlimited **10** continuous, longwinded **11** illimitable **12** longdrawn-out

intermingle 3 mix **4** fuse **5** blend, merge, mix up, unite **6** commix **7** combine **8** emulsify, intermix **9** commingle, interfuse, interlace **10** amalgamate, homogenize, interblend **12** conglomerate

intermission 3 gap **4** halt, rest, stop **5** break, pause **6** hiatus, recess **7** interim **8** interval, stoppage **9** interlude **10** suspension

intermittent 6 fitful **8** on and off, periodic, sporadic **9** irregular, recurrent, spasmodic **10** occasional **13** discontinuous **15** on-again-off-again

intermix 3 mix **5** blend, cross, mix in **6** mingle **10** crossbreed, interbreed **11** intermingle, intersperse

intern 6 commit, detain **7** confine, impound **8** imprison, restrain

internal 5 inner, state **6** inmost **8** domestic, interior **9** executive, political, sovereign **12** governmental **14** administrative

international 9 worldwide **12** cosmopolitan

international affairs
god of: **6** Sancus **10** Dius Fidius, Semo Sancus

internment 9 detention **10** commitment, impounding **11** confinement **12** imprisonment

inter nos 16 between ourselves

interpolate 3 add **5** put in **6** inject, insert, work in **7** implant, intrude, stick in, throw in, wedge in **8** sandwich **9** insinuate, interject, interlard, interline, intervene, introduce **11** intercalate, intersperse

interpose 3 butt in, impose, inject, insert, meddle, step in **7** intrude, mediate, obtrude

---

9 arbitrate, insinuate, intercede, interfere, interject, interrupt, intervene, negotiate **11** come between, interpolate

interpret 3 see **4** read, take **6** accept, define, render, reword **7** clarify, explain, make out, restate, unravel **8** construe, decipher **9** elucidate, explicate, figure out, make clear, puzzle out, translate **10** account for, paraphrase, understand

interpretation 7 reading, version **8** analysis **9** rendition **10** commentary **11** explanation **12** construction

interpreter 7 analyst **9** explainer **10** translator **11** commentator

interrelated 9 companion, connected **10** compatible, correlated **13** complementary, correspondent, corresponding

interrelation 10 connection **11** association, correlation **12** relationship

interrogate 3 ask **4** test **5** grill, probe, query **7** examine **8** question **9** catechize **11** investigate **12** crossexamine **18** give the third degree

interrogation 4 quiz **5** probe, query **7** inquiry **8** grilling, querying, question, quizzing **9** catechism, inquiring **11** examination, inquisition, questioning

interrupt 4 stop **5** sever **7** cut in on, disjoin, disturb **8** break off **9** break in on, intersect, punctuate **10** disconnect **11** discontinue **13** interfere with

interrupted 6 broken, cut off, halted **7** checked, stalled, stopped **8** arrested, broke off, deferred **9** broken off, disturbed, suspended **11** broke in upon, intercepted **12** discontinued

interruption 3 gap **4** halt, rift, stop **5** break, pause **6** hiatus, lacuna **9** hindrance, interlude **11** obstruction **12** interference, intermission **13** disconnection, discontinuity

inter se 15 among themselves **17** between themselves

intersect 4 meet **5** cross **6** bisect, divide **7** overlap **8** crosscut, transect, traverse **9** cut across **10** crisscross

intersection 6 corner **8** crossing, junction **10** crossroads **11** interchange

intersperse 3 dot, mix
5 strew 6 mingle, pepper
7 bestrew, scatter, wedge in
8 disperse, intermix, sprinkle
9 broadcast, interfuse, interject, interlard, interpose
11 intercalate, interpolate

interstice 4 slit, slot 5 crack,
space 7 opening, orifice 8 aperture, interval

intertwine 4 lace 5 braid,
plait, twine, twist, weave
7 entwine 8 entangle
9 interlace

interval 3 gap 4 gulf, rest, rift
5 break, cleft, pause, space,
spell 6 breach, hiatus, recess,
season 7 interim, opening
9 interlude 10 interspace, separation 12 intermission,
interruption

intervene 4 pass 6 befall, butt
in, step in 7 break in, intrude,
mediate 9 arbitrate, intercede,
interfere, interpose, interrupt,
take place 10 come to pass
11 come between

intervention 9 butting in, intrusion, mediation 10 breaking
in, stepping in 11 arbitration
12 intercession, interference
13 interposition
14 intermediation

interview 4 chat, talk 6 parley
7 meeting 8 audience
10 conference, evaluation,
round table 11 questioning
12 consultation,
conversation

interweave 3 mix 4 fuse, join,
knit, lace, link 5 blend, braid,
plait, twine, twist 6 splice
7 wreathe 9 interlace, interknit 10 intertwine
11 intersperse

intestinal 5 inner 7 enteric
8 internal, visceral

intestines 4 guts 6 bowels
7 insides, viscera 8 entrails

in the air 2 up 5 above, aloft
7 skyward 8 all about, in the
sky, overhead 10 everywhere
11 in the clouds

in the doghouse 9 in bad
odor 10 in disfavor, in disgrace, in ill favor 11 in
disrepute

in the end 6 one day 7 finally 8 sometime 10 eventually, ultimately 13 sooner or
later 17 in the course of time
French: 5 enfin

in the family
French: 9 en famille

in the first place
Latin: 8 imprimis

in the future
Latin: 8 in futuro
Spanish: 6 manana

In the Heat of the Night
director: 13 Norman Jewison
cast: 8 Lee Grant 10 Rod
Steiger 11 Warren Oates
13 Sidney Poitier (Virgil
Tibbs)
score: 11 Quincy Jones
Oscar for: 5 actor (Steiger)
7 picture 10 screenplay

in the know 9 cognizant
11 on the inside 13 fully informed, knowledgeable
23 having inside information

in the manner of
French: 3 a la 7 a la mode

in the matter of
Latin: 4 in re

in the meantime
Latin: 9 ad interim

in the middle of things
Latin: 11 in medias res

in the midst of 5 among
7 amongst 12 surrounded by
13 in the middle of

in the nature of things
Latin: 13 in rerum natura

in the neighborhood of
6 almost, around, nearly
7 close to 9 generally, just
about 10 more or less, not far
from 13 approximately 15 in
the vicinity of

in the place cited
Latin: 6 loc cit 10 loco citato

in the place of a parent
Latin: 14 in loco parentis

in the same manner that
Latin: 7 quo modo

in the same place
Latin: 4 ibid 6 ibidem

in the state in which
Latin: 10 in statu quo

in the style of
French: 7 a la mode

**in the very act of commit-
ting the crime**
Latin: 18 in flagrante delicto

in the vicinity of 4 near 6 almost, around, nearly 7 close
to 9 just about 10 more or
less, not far from 13 approximately 19 in the neighborhood of

in the way
French: 6 de trop

in the whole
Latin: 6 in toto

in the work cited
Latin: 5 op cit 11 opere
citato

in the year of the reign
Latin: 9 anno regni

in the year of the world
Latin: 9 anno mundi

In This House of Brede
author: 11 Rumer Godden

**in this sign shalt thou
conquer**
Latin: 16 in hoc signo vinces
motto of: 19 Constantine the
Great
from vision of: 5 cross

intimacy 5 amity 6 caring,
warmth 8 dearness, fondness
9 affection, closeness
10 chumminess, endearment,
fraternity, lovemaking, tenderness 11 brotherhood, camaraderie, familiarity
12 friendliness

intimate 3 pal 4 chum, dear,
deep, hint 5 bosom, buddy,
close, crony, imply, rumor
6 allude, direct 7 guarded, private, special, suggest 8 detailed, familiar, indicate,
personal, profound, thorough
9 cherished, confidant, firsthand, innermost, insinuate
12 confidential
French: 6 intime

intimately 7 closely 8 secretly,
very well 9 privately 10 familiarly, personally 11 essentially 13 intrinsically
14 confidentially

intimation 4 clue, hint, sign
5 rumor 7 inkling, portent
8 allusion, innuendo 10 indication, suggestion 11 insinuation 13 veiled comment

Intimations of Immortality
author: 17 William
Wordsworth

intime 4 cozy 8 intimate

in time 6 before, sooner 7 earlier 9 before now, in advance
10 beforehand, eventually
11 ahead of time 13 before
the fact, sooner or later

intimidate 3 cow 5 alarm,
bully, daunt, scare 6 coerce,
menace, subdue 7 buffalo, terrify 8 browbeat, frighten
9 terrorize

intimidated 5 cowed, fazed
6 scared 7 crushed, daunted,
subdued 10 browbeaten,
frightened, terrorized

intimidation 7 tyranny 8 bullying, coercion 9 despotism
11 browbeating, terrorizing,
tyrannizing 12 scare tactics

intimidator 5 bully 6 despot
7 coercer 9 oppressor, tormenter, tormentor 10 browbeater

into 2 in, to **5** among **6** inside, toward, within **7** against

intolerable 7 hateful, racking **9** abhorrent, agonizing, excessive, loathsome, torturous **10** abominable, outrageous, unbearable **11** unendurable **12** excruciating, insufferable, unreasonable **13** insupportable

intolerance 4 bias **6** racism **7** bigotry **8** weak spot **9** no stomach, prejudice **10** chauvinism, xenophobia **12** low tolerance **16** hypersensitivity, narrow-mindedness

Intolerance
    director: **10** D W Griffith
    cast: **8** Mae Marsh **11** Lillian Gish **12** Robert Harron **17** Constance Talmadge

intolerant 7 bigoted, hostile, jealous **9** fanatical, parochial, resentful, sectarian **10** prejudiced, xenophobic **11** mistrustful **12** chauvinistic, closedminded, narrow-minded

intonation 4 tone **5** pitch **6** accent **8** chanting **10** modulation, inflection

intone 3 hum, say **4** song **5** chant, croon, drawl, mouth, speak, utter, voice **6** murmur, recite **8** intonate, modulate, singsong, vocalize **9** enunciate, pronounce **10** articulate

in toto 5 in all, uncut **6** entire, wholly **7** totally **8** as a whole, entirely, outright **10** completely, in the whole, unabridged **11** all together, uncondensed

intoxicant 3 gin, rum **4** beer, grog, wine **5** booze, drink **6** liquor, tipple, whisky **7** alcohol, spirits, whiskey **8** cocktail, highball **9** inebriant

intoxicated 4 high, rapt **5** drunk, oiled, tight, tipsy **6** bombed, elated, loaded, stewed, stinko, stoned, zonked **7** drunken, exalted, smashed, wrecked **9** delighted, enchanted, entranced, plastered **10** enthralled, inebriated, infatuated, in one's cups **11** exhilarated, transported

intoxicating 4 hard **5** heady **6** potent **7** elating **9** alcoholic, spiritous **11** inebriating **12** exhilarating

intoxication 3 joy **5** bliss **7** elation, rapture **8** euphoria **9** poisoning, tipsiness **10** excitement, insobriety **11** drunkenness, inebriation **12** befuddlement, stupefaction

intractable 6 mulish, ornery, unruly **7** froward, willful **8** obdurate, perverse, stubborn **9** fractious, obstinate **10** headstrong, inflexible, refractory **11** unmalleable **12** contumacious, incorrigible, ungovernable, unmanageable **14** hard to cope with, uncontrollable

intransigent 7 diehard **8** obdurate, stubborn **9** steadfast, unmovable **10** inflexible, ironwilled, unyielding **11** intractable, unbudgeable **14** uncompromising

intrepid 4 bold **5** brave **6** daring, heroic **7** doughty, valiant **8** fearless, resolute, valorous **9** audacious, dauntless **10** courageous, undismayed **11** adventurous

intrepidity 4 guts **5** spunk, valor **6** mettle **7** bravery, courage **8** backbone **9** fortitude, sangfroid **12** fearlessness **13** dauntlessness

intricacy 10 complexity **11** involvement **12** complication, entanglement **15** complicatedness

intricate 6 knotty, tricky **7** complex, devious, tangled **8** involved **9** entangled **11** complicated

intrigue 3 spy **4** fire, plot **5** amour **6** absorb, arrest, scheme **7** attract, collude, knavery, romance **8** conspire, enthrall, scheming **9** fascinate, machinate, titillate **10** conspiracy, love affair **11** machination **13** double-dealing **15** interest greatly, tickle one's fancy

intriguer 7 cheater, plotter, schemer **8** conniver, finagler **9** trickster **10** machinator, wirepuller **11** conspirator, Machiavelli, manipulator

intriguing 8 engaging, exciting **9** absorbing, beguiling **11** captivating, enthralling, fascinating, interesting

intrinsic 5 basic, per se **6** inborn, inbred, innate, native **7** natural **8** inherent **9** essential, ingrained **10** indigenous, underlying **11** fundamental

introduce 3 add **4** show, urge **5** begin, offer, put in, start **6** create, expose, import, inform, infuse, insert **7** advance, bring in, kick off, lead off, present, propose, sponsor, throw in **8** acquaint, initiate, lead into **9** establish, institute, interject, interpose, make known, originate, recommend **10** put forward **11** familiarize, interpolate

introduction 6 change **7** novelty, opening, preface, prelude **8** foreword, preamble, prologue **9** insertion, precursor **10** bringing in, conducting, innovation, ushering in **11** instituting, institution

introductory 7 initial **9** beginning, prefatory **10** initiatory, precursory **11** acquainting, preliminary **13** get-acquaint

introspection 8 brooding **10** meditation, reflection, rumination **12** deliberation, selfanalysis, self-scrutiny **13** contemplation, soul-searching **15** self-examination, self-observation, self-questioning

introspective 7 pensive **10** reflective **13** contemplative, lost in thought

introversion 7 reserve **8** brooding **10** constraint, diffidence, withdrawal **13** introspection

introvert 5 loner **7** brooder, thinker **13** contemplative, private person

introverted 3 shy **5** stiff **8** reserved **9** inhibited, repressed, withdrawn **10** antisocial, restrained **13** inner-directed, introspective

intrude 4 push **6** butt in, impose, meddle, thrust **7** obtrude **8** encroach, trespass **9** interfere, interlope, interpose, intervene

intruder 10 encroacher, interferer, interloper, intervener, trespasser **11** gate-crasher

Intruder in the Dust
    author: **15** William Faulkner

intrusive 4 nosy **5** pushy **6** prying, snoopy **8** in the way, invasive **9** hindering, obtrusive, officious, unwelcome **10** meddlesome **11** impertinent, interfering, interruptive

intuition 5 flash, hunch **7** insight, surmise **8** instinct **9** guesswork, telepathy **10** sixth sense **11** second sight **12** clairvoyance, precognition

intuitive 6 inborn, inbred, innate, native **7** natural, psychic **10** telepathic **11** clairvoyant, instinctive, intuitional, nonrational **12** extrasensory

Inuit see **6** Eskimo

inundate 4 glut **5** drown, flood, swamp **6** deluge, drench, engulf **8** load down, overcome, overflow, saturate, submerge **9** overwhelm **10** overburden, overspread

inundation 4 glut **5** flood **6** deluge **9** avalanche

in unison 5 as one **8** in chorus **9** all at once **11** all together

inure 5 adapt, steel, train **6** adjust, custom, harden, season, temper **7** toughen **8** accustom **9** acclimate, get used to, habituate **10** discipline, naturalize, strengthen **11** acclimatize, desensitize, familiarize **12** become used to **15** learn to live with **16** become hardened to

in use 8 employed **9** operating **11** functioning, operational

in vacuo 9 in a vacuum **11** in isolation

invade 5 flood, limit **6** assail, attack, engulf, infect, infest **7** assault, overrun, violate **8** permeate, restrict, strike at, trespass **9** intrude on, march into, penetrate

invader 6 raider **8** attacker, intruder, marauder **9** aggressor, assailant **10** trespasser

invalid 4 null, sick, void, weak **5** false **6** ailing, infirm, sickly, unwell **7** amputee, cripple, unsound, useless **8** disabled, not valid, nugatory, weakened **9** enfeebled, forceless, illogical, paralytic, powerless, worthless **10** dead letter, fallacious, paraplegic **11** debilitated, ineffective, inoperative, unsupported **12** unconvincing **13** incapacitated, unsupportable **14** good-for-nothing, valetudinarian

invalidate 5 annul **6** cancel, refute, repeal, weaken **7** nullify, vitiate **8** abrogate, make void, undercut **9** discredit, undermine **11** countermand

invalidation 7 voiding **9** annulment **10** abrogation **12** cancellation **13** nullification

invaluable 4 rare **6** choice **9** priceless **11** beyond price, inestimable

invariable 7 uniform **8** constant **9** immutable, unfailing, unvarying **10** changeless, consistent, unchanging, unwavering **11** unalterable, undeviating **12** unchangeable

invariably 4 ever **6** always **7** forever **9** every time, uniformly **10** all the time, constantly **11** perpetually,

universally **15** in every instance **16** without exception

invasion 4 raid **5** foray **6** attack, breach, inroad, sortie **7** assault **8** trespass **9** incursion, intrusion, onslaught **10** aggression, juggernaut, usurpation **11** penetration **12** encroachment, infiltration, infringement, overstepping

Invasion of the Body Snatchers
　　director:
　　　　1956 version: **9** Don Siegel
　　　　1978 version: **13** Philip Kaufman
　　cast:
　　　　1956 version: **10** Dana Wynter, Larry Gates **11** King Donovan **13** Kevin McCarthy
　　　　1978 version: **11** Brooke Adams **12** Jeff Goldblum, Leonard Nimoy **16** Donald Sutherland

invective 4 rant **5** venom **6** insult **7** censure, railing, sarcasm **8** diatribe **9** contumely **10** execration, harsh words, revilement **11** verbal abuse **12** billingsgate, denunciation, vilification, vituperation

inveigh 4 rail, slam **5** abuse, knock, scold **6** rebuke, revile **7** censure, put down, run down, upbraid **8** belittle, denounce, harangue, reproach **9** castigate, criticize, dress down **10** vituperate

inveigh against 5 abuse **6** defame, rail at, revile **7** protest **8** denounce **9** castigate

inveigle 4 coax, lure **5** tempt, trick **6** allure, cajole, entice, rope in, seduce, suck in **7** beguile, ensnare, flatter, mislead, wheedle **8** persuade, soft-soap **9** bamboozle, sweet-talk

inveiglement 7 coaxing **8** cajolery, flattery **9** wheedling **10** enticement, persuasion **13** blandishments

invent 4 coin **6** cook up, create, devise, make up **7** concoct, develop, fashion, think up, trump up **8** conceive, contrive **9** conjure up, fabricate, formulate, originate **10** come up with **11** put together

invented 6 fabled, made up **8** fabulous, fanciful, mythical **9** fantastic, imaginary, legendary **10** apocryphal, fictitious

Inventing America
　　author: **10** Garry Wills

invention 3 lie **4** fake, sham **6** design, device, gadget **7** fic-

tion, forgery, machine **8** creation, trumpery **9** apparatus, discovery, fertility, implement, ingenuity, inventing **10** concoction, creativity, production **11** contraption, contrivance, development, fabrication, imagination, originality, origination **13** dissimulation, inventiveness, prevarication **15** resourcefulness

invention
　　god of: **6** Hermes

inventive 6 bright, clever **9** ingenious **11** resourceful

inventiveness 9 ingenuity **10** cleverness, creativity **11** imagination, orgininality **15** imaginativeness

inventor 5 maker **6** author **7** creator, deviser **8** engineer, producer, tinkerer **9** architect, generator, innovator **10** discoverer, originator
　　of air brake:
　　　　12 Westinghouse
　　of automobile: **7** Daimler
　　of barometer: **10** Torricelli
　　of camera: **7** Eastman
　　of cotton gin: **7** Whitney
　　of cylinder lock: **4** Yale
　　of dynamite: **5** Nobel
　　of elevator: **4** Otis
　　of gyrocompass: **6** Sperry
　　of helicopter: **8** Sikorsky
　　of linotype: **12** Mergenthaler
　　of machine gun: **7** Gatling
　　of movable type:
　　　　9 Gutenberg
　　of phonograph, incandescent lamp, mimeograph, dictating machine, fluoroscope:
　　　　6 Edison
　　of photography: **6** Niepce, Talbot **8** Daguerre
　　of reaper: **9** McCormick
　　of radio: **7** Marconi
　　of revolver: **4** Colt
　　of rocket engine: **7** Goddard
　　of sewing machine: **4** Howe
　　of sleeping car: **7** Pullman
　　of steamboat: **6** Fulton
　　of steam engine: **4** Watt
　　of steam locomotive:
　　　　10 Stephenson
　　of telegraph: **5** Morse
　　of telephone: **4** Bell
　　of wireless telegraph:
　　　　7 Marconi
　　of vulcanized rubber:
　　　　8 Goodyear

inventory 4 roll **5** goods, index, stock **6** roster, supply **7** catalog **8** register, schedule **9** stock list **10** accounting **11** merchandise, stock-taking

inverse 8 backward, contrary, converse, indirect, inverted, opposite, reversed **11** back to front, bottom-to-top, right-to-left

inversion 7 turning **8** reversal **9** ectropion, turnabout **10** transposal **12** resupination **13** transposition

inverted 7 inverse **8** bottom up **10** upside-down

invest 4 fill, garb, give **5** adorn, allot, array, color, cover, dress, endow, imbue **6** clothe, devote, enable, enrich, infuse, supply **7** appoint, license **8** set aside **9** apportion

investigate 4 sift **5** probe, query, study **6** survey **7** analyze, dissect, explore, inspect **8** ask about, look into, pore over, question, research **9** anatomize, delve into **10** scrutinize

investigation 5 probe, study **6** review, search, survey **7** anatomy, inquiry **8** analysis, research, scrutiny **10** dissection, inspection **11** fact-finding

investigator 6 shamus **7** analyst, gumshoe **8** examiner, inquirer, observer **9** detective **10** private eye, researcher

investment 4 ante, risk **5** share, stake **7** venture **8** offering

inveterate 6 inured **7** adamant, chronic, diehard **8** constant, habitual, hardened **9** confirmed, incurable, ingrained, recurrent, steadfast **10** continuous, deep-rooted, deep-seated **11** established **12** long-standing, unregenerate **15** unreconstructed

invidious 7 vicious **8** spiteful **9** insulting, malicious, offensive, rancorous, resentful, slighting **10** malevolent

invigorate 4 stir **5** brace, cheer, liven, pep up, renew, rouse, zip up **6** jazz up, vivify **7** animate, enliven, fortify, refresh, restore **8** energize, vitalize **9** stimulate **10** exhilarate, rejuvenate, strengthen

invigorated 6 braced **7** revived **8** animated, restored, vivified **9** energized, full of pep, quickened, refreshed **10** stimulated **11** rejuvenated **12** strengthened **17** full of vim and vigor

invigorating 7 bracing **9** animating, healthful **10** energizing, enlivening, quickening, refreshing, vitalizing **11** restorative, stimulating **12** rejuvenating **13** strengthening

invincible 10 unbeatable **11** impregnable, indomitable, insuperable **12** invulnerable, undefeatable **13** irrepressible,

unconquerable **14** insurmountable

in vino veritas 18 in wine there is truth

inviolable 4 holy, pure **6** chaste, divine, sacred, secret **7** blessed **8** hallowed **9** dedicated, inviolate, undefiled **10** sacrosanct **11** consecrated, impregnable, trustworthy **12** impenetrable, invulnerable, unassailable **13** incorruptible

inviolate 4 pure **6** intact, sacred, secret **8** hallowed **9** unaltered, unchanged, undefiled, unstained **10** inviolable, sacrosanct

invisible 6 covert, hidden, unseen, veiled **7** obscure **9** concealed, unseeable **10** unapparent **13** imperceptible, undiscernible

Invisible Man
author: **12** Ralph Ellison

Invisible Man, The
author: **7** H G Wells

invitation 3 bid **4** call, lure **5** offer **7** bidding, summons **8** open door **9** challenge **10** allurement, enticement, inducement, temptation **12** solicitation

invite 3 bid **4** call, lure, urge **5** tempt **6** entice, induce **7** attract, solicit, welcome **9** encourage

inviting 4 warm **8** alluring, charming, engaging, enticing, magnetic, tempting **9** appealing, welcoming **10** attractive, intriguing

invocation 4 plea **6** appeal, orison, prayer **8** petition **9** summoning **12** supplication

in vogue 2 in **6** modish **7** a la mode, current, in style, stylish **9** in fashion **11** fashionable **12** le dernier cri

invoke 3 beg, use **5** apply **6** ask for, employ **7** beseech, conjure, entreat, implore, pray for **8** call upon, petition, resort to **9** appeal for, call forth, implement, importune, introduce **10** supplicate

involuntary 6 forced, reflex **7** coerced **8** unchosen, unwilled **9** automatic, reluctant, unwilling **10** compulsory **11** inadvertent, instinctive, spontaneous, unconscious **13** unintentional **15** against one's will

involve 5 imply, mix up **6** commit, engage, entail, wrap up

7 contain, embroil, include **8** comprise, depend on, entangle **9** implicate, preoccupy

involved 7 complex, engaged, mixed up, wound up **8** absorbed, immersed **9** committed, elaborate, embroiled, engrossed, entangled, intricate, wrapped up **10** implicated **11** complicated, preoccupied

involve deeply 5 mix up **6** absorb, commit, wrap up **7** embroil, engross, immerse **8** entangle **9** implicate, preoccupy

invulnerable 10 formidable, invincible, unbeatable **11** impregnable, indomitable, insuperable **12** imperishable, inexpugnable, unassailable, undefeatable **13** unconquerable, undestroyable

inward, inwards 5 inner **6** mental, toward **7** going in, ingoing, private **8** incoming, interior, inwardly, personal **9** spiritual, the inside **10** interiorly

in what way
Latin: **7** quo modo

in which case 4 then, when **6** thence **9** whereupon **11** accordingly **12** at which point

In Which We Serve
director: **9** David Lean **10** Noel Coward
script: **10** Noel Coward
cast: **9** John Mills **10** Noel Coward **12** Bernard Miles, Celia Johnson

in wine there is truth
Latin: **13** in vino veritas

Io
father: **7** Inachus
husband: **9** Telegonus
loved by: **4** Zeus
son: **7** Epaphus
changed into: **6** heifer
color of heifer: **5** white
guarded by: **5** Argus
pursecuted by: **6** gadfly
  sent by: **4** Hera
corresponds to: **4** Isis

Iobates
king of: **5** Lycia
son-in-law: **7** Proteus
commissioned to kill: **11** Bellerophon

Iodama
priestess of: **6** Athena

iodine
chemical symbol: **1** I

Iolanthe
author: **9** W S Gilbert

Iolaus
father: **8** Iphicles

Iole
mother: 10 Automedusa
uncle: 8 Hercules
companion: 8 Hercules
charioteer of: 8 Hercules

Iole
father: 7 Eurytus
loved by: 8 Heracles
husband: 6 Hyllus

Ion
author: 9 Euripides
character: 6 Apollo, Athene,
Crensa, Xuthus

Iormungandr *see*
11 Jormungandr

iota 3 bit, jot 4 atom, spot,
whit 5 shred, spark, speck
7 smidgin 8 particle 9 scintilla
11 faint degree, small
amount 15 tiniest quantity

IOU 4 chit, debt, note 10 obligation 12 promise to pay
14 promissory note

Iowa *see box*

Iowa, Ioway
language family: 6 Siouan
location: 4 Iowa
related to: 3 Oto 8 Missouri

Ioxus
father: 10 Melanippus
grandfather: 7 Theseus
grandmother: 8 Perigune

Iphicles
father: 10 Amphitryon
mother: 7 Alcmene
half-brother: 8 Hercules
son: 6 Iolaus

Iphidamas
father: 7 Antenor
mother: 6 Theano
killed by: 9 Agamemnon

Iphigenia
father: 9 Agamemnon
mother: 12 Clytemnestra
brother: 7 Orestes
sister: 7 Electra
12 Chrysothemis
saved by: 7 Artemis

Iphigenia in Aulis
author: 9 Euripides
character: 8 Achilles, Menelaus 9 Agamemnon
12 Clytemnestra

Iphigenia in Tauris
author: 9 Euripides
character: 5 Thoas 6 Athena
7 Orestes, Pylades

Iphigenie en Aulide
also: 16 Iphigenia in Aulis
opera by: 5 Gluck
character: 7 Artemis, Calchas 8 Achilles 9 Agamem-
non 12 Clytemnestra

Iphigenie en Tauride
also: 17 Iphigenia in Tauris
opera by: 5 Gluck
character: 5 Diana, Thoas
(King of Scythia) 7 Orestes,
Pylades 9 the Furies

Iphitus
father: 7 Eurytus
sister: 4 Iole

Ipoctonus
epithet of: 8 Hercules
means: 10 worm-killer

ipse dixit 15 he himself said
it 21 assertion without proof

ipsissima verba 8 verbatim
12 the very words

ipso facto 15 by the fact itself 24 by the very nature of
the deed

ipso jure 14 by the law itself
16 by operation of law

Iraklion
capital of: 5 Crete

Iran *see box*

Iraq *see box*

irascibility 8 acerbity 9 bad
temper, crossness, testiness
10 crabbiness, crankiness
11 peevishness, waspishness
12 irritability
16 cantankerousness

irascible 5 cross, testy
6 cranky, grumpy, ornery,
touchy 7 grouchy, peevish,
waspish 8 choleric 9 irritable,
splenetic 10 ill-humored
11 bad-tempered, hot-
tempered, intractable
12 cantankerous

irate 3 mad 5 angry, livid,
rabid, riled, vexed 6 galled
7 angered, annoyed, enraged,
furious 8 burned up 9 indignant, irritated 10 infuriated

ire 4 fury, rage 5 anger, wrath
6 choler 7 outrage, umbrage
8 vexation 10 resentment
11 indignation

Ireland *see box, p. 506*

Ireland forever
Gaelic: 11 Erin go bragh

I Remember Mama
director: 13 George Stevens
based on play by: 13 John
Van Druten

Iowa
abbreviation: 2 IA
nickname: 7 Hawkeye
capital/largest city: 9 Des Moines
others: 4 Ames 5 Amana, Mason, Perry 6 Algona, Keokuk,
Le Mars, Marion, Newton 7 Anamosa, Clinton, Dubuque,
Ft Dodge, Ottumwa 8 Waterloo 9 Davenport, Ft Madison,
Marquette, Mason City, Sioux City 10 Burlington, Cedar
Falls, West Branch 11 Cedar Rapids 12 Marshalltown
13 Council Bluffs
college: 3 Coe 5 Corot, Drake, Loras 7 Cornell, Parsons
8 Grinnell, Wartburg 12 Iowa Wesleyan
explorer: 6 Joliet 7 Jolliet 9 Marquette 13 Lewis and Clark
feature: 13 Amana Colonies 17 first apple orchard
  church: 11 Little Brown
  national historical site: 13 Herbert Hoover
  national monument: 12 Effigy Mounds
  state fair: 4 Iowa
tribe: 3 Fox 4 Sauc 5 Ioway, Omaha 9 Muscoutin,
Winnebago
people: 7 Hawkeye 9 Grant Wood 10 John L Lewis
11 Billy Sunday 15 Buffalo Bill Cody, Charles Ringling
lake: 5 Clear, Storm 6 Spirit 7 Rathbun 11 East Okoboji,
West Okoboji
land rank: 11 twenty-fifth
president: 13 Herbert Hoover
river: 4 Iowa 5 Cedar, Floyd, Skunk 8 Big Sioux, Missouri
9 Des Moines 11 Mississippi, Nishnabotna
12 Wapsipinicon
state admission: 11 twenty-ninth
state bird: 16 eastern goldfinch
state flower: 8 wild rose
state motto: 45 Our Liberties We Prize and Our Rights
We Will Maintain
state song: 13 The Song of Iowa
state tree: 3 oak

Iran

name means: 15 land of the Aryans
other name: 6 Persia
capital/largest city: 6 Tehran **7** Teheran
others: 3 Qum **4** Shah **5** Ahwaz, Urmia **6** Abadan, Bandar, Kashan, Meshed, Shiraz, Tabriz **7** Birjand, Hamadan, Isfahan, Mashhad, Zahidan **11** Bandar Abbas
supreme head of state: 5 faghi **17** religious guardian
measure: 3 gaz, zar, zer **4** cane **5** gareh, kafiz, makuk, qasab **6** charac, chebel, ghalva **7** capicha, chenica, farsakh, mansion, mishara **8** parasang, piamaneh, stathmos
monetary unit: 3 pul **4** asar, gran, rial **5** bisti, daric, dinar, larin, shahi, toman **6** stater **7** ashrafi, pahlavi
weight: 3 ser **4** dung, rotl, seer **5** abbas, artel, pinar, ratel **6** batman, dirhem, karwar, miscal, nimman **7** abbassi **8** tcheirek
lake: 5 Niris, Tasht, Tuzlu, Urmia **6** Sahweh, Sistan **7** Maharlu **8** Nemekser, Urumiyeh
mountain: 6 Elburz, Zagros
highest point: 8 Demavend
river: 4 Aras **5** Araks, Atrak, Atrek, Karun, Safid, Sefid **6** Gargan
sea: 7 Arabian, Caspian
physical feature:
   desert: **9** Dasht-i-Lut **11** Dasht-i-Kavir
   gulf: **4** Oman **7** Persian
   strait: **6** Hormuz
people: 3 Lur, Tat **4** Arab, Kurd, Turk **5** Medes **6** Galcha, Gilani, Jewish, Shugni **7** Baluchi, Persian **8** Armenian, Bactrian, Bartangi, Parthian, Scythian **9** Bakhtiari **11** Azerbaijani, Mazandarani
   dynasty: **5** Qajar **7** Arsacid, Pahlavi, Safavid **8** Parthian, Seleucid **9** Sassanian **10** Achaemenid
   poet: **11** Omar Khayyam
   ruler: **5** Abbas, Cyrus **6** Darius, Xerxes **10** Rafsanjani **23** Shah Mohammed Reza (Riza) Pahlavi **25** Ayatollah Ruhollah Khomeini
language: 4 Luri, Zend **5** Farsi, Turki **6** Arabic **7** Baluchi, Kurdish, Persian **8** Armenian **11** Azerbaijani
religion: 5 Baha'i, Islam **7** Judaism **9** Shia Islam **11** Zoroastrian **12** Christianity
place:
   dam: **5** Karaj
   mosque: **4** Shad **5** Royal **12** Masjidi-i-Shah **18** Madreseh Chahar Bagh
   ruins: **4** Susa **10** Persepolis
feature: 13 Peacock Throne
   head cloth: **6** chador **7** chawdar
   parliament: **6** majlis
   underground water channel: **5** qanat
food: 5 kabob
   soured milk: **4** mast
   stuffed vegetables/leaves: **5** dolma **6** dolmeh

Iraq

capital/largest city: 7 Baghdad
others: 2 Ur **3** Kut **5** Al Faw, Amara, Ashur, Basra, Erbil, Mosul, Najaf, Qurna **6** Hillah, Kirkuk, Tikrit **7** Karbala, Mandali, Samarra, Umm Qasr **8** Al Zubair
division:
   ancient: **5** Akkad, Sumer **7** Assyria **9** Babylonia **11** Mesopotamia
monetary unit: 4 fils **5** dinar
lake: 6 al-Milh **7** Sanniya **8** al-Hammar
mountain: 6 Qalate, Zagros **7** Qaarade **9** Kurdistan
highest point: 7 Halgurd
river: 6 Diyala, Hawran, Tigris **8** Great Zab **9** al-Ubayyid, Euphrates, Little Zab **11** Shatt-al-Arab
physical feature:
   desert: **6** Syrian **8** al-Hajava
   gulf: **7** Persian
people: 4 Arab, Kurd **7** Bedouin
   leader: **6** Faisal, Sargon **7** Abbasid, Hussein, Ottoman **9** Hammurabi **13** Harun al-Rashid, Saddam Hussein **14** Nebuchadnezzar **16** Abbasid Caliphate
language: 5 Farsi **6** Arabic **7** Kurdish, Persian, Turkish
religion: 5 Islam **12** Christianity
place:
   ancient: **14** Hanging Gardens
   arch: **9** Ctesiphon
   mosque: **5** Great **9** Kadhimain
   ruins: **2** Ur **7** Babylon, Nineveh, Samarra
   Sumerian temple tower: **8** Ziggurat
feature:
   marketplace: **4** souk
   war: **4** Gulf **11** Desert Storm **12** Desert Shield

cast: 10 Ellen Corby, Irene Dunne, Philip Dorn **12** Oscar Homolka **16** Barbara Bel Geddes
setting: 12 San Francisco

Irene

member of: 5 Horae
personifies: 5 peace
corresponds to: 3 Pax

iridescence 7 glitter **11** opalescence, pearliness **12** nacreousness, play of colors

iridescent 5 shiny **7** glowing **8** colorful, nacreous **9** prismatic **10** changeable, opalescent **11** rainbowlike

iris

varieties: 3 fan, red **4** roof, wall, wild **5** Dutch, dwarf, house **6** copper, German, orchid, Sierra, Spuria, violet, yellow **7** African, bearded, crested, English, Evansia, Lamance, peacock, Persian, Prairie, Spanish, walking **8** Japanese, mourning, Siberian, stinking **9** beachhead, beardless, butterfly, Palestine **10** snake's-head

Iris

goddess of: 7 rainbow
messenger of: 4 gods
father: 7 Thaumas
mother: 7 Electra
sisters: 7 Harpies
husband: 8 Zephyrus

Ireland
  other name: 4 Eire, Erin 5 Ierne 8 Hibernia 9 Innisfail 11 Emerald Isle
  capital/largest city: 6 Dublin
  others: 4 Cobh, Cork, Erne, Suir, Tara 5 Adare, Ennis, Sligo 6 Bangor, Galway, Lurgan, Mallow, Tralee, Ulster 7 Athlone, Belfast, Donegal, Dundalk, Kildare, Wexford 8 Drogheda, Kilkenny, Limerick 9 Craigavon, Tipperary, Waterford 10 Queenstown 11 Londonderry
  school: 7 Trinity
  division: 4 Cork, Down, Mayo 5 Clare, Kerry, Meath 6 Antrim, Armagh, Galway, Tyrone, Ulster 7 Donegal, Kildare, Wexford, Wicklow 8 Kilkenny, Limerick 9 Fermanagh, Killarney, Tipperary, Waterford 11 Londonderry
    ancient: 6 Ulster 7 Munster 8 Connacht, Leinster
  head of government: 9 taoiseach (prime minister)
  measure: 4 mile 6 bandle 8 crannock
  monetary unit: 3 rap 4 real 5 pence, pound 6 turney 8 shilling
  island: 3 Man 4 Aran, Bear, Holy, Tory 5 Clare, Clear, Magee 6 Achill, Saltee, Whiddy 7 Blasket, Gorumna, Rathlin 8 Aranmore, Inisheer 9 Inishmore 10 Inishbofin
  lake: 3 Doo, Key, Ree, Tay 4 Conn, Derg, Erne, Mask 5 Allen, Barra, Capra, Gowna, Leane, Lough, Neagh 6 Boderg, Cooter, Corrib, Ennell 7 Dromore, Gougane, Oughter, Sheelin 9 Killarney
  mountain: 5 Galty 6 Croagh, Mourne 7 Errigal, Muckish, Patrick, Wicklow 8 Comeragh 10 Benna Beola, Twelve Bens, Twelve Pins 13 Knockmealdown 19 Macgillycuddy's Reeks
  highest point: 13 Carrantuohill
  river: 3 Lee, May 4 Bann, Deel, Erne, Nore, Suir 5 Boyne, Clare, Feale, Flesk, Foyle, Laune 6 Bandon, Barrow, Corrib, Liffey, Slaney 7 Kenmare, Munster, Shannon 10 Blackwater
  sea: 5 Irish 8 Atlantic
  physical feature:
    bay: 4 Clew 5 Sligo 6 Bantry, Dingle, Galway, Tralee 7 Donegal, Dundalk
    cape: 5 Clear
    channel: 5 North 9 St George's
    cliffs: 5 Moher
    point: 6 Cahore 8 Carnsore
  people: 4 Celt, Erse, Gael 6 Celtic 9 Hibernian
    author: 4 Shaw 5 Behan, Burke, Joyce, Swift, Synge, Wilde, Yeats 6 O'Casey, Steele 7 Beckett, O'Connor 8 O'Faolain, Sheridan, Stephens 9 Goldsmith, O'Flaherty 13 St John Gogarty
    leader: 4 Tone 6 Devlin, Valera 7 Grattan, Parnell, Redmond 8 O'Connell 9 Brian Boru 12 Saint Patrick
    legend: 9 Cuchulain 11 Finn MacCool
  language: 5 Irish 6 Gaelic 7 English
  religion: 8 Anglican 13 Roman Catholic
  feature:
    airport: 7 Shannon
    castle: 4 Tara 7 Blarney
    crystal: 9 Waterford
    dance: 3 jig 4 reel
    game: 7 hurling
    lottery: 16 Irish Sweepstakes
    manuscript: 11 Book of Kells
    museum: 10 James Joyce
    political movement: 8 Sinn Fein
    race: 10 Irish Derby
    relic: 13 Ardagh Chalice
    revolutionary society: 6 Fenian
    stone: 7 Blarney
    street: 8 O'Connell
    theater: 5 Abbey
  food:
    beer: 5 stout

Irish 4 Erse 4 Celtic, dander, Gaelic, temper
  accent: 6 brogue
  death spirit: 7 banshee
  flower: 8 shamrock
  girl: 7 colleen
  king: 9 Brian Boru
  legislature: 4 Dail
  saint: 7 Patrick
  society: 8 Sinn Fein
  theater: 5 Abbey

Irish gods 14 Tuatha De Danann

Irishman 4 Celt, Gael, Kelt, Mick 5 Paddy 7 Irisher 9 Hibernian, orangeman 10 bogtrotter

Irish Mist
  origin: 7 Ireland
  ingredient: 5 cream 12 Irish whiskey

Irish Mythology *see box*

irk 3 bug, vex 4 gall 5 annoy 6 bother, pester, ruffle 7 provoke 8 irritate

irksome 5 pesky 6 plaguy, vexing 7 plaguey, tedious 8 annoying, tiresome, wearying 9 difficult, provoking, vexatious, wearisome 10 bother-

some, irritating, nettlesome
11 troublesome

iron
chemical symbol: **2** Fe

Iron Age
period of: **4** time
followed age of: **6** Bronze

ironclad 5 fixed **6** strict **9** immutable, permanent **10** inexorable, inflexible, rigoristic,
unchanging **11** irrevocable,
unalterable **12** irreversible, unchangeable, unmodifiable

Iron Horse
nickname of: **9** Lou Gehrig

ironic, ironical 3 odd **5** funny,
weird **6** biting **7** abusive, caustic, curious, cutting, mocking,
strange **8** derisive, sardonic,
sneering, stinging **9** facetious,
insincere, pretended, sarcastic
10 surprising, unexpected
11 implausible, incongruous
12 inconsistent
13 contradictory

irons 5 bonds **6** chains **7** fetters, presses, smooths **8** manacles, shackles **9** golf clubs,
handcuffs **10** restraints

Ironside
character: **7** (Det Sgt) Ed
Brown **10** Mark Sanger
11 Fran Belding **12** Eve
Whitfield **14** Robert Ironside
cast: **11** Don Galloway, Don
Mitchell, Raymond Burr
13 Elizabeth Baur **15** Barbara Anderson

irony 7 mockery, sarcasm **9** absurdity **11** incongruity, indirection **12** contrariness
13 facetiousness
14 implausibility

Iroquoian
tribe: **6** Cayuga, Mohawk,
Oneida, Seneca **8** Cherokee,
Iroquois, Onandaga **9** Tuscarora **12** Kaniengehaga

Iroquois
language family: **9** Iroquoian
tribe: **6** Cayuga, Mohawk,
Oneida, Seneca **8** Onondaga
9 Tuscarora
location: **6** Canada **7** New
York **11** Connecticut
13 Massachusetts
leader: **11** Cornplanter, Joseph Brant
formed: **10** Six Nations
19 League of the Iroquois
supernatural force: **6** Orenda
prophet: **10** Ganiodaiyo

Irra
origin: **8** Akkadian
god of: **10** pestilence

irrational 6 absurd **7** foolish,
unsound **8** baseless **9** illogical,
unfounded **10** ill-advised, unthinking **11** nonsensical, unreasoning **12** unreasonable

irreclaimable 4 lost **.6** wicked
7 corrupt, debased **9** abandoned, reprobate **12** disreputable, irredeemable,
irreformable **16** beyond
redemption

irreconcilable 7 opposed
12 incompatible, inconsistent,
intransigent, unadjustable, unappeasable, unbridgeable

irreformable 6 wicked **7** corrupt **9** abandoned, reprobate,
shameless **11** unrepentant
12 disreputable
13 irreclaimable

irrefutable 10 undeniable
12 indisputable, not refutable
13 proof positive **14** unquestionable **16** incontrovertible

irrefutably 6 surely **10** definitely, positively, undeniably
12 conclusively, indisputably
13 incontestably **14** unquestionably **16** incontrovertibly

irregular 3 odd **5** bumpy,
queer, rough **6** broken, uneven **7** crooked, unusual
8 aberrant, abnormal, improper, peculiar, singular
9 anomalous, desultory, eccentric, haphazard, not smooth,
out of line, unaligned, unfitting **10** indecorous, unex-

pected, unsuitable
12 asymmetrical, unmethodical, unsystematic **13** inappropriate, nonconforming
14 unconventional
16 uncharacteristic

irregularity 7 anomaly
9 asymmetry, deviation **10** aberration, divergence, unevenness **11** abnormality,
peculiarity **12** constipation,
eccentricity

irrelevant 5 inapt **7** foreign,
off base **9** unfitting, unrelated
10 extraneous, immaterial,
malapropos, not apropos, not
germane **11** impertinent, unconnected **12** nonpertinent
14 beside the point

irreligion 7 atheism **8** apostasy,
unbelief **9** disbelief
11 godlessness

irreligious 6 unholy **7** godless,
impious, profane, ungodly
8 agnostic **9** atheistic **10** irreverent **11** unbelieving **12** not
religious, sacrilegious

irremediable 8 hopeless **9** incurable **11** irreparable **12** beyond remedy

irreparable 9 unfixable
10 remediless **12** irremediable,
irreversible **13** beyond redress,
uncompensable, uncorrectable

irreplaceable 6 unique **9** essential **13** indispensable

irrepressible 7 vibrant **8** bubbling, galvanic, undamped
9 ebullient **10** boisterous, full
of life **11** tempestuous **12** unquenchable **13** unsquelchable
14 uncontrollable,
unrestrainable

irreproachable 8 flawless
9 blameless, faultless, stainless,
unspotted **10** impeccable, inculpable **11** unblemished
12 above reproof, without
fault **13** unimpeachable

irresistible 8 alluring, enticing **9** beckoning, seductive
10 enchanting, superhuman
11 tantalizing **12** overpowering, overwhelming

irresolute 4 weak **6** fickle, unsure **8** doubtful, hesitant, unsteady, wavering **9** faltering,
uncertain, undecided, unsettled **10** changeable, hesitating,
indecisive, unresolved
11 vacillating

irresolution 5 doubt **9** hesitancy **10** hesitation, indecision

irresponsibility 8 rashness
10 immaturity, imprudence

11 foolishness 12 carelessness, heedlessness, indifference, indiscretion, recklessness 13 unreliability 15 thoughtlessness, undependability 17 untrustworthiness

irresponsible 4 rash 7 foolish 8 careless, immature, reckless 9 imprudent, overhasty 10 capricious, incautious, unreliable 11 harebrained, indifferent, injudicious, thoughtless 12 undependable 13 illconsidered, untrustworthy 14 not responsible, scatterbrained

irresponsible person
  French: 14 enfant terrible

irreverence 7 impiety 9 blasphemy, sacrilege 10 irreligion

irreverent 5 saucy 6 brazen 7 impious, profane 8 critical, impudent, sneering 9 debunking, shameless, skeptical, slighting 11 blasphemous, disparaging, irreligious 12 nosethumbing 13 disrespectful

irrevocable 5 final 10 conclusive 11 unalterable 12 irreversible, unchangeable

irritability 6 spleen 8 acerbity, edginess 9 crossness, huffiness, petulance, testiness 10 crabbiness, crankiness, impatience 11 fretfulness, peevishness, short temper, waspishness 12 irascibility

irritable 5 testy 6 grumpy, touchy 7 fretful, grouchy, peevish, pettish, waspish 8 snappish 9 impatient, irascible 10 ill-humored 11 easily vexed, ill-tempered

irritate 3 irk, vex 5 anger, annoy, chafe, peeve 6 nettle, worsen 7 inflame, provoke 8 make sore 9 aggravate, make angry 10 exasperate

irritated 3 mad, raw 4 sore 5 cross, irked, irate, testy, vexed 6 chafed, crabby, galled, miffed, peeved, piqued, put out 7 annoyed, burning, nettled, peevish 8 burned up, choleric, incensed, inflamed, provoked 9 impatient, irascible 10 aggravated 11 exasperated

irritating 5 acrid, harsh, rough 7 caustic, chafing, galling, irksome, rasping 8 abrasive, annoying 9 provoking, vexatious 10 bothersome 11 infuriating, troublesome 12 exasperating

irritation 6 bother 7 chafing 8 distress, vexation 9 annoy-

ance 10 discomfort 11 irksomeness

irruption 4 raid 5 break, foray 6 inroad 7 upsurge 8 bursting, invasion 9 incursion, intrusion

Irus *see* 7 Arnaeus

Irving, John
  author of: 20 The Hotel New Hampshire 23 The World According to Garp

Irving, Washington
  author of: 10 Salmagundi 12 Rip Van Winkle 13 The Sketch Book 23 The Legend of Sleepy Hollow

Isaac
  father: 7 Abraham
  mother: 5 Sarah
  brother: 7 Ishmael
  wife: 7 Rebekah
  son: 4 Esau 5 Jacob
  birthplace: 5 Gerar
  burial place: 9 Machpelah
  blessed: 5 Jacob
  sacrificed at: 6 Moriah

Isaac of York
  character in: 7 Ivanhoe
  author: 5 Scott

Isabella
  character in: 17 Measure for Measure
  author: 11 Shakespeare

Isaiah
  means: 12 Jehovah saves
  father: 4 Amoz
  son: 11 Shearzashub 18 Maharshalalhashbaz

Iscariot *see* 5 Judas

Ischepolis
  father: 9 Alcathous

Ischys
  killed because of: 10 infidelity
  loved: 7 Coronis
    Coronis loved by: 6 Apollo

Isenstein
  origin: 12 Scandinavian
  home of: 8 Brunhild
  location: 8 Isenland

I serve
  German: 7 ich dien
  motto of: 13 Prince of Wales

Iseult, Isolde
  character in: 16 Arthurian romance

I shall rise again
  Latin: 8 resurgam

Ishbosheth
  father: 4 Saul
  killed by: 6 Baanah, Rechab
  burial place: 6 Hebron

Isherwood, Christopher
  author of: 13 Berlin Stories 17 Down There on a Visit
  character: 11 Sally Bowles

Ishmael
  character in: 8 Moby Dick
  author: 8 Melville

Ishmael
  father: 7 Abraham
  mother: 5 Hagar
  means: 11 God will hear
  brother: 5 Isaac
  son: 5 Kedar 7 Kedemah
  descendant of: 10 Ishmaelite

Ishtar
  also: 7 Mylitta
  origin: 8 Assyrian 10 Babylonian
  goddess of: 3 war 4 love
  queen of: 6 heaven
  corresponds to: 6 Inanna 7 Astarte 9 Ashtoreth

Ishum
  origin: 8 Akkadian
  god of: 4 fire
  companion: 4 Irra

Isis
  origin: 8 Egyptian
  goddess of: 9 fertility
  hieroglyphic symbol: 6 throne
  husband: 6 Osiris
  brother: 6 Osiris
  son: 5 Horus
  father: 3 Geb, Keb
  mother: 3 Nut
  horns of: 3 cow
  headdress: 9 solar disk
  corresponds to: 2 Io

Iskowitz, B Edward Israel
  real name of: 11 Eddie Cantor

Islam
  adherent: 4 Sufi 5 Shiah 6 Moslem, Muslim, Shiite, Wahabi 7 Sunnite 8 Islamite 9 Mussulman 10 Mohammedan
  crusade: 5 Jahad, Jihad
  deity: 5 Allah
  flight from Mecca: 6 hegira
  founder/prophet: 8 Mohammed, Muhammad
  holy city: 5 Mecca 6 Medina
  other names: 9 Moslemism 13 Mohammedanism
  pilgrimage to Mecca: 4 hadj
  priest: 4 imam
  scripture: 5 Koran

Islamabad
  capital of: 8 Pakistan

Islamic 6 Moslem, Muslim 10 Mohammedan

island 4 isle 5 atoll, haven, islet, oasis 6 refuge 7 enclave, retreat, shelter 9 sanctuary

Islands of the Blessed *see* 10 Hesperides

isle, islet 3 ait, cay, key 4 holm 5 islet 6 island

Isle of Cloves *see* 8 Tanzania

Isle of Spice *see* 7 Grenada

Isleta (Tuei)
language family: 6 Pueblo, Tanoan
location: 9 New Mexico, Rio Grande

Ismene
father: 7 Oedipus
mother: 7 Jocasta
uncle: 5 Creon
sister: 8 Antigone
brother: 9 Polynices

isn't that so?
French: 9 n'est-ce pas?
German: 9 nicht wahr?

isolate 6 banish, detach 7 seclude 8 insulate, separate, set apart 9 segregate, sequester 10 disconnect, place apart, quarantine

isolated 4 lone, solo 5 alone, apart 6 cut off, lonely, remote, unique 7 insular, removed 8 detached, secluded, set apart, solitary 9 separated, unrelated 10 segregated 11 out-of-the-way, quarantined, sequestered

isolation 7 privacy 8 solitude 9 aloneness, apartness, hermitism, seclusion 10 desolation, detachment, insularity, insulation, quarantine, separation 11 confinement, segregation 12 separateness

isoptera
class: 8 hexapoda
phylum: 10 arthropoda
group: 7 termite 8 white ant

Ispahan
also: 7 Isfahan 8 Aspadana
location: 4 Iran
capital of: 6 Persia
river: 8 Zayandeh

I Speak for Thaddeus Stevens
author: 15 Elsie Singmaster

I Spy
character: 13 Kelly Robinson 14 Alexander Scott
cast: 9 Bill Cosby 10 Robert Culp
Kelly's cover: 9 tennis pro

Israel
former name: 5 Jacob
means: 12 soldier of God
wrestled with: 5 angel

Israel *see box*

Israel, tribes of 3 Dan, Gad 4 Levi 5 Asher, Judah 6 Joseph, Reuben, Simeon 7 Zebulun 8 Benjamin, Issachar, Naphtali

Israel-born
Hebrew: 5 sabra

Israelite 3 Jew 6 Hebrew, Jewish, Semite 7 Judaist 8 Hebraist
descended from: 5 Jacob

Israel
other name: 4 Zion 6 Canaan, Yishuv 9 Palestine 12 Promised Land

capital: 9 Jerusalem

largest city: 12 Tel Aviv-Jaffa

others: 4 Acre, Elat, Gaza 5 Eilat, Elath, Haifa, Holon, Jaffa, Jenin 6 Ashdod, Bat Yam, Dimona, Hebron, Nablus 7 Netanya, Rehovot, Tel Aviv 8 Nazareth, Ramallah, Ramat Gan 9 Beersheba, Bene Beraq, Bethlehem

school: 6 Hebrew 14 Technion-Israel 26 Weizmann Institute of Science

division: 5 Judea, Negev, Sinai 7 Galilee 8 West Bank 9 Gaza Strip 12 Golan Heights

government:
legislature: 7 Knesset
political parties: 5 Labor, Likud, Mapam

measure: 3 cab, car, hin, kab, kor 4 bath, ezba, omer, reed 5 cubit, donum, dunam, ephah, ganeh, homer, kaneh

monetary unit: 3 mil 5 agora, agura, pound, pruta 6 agorot, shekel

lake: 5 Huleh 7 Dead Sea 8 Kinneret, Tiberias 12 Sea of Galilee

mountain: 4 Nafh, Sagi 5 Harif, Ramon, Tabor 6 Atzmon, Carmel, Hatira

highest point: 5 Meron 6 Meiron

river: 4 Qarn 5 Faria, Malik, Sareq 6 Hadera, Jordan, Kishon, Qishon, Sarida, Yarkon, Yarmuk 7 Lakhish

sea: 3 Red 4 Dead 7 Galilee 13 Mediterranean

physical feature:
bay: 5 Haifa
desert: 5 Negev, Sinai
gulf: 5 Aqaba
plain: 5 Judea 6 Sharon 7 Zebulun 9 Esdraelon

people: 3 Jew 4 Arab 5 Druze 10 Circassian
ancient: 6 Hebrew
immigrant: 4 olim
Jew born in Israel: 5 sabra
leader: 4 Eban, Meir 5 Begin, Dayan, Herzl, Peres, Rabin 6 Ben-Zvi, Eshkol 7 Sharett 8 Weizmann 9 Ben-Gurion

language: 6 Arabic, French, Hebrew 7 English, Yiddish

religion: 5 Baha'i, Islam 7 Judaism 12 Christianity

place:
church: 13 Holy Sepulcher
gates to Old Jerusalem: 3 New 4 Dung, Zion 5 Jaffa 6 Herod's 8 Damascus 10 St Stephen's
mosque: 13 Dome of the Rock
mount: 4 Zion 6 Olives, Scopus
shrine: 3 Bab 4 Book 11 Wailing Wall, Western Wall 18 Garden of Gethsemane
tomb: 9 Sanhedrin 10 King David's
way of sorrows: 11 Via Dolorosa

feature: 14 Dead Sea Scrolls
collective village: 7 kibbutz 9 kibbutzim
cooperative village: 6 moshav 8 moshavim
dance: 4 hora
movement: 7 Zionism
Palestinian uprising: 8 intifada
peace agreement: 16 Camp David Accords
tree: 5 judas
wave of immigration: 5 aliya 6 aliyot

food:
dish: 4 pita 6 hummus 7 falafel

king: 4 Ahab, Elah, Jehu, Omri, Saul 5 David, Hosea, Nadab, Zimri

Issachar
　father: 5 Jacob
　mother: 4 Leah
　brother: 3 Dan, Gad 4 Levi 5 Asher, Judah 6 Joseph, Reuben, Simeon 7 Zebulun 8 Benjamin, Naphtali
　sister: 5 Dinah
　descendant of:
　　11 Issacharite

Is Sex Necessary?
　author: 7 E B White 12 James Thurber

issuance 8 emission 9 allotment, discharge, emanation 12 dispensation, distribution

issue 4 gush, rise, stem 5 allot, arise, ensue, erupt, go out, heirs, spout, yield 6 emerge, follow, number, result, spring 7 dispute, emanate, flow out, give out, outcome, outflow, pass out, problem, proceed, product, progeny 8 children, dispense, drainage, eruption, granting, heritors, issuance, question 9 circulate, discharge, effluence, grow out of, offspring, posterity, pour forth

10 distribute, outpouring 11 consequence, descendants, publication 12 dispensation, distributing

Istanbul
　area: 7 Beyoglu 8 Stamboul
　capital of: 6 Turkey
　formerly: 9 Byzantium 14 Constantinople
　landmark: 10 Hippodrome 11 Hagia Sophia 12 Galata Bridge 14 Bosporus Bridge 26 Palais de la Culture d'Istanbul
　mosque: 3 New 8 Mihrimah 9 Yeni Camii 11 Suleymaniye

Italy
　also: 8 Hesperia
　capital/largest city: 4 Roma, Rome
　others: 4 Pisa 5 Genoa, Milan, Padua, Turin, Udine 6 Amalfi, Ancona, Assisi, Naples, Rimini, Savona, Venice, Verona 7 Bologna, Bolzano, Brescia, Catania, Messina, Palermo, Ravenna, Taranto, Trieste 8 Florence
　division: 6 Apulia, Latium, Marche, Molise, Umbria, Veneto 7 Abruzzi, Liguria, Tuscany 8 Calabria, Campania, Lombardy, Piedmont 10 Basilicata 12 Valle d'Agosta 13 Emilia-Romagna 17 Trentino-Alto Adige 19 Friuli-Venezia Giulia
　　independent enclave: 9 San Marino 11 Vatican City
　measure: 3 pie 4 orna 5 palma, palmo, punto, salma, stero 6 barile, miglie, moggio, rubbio, tomolo 7 braccio, secchio 8 giornata, quadrato
　monetary unit: 4 lira, lire, tara 5 grano, paolo, soldo 6 danaro, denaro, ducato 7 testone 8 zecchino 9 centesini
　weight: 5 carat, libra, oncia, pound 6 denaro, libbra
　island: 4 Elba 5 Capri, Egadi, Eolie 6 Ischia, Istria, Linosa, Lipari, Sicily, Ustica 7 Aeolian, Trieste, Vulcano 8 Lampione, Sardinia 9 Borromean, Lampedusa, Stromboli 10 Isola Bella 11 Pantelleria
　lake: 4 Como, Iseo, Nemi 5 Garda 6 Albano, Lesina, Lugano, Varano 7 Bolsena, Perugia 8 Maggiore 9 Bracciano, Trasimeno
　mountain: 4 Alps, Etna, Visa 5 Amaro, Blanc, Corno, Somma 6 Cimone, Ortles 9 Apennines, Dolomites, Maritimes 11 Gennargentu 12 Gran Paradiso 16 Abruzzi Apennines
　　Alps: 6 Apuane, Carnic, Julian, Otztal 7 Bernina 8 Ligurian 9 Lepontine
　　volcano: 7 Vulcano 8 Vesuvius 9 Stromboli
　highest point: 4 Rosa
　river: 2 Po 4 Adda, Agri, Arno, Liri, Nera, Reno, Sele, Taro 5 Adige, Crati, Mannu, Oglio, Parma, Piave, Salso, Stura, Tiber, Tirso 6 Aniene, Belice, Isonzo, Mincio, Ofanto, Panaro, Rapido, Sangro, Simeto, Tanaro, Tevere, Ticino 7 Biferno, Bradano, Chienti, Metauro, Montone, Ombrone, Pescara, Rubicon, Secchia, Trebbia 8 Volturno
　sea: 6 Ionian 8 Adriatic, Ligurian 10 Tyrrhenian 13 Mediterranean
　physical feature:
　　bay: 6 Naples
　　channel: 5 Malta
　　grotto: 4 Blue
　　gulf: 5 Gaeta, Genoa 6 Venice 7 Salerno, Taranto 11 Manfredonia
　　hills of Rome: 7 Caelian, Viminal 8 Aventine, Palatine, Quirinal 9 Esquiline 10 Capitoline
　　lagoon: 6 Venice
　　pass: 5 Resia 6 Maloja 7 Bernina, Brenner, Simplon 9 Mont Cenis 13 Saint Gotthard 17 Great Saint Bernard
　　resort: 14 Italian Riviera
　　strait: 6 Sicily 7 Messina, Otranto 9 Bonifacio
　people: 7 Italian
　　ancient: 5 Latin, Remus 6 Sabine 7 Lombard, plebian, Romulus 8 Etruscan 9 patrician
　　architect: 5 Nervi, Ponti, Salvi 6 Vasari 7 Alberti, Guarini, Juvarra, Vignola 8 Ammanati, Bramante, Palladio 9 Borromini, De Sanctis 12 Brunelleschi, Michelangelo
　　artist: 5 Balla, Carra 6 Batoni, Gaulli, Guardi, Titian 7 Bellini, Chirico, Cimabue, Cortona, Da Vinci, Raphael, Tiepolo, Uccello 8 Carracci, Mantegna, Masaccio, Severini 9 Benvenuti, Canoletto, Giorgione 10 Botticelli, Caravaggio, Modigliani, Tintoretto 11 Buoninsegna, Fra Angelico 12 Michelangelo 13 Giotto Bondone 14 della Francesca
　　composer: 5 Verdi 7 Bellini, Cavalli, Corelli, Puccini, Rossini, Vivaldi 8 Mascagni, Piccini 9 Donizetti, Scarlatti 10 Monteverdi, Palestrina 11 Leoncavallo

museum: 13 Topkapi Palace **14** Archaeological **20** Turkish and Islamic Art
rulers: 4 Rome **6** Athens, Darius, Rhodes, Sparta **8** Persians, Suleiman **9** Macedonia **11** Latin Empire **12** Ottoman Turks **15** Byzantine Empire, Turkish Republic **19** Constantine the Great
sea: 5 Black **7** Marmara **8** Bosporus **10** Golden Horn

isthmus 4 neck, spit **5** point, strip **6** narrow, strait, tongue **7** narrows

name: 4 Suez **6** Panama **7** Corinth

Isus
father: 5 Priam
killed by: 9 Agamemnon

I sustain the wings
Latin: 12 sustineo alas
motto of: 10 US Air Force

Italiano, Anna Maria Louise
real name of: 12 Anne Bancroft

Italic
language family: 12 Indo-European

branch: 5 Latin, Oscan **7** Umbrian

Italy see box

itch 3 yen **4** ache, long, pine **5** crave, crawl, creep, yearn **6** desire, hanker, hunger, thirst, tickle **7** craving, prickle **8** appetite, have a yen, pruritis, tingling, yearning **9** hankering

it does not follow
Latin: 11 non sequitur

item 4 unit **5** entry, piece, point, story, thing **6** detail, matter, notice, report **7** ac-

---

emperor: 4 Nero, Otho **5** Galba, Nerva, Titus **6** Trajan **7** Hadrian **8** Caligula, Claudius, Commodus, Domitian, Octavian, Tiberius **9** Caracalla, Vespasian, Vitellius **10** Diocletian **11** Constantine **13** Antoninus Dius **14** Caesar Augustus, Marcus Aurelius
film director: 6 de Sica **7** Fellini **8** Visconti **9** Antonioni **10** Bertolucci, Rossellini, Wertmuller, Zeffirelli
god: 4 Juno, Mars **5** Ceres, Diana, Janus, Lares, Venus **6** Apollo, Vulcan **7** Bacchus, Jupiter, Minerva, Neptune, Penates **8** Quirinus
Italian author: 4 Levi **5** Bembo, Bruno, Pulci, Tasso **6** Artino, Vasari **7** Ariosto, Bassani, Deledda, Moravia **8** Bandello, Petrarch **9** Boccaccio, D'Annunzio, Sannazaro **10** Cavalcanti, Guinicelli, Metastasio, Pirandello, Straparola **11** Castiglione, Machiavelli **12** Guicciardini, Michelangelo **14** Dante Alighieri
Latin author: 4 Cato, Livy, Ovid **5** Pliny, Varro **6** Cicero, Gallus, Horace, Seneca, Vergil, Virgil **7** Donatus, Juvenal, Martial, Plautus, Sallust, Tacitus, Terence **8** Boethius, Catullus, Lucilius, St Jerome **9** St Ambrose, Suetonius **11** St Augustine
ruler: 4 Moro **6** Cavour, Enrico **7** Mazzini **9** Mussolini **10** Berlinguer **14** Victor Emmanuel **15** Alcide de Gasperi
ruler/military leader: 5 Sulla **6** Brutus, Pompey, Seneca **7** Crassus, Lepidus **8** Gracchus **10** Mark Antony **12** Gaius Marious, Julius Caesar **15** Cassius Longinus, Scipio Africanus **18** Tarquinius Superbus
ruling family of city-state: 4 Este **6** Medici, Sforza **8** Visconti
sculptor: 6 Canova, Marini, Pisano **7** Bernini, Bologna, Cellini **8** Antelami, Boccioni, Ghiberti **9** Donatello, Sansovino **10** Giacometti, Pollaiuolo, Verrocchio **11** Della Robbia **12** Michelangelo
wife: 7 Poppaea **9** Agrippina, Messalina **13** Livia Drusilla
language: 5 Ladin, Latin **6** French, German **7** Italian, Slovene **8** Friulian **9** Sardinian
religion: 13 Roman Catholic
place:
  arch: 11 Constantine
  baths: 9 Caracalla
  bridge: 5 Sighs **12** Ponte Vecchio
  cathedral/church: 5 Siena **7** St Mark's, Vatican **8** San Marco, St Peter's **13** Sistine Chapel
  fountain: 5 Trevi
  museum: 5 Duomo **6** Uffizi **8** Bargello, National **10** Capitoline **11** Pitti Palace, Villa Giulia **16** Gallerio Borghese
  opera house: 7 La Scala
  palace: 5 Doges
  road: 9 Appian Way
  ruins: 5 Forum **7** Capitol, Pompeii **8** Pantheon **9** Catacombs, Colosseum **11** Herculaneum **13** Circus Maximus
  steps: 7 Spanish
  tower: 18 Leaning Tower of Pisa
feature:
  unification movement: 12 Risorgimento
food:
  cheese: 6 romano **7** fontina, ricotta **8** parmesan
  dish: 5 pizza **6** scampi **7** gnocchi, lasagna, lasagne, polenta, ravioli, risotto **9** antipasti, antipasto **17** chicken cacciatora, cacciatore
  ice cream: 6 gelato **7** spumoni
  meat: 6 salami **9** pepperoni **10** mortadella, prosciutto
  soup: 8 caciucco **10** minestrone
  wine: 7 Chianti

count, article, feature, subject
8 dispatch, notation **9** paragraph **10** particular **11** news article

itemization 4 list **7** listing
11 enumeration

itemize 6 detail **7** specify
8 spell out **9** enumerate

items of business 4 list
6 agenda, docket **7** program
8 schedule

iterate 6 repeat **7** restate
9 reiterate

It Girl
  nickname of: 8 Clara Bow

it grows as it goes
  Latin: 12 crescit eundo
  motto of: 9 New Mexico

It Happened One Night
  director: 10 Frank Capra
  cast: 8 Alan Hale, Ward
  Bond **10** Clark Gable
  11 Roscoe Karns **14** Walter
  Connolly **16** Claudette
  Colbert
  Oscar for: 5 actor (Gable)
  7 actress (Colbert), picture
  8 director
  remade as: 16 Eve Knew
  Her Apples **20** You Can't
  Run Away from It

I think therefore I am
  Latin: 13 cogito ergo sum
  said by: 9 Descartes

Ithomatas *see* **4** Zeus

Ithun, Ithunn *see* **4** Idun

itinerant 5 nomad, rover
6 roamer, roving **7** migrant,
nomadic, roaming, vagrant
8 vagabond, wanderer, wayfarer **9** footloose, transient,
traveling, wandering, wayfaring **11** peripatetic

itinerary 3 log **5** diary, route
6 course **7** account, circuit,
day book, journal **8** schedule
9 timetable **10** travel plan

**it is not clear; it is not
evident**
  Latin: 9 non liquet

**it is not lawful; it is not
permitted**
  Latin: 8 non licet

it is sweet to do nothing
  Italian: 14 dolce far niente

Itonia
  epithet of: 6 Athena

It's a Gift
  director: 13 Norman Z
  McLeod
  cast: 8 W C Fields **9** Baby
  LeRoy, Tommy Bupp **10** T
  Roy Barnes **13** Charles Sellon, Morgan Wallace
  14 Kathleen Howard

remake of: 17 It's the Old
Army Game

It's a Wonderful Life
  director: 10 Frank Capra
  cast: 9 Donna Reed **11** Beulah Bondi **12** Henry Travers,
  James Stewart **13** Gloria
  Grahame **15** Lionel
  Barrymore
  remade as: 22 It Happened
  One Christmas

itsy-bitsy 3 wee **4** tiny
5 dwarf, pygmy, small, teeny
6 bantam, little, minute, petite **9** miniature, miniscule
10 diminutive, teeny-weeny
11 microscopic, pocket-sized

It Takes a Thief
  character: 8 Noah Bain
  12 Alister Mundy, Wallie
  Powers **14** Alexander Mundy
  cast: 11 Edward Binns, Fred
  Astaire **12** Robert Wagner
  13 Malachi Throne

Itylus
  father: 6 Zethus
  mother: 5 Aedon
  killed by: 5 Aedon

Itys
  father: 6 Tereus
  mother: 6 Procne
  killed by: 6 Procne
  to revenge: 9 Philomela

Itza
  language family: 6 Toltec
  location: 6 Mexico **7** Chichen,
  Yucatan **14** Central America

Iulus *see* **8** Ascanius

Ivanhoe
  author: 14 Sir Walter Scott
  character: 7 Rebecca **8** Guilbert **9** Robin Hood **10** Lady
  Rowena **11** Isaac of York
  12 King Richard I **14** Cedric
  the Saxon, Sir Brian de
  Bois **16** Wilfred of Ivanhoe
  19 King Richard the First

Ivanhoe, Burle Icle
  real name of: 8 Burl Ives

I've Got a Secret
  host: 10 Bill Cullen, Garry
  Moore, Steve Allen

Ives, Burl
  real name: 16 Burle Icle
  Ivanhoe
  nickname: 17 Wayfaring
  Stranger
  born: 6 Hunt IL
  roles: 8 Big Daddy **10** East of
  Eden **13** The Big Country
  14 Our Man in Havana
  16 Cat on a Hot Tin Roof
  18 Desire Under the Elms

Ives, Charles
  born: 9 Danbury CT
  composer of: 11 Putnam's
  Camp **13** Concord Sonata
  19 Washington's Birthday

20 Central Park in the
Dark **21** The Unanswered
Question **23** Three Places in
New England

Ivory Coast
  capital/largest city:
  7 Abidjan
  new capital:
  12 Yamoussoukro
  others: 3 Man **4** Divo
  5 Daloa, Tabou **6** Adzobe, Bonoua, Bouake,
  Danane, Gagnoa **7** Korhogo, Odienne, Seguela **8** Dimbokro
  9 Agboville, Bondoukou, Sassandra
  10 Abengourou
  11 Grand Bassam
  14 Ferkessedougou
  monetary unit: 5 franc
  7 centime
  highest point: 5 Nimba
  river: 3 Bia **5** Comoe,
  Komoe **7** Bandama,
  Cavally **9** Sassandra
  ocean: 8 Atlantic
  physical feature:
    cape: **6** Palmas
    gulf: **6** Guinea
    lagoon: **3** Aby **5** Ebrie
    wind: **9** harmattan
  people: 3 Abe, Dan, Kru,
  Kwa **4** Akan, Bete,
  Dida, Guro, Koua, Lobi,
  Wobe **5** Abron, Abure,
  Attie, Baule, Guere,
  Mande, Mossi **6** Baoule,
  Lagoon, Senufo, Senufu **7** Dan Guro, Kroumen, Malinke, Voltaic
  10 Anyi-Baoule
  11 Lobi-Kulango
  12 Agnis-Ashanti
  language: 4 Akan
  6 Dioula, French
  religion: 5 Islam **7** animism **13** Roman
  Catholic
  place:
    canal: **5** Vridi
    dam: **7** Bandama
    game reserve:
      9 Sassandra
  feature: 7 kola nut

Ivory Coast *see* **11** Sierra
Leone

ivory-towered 6 remote **8** academic, romantic **11** conjectural, impractical, theoretical,
unrealistic **12** hypothetical

ivy 6 Cissus, Hedera **15** Kalmia
latifolia
  varieties: 3 fan, red **4** baby,
  tree **5** grape, Irish, Nepal,

water 6 aralia, Baltic, Boston, canary, devil's, German, ground, marine, parlor, poison, spider, switch 7 colchis, English, Italian, Madeira, Mexican, parsley, Persian, Swedish 8 Algerian, American, coliseum, fragrant, Japanese, red-flame 9 bird's-foot, ghost-tree, heart-leaf 10 five-leaved, Kenilworth, variegated 12 Hagenburger's 13 Solomon Island 14 miniature grape 15 Gloire-de-Marengo

Ivy League colleges 4 Yale **5** Brown **7** Cornell, Harvard **8** Columbia **9** Dartmouth, Princeton **12** Pennsylvania (Penn)

I Want to Live!
  director: 10 Robert Wise
  cast: 12 Simon Oakland, Susan Hayward (Barbara Graham) 13 Theodore Bikel 15 Virginia Vincent
  score: 12 Johnny Mandel
  Oscar for: 7 actress (Hayward)

I will defend
  Latin: 6 tuebor

IWW 8 Wobblies **10** labor union **27** Industrial Workers of the World
  leader: 4 Debs 6 DeLeon 7 Haywood
  members: 6 miners 9 lumbermen 16 migratory workers

Ixion
  king of: 8 Lapithae
  wife: 3 Dia
  son: 9 Pirithous
  children: 8 centaurs
  loved: 4 Hera
  punished by: 4 Zeus
  bound to: 5 wheel

Iyar 17 second Hebrew month

Iynx
  father: 3 Pan
  mother: 4 Echo

Izmir
  formerly: 6 Smyrna
  location: 6 Turkey 9 Aegean Sea 11 Gulf of Izmir
  settle by: 7 Ionians 8 Aeolians
  ruled by: 13 Ottoman Empire

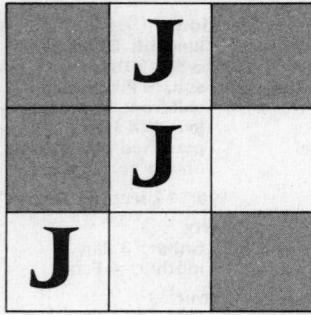

ja 3 yes

jab 3 cut, dig, hit, rap, tap
4 belt, blow, bump, clip, goad,
lick, pelt, plug, poke, poke,
prod, sock, stab, swat 5 elbow,
nudge, paste, swing 6 strike,
stroke

Jabal
father: 6 Lamech
mother: 4 Adah
brother: 5 Jubal

jabber 3 gab, gas 4 blab 5 clack,
prate 6 babble, cackle, drivel,
gibber, gossip, hot air, patter,
ramble, rattle, raving 7 blabber,
blather, chatter, gushing,
maunder, palaver, prating,
prattle, ranting, twaddle, twattle 8 chitchat, idle talk, nonsense, talk idly 9 gibberish
10 maundering 14 chitter-
chatter

jack 4 flag 5 knave 6 ensign

jackass 3 ass 4 fool, mule
5 burro, dummy, idiot
6 donkey

Jack Benny Show, The
cast: 8 Mel Blanc 9 Dennis
Day, Don Wilson 11 Frank
Nelson 13 Artie Auerbach,
Eddie (Rochester) Anderson
14 Mary Livingston
Jack's car: 7 Maxwell
Jack played: 6 violin

jacket 4 case, coat 5 cover
6 blazer, casing, folder, sheath
7 wrapper 8 envelope, mackinaw, wrapping 9 container,
enclosure, short coat, sport
coat 10 dinner coat
11 windbreaker 12 balero

Jack Sheppard
author: 16 William Ainsworth

Jackson, Andrew *see box*

Jackson, Anne
husband: 10 Eli Wallach
born: 10 Millvale PA
roles: 3 Luv 10 The Typists

Jackson, Charles
author of: 14 The Lost
Weekend

Jackson, Glenda
born: 7 England
10 Birkenhead
roles: 10 Elizabeth R
11 Women in Love (Oscar)
13 A Touch of Class (Oscar)
14 The Music Lovers
16 Mary Queen of Scots
18 Sunday Bloody Sunday
politics: 11 Labour Party
18 Member of Parliament

Jackson, Jesse Louis
party: 10 Democratic
born: 12 Greenville SC
education: 20 University of Illinois 26 Chicago Theological
Seminary 49 North Carolina
Agricultural and Technical
State College
religion: 7 Baptist
political career: 17 Democratic
primary
civilian career: 4 SCLC 9 PUSH
Excel 13 Operation PUSH
20 Operation Breadbasket
24 National Rainbow Coalition 37 Southern Christian
Leadership Conference

Jackson, Michael
born: 2 IN 4 Gary
father: 6 Joseph
mother: 9 Katherine
siblings: 4 Tito 5 Janet, Randy
6 Jackie, La Toya, Marlon
7 Maureen 8 Jermaine
wife: 16 Lisa Marie Presley
trademark: 5 glove
recordings: 3 Bad 7 Triumph,
Victory 8 Thriller 9 Dangerous 10 Off the Wall
film: 6 The Wiz
group: 8 Jacksons 11 Jackson
Five

Jackson, Reggie
nickname: 13 Mister October
sport: 8 baseball
position: 8 outfield
team: 9 Oakland A's 14 New

York Yankees 16 Los Angeles
Angels

Jackson, Shirley
author of: 10 The Lottery
28 We Have Always Lived in
the Castle

**Jackson, Stonewall
(Thomas)**
served in: 8 Civil War
10 Mexican War
side: 11 Confederate
battle: 7 Bull Run 8 Antietam,
Richmond 9 Seven Days
14 Fredericksburg 16 Chancellorsville, Shenandoah
Valley

Jacksonville
football team: 5 Bulls
7 Jaguars

Jacob
father: 5 Isaac
mother: 7 Rebekah
brother: 4 Esau
wives: 4 Leah 6 Rachel
concubines: 5 Bilah 6 Zilpah
son: 3 Dan, Gad 4 Levi
5 Asher, Judah 6 Joseph,
Reuben, Simeon 7 Zebulun
8 Benjamin, Issachar,
Naphtali
daughter: 5 Dinah
dream of: 6 ladder
wrestled with: 5 angel
name changed to: 6 Israel
burial place: 9 Machpelah

Jacob, Francois
field: 7 biology
nationality: 6 French
discovered: 3 RNA
awarded: 10 Nobel Prize

Jacobs, Amos Muzyad
real name of: 11 Danny
Thomas

jade
species: 7 jadeite 8 nephrite
source: 5 Burma, China
6 Mexico 7 Mogaung 10 New
Zealand 12 United States

jaded 5 blase, bored, sated,
spent, stale, tired, weary

514

Jackson, Andrew
  nickname: 10 Old Hickory
  presidential rank: 7 seventh
  party: 10 Democratic
  state represented: 2 TN **9** Tennessee
  defeated: 4 (Henry) Clay **5** (John Quincy) Adams
  vice president: 7 (John Caldwell) Calhoun **8** (Martin) Van Buren
  cabinet:
    state: **6** (Louis) McLane **7** (John) Forsyth **8** (Martin) Van Buren **10** (Edward) Livingston
    treasury: **5** (William John) Duane **6** (Louis) McLane, (Samuel Dulucenna) Ingham **8** (Levi) Woodbury
    war: **4** (Lewis) Cass **5** (John Henry) Eaton
    attorney general: **5** (Roger Brooke) Taney **6** (Benjamin Franklin) Butler **7** (John McPherson) Berrien
    navy: **6** (John) Branch **8** (Levi) Woodbury **9** (Mahlon) Dickerson
    postmaster general: **5** (William Taylor) Barry **7** (Amos) Kendall
  born: 8 Waxhaw SC
  died/buried: 11 Nashville TN
  education:
    college: **4** none
    studied: **3** law
    admitted to: **3** bar
  religion: 12 Presbyterian
  political career: 8 US Senate **24** US House of Representatives
    judge: **22** Tennessee Superior Court
  civilian career: 6 lawyer
  military service: 12 major general **16** brigadier general
    defeated: **6** Creeks **9** Cherokees
    captured: **9** Pensacola
    military governor of: **7** Florida
  notable events of lifetime/term:
    battle: **5** Alamo **10** New Orleans
    fought: **5** duels
    scandal/wife suspected of: **6** bigamy
    war: **8** Creek War **13** Revolutionary **16** First Seminole War **19** War of Eighteen Twelve
  father: 6 Andrew
  mother: 9 Elizabeth (Hutchinson)
  siblings: 4 Hugh **6** Robert
  wife: 6 Rachel (Donelson Robards)
  children:
    adopted: **11** wife's nephew **15** Andrew Jackson Jr

house **10** guardhouse **11** incarcerate, reformatory **12** halfway house, penitentiary, reform school, station house **13** hold in custody, police station **14** detention house **16** penal institution **17** house of correction

jailbird 3 con **5** felon **7** convict **8** prisoner

jailer 5 guard, screw **6** gaoler, keeper, warden **7** turnkey **9** custodian

Jair 11 Hebrew judge

Jakarta, Djakarta
  capital of: 9 Indonesia

Jake's Thing
  author: 12 Kingsley Amis

jalopy 3 car **4** auto, heap **5** motor **6** wheels **7** flivver, machine, vehicle **8** motorcar **9** tin lizzie **10** automobile

jam 3 fix, mob, ram, sea **4** army, cram, herd, host, mess, pack, push, stop **5** block, cease, crowd, crush, drove, flock, horde, pinch, press, shove, stall, stick, stuff, swarm, tie-up, wedge **6** arrest, edge in, pickle, plight, scrape, strait, throng, thrust, work in, worm in **7** congest, dilemma, foist in, force in, squeeze, suspend, trouble **8** hot water, obstruct, quandary, sandwich **9** interrupt, multitude, overcrowd **11** malfunction, predicament **13** agglomeration

Jamaica *see box, p. 516*

jamboree 2 do **4** bash, gala **5** party, revel, spree **6** fiesta, frolic **7** blowout, jubilee, shindig **8** carnival, carousal, festival **9** festivity **11** celebration **French: 4** fete **13** fete champetre

James 7 apostle
  also called: 12 James the Less
  father: 7 Zebedee **8** Alphaeus
  brother: 4 John, Levi **5** Judas
  disciple of: 5 Jesus
  killed by: 12 Herod Agrippa
  with John called: 13 sons of thunder

James, Henry
  author of: 11 Daisy Miller, The American **13** The Bostonians, The Golden Bowl **14** Roderick Hudson, The Ambassadors **15** The Aspern Papers **16** Washington Square **17** The Turn of the Screw, The Wings of the Dove **18** The Portrait of a Lady **19** Princess Casamassima

6 cloyed, dulled, fagged **7** glutted, satiate, spoiled, wearied, worn-out **8** dog-tired, fatigued, overused, satiated, shopworn, tired out **9** exhausted, played out, surfeited **11** overwearied **12** overindulged

jadeite
  variety: 4 jade

Jael
  husband: 5 Heber
  killed: 11 Sisera

jagged 5 jaggy, rough, spiny **6** barbed, broken, craggy, nicked, ridged, rugged, snaggy, spiked, thorny, uneven, zigzag **7** angular, bristly, cragged, notched, pointed, spinous, studded **8** indented, serrated

9 irregular, knifelike **10** crenulated, saw-toothed **12** sharptoothed

Jaggers, Mr
  character in: 17 Great Expectations
  author: 7 Dickens

jaguar 3 cat **5** tiger **6** feline **7** panther **8** uturuncu

jail 3 bag, can, jug, nab, pen **4** book, brig, bust, cell, keep, stir **5** clink, pinch, pound, run in, seize **6** arrest, collar, cooler, lockup, prison, take in **7** arraign, bring in, capture, confine, dungeon, slammer **8** bastille, big house, hoosegow, imprison, stockade **9** apprehend, black hole, calaboose, guardroom, work-

Jamaica
name means: 18 land of wood and water
capital/largest city: 8 Kingston
others: 6 May Pen 8 Ocho Rios 9 Morant Bay, Port Maria, Port Royal 10 Mandeville, Montego Bay 11 Port Antonio, Spanish Town 12 Saint Ann's Bay, Savanna-la-Mar
head of state: 14 British monarch 15 governor general
monetary unit: 7 quattie
island: 4 Navy 15 Greater Antilles
mountain: 8 Sir John's
highest point: 4 Blue
river: 5 Black, Cobre, Great, Minho, White 9 Rio Grande
sea: 8 Atlantic 9 Caribbean
physical feature: 13 Portland Bight
  area: 14 Cockpit Country
  bay: 4 Buff, Hope, Long 6 Morant 9 Discovery 10 Black River, Bluefield's, Old Harbour
  point: 6 Galina 8 Portland 9 North East, North West, South East 11 North Negril, South Negril
people: 7 African, Chinese 10 East Indian
  ancient: 6 Arawak 7 Ciboney
  discoverer: 8 Columbus
  leader: 5 Seaga 6 Garvey, Manley 10 Bustamente
language: 6 Creole 7 English
religion: 7 Baptist 8 Anglican 9 Methodist 11 Church of God, Rastafarian 13 Roman Catholic
place:
  beach: 11 Doctor's Cave
  botanical garden: 4 Hope
  racetrack: 12 Caymanas Park
feature:
  evil spirits: 7 duppies
  guerrilla fighters: 7 Maroons
  tree: 4 poui 5 cedar, ceiba, mahoe, saman 6 cassia, guango 7 logwood 8 mahogany 9 casuarina, poinciana 10 silkcotton 11 lignum vitae
  witch doctor: 8 obeah man
food:
  coffee: 12 Blue Mountain
  drink: 3 rum 4 jake 8 tia maria
  fruit: 5 guava, mango 6 pawpaw
  spicy soup: 9 pepper pot

noy, chime, clang, clank, clash, crash, upset 6 jingle, racket, rattle 7 clangor, clatter, grate on 8 irritate 9 cacophony 11 reverberate 13 reverberation 14 tintinnabulate

janitor 5 super 6 porter 8 handyman 9 caretaker, custodian, janitress 11 cleaning man 12 cleaning lady 13 cleaning woman 14 maintenance man, superintendent

Janssen, David
real name: 16 David Harold Meyer
born: 9 Naponee NE
roles: 6 Harry O 11 The Fugitive 14 Richard Diamond 15 Dr Richard Kimble

January
event: 15 Inauguration Day (every 4 years)
flower: 8 snowdrop 9 carnation
French: 7 Janvier
gem: 6 garnet
German: 6 Januar
holiday: 8 Epiphany (6) 11 New Year's Day (1) 12 Twelfth Night (5)
Italian: 7 Gennaio
number of days: 9 thirty-one
origin of name: 5 Janus
  Roman god of: 5 doors 8 doorways 10 beginnings
place in year:
  Gregorian: 5 first
  Julian/Roman: 8 eleventh
Spanish: 5 Enero
Zodiac sign: 8 Aquarius 9 Capricorn

James, P D
author of: 12 Cover Her Face 13 Innocent Blood 15 Unnatural Causes 21 Shroud for a Nightingale 22 Death of an Expert Witness
character: 13 Adam Dalgliesh

James the Less *see* 5 James

jammed 4 full 5 stuck 6 filled, loaded, massed, packed, rammed, wedged 7 blocked, crammed, crowded, crushed, pressed, stuffed 8 overfull, squeezed 10 obstructed, sandwiched 11 overcrowded

Janacek, Leos
born: 8 Hukvaldy 14 Czechoslovakia
composer of: 5 Mladi, Youth 6 Jenufa 9 In the Mist 10 Taras Bulba 13 Katya Kabanova 14 Glagolitic Mass 17 On an Overgrown Path 18 The Makropoulus Case 21 From the House of the Dead, The Cunning Little Vixen 24 The Diary of One Who Vanished, The Excursions of Mr Broucek

Jane
character in: 6 Tarzan
author: 9 Burroughs

Jane Eyre
author: 15 Charlotte Bronte
character: 5 Mason 7 Mrs Reed 10 Grace Poole, Mary Rivers, Mrs Fairfax 11 Adele Varens, Bertha Mason, Diana Rivers 12 Bessie Leaven, St John Rivers 13 Blanche Ingram 15 Edward Rochester
school: 6 Lowood
house: 10 Thornfield
director: 15 Robert Stevenson
cast: 11 Orson Welles 12 Joan Fontaine 14 Margaret O'Brien

jangle 3 din, jar 4 ring 5 an-

Janus
origin: 5 Roman
god of: 8 doorways 9 rising sun 10 beginnings, setting sun

Japan *see box*

Japanese
independent language of: 5 Japan 13 Ryukyu Islands

jape 4 gibe, joke 5 antic, caper, prank 7 mockery

Japheth
father: 4 Noah
brother: 3 Ham 4 Shem

Jaques
character in: 11 As You Like It
author: 11 Shakespeare

Japan
other name: 5 Nihon 6 Nippon
name means: 18 Land of the Rising Sun
capital/largest city: 3 Edo 5 Tokyo
others: 4 Kobe, Naha 5 Kyoto, Osaka 6 Nagoya, Sendai 7 Fukuoka, Niigata, Sapporo 8 Kanazawa, Kawasaki, Nagasaki, Yokohama 9 Hiroshima, Kagoshima 10 Kitakyushu
school: 4 Chuo, Keio 5 Hosei, Kyoto, Nihon, Tokyo 6 Sophia, Waseda 7 Fukuoka 8 Doshisha
head of state: 7 emperor
measure: 2 go 3 boo, cho, djo, fun, inc, ken, kin, kon, rin, shi, sho, sun, tan 4 hiro, isse, kati, koku, niyo, shoo 5 carat, catty, issho, ittan, momme, picul, shaku 6 kwamme 8 hiyak-kin 9 hiyak-hiro 11 komma-ichida, kujira-shaku
monetary unit: 2 bu 3 mon, rin, rio, sen, shu, yen 4 cash, mibu, oban 5 koban, obang, tempo 6 cobang, ichebu, ichibu, itzebu, kobang 7 itzeboo, itziboo
weight: 2 mo 3 fun, kon, rin 4 kati, kwan 5 carat, catty, momme 8 hiyakkin
island: 3 Iki, Izu, Oki, Tsu 4 Oita, Sado, Yaku 5 Amami, Awaji, Bonin, Hondo, Kuril, Rebun, Sikok 6 Honshu, Kiushu, Kyushu, Loochu, Marcus, Riukiu, Tanega, Tyukyu 7 Cipango, Hachijo, Iwo Jima, Okinawa, Rishiri, Shikoko, Shikoku, Volcano 8 Hokkaido, Miyajima, Okigunto, Okushiri, Tsushima, Yakujima
lake: 4 Biwa, Suwa, Toya 6 Towada 8 Kutchawa, Shikotsu
mountain: 3 Uso, Zao 5 Asahi, Asama, Hondo, Yesso 6 Asosan, Enasan, Hiuchi, Kiusiu, Yariga 7 Hakusan, Kujusan, Tokachi 8 Fujiyama 9 Japan Alps
highest point: 4 Fuji 7 Fujisan
river: 4 Tone, Yalu 8 Ishikari, Tonegawa 11 Shinano-gawa
sea: 3 Suo 5 Japan 6 Inland 7 Amakusa, Okhotsk, Pacific 8 Tsushima
physical feature:
  bay: 3 Ise 4 Miku, Tosa, Yedo 5 Amort, Mutsu, Osaka, Otaru, Tokyo 6 Ariake, Atsumi, Sendai, Suruga, Toyama, Wakasa 7 Uchiura
  cape: 3 Iro, Oki, Oma, Toi 4 Daio, Esan, Jizo, Mela, Mino, Noma, Nomo, Sada, Sawa, Shio, Soya, Suzu 5 Erimo, Kyoga, Rurui 6 Todoga 7 Shiriya 8 Ashizuri, Shakotan 12 Muroto Nojima
  channel: 3 Kii 5 Bungo
  current: 5 Japan 7 Okhotsk 8 Kuro Shio
  divine wind: 8 kamikaze
  gulf: 6 Sagami
  plain: 4 Nobi 5 Kanto
  strait: 4 Soya 5 Korea, Osumi 6 Nemuro, Tanega, Tokara 7 Tsugaru 8 Tsushima 9 La Perouse
people: 3 Eta 6 Korean 8 Japanese, Okinawan 10 Buramkumin
  ancient: 4 Ainu 5 Jomon, Yayoi
  artist: 4 Okyo 5 Buson, Jocho, Korin, Taiga, Unkei 6 Bun:ho, Eitoku, Kenzan, Koetsu, Reisai, Sesshu, Sesson, Shubun 7 Baiitsu, Choshun, Foujita Gyokudo, Hokusai, Josetsu, Sanraku, Sharaku, Sotatsu, Utamaro 8 Harunobu, Kiyonaga, Motonobu 9 Hiroshige, Mitsunobu
  author: 5 Basho 7 Abe Kobo 8 Mori Ogai 11 Ueda Akinari 12 Ihara Saikaku, Mishima Yukio, Sakyo Komatsu 13 Natsume Soseki, Zeami Motokiyo 14 Shimazaki Toson, Tsubouchi Shoyo 15 Motoori Norinaga, Murasaki Shikibu 16 Fujiwara Nokisaki, Kawabata Yasunari 17 Tanizaki Junichiro 19 Chikamatsu Monzaemon
  dynasty: 5 Meiji, Taira 6 Yamato 8 Fujiwara, Minamoto
  leader: 4 Hojo 5 Kammu, Meiji 6 Go-Toba, Ieyasu 7 Akihito, Go-Daigo 8 Hirohito, Nobunaga, Yoritomo 9 Hideyoshi, Yoshimasa 10 Tojo Hideki, Yoshimitsu 11 Hara Takashi, Ito Hirobumi 12 Tanaka Kakuei 13 Konoe Fumimaro, Shotoku Taishi 14 Yoshida Shigeru 15 Ashikaga Takauji 18 Matsukata Mayayoshi
  legendary ruler: 5 Jimmu, Jingo 7 Izanagi
  shogunate: 8 Ashikaga, Kamakura, Tokugawa
language: 8 Japanese
  alphabet/characters: 4 kana 5 kanji 8 hiragana, katakana
  dialect: 5 Kanto
religion: 6 Tendai 7 Shingon 8 Buddhism 9 Shintoism 12 Confucianism
place:
  castle: 4 Nijo
  hall: 5 Hoodo 7 Phoenix 12 Golden Buddha
  mausoleum: 4 Ojin 7 Nintoku
  palace: 7 Akasaka, Katsura
  shrine: 5 Heian 11 Itsukushima 16 Grand Shrine of Ise
  temple: 6 Kotoku 7 Byodoin, Horyuji, Ryoanji, Senso-ji, Todaiji 8 Enkakuji, Kenchoji, Kofukuji 9 Kinkakin 13 Asakusa Kannon
feature:
  abacus: 7 soroban
  bed: 5 futon
  clothing: 6 kimono
  festival: 13 Cherry Blossom

(continued)

Japan *(continued)*
   firm: **4** Sony **5** Honda **6** Mitsui, Nissan, Toyota, Yasuda **7** Iwasaki **8** Sumitomo **10** Mitsubishi
   flower arranging: **7** ikebana
   painting style: **4** kano, tosa **5** nanga, nisee, onnae, rarae, rimpa, shijo **6** chinso, otokoe, sesshu, ukiyoe **7** konpeki, nihonga, yamatoe
   paper folding art: **7** origami
   poem: **4** waka **5** haiku, tanka
   puppet theater: **7** bunraku
   rush floor covering: **6** tatami
   sport: **4** judo **6** karate **13** sumo wrestling
   statue: **8** Daibutsu **11** Great Buddha
   tea ceremony: **7** chanoyu
   theater: **2** no **3** noh **6** kabuki
   the way of the warrior/code of honor: **7** bushido
   tree: **6** bonsai
   wood block print: **6** ukiyoe
  food:
   beverage: **4** sake **8** green tea
   dish: **5** sushi **7** sashimi, tempura **8** sukiyaki, teriyaki, yakitori
   noodle: **4** soba

jar **3** din, jug, pot, urn **4** bong, bray, buzz, daze, faze, jolt, rock, stir, stun **5** blare, blast, brawl, clang, clank, crash, crock, flask, floor, quake, shake, shock, throw, upset **6** beaker, bottle, impact, jangle, jiggle, joggle, racket, rattle, vessel **7** agitate, astound, clangor, clatter, confuse, disturb, fluster, perturb, shake up, startle, stupefy, trouble, upheave, vibrate **8** befuddle, bewilder, bleating, canister, clashing, convulse, decanter, demijohn, disquiet, distract, unsettle **9** agitation, cacophony, container **10** concussion, discompose, disconcert, receptacle **11** discordance
  Spanish: **4** olla

jargon **4** bosh, bull, bunk, cant **5** argot, fudge, hooey, idiom, lingo, prate, usage **6** babble, brogue, drivel, patois, pidgin, piffle **7** baloney, blabber, blather, dialect, fustian, hogwash, prattle, rubbish, twaddle **8** folderol, malarkey, nonsense, parlance, tommyrot, verbiage **9** gibberish, moonshine, poppycock, rigmarole **10** balderdash, flapdoodle, hocus-pocus, rigamarole, vernacular, vocabulary **11** abracadabra, jabberwocky, phraseology, shibboleths **12** gobbledygook, lingua franca **14** grandiloquence

Jarley, Mrs
  character in: **19** The Old Curiosity Shop
  author: **7** Dickens

Jarndyce, John
  character in: **10** Bleak House
  author: **7** Dickens

jarring **4** rude **5** harsh, rough **6** jangly **7** grating, jolting, rasping, shaking **8** clashing, grinding, jangling, rattling, strident **9** dissonant, wrenching **10** discordant **12** nerveracking **13** nerve-wracking

Jarry, Alfred
  author of: **7** King Ubu **11** Ubu in Chains **13** Ubu the Cuckold

jasmine **8** Jasminum
  varieties: **4** blue, cape, rock, star **5** crape, night, royal

Java
  other name: **5** Djawa
  capital/largest city: **7** Jakarta **8** Djakarta
  others: **5** Bogor, Dessa **6** Kediri, Malang **7** Bandung, Batavia **8** Semarang, Surabaja, Surabaya **9** Surakarta **11** Djokjakarta **13** Pelabuhanratu
  government: **17** island of Indonesia
  measure: **3** kan **4** paal, rand **5** palen
  weight: **4** amat, pond, tali **5** pound **6** soekel
  island: **4** Bali **5** Sunda **6** Lombok, Madura
  mountain: **4** Amat, Gede **5** Lawoe, Murjo, Prahu **6** Raoeng, Slamet **8** Soembing
  highest point: **6** Semuru **7** Semeroe
  river: **4** Solo **7** Brantas
  sea: **4** Java **6** Indian **7** Pacific
  physical feature:
   plateau: **4** Ijen
   strait: **5** Sunda
  people: **5** Krama, Kromo **6** Kalang **8** Javanese, Madurese **9** Sundanese
   dynasty: **7** Mataram **9** Majapahit, Srivijaya
  language: **4** Kavi, Kawi **5** Malay **6** Sassak **8** Balinese, Madurese, Sudanese **16** Bahasa Indonesian
  religion: **5** Hindu, Islam **7** animism **8** Buddhism
  place:
   temple: **6** Chandi, Thandi **9** Borobudur, Prambanan
  feature:
   cloth: **3** kat **5** batik, kapok
   dance: **7** seri mpi
   dancer: **6** bedoyo
   fishing boat: **4** prau
   ornamental dagger: **4** kris
   puppet play: **6** wajang, wayang
  food:
   fruit: **6** durian, lomboy, nangca **7** gondang

6 orange, yellow 7 Arabian, Chilean, Italian, Spanish 8 Carolina, cinnamon, Japanese, Paraguay, pinwheel, primrose, windmill 9 angelwing 10 Catalonian, Madagascar 11 Confederate

Jason
leader of: 9 Argonauts
father: 5 Aeson
mother: 8 Alcimede, Polymede
half-brother: 6 Pelias
son: 5 Thoas 6 Euneus, Pheres 7 Medeius 8 Mermerus, Tisander 9 Alcimenes, Thessalus
daughter: 7 Eriopis
teacher: 6 Chiron 7 centaur, Cheiron
retrieved: 12 Golden Fleece
ship: 4 Argo
loved by: 5 Medea
loved: 6 Glauce

Jasper, John
character in: 22 The Mystery of Edwin Drood
author: 7 Dickens

jaundiced 5 blase, bored 6 bitter 7 cynical, envious, hostile, jealous 8 covetous, doubting, satiated 9 green-eyed, resentful, skeptical 10 embittered, suspicious 11 mistrustful

jaunt 4 spin, tour, trip 6 airing, flight, junket, outing, ramble, stroll 9 adventure, excursion, promenade, short trip 10 expedition

jaunty 4 airy, neat, trim 5 natty, perky 6 blithe, bouncy, breezy, dapper, lively, sporty, spruce 7 buoyant 8 carefree, debonair 9 sprightly, vivacious 12 lighthearted, high-stepping, high-spirited

Java *see box*

javelin 4 dart 5 lance, shaft, spear 10 projectile

jaw 3 gab, rap 4 chat, chin, talk 7 jawbone, palaver 8 chitchat, converse, mandible 10 chew the fat, chew the rag 11 confabulate

Jaws
author: 13 Peter Benchley
director: 15 Steven Spielberg
cast: 10 Robert Shaw 11 Roy Scheider 12 Lorraine Gary 15 Richard Dreyfuss
score: 12 John Williams
Oscar for: 5 score

Jayhawker State
nickname of: 6 Kansas

jazz musician 8 Art Tatum 10 Miles Davis 11 Lester

Young 12 Benny Goodman, John Coltrane 13 Charlie Parker, Duke Ellington 14 Dizzy Gillespie, Louis Armstrong, Ornette Coleman

jealous 4 wary 7 anxious, envious, mindful 8 covetous, grudging, watchful 9 concerned, green-eyed, regardful, resentful 10 possessive, protective, suspicious 11 mistrustful, mistrusting 12 apprehensive

jealousy 4 envy 8 distrust, jaundice, mistrust 9 suspicion 10 resentment 12 covetousness 14 possessiveness 16 green-eyed monster
color: 5 green

Jebus
city captured by: 5 David
renamed: 9 Jerusalem
inhabitant: 8 Jebusite

jeer 3 boo, bug, dig, rap 4 barb, hiss, hoot, mock, razz, slam, slur 5 abuse, flout, hound, knock, scoff, scorn, sneer, taunt, whoop 6 deride, harass, heckle, hector, insult, revile 7 catcall, laugh at, mockery, obloquy 8 derision, ridicule, scoffing 9 aspersion, contumely, poke fun at, whistle at

Jeffers, Robinson
author of: 5 Medea, Tamar 6 Cawdor 8 Solstice 9 Dear Judas 12 Roan Stallion 14 Thurso's Landing 18 The Women at Point Sur 21 The Tower Beyond Tragedy

Jefferson, Arthur Stanley
real name of: 10 Stan Laurel

Jefferson, Thomas *see box*

Jeffersons, The
character: 8 Florence 9 Tom Willis 11 Helen Willis 12 Harry Bentley 15 George Jefferson, Lionel Jefferson, Louise Jefferson, Ralph the Doorman 20 Jenny Willis Jefferson
cast: 9 Mike Evans 10 Da-

Jefferson, Thomas
nickname: 16 Sage of Monticello
presidential rank: 5 third
party: 20 Democratic-Republican
state represented: 2 VA
defeated: 5 (John) Adams 8 (Charles Cotesworth) Pinckney
vice president: 4 (Aaron) Burr 7 (George) Clinton
cabinet:
  state: 7 (James) Madison
  treasury: 6 (Samuel) Dexter 8 (Albert) Gallatin
  war: 8 (Henry) Dearborn
  attorney general: 6 (Caesar Augustus) Rodney 7 (Levi) Lincoln 12 (John) Breckenridge
  navy: 5 (Robert) Smith
born: 2 VA 14 Shadwell estate 15 Goochland (Albemarle) County
died/buried: 10 Monticello
education: 14 William and Mary
interests: 6 violin 7 writing 11 agriculture 12 architecture
favorite foods: 10 French food 11 French wines
vacation: 12 Poplar Forest
author: 25 Declaration of Independence, Notes on the State of Virginia 39 A Summary View of the Rights of British America
political career: 8 governor 16 House of Burgesses 19 Virginia legislature 25 Declaration of Independence, Second Continental Congress
  secretary of: 5 state
  minister to: 6 France
civilian career: 6 farmer, lawyer
notable events of lifetime/term:
  expedition: 13 Lewis and Clark
  prohibition of: 19 importation of slaves
  purchase: 9 Louisiana
father: 5 Peter
mother: 4 Jane (Randolph)
siblings: 4 Jane, Lucy, Mary 6 Martha 8 Randolph 9 Anna Scott, Elizabeth 10 Peter Field
wife: 6 Martha (Wayles Skelton)
children: 4 Mary 6 Martha

mon Evans, Marla Gibbs,
Roxie Roker **11** Ned Werti-
mer **12** Paul Benedict
13 Franklin Cover, Isabel
Sanford **14** Sherman Hem-
sley **15** Berlinda Tolbert
George's business: 11 dry
cleaning
spinoff from: 14 All in the
Family

Jeffreys, Harold
field: 7 physics **9** astronomy
nationality: 7 British
explained: 7 weather
studied: 10 Earth's core
11 solar system

Jeffries, James Jackson
nickname: 14 The Boilermaker
sport: 6 boxing
class: 11 heavyweight

jehad, jihad 6 strife **7** holy
war **8** struggle

Jehioada
father: 7 Paseach
son: 7 Benaiah
means: 12 Jehovah knows

Jehoshaphat
father: 3 Asa **6** Ahitub, Nim-
shi, Parnah
mother: 8 Jehorani
means: 13 Jehovah judges

Jehova 3 god **5** diety

Jehu
father: 6 Hanani
11 Jehoshaphat

jejune 4 dull **5** banal, inane,
stale, trite, vapid **7** humdrum,
insipid, puerile **8** ordinary
9 hackneyed **10** pedestrian,
unexciting, unoriginal, wishy-
washy **11** commonplace
12 conventional
13 uninteresting

jell 3 gel, jam, set **4** clot, firm
5 jelly **7** congeal, thicken
9 coagulate **10** gelatinize

Jellyby, Mrs
character in: 10 Bleak House
author: 7 Dickens

jellyfish 5 hydra, polyp, softy
6 coward, medusa, nettle
7 sunfish **8** weakling **10** cten-
ophore, pantywaist **11** milquetoast, mollycoddle
12 coelenterate, invertebrate,
siphonophore **18** Portuguese
man-of-war

je ne sais quoi 13 I don't
know what **18** indefinable
quality

Jenkins, Richard Walter, Jr
real name of: 13 Richard
Burton

Jenner, Bruce
sport: 13 track and field
known for: 9 decathlon
won: 8 Olympics

Jenner, Edward
nationality: 7 British
discovered: 11 vaccination
19 smallpox inoculation

Jenney, William Le Baron
architect of: 21 Home Insurance Building (Chicago)

jeopardize 4 risk **6** expose,
hazard **7** imperil **8** endanger
10 compromise **11** put into
danger

jeopardy 4 risk **5** peril **6** danger, hazard **8** exposure, unsafety **9** liability **10** insecurity
11 imperilment **12** endangerment **13** vulnerability
14 precariousness

Jephthah 11 Hebrew judge
father: 6 Gilead

Jeremiah
father: 7 Hilkiah
10 Habazaniah
daughter: 7 Mamutal
grandson: 7 Jehohaz
friend, scribe: 6 Baruch

jerk 3 ass, tic, tug **4** dope,
dupe, fool, pull, snap, yank
5 dummy, dunce, idiot, klutz,
pluck, shake, spasm, start,
twist **6** quiver, reflex, thrust,
twitch, wrench **7** tremble
8 convulse **9** trembling

jerky 4 beef, meat **5** jolty,
jumpy **6** choppy, elboic,
jouncy **7** biltong, charqui, fidgety, twitchy **9** dried beef, spasmodic, twitching

Jeroboam
father: 5 Joash, Nebat
successor: 9 Zachariah

jerry-built 4 weak **5** frail, run-
up, shaky, tacky **6** faulty,
flimsy, shoddy, sleazy **7** rickety, unsound **8** gimcrack, slipshod, thrown-up, unstable
9 cheap-jack, defective
10 ramshackle **13** unsubstantial **14** thrown-together

jersey 3 cow **5** maillot, shirt
6 tricot **7** sweater **8** camisole,
guernsey, pullover
10 undershirt

Jersey Joe
nickname of: 10 Joe Walcott

Jerubbaal *see* **6** Gideon

Jerusalem
author: 12 William Blake

Jerusalem
former name: 5 Jebus
pool of: 6 Siloam **8** Bethesda

Jerusalem
Arabic: 14 Bayt al-Muqaddas
capital of: 6 Israel
Hebrew: 12 Yerushalayim
hills: 7 Judaean
landmark: 6 al-Aqsa **11** Wail-

ing Wall, Western Wall
12 Israel Museum **13** Dome
of the Rock **14** Dead Sea
Scrolls **15** Shrine of the
Book **17** Rockefeller Museum **24** Church of the Holy
Sepulcher
mount: 6 Olives, Scopus
river: 6 Kidron
ruler: 5 Arabs, David, Herod
6 Persia, Romans **7** British,
Saladin, Seljuks, Solomon
8 Ayyubids, Fatimids, Ptolemy I **9** Crusaders, Maccabees, Mamelukes **10** Ca-
naanites **12** Antiochus III
13 Pontius Pilate **15** Byzantine Empire **17** Alexander
the Great, Antiochus the
Third
street: 11 Via Dolorosa

Jerusalem Delivered
author: 13 Torquato Tasso

Jervis, Mrs
character in: 6 Pamela
author: 10 Richardson

jessamine 8 Jasminum
varieties: 3 day **5** night,
poet's **6** orange, yellow
12 willow-leaved **13** night-
blooming **14** Carolina yellow

Jesse
father: 4 Obed
grandfather: 4 Boaz
grandmother: 4 Ruth
great-grandfather: 5 Rahab
son: 5 David, Eliab **7** Shammah **8** Abinadab

jest 3 gag, pun **4** fool, game,
gibe, jape, joke, josh, quip
5 act up, crack, laugh, prank,
tease, trick **6** banter, bon mot
9 wisecrack, witticism **10** crack
jokes, pleasantry **11** horse
around

jester 3 wag, wit **4** card, fool,
mime, zany **5** clown, comic,
joker, mimer, mimic **6** madcap, mummer **7** buffoon **8** comedian, funnyman, humorist,
quipster **9** harlequin **10** motley
fool **11** merry-andrew, panto-
mimist, punchinello

jesting 6 joking **7** teasing
8 sportive **9** bantering, unserious **12** wisecracking

Jesus
also called: 7 Holy One, Messiah **8** Nazarene, Son of
God **9** the Christ **12** Man of
Sorrows **13** Prince of Peace
14 Savior Anointed
mother: 4 Mary
stepfather: 6 Joseph
birthplace: 9 Bethlehem
lived in: 8 Nazareth
death place: 9 Jerusalem
buried by: 17 Joseph of
Arimathea
disciples: 4 John, Jude

5 James, Peter, Simon
6 Andrew, Philip, Thomas
7 Matthew **12** James the
Less **13** Judas Iscariot
20 Bartholomew Nathanael
secret follower: 9 Nicodemus
famous discourse: 16 Sermon
on the Mount

jet 4 gush **5** flush, issue, shoot,
spout, spray, spurt, surge,
swash **6** effuse, nozzle, rush
up, squirt, stream **7** sparger,
sprayer, Spritze, syringe **8** atomizer, fountain, shoot out,
Spritzer **9** discharge, sprinkler

Jethro
daughter: 8 Zipporah
son-in-law: 5 Moses

Jetsons, The
character: 5 Astro **10** Jane
Jetson, Judy Jetson **11** Elroy Jetson **12** George Jetson **13** Cosmo G Spacely
voices: 8 Mel Blanc **10** Daws
Butler, Don Messick, Janet
Waldo **13** George O'Hanlon
14 Penny Singleton

jettison 4 dump **5** eject, scrap
6 unload **7** cast off, discard
8 throw out **9** discharge, eliminate, pitch over, throw over
13 toss overboard

jetty 4 dike, dock, mole, pier,
quay, slip **5** black, ebony,
groin, levee, raven, sable,
wharf **6** bridge **7** sea wall
8 buttress **10** breakwater

jeu de mots 3 pun **11** play
on words

jeu d'esprit 9 witticism
17 witty literary work
literally: 12 play of spirit

jeune fille 4 girl **9** young girl
13 unmarried girl

jeunesse doree 11 gilded
youth, golden youth

Jeven 3 God

Jew 6 Essene, Hebrew, Judean,
Semite **7** Edomite, Judaist,
Moabite **8** Hebraist, Sephardi
9 Israelite

jewel 3 ace, gem, pip **4** bead,
dear, find, ring, whiz **5** honey,
pearl, prize, stone, tiara
6 bangle, bauble, brooch,
locket, winner **7** earring, pendant, trinket **8** bracelet, knockout, necklace, ornament, pure
gold, treasure **9** humdinger,
lavaliere **10** topnotcher
11 crackerjack, masterpiece

jewelry 4 gems, gold **6** silver
7 bangles, gewgaws, regalia
8 trinkets **10** adornments
14 precious stones

Jewett, Sarah Orne
author of: 26 The Country of
the Pointed Firs

Jewish 6 Hebrew, Judaic
7 Hebraic, Semitic
bread: 5 matzo **6** matzoh
7 challah
candelabrum: 7 menorah
ceremonial robe: 5 kitel
color: 5 white
coming of age: 10 bar mitzvah, bat mitzvah
dietary laws: 7 kashrut
8 kashruth
group: 8 Hadassah **9** B'nai
B'rith
holy day/festival: 5 Purim,
seder **6** Sukkot **7** Shavuot
8 Chanukah, Hanukkah,
Passover **9** Yom Kippur
12 Rosh Hashanah
law/scripture: 5 Torah **6** Ge-
mara, Talmud, Tanach
7 Mishnah
liturgical prayer: 6 Yigdal
8 Kol Nidre
recited on eve of: 9 Yom
Kippur
marriage canopy: 6 chupah
prayerbook: 6 mahzor, siddur **7** machzor
quarter: 6 ghetto, mellah
school: 5 heder **6** cheder
skullcap: 5 kipah **8** yarmulka
**service to commemorate the
dead: 6** Yizkor
synagogue: 4 shul **5** schul
toast: 8 mazel tov

Jewkes, Mrs
character in: 6 Pamela
author: 10 Richardson

Jew of Malta, The
author: 18 Christopher
Marlowe
character: 7 Abigail, Barabas
8 Ithamore **15** Governor of
Malta

Jezebel
director: 12 William Wyler
cast: 10 Bette Davis, Fay
Bainter, Henry Fonda
11 Donald Crisp, George
Brent **15** Margaret Lindsay
Oscar for: 7 actress (Davis)
17 supporting actress
(Bainter)

Jezebel
father: 7 Ethbaal
husband: 4 Ahab
daughter: 8 Athaliah
opposed: 6 Elijah
killed: 6 Naboth
father-in-law: 4 Omri

jib 3 arm, shy **4** balk, boom,
sail, tack **5** demur, gigue,
stick **6** recoil **7** scruple

Jibaro *see* **6** Jivaro

jibe 2 go **3** fit **4** mesh, tack
5 agree, fit in, match, shift,
tally **6** accord, concur, square

7 conform **8** coincide, dovetail **9** harmonize **10** correspond, go together **11** fit
together

jiffy 4 jiff **5** flash, shake, trice
6 minute, moment, second
7 half a mo, instant **9** twinkling **10** nanosecond **11** microsecond, millisecond, split
second

jigger 4 dram, shot **5** glass
6 device, doodad, gadget, object **7** bicycle, gimmick, measure **9** doohickey, shot glass
10 boneshaker **11** contraption,
thingumabob

jiggle 4 jerk **5** shake **6** bounce,
fidget, joggle, jostle, twitch,
wiggle **7** agitate, wriggle

jihad *see* **5** jehad

jilt 5 leave **6** betray, desert
7 forsake, let down **12** break
off with **17** break an
engagement

Jim
character in: 15 (The Adventures of) Huckleberry Finn
author: 5 Twain

jimmy 3 bar, pry **5** force, lever **7** crowbar

jingle 4 ring **5** clang, clank,
clink, ditty **6** jangle, tinkle
7 clatter, ringing **8** doggerel,
facetiae, limerick **10** catchy
poem, catchy song **12** product
theme **13** reverberation
14 commercial tune
16 tintinnabulation

Jingle, Alfred
character in: 14 Pickwick
Papers
author: 7 Dickens

jingoism 10 chauvinism, flagwaving, patriotics **11** nationalism **14** overpatriotism, spread-
eagleism **15** superpatriotism
16 ultranationalism

jinn 3 imp **5** afrit, demon, ge-
nie, jinni **6** afreet, spirit
8 jinniyeh

jinx 3 hex **5** curse **6** plague,
whammy **7** bugaboo, bugbear,
evil eye, ill wind, nemesis
9 evil spell
French: 9 bete noire

jitterbug 5 dance, lindy **8** lindy
hop **12** boogie-woogie

jitters 6 shakes **7** anxiety, fidgets, jim-jams, shivers, willies
9 jumpiness, quivering, shakiness, tenseness, the creeps,
whim-whams **10** uneasiness
11 butterflies, fidgetiness, nervousness **12** skittishness
13 heebie-jeebies
16 screaming-meemies

jittery 5 jumpy 6 uneasy 7 anxious, nervous

Jivaro, Shuara, Jibaro
  tribe: 6 Achual, Antipa 8 Aguaruna, Huambiza
  location: 4 Peru 7 Ecuador 12 South America
  noted for: 7 tsantsa (shrunken heads)

Joab
  mother: 7 Zeruiah
  brother: 6 Asahel 7 Abishai
  commanded: 10 David's army
  killed: 5 Abner, Amasa 7 Absalom
  killed by: 7 Benaiah
  conspired to overthrow: 5 David

Joad family
  characters in: 16 The Grapes of Wrath
  members: 2 Ma, Pa 3 Tom 4 Noah 6 Connie 12 Rose of Sharon
  author: 9 Steinbeck

Joakim
  wife: 7 Susanna

Joash
  means: 15 Jehovah is strong
  father: 4 Ahab 7 Ahaziah, Jehohaz
  son: 6 Gideon, Shelah 7 Amaziah
  succeeded: 8 Athaliah

job 3 lot 4 care, duty, part, role, spot, task, work 5 chore, craft, field, place, quota, share, stint, trade, trust 6 affair, career, charge, errand, living, metier, office, output 7 calling, concern, mission, opening, portion, product, pursuit 8 activity, business, capacity, contract, exercise, function, position, province, vocation 9 allotment, piecework, situation 10 assignment, commission, engagement, enterprise, livelihood, occupation, profession 11 achievement, appointment, performance, undertaking 14 accomplishment, responsibility

Job
  father: 8 Issachar
  friend: 5 Elihu 6 Bildad, Zophar 7 Eliphaz

job holder 6 worker 8 employee, hireling

job seeker 7 hopeful 8 aspirant 9 applicant, candidate

Jocasta
  also: 8 Epicaste
  queen of: 6 Thebes
  father: 9 Menoeceus
  brother: 5 Creon

  husband: 5 Laius 7 Oedipus
  son: 7 Oedipus 8 Eteocles 9 Polynices
  daughter: 6 Ismene 8 Antigone
  death by: 7 hanging, suicide

Jochebed
  father: 4 Levi
  husband: 5 Amram
  nephew: 5 Amram
  son: 5 Aaron, Moses

jockey 5 Baeza, Krone 6 Arcaro, Pincay 7 Cauthen, Cordero, Cruguet, Hartack 8 McCarron, McHargue, Turcotte 9 Shoemaker, Velasquez

jocose 3 fun 4 arch 5 comic, droll, funny, jolly, merry, witty 6 joking, jovial 7 amusing, comical, jesting, jocular, playful, roguish, teasing, waggish 8 humorous, mirthful, prankish, sportive 9 facetious

jocular 3 gay 5 droll, funny, jolly, merry, witty 6 jocose, jocund, joking, jovial 7 amusing, jesting, playful, roguish, rompish, waggish 8 humorous, mirthful, prankish, sportive 9 facetious 10 frolicsome 12 entertaining, lighthearted

jocund 5 jolly, merry 6 breezy, cheery, elated, jovial, lively 8 cheerful, debonair, pleasant 9 easygoing 10 untroubled 12 happy-go-lucky, lighthearted

Joel
  means: 12 Jehovah is God
  father: 4 Nebo 6 Samuel 7 Azariah, Pedaiah, Pethuel
  brother: 6 Nathan

Joe Palooka
  creator: 9 Ham Fisher 11 Tony DiPreta
  character:
    children: 3 Joe 5 Buddy 7 Joannie
    friend: 9 Little Max 10 Jerry Leemy
    manager: 11 Knobby Walsh
    valet: 6 Smokey
    wife: 8 Anne Howe
  profession: 5 boxer

jog 3 bob, jar, tug 4 jerk, pull, rock, stir, trot, yank 5 nudge, shake, twist 6 bounce, jiggle, jostle, jounce, prompt, twitch, wrench 7 actuate, animate 8 activate, energize 9 stimulate

jogger 4 memo 6 layboy, runner 7 trotter 8 reminder 10 memorandum

Johannesburg
  airport: 8 Jan Smuts
  area: 4 Rand 9 Transvaal
  capital of: 11 South Africa

  landmark: 13 Carlton Centre 14 Africana Museum 16 Union Observatory 17 Zoological Gardens 20 Melrose Bird Sanctuary
  township: 6 Soweto 7 Lenasia 10 Nancefield
  university: 13 Rand Afrikaans, Witwatersrand

John
  father: 7 Zebedee
  brother: 5 James
  son: 5 Peter
  called, with brother: 9 Boanerges 13 sons of thunder
  pertaining to John or his writings: 9 Johannine

John Brown's Body
  author: 19 Stephen Vincent Benet

John Gabriel Borkman
  author: 11 Henrik Ibsen

John Mark *see* 4 Mark

Johnny Belinda
  director: 13 Jean Negulesco
  cast: 8 Lew Ayres 9 Jane Wyman 15 Charles Bickford
  Oscar for: 7 actress (Wyman)

Johnny Cash Show, The
  cast: 9 Jim Varney 10 Howard Mann 11 Carl Perkins, Steve Martin 14 June Carter Cash, Tennessee Three 15 Statler Brothers 32 Mother Maybelle and the Carter Family

Johnny-come-lately 8 newcomer 9 latecomer 10 new arrival 11 late arrival

Johnny U
  nickname of: 12 Johnny Unitas

Johns, Glynis
  born: 8 Pretoria 11 South Africa
  roles: 11 Mary Poppins 13 The Sundowners 17 A Little Night Music 26 Around the World in Eighty Days

Johns, Jasper
  born: 9 Augusta GA
  artwork: 4 Flag 6 Studio, Target 8 Watchman 10 Fool's House 12 Device Circle 13 Painted Bronze (Beer Cans) 14 The Barber's Tree 19 Target with Four Faces 22 Target with Plaster Casts

Johnson, Andrew *see box*

Johnson, Earvin
  nickname: 5 Magic
  sport: 10 basketball
  position: 5 guard
  team: 16 Los Angeles Lakers

Johnson, Andrew
  presidential rank: 11 seventeenth
  party: 8 Democrat
  state represented: 2 TN
  defeated: 5 no one
    succeeded upon death of: 7 Lincoln
  vice president: 4 none
  cabinet:
    state: 6 (William Henry) Seward
    treasury: 9 (Hugh) McCulloch
    war: 7 (Edwin McMasters) Stanton 9 (John McAllister) Schofield
    attorney general: 5 (James) Speed 6 (William Maxwell) Evarts 8 (Henry) Stanbery
    navy: 6 (Gideon) Welles
    postmaster general: 7 (Alexander Williams) Randall 8 (William) Dennison
    interior: 5 (John Palmer) Usher 6 (James) Harlan 8 (Orville Hickman) Browning
  born: 9 Raleigh NC
  died: 16 Carter's Station TN
  buried: 13 Greeneville TN
  education: 9 no college 12 self-educated
  political career: 8 US Senate 13 vice president 22 House of Representatives
    only president to be: 9 impeached (1868)
    found: 9 not guilty
    mayor of: 11 Greeneville (TN)
    governor of: 9 Tennessee
  civilian career: 6 tailor
  military service: 8 Civil War 12 US Volunteers 16 brigadier general
    military governor of: 9 Tennessee
  notable events of lifetime/term: 14 Reconstruction
    Purchase: 6 Alaska
  father: 5 Jacob
  mother: 4 Mary (McDonough)
    stepfather: 15 Turner Dougherty
  sibling: 7 William
  wife: 5 Eliza (McCardle)
  children: 4 Mary 6 Andrew, Martha, Robert 7 Charles

Johnson, Jack (John Arthur)
  nickname: 11 Little Artha 14 Galveston Giant
  sport: 6 boxing
  class: 11 heavyweight

Johnson, Lyndon Baines
see box, p. 524

Johnson, Philip Cortelyou
  architect of: 10 Glass House (New Canaan CT), Wiley House (New Canaan CT) 12 Hodgson House (New Canaan CT) 13 Pennzoil Place (Houston TX) 14 Bolssonas House (New Canaan CT) 16 Amon Carter Museum (Ft Worth TX) 17 Sheldon Art Gallery (Lincoln NE) 18 A T and T Headquarters (NYC), Kline Science Center (Yale) 19 New York State Theater (Lincoln Center)

Johnson, Samuel
  author of: 8 Rasselas, The Idler 18 The Lives of the Poets 22 The Vanity of Human Wishes 30 Dictionary of the English Language

Johnson, Walter
  nickname: 8 Big Train
  sport: 8 baseball
  position: 7 pitcher
  team: 18 Washington Senators

John the Baptist
  father: 9 Zechariah
  mother: 9 Elizabeth
  descendant of: 5 Aaron
  precurser of: 5 Jesus 10 the Messiah

joie de vivre 11 joy of living 19 delight in being alive

join 3 hug, mix 4 abut, ally, band, bind, fuse, glue, link, meet, pool 5 affix, brush, chain, enter, graze, marry, merge, paste, reach, skirt, stick, touch, unify, unite 6 adjoin, attach, bridge, cement, cohere, couple, fasten, scrape, solder, splice 7 combine, connect, verge on 8 border on, enlist in, enroll in, federate, hold fast 9 associate, cooperate, syndicate 10 amalgamate, fraternize 11 confederate, consolidate 12 conglomerate

joined 3 met, wed 4 tied 5 bound, fused, glued, mated, yoked 6 allied, bonded, linked, merged, paired, seamed, united, welded 7 coupled, married, related, spliced 8 attached, cemented, combined, enlisted, fastened 9 bracketed, connected 10 associated, hand-in-hand, integrated 11 hand-in-glove

join forces 4 ally 5 merge, unite 6 league, team up 7 combine 8 coalesce 9 affiliate, cooperate 11 consolidate 12 band together

joint 4 hock, knee, knot, link 5 elbow, hinge, nexus 6 allied, common, mutual, shared, united 7 knuckle, unified 8 combined, communal, coupling, junction, juncture 9 associate, community, conjoined, corporate, unanimous 10 associated, collective, connection, hand-in-hand, like-minded 11 coalitional, conjunctive, cooperative 12 articulation, consolidated 13 collaborative
  kind:
    ball and socket: 3 hip 8 shoulder
    fused: 5 skull 11 base of spine
    hinged: 4 knee 5 elbow
    unfused: 3 hip, jaw 4 knee 5 elbow 8 shoulder

joint action 7 concert 8 teamwork 11 cooperating, cooperation, give-and-take 13 collaboration, participation

joint effort 7 concert 8 teamwork 11 cooperation 13 collaboration

jointly 8 arm in arm, in common, in unison, mutually, together, unitedly 10 conjointly, hand-in-hand, side by side 12 collectively 13 in association, in conjunction

join together 3 wed 4 fuse, weld 5 marry, unify, unite 6 solder 9 integrate 10 amalgamate 11 consolidate, incorporate

Johnson, Lyndon Baines
   nickname: **3** LBJ **15** Landslide Lyndon
   presidential rank: **11** thirty-sixth
   party: **10** Democratic
   state represented: **2** TX
   succeeded upon death of: **7** Kennedy
   defeated: **4** (Earle Harold) Munn, (Eric) Hass **6** (John) Kasper **7** (Clifton) DeBerry **9** (Barry Morris) Goldwater
   vice president: **4** none (first term) **8** (Hubert Horatio) Humphrey
   cabinet:
      state: **4** (David Dean) Rusk
      treasury: **4** (Joseph William) Barr **6** (Clarence Douglas) Dillon, (Henry Hamill) Fowler
      defense: **8** (Clark McAdams) Clifford, (Robert Strange) McNamara
      attorney general: **5** (William Ramsey) Clark **7** (Robert Francis) Kennedy **10** (Nicholas deBelleville) Katzenbach
      postmaster general: **6** (Lawrence Francis) O'Brien, (William Marvin) Watson **9** (John Austin) Gronouski
      interior: **5** (Stewart Lee) Udall
      agriculture: **7** (Orville Lothrop) Freeman
      commerce: **5** (Cyrus Rowlett) Smith **6** (John Thomas) Connor, (Luther Hartwell) Hodges **10** (Alexander Buel) Trowbridge
      labor: **5** (William Willard) Wirtz
      HEW: **5** (Wilbur Joseph) Cohen **7** (John William) Gardner **10** (Anthony Joseph) Celebrezze
      HUD: **4** (Robert Colwell) Wood **6** (Robert Clifton) Weaver
      transportation: **4** (Alan Stevenson) Boyd
   born: **11** (near) Stonewall TX
   died/buried: **13** (near) Johnson City TX
   education:
      teachers' college: **19** Southwest Texas State
      law school: **10** Georgetown
   religion: **17** Disciples of Christ
   vacation spot: **8** LBJ Ranch
   author: **15** The Vantage Point
   political career: **8** US Senate **13** vice president **24** US House of Representatives
   civilian career: **7** teacher
   military service: **6** US Navy **10** World War II **11** World War Two
   notable events of lifetime/term: **9** race riots **12** Great Society
      act: **11** Civil Rights **12** Voting Rights **19** Economic Opportunity
      assassination of: **14** Robert F Kennedy **18** Martin Luther King Jr
      capture of: **6** Pueblo
      Pueblo captured by: **10** North Korea
      treaty: **23** Nuclear Non-Proliferation
      war: **7** Vietnam **11** Arab-Israeli
   father: **7** Sam Ealy
   mother: **7** Rebekah (Baines)
   siblings: **10** Sam Houston **12** Lucia Huffman **13** Josefa Hermine, Rebekah Luruth
   wife: **7** Claudia (Alta Taylor)
      nickname: **8** Lady Bird
   children: **9** Lynda Bird **10** Luci Baines
   First Lady:
      responsible for: **24** Highway Beautification Act
      author: **16** A White House Diary

6 solder **9** integrate **10** amalgamate **11** consolidate, incorporate

join up 6 enlist, enroll, sign up **9** volunteer

joist 4 beam **5** brace **6** timber **7** support

joke 3 gag, pun, wit **4** butt, dupe, fool, gibe, goof, gull, jape, jest, josh, lark, mock, quip **5** antic, caper, cinch, clown, farce, prank, put-on, roast, tease, trick **6** banter, bon mot, deride, frolic, gambol, gibe at, jeer at, parody, satire, take in, target, trifle, whimsy **7** buffoon, bumpkin, chortle, lampoon, laugh at, nothing, scoff at, smile at, snicker **8** anecdote, badinage, pooh-pooh, pushover, repartee, ridicule, town fool, travesty **9** burlesque, diversion, horseplay, simpleton, wisecrack, witticism **10** pleasantry **11** horse around, monkeyshine **13** facetiousness, laughingstock

joker 3 wag, wit **4** snag, trap, zany **5** catch, clown, hitch, mimic, rider, snare, trick **6** jester, madcap **7** codicil, pitfall, punster **8** addendum, comedian, funnyman, humorist **10** subterfuge, supplement **11** wisecracker
   French: **7** farceur

jokester 3 wag **5** comic, cutup, joker **8** comedian **9** prankster

Joliba *see* **5** Niger

Joliot-Curie, Frederic
   field: **9** chemistry
   nationality: **6** French
   discovered: **23** artificial radioisotopes
   awarded: **10** Nobel Prize
   wife: **16** Irene Joliot-Curie

Joliot-Curie, Irene
   field: **7** physics
   nationality: **6** French
   discovered: **23** artificial radioisotopes
   awarded: **10** Nobel Prize
   husband: **14** Frederic Joliot
   father: **11** Pierre Curie
   mother: **10** Marie Curie

jollity 3 fun **4** glee, play, romp **5** cheer, mirth, revel, sport **6** frolic, gaiety **7** revelry, whoopee **8** hilarity **9** amusement, festivity, jocundity, joviality, merriment, pleasure **10** jocularity **11** merrymaking **12** conviviality

jolly 3 gay **5** droll, funny, happy, merry **6** jocund, jovial **7** gleeful, jocular, playful **8** cheerful, mirthful, sportive

9 fun-loving **10** delightful, rollicking **12** high-spirited

jolt 3 bob, jar, jog **4** bump, jerk, jump, stun **5** lurch, quake, shake, shock, start, throw, upset **6** bobble, bounce, jiggle, joggle, jostle, jounce, quiver, trauma, twitch **7** disturb, perturb, setback, shake up, shaking, startle **8** convulse, reversal **9** agitation, take aback **11** thunderbolt

Joltin' Joe
nickname of: **11** Joe DiMaggio

Jonah
father: **7** Amittai
swallowed by: **9** large fish
preached in: **7** Nineveh
hometown: **10** Gathhepher

Jonathan
means: **11** Jehovah gave
father: **4** Jada, Saul **6** Joiada, Kereah **8** Abiathar
friend: **5** David
son: **9** Meribkaal **12** Mephibosheth

Jonathan Livingston Seagull
author: **11** Richard Bach

Jonathan Wild
author: **13** Henry Fielding

Jones, Carolyn
born: **10** Amarillo TX
roles: **8** Morticia **15** The Addams Family

Jones, Inigo
architect of: **11** Queen's House (Greenwich) **14** Banqueting Hall (Whitehall Palace, London)
restoration: **16** St Paul's Cathedral

Jones, James
author of: **7** Whistle **14** The Thin Red Line **15** Some Came Running **18** From Here to Eternity

Jones, James Earl
born: **11** Arkabutla MS
roles: **6** The Man **7** Othello **8** Star Wars **15** The Emperor Jones **17** The Great White Hope
voice of: **10** Darth Vader

Jones, John Paul
served in: **11** Russian navy **16** Revolutionary War **21** British merchant marine
commander of ship: **6** Ranger **10** Providence **15** Bonhomme Richard
defeated ship: **7** Serapis
saying: **23** "I have not yet begun to fight"

Jones, Shirley
husband: **11** Jack Cassidy, Marty Ingels
born: **10** Smithton PA

roles: **8** Carousel, Oklahoma **11** Elmer Gantry, The Music Man **18** The Partridge Family

Jong, Erica
author of: **5** Fanny **12** Fear of Flying **18** At the Edge of the Body **20** How to Save Your Own Life

jonquil 4 bulb, lily **8** daffodil **9** narcissus

Jonson, Ben
author of: **6** The Fox **7** Sejanus, Volpone **11** A Tale of a Tub **12** The Alchemist **15** Bartholomew Fair **18** Every Man in His Humo(u)r **21** Every Man out of His Humo(u)r **23** Epicene or the Silent Woman

Jordan *see box*

Jordan, Robert
character in: **19** For Whom the Bell Tolls
author: **9** Hemingway

Jormungandr
also: **10** Jormungand **11** Iormungandr **14** Midgard Serpent
origin: **12** Scandinavian
form: **7** serpent
father: **4** Loki
mother: **9** Angerboda, Angrbodha, Angurboda
brother: **6** Fenrir, Fenris
sister: **3** Hel
wrapped around: **5** world
killed by: **4** Thor
death place: **6** Vigrid
killed: **4** Thor

Jo's Boys
author: **15** Louisa May Alcott

Jordan
other name: **24** Hashemite Kingdom of Jordan
capital/largest city: **5** Amman
ancient name: **12** Philadelphia
others: **4** Krak, Ma'an, Salt **5** Agaba, Ariha, Irbid, Jenin, Karak, Kerak, Sarga, Zarga, Zerke **6** Bethel, Hebron, Jarash, Jerash, Madaba, Nablus, Ramtha **7** Al-Agaba, Bethany, El-Kerak, El Zerga, Jericho, Kirmoab, Nabulus, Samaria **8** Al-Khalil, Ram Allah **9** Bethlehem, Jerusalem
school: **7** yarmouk
division: **8** East Bank, West Bank **11** Transjordan
ancient state: **4** Edom, Moab **5** Ammon, Judah **6** Gilead
head of state: **4** king
monetary unit: **4** fils **5** dinar
mountain: **3** Hor **4** Nebo **5** Bukka, Dabab **6** Ataiba, Gilead, Mubrak
highest point: **9** Jabal Ramm, Jebel Ramm
river: **6** Jordan, Yarmuk **11** Nahr-az-Zarga
sea: **3** Red **4** Dead **7** Galilee **13** Mediterranean
physical feature:
  desert: **6** Syria
  gulf: **5** Aqaba
  plateau: **11** Transjordan
  valley: **4** Ghor **9** Great Rift
  wind: **7** Khamsin
people: **4** Arab, Kurd **7** Bedouin, Checher **8** Armenian, Assyrian **10** Circassian **11** Palestinian
  ancient: **8** Armonite **9** Nabataean
  ruler: **5** Talal **6** Faisal, Greeks, Romans **7** Hussein **8** Abdullah, Selucidas **9** Crusaders **10** Ibn Hussein, Nabataeans **12** Ottoman Turks **18** Abdullah Ibn Hussein
  tribe: **5** Qaysi **6** Yamani
language: **6** Arabic
religion: **5** Islam **13** Greek Orthodox
place:
  canal: **8** East Gher
  ruins: **5** Ajlun, Petra **6** Jarash **7** Al Karak
feature:
  headdress: **8** kaffiyeh
  village headman: **7** mukhtar
  village square: **5** sahah
food:
  dessert: **7** baklava
  pastry: **7** katayif

Joseph
father: 4 Bani 5 Aseph, Jacob 10 Mattathias
mother: 6 Rachel
brother: 3 Dan, Gad 4 Levi 5 Asher, Judah 6 Reuben, Simeon 7 Zebulun 8 Benjamin, Issachar, Naphtali
wife: 4 Mary 7 Asenath
stepson: 5 Jesus
also called: 20 Barsabbas of Arimathea 21 Barsabbas of Arimathaea
buried: 5 Jesus
slave of: 8 Potiphar

Joseph Andrews
author: 13 Henry Fielding
character: 5 Fanny 9 Lady Booby 11 Mrs Slipslop, Parson Adams, Peter Pounce 13 Pamela Andrews

josh 3 guy, kid, rag, rib 4 dish, haze, jape, jest, jive, joke, quiz, razz, ride, twit 5 chaff, jolly, put on, roast, tease 6 banter, needle 8 ridicule

Joshua
means: 18 Jehovah is salvation
father: 3 Nun
succeeded: 5 Moses
captured: 7 Jericho, Lachish
hid spies: 5 Rahab

Josiah
means: 12 Jehovah heals
father: 9 Zephaniah
succeeded: 4 Amon

jostle 3 jab 4 bump, butt, poke, prod, push 5 crowd, elbow, shove 7 collide 8 shoulder 10 hit against, run against 12 knock against

jot 3 bit, dot 4 list, mite, note, snip, whit 5 enter, speck, trace 6 record, trifle 7 modicum, one iota, put down, set down, smidgen, snippet 8 flyspeck, particle, register, scribble, take down 9 scintilla

Jotham
son: 4 Ahaz

Jo the crossing sweeper
character in: 10 Bleak House
author: 7 Dickens

jotting 4 memo, note 6 doodle 8 scribble 10 memorandum, scribbling

Jotun
origin: 12 Scandinavian
form: 5 giant
conflicts with: 4 gods
enemy: 4 Asar 5 Aesir

Jotunheim
origin: 12 Scandinavian
realm of: 6 giants

Joukahainen
origin: 7 Finnish
form: 8 magician

location: 7 Lapland
tried to kill: 11 Vainamoinen

Joule, James Prescott
field: 7 physics
nationality: 7 British
established law of: 20 conservation of energy
named for him: 10 unit of work

jounce 3 bob 6 bounce 7 rebound 8 ricochet

Jourdain, Monsieur
character in: 21 The Bourgeois Gentleman 22 Le Bourgeois Gentilhomme
author: 7 Moliere

Jourdan, Louis
real name: 11 Louis Gendre
born: 6 France 9 Marseille
roles: 4 Gigi 6 Can Can 9 Octopussy 15 The Paradine Case 23 Three Coins in the Fountain 24 Letter from an Unknown Woman

journal 3 log 5 album, daily, diary, paper, sheet 6 annual, ledger, memoir, record, weekly 7 almanac, daybook, gazette, history, logbook, monthly, tabloid 8 calendar, magazine, notebook, register, yearbook 9 chronicle, newspaper, quarterly, scrapbook 10 chronology, confession, memorandum, memory book, periodical, record book 11 account book, daily record, publication 13 autobiography

journalist 6 author, editor, writer 7 byliner, diarist, newsman 8 reporter 9 columnist, newswoman 12 newspaperman 13 correspondent 14 newspaperwoman

Journal of the Plague Year, A
author: 11 Daniel Defoe

journey 3 fly, way 4 roam, rove, sail, tour, trek, trip, wend 5 jaunt, quest, route, tramp 6 course, cruise, flight, junket, outing, ramble, roving, travel, voyage, wander 7 circuit, meander, odyssey, passage, transit 8 divagate, navigate, sightsee, vagabond 9 excursion, itinerary, take a trip, wandering 10 divagation, expedition, pilgrimage 11 peregrinate 13 peregrination

Journey Into Fear
author: 10 Eric Ambler

journey's end 4 goal 9 objective 11 destination

Journey to the End of the Night
author: 20 Louis-Ferdinand Celine

joust 4 tilt 5 combat, jostle 7 contend, contest, tourney 8 run a tilt 10 contention, tournament

Jove see 7 Jupiter

jovial 3 gay 5 jolly, merry, sunny 6 blithe, cheery, hearty, jocose, jocund 7 buoyant, gleeful, jocular, playful, zestful 8 cheerful, humorous, laughing, mirthful, sportive 9 convivial, fun-loving, hilarious 10 delightful, frolicsome, rollicking

joviality 3 fun 4 glee 5 cheer, gaity, mirth 7 delight, jollity, revelry 8 buoyancy 9 jocundity, merriment 10 joyfulness, liveliness 11 high spirits

jowl 3 jaw 5 cheek, chops 6 muzzle 8 mandible

joy 3 gem 4 glee 5 jewel, pride, prize 6 gaiety 7 delight, ecstasy, elation, rapture 8 gladness, pleasure, treasure 9 enjoyment, happiness 10 excitement, exultation, jubilation 11 contentment, delectation 12 cheerfulness, exhilaration, satisfaction
goddess of: 6 Hathor

Joyce, James
author of: 7 Ulysses 9 Dubliners 13 Finnegan's Wake 31 A Portrait of the Artist as a Young Man

joyful 4 glad, rosy 5 happy 6 bright, elated 7 blessed, pleased 8 cheerful, ecstatic, exultant, gladsome, jubilant, pleasing 9 delighted, full of joy, overjoyed 10 delightful, enraptured, gratifying, heartening 11 pleasurable, transported 12 heartwarming

joyless 3 sad 4 glum, grim 5 black 6 dismal, gloomy, morbid, woeful 7 doleful, forlorn, unhappy 8 dejected, desolate, dolorous, downcast, mournful 9 cheerless, depressed, sorrowful, woebegone 10 despondent, in the dumps, lugubrious, melancholy 11 downhearted, pessimistic 12 disconsolate, heavyhearted 14 down in the mouth

joy of living
French: 11 joie de vivre

Joy of Sex, The
author: 11 Alex Comfort

joyous 3 gay 4 glad 5 happy, merry 7 festive, gleeful 8 cheerful, gladsome, mirthful 9 rapturous, wonderful 10 delightful, gratifying, hearten-

ing **11** pleasurable
12 heartwarming, lighthearted

joyousness 4 glee **8** gladness
9 happiness, merriment
10 blitheness, exuberance
11 high spirits
16 lightheartedness

Jubal
father: **6** Lamech
mother: **4** Adah
brother: **5** Jabal

jubilant 3 gay **4** glad **5** happy,
jolly, merry **6** blithe, cheery,
elated, enrapt, joyful, joyous
7 buoyant, charmed, gleeful,
pleased, radiant, smiling
8 cheerful, ecstatic, exultant,
gladsome, laughing, mirthful
9 delighted, delirious, exuberant, gladdened, gratified, overjoyed, rapturous, rejoicing,
rhapsodic **10** blithesome, captivated, enraptured **11** exhilarated, intoxicated, tickled
pink **12** happy as a lark, lighthearted **13** in high spirits

jubilation 5 bliss **9** rejoicing
11 celebration **12** exhilaration

jubilee 2 do **4** bash, fete, gala
5 blast, party **6** frolic, revels
7 blowout, holiday, revelry,
shindig **8** festival, wingding
9 festivity **10** jubilation, observance **11** anniversary, celebration, merrymaking
12 conviviality
13 commemoration

Juda
father: **6** Joanna, Joseph
8 Hananiah

Judah
father: **5** Jacob
mother: **4** Leah
brother: **3** Dan, Gad **4** Levi
5 Asher, Judah **6** Joseph,
Reuben, Simeon **8** Benjamin,
Issachar, Naphtali
sister: **5** Dinah
wife: **5** Shuah
son: **2** Er **4** Onan **5** Perez,
Zerah **6** Baruch, Shelah
daughter-in-law: **5** Tamar
last king of: **8** Zedekiah
descendant of: **8** Judahite

Judah, tribes of *see* **14** Israel, tribes of

Judas
brother: **5** James
also called: **8** Thaddeus
disciple of: **5** Jesus

Judas Iscariot 8 betrayer
disciple of: **5** Jesus
betrayed: **5** Jesus
replaced by: **8** Matthias

Jude 7 apostle
brother: **5** James

Jude the Obscure
author: **11** Thomas Hardy

character: **10** Jude Fawley
12 Arabella Donn, Sue
Bridehead **14** Drusilla Fawley **16** Little Father Time
17 Richard Phillotson

judge 3 try **4** deem, find, hear,
rank, rate **5** fancy, gauge,
guess, infer, juror, value,
weigh **6** assess, assume, censor, critic, decide, deduce, expert, reckon, regard, review,
rule on, settle, size up, umpire **7** adjudge, analyze, arbiter, believe, conduct, discern,
imagine, justice, referee, resolve, suppose, surmise **8** appraise, assessor, conclude,
consider, estimate, official, reviewer **9** appraiser, arbitrate,
ascertain, authority, determine,
evaluator, moderator **10** adjudicate, arbitrator, conjecture,
magistrate **11** adjudicator, connoisseur, distinguish **12** pass
sentence

judgment, judgement
4 view **5** sense, taste **6** acumen, belief, decree, ruling
7 finding, opinion, verdict
8 decision, estimate, sentence
9 appraisal, deduction, valuation **10** assessment, conclusion, conviction, discretion,
perception, persuasion,
shrewdness **11** arbitration, discernment, percipience **14** discrimination, perceptiveness

Judgment at Nuremberg
director: **13** Stanley Kramer
cast: **11** Judy Garland
12 Spencer Tracy **13** Burt
Lancaster **14** Richard Widmark, William Shatner
15 Marlene Dietrich, Montgomery Clift **16** Maximilian
Schell
Oscar for: **5** actor (Schell)

Judgment Day 8 doomsday
13 end of the world **14** day of
reckoning **15** the Last
Judgment

Judgment Day
author: **13** James T Farrell

Judgment of Paris *see*
5 Paris

judicial 5 legal **8** imposing, juristic, majestic, official **9** mag-
istral **11** magisterial
13 distinguished

judiciary 5 bench, court
11 court system

judicious 4 just, sage, wise
5 acute, sober, sound **6** astute,
shrewd **7** knowing, politic,
prudent, tactful **8** sensible
9 sagacious **10** diplomatic, discerning, percipient, reasonable,
reflective, thoughtful **11** level-

headed **13** perspicacious
14 discriminating

judiciousness 4 tact **6** acumen,
wisdom **8** prudence, sagacity
9 good sense **10** discretion
11 discernment, percipience
12 perspicacity
14 discrimination

Judique, Mrs Tanis
character in: **7** Babbitt
author: **5** Lewis

Judith
husband: **4** Esau
killed: **10** Holofernes

Judith Paris
author: **11** Hugh Walpole

jug 3 jar, urn **4** ewer **5** crock,
stein **6** bottle, carafe, flagon,
vessel **7** pitcher, tankard **8** decanter, demijohn **9** container

juggle 4 redo **5** alter **6** modify
7 falsify **8** disguise, fool with
9 keep aloft **10** manipulate,
meddle with, reorganize,
tamper with, tinker with
12 misrepresent

juggler 5 cheat **6** jester **8** con-
juror, deceiver, jongleur, magician, shuffler **15** prestidigitator

Juice
nickname of: **9** O J Simpson

juicy 3 wet **4** lush, racy **5** fluid,
lurid, moist, pulpy, runny,
sappy, spicy, vivid **6** fluent,
liquid, risque, watery **7** flowing, graphic **8** colorful, dripping, exciting, luscious
9 succulent, thrilling **10** intriguing **11** captivating, fascinating, picturesque,
provocative, sensational,
tantalizing

Jules and Jim
director: **16** Francois Truffaut
cast: **10** Henri Serre
11 Marie Dubois, Oskar
Werner **12** Jeanne Moreau

Julia
character in: **20** Two Gentlemen of Verona
author: **11** Shakespeare

Julia
character: **10** Corey Baker,
Eddie Edson, Julia Baker
11 Hannah Yarby **14** Earl J
Waggedorn, Marie Wagge-
dorn **15** Dr Morton Chegley
cast: **10** Lloyd Nolan, Marc
Copage **11** Betty Beaird, Michael Link **12** Eddie Quillan,
Lurene Tuttle, Paul Win-
field **14** Diahann Carroll

Julia
director: **13** Fred Zinnemann
based on story by: **14** Lillian
Hellman (Pentimento)
cast: **9** Jane Fonda (Lillian

Hellman) **11** Hal Holbrook **12** Jason Robards (Dashiell Hammett) **15** Vanessa Redgrave (Julia) **16** Maximilian Schell
Oscar for: 12 screenwriter **15** supporting actor (Robards) **17** supporting actress (Redgrave)

Julius Caesar
author: 18 William Shakespeare
character: 6 Brutus (Marcus Brutus), Portia **7** Cassius (Gaius Cassius) **9** Calpurnia **10** Mark Antony (Marcus Antonius)
director: 17 Joseph L Mankiewicz
cast: 10 James Mason **11** Deborah Kerr, Greer Garson, John Gielgud **12** Edmond O'Brien, Louis Calhern, Marlon Brando

July
flower: 8 larkspur **9** water lily
French: 7 Juillet
holiday: 11 Bastille Day (14), Dominion Day (1) **15** Independence Day (4) **16** Saint Swithin's Day (15)
gem: 4 ruby
German: 4 Juli
Italian: 6 Luglio
number of days: **9** thirty-one
origin of name: 12 Julius Caesar
place in year:
Gregorian: **7** seventh
Roman: **5** fifth
Spanish: 5 Julio
Zodiac sign: 3 Leo **6** Cancer

jumble 3 mix **4** heap, mess, olio, stew **5** bunch, chaos, mix up, pitch, snarl **6** ball up, medley, muddle, pile up, tangle, tumble **7** clutter, farrago, melange, mixture, scatter **8** disarray, mishmash **9** aggregate, confusion, patchwork, potpourri **10** hodgepodge, miscellany, salmagundi **11** gallimaufry **12** accumulation **14** conglomeration

jumbled 5 messy **7** chaotic, mixed up, snarled, tangled **8** confused **9** cluttered, illogical **10** disjointed, incoherent **11** disarranged **12** disconnected, disorganized

jumbo 4 huge, vast **5** giant **6** mighty **7** immense, mam-

moth, titanic **8** colossal, enormous, gigantic, towering **9** cyclopean, monstrous, oversized **10** monumental, stupendous **11** elephantine, mountainous

jump 3 hop **4** buck, leap, pass, skip **5** boost, bound, pitch, start, surge, vault, wince **6** ambush, attack, blench, bounce, flinch, gambol, go over, hurdle, prance, recoil, spring, switch, upturn, zoom up **7** advance, barrier, digress, maunder, overrun, upsurge **8** fall upon, obstacle **9** barricade, increment, skyrocket **10** impediment **11** obstruction **12** augmentation

jumper 4 frog, sled, toad **5** dress, horse, shirt, smock **6** blouse, hopper, jacket, leaper **7** overall **8** coverall, kangaroo

jump for joy 5 exult **7** rejoice

jumpy 5 nervy, shaky **6** goosey, uneasy **7** alarmed, anxious, fidgety, fretful, jittery, nervous, panicky, twitchy, uptight **8** aflutter, agitated, fluttery, skittish **9** trembling, twitching **10** frightened **12** apprehensive

junction 6 linkup **7** conflux, joining **10** confluence, crossroads **11** concurrence, convergence, interchange **12** intersection

juncture 4 pass, seam **5** joint **6** crisis, linkup, moment **7** closure, joining, meeting **8** interval, occasion **10** confluence, connection **11** convergence, point in time **12** intersection **13** critical point

June *see box*

jungle 4 bush, wild **5** woods **10** rain forest, wilderness **11** undergrowth **12** swampy forest, virgin forest

Jungle, The
author: 13 Upton Sinclair
character: 3 Ona **5** Jonas **6** Marija **8** Elzbieta **12** Jurgis Rudkus **13** Antanas Rudkus
criticism of: 19 meat-packing industry

Jungle Books, The
author: 14 Rudyard Kipling
character: 3 Kaa **5** Akela, Baloo, Hathi **6** Buldeo, Messau, Mowgli **8** Bagheera **9** Shere Khan **11** Gray Brother

Jungle Jim
creator: 11 Alex Raymond
character: 4 Joan, Kolu

junior 5 later, lower, minor, newer **6** lesser **7** younger

June
characteristic:
8 weddings
event: 12 Midsummer Day (24), Midsummer Eve (23) **14** summer solstice (21)
flower: 4 rose
French: 4 Juin
gem: 5 pearl **9** moonstone **11** alexandrite
German: 4 Juni
holiday: 7 Flag Day (14) **10** Father's Day (third Sunday) **13** Kamehameha Day (11) **22** Jefferson Davis' birthday (3)
Italian: 6 Giugno
number of days: 6 thirty
origin of name: 4 Juno (Roman goddess) **6** Junius (Roman clan) **8** juniores (youths)
place in year:
Gregorian: **5** sixth
Roman: **6** fourth
saying: 24 What is so rare as a day in June
Spanish: 5 Junio
Zodiac sign: 6 Cancer, Gemini

8 inferior **9** secondary **11** subordinate

juniper 9 Juniperus
varieties: 4 ashe, plum **5** Greek, Irish, shore **6** common, ground, needle, Polish, Sierra, Syrian **7** African, incense, prickly, Sargent **8** creeping, drooping, mountain, red-berry, Waukegan **9** alligator, blue-spire, Himalayan, prostrate **10** California **11** cherrystone **12** Canary Island, sweet-fruited **13** Rocky Mountain

junk 4 dump **5** scrap, trash, waste **6** debris, litter, refuse **7** clutter, discard, garbage, rubbish, rummage **8** castoffs, oddments, throw out **9** dispose of, throw away **11** odds and ends

junket 4 tour, trip **7** journey **9** excursion

Juno
origin: 5 Roman
queen of: 6 heaven
father: 6 Saturn
brother: 7 Jupiter
husband: 7 Jupiter
son: 4 Mars
protectress of: 5 women **8** marriage
epithet: 6 Lucina, Moneta **7** Curitis, Pronuba, Sospita
festival: 10 Matronalia
corresponds to: 4 Hera, Here

Juno and the Paycock
author: **10** Sean O'Casey

junta 5 cabal **7** council **9** committee **18** military government

Jupe, Sissy
character in: **9** Hard Times
author: **7** Dickens

Jupiter
also: **4** Jove
god of: **5** light **7** heavens, weather **9** lightning **11** thunderbolt
epithet: **5** Ultor **7** Elicius, Pluvius
corresponds to: **4** Zeus

Jupiter
position: **5** fifth
satellite: **2** Io **6** Europa **8** Amalthea, Callisto, Ganymede
characteristic: **7** red spot

Jurassic period
dinosaur from: **10** Diplodocus **11** Apatosaurus, Stegosaurus **12** Brontosaurus, Camarasaurus, Camptosaurus, Ceratosaurus, Megalosaurus **13** Brachiosaurus, Compsognathus, Ornitholestes

Jurgen
author: **17** James Branch Cabell

Jurgens, Curt
also: **11** Curd Jurgens
born: **6** Munich **7** Germany
roles: **12** The Blue Angel **16** The Spy Who Loved Me

jurisdiction 3 say **4** area, beat, rule, sway, zone **5** field, range, reach, scope **6** bounds, domain, sphere **7** circuit, command, compass, control, quarter **8** district, dominion, hegemony, latitude, precinct, province **9** authority, bailiwick **10** legal right **11** prerogative

jurist 5 judge **6** lawyer **7** counsel, justice **8** advocate, attorney **9** barrister, counselor, solicitor **10** magistrate **12** legal adviser **13** attorney-at-law

jury 5 panel, peers **6** assize, twelve **9** committee, makeshift, veniremen

jury-rigged 9 improvised, makeshift, temporary

jus 3 law **5** right

jus civile 8 civil law

jus gentium 12 law of nations

jus naturale 11 law of nature

jus sanguinis 12 right of blood
(law) citizenship of child is same as: **7** parents

jus soli 11 right of land, right of soil
(law) citizenship of child based on place of: **5** birth

just 3 but, due **4** fair, firm, good, only, sane **5** fully, moral, quite, solid, sound **6** at most, barely, decent, hardly, honest, lately, merely, proper, simply, strong, worthy **7** condign, ethical, exactly, fitting, logical, merited, only now, upright **8** adequate, balanced, deserved, entirely, narrowly, recently, scarcely, sensible, suitable, unbiased **9** befitting, blameless, equitable, honorable, impartial, justified, objective, perfectly, precisely, reputable, righteous, unbigoted, uncorrupt **10** aboveboard, absolutely, acceptable, completely, evenhanded, fairminded, high-minded, no more than, nothing but, not long ago, principled, reasonable, scrupulous, upstanding **11** appropriate, justifiable, trustworthy, well-founded **12** conscionable, open to reason, unprejudiced, well-grounded **13** conscientious, disinterested, dispassionate

just about 6 almost, around, barely, nearly **7** close to **10** not far from **12** on the point of **13** approximately

Just Above My Head
author: **12** James Baldwin

just a moment ago
French: **11** tout a l'heure

justice 5 honor, right, truth **6** amends, equity, the law, virtue **7** honesty, payment, penalty, probity, redress **8** fair play, fairness, goodness, legality **9** atonement, integrity, rightness **10** correction, lawfulness, legitimacy, reparation **11** just desserts, proper cause, uprightness **12** chastisement, compensation, equitability, remuneration, satisfaction **13** due punishment, equitableness, justification, righteousness **17** constitutionality
god of: **7** Forsete, Forseti
goddess of: **4** Dice, Dike **6** Astrea **7** Astraea

Justice
author: **14** John Galsworthy

Justice Clement
character in: **19** Every Man in His Humour
author: **6** Jonson

justice to all
Latin: **15** justitia omnibus
motto of: **18** District of Columbia

justifiable 9 excusable **10** defensible **11** explanatory, extenuating, supportable

justification 5 alibi **6** excuse **7** apology, defense, pretext, support **8** sanction **10** accounting, adjustment, validation **11** explanation, vindication **12** confirmation **13** rectification **14** reconciliation

justification for existence
French: **11** raison d'etre

justify 6 back up, defend, excuse, uphold **7** bear out, confirm, explain, support, sustain, warrant **8** sanction, validate **9** vindicate **10** account for, prove right

justitia omnibus 12 justice to all
motto of: **18** District of Columbia

just now
French: **11** tout a l'heure

just the same 6 anyhow, anyway **12** nevertheless

just the thing 7 apropos **8** suitable **11** appropriate **12** exactly right

Justus see **5** Titus

jut 5 bulge **6** beetle, extend **7** poke out, project **8** overhang, protrude, shoot out, stand out, stick out **13** thrust forward

jute 19 Corchorus capsularis
varieties: **5** Bimli, China, Tossa, white **7** bastard **10** Bimlipatum

Juturna
form: **5** nymph
goddess of: **5** lakes **7** streams
father: **6** Daunus
brother: **6** Turnus
loved by: **7** Jupiter

juvenile 5 child, minor, young, youth **6** boyish, callow, infant, junior **7** girlish **8** childish, immature, teenager, youthful **9** childlike, pubescent, stripling, youngster **10** adolescent, sophomoric **15** unsophisticated

Juventas
protectress of: **14** military age men

juxtaposed 6 next to **8** adjacent, touching **9** proximate **10** contiguous, side by side **12** conterminous

juxtaposition 5 touch **7** balance, contact **8** contrast, nearness **9** adjacency, proximity **10** apposition, contiguity

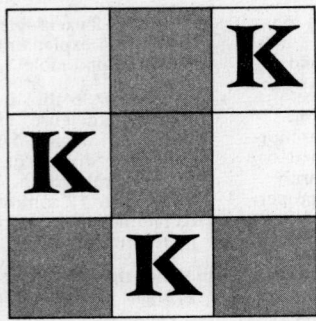

K
character in: 9 The Castle
author: 5 Kafka

Ka
origin: 8 Egyptian
form: 6 spirit
trait: 11 immortality

kabob 5 cabab, cabob, kabab, kebab, kebob 7 shaslik 8 shashlik 9 shashlick

Kabul
capital of: 11 Afghanistan

Kafka, Franz
author of: 7 Amerika 8 The Trial 9 The Castle 16 The Metamorphosis

kahlua
type: 6 brandy
origin: 6 Mexico
flavor: 6 coffee
with rum: 10 Black Maria
with tequila: 9 Brave Bull
with vodka: 12 Black Russian

Kahn, Albert
architect of: 15 River Rouge Plant 17 Highland Park Plant 20 Athletic Club Building (Detroit) 21 General Motors Building (Detroit)

Kahn, Louis Isadore
architect of: 16 Kimbell Art Museum (Ft Worth TX) 23 Yale Center for British Art 24 Yale University Art Gallery 28 Phillips Exeter Academy Library (NH) 31 Richards Medical Research Building (U of PA) 33 Salk Institute for Biological Studies (La Jolla CA)

Kahn, Madeline
born: 8 Boston MA
roles: 9 Paper Moon 10 What's Up Doc? 14 Blazing Saddles 17 Young Frankenstein

kaiser 5 ruler 7 emperor, Wilhelm 8 autocrat

kakemono 6 scroll 13 hanging object

kale 16 Brassica oleracea (Acephala Group)
varieties: 3 sea 4 Ruvo, tall, tree 6 Indian, Scotch 7 cabbage, Chinese, Italian, kitchen 8 Siberian 9 flowering, Tronchuda 10 decorative, ornamental, Portuguese 13 dwarf Siberian 16 ornamental-leaved

kaleidoscopic 6 mobile, motley 7 protean 8 shifting, unstable, variable 9 checkered 10 changeable, variegated 11 fluctuating, many colored, rainbowlike, vacillating 12 ever-changing

Kaleva 8 folk hero
origin: 7 Finnish 8 Estonian

Kalevala
origin: 7 Finnish
form: 4 epic

Kali
also: 3 Uma 5 Durga 7 Parvati
husband: 4 Siva 5 Shiva
festival: 6 dewali
goddess of: 5 death 7 disease

Kalidasa
author of: 9 Meghaduta, Sakuntala 10 Shakuntala 14 Cloud Messenger

Kalimantan see 6 Borneo

Kalki
author: 9 Gore Vidal

Kampala
capital of: 6 Uganda

Kampuchea see 8 Cambodia

Kandinsky, Wassily (Vasily)
born: 6 Moscow, Russia
artwork: 7 Striped 8 Twilight 10 Black Lines 11 Impressions 12 Blue Mountain (no 84), Compositions, Violet Orange

13 Black Relation 14 Improvisations 15 Capricious Forms 17 Bavarian Mountains, The Street in Murnau 23 Painting with White Border

Kanga
character in: 13 Winnie the Pooh
author: 5 Milne

kangaroo
young: 4 joey
group of: 3 mob 5 troop

Kaniengehaga *see* 6 Mohawk

Kansas *see* box

Kansas City
baseball team: 6 Royals
basketball team: 5 Kings
football team: 6 Chiefs
landmark: 12 Union Station 22 Nelson-Atkins Art Gallery
river: 6 Kansas 8 Missouri

Kant, Immanuel
author of: 20 Critique of Pure Reason

Kantor, MacKinlay
author of: 13 Andersonville

Karloff, Boris
real name: 17 William Henry Pratt
born: 7 Dulwich, England
roles: 12 Frankenstein

karma 3 act 4 aura, deed, duty, fate, rite 5 force, power 6 action, kismet, spirit 7 destiny 9 vibration

Kasdan, Lawrence
director of: 11 The Big Chill

Kashmiri
language family: 12 Indo-European
branch: 11 Indo-Iranian
group: 5 Indic
spoken in: 5 (northern) India

kashruth, kashrut 7 fitness 17 Jewish dietary laws

Kansas
  abbreviation: 2 KS **4** Kans
  nickname: 5 Wheat **9** Jayhawker, Sunflower **15** Garden of
    the West
  capital: 6 Topeka
  largest city: 7 Wichita
  others: 4 Hays, Iola **5** Colby, Dodge **6** Salina **7** Abilene,
    Chanute, Emporia, Liberal **8** Atchison, Lawrence **9** Great
    Bend **10** Belleville, Hutchinson, Kansas City **11** Coffeeville,
    Leavenworth **12** Junction City
  college: 5 Baker, Tabor **7** Bethany **8** Sterling, Washburn
  explorer: 8 Coronado
  feature: 16 Eisenhower Center
    fort: **5** Riley, Scott
    Indian training school: **16** Haskell Institute
    penitentiary: **11** Leavenworth
    reservoir: **11** Tuttle Creek
  tribe: 3 Kaw **4** Pani **5** Kansa, Kiowa, Osage **6** Pawnee
    7 Arapaho, Wichita **8** Cheyenne, Comanche, Kickapoo
  people: 7 Jayhawk **11** Damon Runyon **13** Amelia Earhart,
    Karl Menninger **14** Walter Chrysler **15** Edgar Lee Masters
  lake: 6 Cheney, Kerwin, Neosho **7** Milford
  land rank: 10 fourteenth
  mountain:
    highest point: **9** Sunflower
  physical feature:
    plains: **5** Great, Osage
  president: 17 Dwight D Eisenhower
  river: 3 Kaw **6** Kansas **8** Arkansas, Cimarron, Missouri
    9 Smoky Hill **10** Republican
  state admission: 12 thirty-fourth
  state bird: 17 western meadowlark
  state flower: 9 sunflower
  state motto: 29 To the Stars Through Difficulties
  state song: 14 Home on the Range
  state tree: 10 cottonwood

Katharina
  character in: 19 The Taming
    of the Shrew
  author: 11 Shakespeare

Katmandu, Kathmandu
  capital of: 5 Nepal

Katzenjammer Kids
  also: 17 Captain and the Kids
  creator: 12 Rudolph Dirks
  character: 4 Hans **5** Fritz,
    Momma **10** der Captain
    12 der Inspector

Kaufman, George S
  author of:
    with Edna Ferber: **9** Stage
    Door **13** Dinner at Eight
    14 The Royal Family
    with Moss Hart: **15** Once
    in a Lifetime **20** You
    Can't Take It with You
    21 The Man Who Came
    to Dinner

Kay (Sir Kay)
  character in: 16 Arthurian
    romance
  foster brother: 6 Arthur

Kaye, Danny
  real name: 19 David Daniel
    Kaminski
  born: 10 Brooklyn NY

  roles: 19 The Inspector Gen-
    eral **21** Hans Christian
    Andersen

Kaye, M M
  author of: 9 Trade Wind
    12 Death in Kenya **15** Death
    in Zanzibar, Shadow of the
    Moon, The Far Pavilions

Kazakhstan
  capital/largest city: 7 Alma-
    Ata
  others: 9 Karaganda **13** Petro-
    pavlovsk, Semipalatinsk
  head of state: 9 president
  government: 8 republic
  monetary unit: 5 ruble
  sea: 4 Aral **7** Caspian
  physical feature: 7 steppes
    12 Lake Balkhash
  people: 6 Kazakh
  language: 6 Kazakh

Kazan, Elia
  director of: 10 East of Eden,
    Viva Zapata **15** On the Wa-
    terfront (Oscar) **18** Splendor
    in the Grass **19** Gentleman's
    Agreement (Oscar) **20** A Tree
    Grows in Brooklyn **21** A
    Streetcar Named Desire

Kazantzakis, Nikos
  author of: 13 Zorba the Greek
    14 Freedom or Death, The
    Greek Passion **25** The Last
    Temptation of Christ

kazoo 5 bazoo, zarah **6** hewgag
  11 eunuch flute
  French: 8 mirliton

Keach, Stacy
  real name: 18 Walter Stacy
    Keach Jr
  born: 10 Savannah GA
  roles: 3 Doc **6** Luther **10** Mike
    Hammer **24** Twinkle Twinkle
    Killer Kane

Kearny, Stephen Watts
  served in: 10 California, Mexi-
    can War
  commander of: 13 Army of
    the West
  occupied: 9 New Mexico
  battle: 10 San Gabriel, San
    Pasqual

Keaton, Buster
  real name: 19 Joseph Francis
    Keaton
  born: 7 Piqua KS
  roles: 6 Go West **7** College
    10 The General **12** The
    Cameraman

Keaton, Diane
  real name: 9 Diane Hall
  born: 12 Los Angeles CA
  roles: 4 Reds **7** Sleeper **8** Baby
    Boom **9** Annie Hall (Oscar)
    12 Shoot the Moon, The
    Godfather **13** The Good
    Mother **14** Play It Again Sam
    19 Looking for Mr Goodbar
    20 The Little Drummer Girl

Keats, John
  author of: 5 Lamia **8** Endymi-
    on, Hyperion, Isabella
    11 Ode to Autumn, Ode to
    Psyche **14** Ode on Indolence
    15 Ode on Melancholy, The
    Eve of St Agnes **16** Ode on a
    Grecian Urn **17** Ode to a
    Nightingale **20** La Belle
    Dame Sans Merci **31** On
    First Looking into Chap-
    man's Homer

Kedemah
  also called: 5 Kedar
  father: 7 Ishmael
  mother: 5 Hagar
  descendant of: 8 Kedarite

Keel (of Argo)
  constellation of: 6 Carina

Keel, Howard
  real name: 17 Harry Clifford
    Leek
  costar: 14 Kathryn Grayson
  born: 11 Gillespie IL
  roles: 6 Dallas, Kismet
    8 Showboat **10** Kiss Me

Kate **13** Clayton Farlow
15 Annie Get Your Gun
27 Seven Brides for Seven
Brothers

Keeler, Ruby
husband: 8 Al Jolson
costar: 10 Dick Powell
born: 6 Canada **7** Halifax
roles: 15 Footlight Parade
17 Forty-Second Street
32 Gold Diggers of Nineteen
Thirty Three

keel over 5 faint, swoon, upset **7** capsize, tip over **8** collapse, fall down, fall flat, flip
over, overturn, turn over
10 turn turtle

keen 4 avid, fine **5** acute, alert,
eager, sharp **6** ardent, astute,
clever, fervid, fierce, shrewd
7 earnest, excited, fervent, intense, zealous **8** incisive **9** impatient, paper thin, razorlike
10 discerning **11** finely honed,
impassioned, penetrating,
quick-witted **12** enthusiastic
13 perspicacious
14 discriminating

keen-eyed 5 alert **8** vigilant,
watchful **9** attentive, eagle-
eyed, observant, sharp-eyed,
wide-awake

keen-minded 5 acute, sharp,
smart **6** astute, clever, shrewd
10 perceptive **11** penetrating

keenness 4 zeal, zest **5** ardor
6 acumen, fervor **7** passion
9 acuteness, eagerness, sharpness **10** astuteness, cleverness,
enthusiasm, excitement,
shrewdness **11** discernment
12 anticipation, intelligence,
perspicacity

keen-sighted 4 sage, wise
5 acute, sharp **6** astute,
shrewd **8** piercing **9** eagle-
eyed, judicious, sagacious,
sharp-eyed **10** discerning
11 intelligent, penetrating
12 clear-sighted, sharp-sighted
13 perspicacious

keep 3 bar **4** clog, fort, have,
heap, hold, mind, pile, stay
5 abide, block, carry, cramp,
delay, deter, guard, honor, lay
in, place, stack, stall, stand,
stick, stock, store, tie up,
tower **6** arrest, castle, detain,
donjon, endure, hamper,
hinder, hobble, hold up,
impede, living, pay for, remain, retain, retard **7** care for,
carry on, citadel, deposit, furnish, inhibit, observe, possess,
prevent, shackle, support, sustain **8** conserve, continue, encumber, fortress, hang on to,
hold back, maintain, obstruct,
preserve, restrain **9** celebrate,
constrain, hamstring, perse-

vere, persist in, ritualize, safeguard, solemnize, watch over
10 accumulate, daily bread,
livelihood, provide for, stronghold, sustenance **11** commemorate, maintenance,
memorialize, subsistence
12 room and board
13 fortification

keep an eye on 5 watch
7 oversee **9** chaperone, look
after, watch over

keep apart 7 isolate **8** separate **9** segregate

keep at bay 7 beat off, fend
off, ward off **8** stave off

keep back 5 check, delay
6 detain, hold up, retain
8 withhold

keep busy 3 use **6** employ, engage, occupy **7** utilize

keep clear of 4 shun **5** avoid,
dodge, elude, evade, skirt
6 escape

keep company 4 date **5** court
7 consort, hang out **8** go
around, go steady **9** accompany, associate **10** fraternize,
go together

keeper 5 guard, nurse
6 duenna, escort, jailer, sentry,
warden **7** curator **8** chaperon,
guardian, retainer, sentinel,
wet nurse **9** attendant, bodyguard, caretaker, chaperone,
custodian, governess, nursemaid, protecter, protector
11 conservator, nurserymaid
13 guardian angel

keep in mind 8 consider, remember **10** think about

keep mum 13 button one's lip

keep off 7 fend off, stay off,
ward off **8** stave off

keep one's counsel 12 remain silent **13** button one's
lip

keep open 8 hold open
16 leave unscheduled

keep out 6 reject **8** prohibit
9 blackball, blacklist

keep out of sight 4 hide
5 cover **6** lay low, lie low
7 conceal, cover up, secrete
10 camouflage

keep private 4 hide **7** conceal,
reserve **8** withhold

keepsake 5 relic, token **6** emblem, memory, symbol **7** memento **8** memorial, reminder,
souvenir **11** remembrance
18 token of remembrance

keep secret 4 hide **6** hush
up **7** conceal, cover up **8** suppress, withhold

keep silent 10 remain dumb
15 not breathe a word

keep steady 5 poise **7** balance **9** stabilize

keep to 5 cling, stick **6** adhere, be true, cleave, hold to
7 be loyal, stand by
8 maintain

keg 3 tub, tun, vat **4** butt,
cask, drum, tank **6** barrel
7 rundlet **8** hogshead, puncheon **9** container, kilderkin

Kellerman, Sally
born: 11 Long Beach CA
roles: 4 MASH **15** Hot Lips
Houlihan

Kelly, Gene
real name: 17 Eugene Curran
Kelly
born: 12 Pittsburgh PA
roles: 7 Pal Joey **9** Brigadoon, On the Town **13** Anchors Aweigh **15** Singin' in
the Rain **17** An American
in Paris **18** The Three
Musketeers

Kelly, Grace
husband: 21 Prince Rainier
Grimaldi
nickname: 11 Ice Princess
born: 14 Philadelphia PA
roles: 7 Mogambo **8** High
Noon **10** Rear Window
11 High Society **13** To Catch
a Thief **14** Dial M for Murder, The Country Girl
(Oscar)

Kelly, Walt
creator/artist of: 4 Pogo

kelp 3 ash **4** agar, alga, leag
5 varec, varic, wrack
7 seaweed
source of: 4 soda **6** iodine
9 potassium

Kelpie
origin: 8 Scottish
form: 5 horse **6** spirit
habitat: 4 lake **5** river
causes: 8 drowning
warns of: 8 drowning

Kelvin
abbreviation: 1 K

Kelvin, William Thomson
field: 7 physics
11 mathematics
nationality: 7 British
worked on: 4 heat
11 electricity
invented: 12 electrometer,
galvanometer **13** tide
predictor
named for him: 22 Kelvin
temperature scale

Kempis, Thomas a
author of: 20 The Imitation
of Christ

Kenaz
father: 7 Eliphaz
son: 5 Caleb 7 Othniel

Keneally, Thomas
author of: 12 Confederates
14 Schindler's List

Kenilworth
author: 14 Sir Walter Scott
character: 6 Alasco, Dudley
(Earl of Leicester) 10 Amy
Robsart 12 Wayland Smith
13 Richard Varney
14 Queen Elizabeth 15 Flibbertigibbet 16 Edmund
Tressilian

Kennedy, Arthur
real name: 17 John Arthur
Kennedy
born: 11 Worcester MA
roles: 6 Becket 9 All My
Sons 11 Peyton Place
12 Blind Victory 16 Death
of a Salesman

Kennedy, Frank
character in: 15 Gone With
the Wind
author: 8 Mitchell

Kennedy, John Fitzgerald
see box

**Kennicott, Dr Will and
Carol**
characters in: 10 Main Street
author: 5 Lewis

Kentucky *see box, p. 534*

Kenya *see box, p. 535*

Kepler, Johannes
nationality: 6 German
invented: 14 convex eye-
piece 21 astronomical
telescope
formulated:
*three laws of planetary
motion (Kepler's Laws):*
10 law of areas 11 har-
monic law 24 elliptical
orbit of planets
author of: 14 Astronomia
nova, Harmonice mundi
16 Rudolphine Tables
23 Mysterium cosmographi-
cum 30 Epitome astronom-
iae Copernicanae

Ker
form: 6 spirit
associated with: 5 death
corresponds to: 6 Furies

kerchief 5 cloth, scarf 7 muffler 8 babushka, neckwear
9 headpiece, neckcloth
11 neckerchief
12 handkerchief

Keres
origin: 5 Greek
spirits of: 4 evil 5 death
6 old age 7 disease

Keres-Siouan
language branch: 5 Keres

Kennedy, John Fitzgerald
nickname: 3 JFK 4 Jack
presidential rank: 11 thirty-fifth
party: 10 Democratic
state represented: 2 MA
defeated: 5 (Richard Milhous) Nixon
vice president: 7 (Lyndon Baines) Johnson
cabinet:
state: 4 (David Dean) Rusk
treasury: 6 (Clarence Douglas) Dillon
defense: 8 (Robert Strange) McNamara
attorney general: 7 (Robert Francis) Kennedy
postmaster general: 3 (James Edward) Day 9 (John
Austin) Gronouski
interior: 5 (Stewart Lee) Udall
agriculture: 7 (Orville Lothrop) Freeman
commerce: 6 (Luther Hartwell) Hodges
labor: 5 (William Willard) Wirtz 8 (Arthur J) Goldberg
HEW: 8 (Abraham Alexander) Ribicoff 10 (Anthony Joseph) Celebrezze
born: 11 Brookline MA
died: 8 Dallas TX
died by: 13 assassination
assassinated by: 6 (Lee Harvey) Oswald
buried: 25 Arlington National Cemetery
education:
prep school: 6 Choate
University: 7 Harvard 9 Princeton 23 London School of
Economics
religion: 13 Roman Catholic
interests: 7 sailing 8 football 13 touch football
vacation spot: 9 Cape Cod MA 13 Hyannis Port MA
author: 15 Strategy of Peace, Why England Slept 17 Profiles in Courage (Pulitzer Prize)
political career: 9 US Senator 24 US House of
Representatives
civilian career: 17 newspaper reporter
military service: 6 US Navy 10 lieutenant 11 World War
Two
commander of: 6 PT boat
notable events of lifetime/term: 9 Bay of Pigs 10 Berlin
Wall, Peace Corps 18 Cuban missile crisis
march: 11 Civil Rights
treaty: 14 Nuclear Test-Ban
quote: 17 Ich bin ein Berliner (I am a Berliner) 35 We
stand today on the edge of a New Frontier 61 Ask not
what your country can do for you ask what you can do
for your country
father: 13 Joseph Patrick
mother: 4 Rose (Fitzgerald)
siblings: 4 Jean 6 Eunice, Joseph 8 Kathleen, Patricia,
Rosemary 11 Edward Moore 13 Robert Francis
wife: 10 Jacqueline (Lee Bouvier)
nickname: 6 Jackie
second marriage to: 7 Onassis
children: 14 John Fitzgerald, Patrick Bouvier (died in infancy) 15 Caroline Bouvier

7 Caddoan 9 Iroquoian
11 Siouan-Yuchi

kernel 3 nub, nut, pip, pit
4 core, germ, gist, pith, seed
5 grain, stone 6 center, marrow 7 nucleus 12 quintessence

Kerouac, Jack
author of: 6 Big Sur 9 On
the Road 13 The Dharma
Bums 16 Lonesome Traveler

Kerr, Deborah
real name: 22 Deborah Jane
Kerr-Trimmer
born: 8 Scotland
11 Helensburgh
roles: 11 Edward My Son,
The King and I 12 The
Hucksters 13 The Sundown-
ers 14 Separate Tables, The
Chalk Garden 18 From Here
to Eternity 19 The Night of

Kentucky
  abbreviation: 2 KY
  nickname: 9 Bluegrass 11 Corncracker
  capital: 9 Frankfort
  largest city: 10 Louisville
  others: 5 Berea 6 Corbin, Hazard 7 Ashland, Glasgow,
    Newport, Paducah, Shively 8 Danville 9 Covington, Hen-
    derson, Lexington, Owensboro 12 Bowling Green, Hop-
    kinsville, Madisonville
  college: 5 Berea 6 Centre 7 Ashbury, Brescia 8 Ursuline
    12 Transylvania
  explorer: 11 Daniel Boone
  feature: 7 Obelisk
    birthplace: 14 Abraham Lincoln
    fort: 4 Knox
    national park: 11 Mammoth Cave
    race: 13 Kentucky Derby
    racetrack: 14 Churchill Downs
    trail: 10 Wilderness
  tribe: 7 Shawnee 8 Cherokee, Iroquois
  people: 11 corncracker, John M Harlan 13 Louis Brandeis
    16 Frederick M Vinson, Robert Penn Warren
  lake: 8 Kentucky 10 Cumberland
  land rank: 13 thirty-seventh
  mountain: 4 Pine 10 Cumberland
    highest point: 5 Black 8 Big Black
  physical feature:
    basin: 9 Bluegrass
    cave: 7 Mammoth
    gap: 10 Cumberland
    plain: 7 Coastal
    plateau: 10 Cumberland
  president: 14 Abraham Lincoln
    Confederate president: 14 Jefferson Davis
  river: 3 Dix 4 Ohio, Salt 5 Green 6 Barren 7 Licking 8 Big
    Sandy, Kentucky 9 Tennessee 10 Cumberland
    11 Mississippi
  state admission: 9 fifteenth
  state bird: 8 cardinal
  state flower: 9 goldenrod
  state motto: 26 United We Stand Divided We Fall
  state song: 17 My Old Kentucky Home
  state tree: 10 coffee tree 11 tulip poplar 12 yellow poplar

the Iguana 20 Heaven
Knows Mr Allison

Kesey, Ken
  author of: 21 Sometimes a
  Great Notion 25 One Flew
  Over the Cuckoo's Nest

Ketcham, Hank
  creator/artist of: 15 Dennis
  the Menace

kettle 3 pan, pot, tub, vat
  6 boiler, teapot, tureen 8 cauldron, crucible, saucepan

Ketubim 8 writings
  11 Hagiographa

Keturah
  husband: 7 Abraham

key 3 cue, fit 4 clue, gear,
  mode, suit 5 adapt, light,
  point, scale 6 adjust, answer,
  direct, opener 7 address, finding, meaning, pointer 8 indi-
  cant, solution, tonality

9 indicator 10 exposition, indication, resolution 11 elucidation, explanation, explication,
translation 14 interpretation

Key, Ted
  creator/artist of: 5 Hazel

keyboard instrument 5 organ, piano 6 spinet 8 psaltery,
virginal 9 harmonium 10 clavichord, pianoforte
11 harpsichord

keyed up 5 tense 7 excited,
nervous 8 volatile 9 emotional,
explosive

key element 9 essential, vital
part 18 primary constituent
20 indispensable element

Key Largo
  director: 10 John Huston
  based on story by: 15 Maxwell Anderson
  cast: 12 Claire Trevor, Lauren Bacall 14 Humphrey Bo-

gart 15 Edward G Robinson,
Lionel Barrymore
Oscar for: 17 supporting ac-
tress (Trevor)

Keynes, John Maynard
  author of: 44 The General
  Theory of Employment Interest and Money

keynote 3 nub 4 core, gist,
pith 5 heart, theme 6 marrow
7 essence, nucleus, pattern
8 main idea, quiddity 9 substance 11 nitty-gritty, salient
idea 12 central point

keystone 4 base, crux, root
5 basis 8 gravamen, linchpin
9 principle 10 foundation,
mainspring

Keystone State
  nickname of:
  12 Pennsylvania

Key to Rebecca, The
  author: 10 Ken Follett

Khachaturian, Aram Ilich
  born: 6 Tiflis 7 (Soviet)
  Georgia
  composer of: 6 Gayane
  9 Spartacus 12 Song of
  Stalin

khaki 5 cloth 6 fabric 7 uniform 9 olive-drab
14 yellowish-brown

khan, kahn 3 inn 4 lord
5 chief, ruler 6 prince 7 emperor 9 chieftain, sovereign
11 caravansary
  famous: 4 Yuan 6 Kublai
  7 Genghis 8 Ghenghis

Khartoum
  capital of: 5 Sudan

Khartvelian
  language family: 9 Caucasian
  includes: 8 Georgian

Khayyam, Omar
  author of: 11 The Rubaiyat

Khnum
  origin: 8 Egyptian
  form: 3 ram
  created: 6 humans
  used: 4 clay

Khoisan
  language spoken by: 3 San
  7 Bushmen 9 Khoikhoin
  10 Hottentots
  includes: 5 Hatsa 7 Sandawe
  distinguishing sound: 5 click

kibitzer 3 pry 5 prier, snoop
6 butt-in 7 meddler, snooper,
watcher 8 busybody
9 buttinsky

kick 3 fun, hit, out, pep, vim,
4 beef, boot, dash, fret, fume,
fuss, life, punt, snap, tang,
zest 5 eject, force, gripe,
growl, power, punch, verve,
vigor 6 flavor, grouch, grouse,

Kenya
  capital/largest city: 7 Nairobi
  others: 5 Nyeri, Thika, Wajir 6 Kisumu, Kitale, Lodwar,
    Moyale, Nakuru, Webuye 7 Eldoret, Kericho, Malindi,
    Mandera, Mombasa, Nanyuki 9 Lokitaung
  measure: 4 wari
  monetary unit: 4 cent 5 pound 8 shilling
  island: 5 Manda, Patta
  lake: 6 Magadi, Nakuru, Natron, Rudolf 7 Turkana 8 Nai-
    vasha, Victoria
  mountain: 5 Elgon, Kulai, Nyira, Nyiru 6 Matian 7 Lo-
    gonot 8 Aberdare
  highest point: 5 Kenya 6 Kinyaa 9 Kirinyaga
  river: 3 Lak 4 Athi, Dawa, Kuja, Tana 5 Nzoia 6 Galana
    8 Turkwell
  sea: 6 Indian
  physical feature:
    bay: 7 Formosa
    desert: 6 Chalbi
    escarpment: 3 Mau
    gulf: 9 Kavirondo
    highlands: 5 Kenya, Kisii, Luyla 7 Kericho
    plain: 4 Kano
    plateau: 5 Nandi, Yatta 6 Elgeyo
    valley: 9 Great Rift
  people: 3 Luo 4 Arab, Meru 5 Bantu, Elgey, Galla, Kamba,
    Kisii, Luhya, Masai, Nandi, Tugen 6 Kikuyu, Ogaden, So-
    mali 7 Baluhya, Hamitic, Hilotic, Kipsigi, Swahili, Tur-
    kana 8 Kalenjin, Marakwet
    god: 4 Ngai
    leader: 5 Mboya 12 Jomo Kenyatta 13 Daniel Arap Moi
  language: 3 Luo 5 Bantu, Luhya, Masai 6 Kikuyu
    7 English, Swahili 8 Guyerati 10 Hindustani
  religion: 5 Islam 7 animism 8 Anglican 13 Roman Catholic
  place:
    archeological excavation: 11 Gamble's Cave
    mosque: 5 Khoja
    museum: 9 Fort Jesus
    national park/wildlife preserve: 4 Meru 5 Nyeri, Tsavo
      6 Arusha 7 Manyara, Nairobi, Samburu 8 Aberdare,
      Amboseli 10 Lake Nakuru, Mount Kenya, Rift Valley
    ruins: 4 Gedi
  feature:
    garment: 5 kanga 7 kitenge
    round house: 6 shamba
    secret organization: 6 Mau Mau
    tree: 6 ayieke, baobab
  food:
    fish: 7 tilapia
    wine: 5 tembo

object, recoil, remove, return,
strike, stroke, thrill 7 boot
out, cast out, grumble, fly
back, protest, rebound, sparkle, turn out 8 backlash, complain, jump back, piquancy,
pleasure, pungency, reaction,
throw out, vitality 9 amusement, animation, complaint,
enjoyment, find fault, grievance, intensity, make a fuss,
objection 10 excitement,
spring back 11 give the gate,
remonstrate, send packing,
show the door 12 protestation 13 gratification,
remonstration

Kickapoo
  language family: 9 Algon-
    kian 10 Algonquian
  location: 5 Texas 6 Kansas,
    Mexico 9 Chihuahua,
    Wisconsin
  related to: 3 Fox, Sac 4 Sauk

kickback 3 cut 5 bribe, graft,
  share 6 boodle, payoff, payola
  9 hush money 10 commission,
  percentage, protection, recompense 12 compensation, remuneration 15 protection money

kick downstairs 4 bust 6 demote 7 degrade

kickoff 5 start 7 opening 9 beginning, inception, launching
  12 inauguration

kick out 4 oust 5 eject, evict,
  expel 8 throw out 9 discharge

kicks 3 fun 7 thrills 8 pleasure
  10 excitement 11 stimulation

kick upstairs 5 boost 7 advance, elevate, promote

Kicva
  origin: 5 Welsh
  husband: 7 Pryderi

kid 3 rag, rib, tot 4 baby, fool,
  gull, jest, joke, josh, mock,
  ride, tyke 5 bluff, child, cozen,
  harry, put on, tease, trick,
  youth 6 delude, infant, moppet, plague, shaver, squirt
  7 beguile, deceive, laugh at,
  mislead 8 goat hide, goatskin,
  hoodwink, juvenile, ridicule,
  teenager, yearling 9 bamboozle, billy goat, little one,
  make fun of, nanny goat, offspring, young goat, youngster
  10 adolescent 11 goat leather,
  young person 12 little shaver

Kid, The
  nickname of: 11 Ted
    Williams

kid around 5 clown, cut up
  10 fool around, play around
  11 clown around

Kidder, Margot
  born: 6 Canada 11 Yellow
    Knife
  roles: 7 Sisters 8 Lois Lane,
    Superman 14 Some Kind of
    Hero 19 The Amityville
    Horror

Kiddush 6 prayer 8 blessing
  14 sanctification

kidnap 5 seize, steal 6 abduct,
  hijack, snatch 7 bear off, capture, impress, skyjack 8 bear
  away, carry off, shanghai
  10 run off with 11 make off
  with 13 hold for ransom

Kidnapped
  author: 20 Robert Louis
    Stevenson
  character: 9 Alan Breck
    10 Rankeillor 12 David Bal-
    four 15 Ebenezer Balfour

Kigali
  capital of: 6 Rwanda

Kiley, Richard
  born: 9 Chicago IL
  roles: 7 Redhead 13 Man of
    La Mancha 16 Advise and
    Consent

Kilkenny Cats
  origin: 5 Irish
  form: 4 cats
  number: 3 two
  left after fight: 5 tails

kill 4 beat, do in, halt, hang, ruin, slay, stay **5** break, check, drown, erase, lynch, quell, shoot, waste **6** behead, defeat, murder, poison, rub out, stifle **7** bump off, butcher, cut down, destroy, execute, garrote, silence, smother, squelch, wipe out **8** blow away, dispatch, get rid of, knock off, massacre, strangle, string up **9** dismember, finish off, shoot down, slaughter, suffocate **10** asphyxiate, decapitate, disembowel, extinguish, guillotine, put a stop to, put an end to, put to death **11** assassinate, burn to death, electrocute, exterminate **13** mortally wound

killer 6 hit man, slayer **7** butcher **8** assassin, murderer **11** executioner **12** exterminator

Killers, The
  director: 13 Robert Siodmak
  based on story by: 15 Ernest Hemingway
  cast: 10 Ava Gardner **12** Edmond O'Brien **13** Burt Lancaster

killer whale 4 orca **7** grampus **11** Orcinus orca

killing 4 coup **5** fatal **6** big hit, deadly, lethal, mortal, murder **7** bonanza, cleanup, deathly, hanging, slaying, success, suicide **8** butchery, fatality, homicide, lynching, massacre, regicide, shooting, smash hit, stabbing, windfall **9** bloodshed, execution, garroting, martyrdom, matricide, murderous, patricide, poisoning, slaughter, uxoricide **10** cleaning up, decimation, fratricide, immolation, impalement, sororicide, strangling **11** crucifixion, devastating, elimination, infanticide **12** annihilation, death-dealing, decapitation, excruciating, guillotining, manslaughter, master stroke, stroke of luck, violent death **13** electrocution, extermination, strangulation **17** capital punishment

Killing Fields
  director: 11 Roland Joffe
  based on article by: 15 Sydney Schanberg (The Death and Life of Dith Pran)
  cast: 10 Haing S Ngor **12** Sam Waterston
  Oscar for: 15 supporting actor (Ngor)

Killing Time
  author: 12 Thomas Berger

killjoy 6 grouch **8** grumbler, sourball, sourpuss **9** Cassandra, gloomy Gus, worrywart

10 complainer, malcontent, spoilsport, wet blanket **11** crapehanger, party-pooper

kill time 4 idle **6** dawdle **9** waste time **10** fool around

Kilmer, Joyce
  author of: 5 Trees

kiln 3 ost **4** bake, burn, fire, oast, oven **5** drier, glaze, stove, tiler **7** furnace **8** calciner, limekiln **9** oasthouse

kiloliter
  abbreviation: 2 kL

kilometer
  abbreviation: 2 km

Kilwich
  origin: 5 Welsh
  form: 6 prince
  performed: 6 labors
  number of labors: 4 five
  married: 5 Olwen

Kim
  author: 14 Rudyard Kipling
  character: 9 Mahbub Ali **11** Tibetan Lama **12** Kimball O'Hara **16** Colonel Creighton **22** Hurree Chunder Mookerjee

kin 4 akin, clan, kith, race **5** folks, tribe **6** family, people **7** kinfolk, kinsmen, related **8** clansmen, kinfolks **9** next of kin, relations, relatives, tribesmen **10** kith and kin **11** connections, consanguine, distaff side, spindle side **13** flesh and blood **14** kissing cousins

kind 3 ilk **4** cast, make, mold, sort, type **5** brand, breed, caste, civil, class, genre, genus, style **6** benign, gentle, kidney, kindly, nature, polite, strain, tender **7** amiable, cordial, variety **8** amicable, friendly, generous, gracious, merciful, obliging **9** courteous **10** bighearted, charitable, neighborly, thoughtful **11** considerate, description, designation, good-hearted, good-humored, good-natured, softhearted, sympathetic, warmhearted, well-meaning **12** affectionate, well-disposed **13** accommodating, compassionate, tenderhearted, understanding
  French: 6 gentil

kindhearted 4 good, warm **6** benign, gentle, humane, kindly, loving **7** helpful **8** amicable, generous, gracious, merciful **10** altruistic, charitable, thoughtful **11** considerate, good-hearted, good-natured, softhearted, sympathetic, warmhearted, well-meaning **12** affectionate, humanitarian **13** accommodating, compas-

sionate, philanthropic, tenderhearted, understanding

kindheartedness 5 mercy **8** altruism, goodness, goodwill, humanity, sympathy **10** compassion, humaneness, tenderness **11** benefaction, benevolence, magnanimity **12** graciousness, philanthropy **13** consideration, understanding, unselfishness **14** charitableness **15** humanitarianism

kindle 4 fire, goad, prod, stir, urge, whet **5** awake, light, rouse, waken **6** arouse, excite, foment, ignite, incite, induce, stir up **7** agitate, animate, inflame, inspire, provoke, quicken, sharpen **8** enkindle **9** call forth, intensify, set fire to, set on fire, stimulate **10** invigorate

kindling 4 fuel **5** brush, paper, twigs **6** firing, tinder **7** burning, flaming **8** firewood, igniting, ignition, lighting, shavings **9** brushwood **10** combustion, enkindling

kindly 4 good, warm **6** benign, gentle, gently, humane, tender, warmly **7** amiable, amiably, civilly, cordial, devoted, patient **8** amicable, amicably, benignly, friendly, generous, gracious, humanely, merciful, tenderly **9** cordially, courteous **10** benevolent, bighearted, charitable, charitably, generously, graciously, mercifully, neighborly **11** considerate, good-humored, good-natured, magnanimous, softhearted, sympathetic, warmhearted, well-meaning **12** affectionate, benevolently, bigheartedly, humanitarian **13** compassionate, considerately, good-humoredly, good-naturedly, magnanimously, philanthropic, softheartedly, tenderhearted, understanding, warmheartedly, well-meaningly **14** affectionately, well-manneredly **15** compassionately, sympathetically, tenderheartedly, understandingly **17** philanthropically

kindness 3 aid **4** gift, help **5** favor, grace, mercy **6** bounty **7** charity **8** good deed, good turn, goodness, goodwill, humanity, patience, sympathy **9** tolerance **10** act of grace, assistance, compassion, generosity, humaneness, kind office, toleration **11** benefaction, beneficence, benevolence, magnanimity **12** act of charity, graciousness, philanthropy **13** consideration, understanding, unselfishness

14 charitableness
15 humanitarianism

Kind of Anger, A
author: **10** Eric Ambler

kindred 4 akin, like **5** alike
6 allied, united **7** related, similar **8** agreeing, familial, matching **9** accordant, analogous, congenial, simpatico **10** harmonious, resembling **11** consanguine, sympathetic
13 corresponding

kine 4 cows, oxen **6** cattle
9 livestock

kinfolk 3 kin **6** family **7** kinsmen **9** relations, relatives
10 kith and kin

king 3 HRH **5** liege, ruler
7 monarch **8** suzerain **9** potentate, protector, sovereign
10 His Majesty **11** crowned head, royal person, the anointed **18** defender of the faith
Latin: **3** rex

king/emperor/dynasty *see box*

King, Frank
creator/artist of: **13** Gasoline Alley

King, Stephen
author of: **2** It **4** Cujo **6** Carrie, Misery **9** Christine, Salem's Lot, The Stand
10 Night Shift, The Shining
11 Firestarter, Pet Sematary, The Dead Zone **12** Skeleton Crew, The Dark Tower
16 Different Seasons, The Tommyknockers

King and I, The
director: **10** Walter Lang
cast: **10** Rita Moreno, Yul Brynner **11** Deborah Kerr
12 Martin Benson
score: **21** Rodgers and Hammerstein
remake of: **20** Anna and the King of Siam
song: **12** Shall We Dance?
16 Getting to Know You, Hello Young Lovers
18 Something Wonderful

King Arthur
opera by: **7** Purcell
character: **6** Merlin, Osmond, Oswald **8** Emmeline, Philadel **14** Duke of Cornwall

kingdom 4 land **5** duchy, field, realm, state **6** domain, empire, nation, sphere **7** country, dukedom **8** dominion, monarchy **9** territory **12** principality

King John
author: **18** William Shakespeare
character: **6** Elinor **9** Constance **11** Prince Henry
13 Hubert de Burgh
15 Blanch of Castile, Lewis the Dauphin
16 Arthur of Bretagne, Cardinal Pandulph, William Longsword, William Mareshall
19 Philip Faulconbridge, Robert Faulconbridge

King Kong
director: **13** Merian C Cooper **17** Ernest B Schoedsack
cast: **7** Fay Wray **10** Bruce Cabot **11** James Flavin
12 Noble Johnson **15** Robert Armstrong
setting (final scene): **19** Empire State Building
score: **10** Max Steiner

King Lear
author: **18** William Shakespeare
character: **5** Edgar, Regan
6 Edmund **7** Goneril **8** Cordelia **10** Earl of Kent
12 Duke of Albany, King of

king / emperor / dynasty (*continued*)
  of Korea: 2 Yi **4** Choe **5** Ki-tse, Koryo **6** Chi-tsi, Chi-tzu, Tangun
  of Kuwait: 5 Ahmad, Sabah, Salem **7** Mubarak **12** Jaber al-Ahmed, Sabah al-Salim **15** Abdullah al-Salim
  of Liechtenstein: 7 Florian **13** Francis Joseph **16** von Liechtenstein
  of Luxembourg: 8 Sigefroi, Wencelas **12** Jean l'Aveugle **21** House of Nassau-Weilburg
  of Madagascar: 6 Merina
  of Malawi: 6 Maravi
  of Maldives: 4 Didi
  of Mexico: 10 Maximilian
  of Monaco: 5 Louis **6** Albert, Honore **7** Antoine, Charles, Rainier **9** Florestan
  of Mongolia: 8 Jahangir, Jehangir **10** Kublai Khan, Tsendenbal **11** Genghis Khan
  of Morocco: 7 Alawite, Almohad **9** Almoravid
  of Nepal: 8 Mahendra **9** Tribhuwan **10** Birenda Bir **12** Bikram Sha Dev **17** Prithwi Narayan Sha
  of the Netherlands: 7 William
  of Nigeria: 3 Ife, Nok, Oyo **6** Fulani **10** Kanem-Borno
  of Norway: 4 Olaf, Olav **5** Olave, Oscar **6** Haakon, Harold, Magnus, Sverre
  of Peru: 7 Huascar **9** Atahualpa **10** Manco Capac
  of Poland: 5 Piast **7** Casimir, Jagello **8** Augustus
  of Portugal: 6 Manuel, Philip, Sancho **7** Alfonso **9** Ferdinand, Sebastian **23** Prince Henry the Navigator
  of Qatar: 18 Ahmad bin Ali al-Thani **22** Khalifa bin Hamad al-Thani
  of Rumania: 5 Carol **7** Michael
  of Russia: 4 Ivan, Paul **5** Peter **6** Alexis **7** Michael **8** Nicholas **9** Alexander **12** Boris Godunov
  of Sardinia: 12 Charles Felix **13** Charles Albert **14** Victor Emmanuel
  of Saudi Arabia: 4 Fahd, Saud **6** Faisal, Khalid **7** Ibn Saud **9** Abdul Aziz
  of Scotland: 5 David, James **6** Duncan **7** Kenneth, Macbeth, Malcolm, Stuarts, William **9** Alexander **14** Robert the Bruce **19** Bonnie Prince Charlie
  of Sicily: 4 Eryx **5** Bomba, Henry, Peter, Roger **7** Charles, Cocalus, Leontes **9** Ferdinand, Frederick
  of Spain: 6 Pelayo, Philip, Ramiro, Sancho, Witiza **7** Alfonso, Almohad, Charles, Umayyad **8** al-Mansur, Reccared, Roderick **9** Almoravid, Ferdinand, Leovigild **10** Juan Carlos **11** Abd al-Rahman, Reccosvinth
  of Swaziland: 3 Kbe **5** Nyama **6** Mswati, Sozisa **7** Sobhuza
  of Sweden: 4 Vosa, Wasa **5** Oscar **6** Gustav **8** Gustavus **10** Carl Gustav **12** Gustav Adolph **13** Charles Gustav **22** Jean Baptiste Bernadotte
  of Syria: 5 Rezin **6** Faisal, Hazael **8** Benhadad **9** Antiochus
  of Thailand: 4 Rama **7** Chakkri, Mongkut **10** Chao Phraya **12** Prahjadhipok **13** Chulalongkorn **17** Bhumibol Adulyadej
  of Tongo: 11 George Tupou **14** Taufaahau Tupou
  of Tunisia: 6 Hafsid **7** Fatimid **8** Aghlabid, Almohade **10** Husseinite
  of Turkey: 8 Mausolus
  of Uganda: 6 Mutesa, Mwanga **8** Kabarega
  of Upper Volta: 4 Naba **5** Mogho
  of Zimbabwe: 9 Lobengula, Mzilikaze

France **14** Duke of Cornwall **16** Earl of Gloucester

kingly 5 grand, noble, regal, royal **6** august, lordly, mighty **7** queenly, stately **8** absolute, despotic, glorious, kinglike, imperial, majestic, princely, splendid **9** imperious, monarchal, patrician, sovereign **10** autocratic, commanding, tyrannical **11** magnificent **12** awe-inspiring

Kingman, Dave
  nickname: 4 Kong
  sport: 8 baseball
  position: 8 outfield **9** first base
  team: 11 Chicago Cubs, New York Mets **14** New York Yankees, San Diego Padres **16** California Angels **18** San Francisco Giants

king of gods 4 Amen, Amon, Finn, Zeus **5** Ammon, Enlil, Fionn, Wotan **6** Marduk **8** Merodach **12** Baal Merodach **13** Fionn MacCumal

King of Hearts
  character in: 28 Alice's Adventures in Wonderland
  author: 7 Carroll

King of Righteousness
  11 Melchizedek

Kingsley, Ben
  roles: 6 Gandhi (Oscar) **8** Betrayal

Kingsley, Charles
  author of: 7 Hypatia **10** Alton Locke **11** Westward Ho! **14** The Water Babies **15** Hereward the Wake

King Solomon's Mines
  author: 13 H Rider Haggard
  character: 5 Twala **6** Gagool, Umbopa **14** Sir Henry Curtis **15** Allan Quatermain, Captain John Good

King's Row
  author: 14 Henry Bellamann
  director: 7 Sam Wood
  cast: 10 Betty Field **11** Ann Sheridan, Claude Rains **12** Ronald Reagan **13** Charles Coburn **14** Judith Anderson, Robert Cummings
  score: 21 Erich Wolfgard Korngold
  character: 11 Drake McHugh, Elise Sandor **13** Randy Monaghan **14** Cassandra Tower, Parris Mitchell

Kingston
  capital of: 7 Jamaica

Kingu
origin: **8** Akkadian
father: **4** Apsu
mother: **6** Tiamet
blood used by: **2** Ea **6** Marduk **8** Merodach **12** Baal Merodach
blood used for: **8** creation

kink 4 coil, flaw, knot, pang **5** cramp, crick, crimp, frizz, gnarl, hitch, quirk, snarl, spasm, twist **6** defect, foible, glitch, oddity, tangle, twinge, vagary **7** crinkle, frizzle **8** crotchet **9** queerness, stiffness, weirdness **10** difficulty **11** peculiarity, singularity **12** charley horse, complication, eccentricity, freakishness, idiosyncrasy, imperfection

kinky 3 odd **4** sick, wiry **5** kooky, queer **6** frizzy, matted, quirky, twisty **7** bizarre, deviant, frizzly, knotted, strange, tangled, twisted, unusual **8** aberrant, abnormal, crinkled, freakish, frizzled, peculiar, perverse **9** eccentric, unnatural **10** unorthodox **13** idiosyncratic

Kinshasa
capital of: **5** Zaire

kinsman 3 sib, son **4** aunt, heir **5** child, uncle **6** cousin, father, mother, parent, sister **7** brother **8** daughter, landsman, relation, relative **9** offspring **10** countryman **11** grandfather, grandmother **13** blood relation, blood relative

Kiowa
language family: **6** Tanoan
location: **6** Plains **7** Montana **8** Colorado, Oklahoma
allied with: **7** Arapaho **8** Comanche **11** Kiowa Apache
deity: **5** Taime

Kiowa Apache
language family: **12** Shapwailutan
location: **6** Plains

Kipling, Rudyard
author of: **3** Kim **8** Gunga Din, Mandalay **11** Danny Deaver **12** The Seven Seas **13** Just So Stories, The Jungle Book **18** Barrack-Room Ballads, Captains Courageous

Kipps
author: **7** H G Wells

Kirchhoff, Gustav Robert
field: **7** physics
nationality: **6** German
discovered: **6** cesium **8** rubidium
developed: **12** spectroscope
named for him: **19** electric circuit laws

Kirchner, Ernst Ludwig
born: **7** Germany **13** Aschaffenburg
artwork: **11** Street Scene **12** Street Berlin **13** Moonlit Winter **21** Self-portrait with Model

---

Kiribati
other name: **14** Gilbert Islands
capital/largest city: **6** Tarawa
others: **5** Betio **7** Bairiki, Bonriki **9** Bikenibeu
school: **12** South Pacific
monetary unit: **4** cent **6** dollar
island: **5** Flint, Ocean **6** Banaba, Canton, Malden, Tarawa **7** Abemama, Fanning, Gilbert, Marakei, Nonouti, Phoenix, Vostock **8** Caroline, Starbuck **9** Christmas, Enderbury, Tabiteuea **10** Butaritari, Equatorial, Washington **12** Northern Line, Southern Line
sea: **7** Pacific
people: **8** Banabans **10** Polynesian **11** Micronesian
language: **6** Samoan **7** English **10** Gilbertese
religion: **5** Baha'i **8** Anglican **9** Methodist **11** Church of God **13** Roman Catholic **19** Seventh Day Adventist

---

kirsch, kirschwasser
type: **6** brandy **7** liqueur
origin: **6** France **7** Germany **11** Switzerland
flavor: **6** cherry
with gin: **7** Florida **10** Lady Finger
with vodka: **12** Volga Boatman

kismet 3 end, lot **4** doom, fate **5** moira **7** destiny, fortune, portion **8** God's will **10** Providence **11** will of Allah **12** circumstance **13** inevitability **14** predestination

kiss 4 buss, neck **6** smooch, salute **8** osculate

Kiss for Cinderella, A
author: **12** James M Barrie

kit 3 rig **4** gear **5** tools **6** outfit, tackle, things **7** devices **8** supplies, utensils **9** equipment, trappings **10** implements, provisions **11** furnishings, impedi-

ments, instruments, necessaries **13** accoutrements, paraphernalia

Kitasato, Shibasaburo
field: **12** bacteriology
nationality: **8** Japanese
isolated: **7** anthrax, tetanus **9** dysentery **13** bubonic plague
developed: **19** diphtheria antitoxin

kitchen 6 bakery, cocina, galley **7** cuisine **8** cookroom, scullery **9** bakehouse, cookhouse

Kitchener, Horatio Herbert
also: **18** first Earl Kitchener
nationality: **7** British
served in: **7** Boer War **15** South African War
battle: **8** Khartoum, Omdurman
governor of: **8** the Sudan
commander in chief of: **5** India **12** Egyptian army
consul general of: **5** Egypt

kitel 20 Jewish ceremonial robe
color: **5** white

Kitely
character in: **19** Every Man in His Humour
author: **6** Jonson

kittenish 3 coy **7** playful **10** coquettish

Klamath
language family: **8** Penutian
location: **6** Oregon **10** California
related to: **5** Modoc **6** Cayuse, Molala

Klee, Paul
born: **11** Switzerland **14** Munchenbuchsee
artwork: **9** Locksmith **11** Ad Parnassum **18** Barbarian Sacrifice, Demon above the Ships **20** The Twittering Machine **22** Revolution of the Viaduct **23** Dance-Play of the Red Skirts **24** Dance Monster to my Soft Song **35** The Vocal Fabric of the Singer Rosa Silber

Kleist, Heinrich von
author of: **11** Penthesilea **14** The Marquise of O **16** The Broken Pitcher **18** The Prince of Homburg

Kline, Kevin
roles: **11** The Big Chill **13** Sophie's Choice **17** Pirates of Penzance

Klugman, Jack
born: **14** Philadelphia PA
roles: **6** Quincy **12** Oscar Madison, The Odd Couple

klutz 5 dummy **9** blockhead **11** satchelfoot **13** fumblefingers

klutzy 4 dumb **6** clumsy, stupid **7** awkward **9** graceless

knack 4 bent, gift, turn **5** flair, forte, skill **6** genius, talent **7** ability, faculty, finesse **8** aptitude, capacity, facility **9** dexterity, expertise, ingenuity, quickness, readiness **10** adroitness, capability, cleverness, competence, efficiency, propensity **11** inclination, proficiency **13** dexterousness

knave 3 cad, cur, dog, rat **5** phony, rogue, scamp **6** con man, rascal, rotter, varlet, wretch **7** bounder, culprit **8** scalawag, swindler **9** charlatan, con artist, reprobate, scoundrel **10** blackguard **11** rapscallion **14** good for nothing

knee breeches 8 breeches, jodhpurs, knickers **9** plus fours

kneel 3 bow **6** curtsy, kowtow, salaam **7** bow down **9** genuflect **13** make obeisance **16** prostrate oneself

knell 4 peal, ring, toll **5** chime, sound **6** stroke **7** pealing, ringing, tolling

Knickerbocker Holiday
   author: **15** Maxwell Anderson

knickknack, nicknack 3 toy **6** bauble, gewgaw, trifle **7** bibelot, trinket **8** frippery, gimcrack **9** bagatelle, bric-a-brac, plaything **11** thingamajig

knife 3 cut **4** dirk, shiv, stab **5** blade, slash, wound **6** cutter, pierce **7** cut down, cutlery **8** cut apart, lacerate, mutilate
   type: **3** pen **4** jack **5** bowie, bread, putty, table **6** dagger, paring, pocket **7** butcher, carving, hunting, machete, palette, pruning, scalpel **8** skinning, stiletto, surgical **11** switchblade

knight 4 hero **7** fighter, gallant, paladin, soldier, Templar, warrior **8** cavalier, champion, defender, guardian, horseman, Lancelot **9** gentleman, man-at-arms, protecter, protector **10** equestrian, vindicator

Knight
   character in: **18** The Canterbury Tales
   author: **7** Chaucer

Knightley, George
   character in: **4** Emma
   author: **6** Austen

Knights, The
   author: **12** Aristophanes
   character: **5** Demus **6** Nicias **11** Demosthenes **20** Cleon the Paphlagonian

knit 3 tat **4** ally, bind, draw, join, knot, link **5** braid, plait, twist, unify, unite, weave **6** attach, crease, fasten, furrow, stitch **7** connect, crochet, wrinkle **10** intertwine, interweave **12** draw together

knob 3 nub **4** bulb, bump, grip, hold, hump, knot, knur, lump, node, snag **5** bulge, gnarl, knurl, latch, lever, swell **6** handle, nubbin **8** handhold, swelling, tubercle **9** convexity **10** projection, prominence, protrusion **12** protuberance, protuberancy

knock 3 bat, hit, pat, rap, tap **4** bang, beat, belt, blow, bomb, bump, clip, cuff, dash, kick, lick, push, slam, slap, sock, swat, thud **5** abuse, cavil, clout, crack, crash, decry, pound, punch, smack, smash, smite, thump, whack **6** batter, carp at, defeat, hammer, jostle, murder, peck at, pummel, strike, stroke, thwack, wallop **7** censure, condemn, failure, setback **8** belittle, lambaste **9** criticism, criticize, deprecate, disparage, reprehend **12** condemnation, faultfinding, reprehension

knock down 4 deck, down, drop, fell **5** floor **7** flatten **8** bowl over, discount **9** take apart **11** disassemble

knock off balance 6 rattle **7** shake up **8** unsettle **9** take aback **11** disorganize

knockout 2 KO **4** doll **5** beaut, Venus **6** beauty, eyeful **7** stunner

knock out of shape 4 maul **5** crush **6** batter, beat up, mangle

knoll 4 hill, rise **5** mound

knot 3 bun **4** bump, frog, heap, hump, loop, lump, mass, pack, pile, star, tuft **5** braid, bunch, clump, group, hitch, knurl, plait, twist **6** bundle, circle **7** cat's-paw, chignon, cluster, epaulet, rosette **8** ornament **9** gathering **10** assemblage, collection, intertwist **13** interlacement
   type: **3** bow, top **4** flat, slip **5** slide **6** double, single, square **7** running **8** hangman's, overhand, shoulder, surgeon's **9** half-hitch **11** figure-eight, midshipman's

Knots Landing
   character: **9** Abby Ewing, Gary Ewing **10** Greg Sumner **11** Valene Ewing **12** Mac Mackenzie **14** Karen Mackenzie, Paige Forrester
   cast: **10** Donna Mills, Joan Van Ark **11** Julie Harris, Kevin Dobson, Michelle Lee **13** William Devane **14** Douglas Sheehan, Ted Shackelford **17** Nicolette Sheridan

knotty 4 hard **5** bumpy, rough, tough **6** coarse, flawed, knobby, knurly, rugged, snaggy, thorny, tricky, uneven **7** complex, gnarled, knurled, nodular **8** baffling, involved, puzzling, ticklish, unsmooth **9** blemished, difficult, intricate **10** perplexing **11** complicated, troublesome **12** rough-grained **13** coarse-grained, problematical

know 3 see **6** be sure, be wise, notice **7** be smart, discern, make out, realize **8** identify, perceive **9** apprehend, be assured, be aware of, be certain, be close to, get wise to, recognize **10** be informed, be positive, understand **11** be confident, be sagacious, be thick with, distinguish, feel certain, have down pat, have no doubt **12** discriminate, have down cold, have the ear of **13** be cognizant of, be intelligent, have knowledge, rub elbows with **14** be familiar with

knowable 9 thinkable **11** conceivable, discernible, perceivable **14** understandable

Knowell, Edward
   character in: **19** Every Man in His Humour
   author: **6** Jonson

know for sure 9 be certain **10** be positive

know-how 3 art **4** bent, gift **5** craft, flair, knack, savvy, skill **6** talent **7** ability, mastery **8** aptitude, capacity, deftness **9** adeptness, expertise, knowledge, technique **10** adroitness, capability, competence, experience, expertness **11** proficiency **12** skillfulness **15** professionalism
   French: **11** savoir-faire

knowing 4 deep, wise **5** aware, canny, sharp, smart, sound **6** astute, brainy, bright, clever, shrewd **7** erudite, fraught, learned, sapient **8** academic, educated, eloquent, highbrow, literary, profound, schooled, sensible **9** conscious, judicious, revealing, sagacious **10** discerning, expressive, meaningful, perceptive, percipient, scholastic, widely read **11** enlightened, intelligent, significant **12** intellectual, well-informed **13** comprehending, knowledgeable, perspicacious, philosophical, sophisticated, understanding

knowing how to live
  French: **11** savoir-vivre

knowing just what to do
  French: **11** savoir-faire

know-it-all 5 brash
13 overconfident

knowledge 3 ken, tip **4** data, hint, news **5** sense **6** memory, notice, report, wisdom **7** inkling, mention, tidings **8** learning **9** awareness, education, erudition, schooling, statement **10** cognizance, intimation, perception **11** cultivation, declaration, familiarity, information, realization, recognition, revelation, scholarship **12** announcement, book learning, intelligence, notification **13** communication, comprehension, consciousness, enlightenment, pronouncement
  god of: 4 Odin **5** Othin

knowledgeable 3 hip **8** at home in, versed in **12** familiar with, well-informed **14** acquainted with, conversant with
  French: **9** au courant

knowledge of the world
  French: **11** savoir-vivre

known 5 noted, plain **6** common, famous, patent **7** evident, obvious, popular **8** apparent, definite, distinct, familiar, manifest, palpable **9** notorious, prominent **10** celebrated, recognized **11** self-evident

know thyself
  Greek: **13** gnothi seauton

knuckle under 5 yield **6** give in, submit **7** bow down **9** surrender **10** capitulate

knurled 5 bumpy, lumpy **6** gnarly, knobby, knotty, knurly, nubbly, ridged **7** bulging, gnarled, knotted, nodular

Koch, Robert
  field: 12 bacteriology
  nationality: 6 German
  isolated: 2 TB **12** tuberculosis
  awarded: 10 Nobel Prize

Kodaly, Zoltan
  born: 7 Hungary **9** Kecskemet
  composer of: 9 Hary Janos **11** Czinka Panna, Missa Brevis, Szekely Fono **14** Budavari Te Deum **15** Dances of Galanta **17** Dances of Marosszek, Peacock Varia-

tions, Psalmus Hungaricus **28** The Spinning Room of the Szekelys

Koestler, Arthur
  author of: 14 Darkness at Noon **15** The Sleepwalkers

Kojak
  character: 5 (Det) Rizzo **7** (Det) Stavros **9** (Lt) Theo Kojak **10** (Det) Saperstein **11** Frank McNeil **12** (Lt) Bobby Crocker
  cast: 9 Dan Frazer **10** Vince Conti **11** Kevin Dobson, Mark Russell **12** Telly Savalas **13** George Savalas (Demosthenes)
  trademark: 8 lollipop
  phrase: 14 Who loves ya baby?

Kollwitz, Kathe
  real name: 12 Kathe Schmidt
  born: 10 Konigsberg **11** East Prussia
  artwork: 3 War **5** Death, Pieta **11** Proletariat **13** Weavers' Revolt (Weaver's Rebellion) **14** Mother and Child, The Peasants' War **18** Death Seizing a Woman

Kol Nidre 4 vows **8** promises **22** Jewish liturgical prayer
  recited on eve of: 9 Yom Kippur

Kong
  nickname of: 11 Dave Kingman

Kon-Tiki
  author: 13 Thor Heyerdahl

kook 3 nut **5** crazy, flake, loony, wacko **6** cuckoo, weirdo **7** dingbat **8** crackpot **9** ding-a-ling, eccentric, fruitcake, harebrain, screwball **10** crackbrain

Korah
  father: 4 Esau **6** Hebron **7** Eliphaz
  conspired with: 6 Abiram, Dathan
  rebelled against: 5 Aaron, Moses

Korea *see box, p. 542*

Koridethianus 16 Greek unical codex

Korman, Harvey
  born: 9 Chicago IL
  roles: 11 High Anxiety **13** Danny Kaye Show **14** Blazing Saddles **16** Carol Burnett Show

Kornberg, Arthur
  field: 12 biochemistry
  sythesized: 3 DNA, RNA **15** ribonucleic acid **20** deoxyribonucleic acid
  awarded: 10 Nobel Prize

kosher 5 right **6** proper **7** ethical **10** aboveboard **12** on the up and up

Kosinski, Jerzy
  author of: 5 Steps **7** Cockpit **9** Blind Date **10** Being There **11** Passion Play **12** The Devil Tree **14** The Painted Bird

Kowalski, Stanley
  character in: 21 A Streetcar Named Desire
  author: 8 Williams

kowtow 4 bend, fawn **5** cower, stoop, toady **6** bow low, cringe, curtsy, grovel, salaam **7** truckle **8** bootlick, butter up, softsoap **9** genuflect **11** applepolish **12** bow and scrape **16** prostrate oneself

kowtowing 7 fawning, servile **8** toadying **9** groveling **10** obsequious

Kraken
  origin: 9 Norwegian
  form: 7 monster
  habitat: 3 sea
  caused: 10 whirlpools

Kramer, Stanley
  director of: 10 On the Beach **11** Ship of Fools **14** Inherit the Wind, The Defiant Ones **19** Judgment at Nuremberg

Kramer vs Kramer
  director: 12 Robert Benton
  based on novel by: 11 Avery Corman
  cast: 10 Howard Duff **11** Justin Henry, Meryl Streep **13** Dustin Hoffman, Jane Alexander
  Oscar for: 5 actor (Hoffman) **7** picture **8** director **10** screenplay **17** supporting actress (Streep)

Krantz, Judith
  author of: 8 Scruples **13** Princess Daisy **16** I'll Take Manhattan, Mistral's Daughter

Krazy Kat
  creator: 14 George Herriman
  character:
    cop: **12** Offissa B Pupp
    mouse: **6** Ignatz
  prop: 5 brick
  place: 4 jail **14** Coconino County **24** Kelly's Exclusive Brick Yard

Krebs, Hans Adolf
  field: 9 chemistry
  nationality: 6 German
  discovered: 15 citric acid cycle
  awarded: 10 Nobel Prize

Korea
other name: 6 Choson 17 land of morning calm
capital:
  North Korea: 9 Pyongyang
  South Korea: 5 Seoul
largest city: 5 Seoul
others: 5 Masan, Mokpo, Pusan, Sinpo, Suwon, Taegu,
  Wonju 6 Chonju, Inchon, Kangso, Kunsan, Taejon, Won-
  san 7 Hanyang, Hungnam, Kaesong, Kangson, Kwangju
  8 Chongjin, Chunchon, Kimchaek
school: 5 Busan 6 Yonsei 7 Hanyang 8 Kim Chaek, Kyung
  Hee 9 Kim Il Sung
division:
  ancient: 5 Silla 6 Choson 7 Koguryo, Paekche
monetary unit: 3 woh, won 4 chun, hwan, kwan
weight: 3 won
island: 4 Chin, Koje 5 Cheju, Sinmi 6 Anmyon, Huksan,
  Namhae 7 Tokchok 8 Quelpart 10 Paengnyong
mountain: 4 Wang 5 Chiri, Halla 6 Kwanmo, Sobaek
  7 Diamond, Kyebang, Nangnim, Taebaek 8 Chang-pai,
  Hamgyong, Myohyang 9 Paektu-san 10 Kumgang-san
highest point: 6 Paektu 9 Paektu-san
river: 3 Han, Kin, Kum, Kun, Nam 4 Lobk, Yalu 5 Am-
  nok, Imjin, Tumen 6 Namhan, Pukhan, Somjin, Soyang,
  Yesong 7 Naktong, Taedong 8 Changjin, Youngsan
  9 Chongchon
sea: 5 Japan 6 Yellow 9 East China
physical feature:
  bay: 5 Korea 6 Yongil 7 Kanghwa, Kyonggi 9 Tongjoson
  cape: 4 Musu
  point: 7 Changgi 8 Changsan
  strait: 5 Korea
  valley: 7 Naktong
people: 6 Korean
  artist: 8 Chong Son 10 Kimtlong-do
  dynasty: 2 Yi 4 Choe 5 Koryo
  leader: 6 Sejong 8 Yi Sung-gy 9 Kim Il Sung 11 Chun
    Doo Hwan, Syngman Rhee 12 Park Chung Hee
  legendary leader: 5 Ki-tse 6 Chi-tse, Chi-tzu, Tangun
  poet: 10 Hwang Chini
language: 6 Korean
  alphabet: 6 hangul
religion: 6 Taoism 7 animism 8 Buddhism 9 Chondogyo
  12 Christianity, Confucianism
place:
  palace: 8 Kyongbok
  temple: 7 Haein-sa 17 Hall of Eternal Life
  tomb: 14 Dancing Figures
feature:
  clothing: 5 chima
  game: 3 yut 5 akoan 6 ho-hpai 7 kol-ye-si 9 ryong-hpai,
    sang-ryouk 10 ke-pouk-hpai, sin-syo-tyen 12 tjak-ma-
    tchi-ki 15 kko-ri-pouk-tchi-ki
  martial art: 9 tae-kwon-do
  musical instrument: 6 chaing 7 kayagum, komungo
  porcelain: 7 Celadon
  porch: 4 maru
  pottery: 8 pun-chong
food:
  bean curd: 4 tubu
  hot pickle: 6 kimchi
  meat-filled dumpling: 5 mandu
  noodle: 5 kuksu

Kreisler, Fritz
born: 6 Vienna 7 Austria
composer of: 7 Allegro
  10 Praeludium 15 Caprice
  Viennois 16 Tambourin
  Chinois

Kreutzer, Rodolphe
born: 6 France 10 Versailles
composer of: 16 Etudes ou
  Caprices

Kreutzer Sonata, The
author: 10 Leo Tolstoy
character: 13 Mme
  Pozdnishef, Trukhashevsky
  16 Vasyla Pozdnishef

Krieg 3 war

Kriemhild
origin: 8 Germanic
mentioned in:
  14 Nibelungenlied
brother: 7 Gunther
husband: 9 Siegfried
slew: 5 Hagan 7 Gunther
avenged: 6 murder 9 Siegfried
corresponds to: 6 Gudrun,
  Kudrun 7 Guthrun

Kristin Lavransdatter
author: 12 Sigrid Undset

Kronos *see* 6 Cronus

Krook
character in: 10 Bleak House
author: 7 Dickens

Kropp, Albert
character in: 25 All Quiet on
  the Western Front
author: 8 Remarque

krypton
chemical symbol: 2 Kr

Kuala Lumpur
capital of: 8 Malaysia

Kubla Khan
author: 15 Samuel Coleridge

Kubrick, Stanley
director of: 6 Lolita 9 Sparta-
  cus 11 Barry Lyndon
  12 Paths of Glory 13 Dr
  Strangelove (or How I
  Learned to Stop Worrying
  and Love the Bomb) 16 A
  Clockwork Orange 30 Two
  Thousand and One A Space
  Odyssey

kudo, kudos 4 fame 5 award,
glory, honor, prize 6 esteem,
praise, renown, repute 7 acclaim, plaudit 8 citation, prestige 9 celebrity, laudation
10 admiration, decoration
12 commendation
14 celebratedness

Kudrun *see* 6 Gudrun

Kukla, Fran & Ollie
hostess: 11 Fran Allison
puppet: 5 Kukla, Ollie (Oliver
  J Dragon) 8 Mercedes
  9 Cecil Bill 10 Col Crackie
  11 Beulah Witch 12 Olivia

Dragon **13** Delores Dragon **14** Fletcher Rabbit **18** Mme Ophelia Oglepuss

Kulla
origin: **8** Egyptian, Sumerian
world of: **4** dead
god of: **6** bricks

Kullervo
origin: **7** Finnish
mentioned in: **8** Kalevala
form: **5** slave
death: **7** suicide

kummel
origin: **7** Germany
flavor: **7** caraway

kumquat 10 Fortunella
varieties: **4** oval **5** round **6** Marumi, Nagami **16** Australian desert

Kung Fu
character: **8** Master Po **9** Master Kan **14** Kwai Chang Caine
cast: **8** Keye Luke **9** Philip Ahn **11** Radames Pera **14** David Carradine
Caine raised in: **13** Shaolin Temple

kunzite
species: **9** spodumene

Kupka, Frank (Frantisek)
born: **6** Opocno **7** Bohemia **14** Czechoslovakia
artwork: **12** Black Accents, The Cathedral **16** Etude pour la Fugue **17** Fugue in Red and Blue **23** Fugue in Two Colors Amorpha **25** Philosophical Architecture

Kuprin, Aleksandr
author of: **7** The Duel **10** Yama the Pit

Kurosawa, Akira
director of: **3** Ran **8** Rashomon **12** Seven Samurai

Kurtz
character in: **15** Heart of Darkness
author: **6** Conrad

Kuwait *see box*

Kwa
language family: **16** Niger-Kordofanian
group: **10** Niger-Congo
includes: **3** Ewe, Ibo, Twi **4** Bini, Nupe, Togo **6** Yoruba **7** Dahomey

Kwakiutl
language family: **8** Wakashan
location: **6** Canada **15** British Columbia, Vancouver Island **20** Queen Charlotte Island
related to: **6** Nootka **10** Bellabella
noted for: **10** totem poles **15** Cannibal Society, wooden sculpture
called: **14** potlatch people

Kyd, Thomas
author of: **17** The Spanish Tragedy

Kyrgyzstan
other name: **9** Kirghizia
capital/largest city: **6** Frunze **7** Bishkek
head of state: **9** president
government: **8** republic
monetary unit: **3** som
mountain: **8** Tian Shan
people: **5** Uzbek **6** Kyrgyz **7** Kirghiz
language: **6** Turkic **7** Kirghiz
religion: **6** Muslim **10** Sunni Islam

Kyrie eleison 13 Lord have mercy

Kuwait
name means: **9** small fort
capital/largest city: **10** Kuwait City
others: **6** Ahmadi **7** Hawalli **8** Abdullah, al-Jahrah, Fahaheel, Shuwaykh **9** al-Shuayba **12** Mena al-Ahmadi, Mina Abd Allah, Mina al-Ahmadi
head of state: **4** emir
monetary unit: **4** fils **5** dinar
island: **5** Warba **7** Bubiyan, Failaka
physical feature:
    bay: **6** Kuwait **12** Khor Abdullah
    duststorm: **4** kaus
    gulf: **7** Persian
    oasis: **6** Jahrah
people: **4** Arab **5** Iraqi, Saudi **6** Indian **7** Bedouin **8** Egyptian **9** Pakistani **11** Palestinian
    ruling family: **5** Sabah
    sheikh (Sabah family): **5** Ahmad, Salem **7** Mubarak **12** Jaber al-Ahmed, Sabah al-Salim **15** Abdullah al-Salim
religion: **5** Islam
war: **4** Gulf **11** Desert Storm, Persian Gulf **12** Desert Shield
    enemy: **4** Iraq **13** Saddam Hussein

Laban
father: 7 Bethuel
grandfather: 5 Nahor
daughter: 4 Leah 6 Rachel
sister: 7 Rebekah
son-in-law: 5 Jacob

Labdacus
king of: 6 Thebes
father: 9 Polydorus
mother: 7 Nycteis
grandfather: 7 Nycteus
brother: 5 Lycus
son: 5 Laius
grandson: 7 Oedipus

label 3 tag 4 mark, name, note, seal, sign, slip 5 brand, stamp, tally, title 6 define, docket, ticket 7 earmark, mark off, sticker 8 classify, describe 9 designate 10 denominate, put a mark on 11 appellation, designation, inscription 12 characterize 13 specification 14 classification, identification 16 characterization

labor, labour 4 plod, toil, work 5 slave, sweat 6 drudge, effort, suffer 7 agonize, travail, workers, workmen 8 drudgery, exertion, laborers, manpower, plodding, plug away, struggle, struggle 9 employees, grind away, work force 10 birth pangs, childbirth, menial work, smart under 11 birth throes, manual labor, parturition 12 accouchement, be affected by, be burdened by, be troubled by 13 be the victim of 14 employ one's time, work like a slave

labored 5 heavy, stiff 6 clumsy, forced, wooden 7 awkward, cramped, halting, studied 8 drawnout, overdone, strained 9 contrived, difficult, laborious, maladroit, ponderous, unnatural 13 self-conscious, unspontaneous

laborer 4 hand 6 coolie,

drudge, menial, toiler, worker 7 plodder, workman 8 handyman, hired man, hireling, workhand 9 hired hand 10 roustabout, wage earner, workingman 11 proletarian 12 manual worker 16 blue-collar worker

laborious 4 hard 6 brutal, severe, uphill 7 arduous, irksome, labored, onerous, wearing 8 rigorous, tiresome, toilsome, wearying 9 demanding, difficult, effortful, fatiguing, herculean, strenuous, wearisome 10 burdensome, oppressive, struggling 11 troublesome

laboriously 4 hard 9 arduously 14 with difficulty 15 with great effort

laboriousness 5 trial 8 tough job 10 difficulty, rough going, uphill work 11 arduousness 12 hard sledding 15 troublesomeness

labor omnia vincit 15 work conquers all
motto of: 8 Oklahoma

Labors of Hercules see 8 Hercules

labyrinth 3 web 4 knot, maze 5 snarl 6 jungle, morass, riddle, tangle 7 complex, network 9 intricacy, mare's nest 10 complexity, perplexity, wilderness 11 convolution

Labyrinth
form: 4 maze
location: 5 Crete
built by: 8 Daedalus
housed: 8 Minotaur

Lacaille, Nicholas Louis de
field: 9 astronomy
nationality: 6 French
mapped: 14 constellations

lace 3 tie 4 beat, bind, cane, dope, lash, whip 5 braid, cinch, close, flail, spank,

spike, strap, tie up, truss 6 dope up, fasten, flavor, infuse, punish, secure, switch, tether, thrash 7 fortify, spice up, suffuse, tighten 8 chastise, make fast, make taut 10 strengthen 11 add liquor to 12 add spirits to, draw together, give a beating

Lacedaemon
father: 4 Zeus
mother: 8 Taygete
wife: 6 Sparta
son: 7 Amyclas
daughter: 8 Eurydice
founder of: 6 Sparta

lacerate 3 cut, rip 4 gash, hurt, pain, scar, stab, tear 5 lance, sever, slash, slice, wound 6 deface 7 agonize, scratch, torment, torture 8 distress, give pain, puncture 10 excruciate 11 inflict pain

lacerating 5 acute 6 fierce, severe 7 cutting, extreme, intense, violent 12 excruciating

laceration 3 cut, rip 4 tear 5 wound 10 mutilation

Lachaise, Gaston
born: 5 Paris 6 France
artwork: 12 Standing Nude 13 Standing Woman 14 Floating Figure

Lachesis
form: 4 Fate
holds: 12 thread of life
determines: 6 length 7 destiny

lachrymose 3 sad 5 teary, weepy 6 crying 7 maudlin, tearful, weeping 8 mournful 10 melancholy

lack 4 miss, need, want 6 dearth 7 absence 8 omission, scarcity, shortage 9 be missing, be short of, depletion, neediness, privation, scantness 10 deficiency, exhaustion 11 deprivation, fall short of 12 be inadequate 13 be

545

caught short, be deficient in **14** be found wanting, be insufficient

lackadaisical 4 idle **7** languid, loafing **8** lifeless, listless, mindless **9** apathetic, lethargic, unexcited **10** inanimated, phlegmatic, spiritless, unaspiring, uninspired **11** indifferent, languishing, unambitious, unconcerned, unexcitable, unmotivated **12** uninterested **13** dillydallying

lackey 4 page **5** slave, toady, usher, valet **6** butler, flunky, helper, menial, minion, squire, waiter **7** servant, steward **8** employee, follower, hanger-on, hireling, inferior, retainer **9** assistant, attendant, cupbearer, mercenary, underling

lacking 7 needing, wanting **9** deficient **10** inadequate **12** falling short, insufficient **French: 6** manque

lackluster 4 blah, dead, drab, dull **5** bland, muted **6** boring, dreary, leaden, pallid, somber **7** humdrum, nothing, prosaic, subdued **8** lifeless, mediocre, ordinary **9** colorless **10** lusterless **11** commonplace **12** run-of-the-mill **13** uninteresting

lack of conviction 5 doubt **8** question **9** misgiving **10** hesitation, indecision **11** uncertainty

lack of faith 5 doubt **7** atheism **8** distrust, mistrust **9** disbelief, suspicion

lack of feeling 6 apathy **8** coldness, numbness **11** impassivity **15** emotionlessness, hardheartedness, passionlessness

lack of interest 5 ennui **6** apathy **7** boredom **9** unconcern **12** indifference

lack of respect 8 contempt, rudeness **9** disregard **10** disrespect **11** discourtesy, irreverence **12** impoliteness

lack of skill 9 inability **10** clumsiness, ineptitude **11** awkwardness **12** incompetency

Laclos, Pierre Choderlos de author of: **22** Les Liaisons Dangereuses

Lacombe, Lucien director: **10** Louis Malle cast: **12** Pierre Blaise **13** Aurore Clement **16** Holger Lowenadler

laconic 4 curt **5** blunt, brief, pithy, short, terse **7** compact, concise, pointed, summary

8 succinct **9** condensed **10** to the point **12** concentrated **14** sparing of words

lacquer 4 coat **5** glaze **7** coating, shellac, varnish

lacrimoso music: **7** tearful

lacrosse Indian name: **9** bagataway circle around goal: **6** crease players/team: **3** ten position: **6** goalie **9** attackman **10** defenseman, midfielder term: **6** riding **8** clearing

lacuna 3 gap, pit **4** gulf, hole, void **5** blank, break, crack, ditch, pause, space **6** breach, cavity, hiatus **7** caesura, fissure, interim, opening, vacancy **8** interval, omission **10** interstice, suspension **12** interruption **13** discontinuity

lacustrine 7 aquatic **11** lake-growing **12** lake-dwelling

lacy 4 fine **5** filmy, gauzy, meshy, netty, sheer, webby **6** barred, frilly, netted, porous, webbed **7** gridded, netlike **8** cobwebby, delicate, filigree, gossamer, lacelike, retiform **9** filigreed **10** diaphanous, reticulate **11** latticelike, transparent

lad 3 boy, kid **5** sprig, youth **6** shaver, sprout **8** juvenile, young man **9** schoolboy, stripling, young chap, youngster **11** young fellow

Ladd, Alan son: **5** David **6** Alan Jr co-star: **12** Veronica Lake born: **12** Hot Springs AR roles: **5** Shane **13** The Blue Dahlia **14** The Great Gatsby, This Gun for Hire

ladies' man 4 beau, stud **5** spark **7** playboy **8** cavalier, gay blade

La Dolce Vita director: **15** Federico Fellini cast: **9** Lex Barker, Nadia Gray **10** Anouk Aimee **11** Anita Ekberg **19** Marcello Mastroianni

Ladon form: **6** dragon father: **6** Typhon mother: **7** Echidna number of heads: **7** hundred guarded: **6** garden garden owned by: **10** Hesperides killed by: **8** Hercules

ladrone 5 thief **6** bandit, outlaw

lady 4 wife **5** woman **6** female, matron, spouse **7** duchess, peeress **8** baroness, countess **10** aristocrat, noblewoman **11** gentlewoman, marchioness, viscountess, woman of rank **13** well-bred woman German: **4** frau Italian: **5** donna Spanish/Portuguese: **4** dona

Lady Chatterley's Lover author: **10** D H Lawrence character: **7** Mellors **19** Constance Chatterley

Lady Eve, The director: **14** Preston Sturges cast: **10** Henry Fonda **13** Charles Coburn **14** Eugene Pallette **15** Barbara Stanwyck, William Demarest

Lady for a Day director: **10** Frank Capra based on story by: **11** Damon Runyon cast: **9** Guy Kibbee, May Robson **13** Warren William remade as: **19** Pocketful of Miracles

Lady from Dubuque, The author: **11** Edward Albee

Lady from the Sea, The author: **11** Henrik Ibsen

Lady in Chair constellation of: **10** Cassiopeia

ladylike 5 civil **6** modest, polite, proper **7** courtly, elegant, genteel, refined **8** cultured, decorous, mannerly, polished, well-bred **9** courteous, dignified **10** cultivated **11** respectable **12** well-mannered **13** well brought up

Lady of the Camellias, The see **7** Camille

Lady of the Lake, The author: **14** Sir Walter Scott character: **9** Allan Bane **11** Roderick Dhu **12** Ellen Douglas **13** Malcolm Graeme **14** James Fitz-James, James of Douglas

Lady Oracle author: **14** Margaret Atwood

lady's maid French: **14** femme de chambre

Lady's Not for Burning, The author: **14** Christopher Fry

lady's-slipper, Lady-slipper 11 Cypripedium **13** Paphiopedilum, Phragmipedium varieties: **4** pink **5** showy **8** mountain, ram's-head **9** two-leaved **10** small

white 11 large yellow, small
yellow

Lady Vanishes, The
director: 15 Alfred Hitchcock
cast: 9 Paul Lukas 13 Dame
May Whitty 15 Michael
Redgrave 16 Margaret
Lockwood

Lady Windermere's Fan
author: 10 Oscar Wilde
character: 10 Mrs Erlynne
14 Lord Darlington, Lord
Windermere 18 Lord Augus-
tus Lorton

Laelaps
form: 5 hound
borrowed from: 8 Cephalus
borrowed by: 10 Amphitryon

Laertes
son: 8 Odysseus

Laertes
character in: 6 Hamlet
author: 11 Shakespeare

Laertiades
epithet of: 8 Odysseus
means: 12 son of Laertes

Laestrygones
form: 6 giants
characteristic: 9 cannibals

La Farge, John
born: 9 New York NY
artwork: 14 Maua Our Boatman 17 The Muse of Paint-
ing 18 Red and White
Peonies

La Fayette, Comtesse de
author of: 19 La Princesse de
Cleves

Lafayette, Marquis de
also: 38 Marie Joseph Paul
Yves Roch Gilbert du Motier
nationality: 6 French
served in: 14 July Revolution 16 French Révolution
18 American Revolution
battle: 8 Yorktown
10 Brandywine

**Lafcadio's Adventures (The
Vatican Swindle)**
author: 9 Andre Gide

La Fontaine, Jean de
author of: 6 Fables

lag 4 drag, halt, inch, limp,
snag 5 dally, delay, hitch,
tarry, trail 6 be idle, be late,
be slow, dawdle, falter, hold
up, linger, loiter, trudge 7 be
tardy, setback, slacken, stagger 8 be behind, hang back,
slowdown 9 be overdue, inch
along 10 drag behind, slackening 11 slowing down 12 bide
one's time, take one's time
13 falling behind,
procrastinate

laggard 4 mope, poke, slow,
slug 5 idler, snail, tardy

6 loafer, remiss 7 dallier, dawdler, lounger 8 lingerer, loiterer, potterer, putterer, slowfoot,
slowpoke, sluggard, sluggish
9 do-nothing, straggler
12 dilly-dallier 13 stick-in-the-
mud

lagniappe, lagnappe 3 tip
4 gift, perk 5 bonus, favor,
prize 7 largess, memento, present 8 gratuity, largesse
9 pourboire

Lagos
former capital of: 7 Nigeria

Lahr, Bert
real name: 14 Irving
Lahrheim
born: 9 New York NY
roles: 12 Cowardly Lion
13 The Wizard of Oz

laic 3 lay 5 civil 6 laical 7 amateur, popular, profane, secular, worldly 8 temporal
11 nonclerical, nonpastoral
12 secularistic 13 inexperienced 15 nonprofessional
17 nonecclesiastical

lair 3 den, lie, mew 4 hole,
nest 5 cover, haunt 6 burrow,
cavern, covert 7 hideout, retreat 8 hideaway 9 sanctuary
12 resting place

laissez-faire, laisser-faire
8 hands off 9 let them be, unconcern 12 indifference 14 let-
alone policy, live and let live
15 noninterference,
nonintervention

laissez-passer 4 pass 6 permit 11 allow to pass

Laius
king of: 6 Thebes
father: 8 Labdacus
great-grandfather: 6 Cadmus
wife: 7 Jocasta
son: 7 Oedipus
killed by: 7 Oedipus

Lajeunesse, Gabriel
character in: 10 Evangeline
author: 10 Longfellow

lake see **box**

Lake, Harriette
real name of: 10 Ann
Sothern

Lake, Veronica
real name: 29 Constance
Frances Marie Ockelman
co-star: 8 Alan Ladd
born: 10 Brooklyn NY
roles: 13 The Blue Dahlia
14 I Married a Witch, This
Gun for Hire 16 Sullivan's
Travels

Lake Isle of Innisfree, The
author: 7 W B Yeats

Lakes
goddess of: 7 Juturna

L'Allegro
author: 10 John Milton
companion piece: 11 Il
Penseroso

**Lalo, (Victor Antoine)
Edouard**
born: 5 Lille 6 France
composer of: 7 Namouna
8 Le Roi d'Ys 11 The King
of Ys 15 Spanish Sym-
phony 18 Symphonie
Espagnole

Lamar, Ruby
character in: 9 Sanctuary
author: 8 Faulkner

Lamarck, Jean B
field: 7 biology
forerunner of theory of:
9 evolution
author of: 21 Philosophie
Zoologique

La Mare, Walter de
author of: 16 Memoirs of a
Midget

Lamarr, Hedy
real name: 21 Hedwig Eva
Maria Kiesler
born: 6 Vienna 7 Austria
roles: 7 Ecstasy 16 Samson
and Delilah

Lamas, Fernando
wife: 10 Arlene Dahl 14 Esther Williams
born: 9 Argentina 11 Buenos
Aires
roles: 13 The Merry Widow
16 Dangerous When Wet
23 The Girl Who Had
Everything

Lamb, Charles
author of: 12 Essays of Elia
13 Dream Children 25 A
Dissertation upon Roast Pig
31 Specimens of English
Dramatic Poets

lambaste 4 beat, drub, lick,
pelt, whip 5 scold, smear
6 berate, defeat, pummel, rebuke, subdue, thrash, wallop
7 bawl out, censure, chew
out, clobber, cuss out, shellac,
trounce 8 bludgeon, denounce,
vanquish 9 castigate, dress
down, light into, overwhelm,
reprimand

lambent 6 bright 7 radiant,
shining 8 luminous, lustrous
10 flickering, shimmering

Lambeosaurus
type: 8 dinosaur
10 ornithopod
location: 6 Canada
period: 10 Cretaceous

Lambert, Constant
born: 6 London 7 England
composer of: 9 Horoscope,
Rio Grande 14 Romeo and
Juliet 17 Music for Orches-

lake

of Afghanistan: 7 Helmand 13 Hamud-i-Helmand
of Albania: 4 Ulze 5 Matia, Ohrid 6 Prespa 7 Ochrida, Scutari, Shkoder 8 Ohridsko
of Algeria: 5 Hodna 6 Sabkha 7 Cherqui, Fedjadj, Meirhir 10 Azzel Matti, Meherrhane
of Andorra: 11 Engolasters
of Argentina: 6 Viedma 7 Cardiel, Fagnano, Musters 11 Buenos Aires, Mar Chiquita, Nahuel Huapi
of Armenia: 3 Van 5 Sevan, Urmia 8 Urumiyah
of Australia: 4 Eyre 5 Carey, Cowan, Frome, Moore, Wells 6 Austin, Barlee, Bulloo, Dundas, Harris, Mackay 7 Amadeus, Blanche, Everard, Torrens 8 Carnegie, Gairdner 9 MacDonald 10 Yammayamma 14 Disappointment
of Austria: 6 Almsee 7 Fertoto, Mondsee 8 Bodensee, Traunsee 9 Constance 10 Neusiedler
of Benin: 5 Aheme 6 Nokoue
of Bolivia: 5 Poopo 7 Allagas, Coipasa, Rogagua 8 Titicaca 10 Desaguader
of Botswana: 3 Dow, Xau 5 Ngami
of Brazil: 4 Aima, Feia 5 Mirim 13 Logo dos Platos
of Burma: 4 Inle
of Burundi: 7 Rugwero 8 Tshohoha 10 Tanganyika
of Cambodia/Kampuchea: 8 Tonle Sap
of Cameroon: 4 Chad
of Canada: 4 Cree, Erie, Gras, Seul 5 Garry, Huron, Rainy 6 Louise, St John 7 Abitibi, Dubawnt, Nipigon, Ontario, Testlin 8 Kootenay, Manitoba, Okanagan, Reindeer, Superior, Winnipeg 9 Athabaska, Great Bear, Nipissing 10 Great Slave, Mistassini 12 Winnipegosis
of Central African Republic: 4 Assa
of Chad: 4 Chad
of Chile: 5 Ranco 6 Yelcho 7 Puyehue, Rupanco 8 Cochrane 10 General Paz, Llanquihue 11 Buenos Aires
of China: 3 Tai 4 Chao, Na-mu 5 Kaoyu, Oling, Telli 6 Bamtso, Bornor, Ebinor, Erhhai, Khanka, Lopnor, Namtso, Poyang 7 Chaling, Hungtse, Karanor, Kokonor 8 Hulunnor, Montcalm, Taroktso, Tellinor, Tienchih, Tsinghai, Tungting
of Colombia: 4 Tota
of the Congo: 5 Mweru, Tumba 6 Albert, Nyanza, Upemba 7 Leopold 11 Stanley Pool
of Costa Rica: 6 Arenal
of Denmark 6 Arreso
of Djibouti: 4 Abbe 5 Assal
of Dominican Republic: 10 Enriquillo
of Egypt: 4 Edku, Idku 5 Qarun 6 Maryut, Moeris, Nasser 7 Manzala 8 Burullus, Mareotis
of El Salvador: 5 Guiha, Guija 8 Ilopango 10 Coatepeque
of England: 8 Grasmere 9 Ennerdale, Ullswater, Wastwater 10 Buttermere, Windermere 12 Derwentwater 13 Coniston Water
of Estonia: 5 Pskov 6 Peipus 9 Vortsjarv
of Ethiopia: 3 Abe 4 Tana 5 Abaya, Shola, Tanna, Tsana, Tzana, Zeway 6 Dambea, Dembea, Rudolf 8 Blue Nile, Stefanie
of Finland: 3 Juo, Muo 4 Kemi, Kiui, Nasi, Oulu, Puru, Pyha, Simo 5 Enara, Enare, Hauki, Inari, Kalla, Lappa, Lesti, Puula, Saima 6 Ladoya, Lentua, Saimaa, Sounne, Syvari 7 Koitere, Nilakka 8 Pielinen 9 Kallavesi, Pielavesi
of France: 6 Annecy, Cazaux, Geneva
of Gabon Republic: 7 Anengue, Azinguo
of Germany, East: 6 Muritz
of Germany, West: 9 Constance 11 Inner Alster, Outer Alster
of Ghana: 5 Volta 8 Bosumtwi
of Greece: 5 Karla, Volve 6 Copais, Kopais, Prespa, Voweis 8 Ioannina, Koroneia, Vistonis 9 Trichonis, Vegoritis
of Grenada: 10 Grand Etang
of Guatemala: 5 Dulce, Guija, Peten 6 Izabal 7 Atitlan 9 Amatitlan, Peten Itza
of Haiti: 8 Saumatre
of Honduras: 5 Criba, Yojoa 6 Brewer
of Hungary: 5 Ferto 7 Balaton, Velence 9 Blatensee 10 Neusiedler, Plattensee
of Iceland: 6 Myvatn 10 Thorisvatn 14 Thingvallavatn
of India: 5 Jheel, Lonar, Wular 6 Chilka, Colair, Dhebar, Kolair 7 Kolleru, Pulicat, Pushkar, Sambahr
of Indonesia: 4 Toba 5 Ranau 6 Towuti
of Iran: 5 Niris, Tasht, Tuzlu, Urmia 6 Sahweh, Sistan 7 Maharlu 8 Nemekser, Urumiyeh
of Iraq: 6 al-Milh 7 Sanniya 8 al-Hammar
of Ireland: 3 Doo, Key, Ree, Tay 4 Conn, Derg, Erne, Mask 5 Allen, Barra, Carra, Gowna, Leane, Lough, Neagh 6 Boderg, Cooter, Corrib, Ennell 7 Dromore, Gougane, Oughter, Sheelin 9 Killarney
of Israel: 5 Huleh 7 Dead Sea 8 Kinneret, Tiberias 12 Sea of Galilee
of Italy: 4 Como, Iseo, Nemi 5 Garda 6 Albano, Lesina, Lugano, Varano 7 Bolsena, Perugia 8 Maggiore 9 Bracciano, Trasimeno

(continued)

lake (*continued*)
  of Japan: 4 Biwa, Suwa, Toya 6 Towada 8 Kutchawa, Shikotsu
  of Kazakhstan: 8 Balkhash
  of Kenya: 6 Magadi, Nakuru, Natron, Rudolf 7 Turkana 8 Naivasha, Victoria
  of Lebanon: 5 Quran 6 Qirawn
  of Lithuania: 5 Dysna
  of Luxembourg: 8 Haut Sure
  of Madagascar: 5 Itasy 7 Alaotra, Kinkony
  of Malawi: 5 Nyasa 6 Chilwa, Malawi
  of Mali: 2 Do 4 Debo 5 Garou 7 Korarou 9 Faguibine
  of Mexico: 7 Chapala, Texcoco 9 Patzcuaro
  of Mongolia: 3 Uvs 5 Har Us 6 Bor Nor 7 Ghirgis, Ubsa Nor 8 Airik Nor, Durga Nor, Hobsogol, Khara Usu 9 Khubsugul, Khukhu-Nur 10 Khirgis Nor
  of Montenegro: 7 Scutari, Shkoder
  of Mozambique: 5 Nyasa 6 Chuali, Nyassa 8 Nhavarre
  of Myanmar: 4 Inle
  of Nauru: 11 Buada Lagoon
  of the Netherlands: 7 Haarlem 10 Ijsselmeer 11 Grevelingen, Hazinguliet
  of New Zealand: 3 Ada 4 Gunn, Ohau 5 Hawea, Taupo 6 Pukaki, Pupuke, Te Anau, Tekapo, Wanaka 7 Brunner, Diamond, Kanieri, Okareka, Rotorua 8 Okataina, Paradise, Rotoaira, Wakatipi 9 Manapouri
  of Nicaragua: 7 Managua 9 Nicaragua
  of Niger: 4 Chad
  of Nigeria: 4 Chad
  of the Nile: 4 Tana 5 Kyoga, Tsana 6 Albert, Edward, Nasser 8 Victoria
  of Norway: 4 Alte 5 Ister, Mjosa, Snasa 6 Femund 7 Rostavn, Tunnsjo
  of Panama: 5 Gatun
  of Paraguay: 4 Vera, Ypoa 8 Ypacarai
  of Peru: 8 Titicaca
  of Poland: 5 Goplo, Mamry 8 Niegocin, Sniardwy 13 Stettin Lagoon
  of Puerto Rico: 5 Loiza 6 Carite 8 Dos Bocas 9 Caonillas, Guatajaca
  of Rumania: 5 Sinoe 6 Snagov
  of Russia: 3 Seg 4 Azor, Kola, Neva 5 Byelo, Chany, Elton, Erara, Ilmen, Lacha, Onega, Vozhe 6 Baikal, Ladoga, Tengiz 10 Caspian Sea
  of Rwanda: 4 Kivu 5 Ihema 6 Bufera, Bulera, Mohasi 7 Rugwero, Ruhnodo 8 Mugesera, Tshohoha
  of Sardinia: 6 Omodeo
  of Scotland: 3 Awe, Dee, Lin, Tay 4 Earn, Fyne, Gair, Gare, Linn, Ness, Oich, Ryan, Sloy 5 Duich, Leven, Lochy, Lough, Morar, Maree, Nevis 6 Laggan, Linnhe, Lomond 7 Katrine, Rannoch, St Marys
  of Senegal: 6 Guiers
  of Sicily: 7 Pergusa 8 Camarina
  of Spain: 4 Lago 9 Albrifera
  of the Sudan: 2 No 4 Chad, Toad 6 Nasser
  of Sweden: 4 Ster 5 Asnen, Malar, Silja, Vaner 6 Vanern, Vatter, Wennen 7 Hielmar, Malaren, Vattern 8 Dalalven 9 Hjalmaren
  of Switzerland: 3 Uri, Zug 4 Biel, Thon, Thun 5 Ageri, Leman, Morat 6 Bienne, Brienz, Geneva, Lugano, Sarnen, Wallen, Zurich 7 Hallwil, Lucerne, Lungern 8 Maggiore, Vierwald 9 Bielersee, Constance, Neuchatel, Sarnersee, Thunersee
  of Syria: 5 Merom 7 Djeboid 8 Tiberias
  of Tanzania: 5 Eyasi, Nyasa, Rukwa 6 Malawi, Natron, Nyassa 7 Manyara 8 Victoria 10 Tanganyika
  of Thailand: 9 Nong Lahan
  of Tibet: 3 Aru, Bam, Bum, Nam 4 Mema, Tosu 5 Jagok, Tabia 6 Dagtse, Garhur, Kashun, Nam Iso, Seling, Tangra, Yamdok 7 Kyaring, Terinam, Tsaring, Zilling 8 Jiggitai 9 Tengrinor 11 Manasarowar
  of Tunisia: 6 Achkel, Djerid 7 Bizerte
  of Turkey: 3 Tuz, Van 7 Egridir 8 Beysehir
  of Uganda: 5 Kioga, Kyoga 6 Albert, Edward, George 8 Victoria
  of the United States: 4 Erie, Mead 5 Huron, Tahoe 6 Cayuga, Finger, George, Itasca, Oneida, Seneca 7 Iliamma, Ontario 8 Michigan, Superior 9 Champlain, Great Salt, Salton Sea, Teshekpuk, Winnebago 10 Okeechobee 11 Yellowstone 13 Pontchartrain, Wallenpaupack, Winnipesaukee 14 Lake of the Woods
  of Uruguay: 5 Merin, Mirim 18 Embalse del Rio Negro
  of Venezuela: 9 Maracaibo, Tacarigua
  of Wales: 4 Bala 6 Vyrnwy
  of Yugoslavia: 4 Bled 5 Ohrid 6 Prespa 7 Ochrida, Scutari
  of Zaire: 4 Kivu 5 Mweru, Tumba 6 Albert, Edward, Upemba 9 Mai-Ndombe 10 Tanganyika
  of Zambia: 5 Mweru 6 Kariba 9 Bangweulu 10 Tanganyika
  of Zimbabwe: 4 Kyle 6 Kariba

tra **27** Summer's Last Will and Testament

lame 4 game, halt, weak **5** sorry **6** clumsy, feeble, flimsy, infirm, maimed **7** failing, halting, hobbled, limping, unsound, wanting **8** crippled, deformed, disabled **9** deficient, faltering **10** inadequate **11** ineffectual **12** insufficient, unconvincing, unpersuasive **14** unsatisfactory

lamebrain 3 ass, sap **4** fool **5** booby, dunce, idiot, moron, ninny **6** dimwit, nitwit **7** fathead, half-wit **8** bonehead, dumb-dumb, imbecile, lunkhead, numskull **9** blockhead, numbskull **10** dunderhead, nincompoop **11** chowderhead

lamebrained 4 dumb **6** stupid **7** asinine, foolish, idiotic, moronic **8** crackpot **9** dimwitted, imbecilic **10** half-witted **12** feeble-minded, simpleminded

Lamech
  father: 9 Methusael **10** Methuselah
  wives: 4 Adah **6** Zillah
  son: 5 Jabal, Jubal **9** Tubalcain
  daughter: 6 Naamah

lament 3 cry, sob **4** moan, wail, weep **5** dirge, mourn **6** bewail, outcry, plaint, regret **7** deplore, keening, requiem, whimper **8** mourning **9** death song **11** condole with, lamentation **12** funeral music **13** complain about **14** express pity for, show concern for, sympathize with **15** commiserate with

lamentable 4 dire **6** woeful **7** piteous **8** dreadful, grievous, pathetic, pitiable, shameful, terrible, wretched **9** miserable **10** deplorable **11** distressing, regrettable, unfortunate **13** disheartening, heartbreaking

Lamia
  author: 9 John Keats

Lamia
  form: 7 monster
  characteristic: 12 bloodsucking

La Motta, Jake (Jacob)
  nickname: 9 Bronx Bull
  sport: 6 boxing
  class: 12 middleweight
  movie biography: 10 Raging Bull

Lamour, Dorothy
  real name: 23 Mary Leta Dorothy Kaumeyer
  trademark: 6 sarong

  co-star: 7 Bob Hope **10** Bing Crosby
  born: 12 New Orleans LA
  roles:
    Road to: **3** Rio **4** Bali **6** Utopia **7** Morocco **8** Hong Kong, Zanzibar **9** Singapore

L'Amour, Louis
  author of: 5 Hondo, Lando **7** Sackett, Shalako **8** Conagher **10** Key-Lock Man, Rivers West **14** The Californios, The Daybreakers **15** Westward the Tide **16** How the West Was Won, Over on the Dry Side **21** The Man from Broken Hills, To the Far Blue Mountains

lamp 4 bulb **5** light, torch **6** beacon **7** blinker, lantern **9** headlight, spotlight **10** chandelier, floodlight, klieg light, night light **11** searchlight **12** ceiling light, reading light **14** ceiling fixture
  invented by:
    arc: **6** Staite
    incandescent: **6** Edison
    incandescent frosted: **6** Pipkin
    incandescent gas: **8** Langmuir
    Kleig: **7** Kleigel
    mercury vapor: **6** Hewitt
    miner's safety: **4** Davy
    neon: **6** Claude

Lampedusa, Giuseppe di
  author of: 10 The Leopard

Lampetia
  father: 6 Helius
  mother: 6 Neaera

lampoon 5 farce, put-on, spoof, squib **6** parody, satire, send up **7** mockery, takeoff **8** diatribe, ridicule, satirize, travesty **9** broadside, burlesque **10** caricature, pasquinade **11** make light of

Lamus
  father: 8 Hercules
  mother: 7 Omphale
  attacked: 5 ships

Lamy of Santa Fe
  author: 10 Paul Horgan

lanai 7 veranda

Lancaster, Burt
  real name: 22 Burton Stephen Lancaster
  born: 9 New York NY
  roles: 5 Moses **9** All My Sons, Local Hero **11** Elmer Gantry (Oscar) **12** Atlantic City, The Rainmaker **13** The Rose Tattoo **14** Seven Days in May **16** Sorry Wrong Number **17** Birdman of Al-

catraz **18** From Here to Eternity **19** Come Back Little Sheba, Sweet Smell of Success

lance 4 gaff, pike **5** shaft, spear **7** assegai, halberd, harpoon, javelin

Lancelot, Launcelot
  character in: 16 Arthurian romance
  lover: 9 Guinevere
  home: 10 Joyous Gard

lancer 8 cavalier, horseman **10** cavalryman **12** horse soldier, horse trooper **14** mounted soldier

Lanchester, Elsa
  real name: 17 Elizabeth Sullivan
  husband: 15 Charles Laughton
  born: 7 England **8** Lewisham
  roles: 15 Come to the Stable **22** The Bride of Frankenstein **24** Witness for the Prosecution **25** The Private Life of Henry VIII **31** The Private Life of Henry the Eighth

land 3 get, lea, nab, net **4** area, dirt, dock, gain, grab, lawn, loam, moor, park, soil, take, ward, zone **5** acres, catch, earth, grass, green, humus, light, put in, realm, seize, shire, snare, state, tie up, tract **6** alight, anchor, canton, clinch, colony, county, debark, domain, empire, fields, ground, meadow, nation, parish, realty, region, secure **7** acreage, capture, country, descend, dry land, grounds, kingdom, pasture, section, set down, subsoil, terrain, win over **8** come down, district, dominion, farmland, homeland, location, mainland, make land, make port, precinct, property, province, republic, vicinity **9** cornfield, disembark, grassland, lay anchor, lay hold of, lead one to, reach land, territory **10** bring one to, carry one to, come to land, drop anchor, fatherland, motherland, native land, native soil, real estate, settle down, settlement, terra firma, wheat field **11** countryside, put into port **12** commonwealth, put into shore, real property, village green **13** the old country

Landau, Lev Davidovitch
  field: 7 physics
  nationality: 7 Russian
  discovered: 12 liquid helium **14** ferromagnetism
  awarded: 10 Nobel Prize

landed property 5 manor
6 estate 8 compound
12 countryplace

land force 4 army 6 legion,
troops 7 legions 8 infantry,
soldiers, soldiery 9 artillery

**Landless, Neville and
Helena**
characters in: 22 The Mystery of Edwin Drood
author: 7 Dickens

landlord 5 owner 6 holder,
squire 8 landlady 9 landowner,
possessor 10 freeholder, landholder, proprietor 13 property
owner 14 lord of the manor

landmark 8 keystone, monument, signpost 9 benchmark,
guidepost, highlight, high
point, milestone, watershed
11 cornerstone 12 turning
point 16 historic building

Landmarks
god of: 8 Terminus

Land of Enchantment
nickname of: 9 New Mexico

Land of Lincoln
nickname of: 8 Illinois

Land of Opportunity
nickname of: 8 Arkansas

Land of Sky-blue Waters
nickname of: 9 Minnesota

Land of Steady Habits
nickname of: 11 Connecticut

**Land of Ten Thousand
Lakes**
nickname of: 9 Minnesota

Land of the Dakotas
nickname of: 11 North
Dakota

Land of the Midnight Sun
nickname of: 6 Alaska

Landon, Michael
real name: 20 Eugene Maurice Orowitz
born: 13 Forest Hills NY
roles: 7 Bonanza 15 Highway
to Heaven 19 Little Joe
Cartwright 20 I Was a
Teenage Werewolf 23 Little
House on the Prairie

landscape 4 view 5 scene,
sight, vista 6 aspect 7 scenery
8 panorama, prospect 9 spectacle 10 rural scene, scenic
view 14 natural scenery

landscape architect 7 Le
Notre, Olmsted

landsman 10 countryman
13 fellow citizen

Landsteiner, Karl
field: 8 medicine 9 pathology
distinguished: 10 blood types
identified: 8 RH factor
awarded: 10 Nobel Prize

lane 3 way 4 pass, path, road
5 alley, byway, drive, route,
track, trail 6 access, avenue,
bypath, course 7 passage,
roadway 8 alleyway, approach,
footpath 10 passageway

Lang, Walter
director of: 7 Desk Set
11 The King and I

Lange, Jessica
born: 9 Cloquet MN
roles: 7 Country, Frances,
Tootsie 8 King Kong 11 All
That Jazz 16 Crimes of the
Heart 26 The Postman Always Rings Twice

Langella, Frank
born: 9 Bayonne NJ
roles: 7 Dracula 23 The Diary
of a Mad Housewife

**Langhanke, Lucille
Vasconcellos**
real name of: 9 Mary Astor

Langland, William
author of: 12 Piers Plowman

Langmuir, Irving
field: 9 chemistry
invented: 15 atomic blowtorch 17 gas-tungsten lights
awarded: 10 Nobel Prize

language *see box*

language, artificial
of James Cooke Brown:
6 Loglan
of Hans Freudenthal: 6 Lincos 13 Lingua Cosmica
of Alexander Gode:
11 Interlingua
of C K Ogden: 12 Basic
English
of J M Schleyer: 7 Volapuk
of Jean Francois Sudre:
8 Solresol
of L L Zamehof: 9 Esperanto

language, extinct 6 Dacian,
Hattic, Lycian, Lydian, Palaic
7 Cornish, Elamite, Hittite,
Hurrian 8 Etruscan, Illyrian,
Phrygian, Sumerian, Thracian,
Urartian 9 Dalmatian 15 Cuneiform Luwian 18 Hieroglyphic Luwian

languid 4 dull, slow, weak
5 faint, heavy, inert, shaky,
spent, weary 6 feeble, infirm,
leaden, sickly, supine, torpid
7 rickety, unsound, worn-out
8 drooping, fatigued, inactive,
lifeless, listless, sluggish, unstable 9 apathetic, declining,
doddering, enervated, exhausted, inanimate, lethargic,
trembling, unhealthy 10 indisposed, spiritless 11 debilitated
12 on the decline
13 lackadaisical

languidness 6 apathy, torpor
7 inertia 8 lethargy 12 listless-

ness, sluggishness
13 indisposition

languish 3 ebb 4 fade, fail,
flag, wane, wilt 5 covet,
droop, faint 6 desire, hunger,
sicken, thirst, wither 7 dwindle, long for, pine for, sigh
for 8 diminish, give away,
take sick, yearn for 9 become
ill, break down, hanker for,
hunger for, thirst for, waste
away 10 go downhill 11 deteriorate, have a yen for, hunger after 12 be desirous of
13 go into decline

Languish, Lydia
character in: 9 The Rivals
author: 8 Sheridan

languor 5 ennui 6 torpor 7 inertia 8 dullness, hebetude,
lethargy 9 indolence, lassitude,
torpidity, weariness 10 dispassion, dreaminess 11 languidness, leisureness
12 lifelessness, listlessness,
sluggishness

lank 4 bony, lean, limp, thin
5 gaunt, spare 6 skinny,
slight 7 angular, scrawny
8 straight

lanky 4 bony, lean 5 gaunt,
gawky, rangy, spare, weedy
6 skinny 7 angular, scrawny
8 gangling, rawboned 11 tall
and thin

La Nouvelle Heloise
author: 10 J J Rousseau

Lansbury, Angela
born: 6 London 7 England
roles: 4 Mame 8 Gaslight
10 JB Fletcher 11 Sweeney
Todd 14 Murder She Wrote
15 Jessica Fletcher 22 The
Manchurian Candidate

Laocoon
vocation: 6 priest
father: 5 Capys
brother: 8 Anchises
son: 10 Thymbraeus
warned: 7 Trojans
warned of: 11 Trojan horse
killed by: 8 serpents

Laodamas
father: 8 Eteocles
defended: 6 Thebes
killed: 9 Aegialeus
killed by: 8 Alcmaeon

Laodamia
father: 7 Acastus
11 Bellerophon
mother: 9 Astydamia
husband: 11 Protesilaus
lover: 4 Zeus
son: 8 Sarpedon

Laodice
father: 5 Priam
mother: 6 Hecuba

language 4 cant, jive 5 argot, idiom, lingo, prose, slang, words 6 jargon, patois, speech, tongue 7 cursing, cussing, dialect, diction, wording 8 parlance, rhetoric, swearing, verbiage 9 discourse, elocution, profanity 10 expression, use of words, vernacular, vocabulary 11 imprecation, phraseology, profane talk 12 mother tongue, native tongue 13 colloquialism 14 public speaking, self-expression 16 manner of speaking, mode of expression 17 oral communication, reading and writing, verbal intercourse

- **of Afghanistan:** 4 Dari 5 Farsi 6 Afghan, Pashto, Pushtu 7 Balochi, Baluchi, Persian
- **of Albania:** 3 Geg 4 Cham, Gheg, Hish, Tosk 5 Greek 8 Albanian
- **of Algeria:** 6 Arabic, Berber, French, Zenata 7 Senhaja
- **of Andorra:** 6 French 7 Catalan, Spanish
- **of Angola:** 5 Bantu 8 Kimbundu, Oumbundu 9 Ovimbundu 10 Portuguese
- **of Antigua and Barbuda:** 7 English
- **of Argentina:** 7 Spanish
- **of Armenia:** 7 Russian 8 Armenian
- **of Australia:** 6 Yabber 7 English 9 aborigine (dialects)
- **of Austria:** 5 Czech 6 German, Magyar 8 Croatian 9 Slovenian
- **of Azerbaijan:** 6 Turkic
- **of the Bahamas:** 6 Creole 7 English
- **of Bahrain:** 4 Urdu 5 Farsi 6 Arabic 7 English, Persian
- **of Bangladesh:** 6 Bihari 7 Bengali, English
- **of Barbados:** 7 English
- **of Belgium:** 5 Dutch 6 French, German 7 Flemish
- **of Benin:** 3 Fon 5 Dendi 6 Bariba, French, Fulani, Yoruba
- **of Bermuda:** 7 English
- **of Bhutan:** 5 Hindi, Lhoke 7 Tibetan 8 Dzongkha, Nepalese
- **of Bolivia:** 6 Aymara 7 Quechua, Spanish
- **of Borneo:** 5 Malay 7 Chinese, English
- **of Bosnia-Herzegovina:** 13 Serbo Croatian
- **of Botswana:** 5 Bantu, Click 6 Tswana 7 English, Khoisan 8 Setswana
- **of Brazil:** 10 Portuguese
- **of Brunei:** 4 Iban 5 Malay 7 Chinese, English
- **of Bulgaria:** 9 Bulgarian
- **of Burkina Faso:** 4 Bobo, Lobi, More, Samo 5 Dyula, Mande, Mossi 6 French
- **of Burundi:** 6 French 7 Kirundi, Swahili
- **of Cambodia/Kampuchea:** 5 Khmer 6 French
- **of Cameroon:** 4 Bulu 5 Bantu, Bassa, Hausa 6 Douala, Ewondo, French, Fulani 7 English 8 Bamileke, Fulfulde
- **of Canada:** 6 Eskimo, French 7 English
- **of Canary Islands:** 7 Spanish
- **of Cape Verde:** 7 Crioulo 10 Portuguese 13 Verdean Creole
- **of Central African Republic:** 5 Sango, Zande 6 French
- **of Chad:** 4 Sara 5 Turku 6 Arabic, French
- **of Chile:** 7 Spanish
- **of China:** 7 Chinese 8 Mandarin, Shanghai 9 Cantonese
- **of Colombia:** 7 Spanish
- **of Comoros:** 6 Arabic, French 7 Swahili 8 Malagasy
- **of Congo:** 4 Susu 5 Bantu, Fiote 6 French, Kituba 7 Bangala, Lingala
- **of Costa Rica:** 7 Spanish
- **of Crete:** 5 Greek 6 Minoan 7 Linear A, Linear B
- **of Croatia:** 8 Croatian 13 Serbo Croatian
- **of Cuba:** 7 Spanish
- **of Cyprus:** 5 Greek 7 Turkish 8 Armenian
- **of Czechoslovakia/Czech Republic:** 5 Czech 6 German, Magyar, Slovak 7 Russian 9 Hungarian
- **of Denmark:** 4 Odan 5 Danish 8 Faeroese 11 Greenlander
- **of Djibouti:** 4 Afar 6 Arabic, French, Somali
- **of Dominican Republic:** 6 French 7 English, Spanish
- **of Ecuador:** 6 Jibaro 7 Quechua, Spanish
- **of Egypt:** 6 Arabic, Coptic, French 7 English
- **of El Salvador:** 7 Spanish
- **of England:** 7 English
- **of Equatorial Guinea:** 4 Bubi, Fang 6 pidgin 7 Spanish
- **of Eritrea:** 7 Amharic
- **of Estonia:** 5 Tartu 10 Finno-Ugric
- **of Ethiopia:** 3 Giz 4 Afar, Agow, Geez, Saho 5 Geeze, Ghese, Smali, Tigre 6 Arabic, Harari 7 Amharic, English, Italian, Russian 8 Gallinya, Irob-Saho, Tigrinya
- **of Fiji:** 5 Hindi 6 Fijian 7 English
- **of Finland:** 4 Avar, Lapp 5 Karen, Ugric, Vogul 6 Magyar, Ostyak, Tarast 7 Finnish, Olonets, Samoyed, Swedish 8 Estonian 10 Olenetsian
- **of France:** 6 French
- **of Gabon Republic:** 6 French
- **of the Gambia:** 4 Fula 5 Wolof 6 Fulani 7 English, Malinke 8 Mandingo
- **of Georgia:** 8 Georgian
- **of Germany:** 6 German 10 High German 11 Hochdeutsch
- **of Ghana:** 2 Ga 3 Ewe, Gur, Kwa, Twi 5 Fanti, Hausa 7 Dagomba, English

(continued)

language (*continued*)
- **of Gibraltar: 7** English, Spanish
- **of Greece: 5** Greek
- **of Greenland: 6** Danish, Eskimo **11** Greenlandic
- **of Grenada: 7** English
- **of Guatemala: 6** Quiche **7** Spanish
- **of Guinea: 5** Fulbe, Mande **6** Arabic, French, Fulani **7** English
- **of Guinea-Bissau: 5** Fulah **7** Balante, Crioulo **8** Mandingo **10** Portuguese **21** Cape Verde-Guinea Creole
- **of Guyana: 5** Hindi **7** English
- **of Haiti: 6** Creole, French, patois
- **of Honduras: 7** English, Spanish
- **of Hong Kong: 7** Chinese, English **9** Cantonese
- **of Hungary: 6** German, Magyar, Slovak **8** Croatian **9** Hungarian **10** Finno-Ugric
- **of Iceland: 5** Norse **9** Icelandic
- **of India: 4** Urdu **5** Hindi, Oriya, Tamil **6** Sindhi, Telugu **7** Bengali, English, Kannada, Malayam, Marathi, Punjabi **8** Assamese, Gujarati, Kashmiri, Sanskrit **9** Malayalam
- **of Indonesia: 5** Tetum **6** Bahasa, Igorot **7** English, Gyarung, Malayan **8** Balinese, Chamorro, Javanese, Madurese, Sudanese **10** Indonesian, Polynesian
- **of Iran: 4** Luri, Zend **5** Farsi, Turki **6** Arabic **7** Baluchi, Kurdish, Persian **8** Armenian **11** Azerbaijani
- **of Iraq: 5** Farsi **6** Arabic **7** Kurdish, Persian, Turkish
- **of Ireland: 5** Irish **6** Gaelic **7** English
- **of Israel: 6** Arabic, French, Hebrew **7** English
- **of Italy: 5** Ladin, Latin **6** French, German **7** Italian, Slovene **8** Friulian **9** Sardinian
- **of Ivory Coast: 4** Akan **6** Dioula, French
- **of Jamaica: 6** Creole **7** English
- **of Japan: 5** Kanto **8** Japanese
- **of Java: 4** Kavi, Kawi **5** Malay **6** Sassak **8** Balinese, Madurese, Sudanese **16** Bahasa Indonesian
- **of Jordan: 6** Arabic
- **of Kazakhstan: 6** Kazakh
- **of Kenya: 3** Luo **5** Bantu, Luhya, Masai **6** Kikuyu **7** English, Swahili **8** Buyerati **10** Hindustani
- **of Kiribati: 6** Samoan **7** English **10** Gilbertese
- **of Korea: 6** Korean
- **of Kuwait: 6** Arabic
- **of Kyrgyzstan: 6** Turkic **7** Kirghiz
- **of Laos: 3** Lao, Man, Meo **6** French **7** English
- **of Latvia: 7** Lettish
- **of Lebanon: 6** Arabic, French, Syriac **7** English, Turkish **8** Armenian
- **of Lesotho: 5** Sotho **7** English, Sesotho
- **of Liberia: 3** Kru, Kwa **5** Mande **7** English
- **of Libya: 6** Arabic, Berber **7** English, Italian
- **of Liechtenstein: 6** German **10** Alemannish
- **of Lithuania: 5** Zmudz **6** Baltic **10** Lithuanian
- **of Luxembourg: 6** French, German **7** English **13** Letzeburgesch
- **of Macao: 7** Chinese, English **9** Cantonese **10** Portuguese
- **of Macedonia: 10** Macedonian
- **of Madagascar/Malagasy Republic: 6** French **8** Malagasy, Malgache
- **of Malawi: 3** Yao **4** Cewa **5** Bantu, Ngoni, Tonga **6** Nyanja **7** English, Tumbuka **8** Chichewa **10** Chitumbuka
- **of Malaysia: 4** Bugi, Dyak **5** Malay, Tamil **6** Battok, Rejang **7** Chinese, English, Lampong, Niasese **8** Achinese, Javanese, Makassar **14** Bahasa Malaysia
- **of Maldives: 6** Arabic, Divehi
- **of Mali: 5** Dogon, Dyula, Feulh, Mande, Marka **6** Berber, French, Fulani **7** Bambara, Malinke, Senoufo, Songhai
- **of Malta: 7** English, Italian, Maltese
- **of Mauritania: 4** Fula **5** Wolof **6** Arabic, French **7** Phoolor, Tukulor **8** Fulfulde, Mandingo **9** Sarakolle **10** Hassaniyya
- **of Mauritius: 4** Urdu **5** Hindi, Tamil **6** Creole, French **7** English
- **of Mexico: 5** Mayan, Otomi **6** Mixtec **7** Mazahua, Mazatec, Nahuatl, Spanish, Totonac, Zapotec **8** Tarascan
- **of Moldova: 8** Romanian **9** Moldovian
- **of Monaco: 6** French **7** English, Italian **10** Monegasque
- **of Mongolia: 6** Kazakh **16** Khalkha Mongolian
- **of Montenegro: 13** Serbo-Croatian
- **of Morocco: 6** Arabic, Berber, French **7** Spanish
- **of Mozambique: 3** Yao **5** Makua **6** Nyanji, Thonga **7** Swahili **10** Portuguese
- **of Myanmar: 3** Lai **4** Chin, Kuki, Pegu, Shan **5** Karen **6** Kachin **7** Burmese
- **of Namibia: 5** Bantu **6** German **7** English, Khoisan **9** Afrikaans
- **of Nauru: 7** English, Nauruan
- **of Nepal: 6** Nepali, Newari **7** English
- **of the Netherlands: 5** Dutch **7** English, Frisian
- **of New Guinea: 4** Motu **7** English **16** Melanesian Pidgin
- **of New Zealand: 5** Maori **7** English
- **of Nicaragua: 7** English, Spanish
- **of Niger: 5** Hausa, Mande **6** Djerma, French, Fulani, Tuareg **8** Mandingo, Tamashek

(*continued*)

language (*continued*)

of Nigeria: 3 Ibo **4** Efik, Igbo **5** Hausa **6** Yoruba **7** English
of Norway: 4 Lapp **5** Norse **6** Bokmal **7** Nynorsk, Riksmal **8** Landsmal, Samnorsk **9** Landsmaal, Norwegian
of Oman: 4 Urdu **5** Hindi **6** Arabic **7** Baluchi
of Pakistan: 4 Urdu **6** Pushtu, Sindhi **7** Baluchi, Bengali, English, Punjabi
of Panama: 7 English, Spanish
of Paraguay: 6 German **7** Guarani, Spanish
of Peru: 6 Aymara **7** English, Quechua, Spanish
of the Philippines: 4 Moro **5** Bicol, Bikol **6** Ibanag **7** Cebuano, English, Ilocano, Spanish, Tagalog, Visayan **8** Filipino **9** Pampangan, Philipino **10** Samar-Leyte **13** Bamboo-English **14** Panay-Hiligayon
of Poland: 6 Kaszub, Polish **10** Pomeranian
of Polynesia: 4 Niue, Uvea **5** Maori **6** Samoan, Tongan **7** Austral, Tagalog, Tokelau **8** Hawaiian, Tahitian **9** Marquesan, Tuamatuan **10** Mangarevan
of Portugal: 10 Portuguese
of Qatar: 6 Arabic
of Romania: 6 French, Magyar **7** Russian **8** Romanian, Rumanian **9** Hungarian
of Russia: 5 Evenk **6** Buriat, Kalmyk **7** Finnish, Russian **8** Ossetian
of Rwanda: 6 French **7** Swahili **11** Kinyarwanda
of Samoa: 6 Samoan **7** English
of San Marino: 7 Italian
of Sao Tome and Principe: 10 Portuguese
of Sardinia: 7 Italian
of Saudi Arabia: 6 Arabic
of Scotland: 4 Erse **6** Celtic, Gaelic, Keltic, Lallan **7** English, Lalland
of Senegal: 5 Wolof **6** French
of the Seychelles: 6 Creole, French **7** English
of Sierra Leone: 4 Krio **5** Limba, Mende, Mendi, Temne **6** Creole **7** English
of Singapore: 5 Malay, Tamil **7** Chinese, English **8** Mandarin
of Slovakia: 6 Slavik, Slovak
of Slovenia: 7 Slovene
of the Solomon Islands: 7 English **13** Pidgin English **16** Melanesian Pidgin
of Somalia: 6 Arabic, Somali **7** English, Italian
of South Africa: 4 Taal, Zulu **5** Bantu, Hindi, Nguni, Sotho, Swazi, Tamil, Venda, Xhosa **6** Telegu, Thonga **7** English, Khoisan, Ndebele, Sesotho **8** Bujarati, Fanakalo **9** Afrikaans **13** Kitchen-Kaffir
of Spain: 6 Basque **7** Catalan, Spanish **8** Balearic, Galician **9** Castilian, Valencian
of Sri Lanka: 4 Pali **5** Tamil **7** English **9** Sinhalese
of Sudan: 2 Ga **3** Efe, Ewe, Ibo, Kru, Vak, Vei **4** Efik, Mole, Tshi **6** Arabic, Nubian, Yoruba **7** English **8** Mandango, Mandingo **9** Ta Bedawie
of Suriname: 5 Carib, Dutch, Hindi **6** Arawak **7** English **8** Javanese, Taki-Taki **10** Hindustani **11** Sranan Tongo **12** Sranang Tongo
of Swaziland: 5 Ngumi **7** English, Siswati **9** Afrikaans **10** Portuguese
of Sweden: 4 Lapp **7** Swedish
of Switzerland: 5 Ladin **6** French, German **7** Italian **8** Romansch **14** Switzerdeutsch
of Syria: 6 Arabic, French, Syriac **7** Aramaic, English, Kurdish, Turkish **8** Armenian
of Taiwan: 4 Amon, Amoy **5** Hakka, Kuo Yu **6** Minnan **9** Taiwanese **15** Mandarin Chinese
of Tajikistan: 5 Tajik **7** Tadzhik
of Tanzania: 5 Bantu **6** Arabic **7** English, Khoisan, Nilotic, Swahili **8** Cushitic, Gujarati
of Thailand: 3 Lao, Tai **4** Ahom, Shan, Thai **5** Kadai **7** Bangkok, English **9** Krung Thep **12** Chinese Malay
of Tibet: 5 Balti **6** Ladkhi **7** Bhutani, Bodskad **8** Sanskrit **9** Bhutanese
of Togo: 3 Ana, Ewe, Twi **4** Mina **5** Hausa **6** French, Kabrai, Kabrie **7** Bassari, Dagomba, Quatchi **8** Kotokoli, Lotocoli
of Tonga: 6 Tongan **7** English
of Trinidad and Tobago: 6 French **7** Chinese, English, Spanish **10** Portuguese **12** French Patois
of Tunisia: 6 Arabic, Berber, French
of Turkey: 6 Arabic **7** Kurdish, Turkish
of Turkmenistan: 6 Turkic **10** West Turkic
of Tuvalu: 6 Samoan **7** English **8** Tuvaluan **10** Polynesian
of Uganda: 5 Ateso, Ganda **7** English, Luganda, Swahili
of Ukraine: 9 Ukrainian
of United Arab Emirates: 5 Farsi **6** Arabic **7** English, Persian
of Uruguay: 7 Italian, Spanish
of Uzbekistan: 5 Uzbek
of Vanuatu: 6 French **7** Bislama, English **16** Melanesian Pidgin
of Venezuela: 4 Pume **7** Spanish
of Vietnam: 3 Yue **4** Cham **5** Khmer, Rhade **6** French **7** Chinese, English **9** Cantonese **10** Vietnamese
of Wales: 5 Welsh **6** Celtic, Cymric, Keltic, Kymric **7** Cymraeg, English
of Western Sahara: 16 Hassaniyya Arabic
of Western Samoa: 6 Samoan **7** English
of Yemen: 6 Arabic

(*continued*)

language (*continued*)
of Yugoslavia: **7** Bosnian, Slovene **8** Albanian, Croatian **9** Hungarian, Slovenian **10** Macedonian
11 Montenegrin **13** Herzegovinian, Serbo-Croatian
of Zaire: **5** Bantu **6** French **7** Chiluba, Kikongo, Lingala, Swahili **8** Sudanese, Tshiluba
of Zambia: **4** Lozi **5** Bemba, Lunda, Tonga **6** Luvale, Nyanja **7** English **9** Afrikaans
of Zimbabwe: **3** Ila **5** Bantu, Shona **7** English, Ndebele

husband: 8 Helicaon
son: 6 Pereus **7** Munitus

Laodocus
father: 6 Apollo
mother: 6 Phthia
killed by: 7 Aetolus

Laomedon
king of: 4 Troy
father: 4 Ilus
wife: 6 Strymo
son: 5 Priam **6** Lampus **7** Clytius **8** Hicetaon, Tithonus
daughter: 7 Hesione **8** Themiste

Laos *see box*

Laothoe
concubine of: 5 Priam
son: 6 Lycaon **9** Polydorus

Lao-tzu
author of: 10 Tao Te Ching

lap 3 sip **4** lick, wash **5** awash, drink, plash, slosh **6** babble, bubble, gurgle, lick up, murmur, ripple, splash, tongue

La Paz
administrative capital of:
7 Bolivia

lapis lazuli
species: 8 lazurite
source: 10 Badakhshan **11** Afghanistan

lapse 3 gap, sag **4** drop, fall, flaw, go by, loss, sink, slip, stop, wane **5** boner, break, cease, droop, error, fault, pause, slump **6** breach, elapse, expire, hiatus, laxity, pass by, period, recede, recess, run out, slip by, wither, worsen **7** blunder, decline, descent, failing, failure, faux pas, interim, passage, relapse, respite, subside **8** collapse, downfall, elapsing, interval, omission, slip away **9** backslide, disregard, interlude, oversight, slump down, terminate **10** degenerate, falling off, forfeiture, infraction, negligence, peccadillo, regression **11** backsliding, delinquency, dereliction, deteriorate, shortcoming **12** degeneration, intermission, interruption, lose validity **13** deterioration, process of time, slight mistake **14** become obsolete, fall into disuse

lapsus linguae 16 a slip of the tongue

lar *see* **5** lares

Lara
character in: 9 Dr Zhivago
author: 9 Pasternak

Laraia, Carol Maria
real name of: 13 Carol Lawrence

larceny 5 fraud, theft **7** bilking, forgery, looting, robbery, sacking **8** burglary, cheating, fleecing, stealing **9** extortion, pilferage, pilfering, swindling **10** absconding, peculation, plagiarism, purloining **11** defalcation, depredation **12** embezzlement, grand larceny, petit larceny, petty larceny, safecracking **13** appropriation, housebreaking **16** misappropriation

larder 5 cuddy **6** pantry, spence **7** buttery **8** food room **9** stillroom, storeroom **10** supply room **11** storage room

Lardner, Ring
author of: 11 The Love Nest, You Know Me Al **12** Treat Em Rough **16** Gullible's Travels

Larentalia
origin: 5 Roman
event: 8 festival

lares
form: 7 spirits
watched over: 5 house **6** hearth **9** community **10** crossroads
single member: 3 lar
companions: 7 penates
correspond to: 8 Dioscuri

large 3 big, fat **4** high, huge, vast, wide **5** ample, broad, grand, great, heavy, hulky, obese, plump, roomy **6** goodly, mighty, portly, rotund **7** copious, immense, liberal, massive, sizable **8** colossal, enormous, gigantic, imposing, man-sized, outsized, spacious, sweeping, towering **9** boundless, capacious, expansive, extensive, giantlike, kingsized, limitless, monstrous, overgrown, ponderous, strapping, unlimited, unstinted **10** exorbitant, gargantuan, stupendous **11** extravagant, far-reaching,

Laos
other name: 7 Lan Xang **23** land of a million elephants
capital/largest city: 9 Viengchan, Vientiane
others: 4 Nape **5** Pakse, Xieng **6** Paklay **7** Thakhek **11** Savannakhet, Xiang Khoang **12** Luang Prabang **14** Louangphrabang
school: 12 Sisavangvong
measure: 3 bak
monetary unit: 2 at **3** att, kip
mountain: 3 Lai, Loi, San **4** Copi, Khat **5** Atwat **6** Khoung, Tiubia **15** Annam Cordillera
highest point: 3 Bia **7** Phou Bia
river: 3 Noi **4** Done **5** Khong **6** Mekong, Sebang
physical feature:
plain: **4** Jars
plateau: **8** Bolovens
people: 2 Lu **3** Kha, Lao, Man, Meo, Tai, Yao, Yun **4** Miao, Thai **5** Hmong **8** Lao Teung **10** Phoutheung
leader: **7** Fa Ngoun **13** Souphanouvong **14** Souligna Vongsa, Souvanna Phouma
language: 3 Lao, Man, Meo **6** French **7** English
religion: 7 animism **8** Buddhism **17** Theravada Buddhism
feature:
Buddhist priest: **5** bonze
Communist guerrilla group: **9** Pathet Lao
musical instrument: **5** khene
temple: **3** wat
trail: **9** Ho Chi Minh

magnificent, substantial 12 considerable **13** comprehensive **14** Brobdingnagian

large-hearted 8 generous **10** altruistic, benevolent, charitable **12** humanitarian **13** philanthropic

largely 6 mainly, mostly, widely **7** chiefly, greatly **9** generally, primarily **10** on the whole **11** extensively, principally **12** considerably **13** predominantly, substantially **14** for the most part, to a great extent

largeness 7 bigness **8** enormity, hugeness **9** amplitude, greatness, immensity **11** massiveness **12** enormousness

large-scale 3 big **4** huge, vast, wide **5** broad, great **6** all-out, mighty **8** colossal, far-flung, gigantic **9** extensive, monstrous **10** gargantuan, stupendous, tremendous **11** far-reaching, wide-ranging **15** all-encompassing

largess, largesse 3 aid **4** boon, gift, help **5** favor, mercy **6** bounty, reward **7** charity, payment **8** bestowal, donation, gratuity, kindness, offering **9** benignity **10** assistance, generosity **11** benefaction, benevolence **12** philanthropy, remuneration

large store 8 emporium **11** supermarket **15** department store

largo
   music: **4** slow **14** dignified tempo

lark 3 gag **4** game, jape, romp, whim **5** antic, caper, fling, prank, spree, trick **6** frolic, gambol **7** caprice **8** escapade **11** high old time **12** sportiveness
   group of: **10** exaltation

larkspur 9 Consolida **10** Delphinium
   varieties: **4** Tall **5** Dwarf **6** Rocket

La Rochefoucauld, Francois
   author of: **6** Maxims **7** Maximes

larva
   insect stage after: **3** egg
   insect stage before: **4** pupa
   legless: **6** maggot

larvae
   form: **6** ghosts
   characteristic: **9** malignant

lascivious 4 foul, lewd **5** bawdy, dirty, gross, lurid **6** coarse, filthy, impure, ribald,

---

sordid, vulgar, wanton **7** immoral, lustful, obscene, ruttish, squalid **8** depraved, immodest, improper, indecent, prurient **9** lecherous, salacious, shameless **10** indelicate, licentious, unblushing **11** dirty-minded, unwholesome

lash 3 fix, hit, tie **4** beat, bind, blow, flog, moor, rope, whip **5** brace, curse, flail, hitch, knock, leash, pound, scold, smack, strap, thong, tie up, truss **6** attach, berate, buffet, fasten, hammer, pinion, revile, secure, strike, stroke, tether, thrash, whip up **7** lecture, scourge, upbraid **8** lambaste, make fast **9** castigate, horsewhip **10** take to task, tongue-lash **11** rail against **13** cat-o'-nine-tails

lashed together 4 tied **5** bound **6** tied up **7** secured, trussed **8** fastened

lash out at 5 fly at **6** assail, attack, strike **8** fall upon

Las Palmas
   capital of: **13** Canary Islands

lass 4 girl, maid, miss **5** wench **6** damsel, female, lassie, lovely, maiden, pretty, virgin **7** colleen **10** schoolgirl, young woman

Lasser, Louise
   father: **8** S J Lasser
   husband: **10** Woody Allen
   born: **9** New York NY
   roles: **22** Mary Hartman Mary Hartman

lassie 4 girl, lass, maid **6** maiden **7** colleen **10** young woman

Lassie
   character: **5** Timmy **9** Doc Weaver **10** Jeff Miller, Paul Martin, Ruth Martin **11** Corey Stuart, Ellen Miller **12** Gramps Miller **17** Sylvester (Porky) Brockway
   cast: **10** Jan Clayton, Jon Provost, Jon Shepodd, Robert Bray **11** Arthur Space, Tommy Rettig **12** Donald Keeler, June Lockhart **14** Cloris Leachman, George Chandler **15** George Cleveland

lassitude 5 ennui **6** apathy, torpor **7** boredom, fatigue, inertia, languor, malaise **8** debility, doldrums, dullness, lethargy, weakness **9** faintness, indolence, tiredness, torpidity, wea-

---

riness **10** droopiness, drowsiness, enervation, exhaustion, feebleness, supineness **11** languidness, prostration **12** indifference, lack of energy, listlessness, sluggishness

lasso 4 lash, rope **5** catch, noose, reata, riata, thong **6** lariat

last 3 end **4** go on, keep, live, stay, wear **5** abide, after, exist, final, stand **6** behind, ending, endure, extend, finale, finish, hold on, hold up, remain, utmost **7** carry on, closing, extreme, finally, hold out, outlive, outwear, persist, stand up, subsist, survive, tailing **8** at the end, continue, doomsday, farthest, final one, furthest, hindmost, hold good, in back of, maintain, rearmost, terminal, terminus, trailing, ultimate **9** in the rear, persevere **10** Armageddon, concluding, conclusion, conclusive, eventually, terminally, ultimately **11** crack of doom, crucial time **12** in conclusion, tagging along **13** Day of Judgment
   French: **7** dernier

Last Days of Pompeii, The
   author: **18** Edward Bulwer-Lytton
   character: **4** Ione **5** Nydia **7** Arbaces, Glaucus **9** Apaecides

Last Frontier
   nickname of: **6** Alaska

lasting 4 firm **5** fixed, solid **7** abiding, chronic, durable, eternal **8** constant, enduring, immortal, lifelong, long-term **9** incessant, lingering, long-lived, permanent, perpetual, steadfast, unceasing **10** continuing, deep-rooted, deep-seated, perdurable, persistent, protracted **11** established, never-ending **12** indissoluble **14** indestructible, of long duration **17** firmly established

lastly 6 at last **7** finally, to sum up **8** after all, in the end **10** on the whole **12** in conclusion **19** all things considered

Last of the Mohicans, The
   author: **19** James Fenimore Cooper
   character: **5** Magua, Uncas **9** Cora Munro **10** Alice Munro **11** Natty Bumppo

12 Chingachgook 18 Major Duncan Heyward

last part 3 end 6 ending, finale, finish 8 third act 10 denouement 12 final chapter

Last Picture Show, The
director: 16 Peter Bogdanovich
based on story by: 13 Larry McMurtry
cast: 10 Ben Johnson 11 Jeff Bridges 12 Ellen Burstyn 13 Eileen Brennan 14 Cloris Leachman, Cybill Shepherd, Timothy Bottoms
Oscar for: 15 supporting actor (Johnson) 17 supporting actress (Leachman)

Last Puritan, The
author: 15 George Santayana

La Strada
director: 15 Federico Fellini
cast: 11 Aldo Silvana 12 Anthony Quinn 15 Giulietta Masina, Richard Basehart
score: 8 Nino Rota
Oscar for: 11 foreign film

last resort
French: 8 pis aller

last resource
French: 8 pis aller

Last Tango in Paris
director: 18 Bernardo Bertolucci
cast: 12 Marlon Brando 14 Maria Schneider

Last Things
author: 6 C P Snow

Last Valley, The
author: 11 A B Guthrie Jr

Last Waltz, The
director: 14 Martin Scorsese
cast: 7 The Band 8 Bob Dylan 9 Neil Young 10 The Staples 11 Eric Clapton, Muddy Waters, Neil Diamond, Van Morrison 12 Joni Mitchell 13 Emmylou Harris

latch 3 bar 4 bolt, clip, hasp, hook, lock, loop, shut, snap 5 catch, clamp, close 6 buckle, button, clinch, fasten, secure 8 make fast 9 fastening

late 3 new 4 dead, gone, slow 5 fresh, tardy 6 held up, put off, recent 7 delayed, newborn, overdue, tardily 8 departed, detained, dilatory, passed on 9 after time, postponed 10 behindhand, behind time, dilatorily, unpunctual 16 recently deceased

late arrival 7 laggard 8 lateness, newcomer 9 immigrant, latecomer, tardiness 16 Johnny-come-lately

Late George Apley, The
author: 10 J P Marquand

lately 6 of late 7 just now 8 latterly, recently, right now 9 currently, presently, yesterday 10 not long ago 13 a short time ago

Late Mattia Pascal, The
author: 15 Luigi Pirandello

latency 8 abeyance, deferral, dormancy, inaction 10 quiescence, suspension

Late Night with David Letterman
feature: 11 Ask Mr Melman 15 Stupid Pet Tricks 18 Brush with Greatness, Stupid People Tricks
bandleader: 10 Paul Shafer
city: 7 New York

latent 6 covert, hidden 7 abeyant, dormant, lurking, passive 8 inactive, sleeping 9 concealed, potential, quiescent, suspended, unaroused, unexposed 10 in abeyance, intangible, unapparent, unrealized 11 not manifest, undeveloped, unexpressed 13 inconspicuous

later 4 next 5 since 6 behind, in time, mature 7 ensuing, tardily 8 in a while, in sequel 9 afterward, following, presently, thereupon 10 consequent, more recent, most recent, subsequent, succeeding, successive, thereafter 11 after a while, consecutive 12 subsequently, successively, toward the end

lateral 4 side 5 sided 7 flanked, oblique, sloping 8 edgeways, edgewise, flanking, sidelong, sideward, sideways, sidewise, skirting, slanting

latest cry
French: 10 dernier cri

latest fashion
French: 10 dernier cri

latest word
French: 10 dernier cri

lather 4 foam, head, scum, soap, suds 5 froth, spume, sweat 6 soap up 8 make foam, soapsuds 9 make froth 11 shaving foam

Latin
language family: 12 Indo-European
branch: 6 Italic
group: 7 Romance
subgroup: 6 French 7 Catalan, Italian, Romansh, Spanish 8 Romanian 9 Provencal 10 Portuguese 13 Rhaeto-Romanic

Latinus
king of: 6 Latium
father: 6 Faunus
mother: 6 Marica
wife: 5 Amata
daughter: 7 Lavinia

latitude 5 range, scope, sweep 6 leeway, margin 7 license 8 free play 9 amplitude, elbowroom, full swing 10 indulgence, liberality 11 opportunity, unrestraint 12 independence 15 freedom of action, freedom of choice 16 unrestrictedness

Latona see 4 Leto

La Tour, Georges de
born: 3 Vic 6 France 8 Lorraine
artwork: 7 Peasant 10 The New Born 12 Peasant's Wife, The Card Cheat 15 St Peter Penitent 16 The Fortune Teller 18 The Denial of St Peter 23 The Education of the Virgin 31 St Sebastian Tended by the Holy Women

Latrobe, Benjamin Henry
architect of: 9 US Capitol 15 Sedgeley Mansion (PA) 18 Baltimore Cathedral 22 Philadelphia Waterworks
style: 12 Greek Revival, Neoclassical 13 Gothic Revival

latter 3 end 4 last 5 final, later 6 ending, latest, modern 7 ensuing 8 terminal 10 most recent, subsequent, succeeding, successive 13 last-mentioned 15 second-mentioned

lattice 4 fret, grid 5 frame, grate 6 grille, screen 7 framing, grating, network, trellis, webwork 8 fretwork, openwork 9 framework, reticulum 11 trelliswork 12 reticulation

Latvia see box

laud 5 extol, honor 6 praise 7 acclaim, commend, glorify

laudable 5 model, noble 8 sterling 9 admirable, estimable, excellent, exemplary 10 creditable 11 commendable, meritorious 12 praiseworthy 13 unimpeachable 17 deserving of esteem 18 worthy of admiration

laudation 6 praise 7 acclaim 8 applause, approval 11 approbation 12 commendation

laudatory 8 admiring, honoring, praising 9 adulatory, approving, extolling, favorable 10 eulogistic, eulogizing, flattering, glorifying 11 acclamatory, approbatory, celebratory, encomiastic, panegyrical

Latvia
former name: **30** Latvian Soviet Socialist Republic
capital/largest city: **4** Riga
others: **5** Cesis, Libau **6** Dvinsk, Libava, Tukums **7** Jelgava, Jurmala, Liepaja, Rezekne **8** Dunaberg, Dunaburg, Valmiera **9** Ventspils **10** Daugavpils
government: **8** republic
measure: **3** let **4** stof **5** stoff, verst **6** arshin, kulmet **7** verchoc, verchok **8** krouchka, pourvete **9** deciatine, lofstelle, pourvette **10** tonnseteel
monetary unit: **3** lat **4** latu **6** rublis, santim **7** kapeika, santima
weight: **9** liespfund
lake: **7** Aluksne
river: **4** Ogre **5** Gauja, Venta **6** Salaca **7** Daugava, Lielupe **12** Western Dvina
sea: **6** Baltic
physical feature:
  cape: **8** Domesnes
  gulf: **4** Riga
  strait: **4** Irbe
people: **3** Kur, Liv **4** Balt, Cour, Lett **7** Latgale, Latvian, Russian, Zemgale
  former ruler: **15** Teutonic Knights
language: **7** Lettish
religion: **8** Lutheran **13** Roman Catholic

---

12 commendatory
13 complimentary

Laudianus 16 Greek unical codex

laugh 4 glee, ha-ha, ho-ho, howl, roar **5** mirth **6** cackle, giggle, guffaw, titter **7** break up, chortle, chuckle, snicker, snigger **10** bellylaugh, horselaugh **12** express mirth **14** roll in the aisle, split one's sides

laughable 5 comic, dopey, droll, funny, inane, merry, silly, witty **6** absurd, stupid **7** amusing, asinine, comical, foolish, risible **8** farcical, tickling **9** diverting, grotesque, hilarious, ludicrous **10** outlandish, outrageous, ridiculous **11** rib-tickling **12** preposterous **13** sidesplitting

Laugh-In, Rowan & Martin's
regular: **8** Dan Rowan **9** Gary Owens, Judy Carne, Ruth Buzzi **10** Dick Martin, Goldie Hawn, Larry Hovis, Lily Tomlin **11** Arte Johnson, Henry Gibson **12** Jo Anne Worley **13** Eileen Brennan
saying: **10** Sock it to me **15** Here come de judge, You bet your bippy **24** Beautiful downtown Burbank **31** Look that up in your Funk and Wagnalls

laughingstock 3 ass **4** butt, dupe, fool, joke **8** fair game **11** figure of fun

laugh off 6 deride **7** dismiss, put down **8** belittle, ridicule **9** disparage

laughter 3 joy **4** glee **5** mirth **6** gaiety **7** jollity, revelry **8** hilarity **9** joviality, merriment **11** merrymaking **12** conviviality, exhilaration

Laughton, Charles
wife: **14** Elsa Lanchester
born: **7** England **11** Scarborough
roles: **9** Rembrandt **10** Jamaica Inn **13** Les Miserables **15** Ruggles of Red Gap, The Paradine Case **16** Advise and Consent **17** Mutiny on the Bounty **23** Barretts of Wimpole Street, The Hunchback of Notre Dame **24** Witness for the Prosecution **25** The Private Life of Henry VIII (Oscar)

launch 4 fire, hurl **5** begin, eject, float, found, impel, shoot, start, throw **6** let fly, propel, unveil **7** fire off, project, send off **8** catapult, initiate, premiere, put to sea **9** cast forth, discharge, establish, institute, introduce, set afloat **10** embark upon, inaugurate, set forth on **11** set in motion, venture upon **13** thrust forward **15** set into the water

launder 4 soak, wash **5** clean, rinse, scour, scrub **7** cleanse, wash out **11** wash and iron

Launfal
knight of: **10** roundtable

Laura
director: **13** Otto Preminger
cast: **11** Clifton Webb, Dana Andrews, Gene Tierney **12** Vincent Price **14** Judith Anderson

laurel 6 Kalmia, Laurus **13** Laurus nobilis **14** Ficus benjamina **15** Cordia alliodora
varieties: **3** bog, pig **4** pale **5** black, dwarf, great, sheep **6** Alpine, cherry, ground, Indian, purple, Sierra, spurge, tropic **7** Chinese, English, red-twig, weeping, western **8** American, drooping, Himalaya, Japanese, mountain, Portugal **9** Tasmanian **10** Australian, California, variegated **11** Alexandrian

Laurel, Stan
real name: **22** Arthur Stanley Jefferson
partner: **11** Oliver Hardy
born: **7** England **9** Ulverston
roles: **8** Pardon Us **9** Saps at Sea **10** Way Out West

laurels 4 fame **5** award, glory, honor, kudos, prize **6** credit, praise, renown, reward **7** acclaim, tribute **8** accolade, applause, citation **9** celebrity **10** decoration, popularity **11** acclamation, distinction, recognition **12** commendation **15** illustriousness

Laurie
also: **16** Theodore Laurence
character in: **11** Little Women
author: **6** Alcott

laus Deo 11 praise to God **13** praise be to God

Lautreamont, Comte de
author of: **19** Les Chants de Maldoror

lavation 7 bathing, washing **8** ablution, cleaning **9** cleansing

lavender 4 herb, mint **5** aspic, behen, lilac, spick, spike **6** purple **7** inkroot **8** amethyst, stichado **9** lavendula
represents: **6** purity
uses: **6** sachet **7** perfume **8** medicine **9** cosmetics

laver 11 footed basin

Laverne and Shirley
character: **12** Frank De Fazio **13** Carmine Ragusa, Lenny Kolowski, Mrs Edna Babish, Shirley Feeney **14** Laverne De Fazio **15** Andrew (Squiggy) Squiggman
cast: **10** Eddie Mekka, Phil

Foster **12** Betty Garrett, David L Lander **13** Cindy Williams, Michael McKean, Penny Marshall
girls worked in: 12 Shotz Brewery
theme song: 23 Making Our Dreams Come True
spinoff from: 9 Happy Days

Lavinia
father: 7 Latinus
mother: 5 Amata
husband: 6 Aeneas

lavish 4 free, lush, wild **5** plush, waste **6** shower **7** copious, opulent, pour out, profuse **8** abundant, effusive, generous, prodigal, squander **9** bounteous, bountiful, dissipate, excessive, exuberant, impetuous, luxuriant, plenteous, plentiful, sumptuous, unsparing **10** immoderate, munificent, profligate, unstinting **11** extravagant, fritter away, intemperate, overindulge, overliberal, spend freely **12** give overmuch, greathearted, overwhelming, unrestrained, without limit

lavishness 6 bounty **8** lushness, opulence **9** profusion **10** luxuriance **11** munificence, prodigality **12** extravagance, immoderation **13** bountifulness, plenteousness, sumptuousness

Lavoisier, Antoine
field: 9 chemistry
nationality: 6 French
founder: 15 modern chemistry
named: 6 oxygen **8** hydrogen

law 3 act **4** bill, code, fuzz, rule, writ **5** axiom, bylaw, canon, dogma, edict, model, truth **6** decree, police **7** justice, mandate, precept, statute, theorem **8** absolute, legality, standard **9** criterion, enactment, gendarmes, legal form, ordinance, postulate, principle **10** civil peace, convention, due process, invariable, regulation **11** commandment, formulation, fundamental, orderliness, working rule **13** jurisprudence, standing order **14** generalization, rules of conduct **15** legal profession
Latin: 3 jus
goddess of: 4 Maat

law-abiding 6 honest **7** upright **9** honorable **10** aboveboard, principled

lawbreaker 3 con **4** hood, thug **5** crook, felon **6** outlaw **7** convict, culprit **8** criminal, jailbird, offender, scofflaw **9** miscreant, wrongdoer **10** delinquent, malefactor, recidivist **11** perpetrator **12** transgressor

lawful 3 due **5** legal, licit **6** proper, titled **7** allowed, granted **8** rightful **9** legalized, statutory, warranted **10** authorized, legitimate, prescribed **11** legitimized, permissible **15** legally entitled **16** legally permitted

lawless 6 unruly, wanton **7** chaotic, defiant, illegal, riotous, wayward **8** anarchic, mutinous, unlawful, wide open **9** insurgent, out of hand, unbridled **10** disorderly, licentious, rebellious, refractory, ungoverned **11** disobedient, lawbreaking, terroristic **12** disorganized, freewheeling, illegitimate, noncompliant, unrestrained **13** insubordinate, transgressive **14** uncontrollable

lawlessness 5 chaos **7** anarchy **8** disorder

lawn 4 park, turf, yard **5** glade, grass, sward **7** grounds, terrace **10** grassy plot, green field, greensward, meadowland **12** grassy ground

law of a place
Latin: 7 lex loci

Law of Moses 5 Torah **10** Pentateuch **15** Ten Commandments

law of nations
Latin: 10 jus gentium

law of nature
Latin: 11 jus naturale

Lawrence, Carol
real name: 16 Carol Maria Laraia
husband: 12 Robert Goulet
born: 13 Melrose Park IL
roles: 5 Maria **13** West Side Story

Lawrence, D H
author of: 10 The Rainbow **11** Women in Love **13** Sons and Lovers **20** Lady Chatterley's Lover

Lawrence, Ernest Orlando
field: 7 physics
invented: 9 cyclotron
awarded: 10 Nobel Prize

Lawrence, Gertrude
real name: 29 Alexandra Dagmar Lawrence Klasen
born: 6 London **7** England
roles: 9 Pygmalion **11** The King and I **17** The Glass Menagerie

Lawrence, T E
also: 16 Lawrence of Arabia
served in: 3 WWI **10** Arab Revolt
advisor to: 6 Faisal **12** Husayn Ibn Ali
fought against: 5 Turks **8** Ottomans
author of: 20 Seven Pillars of Wisdom

Lawrence of Arabia
director: 9 David Lean
cast: 10 Jose Ferrer, Omar Sharif **11** Claude Rains, Jack Hawkins, Peter O'Toole (T E Lawrence) **12** Alec Guinness, Anthony Quinn **13** Arthur Kennedy, Anthony Quayle
Oscar for: 7 picture **8** director **14** cinematography

Lawrence Welk Show, The
champagne lady: 8 Alice Lon **11** Norma Zimmer
cast: 7 Aladdin **11** Larry Hooper, Myron Floren **12** Bobby Burgess **13** Barbara Boylan, Lennon Sisters
Welk played: 9 accordion

lawyer 6 jurist, legist **7** counsel, shyster **8** advocate, attorney **9** barrister, counselor, solicitor **10** mouthpiece, prosecutor **11** pettifogger **12** legal advisor **14** special pleader **15** ambulance chaser

lax 4 hazy, limp, weak **5** agape, loose, slack, vague **6** casual, flabby, floppy, remiss **7** cryptic, flaccid, inexact, lenient, not firm, relaxed **8** careless, derelict, drooping, heedless, nebulous, slipshod, uncaring, yielding **9** confusing, imprecise, negligent, oblivious, undutiful, unheeding, unmindful **10** ill-defined, incoherent, neglectful, permissive **11** hanging open, indifferent, thoughtless, unconcerned **12** loose-muscled, unstructured **13** irresponsible **15** unconscientious

laxness 7 neglect **9** looseness, slackness **10** negligence **11** imprecision **12** carelessness, indifference

Laxness, Halldor Kiljan
author of: 12 Iceland's Bell **14** The Atom Station **17** Independent People **25** The Great Weaver from Kashmir

lay 3 air, bet, put, set **4** bear, fell, fine, form, give, laic, lend, levy, make, plan, poem, raze, rest, seat, song, tune **5** align, allot, apply, ditty, exact, floor, hatch, level, offer, place, stage, wager **6** assess, assign, ballad, charge, demand, depict, devise, gamble, ground, hazard, impose, impute, laical, layout, locate, melody, repose, strain **7** amateur, arrange, concoct, contour, deposit, dispose, forward, present, produce, profane, proffer, refrain, secular, set down, situate, station 8 allocate, assemble, beat down, give odds, inexpert, organize, oviposit, position 9 attribute, elucidate, enunciate, formulate, knock down, knock over, prostrate, roundelay, situation 10 cause to lie, topography 11 arrangement, disposition, nonclerical, orientation, put together 12 conformation 13 configuration, inexperienced, nonspecialist 14 partly informed, unprofessional 15 nonprofessional 17 nonecclesiastical

lay at the door of 6 assign 7 ascribe 8 charge to 9 attribute

lay bare 4 bare, show 6 expose, reveal, unmask, unveil, unwrap 7 divulge, exhibit, publish, uncover 8 disclose 9 broadcast, make known 10 make public 11 communicate

lay down arms 5 yield 6 give up 7 succumb 8 cry quits 9 surrender 10 capitulate 11 come to terms, sue for peace 13 declare a truce 17 acknowledge defeat

layer 3 bed, lap, ply 4 coat, fold, leaf, seam, slab, tier, zone 5 level, plate, scale, sheet, stage, story 6 lamina 7 stratum 9 thickness

layman 4 laic 6 sister 7 amateur, brother 8 outsider 9 churchman 10 catechumen 11 churchwoman, communicant, parishioner 15 nonprofessional 16 member of the flock

layoff 4 fire 6 firing, idling, ouster, the axe 7 dismiss, release, sacking, the boot, the gate, the sack 8 pink slip, shutdown 9 closedown, discharge, dismissal, hard times, the bounce 10 cashiering, depression, the heave-ho 11 furloughing, termination 12 unemployment 13 disemployment, walking papers 20 discharge temporarily

lay off 7 dismiss, forfeit, release, set free 8 get rid of, liberate 9 discharge, terminate 11 give the gate, send packing

Lay of the Last Minstrel, The
  author: 14 Sir Walter Scott
  character: 8 Margaret, The Dwarf 13 Lady Buccleuch, Lord Cranstoun 17 Master of Buccleuch 19 Ghost of Michael Scott 21 Sir William of Deloraine

lay on 6 bestow, confer, supply 7 present, provide

lay open 4 open 6 expose, open up 7 clarify 9 make plain 18 make understandable

layout 4 form, plan 5 chart, draft, dummy, model, motif, spend 6 design, expend, pay out, sketch, spread 7 diagram, drawing, fork out, outline, pattern 8 disburse, shell out 9 blueprint, delineate, placement, spread out, structure 11 arrangement, composition

lay waste 4 ruin 5 level, wreck 6 ravage 7 despoil, destroy, wipe out 8 demolish, desolate 9 devastate, eradicate 10 annihilate, obliterate

Lazarus 6 beggar
  means: 8 God helps
  sister: 4 Mary 6 Martha
  hometown: 7 Bethany
  resurrected by: 5 Jesus

Lazarus
  author: 14 Leonid Andreyev

Lazarus, Mell
  creator/artist: 5 Momma 9 Miss Peach

lazurite
  variety: 11 lapis lazuli

lazy 3 lax 4 idle, slow 5 inert, slack 6 drowsy, sleepy, torpid 7 laggard, languid 8 inactive, indolent, listless, slothful, sluggish 9 apathetic, easygoing, lethargic, shiftless 10 languorous, slow-moving 13 unindustrious 15 unwilling to work

lazy person 5 drone, idler 6 loafer 14 good-for-nothing

Leach, Archibald Alexander
  real name of: 9 Cary Grant

Leachman, Cloris
  born: 11 Des Moines IA
  roles: 7 Phyllis 11 High Anxiety 12 Kiss Me Deadly 17 Young Frankenstein 18 Mary Tyler Moore Show, The Last Picture Show

lead 2 go 3 aim, top 4 clue, draw, edge, have, head, hero, hint, live, lure, pass 5 charm, excel, guide, model, outdo, pilot, steer, tempt 6 allure, convey, direct, entice, extend, induce, manage, margin, pursue, seduce 7 advance, attract, bring on, command, conduct, control, example, go first, incline, issue in, marshal, pioneer, precede, proceed, produce, stretch, surpass, undergo 8 domineer, go before, guidance, moderate, outstrip, persuade, priority, result in, shepherd, star part 9 advan-

tage, come first, direction, go through, headliner, influence, plurality, rank first 10 branch into, experience, first place, indication, precedence, precedency, set the pace, show the way, tend toward 11 antecedence, be in advance, leading role, preside over, protagonist

lead
  chemical symbol: 2 Pb

lead astray 4 dupe, lure 6 delude 7 beguile, deceive, ensnare, mislead 19 lead up the garden path

leaden 4 dark, dull, glum, gray 5 inert, murky 6 dreary, gloomy, numbed, somber, torpid 7 grayish, languid 8 burdened, careworn, darkened, deadened, listless, sluggish, unwieldy 9 depressed, inanimate 10 cumbersome, hard to move

leader 4 boss, guru, head 5 chief, guide, mogul 6 bigwig, honcho, master, mentor, tycoon 7 captain, foreman, kingpin, magnate, manager, pioneer, prophet 8 director, superior 9 chieftain, commander, conductor, godfather, pacemaker, patriarch 10 forerunner, pacesetter, pathfinder, supervisor 11 frontrunner, torchbearer, trailblazer

leadership 4 helm, lead, sway 5 reins, wheel 7 command, primacy 8 charisma, guidance, headship, hegemony 9 captaincy, supremacy 10 domination, mastership 11 managership, preeminence, stewardship 12 directorship, governorship, guardianship, self-reliance 13 ability to lead, self-assurance 14 administration 15 managerial skill, superintendency 17 authoritativeness

leading 3 top 4 head, main 5 basic, chief, first, great, prime 6 ruling 7 advance, guiding, initial, leadoff, notable, primary, ranking, stellar, supreme, topmost 8 advanced, dominant, foremost 9 directing, essential, governing, nonpareil, paramount, principal, prominent, sovereign, unrivaled 10 motivating, preeminent, underlying 11 controlling, outstanding, pacesetting 12 unchallenged, unparalleled 13 most important 14 quintessential 15 most influential, most significant

lead on 4 goad 5 egg on 6 entice 7 mislead, support 9 encourage **19** lead up the garden path

lead the way 4 lead, show, take **5** guide **6** escort **7** conduct

leaf 4 flip, foil, page, skim **5** blade, bract, folio, frond, green, inset, petal, sheet, thumb **6** browse, glance, insert, needle **7** foliole, lamella, leaflet **8** cotyledon, extension, turn green **10** lamination **12** sheet of metal

leaflet 2 ad **4** bill **5** flier, flyer, tract **6** folder, notice **7** booklet, handout **8** brochure, bulletin, circular, handbill, pamphlet **9** broadside, throwaway **10** broadsheet **12** announcement **13** advertisement

league 4 ally, band **5** cabal, group, guild, merge, union **6** cartel **7** combine, compact, company, network, society **8** alliance **9** coalition **10** conspiracy, federation, fraternity, join forces **11** association, confederacy, confederate, consolidate, cooperative, partnership **13** collaboration, confederation, confraternity

Leah
 means: **7** wild cow
 father: **5** Laban
 husband: **5** Jacob
 sister: **6** Rachel
 slave: **6** Zilpah
 son: **4** Levi **5** Judah **6** Reuben, Simeon **7** Zebulun **8** Issachar
 daughter: **5** Dinah
 burial place: **9** Machpelah

leak 3 ebb, rip **4** blab, gash, hole, ooze, rent, rift, seep, vent **5** break, chink, cleft, crack, drain, exude, fault, spill **6** breach, efflux, escape, filter, let out, reveal, take in **7** confide, crevice, divulge, dribble, fissure, let slip, opening, outflow, rupture, seepage **8** aperture, disclose, draining, give away, puncture **9** discharge, percolate **10** interstice, make public **11** be permeable, perforation **12** admit leakage **16** let enter or escape

leakage 5 issue **7** outflow, seepage **9** discharge

Leakey, Louis S Bazett
 field: **12** anthropology
 discovered: **8** early man
 worked at: **8** Tanzania **12** Olduvai Gorge
 wife: **4** Mary
 son: **7** Richard

lean 3 aim, bow, tip **4** bend, cant, lank, list, poor, rely, rest, slim, tend, thin, tilt

5 gaunt, lanky, lurch, scant, slant, slope, small, spare, weedy **6** barren, depend, meager, modest, nonfat, prefer, scanty, skinny, sparse, svelte **7** angular, count on, incline, recline, scraggy, scrawny, slender, spindly, trust in, willowy **8** exiguous, rawboned, resort to, skeletal **9** emaciated **10** inadequate, set store by **11** be partial to, have faith in, prop oneself **12** insufficient, seek solace in **14** rest one's weight, support oneself

Lean, David
 director of: **10** Summertime **11** Oliver Twist **13** Doctor Zhivago, Ryan's Daughter **15** A Passage to India **16** Lawrence of Arabia (Oscar) **17** Great Expectations **23** The Bridge on the River Kwai (Oscar)

Leander
 loved: **4** Hero
 swam nightly: **10** Hellespont
 death by: **8** drowning

leaning 4 bent, turn **5** slant **7** relying **8** affinity, tendency **9** proneness **10** dependence, partiality, preference, proclivity, propensity **11** inclination **14** predisposition

leap 3 hop **4** jete, jump, romp, rush, skip **5** bound, caper, frisk, vault **6** bounce, cavort, frolic, gambol, hasten, hurtle, prance, spring **7** hop over **8** jump over **9** bound over, saltation **10** hurtle over, jump across, spring over

Learchus
 father: **7** Athamas
 mother: **3** Ino
 killed by: **7** Athamas

learn 3 con **4** hear **6** detect, master, pick up **7** find out, uncover, unearth **8** discover, memorize **9** ascertain, determine, ferret out **10** become able **12** find out about

learned 4 deep, wise **7** erudite **8** cultured, educated, informed, lettered, literate, profound, schooled, well-read **9** scholarly **10** cultivated **12** accomplished, intellectual, well-educated **13** knowledgeable

Learned, Michael
 roles: **5** Nurse **10** The Waltons

learner 4 tyro **5** pupil **6** novice, rookie **7** draftee, recruit, scholar, student, trainee **8** beginner, disciple, enlistee, follower, freshman, neophyte **9** fledgling, greenhorn, novitiate, proselyte, schoolboy

10 apprentice, schoolgirl, tenderfoot **11** schoolchild

learning 5 study **6** wisdom **7** culture **8** teaching **9** education, erudition, knowledge, schooling **11** cultivation, edification, information, instruction, scholarship **13** comprehension, enlightenment, understanding

Learning
 god of: **5** Thoth

leash 4 curb, lead, line, rein, ruin **5** strap, thong **6** bridle, choker, fasten, hold in, stifle, string, tether **7** contain, control, harness **8** restrain, suppress

Leather-Stocking Tales
 author: **19** James Fenimore Cooper
 includes: **10** The Prairie **11** The Pioneers **13** The Deerslayer, The Pathfinder **20** The Last of the Mohicans
 hero of: **7** Hawkeye **10** Pathfinder, The Trapper **11** Natty Bumppo **13** The Deerslayer **15** Leather-stocking **16** Le Longue Carabine

leave 2 go **3** fly **4** cede, exit, flee, keep, quit, will **5** allot, be off, cause, endow, forgo, going, split, waive, yield **6** assign, bug out, commit, decamp, depart, desert, eschew, forego, give up, legate, move on, recess, resign, retain, set out **7** abandon, abscond, bequest, consent, consign, deposit, entrust, forsake, holiday, let stay, liberty, parting, produce, push off, release, respite, retreat, sustain, take off, time off **8** approval, bequeath, farewell, furlough, generate, give over, maintain, result in, sanction, shove off, vacation **9** allowance, apportion, departure, hotfoot it, let remain, surrender, tolerance **10** concession, depart from, embark from, go away from, indulgence, permission, relinquish, retire from, sabbatical, sufferance, withdrawal **11** bid farewell, endorsement **13** absent oneself, understanding

leave a ship 4 land **6** debark **8** go ashore **9** disembark **11** abandon ship

leave behind 6 desert, vacate **7** abandon, discard, forsake **8** evacuate **9** cast aside **10** relinquish **11** outdistance

leave cold 4 bore **12** leave unmoved **15** leave unaffected

Leave It To Beaver
  character: **11** June Cleaver, Ward Cleaver **12** Eddie Haskell, Wally Cleaver **13** Beaver (Theodore) Cleaver
  cast: **7** Tony Dow **9** Ken Osmond **12** Hugh Beaumont, Jerry Mathers **18** Barbara Billingsley

leave off 3 end **4** halt, quit, stop **5** cease **6** desist, finish **7** suspend **8** conclude **11** discontinue, refrain from

leave out 4 drop, omit **6** except, reject **7** exclude

Leaves of Grass
  author: **11** Walt Whitman

leave suddenly 3 fly **4** flee **6** cut out, decamp, run off **7** abscond, make off, run away, rush off, take off **11** take a powder **15** be off and running

leave-taking 4 exit **5** adieu **7** good-bye, leaving, parting, send-off **8** au revoir, farewell **9** departure **10** withdrawal

leave undone 4 quit **6** give up **7** abandon, forsake, neglect **8** give up on

Lebanon *see box*

Le Bel, Joseph Achille
  field: **9** chemistry
  nationality: **6** French
  founded: **15** stereochemistry

Le Bourgeois Gentilhomme
  author: **7** Moliere
  character: **7** Cleonte, Dorante **9** M Jourdain **16** Monsieur Jourdain

Le Carre, John
  real name: **13** David Cornwell
  author of: **11** A Perfect Spy **13** Smiley's People **18** The Looking Glass War **19** A Small Town in Germany **20** The Little Drummer Girl **21** The Honorable Schoolboy **22** Tinker Tailor Soldier Spy **26** The Spy Who Came in from the Cold

lechayim, lehayim 6 to life

Lecheates
  epithet of: **4** Zeus
  means: **10** in childbed

lecherous 4 lewd **5** randy **6** carnal **7** goatish, lustful, ruttish **8** prurient **9** salacious, satyrlike **10** lascivious, libidinous, licentious, lubricious

lechery 4 lust **8** lewdness **9** carnality, prurience **10** satyriasis **11** lustfulness, nymphomania **13** salaciousness **14** lasciviousness

Le Cid
  author: **9** Corneille
  composer: **13** Jules Massenet

Leconte de Lisle, Charles
  author of: **14** Poemes Antiques, Poemes Barbares

Le Corbusier
  real name: **23** Charles Edouard Jeanneret
  architect of: **10** La Tourette (monastery) **15** Notre Dame du Haut (Ronchamp France) **16** Unite d'Habitation (Marseilles)
  planned city of: **10** Chandigarh (capital of the Punjab)

style: **6** Purism **12** New Brutalism

lecture 4 talk **5** chide, scold, speak **6** homily, preach, rail at, rebuke, sermon, speech **7** address, censure, chiding, expound, oration, reading, reproof, reprove, upbraid, warning **8** admonish, call down, harangue, moralize, reproach **9** discourse, hold forth, reprimand, sermonize, talking-to **10** preachment, take to task **12** chastisement, disquisition, remonstrance

lecture hall 9 classroom

Lebanon
  ancient name: **9** Phoenicia
  capital/largest city: **6** Beirut **8** Beyrouth
  others: **3** Sur **4** Arca, Tyre **5** Ehden, Halba, Hamat, Sahle, Saida, Sayda, Sidon, Sofar, Zahla, Zahle **6** Byblos, Ghazir, Juniye, Tibnin **7** Baalbek, Batroun, Bsherri, Rachaya, Tripoli, Zgharta **8** Djezzine, El Hermel, Hasbaiya, Merjuyun **9** Broummana, Marjayoun **10** Beited Dine, Heliopolis
    ancient city:
      8 Carthage
  school: **4** Arab **8** American, Lebanese **11** Saint Joseph
  division:
    ancient: **4** Tyre **5** Arwad, Sidon **6** Byblos, Jubayl
  monetary unit: **5** livre, pound **7** piastre
  lake: **5** Quran **6** Qirawn
  mountain: **4** Mzar **5** Aruba **6** Hermon **7** Lebanon, Sannine **8** Kadischa, Kenisseh **9** Kennisseh **10** al-Mukammal **11** Anti-Lebanon
  highest point: **7** es Sauda **13** Qurnat al-Sawda
  river: **3** Dog, Joz **5** Barid, Kebir, Lycos **6** Auwali, Barada, Damour, Litani **7** Hasbani, Leontes, Orontes **8** Kasemieh
  sea: **13** Mediterranean
  physical feature:
    cape: **10** Pigeon Rock **11** Ras esh Shiqa **12** Qadisha Gorge
    plain: **4** Bika **5** Bekaa
    valley: **5** Beqaa **6** al-Biqa **9** Great Rift
    wind: **7** khamsin
  people: **4** Arab **11** Palestinian
    ancient: **9** Canaanite **10** Phoenician
    leader: **6** Bashir, Sarkis **7** Chamoun **8** Franjieh **9** al-Din Maan **11** Amin Gemayel **13** Bashir Gemayel
    poet: **11** Kahil Gibran
    rulers: **5** Arabs **6** French, Greeks, Romans **8** Hittites, Ottomans, Persians **9** Assyrians, Crusaders, Egyptians, Mamelukes **11** Babylonians
  language: **6** Arabic, French, Syriac **7** English, Turkish **8** Armenian
  religion: **5** Druse, Druze, Islam **8** Maronite, Melchite **10** Protestant **11** Monophysite **12** Christianity **13** Greek Catholic **14** Greek Orthodoxy **17** Armenian Orthodoxy
  place:
    dam: **5** Qarun
    ruins: **7** Baalbek **15** Temple of Bacchus, Temple of Jupiter
  feature:
    Christian group: **10** Phalangist
    dance: **6** dabkeh, dabkey
    tree: **5** cedar
  food:
    dish: **6** kibbeh **8** tabouleh
    drink: **4** arak **6** arrack

10 auditorium 12 amphitheater, assembly hall

lecturelike 7 donnish, preachy 8 academic, didactic, pedantic 9 homiletic 10 moralizing

Leda
father: 8 Thestius
husband: 9 Tyndareus
lover: 4 swan, Zeus
son: 6 Castor, Pollux 8 Dioscuri 10 Polydeuces
daughter: 5 Helen 6 Phoebe 8 Philonoe, Timandra 12 Clytemnestra

Leda and the Swan
author: 7 W B Yeats

ledge 4 sill, step 5 ridge, shelf 6 mantel, offset 8 foothold, shoulder 10 projection 11 mantelpiece, mantelshelf, outcropping

Lee, Henry
nickname: 15 Light Horse Harry
served in: 16 Revolutionary War
member of: 10 US Congress 19 Continental Congress
governor of: 8 Virginia
suppressed: 16 Whiskey Rebellion
son: 7 Robert E

Lee, Robert E
father: 5 Henry 15 Light Horse Harry
born: 11 Stratford VA 18 Westmoreland County
wife: 21 Mary Ann Randolph Custis
served in: 8 Civil War 10 Mexican War
commander of: 22 Army of Northern Virginia
suppressed raid: 9 John Brown 12 Harper's Ferry
battle: 7 Bull Run 8 Antietam 10 Gettysburg 14 Fredericksburg 16 Chancellorsville, Seven Days' Battles
surrendered at: 20 Appomattox Court House
president of: 17 Washington College

Lee, Spike
original name: 17 Sheldon Jackson Lee
born: 2 GA 7 Atlanta
wife: 17 Tonya Linette Lewis
films: 8 Malcolm X 10 School Daze 11 Jungle Fever 15 Do the Right Thing, She's Gotta Have It 31 Joe's Bed-Stuy Barbership We Cut Heads
company: 18 Forty Acres and A Mule
ads for: 4 Nike

leek 18 Allium ampeloprasum

varieties: 4 lily, rose, sand, wild 5 lady's 6 meadow

leer 4 ogle 5 fleer, smirk 6 goggle

leery 4 wary 5 cagey, chary 6 unsure 7 guarded 8 cautious, doubtful, hesitant 9 skeptical, undecided 10 suspicious 11 circumspect, distrustful, mistrustful

Leeuwenhoek, Anton van
field: 10 microscopy
father of: 12 microbiology
discovered: 13 red blood cells

leeway 4 play 5 scope, slack 6 margin 7 cushion, headway, reserve 8 headroom, latitude 9 allowance, clearance, elbowroom, extra time, tolerance 11 flexibility 13 room for choice 14 margin for error 15 maneuverability

left behind 7 vacated 8 deserted, forsaken, forsook 9 abandoned, discarded, evacuated 12 relinquished

leftover 6 excess, legacy, unused 7 overage, residue, surplus, uneaten 8 leavings, oddments, residual, survivor 9 carry-over, remainder, remaining

left-wing 7 leftist, liberal, radical 9 socialist 11 progressive

left-winger 7 leftist, liberal, radical 9 socialist 11 progressive

Lefty
nickname of: 5 Gomez 12 Steve Carlton

leg 3 gam, lap, pin 4 limb, part, post, prop 5 brace, femur, shank, stage, stump, tibia 6 column, fibula, member, pillar 7 portion, section, segment, stretch, support, upright

legacy 4 gift 6 devise, estate 7 bequest, vestige 8 heirloom, heritage, leftover, survivor 9 carry-over, throwback, tradition 10 birthright, hand-me-down 11 inheritance

legal 4 fair 5 licit, of law, valid 6 kosher, lawful 7 cricket 8 forensic, judicial, juristic, rightful 9 courtroom, juridical 10 legitimate, sanctioned 11 permissible

legal advisor 6 lawyer 7 counsel 8 advocate, attorney 9 barrister, counselor, solicitor 13 attorney-at-law 14 counselor-at-law

legal form 4 writ 8 document 10 instrument

legality 8 validity 9 licitness

10 lawfulness, legitimacy 17 constitutionality

legalization 8 sanction 9 enactment 10 permission, validation 13 authorization 14 legitimization

legalize 5 enact 6 permit 8 sanction, validate 9 authorize 10 legitimize

legal residence 4 home 8 domicile, dwelling

legal tender 4 cash 5 money 8 currency

legate 5 agent, envoy 6 deputy 8 emissary 14 representative

legatee 4 heir 9 inheritor 11 beneficiary

legation 7 embassy, mission 8 ministry 9 consulate 10 delegation 11 chancellery

legend 3 key 4 edda, lore, myth, saga, tale 5 fable, motto, story, title 7 caption, fiction, proverb 8 folklore 11 inscription

legendary 5 famed 6 fabled, famous, mythic 7 storied 8 fabulous, fanciful, mythical 9 imaginary 10 apocryphal, celebrated, fictitious, proverbial

Legend of Good Women, The
author: 15 Geoffrey Chaucer
character: 4 Dido 5 Medea 6 Thisbe 7 Alceste, Ariadne, Lucrece, Phyllis 9 Cleopatra, Hypsipyle, Philomela 12 Hypermnestra

Legend of Sleepy Hollow, The
author: 16 Washington Irving
character: 12 Brom Van Brunt (Brom Bones), Ichabod Crane 16 Katrina Van Tassel

Leger, Fernand
born: 6 France 8 Argentan
artwork: 8 Bargeman 10 Adam and Eve, The Wedding, Three Women 11 The Builders, The Cyclists, The Mechanic, The Stairway 14 The Great Parade 15 Le Grand Dejeuner 16 Contrasting Forms, Nudes in the Forest 21 Butterflies and Flowers

legerdemain 7 cunning 8 deftness, jugglery, juggling, trickery 9 deception 10 adroitness, artfulness 11 maneuvering 13 sleight of hand 16 prestidigitation

legible 4 neat 5 clear, plain 7 visible 8 clear-cut, distinct, readable 12 decipherable

14 comprehensible, understandable

legion 3 mob, sea **4** army, host, mass **5** corps, drove, horde, spate, swarm **6** myriad, throng, troops **7** brigade **8** division **9** multitude

leg irons 5 bonds, irons **6** chains **7** fetters **8** shackles

legislation 3 act **4** bill **6** ruling **7** measure, statute **9** amendment, enactment, lawmaking, ordinance

legislator 7 senator **8** alderman, delegate, lawgiver, lawmaker **10** councilman **11** assemblyman, congressman **13** congresswoman **14** representative **15** parliamentarian

legislature 4 diet **5** house **6** senate **7** chamber, council **8** assembly, congress **10** parliament

legitimacy 8 legality, validity **10** lawfulness **11** correctness, genuineness **12** authenticity, rightfulness **15** appropriateness

legitimate 4 fair, just, true **5** legal, licit, sound, valid **6** lawful, proper **7** correct, genuine, logical, tenable **8** rightful **9** authentic, justified, plausible **10** believable, reasonable **11** appropriate, wellfounded

leg-pull 4 hoax **9** deception **13** practical joke

Legree, Simon
character in: **14** Uncle Tom's Cabin
author: **5** Stowe

LeGuin, Ursula K
author of: **13** Lathe of Heaven **14** Rocannon's World **15** The Dispossessed **16** Always Coming Home **21** The Left Hand of Darkness

Lehar, Franz (Ferencz)
born: **7** Komarno (then Hungary, now Czechoslovakia)
composer of: **9** Gipsy Love **13** The Merry Widow **20** The Count of Luxembourg

Lehmbruck, Wilhelm
born: **7** Germany **9** Meiderich
artwork: **11** Rising Youth **12** Man Flung Down, Praying Woman, Seating Youth **13** Kneeling Woman, Standing Woman, Standing Youth

Leigh, Janet
husband: **10** Tony Curtis
daughter: **14** Jamie Lee Curtis

born: **8** Merced CA
roles: **6** Psycho, The Fog **10** The Vikings **11** Little Women, Touch of Evil

Leigh, Vivien
real name: **17** Vivian Mary Hartley
husband: **15** Laurence Olivier
born: **5** India **10** Darjeeling
roles: **11** Ship of Fools **12** Anna Karenina **13** Blanche du Bois, Scarlett O'Hara **14** Waterloo Bridge **15** Gone With the Wind (Oscar) **17** That Hamilton Woman **21** A Streetcar Named Desire (Oscar), Roman Spring of Mrs Stone

Leighton, Margaret
husband: **12** Max Reinhardt **14** Laurence Harvey, Michael Wilding
born: **7** England **10** Barnt Green **14** Worcestershire
roles: **12** The Go-Between **13** The Winslow Boy **14** Separate Tables **19** The Night of the Iguana

leisure 4 ease, rest **6** recess, repose **7** holiday, respite, time off **8** free time, vacation **9** diversion, idle hours, spare time **10** recreation, relaxation

leisurely 4 idle, slow **6** casual, slowly **7** languid, relaxed, restful **9** unhurried **10** slowmoving **11** lingeringly, unhurriedly **12** without haste **13** lackadaisical

Lemminkainen
origin: **7** Finnish
mentioned in: **8** Kalevala
role: **4** hero

Lemmon, Jack
real name: **18** Jack Uhler Lemmon III
wife: **11** Felicia Farr
born: **8** Boston MA
roles: **7** Missing **10** April Fools **12** Save the Tiger (Oscar), The Apartment, The Great Race, The Odd Couple **13** China Syndrome, Mister Roberts, Some Like It Hot **18** Days of Wine and Roses, Under the Yum-Yum Tree **19** How to Murder Your Wife

lemon 11 Citrus limon
varieties: **4** wild **5** dwarf, giant, Meyer, water **6** garden, wonder **9** wild water **12** Chinese dwarf **14** American wonder

Lemuralia
origin: **5** Roman
event: **8** festival
to exorcise: **6** ghosts

lemures
form: **6** ghosts
characteristic: **10** maleficent **11** troublesome

Lenaea
origin: **8** Athenian
event: **8** festival

lend 4 give, loan **6** impart, invest, supply **7** advance, furnish **10** contribute

lend a hand 3 aid **6** assist **7** help out

lend assistance 3 aid **4** abet, help **6** succor **7** relieve **16** give a helping hand

lend one's name to 7 endorse, support **9** recommend

length 3 run **4** span, term, time **5** piece, range, reach **6** extent, period **7** compass, measure, portion, section, segment, stretch **8** distance, duration, end to end **9** longitude, magnitude **11** elapsed time, measurement

lengthen 3 pad **5** add to **6** expand, extend, let out, pad out **7** augment, drag out, draw out, fill out, prolong, spin out, stretch **8** elongate, flesh out, increase, protract **9** attenuate, string out

lengthened 8 drawn out, extended **9** augmented, elongated, prolonged, stretched **10** attenuated, grew longer

lengthening 8 full form **9** extending, extension **10** elongation, stretching **11** extenuation, protraction **12** prolongation

lengthy 5 windy, wordy **6** padded, prolix **7** endless **8** drawn out, extended, overlong, rambling **9** elongated, extensive, garrulous, long-drawn, prolonged **10** digressive, discursive, long-winded, protracted **12** interminable

leniency 5 mercy **7** charity **8** clemency **9** tolerance **10** compassion **11** forbearance, magnanimity **12** mercifulness **13** forgivingness

lenient 4 kind, mild, soft **6** gentle **7** clement, liberal, patient, sparing **8** merciful, moderate, tolerant **9** easygoing, forgiving, indulgent **10** benevolent, charitable, forbearing, permissive **11** kindhearted, soft-hearted, sympathetic **13** compassionate, tenderhearted

Lenni-Lenape *see* **8** Delaware

Lenny
director: **8** Bob Fosse

cast: 8 Jan Miner **11** Stanley Beck **13** Dustin Hoffman (Lenny Bruce) **14** Valerie Perrine (Honey Harlowe)

Le Notre, Andre
landscape architect of:
6 Clagny **9** Tuileries **10** Versailles **12** Saint Germain **13** Fontainebleau **22** Chateau de Vaux-le-Vicomte

lens
invented by:
achromatic: **7** Dollond
bifocal: **8** Franklin
fused bifocal: **6** Borsch

Lenya, Lotte
real name: **16** Karoline Blamauer
husband: **9** Kurt Weill
born: **7** Austria, Hitzing
roles: **5** Jenny **18** From Russia with Love, The Seven Deadly Sins, The Three-penny Opera

Leo
symbol: **4** lion
planet: **3** Sun
rules: **7** romance **10** creativity
born: **4** July **6** August

Leonard, Elmore
author of: **4** Swag **5** Glitz, Stick **6** Hombre **7** La Brava **9** Cat Chaser, Gold Coast, Gunsights, The Hunted **10** Mr Majestyk **12** The Big Bounce **14** Fifty-Two Pick-Up, Valdez Is Coming **16** Double Dutch Treat, The Bounty Hunters **18** Forty Lashes Less One

Leonardo da Vinci
born: **5** Italy, Vinci
artwork: **8** Mona Lisa **13** The Last Supper **15** The Annunciation **19** The Battle of Anghiari **21** The Adoration of the Magi

Leonato
character in: **19** Much Ado About Nothing
author: **11** Shakespeare

Leoncavallo, Ruggiero
born: **5** Italy **6** Naples
composer of: **8** Serafita **9** Pagliacci

Leontes
character in: **14** The Winter's Tale
author: **11** Shakespeare

Leonteus
leader of: **6** Greeks
leader at: **4** Troy
suitor of: **5** Helen

leopard 3 cat **7** panther **10** spotted cat
group of: **4** leap

Leos
occupation: **6** herald

father: 7 Orpheus
sacrificed: 9 daughters

Leo the Lip
nickname of: **11** Leo Durocher

lepidoptera
class: **8** hexapoda
phylum: **10** arthropoda
group: **4** moth **9** butterfly

leprechaun 3 elf, imp **5** dwarf, gnome **6** sprite **12** little person

Ler
also: **3** Lir
origin: **5** Irish
personifies: **3** sea
son: **8** Manannan
corresponds to: **4** Llyr

Lesage, Alain
author of: **7** Gil Blas **8** Turcaret

Lescaze, William
architect of: **18** Borg-Warner Building (Chicago) **38** Philadelphia Savings Fund Society Building

Lescot, Pierre
architect of: **10** Cour Carree **20** Fontaine des Innocents
rebuilding of: **6** Louvre

Lesotho *see box*

less 6 barely, little **7** smaller **8** meagerly, slighter **10** not as great **11** more limited

lessen 3 ebb **4** ease, sink, thin, wane **5** abate, lower **6** dilute, reduce, shrink **7** abridge, decline, dwindle, lighten, slacken, subside **8** contract, decrease, diminish, mitigate, wind down **9** alleviate **10** depreciate

lessening 6 waning **8** decrease, dilution **9** abatement, deduction, dwindling, reduction, shrinkage **10** diminution, lightening, mitigation, shortening, slackening **11** abridgement, alleviation, contraction, diminishing, slacking off **12** abbreviation, condensation, depreciation

lesser 4 less **5** minor **7** humbler, smaller **8** inferior, slighter **9** secondary **11** secondarily

Lesser Dionysia
also: **13** Rural Dionysia
event: **8** festival
origin: **6** Attica

Lessing, Doris
author of: **8** Shikasta **16** The Four-Gated City **17** The Golden Notebook **20** The Sirian Experiments **21** The Children of Violence **37** Marriages Between Zones Three Four and Five **42** The Making of the Representative for Planet Eight

lesson 5 class, drill, guide, model, moral, study **6** caveat, notice, rebuke **7** caution, example, message, reading, segment, warning **8** exemplar, exercise, homework **9** deterrent **10** admonition, advisement, assignment, punishment, recitation, Scrip-

Lesotho
other name: **10** Basutoland
capital/largest city: **6** Maseru
others: **4** Roma **5** Joels **6** Leribe, Morija **7** Quthing, Sekakes **8** Mafeteng, Matsieng **9** Marakabei, Qachas Nek, Semonkong **10** Butha Buthe, Mokhotlong, Thaba Bosiu **11** Mohales Hoek **12** Sehlabathebe, Teyateyaneng
head of state: **4** king
monetary unit: **4** cent, rand
mountain: **6** Maloti, Maluti **7** Central **8** Injasuti, Machache **10** Ben Macdhui **11** Drakensberg, Thaba Putsoa
highest point: **16** Thabana Ntlenyana
river: **5** Senqu **6** Orange, Tugela **7** Caledon **9** Makhaleng
physical feature:
gorge: **5** Oxbow
people: **4** Zulu **5** Bantu, Tembu **6** Basuto **7** Basotho
leader: **7** Moshesh **9** Mosheshwe **10** Moshoeshoe **14** Leabua Jonathan
language: **5** Sotho **7** English, Sesotho
religion: **7** animism **13** Roman Catholic **18** Lesotho Evangelical
feature:
blanket: **4** kobo
house: **8** rondavel
water project: **11** Malibamatso

tures **11** instruction
12 remonstrance

Lestrade, Inspector
character in: **14** (The Adventures of) Sherlock Holmes
author: **10** Conan Doyle

Le Sueur, Lucille Fay
real name of: **12** Joan Crawford

let 4 make, rent **5** admit, allow, cause, grant, lease, leave **6** enable, permit, sublet, suffer **7** approve, charter, concede, empower, endorse, hire out, license, warrant **8** sanction, sublease, tolerate **9** authorize

let down 4 drop **5** lower **6** betray **8** push down **10** disappoint **11** disillusion

letdown 3 rue **4** balk, blow **6** fizzle, regret **7** chagrin, setback **8** comedown **10** anticlimax, bafflement, bitter pill, dashed hope, discontent **11** frustration **12** blighted hope, discomfiture **13** mortification **14** disappointment, disenchantment, disgruntlement **15** disillusionment, dissatisfaction

let fall 4 drop **5** let go **7** release

let fly 4 cast, hurl **5** eject, fling, heave, sling, throw **6** launch, propel

let go 3 axe, can **4** fire, free, lose, oust, sack **6** bounce, give up

lethal 5 fatal, toxic **6** deadly, mortal **7** baneful, killing **8** venomous, virulent **9** dangerous, malignant, poisonous **11** destructive **13** mortally toxic

lethargic 4 dull, idle, lazy **5** inert **6** drowsy, sleepy, torpid **7** languid, passive **8** comatose, indolent, listless, slothful, sluggish **9** apathetic, enervated, somnolent, soporific **10** dispirited, lackluster, unspirited **11** debilitated, indifferent

lethargy 5 sloth **6** apathy, stupor, torpor **7** inertia, languor **8** dullness, laziness **9** indolence, lassitude, torpidity **10** drowsiness, inactivity **12** indifference, listlessness, slothfulness, sluggishness

Lethe
form: **5** river
location: **5** Hades
caused: **13** forgetfulness

let in 5 admit **7** receive **12** allow to enter

let loose 4 free **5** let go **6** let

fly **7** release, set free, unleash **8** give vent, liberate **12** give free rein

Leto
also: **6** Latona
form: **7** goddess
father: **5** Coeus
mother: **6** Phoebe
son: **6** Apollo
daughter: **7** Artemis

let off 5 let go **6** acquit, excuse, exempt **7** release, set free **8** liberate **9** discharge

let slip 6 betray, expose, reveal **7** divulge, uncover **8** blurt out, disclose, give away

Let's Make a Deal
host: **9** Monty Hall
announcer: **10** Jay Stewart

letter 4 note **7** epistle, message, missive **8** dispatch, document **9** substance **10** billet-doux

Letter, The
director: **12** William Wyler
based on story by: **15** Somerset Maugham
cast: **10** Bette Davis **14** Frieda Inescort **15** Gale Sondergaard, Herbert Marshall, James Stephenson
setting: **6** Malaya

letter ordering imprisonment
French: **14** lettre de cachet
carried seal of: **4** king **9** sovereign

letters 8 learning **9** erudition **10** literature **13** belles lettres

Letters from the Underground
author: **16** Fyodor Dostoevsky

Letter to Three Wives, A
director: **17** Joseph L Mankiewicz
cast: **10** Ann Sothern **11** Jeanne Crain, Jeffrey Lynn, Kirk Douglas, Paul Douglas **12** Linda Darnell, Thelma Ritter
Oscar for: **6** script **8** director

let the buyer beware
Latin: **12** caveat emptor

let the people rule
Latin: **13** regnat populus
motto of: **8** Arkansas

let there be light
Latin: **7** fiat lux

lettre de cachet 26 letter ordering imprisonment **28** letter under the sovereign's seal

lettuce 7 Lactuca
varieties: **3** cos **5** chalk, frog's, lamb's, water **6** Boston, garden, miner's **7** iceberg, prickly, romaine

8 escarole **9** asparagus **11** common lamb's

letup 4 lull **5** pause **6** relief **7** respite **8** decrease, interval, slowdown, stopping, surcease, vacation **9** abatement, cessation, interlude, lessening, remission **10** slackening **11** retardation

Let Us Now Praise Famous Men
author: **9** James Agee

Let us therefore be joyful
Latin: **15** Gaudeamus igitur

Leucaeus
epithet of: **4** Zeus
means: **16** of the white poplar

Leuce
form: **5** nymph
changed into: **6** poplar
color of poplar: **5** white

Leucippe
father: **6** Minyas **7** Thestor
mother: **10** Orchomenus
son: **8** Teuthras

Leucippides
refers to: **6** Phoebe **7** Hilaira

Leucippus
father: **8** Perieres
mother: **10** Gorgophone
brother: **8** Aphareus
fathered: **11** Leucippides
daughter: **6** Phoebe **7** Arsinoe, Hilaira
pursued: **6** Daphne
disguised as: **4** girl
killed by: **6** nymphs

Leucophryne
epithet of: **7** Artemis

Leucothea *see* **3** Ino

Leucus
mentioned in: **5** Iliad
companion of: **8** Odysseus
usurped throne of: **9** Idomeneus
killed by: **8** Antiphus

Le Vau, Louis
architect of: **6** Louvre **10** Versailles **12** Hotel Lambert **22** Chateau de Vaux-le-Vicomte **24** College des Quatres Nations

levee 3 dam **4** bank, dike, pier, quay, wall **5** ditch, jetty, ridge, wharf **6** durbar **9** reception **10** embankment

level 3 aim, bed **4** even, flat, rank, raze, tied, vein, zone **5** align, floor, flush, grade, layer, plane, point, stage, story, wreck **6** direct, height, lay low, reduce, smooth, topple **7** aligned, even out, flatten, landing, on a line, station, stratum, uniform **8** equalize, make even, posi-

tion, tear down, together
9 devastate, elevation, knock
down **10** consistent, horizontal, on a par with, unwrinkled **11** achievement, neck
and neck **12** on an even keel

level-headed 4 sage **5** sound
6 poised, stable, steady **7** prudent **8** balanced, cautious,
composed, sensible **9** collected,
judicious, practical, unruffled
10 cool-headed, dependable,
thoughtful **11** circumspect
12 even-tempered **13** dispassionate **14** self-controlled

levelheadedness 6 aplomb
9 good sense, soundness, stability **10** equanimity **11** common sense **13** judiciousness

Levene, Sam
real name: **12** Samuel Levine
born: **6** Russia
roles: **12** Guys and Dolls
13 Nathan Detroit **15** The
Sunshine Boys

lever 3 bar, pry **5** jimmy,
raise **7** crowbar

Lever, Charles
author of: **14** Charles
O'Malley

**Leverrier, Urbain Jean
Joseph**
field: **9** astronomy
nationality: **6** French
co-discovered: **7** Neptune
worked with: **14** John Couch
Adams

Levi
father: **5** Jacob **6** Melchi,
Symeon
mother: **4** Leah
son: **6** Kohath, Merari
7 Gershom
brother: **3** Dan, Gad **5** Asher,
Judah **6** Joseph, Reuben,
Simeon **7** Zebulun **8** Benjamin, Issachar, Naphtali
sister: **5** Dinah
violated: **5** Dinah
also called: **7** Matthew
descendant of: **6** Levite

Leviathan 6 dragon **10** sea
monster
means: **13** spirally bound
represents: **14** terrible
powers

Leviathan
author: **12** Thomas Hobbes

Levin, Ira
author of: **13** Rosemary's
Baby

Levin, Konstantin
character in: **12** Anna
Karenina
author: **7** Tolstoy

Levi-Strauss, Claude
method: **13** structuralism
author of: **13** Mythologiques,

The Savage Mind **16** Tristes
Tropiques **22** Structural An-
thropology **29** Elementary
Structures of Kinship

Levitch, Joseph
real name of: **10** Jerry Lewis

levity 3 fun **5** mirth **6** joking,
whimsy **8** hilarity, trifling
9 flippancy, frivolity, lightness,
silliness **10** jocularity, pleasantry, triviality **11** flightiness,
foolishness **16** lightheartedness

levy 3 fee, tax **4** duty, make,
toll, wage **5** draft, exact, start
6 assess, call up, charge, demand, enlist, excise, impose,
muster, pursue, tariff **7** carry
on, collect **9** calling up, conscript, prosecute **10** assessment, imposition
12 conscription

Levy, Marion
real name of: **15** Paulette
Goddard

**Lew Archer, Private
Detective**
author: **13** Ross MacDonald

lewd 5 bawdy **6** ribald, risque,
vulgar, wanton **7** goatish, immoral, lustful, obscene **8** indecent, prurient **9** lecherous,
libertine, salacious **10** lascivious, libidinous, licentious, lubricious **11** Rabelaisian
12 pornographic

Lewis, C S
author of: **10** Perelandra
13 Prince Caspian, The Last
Battle **14** Surprised by Joy,
The Silver Chair, Til We
Have Faces **17** The Horse
and His Boy **18** The Magi-
cian's Nephew **19** The
Screwtape Letters **20** Out of
the Silent Planet **21** The
Chronicles of Narnia **25** The
Voyage of the Dawn
Treader **29** The Lion the
Witch and the Wardrobe

Lewis, Jerry
real name: **13** Joseph Levitch
partner: **10** Dean Martin
born: **8** Newark NJ
roles: **8** The Caddy **10** The
Bellboy, The Sad Sack
11 Cinderfella **12** The
Geisha Boy **16** Artists and
Models **17** The Nutty Professor **20** The Disorderly
Orderly

Lewis, Sinclair
author of: **7** Babbitt **9** Dodsworth **10** Arrowsmith, Main
Street **11** Elmer Gantry
14 Cass Timberlane

lexicon 5 gloss, index **8** code
book, glossary, synonymy,
wordbook, wordlist **9** thesaurus, wordstock **10** dictionary,

vocabulary **11** concordance,
onomasticon

lex loci 11 law of a place

lex non scripta 9 common
law **12** unwritten law

lex scripta 10 statute law,
written law

Leyden, Lucas (Lukas) van
born: **6** Leiden, Leyden
14 The Netherlands
artwork: **12** Last Judgment
14 The Card Players, The
Game of Chess **26** Mo-
hammed and the Murdered
Monk

Lhasa, Lassa
capital of: **5** Tibet

liability 4 debt, drag, duty,
onus **5** debit, minus **6** arrear,
burden **8** drawback, handicap,
obstacle **9** hindrance **10** impediment, obligation **11** encumbrance, shortcoming
12 disadvantage, indebtedness
13 inconvenience **14** responsibility, stumbling block

liable 3 apt **4** open **5** prone
6 likely **7** exposed, ripe for,
subject **8** disposed, inclined
9 obligated, sensitive **10** answerable, chargeable, vulnerable **11** accountable,
responsible, susceptible

liaison 4 bond, link **5** amour,
union **7** contact **8** alliance, intrigue, mediator **9** adventure,
dalliance, go-between **10** connection, flirtation, love affair
11 association, cooperation, interchange **12** coordination, entanglement **13** communication

liar 6 fibber **8** perjurer **9** falsi-
fier **10** fabricator **11** storyteller **12** prevaricator

libation 4 wine **5** drink, water
6 liquid **8** ambrosia, beverage,
offering, potation **9** sacrifice

Libation Bearers, The see
10 Choephoroe

libel 4 slur **5** smear **6** defame,
malign, revile, vilify **7** asperse,
blacken, calumny, obloquy,
slander **8** derogate **9** aspersion,
discredit, disparage **10** calumniate, defamation
12 vilification

Libeled Lady
director: **10** Jack Conway
cast: **8** Myrna Loy **10** Jean
Harlow **12** Spencer Tracy
13 William Powell **14** Walter Connolly
remade as: **9** Easy to Wed

Libera
origin: **7** Italian
goddess of: **4** wine **9** fertility,
vineyards

husband: 5 Liber
**corresponds to:
10** Persephone

liberal 5 ample, broad **6** casual,
lavish **7** leftist, lenient
8 abundant, advanced, flexible,
generous, handsome, left-wing,
prodigal, reformer, tolerant,
unbiased **9** bounteous, bountiful, impartial, not strict, plenteous, reformist, unbigoted,
unsparing **10** fair-minded, forbearing, left-winger, munificent, not literal, openhanded,
open-minded, unrigorous, unstinting **11** broad-minded, enlightened, extravagant,
libertarian, magnanimous, progressive **12** freethinking, humanitarian, open to reason,
unprejudiced **14** latitudinarian

Liberalia
origin: 5 Roman
event: 8 festival

liberality 10 generosity **11** benevolence, munificence
12 philanthropy **13** bountifulness **14** openhandedness

liberate 5 let go **6** let out, redeem, rescue, spring **7** absolve,
deliver, manumit, release, set
free **8** let loose **9** discharge,
disengage, extricate, unshackle **10** emancipate
11 disencumber

liberated 5 freed, let go **7** rescued, set free **8** let loose, released **10** discharged,
extricated **11** emancipated

liberation 6 escape, rescue
7 freedom, freeing, release
8 delivery **9** letting go, releasing **11** manumission
12 emancipation

Liberia *see box*

Libertas
origin: 5 Roman
personifies: 7 liberty

liberte egalite fraternite
25 liberty equality fraternity
motto of: 16 French
Revolution

liberties 6 misuse **7** license
9 violation **10** distortion
11 familiarity, impropriety
13 falsification

libertine 4 goat, lewd, rake,
roue **5** loose, satyr **6** lecher,
wanton **7** immoral, lustful,
seducer **8** unchaste **9** debauchee, dissolute, lecherous, reprobate, womanizer
10 immoralist, lascivious, libidinous, licentious, profligate,
sensualist, voluptuary

liberty 5 leave, right **7** freedom, license **8** autonomy, delivery, free time, furlough,
sanction, vacation **9** privilege

10 liberation, permission,
shore leave **11** citizenship,
manumission **12** carte blanche,
dispensation, emancipation, independence **15** enfranchisement **17** self-determination

liberty equality fraternity
French: 24 liberte egalite
fraternite
motto of: 16 French
Revolution

Libra
symbol: 6 scales **7** balance
planet: 5 Venus
rules: 8 marriage
born: 7 October **9** September

Libreville
capital of: 13 Gabon Republic

Libya *see box, p. 568*

lice
variety: 4 bird, crab **5** human, pubic, spiny **7** chewing, sucking **8** barklice,
booklice **9** guinea pig
13 mammal chewing

license 3 let **4** pass, visa **5** allow, grant, leave, right **6** enable, laxity, permit **7** anarchy,
approve, certify, charter, empower, endorse, freedom, liberty, warrant **8** accredit,
audacity, disorder, latitude,
passport, sanction, temerity
9 admission, allowance, authorize, franchise, looseness,
privilege, slackness **10** brazenness, commission, debauchery,
unruliness **11** certificate, free
passage, lawlessness, libertinism, presumption, safe-
conduct **12** carte blanche, dispensation, recklessness

licentious 4 lewd **5** dirty,
loose **6** amoral, sleazy, wanton **7** brutish, goatish, immoral, lawless, lustful,
raunchy, ruttish **8** depraved,
prodigal **9** abandoned, debauched, dissolute, excessive,
lecherous, libertine, salacious
10 dissipated, lascivious, libidinous, lubricious, profligate,
ungoverned **11** promiscuous
12 unprincipled, unrestrained,
unscrupulous **13** irresponsible,
unconstrained

licentiousness 7 abandon
8 lewdness **10** immorality,
wantonness

licit 5 legal, legit, valid **6** kosher, lawful **9** allowable, statutory **10** acceptable, admissible,
authorized, legitimate, sanctioned **11** permissible **12** au-
thorizable, sanctionable
14 constitutional

lick 3 bit, dab, hit, jot, lap
4 beat, blow, drub, fire, hint,
iota, rout, slap, snip, sock,

Liberia
capital/largest city: 8 Monrovia
others: 4 Sino **5** Gribo, Rebbo **6** Bopora, Gbanga, Harper,
Kakata **7** Bgarnga, Kolahun, Nanakru, Tappita, Vonjama
8 Buchanan, Garraway, Marshall, Nanakaru, Sass Town
9 Grand Cess, River Cess, Roysville **10** Careysburg, Greenville, Sanoquelli **11** Robertsport **12** Sanniquellie
school: 7 Liberia **10** Cuttington **15** Our Lady of Fatima
16 Booker Washington
religious school/secret society: **4** poro **5** sande
measure: 4 kuba
monetary unit: 4 cent **6** dollar
mountain: 3 Uni **4** Bong, Putu **5** Niete, Nimba **9** Bomi Hills
highest point: 6 Wutivi
river: 4 Cess, Lofa, Mano **5** Duobe, Lotta, Manna, Morro,
Sinoe **6** Cestos, Douobe **7** Cavalla, Cavally **8** San Pedro
9 Saint John, Saint Paul, Sehnkwehn
sea: 8 Atlantic
physical feature:
wind: **9** harmattan
people: 2 Gi **3** Gio, Kra, Kru, Kwa, Vai, Vei **4** Gola, Kroo,
Krou, Loma, Mano, Toma **5** Bassa, Gibbi, Gissi, Grebo
6 Gbande, Kpelle, Kpuesi, Krooby, Kruman **7** Krooboy,
Krooman **8** Mandingo **15** Americo-Liberian
leader: **3** Doe **6** Tubman **7** Roberts, Tolbert
language: 3 Kru, Kwa **5** Mande **7** English
religion: 5 Islam **7** animism **10** Protestant **12** Christianity
feature:
clothing: **5** lappa
rubber plantation: **9** Firestone

Libya
  capital/largest city: 7 Tripoli
    summer capital: 8 Benghazi
  others: 4 Homs, Marj, Surt 5 Beida, Darna, Derna, Khums, Kufra, Sebha, Sidri, Zawia 6 Garian, Murzuq, Tobruk 7 Es Sidar, Gharyan, Misrata 8 Ajdabiya, Misurata, Rashanuf 12 Marsa el Brega
  school: 7 Alfateh 9 Garyounis
  division: 6 Fezzan 9 Cyrenaica 12 Tripolitania
  measure: 3 dra, pik, saa 4 kele 5 bozze, donum, jabia, teman, uckia 6 barile, gorraf, misura 7 mattaro, termino 8 kharouba
  weight: 4 kele 6 gorraf 8 kharouba
  monetary unit: 5 dinar
  mountain: 5 Green 13 Jabal al Akhdar, Tibesti Massif
  highest point: 9 Bette Peak
  sea: 13 Mediterranean
  physical feature:
    desert: 6 Libyan, Sahara 9 Calanscio
    gulf: 5 Bomba, Sidra, Sirte
    oasis: 4 Ghat 5 Kufra, Sebha 7 Tazerbo 8 Al-Kufrah, Ghudamis
    plain: 6 al Marj, Gefara 7 Jaffara
    plateau: 12 Gebel Nefuisa, Jabal Nafusah
    wind: 6 ghibli
  people: 4 Arab, Tebu 6 Berber, Tuareg 7 Gaetuli 8 Getulans, Harratin
    leader: 6 Battus 7 Jalloud, Qadhafi 8 Aegyptus 9 al-Qaddafi, Karamanli 13 Idris al-Senusi
    religious leader: 8 al-Senusi
    ruler: 4 Rome 5 Italy 6 Greece 9 Phoenicia 12 Ottoman Turks
  language: 6 Arabic, Berber 7 English, Italian
    alphabet: 8 tifinagh
  religion: 5 Islam
  feature: 14 Tropic of Cancer
    clothing: 5 lanaf 9 barracano
    festival: 3 Mez 7 Fantasi
    Islamic law: 6 sharia
    leader: 6 sheikh
    ruins: 11 Leptis Magna
  food:
    dish: 5 bazin 8 couscous
    red pepper: 6 filfil

ism, survival, vitality, vivacity 9 animation, biography, existence, life story, longevity 11 subsistence 13 autobiography
  French: 3 vie

Life at the Dakota
  author: 17 Stephen Birmingham

Life Before Man
  author: 14 Margaret Atwood

Lifeboat
  director: 15 Alfred Hitchcock
  cast: 10 John Hodiak 12 Mary Anderson 13 William Bendix 16 Tallulah Bankhead

life-giving 5 vital 9 vivifying 12 invigorating

lifeless 4 dead, dull, flat, late 5 inert, stiff, vapid 6 boring, hollow, static, torpid, wooden 7 defunct 8 deceased, departed, inactive, lifeless, sluggish 9 colorless, inanimate 10 lackluster, spiritless

Liechtenstein
  capital/largest city: 5 Vaduz
  others: 4 Haag 6 Balzer, Eschen, Iradug, Schaan 7 Balzers, Bendern, Nendeln, Planken, Triesen 12 Schellenberg
  division:
    ancient province: 6 Rhaeti 7 Rhaetia
  government:
    legislature: 7 Landtag
  monetary unit: 6 rappen 7 franken
  mountain: 4 Alps 8 Naafkopf, Rhatikon 12 Three Sisters
  highest point: 15 Vorder-Grauspitz
  river: 5 Rhine
  physical feature:
    valley: 6 Lavena, Samina
  people: 8 Alemanni
    leader: 7 Florian 15 Francis Joseph II 16 von Liechtenstein
  language: 6 German 10 Alemannish
  religion: 13 Roman Catholic
  place:
    castle: 9 Gutemburg, Gutenberg
  feature:
    legendary dwarf: 10 wildmannli
    wine: 7 Vaduzer

suck, whip 5 crack, punch, sally, shred, spank, speck, taste, touch, trace 6 defeat, ignite, kindle, master, sample, stroke, subdue, thrash, tongue, wallop 7 clobber, conquer, modicum, smidgen, trounce 8 outmatch, overcome, particle, vanquish 9 overpower, overthrow, scintilla, subjugate 10 smattering 12 denunciation

Licymnius
  father: 9 Electryon
  mother: 5 Midea
  wife: 8 Perimede
  son: 5 Melas 6 Oeonus 7 Argeius
  nephew: 8 Hercules

lid 3 cap, top 4 cork, curb, plug 5 cover, limit 7 ceiling, maximum, stopper, stopple 9 operculum, restraint

lie 3 fib 4 loll, rest, stay

5 abide, exist, range, story 6 belong, deceit, extend, inhere, lounge, obtain, remain, repose, sprawl 7 falsify, fiction, perjury, recline, romance, untruth 8 misstate, tall tale 9 deception, embellish, embroider, fabricate, falsehood, invention 10 equivocate 11 fabrication, prevaricate 12 equivocation 13 falsification, prevarication 17 misrepresentation

Liechtenstein *see box*

lie down 6 retire 7 go to bed, recline 8 take a nap 11 take a snooze 15 catch forty winks

life 4 path, soul, zest 5 being, human, plant, story, verve, vigor 6 animal, career, course, energy, memoir, person, spirit 8 creature, duration, life span, lifetime, lifework, organ-

569

lifelessness 5 death **7** inertia **8** dullness, limpness, vapidity **9** blandness **10** flaccidity, inactivity **13** colorlessness

Life of Dante
author: **17** Giovanni Boccaccio

Life of Emile Zola
director: **15** William Dieterle
cast: **8** Paul Muni **11** Donald Crisp **12** Gloria Holden **15** Gale Sondergaard **17** Joseph Schildkraut (Dreyfus)
Oscar for: **7** picture

Life of Man, The
author: **14** Leonid Andreyev

Life of Riley, The
character: **4** Babs **6** Dangle, Junior **8** Peg Riley **9** Jim Gillis **10** Cunningham, Digby (Digger) O'Dell **11** Waldo Binney **13** Chester A Riley **14** Honeybee Gillis
cast: **9** John Brown, Lanny Rees, Sid Tomack **10** Tom D'Andrea **12** Emory Parnell, Wesley Morgan **13** Gloria Winters, Jackie Gleason, Lugene Sanders, Robert Sweeney, William Bendix **14** Gloria Blondell, Rosemary DeCamp **16** Douglas Dumbrille, Marjorie Reynolds, Sterling Holloway

Life of Samuel Johnson, The
author: **12** James Boswell

life of the party 7 show-off **9** extrovert **13** exhibitionist **17** hail-fellow-well-met

Life on the Mississippi
author: **9** Mark Twain

life span 4 life **8** lifetime **14** life expectancy

Life Studies
author: **12** Robert Lowell

Life With Father
author: **13** Clarence Day Jr
director: **13** Michael Curtiz
cast: **9** ZaSu Pitts **10** Irene Dunne **11** Edmund Gwenn **13** William Powell **15** Elizabeth Taylor
setting: **11** New York City

lifework 6 career **7** calling **8** vocation **10** livelihood, occupation, profession

lift 4 high, palm, pick, rear, rise, soar, take **5** boost, climb, exalt, filch, heave, hoist, pinch, raise, steal, swipe **6** ascend, ascent, banish, cancel, pilfer, pirate, pocket, remove, revoke, snatch, thieve, uplift, vanish **7** elation, elevate, purloin, raise up, raising, rescind, scatter, upraise **8** disperse **9** disappear, dissipate, float

away **10** ascendance, move upward, plagiarize, put an end to **11** appropriate, countermand, inspiration, make off with, reassurance **12** give a boost to, shot in the arm **13** encouragement, enheartenment

ligament
holds: **5** bones

Ligeia
author: **13** Edgar Allan Poe
character: **19** Lady Rowena Trevanion

Ligeti, Gyorgy
composer of: **7** Lontano **11** Atmospheres **13** Ramifications

light *see box*

light-colored 4 pale **5** beige, blond **6** blonde, flaxen, pastel **7** neutral, whitish **9** yellowish

light-complexioned 4 fair, pale **12** white-skinned

lighten 4 buoy, ease, lift **5** abate, allay, blaze, elate, flare, flash, gleam, shine **6** buoy up, lessen, reduce, revive, temper, unload, uplift **7** assuage, enliven, gladden, inspire, light up, relieve **8** brighten, mitigate, moderate, unburden **9** alleviate, coruscate, disburden, irradiate **10** illuminate, make bright **11** become light, disencumber, make lighter, scintillate

light-filled 5 sunny **6** bright **7** well-lit **11** illuminated

lighthearted 3 gay **4** airy, glad **5** jolly, merry, sunny **6** blithe, cheery, joyful, joyous, lively **7** buoyant, cheered, chipper **8** carefree, cheerful, sanguine **9** sprightly **10** insouciant, untroubled **11** free and easy **12** effervescent

lightheartedness 3 joy **4** glee **5** mirth **6** gladness **9** happiness, merriment **10** blitheness, exuberance, joyfulness, joyousness **11** high spirits

Light in August
author: **15** William Faulkner
character: **8** Doc Hines, Joe Brown **9** Lena Grove, McEachern **10** Byron Bunch **12** Joanna Burden, Joe Christmas

lightless 4 dark **5** black, murky **7** stygian **9** unlighted **13** unilluminated

lightly 6 airily, easily, gently, nimbly, softly, thinly, weakly **7** blandly, faintly, quickly, readily, swiftly, timidly **8** blithely, facilely, gingerly, meagerly, slightly, sparsely **9** buoyantly, sparingly **10** carelessly, flippantly, hesitantly, moderately **11** frivolously, slightingly **13** indifferently, thoughtlessly, unconcernedly, without effort **14** without concern

---

light 3 gay **4** airy, beam, easy, fair, fall, find, fire, glow, lamp, land, pale, puny, side, soft, stop **5** aglow, angle, blaze, blond, faint, flame, funny, glare, guide, happy, jolly, match, model, perch, petty, put on, roost, shine, slant, small, spare, spark, sunny, torch **6** alight, aspect, beacon, blithe, bright, candle, chance, frugal, gentle, get off, ignite, jaunty, kindle, luster, meager, paltry, scanty, settle, simple, slight, turn on **7** amusing, buoyant, chipper, clarify, come off, descend, get down, gleeful, insight, lantern, lighten, lighter, lucifer, not dark, not rich, paragon, radiant, radiate, sparkle, sunbeam, trivial **8** approach, attitude, bleached, blondish, brighten, carefree, cheerful, come upon, discover, dismount, ethereal, exemplar, gossamer, graceful, illumine, jubilant, luminous, meet with, moderate, moonbeam, not heavy, paradigm, radiance, sportive, step down, switch on, trifling, untaxing **9** brilliant, catch fire, direction, encounter, frivolous, irradiate, light-hued, set fire to, sprightly, stumble on, sylphlike, viewpoint **10** abstemious, brightness, brilliance, burdenless, come across, come to rest, effortless, effulgence, floodlight, happen upon, illuminate, light-toned, luminosity, manageable, restricted, set burning, weightless **11** conflagrate, elucidation, illuminated, information, make radiant, superficial, undemanding, underweight **15** inconsequential
god of: **6** Apollo **7** Mithras, Phoebus, Pythius **8** Heimdall **9** Musagetes
Latin: **3** lux
measurement: **7** candela **11** candlepower

lightness 8 airiness, radiance
10 brightness, fluffiness, luminosity **12** illumination,
luminousness

lightning rod
invented by: **8** Franklin

light of day 8 daylight, sunlight, sunshine

light sleep 3 nap **4** doze
6 catnap, snooze **10** forty
winks

light wind 4 waft **6** breeze,
zephyr **10** gentle wind
11 breath of air

Lightwood, Mortimer
character in: **15** Our Mutual
Friend
author: **7** Dickens

lignum vitae 10 wood of life
tree species: **8** Guaiacum

Ligure 8 gemstone

likable, likeable 4 nice **6** genial **7** amiable, lovable, winsome **8** charming, engaging,
loveable, pleasant, pleasing
9 agreeable, appealing, simpatico **10** attractive **11** complaisant, sympathetic

like 4 akin, care, dote, same,
wish **5** enjoy, equal, fancy, favor, savor **6** admire, allied,
choose, esteem, relish **7** approve, cognate, endorse,
matched, related, similar, support, uniform **8** be fond of,
parallel, selfsame, think fit
9 analogous, congruent, have
a mind, identical **10** comparable, equivalent, homologous,
resembling **11** be partial to,
much the same **12** feel inclined, have a crush on, take
a shine to **13** corresponding,
find agreeable **14** take pleasure in

Like a Bulwark
author: **13** Marianne Moore

likelihood 8 prospect **10** good
chance **11** possibility, probability **12** potentiality

likely 3 apt, fit **4** able **6** liable,
proper **8** credible, destined,
inclined, probable, probably,
rational, reliable, suitable
9 befitting, plausible, promising, qualified **10** believable,
presumably, reasonable **11** appropriate, verisimilar **16** in all
probability

like-mindedness 6 accord
7 concord, harmony, rapport
8 affinity **9** agreement **12** congeniality **13** compatibility

likeness 5 image, model,
study **6** effigy **7** analogy, picture, replica **8** affinity, portrait **9** agreement, depiction,

facsimile, portrayal, rendition,
semblance **10** similarity, similitude **11** delineation, resemblance **14** correspondence,
representation

likes 9 favorites **10** prejudices
11 preferences **12** inclinations,
partialities

likewise 3 and, eke, too
4 also **5** ditto **6** as well **7** besides, equally, the same
8 moreover **9** similarity **10** in
addition

liking 4 bent **5** fancy, taste
7 leaning **8** affinity, appetite,
fondness, penchant, soft spot,
weakness **9** affection **10** partiality, preference, proclivity,
propensity **11** inclination
12 predilection

Li'l Abner
creator: **6** Al Capp
character: **5** Pappy **7** Wolf
Gal **10** Joe Btfsplk, Mammy
Yokum, Marryin' Sam
11 Adam Lazonga, Hairless
Joe **12** Tobacco Rhoda
13 Joanie Phoanie **14** Daisy
Mae Scragg, Evil-Eye Fleegle, Stupefyin' Jones
15 Fearless Fosdick, Henry
Cabbage Cod, Lonesome
Polecat, Moonbeam McSwine **16** General Bullmoose, Sir Cecil Cesspool
17 Sen Jack S Phogbound
18 J Roaringham Fatback
21 Appassionata von
Climax
brewery: **23** Big Barnsmell's
Skonk Works
event: **15** Sadie Hawkins
Day
juice: **16** Kickapoo Joy Juice
kingdom: **14** Lower Slobbovia
mountain: **11** Onnecessary
people: **7** Schmoos
8 Kingmies
place: **8** Dogpatch
railroad: **11** West Po'k Chop
ruler: **14** King Nogoodnick

lilac 7 Syringa
varieties: **4** late, vine, wild
6 common, Indian, summer
7 Chinese, cut-leaf, Persian
9 Himalayan, Hungarian
12 Japanese tree **16** Catalina
mountain

Lili
director: **14** Charles Walters
cast: **9** Mel Ferrer **11** Leslie
Caron, Zsa Zsa Gabor
16 Jean-Pierre Aumont

Lilies of the Field
director: **11** Ralph Nelson
cast: **8** Lisa Mann **10** Lilia
Skala **13** Sidney Poitier
Oscar for: **5** actor (Poitier)

Liliom
author: **12** Ferenc Molnar

lillet
type: **8** aperitif
origin: **6** France
flavor: **6** orange
color: **3** red **5** white

Lilliput
fictional land in: **16** Gulliver's
Travels
author: **5** Swift

lilliputian 3 wee **4** tiny
5 dwarf, short, small, teeny,
weeny **6** little, midget, minute,
petite **9** miniature **10** diminutive, teeny-weeny **11** pocket-sized

Lilongwe
capital of: **6** Malawi

lily see box

lily-livered 6 afraid, craven,
scared, yellow **7** chicken, fearful, gutless **8** cowardly **9** dastardly **12** fainthearted
13 pusillanimous, yellow-bellied **14** chicken-hearted,
chicken-livered **22** showing
the white feather

lily-white 4 good, pure
6 biased, decent, proper, racist **7** bigoted, upright **8** all-white, innocent, virtuous
9 blameless, exclusive, exemplary, faultless, guiltless, honorable, righteous
10 impeccable, inculpable,
prejudiced, segregated, upstanding **11** uncorrupted
12 unintegrated **13** unimpeachable **14** discriminatory,
irreproachable

Lima
capital of: **4** Peru
foothills of: **5** Andes
founder: **7** Pizarro
nickname: **11** city of kings
ocean: **7** Pacific
port: **6** Callao
river: **5** Rimac
square: **12** Plaza de Armas

limb 3 arm, gam, leg, pin
4 part, spur, twig, wing
5 bough, shoot, sprig
6 branch, member **9** appendage, extension, outgrowth
10 projection, prosthesis

limber 5 agile, lithe, relax
6 loosen, pliant, supple
7 bending, elastic, lissome, pliable **8** flexible **9** lithesome,
malleable

lime 18 Citrus aurantifolia
varieties: **3** key **4** wild
7 Mexican, Persian, Rangpur, Spanish **8** Mandarin
10 West Indian **14** Australian wild **15** Australian
round **16** Australian desert,
Australian finger

lily 6 Lilium
varieties: 3 Alp, cow, day, pig **4** Arum, bell, boat, corn, fawn, fire, flax, herb, palm, pine, pond, rain, roan, rock, sand, Sego, star, toad, wood **5** adobe, Aztec, blood, bugle, calla, coast, cobra, crane, Cuban, fairy, globe, glory, Gray's, Ifafa, lemon, magic, natal, queen, regal, royal, showy, snake, spear, swamp, sword, tiger, torch, trout, water, wheel **6** Alpine, Amazon, Canada, Crinum, desert, Easter, eureka, ginger, hidden, Kaffir, Marhan, meadow, one-day, orange, Oregon, shasta, Sierra, spider, sunset, tartar, turban, voodoo, yellow, Zephyr **7** African, Bermuda, chamise, checker, garland, leopard, madonna, Nankeen, panther, redwood, thimble, toad-cup, triplet, trumpet, western **8** Atamasco, Barbados, bluebead, Carolina, climbing, Columbia, flamingo, gloriosa, Guernsey, Humboldt, Jacobean, Japanese, long's red, Mariposa, Martagon, Michigan, mountain, paradise, Peruvian, plantain, Siberian, Solomon's, St Bruno's, St James's, turk's cap **9** alligator, avalanche, butterfly, caucasian, celestial, chaparral, checkered, Eucharist, Kamchatka, naked-lady, orange-cup, pineapple, pinewoods, pot-of-gold, red ginger, red spider, St Joseph's **10** belladonna, blackberry, blue funnel, fairy water, giant water, globe spear, goldbanded, Josephine's, orange-bell, pink Easter, pygmy water, royal water, small tiger, St Bernard's, Washington, white water, wild yellow, yellow-bell, yellow pond **11** African corn, Amazon water, blue African, candlestick, dwarf ginger, golden-rayed, milk-and-wine, Palmer spear, Scarborough, southern red, yellow water **12** African blood, Chinese white, golden spider, prickly water, resurrection, speckled wood, white trumpet **13** Bermuda Easter, cape blue water, Chinese sacred, Egyptian water, fragrant water, India red water, lavender globe, magnolia water, minor Turk's-cap, perfumed fairy, pink porcelain, scarlet ginger, showy Japanese, tuberous water, wild orange-red **14** Chinese-lantern, lesser Turk's cap, little Turk's-cap, Santa Cruz water, yellow Turk's-cap **15** Australian water, backhouse hybrid, golden hurricane, scarlet Turk's-cap **16** American Turk's cap, Bellingham hybrid, Cape Cod pink water, fragrant plantain, Japanese Turk's-cap, western orange-cup **17** midsummer plantain **18** European white water, seersucker plantain **20** narrow-leaved plantain

Limenia
epithet of: 9 Aphrodite
means: 11 of the harbor

limit 3 end **4** curb **8** boundary, end point, restrain, ultimate **13** breaking point

limitation 4 curb **5** quota **8** boundary, decrease **9** lessening, reduction, restraint **10** shortening **11** abridgement, restriction, shortcoming **13** qualification, specification

limited 5 fixed **6** finite, narrow **7** bounded, cramped, defined, minimal, special **8** confined **9** delimited, specified **10** controlled, restrained, restricted **13** circumscribed

limitless 7 endless, eternal, unbound **8** infinite, unending **9** boundless, unlimited **11** measureless **12** immeasurable

limits 3 rim, top **4** curb, edge **5** bound, check, quota **6** border, define, fringe, margin, narrow **7** ceiling, confine, delimit, inhibit, maximum, qualify **8** confines, frontier, restrain, restrict **9** perimeter, periphery, prescribe, restraint **10** boundaries **11** limitations **12** restrictions

limn 4 draw **6** sketch **7** picture **9** delineate

Limnaea
epithet of: 7 Artemis
means: 9 of the lake

Limnoria
member of: 7 Nereids

Limon
father: 8 Tegeates
mother: 5 Maera
brother: 8 Scephrus
killed: 8 Scephrus

limp 3 lax **4** gimp, halt, soft,

weak **5** crawl, loose, skulk, slack **6** droopy, falter, flabby, floppy, hobble **7** flaccid **8** drooping, lameness, yielding **9** dead tired, enervated, exhausted

limpid 4 pure **5** clear, lucid **8** clear-cut, pellucid, vitreous **11** crystalline, perspicuous, translucent, transparent, unambiguous **15** straightforward

Lincoln, Abraham *see box, p. 572*

Lind, James
field: 8 medicine
nationality: 8 Scottish
eliminated: 6 scurvy

Lindbergh, Anne Morrow
author of: 14 Gift from the Sea **15** Bring Me a Unicorn **16** North to the Orient **19** War Within and Without

linden 5 Tilia
varieties: 6 Indoor **7** Crimean **8** American, Japanese **9** Mongolian **10** Manchurian **11** Large-leaved **13** Pendent silver **19** Small-leaved European

lindy 5 dance **8** lindy hop **9** jitterbug

line, lines 4 card, cord, dash, draw, file, idea, mark, note, part, race, rank, rope, rule, tier, word **5** align, array, breed, cable, craft, front, house, model, queue, range, score, slash, stock, trade **6** belief, border, column, crease, family, furrow, letter, method, metier, policy, report, scheme, series, stance, strain, strand, streak, stripe, system, thread **7** calling, circuit, conduit, contour, cordage, example, lineage, marshal, outline, pattern, purpose, pursuit, queue up, routine, towline, wrinkle **8** ancestry, business, dialogue, doctrine, fishline, ideology, inscribe, position, postcard, trenches, vanguard, vocation **9** conductor, crow's foot, direction, frontline, genealogy, intention, principle **10** barricades, convention, firing line, livelihood, long stroke, occupation, procession, profession, underscore **11** demarcation

lineage 4 line **5** blood, stock **7** descent **8** ancestry, heredity, pedigree **9** genealogy, parentage **10** derivation, extraction

linen
fabric: 6 canvas, damask **7** butcher, cambric **8** birds-eye **9** huckaback
plant: 4 flax

Lincoln, Abraham
  nickname: 9 Honest Abe 20 Illinois Rail Splitter
  presidential rank: 9 sixteenth
  party: 4 Whig 10 Republican
  state represented: 2 IL
  defeated: 4 (John) Bell 7 (John Charles) Fremont, (Stephen Arnold) Douglas 9 (George Brinton) McClellan 12 (John Cabell) Breckinridge
  vice president: 6 (Hannibal) Hamlin 7 (Andrew) Johnson
  cabinet:
    state: 6 (William Henry) Seward
    treasury: 5 (Salmon Portland) Chase 9 (Hugh) McCulloch, (William Pitt) Fessenden
    war: 7 (Edwin McMasters) Stanton, (Simon) Cameron
    attorney general: 5 (Edward) Bates, (James) Speed
    navy: 6 (Gideon) Welles
    postmaster general: 5 (Montgomery) Blair 8 (William) Dennison
    interior: 5 (Caleb Blood) Smith, (John Palmer) Usher
  born: 2 KY 8 log cabin 11 Larue County 17 Sinking Spring farm
  died: 12 Washington DC, Fords Theater
    died by: 13 assassination
    assassinated by: 15 John Wilkes Booth
  buried: 13 Springfield IL
  education:
    educated by: 4 self
    studied: 3 law
  interests: 7 theater
    received patent for: 25 adjustable buoyant chambers (for lifting boats)
  political career: 16 state legislature 24 US House of Representatives
  civilian career: 6 lawyer 8 surveyor 10 postmaster
  military service:
    War: 9 Black Hawk
    US Army: 7 private
    captain of company of: 10 volunteers
  notable events of lifetime/term: 8 Civil War 24 Emancipation Proclamation
    Act: 9 Homestead, Income Tax, Judiciary 12 Conscription
    debates: 14 Lincoln-Douglas
    speech: 17 Gettysburg Address
  father: 6 Thomas
  mother: 5 Nancy (Hanks)
    stepmother: 5 Sarah (Bush Johnston)
  siblings: 5 Sarah 6 Thomas
    stepbrother: 4 John
    stepsister: 7 Matilda 9 Elizabeth
  wife: 4 Mary (Ann Todd)
  children: 6 Thomas 10 Robert Todd 11 Edward Baker 14 William Wallace

finest from: 7 Belgium, Ireland
processing term: 6 shives, sliver 7 carding, hackled, retting 8 beetling, breaking, rippling, spinning 9 scutching

line of march 4 path 5 route, track 11 parade route

line of reasoning 4 case 7 premise 8 argument 10 hypothesis

line up 4 book 5 align 6 engage, even up 7 arrange, procure, program, queue up 8 schedule 9 form a line, put in a row 10 arrange for

line-up 5 slate 6 roster 8 schedule

linger 3 lag 4 idle, last, stay, wait 5 dally, delay, tarry, trail 6 dawdle, hang on, loiter, remain 7 persist, survive 9 die slowly 10 dillydally, hang around

lingering 4 slow 7 abiding, chronic, delayed, lagging, lasting, staying, waiting 8 dawdling, delaying, dragging, drawn out, dwelling, enduring, hovering, tarrying 9 loitering, remaining 10 protracted, sauntering 15 procrastinating

lingo 4 cant, talk 5 argot, idiom, slang 6 jargon, patois, tongue 7 dialect 8 language, parlance 10 vernacular

linguist 8 polyglot 10 grammarian, translator 11 etymologist, interpreter, philologist, phonetician, phonologist, semanticist 12 morphologist 13 lexicographer

liniment 4 balm 5 salve 7 unguent 8 ointment 9 emollient

link 3 tie 4 bind, bond, fuse, loop, ring 5 group, joint, tie in, unite 6 couple, relate, splice 7 bracket, combine, conjoin, connect, involve, liaison 8 junction, relation 9 associate, implicate 10 connection, connective 11 association 12 interconnect, relationship

linkage 3 tie 4 bond 6 hookup 10 connection 11 affiliation, association, correlation

link up 4 dock, join 6 couple, hook up 7 connect 9 affiliate 14 fasten together

Linnaeus, Carolus
  field: 6 botany
  nationality: 7 Swedish
  developed: 8 taxonomy 18 nomenclature system

linotype
  invented by: 12 Mergenthaler

Linton, Edgar
  character in: 16 Wuthering Heights
  author: 6 Bronte

Linus
  vocation: 4 poet 8 musician
  father: 6 Apollo
  mother: 8 Psamathe
  inventor of: 6 melody, rhythm
  identified with: 5 crops 9 withering 10 harvesting
  student: 8 Hercules
  killed by: 8 Hercules

Liod
  also: 4 Ljod 5 Hliod
  origin: 12 Scandinavian
  mentioned in: 8 Volsunga
  husband: 7 Volsung
  daughter: 5 Signy
  son: 7 Sigmund

lion 3 cat 6 cougar 7 wildcat 9 celebrity 12 man of the hour 15 king of the jungle
  group of: 5 pride
  constellation of: 3 Leo

lionhearted 4 bold 5 brave

6 heroic **7** valiant **8** fearless, intrepid, stalwart, unafraid, valorous **9** audacious, dauntless **10** courageous **11** indomitable **12** stouthearted

Lion in Winter, The
  director: **13** Anthony Harvey
  cast: **10** Jane Merrow **11** Peter O'Toole (Henry II) **13** Timothy Dalton **14** Anthony Hopkins **16** Katharine Hepburn (Eleanor of Aquitaine)
  Oscar for: **7** actress (Hepburn)

lionize 5 deify, exalt **6** admire, praise, revere **7** acclaim, adulate, ennoble, flatter, glorify **8** enshrine, eulogize **9** celebrate, glamorize **10** aggrandize **11** immortalize

lion's share 4 bulk, most **8** majority **9** major part **11** greater part **13** preponderance

lip 3 lap, rim **4** brim, edge, kiss, lick, wash **5** apron, mouth, spout, utter **6** labial, labium, margin **8** backtalk, labellum **9** insincere **10** embouchure, mouthpiece **11** superficial

Lipchitz, Jacques
  real name: **17** Chaim Yakob Lipchiz
  born: **9** Lithuania **11** Druskieniki **12** Druskininkai
  artwork: **4** Head **6** Bather, Figure **7** Harpist **9** Sacrifice **10** Prometheus **11** Benediction, Joie de Vivre **12** Peace on Earth **14** Man with a Guitar **15** Acrobats on a Ball, Man with Mandolin, Song of the Vowels **17** Notre Dame de Liesse, Sailor with a Guitar **19** Pierrot with Clarinet, Return of the Prodigal **24** Virgin of the Inverted Heart

Lipmann, Fritz Albert
  field: **12** biochemistry
  discovered: **9** Coenzyme A
  awarded: **10** Nobel Prize

Lippi, Filippino
  born: **5** Italy, Prato
  father: **15** Fra Filippo Lippi
  artwork: **20** The Vision of St Bernard **24** The Life of St Thomas Aquinas **26** The Lives of Sts Philip and John

Lippi, Fra Filippo
  born: **5** Italy **8** Florence
  son: **9** Filippino
  artwork: **15** Madonna and Child, The Feast of Herod **19** The Tarquinia Madonna **21** Coronation of the Virgin **25** The Madonna Adoring Her Child

liqueur 3 ale **4** beer, grog **5** booze, drink, hooch **7** alcohol, potable, spirits **8** beverage, potation **9** aqua vitae, drinkable, inebriant, moonshine **10** intoxicant
  almond: **8** amaretto
  anise: **8** absinthe
  apple: **8** calvados
  apricot: **10** abricotine
  caraway: **6** kummel **7** aquavit
  chocolate: **12** creme de cacao
  citrus: **10** goldwasser, liquor d'or
  coffee: **6** Kahlua
  grape: **6** Metaxa
  herb: **6** pernod **7** raspail **10** vielle cure **11** fiori alpini
  honey: **8** Drambuie
  medicinal: **11** Benedictine
  mint: **13** creme de menthe
  orange: **6** strega **7** curacao **9** cointreau **12** Grand Marnier
  raspberry: **9** framboise

liquid 5 drink, fluid **6** melted, molten, thawed **7** potable **8** beverage, solution

liquidate 3 hit, pay **4** kill **5** clear, erase, waste **6** cancel, murder, pay off, rub out, settle, wind up **7** abolish, break up, destroy, wipe out **8** close out, conclude, demolish **9** discharge, dispose of, eradicate, put to rest, terminate **10** account for, do away with **11** assassinate

liquor 3 gin, rum, rye **5** booze, broth, hooch, juice, sauce, vodka **6** brandy, liquid, Scotch **7** bourbon, extract, spirits, whiskey **9** drippings **10** inebriants **11** intoxicants
  measure: **4** pint, pony, shot **5** fifth, quart **6** jigger, magnum

Lir *see* **3** Ler

Lisbon
  capital of: **8** Portugal
  landmark:
    castle: **11** Saint George
    monastery: **9** Jeronimos
    square: **10** Black Horse
    tower: **5** Belem
  Moorish name: **7** Lixbuna
  ocean: **8** Atlantic
  Portuguese: **6** Lisboa
  river: **5** Tagus
  Roman name: **14** Felicitas Julia
  rulers: **5** Moors **6** French, Romans **7** British, Germans, Spanish **11** Phoenicians

lissome 5 agile, lithe, quick **6** limber, lively, nimble, pliant, supple **7** slender **8** flexible, graceful **9** lithesome, sprightly **11** light-footed

list 3 tip **4** bend, heel, lean,

roll, tilt **5** index, slant, slate, slope, table **6** career, muster, record, roster **7** catalog, incline, leaning **8** register, schedule, tabulate **9** catalogue, inventory

listen 4 hark, hear, heed, list **6** attend **7** give ear, hearken **8** give heed, listen in, overhear **9** be all ears, bend an ear, eavesdrop **10** take notice **12** pay attention

listener 3 ear **6** hearer **7** auditor **10** overhearer **12** eavesdropper

Lister, Joseph
  field: **7** surgeon **8** medicine
  nationality: **7** British
  pioneer of: **17** antiseptic surgery

listless 4 down, dull, lazy **6** dreamy, drowsy, leaden, mopish, torpid **7** languid **8** inactive, indolent, lifeless, sluggish **9** apathetic, enervated, lethargic, soporific **10** phlegmatic, spiritless **11** indifferent, unconcerned **12** uninterested **13** lackadaisical

Liston, Charles
  nickname: **5** Sonny
  sport: **6** boxing
  class: **11** heavyweight

Liszt, Franz (Ferencz)
  born: **7** Hungary, Raiding
  composer of: **5** Dante (symphony), Faust (symphony) **8** Christus **9** Psalm XIII **10** Nuages gris **13** Psalm Thirteen **17** Years of Pilgrimage **18** Annees de Pelerinage **19** Hungarian Rhapsodies **22** The Legend of St Elizabeth

Litae
  daughters of: **4** Zeus
  personify: **6** prayer

litany 4 list **7** account, catalog, recital **9** catalogue, narration, rendition **10** recitation, repetition **11** description, enumeration

lit de justice 32 formal sessions of French parliament
  literally: **12** bed of justice

literacy 7 culture **8** learning **9** erudition **11** edification, eruditeness, learnedness, scholarship **12** intelligence **13** enlightenment

literal 4 real, true **5** exact **6** actual, direct, honest, strict **7** correct, factual, precise, prosaic **8** accurate, faithful, reliable, truthful, verbatim **9** authentic **10** ad litteram, dependable, meticulous, scrupulous, undisputed

11 trustworthy, undeviating, word-for-word **12** matter-of-fact **13** authoritative, conscientious, unimaginative, unimpeachable

literary 6 poetic **7** bookish, of books **8** artistic, lettered, literate **12** intellectual

literate 7 learned **8** cultured, educated, lettered, literary, schooled, well-read **12** well-informed **13** knowledgeable

literati 9 highbrows **12** connoisseurs **13** intellectuals **14** intelligentsia

literature 4 lore **5** books, works **6** papers, theses **7** letters **8** classics, writings **9** treatises **11** scholarship **12** publications **13** belles lettres, dissertations

lithe 5 agile **6** limber, nimble, pliant, supple **7** lissome, pliable **8** bendable, flexible, graceful

Lithgow, John
roles: **9** Footloose **17** Terms of Endearment **21** Harry and the Hendersons **23** The World According to Garp

lithium
chemical symbol: **2** Li

Lithuania *see box*

litigation 4 suit **7** contest, dispute, lawsuit **10** contention, day in court **11** controversy, disputation, legal action, prosecution

litter 3 bed **4** heap, junk, lair, mess, nest, pile **5** issue, strew, trash, young **6** debris, jumble, pallet, refuse **7** bedding, clutter, kittens, progeny, puppies, rubbish, scatter **8** leavings **9** offspring, stretcher

little 3 bit, dot, jot, wee **4** dash, drop, hint, iota, mean, mild, tiny, whit **5** brief, crumb, elfin, faint, fleet, hasty, never, petty, pinch, pygmy, quick, scant, short, small, speck, trace **6** bantam, hardly, meager, minute, narrow, paltry, petite, rarely, seldom, skimpy, slight, trifle **7** minimum, modicum, not much, passing, stunted, trivial **8** dwarfish, fragment, inferior, mediocre, not at all, not often, particle, piddling, pittance, scarcely, slightly, somewhat, trifling, unworthy **9** by no means, deficient, hardly any, itsy-bitsy, itty-bitty, miniature, momentary, pint-sized, third-rate, worthless **10** diminutive, inflexible, negligible, short-lived, suggestion, under-

sized **11** commonplace, Lilliputian, microscopic, of no account, opinionated, pocket-sized, scarcely any, small amount, unimportant **12** insufficient, run-of-the-mill, short-sighted **13** infinitesimal, insignificant, next to nothing

Little Annie Rooney
creator: **14** Darrell McClure

Little Artha
nickname of: **11** Jack Johnson

Little Big Man
author: **12** Thomas Berger
director: **10** Arthur Penn
cast: **11** Faye Dunaway **12** Martin Balsam **13** Dustin Hoffman (Jack Crabb) **14** Chief Dan George **15** Richard Mulligan

---

Lithuania
other/former name: **5** Litva **7** Lietuva **33** Lithuanian Soviet Socialist Republic
capital/largest city: **5** Vilna **6** Kaunas **7** Vilnius
others: **4** Balt, Lett **5** Aesti, Kouno, Memel **6** Kovnac **7** Jelgava, Palanga, Telsiai **8** Ignalina, Kapsukas, Klaipeda, Siauliai **9** Panevezys **10** Elektrenai
government: **8** republic
monetary unit: **3** lit **5** marka **6** centas **7** ostmark, skatiku **8** auksinas
lake: **5** Dysna
mountain: **15** Samogitian Hills
highest point: **9** Juozapine
river: **5** Neman, Neris, Rusne **6** Dubysa, Nieman, Viliya **7** Nemunas, Nevezis, Nevezys **8** Pregolya
sea: **6** Baltic
physical feature:
lagoon: **8** Courland, Kuronian
people: **4** Balt, Lett **5** Zhmud **6** Jewish, Litvak, Polish **7** Aistian, Russian, Yatvyag **10** Lithuanian, Samogitian **11** Belorussian
language: **5** Zmudz **6** Baltic **10** Lithuanian
religion: **8** Lutheran **13** Roman Catholic

---

little by little
French: **7** peu a peu
Spanish: **9** poco a poco

Little Caesar
director: **11** Mervyn LeRoy
cast: **13** Glenda Farrell **15** Edward G Robinson (Caesar Enrico Bandello) **18** Douglas Fairbanks Jr

Little Daedala
origin: **7** Boeotia
event: **8** festival
honoring: **4** Hera, Zeus

Little Dorrit
author: **14** Charles Dickens
character: **3** Amy (Little Dorrit), Tip **4** Rugg **5** Casby, Fanny, Flora, Gowan **6** Affery, Merdle, Pancks, Rigaud (Blandois) **7** Meagles **8** Mr F's Aunt **9** Mrs Merdle **10** Flintwinch **13** Arthur Clennam, William Dorrit **16** Monsieur Blandois, Young John Chivery

Little Drummer Girl, The
author: **11** John Le Carre

Little Emily, Little Em'ly
character in: **16** David Copperfield
author: **7** Dickens

Little Fox
constellation of: **9** Vulpecula

Little Foxes, The
author: **14** Lillian Hellman
character: **13** Regina Giddens
director: **12** William Wyler
cast: **10** Bette Davis (Regina) **12** Teresa Wright **14** Richard Carlson **15** Herbert Marshall
prequel: **22** Another Part of the Forest

Little Gidding
author: **7** T S Eliot

Little Girls
author: **14** Elizabeth Bowen

Little House on the Prairie
author: **18** Laura Ingalls Wilder
character: **6** Albert **7** Dr Baker **8** Rev Alden **9** Mr Edwards **10** Andy Garvey, Lars Hanson, Nels Oleson **11** Adam Kendall, Alice Garvey, Mary Ingalls **12** Grace Ingalls, Laura Ingalls, Nellie Oleson, Willie Oleson **13** Carrie Ingalls, Harriet Oleson **14** Charles Ingalls, Eva Beadle Simms, Jonathan Garvey **15** Caroline Ingalls
cast: **10** Dabbs Greer, Kevin Hagen **11** Karl Swenson, Merlin Olsen, Richard Bull **12** Hersha Parady, Karen Grassle, Victor French **13** Alison Arngrim, Linwood Boomer, Michael Landon

14 Melissa Gilbert 15 Jonathon Gilbert, Sidney Greenbush, Wendy Turnbeaugh 16 Brenda Turnbeaugh, Charlotte Gilbert, Lindsay Greenbush 17 Katherine McGregor, Matthew Laborteaux, Patrick Laborteaux 18 Melissa Sue Anderson
setting: 6 Winoka 9 Minnesota, Plum Creek 11 Walnut Grove

Little John
character in: 9 Robin Hood

Little King, The
creator: 10 Otto Soglow
technique: 9 pantomine

little-known 6 unsung 7 obscure, unnoted 10 unrenowned

Little Learning, A
author: 11 Evelyn Waugh

Little Lord Fauntleroy
author: 15 Frances H Burnett

Little Lulu
creator: 14 Marge Henderson

Little Match Girl, The
author: 21 Hans Christian Andersen

Little Men
author: 15 Louisa May Alcott

Little Mermaid, The
author: 21 Hans Christian Andersen

Little Minister, The
author: 12 James M Barrie

Little Mo
nickname of: 15 Maureen Connolly

Little Nemo in Slumberland
creator: 11 Winsor McCay
character: 6 Dr Pill 8 cannibal, princess
  clown: 4 Flip
  dog: 6 Blutch

little one 3 tot 4 babe, baby, tyke 5 child 6 infant, wee one 7 toddler

Little Orphan Annie
creator: 10 Harold Gray
character:
  foster father: 13 Daddy Warbucks
  dog: 5 Sandy
saying: 13 Leapin' Lizards

Little Prince, The
author: 21 Antoine de Saint-Exupery

Little Rhody
nickname of: 11 Rhode Island

Little Tramp
nickname of: 14 Charlie Chaplin

Little Women
author: 15 Louisa May Alcott

character: 6 Laurie (Theodore Lawrence), Marmee 10 John Brooke 14 Professor Bhaer
  March sisters: 2 Jo 3 Amy, Meg 4 Beth
director:
  1933 version: 11 George Cukor
  1949 version: 11 Mervyn LeRoy
cast (1933): 9 Paul Lukas 10 Frances Dee, Jean Parker 11 Joan Bennett 16 Katharine Hepburn (Jo)
cast (1949): 9 Mary Astor 10 Janet Leigh 11 June Allyson 12 Peter Lawford 14 Margaret O'Brien 15 Elizabeth Taylor

liturgical 6 ritual 10 ceremonial 11 ceremonious, sacramental

liturgy 4 mass, rite 6 ritual 7 service, worship 8 ceremony, services 9 communion, sacrament

lituus
form: 5 staff
shape: 7 crooked

Lityerses
father: 9 King Midas
held: 15 reaping contests
killed: 6 losers

livable, liveable 4 cozy, snug 5 comfy, homey 8 bearable, passable, pleasant, suitable 9 agreeable, endurable, enjoyable, habitable, tolerable 10 acceptable, convenient, gratifying, satisfying, worthwhile 11 comfortable

live 2 be 3 hot 4 bunk, feed, stay 5 abide, afire, aglow, alive, dwell, exist, fiery, lodge, quick, stand, vital 6 ablaze, active, aflame, alight, at hand, billet, bodily, endure, hold on, living, obtain, occupy, red-hot, remain, reside, settle, thrive 7 animate, at issue, be alive, blazing, breathe, burning, current, flaming, fleshly, going on, ignited, persist, prevail, subsist, survive 8 existent, flourish, get ahead, get along, have life, increase, multiply, physical, pressing, take root, up-to-date, white-hot 9 breathing, corporeal 10 draw breath

live and keep well
Latin: 11 vive valeque

Live and Let Die
author: 10 Ian Fleming

live dissolutely 7 carouse, debauch 9 dissipate 11 overindulge

livelihood 3 job 5 trade 6 career, living, metier 7 calling,

support, venture 8 business, position, vocation 9 situation 10 enterprise, line of work, occupation, profession, sustenance 11 maintenance, subsistence, undertaking

liveliness 3 pep, zip 5 vigor 7 agility 8 alacrity, vitality, vivacity 9 animation, briskness, eagerness 10 ebullience, nimbleness 13 sprightliness

lively 5 alert, brisk, eager, peppy, perky, vivid 6 active, ardent, bouncy 7 buoyant, excited, fervent, intense 8 animated, spirited, vigorous 9 energetic, excitable, sprightly, vivacious 12 enthusiastic

liven 4 buoy 5 cheer, elate, pep up 6 perk up, vivify 7 animate, delight, enliven, fortify, gladden, hearten, punch up, quicken 8 brighten, embolden, energize, inspirit 10 exhilarate, invigorate, strengthen

liver
stores: 8 glycogen
color: 3 red 5 brown
produces: 4 bile 10 blood cells

Livermore Larruper
nickname of: 7 Max Baer

livery 4 garb, suit 5 dress 6 attire 7 costume, raiment, regalia, uniform 8 clothing 9 vestments

Lives of a Bengal Lancer
director: 13 Henry Hathaway
cast: 10 Gary Cooper 12 Franchot Tone 14 Sir Guy Standing 15 Richard Cromwell

Lives of the Poets, The
author: 13 Samuel Johnson

live through 4 know 7 survive, undergo 9 go through 10 experience

livid 3 mad 5 angry, irate, riled, vexed 6 fuming, galled, purple, raging 7 bruised, enraged, furious 8 contused, incensed, inflamed, outraged, provoked, wrathful 9 indignant, steamed up, ticked off 10 discolored, infuriated 11 exasperated

living 3 job 4 life, live, work 5 alive, being, quick, trade 6 active, bodily, career, extant, income 7 animate, calling, fleshly, going on, organic, venture 8 business, embodied, enduring, existent, existing, material, up-to-date, vocation 9 animation, breathing, corporeal, existence, incarnate, lifestyle, operative, permanent, remaining, surviving, way of life **10** employment, enterprise, having life, in the flesh, line of work, livelihood, occupation, persisting, prevailing, profession, subsisting, sustenance **11** maintenance, subsistence **13** drawing breath

living being 8 creature, organism

living conditions 10 atmosphere **11** environment **13** circumstances

living picture
   French: **13** tableau vivant

living quarters 4 home **5** abode, house **6** billet **7** housing, lodging, shelter **8** domicile, dwelling, quarters **9** apartment, residence **10** habitation **13** dwelling place

Livy
   also: **11** Titus Livius
   author of: **13** Ab urbe condita **26** From the Foundation of the City

lizard 3 dab, eft, uma **4** adda, gila, newt, seps, tegu **5** agama, anole, anoli, gecko, idler, shrink **6** aguana, dragon, iguana, komodo, moloch **7** lounger, monitor, reptile, saurian **8** dinosaur, lacerata, scorpion **9** alligator, blindworm, chameleon, crocodile, galliwasp **10** chuckwalla, glass snake, horned toad, salamander **11** gila monster **12** Komodo dragon
   characteristic: **6** scales **7** molting **9** oviparous **11** cold-blooded **12** regeneration
   constellation of: **7** Lacerta

Ljod *see* **4** Liod

llama 6 alpaca, kechua, mammal, vicuna **7** guanaco **8** ungulate **13** Peruvian sheep

Llewellyn, Richard
   author of: **19** How Green Was My Valley

Llew Llaw Gyffes
   origin: **5** Welsh
   father: **7** Gwydion
   mother: **9** Arianrhod
   wife: **10** Blodenwedd
   curses bestowed by: **9** Arianrhod

Lloyd
   origin: **5** Welsh
   form: **8** magician
   cast spells upon: **7** Pryderi

Lloyd, Harold
   born: **10** Burchard NE
   roles: **9** Feet First **10** Safety Last **11** The Freshman **13** The Kid Brother

Llud
   also: **4** Ludd, Nudd
   origin: **5** Welsh
   king of: **7** Britain
   rid kingdom of: **6** plague
   famous for: **10** generosity

Llyr
   origin: **5** Welsh
   son: **10** Manawyddan
   corresponds to: **3** Ler, Lir

load 3 try, vex **4** care, fill, haul, heap, lade, pack, pile **5** cargo, crush, stack, stuff, worry **6** burden, hamper, hinder, lading, misery, strain, weight **7** afflict, carload, freight, oppress, trouble **8** capacity, contents, encumber, handicap, pressure, shipload, shipment **9** overwhelm, planeload, truckload, wagonload, weigh down **10** affliction, deadweight, depression, misfortune, oppression **11** encumbrance

loads 4 lots, much **5** heaps, piles, scads **6** oodles, plenty **14** more than enough

loaf 4 idle, loll **5** dally **6** be lazy **7** goof off **8** kill time, malinger **9** do nothing, goldbrick, laze about, waste time **10** take it easy **12** lounge around

loafer 3 bum **4** shoe **5** idler **6** no-good **7** laggard, shirker, sponger, wastrel **8** deadbeat, loiterer, sluggard **9** goldbrick, lazybones **10** lazy person, malingerer, ne'er-do-well **11** couch potato **12** lounge lizard **15** drugstore cowboy
   French: **7** flaneur

loan 4 lend **5** allow **6** credit **7** advance, lending **8** mortgage **9** advancing

loath 4 loth **6** averse **7** against, counter, hostile, opposed **8** inimical **9** reluctant, resisting, unwilling **10** indisposed, set against **11** disinclined

loathe 4 hate **5** abhor, scorn **6** detest, eschew **7** deplore, despise, disdain, dislike **9** abominate **10** blench from, flinch from, recoil from, shrink from **11** keep clear of, shy away from **12** draw back from **14** be unable to bear, find disgusting, view with horror **16** have no stomach for

loathing 4 hate **5** odium **6** hatred **7** disgust, dislike **8** aversion, distaste **9** antipathy, repulsion, revulsion **10** abhorrence, repugnance **11** abomination, detestation

loathsome 4 foul, mean, rank, vile **5** nasty **6** odious **7** hateful **9** abhorrent, invidious, obnoxious, offensive, repugnant, repulsive, revolting, sickening **10** abominable, despicable, detestable, disgusting, nauseating, unbearable **11** distasteful

lobby 5 foyer **8** anteroom, politick **9** vestibule **11** antechamber, pull strings, waiting room **12** entrance hall

local 6 narrow, native, nearby **7** insular, limited **8** citywide, confined, regional **9** adjoining, homegrown, parochial, sectional **10** provincial **11** territorial **12** neighborhood **13** circumscribed

locale 4 area, site, spot, zone **6** region **7** quarter, section, setting **8** locality, location, precinct, province, vicinity **12** neighborhood

locality 4 area, site, spot, zone **5** place **6** locale, region **7** quarter, section **8** district, location, precinct, province, vicinity **9** territory **12** neighborhood

locate 3 fix, put **4** find, live, post, seat, stay **5** dwell, place **6** detect, move to, reside, settle **7** deposit, discern, hit upon, set down, situate, station, uncover, unearth **8** come upon, meet with, pinpoint **9** establish, ferret out, light upon, search out, stumble on, track down **10** settle down **12** put down roots

location 4 site, spot **5** place **6** locale **8** district, position **9** situation **11** whereabouts **12** neighborhood

Lochinvar
   character in: **7** Marmion
   author: **5** Scott

lock 3 bar, dam, pen **4** bang, bolt, cage, coil, curl, grab, grip, hank, hold, hook, jail, join, link, tuft **5** catch, clamp, clasp, grasp, latch, seize, skein, tress, unite **6** clinch, coop up, fasten, lock up, secure, shut in **7** confine, embrace, entwine, grapple, impound, padlock, ringlet **8** dock gate, imprison **9** canal gate, fastening, floodgate, interlink **10** intertwine, sluice gate **11** incarcerate

lock, cylinder
   invented by: **4** Yale

Lockhart, Gene
   daughter: **12** June Lockhart
   granddaughter: **11** Ann Lockhart
   born: **6** Canada, London **7** Ontario
   roles: **12** Madame Bovary

16 Death of a Salesman
19 The Inspector General
20 Abe Lincoln in Illinois

lock horns 4 feud, tiff **5** argue, brawl, clash, fight **7** dispute, quarrel, wrangle **8** squabble **9** altercate

Lockit
  character in: 12 Beggar's Opera
  author: 3 Gay

lockup 3 jug, pen **4** jail, stir **5** clink, pokey **6** cooler, prison **7** slammer **8** big house, hoosegow **11** reformatory **12** penitentiary

lock up 3 pen **4** cage, jail **6** coop up, secure **7** confine, impound **8** imprison, restrain, restrict **11** incarcerate

Lockyer, Joseph Norman
  field: 9 astronomy
  nationality: 7 British
  discovered: 6 helium

loco citato 15 in the place cited
  abbreviation: 6 loc cit

locomotive
  invented by:
    electric: 4 Vail
    experimental: 6 Fenton, Hedley **10** Stephenson, Trevithick
    first US: 6 Cooper
    practical: 10 Stephenson

Locrian Ajax see **4** Ajax

Locrus
  king of: 8 Locrians

locust 7 Robinia
  varieties: 4 moss **5** black, honey, mossy, swamp, sweet, water **6** clammy, yellow **7** African, bristly **8** shipmast **10** West Indian **13** Allegheny moss, South American

locution 4 term **5** idiom, trope, usage **6** phrase, saying **7** wording **8** idiolect, phrasing **9** set phrase, utterance, verbalism **10** expression **11** phraseology, regionalism **12** turn of phrase **14** figure of speech

lode 3 bed **4** seam **7** deposit

lodge 3 bed, hut **4** camp, file, room, stay **5** cabin, catch, hotel, house, motel, put up **6** billet, harbor, resort, submit **7** cottage, quarter, shelter, sojourn **8** register

lodging 4 room **8** quarters **13** accommodation

Lofn
  origin: 12 Scandinavian
  goddess of: 18 forbidden marriages

permission given by: 4 Odin **5** Othin

loft 3 lob **5** attic, pop up **6** belfry, garret **7** balcony, gallery, hit high, mansard **8** top floor **9** attic room, throw high **10** clerestory

loftiness 5 pride **9** arrogance **11** haughtiness **13** imperiousness **16** superciliousness

Lofting, Hugh
  author of: 11 Dr Doolittle

lofty 4 cold, high, tall **5** aloof, grand, great, noble, proud **6** lordly, mighty, remote, snooty **7** distant, eminent, exalted, haughty, leading, soaring, stately, stuck-up, sublime **8** arrogant, elevated, glorious, imposing, insolent, majestic, puffed-up, scornful, snobbish, superior, towering **9** conceited, dignified, imperious, important **10** disdainful, hoity-toity, preeminent **11** high ranking, illustrious, patronizing **12** high-reaching **13** condescending, distinguished, high-and-mighty, self-important

lofty bearing 7 dignity, majesty **10** augustness **11** stateliness

log 5 block, diary, stump **6** docket, lumber, record, timber **7** account, daybook, journal, logbook **8** calendar, schedule

loges 5 boxes **7** balcony **9** mezzanine

loggia 5 lanai, porch **6** arcade, piazza **7** balcony, gallery

Logi
  origin: 12 Scandinavian
  form: 3 man
  personifies: 4 fire
  defeated: 4 Loki

logic 5 sense **6** reason **7** cogency **8** analysis, argument **9** coherence, deduction, good sense, induction **10** dialectics

logical 5 clear, sound, valid **6** cogent, likely **7** germane **8** coherent, rational, relevant, sensible **9** deducible, pertinent, plausible **10** analytical, consistent, most likely, reasonable **11** enlightened, intelligent **13** well-organized

logos 4 word **5** ratio **6** saying, speech **7** thought **9** discourse, reckoning **10** proportion

logy 4 dull **5** inert, tired, weary **6** drowsy, groggy, sleepy, torpid **8** comatose, lifeless, listless, sluggish **9** enervated, inanimate, lethargic **10** phlegmatic **12** hebetudinous

Lohengrin
  opera by: 6 Wagner
  character: 4 Elsa **6** Ortrud **9** Gottfried (Duke of Brabant) **25** Count Frederick of Telramund

Lohengrin
  origin: 8 Germanic
  knight of: 9 Holy Grail
  father: 8 Parsifal, Parzival

loiter 4 idle, laze, loaf, loll, lurk **5** dally, skulk, slink, tarry **6** dawdle **10** dillydally, hang around **11** hover around **12** shilly-shally

Loki
  origin: 12 Scandinavian
  mentioned in: 9 Lokasenna
  god of: 4 fire
  son: 6 Fenrir, Fenris
  daughter: 3 Hel
  fathered: 10 Jormungand **11** Iormungandr, Jormungandr **14** Midgard Serpent
  mother of his children: 9 Angerboda, Angrbodha, Angurboda
  caused death of: 5 Baldr **6** Balder, Baldur
  form: 5 giant
  extorted treasure from: 7 Andvari
  function: 4 evil **6** strife

Lolita
  author: 15 Vladimir Nabokov
  character: 14 Humbert Humbert
  director: 14 Stanley Kubrick
  based on novel by: 15 Vladimir Nabokov
  cast: 7 Sue Lyon (Lolita) **10** James Mason (Humbert Humbert) **12** Peter Sellers **14** Shelley Winters

loll 3 sag **4** drag, drop, flap, flop, idle, lean, loaf **5** droop, relax, slump **6** dangle, dawdle, lounge, repose, slouch, sprawl **7** goof off, recline **8** flop over, languish

Lollobrigida, Gina
  born: 5 Italy **7** Subiaco
  roles: 7 Trapeze **14** Anne of Brooklyn, The Wayward Wife **15** Solomon and Sheba **20** Buona Sera Mrs Campbell **27** The World's Most Beautiful Woman

Loman, Willy
  character in: 16 Death of a Salesman
  author: 6 Miller

Lombard, Carole
  real name: 15 Jane Alice Peters
  husband: 10 Clark Gable
  born: 11 Fort Wayne IN
  roles: 12 My Man Godfrey **13** Nothing Sacred, To Be

Or Not To Be **16** Twentieth
Century

Lome
  capital of: **4** Togo

London *see box*

London, Jack
  author of: **9** White Fang
  10 The Sea Wolf **16** The
  Call of the Wild

lone 4 only, sole **5** alone **6** single, unique **8** isolated, singular, solitary, unpaired
  9 unabetted **10** individual, unattended, unescorted **13** companionless, unaccompanied

loneliness 9 isolation, seclusion **12** lonesomeness, solitariness **14** friendlessness

**Loneliness of the Long Dis-
  tance Runner, The**
  director: **14** Tony Richardson
  cast: **11** Avis Bunnage, Peter
  Madden **12** Tom Courtenay
  15 Michael Redgrave

lonely 6 remote **7** forlorn **8** deserted, desolate, forsaken, hermitic, isolated, lonesome,
  secluded, solitary, unsocial
  9 by oneself, reclusive, withdrawn **10** friendless, unattended **11** uninhabited,
  unpopulated **12** unfrequented
  13 companionless,
  unaccompanied

Lone Ranger, The
  character: **5** Tonto
  cast: **8** John Hart **12** Clayton
  Moore **14** Jay Silverheels
  horse: **5** Scout **6** Silver

Lone Ranger used: 13 silver
  bullets
  theme: **19** William Tell
  Overture

lonesome 5 alone, aloof
  6 lonely **7** forlorn, insular
  8 desolate, detached, forsaken
  9 alienated, withdrawn
  10 friendless, unfriended
  13 companionless

Lone Star State
  nickname of: **5** Texas

long 4 hope, lust, pine, sigh,
  want, wish **5** covet, crave,
  yearn **6** aspire, hanker, hunger, thirst **7** lengthy, spun
  out **8** drawn-out, extended,
  have a yen, in length, unending **9** elongated, extensive,
  prolonged **10** be bent on, protracted **11** far-reaching, have a
  desire **12** from end to end, interminable, outstretched

Long, Crawford Williamson
  field: **8** medicine
  first used: **5** ether

Longaville
  character in: **16** Love's Labour's Lost
  author: **11** Shakespeare

**Long Day's Journey into
  Night**
  author: **12** Eugene O'Neill
  director: **11** Sidney Lumet
  cast: **13** Dean Stockwell
  14 Jason Robards Jr
  15 Ralph Richardson
  16 Katharine Hepburn

Longest Day, The
  director: **10** Ken Annakin

  12 Andrew Marton, Bernard
  Wicki
  cast: **9** John Wayne, Mel
  Ferrer **10** Henry Fonda, Red
  Buttons, Robert Ryan, Rod
  Steiger **12** Peter Lawford
  setting: **8** Normandy (Allied
  invasion)

Longevity
  goddess of: **11** Anna
  Perenna

long-faced 4 glum **6** dismal,
  gloomy **7** doleful, unhappy
  8 dejected, mournful **10** lugubrious **14** down in the
  mouth

**Longfellow, Henry
  Wadsworth**
  author of: **8** Hyperion, (The
  Song of) Hiawatha
  10 Evangeline **15** Paul Revere's Ride **18** Tales of a
  Wayside Inn **21** The Wreck
  of the Hesperus **27** The
  Courtship of Miles Standish

longing 3 yen **4** wish **6** ardent,
  pining, thirst **7** craving, wishful **8** desirous, yearning
  9 hankering, hungering **10** aspiration **11** languishing

long-lasting 7 chronic,
  lengthy, tedious **8** enduring,
  extended **9** prolonged **10** continuing, protracted

long live
  French: **4** vive

long past 3 old **5** olden **6** gone
  by, of yore **7** ancient, long
  ago **8** long gone

long-standing 4 long **5** hardy,
  hoary **6** rooted **7** abiding, ancient, chronic, durable, lasting **8** enduring, habitual,
  hallowed, unfading **9** confirmed, continual, long-lived,
  perennial, perpetual, venerable **10** continuous, deep-
  rooted, deep-seated, inveterate,
  persistent, persisting **11** long-
  lasting, time-honored **15** long-
  established

Longstreet, James
  served in: **8** Civil War
  side: **11** Confederate
  battle: **7** Bull Run **10** Gettysburg **11** Chickamauga
  14 Fredericksburg **18** Wilderness Campaign
  after war joined:
  11 Republicans
  US minister to: **6** Turkey

Long Voyage Home, The
  director: **8** John Ford
  based on play by: **12** Eugene
  O'Neill
  cast: **9** Ian Hunter, John
  Wayne **13** Wilfrid Lawson
  14 Thomas Mitchell
  15 Barry Fitzgerald

London
  airport: **7** Gatwick **8** Heathrow, Stansted
  architect: **4** Wren
  area: **4** Soho **6** Camden **7** Brixton, Chelsea, Holborn, Pimlico **8** Vauxhall **9** Bayswater, Belgravia, Islington, Southwark **10** Bloomsbury, Kensington, Paddington,
  Shoreditch **11** Notting Hill, St John's Wood
  13 Knightsbridge
  capital of: **7** England **12** Great Britain **13** United Kingdom
  landmark: **6** Big Ben **8** Hyde Park **9** Whitehall, Wimble-
  don **11** Regent's Park, Saint James's, Tate Gallery, Tower
  Bridge **12** Covent Garden, London Bridge **13** British Museum, Tower of London **14** British Library, Speaker's Corner **15** National Gallery, Trafalgar Square **16** Buckingham
  Palace, Piccadilly Circus, Westminster Abbey **17** Kensington Gardens, Royal Festival Hall, Westminster Palace
  18 Houses of Parliament **19** Saint Paul's Cathedral
  23 Victoria and Albert Museum
  police: **7** bobbies
    established by: **13** Sir Robert Peel
  prime minister's residence: **16** Ten Downing Street
  river: **6** Thames
  Roman name: **9** Londinium
  subway: **11** Underground

long-wearing 5 tough
6 strong, sturdy 7 durable,
lasting 8 enduring
11 substantial

long-winded 5 wordy 6 prolix
7 lengthy, tedious, verbose
8 rambling 9 garrulous 10 digressive, discursive

long-windedness 8 rambling
9 garrulity, prolixity, verbosity,
wordiness 14 discursiveness

Lonnrot, Elias
author of: 8 Kalevala

look 3 air, see 4 cast, face,
gape, gaze, mien, ogle, peek,
peep, scan, seem, show, view
5 front, glare, guise, sight,
stare, study, watch 6 appear,
behold, glance, regard, survey
7 bearing, examine, exhibit,
glimpse 8 demeanor, manifest,
once-over, presence, scrutiny
10 appearance, be directed,
cut a figure, expression, scrutinize 11 contemplate, countenance, observation

look after 4 help 6 assist, defend 7 help out, protect
10 minister to 11 watch out
for 17 take under one's wing

look askance at 7 condemn
8 object to 9 frown upon
10 disapprove 14 discountenance 15 take exception to
16 find unacceptable, view
with disfavor

look at 3 see 4 view 6 behold,
notice, regard 7 examine, inspect, witness 10 scrutinize

Look Back in Anger
director: 14 Tony Richardson
based on play by: 11 John
Osborne
cast: 7 Mary Ure 10 Edith
Evans 11 Claire Bloom
13 Richard Burton 15 Donald Pleasance

look down on 7 despise, disdain 9 frown upon, patronize
10 condescend 13 put on airs
with 14 hold in contempt

looker-on 6 viewer 7 watcher,
witness 8 beholder, observer,
onlooker 9 bystander, spectator

look for 4 seek 5 await 6 expect, pursue 7 hunt for
9 search for 10 anticipate

look for the woman
French: 15 cherchez la
femme

Look Homeward, Angel
author: 11 Thomas Wolfe
character: 7 Ben Gant 9 Eliza

Gant 10 Eugene Gant, Laura
James, Oliver Gant 15 Margaret Leonard

Looking Backward
author: 13 Edward Bellamy

look in the eye 4 defy, face
5 brave 8 confront 9 challenge

look into 5 probe 7 examine,
explore 10 scrutinize 11 inquire into, investigate

lookout 4 heed 5 guard, scout,
vigil 6 patrol, sentry 7 spotter
8 observer, sentinel, watchdog,
watchman 9 alertness, attention, awareness, readiness, vigilance 10 precaution
11 guardedness, mindfulness,
watchkeeper 12 surveillance,
watchfulness

look out 4 mind 6 beware
8 take care, watch out 9 be
careful, be on guard 11 take
warning 12 be on the alert

look over 4 scan, skim
5 judge 6 assess, peruse, survey 7 dip into 8 appraise,
evaluate 13 browse through,
glance through

look through 4 scan, skim
6 browse, peruse 7 dip into
8 look over 9 check over
13 glance through

look toward 7 count on
10 anticipate 13 look forward
to

look upon 3 see 4 view 6 behold, gaze at, look at 7 observe, stare at

look upon as 4 deem, hold
5 count, judge, think 6 regard,
view as 7 account, believe
8 consider, take to be

look up to 5 honor 6 admire,
esteem, revere 7 respect
8 venerate

loom 4 hulk, rise, soar
5 tower 6 appear, ascend,
emerge 8 stand out 9 take
shape

loom, power
invented by: 10 Cartwright

loop 3 eye 4 bend, coil, curl,
furl, ring, roll, turn 5 braid,
curve, noose, plait, twirl,
twist, whorl 6 circle, eyelet,
spiral 7 opening, ringlet 8 aperture, encircle, loophole
10 wind around 11 convolution, curve around

Loos, Anita
author of: 22 Gentlemen Prefer Blondes

loose 4 fast, free, lewd, undo,
wild 5 freed, let go, slack, untie, vague 6 freely, loosen, unbind, undone, untied, wanton

7 immoral, inexact, loosely,
release, set free, slacken, unbound, uncaged, unchain, unleash, unloose, unyoked
8 careless, heedless, liberate,
not tight, rakehell, unbridle,
unchaste, unfasten, unjoined,
untether 9 abandoned, debauched, dissolute, imprecise,
liberated, libertine, unbridled,
unchained, unleashed, unmanacle, unshackle 10 dissipated,
inaccurate, licentious, not
binding, profligate, unattached,
unexacting, unfastened, unfettered, unhandcuff, untethered
11 not fastened, unconnected
12 unimprisoned
13 unconstrained

loose-fitting 4 limp 5 baggy,
loose, slack 6 draped, droopy
7 sagging 9 overlarge,
oversized

loosely connected 5 jerky
6 fitful 8 episodic, rambling
9 spasmodic, wandering 10 digressive, discursive,
meandering

loosen 3 lax 4 ease, free,
undo 5 break, relax, untie
6 limber, unbend, unbind
7 release, relieve, slacken, unchain, unscrew 8 liberate, unbuckle, unfasten, work free
10 emancipate

looseness 8 fastness, lewdness,
wildness 9 slackness, vagueness 10 debauchery, immorality, inaccuracy, profligacy,
wantonness 11 dissipation, dissolution, imprecision 12 carelessness, heedlessness,
inexactitude 14 licentiousness

loot 3 rob 4 haul, raid, sack,
swag, take 5 booty, prize,
strip 6 boodle, fleece, pilfer,
ravage, spoils 7 pillage, plunder, ransack 11 stolen goods

looter 5 thief 6 robber, vandal
7 brigand 8 pillager 9 despoiler, plunderer

lop 3 cut 4 chip, chop, crop,
dock, flop, sned, snip, trim
5 droop, prune, sever 6 cut
off, deduct, detach, remove,
slouch 7 cut back 8 amputate,
truncate

Lopez, Nancy
sport: 4 golf
husband: 9 Ray Knight
plays: 8 baseball

lopsided 4 awry 5 askew
6 aslant, tipped, uneven
7 crooked, leaning, listing,
slanted, tilting, unequal
8 cockeyed, inclined, slanting
9 irregular 10 asymmetric, offbalance, unbalanced 15 dis-

proportional
16 disproportionate

loquacious 5 gabby, talky, windy, wordy **6** blabby, chatty, prolix **7** prating, verbose, voluble **8** babbling, chattery **9** garrulous, prattling, talkative **10** chattering, long-winded

loquitur 8 he speaks **9** she speaks

lord 4 king **5** chief, crown, ruler **6** leader, master **7** monarch **8** overlord, seignior, superior **9** commander, landowner, sovereign **10** landholder, proprietor
  Japanese: 6 daimyo
  Turkish: 3 beg, bey

Lord
  Latin: 7 Dominus

Lord be with you, the
  Latin: 15 Dominus vobiscum

Lord have mercy
  Greek: 12 Kyrie eleison

Lord Jim
  author: 12 Joseph Conrad
  character: 5 Stein **6** Marlow **9** Dain Waris **14** Gentleman Brown

lordliness 7 disdain **8** contempt **9** arrogance, insolence, loftiness **11** haughtiness **13** imperiousness **16** superciliousness

lordly 4 cold **5** aloof, bossy, grand, lofty, noble, proud, regal **6** august, remote, snooty **7** distant, elegant, eminent, exalted, haughty, stately, stuck-up **8** arrogant, despotic, imposing, majestic, princely, puffed-up, scornful, snobbish **9** conceited, dignified, imperious, sumptuous **10** disdainful, hoity-toity, tyrannical **11** dictatorial, domineering, magisterial, magnificent, patronizing **13** condescending, high-and-mighty, self-important

Lord of the Flies
  author: 14 William Golding

Lord of the Rings, The
  author: 10 J R R Tolkien

Lord Raingo
  author: 13 Arnold Bennett

Lord Weary's Castle
  author: 12 Robert Lowell

lore 7 beliefs, legends **10** traditions

Lorelei
  also: 7 Lurelei
  origin: 8 Germanic
  form: 5 nymph
  dwelling place: 5 cliff, Rhine

lured: 7 boatmen
caused shipwrecks by: 7 singing

Loren, Sophia
  real name: 14 Sofia Scicolone
  husband: 10 Carlo Ponti
  born: 4 Rome **5** Italy
  roles: 5 El Cid **8** Two Women (Oscar) **9** Arabesque, Houseboat **13** Man of La Mancha **14** The Black Orchid **18** Desire Under the Elms **20** Marriage Italian Style **21** A Countess from Hong Kong, The Pride and the Passion

Lorentz, Hendrik Anton
  field: 7 physics
  nationality: 5 Dutch
  discovered: 17 special relativity
  named for him: 21 Lorentz transformation **34** Lorentz-Fitzgerald Length Contraction
  awarded: 10 Nobel Prize

Loring, Eugene
  choreographer of: 11 Billy the Kid

Lorna Doone
  author: 11 R D Blackmore
  character: 8 John Ridd **9** Tom Faggus **11** Carver Doone **13** Sir Ensor Doone **14** Jeremy Stickles **15** Reuben Huckaback

Lorre, Peter
  real name: 16 Laszlo Lowenstein

born: 7 Hungary **9** Rosenberg
roles: 1 M **7** Mad Love **10** Casablanca, The Verdict **12** The Big Circus **14** Three Strangers **16** The Maltese Falcon **18** Crime and Punishment, The Mask of Dimitrios

Lorry, Jarvis
  character in: 16 A Tale of Two Cities
  author: 7 Dickens

Los Angeles *see box*

lose 4 fail, miss **6** forget, ignore, mislay **7** confuse, forfeit **8** misplace **9** fail to win, stray from **10** be the loser, fail to heed **11** be thrown off **12** be defeated in, be deprived of, suffer loss of, take a licking

lose control 5 break, crack **7** crack up **9** fall apart **10** go to pieces **15** go off the deep end

lose faith 6 give up **7** despair **9** lose heart **10** have no hope **18** become disenchanted

lose force 3 die **7** run down **9** lose power

lose heart 6 give up **7** despair **17** become discouraged

lose one's cool 12 fly into a rage **13** become enraged, throw a tantrum **14** lose one's temper **15** fly off the handle

loser 4 flop **7** failure **8** de-

Los Angeles
  airport: 3 LAX **7** Burbank **23** Los Angeles International
  area: 5 Watts **6** Bel Air, Downey, Venice **7** Anaheim, Compton, Norwalk **8** Mar Vista, Pasadena, Torrance, Westwood **9** Brentwood, Hollywood, Inglewood, Long Beach **10** Culver City **11** Century City, Garden Grove, Palos Verdes, Santa Monica **12** Beverly Hills, Marina del Rey **16** Pacific Palisades
    San Fernando Valley: **6** Encino **7** Tarzana, Van Nuys, Ventura **10** Northridge **11** Sherman Oaks
  baseball team: 7 Dodgers
  basketball team: 6 Lakers **8** Clippers
  football team: 4 Rams **7** Express, Raiders
  hockey team: 5 Kings
  landmark: 5 Forum **10** Disneyland **11** Civic Center, Getty Museum, Watts Towers **12** Griffith Park **13** Farmers' Market, Hollywood Bowl, Hollywood Park, La Brea Tar Pits, Magic Mountain **15** Knott's Berry Farm **16** Bonaventure Hotel **17** Norton Simon Museum **22** Grauman's Chinese Theater **23** Griffith Park Observatory
  mountains: 10 San Gabriel **11** Santa Monica
  nickname: 15 City of the Angels
  street: 4 Vine **10** Rodeo Drive **12** Olvera Street **15** Mulholland Drive **16** Van Nuys Boulevard **17** Wilshire Boulevard **18** Hollywood Boulevard **20** Santa Monica Boulevard
  university: 3 USC **4** UCLA **7** Caltech **10** Pepperdine **17** Occidental College **31** California Institute of Technology

feated **9** conquered
10 vanquished

lose track of 4 lose **9** let escape **11** lose sight of

lose vigor 4 flag **5** droop
6 sicken, weaken, wither
7 decline

Losing Battles
author: **11** Eudora Welty

loss 4 ruin **5** wreck **6** defeat,
losing **7** licking, removal, undoing **8** overturn, riddance,
wrecking **9** abolition, mislaying, privation **10** amount lost,
demolition, extinction, forfeiture, misplacing, number lost
11 bereavement, deprivation,
destruction, dissolution, eradication, expenditure,
extirpation

loss of life 5 death **8** fatality
9 mortality

lost 5 stray **6** absent, astray,
killed, ruined, wasted **7** lacking, mislaid, missing, misused,
strayed, wrecked **8** absorbed,
murdered, perished, vanished,
wiped out **9** abolished, destroyed, engrossed, misplaced,
off-course **10** demolished, eradicated, extirpated, gone astray,
misapplied, squandered **11** annihilated, misdirected, obliterated, preoccupied
12 exterminated

**Lost Honor of Katharina
Blum, The**
author: **12** Heinrich Boll

Lost Horizon
author: **11** James Hilton
character: **10** Hugh Conway,
Rutherford **12** Henry Barnard, Miss Brinklow **14** Father Perrault **20** Captain
Mallison Chang
director: **10** Frank Capra
cast: **5** Margo **8** H B Warner,
Sam Jaffe **9** Jane Wyatt
10 John Howard **12** Isabel
Jewell, Ronald Colman
14 Thomas Mitchell **19** Edward Everett Horton
setting: **5** Tibet

Lost Illusions
author: **14** Honore de Balzac

Lost in America
director: **12** Albert Brooks
cast: **12** Albert Brooks, Julie
Hagerty

Lost in Space
character: **5** Robot **7** Don
West **12** Judy Robinson,
Will Robinson **13** Penny
Robinson **14** Dr Zachary
Smith **15** Maureen Robinson **16** Prof John Robinson
cast: **9** Billy Mumy **11** Guy
Williams, Mark Goddard

12 June Lockhart, Marta
Kristen **14** Jonathan Harris
16 Angela Cartwright
ship: **9** Jupiter II

Lost in the Funhouse
author: **9** John Barth

Lost in the Stars
author: **15** Maxwell Anderson

lost in thought 7 pensive
8 absorbed **9** engrossed,
wrapped up **13** contemplative,
in a brown study,
introspective

Lost Lady, A
author: **11** Willa Cather

Lost Ones, The
author: **13** Samuel Beckett

Lost Patrol, The
director: **8** John Ford
cast: **8** Alan Hale **11** Wallace
Ford **12** Boris Karloff
14 Victor McLaglen
score: **10** Max Steiner

Lost Weekend, The
author: **14** Charles Jackson
director: **11** Billy Wilder
cast: **9** Jane Wyman, Mary
Young **10** Frank Falen, Ray
Milland **11** Philip Terry
12 Doris Dowling **13** Howard da Silva
Oscar for: **5** actor (Milland)
7 picture **8** director
10 screenplay

lot 4 fate, lots, many, much,
plot **5** field, patch, quota,
share, straw, tract **6** oceans,
oodles, ration **7** counter, measure **8** beaucoup, property
9 allotment, allowance, great
deal

Lot
grandfather: **5** Terah
father: **5** Haran
uncle: **7** Abraham
son: **5** Ammon
hometown: **5** Sodom
rescued by: **6** angels
fled to: **4** Zoar

lothario 3 rip **4** rake, roue,
wolf **5** lover, Romeo, sheik
6 lecher **7** Don Juan, seducer,
swinger **8** Casanova, loverboy **9** debauchee, debaucher,
libertine, womanizer **10** ladykiller, profligate, sensualist
11 philanderer, skirt-chaser

Lothario
character in: **15** The Fair
Penitent
author: **4** Rowe

Loti, Piere
author of: **18** An Iceland
Fisherman

lotion 4 balm, wash **5** salve
6 liquid **7** unction, unguent
8 cosmetic, liniment, ointment,

solution **9** demulcent, emollient, freshener, skin cream
10 after-shave, astringent
11 conditioner, embrocation,
moisturizer

Lotis
form: **5** nymph
changed into: **4** tree **5** lotus

lotophagi
means: **11** lotus-eaters

lots 4 much **5** heaps, loads,
plots, scads **10** quantities

lotus 7 Nelumbo **13** Nymphaea
lotus
varieties: **4** blue **5** water,
white **6** sacred **8** American,
Egyptian **10** East Indian

lotus-eaters 9 lotophagi

loud 4 gaudy, noisy, showy,
vivid **6** bright, flashy, garish
7 blatant, booming, intense,
splashy **8** colorful, sonorous
9 clamorous, deafening **10** resounding, stentorian, thundering, vociferous **11** ear-piercing,
loudmouthed **12** earsplitting,
ostentatious

loud sound 4 bang, boom,
clap, honk, howl, peal, roar,
slam, toot **5** blare, blast, burst,
crash **6** bellow, report, scream,
shriek **7** clatter, thunder **9** explosion **10** detonation

Lou Grant
character: **6** Animal **8** Joe
Rossi **10** Art Donovan
11 Charlie Hume **12** Billie
Newman **15** Margaret
Pynchon
cast: **10** Jack Bannon, Mason
Adams **11** Edward Asner,
Linda Kelsey **12** Robert
Walden **13** Nancy Marchand **14** Darryl Anderson
paper: **17** Los Angeles
Tribune
spinoff of: **18** Mary Tyler
Moore Show

Louhi
origin: **7** Finnish
form: **9** sorceress
mistress of: **7** Pohjola
defeated by: **11** Vainamoinen
enemy of: **5** Finns

Louis, Joe
real name: **14** Joe Louis
Barrow
nickname: **11** Brown Bomber
sport: **6** boxing
class: **11** heavyweight

Louis, Morris
born: **11** Baltimore MD
artwork: **4** Veil **5** Signa
7 Stripes **8** Unfurled
15 Mountains and Sea

Louise
opera by: **11** Charpentier
character: **6** Julian

Louisiana
abbreviation: 2 LA
nickname: 5 Bayou, Sugar 6 Creole 7 Pelican
capital: 10 Baton Rouge
largest city: 10 New Orleans
others: 5 Houma 6 Bunkie, Gretna, Kenner, Minden, Monroe, Ruston 7 Bastrop 8 Bogalusa 9 Lafayette, Opelousas 10 Alexandria, Shreveport 11 Lake Charles
college: 3 LSU 6 Loyola, Tulane 7 Dillard, Newcomb 9 Grambling
explorer: 7 La Salle 9 Iberville 13 Pierre Lemoyne
feature:
　area: 5 bayou 13 French Quarter
　festival: 9 Mardi Gras
　music: 4 jazz
　stadium: 9 Sugar Bowl
　street: 7 Bourbon
tribe: 4 Adai, Ioni, Rees, Waco 5 Caddo, Haini, Washa 6 Eyeish, Pawnee 7 Andarko, Arikara, Atakapa 8 Ovachita 9 Bayogoula, Nachitoch
people: 5 Cajun 6 Creole 7 Acadian, pelican 8 Huey Long 14 Lillian Hellman, Louis Armstrong
island: 5 Avery
lake: 3 Iat 4 Iatt 5 Caddo, Clear, Cross, Larto, White 6 Borgne, Saline 8 Darbonne, Maurepas 9 Bistineau, Calcasieu, Catahoula 10 False River 13 Pontchartrain
land rank: 11 thirty-first
mountain:
　highest point: 8 Driskill
physical feature: 15 Head of the Passes 17 coastal marshlands
　delta: 11 Mississippi
　gulf: 6 Mexico
　salt domes: 11 Five Islands
river: 3 Red 5 Amite, Bayou, Pearl 6 Tensas 8 Ouachita 11 Mississippi
state admission: 10 eighteenth
state bird: 19 eastern brown pelican
state flower: 8 magnolia
state motto: 5 Union 7 Justice 10 Confidence
state song: 15 Give Me Louisiana 16 You Are My Sunshine
state tree: 11 bald cypress

Louisiana Lightning
nickname of: 9 Ron Guidry

lounge 4 flop, idle, laze, loaf, loll, rest, sofa 5 couch, dally, divan, lobby, relax, sleep, slump 6 dawdle, daybed, repose, slouch, sprawl 7 recline, slumber 8 kill time, languish 9 davenport, do nothing, lie around, vestibule 10 dillydally, stretch out, take it easy

lourd
music: 5 heavy

Lourenco Marques
capital of: 10 Mozambique

louse 3 cad, rat 4 heel 5 churl, knave 6 rascal, rotter, vermin 8 parasite 9 scoundrel

louse up 3 mar 4 goof, muff, ruin 5 botch, spoil 6 bungle, foul up, mess up 7 butcher, do badly, screw up 9 mismanage 11 make a mess of

lousiness 9 nastiness 10 crumminess, horridness, rottenness 11 inferiority, infestation 13 despicability, unsuitability 14 unpleasantness

lousy 3 bad 4 mean 5 awful, nasty 6 crummy, rotten, shabby, unkind 7 hateful, vicious 8 dreadful, inferior, infested, terrible 9 unethical, worthless 10 pediculous, second-rate, unpleasant 12 contemptible

lout 3 ape, oaf 4 boor, clod 5 booby, churl, clown, dummy, dunce, klutz, yokel 6 lummox, rustic 7 bumpkin, dullard

loutish 4 rude 5 crude 6 coarse, gauche, oafish, vulgar 7 boor-ish, uncouth 9 unrefined 10 unpolished 11 peasantlike

lovable, loveable 4 cute 5 sweet 6 cuddly, lovely, taking 7 darling, winning, winsome 8 adorable, charming, engaging, fetching 9 endearing 10 enchanting 11 captivating

Lovberg, Eilert
character in: 11 Hedda Gabler
author: 5 Ibsen

love 3 man 4 beau, bent, dear, girl, mind, turn 5 adore, amity, amour, angel, ardor, enjoy, fancy, flame, honey, lover, savor, taste, woman 6 admire, bask in, choice, esteem, fellow, relish 7 beloved, charity, cherish, concord, darling, dearest, emotion, leaning, passion, rapture, revel in, sweetie 8 affinity, be fond of, devotion, fondness, goodwill, hold dear, loved one, mistress, paramour, penchant, precious, sympathy, treasure, truelove, weakness 9 adoration, affection, boyfriend, delight in, inamorata, rejoice in, sentiment 10 admiration, appreciate, attachment, cordiality, friendship, girlfriend, partiality, proclivity, solicitude, sweetheart, sweetie pie, tenderness 11 amorousness, benevolence, brotherhood, inclination, infatuation 12 be enamored of, congeniality, predilection
god of: 4 Amor, Eros 5 Cupid 7 Angus Og
goddess of: 5 Freia, Freya 6 Hathor, Inanna, Ishtar 7 Mylitta 9 Aphrodite

Love, the Magician
also: 11 El Amor Brujo
ballet by: 5 Falla

love affair 5 amour 7 liaison, romance 14 affaire de coeur

Love Boat, The
character: 3 Ace 10 (Cruise Director) Julie McCoy 11 (Dr) Adam Bricker, (Purser Burl) Gopher Smith 14 (Captain) Merrill Stubing 15 (Bartender) Isaac Washington
cast: 8 Ted Lange 10 Fred Grandy 11 Lauren Tewes 12 Bernie Kopell, Gavin MacLeod
ship: 15 Pacific Princess

love child 7 bastard 12 natural child 17 illegitimate child

love conquers all
Latin: 15 omnia vincit amor

loved one 4 love, wife

5 lover **6** fiance, spouse **7** beloved, dearest, fiancee, husband **9** boyfriend **10** girlfriend, sweetheart **12** family member

Love for Three Oranges, The
 opera by: 9 Prokofiev

Love in the Afternoon
 director: 11 Billy Wilder
 cast: 10 Gary Cooper **13** Audrey Hepburn **16** Maurice Chevalier
 setting: 5 Paris

Lovelace, Richard
 author of: 18 To Althea from Prison **23** To Lucasta Going to the Wars

loveliness 6 beauty **9** good looks **11** pulchritude **14** attractiveness

lovely 4 cute, fine, good **5** sweet **6** comely **7** elegant, lovable, winning, winsome **8** adorable, alluring, charming, engaging, fetching, handsome, pleasant, pleasing **9** agreeable, beautiful, endearing, enjoyable, exquisite **10** attractive, delightful, enchanting **11** captivating, fascinating **12** irresistible

Love Machine, The
 author: 16 Jacqueline Susann

Love Me Tonight
 director: 15 Rouben Mamoulian
 cast: 8 Myrna Loy **14** Charlie Ruggles **16** Maurice Chevalier **17** Jeanette MacDonald
 score: 14 Rodgers and Hart
 song: 4 Mimi **5** Lover **14** Isn't It Romantic

love of country
 Latin: 11 amor patriae

Love of One's Neighbor
 author: 14 Leonid Andreyev

lover 3 fan, man, nut **4** beau, buff, dear, girl, love **5** freak, honey, swain, woman, wooer **6** fellow, suitor **7** admirer, beloved, darling, devotee, fanatic, sweetie **8** follower, loved one, lover boy, mistress, paramour, truelove **9** boyfriend, inamorata **10** aficionado, enthusiast, girlfriend, sweetheart **11** afficionado
 French: 6 bon ami **9** bonne amie
 Italian: 8 cicisbeo

Lovers and Other Strangers
 director: 8 Cy Howard
 cast: 8 Gig Young **9** Anne Meara, Bea Arthur **11** Anne Jackson **13** Bonnie Bedelia, Harry Guardino **14** Cloris

Leachman, Michael Brandon **17** Richard Castellano

love seat 4 sofa **5** couch **6** settee **13** courting chair

lovesick 7 amorous **8** yearning **10** moonstruck

Love's Labour's Lost
 author: 18 William Shakespeare
 character: 4 Dull **5** Maria **7** Berowne, Costard, Dumaine **8** Rosaline **9** Ferdinand, Katherine **10** Holofernes, Jaquenetta, Longaville **16** Princess of France **18** Don Adriano de Armado

Love Song of J Alfred Prufrock, The
 author: 7 T S Eliot

Love Story
 author: 10 Erich Segal

Love-wit
 character in: 12 The Alchemist
 author: 6 Jonson

loving 4 fond, kind, warm **6** ardent, caring, doting, erotic, tender **7** amatory, amorous, devoted **8** enamored, friendly **10** benevolent, passionate, solicitous **11** sympathetic, warmhearted **12** affectionate

loving word 9 sweet talk **10** endearment **12** sweet nothing

low 4 base, blue, deep, down, evil, glum, mean, soft, vile **5** awful, cruel, dirty, dumpy, faint, gross, lower, lowly, muted, prone, quiet, short, small, squat **6** brutal, coarse, common, cruddy, crummy, feeble, gentle, gloomy, humble, hushed, little, paltry, scurvy, softly, sordid, stubby, stumpy, sunken, vulgar, wicked **7** coastal, concave, corrupt, doleful, heinous, muffled, obscene, quietly, snubbed, squalid, subdued, unhappy **8** cowardly, degraded, dejected, depraved, downcast, inferior, low-lying, low-slung, mediocre, murmured, sawed-off, soothing, terrible, trifling, undersea, unworthy **9** dastardly, depressed, lethargic, nefarious, prostrate, repugnant, repulsive, submarine, submerged, truncated, unethical, whispered **10** abominable, despicable, despondent, dispirited, melancholy, outrageous, scandalous **11** ignominious, scoundrelly, underground, unimportant **12** contemptible, disheartened, dishonorable **14** down in the mouth

lowbred 6 coarse, common, vulgar **7** lowbrow, peasant **10** lower-class, uncultured

low-down 4 base, mean **5** dirty **10** despicable **12** contemptible **13** reprehensible

Lowell, James Russell
 author of: 12 The Cathedral **15** The Biglow Papers **16** A Fable for Critics **21** The Vision of Sir Launfal

Lowell, Robert
 author of: 8 Day by Day **9** Skunk Hour **10** The Dolphin **11** Life Studies **15** For the Union Dead **16** Lord Weary's Castle

Lowenstein, Laszlo
 real name of: 10 Peter Lorre

lower 3 cut, dim **4** damp, drop, duck, mute, pare, sink, sulk **5** frown, glare, pared, prune, scowl **6** deduct, glower, lop off, muffle, reduce, soften, subdue **7** curtail, depress, immerse, let down, put down, reduced, repress, shorten **8** decrease, diminish, grow dark, lessened, make less, pare down, pull down, submerge, take down, tone down **9** curtailed, decreased, make lower, pared down **10** abbreviate, diminished

lower-case letter 9 minuscule **11** small letter

lower-class 4 poor **6** common **7** lowbred, lowbrow, peasant **9** unrefined **10** blue-collar **12** working-class

lower classes 6 proles, rabble **8** canaille, riffraff **9** hoi polloi, peasantry **11** proletariat **13** the common herd, working people **16** the great unwashed

lower depths 4 pits, scum **5** dregs **6** rabble **8** canaille, riffraff **14** scum of the earth

Lower Depths, The
 also called: 11 At the Bottom **14** A Night's Lodging
 author: 10 Maxim Gorky

lower in rank 4 bust **6** demote **7** degrade

lower in spirits 6 deject, sadden **7** depress **8** dispirit **10** dishearten

low-key 4 soft **5** loose, muted **6** gentle, subtle **7** muffled, relaxed, subdued **8** laid-back, softened, soft-sell **9** modulated, toned-down **10** low-pitched, restrained **11** low-pressure, understated, unobtrusive **14** unostentatious

lowliness 8 baseness **9** obscurity **10** humbleness

lowly 3 low **6** humble, modest, simple, softly **7** ignoble, lowborn, lowbred, obscure **8** baseborn, plebeian **10** unassuming **11** proletarian **13** unpretentious

low-minded 4 lewd, vile **5** crude, gross **6** coarse, smutty, vulgar **7** obscene, uncouth **9** obnoxious, offensive **11** disgraceful **12** contemptible

low point, lowest point 4 base, foot, zero **5** depth, nadir, worst **6** bottom **7** perigee **10** rock bottom

low-priced 5 cheap, token **6** budget, modest **7** bargain, cut-rate, low-cost, nominal, reduced **8** closeout, moderate **9** dirt-cheap **10** discounted, economical, marked-down, reasonable **11** inexpensive **15** bargain-basement

low-ranking 5 minor, petty **11** subordinate, unimportant

low-spirited 3 low, sad **4** blue, down, glum **6** gloomy, morose, woeful **7** doleful, forlorn, unhappy **8** dejected, desolate, downcast **9** depressed, heartsore, sorrowful, woebegone **10** despondent, dispirited, melancholy **11** crestfallen, discouraged, downhearted **12** disconsolate, disheartened **14** down-in-the-mouth

low spirits 4 funk **5** gloom **6** dismay, sorrow **7** despair **8** dejected **9** pessimism **10** depression, desolation, melancholy, moroseness **11** despondency **12** hopelessness **14** discouragement **15** downheartedness

Loxias
   epithet of: **6** Apollo
   means: **9** ambiguous

Loy, Myrna
   real name: **13** Myrna Williams
   co-star: **13** William Powell
   born: **13** Raidersburg MT
   roles: **10** The Thin Man **11** Nora Charles **17** Cheaper by the Dozen **22** The Best Years of Our Lives

loyal 4 firm, true **6** trusty **7** devoted, dutiful, staunch **8** constant, faithful, reliable, resolute, true-blue **9** steadfast **10** dependable, scrupulous, unswerving, unwavering **11** trustworthy **12** tried and true

loyalist 4 tory **12** conservative

Loyalties
   author: **14** John Galsworthy

loyalty 6 fealty **8** devotion, fidelity, firmness **9** adherence, constancy **10** allegiance **11** reliability, staunchness **12** faithfulness **13** dependability, steadfastness **15** trustworthiness

lozenge 4 drop, pill **6** tablet, troche **8** pastille **9** cough drop

Luanda
   capital of: **6** Angola

Lubitsch, Ernst
   director of: **9** Ninotchka **13** Heaven Can Wait, To Be or Not To Be

Lucas, Charlotte
   character in: **17** Pride and Prejudice
   author: **6** Austen

Lucentio
   character in: **19** The Taming of the Shrew
   author: **11** Shakespeare

Lucerne
   German: **6** Luzern
   river: **5** Reuss
   landmark: **9** Hofkirche **11** Am Rhyn House **15** Mariahilf Church

Lucia di Lammermoor
   opera by: **9** Donizetti
   based on novel by: **14** Sir Walter Scott
      called: **20** The Bride of Lammermoor

Luciana
   character in: **17** The Comedy of Errors
   author: **11** Shakespeare

Luciani, Albino 13 Pope John Paul I **20** Pope John Paul the First

lucid 5 clear **6** bright, direct, normal **7** certain, precise, radiant, shining **8** accurate, apposite, dazzling, luminous, lustrous, pellucid, positive, rational, specific **9** brilliant, sparkling **10** articulate, perceptive, responsive, to the point **11** clearheaded, crystalline, illuminated, resplendent, transparent **12** crystal clear, intelligible **13** clear thinking, scintillating, well-organized **14** comprehensible, understandable **15** straightforward

Lucifer
   means: **5** Satan **11** fallen angel, light bearer

Lucina
   origin: **5** Roman
   goddess of: **10** childbirth
   corresponds to: **4** Juno **8** Ilithyia **10** Eileithyia

Lucio
   character in: **17** Measure for Measure
   author: **11** Shakespeare

luck 3 lot **4** fate **5** karma **6** chance, kismet **7** destiny, fortune, success, triumph, victory **8** accident, fortuity, good luck, Lady Luck **11** good fortune, piece of luck **12** happenstance
   god of: **12** Bonus Eventus

lucky 4 good **5** happy **6** in luck, timely **7** blessed, favored **9** favorable, fortunate, opportune, promising **10** auspicious, beneficial, felicitous, of good omen, propitious **12** providential

Lucky Jim
   author: **12** Kingsley Amis

lucky piece 5 charm **6** amulet **8** talisman **10** lucky charm

lucrative 7 gainful **8** fruitful **10** beneficial, high-income, high-paying, profitable **11** moneymaking **12** remunerative

Lucretia
   husband: **26** Lucius Tarquinius Collatinus
   raped by: **16** Sextus Tarquinius
   death by: **7** suicide

Lucretius
   author of: **13** De rerum natura **19** On the nature of things

Lucullan 4 rich **6** lavish **7** gourmet **9** epicurean, luxurious

Lucy Show, The
   also: **9** Here's Lucy
   character: **9** Kim Carter **10** Lucy Carter **11** Craig Carter **12** Harry Conners, Vivian Bagley **13** Mary Jane Lewis, Sherman Bagley **14** Lucy Carmichael **15** Chris Carmichael, Harrison Cheever, Jerry Carmichael, Theodore J Mooney **18** Harrison Otis Carter
   cast: **9** Ralph Hart **10** Candy Moore, Dick Martin, Gale Gordon, Lucie Arnaz, Roy Roberts **11** Desi Arnaz Jr, Lucille Ball, Vivian Vance **12** Jimmy Garrett **13** Mary Jane Croft

Ludd *see* **4** Llud

ludicrous 4 wild **5** comic, crazy, funny **6** absurd, far-out **7** amusing, comical **8** farcical **9** laughable **10** outlandish, ridiculous **11** nonsensical **12** preposterous

Ludlum, Robert
  author of: **15** The Matlock
  Paper **17** The Bourne Identity, The Parsifal Mosaic,
  The Road to Gandolfo
  18 The Osterman Weekend
  19 The Gemini Contenders
  20 The Rhinemann Exchange **23** The Chancellor
  Manuscript, The Scarlatti
  Inheritance

Luftwaffe 9 air weapon
  18 German Nazi air force

lug 3 tow, tug **4** bear, drag,
  draw, haul, pull, tote **5** carry,
  heave **9** transport

Lug
  origin: **5** Irish
  habitat: **5** solar

luggage 4 bags, gear **6** trunks
  7 baggage, effects, valises
  9 suitcases **13** accouterments

Luggnagg
  fictional land in: **16** Gulliver's
  Travels
  author: **5** Swift

Lugnasad
  origin: **5** Irish
  feast date: **11** August first

Lugosi, Bela
  real name: **10** Bela Blasko
  born: **5** Lugos **7** Hungary
  roles: **7** Dracula **21** Murders
  in the Rue Morgue

lugubrious 4 dour, glum
  6 gloomy, morose, rueful,
  somber, woeful **7** doleful, elegiac **8** dolorous, downcast, funereal, mournful **9** miserable,
  sorrowful, woebegone **10** depressing, melancholy

Lukas, George
  director of: **8** Star Wars
  16 American Graffiti

Luke
  birthplace: **7** Antioch
  companion: **4** Paul
  wrote: **6** Gospel

lukewarm 4 cool, mild, warm
  5 aloof, tepid **8** detached, uncaring **9** apathetic, temperate
  11 halfhearted, indifferent,
  perfunctory, unconcerned
  12 uninterested **13** lackadaisical **14** unenthusiastic **15** body-
  temperature, room-temperature

lull 3 gap **4** calm, ease, halt,
  hush **5** break, pause, quell,
  quiet, still **6** hiatus, lacuna,
  pacify, recess, soothe, subdue
  7 assuage, caesura, compose,
  mollify, respite **8** breather,
  calmness **9** interlude **12** brief
  silence, interruption

Lully, Jean-Baptiste
  born: **5** Italy **8** Florence
  composer of: **4** Atys, Isis

6 Persee, Psyche, Roland,
  Thesee **7** Alceste, Phaeton
  10 Le Sicilien, Proserpine
  11 Bellerophon **13** Acis et
  Galatee, Amadis de Gaule,
  L'Amour medecin **14** Acis
  and Galatea, Armide et Re-
  naud, Le mariage force
  16 Cadmus et Hermione
  17 Achille et Polyxene, Cadmus and Hermione
  19 Achilles and Polyxene
  20 Les Amants magnifiques
  22 Le Bourgeois Gentilhomme, Monsieur de
  Pourceaugnac

lulu 3 pip **5** dandy, doozy **8** Jim
  Dandy **9** allowance, hum-
  dinger, wonderful
  10 remarkable

lumber 3 log **4** plod, wood
  5 barge, clump, stamp
  6 boards, planks, trudge, waddle **7** shamble, shuffle **8** flounder **9** fell trees

Lumber State
  nickname of: **5** Maine

Lumet, Sidney
  director of: **7** Network, Serpico **13** The Pawnbroker
  14 Twelve Angry Men
  15 Dog Day Afternoon
  24 Long Day's Journey Into
  Night

luminary 3 VIP **5** light, wheel
  6 bigwig **7** big shot, notable
  8 somebody **9** celebrity, dignitary, personage **10** luminosity
  11 illuminator

luminescent 5 aglow **7** glowing **8** gleaming, luminous
  9 twinkling **10** flickering, glimmering, glistening, shimmer-
  ing **11** fluorescent
  14 phosphorescent

luminosity 4 glow **5** gleam,
  sheen, shine **6** luster **8** radiance **10** brightness,
  brilliance

luminous 6 bright **7** glowing,
  radiant, shining **8** lustrous
  9 brilliant **10** irradiated **11** illuminated, luminescent **15** reflecting light

lump 3 gob, mix **4** bump, cake,
  clod, fuse, heap, hunk, knob,
  knot, mass, node, pile, pool
  5 amass, batch, blend, bunch,
  chunk, clump, group, knurl,
  merge, tumor, unite **6** gather,
  growth, nodule **7** collect, combine, compile **8** assemble,
  swelling **9** aggregate **10** protrusion, tumescence **11** excrescence **12** protuberance

lumpish 4 dull, slow **5** bulky,
  dumpy, heavy, lumpy
  6 clumsy **7** awkward **8** cloddish, ungainly, unwieldy

9 corpulent **10** cumbersome,
  overweight

Lumpkin, Tony
  character in: **18** She Stoops
  to Conquer
  author: **9** Goldsmith

lump together 4 fuse, pool
  7 combine **10** amalgamate
  11 consolidate, incorporate

Luna
  personifies: **4** moon

lunacy 5 folly, mania **6** idiocy
  7 madness **8** dementia, insanity **9** absurdity, asininity, craziness, silliness, stupidity
  10 imbecility, imprudence, in-
  saneness **11** foolishness
  13 foolhardiness, senselessness

lunatic 3 mad, nut **4** daft,
  loco **5** batty, crazy, loony,
  nutty, potty **6** cuckoo, insane,
  madman, maniac, screwy
  7 bonkers, cracked, touched
  8 crackers, demented, demoniac, deranged, maniacal, unhinged **9** psychotic, senseless
  10 irrational, psychopath, rea-
  sonless **11** crazy
  person, mentally ill, not all
  there **12** crackbrained, insane
  person, psychopathic, round
  the bend **13** off one's rocker,
  of unsound mind, out of one's
  mind

lunch
  French: **8** dejeuner

luncheonette 4 cafe **5** diner
  7 beanery **8** snack bar **9** hash
  house, lunchroom **10** coffee
  shop **11** eating house
  12 lunch counter, sandwich
  shop

lunchroom 4 cafe **5** diner,
  grill **8** snack bar **9** cafeteria
  12 luncheonette

lunge 3 cut, jab **4** dash, dive,
  pass, rush, stab **5** hit at, lurch,
  swing, swipe **6** attack, charge,
  plunge, pounce, thrust **7** set
  upon **8** fall upon, strike at
  9 make a pass

lunkhead 3 ass **4** dope, fool
  5 booby, dunce, idiot, moron,
  ninny **6** dimwit, nitwit **7** fathead, halfwit **8** bonehead,
  dumb-dumb, imbecile, numskull **9** blockhead, lamebrain,
  numbskull **10** dunderhead,
  nincompoop
  11 chowderhead

Lunt, Alfred
  wife: **12** Lynn Fontanne
  born: **11** Milwaukee WI
  roles: **12** The Guardsman
  13 The Ragged Edge

Lupercalia
  origin: **5** Roman
  event: **8** festival

honoring: 6 Faunus
8 Lupercus
to procure: 9 fertility

Lupercus
origin: 5 Roman
god of: 9 fertility
corresponds to: 3 Pan
6 Faunus

Lupino, Ida
husband: 10 Howard Duff
12 Collier Young, Louis
Hayward
born: 6 London **7** England
roles: 8 Devotion **10** The
Hard Way **12** Junior Bonner, Women's Prison **13** Escape Me Never **15** Strange
Intruder **17** On Dangerous
Ground **18** The Light That
Failed, While the City
Sleeps

lurch 4 cant, keel, list, reel,
roll, sway, tilt, toss **5** lunge,
pitch, slant **6** careen, plunge,
swerve, teeter, totter **7** incline,
stagger, stumble

lure 4 bait, coax, trap **5** bribe,
decoy, snare, tempt **6** allure,
cajole, come-on, entice, induce, seduce **7** attract, beguile **8** cajolery, persuade
9 fascinate, tantalize **10** allurement, attraction, enticement,
inducement, temptation
11 drawing card
12 blandishment

Lurelei *see* **7** Lorelei

lurid 4 gory, grim **5** eerie, fiery,
vivid **6** bloody **7** carmine,
flaming, ghastly, glaring,
glowing, graphic, scarlet, shining **8** dramatic, rubicund, sanguine, shocking **9** appalling,
bright-red **11** sensational
12 melodramatic
13 bloodcurdling

lurk 4 hide **5** prowl, skulk,
slink, sneak **9** lie in wait

Lusaka
capital of: 6 Zambia

luscious 5 tasty **6** savory
7 scented **8** aromatic, fragrant,
perfumed **9** delicious, flavorful,
succulent, toothsome **10** appetizing, delectable **13** mouth-
watering

lush 4 posh, rich **5** dense,
fancy, grand **6** ornate **7** elegant, profuse **8** abundant, prolific, splendid **9** elaborate,
luxuriant, luxurious, sumptuous **11** flourishing,
magnificent

Lusia
epithet of: 7 Demeter
means: 6 bather

lust 5 covet, crave **6** be lewd
7 craving, lechery, passion

8 lewdness **9** carnality, hunger
for, sexuality **10** satyriasis
14 lasciviousness,
libidinousness

lust after 4 want **5** covet,
crave **6** desire **11** have a yen
for, have an eye on, hunger
after, thirst after

luster 4 fame, glow **5** gleam,
glory, gloss, honor, merit,
sheen, shine **6** dazzle **7** burnish, glimmer, glitter, sparkle
8 prestige, radiance **9** radiation **10** brightness, brilliance,
luminosity, notability, refulgence **11** distinction **12** luminousness, resplendence
15 illustriousness

lusterless 3 dim, wan **4** dead,
drab, dull, flat **5** faded, matte,
muted **7** prosaic **9** colorless,
tarnished

Lust for Life
author: 11 Irving Stone
director: 16 Vincente
Minnelli
based on story by: 11 Irving
Stone
cast: 11 James Donald, Kirk
Douglas (Vincent Van
Gogh), Pamela Brown
12 Anthony Quinn (Gaugin)
Oscar for: 15 supporting actor (Quinn)

lustful 4 lewd **6** carnal **8** pru-

rient **9** lecherous, salacious
10 lascivious, libidinous

lustrous 6 bright, glossy
7 glowing, radiant, shining
8 dazzling, gleaming, luminous, polished **9** burnished, effulgent **10** glistening
11 coruscating, illuminated
12 incandescent

lusty 4 hale **5** husky, sound
6 brawny, hearty, robust, rugged, sturdy, virile **7** healthy
8 vigorous **9** exuberant, strapping **10** full of life **11** uninhibited **12** unrestrained,
wholehearted **13** irrepressible

Luther, Martin
born: 7 Germany **8** Eisleben
author: 16 Ninety-Five
Theses **27** On the Freedom
of a Christian Man **46** Address to the Christian Nobility of the German Nation
51 A Prelude Concerning
the Babylonian Captivity of
the Church
excommunicated by: 8 Pope
Leo X **15** Pope Leo the
Tenth
summoned before: 11 Diet of
Worms
founded: 11 Lutheranism,
Reformation
13 Protestantism

lux 5 light

Luxembourg *see box*

Luxembourg
other name: 9 Luxemburg **13** Lucilinburhuc
name means: 10 little fort
capital/largest city: 10 Luxembourg
others: 4 Hamm **5** Roodt, Wiltz **6** Mersch, Remich **7** Kop-
stal, Lintgen, Petange, Redange, Vianden **8** Capellen, Cler-
vaux, Diekirch, Frisange **9** Dudelange **10** Echternach,
Ettelbruck, Hesperange, Larochette **11** Differdange, Wor-
meldange **12** Grevenmacher, Troisvierges, Wasserbillig
14 Esch-sur-Alzette
division: 6 Esleck **7** Bon Pays, Gutland, Oesling
measure: 5 fuder
monetary unit: 5 franc **7** centime
lake: 8 Haut Sure
mountain: 8 Ardennes
highest point: 8 Huldange **9** Burgplatz **11** Wemperhardt
river: 3 Our **4** Sure, Syre **5** Alert, Clerf, Eisch, Mosel,
Sauer, Wiltz **6** Chiers **7** Alzette, Moselle **8** Petrusse
11 Ernz Blanche
physical feature:
plateau: **4** Bock **8** Ardennes, Lorraine
valley: **7** Moselle
people: 6 French, German **12** Luxembourger
ruler: **8** Sigefroi, Wencelas **12** Jean l'Aveugle **21** House
of Nassau-Weilburg
saint: **10** Willibrord
language: 6 French, German **7** English **13** Letzeburgesch
religion: 13 Roman Catholic
food:
pastry: **20** les pensees brouillees

luxuriant 4 lush, rank **5** dense, fancy, grand **6** florid, ornate **7** elegant, flowery, profuse, teeming **8** abundant, splendid **9** elaborate, exuberant, luxurious, overgrown, sumptuous **10** flamboyant **11** extravagant, flourishing, magnificent

luxuriate 4 bask **6** relish **7** delight **8** wallow in **9** indulge in

luxurious 4 rich **5** grand **6** costly, effete **7** elegant, wealthy **8** decadent, pampered **9** enjoyable, expensive, indulgent, sumptuous **10** gratifying **11** comfortable, pleasurable

luxuriousness 4 ease **6** luxury **7** comfort **8** richness **10** costliness **13** sumptuousness

luxury 5 bliss **6** heaven, riches, wealth **7** delight **8** paradise, pleasure **9** enjoyment **10** high living, indulgence **12** extravagance, nonessential, nonnecessity, satisfaction **13** gratification

LXX *see* **15** Septuagint

Lyaeus
epithet of: **8** Dionysus
means: **8** loosener

Lycaeus
epithet of: **4** Zeus
means: **7** wolfish

Lycaon
king of: **7** Arcadia
father: **8** Pelasgus
son: **8** Maenalus, Tegeates
tested: **4** Zeus
turned into: **4** wolf

Lycidas
author: **10** John Milton
elegy for: **10** Edward King

Lycomedes
king of: **6** Scyrus
daughter: **8** Deidamia
pushed over cliff: **7** Theseus

Lycon
mentioned in: **5** Iliad
vocation: **7** warrior

home: **4** Troy
killed by: **8** Peneleus

Lycophron
origin: **5** Greek
father: **9** Periander
exiled to: **7** Corcyra
killed by: **10** Corcyreans
committed: **6** murder
went to: **4** Troy
killed by: **6** Hector

Lycotherses
king of: **7** Illyria
wife: **5** Agave
killed by: **5** Agave

Lycurgas
king of: **6** Edones, Thrace
son: **5** Dryas
persecuted: **8** Dionysus
killed: **5** Dryas

Lycus
king of: **6** Thebes **7** Cilicia
father: **7** Pandion **9** Chthonius
mother: **5** Pylia
brother: **7** Nycteus
wife: **5** Dirce
niece: **7** Antiope
son: **5** Lycus
succeeded: **8** Sarpedon
killed by: **6** Zethus **7** Amphion **12** Antiope's sons

Lygodesma
epithet of: **7** Artemis
means: **11** willow-bound

lying down 5 in bed, prone **6** supine **7** napping, resting **8** snoozing **9** reclining, recumbent **10** taking a nap **13** taking a snooze

Lyle, Albert Walter
nickname: **6** Sparky
sport: **8** baseball
position: **7** pitcher
team: **12** Boston Red Sox **14** New York Yankees
author of: **11** The Bronx Zoo

Lyly, John
author of: **20** Euphues and His England **22** Euphues the Anatomy of Wit

lynch 4 hang **6** gibbet **8** string up

Lynde, Paul
born: **13** Mount Vernon OH
roles: **12** Bye Bye Birdie **16** Hollywood Squares **17** Beach Blanket Bingo **18** Under the Yum-Yum Tree

Lyngi
origin: **12** Scandinavian
mentioned in: **8** Volsunga
rival of: **7** Sigmund
sought: **7** Hiordis, Hjordis
killed: **7** Sigmund
killed by: **6** Sigurd

lynx 3 cat **6** bobcat **7** wildcat

Lyonnesse
place in: **16** Arthurian romance
birthplace of: **8** Tristram

Lyre
constellation of: **4** Lyra

lyric, lyrical 6 poetic **7** lilting, melodic, musical, singing, tuneful **8** songlike **9** melodious **10** euphonious **11** mellifluent, mellifluous **13** sweet-sounding

Lyrical Ballads
author: **17** William Wordsworth **21** Samuel Taylor Coleridge

lyrics 4 poem **5** words

Lyrus
father: **8** Anchises
mother: **9** Aphrodite

Lysander
character in: **21** A Midsummer Night's Dream
author: **11** Shakespeare

Lysippe
father: **7** Proetus
mother: **5** Antia

Lysistrata
author: **12** Aristophanes
character: **7** Lampito **8** Cinesias, Cleonice, Myrrhine **10** Magistrate **14** Old Men of Athens (Chorus)

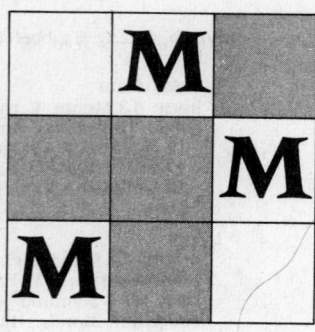

M
director: **9** Fritz Lang
cast: **10** Peter Lorre **11** Inge
Landgut **12** Ellen Widmann
15 Gustav Grundgens
setting: **6** Berlin

Maat
origin: **8** Egyptian
goddess of: **3** law
13 righteousness
symbol: **7** feather

Mabinogian
origin: **5** Welsh
tales of: **7** romance

macabre 4 grim **5** eerie, weird
6 grisly, horrid **7** ghastly,
ghostly **8** dreadful, gruesome,
horrible, horrific **9** frightful,
ghostlike, unearthly
11 frightening

Macao *see box*

Macareus
father: **6** Aeolus
mother: **7** Encrete
sister: **6** Canace

MacArthur, Douglas
served in: **3** WWI **4** WWII
9 Korean War, World War I
10 World War II **11** World
War One, World War Two
commander of: **15** Rainbow
(42nd) Division **19** United
Nations forces **24** US army
forces in the Pacific
rank: **15** five-star general
16 army chief of staff
battle: **5** Luzon, Pusan **6** Inchon **9** New Guinea **11** Leyte
Island, Philippines **14** Bis-
mark Islands, Solomon Is-
lands **15** Bataan Peninsula
16 Admiralty Islands, Corregidor Island
accepted surrender of:
5 Japan
   surrender occurred
   aboard: **8** Missouri
chairman of: **13** Remington
Rand
author of: **13** Reminiscences

smoked: **11** corncob pipe
saying: **12** "I shall return"

Macbeth
author: **18** William
Shakespeare
character: **6** Banquo, Duncan
(King of Scotland) **7** Mac-
Duff, Malcolm **11** Lady Macbeth **12** Three Witches
director: **13** Roman Polanski
cast: **8** Jon Finch **10** Martin
Shaw **13** Nicholas Selby
14 Francesca Annis

Maccabees
title of: **5** Judas
patriarch: **10** Mattathias
means: **8** hammerer

MacDonald, John D
author of: **11** Condominium
character: **11** Travis McGee

MacDonald, Ross
real name: **13** Kenneth Millar
author of: **8** The Chill
10 Black Money **13** The Blue

Macao
other name: **5** Ao-men,
Macau
territory of: **8** Portugal
monetary unit: **3** avo
6 pataca, pataco
island: **5** Taipa **7** Coloane
highest point: **5** Hag-Sa
river: **5** Pearl **6** Canton
sea: **10** South China
people: **7** Chinese, Ma-
caoan **10** Portuguese
language: **7** Chinese,
English **9** Cantonese
10 Portuguese
religion: **6** Taoism **8** Buddhism **13** Roman
Catholic
place:
   street: **11** Praia Grande
feature:
   houseboat: **6** sampan

Hammer **14** The Goodbye
Look
character: **9** Lew Archer

**MacDowell, Edward
Alexander**
born: **9** New York NY
composer of: **9** Sea Pieces
11 To a Wild Rose **13** Fireside Tales **15** Poems after
Heine **16** Hamlet and Ophelia, New England Idylls,
Woodland Sketches

MacDuff
character in: **7** Macbeth
author: **11** Shakespeare

mace
origin: **9** Indonesia
from same tree as: **6** nutmeg
tree: **17** Myristica fragrans
use: **4** fish **7** seafood **9** cherry
pie, pound cake **16** chicken
fricassee

Macedonia
capital/largest city: **6** Skopje
head of state: **9** president
government: **8** republic
monetary unit: **5** denar
river: **4** Crna **6** Vardar
people: **4** Turk **9** Albanian
10 Macedonian
language: **10** Macedonian
religion: **27** Macedonian Orthodox Christian

macerate 4 fade, mash, pulp,
soak **5** souse, steep **6** shrink,
soften, squash, wither **7** decline, liquefy, shrivel **8** dissolve, emaciate, fluidize,
permeate, saturate **9** liquidize,
waste away **10** lose weight

MacGraw, Ali
real name: **12** Alice MacGraw
husband: **8** Bob Evans
12 Steve McQueen
born: **12** Pound Ridge NY
roles: **7** Dynasty **9** Love Story
10 The Getaway

13 The Winds of War
15 Goodbye Columbus

Machaerus
killed: 11 Neoptolemus

Machaon
father: 9 Asclepius
brother: 10 Podalirius
wife: 8 Anticlea
son: 8 Alexanor, Gorgasus
10 Nicomachus
vocation: 9 physician
served in: 9 Trojan War

Macheath, Captain
character in: 12 Beggar's
Opera
author: 3 Gay

ma chere 6 my dear

Machiavelli, Niccolo
author of: 9 The Prince
11 The Art of War 16 Dis-
courses on Livy

Machiavellian 6 amoral,
crafty 7 cunning, devious
8 scheming 9 deceitful,
designing 10 perfidious 11 self-
serving, treacherous, underhanded 12 falsehearted,
unscrupulous

machination 4 plot, rule, ruse
5 dodge 6 design, device,
scheme 8 artifice, intrigue,
maneuver 9 stratagem 10 conspiracy 11 contrivance

machine 3 set 4 army, body,
camp, club, gang, pool, ring
5 corps, crowd, force, group,
setup, trust, union 6 device,
system 7 combine, coterie, faction, society 9 apparatus, appliance, machinery 11 association 12 organization
13 establishment

machine gun
invented by: 7 Gatling
improved by: 5 Maxim
9 Hotchkiss

machinery 4 gear 5 setup,
tools 6 agency, makeup, system, tackle, wheels 9 apparatus, mechanism, resources,
structure 12 contrivances,
organization

macho 5 he-man, manly
6 strong, virile

Machpelah
location: 6 Hebron
burial place of: 4 Leah
5 Isaac, Jacob, Sarah
7 Abraham, Rebekah

Macilente
character in: 22 Every Man
out of His Humour
author: 6 Jonson

MacInnes, Helen
author of: 13 North from
Rome 14 Above Suspicion

16 Decision at Delphi
17 The Venetian Affair
21 The Salzburg Connection

macintosh, mackintosh
7 slicker 8 raincoat
10 waterproof

Mack, Connie
real name: 30 Cornelius
Alexander McGillicuddy
sport: 8 baseball
position: 7 manager
team: 21 Philadelphia
Athletics

MacKellar
character in: 21 The Master
of Ballantrae
author: 9 Stevenson

mackerel
young: 5 spike 6 tinker
7 blinker

mackinaw 4 coat 6 jacket
8 overcoat

MacLaine, Shirley
real name: 19 Shirley Mac-
Lean Beaty
brother: 12 Warren Beatty
born: 10 Richmond VA
roles: 6 Can Can 10 Being
There 11 Irma La Douce
12 Sweet Charity, The
Apartment 15 Some Came
Running, The Turning
Point, Two for the Seesaw
16 The Children's Hour
17 Terms of Endearment
(Oscar) 19 The Trouble with
Harry 20 The Bliss of Mrs
Blossom

MacMurray, Fred
wife: 9 June Haver
born: 10 Kankakee IL
roles: 11 My Three Sons
12 The Apartment 14 Above
Suspicion, The Caine Mu-
tiny 15 Double Indemnity
20 The Miracle of the Bells

Macro-Chibchan
language branch: 6 Paezan
8 Chibchan

macrocosm 6 cosmos, nature
7 heavens 8 creation, universe 9 firmament

Macro-Ge
language family: 11 Ge-
Pano-Carib
group: 2 Ge 6 Bororo, Caraja

Macro-Panoan
language family: 11 Ge-
Pano-Carib
group: 6 Panoan
10 Guaycuruan

mad 4 avid, daft, loco, nuts,
wild 5 angry, balmy, crazy,
irate, nutty 6 ardent, crazed,
cuckoo, fuming, insane,
miffed, screwy, ticked
7 cracked, enraged, excited, fanatic, furious, in a huff, luna-

tic, riled up, teed off,
touched 8 crackers, demented,
deranged, frenzied, incensed,
maniacal, provoked, unhinged,
up in arms, worked up,
wrathful 9 devoted to, non
compos, seeing red, ticked off,
wrought up 10 distracted, distraught, infatuated, infuriated,
in love with, irrational, unbalanced 11 boiling over, exasperated, impassioned, not all
there 12 enthusiastic, round
the bend 13 beside oneself, in
high dudgeon, not quite right,
off one's rocker, out of one's
mind

Madagascar see box, p. 590
Madagascar see box, p. 590

madam, madame 3 Mrs
4 dame, lady 6 matron 7 dow-
ager 8 mistress
German: 4 Frau
Spanish: 6 senora
Italian: 7 signora
Spanish/Portuguese: 4 dona
Italian: 5 donna

Madame Bovary
author: 15 Gustave Flaubert
character: 10 Emma Bovary,
Leon Dupuis 13 Charles
Bovary 17 Rodolphe
Boulanger

Madame Butterfly
also: 15 Madama Butterfly
opera by: 7 Puccini
character: 5 Bonze 6 Suzuki
9 Cho-Cho-San, Cio-Cio-San,
Sharpless 14 Prince Yama-
dori 19 Lieutenant
Pinkerton

mad as a hatter 3 mad
4 daft, nuts 5 crazy, nutty
6 insane 7 cracked, touched
8 demented, deranged, un-
hinged 10 unbalanced 13 off
one's rocker, out of one's
head 14 off one's trolley
15 mad as a March hare
17 nutty as a fruitcake

mad as a March hare
3 mad 4 daft, nuts 5 crazy,
nutty 6 insane 7 cracked,
touched 8 demented, deranged,
unhinged 10 unbalanced
12 mad as a hatter 13 out of
one's head 14 off one's trolley 17 nutty as a fruitcake

madcap 4 rash, wild, zany
5 brash, clown, giddy, joker
6 unruly 7 erratic, flighty,
foolish 8 reckless 9 hotheaded,
impetuous, impulsive, senseless 10 incautious 11 impractical, thoughtless
12 unconsidered 13 inconsiderate, undisciplined

madden 3 vex 4 gall 5 anger,
craze, pique, upset 6 enrage,
frenzy 7 derange, incense, inflame, outrage, provoke, tor-

Madagascar
other name: 16 Malagasy Republic
capital/largest city: 10 Tananarive 12 Antananarivo
others: 6 Tulear 7 Majanga, Nossibe, Toliary 8 Manakara, Tamatave 9 Faradofay, Mananjory, Toamasina 10 Antisirabe 11 Antsiranana, Diego-Suarez, Fort Dauphin
measure: 7 gantang
monetary unit: 5 franc 7 centime
island: 6 Barren, Radama 7 Nossi-Be 11 Sainte-Marie 12 Chesterfield
lake: 5 Itasy 7 Alaotra, Kinkony
mountain: 4 Boby 9 Ankaratra 12 High Plateaus, Tsiafajavona 17 Tsaratanana Massif
highest point: 11 Maromokotro
river: 5 Ikopa, Mania, Sofia 7 Mangoky, Mangoro, Onilahy 8 Ivoloina, Manambao, Mananara 9 Betsiboka, Manambolo 10 Manarandra 11 Tsiribihina
ocean: 6 Indian
physical feature:
  bay: 6 Radama 8 Antongil 9 Mahajamba 10 Sahamalaza
  cape: 5 Amber 10 Saint-Andre 11 Sainte-Marie 14 Saint-Sebastien
  channel: 10 Mozambique
  lagoon: 9 pangalane
  plateau: 9 Ankaizina
people: 4 Arab, Bara, Hova 5 Malay 6 Merina, Tanala 7 African 8 Betsileo, Mahafaly, Malagasy, Sakalava 9 Antaimoro, Antaisaka, Antandroy, Tsimihety 10 Indonesian, Polynesian 13 Betsimisaraka
  dynasty: 6 Merina
  leader: 9 Ratsiraka, Tsiranana 11 Ranamantsoa
language: 6 French 8 Malagasy, Malgache
religion: 5 Islam 7 animism 10 Protestant 13 Roman Catholic
place:
  market: 4 Zoma
  royal estate: 4 Rova
feature:
  animal: 4 zebu 5 lemur 6 foussa
  musical instrument: 11 jego vaotavo
  proverb: 8 hainteny
  shawl: 5 lamba
food:
  vegetable: 7 brettes

Mad Max
director: 12 George Miller
cast: 9 Mel Gibson
sequel: 14 The Road Warrior 17 Beyond Thunderdome (with Tina Turner)

madness 6 lunacy, oddity 8 delusion, dementia, illusion, insanity 9 craziness 11 derangement

Madonna
nickname: 15 The Material Girl
husband: 8 Sean Penn
recordings: 7 Madonna 8 True Blue 11 Like A Prayer, Like A Virgin
films: 9 Dick Tracy 11 Truth or Dare 12 Who's That Girl 14 Body of Evidence 16 Shanghai Surprise 17 A League of Their Own 23 Desperately Seeking Susan
tour: 6 Girlie 13 Blond Ambition
books: 3 Sex

Madrid
area: 9 Salamanca 19 Ciudad Universitaria
capital of: 5 Spain
landmark: 14 National Palace 18 Biblioteca Nacional
  bull ring: 22 Plaza de Toros Monumental
  museum: 5 Prado
mountain: 18 Sierra de Guadaramma
river: 10 Manzanares
square: 10 Plaza Mayor 11 Plaza del Sol 13 Plaza de Espana
street: 13 Paseo del Prado

Madwoman of Chaillot
author: 13 Jean Giraudoux

Mael
origin: 5 Irish
father: 5 Ronan
killed by: 5 Ronan

maelstrom 4 eddy 5 shoot, swirl 6 bedlam, rapids, tumult, uproar, vortex 7 riptide, torrent 8 disorder, madhouse, undertow, upheaval 9 confusion, whirlpool 10 white water 11 pandemonium

maenad, menad 5 lenae 7 bacchae, bassara 8 clodones, thyiades 9 bacchante 10 mimallones
companion of: 7 Bacchus 8 Dionysus

Maenalus
father: 6 Lycaon

Maeterlinck, Maurice
author of: 8 The Blind 11 The Blue Bird, The Intruder 19 Pelleas and Melisande

ment, unhinge 9 aggravate, infuriate, unbalance 10 exasperate

made 5 built 6 formed 7 created 8 composed, produced 9 assembled, developed 10 fabricated 11 constructed 12 manufactured

madeira
type: 4 wine 6 brandy 7 liqueur 8 aperitif
origin: 7 Madeira

Madeira Islands
capital: 7 Funchal
city: 5 Monte
island: 6 Grande 7 Dezerte, Madeira 8 Desertas 9 Selvagens 10 Porto Santo
ocean: 8 Atlantic
owned by: 8 Portugal
stone aqueduct: 7 levadas
wine: 4 Bual 5 Tinta, Tinto

6 Canary, Gomera 7 Malmsey, Marsala, Sercial 8 Verdelho

made-up 5 false 7 assumed, created 8 fanciful, invented 9 fictional, imaginary, pretended, thought-up 10 fictitious 11 make-believe, theoretical 12 hypothetical

Mad Hatter
character in: 28 Alice's Adventures in Wonderland
author: 7 Carroll

madhouse 6 asylum, bedlam, uproar 7 turmoil 8 loony bin, nuthouse

Madison, James *see box*

madman 3 nut 5 loony 6 maniac 7 lunatic 8 demoniac 9 psychotic 10 psychopath 11 crazy person

Madison, James
nickname: 23 Father of the Constitution
presidential rank: 6 fourth
party: 20 Democratic-Republican
state represented: 2 VA
defeated: 7 (DeWitt) Clinton 8 (Charles Cotesworth) Pinckney
vice president: 5 (Elbridge) Gerry 7 (George) Clinton
cabinet:
  state: 5 (Robert) Smith 6 (James) Monroe
  treasury: 6 (Alexander James) Dallas 8 (Abraham Alfonse Albert) Gallatin, (George Washington) Campbell, (William Harris) Crawford
  war: 6 (James) Monroe, (William) Eustis 8 (William Harris) Crawford 9 (John) Armstrong
  attorney general: 4 (Richard) Rush 6 (Caesar Augustus) Rodney 7 (William) Pinkney
  navy: 5 (William) Jones 8 (Paul) Hamilton 13 (Benjamin Williams) Crowninshield
born: 12 Port Conway VA 16 King George County
died/buried: 2 VA 12 Orange County 16 Montpelier estate
education:
  tutored at home by: 15 Rev Thomas Martin
  school: 15 Donald Robertson
  college of: 9 New Jersey (now Princeton University)
religion: 12 Episcopalian
interests: 3 law 11 agriculture 14 natural history
author: 16 Federalist Papers (with Hamilton and Jay) 24 Memorial and Remonstrances 29 Journal of the Federal Convention
political career: 24 US House of Representatives 25 Second Continental Congress
  secretary of: 5 state
  signed: 12 Constitution
civilian career: 6 farmer 7 planter
military service:
  colonel of: 19 Orange County militia
notable events of lifetime/term: 19 War of Eighteen Twelve
  battle of: 10 New Orleans
  treaty of: 5 Ghent
  Washington DC burned by: 7 British
father: 5 James
mother: 7 Eleanor (Rose Conway)
siblings: 5 Sarah 6 Reuben 7 Ambrose, Catlett, Francis, William 9 Elizabeth 11 Nelly Conway 13 Frances Taylor
wife: 8 Dorothea (Payne Todd)
  nickname: 6 Dolley
first lady:
  saved: 11 state papers 25 George Washington's portrait

ma foi 6 my word, really 7 my faith

magazine 6 weekly 7 arsenal, journal, monthly 9 quarterly 10 periodical, powder room 13 military depot, munitions room

Magdalene see 4 Mary

magenta 6 maroon 7 carmine, crimson, fuchsia 9 vermilion 12 purplish rose 13 reddish purple

Maggie
character in: 16 Cat on a Hot Tin Roof
author: 8 Williams

Maggie: A Girl of the Streets
author: 12 Stephen Crane

maggot 4 grub, worm 5 larva 8 mealworm

Magi
also called: 7 Wisemen 11 astrologers
followed: 15 Star of Bethlehem
visited: 5 Jesus
gifts: 4 gold 5 myrrh 12 frankincense
singular: 5 magus

magic 4 lure 5 charm, spell 6 hoodoo, voodoo 7 sorcery 8 charisma, jugglery, witchery, wizardry 9 occultism, voodooism 10 allurement, black magic, demonology, divination, hocus-pocus, witchcraft 11 captivation, conjuration, enchantment, fascination, legerdemain, the black art 12 entrancement 13 sleight of hand 16 prestidigitation
god of: 5 Thoth

Magic
nickname of: 13 Earvin Johnson

Magic Flute, The
also: 14 Die Zauberflöte
opera: 6 Mozart
character: 6 Pamina, Tamino 8 Papagena, Papageno, Sarastro 10 Monostatos 12 Queen of Night

magician 5 magus 6 shaman, wizard 7 juggler, warlock 8 conjurer, sorcerer 9 alchemist 11 illusionist, medicine man, necromancer, witch doctor 12 escape artist 15 prestidigitator

Magic Mountain, The
author: 10 Thomas Mann
character: 6 Naphta 7 Clavdia 11 Hans Castorp, Settembrini 15 Joachim Ziemssen

magisterial 9 imperious 10 autocratic, peremptory 11 dictatorial, domineering, overbearing 13 condescending

Magister Ludi: The Glass Bead Game
author: 12 Hermann Hesse

magistrate 2 JP 5 judge 7 prefect 17 justice of the peace

magna cum laude 15 with great praise

Magna Graecia 27 ancient Greek colonies in Italy

Magna Mater 3 Ops 4 Rhea 6 Cybele

Magnani, Anna
nickname: 10 Nannerella
roles: 8 Open City 13 The Rose Tattoo (Oscar) 15 The Fugitive Kind 21 Secret of Santa Vittoria

magnanimous 7 liberal 8 generous, princely 9 forgiving, unselfish 10 altruistic, beneficent, charitable 12 largehearted 13 philanthropic

magnate 3 VIP 5 giant, mogul, nabob 6 big gun, bigwig, leader, tycoon 7 big shot, notable 8 big wheel, great man 9 celebrity 13 empire builder, industrialist

magnesium
chemical symbol: 2 Mg

magnetic 8 alluring, charming, inviting 9 of a magnet, seductive 10 attractive, enchanting, entrancing, persuasive 11 captivating, charismatic, fascinating 12 irresistible

magnetism 4 lure 5 charm 6 allure 8 charisma 9 mesmerism, seduction 10 allurement, attraction, enticement 11 captivation, enchantment, fascination

magnification 5 honor 7 worship 9 adoration, blowing up, expansion, inflation, reverence 11 acclamation, enlargement, idolization 12 exaggeration 13 amplification, glorification, overstatement

magnificence 4 pomp 5 glory, state 6 luxury 7 glitter, majesty, royalty 8 grandeur, richness, splendor 10 brilliance 13 sumptuousness

magnificent 4 fine 5 grand, noble 6 august, superb 7 elegant, exalted, stately, sublime 8 glorious, imposing, majestic, splendid 9 brilliant, exquisite, wonderful 10 commanding, impressive 11 resplendent 12 transcendent 13 extraordinary

Magnificent Ambersons, The
director: 11 Orson Welles
based on novel by: 15 Booth Tarkington
cast: 7 Tim Holt 10 Anne Baxter 12 Joseph Cotten 14 Agnes Moorehead 15 Dolores Costello

Magnificent Obsession, The
author: 13 Lloyd C Douglas

Magnificent Seven, The
director: 11 John Sturges
cast: 10 Brad Dexter, Eli Wallach, Yul Brynner 11 James Coburn 12 Robert Vaughn, Steve McQueen 13 Horst Buchholz 14 Charles Bronson
setting: 6 Mexico
score: 14 Elmer Bernstein
remake of: 12 Seven Samurai
sequel: 16 Return of the Seven 20 Magnificent Seven Ride

magnify 4 laud 5 adore, boost, exalt, extol 6 blow up, double, expand, praise, puff up, revere 7 acclaim, amplify, enlarge, glorify, greaten, inflate, stretch, worship 8 heighten, maximize, overrate 9 embroi-

der, overstate, reverence 10 exaggerate

magniloquence 7 bombast, fustian 8 euphuism, tumidity 9 pomposity, turgidity 10 orotundity 11 fanfaronade, grandiosity 14 grandiloquence 15 pretentiousness

magniloquent 5 tumid, windy, wordy 6 turgid 7 pompous, verbose 8 inflated 9 bombastic 13 grandiloquent

magnitude 4 bulk, fame, mass, size 6 extent, renown, repute, volume 7 bigness, expanse, measure 8 eminence, enormity, hugeness, vastness

magnolia
varieties: 4 ashe, star 6 saucer 7 Chinese 8 southern, umbrella 11 great-leaved

Magnum, P. I.
character: 2 TC 4 Rick 7 Higgins 12 Thomas Magnum
cast: 10 Tom Selleck 12 Roger E Mosley 13 John Hillerman
setting: 6 Hawaii

Magog
father: 7 Japheth

Magritte, Rene Francois Ghislain
born: 7 Belgium 8 Lessines
artwork: 14 La Belle Captive, The False Mirror, The Key of Dreams 15 Memory of a Voyage 18 L'Empire des Lumieres (The Empire of Light), The Menaced Assassin

Magua
character in: 20 The Last of the Mohicans
author: 6 Cooper

Magus see 4 Magi

Magwitch, Abel
character in: 17 Great Expectations
author: 7 Dickens

Magyar 9 Hungarian

Mahican see 7 Mohican

Mahler, Gustav
born: 7 Austria, Bohemia
composer of: 12 Resurrection (symphony No 2) 15 Das Klagendelied 16 Songs of a Wayfarer 17 Das Lied von der Erde, Kindertotenlieder, The Song of the Earth 19 Des Knaben Wunderhorn 28 Lieder eines fahrenden Gesellen

mahogany 4 tree, wood 5 brown 8 hardwood 9 Swietenia 12 reddish-brown
varieties: 3 red 5 swamp,

white 7 African, big-leaf, Florida, Senegal, Spanish 8 Honduras, mountain 9 Nyasaland, Venezulan 10 West Indian

Mahon, Christopher
character in: 27 The Playboy of the Western World
author: 5 Synge

mahzor, machzor 16 Jewish prayer book

Maia
member of: 8 Pleiades
place in group: 6 eldest
father: 5 Atlas
mother: 7 Pleione
son: 6 Hermes

maid 6 tweeny 7 servant 8 domestic 9 hired girl, housemaid, lady's maid, nursemaid 10 parlor maid 11 maidservant 12 upstairs maid 13 female servant
French: 6 au pair

maiden, maidenly 4 girl, lass, maid, miss 5 chick, first 6 chaste, damsel, lassie, virgin 7 colleen, girlish, ingenue, initial, untried 8 original, virginal, youthful 9 inaugural, soubrette, unmarried 10 demoiselle, initiatory 12 introductory

Maid Marian
beloved of: 9 Robin Hood

maidservant 4 amah, ayah, char, lass, maid 5 bonne 6 au pair, tweeny 7 abigail 8 charlady, domestic 9 hired girl, lady's maid, tirewoman 10 handmaiden, parlormaid

Maidu
language family: 8 Penutian
location: 10 California
noted for: 8 basketry

mail 4 arms, post 5 armor 6 get out 7 airmail, harness, letters, panoply 8 dispatch, packages 9 postcards 10 send by mail, send by post, suit of mail 11 surface mail 12 mail delivery, put in the mail 13 postal service 14 defensive armor, drop in a mailbox 17 post-office service

Mailer, Norman
author of: 15 An American Dream 16 Armies of the Night 18 The Naked and the Dead 19 The Executioner's Song

Maillol, Aristide
born: 6 France 13 Banyuls-sur-mer

artwork: 5 Night, Torso **7** Le Desir (Desire) **11** Ile de France **12** Young Cyclist **14** Action in Chains, The Three Nymphs **16** The Mediterranean (Seated Woman) **17** Monument to Cezanne, Monument to Debussy **18** Venus with a Necklace

maim 3 cut, rip **4** gash, lame, maul, rend, tear **5** slash, wound **6** deface, hobble, injure, mangle, savage **7** cripple, disable **8** lacerate, mutilate **9** disfigure, dismember, hamstring **12** incapacitate

main 4 head **5** chief, prime, vital **6** urgent **7** capital, central, crucial, leading, primary, special, supreme **8** critical, foremost, pressing **9** essential, important, necessary, paramount, principal, requisite **10** particular, preeminent **11** outstanding, predominant **13** consequential, indispensable

Main, Marjorie
    real name: **13** Mary Tomlinson

partner: 12 Wallace Beery **13** Percy Kilbride
born: 7 Acton IN
roles: 7 Dead End **8** Ma Kettle

Maine *see box*

mainly 6 mostly **7** chiefly **8** above all **9** in the main, most of all, primarily **10** on the whole **11** principally **13** predominantly **14** for the most part, in great measure **16** first and foremost

main point 3 nut **4** core, crux, gist, meat **5** basis, heart, theme **6** kernel **7** essence **10** brass tacks **11** nitty-gritty **15** sum and substance

mainspring 5 agent, cause **6** motive **9** incentive **10** motivation

mainstay 4 prop **6** anchor, pillar **7** bulwark **8** backbone, buttress **16** pillar of strength

Main Street
    author: **13** Sinclair Lewis

character: 14 Carol Kennicott **15** Dr Will Kennicott

maintain 4 aver, avow, hold, keep **5** claim, state, swear **6** affirm, allege, assert, defend, insist, keep up, uphold **7** care for, contend, declare, finance, profess, stand by, support, sustain **8** conserve, continue, preserve **9** keep alive, keep going **10** provide for, take care of

maintenance 4 keep **6** living, repair, upkeep **7** keeping, support **10** livelihood, protection, sustenance **11** safekeeping, subsistence, sustainment **12** conservation, preservation, safeguarding

Main-Travelled Road
    author: **13** Hamlin Garland

maison de sante 10 sanitarium **13** house of health

maize 4 corn, milo **5** grain **6** cereal, silage, yellow **7** zea mays **10** Indian corn

majestic, majestical 5 grand, lofty, noble, regal, royal **6** august, famous, superb **7** elegant, eminent, stately, sublime **8** esteemed, glorious, imperial, imposing, princely, renowned, splendid **10** impressive **11** illustrious, magnificent **13** distinguished

majesty 4 pomp **5** glory **6** luster **7** dignity **8** elegance, eminence, grandeur, mobility, splendor **9** elevation, loftiness, solemnity, sublimity **10** augustness **11** distinction, stateliness **12** gloriousness, magnificence **14** impressiveness

major 4 main **5** chief, prime, vital **6** larger, urgent **7** capital, crucial, greater, leading, primary, ranking, serious, supreme **8** critical, foremost, pressing **9** essential, important, necessary, paramount, principal, requisite **10** preeminent **11** outstanding, predominant, significant **13** consequential, indispensable

Major Barbara
    director: **13** Gabriel Pascal
    based on play by: **17** George Bernard Shaw
    cast: **11** Deborah Kerr, Rex Harrison, Wendy Hiller **12** Robert Morley, Robert Newton **14** Sybil Thorndike

majority 4 bulk, mass **8** best part, legal age, maturity **9** adulthood, seniority, woman-

---

Maine
    abbreviation: **2** ME
    nickname: **6** Lumber **8** Pine Tree **10** Wonderland
    capital: **7** Augusta
    largest city: **8** Portland
    others: **4** Bath, Saco **5** Hiram, Orono **6** Auburn, Bangor **7** Kittery **8** Boothbay, Lewiston, Ogunquit **9** Bar Harbor, Biddeford, Brunswick, Skowhegan **10** Waterville **11** Millinocket, Presque Isle
    college: **5** Bates, Colby **7** Bowdoin
    explorer: **6** Cabots **8** Norsemen
    feature: **8** lobsters **19** West Quoddy Headlight
        beach: **10** Old Orchard
        national park: **6** Acadia
        waterway: **18** Allagash Wilderness
    tribe: **6** Abnaki **7** Wewenoc
    people: **10** downeaster **11** Dorothea Dix **19** Edna St Vincent Millay **24** Henry Wadsworth Longfellow
    island: **4** Orrs **8** Mt Desert **10** Campobello
    lake: **5** Sebec, Wyman **6** Sebago **8** Rangeley, Schoodic **9** Flagstaff, Moosehead **10** Chesuncook
    land rank: **11** thirty ninth
    mountain: **5** Kineo, White **7** Bigelow **8** Cadillac
        highest point: **8** Katahdin
    physical feature:
        bay: **5** Casco **9** Penobscot **12** Merrymeeting **13** Passamaquoddy
        sand dunes: **13** Desert of Maine
    river: **4** Saco **6** St John **7** St Croix **8** Allagash, Kennebec **9** Aroostook, Kennebago, Penobscot **12** Androscoggin
    state admission: **11** twenty third
    state bird: **9** chickadee
    state fish: **16** land-locked salmon
    state flower: **7** thistle **8** pine cone **22** white pine cone and tassel
    state motto: **7** I Direct
    state song: **16** State of Maine Song
    state tree: **16** eastern white pine

hood **10** lion's share
13 preponderance

major key (in music)
German: **3** dur

Major prophets *see*
8 prophets

majuscule 7 capital **11**
large letter **13** capital letter
15 upper-case letter

make 3 fix **4** form, kind, mark,
meet, pass **5** beget, brand,
build, catch, cause, enact,
erect, force, frame, impel,
press, reach, shape, speak, utter **6** attain, compel, create,
devise, draw up, effect, foment, makeup, oblige, render
7 appoint, compose, deliver,
dragoon, fashion, produce, require **8** arrive at, assemble,
engender **9** cause to be, constrain, construct, establish,
fabricate, formation, legislate,
pronounce, structure **10** bring
about, fashioning **11** composition, manufacture

make a bet 3 bet **4** risk
5 stake, wager **6** chance, gamble, hazard, plunge
7 venture

make a clean breast of
7 confess, lay bare, own up
to **8** blurt out **14** come clean
about

make a dash 3 fly, run
4 flee **6** escape **7** get away
8 make a run **10** make a
break, take flight **12** make a
getaway

make a deal 5 agree **6** settle
10 compromise **11** come to
terms, meet halfway **14** strike
a bargain

make advances 8 approach,
come on to, sound out
11 proposition **13** make overtures, put the moves on

make a fuss over 6 dote on
7 protest **8** crow over

make again 4 copy **6** remake,
repeat **9** duplicate
11 reconstruct

make a getaway 4 bolt, flee,
skip **6** escape **7** get away,
make off, run away **8** make a
run, slip away **9** break free,
cut and run, make a dash
10 break loose, fly the coop,
take flight

make a gift of 4 give **6** donate **7** present **8** bequeath
10 contribute

make allowance for 6 excuse, pardon **7** forgive, indulge **8** bear with, pass over

make amends 5 atone **6** make

up, square **7** expiate **9** do penance **10** compensate

make a mess of 3 mar
4 goof, muff, ruin **5** botch,
spoil **6** bungle, foul up, mess
up **7** butcher, do badly, louse
up, screw up **9** mismanage

make a mistake 3 err **4** goof
6 mess up, slip up
12 miscalculate

make an effort 3 try **5** essay
6 strive, work at **7** attempt
8 endeavor

make appear 5 evoke **6** elicit
7 produce **9** conjure up
10 bring forth

make a racket 3 cry **4** howl,
yell **5** shout **6** bellow, clamor,
holler, scream **7** bluster
8 make a din **10** vociferate
12 raise a rumpus

make a stab at 3 try **5** essay,
guess **6** reckon, take on **7** attempt, surmise, venture **8** estimate, give a try **9** undertake
10 conjecture **11** approximate
12 take a crack at, take a
fling at

make a stand 9 stand fast
13 refuse to yield **17** fight to
the last man

make a statement 6 remark
7 clarify, comment, discuss,
explain, expound **9** elucidate,
talk about

make aware 4 tell **5** edify
6 advise, inform, notify, reveal **7** apprise **8** acquaint, disclose **9** divulge to, enlighten,
introduce **11** familiarize
16 bring to (one's) attention

make away with 3 eat **4** kill,
take **5** spend, steal **6** kidnap,
murder **7** abolish, consume,
destroy **8** carry off, embezzle,
get rid of **9** dissipate

make-believe 4 fake, sham
5 false, phony **6** made-up,
make-up, unreal **7** assumed,
charade, fantasy, feigned, fiction **8** creation, imagined, invented, pretense, spurious
9 fantastic, imaginary, invention, pretended, simulated
10 artificial, fictitious
11 counterfeit, fabrication
13 falsification

make certain of 6 assure,
clinch, ensure **8** be sure of
10 make sure of

make damp 5 bedew
6 dampen **7** moisten **8** sprinkle

make dark 3 dim **6** darken
7 blacken, obscure

make different 4 vary **5** alter,
amend **6** change, modify, mu-

tate **7** convert, remodel
9 transform, transmute
12 metamorphose

make distinctive 8 set apart
9 single out **11** distinguish
12 characterize **13** differentiate

make easy 4 ease **6** smooth
7 explain, lighten **8** simplify
10 clear a path, facilitate

make eligible 5 allow **6** permit **7** entitle, qualify
9 authorize

make evident 4 show
5 prove **6** reveal **7** exhibit
8 manifest **9** establish, make
clear, make plain
11 demonstrate

make fast 3 fix **4** moor **5** affix,
tie up **6** attach, fasten, secure
7 connect

make feeble 6 weaken **7** wear
out **8** enervate **10** debilitate,
devitalize

make furious 5 anger **6** enrage, madden **7** incense, inflame **9** infuriate

make giddy 5 dizzy **12** make
unsteady **15** make lightheaded

make good 5 repay **6** arrive,
make it **7** fulfill, succeed
11 reach the top **15** make
restitution

make happy 5 amuse, cheer
6 please **7** delight, gratify
9 entertain

make haste slowly
Latin: **12** festina lente

make hostile 5 repel **6** offend
7 provoke **8** alienate
10 antagonize

make ill 5 repel **6** infect, revolt, sicken **7** afflict, disgust,
repulse **8** disagree, distress,
make sick, nauseate **9** discomfit **14** turn the stomach

make ill at ease 5 upset
6 rattle **7** fluster **8** distress
9 discomfit, embarrass
10 disconcert

make impure 4 foul, soil
5 dirty, spoil, taint **6** befoul,
blight, defile, infect, poison
7 corrupt, pollute **10** adulterate **11** contaminate

make inroads 6 invade **7** impinge, intrude **8** encroach, infringe, trespass **9** penetrate

make known 4 tell **6** advise,
impart, inform, notify, report,
reveal, unveil **7** apprise, divulge, lay bare, publish, uncover **8** disclose **9** broadcast
10 give notice, make public
11 communicate

make less forceful 6 soften,

weaken 9 undermine 10 devitalize, emasculate

make light of 8 belittle, minimize, pooh-pooh, sneeze at 9 deprecate, disparage, underrate 10 depreciate, undervalue 13 underestimate

make merry 5 revel 7 carouse, roister 9 celebrate, have a ball 15 paint the town red

make much of 5 honor 6 praise 7 acclaim, applaud, commend, flatter 8 fuss over

make nervous 5 annoy, upset 7 agitate, disturb, perturb, trouble, unnerve 10 disconcert

make off with 5 steal 6 abduct, kidnap, snatch 7 bear off 8 carry off 10 run off with 11 get away with

make one's blood boil 5 anger 6 enrage, madden 7 incense, inflame 9 infuriate

make one's eyes pop 4 stun 5 shock 6 dazzle 7 stagger, startle 8 astonish 9 electrify 11 flabbergast

make out 3 see 4 espy 6 behold, descry, detect, fill in, notice 7 discern, observe, pick out 8 get along, perceive, write out 12 catch sight of

make plain 7 clarify, clear up, explain, lay open 8 elucidate, explicate, make clear 10 illuminate 11 disentangle, shed light on 12 bring to light

make possible for 5 allow 6 enable, permit 7 empower, qualify 10 capacitate

make public 3 air 4 tell, vent 5 print, utter, voice 6 expose, inform, reveal, spread 7 declare, display, divulge, exhibit, express, give out, publish 8 announce, disclose, proclaim, televise 9 broadcast, circulate, publicize

maker, Maker 3 god 4 poet 5 smith 6 author, forger 7 builder, creator, founder 8 declarer, inventor, producer 9 architect, generator 10 originator 12 manufacturer

make ready 5 prime 7 arrange, forearm, prepare

make reparation for 5 atone, repay 6 pay for 10 compensate, recompense, remunerate

make restitution 5 repay 7 pay back 9 reimburse 10 compensate, recompense

make right 3 fix 5 amend, emend 6 remedy, repair 7 correct, improve, rectify

make self-conscious 5 abash 6 rattle 7 chagrin, fluster 9 discomfit, embarrass 10 disconcert

makeshift 6 make-do 7 standby, stopgap 8 slapdash 9 alternate, expedient, temporary, tentative 10 substitute 11 provisional

make sick 6 revolt 7 disgust 8 nauseate

make smaller 6 lessen, reduce, shrink, take in 8 decrease, diminish

make sure 5 cinch 6 assure, clinch, decide, ensure, secure, settle 9 ascertain 11 double-check

make thinner 4 thin 6 dilute 9 water down 10 adulterate

make tracks 2 go 4 scat, shoo 5 be off, leave, scram 6 beat it, cut out, depart, go away 8 withdraw 10 hit the road

make uncomfortable 3 try 7 agitate, perturb 8 disquiet, distress 9 discomfit, embarrass 10 discompose

make uneasy 7 disturb, perturb, trouble, unnerve 8 disquiet, distress 9 discomfit, embarrass 10 discomfort, discompose, disconcert

make uniform 4 even 5 equal 6 smooth 7 balance 8 equalize 10 straighten

makeup 5 frame 9 character, cosmetics, framework, structure 11 composition, personality 12 constitution, organization

make up 4 form 5 cover 6 invent 7 arrange, concoct 8 assemble 9 improvise, reconcile 10 compensate, constitute 11 put together

make up for 5 atone 7 expiate 8 make good 10 make amends 13 compensate for

make up one's mind 6 decide 7 resolve 9 determine

make use of 3 use 5 apply 6 employ, engage, occupy 7 exploit, utilize 8 keep busy, put to use 13 turn to account

make weary 4 do in, poop, tire 7 exhaust, wear out 8 enervate

makeweight 6 weight 7 ballast

make well 4 cure, heal

make wider 5 widen 6 dilate, expand 7 broaden, stretch 9 spread out

make worse 6 worsen 8 heighten, increase 9 aggravate, intensify 10 exacerbate

making excuses 8 alibiing 9 defending 10 justifying 11 apologizing

Making of the President, The (series)
author: 14 Theodore H White

making the rounds 5 about 6 abroad 11 circulating, going around 13 going the route

Malachi
means: 11 my messenger
identified with: 4 Ezra 8 Mordecai, Nehemiah 10 Zerubbabel

maladroit 5 inept 6 clumsy, gauche 7 awkward, unhandy 8 bumbling, bungling, tactless 9 impolitic, unskilled 10 blundering, left-handed, ungraceful

maladroitness 9 gaucherie, inability 10 clumsiness, ineptitude 11 awkwardness, unhandiness 12 incompetence

malady 7 ailment, disease, illness 8 disorder, sickness 9 affection, complaint, infirmity 10 affliction, disability

mala fide 10 in bad faith, not genuine

malaise 4 pang 5 throb 6 twinge 7 anxiety 8 disquiet 9 lassitude 10 uneasiness, discomfort 11 nervousness

Malamud, Bernard
author of: 8 The Fixer 9 God's Grace 10 The Natural, The Tenants 11 Dubin's Lives 12 The Assistant

Malaprop, Mrs
character in: 9 The Rivals
author: 8 Sheridan

Malawi *see box, p. 596*

Malaysia *see box, p. 597*

Malcolm
character in: 7 Macbeth
author: 11 Shakespeare

Malcolm X
original name: 13 Malcolm Little
born: 2 NE 5 Omaha
religion: 5 Islam 11 Black Muslim 13 Nation of Islam
assassinated in: 6 Harlem 11 New York City
book about: 26 The Autobiography of Malcolm X
author: 9 Alex Haley
film about: 8 Malcolm X
director: 8 Spike Lee

malcontent 4 glum, sour 5 rebel 6 grouch, grumpy, morose, sullen, uneasy 7 grouchy, growler, repiner, restive 8 de-

---

Malawi
  other name: 9 Nyasaland
  capital: 8 Lilongwe
  largest city: 8 Blantyre
  others: 4 Bana 5 Dedza, Limbe, Mzuzu, Zomba 6 Kasese, Mzimba, Salima 7 Chipoka, Chiromo, Deep Bay, Karonga, Katumbi 8 Chikwawa, Chilumbe, Kota Kota, Nkata Bay 9 Monkey Bay 10 Port Herald 12 Fort Johnston, Livingstonia
  monetary unit: 6 kwacha 7 tambala
  lake: 5 Nyasa 6 Chilwa, Malawi
  mountain: 11 Livingstone
  highest point: 6 Mlanje 7 Mulanje
  river: 3 Bua 5 Shire 7 Dwangwa 11 South Rukuru
  physical feature:
    highlands: 5 Shire
    plateau: 5 Nyika
    valley: 5 Shire 9 Great Rift
  people: 3 Yao 4 Sena 5 Bantu, Lomwe, Ngoni 6 Cheiva, Maravi, Ngonde, Nyanja 7 Tumbuka
    dynasty: 6 Maravi
    explorer: 16 David Livingstone
    leader: 5 Banda
  language: 3 Yao 4 Cewa 5 Bantu, Ngoni, Tonga 6 Nyanja 7 English, Tumbuka 8 Chichewa 10 Chitumbuka
  religion: 5 Islam 7 animism 10 Protestant 12 Presbyterian 13 Roman Catholic
  feature:
    village: 5 mudzi

---

jected, downcast, grumbler, restless 9 insurgent, irritable 10 complainer, despondent 11 faultfinder 12 discontented, dissatisfied, faultfinding, hard to please

mal de mer 11 seasickness

Malden, Karl
  real name: 16 Mladen Sekulovich
  born: 6 Gary IL
  roles: 6 Patton 8 Baby Doll 15 On the Waterfront 21 A Streetcar Named Desire 24 The Streets of San Francisco

Maldives *see box*

male 3 boy, man, ram 4 bull 5 manly, youth 6 tomcat 7 manlike, rooster 8 stallion 9 billy goat, masculine

Male
  capital of: 8 Maldives

male bird 4 cock 5 drake 6 gander 7 rooster

maledict 4 damn 5 curse 8 denounce 9 proscribe 12 anathematize

malediction 5 curse 8 anathema, diatribe 9 damnation, evil spell 10 execration 11 fulmination, imprecation 12 denunciation, proscription

malefactor 5 felon, knave,

rogue 6 sinner 7 culprit 8 criminal, evil-doer, offender 9 miscreant, scoundrel, wrongdoer 10 malfeasant

male hairdresser
  French: 8 coiffeur

malentendu 7 mistake 16 misunderstanding

male power
  god of: 7 Priapus

Malevich, Kasimir Severinovich
  born: 4 Kiev 6 Russia
  artwork: 11 Black Square 15 The Knife Grinder 18 Eight Red Rectangles 19 Woman with Water Pails 34 Suprematist Composition White on White

malevolence 4 evil, hate 5 spite 6 enmity, grudge, hatred, malice, rancor, spleen 7 despite, ill will 9 hostility, malignity 10 antagonism, malignance, malignancy 12 spitefulness 13 maliciousness

malevolent 5 surly 6 malign, sullen 7 baleful, vicious 8 sinister, spiteful, venomous 9 invidious, malicious, malignant, rancorous, resentful 10 illnatured, pernicious, revengeful 11 acrimonious, illdisposed 14 ill-intentioned

malfeasance 5 crime 8 mis-

deeds 10 misconduct, wrongdoing

malformation 9 deformity 10 aberration, distortion 11 abnormality, monstrosity, peculiarity 12 grotesquerie, irregularity 13 disfigurement

malformed 7 twisted 8 deformed 9 contorted, distorted, grotesque, irregular, misshapen

malfunction 6 glitch, malady 7 problem 9 complaint

malgre lui 16 in spite of himself

Mali *see box, p. 598*

malice 4 hate 5 spite, venom 6 enmity, grudge, hatred, rancor 7 ill will 8 acrimony 9 animosity, malignity 10 antagonism, bitterness, evil intent, resentment 11 malevolence 12 spitefulness

malice aforethought
  legal term: 51 planning to commit a crime without just cause or provocation

malicious 7 baleful, harmful, hateful, vicious 8 spiteful 9 invidious, malignant, rancorous, resentful 10 malevolent, revengeful, vindictive 11 acrimonious, ill-disposed

malign 3 bad 4 evil 5 abuse, black 6 defame, revile, vilify 7 baneful, harmful, hateful, noxious, ominous, put down, run down, slander 8 backbite, bad mouth, belittle, derogate, menacing, sinister 9 denigrate, deprecate, disparage, injurious, malicious, malignant 10 malevolent, pernicious, speak ill of 11 deleterious, detrimental, threatening 14 inveigh against

malignancy 5 spite, tumor 6 cancer, malice, rancor 7 ill will, sarcoma 8 acrimony, neoplasm, toxicity 9 carcinoma, hostility, virulence 10 bitterness 11 malevolence, viciousness 12 hard feelings, spitefulness, vengefulness 13 poisonousness

malignant 4 evil 5 fatal, toxic 6 bitter, deadly 7 hateful, hostile, vicious 8 fiendish, spiteful, venomous, virulent 9 invidious, malicious, poisonous, rancorous, resentful 10 diabolical, evil-minded, malevolent, pernicious, revengeful, vindictive 11 acrimonious, ill-disposed

malignant spirit 3 imp 5 demon, devil 7 gremlin

malignity 4 evil 5 spite, venom 6 animus, rancor,

Malaysia
capital/largest city: 11 Kuala Lumpur
others: 4 Ipoh, Sibu 5 Anson, Davao, Telok 6 Iloilo, Johore, Kupang, Manado, Penang, Pinang 7 Bintulu, Kuantan, Kuching, Melalap 8 Port Weld, Sandakan 10 Georgetown, Kota Baharu 11 Johor Baharu, Port Dickson 12 Kota Kinabulu 14 Port Swettenham
division: 5 Sabah 6 Malaya 7 Malacca, Sarawak
head of state:
  supreme head of state: 18 yang di-pertuan agong
measure: 3 pau, tun 4 para, pipe, tael, wang 5 parah 6 chupak, parrah 7 gantang
monetary unit: 3 sen, tra 4 taro, trah 7 ringgit, tampang
weight: 4 chee, mace, tael, wang 7 tampang
island: 6 Banggi, Borneo, Labuan, Penang, Pinang, Tioman 7 Pangkor, Sebatik 8 Langkawi 10 Perhentian 11 Balambangan
mountain: 4 Bulu, Hose, Iban, Iran, Main, Mulu, Niut, Raja 5 Murjo, Niapa, Ophir 6 Blumut, Kapuas, Leuser, Slamet 7 Binaija, Brassey, Crocker 8 Rindjani 11 Gunong Korbu, Gunong Tahan
highest point: 8 Kinabalu
river: 5 Klang, Kutai, Perak 6 Barito, Pahang, Rajang, Rejang 7 Sarawak 12 Kinabatangan
sea: 4 Sulu 7 Celebes 10 South China
physical feature:
  bay: 5 Labuk
  cape: 5 Sirik
  highlands: 7 Cameron
  passage: 6 Sibutu
  peninsula: 5 Malay
  point: 13 Tanjong Gelang
  strait: 6 Johore 7 Balabac, Malacca
people: 4 Iban 5 Dayak, Malay 6 Indian 7 Chinese, Kadazan 9 Pakistani, Sri Lankan 10 Bangladesh, Indonesian
language: 4 Bugi, Dyak 5 Malay, Tamil 6 Battok, Rejang 7 Chinese, English, Lampong, Niasese 8 Achinese, Javanese, Makassar 14 Bahasa Malaysia
  alphabet: 5 tagal
religion: 5 Hindu, Islam 6 Taoism 7 animism 8 Buddhism 12 Christianity, Confucianism
place:
  mosque: 8 National
feature:
  cap: 7 songkok
  cloth: 4 tapa 5 batik
  clothing: 4 baju, malo, sari 5 badju, pareu 6 cabaya, kebaya, sam-foo, sarong 9 cheongsam
  dance: 4 haka, hula 5 joget
  game: 9 sepakraga
  hamlet: 7 kampong
  parish: 5 mukim
  rice paddy: 4 padi
  scarf: 9 selendang
  self-defense: 5 silat
  shadow play: 6 menora
  spirit: 5 hantu
food:
  drink: 4 kava
  fruit: 6 durian 8 rambutan 10 mangosteen

Maldives
capital/largest city:
  4 Male
government:
  legislature: 6 Majlis
monetary unit: 5 laree, rupee
island: 3 Ari, Gan 4 Addu, Male 5 Rasdu 6 Felidu, Hulele, Mulaku 7 Malcolm, Minicoy, Nilandu 8 Maldives, Suvadiva 9 Fadiffolu, Wilingili 10 Haddummati, Kolumadulu 11 Tiladummati 13 Ihavandiffulu, Miladummadulu 16 North Malosmadulu, South Malosmadulu
sea: 6 Indian 7 Arabian 9 Laccadive
physical feature:
  channel: 4 Wadu 7 Kardiva 8 Veimandu 10 Equatorial 11 Eight Degree 17 One and a Half Degree
people: 4 Arab 6 Indian 9 Sinhalese 10 Singhalese
  ruling family/sultans: 4 Didi
language: 6 Arabic, Divehi
religion: 5 Islam
feature:
  coconut fiber: 4 coir
  dried coconut: 5 copra

Malle, Louis
  director of: 10 Pretty Baby 12 Atlantic City 13 Lacombe Lucien 16 Murmur of the Heart

malleable 6 docile, pliant 7 ductile, plastic, pliable 8 flexible, moldable, workable 9 adaptable, compliant, teachable, tractable 10 governable, manageable 12 easily shaped 13 easily wrought 14 impressionable

mallet
  type: 6 rubber, wooden 12 plastic-faced

mallophaga
  class: 8 hexapoda
  phylum: 10 arthropoda
  group: 8 bird lice 10 biting lice

malnutrition 10 emaciation, starvation 16 undernourishment

spleen 7 ill will 8 acrimony 9 animosity 12 hard feelings, spitefulness, venomousness

malinger 4 loaf 5 dodge, evade, shirk, slack 7 goof off 9 goldbrick

mall 4 yard 5 court, plaza 6 arcade, circus, piazza, square 8 cloister 9 colonnade, esplanade, promenade 10 quadrangle 12 parade ground

Mallarme, Stephane
  author of: 8 Herodias 18 L'Apres Midi d'un faune 19 The Afternoon of a Faun

malodorous 4 rank 5 acrid, fetid, musty 6 putrid, smelly

Mali
  other name: 11 French Sudan 12 French Soudan 16 Sudanese Republic
  capital/largest city: 6 Bamako
  others: 3 Gao 5 Kayes, Mopti, Segou 6 Djenne 7 Sikasso 8 Taoudeni, Timbuktu 10 Tombouctou
  division: 5 Sahel 7 Azaouad
  monetary unit: 5 franc 7 centime
  lake: 2 Do 4 Debo 5 Garou 7 Korarou 9 Faguibine
  mountain: 4 Mina 6 Iforas 7 Manding
  highest point: 12 Hombori Tondo
  river: 4 Bani 5 Bagoe, Bakoy, Diaka, Niger 6 Bafing, Bakoye, Baoule, Faleme 7 Azaouak, Senegal
  physical feature:
    desert: 6 Sahara 8 Chech Erg 10 Sekkane Erg 13 Haricha Hamada
    plateau: 14 Adrar des Iforas
    valley: 5 Niger 7 Tilemsi
  people: 3 Bwa 4 Fula, Kyan, Moor, Peul 5 Dogon, Dyula, Fulbe, Marka 6 Berber, Dognon, Fulani, Senufo, Tuareg 7 Bambara, Fellata, Malinke, Miniaka, Songhai, Soninke 8 Khasonke, Mandingo, Senoulfo
    leader: 4 Umar 5 Keita 6 Traore 9 Mansa Musa
  language: 5 Dogon, Dyula, Feulh, Mande, Marka 6 Berber, French, Fulani 7 Bambara, Malinke, Senoufo, Songhai
  religion: 5 Islam 7 animism
  place:
    ruins: 8 Terhazza
  feature:
    empire: 4 Mali 5 Ghana 7 Bambara, Songhai

7 noisome, reeking 8 stinking 12 foul-smelling

Malone, Dorothy
  real name: 20 Dorothy Eloise Maloney
  husband: 15 Jacques Bergerac
  born: 9 Chicago IL
  roles: 11 Peyton Place 14 Too Much Too Soon 16 Written on the Wind

Malory, Sir Thomas
  author of: 14 Le Morte d'Arthur

Malpighi, Marcello
  field: 10 physiology
  nationality: 7 Italian
  founded: 18 microscopic anatomy

malpractice 10 negligence

Malraux, Andre
  author of: 8 Man's Fate 11 Anti-Memoirs, Days of Wrath, The Royal Way 13 The Conquerors 18 The Voices of Silence

Malta see box

Maltese Falcon, The
  author: 15 Dashiell Hammett
  director: 10 John Huston
  cast: 9 Mary Astor (Bridget O'Shaughnessy) 10 Peter Lorre (Joel Cairo) 12 Elisha Cook Jr (Wilmer), Gladys George 14 Humphrey Bogart

(Sam Spade) 17 Sydney Greenstreet (the Fat Man)
  character: 6 Wilmer 8 Sam Spade 9 Joel Cairo 11 Miles Archer 12 Casper Gutman, Floyd Thursby 18 Brigid O'Shaughnessy

Malta
  capital: 8 Valletta
  largest city: 6 Sliema
  others: 5 Marfa, Mdina, Mgarr, Mosta, Nadut, Paola, Rabat 6 Zejtun 7 Senglea, Zeibrun 8 Cospicua, Floriana, Mellieha, Victoria 10 Birkirkara, Birzebbuga, Vittoriosa
  measure: 4 rotl 5 artal, canna, parto, ratel, salma 6 kantar 7 caffiso
  monetary unit: 4 cent 5 grain, grano, pound
  island: 4 Gozo 5 Malta 6 Comino, Filfla 7 Filfola 9 Cominotto 10 Comminotto
  highest point: 12 Dingli Cliffs
  sea: 13 Mediterranean
  physical feature:
    bay: 7 St Paul's 8 Mellieha 10 Marsaxlokk
    channel: 11 North Comino, South Comino
    harbor: 5 Grand 10 Marsamxett
  people: 7 Maltese
    leader: 7 Mintoff 9 Buttigieo 18 Parisot de La Valette
    ruler: 5 Arabs 6 Romans 7 British 8 Napoleon 10 Byzantines 11 Hospitalers, Phoenicians 13 Carthaginians 15 Holy Roman Empire, Knights of St John
  language: 7 English, Italian, Maltese
  religion: 13 Roman Catholic
  feature:
    gondola boat: 7 dghaisa

remade as: 13 Satan Met a Lady

malt liquor 3 ale 4 beer, bock, brew 5 stout 6 porter

maltreat 4 harm, hurt 5 abuse 6 ill-use, injure 8 mistreat

maltreatment 5 abuse 6 ill-use, injury 7 assault, cruelty 10 bodily harm, oppression 11 manhandling, molestation, persecution 12 mistreatment

Malvolio
  character in: 12 Twelfth Night
  author: 11 Shakespeare

Mama
  character: 4 Nels 6 Dagmar, Katrin, TR Ryan 9 Aunt Jenny 10 (Papa) Lars Hansen 11 (Mama) Marta Hansen
  cast: 8 Iris Mann 9 Peggy Wood, Ruth Gates 11 Judson Laire, Robin Morgan 12 Rosemary Rice 13 Dick Van Patten, Kevin Coughlin
  dog: 6 Willie
  based on book: 16 Mama's Bank Account
  setting: 12 San Francisco
  theme: 12 Holverg Suite 13 The Last Spring

Mamers see 4 Mars

mamma, mama 2 ma 3 mam, mom, mum 4 wife 5 madre, mammy, mater, mommy,

mummy, mumsy, woman
6 mother, parent

mammal *see box*

mammon, Mammon 4 gain,
gold 5 money 6 profit, riches,
wealth 9 affluence 11 possessions 13 material goods, the
god of money

Mammon, Sir Epicure
character in: 12 The
Alchemist
author: 6 Jonson

mammoth 4 huge 5 great
6 mighty 7 immense, massive

8 colossal, enormous, gigantic,
whopping 9 cyclopean, herculean, monstrous, ponderous,
very large 10 gargantuan,
monumental, prodigious, stupendous, tremendous 11 elephantine, mountainous

Mammy
character in: 15 Gone With
the Wind
author: 8 Mitchell

Mamoulian, Rouben
director of: 13 Love Me Tonight, Silk Stockings
14 Queen Christina, The
Mark of Zorro

---

mammal
bat (chiroptera): 4 tomb 5 fruit, naked, smoky 7 mastiff,
vampire 9 fisherman, horseshoe, leaf-nosed, sac-winged,
slit-faced, thumbless 10 disk-winged, free-tailed, mous-
tached 11 funnel-eared, hollow-faced, mouse-tailed
12 false vampire, sheath-tailed, sucker-footed, yellow-
winged 14 vespertilionid 21 New Zealand short-tailed
carnivore: 3 cat, dog, fox 4 bear, lion, lynx, mink, puma,
wolf 5 civet, dingo, fossa, hyena, otter, panda, skunk,
tayra, tiger 6 badger, bobcat, coyote, ferret, grison,
hyaena, jackal, jaguar, marten, olingo, weasel 7 polecat,
raccoon 8 aardwolf, kinkajou, mongoose, suricate 9 wolverine 10 cacomistle, coatimundi
cetacea: 4 gray 5 pilot, right, whale 6 beluga, killer 7 dolphin, rorqual 8 humpback, narwhale, porpoise 10 sperm
whale 11 beaked whale 16 bottle-nosed whale
edentata: 5 sloth 8 anteater 9 armadillo, tree sloth
egg-laying: 7 echidna 13 spiny anteater 18 duck-billed
platypus
even-toed ungulate: 2 ox 3 elk, hog, pig 4 deer, goat,
oxen 5 bison, camel, llama, moose, okapi, sheep 6 alpaca,
cattle, duiker, vicuna 7 buffalo, caribou, gazelle, giraffe,
guanaco, muntjak, peccary 8 antelope 9 mouse deer
10 chevrotain 12 hippopotamus
hyracoidea: 5 hyrax
insect-eating: 4 mole 5 shrew 6 desman, tenrec 7 gym-
nure, moon rat 8 hedgehog 9 shrew-mole, solenodon
10 golden mole, otter shrew, water shrew 13 elephant
shrew
lagomorpha: 4 hare, pika 6 rabbit
marsupials/pouched: 5 koala 6 cuscus, numbat, possum,
wombat 7 opossum, wallaby 8 kangaroo 9 bandicoot,
phalanger 14 Tasmanian devil
odd-toed ungulate: 3 ass 5 horse, kiang, tapir, zebra 6 onager, quagga 10 rhinoceros
pinnipedia: 4 seal 6 walrus 7 sea lion
primate: 5 lemur, loris, potto 6 avahis, aye-aye, baboon,
galago, gibbon, indris, monkey, people 7 gorilla, tamarin,
tarsier 8 marmoset, simpoona 9 orangutan, tree shrew
10 chimpanzee
proboscidea: 8 elephant
rodent: 4 cavy, vole 5 coypu, gundi, hutia, mouse
6 agouti, beaver, coruro, gerbil, gopher, jerboa, nutria
7 blesmol, cane rat, hamster, lemming, mole-rat, rock
rat 8 capybara, chipmunk, dormouse, sewellel, spiny rat,
squirrel, tucu-tuco, viscacha 9 chozchori, false paca, pa-
caranas, porcupine, woodchuck 10 chinchilla, prairie dog,
springhare 11 kangaroo rat, pocket mouse, viscacha rat
13 kangaroo mouse 16 Speke's pectinator
sirenia: 6 dugong, sea cow 7 manatee
tubulidentata: 8 aardvark

Mamurius
copied: 6 Ancile

man 3 boy, guy, one 4 chap,
gent, hand, male, soul
5 equip, hubby, human, staff
6 anyone, attend, butler, fellow, fit out, helper, outfit,
people, person, spouse, waiter,
worker 7 footman, husband,
laborer, mankind, someone,
subject, workman 8 employee,
garrison, handyman, henchman, humanity, liegeman,
somebody 9 assistant, gentleman, hired hand, humankind
11 Homo sapiens
Spanish: 6 hombre

Man, first 4 Adam
12 Alalcomeneus
Nordic: 3 Ask

Man, Woman and Child
author: 10 Erich Segal

man-about-town 5 blade
7 playboy 8 cavalier, gay
blade 12 boulevardier

manacle, manacles 3 ply,
run, use 4 cope, fare, head,
rule, work 5 bonds, get on,
guide, irons, order, pilot, shift,
steer, wield 6 chains, direct,
fetter, govern, handle, make
go 7 command, conduct, control, operate, oversee, shackle,
succeed, survive, work out
8 cope with, deal with, dominate, get along, handcuff, maneuver, shackles 9 bracelets,
handcuffs, look after, supervise, watch over 10 accomplish, administer, bring about,
manipulate, put in irons, take
care of 11 be at the helm,
hand-fetters, preside over, put
in chains, superintend 12 have
charge of, hold the reins

manage 4 care, rule 6 bosses,
charge, wheels 7 bigwigs,
command, conduct, control,
dealing, running, tactics 8 big
shots, guidance, handling, ordering, planning, strategy, top
brass 9 direction, directors, operation 10 conducting, executives, overseeing, regulation
11 generality, negotiation,
supervision, supervisors, transaction 12 manipulation, organization 14 administration,
administrators
15 superintendence

manageable 4 easy 6 docile,
pliant, wieldy 8 amenable,
flexible 9 compliant, tractable
10 governable, submissive
12 controllable

management 4 boss, head
5 agent, chief 7 foreman, planner 8 overseer 9 budgeteer,
majordomo, organizer, tactician 10 impresario, negotiator,

supervisor **11** manipulator
13 administrator
14 superintendent

manager 4 boss, head **5** agent, chief **7** foreman, planner **8** overseer **9** budgeteer, majordomo, organizer, tactician **10** impresario, negotiator, supervisor **11** manipulator **13** administrator **14** superintendent

managerial 9 executive **10** management **11** supervisory **14** administrative, organizational

Managua
capital of: **9** Nicaragua

Manala *see* **7** Tuonela

Manama
capital of: **7** Bahrain

manana 6 future **8** tomorrow **11** in the future

Man and Superman
author: **17** George Bernard Shaw

Manannan
origin: **5** Irish
god of: **3** sea
father: **3** Ler, Lir

Manassa Mauler
nickname of: **11** Jack Dempsey

Manasseh
father: **6** Joseph
mother: **7** Asenath
great uncle: **4** Esau
grandfather: **5** Jacob
descendant of: **9** Manassite

man-at-arms 7 fighter, soldier, warrior **9** combatant **10** cavalryman

Manawyddan
origin: **5** Welsh
father: **4** Llyr
sister: **7** Branwen
brother: **4** Bran **9** Evnissyen
wife: **8** Rhiannon
rescued: **7** Pryderi

Manchester, William
author of: **11** The Last Lion **14** American Caesar **15** Goodbye Darkness

Manchuria *see box*

Mandalay
found in: **18** Barrack-Room Ballads
author: **14** Rudyard Kipling

mandamus
legal term: **48** writ from a superior court commanding that a thing be done
literally: **9** we command

Mandan
language family: **6** Siouan

Manchuria
also: **7** Manchow
city: **5** Aigun, Hulan, Kirin, Peian, Penki **6** Anshan, Antung, Dairen, Fu-Shun, Hailar, Harbin, Hokang, Mukden, Penchi, Yenchi **7** Hulutao, Ikuliho, Ssuping, Tantung **8** Chinchao, Paicheng, Shenyang **9** Changchun, Chiamussu, Manchouli, Miuchwang **10** Port Arthur **11** Chichihaerh, Mutanchiang
peninsula: **8** Liaotung
province: **5** Jehol, Jilin, Kirin **8** Liaoning **12** Heilongjiang, Heilungkiang
river: **4** Amur, Liao, Yalu **5** Argun, Mutan, Nonni, Tumen **6** Ussuri **7** Sungari
tribe: **5** Tungu **6** Manchu, Mongol

---

location: **11** North Dakota
ceremony: **5** Okipa

Mandarins, The
author: **16** Simone de Beauvoir

Mandasuchus
type: **8** dinosaur
period: **8** Triassic

mandate 5 edict, order **6** behest, charge, decree **7** bidding, command, dictate **8** approval, sanction **9** authority, direction, directive **10** commission, dependency **11** instruction, requisition **12** protectorate **13** authorization

mandatory 7 binding, exigent, needful **8** required **9** called for, essential, necessary, requisite **10** compulsory, imperative, obligatory, peremptory

Mande
language family: **16** Niger-Kordofanian
group: **10** Niger-Congo
includes: **3** Vai **5** Mende **7** Bambara, Malinke

Mandelbaum Gate, The
author: **11** Muriel Spark

Manderly
house in: **7** Rebecca
author: **9** Du Maurier

mandible 3 jaw **4** beak, bill, jowl **7** maxilla **8** lower jaw
part: **4** mala **5** angle, molar, ramus **6** corpus

Mandrake the Magician
creator: **7** Lee Falk **9** Phil Davis
character: **5** Narda **6** Lothar

Manes
spirits or souls of: **4** dead

Manet, Edouard
born: **5** Paris **6** France
artwork: **7** Olympia **8** The Fifer **9** Emile Zola **10** Argenteuil **12** The Guitarist **19** Le Dejeuner sur l'Herbe (Luncheon on the Grass) **25** The Bar at the Folies-Bergeres **31** Execution of the Emperor Maximilian

Manette, Dr and Lucie
characters in: **16** A Tale of Two Cities
author: **7** Dickens

maneuver 4 move, plot, ploy **5** dodge, guide, pilot, steer, trick **6** deploy, device, gambit, scheme, tactic **7** finagle **8** artifice, contrive, intrigue **9** stratagem **10** manipulate **11** contrivance, machination, pull strings

Man for All Seasons, A
director: **13** Fred Zinnemann
based on play by: **10** Robert Bolt
cast: **9** Leo McKern **10** Robert Shaw **11** Orson Welles, Wendy Hiller **12** Paul Scofield (Sir Thomas More), Susannah York **14** Nigel Davenport **15** Vanessa Redgrave
Oscar for: **5** actor (Scofield) **7** picture **8** director

Manfred
author: **21** George Gordon Lord Byron

man Friday 4 aide **8** adjutant, employee **9** assistant **10** aide de camp **12** right-hand man

Man from St Petersburg, The
author: **10** Ken Follett

Man from UNCLE, The
character: **9** Mr Waverly **12** Napoleon Solo **13** Illya Kuryakin
cast: **11** Leo G Carroll **12** Robert Vaughn **13** David McCallum
foe: **6** THRUSH

manful 5 brave **8** resolute **10** courageous

manganese
chemical symbol: **2** Mn

mangle 3 cut **4** harm, hurt, lame, maim, maul, ruin, tear **5** crush, press, slash **6** damage, impair, injure **7** flatten **8** lacerate, mutilate **9** disfigure

manhandle 4 maul 5 abuse 6 batter 7 rough up 8 maltreat, mistreat 9 pull about, push about 10 knock about, slap around

Manhattan
director: 10 Woody Allen
cast: 9 Anne Byrne
10 Woody Allen 11 Diane Keaton, Meryl Streep
13 Michael Murphy
15 Mariel Hemingway

Manhattan Transfer
author: 13 John Dos Passos

manhood 5 prime 8 legal age, machismo, majority, maleness, maturity, virility 9 adulthood, manliness, mature age
10 manfulness 11 masculinity

mania 4 rage 5 craze 6 frenzy, lunacy, raving 7 craving, madness, passion 8 delirium, delusion, dementia, fixation, hysteria, insanity 9 monomania, obsession 10 aberration, compulsion, enthusiasm, fanaticism 11 fascination, infatuation

maniac 3 ass, nut 4 fool 5 loony 6 cuckoo, madman, nitwit 7 half-wit, lunatic 9 psychotic, screwball, simpleton 10 crackbrain, psychopath

manic 2 up 4 high 7 excited, frantic, hyped up 8 agitated, frenzied, worked up 9 wrought up 10 freaked out, switched on 11 hyperactive

manifest 4 bare, open, show 5 clear, frank, plain 6 candid, evince, expose, patent, reveal, unveil 7 display, divulge, evident, exhibit, express, obvious, uncover, visible 8 apparent, disclose, evidence, indicate, palpable 9 make known 10 noticeable 11 demonstrate, make visible, self-evident, transparent, unconcealed, undisguised

manifestation 4 show 7 display, example, symptom 8 evidence, instance 10 exhibition, expression, indication, revelation 12 illustration, presentation, proclamation, public notice 13 demonstration

manifesto 4 bull 5 edict, ukase 6 notice 9 broadside, statement 10 communique, encyclical 11 declaration 12 announcement, annunciation, notification, proclamation, public notice 13 position paper, pronouncement
14 pronunciamento

manifold 4 many 6 myriad, varied 7 complex, diverse

8 multiple, numerous 9 manysided, multiform 10 variegated 11 diversified, innumerable 12 multifarious
13 multitudinous

Manila
capital of: 11 Philippines
former name: 8 Maynilad
island: 5 Luzon
landmark: 9 Rizal Park
16 San Agustin Church
river: 5 Pasig
section: 10 Quezon City
university: 10 Santo Tomas

Man in the Gray Flannel Suit, The
author: 11 Sloan Wilson

manipulate 3 pat, ply, use 4 feel, work 5 drive, pinch, wield 6 employ, finger, handle, manage, stroke 7 control, deceive, defraud, massage, operate, squeeze

Manitoba *see box*

Mankiewicz, Joseph L
director of: 6 Sleuth 9 Cleopatra 11 All About Eve (Oscar) 12 Guys and Dolls, Julius Caesar 18 The Ghost and Mrs Muir 19 A Letter to Three Wives (Oscar)

mankind 3 man 6 people 7 mortals, persons, society 8 humanity 9 humankind 11 Homo sapiens

manlike 5 macho, manly 6 virile 8 hominoid 9 masculine

manly 4 bold, male 5 brave, hardy, husky, noble 6 brawny,

daring, heroic, manful, plucky, robust, strong, sturdy, virile 7 gallant, staunch, valiant 8 athletic, fearless, malelike, muscular, powerful, resolute, stalwart, vigorous 9 masculine, strapping 10 chivalrous, courageous 11 gentlemanly, indomitable, self-reliant
12 stouthearted
Spanish: 5 macho

man-made 4 mock, sham 6 formed 7 crafted, created 8 produced 9 fashioned, ready-made, simulated, synthetic 10 artificial, fabricated, factitious, originated 11 constructed, handcrafted
12 manufactured

Mann, Delbert
director of: 5 Marty (Oscar) 14 Separate Tables

Mann, Thomas
author of: 12 Buddenbrooks 13 Death in Venice, Doctor Faustus 16 The Magic Mountain

manna, Manna 4 boon 5 award 6 reward 7 bonanza 16 divine sustenance

mannequin 4 form 5 dummy, model 6 figure

manner 3 air, way 4 form, kind, make, mode, mold, race, rank, sort, type 5 brand, breed, caste, genre, grade, guise, habit, stamp, style 6 aspect, custom, method, strain 7 bearing, conduct, fashion, species, variety 8 behavior, carriage, category, demeanor,

---

Manitoba
bay: 6 Hudson
capital: 8 Winnipeg
city: 6 Carman, The Pas 7 Brandon, Caribou, Dauphin, Selkirk 8 Flin Flon, Lynn Lake, Wabowden, Winnipeg 9 Churchill, Killarney, Sherridon, Swan River 10 St Boniface 11 Norway House, York Factory 16 Portage La Prairie
flower: 11 windflower 13 prairie crocus
Indian tribe: 4 Cree 6 Eskimo, Ojibwa 8 Chippewa 10 Assiniboin
lake: 4 God's, Swan 5 Cedar, Moose 6 Island 7 Dauphin, Red Deer 8 Manitoba, Reindeer, St Martin, Waterhen, Winnipeg 9 Granville
mountain: 4 Hart 5 Baldy
name means: 16 lake of the prairies 18 Great Spirit's strait 19 Great Spirit's narrows
nickname: 15 Prairie Province 16 Keystone Province
province of: 6 Canada
river: 3 Red 4 Seal, Swan 5 Hayes 6 Nelson, Roseau, Souris 7 Pembina 8 Winnipeg 9 Churchill 11 Assiniboine 12 Saskatchewan
university: 7 Brandon 10 St Boniface

practice, presence **9** character **10** appearance, deportment **14** classification

mannered 6 formal **7** stilted, studied **8** affected **9** contrived, unnatural **10** artificial **11** ceremonious

mannerism 4 airs, pose **5** habit **8** pretense **10** pretension **11** affectation, singularity **12** eccentricity, idiosyncrasy

mannerly 5 civil **6** polite **7** courtly, gallant, genteel, refined **8** well-bred **9** courteous **10** chivalrous **11** gentlemanly, well-behaved

manner of living
Latin: **12** modus vivendi

manner of looking at the world
German: **14** Weltanschauung

manner of speaking 7 diction **9** elocution **10** intonation **13** pronunciation

manners 6 polish **7** decorum **8** behavior, breeding, courtesy **9** amenities, deference, etiquette, gallantry, gentility, politesse, propriety **10** deportment, politeness, refinement **11** courtliness

Mannix
character: **9** Joe Mannix, Peggy Fair **10** (Lt) Adam Tobias **13** Lou Wickersham
cast: **10** Gail Fisher, Robert Reed **11** Mike Connors **16** Joseph Campanella

Mannon family
members: **4** Ezra, Orin **7** Lavinia **9** Christine
characters in: **22** Mourning Becomes Electra
author: **6** O'Neill

Manoah
son: **6** Samson

mano a mano 5 alone **8** conflict **13** confrontation, in a small group
literally: **10** hand to hand

Man of a Thousand Faces
nickname of: **9** Lon Chaney

Man of Nazareth
author: **14** Anthony Burgess

Man of Property, The
author: **14** John Galsworthy

Man of Sorrows see **5** Jesus

Manolin
character in: **18** The Old Man and the Sea
author: **9** Hemingway

Manon Lescaut
author: **11** Abbe Prevost

Manor, The
author: **19** Isaac Bashevis Singer

manor house 6 estate, manoir **7** chateau, mansion **11** stately home

manpower 4 help **5** brawn, labor **9** work force, employees

manque 6 failed, missed **7** lacking **11** fallen short, unfulfilled

Mansart, Francois
architect of: **14** Chateau de Berny **18** Hotel de la Vrilliere **33** Church of Sainte Marie de la Visitation
feature: **11** mansard roof

manservant 5 groom, valet **6** butler **7** footman **8** factotum **9** chauffeur

Man's Fate
author: **12** Andre Malraux

Mansfield, Jayne
real name: **14** Vera Jane Palmer
husband: **14** Mickey Hargitay
born: **10** Bryn Mawr PA
roles: **15** Hell on Frisco Bay **26** Will Success Spoil Rock Hunter

Mansfield, Katherine
author: **5** Bliss **12** The Dove's Nest **14** The Garden Party

Mansfield Park
author: **10** Jane Austen
character: **5** Yates **8** Mrs Grant **9** Mrs Norris, Rushworth **10** Fanny Price **11** Lady Bertram **12** Mary Crawford **13** Henry Crawford **16** Sir Thomas Bertram
Bertram children: **3** Tom **5** Julia, Maria **6** Edmund

mansion 5 manor, villa **6** castle, estate, palace **7** chateau **10** manor house

manslaughter 6 murder **7** killing **8** homicide

manta 3 ray **4** cape **5** cloak, shawl **9** devilfish

Mantegna, Andrea
born: **5** Italy **14** Isola di Carturo
artwork: **9** Parnassus **16** Camera degli Sposi (Bridal Chamber) **18** The Triumph of Caesar, The Triumph of Virtue **20** Madonna della Vittoria

Man That Corrupted Hadleyburg, The
author: **9** Mark Twain

Mantius
father: **8** Melampus
son: **6** Clitus

mantle 4 cape, film, mask, pall, veil **5** cloak, cloud, cover, scarf, tunic **6** canopy, screen, shroud **7** blanket, curtain, wrapper **8** covering, envelope, mantilla

Mantle, Mickey (Charles)
sport: **8** baseball
position: **8** outfield
team: **14** New York Yankees

manual 6 primer **8** handbook, physical, textbook, workbook **9** guidebook **10** done by hand **12** hand-operated, nonautomatic **15** instruction book

manual skill 8 deftness **9** dexterity, handiness **10** adroitness **12** coordination

manufacture 4 form, make, mold **5** build, frame **6** cook up, create, devise, invent, make up **7** concoct, fashion, produce, think up, trump up **8** assemble **9** construct, fabricate **11** mass-produce, put together

manufacturing 8 devising **9** inventing, producing **10** industrial **11** fabricating, nonagrarian

manumission 7 freeing **10** liberation **11** setting free **12** emancipation

manumit 4 free **7** set free **8** liberate **10** emancipate

manure 4 dung **5** feces **6** ordure **7** compost, excreta **8** dressing **10** fertilizer

manuscript 6 script **10** typescript **14** shooting script **15** written document

Manvah
son: **6** Samson

Man Who Came to Dinner, The
director: **15** William Keighley
based on play by: **8** Moss Hart **14** George S Kaufman
cast: **10** Bette Davis **11** Ann Sheridan, Billie Burke **12** Monty Woolley **13** Richard Travis

Man Who Fell to Earth, The
director: **12** Nicholas Roeg
cast: **7** Rip Torn **9** Buck Henry **10** Candy Clark, David Bowie

Man Who Shot Liberty Valence, The
director: **8** John Ford
cast: **9** John Wayne, Lee Marvin, Vera Miles **12** Edmund O'Brien, James Stewart

Man Who Was Thursday, The
author: **12** G K Chesterton

Man Without a Country, The
author: **17** Edward Everett Hale
character: **11** Philip Nolan

many 4 a lot, lots **5** a heap, heaps, piles **6** divers, dozens, myriad, scores, sundry **7** numbers, several, various **8** numerous **9** countless **10** a profusion, numberless **11** an abundance, innumerable **13** multitudinous

manzanita 14 Arctostaphylos
varieties: **4** dune, Ione, Otay **5** hairy, hoary, Morro, Parry, Pecho **6** island, Sonoma, woolly **7** Mexican, Pajarro, pine-mat **8** big-berry, Del Norte, Eastwood, Mariposa, Monterey, shagbark, Stanford **9** Fort Bragg, green-leaf, heart-leaf, little Sur, white-leaf **10** serpentine, silver-leaf **11** brittle-leaf, pink-bracted

map 4 plan, plot **5** chart, graph, ready **6** design, devise, lay out **7** arrange, diagram, prepare, project **8** contrive, organize **9** elevation **10** make a map of, projection **14** representation **18** topographical chart

maple 4 Acer
varieties: **3** red **4** Amur, hard, rock, soft, vine **5** black, chalk, field, hedge, Nikko, river, sugar, swamp, white **6** Balkan, canyon, Norway, Oregon, parlor, sierra, silver, Triden **7** bigleaf, Florida, Persian, scarlet, striped **8** big-tooth, Drummond, full-moon, Hawthorn, Hornbeam, Japanese, mountain, Shantung, Sycamore, Tatarian **9** ash-leaved, eagleclaw, flowering, paperbark, Schwedler, Tartarian **11** Montpellier **12** Pennsylvania **13** Rocky Mountain, Southern sugar **18** Rocky Mountain sugar

map out 3 map **5** chart, draft **6** devise, lay out **7** diagram, outline **8** block out **9** delineate, formulate

Maputo
capital of: **10** Mozambique

mar 4 hurt, maim, mark, nick, ruin, scar **5** botch, spoil, stain, taint **6** blight, damage, deface, defile, impair **7** blemish, destroy, scratch **8** diminish, mutilate **9** disfigure

Marabar Caves
setting in: **15** A Passage to India
author: **7** Forster

Maranatha
means: **9** O Lord come

maraschino
type: **7** liqueur
origin: **5** Italy
flavor: **6** cherry
color: **3** red **5** white

Marathi
language family: **12** Indo-European
branch: **11** Indo-Iranian
group: **5** Indic
spoken in: **5** (northern) India

Marathonian bull see **10** Cretan bull

marauder 6 looter, pirate, ranger **7** corsair, ravager, spoiler **8** pillager **9** buccaneer, despoiler, guerrilla, plunderer, privateer **10** depradator, freebooter

marble 3 jet **4** vein **5** agate **6** basalt, blotch, mottle, streak **7** calcite **8** dolomite **9** limestone **10** serpentine, travertine **12** anthraconite
quarry: **7** Carrara

Marble Faun, The
author: **18** Nathaniel Hawthorne
character: **5** Hilda **6** Kenyon, Miriam **9** Donatello

marbles
type: **3** mib, taw **4** aggy, duck, immy, migg **5** agate, monny, scrap **6** commie, glassy, hoodle, marine **7** cat's eye, rainbow, shooter **9** carnelian **16** peppermint stripe
term: **3** hit **4** shot **6** edgers, ringer **7** bowling, for fair, histing, lagging, lag line, lofting **8** circling, for keeps, hunching **9** pitch line **10** roundsters **11** knuckle down **13** knuckling down

Marc, Franz
born: **6** Munich **7** Germany
artwork: **10** Blue Horses **12** Yellow Horses **13** Fighting Forms

Marceline
character in: **19** The Marriage of Figaro
author: **12** Beaumarchais

march 2 go **4** hike, rise, step, trek, walk **5** tramp **6** file by, growth, parade **7** advance, proceed **8** progress **9** group walk **10** go directly, procession, walk in step **11** advancement, development, progression **12** martial music

March
event: **8** Passover **9** Mardi Gras **11** Ides of March (15) **12** Ash Wednesday **13** vernal equinox (21)
flower: **7** jonquil **8** daffodil
French: **4** Mars
gem: **10** aquamarine, bloodstone
German: **4** Marz
holiday: **6** Easter **12** St Joseph's Day (19) **13** St Patrick's Day (17)
Italian: **5** Marzo
number of days: **9** thirty-one
origin of name: **4** Mars
Roman god of: **3** war
place in year:
   Gregorian: **5** third
   Roman: **5** first
saying: **20** Beware the Ides of March **40** March comes in like a lion and goes out like a lamb
Spanish: **6** Marcha
Zodiac sign: **5** Aries **6** Pisces

March, Fredric
real name: **29** Ernest Frederick McIntyre Bickel
born: **8** Racine WI
roles: **11** A Star Is Born **12** Anna Karenina, The Buccaneer **13** Les Miserables **14** Anthony Adverse, Inherit the Wind, Mary of Scotland, Seven Days in May **16** Death of a Salesman **17** Alexander the Great, Dr Jekyll and Mr Hyde (Oscar), The Desperate Hours **18** Death Takes a Holiday **19** The Affairs of Cellini **22** The Best Years of Our Lives (Oscar) **23** Barretts of Wimpole Street

Marchen 8 folk tale **9** fairy tale

Marcheshvan 17 eighth Hebrew month

March family
members: **2** Jo **3** Amy, Meg **4** Beth **6** Marmee
characters in: **11** Little Women
author: **6** Alcott

March Hare
character in: **28** Alice's Adventures in Wonderland
author: **7** Carroll

Marchmain family
characters in: **19** Brideshead Revisited
author: **5** Waugh

Marciano, Rocky
real name: **23** Rocco Francis Marchegiano
nickname: **19** Brockton Blockbuster
sport: **6** boxing
class: **11** heavyweight

Marconi, Guglielmo
nationality: **7** Italian
nickname: **16** father of wireless
invented/discovered: **5** radio **12** radio signals **16** magnetic detector **30** wireless high frequency telegraph
shared (1919): **20** Nobel Prize for physics

Marcus Welby MD
character: **11** (Dr) Steven Kiley **13** Consuelo Lopez
cast: **11** James Brolin, Robert Young **12** Elena Verdugo

Mardi (and a Voyage Thither)
author: **14** Herman Melville
character: **4** Alma, Jarl, Mohi, Taji **5** Media, Samoa, Yoomy **6** Yillah **7** Annatoo **10** Babbalanja, Braidbeard **11** Queen Hautia

Mardi Gras 7 holiday **8** carnival, festival, jamboree **10** fat Tuesday

Marduk
also: **8** Merodach **12** Baal Merodach
origin: **10** Babylonian
chief of: **4** gods

mare 3 sea **9** brood-mare **11** female horse

mare nostrum 6 our sea
ancient Roman name for: **13** Mediterranean

mares of Diomedes see **8** Diomedes

margin 3 hem, rim **4** edge, side **5** bound, skirt, verge **6** border, fringe, leeway **7** confine **8** boundary **9** allowance, extra room, safeguard

marginal 9 on the edge **11** in the margin **12** barely useful

mariage de convenance 21 marriage of convenience

Marica
also: **9** Dea Marica
origin: **5** Roman
goddess of: **7** marshes

marigold 7 Tagetes
varieties: **3** big, bur, fig, pot **4** cape, corn, wild **5** Aztec, fetid, field, marsh, water

6 desert, French, signet **7** African **12** sweet-scented

marijuana, marihuana 3 boo, kif, pot, tea **4** hash, hemp, herb, weed **5** bhang, dagga, ganja, grass, joint **6** moocah, reefer **7** hashish **8** cannabis, locoweed, mary jane

Marin, John Cheri (3rd)
born: **12** Rutherford NJ
artwork: **8** Sea Piece **12** Maine Islands **13** Tunk Mountains **16** Beach Flint Island **19** Movement Fifth Avenue **21** Seaside Interpretation **26** Camden Mountain across the Bay

marine 3 sea **5** naval **7** aquatic, oceanic, of ships, pelagic **8** maritime, nautical, of the sea, seagoing **9** salt-water, seafaring **10** oceangoing **13** oceanographic

mariner 3 gob, tar **4** salt **5** pilot **6** sailor, sea dog, seaman **7** boatman **8** deck hand, helmsman, seafarer **9** navigator, yachtsman **10** bluejacket **12** seafaring man **16** able-bodied seaman

Marion, Francis
nickname: **8** Swamp Fox
served in: **16** Revolutionary War
type of warfare: **9** guerrilla
area fought in: **13** South Carolina
battle: **12** Eutaw Springs

marionette 6 puppet **10** fantoccino

Maris
companion of: **8** Sarpedon

marital 6 wedded, wifely **7** married, nuptial, spousal **8** conjugal **9** connubial, husbandly **10** of marriage **11** matrimonial

maritime 5 naval **6** marine **7** aquatic, coastal, oceanic, of ships **8** nautical, of the sea, seagoing **9** seafaring

marjoram
botanical name: **8** Majorana, O vulgare, Origanum **16** M hortensis moench
origin: **4** Asia **13** Mediterranean
family: **4** mint
symbol of: **5** honor **9** happiness
charm against: **10** witchcraft
used as: **12** air sweetener
use: **4** eggs, fish, meat **5** salad **8** stuffing **9** vegetable

Marjorie Morningstar
author: **10** Herman Wouk

mark 3 cut, mar, pit **4** dent, goal, harm, heed, line, mind,

nick, note, pock, rate, scar, show, sign, spot **5** badge, brand, grade, judge, label, notch, point, proof, score, stain, stamp, token, track **6** attend, bruise, deface, denote, emblem, evince, injure, intent, rating, regard, reveal, streak, symbol, target, typify **7** betoken, blemish, correct, imprint, measure, scratch, signify, suggest, symptom, write in, write on **8** bull's-eye, colophon, disclose, evidence, hallmark, indicate, manifest, point out, standard, stand for **9** be a sign of, criterion, designate, disfigure, objective, symbolize, yardstick **10** impression, indication, touchstone **11** distinguish **12** characterize **13** differentiate

Mark
also: **8** John Mark
mother: **4** Mary
cousin: **8** Barnabas
wrote: **11** Gospel

Mark (King Mark)
character in: **16** Arthurian romance

Mark Antony
also: **14** Marcus Antonius
character in: **12** Julius Caesar
author: **11** Shakespeare

mark down 4 note **5** enter, lower **6** record, reduce **7** put down **9** write down

marked 5 clear, great, noted, plain **6** dotted, scored, severe, showed, spotty, tabbed, tagged, traced **7** branded, labeled, pointed, specked, spotted, stained, tracked **8** destined, speckled, striking, targeted **9** indicated, prominent **10** emphasized, identified, made note of, noticeable, remarkable, singled out **11** conspicuous, distinctive, outstanding **12** considerable **13** distinguished

marker 3 IOU, peg, run, tab **4** chip, flag, sign **5** score **6** etcher, scorer, tablet, ticket **7** counter **8** bookmark, memorial, monument, recorder

market 4 hawk, sell, vend **5** stand **6** bourse, peddle, retail **7** grocery **9** dispose of **10** curb market, meat market **11** butcher shop, grocer's shop, marketplace

marketplace 4 mart **5** agora, arena, plaza **6** bazaar, market, square **8** exchange

Mark of Zorro, The
director: **15** Rouben Mamoulian

cast: 11 Tyrone Power
12 Linda Darnell 13 Basil
Rathbone 15 Gale
Sondergaard
score: 12 Alfred Newman

mark out 8 describe
9 delineate

marksman 8 dead shot, good
shot, sure shot 9 crack shot
12 sharpshooter

marksmanship 3 aim 5 skill
8 accuracy 13 sharpshooting

Marley's Ghost
character in: 15 A Christmas
Carol
author: 7 Dickens

Marlow
character in: 7 Lord Jim
author: 6 Conrad

Marlowe
character in: 15 Heart of
Darkness
author: 6 Conrad

Marlowe, Christopher
author of: 8 Edward II
13 Doctor Faustus, The Jew
of Malta 14 Hero and Leander 15 Edward the Second
19 Tamburlaine the Great

Marmax
suitor of: 10 Hippodamia
murdered by: 8 Oenomaus

Marmee
character in: 11 Little
Women
author: 6 Alcott

Marmion
author: 14 Sir Walter Scott
character: 11 Lord Marmion
13 Ralph de Wilton 14 Clare
Fitz-Clare 16 Archibald
Douglas 19 Constance de
Beverley

Marnie
director: 15 Alfred Hitchcock
cast: 10 Diane Baker 11 Sean
Connery, Tippi Hedren

maroon 4 plum, wine 6 desert,
strand 7 abandon, forsake, magenta 8 cast away, jettison
9 put ashore 10 cast ashore,
terra cotta 11 brownish-red,
leave behind 15 leave high
and dry

Marpessa
origin: 5 Greek
father: 6 Euenos
loved by: 4 Idas 6 Apollo
chose: 4 Idas

Marple, Miss Jane
detective created by:
14 Agatha Christie

Marquand, J P
author of: 13 Wickford

Point 18 The Late George
Apley
character: 6 Mr Moto

marquee 4 tent 6 awning, canopy 8 marquise

marred 6 ruined 7 damaged,
injured, spoiled 8 impaired
9 blemished, destroyed
10 disfigured

Marrener, Edythe
real name of: 12 Susan
Hayward

marriage 7 wedding, wedlock
8 nuptials 9 matrimony
god of: 4 Frey 5 Freyr, Hymen 9 Hymenaeus
goddess of: 3 Fri 5 Frigg,
Frija 6 Frigga, Tellus

Marriage a la Mode
author: 10 John Dryden

marriage broker
Yiddish: 8 shadchan
9 schatchen

marriage of convenience
French: 19 mariage de
convenance

Marriage of Figaro, The
also: 15 Le Nozze di Figaro
opera: 6 Mozart
character: 7 Susanna
8 Countess 9 Cherubino, Dr
Bartolo 10 Marcellina
13 Count Almaviva

Marriage of Figaro, The
author: 12 Beaumarchais
character: 6 Figaro 7 Su-
zanne 8 Cherubin 9 Marce-
line 10 Dr Bartholo
13 Count Almaviva
16 Countess Almaviva

Marriages Between Zones
Three, Four and Five
author: 12 Doris Lessing

married 3 wed 5 mated
6 joined, united, wedded
7 hitched, marital 8 combined,
espoused 9 connubial 11 matrimonial, tied the knot

married woman
German: 4 frau

marry 3 wed 7 espouse, make
one 10 get spliced, tie the
knot 13 join in wedlock
14 join in marriage, lead to
the altar, take in marriage

Marryat, Frederick
author of: 11 Peter Simple
16 Mr Midshipman Easy

Mars
also: 6 Mamers, Mavors
origin: 5 Roman
god of: 3 war
mother: 4 Juno
wife: 5 Nerio
epithet: 5 Ultor 8 Gradivus
corresponds to: 4 Ares

Mars
position: 6 fourth
nickname: 9 Red Planet
satellite: 6 Deimos, Phobos

Marseillaise 20 French national anthem

marsh 3 bog, fen 5 swamp
6 morass, slough 7 bottoms,
wetland 8 quagmire 9 everglade, marshland, quicksand

Marsh, Dame Ngaio
author of: 9 Dead Water
12 Final Curtain 13 Death
at the Bar 14 Enter a Murderer 19 Singing in the
Shrouds
character: 10 Troy Alleyn
14 Roderick Alleyn

Marsh, Reginald
born: 5 Paris 6 France
artwork: 9 The Bowery
10 Pip and Flip 14 Why Not
Use the El? 16 Tattoo and
Haircut 17 Twenty-Cent
Haircut

marshal 5 align, array, chief,
group, order 6 deploy, draw
up, gather, leader, line up,
muster 7 arrange, collect,
manager, sheriff 8 assemble,
director, marechal, mobilize,
organize 9 fire chief 10 law officer, supervisor 11 police
chief 12 chief officer, field
marshal 13 generalissimo

Marshall, George C
served in: 3 WWI 4 WWII
9 Korean War, World War
I 10 World War II
11 World War One, World
War Two
rank: 12 chief of staff
16 general of the army
author of: 12 Marshall Plan
secretary of: 5 state
7 defense
winner of: 15 Nobel Peace
Prize (1953)

Marshall, Penny
husband: 9 Rob Reiner
born: 7 Bronx NY
roles: 5 Myrna 12 The Odd
Couple 14 Laverne DeFazio
17 Laverne and Shirley
director: 3 Big

marshy 3 wet 4 miry 5 boggy,
fenny, muddy 6 swampy
7 paludal, paludic
11 waterlogged

marsupial 5 koala 6 numbat,
possum, wombat 7 cuscuse,
opossum, wallaby 8 kangaroo
9 bandicoot, phalanger
14 Tasmanian devil

Marsyas
form: 5 satyr
played: 5 flute

mart 4 show 6 market 8 exchange **9** trade fair, trade show **10** exposition

Martha
sister: **4** Mary
brother: **7** Lazarus
hometown: **7** Bethany

martial 7 hostile, Spartan, warlike **8** militant, military **9** bellicose, combative, soldierly **10** pugnacious **11** belligerent, contentious

Martian Chronicles, The
author: **11** Ray Bradbury

Martin, Dean
real name: **16** Dino Paul Crocetti
partner: **10** Jerry Lewis
born: **14** Steubenville OH
roles: **8** Matt Helm, Rio Bravo, The Caddy **9** The Stooge **10** Living It Up **12** Four for Texas, Sailor Beware **14** Toys in the Attic **15** Some Came Running **16** Artists and Models

Martin, Mary
son: **11** Larry Hagman
born: **13** Weatherford TX
roles: **6** I Do I Do **8** Peter Pan **12** Sound of Music, South Pacific

Martin, Steve
born: **6** Waco TX
roles: **7** The Jerk **17** Pennies From Heaven, Saturday Night Live **19** The Man with Two Brains **20** Dead Men Don't Wear Plaid **26** Planes Trains and Automobiles

Martin Chuzzlewit
author: **14** Charles Dickens
character: **5** Mercy **7** Charity **8** Tom Pinch **9** Pecksniff, Ruth Pinch, Sarah Gamp **10** Mark Tapley, Mary Graham **15** Jonas Chuzzlewit **17** Anthony Chuzzlewit

martinet 6 despot, tyrant **8** dictator **10** hard master, taskmaster **11** drillmaster, Simon Legree **12** little Caesar **13** authoritarian, drill-sergeant

Marty
director: **11** Delbert Mann
cast: **10** Betsy Blair **11** Joe De Santis **14** Ernest Borgnine **15** Esther Minciotti
Oscar for: **5** actor (Borgnine) **7** picture
script: **14** Paddy Chayefsky

martyr 5 saint **8** sufferer

martyrdom 5 agony **6** ordeal **7** anguish, torment, torture **9** bitter cup, suffering **10** affliction **11** cup of sorrow **13** crown of thorns

marvel 4 gape **6** be awed, rarity, wonder **7** miracle **8** be amazed **9** spectacle **10** phenomenon

Marvell, Andrew
author of: **9** The Garden **16** To His Coy Mistress

marvelous, marvellous 4 A-one, fine **5** grand, great, super **6** divine, lovely, superb **7** amazing **8** colossal, fabulous, heavenly, smashing, splendid **9** fantastic, first-rate, wonderful **10** phenomenal, remarkable, stupendous **11** astonishing, magnificent, outstanding, sensational **13** extraordinary

marvelous to relate
Latin: **13** mirabile dictu

Marwood, Mrs
character in: **16** The Way of the World
author: **8** Congreve

Marx, Bernard
character in: **13** Brave New World
author: **6** Huxley

Marx, Karl
author of: **10** Das Kapital **18** Communist Manifesto (with Friedrich Engels)

Marx Brothers 5 Chico (Leonard), Gummo (Milton), Harpo (Adolph, Arthur) Zeppo (Herbert) **7** Groucho (Julius)
costar: **14** Margaret Dumont
born: **9** New York NY
roles: **8** Coconuts, Duck Soup **11** The Big Store **13** Horse Feathers **14** A Day at the Races, Animal Crackers, Monkey Business **16** A Night at the Opera
Groucho's TV show: **14** You Bet Your Life

Mary 6 Virgin **7** Madonna **8** Holy Mary **9** Magdalene, of Cleopas **10** Virgin Mary **11** Mother of God, Regina Coeli **13** Queen of Heaven **15** Mother of Sorrows **17** Mother of the Church
mother: **4** Anna, Anne
husband: **6** Joseph **7** Alpheus, Cleopas
son: **4** Jude, Mark **5** Jesus, Moses, Simon **12** James the Less
sister: **6** Martha
brother: **7** Lazarus **8** Barnabas
cousin: **9** Elizabeth
hometown: **8** Nazareth
visitor: **7** Gabriel
flower: **4** lily **8** marigold

Mary
author: **10** Sholem Asch

Maryland see box

Mary Poppins
director: **15** Robert Stevenson
based on story by: **9** P L Travers
cast: **6** Ed Wynn **11** Dick Van Dyke (Bert), Glynis Johns **12** Julie Andrews **14** David Tomlinson **16** Hermione Baddeley
score: **13** Robert Sherman **14** Richard Sherman
Oscar for: **4** song **5** score **7** actress (Andrews) **13** visual effects
song: **14** Chim-chim-cheree

Mary Queen of Scots
director: **14** Charles Jarrott
cast: **12** Trevor Howard **13** Glenda Jackson (Elizabeth I), Timothy Dalton **14** Nigel Davenport **15** Patrick McGoohan, Vanessa Redgrave (Mary of Scotland)

Mary Tyler Moore Show, The
character: **8** Lou Grant **9** Ted Baxter **12** Gordon (Gordy) Howard, Mary Richards, Sue Ann Nivens **13** Bess Lindstrom **14** Marie Slaughter **15** Murray Slaughter **16** Phyllis Lindstrom, Rhoda Morgenstern **23** Georgette Franklin Baxter
cast: **8** John Amos **9** Ted Knight **10** Betty White **11** Edward Asner **12** Gavin MacLeod, Georgia Engel **13** Joyce Bulifant, Lisa Gerritsen, Valerie Harper **14** Cloris Leachman
setting: **11** Minneapolis

Mary Worth
creator: **8** Carey Orr **9** Dale Allen **10** Dale Connor **13** Allen Saunders
character: **4** Bill, Slim

Masaccio
real name: **26** Tommaso di Ser Giovanni di Mone
born: **5** Italy **27** Castel San Giovanni di Valdarno
artwork: **14** The Holy Trinity **15** The Tribute Money **24** The Expulsion from Paradise

Mascagni, Pietro
born: **5** Italy **7** Leghorn
composer of: **4** Iris **6** Nerone **7** Isabeau **10** Le Maschere **11** L'Amico Fritz **14** Il Piccolo Marat **19** Cavalleria Rusticana

masculine 4 bold, male **5** brave, hardy, husky, macho, manly **6** brawny, daring, manful, plucky, robust, strong, sturdy, virile **7** staunch, valiant **8** athletic, fearless, forceful, intrepid, muscular,

Maryland
 abbreviation: **2** MD
 nickname: **4** Free **7** Cockade **12** Old Line State
 capital: **9** Annapolis
 largest city: **9** Baltimore
 others: **5** Essex **6** Easton, Laurel, Towson **8** Aberdeen, Bethesda, Pocomoke **9** Frederick, Ocean City, Rockville **10** Cumberland, Hagerstown, Pikesville **11** Catonsville, College Park
 college: **4** Hood **7** Goucher, St John's **10** Washington **11** Towson State **12** Johns Hopkins **21** Annapolis Naval Academy
 feature:
  fort: **7** McHenry
  national battlesite: **8** Antietam
  presidential retreat: **9** Camp David
  race: **9** Preakness **12** Steeplechase
  racetrack: **5** Bowie **6** Butler, Laurel **7** Pimlico
 tribe: **5** Conoy **9** Nanticoke
 people: **6** Wesort **8** Terrapin **10** Spiro Agnew **11** crawthumper **14** Sargent Shriver **15** Francis Scott Key
  explorer: **7** Calvert
 lake: **8** Patapsco **9** Deep Creek, Loch Raven, Pretty Boy **10** Rocky Gorge **11** Triadelphia
 land rank: **11** forty second
 mountain: **4** Dans **8** Piedmont **9** Blue Ridge **11** Appalachian
  highest point: **8** Backbone
 physical feature:
  bay: **10** Chesapeake
  sea: **8** Atlantic
  swamp: **7** Pocoson
  valley: **5** Great **10** Hagerstown
 river: **3** Elk **7** Chester, Potomac **8** Choptank, Patapsco, Patuxent, Pocomoke **11** Susquehanna
 state admission: **7** seventh
 state bird: **15** Baltimore oriole
 state fish: **11** striped bass
 state flower: **14** black-eyed Susan
 state motto: **22** Manly Deeds Womanly Words **43** Thou Hast Crowned Us With the Shield of Thy Good Will
 state song: **18** Maryland My Maryland
 state tree: **8** white oak

powerful, resolute, vigorous **9** strapping **10** courageous **11** indomitable, self-reliant **12** stouthearted

Masefield, John
 author of: **7** Cargoes **8** Sea Fever **16** Salt Water Ballads

Maseru
 capital of: **7** Lesotho

mash 4 mush **5** crush, paste, puree, smash **6** squash **8** mishmash **9** pulverize

M*A*S*H
 character: **10** (Capt) BJ Hunnicut, (Lt Col) Henry Blake, (Maj) Frank Burns **12** (Corp) Radar O'Reilly **13** Father (John) Mulcahy, (Capt Benjamin Franklin) Hawkeye Pierce, (Col) Sherman Potter **14** (Corp) Maxwell Klinger **15** (Maj Margaret) Hot Lips Houlihan **19** (Capt

John) Trapper John McIntyre **24** (Maj) Charles Emerson Winchester
 cast: **8** Alan Alda **9** Jamie Farr **11** Harry Morgan, Loretta Swit, Mike Farrell, Wayne Rogers **12** Gary Burghoff **13** Larry Linville **15** McLean Stevenson **16** David Ogden Stiers **18** William Christopher
 war: **6** Korean
 MASH stands for: **26** Mobile Army Surgical Hospital
 tent: **5** Swamp
 theme: **17** Suicide Is Painless

M*A*S*H
 director: **12** Robert Altman
 cast: **10** Jo Ann Pflug **11** Elliot Gould (Trapper John McIntyre), Tom Skerritt (B J Hunnicut) **12** Gary Burghoff (Radar O'Reilly), Robert Duvall (Frank Burns) **14** Sally Kellerman (Margaret Hot

Lips Houlihan) **16** Donald Sutherland (Hawkeye Pierce)

masjid 6 mosque

mask 4 hide, veil **5** blind, cloak, cover **6** domino, screen, shroud **7** conceal, cover-up, curtain, obscure **8** disguise **9** face guard, false face **10** camouflage, keep secret

Mask
 director: **16** Peter Bogdanovich
 cast: **4** Cher **10** Eric Stoltz (Rocky Dennis), Sam Elliott

masked 9 concealed, covered up, disguised **10** in disguise, masquerade

Masked Ball, A
 also: **17** Un Ballo in Maschera
 opera by: **5** Verdi
 character:
  first version: **9** Count Horn **10** King Gustav **12** Count Ribbing
  second version: **3** Sam, Tom **13** Count Riccardo

masking 6 hiding **7** veiling **8** covering **9** eclipsing, obscuring **10** concealing, covering up

Mason, Bertha
 character in: **8** Jane Eyre
 author: **6** Bronte

Mason, James
 wife: **6** Pamela
 born: **7** England **12** Huddersfield
 roles: **6** Lolita **7** Lord Jim **9** Bloodline **10** Georgy Girl **13** Heaven Can Wait **14** Humbert Humbert, Murder by Decree, The Seventh Veil **15** Prisoner of Zenda **16** North by Northwest **17** The Boys from Brazil

Mason, Marsha
 husband: **9** Neil Simon
 born: **9** St Louis MO
 roles: **10** Chapter Two **11** Blume in Love **14** The Goodbye Girl **15** Max Dugan Returns **17** Cinderella Liberty

Masque of the Red Death, The
 author: **13** Edgar Allan Poe

masquerade 4 mask, ruse, veil **5** cloak, cover, guise, trick **6** masque, pose as, screen, shroud **7** cover-up, pretext **8** artifice, pretense **9** bal masque **10** camouflage, masked ball, subterfuge **11** impersonate **12** harlequinade

Masquerade Party
 host: **9** Bert Parks **10** Bud

Collier **11** Peter Donald
12 Eddie Bracken, Robert Q
Lewis **14** Douglas Edwards

mass, Mass 3 jam, lot, mob
4 body, bulk, cake, clot, heap,
host, hunk, knot, lump, pack,
pile **5** amass, batch, block,
bunch, chunk, clump, corps,
crowd, crush, group, horde,
press, stack, troop **6** bundle,
gather, matter, throng,
weight **7** collect, pyramid
8 assemble, best part, main
body, majority, material **9** aggregate, Eucharist, gathering,
plurality **10** accumulate, assemblage, assortment, collection, concretion, congregate,
cumulation, lion's share
11 aggregation, consolidate,
greater part **12** accumulation,
congregation **13** Holy Communion, holy sacrament, preponderance **14** conglomeration

Massachusetts *see box*

massacre 7 butcher, carnage
8 butchery, decimate **9** bloodbath, slaughter **10** mass murder **12** bloodletting

massage 3 rub **4** flex **5** chafe,
knead **6** finger, handle, stroke
7 rubbing, rub down, stretch
8 kneading, stroking **10** manipulate **12** manipulation

Massasoit *see*
10 Wampanoags

**Massenet, Jules Emile
Frederic**
born: **6** France **9** St Etienne
composer of: **5** Le Cid,
Manon, Thais **7** Werther
9 Herodiade **11** David Riz-
zio **12** Don Quichotte **13** Le
Roi de Lahore **21** Le Jongleur de Notre-Dame

masses 6 plebes, proles, rabble, the mob **7** the many
8 the crowd **9** hoi polloi, plebeians **11** the populace, the
riffraff **12** the multitude **13** the
common herd **14** the proletariat, the rank and file **15** the
common people, the lower
classes, the working class
16 the great unwashed

Masset *see* **10** Skidegatta

massive 4 huge, vast **5** ample,
bulky, great, heavy, hefty,
massy, solid **7** hulking, immense, mammoth, titanic,
weighty **8** colossal, enormous,
gigantic, imposing, towering,
whopping **9** cyclopean, extensive, monstrous, ponderous
10 gargantuan, impressive,
monumental, stupendous
11 elephantine, substantial

massiveness 4 bulk, size

Massachusetts
abbreviation: **2** MA **4** Mass
nickname: **3** Bay **7** Puritan **9** Baked Bean, Old Colony
capital/largest city: **6** Boston
others: **4** Ayer, Lynn, Otis **5** Athol, Barre, Lenox, Salem
6 Agawam, Dedham, Groton, Nahant, Natick, Revere,
Saugus, Woburn **7** Belmont, Beverly, Concord, Danvers,
Everett, Holyoke, Ipswich, Medford, Peabody, Taunton,
Waltham **8** Brockton, Chicopee, Cohasset, Plymouth, Sci-
tuate, Yarmouth **9** Arlington, Attleboro, Braintree, Brookline, Cambridge, Lexbridge, Lexington, Worcester
10 Gloucester, New Bedford, Pittsfield **11** Springfield
12 Provincetown, Williamstown
college: **3** MIT **5** Clark, Curry, Smith, Tufts **6** Babson
7 Amherst, Harvard, Simmons, Wheaton **8** Brandeis, Williams **9** Hampshire, Holy Cross, Merrimack, Radcliffe,
Wellesley **11** Springfield **12** Mount Holyoke, Northeast-
ern **13** Boston College
feature: **10** Walden Pond **12** Plymouth Rock
national seashore: **7** Cape Cod
village: **13** Old Sturbridge
tribe: **6** Nauset **8** Pocomtuc **10** Wampanoags
people: **8** Pilgrims **9** Amy Lowell, Elias Howe **10** Cyrus
Field, Eli Whitney **11** Clara Barton, John Hancock, Samuel Adams, Samuel Morse **12** Henry Thoreau, Robert
Lowell, Winslow Homer **13** James Whistler, Joseph Kennedy, Robert Kennedy **14** Emily Dickinson **15** Henry Cabot Lodge **16** Benjamin Franklin, Edward "Ted"
Kennedy **17** Ralph Waldo Emerson **18** Bartholomew Gos-
nold, James Russell Lowell, Nathanial Hawthorne
19 Oliver Wendell Holmes, William Cullen Bryant
21 John Greenleaf Whittier
explorer: **8** Norsemen
island: **5** Duke's **9** Nantucket **13** Chappaquidick **15** Martha's Vineyard
lake: **5** Onota **7** Quabbin, Rohunta, Webster **8** Long Pond
11 Watuppa Pond **16** Assawompsett Pond
17 Chaubunagungamaug
land rank: **10** forty-fifth
mountain: **3** Tom **6** Brodie, Potter **7** Alander, Everett, Taconic **10** Berkshires
highest point: **8** Greylock
physical feature:
bay: **8** Buzzard's
cape: **3** Ann, Cod
sea: **8** Atlantic
president: **9** John Adams **14** Calvin Coolidge **15** John
Quincy Adams **21** John Fitzgerald Kennedy
river: **6** Nashua **7** Charles, Concord, Quaboag, Taunton
8 Chicopee **9** Deerfield, Merrimack **10** Blackstone, Housatonic **11** Connecticut
state admission: **11** thirty-sixth
state bird: **9** chickadee
state flower: **9** mayflower **15** trailing arbutus
state motto: **37** With the Sword She Seeks Peace Under
Liberty **45** By the Sword We Seek Peace But Peace Only
Under Liberty
state song: **22** All Hail to Massachusetts
state tree: **11** American elm

8 enormity, hugeness, vastness **9** amplitude, bulkiness,
greatness, immensity, largeness, magnitude

mast 4 main, nuts, pole, post,
spar **5** spirit, staff, stick, stuff
6 acorns, pillar **9** beechnuts,
chestnuts

type: **4** fore, main **6** jigger,
mizzen
support: **4** bibb

master 3 ace **4** able, A-one,
best, boss, curb, deft, head,
lord, main, tame, whiz
5 check, chief, crack, grasp,
owner, prime, ruler **6** bridle,

choice, expert, genius, gifted, govern, leader, manage, subdue, wizard **7** conquer, control, excel at, head man, manager, primary, skilled, skipper, supreme **8** director, dominate, finished, governor, masterly, overcome, overlord, overseer, regulate, suppress, talented, virtuoso **9** authority, conqueror, craftsman, firstrate, paramount, practiced, principal **10** controller, proficient, supervisor **12** get the hang of, ship's captain

Master Builder, The
  author: **11** Henrik Ibsen

master craftsman 7 artisan **12** masterworker **13** skilled worker

masterful 4 able, deft **5** bossy **6** expert, superb **7** dynamic, skilled **8** finished, forceful, masterly, resolute, skillful, virtuoso **9** excellent **10** commanding **11** domineering, selfreliant **12** accomplished, strong-willed **13** authoritarian, self-confident

masterfulness 6 genius **10** capability, competence, excellence **11** proficiency

Master Melvin
  nickname of: **6** Mel Ott

mastermind 4 plan, sage **6** direct, expert, genius, master, pundit, wizard **7** old hand, planner **8** conceive, director, engineer, organize, virtuoso **9** authority, initiator, organizer **10** specialist **11** moving force

Master of Ballantrae, The
  author: **20** Robert Louis Stevenson
  character: **4** Chew **5** Teach **9** MacKellar **11** Henry Durrie, James Durrie **12** Alison Graeme, Francis Burke, Secundra Dass

master of the family
  Latin: **13** paterfamilias

masterpiece 5 jewel, prize **7** classic, paragon **8** monument, treasure **9** nonpareil **10** brainchild **11** chef d'oeuvre, ne plus ultra, prizewinner

Masterpiece Theater
  host: **13** Alistair Cooke

master race
  German: **10** Herrenvolk

Masters, Edgar Lee
  author of: **19** Spoon River Anthology

Mastersingers of Nuremberg, The
  also: **27** Die Meistersinger von Nurnberg
  opera by: **6** Wagner
  character: **9** Eva Pogner, Hans Sachs **10** Beckmesser **18** Walther von Stolzing

mastery 4 rule, sway **5** grasp **7** ability, command, control **8** deftness, whip hand **9** dominance, supremacy, upper hand **10** adroitness, attainment, domination, leadership **11** achievement, acquirement, proficiency, superiority **14** accomplishment

masticate 4 chew, gnaw **5** champ, munch **6** nibble

Mastroianni, Marcello
  born: **5** Italy **11** Fontana Liri
  roles: **13** Eight and a Half **7** La Notte **11** La Dolce Vita, The Stranger, White Nights **19** Divorce Italian Style

mat 3 dim, pad, rug **4** dead, dull, flat **5** doily, muted **6** carpet, matrix, tangle **7** bedding, bolster, coaster, cushion, support **8** entangle **10** lackluster, lusterless
  Japanese: **6** tatami

Mata Hari
  real name: **21** Gertrud Margarete Zelle
  worked as: **3** spy **6** dancer
  worked for: **7** Germans
  executed by: **6** French

match 3 fit **4** game, join, mate, meet, pair, peer, suit, twin, yoke **5** adapt, agree, equal, event, unite **6** couple, double, oppose **7** be alike, be equal, combine, connect, contend, contest, vie with **8** parallel **9** companion, duplicate, harmonize **10** correspond, equivalent, tournament **11** competition, counterpart

matched 5 equal **8** of a piece **9** identical **11** coordinated

matching 4 twin **5** equal **6** paired **10** equivalent **11** harmonizing **13** corresponding

matchless 4 rare **7** supreme **8** crowning, foremost, peerless, sterling, superior **9** exemplary, first rate, priceless, paramount, unequaled, unmatched, unrivaled **10** invaluable, preeminent, unbeatable, unexcelled **11** inestimable, superlative, unsurpassed **12** incomparable, unparalleled

matchmaker
  Yiddish: **8** shadchan **9** schatchen

mate 3 pal **4** chum, twin,

wife **5** buddy, crony, hubby, match **6** couple, friend, spouse **7** cohabit, comrade, consort, husband, pair off, partner **8** copulate, coworker, sidekick **9** associate, colleague, companion, duplicate **10** better half, equivalent **11** confederate, counterpart **12** fellow worker, ship's officer

materfamilias 15 mother of a family

material 5 stuff **6** matter **8** elements **9** substance **12** constituents

materialism 5 greed **12** covetousness **15** acquisitiveness

materialistic 6 greedy **8** covetous, grasping **11** acquisitive, unspiritual

materiality 9 existence **11** tangibility

materialization 5 ghost, shade **6** coming, wraith **7** phantom, specter **9** emergence **10** apparition, appearance **13** manifestation

materialize 4 loom, rise, show **5** bob up, issue, pop up **6** appear, crop up, emerge, turn up **9** come forth **10** burst forth **11** come to light, spring forth **12** come into view

materially 7 vitally **8** palpably, tangibly **9** in the main, seriously **10** monetarily **11** corporeally, essentially, financially, in substance **12** considerably, emphatically **13** significantly, substantially **14** for the most part

material possessions 6 assets, estate, wealth **7** fortune **8** property **10** belongings **12** worldly goods

material proof 8 evidence **13** documentation

materials 4 data **5** cloth, facts, notes, tools **6** stocks, stores, timber **7** fabrics, figures **8** concrete, dry goods, supplies, textiles **9** citations, equipment, machinery, yard goods **10** essentials, piece goods, quotations, references **11** impressions **12** observations **15** bricks and mortar

materiel 4 gear **6** stores **8** supplies **9** equipment, materials **10** provisions **16** military supplies

Mater Matuta *see* **6** Matuta

maternal 4 fond **6** doting **8** motherly **9** of a mother, shielding **10** motherlike, protective, sheltering

maternity 5 labor **8** delivery
9 pregnancy **10** childbirth,
motherhood **11** parturition
12 accouchement, childbearing

Mater Turrita *see* **6** Cybele

**mathematical, mathematic
5** exact, rigid **6** strict **7** precise **8** accurate, rigorous, unerring **10** meticulous,
scientific, scrupulous **11** punctilious, well-defined
13 computational

mathematician
American: 5 Aiken **6** Wiener
British: 6 Newton **7** Babbage
French: 6 Fermat **9** D'Alembert, Descartes
German: 5 Frege, Gauss
6 Bessel **7** Hilbert
Greek: 6 Euclid, Thales
11 Anaximander
Norwegian: 4 Abel
Swiss: 5 Euler **9** Bernoulli

Mathewson, Christy
nickname: 5 Matty **6** Big Six
sport: 8 baseball
position: 7 pitcher
team: 13 New York Giants

Matholwych
king of: 7 Ireland
wife: 7 Branwen

matinee 9 early show **16** early
performance **20** afternoon
performance

Mating Season, The
author: 11 P G Wodehouse

Matisse, Henri Emile Benoit
born: 6 France **16** Chateau
Cambresis (Le Cateau)
artwork: 5 Dance, Music
8 The Slave **10** Odalisques
11 Joie de Vivre **12** Harmony in Red, La Serpentine **13** Head with Tiara,
The Open Window **15** Bathers by a River, Memory of
Oceanie, Woman with the
Hat **16** Heads of Jeannette
19 Torso with Arms Raised
20 Goldfish and Sculpture

Matralia
origin: 5 Roman
event: 8 festival

matriarch 7 dowager **10** female head, grande dame
11 female ruler **12** female
leader **13** materfamilias

matriculate 4 join **5** enter
6 enlist, enroll, sign up
7 check in **8** register

matriculation 9 signing up
10 enrollment **12** registration

matrimonial 6 bridal, wedded,
wifely **7** marital, married, nuptial, spousal **8** conjugal, hymeneal **9** affianced, connubial,
husbandly **11** epithalamic

matrimony 7 wedlock **8** marriage **11** holy wedlock

matrix 3 die **4** cast, form,
mold **5** frame, punch, stamp

matron 4 dame **5** madam
7 dowager **8** forelady, mistress,
overseer **9** forewoman **10** directress **11** housekeeper
12 married woman
14 superintendent

Matronalia
origin: 5 Roman
event: 8 festival

matter 3 fix **4** gist, snag, text
5 count, drift, event, sense,
stuff, theme, thing, topic **6** affair, crisis, import, moment,
object, scrape, strait, thesis
7 content, dilemma, episode,
essence, purport, signify, subject, trouble **8** argument, business, elements, exigency,
material, obstacle, quandary
9 adventure, emergency, happening, situation, substance
10 difference, difficulty, experience, impediment, importance,
occurrence, perplexity, proceeding **11** carry weight, consequence, predicament,
transaction **12** circumstance,
significance

matter-of-course 5 usual
6 common **7** routine **8** everyday, ordinary, standard **9** customary **11** commonplace,
established

matter-of-fact 4 real **5** blunt,
frank **6** candid, direct **7** factual, literal, mundane, natural,
prosaic **8** ordinary, sensible
9 outspoken, practical, pragmatic, realistic **10** hardheaded,
no-nonsense, unaffected, uninspired, unromantic **11** commonplace, common-sense,
down-to-earth, straight-out
13 unimaginative, unsentimental **15** straightforward

matter-of-factness 10 detachment **11** impassivity
12 practicality **13** impassiveness **17** unimaginativeness

Matter of Time, A
author: 12 Jessamyn West

Matthau, Walter
real name: 13 Walter Matthow **23** Walter
Matuschanskavasky
born: 9 New York NY
roles: 5 Kotch **8** A New Leaf
10 Plaza Suite **11** Pete n Tillie **12** Bad News Bears, Ensign Pulver, Oscar Madison,
The Front Page, The Odd
Couple **15** California Suite,
The Sunshine Boys **16** The
Fortune Cookie **22** A Guide
for the Married Man

Matthew 7 apostle
father: 7 Alpheus
also called: 4 Levi
wrote: 6 Gospel

Matthiessen, Peter
author of: 10 Sand Rivers
14 The Snow Leopard

maturation 6 growth **8** fruition, ripening **9** growing up

mature 4 ripe **5** adult, bloom,
grown, manly, of age, ready,
ripen **6** flower, grow up, mellow, nubile, virile **7** blossom,
develop, grown-up, matured,
womanly **8** finished, maturate,
seasoned **9** come of age, completed, full-blown, full-grown,
perfected, practiced **10** middle-aged **11** become adult, experienced, full-fledged, in one's
prime **12** marriageable

Mature, Victor
born: 12 Louisville KY
roles: 7 The Robe **11** After
the Fox, Kiss of Death
12 Cry of the City, One
Million BC **16** Samson and
Delilah **19** Androcles and
the Lion

matured 3 big **4** aged, ripe
5 adult, grown **6** formed **7** ripened **8** flowered, mellowed,
seasoned **9** blossomed, developed, full-blown, full-grown
11 full-fledged

maturity 7 manhood **8** legal
age, majority, practice, ripeness **9** adulthood, composure,
full bloom, readiness, seasoning, womanhood **10** completion, experience, full growth,
maturation, matureness, perfection **11** culmination, fulfillment **12** age of consent

Matuschanskavasky, Walter
real name of: 13 Walter
Matthau

Matuta
origin: 5 Roman
goddess of: 3 sea **4** dawn
7 harbors **10** childbirth
called: 11 Mater Matuta

Maud
author: 18 Alfred Lord
Tennyson

Maude
character: 5 Carol **7** Phillip
10 Henry Evans **12** Florida
Evans, Maude Findlay, Mrs
Naugatuck **13** Walter Findlay **14** Dr Arthur Harmon
20 Vivian Cavender Harmon
cast: 8 Bill Macy, John
Amos **10** Conrad Bain
11 Esther Rolle **13** Brian
Morrison, Rue McClanahan
14 Beatrice Arthur, Kraig
Metzinger **15** Adrienne Barbeau **16** Hermione Baddeley

spinoff from: 14 All in the Family
spinoff: 9 Good Times

maudlin 5 gushy, mushy, teary **6** slushy **7** gushing, mawkish, tearful **8** bathetic **9** emotional **10** lachrymose **11** sentimental **13** overemotional

maudlinism 6 bathos **11** mawkishness **14** sentimentalism, sentimentality

Maugham, W Somerset
author of: 9 The Circle **10** Our Betters **11** Cakes and Ale **12** Miss Thompson **13** The Razor's Edge **14** Of Human Bondage **15** The Constant Wife **18** The Moon and Sixpence **21** Lady Frederick Ashenden

maul 4 beat **5** stomp **6** batter, beat up, bruise, mangle, pummel, thrash **7** rough up **9** manhandle **10** knock about

Mauldin, Bill
creator/artist of: 7 Up Front **12** Willie and Joe

maunder 4 loaf **5** drift, run on, stray **6** babble, dawdle, gabble, gibber, ramble, wander **7** blather, meander, prattle, saunter **8** flounder, ramble on, straggle **9** go on and on, hem and haw **10** dillydally

maundering 7 diffuse **8** rambling **9** wandering **10** digressive, disjointed, roundabout **14** drift, run on, stray **6** babble, dawdle, gabble, gibber, ramble, wander **7** blather, meander, prattle, saunter **8** flounder **9** go on and on, hem and haw **10** dillydally

Maupassant, Guy de
author of: 6 Belami **9** Ball of Fat, Mont-Oriol **11** A Woman's Life, The Necklace **12** Ball of Tallow **16** Mademoiselle Fifi

Mauriac, Francois
author of: 8 Genitrix **10** The Egoists **12** Viper's Tangle **15** A Kiss to the Leper, The Desert of Love **20** A Woman of the Pharisees

Mauritania *see box*

Mauritius *see box*

mausoleum 10 family tomb **11** stately tomb **18** sepulchral monument

mauve 4 plum, puce **5** lilac **6** violet **8** lavender **11** light purple **12** bluish purple

maverick 5 loner **8** yearling **9** dissenter, dissident, eccentric **11** independent **13** individualist, noncomformist

Maverick
character: 12 Bart Maverick,

Mauritius
other name: 11 Ile de France
capital/largest city:
9 Port Louis
others: 6 Reduit **8** Curepipe **9** Mahebourg **13** Quartre Bornes **19** Grande Riviere Sud-Est
head of state: 14 British monarch **15** governor general
monetary unit: 4 cent **5** rupee
island: 3 Est **4** Flat **5** Ambre, Cerf's, Morne, Round **7** Agalega, Serpent **9** Mauritius, Rodrigues, Rodriguez, St Brandon **12** Gunner's Quoin **15** Cargados Carajos
highest point: 27 Piton de la Petite Riviere Noire
sea: 6 Indian
people: 6 Creole, French, Indian **7** African, Chinese **8** European **13** Indo-Mauritian
  leader: **8** Jugnauth **9** Ramgoolam
  ruler: **5** Dutch **6** French **7** English
language: 4 Urdu **5** Hindi, Tamil **6** Creole, French

Mauritania
capital/largest city: 10 Nouakchott
others: 4 Atar **5** Kaedi, Rosso **6** Fderik **7** Akjoujt **10** Nouadhibou
division: 5 Sahel **7** Chemama
monetary unit: 5 khoum **7** ouguiya
highest point: 11 Kediat Idjil
river: 7 Senegal
sea: 8 Atlantic
physical feature:
  desert: **6** Sahara
  valley: **7** Chemama **12** Senegal River
people: 4 Arab, Fula, Moor **5** Black, Fulbe, Wolof **6** Bafour, Berber, Fulani **7** African, Soninke, Tukulor **8** Sarakole **9** Sarakolle **10** Toucouleur **12** Halphoolaren
  leader: **4** Luly **5** Salek **6** Daddah **8** Haidalla
  ruler: **6** France **9** Almoravid **14** Kingdom of Ghana
language: 4 Fula **5** Wolof **6** Arabic, French **7** Phoolor, Tukulor **8** Fulfulde, Mandingo **9** Sarakolle, Hassaniya
religion: 5 Islam
place:
  mosque: **5** Grand
feature:
  beehive hut: **4** ruga
  priest-teacher: **8** marabout
  waterskin: **6** guerba
food:
  dish: **7** meshuri
  tea: **5** attay

Bret Maverick **13** Brent Maverick **16** Samantha Crawford **24** Cousin Beauregard Maverick
cast: 9 Jack Kelly **10** Roger Moore **11** James Garner **13** Diane Brewster, Robert Colbert

Mavors *see* **4** Mars

maw 4 craw, crop, jaws **5** mouth **6** gullet, muzzle, throat

mawkish 5 gushy, mushy, teary **7** maudlin, tearful **9** emotional, nostalgic, schmaltzy **10** lachrymose **11** sentimental **15** oversentimental

mawkishness 4 mush **5** slush **6** bathos **9** mushiness, soppiness **10** maudlinism, slushiness **14** sentimentalism, sentimentality

maxim 3 saw **4** rule **5** adage, axiom, motto **6** old saw, saying, truism **7** proverb **8** aphorism, apothegm **9** platitude

MAX-VON Sydow

Maximes
author: 23 Francois La Rochefoucauld

Maxims of the Law
author: 12 Francis Bacon

maximum 3 top 4 most 6 utmost 7 highest, largest, maximal, optimum, supreme 8 foremost, greatest 9 paramount 11 unsurpassed

---

May
characteristic: 7 Maypole 13 queen of the May
flower: 8 hawthorn 15 lily of the valley
French: 3 Mai
gem: 7 emerald
German: 3 Mai
holiday: 6 May Day (1) 10 Mother's Day (2nd Sunday) 11 Memorial Day (last Monday) 14 Armed Forces Day (3rd Saturday)
Italian: 6 Maggio
number of days: 9 thirty-one
origin of name: 4 Maia
  Roman goddess of: 6 spring
place in year:
  Gregorian: 5 fifth
  Roman: 5 third
saying: 27 April showers bring May flowers
Spanish: 4 Mayo
Zodiac sign: 6 Gemini, Taurus

May, Elaine
real name: 12 Elaine Berlin
partner: 11 Mike Nichols
born: 14 Philadelphia PA
roles: 8 A New Leaf 15 California Suite
director of: 16 The Heartbreak Kid
writer/director of: 8 A New Leaf

Maya
city: 4 Coba 5 Tulum, Uxmal 6 Akumal, Cuello, Izamal 8 Calakmul, Palenque 11 Chichen Itza
conqueror: 8 Alvarado
day: 5 uayeb
language family: 5 Mayan 10 Maya-Quiche
location: 5 Tikal 6 Belize, Mexico 7 Chiapas, Mayapan, Tabasco, Yucatan 8 Honduras 9 Guatemala 11 Chichen Itza 14 Central America
month: 5 uinal 6 uninal
noted for: 9 astronomy

12 architecture 19 hieroglyphic writing
rain god: 4 Chac 5 Chaac 7 Chac Mol 8 Chac Mool
ruins: 9 Yaxchilan 20 Temple of Inscriptions
underworld: 7 Xibalba
year: 4 haab

maybe 6 mayhap 7 perhaps 8 feasibly, possibly 9 perchance 10 God willing, imaginably 11 conceivably 12 peradventure

Maybe
author: 14 Lillian Hellman

Mayberry RFD
character: 5 Alice 7 Aunt Bee 8 Sam Jones 9 Mike Jones 10 Goober Pyle 11 Emmett Clark 13 Howard Sprague, Millie Swanson
cast: 8 Ken Berry 10 Jack Dodson 11 Buddy Foster, Paul Hartman 13 Alice Ghostley, Arlene Golonka, Frances Bavier, George Lindsey

mayfly
varieties: 5 small 6 stream 9 burrowing

mayhem 4 maim 6 felony 7 battery, cripple 8 mutilate, violence 9 crippling, dismember 10 mutilation 13 disfigurement

may he rest in peace
Latin: 16 requiescat in pace

may it do good
Latin: 6 prosit

Maylie, Mrs and Rose
characters in: 11 Oliver Twist
author: 7 Dickens

Mayo, Virginia
real name: 13 Virginia Jones
husband: 12 Michael O'Shea
born: 9 St Louis MO
roles: 17 The West Point Story 22 The Best Years of Our Lives 26 The Secret Life of Walter Mitty

Mayor of Casterbridge, The
author: 11 Thomas Hardy
character: 13 Donald Farfrae, Richard Newson 14 Lucetta Le Sueur 15 Michael Henchard 19 Elizabeth Jane Newson, Susan Henchard-Newson

Mays, Willie
nickname: 9 Say Hey Kid
sport: 8 baseball
position: 11 center field
team: 11 New York Mets 13 New York Giants 18 San Francisco Giants

may she live forever
Latin: 12 esto perpetua
motto: 5 Idaho

may she rest in peace
Latin: 16 requiescat in pace

maze 5 snarl 6 jungle, tangle 7 complex, meander, network 9 labyrinth 11 convolution

mazel tov 8 good luck

Mbabane
capital of: 9 Swaziland

McCambridge, Mercedes
real name: 32 Carlotta Mercedes Agnes McCambridge
born: 8 Joliet IL
roles: 5 Giant 8 Cimarron 11 Touch of Evil 14 All the King's Men 15 A Farewell to Arms 18 Suddenly Last Summer

McCarey, Leo
director of: 8 Duck Soup 10 Going My Way (Oscar) 13 The Awful Truth (Oscar) 15 Ruggles of Red Gap 17 The Bells of St Mary's

McCarthy, Mary
author of: 8 The Group

McCay, Winsor
creator/artist of: 23 Little Nemo in Slumberland

McClellan, George B
nickname: 25 Little Mac the Young Napoleon
served in: 8 Civil War 10 Mexican War
side: 5 Union
commander of: 16 Army of the Potomac
battle: 8 Antietam 18 Peninsular campaign
governor of: 9 New Jersey

McCloud
character: 10 Sam McCloud 13 Chris Coughlin, (Sgt) Joe Broadhurst 14 Peter B Clifford
cast: 8 JD Cannon 11 Terry Carter 12 Dennis Weaver, Diana Muldaur

McClure, Darrell
creator/artist of: 17 Little Annie Rooney

McCrea, Joel
wife: 10 Frances Dee
born: 12 Los Angeles CA
roles: 11 Buffalo Bill 14 Palm Beach Story 16 Sullivan's Travels, The Great Man's Lady 17 Reaching for the Sun, The More the Merrier 20 Foreign Correspondent

McCreary, Fainy (Mac)
character in: 3 USA
author: 9 Dos Passos

McCullers, Carson
author of: 17 The Mortgaged Heart 18 Member of the Wedding 21 The Ballad of the Sad Cafe 23 Reflections

in a Golden Eye, The Heart Is a Lonely Hunter

McCullough, Colleen
author of: **13** The Thornbirds **19** An Indecent Obsession

McCutcheon, George Barr
author of: **9** Graustark

McEvoy, JP
creator/artist of: **10** Dixie Dugan

McFee, William
author of: **15** Casuals of the Sea

McGillicuddy, Cornelius Alexander
real name of: **10** Connie Mack

McGinley, Phyllis
author of: **12** Three Decades **15** A Pocketful of Wry **24** The Horse Who Lived Upstairs

McHale's Navy
character: **7** Christy **9** Willy Moss **11** Fuji Kobiaji, Happy Haines **12** Harrison (Tinker) Bell, Lester Gruber **13** Virgil Farrell, (Ensign) Charles Parker, (Lt Cdr) Quinton McHale **14** (Lt) Elroy Carpenter **18** (Capt) Wallace B Binghamton
cast: **8** Joe Flynn **9** Tim Conway **10** Billy Sands, Gary Vinson, John Wright, Yoshio Yoda **11** Bob Hastings, Edson Stroll **12** Gavin MacLeod **14** Carl Ballantine, Ernest Borgnine

McKenna, Siobhan
born: **7** Belfast, Ireland
roles: **11** King of Kings **13** Doctor Zhivago **14** Of Human Bondage **24** Playboy of the Western World

McKim, Charles M
architect of: **27** Lutheran Church of the Redeemer (Houston)

McKim, Mead, and White
partners: **13** Stanford White **18** Charles Follen McKim **21** William Rutherford Mead
architects of: **11** Century Club **14** University Club, Washington Arch **17** Vanderbilt Mansion **18** Columbia University (NYC) **19** Boston Public Library, Pennsylvania Station (NYC), (first) Madison Square Garden (NYC) **21** New York Herald Building, Pierpont Morgan Library (NYC) **31** Madison Square Presbyterian Church
style: **7** Shingle **18** Italian Renaissance

McKinley, William
nickname: **13** Major McKinley
presidential rank: **11** twenty-fifth
party: **10** Republican
state represented: **2** OH
defeated: **4** (Eugene Victor) Debs **5** (Seth Hockett) Ellis, (William Jennings) Bryan **6** (John McCauley) Palmer, (Wharton) Barker **7** (Charles Eugene) Bentley, (John Granville) Woolley, (Jonah Fitz Randolph) Leonard **8** (Charles Horatio) Matchett, (Joseph Francis) Malloney, (Joshua) Levering
vice president: **6** (Garret Augustus) Hobart **9** (Theodore) Roosevelt
cabinet:
  state: **3** (John Milton) Hay, (William Rufus) Day **7** (John) Sherman
  treasury: **4** (Lyman Judson) Gage
  war: **4** (Elihu) Root **5** (Russell Alexander) Alger
  attorney general: **4** (Philander Chase) Knox **6** (John William) Griggs **7** (Joseph) McKenna
  navy: **4** (John Davis) Long
  postmaster general: **4** (James Albert) Gary **5** (Charles Emory) Smith
  interior: **5** (Cornelius Newton) Bliss **9** (Ethan Allen) Hitchcock
  agriculture: **6** (James) Wilson
born: **7** Niles OH
died: **9** Buffalo NY
  died by: **13** assassination
buried: **8** Canton OH
education:
  college: **10** Allegheny
  law school: **6** Albany
religion: **9** Methodist
author: **37** The Tariff in the Days of Henry Clay and Since
political career: **24** US House of Representatives
  governor of: **4** Ohio
civilian career: **6** lawyer
military service: **7** captain **8** Civil War **11** brevet major
notable events of lifetime/term:
  Act: **13** Dingley Tariff
  Peace Conference: **5** Hague
  Treaty of: **5** Paris
  war with: **5** Spain
father: **7** William
mother: **5** Nancy (Campbell Allison)
siblings: **4** Anna, Mary **5** Abner, Helen, James **10** Abbie Celia **12** David Allison **14** Sarah Elizabeth
wife: **3** Ida (Saxton)
children: **3** Ida **9** Katherine

McManus, George
creator/artist of: **12** The Newlyweds **16** Bringing Up Father

McMath, Virginia Katherine
real name of: **12** Ginger Rogers

McMeekan, Wayne
real name of: **10** David Wayne

McMillan, Edwin Mattison
field: **7** physics **9** chemistry
developed:
  16 synchrocyclotron
awarded: **10** Nobel Prize

McMillan and Wife
character: **7** Mildred **13** Sally McMillan **14** (Sgt) Charles Enright **15** (Commissioner) Stewart McMillan
cast: **10** John Schuck, Rock Hudson **11** Nancy Walker **15** Susan Saint James

McMurtry, Larry
author of: **10** Texasville **12** Lonesome Dove **14** Horseman Pass By **18** The Last Picture Show

McPhee, John
author of: **16** In Suspect Terrain **20** Coming into the

Country **23** The Curve of Binding Energy **26** Encounters with the Archdruid

McQueen, Steve
real name: **21** Terrence Steven McQueen
wife: **10** Ali MacGraw
born: **8** Slater MO **14** Indianapolis IN
roles: **7** Bullitt, The Blob **8** Papillon **14** The Great Escape, The Sand Pebbles **16** The Cincinnati Kid **17** Thomas Crown Affair, Wanted Dead or Alive **19** The Magnificent Seven

McTeague
author: **11** Frank Norris

mea culpa 7 my fault **14** through my fault

Mead, Margaret
author of: **14** My Earlier Years **16** Blackberry Winter **18** Coming of Age in Samoa **20** Growing Up in New Guinea **42** Sex and Temperament in Three Primitive Societies
husband: **14** Gregory Bateson

Meade, Dr and Mrs
characters in: **15** Gone With the Wind
author: **8** Mitchell

Meade, George Gordon
served in: **8** Civil War **10** Mexican War
side: **5** Union
battle: **7** Bull Run **8** Antietam **10** Gettysburg **13** South Mountain **14** Fredericksburg **16** Chancellorsville **18** Peninsular campaign
commander of: **16** Army of the Potomac

meadow 3 lea **4** mead, park

5 field, green **6** forage **7** herbage, pasture, savanna **9** grassland, pasturage

meager 4 bare, lean, slim, thin **5** scant, short, spare, token **6** little, paltry, scanty, scarce, skimpy, slight, sparse **7** scrimpy, slender, stinted, wanting **9** deficient **10** inadequate **12** insufficient **13** insubstantial

meagerness 8 sparsity **9** smallness **10** inadequacy, measliness, scantiness, skimpiness, sparseness **13** insufficiency **14** insignificance

Meagles
character in: **12** Little Dorrit
author: **7** Dickens

meal 4 bran, chow, diet, eats, fare, food, grub, menu **5** feast, flour, grits **6** farina, groats, repast, spread **7** banquet, cooking, cuisine, oatmeal **8** cornmeal, victuals **10** bill of fare **11** nourishment, refreshment

mealymouthed 6 unsure **7** devious **8** hesitant **9** deceptive, insincere

mean see box

meander 4 loop, rove, wind **5** snake, stray, twist **6** circle, ramble, spiral, wander, zigzag **8** undulate **9** convolute, corkscrew

meandering 7 devious, sinuous, turning, winding **8** indirect, rambling, tortuous, twisting **9** wandering **10** circuitous, roundabout, serpentine

meaning 3 aim, end **4** gist, goal, hint, meat, pith, plan,

view **5** drift, force, point, sense, value, worth **6** burden, design, intent, object, scheme, thrust, upshot **7** content, essence, pointer, purport, purpose **9** intention, substance **10** denotation, indication, intimation, suggestion **11** implication **12** significance **15** sum and substance

meaningful 4 deep **5** meaty, pithy **6** useful **7** pointed, serious **8** eloquent, explicit, pregnant **9** designing, important **10** expressive, gratifying, portentous, purposeful, suggestive, worthwhile **11** significant, substantial **13** consequential

meaningless 5 trite **6** absurd, paltry, stupid **7** aimless, fatuous, foolish, idiotic, shallow, trivial, useless **8** baffling, piddling, puzzling **9** enigmatic, facetious, frivolous, illegible, senseless, valueless, worthless **10** incoherent, mystifying, perplexing **11** bewildering, inscrutable, nonsensical, purposeless, unessential, unimportant **12** impenetrable, inexplicable, inexpressive, preposterous **13** insignificant, unsubstantial **14** undecipherable

Mean Joe
nickname of: **9** Joe Greene

means 3 way **4** jack, mode **5** bread, dough, funds, money **6** avenue, course, income, method, resort, riches, wealth **7** capital, dollars, measure, process, revenue **8** property **9** affluence, long green, resources, substance **11** alternative, wherewithal

mean-spirited 3 low **4** base, poor, vile **5** cheap, nasty, petty, small, snide, sorry, tight, venal **6** abject, measly, paltry, scurvy, shabby, sordid, stingy **7** ignoble, miserly, selfish, vicious **8** tightwad, wretched **9** miserable, penurious **10** ungenerous **12** parsimonious

Mean Streets
director: **14** Martin Scorsese
cast: **11** Amy Robinson, David Proval **12** Harvey Keitel, Robert DeNiro

meantime 7 interim **8** interval **9** meanwhile

meanwhile 8 meantime **12** concurrently, in the interim **13** at the same time **14** simultaneously

measurable 10 assessable, computable, mensurable, reckonable **11** appraisable **12** determinable

---

mean 3 low, par, say **4** base, evil, norm, plan, poor, rude, rule, vile, want, wish **5** aim at, cheap, close, cruel, imply, nasty, petty, small, tight, venal **6** denote, flimsy, greedy, hint at, intend, malign, medium, menial, normal, paltry, sleazy, sordid, stingy, tell off, trashy, unfair **7** average, balance, betoken, dream of, drive at, express, hoggish, inhuman, miserly, point to, propose, purpose, regular, resolve, selfish, signify, squalid, suggest, think of, trivial, vicious **8** aspire to, gimcrack, grasping, indicate, inferior, inhumane, intimate, low-grade, picayune, piddling, pitiless, rubbishy, say truly, shameful, standard, stand for, trifling, uncaring, wretched **9** illiberal, low-paying, malicious, mercenary, merciless, miserable, niggardly, penurious, symbolize, unfeeling **10** avaricious, compromise, despicable, have in mind, have in view, jerry-built, low-ranking, malevolent, pinchpenny, second-rate, ungenerous, villainous **11** closefisted, commonplace, disgraceful, happy medium, hardhearted, self-seeking, small-minded, tightfisted, unimportant **12** contemptible, disagreeable, dishonorable **13** insignificant, unsympathetic **15** inconsequential

measure 3 act, law **4** bill, plan, rule, size, step, time **5** bound, clock, gauge, judge, limit, means, plumb, quota, range, scale, scope, share, sound, value **6** amount, assess, course, degree, design, extent, method, resort, scheme, survey **7** portion, project **8** appraise, evaluate, proposal, quantity **9** allotment, allowance, enactment, procedure, restraint, yardstick **10** limitation, moderation, proceeding, temperance

measure, unit of *see box, p. 616*

measured 5 equal, exact **6** steady **7** precise, regular, studied, uniform **8** verified **10** calculated, deliberate **11** cold-blooded, intentional, well-planned **12** premeditated **13** predetermined

Measure for Measure
author: **18** William Shakespeare
character: **5** Lucio **6** Angelo, Juliet **7** Claudio, Escalus, Mariana **8** Isabella **9** Vincentio

measureless 7 endless **8** infinite **9** boundless, unlimited **12** immeasurable

measurement *see box, p. 618*

measure out 6 ration **7** dole out, mete out **9** apportion

meat 3 nut **4** core, fare, food, gist, grub **5** heart, point **6** kernel **7** edibles, essence, nucleus **8** victuals **9** provender, substance **10** provisions, sustenance **11** comestibles, nourishment

Mechaneus
epithet of: **4** Zeus
means: **9** contriver

mechanic 6 joiner **7** artisan **9** automatic, craftsman, machinist **11** uninspired **12** grease monkey

mechanical 4 cold **7** routine **9** automatic, unfeeling **10** impersonal, self-acting, unthinking **11** instinctive, involuntary, machinelike, perfunctory, unconscious **13** machine-driven

mechanism 4 tool **5** motor, works **7** machine, utensil **9** apparatus, appliance, implement, machinery **10** instrument **11** contrivance

Meda
husband: **9** Idomeneus
lover: **6** Leucus

medal 5 award, honor, prize

6 laurel, reward, ribbon, trophy **8** citation **9** medallion **10** decoration

Medawar, Peter Brian
field: **7** biology
nationality: **7** British
discovered: **23** acquired immune tolerance
awarded: **10** Nobel Prize

meddle 5 mix in **6** butt in, horn in, kibitz **7** intrude, pry into **9** interfere, interlope, intervene **10** tamper with

meddler 3 pry **5** snoop **7** Paul Pry **8** busybody **10** interferer, Nosy Parker

meddlesome 4 nosy **5** pushy **6** prying, snoopy **7** pushing **8** meddling, snooping **9** intrusive, obtrusive, officious **11** impertinent, interfering **12** presumptuous

Medea
author: **9** Euripides
character: **5** Creon, Jason **6** Aegeus, Glauce

Medea
form: **9** sorceress
father: **6** Aeetes
mother: **5** Idyia
aunt: **5** Circe
brother: **8** Apsyrtus
sister: **9** Chalciope
lover: **5** Jason
son: **6** Medeus, Pheres **8** Mermerus, Tisander **9** Alcimenes, Thessalus
killed: **7** her sons
escaped to: **6** Athens

Medeus
father: **6** Aegeus
mother: **5** Medea

media 5 press, radio **9** magazines **10** billboards, journalism, newspapers, television **11** journalists
singular: **6** medium

medial 4 mean **6** median **7** average

median 3 mid, par **4** mean, norm **5** mesne **6** center, medial, medium, middle **7** average, central, halfway **8** middling, midpoint, moderate **12** intermediate

mediate 6 pacify, step in, umpire **7** referee **8** moderate **9** arbitrate, intercede, interpose, intervene, negotiate, reconcile **10** conciliate, propitiate

mediation 6 parley **10** adjustment, compromise, discussion **11** arbitration, give-and-take, negotiation, peacemaking **12** conciliation, intercession, intervention, pacification **14** reconciliation

mediator 6 umpire **7** referee **9** go-between, moderator **10** arbitrator, negotiator, peacemaker, reconciler **12** intermediary

medical 7 healing **8** curative, remedial, salutary, sanative **9** medicinal **10** medicative **11** restorative, therapeutic

medical abbreviation *see box, p. 618*

Medical Center
character: **9** (Dr) Joe Gannon **11** Nurse Wilcox, (Dr) Paul Lochner **13** Nurse Chambers **14** Nurse Courtland, (Dr) Jeanne Bartlett
cast: **9** James Daly **11** Chad Everett, Chris Hutson **12** Audrey Totter, Jayne Meadows **14** Corinne Camacho

medical practitioner 6 doctor, medico **9** physician

medication 4 balm **5** tonic **6** elixir, remedy **7** nostrum, panacea **8** medicine **10** medicament, palliative **11** restorative

Medici, Giovanni de' 8 Pope Leo X **15** Pope Leo the Tenth

Medici, Giulio 14 Pope Clement VII **21** Pope Clement the Seventh

medicine 4 balm, drug, pill **5** salve, tonic **6** remedy **7** nostrum **10** healing art, medication **11** restorative **12** therapeutics **13** materia medica
god of: **9** Asclepius **11** Aesculapius

medieval 8 Dark Ages **10** antiquated, Middle-Ages **12** old-fashioned **14** pre-Renaissance

mediocre 4 so-so **5** petty **6** common, meager, medium, normal, paltry, slight **7** average **8** inferior, ordinary, passable, trifling **9** tolerable **10** negligible, pedestrian, second-rate **11** commonplace, indifferent, unimportant **12** run-of-the-mill **13** inappreciable, insignificant **14** fair-to-middling, inconsiderable **15** inconsequential, undistinguished

mediocrity 8 poorness **9** pettiness **10** low-quality, meagerness, paltriness, triviality **11** inferiority **12** indifference, ordinariness, unimportance **14** insignificance **15** commonplaceness

meditate 4 muse, plan **5** aim at, study, think **6** devise, ponder **7** concoct, dream of, propose, reflect **8** cogitate,

measure, unit of
    of Afghanistan: 3 paw, sir **5** jerib, karoh **6** khurds **7** kharwar
    of Algeria: 3 pik **5** rebis, tarri **6** termin
    of Argentina: 4 sino **5** legua **6** cuadra, lastre **7** manzana
    of Australia: 4 arna, naut, saum
    of Austria: 4 fass, fuss, joch, mass, muth, yoke **5** halbe, linie, meile, metze, pfiff, punkt **6** achtel, becher, leipoa, seidel **7** klafter, viertel **8** dreiling **12** futtermassel
    of Belgium: 3 vat **4** aune, pied **5** carat **6** perche **8** boisseau
    of Bolivia: 6 league **7** celemin
    of Borneo: 7 gantang
    of Brazil: 2 pe **4** moio, sack, vara **5** braca, legoa, milha, tonel **6** canada, cuarto, quarto, tarefa **7** garrafa **8** alqueire
    of Bulgaria: 3 oka, oke **5** krine, lekhe, likhe
    of Canada: 3 ton **5** minot, perch, point **6** arpent **7** chainon
    of the Canary Islands: 8 fanegada
    of Chile: 4 vara **5** legua, linea **6** cuadra **7** fanega
    of China: 3 cho, fan, fen, pau, tou, tun, yan, yin **4** chek, chih, fang, kish, papa, quei, shih, teke, tsan, tsun **5** catty, chang, ching, sheng, shing **6** chupak, gungli, kungho, kungmu, tching **7** kungfen, kungyin **8** kungchih, kungshih **9** kungching
    of Colombia: 4 vara **7** azumbre, celemin
    of Costa Rica: 4 vara **5** cafiz, cahiz **6** fanega, tercia **7** cajuela, cantaro, manzana **10** caballeria
    of Cuba: 4 vara **5** bocoy, cocoy, tarea **6** cordel, fanega **10** caballeria
    of Czechoslovakia: 3 lan **4** mira **5** korec, liket, stopa **6** merice, strych
    of Denmark: 3 ell, fod, mil, pot **4** alen **5** album, anker, kande, linje, paegl **7** landmil, oltonde, ortonde, skieppe, viertel **8** fjerding **9** ottingkar **10** korntonde
    of the Dominican Republic: 3 ona **5** tarea **6** fanega
    of Ecuador: 5 libra **6** cuadra, fanega
    of Egypt: 3 apt, dra, hen, rob **4** arab, dira, draa, khet, nief, ocha, roub, theb, wudu **5** abdat, ardab, cubit, farde, fedan, keleh, kerat, kilah, sahme **6** artaba, aurure, baladi, kantar, keddah, robhah, schene **7** choryos, daribah, malouah, roubouh, toumnah **8** kassabah, kharouba **10** diramimari, diribaladi
    of El Salvador: 4 vara **5** cafiz, cahiz **6** fanega **7** batella, botella, cantara, manzana
    of England: 3 cut, ell, lea, pin, rod, ton, tun, vat **4** acre, bind, butt, comb, coom, cran, foot, gill, goad, hand, hank, heer, hide, inch, last, line, mile, nail, pace, palm, peck, pint, pipe, pole, pool, rood, rope, sack, seam, span, trug, typp, wist, yard, yoke **5** bodge, chain, cubit, digit, float, floor, fluid, hutch, jugum, minim, ounce, perch, point, prime, quart, skein, stack, truss **6** barrel, bovate, bushel, cranne, fathom, firkin, gallon, hobbet, hobbit, league, manent, oxgang, pottle, runlet, square, strike, sulung, thread, tierce **7** auchlet, furlong, kenning, quarter, rundlet, seamile, spindle, tertian, virgate **8** carucate, chaldron, hogshead, landyard, puncheon, quadrant, standard
    of Estonia: 3 tun **4** elle, liin, sund, toll, toop **5** verst **6** sagene, versta **7** kulimet **8** tonnland
    of Ethiopia: 3 tat **4** cubi, kuba **5** derah, messe **6** cabaho, sinjer, sinzer, tanica **7** entelam, farsakh, farsang, ghebeta
    of Finland: 3 kannu, verst **6** fathom, kannor **8** ottinger, skalpund, tunnland
    of France: 3 pot, sac **4** aune, mine, pied, velt **5** arpen, carat, ligne, minot, pinte, point, pouce, velte **6** arpent, hemine, league, quarte, setier
    of Greece: 3 pik **4** bema, piki, pous **5** baril, chous, cubit, diote, doron, maris, pekhe, podos, pygon, xylon **6** acaena, bacile, barile, cotula, dichas, gramme, hemina, koilon, lichas, milion, orgyia, palame, pechys, schene, xestes **7** bacvhel, chenica, choenix, cyathos, diaulos, metreta, stadium, stremma **8** condylos, daktylos, dekapode, dolichos, medimnos, medimnys, metretes, palaiste, plethron, plethrum, stathmos **9** hemiekton, oxybaphon
    of Guatemala: 4 vara **6** cuarta, tercia **7** cajuela, manzana **10** caballeria
    of Guinea: 7 jacktan
    of Honduras: 4 vara **5** milla **6** mecate **7** cajuela
    of Hungary: 3 ako **4** hold, yoke **5** itcze, marok, metze **7** huvelyk
    of Iceland: 3 set **4** alin **5** almud **6** almenn, ferfet, pottur **7** fathmur, fermila, oltunna
    of India: 3 ady, gaz, gez, jow, lan **4** byee, coss, depa, doph, hath, koss, kunk, raik, rati, seit, taun, tola **5** bigha, covid, crosa, danda, depoh, drona, erosa, garce, hasta, krosa, parah, ratti, salay, yojan **6** adhaka, amunam, covido, cudava, cumbha, geerah, moolum, mushti, ouroub, palgat, parran, prasha, ropani, tipree, unglee, yojana **7** dhanush, gavyuti, khahoon, niranga, prastha **8** okthabah
    of Indonesia: 5 depah, depoh
    of Iran: 3 gaz, zar, zer **4** cane **5** gareh, kafiz, makuk, qasab **6** charac, chebel, ghalva **7** capicha, chenica, farsakh, mansion, mishara **8** parasang, piamaneh, stathmos
    of Ireland: 4 mile **6** bandle **8** crannock
    of Israel: 3 cab, car, hin, kab, kor **4** bath, ezba, omer, reed **5** cubit, donum, dunam, ephah, ganeh, homer, kaneh
    of Italy: 3 pie **4** orna **5** palma, palmo, punto, salma, stero **6** barile, miglie, moggio, rubbio, tomolo **7** braccio, secchio **8** giornata, quadrato

of Japan: 2 go **3** boo, cho, djo, fun, inc, ken, kin, kon, rin, shi, sho, sun, tan **4** hiro, isse, kati, koku, niyo, shoo **5** carat, catty, issho, ittan, momme, picul, shaku **6** kwamme **8** hiyak-kin **9** hiyak-hiro **11** komma-ichida, kujira-shaku
of Java: 3 kan **4** paal, rand **5** palen
of Kenya: 4 wari
of Laos: 3 bak
of Latvia: 3 let **4** stof **5** stoff, verst **6** arshin, kulmet **7** verchoc, verchok **8** krouchka, pourvete **9** deciatine, lofstelle, pourvette **10** tonnseteel
of Liberia: 4 kuba
of Libya: 3 dra, pik, saa **4** kele **5** bozze, donum, jabia, teman, uckia **6** barile, gorrah, misura **7** mattaro, termino **8** kharouba
of Luxembourg: 5 fuder
of Madagascar: 7 gantang
of Malaysia: 3 pau, tun **4** para, pipe, tael, wang **5** parah **6** chupak, parrah **7** gantang
of Malta: 4 rotl **5** artal, canna, parto, ratel, salma **6** kantar **7** caffiso
of Mexico: 3 bag, pie **4** alma, onza, vara **5** almud, baril, carga, jarra, labor, legua, libra, linea, marco, sitio **6** adarme, almude, arroba, carega, fanega, ochaua, terceo **7** pulgada, quintal **9** cuarteron, cuartillo **10** caballeria
of Morocco: 4 kala, muhd, rotl, saah, sahh, ueba **5** artal, cadee, gerbe, ratel **6** covado, dirhem, fanega, izenbi, kintar, tangin, tomini **8** quintral
of Myanmar: 2 ly **3** dha, gon, mau, sao, tao, tat **4** byee, phan, seit, taun, that **5** shita, thuoc **6** lamany, palgat **7** chaivai **8** okthabah
of the Netherlands: 2 el **3** aam, ahm, ell, kan, vat **4** duim, mijl, rood, rope **5** anker, roede, wisse **6** bunder, legger, maatje, mutsje, streep **7** schepel **8** mimgelen, steekkan
of Nicaragua: 4 vara **5** cahiz **6** suerte **7** cajuela, manzana **10** cabelleria
of Norway: 3 fot, mal **4** alen **5** kande **6** fathom **7** skieppe **9** korntonde
of Panama: 7 celemin
of Paraguay: 3 pie **4** lino, lira, lire, vara **5** legua **6** cuadra, fanega
of Peru: 4 topo **5** galon **7** celemin **8** fanegada
of the Philippines: 4 loan **5** braza, catty, cavan, chupa, fardo, ganta, picul, punto **6** apatan, balita, lachsa, quinon **7** quilate **8** chinanta
of Poland: 3 cal **4** mila, pret **5** morga, sazen, vloka, wloka **6** cwierc, cwierk, kwarta, lokiec **7** garniec **9** kwarterka
of Portugal: 2 pe **4** bota, moio, vara **5** almud, fanga, geira, linha, milha **6** almude, covado **7** alquier, ferrado, selamin **8** alqueire
of Puerto Rico: 6 cuerda **10** cabelleria
of Rumania: 7 faltche
of Russia: 3 fut, lof **4** duim, fass, loof, pood, quar, stof **5** duime, foute, korec, korek, ligne, osmin, pajak, stoff, stoof, vedro, verst **6** charka, liniya, osmina, paletz, sagene, stekar, tchast, tsarki, versta, verste **7** archine, arsheen, botchka, chkalik, garnetz, verchoc, verchok **8** boutylka, chetvert, krouchka, kroushka **9** chetverik **10** dessiatine **11** polugarnetz
of Scotland: 3 cop **4** boll, cran, fall, mile, peck, pint, rood, rope, span **5** crane, lippy **6** audlet, davach, firlot, lippie, noggin **7** chalder, choppin **8** mutchkin, stimpart, stimpert **9** particate, shaftment, shathmont
of Sicily: 5 salma **7** caffiso
of Sierra Leone: 4 load **6** kettle
of Somalia: 3 top **4** caba **5** chela, darat, tabla **6** cubito **8** parsalah
of South Africa: 4 vara
of Spain: 3 pie **4** codo, dedo, paso, vara **5** braza, cahiz, carga, legua, medio, palmo, sesma **6** cordel, cuarta, fanega, racion, yugada **7** azumbre, celemin, estadel, pulgada **8** fanegada
of Sri Lanka: 4 para, seer **5** parah **6** amunam, parrah
of Sudan: 2 ud
of Suriname: 7 ketting
of Sweden: 3 aln, fot, ref, tum **4** alar, amar, famn, kapp, last, stop **5** carat, foder, kanna, linje, nymil, spann **6** fathom, jumfru **7** oxhuvud, tunland **8** fjarding, koltunna, tunnland
of Switzerland: 3 imi, pot **4** aune, fuss, muid, pied, zoll **5** lieue, linie, maass, pouce, staab, toise **6** perche, strich **7** klafter, viertel **9** quarteron **10** holzlafter **11** holzklafter
of Syria: 5 makuk **6** garava
of Thailand: 2 wa **3** can, ken, niv, rai, sat, sok, wah **4** cohi, keup, niou, tang **5** kwien, leeng, sesti, vouah **6** kabiet, kanahn **7** chaimeu **8** changawn **9** anukabiet
of Tunisia: 3 saa **4** saah **5** cafiz **6** mettar **8** milerole
of Turkey: 3 dra, oka, pik **4** draa, khat, kile, zira **5** berri, kileh, zirai **6** arshin, chinik, fortin, halebi **7** nocktat
of Uruguay: 4 vara **6** cuadra, suerte
of Venezuela: 5 galon, milla **6** fanega **7** estadel
of Vietnam: 4 gang, phan, thon
of Wales: 5 cover **7** cantred, crannoc, listred
of Yugoslavia: 3 oka, rif **4** akov, ralo **5** donum, khvat, lanaz, plaze, stopa **6** motyka, ralico **9** danoranja

measurement 4 area, mass, size 5 depth, width 6 extent, height, length, volume, weight 7 breadth, content, gauging 8 capacity, plumbing, sounding 9 amplitude, appraisal, dimension, magnitude, measuring, reckoning, surveying 10 assessment, estimation, evaluation 11 mensuration

  Biblical: 4 omer 5 cubit, ephah 6 shekel
  champagne: 6 magnum 8 jeroboam, rehoboam 9 balthazar 10 methuselah, salmanazar 14 Nebuchadnezzar
  cloth: 4 bolt
  cotton: 4 bale
  electricity: 3 ohm 4 volt, watt 5 joule 6 ampere 10 horsepower
  energy: 3 BTU 5 joule 7 calorie 11 kilocalorie 18 British thermal unit
  firewood: 4 cord
  force: 4 dyne 6 newton 7 poundal
  gold/jewelry: 5 carat, karat, point
  Greek: 4 mina 5 cubit 6 obolos, talent 7 drachma, stadion
  gun: 5 gauge 7 caliber
  light: 7 candela 11 candlepower
  liquor/spirits: 4 pint, pony, shot 5 fifth, quart 6 jigger, magnum
  metric system: 5 liter, meter 9 deciliter, decimeter, dekaliter, dekameter, kiloliter, kilometer, nanometer 10 centiliter, centimeter, cubic meter, hectoliter, hectometer, milliliter, millimeter 11 square meter 14 cubic dekameter 15 cubic centimeter, cubic millimeter, square decimeter, square dekameter, square kilometer 16 square centimeter, square hectometer, square millimeter
  metric weight: 3 ton 4 gram 5 tonne 7 quintal 8 dekagram, kilogram 9 centigram, hectogram, microgram, milligram
  paper: 4 ream 5 quire
  pressure: 6 pascal 10 atmosphere
  Roman: 2 as 5 cubit, libra 6 pondus 7 stadium
  sound: 7 decibel
  temperature: 6 degree, Kelvin 7 Celsius 10 Fahrenheit
  time: 3 day 4 hour, week, year 5 month, score 6 decade, minute, second 7 century 10 millennium, nanosecond 11 microsecond, millisecond
  typography: 2 em, en 4 pica 5 point
  unit: 3 cup, rod 4 acre, dram, foot, gill, inch, link, mile, peck, pint, yard 5 chain, minim, ounce, quart 6 barrel, bushel, circle, degree, fathom, gallon 7 furlong, hectare 8 angstrom, hogshead, teaspoon 9 cubic foot, cubic inch, cubic yard, square rod 10 fluid ounce, right angle, square foot, square inch, square mile, square yard, tablespoon 25 international nautical mile
  weight: 3 ton 4 dram 5 grain, ounce, pound 7 scruple 8 short ton 9 ounce troy, pound troy 11 pennyweight 13 hundredweight

medical abbreviation
  a c: 11 before meals
  ad lib: 8 as needed 9 as desired
  agit: 5 shake
  aq: 5 water
  b i d: 9 twice a day
  cap: 4 take 7 capsule
  coch: 8 spoonful
  dil: 6 dilute 8 dissolve
  fldxt: 12 fluid extract
  ft: 4 make
  ft mist: 12 make a mixture
  ft pulv: 11 make a powder
  gr: 5 grain
  gt: 4 drop
  gtt: 5 drops
  h s: 9 at bedtime
  in d: 5 daily
  lot: 6 lotion
  mod praesc: 21 in the manner prescribed
  O: 4 pint
  O D: 8 right eye
  O S: 7 left eye
  O U: 9 in each eye
  ol: 3 oil
  p c: 9 after food 10 after meals
  p o: 7 by mouth
  p r n: 25 as circumstances may require
  pil: 3 pill
  pulv: 6 powder
  q i d: 14 four times daily
  rep: 6 repeat
  s o s: 11 if necessary
  ss: 7 one half
  tab: 6 tablet
  t i d: 15 three times daily
  ut dict: 10 as directed

consider, contrive, mull over, ruminate 9 dwell upon 10 deliberate 11 contemplate

meditation 4 yoga 5 study 6 musing, poring 7 mulling, reverie, thought 8 brooding 9 discourse, pondering 10 cogitation, reflection, rumination 12 deliberation 13 consideration, contemplation

Mediterranean
  called by ancient Romans: 11 mare nostrum
  coast: 7 Riviera
  gulf: 5 Lions, Sidra, Tunis 7 Antalya, Catania, Taranto 8 Hammamet 9 Iskenderon

  island: 4 Elba 5 Capri, Corfu, Crete, Ibiza, Malta 6 Cyprus, Euboea, Lesbos, Rhodes, Sicily 7 Corsica, Majorca, Minorca 8 Balearic, Sardinia
  resort: 4 Nice 5 Capri 6 Cannes 7 Riviera 9 Cote d'Azur 10 Costa Brava
  river into: 2 Po 4 Ebro, Nile 5 Rhone
  sea: 5 Black 6 Aegean, Ionian 8 Adriatric, Ligurian 10 Tyrrhenian
  strait: 8 Bosporus 9 Bosphorus, Gibraltar 11 Dardanelles
  wind: 7 mistral, sirocco

medium 3 way 4 form, mean, mode, tool 5 means, organ 6 agency, avenue, common, milieu, normal 7 average, balance, channel, diviner, psychic, setting, vehicle 8 middling, moderate, ordinary 9 go-between, middle way, mid-course 10 atmosphere, compromise, golden mean, instrument, moderation 11 clairvoyant, environment, happy medium 12 crystal-gazer, intermediary, intermediate, middle ground, spiritualist, surroundings 13 fortuneteller 15 instrumentality

medley 4 hash, mess, olio 6 jumble, mosaic 7 farrago, melange, mixture 8 mishmash, pastiche 9 patchwork, potpourri 10 assortment, hodgepodge, miscellany 11 gallimaufry

Medon
mentioned in: **5** Iliad
7 Odyssey
father: **6** Oileus
mother: **5** Rhene
position: **6** herald
friend of: **8** Penelope
killed by: **6** Aeneas

medulla
part of: **5** brain
controls: **6** glands **7** muscles

Medusa
form: **6** Gorgon
father: **7** Phorcys
mother: **4** Ceto
sisters: **6** Graiae
loved by: **8** Poseidon
children: **7** Pegasus
8 Chrysaor
sight of her caused people
to turn to: **5** stone
killed by: **7** Perseus

meek 4 mild **6** docile, gentle,
humble, modest **8** lamblike,
retiring, tolerant, yielding
9 compliant, spineless, tractable, weak-kneed **10** spiritless,
submissive, unassuming **11** acquiescent, complaisant, deferential, unassertive,
unresisting **13** long-suffering,
tenderhearted, unpretentious

meekness 7 pliancy, shyness
8 docility, humility **9** passivity
10 diffidence, humbleness
11 bashfulness **13** nonresistance **14** self-effacement

meet 3 apt, fit **4** abut, face,
good, heed, obey **5** cross,
equal, greet, match, rally,
right **6** adjoin, answer, border,
follow, gather, muster, proper,
seemly **7** abide by, collect,
convene, execute, fitting, fulfill, observe, perform, respect,
run into, satisfy, welcome
8 assemble, becoming, bump
into, confront, converge, decorous, opposite, relevant, suitable **9** agreeable, allowable,
befitting, congruous, discharge,
encounter, intersect, permitted,
pertinent **10** admissable, comply with, congregate, felicitous **11** acknowledge,
appropriate, permissible
12 come together

meet eye to eye 4 face
8 confront, face up to **11** meet
vis-a-vis

meet halfway 6 settle **9** make
a deal **10** compromise
11 come to terms **14** strike a
bargain **18** split the difference

meet head on 4 face **5** crash
6 oppose **7** collide, crack up
8 confront, face up to **9** challenge, encounter

meeting 4 date **5** group, tryst

6 caucus **7** council **8** assembly,
conclave, congress **9** encounter, gathering **10** conference,
convention, engagement, rendezvous **11** assignation, convocation, get-together
12 introduction, presentation
13 confrontation

Meeting at Telgte
author: **11** Gunter Grass

meeting of the minds
7 concert, concord, harmony
9 agreement **11** concordance
13 understanding

meeting place 5 mecca **10** focal point, rendezvous

Meet Me in St Louis
director: **16** Vincente
Minnelli
cast: **8** Leon Ames, Tom
Drake **9** Mary Astor **11** Judy
Garland **12** June Lockhart,
Marjorie Main **13** Lucille
Bremer **14** Margaret O'Brien
song: **11** Trolley Song **14** The
Boy Next Door **33** Have
Yourself a Merry Little
Christmas

Meet the Press
moderator: **9** Ned Brooks
10 Bill Monroe **11** Edwin
Newman **14** Lawrence Spi-
vak, Martha Rountree

meet with 4 meet **6** endure
7 undergo **8** come upon **9** encounter **10** come across,
experience

Mefitis
also: **8** Mephitis
prevented: **5** winds
kind of winds: **7** harmful

Megaera
member of: **6** Furies

Megalosaurus
type: **8** dinosaur
means: **11** great lizard
found by: **15** William
Buckland
period: **8** Jurassic

Megamede
husband: **12** King Thespius
number of daughters: **5** fifty

Megapenthes
father: **7** Proetus **8** Menelaus
mother: **10** Stheneboea

Megara
father: **5** Creon
husband: **8** Hercules
son: **11** Therimachus

Mehuman 6 eunuch

Meilichius
epithet of: **4** Zeus
means: **8** gracious

Mein Kampf
author: **11** Adolf Hitler

means: **7** my fight **8** my
battle

Meitner, Lise
field: **7** physics
nationality: **8** Austrian
contributed to: **21** atomic
bomb development
discovered: **12** protactinium
16 fission of uranium

Melaenis
epithet of: **9** Aphrodite
means: **5** black

Melampus
father: **8** Amythaon
mother: **7** Idomene
brother: **4** Bias
wife: **7** Lysippe
son: **4** Abas **7** Mantius
10 Antiphates
vocation: **4** seer **6** healer

melancholia 7 despair
10 depression, desolation, melancholy **11** despondency

melancholy 4 blue, glum
5 blues, dumps, gloom,
moody **6** dismal, dreary,
gloomy, mopish, morose, somber **7** despair, doleful, forlorn,
joyless, unhappy **8** dejected,
desolate, doldrums, dolorous,
downcast, funereal, mournful
9 cheerless, dejection, depressed, heartsick, moodiness,
plaintive **10** calamitous, depressing, depression, despondent, dispirited, gloominess,
low spirits **11** despondency,
discouraged, downhearted, forlornness, languishing, melancholia, sick at heart,
unfortunate **12** disconsolate,
heavyhearted **14** down in the
dumps, down in the mouth
16 disconsolateness
French: **6** triste **9** tristesse

melange 3 mix **6** jumble, medley **7** mixture **8** compound,
mishmash, pastiche **9** pasticcio,
patchwork, potpourri **10** assemblage, assortment, hodgepodge, miscellany
11 gallimaufry

Melanion
suitor of: **8** Atalanta

Melanippe
form: **4** foal
foal born to: **6** Euippe
transformed into: **4** Arne,
girl
father: **4** Ares
queen of: **7** Amazons

Melanosaurus
type: **8** dinosaur
period: **8** Triassic

Melanthius
goatherd for: **8** Odysseus

Melantho
handmaiden for: **8** Penelope

Melas
father: **7** Phrixus
mother: **10** Chalciiope
brother: **5** Argus **8** Phrontis
10 Cytissorus

Melbourne
bay: **7** Hobson's **11** Port
Phillip
landmark: **20** Flemington
Racecourse
river: **5** Yarra **6** Plenty
9 Mary Creek, Patterson
11 Maribyrnong **12** Diamond
Creek **13** Kororoit Creek
14 Dandenong Creek, Gardiner's Creek **16** Moonee
Ponds Creek
state: **8** Victoria
university: **6** Monash **7** La
Trobe

Melchizedek
means: **19** king of
righteousness
hometown: **5** Salem
contemporary: **7** Abraham

meld 3 mix **4** fuse, join
5 blend, merge, unite **6** jumble, mingle **7** combine **8** coalesce, intermix, scramble
9 commingle **10** amalgamate,
intertwine, interweave
11 consolidate, incorporate,
intermingle

Meleager
father: **4** Ares **6** Oeneus
mother: **7** Althaea
uncle: **9** Plexippus
slew: **14** Calydonian boar
loved: **8** Atalanta
killed: **15** mother's brothers
sisters: **11** Meleagrides

Meleagrides
sisters of: **8** Meleager
transformed into: **10** guinea
hens
transformed by: **7** Artemis

melee 3 row **4** fray, riot
5 brawl, scrap, set-to **6** fracas,
rumpus, tussle **7** scuffle **8** disorder, dogfight **9** commotion,
fistfight **10** free-for-all **11** altercation, pandemonium

Melete
member of: **5** Muses
personifies: **10** meditation

Melia
form: **5** nymph
born from: **5** blood
blood of: **6** Uranus

Meliad
form: **5** nymph
nymph of: **6** flocks **10** fruit
trees

Meliae
nymphs of: **5** Melic

Meliboea
form: **6** maiden

Melicertes
father: **7** Athamas
mother: **3** Ino
changed into: **8** Palaemon

Melie
form: **5** nymph
son: **6** Amycus

Melissa
sister: **8** Amaethea
nourished: **4** Zeus

mellifluous 4 soft **5** sweet
6 dulcet, mellow, smooth
7 musical **8** resonant **9** full-
toned, melodious **10** euphonious, harmonious, sweet-
toned **13** sweet-sounding

Mellors
character in: **20** Lady Chatterley's Lover
author: **8** Lawrence

mellow 4 rich, ripe, soft
5 drunk, sweet **6** mature, season, soften **7** matured, relaxed **8** luscious, tolerant
9 delicious **10** full-bodied
11 sympathetic **12** full-
flavored **13** compassionate,
understanding

mellowness 8 full body, fullness, maturity, richness, ripeness, softness **9** tolerance
10 compassion, smoothness
12 lusciousness, pleasantness

melodic 5 lyric **7** tuneful

melodious 4 rich, soft **5** clear,
lyric, sweet **6** dulcet, mellow,
smooth **7** melodic, musical,
ringing, tuneful **8** resonant
9 full-toned **10** euphonious,
sweet-toned **11** mellifluent,
mellifluous

melodrama 9 theatrics
12 emotionalism
13 theatricality

melodramatic 5 corny,
hammy, hokey, stagy **7** maudlin, mawkish **8** cornball, frenzied **10** flamboyant, histrionic
11 exaggerated, overwrought,
sensational, sentimental, spectacular **13** overemotional

melody 3 air **4** aria, song,
tune **5** ditty, theme **6** ballad,
strain, timbre **7** concord, euphony **10** musicality **11** tunefulness **12** mellifluence
13 melodiousness **14** harmoni-
ousness **15** mellifluousness

melon
varieties: **4** pear **5** mango,
snake, stink **6** casaba, citron,
Dudaim, netted, nutmeg, orange, winter **7** Persian, serpent **8** honeydew
10 cantaloupe, preserving,
watermelon **11** pomegranate **16** Oriental pickling,

Queen Anne's pocket
17 Chinese preserving

Melpomene
member of: **5** Muses
personifies: **7** tragedy

melt 4 fade, fuse, pass, thaw
5 blend, merge, shade, touch
6 affect, disarm, dispel, soften,
vanish **7** appease, dwindle, liquefy, mollify, scatter **8** dissolve **9** disappear, dissipate,
evaporate, waste away
10 arouse pity, conciliate,
propitiate

melt away 5 dry up **8** vaporize **9** evaporate

Melus
father: **7** Cinyras
mother: **6** Cyprus
changed into: **9** apple tree

Melville, Herman
author of: **4** Omoo **5** Mardi,
Typee **7** Redburn **8** Moby
Dick **9** Billy Budd **12** Benito
Cereno **16** The Confidence
Man **20** Bartleby the
Scrivener

Melville, Julia
character in: **9** The Rivals
author: **8** Sheridan

Melvin and Howard
director: **13** Jonathan
Demme
cast: **9** Paul LeMat **12** Jason
Robards **15** Mary
Steenburgen
Oscar for: **6** script **17** sup-
porting actress
(Steenburgen)

member 3 arm, leg, toe **4** foot,
hand, limb, part, tail, wing
5 bough, digit, organ, piece,
shoot **6** branch, finger, pinion
7 element, portion, section,
segment **8** fragment **9** appendage, component, extremity
10 ingredient **11** constituent

member
of the bar: **4** beak **7** counsel
8 advocate, attorney **9** barrister, counselor **10** mouthpiece **12** legal advisor
13 attorney-at-law
of a crew: **4** hand, mate
6 ensign, ganger, gunner,
purser, yeoman **7** bowsman,
oarsman, steward, swabbie
8 cabin boy, coxswain, deckhand, helmsman **9** first
mate, navigator
of faculty: **3** don, PhD
4 prof **5** tutor **6** doctor, master **7** teacher **8** lecturer
9 professor **10** instructor
of family: **3** son **4** aunt
5 niece, uncle **6** cousin, father, mother, nephew, sis-
ter **7** brother **8** daughter,
grandson **11** grandfather,

grandmother
13 granddaughter
of legislature: 4 whip **6** deputy **7** senator, speaker **8** delegate, lawmaker
10 legislator, politician
11 congressman **12** congresswoman
14 representative
of religious order: 3 nun
4 dame, monk **5** Clare, friar, priest **6** father, hermit, Jesuit, sister **7** Alexian, ascetic, brother, Cluniac, Templar
8 Capuchin, cenobite, minister, Trappist **9** Carmelite, Dominican **10** Carthusian, Cistercian, Franciscan
11 Augustinian, Benedictine
14 mother superior

Member of the Wedding, The
author: 15 Carson McCullers
character: 6 Jarvis **11** Janice Evans **13** Frankie Addams, John Henry West **16** Honey Camden Brown **18** Berenice Sadie Brown

membership 4 club **6** league, roster **7** company, society
9 community, personnel
10 connection, fellowship, fraternity **11** affiliation, association, brotherhood

membrane 3 web **4** film, skin
6 lining, sheath **7** coating
8 envelope, pellicle **9** thin sheet **10** integument

memento 5 favor, relic, token
6 record, trophy **8** keepsake, memorial, reminder, souvenir
11 memorabilia, remembrance **12** remembrancer
13 commemoration

memento mori 23 remember that thou must die **31** object serving as a reminder of death

Memnon
origin: 8 Oriental **9** Ethiopian
father: 8 Tithonus
mother: 3 Eos **4** Dawn
brother: 8 Emathion
companions: 10 Memnonides
fought with: 7 Trojans
killed by: 8 Achilles

Memnonides *see* **6** Memnon

memo
French: 11 aide memoire

memoir 4 life **5** diary **7** journal **9** biography, life story
10 adventures **11** confessions, experiences, reflections **13** autobiography, recollections, reminiscences

Memoirs of a Dutiful Daughter
author: 16 Simone de Beauvoir

memorabilia 6 papers **7** records **8** archives **9** documents

memorable 6 famous **7** eminent, notable, salient **8** historic, stirring, striking
9 important, momentous, prominent, red-letter **10** celebrated, impressive, noteworthy, remarkable **11** illustrious, outstanding, significant **13** distinguished, extraordinary, unforgettable

memorandum 4 memo, note
5 brief **6** agenda, minute, record **7** jotting **8** reminder
11 brief report, list of items

memorial 6 homage **7** tribute
8 monument **10** monumental
11 testimonial
13 commemorative

memorialization 11 celebration **13** commemoration

memorialize 4 mark **5** honor
9 celebrate **11** commemorate, pay homage to **12** pay tribute to

memory 4 fame, mark, name, note **5** glory, honor, token
6 esteem, recall, regard, renown, repute **7** memento, respect **8** eminence, keepsake, memorial, prestige, reminder, souvenir **10** estimation, reputation **11** distinction, remembering, remembrance, testimonial **12** recollection, remembrancer, reminiscence
13 commemoration
goddess of: 9 Mnemosyne

Memphis
football team: 9 Showboats

menace 3 cow **4** risk **5** bully, daunt, peril **6** danger, hazard, threat **7** imperil, pitfall, portend, presage, terrify **8** browbeat, endanger, forebode, jeopardy, threaten **9** terrorize
10 intimidate, jeopardize **11** be a hazard to, imperilment
12 endangerment

menacing 7 hostile **9** dangerous **11** belligerent, threatening, treacherous
12 antagonistic

Menaechmi
author: 7 Plautus

menage a trois 9 threesome
16 household of three

Menander
author of: 5 Heros **13** Perikeiromene **14** The Arbitration, The Misanthrope
16 The Rape of the Lock

Men at Arms
author: 11 Evelyn Waugh

Mencken, H L
author of: 10 Prejudices
19 The American Language
editor of: 10 The Mercury
11 The Smart Set

mend 3 fix **4** cure, darn, heal, knit **5** amend, emend, patch
6 better, reform, remedy, repair, revise **7** correct, improve, rectify, restore, retouch, touch up **8** overhaul, renovate
9 meliorate **10** ameliorate
11 recondition

mendacious 5 false, lying
8 spurious **9** deceptive **10** misleading, untruthful

mendacity 5 fraud, lying **6** deceit **7** falsity, perfidy **9** chicanery, deception, duplicity, falsehood, hypocrisy **10** dishonesty **11** insincerity
13 double-dealing, falsification, prevarication **14** untruthfulness **17** misrepresentation

Mendel, Gregor Johann
field: 6 botany
nationality: 8 Austrian
discovered: 14 laws of heredity
founded: 8 genetics

Mendeleyev (Mendeleev), Dimitri Ivanovich
field: 9 chemistry
nationality: 7 Russian
devised: 11 periodic law
13 periodic table

Mendelssohn, (Jakob Ludwig) Felix
born: 7 Germany, Hamburg
composer of: 6 Elijah, St Paul **7** Athalie, Italian (symphony No 4), Lorelei, Ruy Blas **8** Antigone, Scottish (symphony No 3) **11** Reformation (symphony No 5), The Hebrides **12** Hymn of Praise (symphony No 2)
17 Songs without Words
21 A Midsummer Night's Dream

mendicant 6 beggar **10** almsseeker, panhandler

Mending Wall
author: 11 Robert Frost

Menelaus
king of: 6 Sparta
father: 6 Atreus
mother: 6 Aerope
brother: 9 Agamemnon
wife: 5 Helen
son: 11 Megapenthes, Nicostratus
daughter: 8 Hermione

mene mene tekel upharsin
30 numbered numbered weighed divided
foretells destruction of:
10 Belshazzar

from Biblical book of:
6 Daniel

Menestheus
regent of: 6 Athens
rejected by: 5 Helen
assisted: 8 Menelaus

Menesthius
father: 9 Areithous
fought with: 6 Greeks
killed by: 5 Paris

menhaden 4 pogy 5 pogie
6 bunker 7 alewife, bugfish,
ellfish, fatback, herring, old-
wife, sardine 8 bonyfish, hardhead, ladyfish 10 mossbunker

menial 3 low 4 mean 5 drone,
lowly, slave, toady 6 abject,
drudge, flunky, helper, humble, lackey 7 fawning, ignoble,
servant, servile, slavish
8 cringing, employee 9 degrading, groveling, sycophant,
truckling, underling 10 apprentice, obsequious 11 bootlicking, subordinate, subservient, sycophantic

menial labor 4 toil 5 grind
8 drudgery

Menjou, Adolphe
born: 12 Pittsburgh PA
roles: 9 Golden Boy, Pol-
lyanna 11 A Star Is Born
12 The Front Page 13 A
Woman of Paris 15 A Fare-
well to Arms, State of the
Union 16 Little Miss
Marker 18 A Bill of
Divorcement

meno
music: 4 less

Menodice
form: 5 nymph
son: 5 Hylas

Menoeceus
descendant of: 6 Sparti
father: 5 Creon
son: 5 Creon
daughter: 7 Jocasta
death by: 7 suicide

Menoetes
occupation: 7 cowherd

Menoetius
member of: 6 Titans
9 Argonauts
father: 7 Iapetus
mother: 7 Clymene
brother: 5 Atlas 10 Epimetheus, Prometheus
son: 9 Patroclus

**Menominee, Menomini,
Menomonie**
language family: 9 Algon-
kian 10 Algonquian
location: 4 Ohio 7 Indiana
8 Illinois, Michigan
9 Wisconsin

menorah 11 candelabrum, candlestick 12 candleholder
number of candles: 5 seven

Menotti, Gian-Carlo
born: 5 Italy 10 Cadigliano
composer of: 9 The Consul,
The Medium 12 The Island
God, The Telephone
19 Amelia Goes to the Ball
24 Amahl and the Night
Visitors

**mens sana in corpore
sano** 22 a sound mind in a
sound body

mental 5 crazy, nutty 6 insane,
psycho 7 cracked, lunatic,
psychic 8 abstract, cerebral,
neurotic, rational 9 disturbed,
in the mind, of the mind,
psychotic 10 disordered, subjective, unbalanced 11 intelligent, mentally ill
12 intellectual, metaphysical
13 psychological

mental application 9 diligence 10 absorption, intentness 11 deep thought,
engrossment, fixed regard
13 concentration 14 close
attention

mental disorder 5 quirk 6 lunacy, oddity 7 madness 8 delusion, insanity, neurosis
9 craziness, psychosis 10 aberration 11 abnormality, derangement, mental lapse,
peculiarity, strangeness 12 eccentricity, idiosyncrasy
13 schizophrenia 15 manic
depression

mental hospital 6 asylum
8 madhouse 11 institution

mental institution 6 asylum
8 madhouse 12 insane asylum

mentality 4 mind 6 acumen,
brains, wisdom 8 judgment,
sagacity 9 intellect 10 gray
matter, perception 11 discernment 12 intelligence,
perspicacity

mental lapse 5 quirk 6 lunacy, oddity 7 madness
8 rambling, straying 9 wandering 10 aberration 11 derangement, peculiarity
12 eccentricity 13 forgetfulness

mentally incapable
Latin: 15 non compos mentis

mentally sound
Latin: 12 compos mentis

Mentes
origin: 7 Taphian
rank: 7 captain

mention 3 say 4 cite, hint,
name, tell 5 imply, state
6 hint at, notice, remark, report, tell of 7 comment, di-

vulge, inkling, narrate,
observe, recount, refer to,
specify 8 allude to, allusion,
disclose, intimate 9 insinuate,
make known, reference, statement, touch upon, utterance
10 advisement, indication, suggestion 11 designation, insinuation, observation
12 acquaintance, announcement, notification 13 communication, enlightenment,
specification

mentor 4 guru 5 guide, tutor
6 master 7 adviser, monitor,
proctor, teacher 9 counselor,
preceptor, professor
10 instructor

Mentor
advisor of: 8 Odysseus
educated: 10 Telemachus

Mephibosheth
father: 4 Saul 8 Jonathan
also called: 9 Meribbaal
grandfather: 4 Saul
son: 5 Micha

Mephistopheles
character in: 5 Faust
author: 6 Goethe

Mephitis see 7 Mefitis

mer 3 sea

Merab
father: 4 Saul
sister: 6 Michal
brother-in-law: 5 David

mercantile 5 trade 8 business
10 commercial 16 buying-and-
selling

mercantilism 5 trade 8 business, commerce, exchange
13 commercialism

Mercedes
character in: 21 The Count
of Monte Cristo
author: 5 Dumas (pere)

mercenary 5 venal 6 for pay,
greedy 7 for gain, selfish
8 covetous, grasping, hireling,
monetary 10 avaricious 11 acquisitive, paid soldier 12 hired
soldier

merchandise 4 sell 5 goods,
stock, trade, wares 6 deal in,
market 7 effects, staples
8 huckster 9 advertise, publicize, traffic in 10 belongings,
buy and sell, distribute
11 commodities 12 stock in
trade

merchant 6 broker, dealer,
hawker, jobber, monger,
trader, vendor 7 peddler
8 chandler, retailer, salesman
9 purchaser, tradesman
10 saleswoman, shopkeeper,
wholesaler 11 storekeeper,
tradeswoman

Merchant of Venice, The
author: **18** William Shakespeare
character: **6** Portia **7** Antonio, Jessica, Lorenzo, Nerissa, Shylock **8** Bassanio, Gratiano

merci 8 thank you

merci beaucoup 16 thank you very much

merciful 4 kind **6** benign, humane, tender **7** clement, feeling, lenient, pitying, sparing **8** gracious **9** forgiving **10** beneficent **11** kindhearted, softhearted, sympathetic **13** compassionate, understanding

mercifulness 8 clemency, kindness, leniency, sympathy **9** benignity **10** compassion, humaneness **11** beneficence, forgiveness **13** understanding

merciless 4 fell **5** cruel, harsh **6** fierce, severe **7** callous, inhuman **8** inhumane, pitiless, ruthless **9** ferocious, heartless, unpitying, unsparing **10** relentless, unmerciful **11** coldblooded, hardhearted, remorseless, unrelenting

Mercouri, Melina
husband: **11** Jules Dassin
born: **6** Athens, Greece
roles: **7** Topkapi **10** Gaily Gaily **13** Never on Sunday **15** Once Is Not Enough

mercurial 6 fickle, lively, mobile **7** erratic, flighty, kinetic, protean **8** electric, spirited, unstable, variable, volatile **9** impetuous, impulsive **10** capricious, changeable, inconstant **11** fluctuating **13** irrepressible, unpredictable

mercury
chemical symbol: **2** Hg

Mercury
origin: **5** Roman
messenger of: **4** gods
god of: **7** science, thieves **8** commerce **9** eloquence
corresponds to: **6** Hermes, Ogmios

Mercutio
character in: **14** Romeo and Juliet
author: **11** Shakespeare

mercy 4 pity **5** grace **6** lenity **7** charity **8** blessing, clemency, humanity, kindness, lenience, leniency, sympathy **9** good thing, tolerance **10** compassion, humaneness, lucky break **11** benevolence, forbearance, forgiveness, piece of luck **13** commiseration, fellow

feeling **15** softheartedness **17** tenderheartedness
Latin: **12** misericordia

Mercy seat see **16** Ark of the Covenant

Merdle
character in: **12** Little Dorrit
author: **7** Dickens

mere 4 bald, bare, sole **5** plain, scant, sheer, utter **6** common, paltry **7** mundane **8** nugatory, ordinary, trifling **10** negligible, uneventful **11** commonplace, unmitigated **13** insignificant, unappreciable **14** inconsiderable

mere 6 mother

Meredith, Burgess
wife: **15** Paulette Goddard
born: **11** Cleveland OH
roles: **5** Magic, Rocky **6** Batman (the Penguin) **7** Madame X **8** Foul Play **12** Hurry Sundown, Of Mice and Men **15** Magnificent Doll, Such Good Friends **16** Advise and Consent

Meredith, George
author of: **9** The Egoist **10** Modern Love **14** Evan Harrington **16** Beauchamp's Career **19** Diana of the Crossways **25** The Ordeal of Richard Feverel

merely 3 but **4** just, only **5** quite **6** barely, in part, purely, simply, solely **7** utterly **8** scarcely, wholly **10** absolutely

meretricious 4 mock, sham **5** bogus, false, phony **6** pseudo, shoddy, tawdry **8** delusive, specious, spurious **9** deceptive **10** fraudulent, misleading **11** counterfeit

merge 4 fuse, join, weld **5** blend, unify, unite **6** link up **7** combine **8** coalesce, converge, intermix **9** associate, become one, integrate, interfuse, interlock **10** amalgamate, synthesize **11** confederate, consolidate **12** band together, interconnect

mergence 3 mix **5** blend **7** merging, mixture **8** mingling **10** concoction **11** combination

Mergenthaler, Ottmar
nationality: **8** American
invented: **8** linotype

merger 5 union **7** wedding **8** marriage **9** coalition **12** amalgamation **13** confederation, consolidation

Meribbaal see
12 Mephibosheth

meridian 3 tip, top **4** acme, apex, brow, peak **5** crest, crown, point, ridge **6** apogee, climax, summit, vertex, zenith **7** heights **8** pinnacle **11** culmination

Merimee, Prosper
author of: **6** Carmen **7** Colomba

Meriones
mentioned in: **5** Iliad
vocation: **6** archer
father: **5** Molus

merit 4 earn, rate **5** value, worth **6** credit, desert, invite, prompt, talent, virtue **7** ability, benefit, deserve, quality, stature, warrant **8** efficacy **9** advantage **10** be worthy of, excellence, worthiness **11** distinction **12** be entitled to, have a right to **13** justification

merited 3 due **5** rated **6** earned **8** deserved, rightful

meritorious 4 fine **6** worthy **8** laudable **9** admirable, estimable, excellent, exemplary **10** creditable, noteworthy **11** commendable, exceptional **12** praiseworthy

Mermaid Tycoon
nickname of: **14** Esther Williams

Merman, Ethel
real name: **20** Ethel Agnes Zimmermann
husband: **14** Ernest Borgnine
born: **9** Astoria NY
autobiography: **6** Merman
roles: **11** Call Me Madam **12** Anything Goes, Panama Hattie **15** Annie Get Your Gun **16** Stage Door Canteen **21** Alexander's Ragtime Band

Mermerus
father: **5** Jason
mother: **5** Medea

Merodach see **6** Marduk

Merope
member of: **8** Pleiades
father: **5** Atlas **8** Oenopion
husband: **7** Polybus **8** Sisyphus **11** Cresphontes, Polyphontes
son: **7** Aepytus
raped by: **5** Orion
raised: **7** Oedipus

merrily 5 gaily **6** gladly **7** briskly, happily, lightly, lustick, quickly **8** blithely, jocundly, jovially, joyfully, joyously **9** festively, gleefully **10** cheerfully, laughingly, mirthfully **11** hilariously, vivaciously **14** lightheartedly

Merrimac see **9** Pennacook

merriment 3 fun **4** glee
5 cheer, mirth **6** frolic, gaiety,
hoopla, levity **7** good fun, jollity, revelry, whoopee **8** hilarity, laughter **9** amusement,
festivity, good humor, jocundity, joviality **10** jocularity, jubilation, liveliness, skylarking
11 celebration, gleefulness,
good spirits, merrymaking
12 conviviality, exhilaration,
sportiveness
16 lightheartedness

Merriweather, Mrs
character in: **15** Gone With
the Wind
author: **8** Mitchell

merry 3 gay **5** happy, jolly
6 blithe, cheery, jocund, jovial,
joyous, lively **7** festive, gleeful,
jocular **8** animated, carefree,
cheerful, gladsome, laughing,
mirthful, partying, reveling,
sportive **9** convivial, fun-
loving, sprightly, vivacious
10 frolicsome, rollicking, skylarking **12** high-spirited,
lighthearted

merrymaking 5 sport **6** frolic,
gaiety, hoopla, revels **7** jollity,
revelry, whoopee **8** carousal
9 festivity, fun-making, high
jinks, merriment, rejoicing,
whoop-de-do **10** saturnalia
11 bacchanalia, celebration,
festivities **12** conviviality

**Merry Wives of Windsor,
The**
author: **18** William
Shakespeare
character: **4** Ford, Page
5 Caius **6** Doctor, Fenton
7 Slender **8** Anne Page
12 Mistress Ford, Mistress
Page **15** Mistress Quickly,
Sir John Falstaff

mesa 4 hill, peak **5** bench,
butte, table **7** plateau, terrace
9 cartouche, tableland

Mescalero
language family: **6** Apache
location: **6** Mexico **9** New
Mexico
related to: **5** Lipan
10 Chiricahua

**Meserve, Margaret
Hamilton**
real name of: **16** Margaret
Hamilton

Meservey, Robert Preston
real name of: **13** Robert
Preston

mesh 3 fib, net, web **4** grid,
jibe **5** agree, sieve, tally **6** engage, enmesh, grille, plexus,
screen **7** connect, engaged,
netting, network, webbing,
webwork **8** dovetail, interact,
lacework, meshwork, open-

work **9** grillwork, interlock,
intermesh **10** coordinate, correspond, interweave, wicker-
work **11** fit together,
latticework **12** reticulation

Meshach
former name: **7** Mishael
companion: **6** Daniel
friend: **8** Abednego, Shadrach

**Mesmer, Franz (Friedrich)
Anton**
nationality: **6** German
developed: **8** hypnosis

mesmerize 5 charm **7** bewitch **8** enthrall, entrance
9 fascinate, hypnotize, magnet-
ize, spellbind, transport

Mesopotamian mythology
god of agriculture/earth:
5 Dagan
*corresponds to Phoeni-
cian:* **5** Dagon

Mesquakie *see* **3** Fox

mess 3 fix **4** hash, stew **5** mix-
up, pinch **6** crisis, jumble, litter, muddle, pickle, plight,
scrape, strait **7** clutter, dilemma, trouble **8** disarray, disorder, hot water, mess hall,
mishmash, quandary **9** cafeteria, confusion, imbroglio, re-
fectory, situation
10 commissary, difficulty, dining hall, dining room, hodgepodge **11** predicament
14 conglomeration

message 4 news, note, word
5 moral, point, theme **6** letter,
notice, report **7** meaning, missive, purport, tidings **8** bulletin, dispatch **9** statement
10 communique, memorandum **12** intelligence
13 communication

mess around with 4 test
6 try out **8** fool with, play
with **10** tinker with **14** experiment with

Messene
husband: **8** Polycaon

messenger 5 envoy **6** bearer,
runner **7** carrier, courier
8 delegate, emissary **9** deliverer, go-between **11** delivery
boy, delivery man
12 intermediary

messenger of gods 4 Iris
6 Hermes **7** Mercury

**Messiaen, Olivier Eugene
Prosper Charles**
born: **6** France **7** Avignon
composer of: **11** Exotic
Birds, Turangalila **13** Chron-
ochromie **20** Le Nativite du
Seigneur **22** Quartet for the
End of Time **27** Vingt Regards sur l'Enfant Jesus
33 Et exspecto resurrecti-

onem mortuorum **41** Transfiguration de Notre Seigneur
Jesus Christ

Messiah
means: **11** anointed one
see also: **10** Jesus

Messick, Dale
creator/artist of: **19** Brenda
Starr Reporter

messiness 5 chaos, mix-up,
upset **6** jumble **7** clutter **8** disarray, disorder, scramble,
shambles **9** confusion **10** disharmony, sloppiness, untidiness **12** dishevelment
14 disarrangement
15 disorganization

mess up 3 mar **4** goof, muff,
ruin **5** botch, spoil **6** bungle,
foul up, jumble **7** blunder,
butcher, disturb, do badly,
louse up, screw up **9** mismanage **10** disarrange **11** disorganize, make a mess of, make
an error **12** make a mistake

messy 4 ugly **6** blowsy, frowsy,
grubby, sloppy, tricky, untidy
7 awkward, chaotic, jumbled,
tangled, unkempt **8** confused,
littered **9** cluttered, difficult
10 bedraggled, disheveled, disordered, slatternly, topsy-turvy,
unenviable, unpleasant **11** disarranged **12** embarrassing,
inextricable **13** uncomfortable

Mesthles
commander of army of:
5 Maeon

mesto
music: **8** mournful

Mestor
father: **7** Perseus
mother: **9** Andromeda
daughter: **9** Hippothoe

Metabus
daughter: **7** Camilla

metal *see* **box**

Metalious, Grace
author of: **11** Peyton Place

metalworking
god of: **6** Vulcan **10** Hephaestus, Hephaistos

metamorphose 6 change, mutate **7** convert **9** transform
11 transfigure

Metamorphoses
author: **4** Ovid

metamorphosis 8 mutation
10 alteration, conversion
11 permutation **12** change of
form, modification **13** radical
change, transmutation
14 transformation **15** series of
changes, startling change,
transfiguration
18 transmogrification

metal
alloy: 5 brass 6 bronze, nickel, pewter, solder
bar: 3 gad 4 risp 5 ingot
bolt: 5 rivet
box: 8 canister
casting: 3 peg
classification: 5 light, noble 6 alkali, common 7 coinage 8 platinum, precious 9 rare earth 10 low-melting, refractory, transition 11 high-melting 14 semiconductors
clippings: 7 scissel
coarse: 5 matte
corrosion: 4 rust
crude: 3 ore 4 slug
cymbals: 3 tal
deposit: 4 lode, vein
design: 7 chasing
disk or plate: 4 shim 5 medal, paten 6 platen, sequin
eyelet: 7 grommet
filings: 5 lemel
god of: 6 Vulcan 10 Hephaestus
heaviest: 6 osmium
kind: 3 tin 4 gold, iron, lead, zinc 6 barium, cerium, cesium, copper, erbium, nickel, osmium, radium, silver, sodium 7 arsenic, bismuth, calcium, holmium, iridium, lithium, rhodium, silicon, terbium, thulium 8 actinium, aluminum, antimony, europium, lutetium, platinum, rubidium, samarium, selenium, titanium, tungsten 9 beryllium, magnesium, palladium, potassium, ruthenium, strontium 10 molybdenum, phosphorus
layer: 7 plating
leaf: 4 foil
lightest: 7 lithium
liquid: 7 mercury
mass: 3 pid 5 ingot 7 bullion
piece: 4 jack, slug
refuse: 4 slag 5 dross
shaper: 5 swage
suit: 4 mail 5 armor 6 armour
thread: 4 lame, wire
trademark: 5 monel
ware: 4 tole 6 Revere
worker: 5 smith 6 forger, welder 7 armorer, riveter 8 armourer 9 goldsmith, ironsmith 10 blacksmith 11 coppersmith, silversmith 12 metallurgist

---

Metamorphosis, The
author: 10 Franz Kafka

Metanira
husband: 6 Celeus
son: 4 Abas 9 Demophoon 11 Triptolemus

metaphor 5 image, trope 6 simile 7 analogy 8 metonymy, parallel 11 equivalence 14 figure of speech, representation

metaphysical 5 basic, lofty, vague 6 far-out 7 eternal 8 abstract, abstruse, esoteric, mystical, ultimate 9 essential, high-flown, recondite, universal 10 impalpable, intangible, jesuitical, oversubtle 11 existential, fundamental, ontological, speculative 12 cosmological, intellectual, unanswerable 13 philosophical 15 epistemological

Metaphysics
author: 9 Aristotle

metaxa
type: 6 brandy 7 liqueur
origin: 6 Greece

mete, mete out 5 allot 6 assign, divide 7 deal out, dole out 8 allocate, disburse, dispense 9 apportion, parcel out 10 administer, distribute, measure out

meteoric 4 fast 5 fiery, rapid, swift 6 speedy, sudden 7 blazing, flaming, instant 8 flashing, unabated 10 inexorable 11 ineluctable, unstoppable

meter
abbreviation: 1 m

Meter
epithet of: 6 Athena
means: 6 mother

method 3 way 4 form, mode, plan, tack 5 means, order, style, usage 6 course, design, manner, scheme, system 7 fashion, formula, process, program, purpose, routine 8 approach, efficacy 9 procedure, technique, viability 13 modus operandi

methodical, methodic 4 neat, tidy 5 exact 7 careful, logical, orderly, precise, regular, uniform 10 analytical, deliberate, meticulous, systematic 12 businesslike 13 well-regulated

methodization 5 order 11 arrangement 12 organization 14 categorization, classification 15 systematization

methodize 5 order 7 arrange 8 classify, organize 11 systematize

Methuselah
father: 5 Enoch
son: 6 Lamech
years lived: 23 nine hundred and sixty nine
known as: 9 oldest man

meticulous 4 nice 5 exact, fussy 7 finical, finicky, precise 8 exacting, sedulous 10 fastidious, particular, scrupulous 11 painstaking, punctilious 13 conscientious, perfectionist

meticulousness 4 care 5 pains 12 sedulousness, thoroughness 14 fastidiousness, scrupulousness 17 conscientiousness

metier 3 job 4 area, line, work 5 craft, field, forte, trade 7 calling, pursuit 8 activity, business, lifework, province, vocation 9 specialty 10 employment, livelihood, occupation, profession

meting out 8 alloting 9 bestowing, doling out 10 allocating, conferring, consigning, dealing out, dispensing 11 designating 12 apportioning, distributing, measuring out

Metioche
father: 5 Orion
sister: 7 Menippe

Metion
father: 10 Erechtheus
mother: 9 Praxithea
brother: 7 Cecrops

Metis
member of: 6 Titans
father: 7 Oceanus
mother: 6 Tethys
consort of: 4 Zeus
daughter: 6 Athena

Metiscus
   charioteer of: **6** Turnus

metrical narrative
   French: **5** roman

Metropolis
   director: **9** Fritz Lang
   cast: **10** Alfred Abel **12** Brigitte Helm

metropolitan area 4 city **8** core city, downtown, environs **9** inner city, precincts, urban area **10** city limits, metropolis **11** central city **16** business district

mettle 3 vim **4** grit, guts **5** nerve, pluck, spunk, valor, vigor **6** spirit **7** bravery, courage, heroism **8** audacity, backbone, boldness, gameness, temerity **9** derring-do, fortitude, gallantry, manliness **10** enthusiasm, resolution **11** intrepidity **12** fearlessness **13** determination

mettlesome 4 bold, edgy **5** brave, fiery **6** ardent, plucky, spunky **7** gingery, peppery

8 restless, skittish, spirited **9** excitable, impatient **10** courageous, high-strung **12** high-spirited

Mexica see **5** Aztec

Mexico see box

Mexico City
   Aztec name: **12** Tenochtitlan
   capital of: **6** Mexico
   landmark: **13** Mercado Merced **15** Chapultepec Park **19** Basilica of Guadalupe
      bull ring: **11** Plaza Mexico
      floating gardens: **10** Xochimilco
      pyramids: **11** Teotihuacan
   square: **6** Zocalo **22** Plaza de las Tres Culturas
   street: **16** Paseo de la Reforma

Meyer, David Harold
   real name of: **12** David Janssen

Meyerbeer, Giacomo
   real name: **17** Jacob Liebmann Beer

born: **6** Berlin **7** Germany
composer of: **7** Dinorah **10** Le Prophete, The African, The Prophet **12** Les Huguenots, The Huguenots, The North Star **14** Robert le Diable, Robert the Devil

Mezentius
   king of: **7** Etruria
   noted for: **7** cruelty
   son: **6** Lausus
   killed by: **6** Aeneas

mezza voce
   music: **9** half voice **10** half volume

mezzo
   music: **4** half

Miami
   bay: **8** Biscayne
   county: **4** Dade
   developer: **7** Flagler
   football team: **8** Dolphins
   museum: **4** Lowe **12** Villa Viscaya
   ocean: **8** Atlantic
   people: **5** Cuban **8** Hispanic
   section: **7** Hialeah **10** Bal Harbour **11** Coral Gables

---

Mexico
   other name: **8** New Spain
   capital/largest city: **10** Mexico City
   others: **4** Leon **5** La Paz, Taxco **6** Cancun, Celaya, Merida, Oaxaca, Puebla, Toluca **7** Durango, Guaymas, Tampico, Tijuana, Torreon **8** Acapulco, Culiacan, Ensenada, Irapuato, Mazatlan, Mexicali, Saltillo, Veracruz **9** Chihuahua, Matamoras, Monterrey, Queretaro, Salamanca, Zacatecas **10** Hermosillo **11** Guadalajara, Nuevo Laredo **12** Ciudad Juarez, Villahermosa **13** Coatzacoalcos, Piedras Negras, San Luis Potosi **14** Puerto Vallarta **15** Netzahualcoyotl
      ancient city: **4** Tula **7** Texcoco **8** Tlacopan **10** Monte Alban **11** Teotihuacan **12** Tenochtitlan **13** Tula de Allende
   division: **6** Colima, Oaxaca, Puebla, Sonora **7** Chiapas, Durango, Hidalgo, Jalisco, Sinaloa, Tabasco, Yucatan **8** Campeche, Coahuila, Tlaxcala, Veracruz **9** Chihuahua, Michoacan, Nuevo Leon, Zacatecas **13** San Luis Potosi **14** Baja California
   measure: **3** bag, pie **4** alma, onza, vara **5** almud, baril, carga, jarra, labor, legua, libra, linea, marco, sitio **6** adarme, almude, arroba, carega, fanega, ochaua, terceo **7** pulgada, quintal **9** cuarteron, cuartillo **10** caballeria
   monetary unit: **4** onza, peso **5** adobe, claco, tlaco **6** azteca, cuarto, dinero **7** centavo, piaster
   weight: **4** onza **5** libra, marco **6** arroba, tercio **7** quintal
   island: **6** Carmen, Cedros **7** San Jose, Tiburon **8** Cerralvo **10** Tres Marias **13** Espiritu Santo **14** Santa Magdalena, Santa Margarita **15** Angel de la Guarda
   lake: **7** Chapala, Texcoco **9** Patzcuaro
   mountain: **6** Colima, Tacana, Toluca **9** Paricutin **11** Ixtacihuatl, Sierra Madre **12** Popocatepetl **14** Sierra Zacateca **16** Chiapas Highlands **24** Transverse Volcanic Sierra
   highest point: **7** Orizaba **12** Citlaltepetl
   river: **4** Mayo **5** Yaqui **6** Balsas, Fuerte, Grande, Panuco **8** Colorado, Grijalva **10** Papaloapan, Usumacinta **13** Bravo del Norte, Coatzacoalcos, Lerma-Santiago
   sea: **7** Pacific **8** Atlantic **9** Caribbean
   physical feature:
      bay: **8** Campeche **9** Olas Atlas
      cape: **10** Corrientes
      desert: **6** Sonora
      gulf: **6** Mexico **8** Campeche **10** California **11** Tehuantepec
      isthmus: **11** Tehuantepec
      peninsula: **7** Yucatan **14** Baja California
      plain: **7** Tabasco
      plateau: **7** Mexican
      valley: **7** Chiapas
   people: **6** Indian **7** mestizo, Spanish
      architect: **7** O'Gorman

stadium: 10 Orange Bowl
tropical garden: 9 Fairchild
university: 5 Barry **8** St
Thomas
zoo: 11 Crandon Park

Miami (Twightwee)
language family: 9 Algonkian **10** Algonquian
tribe: 3 Wea **5** Miami
10 Piankashaw
location: 4 Ohio **7** Indiana
8 Illinois, Michigan
9 Wisconsin
leader: 12 Little Turtle
allied with: 6 Peoria

Miami Vice
character: 4 Gina **5** Trudy
8 (Capt) Castillo **13** Riccardo
Tubbs, Sonny Crockett
cast: 10 Don Johnson
11 Olivia Brown **15** Saundra
Santiago **16** Edward James
Olmos **20** Phillip Michael
Thomas

Micah Clarke
author: 19 Sir Arthur Conan
Doyle

Micawber, Mr
character in: 16 David
Copperfield
author: 7 Dickens

Micha
father: 9 Meribbaal
12 Mephibosheth
grandfather: 8 Jonathan
great-grandfather: 4 Saul

Michael
author: 17 William
Wordsworth

Michael
means: 12 Who is like God
father: 8 Izrahiah
11 Jehoshaphat
son: 4 Omri **8** Zabadiah
also: 9 archangel

Michel
father: 4 Saul
husband: 5 David, Palti
sister: 5 Merab

**Michelangelo di Buonarotti
(Simoni)**
architect of: 11 Campidoglio
(Capitoline Hill) **12** Medici
Chapel (Florence)

13 Farnese Palace **21** Palazzo Medici-Riccardi (Florence) **22** Palazzo dei
Conservatori (Capitoline
Hill) **24** Convent of San
Marco Library
born: 5 Italy **7** Caprese
patron: 12 Pope Julius II
14 Lorenzo d'Medici
19 Pope Julius the Second
21 Lorenzo the Magnificent
artwork: 5 David, Moses,
Pieta **6** Brutus, Slaves **7** Bacchus **9** The Victor **10** Holy
Family **12** Madonna Pitti
15 The Last Judgment
18 Conversion of St Paul
20 Madonna Seated on a
Step, Sistine Chapel Ceiling
21 The Flight of the Lapites,
The Martyrdom of St Peter

Michelozzo
architect of: 21 Palazzo
Medici-Riccardi (Florence)
24 Convent of San Marco
Library

Michelson, Albert A
field: 7 physics

Mexico (*continued*)
composer: 6 Chavez
emperor: 10 Maximilian
explorer: 6 Cortes, Cortez **7** Cordoba **8** Alvarado, Grijalva
god: 6 Tlaloc **12** Quetzalcoatl **14** Huitzilopochtl
leader: 3 Gil **4** Diaz **5** Lopez, Rubio, Villa **6** Calles, Huerta, Juarez, Madero, Valdes, Zapata
7 Obregon **8** Carranza, Iturbide, Portillo, Santa Ana **9** Diaz Ordaz, Montezuma, Rodriguez
13 Madrid Hurtado **16** Salinas de Gortari
revolutionary/priest: 13 Morelos y Pavon **16** Hidalgo y Costilla
soldier/explorer: 12 conquistador
viceroy: 7 Mendoza
writer: 3 Paz **5** Nervo, Reyes, Yanez **6** Azuela, Guzman, Najera **7** Fuentes
language: 5 Mayan, Otomi **6** Mixtec **7** Mazahua, Mazatec, Nahuatl, Spanish, Totonac, Zapotec
8 Tarascan
religion: 13 Roman Catholic
place:
cathedral: 10 Assumption
center of Mexico City: 6 Zocalo **21** Plaza de la Constitucion
floating gardens: 10 Xochimilco
museum: 28 Shrine of the Virgin of Guadalupe
park: 7 Alameda **11** Chapultepec
ruins: 5 Mitla, Uxmal **8** Palenque **10** Monte Alban **11** Chichen Itza, Teotihuacan **20** Temple
of Quetzalcoatl
street: 13 Avenida Juarez **16** Paseo de la Reforma
temple/pyramid: 7 Cholula **8** Castillo
feature:
agreement: 5 NAFTA
Christmas tradition: 6 pinata
coffee plantation: 5 finca
empire: 4 Maya **5** Aztec, Olmec **6** Mixtec, Toltec **7** Zapotec
large estate: 8 hacienda
musician: 8 mariachi
small farm/commune: 6 ejidos
sport: 7 jai alai **12** bullfighting
tree: 9 sapodilla **11** chicozapote
food:
corn cake: 8 tortilla
dish: 4 mole, taco **5** huevo, pollo **6** tamale **7** burrito, chorizo, taquito, tostada **8** empanada
9 enchilada, guacamole, sopadilla **10** chili verde, quesadilla **11** chimichanga **12** chili relleno
drink: 6 pulque **7** tequila

established: 12 speed of light **15** velocity of Earth
awarded: 10 Nobel Prize

Michener, James A
author of: 5 Space **6** Alaska, Hawaii, Iberia, Legacy, Poland **8** Caravans, Sayonara **9** The Source **10** Centennial, Chesapeake **11** The Covenant, The Drifters **16** The Fires of Spring **18** The Bridges at Toko-ri **22** Tales of the South Pacific

Mickey Mouse
creator: 10 Walt Disney
character: 5 Morty **6** Ferdie **11** Minnie Mouse
cow: **10** Clarabelle

Micklewhite, Maurice Joseph
real name of: 12 Michael Caine

Micmac
language family: 9 Algonkian **10** Algonquian
location: 6 Canada **10** Nova Scotia **12** Newfoundland,

New Brunswick **14** Gaspe Peninsula **16** Cape Breton Island **18** Prince Edward Island

microbe 4 germ **5** virus **6** gamete, zygote **8** bacillus, parasite **9** bacterium **10** spirochete **13** microorganism, streptococcus **14** staphylococcus

microbiologist
American: 7 Waksman **9** Baltimore
Dutch: 11 (van) Leeuwenhoek

Micronesia
part of: 7 Oceania
island: 3 Nui **4** Guam, Rota, Truk, Wake **5** Makin, Nauru, Wotho **6** Bikini, Ellice, Majuro, Ponape **7** Gilbert, Mariana **8** Caroline, Kiribati, Marshall

microorganism 3 bug **4** germ **5** virus **7** microbe **8** bacillus, pathogen **9** bacterium

microphobia
fear of: 12 small objects

microscope
invented by:
compound: **7** Janssen
electronic: **5** Knoll, Ruska
field ion: **7** Mueller
single lens model improved by: 11 (van) Leeuwenhoek
first observed: **8** protozoa **13** red blood cells **19** single-celled animals

microscopic, microscopical 4 tiny **5** teeny **6** atomic, minute **9** invisible **10** diminutive, very little **13** imperceptible, infinitesimal

microscopy
founder: 11 Robert Hooke **13** Jan Swammerdam **16** Marcello Malpighi **19** Anton van Leeuwenhoek

Midas
king of: 7 Phrygia
father: 7 Gordius
gift: 11 golden touch
gift from: 7 Silenus
ears changed to those of: 3 ass
changed by: 6 Apollo

midday 4 noon **7** noonday **8** meridian, noontide, noontime

middle 3 act, gut, hub, mid **4** core, main **5** belly, heart, midst, waist **6** center, course, medial, median, midway, throes **7** central, halfway, midmost, midriff, nucleus, process, stomach **8** midpoint **9** heartland **10** midsection **12** intermediate

Michigan
abbreviation: 2 MI **4** Mich
nickname: 4 Lake **9** Wolverine **10** Automobile **15** Water Wonderland **16** Winter Wonderland
capital: 7 Lansing
largest city: 7 Detroit
others: 4 Caro, Troy **5** Flint, Niles, Wayne **6** Adrien, Alpena, Bad Axe, Monroe, Owosso, Warren, Wassar **7** Bay City, Holland, Jackson, Livonia, Midland, Pontiac, Saginaw, Trenton, Wyoming **8** Ann Arbor, Cadillac, Dearborn, Escanaba, Ironwood, Manistee, Muskegon, Petoskey, Royal Oak **9** Cheboygan, Hillsdale, Kalamazoo, Marquette, Port Huron, Roseville, Wyandotte **10** Birmingham, River Rouge **11** Battle Creek, Grand Rapids **12** Benton Harbor, Traverse City **13** Sault Ste Marie, St Clair Shores
college: 4 Alma, Hope **5** Wayne **6** Adrian, Albion, Calvin, Olivet, Owosso **7** Detroit, Oakland **9** Hillsdale, Kalamazoo, Marygrove
feature:
bridge: **8** Mackinac
canal: **3** Soo **12** Sault St Marie
festival: **12** Holland Tulip
national park: **10** Isle Royale
village: **10** Greenfield
tribe: 6 Ojibwa, Ottawa **8** Chippewa **10** Potawatomi
people: 9 Henry Ford, wolverine **11** Bruce Catton, Edgar A Guest, Julie Harris, Ralph Bunche, Ring Lardner **16** Charles Lindburgh
explorer: **6** Joliet **7** La Salle, Nicolet **9** Marquette **12** Etienne Brule, Sault St Marie
island: 8 Mackinaw
lake: 4 Burt, Erie **5** Clear, Huron, Round, Torch **6** Austin, Devils, Moline **7** Bawbees, St Clair **8** Houghton, Michigan, Superior
land rank: 11 twenty-third
mountain: 6 Copper **7** Gogebic **9** Menominee, Porcupine
highest point: **12** Mount Curwood
physical feature:
bay: **7** Saginaw, Thunder **8** Keweenaw, Sturgeon
straits: **8** Mackinac
president: 10 Gerald Ford
river: 4 Cass **5** Grand, Huron **6** Raisin **7** Detroit, Saginaw, St Clair, St Mary's **8** Escanaba, Muskegon **9** Menominee
state admission: 11 twenty-sixth
state bird: 5 robin
state fish: 5 trout
state flower: 12 apple blossom
state motto: 11 I Will Defend **39** If You Seek a Pleasant Peninsula Look About You
state song: 18 Michigan My Michigan
state tree: 16 eastern white pine

Middle Ages
French: **8** moyen age

middle-class 4 mass **8** ordinary **9** bourgeois **10** mainstream, middlebrow

middle Europe
German: **12** Mitteleuropa

middle ground 4 mean **7** balance **8** midpoint **11** equilibrium **12** common ground

Middle Kingdom see **5** China

middleman 5 agent **6** broker, dealer, jobber **7** liaison **8** mediator **9** go-between **10** wholesaler **11** distributor, intercessor **12** entrepreneur, intermediary

Middlemarch
author: **11** George Eliot
character: **5** Celia **12** Will Ladislaw **13** Rosamond Viney **14** Dorothea Brooke, Edward Casaubon, Tertius Lydgate **15** Sir James Chettam

middlemost 4 mean **5** inner **6** inmost, median **7** central, midmost **8** interior

middle-of-the-road 8 moderate **10** mainstream

middle-of-the-roader 8 moderate **12** mainstreamer

middle way
Latin: **8** via media

middling 4 fair, so-so **6** medium **7** average, fairish, minimal **8** mediocre, moderate, ordinary, passable **9** tolerable **10** pretty good, second-rate **11** indifferent **12** run-of-the-mill, unremarkable

Midea see **9** Licymnius

Midgard
also: **10** Mithgarthr
origin: **10** Scandinavian
means: **10** abode of man
located between: **8** Niflheim **10** Muspelheim
connected to Asgard by: **7** bifrost **13** rainbow bridge
formed from brow of: **4** Ymir

Midgard Serpent see **11** Jormungandr

midget 4 doll, runt **5** dwarf, pygmy **6** peewee, puppet, shrimp, squirt **7** manikin **8** half-pint, munchkin, small fry, Tom Thumb **9** pipsqueak **10** fingerling, homunculus **11** hop-o'-my-thumb, lilliputian

Midian
father: **7** Abraham
mother: **7** Keturah
descendant of: **9** Midianite

midlands 8 interior **10** hinterland **13** central region

midmost 5 inner **6** inmost, middle **7** central, pivotal **8** interior **10** middlemost

Midnight Cowboy
director: **15** John Schlesinger
cast: **9** Jon Voight **11** John McGiver, Sylvia Miles **13** Brenda Vaccaro, Dustin Hoffman (Ratso Rizzo)
Oscar for: **7** picture

Midnight Express
director: **10** Alan Parker
cast: **8** John Hurt **9** Bo Hopkins, Brad Davis (Billy Hayes) **10** Randy Quaid **12** Irene Miracle
setting: **13** Turkish prison
score: **14** Giorgio Moroder
Oscar for: **5** score **6** script

midori
type: **7** liqueur
origin: **5** Japan
flavor: **5** melon

midpoint 4 core, mean **5** focus **6** center, middle **15** point of no return

midriff 3 gut **4** guts **5** belly, tummy **6** paunch **7** abdomen, stomach **9** diaphragm **10** midsection **11** breadbasket

midst 3 eye, hub **4** core **5** bosom, heart, thick **6** center, depths, middle **7** nucleus **8** interior

Midsummer Night's Dream, A
author: **18** William Shakespeare
character: **4** Puck (Robin Goodfellow) **6** Bottom, Helena, Hermia, Oberon **7** Theseus, Titania **8** Lysander **9** Demetrius, Hippolyta

midterm 4 exam, test **6** review **11** examination

midwife
French: **11** accoucheuse

mien 3 air **4** look **5** guise, style **6** aspect, manner, visage **7** bearing, feature **8** attitude, behavior, carriage, demeanor, presence **9** semblance **10** appearance, deportment, expression **11** countenance

Mies van der Rohe, Ludwig
architect of: **14** German Pavilion (1929 International Exposition, Barcelona), Lake Shore Drive (apartment towers, Chicago), Tugendhat House (Brno Czechoslovakia) **15** National Gallery (West Berlin), Seagram Building (NYC)

style: **13** International
principle: **10** less is more

miff 3 irk, vex **4** rile **5** anger, annoy, chafe, pique **6** nettle, offend, rankle **7** affront, provoke **8** irritate **9** put one off **10** exasperate **11** make one sore **14** rub the wrong way **15** raise one's dander

Mifune, Toshiro
born: **5** China **8** Tsingtao
roles: **6** Midway, Shogun **8** Rashomon **12** Seven Samurai **13** Throne of Blood

Miggs, Miss
character in: **12** Barnaby Rudge
author: **7** Dickens

might 3 may **5** brawn, clout, force, power, vigor **6** energy, muscle **7** potency, prowess **8** strength **9** influence, lustihood, puissance, toughness **10** capability, competence, durability, robustness, sturdiness **11** capableness **12** forcefulness

mighty 4 able, bold, huge, vast, very **5** brave, hardy, husky, lusty, stout, truly **6** brawny, manful, potent, really, robust, strong, sturdy **7** immense, massive, titanic, valiant **8** colossal, enormous, forceful, gigantic, imposing, majestic, powerful, puissant, stalwart, towering, valorous, vigorous **9** monstrous, strapping **10** courageous, gargantuan, invincible, monolithic, monumental, prodigious, stupendous **11** elephantine, exceedingly, indomitable, of great size **12** overpowering, particularly **13** exceptionally **14** Brobdingnagian

Migonitis
epithet of: **9** Aphrodite
means: **6** uniter

migrate 4 move, trek **6** travel **7** journey **8** emigrate, relocate, resettle **9** immigrate

migration 4 trek **6** exodus, flight, moving **7** passage **8** diaspora, movement

mikado 5 ruler **7** emperor, monarch **9** sovereign **15** Japanese emperor

Mikado, The
subtitle: **15** The Town of Titipu
operetta by: **18** Gilbert and Sullivan
character: **4** Ko-Ko **6** Peep-Bo, Yum-Yum **7** Katisha, Pooh-Bah **8** Nanki-Poo, Pish-Tush **9** Pitti-Sing

Mikkelsen, Dahl
also: 3 Mik
creator/artist of:
8 Ferd'nand

mikrophobia
fear of: 5 germs

mikvah 35 public establishment
for ritual bathing
used by: 12 Orthodox Jews

mild 4 calm, easy, soft, warm
5 balmy, bland 6 docile, gentle, placid, serene, smooth
7 pacific, summery 8 delicate,
moderate, not sharp, pleasant,
soothing, tranquil 9 easygoing,
emollient, not severe, not
strong, temperate 10 forbearing, not extreme, springlike
11 complaisant, uninjurious
12 good-tempered

mildew 4 mold 6 blight,
fungus

mildewed 5 fusty, moldy
10 discolored

mildness 8 calmness, delicacy,
serenity, softness 9 placidity
10 gentleness, good temper

Mildred Pierce
director: 13 Michael Curtiz
based on novel by: 10 James
M Cain
cast: 8 Ann Blyth, Eve Arden 10 Jack Carson
12 Bruce Bennett, Joan
Crawford, Zachary Scott
Oscar for: 7 actress
(Crawford)

mild-tempered 7 equable, patient 9 easygoing 11 good-
natured, unflappable

mile
abbreviation: 2 mi

Miles, Sarah
brother: 11 Christopher
husband: 10 Robert Bolt
born: 7 England
11 Ingatestone
roles: 6 Blow-Up 10 The Servant 11 The Hireling
13 Ryan's Daughter 16 Lady
Caroline Lamb

miles gloriosus 15 boastful
soldier

Miles Gloriosus
author: 7 Plautus

Milesian
origin: 5 Irish
invaders from: 5 Spain
invaded: 7 Ireland
defeated: 14 Tuatha De
Danann
ancestors of: 5 Irish

milestone 7 jubilee 8 milepost,
signpost 10 road marker
11 anniversary 12 red-letter
day, turning point

Milestone, Lewis
director of: 12 Of Mice and
Men, The Front Page 13 A
Walk in the Sun 17 Mutiny
on the Bounty 25 All Quiet
on the Western Front
(Oscar)

Milestones
author: 13 Arnold Bennett

Miletus
father: 6 Apollo
mother: 4 Aria
son: 6 Caunus
daughter: 6 Byblis

milieu 5 scene 7 culture, element, setting 8 ambience,
backdrop 10 background
11 environment, mise-en-
scene 12 surroundings

militant 7 defiant, extreme,
martial, warlike, warring
8 fighting, military 9 assertive,
bellicose, combatant, combative 10 aggressive, pugnacious
11 belligerent, contentious
12 disputatious, paramilitary,
warmongering
14 uncompromising

military 4 army 5 armed, crisp
6 strict, troops 7 martial, militia, Spartan, warlike 8 generals, soldiers 9 combative,
defensive, regulated, soldierly,
warmaking 10 regimented
11 armed forces, belligerent,
soldierlike

military force 4 army, navy
6 legion, troops 7 legions, militia 8 military, regiment, soldiers, soldiery 9 battalion
11 fighting men 13 fighting
force

military machine 4 army
6 legion, troops 11 armed
forces 13 fighting force

military rank abbreviation
see box

military storehouse 6 armory 7 arsenal 8 magazine
9 arms depot 13 ordnance depot 14 ammunition dump

military stores 7 arsenal,
weapons 8 ordnance 9 munitions 10 ammunition

military unit 4 army, crew,
unit 5 corps, force, squad
6 legion, outfit 7 brigade, company 8 regiment, squadron
9 battalion, task force 10 contingent, detachment

milksop 4 baby, wimp
5 mouse, pansy, sissy, softy
6 coward 7 crybaby, nebbish
8 mama's boy, poltroon, weakling 9 fraidy-cat 10 namby-
pamby, pantywaist, scaredy-
cat, weak sister
11 milquetoast, mollycoddle

military rank	
abbreviation	
admiral:	3 adm
brigadier general:	2 bg
7 brig gen	
captain:	3 cpt 4 capt
chief petty officer:	
3 CPO	
colonel:	3 col
commander:	5 comdr
corporal:	3 cpl
ensign:	3 ens
general:	3 gen
lieutenant:	2 lt 5 lieut
lieutenant colonel:	3 ltc
5 lt col	
lieutenant general:	5 lt
gen 8 lieut gen	
major:	3 maj
master sergeant:	4 msgt
private:	3 pvt
private first class:	3 pfc
sergeant:	3 sgt
sergeant first class:	
3 sfc	
sergeant major:	4 smaj
6 sgt maj	
specialist:	4 spec

mill 4 roam, teem 5 crush,
grind, shape, swarm, works
6 finish, groove 7 factory,
meander 8 converge 9 granulate, pulverize

Mill, John Stuart
author of: 9 On Liberty
14 Utilitarianism 20 The
Subjection of Women
28 Principles of Political
Economy

Millais, Sir John Everett
born: 7 England
12 Southhampton
artwork: 7 Bubbles 9 Blind
Girl 12 Autumn Leaves,
Chill October 13 My First
Sermon 18 Lorenzo and Isabella 25 Christ in the Carpenter's Shop 36 Young
Men of Benjamin Seizing
Their Brides

Millament, Mrs
character in: 16 The Way of
the World
author: 8 Congreve

Milland, Ray
real name: 21 Reginald
Truscott-Jones
born: 5 Neath, Wales
roles: 9 Beau Geste
11 Blonde Crazy 14 Dial M
for Murder, The Lost Weekend (Oscar) 22 Bulldog
Drummond Escapes

Millar, Kenneth
real name of: 13 Ross
MacDonald

Millay, Edna St Vincent
author of: **11** Second April
13 The Harp Weaver
19 Make Bright the Arrows
20 A Few Figs from Thistles

Mille, Agnes de
choreographer of: **5** Rodeo
15 Fall River Legend

millennium 13 thousand
years **9** age of gold **21** one-
thousandth anniversary

Miller
character in: **18** The Canterbury Tales
author: **7** Chaucer

Miller, Ann
real name: **17** Lucille Ann
Collier
autobiography: **15** Miller's
High Life
born: **9** Chireno TX
roles: **9** On the Town, Stage
Door **10** Hit the Deck, Kiss
Me Kate **11** Sugar Babies
16 The Kissing Bandit

Miller, Arthur
wife: **13** Marilyn Monroe
author of: **8** The Price
11 The Crucible **12** After
the Fall **16** Death of a
Salesman **18** A View from
the Bridge

Miller, Henry
author of: **5** Nexus, Sexus
6 Plexus **14** Tropic of Cancer **17** Tropic of Capricorn
18 The Rosy Crucifixion
21 The Colossus of Maroussi

Milles, Carl
real name: **23** Wilhelm Carl
Emil Anderson
born: **5** Lagga **6** Sweden
artwork: **5** Diana, Jonah
6 Europa **12** Man and Nature, Playing Bears **13** Peace
Monument **15** Orpheus
Fountain **18** Meeting of the
Waters, Saltsjobaden Church
(bronze doors)

millet 16 Panicum miliaceum
varieties: **3** hog **5** pearl,
Sanwa **6** finger, Indian
7 African, foxtail, Italian
8 barnyard, browntop, Japanese **16** Japanese barnyard

Millet, Jean-Francois
born: **6** France, Gruchy
artwork: **5** Sower **7** Angelus
11 The Gleaners, The Win-
nower **14** Potato Planters,
The Man with a Hoe
23 Oedipus Taken from the
Tree

Millett, Kate
author of: **6** Flying **14** Sexual
Politics

milligram
abbreviation: **2** mg

milliliter
abbreviation: **2** mL

millimeter
abbreviation: **2** mm

Millionaire, The
character: **14** Michael
Anthony
cast: **12** Marvin Miller

Mill on the Floss, The
author: **11** George Eliot
character: **8** Bob Jakin, Mrs
Glegg **9** Lucy Deane, Mrs
Pullet **11** Philip Wakem,
Tom Tulliver **12** Stephen
Guest **14** Maggie Tulliver

Mills, Hayley
real name: **15** Rose Vivian
Mills
father: **4** John
sister: **6** Juliet
husband: **11** Ray Boulting
born: **6** London **7** England
roles: **8** Tiger Bay **9** Pollyanna **11** Summer Magic
13 The Parent Trap **14** The
Chalk Garden **15** The Moon-
Spinners **19** In Search of
Castaways **20** The Trouble
with Angels

Mills, John
daughter: **6** Hayley, Juliet
born: **7** England
10 Felixstowe
roles: **12** Tunes of Glory
13 Ryan's Daughter **14** The
Chalk Garden **17** Great Expectations **19** Swiss Family
Robinson

Mills, Robert
architect of: **10** Post Office
(Washington DC) **12** Patent
Office (Washington DC)
14 Circular Church (Charleston) **15** Unitarian Church
(Philadelphia) **16** Treasury
Building (Washington DC)
18 Washington Monument
25 Sansom Street Baptist
Church (Philadelphia)
29 Egyptian Revival Monument Church (Richmond
VA)
style: **12** Greek Revival

millstream 3 run **4** race
5 brook, canal, creek, river
6 branch

Milne, A A
author of: **13** Winnie-the-
Pooh **20** The House at Pooh
Corner
character: **3** Roo **4** Pooh
5 Kanga **6** Eeyore, Piglet,
Tigger **16** Christopher Robin

Milosz, Czeslaw
author of: **11** Native Realm,
The Usurpers **13** Bells in
Winter **14** Seizure of Power,
The Captive Mind

milquetoast 4 wimp **7** milksop,
nebbish **11** mollycoddle

Milton
author: **12** William Blake

Milton, George
character in: **12** Of Mice and
Men
author: **9** Steinbeck

Milton, John
author of: **7** Lycidas **8** L'Allegro **11** Il Penseroso **12** Areopagitica, Paradise Lost
15 Samson Agonistes
16 Paradise Regained **29** On
the Morning of Christ's
Nativity

Milton Berle Show, The
host: **11** Milton Berle
regulars: **10** Fatso Marco
11 Arnold Stang, Jack Collins, Milton Frome, Ruth
Gilbert **12** Irving Benson
13 Bobby Sherwood
announcer: **8** Sid Stone
11 Jimmy Nelson **13** Jack
Lescoulie
orchestra: **8** Alan Roth, Billy
May **11** Victor Young
theme: **7** Near You
Milton Berle's nickname:
12 Mr Television
sponsor: **5** Buick **6** Texaco

Milwaukee
baseball team: **7** Brewers
basketball team: **5** Bucks
Indian name: **16** Mahn-a-
waukee Seepe
lake: **8** Michigan
river: **9** Milwaukee, Menomo-
nee, **12** Kinnickinnic
university: **9** Marquette

mimic 3 ape **4** aper, copy,
echo, mime **6** mirror, parrot
7 copycat, copyist, feigner, imitate, take off **8** imitator, simulate **9** reproduce
10 burlesquer **11** counterfeit,
impersonate **13** impressionist

Mimir
origin: **12** Scandinavian
god of: **3** sea
decapitated by: **5** Vanir
head sent to: **4** Odin **5** Othin
oracle for: **4** Asar **5** Aesir

mimosa 14 Acacia dealbata
18 Albizia Julibrissin
varieties: **5** Texas **6** golden
7 prairie **8** Egyptian

mince 4 dice, pose **5** grate,
shred **6** refine, soften **7** posture, qualify **8** chop fine, hold
back, mitigate, moderate, palliate **9** gloss over, put on airs,
whitewash **12** attitudinize
14 affect delicacy, affect primness **15** give oneself airs **16** affect daintiness, soften one's
speech **18** cut into small
pieces **19** be mealymouthed

about **20** cut into tiny particles

mince words 5 dodge, hedge, stall **10** equivocate **11** be ambiguous **13** avoid the issue **17** beat around the bush

mind 4 hate, heed, note, obey, tend, will, wits **5** abhor, bow to, brain, focus, sense, watch **6** brains, choice, detest, eschew, follow, intent, liking, memory, notice, notion, reason, recall, regard, resent, sanity **7** dislike, marbles, observe, opinion, outlook, thought **8** adhere to, attend to, be wary of, judgment, object to, reaction, response, submit to, take care, thinking **9** attention, awareness, be careful, cognition, faculties, intellect, intention, look after, sentiment **10** be cautious, comply with, conception, conclusion, gray matter, impression, perception, propensity, recoil from, reflection, shrink from, take care of **11** acquiesce to, be wary about, inclination, percipience, point of view, rationality, remembrance **12** apprehension, disapprove of, intelligence, recollection, reminiscence, take charge of, take notice of **13** be conscious of, comprehension, concentration, consciousness, consideration, contemplation, look askance at, preoccupation, ratiocination, retrospection, understanding **14** pay attention to **German: 5** Geist

mindful 4 wary **5** aware **7** alert to, alive to, careful, heedful **8** cautious, sensible, watchful **9** cognizant, conscious, observant, regardful **10** absorbed in, open-eyed to, thoughtful **11** attentive to, engrossed in, taken up with **12** occupied with **15** preoccupied with

mindfulness 9 alertness, awareness **10** perception **12** acquaintance **13** attentiveness, consciousness, understanding

mindless 6 insane, obtuse, stupid **7** asinine, doltish, idiotic, unaware, witless **8** careless, heedless **9** apathetic, cretinous, imbecilic, oblivious, unattuned, unheeding **10** neglectful, regardless, sophomoric, unthinking **11** inattentive, indifferent, nonsensical, thoughtless, unobservant, unreasoning **12** disregardful, simple-minded **13** inconsiderate, unintelligent **14** indiscriminate

mine 3 pit **4** fund **5** cache, hoard, shaft, stock, store **6** dig

for, quarry, supply, tunnel, wealth **7** extract, reserve **8** dig under, excavate, treasure **9** abundance, booby-trap **10** excavation **12** accumulation

Mineo, Sal
　real name: 14 Salvatore Mineo
　born: 7 Bronx NY
　roles: 5 Giant, Tonka **6** Exodus **18** Rebel Without a Cause, Who Killed Teddy Bear?

mineral *see box*

Minerva
　origin: 5 Roman
　goddess of: 3 war **4** arts **6** wisdom **11** handicrafts
　corresponds to: 6 Athena

mingle 3 mix **4** fuse, join **5** blend, merge, unite **6** hobnob **7** combine, consort **8** coalesce, intermix **9** associate, circulate, commingle, interfuse, interlard, socialize **10** amalgamate, fraternize, intertwine, interweave **11** intermingle, intersperse **12** rub shoulders

miniature 3 wee **4** tiny **5** elfin, pygmy **6** bantam, little, petite **9** minuscule **10** diminutive, pocket-size, small-scale **11** Lilliputian, microcosmic, microscopic

minim
　abbreviation: 3 min

minimal 5 token **7** minimum, nominal **13** least possible, unappreciable

minimize 5 dwarf **6** reduce, shrink **8** belittle, mitigate **9** underrate **10** depreciate, undervalue

minimum 4 base **5** basic, least **7** modicum **8** smallest

minister 4 abbe, tend **5** padre, rabbi, serve, vicar **6** answer,

cleric, father, oblige, parson, pastor, priest **7** care for, cater to **8** attend to, chaplain, pander to, preacher, reverend **9** clergyman, secretary **10** evangelist, revivalist, take care of **11** accommodate **12** ecclesiastic **13** cabinet member

ministerial 6 cleric **8** churchly, clerical, pastoral, priestly **14** ecclesiastical

ministration 3 aid **4** care **6** charge **7** comfort **9** attention **10** protection **11** supervision

Ministry of Fear, The
　author: 12 Graham Greene

Minitari *see* **7** Hidatsa

Minnehaha
　character in: 8 Hiawatha
　author: 10 Longfellow

Minnelli, Liza
　father: 8 Vincente
　mother: 11 Judy Garland
　born: 12 Los Angeles CA
　roles: 6 Arthur **7** Cabaret (Oscar) **14** New York New York **16** The Sterile Cuckoo **17** Flora the Red Menace

Minnelli, Vincente
　director of: 4 Gigi (Oscar) **9** Brigadoon **11** Lust for Life **15** Bells Are Ringing, Meet Me in St Louis **16** Father of the Bride **17** An American in Paris

Minnesota *see box*

Minni *see* **7** Armenia

minor 5 child, light, petty, small, youth **6** infant, lesser, paltry, slight **7** trivial **8** nugatory, picayune, piddling, teenager, trifling **9** secondary, youngster **10** adolescent **11** subordinate, unimportant **13** insignificant **14** inconsiderable **15** inconsequential

---

mineral 3 jet, ore **4** coal, gold, iron, mica, opal, spar, talc **5** beryl, topaz **6** augite, barite, blende, cerine, copper, galena, garnet, iolite, pinite, rutile, sandix, silver, sphene, spinel, sulfur **7** amesite, apatite, azurite, biotite, bornite, calcite, citrine, coesite, crystal, cuprite, cyanite, element, gahnite, helvite, jadeite, kernite, kunzite, niobite, olivine, prasine, zeolite, zircon **8** asbestos, borocite, chlorite, cinnabar, corundum, dolomite, epsomite, fayalite, feldspar, fluorite, graphite, hematite, lazulite, siderite, sodalite, stibnite, triplite, wellsite **9** aragonite, argentite, carnelian, celestite, cerussite, danburite, fosterite, kaolinite, lawsonite, magnetite, malachite, muscovite, petroleum, phenakite, scapolite, tridymite, turquoise, wulfenite **10** calaverite, chalcedony, orthoclase, pyrrhotite, sphalerite, tourmaline, wolfachite **11** alexandrite, chrysoberyl, melanterite **12** brazilianite, chalcopyrite, fincalconite, fluorapatite **13** rhodochrosite

Minnesota
abbreviation: 2 MN **4** Minn
nickname: 6 Gopher **9** North Star **19** Land of Sky-blue Waters **22** Land of Ten Thousand Lakes
capital: 6 St Paul
largest city: 11 Minneapolis
others: 3 Ada, Ely **4** Mora **5** Edina **6** Austin, Duluth, Newulm, Winona **7** Babbitt, Bemidji, Fosston, Hibbing, Mankato, Red Wing, St Cloud **8** Brainerd, Moorhead **9** Albertlea, Blue Earth, Richfield, Rochester, Roseville **10** Minnetonka, Robinsdale **11** Bloomington, St Louis Park **14** Brooklyn Center **18** International Falls
college: 6 Bethel, St Olaf, Winona **7** Bemidji, Hamline **8** Adolphus, Augsburg, Carleton, St Thomas **10** Macalester
feature:
  monument: 10 Paul Bunyan
  national monument: 9 Pipestone **12** Grand Portage
  national park: 9 Voyageurs'
  Norse artifact: 19 Kensington Rune Stone
tribe: 5 Sioux **6** Dakota, Ojibwa, Santee **8** Chippewa **9** Menominee
people: 11 Judy Garland **12** Mayo brothers **13** Harold Stassen, Lauris Norstad, Sinclair Lewis **16** F Scott Fitzgerald
  explorer: 8 Hennepin, Norsemen, Radisson **9** Greysolon **12** Groseilliers **19** Sieur Duluth of du Lhut
lakes: 3 Red **5** Leech, Rainy **6** Itasca **7** Bemidji **8** Superior **9** Mille Lacs **10** Minnewaska **14** Lake of the Woods, Winnibigoshish
land rank: 7 twelfth
mountain: 6 Cuyuna, Mesabi **7** Misquah **9** Vermilion
  highest point: 5 Eagle
physical feature: 6 Big Bog **14** Northwest Angle
  falls: 9 Minnehaha
river: 3 Red **5** Rainy **6** Pigeon **7** St Croix, St Louis **9** Des Moines, Minnesota **10** St Lawrence **11** Mississippi
state admission: 12 thirty-second
state bird: 10 common loon
state fish: 7 walleye
state flower: 14 moccasin flower **24** pink and white lady's slipper
state motto: 17 The Star of the North
state song: 13 Hail Minnesota
state tree: 13 Norway red pine
baseball team: 5 Twins
football team: 7 Vikings
hockey team: 10 North Stars

ing, Japanese, mountain **9** pineapple
flavor: 7 menthol **9** spearmint **10** peppermint
liqueur: 13 creme de menthe
botanical name: 6 Mentha **8** Labiatae, M spicata **9** M piperita
origin: 13 Mediterranean
related herb: 7 oregano **8** marjoram, rosemary
symbol of: 11 hospitality
mythical nymph: 6 Mintha
  beloved of: 5 Pluto
  Mintha trod underfoot by: 10 Persephone
cure for: 7 hiccups
antidote for: 16 sea serpent stings
use: 4 lamb **5** salad **6** fruits

Minthe
form: 5 nymph
changed into: 9 mint plant
changed by: 10 Persephone

minuscule 3 wee **4** tiny **5** small **6** minute **10** teeny-weeny **11** small letter **13** infinitesimal **15** lower-case letter

minute 3 wee **4** fine, puny, tiny, wink **5** close, exact, flash, jiffy, petty, scant, shake, teeny, trice **6** breath, little, moment, petite, second, slight, strict **7** careful, instant, minikin, precise **8** detailed, itemized, trifling **9** miniature, twinkling **10** a short time, diminutive, exhaustive, meticulous, negligible, scrupulous **11** Lilliputian, microscopic **12** sixty seconds **13** conscientious, imperceptible, inappreciable, infinitesimal, insignificant **14** extremely small, inconsiderable
abbreviation: 3 min

minute portion 3 bit, sip **4** bite **5** crumb, grain, scrap, shred, speck **6** morsel, sliver **7** swallow **8** fragment, mouthful, particle

minutiae 6 trivia **7** trifles **8** niceties **10** bagatelles, pedantries, subtleties **11** odds and ends, particulars **12** minor details, trivialities **15** particularities

minx 4 jade, slut **5** hussy, huzzy, wench **7** baggage **10** prostitute

Minyades
daughters of: 6 Minyas

Miolnir
hammer of: 4 Thor

mir 5 peace, world **21** Russian village commune

mirabile dictu 12 strange to say **17** marvelous to relate

miracle 4 omen, sign **6** marvel,

minority 4 less **5** youth **6** lesser, nonage **7** boyhood, infancy **8** girlhood **9** childhood, juniority **10** immaturity **11** adolescence

minor-league 4 punk **5** dinky, seedy, tacky **6** cheesy, common, lesser, shabby **8** inferior, small-fry **9** secondary, small-time **10** bush-league, second-rate **13** insignificant

Minos
king of: 5 Crete
father: 4 Zeus
mother: 6 Europa
brother: 8 Sarpedon **12** Rhadamanthys
wife: 8 Pasiphae
daughter: 7 Ariadne, Phaedra
ordered: 9 Labyrinth
became: 5 judge
  in: 5 Hades

Minotaur
form: 7 monster
combined: 3 man **4** bull
father: 10 Cretan bull
mother: 8 Pasiphae
home: 9 Labyrinth
ate flesh of: 6 humans
killed by: 7 Theseus

minstrel 4 bard, poet **6** dancer, end man, lyrist, player, singer **8** comedian, songster **9** blackface, poetaster, serenader, versifier **10** troubadour **11** entertainer **12** interlocutor, vaudevillian **15** song-and-dance man

mint
varieties: 3 dog, red **4** wood **5** apple, field, lemon, stone, water **6** coyote, dotted, orange, Scotch **7** Meehan's **8** bergamot, Corsican, creep-

wonder **7** mystery, portent, prodigy **9** divine act, sensation, spectacle **10** phenomenon **11** masterpiece

Miracle of Morgan's Creek, The
director: **14** Preston Sturges
cast: **9** Diana Lynn **11** Betty Hutton **12** Brian Donlevy, Eddie Bracken **15** William Demarest

Miracle on 34th Street
director: **12** George Seaton
based on story by: **15** Valentine Davies
cast: **9** John Payne **11** Edmund Gwenn (Kris Kringle), Natalie Wood **12** Gene Lockhart, Maureen O'Hara, Thelma Ritter
Oscar for: **12** screenwriter **15** supporting actor (Gwenn)

Miracle Worker, The
director: **10** Arthur Penn
cast: **9** Patty Duke (Helen Keller) **10** Victor Jory **11** Inga Swenson **12** Anne Bancroft (Anne Sullivan)
Oscar for: **7** actress (Bancroft) **17** supporting actress (Duke)

miraculous 6 divine **7** amazing, magical **9** marvelous, visionary, wonderful **10** incredible, mysterious, phenomenal, prodigious, remarkable **11** astonishing, astounding, exceptional, spectacular, supernormal **13** extraordinary, preternatural, wonderworking **14** thaumaturgical

miraculous food 5 manna

Miraculous writing
also: **4** mene **5** perez, tekel **8** upharsin
means: **7** divided, weighed **8** numbered
interpreted by: **6** Daniel

mirage 5 fancy **7** fantasy **8** delusion, illusion, phantasm **9** unreality **12** will-o'-the-wisp **13** hallucinations, misconception **14** castle in the air **15** optical illusion

Miranda
character in: **10** The Tempest
author: **11** Shakespeare

Miranda, Carmen
real name: **26** Maria do Carmo Miranda da Cunha
nickname: **18** Brazilian Bombshell
born: **8** Portugal **16** Marco de Canavezes
roles: **10** Copacabana **14** That Night in Rio **15** Weekend in Havana **16** Down Argentine Way **22** Springtime in the Rockies

mire 3 bog, fen, mud **4** cake, muck, ooze, soil **5** marsh, muddy, slime, slush, smear **6** enmesh, sludge **7** begrime, bog down, ensnare, spatter **8** besmirch, entangle, quagmire

Miriam
father: **5** Amram
mother: **8** Jochebed
brother: **5** Aaron, Moses

Miro, Joan
born: **5** Spain **8** Montroig **9** Barcelona
artwork: **9** Help Spain, The Reaper **13** Dutch Interior **14** Constellations **16** Catalan Landscape **19** Dog Barking at the Moon **20** Still Life with Old Shoe **26** Woman and Bird in the Moonlight

mirror 4 copy, show **5** glass, image, model **7** epitome, example, paragon, reflect **8** exemplar, manifest, paradigm, standard **10** reflection **11** cheval glass **12** looking glass

mirth 4 glee **6** gaiety, levity **7** jollity **8** drollery, hilarity, laughter **9** amusement, festivity, happiness, jocundity, joviality, merriment **10** jocularity **11** good spirits, merrymaking, playfulness **12** cheerfulness

mirthful 3 gay **4** glad **5** happy, jolly, merry **6** blithe, jocose, jovial, joyful, joyous **7** gleeful, jocular, risible

mirthless 3 sad **4** dour, glum **6** gloomy, morose **7** joyless, unhappy **8** dejected **9** cheerless, sorrowful **10** in the dumps, melancholy **14** down in the mouth

miry 3 wet **4** oozy **5** boggy, mucky, muddy, slimy, slushy, soggy **6** claggy, swampy **7** sloughy

misadventure 3 ill **4** slip **6** mishap **7** debacle, failure, reverse, setback **8** bad break, calamity, casualty, disaster **9** adversity, mischance **10** infelicity, misfortune **11** catastrophe, contretemps

misanthrope 5 cynic **7** skeptic **9** pessimist **10** misogynist

Misanthrope, Le
author: **7** Moliere
character: **7** Alceste, Arsinoe, Eliante **8** Celimene, Philinte

misanthropic 4 cold **5** surly **6** morose **7** cynical, distant **10** antisocial, unfriendly, unsociable **11** distrustful **12** discourteous, inhospitable, unneighborly, unpersonable,

unresponsive **14** unapproachable **15** unaccommodating

misapplication 5 abuse **6** misuse **11** improper use **13** misemployment

misapply 5 abuse **6** misuse **9** misemploy **13** use improperly

misapprehension 5 mixup **7** mistake **11** misjudgment **13** misconception **14** miscalculation **15** false impression, misconstruction **16** misunderstanding **17** misinterpretation

misappropriate 4 bilk **5** abuse, cheat, mulct, steal **6** misuse **7** defraud, purloin, swindle **8** embezzle, misapply, peculate **9** defalcate, misemploy

misappropriation 6 misuse, taking **11** defalcation **12** embezzlement

misbehave 5 act up **7** disobey, do wrong **10** transgress **15** get into mischief

misbehavior 5 lapse **7** misdeed, offense **8** acting up, trespass **9** impudence **10** bad conduct, bad manners, disrespect, misconduct **11** delinquency, dereliction, impropriety, misdemeanor **12** indiscretion **13** transgression **16** obstreperousness, unmanageableness

misbelief 8 delusion, illusion **13** misconception

miscalculate 3 err **8** misjudge **10** guess wrong **11** misestimate

miscalculation 5 error **10** inaccuracy **13** misestimation

miscarriage 4 slip **5** botch **6** fizzle **7** default, failing, failure, misfire, undoing, washout **8** casualty, collapse

miscarry 4 fail **5** abort, botch **6** fizzle, go awry **9** terminate **12** come to naught

miscellanea 8 analects **9** anthology, gleanings, scrapbook **10** collection, miscellany, selections **11** collectanea

miscellaneous 5 mixed **6** divers, motley, sundry, varied **7** diverse, mingled, various **8** assorted, manifold **9** different **11** diversified **13** heterogeneous

miscellaneous collection
Latin/pseudo Latin: **14** omnium-gatherum

miscellany 5 blend **6** jumble, medley **7** melange, mixture, variety **8** analects, extracts, mishmash, pastiche **9** anthology, gleanings, potpourri

10 assortment, collection, hodgepodge, salmagundi, selections **11** collectanea, compilation, gallimaufry, miscellanea **14** conglomeration, omnium-gatherum

mischance 6 ill lot, mishap **7** bad luck, ill luck, ill wind **8** accident **9** adversity **10** infelicity, misfortune **12** misadventure

mischief 4 evil **5** wrong **6** injury, malice **7** devilry, knavery, roguery **8** deviltry, foul play, plotting, scheming, villainy **9** depravity, devilment, rascality **10** orneriness, wrongdoing **11** naughtiness, playfulness, roguishness, shenanigans, willfulness **12** prankishness, sportiveness **14** capriciousness

mischief-maker 3 imp **5** demon, devil, scamp **7** gremlin, hellion **9** scoundrel **10** hell-raiser

mischievous 3 sly **5** elfin **6** elfish, impish, malign, vexing, wicked **7** harmful, naughty, noxious, playful, roguish, teasing, vicious, waggish **8** annoying, devilish, prankish, spiteful, sportive **9** injurious, malicious, malignant, uninvited **10** frolicsome, gratuitous, pernicious **11** deleterious, destructive, detrimental, uncalled for **12** exacerbating

misconceive 3 err **4** lose, miss **8** misjudge **12** misinterpret **13** misunderstand

misconception 5 error **8** delusion **11** misjudgment **13** erroneous idea **14** misinformation **15** misapprehension, misconstruction **16** misunderstanding **17** misinterpretation, misrepresentation

misconduct 7 misdeed, misstep **10** misprision, peccadillo, wrongdoing **11** delinquency, dereliction, impropriety, malefaction, malfeasance, misbehavior, misdemeanor **13** transgression

misconstrue 7 distort, mistake **8** misjudge **9** misreckon, misrender **12** misapprehend, miscalculate, misinterpret, mistranslate **13** misunderstand

miscreant 3 bum **4** heel **5** knave, scamp **6** bad egg, rascal, sinner, wretch **7** villain **8** evildoer, lost soul, scalawag **9** reprobate, scoundrel **10** blackguard, black sheep, malefactor

misdeed 3 sin **4** slip **5** crime, lapse, wrong **6** felony **7** faux

pas, offense, outrage **8** atrocity, trespass **9** violation **10** misconduct, peccadillo **11** malfeasance, misbehavior, misdemeanor **12** indiscretion, infringement **13** transgression

misdemeanor 3 sin **5** crime, fault **7** offense, misdeed **8** disorder **10** peccadillo **11** misbehavior **13** transgression

misdoer 5 crook **8** criminal **9** miscreant, wrongdoer **10** delinquent

mise en scene 6 milieu **7** setting **8** ambience **10** atmosphere, background **11** environment **12** stage setting, surroundings

misemployment 6 misuse **14** misapplication

Misenus
    father: 6 Aeolus

miser 5 piker **7** hoarder, niggard, Scrooge, skimper **8** tightwad **9** skinflint **10** cheapskate, pinchpenny **12** pennypincher, stingy person

Miser, The
    also: 6 L'Avare
    author: 7 Moliere
    character: 5 Elise **6** Valere **7** Anselme, Cleante, Mariane **8** Harpagon

miserable 3 sad **4** mean **5** inept, needy, sorry **6** abject, scurvy, shabby, sordid, woeful **7** abysmal, crushed, doleful, forlorn, grieved, hapless, unhappy **8** beggarly, degraded, dejected, desolate, dolorous, feckless, inferior, mournful, pathetic, pitiable, rubbishy, very poor, wretched **9** appalling, atrocious, cheerless, depressed, desperate, heartsick, sorrowful, woebegone **10** chapfallen, deplorable, despicable, despondent, heavy-laden, lamentable, second-rate, unbearable **11** crestfallen, heartbroken, unfortunate **12** contemptible, disconsolate, impoverished **13** brokenhearted **14** down in the mouth

Miserables, Les
    author: 10 Victor Hugo
    character: 6 Javert **7** Cosette, Fantine **10** Thenardier **11** Jean Valjean **15** Father Madeleine, Marius Pontmercy **17** Eponine Thenardier

misericordia 5 mercy **10** compassion

miserliness 6 penury **9** frugality, parsimony **10** stinginess

13 niggardliness, penny-pinching **15** tight-fistedness

miserly 4 mean, near **5** cheap, tight **6** frugal, greedy, meager, stingy **7** selfish **8** grasping, grudging, pinching **9** illiberal, niggardly, penurious, scrimping **10** avaricious, ungenerous **11** closefisted, closehanded, tight-fisted **12** parsimonious **13** penny-pinching

misery 3 woe **4** blow **5** agony, curse, grief, trial **6** ordeal, regret, sorrow **7** anguish, bad deal, bad news, chagrin, despair, sadness, torment, trouble **8** bad scene, calamity, disaster, distress, exaction, hardship **9** dejection, heartache, privation, suffering **10** affliction, bitter pill, depression, desolation, melancholy, misfortune **11** catastrophe, despondency, tribulation **12** wretchedness

Misfits, The
    director: 10 John Huston
    based on story by: 12 Arthur Miller
    cast: 10 Clark Gable, Eli Wallach **12** Thelma Ritter **13** Marilyn Monroe **15** Montgomery Clift

misfortune 4 blow, loss **6** misery, mishap **7** bad luck, reverse, setback, tragedy, trouble **8** calamity, casualty, disaster, downfall, hard luck, hardship **9** adversity, hard times, ruination **10** affliction, ill fortune **11** catastrophe, tribulation **12** misadventure

misgiving, misgivings 4 fear **5** alarm, doubt, dread, qualm, worry **7** anxiety, dubiety **8** disquiet, mistrust **9** suspicion **10** foreboding, skepticism **11** dubiousness, uncertainty **12** apprehension, doubtfulness, presentiment, reservations **14** second thoughts

misguided 5 at sea **6** adrift, faulty, misled, unwise **7** in error **8** mistaken **9** erroneous, imprudent, led astray, off course **10** ill-advised, indiscreet, misadvised **11** injudicious, misdirected, misinformed

Mishael *see* **7** Meshach

mishap 4 slip, snag **5** botch **6** fiasco, slipup **7** reverse, setback **8** casualty, disaster **9** mischance **10** difficulty, misfortune **11** miscarriage **12** misadventure

mishmash 3 mix **4** hash, stew **5** salad **6** jumble, medley, muddle **7** melange **8** mixed bag, pastiche, scramble **9** patchwork **10** assemblage, crazy quilt, hodgepodge, miscellany, salmagundi **14** conglomeration, omnium-gatherum

misinform 7 deceive, mislead **8** misguide **9** misdirect **10** lead astray **12** misrepresent

misinterpret 11 misconstrue **12** misapprehend **13** misunderstand

misinterpretation 13 misconception **16** misunderstanding **17** misrepresentation

misjudge 3 err **7** mistake **10** exaggerate, understate **11** misconceive, misconstrue **12** misapprehend, miscalculate, misinterpret, overestimate **13** misunderstand, underestimate

mislay 4 lose, miss **8** displace, misplace

mislead 4 dupe, fool, gull **6** betray, delude, entice, seduce, take in **7** beguile, deceive **8** hoodwink, inveigle, misguide **9** bamboozle, misdirect, misinform, play false, victimize **10** lead astray **11** double-cross, string along

misleading 6 luring **8** deluding **9** deceiving **10** misguiding **11** hoodwinking

mismanage 3 mar **4** flub, muff, ruin **5** botch, spoil **6** bollix, bungle, foul up, mess up **7** louse up, screw up **9** mishandle **11** make a hash of, make a mess of

misnomer 8 misusage, solecism **9** barbarism, misnaming **11** malapropism

misogynic 7 cynical **11** woman-hating **12** misanthropic

misogynist 5 cynic **10** woman-hater **11** misanthrope

misplace 4 lose **5** abuse **6** mislay **11** lose track of

misreckon 8 misjudge **10** guess wrong, miscompute **11** misestimate **12** miscalculate

misrepresent 7 falsify, mislead **8** disguise

misrepresentation 7 mockery **8** altering, travesty, twisting **9** burlesque, doctoring **10** caricature, distortion, falsifying **12** adulteration, exaggeration, misstatement **13** falsification

miss 4 blow, girl, lack, lady, lass, lose, loss, maid, muff, skip, slip, want **5** avert, avoid, error, forgo, let go, woman **6** bypass, damsel, escape, forego, lassie, maiden, miscue, pass by **7** blunder, colleen, default, failure, fly wide, let pass, let slip, long for, mistake, neglect, old maid, overrun, pine for **8** leave out, omission, overlook, pass over, senorita, slip up on, spinster, yearn for **9** disregard, fall short, false step, gloss over, go without, overshoot, oversight, surrender, young lady **10** demoiselle, schoolgirl **12** be absent from **13** feel the loss of, mademoiselle

missal 10 prayer book

missed
  French: **6** manque

misshapen 7 twisted **8** deformed **9** contorted, distorted

missile 4 ball, dart **5** arrow, lance, shaft, shell, spear, stone **6** bullet, rocket **7** harpoon, javelin **10** projectile

missing 4 AWOL, gone, lost **6** absent **7** lacking, left out, not here **8** avoiding, skipping **10** longing for, not present **11** overlooking, yearning for **12** disregarding

Missing
  director: **22** Constantine Costa-Gavras
  cast: **8** John Shea **10** Jack Lemmon **11** Sissy Spacek **13** Melanie Mayron

Missing Persons and Other Essays
  author: **12** Heinrich Boll

mission 3 end, job **4** task **5** quest **6** charge **7** calling, mandate, pursuit **8** legation, ministry **9** objective **10** assignment, commission, delegation, enterprise **11** raison d'etre, undertaking

Mission
  tribe: **7** Chumash, Juaneno, Luiseno **8** Diegueno **9** Costanoan **10** Gabrielino **11** Fernandario
  location: **10** California

Mississippi
  abbreviation: **2** MS **4** Miss
  nickname: **5** Bayou **6** Mudcat **8** Magnolia
  capital/largest city: **7** Jackson
  others: **6** Biloxi, Helena, Laurel, Tupelo, Winona **7** Belzoni, Corinth, Grenada, Natchez **8** Bogalusa, Columbus, Gulfport, Meridian **9** Kosciusko, Vicksburg **10** Clarksdale, Pascagoula **11** Hattiesburg **13** Pass Christian
  college: **4** Rust **6** Alcorn **7** Jackson **8** Belhaven, Millsaps, Tougaloo **11** Mississippi **12** Blue Mountain, William Carey
  feature: **12** Natchez Trace
    national military park: **9** Vicksburg
    national seashore: **11** Gulf Islands
  tribe: **3** Sac **5** Tious **6** Biloxi, Mandan, Tunica **7** Choctaw, Natchez, Tonikan **8** Chicksaw
  people: **11** Eudora Welty **15** William Faulkner **17** Tennessee Williams
    explorer: **6** DeSoto, Joliet **9** Iberville, Marquette
  island: **3** Cat **4** Horn, Ship **9** Petit Bois
  lake: **4** Enid **6** Sardis **7** Barnett, Grenada **8** Pickwick **9** Arkabutla, Okatibbee
  land rank: **12** thirty-second
  highest point: **7** Woodall
  physical feature:
    delta: **10** Yazoo Basin
    hills: **8** Fall Line **9** Tennessee **11** Loess Bluffs
    prairie: **5** Black **7** Jackson
    sound: **11** Mississippi
  river: **4** Leaf **5** Pearl, Yazoo **8** Big Black **9** Tombigbee, Yalobusha **10** Homochitto, Pascagoula **11** Mississippi **12** Tallahatchie
  state admission: **9** twentieth
  state bird: **11** mockingbird
  state flower: **8** magnolia
  state motto: **14** By Valor and Arms
  state song: **13** Go Mississippi
  state tree: **8** magnolia

Mission: Impossible
character: 5 Casey, Paris 10 Rollin Hand 11 Dana Lambert, James Phelps 12 Daniel Briggs 13 Barney Collier 14 Cinnamon Carter, Willie Armitage
cast: 10 Greg Morris, Peter Lupus, Steven Hill 11 Barbara Bain, Peter Graves 12 Leonard Nimoy, Martin Landau 14 Lynda Day George 15 Lesley Ann Warren

Mississippi *see box*

missive
4 note 6 billet, letter 7 epistle, message 13 communication 14 correspondence

Miss Julie
author: 16 August Strindberg

Miss Lonelyhearts
author: 13 Nathanael West

Missouri *see box*

Miss Peach
creator: 11 Mell Lazarus
character: 3 Ira 6 Arthur, Lester, Marcia 8 Francine
place: 9 Kamp Kelly 11 Kelly School

misspend
5 waste 8 squander 9 dissipate, throw away 11 fritter away

misspent
6 wasted 8 depraved 9 debauched, dissolute, idled away 10 misapplied, profitless, squandered, thrown away

misstate
5 alter 6 bollix, garble 7 confuse, distort, falsify, pervert 8 misquote 9 misreport 12 misrepresent

misstatement
3 fib, lie 4 tale 5 error 7 falsity, untruth 9 falsehood 13 prevarication 17 misrepresentation

misstep
3 sin 4 goof, slip, vice 5 boner, error, fault, gaffe, lapse 6 boo-boo, defect, foul-up 7 blooper, faux pas, offense, screw-up 11 delinquency, dereliction, shortcoming 12 indiscretion 13 transgression

miss the mark
4 fail 9 fall short 11 come up short

miss the point
7 mistake 11 fail to catch, misconceive 12 misapprehend 13 misunderstand

mist
3 fog 4 haze, murk, smog 5 steam, vapor 7 drizzle

mistake
4 slip 5 boner, error, gaffe, mix-up 6 slipup 7 blooper, blunder, confuse, faux pas, misstep 8 confound, misjudge 9 misreckon, oversight 11 misconstrue, misidentify 12 misapprehend, miscalculate, misinterpret 13 misunderstand 14 miscalculation
French: 10 malentendu

mistaken
5 at sea, false, wrong 6 faulty, untrue 7 at fault, in error, unsound 8 deceived 9 erroneous, illogical, incorrect, off course, unfounded 10 fallacious, groundless, inaccurate, ungrounded 11 unjustified

Mister
Yiddish: 3 Reb

Mister Roberts
author: 12 Thomas Heggen
director: 8 John Ford 11 Mervyn LeRoy
cast: 8 Ward Bond 10 Henry Fonda, Jack Lemmon (Ensign Pulver) 11 Betsy Palmer, James Cagney 13 William Powell
Oscar for: 15 supporting actor (Lemmon)

Mister Saturday Night
nickname of: 13 Jackie Gleason

mistreat
4 harm 5 abuse, bully, hound, wrong 6 harass, ill-use, injure, misuse, molest 7 assault, oppress, outrage, pervert, torment, violate 8 illtreat, maltreat 9 brutalize, manhandle, mishandle, persecute

mistreatment
5 abuse 6 illuse, injury 7 assault, cruelty, harming 10 bodily harm, oppression 11 manhandling, molestation, persecution 12 maltreatment

mistress
3 Mrs 4 doxy, lady, Miss 5 lover, Madam 6 matron 8 ladylove, paramour 9 concubine, headwoman, housewife, inamorata, kept

---

Missouri
abbreviation: 2 MO
nickname: 5 Ozark 6 Show-Me 7 Bullion 15 Mother of the West
capital: 13 Jefferson City
largest city: 7 St Louis
others: 5 Eldon, Hayti, Lamar, Macon, Rolla 6 Butler, Joplin, Mexico 7 Bethany, Bolivar, Cameron, Clayton, Lebanon, Moberly, Sedalia 8 Berkeley, Columbia, Hannibal, Kirkwood, Sikeston, St Joseph 10 Bonne Terre, Kansas City 11 Springfield, Warrensburg 12 Independence 13 Cape Girardeau, Webster Groves
college: 5 Avila, Drury 6 Tarkio 7 Lincoln, St Louis, Webster 8 Stephens 10 Washington 11 Westminster
feature:
  dam: 5 Osage
tribe: 3 Fox, Sac 4 Sauk 5 Osage 7 Shawnee 8 Cherokee, Missouri
people: 7 TS Eliot 9 Mark Twain 10 Jesse James 11 Omar Bradley 12 Helen Traubel, Sara Teasdale 13 John J Pershing, Marianne Moore, Samuel Clemens 15 Reinhold Niebuhr 22 George Washington Carver
  explorer: 6 Joliet 7 La Salle 9 Marquette
lake: 7 Norfolk 9 Tablerock, Taneycomo 10 Bull Shoals 14 Kaysinger Bluff 15 Lake of the Ozarks
land rank: 10 nineteenth
mountain: 6 Ozarks 10 St Francois
  highest point: 8 Taumsauk
physical feature: 8 Bootheel 9 Big Spring
  plains: 4 Till 5 Osage
  plateau: 5 Ozark
president: 12 Harry S Truman
river: 4 Salt 5 Grand, Osage, White 6 Platte 7 Current, Meramec 8 Big Muddy, Chariton, Missouri 9 Des Moines, Gasconade, St Francis 11 Mississippi
state admission: 12 twenty-fourth
state bird: 8 bluebird
state flower: 8 hawthorn
state motto: 41 The Welfare of the People Shall Be the Supreme Law
state song: 13 Missouri Waltz
state tree: 7 dogwood

woman **10** chatelaine, girl-friend, sweetheart

mistrust 5 doubt, qualm
7 anxiety, dubiety, suspect
8 distrust, question, wariness
9 challenge, chariness, leeri-ness, misgiving, suspicion
10 disbelieve, skepticism

misty 4 dewy, hazy **5** filmy, foggy, murky **6** cloudy, opaque, steamy **8** nebulous, overcast, vaporous
10 indistinct

misunderstand 7 confuse, mis-read, mistake **8** misjudge
9 misreckon **11** misconceive, misconstrue **12** misapprehend, miscalculate, misinterpret, miss the point

misunderstanding 4 rift, spat
5 set-to **7** discord, dispute, quarrel, wrangle **8** conflict, squabble **10** difference, dissen-sion, misreading **11** alterca-tion, contretemps, misjudgment **12** disagreement
13 misconception **15** false impression, misapprehension
16 miscomprehension
17 misinterpretation
French: **10** malentendu

misuse 4 harm, hurt **5** abuse, waste, wrong **6** debase, injure
7 corrupt, exploit, outrage, pervert, profane **8** ill-treat, maltreat, misapply, mistreat, wrong use **9** misemploy
10 corruption, perversion, prostitute **11** desecration, prof-anation, squandering **12** ill treatment, maltreatment, mis-treatment, prostitution
13 misemployment **14** misap-plication **15** take advantage of

Mitchell, Billy (William Lendrum)
advocate of: **8** air power
court-martialed for:
15 insubordination
served in: **3** WWI
rank: **16** brigadier general
commander of: **15** US army air forces

Mitchell, Margaret
author of: **15** Gone With the Wind

Mitchell, Silas Weir
author of: **9** Hugh Wynne (Free Quaker) **11** Roland Blake

Mitchell, Thomas
born: **11** Elizabeth NJ
roles: **7** Our Town **8** Doc Boone **9** The Outlaw
10 Stagecoach **11** Gerald O'Hara, Lost Horizon
15 Gone With the Wind
19 Only Angels Have Wings

Mitchell, William
real name of: **10** Peter Finch

Mitchum, Robert
born: **12** Bridgeport CT
roles: **6** Midway **10** Winds of War **11** Thunder Road
13 Ryan's Daughter, The Longest Day, The Sundown-ers **15** The Story of G I Joe **16** Farewell My Lovely
20 Heaven Knows Mr Allison

mite 3 bit, jot **4** atom, iota, whit **5** scrap, speck **6** spider
7 smidgen **8** arachnid, particle

Mitford, Jessica
author of: **21** The American Way of Death **22** Kind and Usual Punishment

Mitford, Nancy
author of: **14** Noblesse Oblige **16** The Pursuit of Love **18** Love in a Cold Climate

Mithgarthr see **7** Midgard

Mithraeum
temple of: **7** Mithras

Mithras
origin: **7** Persian
god of: **5** light, truth
corresponds to: **3** Sol

mitigate 4 ease **5** allay, blunt
6 lessen, reduce, soften, soothe, temper, weaken **7** as-suage, lighten, mollify, pla-cate, relieve **8** diminish, moderate, palliate **9** alleviate, extenuate **10** ameliorate

mitigating 6 easing **8** allaying, blunting, reducing **9** assuaging, lessening, relieving, softening, tempering **10** lightening, mod-erating, palliating, palliative
11 diminishing, extenuating
12 ameliorating

Mitrephorus
epithet of: **8** Dionysus
means: **15** headband-bearing

Mitteleuropa 12 middle Europe

mitzvah, mitsvah 8 good deed **11** commandment

mix 3 add **4** beat, club, fold, fuse, join, stir, whip **5** admix, alloy, blend, merge, put in, unite **6** commix, fusion, hob-nob, mingle **7** combine, con-sort, include, mixture
8 assembly, coalesce, com-pound, intermix, mingling
9 associate, commingle, inter-fuse, interlard, introduce, so-cialize **10** amalgamate, fraternize, intertwine, inter-weave **11** incorporate, inter-mingle, intersperse, put together

mixed 4 coed **5** fused **6** hybrid, motley **7** alloyed, blended, in-mixed, mingled, mongrel, not pure **8** combined **9** composite, uncertain **10** ambivalent, inde-cisive, interwoven, variegated
11 adulterated, diversified, half and half, put together **12** con-glomerate, inconclusive
13 heterogeneous, male-and-female, miscellaneous

mixed-up 6 addled **7** chaotic, jumbled, muddled, tangled
8 confused, rambling **9** befud-dled, illogical, nonplused, per-plexed **10** bewildered, disjointed, incoherent, irra-tional, nonplussed **12** discon-nected, disorganized
13 disharmonious, heter-ogeneous

Mixtec
tribe: **7** Zapotec

mixture 3 mix **4** hash, stew
5 alloy, blend, union **6** fusion, jumble, medley **7** amalgam, melange **8** compound, mish-mash, pastiche **9** admixture, composite, potpourri **10** com-mixture, hodgepodge, salma-gundi **11** association, combination **12** adulteration, amalgamation, intermixture

mixup 4 mess, riot **5** fight, me-lee **6** fracas, muddle, tangle
7 mistake **8** disorder **9** confu-sion, imbroglio **11** misjudg-ment **14** miscalculation
16 miscomprehension, misunderstanding

mix up 5 addle **6** mess up, muddle **7** confuse, nonplus, perplex **8** befuddle, bewilder
10 disarrange

Mneme
member of: **5** Muses
personifies: **6** memory

Mnemosyne
origin: **5** Greek
member of: **6** Titans
goddess of: **6** memory
father: **6** Uranus
mother: **4** Gaea
daughters: **5** Muses

Moabite god 7 Chemosh

moan 3 sob **4** keen, wail
5 groan **6** bemoan, bewail, la-ment, plaint **7** grumble
11 lamentation

moan over 5 mourn **6** be-moan, bewail, lament **7** cry over **8** weep over **10** grieve over

moat 4 foss **5** ditch, fosse, graff **6** gutter, rundel, trench

mob 4 gang, herd **5** crowd, crush, horde, Mafia, swarm
6 masses, rabble, throng

7 flock to **8** assembly, populace, surround **9** gathering, hoi polloi, multitude, plebeians, syndicate **10** converge on **11** proletariat, rank and file **14** organized crime

mobile 6 active, motile **7** kinetic, movable **8** portable, rootless **9** footloose, traveling, wandering **10** ambulatory, locomotive

mobilize 6 call up, muster, summon **7** marshal **8** activate, organize **10** call to arms **11** put in motion

mobster 4 hood **6** hitman **7** hoodlum, Mafioso **8** gangster **10** gang member

Moby Dick
author: **14** Herman Melville
character: **4** Ahab **5** Stubb **7** Ishmael **8** Fedallah, Queequeg, Starbuck

mock 3 ape **4** copy **5** belie, mimic, scorn, spurn, taunt **6** deride, insult, jeer at, parody, revile, show up **7** imitate, laugh at, let down, profane, scoff at, sneer at **8** ridicule **9** burlesque, frustrate, make fun of, poke fun at **10** caricature, disappoint, make game of **11** make sport of

mockery 4 joke, sham **5** farce, scorn **7** jeering, mimicry, sarcasm **8** derision, raillery, ridicule, scoffing, travesty **9** burlesque, contumely **10** disrespect, ridiculing **13** laughingstock

Mock Turtle
character in: **28** Alice's Adventures in Wonderland
author: **7** Carroll

mode 3 cut, fad, way **4** form, rage, rule **5** craze, means, style, taste, trend, vogue **6** course, custom, manner, method, system **7** fashion, process **8** approach, practice **9** condition, procedure, technique **10** appearance

model 4 cast, copy, form, mold, show, type **5** build, dummy, ideal, shape, sport, style **6** design, mirror, mockup **7** display, example, fashion, outline, paragon, pattern, perfect, replica, subject, variety, version **8** exemplar, paradigm, peerless, standard **9** archetype, criterion, exemplary, facsimile, mannequin, prototype, simulated **10** simulacrum **14** representation, representative

model on 6 base on **7** found on **10** derive from

mode of operating
Latin: **2** mo **13** modus operandi

moderate 4 calm, cool, curb, fair, hush, mild, tame **5** abate, chair, sober **6** direct, gentle, lessen, manage, medium, modest, soften, subdue, temper **7** average, careful, conduct, control, oversee **8** diminish, measured, mediocre, middling, ordinary, passable, rational, regulate, restrain, tone down **9** judicious, peaceable, temperate, unruffled **10** not violent, reasonable **11** inexpensive, preside over **12** mainstreamer, medium-priced

moderation 7 abating, economy **8** allaying **9** abatement, frugality, lessening, remission, restraint **10** continence, diminution, mitigation, palliation, relaxation, temperance **11** alleviation, forbearance, self-control **12** moderateness **13** temperateness **14** abstemiousness **19** avoidance of extremes

moderator 8 chairman, mediator **10** chairwoman, negotiator

modern 3 new **6** modish, recent **7** current, in vogue **8** up-to-date **10** present-day **11** fashionable, streamlined **12** contemporary **15** contemporaneous **16** twentieth-century

Modern Comedy, A
author: **14** John Galsworthy

modernistic 6 modern **7** moderne **10** new-fangled **12** contemporary

modernity 5 vogue **7** fashion, new look, novelty, the rage **8** last word **14** newfangledness **15** contemporaneity **16** new fashionedness

modernize 4 redo **5** renew **6** do over, revamp, update **7** restore **8** redesign, renovate **9** refurbish **10** regenerate, rejuvenate, streamline **11** recondition **13** bring up to date **16** move with the times

modern times 5 today **8** nowadays **10** the present **13** the here and now

Modern Times
director: **14** Charles Chaplin
cast: **12** Henry Bergman **14** Charlie Chaplin, Chester Conklin **15** Paulette Goddard **19** Stanley "Tiny" Sandford

modest 3 coy, shy **4** meek, prim **5** plain, quiet, timid

6 demure, humble, proper, simple **7** bashful, limited, nominal, prudish, unshowy **8** blushing, discreet, moderate, reserved, timorous **9** diffident, shrinking **10** unassuming **11** circumspect, constrained, inexpensive, puritanical, straitlaced, unassertive, unobtrusive **12** medium-priced, not excessive, self-effacing, unpretending **13** unpretentious **14** unostentatious

modesty 7 coyness, prudery, reserve, shyness **8** humility, plainess, timidity **9** propriety, restraint, reticence **10** constraint, demureness, diffidence, humbleness, simplicity **11** bashfulness, naturalness **12** timorousness **14** reasonableness, self-effacement **15** inexpensiveness

modicum 3 bit, dab, jot **4** atom, dash, drop, inch, iota, mite, whit **5** crumb, grain, pinch, scrap, speck, tinge, touch **6** morsel, sliver, snatch, trifle **7** handful, minimum, smidgen **8** fraction, fragment, particle **9** little bit **10** sprinkling **11** small amount **13** small quantity

modification 6 change **8** revision **9** variation **10** adjustment, alteration, conversion, emendation, regulation **14** transformation **15** differentiation

modify 4 redo, vary **5** adapt, alter, limit, lower, remit **6** adjust, change, narrow, reduce, remold, revise, rework, soften, temper **7** control, convert, qualify, remodel, reshape **8** moderate, modulate, restrain, restrict, tone down **9** condition, refashion, transform, transmute **10** reorganize **12** transmogrify

Modigliani, Amedeo
born: **5** Italy **7** Leghorn, Livorno
artwork: **10** Seated Nude **13** Reclining Nude, Yellow Sweater **15** Jeanne Hebuterne

modish 2 in **3** now **4** chic **5** natty, nifty, sharp, smart, today **6** dapper, snazzy, spiffy, trendy, with it **7** a la mode, current, faddish, in style, in vogue, stylish, voguish **9** highstyle **11** fashionable **13** up-to-the-minute

Modoc
language family: **12** Shapwailutan
division: **10** Lutuamnian
location: **6** Oregon **10** California

leader: **14** Chief Kintpuash
(Captain Jack)
related to: **7** Klamath

Modred
character in: **16** Arthurian
romance

Mod Squad, The
character: **9** Linc Hayes,
(Capt) Adam Greer **11** Julie
Barnes, Pete Cochran
cast: **11** Michael Cole, Peggy
Lipton, Tige Andrews
19 Clarence Williams III

modulate 4 pass **5** lower **6** accord, attune, change, reduce,
soften, temper **8** moderate,
progress, regulate, tone down,
turn down **9** harmonize

modulation 4 tone **5** pitch **6** accent **9** reduction **10** expression,
regulation, transition

modus operandi 15 mode of
operating
abbreviation: **2** mo

modus vivendi 14 manner of
living

Moerae *see* **5** Fates

Mogadishu, Mogadiscio
capital of: **7** Somalia

mogul 3 VIP **4** czar, lord
5 baron, power, wheel **6** bigwig, tycoon **7** big shot, magnate, notable **8** big wheel
9 personage, potentate

Mohammed *see box*

Mohammedan 4 Sufi **6** Moslem, Muslim, Shiite **7** Islamic,
Moorish, Sunnite **10** Mahome-
tan, Muhammadan,
Muhammedan

Mohave, Mojave
language family: **5** Yuman
location: **7** Arizona
10 California

Mohawk (Kaniengehaga)
language family: **9** Iroquoian
location: **6** Canada, Quebec
7 New York **11** Lake Ontario
leader: **8** Hiawatha **11** Joseph
Brant
member of: **19** League of the
Iroquois

Mohegan, Mohican, Mahican
language family: **9** Algonkian
10 Algonquian
location: **7** New York **9** Wisconsin **11** Connecticut
12 Hudson Valley
leader: **5** Occom, Uncas
12 Chingachgook
allied with: **6** Pequot
with Delaware: **11** Loup Indians, Wolf Indians

Mohammed
also: **7** Mahomet, Prophet
8 Muhammad
born: **5** Mecca
clan: **6** Hashim
daughter: **6** Fatima
deity: **5** Allah
died: **6** Medina
father: **8** Abdallah,
Abdullah
father-in-law: **7** Abu Bakr,
Abubekr
flight: **4** hadj **6** hegira,
hejira
follower: **6** Moslem, Muslim, Wahbi
10 Mohammedan
grandfather: **13** Abd al-
Muttalib
horse: **5** Buraq **7** Alborrak
mother: **5** Amina
religion: **5** Islam
shrine: **5** Kaaba
son: **7** Ibrahim
adopted: **3** Ali
successor: **4** imam **5** calif
6 caliph **7** Abu Bakr
tribe: **7** Koreish, Quraysh
uncle: **5** Abbas **8** Abu
Talib
wife: **5** Aisha **6** Ayesha,
Safiya **7** Khadija **8** Khad-
idja, Kadijah

---

subject of novel: **20** The Last
of the Mohicans
author: **19** James Fenimore
Cooper

Moira
personifies: **4** fate

Moirai *see* **5** Fates

moist 3 wet **4** damp, dank,
dewy **5** humid, misty, muggy,
rainy **6** clammy, drippy, watery
7 aqueous, drizzly, tearful,
wettish, wet-eyed **8** dripping,
vaporous **10** lachrymose

moisten 3 dew, wet **4** damp,
hose, mist, soak **5** spray, water
6 dampen, douche, splash,
sponge **8** humidify, irrigate,
saturate, vaporize **10** moisturize

moisture 3 dew, wet **4** damp,
mist **5** sweat, vapor **7** drizzle,
exudate, wetness **8** dampness,
dankness, humidity **9** moistness, mugginess **10** wateriness
11 evaporation **12** perspiration

Mojave *see* **6** Mohave

Moki *see* **4** Hopi

mold 3 cut, die, ilk **4** cast,
form, kind, line, make, rust,

---

sort, turn, type **5** brand, frame,
knead, model, shape, stamp,
train **6** blight, create, figure,
fungus, kidney, lichen, matrix,
mildew, render, sculpt, shaper
7 contour, convert, develop,
fashion, outline, pattern, quality, remodel **9** character, construct, formation, structure,
transform

Moldova
other name: **8** Moldavia
capital/largest city: **8** Chisinau, Kishinev
head of state: **9** president
government: **8** republic
monetary unit: **5** ruble
river: **8** Dniester
people: **7** Gagauzi **8** Moldovan
9 Moldavian
language: **8** Romanian
9 Moldavian
religion: **15** Russian Orthodox

moldy 5 fusty, hoary, musty,
stale **7** spoiled **8** mildewed

molest 3 irk, vex **4** fret, harm,
hurt **5** abuse, annoy, beset,
harry, worry **6** attack, bother,
harass, hector, injure, pester,
plague **7** assault, disturb, torment, trouble **8** maltreat

**Moliere (Jean-Baptiste
Poquelin)**
author of: **6** Scapin **8** Tartuffe,
The Miser **10** Amphitryon
13 Le Misanthrope **17** The
School for Wives **19** The
Imaginary Invalid **20** The
School for Husbands **22** Le
Bourgeois Gentilhomme

Moll Flanders
author: **11** Daniel Defoe
character: **5** Robin
6 Jemmy E **10** Sea Captain

mollification 8 soothing **9** pla-
cation **11** appeasement, assuagement **12** conciliation

mollify 4 calm, curb, dull, ease,
lull **5** abate, allay, blunt, check,
quell, quiet, still **6** lessen, pacify, reduce, soften, soothe,
temper **7** appease, assuage,
lighten, placate **8** decrease,
mitigate, moderate, palliate,
tone down

mollusk 4 clam, slug **5** conch,
cowry, murex, snail, squid,
whelk **6** chiton, cockle, cowrie,
limpet, mussel, oyster, teredo,
triton **7** abalone, bivalve, geoduck, octopus, scallop **8** argo-
naut, nautilus, shipworm
9 shellfish **10** cuttlefish, nudi-
branch, periwinkle

mollycoddle 3 pet **4** baby,
wimp **5** sissy, spoil **6** cosset,
coward, pamper **7** cater to,
crybaby, indulge, milksop
8 give in to, mama's boy,

weakling **9** cream puff
11 milquetoast, overindulge

Molnar, Ferenc
author of: **6** Liliom **7** The
Swan **12** The Guardsman

Moloch 3 god **5** diety
also: **6** Molech
worshiped by: **9** Ammonites

Molorchus
form: **7** peasant

Molossus
father: **11** Neoptolemus
mother: **10** Andromache

molt 4 cast, shed, slip
6 change, slough **7** castoff, discard, ecdysis **8** exuviate

molten 6 melted, red-hot **7** fu-
sible, igneous, smelted **8** mag-
matic **9** liquefied

molto
music: **4** very

Molus
father: **4** Ares
mother: **8** Demonice
son: **8** Meriones

Moly
form: **4** herb
given to: **8** Odysseus
given by: **6** Hermes
to counteract spells of:
5 Circe

Momaday, N Scott
author of: **18** The House
Made of Dawn **21** The Way
to Rainy Mountain

moment 5 flash, jiffy, trice,
value, worth **6** import, minute,
second, weight **7** concern,
gravity, instant **8** interest,
juncture **9** twinkling **10** importance **11** consequence,
weightiness **12** significance

momentary 5 brief, hasty,
quick, short **6** sudden **7** instant, passing **8** flashing, fleeting, fugitive, imminent
9 ephemeral, immediate, temporary, transient **10** short-
lived, transitory
13 instantaneous

momentous 5 grave **7** crucial,
fateful, salient, serious,
weighty **8** critical, decisive,
eventful **9** essential, important,
ponderous **11** far-reaching, influential, significant, substantial **12** earthshaking
13 consequential

momentous occurrence
5 event **8** occasion **9** milestone **12** red-letter day, turning point

momentum 2 go **4** dash, push
5 drive, force, speed, vigor
6 energy, moment, thrust

7 headway, impetus, impulse
8 velocity **10** propulsion

Mommsen, Theodor
author of: **16** The History of
Rome

Momus
also: **5** Momos
god of: **7** censure **8** ridicule

Monaco *see box*

Monaco-Ville
capital of: **6** Monaco

monarch 3 HRH **4** czar, doge,
emir, khan, king, rani, shah
5 rajah, ruler, queen **6** kaiser,
prince **7** czarina, emperor, empress, majesty, pharaoh
8 kaiserin, princess **9** chieftain,
potentate

monarchical 9 czaristic **10** autocratic **11** dictatorial

monastery 5 abbey **6** friary,
priory **7** convent, nunnery, retreat **8** cloister

monastic 7 ascetic, monkish,
recluse **8** celibate, hermitic, secluded, solitary **9** cloistral, reclusive, unworldly
10 cloistered, hermitlike
11 sequestered
13 contemplative

mon cher 6 my dear

Moncrieff, Algernon (Algy)
character in: **27** The Importance of Being Earnest
author: **5** Wilde

Mond, Mustapha
character in: **13** Brave New
World
author: **6** Huxley

Monday
French: **5** lundi
German: **6** montag
heavenly body: **4** moon
Italian: **6** lunedi
means: **12** day of the moon
Spanish: **5** lunes

Mondrian, Piet
real name: **23** Pieter Cornelis
Mondriaan
born: **10** Amersfoort **14** The
Netherlands
artwork: **5** Trees **10** The Red
Tree **12** Ocean and Pier
17 Evening Landscapes
18 Landscape with a Mill
20 Broadway Boogie-
Woogie **29** Composition in
Red Yellow and Blue

Monet, Claude Oscar
born: **5** Paris **6** France
artwork: **7** Poplars **9** Hay-
stacks, The Thames **11** Water Lilies **14** Rouen
Cathedral **16** Women in the
Garden **17** Impression Sunrise **18** Mornings on the
Seine **21** The Bridge at
Argenteuil

Moneta
epithet of: **4** Juno
means: **7** advisor

monetary 6 fiscal **9** budgetary,

Monaco
capital: **11** Monaco-Ville
largest city: **10** Monte Carlo
others: **9** Fontville
division: **9** Fontville **10** Monte Carlo **11** La Condamine,
Monaco-Ville
head of government: **15** minister of state
head of state: **6** prince
monetary unit: **5** franc **7** centime
river: **7** Vesubie
sea: **13** Mediterranean
physical feature: **9** Cote d'Azur
people: **6** French **7** Italian **10** Monegasque
oceanographer: **15** Jacques Cousteau
prince: **5** Louis **6** Albert, Honore **7** Antoine, Charles,
Rainier **9** Florestan
princess: **10** Grace Kelly
ruler: **4** Rome **5** Genoa **6** Greece **8** Grimaldi, Saracens
9 Phoenicia
language: **6** French **7** English, Italian **10** Monegasque
religion: **13** Roman Catholic
place:
beach: **8** Larvotto
casino: **10** Monte Carlo
gardens: **6** Exotic
museum: **12** Oceanography
park: **18** Princess Antoinette
feature:
auto race: **15** Monaco Grand Prix

financial, pecuniary,
sumptuary

money 4 cash, coin **5** bread,
bucks, dough, funds **6** assets,
riches, specie, wealth **7** capital,
coinage, payment, revenue,
scratch **8** currency, hard cash,
proceeds **9** affluence, long
green **10** collateral, green-
backs **11** wherewithal

money-carrier
French: **12** porte-monnaie

moneyed, monied 4 rich
5 flush, swell **6** flashy, loaded
7 elegant, opulent, solvent,
wealthy **8** affluent
10 prosperous

money-grubbing 5 venal
6 greedy **8** covetous, grasping
9 mercenary **10** avaricious

money lender 6 banker,
lender, usurer **7** lombard, shylock **9** loanshark
10 pawnbroker

money saved 7 nest egg, savings **10** investment

money spent 6 outlay **7** payment **8** expenses
11 expenditure

Mongolia *see box*

Mongolian
language family: **6** Altaic
group: **6** Buryat **7** Khalkha

Mongoose, The
nickname of: **11** Archie
Moore

mongrel 3 cur **4** mutt **5** mixed
6 hybrid **7** bastard **8** offshoot
9 anomalous, crossbred
10 crossbreed

moniker 3 tag **4** name **5** label,
title **6** eponym, handle **7** epithet, surname **8** cognomen,
nickname, taxonomy **9** sobriquet **11** appellation, designation **12** denomination

monitor 2 TV **4** tend **5** guide,
teach **6** censor, direct, pickup,
police, screen, sensor **7** oversee, proctor, scanner **8** overseer, watchdog **9** supervise
14 disciplinarian

monk 4 abbe **5** abbot, friar
6 hermit **7** brother, holy man,
recluse **8** cenobite, monastic
9 anchorite
French: **5** frere

Monk, The
author: **19** Matthew Gregory
Lewis

Monkees, The
cast/musician: **9** Davy Jones,
Peter Tork **10** David Jones
11 Micky Dolenz, Mike
Nesmith

Mongolia
other name: **13** Outer Mongolia
capital/largest city: **9** Ulan Bator
others: **5** Kobdo **6** Darhan **10** Choibalsan, Sukhe Bator,
Tsetserlik, Uliassutai
ancient capital: **9** Karakoram
government:
legislature: **17** People's Great Hural **18** People's Great
Khural
monetary unit: **5** mongo, mungo **6** tugrik **7** tughrik
weight: **3** lan
lake: **3** Uvs **5** Har Us **6** Bor Nor **7** Ghirgis, Ubsa Nor
8 Airik Nor, Durga Nor, Hobsogol, Khara Usu **9** Khubsugul, Khukhu-Nur **10** Khirgis Nor
mountain: **4** Cast, Orog **5** Altai **6** Kentei, Sevrej **7** Ich
Ovoo, Khangai, Khentei **8** Tannu-Ola **9** Edrengijn **10** Ca-
gaan Bogd **11** Munky Sardyk **14** Hangayn-Hentiyn,
Monch Chajrchan
highest point: **10** Tabun Bogdo
river: **3** Tes **4** Egin, Onon, Tuul, Uldz **5** Kobdo, Tesin
6 Orkhon **7** Kerulen, Selenga, Selenge **8** Dzabkhan,
Dzavchan
physical feature:
desert: **4** Gobi **5** Ordos, Shamo
plateau: **8** Mongolia
region: **10** Great Lakes
people: **5** Oirat, Tungu **6** Buryat, Darbet, Khoton, Mongol
7 Kazakhs, Khalkha **8** Tuvinian **9** Dariganga
leader: **8** Jahangir, Jehangir **10** Kublai Khan, Tsendenbal **11** Genghis Khan
ruler: **4** Huns **5** Ching **6** Manchu **7** Kirghiz, Uighurs
8 Hsiung-nu
spiritual/secular ruler: **12** Living Buddha **21** Jebtsun
Damba Khutu Khtu
language: **6** Kazakh **16** Khalkha Mongolian
religion: **7** Lamaism **9** Shamanism **15** Tibetan Buddhism
place:
monastery: **6** Gandun
feature:
felt tent: **4** yurt
nomadic herder: **4** arat
food:
fermented mare's milk: **5** airag

---

monkey 3 ape, ass, toy **4** butt,
dupe, fool, jerk **5** clown,
jimmy **6** baboon, fiddle, meddle, simian, tamper, tinker,
trifle **7** buffoon, primate
13 laughingstock
group of: **5** troop
god: **7** Hanuman
kind: **3** owl **4** saki, titi
5 aotus, lemur **6** baboon,
guenon, howler, langur,
rhesus, spider **7** colobus,
Goeldi's, guereza, macaque,
tamarin, tarsier, uakaris
8 capuchin, mandrill, marmoset, squirrel, talapoin
11 douroucouli

monkey business 6 capers
9 highjinks **11** shenanigans

monkeyshines 6 antics, capers, pranks **7** hijinks **10** buffoonery, tomfoolery
11 foolishness

Monks (Edward Leeford)
character in: **11** Oliver Twist
author: **7** Dickens

monocle 4 quiz **5** glass **7** lorg-
non **8** eyeglass

Monoclonius
type: **8** dinosaur
10 ceratopsid
location: **12** North America
characteristic: **6** horned

Monod, Jacques
field: **7** biology
nationality: **6** French
researched: **3** RNA **8** genetics
awarded: **10** Nobel Prize

monograph 8 tractate, treatise
9 discourse **12** disquisition,
dissertation

monolith 5 stone **6** column,
menhir, pillar, statue **7** obelisk **8** memorial, monument

monologue, monolog
6 screed, sermon, speech 7 address, lecture, oration 9 discourse, soliloquy
11 expatiation 12 disquisition

monopolize 3 own 6 absorb, corner, manage, take up
7 consume, control, preempt
8 arrogate, dominate, regulate, take over 9 cartelize
11 appropriate

monopoly 4 bloc 5 trust 6 cartel, corner 7 combine, control
8 dominion 9 copyright, ownership, syndicate 10 consortium, domination
11 sovereignty 12 jurisdiction
14 proprietorship

monotonous 3 dry 4 dull, flat
5 banal 6 boring, dreary, jejune, stodgy, torpid 7 droning, humdrum, insipid, mundane, prosaic, routine, tedious
8 plodding, singsong, tiresome, toneless, unvaried 9 colorless, soporific, wearisome 10 pedestrian 11 repetitious, somniferous 13 uninteresting

monotony 3 rut 5 ennui 6 tedium 7 boredom, humdrum
8 dullness, flatness, prosaism, sameness 9 iteration 10 dreariness, redundancy, uniformity
11 reiteration, tediousness
13 wearisomeness
14 predictability

Monroe, Earl
nickname: 12 Earl the Pearl
sport: 10 basketball
position: 5 guard
team: 16 Baltimore Bullets
21 New York
Knickerbockers

Monroe, James *see box*

Monroe, Marilyn
real name: 23 Norma Jean Mortenson Baker
husband: 11 Joe DiMaggio
12 Arthur Miller
born: 12 Los Angeles CA
roles: 7 Bus Stop, Niagara
10 The Misfits 13 Some Like It Hot 16 The Seven-Year Itch 22 Gentlemen Prefer Blondes, How To Marry a Millionaire 23 The Prince and the Showgirl

Monrovia
capital of: 7 Liberia

monseigneur 6 my lord

monsieur 2 Mr 3 sir 6 mister, my lord

Monsieur Beaucaire
author: 15 Booth Tarkington

Monsignor Quixote
author: 12 Graham Greene

Monroe, James
presidential rank: 5 fifth
party: 20 Democratic-Republican
state represented: 2 VA
defeated: 4 (Rufus) King 5 (John Quincy) Adams
vice president: 8 (Daniel D) Tompkins
cabinet:
  state: 5 (John Quincy) Adams
  treasury: 8 (William Harris) Crawford
  war: 7 (John Caldwell) Calhoun
  attorney general: 4 (Richard) Rush, (William) Wirt
  navy: 8 (Samuel Lewis) Southard, (Smith) Thompson
  13 (Benjamin Williams) Crowninshield
born: 2 VA 18 Westmoreland County
died: 13 New York City NY
buried: 10 Richmond VA
education: 14 William and Mary (did not graduate)
religion: 12 Episcopalian
author: 67 A View of the Conduct of the Executive in the Foreign Affairs of the United States
political career: 8 US Senate
  governor of: 8 Virginia
  minister: 5 Spain 6 France 12 Great Britain
  secretary of: 3 war 5 state
civilian career: 6 lawyer
military service: 5 major 7 captain 10 lieutenant 16 Revolutionary War 17 lieutenant colonel
  wounded in Battle of: 7 Trenton
notable events of lifetime/term: 5 Panic (of 1819)
  14 Monroe Doctrine
  Agreement: 9 Rush-Bagot
  Compromise: 8 Missouri
  war: 8 Seminole
father: 6 Spence
mother: 9 Elizabeth (Jones)
siblings: 6 Andrew, Spence 9 Elizabeth 11 Joseph Jones
wife: 9 Elizabeth (Kortright)
  nickname: 5 Eliza
children: 11 Maria Hester 14 Eliza Kortright

---

monster 4 Fury 5 beast, brute, demon, devil, fiend, freak, ghoul, giant, golem, harpy, hydra, satyr, titan 6 dragon, gorgon, marvel, oddity, savage, threat, wonder, wretch, zombie 7 anomaly, caitiff, centaur, chimera, deviant, incubus, mammoth, mermaid, vampire, variant, villain 8 bogeyman, colossus, gargoyle, succubus, werewolf 9 barbarian, curiosity, cutthroat, scoundrel 10 blackguard, phenomenon 11 abnormality, miscreation 12 Frankenstein, lusus naturae

monstrosity 5 freak 7 monster

monstrous 4 bald, evil, huge
5 cruel, giant 6 grisly, mighty, odious 7 ghastly, harried, heinous, hideous, hulking, immense, mammoth, obscene, obvious, satanic, titanic, vicious 8 colossal, enormous, fiendish, flagrant, gigantic, gruesome, horrible, outright, shocking 9 atrocious, egregious, nefarious, revolting
10 diabolical, gargantuan, outrageous, prodigious, scandalous, stupendous, tremendous, villainous 14 Brobdingnagian

monstrousness 8 baseness, enormity, evilness, vileness, villainy 9 barbarity, depravity, malignity 10 inhumanity, wickedness 11 heinousness, viciousness 13 atrociousness, offensiveness 14 outrageousness

Montagnais-Naskapi (Innu)
language family: 9 Algonkian 10 Algonquian
tribe: 8 Nascapee 9 Mistassin
10 Bersiamite, Montagnais
11 Papinachois
location: 5 Maine 6 Canada, Quebec 17 Maritime Provinces
occupation: 7 hunters 10 fur traders

Montague family
characters in: 14 Romeo and Juliet
author: 11 Shakespeare

Montaigne, Michel de
author of: 6 Essais, Essays

Montalban, Ricardo
born: 6 Mexico 10 Mexico City
roles: 4 Khan 8 Mr Roarke 9 The Colbys 13 Fantasy Island 24 Star Trek II The Wrath of Khan

Montalvo, Garcia de
author of: 12 Amadis of Gaul

Montana see box

Montana, Bob
creator/artist of: 6 Archie

Montand, Yves
real name: 7 Ivo Livi
wife: 14 Simone Signoret
born: 5 Italy 14 Monsummano Alto
roles: 1 Z 12 Let's Make Love 14 Is Paris Burning?

montani semper liberi
28 mountaineers are always free men
motto of: 12 West Virginia

Montcalm, Louis Joseph
also: 17 Marquis de Montcalm
nationality: 6 French
served in: 18 French and Indian War
battle: 6 Oswego, Quebec (siege) 8 Carillon 11 Ticonderoga 16 Fort William Henry
killed in battle at: 6 Quebec 15 Plains of Abraham

mont-de-piete 10 pawnbroker
literally: 10 bank of pity

Montenegro see box

Monteverdi, Claudio
born: 5 Italy 7 Cremona
composer of: 5 Adone, Orfeo 7 Arianna 14 La Favola d'Orfeo 17 The Fable of Orpheus 21 The Coronation of Poppea 22 L'incoronazione di Poppea 24 Il Ritorno d'Ulisse in patria 34 Il Combattimento di Tancredi e Clorinda

Montevideo
capital of: 7 Uruguay

Montenegro
name means: 13 black mountain
other name: 4 Zeta 8 Crna Gora
capital: 7 Cetinje 8 Titograd 9 Podgorica
cities: 3 Bar 5 Kotor, Tivat 6 Niksic, Ulcinj 8 Antivari, Dulcigno, Ivangrad, Pljevlja 10 Hercegnovi 11 Sveti Stefan
division:
  Roman province:
    7 Illyria
governed by:
  10 Yugoslavia
monetary unit: 4 para 6 florin 7 perpera
lake: 7 Scutari, Shkoder
mountain: 8 Durmitor 11 Dinaric Alps
river: 3 Lim 4 Piva, Tara, Zeta 6 Moraca 7 Ceotina
sea: 8 Adriatic
physical feature:
  gulf: 5 Kotor
people: 4 Serb, Slav 11 Montenegrin
  former ruler (Orthodox bishop): 7 vladike 8 vladlika
language: 13 Serbo-Croatian
religion: 16 Serbian Orthodoxy

Montana
abbreviation: 2 MT 4 Mont
nickname: 6 Big Sky 7 Bonanza, Stubtoe 8 Mountain, Treasure
capital: 6 Helena
largest city: 8 Billings
others: 4 Kipp 5 Butte, Havre, Malta 6 Hardin 7 Bozeman, Chinook, Choteau, Forsyth, Glasgow, Roundup 8 Anaconda, Missoula 9 Kalispell 10 Great Falls
college: 7 Carroll 10 Great Falls 13 Rocky Mountain
feature: 17 Continental Divide
  cemetery: 6 Custer
  national park: 7 Glacier 11 Yellowstone
tribe: 4 Cree, Crow, Hohe 5 Sioux 6 Atsima, Atsina, Salish 7 Arapaho, Bannock, Kutenai, Siksika 8 Cheyenne, Chippewa, Flatfoot, Flathead, Shoshone 9 Blackfeet 11 Assiniboine
people: 8 Myrna Loy 9 Will James 10 Gary Cooper 14 Charles Russell 15 Jeannette Rankin
  explorer: 13 Lewis and Clark 16 Pierre Jean de Smet
lake: 5 Tiber 6 Hebgen 8 Flathead, Fort Peck, Medicine 10 Yellowtail 11 Canyon Ferry, Hungry Horse
land rank: 6 fourth
mountain: 4 Ajax 5 Baldy, Cowan, Crazy, Lewis 6 Sphinx, Torrey 7 Bighorn, Big Belt, Hilgard, Purcell, Rockies, Trapper 8 Absaroka, Gallatin, Pentagon, Snowshoe
  highest point: 11 Granite Peak
physical feature: 10 Great Falls
river: 3 Sun 4 Milk 5 Clark, Teton 6 Marias, Powder, Tongue, Willow 7 Madison, Shields 8 Columbia, Kootenai, Missouri 9 Blackfoot 10 Bitterroot 11 Musselshell, Yellowstone
state admission: 10 forty-first
state bird: 17 western meadowlark
state fish: 26 black-spotted cutthroat trout
state flower: 10 bitterroot
state motto: 13 Gold and Silver
state song: 7 Montana
state tree: 13 Ponderosa pine

Montgomery, Bernard Law see box

Montgomery, Robert
real name: 17 Henry Montgomery Jr
daughter: 9 Elizabeth
born: 8 Beacon NY
roles: 11 The Big House 13 Night Must Fall 17 Here Comes Mr Jordan

month
abbreviation: 2 mo

Month in the Country, A
author: 12 Ivan Turgenev

months, Hebrew see box

Mont-Oriol
author: 15 Guy de Maupassant

Montreal see box

Montresor
character in: 20 The Cask of Amontillado
author: 3 Poe

Mont Saint Michel and Chartres
author: 10 Henry Adams

Montgomery, Bernard Law
also: 27 (first) Viscount Montgomery of Alamein
author of: 7 Memoirs 17 A History of Warfare
battle: 9 El Alamein
chief: 19 British general staff
commander of: 17 British Eighth Army 32 British occupation forces in Germany
commando raid: 6 Dieppe
deputy supreme commander: 4 NATO
Eighth Army called: 10 Desert Rats
evacuation of: 7 Dunkirk
fought against: 6 Rommel 11 Africa Corps, Afrika Korps
invasion: 6 Sicily 8 Normandy
member: 12 House of Lords
nationality: 7 British
nickname: 5 Monty
served in: 3 WWI 4 WWII

months, Hebrew
first: 4 Ahib, Nisn 6 Ehanim, Tishri
second: 3 Bul, Civ 4 Iyar 7 Heshvan
third: 5 Sivan 6 Kislev
fourth: 5 Tebet 6 Tammuz, Tebeth
fifth: 2 Ab 7 Shelbat
sixth: 4 Adar, Elul 6 Veadar
seventh: 4 Abib 5 Nisan 6 Tishri 7 Ethanim
eighth: 3 Zif 4 Iyar 11 Marcheshvan
ninth: 5 Sivan 7 Chislev
tenth: 6 Tebeth, Tammuz
eleventh: 2 Ab 6 Shabat
twelfth: 4 Adar, Elul

Monty
nickname of: 15 Montgomery Clift 17 (General) Bernard Montgomery

monument 4 slab 5 token 6 shrine 7 memento, obelisk, witness 8 cenotaph, memorial, monolith, reminder 9 testament, tombstone 10 gravestone 11 remembrance, testimonial 13 commemoration

Montreal
airport: 6 Dorval 8 St Hubert 12 Cartierville
baseball team: 5 Expos
founder: 11 Maisonneuve
hill: 10 Mount Royal
hockey team: 9 Canadiens
island: 5 Jesus 6 Bizard, Perrot 8 Montreal 9 des Soeurs 14 de Boucherville
lake: 7 St Louis
landmark: 12 Place des Arts 13 Molson Stadium 16 Chateau de Ramezay 17 Church of Notre Dame, St Sulpice Seminary 21 Man and His World Exhibit
original name: 10 Ville-Marie
province: 6 Quebec
river: 6 Ottawa 10 St Lawrence 11 des Prairies 14 des Milles Isles
subway: 5 Metro
university: 6 McGill

monumental 4 huge 5 fatal, heavy 7 awesome, classic, epochal, immense, lasting, massive 8 colossal, decisive, enduring, gigantic, historic, immortal, statuary 9 cyclopean, egregious, memorable 10 horrendous, monolithic, shattering, stupendous 11 inestimable 12 catastrophic 13 unprecedented

mooch 3 beg, bum 5 cadge 6 hustle, sponge 7 solicit 8 freeload

mood 5 blues, dumps, humor 6 spirit, temper 7 feeling 8 doldrums, vexation 9 condition 10 depression, gloominess, melancholy 11 disposition, melancholia, temperament 14 predisposition 16 hypersensitivity

moody 4 mean 5 sulky, surly, testy 6 crabby, dismal, fickle, gloomy, mopish, morbid, morose, sullen 7 erratic, flighty, peevish, unhappy 8 brooding, dejected, notional, variable, volatile 9 impetuous, impulsive, irascible, irritable, mercurial, saturnine, whimsical 10 capricious, changeable, despondent, inconstant, lugubrious, melancholy 11 pessimistic 12 inconsistent 13 temperamental, unpredictable

Mookerjee, Hurree Chunder
character in: 3 Kim
author: 7 Kipling

moon 4 gape, lamp, luna, roam 5 dream, month, stare 6 dawdle, wander 8 daydream 9 satellite
god of: 3 Sin 5 Nanna 6 Meztli
goddess of: 4 Luna 5 Diana, Holle, Tanit 6 Hecate, Hekate, Phoebe, Selena, Selene, Tanith 7 Artemis, Astarte, Cynthia
full: 9 plenilune
new: 5 prime
waning: 7 waiand

Moon and Sixpence, The
author: 16 W Somerset Maugham

moonless 4 dark 5 black, murky 7 stygian 9 lightless, unlighted 13 unilluminated

Moonlighting
character: 11 Maddie Hayes 12 Agnes Dipesto, David Addison
cast: 11 Bruce Willis 13 Allyce Beasley 14 Cybill Shepherd
detective agency: 8 Blue Moon

Moon Mullins
creator: 12 Frank Willard
character: 4 Kayo 5 Mamie 9 Mushmouth 11 Uncle Willie 15 Lady Plushbottom, Lord Plushbottom 16 Moonshine Mullins

Moon of the Caribbees, The
author: 12 Eugene O'Neill

moonshine 5 hokum 6 bunkum, humbug 7 bootleg 8 clockade, homebrew, malarky, nonsense 10 balderdash, bathtub gin 11 mountain dew

moonstone
species: 8 feldspar
source: 5 Burma, Mogok

Moonstone, The
author: 13 Wilkie Collins
character: 7 Dr Candy 12 Lady Verinder, Sergeant Cuff 13 Franklin Blake 14 John Herncastle, Rachel Verinder 15 Rosanna Spearman 16 Godfrey Ablewhite

moor 3 fen 4 dock, down, fell, lash, wold 5 affix, berth, chain, heath, marsh, tie up 6 anchor, attach, fasten, secure, steppe, tether, tundra, upland 7 savanna, tie down 8 make fast 9 wasteland

Moore, Archie
nickname: 11 The Mongoose

Moore, Clement C
real name: 18 Archibald Lee Wright
sport: 6 boxing
class: 16 light-heavyweight

Moore, Clement C
author of: 23 A Visit from Saint Nicholas

Moore, Dick
creator/artist of: 13 Gasoline Alley

Moore, Dudley
nickname: 12 Cuddly Dudley
wife: 11 Suzy Kendall, Tuesday Weld
born: 5 Essex 7 England 8 Dagenham
roles: 3 Ten 6 Arthur 8 Lovesick, Six Weeks 9 Bedazzled 13 Micki and Maude 16 Arthur on the Rocks 17 Like Father Like Son
plays: 5 piano

Moore, George
author of: 12 Esther Waters 15 Hail and Farewell

Moore, Henry
born: 7 England 10 Castleford
artwork: 4 Mask 8 Two Forms 9 North Wind 10 Bird Basket 11 Family Group, Head of a Girl 12 Locking Piece 13 Nuclear Energy 15 Reclining Figure 20 Four-Piece Composition

Moore, Marianne
author of: 12 Like a Bulwark, Nevertheless, O To Be a Dragon, Tell Me Tell Me

Moore, Mary Tyler
husband: 11 Grant Tinker
born: 10 Brooklyn NY
roles: 4 Mary 12 Mary Richards 14 Ordinary People 18 The Dick Van Dyke Show 21 The Mary Tyler Moore Show

Moore, Mrs
character in: 15 A Passage to India
author: 7 Forster

Moore, Roger
born: 6 London 7 England
roles: 8 The Saint 12 Simon Templar
as James Bond: 9 Moonraker, Octopussy 13 Live and Let Die 16 The Spy Who Loved Me 22 The Man with the Golden Gun

Moorehead, Agnes
born: 9 Clinton MA
roles: 6 Endora 9 Bewitched 11 Citizen Kane 13 Johnny Belinda 15 Dear Dead Delilah 20 Magnificent Obsession 23 The Magnificent Ambersons

mooring 4 hook, line, rope 5 cable, chain 6 anchor, hawser

moot 4 open 7 eristic 8 arguable, disputed 9 debatable, undecided, unsettled 10 disputable, unresolved 11 conjectural 12 questionable 13 controversial, problematical 14 controvertible

mope 4 fret, pine, pout, sulk 5 brood, worry 6 grieve, grouse, lament, repine 7 grumble 8 languish

Mopsus
occupation: 4 seer
mother: 5 Manto
grandfather: 8 Tiresias
member of: 9 Argonauts
founded: 6 oracle
location: 6 Mallus 7 Cilicia
cofounder: 11 Amphilochus
epithet: 9 Ampycides

moral 3 tag 4 fair, just, pure 5 adage, maxim, motto, noble, right 6 honest, lesson, proper, saying 7 epigram, ethical, message, proverb, saintly 8 aphorism, didactic, personal, virtuous 9 estimable, homiletic, honorable, preaching 10 aboveboard, high-minded, principled 11 meritorious, sermonizing, tendentious 12 conscionable

moral code 6 ethics 9 integrity, standards 10 principles

morale 4 mood 6 spirit, temper 10 confidence, resolution 11 disposition
French: 13 esprit de corps

morality 5 honor 6 ethics, habits, tastes, virtue 7 modesty, probity 8 fairness, goodness 9 integrity, rectitude 10 chasteness 11 uprightness 13 righteousness

moralize 6 preach 7 lecture

moralizing 7 preachy 8 didactic 9 homiletic

morally corrupt 6 effete 8 decadent, depraved 10 degenerate

moral sense 9 integrity 10 conscience

morass 3 bog, fen 4 mire 5 marsh, swamp 6 slough 8 quagmire, wetlands 9 quicksand

morbid 3 sad 4 dour, glum, grim 5 moody 6 gloomy, morose, somber 8 brooding 9 depressed, saturnine 10 despondent, lugubrious 11 melancholic, pessimistic, unwholesome

morbid condition 6 malady 7 ailment, disease, illness 8 sickness 9 infirmity

Morcerf, Comte de (Fernand)
character in: 21 The Count of Monte Cristo
author: 5 Dumas (pere)

mordant 6 biting, bitter 7 acerbic, caustic, cutting, waspish 8 incisive, piercing, scathing, scornful, stinging, venomous, virulent 9 acidulous, malicious, sarcastic, trenchant 11 acrimonious

Mordecai
cousin: 6 Esther
served: 15 Ahasuerus Xerxes
enemy: 5 Haman

more 5 added, extra, other, spare 6 longer 7 further, reserve 10 additional 12 additionally, supplemental 13 supplementary

More, Thomas
author of: 6 Utopia

Moreau, Frederic
character in: 21 A Sentimental Education
author: 8 Flaubert

Moreau, Gustave
born: 5 Paris 6 France
artwork: 7 Orpheus 13 Dance of Salome (Salome Dancing), The Apparition 16 Hesiod and the Muse 18 The Poet and the Siren 19 Oedipus and the Sphinx 27 Diomedes Devoured by His Horses

Morehouse, J Ward
character in: 3 USA
author: 9 Dos Passos

Morel, Paul
character in: 13 Sons and Lovers
author: 8 Lawrence

Moreno, Rita
real name: 20 Rosita Dolores Alverio
born: 7 Humacao 10 Puerto Rico
roles: 13 Pagan Love Song, The Deerslayer, West Side Story 15 Singin' in the Rain

more or less 5 about 6 around 8 somewhat 9 generally, just about 13 approximately

moreover 3 too 4 also 7 besides, further 11 furthermore 12 more than that

mores 4 code 5 ethos, forms, rules 6 usages 7 customs, rituals 9 etiquette, practices, standards 10 traditions

11 conventions, observances, proprieties

more than enough 5 ample **6** excess, plenty **7** copious, profuse **8** plethora **9** abundance, amplitude, bountiful, excessive, profusion **10** oversupply

Morgan, Daniel
served in: **16** Revolutionary War
commander of: **8** riflemen **13** sharpshooters
battle: **7** Cowpens **8** Saratoga **12** Bemis Heights, Freeman's Farm
helped suppress: **16** Whiskey Rebellion

Morgan, Thomas Hunt
founder of: **8** genetics
awarded: **10** Nobel Prize

Morgan, William De
author of: **11** Joseph Vance

Morgan family
characters in: **19** How Green Was My Valley
members: **4** Beth, Davy, Huur, Ivor, Owen **5** Ianto **6** Gwilym **8** Angharad
author: **9** Llewellyn

morganite
color: **4** pink **5** peach

Morgan le Fay
character in: **16** Arthurian romance

Moriae Encomium (In Praise of Folly)
author: **7** Erasmus

Moriarty, Professor
character in: **14** (The Adventures of) Sherlock Holmes
author: **10** Conan Doyle

moribund 5 dying **6** doomed, waning **10** stagnating

Morier, James
author of: **18** Hajji Baba of Ispahan

morituri te salutamus 28 we who are about to die salute thee
said by: **15** Roman gladiators
said to: **13** Roman emperors

Mork & Mindy
character: **4** Mork **6** Eugene **10** Cora Hudson **13** Mindy McConnel **17** Frederick McConnel
cast: **9** Pam Dawber **11** Conrad Janis **13** Elizabeth Kerr, Robin Williams **14** Jeffrey Jacquet
Mork's planet: **3** Ork
phrase: **8** nanu nanu
spinoff from: **9** Happy Days

Morland, Catherine
character in: **15** Northanger Abbey
author: **6** Austen

Morley, Robert
born: **6** Semley **7** England
roles: **5** Melba **10** Oscar Wilde **11** Beau Brummel, Edward My Son **12** Major Barbara **15** Marie Antoinette, The African Queen **21** The Man Who Came to Dinner

Mormon State
nickname of: **4** Utah

morning 4 dawn **5** early, sunup **7** sunrise **8** daybreak, daylight, forenoon **9** matutinal

morning-glory 7 Ipomoea **10** Calystegia **11** Convolvulus
varieties: **3** red **4** wild **5** beach, dwarf **6** Ceylon, common, silver, woolly, yellow **9** Brazilian **16** Imperial Japanese

Morocco *see box*

moron 3 ass, nut, oaf, sap **4** boob, dolt, dope, fool **5** dummy, dunce, idiot, loony, ninny **6** dimwit, nitwit **7** halfwit, jackass **8** bonehead, dumbbell, dumbhead, imbecile,

---

Morocco
other name: **7** Barbary **8** Maroquin **9** Al Maghrib **13** Maghrib el Aksa **19** Mauretania Tingitana
capital: **5** Rabat **6** Rabbat
largest city: **10** Casablanca
others: **3** Fes, Fez, Sla **4** Ifni, Safi, Sale, Sali, Taza **5** Ceuta, Oujda, Porte, Saffi **6** Agadir, Meknes, Semara, Tetuan **7** Elarish, Kenitra, Larache, Mazagan, Mililla, Mogador, Tangier, Tetouan **8** Kouribga, Tinerhir **9** Marrakech, Marrakesh **10** Youssoufia **11** Port-Lyautey
division:
  disputed territory: **13** Western Sahara
head of state: **4** king
measure: **4** kala, muhd, rotl, saah, sahh, ueba **5** artal, cadee, gerbe, ratel **6** covado, dirhem, fanega, izenbi, kintar, tangin, tomini **8** quintral
monetary unit: **4** flue, okia, rial **5** floos, franc, okieh, ounce **6** dirham, miskal **8** mouzouna
weight: **4** rotl **5** artel, ratel **6** dirhem, kintar **7** quintal
island: **7** Madeira
mountain: **3** Rif **4** Bani **5** Abyla, Atlas, Sarro **8** Tidiguin **9** Anti-Atlas, High Atlas, Jebel-Musa **11** Middle Atlas
highest point: **12** Jebel Toubkal **13** Djebel Toubkal
river: **3** Dra, Ziz **4** Sous **5** Sebou **6** Gheris **7** Tensift **8** Moulouya **9** Oum er Rbia
sea: **8** Atlantic **13** Mediterranean
physical feature:
  cape: **3** Nun, Sim **4** Juby, Noun, Rhir **6** Cantin
  desert: **6** Sahara
  oasis: **8** Tafilelt
  plain: **5** Rharb
  strait: **9** Gibraltar
  valley: **7** Ouergha
  wind: **5** leste **7** charqui
people: **4** Arab, Moor **6** Berber, French **7** Spanish
  dynasty: **7** Alawite, Almohad **9** Almoravid
  leader: **5** Idris **7** Lyautey **8** Hassan II **9** Abd el-Krim
  philosopher: **8** Averroes
language: **6** Arabic, Berber, French **7** Spanish
religion: **5** Islam
place:
  ruins: **9** Volubilis
feature:
  clothing: **4** haik **7** jellaba
  hat: **3** fez
  Islamic holy war: **5** jehad, jihad
  shanty town: **10** bidonville
food:
  dish: **8** couscous

numskull 9 blockhead, numbskull, simpleton 10 muttonhead, nincompoop

Moroni
  capital of: 7 Comoros

Moros
  mother: 3 Nyx
  personifies: 4 fate

morose 3 low, sad 4 blue,
dour, glum, sour 5 cross,
moody, sulky, surly, testy
6 cranky, gloomy, grumpy,
mopish, solemn, sullen
7 waspish 8 churlish, downcast, mournful 9 depressed,
irascible, saturnine 10 despondent, melancholy
11 crestfallen

moroseness 5 gloom 8 glum-
ness 9 pessimism, sulkiness,
surliness 10 sullenness

Morpheus
  god of: 6 dreams
  father: 6 Hypnos

morphology
  study of: 9 structure

Morris, Dinah
  character in: 8 Adam Bede
  author: 5 Eliot

Morris, Willie
  author of: 5 Yazoo 10 Good
  Old Boy 15 North Toward
  Home

Morris, Wright
  author of: 8 Will's Boy
  10 Plain's Song 13 Field of
  Vision, My Uncle Dudley

Morrison, Jeanette Helen
  real name of: 10 Janet Leigh

Morrison, Marion Michael
  real name of: 9 John Wayne

Morrison, Toni
  real name: 19 Chloe An-
  thony Wofford
  author of: 4 Sula, Jazz 7 Beloved, Tar Baby 12 The Blu-
  est Eye 13 Song of Solomon
  honor: 10 Nobel Price 13 Pulitzer Prize

Morrow, Vic
  born: 7 Bronx NY
  roles: 6 Combat 8 Cimarron
  14 God's Little Acre 15 The
  Twilight Zone 18 Portrait of
  a Mobster 19 The Black-
  board Jungle

Morse, Samuel F B
  nationality: 8 American
  invented: 9 Morse code
  17 electric telegraph
  24 electromagnetic telegraph

morsel 3 bit, nip, sip 4 bite,
drop, iota, whit 5 crumb,
grain, piece, scrap, snack,
speck, taste, touch, trace
6 dollop, nibble, sliver, tidbit

7 modicum, segment, swallow
8 fraction, fragment, mouthful,
particle 9 scintilla

mortal 4 deep, type 5 fatal,
grave, human 6 deadly, lethal,
living, person, severe
7 earthly, extreme, intense,
mundane 8 creature, enor-
mous, fleeting, temporal
9 character, corporeal, ephemeral 10 individual, transitory
12 unimaginable

mortality 7 carnage 8 fatality
9 bloodshed, ephemeral,
slaughter 10 transience 11 evanescence 12 impermanence
13 extermination
14 transitoriness

mortar 6 cannon, cement, vessel 7 plaster 8 adhesive

Morte d'Arthur, Le
  author: 12 Thomas Malory

Mortgaged Heart, The
  author: 15 Carson McCullers

mortification 3 rot 5 decay,
shame 7 chagrin, penance
8 ignominy 11 humiliation
12 putrefaction
13 embarrassment

mortified 6 rotted 7 abashed,
ashamed, debased 8 dismayed,
festered, tortured 9 chagrined,
putrefied 11 discomfited,
embarrassed

mortify 3 rot 4 deny, fast
5 abash, decay, shame 6 appall, fester 7 chagrin, horrify,
putrefy 9 discomfit, embarrass
10 discipline, disconcert

Mosaic law 10 Pentateuch
15 Ten Commandments

Mosan
  language family:
    14 Algonkian-Mosan
  subgroup: 6 Nootka 8 Che-
    makum, Kwakiutl, Quileute,
    Salishan, Wakashan
    9 Chemakuan

Moscow
  airport: 12 Sheremetyevo
  canal: 11 Moscow-Volga
  capital of: 4 USSR 6 Russia
    11 Soviet Union
  hills: 5 Lenin
  landmark: 7 Kremlin 9 Gorky
    Park, Red Square 12 Lenin
    Library 13 Izmailovo Park,
    Sokolniki Park 14 Bolshoi
    Theater 16 Moscow Art
    Theater 21 Luzhniki Sports
    Complex
  museum: 6 Armory 7 Push-
    kin 10 Historical 16 Tretya-
    kov Gallery 28 Central
    Museum of the Soviet Army
  river: 5 Setun, Volga, Yauza
    6 Moscow
  Russian: 6 Moskva

Moses
  father: 5 Amram
  mother: 8 Jochebed
  sister: 6 Miriam
  brother: 5 Aaron
  wife: 8 Zipporah
  son: 7 Eliezar, Gershom
  father-in-law: 6 Jethro
  received: 15 Ten
    Commandments
  patriarch of:
    10 Israelites
  saw: 11 burning bush
  successor: 6 Joshua
  pertaining to: 6 Mosaic

Moses, Grandma
  real name: 17 Anna Mary
    Robertson, Mary Anne
    Robertson
  born: 11 Greenwich NY
  artwork: 23 Out for the
    Christmas Trees

mosey 4 poke 5 amble 6 stroll
7 saunter, shuffle

Moslem 4 Moor 5 Islam,
Sunni 6 Muslim, Shiite 7 Is-
lamic 10 Mohammadan,
Muhammadan

mosque 6 temple
  Arabic: 6 masjid, musjid

Mosquito Coast, The
  author: 11 Paul Theroux

Mosquito State
  nickname of: 9 New Jersey

moss
  varieties: 4 ball, club, gold,
    rose 5 broom, bunch, coral,
    ditch, fairy, Irish, spike, wa-
    ter 6 Scotch, spring 7 cush-
    ion, haircap, peacock,
    Spanish 8 floating, fountain,
    Japanese, mat spike 9 dwarf
    club, flowering 10 little
    club, pincushion 11 basket
    spike, meadow spike, shin-
    ing club 12 treelet spike
    13 Douglas's spike

Mossbauer, Rudolph Ludwig
  field: 7 physics
  nationality: 6 German
  discovered: 15 Mossbauer ef-
    fect 28 recoil-free gamma
    ray absorption
  awarded: 10 Nobel Prize

Mosses from an Old Manse
  author: 18 Nathaniel
    Hawthorne

most 4 best, very 6 degree
7 maximum 9 extremely

most distant point 5 limit,
reach 8 boundary 9 extremity

Mostel, Zero
  real name: 16 Samuel Joel
    Mostel
  born: 10 Brooklyn NY
  roles: 8 The Front 10 Rhi-
    noceros 11 The Enforcer
    12 The Producers 15 Du

Barry Was a Lady **16** Fiddler on the Roof **17** Panic in the Streets

most important 3 key, top **4** head, main **5** chief **7** central, highest, leading **8** cardinal, dominant, foremost, greatest **9** paramount, principal, uppermost **10** preeminent **11** outstanding, predominant

mostly 6 mainly **7** as a rule, chiefly, greatly, largely **8** above all **9** generally, primarily, specially **10** especially **11** principally **12** particularly **13** predominantly

most prominent 7 leading **8** dominant **10** preeminent **11** outstanding

most successful 6 banner, record **7** winning **10** triumphant **11** outstanding

mote 3 dot **4** iota **5** speck **8** particle **9** scintilla

moth
  varieties: **4** hawk, luna, tent **5** ghost, gypsy, plume, royal, swift, yucca **6** hornet, lappet, miller, urania **7** clothes, emperor, flannel, hook tip, leopard, tussock **8** army worm, forester, imperial, polka dot **9** carpenter, clearwing **10** forest tent **11** pseudosphex **12** African peach **13** American tiger, giant Hercules **14** tropical sphinx **15** Chinese silkworm, glover's silkworm **20** striped morning sphinx

moth-eaten 5 holey **6** old-hat **7** worn-out **8** outmoded **10** antiquated, threadbare **11** dilapidated

mother 3 mom, mum **4** bear, mama, mind, mums, rear, tend **5** beget, breed, mater, momma, mommy, mummy, nurse, raise **6** origin, source **7** care for, indulge, nurture, old lady, produce, protect **8** conceive, stimulus **10** wellspring **11** inspiration
  French: **4** mere
  Spanish: **5** madre
  of wind: **3** Eos
  of stars: **3** Eos
  of gods: **5** Nammu

mother country 8 homeland **10** fatherland, native land, native soil, old country **13** native country

Mother Goose in Prose
  author: **14** Lyman Frank Baum

motherly 4 kind **6** gentle, loving, tender **7** devoted **8** mater-

nal, parental **9** indulgent **10** protective, sheltering

mother of a family
  Latin: **13** materfamilias

Mother of the West
  nickname of: **8** Missouri

mother's helper
  French: **6** au pair

motif 4 form, idea **5** shape, style, theme, topic **6** design, figure, thread **7** pattern, refrain, subject **9** treatment

motion 3 cue, nod **4** flow, flux, move, sign, stir **5** drift **6** action, beckon, signal, stream **7** gesture, kinesis, passage, request **8** mobility, movement, progress **10** indication, suggestion **11** gesticulate, proposition **13** gesticulation **14** recommendation

motionless 4 calm, dead, idle **5** fixed, inert, still **6** at rest, frozen, stable, static **8** immobile, inactive, lifeless, tranquil, unmoving **9** immovable, quiescent **10** stationary, transfixed **11** immobilized **12** unresponsive

motion picture 3 pic **4** cine, film, show **5** flick, movie **6** cinema, talkie **8** flickers **10** photodrama **11** picture show **13** moving picture

motivate 4 goad, move, stir **5** egg on, impel **6** arouse, induce, prompt, stir up, turn on **7** actuate, provoke **8** activate, persuade **9** influence, stimulate

motivation 5 cause **6** reason **7** impetus, impulse **9** causation, impulsion **11** provocation

motive 3 aim, end **4** goal, spur **5** cause **6** design, object, reason **7** grounds, purpose **8** occasion, stimulus, thinking **9** incentive, intention, prompting, rationale **10** enticement, incitement, inducement **11** inspiration, instigation, provocation

motley 4 pied **5** mixed, tabby **6** hybrid, sundry, unlike, varied **7** dappled, piebald, watered **8** assorted, brindled, speckled **9** checkered, composite, different, disparate, divergent, harlequin, patchwork **10** dissimilar, iridescent, polychrome, variegated **11** diversified, incongruous, varicolored **12** multicolored **13** heterogeneous, kaleidoscopic, miscellaneous

motor 3 car **4** auto, ride, tour **5** drive, pilot, wheel **6** engine,

turbine **7** machine **8** efferent **10** automobile

motorcar 4 auto, heap **6** jalopy, wheels **7** flivver, machine, vehicle **9** tin lizzie **10** automobile

motor vehicle 3 bus, car, van **4** auto, heap, limo **5** motor, truck, wagon **6** jalopy, pickup, wheels **7** flivver, hardtop, machine, omnibus, town car, vehicle **8** limosine **9** tin lizzie **10** automobile **11** convertible

mottled 4 pied **5** tabby **7** blotchy, flecked, piebald, specked **8** brindled, speckled, stippled **10** iridescent, multicolor, variegated **11** varicolored **12** parti-colored **13** kaleidoscopic, polychromatic

motto 3 saw **4** rule **5** adage, axiom, maxim **6** byword, dictum, saying, slogan, truism **7** epigram, precept, proverb **8** aphorism **9** catchword, principle, watchword

moue 4 pout **7** grimace

Moulin Rouge
  director: **10** John Huston
  cast: **10** Jose Ferrer (Toulouse-Lautrec) **11** Suzanne Flon, Zsa Zsa Gabor **12** Eric Pohlmann
  setting: **5** Paris **10** Montmartre

mound 4 bump, dune, heap, hill, pile, rick **5** knoll, mogul, ridge, stack **7** bulwark, hillock, hummock, rampart **9** earthwork **10** embankment **12** entrenchment

Mound Builders
  location: **15** Ohio River Valley **22** Mississippi River Valley
  known for: **13** earthen mounds

mount 3 fit, fix, rig, set, wax **4** go up, grow, pony, rise, soar **5** affix, camel, climb, equip, frame, horse, scale, steed, surge, swell **6** ascend, fit out, outfit, set off **7** augment, charger, climb up, get over, get upon, install, set into **8** elephant, increase, multiply, straddle **9** intensify

mountain *see box, p. 650*

Mountain
  constellation of: **5** Mensa

mountaineers are always free men
  Latin: **19** montani semper liberi
  motto of: **12** West Virginia

mountain 3 alp 4 peak 5 bluff, butte, range, ridge 6 height, massif 7 volcano 8 eminence, highland 9 elevation
   of Afghanistan: 3 Koh 5 Safeo 6 Chagai, Pamirs 7 Nowshak 8 Koh-i-Baba, Safed Koh, Sulaiman 9 Himalayas, Hindu Kush, Istoro Nal 11 Khwaja Amran, Paropamisus
   of Albania: 5 Shala 6 Pindus 8 Koritnjk 10 Mount Korab 12 Albanian Alps
   of Algeria: 5 Aissa, Atlas, Aures, Dahra, Tahat 6 Chelia 7 Ahaggar, Kabylia, Mouydir 8 Djurjura 9 Djurdjura, Tell Atlas 12 Saharan Atlas
   of Andorra: 6 d'Etats 8 l'Estanyo 8 Pyrenees 10 Cataperdis 11 Como Pedrosa
   of Angola: 4 Moco 5 Chela 6 Loviti 16 Humpata Highlands
   of Antigua and Barbuda: 9 Boggy Peak
   of Argentina: 4 Toro 5 Andes, Chato, Laudo, Potro 6 Conico, Pissis, Rincon 8 Famatina, Murallon, Olivares, Tronador, Zapaleri 9 Aconcagua, Tupungato 10 Cordillera 13 Ojos del Salado 15 Cerro Mercedario, Sierra de Cordoba
   of Armenia: 6 Ararat, Taurus 7 Karabekh 7 Aladagh 12 Mount Aragats
   of Australia: 3 Ise 4 Blue, Olga, Ossa, Zeil 5 Bruce, Snowy 6 Cradle, Doreen, Garnet, Gawler, Magnet, Morgan 7 Bongong, Gregory 8 Augustus, Brockman, Cuthbert, Herbert, Jusgrave, Mulligan, Surprise 9 Murchison, Kosciusko, Woodroffe 14 Australian Alps 15 New England Range 18 Great Dividing Range
   of Austria: 4 Alps 6 Tirols, Tyrols, Stubai 8 Eisenerz, Rhatikon 9 Dolomites, Kitzbuhel 10 Hohe Tauern 13 Grossglockner 14 Silvretta Group
   of Azerbaijan: 8 Caucasus
   of Bangladesh: 10 Keokradong 15 Chittagong Hills
   of Barbados: 6 Chalky 7 Hillaby
   of Belgium: 8 Ardennes 16 Signal de Botrange
   of Benin: 7 Atakora
   of Bhutan: 5 Black 9 Himalayas 10 Chomo Lhari, Kula Kangri
   of Bolivia: 4 Jara 5 Andes, Cusco, Cuzco 6 Sajama, Sorata, Sunsas 7 Illampu 8 Ancohuma, Illimani, Mururata, Sansimon, Santiago, Zapaleri 12 Eastern Range, Western Range 18 Cordillera Oriental 20 Cordillera Occidental
   of Borneo: 4 Iran, Raja 5 Saran 6 Kapuas, Muller, Nijaan, Tebang 8 Kinabalu, Kinibalu, Schwaner
   of Bosnia-Herzegovina: 11 Dinaric Alps
   of Brazil: 3 Mar 5 Geral, Organ, Piaui 6 Acarai, Gurupi, Parima, Urucum 7 Amambai, Carajas, Gradaus, Neblina, Oragaos, Roraima 8 Bandeira, Itatiaia, Roncador, Tombador 9 Pacaraima, Sugar Loaf 10 Tumuc-Humac
   of Brunei: 6 Teraja 9 Ulu Tutong 10 Pagon Priok
   of Bulgaria: 3 Kom 5 Botev, Pirin, Sapka 6 Balkan, Musala, Sredna 7 Vikhren 8 Musallah 11 Rila-Rhodope
   of Burkina Faso: 4 Tema 8 Nakourou 10 Tenakourou, Tenekourou
   of Burundi: 8 Nyarwana 9 Nyamisana
   of Cambodia: 3 Pan 7 Dangrek, Dong Rek 8 Cardamom, Elephant 10 Phnom Aoral, Phnom Aural
   of Cameroon: 5 Mbabo 7 Bambuto, Kapsiki, Mandara 8 Batandji, Cameroon 9 Atlantika
   of Canada: 5 Coast, Logan, Royal 6 Robson, Skeena 7 Cariboo, Cascade, Purcell, Rockies, Selkirk, Stelias, St Elias 8 Columbia, Hazelton, Monashee 9 Mackenzie, Notre Dame, Tremblant 10 Laurentian, Richardson, Shickshock 14 Jacques Cartier
   of Canary Islands: 5 Teide, Teyde 6 La Cruz 8 El Cumbre, Tenerife
   of Cape Verde: 4 Cano, Fogo 10 Pico de Cano
   of Central African Republic: 5 Karre, Tinga 6 Mongos 9 Dar Challa 11 Kayagangiri
   of Chad: 7 Tibesti, Touside 8 Emi Koussi
   of Chile: 4 Maca, Toro 5 Chato, Maipo, Maipu, Paine, Potro, Pular, Torre, Yogan 6 Apiwan, Burney, Conico, Jervis, Poquis, Rincon 7 Chaltel, Copiapo, Fitzroy, Palpana, Velluda 8 Cochrane, Tronador, Yanteles 9 Tupungato 13 Ojos del Salado
   of Colombia: 5 Abibe, Andes, Baudo, Chita, Cocuy, Huila, Pasto 6 Ayapel, Perija, Purace, Tolima, Tunahi 7 Chamusa, del Ruiz 8 Oriengal 10 Santa Marta 14 Cristobal Colon 17 Central Cordillera, Eastern Cordillera, Western Cordillera
   of Costa Rica: 4 Poas 5 Barba, Irazu 6 Blanco 7 Central, Gongora 9 Talamanca, Turrialba 10 Guanacaste 14 Chirripo Grande
   of Crete: 3 Ida 5 Dikte, Phino 6 Juktas 7 Lasithi, Madaras 8 Leuka Ori, Theodore, Thriphte 9 Psiloriti
   of Croatia: 10 Julian Alps 11 Styrian Alps
   of Cuba: 6 Copper 7 Cristal, Maestra, Organos 8 Camaguey, Trinidad, Turquino 9 Las Villas 11 Pinar del Rio 12 Guaniguanico 14 Sancti-Spiritus
   of Czechoslovakia/Czech Republic: 3 Ore 5 Grant, Tatra 6 Sumava 7 Gerlach, Sudeten 8 Krkonose 9 High Tatra 10 Carpathian 11 Gerlachovka
   of Denmark: 12 Ejer Bavnehoj, Yding Skovhoj 14 Himmelbjaerget
   of Djibouti: 5 Gouda 9 Moussa Ali
   of Dominican Republic: 4 Tina 5 Gallo, Neiba 6 Duarte 7 Baoruco, Central 8 Bahoruco, Oriental 13 Septentrional

of Ecuador: 5 Andes **6** Condor, Sangay **7** Cayambe **8** Antisana, Cotopaxi **9** Cotacachi, Pichincha **10** Chimborazo

of Egypt: 5 Sinai, Uekia **6** Gharib **8** Katerina **9** Katherina **13** Shayib al-Banat

of El Salvador: 6 Izalco **8** Santa Ana

of England: 5 Black **7** Pennine, Snowdon **8** Cambrian, Cumbrian **11** Scafell Pike

of Ethiopia: 4 Amba, Batu, Guge, Guna, Talo **5** Ahmar, Choke **9** Rasdashan, Ras Deshen

of Finland: 6 Haltia **7** Laltiva **10** Saari Selka **11** Haldetsokka

of France: 4 Alps, Jura **5** Blanc, Pelat **6** Vosges **8** Ardennes, Pyrenees **9** Mont Blanc **10** French Alps **11** Pic Montcalm

of Gabon Republic: 5 Mpele **7** Chaillu, Cristal, Mikongo **8** Balaquri, Birougou, Iboundji

of Georgia: 8 Caucasus

of Germany: 3 Ore **4** Harz **8** Feldberg **9** Zugspitze **10** Erzgebirge **11** Black Forest, Fichtelberg **12** Bavarian Alps

of Ghana: 8 Afadjato **12** Akwapim Hills

of Gibraltar: 6 Misery

of Greece: 3 Ida **4** Idhi, Oeta, Oite, Ossa **5** Athos **6** Ithome, Peleon, Pelion, Pindus **7** Grammos, Helicon, Olympus, Rhodope **8** Hymettos, Smolikas, Targetos, Taygetus **9** Parnassus **10** Hagion Oros, Lycabettus, Pentelicus

of Greenland: 5 Forel, Payer **7** Khardyu **8** Peterman **9** Gunnbjorn **15** Petermannsbjerg

of Guatemala: 4 Agua, Mico **5** Fuego, Madre **6** Pacaya, Tacana **7** Atitlan, Toliman **8** La Candon, Las Minas, Tajumuko **9** Tajamulco **10** Acatenango, Santa Maria **12** Cuchumatanes

of Guinea: 4 Loma **5** Nimba **6** Tamgue **11** Fouta Djalon

of Guyana: 5 Amuku, Ariwa, Kamoa **6** Akarai, Kanuku **7** Caburai **9** Pacaraima

of Haiti: 4 Nord **5** Cahos **6** Macaya, Noires **7** Lahotte, Laselle **8** Troudeau

of Honduras: 4 Pija **6** Agalta **7** Celaque **8** Las Minas **9** Esperanza **25** Central American Cordillera

of Hong Kong: 6 Castle **8** Victoria **9** Tai Mo Shan

of Hungary: 4 Alps, Bukk **5** Kekes, Matra, Tatra, Vetes **6** Bakony, Mecsek **7** Cserhat, Gerecse **8** Borzsony, Zempleni **9** Korishegy **10** Carpathian

of Iceland: 4 Laki **5** Askja, Hekla, Jokul, Katla **7** Surtsey **10** Orafajokul **16** Hvannadalshnukur

of India: 8 Aravalli **9** Broad Peak, Distaghil, Himalayas, Karakoram, Nanda Devi, Rakaposhi **10** Gasherbrum, Masherbrum **11** Nanga Parbat **12** Eastern Ghats, Godwin Austen, Kanchenjunga, Western Ghats

of Iran: 6 Elburz, Zagros **8** Demavend

of Iraq: 6 Qalate, Zagros **7** Halgurd, Qaarade **9** Kurdistan

of Ireland: 5 Galty **6** Croagh, Mourne **7** Errigal, Muckish, Patrick, Wicklow **8** Comeragh **10** Benna Beola, Twelve Bens, Twelve Pins **13** Carrantuohill, Knockmealdown **19** Macgillycuddy's Reeks

of Israel: 4 Nafh, Sagi **5** Harif, Meron, Ramon, Tabor **6** Atzmon, Carmel, Hatira, Meiron

of Italy: 4 Alps, Etna, Rosa, Viso **5** Amaro, Blanc, Corno, Somma **6** Cimone, Ortles **7** Vulcano **8** Vesuvius **9** Apennines, Dolomites, Maritimes, Stromboli **10** Apuane Alps, Carnic Alps, Julian Alps, Otztal Alps **11** Bernina Alps, Gennargentu **12** Gran Paradiso, Ligurian Alps **13** Lepontine Alps **16** Abruzzi Apennines

of Jamaica: 4 Blue **8** Sir Johns

of Japan: 3 Uso, Zao **4** Fuji **5** Asahi, Asama, Hondo, Yesso **6** Asosan, Enasan, Hiuchi, Kiusiu, Yariga **7** Fujisan, Hakusan, Kujusan, Tokachi **8** Fujiyama **9** Japan Alps

of Java: 4 Amat, Gede **5** Lawoe, Murjo, Prahu **6** Raoeng, Semuru, Slamet **7** Semeroe **8** Soembing

of Jordan: 9 Jabal Ramm, Jebel Ramm

of Kenya: 5 Elgon, Kenya, Kulai, Nyira, Nyiru **6** Kinyaa, Matian **7** Logonot **8** Aberdare **9** Kirinyaga

of Korea: 4 Wang **5** Chiri, Halla **6** Kwanmo, Paektu, Sobaek **7** Diamond, Kyebang, Nangnim, Taebaek **8** Chang-pai, Hamgyong, Myohyang **9** Paektu-san **10** Kumgang-san

of Kyrgyzstan: 8 Tian Shan

of Laos: 3 Bia, Lai, Loi, San **4** Copi, Khat **5** Atwat **6** Khoung, Tiubia **7** Phou Bia **15** Annam Cordillera

of Lebanon: 4 Mzar **5** Aruba **6** Hermon **7** es Sauda, Lebanon, Sannine **8** Kadischa, Kenisseh **9** Kennisseh **10** al-Mukammal **11** Anti-Lebanon **13** Qurnat al-Sawda

of Lesotho: 6 Maloti, Maluti **7** Central **8** Injasuti, Machache **10** Ben Macdhui **11** Drakensberg, Thaba Putsoa **16** Thabana Ntlenyana

of Liberia: 3 Uni **4** Bong, Putu **5** Niete, Nimba **6** Wutivi **9** Bomi Hills

of Libya: 5 Green **9** Bette Peak **13** Jabal al Akhdar, Tibesti Massif

of Liechtenstein: 4 Alps **8** Naafkopf, Rhatikon **12** Three Sisters **15** Vorder-Grauspitz

of Lithuania: 9 Juozapine **15** Samogitian Hills

of Luxembourg: 8 Ardennes, Huldange **9** Burgplatz **11** Wemperhardt

of Madagascar: 4 Boby **9** Ankaratra **11** Maromokotro **12** High Plateaus, Tsiafajavona **17** Tsaratanana Massif

of Malawi: 6 Mlanje **7** Mulanje **11** Livingstone

of Malaysia: 4 Bulu, Hose, Iban, Iran, Main, Mulu, Niut, Raja **5** Murjo, Niapa, Ophir **6** Blumut, Kapuas, Leuser, Slamet **7** Binaija, Brassey, Crocker **8** Kinabalu, Rindjani **11** Gunong Korbu, Gunong Tahan

(continued)

mountain (*continued*)
    of Mali: **4** Mina **6** Iforas **7** Manding **12** Hombori Tondo
    of Mexico: **6** Colima, Tacana, Toluca **7** Orizaba **9** Paricutin **11** Ixtacihuatl, Sierra Madre **12** Cit-
    laltepetl, Popocatepetl **14** Sierra Zacateca **16** Chiapas Highlands **24** Transverse Volcanic Sierra
    of Mongolia: **4** Cast, Orog **5** Altai **6** Kentei, Sevrej **7** Ich Ovoo, Khangai, Khentei **8** Tannu-Ola
    9 Edrengijn **10** Cagaan Bogd, Tabun Bogdo **11** Munky Sardyk **14** Hangayn-Hentiyn, Monch
    Chajrchan
    of Montenegro: **8** Durmitor **11** Dinaric Alps
    of Morocco: **3** Rif **4** Bani **5** Abyla, Atlas, Sarro **8** Tidiguin **9** Anti-Atlas, High Atlas, Jebel-Musa
    11 Middle Atlas **12** Jebel Toubkal **13** Djebel Toubkal
    of Mozambique: **5** Binga **7** Lebombo
    of Myanmar: **4** Chin, Naga, Pegu, Popa **5** Dawna **6** Arakan, Kachin, Lushai, Patkai **7** Karenni
    8 Nattaung, Peguyona, Saramati, Victoria **10** Tenasserim **11** Hkakabo Razi, Manipur Hill **12** Ta-
    nen Taunggi
    of Namibia: **9** Brandberg **14** Khomas Highland, Koakoveld Hills
    of Nepal: **6** Cho Oyu, Churia, Makalu **7** Everest, Lhotse I, Manaslu, Siwalik **8** Lhotse II **9** An-
    napurna, Himalayas **10** Dhaulagiri, Gosainthan, Himalchuli **11** Ganesh Himal **12** Kanchenjunga
    14 Mahabharat Lekh
    of New Guinea: **4** Snow **6** Orange **7** Bismark, Wilhelm **8** Victoria **9** Carstensz **10** Puncak Jaya
    11 Owen Stanley **12** Albert Edward
    of New Zealand: **4** Cook, Eden, Flat, Owen **5** Allen, Chope, Lyall, Mitre, Ohope, Otari, Young
    6 Egmont, Stokes, Tasman **7** Aorangi, Cameron, Coronet, Ernslaw, Huiarau, Pihanga, Ru-
    ahine, Ruapehu, Tauhera, Tutamee, Tyndall **8** Aspiring, Richmond, Tauranga **9** Messenger,
    Murchison, Ngauruhoe, Raukumara, Tongariro **11** Remarkables **12** Southern Alps
    of Nicaragua: **4** Leon **5** Negro, Viejo **6** Madera, Telica **7** Managua, Mogoton, Saslaya
    9 Momotombo
    of Norway: **5** Sogne **6** Kjolen **7** Numedal **8** Blodfjel, Snohetta, Telemark, Ustetind **9** Harteigen,
    Jotunheim, Langfjell, Ramnanosi **10** Dovrefjell, Galdhoepig, Glitretind, Vibmesnosi **11** Myrda-
    lfjell **12** Galdhopiggen **13** Glittertinden **14** Aardangerjokul, Hallingskarvet, Skagastolstind
    of Pakistan: **3** Pab, Pub **4** Salt **6** Makran **7** Kirthar **8** Himalaya, Safed Koh, Sulaiman **9** Hindu
    Kush, Karakoram, Tirich Mir **11** Makran Coast **12** Godwin Austin **13** Central Makran
    14 Takht-i-Sulaiman
    of Panama: **4** Baru, Maje **5** Chico, Gandi **6** Darien **7** Columan, San Blas, Veragua **8** Chiriqui,
    Santiago, Tabasara **10** Costa Rican **14** Serrania de Sapo **15** Aspave Highlands **17** Cordillera
    Central
    of Peru: **5** Andes **7** El Misti, Huamina **8** Coropuna **9** Huascaran
    of Philippines: **3** Apo, Iba **4** Mayo, Taal **5** Albay, Askja, Hibok, Mayon, Pulog **6** Pagsan **7** Bana-
    hao, Canlaon
    of Poland: **4** Rysy **5** Tatra **6** Beskid **7** Pieniny, Sudeten **9** Beshchady, High Tatra, Holy Cross
    10 Carpathian
    of Portugal: **4** Acor, Lapa **5** Gerez, Marao, Mousa **6** Bornes, Peneda **7** Larouco **8** Caramulo
    9 Caldeirao, Monchique **11** Pico da Serra **14** Serra da Estrela
    of Puerto Rico: **4** Toro **5** Cayey, Punta **6** Yunque **8** Guilarte, Luquilla **10** Torrecilla **17** Cordillera
    Central
    of Rumania: **5** Banat, Bihor, Negoi **6** Codrul, Rodnei **7** Apuseni, Balkans, Caliman, Fagaras
    8 Pietrosu **9** Moldavian **10** Carpathian, Moldoveanu **17** Transylvanian Alps
    of Russia: **5** Altai, Lenin, Sayan, Urals **6** Anadyr, Elbrus, Koryak, Pamirs, Pobedy **7** Belukha,
    Crimean, Khibiny, Stanovi, Zhiguli **8** Caucasus, Dzhughur, Stanavoi, Tien Shan **9** Kopet Dagh,
    Narodnaya, Pamir-Alai, Yablonovy **10** Carpathian **11** Sikhote-Alin, Verkhoyansk
    of Rwanda: **7** Mitumba, Virunga **8** Muhavura **9** Karisimbi
    of Samoa: **4** Fito, Vaea **5** Alava **6** Savaii **7** Matafao **8** Silisili **9** Rainmaker
    of San Marino: **6** Titano **9** Apennines
    of Sardinia: **4** Rasu **5** Ferry, Linas **7** Gallura, Limbara **8** Marghine, Serpeddi, Vittoria
    11 Gennargentu
    of Saudi Arabia: **5** Razih **6** Tuwayq **10** Jebal Sawda
    of Scotland: **5** Attow, Ochil **6** Sidlaw **7** Cheviot **8** Ben Nevis, Grampian **9** Ben Lomond, High-
    lands, Trossachs
    of Senegal: **6** Gounou **12** Fouta Djallon
    of Sicily: **4** Erei, Etna, Moro, Sori **5** Aetna, Atlas, Erici, Hybla, Iblei, Ibrei **7** Nebrodi, Vulcano
    9 Apennines, Le Madonie, Stromboli **10** Peloritani
    of Sierra Leone: **4** Loma **9** Bintimani **10** Tingi Hills
    of Sikkim: **7** Dongkya, Donkhya **9** Himalayas, Singalili **10** Darjeeling **12** Kanchenjunga
    of Singapore: **6** Mandai **7** Panjang **10** Bukit Timah
    of Slovakia: **7** Sudetes **8** Low Tatra **9** High Tatra, Slovak Ore **10** Carpathian, Nizke Tatry **11** Vi-
    soke Tatry **15** White Carpathian
    of the Solomon Islands: **5** Balbi **11** Popomanasiu
    of Somalia: **5** Guban **7** Surud Ad **11** Migiurtinia, Ogo Highland
    of South Africa: **3** Aux, Kop **5** Table **7** Kathkin **8** Injasuti **9** Stormberg **10** Devil's Peak,
    Sneeuwberg **11** Drakensberg **12** Giant's Castle **13** Witwatersrand **14** Mont-aux-Sources **15** Great
    Escarpment

of Spain: 4 Gata **5** Aneto, Rouch, Teide **6** Cuenca, Estats, Europa, Gredos, Magina, Morena, Nethou, Nevada, Teleno, Toledo **7** Alcaraz, Banuelo, Catalan, Cerredo, Demanda, Iberian, La Sagra, Moncayo, Perdido **8** Almanzor, Asturias, Galician, Maladeta, Monegros, Montseny, Mulhacen, Penalara, Pyrenees **10** Albarracin, Cantabrian, Guadarrama, Torrecilla

of Sudan: 4 Nuba **6** Red Sea **7** Imatong, Kinyeti **9** Dongotona **10** Jabal Marra, Jebel Marra **18** Ethiopian Highlands

of Suriname: 4 Emma **6** Kayser, Oranje **10** Julianatop, Tumuc-Humac, Wilhelmina **13** Eilert's Il Haan, Van Ach Van Wyck **15** Guiana Highlands

of Swaziland: 7 Emlembe **8** Highveld **11** Drakensberg

of Sweden: 4 Sarv **5** Ammar, Kebne **6** Helags, Kjolen, Ovniks, Sarjek **7** Kjollen **10** Kebnekaise

of Switzerland: 3 Dom **4** Alps, Jura, Rigi, Rosa, Todi **5** Adula, Blanc, Cenis, Eiger, Genis, Karpf, Righi **6** Linard, Pizela, Sentis **7** Bernina, Beverin, Grimsel, Pilatus, Rotondo **8** Balmhorn, Jungfrau **9** Weisshorn **10** Diablerets, Matterhorn, St Gotthard, Wetterhorn **11** Burgenstock **12** Dufourspitze **13** Rheinwaldhorn **14** Finsteraarhorn

of Syria: 6 Carmel, Hermon **7** Alawite, Libanus **10** Nusairiyya **11** Anti-Lebanon

of Taiwan: 5 Tatun **6** Tzukao, Yu Shan **7** Taitung **8** Morrison **10** Sinkao Shan **11** Hsin-Kao Shan **15** Chungyang Shanmo

of Tajikistan: 13 Communism Peak

of Tanzania: 4 Kibo, Mero **8** Usambara **11** Kilimanjaro

of Thailand: 5 Dawna, Khieo **6** Phanom **8** Dang Raek, Inthanon, Kao Prawa, Maelamun **9** Khao Luang **11** Bilauktaung, Doi Inthanon

of Tibet: 5 Kamet, Sajum **6** Kailas, Kunlun **7** Bandala, Everest **9** Himalayas, Karakoram

of Tunisia: 6 Atlas **6** Chambi, Mrhila **7** Tebessa **8** High Tell, Zaghouan **12** Northern Tell **18** Dorsale Tunnisienne

of Turkey: 2 Ak **3** Ala **4** Alai, Dagh, Kara **5** Hasan, Hinis, Honaz, Murat, Murit **6** Ala Dag, Ararat, Bingol, Bolgar, Pontic, Suphan, Taurus **7** Aladagh, Erciyas **8** Karacali **10** Kackar Dagi

of Uganda: 4 Oboa **5** Elgon **7** Virunga **9** Mufumbiro, Ruwenzori **10** Margherita **18** Mountains of the Moon

of Ukraine: 7 Crimean **10** Carpathian

of United States: 4 Hood **5** Coast, Green, Kenai, Ozark, Rocky, White **6** Alaska, Brooks, De-Long, Elbert, Helena, Mesabi, Pocono, Shasta **7** Cascade, Chugach, Foraker, Harvard, Kilauea, Massive, Olympic, Olympus, Rainier, St Elias, Whitney **8** Catskill, Davidson, Endicott, Katahdin, Mauna Loa, McKinley, Mitchell, Ouachita, St Helens, Wrangell **9** Allegheny, Blue Ridge, Kuskokwim, North Peak, Pike's Peak **10** Black Hills, Blanca Peak, Grand Teton, Washington, Williamson **11** Appalachian, Santa Monica **12** Sierra Nevada **14** Berkshire Hills

of Uruguay: 6 Animas **10** Grand Hills **14** Cuchilla Grande **15** Mirador Nacional

of Venezuela: 3 Pao **4** Pava, Yair **5** Andes, Duida, Icutu **6** Concha, Cuneva, Merida, Parima, Sierra, Yumari **7** Bolivar, Imutaca, Masaiti, Roraima **8** Gurupira **9** Pacaraima **10** Auyan-Tepui **11** Turimiquire **18** Cordillera del Norte

of Vietnam: 6 Badinh, Badink **7** Nindhoa, Ninhhoa **8** Fansipan, Knontran, Ngoklinh, Ngoklink, Tchepone, Tclepore **18** Annamese Cordillera

of Wales: 6 Berwyn **7** Snowdon **8** Cambrian **9** Prescelly **13** Brecon Beacons

of Western Samoa: 4 Fito, Vaea **13** Mauga Silisili

of Yemen: 6 Shuayb, Thamir **7** Djehaff

of Yugoslavia: 5 Karst **6** Balkan **7** Rhodope, Triglav **8** Crna Gora, Durmitor **9** Sar-Pindus **10** Carnic Alps, Julian Alps, Karawanken **11** Dinaric Alps **13** Slovenian Alps **20** Northern Albanian Alps

of Zaire: 7 Crystal, Mitumba, Virunga **9** Ruwenzori **10** Margherita, Nyaragongo **18** Mountains of the Moon

of Zambia: 8 Muchinga **12** Mafinga Hills

of Zimbabwe: 5 Vumba **6** Manica **7** Inyanga **9** Inyangani **11** Chimanimani, Matopo Hills

---

humbug **7** hustler, sharper **8** huckster, operator, swindler **9** charlatan, con artist **11** quacksalver

mounted soldier 6 hussar, lancer **7** dragoon **8** cavalier, horseman **10** cavalryman

mourn 3 cry, rue, sob **4** keen, pine, wail, weep **6** bemoan, bewail, grieve, lament, regret, sorrow **7** deplore, despair **8** languish, weep over

mournful 3 sad **5** black, sorry, weepy **6** dismal, rueful, som-ber, triste, woeful **7** doleful, joyless, unhappy **8** dejected, dirgeful, dolorous, funereal, grevious, saddened **9** depressed, plaintive, sorrowful **10** depressing, dispirited, lamentable, lugubrious, melancholy **11** distressing,

melancholic 12 heavy hearted

mourning 3 woe **5** black, crape, dolor, grief, weeds **6** sorrow **7** anguish, despair **8** grieving **9** lamenting, sorrowing **11** bereavement, lamentation

Mourning Becomes Electra
author: **12** Eugene O'Neill
character: **4** Seth **10** Hazel Niles, Peter Niles **16** Captain Adam Brant
Mannon family: **4** Ezra, Orin **7** Lavinia **9** Christine

mourning period
Hebrew: **6** shibah, shivah

mouser 3 cat **4** puss **5** kitty, pussy **6** feline **8** pussycat

Mousetrap, The
author: **14** Agatha Christie

mousseline 6 muslin

mousy 3 shy **4** drab, dull **5** timid, wimpy **7** bashful, fearful **8** timorous **9** colorless, unnoticed, withdrawn **11** unobtrusive **13** inconspicuous

mouth 3 bay, say **4** bell, jaws, lips **5** inlet, speak, voice **6** outlet, portal **7** declare, estuary, opening **8** aperture, propound **9** pronounce

mouthful 3 dab **4** bite **5** taste **6** morsel, nibble

mouthpiece 4 reed **6** lawyer **7** counsel **8** advocate, attorney **9** counselor

mouth-watering 8 inviting, tempting **9** appealing **10** appetizing **11** tantalizing

movable, moveable 4 free **5** loose **6** mobile, motile, moving **8** portable **10** changeable

movables 4 gear **5** goods **7** baggage, effects, luggage **9** equipment **10** belongings **11** impedimenta, possessions **13** accoutrements, paraphernalia

move 2 go **3** act, ask, get **4** bear, deed, fire, lead, pass, ploy, step, stir, sway, turn, urge **5** begin, budge, carry, cause, drive, impel, plead, rouse, shift, touch **6** action, affect, arouse, attack, convey, excite, exhort, incite, induce, motion, prompt, strike, stroke, switch **7** advance, budging, gesture, go ahead, impress, inspire, measure, operate, proceed, propose, provoke, request, suggest **8** function, interest, locomote, maneuver, motivate, persuade, relocate, start off, stirring, transfer,

transmit **9** impassion, influence, recommend, stimulate, transport, transpose **10** transplant **11** opportunity

move downward 3 dip **4** dive, drop, fall, sink **6** plunge, tumble **7** decline, descend, plummet **8** decrease

movement 4 part **5** drive, steps, works **6** action, effort, motion **7** crusade, measure, program, section **8** activity, division, gestures, maneuver, progress, stirring **9** agitation, execution, mechanism, operation **10** locomotion **11** undertaking

move out 5 leave **6** depart, vacate **8** evacuate

move quickly 3 fly, run **4** bolt, dash, race, rush, tear **5** hurry **6** hasten, sprint

move sideways 4 edge **5** sidle **8** sidestep

move slyly 4 edge, lurk **5** sidle, skulk, slink, sneak, steal

move up 5 boost, climb, heave, hoist, raise, scale **6** ascend, uplift **7** advance, elevate, promote, upraise

move upward 4 rise, soar **5** climb, mount **6** ascend **7** take off

movie 4 film, show **5** flick **6** cinema **7** feature, picture, showing **9** screening
invented by:
machine: **7** Jenkins
panoramic: **6** Waller
projector: **6** Edison
talking: **14** Warner Brothers

moving 5 motor **6** mobile, motile **8** exciting, poignant, spurring, stirring, touching **9** affecting, inspiring **10** impressive, locomotive, motivating **11** interacting, stimulating

moving about 5 astir **6** active **7** on the go

Moving Target, A
author: **14** William Golding

Mowgli
character in: **14** The Jungle Books
author: **7** Kipling

moxie 4 grit, guts, sand **5** nerve, pluck, spunk **6** mettle, spirit **7** courage, stamina **8** audacity, backbone **9** hardihood,

Mozambique
capital/largest city: **6** Maputo **15** Lourenco Marques
others: **4** Tete **5** Beira, Pemba, Zumbo **6** Chemba, Nacala, Pafuri, Sofala **7** Nampula **8** Mutarara **9** Inhambane, Quelimane **11** Porto Amelia
school: **15** Eduardo Mondlane
monetary unit: **6** escudo **7** centavo, metical
island: **6** Inhaca **7** Angoche **8** Bazanuto **9** Benguerua
lake: **5** Nyasa **6** Chuali, Nyassa **8** Nhavarre
mountain: **7** Lebombo
highlands: **6** Namuli **9** Gorongosa
highest point: **5** Binga
river: **4** Buzi, Save **5** Lurio, Msalu **6** Rovuma, Ruvuma **7** Ligonha, Limpopo, Lugenda, Messaio, Zambezi **8** Changane
ocean: **6** Indian
physical feature:
cape: **7** Delgado
channel: **10** Mozambique
people: **3** Yao **5** Bantu, Chopi, Lomue, Lomwe, Macua, Makua, Ngoni, Nguni, Shona **6** Maravi, Thouga **7** Maconde, Makonde **10** Portuguese
explorer: **11** Vasco de Gama
leader: **8** Chissano **9** Dos Santos **12** Samora Machel **15** Eduardo Mondlane
language: **3** Yao **5** Makua **6** Nyanji, Thonga **7** Swahili **10** Portuguese
religion: **5** Islam **7** animism **13** Roman Catholic
place:
game reserve: **8** Marromeu **9** Gorongosa, Gorongoza **18** Maputo Elephant Park
reservoir: **11** Cabora Bassa
feature:
bride price: **6** lobolo

toughness **10** pluckiness **13** dauntlessness

moyen age 10 Middle Ages

Mozambique *see box*

Mozart, Wolfgang Amadeus *see box*

Mr, Mister
Russian: **8** gospodin
French: **8** monsieur
Yiddish: **3** Reb

Mr B
character in: **6** Pamela
author: **10** Richardson

Mr Basketball
nickname of: **8** Bob Cousy

Mr Britling Sees It Through
author: **7** H G Wells

Mr Cub
nickname of: **10** Ernie Banks

Mr Deeds Goes to Town
director: **10** Frank Capra
cast: **10** Gary Cooper (Long-fellow Deeds), Jean Arthur **14** George Bancroft

Mr Ed
character: **9** Carol Post **10** Kay Addison, Wilbur Post **12** Roger Addison **14** Gordon Kirkwood, Winnie Kirkwood
cast: **8** Leon Ames **9** Alan Young **11** Connie Hines, Edna Skinner **12** Larry Keating **18** Florence MacMichael
Mr Ed was: **12** talking horse

Mr Flood's Party
author: **22** Edwin Arlington Robinson

Mr Midnight
nickname of: **10** Steve Allen

Mr Peepers
character: **9** Mrs Gurney **11** Marge Weskit, Mr Remington **12** Harvey Weskit **14** Nancy Remington **15** Robinson Peepers **20** Superintendent Bascom
cast: **8** Wally Cox **9** Gage Clark **11** Ernest Truex, Marion Lorne, Tony Randall **14** Patricia Benoit **16** Georgiann Johnson
Mr Peepers taught: **7** science
school: **13** Jefferson High

Mr Sammler's Planet
author: **10** Saul Bellow

Mrs Dalloway
author: **13** Virginia Woolf
character: **10** Miss Kilman, Peter Walsh, Sally Seton **15** Richard Dalloway **16** Clarissa Dalloway **17** Elizabeth Dalloway

Mrs Miniver
director: **12** William Wyler
cast: **11** Greer Garson **12** Teresa Wright **13** Dame May Whitty, Walter Pidgeon
Oscar for: **7** actress (Garson), picture **8** director **17** supporting actress (Wright)

Mr Smith Goes to Washington
director: **10** Frank Capra
cast: **9** Guy Kibbee **10** Jean Arthur **11** Claude Rains **12** Edward Arnold, James Stewart **14** Thomas Mitchell

Mrs Parkington
author: **14** Louis Bromfield

Mrs Stevens Hears the Mermaids Singing
author: **9** May Sarton

Mrs Warren's Profession
author: **17** George Bernard Shaw

Mr Television
nickname of: **11** Milton Berle

much 3 far **4** a lot, lots **5** about, ample, heaps, loads, often **6** almost, indeed, nearly, overly, rather, scores **7** copious, greatly **8** abundant, good deal, plenty of, quantity, somewhat, striking **9** decidedly, important, plenteous, plentiful, regularly **10** frequently, impressive, noteworthy, oftentimes, satisfying, sufficient, worthwhile **11** appreciable, exceedingly, excessively, sufficiency **12** considerable **13** approximately, consequential

Much Ado About Nothing
author: **18** William Shakespeare
character: **4** Hero **7** Claudio, Don John, Leonato **8** Beatrice, Benedick, Dogberry, Don Pedro

much in little
Latin: **13** multum in parvo

much loved 4 dear **7** beloved, darling, dearest **8** precious **9** cherished, treasured

mucilage 3 gum **4** glue **5** paste **6** cement **8** adhesive

mucilaginous 5 gluey, gummy, gunky **6** gloppy, sticky **8** adhesive

muck 3 mud **4** dirt, dung, gunk, mire, ooze, slop **5** filth, slime **6** sewage, sludge **7** compost, garbage

muck up 4 soil **5** dirty, muddy **7** pollute

mud 4 dirt, muck, soil, wire

Mudcat State
nickname of: **11** Mississippi

muddied 5 dirty, grimy **6** grubby, soiled **7** stained **8** begrimed, confused

muddle 3 fog **4** blow, daze, haze, mess, muff, ruin **5** botch, chaos, mix up, spoil, throw **6** boggle, bungle, fumble, goof up, jumble, mess up, pother, rattle **7** blunder, clutter, confuse, nonplus, stupefy **8** bewilder, confound, disarray, disorder **13** disconcertion **14** disarrangement

muddlebrained 5 inept **7** witless **8** confused **11** lamebrained

muddled 5 fuzzy **7** bemused **8** confused **10** bewildered

---

Mozart, Wolfgang Amadeus
born: **7** Austria **8** Salzburg
composer of: **4** Linz (symphony No 36) **5** Paris (symphony No 31) **6** Prague (symphony No 38) **7** Don Juan, Haffner (symphony No 35), Jupiter (symphony No 41), Requiem, Turkish (concerto) **8** Idomeneo **9** Credo Mass, Mitridate **10** Lucio Silla **11** Don Giovanni, Hunt Quartet, Il Re Pastore, Sparrow Mass **12** A Musical Joke, Cosi Fan Tutte (So Do They All or Women Are Like That), Haydn Quartet, Spatzenmesse **13** The Magic Flute, Trumpet Sonata, Turkish Sonata **14** Coronation Mass, Stadler Quintet, Die Zauberflote **15** Haffner Serenade, La Finta Semplice, Prussian Quartet **16** Dissonant Quartet, La Clemenza di Tito, Posthorn Serenade, Serenata Notturna **17** A Little Night Music **18** Jeunehomme Concerto, La Finta Giardiniera, The Clemency of Titus **19** Bastien und Bastienne, The Marriage of Figaro **20** Eine Kleine Nachtmusik, The Pretender Gardener **21** Der Schauspieldirektor, Ein Musikalischer Spass **22** The Pretending Simpleton **25** Die Entfuhrung aus dem Serail **27** The Abduction from the Seraglio

muddy 4 dull **5** dirty, grimy, vague **6** filthy, grubby **7** obscure **8** begrimed, confused

muff 5 botch, spoil **6** bungle **10** handwarmer

muffle 3 gag **4** dull, hush, mask, mute, veil, wrap **5** cloak, cover, quell, quiet, still **6** dampen, deaden, shroud, soften, stifle, swathe **7** conceal, enclose, envelop, silence, swaddle

muffled 3 low **4** dull, soft **5** faint, muted **6** dulled, feeble, hushed, veiled **7** cloaked, covered, quelled, quieted, stilled, subdued, swathed, wrapped **8** deadened, shrouded, silenced, softened, swaddled **9** concealed, enveloped, inaudible **10** indistinct, suppressed

mug 3 cup **4** face, puss, toby **5** stein, stoup **6** beaker, flagon, goblet, kisser, visage **7** chalice, tankard, toby jug, tumbler **11** countenance

mugger 8 assailer, attacker **9** assailant, assaulter

mugginess 4 damp **8** dampness, dankness, humidity **9** humidness **10** sultriness **14** oppressiveness

muggy 5 close, humid **6** clammy, steamy, sticky, stuffy, sultry, sweaty **8** steaming, vaporous **10** oppressive, sweltering

Muisca *see* **7** Chibcha

mulberry 5 Morus
  varieties: 3 red **4** Aino **5** black, paper, white **6** French, Indian **7** Russian **8** American, silkworm

Mulciber
  epithet of: 6 Vulcan
  means: 6 melter

mulct 4 bilk **6** extort **7** defraud, swindle

mule 3 ass **5** burro **6** donkey **7** jackass
  group of: 4 span

mulish 5 balky **6** ornery **8** perverse, stubborn **9** fractious, obstinate **10** refractory **11** intractable **12** recalcitrant

Mulius
  wife: 7 Agamede
  father-in-law: 6 Augeas
  position: 8 spearman
  killed by: 6 Nestor

mull, mull over 5 study, weigh **6** ponder **8** consider, meditate, pore over, ruminate **10** deliberate

Muller
  character in: 25 All Quiet on the Western Front
  author: 8 Remarque

Muller, Hermann Joseph
  field: 8 genetics
  researched: 5 X-rays **8** mutation
  awarded: 10 Nobel Prize

Muller, Paul
  field: 9 chemistry
  nationality: 5 Swiss
  established: 16 DDT as insecticide
  awarded: 10 Nobel Prize

Mulligan, Buck
  character in: 7 Ulysses
  author: 5 Joyce

multicolored 10 variegated

multifarious 4 many **5** mixed **6** divers, motley, sundry, varied **7** diverse, protean, several, various **8** manifold, numerous **9** different, multiplex **10** variegated **11** diversified **13** heterogeneous, miscellaneous

multiple 4 many **7** various **8** manifold

multiply 5 add to, beget, breed, raise **6** extend, spread **7** augment, enhance, enlarge, magnify **8** generate, heighten, increase **9** intensify, procreate, propagate, reproduce **11** proliferate

multitude 3 mob **4** army, herd, host, mass, pack, slew **5** array, crowd, crush, drove, flock, flood, horde, troop **6** legion, myriad, scores, throng **7** conflux

multum in parvo 12 much in little **23** a great deal in a small space

mum 4 mute **5** quiet, still, tacit **6** silent **8** taciturn, wordless **9** secretive **12** closemouthed **15** uncommunicative

mumble 5 growl, grunt, mouth **6** murmur, mutter, rumble **7** stammer **9** hem and haw

mumbo jumbo 3 rot **4** blah, bosh, cant, tosh **5** bilge, hokum, hooey, tripe **6** hot air, humbug **7** baloney **8** flummery **9** gibberish, sophistry **10** double talk, hocus pocus **11** doublespeak, jabberwocky, obfuscation **12** fiddle-faddle, gobbledygook, obscurantism

Mummy, The
  director: 10 Karl Freund
  cast: 10 Zita Johann **12** Boris Karloff, David Manners **16** Bramwell Fletcher

munch 4 chew, gnaw **5** champ, chomp, crush, grind **9** masticate

Munch, Edvard
  born: 5 Loten **6** Norway **10** Hedemarken
  artwork: 6 The Cry **7** Puberty, The Kiss **9** The Scream **11** Dance of Life **12** Frieze of Life **21** Death in the Sick Chamber

Munchkins
  characters in: 13 The Wizard of Oz
  author: 4 Baum

mundane 5 petty **7** earthly, humdrum, prosaic, routine, worldly **8** day-to-day, everyday, ordinary **9** practical **10** pedestrian **11** commonplace, down-to-earth, terrestrial

Muni, Paul
  real name: 16 Muni Weisenfreund
  born: 7 Austria, Lemberg (now Lvov USSR)
  roles: 6 Juarez **8** Scarface **10** The Valiant **12** The Good Earth **14** Clarence Darrow, Inherit the Wind **15** The Last Angry Man **18** The Life of Emile Zola **22** The Story of Louis Pasteur (Oscar) **26** I Am a Fugitive from a Chain Gang

municipal 4 city **5** civic **6** public **9** community **14** administrative

municipality 4 city, town **6** parish **7** village **8** township **9** bailiwick

munificence 6 bounty **7** charity **8** largesse **9** patronage **10** generosity, liberality **11** benefaction, beneficence, benevolence **12** philanthropy **13** bounteousness, bountifulness **14** charitableness **15** humanitarianism

munificent 4 free **6** kindly, lavish **7** liberal, profuse **8** generous, princely **9** bounteous, bountiful **10** altruistic, beneficent, benevolent, charitable, freehanded, open-handed **11** extravagant, magnanimous **12** eleemosynary, humanitarian **13** philanthropic

Munin
  origin: 12 Scandinavian
  form: 5 raven
  owned by: 4 Odin **5** Othin
  personifies: 6 memory
  duty: 10 newsbearer
  other raven: 5 Hugin

Munitus
  father: 6 Acamas
  mother: 7 Laodice

Muppet Show, The
character: **4** Rolf **5** Gonzo
6 Animal, Beaker **7** Scooter
9 Miss Piggy **10** Fozzie Bear
13 Kermit the Frog (Kermie)

Murasaki, Lady
author of: **14** The Tale of
Genji

murder 4 kill, slay **5** abuse,
waste **6** mangle, misuse
7 butcher, corrupt, cut down,
killing **8** homicide, knock off
9 agonizing, slaughter **10** bastardize, formidable, impossible,
oppressive, unbearable **11** assassinate, intolerable **12** manslaughter **13** assassination, very
difficult **14** commit homicide,
use incorrectly

murderer 4 Cain **6** killer, slayer
7 butcher **8** assassin, Barabbas,
homicide **9** cutthroat

Murder in the Cathedral
author: **7** T S Eliot

**Murder of Roger Ackroyd,
The**
author: **14** Agatha Christie

**Murder on the Orient
Express**
author: **14** Agatha Christie

murderous 4 gory **5** cruel,
rough **6** bloody, brutal, deadly,
savage, trying **7** killing **9** dangerous, difficult, ferocious
11 devastating **12** bloodthirsty,
disaggreeable

Murdoch, Iris
author of: **7** The Bell **11** Under the Net **12** A Severed
Head, The Sea the Sea
14 The Black Prince **15** Nuns
and Soldiers **17** The Good
Apprentice, The Nice and
the Good

**Murillo, Bartolome (Bartolo-
meo) Esteban**
born: **5** Spain **7** Seville
artwork: **13** Angels' Kitchen
14 Death of St Clare **15** The
Two Trinities **17** Vision of St
Anthony **23** The Immaculate
Conception **24** Dream of the
Roman Patrician

murk 3 fog **4** haze, mist
5 gloom **6** miasma **8** darkness

murky 3 dim **4** dark, gray, hazy
5 dusky, foggy, misty **6** cloudy,
dismal, dreary, gloomy, somber
7 obscure, sunless **8** lowering,
overcast, vaporous **9** cheerless

murmur 3 hum **4** buzz, purl,
purr, sigh **5** drone, sough,
swish **6** lament, mumble, mutter, rumble, rustle **7** grumble,
lapping, whimper, whisper
8 low sound, susurrus **9** complaint, undertone

murophobia
fear of: **4** mice

Murphy, Eddie
roles: **3** Raw **13** Trading Places
14 The Golden Child
15 Coming to America,
Forty-Eight Hours **16** Beverly
Hills Cop **17** Saturday Night
Live **19** Beverly Hills Cop
Two

Murray, Bill
roles: **7** Stripes **9** Meatballs
10 Caddyshack **12** Ghostbusters **13** The Razor's Edge
17 Saturday Night Live
27 Not Ready for Prime Time
Players

Muscat, Masqat
capital of: **4** Oman

muscle *see box*

muscular 3 fit **5** burly, husky,
tough **6** brawny, sinewy,
strong **8** athletic, powerful
9 strapping

muscular contraction
5 cramp, crick, spasm **6** stitch
12 charley horse

---

muscle 4 grit, thew **5** bi-
cep, brawn, force, might,
power, sinew, vigor **6** energy, flexor, tendon **7** potency, prowess, stamina
8 virility **9** puissance
10 sturdiness **16** muscular
strength
kind: **4** limb **5** axial
6 smooth **7** dynamic,
flexors, special, striped
8 postural, striated **9** ab-
ductors, extensors, vol-
untary **11** involuntary
fuel: **4** food
action: **4** pull
specific: **6** rectus **7** deltoid,
oblique **8** omohyoid **9** ab-
dominal, abdominis, sar-
torius **10** pectoralis
11 intercostal, sternohy-
oid **13** biceps brachii,
rectus femoris **14** vastus
medialis **15** brachioradi-
alis, vastus lateralis
16 serratus anterior, ten-
sor fascia lata **17** quadri-
ceps femoris
18 transverse thoracic
19 sternocleidomastoid
20 transversus abdominis
supplementary structure:
6 sheath **10** deep fascia,
retinacula **14** synovial
bursae, synovial sheath

---

musculoskeletal system
component: **4** bone **6** muscle,
tendon **8** ligament

muse 4 mull **6** ponder, review
7 reflect **8** cogitate, consider,
meditate, ruminate **9** speculate
10 deliberate **11** contemplate

Muses
also: **7** the Nine **8** Pierides
10 Castalides
form: **9** goddesses
names: **4** Clio **5** Aoede, Erato,
Mneme **6** Melete, Thalia,
Urania **7** Euterpe **8** Calliope
9 Melpomene **10** Polyhymnia
11 Terpsichore
father: **4** Zeus
mother: **9** Mnemosyne
corresponds to: **7** Camenae

mush 5 slush **6** drivel **8** porridge **14** sentimentalism,
sentimentality

mushiness 5 slush **6** bathos
10 sponginess **11** mawkishness
14 sentimentalism,
sentimentality

---

mushroom 4 grow
5 burst, fungi **6** blow up,
expand, fungus, spread,
sprout **7** burgeon, explode,
shoot up **8** flourish, increase, spring up **9** toadstool **11** proliferate
part: **3** cap **4** veil **5** gills,
stalk, tubes, volva **6** button, hyphae, spores
7 annulus, basidia
10 rhizomorph
non-poisonous: **5** field,
honey, morel, table
6 oyster **7** inky cap, parasol **8** puffball, shiitake
9 fairy-ring, morchella,
shaggy cap, stinkhorn
10 champignon **11** chan-
terelle **12** edible bolete,
slippery jack **16** old man
of the woods
poisonous: **7** amanita
8 death cap, sickener
9 fly agaric **12** jack-o-lan-
tern **13** devil's boletus
15 destroying angel
study of: **8** mycology

---

mushy 4 soft **5** foggy, misty,
pappy, pulpy, vague **6** cloudy,
quaggy, spongy **7** maudlin,
mawkish, squashy, squishy
8 effusive, romantic, squelchy
10 lovey-dovey **11** sentimental,
tear-jerking **12** affectionate

Musial, Stan
nickname: **10** Stan the Man

sport: 8 baseball
team: 16 St Louis Cardinals

music 4 song, tune **5** score
6 melody **7** euphony, harmony
8 lyricism **10** minstrelsy
11 tunefulness
13 melodiousness
  god of: 5 Brage, Bragi
  6 Apollo **7** Phoebus, Pythius
  9 Musagetes

musical 5 lyric, sweet **6** dulcet
7 lilting, lyrical, melodic, tuneful **9** melodious **10** euphonious, harmonious **11** mellifluent

musical instrument *see box*

musical terms *see box*

musician 4 bard **5** piper **6** artist,
player, singer, violer **7** bandman, cellist, drummer, pianist,
twanger **8** minstrel, organist,
virtuoso **9** performer, trumpeter, violinist **11** saxophonist

Music Man, The
  director: 13 Morton Da Costa
  cast: 12 Buddy Hackett, Shirley Jones (Marian the librarian) **13** Robert Preston
  (Professor Harold Hill)
  15 Hermione Gingold
  setting: 9 River City
  score: 15 Meredith Willson
  song: 15 Till There Was You
  19 Seventy-six Trombones

music school 12 conservatory
  French: 13 conservatoire

musing 6 absent, dreamy
7 mulling **8** absorbed **9** pondering **10** meditating, meditative,
reflecting, reflective

musjid 6 mosque

Muskogean, Muskhogean
  tribe: 4 Cree **7** Alabama, Alibamu, Choctaw, Natchez
  8 Seminole **9** Chickasaw

Muslim *see* **6** Moslem

muslin
  French: 10 mousseline

muss 4 mess **6** foul up, jumble,
ruffle, rumple, tangle, tousle
7 crumple, disturb **8** dishevel,
disorder **9** bedraggle
10 disarrange

mussed 5 messy **6** frowzy, untidy **7** ruffled, rumpled, tousled, unkempt **8** uncombed
10 disarrayed, disheveled, disordered, disorderly
11 disarranged

**Mussorgsky (Moussorgsky),
Modest Petrovich**
  born: 5 Pskov **6** Russia
  member of: 7 The Five
  composer of: 7 Sunless **10** The
  Nursery **12** Boris Godunov
  13 Khovanshchina **19** Night on Bald
  Mountain

mustard
  botanical name: 5 B alba **6** B
  hirta, B nigra **7** B juncea
  8 Brassica
  also called: 7 sinapis
  origin: 4 Asia **5** China
  use: 6 hotdog, sauces **7** egg
  roll **9** hamburger **13** salad
  dressing

muster 4 call **5** amass, raise,
rally **6** gather, line up, summon **7** collect, company, convene, convoke, marshal,
meeting, round up, turnout
8 assemble, assembly, mobilize
9 convocate, gathering **10** assemblage, confluence, congregate, inspection **11** aggregation
12 accumulation
13 agglomeration

musty 3 old **4** damp, dank,
worn **5** banal, dirty, dusty,
moldy, stale, tired, trite

musical terms
  agitated: 7 agitato
  all players/singers together: 5 tutti
  becoming quicker:
  11 accelerando
  continue without a break:
  5 segue
  **disconnected/each note
  separate: 8** staccato
  end: 4 fine
  expressively: 10 espressivo
    abbreviation: **4** espr
  fast: 6 veloce **7** allegro
  gentle: 5 soave
  gently: 9 doucement
  getting slower:
  10 allargando
  **getting weaker and
  slower: 7** calando
  gradually getting louder:
  9 crescendo
    abbreviation: **5** cresc
  gradually getting softer:
  10 diminuendo
  11 decrescendo
    abbreviation: **3** dim
    4 decr
  gradually slowing:
  11 rallentando
    abbreviation: **4** rall
  half: 5 mezzo
  half voice/half volume:
  9 mezza voce
  heavy: 5 lourd
  **in an undertone/in a low
  voice: 9** sotto voce
  leisurely: 6 comodo
  less: 4 meno
  light: 8 leggiero
  little: 4 poco
  lively: 3 vif
  loud: 5 forte
    abbreviation: **1** f
  **moderately slow and
  even: 7** andante
  more: 3 piu
  mournful: 5 mesto

musical instrument 3 lur, sax, saz **4** bass, bell, drum, fife,
gong, harp, horn, lute, lyre, oboe, outi, pipe, tuba, viol **5** argul, banjo, bugle, cello, cobza, flute, kazoo, organ, piano,
guena, rabob, sansa, shawm, sheng, sitar, viola **6** bagana,
chimes, cornet, cymbal, fiddle, guitar, spinet, treble, violin,
zither **7** bagpipe, bassoon, cittern, clavier, kithara, marimba,
panpipe, pibcorn, piccolo, samisen, strings, tambura, theorbo,
timpani, trumpet, ukulele **8** autoharp, bass drum, calliope,
clarinet, dulcimer, Jew's harp, mandolin, psaltery, recorder,
talharpa, triangle, trombone, virginal **9** accordion, balalaika,
castanets, harmonica, harmonium, krummhorn, rommelpot,
saxophone, snare drum, xylophone **10** bongo drums, clavichord, concertina, flugelhorn, French horn, kettledrum, sousaphone, tambourine, vibraphone **11** English horn,
harpsichord **12** jouhikantele
  classification: 4 horn, reed, wind **5** brass **6** string **8** keyboard, woodwind **10** electronic, percussion

6 frousy, frouzy, frowsy,
frowzy, old hat, stuffy **7** wornout **8** familiar, mildewed
9 hackneyed **10** antiquated,
threadbare **11** commonplace

mutable 6 fickle **7** pliable
8 flexible, variable **9** adaptable,
alterable, mercurial, versatile
10 adjustable, changeable, inconstant, modifiable, permutable **11** convertible,
metamorphic **13** transformable

mutate 4 turn **5** alter **6** change
7 convert **9** transform

mutation 6 change **7** anomaly
9 deviation, variation **10** alteration **12** modification **13** metamorphosis **14** transformation

not too much: 9 non troppo
plucked instead of bowed: 9 pizzicato
   abbreviation: **4** pizz
quick/vivacious: 6 vivace
repeat from beginning: 6 da capo
   abbreviation: **2** D C
shaking and quavering/ rapid alternation of notes: 5 trill
silent: 4 tace
singing/songlike/flowing: 9 cantabile
sliding: 9 glissando
slow: 5 lento **6** adagio
slow dignified tempo: 5 largo
slow down: 5 cedez
smooth/connected: 6 legato
soft: 5 piano
   abbreviation: **1** p
solemn/serious: 5 grave
sorrowful: 7 dolente
strict time: 10 tempo gusto
sudden accent: 9 sforzando
   abbreviation: **2** sf
sweetly: 5 dolce
tearful: 9 lacrimoso
tenderly: 10 affettuoso
trembling vibrating effect/ rapid reiteration of a single pitch: 7 tremolo
very: 5 molto
very loud: 10 fortissimo
   abbreviation: **2** ff
very soft: 10 pianissimo
   abbreviation: **2** pp
with fire: 8 con fuoco
with spirit/vigor: 7 con brio
with style/taste: 8 con gusto
with the mute: 10 con sordino

15 transfiguration
18 transmogrification

mutatis mutandis 30 necessary changes having been made

mute 3 mum **4** dumb **5** quiet, tacit **6** silent **8** aphasiac, nonvocal, reserved, reticent **9** unsounded, unuttered, voiceless **10** speechless **12** inarticulate, noncommittal, unpronounced **13** unarticulated **15** uncommunicative

muted 3 dim, low **4** dull, soft, weak **5** quiet **6** dulled, feeble **7** muffled **8** deadened, softened **10** indistinct, lackluster

mutilate 4 lame, maim **6** cut off, deform, excise, mangle **7** butcher, cripple **8** amputate, lacerate, truncate **9** disfigure, dismember

mutineer 5 rebel **9** dissident, insurgent **10** malcontent **15** insurrectionist

mutinous 6 unruly **10** dissenting, rebellious **13** revolutionary

Mutinus
origin: 5 Roman **7** Italian
god of: 9 fertility
fertility in: 8 marriage
corresponds to: 7 Priapus

mutiny 4 coup **5** rebel **6** revolt, rise up **8** takeover, upheaval, uprising **9** overthrow, rebellion **10** insurgency **12** insurrection

Mutiny on the Bounty
author: 15 Charles Nordhoff, James Norman Hall
character: 6 Tehani **9** Roger Byam **12** William Bligh (Captain Bligh) **13** George Stewart **17** Fletcher Christian
director: 10 Frank Lloyd
cast: 10 Clark Gable (Fletcher Christian) **12** Eddie Quillan, Franchot Tone **13** Herbert Mundin **15** Charles Laughton (Captain Bligh)
Oscar for: 7 picture

mutt 3 cur, dog, pup **5** puppy **7** mongrel

mutter 4 carp **5** gripe, growl, grunt **6** grouch, grouse, kvetch, mumble, murmur, rumble **7** grumble, whisper **8** complain

mutual 5 joint **6** common, shared **7** related **8** communal, returned **10** coincident, reciprocal **11** correlative, interactive

mutual understanding 6 accord **9** agreement

muzzle 3 gag **4** bind, curb **5** check, quiet, still **6** bridle, rein in, stifle **7** harness, silence **8** strangle, suppress, throttle

Myanmar *see box*

My Antonia
author: 11 Willa Cather

My Darling Clementine
director: 8 John Ford
cast: 7 Tim Holt **8** Ward Bond **10** Henry Fonda (Wyatt Earp) **12** Linda Darnell, Victor Mature (Doc Holliday) **13** Walter Brennan

my dear
French: 7 ma chere, mon cher

My Fair Lady
director: 11 George Cukor
based on play by: 17 George Bernard Shaw (Pygmalion)
cast: 11 Rex Harrison (Professor Henry Higgins) **13** Audrey Hepburn (Eliza Doolittle) **15** Stanley Holloway **16** Wilfrid Hyde-White
score: 14 Lerner and Loewe
Oscar for: 7 picture
song: 14 The Rain in Spain **24** I Could Have Danced All Night

my faith
French: 5 ma foi

my fault
Latin: 8 mea culpa

Mygdon
king of: 8 Bebryces
killed by: 8 Hercules

Myles
king of: 7 Laconia
invented: 9 grain mill

Mylitta *see* **6** Ishtar

My Little Margie
character: 7 Charlie **9** Mrs Odetts **11** Mr Honeywell **13** Freddie Wilson **14** Margie Albright, Vernon Albright **15** Roberta Townsend

my lord
French: 8 monsieur **11** monseigneur
Italian: 9 monsignor **10** monsignore

My Man Godfrey
director: 13 Gregory La Cava
cast: 10 Alice Brady, Mischa Auer **11** Gail Patrick **13** Carole Lombard, William Powell

Mynes
king of: 9 Lyrnessus
wife: 7 Briseis
killed by: 8 Achilles

myriad 6 untold **7** endless **8** infinite, manifold **9** boundless, countless, limitless, uncounted **11** innumerable, measureless **12** immeasurable, incalculable **13** multitudinous

myrmidon 6 cohort **8** follower, henchman

Myrmidons
people of: 6 Aegina **8** Thessaly
created by: 4 Zeus
created from: 4 ants
characteristic: 7 warlike
leader: 6 Peleus **8** Achilles

Myrrha
also: 6 Smyrna
father: 11 King Cinyras
loved: 7 Cinyras

Myanmar

former name: 5 Burma
other name: 16 Land of the Pagodas
capital: 6 Yangon 7 Rangoon
   ancient capital: 3 Ava 4 Pegu 8 Mandalay
largest city: 7 Rangoon
others: 2 Ye 3 Ava 4 Pegu 5 Akyab, Bhamo, Katha, Minbu, Namtu, Papun, Prome, Tavoy 6 Hsenwi, Hsipaw, Lashio, Maymyo, Monywa, Shwebo 7 Bassein, Henzada, Pakokku, Toungoo 8 Moulmein, Myingyan
measure: 2 ly 3 dha, gon, mau, sao, tao, tat 4 byee, phan, seit, taun, that 5 shita, thuoc 6 lamany, palgat 7 chaivai 8 okthabah
monetary unit: 3 pya 4 kyat
weight: 2 ta 3 can, pai, vis 4 binh, kyat, ruay, viss 5 behar, candy, ticul 6 abucco 7 peiktha
lake: 4 Inle
mountain: 4 Chin, Naga, Pegu, Popa 5 Dawna 6 Arakan, Kachin, Lushai, Patkai 7 Karenni 8 Nattaung, Peguyoma, Saramati, Victoria 10 Tenasserim 11 Manipur Hill 12 Tanen Taunggi
highest point: 11 Hkakabo Razi
river: 3 Hka 6 Salwin, Sutang 7 Irawadi, Kaladan, Myitnge, Salween, Schweli, Sittang 8 Chindwin, Indawgyi 9 Irrawaddy
sea: 7 Andaman
physical feature:
   bay: 4 Siam 6 Bengal, Hunter 7 Heanzay 8 Thailand
   gulf: 8 Martaban
   plateau: 4 Shan
   port: 5 Akyab 7 Bassein, Henzada 8 Moulmein
people: 2 Ao, Vu, Wa 3 Kaw, Lai, Lao, Mon, Pyu, Tai, Was 4 Akha, Chin, Juki, Kadu, Laos, Lolo, Miao, Naga, Sema, Shan, Thai, Tsin 5 Karen, Lhota 6 Birman, Burman, Kachin, Peguan, Rengma 7 Akhlame, Burmese, Kakhyen, Palauna, Palaung, Siamese 8 Mon-Khmer 9 Arakanese 12 Tibeto-Berman
language: 3 Lai 4 Chin, Kuki, Pegu, Shan 5 Karen 6 Kachin 7 Burmese, English
religion: 5 Hindu, Islam 8 Buddhism 12 Christianity
place:
   mines: 6 Mawchi 7 Bawdwin
   pagoda: 9 Shwe Dagon
   road: 4 Ledo 5 Burma 9 Stillwell
feature:
   ball game: 7 chin-lon
   festival: 5 Water 6 Lights 10 Thadin-gyut
   silk headband: 10 gaungbaung
   skirt: 6 longyi
   traveling theatrical group: 4 Pwes

crime: 6 incest
son: 6 Adonis
changed into: 6 myrtle 9 myrrh tree

myrtle 6 Myrtus 10 Vinca minor 14 Myrtus communis 18 Cyrilla racemiflora 23 Umbellularia californica
  varieties: 3 bog, gum, sea, wax 4 cape, Jew's, sand 5 crape, crepe, downy, dwarf, Greek, honey, scent 6 German, Oregon, Polish, willow 7 box sand, classic, running, Swedish 10 Western tea 11 candleberry, Queen's crape, sandverbena 13 Allegheny sand, bracelet honey, California wax 16 Australian willow

mysophobia
fear of: 4 dirt

mysterious 4 dark 6 cloudy, covert, hidden, secret 7 cryptic, obscure, strange, unknown 8 baffling, puzzling 9 enigmatic, secretive 10 perplexing, sphinxlike, undercover 11 clandestine, inscrutable 12 impenetrable, inexplicable, supernatural, unfathomable 13 surreptitious 14 undecipherable

Mysterious Stranger, The
author: 9 Mark Twain

mystery 6 enigma, occult, puzzle, riddle, secret 7 problem, secrecy 9 conundrum, obscurity, symbolism, vagueness 11 ambivalence, elusiveness 12 ineffability, quizzicality 13 ineffableness, mystification

Bird- RDC

mystical, mystic 5 inner 6 hidden, occult 7 cryptic, obscure 8 abstruse, esoteric, ethereal, symbolic 9 enigmatic, secretive 10 cabalistic, symbolical, unknowable 11 inscrutable, nonrational 12 metaphysical, otherworldly 14 transcendental

mystification 9 confusion 10 bafflement, perplexity, puzzlement 12 bewilderment

mystify 4 fool 5 elude 6 baffle, puzzle 7 confuse, deceive, mislead, perplex 8 bewilder, confound 9 bamboozle

myth 3 fib, lie 4 tale, yarn 5 error, fable, story 6 canard, legend 7 fantasy, fiction, hearsay, parable 8 allegory, delusion, illusion, tall tale 9 fairy tale, falsehood 10 shibboleth 13 prevarication

mythical, mythic 6 fabled, unreal 8 illusory 9 imaginary, legendary, pretended 10 conjured-up, fabricated, fantasized, fictitious 13 unsubstantial

mythological, mythologic 6 unreal 8 fabulous, illusory, imagined 9 fantastic, imaginary, legendary, unfactual 10 fictitious

My Three Sons
character: 11 Chip Douglas, Mike Douglas 12 Steve Douglas 13 Robbie Douglas 18 Katie Miller Douglas, Uncle Charley O'Casey 20 Ernie Thompson Douglas, Michael Francis (Bub) O'Casey
cast: 8 Don Grady, Tina Cole 12 Tim Considine 13 Fred MacMurray 14 William Frawley 15 Barry Livingston, William Demarest 17 Stanley Livingston
dog: 5 Tramp

my word
French: 5 ma foi

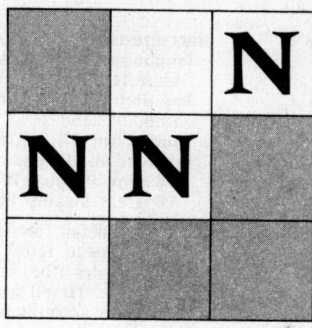

nab 4 bust, grab, nail, snag **5** catch, pinch, seize, snare **6** arrest, collar, detain, haul in, pick up, pull in, snatch **7** capture **9** apprehend

nabob 4 lord **5** mogul, nawab **6** deputy, tycoon **7** magnate **8** governor **9** plutocrat **10** capitalist **11** billionaire, millionaire

Nabokov, Vladimir
  author of: **3** Ada **6** Lolita **8** Pale Fire

Nabonidus
  son: **10** Belshazzar

Nadab
  father: **5** Aaron **6** Gibeon **7** Shammai **8** Jeroboam
  mother: **8** Elisheba
  brother: **5** Abihu **7** Eleazar, Ithamar

nadir 4 base, zero **5** floor **6** apogee, bottom **7** nothing **8** low point **10** rock bottom **11** lowest point

Nadja
  author: **11** Andre Breton

nag 4 fury, goad, harp **5** annoy, devil, harpy, scold, shrew, vixen **6** badger, bicker, harass, hassle, heckle, hector, nettle, peck at, pester, pick at, pick on, plague, rail at, tartar, virago **7** bedevil, upbraid **8** battle-ax, irritate **9** importune, termagant, Xanthippe

Nahua *see* **5** Aztec

Nahuatl *see* **10** Uto-Aztecan

Naiad
  form: **5** nymph
  location: **5** water

nail 3 fix, pin **4** claw **5** talon **6** fasten, hammer, secure
  part: **3** bed **4** root

Naipaul, V S
  author of: **10** Guerrillas **15** A Bend in the River **17** A House for Mr Biswas

19 The Return of Eva Peron, The Suffrage of Elvira

Nairobi
  capital of: **5** Kenya

naive 4 open **5** green, plain **6** candid, simple, unwary, unwise **7** artless, foolish, natural, unjaded **8** gullible, immature, innocent **9** childlike, credulous, guileless, ingenuous, unspoiled, unworldly **10** unaffected, unassuming **11** susceptible **12** unsuspecting, unsuspicious **15** unsophisticated

naivete, naivete 6 candor **7** modesty **8** openness **9** credulity, frankness, greenness, innocence, sincerity **10** callowness, simplicity **11** artlessness, foolishness, naturalness **12** childishness, inexperience **13** ingenuousness **14** unaffectedness **16** simplemindedness

naked 4 bald, bare, nude, pure **5** bared, frank, plain, sheer **6** patent, simple, unclad **7** blatant, exposed **8** disrobed, laid bare, manifest, palpable, undraped, wide-open **9** in the buff, unclothed, uncovered, undressed **11** perceptible, unapparel ed, unqualified, unvarnished **15** in the altogether

Naked and the Dead, The
  author: **12** Norman Mailer

Naked City
  character: **5** Libby **9** (Det) Adam Flint **10** (Det Lt) Dan Muldoon, (Lt) Mike Parker **11** (Det) Jim Halloran, (Ptlm/Sgt) Frank Arcaro **13** Janet Halloran
  cast: **9** Paul Burke **11** Nancy Malone **12** John McIntire **13** Harry Bellaver, Horace McMahon, Suzanne Storrs **15** James Franciscus
  setting: **11** New York City
  theme: **19** Somewhere in the Night

Namath, Joe (Joseph William)
  nickname: **11** Broadway Joe
  sport: **8** football
  position: **11** quarterback
  team: **11** New York Jets

namby-pamby 3 coy **4** dull, prim, weak **5** banal, inane, vapid **6** prissy **7** insipid, mincing, sapless **9** colorless, innocuous, simpering **10** indecisive, wishy-washy **13** characterless

name 3 tag **4** call, term **5** label, title **6** choose, ordain, select **7** appoint, baptize, epithet, specify **8** christen, cognomen, delegate, deputize, nominate, taxonomy **9** authorize, designate, signature, sobriquet **10** commission **11** appellation, designation **12** denomination, nomenclature

nameless 5 minor **7** obscure, unknown, unnamed **8** untitled **9** anonymous, unheard-of, unhonored **12** undesignated

namely
  Latin: **3** viz **9** videlicet

Name of the Game
  character: **8** Andy Hill **9** Joe Sample, Ross Craig **10** Dan Farrell, Jeff Dillon **11** Glenn Howard **12** Peggy Maxwell
  cast: **9** Ben Murphy, Gene Barry **10** Mark Miller **11** Cliff Potter, Robert Stack **13** Tony Franciosa **15** Susan Saint James
  business: **8** magazine **10** publishing

Name of the Rose, The
  author: **10** Umberto Eco

Name That Tune
  host: **9** Red Benson **10** Bill Cullen **12** George de Witt
  orchestra: **11** Harry Salter

Namibia *see box, p. 662*

Nammu
  origin: **8** Sumerian

Namibia
    other name: 15 South
        West Africa
    capital/largest city:
        8 Windhoek
    others: 6 Tsumeb 8 Lu-
        deritz 9 Walvis Bay
        10 Oranjemund, Swak-
        opmund
        12 Keetmanshoop
    monetary unit: 4 cent,
        rand
    mountain: 14 Khomas
        Highland, Koakoveld
        Hills
    highest point:
        9 Brandberg
    river: 4 Fish 6 Cunene,
        Orange 7 Zambezi
        8 Okavango
    sea: 8 Atlantic
    physical feature:
        bay: 6 Walvis
        desert: 5 Namib
            8 Kalahari
        region: 12 Caprivi
            Strip
    people: 4 Nama
        5 Bantu 6 Damara, Her-
        ero, Ovambo, Tswara
        7 Bushman, colored
        8 Okavango 9 Hottentot
    language: 5 Bantu
        6 German 7 English,
        Khoisan 9 Afrikaans
    religion: 7 animism
        8 Lutheran
    feature:
        homeland: 9 bantustan

mother of: 4 gods
personifies: 3 sea

Namtar
    origin: 8 Akkadian, Sumerian
    form: 5 demon
    personifies: 5 death

Nana
    author: 9 Emile Zola

Nana (Nurse)
    character in: 8 Peter Pan
    author: 6 Barrie

Nancy
    character in: 11 Oliver Twist
    author: 7 Dickens

Nancy
    creator: 15 Ernie Bushmiller
    character: 6 Sluggo 10 Aunt
        Fritzi

Nanna
    origin: 12 Scandinavian
    husband: 5 Baldr 6 Balder,
        Baldur
    habitat: 4 moon

Nannerella
    nickname of: 11 Anna
        Magnani

nanometer
    abbreviation: 2 nm

Naoise
    origin: 5 Irish
    wife: 7 Deirdre
    uncle: 9 Conchobar
    killed by: 9 Conchobar
    father: 6 Usnach, Usnech

Naomi
    husband: 9 Elimelech
    daughter-in-law: 4 Ruth
    son: 6 Mahlon 7 Chilion

nap 3 nod 4 doze, rest 6 cat-
    nap, drowse, siesta, snooze
    7 doze off, drop off, goof off,
    shut-eye, slumber 8 drift off
    10 forty winks

Napaeae
    form: 6 nymphs
    location: 4 dell

napery 5 doily 6 linens, nap-
    kin 10 tablecloth

Naphtali
    father: 5 Jacob
    mother: 6 Bilkah
    brother: 3 Dan, Gad 4 Levi
        5 Asher, Judah 6 Joseph,
        Reuben, Simeon 7 Zebulun
        8 Benjamin, Issachar
    sister: 5 Dinah
    descendant of: 10 Naphtalite

Napoleon Bonaparte *see
box*

**Napoleon of Notting Hill,
The**
    author: 12 G K Chesterton

Narcaeus
    father: 8 Dionysus
    mother: 7 Physcoa

narcissism 6 egoism, vanity
    7 conceit 8 self-love 11 ego-
    centrism 16 self-centeredness

narcissist 6 egoist 7 egotist
    11 egocentrist 12 self-absorbed,
    self-admiring

narcissistic 4 smug, vain
    6 vanity 7 conceit, selfish
    8 egotistic, puffed-up 9 con-
    ceited 10 egocentric, egoisti-
    cal 11 egomaniacal, egotistical

narcissus
    varieties: 5 poet's 6 poetaz
        7 leedsii, trumpet 10 paper-
        white, polyanthus 16 prim-
        rose peerless

Narcissus
    father: 8 Cephisus
    mother: 8 Leiriope
    loved: 7 himself
    loved by: 4 Echo
    punished by: 9 Aphrodite
    changed into: 6 flower

narcotic 4 drug 6 opiate
    8 medicine, sedative 9 soporif-
    ic 10 medicament, medication,
    painkiller 12 tranquilizer
    14 pharmaceutical

Narragansett
    language family: 9 Algon-
        kian 10 Algonquian
    location: 11 Connecticut,
        Rhode Island
    related to: 7 Niantic
    involved in: 9 Pequot War
        14 King Philip's War
        15 Great Swamp Fight

narrate 6 detail, recite, relate,
    render, repeat, retell 7 portray,
    recount 8 describe, set forth
    9 chronicle 10 tell a story
    15 give an account of

narration 7 recital, telling
    8 relating, speaking 9 voice-
    over 10 recitation, recounting
    11 chronicling, description
    12 storytelling

narrative 4 tale 5 story 6 re-
    port 7 account, recital 8 dia-
    logue, episodic 9 anecdotal,
    chronicle, statement 10 histor-
    ical 12 storytelling

**Narrative of Arthur Gordon
Pym, The**
    author: 13 Edgar Allan Poe

Napoleon Bonaparte
    also: 9 Napoleon I
        18 Emperor of the
        French
    battle: 3 Ulm 5 Eylau
        6 Lutzen, Moscow, Tou-
        lon (siege), Wagram
        7 Bautzen, Dresden,
        Leipzig, Marengo, Mon-
        dovi 8 Borodino, Water-
        loo 9 Friedland
        10 Austerlitz 13 Aspern-
        Essling, Jena-Auerstadt,
        Peninsular War 22 War
        of the Fifth Coalition
    born: 7 Corsica
    exile to: 4 Elba 11 Saint
        Helena
    fought against: 7 Kutu-
        zov 10 von Blucher,
        Wellington 14 Barclay
        de Tolly
    French fleet destroyed
        at: 9 Trafalgar
        destroyed by:
            6 Nelson
    laws: 14 Napoleonic
        Code
    marshal/general under:
        3 Ney 5 Murat 7 Mas-
        sena 10 Bernadotte
    position: 7 emperor
        11 first consul 13 con-
        sul for life
    tomb: 5 Paris 9 Invalides
    wife: 9 Josephine
        20 Marie-Louise of
        Austria

narrow 3 set **4** fine, slim
5 close, scant, small, tight
6 biased, scanty **7** bigoted,
cramped, pinched, shallow,
slender, tapered **8** confined,
dogmatic, isolated, squeezed
9 hidebound, illiberal, parochial **10** attenuated, compressed, intolerant, provincial,
restricted **11** constricted, inca-
pacious, opinionated, reactionary **12** conservative

narrowing 5 taper **8** tapering
9 squeezing **11** compressing
12 constricting

narrow-minded 5 petty **7** bigoted, prudish **8** one-sided
9 hidebound, parochial, unworldly **10** provincial **11** opinionated, reactionary,
straitlaced **12** conservative
15 unsophisticated

narrow-mindedness 4 bias
7 bigotry **9** prejudice **10** unfairness **11** intolerance

narrows 4 neck, pass **5** canal
6 ravine, strait **7** channel, isthmus, passage

Nasca see **5** Nazca

**Nascimento, Edson Arantes
do**
real name of: **4** Pele

Nash, Ogden
author of: **6** Versus **9** Hard
Lines **20** The Private Dining
Room **21** I'm a Stranger
Here Myself

Nashville
director: **12** Robert Altman
cast: **10** Karen Black, Lily
Tomlin **11** Henry Gibson
12 Ronee Blakley **13** Barbara Harris, Michael Mur-
phy **14** Keith Carradine
16 Geraldine Chaplin
Oscar for: **4** song
song: **6** I'm Easy

Nassau
capital of: **7** Bahamas

nasty 4 foul, mean, vile **5** awful **6** odious **7** beastly, hateful,
vicious **8** horrible **9** repellent,
revolting **10** abominable, disgusting, nauseating, unpleasant **11** distasteful
12 disagreeable

Natchez
language family:
10 Muskhogean
tribe: **6** Avoyel, Taensa
location: **11** Mississippi
13 South Carolina
allied with: **7** Choctaw
practiced: **14** head flattening

nates 4 buns, rear, rump, seat
7 rear end **8** buttocks,
haunches **9** fundament, posterior **12** hindquarters

Nathan
father: **5** Attai
served: **5** David **7** Solomon

Nathanael see **5** Jesus **8** Apostles **11** Bartholomew

nation 4 host, race **5** realm,
state, tribe **6** empire, people
7 country, kingdom **8** republic **9** community **11** sovereignty **12** commonwealth

national park see box

National Velvet
director: **13** Clarence Brown
cast: **10** Anne Revere
11 Donald Crisp **12** Mickey
Rooney **14** Angela Lansbury **15** Elizabeth Taylor
Oscar for: **17** supporting actress (Revere)
sequel: **19** International
Velvet

native 4 home **5** basic, local,
natal **6** inborn, inbred, innate,
savage **7** citizen, endemic, natural **8** domestic, inherent, national, paternal **9** aborigine,
elemental, homegrown, in-
grained, inherited, intrinsic,
primitive **10** congenital, countryman, hereditary, indigenous **11** instinctive
12 countrywoman
13 autochthonous

native country 7 country
8 homeland **10** fatherland
13 mother country

native-grown 5 local **8** domestic **9** homegrown
10 indigenous

native land 8 homeland
10 birthplace, fatherland, native soil **13** mother country,
native country

native of Israel
Hebrew: **5** sabra

native soil 8 homeland **10** fatherland, native land
13 mother country, native
country

Native Son
author: **13** Richard Wright

natty 4 chic, neat, posh, tidy,
trim **5** smart **6** dapper,
jaunty, snappy, spruce **7** dashing, modish, stylish
11 fashionable

Natty Bumppo
also: **7** Hawkeye **10** Pathfinder, The Trapper **13** The
Deerslayer **15** Leatherstocking **16** Le Longue Carabine
character in: **23** The Leather-
stocking Tales
friend: **5** Uncas
12 Chingachgook
author: **6** Cooper

national park
Alaska: 13 Mount McKinley
Arizona: 11 Grand Canyon **15** Petrified Forest
Arkansas: 10 Hot Springs
California: 7 Redwood, Sequoia **8** Yosemite **11** Kings Can-
yon **14** Channel Islands, Lassen Volcanic
Canada: 4 Yoho **5** Banff, Fundy **6** Jasper, Kluane **8** Koo-
tenay **9** Auyuittuq **13** Waterton Lakes
Colorado: 5 Estes **9** Mesa Verde **13** Rocky Mountain
Florida: 10 Everglades
Hawaii: 9 Haleakala **15** Hawaii Volcanoes
Kentucky: 11 Mammoth Cave
Maine: 6 Acadia
Michigan: 10 Isle Royale
Minnesota: 9 Voyageurs
Montana: 7 Glacier **11** Yellowstone
New Mexico: 15 Carlsbad Caverns
North Carolina: 19 Great Smoky Mountains (with
Tennessee)
North Dakota: 17 Theodore Roosevelt
Oklahoma: 6 Platte
Oregon: 10 Crater Lake
South Dakota: 8 Badlands, Wind Cave
Tennessee: 6 Shiloh **13** Cumberland Gap **19** Great Smoky
Mountains (with North Carolina)
Texas: 7 Big Bend **18** Guadalupe Mountains
Utah: 4 Zion **6** Arches **11** Bryce Canyon, Canyonlands,
Capital Reef
Virginia: 10 Shenandoah **26** Colonial National Historical
Washington: 7 Olympic **12** Mount Rainier **13** North
Cascades
Wyoming: 10 Grand Teton **11** Yellowstone

natural 5 plain **6** inborn, native, normal **7** earthly, genuine, regular **8** God-given, inherent **9** essential, intuitive, unstudied **10** unaffected, unmannered **11** instinctive, spontaneous, terrestrial **13** unpretentious **14** characteristic **15** straightforward

Natural, The
    director: 13 Barry Levinson
    based on story by: 14 Bernard Malamud
    cast: 10 Glenn Close **12** Robert Duvall **13** Robert Redford

natural child 7 bastard **9** love child **17** illegitimate child

natural gift 5 flair **6** talent **7** ability, faculty **8** aptitude **9** attribute, endowment

natural habitat 5 range **6** domain, milieu **7** element **9** territory **11** environment

naturalize 5 adapt, adopt **6** adjust **8** accustom **9** acclimate **11** domesticate, familiarize

naturalness 4 ease **9** sincerity **10** simplicity **11** artlessness, genuineness **12** unconstraint **14** unaffectedness

nature 4 bent, kind, mood, sort, type **5** birth, earth, globe, humor, stamp, style, trait **6** cosmos, spirit **7** essence, feature, variety **8** category, creation, instinct, property, universe **9** character **11** disposition, peculiarity **12** constitution **13** particularity **14** characteristic
    goddess of: 6 Cybele **9** Dindymene **10** Berecyntia

Nature
    author: 17 Ralph Waldo Emerson

naught 3 nil **4** zero **5** nihil, zilch **6** cipher **7** nothing, useless **9** worthless

naughty 3 bad **4** blue **5** bawdy, dirty **6** ribald, risque, vulgar **7** wayward, willful **8** devilish, off-color, perverse **9** fractious, obstinate **11** disobedient, misbehaving, mischievous **12** pornographic, recalcitrant, unmanageable **13** disrespectful

Naum
    son: 4 Amos

Nauru *see box*

nausea 7 disgust, heaving **8** contempt, loathing, retching, sickness, vomiting **9** repulsion, revulsion **10** queasiness **11** airsickness, biliousness, car sickness, seasickness **12** upset stomach **14** motion sickness, travel sickness

---

Nauru
    other name: 14 Pleasant Island
    capital: 13 Yaren District
    cities: 3 Boe, Ewa **4** Aiwo, Ijuw **5** Baiti, Buada, Nibok, Uaboe, Yaren **6** Anabar, Anetan, Meneng **7** Anibare **10** Denigomodu
    monetary unit: 4 cent **6** dollar
    lake: 11 Buada Lagoon
    sea: 7 Pacific
    physical feature:
        bay: **7** Anibare
        lagoon: **5** Buada
        point: **4** Anna **6** Meneng
    people: 7 Chinese **10** Melanesian, Polynesian **11** Micronesian
        explorer: **9** John Fearn
    language: 7 English, Nauruan
    religion: 10 Protestant **13** Roman Catholic
    feature: 9 phosphate

Nausea
    author: 14 Jean-Paul Sartre

nauseate 5 repel, upset **6** offend, revolt, sicken **7** disgust, repulse **8** make sick **15** turn one's stomach

nauseated 3 ill **4** sick **5** upset **6** queasy **8** repelled, revolted **9** disgusted

nauseating 9 offensive, repellent, repulsive, revolting, sickening **10** disgusting

nauseous 4 sick **5** upset **6** queasy **9** abhorrent, nauseated, offensive, repellent, repulsive, revolting, sickening, upsetting **10** disgusting, nauseating **12** unappetizing

Nausicaa
    father: 8 Alcinous
    position: 8 princess
    aided: 8 Odysseus

Nausithous
    father: 8 Poseidon
    mother: 8 Periboea
    occupation: 8 helmsman
    employer: 7 Theseus
    became: 4 king
    realm: 8 Phaeacia

Nautes
    advisor to: 6 Aeneas

nautical 5 naval **6** marine **7** aquatic, boating, oceanic **8** maritime, of the sea, seagoing, yachting

---

nautical mile
    abbreviation: 3 nmi

Nautilus
    submarine in: 32 Twenty Thousand Leagues Under the Sea
    author: 5 Verne

Navajo, Navaho (Dine)
    language family: 10 Athapascan, Athapaskan
    location: 4 Utah **7** Arizona **9** New Mexico
    noted for: 7 weaving **14** silversmithing
    dwelling: 5 hogan

navigate 3 fly **4** ride, sail, ship **5** cross, steer **6** cruise, voyage **8** maneuver, sail over **11** plot a course **12** chart a course

navigation 7 boating, sailing **8** cruising, piloting, voyaging **9** traveling **10** seamanship
    god of: 5 Niord, Njord

Navigators Islands *see* **12** Western Samoa

navy 5 fleet **6** armada, convoy **8** flotilla, warships

navy-blue 6 indigo **8** dark blue, deep blue

nay 4 also, deny, vote **5** never **6** denial, refuse **7** against, but also, refusal **8** negative

Nazarene *see* **5** Jesus

Nazarene, The
    author: 10 Sholem Asch

Nazca, Nasca
    location: 4 Peru **12** South America
    noted for: 8 ceramics, textiles **10** Nazca lines (sketches on plain)

Nazi air force
    German: 9 Luftwaffe

Nazi swastika
    German: 10 Hakenkreuz

N'Djamena
    capital of: 4 Chad

Neaera
    mentioned in: 7 Odyssey
    form: 5 nymph
    father: 6 Pereus
    cousin: 9 King Aleus
    husband: 9 King Aleus
    son: 7 Cepheus
    daughter: 4 Auge **6** Evadne **8** Lampetia

Neal, Patricia
    husband: 9 Roald Dahl
    born: 9 Packard KY
    roles: 3 Hud (Oscar) **15** A Face in the Crowd, The Fountainhead **18** The Subject Was Roses

near **4** nigh **5** about, close **6** all but, almost **7** close by, close to, looming **8** approach, come up to, imminent, next door **9** alongside, close with, impending **10** hereabouts **11** approaching, practically, proximately, threatening **13** approximately

nearby **5** close, handy **6** at hand **7** close by **8** next door **9** adjoining **10** accessible, hereabouts

near death
 Latin: **10** in extremis

near home **5** close **7** close by **10** hereabouts

nearly **4** nigh **5** about **6** all but, almost **7** close to, roughly **11** practically **13** approximately

nearly equal **5** close **7** similar **10** nip-and-tuck **11** approaching

nearly even **5** close **10** head to head, nip-and-tuck **11** neck and neck

nearness **8** intimacy, vicinity **9** adjacency, closeness, handiness, immediacy, proximity **10** contiguity **11** propinquity **12** availability, neighborhood **13** accessibility, approximation

neat **4** tidy **5** clean, great **6** groovy **7** concise, correct, orderly **8** accurate, exciting, original, straight, striking, succinct **9** competent, dexterous, efficient, ingenious, organized, purposive, shipshape **10** controlled, immaculate, methodical, systematic **11** imaginative, intelligent, uncluttered

neatness **5** order **8** tidiness **11** orderliness **12** organization

Nebraska *see box*

nebris
 skin of: **4** fawn

Nebrophonus *see* **5** Thoon

Nebuchadnezzar
 father: **12** Nabopolassar
 son: **12** Evilmerodach

nebula **4** Crab, Ring, Veil **5** Great **6** Lagoon **7** Rosette **9** Horsehead

nebulous **3** dim **4** dark, hazy **5** murky, vague **6** cloudy **7** obscure, unclear **8** confused **9** ambiguous, uncertain **10** impalpable, indefinite, indistinct, intangible **13** indeterminate

necessarily **8** perforce **9** naturally **10** inevitably, inexorably **11** accordingly **12** compulso-

---

Nebraska
 abbreviation: **2** NE **4** Nebr
 nickname: **4** Beef **8** Antelope **10** Blackwater, Cornhusker **12** Treeplanter's
 capital: **7** Lincoln
 largest city: **5** Omaha
 others: **5** Cozad **6** Gering **7** Kearney **8** Beatrice, Hastings **9** Broken Bow **11** Grand Island, North Platte, Scottsbluff
 college: **4** Dana **5** Doane **8** Duchesne, Hastings **9** Creighton **15** Midland Lutheran
 feature: **8** Boys' Town
  national monument: **11** Scott's Bluff **15** Agate Fossil Beds
 tribe: **3** Oto **4** Otoe **5** Kiowa, Omaha, Ponca, Sioux **6** Pawnee
 people: **10** Henry Fonda **11** Fred Astaire, Roscoe Pound
 lake: **7** Merritt, Sherman, Swanson **10** McConaughy **13** Lewis and Clark
 land rank: **9** fifteenth
 physical feature: **8** Badlands
  hills: **4** Sand **5** Drift, Loess
  plains: **5** Great
 river: **4** Loup **5** Logan **6** Dismal, Nemaha, Platte **7** Big Blue, Elkhorn **8** Missouri, Niobrara **10** Little Blue, Republican **12** Harlan County
 state admission: **13** thirty-seventh
 state bird: **17** western meadowlark
 state flower: **9** goldenrod
 state motto: **20** Equality Before the Law
 state song: **17** Beautiful Nebraska
 state tree: **3** elm **10** cottonwood

---

rily **13** automatically, axiomatically, unqualifiedly **16** incontrovertibly

necessary **6** needed, urgent, wanted **7** crucial, desired, exigent, fitting, needful **8** required **9** called for, essential, requisite **10** compulsory, imperative, obligatory **13** indispensable

necessary changes having been made
 Latin: **15** mutatis mutandis

necessitate **5** cause, force, impel **6** compel, demand, oblige **7** call for, enforce, require **9** constrain, prescribe

necessitation **5** cause, force **6** demand, duress **8** coercion, pressure **10** compulsion, constraint, obligation **11** enforcement, requirement

necessity, necessities **4** must, need **6** demand, needed **7** urgency **8** exigency, pressure **9** essential, requisite **10** sine qua non **11** requirement **13** indispensable
 Latin: **10** sine qua non

neck **3** pet **4** kiss, nape, pass **6** caress, cervix, cuddle, fondle, smooth, strait **7** channel, isthmus, make out **9** narrowing

neckerchief **5** scarf **8** bandanna, kerchief

necklace **3** tie **5** beads, chain, noose **6** choker, collar, locket, pearls, string **7** jewelry, pendant **8** ornament **9** lavaliere

necktie **3** bow **4** band **5** ascot, black, scarf **6** cravat, string **7** Windsor **10** four in hand **11** half Windsor **12** hangman's rope

necromancer **5** hexer, magus, witch **6** wizard **7** charmer, warlock **8** conjurer, exorcist, magician, sorcerer **9** enchanter, occultist, voodooist **10** soothsayer **13** black magician, thaumaturgist

necromancy **5** magic, spell **7** sorcery **8** black art **10** witchcraft **11** enchantment, foretelling

necrophobia
 fear of: **5** death **10** dead bodies

necropolis **8** cemetery **9** graveyard **12** burial ground **13** burying ground

Nectar
 drink of: **4** gods
 gives: **4** life

Neda
 form: **5** nymph, river
 location: **11** mountaintop

need 4 lack, want, wish
5 crave, exact 6 demand, penury 7 call for, longing, poverty, require, straits 8 distress, exigency, yearn for 9 essential, extremity, indigence, necessity, requisite 10 bankruptcy, insolvency 11 desideratum, destitution, necessitate, requirement 13 impecuniosity, pennilessness

needed 5 vital 7 crucial 9 essential, necessary, requisite 13 indispensable

needful 7 wishful 8 required 9 essential, necessary, requisite 10 imperative 13 indispensable

needle 3 vex 4 josh, leaf, ride, twit 5 annoy, chaff, harry, taunt, tease 6 badger, harass, hector 7 torment 9 indicator

needle-shaped 5 sharp 6 peaked, spiked 7 pointed 8 piercing 10 bodkin-like

needless 7 useless 9 excessive, pointless, redundant 10 gratuitous, pleonastic, unavailing 11 dispensable, purposeless, superfluous, uncalled-for, unessential, unnecessary 12 overabundant

needlework 6 sewing 7 basting, brocade, darning, tacking, tatting 8 applique, knitting, quilting 9 stitching 10 embroidery 11 cross stitch, needle point

needy 4 poor 5 broke 6 hard-up, in want 8 indigent, strapped 9 destitute, moneyless, penniless 10 down-and-out 12 impoverished 15 poverty-stricken

ne'er-do-well 3 bum 5 idler, loser 6 loafer, no-good 7 goof-off, sad sack, wastrel 8 layabout 9 do-nothing, no-account 10 black sheep 14 good-for-nothing

nefarious 3 bad, low 4 base, evil, foul, vile 6 odious, wicked 7 beastly, ghastly, heinous, hellish, ungodly, vicious 8 depraved, devilish, infamous, infernal, shameful 9 atrocious, execrable 10 abominable, despicable, detestable, iniquitous, scandalous, villainous 11 disgraceful, opprobrious, unspeakable 12 dishonorable 13 unmentionable

Nefertem
origin: 8 Egyptian
personifies: 5 lotus
true identity: 4 Ptah

negate 4 deny, veto, void

5 quash, quell, rebut 6 defeat, disown, refute, repeal, revoke, squash 7 blot out, destroy, disavow, gainsay, nullify, retract, reverse, squelch, wipe out 8 abrogate, disallow, disclaim, set aside, vanquish 9 overthrow, overwhelm, repudiate 10 contradict, invalidate

negating 7 denying, voiding 8 refuting, revoking 9 reversing 10 cancelling, nullifying 11 disallowing 12 invalidating, setting aside 13 contradicting

negation 6 denial 7 counter 8 reversal 9 rejection 10 abrogation, disclaimer, refutation 11 confutation, repudiation 12 invalidation 13 contradiction, nullification

negative 4 blue, dark 5 bleak 6 at odds, gloomy 7 dubious, opposed 8 contrary, doubtful, downbeat, inimical, opposing, refusing 9 declining, demurring, dissident, jaundiced, objecting, rejecting, reluctant, skeptical, unwilling 10 dissenting, fatalistic 11 disagreeing, pessimistic 12 antagonistic, disapproving 13 uncooperative 14 unenthusiastic

neglect 4 fail, omit 5 let go, shirk 6 forget, ignore, laxity, pass by, pass up, slight 7 abandon, default, laxness, let pass, let ride, let slip 8 be remiss, idleness, let slide, omission, overlook, pass over, shake off 9 disregard, oversight, passivity, slackness 10 inaccuracy, negligence, remissness 11 dereliction, inattention, inexactness 12 carelessness, fecklessness, indifference, slovenliness 13 noncompliance, unfulfillment 14 nonpreparation 16 underachievement

neglected 7 dropped, ignored, omitted, shirked, unkempt 8 forsaken, untended 9 abandoned, cast aside, forgotten 10 overlooked, uncared for 11 disregarded

neglectful 4 lazy 5 slack 6 remiss, untrue 8 careless, derelict, heedless 9 forgetful, negligent, oblivious, unheeding, unmindful 10 inconstant, thriftless, unfaithful, unthinking, unwatchful 11 improvident, inattentive, indifferent, respectless, thoughtless, unobservant 12 devil-may-care, disregardant, disregardful, happy-go-lucky 15 procrastinating

negligee, neglige 4 robe 6 kimono 7 wrapper 8 bathrobe,

peignoir 9 housecoat 12 dressing gown

negligence 6 laxity 7 neglect 11 disregarded 12 carelessness

negligent 3 lax 5 slack 6 remiss, untidy 8 careless, heedless, slovenly 9 forgetful, unheeding, unmindful 10 neglectful, unthinking, unwatchful 11 inattentive, indifferent, thoughtless, unobservant 13 inconsiderate

negligible 5 minor, petty, small 6 minute, paltry, slight 7 trivial 8 piddling, trifling 11 unimportant 13 insignificant 15 inconsequential

negotiate 4 cash, make, pass 6 barter, cash in, convey, dicker, haggle, handle, manage, redeem, settle 7 arrange, consign, deliver, discuss, get over 8 contract, cope with, deal with, hand over, make over, pass over, sign over, transact, transfer, transmit, turn over 10 bargain for 11 come to terms, meet halfway

negotiation 4 deal 6 treaty 8 argument, haggling 9 dickering 10 bargaining 11 arbitration, arrangement 12 compromising

negotiator 7 arbiter 8 mediator 9 go-between 10 arbitrator 12 intermediary

Negrette, Lolita Dolores
real name of: 13 Dolores Del Rio

Nehemiah
father: 5 Azbuk 14 Hachaliah

neigh 5 hinny 6 nicker, whinny

neighbor 4 abut, meet 5 touch 6 adjoin, be near, border, friend 7 conjoin 8 borderer, border on 9 associate 12 acquaintance

neighborhood 4 area, part, side, ward 5 place, range 6 locale, parish, region, sphere 7 quarter, section 8 confines, district, environs, precinct, purlieus, vicinity 9 community

neighboring 4 near, next 5 close 6 at hand, nearby 7 close by 8 abutting, adjacent 9 adjoining, bordering 10 contiguous 11 surrounding 12 circumjacent

neighborly 4 kind 5 civil 6 chummy, kindly, polite 7 affable, amiable, cordial, helpful 8 amicable, friendly, gracious, obliging 9 courteous 10 hospitable 11 considerate, warmhearted 12 well-disposed

Neighbors
author: **12** Thomas Berger

Neith
origin: **8** Egyptian
personifies: **10** femininity
son: **2** Ra
corresponds to: **6** Athena

Nekhbet
origin: **8** Egyptian
form: **7** vulture
guardian of: **5** Egypt **10** Upper Egypt

Neleus
king of: **5** Pylos, Pylus
father: **8** Poseidon
mother: **4** Tyro
twin brother: **6** Pelias
wife: **7** Chloris
son: **6** Nestor **12** Periclymenus
daughter: **4** Pero
refused purification to: **8** Hercules
killed by: **8** Hercules

Nelides
epithet of: **6** Nestor

Nelson, Harriet Hilliard
real name: **14** Peggy Lou Snyder
husband: **5** Ozzie
son: **4** Rick **5** David
born: **11** Des Moines IA
roles: **30** The Adventures of Ozzie and Harriet

Nelson, Horatio
also: **14** Viscount Nelson
nationality: **7** British
battle: **9** Trafalgar **11** Bay of Abukir **15** Battle of the Nile **16** Cape Saint Vincent **18** Battle of Copenhagen
defeated: **5** Danes **6** French **7** Spanish
flagship: **7** Victory
killed at: **9** Trafalgar
lover: **16** Emma Lady Hamilton

Nelson, Ozzie
real name: **18** Oswald George Nelson
wife: **15** Harriet Hilliard
son: **4** Rick **5** David
born: **12** Jersey City NJ
roles: **30** The Adventures of Ozzie and Harriet

Nemean
epithet of: **4** Zeus

Nemean lion
strangled by: **8** Hercules

nemesis 4 ruin **5** match, rival **7** avenger, justice, revenge, undoing **8** downfall, punisher, Waterloo **9** overthrow, vengeance **10** punishment **11** destruction, retaliation, retribution **16** instrument of fate

Nemesis *see* **8** Adrastea

**nemine contradicente
11** unanimously **18** no one contradicting

**nemine dissentiente
11** unanimously **15** no one dissenting

Nemo
character in: **10** Bleak House
author: **7** Dickens

Nemo, Captain
character in: **32** Twenty Thousand Leagues Under the Sea
author: **5** Verne

neologism, neology 7 coinage **9** nonce word

neon
chemical symbol: **2** Ne

neonate 4 baby **6** infant **7** newborn

neophyte 4 tyro **5** pupil **6** novice, rookie **7** convert, entrant, learner, recruit, student, trainee **8** beginner, disciple, newcomer **9** greenhorn, novitiate, proselyte **10** apprentice, tenderfoot **11** probationer

neoplasm 5 tumor **6** cancer, growth **7** sarcoma **9** carcinoma **10** malignancy **14** carcinosarcoma

Nepal *see box*

Nepali
language family: **12** Indo-European
branch: **11** Indo-Iranian
group: **5** Indic
spoken in: **5** Nepal

nepenthe 4 drug **5** drink, opium **6** heroin, opiate **7** hashish **8** narcotic

Nephele
counterfeit of: **4** Hera
formed by: **4** Zeus
husband: **7** Athamas
children: **8** centaurs
son: **7** Phrixus
daughter: **5** Helle

nephrite
variety: **4** jade

ne plus ultra 4 acme **12** highest point

Neptune
origin: **5** Roman

Nepal
other name: **9** Shangri-La
capital/largest city: **8** Katmandu **9** Kathmandu
others: **5** Patan, Patna **6** Gurkha **7** Birganj **8** Bhadgaon, Lalitpur **9** Bhaktapur **10** Biratnagar
university: **9** Tribhuvan
division: **5** Terai **13** High Himalayas
monetary unit: **4** anna, pice **5** mohar, paisa, rupee
mountain: **6** Cho Oyu, Churia, Lhotse, Makalu **7** Manaslu, Siwalik **9** Annapurna, Himalayas **10** Dhaulagiri, Gosainthan, Himalchuli **11** Ganesh Himal **12** Kanchenjunga **14** Mahabharat hekh
highest point: **9** Mt Everest
river: **4** Kali, Kosi, Mugu, Seti **5** Babai, Bheri, Rapti, Sarda, Tamur **6** Gandak **7** Karnali **8** Narayani
physical feature:
  plain: **5** Terai
  valley: **5** Nepal **8** Katmandu
people: **3** Rai **4** Aoul **5** Bhote, Limbu, Magar, Murmi, Newar, Tharu **6** Bhutia, Gurkha, Gurung, Nepali, Sherpa, Tamang **7** Kiranti, Tibetan **8** Gorkhali, Nepalese
  birthplace of: **6** Buddha **13** Gautama Buddha **17** Siddhartha Gautama
  king: **8** Mahendra **9** Tribhuwan **18** Prithwi Narayan Shah **23** Birenda Bir Bikram Shah Dev
  ruler: **4** Rana **5** Malla **6** Rajput
language: **6** Nepali, Newari
religion: **8** Buddhism, Hinduism
place:
  dam: **6** Gandak
  shrine: **9** Swayambhu **10** Gorakhnath
feature:
  animal: **3** dzo, yak **7** dzopkyo
  arch: **6** Juddha
  god/goddess: **5** Indra **6** Kumari
  legend: **4** Yeti **17** abominable snowman
  soldiers: **6** Gurkha

Neptune
god of: 3 sea
corresponds to: 8 Poseidon

Neptune
position: 6 eighth
satellite: 6 Nereid, Triton
color: 5 green

Nereid
form: 5 nymph
location: 3 sea
father: 6 Nereus

Nereus
god of: 3 sea
father: 6 Pontus
mother: 4 Gaea
father of: 7 Nereids
number of Nereids: 5 fifty
son: 7 Nerites

Nergal
origin: 8 Akkadian
ruler of: 4 dead
consort of: 10 Ereshkigal

Nerissa
character in: 19 The Merchant of Venice
author: 11 Shakespeare

Nerites
father: 6 Nereus
mother: 5 Doris
transformed into: 6 mussel
transformed by: 9 Aphrodite

neritic 7 aquatic, coastal 8 offshore

Nero
name: 18 Nero Claudius Caesar
emperor of: 4 Rome
mother: 9 Agrippina
father: 19 Domitius Ahenobarbus
stepfather: 8 Claudius
tutor: 6 Seneca
son: 11 Britannicus
wife: 7 Octavia 13 Poppaea Sabina

nerve 4 dash, gall, grit, guts, sass 5 brass, cheek, crust, pluck, spunk, valor 6 mettle, spirit 7 bravery, courage 8 backbone, boldness, coolness, gameness, strength, tenacity 9 arrogance, assurance, derring-do, endurance, flippancy, fortitude, gallantry, hardihood, hardiness, impudence, insolence, sauciness 10 assumption, brazenness, confidence, effrontery, steadiness 11 intrepidity, presumption 12 fearlessness, impertinence, resoluteness 13 determination 16 stoutheartedness

nerveless 4 calm, dead, weak 5 brave, frail, inert 6 feeble, flabby 7 flaccid 8 cowardly 9 powerless 10 courageous 12 fainthearted

nervous 4 wild 5 jumpy, shaky, tense 6 touchy, uneasy 7 alarmed, anxious, excited, fearful, fidgety, jittery, peevish, ruffled 8 feverish, neurotic, skittish, startled, timorous, unstrung 9 delirious, disturbed, excitable, impatient, irritable, sensitive, trembling, tremulous, unsettled 10 high-strung, hysterical 12 apprehensive

nervousness 6 tremor 7 anxiety, flutter, shaking, tension 8 hysteria, timidity 9 agitation, quivering, the creeps, the shakes, trembling, twitching 10 the fidgets, touchiness 11 disturbance, fidgetiness, stage fright 12 apprehension, excitability, irascibility, irritability, perturbation, timorousness 16 hypersensitivity

nervous system
component: 4 ears, eyes 5 brain, taste, touch 7 ganglia 8 nerve end 10 nerve fiber, spinal cord

nervy 4 bold, firm, rude 5 brash, gutty, gutsy, sassy 6 brassy, brazen, cheeky, gritty, plucky, strong 7 assured, nervous 10 courageous, determined 12 stouthearted

Nesbitt, Cathleen
born: 7 England 8 Cheshire
roles: 10 My Fair Lady 18 Upstairs Downstairs 23 Three Coins in the Fountain

Nessus
form: 7 centaur
shot by: 8 Hercules
caused death of: 8 Hercules

n'est-ce pas? 10 isn't that so?

nestle 3 lie, pet 4 live, snug, stay 5 clasp, dwell, lodge 6 bundle, caress, coddle, cosset, cuddle, enfold, fondle, huddle, nuzzle, occupy, remain, settle 7 embrace, inhabit, lie snug, snuggle 8 lie close 10 settle down

Nest of Gentlefolk
author: 23 Ivan Sergeyevich Turgenev

Nest of Simple Folk, A
author: 12 Sean O'Faolain

Nestor
origin: 5 Greek
attributes: 6 oldest, wisest
father: 6 Neleus
son: 10 Thasymedes 11 Pisistratus
epithet: 7 Nelides

net 3 web 4 earn, gain, grab, grid, grip, mesh, snag, take, trap 5 catch, clasp, grate, seize, snare 6 clutch, enmesh, gather, grille, obtain, pick up, screen, snap up, take in 7 acquire, bring in, capture, collect, ensnare, grating, lattice 8 entangle, gather in, gridiron, meshwork 9 apprehend, grillwork, lay hold of, screening 10 accumulate 11 latticework
constellation of: 9 Reticulum

nether 5 basal, below, lower, under 6 bottom, lowest 8 downward, inferior 9 subjacent 10 bottommost

Netherlands see box

Netherlands East Indies see 9 Indonesia

netherworld 4 hell 5 Hades 10 underworld 14 infernal region

nettle 3 vex 4 bait, gall, miff, rile 5 annoy, beset, chafe, harry, pique, sting 6 bother, harass, ruffle 7 perturb, prickle, provoke 8 irritate 9 displease 10 exasperate

nettle 6 Urtica
varieties: 4 dead, dumb, hemp, rock 5 false, flame, hedge, horse, Roman 6 spurge 7 painted 8 stinging 9 white dead 11 spotted dead 12 western horse

network 3 web 4 grid, mesh, trap 5 grate, group, snare 6 grille, scheme, system 7 complex, netting, station

Network
director: 11 Sidney Lumet
based on story by: 14 Paddy Chayefsky
cast: 9 Ned Beatty 10 Peter Finch, Wesley Addy 11 Faye Dunaway 12 Robert Duvall 13 William Holden 16 Beatrice Straight
Oscar for: 5 actor (Finch) 7 actress (Dunaway) 17 supporting actress (Straight)

neuroptera
class: 8 hexapoda
phylum: 10 arthropoda
group: 7 ant lion, fishfly 8 alderfly, lacewing, snakefly

neurotic 4 sick 7 anxious, intense, nervous 8 abnormal, unstable 9 disturbed, obsessive, unhealthy 10 distraught, immoderate 11 overwrought

neuter 5 fixed 6 barren, fallow, gelded, spayed 7 asexual, sexless, sterile 8 impotent 9 infertile

Neutra, Richard J
architect of: 15 Mathematics Park (Princeton) 16 Lovell Heath House (Los Angeles

Netherlands
other name: 7 Holland 12 Low Countries
capital/largest city: 9 Amsterdam
others: 3 Urk 5 Delft, Lisse 6 Almelo, Arnhem, Leiden, Velsen 7 Haarlem, Helmond, Hengelo, Limburg, Tilberg, Tilburg, Utrecht 8 Aalsmeer, Enschede, Ijmuiden, Nijmegen, The Hague 9 Apeldoorn, Dordrecht, Eindhoven, Groningen, Rotterdam 12 Scheveningen
division: 6 Twente 7 Drenthe, Limburg, Utrecht, Zeeland 9 Friesland, Groningen 10 Gelderland, Overijssel 12 North Brabant, North Holland, South Holland 19 Netherlands Antilles
government:
  legislature: 4 Raad 11 Eerste Kamer, Tweede Kamer
head of state: 5 queen
measure: 2 el 3 aam, ahm, ell, kan, vat 4 duim, mijl, rood, rope 5 anker, roede, wisse 6 bunder, legger, maatje, mutsje, streep 7 schepel 8 mimgelen, steekkan
monetary unit: 4 doit, oord, raps 5 crown, daler, rider, ryder 6 florin, gulden, stiver, suskin 7 daalder, ducaton, escalan, escalin, guilder, stooter, stuiver 8 albertin, ducatoon 9 dubbeltje 12 rijksdaalder 13 albertustaler
weight: 3 ons 4 last, pond 5 bahar 6 korrel 7 wichtje
island: 5 Texel 7 Ameland, Frisian 8 Antilles, Vlieland
lake: 7 Haarlem 10 Ijsselmeer 11 Grevelingen, Havingvliet
highest point: 11 Vaalserberg
river: 3 Eem, Lek 4 Leck, Maas, Waal, Ysel 5 Donge, Hunse, Meuse, Rhine, Schie, Yssel 6 Dintel, Dommel, Ijssel, Kromme 7 Scheldt
sea: 5 North
physical feature:
  canal: 6 Oranje 7 Juliana, Merwede 8 Drentsch, North Sea 10 Wilhelmina 11 New Waterway
  former bay: 9 Zuider Zee
  port: 9 Europoort
people: 5 Dutch 7 Frisian 9 Hollander 10 Surinamese 12 Netherlander 13 South Moluccan
  artist: 4 Eyck, Hals 5 Appel, Bosch 7 Van Gogh, Vermeer 8 Mondrian, Ruisdael 9 Rembrandt
  author: 6 Vondel 7 Erasmus, Grotius, Spinoza 8 Vestdijk 9 Anne Frank
  explorer: 6 Tasman
  king: 7 William
  queen: 7 Beatrix, Juliana 10 Wilhelmina
  ruler: 5 Spain 13 House of Orange 15 Holy Roman Empire
  scientist: 7 Huygens 11 Leeuwenhoek
language: 5 Dutch 7 English, Frisian
religion: 13 Dutch Reformed, Protestantism 16 Roman Catholicism
place:
  airport: 8 Schiphol
  bird sanctuary: 9 Waddenzee
  miniature town: 9 Madurodam
  museum: 9 Frans Hals, Stedelijk 11 Mauritshuis, Rijksmuseum 14 Vincent Van Gogh 19 Boymans-van Beuningen
  seat of government: 7 Den Haag 8 The Hague 11 'sGravenhage
  tower: 14 Schreierstoren
feature:
  cheese market: 9 kaasmarkt
  earth mounds: 6 terpen
  flower: 5 tulip
  flower parade: 12 Bloemencorso
  pottery: 5 Delft
  reclaimed land: 6 polder
  wooden shoes: 7 klompen
food:
  cheese: 4 Edam 5 Gouda 6 Leyden 7 cottage
  dish: 10 nasi goreng, rijsttafel
  drink: 3 gin 8 anisette, schnapps
  pea soup: 10 erwtensoep

CA) 17 von Sternberg House (Northridge CA) 22 Orange County Courthouse (Santa Ana CA)

neutral 4 mean 5 aloof 6 medium, middle, normal, remote 7 average 8 pacifist, peaceful, unbiased 9 impartial, in-between, peaceable, withdrawn 10 achromatic, indefinite, of two minds, unaffected, uninvolved 11 half-and-half, indifferent, nonpartisan, unconcerned 12 fence sitting, intermediate, noncombatant 13 disinterested, dispassionate 14 nonbelligerent, noninterfering 16 nonparticipating 18 noninterventionist

neutralize 4 halt, stop 5 annul, block, check 6 cancel, defeat, impede, negate, offset, stymie 7 balance, disable, nullify, prevent 8 overcome, suppress 9 frustrate, overpower

Nevada
abbreviation: 2 NV **3** Nev
nickname: 6 Silver **9** Sagebrush
capital: 10 Carson City
largest city: 8 Las Vegas
others: 3 Ely, Nye **4** Elko, Reno **6** Fallon, Nellis, Sparks, Storey, Washoe **7** Boulder, Gerlach **9** Hawthorne, Henderson **11** Weed Heights **12** Virginia City
explorer: 7 Fremont **13** Jedediah Smith
feature: 12 Comstock Lode
 dam: **5** Davis **6** Hoover
 hot springs: **4** Tule **9** Punch Bowl, Steam Boat
 national monument: **11** Death Valley
tribe: 5 Modoc, Washo **6** Digger, Mohave, Paiute **7** Klamath **8** Achomawi, Atsugewi, Shoshone
lake: 4 Mead, Ruby **5** Tahoe, Weber **6** Mohave, Walker **7** Pyramid **8** Lahontan, Rye Patch **9** Wild Horse
land rank: 7 seventh
mountain: 4 East, Pine, Ruby **5** White **7** Rockies, Toiyabe, Wasatch **13** Sierra Nevadas
 highest point: **12** Boundary Peak
physical feature: 7 geysers **10** hot springs
 basin: **5** Great
 cave: **6** Gypsum
 desert: **7** Sonoran
 plateau: **8** Columbia
river: 5 Reese **6** Carson, Walker **7** Truckee **8** Colorado, Humboldt
state admission: 11 thirty-sixth
state bird: 7 sagehen **16** mountain bluebird
state flower: 9 sagebrush
state motto: 16 All for Our Country
state song: 15 Home Means Nevada
state tree: 9 pinon pine **15** single-leaf pinon

---

10 counteract **12** counterpoise, incapacitate **14** counterbalance

neutralizer 7 blocker **9** nullifier **12** counteractor, counteragent **15** counterbalancer

Neuvillette, Christian de
character in: **16** Cyrano de Bergerac
author: **7** Rostand

Nevada *see box*

never 4 ne'er **7** not ever **8** at no time, not at all

never-ending 6 steady **7** abiding, eternal, lasting, nonstop **8** constant, enduring, immortal, infinite, repeated, unbroken **9** ceaseless, continual, incessant, perennial, perpetual,

recurring, unceasing **10** continuous, persistent, relentless **11** everlasting, unremitting **12** interminable, undiminished **13** uninterrupted

never-failing 4 firm, sure **6** proven, trusty **7** abiding **8** enduring, reliable **9** steadfast **10** dependable **11** trustworthy, undeviating, unfaltering **12** unhesitating, tried-and-true

nevermore 6 no more **10** never again

Never on Sunday
director: **11** Jules Dassin
cast: **11** Jules Dassin, Titos Vandis **14** Georges Foundas, Melina Mercouri
setting: **6** Greece

nevertheless 3 but, yet **6** anyhow, anyway, even so, though **7** however **8** after all, although **10** contrarily, in any event, regardless **12** contrariwise **15** notwithstanding

Neville, Constance
character in: **18** She Stoops to Conquer
author: **9** Goldsmith

new 4 late **5** fixed, fresh, green, novel **6** modern, reborn, recent, remote, unused **7** altered, changed, current, just out, rebuilt, resumed, untried **8** original, reopened, repaired, restored, up-to-date **9** recreated, refreshed, remodeled, renovated, uncharted, unessayed, untouched **10** revivified, unexplored, unfamiliar, ungathered, unseasoned, unventured **11** regenerated, uncollected, unexercised **12** unaccustomed **13** reconstructed, reinvigorated

New Atlantis
author: **12** Francis Bacon

New Brunswick *see box*

New Centurions, The
author: **14** Joseph Wambaugh

newcomer 4 tyro **5** alien **6** novice **7** entrant **8** intruder, neophyte, outsider, stranger **9** foreigner, immigrant, outlander **10** interloper, trespasser

Newcomes, The
author: **25** William Makepeace Thackeray

New Deal Agency 3 AAA, CCC, CWA, FCA, FHA, FSA, NRA, NYA, PWA, REA, SEC, SSB, TVA, WPA **4** FCIC, FDIC, FERA, HOLC, NLRD, USHA

New Brunswick
abbreviation: 2 NB
bay: 5 Fundy, Maces **7** Shepody **9** Chignecto, Miramichi **13** Passamaquoddy
channel: 5 Minas **10** Grand Manan
city: 7 Moncton **8** Bathurst **9** Riverview **10** Edmundston, Saint John **11** Fredericton
island: 4 Deer **6** Miscou **7** Machias **10** Campobello, Grand Manan
known as: 16 Atlantic province, maritime province
lake: 5 Grand **8** Oromocto **12** Magaguadavic **14** Chiputneticook
people: 5 Irish **6** French **7** Acadian, English **8** American, Scottish **9** Algonkian **10** Anglo Saxon
religion: 6 Canaan **7** Baptist **8** Anglican **10** Protestant **12** Presbyterian, United Church **13** Roman Catholic
river: 5 Cains, Green **6** Renous, Salmon **7** Tobique **8** Kedgwick, Nashwak, Oromocto **9** Miramichi, Patapedia, Saint John **10** Nepisiguit, Richibucto, Saint Croix **11** Petitcodiac, Restigouche, Upsalguitch **12** Kennebecasis

New Delhi
capital of: 5 India
designed by: 7 Lutyens
earlier city: 5 Dilli
8 Dhillika, Din Panah,
Kilookai **9** Firozabad
11 Tughlukabad **12** Indraprastha **13** Shah
Jahanabad
invader: 5 Timur **6** Abdali **7** British, Rohilas
8 Marathas **9** Nadir
Shah
landmark: 7 Red Fort
9 India Gate, Qutb
Minar **10** Iron Pillar,
Jama Masjid **12** Humayun's Tomb **14** Connaught Place
15 Rajghat Memorial
17 Rashtrapati Bhavan
(Presidential Palace)
23 Jantar Mantar Observatory **30** Gandhi
National Museum and
Library
river: 6 Yamuna
street: 7 Raj Path
(Kingsway)
university: 15 Jawaharlal
Nehru

New England
capital: 6 Boston **7** Augusta, Concord **8** Hartford **10** Montpelier, Providence
city: 4 Lynn **5** Barre **6** Bangor, Lowell, Nashua **7** Hyannis,
Rutland, Warwick **8** Brockton, Cranston, Lawrence, Lewiston, New Haven, Portland, Stamford **9** Cambridge, Fall
River, New London, Pawtucket, Waterbury, Worcester
10 Bridgeport, Burlington, Manchester, Pittsfield, Portsmouth, Woonsocket **11** Brattleboro, Springfield
football team: 8 Patriots
Indians: 6 Abnaki, Pequot **7** Mahican, Mohegan, Niantic,
Nipmuck, Wangunk **8** Algonkin, Iroquois **9** Algonquin,
Pennacook **10** Quinnipiac **12** Narragansett
lake: 6 Sebago, Tiogue **7** Sunapee **9** Champlain, Moosehead **10** Candlewood **11** Pemaduncook **13** Winnipesaukee
mountain: 5 Green, White **8** Greylock, Katahdin **9** Berkshire, Mansfield **10** Washington **11** Appalachian
river: 5 Otter **6** Thames **7** Charles **8** Kennebec, Pawtucket,
Winooski **9** Merrimack, Missiquoi, Naugatuck, Pawcatuck,
Penobscot, Saint John **10** Housatonic, Providence, Quinnipiac **11** Connecticut **12** Androscoggin
state: 5 Maine **7** Vermont **11** Connecticut, Rhode Island
12 New Hampshire **13** Massachusetts

New England *see box*

newfangled 5 novel **6** modern,
modish **7** stylish

new-fashioned 6 modern,
modish **7** stylish
8 up-to-date

Newfoundland
abbreviation: 4 Nfld
capital: 10 Saint Johns
city: 19 Happy Valley Goose
Bay
lake: 7 Jeddore, Melville
8 Meelpaeg
10 Michikamau
mountain: 9 Long Range
river: 5 Eagle **6** Fraser, Gander **8** Exploits, Naskaupi
9 Churchill
section: 8 Labrador

New Granada *see*
8 Colombia

New Guinea *see box*

New Hampshire *see box,*
p. 672

Newhart
character: 4 Dick **6** Joanna
7 Michael **9** Stephanie
cast: 9 Mary Frann **10** Bob
Newhart, Julia Duffy **12** Peter Scolari

New Guinea
other name: 14 Papua New Guinea
capital/largest city: 11 Port Moresby
others: 3 Lae, Wau **4** Daru **5** Soron, Wewak **6** Aitape, Kikori, Medang, Rabaul **7** Gorolka, Kitbadi
division:
eastern half of island: **9** Indonesia, Irian Jaya
western half of island: **14** Papua New Guinea
government: 22 constitutional monarchy
head of state: 14 British monarch **15** governor-general
monetary unit: 4 kina, toea
island: 3 Aru **4** Aroe, Buka **5** Arroe, Ceram, Japen, Jobie,
Manus **6** Cretin, Mussau, Ninigo, Waigeu **7** Sainson, Solomon **8** Bismarck, Kiriwina, Schouten, Woodlark **9** Admiralty, Trobriant **10** Louisiande, New Britain, New Ireland
12 Bougainville **14** D'Entrecasteaux
mountain: 4 Snow **6** Orange **8** Bismarck, Victoria **9** Carstensz **11** Owen Stanley **12** Albert Edward
highest point:
Irian Jaya: **9** Carstensz **10** Puncak Jaya
Papua New Guinea: **7** Wilhelm
river: 4 Fly, Hamu, Hany, Ramu **5** Degul, Sepik **6** Kikori,
Purari **7** Amberno, Markham
sea: 5 Ceram, Coral, Sepik **6** Indian **7** Arafura, Pacific, Solomon **8** Bismarck
physical feature:
bay: **3** Oro **5** Milne **8** Geelvink
gulf: **4** Huon **5** Papua
strait: **6** Torres, Vitiaz
people: 5 Pygmy **6** Papuan **7** Negrito **10** Melanesian
explorer: **15** Jorge de Menesses
ruler: **7** Germany **9** Australia **12** Great Britain
language: 4 Motu **7** English **16** Melanesian Pidjin
religion: 7 animism **10** Protestant **13** Roman Catholic
feature:
bird: **7** mudlark **9** cassowary
food:
dried coconut meat: **5** copra

Newhart, Bob
born: 9 Chicago IL
roles: 7 Newhart **10** Cold
Turkey **17** The Bob Newhart
Show

New Hebrides *see*
7 Vanuatu

New Jersey *see box,*
p. 672

New Hampshire
abbreviation: 2 NH
nickname: 7 Granite
capital: 7 Concord
largest city: 10 Manchester
others: 5 Dover, Keene 6 Berlin, Durham, Exeter, Nashua 7 Hanover, Laconia 8 Sandwich
9 Claremont, Rochester 10 Portsmouth 12 Bretton Woods
college: 5 Keene 6 Rivier 9 Dartmouth, St Anselms 10 New England
feature: 14 Great Stone Face
  notch: 7 Kinsman, Pinkham 8 Crawford 9 Franconia
tribe: 6 Abnaki 9 Pennacook
people: 11 Robert Frost 12 Daniel French 13 Daniel Webster, Horace Greeley, Mary Baker
Eddy
  explorer: 9 Champlain 16 Captain John Smith
island: 4 Star 5 White 6 Shoals 7 Lunging
lake: 5 Squam 7 Ossipee, Sunapee, Umbagog 8 Newfound 10 Winnisquam 13 Winnipesaukee
land rank: 11 forty-fourth
mountain: 5 Flume, White 6 Moriah, Paugus 7 Waumbek 8 Chocorua, Sandwich 9 Franconia,
Monadnock 11 Profile Peak 12 Presidential
  highest point: 10 Washington
physical feature:
  bay: 5 Great
president: 14 Franklin Pierce
river: 4 Saco 6 Israel 7 Bellamy 8 Souhegan 9 Merrimack 10 Piscataqua 11 Connecticut,
Salmon Falls 12 Androscoggin
state admission: 5 ninth
state bird: 11 purple finch
state flower: 11 purple lilac
state motto: 13 Live Free Or Die
state song: 15 Old New Hampshire 26 New Hampshire My New Hampshire
state tree: 10 paper birch, white birch

New Jersey
abbreviation: 2 NJ
nickname: 6 Garden 8 Mosquito
capital: 7 Trenton
largest city: 6 Newark
others: 4 Lodi 5 Ewing, Ft Lee 6 Camden, Dumont, Haddon, Kearny, Linden, Nutley, Orange,
Rahway, Totowa 7 Bayonne, Cape May, Clifton, Hoboken, Hohokus, Keyport, Madison, Mat-
awan, Netcong, Oradell, Paramus, Passaic, Raritan, Teaneck, Tenafly, Wyckoff 8 Carteret,
Cranford, Freehold, Garfield, Hillside, Metuchen, Paterson, Secaucus, Watchung 9 Bridgeton,
Elizabeth, Englewood, Hawthorne, Irvington, Maplewood, Montclair, Ocean City, Princeton
10 Asbury Park, Belleville, Ft Monmouth, Hackensack, Jersey City, Livingston, Long Branch,
Morristown, Perth Amboy 11 Bergenfield 12 Atlantic City, Collingswood, New Brunswick
colleges: 4 Drew 6 Upsala 7 Rutgers 8 Caldwell, Monmouth, St Peter's 9 Princeton, Seton
Hall 10 Bloomfield 18 Fairleigh-Dickinson
feature: 9 Boardwalk 16 Delaware Water Gap
tribe: 8 Delaware 11 Lenni-Lanape
people: 9 Aaron Burr 11 Joyce Kilmer, Paul Robeson 12 Stephen Crane, Thomas Edison
13 James Lawrence 19 James Fenimore Cooper
  explorer: 6 Hudson 9 Verrazano
lake: 6 Mohawk 9 Greenwood, Hopatcong
land rank: 10 forty-sixth
mountain: 8 Piedmont 10 Kittatinny 13 First Watchung 14 Second Watchung
  highest point: 9 High Point
physical feature: 9 Palisades, Sandy Hook
  bay: 8 Delaware
  cape: 3 May
  sea: 8 Atlantic
president: 15 Grover Cleveland
river: 4 Toms 6 Dennis, Haynes, Hudson, Mantua, Ramapo 7 Mullica, Passaic, Raritan 8 Co-
hansey, Delaware, Tuckahoe 10 Hackensack
state admission: 5 third
state bird: 16 eastern goldfinch
state flower: 6 violet
state motto: 20 Liberty and Prosperity
state tree: 6 red oak
basketball team: 4 Nets
football team: 8 Generals
hockey team: 6 Devils

New Mexico
  abbreviation: **2** NM **4** N Mex
  nickname: **8** Sunshine **17** Land of Enchantment
  capital: **7** Santa Fe
  largest city: **11** Albuquerque
  others: **3** Jal **4** Taos **5** Aztec, Belen, Hobbs, Raton **6** Clovis, Deming, Gallup, Grants **7** Artesia, Bananea, Roswell, Socorro, Torreon **8** Carlsbad **9** Las Cruces, Los Alamos **10** Alamogordo **13** Piedras Negras
  college: **7** Sante Fe **11** Albuquerque
  feature: **11** Four Corners
    dam: **5** Butte **8** Elephant
    labs: **6** Sandia **17** Los Alamos National
    national monument: **10** Aztec Ruins, White Sands **11** Chaco Canyon **17** Gila Cliff Dwelling
    national park: **15** Carlsbad Caverns
    observatory: **14** Sacramento Peak
  tribe: **3** Sia **4** Hano, Piro, Tano, Taos, Tewa, Tiwa, Zuni **5** Acoma, Jemez, Kares, Manso, Pecos, Tiqua, Tonoa **6** Apache, Isleta, Laguna, Navaho, Navajo, Pueblo **7** Anasazi, Picuris **8** Santa Ana **9** Mescalero **12** Santo Domingo
  people: **9** Kit Carson, Peter Hurd **11** Bill Mauldin
    explorer: **5** Onate **6** de Niza, de Vaca **8** Coronado
  lake: **6** El Vado, Navajo, Sumner **7** Conchas **8** McMillan **10** Alamogordo **13** Elephant Butte
  land rank: **5** fifth
  mountain: **5** Jemez **6** Sandia **7** Manzano, Mimbres, Rockies, Truchas **8** Mogollon **9** Guadalupe, San Andres **10** Nacimiento, Sacramento **11** Mount Taylor **15** Sangre de Christo
    highest point: **11** Wheeler Peak
  physical feature:
    basin: **8** Tularosa
    desert: **15** Jornada de Muerto
    plains: **5** Great
  river: **3** Ute **4** Gila **5** Pecos **7** San Jose, San Juan **8** Canadian **9** Rio Grande
  state admission: **12** forty-seventh
  state bird: **10** roadrunner
  state fish: **14** cutthroat trout
  state flower: **5** yucca
  state motto: **15** It Grows as It Goes
  state song: **14** O Fair New Mexico **16** Asi es Nuevo Mexico
  state tree: **5** pinon **8** tarantah **15** velvet ash pinyon

Malice, The Color of Money **16** Cat on a Hot Tin Roof, The Left-Handed Gun, The Long Hot Summer, The Silver Chalice **29** Butch Cassidy and the Sundance Kid

New Mexico *see box*

New Orleans
  basketball team: Jazz
  event: **9** Mardi Gras, Sugar Bowl **25** International Jazz Festival
  football team: **6** Saints
  landmark: **7** Cabildo **9** Old Square, Superdome **10** Vieux Carre **12** Pirate's Alley **13** French Quarter
  noted for: **4** jazz
  people: **5** Cajun **6** Creole **7** Acadian
  river: **11** Mississippi
  street: **5** Royal **7** Bourbon
  university: **6** Loyola, Tulane

news 4 dirt, dope, talk, word **5** flash, libel, piece, rumor, story **6** babble, expose, gossip, report **7** account, article, chatter, hearsay, lowdown, mention, message, release, scandal, slander, tidings **8** bulletin, dispatch, exposure **9** statement **10** communique, disclosure, divulgence, revelation **11** information **12** announcement, intelligence

news account 4 item **5** story **6** report **7** release **8** bulletin, dispatch **10** communique

newsmonger 6 gossip **8** busybody, reporter

News of the Day
  also: **12** Neues vom Tage
  opera by: **9** Hindemith
  character: **5** Laura **12** Eduoard

Newsome, Chadwick
  character in: **14** The Ambassadors
  author: **5** James

New Spain *see* **6** Mexico

newspaper 3 rag **5** daily, paper, sheet **6** herald, weekly **7** courant, gazette, journal, tabloid, tribune **10** periodical **11** publication

New Testament
  books of: **4** Acts, John, Jude, Luke, Mark **5** James, Peter, Titus **6** Romans **7** Hebrews, Matthew, Timothy **8** Philemon **9** Ephesians, Galatians **10** Colossians, Revelation **11** Corinthians, Philippians **13** Thessalonians
  books: **12** Humologumena

Newton, Isaac
  field: **11** mathematics
  nationality: **7** British

Newley, Anthony
  wife: **11** Joan Collins
  born: **6** London **7** England
  roles: **11** Oliver Twist **25** Stop the World I Want to Get Off **41** The Roar of the Greasepaint The Smell of the Crowd

newly 4 anew **6** afresh, lately, of late **7** freshly, just now **8** recently

newly rich person
  French: **12** nouveau riche

Newlywed Game, The
  host: **10** Bob Eubanks
  executive producer: **11** Chuck Barris

Newlyweds, The
  creator: **13** George McManus
  character: **12** Baby Snookums

Newman, Barnett
  born: **9** New York NY
  artwork: **7** Abraham, The Wild **8** Onement I **18** Stations of the Cross **19** Vir Heroicus Sublimis

Newman, Christopher
  character in: **11** The American
  author: **5** James

Newman, John Henry (Cardinal)
  author of: **18** Apologia pro Vita Sua

Newman, Paul
  wife: **14** Joanne Woodward
  born: **11** Cleveland OH
  roles: **3** Hud **6** Harper, Picnic **8** The Sting **10** The Hustler, The Verdict **12** Cool Hand Luke **15** Absence of

Newt- Salamander

New York
  abbreviation: 2 NY
  nickname: 6 Empire **9** Excelsior
  capital: 6 Albany
  largest city: 7 New York
  others: 3 Rye **4** Rome, Troy **5** Ilion, Islip, Nyack, Olean, Owego, Utica **6** Attica, Auburn, Cohoes, Elmira, Goshen, Ithaca, Oneida, Oswego, Tappan **7** Ardsley, Babylon, Batavia, Buffalo, Congers, Endwell, Geneseo, Hewlett, Mahopac, Merrick, Messena, Mineola, Montauk, Oneonta, Pennyan, Suffern, Syosset, Wantagh, Yaphank, Yonkers **8** Bethpage, Catskill, Endicott, Herkimer, Kingston, Ossining, Pottsdam, Saratoga, Tuckahoe **9** Rochester, Scarsdale **10** Binghamton, Bronxville, Mamaroneck **11** Cooperstown, New Rochelle, Schenectady, White Plains **12** Poughkeepsie
  college: 4 Bard, CUNY, Iona, Pace, SUNY **5** Finch, Keuka **6** Hobart, Hunter, Vassar **7** Adelphi, Barnard, Colgate, Cornell, Fordham, St John's **8** Columbia, Skidmore, Syracuse **9** Juilliard, Rochester, West Point **13** Sarah Lawrence **30** Rensselaer Polytechnic Institute
  feature:
    building: 11 Empire State
    hall of fame: 8 baseball
    park: 7 Central
    prison: 6 Attica **8** SingSing
    square: 5 Times **6** Herald
    statue: 7 Liberty
    street/avenue: 4 Park, Wall **5** Fifth **7** Madison **8** Broadway
    tomb: 6 Grant's
  tribe: 4 Erie **6** Cayuga, Mohawk, Oneida, Seneca **7** Mohican, Montauk **8** Iroquois, Onondaga **9** Manhattan, **people: 7** John Jay **8** Walloons **9** Jonas Salk **10** Henry James **11** Rockefeller, Walt Whitman **12** Eugene O'Neill **13** DeWitt Clinton, John Burroughs **14** Herman Melville **15** Peter Stuyvesant **16** Eleanor Roosevelt, Washington Irving **17** Fiorello La Guardia
    explorer: 6 Hudson **9** Champlain, Verrazano **16** Dutch West India Co
  island: 4 Fire, Long **5** Ellis **6** Staten **7** Bedloe's, Fisher's, Liberty, Shelter, Welfare **8** Thousand **9** Governors, Manhattan
  lake: 4 Erie **6** Cayuga, Finger, George, Oneida, Otisco, Otsego, Owasco, Placid, Seneca **7** Conesus, Ontario, Saranac, Schroon **8** Saratoga **9** Champlain
  land rank: 9 thirtieth
  mountain: 4 Bear **5** Slide **7** Taconic **9** Catskills **11** Adirondacks
    highest point: 5 Marcy
  physical feature:
    bay: 7 Jamaica, Peconic **8** Moriches
    canal: 4 Erie **7** Gowanus
    falls: 7 Niagara
    valley: 6 Mohawk
  president: 14 Martin Van Buren **14** Teddy Roosevelt **15** Millard Fillmore **17** Theodore Roosevelt **23** Franklin Delano Roosevelt
  river: 4 East **5** Black, Tioga **6** Harlem, Hoosic, Hudson, Mohawk, Oswego **7** Ausable, Genesee, Niagara **10** St Lawrence **11** Susquehanna
  state bird: 8 bluebird
  state fish: 10 brook trout
  state flower: 4 rose
  state motto: 9 Excelsior (Ever upward, Still higher)
  state tree: 10 sugar maple

discovered laws of: 6 motion **7** gravity **8** calculus
discovered: 13 color spectrum **15** binomial theorem **16** method of fluxions
invented: 21 infinitesimal calculus

New York *see box*

New York City *see box*

New Zealand *see box, p. 676*

next-door 8 adjacent **9** adjoining **10** connecting, contiguous, juxtaposed, side-by-side, **12** conterminous

next to 6 beside **8** abutting, adjacent **9** adjoining, bordering **10** contiguous, juxtaposed **12** conterminous

next world, the 6 Heaven **8** eternity, paradise **12** the hereafter **14** the world to come

Nez Perce (Numipu)
  language family:
    10 Shahaptian
  location: 5 Idaho **6** Oregon **10** Washington
  leader: 11 Chief Joseph

Niamey
  capital of: 5 Niger

nib 3 end, tip, top **4** apex, peak **5** point **6** height, tiptop, vertex **7** extreme **8** pinnacle **9** extremity

nibble 3 nip **4** bite, chew, gnaw, peck **5** crumb, munch, speck, taste **6** crunch, morsel, peck at, tidbit **8** fragment, particle

Nibelung, ring of
  origin: 8 Germanic
  mentioned in:
    14 Nibelungenlied
  stolen by: 8 Alberich

Nibelungenlied
  origin: 8 Germanic
  form: 4 epic

New York City

airport: 3 JFK 6 Newark 9 La Guardia 12 John F Kennedy
area: 4 Soho 6 Harlem 7 Chelsea, Midtown, Tribeca 9 Chinatown, Manhattan 10 Stuyvesant 11 Brownsville, Little Italy 13 Spanish Harlem 16 Greenwich Village 17 Bedford-Stuyvesant
baseball team: 4 Mets 7 Yankees
basketball team: 6 Knicks 14 Knickerbockers
borough: 5 Bronx 6 Queens 8 Brooklyn, Richmond 9 Manhattan
early governor: 10 Stuyvesant
football team: 4 Jets 6 Giants
former name: 12 New Amsterdam
hockey team: 7 Rangers 9 Islanders
island: 4 City, Long 5 Ellis, Ward's 6 Riker's, Staten 7 Liberty 8 Randall's 9 Governor's, Manhattan, Roosevelt
landmark: 5 Macy's 8 Bronx Zoo 11 Battery Park, Central Park, Penn Station, Shea Stadium, Times Square 12 Carnegie Hall 13 Gracie Mansion, Lincoln Center, Port Authority, Trinity Church, United Nations, Yankee Stadium 14 Waldorf-Astoria 15 NY Public Library, NY Stock Exchange, Seagram Building, Statue of Liberty 16 Bellevue Hospital, Chrysler Building, World Trade Center 17 Hayden Planetarium, Rockefeller Center, Woolworth Building 18 Radio City Music Hall 19 Empire State Building, Grand Central Station, Madison Square Garden, St Patrick's Cathedral 22 Metropolitan Opera House 26 Sloan-Kettering Cancer Center 29 Cathedral of Saint John the Divine
mayor: 4 Koch 6 Walker 9 La Guardia
museum: 6 Jewish 7 Whitney 9 Cloisters 10 Guggenheim 12 Cooper-Hewitt, Metropolitan 15 Frick Collection 17 Museum of Modern Art (MOMA) 30 American Museum of Natural History
river: 4 East 6 Harlem, Hudson
street: 6 Bowery 8 Broadway 9 Lexington 10 Park Avenue, Wall Street 11 Central Park, Fifth Avenue, Sutton Place 13 Madison Avenue 17 Forty-Second Street
university: 3 NYU 6 Queens 7 Barnard, Fordham, Yeshiva 8 Brooklyn, Columbia 13 Hunter College 22 Juilliard School of Music 23 City University of New York

date written: 17 thirteenth century
related to: 8 Volsunga
author: 7 unknown
character: 5 Etzel (Attila), Hagen 6 Gernot 7 Gunther 8 Brunhild, Dankwart, Giselher 9 Kriemhild, Siegfried

Nibelungs, Niblungs
origin: 8 Germanic, Teutonic
followers of: 9 Siegfried
race: 6 dwarfs
possessed: 8 treasure
captured by: 9 Siegfried
family of: 7 Gunther

Nicaragua see box, p. 677

nice 4 deft, fine, good, kind 5 dandy, exact, fussy, great, swell 6 divine, genial, lovely, proper, seemly, strict, subtle 7 amiable, amusing, careful, cordial, correct, finicky, genteel, likable, precise, refined, winning 8 accurate, charming, cheerful, delicate, friendly, gracious, jim-dandy, ladylike, pleasant, pleasing, rigorous, skillful, unerring, virtuous, well-bred 9 agreeable, congenial, excellent, fantastic, marvelous, sensitive, wonderful 10 attractive, delightful, enchanting, entrancing, fastidious, methodical, meticulous, scrupulous 11 interesting, painstaking, pleasurable, punctilious, respectable, sympathetic, warmhearted 13 compassionate, understanding, well brought up 17 overconscientious

Nice and the Good, The
author: 11 Iris Murdoch

nicely 6 neatly 7 exactly, fussily, happily 9 carefully, precisely 10 accurately, critically, pleasantly, unerringly 11 faultlessly, fortunately, opportunely 12 attractively, fastidiously

nicety 4 care, tact 5 flair, grace 6 acumen, polish 7 culture, finesse, insight 8 accuracy, delicacy, elegance,

subtlety 9 attention, exactness, precision 10 refinement 11 cultivation, penetration, preciseness, sensitivity 12 perspicacity, subtle detail; tastefulness 13 elaborateness, particularity 14 discrimination, fastidiousness, meticulousness

niche 4 cove, nook, slot 5 berth, trade 6 alcove, cavity, corner, cranny, dugout, hollow, metier, recess 7 calling 8 position, vocation 9 cubbyhole 10 depression, pigeonhole 11 proper place 13 hole in the wall

Nicholas Nickleby
author: 14 Charles Dickens
character: 5 Smike 11 Arthur Gride, Newman Noggs 12 Kate Nickleby, Madeline Bray 13 Lord Verisopht, Ralph Nickleby 14 Frank Cheeryble 15 Sir Mulberry Hawk, Vincent Crummles, Wackford Squeers 17 Cheeryble Brothers

Nichols, Mike
director of: 7 Catch-22 11 The Graduate (Oscar) 15 Carnal Knowledge 25 Who's Afraid of Virginia Woolf?

Nicholson, Ben
born: 6 Denham 7 England
artwork: 9 Fireworks 11 White Relief 12 Tuscan Relief 13 Painted Relief 14 At the Chat Botte

Nicholson, Jack
born: 9 Neptune NJ
roles: 8 Ironweed 9 Chinatown, Easy Rider 10 The Shining 12 Prizzi's Honor, The Passenger 13 The Last Detail 14 Five Easy Pieces 15 Carnal Knowledge 17 Terms of Endearment 20 The Witches of Eastwick 22 The King of Marvin Gardens 25 One Flew Over the Cuckoo's Nest (Oscar) 26 The Postman Always Rings Twice

nicht wahr? 10 isn't that so?

Nicippe
father: 6 Pelops
son: 10 Eurystheus

nick 3 cut, jag, mar 4 chip, dent, gash, mark, scar 5 cleft, gouge, notch, score, wound 6 damage, deface, indent, injure, injury 7 marking, scarify, scoring, scratch 8 incision, lacerate 10 depression 11 indentation

nickel
chemical symbol: 2 Ni

New Zealand
  other name: 8 Aotearoa 12 Nieuw Zeeland 23 Land of the Long White Cloud
  capital: 10 Wellington
  largest city: 8 Auckland
  others: 5 Leuin, Oreti, Otaki, Taupo 6 Clutha, Foxton, Oamaru, Picton, Timaru 7 Dunedin,
    Manu Kau, Raetihi, Rotorua 8 Hamilton, Kawakawa, Touranga 9 Lyttelton 10 Queenstown
    12 Christchurch, Invercargill, Port Chalmers 13 Port Nicholson 14 Napier-Hastings 15 Pal-
    merston North
  school: 5 Otago 6 Massey 7 Waikato 8 Auckland, Victoria 10 Canterbury
  division: 11 North Island, South Island
  head of state: 14 British monarch 15 governor general
  monetary unit: 4 cent 6 dollar
  island: 4 Cook, Niue, Otea 5 North, South 6 Bounty, Chatam, Snares 7 Stewart, Tokelau
    8 Auckland, Campbell, Kermadec, Puketutu 9 Antipodes 10 Resolution, Three Kings 12 Great
    Barrier
  lake: 3 Ada 4 Gunn, Ohau 5 Hawea, Taupo 6 Pukaki, Pupuke, Te Anau, Tekapo, Wanaka
    7 Brunner, Diamond, Kanieri, Okareka, Rotorua 8 Okataina, Paradise, Rotoaira, Wakatipu
    9 Manapouri
  mountain: 4 Eden, Flat, Owen 5 Allen, Chope, Lyall, Mitre, Ohope, Otari, Young 6 Egmont,
    Stokes, Tasman 7 Cameron, Coronet, Ernslaw, Huiarau, Pihanga, Ruahine, Ruapehu, Tau-
    hera, Tutamoe, Tyndall 8 Aspiring, Richmond, Tauranga 9 Messenger, Murchison, Ngauru-
    hoe, Raukumara, Tongariro 11 Remarkables 12 Southern Alps
  highest point: 4 Cook 7 Aorangi
  river: 4 Avon 5 Mokau, Waipa 6 Clutha, Rakaia, Tamaki, Waihou, Wairau, Wairoa 7 Waikato,
    Waitaki 8 Clarence, Manawatu, Wanganui 10 Rangitikei
  sea: 6 Tasman 12 South Pacific
  physical feature:
    bay: 4 Ohua 5 Evans, Hawke, Lyall 6 Awarua, Cloudy, Golden, Plenty, Tasman 7 Fitzroy,
      Pegasus, Poverty 8 Halfmoon, Rangaunu
    bight: 7 Karamea 10 Canterbury 13 North Taranaki, South Taranaki
    cape: 4 East, West 5 North 6 Egmont 8 Farewell, Foulwind, Palliser 9 Southwest
    channel: 8 Colville
    falls: 10 Sutherland
    glacier: 3 Fox 6 Tasman 11 Franz Joseph
    gulf: 7 Hauraki
    harbor: 7 Kaipara, Manukau 9 Waitemata
    peninsula: 5 Mahia, Otago
    plains: 10 Canterbury
    sound: 8 Doubtful
    strait: 4 Cook 7 Foveaux
  people: 3 Ati 5 Arawa, Dutch, Maori 7 British, Ringatu 10 Polynesian
    author: 5 Frame 9 Mansfield 10 Ngaio Marsh 12 Ashton-Warner
    explorer: 4 Cook 6 Tasman
    mountain climber: 7 Hillary
  language: 5 Maori 7 English
  religion: 8 Anglican 9 Methodist 10 Protestant 12 Presbyterian 13 Roman Catholic
  place:
    national park: 9 Fiordland, Fjordland, Tongariro
  feature:
    animal: 7 tuatara
    bird: 3 kea, tui 4 kiwi, weka 6 takahe 7 apteryx 8 bellbird
    tree: 4 rimu, tawa 5 kauri, matai 6 totara
  food:
    fish: 4 mako
    fruit: 4 kiwi 9 tamarillo 17 Chinese gooseberry

Nickel Mountain
  author: 11 John Gardner

nickname 6 handle 7 agno-
men, epithet, moniker, pet
name 8 baby name, cogno-
men 9 pseudonym, sobriquet
10 diminutive 11 appellation,
designation

Nicomachean Ethics
  author: 9 Aristotle

Nidhogg
  origin: 12 Scandinavian

  form: 7 serpent
  domain: 8 Niflheim
  gnaws on lowest root of:
    9 Iggdrasil, Yggdrasil

Nielsen, Carl August
  born: 6 Odense 7 Denmark
  composer of: 9 Maskarade
    12 Saul and David 16 Inex-
    tinguishable (symphony No
    4)

Nietzsche, Friedrich
  author of: 14 The Will to
  Power 17 Beyond Good and

  Evil, The Birth of Tragedy
    20 Thus Spake Zarathustra

Niflheim
  origin: 12 Scandinavian
  ruler of: 3 Hel
  purpose: 10 punish dead
  climate: 3 fog 4 cold

nifty 4 chic, fine, neat, posh
5 natty, smart 6 clever, dapper 7 dashing, stylish 8 splendid 10 attractive
11 fashionable

Niger *see box*

Nicaragua
capital/largest city: 7 Managua
others: 4 Leon, Rama 6 Masaya 7 Corinto, Granada 8 Jinotega 9 Matagalpa 10 Bluefields, Chinandega
division: 13 Mosquito Coast
measure: 4 vara 5 cahiz 6 suerte 7 cajuela, manzana 10 cabelleria
monetary unit: 4 peso 7 centavo, cordoba
weight: 3 bag 4 caha, caja 8 tonelada
island: 7 Ometepe
lake: 7 Managua 9 Nicaragua
mountain: 4 Leon 5 Negro, Viejo 6 Madera, Telica 7 Managua, Saslaya 9 Momotombo
highest point: 7 Mogoton
river: 4 Coco, Tuma 5 Wanks 6 Grande, Poteca 7 San Juan 8 Tipitapa 9 Escondido
sea: 7 Pacific 9 Caribbean
physical feature:
  gulf: 7 Fonseca
people: 4 Mico, Mixe, Rama, Smoo, Ulva 5 Cukra, Diria, Lenca, Sambo, Toaca 6 Mangue 7 mestizo, Miskito 8 Mosquito 9 Matagalpa
  author: 5 Dario
  explorer: 6 Davila 7 Cordoba 8 Columbus
  group: 6 Contra 10 Sandinista
  leader: 6 Somoza, Walker, Zelaya 7 Nicardo 8 Chamorro
language: 7 English, Spanish
religion: 13 Roman Catholic
place:
  cathedral: 12 Metropolitan
feature:
  dance: 5 sones 10 zapateados, zarabandas
food:
  beans: 8 frijoles
  dish: 10 naca tamale
  drink: 5 tiste 9 pinolillo
  fruit: 6 zapote

Niger
other name: 6 Joliba, Kworra, Ramtil
capital/largest city: 6 Niamey
others: 5 Goure 6 Agadex, Agadez, Maradi, Tahoua, Zinder
division:
  region: 3 Air 5 Arlit, Sahel
monetary unit: 5 franc 7 centime
lake: 4 Chad
mountain: 7 Bagzane 9 Air Massif
highest point: 7 Greboun
river: 5 Niger 6 Dillia
physical feature:
  desert: 6 Sahara
  oasis: 6 Kaouar
  plateau: 5 Djado 6 Tegama 7 Tchigai 8 Mengueni 11 Adar Doutchi, Djerma Ganda
people: 4 Daza, Idjo, Idyo, Idzo, Peul, Teda 5 Hausa, Warri 6 Djerma, Fulani, Kanuri, Songha, Toubou, Tuareg 13 Djerma-Songhai
  conqueror: 13 Usman Dan Fodio
  leader: 5 Diori 6 Saibou 7 Ousmane 8 Kountche
language: 5 Hausa, Mande 6 Djerma, French, Fulani, Tuareg 8 Mandingo, Tamashek
religion: 5 Islam 7 animism 12 Christianity
place:
  ruins: 6 Agadez
feature:
  cavalry: 5 Dosso
  empire: 4 Mali 6 Fulani 7 Songhai 10 Kanem-Borno
  tree: 6 acacia, baobab

Nigeria *see box, p. 678*

niggard 4 mean 5 cheap, miser, tight 6 stingy 7 miserly 8 scrimper 9 skinflint 10 ungenerous 12 parsimonious

niggardliness 6 penury 8 meanness 9 closeness, parsimony 10 stinginess 11 miserliness 13 penny-pinching 15 tight-fistedness

niggardly 4 mean, poor 5 cheap, close, sorry, tight 6 flimsy, frugal, meager, measly, paltry, saving, scanty, shabby, stingy, tawdry 7 miserly, scrubby, sparing, thrifty 8 beggarly, grubbing, grudging, stinting, wretched 9 illiberal, mercenary, miserable, penurious 10 hardfisted, second-rate, ungenerous 11 closefisted 12 contemptible, insufficient, parsimonious

Nigger of the Narcissus, The
  author: 12 Joseph Conrad
  character: 5 Baker 6 Donkin 9 James Wait 12 Old Singleton

niggling 5 fussy, minor, petty, small 7 finicky 8 caviling, nugatory, picayune, piddling, trifling 9 quibbling 10 negligible, nit-picking 12 pettifogging 13 insignificant 15 inconsequential

nigh 4 near 5 close, handy 6 almost, at hand, nearly 7 close by 8 adjacent 9 bordering 11 neighboring, practically

night 4 dark, dusk 7 bedtime, evening, sundown 8 darkness, eventide 9 murkiness, obscurity 13 tenebrousness
  goddess of: 3 Nox

nightclub
  French: 5 boite 11 boite de nuit

nightfall 4 dark, dusk 6 sunset 7 evening, sundown 8 darkness, eventide, gloaming, moonrise, twilight
  French: 10 crepuscule

Night Gallery
  host: 10 Rod Serling

nightingale
  group of: 5 watch

Nightline
  host: 9 Ted Koppel

nightly 4 dark 7 evening, obscure 9 nocturnal 11 nocturnally

nightmare 7 incubus 8 bad dream, succubus 13 hallucination

Nigeria
capital: 5 Abuja
largest city: 5 Lagos
others: 3 Aba, Ado, Ede, Isa, Iwo, Jos, Oyo 4 Bida, Bidi, Buea, Kano, Offa, Yola 5 Benin, Bonny, Enugu, Warri, Zaria 6 Burutu, Ibadan, Ilesha, Ilorin, Kachia, Kaduna, Kadune, Kokoto, Mushin, Takoba 7 Calabar, Onitsha, Oshogbo 8 Abeokuta 9 Maiduguri, Ogbomosho 12 Port Harcourt
division: 3 Air, Isa, Oyo 4 Kano, Nupe, Ondo 5 Asben, Benin, Bornu, Ijebu, Ogoja, Warri 6 Biafra, Degema, Owerri, Sokoto 7 Adamawa
monetary unit: 4 kobo 5 naira
lake: 4 Chad
highest point: 7 Dimlang
river: 3 Oli 4 Gana, Yobe 5 Benin, Benue, Cross, Niger 6 Kaduna, Sokoto 7 Calabar, Gongola 8 Komadugu 9 Sambreiro
sea: 8 Atlantic
physical feature:
  bight: 5 Benin, Bonny 6 Biafra
  delta: 5 Niger
  gulf: 6 Guinea
  plains: 5 Bornu 9 Hausaland
  plateau: 3 Jos, Udi 6 Bauchi
  port: 5 Lagos 7 Calabar 8 Harcourt
people: 3 Abo, Aro, Djo, Ebo, Edo, Ibo, Ijo, Tiv, Vai 4 Beni, Bini, Eboe, Efik, Egba, Ejam, Ekoi, Idyo, Igbo, Ijaw, Nupe 5 Angas, Benin, Gwari, Hausa 6 Chamba, Fulani, Ibibio, Kanuri, Yoruba 11 Hausa-Fulani
  author: 6 Achebe
  British colonial ruler: 6 Goldie, Lugard
  kingdom: 3 Ife, Nok, Oyo 5 Benin 6 Fulani 10 Kanem-Borno
  leader: 5 Gowon 6 Balewa, Ojukwu, Schick 7 Awolowo, Azikine, Azikiwe, Shagari 8 Obasanjo 9 Babangida 13 Usman dan Fodio
language: 3 Ibo 4 Efik, Igbo 5 Hausa 6 Yoruba 7 English
religion: 5 Islam 7 animism 12 Christianity
place:
  dam: 6 Kainji
  mosque/walled city: 4 Kano
feature:
  dress: 4 riga 7 agbados
  tree: 5 abura, afara 6 obeche 10 terminalia
  war: 7 Biafran

Nile
boat: 5 baris 6 cangia, nuggar, sandal 7 felucca, gaiassa 8 dahabeah
cities: 3 Qus 4 Abri, Argo, Idfu, Isna, Juba, Qina 5 Aswan, Asyut, Cairo, Kokka, Kusti, Luxor, Meroe, Minya, Rejaf, Saite, Tanis, Tanta 6 Atbara, Faiyum 7 Malakel, Mansura, Rosetta 8 Khartoum, Omdurman, Rusayris 9 Was Madani 10 Alexandria
dam: 6 Sannar 9 Aswan High, White Nile
desert bordering: 6 Libyan, Nubian 7 Arabian
falls: 5 Ripon 8 Kabalega 9 Murchison
feature: 6 Sphinx
  pyramid: 4 Giza
  temple: 8 Ramses II 9 Abu Simbel 11 Deir el-Bahri, Medinet Habu
flows into:
  13 Mediterranean
flows through: 5 Egypt, Kenya, Sudan, Zaire 6 Rwanda, Uganda 7 Burundi 8 Ethiopia, Tanzania
island: 4 Roda 6 Philae
lake: 4 Tana 5 Kyoga, Tsana 6 Albert, Edward, Nasser 8 Victoria
other name: 4 Hapi 20 The Father of the Rivers
people: 3 Jur, Luo, Lwo, Nuo, Suk 4 Bari, Beja, Golo, Luoh, Madi 5 Nilot 7 Shilluk
plain: 6 Gezira
plant: 4 sudd 5 lotus
starting point: 5 Tsana 8 Victoria
swamp: 4 Sudd
tributary: 4 Arab 5 Rahad, Sobat 6 Atbara, Ghazai, Kagera 7 Rosetta 8 Blue Nile, Damietta 9 Bahr Jebel, White Nile

Night of the Iguana, The
director: 10 John Huston
based on play by: 17 Tennessee Williams
cast: 7 Sue Lyon 8 Skip Ward 10 Ava Gardner 11 Deborah Kerr 13 Richard Burton
setting: 6 Mexico

nightshade 16 Solanum dulcamara
varieties: 4 ball 5 black 6 common, deadly, sticky 7 Malabar 8 stinking 9 melon-leaf, poisonous, soda-apple 10 enchanter's

Nights of Cabiria
director: 15 Federico Fellini
cast: 13 Amedeo Nazzari 14 Francois Perier 15 Giulietta Masina
remade as: 12 Sweet Charity

nightstick 3 rod 4 mace, wand 5 baton, staff 6 cudgel 7 scepter 8 bludgeon 9 billy club, truncheon 10 shillelagh

nighttime 4 late 5 night 9 latenight, nighttide, nocturnal

Night to Remember, A
director: 8 Roy Baker
based on story by: 10 Walter Lord
cast: 9 Jill Dixon 11 Kenneth More 13 David McCallum 16 Laurence Naismith
setting: 7 Titanic

nihil 7 nothing

nihilism 5 chaos 6 anomie 7 license 9 amorality, anarchism, emptiness, terrorism 10 alienation, iconoclasm, radicalism, skepticism 11 agnosticism, lawlessness, nothingness

12 nonexistence
16 irresponsibility

nihilist 5 rebel 9 anarchist, terrorist 13 revolutionary

Nihon *see* 5 Japan

Nike
origin: 5 Greek
goddess of: 7 victory
father: 11 Titan Pallas
mother: 4 Styx

brother: 5 Zelos
corresponds to: 6 Athena **8** Victoria

nil 4 none, null, zero **6** cipher, naught **7** nothing, nullity **11** nonexistent

Nile *see* box, p. 678

Niles, Hazel and Peter
characters in: 22 Mourning Becomes Electra
author: 6 O'Neill

nil nisi bonum 21 nothing unless it is good

nil sine numine 27 nothing without the divine will
motto of: 8 Colorado

nimble 4 deft, spry **5** agile, fleet, light, quick, rapid, ready, swift **6** active, expert, lively, prompt, speedy, supple **8** animated, skillful, spirited **9** dexterous, mercurial, sprightly **10** proficient

nimbleness 7 agility **8** alacrity, spryness **9** dexterity, quickness **10** limberness, suppleness

nimble-witted 5 droll, witty **6** clever **11** resourceful

nimbus 4 aura, disk, halo **5** cloud, vapor **7** aureole **8** radiance

Nimitz, Chester
served in: 3 WWI **4** WWII
commander of: 12 Pacific fleet
rank: 12 fleet (five-star) admiral **22** chief of naval operations
battle: 6 Midway **9** Leyte Gulf **13** Philippine Sea

Nimoy, Leonard
born: 8 Boston MA
roles: 7 Mr Spock **8** Star Trek **17** Mission Impossible **21** Star Trek: The Voyage Home **22** Star Trek: The Wrath of Khan **25** Star Trek: The Search for Spock

Nimrod
father: 4 Cush
grandfather: 3 Ham
great grandfather: 4 Noah
founded: 5 Calah, Resen **7** Nineveh **8** Rehoboth

nincompoop 4 boob, dolt, dope, fool, jerk **5** dummy, dunce, idiot, klutz, moron, ninny **6** dimwit, lummox, nitwit **7** half-wit, jackass **8** bonehead, dummkopf, imbecile, lunkhead, numskull **9** blockhead, dumb bunny, harebrain, numbskull, simpleton **10** dunderhead, dunderpate, muddlehead, noodlehead **11** knucklehead, rattlebrain **12** featherbrain, scatterbrain

Nine, the *see* **5** Muses

Nineteen Eighty-Four
author: 12 George Orwell
character: 5 Julia **6** O'Brien **11** Charrington **12** Winston Smith

1919
author: 13 John Dos Passos

Ninety-Five Theses
author: 12 Martin Luther

Nineveh
founder: 6 Nimrod

Nine worthies
mentioned in: 16 medieval romances
three each of: 4 Jews **6** Pagans **10** Christians
names: 5 David **6** Arthur, Hector, Joshua **11** Charlemagne **12** Julius Caesar **15** Judas Maccabaeus **17** Alexander the Great **18** Godefroy de Bouillon

Ningal
origin: 8 Sumerian
son: 3 Utu
consort of: 5 Nanna

Ninib *see* **7** Ninurta

Ninlil
origin: 8 Sumerian
goddess of: 3 air

ninny 3 ass, sap **4** fool, simp **5** booby, dunce, idiot, moron **6** dimwit, nitwit **7** fathead, half-wit **8** bonehead, dumb-dumb, imbecile, lunkhead, numskull **9** blockhead, dumb bunny, lamebrain, numbskull **10** dunderhead, nincompoop **11** chowderhead

Ninotchka
director: 13 Ernst Lubitsch
cast: 9 Ina Claire **10** Bela Lugosi, Greta Garbo **13** Melvyn Douglas
setting: 5 Paris
remade as: 13 Silk Stockings

Ninurta
also: 5 Ninib
origin: 8 Sumerian **10** Babylonian
type of god: 4 hero
personifies: 4 wind **9** south wind
father: 5 Enlil
avenger of: 5 Enlil

Ninus
wife: 9 Semiramis
founder of: 7 Nineveh

Niobe
father: 8 Tantalus
mother: 5 Dione
brother: 6 Pelops
husband: 7 Amphion
children: 9 seven sons **14** seven daughters
children called: 6 Niobid

taunted: 4 Leto
children killed by: 6 Apollo **7** Artemis
changed into: 5 stone
changed by: 4 Zeus

Niord
also: 5 Njord
origin: 12 Scandinavian
god of: 4 wind **10** navigation, prosperity
king of: 5 Vanir
son: 4 Frey **5** Freyr
daughter: 5 Freia, Freya

nip 3 cut, lop **4** bite, clip, crop, dock, grab, grip, ruin, snag, snap, snip **5** blast, check, chill, clamp, clasp, crack, crush, frost, grasp, pinch, quash, seize, sever, shear, snare, tweak **6** benumb, clutch, cut off, freeze, pierce, snatch, sunder, thwart **7** curtail, destroy, shorten, squeeze **8** compress, cut short, demolish **9** frustrate **10** abbreviate

nip-and-tuck 5 close

nip in the bud 7 prevent **8** preclude **9** forestall, frustrate

Nipper, Susan
character in: 12 Dombey and Son
author: 7 Dickens

Nippon *see* **5** Japan

nippy 3 raw **5** brisk, chill, crisp, sharp **6** biting, chilly **7** cutting

Nisn 16 first Hebrew month

nit-pick 4 carp, pick **5** cavil **9** criticize

nitrate 4 salt **5** ester **6** sodium **9** potassium **10** fertilizer

nitrogen
chemical symbol: 1 N

nitty-gritty 4 core, crux, gist, meat, pith **5** heart **7** essence **9** substance

nitwit 3 ass **4** clod, dolt, fool **5** booby, dummy, dunce, idiot, klutz, moron, ninny **7** fathead, pinhead **8** bonehead, dumb-dumb, imbecile, lunkhead, meathead, numskull, peabrain **9** birdbrain, blockhead, lamebrain, numbskull **10** dunderhead, nincompoop, noodlehead **11** chowderhead

Niven, David
real name: 21 James David Graham Niven
autobiography: 16 The Moon's a Balloon **21** Bring on the Empty Horses
born: 8 Scotland **10** Kirriemuir
roles: 11 Phileas Fogg **12** Casino Royale, My Man Godfrey **14** The Pink Panther,

Nixon, Richard Milhous
presidential rank: 13 thirty-seventh
party: 10 Republican
state represented: 2 NY
defeated: 7 (George Corley) Wallace **8** (Hubert Horatio) Humphrey
vice president: 4 (Gerald Rudolph) Ford **5** (Spiro Theodore) Agnew
cabinet:
  state: **6** (William Pierce) Rogers **9** (Henry A) Kissinger
  treasury: **5** (William E) Simon **6** (George P) Shultz **7** (David Matthew) Kennedy **8** (John Bowden) Connally
  defense: **5** (Melvin Robert) Laird **10** (Elliot L) Richardson **11** (James R) Schlesinger
  attorney general: **5** (William B) Saxbe **8** (John Newton) Mitchell **10** (Elliot L) Richardson **11** (Richard G) Kleindienst
  postmaster general: **6** (Winton Malcolm) Blount
  interior: **6** (Rogers Clark Ballard) Morton, (Walter Joseph) Hinkel
  agriculture: **4** (Earl Lauer) Butz **6** (Clifford Morris) Hardin
  commerce: **4** (Frederick B) Dent **5** (Maurice Hubert) Stans
  labor: **6** (George Pratt) Shultz **7** (James Day) Hodgson, (Peter J) Brennan
  HEW: **5** (Robert Hutchinson) Finch **10** (Caspar W) Weinberger, (Elliot Lee) Richardson
  HUD: **4** (James T) Lynn **6** (George Wilcken) Romney
  transportation: **5** (John Anthony) Volpe **8** (Claude S) Brinegar
born: 2 CA **10** Yorba Linda
died: 7 New York **11** New York City
education:
  college: **8** Whittier
  law school: **14** Duke University
religion: 6 Quaker **16** Society of Friends
interests: 8 football
vacation spot: 11 Key Biscayne (FL), San Clemente (CA)
dog: 8 Checkers **11** King Timahoe
author: 9 Six Crises **10** The Real War **11** Beyond Peace **27** RN: The Memoirs of Richard Nixon
political career: 8 US Senate **13** Vice President **24** US House of Representatives
civilian career: 6 lawyer
military service: 6 US Navy **10** lieutenant, World War II
notable events of lifetime/term:
  Calley court martialed for: **13** Mylai Massacre
  court martial of: **6** Calley
  creation of: **10** Bangladesh
  crisis: **3** oil **6** energy
  embargo on: **3** oil
  first men on: **4** moon
  incident: **11** Wounded Knee
  pardon of Nixon by: **4** Ford
  publication of: **14** Pentagon Papers
  resignation of: **5** Agnew, Nixon
  scandal: **9** Watergate
  student deaths at: **9** Kent State
  treaty: **10** Seabed Arms **32** Nonproliferation of Nuclear Weapons
  trip to: **5** China
  war: **7** Vietnam **10** Middle East **12** East Pakistan
quotes: 31 A respectable Republican cloth coat **35** You won't have Nixon to kick around any more
father: 14 Francis Anthony
mother: 6 Hannah (Milhous)
siblings: 11 Arthur Burdg **12** Harold Samuel **13** Edward Calvert, Francis Donald
wife: 8 (Thelma Catherine) Patricia (Ryan)
  nickname: **3** Pat
children: 5 Julie **8** Patricia
  Julie married: **15** David Eisenhower
  Patricia married: **9** Edward Cox
  Patricia's nickname: **6** Tricia

Separate Tables (Oscar)
16 Stairway to Heaven,
Wuthering Heights **18** The
Prisoner of Zenda
26 Around the World in
Eighty Days

Nix
  origin: 8 Germanic
  form: 6 spirit
  habitat: 5 water

Njord *see* **5** Niord

no 3 nay, nix, not **4** none, veto

Noah
  father: 6 Lamech
  grandfather: 10 Methuselah
  son: 3 Ham **4** Shem **7** Japheth
  grandson: 3 Put **4** Cush **6** Canaan **7** Misraim
  great grandson: 6 Nimrod
  built: 3 ark

collected: 7 animals
survived: 5 flood
pertaining to: 8 Noachian

Noah's Ark
made of: 10 gopherwood

nob 4 peer, toff **5** swell **9** patrician **10** aristocrat

Nobel, Alfred
nationality: 7 Swedish
invented: 8 dynamite
originated: 10 Nobel Prize

Nobel Prizes *see box,*
p. 682

nobility 5 elite, lords **7** dignity, majesty, peerage, primacy, royalty **8** breeding, eminence, grandeur, high rank, prestige, splendor **9** gentility, grandness, greatness, loftiness, sublimity, supremacy **10** blue bloods, mightiness, patricians, patriciate, upper crust **11** aristocracy, distinction, exaltedness, preeminence, stateliness, superiority **12** magnificence

nobility obliges
French: 14 noblesse oblige

noble 3 don **4** high, just, lord, peer **5** famed, grand, great, lofty, moral, regal, royal **6** famous, gentle, honest, knight, lordly, squire, superb, worthy **7** awesome, courtly, eminent, ethical, exalted, grandee, stately, sublime, supreme, upright **8** baronial, cavalier, elevated, glorious, handsome, highborn, imperial, imposing, lordlike, majestic, princely, renowned, selfless, splendid, superior, virtuous **9** chevalier, dignified, estimable, excellent, exemplary, gentleman, honorable, patrician, personage, reputable **10** aristocrat, impressive, preeminent **11** magnanimous, magnificent, meritorious, pureblooded, trustworthy **12** aristocratic, thoroughbred **13** distinguished, incorruptible
French: 6 gentil

Noble House
author: 12 James Clavell

nobleman 4 lord, peer **7** grandee **9** patrician **10** aristocrat

noblesse oblige 15 nobility obliges

noblewoman 4 dame, lady, rani **5** begum, queen **6** milady **7** czarina, duchess, empress, peeress, sultana **8** baroness, contessa, countess, maharani, princess **11** marchioness

Nobody Knows My Name
author: 12 James Baldwin

nocturnal 4 dark **5** night **7** nightly, obscure **8** darkling **9** nighttime

Nocturne
author: 15 Frank Swinnerton

nod 3 bob **4** doze, hail, show, sign **5** agree, greet, lapse, let up **6** assent, beckon, concur, drowse, motion, reveal, salute, signal **7** consent, drop off, fall off, gesture, signify **9** recognize

node 3 bud **4** bump, burl, hump, knob, knot, lump **5** bulge, joint **6** button **8** swelling **10** prominence, tumescence **11** excrescence **12** protuberance

Nodosaurus
type: 8 dinosaur
10 ornithopod
location: 12 North America

nodule 3 sac, wen **4** bump, cyst, knob, knot, lump, stud **5** bulge **6** growth **8** swelling **9** outgrowth **10** projection, prominence, protrusion, tumescence **11** excrescence **12** protuberance

noel, Noel 4 yule **5** carol **8** yuletide **9** Christmas **13** Christmastide

Noemon
mentioned in: 7 Odyssey
supplied: 4 ship
supplied ship to:
10 Telemachus

No Exit
author: 14 Jean-Paul Sartre

noggin 3 cup, mug **4** bean, head, pate **5** gourd **6** noodle

Noggs, Newman
character in: 16 Nicholas Nickleby
author: 7 Dickens

Noguchi, Hideyo
field: 12 bacteriology
nationality: 8 Japanese
isolated: 8 syphilis

noise 3 ado, din **4** bang, blab, boom, echo, pass, roar, stir, wail **5** babel, blare, blast, bruit, rumor, sound, voice **6** bedlam, clamor, hubbub, racket, repeat, report, rumble, tumult, uproar **7** barrage, bluster, clatter, thunder **8** brawling, gabbling, rumbling, shouting **9** cacophony, cannonade, circulate, commotion, discharge **10** dissonance, hullabaloo **11** pandemonium **12** caterwauling, vociferation **13** reverberation

noiseless 5 quiet, still, tacit **6** hushed, silent **9** soundless, voiceless

noisemaker 4 bell, horn **5** siren **6** rattle **7** clacker, clapper, snapper, whistle

noisome 4 foul, rank **5** acrid, fetid, toxic **6** putrid, rotten, smelly **7** baneful, harmful, hurtful, noxious, reeking **8** mephitic, stinking **9** injurious, offensive, poisonous, unhealthy **10** malodorous, nauseating, pernicious **11** deleterious, detrimental **12** evil-smelling

noisy 4 loud **5** alive **6** lively, raging, shrill, stormy **7** blaring, blatant, furious, grating, jarring, rackety **8** animated, piercing, strident **9** clamorous, deafening, dissonant, turbulent **10** boisterous, clangorous, discordant, rampageous, resounding, thundering, thunderous, tumultuous, uproarious **11** cacophonous, tempestuous **12** earsplitting

Nolan, George Brendan
real name of: 11 George Brent

Nolan, Lloyd
born: 14 San Francisco CA
roles: 22 Lieutenant Colonel Queeg **26** The Caine Mutiny Court Martial

Nolde, Emil
real name: 10 Emil Hansen
born: 7 Nolde **7** Germany
artwork: 7 Prophet **10** Papua Youth **11** Tropical Sun **12** The Magicians, The Pentecost **13** The Last Supper, Three Russians **14** Doubting Thomas **20** Life of Maria Aegyptica **22** Christ Among the Children, Christ and the Adulteress

nolens volens 10 willy-nilly **19** whether willing or not

noli me tangere 10 touch me not

nolle prosequi 14 do not prosecute **19** be unwilling to pursue

nolo contendere 21 I am unwilling to contend

no longer able to fight
French: 12 hors de combat

no longer in existence
4 dead, gone, lost **7** defunct, died out, extinct **8** vanished

Nolte, Nick
born: 7 Omaha NE
roles: 5 Weeds **7** The Deep **10** Cannery Row **12** I Love Trouble **13** Prince of Tides **14** Rich Man Poor Man **15** Forty-Eight Hours **16** North Dallas Forty, Jefferson in Paris

Nobel Prizes

Literature:

1901: 20 Rene F A Sully-Prudhomme
1902: 14 Theodor Mommsen
1903: 20 Bjornstjerne Bjornson
1904: 13 Jose Echegaray
15 Frederic Mistral
1905: 17 Henryk Sienkiewicz
1906: 14 Giosue Carducci
1907: 14 Rudyard Kipling
1908: 13 Rudolf C Eucken
1909: 13 Selma Lagerlof
1910: 12 Paul von Heyse
1911: 18 Maurice Maeterlinck
1912: 16 Gerhart Hauptmann
1913: 21 Sir Rabindranath Tagore
1915: 13 Romain Rolland
1916: 19 Verner von Heidenstam
1917: 11 K A Gjellerup
17 Henrik Pontoppidan
1919: 15 Carl F G Spitteler
1920: 10 Knut Hamsun
1921: 13 Anatole France
1922: 25 Jacinto Benavente y Martinez
1923: 18 William Butler Yeats
1924: 17 Wladyslaw S Reymont
1925: 17 George Bernard Shaw
1926: 13 Grazia Deledda
1927: 12 Henri Bergson
1928: 12 Sigrid Undset
1929: 10 Thomas Mann
1930: 13 Sinclair Lewis
1931: 14 Erik A Karlfeldt
1932: 14 John Galsworthy
1933: 10 Ivan A Bunin
1934: 15 Luigi Pirandello
1936: 12 Eugene O'Neill
1937: 17 Roger Martin du Gard
1938: 10 Pearl S Buck
1939: 15 Frans E Sillanpaa
1944: 15 Johannes V Jensen
1945: 15 Gabriela Mistral
1946: 15 Hermann Hesse
1947: 9 Andre Gide
1948: 7 T S Eliot
1949: 15 William Faulkner
1950: 15 Bertrand Russell (Earl Russell)
1951: 14 Par F Lagerkvist
1952: 15 Francois Mauriac
1953: 21 Sir Winston L S Churchill
1954: 15 Ernest Hemingway
1955: 15 Halldor K Laxness
1956: 16 Juan Ramon Jimenez
1957: 11 Albert Camus
1958: 15 Boris L Pasternak
1959: 18 Salvatore Quasimodo
1960: 14 Saint-John Perse
1961: 9 Ivo Andric
1962: 13 John Steinbeck
1963: 13 George Seferis
1964: 14 Jean Paul Sartre
1965: 17 Mikhail A Sholokhov
1966: 10 Nelly Sachs
17 Samuel Joseph (Shmuel Y) Agnon
1967: 19 Miguel Angel Asturias
1968: 16 Yasunari Kawabata
1969: 13 Samuel Beckett
1970: 22 Aleksandr I Solzhenitsyn
1971: 11 Pablo Neruda
1972: 12 Heinrich Boll
1973: 12 Patrick White
1974: 13 Eyvind Johnson
14 Harry Martinson
1975: 14 Eugenio Montale
1976: 10 Saul Bellow
1977: 17 Vicente Aleixandre
1978: 19 Isaac Bashevis Singer
1979: 14 Odysseus Elytis
1980: 13 Czeslaw Milosz
1981: 12 Elias Canetti
1982: 20 Gabriel Garcia Marquez
1983: 14 William Golding
1984: 15 Jaroslav Seifert
1985: 11 Claude Simon
1986: 11 Wole Soyinka
1987: 13 Joseph Brodsky
1988: 13 Naguib Mahfouz
1989: 10 Camilo Cela
1990: 10 Octavio Paz
1991: 14 Nadine Gordimer
1992: 12 Derek Walcott
1993: 12 Toni Morrison
1994: 11 Kenzaburo Oe
1995: 12 Seamus Heaney
1996: 17 Wislawa Szymborska

Physiology/Medicine:

1901: 15 Emil A von Behring
1902: 13 Sir Ronald Ross
1903: 12 Niels R Finsen
1904: 11 Ivan P Pavlov
1905: 10 Robert Koch
1906: 12 Camillo Golgi
19 Santiago Ramon y Cajal
1907: 16 Charles L A Laveran
1908: 11 Paul Ehrlich
15 Elie Metchnikoff
1909: 11 Emil T Kocher
1910: 14 Albrecht Kossel
1911: 16 Allvar Gullstrand
1912: 12 Alexis Carrel
1913: 14 Charles R Richet
1914: 12 Robert Barany
1919: 11 Jules Bordet
1920: 12 Shack A S Krogh
1922: 12 Otto Meyerhof
14 Archibald V Hill
1923: 13 John J R Macleod
20 Sir Frederick G Banting
1924: 15 Willem Einthoven
1926: 15 Johannes Fibiger
1927: 19 Julius Wagner-Jauregg
1928: 16 Charles J H Nicolle
1929: 17 Christiaan Eijkman
20 Sir Frederick G Hopkins
1930: 15 Karl Landsteiner
1931: 12 Otto H Warburg
1932: 12 Edgar D Adrian
21 Sir Charles Sherrington
1933: 13 Thomas H Morgan
1934: 12 George R Minot
14 George H Whipple, William P Murphy
1935: 11 Hans Spemann
1936: 9 Otto Loewi 13 Sir Henry H Dale
1937: 31 Albert Szent-Gyorgyi von Nagyrapolt
1938: 16 Corneille Heymans
1939: 13 Gerhard Domagk
1943: 9 Henrik Dam 12 Edward A Doisy
1944: 14 Herbert S Gasser, Joseph Erlanger
1945: 11 Ernst B Chain
16 Sir Howard W Florey
19 Sir Alexander Fleming
1946: 14 Hermann J Muller
1947: 9 Carl F Cori
10 Gerty T Cori 16 Bernardo A Houssay
1948: 11 Paul H Muller
1949: 11 Walter R Hess
21 Antonio C de A F Egas Moniz
1950: 12 Philip S Hench
14 Edward C Kendall
16 Tadeus Reichstein
1951: 10 Max Theiler
1952: 14 Selman A Waksman
1953: 13 Fritz A Lipmann, Sir Hans A Krebs
1954: 11 John F Enders
13 Thomas H Weller
17 Frederick C Robbins
1955: 14 Axel H T Theorell
1956: 13 Andre Cournand
15 Werner Forssmann
20 Dickenson W Richards Jr
1957: 11 Daniel Bovet
1958: 12 Edward L Tatum
13 George W Beadle
15 Joshua Lederberg
1959: 11 Severo Ochoa
14 Arthur Kornberg
1960: 13 Peter B Medawar
15 Sir Frank M Burnet

1961: 14 Georg von Bekesy
1962: 12 James D Watson 14 Francis H C Crick 16 Maurice H F Wilkins
1963: 16 Alan Lloyd Hodgkin 18 Sir John Carew Eccles 20 Andrew Fielding Huxley
1964: 11 Feodor Lynen 12 Konrad E Bloch
1965: 10 Andre Lwoff 12 Jacques Monod 13 Francois Jacob
1966: 17 Francis Peyton Rous 21 Charles Brenton Huggins
1967: 10 George Wald 12 Ragnar Granit 20 Haldan Keffer Hartline
1968: 13 Robert W Holley 14 H Gobind Khorana 18 Marshall W Nirenberg
1969: 11 Max Delbruck 14 Alfred D Hershey, Salvador E Luria
1970: 11 Ulf von Euler 13 Julius Axelrod 14 Sir Bernard Katz
1971: 17 Earl W Sutherland Jr
1972: 13 Rodney R Porter 14 Gerald M Edelman
1973: 12 Konrad Lorenz 13 Karl von Frisch 17 Nikolaas Tinbergen
1974: 12 Albert Claude 15 Christian de Duve 16 George EmilPalade
1975: 12 Howard M Temin 14 David Baltimore, Renato Dulbecco
1976: 15 Baruch S Blumberg 22 Daniel Carleton Gajdusek
1977: 13 Andrew Schally, Rosalyn S Yalow 14 Roger Guillemin
1978: 11 Werner Arber 13 Daniel Nathans, Hamilton Smith
1979: 13 Allan M Cormack 17 Godfrey Hounsfield
1980: 11 Jean Dausset 12 George D Snell 15 Baruj Benacerraf
1981: 11 David H Hubel 12 Roger W Sperry 14 Torsten N Wiesel
1982: 9 John R Vane 15 Bengt Samuelsson 17 Sune Karl Bergstrom
1983: 17 Barbara McClintock
1984: 11 Niels K Jerne 13 Cesar Milstein 16 Georges J F Koehler
1985: 13 Michael S Brown 16 Joseph L Goldstein

1986: 12 Stanley Cohen 18 Rita Levi-Montalcini
1987: 14 Susumu Tonegawa
1988: 10 James Black 14 Gertrube B Elion 16 George H Hitchings
1989: 12 Harold Varmas 14 J Michael Bishop
1990: 12 Joseph Murray 14 E Donnall Thomas
1991: 10 Edwin Neher 11 Bert Sakmann
1992: 12 Edwin Krebs 12 Edmond Fisher
1993: 12 Phillip Sharp 14 Richard Roberts
1994: 12 Alfred Gilman 13 Martin Rodbell
1995: 12 Edward B Lewis 14 Eric F Wieschaus 26 Christiane Nuesslein-Volhard
1996: 13 Peter C Doherty 16 Rolf M Ziwkernagel

Chemistry:
1901: 16 Jacobus H van't Hoff
1902: 11 Emil Fischer
1903: 16 Svante A Arrhenius
1904: 16 Sir William Ramsay
1905: 17 J F W Adolf von Baeyer
1906: 12 Henri Moissan
1907: 13 Eduard Buchner
1908: 19 Sir Ernest Rutherford
1909: 14 Wilhelm Ostwald
1910: 11 Otto Wallach
1911: 11 Marie S Curie
1912: 12 Paul Sabatier 14 Victor Grignard
1913: 12 Alfred Werner
1914: 17 Theodore W Richards
1915: 18 Richard Willstatter
1918: 10 Fritz Haber
1920: 13 Walther Nernst
1921: 14 Frederick Soddy
1922: 13 Francis W Aston
1923: 10 Fritz Pregl
1925: 16 Richard Zsigmondy
1926: 15 Theodor Svedberg
1927: 15 Heinrich Wieland
1928: 12 Adolf Windaus
1929: 15 Sir Arthur Harden 19 Hans von Euler-Chelpin
1930: 11 Hans Fischer
1931: 9 Carl Bosch 16 Friedrich Bergius
1932: 14 Irving Langmuir
1934: 11 Harold C Urey
1935: 16 Irene Joliot-Curie 19 Frederic Joliot-Curie
1936: 12 Peter J W Debye
1937: 10 Paul Karrer 17 Sir Walter N Haworth

1938: 11 Richard Kuhn
1939: 14 Adolf Butenandt, Leopold Ruzicka
1943: 14 Georg von Hevesy
1944: 8 Otto Hahn
1945: 16 Artturi I Virtanen
1946: 12 James B Sumner 13 John H Northrop 15 Wendell M Stanley
1947: 17 Sir Robert Robinson
1948: 12 Arne Tiselius
1949: 15 William F Giauque
1950: 9 Kurt Alder, Otto Diels
1951: 13 Glenn T Seaborg 14 Edwin M McMillan
1952: 14 Archer J P Martin, Richard L M Synge
1953: 17 Hermann Staudinger
1954: 13 Linus C Pauling
1955: 17 Vincent du Vigneaud
1956: 15 Nikolai N Semenov 20 Sir Cyril N Hinshelwood
1957: 17 Sir Alexander R Todd (Baron Todd)
1958: 15 Frederick Sanger
1959: 17 Jaroslav Heyrovsky
1960: 11 Willard F Libby
1961: 12 Melvin Calvin
1962: 10 Max F Perutz 12 John C Kendrew
1963: 11 Giulio Natta, Karl Ziegler
1964: 26 Dorothy Mary Crowfoot Hodgkin
1965: 19 Robert Burns Woodward
1966: 15 Robert S Mulliken
1967: 12 Manfred Eigen 15 Sir George Porter 27 Ronald George Wreyford Norrish
1968: 11 Lars Onsager
1969: 9 Odd Hassel 13 Derek H R Barton
1970: 18 Luis Federico Leloir
1971: 15 Gerhard Herzberg
1972: 15 Stanford Moore 18 Christian B Anfinsen, William Howard Stein
1973: 16 Ernst Otto Fischer 17 Geoffrey Wilkinson
1974: 10 Paul J Flory
1975: 14 John W Cornforth, Vladimir Prelog
1976: 16 William N Lipscomb
1977: 13 Ilya Prigogine
1978: 13 Peter Mitchell
1979: 11 Georg Wittig 13 Herbert C Brown
1980: 8 Paul Berg 13 Walter Gilbert 15 Frederick Sanger

(continued)

Nobel Prizes (*continued*)
1981: **12** Kenichi Fukui
13 Roald Hoffmann
1982: **9** Aaron Klug
1983: **10** Henry Taube
1984: **21** Robert Bruce Merrifield
1985: **11** Jerome Karle
16 Herbert A Hauptman
1986: **8** Yuan T Lee
12 John C Polanyi **16** Dudley Herschbach
1987: **11** Donald J Cram
16 Charles J Pederson
1988: **11** Robert Huber
13 Hartmut Michel **17** Johann Deisenhofer
1989: **10** Thomas Cich
12 Sidney Altman
1990: **10** Elias Corey
1991: **12** Richard Ernst
1992: **13** Rudolph Marcus
1993: **10** Kary Mullis **Michael Smith**
1994: **10** George Olah
1995: **11** Paul Crutzen, Mario Molina **16** F Sherwood Rowland
1996: **11** Robert F Curl
15 Richard E Smalley, Sir Harold W Kroto

Physics:
1901: **16** Wilhelm K Roentgen
1902: **12** Pieter Zeeman
15 Hendrik A Lorentz
1903: **11** Marie S Curie, Pierre Curie **15** A Henri Becquerel
1904: **11** John W Strutt (Lord Rayleigh)
1905: **13** Philipp Lenard
1906: **16** Sir Joseph Thomson
1907: **16** Albert A Michelson
1908: **15** Gabriel Lippmann
1909: **10** Karl F Braun
16 Guglielmo Marconi
1910: **20** Johannes D van der Waals
1911: **11** Wilhelm Wien
1912: **10** Nils G Dalen
1913: **20** Heike Kamerlingh Onnes
1914: **10** Max von Laue
1915: **16** Sir William H Bragg, Sir William L Bragg
1917: **14** Charles B Barkla
1918: **9** Max Planck
1919: **13** Johannes Stark
1920: **17** Charles E Guillaume
1921: **14** Albert Einstein
1922: **10** Nils H D Bohr
1923: **15** Robert A Millikan
1924: **14** Karl M G Siegbahn

1925: **11** Gustav Hertz, James Franck
1926: **11** Jean B Perrin
1927: **14** Arthur H Compton **15** Charles T R Wilson
1928: **18** Sir Owen W Richardson
1929: **15** Louis V de Broglie
1930: **23** Sir Chandrasekhara V Raman
1932: **16** Werner Heisenberg
1933: **11** Paul A M Dirac
16 Erwin Schrodinger
1935: **16** Sir James Chadwick
1936: **11** Victor F Hess
13 Carl D Anderson
1937: **16** Clinton J Davisson **17** Sir George P Thomson
1938: **11** Enrico Fermi
1939: **15** Ernest O Lawrence
1943: **9** Otto Stern
1944: **11** Isidor I Rabi
1945: **13** Wolfgang Pauli
1946: **14** Percy W Bridgman
1947: **18** Sir Edward V Appleton
1948: **17** Patrick M S Blackett
1949: **12** Hideki Yukawa
1950: **12** Cecil F Powell
1951: **14** Ernest T S Walton **17** Sir John D Cockcroft
1952: **10** Felix Bloch **14** Edward M Purcell
1953: **12** Frits Zernike
1954: **7** Max Born
12 Walther Bothe
1955: **13** Polykarp Kusch, Willis E Lamb Jr
1956: **11** John Bardeen
15 Walter H Brattain
16 William B Shockley
1957: **11** Tsung Dao Lee
12 Chen Ning Yang
1958: **9** Igor Y Tamm
10 Ilya M Frank **15** Pavel A Cherenkov
1959: **11** Emilio Segre
15 Owen Chamberlain
1960: **13** Donald A Glaser
1961: **16** Robert Hofstadter, Rudolf L Mossbauer
1962: **10** Lev D Landau
1963: **11** J Hans Jensen
16 Eugene Paul Wigner
18 Maria Goeppert Mayer
1964: **17** Charles Hard Townes **25** Nikolai Gennadiyevich Basov **30** Aleksandr Mikhailovich Prokhorov
1965: **18** Shinichiro Tomonaga **22** Julian Seymour Schwinger, Richard Phillips Feynman
1966: **13** Alfred Kastler

1967: **17** Hans Albrecht Bethe
1968: **12** Luis W Alvarez
1969: **14** Murray Gell-Mann
1970: **12** Hannes Alfven
15 Louis Eugene Neel
1971: **11** Dennis Gabor
1972: **11** John Bardeen, Leon N Cooper **20** John Robert Schreiffer
1973: **8** Leo Esaki **11** Ivar Giaever **15** Brian D Josephson
1974: **12** Antony Hewish
13 Sir Martin Ryle
1975: **8** Aage Bohr **13** Ben R Mottelson **15** L James Rainwater
1976: **12** Samuel C C Ting
13 Burton Richter
1977: **13** John H Van Vleck, Sir Nevill Mott **15** Philip W Anderson
1978: **12** Arno A Penzias, Peter Kapitza (Pyotr Kapitsa) **13** Robert W Wilson
1979: **10** Abdus Salam
14 Sheldon Glashow, Steven Weinberg
1980: **9** Val L Fitch
12 James W Cronin
1981: **12** Kai M Siegbahn
14 Arthur Schawlow **19** Nicolaas Bloembergen
1982: **14** Kenneth G Wilson
1983: **14** William A Fowler
25 Subrahmanyan Chandrasekhar
1984: **11** Carlo Rubbia
15 Simon van der Meer
1985: **16** Klaus von Klitzing
1986: **10** Ernst Ruska, Gerd Binner **14** Heinrich Rohrer
1987: **12** K Alex Mueller
13 J Georg Bednorz
1988: **13** Leon M Lederman
14 Melvin Schwartz
15 Jack Steinberger
1989: **11** Hans Dehmelt
12 Norman Ramsey, Wolfgang Paul
1990: **12** Henry Kendall
13 Richard Taylor **14** Jerome Friedman
1991: **12** Pierre Gennes
1992: **13** George Charpak
1993: **12** Joseph Taylor, Russell Hulse
1994: **13** Clifford Shull
17 Bertram Brockhouse
1995: **11** Martin L Perl
15 Frederick Reines
1966: **9** David M Lee
16 Douglas D Osheroff
17 Robert C Richardson

Peace:
1901: **13** Frederic Passy
15 Jean Henri Dunant

1902: **12** Elie Ducommun **18** Charles Albert Gobat
1903: **17** Sir William R Cremer
1904: **27** Institute of International Law
1905: **24** Baroness Bertha von Suttner
1906: **17** Theodore Roosevelt
1907: **12** Louis Renault **14** Ernesto T Moneta
1908: **12** Fredrik Bajer **14** Klas P Arnoldson
1909: **16** Auguste Beernaert **35** Paul H Balluat d'Estournelles de Constant
1910: **24** International Peace Bureau
1911: **12** Alfred H Fried **13** Tobias M C Asser
1912: **9** Elihu Root
1913: **15** Henri La Fontaine
1917: **30** International Red Cross Committee
1919: **13** Woodrow Wilson
1920: **13** Leon Bourgeois
1921: **15** Christian L Lange **19** Karl Hjalmar Branting
1922: **14** Fridtjof Nansen
1925: **13** Charles G Dawes **26** Sir Joseph Austen Chamberlain
1926: **14** Aristide Briand **16** Gustav Stresemann
1927: **12** Ludwig Quidde **17** Ferdinand E Buisson
1929: **13** Frank B Kellogg
1930: **15** (Lars Olof Jonathan) Nathan Soderblom
1931: **10** Jane Addams **20** Nicholas Murray Butler
1933: **15** Sir Norman Angell
1934: **15** Arthur Henderson
1935: **16** Carl von Ossietzky
1936: **19** Carlos Saavedra Lamas
1937: **13** E A Robert Cecil (Viscount Cecil)
1938: **36** Nansen International Office for Refugees
1944: **30** International Red Cross Committee
1945: **11** Cordell Hull
1946: **9** John R Mott **11** Emily G Balch
1947: **21** Friends Service Council **31** American Friends Service Committee

1949: **11** John Boyd Orr (Baron Orr)
1950: **12** Ralph J Bunche
1951: **11** Leon Jouhaux
1952: **16** Albert Schweitzer
1953: **15** George C Marshall
1954: **51** Office of the United Nations High Commissioner for Refugees
1957: **14** Lester B Pearson
1958: **28** Rev Dominique Georges Henri Pire
1959: **16** Philip J Noel-Baker
1960: **14** Albert J Luthuli
1961: **15** Dag Hammarskjold
1962: **13** Linus C Pauling
1963: **25** League of Red Cross Societies **30** International Red Cross Committee
1964: **18** Martin Luther King Jr
1965: **26** United Nations Children's Fund (UNICEF)
1968: **10** Rene Cassin
1969: **30** International Labor Organization (ILO)
1970: **14** Norman E Borlaug
1971: **11** Willy Brandt
1973: **8** Le Duc Tho **15** Henry A Kissinger
1974: **10** Eisaku Sato **12** Sean MacBride
1975: **15** Andrei D Sakharov
1976: **13** Betty Williams **15** Mairead Corrigan
1977: **20** Amnesty International
1978: **10** Anwar Sadat **13** Menachem Begin
1979: **12** Mother Teresa
1980: **19** Adolfo Perez Esquivel
1981: **51** Office of the United Nations High Commissioner for Refugees
1982: **10** Alva Myrdal **19** Alfonso Garcia Robles
1983: **10** Lech Walesa
1984: **17** Bishop Desmond Tutu
1985: **51** International Physicians for the Prevention of Nuclear War
1986: **10** Elie Wiesel
1987: **17** Oscar Arias Sanchez

1988: **31** United Nations peacekeeping troops
1989: **9** Dalai Lama
1990: **16** Mikhail Gorbachev
1991: **13** Aung San Suu Kyi
1992: **15** Rigoberta Menchu
1993: **9** F W de Klerk **13** Nelson Mandela
1994: **11** Yasir Arafat, Shimon Peres **12** Yitzhak Rabin
1995: **13** Joseph Rotblat
1996: **14** Jose Ramos Horta **23** Carlos Filepe, Ximenes Belo

Economics:
1969: **12** Jan Tinbergen, Ragnar Frisch
1970: **14** Paul A Samuelson
1971: **13** Simon S Kuznets
1972: **13** Kenneth J Arrow, Sir John R Hicks
1973: **15** Wassily Leontief
1974: **12** Gunnar Myrdal **18** Friedrich A von Hayek
1975: **17** Tjalling C Koopmans **18** Leonid V Kantorovich
1976: **14** Milton Friedman
1977: **11** Bertil Ohlin, James E Meade
1978: **13** Herbert A Simon
1979: **14** Sir Arthur Lewis **15** Theodore Schultz
1980: **14** Lawrence R Klein
1981: **10** James Tobin
1982: **14** George J Stigler
1983: **12** Gerard Debreu
1984: **15** Sir Richard Stone
1985: **16** Franco Modigliani
1986: **19** James McGill Buchanan
1987: **12** Robert M Solow
1988: **13** Maurice Allais
1989: **14** Trygve Haavelmo
1990: **12** Merton Miller **13** William Sharpe **14** Harry Mrkowitz
1991: **11** Ronald Coase
1992: **14** Gary Becker
1993: **11** Robert Fogel **12** Douglas North
1994: **8** John Nash **12** John Harsanyi **14** Reinhard Selten
1995: **14** Robert E Lucas Jr
1996: **14** James A Mirrlees **15** William S Vickrey

nomad 4 hobo 5 gypsy, mover, rover, stray, tramp 6 roamer 7 migrant, rambler, refugee, runaway, strayer, vagrant 8 bohemian, emigrant, migrator, renegade, traveler, vagabond, wanderer 9 immigrant, itinerant, straggler

nomadic 6 roving 7 migrant, roaming, vagrant 8 drifting, vagabond 9 footloose, itinerant, migratory, strolling, traveling, wandering

nom de guerre 5 alias 7 war name 9 pseudonym 11 assumed name

nom de plume 5 alias 7 pen name 9 false name, pseudonym 11 assumed name, writing name

nomenclature 5 lingo, terms 6 jargon, naming 8 language, taxonomy 10 nomination, vocabulary

nominal 3 low 5 cheap, small 6 puppet 7 minimum, titular 8 baseless, moderate, official, so-called 9 pretended, professed, purported, suggested 10 groundless, ostensible, reasonable

nominate 3 tag 4 call, name, pick, term 5 elect, label, style 6 choose, invest, select 7 elevate, install, propose, suggest 9 authorize, recommend

nomination 8 election 9 accession, selection 10 suggestion

nominee 7 hopeful 8 aspirant, eligible 9 applicant, candidate 10 competitor, contestant

nonadjustable 5 fixed, rigid 9 immovable 10 inflexible

nonalcoholic 4 soft 15 nonintoxicating

nonattendance 3 cut 7 absence, truancy 11 absenteeism

nonbeliever 5 cynic, pagan 7 atheist, doubter, heathen, infidel, skeptic 8 agnostic, apostate 10 backslider, empiricist, questioner, unbeliever 11 disbeliever, freethinker 14 doubting Thomas

nonbinding 8 optional 9 voluntary 12 unimperative 13 discretionary

nonchalance 9 composure, unconcern 13 offhandedness
French: 11 insouciance

nonchalant 3 lax 4 cool, idle, lazy 5 blase, slack 6 casual 7 languid, offhand, unmoved 8 careless, heedless, indolent, listless 9 apathetic, collected, easygoing, lethargic, unexcited, unheeding, unmindful, unruffled, unstirred, withdrawn 10 insensible, insouciant, phlegmatic, unaffected

noncombatant 7 neutral 8 civilian

noncommittal 3 mum 4 cool, mute, safe, wary 5 vague 7 careful, evasive, guarded, neutral, politic, prudent 8 cautious, discreet, reserved 9 ambiguous, equivocal, tentative 10 indecisive, indefinite, unspeaking 11 circumspect, temporizing

noncompliance 6 breach 7 failure, neglect 9 disregard 10 resistance 11 dereliction

noncompliant 6 unruly 7 defiant, froward, naughty, wayward 8 contrary, mutinous, perverse, stubborn 9 differing, dissident, fractious, objecting, obstinate, resistant, resistive, undutiful 10 disorderly, dissenting, rebellious, refractory, unorthodox, unyielding

non compos mentis 14 not of sound mind 17 mentally incapable

nonconfirming 7 denying 8 negating, refuting 9 rejecting 10 disavowing 11 disclaiming, repudiating

nonconformist 3 nut 4 beat, card 5 freak, hippy, loner, rebel 6 oddity, weirdo 7 heretic, oddball, radical 8 bohemian, crackpot, deserter, maverick, original, reformer, renegade, vagabond 9 character, dissenter, dissident, eccentric, exception, insurgent, protester, screwball 10 dissenting, iconoclast, rebellious, schismatic 13 individualist, revolutionary

nonconformity 5 quirk 6 oddity 7 anomaly 9 deviation, rebellion 10 aberration, divergence, resistance

noncongenial 6 unlike 8 opposite 9 different, disparate, ill-suited, unrelated 10 dissimilar 11 disagreeing 12 disagreeable, incompatible 13 unsympathetic

nondescript 5 usual, vague 8 ordinary 9 amorphous, colorless 11 stereotyped 12 unimpressive 13 characterless, undistinctive, unexceptional 15 undistinguished

nonentity 4 zero 6 cipher, nobody 7 nothing, no-count, nullity 8 small-fry, unperson 10 mediocrity

nonessential 6 luxury, trivia 7 trivial 9 extrinsic, secondary, trimmings 10 accidental, extraneous, incidental, irrelevant, peripheral, subsidiary

nonexclusive 4 open 6 public, shared 7 divided 12 unrestricted

nonexistence 4 lack, void 7 absence 8 oblivion 11 nothingness

nonexistent 4 gone 5 short 6 absent 7 lacking, missing, wanting 11 unavailable 12 insufficient

nonirritating 4 calm 5 bland 6 benign 7 calming 8 soothing, tranquil 9 temperate

nonmaterialistic 9 spiritual 10 idealistic 12 intellectual

nonmember 5 guest 7 outcast, visitor 8 outsider

nonnatural 7 manmade 9 synthetic 10 artificial, fabricated, factitious 12 manufactured

nonobservance 6 breach 7 failure, neglect 9 disregard 11 dereliction 13 noncompliance

non obstante 15 notwithstanding

no-nonsense 4 grim, hard 5 grave, harsh, rigid, sober, stern 6 ardent, intent, severe, solemn, strict 7 earnest, serious 8 critical, diligent, exacting, resolute 9 committed, dedicated, demanding, hardnosed, practical, pragmatic, unbending, unsparing 10 determined, hard headed, purposeful, sobersided 12 businesslike

nonpareil 5 elite, ideal, model, super 6 symbol, unique 7 epitome, paragon, pattern, supreme 8 exemplar 9 unequaled, unmatched, unrivaled 10 apotheosis 11 exceptional, unsurpassed 13 extraordinary 14 representative
French: 11 ne plus ultra 14 creme de la creme

nonparticipation 7 refusal 8 eschewal, forgoing 9 avoidance, eschewing 10 abstaining, abstention, refraining, sitting out 11 forbearance

nonpartisan 4 fair, just 8 unbiased, unswayed 9 equitable, impartial, objective, unbigoted 10 impersonal, uninvolved 12 freethinking, unaffiliated, unimplicated, uninfluenced, unprejudiced 13 disinterested

nonpermissible 9 forbidden 10 disallowed 11 intolerable 12 inadmissible, unacceptable

nonplus 4 balk, faze, foil, halt, stop 5 abash, stump, upset

6 baffle, bother, dismay, muddle, puzzle, stymie **7** astound, confuse, disturb, mystify, perplex **8** astonish, bewilder, confound, deadlock **9** dumbfound, embarrass **10** disconcert **11** flabbergast **14** discountenance

nonplussed, nonplused 5 at sea, fazed **7** at a loss, baffled, floored, mixed-up, muddled, puzzled, stumped **8** confused **9** befuddled, mystified, unsettled **10** bewildered, confounded **12** disconcerted

nonpoisonous 4 safe **8** nontoxic **11** nonvenomous, nonvirulent

nonpresence 3 cut **7** absence, truancy **11** absenteeism

nonprofessional 3 lay **4** laic **7** dabbler
   French: 7 amateur **10** dilettante

nonresident 7 tourist, visitor **9** transient **11** out-of-towner

nonresistance 6 assent **7** pliancy **8** docility, giving in, meekness, yielding **9** deference, obedience, passivity **10** compliance, conforming, conformity, pliability, submission **12** acquiescence, complaisance

nonresistant 4 meek **6** docile, pliant **7** passive, pliable **8** deferent, obedient, yielding **9** compliant **10** conforming, submissive **11** acquiescent, complaisant, deferential

nonscholarly 8 untaught **9** unlearned **10** uneducated, unlettered, unpedantic, unschooled

nonsectarian 10 ecumenical **11** interchurch **16** undenominational **17** nondenominational **19** interdenominational

nonsense 3 rot **4** bosh, bunk **5** folly, trash **6** antics, babble, drivel, joking, piffle **7** baloney, blather, bombast, chatter, fooling, garbage, hogwash, inanity, prattle, rubbish, trifles, twaddle **8** claptrap, flummery **9** absurdity, frivolity, gibberish, high jinks, horseplay, moonshine, silliness, stupidity **10** balderdash, flapdoodle, tomfoolery, triviality **11** foolishness, shenanigans **12** childishness, extravagance **13** facetiousness, ludicrousness, senselessness **14** ridiculousness **15** meaninglessness

nonsensical 4 wild **5** crazy, funny, inane, silly **6** absurd, stupid **7** asinine, comical, foolish **8** farcical **9** facetious,

laughable, ludicrous **10** irrational, ridiculous

non sequitur 15 it does not follow

nonspecialized 11 generalized

nonspecific 4 hazy **5** vague **7** general, inexact **9** imprecise, uncertain **10** indefinite, undetailed **11** approximate, generalized

nonspiritual 7 earthly, profane, secular, worldly **8** material, temporal **13** materialistic

nonstop 7 endless, express **8** constant, unbroken **9** incessant **10** continuous, unrelieved **11** unremitting **12** interminable

nonstudious 9 unlearned **10** uneducated, unlettered, unpedantic, unschooled

nontaxable 9 sheltered **10** deductible

nontechnical 6 simple **8** academic **13** uncomplicated

nontypical 7 unusual **8** abnormal, uncommon **9** anomalous, irregular **16** unrepresentative

nonuniform 5 mixed **6** unlike **7** altered, changed, erratic, unalike **8** changing, variable **9** deviating, different, irregular, multiform **10** dissimilar **11** fluctuating, nonstandard **12** inconsistent

nonvital 9 accessory, extrinsic **10** disposable, expendable, incidental **11** dispensable, superfluous, unessential, unimportant, unnecessary

nonvocational 8 academic

nonvolitional 6 reflex **8** unwilled **9** automatic **11** instinctive, involuntary, spontaneous **12** uncontrolled

noodle 4 bean, head, pate **5** gourd, pasta **6** noggin **8** practice **9** improvise

nook 3 den **4** cove, lair **5** haven, niche **6** alcove, cavity, corner, cranny, dugout, recess, refuge **7** retreat, shelter **8** hideaway **9** cubbyhole **10** depression **11** hiding place

noon 6 midday, zenith **8** high noon, meridian

noose 3 tie **4** bond, hang, loop **5** catch, hitch, lasso, snare **6** choker, entrap, halter, lariat, tether

Nootka
   language family: 8 Wakashan
   tribe: 5 Makah **6** Hoiath, Ozette **7** Ahosath, Nitinat

8 Machlath, Otsosath, Tokwaath **9** Ihatisath, Mowachath, Nochalath, Qayokwath, Tsishaath, Yoloilath **10** Hishkwiath, Hochoqtlis, Manohisath, Tlaokwiath **11** Chiqtlisath, Hopachasath, Qiltsamaath
   location: 10 Washington **15** Vancouver Island
   leader: 8 Maquinna **10** Wikaninish
   related to: 5 Makah
   noted for: 7 whaling

Nordhoff, Charles
   author of: 17 Mutiny on the Bounty (with James Norman Hall)

Nordic Mythology see **21** Scandinavian Mythology

norm 3 par **4** rule, type **5** gauge, model **7** average, measure, pattern **8** standard **9** measure, criterion, yardstick **12** measuring rod

norm, the norm 7 the mean, the rule **9** the median **10** the average **14** the common thing

normal 3 fit, par **4** sane **5** sound, usual **6** steady **7** average, healthy, natural, regular, typical, uniform **8** constant, expected, mediocre, middling, ordinary, rational, reliable, standard **9** incessant, steadfast, unceasing **10** conforming, consistent, continuous, dependable, reasonable, unchanging **11** conformable, right-minded, unremitting **12** conventional **13** uninterrupted **14** representative

Normandy, Normandie
   beach: 4 Gold, Juno, Utah **5** Omaha, Sword
   borders: 7 Picardy **8** Brittany **14** English Channel
   church/shrine: 12 Saint Etienne **15** Mont Saint Michel
   city: 4 Caen **5** Rouen **7** Le Havre **9** Cherbourg
   event: 4 D Day **17** Operation Overlord
   region of: 6 France
   river: 5 Seine

Norn
   origin: 12 Scandinavian
   form: 6 virgin **7** goddess
   personifies: 4 fate
   original Norn: 5 Urdar
   the three: 3 Urd **5** Skuld **8** Verdandi
   known as: 12 weird sisters

Norris, Frank
   author of: 6 The Pit **8** McTeague **10** The Octopus

Norse Mythology see **21** Scandinavian Mythology

north 5 polar, upper **6** arctic

North America *see box*

Northanger Abbey
author: **10** Jane Austen
character: **8** Mrs Allen
10 John Thorpe **12** James
Morland **14** Isabella Thorpe
16 Catherine Morland
Tilney family: **5** Henry
7 Captain, Eleanor, General

North by Northwest
director: **15** Alfred Hitchcock
cast: **9** Cary Grant **10** James
Mason **11** Leo G Carroll
12 Martin Landau **13** Eva
Marie Saint **17** Jessie Royce
Landis
setting (climax): **13** Mount
Rushmore
score: **15** Bernard Herrmann

North Carolina *see box*

North Dakota *see box,*
p. 690

North Dallas Forty
director: **11** Ted Kotcheff

based on story by: **9** Peter
Gent
cast: **8** Mac Davis **9** Nick
Nolte **11** Dayle Haddon
14 Charles Durning

Northern Crown
constellation of: **14** Corona
Borealis

Northern Rhodesia *see*
6 Zambia

North Korea *see* **5** Korea

North Star State
nickname of: **9** Minnesota

North Toward Home
author: **12** Willie Morris

North Vietnam *see* **7** Vietnam

Northwest Passage
director: **9** King Vidor
author: **14** Kenneth Roberts
cast: **10** Ruth Hussey
11 Robert Young **12** Spencer
Tracy **13** Walter Brennan

Northwest Territories *see*
box, p. 690

North wind
associated with: **6** Boreas

Norton, Thomas
author of: **8** Gorboduc (with
Thomas Sackville)

Norway *see box, p. 691*

Norwegian Mythology *see*
21 Scandinavian Mythology

nose
sense of: **5** smell
part: **7** nostril **14** olfactory
patch

nosegay 4 posy **7** bouquet
10 tussy-mussy

nosiness 6 prying **9** curiosity
15 inquisitiveness

nostalgia 6 pining, regret **7** remorse **11** languishing, remembrance **12** homesickness
13 regretfulness

Nostradamus
name: **7** Michael **17** Michelde
Notredame
occupation: **7** prophet **9** physician **10** astrologer
13 metaphysicist
wrote: **9** Centuries

Nostromo
author: **12** Joseph Conrad

nostrum 4 balm, cure, dose,
drug **5** draft **6** elixir, physic,
potion, remedy **7** cure-all, formula, panacea **8** medicine
9 treatment **10** medicament
12 prescription

nosy, nosey 6 prying, snoopy
7 all ears, curious **8** snooping
9 intrusive **11** inquisitive, overcurious **13** eavesdropping

nota bene 8 note well **10** take
notice

notability 4 fame **6** import,
moment, renown **8** eminence
9 celebrity **10** importance,
prominence **11** consequence,
distinction, preeminence
12 significance

notable 3 VIP **4** name **5** famed,
wheel **6** biggie, bigwig, famous, marked **7** eminent, salient **8** luminary, renowned,
striking **9** celebrity, dignitary,
personage, prominent, reputable **10** celebrated, pronounced,
remarkable **11** conspicuous,
outstanding, personality
13 distinguished

notably 7 visibly **8** markedly
10 distinctly, strikingly
11 prominently **12** unmistakably **13** conspicuously,
outstandingly

not alike 8 distinct **9** different,
differing, disparate, divergent
10 dissimilar **11** contrasting

North America
nation: **4** Cuba **5** Haiti **6** Belize, Canada, Mexico, Panama
7 Bahamas, Jamaica **8** Barbados, Honduras **9** Costa Rica,
Guatemala, Nicaragua **10** El Salvador, Puerto Rico, Saint
Lucia **12** Saint Vincent, United States **17** Dominican Republic, Trinidad and Tobago **28** Saint Vincent and the
Grenadines
desert: **7** Sonoran
island: **4** Long **6** Baffin, Cayman, Kodiak **7** Antigua, Bermuda, Iceland **8** Aleutian, Catalina, Thousand **9** Antilles,
Greenland, Nantucket, Vancouver **10** Cape Breton
12 Newfoundland, Prince Edward **14** Queen Charlotte
ocean/sea/bay: **6** Arctic, Baffin, Bering, Hudson, Mexico
7 Chukchi, Lincoln, Pacific **8** Amundsen, Atlantic, Beaufort, Labrador **9** Caribbean, Greenland **10** California,
Chesapeake, St Lawrence
river: **3** Red **4** Ohio **5** Peace, Snake, Yukon **6** Hudson
8 Arkansas, Colorado, Columbia, Missouri **9** Churchill,
Mackenzie, Rio Grande **10** St Lawrence **11** Mississippi
12 Saskatchewan
lake: **4** Erie **5** Huron **7** Ontario **8** Michigan, Superior, Winnipeg **9** Great Bear, Nicaragua **10** Great Lakes, Great
Slave
mountain range: **5** Ozark, Rocky **6** Alaska **7** Cascade
9 Blue Ridge **10** Laurentian **11** Appalachian, Sierra
Madre **12** Sierra Nevada
highest point: **13** Mount McKinley
lowest point: **11** Death Valley
city: **4** Nome **5** Miami **6** Boston, Dallas, Denver, Havana,
Ottawa, Quebec **7** Atlanta, Calgary, Chicago, Detroit,
Houston, Memphis, New York, Phoenix, Seattle, Toronto
8 Montreal, Portland, San Diego **9** Anchorage, Milwaukee, Reykjavik, Vancouver **10** Kansas City, Los Angeles,
Mexico City, New Orleans, Washington **11** Philadelphia,
San Antonio, San Francisco
mineral: **3** oil, tin **4** coal, gold, lead, salt, zinc **6** cobalt,
copper, nickel, quartz, silver **7** iron ore, mercury, sulphur, uranium **8** aluminum, antimony, asbestos, chromium, platinum, titanium, tungsten **9** magnesium,
manganese, petroleum **10** molybdenum, natural gas

North Carolina
abbreviation: 2 NC 4 N Car
nickname: 7 Tar Heel 8 Old North 10 Turpentine
capital: 7 Raleigh
largest city: 9 Charlotte
others: 4 Bath 6 Durham, Lenoir, Shelby, Wilson 7 Edenton, Hickory, Kinston, New Bern, Roxboro, Tarboro 8 Gastonia 9 Albemarle, Asheville, Goldsboro, Henderson, Kitty Hawk, Lumberton 10 Chapel Hill, Greensboro, Greenville, Kannapolis, Wilmington 11 Statesville, Thomasville, Williamston 12 Fayetteville, Jacksonville, Winston-Salem
college: 4 Duke, Elon 7 Catawba 8 Davidson 10 Wake Forest
feature:
  battle site: 18 Guilford Courthouse
  national park: 19 Great Smoky Mountains (with Tennessee)
  national seashore: 11 Cape Lookout 12 Cape Hatteras
tribe: 3 Eno 5 Coree 6 Cheraw 7 Buffalo, Moratok, Pamlico 8 Chowanoc, Hatteras 9 Tuscarora
people: 6 O Henry (William Sidney Porter) 7 tarheel 11 Billy Graham, Thomas Wolfe 13 Dolley (Dolly) Madison, Edward R Murrow 14 Richard Gatling
  explorer: 6 de Soto 8 de Ayllon 9 Verrazano
island: 7 Roanoke
lake: 6 Norman, Phelps 7 Fontana 8 Waccamaw 12 Mattamuskeet
land rank: 12 twenty-eighth
mountain: 5 Black, Unaka 6 Harris 9 Blue Ridge 10 Great Smoky 13 Clingman's Dome
  highest point: 8 Mitchell
physical feature: 10 Outer Banks 11 French Broad 15 Little Tennessee
  cape: 4 Fear 7 Lookout 8 Hatteras
  plateau: 8 Piedmont
  sea: 8 Atlantic
  sound: 4 Core 5 Bogue 7 Croatan, Pamlico
  swamp: 6 Dismal
president: 9 James Polk 13 Andrew Johnson
river: 3 Haw, Tar 4 Fear 5 Neuse 6 Chowan, Lumber, Peedee, Yadkin 7 Roanoke, Wateree
state admission: 7 twelfth
state bird: 8 cardinal
state fish: 11 channel bass
state flower: 7 dogwood 9 goldenrod
state motto: 20 To Be Rather Than To Seem
state song: 16 The Old North State
state tree: 4 pine
state dance: 4 shag

notation 5 entry 10 memorandum

not bright 3 dim 4 dark, dull 5 dense, dusky, murky 6 cloudy, stupid 7 clouded 8 obscured 13 unilluminated

notch 3 cut 4 dent, mark, nick 5 grade, level, score 6 degree 7 scoring, scratch 11 indentation

not disclosed
Italian: 7 in petto

note 4 bill, fame, line, mark 5 bread, draft, enter, green, money, write 6 regard, renown 7 epistle, jot down, lettuce, message, missive, put down, scratch, set down, voucher 8 currency, dispatch, eminence, mark down, perceive 9 bank draft, celebrity, greenback 10 communique, importance, memorandum, prominence, reputation 11 certificate, consequence, distinction

notebook 3 log 5 diary 6 record 7 journal 9 looseleaf
French: 6 cahier

noted 6 famous 7 eminent 8 renowned 9 prominent, reputable 10 celebrated, remarkable 11 illustrious, outstanding 13 distinguished

Notes from the Underground
author: 16 Fyodor Dostoevsky

note well
Latin: 8 nota bene

noteworthy 7 unusual 8 singular 9 important 10 remarkable 11 outstanding, significant, substantial 12 considerable 13 distinguished, exceptional

not far from 4 near 6 all but, almost, nearly 7 close to 8 not quite 13 approximately

not genuine 4 fake, sham 5 bogus, false, phony 6 ersatz, unreal 7 feigned 8 spurious 9 imitation, insincere, pretended, synthetic 10 artificial, fraudulent 11 counterfeit 12 hypocritical
Latin: 8 mala fide

not germane 9 extrinsic, unrelated 10 extraneous, immaterial, irrelevant 11 incongruous, inconsonant, unconnected 12 incompatible, nonessential 13 inappropriate

not guilty 5 clear 8 innocent 9 blameless 10 inculpable, unblamable

nothing 3 air, nix, zip 4 none, zero 5 stuff, trash, zilch 6 bauble, bubble, cipher, gewgaw, naught, trifle, trivia 7 duck egg, nullity, rubbish, trinket 8 goose egg 9 bagatelle, obscurity 14 insignificance 16 inconsequentials
Latin: 5 nihil

nothing is created from nothing
Latin: 16 ex nihilo nihil fit

nothingness 4 void 5 death 8 oblivion 9 emptiness 10 triviality 12 nonexistence 14 insignificance

Nothing Sacred
director: 14 William Wellman
cast: 13 Carole Lombard, Frederic March 14 Walter Connolly
score: 11 Oscar Levant
remade as: 10 Living It Up
script: 8 Ben Hecht

nothing unless it is good
Latin: 12 nil nisi bonum

nothing without the divine will
Latin: 13 nil sine numine
motto of: 8 Colorado

notice 3 eye, see 4 dope, heed, info, mark 5 goods 6 poster, rating, regard, review, take in 7 leaflet, mention, observe, warning 8 brochure, circular, critique, handbill, pamphlet

North Dakota
  abbreviation: 2 ND **4** N Dak
  nickname: 5 Sioux **11** Flickertail **16** Land of the Dakotas
  capital: 8 Bismarck
  largest city: 5 Fargo
  others: 5 Minot **9** Bottineau, Jamestown, Williston
    10 Grand Forks
  college: 4 Mary **9** Jamestown
  feature:
    dam: **4** Oahe **8** Garrison
    garden: **18** International Peace
    national park: **17** Theodore Roosevelt
  tribe: 5 Sioux **6** Mandan **7** Arikara, Hidatsa **8** Chippewa
  people: 12 Eric Sevareid
    explorer: **6** Carver **8** Thompson, Varennes **13** Lewis and
    Clark
  lake: 5 Stump **6** Devils **9** Sakakawea
  land rank: 11 seventeenth
  mountain: 6 Turtle **8** Killdeer **10** Black Butte
    highest point: **10** White Butte
  physical feature:
    basin: **9** Williston
    plain: **8** The Slope
    valley: **8** Red River
  river: 3 Red **4** Park, Rush **5** Cedar, Goose, Heart, James,
    Knife, Mouse **6** Souris **7** Deslacs, Pembina **8** Missouri,
    Cheyenne, Wild Rice **9** Otter Tail **10** Cannonball **11** Yel-
    lowstone **12** Boise de Sioux **14** Little Missouri **18** Red
    River of the North
  state admission: 8 fortieth **11** thirty-ninth (with South
    Dakota)
  state bird: 17 western meadowlark
  state fish: 12 northern pike
  state flower: 15 wild prairie rose
  state motto: 45 Liberty and Union Now and Forever One
    and Inseparable
  state song: 15 North Dakota Hymn
  state tree: 11 American elm

Notorious
  director: 15 Alfred Hitchcock
  cast: 9 Cary Grant **11** Claude
  Rains **12** Louis Calhern
  13 Ingrid Bergman

not pertinent 9 unrelated
  10 extraneous, immaterial, irrelevant **11** incongruous, unconnected **13** inappropriate

not quite 6 all but, almost,
  nearly

not required 8 elective, optional **9** voluntary

not too seriously
  Latin: 13 cum grano salis

Notus
  origin: 5 Greek
  personifies: 9 south wind

not wanted
  French: 6 de trop

notwithstanding
  Latin: 11 non obstante

not working 4 dead **8** inactive **10** unemployed **11** inoperative **12** unresponsive

Nouakchott
  capital of: 10 Mauritania

nourish 4 feed **5** nurse
  6 suckle **7** nurture, sustain

nourishing 4 rich **6** hearty
  7 healthy **9** fostering, nurtur-
  ing, wholesome **10** nutritious,
  sustaining **11** maintaining

9 appraisal, attention, knowledge, statement **10** advisement, cognizance, disclosure
11 declaration, information
12 announcement, intelligence **13** advertisement,
communication,
specification

noticeable 5 clear, plain **7** evident, obvious **8** definite, distinct, manifest, palpable,
striking **10** observable **11** appreciable, conspicuous, perceivable, perceptible
12 unmistakable

notification 4 news, word
6 advice, report **7** message, release **8** bulletin, dispatch
9 statement **10** communique
11 information **12** announcement, intelligence
13 communication

notify 4 tell, warn **6** advise, inform **7** apprise, let know **8** acquaint, send word **9** enlighten

not indigenous 5 alien **6** exotic **7** foreign **8** imported
9 nonnative **10** extraneous
11 naturalized

notion 4 idea, view, whim
5 fancy, humor, quirk **6** belief,
vagary, whimsy **7** caprice, conceit, concept, opinion
8 crotchet **9** suspicion **10** conception, intimation
12 eccentricity

not native 5 alien **6** exotic
7 foreign **8** imported **10** extraneous **11** naturalized

not of sound mind
  Latin: 15 non compos mentis

not ordinary 4 rare **6** exotic,
unique **7** bizarre, foreign,
strange, unusual **8** peculiar,
singular, uncommon **9** anomalous, different, fantastic
11 distinctive, outstanding
14 unconventional

notoriety 4 blot **5** shame,
stain **6** infamy, stigma **7** scandal **8** disgrace, dishonor, ignominy **9** discredit, disrepute
11 degradation

notorious 6 arrant **7** blatant,
glaring **8** infamous, renowned
9 egregious **10** celebrated, outrageous **11** outstanding

Northwest Territories
  abbreviation: 3 NWT
  borders: 7 Alberta
    8 Manitoba **9** Baffin
    Bay, Hudson Bay
    11 Arctic Ocean, Beau-
    fort Sea, Labrador Sea
    12 Saskatchewan
    15 British Columbia
  city: 6 Inuvik **8** Hay
    River **9** Fort Smith
    11 Yellowknife
    12 Frobisher Bay
  country: 6 Canada
  Inuit land: 7 Nunavut
  island: 5 Banks, Devon
    6 Baffin **7** Melville
    8 Bathurst, Somerset,
    Victoria **9** Ellesmere
    11 King William
    13 Prince of Wales,
    Prince Patrick
    14 Queen Elizabeth
  mineral: 3 oil **4** gold,
    lead, zinc **6** silver
    8 tungsten **9** petroleum
  mountain: 21 Mount Sir
    James Mac Brien
  native: 5 Inuit **6** Eskimo
  territory: 8 Franklin,
    Keewatin **9** Mackenzie

Norway

other name: 5 Norge 20 Land of the Midnight Sun
capital: 4 Oslo 11 Christiania
largest city: 4 Oslo
others: 3 Gol, Nes 4 Bodo, Moss, Odda, Rena, Voss 5 Bjort, Floro, Hamar, Molde, Skien, Skjak, Vadso 6 Bergen, Horton, Larvik, Narvik, Tromso 7 Alesund, Arendal, Drammen, Harstad, Sandnes 8 Aalesund, Kirkenes 9 Stavanger, Trondheim 10 Hammerfest 12 Kristiansand
division: 3 Amt 4 Oslo 5 Fylke, Troms 6 Bergen, Opland, Tromso 7 Finmark, Hedmark, Ostfold 8 Letemark, Nordland, Rogaland, Vestfold 9 Ostlandet
  former: 11 Kalmar Union
  province called: 6 fylker
government:
  legislature: 8 Storting
head of state: 4 king
measure: 3 fot, mal 4 alen 5 kande 6 fathom 7 skieppe 9 korntonde
monetary unit: 3 ore 5 krone
weight: 3 lod 4 mark, pund 10 bismerpund
island: 4 Vega 5 Bomlo, Donna, Froya, Hitra, Hopen, Senja, Smola, Soroy 6 Alsten, Averoy, Bouvet, Hinnoy, Karmoy, Kvaloy, Solund, Vannoy 7 Gurskoy, Lofoten, Mageroy, Seiland 8 Jan Mayen, Svalbard
lake: 4 Alte 5 Ister, Mjosa, Snasa 6 Femund 7 Rostavn, Tunnsjo
mountain: 5 Sogne 6 Kjolen 7 Numedal 8 Blodfjel, Snohetta, Telemark, Ustetind 9 Harteigen, Jotunheim, Langfjell, Ramnanosi 10 Dovrefjell, Galdhoepig, Glitretind, Vibmesnosi 11 Myrdalfjell 14 Aardangerjokul, Hallingskarvet, Skagastolstind
highest point: 12 Galdhopiggen 13 Glittertinden
river: 3 Ena 4 Alta, Klar, Otra, Rana, Tana, Teno 5 Bardu, Begna, Glama, Lagen, Orkla, Otter, Rauma, Reisa 6 Glomma, Lougen, Namsen, Pasvik
sea: 5 North 6 Arctic 7 Barents 8 Atlantic 9 Norwegian, Skagerrak
physical feature:
  cape: 4 Naze 7 Nordkyn 8 Nordkapp 9 Lindesnes
  fjord: 4 Oslo 5 Sogne
  glacier: 12 Jostedalsbre
  inlet: 2 Is 3 Kob, Ran 4 Alst, Ands, Bokn, Nord, Ofot, Salt, Sunn, Tyri, Vest 5 fiord, fjord, Folda, Lakse, Sogne 6 Bjorna, Hadsel 7 Hortens 9 Trondheim
  plateau: 5 Doure, Dovre, Fjeld 9 Hardanger
people: 4 Lapp 5 Samme 6 Nordic, Viking
  artist: 5 Munch
  author: 5 Ibsen 6 Hamsun, Undset 7 Holberg 8 Bjornson 9 Wergeland
  composer: 5 Grieg 7 Sinding 8 Svendsen
  explorer: 4 Eric, Leif, Mohn, Sars 6 Nansen 8 Amundsen
  explorer/statesman: 6 Nansen 8 Amundsen 9 Heyerdahl
  king: 4 Olaf, Olav 5 Olave, Oscar 6 Haakon, Harold, Magnus, Sverre
  Nazi collaborator: 8 Quisling
  Norse god/goddess: 3 Sif, Tyr 4 Frey, Idun, Loki, Odin, Thor 5 Bragi, Freya, Hoder, Woden 6 Balder, Eostre, Frigga, Hermod
  sculptor: 8 Vigeland
language: 4 Lapp 5 Norse 6 Bokmal 7 Nynorsk, Riksmal 8 Landsmal, Samnorsk 9 Landsmaal, Norwegian
religion: 19 Evangelical Lutheran 22 National Church of Norway
place:
  castle: 8 Akershus
  cathedral: 7 Nidaras
  museum: 7 Kon Tiki 10 Viking Ship 15 Polar Expedition
  park: 7 Frogner
former colony: 7 Vinland
feature:
  dance: 6 gangar 7 halling 8 springar 9 spingleik
  literature form: 4 edda, saga
food:
  bread: 8 flat brod
  cheese: 3 Ost 7 gjetost 9 gammelost, Jarlsberg
  drink: 7 aquavit

---

12 invigorating
13 strengthening

nourishment 4 chow, eats, food, grub, meat 5 bread 6 viands 8 victuals 9 nutriment, nutrition 10 sustenance 11 comestibles

nouveau riche 9 newly rich (person)

Novak, Kim
  real name: 19 Marilyn Pauline Novak
  born: 9 Chicago IL
  roles: 6 Picnic 7 Pal Joey,

Vertigo 14 Of Human Bondage 17 Bell Book and Candle 20 The Jeanne Eagels Story 22 The Man with the Golden Arm 31 Amorous Adventures of Moll Flanders

Nova Scotia *see box,* p. 692

Nova Scotia
  borders: **10** Bay of Fundy **12** New Brunswick **13** Atlantic Ocean **16** Gulf of St Lawrence **20** Northumberland Strait
  city: **5** Truro **6** Sydney **7** Amherst, Halifax **8** Glace Bay, Yarmouth **9** Dartmouth **10** New Glasgow
  country: **6** Canada
  island: **10** Cape Breton
  means: **11** New Scotland
  mineral: **3** oil **4** lead, salt, sand, zinc **6** barite, gravel, gypsum, silver **9** celestite, petroleum **10** natural gas
  mountain: **5** North **8** Cobequid
  part of: **12** Appalachians **17** Maritime Provinces **18** Atlantic Provinces
  river: **4** Avon **5** Clyde **6** LaHave, Medway, Mersey **7** St Mary's **12** Shubenacadie

novel 3 new **6** unique **7** unusual **8** original, singular, uncommon **9** different **10** innovative, unorthodox **14** unconventional
  French: **5** roman

novelty 5 token **6** bauble, change, gewgaw **7** memento, newness, trinket **8** gimcrack, souvenir, surprise **9** bagatelle, variation **10** innovation, knickknack, uniqueness **11** originality

November *see box*

novice 4 tyro **5** pupil **7** amateur, learner, student **8** beginner, disciple, newcomer **9** greenhorn **10** apprentice, tenderfoot

Novum Organum
  author: **12** Francis Bacon

novus ordo seclorum 24 a new order of the ages is born
  author: **6** Vergil, Virgil
    work: **8** Eclogues
  motto of: **11** US Great Seal

Now, Voyager
  director: **12** Irving Rapper
  cast: **10** Bette Davis **11** Claude Rains, Janis Wilson, Paul Henreid **12** Gladys Cooper
  score: **10** Max Steiner

now and then 8 on-and-off, periodic, sometime, sporadic **9** irregular, sometimes, temporary **10** infrequent, occasional **11** irregularly **12** infrequently, occasionally, periodically, sporadically

Now Playing at Canterbury
  author: **14** Vance Bourjaily

Nox
  goddess of: **5** night

noxious 4 foul **6** deadly, lethal, putrid **7** baneful, beastly, harmful, hurtful, noisome **8** damaging, virulent **9** injurious, loathsome, poisonous, revolting **10** abominable, disgusting, pernicious, putrescent **11** deleterious **12** foulsmelling

nth degree 5 limit **6** utmost **7** extreme

nuance 5 shade, touch **6** nicety **7** finesse **8** delicacy, fineness, keenness, subtlety **9** sharpness, variation **10** modulation, refinement **11** discernment

nub 4 core, crux, gist, hump, knob, knot, lump, node **5** bulge, heart **6** kernel **7** essence **8** swelling **10** projection, prominence, tumescence **11** nitty-gritty **12** protuberance

nubbin 3 ear **4** corn, lump, stub **5** bulge, fruit, piece, stump **10** diminutive

Nubbles, Kit
  character in: **19** The Old Curiosity Shop
  author: **7** Dickens

nubbly 5 lumpy, rough **6** coarse, knobby, pebbly

nucleus 3 nub **4** core, pith, seed **5** heart **6** center, kernel

Nudd *see* **4** Llud

nude 3 raw **4** bare **5** bared, naked **6** unclad **7** exposed **8** in the raw, stripped **9** unadorned, unarrayed, unclothed, uncovered, undressed
  French: **9** au naturel

nudge 3 jab, jog, nod **4** bump, jolt, poke, prod, push **5** elbow, press, punch, shove, touch **6** jostle, motion, signal **8** indicate

nugatory 4 idle **5** empty **6** hollow, otiose, paltry **7** trivial, useless **8** piddling, trifling **9** meritless, valueless, worthless **10** profitless **11** ineffec-

tual **12** functionless **15** inconsequential

nugget 4 hunk, lump **5** chunk, piece

nuisance 4 bore, fret, hurt, pain, pest **5** curse, thorn, worry **6** blight, bother, burden, plague **7** scourge, torment, trouble **8** handicap, vexation **9** annoyance, grievance **10** affliction, irritation, misfortune, pestilence **11** aggravation, botheration **13** inconvenience

Nuk
  capital of: **9** Greenland

Nukualofa
  capital of: **5** Tonga

null 2 NG **4** void **6** no good **7** invalid **9** valueless, worthless **10** immaterial **11** inoperative, nonexistent, unimportant **13** insignificant

nullification 6 repeal **7** voiding **8** recision **9** abolition, annulment **10** abrogation, rescinding **11** abolishment **12** cancellation, invalidation

nullify 4 veto, void **5** annul **6** cancel, repeal, revoke **7** abolish, rescind, retract **8** abrogate, make void, override, set aside **10** invalidate

nullity 6 cipher, naught **7** nothing **9** nonentity

Numanus
  brother-in-law: **6** Turnus

numb 4 dead **6** frozen **8** dead-

November
  event: **11** Election Day
  flower: **13** chrysanthemum
  French: **8** Novembre
  gem: **5** topaz
  German: **8** November
  holiday: **11** All Souls' Day (2), Veterans Day (11) **12** All Saints' Day (1), Guy Fawkes Day (5), Thanksgiving (4th Thursday)
  Italian: **8** Novembre
  number of days: **6** thirty
  origin of name: **5** novem (Latin meaning nine)
  place in year:
    Gregorian: **8** eleventh
    Roman: **5** ninth
  Spanish: **9** Noviembre
  Zodiac sign: **7** Scorpio **11** Sagittarius

ened **9** insensate, unfeeling **10** insensible, narcotized **12** anesthetized

number 3 mob, sum, tot **4** army, bevy, book, herd, host, mass, part **5** array, bunch, count, crowd, digit, group, issue, swarm, tally, total **6** amount, cipher, figure, reckon, scores, symbol **7** chapter, company, compute, edition, foliate, integer, numeral, passage, section **8** division, estimate, magazine, numerate, paginate, quantity **9** abundance, aggregate, calculate, character, enumerate, multitude, paragraph, quarterly **10** assemblage, quantities **13** preponderance

numbered numbered weighed divided
Aramaic: 21 mene mene tekel upharsin
foretells destruction of:
10 Belshazzar
Biblical book of: 6 Daniel

numberless 6 myriad **7** copious, umpteen **8** unending, zillions **9** countless, plenteous, unbounded, uncounted **11** illimitable, uncountable **12** immeasurable **13** multitudinous

numbness 8 deadness **11** insentience

numeral 5 digit **6** cipher, figure, letter, number, symbol **7** integer **9** character

numerate 3 add **5** count, tally, total **6** number, reckon **7** compute, tick off **9** calculate

numerophobia
fear of: 7 numbers

numerous 4 many **6** myriad **7** copious, profuse **8** abundant **9** plentiful **13** multitudinous

Numidia *see* **7** Algeria

Numipu *see* **8** Nez Perce

Numitor
king of: 9 Alba Longa
father: 5 Proca
brother: 7 Amulius
daughter: 10 Rhea Silvia
grandson: 5 Remus
7 Romulus

numskull, numbskull 3 sap **4** dolt, dope, fool, jerk **5** dummy, dunce, idiot, klutz, ninny **6** dimwit, nitwit **7** dullard, half-wit **8** bonehead, dummkopf, imbecile, lunkhead, silly ass **9** blockhead, simpleton **10** dunderhead, muttonhead, nincompoop,

noodlehead **11** chowderhead, knucklehead **12** scatterbrain

Nun *see* **4** Nunu

nuncio 5 envoy **6** legate **8** diplomat, minister **9** messenger **10** ambassador **11** papallegate **14** representative

nunnery 5 abbey, order **6** priory **7** cenacle, convent **8** cloister **9** hermitage, monastery **10** sisterhood

Nun's Story, The
director: 12 Fred Zinneman
based on story by: 12 Kathryn Hulme
cast: 10 Dean Jagger, Edith Evans, Peter Finch **13** Audrey Hepburn, Peggy Ashcroft **15** Colleen Dewhurst

Nunu
also: 3 Nun
origin: 8 Egyptian
god of: 5 ocean
personifies: 5 chaos

nuptial 7 marital **8** conjugal, hymeneal **9** connubial **11** matrimonial

nuptials 7 wedding **8** marriage **9** espousals, hymeneals **12** matrimonials

Nurmi, Paavo
nickname: 13 The Flying Finn
sport: 5 track
won: 8 Olympics

nurse 4 feed **5** nanny, treat **6** attend, doctor, foster, harbor, remedy, sister, succor, suckle **7** care for, nourish, nurture, promote **8** attend to, guardian **9** attendant, cultivate, encourage, governess
Hindi/Indian: 4 ayah

nursery 6 hotbed **9** incubator, preschool **10** greenhouse, schoolroom **12** conservatory, kindergarten

nurture 4 feed, mess, rear, tend **5** breed, raise, teach, train, tutor **6** foster, school **7** bring up, develop, educate, nourish, prepare, sustain, victual **8** instruct, maintain **9** cultivate, provision **10** discipline, strengthen

Nusantara *see* **9** Indonesia

Nusku
origin: 8 Sumerian
10 Babylonian
visier of: 5 Enlil

nut 3 fan, pit **4** buff, seed **5** freak, idiot, loony, stone **6** madman, maniac, zealot **7** devotee, fanatic, lunatic,

oddball **8** crackpot **9** eccentric, screwball **10** aficionado, enthusiast, psychopath **11** afficionado

Nut
origin: 8 Egyptian
goddess of: 3 sky

nut-brown 5 tawny **6** auburn, brunet **8** brunette, cinnamon

Nutcracker, The
also: 13 Shchelkunchik
ballet by: 11 Tchaikovsky
based on fairy tale by:
11 E T A Hoffmann
contains: 17 Waltz of the Flowers **24** Dance of the Sugar-Plum Fairy

nutmeg
botanical name: 17 Myristica fragrans
from same plant as: 4 mace
origin: 9 Indonesia
use: 5 punch **6** eggnog **8** desserts **10** vegetables **11** baked dishes

Nutmeg State
nickname of: 11 Connecticut

nutriment 4 chow, eats, fare, feed, food, meat, mess **5** board **6** fodder, forage **7** aliment, edibles **8** eatables, victuals **9** foodstuff, groceries, provender **10** provisions, sustenance **11** nourishment, subsistence

nutrition 4 chow, feed, food, grub **6** fodder, forage, silage **7** edibles, rations **8** eatables **9** groceries, pasturage, provender **10** foodstuffs, provisions, sustenance **11** nourishment, subsistence

nutritious 9 wholesome **10** nourishing, sustaining

nuts 3 mad **4** bats, daft **5** balmy, crazy, dotty, loony, potty, wacko, wacky **6** insane **7** bananas, bonkers, cracked, touched **8** demented, deranged, unhinged **10** unbalanced

nutty 3 mad **4** daft **5** balmy, crazy, dippy, dotty, goofy, inane, loony, silly, wacko, wacky **6** cuckoo, insane, screwy, weirdo **7** bonkers, cracked, foolish, lunatic, meshuga, touched **8** bughouse, demented **9** senseless **10** addlepated, squirrely **11** harebrained **12** crackbrained

nuzzle 3 pat, pet **4** buss, kiss **5** smack **6** caress, coddle, cosset, cuddle, fondle, nestle **7** embrace, snuggle

Nyasaland *see* **6** Malawi

Nycteus
  father: **9** Chthonios
  brother: **5** Lycus
  daughter: **7** Antiope, Nycteis

Nyctimus
  father: **6** Lycaon

nyctophobia
  fear of: **8** darkness **14** the
    dark of night

nymph 5 belle, dryad, naiad,
  sylph **6** beauty **7** charmer

Nymphaea
  epithet of: **9** Aphrodite
  means: **6** bridal

Nyx
  form: **7** goddess
  personifies: **5** night
  originated from: **5** Chaos

children: 3 Ker **4** Eris **5** Fates,
  Geras, Momus, Moros,
  Oizys **6** Aether, Hemera,
  Hypnos, Somnus **7** Nemesis,
  Oneiroi **8** Thanatos

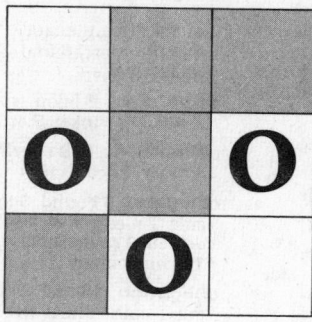

oaf 3 sap 4 boob, boor, clod, dolt, dope, fool, jerk, lout 5 booby, dummy, dunce, idiot, klutz, moron, ninny 6 lummox, nitwit 7 dullard, halfwit 8 bonehead, imbecile, numskull 9 blockhead, ignoramus, numbskull, simpleton 10 dunderhead, nincompoop

oafish 4 rude 5 crude 6 coarse, gauche, vulgar 7 boorish, doltish, loutish, uncouth 9 unrefined 10 unpolished

oak *see box*

Oak, Gabriel
   character in: 22 Far From the Madding Crowd
   author: 5 Hardy

Oakie, Jack
   real name: 19 Lewis Delaney Offield
   born: 9 Sedalia (Sadalia) MO
   roles: 16 The Great Dictator 17 Alice in Wonderland

Oakland
   baseball team: 2 As 9 Athletics
   football team: 8 Invaders

oar 3 row 4 pole 5 blade, rower, scull 6 paddle, propel 9 propeller
   blade: 4 palm, peel
   fulcrum: 5 thole 7 oarlock, rowlock
   part: 4 loom 5 shaft 6 collar

oarsman 5 pilot, rower 6 bowman 7 mariner, sculler 8 helmsman 9 gondolier, propeller

oasis 5 haven 6 asylum, harbor, refuge 7 retreat, sanctum, shelter 9 green spot, sanctuary, water hole 11 fertile area 13 watering place

oast 4 kiln, oven

oat, oats 5 Avena 11 Avena sativa
   varieties: 3 sea 4 wild 6 potato 8 animated 9 Tartarian 11 slender wild

Oates, Joyce Carol
   author of: 4 Them 9 Childwold 10 Bellefleur, Wonderland 11 Unholy Loves, Wheel of Love 15 Son of the Morning 18 A Bloodsmoor Romance 19 Do With Me What You Will

oath 3 vow 5 curse 6 avowal, pledge 8 cuss word, swearing 9 affidavit, blasphemy, expletive, obscenity, profanity 10 adjuration, deposition 11 affirmation, attestation, declaration, imprecation, malediction

oaths
   god of: 6 Horcus, Sancus 10 Dius Fidius, Semo Sancus

oatmeal 6 cereal 7 pottage 8 drammock, porridge

Obadiah 4 Obad 7 prophet 12 minor prophet
   father: 4 Azel 6 Jehiel 8 Izrahiah, Shemaiah
   son: 8 Ishmaiah
   predicted fall of: 4 Edom

Obata, Gyo
   architect of: 20 Dallas-Ft Worth Airport 25 National Air and Space Museum (Smithsonian Institute)

obdurate 5 cruel, harsh 6 mulish 7 adamant, callous, unmoved, willful 8 hardened, pitiless, stubborn, uncaring 9 immovable, merciless, obstinate, pigheaded, unfeeling, unpitying, unsparing, untouched 10 bullheaded, headstrong, inflexible, unmerciful, unyielding 11 cold-blooded, hardhearted, intractable 12 ungovernable, unmanageable 13 unsympathetic 14 uncontrollable 15 uncompassionate

---

oak 7 Quercus
   varieties: 3 bur, cow, pin, red, she 4 bear, blue, cork, deer, Holm, jack, live, maul, post, silk 5 black, Emory, holly, scrub, ubame, water, white 6 basket, Belote, canyon, Ceylon, Daimyo, gambel, gander, Havard, Indian, island, Kermes, Konara, laurel, Oregon, poison, possum, Turkey, Turner, valley, willow, yellow 7 Ballota, Bartram, Belloot, Catesby, Durmast, English, Georgia, Italian, Kellogg, leather, Lebanon, overcup, scarlet, shingle, Spanish, tanbark, truffle, western 8 Arkansas, bluejack, chestnut, McDonald, mossy-cup, shinnery, Texas red 9 blackjack, Engelmann, flowering, Jerusalem, Mongolian, pubescent, swamp post 10 Chinquapin, Darlington, ring-cupped, Spanish red, swamp white 11 huckleberry, Japanese red, northern pin, northern red, Shumard's red 12 interior live, laurel-leaved, rock chestnut, southern live, yellowbarked 13 dwarf chestnut, oriental white, swamp chestnut 14 Austrian turkey, California live, yellow chestnut 15 California black, California field, California scrub, California white 16 high-ground willow 17 Japanese evergreen 18 Rocky Mountain scrub

obedience 8 docility, yielding
9 deference, ductility, obeisance 10 accordance, allegiance, compliance, subjection, submission 11 conformance, dutifulness, willingness 12 acquiescence, subservience, tractability 14 conformability, submissiveness

obedient 5 loyal 6 docile 7 devoted, dutiful 8 amenable, faithful, obeisant, yielding 9 compliant, tractable 10 governable, law-abiding, respectful, submissive 11 acquiescent, deferential, subservient

obeisance 3 bow 5 honor 6 curtsy, esteem, fealty, homage, regard 7 loyalty, respect 8 courtesy, fidelity, humility, kneeling 9 deference, obedience, reverence 10 allegiance, humbleness, subjection, submission, veneration 11 prostration 12 genuflection 13 self-abasement

obelisk 5 pylon, shaft, tower 6 column, dagger, needle, pillar 8 memorial, monolith, monument

Oberon
character in: 21 A Midsummer Night's Dream
author: 11 Shakespeare

Oberon
opera by: 5 Weber
character: 5 Reiza
setting: 18 court of Charlemagne 21 court of Haroun al Rashid

Oberon, Merle
real name: 26 Estelle Merle O'Brien Thompson
husband: 14 Alexander Korda
born: 8 Tasmania
roles: 5 Hotel 7 Desiree 15 A Song to Remember 16 Wuthering Heights 19 The Scarlet Pimpernel 25 The Private Life of Henry VIII 30 The Private Life of Henry the Eighth

obese 3 fat 5 gross, heavy, plump, porky, pudgy, stout, tubby, 6 chubby, fleshy, portly, rotund 7 paunchy 9 corpulent 10 overweight, potbellied

obesity 3 fat 7 fatness, liposis 8 adiposis, enormity 9 heaviness, plumpness, stoutness 10 corpulence, overweight

obey 4 heed, mind 5 bow to, serve 6 assent, concur 7 abide by, observe, respect, yield to 8 accede to, submit to 9 acquiesce, conform to, succumb to 10 comply with, toe the line 12 follow orders

obfuscate 4 blur 5 befog

6 garble, mess up, muddle 7 becloud, confuse, distort, fluster, obscure, stupefy 8 confound, scramble 10 complicate

obfuscation 8 flummery 9 confusion 10 doubletalk, mumbo jumbo

obi 4 sash 5 obeah 6 girdle

obiit 6 he died 7 she died

obiter dictum 9 diversion 10 digression, divagation, side remark

object 3 aim, end, use 4 body, butt, dupe, form, gist, goal, pith, prey 5 abhor, basis, cause, knock, point, sense, thing 6 balk at, carp at, design, device, dingus, gadget, intent, loathe, motive, oppose, quarry, reason, target, victim 7 article, cavil at, condemn, dislike, essence, frown on, meaning, mission, protest, purpose, subject 8 be averse, cynosure, denounce 9 abominate, criticize, doohickey, incentive, intention, objective, principle, recipient, substance 10 inducement, phenomenon 11 contrivance, explanation, thingamabob, thingamajig 12 be at odds with, disapprove of, significance 13 find fault with, take exception 18 remonstrate against

objection 4 beef, kick 5 cavil 7 protest 8 demurral, rebuttal 9 challenge, complaint, criticism, exception 10 dissension, opposition 11 disapproval, reservation 12 disagreement 13 contradiction 14 disapprobation, opposing reason 15 counter argument

objectionable 4 foul, vile 5 nasty 6 odious 8 unseemly 9 abhorrent, loathsome, obnoxious, offensive, revolting 10 abominable, despicable, disgusting, unbearable, unpleasant 11 displeasing, distasteful, intolerable, unendurable 12 disagreeable, unacceptable 13 inappropriate

objective 3 aim, end 4 fair, goal, just, mark, real 6 actual, design, intent, target 7 mission, purpose 8 detached, unbiased, unswayed 9 impartial, intention, uncolored 10 impersonal, open-minded 11 destination 12 uninfluenced, unprejudiced 13 disinterested, dispassionate

objectivity 8 fairness 10 detachment, neutrality 12 impartiality

object to 7 condemn, dislike 9 frown upon 12 disapprove

of 14 discountenance 15 take exception to 16 find unacceptable

objet d'art 5 bijou, curio 7 bibelot, trinket 9 art object

oblation 4 gift 8 offering 9 offertory 10 collection

obligated 5 bound 6 forced, liable 7 pledged 8 beholden, indebted 9 committed 11 constrained

obligation 4 bond, care, debt, duty, oath, onus, word 6 charge, pledge 7 compact, promise 8 contract, guaranty, warranty 9 agreement, guarantee, liability 10 a favor owed, commitment, constraint 12 indebtedness 13 answerability, understanding 14 accountability, responsibility

obligatory 7 binding 8 coercive, enforced, required 9 mandatory, necessary, requisite 10 compulsory, imperative, peremptory 11 unavoidable

oblige 3 aid 4 bind, help, make 5 favor, force, impel, serve 6 assist, coerce, compel 7 require, support 8 obligate 9 constrain 11 accommodate, do a favor for, necessitate 13 do a service for, to be duty bound

obliged 5 bound 7 favored, pleased 8 assisted, beholden, indebted, required, thankful 9 compelled 12 accommodated

obliging 4 kind 6 polite 7 amiable, helpful 8 cheerful, friendly, gracious 9 agreeable, courteous 10 solicitous 11 complaisant, considerate, cooperative, good-natured, sympathetic 12 well-disposed 13 accommodating

oblique 3 sly 4 awry 5 askew 6 aslant, covert, hinted, masked, tilted, veiled 7 cloaked, devious, furtive, implied, slanted, sloping 8 allusive, diagonal, inclined, indirect, slanting, sneaking 9 suggested, underhand

obliterate 4 raze 5 erase, level 6 cancel, delete, efface, remove, rub out 7 abolish, blot out, destroy, expunge, wipe out 9 eradicate, write over 10 annihilate, strike over

obliteration 8 deletion 9 abolition, expunging, wiping out 11 blotting out, destruction, eradication 12 annihilation

oblivion 5 limbo 7 the void 9 blankness, disregard, obscurity, unconcern 11 blotting out, nothingness **12** nonexistence **13** forgetfulness, insensibility, obliviousness **14** insignificance **15** unconsciousness

oblivious 8 careless **9** forgetful, unaware of, unmindful **10** heedless of, insensible **11** inattentive, unconcerned, unobservant **12** disregardful, undiscerning **13** unconscious of

Oblonsky, Prince Stepan
  character in: 12 Anna Karenina
  author: 7 Tolstoy

obloquy 5 abuse, odium, shame **6** infamy, rebuke **7** calumny, censure, railing **8** contempt, disfavor, disgrace, ignominy, reviling **9** discredit, invective **10** defamation, opprobrium, scurrility **11** degradation, humiliation, verbal abuse **12** billingsgate, condemnation, denunciation, dressing-down, vilification

obnoxious 4 foul, vile **5** nasty **6** odious **7** hateful **8** unseemly **9** abhorrent, loathsome, offensive, repellent, repugnant, revolting **10** abominable, despicable, detestable, disgusting, nauseating, unbearable, unpleasant **11** displeasing, intolerable, unendurable **12** disagreeable, insufferable **13** inappropriate, objectionable

oboe family
  instruments: 5 shawm **6** curtal, pommer, racket **7** bassoon, bombard, curtall, hautboy **8** crumhorn, schalmey, tenoroon **10** Cor Anglais, oboe d'Amore **11** English horn, heckelphone, sarusophone **12** oboe da caccia, sarrusophone **13** contra bassoon, double bassoon

O'Brian, Hugh
  real name: 11 Hugh J Krampe
  born: 11 Rochester NY
  roles: 9 Wyatt Earp **27** The Life and Legend of Wyatt Earp

O'Brien, Edna
  author of: 5 Night **11** A Pagan Place **13** The Lonely Girl **14** The Country Girl **20** August Is a Wicked Month **24** Girls in Their Married Bliss

O'Brien, Margaret
  real name: 18 Angela Maxine O'Brien
  born: 12 Los Angeles CA
  roles: 8 Jane Eyre **11** Little Women **15** Meet Me in St

Louis **24** Our Vines Have Tender Grapes

O'Brien, Pat
  real name: 26 William Joseph Patrick O'Brien
  born: 11 Milwaukee WI
  roles: 12 Hildy Johnson, The Front Page **13** Some Like It Hot, The Last Hurrah **20** Angels with Dirty Faces **22** Knute Rockne All American
  autobiography: 12 Wind on My Back

obscene 4 blue, foul, lewd **5** dirty **6** filthy, smutty, vulgar **8** indecent, prurient **9** salacious **10** lascivious, lubricious **12** pornographic, scatological **16** morally offensive

obscenity 8 cuss word, lewdness **9** dirtiness, indecency, profanity, prurience, swear word, taboo word, vulgarity **10** filthiness, smuttiness **11** pornography **13** salaciousness **14** four-letter word, lasciviousness

obscuration 7 eclipse, masking, veiling **8** cloaking, clouding, covering **9** darkening, shadowing **10** concealing **11** concealment

obscure 3 dim, fog **4** blur, dark, hide, mask, veil **5** bedim, befog, block, cloak, cloud, cover, dingy, dusky, faint, murky, vague **6** cloudy, darken, hidden, muddle, screen, shadow, shroud, somber, unsung **7** becloud, conceal, confuse, cryptic, curtain, eclipse, shadowy, unclear, unknown, unnoted **8** befuddle, confused, disguise, nameless, puzzling **9** confusing, enigmatic, forgotten, lightless, obfuscate, uncertain, unheard of, unlighted **10** indefinite, indistinct, overshadow, perplexing, unrenowned **11** indefinable, inscrutable, little known, out-of-the-way, unimportant **12** unfathomable **13** inconspicuous, insignificant, unilluminated **15** inconsequential

obscurity 3 fog **4** mist **5** cloud, shade **6** shadow **7** dimness, mystery, opacity, privacy **8** darkness **9** ambiguity, seclusion, vagueness **10** cloudiness

obsequies 5 rites **6** burial **7** funeral **15** memorial service

obsequious 6 menial **7** fawning, servile, slavish **8** cowering, cringing, toadying **9** kowtowing, truckling **11** bootlicking, deferential,

subservient, sycophantic **12** ingratiating, mealy-mouthed **14** apple-polishing

observance 4 rite **6** custom, regard, ritual **7** heeding, keeping, obeying **8** ceremony, practice **9** adherence, attending, attention, following, formality, solemnity **10** ceremonial, compliance **11** celebration, observation **13** commemoration **15** memorialization

observant 5 alert, awake, aware **7** careful, heedful, mindful **8** vigilant, watchful **9** attentive, conscious, regardful, wide-awake **10** perceptive **12** on the lookout

observation 4 heed, idea, view **5** probe **6** eyeing, notice, remark, search, seeing, survey, theory **7** comment, finding, opinion, viewing **8** interest, judgment, scrutiny, spotting, watching **9** assertion, attention, beholding, detection, diagnosis, discovery, glimpsing, observing, statement **10** cognizance, commentary, inspection, reflection **11** description, examination, heedfulness **12** surveillance, watchfulness **13** pronouncement **20** firsthand information

observatory 5 tower **7** lookout **9** satellite **11** planetarium
  name: 4 Hale, Lick **6** Yerkes **7** Palomar, Whipple **8** Kitt Peak, Mt Wilson **11** Las Campanas, Mount Wilson **12** Big Bear Solar **14** Royal Greenwich

observe 3 eye, say, see **4** espy, heed, keep, mark, note, obey, ogle, spot, view **5** honor, opine, state, watch **6** assert, behold, detect, follow, notice, peer at, regard, remark, size up, survey **7** abide by, comment, declare, defer to, execute, fulfill, glimpse, inspect, make out, mention, perform, reflect, respect, stare at **8** adhere to, announce, carry out, discover, perceive, sanctify, theorize **9** celebrate, recognize, solemnize **10** be guided by, comply with, consecrate **11** acknowledge, acquiesce to, commemorate, take stock of **12** catch sight of **14** pay attention to

observer 6 viewer **7** watcher **8** onlooker **12** investigator

obsessed 5 beset **7** haunted **8** hung up on, maniacal **9** dominated, possessed **10** controlled **15** having a fixation

obsession 5 craze, mania, quirk 6 phobia 8 fixation 9 fixed idea, monomania 11 infatuation 13 preoccupation 16 overwhelming fear 18 neurotic conviction

obsolescent 8 dying out 9 declining 11 on the way out 12 disappearing 16 becoming obsolete 17 becoming out-of-date

obsolete 3 out 5 dated, passe 6 bygone 7 antique, archaic, extinct 8 outdated, out of use, outmoded 9 out-of-date 10 antiquated 12 old-fashioned, out of fashion

obstacle 3 bar 4 curb, snag 5 block, catch, check 6 hurdle 7 barrier, problem 8 blockade, stoppage 9 barricade, hindrance, roadblock 10 difficulty, impediment, limitation 11 obstruction, restriction 12 interference 14 stumbling block

obstetrician
French: 10 accoucheur

obstinacy 8 rigidity 10 mulishness, resistance 11 willfulness 12 stubbornness 13 inflexibility, intransigence, pigheadedness

obstinate 6 dogged, mulish 7 staunch, willful 8 obdurate, resolute, stubborn 9 pigheaded, steadfast, tenacious, unbending 10 headstrong, inflexible, refractory, self-willed, unyielding 11 intractable 12 recalcitrant, ungovernable, unmanageable 14 uncontrollable 20 unreasonably stubborn

obstreperous 4 loud 5 noisy 6 unruly 8 perverse 9 clamorous, rampaging 10 boisterous, disorderly, refractory, roistering, uproarious, vociferous 11 disobedient 12 uncontrolled, ungovernable, unmanageable, unrestrained 14 uncontrollable

obstruct 3 bar 4 curb, halt, hide, mask, stop 5 block, check, cloak, close, cover, dam up, debar, delay, limit, stall 6 arrest, hinder, hobble, impede, plug up, retard, shroud, stifle, thwart 7 eclipse, inhibit, shut off 8 blockade, choke off, close off, restrict, suppress, throttle 9 barricade, frustrate 18 bring to a standstill

obstruction 3 bar 4 curb, snag, stop 5 block, check, hitch 6 hurdle 7 barrier 8 blockage, obstacle, stoppage 9 barricade, hindrance 10 bottleneck, impediment 11 encumbrance

obtain 3 get 4 earn, gain, hold, take 5 exist, glean, stand 6 attain, come by, gather, pick up, secure 7 achieve, acquire, prevail, procure, receive 9 get hold of 14 get one's hands on 16 gain possession of

obtainment 11 achievement, acquirement, acquisition, procurement

obtrude 5 eject, expel, force 6 butt in, impose, meddle, thrust 7 presume, project 9 interfere

obtrusive 4 nosy 5 brash 6 prying, snoopy 7 bulging, forward, salient 8 familiar, meddling 9 intruding, intrusive, prominent 10 aggressive, jutting out, meddlesome, projecting, protruding 11 conspicuous, impertinent, interfering, outstanding, protuberant, sticking out, trespassing 12 interrupting, presumptuous

obtuse 4 dull, slow 5 blunt, dense, thick 6 simple, stupid 7 blunted 8 ignorant, not sharp 9 unpointed 10 insensible, not pointed, slow-witted 11 insensitive, unsharpened 12 imperceptive, thick-skinned 15 uncomprehending

obtuseness 8 dullness 9 denseness, ignorance, stupidity 13 insensitivity 14 slow-wittedness 15 thick-headedness 16 lack of perception, simplemindedness 19 lack of comprehension

obverse 4 face 5 front 10 complement 11 counterpart of coin: 4 head

obviate 5 avert, avoid, parry 6 divert, remove 7 fend off, prevent, ward off 8 preclude, stave off 9 forestall, sidetrack, turn aside 10 circumvent, do away with 11 nip in the bud

obvious 5 clear, plain 6 patent 7 evident, glaring, visible 8 apparent, distinct, manifest, palpable, striking, unhidden, unmasked, unveiled 10 undeniable 11 conspicuous, discernible, perceptible, self-evident, unconcealed, undisguised 12 in plain sight, unmistakable 24 plain as the nose on your face

O'Casey, Sean
author of: 10 Purple Dust 12 The Green Crow 17 Juno and the Paycock 18 The Shadow of a Gunman 20 The Plough and the Stars

occasion 4 base, time 5 basis, cause, event 6 advent, affair, chance, elicit, ground, lead to, motive, prompt, reason 7 episode, grounds, inspire, opening, provoke, venture 8 incident, instance 9 adventure, happening, rationale, situation 10 bring about, experience, motivation, occurrence 11 celebration, explanation, opportunity, provocation 12 circumstance, special event, suitable time 13 justification, opportune time 14 convenient time, important event, particular time

occasional 4 rare 6 fitful, random 8 sporadic, uncommon 9 irregular, recurring, scattered, spasmodic, uncertain 10 incidental, infrequent, now and then, unreliable 12 intermittent

occasionally 6 rarely, seldom 7 at times 8 fitfully 9 sometimes 10 now and then 11 irregularly 12 infrequently, once in a while, periodically, sporadically 14 from time to time, intermittently 15 every now and then, once in a blue moon

occidental 7 Western 8 American, European 9 Hesperian, Westerner

occlude 4 clog, plug 5 block, choke, close 6 shut up, stop up 7 congest, shut off, stopper 8 choke off, obstruct 9 barricade, constrict 11 strangulate

occult 4 dark 5 magic 6 arcane, hidden, mystic, secret, veiled 7 obscure, private 8 esoteric, mystical, shrouded 9 concealed 10 cabalistic, mysterious, unrevealed 11 undisclosed 12 supernatural

occupancy 3 use 6 tenure 7 tenancy 8 lodgment 9 enjoyment, habitancy 10 engagement, habitation, occupation, possession 11 inhabitancy

occupant 5 owner 6 lessee, lodger, native, renter, roomer, tenant 7 dweller, settler 8 colonist, occupier, resident 9 addressee 10 inhabitant 11 householder

occupation 3 job 4 line, work 5 craft, forte, trade 6 career, living, metier, sphere 7 calling, control, pursuit, seizure 8 activity, business, capacity, conquest, lifework, vocation 9 specialty 10 employment, line of work, livelihood, possession, profession, subjection 11 foreign rule, subjugation 14 specialization 15 military control 18 military occupation

occupied 5 in use **6** amused, took up, used up **7** dwelt in, engaged, lived in, overran, overrun, taken up **8** absorbed, tenanted **9** concerned, conquered, inhabited, resided in **12** had control of, held in thrall **13** was situated in **16** took possession of

occupy 3 use **4** be in, be on, busy, fill, hold **5** amuse, sit in **6** absorb, employ, engage, fill up, room in, take up **7** concern, conquer, dwell in, engross, enslave, inhabit, lodge in, overrun, pervade, possess **8** permeate, reside in, saturate **9** entertain, subjugate **10** monopolize **11** have control **12** be situated in, hold in thrall **14** be the tenants of **16** take possession of

occur 3 hit **4** rise **5** arise, ensue **6** appear, befall, crop up, emerge, happen, result, strike, turn up **7** be found, come off, develop **8** spring up **9** come about, eventuate, take place, transpire **10** come to pass **11** materialize **13** cross one's mind, enter one's mind

occurrence 5 event **6** affair **7** episode, venture **8** business, incident, instance, occasion **9** adventure, emergence, happening, situation, unfolding **10** appearance, experience, proceeding **11** development, transaction **12** circumstance **13** manifestation **15** materialization

ocean 3 sea **4** deep, main, pond **5** flood, water **7** big pond, high sea **9** briny deep
god of: 3 Nun **4** Nanu **7** Neptune, Oceanus **8** Poseidon

Oceania, Oceanica 9 Melanesia, Polynesia **10** Micronesia **11** Australia
ocean: 12 South Pacific
island: 4 Cook, Guam, Fiji, Maui, Niue, Wake **5** Aunuu, Bonin, Kauai, Lanai, Tonga **6** Bikini, Futuna, Hawaii, Marcus, Midway, Rurutu, Tahiti, Tubuai, Tuvalu, Wallis **7** Gambier, Gilbert, Iwo Jima, Leeward, Mariana, Molokai, Phoenix, Solomon, Tokelau, Tuamotu, Tutuila, Vanuatu, Volcano **8** Aitutaki, Bismarck, Bora-Bora, Johnston, Kiribati, Marshall, Pitcairn, Windward **9** Australia, Christmas, Marquesas, Trobriand **10** New Zealand **12** New Caledonia, Western Samoa **14** Papua New Guinea **15** French Polynesia

oceanic 6 marine **7** aquatic, pelagic **8** seagoing **9** thalassic

Oceanid
form: 5 nymph
location: 3 sea
father: 7 Oceanus
mother: 6 Tethys

Oceanus
member of: 6 Titans
father: 6 Uranus
mother: 4 Gaea
consort of: 6 Tethys
father of: 8 Oceanids **9** river gods
son: 7 Proteus
daughter: 5 Doris, Persa **7** Philyra
form: 6 stream

ocelot 3 cat **7** wildcat

Ochimus
king of: 6 Rhodes
father: 6 Helius
wife: 9 Hegetoria
daughter: 7 Cydippe

ochlophobia
fear of: 6 crowds

Ockelman, Constance Frances Marie
real name of: 12 Veronica Lake

Ocnus
origin: 6 Tuscan
father: 8 river god
mother: 5 Manto
founded: 6 Mantua
personifies: 16 unavailing effort

O'Connor, Carroll
born: 7 Bronx NY
roles: 12 Archie Bunker, Archie's Place **14** All in the Family
restaurant: 12 The Ginger Man

O'Connor, Donald
born: 9 Chicago IL
roles: 9 Beau Geste **15** Singin' in the Rain **18** Tom Sawyer Detective **21** Francis the Talking Mule

O'Connor, Flannery
author of: 9 Wise Blood **15** The Habit of Being **17** Mystery and Manners **20** A Good Man Is Hard to Find, The Violent Bear It Away

Ocrisia
position: 5 slave
slave to: 7 Tarquin **8** Tanaquil
son: 14 Servius Tullius

Octavia
brother: 8 Augustus
husband: 4 Nero **10** Mark Antony
grandson: 8 Caligula

October
flower: 6 cosmos **9** calendula
French: 7 Octobre
gem: 4 opal **10** tourmaline
German: 7 Oktober
holiday: 9 Halloween (31), Yom Kippur **11** Columbus Day (12) **12** Rosh Hashanah **16** United Nations Day (24)
Italian: 7 Ottobre
number of days: 9 thirty-one
origin of name: 4 octo (Latin meaning eight)
place in year:
Gregorian: 5 tenth
Roman: 6 eighth
Spanish: 7 Octubre
Zodiac sign: 5 Libra **7** Scorpio

October Light
author: 11 John Gardner

Octopus, The
author: 11 Frank Norris

odd 4 rare **5** extra, funny, queer, spare, weird **6** casual, far-out, quaint, single, sundry, unique **7** bizarre, curious, not even, strange, surplus, unusual, various **8** freakish, leftover, peculiar, periodic, singular, sporadic, uncommon **9** irregular, remaining, spasmodic, unmatched **10** occasional, outlandish **13** miscellaneous **15** being one of a pair **16** out of the ordinary **17** not divisible by two

oddball 3 nut **4** kook **5** freak **6** weirdo **8** crackpot, original **9** character, eccentric, screwball **10** one-of-a-kind

Odd Couple, The
character: 3 Roy **5** Myrna, Roger, Speed **6** Miriam, Murray, Vinnie **10** Felix Unger **11** Gloria Unger **12** Cecily Pigeon, Oscar Madison **14** Blanche Madison **15** Gwendolyn Pigeon, (Dr) Nancy Cunningham
cast: 10 Al Molinaro, Archie Hahn **11** Brett Somers, Carol Shelly, Jack Klugman, Larry Gelman, Monica Evans, Tony Randall **12** Garry Walberg, Janice Hansen, Ryan McDonald **13** Elinor Donahue, Joan Hotchkiss, Penny Marshall
setting: 11 New York City
Felix's job: 12 photographer
Oscar's job: 12 sportswriter

Odd Couple, The
based on play by: **9** Neil Simon

Odd Couple, The
director: **8** Gene Saks
based on play by: **9** Neil Simon
cast: **10** Jack Lemmon (Felix Unger) **11** Herb Edelman, John Fiedler **13** Walter Matthau (Oscar Madison)

oddity 5 freak, sight **6** marvel, rarity, wonder **9** curiosity, queerness **10** phenomenon, uniqueness **11** abnormality, bizarreness, peculiarity, singularity, strangeness, unusualness **12** eccentricity, freakishness **13** individuality, unnaturalness **14** outlandishness
Latin: **8** rara avis

oddly amusing 5 droll, kooky **9** laughable, whimsical **10** ridiculous

odd person 3 nut **4** kook **5** flake, freak **6** looney, weirdo **7** oddball **8** crackpot **9** character, eccentric, screwball

odds and ends 4 olio **6** scraps **8** remnants **9** leftovers **10** hodgepodge, miscellany **11** this and that **13** bits and pieces **18** miscellaneous items

ode 4 epic, hymn, poem **5** lyric, paean, psalm, verse **6** ballad **8** canticle
type: **8** Horatian, Pindaric

Ode on a Grecian Urn
author: **9** John Keats

Ode on Indolence
author: **9** John Keats

Ode on Melancholy
author: **9** John Keats

Ode to a Nightingale
author: **9** John Keats

Ode to Autumn
author: **9** John Keats

Ode to Duty
author: **17** William Wordsworth

Ode to Psyche
author: **9** John Keats

Ode to the West Wind
author: **18** Percy Bysshe Shelley

Odets, Clifford
author of: **9** Golden Boy **12** Awake and Sing **14** The Country Girl **15** Waiting for Lefty **17** The Flowering Peach

Odin *see box*

odious 4 evil, foul, vile **5** hated, nasty **6** rotten **7** hate-ful, heinous, hideous **8** infamous **9** invidious, loathsome, monstrous, obnoxious, offensive, repugnant, repulsive, revolting, sickening **10** abominable, despicable, detestable, disgusting, nauseating, unbearable **11** intolerable, unendurable **12** contemptible **13** objectionable

odium 5 shame **6** hatred, infamy **7** disgust **8** contempt, disfavor, disgrace, dishonor, ignominy **9** antipathy, discredit, disesteem, disrepute **10** abhorrence, disrespect, opprobrium, repugnance **11** detestation, disapproval **14** disapprobation

odonata
class: **8** hexapoda
phylum: **10** arthropoda
group: **9** damselfly, dragonfly

odor 4 aura **5** aroma, scent, smell, stink **6** flavor, stench **7** bouquet, essence, perfume **9** effluvium, fragrance **10** atmosphere

odoriferous 4 rank **5** acrid, fetid **6** putrid, smelly **7** noisome, odorous, pungent, reeking, scented **8** aromatic, fragrant, perfumed, stinking **10** malodorous

odorous 4 rank **5** acrid, fetid **6** smelly **7** noisome, pungent, reeking, scented **8** aromatic, fragrant, perfumed, stinking

Odysseus
also: **7** Ulysses
king of: **6** Ithaca

Odin
also: **5** Othin
brother: **2** Ve **4** Vili
children: **4** Hodr, Thor **5** Baldr **6** Balder, Baldur
corresponds to: **5** Wotan
counterpart: **5** Wotan
court: **8** Valhalla
father: **3** Bor
god of: **3** war **6** poetry, wisdom **9** knowledge
grandson: **7** Volsung
home: **9** Gladsheim
horse: **8** Sleipnir
magic ring: **8** Draupnir
origin: **12** Scandinavian
raven: **5** Hugin, Munin
remaining eye: **3** sun
ruler of: **5** Aexir
spear: **7** Gungnir
throne: **10** Hlidskjalf
wife: **3** Fri **5** Frigg, Frija **6** Frigga
wolf: **4** Geri **5** Freki

---

father: **7** Laertes
mother: **8** Anticlea
hero of: **5** Iliad **7** Odyssey
wife: **8** Penelope **9** Callidice
son: **9** Telegonus **10** Polypoetes, Telemachus **11** Polyporthis
seduced by: **5** Circe
killed by: **9** Telegonus
epithet: **10** Laertiades

Odyssey
author: **5** Homer
character: **4** Zeus **5** Arete, Circe, Helen **6** Athene, Nestor, Scylla, Sirens **7** Calypso, Cyclops **8** Alcinous, Menelaus, Nausicaa, Odysseus, Penelope, Poseidon, Tiresias **9** Charybdis **10** Telemachus **11** Lotus-eaters

Oedipus
king of: **6** Thebes
father: **5** Laius
mother: **7** Jocasta
foster father: **7** Polybus
foster mother: **6** Merope **8** Periboea
wife: **7** Jocasta
son: **8** Eteocles **9** Polynices
daughter: **6** Ismene **8** Antigone
killed: **5** Laius
defeated: **6** Sphinx

Oedipus at Colonus
author: **9** Sophocles
character: **5** Creon **6** Elders, Ismene **7** Theseus **8** Antigone **9** Polynices

Oedipus Rex (Oedipus Tyrannus)
author: **9** Sophocles
character: **5** Creon, Laius **7** Jocasta **8** Tiresias

oeil-de-boeuf 16 small round window
literally: **8** bull's eye

Oeneus
king of: **7** Calydon
wife: **7** Althaea
son: **8** Meleager

Oenomaus
king of: **4** Elis, Pisa
father: **4** Ares
mother: **7** Sterope
daughter: **10** Hippodamia
murdered: **6** Marmax

Oenone
form: **5** nymph
father: **6** Cebren
husband: **5** Paris

Oenopion
king of: **5** Chios
father: **8** Dionysus
mother: **7** Ariadne
daughter: **6** Merope
blinded: **5** Orion

Oersted, Hans Christian
field: **7** physics
nationality: **6** Danish

founded: 16 electromagnetism
isolated: 16 metallic
  aluminum
named for him: 11 oersted
  unit

oeuvre 4 work **5** works **13** artist's output

O'Faolain, Sean
  author of: 15 The Heat of
  the Sun **17** A Nest of Simple Folk **22** Midsummer
  Night's Madness

of a piece 5 alike, equal
7 matched, the same **8** all in
one **9** analogous, identical
10 equivalent, homogenous,
synonymous **13** evenly
matched, one and the same

of bad character 5 shady
8 unsavory **11** of ill repute
12 disreputable, unprincipled

off 2 by **3** bad, far, ill, odd
4 afar, away, down, from, kill,
poor, stop **5** amiss, apart,
aside, crazy, wrong **6** absent,
begone, lessen, remote **7** distant, further, in error,
stopped, tainted **8** abnormal,
canceled, inferior, mistaken
9 imperfect

offal 4 junk, slag **5** dregs, trash,
waste **6** debris, refuse **7** carcass, carrion, garbage,
grounds, remains, residue, rubbish **8** leavings

off base 5 amiss, wrong **8** improper, mistaken **10** out of order, unsuitable
13 inappropriate

offbeat 3 odd **7** strange **8** peculiar **9** different, eccentric
14 unconventional

off-center 6 askew **7** strange
9 eccentric **10** imbalanced,
nonaligned, unbalanced
12 unreasonable
14 unconventional

off-color 4 blue, lewd, racy,
sexy **5** bawdy, dirty, salty,
spicy **6** earthy, risque, smutty,
wicked **7** naughty, obscene,
raunchy **8** improper, indecent,
scabrous **9** offensive **10** indelicate, indiscreet, suggestive

off duty 8 inactive **9** at leisure **10** unoccupied **13** on
one's own time

Offenbach, Jacques
  born: 7 Cologne, Germany
  composer of: 13 La Belle Helene **15** Tales of Hoffmann,
  La Vie Parisienne **22** Orpheus in the Underworld

offend 3 err, sin, vex **4** fret,
gall, miff, rile **5** anger, annoy,
chafe, lapse, pique, wound
6 insult, madden, nettle, ran-

kle **7** affront, disgust, incense,
inflame **8** irritate **9** aggravate,
displease, misbehave **10** antagonize, disgruntle, exasperate,
transgress **13** fall from grace

offender 5 crook, felon **6** sinner **7** culprit **8** criminal, violator **9** wrong doer
10 malefactor, trespasser

offense 3 sin **4** gibe, harm,
slap, slip, snub, twit **5** abuse,
crime, lapse, taunt **6** attack,
charge, felony, insult **7** affront,
assault, misdeed, outrage, umbrage **8** atrocity, enormity, evil
deed, rudeness **9** impudence,
indignity, insolence, offensive,
violation **10** aggression, disrespect, infraction, peccadillo,
wickedness **11** delinquency,
humiliation, malfeasance, misdemeanor, shortcoming
13 embarrassment, transgression **15** breach of conduct

offensive 4 foul, rank, rude,
ugly **5** nasty, onset **6** attack,
horrid **7** abusive, assault, hideous, offense, uncivil **8** charging, impudent, insolent,
storming **9** abhorrent, assailing, attacking, insulting, loathsome, obnoxious, onslaught,
repugnant, repulsive, revolting,
sickening, ungallant **10** abominable, aggression, aggressive,
assaulting, bombarding, detestable, disgusting, nauseating,
unmannerly, unpleasant
11 belligerent, distasteful, intolerable **12** disagreeable, embarrassing, insufferable
13 disrespectful, objectionable

offensiveness 8 rudeness
9 impudence, insolence, nastiness **10** disrespect, horridness,
incivility **13** repulsiveness
14 unpleasantness
15 distastefulness

offer 3 bid **5** put up **6** bestow,
extend, render, submit,
tender **7** advance, hold out,
present, proffer, propose, suggest **8** bestow on, offering,
overture, proposal, propound,
put forth **9** be willing, volunteer **10** invitation, put forward, submission, suggestion
11 make a motion, proposition **12** bring forward **14** put
on the market **19** place at
one's disposal

offer hospitality 4 host
7 welcome **8** play host **9** entertain **10** give a party, have
guests **13** keep open house

offering 3 bid **4** alms, gift
5 goods, wares **6** course
7 charity, present, tribute
8 anathema, bestowal, donation, oblation **9** sacrifice

11 beneficence **12** contribution
  to God: 6 corban **7** deodate
  to household deities: 4 bali

offertory 4 gift **8** oblation, offering **10** collection

offhand, offhanded 5 ad-lib,
hasty **6** casual, chance, random **7** relaxed **8** careless, cavalier, heedless **9** facetious,
haphazard, impromptu, unplanned, unstudied **10** improvised, nonchalant, off-the-cuff,
unprepared **11** spontaneous,
thoughtless, unconcerned, unrehearsed **12** off-the-record
14 extemporaneous,
unpremeditated

office 3 job **4** post, role **8** capacity, function, position
10 commission, occupation
11 appointment

officer 3 cop **4** head **7** manager **8** director, gendarme,
governor **9** constable, detective, executive, patrolman, policeman, president, secretary,
treasurer **10** bureaucrat
12 commissioner **13** administrator, vice-president

officers 8 managers **10** executives, management
14 administration

Officers and Gentlemen
  author: 11 Evelyn Waugh

offices 4 duty, help, task **5** favor, trust **6** charge **7** service
8 function, province
10 assistance

office seeker 7 hopeful, nominee **8** aspirant **9** candidate

office worker 5 clerk, steno
6 typist **9** file clerk, secretary
10 bookkeeper, keypuncher
13 data processor **14** clerical
worker

official 5 agent **6** formal,
vested **7** manager, officer
8 approved, chairman, director,
licensed **9** authentic, certified,
dignitary, executive, warranted **10** accredited, authorized, sanctioned, supervisor
11 functionary **13** administrator, authoritative **14** administrative **18** administrative head

**official communication
5** edict, order, ukase **6** report
7 release **8** bulletin **10** communique **12** proclamation

officialdom 10 government
11 authorities, bureaucracy
14 administration

official paper 4 writ **5** order
8 document **10** instrument

officiate 3 run **4** head, lead
5 chair, emcee **6** direct, handle, manage **7** oversee, pre-

side **8** moderate, regulate
9 supervise **10** administer
11 superintend **12** be in
charge of

officious 6 prying **7** pompous
8 meddling **9** intrusive, kibitz-
ing, obtrusive **10** high-handed,
meddlesome **11** domineering,
interfering, overbearing, patronizing **13** high and mighty,
self-assertive, self-important
16 poking one's nose in

Offield, Lewis Delaney
real name of: 9 Jack Oakie

offset 6 redeem **7** balance, nullify **8** equalize, knock out
9 cancel out, make up for
10 counteract, neutralize
11 countervail **13** compensate
for, counterweight
14 counterbalance

offshoot 4 limb **5** scion, shoot
6 branch **7** adjunct **9** aftermath, by-product, outgrowth
10 descendant

offspring 3 fry **4** heir, seed
5 brood, child, issue, scion,
spawn, young **6** family, litter
7 progeny **8** children, increase
9 posterity **10** descendant,
succession **11** descendants

off the mark 5 amiss **6** afield,
astray **9** off target **16** off the
right track

off-the-record 5 privy **6** secret **7** private **11** undisclosed
12 confidential **16** not to be
disclosed **17** not for
publication

off the top of one's head
5 ad-lib **7** offhand **9** extempore, impromptu **10** improvised, unprepared
11 extemporary, unrehearsed
14 extemporaneous,
unpremeditated

of good quality 4 good
6 worthy **8** superior **9** excellent **10** creditable

of high rank 5 noble, regal,
royal **6** lordly, titled **7** courtly
11 blue-blooded **12** aristocratic

Of Human Bondage
author: 16 W Somerset
Maugham
director: 12 John Cromwell
character: 5 Weeks **7** Hayward **11** Louisa Carey,
Philip Carey **12** Sally
Athelny, William Carey
13 Mildred Rogers, Miss
Wilkinson, Thorpe Athelny
cast: 10 Bette Davis, Frances
Dee, Kay Johnson **12** Leslie
Howard

of its own kind
Latin: 10 sui generis

Of Mice and Men
author: 13 John Steinbeck
director: 14 Lewis Milestone
character: 4 Slim **5** Candy
6 Crooks, Curley **11** Lennie
Small **12** George Milton
cast: 10 Betty Field **11** Lon
Chaney Jr (Lenny) **15** Burgess Meredith, Charles
Bickford
score: 12 Aaron Copland

of one's own right
Latin: 8 sui juris

of poor quality 5 junky
6 flimsy, shoddy, sleazy,
trashy **8** inferior
11 substandard

of secondary importance
8 nonvital **9** accessory, extrinsic **10** incidental **11** dispensable, unnecessary
12 nonessential

often 3 oft **4** much **7** usually
8 commonly, ofttimes **9** generally, regularly **10** constantly,
frequently, habitually, oftentimes, repeatedly **11** continually, customarily, over and
over, recurrently **12** periodically, time and again

**of the dead say nothing
but good**
Latin: 21 de mortuis nil nisi
bonum

of the faith
Latin: 6 de fide

of their own kind
Latin: 10 sui generis

of the old school 5 passe
8 outdated, outmoded
9 out-of-date **12** conservative,
old-fashioned **18** establish-
mentarian

Of Time and the River
author: 11 Thomas Wolfe
character: 10 Eugene Gant

oft-repeated 5 trite **7** popular
8 constant, familiar, frequent,
habitual, well-worn **9** continual, recurring, well-known
10 persistent **11** widely-known

of what good
Latin: 7 cui bono

Ogdoad
also: 3 Heh
origin: 8 Egyptian
number of gods: 5 eight

ogle 3 eye **6** gape at, gawk at,
goggle, leer at **7** stare at
8 goggle at **10** give the eye,
scrutinize **15** give the once-
over, stare at greedily **16** cast
sheep's eyes at, gaze at with
desire

Ogma
origin: 5 Irish

god of: 6 poetry **9** eloquence
inventor of: 12 Ogham letters

Ogmios
origin: 6 Gaelic
god of: 9 eloquence
corresponds to: 7 Mercury

ogre, ogress 5 brute, demon,
fiend, ghoul, harpy **6** despot,
tyrant **7** bugbear, monster
8 bogeyman, dictator, martinet **11** slave driver

Ogygia
island of: 7 Calypso

Ogygus
king of: 7 Boeotia
father: 8 Poseidon

O'Hara, John
author of: 7 Pal Joey **11** A
Rage to Live **13** The Instrument **14** From the Terrace,
The Hat on the Bed
16 Butterfield Eight **17** Ten
North Frederick **19** The
Horse Knows the Way
20 Appointment in Samarra

O'Hara, Maureen
real name: 18 Maureen
Fitzsimmons
nickname: 18 Queen of
Technicolor
born: 7 Ireland **8** Milltown
roles: 10 Lady Godiva **11** The
Quiet Man **13** North to
Alaska, The Parent Trap
16 The Foxes of Harrow
19 How Green Was My Valley **20** Hunchback of Notre
Dame **27** Miracle on Thirty-
fourth Street

O'Hara, Scarlett
character in: 15 Gone With
the Wind
family: 6 Gerald **7** Carreen,
Suellen
author: 8 Mitchell

O Henry
real name: 19 William Sidney Porter
author of: 11 The Last Leaf
16 Cabbages and Kings, The
Gift of the Magi **18** The
Cop and the Anthem
19 The Ransom of Red
Chief

Ohio *see box*

Ohm, Georg Simon
field: 7 physics
nationality: 6 German
discovered: 20 electrical
resistance
named for him: 7 ohm unit

oil 4 balm, lard **5** cream, salve
6 anoint, grease, pomade
7 unguent **8** liniment, ointment **9** lubricant, lubricate,
melted fat, petroleum
12 melted grease
type: 4 corn, fuel, hair

Ohio
abbreviation: 2 OH
nickname: 7 Buckeye
capital: 8 Columbus
largest city: 9 Cleveland
others: 3 Ada 4 Kent, Lima 5 Akron, Berea, Cadiz, Niles, Parma, Piqua, Xenia 6 Athens, Canton, Dayton, Elyria, Lorain, Marion, Newark, Tiffin, Toledo, Warren 7 Ashland, Findlay, Fremont, Norwood, Wooster 8 Alliance, Bluffton, Fostoria, Lakewood, Marietta, Sandusky 9 Ashtabula, Kettering, Lancaster, Massillon, Struthers, Vermilion, Willowick 10 Cincinnati, Huntington, Portsmouth, Rocky River, Willoughby, Youngstown, Zanesville 11 Painesville, Springfield 12 Steubenville
college: 4 Kent 5 Akron, Hiram, Miami 6 Dayton, Kenyon, Xavier 7 Antioch, Oberlin, Wooster 8 Defiance, Dennison, Marietta, Ursuline 10 Wittenberg 11 Case Western 12 Bowling Green, Ohio Wesleyan
feature:
   hall of fame: 11 Pro Football
   race: 12 Soap Box Derby
tribe: 4 Erie 7 Wyandot 13 Mound Builders
people: 7 buckeye, Cy Young 8 Zane Grey 10 Clark Gable, T Hart Crane 11 Annie Oakley, Lillian Gish 12 James Thurber, Lowell Thomas, Norman Thomas 13 Neil Armstrong, Orville Wright, Thomas A Edison 14 Barney Oldfield, Clarence Darrow 15 William T Sherman 16 Sherwood Anderson 18 Norman Vincent Peale
   explorer: 7 La Salle
lake: 4 Erie 5 Grand 6 Berlin, Dillon, Hoover, Indian 8 Delaware 13 Mosquito Creek
land rank: 35 thirty-fifth
mountain:
   highest point: 12 Campbell Hill
physical feature:
   caverns: 4 Ohio, Zane 6 Seneca
   spring: 8 Blue Hole
president: 13 Ulysses S Grant 14 James A Garfield, Warren G Harding 15 William McKinley 16 Rutherford B Hayes 17 William Howard Taft 20 William Henry Harrison
river: 5 Grand, Miami 6 Maumee, Scioto, Wabash 7 Hocking 8 Cuyahoga, Sandusky 9 Muskingum, Tennessee 10 Cumberland 11 Monongahela
state admission: 11 seventeenth
state bird: 8 cardinal
state flower: 16 scarlet carnation
state motto: 27 With God All Things Are Possible
state song: 13 Beautiful Ohio
state tree: 7 buckeye

5 crude, motor, olive, whale 7 cooking, mineral 9 safflower, vegetable

Oilean Ajax *see* 4 Ajax

Oileus
king of: 6 Locris
member of: 9 Argonauts
father: 10 Hodoedocus
mother: 9 Agrianome
son: 5 Medon 13 Ajax the Lesser

oily 5 fatty, lardy, slick 6 greasy, smarmy 7 buttery, fawning, servile 8 slippery, slithery, toadying, unctuous 9 groveling, sebaceous 10 lubricious, oleaginous 11 bootlicking, subservient 12 ingratiating

ointment 4 balm 5 salve 6 lotion, pomade 7 pomatum, unguent 8 liniment 9 emollient, spikenard

Oizys
mother: 3 Nyx
personifies: 4 pain

Ojibwa, Ojibway *see* 8 Chippawa

OK 4 fine, good 7 approve, endorse 8 all right, approval 9 authorize 11 endorsement 13 authorization
   French: 7 d'accord

O'Keeffe, Georgia
born: 12 Sun Prairie WI
artwork: 7 Stables 9 Black Iris 14 Patio with Cloud 15 Lake George Barns 22 Light Coming on the Plains 26 Black Flower and Blue Larkspur

Oklahoma *see box, p. 704*

Oklahoma!
director: 13 Fred Zinnemann
cast: 10 Rod Steiger 11 Eddie Albert 12 Gordon MacRae, Shirley Jones 13 Gloria Grahame, James Whitmore 18 Charlotte Greenwood
score: 21 Rodgers and Hammerstein
song: 23 People Will Say We're in Love 24 Surrey with the Fringe on Top

Olbers, Heinrich Wilhelm Matthaus
field: 9 astronomy
nationality: 6 German
discovered: 5 Vesta 6 comets, Pellas 9 asteroids

old 4 aged, used 5 hoary, of age 6 beat-up, bygone, of yore 7 ancient, antique, archaic, elderly, outworn, rundown, vintage, wornout 8 battered, decrepit, familiar, grizzled, much-used, obsolete, outdated, timeworn 9 crumbling, hackneyed, out-of-date, venerable, weathered 10 antiquated, broken-down, grayheaded, ramshackle, tumbledown 11 dilapidated, from the past, gray with age, obsolescent, time-honored, traditional 12 deteriorated, old-fashioned, white with age 13 weather-beaten 14 of long standing 15 long established

Old Aches and Pains
nickname of: 11 Luke Appling

old age 6 dotage 7 ripe age 8 maturity, senility 11 advanced age 15 second childhood

Old and the Young, The
author: 15 Luigi Pirandello

Old Bay State
nickname of:
13 Massachusetts

Old Bulgarian
also: 15 Old Church Slavic
language family: 12 Indo-European
group: 11 Balto-Slavic
status: 7 archaic
used in: 14 Orthodox church

Old Chinook
nickname of: 10 Washington

Oklahoma
   abbreviation: 2 OK 4 Okla
   nickname: 6 Boomer, Sooner
   capital/largest city: 12 Oklahoma City
   others: 3 Ada 4 Alva, Enid, Hugo 5 Altus, Miami, Ponca, Tulsa 6 Duncan, El Reno, Guymon, Idabel, Lawton 7 Ardmore, Guthrie, Sapulpa, Shawnee 8 Anadarko, Fort Sill, Muskogee 9 Blackwell, Claremore, McAlester 10 Stillwater 12 Bartlesville
   college: 5 Tulsa 6 Norman 7 Cameron 8 Langston, Phillips 10 Stillwater 11 Oral Roberts 12 Oklahoma City 15 Bethany Nazarene 17 American Christian
   feature:
      hall of fame: 14 American Indian
      national park: 6 Platte
   tribe: 3 Kaw, Oto 4 Iowa, Loup, Otoe, Waco 5 Caddo, Kansa, Osage, Ponca 6 Apache, Ottawa, Pawnee, Quapaw 7 Shawnee, Wichita 8 Arapahoe, Tawakoni
      Five Civilized Tribes: 5 Creek 7 Choctaw 8 Cherokee, Seminole 9 Chickasaw
   people: 4 Okie 6 sooner 9 Jim Thorpe 10 Will Rogers 12 Mickey Mantle 14 Maria Tallchief
      explorer: 8 Coronado
   lake: 5 Atoka, Grand, Hulah 6 Texoma, Wister 7 Eufaula, Heyburn, Oologah 8 Keystone 9 Pensacola, Tenkiller 10 Fort Gibson 11 Thunderbird 12 Markham Ferry 17 Lake O' The Cherokees
   land rank: 10 eighteenth
   mountain: 6 Ozarks 8 Ouachita
      highest point: 9 Black Mesa
   physical feature: 9 Panhandle
      plains: 5 Great
   river: 3 Red 5 Grand 6 Little, Neosho 7 Washita 8 Arkansas, Canadian, Cimarron 9 Verdigris 15 Muddy Boggy Creek
   state admission: 10 forty-sixth
   state bird: 23 scissor-tailed flycatcher
   state fish: 9 white bass
   state flower: 9 mistletoe
   state motto: 22 Labor Conquers All Things
   state song: 8 Oklahoma
   state tree: 6 redbud

Old Colony State
   nickname of:
   13 Massachusetts

Old Curiosity Shop, The
   author: 14 Charles Dickens
   character: 5 Quilp 9 Fred Trent, Mrs Jarley 10 Kit Nubbles, Sally Brass 11 Grandfather 12 Sampson Brass 13 Dick Swiveller 15 Little Nell Trent 18 The Single Gentleman

Old Dominion
   nickname of: 8 Virginia

olden 4 past 6 bygone, former, of yore 7 ancient, long-ago 8 departed

Oldest Man 10 Methuselah

old-fashioned 5 corny, dated, passe 7 antique, archaic 8 obsolete, outdated, outmoded 9 out-of-date 10 antiquated, out of style 11 obsolescent,

traditional 12 long-standing, out of fashion 13 unfashionable 14 behind the times

Old-Fashioned Girl, An
   author: 15 Louisa May Alcott

Old Franklin State
   nickname of: 9 Tennessee

old hand 3 pro 6 expert, master 8 virtuoso 9 authority 12 professional

old hat 5 passe, stale 6 demode 7 archaic, outworn 8 obsolete, outdated, outmoded 9 out-of-date 10 antiquated, superseded 11 obsolescent 12 old-fashioned 13 unfashionable 14 behind the times

old-line 11 established, traditional 12 conservative

Old Line State
   nickname of: 8 Maryland

Old Love
   author: 19 Isaac Bashevis Singer

Old Maid, The
   author: 12 Edith Wharton

Old Man and the Sea, The
   author: 15 Ernest Hemingway
   character: 7 Manolin 8 Santiago

Old Mortality
   author: 14 Sir Walter Scott
   character: 5 Edith 11 Henry Morton 12 Basil Olifant, Lord Evandale 19 John Balfour of Burley 21 Lady Margaret Bellenden 27 Colonel Grahame of Claverhouse

Old Mortality
   author: 19 Katherine Anne Porter

Old North
   nickname of: 13 North Carolina

Old Patagonian Express, The
   author: 11 Paul Theroux

old saw 5 adage, maxim 6 cliche, saying, truism 7 bromide, proverb 9 old saying 10 expression 11 old chestnut

oldster 5 elder 6 codger, old man 7 ancient 8 old woman 13 senior citizen

Old Testament
   first five books:
      10 Pentateuch
   first six books: 9 Hexateuch
   first seven books:
      10 Heptateuch
   books of: 3 Job 4 Amos, Ezra, Joel, Ruth 5 Hosea, Jonah, Kings, Micah, Nahum, Songs, Tobit 6 Baruch, Daniel, Esther, Exodus, Haggai, Isaiah, Joshua, Judges, Judith, Psalms, Samuel, Sirach, Wisdom 7 Ezekiel, Genesis, Malachi, Numbers, Obadiah 8 Habakkuk, Jeremiah, Macabees, Nehemiah, Proverbs 9 Leviticus, Zechariah, Zephaniah 10 Chronicles 11 Deuteronomy 12 Ecclesiastes 13 Song of Solomon 14 Ecclesiasticus

Oldtown Folks
   author: 19 Harriet Beecher Stowe

Old Wives' Tale, The
   author: 13 Arnold Bennett

old-world 6 formal 7 courtly, gallant, old-line 8 European, orthodox 10 ceremonial, chivalrous, prescribed 11 ceremonious, continental, established, traditional 12 conservative, conventional, old-fashioned

Ole
  character in: **16** Giants of the Earth
  author: **7** Rolvaag

Olen
  occupation: **4** poet
  location: **5** Lycia

Olenska, Ellen
  character in: **17** The Age of Innocence
  author: **7** Wharton

oleoresin 3 gum **5** anime, apiol, elemi **6** balsam **7** solvent **10** turpentine

olio 4 stew **6** jumble, medley **7** melange, mixture **8** mishmash **9** potpourri **10** assortment, collection, hodgepodge, hotchpotch, miscellany

olive 12 Olea europaea
  varieties: **3** tea **4** wild **5** black, false, holly, sweet **6** common, desert, spurge **7** Russian **8** American, fragrant **11** Californian

olive-drab 5 khaki **13** greenish-brown

Oliver
  character in: **11** As You Like It
  author: **11** Shakespeare

Oliver!
  director: **9** Carol Reed
  based on story by:
    14 Charles Dickens (Oliver Twist)
  cast: **8** Jack Wild, Ron Moody (Fagin) **10** Mark Lester (Oliver), Oliver Reed **11** Shani Wallis
  Oscar for: **7** picture **8** director
  remake of: **11** Oliver Twist
  song: **16** Consider Yourself, Food Glorious Food **17** As Long As He Needs Me

Oliver Twist
  author: **14** Charles Dickens
  character: **5** Fagin, Monks (Edward Leeford), Nancy **6** Bumble **9** Bill Sikes, Mrs Maylie **10** Mr Brownlow, Rose Maylie
  director: **9** David Lean
  cast: **8** Kay Walsh **12** Alec Guinness (Fagin), Robert Newton **13** Anthony Newley (Artful Dodger) **16** Francis L Sullivan, John Howard Davies
  remade as: **7** Oliver!

Olivia
  character in: **12** Twelfth Night
  author: **11** Shakespeare

Olivier, Sir Laurence
  born: **7** Dorking, England

wife: **11** Vivien Leigh **13** Joan Plowright
  roles: **6** Becket, Hamlet (Oscar), Henry V, Sleuth **7** Rebecca **11** Marathon Man **16** Wuthering Heights **17** Pride and Prejudice, The Boys from Brazil, The Devil's Disciple **19** Shoes of the Fisherman **23** The Prince and the Showgirl

olivine
  variety: **7** peridot

olla 3 jar, pot **10** earthen pot

Olmsted, Frederick Law
  landscape architect of:
    11 Central Park (NYC, with Calvert Vaux) **12** Prospect Park (Brooklyn NY) **13** Fairmount Park (Philadelphia) **14** Biltmore Estate (Asheville NC), Mount Royal Park (Montreal)

Olsen, Merlin (Jay)
  sport: **8** football
  team: **14** Los Angeles Rams
  TV roles: **12** Father Murphy **15** Highway to Heaven **23** Little House on the Prairie

Olsson, Ann-Margret
  real name of: **10** Ann-Margret

O Lucky Man
  director: **15** Lindsay Anderson
  cast: **9** Alan Price **13** Rachel Roberts **15** Malcolm McDowell, Ralph Richardson
  score: **9** Alan Price

Olwen
  origin: **5** Welsh
  form: **8** princess
  father: **16** Yspadaden Penkawr

Olympic Games *see box*

Omaha
  language family: **6** Siouan **7** Dhegiha
  location: **4** Iowa **8** Nebraska, Oklahoma

Oman *see box, p. 706*

omega 3 end **4** last **5** final **6** ending **8** terminus
  opposite: **5** alpha

omen 4 sign **5** token **6** augury, herald **7** auspice, portent, presage, warning **9** foretaste, harbinger, precursor **10** foreboding, indication

Omet 15 Biblical measure

ominous 7 unlucky **8** menacing, minatory, monitory, sinister **9** dismaying, ill-omened **10** foreboding, ill-starred, portentous

Olympic Games
  site:
    1896: **6** Athens
    1900: **5** Paris
    1904: **7** St Louis
    1906: **6** Athens
    1908: **6** London
    1912: **9** Stockholm
    1920: **7** Antwerp
    1924: **5** Paris
      8 Chamonix
    1928: **8** St Moritz
      9 Amsterdam
    1932: **10** Lake Placid, Los Angeles
    1936: **6** Berlin
      21 Garmisch-Partenkirchen
    1948: **6** London **8** St Moritz
    1952: **4** Oslo
      8 Helsinki
    1956: **9** Melbourne
      15 Cortina d'Ampezzo
    1960: **5** Tokyo
      11 Squaw Valley
    1968: **8** Grenoble
      10 Mexico City
    1972: **6** Munich
      7 Sapporo
    1976: **8** Montreal
      9 Innsbruck
    1980: **6** Moscow
      10 Lake Placid
    1984: **8** Sarajevo
      10 Los Angeles
    1988: **5** Seoul
      7 Calgary
    1992: **9** Barcelona
      11 Albertville
    1994: **11** Lillehammer
    1996: **7** Atlanta

omission 3 gap **4** hole **7** neglect **9** exception, exclusion, oversight **10** leaving out, negligence **11** delinquency, elimination **12** noninclusion **13** neglected item **16** something omitted

omit 3 cut **4** drop, fail, jump, miss, shun, skip **5** avoid, elide **6** bypass, delete, except, forget, ignore, slight **7** excerpt, exclude, let slip, neglect **8** leave out, overlook, pass over, preclude, set aside **11** forget about

omnia vincit amor 15 love conquers all

Omnibus
  host: **13** Alistair Cooke

omnipotent 6 mighty **7** supreme **8** almighty, powerful, puissant **11** all-powerful

omniscient 7 all-wise, su-

Oman
other name: 13 Muscat and Oman
capital: 6 Masqat, Muscat
largest city: 5 Matra **6** Matrah
others: 3 Sur **4** Fida **5** Dubai, Nazwa, Nigwa, Sohar, Wazit **6** Khasab, Marbat, Murbat, Suwaih, Tinouf **7** Khabura, Salalah **8** Ashkhara
government: 9 Sultanate
head of state/government: 6 sultan
monetary unit: 3 gaj, gaz **4** rial **5** baiza, ghazi **7** mahmudi
island: 6 Masera, Masira **7** Masirah **10** Kuria Muria
mountain: 4 Qara **5** Hafit, Harim, Nakhl, Tayin **8** el-Akhdar **11** Jabal Akhdar **13** Green Mountain
highest point: 6 al-Sham
sea: 6 Indian **7** Arabian
physical feature:
  cape: **7** Madraka **9** Ras Al Hadd **13** Ras Dharbat 'Ali
  gulf: **4** Oman
  peninsula: **7** Arabian **8** Musandam
  plain: **6** Dhofar **7** Batinah
  strait: **6** Hormuz
people: 4 Arab
  ruler: **12** Qabus Bin Said **13** Said Bin Taimur
language: 4 Urdu **5** Hindi **6** Arabic **7** Baluchi
religion: 5 Islam
war: 4 Gulf **11** Desert Storm

preme **8** infinite **9** all-seeing **10** all-knowing, preeminent

omnium gatherum 23 miscellaneous collection

omnivorous 7 hoggish **8** edacious, ravenous **9** crapulous, rapacious, voracious **10** gluttonous, polyphagic, predacious **12** pantophagous

Omoo
author: 14 Herman Melville
character: 10 Captain Bob **15** Doctor Long Ghost

Omphale
queen of: 5 Lydia
father: 8 Iardanus
husband: 6 Tmolus
son: 5 Lamus
served by: 8 Hercules

Omri
father: 6 Becher **7** Michael
son: 4 Ahab
daughter-in-law: 7 Jezebel

on 2 at **4** atop, near, over, upon **5** about, above, ahead, along, anent **7** against, forward, planned **8** abutting, adjacent, attached, intended, touching **9** occurring **10** concerning, juxtaposed

On
father: 6 Peleth
city of: 10 Heliopolis

on-and-off 6 spotty **8** episodic **9** irregular, spasmodic, temporary **10** now-and-then, occasional

On Beginning and Perishing
author: 9 Aristotle

once 7 ages ago, long ago, one time **8** formerly, hitherto, years ago **9** at one time **10** heretofore, previously **11** a single time, for the nonce, in times past, some time ago **12** in the old days, some time back **13** once upon a time, on one occasion

once-in-a-lifetime 6 unique **7** special **8** singular **11** one-time-only

once more 4 anew **5** again **9** once again, over again **11** one more time

on cloud nine 6 elated, joyful, joyous **8** ecstatic, euphoric **9** exuberant, rapturous **15** in seventh heaven

oncoming 5 close **7** looming, nearing **8** imminent **9** advancing, impending, onrushing **11** approaching, bearing down

on course 8 on target **15** on the right track

Ondine
author: 13 Jean Giraudoux

one 2 an **3** you **4** a man, lone, only, sole **5** a body, a soul, whole **6** a thing, entire, single, unique **7** a person, someone **8** complete, singular, solitary, somebody **10** individual, unrepeated

One, Two, Three
director: 11 Billy Wilder
cast: 11 James Cagney **12** Pamela Tiffin **13** Arlene Francis, Horst Buchholz

setting: 10 West Berlin
score: 11 Andre Previn

O'Neal, Ryan
real name: 16 Patrick Ryan O'Neal
born: 12 Los Angeles CA
daughter: 10 Tatum O'Neal
roles: 9 Love Story, Paper Moon **10** What's Up Doc **11** Barry Lyndon, Peyton Place **16** Rodney Harrington

O'Neal, Tatum
born: 12 Los Angeles CA
father: 9 Ryan O'Neal
roles: 9 Paper Moon **12** Bad News Bears **14** Little Darlings **19** International Velvet
husband: 11 John McEnroe

one and the same 5 equal **7** matched **9** identical

one by one 6 singly **10** one at a time, separately, single file **12** individually

One Day at a Time
character: 9 Ann Romano **11** Julie Cooper **13** Barbara Cooper **15** Dwayne Schneider
cast: 14 Bonnie Franklin **15** Pat Harrington Jr **17** Mackenzie Phillips, Valerie Bertinelli

One Day in the Life of Ivan Denisovich
author: 23 Aleksandr Solzhenitsyn Jr

One Fat Englishman
author: 12 Kingsley Amis

One Flew Over the Cuckoo's Nest
director: 11 Milos Forman
based on story by: 8 Ken Kesey
cast: 13 Jack Nicholson **14** Louise Fletcher, Michael Beryman **15** William Redfield
Oscar for: 5 actor (Nicholson) **7** actress (Fletcher), picture **8** director **10** screenplay

One Hour with You
director: 11 George Cukor **13** Ernst Lubitsch
cast: 14 Genevieve Tobin **16** Maurice Chevalier **17** Jeanette MacDonald
remake of: 17 The Marriage Circle
song: 14 What Would You Do

one-hundred percent 5 sheer, total, utter, whole **7** supreme **8** absolute, complete **10** consummate **17** through-and-through

O'Neill, Eugene
author of: 8 The Straw **11** The Hairy Ape **12** Ah

Wilderness, Anna Christie
13 Marco Millions **14** Glencairn Cycle **15** The Emperor Jones, The Iceman Cometh **16** Beyond the Horizon, Strange Interlude, The Great God Brown **18** Desire Under the Elms **20** The Moon of the Caribees **22** A Moon for the Misbegotten, All God's Chillun Got Wings, Mourning Becomes Electra **24** Long Day's Journey into Night

Oneiros
  also: 6 Oniros
  origin: 5 Greek
  god of: 6 dreams

oneness 5 union, unity **7** concord, harmony **8** entirety, identity, sameness, totality **9** agreement, aloneness, integrity, wholeness **10** uniformity, uniqueness **11** singularity **12** completeness **13** individuality

one-of-a-kind 4 rare **6** unique **7** strange, unusual **8** original **9** eccentric

onerous 5 heavy **6** taxing **7** arduous, painful, weighty **8** crushing, grievous **9** demanding, wearisome **10** burdensome, exhausting, oppressive **11** distressing **12** hard to endure

one thing in return for another
  Latin: 10 quid pro quo

one-time 3 old **4** past **5** early, prior **6** former, recent **7** earlier, quondam **8** previous **9** erstwhile
  French: 8 ci-devant

one voice 4 solo **6** unison **7** concert

one who has a fixed income
  French: 7 rentier

On First Looking Into Chapman's Homer
  author: 9 John Keats

on foot
  French: 5 a pied

ongoing 7 endless, lasting **8** enduring, unbroken, unending **10** continuing, proceeding **11** never-ending, unremitting **13** uninterrupted

On Golden Pond
  director: 10 Mark Rydell
  based on play by: 14 Ernest Thompson
  cast: 9 Jane Fonda **10** Doug McKeon, Henry Fonda (Norman Thayer Jr) **16** Katharine Hepburn
  setting: 5 Maine

Oscar for: 5 actor (Fonda) **7** actress (Hepburn)

on guard 4 wary **5** alert **7** careful, heedful **8** cautious, vigilant, watchful

on hand 5 handy, on tap **6** at hand **9** available **10** accessible, convenient **14** at one's disposal

on horseback
  French: 7 a cheval

onion 6 Allium **10** Allium cepa
  varieties: 3 red, sea, top **4** leek, tree, wild **5** green, gypsy, pearl, swamp, Welsh, white **6** German, potato, yellow **7** Bermuda, Danvers, nodding, prairie, shallot, Spanish **8** climbing, Egyptian, false sea, scallion, Valencia **9** Catawissa, ever-ready, flowering, two-bladed **10** multiplier, red-skinned **16** Japanese bunching
  origin: 9 Asia Minor
  called by Robert Louis Stevenson: 14 rose among roots

Onion Field, The
  author: 14 Joseph Wambaugh

Oniros *see* **7** Oneiros

On Liberty
  author: 14 John Stuart Mill

onlooker 5 gazer, ogler **6** viewer **7** watcher, witness **8** beholder, kibitzer, observer **9** bystander, spectator **10** eyewitness, rubberneck

only 4 just, lone, sole **5** alone **6** barely, merely, purely, simply, single, singly, solely, unique **7** at least **8** by itself, singular, solitary **9** by oneself, exclusive, unmatched **10** individual, no more than, nothing but, one and only, unrepeated **11** exclusively **12** individually, unparalleled

on one's uppers 5 broke **9** destitute **10** down and out

On Plants
  author: 9 Aristotle

On Revolution
  author: 12 Hannah Arendt

onrush 4 flow, flux, gush, tide, wave **5** flood, onset, storm, surge **6** attack, charge, deluge, spring, stream **7** assault, cascade, current, torrent **9** avalanche

onset 4 push, raid **5** birth, sally, start **6** attack, charge, onrush, outset, thrust **7** assault, genesis, infancy, offense **8** founding, invasion, outbreak, storming **9** beginning, inception, incursion, offensive, onslaught **10** incipience, initiation **12** commencement, inauguration

onslaught 4 coup, push, raid **5** blitz, foray, onset, sally **6** attack, charge, putsch, thrust **7** assault, offense **8** invasion **9** incursion, offensive **10** aggression, blitzkrieg

on tap 5 handy **6** at hand, on hand **9** available **10** accessible, convenient

Ontario
  bay: 6 Hudson
  canal: 5 Trent **6** Rideau
  capital: 7 Toronto
  city: 3 Emo **4** Galt **6** London, Ottawa **7** Windsor **8** Hamilton, Kingston **9** Kitchener
  explored by: 5 French **6** British
  industry: 6 mining **11** agriculture **13** manufacturing
  lake: 6 Simcoe
  province of: 6 Canada
  river: 6 Ottawa, Thames **7** Niagara **10** St Lawrence
  settled by: 9 Loyalists
  university: 4 York **5** Brock, Trent **8** McMaster

on the alert 4 wary **7** careful, mindful, on guard **8** cautious, watchful **9** wide awake **12** on the lookout

On the Beach
  author: 10 Nevil Shute
  director: 13 Stanley Kramer
  cast: 10 Ava Gardner **11** Fred Astaire, Gregory Peck **13** Donna Anderson **14** Anthony Perkins

on the contrary
  French: 11 au contraire

on the dot 7 exactly **8** promptly **9** on the nose, precisely **10** punctually

on the face
  Latin: 7 ex facie

on the go 4 busy **6** active, mobile **8** in motion **9** energetic, on the move **13** indefatigable

On the Heavens
  author: 9 Aristotle

On the Morning of Christ's Nativity
  author: 10 John Milton

on the move 5 astir **6** active, mobile **7** on the go **8** in motion

on the nose 5 exact **7** exactly, precise **8** accurate, on target **9** precisely **10** accurately, on the money

on the outer edges
Latin: 10 in extremis

on the right track 8 on course, on target

On the Soul
author: 9 Aristotle

On the Town
director: 9 Gene Kelly 12 Stanley Donen
cast: 9 Ann Miller, Gene Kelly, Vera-Ellen 12 Betty Garrett, Frank Sinatra
setting: 11 New York City
score: 11 Adolph Green, Betty Comden 16 Leonard Bernstein
song: 14 New York New York

On the Waterfront
director: 9 Elia Kazan
cast: 8 Lee J Cobb 10 Karl Malden, Pat Henning, Rod Steiger 12 Leif Erickson, Marlon Brando 13 Eva Marie Saint
Oscar for: 5 actor (Brando) 7 picture 8 director 10 screenplay 17 supporting actress (Saint)

on the whole 9 in general 10 by and large 27 considering the circumstances

onto 4 atop, upon 5 aware, privy 6 aboard

onus 4 duty, load 5 cross 6 burden, strain, weight 9 liability 10 obligation 11 encumbrance 13 burden of proof 14 responsibility

onus probandi 13 burden of proof

onward, onwards 5 ahead, along 7 forward, ongoing 9 advancing, frontward 11 moving ahead, progressive
French: 7 en avant, en route

On Wings of Eagles
author: 10 Ken Follett

oodles 4 gobs, lots, many 5 heaps, loads, scads 6 plenty

ooze 4 drip, leak, mire, muck, seep, silt 5 bleed, drain, exude, slime, sweat 6 filter, sludge 7 dribble, leakage, seepage, soft mud, trickle 8 alluvium 9 discharge, exudation, percolate, secretion, transpire

oozing 5 leaky, weepy 6 sweaty 7 exuding, seepage, seeping 8 bleeding, sweating

opal
color: 3 red 5 black, white 6 orange 11 transparent
source: 6 Mexico 9 Australia 14 Lightning Ridge
variety: 8 fire opal

opalescent 5 milky 6 pearly 8 irisated, luminous 10 iridescent

opaque 4 dark, dull, hazy 5 muddy, murky 7 clouded, muddied, obscure, unclear 8 abstruse 9 difficult 12 impenetrable, unfathomable 14 nontranslucent, nontransparent, unintelligible 16 incomprehensible

opaqueness 7 opacity 8 dullness 9 denseness, muddiness, murkiness, obscurity 10 cloudiness 11 unclearness 15 impenetrability 17 unintelligibility 19 incomprehensibility

---

open 4 ajar, fair, just, wide 5 agape, begin, clear, crack, found, frank, plain, unbar 6 candid, create, direct, expand, gaping, honest, launch, unfold, unlock, unseal, unshut 7 artless, exposed, lay open, natural, not shut, sincere, unblock, unclose, yawning 8 commence, extended, outgoing, unbiased, unclosed, unfasten, unfenced, unfolded, unlocked, unsealed 9 available, coverless, establish, expansive, impartial, institute, not closed, objective, originate, receptive, unbigoted, unbounded, uncovered, uncrowded, undertake, welcoming 10 accessible, forthright, impersonal, inaugurate, responsive, unenclosed, unfastened 11 extroverted, uncluttered, uninhabited 12 permit access, unobstructed, unprejudiced 13 disinterested, doing business 15 straightforward

---

open-air 7 outdoor, outside 10 unconfined
Italian: 8 al fresco

open and aboveboard 6 candid, honest 7 ethical 10 forthright 12 on the up and up 15 straightforward

Open Boat, The
author: 12 Stephen Crane

Open City
director: 17 Roberto Rossellini
cast: 11 Aldo Fabrizi, Anna Magnani 16 Marcello Pagliero
setting: 4 Rome

open-eyed 5 alert, awake, aware 7 heedful, mindful 8 vigilant, watchful, wide-eyed 9 attentive, wide-awake

open-handed 6 lavish 7 liberal 8 generous, prodigal 9 bounteous, bountiful 10 altruistic, beneficent, benevolent, ungrudging, unstinting 11 magnanimous

openhandedness 10 generosity, liberality 11 benevolence, generousity, munificence 12 extravagance

openhearted 7 artless, sincere 8 trusting 9 ingenuous

opening 3 gap, job 4 gash, hole, rent, rift, slit, slot, spot, tear, vent 5 break, chink, cleft, crack, place, space, start 6 breach, chance 7 fissure, kickoff, preface, prelude, send-off, vacancy 8 aperture, occasion, overture, position 9 beginning, first part, launching, situation 10 initiation 11 opportunity, possibility 12 commencement, inauguration, installation, introduction

openly 6 freely 7 frankly 8 directly, honestly, publicly 9 obviously

open-minded 4 fair 7 liberal 8 amenable, flexible, tolerant, unbiased 9 adaptable, impartial, objective, receptive 10 responsive, undogmatic 11 broad-minded 12 unprejudiced 13 disinterested, nonjudgmental

openmouthed 4 agog, awed 5 agape 6 aghast, amazed 8 wide-eyed 9 awestruck, bewitched, marveling, staggered, stupefied, surprised 10 astonished, confounded 10 dumbstruck, enthralled, spellbound 11 dumbfounded 12 wonderstruck 13 flabbergasted, thunderstruck

openness 6 candor 7 honesty 8 daylight 9 frankness, sincerity 11 artlessness 13 guilelessness 14 forthrightness 19 straightforwardness

open sanction 8 free hand, free rein 13 full authority
French: 12 catre blanche

open the eyes of 8 disabuse 11 set straight

open to choice 8 elective, optional 9 voluntary

openwork 3 net 4 lace 6 eyelet 7 lattice, Madeira, tracery 8 filigree

oolong-tea

opera 5 score **7** musical **8** libretto **11** composition
  by Bizet: 6 Carmen
  by Delibes: 5 Lakme
  by Gounod: 5 Faust
  by Leoncavallo: 10 I Pagliacci
  by Mozart: 8 Idomeneo **10** Magic Flute **11** Don Giovanni **12** Cosi fan tutte **16** Marriage of Figaro
  by Offenbach: 15 Tales of Hoffmann
  by Ponchielli: 10 La Gioconda
  by Puccini: 5 Tosca **8** La Boheme **12** Manon Lescaut **15** Madame Butterfly
  by Rossini: 8 Tancredi **11** William Tell **15** The Barber of Seville
  by Smetana: 13 The Bartered Bride
  by Strauss: 6 Salome **7** Elektra **15** Ariadne auf Naxos **16** Der Rosenkavalier
  by Tchaikovsky: 12 Eugene Onegin
  by Verdi: 4 Aida **6** Otello **8** Falstaff **9** Rigoletto **10** La Traviata **11** Il Trovatore
  by Wagner: 8 Parsifal **9** Lohengrin **10** Tannhauser **16** Tristan and Isolde **17** The Flying Dutchman **21** The Ring of the Nibelungs
  comic: 5 buffa **7** comique
  glass: 9 lorgnette
  hat: 5 crush, gibus
  house: 3 Met **6** Sydney **7** La Scala **12** Covent Garden, Metropolitan
  singer: 4 bass, diva **5** buffa, buffo, tenor **7** soprano **10** coloratura, prima donna
  singular: 4 opus
  solo: 4 aria
  text: 8 libretto

operate 2 go **3** run **4** go in, work **6** behave, manage, open up **7** oversee, perform **8** function **11** superintend **14** perform surgery **18** perform an operation

operating 6 active **7** working **8** in motion **9** operative **10** responsive

operation 5 force **6** action, agency, effect **7** conduct, pursuit, running, surgery, working **8** activity, exertion **9** influence, procedure **10** management, overseeing **11** exploratory, performance, supervision **15** instrumentality, superintendence

operative 3 spy **4** dick **5** agent, in use **6** acting, active, shamus, worker **7** in force, working **8** in effect, in motion, workable **9** activated, detective, effective, effectual, operating **10** functional, private eye, responsive **11** efficacious, secret agent

operator 4 doer, user **5** agent, pilot **6** driver, worker **7** manager **9** performer

opere citato 14 in the work cited
  abbreviation: 5 op cit

Ophelia
  character in: 6 Hamlet
  author: 11 Shakespeare

Opheltes
  also: 10 Archemorus

ophidiophobia
  fear of: 6 snakes

Ophion
  form: 7 serpent
  created from: 9 north wind
  created by: 8 Eurynome

Ophir
  father: 6 Joktan
  source of: 4 gold

opiate 4 dope **6** downer **7** anodyne **8** hypnotic, narcotic, nepenthe, sedative **9** analgesic, calmative, soporific, stupefier **10** depressant, painkiller, palliative **12** somnifacient, stupefacient, tranquilizer

opine 3 say **4** deem **5** allow, guess, offer, state, think **6** assume, reckon **7** believe, imagine, presume, suggest, surmise **8** conclude, consider, estimate **9** speculate, volunteer **10** conjecture, have a hunch

opinion 4 idea, view **6** belief, notion, theory **7** surmise **8** estimate, judgment, thinking **9** sentiment, suspicion **10** assessment, assumption, conception, conclusion, conjecture, conviction, estimation, evaluation, impression, persuasion **11** speculation

opinionated 8 dogmatic, obdurate, stubborn **9** obstinate, pigheaded, unbending **10** bullheaded, headstrong, inflexible, unyielding **12** closedminded **14** uncompromising

O Pioneers!
  author: 11 Willa Cather

Opis
  companion of: 7 Artemis

Opobalsammum 12 Biblical tree

Oppenheimer, Julius Robert
  field: 7 physics
  directed development of: 10 atomic bomb
    location: 9 Los Alamos, New Mexico
  chaired: 3 AEC **22** Atomic Energy Commission

Opper, Frederick
  creator/artist of: 13 Happy Hooligan **17** Alphonse and Gaston, And Her Name Was Maud

opponent 3 foe **5** enemy, rival **8** resister **9** adversary, assailant, contender, disputant **10** antagonist, challenger, competitor, opposition

opportune 3 apt **5** happy, lucky **6** proper, timely **7** fitting **8** suitable **9** expedient, favorable, fortunate, well-timed **10** auspicious, convenient, felicitous, profitable, propitious, seasonable **11** appropriate **12** advantageous

opportunity 4 time, turn **5** means **6** chance, moment **7** opening **8** occasion **9** situation **10** good chance **11** contingency

oppose 4 buck, defy **5** fight **6** battle, combat, resist, thwart **7** contest **8** obstruct **9** withstand **12** be set against, speak against

opposed 3 con **4** anti **6** averse, pitted **7** adverse, against, counter, hostile **8** contrary, disputed, objected, resisted **9** contested, countered **10** confronted, contrasted, reciprocal **12** contradicted

opposer 5 rival **8** opponent **9** adversary **10** antagonist, competitor

opposite 5 other **6** facing **7** adverse, counter, reverse **8** contrary, converse, oppos-

ing 9 differing **11** conflicting **12** antagonistic, antithetical **13** contradictory, counteractive

opposite number 5 equal **8** parallel **10** equivalent **11** correlative, counterpart

opposition 3 foe **5** enemy, rival **6** enmity **8** aversion, defiance, opponent **9** adversary, contender, hostility, other side, rejection **10** antagonism, antagonist, competitor, negativism, resistance **11** contrariety, disapproval **12** disagreement

oppress 3 tax, try, vex **4** pain **5** abuse, worry **6** burden, deject, grieve, sadden, sorrow **7** depress, trouble **8** cast down, dispirit, maltreat **9** despotize, persecute, tyrannize, weigh down **10** discourage, dishearten

oppressed 7 crushed **9** exploited **10** tyrannized **11** downtrodden, subservient

oppressive 5 cruel, harsh **6** brutal, severe, trying, vexing **7** onerous, painful, wearing **8** despotic, grievous, pressing **9** worrisome **10** burdensome, depressing, repressive, tyrannical, unbearable **11** distressing, hardhearted, troublesome **12** discouraging **13** uncomfortable

oppressor 6 despot, tyrant **8** autocrat, dictator

opprobrious 4 base **6** wicked **7** abusive, corrupt, damning **8** infamous, reviling, shameful, shocking **9** malicious, maligning, nefarious, vilifying, vitriolic **10** censorious, deplorable, despicable, malevolent, outrageous, scandalous, scurrilous, unbecoming **11** acrimonious, disgraceful, fulminating **12** condemnatory, denunciatory, dishonorable, disreputable, faultfinding **13** hypercritical, objectionable, reprehensible

opprobrium 5 shame **6** infamy **8** disgrace, dishonor **9** disrepute **12** denunciation

Ops
origin: **5** Roman
goddess of: **6** plenty
husband: **6** Saturn
son: **7** Jupiter
called: **10** Magna Mater
corresponds to: **4** Rhea
6 Cybele **9** Dindymene
10 Berecyntia

opt 4 pick, take **5** elect, fix on, go for **6** choose, prefer, select **7** vote for **8** decide on, settle on

opt for 4 pick, take **5** adopt **6** choose, select, take up **7** embrace, espouse, fix upon, pick out **8** decide on, settle on

optimism 10 confidence **11** hopefulness **12** cheerfulness, sanguineness **13** bright outlook, encouragement

optimistic 6 bright **7** hopeful, roseate **8** buoyed up, cheerful, sanguine **9** confident, favorable, heartened, promising **10** auspicious, encouraged, heartening, propitious **11** encouraging, rose-colored **12** enthusiastic

Optimist's Daughter, The
author: **11** Eudora Welty

optimum 4 acme, A-one, best, peak **5** crest, ideal, prime **6** choice, height, select, zenith **7** capital, perfect, supreme **8** flawless **9** faultless, first-rate **10** perfection, unexcelled **11** superlative **12** quintessence

option 4 will **5** voice **6** choice, liking **8** decision, election, free will, pleasure **9** franchise, privilege, selection **10** discretion, partiality, preference **11** alternative **12** predilection

optional 4 open **8** elective, unforced **9** allowable, open-ended, voluntary **10** volitional **11** not required **12** discretional **13** discretionary, nonobligatory

opulence 6 bounty, plenty, riches, wealth **7** fortune **8** elegance, luxuries, richness **9** abundance, affluence, amplitude, profusion **10** cornucopia, lavishness, plentitude, prosperity **11** copiousness, great wealth **13** sumptuousness

opus 4 work **5** piece **6** effort **7** attempt, product **8** creation **9** handiwork, invention **10** brainchild, production **11** composition

oracle, Oracle 4 sage, seer **5** augur, sibyl **6** wizard **7** adviser, diviner, prophet **9** predictor, Scripture **10** forecaster, soothsayer **11** clairvoyant

oral 5 vocal **6** spoken, verbal, voiced **7** uttered **8** ingested **9** swallowed **10** of the mouth, verbalized **11** articulated, using speech
Latin: **8** viva voce

orange
varieties: **4** king, mock, sour, wild **5** blood, hardy, natal, navel, Osage, sweet **6** bitter, common, Panama, Temple **7** Florida, Mexican, Satsuma,

Seville, Spanish **8** Bergamot, Mandarin, Otaheite, Valencia **9** Tachibana, vegetable **10** Chinese box, trifoliate **13** African cherry, Mediterranean **15** Jamaica mandarin **17** house-blooming mock
liqueur: **7** Curacao

orangutan, orang-outang 3 ape **4** mias **5** satyr **6** primate **10** anthropoid
characteristic: **8** arboreal
11 herbivorous
native land: **6** Borneo
7 Sumatra
species: **13** Pongo pygmaeus

ora pro nobis 9 pray for us

orate 6 recite, speak **7** declaim **11** make a speech

oration 4 talk **5** spiel **6** eulogy, sermon, speech **7** address, lecture, recital **9** discourse, monologue, panegyric **10** peroration **11** declamation **12** disquisition, formal speech

orator 6 talker **7** speaker **8** lecturer, preacher **9** declaimer **10** sermonizer **11** rhetorician, speechmaker, spellbinder **12** elocutionist **13** public speaker

oratory 6 speech **7** bombast **8** delivery, rhetoric **9** elocution, eloquence, preaching **11** declamation **12** speechifying, speechmaking **14** grandiloquence

orb 4 ball, moon **5** globe **6** sphere **7** globule **8** spheroid

orbit 3 way **4** path **5** cycle, route, track **6** circle, course **7** channel, circuit, pathway **10** trajectory **13** revolve around **14** circumnavigate

orchards
god of: **9** Vertumnus

orchestra 3 pit **4** band **6** stalls **7** parquet **8** ensemble, parterre **12** Philharmonic

orchestrate 5 adapt, score **7** arrange, compose

orchestration 5 score **10** adaptation **11** arrangement **12** organization

orchid *see* **box**

Orcus
god of: **10** underworld
punishes: **7** perjury
corresponds to: **3** Dis
5 Hades, Pluto **8** Dis Pater

ordain 4 name, rule, will **5** elect, enact, frock **6** decree, invest **7** adjudge, appoint, command, dictate **8** delegate, deputize, instruct **9** determine,

orchid
  varieties: 3 bat, bee, fen, fly, nun, nut **4** baby, blue, dove, moth, nun's, rein, swan **5** black, chain, cigar, cobra, coral, giant, jewel, pansy, Salep, showy, snowy, spice, tiger, water, widow **6** bamboo, bottle, cradle, dollar, Easter, helmet, mirror, monkey, pigeon, ragged, sawfly, shower, spider, stream, virgin **7** Alaskan, cow-horn, fringed, hooker's, jumping, peacock, rainbow, rosebud, scarlet, soldier **8** bee-swarm, Cooktown, cranefly, fried-egg, gold-lace, green-fly, hyacinth, nun's-hood, poor-man's, Savannah, scorpion, white nun, windmill, woodland **9** blunt-leaf, butterfly, chocolate, Christmas, clam-shell, green rein, green swan, white rein **10** buttonhole, five-leaved, golden swan, hay-scented, late spider, leafy white, Sierra rein, slender bog **11** cockle-shell, crested rein, dancing-doll, dancing-lady, early spider, golden chain, green-winged, one-leaf rein, pink slipper, purple-spire, rattlesnake, round-leaved **12** green fringed, pink scorpion, purple-hooded, Southern rein, tall white bog, white fringed **13** crested yellow, golden fringed, green woodland, Northern green, ragged fringed, yellow fringed **14** crested fringed, large butterfly, little club-spur, white butterfly **15** lesser butterfly, lily-of-the-valley **16** downy rattlesnake, Florida butterfly, Northern small bog, purple fringeless, small round-leaved, white-flowered bog **18** large purple fringed, leafy Northern green, small purple fringed, Southern small white **19** lesser purple fringed **20** greater purple fringed

legislate, prescribe, pronounce **10** commission, consecrate

ordeal 4 care, pain **5** agony, grief, trial, worry **6** burden, misery, sorrow, strain, stress **7** anguish, concern, torment, tragedy, trouble **8** calamity, distress, pressure, vexation **9** heartache, nightmare, suffering **10** affliction, oppression **11** tribulation, unhappiness **12** wretchedness **16** trying experience

Ordeal of Richard Feverel, The
  author: 14 George Meredith

order 3 bid, law **4** body, book, calm, club, fiat, form, kind, rank, rule, sort, type **5** breed, caste, class, grade, group, guild, house, lodge, quiet, ukase **6** adjure, ask for, charge, decree, degree, demand, dictum, direct, engage, enjoin, family, status, stripe, system **7** agree to, bidding, caliber, call for, command, company, control, dictate, harmony, pattern, quality, request, reserve, silence, society, species, station **8** alliance, category, division, grouping, instruct, neatness, position, purchase, sorority, standing, tidiness **9** framework, structure, ultimatum **10** discipline, federation, fraternity, imperative, sisterhood, tabulation **11** arrangement, association, broth-

erhood, commandment, confederacy, designation, instruction, tranquility **12** codification, organization, peacefulness, tranquillity **13** pronouncement **14** categorization, classification

ordered 4 bade, neat, trim **7** regular, uniform **8** arranged **9** shipshape **10** systematic

orderliness 8 neatness, tidiness **10** discipline **12** organization

orderly 4 neat, tidy **5** civil, quiet **6** proper, spruce **8** peaceful **9** organized, peaceable, shipshape, tractable **10** classified, controlled, methodical, restrained, systematic **11** disciplined, uncluttered, well-behaved

ordinance 3 act, law **4** bull, fiat, rule, writ **5** canon, edict, order **6** decree, dictum, ruling **7** command, mandate, statute **9** enactment **10** regulation **11** commandment

ordinarily 7 as a rule, usually **8** commonly, normally **9** generally, regularly, routinely **10** habitually **11** customarily **12** on the average **14** conventionally

ordinary 4 dull, so-so **5** usual **6** common, normal **7** average, humdrum, routine, trivial, typical **8** everyday, familiar, habitual, mediocre, standard

9 customary **10** pedestrian, uninspired **11** commonplace, indifferent, stereotyped, traditional, unimportant **12** conventional, run-of-the-mill, unimpressive **13** insignificant, unexceptional, unimaginative, uninteresting **15** inconsequential, undistinguished

Ordinary People
  director: 13 Robert Redford
  author: 11 Judith Guest
  cast: 10 Judd Hirsch **13** Timothy Hutton **14** Mary Tyler Moore **16** Donald Sutherland
  Oscar for: 7 picture **8** director **12** screenwriter **15** supporting actor (Hutton)

ordinary wine
  French: 12 vin ordinaire

ordnance 4 arms **6** cannon **9** armaments, artillery, munitions

ordnance depot 6 armory **7** arsenal **18** military storehouse

ore 3 tin **4** gold, iron, lead, paco, rock, zinc **5** metal **6** bronze, copper, galena, sulfur **7** halvans, mineral **8** aluminum, cinnabar, hematite **9** melachite
  byproduct: 6 gangue
  deposit: 3 bed **4** lode, mine, vein **7** bonanza
  layer: 4 seam **5** stope
  trough: 6 strake
  worthless: 4 slag **5** dross, matte

Oread
  form: 5 nymph
  location: 8 mountain
  companion of: 7 Artemis

oregano
  name means: 16 joy of the mountain
  botanical name: 8 O vulgare, Origanum
  also: 6 organy, origan **8** marjoram **9** pizza herb **11** Mexican sage, winter sweet
  origin: 13 Mediterranean
  family: 4 mint
  cure for: 11 indigestion **14** loss of appetite
  first aid for: 12 spider stings **14** scorpion stings
  use: 5 pizza **6** broths **8** stuffing **12** tomato dishes **13** Italian dishes

Oregon *see box, p. 712*

Oregon Trail, The
  author: 14 Francis Parkman

Oresteia
  author: 9 Aeschylus
  trilogy includes: 9 Agamemnon, Eumenides **10** Choephoroe

Oregon
  abbreviation: **2** OR **4** Oreg
  nickname: **6** Beaver, Sunset **7** Webfoot **13** Sawdust Empire
  capital: **5** Salem
  largest city: **8** Portland
  others: **5** Nyssa **6** Albany, Eugene **7** Ashland, Astoria,
    Medford **8** Portland, Roseburg **9** Corvallis, Pendleton
    10 Grant's Pass, Willamette **12** Klamath Falls
  college: **4** Reed **7** Pacific **8** Linfield, Portland **10** Willa-
    mette **13** Lewis and Clark
  feature:
    fort: **5** Boise **6** Casper **7** Kearney, Laramie
    national park: **10** Crater Lake
  tribe: **4** Coos **5** Alsea, Kusan, Modoc, Wasco, Yanan,
    Yunca **6** Cayuse, Chetco, Chinoo, Kuitsh, Molala, Siletz,
    Tenino, Umpqua **7** Bannock, Clatsop, Klamath, Sastean,
    Shastan, Takelma, Walpapi, Yaquina **8** Clackama, Klikitat,
    Nez Perce, Sahaptin, Umatilla **9** Kalapuyan, Tillamook
    10 Kalapooian, Wallawalla
  people: **10** Wayne Morse **12** Linus Pauling **15** Phyllis
    McGinley
    explorer: **13** Lewis and Clark
  lake: **5** Abert, Waldo **6** Harney, McNary **7** John Day, Kla-
    math, Malheur
    deepest in US: **6** Crater
  land rank: **5** tenth
  mountain: **6** Mazama, Tacoma, Walker, Wilson **7** Elkhorn,
    Grizzly, Jackass, Rainier, Tidbits, Wallowa **8** Cascades
    9 Blue Coast, Marys Peak **10** Strawberry
    highest point: **4** Hood
  physical feature:
    bay: **4** Coos
    caves: **11** Marble Halls
    wind: **7** Chinook
  river: **5** Rogue, Snake **6** Imnaha, Owyhee, Powder,
    Umpqua **7** Blitzen, John Day, Klamath, Silvie's **8** Colum-
    bia **9** Deschutes **10** Willamette
  state admission: **11** thirty-third
  state bird: **17** western meadowlark
  state fish: **13** chinook salmon
  state flower: **7** mahonia **11** Oregon grape
  state motto: **8** The Union
  state song: **14** Oregon My Oregon
  state tree: **10** Douglas fir

Orestes
  author: **9** Euripides
  character: **5** Helen **6** Apollo,
    Furies **7** Electra, Pylades
    8 Menelaus

Orestes
  father: **9** Agamemnon
  mother: **12** Clytemnestra
  sister: **7** Electra **9** Iphigenia
  wife: **8** Hermione
  son: **9** Tisamenus
  killed: **9** Aegisthus
    12 Clytemnestra
  pursued by: **6** Furies

Orfeo, L'
  also: **17** The Story of
    Orpheus
  opera by: **10** Monteverdi

Orfeo ed Euridice
  also: **18** Orpheus and
    Eurydice
  opera by: **5** Gluck

  character: **4** Amor, Zeus
    6 Furies

Orff, Carl
  born: **6** Munich **7** Germany
  composer of: **7** Der Mond,
    The Moon **8** Antigone, Die
    Kluge **9** Schulwerk **10** Pro-
    metheus **13** Carmina Bur-
    ana, The Clever Girl
    14 Catulli Carmina **16** Oedi-
    pus der Tyrann, Oedipus the
    Tyrant

organ 6 agency **7** journal, vehicle **9** harmonium **10** hurdy-
  gurdy, instrument
  11 publication

organic 5 alive, quick **6** living
  7 animate, natural, ordered,
  planned, unified **8** designed,
  physical **9** patterned **10** ana-
  tomical, harmonious, methodical, systematic

  12 nonsynthetic **13** physiological **14** constitutional

organism 4 cell **5** plant,
  whole **6** animal, entity, system **7** complex, network, society **8** creature **9** bacterium
  10 federation **11** association,
  corporation, institution, living
  thing **13** microorganism

organization 4 club, firm,
  sect **5** corps, group, order,
  party, union **6** design, league,
  making, outfit **7** company,
  forming, harmony, pattern, society **8** alliance, assembly,
  business, grouping, ordering
  9 arranging, formation **10** federation, fellowship, fraternity
  11 arrangement, association,
  composition, corporation, formulation, structuring **12** constitution, coordination
  13 establishment,
  incorporation

organizational 10 managerial
  13 developmental
  14 administrative

organize 4 file, form, tidy
  5 found, group, index, order,
  set up **6** codify, create, neaten,
  tidy up **7** arrange, catalog, develop **8** classify, tabulate **9** establish, formulate, originate
  10 categorize, coordinate
  11 make orderly, systematize

organized 4 neat, tidy **7** logical, orderly **8** coherent **10** methodical, systematic

orgiastic 4 wild **6** wanton
  7 drunken, riotous **9** abandoned, debauched, Dionysian,
  dissolute, libertine **10** dissipated, licentious **12** bacchanalian, unrestrained
  13 overindulgent, undisciplined

orgy 7 debauch, wassail **8** carousal **9** bacchanal **10** saturnalia **11** bacchanalia

orient, the Orient 3 fix, set
  4 Asia, find **6** locate, relate,
  square **7** situate **8** accustom
  9 acclimate, reconcile **10** the
  Far East **11** Eastern Asia,
  familiarize

oriental 4 Arab, fine, Thai,
  Turk **5** Asian **6** bright, Indian,
  Korean **7** Asiatic, Chinese,
  Eastern, Iranian, shining
  8 Japanese, lustrous, precious,
  superior **10** Vietnamese
  animal: **4** zebu **5** rasse
  building: **6** pagoda
  dish: **5** pilau, pilaw **6** pilaff
  drum: **6** tomtom
  food fish: **3** tai
  garment: **3** aba **6** sarong
  inn: **4** Khan **5** serai **6** imaret
    11 caravansary

laborer: 6 coolie
market: 3 suk, sug 4 souk
   6 bazaar
nurse: 4 amah, ayah
prince: 4 amir, haja
sail: 6 lateen
sash: 3 obi
shrub: 3 tea 5 henna
   8 oleander
wagon: 5 araba
weight: 2 mo 4 rotl, tael
   5 catty, liang 6 cantar

orientation 8 location 9 alignment, direction, situation
10 adjustment 11 acclimation
15 acclimatization,
familiarization

orifice 3 gap, pit 4 hole, slit,
slot, vent 5 cleft, inlet,
mouth 6 cavity, cranny, hollow, lacuna, pocket, socket
7 crevice, fissure, opening,
passage 8 alveolus, aperture,
entrance

origin 4 base, line, race, rise,
root 5 agent, basis, birth,
breed, cause, house, stock
6 author, family, father,
ground, growth, mother, reason, source, spring, strain
7 creator, descent, genesis, lineage, taproot 8 ancestry, nativity, producer 9 beginning,
emergence, evolution, generator, inception, parentage, principle 10 derivation, extraction,
foundation 12 commencement,
fountainhead

Origin, The
author: 11 Irving Stone

original 3 new 4 bold 5 basic,
basis, first, fresh, novel 6 daring, primal, unique 7 example,
initial, pattern, primary, seminal, strange, unusual 8 atypical, creative, earliest,
germinal, primeval, singular,
uncommon 9 different, essential, first copy, formative, inaugural, ingenious, inventive,
prototype 10 aboriginal, new-
fangled, primordial, underlying, unfamiliar, unorthodox
11 fundamental, imaginative
12 introductory 13 extraordinary 14 unconventional

**Original Amateur Hour,
The**
host: 7 Ted Mack

originality 6 daring 7 newness,
novelty 8 boldness 9 freshness,
ingenuity 10 cleverness, creativity, uniqueness 11 imagination, singularity, unorthodoxy
13 individuality, inventiveness
17 unconventionality

originally 7 at first, by birth
8 uniquely 9 initially, unusually 10 creatively 11 differ-

ently, inventively
13 imaginatively

originate 4 come, flow, rise,
stem 5 arise, begin, draft,
found, issue, start 6 create,
crop up, derive, design, devise,
emerge, evolve, father, invent,
sprout 7 develop, emanate,
proceed 8 commence, con-
ceive, envision, initiate, organize, spring up 9 establish,
fabricate, formulate, germinate 10 inaugurate

origination 5 birth 7 genesis
9 inception, invention 10 conception, initiation 11 germination 12 commencement
13 establishment

Origin of Species, The
author: 13 Charles Darwin

**Origins of Totalitarianism,
The**
author: 12 Hannah Arendt

Orion
form: 5 giant
vocation: 6 hunter
pursued: 8 Pleiades
killed by: 7 Artemis
became: 13 constellation

Orithyia
father: 10 Erechtheus
mother: 9 Praxithea
abducted by: 6 Boreas
son: 5 Zetes 6 Calais
daughter: 6 Chione
   9 Cleopatra

Oriya
language family: 12 Indo-
European
branch: 11 Indo-Iranian
group: 5 Indic
spoken in: 5 (northern) India

Orkney Islands
county seat: 8 Kirkwall
country: 8 Scotland
firth: 8 Pentland
island: 3 Hay 6 Rousay, San-
day 7 Westray 8 Stronsay
14 South Ronaldsay
largest city: 6 Pomona

Orlando
author: 13 Virginia Woolf
character: 5 Sasha 14 Nicholas Greene 28 Archduchess
Harriet of Roumania, Mar-
maduke Bonthrop
Shelmerdine

Orlando
character in: 11 As You Like
It
author: 11 Shakespeare

Orlando Furioso
author: 7 Ariosto
character: 6 Rogero 7 Rinaldo 8 Agramant, Angelica,
Rodomont 9 Bradamant
11 Charlemagne

Orley Farm
author: 15 Anthony Trollope

ormolu 5 alloy, brass, paste
6 bronze 7 gilding 8 ornament
imitation of: 4 gold
used to decorate: 5 clock
   9 furniture

ornament 4 deck, gild, trim
5 adorn 6 bedeck, enrich, finery, frills 7 festoon, furbish,
garnish 8 beautify, decorate,
furbelow, trick out, trimming
9 accessory, adornment, embellish 10 decoration, enrichment 11 elaboration
13 embellishment
14 beautification

ornamental 4 gilt 5 fancy
6 chichi, rococo 10 decorative
ball: 4 bead 6 pompom
button: 4 stud
grass: 4 neti
loop: 5 picot
metal: 5 niello

ornamentation 7 garnish
8 trimming 9 adornment
10 decoration
13 embellishment

ornate 5 fancy, showy 6 flashy,
florid, lavish, rococo
7 adorned, baroque, flowery
9 decorated, elaborate, sumptuous 10 flamboyant 11 embellished, pretentious
12 ostentatious

ornery 4 curt, mean 5 surly,
testy 6 crabby, grumpy, shirty
7 grouchy, peevish, waspish
8 snappish 9 dyspeptic, irascible, irritable 10 ill-natured
11 ill-tempered, quarrelsome
12 cantankerous

Orneus
father: 10 Erechtheus
brother: 6 Metion 7 Cecrops
son: 6 Peteos

Ornitholestes
type: 8 dinosaur
period: 8 Jurassic

Ornithomimus
type: 8 dinosaur
period: 10 Cretaceous

ornithophobia
fear of: 5 birds

ornithopod
type of: 8 dinosaur
member: 9 Iguanodon 10 Edmontonia, Nodosaurus
11 Anatosaurus, Polacan-
thus, Saurolophus, Scolosaurus, Stegosaurus
12 Ankylosaurus, Campto-
saurus, Lambeosaurus, Pisanosaurus 13 Acanthopholis,
Corythosaurus, Hypsilophodon, Palaeoscincus 14 Thescelosaurus

15 Parasaurolophus, Procheneosaurus **17** Heterodontosaurus

Ornytus see **7** Teuthis

orotund 4 full, rich **5** clear **6** strong **7** pompous, ringing, vibrant **8** resonant, sonorous **9** bombastic **10** resounding, rhetorical, stentorian **Latin: 10** ore rotundo

Orowitz, Eugene Maurice
real name of: **13** Michael Landon

oro y plata 13 gold and silver motto of: **7** Montana

Orozco, Jose Clemente
born: **6** Mexico **7** Jalisco (Zapotlan) **12** Ciudad Guzman
artwork: **5** Grief **9** Catharsis **11** Omniscience **12** House of Tears **16** National Allegory, Social Revolution **18** Hidalgo and Castillo

Orphans of the Storm
director: **10** D W Griffith
cast: **11** Dorothy Gish, Lillian Gish **17** Joseph Schildkraut

Orpheus
vocation: **4** poet **8** musician
mother: **8** Calliope
wife: **8** Eurydice
member of: **9** Argonauts
went into: **5** Hades
killed by: **7** Maenads

Orpheus in the Underworld
also: **15** Orphee aux Enfers
operetta by: **9** Offenbach

Orsino
character in: **12** Twelfth Night
author: **11** Shakespeare

ort 3 bit **5** crumb, dregs, scrap **6** morsel, refuse, trifle **7** remnant **8** leavings, leftover

Orthaea
father: **10** Hyacinthus

Orthia
epithet of: **7** Artemis
means: **7** upright

orthodox 5 fixed, pious, usual **6** devout, narrow **7** limited, regular, routine **8** accepted, approved, official, ordinary, standard **9** customary, religious **11** commonplace, conformable, established, traditional **12** conventional **13** authoritative, circumscribed

orthoptera
class: **8** hexapoda
phylum: **10** arthropoda
group: **4** leaf **5** stick **6** locust, mantid **7** cricket **9** cockroach **11** grasshopper

Orwell, George
real name: **15** Eric Arthur Blair
author of: **4** 1984 **10** Animal Farm **18** Nineteen Eighty Four **29** Politics and the English Language

oryx 5 beisa **6** pickax **7** gazelle, gemsbok **8** antelope, leucoryx

Osage (Wazhazhe)
language family: **6** Siouan
location: **6** Kansas **8** Arkansas, Missouri, Oklahoma

Oscan
language family: **12** Indo-European
branch: **6** Italic

Oschophoria
origin: **8** Athenian
event: **8** festival
honoring: **7** vintage **8** Dionysus

oscillate 4 vary **5** pulse, swing, waver **6** change, seesaw **7** librate, pulsate, vibrate **8** hesitate **9** alternate, come and go, fluctuate, hem and haw, vacillate **10** ebb and flow, equivocate **12** shilly-shally **16** move back and forth

O'Shaughnessy, Brigid
character in: **16** The Maltese Falcon
author: **7** Hammett

osier 3 rod **4** wand **5** salix, withe **6** willow **7** dogwood, wilgers **9** twigwithy
species: **14** Salix viminalis
use: **6** wicker **8** basketry

Osiris
origin: **8** Egyptian
god of: **4** dead, Nile
judge of: **4** dead
king of: **4** dead
wife: **4** Isis
sister: **4** Isis
son: **5** Horus
brother: **3** Set **4** Seth **5** Horus
killed by: **3** Set **4** Seth

Oskar Matzerath
character in: **7** Tin Drum
author: **5** Grass

Oslo
capital of: **6** Norway
former name: **11** Christiania
landmark: **8** Storting (Parliament) **11** Royal Palace
mountain: **12** Holmenkollen
park: **7** Frogner
peninsula: **8** Akershus
street: **14** Karl Johansgate

Osmond, Gilbert
character in: **18** The Portrait of a Lady
author: **5** James

Ossian
character in: **12** Gaelic poetry

ossify 6 harden **7** stiffen **9** fossilize

ossuary 8 boneyard **10** depository, receptacle

ostensible 6 avowed **7** alleged, assumed, feigned, implied, nominal, outward, seeming, surface, titular, visible **8** apparent, declared, illusory, manifest, specious **9** pretended, professed **10** presumable **11** perceivable

ostentation 4 airs, dash, fuss, pomp, ritz, show **5** glitz, gloss, swank **6** splash **7** display, glitter **8** flourish, pretense **9** pageantry, pomposity, showiness, spectacle
French: **7** etalage

ostentatious 4 loud **5** gaudy, showy **6** flashy, florid, garish **7** pompous **8** affected, immodest, overdone **9** grandiose, obtrusive **10** flamboyant, showing off **11** conspicuous, exaggerated, pretentious **15** flaunting wealth

Osterreich see **7** Austria

ostracize 3 cut **4** oust, shun, snub **5** avoid, expel **6** banish, disown, reject **7** exclude, shut out **9** blackball, blacklist

Ostwald, Wilhelm
field: **9** chemistry
nationality: **6** German
founded: **17** physical chemistry

O'Sullivan, Maureen
born: **5** Boyle **7** Ireland **15** County Roscommon
daughter: **9** Mia Farrow
roles: **4** Jane (Tarzan movies) **16** David Copperfield **17** Pride and Prejudice **19** Hannah and her Sisters

Otello
also: **7** Othello
opera by: **5** Verdi **7** Rossini

O tempora! O mores! 14 O times! O customs!

Othello
director: **11** Stuart Burge
author: **18** William Shakespeare
character: **4** Iago **6** Cassio, Emilia **9** Desdemona
cast: **11** Frank Finlay, Joyce Redman, Maggie Smith **15** Laurence Olivier

other 4 more **5** added, extra, spare **6** unlike **7** further, reverse **8** contrary, opposite **9** alternate, auxiliary, different, remaining **10** additional, contrasted, dissimilar **11** contrasting **13** contradictory, supplementary **14** differentiated

Other Gods
author: 9 Pearl Buck

Other Side of Midnight, The
author: 13 Sidney Sheldon

other than 3 but 4 save 6 except, saving 7 barring, besides 9 excepting, excluding

otherwise 5 if not 6 or else 9 inversely 10 contrarily 11 differently 12 contrariwise

otherworldly 7 sublime 8 heavenly 10 celestial 14 transcendental

Othin see 4 Odin

Othniel 11 Hebrew judge
father: 5 Kenaz
brother: 5 Caleb
wife: 6 Achsah

O times! O customs!
Latin: 14 O tempora! O mores!

Otionia
father: 10 Erechtheus
sister: 10 Protogonia
death by: 9 sacrifice
  for victory of: 9 Athenians
  over: 11 Eleusinians

otiose 4 idle, lazy 6 futile 7 laggard, resting, useless, worn-out 8 abortive, impotent, inactive, indolent, listless, slothful, sluggish 9 fruitless, lethargic, powerless, somnolent 10 unavailing 11 incompetent, ineffective, inoperative, unrewarding 12 unproductive

Otomi
tribe: 7 Capotec

O'Toole, Peter
born: 7 Ireland 9 Connemara
roles: 6 Becket 7 Creator, Lord Jim 13 Man of La Mancha 14 Goodbye Mr Chips, My Favorite Year, The Last Emperor 15 The Lion in Winter 16 Lawrence of Arabia, What's New Pussycat 18 How to Steal a Millon

O'Trigger, Sir Lucius
character in: 9 The Rivals
author: 8 Sheridan

Ott, Mel
nickname: 9 Boy Wonder 12 Master Melvin
sport: 8 baseball
position: 8 outfield
team: 13 New York Giants

Ottawa
capital of: 6 Canada
early name: 6 Bytown
falls: 6 Rideau 9 Chaudiere
landmark: 9 National Arts Centre 19 Dominion Observatory, Parliament Buildings
river: 6 Ottawa, Rideau 8 Gatineau
university: 8 Carleton

Ottawa
language family: 9 Algonkian 10 Algonquian
location: 4 Ohio 6 Canada, Kansas 7 Ontario 12 Lake Michigan
leader: 7 Pontiac

Otter
origin: 12 Scandinavian
mentioned in: 8 Volsunga
form: 5 otter
father: 8 Hreidmar
killed by: 4 Loki

ottoman, Ottoman 4 seat, Turk 5 couch, divan, stool 7 sultane, Turkish 9 footstool
color: 3 red 9 vermilion
governor: 3 bey, dey 5 pasha
ruler: 5 Osman 8 Suleiman
standard: 4 ale

Otus
form: 5 giant
member of: 7 Aloidae
father: 8 Poseidon
mother: 9 Iphimedia
brother: 9 Ephialtes

Ouagadougou
capital of: 10 Upper Volta 11 Burkina Faso

oui 3 yes

ounce
abbreviation of: 2 oz

ounce troy
abbreviation of: 3 oz t

Our Bill
creator: 14 Harry Haenigsen
character: 6 Walter

Our Crowd
author: 17 Stephen Birmingham

Our Miss Brooks
character: 8 Mrs Davis 12 Connie Brooks, Walter Denton 13 Osgood Conklin, Philip Boynton 14 Harriet Conklin
cast: 8 Eve Arden 10 Dick Crenna, Gale Gordon, Jane Morgan 14 Gloria McMillan, Robert Rockwell
Miss Brooks taught: 7 English
school: 11 Madison High

Our Mutual Friend
author: 14 Charles Dickens
character: 4 Wegg 5 Venus 6 Boffin 11 Bella Wilfer 17 Mortimer Lightwood, Young John Harmon (Handford, Rokesmith)

our sea
Latin: 11 mare nostrum
ancient Roman name for: 13 Mediterranean

Our Town
author: 14 Thornton Wilder
character: 12 Simon Stimson
  Gibbs family: 2 Dr 3 Mrs 6 George 7 Rebecca
  Webb family: 2 Mr 3 Mrs 5 Emily, Wally
director: 7 Sam Wood
cast: 10 Fay Bainter 11 Martha Scott 13 William Holden

oust 4 fire, sack 5 eject, evict, expel 6 banish, bounce, put out, remove, unseat 7 boot out, cashier, cast out, dismiss, kick out 8 throw out 9 discharge, give the ax 11 give the gate, send packing

ouster 6 firing 7 removal, sacking 8 bouncing, ejection, eviction 9 discharge, dismissal, expelling, expulsion, overthrow 10 banishment, cashiering 11 dislodgment, drumming out, throwing out 13 dispossession

out 2 ex 4 away 5 aloud, eject, forth, not in, passe 6 absent, begone, excuse, public 7 outside 8 exterior, external, revealed 9 in society, in the open, published 10 extinguish

out-and-out 4 pure, sure 5 sheer, total, utter 6 arrant 7 perfect 8 absolute, complete, hardened, outright, positive, thorough 9 confirmed, downright, unlimited 10 inveterate 11 straight out, unequivocal, unmitigated, unqualified 12 unregenerate, unrestricted 13 dyed-in-the-wool, thoroughgoing, unadulterated, unconditional 14 unquestionable

outbrazen 4 dare, defy, face 8 confront 9 challenge, stand up to

outbreak 5 burst 7 display 8 epidemic, eruption, invasion, outburst 9 explosion 10 outpouring 13 demonstration

outbuilding 4 barn, shed 5 privy 6 garage, stable 7 latrine 8 outhouse, woodshed

outburst 5 blast, burst 7 display, thunder 8 eruption, outbreak 9 explosion 10 outpouring 11 fulmination 13 demonstration

outcast 5 exile, rover 6 ousted, outlaw, pariah, roamer 7 refugee, runaway 8 banished, castaway, deportee, derelict, expelled, fugitive, rejected, vagabond 9 discarded 10 expatriate

Outcast of the Islands, The
author: 12 Joseph Conrad

Outcault, R F
creator/artist of: **11** Buster
Brown **12** The Yellow Kid

outcome 3 end **5** fruit, issue
6 effect, payoff, result, upshot
9 aftermath, outgrowth **11** aftereffect, consequence

outcry 3 cry **4** howl, roar, yell,
yelp, yowl **5** noise, shout,
whoop **6** bellow, clamor, hubbub, scream, shriek, uproar
7 clangor, protest, screech
9 commotion, complaint,
crying out, hue and cry, objection **10** cry of alarm, hullabaloo **12** caterwauling,
remonstrance

outdated 5 passe **7** antique
8 outmoded **9** out-of-date
10 antiquated **12** old-fashioned

outdo 3 top **4** beat, best **5** excel, worst **6** better, defeat, exceed, outfox, outwit **7** eclipse,
outplay, outrank, surpass
8 outclass, outshine, outstrip,
overcome **9** transcend

outdoor festival
French: **13** fete champetre

outdoor market 5 agora
6 bazaar **10** flea market
11 marketplace

outer 6 distal, remote **7** extreme, farther, outside, outward, without **8** exterior,
external, outlying **9** outermost **10** farther out, peripheral

outer edge 3 lip, rim, tip
5 bound **6** margin **8** boundary
9 extremity

Outer Mongolia
also: **24** Mongolian People's
Republic
border: **5** China **6** Russia
11 Soviet Union
capital: **4** Urga **5** Kulun
9 Ulan Bator
currency: **5** mongo **6** tugrik
desert: **4** Gobi **5** Shamo
language: **7** Khalka
mountain range: **5** Altai, Altay **7** Khangai

outermost 5 outer **6** utmost
7 extreme, outside, outward,
surface **8** exterior, external
11 farthest out, most distant,
superficial

outfit 3 fit, rig **4** gear **5** array,
dress, equip, getup, habit, rig
up **6** clothe, supply **7** appoint,
costume, furnish **8** accouter,
ensemble, wardrobe **9** equipment, provision, trappings
13 accoutrements,
paraphernalia

outflow 5 issue **7** leakage,
seepage **8** drainage **9** discharge

outgo 4 beat, cost, exit, pass

5 excel, issue, outdo **6** efflux,
egress, outlay, outlet **7** outflow, surpass **8** outstrip **9** departure **11** expenditure

outgoing 4 warm **6** genial, social **7** amiable, cordial, exiting,
leaving **8** friendly, going out,
outbound, sociable **9** convivial,
departing **10** gregarious **11** extroverted, sympathetic,
warmhearted

outgoing person 9 extrovert
17 hail-fellow-well-met

outgrowth 3 end **4** knob,
knot, node **5** bulge, fruit, issue, shoot **6** result, sequel,
sprout, upshot **7** product **8** offshoot **9** aftermath **10** conclusion, projection **11** aftereffect,
consequence, culmination, excrescence, outcropping
12 protuberance

outing 4 hike, ride, spin, tour,
trip, walk **5** drive, jaunt,
tramp **6** airing, junket, ramble **7** holiday **9** excursion
10 expedition

outlander 5 alien, exile
6 emigre **7** invader, settler
8 intruder, newcomer,
stranger, wanderer **9** Auslander, barbarian, foreigner, immigrant **10** tramontane
12 ultramontane

outlandish 3 odd **5** kooky,
queer, weird **6** far-out **7** bizarre, curious, strange, unusual **8** freakish, peculiar
9 eccentric, fantastic, grotesque, unheard-of **10** incredible, outrageous, ridiculous
12 preposterous, unbelievable,
unimaginable, unparalleled
13 inconceivable
14 unconventional

outlast 6 endure, hold on,
keep on, remain, stay on
7 carry on, hold out, outstay,
outwear, perdure, persist, prevail, survive **8** continue

outlaw 3 ban, bar **4** deny,
stop **5** felon **6** bandit, forbid,
pariah **7** exclude, outcast
8 criminal, disallow, fugitive,
prohibit, suppress **9** desperado,
interdict, miscreant, proscribe
10 highwayman

outlay 3 fee **4** cost **5** outgo,
price **6** charge **7** expense, payment **8** spending **11** amount
spent, expenditure
12 disbursement

outlet 3 way **4** door, duct, exit,
gate, path, vent **5** means
6 avenue, egress, escape, portal **7** channel, conduit, gateway, opening, passage

outline 4 plot **5** brief, trace

6 digest, limits, resume, review **7** contour, diagram, profile, summary, tracing
8 abstract, synopsis **9** blueprint, delineate, lineation, perimeter, periphery, sketch out
10 abridgment, silhouette
11 delineation **12** condensation
French: **6** apercu

outlook 4 view **5** scene, sight,
vista **6** aspect, chance **7** picture, promise **8** attitude, forecast, panorama, prospect
9 spectacle, viewpoint **10** assumption **11** expectation,
frame of mind, perspective,
point of view, presumption,
probability **12** anticipation

outlying 5 outer, rural **6** far-off,
remote **7** distant, exurban
8 exterior, suburban
10 peripheral

outmoded 5 corny, dated,
passe, tired **6** demode, old
hat **7** antique, archaic, vintage **8** obsolete, old-timey, outdated **9** out-of-date
10 antiquated **12** old-
fashioned, out-of-fashion
14 behind the times
French: **6** demode

Out of Africa
director: **13** Sydney Pollack
cast: **11** Meryl Streep (Baroness Karen Blixen, Isak
Dinesen) **13** Robert Redford
(Denys Finch Hatton)
19 Klaus Maria Brandauer
(Baron Bror von Blixen)

out of bed 2 up **5** astir **9** up
and at 'em **10** on one's feet,
up and about **12** rise and
shine

out-of-date 5 dated, passe
8 outmoded **10** antiquated
12 old-fashioned
French: **6** demode

out of doors 3 out **5** forth
6 abroad **7** outside **8** alfresco
12 in the open air

out-of-fashion 5 passe **8** obsolete, outmoded **9** out-of-date
12 old-fashioned
French: **6** demode

out of hand 4 wild **5** rowdy
6 unruly **10** disorderly **12** obstreperous, out of control, unmanageable, unrestrained
14 uncontrollable

out of keeping 8 atypical, peculiar, unseemly **9** anomalous,
irregular **11** incongruous
12 inconsistent
13 inappropriate

out of kilter 4 awry **5** askew
6 uneven **7** crooked, oblique

out of line 6 unruly **9** excessive 10 exorbitant 12 presumptuous, unreasonable

out of many one
Latin: 13 e pluribus unum
motto of: 12 United States

out of one's head 3 mad
4 daft, nuts 5 crazy, nutty
6 insane 7 cracked, touched
8 demented, deranged, unhinged 10 unbalanced 12 mad
as a hatter, off his rocker
15 mad as a March hare
17 nutty as a fruitcake

out of operation 4 dead,
down 8 inactive 10 not working, out of order
11 inoperative

out of order 5 amiss 6 faulty
10 not working 11 inoperative, uncalled-for
13 inappropriate

out of place 3 odd 8 unseemly 10 unsuitable 11 incongruous, inconsonant
13 inappropriate

out of shape 4 bent 5 unfit
6 flabby, warped 7 crooked
8 deformed 9 distorted,
untrained

out of sorts 5 cross, huffy,
testy 6 crabby, cranky,
touchy 7 bearish, grouchy,
peevish 8 petulant, snappish
9 crotchety, irritable 10 illhumored 11 ill-tempered
12 cantankerous 13 shorttempered

out of the books of
Latin: 8 ex libris

out of the fight
French: 12 hors de combat

out of the ordinary 4 rare
6 unique 7 notable, unusual
8 singular, uncommon
10 phenomenal, remarkable
11 exceptional
13 extraordinary

Out of the Past
director: 15 Jacques
Tourneur
based on novel by: 13 Geoffrey Homes (Daniel Mainwaring) (Build My Gallows
High)
cast: 9 Jane Greer 11 Kirk
Douglas, Richard Webb
13 Rhonda Fleming, Robert
Mitchum

out of touch 7 mixed-up
8 unstable 11 disoriented
12 out of contact
13 incommunicado

out-of-towner 7 tourist, visitor 9 sojourner, transient
11 nonresident

outpace 4 pass 5 outdo 6 exceed, outrun 8 outstrip

outpouring 6 deluge 7 barrage,
gushing, outflow 8 effusion

output 4 crop, gain, take
5 yield 6 profit 7 harvest, produce, product, reaping, turnout 8 gleaning, proceeds
9 gathering 10 production
11 achievement 12 productivity 14 accomplishment

outrage 4 evil, gall, rile 5 anger, shock, wrong 6 arouse,
enrage, insult, madden, offend,
ruffle 7 affront, incense, provoke, steam up 8 atrocity, disquiet, enormity, iniquity
9 barbarity, indignity, infuriate 10 discompose, disrespect,
exasperate, gross crime, scandalize 11 desecration, monstrosity, profanation
13 barbarousness, get one's
back up, make one see red,
slap in the face, transgression
17 make one's blood boil

outraged 3 mad 5 angry, irate,
riled 6 fuming, raging 7 enraged, furious 8 incensed, inflamed, offended 9 affronted,
indignant 10 displeased,
infuriated

outrageous 4 base, foul, rank,
rude, vile 5 gross 6 brutal,
odious, wicked 7 abusive, extreme, galling, heinous, immense, inhuman 8 enormous,
flagrant, inhumane, insolent,
scornful, shocking 9 atrocious,
barbarous, excessive, insulting,
maddening, monstrous, nefarious, offensive, shameless
10 despicable, exorbitant, horrifying, immoderate, iniquitous, scandalous
11 disgraceful, infuriating, unspeakable, unwarranted
12 contemptible, contemptuous, exasperating, preposterous, unreasonable
13 disrespectful, reprehensible
14 unconscionable

outrageousness 8 enormity
9 immensity 10 wickedness
13 atrociousness, monstrousness, offensiveness
16 preposterousness

outre 8 improper

outreach 6 exceed 7 surpass

outright 4 full 5 sheer, total,
utter 6 at once, entire,
openly 7 utterly, visibly 8 absolute, complete, entirely, patently, promptly, thorough
9 downright, forthwith, instantly, on the spot, out-and-out 10 absolutely, altogether,
completely, manifestly, thoroughly, unreserved 11 immediately, unmitigated,
unqualified 12 demonstrably,

undiminished 13 thoroughgoing, unconditional

outrival 3 dim 5 excel, outdo
6 exceed 7 eclipse, surpass
8 outshine 9 transcend
10 overshadow, tower above

outrush 4 gust 8 overflow

outset 4 dawn 5 birth, start
7 dawning 9 beginning, departure, threshold
12 commencement

outshine 3 dim 5 excel, outdo
6 exceed 7 eclipse, surpass
9 transcend 10 overshadow

outside 4 case, face, skin
5 alien, faint, outer 6 facade,
remote, sheath, slight 7 coating, distant, foreign, obscure,
outdoor, outward, strange, surface 8 covering, exterior, external, outdoors 9 nonnative,
outer side, outermost 10 extraneous, out-of-doors,
unfamiliar

outsider 5 alien 7 outcast
8 onlooker, stranger 9 bystander, foreigner, nonmember 14 nonparticipant

outskirts 3 rim 4 edge 6 limits,
verges 7 borders, fringes, margins, suburbs 8 environs 9 periphery, precincts
10 perimeters 11 extremities

outspoken 5 blunt, frank
6 candid, direct, honest 7 artless 9 guileless, ingenuous, unsparing 10 forthright,
unreserved 11 opinionated,
plainspoken 13 undissembling
15 straightforward,
undissimulating

outspread 5 broad 6 opened,
spread 7 laid out 8 expanded,
extended, unfolded, unfurled,
unrolled 9 spread out,
stretched 12 outstretched

outstanding 3 due 5 famed,
great, owing 6 famous, unpaid 7 eminent, notable, payable 8 foremost, renowned,
striking 9 best known, exemplary, in arrears, marvelous,
memorable, prominent, unsettled 10 celebrated, noteworthy,
phenomenal, remarkable
11 exceptional, magnificent,
uncollected 13 distinguished,
extraordinary, unforgettable

outstrip 4 pass 6 exceed, outrun 7 outpace, surpass
11 leave behind

outward 5 outer 7 evident,
outside, surface, visible 8 apparent, exterior, external,
manifest 10 observable, ostensible 11 perceivable, perceptible, superficial

outward appearance 4 mien 6 aspect, facade, manner 7 bearing 8 demeanor, exterior

Outward Bound
author: 10 Sutton Vane

outwardly 7 clearly, visibly 9 evidently, seemingly 10 apparently, manifestly, ostensibly 13 on the face of it 16 to all appearances

outwards 3 out 4 away

outweigh 6 exceed 7 eclipse, surpass 8 override 9 rise above 10 overshadow 11 predominate, prevail over 13 be heavier than, weigh more than

outwit 4 dupe, foil, fool, trap 5 trick 6 baffle, outfox, take in, thwart 7 ensnare 8 outsmart 9 get around 10 circumvent 11 outmaneuver

outworn 5 dated, passe 6 bygone 7 defunct, disused, extinct 8 obsolete, rejected 9 abandoned, discarded, forgotten, out-of-date 10 antiquated, superseded 12 old-fashioned 13 unfashionable

ouzo
type: 7 liqueur
origin: 6 Greece
flavor: 5 anise
substitute for: 8 absinthe

oval 5 ovate, ovoid 6 curved, ovular 7 obovate, oviform, rounded 9 egg-shaped 10 elliptical 11 ellipsoidal

ovation 6 cheers, homage, hurrah, hurray, huzzah 7 acclaim, fanfare, tribute 8 applause, cheering 9 adulation 11 acclamation

oven 3 umu 4 kiln, oast 5 baker, range, stove 6 hearth 7 broiler, chamber, kitchen, roaster
clay: 7 tandoor
fork: 7 fruggan, fruggin
mop: 6 scovel

over 3 too 4 also, anew, done, else, gone, past 5 above, again, ended, extra, often 6 afresh, bygone, lapsed, no more, to boot 7 at an end, elapsed, expired, settled, surplus 8 finished, in excess, once more, too great 9 completed, concluded, excessive, remaining 10 additional, all through, in addition, passed away, repeatedly, terminated 11 a second time, superfluous

overabundance 4 glut 6 excess 7 surfeit, surplus 8 plethora 9 abundance, profusion 10 oversupply 11 superfluity 14 superabundance 15 super-

saturation 21 embarrassment of riches
French: 19 embarras de richesses

over again 4 anew 5 again 7 all over 8 once more 9 once again

overall 5 total 6 entire 7 general 8 complete, long-term, sweeping 9 extensive, long-range, panoramic 10 exhaustive, widespread 12 all-embracing, all-inclusive 13 comprehensive, thoroughgoing

over-and-above 5 added, extra 7 added on, besides 10 additional, in addition 13 supplementary

overawe 6 dazzle 9 overpower, overwhelm 10 intimidate

overbalance 5 upset 6 topple 8 outweigh

overbearing 5 cocky 6 lordly, snooty 7 haughty, high-hat, pompous, stuck-up 8 arrogant, despotic, egoistic 9 conceited, imperious, know-it-all 10 autocratic, disdainful, egoistical, high-handed, tyrannical 11 dictatorial, domineering, egotistical 13 high-and-mighty, self-assertive, self-important

overburden 3 tax 4 load, task, tire 5 whelm 7 exhaust, wear out 8 encumber, overwork, surcharge 9 overwhelm

overcast 4 dark, dull, gray, hazy 5 foggy, misty, murky 6 cloudy, dreary, gloomy, leaden 7 sunless 8 lowering 11 overclouded, threatening

overcharge 3 gyp, pad 4 rook, skin, soak 5 bleed, cheat, gouge, stick, sting, usury 6 extort, fleece 7 exploit 10 exaggerate

overcoat 3 mac 5 parka 6 duster, poncho, raglan, tabard, ulster 7 oilskin, paletot, topcoat 8 burberry, mackinaw 9 greatcoat, inverness, pea jacket 10 mackintosh, trenchcoat 12 chesterfield, Prince Albert

Overcoat, The
author: 12 Nikolai Gogol
character: 9 Petrovich 26 A Certain Important Personage 28 Akakii Akakiievich Bashmachkin

overcome 4 beat, best, lick 5 crush, quell 6 defeat, master, subdue 7 conquer, put down, survive, win over 8 suppress, surmount, vanquish 9 overpower, overthrow, overwhelm, transcend 11 prevail over,

triumph over 14 get the better of

overconfident 5 brash 6 cheeky 8 arrogant, cocksure, egoistic, immodest, impudent 9 conceited 10 egoistical 11 egotistical, self-assured 12 presumptuous

overcrowd 3 jam 4 cram, fill, pack 5 stuff 7 congest

overcrowded 6 filled, jammed, packed 7 crammed, stuffed 9 congested, jampacked

overdecorated 5 gaudy, showy 6 flashy, garish 9 unsightly 12 ostentatious

overdelicacy 11 genteelness, prudishness 12 priggishness 14 overrefinement

overdo 4 gild 6 expand 7 amplify, ham it up, magnify, overact 8 overplay 9 embroider, overstate 10 do to excess, exaggerate 11 carry too far, hyperbolize 12 lay it on thick 13 stretch a point

overdue 4 late, slow 5 tardy 7 belated, delayed, past due 8 dilatory 10 behindhand, behind time, unpunctual 11 long delayed

overdue debt 7 arrears 10 balance due 18 balance outstanding

overflow 4 glut 5 flood 6 excess 7 run over, surplus 8 flow over, inundate, plethora, slop over 9 overspill, profusion 10 overspread, oversupply 11 copiousness, superfluity 13 overabundance 14 superabundance

overflowing 4 full 5 flush 7 replete, swamped 8 abundant, flooding 9 abounding, inundated 11 running over

overgarment 4 cape, coat, robe 5 cloak, habit, parka, shawl, smock 6 blazer, blouse, duster, jacket, kimono, mantle, poncho 7 sweater, topcoat, wrapper 8 cardigan, raincoat 9 gaberdine, housecoat

overgrown 4 rank 5 giant 7 blown-up 8 colossal, enlarged, forested, gigantic 9 luxuriant, oversized

overhang 3 jut 4 eave 5 bulge, drape, eaves, jetty 6 beetle, impend, sadden, shelve 7 project, suspend 8 protrude, threaten 9 projection

overhaul 4 beat, pass 5 catch 6 revamp 7 rebuild, remodel, restore, service 8 overtake, renovate 11 catch up with, recondition, reconstruct

overhead 3 nut 4 atop, roof 5 above, aloft, on top, upper 6 upward 7 ceiling, topmost, up above 8 superior 9 overlying, uppermost 11 overhanging

overindulge 4 baby 5 spoil, stuff 6 overdo, pamper, pig out 7 carouse, overeat 9 dissipate 11 mollycoddle

overjoyed 6 elated, joyous 8 ecstatic, euphoric, exultant, jubilant, thrilled 9 delighted, enchanted, exuberant, gratified 10 enraptured, enthralled 11 carried away, tickled pink, transported 12 happy as a lark

overlay 4 coat 5 cover, layer 6 carpet, veneer 7 blanket, coating 8 covering 11 superimpose

overload 3 tax 4 glut 5 flood, whelm 6 deluge, excess 7 burnout, surfeit 8 encumber 9 innundate, surcharge

overlook 4 miss, omit, skip 6 excuse, forget, give on, ignore, pass up, slight, survey, wink at 7 blink at, command, forgive, let ride, neglect 8 leave out, look over, pass over, shrug off 9 disregard, look out on 10 tower above 11 forget about, have a view of, leave undone

overlord 4 czar, tsar 7 emperor, monarch 8 autocrat 12 supreme ruler 13 absolute ruler

overly 3 too 4 very 6 highly, unduly 7 acutely, too much 8 overmuch, severely, to a fault, unfairly 9 extremely, intensely 10 needlessly 11 exceedingly, excessively 12 exorbitantly, immoderately, inordinately, unreasonably 18 disproportionately

overly trusting 5 naive 8 gullible 9 credulous 12 unsuspicious

overmodest 3 coy 4 prim 7 prudish 8 priggish 11 puritanical

overmuch 3 too 6 excess 7 surplus 8 plethora 9 profusion

overpass 4 span 6 bridge 9 crossover

overpower 4 beat, best, move, sway 5 crush, quell, worst 6 defeat, master, subdue 7 conquer 8 overcome, vanquish 9 influence, overwhelm

overpowering 6 mighty, strong 8 crushing 10 astounding 12 overwhelming

overpraise 4 line 7 blarney, fawning 8 flattery 11 fulsomeness

overpriced 6 costly 7 too high 9 expensive 10 exorbitant

overproud 4 vain 8 arrogant, egoistic 9 conceited 10 egoistical 11 egotistical, swellheaded 13 self-important

overrate 9 overprize, overvalue 10 overesteem, overpraise 12 overestimate 13 make too much of

overrefined 7 genteel, prudish 8 priggish 12 overdelicate

override 5 crush, quash 7 reverse 8 set aside 10 commission 11 countermand

overrule 4 deny, veto 5 annul, eject, repel, waive 6 cancel, refuse, reject, revoke 7 dismiss, nullify, outvote 8 disallow, outweigh, override, overturn, preclude, set aside, throw out 9 repudiate 10 invalidate 11 countermand

overrun 4 loot, raid, sack 5 choke 6 deluge, engulf, infest, invade 7 despoil, pillage, plunder, surplus 8 inundate, overgrow, pour in on, rove over 9 overwhelm, surge over, swarm over

overseas, oversea 5 alien 6 abroad, exotic 7 foreign 8 external 11 ultramarine 12 transoceanic 14 in foreign lands

oversee 3 run 4 boss, rule 5 guide, pilot, see to, steer, watch 6 direct, govern, handle, manage 7 carry on, command 8 attend to, overlook, regulate 9 supervise 10 administer 11 keep an eye on, preside over, superintend 12 have charge of

overseeing 7 bossing, guiding, running 8 guidance, handling, managing 10 leadership, management 11 attending to, supervising, supervision 13 administering 14 administrating, administration, superintending 15 superintendence

overseer 4 boss, head 5 chief 7 captain, foreman, manager 8 director, governor 10 supervisor, taskmaster 11 slave driver 13 administrator 14 superintendent

overshadow 3 fog 4 hide, mask, veil 5 cover, dwarf, shade 6 darken, screen, shroud 7 conceal, eclipse, obscure 8 outshine 9 tower over

overshadowing 7 eclipse, masking, shading, veiling 8 cloaking 9 darkening, eclipsing, obscuring 10 concealing, surpassing 11 concealment, obscuration 12 towering over

overshoe 3 gum 4 boot 6 arctic, gaiter, galosh, patten, rubber 7 galoshe

overshoot 4 pass 6 exceed, go over 8 go beyond

oversight 6 laxity, slight 7 blunder, mistake, neglect 8 omission 9 disregard 10 negligence 11 inattention 12 carelessness, heedlessness, inadvertence 13 careless error 14 neglectfulness 15 thoughtlessness

oversized 4 huge, vast 7 immense, mammoth 8 colossal, enormous, gigantic 10 monumental 14 Brobdingnagian

overspending 12 extravagance, throwing away

overspread 3 fog 4 coat, fill, pave 5 bathe, cloud, cover, paint, plate, smear 6 clothe, infest 7 blanket, diffuse, overlay, overrun, pervade, suffuse 8 disperse 9 whitewash

overstate 6 overdo, play up 7 enlarge, inflate, lay it on, magnify, stretch, touch up 8 increase, overdraw, oversell 9 embellish, embroider, enlarge on, overpaint 10 exaggerate, overstress 15 spread it on thick

overstep 6 exceed 7 violate 10 transgress

oversupply 4 glut 6 excess 7 surfeit, surplus, too much 8 plethora 11 undue amount 13 overabundance 14 superabundance

overt 4 open 5 plain 6 public 7 evident, obvious, visible 8 apparent, manifest, palpable, revealed 10 easily seen, noticeable, observable, ostensible 11 perceivable, perceptible, unconcealed, undisguised

overtake 4 go by, pass 5 catch, reach 6 befall, gain on 7 run down 8 approach, overhaul 11 catch up with

overtax 4 tire 5 abuse, hoist 6 burden, exceed, strain, stress 7 exhaust 8 overload, overwork 9 misemploy 10 overburden

over the hill 3 old 4 aged 5 aging 7 elderly 11 past the peak 13 past one's prime

overthrow 4 undo 5 crush 6 defeat, mutiny, topple

7 abolish, undoing **8** downfall, overcome, overturn, toppling **9** abolition, bring down, overpower, rebellion **10** do away with, revolution

overtire 3 fag **4** bush, do in, poop **5** drain **7** exhaust, fatigue, wear out **8** enervate

overtone 3 hue **4** hint **5** drift **8** coloring, innuendo **10** intimation, suggestion **11** connotation, implication, insinuation

overtrustful 8 gullible **9** credulous **12** unsuspecting, unsuspicious **13** unquestioning

overture 3 bid **6** motion, signal, tender **7** advance, gesture, preface, prelude **8** approach, foreword, offering, preamble, prologue, proposal **9** beginning **10** invitation, suggestion **11** opening move, proposition **12** introduction

overturn 4 beat, oust **5** crush, upend, upset **6** defeat, depose, thrash, topple **7** capsize, conquer, turn out **8** overcome, push over, vanquish **9** knock down, knock over, overpower, overthrow, overwhelm **14** turn topsy-turvy, turn upside down

overturning
French: **14** bouleversement

overweening 5 bossy, cocky, pushy **6** brassy **7** haughty, pompous **8** arrogant, egoistic **9** bigheaded, imperious **10** disdainful, egoistical, highhanded, immoderate **11** domineering, egotistical, overbearing, patronizing **12** presumptuous **13** high-and-mighty, overconfident, self-important

overweight 3 fat **5** dumpy, fatty, gross, hefty, obese, piggy, plump, pudgy, stout, tubby **6** chubby, chunky, fleshy, portly, rotund **7** fattish, well-fed **8** roly-poly **9** corpulent **10** potbellied, well-padded **11** beer-bellied, overstuffed **15** well-upholstered

overwhelm 4 beat, bury **5** crush, quash, quell, swamp **6** defeat, engulf **7** conquer, overrun, stagger **8** bowl over, confound, inundate, overcome, vanquish **9** devastate, overpower, overthrow, subjugate

overwhelming 8 crushing **10** staggering **11** astonishing, devastating **12** overpowering

overwork 3 tax **4** task, tire, toil **5** labor **6** burden, strain **7** exhaust, overtax, wear out **9** misemploy **10** overburden

overwrought 4 wild **5** riled **6** touchy, uneasy **7** excited, nervous, ruffled **8** agitated, frenzied, inflamed, wild-eyed, worked up **9** perturbed, wrought up **10** distracted, high-strung **11** carried away, overexcited

Ovid
author of: **6** Amores **7** Tristia **8** Heroides **11** Ars Amatoria **12** The Art of Love **13** Metamorphoses

ovule 3 egg, nit **4** germ, ovum **6** embryo **7** seedlet

ovum 3 egg **4** cell, germ, seed **5** spore **6** gamete **8** oosphere

owe 8 be in debt **11** be obligated **12** be beholden to, be indebted to

owed 3 due **5** owing **6** unpaid **9** in arrears **11** outstanding

Owen Marshall, Counselor at Law
character: **11** Jess Brandon **12** Frieda Krause **15** Melissa Marshall
cast: **9** Lee Majors **10** Arthur Hill **11** Joan Darling **17** Christine Matchett

owing 3 due **4** owed **6** unpaid **9** in arrears **11** outstanding

own 4 avow, have, hold, keep, tell **5** admit, allow, grant, yield **6** assent, concur, retain **7** concede, possess, private **8** disclose, maintain, personal **9** acquiesce, confess to, consent to, recognize **10** individual, particular **11** acknowledge

owner 6 holder, master **7** partner **8** landlady, landlord, mistress **9** copartner, landowner, possessor **10** landholder, proprietor **11** householder, titleholder **12** proprietress

own up to 5 admit **6** accept **7** confess **8** blurt out **9** recognize **11** acknowledge **14** come clean about

ox 3 oaf **4** bull, clod, musk, urus, zebu **5** aiver, beast, bison, gayal, steer **6** auroch, bantin, bovine **7** banteng, buffalo **10** clodhopper
Cambodian: **7** Kouprey, Kouproh
Celebesian: **3** goa, noa **4** anoa
extinct: **4** urus **7** aurochs
family: **7** bovidae
genus: **3** bos
horned: **4** reem
hornless: **4** moil
Indian: **4** gaur
Paul Bunyan's: **4** Babe
  color: **4** blue

stall: **4** crib
team: **4** yoke
Tibetan: **3** yak
wild: **3** ure **4** anoa
young: **4** stot **5** stirk

Ox-Bow Incident, The
author: **21** Walter Van Tilburg Clark
character: **5** Canby, Croft **6** Davies, Gerald, Martin, Tetley **9** Gil Carter
director: **14** William Wellman
cast: **10** Henry Fonda **11** Dana Andrews **12** Anthony Quinn **13** William Blythe **14** Mary Beth Hughes

oxen
group of: **4** yoke

oxide 8 compound
afterburn: **4** calx
calcium: **4** calx, lime
cobalt: **6** zaffer, zaffre
element: **6** oxygen
iron: **4** rust **8** hematite, limonite **9** colcothar, magnetite
make by heat: **7** calcine
sodium: **4** soda
zinc: **6** cadmia

oxidize 4 burn, char, rust **7** corrode

Oxyderces
epithet of: **6** Athena
means: **10** bright-eyed

oxygen
chemical symbol: **1** O

Oxylus
origin: **8** Aetolian
punishment: **5** exile
chosen leader of: **10** Heraclidae
led invasion of: **12** Peloponnesus

oyez 4 hear **6** attend
cry used by: **10** court crier
preceded: **12** proclamation

Ozark Jubilee
host: **8** Red Foley **10** Webb Pierce
theme: **12** Sugarfoot Rag

Ozark State
nickname of: **8** Missouri

Ozick, Cynthia
author of: **10** Levitation **17** The Cannibal Galaxy **21** The Messiah of Stockholm

Ozzie and Harriet, The Adventures of
cast: **11** David Nelson, Ozzie Nelson, Ricky (Eric) Nelson **13** Harriet Nelson

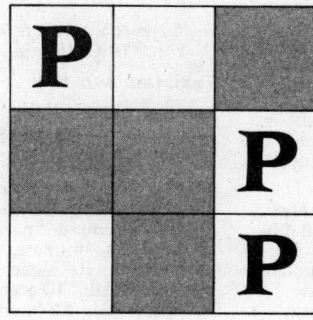

pa 3 dad, paw, pop 4 papa
5 daddy 6 father
   mate: 2 ma

pace 4 clip, flow, gait, rate,
step, walk 5 amble, speed,
tread 6 motion, stride, stroll
7 saunter 8 momentum, slow
gait, velocity

**Pacelli, Eugenio Maria Giu-
seppe Giovanni** 11 Pope
Pius XII

pachyderm 5 hippo, rhino
8 elephant, ungulate 10 rhinoceros 12 hippopotamus
   characteristic: 4 tusk 5 ivory,
   trunk 12 thick-skinned
   prehistoric: 7 mammoth
   8 mastodon

pachydermatous 4 hard
5 horny, tough 7 callous
8 callused, hardened, leathery
12 thick-skinned 13 elephant-
hided

pacific 4 calm 5 quiet, still
6 gentle, placid, serene,
smooth 7 halcyon, restful
8 dovelike, peaceful, tranquil
9 pacifying, peaceable, reposeful, unruffled 10 harmonious,
untroubled 11 inoffensive, undisturbed 12 conciliatory

pacification 8 soothing 11 appeasement, peacemaking
12 conciliation, nonagression
14 reconciliation

pacify 4 calm 5 allay, quiet
6 soothe 7 appease, assuage,
compose, mollify, placate
9 reconcile 10 conciliate,
propitiate

Pacino, Al
   real name: 13 Alberto Pacino
   born: 9 New York NY
   roles: 7 Serpico 8 Scarface
   12 Author Author, The Godfather 15 Dog Day Afternoon, Michael Corleone
   16 And Justice for All

pack 3 box, jam, kit, lot, mob,
set, tie 4 bevy, bind, cram,
fill, heap, herd, load, mass
5 batch, bunch, clump, covey,
crowd, drove, flock, group,
horde, stuff, swarm, truss
6 bundle, gaggle, gather,
packet, parcel, passel, throng
7 cluster, package 8 assemble
9 container, multitude 10 assortment, collection, miscellany 12 accumulation

package 3 box, kit 4 case,
pack, wrap 6 bundle, carton,
encase, packet, parcel, wrap
up 9 container, wrappings

packed 4 full 6 filled, jammed,
loaded, massed, rammed,
wedged 7 crammed, crowded,
crushed, pressed, stuffed
8 overfull, squeezed 10 sandwiched 11 overcrowded

packet 3 bag, box 4 bale, pack,
roll 5 pouch, sheaf 6 bundle,
parcel, quiver 7 package

pack closely 4 cram, pack
5 press, stuff 7 compact
8 compress

pact 4 bond 6 treaty 7 compact 8 alliance, contract, covenant 9 agreement, concordat
10 convention 11 concord-
ance 13 understanding

pad 3 mat 4 fill 5 stuff 6 blow
up, fatten, tablet 7 bolster,
cushion, inflate, protect, puff
out 8 mattress, notebook
9 upholster 10 cushioning,
stretch out

padding 6 filler, lining 7 filling,
packing, surfeit, surplus, wadding 8 stuffing, verbiage,
wrapping 9 prolixity, verbosity,
wordiness 10 redundancy
11 verboseness 12 extravagance 14 superabundance

**Paderewski, Ignace (Ignacy
Jan)**
   born: 6 Poland 9 Kurilowka
   composer of: 5 Manru
   9 Minuet in G

pad out 5 add to 6 expand, extend 7 amplify, augment, enlarge, stretch 8 elongate,
increase, lengthen

padre 6 cleric, father, priest
8 chaplain 9 clergyman

paean 6 anthem, eulogy 7 hosanna 9 laudation, panegyric
10 hallelujah 11 acclamation
12 hymn of praise
   form: 4 hymn, song
   characteristic: 6 joyful
   12 thanksgiving

Paeon
   form: 3 god
   position: 9 physician
   served gods of: 7 Olympia
   corresponds to: 6 Apollo

Paeonia
   epithet of: 6 Athena
   means: 6 healer

Paezan
   language family: 13 Macro-
   Chibchan
   group: 4 Paez 5 Choco
   6 Warrau 8 Colorado

pagan 7 atheist, heathen, infidel 8 idolator 9 barbarian
10 heathenish, idolatrous,
polytheist, unbeliever 11 nonbeliever 12 polytheistic

Paganini, Niccolo
   born: 5 Genoa, Italy
   played: 6 violin
   composer of: 19 The Carnival of Venice

page 3 boy, lad 4 beep, call,
girl, leaf 5 folio, groom, sheet,
youth 6 knight, number, summon 7 callboy, contact 8 announce 9 attendant,
messenger 10 apprentice,
manservant
   blank: 7 flyleaf
   left-hand: 5 verso
   right-hand: 5 recto

Page, Geraldine
   born: 12 Kirksville MO
   husband: 7 Rip Torn

roles: 5 Hondo **9** Interiors **11** Pete-n-Tillie **14** Summer and Smoke **16** A Trip to Bountiful (Oscar), Sweet Bird of Youth

Page and Mistress Page
characters in: 22 The Merry Wives of Windsor
author: 11 Shakespeare

pageant 4 pomp, rite, show **6** parade, ritual **7** display **8** ceremony **9** spectacle **10** exhibition, procession **12** extravaganza

pageantry 4 pomp, rite, show **5** drama, flair **6** ritual, splash **7** display, glitter, pageant **8** ceremony, grandeur, splendor **9** showiness, spectacle, theatrics **10** flashiness **11** ostentation **12** extravagance, magnificence

Paget, James
field: 7 surgery **8** medicine
nationality: 7 British
founder of: 9 pathology

Pagliacci, I
also: 9 The Clowns
opera by: 11 Leoncavallo
character: 5 Canio, Nedda, Tonio **6** Silvio

Pagnol, Marcel
author of: 5 Cesar, Fanny **6** Marius, Topaze

Pago Pago
capital of: 13 American Samoa

Paige, Leroy
nickname: 7 Satchel
sport: 8 baseball
position: 7 pitcher

pain 3 vex, woe **4** ache, gall, hell, hurt, pang, rile **5** agony, annoy, chafe, grief, pinch, pique, smart, sting, throb, worry **6** aching, grieve, harass, misery, ordeal, sadden, sorrow, stitch, twinge **7** agonize, anguish, disturb, hurting, malaise, sadness, torment, torture, trouble **8** distress, smarting, soreness **9** displease, heartache, suffering **10** affliction, discomfort, exasperate, heartbreak **11** unhappiness **12** wretchedness

Paine, Thomas
author of: 9 The Crisis **11** Common Sense **14** The Rights of Man

painful 3 sad **4** dire **5** sharp **6** aching, dismal, dreary, trying **7** arduous, hurtful, racking **8** grievous, grueling, pathetic, piercing, smarting, stinging, very sore **9** agonizing, difficult, sorrowful, throbbing, torturous **10** afflictive,

disturbing, lamentable, unpleasant **11** disquieting, distasteful, distressful, distressing **12** disagreeable, excruciating

pain in the neck 4 bane **6** bother **7** torment **8** headache, nuisance **9** annoyance **10** affliction

painstaking 5 fussy **7** careful, earnest, finicky, precise **8** diligent, exacting, thorough **9** assiduous, energetic, strenuous **10** meticulous, scrupulous **11** industrious, persevering, punctilious **13** conscientious, thoroughgoing

paint 4 coat, daub, draw, limn, swab, tint **5** adorn, brush, color, cover, horse, rouge, shade, stain **6** depict, enamel, makeup, opaque, sketch **7** pigment, portray, stipple, touch up **8** cosmetic, decorate, describe, variegate **9** delineate, represent

Painted Bird, The
author: 13 Jerzy Kosinski

painter 6 artist, drawer **8** sketcher **9** old master **10** delineator **11** illustrator, landscapist, miniaturist **13** watercolorist

Painter, Painter's Easel
constellation of: 6 Pictor

painting 3 art, oil **5** draft, mural, piece **6** canvas, design, tablet **7** cartoon, daubing, drawing, graphic, picture, tableau **8** panorama, portrait, seascape **9** depiction, landscape, still life **10** cerography, watercolor **11** perspective **12** illustration
colloidal: 7 tempera
method: 9 encaustic
on plaster: 5 secco **6** fresco
one-color: 8 monotint **10** monochrome
opaque: 7 gouache
religious: 5 Pieta
style: 5 genre
tool: 5 brush, easel, knife **6** canvas, roller, sponge **7** palette **8** spraygun

pair 3 duo **4** dyad, mate, span, team, yoke **5** brace, match, unite **6** couple **7** combine, doublet, match up, pair off, twosome

pair off 10 go two by two **11** form couples

Paiute
language family: 10 Shoshonean
tribe: 12 Mono-Paviosto, Snake Indians **13** Digger Indians **14** Northern Paiute, Southern Paiute
location: 4 Utah **5** Idaho

6 Nevada, Oregon **7** Arizona **10** California

Pakistan *see box*

Pakula, Alan
director of: 19 All the President's Men

pal 4 chum, mate, pard **5** buddy, crony **6** cohort, friend **7** comrade, partner **8** alter ego, intimate, sidekick **9** associate, colleague, companion, confidant **10** accomplice, bosom buddy **13** boon companion

palace 5 villa **6** castle **7** chateau, mansion **8** hacienda
French: 6 palais
Italian: 7 palazzo

Palaeoscincus
type: 8 dinosaur **10** ornithopod
location: 12 North America
period: 10 Cretaceous

palais 6 palace **17** municipal building **18** government building

Palamedes
lieutenant of: 9 Agamemnon

pal around 7 consort, hang out **9** associate, be friends, run around **10** fraternize

palatable 5 tasty **6** savory **8** pleasant **9** agreeable, toothsome **10** appetizing

palatial 4 posh, rich **5** grand, noble, plush, regal, ritzy, showy **6** swanky **7** elegant, opulent, stately **8** imposing, splendid **9** grandiose, luxurious, sumptuous **10** monumental **11** magnificent

palaver 3 gab **4** chat, talk **5** prate **6** confer, gossip, parley **7** consult, discuss, prattle **8** chitchat, idle talk **10** chew the fat, chew the rag, conference, discussion

palazzo 6 palace

pale 3 pen, wan **4** fold, post **5** ashen, close, light, pasty, stake, white **6** anemic, blanch, paling, pallid, picket, sallow, whiten **7** closure, confine, deathly, ghastly, upright, whitish **8** bleached, palisade **9** bloodless, colorless, deathlike, enclosure, ghostlike **10** ash-colored, cadaverous, light-toned

Pale Horse, Pale Rider
author: 19 Katherine Anne Porter

paleness 6 pallor **7** wanness **8** dullness **9** whiteness **13** colorlessness

Pakistan
name means: 13 Land of the Holy, Land of the Pure
capital: 9 Islamabad
largest city: 7 Karachi
others: 3 Dir, Sui 4 Mari, Sidi 5 Dacca, Qasim, Ralat
6 Chalna, Khulna, Lahore, Multan, Quetta 7 Larkana,
Sialkot 8 Jamalpur, Lyallpur, Peshawar, Sargodha 9 Hyderabad 10 Gujranwala, Rawalpindi
school: 9 U of Punjab 10 U of Karachi 12 U of Hyderabad 16 Allama Iqbal Open U 22 Pakistan U of Agriculture 39 Pakistan Institute of International Affairs
division: 3 Dir 4 Sind, Swat 5 Hunza, Kalat 6 Bengal,
Kharan, Punjab 7 Chitral 8 Khairpur, Peshawar 10 Baha-
walpur, Waziristan 11 Baluchistan
  empire: 5 Gupta, Mogul 6 Kushan, Maurya 7 British,
  Magadha
  seceded state: 10 Bangladesh
monetary unit: 4 anna, pice 5 paisa, rupee
weight: 4 seer, tola 5 maund
mountain: 3 Pab, Pub 4 Salt 6 Makran 7 Kirthar 8 Himalaya, Safed Koh, Sulaiman 9 Hindu Kush, Karakoram
11 Makran Coast 13 Central Makran 14 Takht-i-Sulaiman
highest point: 9 Tirich Mir 12 Godwin Austin
river: 3 Nal 4 Bado, Beas, Ravi, Swat, Zhob 5 Dasht, Indus, Kabul 6 Chenab, Ganges, Jamuna, Jhelum, Kundar,
Porali, Sutlej 7 Jamunna
sea: 7 Arabian
physical feature:
  bay: 8 Soymiani
  canal: 4 Nara 5 Rohri
  cape: 5 Fasta, Jaddi 6 Jiwani
  delta: 6 Ganges 11 Char-Manpura
  desert: 4 Sind, Thal, Thar
  mountain pass: 5 Bolan 6 Khyber
  plateau: 11 Baluchistan
  valley: 5 Kohat
people: 5 Sindi, Wazir 6 Afridi, Bengal, Mahsud, Pathan,
Sindhi 7 Baluchi, Brahuis, Puktuns, Punjabi, Sherani
8 Khattack, Pushtuns, Shinwari, Yusefazi
11 Mohammedzai
  leader: 6 Jinnah 7 Aly Khan 8 Ayub Khan, Zia Ul-Haq
  9 Ali Bhutto, Yahya Khan 13 Benazir Bhutto, Mujibur
  Rahman 15 Mahmud of Ghaznbi
  poet: 5 Igbal, Iqbal
language: 4 Urdu 6 Pushtu, Sindhi 7 Baluchi, Bengali,
English, Punjabi
religion: 5 Hindu, Islam 8 Buddhism 12 Christianity
place:
  dam: 6 Mangla 7 Tarbela
  gardens: 8 Shalamar
  mosque: 8 Badshahi
  tomb: 15 Emperor Jahangir
feature:
  clothing: 5 kurta, pugri, qamis 6 jinnah 7 dupatta, shal-
  war 8 sherwani 9 churidars
food:
  bread: 8 chappati
  dish: 5 kebab, pilaf 6 qormas, salans, sautes
  10 vermicelli
  yogurt: 4 dahi

paleontology
study of: 18 correlation of
parts
founder: 13 Georges Cuvier

Palermo
capital of: 6 Sicily

Pales
origin: 5 Roman

protector of: 6 flocks
9 shepherds
festival: 7 Parilia

Palestine *see* 6 Israel

**Palestrina, Giovanni Pier-
luigi da**
born: 5 Italy 10 Palestrina
composer of: 11 Stabat Mater 18 Missa Papae
Marcelli

Paley, Grace
author of: 26 The Little Dis-
turbances of Man 30 Enor-
mous Changes at the Last
Minute

Palici
origin: 5 Roman
form: 4 gods 5 twins
gods of: 14 sulphur springs

Palilicium *see* 6 Hyades

paling 4 pale, rail 5 fence,
stake 6 picket

Palinurus
steersman of: 6 Aeneas

palisade 5 close, fence 7 bulwark, rampart 8 stockade
9 enclosure

palisades 4 crag 5 ledge
6 bluffs, cliffs 10 escarpment,
promontory

pall 4 cloy, haze, sate 5 gloom,
weary 6 shadow, sicken
7 dimness, satiate 8 darkness
10 become dull, be tiresome,
depression, desolation, melancholy, moroseness, oppression

Palladio, Andrea
real name: 26 Andrea di Pietro della Gondola
architect of: 12 Villa Ro-
tunda (Vicenza Italy)
14 Teatro Olimpico (Vi-
cenza) 19 Church of Il Re-
dentore (Venice) 26 Church
of San Giorgio Maggiore
(Venice)
style: 9 Palladian

Pallas *see* 6 Athena

Pallas Athena *see* 6 Athena

pallet 3 bed, cot 4 bunk, tick
5 berth 8 mattress, platform

palliate 4 calm, curb, ease,
hush, lull, tame 5 abate, allay,
check, quiet, sooth, still
6 lessen, modify, reduce,
soften, subdue, temper 7 assuage, comfort, cushion,
lighten, relieve 8 decrease, diminish, minimize, mitigate,
moderate 9 alleviate
10 ameliorate

palliative 4 balm 6 solace
7 anodyne, comfort
10 comforting

pallid 3 wan 4 ashy, blah, dull,
pale 5 ashen, bland, pasty,
vapid, waxen 6 boring, chalky,
peaked, sallow 7 ghostly, humdrum, insipid, tedious
8 blanched, lifeless 9 bloodless,
colorless 10 monotonous
13 anemic looking, unimaginative, uninteresting

pallor 7 wanness 8 paleness

9 pastiness, whiteness
10 ashen color, pallidness
11 ghostliness 13 bloodless-
ness, colorlessness

palm *see box*

Palm Beach Story, The
director: 14 Preston Sturges
cast: 9 Mary Astor 10 Joel
McCrea, Rudy Vallee
15 William Demarest
16 Claudette Colbert

Palmer, Arnold
sport: 4 golf
noted for: 10 Arnie's Army

Palmer, Lilli
real name: 17 Lillie Marie
(Maria Lilli) Peiser
born: 5 Posen 7 Germany
husband: 11 Rex Harrison
14 Carlos Thompson
roles: 11 Body and Soul
autobiography: 22 Change
Lobsters and Dance

Palmer, Vera Jane
real name of: 14 Jayne
Mansfield

Palmetto State
nickname of: 13 South
Carolina

Palm Sunday
author: 12 Kurt Vonnegut

palmy 4 rosy 5 balmy, sunny
6 golden 7 booming, halcyon
8 blooming, pleasant, thriving
9 agreeable, bounteous, congenial 10 prosperous, successful 11 flourishing,
pleasurable

Palmyra
Biblical name: 6 Tadmor

palpable 5 clear, plain 7 evident, obvious, tactile, visible
8 apparent, definite, distinct,
feelable, manifest, tangible
9 touchable 10 noticeable
11 discernible, perceivable,
perceptible 12 recognizable,
unmistakable

palpitate 4 beat 5 pound,
shake, throb 6 quaver, quiver,
shiver 7 flutter, tremble, vibrate 9 go pit-a-pat

palsied 7 quaking, shaking,
spastic 9 trembling

palsy-walsy 5 close, palsy,
thick 6 chummy 8 friendly, intimate 10 buddy-buddy
14 thick as thieves

paltriness 10 triviality 12 unimportance 14 insignificance
18 inconsequentiality

paltry 4 poor, puny 5 petty,
sorry 6 measly, shabby
7 scrubby, trivial 8 inferior,
picayune, piddling, trifling,
wretched 11 unimportant
13 insignificant, of little
value 14 inconsiderable
15 inconsequential

Pama-Nyungan
language spoken by:
10 aborigines
spoken in: 9 Australia

Pamela
author: 16 Samuel
Richardson
character: 3 Mr B 9 Mrs Jervis, Mrs Jewkes 10 Lady
Davers 13 Pamela Andrews

pamper 5 humor, spoil 6 coddle, cosset 7 cater to, indulge
8 give in to 11 mollycoddle

pampered 7 coddled, humored 8 indulged 9 catered-to,
cossetted

pamphlet 5 tract 6 folder
7 booklet, leaflet 8 brochure,
bulletin, circular 9 monograph,
throwaway

pan 3 boo, map, mug, pot
4 face, hiss 6 kisser 8 ridicule,
saucepot 9 criticize

Pan
also: 7 Sinoeis
origin: 5 Greek
form combined: 3 man
4 goat
god of: 6 flocks 7 forests
8 pastures 9 shepherds
father: 4 Zeus 6 Hermes
loved: 4 Echo 5 Pitys
6 Syrinx
invented: 5 pipes 6 syrinx
corresponds to: 6 Faunus

panacea 6 elixir 7 cure-all,
nostrum 13 universal cure

panache 4 dash, tuft 5 flair,
plume, style, verve
11 flamboyance

Panama *see box*

Panama City
capital of: 6 Panama

pancake 4 blin 5 blini, crepe,
kisra, latke, lefse 6 blintz,
makeup 7 fritter, hotcake
8 flapjack, slapjack 11 griddle-
cake 12 silver dollar
day: 13 Shrove Tuesday

---

palm
varieties: 3 Fan, Ita, Key, Nut, Oil, Wax 4 Cane, Date,
Doom, Doub, Doum, Fern, Hair, Hemp, King, Lady, Nipa,
Nypa, Rock, Sago, Step, Tala, Wine 5 Areca, Areng, As-
sai, Betel, Black, Bread, Broom, Curly, Grass, Honey, In-
aga, Ivory, Jelly, Latan, Manac, Nikau, Peach, Queen,
Royal, Snake, Spine, Sugar, Syrup, Toddy, Yatay, Zombi
6 Bamboo, Barbel, Barrel, Bottle, Cherry, Cohune, Coyoli,
Gebang, Gomuti, Gru-gru, Hesper, Kentia, Licuri, Manila,
Mazari, Needle, Nibung, Parlor, Pignut, Raffia, Rattan,
Ruffle, Sagisi, Sentry, Silver, Thatch, Thread, Yellow
7 Arikury, Cabbage, Calappa, Coconut, Coquito, Feather,
Fiji fan, Funeral, Jaggery, Leopard, Mexican, Moriche,
Overtop, Palmyra, Prickly, Spindle, Talipot, Weddell
8 Betel nut, Carnauba, Cucurite, Dwarf fan, Fishtail,
Good luck, Ivory-nut, Mangrove, Pandanus, Peaberry,
Princess, Roebelin, Umbrella, Wild date, Windmill
9 Alexander, Alexandra, Butterfly, Christmas, Desert fan,
Gippsland, Guadalupe, Hurricane, India date, Macarthur,
Ouricouri, Panama-hat, Petticoat, Piccabeen, Porcupine,
Pygmy date, Silver saw, Solitaire, Spiny-club, Traveler's
10 African oil, Black-fiber, Canary date, Chinese fan, Cuban belly, Cuban royal, Everglades, Franceschi, Saw cabbage, Sealing-wax, Thatch-leaf, Washington 11 American
oil, Chilean wine, European fan, Gingerbread, Mexican
blue, Morass royal, Senegal date, Slender lady, Woolly
butia 12 Caribee royal, Egyptian doum, Florida royal,
Miniature fan, Walking-stick 13 Australian fan, Australian ivy, Australian nut, Belmore sentry, Feather-duster,
Florida silver, Florida thatch, Forster sentry, Golden
feather, Miniature date, San Jose hesper 14 Common
princess, East Indian wine, Puerto Rican hat, Tufted fishtail, Yellow princess 15 Burmese fishtail, Chinese fountain, Chinese windmill, Yellow butterfly 16 Hispaniolan
royal, Northern bangalow, Puerto Rican royal 17 Australian cabbage, Clustered fishtail, Mexican Washington, Piccabeen bangalow 18 South American royal

Panama
  capital/largest city: 10 Panama City
  others: 4 Daid **5** Ancon, Colon **6** Azuero, Balboa, Gamboa
    8 Dos Bocas, Penonome, Santiago **9** Cristobal
    10 Portobello
  division: 5 Cocle, Colon **6** Darien, Panama **7** Herrera
    8 Chiriqui, Veraguas **9** Los Santos **12** Bocas del Toro
  measure: 7 celemin
  monetary unit: 4 cent **6** balboa **10** centesimos
  island: 5 Coiba, Pearl **6** Cebaco, Multas, Taboga **7** San
    Blas **10** Isla Del Rey **12** Bocas del Toro, Juan Gallegos
    13 Barro Colorado
  lake: 5 Gatun
  mountain: 4 Baru, Maje **5** Chico, Gandi **6** Darien **7** Colu-
    man, San Blas, Veragua **8** Santiago, Tabasara **10** Costa Ri-
    can **14** Serrania de Sapo **15** Aspave Highlands
    17 Cordillera Central
  highest point: 8 Chiriqui
  river: 5 Chepo, Sambu, Tuira **6** Bayano, Panugo **7** Chagres
  sea: 7 Pacific **9** Caribbean
  physical feature:
    bay: **5** Limon **6** Panama
    dam: **5** Gatun
    gulf: **6** Darien, Panama, Parita **7** Montijo, San Blas
      8 Chiriqui **9** Mosquitos, San Miguel
    isthmus: **6** Darien, Panama **7** San Blas
    lagoon: **8** Chiriqui
    peninsula: **6** Azuero **8** Valjente
  people: 4 Cuna **5** Choco **6** Guaymi **7** mestizo
    canal builder: **7** Lesseps
    explorer: **6** Balboa **8** Bastidas, Columbus
    leader: **4** Royo **5** Arias **7** Noriega **8** Guerrero, Torrijos
      9 Espriella **12** Simon Bolivar
    poet: **4** Miro **5** Korsi, Sinan
  language: 7 English, Spanish
  religion: 13 Roman Catholic
  place:
    church: **7** San Jose **15** Virgen del Carmen
    plaza: **13** Independencia
    ruins: **9** Old Panama
  feature:
    clothing: **7** montuno, pollera
    dance: **4** caja **7** pujador **9** tamborito
    tree: **4** yaya **5** maria, quira **6** alfaje, cativo
    US operation: **9** Just Cause
  food:
    meat: **6** tazajo
    soup: **8** sancocho

Pancks
  character in: 12 Little Dorrit
  author: 7 Dickens

pancreas
  produces: 7 insulin

Pandareus
  father: 6 Lycaon, Merops
  daughter: 5 Aedon **6** Merope
    9 Cleothera
  wounded: 8 Menelaus
  stole: 9 golden dog
  turned to: 5 stone
  killed by: 8 Diomedes

Pandarus
  character in: 18 Troilus and
    Cressida, Troilus and
    Criseyde
  author: 7 Chaucer
    11 Shakespeare

Pandarus
  son: 7 Alcanor
  companion of: 6 Aeneas

pandemic 4 rife **7** rampant
  8 epidemic **10** prevailing,
  widespread **21** dangerously
  contagious

pandemonium 3 din **5** chaos
  6 bedlam, clamor, hubbub,
  racket, rumpus, tumult, uproar **7** turmoil **8** disorder
  9 commotion **10** hullabaloo
  11 disturbance

Pandemos
  epithet of: 9 Aphrodite

pander, panderer 4 mack,
  pimp **5** cadet **7** hustler **8** procurer **9** maquereau, souteneur
  12 flesh-peddler

Pandion the Younger
  king of: 6 Athens
  later reigned in: 6 Megara

Pandora
  form: 10 first woman
  created by: 10 Hephaestus
  presented to: 10 Epimetheus
  daughter: 6 Pyrrha
  given by gods: 3 box
    box contained: **4** hope
      5 evils

Pandrosos
  position: 9 priestess
  first priestess of: 6 Athena
  father: 7 Cecrops
  mother: 8 Agraulos

panegyric 6 eulogy, homage,
  praise **7** tribute **8** citation, encomium, good word **9** extol-
  ment, laudation
  10 compliment **11** testimonial
  12 commendation

panegyrize 4 laud **5** extol
  6 praise **8** eulogize

panel 4 jury, pane **5** board,
  group, piece **6** insert **7** divider
  8 bulkhead **9** committee, partition **10** round table **11** compartment, expert group, select
  group **13** advisory
  group

pang 4 ache, pain **5** agony,
  pinch, smart, stick, sting,
  throb **6** stitch, twinge **7** anguish **8** distress **9** suffering
  10 discomfort

Pangloss
  character in: 7 Candide
  author: 8 Voltaire

pang of conscience 5 demur,
  qualm **6** unease **7** remorse,
  scruple **9** misgiving **10** uneasiness **11** compunction

panhandle 3 beg, bum
  5 cadge, mooch **6** hustle **7** solicit **9** importune

Panhandle State
  nickname of: 12 West
    Virginia

Panhellenius
  epithet of: 4 Zeus
  means: 14 god of all Greeks

panic 5 alarm, dread, go ape,
  scare **6** fright, horror, terror
  7 anxiety **8** affright, hysteria
  9 cold sweat, confusion, fall
  apart **10** go to pieces **11** nervousness, trepidation **12** apprehension, perturbation
  13 consternation

panicky 6 scared **7** alarmed,
  anxious **9** terrified **10** frightened **13** panic-stricken, scared
  to death **14** terror-stricken

panic-stricken 6 afraid,
  scared **7** alarmed, anxious,
  fearful, panicky **9** terrified

13 scared to death 14 terror-stricken

Panjabi
language family: 12 Indo-European
branch: 11 Indo-Iranian
group: 5 Indic
spoken in: 5 (northern) India

Pankrits
language family: 12 Indo-European
branch: 11 Indo-Iranian
form of: 5 Indic
followed use of: 8 Sanskrit

pannier 3 bag 4 hoop 6 basket, dossel, pantry 7 corbeil, drapery 9 framework, overskirt literally: 11 breadbasket

Panomphaeus see 4 Zeus

Panopeus
father: 6 Phocus
mother: 7 Asteria
twin brother: 6 Crisus

Panoptes
epithet of: 5 Argus
means: 7 all eyes

panorama 5 scene, vista 6 survey 7 diorama, picture, scenery, tableau 8 long view, overview, prospect 10 scenic view 11 perspective 12 bird's-eye view

panoramic 3 ide 7 overall 8 bird's-eye, extended, sweeping 9 extensive 10 far-ranging 11 far-reaching 12 all-embracing, all-inclusive 15 all-encompassing

pansy 5 Viola
varieties: 4 Wild 5 Field 6 Garden, Orchid 8 Japanese 9 Miniature 11 Monkey-faced 12 European wild

pant 4 blow, gasp, huff, puff 6 wheeze

pant after 4 seek 5 covet, crave 6 desire, pursue 7 hope for, long for, lust for, wish for 8 yearn for 9 hanker for, hunger for, lust after 11 thirst after, have a yen for 14 set one's heart on

Pantagruel see 22 Gargantua and Pantagruel

panther 3 cat 6 cougar 7 leopard

Panthous
priest of: 6 Apollo
counselor of: 5 Priam
father: 8 Othrys
son: 9 Euphorbus, Hyperenor, Polydamas

Pantomime Quiz
host: 10 Mike Stokey 15 Pat Harrington Jr

pantry 5 ambry, store 6 closet,

galley, larder 7 butlery, buttery, pannier, spicery 8 cupboard, scullery

pants 5 jeans 6 denims, shorts, slacks 7 drawers, panties 8 breeches, britches, knickers, trousers 9 bluejeans, dungarees 10 underpants 11 undershorts 12 underdrawers

pantywaist 4 wimp 5 sissy, softy 7 crybaby, milksop 8 mama's boy, weakling 10 namby-pamby, sissy-pants, weak sister 11 Milquetoast, mollycoddle 13 sissy-britches

Panurge
character in: 22 Gargantua and Pantagruel
author: 8 Rabelais

Panza, Sancho
character in: 10 Don Quixote
author: 9 Cervantes

pap 3 rot 4 bosh, junk, mash, mush, pulp, tosh 5 gruel, paste 6 cereal, drivel, Pablum, trivia 7 rubbish, twaddle 8 soft food 10 balderdash, flapdoodle, triviality

papa 2 pa 3 dad, doc, paw, pop 5 daddy, poppy 6 father, priest 9 Hemingway
mate: 4 mama

Papa Bear
nickname of: 11 George Halas

Papago
language family: 5 Piman 10 Uto-Aztecan
location: 6 Mexico 7 Arizona
related to: 4 Pima

papal 9 apostolic, of the pope 10 pontifical

Papaleo, Anthony
real name of: 16 Anthony Franciosa

paper 4 bond, deed, news, opus, pulp, work 5 daily, draft, essay, stock, theme 6 record, report, tissue, weekly 7 article, gazette, journal, monthly, tabloid, writing 8 document, gift wrap 9 cardboard, chronicle, newspaper, newsprint, onionskin 10 instrument, manuscript, paperboard, periodical, stationery, typescript 11 certificate, composition, publication

Paper Chase, The
character: 10 James T Hart, Willis Bell 13 Asheley Brooks 14 Elizabeth Logan, Jonathan Brooks 15 Franklin Ford III 19 Thomas Craig Anderson 29 Professor Charles W Kingsfield Jr
cast: 10 James Keane 11 Robert Ginty 12 Deka

Beaudine, John Houseman 13 James Stephens, Jonathan Segal 14 Francine Tacker, Tom Fitzsimmons
subject: 9 law school
Kingsfield's specialty: 11 contract law

paper measure 4 ream 5 quire

Paper Moon
director: 16 Peter Bogdanovich
cast: 9 Ryan O'Neal 10 Tatum O'Neal 12 Madeline Kahn (Trixie Delight) 13 John Hillerman
Oscar for: 17 supporting actress (O'Neal)

Paphian see 9 Aphrodite

Paphos
also: 6 Paphus
father: 9 Pygmalion
mother: 7 Galatea

Paphus see 6 Paphos

Papua New Guinea
formerly: 16 British New Guinea
capital: 11 Port Moresby
town: 3 Thu, Lae 4 Ioma 6 Kikori, Madang
province of: 9 Indonesia
province: 9 West Irian
monetary unit: 4 kina
island: 6 Misima 10 New Britain
archipelago: 8 Bismarck
lake: 6 Murray
river: 3 Fly 4 Ramu
sea: 5 Coral 7 Solomon
strait: 6 Torres
people: 4 Hula, Kate 5 Kiwai, Kwoma 6 Banaro 7 Arapesh 10 Melanesian
language: 7 English

papyrus 4 pith, reed 5 paper, sedge 6 scroll 7 bulrush 8 document 10 manuscript
accordion pleated: 6 orihon
genus: 7 Cyperus
origin: 5 Egypt 9 Nile delta 10 Nile valley
use: 3 mat 4 rope, shoe, sail 5 paper

par 5 level, usual 6 normal, parity 7 average, balance, the norm 8 equality, evenness, identity, sameness, standard 9 stability 11 equilibrium, equivalency 12 equal footing 13 identicalness

parable 4 myth, tale 5 fable, story 6 homily, legend 8 alle-

gory, apologue, folk tale
9 folk story 12 morality tale

Paracelsus
author: 14 Robert Browning

parade 4 line, pomp, show
5 array, march, strut, train,
vaunt 6 column, defile, flaunt,
review, string 7 caravan, cortege, display, show off
8 vaunting 9 cavalcade, flaunting, march past, motorcade,
pageantry, put on airs, spectacle 10 exposition, grandstand,
procession 11 progression
13 demonstration

paradigm 5 ideal, model 6 matrix, sample 7 example, paragon, pattern 8 exemplar,
original, standard 9 archetype,
criterion, prototype, yardstick

paradise 3 joy 4 Eden 5 bliss
6 heaven, utopia 7 delight, ecstasy, nirvana, rapture
8 pleasure 9 enjoyment, happiness, Shangri-la, transport
11 happy valley 12 Garden of
Eden, satisfaction 13 gratification, seventh heaven 15 Land
of Cockaigne

Paradise 5 Annwn 6 Annfwn

Paradise
also: 9 Paradisio
part three of: 12 Divine
Comedy
author: 14 Dante Alighieri

Paradise Lost
author: 10 John Milton
character: 3 Eve, God
4 Adam 5 Satan 6 Christ
7 Lucifer

Paradise of the Pacific
nickname of: 6 Hawaii

Paradise Regained
author: 10 John Milton

paradisiacal 7 elysian, sublime 8 blissful, empyreal, empyrean, ethereal, heavenly
9 celestial, unearthly
12 otherworldly

paradox 5 poser 6 enigma,
oddity, puzzle, riddle 7 anomaly 11 incongruity
13 inconsistency

paradoxical 9 ambiguous,
enigmatic, equivocal
13 contradictory

paragon 4 norm 5 ideal,
model 6 symbol 7 example,
pattern 8 exemplar, paradigm,
standard 9 archetype, criterion,
prototype, yardstick
10 apotheosis

Paraguay *see box*

parallel 4 akin, like, same,
twin 5 alike, equal, match
6 follow 7 abreast, analogy, be

alike, similar 8 analogue, likeness, relation 9 alongside,
analogous, corollary, duplicate 10 collateral, comparable,
comparison, concurrent, connection, equivalent, similarity
11 coextensive, coincidence,
comparative, compare with,
correlation, correlative, counterpart, equidistant, resemblance 12 correspond to
13 corresponding
14 correspondence

parallelism 8 affinity, likeness,
sameness 9 agreement
10 comparison, similarity, similitude 11 resemblance
14 correspondence

parallelogram 5 rhomb
6 square 7 diamond, rhombus
8 rhomboid 9 rectangle
11 plane figure
13 quadrilateral

paralyze 4 stun 6 benumb,
deaden, disarm, freeze,

Paraguay
capital/largest city: 8 Asuncion
others: 3 Ita 4 Rica, Yuty 5 Belen, Luque, Pilar, Villa
7 Caacupe 8 Trinidad 9 Paraguari 10 Concepcion, Villarrica 11 Encarnacion 26 Puerto Presidente Stroessner
division: 6 Guaira, Itapua, Olimpo 7 Caazapa 8 Boqueron
10 Concepcion
measure: 3 pie 4 lino, lira, lire, vara 5 legua 6 cuadra,
fanega
monetary unit: 4 peso 7 guarani, centimo
weight: 7 quintal
island:
 floating island: 8 camalote
lake: 4 Vera, Ypoa 8 Ypacarai
river: 3 Apa 5 Guazu, Negro, Plata, Verde, Ypane
6 Acaray, Parana 7 Aguaray, Confuso 8 Paraguay
9 Aquidaban, Pilcomayo, Tebicuary, Tibiquare 10 Monte
Lindo 14 Riacho Gonzales 15 Riacho Mosquitos
physical feature:
 falls: 6 Guaira
 plains: 5 Chaco
 plateau: 6 Parana
people: 6 Abipon, Moskoi 7 Guarani, mestizo 8 Guayaqui
 artist: 7 Bestard
 author: 3 Pla 4 Baez 6 Alcala, Bastos, Correa, O'Leary
 7 Cervera 8 Casaccia
 composer: 8 Asuncion
 leader: 5 Lopez 7 Francia 10 Stroessner 16 Antequera y
 Castro
 sculptor: 8 Guggiari
language: 6 German 7 Guarani, Spanish
religion: 9 Mennonite 13 Roman Catholic
place:
 church: 10 Villarrica 11 Incarnation
 dam: 6 Itaipu
 memorial: 16 Pantheon of Heroes
 museum: 5 Godoi
 palace: 10 Government
feature:
 animal: 4 puma 5 tapir 6 iguana, jaguar 7 peccary
 bird: 6 toucan
 clothing: 5 fajas, typoi 6 poncho 7 rebozos 9 bombachas
 10 alpargatas
 communes: 11 reducciones
 dance: 7 Sante Fe 15 Paraguayan polka
 fish: 7 piranha
 lace: 7 nanduti
 music: 8 quarania
 townspeople: 9 comuneros
 tree: 5 ceiba 7 lapacho 9 quebracho
food:
 bread: 5 chipa, mbeyu
 dish: 12 sopa paraguay
 tea: 9 yerba mate
 vegetable: 8 mandioca

weaken **7** cripple, destroy, disable, petrify, stupefy, wipe out **8** demolish, enfeeble **10** debilitate, immobilize, neutralize **12** incapacitate

Paramaribo
  capital of: **8** Suriname

paramount 4 main **5** chief **6** utmost **7** capital, highest, leading, premier, supreme **8** cardinal, dominant, foremost, greatest, peerless, superior **9** essential, principal, unmatched **10** preeminent **11** outstanding, predominant **12** incomparable, preponderant, transcendent

paramour 3 man **4** doxy **5** lover, Romeo **6** gigolo **7** Don Juan **8** Casanova, fancy man, lothario, lover boy, mistress **9** boyfriend, concubine, courtesan, inamorata, inamorato, kept woman **10** girl friend, lady friend, sugar daddy

paranoid 4 wary **7** deluded **9** paranoiac **11** distrustful **14** oversuspicious

parapet 7 bulwark, rampart **8** abutment, palisade **9** barricade, earthwork **10** battlement, breastwork

paraphernalia 3 rig **4** gear **5** stuff **6** outfit, tackle, things **7** effects, harness, regalia **8** fittings, material, supplies, utensils **9** apparatus, equipment, trappings **10** belongings, implements, properties, provisions **11** accessories, furnishings **13** accoutrements

paraphrase 5 recap **6** rehash, reword **7** restate **8** rephrase **12** recapitulate

Parasaurolophus
  type: **8** dinosaur
    10 ornithopod
  location: **6** Canada
  period: **10** Cretaceous

parasite 5 leech **6** beggar, cadger, loafer **7** moocher, shirker, slacker, sponger **8** deadbeat **9** goldbrick, scrounger **10** freeloader **11** bloodsucker
  inside host: **12** endoparasite
  outside host: **12** ectoparasite

parasol 5 shade **6** shadow **7** roundel **8** sunshade, umbrella
  mushroom: **7** lepiota

par avion 5 by air

parboil 4 boil **5** scald **6** blanch **7** precook

Parca
  origin: **5** Roman
  member of: **6** Parcae

  goddess of: **7** destiny
    10 childbirth

Parcae *see* **5** Fates

parcel 3 lot **4** bale, pack, part, plot **5** allot, piece, tract **6** bundle, divide, packet **7** carve up, deal out, dole out, package, portion, section, segment, split up **8** allocate, dispense, disperse, division, fraction, fragment, property **9** allotment, allowance, apportion, partition **10** distribute **11** piece of land

parceling out 9 allotment, doling out, meting out **10** allocation, assignment, dealing out **12** distribution **13** apportionment

parcel out 5 allot **7** dole out, give out, mete out **8** allocate, dispense, divide up **9** apportion **10** distribute, portion out

parch 4 bake, burn, char, sear **5** dry up, singe **6** dry out, scorch, sun-dry, wither **7** blister, shrivel **9** dehydrate, dessicate, evaporate

parched 3 dry **4** arid **6** barren **8** withered **9** shriveled **10** dehydrated, desiccated

parchment 6 scroll, vellum **7** papyrus **8** goatskin **9** sheepskin

pardon 5 grace, mercy **6** excuse, wink at **7** absolve, amnesty, blink at, forbear, forgive, indulge, release, set free **8** overlook, reprieve, shrug off **9** discharge, disregard, exculpate, exonerate, remission, vindicate **10** absolution, indulgence **11** deliverance, exculpation, forbearance, forgiveness **12** grant amnesty **16** forgive and forget

Pardoner
  character in: **18** The Canterbury Tales
  author: **7** Chaucer

pare 3 cut, lop **4** clip, crop, dock, hull, husk, peel, skin, trim **5** lower, prune, shave, shear, shell, shuck, slash, strip **6** lessen, reduce, shrink **7** curtail, cut back **8** decrease, diminish **11** decorticate

pare down 3 cut **4** trim **5** shave **6** reduce **7** abridge, curtail, cut down, shorten **8** condense, cut short, diminish **10** abbreviate

parent 3 dam **4** sire **5** model **6** father, mother **7** creator **8** ancestor, begetter, exemplar, original, producer **9** precursor, prototype **10** antecedent, fore-

runner, originator, procreator, progenitor **11** predecessor

parentage 5 birth, roots, stock **6** family, origin, strain **7** descent, lineage **8** ancestry, forbears, heredity, pedigree **9** ancestors, genealogy **10** background, derivation, extraction, family tree **11** antecedents

Parentalia
  origin: **5** Roman
  event: **8** festival

parenthetical 5 aside **6** braced, casual **8** inserted **9** bracketed **10** extraneous, immaterial, incidental, interposed, irrelevant **11** impertinent, intervening, superfluous

par excellence 8 superior **10** preeminent

parfait d'amour
  type: **7** liqueur
  flavor: **7** violets
  color: **6** purple

Paria
  form: **5** nymph
  loved by: **5** Minos
  children: **7** Chryses **9** Eurymedon, Nephalion, Philolaus

pariah 5 exile, rover, stray **6** outlaw, roamer **7** outcast **8** vagabond, wanderer **10** expatriate **11** undesirable, untouchable

paring 4 chip, snip **5** scrap, shred, slice **6** sliver **7** cutting, peeling, shaving **8** fragment

pari passu 6 fairly **7** equably **10** side by side **13** equal progress **17** without partiality

Paris *see box*

Paris
  character in: **14** Romeo and Juliet
  author: **11** Shakespeare

Paris
  postion: **6** prince
  father: **5** Priam
  mother: **6** Hecuba
  brother: **6** Hector **9** Polydorus
  sister: **9** Cassandra
  wife: **6** Oenone
  abducted: **5** Helen
  judgment of: **14** apple of discord
  awarded apple to:
    9 Aphrodite
  killed by: **11** Philoctetes

parish 4 fold **5** flock, shire **6** canton, county **7** diocese, section **8** brethren, district, precinct, province **9** community, pastorate **10** department **11** archdiocese **12** congregation, neighborhood

parity 7 balance **8** equality,

Paris

airport: 4 Orly 9 Le Bourget 15 Charles de Gaulle
area: 5 Passy 6 Clichy, Marais, Ternes, Wagram 7 Auteuil 8 Chaillot, Gobelins, Left Bank, St Honore 9 Les Halles, Right Bank, St Germain 10 Montmartre, Rive Droite, Rive Gauche, Val de Grace 11 Ile de la Cite 12 Hotel de Ville, Latin Quarter, Montparnasse
capital of: 6 France
city planner: 9 Haussmann
island: 10 Ile St Louis 11 Ile de la Cite
landmark: 8 Pantheon 9 Notre Dame 10 Paris Opera, Sacre Coeur 11 Eiffel Tower, La Madeleine, Palais Royal 12 Elysee Palace, Hotel de Ville, Place Vendome 13 Arc de Triomphe, Palais Bourbon 14 Bois de Boulogne, Place de l'Etoile, Pompidou Center, Sainte Chapelle, Tomb of Napoleon 15 Bois de Vincennes 16 Luxembourg Palace 17 Hotel des Invalides, Place de la Bastille, Place de la Concorde 18 Jardin des Tuileries 20 Place Charles de Gaulle
nickname: 11 city of light
river: 5 Seine
street: 9 Haussmann, Invalides 10 Grand Armee 11 Saint Michel 12 Montparnasse, Saint Germain 13 Champs Elysees 15 Charles de Gaulle
subway: 5 Metro
university: 8 Sorbonne

---

sameness 10 coequality, uniformity 11 equivalence, equivalency 14 correspondence

park 4 lawn 5 field, green, grove, woods 6 common, meadow, square 7 grounds, reserve 8 parkland, preserve, woodland 9 grassland, sanctuary 10 public park, quadrangle

Parker, Dorothy
  author of: 9 Big Blonde 10 Enough Rope 13 Death and Taxes 18 After Such Pleasures 19 Laments for the Living

Parkman, Francis
  author of: 30 France and England in North America

parkway 6 avenue 9 boulevard 12 thoroughfare

parlance 4 talk 5 idiom, lingo 6 speech 16 manner of speaking

Parlement of Fowles, The
  author: 15 Geoffrey Chaucer

parley 4 talk 6 confab, powwow, summit 7 council, meeting, palaver 8 conclave 9 discourse, mediation, peace talk 10 conference, discussion 11 arbitration, negotiation 12 conversation

parliament 4 diet 5 court, house, junta 6 fan-tan, senate, sevens 7 cabinet, council 8 assembly, congress 9 high court 11 legislature 12 three estates

Communist: 6 Soviet 9 politburo, presidium
estate: 12 House of Lords 14 House of Commons
Germanic: 9 Bundesrat, Bundestag, Bolksraad 11 Volkshammer
Greek: 5 Boule
Icelandic: 7 Althing
Israeli: 7 Knesset 8 Knesseth
Scandinavian: 7 Lagting, Riksdag 8 Lagthing, Storting 9 Odelsting, Storthing
Spanish: 6 Cortes

parlor 5 salon 6 saloon 8 best room 9 front room 10 living room 11 drawing room, sitting room

Parnopius
  epithet of: 6 Apollo
  means: 9 locust god

parochial 5 local, petty, small 6 church, little, narrow, parish 7 insular, limited 8 regional 9 hidebound, illiberal, religious, sectional, smalltown 10 provincial, restricted 11 countrified 12 narrowminded

parodos
  from Greek drama: 9 choral ode

parody 5 mimic 6 satire 7 lampoon, takeoff 8 satirize, travesty 9 burlesque, take off on 10 caricature

Parolles
  character in: 20 All's Well That Ends Well
  author: 11 Shakespeare

paroxysm 3 fit 5 spasm, spell 7 seizure 10 convulsion

parrot 3 ape 4 bird, echo, lory 5 macaw, mimer, mimic 6 chorus, monkey 7 copycat, imitate 8 cockatoo, imitator, parakeet 9 reiterate

parry 4 duck, shun 5 avert, avoid, dodge, elude, repel 7 beat off, fend off, repulse, ward off 8 sidestep, stave off 10 circumvent, fight shy of

Parsifal
  opera by: 6 Wagner
  character: 6 Kundry 8 Amfortas, Klingsor 9 Gurnemanz

Parsifal Mosaic, The
  author: 12 Robert Ludlum

parsimonious 5 close, tight 6 frugal, saving, stingy 7 miserly, sparing, thrifty 9 niggardly, penurious 10 economical, ungenerous 11 closefisted, tightfisted 13 money-grubbing, penny-pinching

parsimony 6 thrift 7 economy 8 meanness 10 stinginess 13 niggardliness 15 tightfistedness

parsley 19 Petroselinum crispum
  varieties: 5 Horse 7 Chinese, Italian 12 Turnip-rooted
  related herb: 4 dill 5 cumin 6 fennel
  garland worn by: 8 Hercules
  gives speed to: 6 horses
  use in: 11 fines herbes 12 bouquet garni

parson 5 clerk, padre 6 cleric, divine, father, pastor, priest, rector 7 dominie 8 minister, preacher, reverend, shepherd, sky pilot 9 clergyman
  French: 4 abbe, cure

parsonage 5 glebe, manse 7 deanery, rectory, Vatican 8 vicarage 9 pastorate

part 2 go 3 bit, job 4 care, chip, duty, hunk, item, open, rend, role, slit, task, tear, unit 5 break, chore, crumb, guise, leave, piece, place, scrap, sever, shard, share, sherd, shred, slice, split 6 branch, charge, cleave, depart, detach, detail, divide, go away, member, morsel, region, sector, set out, sliver, sunder 7 concern, cutting, disjoin, element, portion, push off, section, segment, snippet 8 break off, business, capacity, disguise, disunite, division, fraction, fragment, function, separate, set forth, start out 9 character, component, disengage, go one's way **10** assignment, break apart, department, disconnect, get up and go, ingredient, mosey along, say good-bye **11** be on one's way, call it quits, constituent, subdivision

partake 5 enjoy, savor, share **6** join in, sample **7** share in **8** engage in **11** participate

part from 5 leave **9** break with **12** separate from

Parthenia
epithet of: **6** Athena
means: **6** virgin

Parthenius see **9** Plexippus

Parthenopaeus
father: **10** Hippomenes
mother: **8** Atalanta
member of: **18** Seven against Thebes

Parthenope
form: **5** siren

Parthenos
means: **6** virgin

partial 6 biased, unfair, unjust **7** limited, slanted **8** one-sided, partisan **9** factional **10** fractional, incomplete, interested, prejudiced, subjective, unbalanced, unfinished **11** fragmentary, inequitable, predisposed, uncompleted **12** inconclusive, prepossessed

partiality 4 bent, bias, love, tilt **5** fancy, slant, taste **6** choice, liking **7** leaning **8** affinity, fondness, penchant, tendency, weakness **9** prejudice **10** attraction, favoritism, preference, proclivity, propensity **11** inclination **12** one-sidedness, partisanship, predilection **14** predisposition

partially 6 in part, partly **7** partway **8** somewhat **9** piecemeal **12** fractionally, incompletely

participant 4 ally **5** party **6** cohort, fellow, helper, member, player, sharer, worker **7** partner **8** confrere, partaker **9** accessory, associate, colleague, performer **10** accomplice **11** contributor, shareholder **12** collaborator, participator

participate 5 share **6** join in **7** partake, perform **8** engage in, take part **9** play a part

particle 3 bit, jot **4** atom, iota, mite, snip, whit **5** crumb, grain, scrap, shred, speck, trace **6** morsel, tittle, trifle **7** granule, modicum, smidgen, snippet **9** scintilla

parti-colored 4 pied **5** plaid

6 motley **7** checked, dappled, mottled **8** colorful **9** checkered **10** variegated **11** manycolored **12** multicolored

particular 4 sole **5** exact, fixed, fussy, picky **6** single, strict **7** express, finicky, special **8** concrete, critical, definite, detailed, distinct, especial, exacting, explicit, itemized, personal, separate, specific **9** demanding **10** fastidious, individual, meticulous, scrupulous **11** painstaking, persnickety, punctilious, welldefined **12** hard to please

particularize 6 detail **7** itemize, specify **9** enumerate

particularly 6 mainly **7** notably **8** markedly **9** eminently, expressly, specially, supremely, unusually **10** definitely, distinctly, especially, explicitly, strikingly **11** principally, prominently **13** exceptionally **15** extraordinarily

particulars 5 facts, items **6** events **7** details **9** specifics **13** circumstances

parti pris 15 position decided **20** preconceived attitude

partisan 3 fan **4** ally **6** backer, biased, rooter, zealot **7** booster, devotee, partial, slanted **8** adherent, advocate, champion, follower, one-sided, upholder **9** guerrilla, insurgent, irregular, jayhawker, supporter **10** bushwacker, enthusiast, prejudiced, subjective, unbalanced **11** sympathizer

partition 4 wall **5** allot, fence, panel **6** assign, divide, screen **7** barrier, deal out, divider, mete out, parting, split up **8** allocate, bulkhead, dispense, disperse, dividing, division, separate **9** allotment, apportion, parcel out, separator, severance, splitting, subdivide **10** allocation, assignment, distribute, separation **11** demarcation, segregation **12** distribution, dividing wall **13** apportionment

partly 6 in part **7** part way **8** somewhat **9** not wholly, partially, to a degree **10** relatively **12** fractionally, incompletely **13** after a fashion, comparatively

partly open 4 ajar **5** agape **6** gaping **7** cracked **8** halfopen, unclosed **9** squinting **10** half-closed

partner 3 aid, pal **4** ally, chum, mate, wife **5** aider, buddy **6** fellow, friend, helper, sharer, spouse **7** comrade, co-

owner, husband **8** confrere, helpmate, partaker, sidekick, teammate **9** accessory, assistant, associate, colleague, companion, co-partner **10** accomplice, better half, joint owner **11** confederate, participant **12** collaborator

Partners, The
author: **16** Louis Auchincloss

Parton, Dolly
roles: **10** Nine to Five, Rhinestone **30** The Best Little Whorehouse in Texas

partridge
group of: **5** covey

Partridge
character in: **8** Tom Jones
author: **8** Fielding

Partridge Family, The
character: **13** Reuben Kinkaid **14** Danny Partridge, Keith Partridge, Tracy Partridge **15** Connie Partridge, Laurie Partridge **20** Christopher Partridge
cast: **8** Susan Dey **11** David Madden **12** Brian Forster, David Cassidy, Shirley Jones **13** Danny Bonaduce, Suzanne Crough **14** Jeremy Gelbwaks
song: **14** I Think I Love You

Parts of Animals
author: **9** Aristotle

parturition 5 birth **8** delivery **10** childbirth **11** giving birth **12** childbearing

party 2 do **4** band, bash, body, crew, fete, gang, team, unit, wing **5** corps, force, group, squad **6** affair, at-home, league, soiree **7** accused, blowout, company, coterie, faction **8** alliance, claimant, conclave, litigant, wingding **9** appellant, coalition, defendant, festivity, gathering, plaintiff, reception **10** contestant, federation, petitioner, respondent **11** celebration, confederacy, get-together, participant, paticipator, perpetrator

party-pooper 4 drag **10** spoilsport, wet blanket

parvenu 4 snob **6** nobody **7** upstart **8** arrivist, mushroom **9** arriviste **12** nouveau riche

Pascal, Blaise
nationality: **6** French
invented: **7** syringe **13** adding machine **14** hydraulic press
author of: **7** Pensees **19** Lettres provinciales **20** Essay pour les coniques

Pascin, Julius
real name: **6** Pincas

born: 5 Vidin **8** Bulgaria
artwork: 6 Femmes **12** Les
Deux Amies **17** Ginette et
Mireille

Pasiphae
father: 6 Helios
mother: 7 Perseis
husband: 5 Minos
daughter: 7 Ariadne, Phaedra **9** Acacallis
became enamored of:
10 Cretan bull
mother of: 8 Minotaur

Pasithea
member of: 6 Graces

Pasolini, Pier Paolo
director of: 13 Arabian
Nights

pass 2 go **3** cap, die, end, gap,
hit, top, use, way **4** best,
busy, fill, flow, give, go by,
go on, hand, kick, lane, meet,
toss **5** canal, exact, excel,
gorge, gulch, leave, outdo,
route, spend, throw, trail
6 accept, affirm, avenue, be
over, canyon, convey, course,
decree, depart, devote, elapse,
employ, engage, exceed, expend, expire, finish, go away,
go past, occupy, ordain, permit, pickle, plight, ratify, ravine, slip by, strait, take up,
vanish **7** achieve, advance, approve, channel, confirm, consume, deliver, die away,
eclipse, freebie, glide by, go
ahead, let have, narrows,
pathway, present, proceed,
qualify, satisfy, slide by, surpass **8** blow over, dissolve, exigency, fade away, furlough,
go onward, go onward, hand
over, juncture, legalize, melt
away, outshine, outstrip, pass
away, peter out, progress,
quandary, sanction, transfer,
transmit, turn over **9** authorize, disappear, evaporate, extremity, hand along, legislate,
situation, terminate **10** accomplish, difficulty, free ticket, get
through, move onward, overshadow, passageway **11** predicament, proposition
12 complication, run its
course, solicitation, stand the
test **13** authorization **15** amorous overture
French: 13 laissez passer

passable 4 fair, open, so-so
5 clear **6** not bad **8** adequate,
fordable, mediocre, middling
9 allowable, crossable, naviga-
ble, tolerable **10** acceptable,
admissible, pretty good
11 presentable, respectable,
traversable **12** unobstructed

passage 3 way **4** hall, pass,
path, road, tour, trek, trip
5 aisle, canal, piece, route,

verse **6** access, clause, column,
course, junket, tunnel, voyage **7** channel, chapter, hallway, journey, passing, portion,
section, transit **8** approach, approval, corridor, movement,
sanction, sentence **9** enactment, excursion, paragraph,
selection, ship's fare **10** acceptance, expedition, ordain-
ment **11** affirmation,
endorsement, legislation, progression **12** confirmation, legalization, ratification
13 authorization

passage out 4 exit **6** egress,
outlet

Passages
author: 10 Gail Sheehy

Passage to India, A
author: 9 E M Forster
character: 6 Dr Aziz **8** Mrs
Moore **12** Adela Quested
13 Cecil Fielding, Ronald
Heaslop **16** Professor
Godbole
setting: 11 Chandrapore
12 Marabar Caves
director: 9 David Lean
cast: 9 Judy Davis **12** Alec
Guinness **13** Peggy Ashcroft **15** Victor Bannerjee
Oscar for: 17 supporting actress (Ashcroft)

passageway 4 exit, hall, lane,
path, walk **5** aisle **6** access, arcade, tunnel **7** doorway, gang-
way, gateway, hallway,
passage **8** corridor, entrance,
entryway, sidewalk
12 companionway

pass away 3 die **6** depart, expire, pass on, perish **7** decease **8** pass over **13** go to
one's glory **14** give up the
ghost

pass by 4 go by, pass **5** lapse
6 elapse, roll by, slip by
7 glide by, slide by **8** slip
away

passe 4 past **5** faded, hoary,
stale **6** demode, lapsed,
quaint **7** ancient, antique, archaic, disused, outworn, retired **8** obsolete, outdated,
outmoded **9** out-of-date **10** antiquated **11** prehistoric **12** antediluvian, old-fashioned, out
of fashion **13** superannuated

passenger 4 fare **5** rider
8 commuter, stowaway, traveler, wayfarer

Passepartout
character in: 26 Around the
World in Eighty Days
author: 5 Verne

pas seul
ballet: 9 solo dance
literally: 8 solo step

passim 12 here and there, repeated item

passing 5 brief, death, dying
6 demise, fickle **7** decease, passage **8** adequate, fleeting **9** enactment, ephemeral, momen-
tary, temporary, transient
10 evanescent, expiration, not
failing, short-lived, transitory
11 impermanent, legislating

**passing the bounds of
propriety**
French: 5 outre

passion 4 fire, idol, love, lust,
rage, urge **5** ardor, craze,
fancy, flame, gusto, heart,
mania **6** desire, fervor, hunger,
thirst, warmth **7** beloved, craving, ecstasy, emotion, feeling,
rapture **8** loved one **9** carnality, eagerness, inamorata, intensity, obsession, sentiment,
transport, vehemence **10** carnal love, enthusiasm **11** amorousness, earnestness,
infatuation

passionate 3 hot **4** sexy
5 fiery **6** ardent, carnal, erotic,
fervid, fierce, heated, loving,
raging **7** amorous, earnest, excited, feeling, fervent, furious,
intense, lustful **8** desirous, ecstatic, inflamed, sensuous, vehement **9** emotional, heartfelt,
wrought-up **11** tempestuous
12 enthusiastic, intoxicating

passionfruit
type: 7 liqueur
origin: 6 Hawaii
flavor: 5 peach

passionless 4 calm, cold
6 placid, serene **7** passive
8 tranquil **9** apathetic, unfeeling **10** spiritless **11** emotionless, indifferent, unemotional

Passion Play
author: 13 Jerzy Kosinski

passive 5 inert **6** docile **7** dormant, patient, pliable **8** enduring, inactive, lifeless, listless,
resigned, yielding **9** apathetic,
compliant, impassive, quiescent, tractable **10** spiritless,
submissive **11** acquiescent, unassertive, unresisting
12 nonresistant

passiveness 6 apathy **7** inertia **8** docility **10** quiescence
11 resignation **12** acquiescence, lifelessness **14** submissiveness **16** unresponsiveness

passivity 6 apathy **7** inertia
8 docility, meekness **11** resignation **12** complaisance, lifelessness **13** nonresistance
14 submissiveness

pass muster 2 do **5** serve
6 answer **8** be enough **10** be

adequate **12** be sufficient **14** be satisfactory

pass on 3 die **6** depart, expire **7** decease **8** pass away **13** go to one's glory **14** give up the ghost, leave this world **15** breathe one's last

pass over 6 ignore, slight **7** neglect **8** overlook **10** brush aside

pass up 4 miss **6** ignore, refuse

password 3 key **4** word **6** byword, slogan **7** keyword, tessera **9** catchword, watchword **10** open sesame, secret word, shibboleth **11** countersign, passe-parole

Password
host: **11** Allen Ludden

past 2 by **4** gone **5** ended, prior **6** beyond, bygone, former, gone by **7** ancient, earlier, elapsed, expired, history, long ago, through **8** departed, finished, previous **9** antiquity, days of old **10** days gone by, days of yore, historical, olden times, passed away, yesteryear **11** dead and gone, former times, times gone by **12** ancient times

pasta 4 orzo, ziti **6** elbows, shells **7** gnocchi, lasagna, pastina, ravioli, rotelli **8** ditalini, linguini, macaroni, rigatoni, tortelli **9** canelloni, cavatelli, fettucine, manicotti, spaghetti **10** tortellini, vermicelli
ingredient: **3** egg **5** flour

past due 4 late **5** tardy **7** belated, overdue **9** in arrears **10** behindhand

paste 3 gum, hit **4** glue, seal, sock **5** affix, punch, stick **6** attach, cement **7** stickum **8** adhesive, mucilage

pastel 3 dim **4** pale, soft **5** chalk, faded, faint, light, muted **6** crayon **9** washed-out **13** coloring stick **14** coloring pencil

Pasternak, Boris
author of: **9** Dr Zhivago

Pasteur, Louis
field: **9** chemistry
nationality: **6** French
originated: **14** anti-rabies shot, pasteurization
founded: **12** microbiology
disproved: **21** spontaneous generation

pastime 3 fun **4** game, play **5** hobby, sport **9** amusement, avocation, diversion **10** relaxation **11** distraction **13** entertainment **14** divertissement

Passover Feast
Seder

pastis
type: **7** liqueur
flavor: **8** licorice
substitute for: **8** absinthe

past one's prime 3 old **4** aged **5** aging **7** elderly **9** venerable **11** over the hill **12** in one's dotage

pastor 4 cure, dean **5** padre, vicar **6** cleric, father, parson, priest, rector **8** chaplain, minister, preacher **9** clergyman

pastoral 5 rural **6** rustic **7** bucolic, idyllic **8** arcadian, clerical, priestly **9** episcopal **10** sacerdotal **11** ministerial **14** ecclesiastical

Pastoral Symphony, The
author: **9** Andre Gide

pastorate 6 clergy **8** ministry, the cloth **10** priesthood

pastures
god of: **3** Pan **6** Dumuzi

pasty 3 wan **4** ashy, gray, pale **5** ashen, gluey, gooey, gummy, white **6** anemic, chalky, doughy, pallid, peaked, sallow, sticky **7** deathly, starchy **8** bloodless, colorless, ghostlike, glutinous, like paste **12** mucilaginous

pat 3 apt, dab, hit, pet, rap, tap **4** cake, daub, easy, glib, slap **5** exact, ideal, ready, slick, thump **6** caress, facile, fondle, simple, smooth, stroke, thwack **7** apropos, fitting, perfect, precise, reliant **8** flippant, suitable **9** contrived, pertinent, rehearsed

patch 3 fix, lot **4** area, darn, mend, plot, spot, zone **5** field, sew up, tract **6** garden, repair, stitch **7** expanse, stretch **8** clearing, insignia **9** reinforce **13** reinforcement

patchwork 4 hash, mess **6** jumble, medley, muddle, tangle **7** grab bag, melange, mixture **8** mishmash, mixed bag, pastiche, scramble **9** confusion, potpourri **10** hodgepodge, miscellany, salmagundi **11** gallimaufry **14** conglomeration, omnium-gatherum

pate 3 pie **4** brow, head **5** brain, crown, paste, pastry, patty, skull **6** noddle, noggin, noodle **9** meat paste

patella
bone of: **7** kneecap

patent 4 bald, bold, open, rank **5** clear, gross, overt, plain **6** permit **7** decided, evident, express, glaring, license, obvious **8** apparent, distinct,

flagrant, manifest, palpable, registry, striking **9** copyright, downright, prominent **10** pronounced, unreserved **11** conspicuous, copyrighted, indubitable, self-evident, trademarked, transparent, unconcealed, undisguised **12** unmistakable **15** nonprescription

paterfamilias 6 father **17** father of the family, master of the family **20** master of the household

paternal 4 kind **6** tender **8** fatherly, parental, vigilant, watchful **9** concerned, indulgent **10** benevolent, fatherlike, interested, solicitous **11** patriarchal

Pater Patriae 18 father of his country

path 3 way **4** lane, plan, road, walk **5** byway, means, orbit, route, track, trail **6** access, bypath, course **7** pathway, process, walkway **8** approach, footpath

pathetic 3 sad **6** moving, rueful, woeful **7** doleful, piteous, pitiful **8** dolorous, grievous, pitiable, poignant, touching, wretched **9** affecting, miserable, plaintive, sorrowful **10** deplorable, lamentable, to be pitied **11** distressing

Pathfinder, The
author: **19** James Fenimore Cooper
character: **9** Arrowhead, Dew-of-June **10** Charles Cap **11** Mabel Dunham, Natty Bumppo **12** Chingachgook **13** Jasper Western **14** Sergeant Dunham **18** Lieutenant Davy Muir

Pathfinders, The
author: **10** Gail Sheehy

pathogen 3 bug **4** germ **5** virus **7** microbe **8** bacillus **9** bacterium **13** microorganism

pathophobia
fear of: **7** disease

pathos 3 woe **5** agony **6** misery **7** anguish, feeling, sadness **8** distress **9** heartache, poignancy, sentiment **10** desolation **12** pitiableness **13** plaintiveness

Paths of Glory
director: **14** Stanley Kubrick
cast: **11** Kirk Douglas, Ralph Meeker **13** Adolphe Menjou

pathway 4 lane, path, road **5** alley, route, track **6** course **7** passage, walkway **8** footpath **10** passageway

patience 5 poise 7 stamina 8 industry, tenacity 9 composure, diligence, fortitude, restraint, tolerance 10 equanimity, resolution, sufferance 11 application, forbearance, longanimity, persistence, self-control 12 perseverance, tirelessness

Patience
  author: 9 W S Gilbert

patient 4 case 6 dogged, serene 8 composed, diligent, enduring, resolute, tireless 9 dauntless, tenacious, undaunted 10 determined, forbearing, persistent, sick person, unflagging, unswerving, unwavering 11 industrious, persevering, unfaltering, unperturbed 13 indefatigable, long-suffering, uncomplaining

patio 4 deck 5 lanai, porch 6 piazza 7 terrace, veranda

patois 5 argot, idiom, lingo 6 jargon 7 dialect 10 vernacular

Paton, Alan
  author of: 19 Too Late the Phalarope 20 Cry the Beloved Country 24 Ah but Your Land Is Beautiful

pat on the back 6 praise 7 plaudit 10 compliment 12 commendation

patriarch 5 elder, ruler 6 father, leader, old man 8 male head 9 chieftain 13 paterfamilias

patrician 4 lord, peer 5 noble 6 lordly 7 genteel, stately 8 highborn, imposing, nobleman, princely, well-bred 9 blueblood, dignified, gentleman 10 aristocrat, upper-class 12 aristocratic, silk-stocking

patrimony 3 lot 5 dower, share 6 devise, estate, legacy 7 portion 8 bestowal, heritage, jointure 9 endowment 10 bequeathal, birthright 11 inheritance 12 hereditament

patriotism
  Latin: 11 amor patriae

Patroclus
  father: 9 Menoetius
  mother: 8 Periapis
  friend: 8 Achilles
  killed by: 6 Hector

patrol 5 guard, scout, watch 6 ranger, sentry, warden 7 protect 8 sentinel 9 safeguard, walk a beat, watchman, watch over 10 stand watch

patron 5 angel, buyer 6 backer, client, friend, helper 7 habitue, shopper, sponsor, visitor 8 advocate, attender, champion, customer, defender, financer, promoter, upholder 9 protector, spectator, supporter 10 benefactor, encourager, frequenter, well-wisher 11 sympathizer 12 benefactress 14 philanthropist

patronage 3 aid 4 help 5 favor, plums, trade 6 buying, custom, spoils 7 backing, charity, clients, dealing, support 8 advocacy, auspices, business, commerce 9 clientele, customers, fosterage 10 assistance, friendship, pork barrel, protection, purchasing 11 benefaction, sponsorship 12 philanthropy 13 encouragement

patronize 5 humor 6 shop at 7 buy from 8 deal with, frequent 9 trade with 10 condescend

patsy 4 dupe, pawn, tool 7 cat's-paw, fall guy

patter 3 pad, pat, rap, tap 4 beat, drum 5 pound, thrum 6 tattoo 7 rat-a-tat, spatter, tapping 8 drumming, sprinkle

pattern 4 copy, form, mold, plan 5 draft, guide, ideal, mimic, model, motif, shape 6 design, follow, sample 7 emulate, example, fashion, imitate, paragon 8 exemplar, original, paradigm, parallel, simulate, specimen, standard 9 archetype, criterion, duplicate, prototype 10 apotheosis, stereotype 12 illustration

Patton
  director: 17 Franklin Schaffner
  cast: 10 Karl Malden (Omar Bradley) 12 George C Scott (George Patton), Stephen Young 13 Michael Strong
  Oscar for: 5 actor (Scott), story 7 picture 8 director 10 screenplay (Francis Ford Coppola and Edmund H North)

Patton, George S
  nickname: 15 Old Blood and Guts
  served in: 3 WWI 4 WWII 11 World War One, World War Two
  commander of: 9 Third Army
  invasion of: 8 Normandy 11 North Africa
  capture of: 6 Sicily
  battle: 5 Bulge
  wore: 21 ivory-handled revolvers
  memoirs: 12 War As I Knew It

Patty Duke Show, The
  character: 7 Richard 8 Ross Lane 9 Cathy Lane, Patty Lane 10 Martin Lane 14 Natalie Masters
  cast: 9 Jean Byron, Patty Duke 10 Paul O'Keefe 14 Eddie Applegate 16 William Schallert

paucis verbis 10 by few words, in few words 12 with few words

paucity 4 lack 6 dearth 7 fewness, poverty 8 exiguity, poorness, puniness, scarcity, shortage, sparsity, thinness 10 deficiency, meagerness, scantiness, scarceness 13 insufficiency

Paul
  former name: 4 Saul
  hometown: 6 Tarsus
  teacher: 8 Gamaliel
  companion: 5 Silas 7 Timothy 8 Barnabas, John Mark 9 Trophimus
  cities visited: 4 Rome 5 Derbe, Perga, Troas 6 Lystra, Paphos 7 Antioch, Corinth, Ephesus, Iconium, Miletus, Salamis 8 Caesarea, Damascus, Neapolis, Philippi 9 Macedonia 12 Thessalonica
  conversion place: 14 road to Damascus
  wrote: 8 epistles

Paul Bunyan
  author: 12 James Stevens
  character: 9 Shanty Boy 10 Hels Helson 11 King Bourbon 12 Sourdough Sam 13 Babe the Blue Ox 14 Hot Biscuit Slim 16 Johnny Inkslinger

Pauli, Wolfgang
  field: 7 physics
  researched: 13 quantum theory
  established: 14 Pauli principle 18 exclusion principle
  awarded: 10 Nobel Prize

Paulina
  character in: 14 The Winter's Tale
  author: 11 Shakespeare

Pauling, Linus Carl
  field: 12 biochemistry
  worked on: 8 proteins 18 molecular structure
  advocated: 8 Vitamin C
  awarded: 10 Nobel Prize
    awarded for: 5 peace 9 chemistry

paunch 3 gut, pot 5 belly, tummy 7 abdomen, stomach 8 potbelly 9 bay window, beer belly, spare tire 10 midsection 11 breadbasket, corporation

pauper 6 beggar 7 almsman
8 bankrupt, indigent 9 insolvent, mendicant 10 poor person, starveling 11 charity
case 12 down-and-outer

pause 3 gap 4 halt, rest, stop,
wait 5 break, cease, delay, let
up 6 hiatus 7 interim, time
out 8 break off, hesitate, interval 9 cessation, interlude
10 deliberate, suspension
12 intermission,
interruption

pave 3 tar 4 face 6 cement
7 asphalt, surface 8 black top
9 resurface 10 macadamize

pavement 4 slab 5 brick 6 cement, hearth, street, tarmac
7 asphalt, cobbles, macadam
8 concrete, driveway, flagging,
sidewalk 9 flagstone

pavilion 4 tent, ward, wing
5 arbor, kiosk 6 gazebo 7 pergola 9 bandshell
11 summerhouse

Pavlov, Ivan Petrovich
  nationality: 7 Russian
  researched: 9 digestion
  studied: 20 behavior condi-
    tioning 21 Pavlovian
    conditioning
  awarded: 10 Nobel Prize

paw 2 pa 3 dad, pop, toe
4 feel, foot, grab, hand, maul,
mitt, papa 5 daddy, flail,
touch 6 caress, clutch, father,
handle, scrape, strike 7 rough
up 8 forefoot 9 mishandle
  mate: 3 maw

pawn 4 bond, dupe, hock,
tool 5 agent, patsy 6 flunky,
lackey, pledge, puppet 7 cat's
paw 8 borrow on, creature,
guaranty, henchman, hireling,
security 9 assurance, guarantee, underling 10 instrument
12 raise money on 14 give as
security

pawnbroker
  French: 11 mont-de-piete

Pawnbroker, The
  director: 11 Sidney Lumet
  cast: 10 Rod Steiger (Sol Na-
    zerman) 11 Brock Peters
    12 Jaime Sanchez 19 Geral-
    dine Fitzgerald
  setting: 6 Harlem

Pawnee (Chahiksichhiks)
  language family: 7 Caddoan
  location: 5 Texas 8 Nebraska,
    Oklahoma 9 New Mexico
  related to: 7 Arikara
  god: 6 Tirawa

Pawtuxet
  location: 13 Massachusetts
  leader: 7 Squanto

Pax
  origin: 5 Roman

  goddess of: 5 peace
  corresponds to: 5 Irene

pax vobiscum 14 peace be
with you

pay 3 fee 4 foot, give, meet
5 grant, honor, remit, repay,
serve, wages, yield 6 ante up,
chip in, extend, income,
profit, render, return, salary,
settle 7 benefit, bring in,
cough up, payment, present,
proffer, stipend 8 be useful,
earnings, paycheck, shell out
9 bear fruit, liquidate, reimburse 10 come across, compensate, make good on,
recompense 12 compensation
13 reimbursement

payable 3 due 4 owed 5 owing 6 mature, unpaid 8 to be
paid 9 in arrears, spendable
10 demandable, expendable,
receivable 11 outstanding

pay attention 4 heed, note
6 attend, notice 7 observe

Payaya
  language family:
    12 Coahuiltecan
  location: 5 Texas

pay back 5 repay 7 counter,
get even 9 reimburse, retaliate 10 recompense, remunerate 15 make restitution

pay for 6 redeem 7 expiate
8 atone for 9 answer for, suffer for 10 compensate, recompense, remunerate 13 make
amends for 17 make reparation for

pay heed 6 notice 8 consider
11 concentrate 12 pay attention 13 put one's mind to

pay homage 5 defer, honor
7 acclaim 10 pay tribute

paying back 9 repayment
11 getting even 12 making
good on 13 reimbursement

paymaster 6 bursar, purser
7 cashier 10 cashkeeper

payment 3 fee, pay 4 debt
6 outlay, paying, salary 7 premium 8 defrayal, spending
9 allowance, discharge 10 recompense, remittance, settlement 11 expenditure,
installment, liquidation
12 compensation, contribution,
disbursement, remuneration
13 reimbursement

pay no heed to 4 defy 6 ignore, slight 7 disobey, neglect,
violate 8 overlook, pass over
9 disregard 10 brush aside, infringe on 14 shut one's eyes
to 16 pay no attention to
17 transgress against

payoff 3 end 4 soap 5 bribe,

graft 6 climax, crunch, finale,
finish, grease, payola, result,
upshot, windup 7 outcome
8 clincher 9 hush money
10 bottom line, conclusion,
denouement, protection, resolution 11 culmination

pay off 5 bribe 6 buy off, suborn 13 grease the palm

payola 5 bribe, graft 6 grease,
payoff

pay out 5 spend 6 expend, lay
out 7 fork out 8 allocate, disburse, dispense, shell out
10 distribute

pay suit 3 woo 5 court 8 pay
court

Payton, Walter
  nickname: 9 Sweetness
  sport: 8 football
  position: 11 running back
  team: 12 Chicago Bears

pay tribute to 4 laud, tout
5 boost, toast 6 praise, salute
7 applaud, commend 8 eulogize 10 compliment 16 sing
the praises of

Payuga
  tribe: 4 Agaz 6 Magach 7 Ca-
    digue, Payagua, Sarigue, Sia-
    cuas, Tacumbu
  location: 8 Paraguay 12 South
    America

pea 5 Pisum 12 Pisum sativum
  varieties: 4 Flat, Love, Snow,
    Wild 5 Beach, Caley, Chick,
    Congo, Coral, Field, Glory,
    Green, Heart, Heath, Hoary,
    No-eye, Rough, Sugar,
    Sweet 6 Angola, Canada,
    Desert, Garden, Marble, Pi-
    geon, Rosary, Scurfy,
    Winged, Winter 7 Catjang,
    Darling, English, Rabbit's,
    Seaside 8 Earthnut, Egyp-
    tian, Princess, Shamrock
    9 Asparagus, Black-eyed,
    Butterfly, Chaparral, Jerusa-
    lem, Partridge, Perennial
    10 Australian, Singletary,
    Wild winter 11 Everlasting,
    Sturt desert, Two-flowered,
    Winter sweet 12 Edible-pod-
    ded 14 Austrian winter
    15 Australian flame

peace 4 calm, ease 5 amity,
truce 6 accord, repose 7 concord, content, entente, harmony 8 serenity 9 agreement,
armistice, composure, placidity 12 pacification, tranquillity 14 reconciliation
  god of: 4 Frey 5 Freyr
  goddess of: 3 Pax
    9 Concordia
  Hebrew: 6 shalom
  Russian: 3 mir

Peace
  author: 12 Aristophanes

peace be with you
Latin: 11 pax vobiscum

peaceful 4 calm **5** quiet, still **6** placid, serene, silent **7** pacific, restful **8** amicable, friendly, tranquil **9** agreeable, peaceable, peacetime **10** harmonious, nonviolent, nonwarring, pacifistic, untroubled **11** undisturbed

peacefulness 4 calm **7** concord, harmony **8** calmness, serenity **9** placidity **11** tranquility

peacemaker 8 diplomat, mediator, placater **9** go-between **10** ambassador, arbitrator, negotiator **11** adjudicator, conciliator, pacificator, peacekeeper, peacemonger **12** intermediary

peacemaking 9 pacifying, placating, placatory **11** reconciling **12** conciliating, conciliatory, pacification

peace offering 6 amends **11** appeasement **12** conciliation

peace of mind 8 security, serenity **11** tranquility **16** freedom from worry

peace to you
Hebrew: **14** shalom aleichem

peach 13 Prunus persica
varieties: **4** Muir, Peak, Sims, Vine, Wild **5** Gaume, Hiley, Pavie **6** Carmen, Crosby, Desert, Foster, J H Hale, Lovell, Orejon, Paloro, Peento, Salwey **7** Dixigem, Dixired, Elberta, Persian, Quadong **8** Champion, Crawford, Isabella, Redhaven, Russelet **9** Alexander, Freestone, Halehaven, Rochester, Southland **10** Clingstone, Goldeneast, Heath Cling, Summer Snow **12** Chinese Cling, Iron Mountain, Mountain Rose, Oldmixon Free **13** Golden Jubilee, Oldmixon Cling, Phillips Cling **14** Belle of Georgia
peach-like: **7** apricot **9** nectarine

Peach State
nickname of: **7** Georgia

Peachum, Polly
character in: **12** Beggar's Opera
author: **3** Gay

peachy 4 fine, keen **5** dandy, super, swell **9** excellent, marvelous, wonderful

peacock
group of: **6** muster

Peacock
constellation of: **4** Pavo

Peacock, Thomas Love
author of: **12** Headlong Hall **14** Crotchet Castle, Nightmare Abbey

Peacock Spring, The
author: **11** Rumer Godden

peak 3 tip, top **4** acme, apex **5** crest, crown, flood, prime **6** apogee, climax, summit, zenith **8** pinnacle **9** culminate **11** culmination

peaked 3 ill, wan **4** lean, pale, thin, weak **5** ashen, drawn, gaunt, spare, spiked, spiny, white **6** ailing, infirm, pallid, pointy, sallow, sickly, skinny, spiked **7** haggard, pinched, pointed, scrawny, tapered, wizened **9** emaciated, shriveled **11** debilitated

peal 3 din **4** boom, clap, ring, roar, roll, toll **5** blare, blast, clang, crack, crash, knell **6** rumble **7** clangor, resound, ringing **10** resounding **11** reverberate **13** reverberation **14** tintinnabulate **16** tintinnabulation

Peale, Charles Willson
born: **17** Queen Anne County MD
son: **9** Raphaelle, Rembrandt **12** Titian Ramsay
artwork: **26** The Exhumation of the Mastodon
portrait: **8** Franklin **9** Jefferson, John Adams **10** Washington

Peale, Raphaelle
born: **13** Bucks County PA
father: **14** Charles Willson
brother: **9** Rembrandt **12** Titian Ramsay
artwork: **12** After the Bath

Peale, Rembrandt
born: **13** Bucks County PA
father: **14** Charles Willson
brother: **9** Raphaelle **12** Titian Ramsay
artwork: **15** The Court of Death
portrait: **9** Jefferson **10** Washington

peal of bells 7 clangor, ringing **16** tintinnabulation

peanut 3 pod, tot **4** puny, seed **5** petty, small **6** goober, legume, measly, paltry **8** earthpea **9** little one
species: **15** Arachis hypogaea

Peanuts
creator: **13** Charles Schulz
character: **4** Lucy **5** Linus **6** Marcie, Snoopy **9** Schroeder **12** Charlie Brown **15** Peppermint Patty
Halloween figure: **12** Great Pumpkin

Snoopy's plane: 12 Sopwith Camel
Snoopy's foe: 8 Red Baron
saying: **9** Good Grief

pear 5 Pyrus **13** Pyrus communis
varieties: **4** Bosc, Sand **5** Anjou, Asian, Blind, Melon, Smith **6** Balsam, Burrel, Butter, Comice, Common, Garber, Garlic, Orient, Seckel, Warden **7** Chinese, Kieffer, Prickly, Vinegar **8** Bartlett, Japanese, Oriental **9** Alligator, Evergreen, Muscadine **10** Beurre Bosc, Brandywine, Chaumontel **11** Birch-leaved, Bon Chretien, Paper-spined, Winter Nelis **12** Beurre d'Anjou, Easter Beurre, Sacred garlic, Willow-leaved **13** Flemish Beauty, Waite Bergamot **15** Doyenne du Comice **18** Duchesse d'Angouleme

pearl
grows in: **6** oyster
genus: **8** Pinctada
source: **6** Red Sea **9** Caribbean **11** Persian Gulf **12** South Pacific **16** Gulf of California
composed of: **5** nacre **9** aragonite **10** conchiolin **13** mother-of-pearl
quality: **6** luster **11** iridescence
color: **4** blue, rose **5** black, brown, cream, green, white **6** yellow
shape: **5** round **7** baroque
type: **8** cultured, Oriental (saltwater) **9** simulated **10** freshwater

Pearl-Fishers, The
also: **19** Les Pecheurs de Perles
opera by: **5** Bizet
setting: **6** Ceylon

Pearl of the Antilles see **4** Cuba

peasant 4 boor, esne, peon, serf **5** churl, knave, yokel **6** farmer, rustic, worker **7** laborer, lowlife, villein **10** countryman, dirt farmer
Arabic: **6** fellah
Indian: **4** ryot **5** kisan **6** raiyat
Irish: **4** kern
Russian: **5** kulak **6** muzhik
Scottish: **6** cotter

peasantlike 5 crude, rough **6** coarse, oafish, rustic, vulgar **7** boorish, loutish, uncouth **9** unrefined **10** unpolished

peccadillo 4 slip **5** lapse **6** booboo **7** blunder, faux pas, misdeed, misstep **8** petty sin, trespass **9** false move, wrong step **10** misconduct, wrongdo-

ing **11** misdemeanor
13 transgression

peck 3 pat, rap, tap **4** buss,
gobs, lots, mess **5** a slew,
batch, bunch, heaps, scads,
smack, snack, stack, thump
6 nibble, oodles, pick at,
strike, stroke, worlds **8** light
jab **9** abundance, light kiss
11 eight quarts
   abbreviation of: 2 pk

Peck, Gregory
   real name: 17 Eldred Gregory
   Peck
   born: 9 La Jolla CA
   roles: 8 Moby Dick **10** On
   the Beach, Spellbound
   11 The Yearling **12** Duel in
   the Sun, Roman Holiday
   15 The Paradine Case
   16 Twelve O'Clock High
   17 The Boys from Brazil,
   The Guns of Navarone
   18 To Kill a Mockingbird
   (Oscar) **19** Gentleman's
   Agreement, The Keys of the
   Kingdom **21** The Snows of
   Kilimanjaro **26** The Man in
   the Gray Flannel Suit
   autobiography: 12 An Actor's
   Life

Peckinpah, Sam
   director of: 9 Straw Dogs
   12 The Wild Bunch

Pecksniff
   character in: 16 Martin
   Chuzzlewit
   author: 7 Dickens

peculiar 3 odd **5** queer, weird
6 far-out, quaint, unique **7** bizarre, curious, erratic, private,
special, strange, typical, unusual **8** abnormal, distinct,
freakish, personal, singular,
specific **9** eccentric, exclusive,
whimsical **10** capricious, individual, outlandish, particular
11 distinctive **13** idiosyncratic
14 characteristic, distinguishing, representative,
unconventional

peculiarity 4 mark **5** badge,
stamp, trait **6** oddity **7** feature,
quality **8** odd trait **9** attribute,
queerness, weirdness **10** erraticism, uniqueness **11** abnormality, bizarreness, distinction,
singularity, strangeness **12** eccentricity, freakishness, idiosyncrasy **13** particularity,
unnaturalness **14** characteristic **21** distinguishing quality

pecuniary 6 fiscal **8** economic,
monetary **9** budgetary,
financial

pedagogic 7 bookish, donnish
8 academic, didactic, pedantic,
tutorial **9** scholarly **11** educational **12** professorial
13 instructional

pedagogue, pedagog 5 tutor
7 teacher **8** academic, educator **9** professor **10** instructor,
schoolmarm **12** educationist,
schoolmaster **13** schoolteacher
14 schoolmistress

pedant 6 purist **8** bookworm
9 dogmatist **13** methodologist

pedantic 5 fussy **7** bookish,
finicky, pompous, stilted **8** academic, didactic, dogmatic
10 nitpicking, scholastic
11 doctrinaire, punctilious
13 hairsplitting
14 overparticular

Pedasus
   mentioned in: 5 Iliad
   twin brother: 7 Aesepus
   killed by: 8 Euryalus

peddle 4 hawk, sell, vend
6 retail **7** deal out **8** dispense

Peder Victorious
   character in: 16 Giants of
   the Earth
   author: 7 Rolvaag

pedestal 4 base, foot **6** bottom,
plinth **10** foundation

pedestrian 6 walker **7** mundane, prosaic, tedious, trekker
8 mediocre, ordinary, stroller
9 itinerant **10** ambulatory, for
walking, unexciting **11** commonplace, peripatetic, unimportant **12** foot-traveler, run-
of-the-mill **13** insignificant,
perambulating, perambulatory,
unimaginative
15 inconsequential

pedigree 4 line **6** family,
strain **7** descent, lineage **8** ancestry **9** bloodline, parentage
10 derivation, extraction, family tree **13** line of descent

peek 3 pry **4** peep, peer
5 watch **6** glance **7** glimpse

peel 4 bark, hull, husk, pare,
rind, skin, tear, zest **5** flake,
scale, shuck, spade, strip **6** remove **7** undress **11** decorticate

peel off 6 remove **7** veer off
8 strip off

peep 4 peek, peer, skim, word
5 cheep, chirp, tweet
6 emerge, glance, murmur,
mutter, squeak **7** chirrup,
glimpse, peeping, peer out,
twitter, whimper, whisper
9 come forth, quick
look

peeper 3 eye **4** frog **6** voyeur
10 peeping Tom

peer 4 gape, gaze, look, lord,
peek, peep **5** equal, noble,
stare **6** appear, emerge,
squint **7** compeer **8** nobleman
9 blue blood, gentleman, patrician **10** aristocrat

peerage 8 nobility **10** blue
bloods, patricians
11 aristocracy

Peer Gynt
   author: 11 Henrik Ibsen
   character: 3 Ase **7** Solveig
   12 The Great Boyg **16** The
   Button Moulder

peerless 7 supreme **8** flawless
9 faultless, matchless, unequaled, unmatched, unri-
valed **10** consummate,
inimitable, preeminent, surpassing, unexcelled **11** superlative, unsurpassed
12 incomparable, transcendent

peeve 3 bug, eat, irk, vex
4 fret, gall, rile **5** annoy,
chafe, eat at, frost, gripe
6 gnaw at, nettle **7** dislike,
perturb, provoke **8** irritate,
vexation **9** aggravate, annoyance, complaint, grievance
10 exasperate, irritation
11 aggravation, provocation
12 exasperation, give one a
pain **13** pain in the neck
14 thorn in the side

peevish 4 mean **5** cross, huffy,
sulky, surly, testy **6** crabby,
cranky, grumpy **7** grouchy,
pettish **8** churlish, petulant,
snappish **9** fractious, irritable,
querulous, splenetic **10** ill-humored, ill-natured **11** bad-tempered, ill-tempered,
quarrelsome **12** cantankerous

peewee 4 tiny **5** dwarf, small,
teeny **6** little, midget, minute
9 itsy-bitsy, itty-bitty, minuscule **10** diminutive, teeny-
weeny **11** Lilliputian

Pee Wee
   nickname of: 11 Harold
   Reese

peg 3 pin **4** nail **5** cleat, dowel,
spike, thole **6** skewer, toggle
8 fastener, tholepin

Pegae
   form: 6 spring
   spring of: 6 Dryope

Pegasus
   form: 5 horse
   characteristic: 6 winged
   mother: 6 Medusa
   ridden by: 11 Bellerophon

Peggotty, Clara
   character in: 16 David
   Copperfield
   author: 7 Dickens

Pei, I M (Ieoh Ming)
   architect of: 12 East Building
   (National Gallery of Art),
   L'Enfant Plaza (Washington
   DC) **14** East-West Center (U
   of Hawaii), Mile High Cen-
   ter (Denver) **15** Place Ville
   Marie (Montreal) **16** John

Hancock Tower (Boston)
18 Everson Museum of Art
(Syracuse NY) **22** Kips Bay
Plaza Apartments (NYC)
36 National Center for Atmospheric Research (Boulder
CO)

peignoir 4 gown **6** kimono
8 negligee **9** nightgown
12 dressing gown

Peiser, Lillie Marie
real name of: **11** Lilli Palmer

pejorative 7 mocking **8** debas-
ing, negative, scornful **9** degrading, demeaning, slighting
10 belittling, derogatory, detracting, disdainful, ridiculing,
unpleasant **11** deprecatory, disparaging, downgrading
12 contemptuous, depreciatory,
disapproving
15 uncomplimentary

Peking
also: **7** Beijing
means: **15** northern capital
capital of: **5** China
landmark: **9** Bell Tower,
Drum Tower, Ming Tombs
10 Pei-hai Park **12** Palace
Museum **13** Forbidden City
14 Hall of Classics, Temple
of Heaven **15** Marco Polo
Bridge **17** Temple of Confucius **18** Old Legation Quarter **19** Temple of
Agriculture **20** Great Hall of
the People, Hall of Supreme
Harmony **21** Mausoleum of
Mao Tse-tung **22** Palace of
Heavenly Purity **26** Monument to the People's He-
roes **32** Revolutionary and
Historical Museum
mountain: **7** Taihang
river: **3** Hai **7** Ch'ao-pai
8 Yungting
square: **9** T'ien-an Men
university: **8** Tsinghua
walled city: **5** Inner, Outer,
Tatar **7** Chinese

pelagic 6 marine **7** aquatic,
oceanic **9** thalassic **11** sea-
dwelling

Pelagon
mentioned in: **5** Iliad
ally of: **8** Sarpedon

Pelasgus
also: **9** Corynetes
son: **6** Lycaon **7** Temenus
first: **3** man
founder of: **10** Pelasgians

Pele
real name: **24** Edson Arantes
do Nascimento
sport: **6** soccer
team: **13** New York Cosmos
nationality: **9** Brazilian

Pelegon
mentioned in: **5** Iliad

god of: **5** river
mother: **8** Periboea
son: **11** Asteropaeus

Peleus
king of: **6** Phthia
9 Myrmidons
father: **6** Aeacus
mother: **6** Endeis
brother: **7** Telamon
half-brother: **6** Phocus
wife: **6** Thetis **8** Antigone
son: **8** Achilles
daughter: **8** Polydora

pelf 4 gain **5** booty, lucre,
money **6** mammon, riches,
spoils

Pelias
father: **8** Poseidon
mother: **4** Tyro
twin brother: **6** Neleus
wife: **8** Anaxibia
son: **7** Acastus
nephew: **5** Jason

Pelican State
nickname of: **9** Louisiana

Pelides
descendant of: **6** Peleus

pelisse 4 cape, coat **5** cloak
6 mantle

Pelleas (King Pelleas)
character in: **16** Arthurian
romance
daughter: **6** Elaine

Pelleas and Melisande
also: **18** Pelleas et Melisande
opera by: **7** Debussy
character: **6** Golaud, Yniold
author: **18** Maurice
Maeterlinck

pellet 3 pea **4** ball, bead, drop,
pill **5** pearl, stone **6** marble,
pebble, sphere **7** globule

pell-mell 6 rashly **7** hastily
8 slapdash **9** hurriedly, posthaste **10** at half cock, carelessly, heedlessly, recklessly
11 hurry-scurry, impetuously,
imprudently **12** incautiously
13 helter-skelter, precipitately,
thoughtlessly

pellucid 5 clear, lucid **10** articulate **11** crystalline, translucent, transparent
12 intelligible
14 understandable

Pelopia
father: **8** Thyestes
raped by: **8** Thyestes
son: **9** Aegisthus

Pelops
father: **8** Tantalus
sister: **5** Niobe
son: **6** Atreus, Sciron **7** Le-
treus **8** Pittheus, Thyestes
9 Alcathous **10** Chrysippus

daughter: **7** Nicippe **8** Lysid-
ice **9** Astydamia
resurrected by: **6** Hermes

pelt 3 fur, hit, rap **4** belt, coat,
hide, skin, sock **5** pound,
punch, whack **6** batter, buffet,
fleece, pepper, pummel, strike,
thrash, thwack **7** clobber

Pemphredo
member of: **6** Graeae, Graiae

pen 3 sty **4** cage, coop, crib,
fold **5** draft, hutch, pound,
quill, stall, write **6** corral, pencil, scrawl **7** compose, pad-
dock **8** compound, scribble,
stockade **9** ballpoint, enclosure

penal 7 of jails **8** punitive
9 punishing **10** corrective, penalizing **11** castigatory, retrib-
utive **12** disciplinary

penalty 4 fine **7** forfeit
8 handicap **9** suffering **10** assessment, forfeiture, infliction,
punishment **11** retribution
12 disadvantage

penance 9 atonement, expiation, hair shirt, penitence
10 contrition, repentance
12 propitiation
13 mortification

Penates
protectors of: **4** home
companions: **5** lares

penchant 4 bent, bias, gift,
turn **5** fancy, flair, knack,
taste **6** liking, relish **7** leaning
8 affinity, fondness, tendency
9 prejudice, proneness, readiness **10** attraction, partiality,
preference, proclivity, propensity **11** disposition, inclination **12** predilection
14 predisposition

pendant 3 fob **6** locket
15 hanging ornament

Pendennis
author: **25** William Makepeace Thackeray
character: **9** Laura Bell
10 Henry Foker **12** Blanche
Amory **13** Emily Costigan
14 Helen Pendennis, Major
Pendennis **15** Arthur
Pendennis

pendent, pendant 7 hanging,
jutting, pensile **8** dangling,
swinging **9** extending, pendulous, suspended **10** projecting,
protruding **11** overhanging,
protuberant

pendente lite 16 during litigation **19** with a lawsuit
pending

pending 8 imminent **9** undecided, unsettled **10** in suspense, unfinished, unresolved,

Pekoe- tea

up in the air **11** in the offing
12 undetermined

pendulous 7 hanging, pendent,
pensile, sagging **8** dangling,
drooping, swinging
9 suspended

pendulum
invented by: **7** Galileo

Penelope
father: **7** Icarius
mother: **8** Periboea
husband: **8** Odysseus
9 Telegonus
son: **6** Ifalus **10** Telemachus
11 Polyporthis
fended off: **7** suitors

penetrate 3 get **4** bore
5 catch, enter, prick **6** decode,
fathom, invade, pierce, seep
in **7** cut into, discern, pervade,
unravel **8** decipher, perceive,
permeate, puncture, saturate,
traverse **9** figure out, perforate **10** comprehend, cut
through, impregnate, infiltrate,
see through, understand
11 pass through

penetrating 4 keen **5** acrid,
alert, alive, aware, harsh,
heady, sharp, smart **6** astute,
biting, clever, shrewd, strong
7 caustic, pungent, reeking
8 piercing, redolent, stinging
9 pervading, pervasive, trenchant **10** discerning, perceptive,
percipient, permeating, saturat-
ing, thoughtful **11** intelligent,
sharp-witted **13** perspicacious

penetration 5 foray, grasp
6 access, boring **7** insight, passage **8** infusion, invasion,
keenness, piercing **9** intrusion,
quickness, sharpness **10** astuteness, cleverness, perception, puncturing, shrewdness
11 discernment, perforation
12 intelligence, perspicacity

Peneus
god of: **5** river
river: **6** Peneus
son: **7** Hypseus
daughter: **6** Daphne

Penguin Island
author: **13** Anatole France

peninsula 4 cape **5** point
8 headland **10** promontory

Peninsular State
nickname of: **7** Florida

penitence 6 regret, sorrow
7 penance, remorse **9** atonement, attrition, expiation
10 contrition, repentance
11 compunction,
humiliation

penitent 5 sorry **6** rueful
7 atoning, devotee, pilgrim
8 contrite **9** regretful, repentant **10** remorseful

penitentiary 3 pen **4** jail, stir
5 joint **6** prison **7** slammer
8 big house

Penn, Arthur
director of: **12** Little Big
Man **14** Bonnie and Clyde
16 The Miracle Worker

Penn, Sean
wife: **7** Madonna
roles: **7** Bad Boys **15** Shanghai Express **22** The Falcon
and the Snowman **24** Fast
Times at Ridgemont High

Pennacook (Merrimac)
language family: **9** Algonkian **10** Algonquian
location: **5** Maine **6** Quebec
7 New York, Vermont
10 New England **12** New
Hampshire **13** Massachusetts
leader: **11** Wannalancet
12 Passaconaway
related to: **6** Abnaki

pen name
French: **10** nom de plume

pennant 4 flag, jack **6** banner,
burgee, colors, ensign, pen-
non **7** bunting **8** ensignia,
standard, streamer **9** bander-
ole, oriflamme

penniless 4 poor **5** broke,
needy **6** busted, ruined
8 bankrupt, indigent, strapped,
wiped out **9** destitute, flat
broke, insolvent, moneyless
10 down-and-out, pauperized
12 impoverished **15** poverty-
stricken

pennon 4 flag, jack **6** banner,
colors, ensign **7** pennant
8 standard, streamer

Pennsylvania see box

penny 3 sum **4** cent **5** cheap,
pence **6** copper, stiver **7** trivial

penny-pinching 5 close, tight
6 stingy **7** miserly **8** grudging
9 niggardly, penurious **10** ungenerous **11** tight-fisted
12 parsimonious

Penny Serenade
director: **13** George Stevens
cast: **9** Cary Grant **10** Irene
Dunne **11** Beulah Bondi
13 Edgar Buchanan

pennyweight
abbreviation of: **3** dwt

Penobscot
language family: **9** Algonkian **10** Algonquian
location: **5** Maine **13** Old
Town Island
members of: **17** Abnaki
Confederacy

Penrod
author: **15** Booth Tarkington
sequel: **12** Penrod and Sam
13 Penrod Jashber

character: **6** Herman, Ver-
man **9** Sarah Crim **11** Rupe
Collins **13** Marjorie Jones
15 Penrod Schofield
dog: **4** Duke

pensee 7 thought **10** reflection

Pensees
author: **12** Blaise Pascal

pension 5 grant **6** income, retire **7** annuity, stipend, subsidy **9** allowance
13 boardinghouse **14** retirement fund

pensive 3 sad **5** grave
6 dreamy, musing, solemn,
somber **7** serious, wistful
8 dreaming **10** meditative,
melancholy, reflective **11** daydreaming **13** contemplative,
introspective **15** sadly
thoughtful

Pentateuch 10 Law of Moses
28 first five books of Old
Testament
see also: **7** books of **12** Old
Testament

Penthesilea
queen of: **7** Amazons
father: **4** Ares
mother: **6** Otrere
sister: **9** Hippolyta
killed by: **8** Achilles

Pentheus
king of: **6** Thebes
father: **6** Echion
mother: **5** Agave
grandfather: **6** Cadmus

pent-up 7 boxed-up, checked,
stifled **8** hedged-in, held back,
penned-in, penned-up, reined
in, stored-up **9** bottled-up, repressed **10** restrained,
suppressed

penurious 5 close **6** frugal,
stingy **7** miserly, sparing
8 stinting **9** niggardly **12** parsimonious **13** penny-pinching

penury 4 need, want **7** poverty **9** indigence, privation
10 bankruptcy, insolvency
11 destitution
14 impoverishment

Penutian
language branch: **4** Coos
5 Huave, Maidu, Mayan,
Miwok **6** Wintun, Yokuts
7 Chinook, Klamath, Tak-
elma, Totonac **8** Sahaptin
9 Mixe-Zoque, Tsimshian
tribe: **5** Maidu **7** Klamath

peon 4 pawn, serf **5** slave
6 drudge, menial, worker
7 footman, laborer, orderly,
peasant, servant

peony 7 Paeonia
varieties: **4** Tree **7** Chinese,

Pennsylvania
  abbreviation: **2** PA **5** Penna
  nickname: **8** Keystone
  capital: **10** Harrisburg
  largest city: **12** Philadelphia
  others: **4** Erie, Etna, Plum, York **5** Avoca, Baden **6** Beaver, Bethel, Butler, Easton, Emmaus, Radnor, Ridley, Sharon **7** Altoona, Baldwin, Bristol, Chester, Ephrata, Hanover, Hershey, Lebanon, Reading **8** Abington, Braddock, Bradford, Bryn Mawr, Carlisle, Clairton, Harrison, Hazelton, Monessen, Scranton, Shamokin **9** Aliquippa, Allentown, Bethlehem, Charleroi, Haverford, Jeannette, Johnstown, Lancaster, Meadville, Mill Creek, Newcastle, Swissvale, Uniontown, Whitehall **10** Carbondale, Gettysburg, McKeesport, Norristown, Pittsburgh **11** Springfield, Wilkes Barre **12** State College, Williamsport
  college: **3** PSU **4** Penn, Pitt **5** Gratz, Thiel **6** Drexel, Lehigh, Temple **7** Juniata, LaSalle, Ursinus **8** Alliance, Bryn Mawr, Bucknell, Duquesne, Lycoming **9** Dickinson, Lafayette, Penn State, St Josephs, Villanova **10** Pittsburgh, Swarthmore **12** Carnegie Tech **17** Pennsylvania State
  feature:
    battle site: **10** Gettysburg
    bell: **7** Liberty
    hall: **12** Independence
    historical site: **11** Valley Forge
  tribe: **6** Seneca **7** Shawnee **8** Delaware **11** Lenni-Lanape **13** Susquehannock
  people: **5** Amish, Dutch **10** Stan Musial **11** Andrew Wyeth, Ethel Waters, Mary Cassatt, Stuart Davis **12** Andrew Mellon, Anthony Wayne, Margaret Mead, Martha Graham, Samuel Barber, Thomas Eakins **13** Clifford Odets, Gertrude Stein **14** George S Kaufman **15** Maxwell Anderson **19** Stephen Vincent Benet
    explorer: **5** Brule **6** Hudson **11** Hendrickson
  lake: **4** Erie **7** Harveys **8** Conneaut **10** Pymatuning **13** Wallenpaupack
  land rank: **11** thirty-third
  mountain: **5** South **6** Pocono **11** Alleghenies
    highest point: **5** Davis
  physical feature:
    peninsula: **11** Presque Isle
    valley: **5** Great
  president: **13** James Buchanan
  river: **4** Ohio **6** Lehigh **7** Clarion, Genesee, Juniata, Licking, Towanda **8** Caldwell, Delaware, Schrader **9** Allegheny **10** Schuylkill **11** Monongahela, Susquehanna
  state admission: **6** second
  state bird: **12** ruffed grouse
  state fish: **10** brook trout
  state flower: **14** mountain laurel
  state motto: **28** Virtue Liberty and Independence
  state tree: **7** hemlock

Tibetan **8** Majorcan **11** Chinese tree **12** Common garden

people 3 kin **5** folks **6** family, humans, the mob **7** kinfolk, mankind, mortals, the herd **8** citizens, humanity, populace, the crowd **9** ancestors, citizenry, commoners, humankind, relatives, the masses, the public, the rabble **10** population **11** homo sapiens, human beings, individuals, inhabitants, John Q Public, men and women, the millions

People Are Funny
  host: **13** Art Linkletter

pep 3 vim, zip **4** dash, life, snap **5** gusto, verve, vigor **6** energy, ginger, spirit **8** vitality, vivacity **9** animation **10** enthusiasm, get-up-and-go, liveliness

Pepe Le Moko
  director: **14** Julien Duvivier
  cast: **9** Jean Gabin **13** Gabriel Gabrio, Mireille Balin
  remade as: **6** Casbah **7** Algiers

peperomia
  varieties: **3** Ivy **6** Prayer, Vining **7** Ivy-leaf, Leather, Rededge **8** Coin-leaf, Platinum **9** Flowering **10** Silver-edge, Silver-leaf, Watermelon **11** Green-ripple **13** Emerald-ripple, Little fantasy

Pepita
  character in: **21** The Bridge of San Luis Rey
  author: **6** Wilder

Peppard, George
  born: **9** Detroit MI
  wife: **15** Elizabeth Ashley
  roles: **6** Tobruk **7** Banacek **8** The A-Team **16** The Carpetbaggers **19** Breakfast at Tiffany's

pepper 3 dot **6** shower, strafe **7** bombard **8** sprinkle **9** condiment, vegetable

pepper, peppercorn
  botanical name: **5** Piper **7** P nigrum **8** Capsicum **10** Piperaceae **11** C frutescens
  color: **3** red **5** black, green, white
  origin: **5** India **6** Brazil, Ceylon **7** Malabar, Sarawak, Sumatra **8** Alleppey, Pandjang, Sri Lanka **11** Tellicherry
  varieties: **3** Red **4** Baby, Bell, Bird, Cone, Long, Wild **5** Betle, Black, Chili, Cubeb, Green, Japan, Sweet, White **6** Cherry **7** Cayenne, Celebes, Cluster, Tabasco **8** Capsicum **9** Mild water **10** Australian, Red cluster **12** Mountain long, Tabasco-sauce
  French: **6** poivre
  German: **7** pfeffer
  Italian: **4** pepe
  Latin: **5** piper
  Persian: **5** biber **6** pilpil
  Spanish: **8** pimienta
  Swedish: **6** peppar
  Sanskrit: **7** pippali

peppermint 6 Mentha
  varieties: **4** Gray **5** Black, River, White **6** Silver, Sydney **9** Blackbutt **10** Robertson's **11** Broad-leaved **15** Mount Wellington **17** Narrow-leaved black **19** Nichol's willow-leaved

peppermint schnapps
  type: **7** liqueur
  flavor: **4** mint

peppery 3 hot **5** fiery, sharp, spicy **7** burning, piquant, pungent **14** highly seasoned

peppy 4 spry **5** brisk, perky **6** active, bouncy, frisky, lively, snappy **7** dynamic **8** animated, spirited, vigorous **9** energetic, full of pep, sparkling,

sprightly, vivacious
12 enthusiastic

pep up 4 fire 6 excite, vivify,
wake up 7 animate, enliven,
quicken 8 vitalize

Pepys, Samuel
author of: 10 Pepys' Diary

Pepys' Diary
author: 11 Samuel Pepys

Pequot
language family: 9 Algon-
kian 10 Algonquian
location: 11 Connecticut,
Rhode Island

perambulate 4 pace, tour,
walk 5 amble, mosey 6 ramble, stroll 7 meander, saunter
9 promenade

perceivable 7 visible 8 apparent, distinct 10 detectable, noticeable, observable
11 discernible, perceptible
13 ascertainable

perceive 3 get, see 4 feel,
hear, know, note 5 grasp,
savvy, sense, smell, taste 6 deduce, detect, gather, notice
7 discern, make out, observe,
realize 8 conclude, discover
9 apprehend, be aware of, recognize 10 comprehend, understand 11 distinguish

perceptible 5 clear, plain
7 evident, notable, obvious,
visible 8 apparent, distinct,
manifest, palpable, tangible,
unhidden 9 prominent 10 detectable, noticeable, observable 11 conspicuous,
discernible, perceivable, unconcealed, well-defined 12 dis-
coverable, unmistakable
13 ascertainable

perception 5 grasp, sense
7 faculty 8 judgment 9 awareness, detection 10 cognizance,
conception 11 discernment,
recognition 12 apprehension
13 comprehension, consciousness, understanding
14 discrimination

perceptive 4 keen 5 acute,
aware, quick, sharp 6 astute,
shrewd 8 sensible 9 sensitive
10 discerning, insightful, responsive 11 intelligent, penetrating, quick-witted
13 understanding

perch 3 sit 4 land, rest, seat
5 eyrie, light, roost 6 alight,
settle

Perchta
also: 7 Berchta
origin: 8 Germanic
goddess of: 5 death 9 fertility
corresponds to: 5 Holle

Percival, Perceval
character in: 16 Arthurian
romance

percolate 4 boil, brew 6 bubble, seethe

percussion instrument
4 gong 5 anvil, bells, tabor
6 chimes, rattle 7 celesta, cymbals, marimba, taboret, timpani 8 bass drum, side drum,
triangle 9 castanets, dulcitone,
snare drum, tenor drum, typo-
phone, xylophone 10 kettledrum, tambourine
12 Glockenspiel, tubular bells

Percy, Walker
author of: 8 Lancelot 12 The
Moviegoer 14 Love in the
Ruins 15 The Second Com-
ing 16 The Last Gentleman

Perdita
character in: 14 The Winter's
Tale
author: 11 Shakespeare

perdition 4 Hell, ruin 8 hellfire 9 damnation, ruination
11 destruction
12 condemnation

Perdix
also: 9 Polycaste
brother: 8 Daedalus
son: 5 Talus
changed into: 9 partridge

pere 6 father, senior

Pere Goriot
author: 14 Honore de Balzac
character: 15 Monsieur Vau-
trin 17 Eugene de Rastig-
nac, Madame de Beauseant
18 Victorine Taillefer
26 Countess Anastasie de
Restaud, Baroness Delphine
de Nucingen

peregrination 4 trip 5 jaunt,
sally 6 hiking, junket, roving,
travel 7 journey, roaming
8 rambling, trekking 9 excursion, wandering 10 expedition

Peregrine Pickle
author: 14 Tobias Smollett

Pereira, William
architect of: 13 Cape Canaveral 20 Transamerica Building (San Francisco)

Perelman, S J
author of: 10 Eastward Ha
15 One Touch of Venus
(with Ogden Nash and Kurt
Weill) 16 The Road to Mil-
town 18 Strictly from Hunger 24 Under the Spreading
Atrophy

peremptory 5 final 6 biased,
lordly 8 absolute, decisive,
dogmatic 9 assertive, imperious 10 aggressive, high-
handed, imperative, obligatory,

undeniable 11 dictatorial,
domineering, irrevocable,
opinionated, overbearing, unavoidable, unequivocal
12 closed-minded, irreversible
13 authoritative 14 unquestionable 16 incontrovertible

perennial 5 fixed 7 durable,
lasting, undying 8 constant,
enduring, timeless 9 ceaseless,
continual, immutable, incessant, long-lived, permanent,
perpetual, unceasing, unfailing 10 changeless, continuous,
persistent, unchanging 11 everlasting, long-lasting, unremitting 12 imperishable
14 indestructible

Pereus
father: 6 Elatus
mother: 7 Laodice

Perez, Manuel Benitez
nickname: 10 El Cordobes

perfect 4 pure, true 5 exact,
ideal, whole 6 effect, entire,
evolve, strict 7 achieve, develop, fulfill, precise, realize,
sublime, supreme 8 absolute,
accurate, complete, faithful,
finished, flawless, peerless,
thorough, unbroken, unerring
9 blameless, faultless, matchless, undamaged, unequaled,
unrivaled, untainted 10 accomplish, consummate, im-
maculate, impeccable,
scrupulous, unimpaired 11 superlative, unblemished, unmitigated, unqualified

perfection 6 purity 9 achiev-
ing, evolution, exactness, precision, sublimity
10 completion, excellence,
ideal state 11 development,
fulfillment, perfectness, realization, superiority 12 accurateness, consummation,
flawlessness 13 faultlessness,
impeccability
14 accomplishment

perfectly 5 fully, quite
6 purely, wholly 7 totally, utterly 8 entirely, superbly
9 downright, supremely
10 absolutely, altogether, completely, flawlessly, impeccably,
infinitely, positively, thoroughly 11 faultlessly, wonderfully 12 consummately,
preeminently, to perfection,
without fault 13 without defect 14 to the nth degree,
without blemish

perfidious 5 false, lying
6 shifty, sneaky 7 corrupt
8 cheating, disloyal, two-faced
9 deceitful, dishonest, faithless 10 traitorous, treasonous,
unfaithful, untruthful
11 treacherous, treasonable

12 dishonorable, undependable, unscrupulous **13** double-dealing, untrustworthy

perfidy 6 deceit **7** treason **8** bad faith, betrayal **9** falseness, recreancy, treachery, two-timing **10** disloyalty, infidelity **11** double-cross, inconstancy **13** breach of faith, deceitfulness, double-dealing, faithlessness **14** unfaithfulness

perforate 4 bore, gash, hole, slit, stab **5** drill, prick, punch, slash, split, stick **6** pierce **8** puncture **9** lancinate, penetrate

perform 2 do **3** act **4** meet, play **5** enact **6** attain, depict, effect, finish, render, troupe **7** achieve, execute, fulfill, portray, present, pull off, realize **8** carry out, knock off **9** discharge, dispose of, polish off, represent **10** accomplish, bring about, consummate, perpetrate, take part in

performance 4 play, show **5** doing, opera **6** ballet **7** concert, conduct, recital **8** ceremony, dispatch, exercise **9** acquittal, discharge, execution, rendering, spectacle **10** attainment, completion, exhibition, performing, production **11** achievement, fulfillment, realization, transaction **12** consummation, effectuation, perpetration, presentation **13** entertainment **14** accomplishment

perfume 4 odor **5** aroma, scent, smell **7** bouquet, cologne, essence, extract, sweeten **9** aromatize, fragrance

perfumed 7 odorous, scented **8** aromatic, fragrant **11** odoriferous **12** sweet-scented **13** sweet-smelling

perfunctory 3 lax **5** hasty **6** casual **7** cursory, offhand, routine **8** careless, listless, lukewarm **9** apathetic, negligent **10** mechanical, spiritless, unthinking **11** halfhearted, inattentive, indifferent, passionless, superficial, unconcerned **13** disinterested

Pergamus
father: **11** Neoptolemus
mother: **10** Andromache

pergola 5 arbor, bower **6** ramada **7** balcony, trellis

Per Hanea
character in: **16** Giants of the Earth
author: **7** Rolvaag

perhaps 5 maybe **6** mayhap **8** peut-etre, possibly **9** per-

chance **10** God willing, imaginably **11** conceivably **12** peradventure

Perialla
form: **9** priestess
priestess of: **6** Delphi

Periapis
also: **8** Periopis
father: **6** Pheres
son: **9** Patrocles

Periboea
father: **9** Alcathous, Hipponous
husband: **6** Oeneus **7** Polybus
son: **6** Tydeus **7** Olenias, Pelegon **14** Telamonian Ajax
foster son: **7** Oedipus

Perichole, La
character in: **21** The Bridge of San Luis Rey
author: **6** Wilder

Pericles, Prince of Tyre
author: **18** William Shakespeare
character: **5** Cleon **6** Marina, Thaisa **7** Dionyza **9** Antiochus **10** Lysimachus

Periclymenus
father: **6** Neleus **8** Poseidon
grandfather: **8** Poseidon
gift: **13** shape-changing
killed by: **8** Hercules

periderm 4 bark **8** covering **9** sheathing

peridot
species: **7** olivine
source: **5** Burma, Mogok **8** Zebirget
color: **11** yellow-green

perigee 5 depth, nadir **8** low point

Perikeiromene (The Rape of the Ringlets)
author: **8** Menander

peril 4 risk **6** danger, hazard, menace, threat **7** pitfall **8** jeopardy, unsafety **10** insecurity **11** uncertainty **13** cause for alarm, vulnerability

Perilaus
father: **7** Icarius
cousin: **12** Clytemnestra

perilous 5 risky, shaky **6** chancy, unsafe, unsure **7** ominous **8** insecure, slippery, ticklish **9** dangerous, hazardous, uncertain **10** precarious, vulnerable **11** threatening, venturesome

Perimedes
mentioned in: **7** Odyssey
companion of: **8** Odysseus
father: **10** Eurystheus

Perimele
father: **10** Hippodamas

ravished by: **8** Achelous
changed into: **6** island

perimeter 4 edge **6** border, bounds, margin **8** confines **9** periphery **10** borderline **13** circumference

period 3 age, end, eon, era **4** halt, stop, term, time **5** close, epoch, limit **6** finale, finish, season **7** curtain **8** duration, interval **9** cessation, interlude
French: **6** siecle

periodic, periodical 6 cyclic **7** regular, routine **8** frequent, repeated, seasonal **9** recurrent, recurring **12** intermittent

periodical 5 daily, paper **6** annual, review, weekly **7** journal, monthly **8** bulletin, magazine **9** newspaper, quarterly **10** newsletter **11** publication **12** newsmagazine

periodically 5 often **9** regularly, routinely **10** frequently, repeatedly **12** occasionally

Periopis see **8** Periapis

peripatetic 6 roving **7** migrant, nomadic, roaming, walking **8** rambling, tramping **9** itinerant, migratory, traveling, wandering **10** ambulating, ambulatory **12** Aristotelian, gallivanting **13** peregrinating

Periphas
mentioned in: **5** Iliad
king of: **6** Attica
father: **6** Epytus
vocation: **6** herald **7** warrior
changed into: **5** eagle
changed by: **4** Zeus

periphery 4 edge **5** bound **6** border **7** fringes **8** boundary **9** outskirts, perimeter **13** circumference

Periphetes
form: **5** giant
father: **7** Copreus
ally of: **7** Trojans
killed by: **7** Theseus

perish 3 die **5** decay **6** expire, vanish **7** crumble **8** pass away **9** disappear **10** come to ruin, wither away **11** be destroyed

perishable 8 fleeting, unstable **9** ephemeral **10** evanescent, short-lived, transitory **12** decomposable

perished 4 dead, died **7** expired **8** lifeless **10** passed away

periwinkle 5 Vinca **12** Catharanthus
varieties: **4** Rose **6** Common, Lesser **7** Greater **10** Madagascar

perjury 13 false swearing 14 lying under oath 20 giving false testimony

Perkins, Anthony
   born: 9 New York NY
   roles: 6 Psycho 11 Norman Bates 14 Catch Twenty-Two 17 Look Homeward Angel 18 Desire Under the Elms, Friendly Persuasion

perk up 4 lift 5 cheer, rally, renew 6 buoy up, lift up, revive 7 animate, enliven, gladden 8 brighten, vitalize 9 stimulate 10 rejuvenate

perky 3 gay 4 pert 5 alert, brisk, happy, saucy, sunny 6 jaunty, lively 7 smiling 8 animated, cheerful, spirited 9 sprightly, vivacious 11 free and easy 12 full of spirit, lighthearted

permanent 3 set 4 perm, wave 6 stable 7 abiding, durable, endless, eternal, lasting, undying 8 constant, enduring, immortal, infinite, unending, unfading 9 deathless, immutable, long-lived, perpetual, unfailing 10 changeless, unyielding 11 everlasting, long-lasting, never-ending, unalterable 12 imperishable

permeate 4 fill 5 imbue 6 infuse 7 pervade 8 saturate 9 penetrate 11 pass through, seep through, soak through

per mensem 10 by the month

permissible 5 legal, licit 6 lawful 7 allowed, granted 8 licensed 9 allowable, permitted, tolerated 10 admissible, authorized, legitimate, sanctioned 12 unprohibited

permission 5 grant, leave 6 assent, permit 7 consent, license 8 approval, sanction 9 agreement, allowance 10 compliance, concession, indulgence 11 approbation, endorsement 12 acquiescence, dispensation 13 authorization

permissive 3 lax 7 lenient 8 allowing, granting, tolerant 9 assenting, easygoing, indulgent 10 consenting, forbearing, permitting 11 acquiescent 13 unprohibitive 14 unproscriptive

permit 2 OK 3 let 5 allow 6 endure, suffer 7 agree to, approve, condone, endorse, let pass, license, warrant 8 bear with, sanction, tolerate 9 authority, authorize, consent to, put up with 11 give leave to 12 give assent to 13 authorization
   French: 13 laissez passer

permit to leave 4 free 5 let go 6 excuse 7 dismiss, release, set free 8 liberate 9 allow to go, discharge, send forth

pernicious 5 fatal, toxic 6 deadly, lethal, mortal 7 baneful, harmful, noxious, serious 8 damaging, venomous 9 dangerous, injurious, malignant, poisonous 10 disastrous 11 deleterious, destructive, detrimental

pernod
   type: 8 aperitif
   flavor: 5 anise
   substitute for: 8 absinthe
   with gin: 7 Dubarry
   with orange juice: 9 Tiger Tail
   with rum: 8 Shanghai
   with rye: 3 TNT

Pero
   father: 6 Neleus
   mother: 7 Chloris
   husband: 4 Bias

peroration 6 sermon, speech, tirade 7 address, lecture, oration 8 diatribe, harangue, jeremiad 9 discourse, philippic 10 filibuster 11 declamation, exhortation

perpendicular 4 sine 5 erect, plumb, sheer, steep 7 upright 8 vertical 10 right angle

perpetrate 2 do 5 enact 6 commit, pursue 7 execute, inflict, perform, pull off 8 carry out, transact

perpetration 5 doing 9 committal 10 commission, committing, performing 11 carrying out, performance

perpetrator 9 performer 11 participant

perpetual 7 abiding, endless, eternal, lasting 8 constant, enduring, repeated, unending 9 ceaseless, continual, incessant, permanent, sustained, unceasing 10 continuous 11 everlasting, never ending, unremitting 12 interminable 13 inexhaustible, uninterrupted

perpetuate 4 save 7 sustain 8 continue, maintain, make last, preserve 10 eternalize 11 immortalize, memorialize

perpetuity 7 all time, forever 8 eternity, infinity 9 end of time 10 permanence 11 endlessness 12 perpetuation, timelessness 13 perdurability, perennialness

perplex 5 mix up, stump 6 baffle, boggle, muddle, puzzle, rattle 7 confuse, mystify, nonplus 8 befuddle, bewilder, confound 9 dumbfound

perplexed 7 anxious, amazed, baffled, bemused, muddled, puzzled 8 confused, doubtful, involved 9 befuddled, intricate, mystified 10 astonished, bewildered, nonplussed

perplexing 4 hard, mazy 6 thorny 7 complex 10 mysterious
   riddle: 9 conundrum

perplexity 9 confusion 10 bafflement, puzzlement 12 bewilderment 13 mystification

perquisite 3 due 4 gift, perk 5 right 6 reward 7 benefit, present 9 advantage, emolument, privilege 10 honorarium, inducement, recompense 13 fringe benefit

Perry, Matthew Calbraith
   served in: 10 Mexican War 19 War of Eighteen Twelve
   rank: 9 commodore
   helped establish: 7 Liberia
   commander of: 17 US African Squadron
   gained treaty with: 5 Japan

Perry, Oliver Hazard
   nickname: 14 Hero of Lake Erie
   served in: 13 Tripolitan War 19 War of Eighteen-Twelve
   battle: 8 Lake Erie
   commander of ship: 7 Niagara 8 Lawrence
   defeated: 7 British
   saying: 31 We have met the enemy and they are ours

Perry, William
   nickname: 12 Refrigerator
   sport: 8 football
   team: 12 Chicago Bears

Perry Como Show, The
   regulars: 8 Don Adams 9 Jack Duffy, Paul Lynde 10 Pierre Olaf 11 Kaye Ballard 12 Sandy Stewart 14 Fontane Sisters 17 Ray Charles Singers 18 Louis Da Pron Dancers 19 Peter Gennaro Dancers
   orchestra: 13 Mitchell Ayres
   theme: 16 Dream Along with Me

Perry Mason
   character: 6 Lt Drum 7 Lt Tragg 9 Paul Drake 10 Lt Anderson 11 Della Street 14 Hamilton Burger
   cast: 9 Wesley Lau 10 Ray Collins 11 Barbara Hale, Raymond Burr 13 William Hopper, William Talman 15 Richard Anderson

Persa
   father: 7 Oceanus
   mother: 6 Tethys

persecute 3 vex **4** bait **5** abuse, annoy, bully, harry, hound **6** badger, harass, harrow, hector, plague **7** oppress, torment **8** maltreat **9** tyrannize, victimize

Persephone
also: **4** Cora, Kore **10** Perserpina, Proserpine
queen of: **5** Hades
father: **4** Zeus
mother: **7** Demeter
husband: **5** Hades
abducted by: **5** Pluto
ate seeds of: **11** pomegranate
epithet: **11** Carpophorus
corresponds to: **5** Brimo **6** Libera **8** Despoena

Perseus
father: **4** Zeus
mother: **5** Danae
grandfather: **8** Acrisius
wife: **9** Andromeda
son: **6** Mestor, Perses **7** Alcaeus, Heleius **9** Electryon, Sthenelus
daughter: **10** Gorgophone
saved: **9** Andromeda
killed: **6** Gorgon, Medusa

perseverance 8 tenacity **10** doggedness, resolution **11** persistence **12** resoluteness **13** determination, steadfastness

persevere 6 hang on, keep on **7** persist **8** keep at it, plug away, work hard **9** not give up, stick to it **10** be resolute, be resolved, hammer away **11** be obstinate, be steadfast, hang in there

persevering 6 dogged **8** constant, diligent, resolute, sedulous **9** keeping on, steadfast, tenacious **10** determined, persistent, unflagging **11** hardworking, industrious, unremitting

Pershing, John J
nickname: **9** Black Jack
served in: **3** WWI **11** Philippines, World War One **18** Spanish-American War
commander of: **21** Mexican border campaign
trained: **27** American Expeditionary Forces
battle: **10** Kettle Hill **11** San Juan Hill
fought against: **5** Moros **11** Pancho Villa
rank: **16** brigadier general **18** general of the armies
memoirs: **26** My Experiences in the World War
won: **13** Pulitzer Prize (for history)

Persia see **4** Iran

Persian Gulf War
caused by: **4** Iraq **13** Saddam Hussein **14** Kuwait invasion

took place in: **4** Iraq **6** Kuwait **10** Middle East **11** Saudi Arabia
leaders:
Allies: **11** Colin Powell **15** Khalid bin Sultan **18** H Norman Schwarzkopf
Iraq: **13** Saddam Hussein
operations: **11** Desert Storm **12** Desert Shield
weapons: **4** Scud **5** AWACS **6** Abrams, Apache **7** Bradley, Patriot, Stealth **8** Tomahawk
battle: **6** Khafji **18** mother of all battles

Persian Mythology
god of light/truth: **7** Mithras

Persians, The
author: **9** Aeschylus
character: **6** Atossa, Xerxes **13** Ghost of Darius

persist 4 go on, last, stay **6** endure, hang on, hold on, remain **7** hold out, survive **8** continue, keep at it, not yield **9** not give up, persevere, stand fast, stick to it **10** be resolute **11** be obstinate, be tenacious, hang in there, never say die

persistence 8 tenacity **9** diligence **11** application **12** perseverance **13** determination

persistent 6 dogged **7** abiding, endless, eternal, lasting **8** constant, enduring, obdurate, resolute, stubborn **9** continual, incessant, obstinate, perpetual, steadfast, sustained, tenacious, unceasing, unfailing **10** continuous, determined, persisting, relentless, unshakable, unswerving **11** persevering, unrelenting, unremitting **12** interminable **13** inexhaustible

Perske, Betty Joan
real name of: **12** Lauren Bacall

persnickety 5 fussy **6** choosy **7** finical, finicky **8** picayune **10** fastidious, fuddy-duddy, meticulous, nitpicking, particular, pernickety **11** overprecise, punctilious **13** overdemanding

person 4 body, soul **5** being, human **6** mortal **8** creature **9** earthling **10** human being, individual, living body, living soul

persona 5 being **6** facade **9** character

personable 4 warm **7** affable, amiable, cordial, likable, tactful **8** amicable, charming, friendly, outgoing, pleasant, sociable **9** agreeable **10** attractive, diplomatic **11** complaisant, sympathetic **12** well-disposed, well-mannered

personage 3 VIP **5** nabob **6** bigwig **7** big name, big shot, notable **8** big wheel, luminary, somebody **9** celebrity, dignitary **11** heavyweight **12** leading light, public figure **13** highmuck-a-muck

persona grata 16 acceptable person **34** acceptable diplomatic representative

personal 3 own **5** privy **6** bodily, inward, secret **7** private, special **8** intimate, physical **9** corporeal, exclusive **10** individual, particular, subjective **12** confidential

personality 5 charm **6** makeup, nature **8** charisma, identity **9** magnetism **10** affability, amiability **11** disposition, temperament **12** friendliness **13** agreeableness, individuality **15** distinctiveness

persona non grata 15 unwelcome person **18** unacceptable person **33** unwelcome diplomatic representative

personification of see box, p. 744

personify 6 embody **7** express **9** exemplify, incarnate, represent, symbolize **11** externalize, incorporate, personalize **12** characterize

personnel 4 crew **5** staff **7** members, workers **8** manpower **9** employees, work force **10** associates

Person to Person
host: **13** Edward R Murrow **18** Charles Collingwood

perspective 4 view **5** scape, scene, vista **7** outlook **8** overview, prospect **9** broad view, viewpoint **12** bird's-eye view

perspicacious 4 keen **5** acute, alert, awake, sharp **6** astute, shrewd **9** clear-eyed, sagacious **10** discerning, perceptive **11** clearheaded, keen-sighted, penetrating, sharp-witted **12** clear-sighted

perspicacity 6 acumen **8** keenness, sagacity **9** acuteness, alertness, sharpness **10** astuteness, perception, shrewdness **11** discernment **14** discrimination

persuadable 7 willing **8** amenable, obliging **9** malleable, tractable **10** open-minded **16** open to suggestion

persuade 3 get **4** coax, lure, move, sway **5** tempt **6** cajole, entice, induce, prompt

Personification of
aging: 4 Elli
air: 4 Amen, Amon
  5 Ammon 6 Aether
astronomy: 6 Urania
breath: 4 Amen, Amon
  5 Ammon
chaos: 4 Nunu
choral song:
  11 Terpsichore
comedy: 6 Thalia
confusion: 5 Chaos
conscience: 5 Aidos
courage: 5 Arete 6 Virtus
dance: 8 Polymnia
  10 Polyhymnia
  11 Terpsichore
death: 4 Mors 6 Namtar
  8 Thanatos
desert: 3 Set 4 Seth
desire: 6 Pothos
divine punishment:
  3 Ate 7 Nemesis
east wind: 5 Eurus
  9 Volturnus
echo: 4 Echo
emulation: 5 Zelos
familial affection:
  6 Pietas
fate: 4 Norn 5 Moira,
  Moras
fear: 6 Deimos
femininity: 5 Neith
fire: 4 Logi
force: 3 Bia
good faith: 5 Fides
grain blight: 7 Robigus
heaven: 6 Uranus
hostile nature:
  8 Fomorian
idyllic poetry: 6 Thalia
liberty: 8 Libertas
longing: 6 Pothos

lotus: 8 Nefertem
meditation: 6 Melete
memory: 5 Mneme,
  Munin
moon: 4 Luna
nature: 7 Eriking
night: 3 Nox
north wind: 6 Boreas
order: 7 Eunomia
pain: 5 Oizys
past: 3 Urd
peace: 5 Irene
prayer: 5 Litae
present: 8 Verdandi
punishment: 5 Poena,
  Poine
recklessness: 3 Ate
revenge: 5 Poena, Poine
Roman nation:
  8 Quirinus
sacred music: 8 Polymnia 10 Polyhymnia
sea: 3 Ler, Lir
  5 Nammu 6 Pontus
  8 Thalassa
sky: 6 Aether, Hathor
soul: 6 Psyche
southeast wind: 5 Eu-
  rus 9 Volturnus
south wind: 5 Notus
  7 Ninurta
strength: 6 Cratus
sun: 3 Sol
thought: 5 Hugin
tragedy: 9 Melpomene
truth: 7 Alethia
unavailing effort:
  5 Ocnus
wealth: 6 Plutus
west wind: 8 Favonius,
  Zephyrus
wind: 7 Ninurta
zeal: 5 Zelos

7 wheedle, win over 8 convince, inveigle, motivate, talk
into 9 influence

Persuasion
  author: 10 Jane Austen
  character: 7 Mrs Clay 8 Mrs
  Croft 11 Lady Russell
  12 Admiral Croft 25 Captain
  Frederick Wentworth
    Elliot family: 4 Anne
    7 William 9 Elizabeth, Sir
    Walter
    Musgrove family: 4 Mary
    6 Louisa 7 Charles
    9 Henrietta

persuasive 6 cogent 7 coaxing,
logical, winning 8 alluring,
credible, forceful, inviting 9 effective, plausible, seductive
10 believable, compelling, convincing 11 influential

pert 4 flip, spry 5 alert, brash,
brisk, fresh, nervy, perky,
quick, saucy 6 brassy, brazen,

cheeky, lively, nimble 7 chipper 8 flippant, impolite, impudent, insolent 9 audacious,
energetic, insulting, sprightly,
wide-awake 11 impertinent,
smart-alecky 12 discourteous

pertain 2 be 5 apply, touch
6 befall, belong, relate 7 concern, connect

pertinacious 6 dogged 8 stubborn 9 obstinate, tenacious
10 persistent, unyielding
11 persevering

pertinacity 9 obstinacy
10 mulishness 11 persistence,
willfulness 12 contrariness, ob-
durateness, perverseness, stubbornness 13 determination,
inflexibility, intransigence, pigheadedness 14 bullheadedness,
intractability

pertinence 9 relevance 11 germaneness 12 appositeness
13 applicability

pertinent 3 apt 4 meet 7 apropos, fitting, germane, related
8 apposite, material, relevant,
suitable 9 befitting, concerned,
congruent, connected 10 applicable, consistent, to the
point
  Latin: 5 ad rem

perturb 5 upset, worry
6 bother 7 disturb, fluster,
trouble 8 disquiet, distress
10 discompose, disconcert

perturbation 5 alarm, upset,
worry 6 dismay 7 anxiety,
concern, turmoil 8 distress
9 agitation, commotion 10 excitement 11 disquietude, trepidation 12 apprehension,
discomposure 13 consternation

perturbed 5 upset 7 annoyed,
worried 8 agitated, troubled
9 disturbed 12 disconcerted

perturbing 6 vexing 7 irksome 8 annoying 9 vexatious
10 bothersome, irritating, unsettling 11 disquieting, distressing, troublesome
13 disconcerting

Peru *see box*

Perugino, Pietro
  real name: 14 Pietro
  Vannucci
  also called: 10 Il Perugino
  14 Pier della Pieve
  born: 5 Italy 15 Citta della
  Pieve
  artwork: 24 The Crucifixion
  with Saints 26 Delivery of
  the Keys to St Peter 27 The
  Giving of the Keys to St Peter 32 Apparition of the Virgin to St Bernard, Christ
  Delivering the Keys to St
  Peter

perusal 5 study 6 review
7 reading 8 scanning, scrutiny
10 inspection, run-through
11 examination, look-through
12 scrutinizing
13 contemplation

peruse 3 con 4 read, scan
5 study 6 search, survey 7 examine, inspect 10 scrutinize

pervade 4 fill 5 imbue 6 infuse 7 suffuse 8 permeate, saturate 9 penetrate 13 spread
through 17 diffuse throughout

pervasive 4 rife 7 rampant
8 dominant 9 prevalent
10 ubiquitous 11 omnipresent,
predominant

perverse 5 balky 6 dogged,
mulish, ornery 7 wayward,
willful 8 contrary, obdurate,
stubborn 9 obstinate, pigheaded 10 hardheaded, headstrong, inflexible, rebellious

Peru

capital/largest city: 4 Lima
  Inca capital: **5** Cuzco

others: 3 Ica **4** Puno **5** Cuzco, Paita, Pisco, Tacna **6** Callao, Talara **7** Huanuco, Iquitos **8** Arequipa, Castilla, Chiclayo, Chimbote, Mollendo, Pucallpa, Trujillo **9** Cajamarca **10** Yurimaguas

school: 8 Trujillo **9** San Marcos

division: 3 Ica **4** Lima, Puno **5** Cusco, Cuzco, Junin, Piura, Tacna **6** Ancash, Loreto, Tumbes
  Inca empire: **13** Tahuantinsuyo

measure: 4 topo **5** galon **7** celemin

monetary unit: 3 sol **5** libra **6** dinero, reseta **7** centavo

weight: 5 libra **7** quintal

island: 6 Chinca **7** Chincha

lake: 8 Titicaca

mountain: 5 Andes **7** El Misti, Huamina **8** Coropuna

highest point: 9 Huascaran

river: 3 Ene, Ica, Ilo **4** Napo, Napu **5** Piura, Rimac **6** Amazon, Oroton, Pampas, Yaguas, Yavari **7** Curaray, Mantaro, Maranon, Pastaza, Tapiche, Ucayali **8** Apurimac, Huallaga, Urubamba **11** Madre de Dios, Paucartambo

sea: 7 Pacific

physical feature:
  current: **6** el nino
  desert: **5** Nazca **7** Atacama, Sechura
  drizzling rain: **8** ilovizna
  fog: **5** garua
  gulf: **9** Guayaquil
  plateau: **7** Tablazo

people: 4 Ande, Boro, Cana, Inca, Inka, Lama, Pano, Peba, Piro, Yutu **5** Campa, Carib, Chana, Colan, Colla, Jwaro, Moche, Nasca, Senci, Yagua, Yunca **6** Atalan, Aymara, Canchi, Chanca, Chanka, Chimer, Cholos, Cocama, Jibaro, Kechua, Omagua, Quiche, Quolla, Setibo, Sipibo **7** Changos, Chincha, Chuncho, Mestizo, Mochica **8** Amahuaca, Criollos, Mayoruma, Quechuia **9** Callawaya **10** Tiahuanaca, Tiatinagua **11** Chumpivilca
  artist: **4** Lazo **7** Montero, Sabogal, Szyszlo **8** Codesido
  author: **4** Vega **5** Palma, Prada **8** Caviedes **10** Mariategui
  explorer: **7** Pizarro
  Inca leader: **7** Huascar **9** Atahualpa **10** Manco Capac
  leader: **5** Balta, Pardo, Prado, Torre **7** Bolivar **8** Castilla, Fujimori **9** Santa Cruz **13** Belaunde Terry **15** Leguiay y Salcedo, Morales Bermudez

language: 6 Aymara **7** English, Quechua, Spanish

religion: 13 Roman Catholic

place:
  bullring: **11** Plaza de Acho
  center of Lima: **12** Plaza de Armas
  church: **10** La Compania
  open market/street: **9** Calle Real
  ruins: **5** Huaco **8** Chan-Chan **9** Cajamarca **11** Machu-Picchu **22** Fortress of Sacsayhuaman

feature:
  animal: **5** llama **6** alpaca, vicuna **7** guanaco
  commune: **6** ayllus
  dance: **5** cueca, kaswa **6** cachua
  farmers: **10** campesinos
  priest: **6** villac
  slums: **9** barriadas
  tree: **8** cinchona

food:
  dish: **3** aji, cuy **7** ceviche **10** anticuchos
  drink: **5** pisco **6** chicha **11** aguardiente

---

11 disobedient, intractable, wrongheaded

perversion 9 depravity **10** corruption, degeneracy, immorality **11** dissipation, dissolution

pervert 4 warp **5** abuse **6** debase, misuse **7** contort, corrupt, degrade, deprave, distort, falsify, subvert **8** misapply **9** desecrate **12** misrepresent

perverted 5 false **6** faulty, untrue, warped **7** corrupt, debased, deviant, twisted, unsound **8** aberrant, abnormal, degraded, depraved **9** contorted, distorted, erroneous, imperfect, unnatural **10** fallacious, unbalanced **12** misconceived, misconstrued **13** misunderstood

Peschkowsky, Michael Igor
  real name of: 11 Mike Nichols

pesky 7 chafing, galling, irksome **8** annoying **9** maddening, obnoxious, offensive, vexatious **10** bothersome, disturbing, nettlesome **11** aggravating, distasteful, infuriating, pestiferous, troublesome **12** disagreeable, exasperating **13** objectionable

pessimism 5 gloom **7** despair **10** gloominess **12** hopelessness **13** gloomy outlook **14** discouragement **15** downheartedness

pessimist 7 kill-joy **8** sourpuss **9** Cassandra, defeatist, gloomy Gus **10** spoilsport, wet blanket **11** crepehanger **13** prophet of doom

pessimistic 6 gloomy **8** hopeless **10** despairing, dispirited **11** discouraged, downhearted

pest 4 bane **5** curse **6** blight, bother **7** scourge **8** nuisance, vexation **9** annoyance **10** irritation **13** pain in the neck

pester 3 irk, nag, vex **4** bait, fret **5** annoy, harry, taunt, worry **6** badger, bother, harass, hector, nettle, plague **7** disturb, provoke, torment, trouble **8** irritate

pesticide 3 DDT **7** biocide **8** fumigant **9** fungicide, germacide, vermicide **11** insecticide
  user: 12 exterminator

pestilence 6 blight, plague **7** disease **8** epidemic
  god of: 4 Irra

pet 3 pat **4** baby, dear **6** caress, choice, fondle, stroke **7** beloved, darling, dearest, favored **8** favorite **9** cherished,

preferred **10** sweetheart
14 apple of one's eye

pet activity 5 hobby **7** passion **8** interest **10** enthusiasm, hobbyhorse

Peter 7 apostle
means: 4 rock
also called: 5 Simon
6 Cephas
father: 4 John **5** Jonas
brother: 6 Andrew
birthplace: 9 Bethsaida
hometown: 9 Capernaum
disciple of: 5 Jesus
companion: 4 John **5** James
rebuked: 7 Ananias
8 Sapphira
secretary: 8 Silvanus
pertaining to: 7 Petrine

Peter and the Wolf
composed by: 9 Prokofiev

Peter Grimes
opera by: 7 Britten
character: 11 Ellen Orford

Peter Heering, Cherry Heering
type: 6 brandy **7** liqueur
origin: 7 Denmark
flavor: 6 cherry
color: 3 red

Peter Ibbetson
author: 15 George Du Maurier

peter out 3 ebb **7** decline, dwindle, fall off, give out
8 diminish

Peter Pan
author: 11 James Barrie
character: 9 Nurse Nana
10 Tinker Bell **11** Captain Hook **12** Wendy Darling

Peter Quince at the Clavier
author: 14 Wallace Stevens

Peters, Jane Alice
real name of: 13 Carole Lombard

petiole 4 stem **5** spine, stalk, stipe **8** peduncle **9** leafstalk

petite 4 wee **4** tiny **5** small
6 little **9** miniature
10 diminutive

petition 3 ask, beg, sue **4** plea, pray, seek, suit, urge **5** press
6 appeal, invoke, orison, prayer **7** apply to, beseech, entreat **8** appeal to, call upon, entreaty, proposal **9** imploring, plead with, request of **10** invocation, supplicate **11** application, beseechment, requisition **12** solicitation, supplication

petitioner 6 suitor **8** claimant
9 solicitor, suppliant
10 supplicant

pet name 8 nickname **9** sobri-

quet **10** diminutive, endearment

pet phrase 5 maxim, motto
6 saying, slogan **9** catchword

Petre (Lord)
character in: 16 The Rape of the Lock
author: 4 Pope

petrified 4 hard **5** dense, solid, stony **6** frozen **8** hardened, rocklike **9** paralyzed **10** solidified **11** hard as a rock, scared stiff **13** turned to stone

Petrified Forest, The
director: 10 Archie Mayo
based on play by: 14 Robert Sherwood
cast: 9 Dick Foran **10** Bette Davis **12** Leslie Howard
14 Humphrey Bogart (Duke Mantee)
setting: 7 Arizona

Petronius
author of: 9 Satyricon

Petruchio
character in: 19 The Taming of the Shrew
author: 11 Shakespeare

Petticoat Junction
character: 10 Floyd Smoot, Sam Drucker **11** Homer Bedloe, Kate Bradley **12** Charlie Pratt, Dr Janet Craig, Steve Elliott, Wendell Gibbs
14 Betty Jo Bradley, Uncle Joe Carson **15** Billie Jo Bradley, Bobbie Jo Bradley
cast: 9 Frank Cady, Linda Kaye, Mike Minor, Rufe Davis **10** Pat Woodell
11 Charles Lane **12** Bea Benaderet, Byron Foulger, June Lockhart, Lori Saunders **13** Edgar Buchanan, Gunilla Hutton, Jeannine Riley **14** Meredith MacRae, Smiley Burnette
setting: 11 Hooterville
14 Shady Rest Hotel
train: 10 Cannonball

petto 5 chest **6** breast

petty 4 mean **5** minor, small
6 flimsy, paltry, shabby, slight **7** ignoble, trivial
8 niggling, picayune, piddling, trifling **10** ungenerous
11 small-minded, unimportant
12 narrow-minded **13** insignificant **14** inconsiderable
15 inconsequential

petulance 9 poutiness, sulkiness **11** fretfulness, peevishness **12** irritability

petulant 4 sour **5** cross, gruff, huffy, sulky, surly, testy
6 grumpy, sullen, tetchy, touchy **7** bearish, crabbed, fretful, grouchy, peevish, pet-

tish, uncivil **8** snappish
9 crotchety, fractious, irascible, irritable **10** ill-natured, out of sorts, ungracious **11** complaining, contentious, ill-tempered, quarrelsome, thin-skinned
12 cantankerous, faultfinding

Petulia
director: 13 Richard Lester
cast: 10 Arthur Hill, Pippa Scott **12** George C Scott, Joseph Cotten **13** Julie Christie, Shirley Knight
18 Richard Chamberlain
setting: 12 San Francisco

petunia
varieties: 4 Wild **7** Mexican, Seaside **10** Large white
12 Common garden **14** Violet-flowered

peu a peu 14 little by little

peu de chose 14 trifling matter **17** unimportant matter

pew 4 seat **5** bench **6** settle

Peychaud Bitters
type: 8 aperitif
origin: 10 New Orleans

Peyton Place
author: 14 Grace Metalious
character: 9 Rita Jacks (Harrington) **10** Hannah Cord, Steven Cord **12** Matthew Swain **13** Betty Anderson (Harrington Cord Harrington), Elliott Carson, Julie Anderson **14** Dr Michael Rossi, Dr Robert Morton, George Anderson **16** Allison Mackenzie (Harrington), Leslie Harrington, Norman Harrington, Rodney Harrington
18 Constance Mackenzie (Carson)
cast (television): 8 Ed Nelson **9** Kent Smith, Mia Farrow, Ryan O'Neal **10** Tim O'Connor **11** Kasey Rogers, Paul Langton, Ruth Warrick **12** Henry Beckman, James Douglas **13** Dorothy Malone **14** Barbara Parkins, Patricia Morrow, Warner Anderson **19** Christopher Connelly
director (movie): 10 Mark Robson
cast (movie): 9 Hope Lange **10** Lana Turner, Lloyd Nolan **13** Arthur Kennedy
score: 11 Franz Waxman

Phaeax
father: 8 Poseidon
mother: 7 Corcyra
ancestor of: 10 Phaeacians

Phaedo
author: 5 Plato

Phaedra
father: 5 Minos
mother: 8 Pasiphae

sister: 7 Ariadne
husband: 7 Theseus
son: 6 Acamas 8 Demophon
stepson: 10 Hippolytus
loved: 10 Hippolytus
death by: 7 hanging, suicide

Phaenna
origin: 5 Greek 7 Spartan
member of: 6 Graces

Phaethon
father: 6 Helios
mother: 7 Clymene

phalanx 6 column, parade
9 formation 13 ranks and files

Phallus
image of: 9 male organ
symbol of: 9 fertility
carried in: 6 comedy
9 festivals
associated with: 3 Pan
6 Hermes 7 Demeter
8 Dionysus

phantasm 5 ghost, shade,
spook 6 mirage, spirit, vision
7 fantasy, figment, incubus,
phantom, specter 8 delusion,
illusion, succubus
10 apparition

Phantasus
origin: 5 Greek
god of: 6 dreams

phantom 5 dream, ghost 6 mirage, spirit, vision, wraith
7 chimera, specter 8 illusion,
phantasm 10 apparition
13 hallucination

Phantom, The
creator: 7 Lee Falk 8 Ray
Moore
nickname: 16 The Ghost
Who Walks
mask: 5 black
costume: 6 purple

Phantom of the Opera, The
director:
1925 version: 12 Rupert
Julian
1943 version: 11 Arthur
Lubin
cast:
1925 version: 9 Lon Chaney 11 Mary Philbin, Nor-
man Kerry
1943 version: 10 Hume
Cronyn, Jane Farrar, Nelson
Eddy 11 Claude Rains
12 Edgar Barrier 13 Susanna
Foster
setting: 10 Paris Opera

Phaon
occupation: 7 boatman
location: 8 Mitylene
given: 5 youth 6 beauty
given by: 9 Aphrodite

pharos 5 light 6 beacon, signal 7 seamark 10 lighthouse,
watchtower

phase 4 side, step, view 5 an-

gle, facet, guise, level, slant,
stage 6 aspect, degree, period
7 feature 8 attitude, juncture
9 condition, viewpoint 10 appearance 11 development
12 circumstance

pheasant
group of: 4 nest, nide

Phedre, Phaedra
author: 6 Racine
character: 6 Aricia 7 Theseus 10 Hippolytus

Phegeus
king of: 7 Psophis
son: 5 Axion 7 Temenus
daughter: 7 Arsinoe
purified: 8 Alcmaeon
ordered death of:
8 Alcmaeon

Phenix *see* 7 Phoenix

phenomenal 5 super 6 unique
7 amazing, unusual 8 singular,
superior, uncommon 9 fantastic, marvelous, unheard-of
10 incredible, miraculous, prodigious, remarkable, stupendous, surpassing
11 astonishing, exceptional,
outstanding, sensational, spectacular 12 overwhelming, unparalleled 13 extraordinary,
unprecedented

phenomenon 5 thing 6 marvel, rarity, wonder 7 episode,
miracle 8 incident, occasion
9 actuality, curiosity, exception, happening, nonpareil,
sensation 10 fact of life, occurrence, proceeding
11 contingency

Phereclus
also: 10 Harmonides
father: 6 Tecton
built: 5 ships

Pheres
king of: 6 Pherae
father: 8 Cretheus
mother: 4 Tyro
son: 7 Admetus, Idomene
daughter: 8 Periapis

Periphetes
epithet: 9 Corynetes

phial 4 vial 6 bottle, vessel
9 container

Phidias
born: 6 Athens, Greece
artwork: 4 Zeus 6 Amazon
13 Lemnian Athene (Athena
Lemnia) 15 Apollo Parno-
pios, Athena Parthenos,
Athena Promachos

Philadelphia
baseball team: 8 Phillies
basketball team: 13 Seventy-
sixers
bay: 8 Delaware
football team: 5 Stars
6 Eagles

founded/planned by: 4 Penn
hockey team: 6 Flyers
landmark: 6 US Mint 8 City
Hall 11 Liberty Bell
12 Christ Church, Congress
Hall 13 Franklin Field, Roosevelt Park 14 Betsy Ross
House, Carpenter's Hall
15 Gloria Dei Church, Veterans Stadium 16 Indepen-
dence Hall
means: 19 city of brotherly
love
museum: 5 Rodin 15 Fels
Planetarium 16 Barnes
Foundation 17 Franklin
Institute
river: 8 Delaware
10 Schuylkill
university: 4 Penn 6 Drexel,
Temple 9 Jefferson, St Joseph's 22 Curtis Institute of
Music

Philadelphia Story, The
director: 11 George Cukor
based on play by: 11 Philip
Barry
cast: 9 Cary Grant 10 Ruth
Hussey 12 James Stewart
16 Katharine Hepburn
Oscar for: 5 actor (Stewart)
remade as: 11 High Society

Philammon
father: 6 Apollo
mother: 6 Chione
half-brother: 9 Autolycus
son: 8 Thamyris
vocation: 8 musician

philanderer 3 rip 4 rake, wolf
5 flirt 6 lecher, tomcat, wanton 7 dallier, Don Juan, gallant, swinger, trifler 8 lothario,
lover boy, rakehell 9 adulterer,
libertine, womanizer 10 lady-
killer 11 woman-chaser

**philanthropic, philanthropi-
cal** 7 liberal 8 generous
9 bounteous 10 almsgiving, beneficent, benevolent, charitable, munificent
11 magnanimous 12 eleemosynary, humanitarian

philanthropist 5 donor, giver
8 do-gooder 9 almsgiver
11 contributor 12 humanitarian 13 Good Samaritan

philanthropy 6 bounty 7 charity 8 goodness 10 almsgiving,
generosity, liberality 11 beneficence, benevolence, munificence 13 unselfishness
14 charitableness, openhandedness 15 humanitarianism
16 largeheartedness 18 public-
spiritedness

Philaster
author: 30 Francis Beaumont
and John Fletcher

Philemon
friend: 4 Paul

Philippines

named for: 15 Philip II of Spain

capital/largest city: 6 Manila

others: 3 Iba 4 Agoa, Bogo, Cebu, Debu, Naga, Palo 5 Albay, Davao, Gapan, Iriga, Lanao, Laoag, Pasay, Vigan 6 Aparri, Baguio, Cavite, Ilagan, Iloilo, Tarlac 7 Bacolod, Basilan, Calapan, Dagupan, Legaspi 8 Batangas, Caloocan, Cotabato, Tacloban 9 Zamboanga 10 Cabanutuan, Dumaguette, Quezon City

school: 10 Santo Tomas 14 Ateneo de Manila

division: 4 Abra, Cebu 5 Aklan, Albay, Bohol, Capiz, Davao, Lanao, Leyte, Rizal, Samar 6 Agusan, Bataan, Cavite, Iloílo, Laguna, Quezon, Tarlac 7 Isabela, Lepanto, Surigao

measure: 4 loan 5 braza, catty, cavan, chupa, fardo, ganta, picul, punto 6 apatan, balita, lachsa, quinon 7 quilate 8 chinanta

monetary unit: 4 peso 6 conant, peseta 7 centavo

weight: 5 catty, picul 6 lachsa 7 quilate 8 chinanta

island: 4 Cebu, Cuyo, Jolo, Poro, Sulu 5 Batan, Bohol, Leyte, Luzon, Panay, Samar, Ticao 6 Culion, Lubang, Negros 7 Babuyan, Batanes, Bisayan, Masbate, Mindoro, Palawan, Paragua, Polillo, Visoyan 8 Mindanao 10 Corregidor, Marinduque

lake: 4 Taal 5 Lanao

mountain: 3 Iba 4 Mayo, Taal 5 Albay, Askja, Hibok, Mayon, Pulog 6 Pagsan 7 Banahao, Canlaon

highest point: 3 Apo

river: 4 Abra, Agno 5 Magat, Pasig 6 Agusan, Laoang 7 Cagayan 8 Mindanao, Pampanga

sea: 4 Sulu 5 Samar 7 Celebes, Pacific, Visayan 10 Philippine, South China

physical feature:

    bay: 6 Manila

    falls: 9 Pagsanjan 14 Maria Christina

    gulf: 4 Moro 5 Albay, Davao, Leyte, Ragay 8 Lingayen

    hot springs: 8 Los Banos

    national park: 12 Mayon Volcano

    ocean trench: 8 Mindanao

    peninsula: 6 Bataan

    storm: 6 bagyos 7 monsoon, typhoon

    volcano: 8 Pinatubo

people: 3 Ati, Eta, Ita, Tao 4 Aeta, Ifil, Moro, Sulu, Tino 5 Abaca, Aripa, Batak, Batan, Bicol, Bikol, Busao, Lutao, Mundo, Sinay, Tagal, Vicol, Yakan 6 Apayao, Baluga, Bilaan, Biscol, Bontoc, Bontok, Busaos, Ibanag, Ibilao, Ifugao, Igalot, Igorot, Illano, Isinai, Lutayo, Manabo, Manobo, Montes, Sambal, Tagala, Timaua, Timawa, Zambal 7 Bagoboo, Bisayan, Cagayan, Ilocano, Itanega, Malanoa, Mangyan, Naboloi, Negrito, Tagalog, Tirurai, Visayan 8 Arupaata, Babaylan, Bukidono, Filipino, Igorotte, Manguian, Pampanga 9 Arupaatta, Dulangane, Macajambo, Pampangao, Tinguiane 10 Magindanao, Pangasinan 11 Calalangane

    author: 5 Rizal

    explorer: 7 Legazpe 8 Magellan 10 Villalobos

    leader: 5 Ramos 6 Aquino, Marcos, Osmena, Quezon 9 Aguinaldo, Bonifacio, Macapagal, Magsaysay 11 Roxas y Acuna

language: 4 Moro 5 Bicol, Bikol 6 Ibanag 7 Cebuano, English, Ilocano, Spanish, Tagalog, Visayan 8 Filipino, Pilipino 9 Pampangan 10 Samar-Leyte 13 Bamboo-English

religion: 7 animism 9 Aglipayan 10 Protestant 13 Roman Catholic 15 Iglesia ni Kristo

place:

    church: 14 Saint Augustine

    esplanade: 6 Luneta

    fort: 4 Cota, Gota, Kota 5 Lotta 10 Corregidor

    president's palace: 10 Malacanang

    street: 7 Escolta

    US bases: 5 Clark 8 Subic Bay

    walled city: 10 Intramuros

feature:

    animal: 7 carabao, tamarau, tarsier 9 mouse deer

    bird: 7 creeper

    clothing: 4 saya 6 camisa 10 balintawak 12 mestiza terno 13 barong tagalog

    dance: 9 tinikling

    drama: 8 moro-moro

    guerrilla fighter: 3 huk

    musicians: 12 musikongbuho

    naval base: 6 Cavite

    song: 8 kundiman

    village: 8 barangay

food:

    dish: 3 poi 4 baha, sabu, taro 5 balut

    drink: 4 beno, vino 5 bubud 6 tampoy 7 pangasi

slave: 8 Onesimus
wife: 6 Baucis
entertained: 4 Hera, Zeus
became: 12 temple priest

Philip
hometown: 9 Bethsaida
disciple of: 5 Jesus

Philippines *see box*

philistine 5 yahoo **6** savage
7 Babbitt, lowbrow, prosaic
8 ignorant **9** barbarian, bourgeois, unrefined, untutored
10 conformist, uncultured, uneducated, uninformed, unlettered **11** commonplace
12 conventional, uncultivated
13 unenlightened **15** conven-
tionalist **16** anti-intellectual

Philistine city 4 Gath

Philius
epithet of: 4 Zeus
means: 8 friendly

Phillotson, Richard
character in: 14 Jude the
Obscure
author: 5 Hardy

Philoctetes
author: 9 Sophocles
character: 8 Heracles, Odysseus **11** Neoptolemus
inherits arms of: 8 Hercules
father: 5 Poeas, Poias
killed: 5 Paris

philodendron
varieties: 5 Dubia, giant
6 common **7** cut-leaf, red-
leaf **8** blushing **9** black-gold,
heart-leaf, horsehead, spade-
leaf, split-leaf **10** fiddle-leaf,
variegated, velvet-leaf
11 leather-leaf

Philoetius
cowherd of: 8 Odysseus

Philomela
position: 8 princess
realm: 6 Athens
father: 7 Pandion
sister: 6 Procne
brother-in-law: 6 Tereus
raped by: 6 Tereus
transformed into: 7 swallow
11 nightingale

Philomelides
king of: 6 Lesbos
defeated by: 8 Odysseus

Philonome *see* **9** Phylonome

philosopher/theologian *see*
box

Philosopher's Pupil, The
author: 11 Iris Murdoch

philosophic, philosophical
4 calm **5** quiet, stoic **6** serene
7 erudite, learned, logical, patient, stoical **8** abstract, composed, rational, resigned,

tranquil **9** impassive, judicious,
sagacious, unexcited, unruffled **10** complacent, fatalistic,
reasonable, theorizing,
thoughtful **11** imperturbed,
theoretical, unemotional
14 self-restrained

philosophy 4 calm, view
5 ideas, logic **6** reason **7** beliefs, opinion, thought **8** doctrine, fatalism, patience,
serenity, stoicism, thinking
9 basic idea, composure, es-
thetics, principle, reasoning,
restraint, viewpoint **10** conception, theorizing **11** complacency, convictions,
forbearance, impassivity, metaphysics, rationalism,
resignation
means: 12 love of wisdom
branch: 6 ethics **8** ontology
10 aesthetics **11** metaphysics **12** epistemology

term: 8 noumenon **9** causal-
ity, dialectic, solipsism
school of: 7 Sophism **8** idealism, Milesian, Stoicism
9 Epicurean, pantheism, Pla-
tonism **10** empiricism, prag-
matism, Skepticism
11 rationalism **12** Aristotelian, neoplatonism **13** Phe-
nomenology, scholasticism
14 existentialism **17** logical
positivism

Phil Silvers Show, The
character: 6 Fender **7** Col
Hall, Henshaw **8** Doberman
9 Sgt Ritzik **12** Sgt Joan Hogan **13** Rocco Barbella, Sgt
Ernie Bilko
cast: 8 Joe E Ross, Paul
Ford **10** Alan Melvin, Her-
bie Faye **13** Harvey Lembeck **15** Elisabeth Fraser,
Maurice Gosfield

---

philosopher/theologian 4 sage **6** savant **7** thinker, wise
man **8** logician, reasoner **9** theorizer **11** rationalist, truth
seeker **12** dialectician **13** metaphysician
Alsatian: 10 Schweitzer
American: 4 Eddy **5** Dewey, James, Royce, Smith, Young
6 Mather, Peirce **7** Edwards, Niebuhr, Russell, Tillich
8 Williams **9** McPherson **14** Elijah Muhammad
Austrian: 12 Wittgenstein
British: 3 Fox **4** Hume, Inge, Knox, More, Owen **5** Bacon,
Burke, Locke, Moore **6** Biddle, Cotton, Hobbes, Huxley,
Newman, Wesley **7** Bentham, Bradley, Carlyle, Cranmer,
Russell, Spencer **8** Berkeley, Wycliffe **9** Whitehead
13 Thomas a Becket **14** William of Occam
Chinese: 6 Lao-tzu **9** Confucius
Christian: 6 Calvin, Luther, Origen, St Paul **7** Abelard **8** St
Anselm **9** St Patrick **10** Duns Scotus, St Benedict **11** St
Augustine **14** William of Occam **15** St Thomas Aquinas
16 St Albertus Magnus
Czech: 3 Hus
Danish: 11 Kierkegaard
Dutch: 7 Erasmus, Spinoza
El Salvadorian: 9 Masferrer
French: 5 Comte **6** Calvin, Pascal, Sartre **7** Abelard, Berg-
son, Diderot **8** Maritain, Rousseau, Voltaire **9** Descartes,
Levy-Bruhl, Montaigne **11** Montesquieu
German: 4 Kant, Marx **5** Buber, Hegel **6** Boehme, Fichte,
Herder, Luther **7** Husserl, Jaspers, Leibniz **9** Heidegger,
Nietzsche, Schelling **10** Muhlenberg **11** Melanchthon
12 Schopenhauer **13** Thomas a Kempis **14** Schleiermacher
Greek: 5 Plato **6** St Paul, Thales **7** Socrates **9** Aristotle
10 Anaxagoras, Anaximenes, Heraclitus, Parmenides, Py-
thagoras **11** Anaximander
Indian: 6 Buddha **16** Siddharta Gautama
Islamic: 7 al Kindi **8** al-Farabi, Averroes, Avicenna **9** al
Ghazali **10** Ibn Khaldun
Italian: 5 Bruno **7** Aquinas, Mazzini **10** St Benedict, Zeno
of Elea **17** St Francis of Assisi
Japanese: 6 Suzuki
Jewish: 7 Spinoza **10** Maimonides
Latin: 8 Plotinus **11** St Augustine
Spanish: 8 Averroes **10** Maimonides **13** Ortega y Gasset
16 Ignatius of Loyola
Swedish: 10 Swedenborg
Swiss: 7 Zwingli

setting: 6 Kansas 10 Fort
Baxter

Philyra
  father: 7 Oceanus
  mother: 6 Tethys
  mother of: 6 Chiron
  changed into: 10 linden
  tree

Phlegethon
  also: 14 Pyriphlegethon
  form: 5 river
  location: 10 underworld

phlegmatic 4 calm, cool, dull
6 serene 7 languid, passive,
stoical 8 listless, sluggish, tranquil 9 apathetic, impassive, lethargic, unfeeling
10 nonchalant, spiritless
11 indifferent, insensitive, unconcerned, unemotional, unexcitable 12 unresponsive
13 imperturbable, unimpassioned 15 undemonstrative

Phlegyas
  king of: 8 Lapithae
  condemned: 6 Apollo

Phlias
  father: 8 Dionysus
  member of: 9 Argonauts

phlox
  varieties: 4 blue, fall, moss,
  sand, star 6 annual, smooth
  7 prickly 8 creeping, drummond, mountain, trailing
  9 perennial, sword-leaf,
  thick-leaf 15 summer
  perennial

Phnom-Penh
  airport: 10 Pochentong
  also: 8 Pnom Penh
  capital of: 8 Cambodia
  9 Kampuchea
  pagoda: 12 Preah Morokot
  river: 6 Mekong 8 Tonle Sap

Phobetor
  epithet of: 6 Icelus
  means: 9 terrifier

phobia *see box*

Phobos
  also: 6 Phobus
  father: 4 Ares

Phocus
  father: 6 Aeacus 8 Ornytion
  mother: 8 Psamathe
  half-brother: 6 Peleus
  7 Telamon
  wife: 7 Antiope
  killed by: 7 Telamon
  burial place: 8 Tithorea

Phoebe
  member of: 6 Titans
  father: 6 Uranus
  mother: 4 Gaea
  sister: 6 Themis
  daughter: 4 Leto 7 Asteria
  identified with: 4 moon
  corresponds to: 5 Diana
  7 Artemis

Phoebus *see* 6 Apollo

Phoenicia *see* 7 Lebanon

Phoenician Mythology
  god of agriculture/earth:
  5 Dagon
    corresponds to Mesopota-
    mian: 5 Dagan
  bird: 6 Phenix 7 Phoenix
  8 Phoeonix
  goddess of fertility/repro-
  duction: 7 Astarte

Phoenissae (The Phoenician
Maidens)
  author: 9 Euripides
  character: 5 Creon 7 Jocasta,
  Oedipus 8 Adrastus, Antigone, Eteocles, Tiresias
  9 Polynices 10 Menoikieus

Phoenix
  basketball team: 4 Suns
  capital of: 7 Arizona
  event: 5 rodeo
  feature: 10 Papago Park
  22 Desert Botanical
  Gardens
  football team: 9 Wranglers
  river: 4 Salt

Phoenix, Phoeonix
  also: 6 Phenix
  origin: 10 Phoenician
  form: 4 bird
  gift: 11 immortality
  king of: 9 Dolopians
  father: 7 Amyntor
  mother: 8 Cleobule
  brother: 6 Cadmus
  sister: 6 Europa
  foster son: 8 Achilles
  ancestor of: 11 Phoenicians

Pholus
  form: 7 centaur
  guarded: 4 wine
  wine a gift from: 8 Dionysus

phonograph 4 hi-fi 5 phono
6 stereo 8 Victrola 9 turntable
10 gramophone 12 record
player

phonophobia
  fear of: 13 speaking aloud

phony, phoney 4 fake, hoax,
mock, sham 5 bogus, false,
fraud, trick 6 forged, pseudo,
unreal, untrue 7 forgery
8 specious, spurious 9 decep-

---

phobia 5 dread 6 horror, terror 7 bugaboo, bugbear 8 aversion, loathing 12 apprehension 16 unreasonable fear
19 overwhelming anxiety
  fear of animals: 9 zoophobia
  fear of birds: 13 ornithophobia
  fear of blushing: 13 erythrophobia
  fear of bridges: 13 gephyrophobia
  fear of cats: 10 gatophobia 12 aelurophobia, ailurophobia
  fear of closed/confined spaces: 14 claustrophobia
  fear of crowds: 11 ochlophobia
  fear of darkness/the dark of night: 11 nyctophobia
  fear of death: 13 thanatophobia
  fear of death/dead bodies: 11 necrophobia
  fear of dirt: 10 mysophobia
  fear of disease: 11 pathophobia
  fear of fire: 10 pyrophobia
  fear of flowers: 11 anthophobia
  fear of flying: 10 aerophobia
  fear of germs: 11 mikrophobia
  fear of hair: 12 trichophobia
  fear of heights: 10 acrophobia
  fear of insanity: 13 dementophobia
  fear of lightning: 11 astraphobia
  fear of men: 11 androphobia
  fear of mice: 10 murophobia
  fear of numbers: 12 numerophobia
  fear of open spaces: 11 agoraphobia
  fear of pain: 10 algophobia
  fear of people: 12 anthrophobia
  fear of reptiles: 13 herpetophobia
  fear of snakes: 13 ophidiophobia
  fear of speaking aloud: 11 phonophobia
  fear of spiders: 13 arachnophobia
  fear of strangers: 10 xenophobia
  fear of thunder: 12 brontophobia
  fear of the number thirteen: 17 triskaidekaphobia
  fear of vehicles/driving: 11 amaxophobia
  fear of water: 10 aquaphobia 11 hydrophobia
  fear of women: 10 gynophobia

tive, imitation, pretended, synthetic **10** artificial, fraudulent, not genuine **11** counterfeit, make-believe, unauthentic

Phorbas
son of: **8** Lapithes
dispelled: **6** plague
plague of: **8** serpents
leader of: **4** Troy
allies of: **9** Phygians
killed by: **4** Ajax
form: **5** boxer
killed: **8** pilgrims
killed by: **6** Apollo

Phorcids
father: **7** Phorcys
mother: **4** Ceto

Phorcys
god of: **3** sea
sister: **4** Ceto
children: **5** Ladon **6** Graiae
7 Echidna, Gorgons
8 Phorcids
harbor in: **6** Ithaca

Phormio
author: **7** Terence

phosphorus
chemical symbol: **1** P

photograph **3** pic **4** film, snap
5 image, print, shoot, still
6 candid, glossy **7** mugshot,
picture, tintype **8** likeness, portrait, snapshot **12** daguerrotype
bath: **5** fixer, toner **7** reducer **9** developer
book: **5** album

photographer
American: **4** Haas, Hine,
Penn, Riis, Rose, Tice
5 (Ansel) Adams, Annan,
Arbus, Brady, Evans, Hawes,
Lange, Lynes, Smith, White
6 Avedon, Coburn, Eakins,
Man Ray, Strand, Turner,
Weston **7** Burrows, Eastman,
Gardner, Jackson, Watkins
8 Bogardus, Davidson,
Steichen **9** Muybridge,
O'Sullivan, Rothstein, Stieglitz **10** Cunningham, Southworth **11** Bourke-White, Eisenstaedt, Turberville
13 Watson-Schutze
British: **5** Evans, Frith **6** Bailey, Beaton, Fenton, Mayall,
Talbot **7** Cameron **8** Brewster, Robinson **9** Rejlander
10 MacPherson
French: **5** Marey, Nadar
6 Baldus, DuCamp, Le Secq,
Newton, Niepce **7** Lumiere
8 Daguerre **12** Sabatier-Blot
14 Cartier-Bresson
German: **4** Hoch **5** Ernst
7 Hausman **8** Stelzner
13 Renger-Patzsch
Hungarian: **7** Kertesz **10** Moholy-Nagy
Japanese: **4** Ikko

Scottish: **4** Hill **7** Adamson
Spanish: **7** Picabia

photostat **4** copy **7** replica
9 duplicate, facsimile
12 reproduction

phrase **3** put, say **4** word
5 couch, idiom, maxim, state,
utter, voice, words **6** cliche,
dictum, impart, remark, saying, truism **7** declare, express,
proverb **8** aphorism, banality,
locution **9** enunciate, find
words, platitude, utterance,
verbalize, word group **10** articulate, expression
11 communicate

phraseology **5** style **7** diction,
wording **13** choice of words
18 manner of expression

Phrixus
father: **7** Athamas
mother: **7** Nephele
stepmother: **3** Ino
sister: **5** Helle
wife: **9** Chalciope
son: **5** Argus, Melas **8** Phrontis **10** Cytissorus

Phrontis
father: **7** Phrixus
mother: **9** Chalciope
brother: **5** Argus, Melus
10 Cytissorus
husband: **8** Panthous

Phthia
mentioned in: **5** Iliad
concubine of: **7** Amyntor
seduced by: **7** Phoenix
son: **5** Dorus **8** Laodocus
10 Polypoetes

Phyleus
king of: **6** Ephyra
father: **6** Auglas
wife: **8** Timandra
children: **5** Meges
10 Astyocheia

Phyllis
father: **8** Phylleus
husband: **8** Demophon
loved: **6** Acamas

Phylomache
son: **7** Acastus
daughter: **8** Alcestis

Phylonome
also: **9** Philonome
husband: **6** Cycnus
stepson: **5** Tenes

physical **4** real **5** human, solid
6 actual, animal, bodily, carnal, living **7** fleshly, natural,
sensual **8** apparent, concrete,
corporal, existent, existing, external, material, palpable, tangible **9** corporeal, essential, of
the body **11** substantive

physical checkup **4** exam
8 physical **11** examination
19 physical examination

physical condition **5** shape
7 fitness, stamina
12 constitution

physical disorder **6** malady
7 ailment, disease, illness
8 sickness **9** ill health,
infirmity

physical training **3** gym
6 sports **8** exercise **9** athletics,
shaping up **10** gymnastics,
working out **12** conditioning

physician **2** GP, MD **3** doc
5 medic **6** doctor, medico
7 surgeon **8** sawbones **10** specialist **11** medicine man, pill
peddler **13** medical doctor
Alsatian: **10** Schweitzer
American: **4** Long, Rush,
Salk **5** Sabin **6** Dooley, Gorgas **7** Huggins, Whipple
8 Williams **9** Blackwell
11 Landsteiner
British: **5** Paget **6** Adrian,
Harvey, Jenner, Lister
Canadian: **4** Best **7** Banting
Dutch: **7** Eijkman
French: **7** Charcot
German: **6** Mesmer **7** Fechner, Virchow
10 Blumenbach
Greek: **10** Herophilus
11 Hippocrates
12 Erasistratus
Italian: **8** Malpighi
Russian: **6** Pavlov
Scottish: **4** Lind
South African: **7** Barnard

**Physician to Olympian
gods** **5** Paeon **6** Apollo

physicist
American: **4** Hess, Rabi
5 Bethe, Gamow, Pauli, Yalow **6** Bekesy, Teller,
Townes, Watson **7** Richter,
Seaborg **8** Einstein, Lawrence, Van Allen **9** Michelson **11** Chamberlain,
Oppenheimer
Austrian: **7** Doppler,
Meitner
British: **4** Born **5** Bragg,
Hooke, Joule **6** Kelvin
7 Gilbert, Thomson **8** Chadwick, Rayleigh **9** Cockcroft
10 Rutherford
Danish: **4** Bohr **7** Oersted
Dutch: **6** Zeeman **7** Lorentz
French: **6** Ampere **7** Broglie,
Coulomb, Fresnel **8** Foucault **9** Becquerel **11** Joliot-Curie
German: **3** Ohm **5** Hertz,
Stark **6** Planck **7** Rontgen,
Wegener **8** Humboldt,
Roentgen **9** Kirchhoff, Mossbauer **10** Fahrenheit,
Fraunhofer
Indian: **5** Raman
Irish: **7** Tyndall **10** Fitzgerald
Italian: **5** Fermi

Russian: 6 Landau **8** Cerenkov, Sakharov
Scottish: 7 Rankine

Physics
author: **9** Aristotle

physiognomy 4 face **5** shape **6** facade, visage **7** contour, outline, profile **8** features **10** silhouette **11** countenance

physiology
founder: **13** William Harvey
study of: **8** function
study of nervous sytem: **15** neurophysiology

Phytalus
hospitable to: **7** Demeter
given: **7** fig tree

Phyteus
epithet of: **6** Apollo

pianissimo
music: **8** very soft
abbreviation: **2** pp

pianist 4 Hess **5** Liszt, Watts **6** Busoni, Chopin, Gilels, Serkin **7** Cliburn, Hofmann, Richter **8** Backhaus, Horowitz, Schnabel, Schumann, Thalberg, von Bulow **9** Barenboim, Casadesus, Gieseking **10** Gottschalk, Rubinstein **12** Rachmaninoff

piano
invented by: **10** Cristofori
player piano: **9** Fourneaux

piano
music: **4** soft
abbreviation: **1** p

piazza 5 patio, porch **6** square **7** gallery, portico, veranda

Piazzi, Giuseppe
field: **9** astronomy
nationality: **7** Italian
discovered: **5** Ceres
catalogued: **5** stars

picaresque 6 daring **7** raffish, roguish, waggish **8** devilish, prankish, rascally, scampish **9** foolhardy **10** roistering **13** adventuresome **14** mischiefloving

Picasso, Pablo
born: **5** Spain **6** Malaga
artwork: **4** Dove **6** Guitar, Jester **7** Ma Jolie, Rooster, She-Goat **8** Guernica **9** Bull's Head, Notre Dame **11** Seated Woman, Woman Diving **12** Head of a Woman **13** Seated Bathers **14** Minotauromachy, Mother and Child, Women of Algiers **15** Ambroise Vollard, Man Holding a Lamb, The Charnel-House, The Large Profile, The Three Dancers **16** Nude in an Armchair **17** Girl Before a Mirror, The

Glass of Absinth, The Three Musicians **20** Still Life with a Candle **22** Les Demoiselles d'Avignon **23** Portrait of Gertrude Stein

picayune, picayunish 5 dinky, petty, small **6** flimsy, little, measly, paltry, slight **7** trivial **8** niggling, nugatory, piddling, trifling **11** unimportant **13** insignificant **14** inconsiderable **15** inconsequential

Piccini, Nicola (Piccinni, Niccola)
born: **4** Bari **5** Italy
composer of: **5** Didon **6** Roland **11** The Good Girl **15** La buona figliola **18** Iphigenie en Tauride

pick 3 cut **4** crop **5** cream, elect, elite, pluck, prize **6** choice, choose, detach, flower, gather, opt for, select **7** collect, fix upon, harvest, pull off, pull out, the best **9** single out **10** decide upon, favored one, preference, settle upon

picket 4 pale, post **5** fence, go out, guard, hem in, pen in, stake, watch **6** corral, paling, patrol, sentry, shut in, strike, tether, wall in **7** boycott, enclose, hedge in, lookout, striker, upright, walk out **8** blockade, palisade, restrain, restrict, sentinel **9** blockader, boycotter, protester, restraint, stanchion

picketing 5 march **7** protest **8** marching, on strike, striking **10** protesting **12** protest march **13** demonstrating, demonstration

Pickett, George E
served in: **8** Civil War **10** Mexican War
side: **11** Confederate
battle: **10** Gettysburg
famous for: **6** charge

Pickford, Mary
real name: **15** Gladys Mary Smith
nickname: **18** America's Sweetheart
born: **6** Canada **7** Toronto
husband: **16** Douglas Fairbanks **18** Charles Buddy Rogers
roles: **4** Rags **8** Coquette (Oscar) **9** Pollyanna **19** The Taming of the Shrew **21** The Poor Little Rich Girl **23** Rebecca of Sunnybrook Farm
home: **8** Pickfair
memoirs: **17** Sunshine and Shadow
formed: **13** United Artists
partners: **10** D W Griffith

14 Charlie Chaplin **16** Douglas Fairbanks

pickings 4 loot **5** booty **6** scraps, spoils **7** plunder, takings **9** leftovers

pickle 3 fix, jam **4** corn, dill, mess, sour **6** crisis, plight, scrape **7** dilemma, gherkin, mustard **8** cucumber, hot water, quandary **9** emergency, extremity, tight spot **10** difficulty, kosher dill, pretty pass **11** predicament **14** bread-and-butter

pickled 5 drunk **6** soused **8** powdered

pick on 5 annoy, bully **6** harass, jibe at **7** torment **8** browbeat

pick out 3 see **4** espy **6** choose, descry, detect, notice, select **7** discern, make out **8** perceive **12** catch sight of

pickup 4 rise **5** boost, truck **7** advance **9** impromptu **11** improvement **12** acceleration

pick up 3 buy, get **6** gather, lift up, look up, obtain, secure **7** acquire, develop, improve, procure **8** contract, retrieve **9** cultivate, get better

Pickwick Papers
author: **14** Charles Dickens
character: **6** Perker, Tupman, Wardle, Winkle **9** Sam Weller, Snodgrass **10** Mrs Bardell **11** Emily Wardle **12** Alfred Jingle, Rachel Wardle **13** Arabella Allen

picky 5 fussy **6** choosy **7** finicky **10** fastidious, particular **11** persnickety **14** discriminating

Picrochole
character in: **22** Gargantua and Pantagruel
author: **8** Rabelais

picture 3 see **4** copy, draw, film **5** fancy, flick, image, model, movie, paint, photo, study **6** cinema, depict, double, mirror, sketch **7** believe, drawing, essence, etching, feature, imagine, paragon, portray, tintype **8** envision, likeness, painting, snapshot **9** delineate, duplicate, facsimile, portrayal, represent **10** call to mind, carbon copy, conceive of, dead ringer, embodiment, illustrate, photograph **11** delineation **12** illustration, see in the mind **13** daguerreotype, motion picture, moving picture, spitting image **14** representation **15** exemplification, personification

Picture of Dorian Gray, The
author: **10** Oscar Wilde
character: **9** James Vane, Sibyl Vane **13** Basil Hallward **15** Lord Henry Wotton

picturesque 6 exotic, quaint **7** unusual **8** artistic, charming, colorful, striking **9** beautiful, pictorial **10** attractive **11** distinctive, imaginative, interesting

Picumnus
also: **8** Pilumnus
origin: **5** Roman
god of: **9** fertility **11** agriculture

Picus
origin: **5** Roman **7** Italian
god of: **11** agriculture
father: **6** Saturn
associated with: **10** woodpecker
loved by: **5** Circe
changed into: **10** woodpecker
son: **6** Faunus

piddling 4 puny **5** petty, small **6** flimsy, little, measly, modest, paltry, skimpy, slight **7** trivial **8** picayune, trifling **9** niggardly **11** unimportant **13** insignificant **15** inconsequential

pie 4 tart **6** pastry, quiche **7** cobbler, dessert **8** turnover
liner: **5** crust, shell
top: **7** lattice **8** meringue

piebald 6 motley **7** dappled, flecked, mottled, spotted **8** many-hued, speckled **10** variegated **11** many-colored, varicolored **12** multicolored, parti-colored

piece 3 bit, cut, fix, pat **4** blob, case, hunk, item, lump, mend, part, play, unit, work **5** chunk, drama, essay, patch, scrap, shard, share, shred, slice, story, study, thing **6** amount, entity, length, member, paring, repair, review, sample, sketch, sliver, swatch **7** article, cutting, example, patch up, portion, restore, section, segment **8** creation, division, fraction, fragment, instance, quantity, specimen **9** component, selection **11** composition

piece de resistance 13 principal dish **14** principal event

piece goods 5 cloth, goods **6** fabric **8** dry goods, material **9** yard goods

piecemeal 9 gradually **10** fragmented, one at a time **14** little by little

piece of the action 3 cut, fee **5** piece **7** portion, rake-off **10** commission, percentage

pied 6 motley **7** checked, dappled, mottled, piebald **8** colorful **9** checkered **10** variegated **11** many-colored **12** parti-colored

pied-a-terre 17 temporary dwelling
literally: **12** foot on ground

Pied Piper of Hamlin, The
author: **14** Robert Browning

Pielus
father: **11** Neoptelemus
mother: **10** Andromache

pier 4 anta, dock, mole, quay, slip **5** jetty, levee, wharf **6** pillar **7** landing, support **10** breakwater

pierce 3 cut **4** hurt, pain, stab **5** drill, lance, prick, spear, spike, stick, sting, wound **6** grieve, impale **7** affront **8** distress, puncture **9** penetrate, perforate **10** cut through, run through

Pierce, Franklin see box

piercing 3 raw **4** keen, loud **5** angry, cruel, sharp **6** biting, bitter, fierce, shrill **7** caustic, cutting, furious, grating, hurtful, intense, painful, probing **8** strident **9** agonizing, deafening, searching, shrieking, torturous **10** screeching **11** penetrating **12** earsplitting, excruciating **13** ear-shattering

Pierian
pertains to: **5** Muses

Pierian Spring
form: **8** fountain

Pierides see 5 Muses

Pierce, Franklin
nickname: **29** Young Hickory of the Granite Hills
presidential rank: **10** fourteenth
party: **8** Democrat
state represented: **2** NH
defeated: **4** (John Parker) Hale **5** (Winfield) Scott
vice president: **4** (William Rufus Devane) King (died in office)
cabinet:
state: **5** (William Learned) Marcy
treasury: **7** (James) Guthrie
war: **5** (Jefferson) Davis
attorney general: **7** (Caleb) Cushing
navy: **6** (James Cochran) Dobbin
postmaster general: **8** (James) Campbell
interior: **10** (Robert) McClelland
born: **14** Hillsborough (Hillsboro) NH
died/buried: **9** Concord NH
education:
Academy: **7** Hancock **11** Francestown
College: **7** Bowdoin
studied: **3** law
religion: **12** Episcopalian
political career: **8** US Senate **16** state legislature **24** US House of Representatives
civilian career: **6** lawyer
military service: **6** US Army **10** Mexican War **16** brigadier general
notable events of lifetime/term:
Act: **6** Tariff (of 1857)
bill: **14** Kansas-Nebraska
civil war in: **6** Kansas
first US: **10** World's Fair
Manifesto: **6** Ostend
Purchase: **7** Gadsden
treaty of: **8** Kanagawa
father: **8** Benjamin
mother: **4** Anna (Kendrick)
siblings: **5** Henry, Nancy **7** Charles, Harriet **9** Charlotte **12** John Sullivan **16** Benjamin Kendrick
half sister: **9** Elizabeth
wife: **4** Jane (Means Appleton)
children: **8** Benjamin, Franklin **11** Frank Robert

Piero della Francesca (Piero dei Franceschi)
  born: 5 Italy **16** Borgo San Sepolcro
  artwork: 12 Duke of Urbino **15** The Resurrection **18** Federigo and His Wife **19** St John the Evangelist **20** Flagellation of Christ **23** The Compassionate Madonna, The Legend of the True Cross, The Old Age and Death of Adam **24** The History of the True Cross **45** The Madonna and Saints with Frederigo da Montefeltro

Pierre
  author: 14 Herman Melville

Piers Plowman
  author: 15 William Langland

Pietas
  personifies: 17 familial affection

piety 7 loyalty, respect **8** devotion, humility **9** godliness, piousness, reverence **10** devoutness **11** dutifulness, religiosity **13** religiousness

pig 3 hog **5** piggy, porky, swine **6** porker **7** glutton, guzzler **8** gourmand **9** chowhound **11** gormandizer
  male: 4 boar
  female: 3 sow
  young: 5 shoat **6** piglet **11** suckling pig

pigeon
  young: 5 squab **8** squeaker

pigeonhole 4 rank, rate, type **5** brand, cubby, group, label, niche **8** category, classify **9** cubbyhole **10** categorize **11** compartment

pigheaded 6 dogged, mulish **7** willful **8** obdurate, perverse, stubborn **9** insistent, obstinate, unbending **10** bullheaded, inflexible, refractory, unyielding **11** opinionated, wrongheaded

Piglet
  character in: 13 Winnie-the-Pooh
  author: 5 Milne

pigment 3 dye **4** tint **5** color **8** coloring, dyestuff **14** coloring matter

pigmentation 5 color **9** skin color **10** coloration

pigtail 5 braid, plait, queue **8** ponytail

pike 4 bill **5** lance, spear, spike **6** poleax **7** assegai, freeway, halberd, harpoon, highway, javelin, parkway, thruway **8** autobahn, hard

road, speedway, toll road, turnpike **10** expressway, interstate, throughway **12** superhighway
  British: 12 King's Highway **13** Queen's highway
  German: 8 autobahn

piker 5 miser **7** niggard, trifler **8** tightwad **9** skinflint **10** cheapskate, pinchpenny **12** penny pincher

Pilar
  character in: 19 For Whom the Bell Tolls
  author: 9 Hemingway

pilaster 4 pier **6** column, pillar **7** support, upright **8** baluster

pile 3 nap **4** heap, mass, pier, post, shag, warp **5** amass, batch, fluff, grain, hoard, mound, plush, stack, store **6** fleece, gather, piling, pillar **7** collect, pyramid, support, surface, upright **8** assemble, quantity **9** abundance, amassment, profusion, stanchion **10** accumulate, assortment, collection, foundation **11** agglomerate, aggregation, fibrousness **12** accumulation

pile up 4 bank, heap **5** amass, hoard, mound, stack **7** collect **10** accumulate

pile-up 3 jam, mob **4** mass **5** snarl **8** crowding, gridlock **10** bottleneck, congestion **11** obstruction **12** overcrowding

pilfer 3 cop, rob **4** hook, lift **5** boost, filch, heist, pinch, steal, swipe **6** finger, pirate, snitch, thieve **7** purloin **8** shoplift **10** plagiarize

pilferer 5 thief **6** robber **7** burglar **10** shoplifter, sneak thief

pilgrim, Pilgrim 4 haji **5** exile, hadji **6** palmer **7** pioneer, Puritan, settler **8** newcomer, traveler, wanderer, wayfarer **9** foreigner
  father: 5 Alden
  founder: 10 Separatist
  interpreter: 7 Squanto
  leader: 8 Standish
  protector: 7 Templar
  ship: 9 Mayflower, Speedwell

Pilgrim, Billy
  character in: 18 Slaughterhouse Five
  author: 8 Vonnegut

pilgrimage 4 hadj, trek **6** ramble, roving, voyage **7** journey, roaming, sojourn **8** long trip **9** excursion, wandering **13** peregrination

Pilgrim's Progress, The
  author: 10 John Bunyan

character: 7 Despair, Hopeful **8** Apollyon, Faithful **9** Christian, Ignorance **10** Evangelist **14** Worldly Wiseman

pill 3 rob **4** ball, pell **5** bolus **6** bullet, pellet, tablet, pilule **7** capsule **8** medicine **9** cigarette

pillage 3 rob **4** loot, raid, sack **5** booty, rifle, strip **6** fleece, maraud, piracy, ravage, spoils **7** despoil, looting, plunder, robbery **9** filchings **10** plundering

pillager 6 looter, vandal **7** brigand **9** despoiler, plunderer

pillar 3 VIP **4** pile, post, rock **5** shaft, wheel **6** column, piling **7** obelisk, support, upright **8** champion, mainstay, pilaster, somebody **9** colonnade, stanchion

Pillars of Society, The
  author: 11 Henrik Ibsen

pillow 3 pad **7** bolster, cushion **8** headrest

pilot 4 lead **5** flyer, guide, steer **6** airman, direct, escort, fly-boy, handle, leader, manage **7** aviator, birdman, conduct, control **8** aeronaut, coxswain, helmsman, navigate, wheelman **9** accompany, sky jockey, steersman

Pilot, The
  author: 19 James Fenimore Cooper

Pima (Aatam, Pima Alto)
  language family: 10 Uto-Aztekan
  location: 7 Arizona
  related to: 6 Papago
  descendants of: 7 Hohokam

Pima Alto *see* **4** Pima

Piman
  tribe: 6 Papago

pin 4 bind, clip, tine **5** affix, badge, clasp, dowel, medal, prong **6** brooch, fasten, pinion, secure, skewer **8** hold down, hold fast, restrain **10** decoration
  type: 3 hat **4** push **5** stick, thole **6** breast, common, diaper, safety **8** straight

pincer 4 claw **5** chela

pinch 3 bit, cop, jam, jot, nab, nip **4** bust, crib, grab, iota, lift, mite, pain, snip, spot **5** catch, cramp, crimp, crush, filch, run in, speck, steal, swipe, trace, trial, tweak **6** arrest, clutch, collar, crisis, misery, ordeal, pickle, plight, snatch, snitch, strait, tittle

7 capture, purloin, squeeze, tighten **8** compress, exigency, hardship **9** apprehend, emergency **10** affliction, difficulty, discomfort **11** predicament

Pinch, Tom
  character in: **16** Martin Chuzzlewit
  author: **7** Dickens

pinch hitter 5 proxy **7** stand-in **9** alternate **10** substitute

pinchpenny 5 miser **6** frugal, stingy **7** niggard, prudent, thrifty
  Dickensian: **7** Scrooge

Pindar
  author of: **4** Odes **8** Epinicea

pine 3 die, ebb **4** flag, long, sigh, wilt **5** covet, crave, droop, yearn **6** desire, expire, hanker, weaken, wither **7** decline, dwindle, pant for **8** languish **9** hunger for, waste away **11** have a yen for, thirst after **12** fail in health

pine *see* **box**

Pine Tree State
  nickname of: **5** Maine

pin hope on 6 bank on **7** count on, long for, wish for **8** aspire to, yearn for **10** anticipate

pink 8 Dianthus
  varieties: **3** Sea **4** fire, moss, pine, rose, wild **5** cameo, clove, dairy, grass, marsh,

swamp **6** button, ground, indian, Kirtle, maiden **7** cheddar, cottage, cushion, Mullein, rainbow **8** Childing, Deptford, election **11** clusterhead **13** fringed indian, spottle kirtle **16** California indian

pinnacle 3 cap, top **4** acme, apex, peak **5** crest, crown, spire, tower **6** belfry, height, summit, tiptop, vertex, zenith **7** steeple **9** bell tower, campanile

pinochle
  also known as: **7** binocle, pinocle **8** penuchle
  derived from: **7** bezique
  points/game: **11** one thousand

pinpoint 3 dot, jot **4** iota, spot **5** speck **6** detail **8** home in on, localize, zero in on **12** characterize

pint
  abbreviation of: **2** pt

pinxit 11 he painted it **12** she painted it

pioneer 5 found, start **6** create, father, herald, invent, leader **7** develop, founder **8** colonist, discover, explorer **9** be a leader, developer, establish, harbinger, innovator, precursor **10** antecedent, forerunner, lead the way, pathfinder, show the way **11** establisher, predecessor, trailblazer **12** first

settler, frontiersman **13** blaze the trail **14** early immigrant, founding father
  Hebrew: **6** halutz **7** chalutz

Pioneers, The
  author: **19** James Fenimore Cooper
  character: **10** Indian John **11** Judge Temple, Natty Bumppo **13** Oliver Edwards **14** Hiram Doolittle **15** Elizabeth Temple

pious 4 holy **5** godly **6** devout, divine **7** sainted, saintly **8** faithful, reverent, unctuous **9** dedicated, insincere, pietistic, religious, spiritual **10** worshipful **11** reverential **12** hypocritical **13** rationalizing, sanctimonious, self-righteous **14** holier-than-thou

Pip
  character in: **17** Great Expectations
  author: **7** Dickens

pipe 4 duct, main, peep, sing, tube **5** cheep, chirp, trill, tweet **6** warble **7** conduit, twitter, whistle **8** conveyor **9** conductor **10** play a flute **12** play a bagpipe

Pippa Passes
  author: **14** Robert Browning

piquant 3 hot **4** acid, racy **5** peppy, salty, sharp, spicy, tangy, zesty **6** biting, bitter, bright, clever, lively, savory **7** mordant, peppery, pungent, rousing **8** animated, incisive, piercing, spirited, stinging, vigorous **9** sparkling, trenchant **11** interesting, provacative, stimulating **13** scintillating **14** highly seasoned, strong-flavored

pique 3 ire, irk, vex **4** gall, goad, miff, snit, spur, stir **5** annoy, peeve, rouse, spite **6** arouse, excite, grudge, kindle, malice, nettle, offend **7** affront, incense,. perturb, provoke, quicken, umbrage **8** disquiet, irritate, vexation **9** annoyance, displease, stimulate **10** discomfort, exasperate, irritation, resentment **11** displeasure, humiliation, ill feelings, indignation **12** exasperation, hurt feelings **13** embarrassment, mortification, put one's back up **14** vindictiveness

piqued 5 angry, riled, vexed **6** galled, miffed, peeved **7** annoyed, aroused, excited, kindled, nettled, stirred **9** affronted, irritated **10** displeased, stimulated

pine 5 Pinus
  varieties: **3** air, nut, red **4** blue, chir, gray, hoop, Huon, Imou, Jack **5** beach, cedar, Cuban, Emodi, giant, house, Kauri, pitch, Scots, screw, shore, slash, stone, sugar, white **6** Aleppo, Apache, Bhutan, Bishop, celery, Dammar, digger, ground, Jersey, Korean, limber, Mallee, Norway, Parana, Pinyon, Scotch, spruce, Torrey, Totara, yellow **7** Amboina, Benguet, big-cone, Chilean, Chinese, cluster, Cypress, Formosa, Georgia, Gerard's, hickory, jointed, long-tag, poverty, prickly, prince's, running, Soledad **8** Austrian, Buddhist, cow's-tail, knob-cone, lace-bark, Loblolly, longleaf, mahogany, Monterey, mountain, Nepal nut, old-field, princess, umbrella **9** Brazilian, Calabrian, Chilghoza, Jerusalem, lodgepole, Oyster Bay, shortleaf, white-bark **10** Australian, Bunya-bunya, dwarf stone, Macedonian, Moreton Bay, red cypress, Swiss stone, Tenasserim **11** African fern, bristlecone, common screw, Japanese red, Parry pinyon, Port Jackson, thatch screw, twisted-leaf, Veitch screw **12** black cypress, Canary Island, Chinese water, eastern white, frankincense, Italian stone, Mexican stone, Mexican white, two-leaved nut, western white **13** dwarf Siberian, Japanese black, Japanese white, Mexican yellow, New Caledonian, Norfolk Island, Swiss mountain, table mountain **14** Himalayan white, Rottnest Island, southern yellow **15** Mueller's cypress **16** Japanese umbrella, single-leaf pinyon **18** Rough-barked Mexican **19** Rocky Mountain yellow

Pirandello, Luigi
   author of: **17** The Old and the Young **18** Tonight We Improvise **19** The Late Mattia Pascal **31** Six Characters in Search of an Author

pirate 3 rob **5** steal **6** raider, robber, sea dog **7** brigand, corsair, plunder **8** marauder **9** buccaneer, privateer **10** freebooter
   flag: **9** blackjack **10** Jolly Roger
   name: **4** Kidd **6** Morgan **7** Lafitte **10** Blackbeard

Pirate Coast *see* **18** United Arab Emirates

Pirates of Penzance, The
   author: **9** W S Gilbert
   comic opera by: **18** Gilbert and Sullivan
   character: **4** Kate, Ruth **5** Edith, Mabel **6** Isabel **8** Frederic, Sergeant **10** Pirate King **14** General Stanley

Pirithous
   prince of: **8** Lapithae
   father: **4** Zeus
   mother: **3** Dia
   son: **10** Polypoetes
   friend of: **7** Theseus

Pirous
   led allies of: **6** Thrace

pis aller 10 last resort **12** last resource

Pisan Cantos
   author: **9** Ezra Pound

Pisander
   rank: **7** captain
   member of: **9** Myrmidons

Pisanio
   character in: **9** Cymbeline
   author: **11** Shakespeare

Pisanosaurus
   type: **8** dinosaur **10** ornithopod
   location: **12** South America
   period: **8** Triassic

Pisces
   symbol: **4** fish
   planet: **7** Jupiter, Neptune
   rules: **7** secrets
   born: **13** February-March

Pisistratidae
   sons of: **11** Pisistratus
   names: **7** Hippias **10** Hipparchus

Pisistratus
   tyrant of: **6** Athens
   father: **11** Hippocrates
   son: **7** Hippias **10** Hipparchus

Pissarro, Camille
   born: **8** St Thomas **16** Danish West Indies
   artwork: **8** Red Roofs **15** Morning Sunlight

21 Lower Norwood Snow Scene **28** Peasant Woman with a Wheelbarrow

pistol (revolver)
   invented by: **4** Colt

pit 3 dip, nut **4** dent, hole, nick, pock, scar, seed **5** gouge, gully, match, notch, stone **6** cavity, crater, dimple, furrow, hollow, indent, kernel, oppose, trough **7** scratch **8** contrast, pockmark **9** concavity, juxtapose **10** depression, set against **11** indentation

Pit, The
   author: **11** Frank Norris

Pitana
   form: **5** nymph
   daughter: **6** Evadne

Pit and the Pendulum, The
   author: **13** Edgar Allan Poe

pitch 3 bob, dip, fix, lob, set, shy, top **4** apex, cant, cast, fall, fire, hurl, jerk, jolt, peak, rock, tone, toss **5** angle, chuck, crown, erect, fling, grade, heave, level, lurch, place, plant, point, raise, set up, shake, slant, sling, slope, sound, throw **6** degree, height, let fly, locate, plunge, propel, settle, summit, topple, tumble, zenith **7** bobbing, incline, rocking, station **8** delivery, harmonic, lurching, pinnacle, undulate **9** declivity, establish, oscillate **10** undulation **11** oscillation **12** fall headlong
   speed of: **9** vibration

pitcher 3 jar, jug **4** ewer **6** carafe **8** decanter **9** container **10** spitballer
   and catcher: **7** battery
   award: **7** Cy Young
   brother duo: **4** Dean **5** Perry **6** Niekro
   Hall of Famer: **4** Ford, Wynn **6** Koufax **8** Drysdale
   left-hander: **8** southpaw
   relief staff: **7** bullpen
   reliever: **7** fireman

pitch in 5 begin **7** share in **8** take part **9** cooperate, get to work, join hands **10** act jointly, contribute, get started **11** collaborate, participate **12** make an effort, pull together, work together

pitch into 5 fly at **6** assail, have at **7** assault, set upon

piteous 3 sad **6** moving, woeful **7** pitiful **8** pathetic, pitiable, poignant, touching **9** affecting **10** deplorable **11** distressing **12** heart-rending **13** heartbreaking

pitfall 4 risk, trap **5** peril,

snare **6** ambush, danger, hazard **7** springe **8** quagmire **9** booby trap, quicksand **14** stumbling block

pith 4 core, gist, meat **5** heart, point **7** essence, meaning **12** significance

pithy 5 terse **6** cogent **7** concise **8** forceful, succinct **9** effective, trenchant **10** expressive, meaningful, to the point **12** concentrated

pitiful 3 sad **4** poor **5** sorry **6** abject, measly, moving, paltry, shabby **7** doleful, forlorn, piteous **8** dreadful, god-awful, mournful, pathetic, pitiable, poignant, touching, wretched **9** miserable, plaintive, worthless **10** abominable, despicable, lamentable **11** distressing **12** arousing pity, contemptible, heartrending

pitiless 5 cruel **6** brutal **7** inhuman, unmoved **8** ruthless, uncaring **9** heartless, merciless, unpitying, unsparing, untouched **10** implacable, relentless, unmerciful **11** cold-blooded, hardhearted, indifferent, insensitive, unrelenting

pittance 4 mite **5** crumb **6** little, trifle **7** minimum, modicum, smidgen

Pittheus
   father: **6** Pelops
   mother: **10** Hippodamia
   brother: **7** Troezen
   daughter: **6** Aethra

Pittsburgh
   baseball team: **7** Pirates
   feature: **14** Fort Pitt Museum **15** Buhl Planetarium
   football team: **8** Steelers
   formerly: **8** Fort Pitt **12** Fort Duquesne
   hockey team: **8** Penguins
   noted for: **5** steel
   river: **4** Ohio **9** Allegheny **11** Monongahela
   university: **8** Duquesne **14** Carnegie-Mellon

Pittypat, Aunt
   character in: **15** Gone With the Wind
   author: **8** Mitchell

pituitary
   located in: **5** brain
   known as: **11** master gland

pity 5 mercy, shame **6** lament, lenity, regret **7** charity, feel for, weep for **8** bleed for, clemency, humanity, leniency, sad thing, sympathy **10** compassion, condolence, indulgence, kindliness, tenderness **11** crying shame, forbearance, magnanimity **12** feel sorry for **13** commiseration

Pityocamptes
epithet of: 5 Sinis
means: 10 pine-bender

Pitys
form: 5 nymph
loved by: 3 Pan
changed into: 8 pine tree

piu
music: 4 more

pivot 4 axis, axle, hang, rely, spin, turn **5** focus, hinge, twirl, wheel, whirl **6** center, circle, depend, rotate, swivel **7** fulcrum, hinge on, revolve **9** pirouette

pivotal 5 vital **7** crucial **8** critical, decisive **9** climactic **11** determining

pivotal point 4 axis **12** turning point **13** crucial moment

pixy 3 elf **5** fairy **6** sprite **10** leprechaun

pizzicato
music: 21 plucked instead of bowed
abbreviation: **4** pizz

placable 7 lenient **8** flexible, tolerant, yielding **9** indulgent, relenting **10** appeasable, forbearing **12** reconcilable

placard 4 bill, sign **6** notice, poster **8** bulletin **13** advertisement

placate 4 calm, lull **5** quiet **6** pacify, soothe **7** appease, assuage, mollify, win over **9** alleviate **10** conciliate, propitiate

placatory 9 appeasing, pacifying **10** mollifying **12** conciliatory **13** accommodative

place 3 fix, job, put, set **4** area, city, digs, duty, farm, firm, home, land, plot, post, rank, rest, shop, site, spot, town, zone **5** abode, affix, array, berth, house, lodge, niche, plant, point, ranch, space, stand, state, store, venue **6** assign, attach, county, harbor, invest, locale, locate, office, region, settle **7** appoint, borough, company, concern, country, deposit, install, quarter, shelter, situate, station, village **8** building, business, classify, district, domicile, dwelling, ensconce, find hire, function, identify, locality, location, lodgings, position, premises, property, province, quarters, remember, standing, township, vicinity **9** recognize, residence, situation, territory **10** commission, get a job for, habitation **11** appointment,

find work for, whereabouts **12** neighborhood **13** establishment
Latin: 4 situ

Place in the Sun, A
director: 13 George Stevens
based on novel by: 15 Theodore Dreiser (An American Tragedy)
cast: 14 Keefe Brasselle, Shelley Winters **15** Elizabeth Taylor, Montgomery Clift
Oscar for: 5 score **9** direction **10** screenplay

placement 8 grouping, location **10** assignment, employment **11** arrangement, disposition, positioning

place of residence 4 home **5** abode, house **7** address, lodging **8** domicile, dwelling **9** residence **10** habitation **14** living quarters

place to stand on
Greek: 6 pou sto

place upright 5 erect, raise **7** stand up

placid 4 calm, mild **5** quiet **6** gentle, poised, serene, smooth **7** pacific, restful **8** composed, peaceful, tranquil **9** collected, unexcited, unruffled **10** untroubled **11** undisturbed, unexcitable **13** imperturbable, self-possessed **15** undemonstrative

plague 3 irk, vex, woe **4** bane, evil, fret, gall, pain, pest **5** agony, chafe, curse, harry, haunt, peeve, worry **6** badger, blight, bother, burden, cancer, harass, misery, nettle **7** afflict, disturb, perturb, scourge, torment, trouble **8** aggrieve, calamity, disquiet, distress, hardship, pandemic **9** embarrass, persecute, suffering **10** affliction, Black Death, pestilence, visitation
French: 5 peste

Plague, The
author: 11 Albert Camus
character: 7 Rambert **10** Jean Tarrou **11** Joseph Grand **14** Father Paneloux, Raymond Cottard **15** Dr Bernard R Rieux

Plague Dogs, The
author: 12 Richard Adams

plain 4 bald, bare, open **5** blunt, clear, frank, naked, vivid **6** candid, common, direct, homely, honest, modest, simple **7** average, glaring, legible, obscure, obvious, plateau, prairie, sincere, visible **8** apparent, clear-cut, distinct, everyday, explicit, manifest, ordinary, palpable, specific,

straight, striking, uncomely, unlovely **9** grassland, outspoken, prominent, tableland, unadorned, undiluted **10** forthright, pronounced, unaffected, unassuming, unhandsome, unreserved, well-marked **11** commonplace, conspicuous, discernible, not striking, open country, outstanding, plain-spoken, unambiguous, undecorated, undisguised, unequivocal, ungarnished, unvarnished, well-defined **12** matter-of-fact, not beautiful, unattractive, unmistakable, unornamented **13** unembellished, unpretentious, without frills **14** comprehensible, understandable **15** straightforward, undistinguished

Plain Dealer, The
author: 16 William Wycherley

plainly 6 baldly, openly, simply **7** bluntly, clearly, frankly, visibly, vividly **8** candidly, directly, honestly, markedly, modestly **9** doubtless, obviously **10** apparently, definitely, distinctly, explicitly, manifestly, ordinarily, positively, strikingly, undeniably **11** beyond doubt, discernibly, prominently, undoubtedly **12** unaffectedly, unassumingly, unmistakably, without doubt **13** conspicuously, unambiguously, unequivocably **14** comprehensibly, unquestionably

plainness 10 homeliness, simplicity **12** ordinariness

plainspoken 4 open **5** bluff, blunt, frank, plain **6** candid, direct, honest **7** genuine, sincere **8** explicit, straight **9** openfaced, outspoken, unsparing **10** above board, forthright, point-blank **11** straight-out **15** straightforward

plaint 3 cry, sob **4** beef, moan, wail **5** gripe **6** charge, grouse, grudge, lament, regret, squawk **7** grumble, reproof **8** reproach **9** complaint, grievance, objection **10** accusation, resentment **12** remonstrance

plaintive 3 sad **6** rueful **7** doleful, moaning, piteous, pitiful, tearful **8** dolorous, grievous, mournful, pathetic, wretched **9** lamenting, sorrowful, woebegone **10** lugubrious, melancholy **12** heartrending

plait 5 braid, queue, twine, twist, weave **7** pigtail **10** intertwine

plan 3 aim, map, way **4** form, idea, plot **5** frame, shape

6 design, devise, intend, lay out, map out, method, scheme, sketch **7** diagram, outline, prepare, program, project, propose, purpose **8** block out, conceive, contrive, organize, proposal, strategy, think out **9** blueprint, fabricate, procedure, stratagem **10** conception, suggestion **11** proposition
French: **8** demarche

Planchet
character in: **18** The Three Musketeers
author: **5** Dumas (pere)

Planck, Max
field: **7** physics
nationality: **6** German
developed: **13** quantum theory **15** Planck's constant
awarded: **10** Nobel Prize

Planctae
form: **5** rocks
characteristic: **8** shifting

plane 3 jet **4** bird, flat **5** level, plumb **6** degree, status **7** regular, station **8** aircraft, airplane, position, standing **9** condition, elevation
type: **4** jack **5** block

planet, planets 13 celestial body
first: **7** Mercury
second: **5** Venus
third: **5** Earth
   satellite: **4** Moon
fourth: **4** Mars
   satellite: **6** Deimos, Phobos
   nickname: **9** Red Planet
fifth: **7** Jupiter
   satellite: **2** Io **6** Europa **8** Amalthea, Callisto, Ganymede
   characteristic: **7** red spot
sixth: **6** Saturn
   satellite: **4** Rhea **5** Dione, Janus, Mimas, Titan **6** Phoebe, Tethys **7** Iapetus **8** Hyperion **9** Enceladus
   characteristic: **5** rings
seventh: **6** Uranus
   satellite: **5** Ariel **6** Oberon **7** Miranda, Titania, Umbriel
   color: **9** blue-green
   characteristic: **5** rings
eighth: **7** Neptune
   satellite: **6** Nereid, Triton
   color: **5** green
ninth: **5** Pluto
   satellite: **6** Charon
asteroid/minor planet/planetoid: **4** Eros, Juno **5** Ceres, Vesta **6** Chiron, Hermes, Icarus, Pallas **7** Astraea, Hidalgo

planetary 6 astral **7** earthly **9** celestial **11** terrestrial **12** astronomical

Planet of the Apes
director: **18** Franklin J Schaffner
based on novel by: **12** Pierre Boulle
cast: **9** Kim Hunter **12** Maurice Evans **13** Roddy McDowall **14** Charlton Heston
script: **10** Rod Serling

plank 4 deal, deck, slab **5** board, shole, stone **8** platform

planned 7 devised, schemed **8** designed, expected, foreseen, intended, prepared **9** mapped out, organized, projected, rehearsed **10** calculated, purposeful, thought out **11** intentional, prearranged, prepared for **12** premeditated

planner 6 author, framer **7** creator, deviser **8** arranger, designer **9** architect, organizer

plant 4 bush, herb, mill, moss, shop, slip, tree, vine, weed, wort, yard **5** algae, flora, fungi, grass, set in, shrub, works **6** flower, foster, infuse, set out **7** factory, foundry, herbage, implant, inspire, instill, scatter, sow seed **8** business, engender, seedling **9** broadcast, cultivate, establish, inculcate, propagate, vegetable **10** transplant, vegetation **13** establishment, sow the seeds of **14** put in the ground

plaster 4 coat, daub, sand **5** grout, smear **6** bedaub, gypsum, lather, stucco **7** overlay, spackle
mixture of: **4** lime **5** water **6** gypsum

plastered 5 drunk **6** coated, daubed, soused **7** covered, crocked, smeared, swacked **8** mortared, polluted, stuccoed **10** inebriated **11** intoxicated

plastic 4 soft **6** pliant, supple **7** ductile, elastic, pliable **8** flexible, formable, moldable, shapable, yielding **9** malleable, tractable

Platanistius
epithet of: **6** Apollo
means: **22** god of the plane-tree grove

plate 4 dish **6** saucer **7** helping, platter, portion, serving **10** platterful **11** serving dish

plateau 4 mesa **5** table **6** upland **8** highland **9** tableland

Plateosaurus
type: **8** dinosaur, sauropod
location: **6** Europe **7** Germany
period: **8** Triassic

platform 4 dais, goal, plan

5 creed, plank, stage, stand **6** podium, policy, pulpit, tenets **7** program, rostrum

Plath, Sylvia
author of: **5** Ariel **10** The Bell Jar

platinum
chemical symbol: **2** Pt

platitude 3 saw **6** cliche, old saw, truism **7** bromide **8** banality, chestnut **11** commonplace

platitudinous 5 banal, corny, stale, tired, trite, vapid **6** jejune **8** bromidic, ordinary **9** hackneyed **10** pedestrian, unexciting, unoriginal **12** cliche-ridden, conventional **13** unimaginative

Plato
author of: **4** Laws **5** Crito **6** Phaedo **7** Apology, Gorgias, Sophist, Timaeus **8** Philebus, Republic **9** Symposium **10** Parmenides

platoon 4 band, body, crew, team, unit **5** corps, force, group **10** detachment

platter 4 dish, disk, lanx **6** salver **7** record **8** trencher **9** recording

plaudit, plaudits 4 rave **5** cheer, kudos **6** hurrah, huzzah, praise **7** acclaim, bouquet, ovation **8** applause, approval, cheering **10** compliment, hallelujah **11** approbation **12** commendation

plauditory 8 admiring, praising **9** extolling, laudatory, praiseful **12** commendatory **13** complimentary

plausible 5 sound, valid **6** likely **7** logical, tenable **8** credible, feasible, possible, probable, rational, sensible **10** acceptable, believable, convincing, persuasive, reasonable **11** conceivable, justifiable

Plautus
author of: **7** Stichus **8** Mercator **9** Amphitruo, Menaechmi, Pseudolus **10** Amphitryon **14** Miles Gloriosus

play 3 act, fun, toy **4** jest, lark, romp, room, show **5** antic, caper, drama, enact, farce, frisk, revel, space, sport, sweep, swing **6** act out, cavort, comedy, frolic, gambol, leeway, trifle **7** disport, have fun, pageant, perform, skylark, tragedy, vie with **8** pleasure, take part **9** amusement, diversion, elbowroom, enjoyment, make merry, melodrama, perform on, personify, represent, spectacle **10** recreation **11** impersonate, merrymaking

playboy 4 rake, wolf **5** Romeo, sheik **6** lecher **7** Don Juan, swinger **8** Casanova, hedonist, Lothario, party boy **9** jet-setter, ladies' man, partygoer, womanizer **10** lady-killer, profligate **14** pleasure seeker **15** good-time Charlie

Playboy of the Western World, The
author: 19 John Millington Synge
character: 8 Old Mahon **9** Widow Quin **10** Shawn Keogh **16** Christopher Mahon, Margaret Flaherty (Pegeen)

play down 9 underplay **11** de-emphasize

played out 4 beat **5** all in, spent, weary **6** bushed, done in, pooped **7** drained, wearied, worn out **8** depleted, dog tired, fatigued, tired out, unreeled **9** dead tired, exhausted

player 4 jock, mime **5** actor **6** mummer **7** actress, athlete, trouper **8** gamester, opponent, thespian **9** adversary, contender, performer **10** antagonist, competitor, contestant, team member **11** entertainer, participant

play false 4 dupe **5** trick **6** betray **7** deceive, two-time **10** be disloyal **12** be unfaithful **13** be treacherous

playfellow 3 pal **4** chum **5** buddy **6** friend **8** playmate

playful 6 frisky, impish, lively **7** amusing, coltish, jesting, waggish **8** humorous, mirthful, prankish, sportive **9** fun-loving, sprightly **10** capricious, frolicsome, rollicking **12** lighthearted
French: **8** espiegle

playful trick
French: **11** espieglerie

play host 4 host **9** entertain **10** give a party, have guests **13** keep open house

playing field 4 bowl **5** arena **7** diamond, stadium **8** gridiron **10** playground **12** amphitheater

playing piece 3 man **4** disk **5** piece **7** counter

play in water 3 dip **4** swim **6** dabble, paddle, splash

play Judas 6 betray **7** sell out, two-time **9** play false **11** double-cross

playmate 3 pal **4** chum

5 buddy **6** friend **10** playfellow

play of spirit
French: **10** jeu d'esprit

play on words
French: **9** jeu de mots

plaything 3 toy **4** dupe **5** patsy, sport **6** bauble, trifle **9** diversion

play truant 3 cut **4** skip **8** be absent **9** play hooky

play with 5 bandy **7** torment, toy with **11** have fun with

playwright 6 author, writer **9** dramatist, scenarist **10** dramatizer, dramaturge, librettist, play doctor **12** dramatic poet, dramaturgist, scriptwriter **13** melodramatist

plea 4 suit **5** alibi **6** appeal, excuse, prayer **7** apology, begging, defense, pretext, request **8** argument, entreaty, petition **10** adjuration, beseeching **11** explanation, extenuation, vindication **12** solicitation, supplication **13** justification

plead 3 ask, beg **6** adjure, enjoin **7** beseech, entreat, implore, request, solicit **8** appeal to, petition **9** importune **10** supplicate

pleader 6 beggar **8** advocate, defender, implorer **9** apologist, beseecher **10** importuner, supplicant

plead with 3 beg **4** pray **6** adjure **7** beseech, implore **10** supplicate

Pleasance, Donald
born: 7 England, Worksop
roles: 12 The Caretaker **14** The Great Escape **16** You Only Live Twice **17** The Eagle Has Landed **24** The Greatest Story Ever Told

pleasant 4 fine, good, mild, nice, soft, warm **6** genial, gentle, lovely, polite **7** affable, amiable, cordial, likable, tactful **8** amicable, charming, cheerful, friendly, inviting, pleasing, sociable **9** agreeable, congenial, enjoyable **10** attractive, felicitous, gratifying, gregarious, satisfying **11** good-humored, good-natured, pleasurable **13** companionable

Pleasant Island see **5** Nauru

pleasantry 4 jape, jest, joke, quip **5** sally **6** bon mot **8** greeting **9** wisecrack, witticism **10** salutation

pleasant-tasting 4 mild **5** sweet, tasty **6** savory **8** luscious **9** delicious, palatable,

succulent **10** appetizing, delectable **11** scrumptious **13** mouth-watering

please 3 opt **4** like, suit, want, will, wish **5** amuse, charm, elate, elect **6** choose, desire, divert, prefer, thrill, tickle **7** content, delight, gladden, gratify, satisfy **8** enthrall, entrance **9** enrapture, entertain, fascinate, make happy **10** be inclined **14** give pleasure to
French: **12** s'il vous plait
German: **5** bitte
Spanish: **8** por favor

pleased 4 glad **5** happy, proud **6** elated **8** thrilled **9** delighted, gratified

please reply
French: **4** rsvp **20** repondez s'il vous plait

pleasing 6 genial, polite **7** affable, amiable, amusing, likable, winning **8** charming, cheerful, friendly, inviting, mannerly **9** agreeable, congenial, diverting, enjoyable **10** attractive, delightful, gladdening, gratifying, satisfying **11** captivating, fascinating, good-humored, good-natured, pleasurable **12** entertaining, well-mannered

pleasing inactivity
Italian: **14** dolce far niente

pleasurable 8 pleasing **9** agreeable, enjoyable **10** delightful

pleasure 3 fun, joy **4** like, will, wish **5** bliss, cheer, mirth **6** choice, desire, gaiety, option **7** delight, elation, rapture **9** amusement, diversion, enjoyment, festivity, happiness, merriment, selection **10** exultation, jubilation, preference, recreation **11** high spirits, inclination **13** entertainment, gratification **15** beer and skittles **16** lightheartedness
goddess of: 8 Voluptas

pleasure-giving 7 amusing **8** pleasing **9** agreeable, enjoyable **10** delightful **11** pleasurable **12** entertaining

Pleasure of His Company, The
author: 19 Cornelia Otis Skinner

pleasure trip 4 tour **5** jaunt **6** outing **8** vacation **9** excursion

pleat 4 fold **5** crimp, frill **6** crease

pleated 6 fluted, folded **7** creased, crimped **10** corrugated

plebeian 3 low 4 base, mean 5 banal 6 coarse, common, vulgar 7 lowborn, lowbrow, popular 8 commoner, everyman, low-class, ordinary 9 bourgeois, common man, unrefined 10 average man, uncultured 11 bourgeoisie, commonplace, proletarian 12 uncultivated

plebs 5 demos 6 masses 7 commons 8 populace 9 commoners, hoi polloi, plebeians 11 bourgeoisie 12 common people

plecoptera
class: 8 hexapoda
phylum: 10 arthropoda
group: 8 stone fly

pledge 3 vow 4 bail, bond, oath, pact, pawn, word 5 swear, troth 6 assert, avowal, surety 7 compact, promise, warrant 8 contract, covenant, guaranty, security, warranty 9 agreement, assurance, guarantee 10 adjuration, collateral

Pleiades
father: 5 Atlas
mother: 7 Pleione
half-sisters: 6 Hyades
names: 4 Maia 6 Merope
  7 Alcyone, Celaeno, Electra, Sterope, Taygete
number of daughters:
  5 seven

plenary 4 full 6 entire 7 perfect 8 absolute, complete

plenitude 4 glut, heap, mass 5 flood 6 bounty, plenty, wealth 7 quality, surfeit, surplus 8 fullness, plethora, totality 9 abundance, amplitude, profusion, repletion, wholeness 10 cornucopia, entireness, quantities 11 ample supply, copiousness, full measure, sufficiency 12 completeness 14 more than enough

plenteous 6 lavish 7 copious, profuse 8 abundant 9 bountiful, plentiful

plentiful 4 lush 5 ample, large 6 lavish 7 copious, liberal, profuse 8 abundant, generous, infinite, prolific 9 abounding, bounteous, bountiful, plenteous, unsparing, unstinted 11 overflowing 13 inexhaustible

plenty 4 gobs, lots, slew 5 scads 6 luxury, oceans, oodles, riches, wealth, worlds 8 opulence 9 abundance, affluence, good times, great deal, plenitude, profusion, wellbeing 10 prosperity 11 ample

amount, good fortune, sufficiency 12 a full measure
goddess of: 3 Ops

plethora 4 glut 5 flood 6 excess, wealth 7 overage, surfeit, surplus 8 fullness 9 abundance, amplitude, plenitude, profusion 10 oversupply, redundancy, surplusage 11 superfluity 13 overabundance 14 more than enough, superabundance

Plexippus
also: 10 Parthenius
father: 7 Phineus 8 Thestius
brother: 7 Pandion
sister: 7 Althaea
nephew: 8 Meleager
killed by: 8 Meleager

pliable 5 lithe 6 limber, pliant, supple 7 elastic, plastic, springy, willing 8 flexible, yielding 9 adaptable, compliant, receptive, resilient, tractable 10 manageable, responsive, submissive 11 acquiescent 13 accommodating 14 easily bendable, impressionable

pliancy 8 docility, meekness, yielding 9 passivity 10 compliance, pliability, submission, suppleness 11 flexibility 12 complaisance

pliant 4 meek 6 supple 7 pliable 8 flexible, yielding 9 compliant 10 submissive 11 deferential

pliers
type: 10 fixed-joint 11 combination, needle-nosed, side-cutting 17 offset combination

plight 3 fix, jam 5 pinch, state, trial 6 crisis, muddle, pickle, scrape 7 dilemma, impasse, straits, trouble 8 distress, exigency 9 condition, emergency, extremity, situation 10 difficulty 11 predicament, tribulation, vicissitude 12 circumstance

Plisthenes
brother/half-brother: 8 Menelaus 9 Agamemnon
father: 6 Atreus
mother: 6 Cleola
sister/half-sister: 8 Anaxibia
sister-in-law: 12 Clytemnestra
uncle: 8 Thyestes

plod 4 drag, grub, moil, plug, slog, toil 5 grind, sweat, tramp 6 drudge, lumber, trudge, waddle 7 peg away, shuffle 8 struggle 9 persevere

plodding 4 dull 6 clumsy 8 trudging 9 laborious 10 pedestrian

plot 3 lot, map 4 area, draw, mark, plan, tale, yarn 5 chart, draft, field, patch, space, story, tract 6 action, design, scheme, sketch 7 collude, compute, diagram, outline, section 8 clearing, conspire, contrive, evil plan, intrigue, maneuver 9 blueprint, calculate, determine, incidents, narrative, story line, stratagem 10 conspiracy, secret plan 11 machination

plotting 4 wily 6 artful, crafty 7 cunning 8 scheming 9 conniving, designing 10 intriguing

Plough and the Stars, The
author: 10 Sean O'Casey

plover
group of: 4 wing
  12 congregation

plow, plough 3 cut, dig 4 push, till, work 5 break, dig up, drive, forge, press, shove, spade 6 furrow, harrow, loosen, plunge, turn up 7 break up 8 bulldoze 9 cultivate
invented by:
  cast iron: 7 Ransome
  disc: 5 Hardy

plowable 6 arable 7 friable 8 farmable, tillable 10 cultivable

Plowright, Joan
born: 5 Brigg 7 England
husband: 15 Laurence Olivier
roles: 13 A Taste of Honey
  15 The Entertainers

ploy 4 game, ruse, wile 5 trick 6 design, gambit, scheme, tactic 7 gimmick 8 artifice, maneuver, strategy 9 stratagem 10 subterfuge

pluck 4 draw, grab, grit, guts, jerk, pick, sand, yank 5 spunk, valor 6 daring, mettle, pull at, snatch, spirit, uproot 7 bravery, courage, pull off, pull out, resolve 8 boldness, temerity, tenacity 9 extirpate, fortitude 10 doggedness, resolution 11 persistence 12 perseverance 13 determination

pluck out 7 extract, pick out, pull out

plucky 4 bold, game 5 brave, gutsy 6 daring, spunky 7 doughty, valiant 8 fearless, intrepid, spirited, unafraid, valorous 9 audacious, dauntless, undaunted 10 courageous, mettlesome 11 lionhearted, unflinching 12 stouthearted

plug 4 bung, cork 5 close, stuff 6 fill up, stanch, stop up 7 shut off, stopper, stopple

plug up 3 dam **4** clog, plug **5** block, choke, dam up, stuff **6** stop up **7** congest **8** obstruct

plum
varieties: **3** hog **4** Coco, date, Duhr, gage, Java, sand, sloe, wild **5** beach, black, goose, Islay, Jaman, Lansa, Moxie, nanny, Natal, shore, Simon **6** August, Batoko, Canada, Cheney, cherry, common, Damson, ground, Indian, Jambul, Kaffir, Kelsey, Lomboy, Pigeon, Sapote, Sierra, Sisson **7** apricot, Burbank, Cheston, Jambosa, Malabar, Orleans, Pacific, Spanish, Wickson **8** American, Assyrian, Burdekin, European, Hortulan, Jambolan, Japanese, Oklahoma, Prunello, Victoria **9** Allegheny, Chickasaw, Governor's, greengage, marmalade, Myrobalan, wild-goose **10** Madagascar **13** Queensland hog

plumb 4 lead, test, true **5** gauge, level, probe, sheer, sound **6** fathom **7** examine, measure, plummet **8** plumb bob, straight, vertical **9** penetrate

plume 3 pen **4** down **5** egret, pique, preen, pride, prize, quill **7** feather
military: **7** panache

Plumed Serpent, The
author: **10** D H Lawrence

Plummer, Christopher
real name: **28** Arthur Christopher Orme Plummer
born: **6** Canada **7** Toronto
wife: **11** Tammy Grimes **12** Elaine Taylor
roles: **14** Murder by Decree **15** The Sound of Music **18** Baron Georg von Trapp **20** The Man Who Would Be King **25** The Return of the Pink Panther

plummet 4 dive, fall **6** plunge, tumble **8** nosedive **12** fall headlong

plump 4 drop, firm, flop, plop, sink **5** blunt, buxom, obese, plunk, pudgy, solid, spill, stout **6** abrupt, chubby, direct, fleshy, portly, rotund, sprawl, stocky, tumble **7** rounded **8** collapse, outright **9** corpulent

plumpness
French: **10** embonpoint

plunder 3 rob **4** haul, loot, raid, sack, swag, take **5** booty, rifle, prize, strip **6** fleece, maraud, pilfer, ravage, spoils **7** despoil, pillage, ransack, takings **9** filchings **10** pilferings

plunderer 6 looter, vandal

7 brigand **8** pillager **9** despoiler

plunge 3 dip, fly, run **4** bolt, cast, dart, dash, dive, drop, duck, fall, jerk, roll, jump, leap, push, reel, rock, rush, sink, sway, tear, toss **5** douse, drive, heave, lunge, lurch, pitch, press, shoot, speed, surge, swarm, whisk **6** charge, hasten, hurtle, hustle, scurry, sprint, streak, thrust, tumble **7** descend, immerse, scuttle **8** scramble, submerge, submerse **12** fall headlong

plunk 4 pick, thud **5** pluck, plumb, strum, twang **6** dollar **7** exactly **8** squarely **9** precisely

plurality 4 bulk, most **8** majority **13** preponderance

plus 5 added, extra, other, spare **6** useful **7** helpful **9** auxiliary, desirable **10** additional, beneficial **12** advantageous, supplemental **13** supplementary

plush 4 lush, posh, rich **5** fancy, grand, ritzy, swank, thick **6** classy, deluxe, lavish, snazzy, swanky **7** elegant, opulent **8** palatial **9** luxurious, sumptuous **11** extravagant

plushy 4 soft **5** cushy, swank **7** opulent, velvety **9** luxurious, sumptuous

Plutarch
author of: **13** Parallel Lives

Plutarch's Lives
author: **8** Plutarch

Pluto
also: **5** Hades
god of: **10** underworld
corresponds to: **3** Dis **5** Orcus **8** Dis Pater

Pluto
position: **5** ninth
satellite: **6** Charon

plutocrat 5 mogul **6** fat cat, tycoon **9** financier **10** capitalist

plutonic 7 abyssal, igneous **9** cimmerian, intrusive, vulcanian

plutonium
chemical symbol: **2** Pu

Plutus
author: **12** Aristophanes
character: **5** Cario **9** Chremylus **11** Blepsidemus
god of: **6** wealth

Plutus
personifies: **6** wealth
father: **6** Iasion
mother: **7** Demeter

Pluvius
epithet of: **7** Jupiter

ply 3 fly, run **4** leaf, sail, work **5** layer, offer, plait, plate, press, sheet, slice, twist, wield **6** employ, follow, handle, lamina, pursue, sheath, strand, supply **7** besiege, carry on, labor at, operate, stratum, utilize **8** exercise, navigate, practice, put to use, urge upon **9** thickness **10** manipulate

poach 3 rob **4** cook **5** shirr, steal **6** plunge, simmer **7** trample **8** encroach, trespass

pocket 3 bag, get, pit **4** gain, lode, sack, vein **5** pouch, purse, pygmy, small, steal, strip, usurp **6** attain, bantam, cavity, come by, hollow, little, obtain, pilfer, strain, streak **7** chamber, compact, handbag, placket, receive **8** arrogate, envelope, portable **9** miniature **10** diminutive, receptacle **11** appropriate, compartment

Pocket, Herbert
character in: **17** Great Expectations
author: **7** Dickens

pocketbook 3 bag **5** pouch, purse **6** clutch, wallet **7** handbag, satchel **8** moneybag, notecase **9** coin purse **10** money purse **11** shoulder bag
French: **12** porte-monnaie

pocket flask 5 flask **6** bottle **7** canteen

pocket-sized 3 wee **4** tiny **5** dwarf, pygmy, small **6** bantam, little, midget, minute, petite **7** compact **9** miniature **10** diminutive, vest-pocket

poco
music: **6** little

Pocock, Mamie
character in: **14** The Ambassadors
author: **5** James

pod 4 case, hull, husk **5** shell **6** jacket, sheath **8** pericarp, seed case **10** seed vessel

Podarces
mentioned in: **5** Iliad
father: **8** Iphiclus
brother: **11** Protesilaus
commanded: **8** Pythians

Podes
home: **4** Troy
occupation: **7** warrior
killed by: **8** Menelaus

Podgorica
capital of: **10** Montenegro

podium 4 dais, foot, wall **5** stipe **7** lectern **8** pedestal, platform **9** footstalk

Poe, Edgar Allan
author of: 6 Ligeia 7 Israfel,
To Helen 8 The Bells, The
Raven 10 Annabel Lee, The
Gold Bug 18 The Purloined
Letter 20 The Cask of
Amontillado, The Pit and
the Pendulum 22 The
Masque of the Red Death
24 The Fall of the House of
Usher, The Murders in the
Rue Morgue 29 The Narra-
tive of Arthur Gordon Pym

Poeas
also: 5 Poias
lit: 11 funeral pyre
pyre of: 8 Hercules
son: 11 Philoctetes

poem 3 lay, ode 4 epic, song
5 elegy, idyll, lyric, rhyme,
verse 6 ballad, jingle, sonnet
8 doggerel, limerick,
madrigal

Poema del Cid *see* 6 The Cid

**Poems Chiefly in the Scot-
tish Dialect**
author: 11 Robert Burns

Poena
also: 5 Poine
personifies: 7 revenge
10 punishment

poet 4 bard 5 maker 6 lyrist,
rhymer, singer 7 reciter 8 lyri-
cist, minstrel, verseman 9 bal-
ladeer, balladist, poetaster,
rhymester, sonneteer, versifier
10 improviser, librettist,
songwriter

poetaster 4 bard, poet
6 rhymer, writer 8 poetizer,
rimester 9 rhymester, versifier

poetic, poetical 5 lyric 7 lilting, lyrical, melodic, musical
8 metrical, rhythmic, songlike
9 melodious 11 imaginative

Poetics
author: 9 Aristotle

poetizer 4 bard, poet 6 rhymer, writer 8 rhymster 9 poetaster, versifier

poetry 5 poesy, rhyme, verse
13 versification
god of: 4 Odin, Ogma
5 Brage, Bragi, Othin
6 Apollo 7 Phoebus, Pyth-
ius 9 Musagetes

Pogo
creator: 9 Walt Kelly
character: 9 Porkypine, Wiley
Catt 10 Boll Weevil 12 PT
Bridgeport 13 Deacon Mush-
rat, Mole MacCarony
alligator: 6 Albert
fox: 11 Seminole Sam
frog: 15 Moonshine Sonata
hound: 18 Beauregard
Bugleboy
possum: 4 Pogo

skunk: 16 Ma'm'selle
Hepzibah
snake: 7 Snavely
sorcerer: 10 Howland Owl
turtle/pirate captain:
14 Churchy La Femme
place: 15 Okefenokee Swamp

Pohjola
origin: 7 Finnish
identified with: 7 Lapland
location: 12 North Finland

poignant 3 sad 5 sharp 6 biting, moving, rueful, woeful
7 cutting, doleful, piquant, piteous, pitiful, pungent, tearful
8 grievous, pathetic, piercing,
pitiable, touching 9 affecting,
sorrowful, trenchant 10 lamentable 11 distressing, penetrating 12 heartrending

Poine *see* 5 Poena

point 3 aim, end, hit, nib, run,
tip, use 4 apex, bend, bode,
core, game, gist, goal, item,
mark, meat, pike, pith, spur,
time, turn, unit 5 argue,
cause, guide, heart, imply,
level, limit, place, prong,
prove, score, sense, slant,
spike, stage, steer, tally, train,
value 6 aspect, basket, degree,
detail, direct, hint at, kernel,
marrow, moment, number, object, reason 7 essence, feature,
instant, portend, presage, purpose, quality, signify, suggest,
testify 8 indicate, intimate,
juncture, main idea, manifest,
offshoot, position, sharp end
9 condition, extension, intention, objective, outgrowth
10 foreshadow, particular, projection, prominence, promontory 11 demonstrate
12 protuberance

point-blank 5 blunt 6 direct
10 forthright 11 plainspoken

Point Counter Point
author: 12 Aldous Huxley

point d'appui 4 prop, stay
24 point of battle line support

pointed 5 acute, blunt, sharp
6 biting, direct, peaked,
pointy 7 cutting, fitting, hint-
ing, telling 8 accurate, incisive, piercing 9 aciculate,
acuminate, cuspidate, pertinent, trenchant 10 empha-
sized, forthright
11 appropriate, conspicuous,
insinuating, penetrating

pointer 3 arm, tip 4 hand,
hint 5 arrow, guide, stick
6 needle 7 caution, warning
9 indicator 10 admonition, advisement, suggestion 13 piece
of advice 14 recommendation
dog breed: 16 German wirehaired 17 German short-

haired 25 wirehaired
pointing griffon

pointless 4 dull 5 blunt 6 absurd, futile, obtuse, stupid
7 aimless, invalid, rounded,
unedged, useless 8 bootless,
worn down 9 fruitless, illogical, senseless, unpointed,
worthless 10 irrational, irrelevant, ridiculous, unavailing
11 ineffectual, meaningless,
purposeless, unsharpened
12 inapplicable, preposterous,
unproductive, unprofitable,
unreasonable

point of view 4 side 5 angle,
slant 6 aspect 7 outlook 8 attitude 9 viewpoint 10 standpoint 11 frame of mind,
perspective

point the way 5 guide, pilot,
usher 6 direct 8 indicate, navigate 14 give directions

point to 5 argue, imply 6 denote 7 express 8 indicate

point up 6 stress 9 emphasize,
underline 10 accentuate,
underscore

Poirot, Hercule
detective created by:
14 Agatha Christie
nationality: 7 Belgian
famed for: 10 moustaches
phrase: 15 little grey cells
played by: 12 Peter Sellers

poise 4 calm 5 raise 6 aplomb
7 balance, elevate 8 presence
9 assurance, composure, hold
aloft, sangfroid 10 equanimity
11 savoir faire, self-command,
self-control 13 self-assurance
14 presence of mind, self-confidence 15 be in equilibrium

poised 7 assured 8 composed
9 confident 10 controlled
11 self-assured 13 self-
possessed

poison 4 bane, evil, harm
5 curse, taint, toxin, venom
6 cancer, canker, debase, defile, impair, infect, plague,
weaken 7 corrode, corrupt, degrade, disease, outrage, pollute 8 enormity, make sick
9 malignity 10 adulterate, corruption, debilitate, malignancy,
pestilence 11 abomination,
contaminate

poisonous 5 fatal, toxic
6 deadly, lethal, mortal
7 baneful, noxious 8 venomous, virulent 10 pernicious
11 deleterious 12 pestilential

Poitier, Sidney
born: 7 Miami FL
wife: 13 Joanna Shimkus
roles: 11 Virgil Tibbs 12 A
Patch of Blue, For Love of

Ivy, Porgy and Bess **13** To
Sir with Love **14** The De-
fiant Ones **15** A Raisin in
the Sun **16** Lilies of the
Field (Oscar) **17** They Call
Me Mr Tibbs **19** In the
Heat of the Night, The
Blackboard Jungle, Uptown
Saturday Night **23** Guess
Who's Coming to Dinner?

Pokanoket *see*
10 Wampanoags

poke 3 dig, hit, jab **4** butt,
drag, gore, idle, jolt, prod,
push, stab **5** crawl, dally, delay, mosey, nudge, punch,
stick, thump **6** dawdle, fiddle,
potter, thrust **7** meander,
saunter, shamble, shuffle
8 hang back **10** dillydally
12 shilly-shally

poker
  derived from: 5 as nas, gilet
  6 brelan **7** primero
  11 brouillotte
  cards/hand: 4 five **5** seven
  bets: 4 ante **5** chips
  hand: 4 pair **5** flush
  8 straight, two pairs **9** full
  house **10** royal flush **11** four
  of a kind **12** three of a
  kind **13** straight flush
  term: 4 call, fold **5** check,
  raise **6** ante up **7** reraise
  variation: 4 draw, stud
  5 jacks **8** jackpots **12** five-
  card draw **13** seven-card
  stud

poky, pokey 4 dull, jail, slow
5 dowdy, small **6** dreary,
shabby, stodgy, stuffy
7 cramped **8** confined, dawdling, dilatory, frumpish
9 puttering **10** monotonous
  creature: 5 sloth, snail **6** turtle **8** slowpoke, tortoise

Polacanthus
  type: 8 dinosaur
  10 ornithopod

Poland *see box, p. 764*

Polanski, Roman
  director of: 4 Tess **7** Macbeth **9** Chinatown **13** Rosemary's Baby

polar 3 icy **6** arctic, frigid, wintry **7** glacial, ice-cold **8** freezing **9** antarctic
11 nothernmost
12 southernmost

pole 3 rod **4** mast, spar **5** shaft,
staff, stick **6** tongue **9** pikestaff
  flax holder: 7 distaff
  pertaining to: 5 nodal
  sacred: 7 Asherah
  Scottish: 5 caber
  tribal: 5 totem
  vehicular: 4 neap

Polias, Poliatas
  epithet of: 6 Athena

police, police officer 4 cops,
dick, fuzz, tidy **5** clean, guard
6 neaten, patrol, tidy up
7 clean up, control, marshal,
officer, protect, sheriff **8** blue-
coat, flatfoot, gendarme, regulate, spruce up, troopers
9 gendarmes, men in blue, pa-
trolmen **10** traffic cop **11** arm
of the law, keep in order
12 constabulary, cop on the
beat
  French: 8 gendarme
  Italian: 11 carabiniere

Police Woman
  character: 9 (Det) Joe Styles,
  (Lt) Paul Marsh **11** (Det)
  Pete Royster, (Lt) Bill Crow-
  ley **12** (Sgt Suzanne) Pepper
  Martin
  cast: 9 Ed Bernard **11** Val
  Bisoglio **12** Earl Holliman
  14 Angie Dickinson, Charles
  Dierkop

policy 3 way **4** plan, rule
5 habit, style **6** custom, design,
method, scheme, system
7 program, routine, tactics
8 behavior, platform, practice,
strategy **9** principle, procedure

Polieus
  epithet of: 4 Zeus
  means: 5 urban

polish 3 oil, wax **4** buff, sand
5 class, emend, glaze, gloss,
grace, rouge, rub up, shine
6 pumice, refine, smooth
7 burnish, correct, culture, enhance, finesse, improve, perfect, sauvity, touch up,
varnish **8** abrasive, courtesy,
elegance, round out, urbanity
9 gentility, politesse, sandpaper **10** politeness, refinement
11 cultivation, good manners

polished 4 able, deft, fine,
oily **5** oiled, suave, waxed
6 buffed, expert, glassy, glazed,
glossy, polite, rubbed, sanded,
shined, urbane **7** capable, elegant, genteel, refined, skilled
8 cultured, finished, mannerly,
masterly, skillful, smoothed
9 brilliant, burnished, courteous, masterful, practiced,
varnished **10** cultivated, proficient **11** experienced
12 accomplished

polish off 6 finish **8** complete,
get rid of **9** dispose of

polite 4 high **5** civil, elite
6 proper **7** courtly, elegant,
gallant, genteel, refined **8** cultured, mannerly, polished,
well-bred **9** civilized, courteous, diffident, patrician
10 cultivated, respectful
11 ceremonious, fashionable,
gentlemanly, well-behaved
12 well-mannered

politeness 7 decorum **8** courtesy **9** gentility, propriety
10 refinement **11** good
manners

Polites
  character in: 7 Odyssey
  brother: 5 Paris **6** Hector
  companion: 8 Odysseus
  father: 5 Priam
  mother: 6 Hecuba
  sister: 9 Cassandra
  transformed by: 5 Aeaea,
  Circe
  transformed into: 3 hog, pig
  5 swine

politic 4 wily, wise **5** chary,
suave **6** artful, astute, shrewd,
subtle **7** mindful, prudent,
tactful **8** cautious, discreet,
scheming **9** designing, expedient, judicious, opportune
10 contriving, diplomatic
11 calculating, circumspect,
machinating **13** Machiavellian

political party 3 GOP **4** Tory,
Whig **5** Labor **7** faction
9 Communist, Greenback, Socialist **10** Democratic, Republican **11** Know-Nothing

political refugee 2 DP **5** exile **6** emigre **10** expatriate
15 displaced person

politician 8 politico **9** incum-
bent, statesman **10** campaigner, legislator
12 officeholder, office seeker
13 public servant

politics 10 government, state-
craft **11** party policy **13** statesmanship **14** affairs of state

Politics
  author: 9 Aristotle

**Politic Would-Be, Lord and
Lady**
  characters in: 7 Volpone
  author: 6 Jonson

Poliuchus
  epithet of: 6 Athena
  means: 14 city-protecting

Polixenes
  character in: 14 The Winter's
  Tale
  author: 11 Shakespeare

Polk, James Knox *see box,
p. 765*

polka 5 dance **10** round dance
13 Bohemian dance

poll 4 head, vote **5** count, tally
6 census, survey, voting
7 canvass, figures, returns
8 register, sampling **9** interview, nose count **10** count
noses, voting list **11** voting
place

Pollack, Sydney
  director of: 11 Out of Africa
  (Oscar) **12** The Way We

Poland
  other name: 6 Polska 17 the land of the plain
  capital/largest city: 6 Warsaw
    medieval capital: 6 Cracow, Krakow
  others: 3 Lwo 4 Kodz, Kolo, Lida, Lodz, Lvov, Lyck, Nysa, Oels, Pila 5 Brest, Bytom, Chelm,
    Dukla, Narev, Opole, Posen, Radom, Sroda, Torun, Vilna 6 Danzig, Elblag, Gdansk,. Gdynia,
    Gnesen, Grodno, Kalisz, Kielce, Kracow, Lublin, Poznan, Tarnow, Zabrze 7 Beuthen, Breslau,
    Chorzow, Garocin, Gliwice, Litousk, Litovsk, Lyublin, Oleztyn, Stettin, Wroclaw 8 Frombork,
    Gleiwitz, Katowice, Lidzbark, Liegnitz, Oswiecim, Przemysl, Szczecin, Tarnopol 9 Auschwitz,
    Bialogard, Bialystok, Bydgoszcz, Sosnowiec, Szcezecin, Walbrzych 11 Czestochowa
  school: 6 Warsaw 12 Jagiellonian
  division: 7 Galicia, Silesia 8 Podlesia, Volhynia 9 Lithuania, Pomerania
  measure: 3 cal 4 mila, pret 5 morga, sazen, vloka, wloka 6 cwierc, cwierk, kwarta, lokiec
    7 garniec 9 kwarterka
  monetary unit: 4 abia 5 dalar, ducat, grosz, marka, zloty 6 fennig, groszy, gulden, halerz, ko-
    rona 8 groschen
  weight: 3 lut 4 funt 6 kamian 7 skrupul
  island: 5 Wolin
  lake: 5 Goplo, Mamry 8 Niegocin, Sniardwy 13 Stettin Lagoon
  mountain: 5 Tatra 6 Beskid 7 Pieniny, Sudeten 9 Beshchady, High Tatra, Holy Cross
    10 Carpathian
  highest point: 4 Rysy
  river: 3 Bug, San 4 Alle, Brda, Gwda, Lyna, Nysa, Oder, Styr 5 Biala, Drana, Dwina, Narev,
    Narew, Notec, Podra, Seret, Warta, Wista 6 Neisse, Niemen, Nyeman, Pilica, Pripet, Prosna,
    Styrpa, Wieprz 7 Nemunas, Vistula, Wistoka 8 Dniester
  sea: 6 Baltic
  physical feature:
    forest: 10 Bialowieza
    gulf: 6 Danzig, Gdansk
    lagoon: 7 Stettin 12 Frischeshaff
    plain: 7 Silesia
    plateau: 6 Lublin
  people: 4 Pole, Slav 5 Mazur 8 Silesian
    astronomer: 10 Copernicus
    author: 7 Reymont 8 Zeromski 10 Mickiewicz, Wyspianski 11 Sienkiewicz
    composer: 6 Chopin 10 Paderewski
    dynasty: 5 Piast 7 Jagello
    king: 7 Casimir 8 Augustus
    leader: 5 Kania 6 Gierek 7 Gomulka, Mieszko 8 Boleslaw 9 Pilsudski, Stanislaw 10 Jaruzel-
      ski, Kosciuszko, Lech Walesa
    pope: 10 John Paul II 20 Cardinal Carol Wojtyla
    queen: 7 Jadwiga
  language: 6 Kaszub, Polish 10 Pomeranian
  religion: 13 Roman Catholic
  place:
    castle: 5 Wawel
    church: 6 St John 10 Panna Maria
    monastery: 9 Jasna Gora
    monument: 17 Heroes of the Ghetto
    national park: 5 Ojcow 10 Bialowieza
    palace: 7 Casimir
  feature:
    folk dance: 5 polka 7 mazurka 9 krakowiak, polonaise
    union: 10 Solidarity
  food:
    dish: 5 bigos 7 kolduny
    drink: 5 vodka 7 Krupnik
    sausage: 8 kielbasa
    soup: 7 barszca

Were 15 Absence of Malice
23 They Shoot Horses Don't
They?

Pollock, Jackson
  born: 6 Cody WY
  artwork: 5 Scent 9 Blue
  Poles 10 The She-Wolf
  11 Convergence 12 Autumn

Rhythm 13 Eyes in the
Heat 17 Easter and the To-
tem 20 Guardians of the
Secret

pollutant 5 fumes, smoke,
waste 7 exhaust 8 emission,
impurity

pollute 4 foul, soil 5 dirty,

sully 6 befoul, debase, defile
7 deprave, profane 9 desecrate 10 adulterate, make
filthy 11 contaminate

polluted 4 foul 5 dirty, drunk
6 impure, soiled 7 corrupt,
profane, smashed, unclean
9 poisonous 12 contaminated

Polk, James Knox
presidential rank: 8 eleventh
party: 8 Democrat
state represented: 2 TN
defeated: 4 (Henry) Clay 6 (James Gillespie) Birney
vice president: 6 (George Mifflin) Dallas
cabinet:
  state: 8 (James) Buchanan
  treasury: 6 (Robert John) Walker
  war: 5 (William Learned) Marcy
  attorney general: 5 (John Young) Mason 6 (Isaac)
    Toucey 8 (Nathan) Clifford
  navy: 5 (John Young) Mason 8 (George) Bancroft
  postmaster general: 7 (Cave) Johnson
born: 2 NC 17 Mecklenburg County
died/buried: 2 TN 9 Nashville
education: 11 prep schools 16 tutored privately
  University: 13 North Carolina
religion: 9 Methodist
political career: 16 state legislature 17 Speaker of the
  House 24 US House of Representatives
  governor of: 9 Tennessee
civilian career: 6 lawyer
notable events of lifetime/term:
  boundary dispute: 9 Northwest
  discovery in California of: 4 gold
  Proviso: 6 Wilmot
  treaty of: 16 Guadalupe Hidalgo
  war: 7 Mexican
father: 6 Samuel
mother: 4 Jane
siblings: 7 John Lee 9 Jane Maria, Naomi Tate 10 Lydia
  Eliza 12 Marshall Tate, Samuel Wilson 14 William Hawkins 15 Franklin Ezekiel, Ophelia Clarissa
wife: 5 Sarah (Childress)
children: 4 none

pollution 7 fouling, soiling
8 defiling, dirtying, foulness,
impurity 9 befouling, pollutant 11 uncleanness 12 adulteration 13 contaminating,
contamination

Pollux *see* 15 Castor and
Pollux

Pollyanna
director: 10 David Swift
based on story by:
13 Eleanor Porter
cast: 9 Jane Wyman 10 Karl
Malden 11 Hayley Mills,
Richard Egan

polo
equipment: 6 mallet
period of play: 7 chukker
championship: 10 Camacho
Cup 13 Coronation Cup
16 Cup of the Americas

Polonius
character in: 6 Hamlet
author: 11 Shakespeare

Polska *see* 6 Poland

poltergeist 5 ghost 6 spirit
literally: 10 noise-ghost
manifestation: 5 knock,
noise, prank

Poltergeist
director: 10 Tobe Hooper
cast: 12 Craig T Nelson
14 Jobeth Williams 16 Beatrice Straight
co-writer/producer: 15 Steven Spielberg

poltroon 6 coward, craven
7 caitiff, chicken, dastard
11 yellow-belly

Polybates
member of: 8 Gigantes

Polycaste *see* 6 Perdix

Polydora
father: 6 Peleus
mother: 8 Antigone
husband: 5 Borus
son: 10 Menestheus

Polydorus
mentioned in: 5 Iliad
father: 5 Priam
10 Hippomedon
mother: 6 Hecuba
killed by: 10 Polymestor
11 Polymnestor
avenged by: 6 Hecuba
member of: 7 Epigoni
descendant of: 18 Seven
against Thebes

polygon 10 multiangle
11 plane figure
eight-sided: 7 octagon
equal angled: 6 isogon
five-sided: 8 pentagon
four-sided: 6 square 7 rhombus 8 tetragon 9 rectangle,
trapezoid
nine-sided: 7 nonagon
seven-sided: 8 heptagon
six-sided: 7 hexagon
ten-sided: 7 decagon
three-sided: 8 triangle
twelve-sided: 9 dodecagon

Polyhymnia
also: 8 Polymnia
member of: 5 Muses
personifies: 5 dance 11 sacred music
mother: 9 Mnemosyne

Polyidus
revived: 7 Glaucus

Polymastus
epithet of: 7 Artemis
means: 12 many-breasted

polymer 5 dimer, nylon 6 hy-
drol 7 hexamer 8 oligomer

Polymnestor
king of: 6 Thrace
killed: 9 Polydorus

Polymnia *see* 10 Polyhymnia

Polyneices *see* 9 Polynices

Polynesia *see box, p. 766*

Polynices
also: 10 Polyneices
father: 7 Oedipus
mother: 7 Jocasta
uncle: 5 Creon
brother: 7 Oedipus 8 Eteocles
sister: 6 Ismene 8 Antigone
killed by: 8 Eteocles

polyp 5 coral, hydra, tumor
6 growth, isopod 7 octopod
10 sea anemone

Polypemon *see* 10 Procrustes

Polyphemus
form: 7 Cyclops 12 one-eyed
giant
father: 6 Elatus 8 Poseidon
mother: 6 Thoosa
joined: 9 Argonauts
killed: 4 Acis
blinded by: 8 Odysseus
loved: 7 Galatea

Polyphides
king of: 6 Sicyon
vocation: 4 seer
protected: 8 Menelaus
9 Agamemnon

Polyphontes
brother: 11 Cresphontes
killed: 11 Cresphontes

polyphony 7 organum 8 fabur-
den 11 fauxbourdon
12 counterpoint

Polynesia
  name means: 11 many islands
  cities: 4 Apia 7 Papeete 8 Auckland, Pago Pago
    9 Nukualofa
  island: 4 Cook, Line 5 Samoa, Tonga 6 Easter, Ellice, Hawaii, Midway, Tahiti, Tubuai, Tuvalu 7 Austral, Maupiti, Phoenix, Society, Tokelau, Tuamotu 8 Pitcairn 9 Marquesas 10 New Zealand 15 French Polynesia
  sea: 7 Pacific
  people: 3 Ati 5 Maori 6 Kanaka, Nivean, Samoan, Tongan 9 Nesogaean 10 Polynesian
    explorer: 4 Cook 6 Tasman, Wallis 8 Magellan 9 Roggeveen 12 Bougainville
  language: 4 Niue, Uvea 5 Maori 6 Samoan, Tongan 7 Austral, Tagalog, Tokelau 8 Hawaiian, Tahitian 9 Marquesan, Tuamatuan 10 Mangarevan
  religion: 12 Christianity
  place:
    legendary origin: 8 Hawaiiki
  feature:
    chief: 5 matai
    clothing: 5 pareu 6 sarong 8 lavalava
    dance: 4 hula, siva
    dwelling: 4 fale
    family social unit: 4 aiga
    priest: 7 kahunas
    supernatural power: 4 mana
  food:
    dish: 3 kai, poi 4 taro 8 palusami
    drink: 3 ava 4 kava, kawa

Polypoetes
  king of: 10 Thesprotia
  father: 6 Apollo 8 Odysseus
    9 Pirithous
  mother: 6 Phthia 9 Callidice
    10 Hippodamia
  leader of: 6 Greeks

Polyporthis
  father: 8 Odysseus
  mother: 8 Penelope

polysaccharide 6 insulin, starch 7 dextrin 8 galactin, lichenin 9 cellulose 12 carbohydrate

Polytechnus
  wife: 5 Aedon

Polyxena
  father: 5 Priam
  mother: 6 Hecuba
  loved by: 8 Achilles

Polyxenus
  grandfather: 6 Augeas

Polyxo
  advisor to: 9 Hypsipyle

Pomaria see 7 Algeria

Pomerania
  capital: 7 Stettin
  city: 5 Thorn, Torun
    6 Anklam
  country: 6 Poland 7 Germany
  island: 5 Rugen 6 Usedom
  province: 7 Pomorze

pommel, pummel 4 beat, hilt, horn, knob, pake 6 finial, strike 9 saddlebow

Pomona
  origin: 5 Roman
  goddess of: 10 fruit trees

pomp 4 show 5 front, glory, style 7 display 8 ceremony, flourish, grandeur, splendor 9 pageantry, showiness, solemnity, spectacle 10 brilliance 11 affectation, grandiosity, ostentation, pompousness 12 magnificence 14 stately display 15 pretentiousness

pompous 4 vain 5 proud 6 lordly, uppish 7 haughty 8 affected, arrogant, mannered, overdone, puffed-up, snobbish 9 conceited, egotistic, grandiose, imperious 10 blustering, swaggering 11 overbearing, patronizing, pretentious 12 ostentatious, presumptuous, supercilious, vainglorious 13 condescending, high and mighty, self-important

Ponchielli, Amilcare
  born: 5 Italy 7 Cremona
  composer of: 10 La Gioconda 15 Dance of the Hours

poncho 4 cape 5 cloak, shawl 6 mantle, serape

pond 4 pool, tarn 5 basin 6 lagoon 9 small lake, water hole

ponder 4 muse 5 study 6 wonder 7 examine, reflect 8 cogitate, consider, mull over, ruminate 9 brood over, cerebrate, reflect on, speculate, think over 10 deliberate, meditate on, puzzle over 11 contemplate

ponderous 3 big 4 dull 5 bulky, heavy, hefty, large, wordy 6 boring, bovine, dreary 7 awkward, droning, hulking, labored, lumpish, massive, tedious, weighty 8 cumbrous, enormous, sluggish, unlively, unwieldy 9 corpulent, graceless, lumbering, wearisome 10 burdensome, cumbersome, long-winded, lusterless, monotonous, unexciting, ungraceful 11 heavy-handed

pontiff 4 pope 6 bishop, priest 8 pontifex

pontifical 7 pompous 8 churchly, clerical, dogmatic, priestly 9 apostolic, episcopal, imperious 11 opinionated, overbearing, patronizing, pretentious 13 authoritarian, condescending 14 ecclesiastical

Pontus
  personifies: 3 sea
  father: 2 Ge
  son: 6 Nereus 7 Phorcys

pony 3 nag 4 crib, trot 5 glass, horse, pinto 7 mustang 9 racehorse
  breed: 6 Exmoor 8 Shetland

pooh-pooh 5 knock 7 disdain, put down, run down, sneer at 8 belittle 9 disparage

Pooka see 4 Puca

pool 3 pot 4 ally, bank, lake, mere, pond, tarn 5 group, kitty, merge, share, union, unite 6 puddle, splash, stakes 7 combine 8 alliance, fishpond, millpool 9 coalition 10 amalgamate, collective 11 association, consolidate, cooperative 13 confederation

Poole, Grace
  character in: 8 Jane Eyre
  author: 6 Bronte

poop 3 fag 4 bush, deck, do in, tire 7 exhaust, fatigue, wear out 8 enervate

pooped 4 beat 5 all in, spent, tired, weary 6 bushed, done in 7 drained, wearied, worn out 8 fatigued, tired out 9 dead tired, exhausted, played out

poor 3 sad 4 bare, dead, vain, worn 5 broke, empty, needy, sorry 6 barren, fallow, faulty, futile, hard up, in need, in want, meager, paltry, wasted **7** forlorn, sterile, unhappy, unlucky, wanting **8** badly off, bankrupt, beggarly, depleted, desolate, devoid of, grieving, indigent, inferior, pathetic, pitiable, strapped, unworthy, wretched **9** defective, deficient, destitute, exhausted, fruitless, imperfect, infertile, insolvent, in straits, miserable, moneyless, penniless, unfertile, worthless **10** distressed, inadequate, pauperized **11** impecunious, unfortunate **12** impoverished, uncultivable, unproductive, unprofitable **15** poverty-stricken

Poor People
author: **16** Fyodor Dostoevsky

Poor Richard's Almanac
author: **16** Benjamin Franklin

Poor White
author: **16** Sherwood Anderson

pop 4 bang, boom, come, shot, snap, soda **5** arise, blast, burst, crack **6** appear, report **7** explode **8** detonate **9** discharge, explosion, soft drink **10** detonation

pope *see box*

Pope, Alexander
author of: **10** The Dunciad **12** An Essay on Man **15** Eloisa to Abelard **16** The Rape of the Lock **18** An Essay on Criticism **20** Epistle to Dr Arbuthnot

Pope, John Russell
architect of: **17** Jefferson Memorial **20** National Gallery of Art **23** Temple of the Scottish Rite **24** National Archives Building

Popeye
character in: **9** Sanctuary
author: **8** Faulkner

popinjay 3 fop **4** beau **5** dandy **7** coxcomb

poplar 7 Populus **22** Liriodendron tulipifera
varieties: **4** gray **5** black, downy, tulip, white **6** balsam, Eugene, yellow **8** Carolina, Lombardy, necklace **10** Queensland **12** Chinese white, silver-leaved **13** Western balsam

poppy 7 Papaver
varieties: **3** sea **4** blue, bush, corn, snow, tree, wind, wood **5** field, opium, plume, satin, tulip, water, Welsh **6** arctic, desert, horned **7** Asiatic, flaming, Iceland, Mexican, prickly, Shirley, Western **8** Flanders, hare-

bell, Matilija, oriental **9** Celandine **10** California, island tree **12** Mexican tulip **13** yellow Chinese **14** California tree
drug: **5** opium **6** heroin **8** morphine

poppycock 3 rot **4** bosh, bunk, jive, tosh **5** froth, fudge, hooey, stuff, trash **6** drivel, humbug **7** baloney, blabber, blather, eyewash, fustian, garbage, hogwash, inanity, prattle, rubbish, twaddle **8** falderal, flummery, nonsense, tommyrot, wish-wash **9** absurdity, gibberish, moonshine, rigmarole **10** applesauce, balderdash, flapdoodle, hocus-pocus, mumbo-jumbo, rigamarole **11** abracadabra, jabberwocky **12** fiddlefaddle, gobbledygook

poppy seed
botanical name: **7** Papaver **11** P somniferum (sleepbearing poppy)
color: **4** blue **5** white
origin: **4** Asia **6** Europe
guards against: **9** creditors
use: **5** bread, cakes, rolls **6** sweets **10** vegetables **11** butter sauce

populace 4 folk **6** people, public **7** society **9** citizenry, community **10** population

popular 5 cheap, civic, civil, stock **6** famous, public, social **7** admired, current, general, in favor **8** accepted, approved, communal, familiar, favorite, in demand, national, orthodox **9** community, preferred, prevalent, well-known, wellliked **10** affordable, celebrated,

---

pope 3 Leo **4** John, Paul, Pius **5** Peter, Urban **6** Adrian, Eugene, Julius, Martin, Sixtus **7** Clement, Gregory **8** Benedict, Innocent, John Paul, Nicholas **9** Alexander, Callistus
also: **12** Bishop of Rome **13** Vicar of Christ **14** Primate of Italy, Supreme Pontiff **16** Archbishop of Rome **18** Metropolitan of Rome, Patriarch of the West **25** Servant of the Servants of God
office: **6** Papacy **7** Holy See **11** Seat of Peter
elected by: **18** College of Cardinals
elected in: **8** conclave
signal that election is concluded: **10** white smoke
resides: **4** Rome **10** the Vatican **11** Vatican City
former residence: **13** Lateran Palace
summer residence: **14** Castel Gondolfo
papal land holding: **9** patrimony **21** patrimony of Saint Peter
first pope: **10** Saint Peter
pope who crowned Charlemagne: **6** Leo III
pope who excommunicated Luther: **4** Leo X
pope who authorized Michelangelo to paint Sistine Chapel: **8** Julius II
"September Pope": **9** John Paul I
real name of pope:
  Alexander VI: **15** Rodrigo de Borgia
  Callistus III: **15** Alfonso de Borgia
  Clement VII: **14** Giulio de' Medici
  John XXIII: **22** Angelo Giuseppe Roncalli
  John Paul I: **13** Albino Luciani
  John Paul II: **12** Karol Wojtyla **18** Archbishop of Krakow
  Leo X: **16** Giovanni de' Medici
  Pius XI: **12** Achille Ratti
  Pius XII: **35** Eugenio Maria Giuseppe Giovanni Pacelli
popes of Avignon papacy: **6** Urban V **8** Clement V, John XXII **9** Clement VI, Gregory XI, Nicholas V **10** Innocent VI **11** Benedict XII
popes during Great Western Schism:
  Avignon: **10** Clement VII **12** Benedict XIII
  Pisa: **9** John XXIII **10** Alexander V
  Rome: **7** Urban VI **10** Boniface IX, Gregory XII **11** Innocent VII
papal bull/encyclical: **11** Unam sanctam **12** Humanae vitae, Rerum novarum, Vox in excelso **13** Pacem in terris **15** Mater et magistra **19** Populorum progressio **22** Sacerdotalis caelibatus

democratic **11** established, fashionable, inexpensive, of the people, sought-after

popularity 4 fame, note **5** favor, glory, kudos, vogue **6** esteem, regard, renown, repute **7** acclaim, fashion **8** approval **9** celebrity, notoriety **10** acceptance, admiration, notability, reputation **11** acclamation

popular opinion
  Latin: **9** vox populi

popular whim 3 fad **4** rage **5** craze, mania **7** passion **11** infatuation

populate 6 occupy, people, settle **7** inhabit

populated 5 urban **7** peopled, settled **8** citified, occupied **9** inhabited

population 4 folk **6** people, public **8** citizens, populace **9** citizenry, habitancy, residents **11** body politic, commonality, inhabitants

populous 5 dense **6** jammed **7** crowded, peopled, teeming **8** swarming, thronged

porcelain 5 china **11** ceramic ware

porch 4 stoa **5** lanai, plaza, stoop **7** balcony, narthex, portico, veranda **8** solarium, verandah **9** colonnade, vestibule

pore 4 hole, read, scan **5** probe, study **6** outlet, peruse, ponder, review, search, survey **7** dig into, examine, explore, inspect, orifice **8** aperture, consider **9** delve into

Porfiry
  character in: **18** Crime and Punishment
  author: **10** Dostoevsky

Porgy
  author: **13** DuBose Heyward

Porgy and Bess
  opera by: **14** George Gershwin
  character: **4** Bess **5** Porgy **11** Sportin' Life

pornographic 4 blue, lewd **5** bawdy, dirty, gross **6** coarse, filthy, smutty, vulgar **7** obscene **8** indecent, off-color, prurient **9** salacious **10** lascivious, licentious

porous 4 lacy **6** spongy **7** riddled **8** cellular, pervious **9** absorbent, permeable, sievelike **10** penetrable **11** honeycombed

Porphyrion
  member of: **8** Gigantes

porpoise 4 leap **5** whale **6** pal-

ach, puffer, seahog **7** cowfish, dolphin, surface **8** cetacean
  genus: **8** Phocaena **9** Delphinus

porridge 4 pobs, samp **5** atole, brose, brout, gruel **6** cereal **7** crowdie, oatmeal, polenta **8** flummery

Porrima *see* **9** Antevorta

porringer 4 bowl, dish **6** vessel **9** container **10** receptacle

port 4 dock, pier, quay **5** haven, wharf **6** harbor, refuge **7** dry dock, landing, mooring, seaport, shelter **9** anchorage, harborage **11** destination

port
  type: **4** wine **6** brandy
  origin: **8** Portugal
  variety: **4** ruby **5** tawny **7** vintage
  with brandy: **9** Betsy Ross
  with vermouth: **10** Broken Spur

portable 5 handy, light, small **6** bantam, pocket **7** compact, folding, movable **8** cartable, haulable, liftable **9** ready-to-go **10** convenient, conveyable, manageable, vest-pocket **11** pocket-sized

portal, portals 4 adit, arch, door, gate **5** entry **6** wicket **7** doorway, gateway, portico **8** approach, entrance **9** threshold, vestibule **10** portcullis **11** entranceway

Port-au-Prince
  capital of: **5** Haiti

porte-monnaie 5 purse **10** pocketbook **12** money-carrier

portend 4 bode **5** augur **6** denote, herald, warn of **7** bespeak, betoken, point to, predict, presage, signify, suggest **8** forebode, forecast, foretell, forewarn, prophesy **9** foretoken, prefigure **10** foreshadow

portent 4 omen, sign **5** token **6** augury, boding, threat **7** presage, warning **9** harbinger **10** foreboding **11** forewarning

portentous 6 superb **7** amazing, fateful, ominous, pompous **8** alarming, menacing **9** bombastic, grandiose, prophetic **10** foreboding, incredible, prodigious, remarkable, stupendous, surprising **11** astonishing, exceptional, frightening, pretentious, significant, superlative, threatening **12** inauspicious, intimidating, unpropitious

porter 4 brew **5** stout **6** bearer, coolie, redcap, skycap **7** carrier **8** conveyer **9** conductor

Porter, Katherine Anne
  author of: **11** Ship of Fools **12** Old Mortality **14** Flowering Judas **15** The Leaning Tower **18** Pale Horse Pale Rider

Porter, William Sidney
  real name of: **6** O Henry

portfolio 4 case, file **5** album **6** binder, folder **7** dossier **8** envelope **9** scrapbook **10** securities

Porthos
  character in: **18** The Three Musketeers
  author: **5** Dumas (pere)

Portia
  character in: **12** Julius Caesar **19** The Merchant of Venice
  author: **11** Shakespeare

portico 4 stoa **5** lanai **6** piazza **7** balcony, veranda, walkway

portion 3 cut, lot, sum **4** dole, doom, fate, luck, part **5** carve, cut up, moira, piece, sever, share, slice, split **6** amount, divide, kismet, parcel, ration, sector **7** break up, deal out, destiny, fortune, helping, measure, section, segment, serving **8** allocate, disperse, division, fraction, fragment, quantity, separate **9** allotment, allowance, demarcate, partition **10** allocation, distribute, percentage

portion out 5 allot **6** ration **7** dole out, mete out, prorate **8** allocate, dispense, divide up **9** apportion, parcel out **10** distribute, measure out

Portland
  basketball team: **12** Trailblazers
  football team: **8** Breakers
  river: **8** Columbia **10** Willamette
  university: **4** Reed

Port Louis
  capital of: **9** Mauritius

portly 3 big, fat **4** full **5** beefy, burly, heavy, large, obese, plump, pudgy, round, stout, tubby **6** brawny, chubby, fleshy, rotund, stocky **9** corpulent

Portman, John
  architect of: **15** Peachtree Center (Atlanta)

portmanteau 3 bag **4** grip **5** cloak **6** mantle, valise **8** suitcase **9** gladstone

Port Moresby
capital of: **9** New Guinea

Portnoy's Complaint
author: **10** Philip Roth

Port of Spain
capital of: **17** Trinidad and Tobago

Porto-Novo
capital of: **5** Benin

portrait 5 cameo **6** sketch **7** drawing, picture **8** likeness, painting, vignette **9** depiction **10** impression, photograph **11** description

Portrait of a Lady, The
author: **10** Henry James
character: **11** Madame Merle, Pansy Osmond **12** Isabel Archer **13** Gilbert Osmond, Lord Warburton, Ralph Touchett **14** Caspar Goodwood **18** Henrietta Stackpole

Portrait of the Artist as a Young Man
author: **10** James Joyce
character: **4** Emma **12** Simon Dedalus **14** Stephen Dedalus

portray 3 ape **4** draw, play **5** carve, enact, mimic, model, paint **6** depict, detail, figure, pose as, sketch **7** imitate, narrate, picture **8** describe, set forth, simulate **9** delineate, represent, sculpture **10** illustrate, photograph **11** impersonate **12** characterize

portrayal 7 picture **8** portrait **9** picturing **11** delineation, description **14** representation **16** characterization

ports
god of: **8** Portunus

Portugal *see box, p. 770*

Portuguese Guinea *see* **12** Guinea-Bissau

Portuguese West Africa *see* **6** Angola

Portunus
origin: **5** Roman
god of: **5** ports **7** harbors

posada 3 inn **12** halting place

pose 3 air, set **4** cast, mien **5** group, order, state, style **6** line up, stance, submit **7** advance, arrange, bearing, bring up, posture, present, propose, show off, suggest **8** attitude, carriage, position, propound, set forth, throw out **9** mannerism, postulate **10** put forward

Poseidon
also: **9** Asphalius
origin: **5** Greek
god of: **3** sea
caused: **11** earthquakes

father: **6** Cronos
mother: **4** Rhea
brother: **4** Zeus
wife: **10** Amphitrite
lover: **2** Ge **6** Aethra, Medusa, Thoosa **7** Demeter
child: **5** Arion **6** Triton **7** Antaeus, Pegasus, Theseus **8** Chrysaor **10** Polyphemus
symbol: **5** horse **7** trident
epithet: **11** Ennosigaeus, Hippocurius **12** Prosclystius
corresponds to: **7** Neptune

poser 5 facer **6** puzzle **7** problem **8** examiner, stickler

posh 4 chic **5** fancy, ritzy, smart, swell **6** chi-chi, classy, deluxe, lavish, swanky **7** elegant, opulent, refined, stylish **9** high-class, luxurious **11** extravagant

position 3 fix, job, put, set **4** duty, pose, post, role, site **5** array, caste, class, locus, lodge, order, place, stand, state **6** career, charge, ground, locate, office, plight, stance, status **7** arrange, deposit, opinion, outlook, posture, situate, station, vantage **8** attitude, capacity, eminence, function, locality, location, prestige, standing **9** condition, elevation, establish, placement, situation, viewpoint **10** assignment, commission, importance, notability, prominence **11** appointment, consequence, disposition, distinction, frame of mind, point of view

position decided upon
French: **9** parti pris

positive 4 firm, good, real, sure **5** total **6** narrow, useful **7** assured, certain, gainful, helpful **8** absolute, cocksure, complete, decisive, definite, dogmatic, explicit, obdurate, salutary **9** assertive, confident, convinced, effective, immovable, practical, satisfied, veritable **10** applicable, autocratic, beneficial, conclusive, definitive, optimistic, undisputed, undoubting **11** affirmative, cooperative, dead certain, dictatorial, irrefutable, opinionated, overbearing, practicable, progressive, self-assured, serviceable, unequivocal, unqualified **12** confirmatory, constructive, contributory, unchangeable **13** corroborative, thoroughgoing **16** incontrovertible

positively 9 assuredly, certainly, decidedly, literally **10** absolutely, definitely **11** confidently, indubitably **12** emphatically, indisputably, unmistakably, without doubt

13 affirmatively, categorically, unqualifiedly **14** beyond question, unhesitatingly, unquestionably

possess 3 own **4** grab, have, hold **5** boast, enjoy **6** absorb, fixate, obsess, occupy **7** acquire, bedevil, bewitch, command, conquer, consume, control, enchant, overrun **8** dominate, dominate, maintain, take over, vanquish **9** fascinate, hypnotize, influence, mesmerize

Possessed, The
author: **16** Fyodor Dostoevsky
character: **5** Marya, Pyotr **6** Shatov **7** Nikolay **16** Varvara Stavrogin **17** Stepan Verhovensky

possession 4 hold **5** asset, poise, title **6** effect, owning **7** command, control, control, custody, tenancy **8** calmness, coolness, dominion, province, resource **9** belonging, composure, occupancy, ownership, placidity, sangfroid, territory **10** equanimity, even temper, occupation, possessing **11** equilibrium, self-control **12** accoutrement, protectorate

possibility 4 hope, odds, risk **6** chance, gamble, hazard **7** promise **8** prospect **9** prospects **10** likelihood **11** contingency, eventuality, feasibility, probability, workability **12** potentiality **14** practicability

possible 8 credible, feasible, workable **9** potential, thinkable **10** achievable, admissible, attainable, cognizable, compatible, contingent, imaginable, manageable, obtainable, reasonable **11** conceivable, performable, practicable **12** hypothetical

possibly 5 at all, maybe **6** mayhap **7** could be, perhaps **8** in any way, normally **9** at the most, perchance **10** by any means, God willing **11** conceivably

post 2 PX **3** fix, job, put, set **4** base, beat, camp, pale, part, pile, pole, role, seat, send, spot, work **5** brace, house, lodge, place, put up, round, shaft, stake **6** advise, column, inform, locate, notify, office, picket, report, settle, splint, tack up **7** apprise, declare, install, mission, publish, quarter, routine, situate, station, support, upright **8** acquaint, announce, capacity, disclose, exchange, fasten up, function, instruct, mainstay, position, proclaim **9** advertise, broad-

Portugal
  capital/largest city: 6 Lisbon
  others: 4 Beja, Faro, Ovar **5** Braga, Evora, Olhao, Porto, Viseu **6** Aveiro, Guarda, Leiria, Oporto, Sintra **7** Algarve, Amadora, Bragama, Cascoes, Coimbra, Covilha, Estoril, Funchal, Granada, Setubal **8** Barreiro, Portimao **9** Lusitania **10** Portalegre **14** Vila Nova de Gaia
   Roman city: **10** Portus Cale
  school: 5 Minho **6** Aveiro, Lisbon, Oporto **7** Coimbra
  division: 3 Goa **4** Tejo, Tete **5** Beira, Evora, Macao, Minho, Timor **6** Azores, Loanda **7** Algarve, Madeira **8** Alemteho, Rebatejo **9** Cape Verde **10** Mozambique **11** Estremadura
   Roman district: **9** Lusitania
  measure: 2 pe **4** bota, moio, vara **5** almud, fanga, geira, linha, milha **6** almude, covado **7** alquier, ferrado, selamin **8** alqueire
  monetary unit: 3 avo, rei **4** peca, real **5** conto, crown, dobra, indio, justo, rupia **6** escudo, macuta, octave, pataca, testad, tostao, vintem **7** angalar, centavo, crusado, miereis, testone **8** equipaga, johannes
  weight: 4 onca, once **5** libra, marco **6** arroba **7** arratel **9** excropulo
  island: 6 Azores **7** Madeira **8** Terceira
  mountain: 4 Acor, Lapa **5** Gerez, Marao, Mousa **6** Bornes, Peneda **7** Larouco **8** Caramulo **9** Caldeirao, Monchique **14** Serra da Estrela
  highest point: 11 Pico da Serra
  river: 3 Sor, Tua **4** Lima, Mino, Mira, Sado, Seda, Tago, Tajo, Tejo, Vara **5** Douro, Duero, Legoa, Micha, Minho, Sabar, Tagus, Vouga, Zatas **6** Cavado, Chanca, Quarto, Tamega, Zezere **7** Mondego, Selamin, Sorraia **8** Quadiana, Tonelada
  ocean: 8 Atlantic
  physical feature:
   bay: **7** Setubal
   cape: **4** Roca **7** Mondego **8** Espichel **9** St Vincent
   peninsula: **7** Iberian
   port: **4** Faro **6** Aveiro, Lisbon, Oporto **7** Leixoes
  people: 4 Celt, Moor **7** Iberian **10** Portuguese
   artist: **7** Pereira **9** Goncalves **13** Soares dos Reis
   author: **5** Dinis **6** Camoes, Vieiva **7** Garrett, Vicente **9** Deus-Ramos
   explorer: **3** Cam, Cao **4** Dias, Diaz **6** Cabral, Da Gama **7** Almeida **8** Magellan **11** Albuquerque **23** Prince Henry the Navigator
   king: **6** Manuel, Philip, Sancho **7** Alfonso **9** Ferdinand, Sebastian
   leader: **5** Eanes **6** Dombal, Soares **7** Caetano, Carmona, Salazar, Spinola
   queen: **5** Maria **9** Elizabeth
  language: 10 Portuguese
  religion: 13 Roman Catholic
  place:
   church: **5** Jesus **6** Christ **11** Os Jeronimos, Sao Lourenco **12** Old Cathedral **13** Santa Engracia **16** Sao Vicente de Fora
   city square: **15** Praca do Comercio
   dam: **6** Belver, Idanha **13** Castelo do Bode
   fortress-church: **12** Leco do Bailio
   monastery: **8** Alcobaca **12** Hieronymites **20** Santa Maria da Victoira
   monument: **11** Discoveries
   museum: **13** Soares dos Reis
   palace: **6** Cintra
   shrine: **6** Fatima
  colony: 5 Macad, Macao
   former colony: **3** Goa **5** Timor **6** Angola **7** Sao Tome **8** Principe, St Thomas **9** Cape Verde **10** Mozambique **12** Guinea Bissau
  feature:
   song: **4** fado
  food:
   dish: **8** bacalhau, bucellas **10** calcavella **11** carcavellos
   sausage: **8** linguica
   wine: **4** port **7** madeira

---

cast, circulate, enlighten, establish, make known, situation **10** assignment, settlement

postdate 6 follow **7** succeed **9** come after

poster 4 bill, sign **6** notice

7 placard **8** bulletin **13** advertisement

posterior 3 bum, can **4** back, butt, prat, rear, rump, seat, tail, tush **5** fanny, stern, tushy **6** behind, bottom, caudal, dorsal, hinder **7** keister **8** backside, buttocks, derriere,

hindmost, rearward **9** aftermost

Posterior Analytics
  author: 9 Aristotle

posterity 5 heirs, issue, young **6** family **7** descent, history, lineage, progeny **8** children **9** offspring **10** succession, successors **11** descendants

post hoc, ergo propter hoc 29 after this therefore because of it
describes: **14** logical fallacy

Posthumus, Leonatus
character in: **9** Cymbeline
author: **11** Shakespeare

Postman Always Rings Twice, The
director: **10** Tay Garnett
based on story by: **10** James M Cain
cast: **10** Hume Cronym, Lana Turner **12** John Garfield **13** Cecil Kellaway

postpone 4 stay **5** defer, delay, table, waive **6** put off, remand, shelve **7** adjourn, lay over, reserve, suspend

postponement 4 stay **5** delay **6** recess **7** tabling **8** abeyance, deferral **9** deferment, extension **10** suspension

postscript 2 ps **5** rider **7** codicil **8** addendum **10** attachment

postulate 5 axiom, guess **6** assume, hazard, submit, theory **7** premise, presume, propose, surmise, theorem **8** put forth, theorize **9** speculate **10** assumption, conjecture, hypothesis, presuppose **11** hypothesize, presumption

posture 3 air, set **4** case, mien, mood, pose, post, tone **5** phase, place, shape, state, tenor **6** aspect, stance, status **7** bearing, contour, station **8** attitude, carriage, position, standing **9** condition, situation **11** predicament **12** circumstance

Postvorta
form: **5** nymph
member of: **7** Camenae
knowledge of: **4** past

posy 5 bloom, motto **6** flower, phrase **7** blossom, bouquet, corsage, garland, nosegay

pot 3 pan **4** ruin **5** crock, kitty **6** vessel **9** container, marijuana **11** rack and ruin
Spanish: **4** olla

potable 3 ale **5** clean, drink, water **6** liquor **8** beverage, quencher **9** drinkable

potage 4 soup **9** thick soup

potassium
chemical symbol: **1** K

potato 16 Solanum tuberosum
varieties: **3** air, yam **4** duck, swan, wild, Zulu **5** Idaho, Irish, Maine, rural, swamp, sweet, white **6** Russet

7 Burbank, epicure, prairie, Telinga
dish: **4** chip **5** baked, salad **6** mashed **8** au gratin **9** lyonnaise, scalloped **11** french fries **12** baked stuffed

Potawatomi
language family: **9** Algonkian **10** Algonquian
location: **4** Ohio **6** Kansas **7** Indiana **8** Illinois, Michigan, Oklahoma **9** Wisconsin
leader: **7** Pontiac
united with: **6** Ojibwa, Ottawa **7** Ojibway

Potemkin
director: **17** Sergei Eisenstein
cast: **14** Vladimir Barsky **16** Alexander Antonov **17** Grigori Alexandrov
famous segment: **11** Odessa Steps

potency 3 vis **5** force, power **6** energy **8** efficacy, strength, virility, vitality

potent 5 solid, tough **6** mighty, strong **7** dynamic **8** forceful, forcible, powerful, vigorous **9** effective, operative **10** compelling, convincing, formidable, impressive, persuasive **11** efficacious, influential **12** overpowering

potentate 4 lord **5** chief, mogul, ruler **6** prince, satrap, sultan **7** emperor, monarch **8** overlord, suzerain **9** chieftain, sovereign

potential 6 covert, hidden, latent **7** dormant, lurking, passive **8** implicit, possible **9** concealed, quiescent, unexerted **10** unapparent, unrealized **11** conceivable, undisclosed, unexpressed

potentiality 7 ability **10** capability **13** possibilities

potentially
Latin: **7** in posse

pother 3 ado **4** fuss, stir, to-do **6** bustle, flurry, hustle, tumult **8** activity **9** agitation, commotion

Pothos
companion of: **9** Aphrodite
personifies: **6** desire **7** longing

potion 4 brew, dram **5** draft, tonic **6** elixir **7** mixture, philter **8** libation, potation **10** concoction

Pot of Gold, The
author: **7** Plautus

Potok, Chaim
author of: **9** The Chosen

10 Wanderings **15** The Book of Lights

potpourri 4 hash, mess, olio, stew **6** jumble, medley, mosaic, motley **7** farrago, goulash, melange, mixture **8** mishmash, pastiche **9** patchwork **10** hodgepodge, miscellany, salmagundi **11** gallimaufry, olla podrida

pottage 4 soup, stew **6** brewis **8** porridge

Potter, Beatrix
author of: **11** (The Tale of) Peter Rabbit **21** The Tailor of Gloucester

Potter, Muff
character in: **9** Tom Sawyer
author: **5** Twain

potter's field 8 boneyard, cemetery **9** graveyard **12** burial ground **13** burying ground

pottery 5 china **8** clayware, crockery **11** ceramic ware, earthenware

pouch 3 bag, kit, sac **4** sack **5** purse **6** pocket, wallet **7** handbag, satchel **8** carryall, ditty bag, reticule, rucksack **9** container **10** pocketbook, receptacle

Poulenc, Francis
born: **5** Paris **6** France
member of: **6** Les Six, The Six
composer of: **9** Les Biches **13** The Carmelites **22** Dialogues des Carmelites

poultice 7 plaster **8** dressing **10** medicament

poultry 3 hen **4** cock, duck, fowl, swan **5** capon, geese, goose, quail **6** grouse, layers, pigeon, turkey **7** chicken, peacock, rooster **8** pheasant **9** partridge **10** guinea fowl
breed: **6** Ancona, Bantam **7** Cornish, Dorking, Leghorn **9** Wyandotte **12** Plymouth Rock **14** Rhode Island Red
disease: **3** pip **4** roup, tick
farm: **7** hennery
house: **4** coop

pounce 4 jump, leap **5** fly at, swoop **6** ambush, dash at, jump at, plunge, snatch, spring **8** downrush, fall upon, surprise

Pounce, Peter
character in: **13** Joseph Andrews
author: **8** Fielding

pound 4 bang, beat, drub, drum, maul **5** clomp, clout, crush, grind, march, paste, smack, stomp, throb, thump,

tramp **6** batter, bruise, cudgel, hammer, pummel, strike, thrash, thwack, wallop **7** clobber, crumble, pulsate, thunder, trounce **8** lambaste **9** fustigate, palpitate, pulverize **13** sixteen ounces
abbreviation: 2 lb

Pound, Ezra
author of: **6** Cantos **8** Personae **11** Exultations, Pisan Cantos

pound troy
abbreviation: 3 lb t

pour 3 tap **4** drip, drop, flow, gush, ooze, rain, seep, slop **5** drain, flood, issue, spill, spout **6** decant, deluge, drench, effuse, squirt, stream **7** cascade, draw off, dribble, lade out **15** rain cats and dogs **16** come down in sheets **17** come down in buckets

pourboire 3 tip **8** gratuity
literally: 11 for drinking

pourparler 29 informal preliminary conference
literally: 10 for talking

Poussin, Nicholas
born: 6 France **10** Les Andelys
artwork: 10 The Seasons **14** Birth of Bacchus, St John on Patmos **17** Bacchanalian Revel **18** The Burial of Phocion **19** The Poet's Inspiration **20** The Arcadian Shepherds **23** Landscape with Polyphemus, The Holy Family on the Steps **27** The Adoration of the Golden Calf

pou sto 14 place to stand on, where I may stand **16** base of operations

pout 4 crab, fret, fume, mope, sulk **5** brood, frown, lower, scowl **6** glower
French: 4 moue

poverty 4 lack, need, want **6** dearth, penury **7** beggary, deficit, paucity **8** scarcity, shortage **9** indigence, neediness, pauperism, privation **10** bankruptcy, deficiency, insolvency, meagerness, mendicancy **11** destitution **13** insufficiency, pennilessness **14** impoverishment

poverty-stricken 4 poor **5** broke, needy **8** indigent **9** destitute, penniless **10** down and out

powder 4 dust, talc **5** emery **6** pollen, talcum **7** crumble **9** pulverize
antiseptic: 6 formin **7** aristol
applier: 4 puff

cookery: 4 soda
cosmetic: 5 blush, rouge **7** compact
poisonous: 5 robin

powder-blue 5 azure **6** pastel **7** sky-blue **8** pale-blue **9** light-blue, robin's egg

powdery 5 dusty, mealy **6** chalky, floury, grated, ground, milled **7** crushed, pestled **8** shredded **10** comminuted, pulverized, triturated

Powell, Dick
real name: 14 Richard E Powell
born: 14 Mountain View AR
wife: 11 June Allyson **12** Joan Blondell
costar: 10 Ruby Keeler
roles: 7 Mrs Mike **8** Cornered **12** Johnny O'Clock **13** Murder My Sweet **15** Footlight Parade **17** Forty-second Street **32** Gold Diggers of Nineteen Thirty-three

Powell, Jane
real name: 12 Suzanne Burce
born: 10 Portland OR
roles: 5 Irene **12** Royal Wedding **13** A Date with Judy **27** Seven Brides for Seven Brothers

Powell, John
nickname: 4 Boog
sport: 8 baseball
team: 16 Baltimore Orioles

Powell, Michael
codirector: 17 Emeric Pressburger
director of: 11 The Red Shoes **14** Black Narcissus **16** Stairway to Heaven

Powell, SR
creator/artist of: 22 Sheena Queen of the Jungle

Powell, William
born: 12 Pittsburgh PA
wife: 13 Carole Lombard
costar: 8 Myrna Loy
roles: 10 Philo Vance, The Thin Man **11** Nick Charles **12** My Man Godfrey **13** Mister Roberts **14** Life with Father **16** The Great Ziegfeld **22** How to Marry a Millionaire

power 4 gift, sway **5** brawn, force, might, right, ruler, skill, vigor **6** energy, genius, muscle, status, talent **7** faculty, license, operate, potency, quality **8** activate, aptitude, capacity, energize, iron grip, pressure, prestige, property, strength, vitality **9** attribute, authority, endowment, influ-

ence, puissance **10** capability, competence
Latin: 3 vis

Power, Tyrone
born: 12 Cincinnati OH
wife: 9 Annabella **14** Linda Christian
roles: 10 Jesse James **12** Blood and Sand **13** The Razor's Edge **14** Nightmare Alley, The Mark of Zorro **15** The Sun Also Rises **18** Captain from Castile

Power and the Glory, The
author: 12 Graham Greene

powerful 5 hardy, husky, stout **6** brawny, cogent, mighty, moving, potent, robust, sturdy **7** intense, rousing **8** athletic, emphatic, exciting, forceful, incisive, muscular, stalwart, vigorous **9** effective, energetic, herculean, strapping **10** able-bodied, commanding, invincible

powerhouse 9 strongman **10** power plant **15** generating plant

powerless 4 weak **6** feeble, infirm **7** unarmed **8** crippled, disabled, feckless, helpless, impotent **9** incapable, pregnable, prostrate, vulnerable, weaponless **11** debilitated, defenseless, immobilized **13** incapacitated

powerlessness 8 debility, weakness **9** impotence, inability, infirmity **10** enervation, feebleness, inadequacy, incapacity **12** helplessness, incapability, inefficiency **13** vulnerability

Power Politics
author: 14 Margaret Atwood

powers that be 9 higher-ups **10** government **11** authorities **13** establishment **14** administration

Powhatan
language family: 9 Algonkian **10** Algonquian
tribe: 11 Confederacy
location: 8 Atlantic, Maryland, Virginia
leader: 8 Powhatan **11** Opechancano **13** Wahunsonacock
member: 10 Pocahontas

powwow 4 meet, talk **5** forum **6** caucus, confer, huddle, parley **7** consult, convene, council, discuss, meeting, palaver **8** assembly, colloquy, conclave, congress **9** discourse, interview **10** colloquium, conference, convention, discussion, round table **12** consultation

Poyser, Martin
character in: 8 Adam Bede
author: 5 Eliot

practicable 6 doable, viable
8 feasible, possible, workable
9 practical 10 achievable, attainable, functional

practical 4 able 5 solid, sound
6 expert, useful, versed
7 skilled, trained, veteran,
working 8 seasoned, sensible,
skillful 9 efficient, judicious,
practiced, pragmatic, qualified,
realistic 10 functional, hardheaded, instructed, proficient,
systematic, unromantic
11 down-to-earth, experienced,
pragmatical, serviceable, utilitarian 12 accomplished, businesslike, matter-of-fact
13 unsentimental

practical joke 4 jape 5 caper,
prank, stunt, trick

practically 6 all but, almost,
nearly 8 actually, in effect
9 basically, in the main, just
about, virtually 11 essentially
13 fundamentally, substantially

practice 2 do 3 use, way
4 deed, mode, play, rule, ruse,
ways, wont 5 apply, dodge,
drill, habit, train, trick, usage
6 action, custom, device, effect, follow, manner, method,
pursue, ritual, work at 7 conduct, fashion, perform, process, qualify, routine, utilize
8 carry out, engage in, exercise, live up to, maneuver, rehearse, tendency, training
9 execution, operation, perform in, procedure, rehearsal,
seasoning, set to work, turn
to use 10 discipline, observance, prepare for, repetition
11 application, be engaged in,
performance, preparation

practiced 4 able, fine 5 adept
6 adroit, expert 7 capable,
drilled, pursued, skilled,
trained 8 masterly, polished,
seasoned, skillful, worked at
9 competent, engaged in, masterful, qualified, rehearsed
10 cultivated, proficient 11 experienced, prepared for
12 accomplished

practice sorcery 5 charm
7 bewitch, conjure, enchant
9 work magic 10 cast a spell

Practicing History
author: 15 Barbara W
Tuchman

practitioner 6 doctor 7 dentist
9 performer 12 professional

pragmatic 5 sober 8 sensible
9 hard-nosed, practical, realistic 10 hardheaded, hardboiled 11 down-to-earth,

utilitarian 12 businesslike,
matter-of-fact, unidealistic
13 materialistic, unsentimental

Praia
capital of: 9 Cape Verde

prairie 3 bay 5 llano, pampa,
plain 6 camass, meadow,
steppe 7 quamash 9 grassland
apple: 9 breadroot
berry: 9 trampillo
chicken: 6 grouse
dog: 6 gopher, marmot
schooner: 12 covered wagon
state: 8 Illinois
wolf: 6 coyote

Prairie, The
author: 19 James Fenimore
Cooper
character: 4 Inez 9 Dr Battius, Ellen Wade, HardHeart, Paul Hover 10 Esther
Bush 11 Abiram White, Ishmael Bush, Natty Bumppo
16 Captain Middleton

Prairie State
nickname of: 8 Illinois

praise 4 laud, tout 5 cheer, exalt, extol, honor 6 esteem, eulogy, hurrah, regard, revere
7 acclaim, applaud, approve,
build up, commend, glorify,
plaudit, respect, root for, tribute, worship 8 accolade, applause, approval, encomium,
eulogize, venerate 9 adoration,
celebrate, good words, laudation, panegyric 10 admiration,
compliment, panegyrize
11 approbation, compliments,
testimonial 12 appreciation,
commendation, congratulate
14 congratulation
Hebrew: 6 hallel

praise be to God
Latin: 7 laus Deo

praiseful 8 praising 9 extolling,
laudatory 10 plauditory
12 commendatory
13 complimentary

praiseworthiness 5 merit
10 excellence 12 admirability,
desirability 14 commendability

praiseworthy 4 fine 6 worthy
8 laudable 9 admirable, estimable, excellent, exemplary
11 commendable, meritorious

pram, praam, prahm 4 boat
5 buggy 6 vessel 7 rowboat
8 carriage, stroller
12 perambulator

prance 4 jump, leap, romp,
skip 5 bound, caper, dance,
frisk, strut, vault 6 bounce, cavort, frolic, gambol, spring
7 swagger

prank 4 joke, lark 5 antic, caper, spoof, stunt, trick 6 gambol 8 escapade, mischief

9 horseplay 10 shenanigan,
tomfoolery

prate 3 gab, yak 4 blab, brag,
chat, crow, talk 5 boast
6 babble, gabble, jabber
7 blabber, chatter, prattle,
twaddle, twattle

Prathet Thai see 8 Thailand

Pratt, William Henry
real name of: 12 Boris
Karloff

prattle 3 gab, yak 4 blab
5 prate 6 babble, gabble, hot
air, jabber 7 blather, chatter,
twaddle 8 cackling, chitchat,
gabbling 9 gibbering, jabbering

Pravda 16 Russian newspaper
literally: 5 truth

Praxithea
husband: 10 Erechtheus
daughters: 8 Orithyia
10 Protogonia

pray 3 beg, bid, sue 4 urge
5 cry to, plead 7 beseech, entreat, implore, request, solicit
8 call upon, invocate, petition
9 importune 10 supplicate

prayer 6 litany, orison, praise
7 worship 9 adoration
12 thanksgiving
13 glorification

prayerful 4 holy 5 godly,
pious 6 devout, solemn 8 reverent 9 pietistic, religious, spiritual 10 worshipful
11 reverential

prayers 4 hope, plea, suit
5 dream 6 appeal 7 request
8 entreaty, petition 10 aspiration, invocation 11 beseechment 12 solicitation,
supplication

prayer service 9 devotions
13 prayer meeting 14 worship
service

pray for us
Latin: 11 ora pro nobis

pray to 3 beg 5 plead 7 address, entreat, worship 8 call
upon, petition, venerate
10 supplicate

preach 4 urge 6 advise, exhort 7 counsel, declare, expound, profess 8 admonish,
advocate, homilize, proclaim,
stand for 9 discourse, hold
forth, preachify, prescribe,
pronounce, propagate, sermonize 10 evangelize, promulgate

preacher 5 vicar 6 curate, parson, pastor 8 chaplain, homilist, minister, reverend, sky
pilot 9 churchman, clergyman
10 evangelist, prebendary, sermonizer 12 ecclesiastic
13 man of the cloth

preachy 8 didactic, pedantic
10 moralistic, moralizing

prearranged 7 planned 10 calculated, deliberate, purposeful
11 intentional 12 premeditated

pre-Cambrian 5 Azoic
6 Eozoic 7 primary 10 Archeozoic 11 Proterozoic

precarious 5 risky, shaky
6 chancy, unsafe 7 dubious
8 alarming, critical, doubtful,
insecure, perilous, sinister,
ticklish, unstable, unsteady
9 hazardous, uncertain
10 touch-and-go, unreliable,
vulnerable 12 questionable,
uncontrolled, undependable
13 problematical

precaution 4 care 7 caution,
defense 8 prudence, security,
wariness 9 foresight, provision,
safeguard 10 protection
11 carefulness, forethought,
heedfulness 12 anticipation
14 circumspection

precede 8 antecede, antedate,
go before 9 go ahead of
10 come before

precedence, precedency
8 priority 10 importance, preference, prevalence 11 antecedence, preeminence
12 predominance, preexistence

precedent 5 model 7 example,
pattern 8 standard 9 criterion,
guideline

preceding 5 prior 6 former
7 earlier 8 anterior, previous
9 aforesaid, foregoing 10 antecedent, first-named, precursory 11 preexistent,
preliminary 14 abovementioned, aforementioned, first-mentioned

precept 3 law 4 bull, code,
rule 5 axiom, canon, edict,
maxim, motto, tenet, truth,
ukase 6 byword, decree, dictum 7 dictate, mandate, statute 8 standard, teaching
9 ordinance, principle, yardstick 10 regulation 11 commandment, declaration

preceptor 5 coach, tutor
6 mentor 7 advisor, teacher
8 director 9 admonitor, counselor, principal 10 headmaster
12 headmistress

precincts 7 suburbs 8 environs 9 districts, outskirts
10 boundaries 12 subdivisions
15 surrounding area

precious 4 dear, rare 5 fussy,
sweet 6 adored, choice, costly,
dainty, prissy, prized, valued
7 beloved, darling, finical, finicky, lovable 8 adorable, affected, uncommon, valuable
9 cherished, expensive, exquisite, priceless, treasured
10 fastidious, high-priced, invaluable, meticulous, particular 11 beyond price,
inestimable, overrefined,
pretentious

Precious Bane
author: 8 Mary Webb

precipice 4 crag 5 bluff, cliff,
ledge 8 headland, palisade
9 cliff edge, declivity
10 escarpment

precipitate 4 cast, hurl, rash,
spur 5 drive, fling, hasty,
throw 6 abrupt, hasten,
launch, let fly, propel, rushed,
speedy, thrust 7 advance,
bring on, hurried, quicken,
speed up 8 catapult, expedite,
headlong, reckless 9 discharge,
foolhardy, impetuous, imprudent, impulsive 10 accelerate,
incautious 11 thoughtless

precipitation 4 hail, rain,
rush, snow 5 haste, sleet
8 rainfall, rashness 9 hastiness 11 impetuously

precipitous 5 hasty, sharp,
sheer, steep 6 abrupt
9 impetuous

precis 5 brief 6 apercu, digest,
resume, sketch 7 epitome, outline, rundown, summary 8 abstract, synopsis 10 abridgment,
compendium 12 condensation
14 recapitulation

precise 4 true 5 exact, fussy,
rigid 6 strict 7 careful, express,
finicky, literal 8 accurate,
clear-cut, definite, distinct, explicit, incisive, specific 9 unbending 10 fastidious,
inflexible, meticulous, particular, to the point 11 painstaking, unequivocal

precision 5 rigor 8 accuracy,
fidelity 9 attention, exactness
11 factuality, preciseness
12 authenticity, truthfulness
14 meticulousness

preclude 3 bar, dam 4 balk,
curb, foil, stop 5 avert, avoid,
block, check, debar, deter
6 arrest, hamper, hinder,
thwart 7 head off, inhibit, prevent 8 stave off 9 forestall,
frustrate 11 nip in the bud

preclusion 9 exclusion, restraint 10 prevention

precocious 3 apt 5 quick,
smart 6 bright, clever, gifted,
mature 8 advanced
9 brilliant

preconception 4 bias 6 notion 9 fixed idea, prejudice
11 prejudgment, presumption
14 predisposition

precursor 4 mark, omen, sign
5 token, usher 6 herald 7 portent, symptom, warning
8 vanguard 9 harbinger, messenger 10 antecedent, forerunner 11 predecessor

precursory 5 prior 8 anterior,
previous 9 precedent 10 antecedent 11 preexistent

predaceous, predacious
9 predatory, rapacious
10 meat-eating 11 carnivorous,
flesh-eating

predate 7 precede 8 antecede,
antedate, go before

predatory 8 thievish 9 larcenous, marauding, pillaging, piratical, rapacious, raptorial,
vulturine 10 plunderous,
predacious

predecessor 7 forbear
8 ancestor, forebear, foregoer
10 antecedent, forefather,
forerunner

predestination 4 fate 6 kismet 7 destiny, fortune 8 God's
will 10 providence 13 inevitability, preordination
16 predetermination

predetermined 5 fated 7 decided, planned 8 destined
10 calculated, deliberate, preplanned 11 intentional, prearranged, predestined
12 foreordained, premeditated

predicament 3 fix, jam 4 bind,
mess 5 pinch 6 corner, crisis,
pickle, plight, scrape, strait
7 dilemma, trouble 8 hot water, quandary 9 imbroglio, sad
plight 10 difficulty,
perplexity

predicate 4 base, real, rest,
true 5 found, imply 6 affirm,
assert 7 commend, connote,
declare 8 proclaim

predict 4 omen 5 augur 6 divine 7 betoken, foresee, presage 8 envision, forecast,
foretell, prophesy 10 anticipate 13 prognosticate

prediction 6 augury 7 portent
8 forecast, prophecy 10 divination 11 declaration, foretelling, soothsaying
12 announcement, anticipation, proclamation 13 crystal
gazing 15 prognostication

predilection 4 bent, bias, love
5 fancy, favor, taste 6 desire,
hunger, liking, relish 7 leaning 8 appetite, fondness, penchant, tendency 9 prejudice,
proneness 10 attraction, partiality, preference, proclivity,
propensity 11 inclination
13 prepossession
14 predisposition

predispose 4 bias, lure, sway, urge 5 tempt 6 entice, induce, prompt, seduce 7 dispose, incline, win over 8 persuade 9 encourage, influence, prejudice

predisposed 3 apt 5 given, prone 8 inclined

predisposition 7 leaning 8 tendency 11 inclination

predominance 7 command, control 9 currency 9 dominance, supremacy 10 ascendancy, importance, prevalence 11 preeminence, superiority 12 universality

predominant 4 main 5 chief, major 6 potent, ruling, strong 7 leading, supreme 8 dominant, forceful, powerful, reigning, vigorous 9 ascendant, important, paramount, sovereign 11 controlling, influential 13 authoritative

predominate 4 lead 7 prevail 8 dominate

predominating 5 chief 6 ruling 8 dominant, superior 9 principal 10 commanding, prevailing 11 controlling, predominant 13 authoritative

preeminence 9 greatness, supremacy 10 ascendancy, importance, leadership, notability, prominence 11 distinction, superiority 12 predominance

preeminent 4 best 5 famed 6 famous 7 eminent, honored, supreme 8 dominant, foremost, greatest, peerless, renowned, superior 9 matchless, paramount, unequaled, unrivaled 10 celebrated, consummate 11 illustrious, predominant, unsurpassed 12 incomparable, second to none, unparalleled 13 distinguished
  French: 13 par excellence

preempt 4 take 5 seize, usurp 8 arrogate, take over 10 commandeer, confiscate 11 appropriate, expropriate

preen 3 pin 4 perk, trim 5 adorn, dress, groom, plume, pride, primp, prink 6 brooch, smooth
  wings: 4 whet

preexistent 5 prior 8 anterior, previous 9 precedent 10 antecedent, precursory

preface 4 open 5 begin, proem, start 6 launch 7 prelude 8 commence, foreword, initiate, lead into, overture, preamble, prologue 9 introduce 12 introduction

prefer 3 opt 4 file 5 adopt, elect, exalt, fancy, favor, lodge, offer 6 select, take to, tender 7 dignify, elevate, ennoble, fix upon, pick out, present, proffer, promote 8 graduate, set forth 9 single out

preference 4 bent, bias, pick 5 fancy 6 liking, option 7 leaning 8 favoring, priority 9 advantage, prejudice, proneness, selection, supremacy 10 ascendancy, partiality, precedence, proclivity, propensity 11 first choice, inclination 12 predilection 13 predomination 14 predisposition
  French: 4 gout

prefigure 4 hint, type 6 shadow, typify 7 foresee, imagine, presage, suggest 9 adumbrate 10 foreshadow

pregnant 4 full, rich 6 fecund, filled, gravid 7 copious, fertile, fraught, replete, seminal, teeming, weighty 8 forceful, fruitful, prolific 9 abounding, expecting, gestating, important, luxuriant, momentous, plenteous, potential, with child, with young 10 impressive, life-giving, meaningful, parturient, productive, suggestive 11 having a baby, proliferous, provocative, significant 12 fructiferous, in a family way
  French: 8 enceinte

prehistoric 3 old 7 ancient 10 immemorial
  continent: 8 Atlantis
  epoch: 6 Eocene 7 Miocene 8 Pliocene 9 Oligocene, Paleocene 11 Pleistocene
  era: 8 Cenozoic, Mesozoic 9 Paleozoic 10 Archeozoic 11 Proterozoic
  implement: 4 celt 6 eolith
  period: 7 Neogene, Permian 8 Cambrian, Devonian, Jurassic, Silurian, Triassic 9 Paleogene 10 Cretaceous, Ordovician, Quaternary
  reptile: 8 dinosaur

prehistoric era 6 Ice Age 8 Cenozoic, Jurassic, Mesozoic, Triassic 9 Paleozoic 10 Cenomanian, Cretaceous 11 Precambrian 15 Upper Cretaceous 16 Pleistocene Epoch

prehistoric man *see* 8 early man

prejudice 3 ill, mar 4 bias, harm, hurt, loss, sway 5 slant, spoil, taint 6 damage, impair, infect, injure, injury, poison 7 bigotry 8 jaundice 9 detriment 10 favoritism, impair-

ment, partiality, predispose, unfairness 11 contaminate, intolerance, prejudgment 12 disadvantage, one-sidedness, predilection 13 preconception 14 discrimination, predisposition

prejudiced 6 biased, unfair, unjust 7 bigoted, slanted 9 arbitrary 10 intolerant 11 close-minded, opinionated 12 narrow-minded

prejudicial 3 bad 6 biased 7 harmful, hurtful 8 damaging, inimical, sinister 9 injurious 11 deleterious, detrimental

prelate 5 abbot 6 bishop, cleric 9 churchman, clergyman 12 ecclesiastic

preliminary 9 prelusive, prelusory 10 initiatory, precursory, prefactory 11 preparative, preparatory 12 introductory

prelude 7 opening, preface 8 overture, preamble, prologue 9 beginning 11 preliminary, preparation 12 introduction

Prelude, The
  author: 17 William Wordsworth

premature 3 raw 5 green, hasty 6 callow, unripe 7 too soon, unready 8 abortive, ill-timed, immature, previous, too early, untimely 9 embryonic, overhasty, unfledged, unhatched, vestigial 10 incomplete, unprepared 11 inopportune, precipitate, rudimentary, undeveloped 12 unseasonable

premeditated 7 planned, plotted, studied, willful 8 intended 9 conscious, contrived, voluntary 10 calculated, considered, deliberate, predevised, purposeful 11 in cold blood, intentional, prearranged, predesigned 13 predetermined 22 with malice aforethought

premeditation 4 plan 6 design 7 purpose 11 calculation, forethought, preplanning 12 deliberation

premier 3 bet 4 head 5 chief, first 6 oldest 7 leading, supreme 8 earliest, foremost 9 principal 13 prime minister

Preminger, Otto
  director of: 5 Laura 11 Carmen Jones 16 Anatomy of a Murder

premise 6 theory 8 argument 9 postulate, principle 10 assumption, hypothesis 11 presumption, proposition, supposition 14 presupposition

premises 4 site 8 environs, property, vicinity 9 precincts

premium 4 gain, gift 5 award, bonus, prize 6 bounty, return, reward 7 benefit, payment 8 priority 9 high value, incentive 10 great stock, recompense, reparation 11 overpayment 12 appreciation, compensation, inflated rate, remuneration 13 consideration, encouragement

premonition 4 omen, sign 5 hunch, token 6 augury 7 auspice, feeling, inkling, portent, presage 9 foretoken 10 foreboding, indication, prediction 11 forewarning 12 presentiment

preoccupation 9 immersion, obsession 10 absorption, detachment, dreaminess, employment 11 abstraction, involvement 16 absent-mindedness

preoccupied 6 absent, dreamy 8 absorbed, immersed, involved, obsessed 9 engrossed, wrapped up 10 abstracted, distracted 12 absent-minded

preoccupy 6 absorb, arrest, obsess, take up, wrap up 7 engross, immerse 9 fascinate

preparation 8 prudence, readying 9 foresight, preparing, provision, safeguard 10 precaution 11 expectation, forethought 12 anticipation

preparations 5 plans 7 elixirs 8 guidance, measures, mixtures, training, tutelage 9 dressings, educaiton, seasoning, tinctures 11 concoctions, confections 12 arrangements 13 preliminaries, prepared foods, prescriptions

prepare 3 fix 5 adapt, prime, ready 7 arrange, be ready, provide 8 get ready 9 make ready, rearrange, take steps

prepared 4 done 5 fixed, ready 6 cooked, primed 7 planned 8 arranged, finished 9 made ready, rehearsed 11 provided for

prepayment 6 credit 7 advance 9 allowance 11 downpayment

preponderance, preponderancy 4 bulk, glut, mass 6 excess 7 surfeit, surplus 8 majority, plethora 9 dominance, plurality, profusion 10 domination, lion's share, oversupply, prevalence, redundance 12 predominance

preponderant 3 key 4 main 5 chief, first, major, prime 7 highest, leading, primary, supreme 8 dominant, foremost, greatest 9 paramount, principal, uppermost 10 prevailing 11 outstanding, predominant

prepossessing 4 nice 7 winsome 8 alluring, charming, engaging, inviting, pleasant, striking 9 beguiling 10 attractive, bewitching, enchanting, entrancing, personable 11 captivating, fascinating, tantalizing

preposterous 5 inane, outre, silly 6 absurd, stupid 7 asinine, bizarre, fatuous, foolish, idiotic 9 imbecilic, laughable, ludicrous 10 irrational, outrageous, ridiculous 11 nonsensical, unthinkable 12 unreasonable

prerequisite 4 need 6 demand 8 demanded, exigency, required 9 called for, condition, de rigueur, essential, mandatory, necessary, necessity, postulate, requisite 10 imperative, sine qua non 11 requirement, stipulation 13 indispensable, qualification

prerogative 3 due 5 claim, grant, right 6 choice, option 7 freedom, liberty, license, warrant 9 advantage, exemption, franchise, privilege 10 birthright

presage 4 bode, omen, osse, sign 5 augur, token 6 augury, herald 7 betoken, portend, portent, predict 8 forecast, foreshow, foretell, indicate 9 foresight 10 foreboding, foreshadow, indication, prediction, prescience, prognostic 11 premonition 12 presentiment

presbyter 5 elder 13 church officer

prescience 7 presage 9 foresight, prevision 13 foreknowledge

prescribe 3 fix, set 4 rule, urge 5 enact, order 6 assign, decree, demand, direct, enjoin, impose, ordain, settle 7 appoint, command, dictate, require, specify 8 advocate, proclaim 9 authorize, establish, institute, legislate, recommend, stipulate

prescribed 3 set 5 fixed 6 thetic 9 formulary

prescript 3 law 4 rule 5 order 7 precept, statute 10 regulation

prescriptive 7 binding 8 demanded, dictated, didactic, required 9 customary,

mandatory, requisite 10 compulsory, imperative, obligatory

presence 3 air 4 life, look, mien 5 being, curse, favor, ghost, group, midst 6 aspect, entity, figure, manner, shadow, spirit, vision, wraith 7 bearing, company, eidolon, phantom, specter 8 carriage, charisma, demeanor, features, phantasm, revenant, vitality 9 character, existence 10 apparition, attendance, deportment, expression, lineaments 11 reification, subsistence 12 neighborhood 13 manifestation

presence of mind 6 aplomb 8 calmness, coolness 9 composure, sangfroid 10 equanimity, steadiness 14 self-possession

present 2 in 3 fee, now, tip 4 alms, aver, boon, cite, gift, give, here, near, nigh, read, show, tell 5 about, award, frame, grant, offer, state, today 6 accord, allege, assert, at hand, bestow, bounty, call up, chip in, coeval, confer, donate, hand in, impart, legacy, nearby, on hand, recite, relate, render, rooted, submit, summon, supply, tender, turn in 7 advance, bequest, bring on, current, declare, deliver, display, dole out, exhibit, expound, give out, instant, largess, mete out, not away, produce, profess, proffer, propose, provide, recount, vicinal 8 donation, embedded, existent, existing, give away, give over, gratuity, hand over, nowadays, oblation, offering, propound, put forth 9 apprise of, attending, draw forth, endowment, ensconced, hold forth, immediate, implanted, in the room, introduce, make known, not absent, on-the-spot, prevalent, pronounce, surrender, the moment, unremoved 10 asseverate, come up with, contribute, here and now, liberality, perquisite, put forward 11 benefaction, communicate 12 accounted for, bring forward, contemporary, in attendance

presentable 4 chic, so-so 6 decent, modish, not bad, proper 7 stylish 8 becoming, passable, suitable 9 tolerable 10 acceptable, good enough 11 appropriate, fashionable, fit to be seen, respectable

presentation 3 fee, tip 4 boon, gift, show 5 favor, grant, offer 6 bounty 7 advance, display, exhibit, largess, present, proffer **8** bestowal, exposure, gratuity, oblation, offering, overture, proposal **9** unfolding **10** appearance, compliment, disclosure, exhibition, exposition, liberality, production, proffering, submission, unfoldment **11** benefaction, performance, proposition **13** demonstration

presentiment 7 feeling **10** foreboding **11** forewarning, premonition **12** apprehension

presently 3 now **4** anon, soon **7** shortly **8** directly, in a while, this week, this year **9** at present, currently, forthwith **10** any time now, before long, pretty soon **11** after a while, at the moment **12** in a short time **French: 11** tout a l'heure

preservation 6 saving **7** defense **9** salvation **10** protection **11** maintenance, safekeeping **12** conservation, safeguarding

preservative 4 salt **5** brine, spice **8** marinade **12** formaldehyde

preserve, preserves 3 can, dry, jam **4** corn, cure, park, salt, save, seal **5** guard, haven, jelly, nurse, put up, smoke, sweet **6** comfit, defend, embalm, foster, freeze, pickle, refuge, season, secure, shield **7** care for, compote, mummify, protect, reserve, shelter **8** conserve, insulate, keep safe, maintain, marinate **9** dehydrate, keep sound, marmalade, safeguard, sanctuary, sweetmeat, watch over **10** confection, keep intact, perpetuate **11** refrigerate, reservation

preside 4 boss, host, rule **5** chair, watch **6** direct, govern, manage **7** command, conduct, control, hostess, oversee **8** chairman, overlook, regulate **9** keep order, supervise **10** administer **11** superintend **12** administrate, take the chair

president, President 4 head **5** ruler **8** chairman **12** chief officer, chief of state, first citizen **14** chief executive **16** commander in chief, executive officer, head of government

president of US *see box*

preside over 5 chair, guide **6** direct, govern, manage **7** con-

---

president of US
first: 16 George Washington
second: 9 John Adams
third: 15 Thomas Jefferson
fourth: 12 James Madison
fifth: 11 James Monroe
sixth: 15 John Quincy Adams
seventh: 13 Andrew Jackson
eighth: 14 Martin Van Buren
ninth: 20 William Henry Harrison
tenth: 9 John Tyler
eleventh: 10 James K Polk
twelfth: 13 Zachary Taylor
thirteenth: 15 Millard Fillmore
fourteenth: 14 Franklin Pierce
fifteenth: 13 James Buchanan
sixteenth: 14 Abraham Lincoln
seventeenth: 13 Andrew Johnson
eighteenth: 13 Ulysses S Grant
nineteenth: 16 Rutherford B Hayes
twentieth: 14 James A Garfield
twenty-first: 17 Chester Alan Arthur
twenty-second: 15 Grover Cleveland
twenty-third: 16 Benjamin Harrison
twenty-fourth: 15 Grover Cleveland
twenty-fifth: 15 William McKinley
twenty-sixth: 17 Theodore Roosevelt
twenty-seventh: 17 William Howard Taft
twenty-eighth: 13 Woodrow Wilson
twenty-ninth: 14 Warren G Harding
thirtieth: 14 Calvin Coolidge
thirty-first: 13 Herbert Hoover
thirty-second: 18 Franklin D Roosevelt
thirty-third: 12 Harry S Truman
thirty-fourth: 17 Dwight D Eisenhower
thirty-fifth: 12 John F Kennedy
thirty-sixth: 14 Lyndon B Johnson
thirty-seventh: 13 Richard M Nixon
thirty-eighth: 11 Gerald R Ford
thirty-ninth: 11 (James E) Jimmy Carter (Jr)
fortieth: 12 Ronald Reagan
forty-first: 10 George Bush
forty-second: 11 (William Jefferson) Bill Clinton

---

duct **8** dominate **9** supervise **10** administer **11** superintend

Presley, Elvis Aron
nickname: 14 Elvis the Pelvis **15** King of Rock n Roll
born: 6 Tupelo **11** Mississippi
wife: 9 Priscilla
daughter: 9 Lisa Marie
father: 6 Vernon
mother: 6 Gladys
twin brother: 11 Jessie Garon
manager: 16 Colonel Tom Parker
home: 9 Graceland
location: 7 Memphis **9** Tennessee
song: 8 Hound Dog **10** All Shook Up **11** Don't Be Cruel **12** Love Me Tender **13** Jailhouse Rock **14** Blue Suede Shoes **15** Heartbreak Hotel **17** That's All Right Mama
film: 7 G I Blues **9** Loving You **10** Blue Hawaii, King Creole **12** Love Me Tender, Viva Las Vegas **13** Jailhouse Rock

press 2 TV **3** beg, bug, dun, hit, hug, jam, mob, pet, tap, tax **4** army, body, cram, duty, heap, herd, host, iron, mash, mill, pack, prod, push, rush **5** beset, bunch, clasp, crowd, crush, drove, exact, flick, force, horde, hound, hurry, media, plead, radio, set on, steam, stuff, surge, swarm **6** appeal, bother, burden, caress, compel, duress, enjoin, exhort, extort, fondle, gather, huddle, legion, mangle, push in, reduce, smooth, strain, stress, throng **7** cluster, collect, depress, embrace, entreat, flatten, implore, newsmen, oppress, snuggle, squeeze, trouble **8** assemble, bear down, bear upon, calender, compress, condense, hot-press, insist on, pressure, printing, push down **9** be hard put, constrain, constrict, final form, force down, force from, importune, multitude, reporters **10** compulsion, congregate, newspapers, obligation, supplicate, television, thrust down **11** journalists, periodicals, publication **12** bear down upon, broadcasting, come together, news services, newspapermen **14** Fourth Estate

Pressburger, Emeric *see* **13** Michael Powell

press down 7 compact, depress **8** push down

press forward 5 drive **6** push on **7** advance **10** forge ahead

press home 6 stress **9** emphasize, underline **10** accentuate, underscore

pressing 5 vital **6** crying, needed, urgent **7** crucial, exigent, needful **8** critical **9** clamoring, demanding, essential, important, insistent, necessary **10** imperative **11** importunate **13** indispensable

pressing necessity 6 crisis **7** urgency **8** exigency **9** emergency

press on 9 move ahead, persevere **10** accelerate, forge ahead **11** move forward

pressure 4 bias, care, load, need, pull, sway, want **5** force, hurry, pinch, power, press, trial **6** burden, demand, strain, stress, weight **7** anxiety, density, gravity, potency, squeeze, straits, tension, trouble, urgency **8** coercion, distress, exigency, interest **9** adversity, grievance, heaviness, influence, necessity **10** affliction, compaction, compulsion, difficulty, oppression

pressure measurement 6 pascal **10** atmosphere

prestige 4 fame, mark, note **5** glory, honor **6** esteem, import, regard, renown, report, repute **7** account, respect **8** eminence **9** authority, celebrity **10** importance, notability, prominence, reputation **11** consequence, distinction, preeminence **12** significance

prestigious 5 famed **6** famous **7** eminent, honored, notable **8** esteemed, renowned **9** acclaimed, important, prominent, reputable, respected, wellknown **10** celebrated **11** illustrious, outstanding **13** distinguished

Preston, Robert
real name: 21 Robert Preston Meservey

born: 17 Newton Highlands MA
roles: 4 Mame **9** Semi-Tough **11** The Music Man **12** Junior Bonner **14** Victor Victoria **16** How the West Was Won

presumable 6 likely **8** apparent, probable **10** ostensible

presumably 6 likely **8** probably **9** assumably, doubtless **10** apparently, ostensibly **13** presumptively **14** unquestionably **15** in all likelihood **16** in all probability

presume 4 dare **5** fancy, guess, posit **6** assume, deduce, gather, have it, impose, take it **7** believe, imagine, suppose, surmise, suspect, venture **8** be so bold, conceive, make bold, make free **9** postulate, take leave **11** hypothesize, rely too much, think likely **12** take a liberty

presumed 7 assumed, deduced, posited **8** believed, imagined, supposed, surmised **9** suspected **10** postulated **13** took advantage **15** taken for granted

presumption 3 lip **4** gall **5** brass, cheek, guess, nerve, pride **6** belief, daring **7** egotism, premise, surmise **8** audacity, boldness, chutzpah, rudeness **9** arrogance, flippancy, impudence, insolence, postulate **10** assumption, conjecture, effrontery **11** forwardness, haughtiness, prejudgment, speculation, supposition **12** impertinence **13** preconception **14** presupposition

presumptuous 4 bold **5** brash, cocky, fresh, lofty, nervy, proud **6** brassy, brazen, daring, lordly **7** forward, haughty, pompous **8** arrogant, assuming, snobbish **9** audacious, imperious, shameless **10** disdainful **11** dictatorial, domineering, overbearing, patronizing **12** contemptuous, overfamiliar **13** overconfident

presuppose 6 assume **7** presume, suppose **9** speculate **10** conjecture **11** hypothesize

presupposed 7 assumed **8** presumed, supposed **10** speculated **11** conjectured

presupposition 7 premise **10** assumption **11** postulation, presumption

pretend 4 fake, sham **5** claim, fancy, feign, mimic, put on **6** affect, assume **7** imagine, imitate, playact, purport, sup-

pose **8** simulate **9** dissemble **10** masquerade **11** counterfeit, dissimulate, impersonate, make believe

pretended
French: 9 soi-disant

pretender 5 faker, fraud, phony **8** claimant, imposter

pretense 4 airs, fake, hoax, mask, sham, show **5** cloak, cover, feint, guile, trick, vaunt **6** deceit **7** bluster, bombast, display, pretext **8** boasting, bragging, disguise, trickery **9** deception, false show, imposture, invention, pomposity **10** camouflage, pretension, showing off, subterfuge **11** affectation, counterfeit, fabrication, fanfaronade, make-believe, ostentation **12** affectedness

pretension 4 airs, pomp, show **5** claim, right, title **7** bombast, display **8** ambition, pretense, snobbery **9** hypocrisy, pomposity, showiness **10** aspiration, showing off **11** affectation, ostentation **13** grandioseness **14** self-importance **16** ostentatiousness

pretentious 4 airy, smug **5** gaudy, lofty, showy, stagy **6** flashy, florid, garish, ornate, tawdry **7** blown-up, fatuous, pompous, stuck-up **8** affected, assuming, boastful, inflated, overdone, pedantic, puffed-up, snobbish **9** bombastic, flaunting, insincere, presuming, unnatural **10** hoity-toity, theatrical **11** exaggerated, extravagant, overbearing **12** ostentatious, self-praising **13** high-and-mighty, self-important

pretentiousness 4 cant **6** humbug **9** hypocrisy **11** insincerity **17** sanctimoniousness

preternatural 5 eerie, weird **6** arcane, occult **7** bizarre, strange, uncanny **8** esoteric, mystical **9** unearthly, unworldly **10** miraculous, mysterious, superhuman **11** hypernormal, preterhuman, supernormal **12** extramundane, metaphysical, supernatural, supranatural **14** transcendental

pretext 5 basis, bluff, feint **6** excuse, ground **8** pretense **9** semblance **10** pretension, subterfuge **11** vindication

pretty 4 fair **5** bonny **6** comely, dainty, fairly, goodly, lovely, rather **7** shapely, sightly, wellset **8** alluring, charming, delicate, engaging, fetching, graceful, handsome, somewhat, well-made **9** beauteous, beautiful **10** adequately, attractive, moderately, reasonably **11** captivating, good-looking, symmetrical, well-favored

pretty child 4 doll **5** cutie **10** living doll

prevail 3 win **4** rule **5** exist, reign **6** abound, obtain, win out **7** conquer, succeed, triumph **8** have sway, hold sway, overcome **9** be a winner, be current **11** be prevalent, be the victor, carry the day, gain the palm, predominate **12** be victorious, be widespread, preponderate

prevailing 3 set **4** main **5** fixed, usual **6** normal **7** current, general, in style, popular **8** definite, dominant **9** customary, prevalent, principal **10** accustomed, widespread **11** established, predominant **12** conventional, preponderant

prevail over 4 beat **5** outdo **6** defeat **7** eclipse, surpass **8** overcome

prevail upon 4 sway **8** convince, persuade **9** influence

prevalent 4 rife **5** usual **6** common, normal **7** general, popular, rampant **8** abundant, everyday, familiar, frequent, habitual, numerous **9** customary, extensive, pervasive, universal **10** prevailing, ubiquitous, widespread **11** commonplace **12** conventional

prevaricate 3 fib, lie **4** fake **6** palter **7** deceive, distort, falsify, mislead, perjure **8** hoodwink, misstate **9** be evasive, dissemble **10** equivocate, tell a story **11** counterfeit **12** be untruthful, misrepresent

prevarication 3 fib, lie **5** fable **7** fiction, untruth, whopper **9** fairy tale, falsehood, fish story, invention **11** fabrication **12** equivocation **16** cock-and-bull story **17** misrepresentation

prevent 3 bar, dam **4** balk, foil, halt, stop, veto **5** avert, avoid, block, deter **6** arrest, forbid, thwart **7** deflect, draw off, fend off, obviate, rule out, ward off **8** hold back, preclude, prohibit, stave off, turn away **9** forestall, frustrate, intercept, sidetrack, turn aside **10** anticipate, counteract **11** nip in the bud

prevention 6 defeat **8** stoppage **9** avoidance, hindrance, obviation, restraint, thwarting **10** deterrence, inhibition, pre-

clusion **11** elimination, frustration **12** interception **13** forestallment

preview 5 sneak **6** sample, survey **8** futurama **9** foretaste **10** inspection

previous 5 early, prior **6** before, former **7** earlier **8** foregone **9** aforesaid, erstwhile, foregoing, preceding **10** antecedent **14** aforementioned

previously 4 once **6** before **7** earlier, long ago **8** back when, formerly **9** at one time, a while ago, earlier on **10** a while back, heretofore **11** in times past **12** sometime back

Prevost, Abbe
  author of: **12** Manon Lescaut

prey 3 eat **4** dupe, food, game, gull, kill **5** patsy, prize, quest **6** devour, infest, pigeon, quarry, sucker, target, victim **7** cat's-paw, consume, fall guy, live off **8** feed upon **9** feast upon **10** fasten upon, fatten upon, parasitize

Priam
  king of: **4** Troy
  father: **8** Laomedon
  brother: **8** Tithonus
  wife: **6** Hecuba
  son: **5** Paris **6** Hector **9** Polydorus
  daughter: **8** Polyxena **9** Cassandra
  number of sons: **5** fifty
  number of daughters: **5** fifty
  killed by: **11** Neoptolemus

Priamid
  father: **5** Priam

Priapus
  god of: **5** herds **7** gardens **9** fertility, male power **11** procreation
  father: **8** Dionysus
  mother: **9** Aphrodite
  corresponds to: **7** Mutinus

price 3 fee **4** cost, fine, rate **5** value, worth **6** amount, assess, charge, outlay **7** expense, penalty **8** appraise, evaluate, par value **9** face value, list price **10** forfeiture, punishment

Price, Fanny
  character in: **13** Mansfield Park
  author: **6** Austen

Price, Vincent
  born: **9** St Louis MO
  wife: **11** Coral Browne **12** Edith Barrett
  roles: **6** The Fly **8** The Raven **10** House of Wax **13** Tower of London **15** The House of Usher **20** The Pit and the Pendulum **22** The

Masque of the Red Death
  expert in: **3** art

Price Is Right, The
  host: **9** Bob Barker **10** Bill Cullen

priceless 4 dear, rare **6** costly, prized, valued **8** peerless, precious, valuable **9** cherished, expensive, treasured **10** high-priced, invaluable **11** beyond price **12** incomparable, without price **13** irreplaceable **17** worth a king's ransom

prick 5 stick **6** pierce **8** puncture

prickle 4 barb, itch **5** point, quill, smart, sting, thorn **6** tingle **7** barbule, bristle, spicule

prickly 5 itchy **6** coarse, thorny **8** scratchy, stinging **9** vexatious

pride 3 joy **4** airs, pomp, show **5** honor **6** egoism, parade, vanity **7** comfort, conceit, delight, dignity, display, egotism, swagger **8** pleasure, self-love, smugness **9** arrogance, be proud of, enjoyment, happiness, immodesty, pomposity, vainglory **10** pretension, self-esteem **11** haughtiness, ostentation, self-respect **14** self-importance

Pride and Prejudice
  author: **10** Jane Austen
  character: **7** Mr Darcy **9** Mr Bingley, Mr Collins, Mr Wickham **14** Charlotte Lucas **15** Caroline Bingley **21** Lady Catherine de Bourgh
    Bennet daughters: **4** Jane, Mary **5** Kitty, Lydia **9** Elizabeth
  director: **14** Robert Z Leonard
  cast: **10** Mary Boland **11** Edmund Gwenn, Greer Garson, Karen Morley **13** Ann Rutherford, Edna May Oliver **15** Laurence Olivier **16** Maureen O'Sullivan

Pride of the Yankees, The
  director: **7** Sam Wood
  cast: **8** Babe Ruth **9** Dan Duryea **10** Gary Cooper (Lou Gehrig) **12** Teresa Wright **13** Walter Brennan

priest 5 padre **6** cleric **8** minister, preacher **9** churchman **13** man of the cloth

priesthood 5 cloth **6** clergy **8** ministry, the cloth **9** pastorage

Priestley, J B
  author of: **9** Bright Day

11 Lost Empires **13** Angel Pavement **17** The Good Companions

Priestley, Joseph
field: **9** chemistry
nationality: **7** British
discovered: **6** oxygen **7** ammonia **13** nitrogen oxide
invented: **11** carbonation

priestly 8 churchly, clerical **10** sacerdotal **14** ecclesiastical

prig 5 bigot, prude **6** pedant **7** puritan **8** bluenose **9** formalist, hypocrite, nitpicker, pretender **10** fuddy-duddy **11** faultfinder **12** bluestocking, precisionist, stuffed shirt **14** attitudinarian

priggish 4 prim, smug **6** stuffy **7** prudish **9** blue-nosed **10** tight-laced **11** puritanical, strait laced **13** self-righteous, self-satisfied

prim 4 smug, tidy **5** fussy **6** prissy, proper, strict, stuffy **7** haughty, prudish **8** priggish, starched **9** squeamish, unbending **10** fastidious, fuddy-duddy, inflexible, no-nonsense, particular **11** overprecise, puritanical, stiff-necked, straitlaced

prima donna 4 diva, lead, star **6** singer **9** principal
literally: **9** first lady

primarily 6 mainly, mostly **7** chiefly, largely **9** basically, generally, in the main **11** essentially, principally **13** fundamentally, predominantly **14** for the most part **16** first and foremost

primary 3 key **4** main, star **5** basal, basic, chief, first, prime, vital **6** innate, native, oldest, primal, ruling, utmost **7** highest, initial, leading, nascent, natural **8** cardinal, dominant, earliest, greatest, inherent, original, primeval **9** beginning, elemental, essential, important, necessary, primitive, principal, prominent **10** aboriginal, elementary, indigenous, primordial, rudimental **11** fundamental, predominant, preparatory, rudimentary **12** introductory

primary constituent 5 basic **9** basic need, essential, necessity, requisite **10** sine qua non

primate 3 ape, man **5** avahi, indri, lemur, loris, potto **6** aye-aye, baboon, bishop, galago, gibbon, mammal, monkey **7** gorilla, tamarin, tarsier **8** marmoset, simpoona **9** orangutan, tree shrew **10** archbishop, chimpanzee

prime 2 A1 **3** ace, fit **4** best, main, peak, pink **5** adapt, basal, basic, bloom, breed, brief, chief, coach, early, first, groom, guide, lucky, raise, ready, train, tutor, vital **6** adjust, choice, fill in, flower, Grade A, height, heyday, inform, innate, native, oldest, primal, prompt, ruling, school, seemly, select, timely, utmost, zenith **7** educate, fitting, highest, leading, maximal, natural, prepare, primary, quality, supreme, top-hole **8** best days, cardinal, crowning, earliest, get ready, greatest, inherent, instruct, maturity, original, peerless, suitable, superior **9** befitting, elemental, essential, expedient, important, intrinsic, make ready, matchless, necessary, opportune, paramount, preferred, principal, provident, top-drawer, topflight, unmatched, well-timed **11** superlative, unsurpassed, without peer **12** unparalleled

prime example 5 model **7** classic **8** exemplar **9** archetype

prime mover 6 author **9** initiator, organizer **10** originator
Latin: **12** primum mobile

Prime of Miss Jean Brodie, The
author: **11** Muriel Spark

primer 3 cap **4** book **5** paint **6** manual, reader **8** hornbook, textbook **9** undercoat

primeval 5 early **6** oldest, primal **7** ancient, archaic **8** earliest, original **9** ancestral, legendary, primitive **10** aboriginal, indigenous, primordial **11** fundamental, prehistoric **12** antediluvian, mythological

primitive 4 bare **5** crude, early, first **6** native, simple **7** antique, archaic, artless, ascetic, austere, primary, Spartan **8** backward, earliest, original **9** beginning, unlearned, unrefined, unskilled **10** aboriginal, elementary **11** rudimentary, uncivilized, undeveloped

primordial 5 first **6** primal **7** initial **8** original, primeval **9** beginning, primitive **10** elementary **11** fundamental, prehistoric

primp 5 groom, plume, preen **6** doll up, make up **7** gussy up **8** prettify, spruce up

primrose 7 Primula **15** Primula vulgaris
varieties: **4** baby, cape, star

5 fairy **6** German, poison **7** Chinese, English, evening **8** bird's-eye **9** buttercup **12** beach evening, white evening **13** desert evening **14** Mexican evening

primum mobile 10 prime mover **16** first moving thing

primus inter pares 16 first among equals

prince
Italian: **8** principe
Turkish: **3** beg, bey

Prince
original name: **18** Prince Rogers Nelson
nickname: **12** Royal Badness
born: **2** MN **11** Minneapolis
recording: **6** For You, Parade, Prince **9** Dirty Mind **10** Purple Rain **11** Controversy **20** Around the World in a Day
film: **10** Purple Rain **13** Sign o' the Times **14** Graffiti Bridge **18** Under the Cherry Moon

Prince, The
author: **18** Niccolo Machiavelli

Prince and the Pauper, The
author: **9** Mark Twain
character: **4** Hugo **8** Tom Canty **9** John Canty **10** Hugh Hendon **11** Miles Hendon **19** Edward Prince of Wales

Prince Edward Island
abbreviation: **3** PEI
bay: **5** Rollo **6** Egmont **7** Bedeque **8** Cardigan, Malpeque **9** Cascumpec **12** Hillsborough
capital: **13** Charlottetown
gulf: **10** St Lawrence
people: **4** Scot **5** Irish, Scots **6** French **7** English
   discoverer: **7** Cartier
province of: **6** Canada
river: **4** Dunk **5** Eliot, Yorke **12** Hillsborough
strait: **14** Northumberland

Prince Igor
also: **9** Kniaz Igor
opera by: **7** Borodin
character: **11** Khan Konchak
contains: **17** Polovetsian dances

princely 3 big **5** noble, royal **8** generous **11** magnificent

prince of darkness 5 Satan **7** Lucifer **8** the Devil **9** Beelzebub

Prince of Peace 5 Jesus **6** Christ

Princess and the Pea, The
author: **21** Hans Christian Andersen

Princess Casamassima
author: 10 Henry James

Princess Daisy
author: 12 Judith Krantz

Princesse de Cleves, La
author: 14 Mme de LaFayette

Princess Flavia
character in: 15 Prisoner of Zenda
author: 4 Hope

Prince Valiant
creator: 12 Harold Foster
character: 5 Ilene 9 Prince Arn 10 King Arthur
wife: 5 Aleta
nickname: 3 Val

principal 4 dean, fund, main, star 5 basic, chief, first, money, prime 6 master 7 capital, leading, primary, supreme 8 cardinal, dominant, foremost, greatest, superior, ultimate 9 essential, paramount, preceptor, prominent 10 capital sum, headmaster, leading man, preeminent 11 fundamental, predominant, protagonist 13 most important

principal constituent 4 base 12 chief feature 14 main ingredient

principal dish of a meal
French: 17 piece de resistance

principal event
French: 17 piece de resistance

principality 5 angel 9 princedom 14 celestial being, heavenly spirit

principally 6 mainly, mostly 7 chiefly, largely 8 above all 9 basically, primarily 10 especially 12 particularly 13 fundamentally, predominantly 14 for the most part 16 first and foremost

principe 6 prince

principle 3 law 4 code, fact, rule, view 5 axiom, basis, canon, credo, creed, dogma, honor, maxim, tenet, truth 6 belief, dictum, ethics, morals, theory, virtue 7 element, formula, honesty, precept, probity, scruple, theorem 8 attitude, doctrine, goodness, morality, position, rudiment, scruples, teaching 9 direction, integrity, rectitude, standards 10 assumption, regulation 11 fundamental, proposition, uprightness

principled 6 honest 7 upright 9 honorable 10 aboveboard, forthright

Pringle, John
real name of: 11 John Gilbert

prink 4 deck, fuss 5 adorn, preen, primp 6 spruce

print 3 die 4 copy, text, type 5 issue, plate, press, stamp, write 7 compose, edition, engrave, etching, gravure, impress, picture, publish, woodcut 10 lithograph, silkscreen 11 letterpress

printing press
invented by:
  rotary: 3 Hoe
  web: 7 Bullock

prior 6 former 7 earlier 8 anterior, previous 9 aforesaid, erstwhile, foregoing, prefatory 10 antecedent, precursory 11 going before, preexistent, preexisting, preparatory 14 aforementioned

Prior Analytics
author: 9 Aristotle

Prioress
character in: 18 The Canterbury Tales
author: 7 Chaucer

priority 7 urgency 9 immediacy, seniority 10 ascendancy, precedence, precedency, preference 11 antecedence, preeminence, superiority

priory 5 abbey 6 friary 7 convent, nunnery 8 cloister 9 hermitage, monastery

Prism, Letitia
character in: 27 The Importance of Being Earnest
author: 5 Wilde

prison 3 can, jug, pen 4 brig, gaol, jail, stir, tank 5 clink, joint, pokey, tower 6 cooler 7 dungeon, slammer 8 bastille, big house 9 calaboose, jailhouse

Prisoner of Zenda
author: 11 Anthony Hope
character: 14 Princess Flavia 17 Lady Rose Burlesdon, Rudolph Rassendyll 18 Antoinette de Mauban, Fritz von Tarlenheim 21 Michael Duke of Strelsau 22 Rudolph King of Ruritania
director: 12 John Cromwell
cast: 9 Mary Astor 10 David Niven 12 C Aubrey Smith, Ronald Colman (Rudolf Rassendyll) 16 Madeleine Carroll 18 Douglas Fairbanks Jr (Rupert of Hentzau)
setting: 9 Ruritania

prissy 4 prim 5 fussy 6 proper, stuffy 7 finicky, prudish 8 overnice 9 sissified 10 effeminate 11 strait-laced

Prissy
character in: 15 Gone With the Wind
author: 8 Mitchell

pristine 4 pure 8 unmarred, virginal 9 undefiled, unspoiled, unsullied, untouched 10 unpolluted 11 untarnished 14 uncontaminated

Pritchett, V S
author of: 11 Midnight Oil 16 Collected Stories, The Spanish Temper 19 On the Edge of the Cliff

privacy 6 secret 7 privity, retreat, secrecy 8 security, solitude 9 integrity, isolation, seclusion 10 retirement, withdrawal 11 privateness 12 dissociation, solitariness 13 sequestration

private 4 dark 5 fixed, privy 6 buried, closed, covert, hidden, lonely, remote, secret 7 cryptic, express, limited, obscure, special 8 confined, desolate, esoteric, hush-hush, isolated, lonesome, personal, secluded, solitary 9 concealed, exclusive, inviolate, invisible, nonpublic, not public, reclusive 10 classified, indistinct, mysterious, restricted, undercover, under wraps, unofficial, unrevealed 11 clandestine, nonofficial, sequestered, underground, undisclosed 12 confidential, off-the-record, unfrequented

privateer 6 pirate 7 brigand, corsair 9 buccaneer

private eye 4 dick 6 shamus 7 gumshoe 9 detective 12 investigator

Private Life of Henry VIII, The
director: 14 Alexander Korda
cast: 11 Merle Oberon, Robert Donat 12 Binnie Barnes 14 Elsa Lanchester (Anne of Cleves) 15 Charles Laughton (Henry VIII)

Private Life of the Master Race, The
author: 13 Bertold Brecht

Private Lives
author: 10 Noel Coward
character: 10 Elyot Chase, Sibyl Chase 12 Amanda Prynne, Victor Prynne

Private Lives of Elizabeth and Essex, The
director: 13 Michael Curtiz
cast: 10 Bette Davis (Elizabeth I), Errol Flynn (Essex) 11 Donald Crisp 12 Vincent Price 13 Nanette Fabray 17 Olivia de Havilland

also known as: 17 Elizabeth the Queen

privately 7 sub rosa **8** in secret, secretly **9** between us, entre nous, in private **12** in confidence **14** confidentially **15** between you and me **16** between ourselves **17** behind closed doors

privation 4 lack, need, want **5** pinch **6** misery, penury **7** beggary, poverty, straits **8** distress, exigency, hardship **9** indigence, neediness, pauperism **10** bankruptcy, mendicancy **11** destitution **14** impoverishment **15** impecuniousness

privilege 3 due **4** boon **5** allow, favor, grant, honor, power, right, title **6** patent, permit **7** benefit, charter, empower, entitle, freedom, liberty, license **8** pleasure **9** advantage, authority, franchise **10** birthright **11** entitlement, prerogative **12** prerequisite

privileged 4 free **6** exempt, immune **7** allowed, excused, granted, limited, special **8** entitled, licensed **9** empowered, not liable, permitted, warranted **10** authorized, sanctioned **13** unaccountable

prize 3 cup, gem, pip **4** like, lulu **5** award, catch, crown, dandy, honey, honor, jewel, medal, peach, pearl, value **6** admire, esteem, honors, regard, reward, ribbon, trophy **7** cherish, diamond, guerdon, honored, laurels, premium, respect, winning **8** accolade, champion, citation, hold dear, look up to, pure gold, treasure **9** humdinger, medallion **10** appreciate, blue ribbon, decoration, set store by **11** crackerjack, masterpiece

prized 4 dear **8** esteemed, precious **9** cherished, treasured

prizefight 2 go **4** bout **5** match **6** boxing **7** contest **10** fisticuffs

prizefighter 3 pug **5** boxer **7** slugger **8** pugilist **9** flyweight **11** heavyweight, lightweight **12** bantamweight, middleweight, welterweight **13** featherweight **16** light heavyweight

pro 3 for **5** forth **6** before, expert, master **8** favoring **9** authority **11** affirmative
opposite: 3 con **7** amateur

probability 4 odds **6** chance **10** likelihood

probable 6 likely **7** logical, seeming, tenable **8** apparent, assuring, credible, expected, possible, presumed, supposed **9** plausible, promising, thinkable **10** believable, in the cards, ostensible, presumable, reasonable **11** conceivable, encouraging, presumptive

probably 6 likely **10** most likely, presumably, supposedly **11** as like as not **15** in all likelihood

probe 4 hunt, quiz, seek, test **5** query, study, trial **6** pursue, review, search, survey **7** examine, fish for, inquest, inquire, inquiry, inspect, pry into, rummage **8** analysis, look into, question, research **9** penetrate **10** inspection, scrutinize **11** examination, exploration, interrogate, investigate **13** investigation

probity 5 honor **6** virtue **7** decency, honesty **8** goodness, morality **9** character, integrity, principle **11** uprightness **12** straightness **13** righteousness **14** high-mindedness **15** trustworthiness **16** incorruptibility

problem 5 poser, query **6** puzzle, riddle, unruly **8** question, stubborn **9** conundrum, difficult **10** difficulty **11** intractable **12** disagreement, hard to manage, incorrigible, unmanageable

problematic 7 dubious, unknown **8** doubtful, puzzling **9** difficult, enigmatic, uncertain, unsettled, worrisome **10** perplexing **11** paradoxical, troublesome **12** questionable, undetermined

pro bono publico 16 for the public good

proboscis 4 beak, nose **5** snoot, snout, trunk **6** siphon, sucker, syphon **7** rostrum
monkey: 4 kaha **5** kahua

procedure 2 MO **3** way **4** mode **6** course, manner, method **7** process, routine **8** approach, strategy **9** technique **11** methodology **13** modus operandi

proceed 2 go **3** act **4** come, flow, go on, grow, move, stem, work **5** arise, begin, ensue, issue, start **6** derive, follow, move on, push on, result, set out, spring **7** advance, carry on, emanate, go ahead, operate, press on, succeed **8** be caused, commence, continue, function, progress, take rise **9** be derived, go forward, move ahead, originate, undertake

proceedings 4 case, suit **5** cause, trial **6** doings, events, report **7** account, actions, affairs, lawsuit, matters, minutes, records, returns **8** activity, archives, goings on **9** incidents, memoranda **10** happenings, litigation, operations **11** occurrences **12** transactions

proceeds 3 net **4** gain, gate, pelf, take **5** gross, lucre, money, yield **6** assets, income, profit, reward **7** returns, revenue **8** earnings, pickings, receipts, winnings **9** box office

process 3 can, dry **4** fill, flow, flux, mode, plan, ship, step, writ **5** alter, candy, smoke, treat, usage **6** change, course, freeze, handle, manner, method, motion, policy, scheme, system **7** convert, measure, passage, prepare, project, summons **8** deal with, function, movement, practice, preserve, progress, subpoena **9** dehydrate, dispose of, freeze-dry, procedure, transform, unfolding **10** court order, proceeding

procession 4 file, line, rank **5** array, march, train **6** column, course, parade **7** caravan, cortege, pageant, passage **8** progress, sequence **9** cavalcade, motorcade **10** succession **11** progression

Procheneosaurus
type: 8 dinosaur **10** ornithopod
location: 6 Canada
period: 10 Cretaceous

proclaim 3 cry **4** tell **5** blare, state, voice **6** affirm, assert, blazon, herald, report, reveal **7** call out, declare, divulge, give out, profess, publish, release, sing out, trumpet **8** announce, disclose, set forth **9** advertise, broadcast, circulate, enunciate, hawk about, make known, publicize **10** make public, promulgate

proclamation 5 edict, ukase **6** decree **12** announcement **13** pronouncement

Proclea
husband: 6 Cycnus
son: 5 Tenes

Procles
twin of: 11 Eurysthenes

proclivity 3 yen **4** bent, bias **5** taste **6** desire, liking **7** impulse, leaning **8** affinity, appetite, penchant, soft spot, tendency **9** affection, prejudice, proneness 10 partiality, propensity 11 disposition, inclination 12 predilection 14 predisposition

Procne
sister: 9 Philomela
husband: 6 Tereus
changed into: 7 swallow

procrastinate 3 lag 5 dally, defer, delay, stall, tarry 6 dawdle, linger, loiter 7 adjourn 8 hang back, hesitate, hold back, kill time, postpone, put on ice 9 temporize, waste time 10 be dilatory, dillydally 11 play for time 12 drag one's feet

procrastinating 4 slow 5 tardy 6 remiss 8 dilatory 9 reluctant 12 foot-dragging 13 dillydallying

procreate 3 get 4 bear, sire 5 beget, breed, spawn 6 create, father, mother 7 produce 8 conceive, engender, generate, multiply 9 propagate, reproduce 10 bring forth 11 give birth to, proliferate

procreation
god of: 7 Priapus

procreator 4 sire 6 father 8 begetter

Procris
father: 8 Thespius 10 Erechtheus
husband: 8 Cephalus

Procrustes
also: 8 Damastes 9 Polypemon
robber who: 6 maimed
killed by: 7 Theseus

procure 3 buy, get, win 4 earn, gain, take 5 evoke, seize 6 attain, come by, effect, elicit, gather, incite, induce, obtain, pick up, secure 7 achieve, acquire, receive 8 contrive, purchase 10 accumulate, bring about, commandeer, lay hands on 11 appropriate

procurement 4 gain 7 seizure 8 purchase 10 attainment, purchasing 11 achievement, acquirement, acquisition 12 accumulation 13 appropriation

prod 3 jab, nag 4 flog, goad, lash, move, poke, push, spur, stir, urge, whip 5 egg on, impel, prick, rouse, shove, speed 6 excite, exhort, incite, needle, prompt, propel, stir up 7 actuate, animate, provoke, quicken 8 motivate, pressure 9 encourage, instigate, stimulate

prodigal 4 lush 5 ample 6 lavish, myriad, wanton 7 copious, profuse, replete, spender, teeming, wastrel 8 abundant, generous, numerous, reckless, swarming, wasteful 9 abounding, bounteous, bountiful, countless, excessive, exuberant, impetuous, luxuriant, plentiful, unthrifty 10 exorbitant, gluttonous, immoderate, inordinate, numberless, profligate, squanderer, thriftless 11 dissipating, extravagant, improvident, innumerable, intemperate, overliberal, precipitate, spendthrift 13 multitudinous

prodigality 10 imprudence, lavishness 12 extravagance, improvidence, overspending, wastefulness

prodigious 3 big 4 huge, rare, vast 5 grand, great, large 6 mighty, unique 7 amazing, immense 8 colossal, enormous, gigantic, renowned, singular, striking, terrific, uncommon, unwonted, wondrous 9 marvelous, monstrous, startling, wonderful 10 astounding, impressive, miraculous, monumental, noteworthy, remarkable, stupendous, surprising, tremendous 11 astonishing, exceptional, far-reaching, uncustomary, unthinkable 12 dumbfounding, overwhelming, unimaginable 13 extraordinary, inconceivable, unprecedented

prodigiously 10 enormously, incredibly, remarkably 12 inordinately, tremendously 13 astonishingly, exceptionally, extravagantly, outstandingly, spectacularly 14 overwhelmingly

prodigiousness 6 rarity 8 enormity, hugeness, vastness 10 uniqueness 11 singularity 12 extravagance

prodigy 4 whiz 6 expert, genius, marvel, master, rarity, wizard, wonder 7 stunner, whiz kid 8 rara avis 9 sensation 10 mastermind, phenomenon, wunderkind 11 wonder child

Prodromia
epithet of: 4 Hera
means: 7 pioneer

produce 4 bear, form, give, make, show 5 beget, bloom, cause, found, frame, hatch, set up, shape, yield 6 adduce, afford, create, devise, effect, evince, evolve, flower, fruits, greens, invent, reveal, sprout, supply, unmask, unveil 7 achieve, advance, bring in, compose, concoct, develop, display, divulge, exhibit, fashion, furnish, present, provide, staples, turn out, uncover 8 bring off, bring out, conceive, disclose, discover, generate, manifest, set forth 9 bear fruit, construct, fabricate, institute, make plain, originate, procreate, put on view, show forth 10 accomplish, bring about, come up with, effectuate, foodstuffs, give life to, give rise to, put in force, vegetables 11 bring to pass, give birth to, manufacture, materialize 14 bring into being

Producers, The
director: 9 Mel Brooks
cast: 9 Dick Shawn 10 Gene Wilder, Zero Mostel 11 Kenneth Mars

production 4 film, play, show 5 drama, movie 6 cinema, circus, making 7 display, exhibit, musical, showing 8 building, carnival, creation 9 execution, formation, producing, stage show 10 appearance, disclosure, revelation 11 fabrication, fulfillment, manufacture, origination, performance 12 construction, effectuation, introduction, presentation 13 demonstration, entertainment, manifestation, manufacturing, motion picture 15 materialization

productive 4 busy, rich 6 active, fecund, paying, useful 7 causing, copious, dynamic, fertile, gainful, teeming 8 creating, creative, fruitful, prolific, valuable, vigorous, yielding 9 effectual, luxuriant, plenteous, plentiful, producing 10 invaluable, profitable, worthwhile 11 efficacious, moneymaking, proliferous 12 contributing, fructiferous, remunerative

Proetus
father: 4 Abas
mother: 6 Aglaia
twin brother: 8 Acrisius
wife: 5 Antia 10 Stheneboea
son: 11 Megapenthes
daughter: 7 Iphinoe, Lysippe 10 Iphianassa
invented: 6 shield
enemy: 8 Acrisius

profanation 9 sacrilege 10 defilement 11 desecration

profane 3 lay 4 evil, foul, lewd, mock, vile 5 abuse, bawdy, crude, nasty, scorn, waste 6 coarse, debase, filthy, ill-use, impure, misuse, offend, revile, ribald, sinful, unholy, vulgar, wicked 7 abusive, earthly, godless, impious, obscene, outrage, pervert, pollute, satanic, secular, ungodly, violate, worldly **8** agnostic, diabolic, off-color, temporal, unchaste, undevout, unseemly **9** atheistic, blaspheme, desecrate, hellbound, heretical, misemploy, shameless, unsaintly **10** irreverent, prostitute **11** blasphemous, contaminate, irreligious, terrestrial, unbelieving **12** nonreligious, sacrilegious

profanity 5 filth, oaths **7** cursing, cussing, impiety **8** swearing **9** blasphemy, obscenity, scatology **10** dirty words, execration, expletives, scurrility, swearwords **11** irreverence, obscenities, ungodliness **12** billingsgate **15** four-letter words

profess 3 act, own, say **4** aver, avow, fake, sham, tell **5** admit, claim, feign, offer, put on, state, vouch **6** affirm, allege, assert, assume, depose **7** advance, certify, confess, confirm, contend, declare, embrace, pretend, purport **8** announce, lay claim, maintain, practice, proclaim, propound, simulate **9** believe in, dissemble, enunciate, hold forth **10** asseverate, put forward **11** acknowledge, counterfeit, dissimulate

professed 6 avowed **7** alleged **8** admitted **9** confessed, purported **12** acknowledged, self-declared **14** self-proclaimed

profession 3 job, law, vow **4** line, post, word, work **5** claim, craft, field, trade, troth **6** avowal, career, metier, office, pledge, plight, sphere **7** calling, promise, pursuit, service **8** averment, business, endeavor, industry, medicine, position, practice, teaching, vocation **9** assertion, assurance, guarantee, situation, specialty, statement, testimony **10** allegation, confession, deposition, employment, line of work, occupation, walk of life **11** affirmation, attestation, declaration, undertaking, word of honor **12** announcement, confirmation **13** pronouncement **15** acknowledgement

professional 4 paid **5** adept **6** expert **9** authority, competent, practiced **10** specialist **11** experienced

professionalism 5 savvy, skill **7** know-how **9** expertise **10** expertness

professor 3 don **6** regent

7 adjoint, teacher **8** lecturer **10** instructor
retired: 8 emeritus

Professor, The
author: **15** Charlotte Bronte

professorial 6 teachy **7** bookish, donnish, preachy **8** academic, didactic, pedantic, teachery **11** pedagoguish **13** schoolmarmish **15** schoolmasterish **16** schoolteacherish

Professor's House, The
author: **11** Willa Cather

proffer 5 offer **6** extend, tender **7** advance, hold out, present

proficiency 5 knack, skill **6** acumen **7** ability, know-how **8** aptitude, capacity, deftness, facility **9** adeptness, dexterity, expertise, handiness **10** adroitness, capability, competence **13** qualification **14** accomplishment

proficient 3 apt **4** able, deft, good **5** adept, handy, quick, ready, sharp **6** adroit, clever, expert, gifted **7** capable, skilled, trained **8** masterly, polished, skillful, talented **9** competent, dexterous, effective, efficient, masterful, practiced, qualified, versatile **11** experienced **12** accomplished, professional

profile 4 form, side, tale **5** shape **6** figure, sketch **7** contour, drawing, outline, picture, skyline **8** half face, portrait, side view, vignette **9** biography **10** lineaments, silhouette **11** delineation **13** configuration

Profiles in Courage
author: **12** John F Kennedy

profit 3 pay, use **4** boon, earn, gain, good, help **5** avail, favor, money, serve, value **6** income, return **7** account, benefit, revenue, service, utility, utilize **8** earnings, interest, proceeds, receipts **9** advantage, make money **11** advancement

profitable 6 paying, useful **7** gainful **8** fruitful, salutary, valuable **9** favorable, lucrative, rewarding **10** beneficial, invaluable, productive, well-paying, worthwhile **11** moneymaking, serviceable **12** advantageous, remunerative

profitmaking 8 business **11** moneymaking **13** noncharitable

profits 4 gate, take **5** gains, yield **6** assets, income **7** returns, revenue **8** earnings, receipts

profligacy 10 lavishness **11** dissipation, dissolution, prodigality, unrestraint **12** extravagance, immoderation, improvidence, recklessness, wastefulness **13** excessiveness

profligate 4 evil, fast, rake, roue, wild **5** loose, satyr **6** erotic, lavish, sinful, sinner, wanton, wicked **7** corrupt, immoral, pervert, satyric, wastrel **8** degraded, depraved, prodigal, reckless, wasteful **9** abandoned, debauched, debauchee, dissolute, libertine, reprobate, sybaritic, unbridled, unthrifty, wrongdoer **10** degenerate, dissipated, dissipater, iniquitous, lascivious, licentious **11** extravagant, improvident, promiscuous, spendthrift **12** unprincipled, unrestrained

pro forma 15 according to form, as a matter of form

profound 4 deep, keen, sage, wise **5** acute, sober, utter **6** abject, hearty, moving, severe **7** decided, erudite, extreme, intense, knowing, learned, radical, serious, sincere **8** complete, educated, informed, piercing, positive, thorough **9** heartfelt, out-and-out, recondite, sagacious, scholarly **10** all-knowing, consummate, deep-seated, omniscient, pronounced, reflective, thoughtful **11** enlightened, far-reaching, penetrating **12** intellectual, soul-stirring **13** comprehensive, knowledgeable, philosophical, thoroughgoing

profundity 5 abyss, depth **6** wisdom **8** deepness, sagacity, sapience **9** erudition **11** learnedness, penetration **12** abstractness, abstruseness, profoundness **13** reconditeness, sagaciousness **16** impenetrableness

profuse 4 rich **5** ample, wordy **6** lavish, prolix **7** copious, diffuse, verbose **8** abundant, generous, prodigal, rambling, wasteful **9** bounteous, bountiful, excessive, garrulous, unthrifty **10** digressive, discursive, immoderate, inordinate, long-winded, loquacious, munificent **11** extravagant, improvident, intemperate, spendthrift

profuseness 9 abundance, diffusion, profusion, prolixity, verbosity, wordiness **10** lavishness **11** copiousness, diffuseness

profusion 4 glut **5** waste **6** excess **7** surfeit, surplus **8** plethora **9** abundance, multitude **10** oversupply **11** superfluity **12** extravagance, multiplicity

progenitor 8 ancestor, forebear **10** forefather

progeny 3 kin, son **4** clan, heir, line, race, seed **5** blood, breed, child, issue, scion, stock, young **6** family **7** kindred, lineage **8** children, offshoot **9** offspring, posterity **10** descendant

prognosticate 7 predict, presage **8** forecast, foretell, prophesy **9** foretoken

prognostication 6 augury **8** forecast, prophecy **10** divination, prediction

prognosticator 4 seer **5** augur **7** prophet **9** predictor **10** forecaster

program 4 bill, book, card, list, plan, show **5** slate **6** agenda, design, docket, expect, intend, line up, notice, series, sketch **7** arrange, outline **8** bulletin, calendar, playbill, register, schedule, syllabus **9** timetable **10** curriculum, production, prospectus **12** presentation

progress 4 gain, grow, rise **5** climb, get on, mount, ripen **6** action, course, grow up, growth, mature, stride **7** advance, develop, headway, improve, proceed, process, success **8** get ahead, increase, movement **9** get better, go forward, move ahead, promotion, unfolding **10** betterment, enrichment, gain ground **11** achievement, advancement, development, enhancement, furtherance, improvement, make headway, make strides

progression 3 run **5** chain, climb, order **6** ascent, course, series, strain, string **7** advance **8** progress, sequence **10** succession **11** advancement, continuance, furtherance **12** continuation **14** continuousness **15** consecutiveness

progressive 7 dynamic, gradual, liberal, ongoing **8** activist, advanced, populist, up-to-date **9** advancing, enlarging, reformist, spreading, traveling **10** ameliorist **11** incremental **12** enterprising

prohibit 3 ban, bar **4** curb, deny, stay, stop, veto **5** block, check, delay, limit **6** enjoin, forbid, hamper, hinder, impede, negate **7** inhibit, obviate, prevent, repress **8** disallow, obstruct, preclude,

restrain, restrict, suppress, withhold **9** proscribe

prohibited
  German: **8** verboten

prohibition 3 ban **4** veto **5** edict **7** embargo, sanction **10** temperance **11** forbiddance **12** interdiction

prohibitive, prohibitory 9 enjoining, hindering **10** forbidding, inhibitive, injunction, preventative, repressive **11** disallowing, obstructive, restraining, restrictive, suppressive **12** inadmissible, unacceptable **13** disqualifying **15** circumscriptive

project 3 aim, job **4** cast, emit, fire, goal, plan, send, task, work **5** draft, eject, expel, fling, frame, shoot, throw **6** beetle, design, devise, extend, hurtle, invent, jut out, launch, map out, propel, scheme **7** concoct, outline, propose **8** activity, ambition, bend over, contrive, forecast, overhang, protrude, stand out, stick out, throw out, transmit **9** calculate, discharge, ejaculate, intention, objective, plan ahead **10** assignment **11** extrapolate, undertaking **12** predetermine

projected 6 hurled **7** hurtled, planned **8** extended, forecast, launched, overhung, proposed, stood out, stuck out **9** mapped out, propelled, protruded **10** catapulted **11** conjectural

projectile 4 dart **5** arrow, spear **6** rocket **7** javelin, missile

projecting part 3 arm, ell, leg **4** eave, limb, tail **6** branch, feeler, member **7** antenna **8** tentacle **9** appendage

projection 4 brow, bump, eave **5** bulge, guess, jetty, jutty, ledge, ridge, shelf **8** estimate, forecast, overhang **9** extension, extrusion **10** estimation, prediction, prospectus, protrusion **11** guesstimate **12** protuberance **13** approximation, extrapolation

Prokofiev, Serge
  born: **6** Russia **9** Sontsovka
  composer of: **6** Lt Kije
    10 Cinderella, The Gambler
    11 War and Peace
    13 Scythian Suite, The Fiery Angel **14** Lieutenant Kije, Romeo and Juliet; The Prodigal Son **15** Alexander Nevsky, Peter and the Wolf **17** Classical Symphony **22** The Love for Three Oranges **57** Cantata for the

Twentieth Anniversary of the October Revolution

proletarian 6 worker **7** laborer **10** working man

proletariat 5 plebs **6** rabble, the mob **7** populus **8** canaille, laborers, populace **9** commonage, commoners, hoi polloi, the masses **10** commonalty **11** lower orders, rank and file, wage earners **12** lower classes, vulgus mobile, working class **15** the common people **16** the great unwashed

proliferate 4 teem **5** breed, hatch, spawn, swarm **8** increase, multiply **9** procreate, propagate, pullulate **10** regenerate **11** overproduce

prolific 4 lush **6** fecund **7** copious, fertile, profuse **8** abundant, breeding, creative, fruitful, yielding **9** luxuriant **11** germinative, multiplying, procreative, progenitive, proliferous, propagating **12** reproductive

prolix 5 wordy **7** verbose **10** long-winded

prolixity 9 verbosity, wordiness **11** profuseness **14** long-windedness

prologue 7 opening, preface, prelude **8** foreword, overture, preamble **9** beginning **12** introduction

prolong 5 delay **6** extend, retard **7** drag out, draw out, spin out, stretch, sustain **8** continue, elongate, lengthen, maintain, protract **9** attenuate **10** perpetuate

prolongation 5 delay **9** extending, extension **10** drawing out **11** attenuation, dragging out, lengthening, protraction, retardation **12** perpetuation **13** streching out

prolonged 7 lengthy **8** drawn-out, extended **9** continued, long-lived **10** continuing, lengthened, persistent, protracted **11** long-lasting

prom 3 hop **4** ball **5** dance **9** cotillion, promenade

Promachorma
  epithet of: **6** Athena
  means: **25** protectress of the anchorage

Promachus
  member of: **7** Epigoni
  leader of: **9** Boeotians
  epithet of: **6** Athena
  means: **8** defender **9** protector

promenade 3 hop **4** ball, prom, walk **5** dance **6** soiree, stroll **9** cotillion

Prometheus
> member of: **6** Titans
> father: **7** Iapetus
> mother: **6** Themis **7** Clymene
> brother: **5** Atlas
> **10** Epimetheus
> son: **9** Deucalion
> created mankind from:
> **4** clay
> stole: **4** fire
> punished by: **4** Zeus
> chained to: **4** rock
> released by: **8** Hercules

Prometheus Bound
> author: **9** Aeschylus
> character: **2** Io **3** Bia
> **6** Hermes, Kratos
> **7** Oceanus **10** Hephaestus

Prometheus Unbound
> author: **18** Percy Bysshe
> Shelley
> character: **4** Asia, Ione
> **5** Earth **7** Jupiter, Mercury,
> Panthea **8** Hercules
> **9** Demogoron

prominence 3 tor **4** bump,
dune, fame, hill, hump, knob,
lump, mark, mesa, name,
node, peak, rise, spur **5** bluff,
bulge, cliff, crest, honor, jetty,
jutty, knoll, knurl, might,
mound **6** credit, height, renown, rising, summit, weight
7 dignity, hillock, majesty,
process **8** eminence, grandeur,
mountain, nobility, outshoot,
overhang, pinnacle, prestige,
salience, splendor, swelling
9 celebrity, convexity, elevation, extension, extrusion,
greatness, influence, notoriety,
precipice **10** brilliance, importance, notability, popularity,
projection, promontory, protrusion, reputation, tumescence **11** distinction,
excrescence, excurvature,
preeminence, superiority
12 protuberance, significance

prominent 6 convex, famous
7 bulging, eminent, evident,
glaring, honored, jutting, leading, notable, obvious, salient,
staring, swollen **8** apparent,
definite, excurved, extended,
renowned, striking, swelling
9 arresting, important, respected, well-known **10** celebrated, easily seen, jutting
out, noticeable, preeminent,
projecting, pronounced, protruding, protrusive, remarkable **11** conspicuous,
discernible, illustrious, outstanding, prestigious, protuberant **12** recognizable
13 distinguished

promiscuous 3 lax **4** fast,
lewd, wild **5** loose, mixed
6 casual, impure, medley, motley, rakish, wanton **7** aimless,

chaotic, diverse, immoral,
jumbled, mingled, mixed-up,
satyric **8** careless, confused,
immodest, sweeping, un-
chaste **9** composite, desultory,
dissolute, haphazard, perplexed, scrambled, wholesale
10 commingled, disordered,
disorderly, dissipated, intermixed, lascivious, licentious,
uncritical, undirected, unvir-
tuous, variegated **11** disarranged, incontinent,
indifferent, intemperate, unselective **12** disorganized, of
easy virtue, undiscerning
13 helter-skelter, heterogeneous, miscellaneous
14 indiscriminate

promise 3 vow **4** aver, avow,
oath, word **5** agree, augur, imply, swear, troth, vouch **6** assure, avowal, oath of, parole,
pledge, plight **7** be bound, betoken, suggest, warrant **8** covenant, indicate, warranty
9 agreement, assurance, guarantee, potential, undertake
11 declaration, stipulation,
swear an oath, word of honor

Promised Land 6 Canaan
> nickname of: **10** California
> **6** Israel

Promises
> author: **16** Robert Penn
> Warren

promising 4 rosy **5** happy,
lucky **6** bright, rising **7** hopeful **8** assuring, cheerful, cheering **9** advancing, favorable,
fortunate, looking up **10** auspicious, of good omen, optimistic, propitious, reassuring
11 encouraging, inspiriting,
up-and-coming

promissory note 3 IOU
4 bond, chit **6** pledge **7** promise **9** agreement **10** obligation
11 certificate

promontory 4 cape, hill, ness,
spur **5** bluff, cliff, jetty, jutty,
point **6** height **8** headland,
overhang **9** peninsula, precipice **10** embankment,
projection

promote 3 aid **4** abet, ease,
help, plug, push **5** raise **6** assist, foster, prefer, refine **7** advance, develop, elevate,
enhance, forward, further,
support, upgrade, work for
8 advocate, expedite, graduate
9 advertise, cultivate, encourage, publicize

promoter 6 backer **8** advocate,
champion **9** proponent,
supporter

promotion 4 hype **5** raise
7 advance, fanfare, puffery

8 ballyhoo, boosting, progress
9 elevation, publicity, upgrad-
ing **10** preferment **11** advancement, advertising,
furtherance **12** promulgation
13 advertisement,
encouragement

promotive 7 helpful **9** conducive **10** beneficial **12** contributive, contributory, instrumental

prompt 3 cue **4** goad, keen,
move, prod, push, spur, stir
5 alert, alive, cause, drive, eager, force, impel, press, quick,
ready, sharp **6** active, assist,
bright, excite, incite, induce,
intent, lively, on time, propel,
remind, thrust, timely **7** actuate, animate, dispose, help
out, incline, inspire, instant,
on guard, provoke, zealous
8 activate, inspirit, motivate,
occasion, open-eyed, persuade,
punctual, vigilant, watchful
9 attentive, determine, efficient, immediate, influence,
instigate, observant, open-
eared, stimulate, wide-awake
10 on one's toes **12** jog the
memory, unhesitating
13 instantaneous

prompting 6 cueing, urging
7 goading **8** egging on **10** motivation **11** exhortation

promptly 3 pat **4** anon, soon,
tite **6** pronto **7** quickly,
swiftly **10** punctually
11 immediately

promptness 5 haste **8** alacrity,
celerity, dispatch **9** quickness,
readiness, swiftness **11** punc-
tuality **15** expeditiousness

promulgate 6 foster **7** explain,
expound, present, promote,
sponsor **8** instruct, set forth
9 elucidate, enunciate, interpret **11** communicate

promulgation 9 fostering, promotion **11** circulation, instruction, sponsorship
12 distribution, presentation,
transmission **13** communication **14** interpretation

Pronaus
> epithet of: **6** Athena
> means: **12** of the pronaos
> *pronaos:* **15** before the
> temple

prone 3 apt **4** flat **5** level **6** liable, likely **7** subject, tending
8 disposed, face-down, inclined **9** prostrate, reclining,
recumbent **10** accustomed, habituated, horizontal **11** predisposed, susceptible

proneness 4 bent, bias, turn
7 leaning **8** penchant, tendency **9** prejudice **10** proclivity, propensity **11** inclination

12 predilection
14 predisposition

prong 4 barb, hook, horn, spur, tine **5** point, spike, tooth **6** branch **10** projection

Pronoea
epithet of: **6** Athena
means: **11** forethought

pronoun 2 he, it, me, my, us, we, ye **3** all, any, few, her, his, one, she, thy, who, you **4** hers, mine, ours, some, thee, them, they, that, this, thou, what, whom **5** no one, their, these, thine, those, which, whose, yours **6** anyone, itself, myself, nobody **7** anybody, herself, himself, nothing, someone, whoever **8** somebody, whomever **9** everybody, something, whosoever **10** everything, themselves
French: **2** il, je, tu **3** lui, mes, moi **4** elle, vous
German: **2** er, es, du **3** ich, mir, sie **4** mein, mich
Italian: **2** io, me, mi, ti, tu, vi **3** cio, lei, lui, mio, tei, voi **4** egli, ella, essa, esse, essi, loro
Spanish: **2** el, la, lo, me, mi, tu, yo **4** ella, ello, suyo, tuyo **5** usted

pronounce 3 say **4** emit, form, rule **5** frame, judge, orate, sound, speak, state, utter, voice **6** decree **7** declare, enounce **8** announce, proclaim, vocalize **9** enunciate **10** articulate

pronounced 4 bold **5** broad, clear, plain, vivid **6** patent **7** decided, evident, obvious, visible **8** apparent, clear-cut, definite, distinct, manifest, positive, unhidden **9** arresting **10** noticeable **11** conspicuous, outstanding, undisguised, well-defined **12** recognizable, unmistakable **14** unquestionable

pronouncement 6 decree **11** declaration **12** announcement, proclamation

pronto 3 now **4** asap, fast, stat **5** quick **7** quickly **8** promptly **11** immediately

Pronuba
epithet of: **4** Juno

pronunciamento 5 edict **12** proclamation **13** pronouncement

pronunciation 6 accent **10** inflection **11** enunciation **12** articulation **16** manner of speaking

proof 4 test **5** essay, proof,

sheet, trial **6** galley, ordeal **8** scrutiny, weighing **9** probation **10** assessment **11** attestation, examination **12** confirmation, ratification, verification **13** certification, corroboration, documentation **14** substantiation

proofreader's mark 3 cap, rom **4** dele, ital, stet **5** caret, space

prop 3 set **4** lean, rest, stay **5** brace, stand **6** hold up, pillar **7** bolster, shore up, support **8** buttress, mainstay, shoulder, underpin **9** stanchion, supporter, sustainer **13** reinforcement
French: **11** point d'appui

propaganda 6 hoopla **8** ballyhoo **9** party line, promotion, publicity **10** persuasion **11** advertising

propagandist 6 zealot **8** activist, exponent **9** apologist, proponent, publicist **12** spokesperson

propagate 3 air, sow **4** bear, tell **5** beget, breed, hatch, issue, rumor, spawn, spray **6** blazon, herald, impart, notify, preach, purvey, repeat, report, spread **7** bestrew, give out, implant, instill, publish, scatter, trumpet **8** disperse, engender, generate, increase, multiply, proclaim, put forth **9** broadcast, circulate, enunciate, give birth, inculcate, make known, procreate, publicize, reproduce

propagation 6 laying, siring **7** bearing **8** breeding, hatching, issuance, spawning, yielding **9** begetting, diffusion, gestation, pregnancy, spreading **10** dispersion, generation **11** circulation, engendering, giving birth, procreation, publication **12** distribution, reproduction, transmission **13** dissemination

pro patria 14 for one's country

propel 4 cast, goad, hurl, poke, prod, push, send, toss **5** drive, eject, force, heave, impel, pitch, shoot, shove, sling, start **6** launch, thrust **7** project **8** catapult **9** discharge **11** precipitate, set in motion

propeller, screw
invented by: **7** Stevens **8** Ericsson

propensity 4 bent, bias, turn **5** fancy, favor, taste **6** liking **7** leaning **8** affinity, penchant, pleasure, sympathy, tendency,

weakness **9** prejudice **10** attraction, partiality, preference, proclivity **11** disposition, inclination **12** predilection **14** predisposition

proper 3 apt, fit, own **4** meet, nice, true **5** per se, right **6** decent, marked, modest, polite, seemly **7** apropos, correct, express, fitting, germane, precise, typical **8** assigned, becoming, decorous, orthodox, peculiar, relevant, specific, suitable **9** befitting, courteous, pertinent **10** acceptable, applicable, individual, particular, respective **11** appropriate, conformable, distinctive **12** conventional **14** characteristic, distinguishing, representative
French: **11** comme il faut

properly 5 aptly, right **7** exactly **8** decently, politely, suitably **9** correctly, perfectly, precisely **10** acceptably, accurately, decorously, tastefully **12** without error **13** appropriately **14** conventionally

property 4 hold, land, mark **5** acres, badge, funds, goods, means, point, stock, title, trait **6** aspect, assets, estate, moneys, realty, wealth **7** acreage, capital, earmark, effects, estates, feature, grounds, quality **8** chattels, holdings, treasure **9** attribute, ownership, resources, territory **10** belongings, real estate **11** investments, peculiarity, possessions, singularity **12** appointments, idiosyncrasy **13** individuality, particularity **14** characteristic, proprietorship

prophecy 6 augury **7** portent **8** forecast **10** divination, prediction, revelation **15** prognostication
god of: **6** Apollo **7** Phoebus, Pythius **9** Musagetes

prophesy 4 warn **5** augur **6** divine **7** forbode, foresee, portend, predict, presage **8** forecast, foretell, forewarn, soothsay **9** apprehend, premonish **13** prognosticate

prophet 4 seer **5** augur, guide, sibyl **6** oracle **7** diviner, palmist, seeress **8** preacher, sorcerer **9** Cassandra, divinator, geomancer, predictor, sorceress **10** evangelist, forecaster, foreteller, prophesier, prophetess, soothsayer **11** clairvoyant, intercessor, interpreter **12** crystal gazer **13** fortune-teller **14** prognosticator

Prophet, major 6 Baruch, Daniel, Elijah, Isaiah 7 Ezekiel 8 Jeremiah

Prophet, minor 3 Gad 4 Amos, Joel 5 Hosea, Jonah, Micah, Nahum 6 Haggai, Nathan 7 Malachi, Obadiah 8 Habakkuk 9 Zechariah, Zephaniah

Prophetess 4 Anna 6 Miriam 7 Deborah

prophetic, prophetical 5 vatic 6 mantic 7 fateful, ominous 8 oracular 10 portentous, predictive, presageful

Prophetic Books
author: 12 William Blake

Prophet of famine 11 Agabus

prophylactic 8 hygienic 10 preventive 13 contraceptive

propinquity 7 kinship 8 affinity, nearness, vicinity 9 closeness, proximity 10 similarity

propitiate 4 calm 5 allay 6 pacify, soothe 7 appease, assuage, mollify, placate 10 conciliate 11 accommodate

propitiation 8 soothing 11 appeasement 12 conciliation, pacification

propitious 3 fit 5 bonny, happy, lucky 6 benign, golden 8 suitable 9 agreeable, favorable, fortunate, opportune, promising, well-timed 10 auspicious, beneficial, felicitous 12 advantageous, providential

Propoetides
form: 7 maidens
home: 6 Cypria
changed into: 5 stone
angered: 9 Aphrodite
denied her: 8 divinity

proponent 6 backer, friend, patron, votary 7 booster 8 advocate, champion, defender, endorser, espouser, exponent, partisan, upholder 9 apologist, spokesman, supporter 10 enthusiast, vindicator 14 representative

proportion 5 ratio 7 balance, harmony 8 evenness, symmetry 9 agreement 11 consistency, correlation, perspective 12 distribution, relationship 14 commensuration, correspondence

proportionate 5 equal 8 balanced 10 comparable, equivalent 12 commensurate 13 commensurable, corresponding

proportions 3 fit, lot 4 area,

bulk, form, gear, mass, part, size, span 5 adapt, gauge, grade, match, order, poise, quota, range, ratio, scope, shape, share, width 6 amount, degree, equate, extent, spread, volume 7 balance, breadth, conform, correct, expanse, measure, portion, rectify, segment 8 capacity, division, equalize, fraction, graduate, modulate, regulate 9 amplitude, apportion, greatness, harmonize, magnitude 10 dimensions 12 measurements

proposal 3 bid 4 idea, plan, plot, suit 5 draft, offer 6 appeal, course, design, motion, scheme, sketch, theory 7 outline, proffer, program, project 8 overture, prospect 9 stratagem 10 conception, invitation, nomination, prospectus, resolution, suggestion 11 proposition 12 presentation 14 recommendation

propose 3 aim, woo 4 hope, mean, plan, plot 6 aspire, design, expect, intend, scheme, submit, tender 7 advance, present, proffer, purpose, suggest, venture 8 affiance, propound, put forth, set about, set forth 9 determine, have a mind, introduce, recommend, undertake 10 come up with, have in mind, have in view, put forward 11 contemplate 14 pop the question 21 offer for consideration

proposition 4 deal, pass, plan 5 issue, offer, point, topic 6 matter, scheme 7 advance, bargain, solicit, subject 8 contract, proposal, question 9 agreement, assurance, guarantee 10 resolution, suggestion 11 make a pass at, negotiation, stipulation, undertaking 14 recommendation

propound 4 pose 5 boost 6 assert 7 advance, profess, propose 8 put forth, set forth

proprieties 7 decorum, manners 8 protocol 9 amenities, etiquette 10 civilities 11 conventions

proprietor 5 owner 6 holder, master 7 manager 8 landlord 9 landowner, possessor 10 landholder 11 titleholder 12 proprietress

propriety 7 aptness, decorum, dignity, fitness 8 courtesy 9 etiquette, formality, rightness 10 seemliness 11 correctness, good manners, savoir faire 12 becomingness, decorousness, good behavior, suit-

ableness 13 applicability 14 respectability 15 appropriateness

propulsion 6 launch, thrust 9 launching 10 propelling

prop up 5 brace 7 bolster, support 8 buttress

prorate 6 divide 9 apportion 10 distribute

Prorsa *see* 9 Antevorta

prosaic 3 dry 4 blah, dull, flat 5 prosy, stale, trite, vapid, wordy 6 common, jejune 7 humdrum, tedious 8 ordinary, plebeian, tiresome 9 hackneyed 10 monotonous, pedestrian, spiritless, unpoetical 12 matter-of-fact 13 platitudinous, unimaginative, uninteresting

Prosclystius
epithet of: 8 Poseidon
means: 7 flooder

proscribe 3 ban 4 damn 5 curse, exile 6 banish, forbid, outlaw 7 boycott, censure, condemn 8 denounce, prohibit 9 interdict, repudiate 10 disapprove 12 anathematize 13 excommunicate

proscription 3 ban 7 barring, censure 8 anathema 9 interdict 11 forbiddance, prohibition 12 condemnation, denunciation, interdiction 15 excommunication

prose 3 dry 4 dull 5 novel 7 fiction, quality, tedious, writing 8 sequence 9 discourse 10 expression 11 commonplace 13 unimaginative

prosecute 3 sue, try 4 wage 6 direct, go with, handle, indict, manage, pursue 7 arraign, carry on, conduct, execute, go to law, perform, prolong, stick to, sustain 8 continue, deal with, follow up, maintain 9 discharge, persist in 10 administer, put on trial, see through 11 take to court 12 bring to trial 14 bring to justice

prosecution 4 suit 6 action 7 conduct, pursuit 11 performance 14 administration

Proserpina *see* 10 Persephone

prosit 11 may it do good
used as: 5 toast

prospect, prospects 4 hope, plan, seek, view 5 scene, vista 6 aspect, design, search, vision 7 chances, explore, go after, look for, outlook, picture, promise, scenery 8 ambition, panorama, proposal

9 candidate, foretaste, intention, landscape, work a mine **10** expectancy, likelihood **11** expectation, possibility, probability **12** anticipation **13** contemplation

prospective 4 to be **6** coming, future, in view, likely, to come **7** looming **8** destined, eventual, expected, foreseen, hoped-for, intended, possible **9** about to be, impending, in the wind, looked-for, potential, promising **10** in prospect **11** approaching, forthcoming, threatening

prosper 4 gain **5** get on **6** flower, thrive **7** advance, succeed **8** fare well, flourish, fructify, get ahead, grow rich, increase, make good, progress **9** bear fruit **15** make one's fortune

prosperity 4 ease, gain **6** luxury, plenty, profit, wealth **7** advance, success, welfare **8** good luck, progress **9** abundance, advantage, affluence, blessings, golden age, good times, palmy days, run of luck, well-being **11** advancement, good fortune
god of: 4 Frey **5** Freyr, Niord, Njord **12** Bonus Eventus
goddess of: 5 Salus

Prospero
character in: 10 The Tempest
author: 11 Shakespeare

prosperous 4 fair, good, rich, rosy **5** happy, lucky, sunny **6** bright, golden, timely **7** hopeful, moneyed, opulent, smiling, wealthy, well-off **8** affluent, cheering, pleasing, thriving, well-to-do **9** favorable, fortunate, opportune, promising **10** auspicious, heartening, of good omen, propitious, reassuring, successful **11** comfortable, encouraging, flourishing **12** on easy street

Pross, Miss
character in: 16 A Tale of Two Cities
author: 7 Dickens

prostitute 4 bawd, jade, slut, tart **5** abuse, hussy, lower, spoil, whore **6** chippy, debase, defile, demean, floozy, harlot, hooker, misuse **7** cheapen, corrupt, debauch, degrade, hustler, pervert, profane, sell out, trollop **8** call girl, misapply, strumpet **9** courtesan, desecrate, misdirect, misemploy **12** streetwalker **14** lady of the night

prostrate 4 deck, flat **5** abase,

floor, prone, spent **6** fagged, kowtow **7** bow down, flatten, laid out, worn out **8** bowed low, overcome **9** bone weary, crouching, dead tired, exhausted, kneel down, lying flat, overthrow, recumbent **10** beseeching, horizontal **11** on one's knees **12** on bended knee, stretched out, supplicating **13** lying face down **15** fall to one's knees

prostration 3 bow, woe **5** grief **6** misery, sorrow **7** anguish, despair **8** distress, kneeling, weakness **9** abasement, dejection, heartache, impotence, lowliness, paralysis, weariness **10** depression, desolation, enervation, exhaustion, subjection, submission **11** desperation, despondency **12** genuflection, helplessness, wretchedness **13** depth of misery

prosy 4 dull, flat **5** banal, inane **6** stupid **7** humdrum, prosaic, tedious **9** wearisome **11** commonplace **13** uninteresting

protagonist 4 diva, hero, lead, star **7** heroine **9** headliner, principal, superstar, title role **10** leading man, prima donna **11** leading lady **12** danseur noble, jeune premier **13** jeune premiere, main character **14** prima ballerina **16** central character

protect 4 hide, keep, save, tend, veil **5** cover, guard **6** defend, harbor, screen, secure, shield **7** care for, shelter, sustain **8** conserve, maintain, preserve **9** look after, safeguard, watch over **10** take care of

protected 4 safe **5** saved **6** immune, secure **7** guarded, secured **8** anchored, defended, shielded **9** sheltered **10** inviolable **12** invulnerable

protection 3 aid **4** care, keep, wall **5** cover, fence, guard, haven, shade **6** asylum, buffer, charge, harbor, refuge, safety, saving, screen, shield **7** barrier, custody, defense, shelter, support **8** guarding, immunity, preserve, security **9** preserver, safeguard, sanctuary **10** assistance **11** safekeeping **12** championship, conservation, guardianship, preservation

protective 7 careful, heedful **8** fatherly, guarding, maternal, motherly, paternal, sisterly, vigilant, watchful **9** avuncular, brotherly, defensive, shielding

10 preventive, sheltering, solicitous **11** safekeeping **12** bigbrotherly, safeguarding

protective covering 4 coat, hust, mail **5** armor, shell **6** shield **7** coating, plating **8** carapace **10** coat of mail **11** suit of armor **12** armor plating

protectorate 6 colony **7** mandate **8** province, dominion **9** satellite, territory **10** dependency, possession, settlement

protege 4 ward **5** pupil **6** charge **7** student, trainee **9** dependent

pro tempore 9 temporary **11** temporarily **15** for the time being

Protesilaus
father: 8 Iphiclus
brother: 8 Podarces
wife: 8 Laodamia

protest 3 vow **4** aver, avow, beef, deny, kick **5** gripe, march, offer, sit-in, speak, state **6** affirm, allege, assert, assure, attest, avouch, cry out, insist, object, oppose, strike **7** boycott, contend, declare, dispute, dissent, hold out, profess, testify **8** announce, complain, demurral, disagree, maintain, propound, put forth, set forth **9** enunciate, objection, picketing, pronounce **10** asseverate, contradict, controvert, disapprove, disclaimer, dissidence, opposition, put forward, resistance **11** beg to differ, deprecation **12** disaffection, disagreement, remonstrance, renunciation **13** contradiction, demonstration, remonstration, take exception **14** discountenance

Protestant 5 Amish **6** Mormon, Quaker, Shaker **7** Baptist, Puritan **8** Anglican, Huguenot, Lutheran **9** Adventist, Calvinist, Methodist, Unitarian **12** Episcopalian, Presbyterian **17** Congregationalist **18** Christian Scientist

protest meeting 5 rally **13** demonstration

Proteus
character in: 20 Two Gentlemen of Verona
author: 11 Shakespeare

Proteus
god of: 3 sea
king of: 5 Egypt
father: 7 Oceanus
mother: 6 Tethys
wife: 8 Psamathe
son: 12 Theoclymenus
daughter: 7 Theonoe

gift: 8 prophesy 12 form-changing 13 shape-changing

Prothoenor
  leader of: 9 Boeotians

Protoceratops
  type: 8 dinosaur 10 ceratopsid
  period: 10 Cretaceous
  location: 8 Mongolia 10 Gobi Desert
  characteristic: 6 horned 7 armored

protocol 5 usage 7 customs, decorum, manners 8 good form 9 amenities, etiquette, formality, standards 11 conventions, proprieties 14 code of behavior, court etiquette, diplomatic code 17 dictates of society

Protogonia
  father: 10 Erechtheus
  mother: 9 Praxithea
  sister: 7 Otionia

prototypal 5 model 7 classic 9 exemplary 10 archetypal, definitive 12 prototypical

prototype 5 model 7 example 8 original 9 archetype

protozoan 4 cell 5 ameba, cilia 6 amoeba 7 euglena 8 flagella, protista 9 eukaryote, pseudopod 10 paramecium, plasmodium 11 microscopic, unicellular 17 nonphotosynthetic

protract 6 extend, keep up 7 drag out, draw out, prolong, spin out 8 lengthen 9 keep going 10 stretch out

protracted 4 long 7 lengthy 8 drawn-out, extended 9 continued, long-lived, prolonged 10 lengthened, persistent 11 long-lasting

protraction 4 stay 7 lasting 9 extension 10 continuing, drawing out 11 continuance, dragging out, persistence 12 perseverance, prolongation

protrude 5 belly, bulge, swell 6 jut out 7 project 8 stand out, stick out 11 push forward

protrusion 4 bump, hump 6 hernia 8 swelling 9 extension 10 projection 12 prolongation, protuberance

protuberance 3 bow 4 bump, hump, knob, knot, lump, node, weal, welt 5 bulge, gnarl, ridge 6 rising 8 swelling 9 convexity, elevation, roundness 10 projection, prominence 11 excrescence, excurvature

protura
  class: 8 hexapoda

  phylum: 10 arthropoda
  characteristic: 5 small 6 minute 7 eyeless 8 wingless

proud 4 fine, smug, vain 5 aloof, cocky, grand, great, happy, lofty, noble 6 august, lordly, snooty, snotty, strict, uppish, uppity 7 bloated, exalted, haughty, high-hat, pleased, pompous, revered, stately, storied, stuck-up, swollen 8 affected, arrogant, assuming, boastful, braggart, bragging, elevated, euphoric, glorious, inflated, insolent, majestic, prideful, puffed up, reserved, snobbish 9 admirable, cherished, conceited, contented, delighted, dignified, flaunting, gratified, honorable, imperious, know-it-all, satisfied, venerable 10 complacent, disdainful, high-minded, intolerant, principled, scrupulous 11 egotistical, independent, magnificent, overbearing, patronizing, punctilious 12 contemptuous, self-praising, supercilious, vainglorious 13 condescending, distinguished, high-and-mighty, self-important, self-satisfied 14 self-respecting, self-sufficient

Proudie, Dr
  character in: 16 Barchester Towers
  author: 8 Trollope

Proust, Marcel
  author of: 23 Remembrance of Things Past 24 A la Recherche du Temps Perdu

prove 3 try 4 test 5 check, end up, probe 6 affirm, attest, result, try out, uphold, verify, wind up 7 analyze, bear out, certify, confirm, examine, justify, support, sustain, warrant, witness 8 document, evidence, look into, make good, manifest, result in, validate 9 ascertain, establish, eventuate, testify to 11 corroborate, demonstrate 12 authenticate, substantiate

proved 5 known 6 proven, upheld 8 affirmed, attested, borne out, verified 9 certified, confirmed, supported, sustained, warranted, witnessed 10 documented 11 established 12 corroborated, demonstrable 13 authenticated, substantiated

prove false 5 belie 6 refute, reject 7 explode 8 disprove 9 discredit 10 invalidate

proven 5 known 6 proved, upheld 8 accepted, affirmed, attested, borne out, verified

9 certified, confirmed, supported, sustained, warranted, witnessed 10 documented, verifiable 11 established 12 corroborated, demonstrable 13 authenticated, substantiated

provender 3 hay 4 chow, corn, eats, feed, food, grub, oats 5 grain 6 fodder, forage, ration, viands 7 nurture 10 provisions 11 subsistence

proverb 3 mot, saw 5 adage, axiom, maxim, moral, motto 6 byword, cliche, dictum, saying, truism 7 bromide, epigram, precept 8 aphorism, apothegm 9 platitude 11 commonplace 13 accepted truth, popular saying

prove wrong 5 belie 6 expose, refute 7 explode 8 disprove 9 discredit

provide 3 arm, fit, pay 4 give, plan 5 allow, award, cater, equip, grant, offer, state, yield 6 accord, afford, bestow, confer, donate, impart, outfit, render, save up, submit, supply, tender 7 arrange, deliver, furnish, prepare, present, produce, require, specify 8 dispense, get ready 9 make plans, postulate, stipulate 10 accumulate, contribute

provide for 7 care for 8 attend to, wait upon 9 look after 10 minister to, take care of

providence 8 prudence 9 foresight, husbandry, provision 11 forethought 14 circumspection, farsightedness, forehandedness

provident 4 wary 5 chary, ready 6 frugal, saving 7 careful, prudent, thrifty 8 cautious, discreet, equipped, vigilant 9 farseeing, judicious 10 discerning, economical, farsighted, forehanded, foreseeing, thoughtful 11 circumspect, foresighted, precautious 12 parsimonious, well-prepared

province 3 job 4 area, duty, part, role, zone 5 field, place, state 6 canton, charge, county, domain, office, region, sphere 7 section, station 8 business, capacity, function 9 authority, bailiwick, territory 10 assignment, department 11 subdivision 12 jurisdiction 13 scope of duties 14 arrondissement, responsibility

provincial 4 rude 5 crude, gawky, local, rough, rural 6 clumsy, gauche, homely, narrow, oafish, rustic 7 awkward, boorish, bucolic, country, hayseed, insular, loutish **8** cloddish, clownish, downhome, homespun, regional, yokelish **9** backwoods, parochial, small-town, unrefined **10** unpolished **11** clodhopping, countrified, territorial **15** unsophisticated

provision 6 giving **8** donation **9** endowment, providing, supplying **10** furnishing

provisional 6 acting, pro tem **7** interim **9** surrogate, temporary, tentative **10** substitute **11** conditional **12** probationary **15** for the time being

provisions 4 feed, food, term **6** clause, fodder, forage, stores, string, viands **7** article, commons, edibles, proviso **8** eatables, supplies, victuals **9** condition, groceries, provender, readiness, requisite **10** limitation, obligation, precaution, sustenance **11** arrangement, comestibles, forethought, preparation, requirement, reservation, restriction, stipulation, wherewithal **12** anticipation, modification **13** qualification **14** forehandedness, prearrangement

proviso 5 rider **6** clause, string **8** addition **9** amendment, condition **10** limitation **11** requirement, restriction, stipulation **12** modification **13** qualification

provocation 4 goad, spur **5** cause, pique **6** insult, slight **7** affront, offense **8** prodding, stimulus, vexation **9** actuation, annoyance **10** excitation, incitement, irritation, motivation **11** aggravation, fomentation, instigation, stimulation **12** perturbation

provocative 4 sexy **6** vexing **7** irksome **8** alluring, annoying, arousing, exciting, inviting, tempting **9** beguiling, provoking, ravishing, seductive, thrilling, vexatious **10** attractive, bewitching, enchanting, entrancing, intriguing, irritating **11** aggravating, captivating, fascinating, stimulating, tantalizing **12** intoxicating, irresistible

provoke 3 irk, vex **4** fire, gall, move, rile, stir **5** anger, annoy, cause, chafe, evoke, grate, impel, pique, rouse **6** arouse, awaken, compel, create, effect, elicit, enrage, excite, foment, incite, induce, kindle, madden, prompt, put out, stir up **7** actuate, agitate,

animate, bring on, incense, inflame, inspire, outrage, produce, quicken **8** generate, get to one, irritate, motivate **9** aggravate, call forth, establish, galvanize, infuriate, instigate, stimulate **10** bring about, exasperate, give rise to **11** get one's goat, put in motion **15** try one's patience **16** get under one's skin

prow 3 bow **4** stem **5** front **10** forward end

prowess 4 grit, guts **5** knack, might, nerve, power, skill, spunk, valor, vigor **6** daring, genius, mettle, spirit, talent **7** ability, bravery, courage, faculty, heroism, know-how, stamina **8** aptitude, boldness, strength **9** adeptness, derring-do, endurance, fortitude, gallantry, hardihood **10** competence, expertness **11** intrepidity, proficiency **12** fearlessness, skillfulness **13** dauntlessness **14** accomplishment

prowl 4 hunt, lurk, roam **5** creep, range, skulk, slink, snack, stalk, steal **6** ramble **8** scavenge

prowler 7 burglar **10** peeping Tom **16** suspicious person

proximate 4 near **5** close **6** beside, nearby, next to **8** adjacent, imminent, nextdoor **11** forthcoming

proximity 7 presence **8** locality, nearness, vicinity **9** closeness **10** contiguity **11** propinquity **12** togetherness

proxy 3 sub **4** vote **5** agent **6** ballot, deputy **7** stand-in **9** alternate **10** substitute

prude 4 prig **6** modest **7** puritan **9** hypocrite **10** goody-goody **13** prim and proper

prudence 4 care, tact **6** thrift, wisdom **7** caution, economy **9** austerity, foresight, frugality, parsimony **10** discretion, precaution **11** calculation, thriftiness **14** thoughtfulness

prudent 4 sage, sane, wary, wise **5** chary **6** frugal, saving, shrewd **7** careful, guarded, heedful, politic, sapient, sparing, thrifty **8** cautious, discreet, prepared, rational, sensible, vigilant **9** expedient, judicious, provident, sagacious, wideawake **10** discerning, economical, farsighted, prudential, reflecting, thoughtful **11** circumspect, considerate, foresighted, levelheaded,

precautious, well-advised **13** self-possessed

Prud'hon, Pierre-Paul
born: 5 Cluny **6** France
artwork: 14 Venus and Adonis **15** The Rape of Psyche **16** Empress Josephine **33** Crime Pursued by Vengeance and Justice **38** Justice and Divine Vengeance Pursuing Crime

prudish 3 shy **4** prim, smug **5** timid **6** demure, modest, prissy, queasy, stuffy **7** finical, mincing, precise, stilted **8** pedantic, priggish, skittish, starched **9** squeamish, Victorian **10** fastidious, old-maidish, overmodest, particular **11** punctilious, puritanical, straitlaced **13** sanctimonious, self-righteous

prudishness 8 primness **10** prissiness, puritanism **11** overmodesty **12** overdelicacy, priggishness ·**14** overrefinement

prudish phrase 9 euphemism **10** bowdlerism

prune 3 cut, lop **4** clip, crop, pull, snip, thin, trim **5** shear **6** reduce **7** abridge, clarify, curtail, shorten, thin out **8** condense, simplify **10** abbreviate

prunelle
type: 7 liqueur
origin: 6 France
flavor: 4 plum

pruning 6 digest **8** clipping, snipping, synopsis, trimming **10** shortening **11** abridgement, cutting back, cut-down form **12** abbreviation, condensation

prurient 4 lewd, sexy **6** carnal **7** fleshy, goatish, immoral, lustful, obscene, priapic, satyric **9** lecherous, salacious **10** hot-blooded, lascivious, libidinous, licentious, lubricious, passionate **12** concupiscent

pry 4 butt, nose, peek, peer, poke, tear, work, worm **5** break, crack, delve, force, jimmy, lever, mix in, prize, probe, smoke, sniff, snoop, wrest, wring **6** butt in, ferret, horn in, meddle, search, winkle, wrench **7** explore, extract, inquire, intrude, squeeze **9** interfere, intervene **15** stick one's nose in

Pryderi
origin: 5 Welsh
father: 5 Pwyll
mother: 8 Rhiannon
stolen by: 5 Gwawl
wife: 5 Kicva

prying 4 busy, nosy **7** peering, raising, seeking **8** levering, snooping **9** searching **10** intrusive, meddling **11** inquisitive

Prylis
father: **6** Hermes

Prynne, Hester
character in: **16** The Scarlet Letter
author: **9** Hawthorne

Pryor, Richard
born: **8** Peoria IL
roles: **6** The Wiz **9** Stir Crazy **12** Silver Streak **17** Lady Sings the Blues **19** Uptown Saturday Night

Prytanis
ally of: **8** Sarpedon
killed by: **8** Odysseus

psalm 3 ode **4** hymn, poem, song **5** canon, chant, verse **6** praise **7** cantata, glorify, introit **8** canticle

Psalter 12 Book of Psalms

Psamathe
member of: **6** Nereid
form: **8** princess
husband: **7** Proteus
son: **5** Linus **6** Phocus **12** Theoclymenus
daughter: **7** Theonoe

pseudo 4 fake, mock, sham **5** bogus, false, phony **6** forged **7** feigned **8** spurious **9** pretended, simulated, soi-disant **10** fictitious, fraudulent, self-styled **11** counterfeit, make-believe **13** self-described

pseudonym 5 alias **6** anonym **7** pen name **8** cognomen, nickname **9** false name, sobriquet, stage name **11** assumed name **16** professional name
French: **10** nom de plume **11** nom de guerre **12** nom de theatre

pseudonymic 7 assumed **10** fictitious **12** pseudonymous

pseudonymous 7 assumed **10** fictitious **11** pseudonymic

Psittacosaurus
type: **8** dinosaur **10** ceratopsid
period: **10** Cretaceous

psocoptera
class: **8** hexapoda
phylum: **10** arthropoda
group: **8** booklice

psyche 2 id **3** ego **4** mind, self, soul **5** anima **6** bowels, make up, spirit **8** superego **10** penetralia **11** personality, unconscious **12** subconscious

Psyche
personifies: **4** soul

loved by: 4 Eros **5** Cupid
daughter: **8** Voluptas

psychic 5 augur **6** medium, mental, mystic, occult, voyant **7** diviner, prophet, voyante **8** cerebral **9** paragnost, sensitive, spiritual **10** soothsayer, telepathic **11** clairvoyant, telekinetic, telepathist **12** extrasensory, intellectual, spiritualist, supernatural, supersensory **13** preternatural

Psycho
director: **15** Alfred Hitchcock
cast: **9** John Gavin, Vera Miles **10** Janet Leigh **12** Martin Balsam **14** Anthony Perkins
score: **15** Bernard Herrmann

psychoanalysis 7 therapy **8** analysis **14** physchotherapy

psychoanalyst 6 shrink **7** analyst **12** headshrinker

psychologist/psychiatrist
American: **4** Hall, Hull **5** Dewey, James, Lewin **6** Harlow, Horney, Miller, Rogers, Terman, Tolman, Watson, Witmer **7** Cattell, Chomsky, Erikson, Goddard, Guthrie, Johnson, Masters, Skinner **8** Brothers, Wechsler **9** Thorndike **10** Westheimer
Austrian: **5** Adler, Freud, Reich
British: **5** Ellis **7** Eysenck **9** Titchener
French: **5** Binet
German: **5** Wundt **6** Koffka, Kohler **7** Fechner **9** Helmholtz, Kraepelin **10** Ebbinghaus, Wertheimer **11** Krafft-Ebing
Russian: **6** Pavlov
Swiss: **4** Jung **6** Piaget

psychology *see box*

psychopomp
conductor of spirits to: **5** Hades **10** otherworld
epithet: **12** psychopompus
epithet of: **6** Charon, Hermes

psychosis 8 dementia, insanity, neurosis, paranoia **9** paranomia, unreality **10** pathomania **12** hallucinosis **13** schizophrenia **14** mental disorder

psychotherapy 7 therapy **8** analysis **14** psychoanalysis

psychotic 3 mad, nut **4** kook, loon **5** crazy, kooky, loony, nutty **6** insane, madman, maniac **7** lunatic **8** demented, deranged **9** disturbed **10** psychopath **12** insane person, psychopathic **15** non compos mentis

psychology 4 head, mind **6** makeup **7** feeling **8** attitude **15** mental processes
problem/illness: **6** phobia **7** obesity, smoking **8** hysteria, neuroses, paranoia, schizoid **9** drug abuse, obsession, psychoses **10** alcoholism, compulsion, depression **11** sociopathic **13** schizophrenia **14** sexual deviance **15** anxiety reaction **17** passive-aggressive
term: **2** id **3** ego **6** libido **7** empathy **8** neuroses, superego **9** catatonic, cognition, psychoses **10** inhibition, repression **11** behaviorism, unconscious **12** conditioning, transference **13** actualization, Rorschach test **14** identification, Oedipus complex **19** operant conditioning **20** behavior modification
type: **6** social **7** Gestalt **8** abnormal, clinical **9** cognitive **10** industrial **11** educational **12** experimental **13** developmental, physiological, psychometrics, psychophysics

Ptah
origin: **8** Egyptian
diety of: **17** universal creation
worshiped at: **7** Memphis

Pterelaus
descendant of: **8** Poseidon
mother: **9** Hippothoe
daughter: **8** Comaetho

Ptolemy
author of: **8** Almagest **9** Geography

Ptous
father: **7** Athamas
mother: **8** Themisto

pub 3 bar, inn **5** local **6** bistro, saloon, lounge, tavern **7** barroom, ginmill, rummery, rumshop, taproom **8** alehouse, grogshop, pothouse **9** roadhouse, speakeasy **10** beer parlor **11** public house

pubescent 7 teenage **8** immature, juvenile **10** adolescent

public *see box*

publication 4 book, news **5** is-

public 3 mob 4 folk, open 5 civic, civil, frank, overt, plain, state, trade 6 buyers, common, in view, masses, nation, patent, people, shared, social 7 evident, exposed, general, in sight, obvious, outward, patrons, popular, society, visible 8 apparent, audience, communal, divulged, everyone, manifest, national, passable, populace, revealed, societal, unbarred, unfenced 9 available, citizenry, clientele, community, disclosed, followers, following, free to all, hoi polloi, multitude, notorious, political, statewide, unabashed, unashamed, unbounded, used by all 10 accessible, attendance, nationwide, not private, observable, population, purchasers, recognized, supporters, unenclosed 11 body politic, bourgeoisie, commonality, conspicuous, countrywide, discernible, perceivable, proletariat, rank and file, unconcealed, undisguised 12 acknowledged, constituency, unobstructed, unrestricted 14 community-owned

sue, paper 6 digest, report 7 edition, gazette, journal, tabloid 8 bulletin, magazine, pamphlet 9 broadcast, newspaper 10 periodical 11 circulation, information 12 announcement, notification

public disturbance 4 riot 6 fracas, ruckus, uproar 7 turmoil 9 commotion

public house 3 bar, pub 5 local 6 saloon, tavern 7 gin mill, taproom 8 alehouse 9 roadhouse

publicity 4 hype, plug, puff 5 blurb, flack 7 build-up, puffery, write-up 8 ballyhoo, currency 9 attention, notoriety, promotion 10 propaganda, publicness 11 advertising, circulation, information 12 promulgation, public notice, salesmanship

publicize 4 hype, plug, puff, push, sell 6 herald 7 acclaim, promote 8 announce, ballyhoo, emblazon, proclaim 9 advertise, broadcast, make known,

propagate 10 make public, promulgate 11 circularize 12 propagandize

publicly
Latin: 11 coram populo

public matter
Latin: 10 res publica

public notice 5 edict, ukase 6 decree 8 bulletin 9 manifesto 12 proclamation 13 pronouncement 14 pronunciamiento
French: 7 affiche

public speaking 7 oratory 9 lecturing 12 speechmaking

public-spirited 8 generous 10 altruistic, benevolent 12 humanitarian

publish 3 air 4 tell, vent 5 issue, print, utter 6 herald, impart, put out, spread 7 declare, diffuse, divulge, give out, placard, promote, release, trumpet 8 announce, bring out, disclose, proclaim 9 advertise, broadcast, circulate, make known, propagate, publicize 10 make public, promulgate, put to press 11 communicate, disseminate

Puca
also: 5 Pooka
origin: 5 Irish
form: 6 spirit
corresponds to: 4 Puck

Puccini, Giacomo
born: 5 Italy, Lucca
composer of: 5 Tosca 8 La Boheme, Turandot 12 Manon Lescaut 14 Madam Butterfly 15 Madama Butterfly 18 La Fanciulla del West 22 The Girl of the Golden West

puce 3 red 7 dark red 13 purplish-brown

Puck
also: 15 Robin Goodfellow
character in: 21 A Midsummer Night's Dream
author: 11 Shakespeare
form: 6 spirit
characteristic:
11 mischievous
corresponds to: 4 Puca 5 Pooka

pucker 4 fold, tuck 5 pinch, pleat, purse 6 crease, gather, ruffle, rumple, shrink 7 crinkle, crumble, squeeze, wrinkle 8 compress, contract 12 draw together

puckered 6 pursed, rucked, tucked 7 creased, crinkly, pinched, pleated 8 crinkled, gathered, wrinkled 10 compressed, corrugated

puckish 5 elfin 6 impish 7 playful 8 annoying 9 whimsical 11 mischievous

pudding 5 jello 6 junket 7 custard, dessert, tapioca 8 pandowdy 9 charlotte, yorkshire 14 floating island

pudgy, podgy 3 fat 5 buxom, dumpy, obese, plump, squat, stout, tubby 6 chubby, chunky, fleshy, rotund, stocky, stubby 7 paunchy 8 roly-poly, thickset

Pueblo (Cliff Dwellers)
language family: 4 Tewa, Zuni 6 Queres, Tanoan 10 Shoshonean
tribe: 4 Hopi, Tiwa, Towa, Tuei 5 Acoma, Kiowa 6 Isleta
location: 4 Utah 7 Arizona 8 Colorado 9 New Mexico
noted for: 5 adobe 12 architecture
spirit: 7 Kachina 8 Katchina

puerile 3 raw 5 green, inane, petty, silly, vapid 6 callow, simple 7 babyish, foolish, trivial 8 childish, immature, juvenile, piddling 9 childlike, frivolous, infantile, senseless, worthless 10 irrational, ridiculous, sophomoric 11 harebrained, nonsensical

Puerto Rico see box, p. 794

puff 3 bow 4 blow, draw, emit, gasp, hump, node, pant, plug, suck, wisp 5 bloat, blurb, bulge, heave, smoke, swell, whiff 6 blow up, breath, dilate, exhale, expand, extend, flurry, inhale, rising, wheeze 7 bluster, bombast, distend, inflate, puffery, stretch 8 ballyhoo, be winded, dilation, encomium, flattery, flummery, swelling 9 convexity, discharge, elevation, euphemism, extension, inflation, panegyric, publicity, sales talk 10 be inflated, distention, exhalation, overpraise, protrusion, tuberosity 11 be distended, breathe hard, excrescence, excurvature 12 exaggeration, inflammation, protuberance, protuberancy 13 overlaudation 16 overcommendation 17 misrepresentation

puffed 5 baggy 7 bulbous, swollen 9 ballooned

puffed up 4 vain 5 proud, puffy 7 swollen 8 inflated 9 conceited 11 swell-headed 12 vainglorious 13 self-important

puffery 4 hype 7 big talk, blus-

Puerto Rico
- **name means:** 8 rich port
- **other name:** 9 Borinquen 15 San Juan Bautista
- **capital/largest city:** 7 San Juan
- **others:** 5 Cayey, Coamo, Lares, Ponce 6 Caguas, Dorado, Manati, Utuado 7 Arecibo, Bayamon, Fajardo, Guanica, Guayama, Humacao 8 Adjuntas, Cabo Rojo, Mayaguez 9 Aquadilla 11 Santa Isabel
- **government:** 32 self-governing commonwealth of the U S
- **measure:** 6 cuerda 10 caballeria
- **island:** 4 Mona 7 Culebra, Vieques 13 Caja de Muertos 15 Greater Antilles
- **lake:** 5 Loiza 6 Carite 8 Dos Bocas 9 Caonillas, Guatajaca
- **mountain:** 4 Toro 5 Cayey 6 Yunque 8 Guilarte, Luquilla 10 Torrecilla 17 Cordillera Central
- **highest point:** 5 Punta
- **river:** 5 Camuy, Canas, Loiza, Yauco 6 Anasco, Manati, Tanama 7 Arecibo, Fajardo, La Plata 9 Caonillas
- **sea:** 8 Atlantic 9 Caribbean
- **physical feature:**
  - *bay:* 5 Sucia 6 Rincon 8 Boqueron 9 Aquadilla 14 Phosphorescent
  - *sound:* 7 Vieques
- **people:** 6 gibaro 10 borinqueno
  - *explorer:* 8 Columbus 11 Ponce de Leon
  - *leader:* 10 Munoz Marin
- **language:** 7 English, Spanish
- **religion:** 10 Protestant 13 Roman Catholic
- **place:**
  - *area of San Juan:* 7 Hato Rey 10 Rio Piedras
  - *beach:* 7 Condado
  - *cathedral:* 15 San Juan Bautista
  - *fortress:* 7 El Morro 11 San Jeronimo 12 San Cristobal
  - *governor's residence:* 11 La Fortaleza
  - *museum:* 14 El Museo de Ponce
  - *reservoir:* 5 Loiza
  - *tomb:* 11 Ponce de Leon
- **feature:**
  - *bird:* 4 rola 7 yeguita
  - *festival:* 6 Casals
  - *housing development:* 14 urbanizaciones
  - *song:* 9 aguinaldo
  - *strolling musicians:* 9 parrandas
  - *tree:* 4 mora 5 yafua, yaray 8 emajagua, guayrote 10 guaranguao
- **food:**
  - *dish:* 4 sama, sisi 9 moreillas 11 lechon asado
  - *drink:* 3 rum 10 anis-golila

ter, bombast 9 hyperbole 11 braggadocio

puff out 5 bloat, bulge, swell 6 billow, expand 7 balloon, distend, enlarge, inflate

puffy 3 fat 5 round 6 fleshy 7 bloated, bulging, swollen 8 enlarged, expanded, inflamed, inflated, puffed up 9 corpulent, distended

pugilist 3 pug 5 boxer 7 battler, bruiser, fighter 12 prizefighter

pugnacious 7 defiant, hostile, warlike 8 menacing, militant 9 bellicose, combative, fractious 10 aggressive, un-

friendly 11 belligerent, contentious, quarrelsome, threatening 12 antagonistic, disputatious 13 argumentative

pugnacity 9 hostility 10 antagonism 12 belligerence 13 combativeness 14 aggressiveness, fighting spirit 15 contentiousness

puissance 5 force, might, power 6 energy 7 potency, prowess 8 strength

pulchritude 6 beauty 8 fairness 9 bonniness, good looks 10 comeliness, loveliness, prettiness 12 gorgeousness, handsomeness 13 beauteousness,

exquisiteness 14 attractiveness, personableness

pulchritudinous 4 fair, fine 5 bonny 6 comely, lovely, pretty 8 gorgeous, handsome 9 beauteous, beautiful, ravishing 10 attractive 11 good-looking

Pulitzer
- **author:** 10 W A Swanberg

Pulitzer Prize
- **originator:** 14 Joseph Pulitzer
- **administered by:** 18 Columbia University
- **awarded for:** 4 play 5 drama, music, novel 6 poetry 7 cartoon, feature, fiction, letters 9 biography, criticism, editorial, reporting 10 commentary, journalism, literature, nonfiction 11 photography 13 autobiography

pull 2 go 3 lug, rip, tow, tug 4 drag, draw, grab, haul, jerk, lure, move, rend, rive, tear, yank 5 drive, sever, shake, split, trawl, troll, twist, wrest, wring 6 allure, appeal, detach, dig out, entice, remove, sprain, strain, uproot, wrench 7 attract, draw out, extract, gravity, stretch, weed out 8 withdraw 9 extirpate, influence, magnetism, take in tow 10 allurement, attraction, enticement 11 fascination 14 attractiveness

pull apart 3 rip, tug 4 drag, rend, tear 6 detach, wrench 7 extract 8 separate 9 criticize, disengage 10 disconnect

pull away 5 wrest 7 remove 8 drawback, withdraw

pull back 7 back off, retreat 8 fall back, withdraw

Pullman, George Mortimer
- **nationality:** 8 American
- **developed:** 9 (railroad) dining car 11 (railroad) sleeping car

pull off 4 pull 6 commit, effect 7 execute, perform 8 carry out 10 perpetuate 13 participate in

pull on 3 don 5 put on 7 get into

pull one's leg 3 kid 4 fool, hoax 5 tease, trick 7 deceive 9 make fun of

pull out 5 leave 7 draw out, extract 8 withdraw

pull over, pullover 4 cite, stop 5 shirt 6 arrest, jersey, slip on, ticket, t-shirt 7 maillot, sweater 8 slip over

pull together 4 join 5 unite

7 pitch in, share in **8** take part **9** cooperate, join hands **10** act jointly, join forces **11** collaborate, participate

pull to pieces 5 shred **6** tear up **7** destroy **9** tear apart

pull up 4 halt, rein, stop, weed **5** check, hoist **6** arrest, uplift, uproot **7** extract, reprove

pulp 4 curd, mash, mush, pith **5** crush, flesh, paste, puree, slush, smash **6** squash, tissue **7** journal **8** magazine **9** masticate

pulsate 4 beat, tick, wave **5** pound, pulse, shake, throb, thump, waver **6** quaver, quiver, shiver **7** flutter, shudder, tremble, vibrate **8** undulate **9** alternate, come and go, oscillate, palpitate **10** ebb and flow **11** reverberate

pulse 4 beat **5** throb, thump **6** quiver, rhythm, stroke **7** cadence, pulsate, shudder, tremble, vibrate **9** oscillate, palpitate, pulsation, vibration **10** recurrence, undulation **11** oscillation, palpitation

pulverize 4 mash, mill **5** crumb, crush, grind, mince, pound **6** powder **7** atomize, crumble **9** comminate, granulate, triturate **12** reduce to dust

pulverized 6 ground, milled **7** crumbed, crushed, pounded **8** atomized, crumbled, crunched, powdered **10** granulated **12** ground to dust

pummel 4 beat, maul **5** pound **6** batter, thrash **7** trounce

pump 4 quiz, shoe, well **5**.grill **7** inflate, slipper **8** question **9** draw water

Pump
    constellation of: **6** Antlia

Pump House Gang, The
    author: **8** Tom Wolfe

pumpkin 5 fruit, gourd, melon **6** squash **9** vegetable **12** jack o'lantern

pun
    French: **9** jeu de mots

punch 3 box, hit, jab **4** beat, blow, chop, clip, conk, cuff, pelt, plug, poke, slam, sock, swat **5** baste, clout, knock, paste, pound, smite, thump, whack **6** pummel, strike, stroke, thrust, thwack, wallop **7** clobber **8** haymaker **10** roundhouse

punchy 3 fat **5** dazed **6** stubby

8 confused, forceful **9** befuddled

punctilious 5 exact, fussy, picky, rigid **6** proper, strict **7** correct, finicky, precise **8** exacting, rigorous **9** demanding **10** meticulous, particular, scrupulous **11** painstaking

punctual 5 early, quick, ready **6** on time, prompt, steady, timely **7** instant, not late, regular **8** constant, on the dot **9** immediate, well-timed **10** in good time, seasonable **11** expeditious **13** instantaneous

punctuate 4 lace **5** break **6** pepper **7** scatter **8** separate, sprinkle **9** interrupt **11** intersperse

punctuation mark 4 dash **5** colon, comma, pause, point, slash **6** accent, ending, hyphen, parens, period, quotes **7** bracket **8** ellipsis **9** semicolon **10** apostrophe **11** parenthesis **12** question mark **13** quotation mark **16** exclamation point

puncture 3 cut **4** bite, hole, nick, pink **5** break, prick, stick, sting, wound **6** pierce **7** deflate, let down, opening, rupture **9** knock down, shoot down **10** depreciate **11** perforation

pundit 4 guru, sage **5** guide **6** critic, expert, master, mentor, savant, wizard **7** thinker **9** authority **13** learned person

pungent 3 hot **4** acid, keen, racy, sour, tart **5** acrid, acute, nippy, salty, sharp, smart, spicy, tangy, tasty, witty **6** biting, bitter, clever, savory, snappy, strong **7** acetous, caustic, cutting, mordent, peppery, piquant, pointed **8** incisive, piercing, poignant, smarting, stinging, stirring, vinegary, wounding **9** brilliant, flavorful, invidious, palatable, sarcastic, sparkling, trenchant **10** astringent, flavorsome, keen-witted **11** acrimonious, penetrating, provocative, stimulating, tantalizing **12** sharp-tasting **13** scintillating, sharp-smelling **14** highly flavored, highly seasoned

punish 4 beat, fine, flog, whip **6** avenge, rebuke **7** chasten, correct, reprove **8** admonish, chastise, imprison, penalize, sentence **9** castigate, dress down, retaliate **10** discipline, take to task **11** get even with, take revenge **14** bring to account **15** take vengeance on

punishing 5 harsh, penal **6** brutal, severe **7** abusive **8** scolding **9** torturing **10** chastizing, tormenting **11** castigating

punishment 4 fine **5** price **7** damages, deserts, flaying, forfeit, hanging, payment, penalty, penance, redress **8** flogging, punition, spanking, whipping **10** chastening, correction, crucifying, discipline, reparation **11** castigation, retribution **12** chastisement, penalization

punk 4 hood, lout, poor **5** bully, lousy, rowdy, tough **6** crummy, rotten **7** hoodlum, ruffian **8** hooligan **9** barbarian, roughneck **10** delinquent

Punt see **7** Somalia

Puntarvolo
    character in: **22** Every Man Out of His Humour
    author: **6** Jonson

punt e mes
    type: **8** aperitif
    origin: **5** Italy
    flavor: **6** orange
    color: **12** reddish-brown

puny 4 poor, thin, tiny, weak **5** frail, light, petty, runty, small **6** bantam, feeble, flimsy, infirm, little, meager, measly, paltry, sickly, slight, weakly **7** fragile, shallow, tenuous, trivial **8** delicate, impotent, picayune, piddling, runtlike, sawed-off, trifling **9** emaciated, miniature, mite-sized, pint-sized, worthless **10** diminutive, inadequate, picayunish, undersized **11** unimportant **12** insufficient **13** insignificant **14** inconsiderable, underdeveloped

pupa 3 egg **5** larva, nymph **6** cocoon **7** wiggler **9** chrysalis **14** transformation

pupil 4 coed, tyro **6** novice **7** learner, scholar, student, trainee **8** beginner, disciple, initiate **9** schoolboy **10** apprentice, schoolgirl **11** probationer **13** undergraduate

puppet 3 toy **4** doll, dupe, pawn, tool **6** flunky, lackey **7** cat's paw, manikin, servant **8** creature, henchman, hireling **9** jackstraw, lay figure, underling **10** figurehead, instrument, man of straw, marionette **11** subordinate

puppy 3 dog, pet, pup **6** canine

Purcell, Henry
    born: **6** London **7** England
    composer of: **9** Fantasias

10 Bell Anthem, Dioclesian, King Arthur (The British Worthy), The Tempest **12** Golden Sonata **13** Dido and Aeneas **14** The Indian Queen

purchase 3 buy **4** edge, hold **6** buying, pay for, pick up **7** footing, support, toehold **8** foothold, leverage **9** advantage, influence **11** acquirement, acquisition

pure 4 full, mere, neat, true **5** basic, clean, fresh, moral, sheer, stark, utter, whole **6** chaste, decent, entire, higher, virgin **7** angelic, ethical, perfect, sincere, sinless, sterile, unmixed, upright **8** absolute, abstract, complete, flawless, germfree, innocent, positive, purebred, sanitary, spotless, straight, thorough, unmarred, virginal, virtuous **9** blameless, downright, faultless, guileless, guiltless, healthful, inviolate, out-and-out, pedigreed, righteous, unalloyed, undefiled, unmingled, unspoiled, unsullied, untainted, wholesome **10** antiseptic, immaculate, inviolable, sterilized, uninfected, unmodified, unpolluted **11** conjectural, disinfected, fundamental, pure-blooded, speculative, theoretical, unblemished, uncorrupted, unqualified, untarnished **12** fullstrength, hypothetical, thoroughbred **13** unadulterated, unimpeachable **14** above suspicion, uncontaminated

puree 4 bisk, pulp, soup **5** paste **6** bisque

purely 4 only **5** fully **6** merely, simply, solely, wholly **7** cleanly, morally, piously, totally **8** chastely, devoutly, entirely, worthily **9** admirably **10** absolutely, completely, flawlessly, in all honor, innocently, virginally, virtuously **11** essentially, faultlessly **13** incorruptibly

Purgatory, Purgatorio
    part II of: **12** Divine Comedy
    author: **14** Dante Alighieri

purge 4 kill, oust **5** crush, ex-

pel **6** banish, emetic, pardon, physic, purify, remove, uproot **7** clean up, cleanse, cleanup, clyster, dismiss, expiate, purging, rout out, shake up **8** aperient, atone for, clean out, get rid of, laxative, sweep out, wash away **9** cathartic, discharge, eliminate, eradicate, liquidate, purgation, purgative **10** do away with **11** exterminate **12** obtain pardon (from), purification **15** obtain remission (from) **16** obtain absolution (from) **17** obtain forgiveness

purification 7 baptism **9** cleansing **13** sterilization

purify 4 boil **5** clear **6** filter **7** clarify, distill **8** make pure, sanitize **9** disinfect, sterilize **10** chlorinate, pasteurize **13** decontaminate

Puritani, I
    also: **11** The Puritans
    opera by: **7** Bellini
    character: **14** Oliver Cromwell, Queen Henrietta **16** Lord Arthur Talbot

puritanical 4 prim **5** rigid, stiff **6** narrow, prissy, severe, strict, stuffy **7** ascetic, austere, bigoted, prudish, puritan, stilted **8** dogmatic, priggish **9** bluenosed, fanatical **11** stiffnecked, straitlaced **13** sanctimonious

Puritan State
    nickname of:
    13 Massachusetts

purity 5 honor, piety **6** virtue **7** clarity, decency, honesty, modesty **8** chastity, fineness, holiness, lucidity, morality, pureness, sanctity **9** cleanness, clearness, innocence, integrity, limpidity, plainness, rectitude, virginity **10** brilliance, chasteness, directness, excellence, immaculacy, simplicity, temperance, uniformity **11** cleanliness, homogeneity, saintliness, uprightness **12** virtuousness **13** guilelessness, guiltlessness **14** immaculateness **15** clear conscience **16** incorruptibility

purlieu 4 area **5** haunt, limit **6** border, locale, region, resort **7** district, environ **8** outskirt **11** surrounding **12** neighborhood

purloin 3 rob **5** steal **6** pilfer **11** appropriate, make off with

Purloined Letter, The
    author: **13** Edgar Allan Poe

purloiner 5 thief **6** robber **7** burglar **8** pilferer

purple 4 plum, puce, racy **5** color, grape, lilac, lurid, mauve, royal **6** florid, orchid, turgid, violet **7** crimson, flowery, furious, fuchsia, magenta **8** amethyst, burgundy, imperial, lavender **9** gastropod

Purple Land see **7** Uruguay

Purple Rose of Cairo, The
    director: **10** Woody Allen
    cast: **9** Mia Farrow **11** Danny Aiello, Jeff Daniels

purport 3 aim, end **4** gist **5** claim, drift, point, sense, tenor, trend **6** allege, burden, design, import, intent, object, reason **7** bearing, meaning, profess, purpose **9** intention, objective, rationale, substance **11** implication **12** significance **13** signification

purpose 3 aim **4** goal, hope, mean, plan, will, wish **5** elect, point, sense **6** aspire, choose, decide, design, desire, intend, intent, motive, object, reason, scheme, target **7** drive at, meaning, mission, persist, project, propose, resolve, think to **8** ambition, conclude, endeavor, function, proposal, set about **9** determine, intention, objective, persevere, rationale, undertake **10** aspiration, motivation, resolution **11** contemplate, disposition, expectation, fixed intent, have a mind to, raison d'etre **13** commit oneself, determination

purposeful 7 decided, studied **8** resolute, resolved **9** committed, conscious **10** calculated, considered, deliberate, determined **11** intentional **12** premeditated, strong-willed

purposefulness 7 purpose, resolve **10** resolution **11** decidedness **12** decisiveness, resoluteness **13** determination

purposeless 6 random **7** aimless, useless **8** needless, plotless **9** desultory, driftless, haphazard, irregular, senseless, unplanned **11** meaningless **12** functionless, undetermined, unprofitable

purposely 8 by design **9** advisedly, expressly, knowingly, on purpose, willfully, wittingly **10** designedly, with intent **11** consciously, voluntarily **12** calculatedly, deliberately **13** intentionally

purse 3 bag **4** fold, fund, knit **5** award, bunch, pinch, pleat, pouch, prize, stake **6** clutch, coffer, gather, pucker, wallet **7** handbag, sporran, wrinkle

8 contract, moneybag, proceeds, treasury, winnings **10** pocketbook **11** shoulder bag
  French: 12 porte-monnaie

purser 6 bursar **7** cashier **9** paymaster **10** cashkeeper

pursue 4 seek **5** aim at, chase, track, trail **6** aim for, follow, try for **7** be after, carry on, go after, perform **8** aspire to, engage in, labor for, run after **9** race after, strive for **10** chase after, push toward

pursuer 5 pupil **6** seeker **7** devotee, student **8** disciple, follower, searcher **10** aficionado

pursuit 4 hunt **5** chase **6** search **7** pastime **8** activity **9** following **10** occupation

purvey 3 get **4** give, hand **5** cater, equip, yield **6** obtain, outfit, supply **7** deliver, furnish, procure, provide

purveyor 4 pimp **6** seller **8** procurer, provider, supplier

purview 3 ken **4** area **5** field, range, reach, realm, savvy, scope, sweep **6** domain, extent **7** compass, horizon, outlook **8** dominion, overview **9** territory, viewpoint **10** commission, experience **11** mental grasp **13** comprehension, understanding **14** responsibility

push 2 go **3** dun, ram **4** butt, goad, jolt, move, plug, prod, spur, sway, urge, work, worm **5** boost, drive, egg on, elbow, fight, foray, force, forge, harry, hound, impel, nudge, press, rouse, shove, stick, stuff, vigor, wedge **6** arouse, badger, coerce, compel, energy, exhort, harass, heckle, hustle, incite, induce, inroad, jostle, plunge, prompt, propel, thrust, wiggle **7** advance, animate, buffalo, inspire, promote, provoke, squeeze **8** ambition, browbeat, motivate, persuade, shoulder, struggle, vitality **9** advertise, constrain, encourage, importune, incursion, instigate, make known, publicize, stimulate, strong-arm **10** get-up-and-go **11** make one's way, prevail upon, vim and vigor **12** force one's way, propagandize **13** determination

pushcart 5 wagon **6** barrow **8** handcart **10** handbarrow **11** wheelbarrow

push forward 4 goad, prod, spur **5** drive, impel, press **9** urge along

Pushkin, Alexander (Aleksandr)
  author of: 12 Boris Godunov, Eugene Onegin **16** The Queen of Spades **17** The Bronze Horseman **19** The Captain's Daughter

push through 6 hasten **7** advance, forward **8** dispatch, expedite **10** accelerate, facilitate

pushy 8 forceful **9** assertive, insistent **10** aggressive **11** domineering **12** strong-willed **13** self-assertive

pusillanimous 7 fearful **8** cowardly, timorous **10** spiritless **11** lily-livered **12** apprehensive, fainthearted, mean-spirited

pusillanimousness 8 timidity **9** cowardice **12** yellow streak **13** yellow feather **16** faintheartedness **18** chickenheartedness

puss 3 cat, mug, pan **4** face **5** kitty **6** feline, kisser, kitten

pussyfoot 5 dodge, evade, hedge, sneak **6** tiptoe, weasel **8** sidestep **13** evade the issue **14** beg the question **15** walk on eggshells **16** straddle the fence

put 3 fix, lay, set **4** cast, pose, rest, word **5** bring, drive, force, heave, offer, pitch, place, state, throw **6** assign, employ, impute, phrase, submit **7** ascribe, deposit, express, present, propose **8** position **9** attribute, enunciate **10** articulate

put a damper on 4 cool, dull **7** depress, squelch **10** discourage, dishearten

put an edge on 4 hone, whet **6** excite **7** sharpen **9** stimulate

put an end to 4 halt, stop **5** annul, quash **6** cancel, finish, repeal, revoke **7** abolish, blot out, rescind, squelch, wipe out **8** abrogate, demolish, dispatch, stamp out **9** eliminate, eradicate, finish off **10** discourage, do away with, put a stop to **12** write finis to

put aside 5 table **6** forget **7** discard, lay away **10** relinquish

put away 3 eat **4** down, stow **5** stash **6** commit **7** confine, consume **9** drink down

put back 4 rout **5** delay **6** defeat, demote, impair, reject, return **7** replace, restore **9** reinstate

put down 4 note, post **5** crush,

enter, knock, quash, quell **6** dispel, enlist, record, subdue **7** deposit, disdain, sneer at, squelch **8** belittle, derogate, laugh off, pooh-pooh, suppress **9** denigrate, disparage, humiliate, write down **10** depreciate

put forth 5 offer **6** extend, put out **7** proffer, send out

put forward 4 pose **6** assert **7** advance, profess, propose **8** propound

put in irons 5 chain **6** fetter **7** manacle, shackle **8** handcuff

put in motion 4 move **5** begin, start **6** arouse, launch **8** activate, carry out, commence, initiate **9** instigate, undertake

put in order 5 array **6** neaten, tidy up **7** arrange **8** organize **10** straighten

put in plain sight 4 show **6** set out **7** display, exhibit

put in shackles 6 fetter, hobble **7** enchain, enslave, manacle **8** handcuff, imprison

put into circulation 4 move **5** issue, print **7** publish **10** pass around

put into effect 6 effect **7** achieve, enforce, execute, fulfill, realize **8** carry out, complete **10** accomplish, administer, consummate, effectuate, perpetrate **12** carry through

put into words 5 voice **7** express **8** describe **9** verbalize **10** articulate **11** communicate

Putnam, Abbie
  character in: 18 Desire Under the Elms
  author: 6 O'Neill

put off 5 delay, repel, stall **6** offend, rebuff, recess **7** adjourn, repulse, set sail, suspend **8** hold back, launched, offended, postpone, rebuffed, repelled, repulsed **9** interrupt **11** discontinue **13** procrastinate

put off guard 4 lull **6** disarm **10** make unwary

put on 3 don **5** affix **6** attach **7** dress in, get into, stick on **8** fasten to

put-on 8 pretense **11** affectation

put on guard 4 warn **5** alert **6** advise, tip off **7** caution **8** forewarn **9** make ready **10** precaution

put out 3 irk **5** annoy, issue

6 quench, retire 7 produce, publish 8 irritate 9 strike out 10 extinguish 11 manufacture 13 leave the shore

put out of order 5 mix up, upset 6 jumble, mess up, muddle 7 confuse, scatter 8 disarray, disorder, displace, put askew, scramble 10 disarrange 11 disorganize

putrefaction 3 rot 5 decay 7 rotting 8 spoilage, spoiling 10 rottenness 12 decompostion

putrefy 3 rot 4 turn 5 decay, spoil, taint 6 molder 8 putresce, stagnate 9 decompose 10 biodegrade 11 deteriorate 12 disintegrate

putrescent 4 foul, rank 5 fetid 6 smelly 7 rotting 8 decaying, spoiling, stinking 9 offensive 10 malodorous, putrefying 11 decomposing

putrid 3 bad 4 foul, rank 5 fetid 6 rancid, rotten, spoiled 7 tainted 8 decaying, polluted, purulent, stinking 9 putrefied 10 putrescent 11 decomposing 12 contaminated, putrefactive

putridity 5 decay, filth, taint 8 foulness, impurity 9 dirtiness, pollution, purulence, rancidity 10 rottenness 11 putrescence, uncleanness 13 contamination, decomposition

putsch 6 revolt 8 uprising

putter 4 fool, idle, laze, loaf, loll 5 dally, drift 6 dawdle, diddle, fiddle, loiter, lounge, piddle, potter, tinker 8 golf club, lallygag 10 dillydally

put to death 4 do in, hang, kill, slay 5 slain 6 done in, hanged, killed, murder, poison, rub out 7 bump off, butcher, execute 8 dispatch, executed, massacre, murdered, poisoned, strangle 9 bumped off, butchered, finish off, massacred, strangled, suffocate 11 assassinate, electrocute, exterminate 12 assassinated, electrocuted, exterminated

put to flight 4 rout, shoo 5 chase 6 dispel 7 cast out, scatter 8 drive off, send away 11 send packing

put together 4 join 5 unite 7 combine 8 assemble

put to shame 6 ashame 7 chagrin, mortify 9 discomfit, embarrass, humiliate

put to sleep 4 lull 5 quiet 6 sedate 8 knock out 9 narcotize 11 anesthetize

put to use 3 use 5 apply 6 employ, engage, occupy 7 exploit, utilize 9 make use of

put under a spell 5 charm 7 bewitch, enchant 8 entrance 9 fascinate, mesmerize, spellbind

put up 3 can 4 hang 5 erect, house, lodge, raise, store 6 billet 7 shelter 8 preserve 11 accommodate 14 furnish room for

put up with 4 bear, take 5 abide, brave, brook, stand 6 endure, suffer 7 stomach, sustain, undergo 8 stand for, submit to, tolerate 9 withstand 11 countenance

Puvis de Chavannes, Pierre Cecile
born: 5 Lyons 6 France
artwork: 6 Summer 13 Shepherd's Song 14 Ludus pro patria 16 The Poor Fisherman 17 Life of St Genevieve, The Inspiring Muses 21 Science Arts and Letters

Puyallop
language family: 8 Salishan, Wakashan 9 Algonkian 10 Algonquian
location: 10 Washington

Puzo, Mario
author of: 12 The Godfather

puzzle 4 foil, mull 5 brood, stump 6 baffle, enigma, outwit, ponder, riddle, wonder 7 confuse, dilemma, mystery, mystify, nonplus, perplex, problem 8 bewilder, confound, hoodwink 9 conundrum 10 bafflement, difficulty, perplexity 12 bewilderment, complication 13 mystification

puzzled 6 amazed 7 baffled 8 befogged, confused, troubled 9 astounded, befuddled, mystified, perplexed 10 bewildered, confounded, nonplussed

puzzling 7 elusive 8 baffling 9 confusing, enigmatic 10 mysterious, mystifying, perplexing 11 bewildering, confounding, enigmatical 12 unfathomable 16 hard to understand, incomprehensible

Pwyll
origin: 5 Welsh
form: 6 prince
steals: 8 Rhiannon
wife: 8 Rhiannon
son: 7 Pryderi

Pyanepsia
origin: 5 Greek 8 Athenian

event: 8 festival
honoring: 6 Apollo 7 harvest

Pygmalion
author: 17 George Bernard Shaw
character: 12 Henry Higgins 14 Eliza Doolittle
basis for: 10 My Fair Lady
director: 14 Anthony Asquith
cast: 11 Wendy Hiller (Eliza Doolittle) 12 Leslie Howard (Professor Henry Higgins) 13 Wilfrid Lawson

Pygmalion
king of: 6 Cyprus
avocation: 8 sculptor
statue named: 7 Galatea
loved: 7 Galatea
statue changed to: 5 woman
wife: 7 Galatea
daughter: 6 Paphos 8 Metharme

pygmy 3 elf, toy, wee 4 mite, runt, tiny 5 dwarf, elfin, short, small 6 bantam, midget, peewee, shrimp 7 manikin 8 dwarfish, half-pint, Tom Thumb 9 miniature, pipsqueak 10 diminutive, homunculus, undersized 11 Lilliputian

Pylades
father: 9 Strophius
mother: 8 Anaxibia
cousin: 7 Orestes
wife: 7 Electra
son: 5 Medon 9 Strophius
friend: 7 Orestes

Pylaemenes
king of: 13 Paphlagonians
killed by: 8 Menelaus

Pylaeus
mentioned in: 5 Iliad
rank: 7 captain

Pylas
king of: 6 Megara
uncle: 4 Bias
gave throne to: 17 Pandion the Younger

Pyncheon family
character in: 24 The House of the Seven Gables
members: 6 Phoebe 8 Clifford, Hepzibah 12 Judge Jaffrey
author: 9 Hawthorne

Pynchon, Thomas
author of: 1 V 15 Gravity's Rainbow 23 The Crying of Lot Forty-Nine

Pyongyang
capital of: 10 North Korea

Pyramus
form: 5 youth
location: 7 Babylon
loved: 6 Thisbe
died at tomb of: 5 Ninus

Pyrigenes
  epithet of: **8** Dionysus
  means: **10** born of fire

Pyriphlegethon *see*
  10 Phlegethon

pyromaniac 7 firebug **8** arsonist **10** incendiary **11** firestarter

Pyronia
  epithet of: **7** Artemis
  means: **11** fire goddess

pyrope
  species: **6** garnet
  color: **3** red

pyrophobia
  fear of: **4** fire

pyrotechnics 9 fireworks
  16 brilliant display **19** dazzling
  performance

Pyrrha
  father: **10** Epimetheus

  mother: **7** Pandora
  husband: **9** Deucalion

Pythia
  priestess of: **6** Apollo
  location: **6** Delphi
  delivered: **7** oracles

Pythias
  friend: **5** Damon

Pythius *see* **6** Apollo

Python *see* **8** Delphyne

quack 4 fake, sham **5** phony
6 pseudo **9** charlatan, pretender **10** fake doctor, fraudulent **11** counterfeit,
quacksalver **15** medical
impostor

quackery 5 bluff, guile **6** deceit **7** cunning **9** deception,
duplicity **12** charlatanism

quaff 4 down, gulp, swig
5 drink, lap up, swill **6** guzzle,
imbibe, tipple **7** swallow, toss
off **8** belt down, chug-a-lug
9 knock back **11** drink deeply

quagmire 3 bog, fen, fix, jam
4 mess, mire, ooze, quag,
sump **5** marsh, pinch, swamp
6 crisis, morass, muddle,
pickle, plight, scrape, slough,
sludge, strait **7** dilemma **8** hot
water, quandary **9** imbroglio,
intricacy, quicksand **10** difficulty, perplexity **11** Gordian
knot, involvement, predicament **12** entanglement

quail 3 shy **5** cower, quake,
shake **6** blanch, flinch, recoil,
shrink **7** run away, shudder,
tremble **8** fight shy, turn tail
9 lose heart **10** be cowardly,
lose spirit, take fright **11** lose
courage **12** have cold feet
16 shake in one's boots
17 shiver in one's shoes, show
a yellow streak

quail
  group of: 4 bevy **5** covey

quaint 3 odd **4** rare **5** droll,
queer **6** unique **7** antique, bizarre, curious, strange, unusual **8** charming, fanciful,
old-timey, original, peculiar,
singular, uncommon **9** eccentric, whimsical **10** antiquated,
outlandish **11** out-of-the-way,
picturesque **12** old-fashioned
13 extraordinary
14 unconventional

quake 4 wave **5** quail, shake,
spasm, throb **6** blanch, quaver,
quiver, ripple, shiver, thrill,
tremor **7** shudder, tremble
9 trembling **10** earthquake
18 seismic disturbance

qualification 4 gift **5** forte,
skill **6** talent **7** ability, faculty,
fitness, proviso **8** aptitude,
bona fide, capacity, property,
standard **9** attribute, condition,
endowment, exception, exemption, objection, postulate, provision, requisite **10** capability,
competency, credential, limitation **11** achievement, arrangement, eligibility, requirement,

reservation, restriction, stipulation **12** escape clause, modification, prerequisite,
suitableness **13** certification
14 accomplishment

qualified 3 fit **4** able, meet
5 adept, equal **6** expert, fitted,
suited, versed **7** capable,
guarded, hedging, knowing,
limited, skilled, trained **8** eligible, equipped, licensed, reserved, skillful, talented
9 ambiguous, certified, competent, efficient, equivocal, practiced **10** authorized, indefinite,
proficient, restricted **11** conditional, efficacious, experienced,
provisional **12** accomplished

qualify 3 fit **4** ease **5** abate,
adapt, alter, endow, equip,
limit, ready, train **6** adjust, enable, ground, modify, narrow,
permit, reduce, soften, temper **7** assuage, certify, empower, entitle, license, make
fit, prepare **8** describe, diminish, mitigate, moderate, restrain, restrict, sanction
9 authorize, condition, give
power, measure up **10** be accepted, be eligible, commission, legitimate
11 accommodate **12** characterize, circumscribe, make
eligible

qualifying 9 tempering **10** mitigating **11** eligibility, extenuating, preparatory

quality 4 mark, rank **5** blood,
class, grade, merit, trait, value,
worth **6** aspect, family, nature **7** caliber, dignity, faculty,
feature **8** capacity, eminence,
position, property, standing
9 attribute, character **11** disposition, distinction, high station, temperament
12 constitution, social status
13 qualification **14** characteristic

Quality Street
  author: 12 James M Barrie

qualm 4 turn **6** nausea **7** scruple, vertigo **9** faintness, giddiness, misgiving **10** dizzy spell, hesitation, queasiness, reluctance, uneasiness **11** compunction, reservation, sick feeling **13** indisposition, unwillingness **14** disinclination **18** twinge of conscience

quandary 3 fix, jam **4** mire **5** pinch **6** crisis, morass, pickle, plight, scrape, strait **7** dilemma, impasse **8** hot water, quagmire **9** imbroglio **10** difficulty **11** involvement, predicament **12** entanglement, kettle of fish

quantities 4 lots, much **5** heaps, loads **7** amounts

quantity 3 sum **4** area, bulk, dose, mass, size **5** quota, share **6** amount, dosage, extent, length, number, volume **7** expanse, measure, portion **8** vastness **9** abundance, aggregate, allotment, amplitude, extension, greatness, magnitude, multitude **10** proportion **11** measurement **13** apportionment

quarantine 7 confine, isolate **9** isolation, segregate, sequester **13** sequestration **15** cordon sanitaire **18** medical segregation

Quare Fellow, The
author: **12** Brendan Behan

quarrel 3 jar, nag, row **4** carp, feud, fuss, spat, tiff **5** argue, brawl, cavil, clash, fight, scrap **6** bicker, differ, strife **7** contend, discord, dispute, dissent, fall out, wrangle **8** argument, be at odds, conflict, squabble **9** altercate, bickering, complaint, find fault, have words, objection **10** contention, difference, dissension, dissidence, falling out **11** controversy **12** disagreement **13** breach of peace, contradiction, misunderstand **14** apple of discord **15** be at loggerheads **16** bone of contention, misunderstanding

quarreling 6 strife **7** discord **8** clashing, conflict, disunity, friction **9** bickering, disputing, scrapping, wrangling **10** contention, dissension, dissidence, squabbling **11** discordance **12** disagreement

quarrelsome 7 peevish **8** captious, churlish, contrary, militant, petulant **9** bellicose, combative, fractious, irascible, querulous, truculent **10** pugnacious **11** belligerent, contentious **12** antagonistic,

cantankerous, disagreeable, disputatious **13** argumentative

quarry 3 bed, dig, pit **4** game, lode, mine, prey **5** catch, stone **6** source, victim **8** excavate

quart
abbreviation: **2** qt

quarter, quarters 4 area, part, pity, post, side, spot, zone **5** board, house, lodge, mercy, place, put up, realm, rooms **6** billet, domain, fourth, locale, region, sphere **7** housing, install, lodging, shelter, station, terrain **8** clemency, district, humanity, leniency, locality, location, lodgings, position, precinct, province, sympathy **9** percent, direction, one-fourth, situation, territory **10** compassion, fourth part, indulgence, quadrisect **11** place to live, place to stay, three months **13** quarter dollar, specific place **14** accommodations **15** twenty-five cents

quarterstaff 4 pole **5** staff **6** cudgel

quartz
varieties: **4** sard **5** agate, topaz **8** amethyst **9** carnelian, tiger's-eye **11** rock crystal

quash 4 ruin, stop, undo, void **5** annul, crush, erase, quell, smash, wreck **6** cancel, delete, dispel, efface, quench, recall, revoke, squash, subdue, vacate **7** blot out, destroy, expunge, nullify, put down, repress, rescind, retract, reverse, squelch **8** abrogate, dissolve, override, overrule, overturn, set aside, suppress **9** devastate, eradicate, extirpate, overthrow, overwhelm, repudiate, strike out **10** annihilate, extinguish, invalidate, obliterate, put an end to **11** countermand, exterminate

quasi 4 near, part, semi **6** almost, ersatz **7** halfway, seeming, virtual **8** apparent, somewhat, so-called **9** imitation, synthetic **10** resembling

Quasimodo
character in: **23** The Hunchback of Notre Dame
author: **4** Hugo

Quatermain, Allan
character in: **17** King Solomon's Mines
author: **7** Haggard

quaver 4 beat, sway, wave **5** quake, shake, throb, trill, waver **6** falter, quiver, shiver, teeter, totter, tremor, wobble, writhe **7** pulsate, shudder, tremble, tremolo, vibrate, vi-

brato, wriggle **9** oscillate, trembling, vibration **14** tremulous shake

quay 4 dock, mole, pier **5** basin, jetty, levee, wharf **6** marina **7** landing **10** waterfront

queasy 5 giddy, upset **6** uneasy **7** bilious, sickish **8** nauseous, qualmish, troubled **9** nauseated, sickening, uncertain **10** nauseating **13** uncomfortable **16** sick to the stomach

Quebec
borders: **7** Ontario **8** Labrador **9** Hudson Bay **12** Newfoundland, United States **13** Atlantic Ocean **16** Gulf of St Lawrence
cape: **5** Gaspe
city: **6** Quebec **8** Montreal **10** Chicoutimi, Sherbrooke **13** Trois Rivieres
highest point: **18** Mont Jacques Cartier
hockey team: **9** Canadiens, Nordiques
island: **9** Anticosti
lake: **5** Gouin **9** Bienville, Eau Claire, Saint Jean **10** Mistassini **11** Manicouagan
mineral: **4** gold, zinc **6** copper **7** iron ore **8** asbestos **9** limestone
mountain: **5** Otish **10** Laurentian, Shickshock **11** Appalachian **12** Monteregians
province of: **6** Canada

Quechua
tribe: **4** Inca

Quedens, Eunice
real name of: **8** Eve Arden

queen 5 ranee **7** czarina, empress **8** princess **13** female monarch
French: **5** reine
German: **7** Konigin
Latin: **6** regina
Spanish: **5** reina

queen / empress / princess
of Egypt: **9** Cleopatra, Nefertari, Nefertiti **10** Hatshepsut, Hetepheres
of England: **3** Mab **4** Anne, Bess, Jane, Mary **7** Eleanor **8** Boadicea, Victoria **9** Catherine, Charlotte, Elizabeth, Guinevere **10** Bloody Mary, Elizabeth I **11** Elizabeth II, Jane Seymour

of France: 7 Eugenie **9** Josephine **11** Marie Louise **14** Marie de Medicis **15** Marie Antoinette
of Italy/Rome: 7 Poppaea **9** Agrippina, Messalina **13** Livia Drusilla
of Monaco: 8 Caroline **9** Stephanie **10** Grace Kelly
of the Netherlands: 7 Beatrix, Juliana **10** Wilhelmina
of Poland: 7 Jadwiga
of Portugal: 5 Maria **9** Elizabeth
of Russia: 9 Alexandra, Catherine **17** Catherine the Great
of Scotland: 4 Mary **13** Saint Margaret **16** Mary Queen of Scots
of Spain: 8 Isabella **16** Elizabeth Farnese
of Sweden: 9 Christina
of Syria: 7 Zenobia

Queen Christina
director: 15 Rouben Mamoulian
cast: 8 Ian Keith **10** Greta Garbo, Lewis Stone **11** John Gilbert **12** C Aubrey Smith

Queen Mab
author: 18 Percy Bysshe Shelley

Queen of Amazons 9 Hippolyta, Hippolyte

Queen of Hearts
character in: 28 Alice's Adventures in Wonderland
author: 7 Carroll

Queen of Heaven 4 Hera, Mary **6** Ishtar **7** Mylitta

Queen of Spades, The
also: 12 Pikovaya Dama
opera by: 11 Tchaikovsky
character: 4 Lisa **6** Herman **8** Countess

Queen of Spades, The
author: 16 Alexander Pushkin

Queen of Technicolor
nickname of: 12 Maureen O'Hara

Queen of the Surf
nickname of: 14 Esther Williams

Queen's Necklace, The
author: 14 Alexandre Dumas (pere)
character: 5 Oliva **13** Count de Charny **15** Cardinal de Rohan, Count Cagliostro, Marie Antoinette **16** Andree de Taverney **18** Philippe de Taverney **21** Jeanne de la Motte Valois

Queequeg
character in: 8 Moby Dick
author: 8 Melville

queer 3 odd **4** daft, harm, hurt,

rare, ruin **5** crazy, dizzy, droll, faint, fishy, funny, giddy, shady, spoil, weird, woozy, wreck **6** absurd, damage, exotic, impair, injure, quaint, qualmy, queasy, thwart, unique **7** bizarre, comical, curious, disrupt, erratic, reeling, strange, touched, unusual **8** abnormal, bohemian, doubtful, fanciful, freakish, original, peculiar, uncommon, unhinged **9** eccentric, fantastic, grotesque, irregular, laughable, ludicrous, unnatural **10** capricious, compromise, farfetched, irrational, outlandish, remarkable, ridiculous, suspicious, unbalanced, unexampled, unorthodox **11** astonishing, exceptional, light-headed, out of the way, slightly ill, vertiginous **12** preposterous, questionable, unparalleled **13** extraordinary, nonconforming, unprecedented **14** unconventional
French: 5 outre

quell 4 calm, dull, ease, hush, lull, rout, ruin, stay, stem **5** abate, allay, blunt, crush, quash, quiet, still, worst, wreck **6** becalm, deaden, defeat, pacify, quench, reduce, soften, soothe, subdue **7** appease, assuage, compose, conquer, destroy, mollify, put down, scatter, silence, squelch **8** beat down, disperse, mitigate, overcome, palliate, stamp out, suppress, vanquish **9** alleviate, overpower, overthrow, overwhelm, subjugate **10** extinguish **11** tranquilize

quench 4 cool, sate **5** allay, crush, douse, quell, slake **6** dampen, put out, stifle **7** appease, blow out, put down, satiate, satisfy, smother **8** stamp out, suppress **10** annihilate, extinguish

Quentin Durward
author: 14 Sir Walter Scott
character: 8 Isabelle **9** Le Balafre **10** Jacqueline **11** King Louis XI **12** Lady Hameline **13** Ludovic Lesley **15** Countess of Croye **16** William de la Marck **18** Hayraddin Maugrabin **20** King Louis the Eleventh **21** Charles Duke of Burgundy **23** Count Philip de Crevecoeur

querulous 4 sour **5** cross, fussy, testy, whiny **6** cranky, touchy **7** crabbed, finical, finicky, fretful, grouchy, peevish, pettish, waspish, whining **8** captious, exacting, petulant, shrewish **9** difficult, grumbling, irascible, irritable, long-faced,

obstinate, resentful, splenetic **10** nettlesome **11** complaining, quarrelsome **12** disagreeable, discontented, disputatious, dissatisfied, faultfinding

query 3 ask **4** quiz **5** doubt, issue, quest **6** demand, impugn, search **7** dispute, examine, impeach, inquest, inquiry, inspect, problem, request, suspect **8** distrust, look into, mistrust, question, sound out **9** catechize, challenge, inquire of **10** controvert **11** examination, inquisition, interrogate, investigate, make inquiry **13** interrogation, investigation

quest 4 hunt, seek **6** pursue, search, voyage **7** crusade, journey, mission, pursuit, seeking **9** adventure **10** enterprise, pilgrimage **11** exploration

Quested, Adela
character in: 15 A Passage to India
author: 7 Forster

Quest for Fire
director: 17 Jean-Jacques Annaud
cast: 10 Ron Perlman **12** Rae Dawn Chong **13** Everett McGill

question 3 ask, rub **4** pump, quiz, test **5** doubt, drill, grill, issue, query **6** impugn, matter, motion, oppose **7** dispute, dubiety, examine, problem, subject, suspect **8** distrust, look into, mistrust, proposal, sound out **9** catechize, challenge, inquire of, misgiving, moot point, objection **10** difficulty, disbelieve **11** controversy, interrogate, investigate, proposition, uncertainty **12** crossexamine **13** consideration

questionable 4 moot **5** fishy, shady **6** unsure **7** dubious, in doubt, suspect **8** arguable, doubtful, puzzling, unproven **9** ambiguous, confusing, debatable, enigmatic, equivocal, in dispute, uncertain, undecided **10** apocryphal, disputable, indefinite, mysterious, mystifying, perplexing, suspicious **12** hypothetical **13** controversial, problematical

queue 3 row **4** file, line, rank **5** chain, train **6** column, string

quibble 3 nag **4** carp, spar **5** argue, cavil, dodge, fence, fudge, shift **6** bicker, haggle, hassle, nicety, niggle, waffle **7** evasion, nitpick, shuffle **8** artifice, pretense, squabble, subtlety, white lie **9** be evasive, duplicity **10** equivocate, pick a fight, subterfuge **11** distraction **12** equivocation

13 dodge the issue, prevarication

Quiche
language family: **5** Mayan
location: **9** Guatemala
12 South America **14** Central America

quick 3 apt **4** able, deft, fast, keen, spry **5** acute, adept, agile, alert, brief, brisk, eager, fiery, fleet, hasty, rapid, sharp, smart, swift, testy **6** abrupt, active, adroit, astute, brainy, bright, clever, expert, facile, flying, frisky, lively, nimble, prompt, shrewd, speedy, sudden, touchy, winged **7** hurried, peppery, waspish **8** animated, choleric, headlong, petulant, skillful, snappish, spirited, vigilant, vigorous **9** dexterous, energetic, excitable, impatient, impetuous, impulsive, irascible, irritable, sagacious, splenetic, sprightly, vivacious, whirlwind, wide-awake **10** discerning, high-strung, hot-blooded **11** accelerated, expeditious, hot-tempered, intelligent, light-footed, penetrating, precipitate **12** nimble-footed **13** perspicacious, temperamental

quicken 4 fire, goad, move, rush, spur, stir, urge **5** drive, egg on, hurry, impel, pique, press, rouse, speed **6** affect, arouse, excite, hasten, hustle, incite, kindle, propel, revive, vivify **7** actuate, advance, animate, enliven, further, hurry on, inspire, provoke, refresh, sharpen **8** activate, dispatch, energize, enkindle, expedite, inspirit, vitalize **9** galvanize, instigate, stimulate **10** accelerate, invigorate **11** precipitate

quick glance
French: **9** coup d'oeil

quickly 4 anon, fast, soon **6** keenly, presto, pronto **7** briefly, hastily, rapidly, swiftly **8** promptly, speedily **9** instantly **11** immediately **12** lickety-split

Quickly, Mistress
character in: **22** The Merry Wives of Windsor
author: **11** Shakespeare

quickness 5 haste, speed **6** acuity **8** alacrity, celerity, keenness, rapidity **9** acuteness, alertness, dexterity, sharpness **10** cleverness, nimbleness, promptness **15** expeditiousness

quick-tempered 5 cross, testy **6** cranky, shirty, touchy **7** grouchy, peevish, waspish **8** choleric, churlish, shrewish, snappish **9** emotional, excitable, irascible, irritable **10** ill-

humored **11** bad-tempered, hot-tempered, quarrelsome **12** cantankerous **13** temperamental

quick-witted 4 keen **5** acute, alert, aware, quick, ready, sharp, smart, witty **6** astute, bright, clever, shrewd **8** incisive **9** brilliant, wide-awake **10** discerning, perceptive **11** clear-headed, intelligent, penetrating **13** perspicacious

quid pro quo 4 swap **5** trade **8** exchange **9** tit for tat **21** something for something

¿quien sabe 8 who knows?

quiescence 7 latency **8** dormancy, inaction **10** inactivity

quiescent 6 latent **7** dormant **8** inactive **10** in abeyance

quiet *see box*

quietly 5 coyly **6** calmly, humbly, meekly, mildly, mutely, softly, tamely **8** demurely, modestly, placidly, serenely, silently **9** bashfully, inaudibly, patiently **10** composedly, moderately, peacefully, tranquilly **11** collectedly, contentedly, diffidently, noiselessly, pacifically, soundlessly, temperately, unexcitedly **12** speechlessly, unassumingly, unboastfully **13** unobtrusively, unperturbedly **15** dispassionately, unpretentiously, without ceremony **16** unostentatiously **17** undemonstratively

Quiet Man, The
director: **8** John Ford
author: **13** Liam O'Flaherty
cast: **9** John Wayne **12** Maureen O'Hara **14** Mildred Natwick, Victor McLaglen **15** Barry Fitzgerald
setting: **7** Ireland
score: **11** Victor Young
Oscar for: **8** director

quietness 5 peace, quiet **7** silence **8** softness **9** stillness **12** peacefulness

quietude 4 calm, rest **6** repose **8** easiness **9** composure

Quigley, Jane
real name of: **13** Jane Alexander

quill 3 pen **4** fold, hair, pick, seta, stem, tube **5** pluck, plume, spike, spine, spool **6** bobbin, needle **7** bristle, feather, spindle **9** toothpick

Quilp
character in: **19** The Old Curiosity Shop
author: **7** Dickens

quilt 5 cover **6** spread **7** blanket **8** coverlet **9** bedspread, comforter

Quin, Widow
character in: **24** Playboy of the Western World
author: **5** Synge

Quincy, M. E.
character: **3** Lee **5** Danny, (Sgt) Brill **11** Sam Fujiyama, (Dr) Robert Astin **12** (Lt) Frank Monahan

---

quiet 3 low, mum **4** calm, curb, dull, ease, hush, lull, meek, mild, mute, rest, soft, stay, stop **5** abate, allay, blunt, check, fixed, inert, peace, plain, quell, still **6** arrest, at rest, deaden, docile, dozing, gentle, humble, hushed, lessen, mellow, modest, muffle, pacify, placid, repose, sedate, serene, settle, silent, simple, soften, soothe, stable, steady, stifle, subdue, weaken **7** assuage, clement, comfort, compose, dormant, halcyon, mollify, not busy, pacific, passive, patient, relieve, restful, silence, smother, subdued, suspend, unmoved **8** becalmed, calmness, comatose, composed, decrease, immobile, inactive, mitigate, moderate, muteness, not rough, not showy, palliate, peaceful, quietude, reserved, reticent, retiring, serenity, sleeping, stagnant, taciturn, tranquil **9** alleviate, collected, contented, easygoing, immovable, lethargic, make quiet, noiseless, not bright, peaceable, placidity, quietness, set at ease, soundless, stillness, temperate, terminate, unruffled, voiceless **10** coolheaded, gentleness, motionless, phlegmatic, put a stop to, relaxation, slumbering, speechless, stationary, stock-still, unassuming, untroubled **11** discontinue, tranquility, tranquilize, undisturbed, unexcitable, unobtrusive, unperturbed **12** bring to an end, even-tempered, inarticulate, peacefulness, tranquillity **13** at a standstill, dispassionate, imperturbable, noiselessness, soundlessness, unimpassioned, unpretentious **14** unostentatious, unpresumptuous **15** uncommunicative, undemonstrative

Quinn, Anthony

cast: 9 Robert Ito 10 John S
Ragin 11 Jack Klugman, Joseph Roman, Val Bisoglio
12 Garry Walberg 13 Ly-
nette Mettey
setting: 10 Los Angeles
11 Danny's Place

Quinn, Anthony

born: 6 Mexico 9 Chihuahua
wife: 16 Katherine DeMille
roles: 8 La Strada 10 Viva
Zapata 11 Lust for Life
13 Zorba the Greek 17 The
Guns of Navarone 22 Re-
quiem for a Heavyweight,
The Shoes of the Fisherman
autobiography: 14 The Original Sin

Quintana and Friends

author: 16 John Gregory
Dunne

quintessence 4 core, gist,
pith, soul 5 heart 6 elixir,
marrow, nature 7 essence
8 exemplar, quiddity, sum total 9 substance 10 embodiment 12 distillation
15 personification, sum and
substance

quip 3 gag, pun 4 barb, gibe,
jape, jeer, jest, joke 5 crack,
sally, spoof, taunt 6 banter, retort 7 epigram, putdown, riposte, sarcasm 8 badinage,
raillery, repartee, wordplay
9 wisecrack, witticism
French: 6 bon mot 14 double
entendre

Quirinus

origin: 5 Roman
god of: 3 war
personifies: 11 Roman nation
identified with: 7 Romulus

quirk 4 kink, turn, whim 6 fetish, foible, oddity, vagary,
whimsy 7 caprice 8 crotchet,
odd fancy 9 mannerism
10 aberration 11 abnormality,
affectation, peculiarity, sudden
twist 12 eccentricity,
idiosyncrasy

quisling 6 puppet 7 traitor
12 collaborator
16 collaborationist

quit 3 end, rid 4 free, stop
5 cease, clear, forgo, leave, let
go, waive, yield 6 depart, desist, disown, exempt, forego,
give up, reject, resign, retire
7 abandon, disavow, drop out,
forsake, take off 8 abdicate,
absolved, forswear, renounce,
withdraw 9 acquitted, foreswear, leave a job, surrender,
terminate 10 discharged, ex-
culpated, exonerated, relinquish 11 discontinue

quite 4 very 5 fully, truly
6 highly, hugely, indeed, in
fact, in toto, really, surely,
vastly, verily, wholly 7 exactly, in truth, totally, utterly
8 actually, entirely, outright
9 assuredly, certainly, extremely, in reality, out-
and-out, perfectly, precisely,
unusually, veritably 10 absolutely, altogether, completely,
enormously, positively, remarkably, throughout 11 exceedingly, excessively
12 considerably
13 exceptionally

Quito

capital of: 7 Ecuador

quiver 3 tic 4 jerk, jolt, jump,
pant 5 quake, shake, spasm,
throb 6 quaver, shiver, totter,
tremor, twitch, wobble
7 flicker, flutter, pulsate, seizure, shudder, tremble, vibrate, wriggle 8 convulse
9 fluctuate, oscillate, palpitate,
pulsation, quivering, twitching,
vibration 10 convulsion
11 palpitation

Quiverful, Mr

character in: 16 Barchester
Towers
author: 8 Trollope

quivering 7 shaking 9 agitating, quavering, shimmying,
shivering, trembling, vibrating 10 flittering, fluttering,
shuddering, twittering
11 palpitating

qui vive? 12 who goes there?

quixotic 4 wild 6 absurd,
dreamy, madcap, poetic 7 utopian 8 fanciful, romantic
9 fantastic, impulsive, visionary, whimsical 10 chimerical,
idealistic, ridiculous, starry-
eyed 11 impractical, ineffective, sentimental, unrealistic
12 preposterous 13 inefficacious

quiz 3 ask, rib 4 exam, joke,
mock, pump, test 5 prank,
query, taunt, tease 6 banter
7 examine, inquest, inquiry
8 question, ridicule, sound
out 9 catechism, eccentric, inquire of 11 examination, inquisition, interrogate,
investigate, questioning
12 cross-examine 13 interrogation, investigation 16 cross-
examination

Quiz Kids

host: 8 Joe Kelly 14 Clifton
Fadiman

quizzical 3 coy 4 arch 6 joking 7 baffled, curious, mocking, puzzled, teasing
8 derisive, impudent, insolent
9 bantering, inquiring, perplexed, searching 11 inquisitive, questioning

quoad hoc 12 as much as
this, to this extent

quod erat demonstrandum
17 which was to be shown
24 which was to be
demonstrated
abbreviation: 3 QED

quod erat faciendum
16 which was to be done

quod vide 8 which see
abbreviation: 2 qv

quo jure? 11 by what right?

quo modo 3 how 9 in what
way 19 in the same manner
that

quondam 4 erst, late, once,
past 6 bygone, former 8 formerly, sometime 9 erstwhile

quota 4 part 5 share 6 ration
7 measure, minimum, portion
8 quantity 9 allotment 10 allocation, assignment, percentage,
proportion 12 distribution
13 apportionment

quotation 5 quote 7 cutting,
excerpt, extract, passage 8 citation, clipping 9 reference, selection 12 illustration

quote 4 cite, name 6 adduce,
recall, repeat, retell 7 excerpt,
extract, refer to 8 instance
9 exemplify, recollect, reproduce 10 paraphrase

quoted passage 7 excerpt, extract 9 quotation

quotidian 5 daily 6 common
8 everyday, ordinary
11 commonplace

Quo Vadis?

author: 17 Henryk
Sienkiewicz
character: 4 Nero 5 Chilo,
Lygia, Peter 8 Vinitius 9 Petronius, Tigellius
director: 11 Mervyn LeRoy
cast: 7 Leo Genn 11 Deborah
Kerr 12 Peter Ustinov, Robert Taylor
setting: 11 ancient Rome

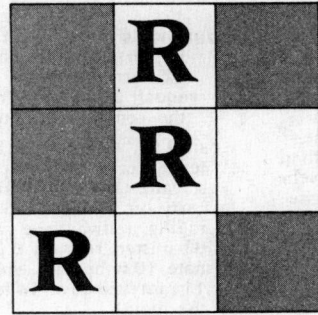

Ra
also: 2 Re
origin: 5 Greek 10 Heliopolis
god of: 3 sun
also worshipped by:
9 Egyptians

Rabat, Rabbat
capital of: 7 Morocco

rabbi 6 master, rabbin
7 scholar, teacher 9 clergyman 15 spiritual leader

rabbinical, rabbinic 8 clerical

rabbit 4 cony, hare, jack, lure
5 bunny, coney, lapin 6 novice, rodent 8 beginner 10 cot-
tontail, pacesetter

Rabbit Is Rich
author: 10 John Updike

Rabbit Redux
author: 10 John Updike

rabble 3 mob 5 swarm 7 the
herd 8 populace, riffraff
9 commoners, hoi polloi, the
masses 11 proletariat, rank
and file 12 lower classes
15 disorderly crowd 16 the
great unwashed
French: 8 canaille
German:
17 Lumpenproletariat

Rabelais, Francois
author of: 22 Gargantua and
Pantagruel

rabid 4 wild 6 ardent, crazed,
raging 7 berserk, fervent, frantic, violent, zealous 8 deranged, frenzied, maniacal,
wild-eyed 9 fanatical 11 hy-
drophobic 17 foaming at the
mouth

race 3 fly, run 4 dart, dash,
heat, rush 5 hurry 6 hasten,
hustle 7 contest, operate
8 campaign 11 competition

racecourse 4 turf 5 track
6 course 9 racetrack

Rachel
father: 5 Laban
husband: 5 Jacob
sister: 4 Leah
son: 6 Joseph 8 Benjamin
slave: 6 Bilhah

Rachmaninov (Rachmani-noff, Rakhmaninov), Sergei
born: 6 Russia 8 Novgorod
composer of: 15 Symphonic
Dances 16 The Isle of the
Dead 19 Second Piano Con-
certo 26 Rhapsody on a
Theme by (of) Paganini

Racine, Jean Baptiste
author of: 6 Phedre
7 Athalie 8 Berenice 10 Andromache 11 Britannicus

racism 7 bigotry 8 color bar
9 color line 10 race hatred, racial bias 11 segregation 15 racial prejudice 20 racial
discrimination

rack 4 buck, gait, hurt, neck,
pace, pain, path 5 agony,
cloud, exert, frame, raise,
track, trail, worry, wreck,
wring 6 canter, holder, strain
7 afflict, agonize, draw off, oppress, stretch, torment, torture 8 distress 9 suffering
10 destruction, excruciate, iron
maiden

racked 4 torn 5 paced
6 framed, pained, traced,
walked 7 annoyed, tracked,
trotted, wronged, worried
8 cantered, suffered, tortured
9 afflicted, anguished, destroyed, oppressed, tormented
10 persecuted

racket 3 din 4 game, line,
roar, stir 5 babel 6 clamor,
hubbub, rumpus, tumult, uproar 7 clangor, clatter, turmoil 8 business, shouting
9 commotion, loud noise
10 hullabaloo, hurly-burly, occupation, turbulence 11 dis-

turbance, pandemonium
12 caterwauling, vociferation

racketeer 4 hood 5 crook
6 bagman, bandit, extort
7 hoodlum, mafioso, mobster
8 criminal, gangster
12 extortionist

racking 7 painful 9 agonizing,
torturous 10 tormenting, unbearable 11 intolerable, unendurable 12 excruciating,
insufferable

raconteur 8 fabulist, narrator,
romancer 10 anecdotist
11 storyteller 13 teller of
tales 14 spinner of yarns

racy 4 keen 5 bawdy, crude,
heady, lurid, zesty 6 erotic,
lively, ribald, risque, smutty,
vulgar 7 buoyant, glowing, obscene, zestful 8 animated, exciting, immodest, indecent,
off-color, prurient, spirited,
vigorous 9 energetic, fast-
paced, salacious, sparkling
10 suggestive 11 stimulating
12 exhilarating, pornographic

radar
invented by: 4 Watt
6 Watson

Radcliffe, Mrs Ann
author of: 10 The Italian
21 The Mysteries of Udolpho

raddle 3 rod 4 reed, scar, twig
5 fence, hedge, rouge, stick,
weave 6 branch, ruddle 8 hematite, red ocher, red ochre
10 interweave

radiance, radiancy 3 joy
5 gleam, gleem, sheen 6 dazzle, luster 7 glitter, rapture,
sparkle 8 lambency, splendor
9 animation, happiness
10 brightness, brilliance, brilliancy, effulgence, luminosity,
refulgence 11 coruscation, iridescence 12 luminousness, resplendence 13 incandescence
god of: 5 Baldr 6 Balder,
Baldur

radiant 5 aglow, happy, sunny 6 bright, elated, joyous 7 beaming, glowing, pleased, shining 8 blissful, dazzling, ecstatic, flashing, gladsome, gleaming, luminous, lustrous 9 brilliant, delighted, effulgent, overjoyed, rapturous, refulgent, sparkling 10 glittering 12 incandescent 13 scintillating

radiate 4 beam, pour, shed 5 carry 6 spread 7 diffuse, diverge, give off, give out, scatter 8 disperse, emit heat, transmit 9 branch out, circulate, emit light, spread out 11 disseminate

radical 4 rash 5 basic, rebel 6 severe 7 drastic, extreme 8 left-wing, militant 9 extremist, firebrand 10 immoderate, inordinate 11 freethinker, fundamental, precipitate 13 revolutionary 22 antiestablishmentarian

radio
   invented by: 7 Donovan, Fleming, Marconi 8 De Forest, Nicolson 9 Armstrong, Fessenden 12 Alexanderson

radium
   chemical symbol: 2 Ra

radon
   chemical symbol: 2 Rn

raffish 3 low 4 fast, wild 5 cheap, rowdy, showy 6 common, flashy, rakish, tawdry, vulgar 7 boorish 8 rakehell 9 worthless 10 dissipated 12 devil-may-care, disreputable

raft 3 lot 4 mass 5 barge, float 6 plenty 7 carrier, pontoon 8 flatboat, platform, quantity 9 abundance, multitude

Raft, George
   real name: 11 George Ranft
   born: 9 New York NY
   roles: 8 Scarface 11 Johnny Angel 12 Guido Rinaldo 13 Some Like It Hot

rag 3 kid, rib 4 scap, song, tune, twit 5 cloth, taunt, taunt, tease 6 harass 7 torment 8 magazine 9 newspaper 11 ragtime tune 14 worn-out garment

ragamuffin 3 bum 4 hobo, waif 5 gamin, tramp 6 beggar, gamine, hoyden, sloven, urchin, wretch 7 vagrant 8 derelict, vagabond 9 itinerant, ragpicker 10 panhandler, street arab 11 guttersnipe 14 tatterdemalion

rage 3 fad, ire 4 boil, fume, fury, mode, rant, rave, roar 5 craze, furor, mania, pique, storm, vogue, wrath 6 blow up, choler, frenzy, seethe, spleen, temper 7 explode, fashion, ferment, flare up, madness, passion, rampage, umbrage 8 paroxysm, the thing 9 animosity, fulminate, raise cain, throw a fit, vehemence 10 bitterness, excitement, irritation, resentment, the "in" thing 11 displeasure, high dudgeon, indignation, the last word 12 current style, le dernier cri, perturbation, violent anger 13 temper tantrum 14 the latest thing 15 fly off the handle, froth at the mouth

Rage of Angels
   author: 13 Sidney Sheldon

ragged 4 rent, torn, worn 5 seedy, tacky 6 beat up, frayed, shabby, shaggy, shoddy 7 patched, run down, worn-out 8 battered, shredded, strained, tattered 9 overtaxed 10 aggravated, threadbare, worn to rags 11 exacerbated

ragging 5 chaff 6 banter 7 kidding, ribbing, teasing 8 chaffing, needling, raillery, taunting, twitting

raging 3 mad 4 wild 5 angry, livid, rabid, rough 6 fierce, raving, stormy 7 fervent, frantic, furious, rampant, violent 8 frenzied, incensed, storming 9 turbulent 10 blustering, ferocious, infuriated 11 tempestuous

Raging Bull
   director: 14 Martin Scorsese
   cast: 8 Joe Pesci 12 Frank Vincent, Robert De Niro (Jake La Motta) 13 Cathy Moriarty
   Oscar for: 5 actor (De Niro)

Ragnarok
   also: 15 Gotterdammerung 17 Twilight of the Gods
   origin: 12 Scandinavian
   event: 11 final battle
   battlefield: 6 Vigrid

ragout 4 hash, stew 7 borscht, goulash 9 fricassee

Ragtime
   author: 10 E L Doctorow

Rahab
   hometown: 7 Jericho
   husband: 6 Solmon
   hid: 12 Joshua's spies

raid 4 bust 5 foray, onset, sally, storm 6 attack, inroad, invade, razzia, sortie 7 assault, round-up 8 invasion 10 pounce upon 14 surprise attack

Raiders of the Lost Ark
   director: 15 Steven Spielberg
   cast: 10 Karen Allen, Wolf Kahler 11 Paul Freeman 12 Harrison Ford
   sequel: 30 Indiana Jones and the Temple of Doom

rail 3 bar 4 rage, rant 5 scold, fence, train 6 blow up, scream, take on 7 barrier, carry on, declaim, inveigh, railing, railway, the cars 8 banister, railroad 9 fulminate 10 vituperate, vociferate 11 rant and rave 14 foam at the mouth

rail at 5 scold 6 berate 7 chew out 9 castigate 14 inveigh against

railing 3 bar 5 fence, grate, rails 6 fender 7 barrier, parapet, support 8 banister 9 enclosing 10 balustrade

raillery 5 chaff, sport 6 banter, japing, joking, satire 7 fooling, jesting, joshing, kidding, ragging, razzing, ribbing, teasing 8 badinage, chaffing, roasting, twitting 10 lampoonery, persiflage, pleasantry

railroad sleeping car
   French: 8 wagon-lit

railroad station 5 depot 8 terminal, terminus

railway 4 tube 5 track, train 6 cogway, subway 7 cogroad, trolley 8 elevated, monorail, railroad 9 streetcar

raiment 4 duds, togs 5 dress 6 attire 7 apparel, clothes, costume, threads 8 clothing, garments 11 habiliments

rain, rains 4 down, drop, mist, pour 5 spate 6 deluge, lavish, shower, squall 7 drizzle, monsoon, torrent 8 downpour, drencher, plethora, rainfall, send down, sprinkle 9 hurricane, rainstorm 10 cloudburst 13 precipitation, thundershower 15 rain cats and dogs 16 come down in sheets 17 come down in buckets
   god of: 4 Thor

Rainbow
   goddess of: 4 Iris

Rainbow, The
   author: 10 D H Lawrence
   character: 10 Anna Lensky 11 Lydia Lensky, Tom Brangwen 12 Will Brangwen 14 Ursula Brangwen 15 Anton Skrebensky

Rainbow Bridge see 7 bifrost

raincoat 3 mac 4 mack 6 poncho, ulster 7 oilskin, slicker 8 burberry 9 tarpaulin 10 mackintosh, trenchcoat, waterproof

rainless 3 dry 4 arid, sere
10 desertlike

Rains, Claude
born: 6 London 7 England
wife: 11 Isabel Jeans
roles: 9 Notorious 10 Casablanca, Now Voyager 13 Mr
Skeffington 14 Anthony Adverse 15 The Invisible Man
16 Lawrence of Arabia
17 Here Comes Mr Jordan
20 The Phantom of the Op-
era 23 Mr Smith Goes to
Washington 24 The Adven-
tures of Robin Hood

rain shower 6 shower 7 drizzle 8 sprinkle 12 thunderstorm

rainstorm 6 deluge, shower
8 downfall, downpour
10 cloudburst 12 thunderstorm

rainy 3 wet 4 damp 7 drizzly,
showery 11 pouring rain
18 raining cats and dogs

raise 3 end 4 grow, hike, lift,
rear, spur, urge 5 amass,
boost, breed, build, erect,
nurse, pique, put up, rouse,
set up, spark 6 arouse,
awaken, excite, foster, hike
up, jack up, kindle, obtain,
stir up 7 advance, bring in,
bring up, canvass, collect, develop, elevate, inflame, inflate,
inspire, nurture, procure, produce, sharpen, solicit 8 increase, summon up
9 construct, cultivate, elevation, promotion, stimulate, terminate 10 make higher, put
forward 11 advancement

raise aloft 5 boost, hoist 6 lift
up, uplift 7 elevate, upraise

raised 4 bred, grew 5 anted,
built, grown 6 anteed, convex,
jacked, lifted, reared, roused
7 aroused, erected, exalted,
hoisted, honored, incited 8 elevated, embossed, leavened,
mustered 9 brought up, collected 10 cultivated
11 resurrected

Raisin in the Sun, A
director: 12 Daniel Petrie
based on play by: 17 Lorraine Hansberry
cast: 7 Ruby Dee 9 Ivan
Dixon 10 Diana Sands
13 Claudia McNeil, Sidney
Poitier
setting: 7 Chicago

rake 4 comb, goat, roue
5 rogue, satyr, scour, sport
6 lecher, pepper, rascal 7 Don
Juan, playboy, ransack, seducer, swinger 8 Casanova, Lothario, enfilade, prodigal,
rakehell 9 debauchee,
libertine, womanizer
10 immoralist,

profligate, sensualist,
voluptuary

rake-off 3 cut, fee 5 piece
10 percentage 16 piece of the
action

Rake's Progress, The
opera by: 10 Stravinsky
character: 10 Ann Trulove,
Nick Shadow 11 Baba the
Turk, Mother Goose, Tom
Rakewell

rakish 4 airy 6 breezy, dapper,
jaunty, sporty 7 dashing, gallant, immoral, lustful 8 cavalier, debonair, depraved,
sporting 9 bumptious, de-
bauched, dissolute, lecherous,
libertine 10 dissipated, lascivious, profligate, sauntering,
swaggering

rally 4 meet, rush 5 score,
unite 6 caucus, gather, muster,
pick up, powwow, revive
7 catch up, collect, get well,
improve, recruit, reunite, revival 8 assemble, assembly, recovery 9 come round,
gathering, get better, reconvene 10 assemblage, convalesce, convention, reassemble,
recuperate 11 convocation, improvement, mass meeting, pull
through, restoration 12 call together, congregation, recuperation 13 convalescence

ram 3 hit, jam 4 beat, bump,
butt, dash, goat, slam 5 crash,
drive, force, smash 6 batter,
hammer, hurtle, strike, thrust
7 run into

Ram
constellation of: 5 Aries

ramble 3 gad 4 hike, roam,
rove, wind 5 amble, drift,
range, snake, twist 6 stroll,
wander, zigzag 7 meander,
saunter, traipse 8 gad about,
idle walk 9 gallivant 11 perambulate, peregrinate

rambling 6 prolix, uneven
7 diffuse 10 circuitous, digressive, discursive, disjointed

rambunctious 4 wild 5 noisy,
rowdy 6 active, unruly 7 raucous, untamed, violent 9 irascible 10 boisterous,
pugnacious 11 quarrelsome
14 uncontrollable

Rameau, Jean-Philippe
born: 5 Dijon 6 France
composer of: 6 Platee 8 Dardanus 13 Les Fetes d'Hebe
14 Castor et Pollux 15 Castor and Pollux 16 Les Indes
Galantes, The Indigo Suitors 17 Hippolyte et Aricie
20 La Princesse de Navarre

ramification 3 arm 4 part,
spur 5 prong 6 branch 8 division, offshoot 9 branching,
outgrowth 10 divergence, separation 11 consequence,
subdivision

rampage 4 rage 5 storm 7 run
amok, run riot

rampant 4 rife 5 erect 6 raging 8 epidemic, pandemic
9 prevalent, unchecked, universal 10 on hind legs, standing up, widespread
12 ungovernable, unre-
strained 14 uncontrollable

rampart 7 barrier, bastion, bulwark, parapet 9 barricade,
earthwork 10 breastwork
13 defensive wall, fortification 14 protective wall

Ramsay, William
field: 9 chemistry
nationality: 7 British
discovered: 4 neon 5 argon
(in air) 6 helium 7 krypton
awarded: 10 Nobel Prize

ramshackle 5 shaky 6 flimsy,
shabby 7 rickety, run-down
8 decrepit, unstable, unsteady
9 crumbling, tottering 10 tumbledown 11 dilapidated
13 deteriorating

Ramtil _see_ 5 Niger

Ran
origin: 12 Scandinavian
goddess of: 3 sea
husband: 5 Aegir

ranch 4 farm 5 range 6 grange,
spread 7 acreage, station 8 hacienda 10 plantation

rancher 6 cowboy, farmer,
gaucho 7 cowhand, cowpoke
8 herdsman, sheepman, stock-
man 9 cattleman
10 cowpuncher

rancid 3 old 4 foul, gamy,
high, rank 6 putrid, strong
8 mephitic, stinking
10 malodorous

rancor 4 hate 5 spite 6 animus,
enmity, hatred, malice,
spleen 7 ill will 8 acrimony
9 animosity, antipathy, hostility 10 antagonism, bitterness,
ill feeling, resentment 11 malevolence 12 spitefulness

rancorous 5 nasty 6 bitter
7 hostile 8 churlish, spiteful,
vengeful, venomous 9 splenetic 10 ill-natured 11 acrimonious 12 antagonistic

Rand, Ayn
author of: 13 Atlas
Shrugged 15 The Fountain-
head 17 Romantic
Manifesto

Randall, Tony
  real name: **16** Leonard
  Rosenberg
  born: **7** Tulsa OK
  roles: **9** Mr Peepers **10** Felix
  Unger, Pillow Talk **12** Harvey Weskit, The Odd Couple **13** The Mating Game
  20 The Seven Faces of Dr
  Lao

random 5 stray **6** casual,
  chance **7** aimless, offhand
  9 haphazard, hit-or-miss, unplanned **10** accidental, fortuitous, occasional, undesigned,
  unexpected, unintended
  12 adventitious **13** unintentional **14** unpremeditated

Ranft, George
  real name of: **10** George Raft

range 3 run **4** roam, rove
  5 field, gamut, limit, orbit,
  reach, ridge, scope **6** bounds,
  domain, extend, massif, plains,
  radius, sierra, sphere, wander
  7 explore, pasture, purview,
  stretch, variety **8** province
  9 selection **11** grazing land
  16 chain of mountains

Rangoon
  capital of: **5** Burma
  former name: **5** Dagon
  6 Yangon
  founder: **10** Alaungpaya
  landmark: **10** Sule Pagoda
  15 Shwe Dagon Pagoda
  name means: **11** end of
  strife
  river: **7** Rangoon
  square: **12** Independence

rangy 4 tall **5** broad, lanky
  9 expansive, extensive

rank 3 row **4** bald, file, foul,
  line, lush, rate, sort, tall, type,
  wild **5** class, crass, dense,
  grade, gross, level, nasty, order, sheer, stale, stand, total,
  utter **6** arrant, coarse, column,
  estate, filthy, jungly, lavish,
  rancid, status **7** come out, echelon, glaring, profuse, quality,
  rampart **8** absolute, complete,
  flagrant, position, standing,
  tropical **9** atrocious, be classed,
  come first, downright, have
  place, luxuriant, monstrous,
  overgrown **10** outrageous,
  scurrilous **11** highgrowing, ill
  smelling, unmitigated **12** overabundant **14** classification, social standing, strong smelling

rank and file 6 troops **17** enlisted personnel, general
  membership

Rankine, William John
  Macquorn
  field: **7** physics
  nationality: **8** Scottish

devised: 12 Rankine Cycle,
  Rankine Scale **26** Fahrenheit
  temperature scale
  author of: **22** Manual of the
  Steam Engine

rankle 4 gall, rile **5** chafe,
  gripe, pique **6** fester **8** irritate
  10 not sit well

ransack 3 gut **4** comb, loot,
  raid, rake, sack **5** rifle, scour,
  strip **6** ravage, search **7** despoil, pillage, plunder **8** lay
  waste **9** devastate, vandalize
  14 rummage through, turn upside down

ransom 3 buy **4** free, save
  5 atone, price **6** redeem, rescue **7** deliver, expiate, reclaim,
  recover, release **8** liberate, retrieve **10** liberation, redemption

Ransom, John Crowe
  member of: **12** the Fugitives
  author of: **14** I'll Take My
  Stand **16** Captain Carpenter
  30 Bells for John White-
  side's Daughter

rant 4 fume, rage, rave, yell
  5 orate, scold, spout, storm
  6 bellow **7** bluster, bombast,
  bravado, explode **8** harangue
  11 declamation
  12 exaggeration

rap 3 jaw, pan, tap **4** bang,
  chat, drum, talk **5** blame,
  knock, roast, speak, thump
  6 dump on **7** clobber **8** converse **9** criticize **10** come down
  on **11** communicate **14** responsibility, shoot the breeze

rapacious 6 greedy **7** looting,
  wolfish **8** covetous, grasping,
  ravenous, thievish **9** marauding, mercenary, pillaging,
  predatory, voracious **10** avaricious, insatiable, plundering,
  ransacking

rapacity 5 greed **7** avarice
  10 greediness **12** covetousness,
  graspingness **13** mercenariness

Rape of Lucrece
  author: **18** William
  Shakespeare
  character: **7** Tarquin
  9 Collatine

Rape of the Lock, The
  author: **13** Alexander Pope
  character: **5** Ariel **7** Belinda,
  Umbriel **9** Lord Petre
  10 Thalestris

Raphael 9 archangel

Raphael
  real name: **14** Raffaello
  Santi **15** Raffaello Sanzio
  born: **5** Italy **6** Urbino
  artwork: **7** Disputa **8** Julius
  II **10** Entombment **14** Sistine Madonna **17** The

School of Athens, The Virgin and Child **18** Madonna
  di Casa Tempi, The Transfiguration **19** The Triumph of
  Galatea **21** Baldassare Castiglione **22** The Marriage of
  the Virgin **24** The Expulsion
  of Heliodorus **28** The Madonna and Child with St
  John (La Belle Jardiniere)
  architect of: **11** Villa Madama (Rome) **16** Pandolfini
  Palace (Florence) **22** Vidoni-
  Caffarelli Palace (Rome)

rapid 4 fast **5** brisk, fleet,
  hasty, quick, swift **6** active,
  flying, prompt, speedy **7** express, hurried, instant, rushing **8** agitated, feverish
  9 galloping, unchecked **11** accelerated, expeditious,
  precipitate

rapidity 5 haste, speed **8** celerity, velocity **9** fleetness, quickness, swiftness **10** promptness

rapidly 4 fast **5** apace **7** briskly,
  hastily, quickly, swiftly **8** pell-
  mell, speedily **9** hurriedly, like
  a shot, overnight **10** in high
  gear **11** at full speed **13** expeditiously, helter-skelter

rapids 5 chute **7** current
  10 white water

rapport 3 tie **4** link **10** connection, fellowship **11** affiliation, camaraderie
  12 relationship **13** understanding **17** interrelationship

rapprochement 6 accord
  7 detente, entente **9** agreement **10** adjustment, compromise, settlement
  11 appeasement, arrangement
  12 conciliation, pacification
  13 accommodation, harmoni-
  zation, reconcilement, understanding **14** reconciliation
  16 mutual concession

rapscallion 5 knave, rogue,
  scamp **6** rascal **7** low-life, villain **8** scalawag **9** scoundrel
  10 blackguard, ne'er-do-well,
  rascallion **14** good-for-nothing

rapt 6 dreamy, enrapt, intent
  7 bemused, charmed **8** absorbed, ecstatic **9** attentive, bewitched, delighted, enchanted,
  engrossed, entranced, rapturous **10** captivated, enraptured,
  enthralled, fascinated, interested, moonstruck, spellbound
  11 transported

rapture 3 joy **5** bliss **6** thrill
  7 delight, ecstasy, elation
  8 euphoria, felicity **9** beatitude

rapturous 4 rapt **8** beatific,
  blissful, ecstatic **9** enthralled
  10 enraptured

rare 3 few **6** scarce, unique **7** unusual **8** uncommon **10** hard to find, infrequent **11** exceptional, seldom found **16** few and far between

rarefied 4 thin **6** dilute, purify, rarify, reduce, refine, subtle **7** inflate **8** diminish **9** attenuate, extenuate

rarely 6 hardly, seldom **8** not often **10** hardly ever, uncommonly **12** infrequently, scarcely ever **15** once in a blue moon, on rare occasions **17** once in a great while

raring 4 agog, avid, keen **5** eager **8** desirous **9** impatient **12** enthusiastic

rarity 6 oddity **7** anomaly **8** scarcity **11** unusualness **12** uncommonness **14** remarkableness

rascal 3 cad, imp **4** rake **5** devil, knave, rogue, scamp **7** villain **8** rakehell, scalawag **9** prankster, reprobate, scoundrel, trickster **10** blackguard, delinquent **11** rapscallion

rash 5 brash, hasty **6** abrupt **7** foolish **8** careless, headlong, heedless, reckless **9** foolhardy, impetuous, imprudent, impulsive, premature, unadvised, unchecked **10** incautious, indiscreet, ungoverned, unthinking **11** adventurous, harebrained, injudicious, precipitate, thoughtless **12** devil-may-care, uncontrolled **13** irresponsible

rashness 8 audacity, boldness **9** riskiness **12** heedlessness, indiscretion, recklessness **13** foolhardiness, impulsiveness **15** precipitousness, thoughtlessness

Rashomon
author: 18 Ryunosuke Akutagawa
director: 13 Akira Kurosawa

Raskolnikov
character in: 18 Crime and Punishment
author: 10 Dostoevsky

rasp 3 irk, nag, rub, vex **4** file **5** chafe, grate, worry **6** abrade, scrape, wheeze **7** grating, scraper, scratch **8** abrasive, irritate **9** huskiness **10** hoarseness

raspberry 11 Rubus idaeus
varieties: 3 red **4** hill **5** black, dwarf **6** Mysore, purple **8** European **9** flowering, Mauritius **11** American red **13** Rocky Mountain

15 Purple-flowering **22** Rocky Mountain flowering
brandy: 9 Framboise

rasping 5 harsh, raspy, rough **6** hoarse **7** chafing, grating, nagging **8** abrading, scraping, worrying **9** offensive **10** irritating

Rasselas
author: 13 Samuel Johnson
character: 5 Imlac **6** Pekuah **7** Nekayah
Rasselas's title: 17 Prince of Abyssinia

Rassendyll, Rudolph
character in: 15 Prisoner of Zenda
author: 4 Hope

rat 3 cad, cur **4** fink, heel **5** churl, knave, louse **6** betray, rascal, rotter, squeal, vermin **7** bounder, villain **8** informer, inform on **9** scoundrel **10** blackguard **11** stool pigeon

rate 3 fee **4** cost, deem, dues, levy, pace, rank, toll **5** class, count, price, speed, tempo **6** charge, figure, look on, regard, tariff **7** expense, measure **8** classify **10** assessment

rate highly 5 prize, value **6** admire, esteem **7** cherish, respect **8** treasure

Rathbone, Basil
real name: 25 Philip St John Basil Rathbone
born: 11 South Africa **12** Johannesburg
roles: 6 Tybalt **7** Karenin **10** Dawn Patrol **11** Mr Murdstone **12** Anna Karenina **14** Romeo and Juliet, Sherlock Holmes, The Mark of Zorro **16** A Tale of Two Cities, David Copperfield **20** The Last Days of Pompeii **24** The Adventures of Robin Hood **25** The Hound of the Baskervilles

rather 4 a bit, very **5** quite **6** fairly, kind of, pretty, sort of **8** slightly, somewhat **10** moderately, more or less, relatively **13** comparatively

ratification 2 OK **4** okay **7** consent **8** approval, sanction **10** validation **11** affirmation, endorsement **12** confirmation **13** authorization, corroboration **14** seal of approval

ratify 2 OK **4** okay **6** affirm, uphold **7** agree to, approve, certify, confirm, endorse, support **8** accede to, make good, sanction, validate **9** authorize, consent to, make valid **11** acknowledge **12** authenticate

rating 4 mark, rank **5** class, grade, ratio, value **6** degree, rebuke, sailor, seaman **7** ranking **8** standing **9** appraisal **10** assessment, evaluation, percentage **14** classification

ratio 8 equation **10** proportion **11** arrangement **12** distribution **13** apportionment, fixed relation **15** proportionality **17** interrelationship **20** proportional relation

ration, rations 3 due **4** dole, food **5** allot **6** stores **7** measure, mete out **8** allocate **9** allotment, apportion, food share, provender, provision **10** provisions **13** apportionment

rational 4 sage, sane, wise **5** lucid, solid, sound **6** normal **7** logical **8** all there, balanced, credible, feasible **9** advisable, judicious, plausible, sagacious **10** reasonable **11** clearheaded, responsible **12** compos mentis **13** perspicacious **15** in one's right mind

rationale 5 basis, logic **6** excuse, reason **7** grounds **9** reasoning **10** key concept, philosophy **11** explanation, foundations **16** underlying reason

rationalize 6 excuse **7** explain, justify **8** palliate **9** whitewash **10** account for **11** explain away **13** put a gloss upon **14** make excuses for **16** make allowance for

rattan, ratan 4 cane, lash, palm, whip **5** thong **6** switch, wicker

Ratti, Achille 10 Pope Pius XI

rattle 3 gab, jar **4** faze **5** clang, clank, clink, prate, shake, throw, upset **6** bounce, flurry, jangle **7** agitate, blather, chatter, clatter, confuse, disturb, fluster, maunder, nonplus, perturb **8** bewilder, clacking, distract **9** discomfit **10** discompose, disconcert **11** roll loosely

rattlebrained 4 dumb **5** silly **6** stupid **7** asinine, doltish, foolish, idiotic, moronic, witless **9** brainless, imbecilic **10** fool-headed, half-witted **11** harebrained, lamebrained

rattled 5 fazed, upset **7** annoyed **9** disturbed, flustered, perturbed, thrown off **10** distracted **11** discomposed **12** disconcerted

rattle on 3 gab **4** blab **5** prate, run on **6** babble, gabble

7 blabber, chatter, prattle **16** run off at the mouth

ratty 4 poor, worn **5** angry, cross, nasty, testy **6** cranky, shabby, touchy **7** tangled, unkempt **8** wretched **9** irascible, motheaten **11** dilapidated

raucous 4 loud **5** harsh, raspy, rough **6** hoarse, shrill **7** blaring, grating, jarring **8** grinding, jangling, piercing, strident **9** dissonant **10** discordant, stertorous **11** cacophonous **12** earsplitting, inharmonious

raunchy 4 lewd **5** dirty, gross **6** coarse, smutty, vulgar **8** off-color

Rauschenberg, Robert
born: 12 Port Arthur TX
artwork: 3 Bed **5** Barge **7** Jammers **8** Monogram **11** Retroactive

ravage 3 gut **4** loot, raid, rape, raze, ruin, sack **5** strip, waste, wreck **6** maraud **7** despoil, destroy, overrun, pillage, plunder, ransack, shatter **8** demolish, desolate, lay waste, spoliate **9** devastate **10** lay in ruins

rave 3 wax **4** fume, go on, gush, rage, rant **5** be mad, kudos, storm **6** babble, bubble, ramble **7** be angry, bluster, carry on, explode, flare up, run amok, sputter, thunder **8** flattery **9** be furious, expatiate, go on and on, good press, laudatory **10** effervesce, high praise, rhapsodize **11** blow one's top, compliments

ravel 4 undo **6** unknit **7** unravel, untwine, untwist

Ravel, Maurice
born: 6 France **7** Ciboure
composer of: 6 Bolero **7** La Valse, Mirrors **8** Jeux d'eau **9** Fountains **11** Mother Goose, Sheherazade **14** Daphnis et Chloe **15** Gaspard de la Nuit, L'Heure Espagnole **17** Rapsodie Espagnole, The Tomb of Couperin **20** Pavane for a Dead Infant **21** Don Quichotte a Dulcinee **22** L'Enfant et les Sortileges, Pavane for a Dead Princess **27** Pavane pour une infante defunte, Valses nobles et sentimentales

raven 3 jet **4** crow, dark, inky, rook **5** black, ebony, sable **6** devour **9** coal-black

Raven, The
author: 13 Edgar Allan Poe

ravenous 6 greedy, hungry **7** piggish, starved **8** covetous, famished, grasping, ravening, starving **9** insatiate, predatory, rapacious, voracious **10** avaricious, gluttonous, insatiable

Ravenshoe
author: 13 Henry Kingsley

ravine 3 gap **4** pass, rift, wadi **5** abyss, break, chasm, cleft, crack, gorge, gulch, gully, split **6** arroyo, breach, canyon, clough, divide, valley **7** fissure **8** crevasse

raving 3 mad **4** wild **6** insane **7** ranting **8** frenzied **9** delirious

ravish 4 rape **5** abuse, charm, cheer **6** defile, snatch, tickle **7** delight, enchant, gladden, outrage, overjoy, violate **8** deflower, enthrall, entrance, knock out **9** captivate, enrapture, fascinate, transport

ravishing 8 alluring, charming, gorgeous, smashing, splendid, striking **9** beautiful **10** bewitching, delightful, enchanting, entrancing **11** captivating, fascinating, sensational

raw 4 bare, cold, damp, rare **5** basic, bleak, crude, frank, fresh, green, harsh, plain, rough, young **6** biting, bitter, brutal, callow, chilly, rookie, unripe **7** cutting, natural, nipping, numbing, unbaked, untried **8** blustery, freezing, ignorant, immature, inexpert, piercing, pinching, uncooked, untaught, untested **9** inclement, underdone, undrilled, unfledged, unrefined, unskilled, untrained, windswept **10** amateurish, unprepared, unseasoned **11** not finished, undercooked, undeveloped, unexercised, uninitiated, unpracticed, unprocessed, unvarnished **13** inexperienced, undisciplined, unembellished **15** not manufactured

rawboned 4 lean **5** gaunt, lanky, spare **7** angular

Rawdon, Captain
character in: 10 Bleak House
author: 7 Dickens

Rawhide
character: 5 Mushy **8** Gil Favor, Ian Cabot, Wishbone **9** Jim Quince, Pete Nolan **10** Rowdy Yates **11** Joe Scarlett, Solomon King **13** Clay Forrester **14** Hey Soos Patines
cast: 10 Sheb Wooley **11** Charles Gray, David Watson, Eric Fleming, Robert Cabal, Rocky Shahan, Steve

Raines **12** James Murdock, Paul Brinegar **13** Clint Eastwood **16** Raymond St Jacques

Rawlings, Marjorie Kinnan
author of: 11 The Yearling

rawness 3 nip **4** bite **5** chill **8** rudeness **9** crudeness, greenness, roughness, sharpness, vulgarity **10** chilliness **12** inexperience

ray 3 arm **4** beam, fish, line **5** gleam, light, shaft, shine, skate, trace **6** branch, streak, stream, stripe **7** radiate **8** particle, plowfish, radiance **9** emanation, radiation

Ray, Man
born: 14 Philadelphia PA
artwork: 4 Gift (Le Cadeau) **7** Manikin **9** The Lovers **13** Observing Time **45** The Rope Dancer Accompanies Herself with Her Shadows

Rayleigh, John William Strutt
field: 7 physics
nationality: 7 British
discovered: 5 argon
awarded: 10 Nobel Prize

rayon
invented by: 4 Swan

raze 4 fell, ruin **5** level, smash, wreck **6** reduce, remove, topple **7** destroy, flatten, wipe out **8** demolish, pull down, tear down **9** break down, dismantle, knock down **10** obliterate

razor
invented by: 6 Schick **8** Gillette

Razorback State
nickname of: 8 Arkansas

Re *see* **2** Ra

reach 3 get, hit **4** find, go to, grab, make, move **5** climb, enter, get to, grasp, seize, touch **6** attain, clutch, come to, extend, grab at, land at, secure, spread **7** contact, stretch **8** amount to, approach, arrive at **9** get hold of, set foot in **10** get as far as, outstretch, stretch out

reachable 6 at hand **8** possible **10** accessible, achievable, attainable, obtainable, procurable

reach the top 6 arrive **7** prosper, succeed **8** make good **13** hit the big time

react 4 work **6** answer, behave, resist, return **9** respond **11** reverberate

reaction 5 reply 6 answer, reflex 8 backlash, response 11 restoration 13 counteraction 14 chemical change 17 counterrevolution, right-wing comeback

reactionary 7 diehard 8 mossback, rightist 9 right-wing 10 regressive 11 right-winger 12 reversionary 17 ultraconservative 20 counterrevolutionary

react to 5 reply 6 answer 7 respond 11 acknowledge

read 2 go 3 say 4 note, scan, show 5 study, utter 6 adduce, peruse, recite 7 analyze, deliver, discern, explain, present 8 construe, decipher, indicate, perceive, pore over 9 apprehend, interpret, translate 10 comprehend, glance over, understand 11 extrapolate

Read, Piers Paul author of: 5 Alive 9 Polonaise 10 Monk Dawson, The Junkers, The Upstart 18 Professor's Daughter

Reade, Charles author of: 13 Peg Woffington 23 The Cloister and the Hearth

readily 6 at once, easily, freely, pronto 7 quickly 8 in no time, promptly, smoothly, speedily 9 expressly, hands down, instantly, willingly 10 graciously 11 immediately, straightway 12 effortlessly, ungrudgingly

readiness 8 alacrity, dispatch 9 alertness 10 promptness 12 preparedness

Reading on the Statute of Uses author: 12 Francis Bacon

read the riot act 5 chide, scold 6 berate, rebuke 7 censure, chasten, correct, lecture, reprove 8 admonish 9 dress down, reprimand 10 take to task

ready 3 apt, fit, set 4 deft, keen, ripe, up to 5 acute, alert, eager, equip, handy, on tap, prone, sharp 6 adroit, all set, artful, astute, at hand, bright, clever, expert, facile, fit out, liable, mature, on hand, primed, prompt, shrewd, speedy 7 cunning, equal to, prepare, present, tending, willing 8 disposed, inclined, masterly, punctual, skillful 9 attentive, dexterous, fitted out, furnished, ingenious, in harness, versatile, wide-awake 10 accessible, discerning, perceptive, put in order 11 acquisitive, expeditious, predisposed, quick-witted, resourceful, serviceable

ready for use 5 handy, on tap 6 at hand, on hand 9 available 10 accessible, convenient 11 at one's elbow 14 at one's disposal

ready-made 10 off-the-rack 11 ready-to-wear, store-bought 17 store manufactured

ready money 4 cash 8 currency 10 cash on hand

ready to go 5 peppy 9 full of pep 10 raring to go 17 full of vim and vigor 24 bright-eyed and bushy-tailed

Reagan, Ronald Wilson *see box, p. 812*

real 4 pure, true 5 solid, valid 6 actual, honest 7 certain, factual, genuine, sincere 8 absolute, bona fide, positive, rightful, tangible, truthful 9 authentic, unalloyed, unfeigned, veracious, veritable 10 legitimate, unaffected 11 not affected, substantial, substantive, unvarnished 12 well-grounded 13 unadulterated 14 unquestionable

realistic 4 real 7 genuine, graphic, natural, precise 8 faithful, lifelike, truthful 9 authentic, depictive, objective, pragmatic 10 true-to-life 11 descriptive, down-to-earth 12 naturalistic 16 representational

reality 4 fact 5 truth 6 verity 9 actuality 11 materiality, tangibility 12 corporeality 14 substantiality 17 physical existence

realization 7 success 8 grasping 10 attainment, perception 11 achievement, culmination, fulfillment 12 appreciation, consummation 13 comprehension, understanding 14 accomplishment

realize 2 do 3 get, net 4 gain 5 clear, grasp 6 absorb, attain, fathom, gather, profit 7 achieve, acquire, cognize, discern, execute, fulfill, imagine, make out, perform, produce 8 carry out, complete, conceive, make good, perceive 9 actualize, apprehend, discharge, make money, penetrate, recognize 10 accomplish, appreciate, bring about, comprehend, consummate, effectuate, understand 11 bring to pass 12 carry through

realized 3 got 6 gained, netted, proved, proven 7 cleared, grasped, made out, saw into 8 absorbed, accepted, effected, executed, existing, fathomed, gathered, imagined, made good, profited 9 completed, conceived, discerned, fulfilled, perceived, performed 10 actualized, penetrated, recognized, understood 11 appreciated, apprehended, consummated, established 12 accomplished, comprehended

really 5 truly 6 indeed, in fact, surely, verily 8 actually 9 certainly, genuinely, literally, veritably 10 absolutely, positively, truthfully 13 categorically 14 unquestionably

realm 4 land 5 field, orbit, state 6 domain, empire, nation, region, sphere 7 country, demesne, kingdom 8 dominion, monarchy, province 11 royal domain

real McCoy, the 4 real 7 genuine 9 authentic 12 the real thing

reap 3 get, win 4 earn, gain 5 glean, score 6 derive, gather, obtain, profit, secure, take in 7 acquire, bring in, harvest, procure, realize

rear 3 aft, end 4 back, heel 5 after, nurse, raise, stern, train 6 dorsal, foster 7 bring up, care for, cherish, develop, educate, nurture, postern, tail end 8 back part, hind part, hindmost 9 aftermost, after part, at the back, cultivate, in the back, posterior

Rear Window director: 15 Alfred Hitchcock based on story by: 15 Cornell Woolrich cast: 10 Grace Kelly 11 Raymond Burr 12 James Stewart, Thelma Ritter, Wendell Corey

Rea Silvia also: 4 Ilia 10 Rhea Silvia form: 12 vestal virgin lover: 4 Mars son: 5 Remus 7 Romulus

reason 3 wit 4 head 5 cause, logic, sense, solve 6 acumen, brains, figure, motive, sanity 7 grounds, insight 8 lucidity, occasion 9 awareness, faculties, intellect, normality, rationale, reasoning 10 perception 11 common sense, discernment, exhortation, explanation, penetration, rationality 12 apprehension, intelligence, perspicacity, think through 13 argumentation, comprehension, justification, mental bal-

Reagan, Ronald Wilson
  nickname: 5 Dutch 6 Ronnie
  presidential rank: 8 fortieth
  party:
    current: 10 Republican
    former: 10 Democratic
  state represented: 2 CA
  defeated: 6 (James Earl) Carter (Jr) 7 (Walter Frederick "Fritz") Mondale 8 (John Bayard) Anderson
  vice president: 4 (George Herbert Walker) Bush
  cabinet:
    state: 4 (Alexander M) Haig (Jr) 6 (George P) Shultz
    treasury: 5 (Donald T) Regan
    defense: 10 (Caspar W) Weinberger
    attorney general: 5 (William French) Smith
    interior: 4 (James) Watt 5 (William P) Clark
    agriculture: 5 (John R) Block
    commerce: 8 (Malcolm) Baldrige
    labor: 7 (Raymond J) Donovan
    health and human services: 7 (Margaret M) Heckler 9 (Richard S) Schweiker
    education: 4 (Terrel H) Bell
    HUD: 6 (Samuel R) Pierce (Jr)
    transportation: 4 (Elizabeth H) Dole 5 (Andrew L) Lewis (Jr)
    energy: 5 (Donald P) Hodel 7 (James B) Edwards
  born: 9 Tampico IL
  education:
    College: 6 Eureka
  religion: 17 Disciples of Christ
  interests: 2 TV 5 track 6 movies 8 football 9 chops wood 10 basketball, jelly beans
    13 weightlifting 15 horseback riding
  vacation spot: 14 Rancho del Cielo (Santa Barbara CA)
  dog: 5 Lucky
  author: 18 Where Is the Rest of Me?
  political career:
    governor of: 10 California
  civilian career: 5 actor 17 radio sportscaster
    host: 15 Death Valley Days 22 General Electric Theater
    president of: 17 Screen Actors Guild
    roles: 8 King's Row 10 Brother Rat 13 John Loves Mary, The Hasty Heart 15 Bedtime for
      Bonzo 19 The Voice of the Turtle 20 Cattle Queen of Montana 21 The Girl from Jones
      Beach 22 Knute Rockne All American
  military service: 6 US Army 7 captain 10 World War II
  notable events of lifetime/term:
    approval of: 10 MX missiles
    assassination attempt on: 6 Reagan 14 Pope John Paul II
    attempted assassination on Reagan by: 15 John W Hinckley Jr
    bombing of: 5 Libya
    hostages freed in: 4 Iran
    invasion of: 7 Grenada
    marines sent to: 7 Lebanon
    nuclear disaster at: 9 Chernobyl
    Russians shot down: 14 Korean airliner
    scandal: 8 Irangate
  father: 10 John Edward
    nickname: 4 Jack
  mother: 5 Nelle (Wilson)
  siblings: 4 (John) Neil
  wife: 4 Jane (Wyman) 5 Nancy (Davis)
    Nancy Davis born: 18 Anne Frances Robbins
  children: 6 Ronald 7 Maureen, Michael (adopted) 8 Patricia
    Patricia also actress known as: 10 Patti Davis
  first lady:
    program: 9 Drug abuse, Just Say No 12 Alcohol abuse 18 Foster Grandparents

ance, understanding
15 clearheadedness

reasonable 4 fair, just, sage, sane, wise **5** sound **6** likely, proper **7** fitting, knowing, le-

nient, logical, natural, patient, prudent **8** credible, moderate, possible, probable, rational, sensible, suitable, thinking **9** equitable, impartial, judicious, objective, plausible,

temperate, tolerable **10** admissible, coolheaded, legitimate, not extreme, reflective, thoughtful **11** circumspect, intelligent, justifiable, levelheaded, not unlikely, of good sense, predictable, well-founded **12** not excessive, well-grounded **13** understanding **14** understandable **15** of sound judgment

reasonableness 5 logic **6** sanity, wisdom **8** fairness, prudence **9** good sense **10** moderation **11** credibility, objectivity, rationality **12** good judgment, impartiality, intelligence **13** judiciousness **14** circumspection, thoughtfulness **15** clearheadedness

reasonably 6 almost, fairly **8** passably, somewhat **10** moderately, more or less **13** approximately

reasoning 5 basis, logic **6** ground **7** thought **8** analysis, argument, thinking **9** deduction, inference, rationale **10** cogitation, reflection **11** penetration **13** ratiocination **14** interpretation

reason out 8 mull over **10** deliberate **12** think through

reassure 5 cheer **6** buoy up, uplift **7** bolster, comfort **8** inspirit **9** encourage **13** inspire hope in

reassured 6 buoyed **9** bolstered, comforted, heartened **10** emboldened, encouraged, inspirited

reassuring 7 hopeful **10** auspicious, comforting, heartening **11** encouraging

Reb 2 Mr **5** Rabbi **6** Mister

rebate 6 refund **8** discount **9** abatement

Rebecca
author: **15** Daphne du Maurier
character: **10** Jack Favell, Mrs Danvers (Danny) **12** Frank Crawley **13** Colonel Julyan, Maxim de Winter
house: **9** Manderley
director: **15** Alfred Hitchcock
cast: **10** Nigel Bruce **12** Joan Fontaine **13** George Sanders **14** Judith Anderson (Mrs Danvers) **15** Laurence Olivier (Maxim de Winter)
Oscar for: **7** picture

Rebecca
character in: **7** Ivanhoe
author: **5** Scott

Rebecca see **7** Rebekah

Rebecca of Sunnybrook Farm
author: **17** Kate Douglas Wiggin
character: **4** Cobb **8** Adam Ladd **11** Aunt Miranda

14 Rebecca Randall
15 Emma Jane Perkins

Rebekah
also: **7** Rebecca
father: **7** Bethuel
husband: **5** Isaac
brother: **5** Laban
son: **4** Esau **5** Isaac, Jacob

rebel 3 shy **4** riot **5** avoid, quail, react, wince **6** flinch, mutiny, recoil, revolt, rise up, shrink **7** seceder, traitor, upstart **8** deserter, maverick, resister, turncoat **9** anarchist, dissenter, insurgent **10** iconoclast, malcontent, separatist **12** secessionist **13** nonconformist, revolutionary, revolutionist **15** insurrectionist

rebellion 6 mutiny, putsch, revolt **8** defiance, sedition, upheaval, uprising **9** coup d'etat **10** insurgency, revolution **12** insurrection

rebellious 6 unruly **7** defiant **8** contrary, mutinous, up in arms **9** alienated, fractious, insurgent, seditious, truculent, turbulent **10** disorderly, pugnacious, refractory **11** disobedient, intractable, quarrelsome **12** contumacious, recalcitrant, ungovernable, unmanageable **13** insubordinate, revolutionary **14** uncontrollable **15** insurrectionary

rebelliousness 8 defiance **9** rebellion **12** disobedience

Rebel Without a Cause
director: **11** Nicholas Ray
cast: **8** Sal Mineo **9** James Dean, Jim Backus **11** Natalie Wood

Rebirth
god of: **4** Gwyn

rebound 3 bob **6** bounce, recoil, re-echo **7** flounce **8** recovery, ricochet **10** spring back

rebounding 7 rubbery, springy **9** resilient **11** ricocheting **12** bouncing back

rebuff 4 deny, snub **5** check, repel, spurn **6** ignore, put off, refuse, reject, slight **7** decline, put-down, refusal, repulse **8** turn down **9** disregard, rejection **10** putting off **12** cold shoulder **13** slap in the face **15** keep at a distance

rebuke 5 blame, chide, scold, score **6** berate **7** censure, chew out, chiding, lecture, reproof, reprove, upbraid **8** admonish, berating, call down, reproach, reproval, scolding **9** dress down, reprimand **10** admonition, chewing out, take to

task, upbraiding **11** castigation, disapproval **12** admonishment, dressing down, remonstrance, reprehension, take down a peg **13** find fault with, tongue-lashing **15** remonstrate with

rebuttal 5 reply **6** answer, denial, retort **7** defense, riposte **8** disproof, negation, response **9** disproval, rejoinder **10** refutation **11** confutation **12** counterreply, disagreement, surrejoinder **13** contradiction **15** counterargument

recalcitrant 5 balky **6** mulish, unruly **7** willful **8** contrary, stubborn **9** obstinate, pigheaded, unwilling **10** bullheaded, headstrong, refractory **11** disobedient, intractable **12** unsubmissive

recall 5 place **6** memory, revive **8** call back, remember **9** reanimate, recognize, recollect **10** reactivate, remobilize **11** reinstitute, remembrance **12** recollection **17** ability to remember

recant 4 deny **5** unsay **6** abjure, disown, recall, renege, repeal, revoke **7** disavow, rescind, retract **8** disclaim, forswear, renounce, take back, withdraw **9** foreswear, repudiate **10** apostatize **12** eat one's words **14** change one's mind

recantation 6 denial **9** disavowal **10** refutation, retraction, revocation **11** repudiation **12** renunciation

recapitulate 5 recap, sum up **6** relate, repeat, reword **7** recount, restate **8** rephrase **9** epitomize, reiterate, summarize **15** repeat in essence

recapture 6 retake **7** reprise **15** experience again

recede 3 ebb **5** abate **6** back up, go back, retire **7** regress, retreat, subside **10** retrogress

receipt 7 arrival, release, voucher **9** admission, discharge, receiving, reception **10** acceptance, admittance, possession, recipience **11** acquisition, transferral

receipts 3 pay **4** gain, gate, take **5** share, split, wages **6** income, recipe, return **7** formula, payment, profits, returns, revenue **8** earnings, proceeds **9** emolument **10** net profits **12** remuneration **13** reimbursement

receive 3 get **4** meet **5** admit, greet, put up **6** accept, come by, obtain, regard, secure, suffer, take in **7** acquire, adjudge, approve, be given, react to, sustain, undergo, welcome **8** meet with, submit to **9** encounter, entertain **10** experience **11** accommodate

receive willingly 6 accept **10** take gladly **16** accept with thanks **18** accept with open arms

receive with favor 6 praise **7** approve **10** appreciate

receive with open arms 6 invite **7** embrace, welcome **13** accept eagerly **19** roll out the red carpet

recent 3 new **4** late **5** fresh, novel **6** modern **8** up-to-date **9** latter-day **12** contemporary **13** up-to-the-minute

receptacle 3 bag, bin, box, can, jar **4** file, tray **6** basket, bottle, hamper, holder, hopper, vessel **7** carrier **8** receiver **9** container **10** depository, repository **11** compartment

reception 2 do **4** fete **5** party **6** affair, soiree **7** welcome **8** greeting **11** recognition **15** social gathering

receptive 8 amenable, friendly **10** accessible, hospitable, interested, open-minded, responsive **11** susceptible **12** approachable **17** favorably disposed

recess 3 bay, gap **4** bend, cell, cove, fold, gulf, lull, nook, pass, rest, slot **5** break, cleft, gorge, inlet, letup, niche, pause **6** alcove, corner, harbor, hiatus, hollow **7** holiday, interim, respite, time out **8** interval, vacation **9** interlude **10** pigeonhole **11** coffee break, indentation **12** intermission **14** breathing spell

recessed 4 sunk **6** paused, sunken **7** delayed **8** deferred, extended, indented **9** adjourned, dissolved, postponed, prolonged, withdrawn **10** terminated
  church wall: 5 ambry
  wall: 6 alcove

recesses 6 depths **10** inmost part, penetralia

recession 10 depression **11** recessional **16** economic downturn

recherche 4 rare **5** prize **6** choice, exotic, scarce, select, unique **7** special, unusual **8** original, superior, uncommon, valuable **9** different, priceless **10** one of a kind **11** exceptional

recipe 2 Rx **4** cure, rule **5** axiom **6** elixir, remedy **7** formula, receipt **12** instructions, prescription

recipient 4 heir **5** donee, taker **6** getter **7** legatee **8** accepter, acquirer, obtainer, receiver **9** presentee **11** beneficiary

reciprocal 6 common, linked, mutual, shared **8** returned **9** bilateral, exchanged, one for one **10** equivalent **11** give-and-take **12** interchanged, interrelated **13** complementary, corresponding, given in return **14** interdependent **15** interchangeable

reciprocate 4 feel **6** return **7** requite, respond **9** retaliate **10** make return **11** act likewise, give and take, interchange **12** give in return **19** return the compliment

reciprocity 8 exchange **11** give and take, interchange

recital 4 talk **6** report **7** concert, telling **8** delivery, reciting **9** discourse, narration, narrative, rendition **10** recitation **11** description, particulars, performance **12** dissertation, oral exercise **13** public reading **14** graphic account, recapitulation

recite 4 tell **5** quote, speak **6** relate, repeat **7** declaim, deliver, narrate, perform, recount **10** say by heart **11** communicate

reckless 4 rash, wild **5** giddy, hasty **6** daring, fickle, madcap, unwary **7** flighty, foolish, unaware **8** careless, cavalier, heedless, mindless, unsteady, volatile **9** daredevil, desperate, foolhardy, imprudent, impulsive, negligent, oblivious, unheeding, unmindful **10** incautious, indiscreet, insensible, neglectful, regardless, unthinking, unwatchful **11** harebrained, inattentive, precipitate, thoughtless, unconcerned **12** devil-may-care, unsolicitous **13** inconsiderate, irresponsible, uncircumspect **14** scatterbrained

recklessly 4 fast **5** blind **6** rashly, wildly **7** hastily **8** headlong **9** headfirst **10** carelessly, heedlessly **11** audaciously, desperately, impetuously, impulsively **12** unmindfully **13** irresponsibly, unconcernedly

recklessness 7 abandon **8** rashness **9** disregard, unconcern **10** imprudence, profli-

gacy **11** impetuosity **12** heedlessness, immoderation **13** foolhardiness **15** thoughtlessness **16** irresponsibility

reckon 3 add **4** bank, cope, deal, deem, plan, rank, rate **5** add up, class, count, fancy, guess, judge, tally, think, total, value **6** assess, decide, esteem, expect, figure, handle, regard **7** account, adjudge, balance, bargain, compute, imagine, presume, suppose, surmise **8** appraise, consider, estimate **9** calculate, determine, speculate

reckoning 3 tab **4** bill, doom **5** count, tally, total **6** adding, charge **7** account **8** estimate, judgment **9** appraisal, summation **10** estimation, evaluation **11** calculation, computation **13** final judgment **19** settling of an account

reclaim 6 reform, rescue **7** correct, recover, rectify, restore

recline 4 lean, loll, rest **6** lounge, repose, sprawl **7** lie back, lie down **12** take one's ease

reclining 7 lolling, resting **8** lounging, reposing **9** lying down, recumbent

recluse 3 nun **4** monk **5** crank, loner **6** hermit, hidden, secret **7** ascetic, eremite, erratic, oddball **8** cenobite, crackpot **9** eccentric **10** cloistered **11** sequestered **13** nonconformist

recognition 6 notice **9** discovery **10** acceptance, validation **13** comprehension, understanding **14** acknowledgment, identification **19** diplomatic relations

recognizable 5 clear, plain **8** distinct **10** detectable **11** discernable, perceivable, perceptible **12** identifiable, intelligible **13** ascertainable **14** comprehensible, understandable **15** distinguishable

recognizance 4 bond **6** pledge **10** obligation **11** recognition **15** acknowledgement

recognize 3 see **4** know, spot **5** admit, place, sight **7** discern, make out, pick out, realize, respect, yield to **8** identify, submit to **9** be aware of, concede to **10** appreciate, comprehend, understand **11** acknowledge **14** give the floor to

recognized 5 known **8** accepted, admitted, approved, familiar, realized **9** customary **10** accredited **11** traditional **12** acknowledged, conventional

recoil 4 fail, kick **5** blink, cower, demur, quail, shirk, start, wince **6** blench, cringe, falter, flinch, revolt **7** fly back, rebound, retreat **8** draw back, hang back, jump back **9** bound back **10** shrink back, spring back

recoil at 4 hate **5** abhor **6** detest, eschew, loathe **7** despise **9** abominate, shudder at **10** shrink from **12** be revolted by **14** view with horror **18** feel aversion toward

recoiling 7 wincing **9** flinching **10** rebounding **11** drawing back **13** shrinking back, springing back

recollect 5 place **6** recall **8** remember **10** call to mind

recollection 4 mind **6** memoir, memory, recall, record **11** remembrance **12** reminiscence **13** retrospection
French: **8** souvenir

recommend 4 urge **5** favor, order **6** advise **7** counsel, endorse, propose, suggest **8** advocate, vouch for **9** encourage, prescribe **10** put forward **11** speak well of

recommendable 9 advisable, favorable **10** worthwhile

recommendation 4 plug **6** behest, praise **8** approval, good word **9** reference **11** endorsement **12** commendation

recompense 3 pay **5** repay **6** return, reward **7** payment **9** reimburse, repayment **10** compensate, remunerate, reparation **12** compensation, remuneration **15** indemnification

reconcile 5 fix up **6** adjust, make up, resign, settle, square **7** correct, patch up, rectify, reunite, win over **8** persuade **9** harmonize **10** conciliate, propitiate **11** set straight

reconcile oneself 6 submit **9** acquiesce **13** resign oneself

reconciliation 8 fixing up, making up, settling, squaring **10** adjustment, correction, patching up, rectifying **11** resignation, winning over **12** conciliation **13** justification, rectification **15** setting straight

recondite 4 deep **6** arcane, hidden **7** obscure **8** abstruse, esoteric **9** concealed **10** mysterious **16** incomprehensible

reconnaissance 6 survey **7** viewing **8** scouting, scrutiny **10** inspection **11** exploration, observation **12** surveillance **13** investigation **14** reconnoitering

reconnoiter 4 look **5** probe, scout **6** patrol, picket, survey **7** examine **8** remember, traverse

reconsider 5 amend **6** modify, ponder, review, revise **7** correct, rethink, sleep on **8** mull over, reassess **9** reexamine, think over **10** reevaluate **13** think better of **15** think twice about

reconstitute 7 restore **9** recompose **10** add water to **11** reconstruct

reconstruct 7 rebuild **8** make over, recreate **10** reassemble **11** reestablish **12** reconstitute

record 3 log **4** copy, file, list, memo, note, post, show, tape **5** admit, enter **6** annals, career, docket, enroll, report **7** account, archive, catalog, conduct, history, jot down, jotting, journal **8** document, indicate, register, take down **9** chronicle, introduce, write down **10** adventures, background, memorandum, transcribe **11** experiences, make an entry, performance, proceedings **12** unbeaten mark **14** top performance
French: **11** compte rendu

record
invented by: **4** Bell **6** Edison **7** Tainter **8** Berliner **10** Goldenmark

recount 4 tell **6** detail, recite, relate **7** explain, narrate **8** describe **9** count over

recoup 5 atone **6** redeem, regain **7** recover, replace **8** make good, retrieve **9** make up for, reacquire **13** make amends for

recourse 6 choice, option, resort **11** alternative, other choice

recover 4 heal, mend **5** rally **6** offset, pick up, recoup, redeem, regain, retake, revive **7** balance, get back, get well, improve, reclaim, restore, win back **8** make good, retrieve, revivify **9** make up for, reacquire, recapture, reconquer, repossess **10** come around, compensate, convalesce, recuperate, rejuvenate **11** pull through, resuscitate

recovery 4 cure **5** rally **6** recoup, rescue, upturn **7** revival, salvage **8** comeback **9** retrieval **10** betterment, regain-

ment **11** improvement, reclamation, reformation, restoration **12** recuperation **13** business cycle, convalescence

recreancy 8 apostasy **9** cowardice, desertion **10** cravenness, disloyalty, infidelity **13** faithlessness, pusillanimity **14** unfaithfulness

recreant 6 coward, craven, yellow **8** apostate, cowardly, deserter, disloyal, renegade **9** undutiful **10** unfaithful **11** lily-livered **12** dishonorable **13** pusillanimous, yellow-bellied

recreation 4 play **5** hobby, sport **7** pastime **9** amusement, avocation, diversion **10** relaxation **13** entertainment **15** leisure activity

recrimination 5 blame **6** charge **10** accusation **13** countercharge

recruit 4 hire **5** raise, renew **6** employ, enlist, enroll, muster, novice, recoup, revive, rookie **7** draftee, provide, recover, restore **8** beginner, newcomer **9** conscript **10** recuperate

rectangle 3 box **6** oblong, square **7** polygon **10** quadrangle **13** parallelogram, quadrilateral

rectangular 4 long **6** square **7** boxlike **11** right-angled **12** quadrangular **13** quadrilateral

rectification 6 fixing, reform **7** redress **8** righting, squaring **9** remedying, repairing **10** adjustment, correction, regulation **12** setting right **15** putting straight, putting to rights **16** straightening out

rectify 3 fix **4** cure, mend **5** amend, emend, focus, right **6** adjust, attune, reform, remedy, repair, revise, square **7** correct, redress **8** put right, regulate, set right **9** make right **10** straighten

rectitude 5 honor **7** decency, probity **8** morality **9** integrity, principle **11** uprightness **12** virtuousness **13** righteousness **14** high-mindedness **15** trustworthiness **16** incorruptibility **17** irreproachability

rector 6 cleric, parson, pastor, priest **8** minister, preacher **9** churchman, clergyman **12** ecclesiastic

recumbent 4 flat **5** prone **6** supine **7** leaning **8** couchant **9** lying down, prostrate, reclining **10** horizontal **12** stretched out

recuperate 4 heal, mend **7** get well, improve, recover **8** come back **9** get better **10** come around, convalesce **11** be on the mend, pull through **14** return to health **16** regain one's health

recuperation 8 recovery **11** restoration **13** convalescence

recuperative 11 restorative **15** health-restoring

recur 6 repeat, resume, return **7** persist **8** come back, continue, reappear **9** come again **10** occur again

recurrence 5 cycle, round **6** repeat, return **7** relapse, renewal, reprise, routine **8** iterance, rotation **10** continuity, repetition **11** periodicity **12** reappearance

recurrent 7 regular **8** frequent, periodic **9** recurring, repeating **10** repetitive **11** reappearing **12** intermittent **14** appearing again

red 4 pink, rose, rosy, ruby, wine **5** aglow, coral, flame, ruddy **6** auburn, cherry, florid, maroon **7** burning, crimson, flaming, flushed, glowing, scarlet **8** blooming, blushing, cardinal, inflamed, reddened, rubicund **9** rubescent, vermilion **12** blood-colored

Red and the Black, The (Le Rouge et le Noir)
   author: **8** Stendhal
   character: **6** Fouque **8** M de Renal **11** Julien Sorel **16** Mathilde de la Mole

Red Badge of Courage, The
   author: **12** Stephen Crane
   character: **6** Wilson **10** Jim Conklin **12** Henry Fleming

red-blooded 5 lusty, peppy, vital **6** ardent, robust, strong, sturdy **7** dynamic, intense **8** forceful, powerful, spirited, vigorous **9** energetic **10** hot-blooded, passionate

Red Branch
   origin: **5** Irish
   warriors of: **9** Conchobar

Redburn
   author: **14** Herman Melville

red-cheeked 4 rosy **5** ruddy **6** robust **8** blushing **12** apple-cheeked

Red Cross Knight
   character in: **15** The Faerie Queene
   author: **7** Spenser

redden 4 burn, glow **5** blush, color, flame, flush **9** go crimson **12** become florid

reddish 4 rosy, ruby **5** ruddy, rufus **6** flushy, rufous **7** roseate **8** rubicund

reddish-brown 4 rust **5** henna **6** auburn, copper, russet, sienna **8** chestnut, cinnamon

Red Earth People see **3** Fox

redeem 4 keep, save **5** cover **6** defray, ransom, recoup, reform, regain, rescue, settle **7** buy back, convert, fulfill, reclaim, recover, satisfy **8** atone for, make good, retrieve **9** discharge, make up for, repossess **10** evangelize, repurchase

redeemed 5 saved **7** claimed, rescued **8** made good, ransomed, reformed **9** atoned for, delivered, fulfilled, recovered **10** carried out, regenerate **11** repossessed

redemption 6 excuse, pardon, ransom, reform, rescue **7** salvage **8** recovery **9** amendment, atonement, exemption, expiation, salvation **10** conversion **11** deliverance, reformation

Redford, Robert
   real name: **20** Charles Robert Redford
   born: **13** Santa Monica CA
   roles: **8** The Sting **10** The Natural **11** Legal Eagles **12** The Candidate, The Way We Were **13** Downhill Racer **14** The Great Gatsby **15** Jeremiah Johnson **17** Barefoot in the Park **19** All the President's Men **20** Three Days of the Condor **29** Butch Cassidy and the Sundance Kid
   director: **14** Ordinary People (Oscar)

Redgrave, Lynn
   born: **6** London **7** England
   father: **18** Sir Michael Redgrave
   sister: **15** Vanessa Redgrave
   roles: **10** Georgy Girl **14** The Happy Hooker

Redgrave, Sir Michael
   born: **7** Bristol, England
   daughter: **4** Lynn **7** Vanessa
   roles: **11** Dan Peggotty **15** The Lady Vanishes **16** David Copperfield **22** Mourning Becomes Electra **27** The Importance of Being Earnest

Redgrave, Vanessa
   born: **6** London **7** England
   father: **18** Sir Michael Redgrave
   sister: **12** Lynn Redgrave

   husband: **14** Tony Richardson
   roles: **5** Julia, Yanks **6** Agatha, Blow-Up, Morgan **7** Camelot, Isadora **9** Guinevere **16** Mary Queen of Scots **17** The Lady from the Sea

red-hot 5 aglow, fiery **6** heated, raging **7** blazing, burning, glowing, intense **12** all-consuming

red-letter 5 happy, lucky **6** banner **10** auspicious, felicitous

redness 4 glow **5** blush, flush **8** rosiness **9** ruddiness **10** floridness

redolence 5 aroma, savor **7** bouquet **9** fragrance, good smell **12** pleasant odor

redolent 5 balmy, spicy **6** savory, smelly **7** mindful, odorous, reeking, scented **8** aromatic, fragrant, perfumed, stinking **9** evocative, odiferous **10** expressive, indicative, suggestive **11** odoriferous, reminiscent **13** sweet-smelling

Redon, Odilon
   born: **6** France **8** Bordeaux
   artwork: **10** In the Dream, The Cyclops **11** Le Vieil Ange **13** Flowers of Evil **15** Violette Heymann

redouble 7 augment, magnify **8** heighten, multiply **9** intensify

redoubtable 7 awesome **8** alarming, imposing **10** formidable **11** illustrious **12** awe-inspiring

redound 4 lead, tend **5** cause, surge **6** abound **7** conduce, incline **8** overflow **10** contribute **11** reverberate

redress 4 ease **5** amend, right **6** amends, reform, relief, remedy **7** correct, payment, rectify, relieve **8** easement, set right **9** make up for **10** recompense, reparation **11** restitution **12** compensation, satisfaction **13** compensate for, rectification **15** indemnification **18** make retribution for

Red River
   director: **11** Howard Hawks
   cast: **9** Joanne Dru, John Wayne **11** John Ireland **13** Walter Brennan **15** Montgomery Clift

Red Rover, The
   author: **19** James Fenimore Cooper

Reds
   director: **12** Warren Beatty
   cast: **11** Diane Keaton

(Louise Bryant), Paul Sorvino **12** Warren Beatty (John Reed) **13** Jack Nicholson, Jerzy Kosinski **14** Edward Herrmann **16** Maureen Stapleton
Oscar for: 8 director **17** supporting actress (Stapleton)

Red Shoes, The
author: 21 Hans Christian Andersen
director: 13 Michael Powell **17** Emeric Pressburger
cast: 12 Marius Goring, Moira Shearer **13** Anton Walbrook **14** Robert Helpmann

Red Skelton Show, The
character: 8 Gertrude **10** Heathcliff **13** Mean Widdle Kid **14** San Fernando Red, Sheriff Deadeye, Willie Lump-Lump **16** Bolivar Shagnasty **17** Cauliflower McPugg **18** Clem Kadiddlehopper **20** Freddie the Freeloader
saying: 7 I dood it
closing line: 8 God bless

Red Sky at Morning
author: 15 Richard Bradford

reduce 3 cut **4** bust, curb, diet, dull, ease, thin **5** abate, blunt, break, check, force, lower, slash, water **6** damage, demote, dilute, lessen, retard, soften, temper, weaken **7** assuage, atrophy, cripple, cut down, leave in **8** diminish, discount, enfeeble, mark down, minimize, mitigate, moderate, modulate, slim down, slow down, tone down, trim down **9** bring down, checkmate, undermine **10** debilitate, devitalize, slenderize **11** lower in rank **12** incapacitate

reduced form 6 digest **7** summary **9** short form **11** abridgement, contraction **12** abbreviation, condensation

reduce speed 4 slow **5** brake **6** rein in **8** slow down **10** decelerate

reduce to nothing 5 erase **7** abolish, destroy, wipe out **8** lay waste **9** eradicate, liquidate **10** annihilate **11** exterminate

reductio ad absurdum
22 reduction to an absurdity

reduction 3 cut **5** break **8** decrease, discount **9** abatement, lessening **10** concession **11** abridgement, subtraction

reduction to an absurdity
Latin: 18 reductio ad absurdum

redundancy 6 excess **7** surplus **8** verbiage **9** tautology **10** repetition **11** diffuseness, superfluity **13** overabundance **14** circumlocution, repetitiveness

redundant 5 extra **6** excess **7** surplus **10** pleonastic **11** dispensable, inessential, overflowing, repetitious, superfluous, unnecessary **12** tautological **13** superabundant

redwood 19 Adenanthera pavonina, Sequoia sempervirens
varieties: 4 dawn **5** coast, giant **7** Madeira

reed
varieties: 3 bur **4** vine **5** Burma, giant **6** common **14** Mauritania vine

reed 9 six cubits

Reed, Sir Carol
director of: 6 Oliver (Oscar) **11** The Third Man

Reed, Walter S
field: 12 bacteriology
discovered cause of: 11 yellow fever

reef 3 bar **4** bank, flat, spit **5** shelf, shoal **7** sandbar, shallow

reek 4 fume **5** smell, smoke, steam, stink **6** stench **7** give off **9** effluvium, emanation

reel 4 rock, roll, spin, sway **5** lurch, pitch, swirl, waver, whirl **6** rotate, teeter, totter, wobble **7** revolve, stagger, stumble

reeling 5 dizzy, giddy, shaky **6** whirly **8** spinning, unsteady **10** staggering **11** vertiginous

Reese, Harold
nickname: 6 Pee Wee
sport: 8 baseball
position: 9 shortstop
team: 15 Brooklyn Dodgers

Reeve
character in: 18 The Canterbury Tales
author: 7 Chaucer

Reeve, Christopher
born: 9 New York NY
roles: 8 Superman **9** Deathtrap **13** The Bostonians **15** Somewhere in Time

refer 2 go **4** cite, send, turn **6** advert, allude, direct, submit **7** consult, deliver, mention **8** hand over, transfer, transmit **9** pass along

referee 5 judge **6** decree, settle, umpire **7** arbiter, mediate **8** judgment, mediator, moderate **9** arbitrate, determine, intercede, intervene, moderator,

pronounce **10** adjudicate, arbitrator **11** adjudicator, intercessor **12** intermediary

reference 4 hint **7** inkling, mention **8** allusion, good word, innuendo **10** deposition, intimation, suggestion **11** affirmation, credentials, endorsement, implication, testimonial **13** certification **14** recommendation

reference book 5 atlas, bible **6** manual **9** guidebook **10** dictionary **12** encyclopedia

refine 6 filter, purify, strain **7** cleanse, develop, improve, perfect, process **9** cultivate

refined 5 clean, suave **6** gentle, polite, urbane **7** courtly, elegant, genteel **8** cleansed, cultured, delicate, finished, graceful, ladylike, mannerly, polished, purified, well-bred **9** civilized, clarified, courteous **10** cultivated, fastidious **11** gentlemanly **14** discriminating

refinement 5 grace **6** finish, nicety, polish, step up **7** advance, culture, dignity, finesse, suavity **8** breeding, civility, cleaning, courtesy, delicacy, elegance, fineness, revision, urbanity **9** amendment, cleansing, gentility, propriety **10** betterment, filtration, gentleness, politeness **11** advancement, cultivation, development, discernment, enhancement, good manners, improvement, progression, savoir faire, step forward **12** amelioration, distillation, graciousness, purification, tastefulness **13** courteousness, rectification **14** discrimination, fastidiousness

refitting 8 adapting **10** adaptation, remodeling **11** reequipping, resupplying

reflect 4 cast, copy, muse, show, undo **5** image, study, think, throw **6** betray, evince, expose, mirror, ponder, reason, return, reveal **7** condemn, display, exhibit, express, imitate, present, rebound, uncover **8** cogitate, consider, disclose, give back, indicate, manifest, meditate, mull over, register, ruminate, send back, set forth **9** bring upon, cerebrate, dwell upon, represent, reproduce, speculate, throw back, undermine **10** deliberate **11** concentrate, contemplate, demonstrate

reflection 4 blot, idea, slur, view **5** image, study **6** insult, musing, notion **7** opinion, re-

proof, thought **8** reproach, thinking **9** attention, pondering, sentiment **10** cogitation, conviction, derogation, impression, imputation, meditation, rumination **11** cerebration, insinuation, mirror image, pensiveness **12** deliberation **13** concentration, consideration, disparagement
French: **6** pensee

reflective 7 pensive **8** thinking **9** judicious, pondering **10** meditative, ruminative, thoughtful **11** speculative **13** contemplative

Reflex
author: **11** Dick Francis

reform 4 mend **5** amend, atone, emend **6** better, remedy, repair, repent, revise **7** convert, correct, improve, rebuild, rectify, remodel, restore **8** progress **9** amendment **10** correction **12** mend one's ways, rehabilitate **13** rectification **16** set straight again, turn over a new leaf

reformation 6 change, reform **9** amendment, reforming **10** alteration, conversion **11** improvement **12** modification **14** reorganization

refractory 5 balky **6** mulish, unruly **7** restive, wayward, willful **8** contrary, stubborn **9** fractious, obstinate, pigheaded **10** rebellious **11** disobedient, intractable **12** unmanageable

refrain 5 avoid, forgo **6** desist, eschew, forego, refuse, resist **7** abstain, forbear, hold off **8** leave off, renounce **11** curb oneself, keep oneself **12** stay one's hand **15** restrain oneself

refrain from 5 avoid, forgo **6** desist, eschew, forego **7** abstain, forbear **8** leave off, renounce

refresh 3 jog **4** prod **5** brace, renew, rouse **6** arouse, awaken, prompt, revive, stir up, vivify **7** cool off, freshen, quicken, recruit, restore **8** activate, energize, recreate **9** reanimate, stimulate **10** invigorate, rejuvenate, strengthen

refreshed 7 revived **8** animated, restored, vivified **9** enlivened, freshened **11** invigorated

refreshing 7 bracing **11** revivifying **12** invigorating **13** strengthening **15** thirst-quenching

refreshment 4 bite, eats **5** drink, snack **6** bracer **7** potable **8** beverage, cocktail, pick-me-up, potation **9** appetizer, drinkable, refresher **10** recreation, relaxation **11** hors d'oeuvre, nourishment, restoration, restorative **12** food and drink, invigoration, rejuvenation **14** reinvigoration, thirst quencher

refrigerate 4 cool **5** chill **6** freeze **7** congeal **8** keep cold, keep cool, put on ice **9** keep on ice

Refrigerator, The
nickname of: **12** William Perry

refuge 4 home **5** haven **6** asylum, harbor, resort **7** hideout, retreat, shelter **8** safehold **9** anchorage, harborage, sanctuary **10** protection **12** port in a storm **14** help in distress, place of shelter

refugee 2 DP **5** exile **6** bolter, eloper, emigre **7** escapee, evacuee, runaway **8** emigrant, fugitive **9** absconder **10** expatriate **15** displaced person

refulgent 6 bright, lucent **7** glowing, lambent, radiant, shining **8** luminous, relucent **9** brilliant

refund 5 remit, repay **6** rebate, return **7** pay back **9** reimburse, repayment **10** recompense, remittance, remunerate **12** amount repaid **13** give back money, reimbursement **18** make restitution for **19** make compensation for

refurbish 4 mend, redo **5** clean, fix up, renew **6** repair, tidy up **7** freshen, improve, remodel, restore **8** overhaul, renovate, spruce up **11** recondition

refusal 2 no **3** nay **4** veto **6** denial **7** regrets **8** turndown **9** declining, rejection **10** nonconsent **11** declination, disapproval **13** nonacceptance, noncompliance, unwillingness

refuse 2 no **4** deny, junk, veto **5** spurn, trash, waste **6** forbid, litter, reject **7** decline, garbage, rubbish, say no to **8** disallow, prohibit, turn down, withhold

refuse pile 4 dump **6** midden **11** rubbish heap

refuse to submit 4 defy **5** rebel **6** resist **7** disobey, hold out, violate **10** transgress **12** fail to comply

refutation 4 veto **6** denial **7** counter **8** negation, rebuttal **9** disavowal **11** confutation, repudiation **12** invalidation **13** contradiction

refutatory 8 contrary, opposing **10** discrepant **11** conflicting, disagreeing **12** antithetical, inconsistent **13** contradictory **14** countervailing, irreconcilable

refute 4 deny **5** rebut **6** answer **7** confute, counter **8** disprove **9** challenge **10** contradict, invalidate **12** give the lie to

regain 6 recoup, redeem, retake **7** get back, reclaim, recover, win back **8** gain anew, get again, retrieve **9** recapture, repossess

regal 5 grand, noble, proud, royal **6** august, kingly, lordly **7** queenly, stately **8** imposing, kinglike, majestic, princely, splendid **9** queenlike **10** princelike **11** magnificent **13** splendiferous

regale 3 ply **4** fete **5** amuse, feast **6** divert, please **7** banquet, delight, lionize **8** enthrall **9** entertain **10** serve nobly **11** wine and dine **15** feed sumptuously

Regan
character in: **8** King Lear
author: **11** Shakespeare

regard 3 eye, see **4** care, heed, hold, mind, note, rate, scan, view **5** judge, point, think, value, watch **6** accept, admire, aspect, behold, detail, esteem, follow, gaze at, look at, matter, notice, reckon, survey, take in **7** account, believe, concern, put down, respect, set down, subject, thought **8** consider, estimate, listen to, look upon, look up to, note well, relation **9** attention, hearken to, reference **10** admiration, connection, estimation, meditation, reflection, scrutinize **11** contemplate, observation, think well of **12** appreciation **13** cast the eyes on, consideration, think highly of **14** pay attention to

regardful 5 civil **6** polite **7** mindful **8** reverent **9** courteous, observant **10** respectful **11** deferential, reverential

regard highly 6 admire, esteem **7** respect **10** appreciate

regarding 4 in re **5** about, anent **7** apropos **10** concerning, respecting

regardless 6 anyhow, anyway **10** for all that **11** nonetheless **12** nevertheless **15** notwithstanding **19** in spite of everything

regard with repugnance
4 hate **5** abhor **6** detest, loathe **7** despise **8** execrate **9** abominate, can't stand, shudder at **10** recoil from, shrink from **11** can't stomach **12** be revolted by **13** be nauseated by, find repulsive **18** feel aversion toward

regard with suspicion
5 doubt **7** suspect **8** distrust, mistrust, question

regenerate 5 renew **6** redeem, reform, revive, uplift **7** restore **8** inspirit, reawaken, retrieve, revivify **9** enlighten, resurrect **10** rejuvenate **11** resuscitate **12** generate anew **13** give new life to, make a new man of

regent 4 king **5** queen, ruler **8** governor **9** protecter, protector

regime 4 rule **5** power, reign **7** command, control, dynasty **8** dominion **9** direction **10** government, leadership, management **12** jurisdiction **14** administration

regimen 4 diet, rule **6** system **10** government

regimentation 5 order, rigor **6** method, system **7** control, regimen **9** orthodoxy **10** discipline, regulation, uniformity **12** rigorousness **13** methodization **19** doctrinaire approach

Regiment of Women
author: **12** Thomas Berger

Regin
origin: **12** Scandinavian
mentioned in: **8** Volsunga
brother: **6** Fafnir
raised: **6** Sigurd

region 4 area, land, zone **5** field, range, realm, space, tract **6** domain, sphere **7** country, expanse **8** district, locality, province, vicinity **9** territory **12** neighborhood

regional 5 areal, local, zonal **7** dialect **10** locational, provincial **11** territorial **12** geographical

register 3 log **4** dial, mark, roll, show **5** diary, gauge, meter, range, scale **6** betray, enlist, enroll, heater, ledger, record, sign up **7** betoken, check in, compass, counter, daybook, exhibit, express, logbook, point to, portray, set down **8** disclose, heat duct, heat vent, indicate, manifest, note down, radiator, recorder, registry, take down **9** indica-

tor, write down **10** calculator, heat outlet, hot-air vent, record book **12** put in writing

Regius 16 Greek unical codex

regnat populus 16 let the people rule
motto of: **8** Arkansas

regress 3 ebb **4** back, exit, fall **6** go back, recede, return, revert **7** relapse, retreat, reverse **8** fall back, pass back, withdraw **9** backslide **10** lose ground, retrogress **11** deteriorate **12** move backward

regressive 8 backward **9** declining, worsening **10** retrograde **13** retrogressive

regret 3 rue, woe **4** moan **5** grief, mourn, qualm **6** bemoan, bewail, lament, repent, sorrow, twinge **7** anguish, apology, deplore, eat crow, remorse, scruple **8** be rueful, grieve at, weep over **9** apologies, grievance, heartache, rue the day **10** be sorry for, contrition, repentance, ruefulness **11** be ashamed of, compunction, lamentation, reservation **12** be remorseful, eat humble pie, eat one's words, self-reproach **13** feel sorrow for, regretfulness, second thought **14** disappointment, feel remorse for, remorsefulness **15** dissatisfaction **16** feel distress over, pang of conscience, self-condemnation

regretful 6 rueful **8** contrite **9** sorrowful **10** apologetic, remorseful **15** self-reproachful

regrettable 6 woeful **7** unhappy **8** grievous, pitiable **10** calamitous, deplorable, lamentable **11** unfortunate

regular 3 set **4** even, fine, real **5** daily, fixed, plain, usual **6** common, normal, proper, smooth, steady, trusty **7** classic, correct, genuine, habitue, natural, typical, uniform **8** absolute, accepted, complete, constant, everyday, faithful, familiar, frequent, habitual, loyalist, ordinary, orthodox, periodic, stalwart, standard, thorough, true blue **9** customary, recurrent, recurring, unvarying **10** consistent, dependable, invariable, periodical, unchanging **11** commonplace, down-to-earth, established, old reliable, symmetrical, undeviating **12** well-balanced **16** well-proportioned

regulate 3 fix **5** guide **6** adjust, direct, govern, handle, manage **7** balance, control, monitor, oversee, rectify

8 moderate, modulate, organize **9** supervise **10** regularize **11** superintend

regulation 4 rule **5** edict, order **6** decree **7** command, control, dictate, statute **8** handling **9** adjusting, direction, ordinance **10** adjustment **11** commandment **13** standing order

regulator 5 guide **7** manager **8** director, governor, overseer **9** moderator, modulator **10** adjustment, supervisor **14** superintendent **15** adjusting device

regurgitate 4 barf **5** vomit **7** throw up **8** disgorge

rehabilitate 3 fix **4** save **6** redeem, remake **7** restore, salvage **8** make over, readjust, renovate **9** reeducate, refurbish, reinstate **11** recondition, reconstruct, resocialize, set straight **13** straighten out **16** restore to society

rehash 6 repeat, retell, reword **7** restate **8** rephrase **9** iteration, rechauffe

rehearsal 5 drill, recap **6** tryout **7** hearing, reading, test run **8** audition, exercise, practice, trial run **9** polishing **10** perfecting, repetition, runthrough **11** preparation, reiteration, walk-through **14** recapitulation

rehearse 5 drill, ready, train **6** go over, polish, recite, relate, repeat, retell **7** narrate, prepare, recount **8** practice **9** reiterate **10** run through **13** read one's lines **14** give a recital of, study one's lines

Rehoboam
father: **7** Solomon
mother: **6** Naamah
son: **6** Abijah

Rehoboth
founder: **6** Nimrod

Reich, Charles
author of: **20** The Greening of America

Reichsfuhrer 11 Reich leader
chief of: **8** SS troops

reign 4 rule **6** govern, regime, regnum, tenure **7** command **8** dominion, hold sway, regnancy, tutelage **9** dominance, influence **10** government, incumbency **11** sovereignty, supervision **12** wear the crown **13** hold authority **14** have royal power, sit on the throne **15** occupy the throne **17** exercise authority **19** exercise sovereignty
Hindu: **3** raj

reign over 4 rule **6** govern **7** command, control **8** dominate

reimburse 5 pay up, remit, repay **6** rebate, refund **7** pay back **8** square up **9** indemnify **10** compensate, recompense, remunerate **15** make restitution

reimbursement 6 refund **9** indemnity, repayment **12** compensation, remuneration

rein, reins 4 curb, hold **5** check, limit, watch **6** bridle **7** control, harness **8** hold back, restrict, suppress **9** restraint **11** keep an eye on

Reiner, Carl
born: 7 Bronx NY
son: 9 Rob Reiner
roles: 15 Your Show of Shows **21** It's a Mad Mad Mad Mad World
created: 15 Dick Van Dyke Show
director: 5 Oh God **7** The Jerk **8** The Comic **11** Where's Poppa?
novel: 13 Enter Laughing

Reiner, Rob
father: 10 Carl Reiner
roles: 8 Meathead **10** Mike Stivik **14** All in the Family

reinforce 4 prop **5** steel **7** bolster, brace up, fortify, support **8** buttress **10** strengthen **12** make stronger

reinforcement 4 stay **5** brace, strut **7** bracing, support **10** assistance **11** buttressing **13** strengthening

reinstate 5 renew **6** revive **7** readmit, restore **11** reestablish, reinstitute, reintroduce

reinstatement 7 renewal, revival **11** restoration **13** reinstitution **14** reintroduction **15** reestablishment

reintroduce 6 revive **8** recreate **9** reinstate **11** reestablish, reinstitute

reintroduction 7 revival **10** recreation **11** restoration **13** reinstatement **15** reestablishment

reiterate 5 resay **6** hammer, rehash, repeat, retell, reword, stress **7** iterate, reprise, restate **8** rephrase **11** pound away at **12** recapitulate **13** go over and over

reject 4 deny **5** repel, spurn **6** rebuff, refuse **7** castoff, decline, discard, disdain, dismiss, flotsam, repulse, say no to **8** castaway, disallow, shrug

off, turn down, turn from **9** repudiate

rejected 6 denied, dumped, jilted **7** cast off, outcast, refused, spurned, unloved **8** disowned, forsaken, lovelorn **9** abandoned, discarded, disproved **10** unaccepted, repudiated **11** invalidated

rejection 6 rebuff **7** disdain, refusal **8** scorning, spurning **9** declining, dismissal, rebuffing, rejecting, ruling out

rejoice 5 exult, glory, revel **6** be glad **7** be happy, delight **8** be elated, jubilate **9** be pleased, celebrate, make merry **10** exhilarate, sing for joy **11** be delighted, be overjoyed **13** be transported

rejoice in 5 eat up, enjoy, savor **6** relish **7** revel in **9** delight in **13** be pleased with, get a kick out of **14** take pleasure in

rejoicing 5 mirth **6** gaiety **7** delight, ecstasy, elation, jollity, jubilee, revelry, triumph **8** cheering, gladness, pleasure, reveling **9** festivity, good cheer, happiness, jubilance, merriment **10** exultation, joyfulness, jubilation, liveliness **11** celebration, merrymaking

rejoin 6 answer, retort **7** respond

rejoinder 5 reply **6** answer, retort, return **7** riposte **8** backtalk, comeback, rebuttal, repartee, response **10** refutation **11** surrebuttal **12** counterblast, remonstrance, surrejoinder **13** countercharge **16** counterstatement

rejuvenate 6 revive **7** restore **8** revivify **9** reanimate **10** revitalize **12** reinvigorate **14** put new life into **17** make youthful again

relapse 4 fall **5** lapse **6** revert, worsen **7** decline, regress, reverse **8** fall back, sink back, slip back, turn back **9** backslide, reversion, worsening **10** degenerate, recurrence, regression, retrogress **11** backsliding, falling back **13** deterioration, retrogression **15** return to illness, turn for the worse

relate 3 say **4** link, tell **5** apply, refer, speak, state, utter **6** attach, belong, convey, detail, impart, recite, report, reveal **7** concern, connect, divulge, narrate, pertain, recount **8** describe, disclose **9** appertain, associate, feel close, make known **10** be rele-

vant **11** communicate, have rapport **12** be responsive, interact well, recapitulate **13** be sympathetic, have reference, particularize **15** feel empathy with, give an account of

related 3 kin **4** akin, said, told **7** kindred, recited **8** narrated, reported **9** recounted **15** of the same family

related by blood 3 kin **4** akin **7** kindred **14** consanguineous, of the same stock **21** having a common ancestor

relation 3 kin, tie **4** bond, link **5** tie-in **6** regard, report **7** account, bearing, concern, kinsman, recital, telling, version **8** relative **9** narrating, narration, narrative, reference, relevance, retelling **10** connection, pertinence, recitation **11** affiliation, application, association, correlation, description **13** applicability, communication **17** interrelationship

relationship 3 kin **5** blood, union **6** affair **7** kindred, kinship, liaison, sibship, society **8** affinity, alliance **10** connection **11** affiliation, association, correlation **13** consanguinity

relative 3 kin **4** clan, kith **5** blood, folks, tribe **6** allied, cousin, family, people **7** cognate, germane, kinfolk, kinsman, related **8** relation, relevant **9** connected, dependent, kinswoman, pertinent, referable **10** affiliated, applicable, associated, comparable, connection, connective, correlated, kith and kin, pertaining, relational, respective **11** appropriate, comparative, correlative, not absolute **12** interrelated **13** flesh and blood **14** interconnected

relax 4 bend, calm, ease, idle, laze, loaf, rest **5** let up, slack **6** be idle, be lazy, ease up, loosen, soften, soothe, unbend, unwind **7** cool off, holiday, make lax, slacken **8** decrease, loosen up, vacation **9** lie around **10** take it easy **12** enjoy oneself **13** make less tense **14** make less severe, make less strict

relaxation 3 fun **5** games, hobby, sport **6** repose **7** bending, leisure, pastime **8** pleasure **9** abatement, amusement, avocation, diversion, enjoyment, loosening, remission **10** recreation, slackening **11** refreshment **12** rest from work **13** entertainment

relaxed 3 lax **4** calm, cool,

easy, slow, soft **5** loose, slack **6** at ease, casual, gentle, remiss **7** flaccid, lenient **8** informal, laid back, unstrict **9** easygoing, leisurely, negligent, nerveless, unnervous **10** unstrained **11** free and easy, thoughtless
French: 6 degage

relaxed manner 4 ease **5** poise **6** aplomb **9** composure **10** confidence **11** naturalness **12** unconstraint **14** unaffectedness

relay 3 leg **4** race, tour **5** shift **6** length **8** transfer, transmit **9** conductor, regulator, satellite **10** retransmit
cylinder: 5 baton
part: 8 armature, receiver **11** transmitter **13** electromagnet
race: 6 medley **10** track event

release 4 free **5** let go, loose, untie **6** detach, let out, unbind **7** freeing, present, relieve, set free, unloose **8** liberate, set loose, unfasten **9** circulate, discharge, disengage, dismissal, extricate, letting go, releasing **10** distribute, liberating, liberation **11** circulation, communicate, extrication, publication, setting free **12** distribution, emancipation, set at liberty, setting loose

relegate 3 bar **5** eject, expel **6** assign, banish, charge, commit, demote, reject **7** cast out, consign, discard, dismiss, exclude, keep out, shut out **8** delegate **9** ostracize

relent 4 bend, melt **5** let up, relax, yield **6** give in, soften, unbend, weaken **7** give way **8** have pity **10** be merciful, capitulate, come around **11** give quarter, grow lenient **12** become milder **14** grow less severe

relentless 4 hard **5** harsh, rigid, stern, stiff **6** severe **7** adamant **8** pitiless, rigorous, ruthless **9** merciless **10** implacable, inexorable, inflexible, unyielding **11** remorseless, undeviating, unrelenting **14** uncompromising

relevance 7 aptness, fitness, meaning **9** propriety **10** pertinence **11** materiality, relatedness, suitability **12** significance **13** applicability **15** appropriateness

relevant 3 apt, fit **6** allied, suited, tied in **7** apropos, bearing, cognate, fitting, germane, related **8** apposite, material, suitable **9** connected, intrinsic,

pertinent, referring **10** applicable, associated, concerning, to the point **11** appropriate, significant **12** on the subject, to the purpose

reliable 4 true **5** solid, sound **6** trusty **7** faithful **9** unfailing **10** dependable **11** responsible, trustworthy **12** tried and true **13** conscientious

reliance 5 faith, trust **6** belief, credit **8** credence **9** assurance **10** confidence, dependence

relic 5 scrap, token, trace **7** antique, memento, records, remnant, vestige **8** artifact, fragment, heirloom, keepsake, reminder, souvenir **11** remembrance

relief 4 balm, cure, dole, rest **5** break, cheer **6** remedy **7** anodyne, elation, panacea, respite, welfare **8** antidote, easement, lenitive **9** abatement, reduction **10** mitigation, palliation, palliative **11** alleviation, assuagement, peace of mind **12** amelioration **13** encouragement **16** public assistance **17** welfare assistance
Italian: 7 rilievo

relieve 3 aid **4** calm, ease, free, help, mark **5** abate, allay, cheer, spell **6** assist, let out, pacify, remove, set off, solace, soothe, subdue, succor, temper **7** appease, assuage, break up, comfort, console, lighten, mollify, release, replace, support, take out **8** contrast, mitigate, palliate, reassure **9** alleviate, encourage, interrupt, punctuate **12** free from fear

relieved 5 freed **6** calmed, exempt **7** cheered, excused, solaced **8** consoled **9** comforted, reassured **10** encouraged

Religio Medici
author: 15 Sir Thomas Browne

religion 4 cult, sect **5** canon, creed, dogma, faith, piety **6** belief, church, homage **7** worship **8** devotion, theology **9** adoration, godliness, reverence **10** devoutness, persuasion, veneration **11** affiliation, belief in God **12** belief in gods, denomination, spirituality **13** system of faith **15** system of worship

religionist 8 believer **16** God-fearing person

religiosity 5 piety **8** devotion **10** fanaticism **15** religious fervor

religious 3 nun **4** holy, monk

5 exact, friar, godly, rigid **6** ardent, devout, divine, priest, sacred **7** devoted, staunch **8** constant, faithful, unerring **9** spiritual, steadfast **10** devotional, fastidious, God-fearing, meticulous, scrupulous, unswerving **11** punctilious, theological, undeviating **12** wholehearted **13** conscientious **14** denominational **15** spiritual-minded

religious belief 5 canon, credo, creed, dogma, tenet **8** doctrine

religious fervor 5 piety **7** ecstasy **8** holiness **9** godliness **10** devoutness **12** religiousity, spirituality

religious group 4 sect **12** denomination

religious orders
Christian: 6 Jesuit **7** Cluniac, Templar **8** Capuchin, Theatine, Trappist, Ursuline **9** Carmelite, Dominican **10** Carthusian, Cistercian, Franciscan **11** Augustinian, Benedictine, Camaldolite **16** Sisters of Charity **20** Order of the Visitation
non-Christian: 4 Sufi **7** Jainism **8** Dasanami

relinquish 4 cede, deny, drop, quit, shed **5** forgo, leave, let go, waive, yield **6** forego, give up, resign, vacate **7** abandon, cast off, discard, dismiss, forbear, forsake, release **8** abdicate, break off, disclaim, hand over, lay aside, put aside, renounce, sign away **9** deliver up, repudiate, surrender

relinquishable 9 forgoable **10** expendable, foregoable **11** dispensable **12** renounceable

relinquished 5 ceded, let go **6** gave up **7** forgone, given up, yielded **8** cast away, foregone, forsaken **9** abandoned, given away, renounced **10** left behind

relinquishment 7 cession **8** giving up, yielding **9** letting go, rejection, surrender **10** abnegation **11** repudiation **12** renunciation

relish 3 dig **4** like, love, tang, want, wish, zest **5** enjoy, fancy, gusto, savor, spice, taste **6** accent, desire, dote on, flavor, liking, palate **7** delight, longing, stomach **8** appetite, fondness, groove on, penchant, piquancy, pleasure **9** condiment, delight in, enjoyment, hankering, rejoice in **10** appreciate, ebullience, en-

thusiasm, exuberance, partiality, propensity **11** luxuriate in **12** appreciation, be crazy about, predilection, satisfaction **13** gratification
type: 4 beef, corn **5** sweet **7** chutney **6** pickle, tomato **10** chili sauce, piccalilli **11** horseradish

reluctance 10 hesitation **13** unwillingness **14** disinclination

reluctant 3 shy **4** slow **5** loath **6** averse **7** laggard **8** hesitant **9** diffident, unwilling **10** indisposed **11** disinclined

rely 3 bet **4** bank, lean, rest **5** count, swear, trust **6** credit, depend, reckon **7** believe **10** feel sure of **11** be dependent **12** give credence

remain 4 go on, last, stay, wait **5** abide, stand **6** be left, endure, hang on, hold up, linger **7** not move, not stir, persist, prevail, stay put, subsist, survive **8** continue, stand pat **10** be left over, stay behind

remainder 4 rest **5** waste **6** excess, refuse **7** balance, overage, remains, remnant, residue, surplus, wastage **8** leavings, residual, residuum **9** leftovers, scourings **10** surplusage **11** superfluity

remains 4 body **5** stiff **6** corpse, scraps **7** cadaver **8** dead body **9** leftovers

remark 3 say, see **4** espy, mark, mind, note, view, word **6** behold, look at, notice, regard, survey **7** comment, mention, observe, pay heed **8** perceive **9** attention **10** commentary, give heed to, make note of, reflection, take note of **11** contemplate, observation **12** fix the mind on, say in passing, take notice of **13** consideration **14** pay attention to

remarkable 6 signal **7** notable, unusual **8** singular, striking **9** memorable **10** impressive, noteworthy, phenomenal **11** conspicuous, exceptional, outstanding **13** distinguished, extraordinary, unforgettable

Remarque, Erich Maria
author of: 25 All Quiet on the Western Front

Rembrandt (Harmensz) van Rijn
born: 6 Leiden, Leyden **14** The Netherlands
artwork: 6 Balaam **9** Bathsheba **13** The Night Watch (The Sortie of the Company of Captain Banning Cocq)

14 The Jewish Bride **15** Old Woman Reading, The Bridal Couple **19** The Blinding of Samson **20** Christ Healing the Sick **21** The Stoning of St Stephen **22** Man with the Golden Helmet, Self-Portrait with Saskia, The Descent from the Cross **24** The Anatomy Lesson of Dr Tulp, The Syndics of the Cloth Hall **36** Aristotle Contemplating the Bust of Homer

remedial 7 healing, helpful, mending **8** curative, salutary, sanative **10** beneficial, corrective **11** meliorative, reformative, restorative, therapeutic **12** advantageous, correctional, prophylactic

remedy 3 aid, fix **4** calm, cure, ease, heal, help, mend **5** amend, emend, right **6** relief, repair, soothe **7** assuage, correct, cure-all, improve, mollify, nostrum, panacea, rectify, redress, relieve, restore **8** make easy, medicine, mitigate, palliate, regulate, set right **9** alleviate, make sound, treatment **10** ameliorate, assistance, corrective, make better, medicament, medication, preventive **13** rectification **15** restore to health

remember 3 tip **6** recall, reward **9** not forget, recognize, recollect **10** appreciate, bear in mind, call to mind, have in mind, keep in mind, take care of, take note of **11** bring to mind **12** bear in memory

remember that thou must die
Latin: 11 memento mori

remembrance 5 favor, relic, token **6** memory, recall **7** memento **8** keepsake, memorial, reminder, souvenir **9** nostalgia **11** recognition, remembering **12** recognizance, recollection, reminiscence **13** commemoration

Remembrance of Things Past
author: 12 Marcel Proust

Remembrance Rock
author: 12 Carl Sandburg

Remick, Lee
born: 8 Quincy MA
roles: 16 Anatomy of a Murder, The Long Hot Summer **18** Days of Wine and Roses

remind 9 put in mind, suggest to **11** bring back to, bring to mind, put in memory **16** awaken memories of

reminder of death
Latin: 11 memento mori

Remington, Frederic Sackrider
born: 8 Canton NY
artwork: 12 Bronco Buster **23** Roping Horses in the Corral **32** Cavalry Charge on the Southern Plains

reminisce 4 mull, muse **6** ponder **7** reflect **8** hark back, look back, remember **9** recollect, think back **12** tell old tales **16** exchange memories, swap remembrances

reminiscent 9 nostalgic, remindful, similar to **11** analogous to, remembering **12** recollecting **13** retrospective

remiss 3 lax **4** idle, lazy, slow **5** loose, slack **6** sloppy **7** laggard, loafing **8** careless, derelict, dilatory, inactive, indolent, slipshod, slothful, uncaring **9** do-nothing, forgetful, negligent, oblivious, shiftless, undutiful, unmindful **10** delinquent, neglectful, unthinking, unwatchful **11** inattentive, indifferent, thoughtless

remission 4 cure **5** lapse, pause **6** hiatus, pardon **7** respite, retreat **8** decrease **9** abatement, acquittal, cessation, reduction, shrinkage **10** absolution, diminution, hesitation, moderation, modulation, subsidence **11** exoneration, forgiveness, vindication

remit 3 pay **4** free, send, ship **5** clear, let go, relax, slack **6** excuse, let out, pardon, reduce **7** absolve, forgive, forward, release, set free, slacken **8** decrease, diminish, dispatch, liberate, make good, moderate, overlook, pass over, transmit **9** discharge, reimburse **10** compensate **11** put to rights **13** send in payment

remnant 3 bit **5** piece, relic, scrap, shred, token, trace **7** discard, remains, residue, vestige **8** fragment, leavings, leftover, monument, residuum, survival **9** remainder **11** odds and ends

remodel 4 redo **5** adapt, alter, fix up **6** change, modify **7** convert, reshape **8** overhaul, renovate **9** refashion, transform **11** recondition

remodeling 6 change **10** alteration, conversion **12** modification **13** transmutation **14** transformation

remonstrance 6 rebuke **7** censure **8** reproach, scolding **9** criticism, reprimand **10** admonition

remonstrate 5 argue, chide,

demur, scold **6** differ, object, rebuke **7** censure, chasten, contend, dispute, dissent, protest, reprove, upbraid **8** admonish, complain, reproach **9** criticize **10** take to task **11** expostulate **13** call to account

remorse 3 rue **4** pang **5** grief, guilt, qualm **6** regret, sorrow **7** anguish **9** penitence **10** contrition, repentance, ruefulness **11** compunction, lamentation, self-reproof **12** self-reproach **13** regretfulness **14** second thoughts

remorseful 8 contrite, penitent **9** chastened, regretful, repentant, sorrowful **10** apologetic **13** grief-stricken **18** conscience-stricken

remote 3 far **4** slim **5** alien, alone, aloof, faint, quiet **6** exotic, far-off, lonely, meager, slight **7** distant, dubious, faraway, foreign, removed, strange **8** detached, doubtful, isolated, secluded, separate, set apart, solitary, unlikely **9** withdrawn **10** far-removed, segregated **11** God-forsaken, implausible, out of the way, sequestered, standoffish

removal 6 moving, ouster **7** doffing **8** deletion, ejection **9** discharge, dismissal, expulsion, taking off, taking out **10** amputation, carting off, cutting away, dislodging, evacuation, lopping off **11** carrying off, chopping off, elimination, transferral **12** cancellation, displacement **14** transportation **15** transplantation

remove 4 doff, drop, fire, move, oust, quit **5** eject, erase, expel, leave, shift **6** cancel, change, cut off, delete, depart, go away, lop off, retire, unseat, vacate **7** blot out, boot out, cart off, chop off, cut away, dismiss, extract, kick out, retreat, take off, take out, wipe out **8** amputate, carry off, dislodge, displace, evacuate, get rid of, sweep out, take away, transfer, withdraw **9** discharge, eliminate, take leave, transport **10** make an exit, transplant

removed 3 off **4** away, took **5** alone, aloof, apart **6** remote **7** distant, faraway **8** abstract, detached, isolated, reticent, secluded **9** alienated, separate, unrelated, withdrawn **10** segregated, unsociable **11** interspaced, standoffish

remove from office 4 oust **6** depose, unseat **9** discharge

remunerate 3 pay **5** award, grant, repay **6** reward **7** requite, satisfy **9** indemnify, reimburse, vouchsafe **10** compensate, recompense **15** make restitution

remuneration 7 payment **9** repayment **10** recompense, reparation **12** compensation **13** reimbursement **15** indemnification

Remus
father: 4 Mars
mother: 4 Ilia **9** Rea Silvia **10** Rhea Silvia
twin brother: 7 Romulus
raised by: 7 she-wolf

renaissance 7 rebirth, renewal, revival **10** rekindling, renascence, resurgence **11** reawakening, reemergence, restoration **12** regeneration, rejuvenation, resurrection, risorgimento **14** revitalization, revivification **15** reestablishment

rend 3 cut, rip **4** hurt, pain, rive, sear, tear **5** break, crack, sever, split, wound **6** cleave, divide, pierce, sunder **7** afflict, rupture, shatter **8** dissever, fracture, lacerate, polarize, splinter **12** disintegrate, fall to pieces **15** break into pieces

render 2 do **4** cede, give, make, play **5** allot, grant, remit, yield **6** accord, donate, give up, supply, tender **7** deal out, dole out, execute, hand out, pay back, perform, present, requite **8** construe, dispense, fork over, hand over, pay as due, shell out, turn over **9** cause to be, interpret, surrender, translate **10** relinquish **12** give in return, make requital **13** cause to become, make available, make payment of

render impotent 6 defuse, weaken **7** disable, unnerve **8** paralyze **9** undermine **10** devitalize, emasculate

render inoperable 6 damage, impair **7** cripple, disable **12** incapacitate

render null and void 4 void **5** annul **6** cancel, repeal, revoke **7** abolish, nullify, rescind, retract, reverse **8** abrogate, dissolve **10** invalidate

rendezvous 4 date **5** focus, haunt, mecca, tryst **6** gather, muster **7** retreat **8** assemble **9** encounter, tete-a-tete **10** engagement, focal point **11** appointment, assignation, get together **12** meeting place,

watering hole **14** gathering place, stamping ground **15** agreement to meet **17** meet by appointment **18** prearranged meeting

rendition 7 edition, reading, version **9** depiction, portrayal, rendering **11** arrangement, performance, translation **14** interpretation

rend the air 3 cry **4** bawl, howl, wail **6** clamor, scream, shriek, squeal **7** screech **9** caterwaul

Renee Mauperin
author: 24 Edmond and Jules de Goncourt

renegade 5 rebel **6** outlaw **7** heretic, runaway, slacker, traitor **8** apostate, betrayer, defector, deserter, forsaker, fugitive, mutineer, mutinous, quisling, recreant, turncoat **9** dissenter, insurgent **10** backslider, traitorous, treasonist, unfaithful

renege 7 back out, fink out, pull out **8** back down, fall back, withdraw **9** repudiate, weasel out **11** get cold feet **12** turn one's back **13** break a promise, break one's word **16** go back on one's word

renew 4 save **6** extend, pick up, redeem, resume, retain, revive **7** prolong, refresh, restore, salvage **8** continue, maintain **9** make sound, reinstate, sign again **10** begin again, offer again, regenerate, rejuvenate, revitalize **11** reestablish, take up again **12** reinvigorate **16** put back into shape

renewal 7 revival **9** extension **10** redemption **11** restoration **12** regeneration **13** reinstatement **14** revitalization

Renoir, Pierre-Auguste
born: 6 France **7** Limoges
artwork: 4 Lise **6** La Loge **10** The Bathers **12** Margot Berard, The Umbrellas **14** La Grenouillere **19** Le Moulin de la Galette **28** Mme Charpentier and Her Children, The Luncheon of the Boating Party

renounce 4 cede, deny, quit **5** forgo, waive **6** abjure, disown, eschew, forego, give up, recant, reject, resign **7** abandon, cast off, disavow, discard, dismiss **8** abdicate, abnegate, abrogate, disclaim, forswear, lay aside, part with, put aside, turn from, write off **9** cast aside, foreswear, repudiate

10 relinquish **13** give up claim to **15** wash one's hands of

renovate 3 fix **4** mend **6** remake, repair, revamp **7** improve, remodel, restore **8** make over **9** modernize, refurbish **10** redecorate

renown 4 fame, mark, note **6** repute, status **7** acclaim **8** eminence **9** celebrity, notoriety **10** popularity, prominence, reputation **11** distinction

renowned 5 famed, noted **6** famous **7** eminent, notable, popular **9** acclaimed, prominent, well-known **10** celebrated, noteworthy **11** outstanding **13** distinguished

rent 3 fee, gap, let, rip **4** dues, gash, hire, hole, rift, slit, tear **5** break, chasm, chink, cleft, crack, lease, split **6** breach, hiatus, rental, schism, tatter, wrench **7** charter, fissure, opening, payment, rent out, rupture **8** cleavage, crevasse, division, fracture **11** buy the use of **12** sell the use of

rente 6 income **7** revenue **12** annual income

rentier 21 one who has a fixed income

renunciation 6 denial **7** refusal **8** forgoing, spurning **9** disavowal, eschewing, foregoing, rejection, repulsion **10** abjuration, renouncing **11** abandonment, disclaiming, forswearing, repudiation **12** foreswearing **14** relinquishment

Renwick, James, Jr architect of: **8** Main Hall (Vassar College) **11** Grace Church (NYC) **15** Corcoran Gallery (now Renwick Gallery, Washington, DC) **19** St Patrick's Cathedral (NYC) **22** Smithsonian Institution (Washington DC) style: **13** Gothic Revival

reopen 7 restart **9** begin anew, reconvene, start anew **10** recommence, reinitiate **11** reestablish, reinstitute **12** reinaugurate

repair 2 go **3** fix **4** mend, move **5** amend, emend, patch, renew, shape, state **6** fixing, remedy, remove, retire **7** correct, mending, patch up, rebuild, rectify, redress, restore **8** make good, overhaul, patching, set right, withdraw **9** condition, make up for, refurbish, repairing **10** rebuilding **11** recondition

12 refurbishing **14** reconditioning

reparation 6 amends, return **7** damages, redress **8** requital **9** quittance **10** recompense **11** restitution **12** compensation, satisfaction **13** peace offering

repartee 6 banter, bon mot **7** riposte **8** badinage, chit chat, word play **10** persiflage, witty reply **11** witty retort **12** pleasantries **14** snappy comeback

repast 4 food, meal **5** board, feast, snack, table **6** spread **7** banquet **8** victuals **9** provision **11** nourishment, refreshment

repay 5 match **6** refund, return, reward **7** pay back, requite **9** get back at, indemnify, pay in kind, reimburse **10** recompense, remunerate **11** get even with, reciprocate **12** make requital **14** give in exchange, make a return for **15** make restitution, make retribution **19** return the compliment

repayment 10 paying back, recompense **12** compensation **13** reimbursement **17** making restitution

repeal 4 void **5** annul **6** cancel, revoke **7** abolish, nullify, rescind, voiding **8** abrogate, set aside **9** abolition, annulment **10** abrogation, invalidate, revocation **11** termination **12** cancellation, invalidation **13** nullification **18** declare null and void

repeat 4 echo, redo, tell **5** mimic, quote, rerun **6** pass on, recite, relate, retell **7** imitate, recount, restate, retread, say over **8** say again **9** duplicate, reiterate, reproduce **10** repetition **11** duplication, reiteration **12** perform again

repeated exercises 4 rote **5** drill **8** practice, training

repel 4 foil, rout **5** check **6** dispel, offend, oppose, put off, rebuff, resist, revolt, sicken **7** deflect, disgust, fend off, forfend, hold off, keep off, keep out, repulse, scatter, turn off, ward off **8** alienate, beat back, disperse, nauseate, push back, stave off, throw off **9** chase away, drive away, drive back, force back, frustrate, keep at bay, withstand

repellent 5 proof **9** abhorrent, loathsome, offensive, repelling, repugnant, repulsive, resisting, revolting, sickening **10** dis-

gusting, nauseating **11** distasteful, impermeable

repent 3 rue **6** bemoan, bewail, lament, regret, repine **7** deplore **8** mea culpa, weep over **9** be ashamed **10** be contrite, be penitent **11** be regretful, feel remorse

repentance 5 grief, guilt **6** regret, sorrow **7** remorse **9** penitence **10** contrition **11** compunction **12** self-reproach **16** self-condemnation **17** pangs of conscience

repercussion 4 echo **6** effect, result **8** backlash, reaction **10** concussion, side effect **11** aftereffect, consequence **13** reverberation **15** boomerang effect

repetition 6 repeat **9** iteration, retelling **11** reiteration, restatement **14** recapitulation

repetitious 5 wordy **6** prolix **8** repeated **9** redundant **10** repetitive

Repin, Ilya Efimovich born: **6** Russia **8** Chuguyev artwork: **15** The Volga Boatmen **18** Zaporozhye Cossacks **19** They Did Not Expect Him **26** Ivan the Terrible Kills His Son

replace 5 spell **6** return **7** put back, restore, succeed **8** supplant **9** supersede

replaceable 10 disposable, expendable **11** dispensable

replenish 5 renew **6** refill, reload **7** refresh, reorder, replace, restock, restore

replenished 7 renewed **8** refilled, replaced, restored **9** restocked

replenishment 7 renewal **9** refilling **10** restocking **11** replacement, restoration

replete 4 full **5** sated **6** gorged, loaded **7** crammed, fraught, stuffed, teeming **8** brimming, satiated **9** abounding, jampacked, surfeited **11** wellstocked

repletion 4 glut **6** excess **7** surfeit, surplus **9** abundance, plenitude, profusion, satiation **11** sufficiency

replica 4 copy **5** model **6** double **8** likeness **9** duplicate, facsimile, imitation **12** reproduction

reply 5 react **6** answer, rejoin, retort **7** counter, respond **8** reaction, response **9** rejoinder **14** acknowledgment

reply if you please
French: **4** rsvp **20** repondez s'il vous plait

reply to 6 answer **7** counter, react to **8** retort to **9** respond to **11** acknowledge

repondez s'il vous plait 11 please reply **16** reply if you please
abbreviation: **4** rsvp

report 4 bang, boom, note, talk, tell, word **5** crack, noise, rumor, sound, state, story **6** appear, detail, expose, gossip, recite, record, relate, reveal, show up, tell on **7** account, article, check in, divulge, hearsay, message, missive, recount, summary, version, write-up **8** announce, denounce, describe, disclose, dispatch, relation **9** discharge, narration **10** communique, detonation, memorandum **11** communicate, description, information
French: **11** compte rendu

reporter 7 newshen, newsman **8** newshawk **9** anchorman, announcer, columnist, newshound, newswoman **10** journalist, newscaster **11** commentator **12** newspaperman **13** correspondent **14** newspaperwoman

repose 3 lie **4** calm, ease, rest **5** quiet, relax **6** be calm, settle **7** leisure, recline, respite **8** quietude **10** inactivity, quiescence, relaxation **11** tranquility **12** peacefulness, tranquillity

repository 5 depot **8** magazine **9** warehouse **10** storehouse

reprehend 5 decry **7** censure, condemn, reprove **8** denounce, reproach **9** criticize **10** disapprove

reprehensible 3 bad **4** base, evil, foul, vile **6** guilty, wicked **7** heinous, ignoble **8** blamable, culpable, infamous, shameful, unworthy **9** nefarious **10** censurable, despicable, villainous **11** blameworthy, condemnable, disgraceful, inexcusable, opprobrious **12** unpardonable **13** objectionable, unjustifiable

reprehension 6 rebuke **7** censure, reproof **8** reproach **9** criticism **11** disapproval **12** condemnation, denunciation **14** disapprobation

represent 2 be **4** mean, show **5** enact, equal, state **6** denote, depict, pose as, sketch, typify **7** betoken, express, outline, picture, portray, present, serve as **8** appear as, describe, indicate, stand for **9** delineate, designate, symbolize **10** illustrate **11** emblematize, impersonate **12** characterize

representation 5 image **6** effigy, emblem, symbol **7** epitome, essence, picture **8** likeness **9** depiction, portrayal **10** embodiment **12** illustration **15** exemplification **16** characterization

representative 2 MP **3** rep **5** agent, envoy, proxy **6** deputy, varied **7** deputed, elected, proctor, typical **8** balanced, delegate, elective, emissary, symbolic **9** delegated, exemplary, spokesman, surrogate, typifying **10** delegatory, democratic, denotative, emblematic, legislator, mouthpiece, republican, substitute, symbolical **11** assemblyman, congressman, delineative, descriptive **12** exemplifying, illustrative **13** assemblywoman, congresswoman **14** characteristic, cross-sectional

repress 4 curb, hide, mask, veil **5** box up, check, cloak, cover, crush, pen up, quash, quell **6** hold in, muffle, shut up, squash, stifle, subdue **7** conceal, control, inhibit, put down, silence, smother, squelch **8** bottle up, hold back, keep down, restrain, strangle, suppress

repression 8 muffling **9** holding in, restraint, retention **10** inhibition, throttling **11** concealment, holding back, suppression

reprieve 4 lull, stay **5** delay, pause **6** pardon, parole **7** amnesty, respite **8** breather **9** remission **10** moratorium, suspension **11** adjournment **12** postponement **14** breathing spell

reprimand 4 trim **5** chide, scold **6** berate, rail at, rebuff, rebuke, revile **7** censure, chew out, chiding, lecture, obloquy, tell off, upbraid **8** admonish, berating, chastise, denounce, reproach, reproval, scolding, take down, trimming **9** castigate, criticism, criticize, disparage, dispraise, dress down, reprehend, reprobate **10** admonition, chewing out, opprobrium, take to task, upbraiding **11** castigation **12** admonishment, denunciation, dressing down, remonstrance **13** disparagement **16** rap on the knuckles

reprisal 7 redress, revenge **8** requital **9** tit for tat, vengeance **11** counterblow, retaliation, retribution **13** counterattack **16** counteroffensive
Latin: **10** quid pro quo

reproach 4 blot, slur, spot **5** blame, chide, scold, shame, stain, taint **6** charge, insult, malign, rail at, rebuke, revile, stigma, tirade, vilify **7** asperse, blemish, censure, condemn, offense, reproof, reprove, scandal, tarnish, upbraid **8** admonish, denounce, diatribe, disgrace, dishonor, scolding **9** castigate, criticism, criticize, discredit, disparage, indignity, reprimand **10** stigmatize, take to task, tonguelash, upbraiding **11** degradation, humiliation **12** remonstrance **13** call to account, embarrassment

reprobate 3 bad, low **4** base, evil, rake, roue, vile **5** scamp **6** pariah, rascal, rotter, sinner, wanton, wicked **7** corrupt, outcast **8** castaway, depraved, derelict, evildoer, prodigal, rakehell **9** abandoned, dissolute, miscreant, shameless, wrongdoer **10** black sheep, degenerate, immoralist, profligate, voluptuary **11** rapscallion, untouchable **12** incorrigible, transgressor, wicked person

reproduce 4 copy, redo, sire **5** beget, breed, match, spawn **6** mirror, repeat, re-echo **7** imitate, reflect **8** generate, multiply **9** duplicate, procreate, propagate, replicate, represent **11** counterfeit, proliferate

reproduction 4 copy **7** replica **8** breeding, likeness **9** duplicate, facsimile, imitation **10** carbon copy, generation, simulation **11** procreation, propagation **13** progeneration, proliferation **14** multiplication, representation
goddess of: **7** Astarte

reproductive system
component: **5** penis **6** testes, uterus, vagina **7** ovaries

reproof 5 blame **6** rebuke **7** censure, chiding **8** reproach, scolding **9** criticism, reprimand **10** admonition **12** condemnation, dressing-down, remonstrance

reprovable 7 at fault **8** blamable, culpable **10** censurable **11** blameworthy **12** reproachable

reprove 5 chide, scold **6** rebuke **7** censure, chasten **8** admonish, reproach **9** castigate, reprimand

reptile 3 asp, eft **4** newt, teju **5** agama, anole, gecko, skink, snake, viper **6** dragon, iguana, lizard, mugger, turtle **7** crawler, creeper, serpent, tuatara **8** basilisk, dinosaur, groveler, terrapin, tortoise **9** alligator, chameleon, crocodile, pterosaur **10** salamander, vertebrate **11** Gila monster, pterodactyl

republic 9 democracy
Latin: **10** res publica

Republic
author: **5** Plato

Republican Party
also called: **3** GOP **13** Grand Old Party
president belonging to:
4 Bush, Ford, Taft **5** Grant, Hayes, Nixon **6** Arthur, Hoover, Reagan **7** Harding, Lincoln, (Andrew) Johnson **8** Coolidge, Garfield, Harrison, McKinley **9** (Theodore) Roosevelt **10** Eisenhower
symbol: **8** elephant

Republic of China *see* **6** Taiwan

repudiate 4 deny, void **5** annul **6** cancel, desert, disown, reject, repeal, revoke **7** abandon, abolish, cast off, disavow, discard, forsake, nullify, protest, rescind, retract, reverse **8** abrogate, disclaim, dissolve, renounce

repudiation 6 denial **9** disavowal, rejection **10** abrogation, disclaimer, retraction

repugnance 4 hate **5** odium **6** hatred **7** disgust **8** aversion, loathing **9** antipathy, revulsion **10** abhorrence **11** abomination, detestation

repugnant 4 foul, vile **5** nasty **6** odious **7** adverse, counter, hateful, opposed **8** contrary, unsavory **9** abhorrent, loathsome, obnoxious, offensive, repellent, repulsive, revolting, sickening **10** abominable, detestable, disgusting, nauseating, unpleasant **11** distasteful, uncongenial, undesirable, unpalatable **12** antipathetic, disagreeable, insufferable, unacceptable, unappetizing **13** objectionable

repulse 4 shun **5** avoid, repel, spurn **6** ignore, rebuff, refuse, reject **7** refusal **8** shunning, spurning **9** rejection

repulsion 6 hatred **7** disgust, dislike **8** aversion, distaste, loathing **9** antipathy **10** ab-

horrence, repugnance **11** abomination, detestation **13** indisposition **14** disinclination

repulsive 4 vile **5** nasty **6** odious **7** hateful **9** abhorrent, loathsome, obnoxious, offensive, repellent, repugnant, revolting **10** abominable, detestable, disgusting, nauseating **11** distasteful **12** disagreeable **13** objectionable

repulsiveness 8 ugliness **13** loathsomeness, offensiveness **14** disgustingness, unpleasantness **16** disagreeableness

reputable 7 honored **8** esteemed, reliable **9** respected **10** creditable **11** respectable, trustworthy

reputation 4 name **7** stature **8** standing

repute 3 say **4** deem, fame, hold, view **5** judge, think **6** esteem, reckon, regard, renown **7** account, believe, suppose **8** consider, estimate, standing **9** celebrity, notoriety **10** prominence **14** respectability

request 3 ask **4** seek **6** ask for, bid for, desire, sue for **7** call for, entreat, solicit **8** petition **9** importune **11** application **12** solicitation

requiem 5 dirge **6** lament **8** threnody

requiescat in pace 11 rest in peace **16** may he rest in peace **17** may she rest in peace

require 3 bid **4** lack, miss, need, want **5** crave, imply, order **6** charge, compel, desire, direct, enjoin, entail, oblige **7** command, dictate **9** constrain **11** necessitate

required 6 forced, needed **7** obliged **9** compelled, essential, necessary **10** compulsory, imperative, obligatory

requirement 4 must **8** standard **9** criterion, essential, guideline, requisite **12** prerequisite **13** specification
Latin: **10** sine qua non **11** desideratum

requisite 4 must, need **6** needed **8** required **9** essential, mandatory, necessary, necessity **10** compulsory, imperative, obligatory **11** requirement **12** prerequisite **13** indispensable
Latin: **10** sine qua non **11** desideratum

requisition 4 form **7** request **11** application

requital 7 redress **9** repayment **11** retaliation **12** compensation **15** indemnification

rescind 4 void **5** annul, quash **6** cancel, recall, repeal, revoke **7** abolish, discard, nullify, retract, reverse **8** abrogate, dissolve, override, overrule **10** invalidate **11** countermand **12** counterorder

rescinding 6 recall **7** voiding **8** recision **9** abolition **10** abrogation, retraction, revocation **11** abolishment, dissolution **12** cancellation, invalidation **13** nullification

rescue 4 save **6** ransom, saving **7** deliver, freeing, recover, release, salvage **8** liberate, recovery **9** extricate **10** liberation **11** deliverance, extrication

research 5 probe, study **7** delving, inquiry **8** analysis, scrutiny **10** inspection **11** examination, exploration, factfinding, investigate, scholarship **13** investigation

resemblance 7 analogy **8** affinity, likeness, parallel **10** congruence, similarity, similitude **14** correspondence

resemble 5 favor **6** be like **8** be akin to, look like, parallel **9** take after

Resen
founder: **6** Nimrod

resent 7 dislike

resentful 5 angry **6** bitter **7** annoyed **8** grudging, offended, provoked **10** displeased **12** dissatisfied

resentfulness 5 anger, spite **10** bitterness **15** dissatisfaction

resentment 3 ire **4** huff **5** anger, pique, spite **6** animus, malice, rancor **7** dudgeon, ill will, offense, umbrage **8** acerbity, acrimony, asperity, jealousy, soreness, sourness **9** animosity, crossness **10** bitterness, irritation **11** displeasure, indignation **12** irritability, vengefulness **14** vindictiveness

reservation 4 date **5** doubt **7** booking, proviso, scruple, strings **8** preserve **9** condition, hesitancy, provision **10** encampment, reluctance, settlement **11** appointment, compunction, stipulation, uncertainty **12** installation **13** accommodation, establishment, qualification **14** prearrangement

reserve 4 book, hold, keep, save **5** amass, delay, extra, hoard, lay up, spare, stock, table **6** backup, engage, retain, shelve, unused **7** husband, nest egg, savings **8** conserve, keep back, postpone, preserve, salt away, schedule, withhold **9** aloofness, reticence, stockpile **10** additional, prearrange

reserved 5 aloof, taken **6** booked, formal **7** distant, engaged **8** bespoken, retained, reticent, strained, unsocial **9** inhibited, spoken for **10** restrained, unsociable **11** ceremonious, constrained, standoffish **12** unresponsive **15** uncommunicative, undemonstrative

reservoir 4 fund, pool, tank, well **5** basin, fount, hoard, stock, store **6** supply **7** backlog, cistern **8** millpond **9** container, stockpile **10** depository, receptacle, repository **12** accumulation

res gestae 5 deeds **10** things done **15** accomplishments

reshape 4 redo **5** adapt, alter, block **6** change, modify, reform, remold, rework **7** convert, reframe, remodel **9** refashion, transform

reside 3 lie **4** live, rest, room **5** dwell, exist, lodge **6** belong, occupy **7** inhabit, sojourn **8** domicile

residence 3 pad **4** digs, flat, home, room, stay **5** abode, house, place **7** address, lodging, sojourn **8** domicile, dwelling, quarters **9** apartment, homestead, household **10** habitation
French: **10** pied a terre

resident 5 local **6** lodger, tenant **7** citizen, denizen, dweller **8** occupant, townsman **9** sojourner **10** inhabitant **11** housekeeper

residual 5 extra **7** abiding, lasting, surplus **8** enduring, leftover **9** lingering, remaining **10** continuing **13** supplementary

residue 4 rest **5** dregs **6** scraps **7** balance, remains, remnant **8** leavings **9** remainder
Latin: **8** residuum

resign 4 quit **5** leave **6** give up, submit **8** abdicate, disclaim, renounce **9** reconcile **10** relinquish

resignation 8 fatalism, patience, quitting, stoicism **9** departure **10** equanimity, retirement, submission, withdrawal **11** passiveness **12** ac-

quiescence **13** nonresistance **14** submissiveness

resign oneself 5 yield **6** submit **9** acquiesce

resilience 6 recoil **7** rebound **8** buoyancy **10** elasticity **11** flexibility **12** adaptability **13** changeability, nonuniformity **16** lightheartedness

resilient 5 hardy **6** supple **7** buoyant, elastic, rubbery, springy **8** flexible **9** adaptable, expansive, resistant, tenacious **10** rebounding, responsive **13** irrepressible

resist 4 balk, foil, stem, stop **5** fight, repel **6** baffle, combat, oppose, refuse, reject, thwart **7** contest, counter, weather **8** beat back, turn down **9** frustrate, withstand **10** counteract

resistance 6 mutiny, rebuff **7** refusal **8** defiance, struggle **9** obstinacy, rebellion, rejection **10** contention, insurgency, opposition **11** obstruction **12** insurrection **13** intransigence, noncompliance, recalcitrance

resolute 5 stern **6** dogged, steady **7** earnest, staunch, zealous **8** decisive, diligent, intrepid, stubborn, untiring, vigorous **9** assiduous, obstinate, purposive, steadfast, tenacious, unbending **10** deliberate, determined, inflexible, persistent, relentless, unflagging, unswerving, unwavering, unyielding **11** industrious, persevering, undeviating, unfaltering, unflinching **12** pertinacious, strong-minded, strong-willed **13** indefatigable **14** uncompromising

resoluteness 7 purpose, resolve **8** decision, tenacity **11** decidedness, persistence **12** decisiveness, perseverance **13** determination, steadfastness **14** purposefulness

resolution 3 aim **4** goal, plan, zeal **6** design, energy, intent, mettle, motion, object, spirit **7** promise, purpose, resolve **8** ambition, proposal, solution, tenacity **9** constancy, intention, objective, resolving, stability **10** resilience, steadiness **11** earnestness, persistence **12** perseverance, resoluteness **13** determination, steadfastness **14** aggressiveness **16** indefatigability

resolve 4 plan **6** answer, decide, design, intend, set out, settle, vote on **7** adjudge, clear

up, explain, purpose **8** decision **9** determine, elucidate **10** commitment, resolution **12** resoluteness **13** determination **14** make up one's mind

resonant 4 full, rich **7** booming, orotund, ringing, vibrant **8** sonorous **10** bellowing **10** resounding, stentorian, thunderous **11** reverberant

resort 3 use **4** hope **5** apply, avail **6** chance, employ, take up **7** utilize **8** exercise, recourse **9** expedient

resound 4 echo, peal, ring **5** clang **6** re-echo **7** vibrate **11** reverberate **14** tintinnabulate

resounding 7 echoing, ringing **9** re-echoing **10** thundering, thunderous **13** reverberating

resource 8 recourse **9** expedient **11** wherewithal

resourceful 4 able **5** ready, sharp, smart **6** adroit, artful, bright, shrewd **7** capable, cunning **8** creative, original, skillful, talented **9** competent, effectual, ingenious, inventive **10** innovative, proficient **11** imaginative **12** enterprising

resourcefulness 9 ingenuity **10** creativity, enterprise **13** inventiveness

resources 5 funds, means, money **6** assets, income **7** capital, effects, revenue **10** belongings, collateral **11** possessions, wherewithal

respect 5 honor, point, sense **6** detail, esteem, matter, notice, praise, regard **7** bearing, feature, viewing **8** approval, courtesy, relation **9** affection, attention, deference, laudation, reference, relevance, reverence **10** admiration, connection, particular, veneration **11** point of view, recognition **12** appreciation, circumstance **13** consideration

respectability 7 decency, decorum **9** gentility, propriety **11** correctness, genteelness

respectable 4 fair **5** ample, civil, noble **6** decent, honest, polite, proper, worthy **7** correct, courtly, passing, refined, upright **8** becoming, decorous, moderate, polished **9** admirable, dignified, estimable, honorable, reputable **10** aboveboard, admissible, sufficient **11** presentable **12** considerable, praiseworthy, satisfactory

respected 6 valued, worthy
7 admired, honored, revered
8 esteemed **9** admirable,
venerated

respectful 5 civil **6** formal,
genial, polite **7** amiable, winning **8** admiring, decorous,
gracious, mannerly, obliging,
reverent **9** attentive, courteous,
regardful **10** personable, solicitous **11** ceremonious, deferential, reverential
13 accommodating

respects 4 heed, obey
5 honor, prize, value **6** admire,
esteem, fealty, follow, regard,
revere **7** abide by, cherish, defer to, observe, regards, tribute **8** adhere to, consider,
venerate **9** greetings **10** appreciate, understand **11** acknowledge, compliments
12 remembrances
13 consideration

Respighi, Ottorino
born: 5 Italy **7** Bologna
composer of: 8 La Fiamma,
The Birds **14** The Pines of
Rome **18** The Fountains of
Rome **19** La Boutique Fan-
tasque, The Fantastic Toy-
shop **27** Ancient Airs and
Dances for Lute

respiration 9 breathing

respiratory system
component: 4 lung, nose
6 larynx **7** pharynx, trachea
8 voice box, windpipe
9 bronchius, diaphragm
action: 9 breathing

respire 7 breathe

respite 4 lull **5** break, delay,
letup, pause **6** recess **8** reprieve **9** extension
12 intermission

resplendence 6 dazzle, luster
7 glitter **8** lambency, radiance
10 brilliance, luminosity, refulgence **12** circumstance,
magnificence

resplendent 6 bright **7** beaming, blazing, glowing, lambent,
radiant **8** dazzling, gleaming,
luminous, lustrous, splendid
9 brilliant, refulgent, sparkling **10** glittering
11 coruscating

respond 5 react, reply **6** answer, rejoin **7** speak up **9** recognize **11** acknowledge

respond to 6 answer **7** act
upon, react to, reply to
8 thank for **11** acknowledge

response 5 reply **6** answer, retort, return **7** riposte **8** comeback, feedback, reaction,
rebuttal **9** rejoinder **10** impression **13** countercharge

14 acknowledgment
16 counterstatement

responsibility 4 duty, task
5 blame, order, trust **6** burden,
charge **8** function **9** liability
10 obligation **11** culpability,
reliability **13** answerability, dependability **14** accountability
15 trustworthiness

responsible 5 adult, of age
6 guilty, liable, mature **7** at
fault, capable **8** culpable, reliable **9** demanding, executive,
important **10** answerable, creditable, dependable **11** accountable, challenging, trustworthy
13 conscientious
14 administrative

responsive 5 alive, awake,
sharp **8** reactive **9** receptive,
sensitive **11** retaliative, retaliatory, susceptible, sympathetic
13 compassionate, understanding **14** impressionable

responsiveness 6 action
7 concern **8** interest **9** attention, awareness **11** sensitivity
13 understanding

res publica 8 republic, the
state **12** commonwealth, public matter

rest 2 be **3** end, lay, lie, nap,
set **4** base, ease, halt, hang,
keep, laze, lean, loaf, loll, lull,
prop, rely, stay, stop **5** break,
death, exist, hinge, let up,
pause, peace, place, quiet, relax, sleep, stand **6** demise, depend, holder, lounge, others,
recess, remain, repose, reside,
scraps, snooze, trivet **7** balance, be based, be found, be
quiet, decease, deposit, holiday, leisure, lie down, recline,
remains, remnant, residue, respite, set down, slumber, support **8** breather, platform,
vacation **9** cessation, departure, leftovers, remainder, stillness **10** complement, quiet
spell, relaxation, standstill,
suspension **11** hibernation,
take time out **12** intermission,
interruption **13** take a
breather
Spanish: 6 siesta
Latin: 8 residuum

restaurant 5 diner **6** eatery
7 beanery, tearoom **9** cafeteria,
chop house, grillroom, hash-
house, lunchroom **11** coffeehouse **12** luncheonette
French: 4 cafe **6** bistro
9 brasserie
German: 11 rathskeller

restful 4 calm **5** quiet **6** placid,
serene **7** pacific, relaxed
8 peaceful, soothing, tranquil
10 unagitated **11** comfortable,
undisturbed

restfulness 4 ease **5** quiet
6 repose **8** serenity, softness
10 relaxation **11** tranquility
12 tranquillity

rest in peace
Latin: 16 requiescat in pace

restitution 6 amends **7** redress,
replevy **8** replevin, requital,
restoral **9** atonement, indemnity, repayment **10** recompense, reparation
11 restoration **12** compensation, remuneration, satisfaction **13** reimbursement,
reinstatement
15 indemnification

restive 5 balky **6** mulish, ornery, unruly **7** fidgety, wayward, willful **8** contrary,
stubborn **9** fractious, pigheaded **10** rebellious, refractory **11** disobedient,
intractable **12** recalcitrant,
unmanageable

restless 5 awake, jumpy **6** fitful, uneasy **7** anxious, fidgety,
fretful, jittery, nervous, on the
go, unquiet, wakeful, worried
8 agitated **9** excitable, impatient, incessant, insomniac, on
the move, sleepless, transient,
unsettled **10** disquieted, high-
strung **11** hyperactive
13 uncomfortable

restoration 7 revival **8** recovery **12** recuperation **13** convalescence, reinstatement
14 rehabilitation, reintroduction, reinvigoration
15 reestablishment

restorative 5 tonic **6** elixir
7 bracing, healing **8** curative
10 beneficial, energizing, fortifying **11** revivifying **12** invigorating, revitalizing
13 strengthening

restore 3 fix **4** cure, dose,
heal, mend **5** rally, renew,
treat **6** do over, recoup, remedy, repair, rescue, return, revive **7** convert, get back, patch
up, put back, rebuild, reclaim,
recover, refresh, remodel, retouch, touch up **8** energize,
give back, make over, make
well, medicate, renovate, retrieve, revivify, recreate
9 reanimate, refurbish, reinstall, reinstate, stimulate
10 exhilarate, revitalize,
strengthen **11** recondition, reconstruct, reestablish, reinstitute, resuscitate
12 rehabilitate, reinvigorate

restored 4 kept **5** saved **7** revived **8** replaced **9** conserved,
pressured **11** replenished
13 rehabilitated

restrain 3 gag **4** bind, curb,

hold, stop **5** check, leash, limit **6** arrest, bridle, fetter, muzzle, pinion, temper, tether **7** chasten, contain, curtail, harness, inhibit, prevent, shackle, trammel **8** handicap, hold back, restrict, suppress, withhold

restrained 4 cool **5** aloof **6** curbed **7** checked, distant **8** held back, reined in, reserved **10** controlled, unfriendly

restraint 4 curb **5** check **7** control **10** limitation

restrict 4 curb, hold **5** check, cramp, crimp, hem in, limit **6** hamper, impede, narrow, thwart **7** confine, inhibit, prevent, squelch **8** hold back, obstruct, straiten, suppress **9** constrain, frustrate **12** circumscribe

restricted 7 cramped, limited **8** confined, hampered, held back **9** exclusive **10** suppressed **13** circumscribed

restriction 4 rule **7** control, curbing, proviso **9** condition, provision **10** limitation, regulation **11** requirement, reservation, stipulation **13** consideration, qualification

restrictive 8 limiting **9** confining, exclusive **10** constraining

result 4 stem **5** arise, end up, ensue, fruit, issue, owe to **6** derive, effect, happen, pan out, report, sequel, spring, upshot, wind up **7** finding, opinion, outcome, product, turn out, verdict **8** decision, judgment, reaction, solution **9** aftermath, culminate, eventuate, originate, outgrowth **10** resolution **11** aftereffect, consequence, development, eventuality **13** determination

resume 2 CV **3** bio **4** go on **5** brief **6** digest **7** epitome, proceed, summary **8** abstract, continue, reembark, synopsis **9** biography, summation **10** abridgment, recommence **11** reestablish **12** condensation **Latin: 15** curriculum vitae **French: 6** precis

resumption 11 recommenced, restoration **12** continuation

resurgam 15 I shall rise again

resurgence 6 return **7** rebirth, renewal, revival **10** renascence **11** reemergence, renaissance **12** rejuvenation **13** recrudescence

retailer 5 store **6** dealer, seller, trader **8** merchant, provider, supplier **9** tradesman

10 wholesaler **11** distributor, storekeeper, tradeswoman **12** merchandiser **French: 9** vivandier **10** vivandiere

retain 4 hold, keep **5** grasp **6** absorb, recall **7** possess **8** hang on to, hold on to, maintain, memorize, remember **9** recollect

retainer 7 servant **8** employee **9** attendant

retainership 4 hire **6** employ **7** service **10** employment

retaliate 5 repay **6** avenge, pay off, return **7** counter, pay back, requite, revenge **11** reciprocate

retaliation 6 talion **7** deserts, revenge **8** reprisal, requital **9** vengeance **10** recompense **11** comeuppance, eye for an eye, interchange, just deserts, lex talionis, retribution **12** compensation **13** reciprocation **14** tooth for a tooth

retard 4 clog, drag **5** block, brake, check, delay **6** arrest, baffle, detain, fetter, hamper, hinder, hold up, impede, slow up **7** draw out, inhibit, prevent, prolong, slacken **8** hold back, obstruct, slow down **10** decelerate

retarded 4 dull, slow **6** simple **7** idiotic, moronic, unsound **8** backward, disabled **9** imbecilic, mongoloid, subnormal **10** slow-witted **11** handicapped **12** simpleminded

reticent 3 shy **5** quiet **6** closed, silent **7** subdued **8** reserved, retiring, taciturn **9** diffident, withdrawn **10** restrained **11** tight-lipped **12** closemouthed **15** uncommunicative

retinue 5 court, staff, suite, train **6** convoy **9** courtiers, employees, entourage, followers, following, personnel, retainers **10** associates, attendance, attendants

retire 6 depart, go away, remove, resign, resort, secede, turn in **7** drop out, retreat **8** abdicate, flake out, withdraw

retired French: 8 ci-devant

retiring 3 shy **4** meek **5** quiet, timid **6** demure, humble, modest **7** bashful **8** reserved, reticent, sheepish, timorous, unsocial **9** diffident, shrinking, withdrawn **10** unassuming **11** unassertive **12** self-effacing **13** inconspicuous, unpretentious **15** uncommunicative

retort 3 say **4** quip **5** rebut, reply **6** answer, rejoin, return **7** counter, respond, riposte **8** fire back, rebuttal **9** rejoinder

retract 4 deny **6** abjure, disown, draw in, recall, recant, recede, recoil, reel in, repeal, revoke **7** disavow, rescind, retreat, reverse **8** abnegate, abrogate, disclaim, draw back, forswear, peel back, pull back, renounce, take back, withdraw **9** foreswear, repudiate

retraction 6 recall **8** recision **9** disavowal **10** disclaimer, refutation, withdrawal

retreat 2 go **3** den **4** bolt, flee, port **5** haunt, haven, leave **6** asylum, depart, escape, flight, harbor, recoil, refuge, resort, retire, shrink **7** abscond, getaway, privacy, sanctum, shelter, shy away **8** back away, draw back, fall back, hideaway, move back, solitude, turn tail, withdraw **9** departure, isolation, reclusion, sanctuary, seclusion **10** evacuation, immurement, retirement, withdrawal **11** hibernation, rustication

retrench 5 slash **6** reduce, scrape, scrimp **7** curtail, cut back, cut down **8** conserve, cut costs **9** economize **15** tighten one's belt

retribution 6 amends, return, reward **7** justice, penalty, redress, revenge **8** reprisal, requital **9** vengeance **10** punishment, recompense, reparation **11** just deserts, restitution, retaliation, vindication **12** satisfaction **13** reciprocation, recrimination

retrieve 4 snag **5** fetch **6** ransom, recoup, redeem, regain, rescue **7** get back, reclaim, recover, salvage **9** recapture, repossess

retriever dog breed: 5 Irish **6** golden, Gordon **7** English **8** Labrador **10** flat-coated **11** curly-coated **13** Chesapeake Bay

retrograde 5 worse **6** worsen **7** inverse, retreat, reverse **8** backward **10** regressive **13** retrogressive

retrogress 6 worsen **9** backslide

retrogression 7 decline, setback **9** worsening **11** backsliding

retrogressive 8 backward **9** declining, worsening **11** backsliding

retrospect 6 review 9 flashback, hindsight 11 remembrance 12 afterthought, reminiscence 15 reconsideration

return 3 net 4 earn, gain 5 gross, recur, repay, yield 6 advent, come to, go back, income, profit, render, reseat, reward 7 arrival, benefit, produce, provide, put back, requite, restore, revenue 8 announce, come back, earnings, give back, hand down, interest, proceeds, reappear, recovery, restoral, send back 9 advantage, reinstall, reinstate, retrieval, reversion 10 homecoming, recurrence 11 reciprocate, reestablish, restoration 12 compensation, reappearance 13 reinstatement 15 reestablishment

Return, The
author: 14 Walter de la Mare

Return of the Native
author: 11 Thomas Hardy
character: 11 Diggory Venn, Eustacia Vye 12 Damon Wildeve 13 Clym Yeobright 17 Thomasin Yeobright

Return to Thebes
author: 10 Allan Drury

Reuben
father: 5 Jacob
mother: 4 Leah
brother: 3 Dan, Gad 4 Levi 5 Asher, Judah 6 Joseph, Simeon 7 Zebulun 8 Benjamin, Issachar, Naphtali
sister: 5 Dinah
descendant of: 9 Reubenite

reunite 5 rewed 7 remarry 9 reconcile

reveal 4 bare, show 6 betray, expose, impart, let out, unfold, unmask, unveil 7 display, divulge, exhibit, give out, lay bare, publish, uncover, unearth 8 disclose, evidence, manifest, point out

revealed 4 open 5 clear, known 7 evident, obvious 8 manifest

revel 4 romp 5 caper, enjoy 6 bask in, frolic, gambol, relish 7 carouse, delight, indulge, rejoice, roister, skylark 8 wallow in 9 celebrate

revelation 6 expose, vision 7 shocker 8 exposure, prophecy 9 admission, bombshell, discovery, eyeopener, unveiling 10 apocalypse, confession, disclosure, divulgence 11 divulgation, divulgement

revelatory 10 expressive

11 informative 13 communicative

reveler 6 barfly, ranter, player 7 drinker 8 bacchant, carouser, drunkard 9 roisterer, rollicker, skylarker 10 merrymaker

revelry 5 spree 7 jollity 8 carnival, carousal, festival, jamboree 9 high jinks, merriment, rejoicing 10 exultation, roistering 11 celebrating, celebration, merrymaking 12 conviviality 13 jollification 14 boisterousness
god of: 5 Comus

revenge 5 repay 7 pay back, requite 8 reprisal, requital 9 repayment, retaliate, vengeance, vindicate 10 recompense 11 eye for an eye, reciprocate, retaliation, retribution 12 satisfaction

revenue 3 pay 4 take 5 gains, wages, yield 6 income, profit, return, salary 7 annuity, pension, subsidy 8 earnings, interest, pickings, proceeds, receipts 9 allowance, emolument 12 compensation, remuneration

revenue, annual
French: 5 rente

reverberate 4 boom, echo, ring 5 carry 6 rumble 7 resound, thunder, vibrate

reverberation 4 boom, echo 6 rumble 7 ringing, thunder 8 rumbling 9 vibration 10 resounding, thundering

revere 5 honor 6 esteem 7 defer to, respect 8 venerate

revered 6 adored 7 admired, honored 9 estimable, respected, venerated, worshiped 10 worshipped

reverence 3 awe 4 fear 5 honor, piety 6 esteem, homage, regard 7 respect, worship 8 devotion 9 adoration, deference 10 admiration, devoutness, observance, veneration 11 prostration, religiosity 12 genuflection

reverent 4 pure 5 pious 6 devout, humble, solemn 7 adoring, awesome, devoted 8 faithful 9 religious, spiritual 10 respectful, worshipful

reverential 4 awed 10 respectful, worshipful 11 deferential

reverie 5 dream, fancy 6 musing 7 fantasy 8 daydream 9 dreamland, quixotism 10 brown study, meditation 12 extravagance 13 woolgathering 14 fantasticality

reverse 4 back, rear, tail, undo, void 5 annul, upend, upset 6 cancel, change, defeat, invert, mishap, negate, recall, recant, repeal, revoke, unmake, upturn 7 counter, failure, nullify, rescind, retract, setback, trouble 8 abrogate, backward, contrary, converse, hardship, inverted, opposite, override, overrule, set aside, turn over, withdraw 9 adversity, mischance, posterior, transpose 10 antithesis, invalidate, misfortune 11 countermand, counterpart, frustration 14 disappointment

revert 5 lapse 6 go back, repeat, return 7 regress, relapse 9 backslide 10 recidivate, retrogress

review 4 show 5 study, sum up 6 notice, parade, rehash, survey 7 analyze, journal, retrace, run over 8 critique, evaluate, hash over, magazine, reassess, report on, scrutiny 9 criticism, criticize, reexamine, reiterate, summarize 10 commentary, evaluation, exhibition, exposition, procession, reconsider, reevaluate, reflection, scrutinize 11 examination 12 presentation, reassessment, recapitulate, reevaluation 13 demonstration, retrospection 14 recapitulation 15 reconsideration
French: 11 compte rendu

revile 4 slur 5 abuse, curse, scold, scorn 6 berate, defame, deride, malign, rebuke, vilify 7 bawl out, chew out, slander, upbraid 8 belittle, denounce, execrate, reproach, sail into 9 blaspheme, castigate, denigrate, disparage 10 vituperate

reviler 6 critic, curser 8 vilifier 9 backbiter, slanderer 10 blasphemer

revise 4 edit, redo 5 alter, amend, emend, fix up 6 change, doctor, modify, recast, redact, revamp, review, update 7 correct, rectify, rewrite 8 emendate, overhaul

revision 6 change 7 edition 9 amendment, recension 10 alteration, correction, emendation 11 improvement 12 modification

revival 7 renewal 11 restoration 13 reinstatement, reinstitution, resuscitation

revive 5 dig up, renew 6 drag up, repeat 7 freshen, refresh, restage 8 reawaken 9 reanimate, reproduce, resurrect 11 resuscitate

revived 7 renewed **8** animated, repeated, restaged **9** enlivened, freshened, refreshed **10** reanimated, reawakened, reproduced **11** invigorated, resurrected **12** resuscitated

revocation 6 repeal **8** recision **9** abolition, annulment **10** abrogation, retraction **11** abolishment, elimination, repudiation **12** cancellation **13** nullification

revoke 4 void **5** annul, erase, quash **6** abjure, cancel, negate, recall, repeal, vacate **7** abolish, dismiss, expunge, nullify, rescind, retract, reverse **8** abrogate, call back, disallow, disclaim, override, overrule, renounce, set aside, take back, withdraw **9** repudiate **10** invalidate **11** countermand

revolt 4 coup, rise **5** rebel, repel, shock **6** appall, mutiny, offend, rise up, sicken **7** disgust, dissent, horrify, repulse **8** disorder, distress, nauseate, sedition, uprising **9** rebellion **10** insurgency, opposition, **12** factiousness, insurrection **German: 6** Putsch

revolting 4 foul, grim, vile **5** nasty **6** horrid, odious **7** hateful, noisome, noxious **8** dreadful, horrible, horrific, shocking, stinking **9** abhorrent, appalling, frightful, invidious, loathsome, obnoxious, offensive, repellent, repugnant, repulsive, sickening **10** abominable, disgusting, malodorous, nauseating **11** distasteful **12** disagreeable **13** objectionable

Revolt of the Angels, The author: 13 Anatole France

revolution 6 mutiny, revolt, rising **8** circling, gyration, rotation, uprising **9** rebellion **12** insurrection **14** circumrotation, circumvolution **French: 4** coup **9** coup d'etat **German: 6** Putsch

revolutionary 7 radical **8** mutinous **9** extremist, insurgent, seditious **10** dissenting, rebellious, subversive **13** superadvanced, unprecedented **15** insurrectionary

revolve 4 spin, turn **5** twist, wheel **6** circle, gyrate, rotate **12** circumrotate

revolver 3 gat, gun, rod **4** colt **6** pistol, weapon **7** firearm, handgun, rotator, sidearm **10** six-shooter **20** Saturday night special

revulsion 8 aversion, distaste,

loathing **10** abhorrence, repugnance **11** detestation

reward 3 due **5** bonus, prize, repay, wages **6** bounty **7** deserts, guerdon, payment, premium, requite **9** reckoning **10** compensate, recompense, remunerate **12** compensation, remuneration **13** consideration **Latin: 10** quid pro quo

rewarding 8 pleasant, valuable **9** enjoyable **10** delightful, gratifying, satisfying **11** pleasurable

rework 4 redo **5** adapt, alter **6** modify **7** remodel, reshape **9** refashion, transform

rex 4 king

Reykjavik capital of: 7 Iceland

Reynolds, Burt born: 10 Waycross GA **wife: 9** Judy Carne **12** Loni Anderson **roles: 6** Shamus **9** Dan August, Semi-Tough **11** Deliverance **14** The Longest Yard **18** Smokey and the Bandit

Reynolds, Debbie real name: 19 Mary Frances Reynolds **born: 8** El Paso TX **husband: 11** Eddie Fisher **roles: 13** The Singing Nun, The Tender Trap **15** Singin' in the Rain **19** Tammy and the Bachelor **23** The Unsinkable Molly Brown

Reynolds, Sir Joshua born: 7 England **8** Plympton **artwork: 14** Lord Heathfield, Miss Jane Bowles **15** Commodore Keppel **18** Mrs Francis Beckford **21** Mrs Abington as Miss Prue **25** Mrs Siddons as the Tragic Muse **38** Lady Sarah Bunbury Sacrificing to the Graces

Rhadamanthus, Rhadamanthys father: 4 Zeus **mother: 6** Europa **brother: 5** Minos **6** Aeacus **8** Sarpedon **became a judge in: 5** Hades

rhapsodic 6 elated **7** beaming, excited **8** blissful, ecstatic, thrilled **9** delirious, overjoyed, rapturous **11** exhilarated, transported

Rhea member of: 6 Titans **father: 6** Uranus **mother: 4** Gaea **brother: 6** Cronos, Cronus, Kronos

husband: 6 Cronos, Cronus, Kronos **son: 4** Zeus **5** Hades **8** Poseidon **daughter: 4** Hera **6** Hestia **7** Demeter **called: 10** Magna Mater **corresponds to: 3** Ops **6** Cybele **9** Dindymene **10** Berecyntia **epithet: 6** Antaea

Rhea Silvia see **9** Rea Silvia

Rhene mistress of: 6 Oileus **son: 5** Medon

Rhesus owned: 6 horses **horses captured by: 8** Diomedes, Odysseus

rhetoric 4 bunk, wind **5** hokum, hooey **6** bunkum, hot air **7** fustian, oratory **8** euphuism **9** discourse, elocution, eloquence, hyperbole **10** hocus-pocus **11** flamboyance **13** magniloquence **14** grandiloquence

Rhetoric author: 9 Aristotle

rhetorical 5 showy, windy **6** florid, ornate, purple, verbal **7** aureate, flowery **8** eloquent, inflated **9** bombastic, grandiose, highflown, stylistic **10** decorative, discursive, euphuistic, expressive, flamboyant, linguistic, oratorical, ornamental **11** disputative, embellished, extravagant **12** disputatious, elocutionary, magniloquent **13** argumentative, grandiloquent

Rhiannon origin: 5 Welsh **husband: 5** Pwyll **10** Manawyddan **son: 7** Pryderi **accused of devouring: 7** Pryderi

Rhigmus origin: 8 Thracian **ally of: 7** Trojans **killed by: 8** Achilles

rhinoceros group of: 5 crash

Rhoda character: 8 Gary Levy **9** Joe Gerard **12** Benny Goodwin **14** Ida Morgenstern, Sally Gallagher **17** Brenda Morgenstern, Martin Morgenstern **22** Rhoda Morgenstern Gerard **cast: 9** Anne Meara, David Groh, Ron Silver **11** Julie Kavner, Nancy Walker **12** Harold J Gould, Ray Buktenica **13** Valerie Harper

Rhode Island
    abbreviation: 2 RI
    nickname: 11 Little Rhody
    capital/largest city: 10 Providence
    others: 7 Bristol, Newport 8 Cranston, Kingston, Westerly
        9 Pawtucket, Wakefield 10 Woonsocket
    college: 5 Brown 6 Bryant 8 Pembroke 10 Barrington,
        Providence 11 Salve Regina 13 Mount St Joseph, Roger
        Williams 15 Johnson and Wales, Naval War College
    feature: 7 Newport
    tribe: 7 Niantic 9 Wampanoag 12 Narragansett
    people: 8 Puritans 12 George M Cohan 13 Gilbert Stuart,
        Matthew C Perry, Roger Williams 15 Ambrose Burnside,
        Nathanael Greene 17 Oliver Hazard Perry
    island: 5 Block, Rhode 8 Prudence 9 Aquidneck, Conanicut
    lake: 8 Scituate
        pond: 7 Wordens 8 Stafford, Watchaug
    land rank: 8 fiftieth
    mountain: 10 Durfee Hill
        highest point: 12 Jerimoth Hill
    physical feature:
        bay: 12 Narragansett
        sea: 8 Atlantic
        sound: 11 Block Island
    river: 7 Seekonk 8 Pawtuxet 9 Pawcatuck, Pawtucket, Poto-
        womut 10 Blackstone, Providence
    state admission: 10 thirteenth
    state bird: 14 Rhode Island Red
    state flower: 6 violet
    state motto: 4 Hope
    state song: 11 Rhode Island
    state tree: 8 red maple

Rhodesia see 8 Zimbabwe

rhodium
    chemical symbol: 2 Rh

rhododendron
    varieties: 4 tree 5 Bluet 6 In-
        dian, Yunnan 7 catawba,
        fringed, Lapland, silvery,
        Smirnow 8 Carolina, Chap-
        man's, Fortune's, Fujiyama,
        piedmont 9 Caucasian,
        honey-bell, West Coast
        11 leather-leaf 12 willow-
        leaved

rhodolite
    species: 6 garnet

Rhodope
    companion of: 7 Artemis
    skill: 7 hunting

Rhodopis
    also: 7 Rhodope
    form: 9 courtesan
    origin: 5 Greek 8 Thracian
    slave in: 5 Egypt
    lost: 7 slipper
    slipper found by:
        12 Psammetichus
    husband: 12 Psammetichus

Rhodus
    father: 8 Poseidon
    mother: 9 Aphrodite

Rhoeo
    father: 9 Staphylus
    mother: 12 Chrysothemis
    seduced by: 6 Apollo

Rhoetus
    member of: 8 Gigantes

rhubarb 5 Rheum 16 Rheum
    rhabarbarum
    varieties: 4 wild 5 monk's
        6 garden, Sikkim 7 spinach
        8 mountain

rhyme 3 pun 4 poem, rune,
    song 5 chime, clink, meter,
    poesy, verse 6 jingle, poetry,
    rhythm 7 measure, poetize,
    versify 8 assonate, doggerel
    10 consonance 12 alliteration
    game: 6 crambo

rhymer, rhymester 4 bard,
    poet 6 writer 8 minstrel, poet-
    izer 9 poetaster, versifier
    10 troubadour

Rhys, Jean
    author of: 7 Quartet 15 Voy-
        age in the Dark, Wide Sar-
        gasso Sea

rhythm 4 beat, lilt, time 5 me-
    ter, pulse, swing, throb 6 ac-
    cent, number, stress
    7 cadence, measure 8 empha-
    sis, movement 9 pulsation
    10 recurrence 11 fluctuation,
    syncopation 12 accentuation

riant 3 gay 4 airy 5 jolly,
    merry 6 blithe, bright, jocund,
    jovial 7 smiling 8 cheerful,
    laughing, mirthful

ribald 4 lewd, racy, rude

    5 bawdy, crude, gross 6 coarse,
    earthy, rakish, risque, vulgar,
    wanton 7 raffish, uncouth
    8 improper, indecent, off-color,
    prurient, shocking 9 salacious,
    unrefined 10 lascivious, libidi-
    nous, licentious, suggestive

ribbon 3 bow, ray 4 band,
    sash 5 award, braid, prize,
    reins, strip 6 cordon, riband
    7 binding, rosette 8 memorial,
    streamer 10 decoration

rice 5 Oryza 11 Oryza sativa
    varieties: 4 wild 6 Indian,
        pampas 8 mountain 9 Ten-
        nessee 10 annual wild
    dish: 5 grits, pilaf 7 pudding,
        risotto 8 porridge
        9 jambalaya
    liquor: 4 sake

Rice, Elmer
    author of: 11 Street Scene
        16 The Adding Machine

Riceyman Steps
    author: 13 Arnold Bennett

rich 4 dark, deep, fine, lush
    5 flush, heavy, loamy, sweet,
    vivid 6 bright, costly, fecund,
    lavish, mellow 7 fertile, filling,
    intense, moneyed, opulent,
    wealthy, well-off 8 abundant,
    affluent, fruitful, in clover,
    precious, prodigal, resonant,
    sonorous, splendid, valuable,
    well-to-do 9 abounding, esti-
    mable, expensive, luxuriant,
    luxurious, priceless, sump-
    tuous 10 euphonious, produc-
    tive, propertied, prosperous
    11 mellifluous 12 on easy
    street

Rich, Adrienne
    author of: 18 Diving into the
        Wreck

Richard, Maurice
    nickname: 6 Rocket
    sport: 6 hockey
    position: 7 forward
    team: 17 Montreal Canadiens

Richard Cory
    author: 22 Edwin Arlington
        Robinson

**Richard Diamond, Private
Detective**
    character: 3 Sam 6 Lt Kile
        9 Lt McGough 10 Karen
        Wells
    cast: 10 Russ Conway
        11 Barbara Bain, Regis
        Toomey 12 David Janssen
        13 Roxanne Brooks 14 Mary
        Tyler Moore
    viewers saw only Sam's:
        4 legs

Richard II
    author: 18 William
        Shakespeare
    character: 11 John of
        Gaunt 13 Edmund Langley,

Thomas Mowbray **16** Henry
Bolingbroke **20** Earl of
Northumberland
  Duke of: **4** York **7** Au-
  merle, Norfolk **8** Here-
  ford **9** Lancaster

Richard III
  author: **18** William
  Shakespeare
  character: **6** George **7** Richard **8** Edward IV, Lady
  Anne **10** Henry Tudor (Earl
  of Richmond) **11** Lord Stanley **12** Lord Hastings
  13 Queen Margaret
  14 Queen Elizabeth **15** Edward the Fourth **17** Sir William Catesby **19** Edward
  Prince of Wales
  Duke of: **4** York **8** Clarence **10** Buckingham,
  Gloucester

Richardson, Henry Hobson
  architect of: **9** Sever Hall
  (Harvard) **11** Grace Church
  (West Medford MA)
  13 Trinity Church (Boston)
  23 State Asylum for the Insane (Buffalo NY) **27** Marshall Field Wholesale Store
  (Chicago)

Richardson, Samuel
  author of: **6** Pamela (or Virtue Rewarded) **8** Clarissa
  (Harlowe) **19** Sir Charles
  Grandison

Richardson, Sir Ralph
  born: **7** England
  10 Cheltenham
  roles: **6** Exodus **10** Oscar
  Wilde, Richard III, The
  Heiress **11** A Doll's House
  12 Anna Karenina **13** Doctor Zhivago **15** Richard the
  Third **20** Little Lord Fauntleroy **24** Long Day's Journey
  into Night **26** Greystoke The
  Legend of Tarzan

Richardson, Tony
  director of: **8** Tom Jones (Oscar) **15** Look Back in Anger **36** The Loneliness of
  the Long Distance Runner

riches 4 pelf **5** lucre, means
  6 assets, mammon, wealth
  7 fortune **8** opulence, treasure
  9 resources **10** prosperity
  11 possessions

richness 6 wealth **8** fullness,
  lushness, opulence **9** amplitude, intensity **10** lavishness,
  mellowness **12** completeness
  13 luxuriousness

Richter, Charles Francis
  field: **10** geophysics,
  seismology
  developed: **12** Richter scale
  24 measurement of
  earthquakes

rickety 4 weak **5** frail, shaky
  6 feeble, flimsy, infirm,
  wasted, weakly, wobbly
  7 fragile **8** decrepit, unsteady,
  withered **9** tottering **10** bro-
  kendown, tumbledown **11** debilitated, dilapidated,
  weakjointed **12** deteriorated

rid 4 free **5** clear, purge **6** remove **8** disabuse, liberate, unburden **9** disburden, eliminate
  11 disencumber

Ridd, John
  character in: **10** Lorna
  Doone
  author: **9** Blackmore

riddance 6 ouster, relief
  7 freeing, removal **8** ejection
  9 clearance, expulsion **11** deliverance, dislodgment

riddle 5 poser, rebus **6** enigma,
  puzzle, secret **7** mystery, problem, puzzler, stumper
  9 conundrum

ride 4 move **5** annoy, carry,
  drive, harry, hound **6** badger,
  handle, harass, hector, manage, needle, travel **7** control,
  journey, support **8** progress
  9 transport

rider 5 affix **6** suffix **7** adjunct,
  codicil **8** addendum, addition,
  appendix **9** amendment, appendage **10** attachment,
  supplement

Riders to the Sea
  author: **19** John Millington
  Synge

ridge 3 bar, rib, rim **4** bank,
  fret, hill, hump, rise, wale,
  weal, welt **5** bluff, crest,
  crimp, knoll, mound, spine
  6 ripple **7** crinkle, hillock,
  wrinkle **10** promontory
  11 corrugation

ridicule 3 guy, rib **4** gibe, jeer,
  josh, mock, razz, ride, twit
  5 mimic, scorn, taunt, tease
  6 deride, gibe at, parody
  7 lampoon, laugh at, mockery,
  ribbing, sarcasm, scoff at,
  sneer at, snicker, teasing
  8 belittle, derision, sneering,
  travesty **9** aspersion, burlesque,
  disparage, humiliate, make fun
  of, poke fun at **10** caricature,
  derogation, lampoonery
  13 disparagement
  god of: **5** Momos, Momus

ridiculous 3 odd **5** crazy, droll,
  funny, inane, nutty, queer,
  silly **6** absurd, screwy **7** amusing, asinine, bizarre, comical,
  fatuous, foolish, idiotic **8** farcical **9** fantastic, frivolous, grotesque, laughable, ludicrous,
  screwball, senseless **10** hysterical, incredible, irrational, out-

landish **11** astonishing,
nonsensical **12** preposterous,
unreasonable

Rienzi
  author: **18** Edward Bulwer-
  Lytton

Riesling, Paul
  character in: **7** Babbitt
  author: **5** Lewis

rife 5 close, dense, solid, thick
  6 common, packed **7** crowded,
  general, studded, teeming
  8 epidemic, pandemic, populous, swarming **9** chock-full,
  extensive, plumbfull, prevalent, universal **10** prevailing,
  widespread **11** predominant

riffraff 3 mob **4** herd, scum
  5 crowd, dregs, trash **6** masses,
  proles, rabble, vermin **9** peasantry **10** commonalty
  11 proletariat
  French: **8** canaille

rifle 3 rob **4** loot, sack **6** ravage **7** despoil, pillage, plunder,
  ransack **8** spoliate
  10 burglarize

rifle, repeating
  invented by: **7** Spencer

Rifleman, The
  character: **10** Lou Mallory,
  Mark McCain **11** Lucas
  McCain **14** Miss Milly
  Scott **20** Marshal Micah
  Torrance
  cast: **7** Paul Fix **10** Joan Tay-
  lor **12** Chuck Connors
  13 Patricia Blair **14** Johnny
  Crawford
  setting: **9** New Mexico, North
  Fork

rift 3 cut, gap **4** gash, gulf,
  rent, slit **5** abyss, break,
  chasm, chink, cleft, crack,
  fault, gorge, gulch, gully,
  split **6** breach, cranny, ravine
  7 breakup, crevice, fissure,
  quarrel, rupture **8** aperture,
  crevasse, division, fracture
  12 disagreement
  16 misunderstanding

rig 4 gear **5** equip **6** fit out,
  outfit **8** carriage **9** apparatus,
  equipment, machinery

Rigaud
  character in: **12** Little Dorrit
  author: **7** Dickens

Rigg, Diana
  born: **7** England **9** Doncaster
  roles: **6** Helena **8** Emma
  Peel **10** Bleak House
  11 Lady Dedlock, The
  Avengers **12** Julius Caesar
  21 A Midsummer Night's
  Dream **26** On Her Majesty's
  Secret Service

right 2 OK **3** due **4** deed, fair, good, just, meet, nice, real, sane, true, well **5** amend, emend, exact, grant, honor, ideal, legal, licit, moral, power, solve, sound, valid **6** actual, at once, decent, honest, lawful, morals, normal, proper, remedy, seemly, square, virtue **7** certain, correct, ethical, exactly, factual, fitting, freedom, genuine, liberty, license, perfect, precise, probity, redress, regular, standup, warrant **8** accurate, becoming, clear-cut, definite, directly, goodness, morality, promptly, properly, rational, sanction, straight, suitable, suitably, truthful, virtuous **9** allowable, authentic, authority, correctly, desirable, equitable, exemplary, favorable, favorably, honorable, integrity, nobleness, opportune, ownership, perfectly, precisely, presently, privilege, propriety, rectitude, veracious, veridical, vindicate **10** aboveboard, accurately, admissible, completely, convenient, infallible, legitimate, permission, preferable, reasonable, recompense, scrupulous, undisputed, unmistaken **11** inheritance, immediately, irrefutable, prerogative, punctilious **12** advantageous, jurisdiction, satisfactory **13** appropriately, authorization, incontestable, justification, unimpeachable **14** proprietorship, satisfactorily, unquestionable
    Latin: 3 jus

right beside 6 next to **8** abutting, adjacent, touching

righteous 4 fair, good, holy, just **5** godly, moral, pious **6** chaste, devout, honest **7** ethical **8** elevated, innocent, reverent, virtuous **9** blameless, equitable, honorable, incorrupt, religious, spiritual, unsullied

righteousness
    goddess of: 4 Maat

righteous person
    Hebrew: 6 zaddik

rightful 3 due **4** just, true **5** legal, valid **6** lawful, proper **7** allowed, condign, correct, fitting, merited **8** deserved **9** deserving, equitable **10** authorized, designated, legitimate, prescribed, sanctioned **11** appropriate, inalienable **14** constitutional

right hand 4 aide, ally **6** helper **7** partner **8** adjutant **9** assistant
    French: 10 aide-de-camp

right of blood
    Latin: 12 jus sanguinis

right of soil/land
    Latin: 7 jus soli

Right People, The
    author: 17 Stephen Birmingham

right side up 7 upright **10** on one's feet

Right Stuff, The
    director: 13 Philip Kaufman
    author: 8 Tom Wolfe
    cast: 8 Ed Harris **10** Sam Shepard
    Oscar for: 5 score

right-wing 7 old-line **10** nonliberal **11** reactionary **12** conservative **14** nonprogressive

right-winger 8 rightist **11** reactionary **12** conservative

rigid 3 set **4** firm, hard, taut **5** fixed, harsh, sharp, stern, stiff, tense **6** formal, severe, strict, strong, wooden **7** austere **8** exacting, obdurate, rigorous, stubborn, unpliant **9** inelastic, stringent, unbending **10** inflexible, unyielding **11** puritanical, unrelenting **14** uncompromising

Rigoletto
    opera by: 5 Verdi
    character: 5 Gilda **9** Maddalena **11** Sparafucile **12** Duke of Mantua **15** Countess Ceprano **16** Count of Monterone

rigorous 5 exact, harsh, stern, tough **6** severe, strict, trying **7** austere, correct, precise **8** accurate, exacting **9** demanding, stringent **10** meticulous, scrupulous **11** challenging, punctilious

rig out 4 garb **5** array, dress **6** attire, clothe

rile 3 irk, vex **4** gall, miff, roil **5** anger, annoy, chafe, gripe, peeve, pique **6** bother, enrage, nettle, offend, plague **7** incense, inflame, provoke **8** irritate **9** aggravate, infuriate

Riley, James Whitcomb
    author of: 18 Little Orphant Annie **25** When the Frost Is on the Punkin

rilievo 6 relief

Rilke, Rainer Maria
    author of: 11 Book of Hours **12** Duino Elegies, Life and Songs **13** Divine Elegies **16** Sonnets to Orpheus **19** Letters to a Young Poet

rill 5 brook, cleft, creek **6** furrow, groove, runnel, stream **7** channel, rivulet **9** streamlet

rim 3 lip **4** edge, side **5** brink, ledge, verge **6** border, margin **9** outer edge

Rima
    character in: 13 Green Mansions
    author: 6 Hudson

Rimbaud, Arthur
    author of: 12 Le Bateau Ivre **13** A Season in Hell **14** The Drunken Boat **16** Les Illuminations **17** Sonnet of the Vowels

rime 3 ice **4** hoar **5** chink, cleft, crack, crust, frost **7** crevice, fissure **9** hoarfrost

Rime of the Ancient Mariner, The
    author: 21 Samuel Taylor Coleridge
    character: 6 Hermit **9** Albatross **12** Wedding Guest **14** Ancient Mariner

Rimsky-Korsakov, Nikolai (Nicholas)
    born: 6 Russia **8** Novgorod
    member of: 7 The Five
    composer of: 5 Mlada, Sadko **6** Kitezh **10** Night in May, Snow Maiden, Tzar Saltan **11** Sheherazade **12** Christmas Eve, Scheherazade **16** Spanish Capriccio **17** Capriccio Espagnol, The Golden Cockerel **21** Russian Easter Overture **29** Russian Easter Festival Overture

rind 4 bark, hull, husk, peel, skin **5** crust, shell **6** cortex, fringe **7** epicarp, surface **8** exterior
    pork: 9 crackling

ring 4 aura, band, bloc, buzz, call, echo, gang, hoop, loop, peal, toll, tone **5** cabal, chime, clang, knell, party, sound **6** cartel, circle, cordon, herald, jangle, jingle, league, signal, strike, summon, tinkle **7** besiege, circuit, combine, enclose, quality, resound, seal off, vibrate **8** announce, blockade, encircle, proclaim, striking, surround **9** broadcast, encompass, perimeter, resonance, syndicate, ting-a-ling, vibration **10** federation **11** reverberate **12** circumscribe **13** circumference, reverbera-

tion **14** tintinnabulate
16 tintinnabulation

Ring and the Book, The
　author: **14** Robert Browning

Ring des Nibelungen, Der
　also: **12** The Ring Cycle
　20 The Ring of the
　Nibelung(s)
　opera by: **6** Wagner
　part one: **12** Das Rheingold,
　The Rhine Gold
　part two: **10** Die Walkure
　11 The Valkyrie
　part three: **9** Siegfried
　part four: **15** Gotterdamme-
　rung **17** Twilight of the
　Gods
　character: **4** Erda, Mime
　5 Freia, Hagen, Wotan
　6 Fafner, Fasolt **7** Gunther,
　Gutrune, Hunding **8** Alber-
　ich, Siegmund **9** Siegfried,
　Sieglinde, Valkyries
　10 Brunnhilde

ring down the curtain
　3 end **4** halt **6** finish **8** con-
　clude **9** terminate

ringleader 5 chief **6** master
10 mastermind

ringlet 4 curl **6** circle

ring-shaped 5 round **8** circular

**Rin Tin Tin, The Adven-
tures of**
　character: **5** Rusty, (Cpl)
　Boone **9** (Sgt) Biff O'Hara
　10 (Lt) Rip Masters
　cast: **8** Lee Aaker **9** Joe Saw-
　yer **10** James Brown, Rand
　Brooks

Rio Bravo
　director: **11** Howard Hawks
　cast: **8** Ward Bond **9** John
　Wayne **10** Dean Martin
　11 Ricky Nelson **13** Walter
　Brennan **14** Angie Dickinson

Rio de Janeiro *see box*

riot 4 rage **5** act up, arise, melee, rebel **6** fracas, mutiny, resist, revolt, rumpus, strife,
tumult, uproar **7** rampage, run
amok, trouble, turmoil **8** disorder, outburst, uprising, violence **9** commotion, confusion,
rebellion **10** Donnybrook, turbulence **11** lawlessness, pandemonium **12** insurrection

rioting 6 tumult, uproar **7** turmoil **8** disorder, outbreak, violence **9** commotion
11 disturbance

riotous 4 loud, wild **5** arroar,
noisy, randy **6** stormy, unruly,
wanton **7** bacchic, rampant,
violent **8** bacchian **9** debauched, dissolute, insurgent,
plentiful, tumultuous, turbulent **10** boisterous, dissipated,
licentious, rebellious **11** in-

Rio de Janeiro
　airport: **6** Galeao
　architect: **5** Costa,
　Reidy **8** Niemeyer
　area: **4** Caju, Lapa **6** Ca-
　tete, Gamboa, Gloria,
　Grajau, Tijuca **7** Ca-
　tumbi, Ipanema **8** Bo-
　tafogo **10** Copacabana,
　Vila Isabel **12** Sao
　Cristovao
　bay: **8** Botafogo, Juru-
　juba **9** Guanabara
　bridge: **11** Costa e Silva
　celebration: **8** Carnival
　9 Mardi Gras
　discovered by: **6** Coelho
　former capital of:
　6 Brazil
　island: **10** Governador
　lake: **16** Rodrigo de
　Freitas
　landmark: **10** Candelaria
　14 Mount Corcovado
　15 Maracana Stadium
　17 Sugarloaf Mountain:
　statue of: **17** Christ
　the Redeemer
　means: **14** river of
　January
　ocean: **8** Atlantic
　people: **8** Cariocas
　replaced as capital by:
　8 Brasilia
　slums: **7** favelas
　suburb: **7** Niteroi

---

temperate, overcopious **12** unrestrained **13** superabundant
15 insurrectionary
party: **4** orgy

rip 3 cut, gap **4** rend, rent, rift,
rive, slit, tear **5** burst, sever,
shred, slash, split **6** cleave
7 fissure, rupture **8** cleavage,
cut apart, fracture, incision,
tear open **10** laceration

ripe 3 due, fit **4** come **5** ideal,
ready **6** mature, mellow,
primed, timely **7** perfect
8 complete, finished, seasoned
9 maturated **10** consummate
12 accomplished

ripen 3 age **4** grow **5** bloom,
fruit **6** flower, mature, mellow **7** develop

Rip Kirby
　creator: **11** Alex Raymond
　12 John Prentice

Ripley, Robert L
　author of: **14** Believe It or
　Not

Rip Van Winkle
　author: **16** Washington Irving

rise 4 bank, defy, dune, face,
gain, go up, grow, hill, lift,

---

meet, soar **5** climb, get up,
knoll, march, mount, rebel,
ridge, spire, stand, surge,
swell, tower **6** ascend, growth,
mutiny, resist, revolt, rocket,
strike, thrive **7** advance, balloon, burgeon, disobey, elevate, headway, improve,
prosper, stand up, succeed, upswing **8** addition, flourish, increase, progress **9** expansion,
extension **10** embankment
11 advancement, enlargement

**Rise and Fall of the Third
Reich, The**
　author: **14** William L Shirer

Rise of Silas Lapham, The
　author: **18** William Dean
　Howells
　character: **5** Irene **8** Mr Rog-
　ers, Penelope, Tom Corey
　9 Mrs Lapham

risible 4 rich **5** comic, droll,
funny, merry, silly, witty
6 absurd, jocose, jovial
7 amusing, comical, jocular
8 farcical, humorous, mirthful
9 facetious, laughable, ludicrous, whimsical **10** ridiculous **11** nonsensical

rising sun
　god of: **5** Janus

risk 4 dare **5** peril **6** chance,
danger, gamble, hazard **7** imperil, venture **8** endanger,
jeopardy **9** speculate **10** jeopardize **11** imperilment, speculation, uncertainty
12 endangerment

risky 6 chancy, daring, unsafe
8 insecure, perilous, ticklish
9 dangerous, daredevil, haphazard, hazardous, hit or miss,
uncertain **10** precarious **11** adventurous, unprotected,
venturesome

risque 4 blue, lewd, racy
5 bawdy, dirty, gross, spicy
6 coarse, daring, ribald,
smutty, vulgar **7** immoral, obscene **8** immodest, improper,
indecent, off-color **9** offensive,
salacious **10** indecorous, indelicate, lascivious, licentious,
suggestive **12** pornographic

rite 6 ritual **7** liturgy, service
8 ceremony **9** formality, solemnity **10** ceremonial, observance

rite of passage 6 ritual
7 baptism **8** ceremony, marriage **10** bar mitzvah, bat
mitzvah, initiation **11** christening **12** confirmation

Rites of Passage
　author: **14** William Golding

Ritt, Martin
　director of: **3** Hud
　7 Sounder **8** Norma Rae,

The Front **26** The Spy Who
Came in From the Cold

Ritter, John
 born: **9** Burbank CA
 father: **9** Tex Ritter
 roles: **9** Hooperman
 11 Americathon, Jack Tripper **13** Three's Company
 14 Captain Avenger

Ritter, Thelma
 born: **10** Brooklyn NY
 roles: **10** Pillow Talk, Rear
 Window, The Misfits **11** All
 About Eve **15** The Mating
 Season **17** Birdman of Alca-
 traz **18** With a Song in My
 Heart **19** A Letter to Three
 Wives, Pickup on South
 Street **21** The Proud and the
 Profane **27** Miracle on
 Thirty-Fourth Street

ritual 4 rite **7** service **9** ceremony **10** observance

ritual bathing place
 Jewish Orthodox: **6** mikvah

ritualistic 6 formal, solemn
 10 ceremonial **11** ceremonious

ritualize 7 observe **9** celebrate,
solemnize **13** ceremonialize

ritzy 4 chic, posh, tony
 5 sharp, swank **6** classy,
 snazzy, spiffy **7** elegant, stylish **9** high-class, high-toned,
 luxurious, sumptuous

rival 3 foe **5** enemy, equal, excel, fight, match, outdo,
 touch **6** strive **7** eclipse, surpass **8** approach, opponent,
 opposing, outshine **9** adversary, competing, contender,
 disputant **10** antagonist, competitor, contending, contestant

Rivals, The
 author: **23** Richard Brinsley
 Sheridan
 character: **8** Bob Acres
 9 Faulkland **11** Mrs Malaprop **13** Julia Melville, Lydia Languish **17** Sir Lucius
 O'Trigger **18** Sir Anthony
 Absolute **19** Captain Jack
 Absolute (Ensign Beverley)

rive 4 rend **5** crack, split
 6 cleave, detach, divide, sunder **7** shatter **8** fracture

riven 4 rent, torn **5** split
 7 cleaved, cracked **8** sundered
 9 fractured, shattered

River, The
 director: **10** Jean Renoir
 based on novel by: **11** Rumer Godden
 cast: **5** Radha **13** Adrienne
 Corri, Arthur Shields, Nora
 Swinburne **15** Patricia
 Walters
 setting: **5** India **6** Bengal

Rivera, Diego
 born: **6** Mexico
 10 Guanajuato
 artwork: **5** Sleep **8** Creation
 11 Mother Earth **14** The Fecund Earth **15** Detroit Industry **18** Man at the
 Crossroads **21** Carnival of
 Mexican Life **23** Life in Pre-
 Hispanic Mexico

river mouth 5 delta, firth
 7 estuary

rivers
 god of: **6** Peneus, Simois
 7 Inachus

Rivers, Reba
 character in: **9** Sanctuary
 author: **8** Faulkner

rivet 3 fix, pin **6** absorb, clinch,
 engage, fasten, occupy **7** engross **8** fastener **9** fascinate

Rivieres du Sud see **6** Guinea

rivulet 3 run **4** rill **5** brook,
 creek **6** stream **9** streamlet

Riyadh
 capital of: **11** Saudi Arabia

Rizzuto, Phil
 nickname: **7** Scooter
 position: **9** shortstop
 sport: **8** baseball
 team: **14** New York Yankees

road 3 way **4** lane, path **5** byway, route, trail **6** avenue,
 street **7** freeway, highway,
 parkway **8** turnpike **9** boulevard **10** expressway, throughway **12** thoroughfare

Road Not Taken, The
 author: **11** Robert Frost

roads
 god of: **6** Hermes

road safety
 god of: **6** Sancus **10** Semo
 Sancus

Road to Gandolfo, The
 author: **12** Robert Ludlum

roam 3 gad **4** rove **5** drift,
 jaunt, prowl, range, stray,
 tramp **6** ramble, stroll, travel,
 wander **7** meander, traipse
 8 divagate **9** gallivant
 11 peregrinate

roan 5 horse **7** grayish, reddish,
 tannish **8** blackish, brownish

Roan Stallion
 author: **15** Robinson Jeffers

roar 3 bay, cry, din **4** bawl,
 boom, howl, roll, yell **5** blare,
 growl, grunt, noise, shout,
 snort **6** bellow, clamor, guffaw, outcry, racket, rumble,
 scream, shriek **7** bluster, resound, thunder **8** outburst
 10 vociferate

roast 3 pan **4** bake **6** berate
 7 scourge **8** barbecue
 9 criticize

rob 4 bilk, lift, loot, raid, sack,
 skin **5** cheat, filch, heist, rifle,
 seize, steal **6** burgle, fleece,
 forage, hold up, pilfer, thieve
 7 despoil, pillage, plunder,
 purloin, ransack, stick up,
 swindle **8** carry off, embezzle
 9 bamboozle **10** burglarize
 11 appropriate

Robards, Jason
 born: **9** Chicago IL
 wife: **12** Lauren Bacall
 roles: **5** Julia **7** Isadora
 9 Dick Diver **10** Ben Brad-
 lee **11** Jamie Tyrone
 12 Hour of the Gun **15** A
 Thousand Clowns, Dashiell
 Hammett, Melvin and How-
 ard, The Disenchanted
 16 Tender Is the Night
 19 All the President's Men
 24 Long Day's Journey into
 Night

Robbe-Grillet, Alain
 author of: **8** Jealousy **9** The
 Voyeur **10** The Erasers
 14 In the Labyrinth **19** Last
 Year at Marienbad

robber, Robber 4 yegg
 5 crook, thief **6** bandit, con
 man, outlaw, pirate, raider
 7 brigand, burglar, forager,
 rustler, sharper **8** Barabbas,
 marauder, swindler **9** buccaneer, despoiler, embezzler, larcenist, plunderer
 10 highwayman,
 pickpocket

Robbins, Harold
 author of: **8** The Betsy
 13 The Inheritors **14** Dreams
 Die First, The Adventurers
 16 The Carpetbaggers
 17 The Dream Merchants
 18 Never Love a Stranger
 20 A Stone for Danny
 Fisher **21** Seventy-Nine Park
 Avenue

Robbins, Jerome
 choreographer of: **8** Les
 Noces **9** Fancy Free,
 Interplay
 director of: **13** West Side
 Story (with Robert Wise,
 Oscar)

robe 4 gown **5** dress, habit,
 smock **6** duster **7** costume,
 garment **8** bathrobe, vestment
 9 housecoat
 French: **8** negligee
 Japanese: **6** kimono

Robe, The
 author: **13** Lloyd C Douglas

robe-de-chambre 12 dressing-
gown

Robert Kennedy and His Times
author: **20** Arthur M Schlesinger Jr

Roberts, Kenneth
author of: **16** Northwest Passage

Roberts, Rachel
born: **5** Wales **8** Llanelly
husband: **11** Rex Harrison
roles: **8** Foul Play **10** Oh Lucky Man **16** This Sporting Life **24** Murder on the Orient Express **29** Saturday Night and Sunday Morning

Robertson, Cliff
real name: **23** Clifford Parker Robertson
born: **9** La Jolla CA
wife: **11** Dina Merrill
roles: **5** PT-109 **6** Charly (Oscar) **9** Obsession **11** Falcon Crest

Robertson, Oscar
nickname: **7** The Big O
sport: **10** basketball
position: **5** guard
team: **14** Milwaukee Bucks **16** Cincinnati Royals

Robeson, Paul
born: **11** Princeton NJ
roles: **7** Othello **8** Show Boat **11** Brutus Jones **15** The Emperor Jones **17** King Solomon's Mines **22** All God's Chillun Got Wings

Robigo
goddess of: **5** grain

Robigus
spirit of: **9** red mildew **11** grain blight

Robin, Christopher
character in: **13** Winnie-the-Pooh
author: **5** Milne

Robin Hood's Adventures
author: **7** unknown
character: **9** Friar Tuck **10** Little John **11** Will Scarlet **14** Band of Merry Men **18** Sir Richard of the Lea **19** Sheriff of Nottingham

robin's-egg-blue 4 aqua **5** azure **7** sky-blue **8** cerulean **9** light blue **10** aquamarine, powder-blue

Robinson, Edward G
real name: **18** Emmanuel Goldenberg
born: **7** Romania **9** Bucharest
roles: **8** Key Largo **12** Little Caesar, Rico Bandello **13** Scarlet Street **15** Double Indemnity, Flesh and Fantasy **16** House of Strangers **19** The Woman in the Window **20** A Dispatch from

Reuters 21 Dr Ehrlich's Magic Bullet

Robinson, Edwin Arlington
author of: **6** Merlin **8** Amaranth, Tristram **10** King Jasper **11** Richard Cory **12** Captain Craig **13** Miniver Cheevy, Mr Flood's Party

Robinson, Jackie
sport: **8** baseball
team: **15** Brooklyn Dodgers
first black in: **12** major leagues

Robinson, Sugar Ray
real name: **19** Walker Smith Robinson
sport. **6** boxing
class: **12** middleweight, welterweight

Robinson Crusoe
author: **11** Daniel Defoe
character: **6** Friday

Rob Roy
author: **14** Sir Walter Scott
character: **11** Diana Vernon **18** Sir Frederick Vernon **23** Rob Roy MacGregor Campbell
Osbaldistone family:
5 Frank **7** William **9** Rashleigh **13** Sir Hildebrand

robust 3 fit **4** firm, hale, well, wiry **5** hardy, husky, lusty, sound, stout, tough **6** active, brawny, hearty, mighty, potent, rugged, sinewy, strong, sturdy, virile **7** healthy, staunch **8** athletic, forceful, muscular, powerful, stalwart, vigorous **9** energetic, healthful, strapping, wholesome **10** able-bodied **12** in fine fettle
French: **8** puissant

robustness 5 vigor **8** strength **10** good health, ruggedness, sturdiness **11** healthiness

Roche, Kevin
architect of: **13** Oakland Museum (CA) **14** Fine Arts Center (U of MA), Ford Foundation (NYC) **17** Knights of Columbus (New Haven CT) **21** One United Nations Plaza (NYC) **24** Union Carbide Headquarters (Danbury CT) **31** Power Center for the Performing Arts (U of Michigan)

Rochester
football team: **8** Panthers

Rochester, Edward
character in: **8** Jane Eyre
author: **6** Bronte

rock 3 bob, jar **4** crag, reef, roll, stun, sway, toss **5** cliff, flint, pitch, quake, shake, stone, swing, upset **6** gravel,

marble, pebble, totter, wobble **7** agitate, bobbing, boulder, disturb, shaking **8** convulse, flounder, undulate, wobbling **9** limestone, oscillate, tottering **10** convulsion, undulation

Rock & Rye
type: **7** liqueur
flavor: **6** citrus
ingredient: **3** rye **9** rock candy

rock crystal
species: **6** quartz
color: **9** colorless

Rocket
nickname of: **14** Maurice Richard

rocket engine
invented by: **7** Goddard

Rockford Files, The
character: **10** John Cooper **11** Angel Martin, Jim Rockford **12** (Det) Dennis Becker **13** Beth Davenport, (Joseph) Rocky Rockford
cast: **9** Bo Hopkins, Joe Santos, Noah Beery **11** James Garner **14** Stuart Margolin **15** Gretchen Corbett

rock of Tarik *see* **9** Gibraltar

Rockwell, Norman
born: **9** New York NY
artwork:
covers: **19** Saturday Evening Post
mural: **15** Freedom of Speech

Rocky
director: **13** John G Avildsen
cast: **9** Burt Young **10** Talia Shire **11** Thayer David **12** Carl Weathers **15** Burgess Meredith **17** Sylvester Stallone (Rocky Balboa, the Italian Stallion)
setting: **12** Philadelphia
Oscar for: **7** editing, picture **8** director
sequel: **7** Rocky II, Rocky IV **8** Rocky III, Rocky Two **9** Rocky Four **10** Rocky Three

rod 4 cane, lash, mace, pale, pole, wand, whip **5** baton, birch, crook, staff, stake, stick **6** cudgel, rattan, switch **7** penalty, scepter, scourge **8** caduceus **9** stanchion **10** alpenstock, punishment **11** retribution **12** swagger stick
abbreviation: **2** rd

rod, Aaron's *see* **9** Aaron's rod

rodent 4 cavy, vole **5** coypu, gundi, hutia, mouse **6** agouti, beaver, cururo, gerbil, gopher, jerboa, nutria **7** blesmol, cane rat, hamster, lemming, molerat, rock rat **8** capybara, chipmunk, dormouse, pacarana, sewellel, spiny rat, squirrel, tucu-tuco, viscacha **9** chozchori, false paca, porcupine, woodchuck **10** chinchilla, prairie dog, springhare **11** kangaroo rat, pocket mouse, viscacha rat **13** kangaroo mouse **16** Speke's pectinator

Roderick Hudson
   author: **10** Henry James

Roderick Random
   author: **14** Tobias Smollett
   character: **5** Strap **8** Narcissa **10** Tom Bowling **12** Miss Williams

Rodin, (Francois) Auguste Rene
   born: **5** Paris **6** France
   artwork: **7** The Kiss **10** Head of Iris, The Thinker, Victor Hugo, Walking Man **14** John the Baptist, The Age of Bronze, The Gates of Hell **16** Monument to Balzac **19** The Burghers of Calais **23** The Man with the Broken Nose

rodomontade 4 rant **5** boast **6** hot air **7** blather, bluster, bombast, fustian **8** bragging, folderol, nonsense, rhetoric **10** balderdash, doubletalk **11** braggadocio **12** boastfulness

roe 3 doe, elk, hen **4** buck, deer, eggs, fawn, fish, hart, hind, milt **5** spawn, sperm **6** caviar **8** fish eggs
   of lobster: **5** coral

Roentgen, Rontgen, Wilhelm Konrad
   field: **7** physics
   nationality: **6** German
   discovered: **5** X-rays
   awarded: **10** Nobel Prize

Roethke, Theodore
   author of: **9** Open House, The Waking **11** The Far Field **15** Straw for the Fire, Words for the Wind

Rogers, Ginger
   real name: **23** Virginia Katherine McMath
   born: **14** Independence MO
   husband: **8** Lew Ayres **15** Jacques Bergerac, William Marshall
   partner: **11** Fred Astaire
   roles: **6** Top Hat **9** Stage Door **10** Hello Dolly, Kitty Foyle (Oscar) **12** Shall We Dance? **14** The Gay Divorcee **15** Flying Down to Rio, Tom Dick and Harry **17** Forty-Second Street **19** The Major and the Minor **21** The Barkleys of Broadway **30** The Story of Vernon and Irene Castle

Rogers, James Gamble
   architect of: **22** Northwestern University (Chicago) **33** Columbia-Presbyterian Medical Center (NYC)

Rogers, Roy
   real name: **11** Leonard Slye
   born: **12** Cincinnati OH
   wife: **9** Dale Evans
   sidekick: **10** Gabby Hayes
   singing group: **17** Sons of the Pioneers
   horse: **7** Trigger
   roles: **10** Apache Rose **11** Song of Texas **12** My Pal Trigger **13** Song of Arizona, Son of Paleface **17** Heart of the Rockies, Under Western Stars **18** Billy the Kid Returns **19** Tumbling Tumbleweeds **20** The Yellow Rose of Texas **22** Springtime in the Sierras

rogue 3 cur **5** devil, fraud, knave, scamp **6** bad man, rascal, rotter, varlet, wretch **7** bounder, hellion, villain **8** deceiver, evildoer, scalawag **9** miscreant, reprobate, scoundrel **10** blackguard, malefactor, mountebank, scapegrace **11** rapscallion **13** mischiefmaker **14** good-for-nothing **15** snake in the grass

Rogue Herries
   author: **11** Hugh Walpole

roguish 3 sly **4** arch **5** saucy **8** devilish, rascally **11** mischievous

Rohe, Vera-Ellen
   real name of: **9** Vera-Ellen

roil 3 irk, vex **4** mill, rile, stir **5** annoy, muddy **6** ruffle, seethe **7** agitate, disturb, perturb, provoke, turmoil **8** irritate **9** aggravate **10** exasperate

role 3 job **4** duty, part, pose, post, task, work **5** chore, guise **7** posture, service **8** capacity, function **9** character, portrayal **10** assignment **13** impersonation **14** representation **15** personification **16** characterization
   Latin: **7** persona

roll 4 boom, coil, curl, echo, flip, flow, furl, knot, list, loop, reel, roar, rock, spin, sway, toss, tube, turn, wind **5** coast, crack, lurch, pitch, sound, spool, surge, swell, swing, swirl, throw, twirl, twist, wheel, whirl **6** billow, gyrate, muster, roster, rotate, rumble, scroll, tumble **7** booming, catalog, entwine, resound, revolve, rocking, thunder, tossing, turning **8** cylinder, drumbeat, drumming, rumbling, sched-

ule, tumbling, undulate **9** inventory **10** undulation **11** reverberate **13** reverberation **15** turn over and over

Rolland, Romain
   author of: **14** Jean-Christophe **16** The Soul Enchanted

rollicking 3 gay **5** happy, jolly, merry, sunny **6** bright, hearty, jocund, jovial, joyous, lively **7** gleeful, jocular, playful, romping **8** cheerful, mirthful, spirited **9** exuberant, gamboling, sparkling, sprightly **10** frolicking, frolicsome, hysterical, rip-roaring **12** lighthearted

Rolvaag, Ole Edvart
   author of: **15** Peder Victorious, Their Father's God **16** Giants in the Earth

roly-poly 3 fat **5** obese, plump, pudgy, round **6** chubby, rotund **9** corpulent

Roma
   father: **7** Evander

roman 5 novel **17** metrical narrative

Roman Catholic church
   council/synod: **4** Pisa **5** Basel, Trent **6** Nicaea, Vienne, Whitby **7** Ephesus, Pistoia, Sardica **9** Chalcedon, Constance **12** First Vatican **13** Fourth Lateran, Second Vatican **14** Constantinople **15** Ferrara-Florence
   official Vatican yearbook: **18** Annuario Pontificio
   first Christian emperor: **11** Constantine
   gifts of territory/sovereignty to papacy: **15** Donation of Pepin **21** Donation of Constantine

romance 4 bosh, call, pull **5** amour, idyll, novel **6** affair, allure **7** fantasy, fiction **8** illusion **9** courtship, exoticism, fairy tale, fish story, invention, love story, melodrama, moonshine, tall story **10** attachment, concoction, flirtation, love affair **11** fabrication, fascination, imagination **12** exaggeration, relationship, self-delusion **13** flight of fancy, tender passion **16** affair of the heart

Romance language see **5** Latin

Romance of the Forest
   author: **12** Ann Radcliffe

Romances sans paroles
   author: **12** Paul Verlaine

Romancing the Stone
   director: **14** Robert Zemeckis

cast: 11 Danny De Vito
14 Kathleen Turner, Michael
Douglas
sequel: 17 The Jewel of the
Nile

Roman Holiday
  director: 12 William Wyler
  cast: 11 Eddie Albert, Gregory Peck **13** Audrey
  Hepburn
  Oscar for: 7 actress (Hepburn)

Romania *see* **7** Rumania

Roman measure 2 as **5** cubit,
libra **6** pondus **7** stadium

Roman Mythology *see box*

romantic 4 fond **5** mushy,
soppy **6** ardent, dreamy, loving, tender, unreal **7** amorous,
devoted, fervent, flighty, idyllic, utopian **8** enamored, fanciful, quixotic **9** fantastic,
idealized, imaginary, sensitive,
visionary, whimsical **10** idealistic, improbable, passionate
11 extravagant, impassioned,
impractical, rhapsodical, sentimental, unrealistic, warmhearted **12** melodramatic,
preposterous

Romantic Comedians, The
  author: 12 Ellen Glasgow

romanticize 8 idealize
9 embroider

Romantic Manifesto
  author: 7 Ayn Rand

Romany Rye, The
  author: 17 George Henry
  Borrow

Rome, ancient *see box,*
p. 841

Rome, Roma *see box,*
p. 841

Rome Haul
  author: 14 Walter D
  Edmonds

Romeo 4 beau **5** lover, sheik,
swain, wooer **7** Don Juan, gallant **8** Casanova, cavalier, Lothario **9** boyfriend, Lochinvar
  French: 8 paramour
  Latin: 9 inamorato

Romeo and Juliet
  author: 18 William
  Shakespeare
  character: 5 Nurse, Paris
  6 Tybalt **8** Benvolio, Mercutio **13** Friar Laurence
    family: **7** Capulet
    8 Montague
  setting: 6 Verona

Romeo and Juliet
  director:
    1936 version: **11** George
    Cukor
    1968 version: **16** Franco
    Zeffirelli

Roman Mythology
  collective name for gods: 6 Superi
  goddess of anguish: 8 Angerona
  goddess of agriculture: 5 Ceres **6** Dea Dia, Vacuna
  13 Acca Laurentia
    Ceres corresponds to Greek: **7** Demeter
  goddess of the arts: 7 Minerva
    corresponds to Greek: **6** Athena
  goddess of baking: 6 Fornax
  goddess of chastity: 5 Fauna **7** Bona Dea
  goddess of childbirth: 5 Parca **6** Lucina, Matuta, Parcae
  11 Mater Matuta
  goddess of the dawn: 6 Aurora, Matuta **11** Mater Matuta
    Aurora corresponds to Greek: **3** Eos
  goddess of destiny: 5 Parca **6** Parcae
  goddess of discord: 9 Discordia
  goddess of door hinges: 6 Cardea
  goddess of the earth: 6 Tellus
    corresponds to Greek: **4** Gaea
  goddess of the family: 6 Cardea
  goddess of fertility: 5 Fauna **6** Libera, Tellus
  7 Bona Dea
    Libera corresponds to Greek: **10** Persephone
    Tellus corresponds to Greek: **4** Gaea
  goddess of flowers: 5 Flora
  goddess of fortune: 7 Fortuna
    corresponds to Greek: **5** Tyche
  goddess of fruit trees: 6 Pomona
  goddess of gardens: 5 Venus
    corresponds to Greek: **9** Aphrodite
  goddess of grain/protectress against grain blight:
  6 Robigo
  goddess of harbors: 6 Matuta **11** Mater Matuta
  goddess of harmony: 9 Concordia
  goddess of the hearth: 4 Caca **5** Salus, Vesta
    Salus corresponds to Greek: **6** Hygeia
  goddess of heaven: 4 Juno
    corresponds to Greek: **4** Hera
  goddess of hunting: 5 Diana
    corresponds to Greek: **6** Phoebe **7** Artemis
  goddess of longevity: 11 Anna Perenna
  goddess of love: 5 Venus
    corresponds to Greek: **9** Aphrodite
  goddess of marriage: 4 Juno **6** Tellus
    corresponds to Greek: **4** Gaea, Hera
  goddess of marshes: 6 Marica **9** Dea Marica
  goddess of the moon: 5 Diana
    corresponds to Greek: **6** Phoebe **7** Artemis
  goddess of peace: 3 Pax **9** Concordia
    Pax corresponds to Greek: **5** Irene
  goddess of pleasure: 8 Voluptas
  goddess of plenty: 3 Ops **10** Magna Mater
  goddess of prosperity: 5 Salus
    corresponds to Greek: **6** Hygeia
  goddess of the sea: 6 Matuta **11** Mater Matuta
  goddess of sleeping infants: 6 Cunina
  goddess of the spring: 5 Venus
    corresponds to Greek: **9** Aphrodite
  goddess of storms: 11 Tempestates
  goddess of victory: 8 Victoria
    corresponds to Greek: **4** Nike
  goddess of vineyards: 6 Libera
    corresponds to Greek: **10** Persephone
  goddess of war: 7 Bellona
    corresponds to Greek: **5** Enyon
  goddess of wine: 6 Libera
    corresponds to Greek: **10** Persephone
  goddess of wisdom: 7 Minerva
    corresponds to Greek: **6** Athena

(continued)

Roman Mythology (continued)

god of agriculture: 5 Picus 6 Saturn 7 Eventus 12 Bonus Eventus
   corresponds to Greek: 6 Cronos, Cronus, Kronos
god of beginnings: 5 Janus
god of boundaries: 8 Terminus
god of commerce: 7 Mercury
   corresponds to Greek: 6 Hermes
god of the dead: 7 Veiovis
god of doorways: 5 Janus
god of drinking/revelry: 5 Comus
god of eloquence: 7 Mercury
   corresponds to Greek: 6 Hermes
god of farm boundaries: 8 Silvanus, Sylvanus
god of fertility: 7 Mutinus, Priapus 8 Lupercus, Picumnus
god of fire/metalworking: 6 Vulcan
   corresponds to Greek: 10 Hephaestus, Hephaistos
god of forest: 7 Virbius
god of gardens: 9 Vertumnus
god of good counsel: 3 Ops 6 Consus
god of grain/protector against grain blight: 7 Robigus
god of healing: 11 Aesculapius
   corresponds to Greek: 9 Asclepius
god of heavens: 4 Jove 7 Jupiter
   corresponds to Greek: 4 Zeus
god of herds: 8 Silvanus, Sylvanus
god of horse racing: 3 Ops 6 Consus
god of hospitality: 6 Sancus 10 Dius Fidius, Semo Sancus
god of the house: 8 Silvanus, Sylvanus
god of hunting: 7 Virbius
god of international affairs: 6 Sancus 10 Dius Fidius, Semo Sancus
god of landmarks: 8 Terminus
god of light: 6 Apollo
god of love: 4 Amor 5 Cupid
   corresponds to Greek: 4 Eros
god of luck: 7 Eventus 12 Bonus Eventus
god of medicine: 11 Aesculapius
   corresponds to Greek: 9 Asclepius
god of music: 6 Apollo
god of oaths: 6 Sancus 10 Dius Fidius, Semo Sancus
god of orchards: 9 Vertumnus
god of ports/harbors: 8 Portunus
god of prosperity: 7 Eventus 12 Bonus Eventus
god of the rising sun: 5 Janus

god of science: 7 Mercury
   corresponds to Greek: 6 Hermes
god of sea: 7 Neptune
   corresponds to Greek: 8 Poseidon
god of seasons: 9 Vertumnus
god of the setting sun: 5 Janus
god of sleep: 6 Somnus
   corresponds to Greek: 6 Hypnos, Hypnus
god of springs: 4 Fons
gods of sulphur springs (twins): 6 Palici
god of the sun: 3 Sol
   corresponds to Greek: 6 Helios 8 Hyperion
god of thievery: 7 Mercury
   corresponds to Greek: 6 Hermes
god of thunder: 7 Taranis
god of thunderstorms: 8 Summanus
god of the Tiber: 9 Tiberinus
god of uncultivated land: 8 Silvanus, Sylvanus
god of underworld: 3 Dis 5 Orcus 8 Dis Pater
   corresponds to Greek: 5 Pluto
god of war: 4 Mars 6 Mamers, Mavors 8 Quirinus
   corresponds to Greek: 4 Ares
god of weather: 4 Jove 7 Jupiter
god of weddings: 8 Talassio
   corresponds to Greek: 5 Hymen 9 Hymenaeus
god of the woods: 6 Faunus 8 Silvanus, Sylvanus
house spirits: 5 lares 7 penates
nymphs/deities with gift of prophecy: 7 Camenae
   names: 6 Egeria 8 Carmenta 9 Antevorta, Postvorta
   correspond to Greek: 5 Muses
protectress of childbirth: 8 Carmenta
protectress of cows/oxen: 6 Bubona
protector of flocks/shepherds: 5 Pales
protectress of military age men: 8 Juventas
   corresponds to Greek: 4 Hebe
protectress of women: 5 Diana
   corresponds to Greek: 6 Phoebe 7 Artemis
protectress of women/marriage: 4 Juno
queen of heaven: 4 Juno
   corresponds to Greek: 4 Hera, Here
staff of Mercury: 8 Caduceus
troublesome ghosts: 7 lemures

---

based on play by: 18 William Shakespeare
cast:
   1936 version: 12 Leslie Howard, Norma Shearer 13 Basil Rathbone, Edna May Oliver, John Barrymore
   1968 version: 9 Milo O'Shea 11 John McEnery, Michael York 12 Olivia Hussey 14 Leonard Whiting
score: 8 Nino Rota

Romeo and Juliet

symphony by: 7 Berlioz

opera by: 6 Gounod
orchestral piece by: 11 Tchaikovsky
ballet by: 9 Prokofiev

Romney, George

born: 7 England 15 Dalton-in-Furness
artwork: 5 Circe 9 Joan of Arc 11 Mrs Robinson, Sensibility 12 Mrs Davenport, Saint Cecilia 19 Mrs Carwardine and Son 22 The Death of General Wolfe 24 The Levenson-Gower Children 26 Sir Christopher and Lady Sykes

Romola

author: 11 George Eliot
character: 5 Bardo, Tessa 10 Tito Melema 15 Baldasarre Calvo

romp 3 hop 4 skip 5 caper, cut up, frisk, sport 6 frolic, gambol 7 disport, rollick

Romulus

father: 4 Mars
mother: 4 Ilia 9 Rea Silvia 10 Rhea Silvia
twin brother: 5 Remus
raised by: 7 she-wolf 9 Faustulus 12 Acca Larentia

Rome, ancient
  emperor: 4 Nero, Otho 5 Galba, Nerva, Titus 6 Trajan
    7 Hadrian 8 Augustus, Caligula, Claudius, Commodus,
    Domitian, Tiberius 9 Caracalla, Vespasian, Vitellius
    10 Diocletian 11 Constantine, Lucius Verus 13 Antoninus
    Pius 14 Marcus Aurelius
  emperor's bodyguard: 15 Praetorian Guard
  first citizen title: 8 princeps
  first triumvirate: 6 Caesar, Pompey 7 Crassus
  foe: 4 Gaul 5 Spain 6 Cimbri 7 Perseus, Philip V, Pyrrhus,
    Teutons 8 Carthage, Hannibal, Iberians, Jugurtha, Sam-
    nites, Tarentum, Umbrians 9 Etruscans, Macedonia, Seleu-
    cids 11 Latin League 12 Antiochus III 13 Achaean
    League, Hamilcar Barca
  general: 5 Sulla 6 Brutus, Marius, Pompey 7 Crassus 8 Oc-
    tavian 10 Flamininus, Mark Antony 12 Julius Caesar
    14 Caesar Augustus 20 Quintus Fabius Maximus, Scipio
    Africanus Major, Scipio Africanus Minor
  king: 12 Ancus Marcius 13 Numa Pompilius 16 Sextus Tar-
    quinius 17 Tarquinius Priscus (Tarquin the Elder) 18 Tar-
    quinius Superbus (Tarquin the Proud)
  reformer: 8 Gracchus
  republican ruler: 6 consul 7 senator, tribune 8 plebeian
    9 optimates, patrician, populares 10 magistrate
  Roman peace: 9 Pax Romana
  second triumvirate: 6 Antony 7 Lepidus 8 Octavian (Cae-
    sar Augustus)

Rome, Roma
  airport: 8 Ciampino 15 Leonardo da Vinci
  area: 9 Cinecitta (Cinema City) 10 Trastevere 11 Vatican
    City
  capital of: 5 Italy 6 Latium 11 Papal States, Roman
    Empire
  church: 8 St Peter's 11 San Giovanni 18 Santa Maria Mag-
    giore 19 San Paolo Fuori le Mura
  Italian: 4 Roma
  landmark: 5 Forum 7 Capitol 8 Pantheon 9 catacombs, Col-
    osseum 12 Palazzo Doria 13 Circus Maximus, Lateran
    Palace, Sistine Chapel, Vatican Palace, Villa Borghese
    14 Palazzo Corsini, Villa Farnesina 16 Baths of Caracalla,
    Castel Sant'Angelo, Palazzo Barberini 17 Arch of Con-
    stantine 19 Saint Peter's Basilica
  legendary founders: 5 Remus 6 Aeneas 7 Romulus
  nickname: 11 Eternal City
  mountain: 8 Apennine
  museum: 5 Doria 7 Colonna, Corsini, Vatican 8 Borghese,
    National 10 Capitoline
  river: 5 Tiber
  school: 33 Conservatorio di Musica Santa Cecilia
  sea: 10 Tyrrhenian
  seven hills: 7 Caelian, Viminal 8 Aventine, Palatine, Quir-
    inal 9 Esquiline 10 Capitoline
  square/piazza: 6 Popolo, Spagna 7 Colonna, Venezia
    9 Quirinale 11 Campidoglio
  state within: 11 Vatican City
  street: 9 Appian Way, Emmanuele 11 Via del Corso
    13 Corso Vittorio
  subway: 13 Metropolitana

first king of: 4 Rome
founder of: 4 Rome

Romus
  father: 6 Aeneas 8 Ascanius
  possible founder of: 4 Rome

Ronan
  origin: 5 Irish
  form: 4 king
  son: 4 Mael
  killed: 4 Mael
  killed by: 13 grandchildren

Roncalli, Angelo Giuseppe
  13 Pope John XXIII 22 Pope
  John the Twenty-Third

Ronsard, Pierre de
  author of: 17 Sonnets pour
    Helene
  member of: 7 Pleiade

roofing 4 tile, turf 5 slate,
  terne 6 thatch 7 asphalt, ceiling, pantile, shingle
  8 housetop

Roof of the World see
  5 Tibet

rook 3 gyp 4 bilk, crow, dupe,
  gull 5 cheat, cozen, raven,
  trick 6 castle, fleece 7 deceive,
  defraud, swindle 8 chessman
  9 bamboozle, victimize

rookie 4 tyro 6 novice 8 beginner 9 fledgling, greenhorn
  10 apprentice, tenderfoot

Rookies, The
  character: 9 Jill Danko, (Offi-
    cer) Mike Danko 10 (Lt) Ed-
    die Ryker, (Officer) Chris
    Owens 12 (Officer) Terry
    Webster, (Officer) Willie
    Gillis
  cast: 11 Kate Jackson, Sam
    Melville 14 Bruce Fairbairn,
    Michael Ontkean 16 Gerald
    S O'Loughlin 18 Georg
    Stanford Brown

room 4 area 5 range, scope,
  space 6 chance, extent, leeway, margin, volume 7 chamber, cubicle, expanse, lodging
  9 allowance, provision, territory 11 compartment
  French: 5 salle
  Spanish: 4 sala

Room at the Top
  director: 11 Jack Clayton
  based on novel by: 10 John
    Braine
  cast: 12 Heather Sears
    14 Laurence Harvey, Simone
    Signoret 16 Hermione
    Baddeley
  Oscar for: 7 actress
    (Signoret)
  sequel: 11 Man at the Top
    12 Life at the Top

Room 222
  character: 6 Bernie 9 Pete
    Dixon 11 Liz McIntyre
    12 Alice Johnson 14 Sey-
    mour Kaufman
  cast: 11 Lloyd Haynes
    13 David Jolliffe 14 Denise
    Nicholas, Karen Valentine
    18 Michael Constantine
  school: 15 Walt Whitman
    High

roomy 3 big 4 huge, long, vast,
  wide 5 ample, broad, large
  7 immense, lengthy, sizable
  8 generous, spacious 9 boundless, capacious, expansive, ex-

Roosevelt, Franklin Delano
   presidential rank: 12 thirty-second
   party: 10 Democratic
   state represented: 2 NY
   defeated: 5 (Jacob Sechler) Coxey, (John W) Aiken, (Thomas Edmund) Dewey, (William)
    Lemke **6** (Alfred Mossman) Landon, (Claude A) Watson, (David Leigh) Colvin, (Herbert Clark)
    Hoover, (Norman) Thomas, (Roger Ward) Babson, (William David) Upshaw, (William Hope)
    Harvey, (William Zebulon) Foster **7** (Earl Russell) Browder, (Wendell Lewis) Willkie **8** (Ed-
    ward A) Teichert, (Verne L) Reynolds
   vice president: 6 (Harry S) Truman, (John Nance) Garner **7** (Henry Agard) Wallace
   cabinet:
    state: **4** (Cordell) Hull **10** (Edward Reilly) Stettinius (Jr)
    treasury: **6** (William Hartman) Woodin **10** (Henry) Morgenthau (Jr)
    war: **4** (George Henry) Dern **7** (Henry Lewis) Stimson **8** (Harry Hines) Woodring
    attorney general: **6** (Francis) Biddle, (Frank) Murphy **7** (Robert Houghwout) Jackson **8** (Ho-
     mer Stille) Cummings
    navy: **4** (Frank) Knox **6** (Charles) Edison **7** (Claude Augustus) Swanson **9** (James Vincent)
     Forrestal
    postmaster general: **6** (Frank Comerford) Walker, (James Aloysius) Farley
    interior: **5** (Harold LeClaire) Ickes
    agriculture: **7** (Claude Raymond) Wickard, (Henry Agard) Wallace
    commerce: **5** (Daniel Calhoun) Roper, (Jesse Holman) Jones **7** (Henry Agard) Wallace,
     (Henry Lloyd) Hopkins
    labor: **7** (Frances) Perkins (Wilson)
   born: 10 Hyde Park NY
   died: 13 Warm Springs GA **16** Little White House
   buried: 10 Hyde Park NY
   education:
    prep school: **6** Groton
    university: **7** Harvard
    law school: **8** Columbia
   religion: 12 Episcopalian
   interests: 3 art **4** polo **6** tennis, travel **7** fishing, hunting **8** shooting
   vacation spot: 13 Warm Springs GA **16** Campobello Island (Canada)
   dog: 4 Fala
   author: 27 The Happy Warrior: Alfred E Smith
   political career: 12 state senator
    assistant secretary of: **4** Navy
    governor of: **7** New York
   civilian career: 6 lawyer **11** bank officer
   notable events of lifetime/term: 4 D-Day, WWII **7** New Deal **10** atomic bomb, Depression,
    World War II **11** World War Two **13** United Nations **15** Atlantic Charter
    act: **9** Lend-Lease
    attack on: **11** Pearl Harbor
    conference: **5** Cairo, Yalta **7** Arcadia, Crimean, Teheran
    scandal: **11** Tammany Hall
   quote: 24 A day that will live in infamy **31** Meet every day's troubles as they come **36** The
    only thing we have to fear is fear itself **50** This generation of Americans has a rendezvous
    with destiny **53** I pledge you I pledge myself to a new deal for the American people
   father: 5 James
   mother: 4 Sara (Delano)
   siblings:
    half-brother: **5** James
   wife: 7 (Anna) Eleanor (Roosevelt)
   children: 5 James **7** Elliott **11** Anna Eleanor **13** John Aspinwell **14** Franklin Delano
   first lady:
    author: **7** On My Own **13** This I Remember, This Is My Story **34** The Autobiography of
     Eleanor Roosevelt
    chairwoman: **25** UN Commission on Human Rights
    codirector: **23** Office of Civilian Defense
    member: **35** Democratic National Campaign Committee
    newspaper column: **5** My Day
    US delegate to: **2** UN

tensive, unlimited
10 commodious

Rooney, Mickey
  real name: 9 Joe Yule Jr
  born: 10 Brooklyn NY

wife: 10 Ava Gardner
 13 Martha Vickers
co-star: 11 Judy Garland
roles: 4 Puck **8** Boys' Town
 9 Andy Hardy **11** Sugar Babies **13** Mickey McGuire

14 Baby Face Nelson, National Velvet, The Human Comedy **21** A Midsummer Night's Dream **30** The Adventures of Huckleberry Finn

Roosevelt, Theodore
  nickname: 5 Teddy
  presidential rank: 11 twenty-sixth
  party: 10 Republican
  state represented: 2 NY
  succeeded: 8 McKinley
  defeated (second term): 4 (Eugene Victor) Debs 6 (Alton Brooks) Parker, (Thomas Edward)
    Watson 7 (Austin) Holcomb, (Silas Comfort) Swallow 8 (Charles Hunter) Corregan
  vice president: 4 none (1st term) 9 (Charles Warren) Fairbanks
  cabinet:
    state: 3 (John Milton) Hay 4 (Elihu) Root 5 (Robert) Bacon
    treasury: 4 (Leslie Mortier) Shaw, (Lyman Judson) Gage 9 (George Bruce) Cortelyou
    war: 4 (Elihu) Root, (William Howard) Taft 6 (Luke Edward) Wright
    attorney general: 4 (Philander Chase) Knox 5 (William Henry) Moody 9 (Charles Joseph)
      Bonaparte
    navy: 4 (John Davis) Long 5 (William Henry) Moody 6 (Paul) Morton 7 (Victor Howard)
      Metcalf 8 (Truman Handy) Newberry 9 (Charles Joseph) Bonaparte
    postmaster general: 5 (Charles Emory) Smith, (George von Lengerke) Meyer, (Henry Clay)
      Payne, (Robert John) Wynne 9 (George Bruce) Cortelyou
    interior: 8 (James Rudolph) Garfield 9 (Ethan Allen) Hitchcock
    agriculture: 6 (James) Wilson
    commerce and labor: 6 (Oscar Solomon) Straus 7 (Victor Howard) Metcalf 9 (George Bruce)
      Cortelyou
  born: 13 New York City NY
  died/buried: 2 NY 9 Oyster Bay 10 Long Island
  education:
    university: 7 Harvard
    law school: 8 Columbia (did not graduate)
  religion: 13 Dutch Reformed
  interests: 7 hunting (African game), writing 9 exploring (South America) 14 natural history
  author: 11 Rough Riders 14 Oliver Cromwell 16 Gouverneur Morris, Thomas Hart Benton
    17 African Game Trails, The New Nationalism 19 The Winning of the West 20 Letters to
    His Children 21 America and the World War 24 The Foes of Our Own Household 25 Fear
    God and Take Your Own Part 27 A Booklover's Holiday in the Open, Ranch Life and the
    Hunting Trail, The Naval War of Eighteen-Twelve 28 Hero Tales from American History
    29 Through the Brazilian Wilderness 33 Life Histories of African Game Animals
  political career: 13 Vice President 15 NY State Assembly 24 US Civil Service Commission
    assistant secretary: 4 Navy
    governor of: 7 New York
    organized party: 9 Bull Moose 11 Progressive
  civilian career: 6 author 7 rancher 14 public lecturer
  military service: 15 NY National Guard 18 Spanish-American War
    organized cavalry regiment: 11 Rough Riders
    led charge up: 11 San Juan Hill
  notable events of lifetime/term: 5 Panic (of 1907) 10 Square Deal 15 Nobel Peace Prize
    22 San Francisco earthquake
    Act: 11 Reclamation 14 Meat Inspection 15 Hepburn Railroad, Pure Food and Drug
    bureau of: 12 Corporations 28 Immigration and Naturalization
    first flight by: 14 Wright Brothers
    revolution: 6 Panama
    treaty: 13 Hay-Pauncefote 15 Hay-Bunau-Varilla
  quotes: 25 Hasten forward quickly there 28 Speak softly and carry a big stick
  father: 8 Theodore
  mother: 6 Martha (Bulloch)
  siblings: 4 Anna 7 Corinne, Elliott
  wife: 5 Alice (Hathaway Lee), Edith (Kermit Carow)
  children: 6 Kermit 7 Quentin 8 Alice Lee, Theodore 10 Ethel Carow 16 Archibald Bulloch

Roosevelt, Franklin Delano
see box, p. 842

Roosevelt, Theodore *see box*

rooster
  young: 8 cockerel

root 3 fix, set 4 back, base,
bind, bulb, clap, hail, nail,
rise, stem 5 basis, boost,
cheer, fount, radix, start, stick,
tubes 6 bottom, fasten,
ground, motive, origin, reason,
second, source, spring 7 acclaim, applaud, bolster, cheer
on, pull for, radicle, support
8 fountain, occasion, shout
for 9 beginning, encourage,
establish, inception, rationale
10 derivation, foundation,
mainspring 11 fundamental
12 commencement,
fountainhead

Root, John Wellborn
  partner: 14 Daniel H
    Burnham
  architect of: 10 The Rook-
    ery 12 Hotel Statler (Wash-
    ington DC), Montauk Block
    13 Hotel Tamanaco (Cara-
    cas) 17 Monadnock Build-

Roots
   author: **9** Alex Haley
   character: **3** Tom **4** Ames, Bell, Noah **5** Binta, Fanta, Grill,
   Irene, Kizzy, Lewis, Mingo, Omoro **6** Justin, Martha, Or-
   dell **7** Fiddler, Gardner, Nyo Boto **8** Kintango, Mathilda,
   Mrs Moore, Tom Moore **9** Evan Brent, Missy Anne
   10 Brima Cesay, Capt Davies, Carrington, Jemmy Brent,
   Kadi Touray, Kunta Kinte, Sam Bennett, Sister Sara
   11 Mrs Reynolds, Squire James **12** John Reynolds
   13 Chicken George **14** Sir Eric Russell, Stephen Bennett
   15 Ol' George Johnson, Third Mate Slater **17** Dr William
   Reynolds
   cast: **8** Burl Ives, John Amos, Ren Woods **9** Ben Vereen,
   Brad Davis, Moses Gunn, O J Simpson, Vic Morrow
   10 Billy Hicks, Ian McShane, John Schuck, Lynne Moody,
   Olivia Cole, Paul Shenar, Ralph Waite, Robert Reed
   11 Beverly Todd, Cicely Tyson, Doug McClure, Edward
   Asner, Gary Collins, Harry Rhodes, Lane Binkley, LeVar
   Burton, Lorne Greene, Maya Angelou, Sandy Duncan
   12 Carolyn Jones, Chuck Connors, Leslie Uggams, Lloyd
   Bridges **13** Louis Gosset Jr, Madge Sinclair, William Wat-
   son **14** George Hamilton, Lynda Day George, Macdonald
   Carey **15** Lillian Randolph, Scatman Crothers, Thalmus
   Rasulala **16** Raymond St Jacques, Richard Roundtree
   18 Georg Stanford Brown **20** Lawrence Hilton-Jacobs

ing, Palmolive Building
(Chicago) **19** Rand-McNally
Building

root for 5 boost **6** urge on
7 cheer on, pull for

root out 5 dig up **6** remove
7 extract, pull out, uncover,
unearth **8** discover **9** extirpate,
ferret out **12** bring to light

Roots *see box*

rope 3 gad, guy, tie, tow
4 bind, cord, fast, guss, hemp,
line, lure, snag, trap, wire,
yarn **5** cable, catch, chord,
lasso, noose, riata, shank,
strap, twine **6** corral, entice,
hawser, lariat, seduce, string,
tether **7** bobstay, cordage, halyard, lanyard, lashing, painter
8 dragline, restrain
   fiber: **5** sisal

Rosaline
   character in: **16** Love's Labour's Lost
   author: **11** Shakespeare

rose 4 Rosa
   varieties: **3** bog, dog, sun, tea,
   wax **4** baby, gold, moss,
   musk, rock, rush, sand,
   wood **5** briar, brier, China,
   fairy, field, malva, Ophir,
   pygmy, swamp **6** Alpine,
   Burnet, copper, cotton, damask, desert, French, ground,
   Karroo, Lenten, mallow,
   Nootka, Scotch, velvet **7** baby
   sun, Banksia, Bourbon, cabbage, cluster, Guelder, Ma-

netti, pasture, prairie,
rambler **8** Burgundy, Champ-
ney, Cherokee, chestnut,
cinnamon, climbing, Japa-
nese, Memorial, mountain,
Noisette **9** Christmas, evergreen, hybrid tea, McCart-
ney, Polyantha, Remontant,
Turkestan **10** California,
Chinquapin, shaggy-rock,
underwater **11** confederate,
giant velvet, hairy alpine
12 green Mexican, Hawaiian
wood, Seven-sisters, white
Mexican **13** Himalayan musk,
Hybrid Bourbon, Persian yellow, Stuart's desert **15** hybrid
perpetual **16** York-and-
Lancaster

Rose, Pete (Peter Edward)
   nickname: **13** Charlie Hustle
   sport: **8** baseball
   position: **7** baseman **8** outfield
   team: **14** Cincinnati Reds
   20 Philadelphia Phillies

Rosedale, Mr
   character in: **15** The House of
   Mirth
   author: **7** Wharton

Rosemary's Baby
   director: **13** Roman Polanski
   based on novel by: **8** Ira
   Levin
   cast: **9** Mia Farrow **10** Ruth
   Gordon **14** John Cassavetes,
   Sidney Blackmer
   Oscar for: **17** supporting actress (Gordon)

Rosenbloom, Maxie
   nickname: **12** Slapsie Maxie
   sport: **6** boxing
   class: **16** light heavyweight

Rosencrantz
   character in: **6** Hamlet
   author: **11** Shakespeare

Rosenkavalier, Der
   also: **18** The Knight of the
   Rose
   opera by: **7** (Richard) Strauss
   character: **6** Sophie **8** Octavian
   9 Baron Ochs **11** Marschallin
   (Princess von Werderberg)

Rose of Sharon
   character in: **16** The Grapes of
   Wrath
   author: **9** Steinbeck

Rose Tattoo, The
   director: **10** Daniel Mann
   based on play by: **17** Tennessee Williams
   cast: **11** Anna Magnani
   13 Burt Lancaster
   Oscar for: **7** actress (Magnani)

Roseanne
   former name: **4** Barr **6** Arnold
   husband: **3** Tom **6** Thomas
   television:
      show: **8** Roseanne
      family:
         husband: **3** Dan
         children: **2** DJ **5** Becky
         7 Darlene
         sister: Jackie
      town: Lanford

rosiness 5 bloom, blush, flush
7 redness **8** pinkness

Rosofsky, Barnet
   real name of: **10** Barney Ross

Ross, Barney
   real name: **14** Barnet Rosofsky
   sport: **6** boxing
   class: **12** welterweight

Ross, Katharine
   born: **12** Los Angeles CA
   aunt: **16** Katharine Hepburn
   roles: **9** The Colbys **11** The
   Graduate **13** Stepford Wives
   29 Butch Cassidy and the
   Sundance Kid

Rossellini, Roberto
   director of: **6** Paisan **8** Open
   City **9** Stromboli **10** The
   Miracle
   wife: **13** Ingrid Bergman

Rossen, Robert
   director of: **11** Body and Soul
   14 All the King's Men

Rossetti, Dante Gabriel
   author of: **17** The Blessed
   Damozel
   born: **6** London **7** England

group: 14 Pre-Raphaelites
artwork: 12 Beata Beatrix
15 The Annunciation
17 Ecce Ancilla Domini

Rossini, Gioacchino Antonio
born: 5 Italy 6 Pesaro
composer of: 5 Moise
6 Otello 8 Tancredi 10 Le
Comte Ory, Semiramide
11 William Tell 12 Mose in
Egitto 13 Guillaume Tell, La
Cenerentola 15 Barber of
Seville 20 Il Barbiere di Si-
viglia 22 La Cambiale di
Matrimonio

Rossner, Judith
author of: 11 Attachments
14 Ordinary People
19 Looking for Mr Goodbar

Rostand, Edmond
author of: 7 L'Aiglon
10 Chantecler 12 The Ro-
mancers 16 Cyrano de
Bergerac

roster 4 list, roll 5 cadre,
panel, slate 6 agenda, docket,
muster, record 7 catalog, listing, posting 8 register, schedule 9 catalogue, directory

rostrum 4 dais 5 stage, stand,
stump 6 podium, pulpit 7 lectern, soapbox 8 platform

rosy 4 pink 5 ruddy 6 bright,
florid 7 flushed, glowing,
hopeful, reddish 8 blooming,
blushing, cheerful, cheering,
flushing, inflamed, rubicund
9 confident, favorable, promising, reddening, rubescent
10 auspicious, felicitous, optimistic, propitious, reassuring
11 encouraging, high-colored,
inspiriting 13 full of promise

Roszak, Theodore
born: 6 Poland, Poznan
artwork: 5 Raven, Surge
7 Anguish 9 Chrysalis,
Scavenger, Sea Quarry
11 Sea Sentinel
12 Amorphic Form, Thorn
Blossom 18 Specter of Kitty
Hawk 20 The Whaler of
Nantucket 27 Recollections
of the Southwest

rot 3 mar 4 bosh, bull, bunk,
harm, hurt, warp 5 decay, go
bad, spoil, stain, taint, trash
6 damage, debase, defile,
drivel, impair, infect, injure,
jabber, molder, poison
7 blather, corrupt, crumble,
deprave, inanity, pervert, pollute, putrefy, rubbish, twaddle 8 flummery, folderol,
nonsense, putresce 9 absurdity,
decompose, gibberish, moonshine, poppycock, purulence,
putridity 10 balderdash, cor-

ruption, degenerate, flapdoodle 11 contaminate,
deteriorate, putrescence
12 disintegrate, fiddle-faddle,
gobbledygook, putrefaction
13 contamination, decomposition, deterioration 14 disintegration 16 stuff and
nonsense

rotate 4 eddy, reel, roll, spin,
turn 5 pivot, swirl, twirl,
twist, wheel, whirl 6 change,
circle, gyrate, swivel 7 revolve 9 alternate, circulate,
pirouette 11 interchange

Roth, Philip
author of: 8 The Facts
15 Goodbye Columbus
16 The Anatomy Lesson,
Zuckerman Unbound
17 Portnoy's Complaint

Rothko, Mark
born: 6 Dvinsk, Latvia, Russia 16 Daugavpils Latvia
artwork: 5 Light 12 Central
Green, Earth and Blue
14 Four Darks in Red

rotten 3 bad 4 base, foul,
rank 5 dirty, fetid, nasty,
reeky, venal 6 filthy, putrid,
rancid, scurvy 7 corrupt,
crooked, decayed, devious, immoral, tainted, very bad, vicious 8 criminal, decaying,
indecent, purulent, two-faced
9 deceitful, dishonest, dissolute, faithless, insincere, mercenary, moldering, putrefied,
worm-eaten 10 decomposed,
iniquitous, putrescent, scurrilous, unpleasant, villainous
11 decomposing, disgraceful,
treacherous 12 contemptible,
dishonorable, unforgivable, unscrupulous 13 double-dealing,
untrustworthy

rotter 3 cad, cur, rat 4 heel
5 knave, louse, rogue 6 no-
good, rascal 7 bounder, caitiff,
villain 9 scoundrel

rotund 3 fat 5 obese, ovate,
ovoid, plump, pudgy, round,
stout, tubby 6 chubby, curved,
fleshy, portly 7 bulbous, lumpish, rounded 8 circular, globular 9 corpulent, egg-shaped,
spherical 10 potbellied 11 full-
fleshed

Rouault, Georges
born: 5 Paris 6 France
artwork: 3 Mr X 5 Clown
8 Le Chahut, Miserere, Twilight 9 The Mirror 10 The
Old King 11 Fleurs du mal,
The Holy Face 12 Head of a
Clown 13 Little Olympia
14 The Three Judges
19 Small Family of Clowns
22 Christ Mocked by Sol-
diers 26 Les Reincarnations
du Pere Ubu 28 The Child
Jesus among the Doctors

roue 3 cad, rip 4 rake, wolf
6 lecher, wanton 7 bounder,
dallier, Don Juan, playboy,
seducer, trifler 8 Casanova, de-
bauche, Lothario, rakehell
9 libertine, womanizer
10 profligate 11 philanderer,
skirt-chaser

rough *see* **box**

rough going 8 struggle 10 difficulty 11 arduousness
13 laboriousness

Roughing It
author: 9 Mark Twain
character: 12 Brigham
Young, Hank Erickson
16 Slade the Terrible

---

rough 3 raw 4 beat, hard, rude, wild 5 bluff, blunt, bumpy,
crude, cruel, draft, green, gruff, harsh, hasty, husky, quick,
raspy, rocky, scaly, sharp, surly, tough, vague 6 abrupt, beaton, broken, brutal, callow, choppy, clumsy, coarse, craggy,
crusty, gauche, hoarse, jagged, knotty, ragged, raging, roiled,
rugged, savage, severe, stormy, thrash, turbid, uneven, vulgar 7 austere, awkward, bearish, boorish, brusque, chapped,
coarsen, drastic, extreme, general, gnarled, grating, ill-bred,
inexact, jarring, loutish, outline, rasping, raucous, scraggy,
sketchy, stubbly, uncouth, unlevel, untamed, violent 8 agitated, churlish, rigorous, scabrous, scratchy, strident, ungentle, unsmooth 9 brutalize, difficult, ferocious, imperfect,
imprecise, inelegant, irregular, manhandle, sketch out, stringent, turbulent, uncourtly, unfeeling, ungenteel, unmusical,
unrefined 10 discordant, incomplete, indelicate, push around,
tumultuous, unfinished, ungracious, unmannerly, unpleasant,
unpolished 11 approximate, cacophonous, ill-mannered, preliminary, rudimentary, tempestuous, unluxurious 12 inharmonious 13 inconsiderate, uncomfortable, ungentlemanly

rough it 4 camp 7 camp out

roughneck 4 hood, lout, punk 5 bully, rowdy, tough 6 vandal 7 hoodlum, ruffian 8 hooligan 9 barbarian 10 delinquent

roughness 7 crudity 8 acrimony, aviation, pungency, violence 9 gruffness, harshness, vulgarity 10 coarseness, inelegance, unevenness, unkindness 11 raucousness 12 irregularity, unsmoothness, unrefinement 13 undevelopment

rough sketch 5 draft 7 cartoon, outline

rough-textured 5 harsh 6 coarse, nubbly, shaggy, tweedy 7 bristly, prickly 8 scratchy 9 bristling 10 sandpapery

round 3 fat 4 full, oval 5 cycle, obese, orbed, ovate, ovoid, plump, pudgy, stout, total, tubby, whole 6 chubby, circle, curved, entire, fluent, intact, portly, rotund, series, smooth 7 flowing, globoid, perfect, rounded 8 circular, complete, globular, resonant, sonorous, spheroid, thorough, unbroken 9 corpulent, egg-shaped, spherical, undivided 10 ball-shaped, elliptical, harmonious, pear-shaped, procession, succession 11 cylindrical, full-fleshed, mellifluent, progression

roundabout 5 wordy 6 random, zigzag 7 devious, erratic, oblique, sinuous, winding 8 indirect, rambling, tortuous, twisting 9 desultory 10 circuitous, discursive, meandering, serpentine 12 labyrinthine 14 circumlocutory

roundaboutness 9 wandering 10 digression, meandering 11 indirection 14 circuitousness, circumlocution

rounded 6 convex 7 curving 11 protuberant

rounding out 10 developing 12 augmentation 13 amplification

rounding-out 10 complement, completion, perfecting 12 consummation

rounds 4 beat 5 route, skirt, watch 7 circuit

roundup 6 muster, resume 7 meeting, summary 8 assembly 9 gathering 11 convocation

round up 6 gather, muster, summon 7 collect, convene, convoke, marshal 8 assemble 10 accumulate 12 call together

rouse 4 call, goad, move, prod, spur, stir, wake 5 arise, awake, get up, pique, rally, waken 6 awaken, excite, foment, kindle, incite, stir up, summon, turn on, wake up 7 animate, inflame, inspire, provoke, shake up 8 activate 9 galvanize, instigate, stimulate

roused 2 up 5 astir, awake 7 excited, incited, kindled, rallied, shook up 8 awakened, inflamed, inspired, out of bed, shaken up 9 stirred up 10 up and about

rousing 5 brisk, peppy 6 active, lively 8 animated, exciting, stirring, vigorous 9 awakening, inspiring 10 energizing, refreshing, remarkable 11 provocative, stimulating 12 exhilarating, intoxicating 13 extraordinary

Rousseau, Henri Julien Felix
nickname: 10 Le Douanier
born: 5 Laval 6 France
artwork: 3 War 8 The Dream 12 Child on Rocks, The Waterfall 13 The Hungry Lion 15 Carnival Evening, The Snake Charmer 16 Bouquet of Flowers, The Sleeping Gypsy 17 The Poet and his Muse

Rousseau, Jean Jacques
author of: 5 Emile 11 Confessions 15 La Nouvelle Heloise, The Social Contract

Rousseau, (Pierre Etienne) Theodore
born: 5 Paris 6 France
artwork: 7 Evening 12 After the Rain 15 Edge of the Forest, Under the Birches 18 Descent of the Cattle, Oak Trees at Apremont 19 The Marsh in the Landes 20 The Valley of Tiffauges 21 Meadow Bordered by Trees

roust 4 bust 5 rouse 6 arrest, hassle 7 capture, seizure 12 apprehension

rout 4 beat, drub, lick, ruin, trim 5 chaos, cream, crush, panic, quell, repel, worst 6 defeat, subdue, thrash 7 beating, clobber, conquer, licking, repulse, scatter 8 drive off, drubbing, lambaste, overcome, vanquish 9 chase away, drive away, overpower, overthrow 11 put to flight 15 disorganization 18 throw into confusion

route 3 run 4 beat, pass, path, road, ship, tack 5 remit, round, track 6 artery, course, detour, direct 7 circuit, highway, parkway, passage, roadway 8 dispatch, transmit, turnpike 9 boulevard, itinerary 10 throughway 12 thoroughfare

Route 66
character: 8 Linc Case 9 Tod Stiles 10 Buz Murdock
cast: 12 Glenn Corbett, Martin Milner 13 George Maharis
car: 8 Corvette

routine 4 dull 5 order, usual 6 boring, custom, method, normal, system 7 formula, regular, tedious, typical 8 habitual, ordinary, periodic, practice 9 customary, operation, technique 11 arrangement, predictable 12 conventional, run-of-the-mill 13 unexceptional

rove 4 roam 5 drift, prowl, range 6 ramble, stroll, travel, wander 7 meander, traipse 9 gallivant

roving 6 errant 7 aimless, gadding, migrant, nomadic, roaming, vagrant 8 errantry, rambling, restless 9 desultory, itinerant, traveling, uncertain, wandering 10 changeable, discursive, meandering, inconstant 11 peripatetic 14 discursiveness

row 4 file, line, rank, spat, tier, tiff 5 brawl, chain, melee, queue, range, scrap, set-to, train, words 6 column, fracas, scrape, series, string 7 echelon, quarrel, wrangle 8 argument, disorder, sequence, squabble 9 imbroglio, wrangling 10 difference, succession 11 altercation, contretemps

rowboat 3 gig 4 bark, dory 5 barge, canoe, dingy, scull, skiff 6 barque, caique, dinghy, wherry
seat: 4 taft

rowdy 6 unruly 7 lawless, raffish 9 roughneck 10 boisterous, disorderly 11 mischievous 12 obstreperous

Rowena, Lady
character in: 7 Ivanhoe
author: 5 Scott

rowing
athlete: 10 James Dietz 14 Anthony Johnson

Rowlands, Gena
real name: 23 Virginia Cathryn Rowlands
born: 9 Cambria WI
husband: 14 John Cassavetes
roles: 5 Faces 12 Opening Night 23 A Woman Under the Influence

Roxana
  subtitle: **20** The Fortunate Mistress
  author: **11** Daniel Defoe

royal 5 grand, regal **6** august, lavish, superb **7** stately **8** imposing, majestic, splendid **9** monarchal, sovereign **10** munificent **11** fit for a king, magnificent, resplendent

royalty 4 sway **7** command, majesty **8** dominion, hegemony, kingship, regality **9** queenship, supremacy **11** divine right, sovereignty

Royaume de Belgique *see* **7** Belgium

Roy Rogers
  ingredient: **9** ginger ale, grenadine
  also called: **13** Shirley Temple

Roy Rogers Show, The
  regular: **8** Pat Brady **9** Dale Evans
  theme: **16** Happy Trails to You
  horse: **7** Trigger
  dog: **6** Bullet
  jeep: **10** Nellybelle
  ranch: **10** Double R Bar

Ruanda *see* **6** Rwanda

rub 4 buff, swab, wipe **5** annoy, braze, catch, chafe, clean, hitch, knead, pinch, scour, scrub, smear, thing, touch, trick **6** abrade, finger, handle, polish, secret, smooth, spread, strait, stroke **7** burnish, dilemma, massage, problem, rubdown, setback, slather, trouble **8** handling, hardship, kneading, obstacle, stroking **10** difficulty, impediment, manipulate **12** manipulation

Rubaiyat of Omar Khayyam, The
  author: **11** Omar Khayyam
  translator: **16** Edward FitzGerald

rubber, vulcanized
  invented by: **8** Goodyear

rubber plant 13 Ficus elastica
  varieties: **4** baby **5** dwarf **7** Chinese **8** American, creeping, Japanese **9** mistletoe **11** small-leaved **16** broad-leaved India

rubberstamp 6 affirm **7** approve, endorse

rubber tree 10 Schefflera
  varieties: **4** Para **5** India **8** Castilla **11** West African

rubbery 5 tough **6** supple **7** elastic **8** flexible **9** resilient **11** stretchable

rubbing 7 chafing **8** abrading, scraping **12** manipulation

rubbish 3 rot **4** bosh, junk **5** dross, offal, trash, waste **6** babble, debris, drivel, idiocy, jetsam, litter, refuse, rubble **7** blather, garbage, inanity, twaddle **8** folderol, nonsense **9** gibberish, rigmarole, silliness **10** balderdash, flapdoodle, rigamarole

rubbish heap 4 dump **6** midden **10** refuse pile

rubble 4 junk, rock **5** brash, chalk, stent, stone, talus, trash **6** debris, refuse **7** rubbish **8** nonsense **9** fragments **11** foolishness

rube 3 oaf **4** boor, clod, hick **5** yokel **6** rustic **7** bumpkin, hayseed, peasant **10** clodhopper

rub elbows 3 mix **4** club **6** hobnob, mingle **7** consort, hang out **9** associate **10** fraternize

Rubens, Peter Paul
  born: **6** Siegen **10** Westphalia
  artwork: **8** Lion Hunt **10** The Rainbow **15** The Garden of Love **17** Laocoon and his Sons **18** Battle of the Amazons **20** The Raising of the Cross **21** Landscape with Het Steen **22** The Descent from the Cross **23** Altarpiece of St Aldefonso **26** The Adoration of the Shepherds **27** Marchesa Brigida Spinola-Doria, Mystic Marriage of St Catherine **29** Rape of the Daughters of Leucippus **34** Helene Fourment with Two of her Children

rubicund 3 red **4** rosy **5** ruddy **6** florid **7** flushed, reddish

rubidium
  chemical symbol: **2** Rb

rub out 4 do in, kill, slay **5** erase **6** efface, murder **7** bump off, destroy, execute, expunge **8** massacre **10** obliterate, put to death **11** assassinate, exterminate

ruby
  species: **8** corundum
  source: **5** Burma, India, Mogok **7** Bangkok, Kashmir **8** Sri Lanka, Thailand
  kind: **4** star
  color: **3** red

ruckus 3 row **4** fray, to-do **5** brawl, broil, clash, fight, melee **6** battle, fracas, rumpus, uproar **7** scuffle **9** imbroglio **10** donnybrook, free-for-all **11** embroilment

ruddy 3 red **4** rosy **6** florid **7** flushed, reddish, roseate, scarlet **8** blushing, rubicund, sanguine **11** rosy-cheeked

rude 3 raw **4** wild **5** blunt, crude, fresh, green, gross, gruff, rough, saucy, sulky, surly **6** abrupt, callow, clumsy, coarse, crusty, gauche, homely, rugged, rustic, sullen, uneven, vulgar **7** abusive, artless, awkward, boorish, brusque, brutish, ill-bred, loutish, profane, scraggy, uncivil, uncouth **8** churlish, homebred, ignorant, impolite, impudent, indecent, insolent, slapdash, untaught **9** inelegant, insulting, makeshift, primitive, roughhewn, uncourtly, ungallant, unlearned, unrefined, untrained, untutored **10** illiterate, indecorous, indelicate, peremptory, provincial, uncultured, uneducated, ungraceful, ungracious, unladylike, unmannerly, unpolished **11** bad-mannered, countrified, impertinent, uncivilized, uncourteous, undignified **12** discourteous, roughly built **13** disrespectful, inconsiderate, ungentlemanly

rudeness 9 bluntness, impudence, insolence, sauciness **10** bad manners, coarseness, disrespect, incivility **11** boorishness, discourtesy **12** impertinence, impoliteness **14** ungraciousness **17** inconsiderateness

rudimentary 5 basic **6** simple **7** initial, primary **8** immature **9** elemental, formative, imperfect, premature, primitive, vestigial **10** elementary, incomplete, prototypal **11** undeveloped

rudiments 6 basics **7** essence **8** elements **9** beginning **10** principles **12** fundamentals

Rudkus, Jurgis and Antanas
  characters in: **9** The Jungle
  author: **8** Sinclair

Rudolph, Paul
  architect of: **16** Jewett Arts Center (Wellesley College) **24** Government Services Center (Boston) **28** School of Architecture Building (Yale)

rue 4 Ruta
  varieties: **4** bush, lady, wall **5** goat's **6** common, meadow **10** tall meadow **11** early meadow **12** Alpine meadow

rue 5 mourn **6** bemoan, lament, regret, repent, repine **7** deplore

rueful 3 sad 5 sorry 6 woeful 7 doleful 8 contrite, mournful, dolorous, penitent, repining 9 depressed, plaintive, regretful, sorrowful, sorrowing 10 deplorable, lamentable, melancholy, remorseful, unpleasant

ruffian 4 hood, thug 5 brute, bully, crook, knave, rogue, rough, rowdy, tough 6 mugger 7 hoodlum, villain 8 gangster, hooligan 9 cutthroat, roisterer, roughneck, scoundrel 10 blackguard

ruffle 4 fold, muss, wave 5 frill, plait, pleat, ruche, upset 6 edging, excite, muss up, pucker, rimple, ripple, rumple 7 agitate, confuse, crinkle, disturb, flounce, perturb, roughen, trouble, wrinkle 8 dishevel, disorder, disquiet, furbelow, unsettle 9 aggravate, agitation, commotion, corrugate 10 disarrange, discompose, disconcert 11 disturbance

ruffled 5 upset, vexed 7 annoyed, frilled, nettled, pleated 8 agitated, flounced, troubled 9 nonplused, unsettled 10 nonplussed

ruffle one's feathers 3 vex 5 anger, annoy, pique 6 enrage, madden, nettle 7 incense, outrage, provoke 9 displease, infuriate

Rugg
  character in: 12 Little Dorrit
  author: 7 Dickens

rugged 4 hale, hard, rude, wiry, worn 5 bumpy, hardy, harsh, husky, lined, rocky, rough, stern, tough 6 brawny, coarse, craggy, jagged, ridged, robust, severe, sinewy, sturdy, taxing, trying, uneven, virile 7 arduous, cragged, onerous, scraggy, uncouth 8 athletic, furrowed, muscular, stalwart, vigorous, wrinkled 9 difficult, graceless, irregular, laborious, masculine, roughhewn, strenuous, unrefined, weathered 12 uncultivated 13 weatherbeaten

Ruggles of Red Gap
  director: 10 Leo McCarey
  cast: 9 ZaSu Pitts 10 Mary Boland 14 Charlie Ruggles 15 Charles Laughton
  remade as: 10 Fancy Pants

ruin, ruins 3 gut, pot 4 doom, fall, fell, harm, raze, seed 5 break, crush, decay, level, quash, quell, shell, spoil, upset, wreck 6 beggar, defeat, ravage, squash 7 destroy, failure, remains, shatter, undoing 8 bankrupt, demolish, downfall, lay waste, make poor, overturn, remnants, wreckage 9 breakdown, devastate, disrepair, overthrow, pauperize 10 impoverish 11 destruction, devastation, dissolution 14 disintegration

ruination 4 ruin 5 wreck 6 fiasco 7 trouble 8 disaster 9 adversity, cataclysm 11 destruction, devastation 12 misadventure

ruinous 4 dire 5 fatal 6 deadly 7 adverse, baneful 8 damaging, ravaging 10 calamitous, disastrous, pernicious 11 cataclysmic, deleterious, destructive, devastating 12 catastrophic

Ruisdael, Jacob (Jakob) van
  born: 7 Haarlem 14 The Netherlands
  uncle: 18 Salomon van Ruysdael
  artwork: 5 Dunes 12 The Waterfall 13 View of Haarlem 14 Bentheim Castle 15 Winter Landscape 17 The Jewish Cemetery 28 View on the Amstel near Amsterdam

rule *see box*

rule out 4 omit 6 delete, except 7 exclude 9 eliminate

ruler 4 boss, czar, emir, head, khan, king, lord, shah, tsar, tzar 5 chief, judge, queen, rajah, sheik 6 dynast, leader, prince, satrap, shogun, sultan 7 arbiter, emperor, manager, measure, monarch, pharaoh, referee, viceroy 8 chairman, director, governor, suzerain 9 chieftain, commander, potentate, president, sovereign, yardstick 10 controller, supervisor 11 coordinator, crowned head, head of state, tape measure 12 straightedge 13 administrator

rules of conduct 6 ethics 9 moral code 10 principles 12 code of ethics

Rules of the Game
  director: 10 Jean Renoir
  cast: 10 Jean Renoir, Mila Parely, Nora Gregor 11 Marcel Dalio

ruling 6 decree 7 regnant 8 decision, dominant, reigning 9 enactment, governing, prescript 10 commanding, widespread 11 controlling, predominant 13 authoritative, predominating

ruling class 11 aristocracy 13 Establishment

Ruling Class, The
  director: 10 Peter Medak

rule 3 law, run 4 find, form, head, lead, sway 5 adage, axiom, canon, guide, judge, maxim, model, order, reign 6 custom, decide, decree, direct, empire, govern, manage, method, policy, regime, settle, system 7 adjudge, command, control, declare, formula, precept, prevail, resolve, routine 8 conclude, doctrine, dominate, domineer, dominion, pass upon, practice, regnancy, regulate, standard 9 authority, criterion, determine, direction, establish, guideline, influence, ordinance, precedent, principle, pronounce, supremacy 10 adjudicate, administer, convention, domination, government, leadership, regulation, suzerainty 11 predominate, preside over, sovereignty 12 jurisdiction, prescription 14 administration
  type: 5 bench 7 folding 9 steel tape
  constellation of: 6 Norma

cast: 10 Arthur Lowe 11 Alastair Sim, Peter O'Toole 12 Harry Andrews

rum *see box*

Rumania *see box, p. 850*

rumble 4 bang, boom, clap, roar, roll 7 booming, resound, thunder 8 drumming 9 resonance 11 reverberate 13 reverberation

Rumford, Benjamin Thomson
  invented: 10 photometer 11 calorimeter

Rumina
  protectress of: 14 nursing mothers

ruminant 3 cow, elk, yak 4 deer, oxen 5 bison, camel, llama, moose, sheep 6 alpaca, cattle, vicuna 7 buffalo, giraffe, pensive 8 antelope 10 chevrotain, meditative, thoughtful 13 contemplative

ruminate 4 mull, muse 5 brood, study, think, weigh 6 ponder 7 reflect 8 cogitate, consider, meditate, mull over 9 speculate, think over 10 deliberate, think about 11 contemplate

ruminating 6 musing 7 pensive 8 thinking 10 meditating,

rum
> **drink: 4** Bolo, Grog **6** Mojito **7** Gauguin **8** Daiquiri, Navy Grog, Pina Fria **9** Borinquen, Hurricane **10** Pina Colada **12** Boston Cooler **13** Planter's Punch **14** Fish House Punch **15** Bacardi Cocktail **18** Barbados Rum Swizzle
> **ingredient: 8** molasses **9** sugar cane
> **origin: 10** West Indies
> **type: 4** dark **5** light
> **with apple brandy: 6** Bolero **8** Apple Pie
> **with apricot brandy: 11** Apricot Lady
> **with black coffee: 9** Black Rose
> **with bouillon: 6** Creole
> **with bourbon: 14** Artillery Punch
> **with brandy: 15** Quaker's Cocktail
> **with Cointreau: 8** Acapulco **10** Casa Blanca **11** Beachcomber **12** Blue Hawaiian
> **with cola: 9** Cuba Libre
> **with creme de cacao: 6** Panama
> **with curacao: 6** Mai-Tai **8** Blue Lady **12** Blue Hawaiian
> **with Dubonnet: 3** BVD **10** Bushranger
> **with Galliano: 9** Bossa Nova
> **with gin: 3** BVD
> **with guava: 8** Ocho Rios
> **with kahlua: 10** Black Maria
> **with milk: 6** Rum Cow **11** Tom-and-Jerry
> **with Pernod: 8** Shanghai
> **with sloe gin: 11** Shark's Tooth
> **with Tia Maria: 10** Black Maria
> **with vermouth: 6** Bolero **8** Apple Pie **10** Black Devil **11** Shark's Tooth

meditative, reflecting, reflective, thoughtful **11** chewing over, mulling over, speculative **13** contemplating, contemplative, introspective

rumination 5 study **6** musing **7** mulling, reverie, thought **8** brooding, thinking **9** pondering **10** cogitation, meditation, reflection **11** speculation **12** deliberation **13** consideration, contemplation **15** reconsideration

rummage 4 root **5** probe **7** examine, explore, ransack **10** disarrange, poke around **11** look through

rummy 3 sot **4** lush, soak **5** drunk, souse, toper **6** barfly, boozer **7** tippler **8** card game, drunkard **9** alcoholic **11** dipsomaniac
also known as: 3 gin, rum **4** rhum **5** romme **8** gin rummy
derived from: 8 conquien

rumor 4 talk **5** story **6** babble, gossip, report **7** hearsay, whisper **8** innuendo, intimate **9** circulate, insinuate **11** insinuation, scuttlebutt, supposition

rump 4 rear, seat **5** croup, stern **6** behind, bottom, breech, dorsum **7** rear end **8** backside, buttocks, derriere, haunches **9** posterior **12** hindquarters

Rumpelstiltskin
origin: 8 Germanic
form: 5 dwarf
spun: 4 flax
made: 4 gold

rumple 4 fold, muss **5** crimp, crush **6** crease, pucker, rimple, ruffle, tousle **7** crinkle, crumple, wrinkle **8** dishevel, disorder **9** corrugate **10** disarrange

rumpus 3 ado, row **4** fray, fuss, stir, to-do **5** brawl, melee, noise **6** affray, fracas, hubbub, pother, racket, ruckus, tumult, uproar **7** rhubarb, scuffle, tempest **8** brouhaha, upheaval **9** agitation, commotion, confusion, imbroglio **10** hullabaloo **11** disturbance, embroilment

run *see box, p. 851*

run aground 7 founder **8** collapse

runaround 4 slip **5** dodge **6** bypass **7** evasion **8** shunning, sidestep **9** avoidance **11** elusiveness, evasiveness **12** equivocation

run around 7 consort, hang out **9** associate, pal around **10** fraternize

runaway 4 pure **6** bolter **7** escapee, perfect, refugee **8** absolute, complete, deserter, fugitive **9** out-and-out, unalloyed **10** skedaddler **11** unmitigated, unqualified

run away 3 fly **4** flee **5** elope **6** decamp, escape, run off **7** abscond, make off **8** sneak off **10** fly the coop, make a break, take flight **12** make a getaway

rundown 5 brief **6** digest, precis, resume, review, sketch **7** outline, summary **8** abstract, synopsis **12** capitulation, condensation

run-down 5 frail, seedy, tacky, tired, weary **6** ailing, beat-up, feeble, shabby, sickly **7** rickety, worn out **8** fatigued, tattered **9** crumbling, exhausted **10** broken-down, tumbledown **11** dilapidated **12** deteriorated

run down 4 scan **5** knock **6** slight **7** detract, put down, run over **8** belittle, derogate, ridicule **9** denigrate, deprecate, discredit, disparage, downgrade, enumerate, underrate **10** depreciate, undervalue

run-in 5 brush, set-to **6** battle, fracas **7** scuffle **8** skirmish **9** encounter **10** engagement

run into 4 meet **8** flow into **9** encounter **10** chance upon, meet up with **11** collide with

run off 3 fly **4** flee **5** elope **6** escape **7** abscond, make off, runaway **9** steal away **10** take flight **15** head for the hills

run off at the mouth 3 gab **5** prate **6** babble, gabble **8** rattle on **11** talk too much

run off with 5 seize **6** abduct, kidnap **7** bear off **8** carry off **9** elope with **11** abscond with, make off with

run-of-the-mill 4 dull, so-so **5** banal, stock, usual **6** common, modest **7** average, humdrum, mundane, routine, typical **8** everyday, mediocre, middling, ordinary, passable, standard **10** second-rate **11** commonplace, indifferent, nondescript **12** unimpressive **13** unimaginative **15** undistinguished

runt 3 elf **4** chit **5** dwarf, pygmy **6** midget, peewee, shrimp **8** half-pint, Tom Thumb **11** Lilliputian
Latin: 10 homunculus

Rumania
   other name: 7 Romania
   capital/largest city: 9 Bucharest
   others: 4 Aiud, Arad, Cluj, Deva, Iasi 5 Bacau, Balta,
     Cerna, Jassy, Neamt, Sibiu, Turnu, Yassy 6 Braila, Brasov,
     Brasso, Eforie, Galatz, Galeti, Lupeni, Mamaia, Oradea,
     Sighet 7 Bendery, Craiova, Focsani, Giurgiu, Ploesti, Sev-
     erin 8 Bloiesti, Cernavti, Chisinau, Irongate, Kishenef,
     Satu-Mare, Temesvar 9 Constanta, Kolozsvar, Timisoara
     10 Czernowitz 11 Klausenburg
   school: 4 Cuza
   division: 4 Alba, Iasi 5 Banat, Bihor, Jassy 6 Ardeal
     7 Dobruja 8 Bucovina, Bukovina, Dobrogea, Moldavia,
     Walachia 9 Maramures 10 Bessarabia 12 Transylvania
     Roman province: 5 Dacia
   measure: 7 faltche
   monetary unit: 3 ban, lei, leu, lev, ley 4 bani 5 uncia
     6 triens
   lake: 5 Sinoe 6 Snagov
   mountain: 5 Banat, Bihor 6 Codrul, Rodnei 7 Apuseni, Bal-
     kans, Caliman, Fagaras 8 Pietrosu 9 Moldavian 10 Carpa-
     thian, Moldoveanu 17 Transylvanian Alps
   highest point: 11 Moldoveanul
   river: 3 Alt, Jui, Olt 4 Prut 5 Aluta, Arges, Buzdu, Moros,
     Mures, Oltul, Schyl, Siret, Somes, Timis, Vedea 6 Crasna,
     Danube 7 Argesul 8 Bistrita, Ialomita, Iniester 9 Dimbov-
     ita, Jiul Mures
   sea: 5 Black
   physical feature:
     canal: 4 Bega
     forest: 6 Snagov 7 Baneasa
     gorge: 8 Iron Gate
     peninsula: 6 Balkan
     plain: 5 Banat 9 Moldavian, Walachian 13 Prahova Valley
     plateau: 7 Dobruja
     wind: 6 crivat
   people: 6 Dacian 8 Romanian, Rumanian
     artist: 8 Brancusi
     author: 7 Ionesco
     composer: 6 Enesco
     leader: 6 Carol I 7 Michael, Iliescu 8 Ioan Cuza 9 Ceau-
     sescu 12 Gheorghiu-Dej, Ion Antonescu
   language: 6 French, Magyar 7 Russian 8 Romanian, Ruma-
     nian 9 Hungarian
   religion: 7 Judaism 8 Lutheran 9 Calvinism, Unitarian
     10 Protestant 13 Roman Catholic 16 Rumanian Orthodox
   place:
     castle: 4 Bran 7 Huniady
     church: 5 Golia 9 Mihaivoda 10 Cretulescu, Patriarchy
     11 Curtea Veche, Stavropdeos, Trei Ierarhi
     monastery: 5 Humor 6 Arbore 7 Voronet 8 Sucerita
     9 Moldovita
     museum: 11 Peles Castle
     palace: 9 mogosoaia
     park: 7 Baneasa
     resort: 5 Venus 6 Eforie, Mamaia, Neptun 7 Jupiter
     10 Costinesti
   feature:
     community gathering: 9 sezatoare
     game: 4 oina
   food:
     dish: 6 ciorba 7 mititei, sarmala 8 mamaliga 11 imam
     bayildi
     plum brandy: 5 tuica

run through 5 spend, waste
  6 expend, pierce 7 deplete, exhaust 8 rehearse, squander

runty 5 short 6 bantam
  7 dwarfed, squatty, stunted
  9 pint-sized

Runyon, Damon
  author of: 12 Guys and
    Dolls 16 Blue Plate Special

rupture 3 pop 4 part, rent, rift,
  snap 5 break, burst, clash,
  cleft, crack, split 6 breach, divide, schism, sunder 7 discord,
  disrupt, fissure 8 breaking,
  bursting, cleavage, dissever,
  disunion, disunite, fracture,
  friction, puncture 9 severance
  10 dissension, falling out, separation 12 disagreement

R U R
  author: 10 Karel Capek

rural 4 hick 6 rustic 7 bucolic,
  country 8 pastoral 10 provincial 11 countrified

rural area 6 sticks 7 boonies,
  country 8 farmland 9 backwater, backwoods, boondocks
  10 hinterland 11 countryside

Rural Dionysia *see* 14 Lesser
  Dionysia

ruse 4 hoax 5 blind, dodge,
  feint, shift, trick 6 deceit, device, scheme 8 artifice, maneuver 9 deception, stratagem
  10 subterfuge 11 contrivance,
  machination

rush 3 hie, run 4 dart, dash,
  goad, leap, push, race, spur,
  tear, urge, whip 5 drive, haste,
  hurry, press, speed, storm
  6 charge, hasten, hustle,
  plunge, scurry, sprint, urgent
  7 scamper, urgency 8 dispatch,
  expedite, pressure, scramble
  9 emergency 10 accelerate
  11 top priority

rush 6 Juncus
  varieties: 3 bog 4 salt, soft,
    wood 5 spike 6 grassy
    8 scouring 9 field wood,
    flowering 10 common wood,
    least spike 11 chair-maker's,
    greater wood, Japanese-mat
    12 slender spike 13 dwarf
    scouring 14 common scour-
    ing 18 variegated scouring

Rush, Benjamin
  field: 8 medicine
  established first: 21 free
    medical dispensary
  signer of: 25 Declaration of
    Independence

rush light 3 dip 5 torch 6 candle, tallow

run 2 be, go **3** fly, get, hie, jog, pen, ply **4** bolt, boss, cost, dart, dash, defy, flee, flow, go by, head, kind, last, meet, melt, pass, pour, push, race, roll, rush, sort, tear, tour, trip, trot, type, vary **5** bleed, bound, class, court, drift, drive, genre, glide, hurry, impel, incur, issue, leave, pilot, print, speed, spell, split, stand, surge, total, while **6** become, canter, course, decamp, direct, elapse, endure, escape, extend, gallop, hasten, hustle, invite, ladder, manage, motion, move on, outing, period, pierce, propel, scurry, series, sprint, streak, stream, thrust, vanish, voyage, wander **7** abscond, add up to, advance, bring on, compete, current, display, freedom, get past, journey, liquefy, meander, operate, oversee, passage, proceed, publish, running, scamper, stretch, take off, vamoose **8** amount to, campaign, continue, dissolve, duration, evanesce, maneuver, meet with, navigate, progress, scramble, separate, tendency **9** direction, disappear, enclosure, encounter, excursion, go quickly, lose color, penetrate, skedaddle, supervise **10** coordinate, pilgrimage **11** continuance **12** beat a retreat, continuation, perpetuation
    baseball: 5 point, score, tally **17** circuit of the bases

Rushworth
character in: **13** Mansfield Park
author: **6** Austen

Ruskin, John
author of: **13** Fors Clavigera **14** Modern Painters **17** The Stones of Venice **27** The Seven Lamps of Architecture

Russell, Bertrand
author of: **19** Why I Am Not a Christian **20** Principia Mathematica (with Alfred North)

Russell, Jane
real name: **29** Ernestine Jane Geraldine Russell
born: **9** Bemidji MN
discovered by: **12** Howard Hughes
roles: **4** Waco **9** The Outlaw **13** The French Line **22** Gentlemen Prefer Blondes, The Revolt of Mamie Stover

Russell, Rosalind
born: **11** Waterbury CT
roles: **5** Gypsy **6** Picnic **8** The Women **9** Hired Wife **10** Auntie Mame **11** Sister Kenny **13** His Girl Friday **14** My Sister Eileen **22** Mourning Becomes Electra

russet 5 apple, umber **6** auburn, copper **10** terra-cotta **11** rust-colored **12** reddish-brown

Russia see box, p. 852

Russian Hide-and-Seek
author: **12** Kingsley Amis

Russian village commune
3 mir

rust 3 rot **5** decay, stain **6** auburn, blight, russet **7** corrode, crumble, decline, oxidize **9** corrosion, oxidation **11** deteriorate **12** reddish-brown **13** reddish-yellow

rust-colored 5 henna **6** auburn, russet **8** cinnamon **12** reddish-brown

rustic 4 rube, rude **5** crude, plain, rough, rural, yokel **6** coarse, gauche, simple **7** awkward, boorish, bucolic, bumpkin, country, hayseed, loutish, peasant, uncouth **8** agrarian, churlish, cloddish, pastoral **9** inelegant, unrefined **10** clodhopper, countryman, provincial, uncultured, unpolished **11** countrified **13** country person **15** unsophisticated

rustle 3 rub **4** hiss, stir **5** swish, whish **6** riffle

rustler 5 thief **6** bandit, outlaw **7** brigand **9** desperado

rusty 5 moldy, stiff **6** rotten, rusted **7** reddish, tainted **8** corroded, sluggish **11** rust-colored **13** out of practice

rut 3 cut **4** mark **5** ditch, habit, score, tread **6** furrow, groove, gutter, hollow, trench, trough **7** channel, depress, dig into, pattern **8** monotony **9** deep track **10** depression **11** dull routine

Ruth
husband: **4** Boaz **6** Mahlon
son: **4** Obed
father-in-law: **9** Elimelech
mother-in-law: **5** Naomi
brother-in-law: **7** Chilion

Ruth, George Herman
nickname: **4** Babe **12** Sultan of Swat
sport: **8** baseball
position: **8** outfield
team: **14** New York Yankees

Rutherford, Dame Margaret
born: **6** London **7** England
roles: **7** The VIPs **10** Jane Marple **12** Blithe Spirit **27** The Importance of Being Earnest

Rutherford, Ernest
field: **7** physics
nationality: **7** British
discovered: **6** proton **13** atomic nucleus, beta radiation **14** alpha radiation, gamma radiation
awarded: **10** Nobel Prize

ruthless 5 cruel, harsh **6** brutal, deadly, savage **7** bestial, brutish, callous, inhuman, vicious **8** pitiless **9** barbarous, ferocious, heartless, merciless, murderous, unfeeling, unpitying, unsparing **10** relentless, sanguinary, unmerciful **11** cold-blooded, hardhearted, remorseless, unforgiving, unrelenting **12** bloodthirsty

ruthlessness 7 cruelty **9** barbarity, brutality, harshness **10** inhumanity, savageness **11** viciousness

Ruysdael, Salomon van
born: **7** Naarden **14** The Netherlands
nephew: **16** Jacob van Ruisdael
artwork: **9** River Bank **10** River Scene **14** River Landscape **18** River with Ferry Boat

Rwanda see box, p. 853

Ryan, Cornelius
author of: **13** A Bridge Too Far, The Last Battle, The Longest Day

Ryan, Robert
born: **9** Chicago IL
roles: **6** Caught **8** The Set-Up **9** Billy Budd, Crossfire **12** Clash by Night, The Wild Bunch **13** Act of Vio-

Russia (includes constituent republics of the former USSR)

other name: 17 Russian Federation
former name: 4 USSR **11** Soviet Union **31** Union of Soviet Socialist Republics
member of: 3 CIS **31** Commonwealth of Independent States
capital/largest city: 6 Moscow
others: 4 Baku, Eisk, Kiev, Okha, Omsk, Poti, Riga **5** Anapa, Batum, Gorki, Gorky, Memel, Minsk, Sochi, Vilna, Yeisk **6** Batumi, Erevan, Frunze, Odessa, Rostov, Samara, Tiflis **7** Alma-Ata, Derbent, Donetsk, Kharkov, Liepaja, Petsamo, Pivonia, Saratov, Tallinn, Tbilisi, Yerevan **8** Dushanbe, Kishinev, Murmansk, Pechenga, Taganrog, Tashkent **9** Ashkhabad, Astrakhan, Balaklava, Kronstadt, Kuibyshev, Leningrad, Nikolayev, Petrograd, Ulyanovsk, Volgograd, Yaroslavl **10** Kronshtadt, Sevastopol, Stalingrad, Sverdlovsk **11** Chelyabinsk, Kaliningrad, Makhachkala, Novorossisk, Novosibirsk, Vladivostok **12** St Petersburg **14** Dnepropetrovsk
division/country: 6 Latvia **7** Armenia, Belarus, Estonia, Georgia, Moldova, Siberia, Ukraine **8** Moldavia **9** Kirghizia, Lithuania, Turkmenia **10** Azerbaijan, Belorussia, Kazakhstan, Kyrgyzstan, Tajikistan, Uzbekistan **12** Tadzhikistan, Turkmenistan
former: **4** Kiev **8** Novgorod
government:
legislature: **4** Duma, Rada **7** Zemstvo **8** Congress
measure: 3 fut, lof **4** duim, fass, loof, pood, quar, stof **5** duime, foute, korec, korek, ligne, osmin, pajak, stoff, stoof, vedro, verst **6** charka, liniya, osmina, paletz, sagene, stekar, tchast, tsarki, versta, verste **7** archine, arsheen, botchka, chkalik, garnetz, verchoc, verchok **8** boutylka, chetvert, krouchka, kroushka **9** chetverik **10** dessiatine **11** polugarnetz
monetary unit: 5 altin, bisti, copec, denga, grosh, kopek, ruble, shaur **6** abassi, copeck, grivna, kopeck, piatak, rouble **7** poltina, valiuta **8** auksinas, deneshka, imperial, polushka **9** poltinnik **10** altininink, chervonets
weight: 3 lof, lot **4** dola, funt, lana, last, loof, loth, once, pood, poud **5** dolia
island: 5 Kuril **7** Hiiumaa, Karagin, Shantar, Vaygach, Wrangel **8** Kolguyev, Saaremaa, Sakhalin **9** Andreanof **12** Novaya Zemlya **13** Komandorskiye **14** Franz Josef Land, Novosibirskiye **15** Severnaya Zemlya
lake: 3 Seg **4** Aral, Azov, Kola, Sego, Topo, Vigo **5** Chany, Elton, Erara, Ilmen, Lacha, Onega, Pskov, Vozhe **6** Baikal, Byeloe, Ladoga, Peipus, Selety, Taymyr, Tengiz, Zaysan **8** Balkhash **10** Caspian Sea
mountain: 5 Altai, Lenin, Sayan, Urals **6** Anadyr, Elbrus, Koryak, Pamirs, Pobedy **7** Belukha, Crimean, Khibiny, Stanovi, Zhiguli **8** Caucasus, Dzhughur, Stanavoi, Tien Shan **9** Kopet Dagh, Narodnaya, Pamir-Alai, Yablonovy **10** Carpathian **11** Sikhote-Alin, Verkhoyansk
highest point: 9 Communism
river: 3 Don, Ili **4** Amur, Lena, Neva, Ural **5** Dvina, Kuban, Neman, Volga **6** Kolyma, Moskva **7** Dnieper, Pechora, Yenisei **8** Amu Darya, Dniester, Ob-Irtysh, Syr Darya **9** Indigirka
sea: 4 Aral, Azov, Kara **5** Black, Japan, White **6** Arctic, Baltic, Bering, Laptev **7** Barents, Caspian, Chukchi, Okhotsk, Pacific
physical feature:
gulf: **4** Azov **5** Mezen **9** Kara-Bogaz, Shelikhov
peninsula: **4** Kola **5** Yamal **6** Crimea, Taymyr **7** Chukchi, Karelia **9** Kamchatka **10** Mangyshlak
strait: **5** Tatar **6** Bering **8** Bosporus **11** Dardanelles
people: 3 Jew **4** Slav **5** Ersar, Kulak, Tatar, Uzbec **6** Kazakh, Soviet, Velika **7** Chukchi, Cossack, Kirghiz, Latvian, Russian, Tadzhik, Turkmen **8** Armenian, Estonian, Georgian, Siberian **9** Moldavian, Ukrainian **10** Lithuanian **11** Azerbaijani, Beloruassian
actor: **12** Stanislavsky
author: **5** Gogol **7** Nabokov, Pushkin, Tolstoy **8** Turgenev **9** Ehrenburg, Pasternak, Sholokhov **10** Dostoevsky **12** Solzhenitsyn
composer: **6** Glinka **7** Borodin **9** Prokofiev **10** Mussorgsky, Stravinsky **11** Tchaikovsky **12** Rachmaninoff, Shostakovich **14** Rimsky-Korsakov
cosmonaut: **11** Yuri Gagarin
czar/tsar/tzar: **4** Ivan, Paul **5** Peter **6** Alexis **7** Michael **8** Nicholas **9** Alexander **12** Boris Godunov
dancer: **7** Nureyev, Pavlova **8** Danilova, Nijinsky **11** Baryshnikov
dynasty: **7** Romanov
early people: **3** Hun **4** Goth **5** Tatar **6** Khazar, Mongol, Tartar **8** Norsemen, Scythian **9** Cimmerian, Sarmatian, Varangian
empress: **9** Alexandra, Catherine
hereditary noble: **5** boyar
leader: **5** Beria, Lenin **6** Stalin, Suslov **7** Gromyko, Kosygin, Molotov, Trotsky, Yeltsin **8** Andropov, Brezhnev, Bukharin, Bulganin, Kerensky, Malenkov, Podgorny **9** Chernenko, Gorbachev **10** Khrushchev
monk: **8** Rasputin
prince: **4** Oleg **5** Rurik **8** Vladimir
revolutionary: **9** bolshevik **10** Decembrist
ruler: **5** Tatar **6** Mongol **8** Batu Khan
scientist: **6** Pavlov **9** Mendeleev **11** Tsiolkovsky

Russia (*continued*)
  language: **5** Evenk, Tatar, Uzbek **6** Buriat, Kalmyk, Kazakh **7** Finnish, Kirghiz, Latvian, Russian, Tadzhik, Turkmen **8** Armenian, Estonian, Georgian, Ossetian **9** Moldavian, Ukrainian **10** Lithuanian **11** Belorussian
    alphabet: **8** cyrillic
  religion: **5** Islam **7** Judaism **8** Buddhism, Lutheran **10** Protestant **13** Roman Catholic **15** Russian Orthodox **16** Armenian Orthodox, Georgian Orthodox
  place: **7** Kremlin **9** Red Square
    art gallery: **9** Tretyakov
    castle: **8** Starosty
    cathedral: **5** Sobor **7** Zagorsk **8** St Basils
    cemetery: **11** Piskarevsky
    museum: **9** Hermitage **12** Petrodvorets **18** Cathedral of St Isaac
    palace: **6** Winter
    park: **5** Gorky
    ruins: **7** Bukhara **10** Echmiadzin **15** Gediminas Castle
    prison: **8** Lubyanka
    street: **11** Kreshchatik **14** Nevski Prospekt
    theater: **7** Bolshoi
  feature:
    collective farm: **7** kolkhoz
    country house: **5** dacha
    dance: **4** kolo **5** gopac, hopak, saber **6** cossac, trepak **7** cosaque, ziganka **8** kozachok **9** tzazatski
    dance company: **5** Kirov **7** Bolshoi
    labor camp: **5** gulag
    musical instrument: **9** balalaika
    secret police: **3** KGB, MGB **4** NKVD, OGPU **5** Cheka
    state farm: **7** sovkhoz
  food:
    caviar: **13** ikra zernistia
    cereal: **5** kasha
    sour cream: **7** smetana
    dessert: **8** vareniki
    dish: **4** plov **5** pirau **6** pelemo **8** osetrina, shashlyk **16** kotleta po kievski
    drink: **4** kvas **5** kvass, vodka **6** chacha, kumiss
    filled pastries: **8** piroshki, pirozhki
    soup: **5** shchi **6** borsch **7** borscht, borshch

Rwanda
  other name: **6** Ruanda
  capital/largest city: **6** Kigali
  others: **6** Biumba, Butare, Kibuye, Nyanza **7** Astrida, Gisenyi, Kibungu **8** Cyangugu **9** Ruhengeri
  division:
    colonial: **12** Ruanda-Urundi
  monetary unit: **5** franc **7** centime
  lake: **4** Kivu **5** Ihema **6** Bufera, Bulera, Mohasi **7** Rugwero, Ruhnodo **8** Mugesera, Tshohoha
  mountain: **7** Mitumba, Virunga **8** Muhavura
  highest point: **9** Karisimbi
  river: **6** Kagera, Ruzizi **7** Akagera **8** Akanyaru **9** Luvironza **10** Nyawarongo
  physical feature:
    forest: **7** Nyungwe
    valley: **11** Western Rift
  people: **3** Twa **4** Hutu **5** Batwa, Pygmy, Tutsi **6** Bahutu, Watusi **7** Batutsi
    explorer: **5** Speke **6** Gotzen
    leader: **9** Kayibanda **11** Habyarimana
  language: **6** French **7** Swahili **11** Kinyarwanda
  religion: **7** animism **13** Roman Catholic
  place:
    game reserve: **6** Gabiro
    park: **6** Albert, Kagera **16** Virunga Volcanoes
  feature:
    clothing: **5** pagne
    king: **5** mwami

lence, The Longest Day **14** About Mrs Leslie, God's Little Acre **17** Bad Day at Black Rock **18** The Woman on the Beach

Ryder, Albert Pinkham
  born: **12** New Bedford MA
  artwork: **12** The Race Track (Death on a Pale Horse) **15** Toilers of the Sea **27** Siegfried and the Rhine Maidens

rye 6 Secale
  varieties: **4** wild **5** giant **6** common **8** Aral wild, blue wild **9** Altai wild, giant wild, Volga wild **10** Canada wild **11** Chinese wild, Russian wild **12** Siberian wild, Virginia wild
  type: **6** liquor **7** whiskey
  origin: **7** Ireland **8** Scotland
  ingredient: **10** mash grains
  drink: **9** Cablegram **11** John Collins, Whiskey Sour
  with Cointreau: **10** Temptation
  with Pernod: **3** TNT
  with vermouth: **8** Brooklyn **9** Algonquin

Saarinen, Eero
father: **5** Eliel
architect of: **11** St Louis
Arch **20** Gateway to the
West Arch (St Louis)
26 Trans World Airlines Terminal (NYC) **28** General Motors Technical Center
(Warren MI) **39** Columbia
Broadcasting Company
Headquarters (NYC)
style: **13** International

Saarinen, Eliel
son: **4** Eero
architect of: **16** Cranbrook
Academy (Bloomfield Hills
MI) **18** Kleinhaus Music
Hall (Buffalo) **19** Tanglewood Music Shed (MA)
20 Christ Lutheran Church
(Minneapolis MN), First
Christian Church (Columbus
IN)

Saba *see* **5** Sheba

Sabaoth 6 armies

Sabbath 8 Lord's Day **9** day of
rest

Sabbatical: A Romance
author: **9** John Barth

saber, sabre 3 cut **4** kill,
stab **5** blade, sword, wound
6 cutlas, rapier, strike **7** cutlass, soldier **8** scimitar
10 broadsword

Sabin, Albert Bruce
field: **8** medicine
developed: **16** oral polio
vaccine

sable 3 fur, jet **4** dark, inky
5 black, ebony, raven

sabotage 3 sap **6** retard **7** cripple, destroy, disable, disrupt,
subvert **8** paralyze **9** undermine, vandalize **10** subversion **12** incapacitate

sabra 11 Israeli-born **14** native
of Israel

Sabra
type: **7** liqueur
origin: **6** Israel
flavor: **6** orange **9** chocolate

Sac *see* **4** Sauk

saccharine 5 gooey, mushy,
soppy, sweet **6** sugary, syrupy
7 candied, cloying, honeyed,
maudlin, mawkish, sugared
9 offensive, oversweet, revolting, sickening **10** disgusting,
nauseating **11** sentimental

sacerdotal 5 papal **8** clerical,
pastoral, priestly **9** apostolic,
canonical, episcopal **10** pontifical **11** ministerial **12** hierarchical **14** ecclesiastical

sack 3 bag, rob **4** loot, pack,
raid **5** pouch, spoil, store,
waste **6** duffel, maraud, rapine,
ravage, tear up **7** despoil, pillage, plunder, ransack **8** spoliate **9** depredate, duffel bag,
gunnysack, haversack, marauding **10** plundering, ravishment **11** depredation,
devastation **12** despoliation

Sackbut 18 Biblical instrument

Sackville, Thomas
author of: **8** Gorboduc (with
Thomas Norton)

sacrament 3 vow **4** rite
5 troth **6** pledge, plight, ritual
7 liturgy, promise, service
8 ceremony, contract, covenant **9** solemnity **10** ceremonial, obligation, observance
11 affirmation **12** ministration

sacramental 4 holy **6** ritual
7 blessed **10** ceremonial,
liturgical

Sacraments, Seven 7 Baptism, Penance **9** Eucharist,
Last Rites, Matrimony **10** Holy
Orders **12** Confirmation
13 Holy Communion **14** Extreme Unction, Reconciliation
18 Anointing of the Sick

sacred 4 holy **6** church

7 blessed, revered **8** Biblical,
hallowed, hieratic **9** religious,
venerable **10** sanctified, scriptural **11** consecrated
14 ecclesiastical

**Sacred and Profane Love
Machine, The**
author: **11** Iris Murdoch

Sacred writings 5 Bible
11 Bibliotheca

sacrifice 4 cede, loss **5** forgo,
waive **6** forego, give up, homage **7** cession, forfeit, offer
up **8** immolate, oblation, offering, renounce **9** surrender
10 concession, immolation,
lustration, relinquish **12** renunciation **14** relinquishment

sacrilege 3 sin **7** impiety,
mockery, outrage **8** iniquity
9 blasphemy, profanity, violation **10** irreligion, sinfulness,
wickedness **11** desecration, impiousness, irreverence, profanation, profaneness

sacrilegious 7 impious, profane **10** irreverent **11** blasphemous, irreligious

sacrosanct 4 holy **5** godly
6 divine, solemn **8** hallowed,
heavenly **9** celestial, inviolate,
religious, spiritual **10** inviolable, unexamined **11** consecrated **12** unquestioned

sacrum
bone of: **11** base of spine

sad 3 low **4** blue, grim, hard,
hurt **5** grave **6** dismal, solemn,
taxing, tragic, trying, woeful
7 adverse, crushed, doleful,
forlorn, grieved, joyless, maudlin, pitiful, serious, unhappy
8 dejected, desolate, downcast,
grievous, mournful, pathetic,
touching, troubled, wretched
9 cheerless, depressed, difficult,
miserable, sorrowful **10** calamitous, chapfallen, despairing, despondent, dispirited,
distressed, lachrymose, lament-

able, melancholy **11** crestfallen, distressing, pessimistic, troublesome, unfortunate **12** disconsolate, heartrending, heavyhearted, inconsolable **13** brokenhearted, griefstricken, heartbreaking **14** down in the dumps, down in the mouth
French: 6 triste

Sadat, Anwar el-
president of: 5 Egypt
awarded: 15 Nobel Peace Prize
author of: 18 In Search of Identity

sadden 4 damp, dash **5** crush **6** burden, deject, grieve, sorrow, subdue **7** depress **8** aggrieve, dispirit **10** discourage, dishearten

saddle with 9 stick with **10** burden with **12** encumber with **18** make responsible for

Sade, Marquis de
author of: 7 Justine
8 Juliette

sadistic 6 brutal **7** vicious **8** fiendish, perverse **9** perverted **12** bloodthirsty

Sadness
author: 15 Donald Barthelme

sadness
French: 9 tristesse

sad poem 5 elegy **6** lament

Sad Sack
creator: 11 George Baker

Saehrimnir
origin: 12 Scandinavian
form: 4 boar
served in: 8 Valhalla
feat: 12 regeneration

safe 4 firm, sure, wary **5** sound, vault, whole **6** intact, modest, secure, stable, steady, unhurt **7** certain, guarded, prudent **8** cautious, defended, discreet, harmless, reliable, unbroken, unharmed **9** innocuous, protected, undamaged, unexposed, unscathed **10** dependable, protecting **11** circumspect, impregnable, out of danger, trustworthy, unscratched **12** conservative, invulnerable, noncommittal

safeguard 4 ward **5** armor, charm **6** amulet, buffer, defend, harbor, screen, secure, shield **7** bulwark, defense, fortify, protect, shelter **8** conserve, garrison, preserve, security, talisman **10** precaution, protection

safekeeping 4 care **6** charge **7** custody **8** security **9** husbandry **10** protection **12** conservation, guardianship, preservation

Safety Net, The
author: 12 Heinrich Boll

saffron
botanical name: 13 Crocus sativus
also called: 6 Krokus
Moorish: 6 Zafran
of all spices most: 6 costly
color: 6 orange, yellow **12** yellow-orange
used as: 8 coloring, cosmetic, medicine **9** fabric dye
origin: 5 Egypt, Syria **8** Holy Land **9** Palestine
use: 4 rice **5** bread, rolls

sag 3 bow, dip **4** drop, fail, flag, flap, flop, keel, lean, list, sink, sway, tilt, tire **5** droop, pitch, slump, weary **6** billow, plunge, settle, weaken **7** decline, descend, give way **8** diminish

saga 4 epic, myth, tale, yarn **6** legend **7** history, romance **9** adventure, chronicle, narrative
French: 11 roman-fleuve

sagacious 4 foxy, wise **5** acute, canny, sharp, smart, sound **6** astute, brainy, clever, shrewd **7** cunning, knowing, prudent, sapient, tactful **8** discreet, rational, sensible **9** judicious, practical **10** diplomatic, discerning, perceptive **11** calculating, intelligent **13** perspicacious **14** discriminating

sagacity 6 acumen, brains, smarts, wisdom **8** sapience **9** canniness, smartness **10** astuteness, braininess, cleverness, shrewdness **11** discernment **12** intelligence, perspicacity **13** judiciousness **14** discrimination

Sagan, Carl
author of: 6 Cosmos **7** Contact **16** The Dragons of Eden

Sagan, Francoise
real name: 16 Francoise Quoirez
author of: 13 A Certain Smile **15** Aimez-vous Brahms **16** Bonjour Tristesse

sage 4 guru, wise **5** sound **6** astute, pundit, savant, shrewd **7** egghead, knowing, prudent, sapient, scholar, wise man **8** mandarin, sensible **11** intelligent, philosopher
French: 6 savant
Latin: 5 magus, solon

sage 6 Salvia **12** S officinalis
varieties: 3 bog **4** baby, blue, gray, rose, sand, wood **5** black, lilac, Texas, white

6 autumn, common, desert, garden, purple, silver, yellow **7** bladder, gentian, scarlet, Spanish, thistle, Vervain **8** creeping, gray ball, mealy-cup, rose-leaf **9** Bethlehem, Jerusalem **11** Mexican bush **16** pineapple-scented
means: 6 to heal, to save
strengthens: 6 memory, wisdom **8** prudence
makes men: 8 immortal
origin: 7 Albania **10** Yugoslavia **13** Mediterranean
use: 4 pork **6** breads, cheese **7** chicken, poultry, seafood **8** stuffing

Sage of Concord
nickname of: 17 Ralph Waldo Emerson

Sagittarius
symbol: 6 archer **7** centaur
planet: 7 Jupiter
rules: 10 philosophy **15** higher education
born: 8 December, November

Sagittary
form: 7 centaur
carried: 3 bow

said 5 above, quoth **6** quoted, spoken, stated **7** related, uttered **8** repeated

Saigon
capital of: 7 Vietnam

sail 3 fly **4** boat, scud, skim, soar **5** drift, float, glide, steam **6** course, cruise, voyage **8** navigate **9** excursion

sailboat 4 saic, yawl **5** craft, ketch, sloop, yacht **6** vessel **7** sunfish **8** schooner **9** catamaran
part: 4 boom, mast **6** canvas **7** rigging **9** mainsheet

sailcloth 4 duck **6** canvas

Sailing to Byzantium
author: 7 W B Yeats

sailor 3 gob, tar **4** salt **6** sea dog, seaman **7** mariner, voyager **8** deckhand, seafarer **9** navigator, yachtsman

sailors
goddess of: 5 Brizo **11** Britomartis

Sails (of Argo)
constellation of: 4 Vela

saint 6 martyr
Buddhist: 5 arhat **11** bodhisattva
Chinese: 8 immortal
Islamic: 3 pir
lives of the saints: 8 menology **9** hagiology **11** hagiography **13** acta sanctorum
process of becoming: 12 canonization

relic box: 6 chasse
remains: 5 relic
symbol: 4 halo

Saint, Eva Marie
born: 8 Newark NJ
roles: 6 Exodus **15** On the
Waterfront **16** North by
Northwest

saint, patron *see box*

Saint, The
author: 16 Antonio Fogazzaro

Saint, The
author: 15 Leslie Charteris
character: 12 Simon Templar **26** Inspector Claude
Eustace Teal
cast: 10 Roger Moore

Saint Anthony's fire
6 herpes **8** ergotism, shingles
10 erysipelas

**Sainte-Beuve, Charles
Augustin**
author of: 19 Monday
Conversations

Saint Elmo's fire 5 flame,
hermo **6** castor, corona, furole,
helena **9** corposant
12 luminescence

Saint Esprit 9 Holy Ghost
10 Holy Spirit

Saint-Exupery, Antoine de
author of: 11 Night Flight
12 Southern Mail **15** The
Little Prince **16** Wind Sand
and Stars

Saint Francis
born: 6 Assisi
called: 9 Poverello

Saint-Gaudens, Augustus
born: 6 Dublin **7** Ireland
artwork: 7 Puritan **13** Mrs
Henry Adams (Grief)
14 General Sherman **15** Admiral Farragut **16** President
Lincoln

Saint Jack
author: 11 Paul Theroux

Saint Joan
author: 17 George Bernard
Shaw

Saint John's bread 5 carob

Saint John's wort 5 amber
6 tutsan **7** ascyrum, cammock
9 androseme, hypericum,
rosin-rose **10** broombrush
11 Aaron's-beard

saintliness 6 purity **8** goodness, holiness **9** beatitude, godliness **11** blessedness
12 spirituality

Saint Lucia, St Lucia
capital: 8 Castries
highest point: 5 Gimie
island group: 8 Windward
14 Lesser Antilles

saint, patron
acolytes: 13 John Berchmans
actors: 8 Genesius
artists: 4 Luke
astronomers: 7 Dominic
athletes: 9 Sebastian
authors: 14 Francis de Sales
aviators: 15 Our Lady of Loreto **16** Therese of Lisieux
17 Joseph of Cupertino
bakers: 8 Nicholas **18** Elizabeth of Hungary
bankers: 7 Matthew
barbers: 5 Louis **6** Cosmas, Damian
barren women: 9 Felicitas **14** Anthony of Padua
beggars/cripples: 5 Giles
blind: 6 Odilia **7** Raphael
bodily ills: 16 Our Lady of Lourdes
boy scouts: 6 George
brides: 14 Nicholas of Myra
builders: 13 Vincent Ferrer
butchers: 4 Luke **7** Hadrian **14** Anthony of Egypt
carpenters: 6 Joseph
cancer patients: 9 Peregrine
children: 10 Santa Claus **14** Nicholas of Myra
comedians: 5 Vitus
cooks: 6 Martha **8** Lawrence
deaf: 14 Francis de Sales
dying: 6 Joseph **7** Barbara
emigrants: 14 Frances Cabrini
England: 6 George
eye sufferers: 4 Lucy
falsely accused: 15 Raymond Nonnatus
farmers: 6 George **7** Isidore
fishermen: 5 Peter **6** Andrew
foreign missions: 13 Francis Xavier **16** Therese of Lisieux
foundlings: 13 Holy Innocents
France: 5 Denis
gardeners: 6 Fiacre, Phocas **7** Adelard, Dorothy, Tryphon
heart patients: 9 John of God
hospitals: 9 John of God **12** Jude Thaddeus **16** Camillus
de Lellis
housewives: 4 Anne
hunters: 6 Hubert **10** Eustachius
invalids: 4 Roch
Ireland: 7 Patrick
Italy: 7 Anthony
laborers: 5 James **7** Isidore **9** John Bosco
lawyers: 3 Ivo **4** Ives **8** Genesius **10** Thomas More
librarians: 6 Jerome
lovers: 9 Valentine
mariners: 7 Michael **19** Nicholas of Tolentino
mentally ill: 6 Dympna

language: 6 patois
location: 9 Caribbean

saintly 4 good, holy **5** godly,
moral, pious **6** devout **7** angelic, blessed, exalted, sinless,
upright **8** beatific, faithful, reverent, virtuous **9** believing, religious, righteous, spiritual
10 benevolent

Saint Paul
born: 6 Tarsus
companion: 4 Luke
epistle: 5 Titus **6** Romans
7 Hebrews, Timothy **8** Philemon **9** Ephesians, Galatians
10 Colossians **11** Corinthians, Philippians
13 Thessalonians

**Saint Paul's Cathedral
(London)**
architect: 4 Wren

Saint Peter
called: 4 Rock **5** Simon
6 Cephas
brother: 6 Andrew

**Saint-Saens, (Charles)
Camille**
born: 5 Paris **6** France
composer of: 12 Danse Macabre **14** Samson et Dalila
16 Samson and Delilah

merchants: **14** Nicholas of Myra **15** Francis of Assisi
metalworkers: **7** Eligius
miners: **7** Barbara
mothers: **6** Monica
musicians: **7** Cecilia, Dunstan **15** Gregory the Great
Norway: **4** Olaf
nurses: **6** Agatha **7** Alexius, Raphael **9** John of God
  16 Camillus de Lellis
painters: **4** Luke
philosophers: **6** Justin **21** Catherine of Alexandria
physicians: **4** Luke **6** Cosmas, Damian **7** Raphael
  9 Pantaleon
pilgrims: **5** James **7** Alexius
poets: **5** David **7** Cecilia
policemen: **7** Michael
poor souls: **19** Nicholas of Tolentino
postal workers: **7** Gabriel
priests: **19** Jean-Baptiste Vianney
printers: **8** Genesius **9** John of God **16** Augustine of Hippo
prisoners: **6** Dismas **7** Barbara **13** Joseph Cafasso
rheumatism: **15** James the Greater
sailors: **4** Elmo **7** Brendan, Erasmus, Eulalia **8** Cuthbert,
  Nicholas **11** Christopher **13** Peter Gonzales
scholars: **6** Brigid
scientists: **6** Albert
Scotland: **6** Andrew
sculptors: **6** Claude
seamen: **14** Francis of Paolo
sick: **7** Michael **9** John of God **16** Camillus de Lellis
singers: **7** Cecilia, Gregory
skiers: **7** Bernard
shoemakers: **7** Crispin
soldiers: **6** George **7** Hadrian **8** Ignatius **9** Joan of Arc, Sebastian **13** Martin of Tours
Spain: **5** James **8** Santiago
students: **13** Thomas Aquinas **21** Catherine of Alexandria
surgeons: **6** Cosmas, Damian
tailors: **9** Homobonus
tax collectors: **7** Matthew
teachers: **15** Gregory the Great **21** Catherine of Alexandria, Jean Baptiste de la Salle
theologians: **9** Augustine **16** Alphonsus Liguori
throat sufferers: **6** Blaise
travelers: **7** Raphael **11** Christopher **14** Anthony of Padua,
  Nicholas of Myra
Wales: **5** David
winegrowers: **7** Vincent
workingmen: **6** Joseph
writers: **14** Francis de Sales
youth: **13** John Berchmans **15** Aloysius Gonzaga, Gabriel
  Possenti

nationality: **7** Russian
researched: **14** nuclear
  fission
defended: **12** civil liberty
exiled to: **5** Gorky
awarded: **10** Nobel Prize

Saki
real name: **7** H H Munro
author of: **8** Reginald
  20 Beasts and Super-Beasts
  21 The Chronicles of Clovis
  23 The Unbearable
  Bassington

salaam 3 bow **6** homage
9 obeisance

Salacia
partner of: **7** Neptune

salacious 4 lewd, sexy **7** lustful, obscene **8** indecent **9** lecherous **10** lascivious, libidinous
12 pornographic

salad days 5 prime, youth
6 heyday **9** flowering

salamander 3 eft **4** newt
5 giant, siren, tiger **6** lizard,
red eft **7** axolotl, urodela
8 congo eel, mudpuppy **9** amphibian, fire-eater, proteidae
10 hellbender, necturidae
14 red-spotted newt

Salamis
father: **6** Asopus
mother: **6** Metope
son: **8** Cychreus

Salammbo
author: **15** Gustave Flaubert
character: **5** Matho **8** Hamilcar, Spendius **9** Narr Havas
setting: **8** Carthage

salary 3 pay **5** wages **6** income **7** stipend **8** earnings
9 allowance, emolument
10 recompense
12 remuneration

sale 3 cut **7** bargain, selling,
special **8** discount, exchange,
markdown, transfer
9 reduction

Salem
home of: **11** Melchizedek

salesperson 5 agent, clerk
6 vendor **8** huckster

salient 6 arrant, marked
7 glaring, notable, obvious
8 flagrant, manifest, palpable,
striking **9** egregious, important, prominent **10** noteworthy, noticeable, pro-
nounced, protruding, remarkable **11** conspicuous,
outstanding, substantial
12 considerable

Salii
also: **6** Salian
form: **7** priests
priests of: **4** Mars

Saints' lives
writer of: **12** hagiographer

Saint Vincent, St Vincent
capital: **9** Kingstown
highest point: **9** Soufriere
Indian: **5** Carib **6** Arawak
island group: **8** Windward
  14 Lesser Antilles
islands: **10** Grenadines
language: **6** patois
location: **9** Caribbean
volcano: **9** Soufriere

Saint Vitus' dance 6 chorea

Saitis see **6** Athena

sake 3 end **4** care, gain, good
5 cause **6** behalf, object, profit,
regard **7** account, benefit, concern, purpose, respect, welfare **8** interest **9** advantage
11 enhancement
13 consideration

sake
type: **4** wine **6** spirit
origin: **5** Japan
ingredient: **4** rice

**Sakharov, Andrei
Dimitrievich**
field: **7** physics

guarded: 7 ancilia **13** sacred shields

saline 4 salt **5** briny, salty **8** brackish

Salinger, J D
author of: **14** Franny and Zooey **18** The Catcher in the Rye

Salisbury
capital of: **8** Zimbabwe

Salisbury, Harrison E
author of: **16** American in Russia **19** A Journey for Our Times, Black Night White Snow

Salish (Flatheads)
language family: **8** Salishan
location: **5** Idaho **6** Oregon **7** Montana **10** Washington **15** British Columbia

Salishan
tribe: **6** Salish **8** Puyallop **9** Flatheads

Salk, Jonas Edward
field: **8** medicine
developed: **12** (inactivated) polio vaccine

salle a manger 10 dining room
literally: **13** hall for eating

sallow 3 wan **4** gray, pale **5** ashen, livid **6** anemic, pallid, sickly, yellow **7** bilious **9** jaundiced, washed-out, yellowish

sallowness 6 pallor **7** wanness **8** paleness **10** sickliness **11** biliousness **13** colorlessness, yellowishness

Sallust
author of: **9** Histories **13** War of Jugurtha **20** Conspiracy of Catiline

sally 3 mot **4** flow, pour, quip, raid, trip **5** erupt, foray, surge **6** attack, banter, charge, outing, retort, sortie, spring, thrust **7** debouch, journey **8** badinage, repartee **9** excursion, wisecrack, witticism **10** expedition **13** counterattack

Salmacis
form: **5** nymph
loved: **14** Hermaphroditus
joined with: **14** Hermaphroditus
became: **13** hermaphrodite **14** bisexual person

Salmagundi
author: **16** Washington Irving

salmon 4 fish, king **5** cohoe **6** silver **7** chinook, Pacific, quinnat, sockeye, spawner **8** Atlantic, humpback
enclosure: **4** yair
female: **4** raun **6** baggit

genus: **12** Oncorhynchus
hatchling: **4** pink **6** alevin
male: **3** gib **4** buck, cock
post-spawning: **4** kelt **7** shedder
pre-spawning: **7** gilling, girling
young: **4** parr **7** essling

Salmoneus
father: **6** Aeolus
mother: **7** Enarete
brother: **8** Sisyphus
wife: **6** Sidero **8** Alcidice
daughter: **4** Tyro
struck by: **9** lightning

Salome
father: **11** Herod Philip
mother: **8** Herodias
husband: **7** Zebedee
opera by: **7** (Richard) Strauss
character: **5** Herod (the Tetrarch) **8** Herodias, Jokanaan (John the Baptist) **9** Narraboth

salon 4 hall **7** gallery **11** drawing room **13** establishment

saloon 3 bar, inn, pub **6** bistro, tavern **7** barroom, ginmill, taproom **8** alehouse **9** roadhouse, speakeasy

salt 3 wit **4** best, corn, cure, pick, save **5** brine, briny, cream, elect, humor, savor, smack, souse, spice **6** choice, flavor, pickle, saline, season, select **8** brackish, marinate, piquancy, pungency **9** seasoning **12** quintessence

Salten, Felix
author of: **5** Bambi

salt water 3 sea **5** brine, ocean

salty 4 racy **5** briny, funny, spicy, terse, witty **6** corned, ribald, risque, saline **7** pungent, zestful **8** brackish, improper

salubrious 7 bracing, healthy **9** healthful, wholesome **10** beneficial, lifegiving **11** therapeutic **12** invigorating

salubriousness 11 healthiness **13** healthfulness, wholesomeness

Salus
origin: **5** Roman
goddess of: **6** health **10** prosperity
corresponds to: **6** Hygeia

salutary 4 good **5** tonic **6** useful **7** healing, healthy **8** curative, sanitary **9** healthful, wholesome **10** beneficial, profitable **12** advantageous

salutation 3 bow **5** hello, howdy, toast **6** curtsy **7** address, welcome **8** greeting **9** reception

Hawaiian: 5 aloha
Italian: 4 ciao
Latin: 3 ave

salute 3 ave **4** hail, kiss **5** bow to, cheer, greet, honor, nod to, salvo **6** accost, homage, praise, wave to **7** address, applaud, respect, welcome **8** accolade, applause, greeting **9** laudation, reverence **11** acclamation, recognition **12** congratulate

Salvador
author: **10** Joan Didion

salvage 4 junk, save **5** scrap **6** debris, rescue **7** recover, remains, restore **8** recovery, retrieve **9** retrieval **11** reclamation **12** rehabilitate

salvation 4 rock **5** grace **6** rescue, saving **8** election, lifeline, mainstay, recovery, survival **9** retrieval **10** protection, redemption **11** deliverance, reclamation **12** preservation

salve 4 balm, calm, ease, hail **5** hello **6** lessen, lotion, pacify, reduce, soothe, temper **7** anodyne, assuage, mollify, relieve, unguent **8** dressing, liniment, mitigate, moderate, ointment **9** alleviate, emollient, greetings **11** alleviative

salver 4 bowl, dish, tray **6** waiter **7** coaster

salvia 4 herb, mint, sage **5** shrub **8** mejorana **9** artemisia

salvo 5 burst **6** volley **7** barrage, battery **8** shelling **9** cannonade, fusillade **11** bombardment

sambuca
type: **7** liqueur
origin: **5** Italy
flavor: **5** anise **10** elderberry

same 4 like, twin, very **5** alike, equal **6** on a par **7** similar, uniform **8** parallel **9** identical, unchanged **10** consistent, equivalent, invariable **13** corresponding

same as previously given
Latin: **4** idem

sameness 6 parity **8** equality, evenness, likeness, monotony **10** similarity, uniformity **11** homogeneity **14** homogenousness

Samoa see box

Samoyed
language family: **6** Uralic
spoken in: **7** Siberia

sample 3 try **4** test **5** model, taste **7** dip into, examine, example, pattern, portion, segment **8** instance, paradigm,

Salmander- Newt

Samoa
  capital:
    American Samoa: 8 Pago Pago
    Western Samoa: 4 Apia
  cities: 6 Utulei 7 Palauli 8 Fagatogo
  division: 12 Western Samoa 13 American Samoa
  monetary unit: 4 tala
  island: 3 Ofu, Tau 4 Rose 5 Aunuu, Manua, Namua,
    Upolu 6 Manono, Nuulua, Savaii, Swains 7 Apolima, Nu-
    utele, Olosega, Tutuila 8 Nuusafee
  mountain: 4 Vaea 5 Alava 6 Savaii 7 Matafao 9 Rainmaker
  highest point: 4 Fito 8 Silisili
  sea: 12 South Pacific
  physical feature:
    bay: 5 Afono, Leone 6 Fagasa, Falefa, Safata 7 Lafanga,
    Masefau, Matautu 8 Massacre, Salealua 9 Saluofata
  people: 6 Samoan 10 Polynesian
    explorer: 9 Roggeveen 12 Bougainville
  language: 6 Samoan 7 English
  religion: 6 Mormon 9 Methodist 13 Roman Catholic
    15 Latter Day Saints 19 Seventh-Day Adventist 26 Con-
    gregational Christianity
  feature:
    bird: 3 iao 4 lulu, lupe 6 manuao, manuma, maomao
    7 manuali 8 manusina, manutagi
    chief: 5 matai
    chief's daughter: 5 taupo
    cloth: 4 para, tapa
    clothing: 5 pareu 8 lavalava, puletasi
    dance: 4 siva
    dwelling: 4 fale
  food:
    drink: 3 ava

specimen 10 experience
12 cross section, illustration
14 representative
15 exemplification

Sampo
  origin: 7 Finnish
  stolen by: 9 Ilmarinen
    11 Vainamoinen
    12 Lemminkainen
  stolen from: 5 Louhi

Samson 11 Hebrew judge
  father: 6 Manoah
  mistress/betrayer: 7 Delilah
  hometown: 5 Zorah

Samson Agonistes
  author: 10 John Milton

Samuel 11 Hebrew judge
  father: 7 Elkanah
  mother: 6 Hannah
  hometown: 5 Ramah
  anointed: 4 Saul 5 David

Sana, Sanaa
  capital of: 10 North Yemen

San Antonio
  basketball team: 5 Spurs
  football team: 11 Gunslingers
  landmark: 8 The Alamo
    9 River Walk

sanctification 8 blessing
9 hallowing 12 consecration
  Hebrew: 7 Kiddush

sanctified 4 holy 6 sacred
7 blessed 8 hallowed
11 consecrated

sanctify 5 bless, exalt 6 anoint,
hallow, purify, uphold 7 absolve, beatify, cleanse 8 dedicate, enshrine, make holy
10 consecrate, legitimate, legitimize 12 legitimatize

sanctimonious 6 solemn
7 canting, pompous, preachy
8 unctuous 9 overblown, pietistic 11 pharisaical, pretentious 14 holier-than-thou

sanctimoniousness 4 cant,
sham 6 humbug 9 hypocrisy
11 insincerity
15 pretentiousness

sanction 5 allow, favor, leave
6 accept, assent, permit, ratify 7 agree to, approve, consent, endorse, liberty, license,
penalty, support 8 approval,
coercion, pressure 9 authority,
authorize 10 legitimate, permission 11 countenance, endorsement 12 commendation,
confirmation, ratification
13 authorization

sanctuary 4 park 5 cover, haven 6 asylum, chapel, church,
refuge, safety, shrine, temple
7 reserve, retreat, shelter
8 preserve 10 protection

Sanctuary
  author: 15 William
    Faulkner
  character: 5 Tommy 6 Pop-
    eye 9 Ruby Lamar 10 Lee
    Goodwin, Reba Rivers
    11 Temple Drake 12 Gowan
    Stevens, Horace Benbow

sanctum sanctorum 12 holy
of holies

sanctus 4 holy

Sancus
  also: 10 Semo Sancus
  origin: 5 Roman
  god of: 5 oaths 10 road
    safety 11 hospitality 20 in-
    ternational affairs
  corresponds to: 8 Hercules
    10 Dius Fidius

sand 4 grit, guts 5 pluck,
spunk 6 mettle 7 bravery,
courage, resolve 8 backbone
9 fortitude 10 resolution
12 resoluteness

Sand, George
  real name: 14 Aurore
    Dudevant
  author of: 5 Lelia 7 Indiana
    8 Consuelo 9 Valentine
    13 Story of My Life 14 The
    Country Waif, The Haunted
    Pool 17 Fanchon the
    Cricket 18 Les Maitres Son-
    neurs 23 The Countess of
    Rudolstadt

sandal 4 clog, flat, shoe, zori
5 scuff, thong 6 loafer 7 slipper 8 flipflop, huarache, moccasin, overshoe 10 espadrille

sandalwood 5 Algum, Almug

sand bank 4 dune, reef
5 shelf, shoal 7 shallow

sandbar 4 bank, flat, reef,
spit 5 shelf, shoal 7 shallow

Sandbox, The
  author: 11 Edward Albee

Sandburg, Carl
  author of: 3 Fog 7 Chicago
    12 Harvest Poems 13 Smoke
    and Steel 14 Abraham Lin-
    coln, The Cornhuskers
    15 Remembrance Rock

Sanders, George
  born: 6 Russia 12 St
    Petersburg
  wife: 10 Benita Hume,
    Magda Gabor 11 Zsa Zsa
    Gabor
  roles: 6 The Fan 7 Ivanhoe,
    Rebecca 8 The Saint 9 The
    Falcon 11 All About Eve
    12 Forever Amber, The Gay
    Falcon 18 The Moon and
    Sixpence 20 Foreign Corre-
    spondent 22 The Picture of

Dorian Gray **24** The House of the Seven Gables
autobiography: 25 Memoirs of a Professional Cad

San Diego
airport: 14 Lindbergh Field
area: 7 La Jolla, Old Town **8** Coronado **9** Point Loma **10** Balboa Park, Mission Bay **13** Mission Valley **14** Gaslamp Quarter
baseball team: 6 Padres
football team: 8 Chargers
founder: 13 Junipero Serra
landmark: 11 San Diego Zoo **14** Wild Animal Park **30** Scripps Institute of Oceanography

sandpiper 3 ree **4** bird, ruff **5** reeve, stint, wader **6** common, oxbird, plover **7** fiddler, haybird, spotted, tipbird **8** graybird, sandpeep, shadbird **10** beachrobin

Sands of Iwo Jima
director: 9 Allan Dwan
cast: 8 John Agar **9** Adele Mara, John Wayne **13** Forrest Tucker

sandwich 3 sub **4** club, deli, hero **5** hogie **6** burger, hoagie, insert **7** grinder, western **8** laminate **9** interpose, submarine **10** lamination **11** combination

sane 5 lucid, sober **7** logical **8** all there, balanced, credible, rational, sensible **9** judicious, plausible, sagacious **10** farsighted, reasonable **11** clearheaded, responsible
Latin: 12 compos mentis

Sanford and Son
character: 5 Bubba **6** Melvin **10** Aunt Esther **11** Donna Harris, Fred Sanford, Grady Wilson, Rollo Larson **12** Julio Fuentes, Officer Smith (Smitty) **13** Lamont Sanford
cast: 8 Redd Foxx **9** Don Bexley **11** Hal Williams, LaWanda Page, Slappy White, Whitman Mayo **12** Demond Wilson, Lynn Hamilton **13** Gregory Sierra **15** Nathaniel Taylor

San Francisco
baseball team: 6 Giants
bay: 12 San Francisco
county: 5 Marin **8** San Mateo **12** San Francisco
football team: 11 Forty-Niners
known as: 12 City by the Bay **19** City by the Golden Gate
landmark: 8 Alcatraz **16** Golden Gate Bridge
noted for: 8 cable car **9** earthquake (1906)

26 crookedest street in the world
street/section: 6 Market **7** Lombard, Nob Hill **8** Presidio **9** Chinatown **10** Montgomery **11** Embarcadero, Russian Hill

Sangallensis 16 Greek uncial codex

sangaree, sangria
flavor: 5 fruit, spice

sangfroid 5 poise **6** aplomb **7** balance **8** coolness **9** composure **10** confidence, equanimity **11** tranquility **12** tranquillity **16** imperturbability

sanguine 3 red **4** rosy **5** happy, ruddy, sunny **6** bright, elated, florid **7** buoyant, crimson, flushed, glowing, hopeful, reddish, scarlet **8** blooming, cheerful, inflamed, rubicund **9** confident **10** optimistic **12** lighthearted

Sanhedrin 7 council

sanitarium, sanitorium
8 hospital **11** institution
French: 13 maison de sante

sanitary 5 clean **7** aseptic, healthy, sterile **8** germ-free, hygienic **9** healthful, wholesome **10** salubrious, sterilized, uninfected, unpolluted **11** disinfected **12** prophylactic

sanitorium *see* **10** sanitarium

sanity 5 sense **6** reason **8** lucidity, saneness **9** coherence, normality **11** rationality **12** sensibleness **14** reasonableness **15** clearheadedness

San Jose
capital of: 9 Costa Rica

San Juan
capital of: 10 Puerto Rico

San Juan Bautista *see* **10** Puerto Rico

San Marino *see box*

San Salvador
capital of: 10 El Salvador

sans doute 12 without doubt

Sansovino, Andrea
real name: 14 Andrea Contucci
born: 5 Italy **14** Monte San Savino
artwork: 15 Baptism of Christ **20** Virgin Child and St Anne

Sansovino, Il
real name: 11 Jacopo Tatti
born: 5 Italy **7** Caprese
artwork: 4 Mars **7** Bacchus, Logetta, Neptune **10** Old Li-

San Marino
capital/largest city: 9 San Marino
others: 10 Serravalle **13** Borgo Maggiore
division: 8 Castelli
government:
legislature: **22** Great and General Council
monetary unit: 4 lira, lire **9** centesimi
mountain: 9 Apennines
highest point: 6 Titano
people: 7 Italian **11** San Marinese
founder: **7** Marinus
language: 7 Italian
religion: 13 Roman Catholic
place: 13 Valloni Palace **17** Palazzo del Governo **19** Basilica of San Marino
church: **5** Pieve **9** St Francis

brary **15** Madonna del Parto **16** St John the Baptist

sans pareil 12 without equal

sans peur et sans reproche 29 without fear and without reproach

sans souci 8 carefree **11** without care

Santa Cruz de Tenerife
capital of: 13 Canary Islands

Santayana, George
author of: 14 The Last Puritan **16** The Realms of Being, The Sense of Beauty **24** Skepticism and Animal Faith

Santiago
capital of: 5 Chile

Santiago
character in: 18 The Old Man and the Sea
author: 9 Hemingway

Santo Domingo
capital of: 17 Dominican Republic

Santo Domingo *see* **5** Haiti

Sao Tome
capital of: 18 Sao Tome and Principe

Sao Tome and Principe *see box*

sap 3 rob, tax **4** ruin, wear **5** bleed, drain **6** impair, reduce, weaken **7** afflict, cripple, deplete, destroy, disable, exhaust, subvert **8** enervate, enfeeble **9** devastate, undermine **10** debilitate, devitalize

Sao Tome and Principe
capital/largest city:
  7 Sao Tome
others: **8** Trindade
  11 Porto Alegre
  12 Santo Antonio
monetary unit: **5** dobra
  6 escudo **7** centavo
highest point: **7** Sao
  Tome
sea: **8** Atlantic
physical feature:
  bay: **11** Ana de
    Chaves
  gulf: **6** Guinea
people: **7** African
  10 Portuguese **11** Cape
  Verdean
  explorer: **7** Escobar
    8 Santarem
language: **10** Portuguese
religion: **7** animism
  13 Roman Catholic
  19 Seventh Day Ad-
  ventist **21** Evangelical
  Protestant

sapient 4 wise **7** knowing
8 profound **9** sagacious **10** discerning, perceptive **11** intelligent **13** knowledgeable

sap one's energy 3 fag
4 bush, poop, tire **5** drain,
weary **6** tucker, weaken **7** deplete, exhaust, fatigue, wash
out **8** enervate, enfeeble
10 debilitate, devitalize

Sapphira
  husband: **7** Ananias
  lied to: **5** Peter

sapphire 3 gem **4** blue **5** azure,
jewel **6** indigo
  species: **8** corundum
  source: **5** Burma, Mogok
    6 Ceylon **7** Kashmir **8** Sri
    Lanka, Thailand **9** Australia
  kind: **4** star

Sappho
  author: **14** Alphonse Daudet

Sarah, Sarai
  father: **5** Asher
  former name: **5** Sarai
  husband: **7** Abraham
  son: **5** Isaac
  slave: **5** Hagar
  burial place: **9** Machpelah

sarcasm 3 rub **4** gibe, jeer,
jest **5** irony, scorn, sneer,
taunt **7** mockery **8** contempt,
derision, ridicule, scoffing
13 disparagement

sarcastic 5 acerb **6** biting, bitter, ironic **7** caustic, cutting,
mocking, mordant **8** derisive,
piercing, sardonic, scornful,
sneering, stinging, taunting

11 disparaging
12 contemptuous

sarcoma 5 tumor **6** cancer,
growth **8** neoplasm
10 malignancy

sarcophagus 4 pall **6** coffin

sard
  species: **6** quartz

sardine 4 bang, cram, fish, lile,
lour, pack **5** crowd **7** alewife,
anchovy, herring **8** pilchard

Sardinia *see box*

Sardius 8 gemstone

sardonic 6 biting **7** caustic,
cynical, jeering, mocking,
mordant, satiric **8** derisive,
scornful, sneering, taunting
9 sarcastic **11** disparaging
12 contemptuous

Sardonyx 8 gemstone

Sargent, John Singer
  born: **5** Italy **8** Florence
  artwork: **6** Madam X (Ma-
    dame Gautreau) **7** El Jaleo
    17 The Wyndham Sisters
    20 Robert Louis Stevenson
    21 Carnation Lily Lily Rose
    22 Daughters of Edward D
    Boit **24** Oyster Gatherers of
    Cancale

Sargom
  captured: **5** Accad
  successor: **11** Sennacherib

Saron
  king of: **7** Troezen

Saroyan, William
  author of: **12** My Name Is
    Aram **14** The Human Com-
    edy **17** The Time of Your
    Life **22** My Heart's in the
    Highlands

Sarpedon
  prince of: **5** Lycia
  father: **4** Zeus
  mother: **6** Europa **8** Laodamia
  uncle: **5** Cilix
  brother: **5** Minos
    12 Rhadamanthys
  ally of: **4** Troy
  friend: **7** Glaucus
  killed by: **9** Patroclus

Sarton, May
  author of: **5** Anger **11** Kinds
    of Love **17** Plant Dreaming
    Deep **20** Faithful Are the
    Wounds **33** Mrs Stevens
    Hears the Mermaids Singing

Sartor Resartus
  author: **13** Thomas Carlyle

Sartre, Jean-Paul
  author of: **6** Nausea, No
    Exit **8** The Words **17** The
    Roads to Freedom **19** Being
    and Nothingness
  philosophy: **14** Existentialism
  quote: **17** Hell is other
    people

sash 3 tie **4** band, belt **5** frame,

Sardinia
  other name: **8** Sardegna
  capital: **8** Cagliari
  cities: **4** Bono, Bosa **5** Nuoro, Olbia **7** Alghero, Bonorva,
    Sassari, Thatari **8** Iglesias, Oristano **11** Porto Torres
  division: **5** Nuoro **7** Arborea, Gallura, Sassari **8** Cagliari,
    Logudoro
  government: **13** region of Italy
  monetary unit: **7** carline
  island: **7** Caprera **8** Tavolara **9** Maddalena
  lake: **6** Omodeo
  mountain: **4** Rasu **5** Ferry, Linas **7** Gallura, Limbara
    8 Marghine, Serpeddi, Vittoria **11** Gennargentu
  river: **5** Mannu, Tirso **6** Lascia **8** Coghinas **10** Flumendosa
  sea: **13** Mediterranean
  physical feature:
    gulf: **6** Orosei, Palmas **7** Asinara **8** Cagliari, Oristano
    plain: **7** Sassari **9** Campidano
    strait: **9** Bonifacio
  people:
    king: **12** Charles Felix **13** Charles Albert **14** Victor
      Emmanuel
    leader: **6** Cavour
    ruler: **4** Pisa **5** Genoa, Spain **7** Austria, Vandals **9** Byzan-
      tium, Phoenicia **12** House of Savoy
  language: **7** Italian
  religion: **13** Roman Catholic
  feature:
    towers: **7** nuraghi
  food:
    cheese: **6** romano **8** pecorino

scarf, strip **6** casing, corset, girdle, ribbon, window **7** baldric **8** casement **9** doorframe, waistband **10** cummerbund **11** windowframe
Japanese: 3 obi
pulley weight: 5 mouse
window: 5 chess

sashay 4 move, skip **5** glide, mince **6** chasse, travel

Saskatchewan 5 river
8 province
boundary: 7 Alberta, Montana **8** Manitoba **11** North Dakota **12** Old Northwest **20** Northwest Territories
capital: 6 Regina
city: 8 Moose Jaw **9** Saskatoon **12** Prince Albert, Swift Current
country: 6 Canada
Indian: 4 Cree **9** Chipewyan **10** Assiniboin
lake: 8 Reindeer **9** Athabasca, Wollaston
mountain: 7 Cypress, Pasquia **9** Porcupine **14** Missouri Coteau
river: 9 Churchill, Frenchman
river mouth: 12 Lake Winnipeg

Sassoon, Siegfried
author of: 26 The Memoirs of a Fox-Hunting Man **26** The Memoirs of George Sherston **29** The Memoirs of an Infantry Officer

sassy 4 bark, bold, flip, rude, tree **5** brash, fresh, saucy **6** mouthy, snippy **7** forward **8** impolite, impudent, insolent **12** discourteous **13** disrespectful

Satan 6 Belial, Moloch **7** Lucifer, Old Nick **8** Apollyon, the Devil **9** Beelzebub **10** Old Scratch, the Evil One, the Tempter **11** fallen angel **12** the Foul Fiend **13** the Old Serpent **14** Mephistopheles **19** the Prince of Darkness

satanic 3 bad **4** evil, vile **5** cruel **6** wicked **7** demonic, heinous, hellish, inhuman, vicious **8** devilish, fiendish, infamous, infernal, sadistic **9** malicious, malignant **10** demoniacal, diabolical, malevolent

satchel, Satchel 3 bag **4** case, grip, sack **5** purse **6** valise **7** handbag **8** reticule, suitcase **9** carpetbag, Gladstone, schoolbag
pitcher, Hall of Famer: 5 Paige

sate 4 cloy, fill, glut **5** gorge, stuff **7** surfeit

satellite 4 moon **5** crony,

toady **6** menial, puppet, vassal **7** servant **8** disciple, follower, hanger-on, parasite, retainer **9** assistant, attendant, companion, sycophant, tributary, underling

satellite state 6 colony **8** dominion **10** possession **12** protectorate

satiate 4 bore, cloy, fill, glut, jade **5** slake, stuff, weary **6** overdo, quench, sicken **7** content, disgust, gratify, suffice, surfeit **8** nauseate, overfill, saturate

Satie, Erik
born: 6 France **8** Honfleur
composer of: 6 Parade **13** Pieces froides **16** The Three Gymnasts **19** Limp Preludes for a Dog **20** Pieces en forme de poire **23** Pieces in the Shape of a Pear

satiny 4 fine **5** shiny, silky **6** smooth

satire 5 irony **6** banter, parody, send up **7** lampoon, mockery, sarcasm, takeoff **8** acrimony, derision, raillery, ridicule, travesty **9** burlesque **10** caricature, persiflage

satirical 5 comic **6** biting, bitter **7** caustic, mocking, mordant **8** derisive, humorous, ironical, sardonic, scornful, sneering **9** malicious, sarcastic

satirize 4 mock **6** parody **7** lampoon **9** burlesque **10** caricature

satisfaction 5 pride **6** amends **7** comfort, content, damages, deserts, justice, payment, redress **8** pleasure, requital **9** answering, atonement, happiness, quittance, reckoning, repayment **10** correction, recompense, remittance, settlement **11** contentment, fulfillment, restitution **12** compensation, remuneration **13** gratification, rectification, reimbursement

satisfactory 2 OK **4** okay **8** adequate, all right, passable, suitable **9** competent **10** acceptable, sufficient

satisfied 5 happy **7** content, pleased **9** gratified **10** complacent **11** comfortable

satisfy 3 pay **4** fill, meet **5** annul, clear, remit, repay, serve, slake **6** answer, assure, pacify, pay off, please, quench, remove, settle **7** appease, content, delight, fulfill, gratify, mollify, requite, suffice **8** convince, persuade, reassure

9 discharge, reimburse **10** compensate, recompense

satisfying 8 pleasant, pleasing **9** agreeable, enjoyable, rewarding **10** delightful, fulfilling, gratifying **11** pleasurable

saturate 4 fill **5** cover, douse, imbue, souse **6** drench, infuse **7** immerse, pervade, suffuse **8** permeate, submerge **10** impregnate, infiltrate

saturated 3 wet **4** full **5** drunk, soggy, soppy **6** soaked, sodden **8** bursting

Saturday
day of: 15 Biblical Sabbath
French: 6 samedi
from: 8 Saturnus
German: 7 samstag
heavenly body: 6 Saturn
Italian: 6 sabato
observance: 13 Jewish Sabbath **20** Seventh Day Adventists
Spanish: 6 sabado

Saturday Night Fever
director: 10 John Badham
cast: 11 Barry Miller **12** John Travolta **15** Karen Lynn Gorney
setting: 8 Brooklyn
score: 7 Bee Gees
sequel: 12 Staying Alive

Saturday Night Live, NBC's
regular: 10 Bill Murray, Chevy Chase, Dan Aykroyd, Jane Curtin **11** Eddie Murphy, Gilda Radner, John Belushi **13** Garrett Morris, Laraine Newman
group: 27 Not Ready For Prime Time Players
bits: 4 Bees **7** Samurai **9** Coneheads **10** Church Lady **13** Blues Brothers, Weekend Update **16** Pathological Liar **18** Rosanne Rosanna-Dana

Saturn
origin: 5 Roman
god of: 11 agriculture
consort of: 3 Ops
son: 5 Picus
corresponds to: 6 Cronos, Cronus, Kronos

Saturn
position: 5 sixth
satellite: 4 Rhea **5** Dione, Janus, Mimas, Titan **6** Phoebe, Tethys **7** Iapetus **8** Hyperion **9** Enceladus
characteristic: 5 rings

saturnalia, Saturnalia
4 orgy **5** revel, spree **7** carouse, debauch, revelry **8** carousal **9** bacchanal **10** debauchery
origin: 5 Roman
event: 8 festival

honoring: 6 Saturn **13** sowing of crops

saturnine 4 dour, glum, grim **5** grave, staid, stern, sulky **6** gloomy, moping, morose, solemn, somber, sullen **7** austere, serious **8** dejected, downcast, reserved, sardonic, taciturn **9** apathetic, cheerless, withdrawn **11** downhearted **15** uncommunicative

satyr
form: 5 deity
location: 8 woodland

Satyricon
author: 9 Petronius
character: 4 Gito **8** Ascyltus, Eumolpus **9** Encolpius **10** Trimalchio

sauce 3 dip **4** sass **5** booze, gravy **6** fillip, flavor **7** alcohol **8** dressing, pertness **9** condiment, flippancy **12** impertinence
basil: 5 pesto
fish: 4 alec

hot: 7 Tabasco
Indian: 5 curry
salty: 3 soy

saucy 4 bold, pert, rude, trim **5** brash, cocky, fresh, natty, smart **6** brazen, cheeky, jaunty, lively, spruce **7** forward **8** flippant, impolite, impudent, insolent **9** audacious, barefaced, unabashed **11** impertinent, smart-alecky **12** discourteous **13** disrespectful

Saudi Arabia *see box*

Sauguet, Henri
born: 6 France **8** Bordeaux
composer of: 6 La Nuit **10** Les Forains, Les Mirages

Sauk, Sac
family: 9 Algonkian **10** Algonquian
tribe: 3 Fox, Sac **8** Kickapoo
location: 4 Iowa, Ohio **6** Kansas **7** Indiana **8** Illinois, Michigan, Oklahoma **9** Wisconsin
leader: 9 Blackhawk

related to: 8 Kickapoo **9** Mesquakie **11** Potawatomie
involved in: 12 Black Hawk War

Saul
king of: 4 Edom **6** Israel
father: 4 Kish
daughter: 5 Merab **6** Michal
son: 7 Abinoam **8** Jonathan **10** Ishbosheth
succeeded: 6 Samlah
anointed by: 6 Samuel
hometown: 6 Gibeah **8** Rehoboth
successor: 5 David
former name: 4 Paul

Saunders, Allen
creator/artist of: 9 Mary Worth

saunter 4 roam **5** amble, mosey, stray **6** loiter, ramble, stroll, wander **7** meander, traipse **8** straggle **9** promenade

Saurolophus
type: 8 dinosaur **10** ornithopod
location: 6 Canada **7** Alberta

sauropod
type of: 8 dinosaur
member: 9 Euhelopus **10** Diplodocus **11** Apatosaurus **12** Brontosaurus, Camarasaurus, Plateosaurus **13** Brachiosaurus, Hypselosaurus

sausage 5 frank, gigot, wurst **6** hot-dog, salami, weenie, wiener **7** baloney, bologna **8** kielbasa **9** bratwurst, pepperoni **10** liverwurst **11** frankfurter
British: 6 banger

sauve qui peut 4 rout **8** stampede **18** every man for himself **23** let him save himself who can

savage 4 boor, wild **5** brute, cruel, feral, fiend, harsh, rough, yahoo **6** animal, bloody, brutal, fierce, maniac, native, rugged, unkind **7** brutish, hoodlum, ruffian, untamed, violent **8** barbaric, hooligan, pitiless, ruthless, sadistic **9** aborigine, barbarian, barbarous, ferocious, merciless, murderous, primitive **10** aboriginal, heathenish, relentless, uncultured, unmerciful **11** uncivilized **12** uncultivated **14** undomesticated

savagery 7 cruelty **8** ferocity **9** barbarism, barbarity, brutality **10** fierceness, inhumanity **12** pitilessness, ruthlessness

savanna, savannah 5 campo, plain **9** grassland

savant 6 genius **7** scholar **13** learned person

Saudi Arabia
capital/largest city: 6 Riyadh
others: 4 Abha, Hail, Taif **5** Hofuf, Hufuf, Jedda, Jidda, Yanbu, Yenbo **6** Anaiza, Dammam, Jiddah, Jubail **7** Al-hofuf, Buraido, Dhahran **9** Ras Tanura
holy city: 5 Mecca **6** Medina
school: 5 Islam **13** King Abd al-Aziz **19** Imam Muhammad bin Saud **20** Petroleum and Minerals
division: 4 Asir, Nejd **5** Hejaz **6** El Hasa
government: 8 monarchy
head of state/government: 4 king
monetary unit: 5 girsh, gursh, pound, riyal
weight: 3 oke
mountain: 6 Tuwayq
highlands: 4 Asir **5** Hejaz
highest point: 5 Razih **10** Jebal Sawda
sea: 3 Red
physical feature:
   desert: 3 Red **5** Dahna, Nafud, Nefud, Nufud **6** al-Dahy, Dahana **10** Rub al Khali
   gulf: 5 Aqaba **7** Persian
   peninsula: 7 Arabian
   plain: 6 Tihama
   plateau: 4 Nejd
people: 4 Arab **7** Bedouin
   king: 4 Fahd, Saud **6** Faisal, Khalid **7** Ibn Saud **9** Abdul Aziz
   religious leader: 8 Mohammed, Muhammad
language: 6 Arabic
religion: 5 Islam
   sect: 5 Sunni **6** Shiite **7** Wahhabi
place:
   shrine: 5 Kaaba **10** Black Stone
feature:
   annual pilgrimage: 4 hadj, hajj
   clothing: 3 aba **4** agal **5** thobe **6** ghutra
   kingdom: 5 Hejaz **7** Minaean, Ottoman, Sabaean **9** Himyarite
   laws of Islam: 6 sharia
   village school: 6 kuttab
   war: 4 Gulf **11** Desert Storm **12** Desert Shield

save 3 but **4** bank, free, help, hold, keep **5** amass, guard, hoard, lay by, lay up, put by, spare, stock, store **6** defend, except, garner, heap up, redeem, rescue, shield **7** deliver, deposit, husband, protect, put away, recover, reserve, salvage **8** conserve, preserve, retrench, withhold **9** economize, safeguard **10** accumulate

save up 5 amass, hoard **7** collect, put away **8** salt away, sock away **10** accumulate **12** squirrel away

saving 5 close, tight **6** frugal, stingy **7** careful, miserly, prudent, sparing, thrifty **8** markdown, stinting **9** illiberal, niggardly, provident, redeeming, restoring **10** economical, reclaiming, redemptory, reparative **12** compensating, conservative

savings 5 hoard **7** nest egg, reserve

savior 5 freer **7** rescuer **8** champion, defender, guardian, redeemer **9** deliverer, liberator, preserver, protecter, protector, salvation **11** emancipator

Savior 5 Jesus **6** Christ **8** Redeemer **10** the Messiah **11** Jesus Christ, the Son of God **13** Prince of Peace

Savior anointed 5 Jesus

savoir-faire 4 tact **5** poise **6** aplomb, polish **7** finesse, know-how, suavity **8** presence, urbanity **9** assurance, composure **10** adroitness, discretion, smoothness **11** worldliness **12** complaisance, graciousness **14** self-possession

savoir-vivre 16 knowing how to live **19** knowledge of the world

savor 3 try **4** aura, gist, like, odor, soul, tang, zest **5** aroma, enjoy, scent, smack, smell, spice, taste, trait **6** flavor, nature, relish, sample, season, spirit **7** essence, quality **8** piquancy, property, pungency **9** character, fragrance, substance **10** appreciate, experience **11** peculiarity **13** particularity **14** characteristic

savory 5 tangy, tasty, yummy **6** honest **7** odorous, piquant, pungent **8** alluring, aromatic, charming, edifying, fragrant, luscious, tasteful **9** delicious, flavorous, palatable, reputable, toothsome **10** appetizing, attractive, delectable **11** inoffen-

sive, respectable, scrumptious **13** mouth-watering

savory
   botanical name: 8 Satureia, S montana **10** S hortensis
   origin: 13 Mediterranean
   varieties: 6 summer, winter
   use: 4 eggs, meat **5** beans, salad **6** sauces **8** dressing **11** chicken soup

savvy 5 catch, get it **7** know-how **10** comprehend, understand **13** understanding

saw 3 cut **4** tool **5** adage, maxim, slash **6** saying **7** proverb **8** aphorism
   type: 3 jig, rip **4** back, band, hack **5** miter **6** coping **7** keyhole **8** circular, crosscut

sawfly
   varieties: 4 stem, wood **5** cedar **6** pergid **7** conifer **8** horntail **11** web spinning

say 2 do **4** hint, hold, read, tell, vote, word **5** bruit, claim, guess, imply, judge, mouth, rumor, speak, state, utter, voice **6** allege, assert, assume, chance, convey, phrase, reason, recite, remark, render, repeat, report, reveal, spread **7** comment, contend, declare, deliver, divulge, express, imagine, mention, perform, suggest, suppose, surmise **8** announce, disclose, intimate, maintain, rehearse, vocalize **9** circulate, franchise, insinuate, pronounce, verbalize **10** articulate, conjecture **11** communicate

Sayers, Dorothy L
   author of: 9 Whose Body **12** Strong Poison **14** Have His Carcase, The Nine Tailors, Unnatural Death **15** Clouds of Witness, Five Red Herrings **16** Busman's

---

Scandinavian Mythology
   abode of man: 7 Midgard **10** Mithgarthr
   afterworld: 6 Manala **7** Tuonela
   began race of giants: 4 Ymir
   blacksmith/hero: 9 Ilmarinen
   boar: 10 Saehrimnir
   bridge of gods: 7 Bifrost
   dragon: 6 Fafnir
   dwarf: 5 Skuld **7** Andvari
   earth is made from: 4 Ymir
   elf: 4 Norn **8** Verdandi
   epic: 8 Kaleva
   final battle: 15 Gotterdammerung **17** Twilight of the Gods
   first god: 4 Buri **7** Forsete, Forseti
   first man: 3 Ask
   first woman: 5 Embla
   folk hero: 8 Kalevala
   giant: 4 Loki **5** Jotun, Thrym **6** Thiazi, Thjazi **7** Skrymir
   giantess: 3 Urd **5** Thokk **9** Angerboda, Angrbodha, Angurboda
   giant's realm: 9 Jotunheim
   goat: 7 Heidrun
   goddesses: 7 Asynjur
   goddess of death: 3 Hel
   goddess of forbidden marriages: 4 Lofn
   goddess of marriage: 4 Frey **5** Freyr
   goddess of peace: 4 Frey **5** Freyr
   goddess of prosperity: 4 Frey **5** Freyr
   goddess of spring: 4 Idun **5** Iduna, Ithun **6** Ithunn
   goddess of the sea: 3 Ran
   god of beauty/radiance: 5 Baldr **6** Balder, Baldur
   god of dawn: 8 Heimdall
   god of farming: 4 Thor
   god of fire: 4 Loki
   god of knowledge: 4 Odin **5** Othin
      corresponds to Germanic: **5** Wotan
   god of justice: 7 Forseti
   god of light: 8 Heimdall
   god of music: 5 Bragi
   god of navigation: 5 Niord, Njord
   god of poetry: 4 Odin **5** Bragi, Othin
      corresponds to Germanic: **5** Wotan
   god of prosperity: 5 Niord, Njord

Honeymoon **19** Murder Must Advertise **30** Unpleasantness at the Bellona Club
character: 6 Bunter **11** Harriet Vane **15** Lord Peter Wimsey

Say Hey Kid
nickname of: 10 Willie Mays

saying 3 saw **5** adage, maxim, moral, motto **6** byword, dictum, truism **7** epigram, precept, proverb **8** aphorism, apothegm **10** expression

Sayonara
director: 11 Joshua Logan
author: 13 James Michener
cast: 9 Miiko Taka **10** Red Buttons **11** James Garner, Martha Scott **12** Marlon Brando, Miyoshi Umeki **16** Ricardo Montalban
score: 12 Irving Berlin
Oscar for: 15 supporting actor (Buttons) **17** supporting actress (Umeki)

scabrous 5 dirty, rough, scaly **7** immoral, leprous **8** indecent, off-color **9** salacious **10** suggestive **12** pornographic

scalding 3 hot **5** harsh **7** boiling, caustic **8** seething, steaming **9** sarcastic

scale, scales 3 key, set **4** chip, film, husk, peel, rise, rule, skin **5** crust, flake, layer, mount, order, plate, range, ratio, scour, shave, shell, weigh **6** adjust, ascend, goupen, ladder, lamina, octave, rub off, scrape, series, spread **7** balance, chip off, clamber, climb up, coating, lamella, measure **8** escalade, membrane, register, regulate, spectrum, surmount **9** continuum, gradation **10** delaminate, graduation, proportion **11** calibration, progression **14** classification

scale down 4 trim **6** reduce **7** abridge, curtail, shorten **8** compress, condense, decrease, diminish, downsize, moderate **10** abbreviate

scale insects
varieties: 3 lac, pit, wax **5** giant **6** ensign **7** armored **8** mealybug, tortoise **12** ground pearls

Scamandrius *see* **8** Astyanax

scamp 3 imp, rip **5** cut-up, knave, rogue, tease **6** rascal, rotter **7** bounder, villain **8** blighter, scalawag **9** miscreant, prankster, scoundrel **10** scapegrace **11** rapscallion **13** mischief-maker

scamper 3 fly, run, zip **4** dart, dash, flit, race, romp, rush, scud **5** frisk, hurry, scoot **6** frolic, gambol, hasten, scurry, sprint **7** scuttle **9** skedaddle **21** running about playfully

scan 4 skim **5** check, probe, scour, study, sweep **6** peruse, search, size up, survey **7** analyze, examine, explore, inspect **10** scrutinize

scandal 4 blot **5** abuse, libel, odium, shame, stain **6** expose, smirch, stigma **7** calumny, obloquy, outrage, slander **8** disgrace, dishonor, ignominy **9** aspersion, discredit, disesteem, sensation **10** debasement, detraction, opprobrium, revilement **12** vituperation **13** disparagement, embarrassment

scandalize 5 shock **6** appall, defame, insult, offend **7** horrify, outrage **10** calumniate

scandalmonger 6 gossip **8** busybody **10** talebearer, tattletale

scandalous 8 libelous, shameful, shocking **9** gossiping, offensive **10** defamatory, outrageous, scurrilous, slanderous **11** disgraceful **12** disreputable **13** reprehensible

Scandinavian
language family: 12 Indo-European
branch: 8 Germanic
group: 15 Western Germanic
language: 6 Danish **7** Swedish **9** Icelandic, Norwegian

Scandinavian Mythology *see box*

scant 3 cut **4** bare **5** limit, short, small, stint **6** in need, meager, paltry, reduce, sparse

---

god of rain: 4 Thor
god of sea: 5 Aegir, Mimir
god of thunder: 4 Thor
god of underworld: 8 Niflheim
god of victory: 3 Tyr
god of war: 4 Odin **5** Othin
  corresponds to Germanic: **5** Wotan
god of wind: 5 Niord, Njord
god of wisdom: 4 Odin **5** Othin
  corresponds to Germanic: **5** Wotan
hero: 11 Vainamoinen **12** Lemminkainen
home of dead: 3 Hel
king: 5 Gjuki
magician: 11 Joukahainen
magic necklace: 11 Brisingamen
misty void: 11 Ginnungagap
mountain: 11 Hindarfjall
nature spirit: 7 Eriking
oak tree: 9 Barnstock, Branstock
Odin's court/hall: 8 Valhalla
Odin's father: 3 Bor
Odin's horse: 8 Sleipnir
Odin's magic ring: 8 Draupnir
Odin's palace: 9 Gladsheim
Odin's raven: 5 Hugin, Munin
Odin's spear: 6 Gungni
Odin's throne: 10 Hlidskjalf
Odin's wolf: 4 Geri **5** Freki
race of gods: 5 Vanir
saga: 8 Vulsunga
sea monster: 6 Kraken
serpent: 7 Nidhogg **11** Jormungandr
Sigmund's sword: 4 Gram
slave: 8 Kullervo
sorceress: 5 Louhi **8** Grimhild
Thor's hammer: 7 Miolnir
Thor's servant: 7 Thialfi
tree with three roots: 9 Iggdrasil, Yggdrasil
Valkyrie: 8 Brynhild **9** Brunhilde, Sigrdrifa **11** Brunnehilde
virgin goddess: 3 Urd **4** Norn **5** Skuld, Urdar **8** Verdandi
warrior: 8 Baresark **9** Berserker
watchdog: 4 Garm
wolf monster: 6 Fenrir, Fenris

7 limited **8** exiguous, hold back **9** deficient **10** inadequate, incomplete **12** insufficient

scantiness 10 deficiency, inadequacy, meagerness, skimpiness **13** insufficiency

scanty 4 thin **5** short, small **6** meager, modest, paltry, skimpy, sparse **7** slender, stunted **9** deficient **10** inadequate, undersized **12** insufficient

scapegoat, Scapegoat 4 butt, dupe, gull **5** patsy **6** Azazel, victim **7** fall guy **11** whipping boy **13** laughingstock

scapolite
source: **5** Burma, Mogok

scapula
bone of: **13** shoulder blade

scar 3 cut, pit **4** dent, flaw, gash, hurt, mark, pock, seam **5** brand, wound **6** affect, bruise, damage, deface, defect, impair, mangle **7** blemish, scratch **8** cicatrix, lacerate, mutilate **9** disfigure, influence

scarce 4 rare **6** scanty, sparse **7** unusual, wanting **8** uncommon **9** deficient

scarcely 4 just **6** at most, barely, hardly **7** but just, faintly **8** slightly

scarcity 4 lack, want **5** stint **6** dearth, rarity **7** fewness, paucity **8** rareness, shortage, sparsity, thinness **10** deficiency, scantiness, sparseness **12** uncommonness **13** insufficiency

scare 4 turn **5** alarm, daunt, panic, shake, shock, start **6** harrow, shiver **7** horrify, jitters, startle, terrify **8** disquiet, frighten **9** terrorize **10** disconcert, dishearten, intimidate **11** nervousness, palpitation **13** consternation

scarecrow 6 effigy **8** straw man

Scarecrow
character in: **13** The Wizard of Oz
author: **4** Baum

scared 5 shaky, timid, upset **6** afraid **7** alarmed, fearful, nervous, spooked **8** startled, timorous **9** diffident, terrified, tremulous **10** frightened **12** apprehensive, fainthearted **13** panic-stricken

scarf 3 boa **4** sash, veil, wrap **5** ascot, shawl, stole **6** choker, cravat, tippet **7** foulard, muffler, overlay **8** babushka, bandanna, mantilla **11** neckerchief

Scarface
director: **11** Howard Hawks
cast: **8** Paul Muni **9** Ann Dvorak **10** George Raft **12** Boris Karloff

scarify 3 cut **6** incise, loosen **7** break up, scratch **8** lacerate **9** cultivate

Scarlatti, Alessandro
born: **6** Sicily **7** Palermo
composer of: **11** Stabat Mater **17** Mitridate Eupatore, The Triumph of Honor **18** Il Trionfo dell Onore **23** Gli equivoci nel sembiante

Scarlatti, Domenico
born: **5** Italy **6** Naples
composer of: **7** Sonatas **9** Cat's Fugue, Essercizi **18** Le Donne di Buon Umore **20** The Good-Humored Ladies **23** Ottavia risituita al trono

scarlet 3 red **6** cherry, claret **7** carmine **8** cardinal

Scarlet Letter, The
author: **18** Nathaniel Hawthorne
character: **5** Pearl **12** Hester Prynne **16** Arthur Dimmesdale **18** Roger Chillingworth

scary 3 bad **5** awful, hairy **6** creepy **7** fearful **8** alarming, menacing, shocking **9** difficult **10** disturbing, terrifying **11** frightening, goosepimply, hair-raising, threatening **12** discomfiting

scat 3 off, out **4** away, shoo **5** be off, leave, scram **6** beat it, be gone, depart, get out, go away **7** get lost, vamoose

scathing 4 keen, tart **5** sharp **6** biting, brutal, savage **7** caustic, cutting, hostile, mordant, pointed, searing **8** incisive, stinging, virulent **9** ferocious, rancorous, scorching, trenchant, vitriolic, withering **10** lacerating **11** acrimonious, excoriating

scatter 3 sow **4** cast, flee, rout **5** strew, throw **6** dispel **8** disperse, sprinkle **9** broadcast, circulate, dissipate **10** distribute **11** disseminate

scatterbrained 4 rash, wild, zany **5** crazy, dizzy, giddy, nutty, silly **6** madcap, stupid **7** flighty, foolish **8** careless, heedless, reckless, unstable, unsteady **9** foolhardy, forgetful, frivolous, imprudent **11** birdbrained, empty-headed, harebrained **12** absent-minded, muddleheaded **13** irresponsible

scattered 6 random, spotty

7 diffuse **9** irregular **10** infrequent, occasional

scattering 6 sowing **7** casting **8** strewing **9** dispersal **10** dispersing, sprinkling **12** broadcasting, distribution **13** dissemination

scavenger 6 magpie **8** salvager **9** collector

scenario 4 book, idea, plan **6** scheme **7** concept, outline, summary **8** abstract, game plan, synopsis, teleplay **10** conception, manuscript, screenplay
French: **6** precis

scene 3 act **4** fuss, part, show, site, spot, to-do, view **5** place, sight, vista **6** locale, region, survey, vision **7** display, episode, picture, scenery, setting **8** backdrop, division, locality, location, panorama, position, prospect, sequence **9** commotion, spectacle **10** background **11** whereabouts

scenery 4 sets, view **5** vista **7** terrain **9** backdrops, landscape, spectacle **11** backgrounds

Scenes from a Marriage
director: **13** Ingmar Bergman
cast: **10** Liv Ullmann **13** Bibi Andersson **15** Erland Josephson

scent 4 odor, path, wake, wind **5** aroma, smell, sniff, spoor, trace, track, trail **6** course, detect, inhale **7** bouquet, breathe, discern, essence, perfume, pursuit, suspect **9** aromatize, fragrance, get wind of, recognize **11** distinguish

scented 5 spicy **7** odorous, piquant, pungent **8** aromatic, fragrant, perfumed **9** odiferous **13** sweet-smelling

Scephrus
father: **8** Tegeates
brother: **5** Limon
killed by: **5** Limon

Schaffner, Franklin
director of: **6** Patton (Oscar) **15** Planet of the Apes

Schedius
father: **7** Iphitus
mother: **9** Hippolyte
suitor of: **5** Helen

schedule 3 fix **4** book, list, plan, roll **5** fit in, slate, table **6** agenda **7** appoint, program, put down, set down **8** calendar **9** inventory, timetable

Scheele, Karl Wilhelm
field: **9** chemistry
nationality: **7** Swedish

discovered: **6** oxygen **8** chlorine **9** glycerine

Scheider, Roy
born: **8** Orange NJ
roles: **4** Jaws **11** All That Jazz, Blue Thunder, The Seven-Ups **14** Fifty-two Pickup **19** The French Connection

Schell, Maria
real name: **15** Margarete Schell
born: **6** Vienna **7** Austria
brother: **16** Maximilian Schell
roles: **8** Cimarron, Gervaise **11** End of Desire, White Nights **13** The Last Bridge **20** The Brothers Karamazov

Schell, Maximilian
born: **6** Vienna **7** Austria
sister: **11** Maria Schell
roles: **5** Julia **13** The Young Lions **19** Judgment at Nuremberg (Oscar) **21** The Man in the Glass Booth

scheme 3 map, way **4** plan, plot, ruse **5** cabal, chart, frame, means, shift, study **6** course, design, device, devise, layout, method, policy, sketch, system **7** complot, concoct, connive, drawing, network, outline, program, project, tactics **8** conspire, contrive, grouping, intrigue, maneuver, organize, strategy **9** machinate, procedure, stratagem **10** connivance, conspiracy **11** arrangement, contrivance, delineation, disposition, machination **12** organization

scheming 3 sly **4** arch, wily **6** artful, crafty, shrewd, tricky **7** cunning **8** slippery **9** conniving, designing, insidious **10** contriving, intriguing **11** calculating **13** Machiavellian

Schiller, (Johann) Friedrich von
author of: **8** Ode to Joy **9** Don Carlos **11** Maria Stuart, William Tell **17** The Bride of Messina **18** The Maiden of Orleans

schism 5 break, split **8** division **10** separation **14** disassociation

Schlegel family
characters in: **10** Howard's End
members: **5** Helen **8** Margaret, Theobald
author: **7** Forster

schlepp 3 lug **4** cart, haul, tote **5** carry **6** convey **9** transport

Schlesinger, Arthur M, Jr
author of: **13** A Thousand Days **15** The Age of Jackson **21** The Imperial Presidency **24** Robert Kennedy and His Times

Schlesinger, John
director of: **7** Darling **14** Midnight Cowboy (Oscar) **22** The Falcon and the Snowman

Schlesinger, Leon
creator/artist of: **9** Bugs Bunny

schmaltz 4 corn **14** sentimentalism, sentimentality

Schmeling, Max (Maxmillian Adolph Otto Siegfried)
nickname: **10** Black Uhlan
sport: **6** boxing
class: **11** heavyweight

Schneider, Romy
real name: **20** Rosemarie Albach-Retty
born: **6** Vienna **7** Austria
roles: **8** The Trial **11** The Cardinal **16** Boccaccio Seventy

Schoenberg, Arnold
born: **6** Vienna **7** Austria
composer of: **9** Erwartung **11** De Profundis, Expectation, Gurrelieder **12** The Lucky Hand **13** Moses and Aaron, Ode to Napoleon **14** Verklarte Nacht **16** Die Glucklich Hand, Resplendent Night **17** Transfigured Night **19** A Survivor from Warsaw, Pelleas and Melisande **26** The Book of the Hanging Gardens

Schoenius
father: **7** Athamas
mother: **8** Themisto
wife: **7** Clymene
daughter: **8** Atalanta

scholar 4 coed, sage **5** brain, grind, pupil **6** pundit, savant **7** egghead, learner, student, studier, wise man **8** bookworm, humanist, mandarin **9** collegian, schoolboy **10** schoolgirl **11** matriculant **12** intellectual **13** undergraduate

Scholar Gypsy, The
author: **13** Matthew Arnold

scholarly 6 humane **7** erudite, learned, liberal **8** academic, educated, informed, lettered, literate, well-read **12** intellectual

scholarship 5 grant **7** stipend **8** learning **9** education, endowment, erudition **12** intelligence, thoroughness **13** enlightenment

scholastic 8 academic, pedantic **9** pedagogic **11** educational **12** professorial **13** instructional

school 3 ism **4** view **5** bunch, crowd, faith, order, style, teach, train **6** belief, lyceum, method, system, theory **7** academy, college, educate, faction, thought **8** doctrine, instruct, seminary **9** institute **10** persuasion, university **12** denomination, kindergarten

schoolbook 3 abc **4** text **5** atlas **6** manual, primer, reader **7** grammar, lessons, speller

School for Scandal, The
author: **23** Richard Brinsley Sheridan
character: **5** Maria **6** Rowley **10** Lady Teazle **13** Joseph Surface, Lady Sneerwell **14** Charles Surface, Sir Peter Teazle **16** Sir Oliver Surface

School for Wives, The
author: **7** Moliere
character: **5** Agnes **6** Horace, Oronte **7** Enrique **8** Arnolphe **9** Chrysalde

schooling 5 drill **8** drilling, training **9** education **11** instruction, preparation **14** indoctrination

schoolmaster 4 head **5** tutor **7** dominie, pedagog, scholar, teacher **9** pedagogue, principal, professor **10** headmaster, instructor **12** disciplinarian
fish: **7** snapper
genus: **8** Lutianus
species: **6** apodus

Schubert, Franz Peter
born: **6** Vienna **7** Austria
composer of: **6** Little (symphony), Tragic (symphony No 4) **8** Sad Waltz **9** Rosamunde **11** Winterreise **12** Trout Quintet **13** Mourning Waltz **17** Die Schone Mullerin **18** Unfinished Symphony (No 8) **24** Death and the Maiden Quartet, Symphony of Heavenly Length

Schulz, Charles
creator/artist of: **7** Peanuts

Schuman, William
born: **9** New York NY
composer of: **8** Undertow **9** Credendum **14** The Mighty Casey **16** American Festival **18** New England Triptych

Schumann, Robert Alexander
born: **7** Germany, Zwickau
composer of: **6** Myrten, Spring (symphony No 1) **7** Rhenish (symphony No 3) **8** Arabeske, Carnival **9** Papillons **10** Novelettes

11 Blumenstuck, Butterflies, Nachtstucke, Nightpieces, Novelletten **12** Bunte Blatter, Dichterliebe, Flower Pieces, Kinderscenen, Kreisleriana, Motley Leaves **14** Fantasiestucke **16** David's Band Dances, Symphonic Studies **18** Davidsbundlertanze **19** Frauenliebe und Leben

Schwann, Theodor
field: **7** biology
nationality: **6** German
established: **10** cell theory

Schwarzenegger, Arnold
roles: **5** Twins **7** Red Heat **8** Commando, Predator, Red Sonja **11** Total Recall **13** The Terminator **15** Kindergarten Cop **17** Conan the Barbarian, Conan the Destroyer
wife: **12** Maria Shriver

Schweitzer, Albert
field: **8** medicine
worked in: **5** Gabon **6** Africa
founded: **17** Lambarene Hospital
awarded: **15** Nobel Peace Prize

Schwitters, Kurt
born: **7** Germany **8** Hannover
artwork: **7** Merzbau
collages called:
   10 Merzbilden

science 3 art **5** skill **6** method **7** finesse **8** aptitude, facility **9** technique **10** discipline **11** acquirement
god of: **7** Mercury

scintilla 3 dot **4** atom, iota **5** shred, spark, speck, trace **7** glimmer **10** smithereen

scintillate 4 joke, snap **5** amuse, charm, flash, gleam, glint, shine, spark **7** glimmer, glisten, glitter, shimmer, sparkle, twinkle **9** coruscate **10** effervesce

scintillating 5 witty **6** bright, lively **8** animated, charming, dazzling **9** brilliant, ebullient, exuberant, sparkling **10** glittering **11** stimulating **12** effervescent

scion 3 son **4** heir, seed **5** child, issue **7** heiress, progeny **8** daughter, offshoot **9** offspring, posterity, successor **10** descendant **11** progeniture

Sciron
vocation: **6** robber
killed by: **7** Theseus

Scirophoria
also: **11** Skirophoria
origin: **5** Greek

event: **8** festival
honoring: **6** Athena

scissors 5 snips **6** blades, cutter, shears **7** clipper, snipper, trimmer
French: **8** secateur

scoff 4 jeer, mock, razz **5** flout, knock, taunt **6** deride, rail at, revile **7** condemn, laugh at, put down, run down **8** belittle, ridicule

Scofield, Paul
real name: **13** David Scofield
born: **7** England **14** Hurstpierpoint
roles: **8** King Lear **13** Sir Thomas More **17** A Man for All Seasons (Oscar)

scold 3 nag **5** chide, shrew **6** berate, carp at, nagger, rail at, rebuke, virago **7** censure, reprove, upbraid **9** castigate, criticize, dress down, reprehend, reprimand, termagant **10** complainer
Yiddish: **6** kvetch

scolding 7 chiding, reproof **8** berating, rebuking **9** reprimand, talking-to **10** admonition, upbraiding **11** castigation **12** admonishment **13** tongue-lashing

Scolosaurus
type: **8** dinosaur **10** ornithopod
location: **12** North America

sconce 11 candlestick **12** candleholder

scoop 4 bail, beat **5** clean, clear, gouge, ladle, spoon **6** burrow, dig out, dipper, hollow, shovel, trowel **7** dish out, lade out, lift out **8** excavate

scoop out 3 dig **5** gouge **8** excavate

scoot 3 run **4** dash, rush **6** scurry, sprint

Scooter
nickname of: **11** Phil Rizzuto

scope 3 aim **4** area, goal, rein, room, span, vent **5** field, force, grasp, range, reach **6** bounds, effect, margin, motive, spread, vision **7** bearing, compass, freedom, liberty, purpose, stretch **8** ambition, confines, latitude **9** extension, influence, intention **10** competence **11** application, destination **13** determination

scorch 3 dry **4** char, sear **5** parch, singe **6** dry out, scathe, wither **7** blacken **8** discolor **9** dehydrate

score, scores 3 cut, mar, run, tab, win **4** bill, debt, gain,

gash, goal, lots, make, mark, nick, slit **5** amass, count, facts, grade, hosts, judge, notch, point, slash, tally, truth **6** basket, charge, damage, deface, droves, groove, grudge, masses, pile up, strike, swarms, twenty **7** account, achieve, arrange, legions, reality, scratch, throngs **8** evaluate, incision, register **9** grievance **10** amount owed, difference, multitudes, obligation **11** orchestrate

scoria 4 slag **5** dross **6** cinder, refuse

scorn 5 spurn **6** ignore, rebuff, refuse, reject, slight **7** condemn, despise, disdain, mockery, repulse, sarcasm **8** contempt, derision, ridicule, scoffing, spit upon **9** arrogance, contumely, disregard, ostracize **10** look down on, opprobrium **11** haughtiness

scorned 7 derided, refused **8** despised, rebuffed, rejected, repulsed **9** disdained **10** deprecated, disparaged

scornful 6 lordly **7** cynical **8** arrogant, derisive, insolent, sardonic, scoffing, sneering **9** sarcastic **10** disdainful, ridiculing **11** disparaging **12** contemptuous, supercilious

Scorpio
symbol: **8** scorpion
planet: **4** Mars **5** Pluto
rules: **5** death **7** passion
born: **7** October **8** November

Scorpion 4 whip **7** scourge
constellation of: **8** Scorpius

Scorsese, Martin
director of: **10** After Hours, Raging Bull, Taxi Driver **11** Mean Streets **12** The Last Waltz

scotch 4 foil, kill, stop **5** crush, quash **6** thwart **7** destroy **8** confound, obstruct, sabotage, suppress **9** undermine **11** nip in the bud

scotch
type: **6** whisky **7** whiskey
origin: **8** Scotland
ingredient: **12** cereal grains
drink: **10** Scotch Mist **14** Highland Cooler
with amaretto: **9** Godfather
with cherry brandy: **12** Blood and Sand
with Drambuie: **9** Rusty Nail
with gin: **12** Barbary Coast
with vermouth: **6** Rob Roy **8** Affinity **10** Bobby Burns

Scotia
epithet of: **9** Aphrodite
means: **7** dark one

Scotland
  Roman name: 9 Caledonia
  capital: 9 Edinburgh
  largest city: 7 Glasgow
  others: 3 Ayr **4** Duns, Oban **5** Alloa, Banff, Brora, Burgh, Cupar, Ellon, Leith, Perth, Salen,
    Troon **6** Dundee, Girvan, Hawick **7** Airdrie, Alloway, Dunkeld, Falkirk, Frunock, Mallaig,
    Paisley, Renfrew **8** Aberdeen, Dumfries, Greenock, Hamilton, Kirkwall, Rothesay, Stirling
    9 Clydebank, Dumbarton, Greenlock, Inverness, Kirkcaldy, Peterhead, St Andrews **10** Coat-
    bridge, Kilmarnock, Motherwell **11** Dunfermline, Grangemouth
  school: 7 Glasgow **8** Aberdeen **9** Edinburgh **12** Saint Andrew's
  division: 3 Ayr **4** Bute, Fife, Ross **5** Angus, Banff, Moray, Nairn, Perth **6** Argyll, Lanark, Ork-
    ney **7** Berwick, Kinross, Lothian, Peebles, Renfrew, Selkirk, Wigtown **8** Aberdeen, Ayrshire,
    Cromarty, Dumfries, Roxburgh, Shetland, Stirling **9** Buteshire, Caithness, Dumbarton **10** Kin-
    cardine, Midlothian, Sutherland **11** Clackmannan, Kincudbight **12** Renfrewshire
    13 Stirlingshire
   kingdom: **8** Dalriada **11** Northumbria, Strathclyde
  government: 13 United Kingdom
  measure: 3 cop **4** boll, cran, fall, mile, peck, pint, rood, rope, span **5** crane, lippy **6** audlet,
    davach, firlot, lippie, noggin **7** chalder, choppin **8** mutchkin, stimpart, stimpert **9** particate,
    shaftment, shathmont
  monetary unit: 3 ecu **4** demy, doit, lion, mark, rial, ryal **5** bodle, broad, groat, plack, rider,
    turne **6** bawbee, folles **7** unicorn **8** atchison, hardhead **9** halfpenny **11** bonnetpiece
  weight: 4 boll, drop **5** trone **6** bushel
  island: 3 Rum **4** Aran, Bute, Eigg, Fair, Inch, Iona, Jura, Lona, Muck, Mull, Rhum, Skye
    5 Arran, Barra, Islay, Lewis **6** Harris, Orkney, Staffa **7** St Kilda **8** Berneray, Cumbraes, Hebri-
    des, Shetland **9** North Uist, South Uist
  lake/loch: 3 Awe, Dee, Lin, Tay **4** Earn, Fyne, Gair, Gare, Linn, Ness, Oich, Ryan, Sloy
    5 Duich, Leven, Lochy, Lough, Morar, Maree, Nevis **6** Laggan, Linnhe, Lomond **7** Katrine,
    Rannoch, St Mary's
  mountain: 4 Hope **5** Attow, Dearg, Nevis, Tinto, Wyvis **7** Cheviot, Macdhui, Merrick **8** Gram-
    pian **9** Ben Lomond, Cairngorm, Highlands, Trossachs
   hills: **5** Ochil **6** Calton, Sidlaw **7** Cheviot
  highest point: 8 Ben Nevis
  river: 3 Ayr, Dee, Don, Esk, Tay **4** Doon, Glen, Nith, Norn, Spey **5** Afton, Annan, Clyde,
    Forth, Garry, North, Tweed, Ythan **6** Affric, Teviot, Tummel **7** Deveron **8** Findhorn
  sea: 5 Irish, North **8** Atlantic, Hebrides
  physical feature:
   bay: **5** Scapa
   canal: **10** Caledonian
   channel: **5** Minch, North
   firth: **3** Tay **4** Kyle, Lorn **5** Clyde, Forth, Lorne, Moray **6** Linnhe, Solway **7** Comarty, Dor-
    noch **8** Pentland
   glen: **8** Glen More **9** Great Glen
   moor: **7** Rannoch
   valley: **8** Trossach
  people: 4 Gael, Pict, Scot **5** Norse
   artist: **7** Raeburn
   author: **5** Burns, Scott **6** Dunbar **7** Barbour, Douglas **8** Henryson **9** Stevenson **10** Conan-
    Doyle, MacDiarmid, Macpherson
   economist: **5** Smith
   historian: **7** Carlyle
   inventor: **4** Bell
   king: **5** David, James **6** Duncan **7** Kenneth, Macbeth, Malcolm, Stuarts, William **9** Alex-
    ander **14** Robert the Bruce
   philosopher: **4** Hume
   prime minister: **9** Macdonald, MacMillan **11** Douglas-Home
   prince: **19** Bonnie Prince Charlie
   queen: **4** Mary **13** Saint Margaret
   religious leader: **8** John Knox
   scientist: **7** Fleming
  language: 4 Erse **6** Celtic, Gaelic, Keltic, Lallan **7** English, Lalland
  religion: 12 Episcopalian, Presbyterian **13** Roman Catholic
  place:
   abbey: **5** Kelso **7** Melrose **8** Dryburgh, Jedburgh
   castle: **8** Stirling **9** Edinburgh **11** Eilean Donan
   church/kirk: **7** St Giles **11** St Cuthbert's
   royal residence: **8** Balmoral
   Scott's home: **10** Abbotsford
   street: **7** Prince's **9** Royal Mile **11** Sauchiehall

(*continued*)

Scotland (*continued*)
feature:
  bird: **3** bae, cae **4** hern, muir, smeu **6** grouse, smeuth, snabby **7** jackdaw **8** throstle
   9 swinepipe
  clothing: **4** kilt **6** tartan **12** Harris tweeds **13** Shetland knits **15** Fair Isle sweater
  dance: **3** bob **4** reel **7** walloch **9** ecossaise **10** petronella **11** strathsprey **12** gilliecallum
   13 Highland fling
  game: **4** golf
  monster: **6** Nessie **8** Loch Ness
  musical instrument: **7** bagpipe
  symbol: **7** thistle
food:
  bread: **5** scone
  cheese: **7** crowdie
  dish: **6** haggis **12** finnan haddie **15** kippered herring
  drink: **12** Scotch whisky
  soup: **11** cock-a-leekie

Scott, George C
  born: 6 Wise VA
  wife: 14 Trish Van Devere
   15 Colleen Dewhurst
  roles: 4 Rage **6** Patton (Oscar, refused) **8** Jane Eyre **16** The New Centurions **18** The Day of the Dolphin

Scott, Sir Walter
  author of: 6 Rob Roy **7** Ivanhoe, Marmion **8** The Abbot, Waverley **10** Kenilworth **11** The Talisman **12** Guy Mannering, Old Mortality, The Antiquary **14** Quentin Durward **16** The Lady of the Lake **20** The Bride of Lammermoor, The Heart of Midlothian **23** The Lay of the Last Minstrel

Scottish Mythology
  spirit/horse: 6 kelpie

scoundrel 3 cad, cur **5** crook, knave, rogue, scamp, thief **6** rascal, rotter, varlet, weasel **7** bounder, ruffian, sharper, varmint, villain **8** scalawag, swindler, turncoat **9** miscreant, trickster **10** blackguard, copperhead, mountebank, ne'er-do-well **11** fourflusher, rapscallion **12** carpetbagger

scoundrelly 3 low **4** mean **7** debased **8** rascally **10** degenerate, despicable, villainous **12** contemptible, disreputable **13** reprehensible

Scoundrel Time
  author: 14 Lillian Hellman

scour 4 buff, comb, rake, scan **5** scrub, shine **6** abrade, polish, scrape **7** burnish, cleanse, ransack, rummage **8** brighten, traverse

scourge, Scourge 3 rod **4** bane, beat, cane, flog, lash, whip **5** birch, blast, curse, flail, strap **6** punish, switch, terror, thrash **7** censure, chasten **8** chastise, scorpion, vexation **9** castigate, excoriate **10** affliction, discipline, flagellate **11** troublement **13** cat-o'-nine-tails

scout 3 spy **4** case **5** guide, pilot **6** escort, spy out, survey **7** lookout, observe **8** outrider, point man, vanguard **9** recruiter **11** reconnoiter **13** reconnoiterer

scowl 4 pout **5** frown, glare, lower **6** glower **7** grimace

scrabble 3 paw **4** claw, rake **5** climb **6** drudge, jostle, scrape, scrawl **7** clamber, grapple, scratch **8** struggle

scram 3 out **4** scat, shoo **5** be off, leave **6** beat it, begone, depart, get out, go away **7** get lost, vamoose **10** make tracks

scramble 3 run, vie **4** race, rush **5** clash, fight, mix up, scrap, upset **6** battle, combat, engage, garble, jostle, jumble, mess up, scurry, strive, tussle **7** collide, confuse, disturb, scatter, scuffle, shuffle **8** disorder, struggle, unsettle **9** scrimmage **10** disarrange, free-for-all **11** competition, disorganize

scramble up 5 climb, mount, scale **7** clamber

scrap 3 bit, dab, jot, row **4** atom, drop, iota, junk, spat **5** brawl, crumb, fight, grain, melee, speck, trace, trash **6** fracas, morsel, refuse, ruckus, sliver **7** abandon, glimmer, minimum, modicum, quarrel, snippet **8** brouhaha, fraction, fragment, jettison, molecule, particle, squabble **10** free-for-all, smattering, sprinkling

scrapbook 5 album **9** portfolio **11** memorabilia, miscellanea

scrape 3 dig **4** buff, gash, mark, rasp, save, skin **5** amass, clean, fight, glean, gouge, grate, graze, grind, plane, run-in, score, scour, scuff, stint **6** abrade, bruise, forage, gather, groove, obtain, pick up, plight, scrimp, secure, smooth, tussle **7** acquire, burnish, dilemma, procure, rub hard, scratch, scuffle, straits **8** abrasion **9** economize, tight spot **10** difficulty **11** predicament **13** confrontation

scratch 3 cut, mar, rub **4** claw, etch, gash, nick, omit, rasp **5** dig at, erase, grate, graze, grind, score **6** cancel, delete, incise, remove, rub out, scrape, scrawl, streak, strike **7** blemish, blot out, exclude, expunge, rule out **8** abrasion, cross out, lacerate, scribble, withdraw **9** eliminate **10** laceration

scratchy 5 rough **6** coarse **7** bristly, prickly **9** irritated **10** irritating

scrawl 4 draw **5** write **6** doodle **7** scratch, writing **8** scrabble, scribble, squiggle **10** penmanship **11** handwriting

scrawniness 8 lankness, leanness, slimness, thinness **10** skinniness, slightness **11** slenderness

scrawny 4 bony, lank, lean, puny **5** drawn, gaunt, lanky, runty, spare **6** sinewy, skinny, wasted **7** angular, scraggy, spindly, stunted **8** rawboned, skeletal **9** emaciated, fleshless **10** attenuated, undersized **11** underweight

screak 4 rasp **5** grate, grind **6** shriek, squeak **7** screech

scream 4 howl, loud, roar, wail, yell, yelp, yowl **5** shout, whine **6** bellow, cry out, holler, outcry, shriek, squawk, squeal **7** screech **11** lamentation

screech 3 cry **4** howl, rasp **6** screak, scream, shriek **9** caterwaul

screen 3 see, web **4** cull, mask, mesh, rate, show, sift, sort, veil, view **5** class, cloak, cover, eject, films, grade, grate, group, guard, order, shade, sieve **6** buffer, cinema, defend, filter, mantle, movies, secure, shield, shroud, sifter, size up, strain, winnow **7** arrange, conceal, curtain, defense, discard, lattice, present, preview, project, protect, secrete, shelter, shutter, weed out **8** colander, coverage, evaluate, jalousie, separate, strainer, withhold **9** eliminate, partition, safeguard **10** protection **11** concealment

screw 4 bolt, join, knot, turn, warp **5** clamp, exact, force, gnarl, rivet, twist, wrest, wring **6** adjust, attach, deform, driver, extort, fasten, garble, wrench **7** contort, distort, pervert, squeeze, tighten **8** fastener, misshape **9** propeller

screwball 3 nut **4** kook **5** flake, freak **6** looney **7** lunatic **8** crackpot **9** character, eccentric

screwdriver
   type: 6 rachet **11** spiral-drive **12** Phillips-head

screwy 3 odd **4** daft **5** batty, dotty, flaky, funny, kinky, kooky, nutty, queer, wacky, weird **6** weirdo **7** oddball **8** peculiar **9** eccentric **10** unbalanced

Scriabin, Aleksandr (Scriabine, Skryabin)
   born: 6 Moscow, Russia
   composer of: 7 Mystery **10** Prometheus **12** Vers la flamme **13** Poem of Ecstasy, The Divine Poem, The Poem of Fire

scribble 4 tear **5** squib **6** doodle, scrawl **7** scratch **8** squiggle **9** pull apart
   fiber: 4 wool
   procedure: 7 carding

scribe, Scribe 3 cut **4** mark, tool **5** clerk, score **6** author, copier, penman, writer **7** copyist, teacher **8** recorder **9** archivist, scrivener, secretary **10** amanuensis, translator **12** newspaperman, stenographer **13** calligraphist

Biblical: 4 Ezra **6** Esdras
French dramatist: 8 Augustin
Palestinian: 5 sofer **6** sopher

scribe of gods 5 Thoth

scrimp 4 save **5** hoard, pinch, skimp, stint **8** begrudge **9** be sparing **12** pinch pennies

scrimping 6 frugal **7** sparing **10** economical **11** economizing **12** cheeseparing **15** pinching pennies

scrip 5 paper **8** document **11** certificate

scripsit 7 he wrote **8** she wrote

script 4 book, hand **5** lines, score **6** dialog **7** cursive **8** dialogue, libretto, longhand, scenario **10** manuscript, penmanship **11** calligraphy, chirography, handwriting

Scriptures, the 5 Bible **6** the Law, oracle **8** holy writ, the Bible, the Torah **10** the Gospels **11** The Good Book **12** New Testament, Old Testament, the Word of God **13** the Pentateuch, the Septuagint **14** sacred writings

scroll of the Torah
   Hebrew: 11 Sepher Torah

Scrooge, Ebenezer
   character in: 15 A Christmas Carol
   author: 7 Dickens

scrub 4 swab **5** brush, scour **8** scouring **9** brushwood, scrubbing

scrubby 4 base **6** brushy **7** stunted **8** inferior **10** undersized

scrumptious 5 juicy, tasty **6** savory, tender **8** luscious, pleasant, pleasing **9** agreeable, delicious, enjoyable, flavorful, succulent, toothsome **10** appetizing, delectable, delightful, flavorsome **13** mouth-watering

scruple 3 shy **4** balk, care, halt **5** demur, pause, qualm, waver **6** blench, ethics, falter **7** anxiety, concern, refrain **8** hesitate **9** fluctuate, misgiving, principle **10** conscience, hesitation **11** compunction, fearfulness, uncertainty **12** apprehension, doubtfulness, protestation **13** squeamishness **17** conscientiousness

Scruples
   author: 12 Judith Krantz

scrupulous 5 exact **6** honest **7** careful, dutiful, precise, upright **8** cautious, exacting, sedulous **9** honorable **10** deliberate, fastidious, meticulous, principled **11** painstaking, punctilious **13** conscientious

scrupulousness 4 care **5** pains **9** exactness **14** meticulousness **17** conscientiousness

scrutinize 4 scan **5** probe, study **6** peruse, search, survey **7** explore, inspect, observe **11** investigate

scrutiny 5 study, watch **7** inquiry, perusal **9** attention **10** inspection **11** examination **12** surveillance **13** investigation

scuffle 3 row **4** spar **5** brawl, clash, fight, melee, scrap **6** fracas, jostle, rumpus, tussle **8** squabble, struggle **9** commotion, imbroglio **10** donnybrook, free-for-all

sculpsit 10 he carved it **11** she carved it **12** he engraved it **13** she engraved it **14** he sculptured it **15** she sculptured it

sculptor 6 artist, carver, caster, imager, molder **7** marbler, modeler **8** chiseler, engraver
   constellation: 19 Apparatus Sculptoris
   French: 5 Rodin
   Greek: 7 Phidias **10** Praxiteles
   Irish-American: 12 Saint-Gaudens
   Italian: 7 Cellini **12** Michelangelo
   tool: 6 chisel, graver **7** spatula **9** ebauchoir

sculpture 3 cut **4** bust, cast, head, work **5** cameo, carve, erode, model, mould **6** chisel, relief, statue **7** carving, erosion, faience **8** intaglio, statuary **9** cloisonne, medallion, statuette
   medium: 4 clay **5** china, stone **6** bronze, enamel, marble **7** ceramic **9** porcelain **10** terra cotta **11** earthenware

scum 4 film, slag **5** crust, dregs, dross, trash **6** rabble, refuse **7** deposit, rubbish, surface **8** riffraff

scurrility 5 abuse **8** rudeness **9** indecency, obscenity, profanity **13** offensiveness, salaciousness

scurrilous 3 low **5** gross **6** coarse, vulgar **7** obscene **8** churlish, derisive, indecent, reviling **9** insulting, offensive, shameless **10** derogatory, detracting, indelicate, slanderous **11** disparaging, foulmouthed **12** contemptuous

scurry 3 hie **4** race, rush,

skim 5 haste, hurry, scoot, speed **6** bustle, hasten, hustle, spring **7** rushing, scamper, scuttle **8** hurrying, scooting, scramble **9** confusion, dispersal **10** scattering

scurvy 3 low **4** base, mean, vile **6** shabby **7** ignoble **9** worthless **10** despicable **12** contemptible, dishonorable

scuttle 4 sink **5** abort, hurry, scrap, speed, wreck **6** hasten, scurry **7** destroy, discard, scamper **8** dispatch, scramble

scuttlebutt 4 talk **5** rumor **6** gossip **7** hearsay, prattle, scandal **8** chitchat

Scylaceus
origin: **6** Lycian
ally of: **7** Trojans
death by: **7** stoning

Scylla
form: **5** nymph **7** monster
location: **3** sea **16** Straits of Messina **20** Whirlpool of Charybdis
father: **7** Phorcys
mother: **6** Hecate
loved by: **8** Poseidon
rival: **10** Amphitrite

Scyphius
first: **5** horse
created by: **8** Poseidon

sea 3 bay, ton **4** deep, gulf, host, lake, leap, lots, main, mass, slew, wave **5** bight, flock, flood, ocean, scads, spate, surge, swarm, swell, waves **6** legion, roller, scores, waters **7** breaker **9** abundance, multitude, profusion
French: **3** mer
god of: **5** Aegir, Memir **6** Nereus, Triton **7** Glaucus, Neptune, Phorcys, Proteus **8** Poseidon **9** Asphalius
goddess of: **3** Ino, Ran **6** Graeae, Graiae, Matuta **8** Dictynna, Menannan **9** Leucothea **10** Amphitrite

Sea, the Sea, The
author: **11** Iris Murdoch

Sea Around Us, The
author: **13** Rachel L Carson

seaboard 5 coast **9** shoreline

Seaborg, Glen Theodore
field: **7** physics
worked with: **14** actinide series **19** transuranic elements
headed: **3** AEC **22** Atomic Energy Commission
awarded: **10** Nobel Prize

seacoast 5 beach, coast, shore **7** seaside **8** littoral **9** coastland, coastline, shoreline, waterside
French: **4** cote
Italian: **4** lido **7** riviera

seafarers 5 salts **7** sailors, seadogs **8** mariners

Seagull, The
author: **12** Anton Chekhov
character: **5** Masha **6** Polina **10** Pyotr Sorin **11** Yevgeny Dorn **12** Ilya Shamraev, Irina Arkadin **13** Boris Trigorin, Nina Zaretchyn **16** Semyon Medvedenko **17** Konstantin Treplev

Seah 15 Biblical measure

Sea Hawk, The
director: **13** Michael Curtiz
cast: **10** Errol Flynn **11** Claude Rains, Donald Crisp **14** Brenda Marshall
score: **21** Erich Wolfgang Korngold

seal 2 OK **3** dam, fix **4** cork, lock, mark, plug, shut, stop **5** brand, close, stamp **6** accept, affirm, emblem, fasten, figure, ratify, secure, settle, shut up, signet, stop up, symbol, verify **7** approve, certify, confirm, endorse, imprint **8** colophon, conclude, fastener, hallmark, insignia, sanction, validate **9** determine, establish, trademark **10** impression **12** authenticate
Latin: **10** imprimatur

seal
young: **3** pup
group of: **3** pod

sea lion
young: **3** pup

seam 3 gap **4** line, lode, mark, scar, vein **5** break, chink, cleft, crack, joint, layer, notch **6** breach, furrow, incise, suture **7** crevice, fissure, joining, opening, rupture, stratum, wrinkle **8** junction, juncture **9** interface

seaman 3 gob, tar **4** hand, mate, salt **5** bosun, middy **6** lubber, merman, sailor, seadog **7** mariner **9** boatswain **10** bluejacket, midshipman

seamark 5 light **6** beacon, pharos, signal **10** lighthouse, watchtower

sea monster 6 dragon **9** Leviathan

seamstress 10 dressmaker
French: **9** midinette **10** couturiere

seamy 3 raw **4** dark **5** dirty, nasty, rough **6** coarse, sordid **7** squalid, unclean **10** unpleasant **11** unwholesome **12** disagreeable

Sea of Grass, The
author: **13** Conrad Richter

sear 4 burn, char, scar **5** blast,

singe, steel **6** harden, scorch **7** blister **9** cauterize **10** caseharden

search 4 comb, drag, fish, hunt, look, seek, sift **5** check, frisk, probe, quest, rifle, scour, snoop, study **6** survey, tracer **7** dragnet, examine, explore, inquiry, inspect, pry into, pursuit, ransack, rummage **8** overhaul, scrutiny **10** inspection, scrutinize **11** examination, exploration **13** investigation

Search, The
director: **13** Fred Zinnemann
cast: **9** Ivan Jandl **13** Aline MacMahon **14** Jarmila Novotna **15** Montgomery Clift
setting: **6** Berlin

Searchers, The
director: **8** John Ford
cast: **8** Ward Bond **9** John Wayne, Vera Miles **11** Natalie Wood **13** Jeffrey Hunter

searching 4 dour, keen, nosy **5** sharp **6** prying, shrewd, snoopy **7** curious, groping **8** exacting, piercing, rigorous, thorough **9** observant, quizzical, unsparing **11** inquisitive, penetrating **13** investigative

Seascape
author: **11** Edward Albee

seashore 5 beach, coast

seasick 3 ill **5** barfy, dizzy, faint, giddy, woozy **6** queasy **8** qualmish, vomitous **9** nauseated, squeamish **11** vertiginous

seasickness
French: **8** mal de mer

seaside 5 beach, coast, shore **9** shoreline

season 3 age, dry **4** fall, lace, tame, term **5** adapt, color, drill, inure, prime, ripen, shape, spell, spice, stage, train **6** accent, autumn, finish, flavor, inform, leaven, mature, mellow, period, refine, soften, spring, summer, temper, winter **7** enhance, enliven, prepare, quarter, stretch **8** accustom, duration, heighten, interval, ornament, practice **9** condition, cultivate, embellish **10** discipline

seasoned 6 herbed, inured, salted, spiced **7** veteran **8** flavored, hardened, peppered **9** competent, qualified **10** acclimated, accustomed, habituated **11** experienced **12** familiarized

seasoning 4 dill, herb, mace, sage, salt, zest **5** aging, basil, clove, gusto, onion, spice, thyme **6** drying, garlic, ginger, nutmeg, pepper, relish **7** oregano, paprika, parsley **8** allspice, cinnamon, marjoram, practice, ripening, rosemary, training **9** condiment, flavoring **10** maturation **11** orientation, preparation **15** familiarization

Season in Hell, A
    author: 13 Arthur Rimbaud

seasons
    god of: 9 Vertumnus
    goddess of: 4 Hour **5** Horae

seat 3 box, hub **4** axis, core, home, rump, site, sofa **5** abode, bench, chair, couch, croup, divan, fanny, heart, house, locus, place **6** behind, bottom, center, locale, settle **7** address, capital, cushion, habitat, housing, nucleus, rear end, situate **8** backside, buttocks, derriere, domicile, dwelling, haunches, location, quarters **9** posterior, residence **10** incumbency, membership **12** hindquarters

seat of justice 5 bench, court **8** tribunal **9** judiciary **10** courthouse

Seattle
    baseball team: 8 Mariners
    basketball team:
        11 Supersonics
    bay: 7 Elliott
    football team: 8 Seahawks
    lake: 10 Washington
    landmark: 11 Space Needle
    site of: 10 World's Fair
    sound: 5 Puget

Sea Wolf, The
    author: 10 Jack London

Sebastian
    character in: 12 Twelfth
      Night
    author: 11 Shakespeare

Seberg, Jean
    born: 14 Marshalltown IA
    husband: 10 Romain Gary
    roles: 6 Lilith **7** Airport
      9 Saint Joan **10** Breathless
      16 Bonjour Tristesse

Secchi, Angelo
    field: 9 astronomy
    nationality: 7 Italian
    classified: 5 stars

secede 4 quit **5** leave **6** resign, retire **7** forsake **8** withdraw **12** disaffiliate

secession 10 separation, withdrawal **14** disaffiliation

seclude 4 hide **6** retire **7** isolate **8** separate **9** sequester **10** dissociate

secluded 6 covert, cut off, lonely, remote, shut in **7** private **8** closeted, confined, isolated, shut away, solitary **9** reclusive, sheltered, unvisited, withdrawn **10** cloistered **11** out-of-the-way, sequestered **12** unfrequented

seclusion 5 exile **6** asylum, hiding **7** retreat **8** cloister, hideaway, solitude **9** hermitage, isolation, reclusion, sanctuary **10** quarantine, retirement, withdrawal **11** concealment **13** sequestration

second 3 aid **4** abet, back, help, wink **5** agent, favor, flash, jiffy, other, proxy, trice **6** assist, back up, deputy, fill-in, helper, minute, moment, uphold **7** advance, another, endorse, further, instant, one more, outdone, promote, stand by, stand-in, support **8** advocate, delegate, exceeded, inferior **9** alternate, assistant, attendant, encourage, surpassed, twinkling **10** additional, lieutenant, substitute, understudy **11** alternating, subordinate **14** representative
    abbreviation: 1 s **3** sec

secondary 5 lower, minor, other **6** backup, lesser **7** smaller **8** inferior, mediocre, middling **9** alternate, ancillary, auxiliary, following, resultant **10** consequent, subsequent, subsidiary **11** subordinate

second childhood 6 dotage **8** senility

secondhand 4 used **8** indirect **10** derivative

second-in-command 6 deputy **8** adjutant **9** assistant **10** lieutenant **13** vice president

second-rate 3 bad **4** poor, soso **5** cheap, tacky **6** shabby **7** average **8** everyday, inferior, mediocre, middling **9** imperfect **10** inadequate, outclassed, pedestrian **11** commonplace, substandard **15** undistinguished

Second Sex, The
    author: 16 Simone de
      Beauvoir

second-story man 5 thief **6** robber **7** burglar **9** cracksman **10** cat burglar

second string 4 subs **5** bench **11** substitutes

second team 5 bench **11** substitutes

secrecy 6 hiding **7** mystery, privacy, private, silence, stealth **8** muteness, solitude **9** closeness, seclusion **10** covertness **11** concealment, furtiveness **13** sequestration

15 clandestineness, confidentiality, underhandedness **17** surreptitiousness **19** uncommunicativeness

secret 3 key, mum **4** dark **6** arcane, covert, enigma, hidden, mystic, occult, puzzle, recipe, unseen **7** formula, furtive, mystery, private, unknown **8** discreet, esoteric, hush-hush, secluded, stealthy **9** concealed, disguised, invisible, secretive **10** confidence, mysterious, undercover, unrevealed **11** camouflaged, clandestine, undisclosed, unpublished **12** confidential, unrevealable **13** surreptitious

Secret Agent
    character: 9 John Drake
    cast: 15 Patrick McGoohan
    theme: 14 Secret Agent Man

secretary 4 aide, desk **5** clerk **6** scribe **7** officer **8** recorder **10** amanuensis **12** stenographer
    French: 10 escritoire

secret council 8 conclave

secrete 4 hide, veil **5** cache, cloak, cover, stash **6** screen, shroud **7** conceal, curtain **8** disguise

secretive 3 mum, sly **4** mute **6** covert, silent **7** cryptic, evasive, furtive, laconic, private **8** discreet, reserved, reticent, stealthy, taciturn **9** enigmatic, withdrawn **10** mysterious **11** tight-lipped, underhanded, unrevealing **13** surreptitious **15** uncommunicative

secretiveness 7 mystery, stealth **9** reticence **11** furtiveness **14** inscrutability, mysteriousness **19** uncommunicativeness

Secret Life of Walter Mitty, The
    author: 12 James Thurber

sect 4 camp, cult **7** faction **8** division **10** persuasion **11** affiliation **12** denomination

sectarian 6 narrow **7** limited **8** clannish **9** exclusive, parochial **10** provincial, restricted

section 4 area, part, side, unit, ward, zone **5** piece, range, share, slice **6** region, sample, sphere **7** chapter, cutting, measure, passage, portion, segment, terrain **8** district, division, province, specimen, vicinity **9** allotment, increment, territory **10** department, proportion **11** installment **12** neighborhood

sector 4 area, zone **7** theater **8** district

secular 3 lay 4 laic 6 carnal 7 earthly, fleshly, mundane, profane, sensual, worldly 8 material, temporal 9 nonsacred 11 nonclerical 12 nonreligious, nonspiritual 17 nonecclesiastical

secundum 11 according to

secure 3 get, set 4 bind, easy, safe, sure 5 fixed, tight 6 at ease, defend, ensure, fasten, immune, insure, obtain 7 acquire, assured, certain, protect, shelter, tie down 8 absolute, carefree, composed, defended, definite, in the bag, positive, surefire 9 confident, guarantee, protected, reassured, safeguard, sheltered 10 guaranteed 11 impregnable 12 invulnerable, unassailable, unattackable, unthreatened

securities 5 bonds, title 6 stocks 12 certificates

security 4 bond, care, hope, keep 5 faith, trust 6 guards, pledge, police, safety, surety, troops 7 defense, deposit, promise, support 8 reliance, sureness, warranty 9 assurance, certainty, guarantee 10 collateral, confidence, conviction, protection, safeguards 11 maintenance, safekeeping 12 absoluteness, decisiveness, definiteness, positiveness, preservation

sedate 4 calm, cool 5 grave, quiet, sober, staid, still 6 poised, serene, solemn, steady 7 serious, subdued 8 composed, decorous, reserved 9 collected, dignified, impassive, unexcited, unruffled 10 cool-headed 11 levelheaded 13 imperturbable 15 undemonstrative

sedateness 7 decorum, dignity, gravity, reserve 8 calmness 9 composure, soberness, solemnity 11 impassivity, seriousness

sedative 6 easing, opiate 7 anodyne, calming 8 allaying, lenitive, narcotic, relaxing, soothing 9 analgesic, assuasive, calmative, composing, mitigator, soporific 10 comforting, palliative 11 alleviative 12 tranquilizer 13 tranquilizing

sedentary 5 fixed, inert, still 6 seated 7 resting, sitting 8 inactive, unmoving 9 quiescent 10 stationary, unstirring

sedge 4 reed 5 grass 10 marsh grass

sediment 4 lees, scum, slag 5 dregs, dross, waste 6 debris,

sludge 7 grounds, remains, residue 8 leavings 9 settlings

sedition 6 mutiny, revolt 7 treason 8 defiance, uprising 9 rebellion 10 disloyalty, insurgency, subversion, unruliness 11 lawlessness 12 disobedience, insurrection 14 rebelliousness, subversiveness

Sedley, Amelia and Joseph characters in: 10 Vanity Fair author: 9 Thackeray

seduce 4 lure, ruin 5 abuse, charm, tempt 6 allure, defile, entice, ravish 7 attract, conquer, corrupt, debauch, deprave, pervert, violate, win over 8 deflower, disgrace, dishonor, persuade 9 captivate

seducer 3 cad 4 wolf 5 letch, Romeo 7 defiler, Don Juan, playboy 8 Casanova, Lothario, lover-boy, ravisher, violater 9 corrupter, debaucher, womanizer 10 deflowerer 11 philanderer 12 heartbreaker **French:** 4 roue

seductive 4 sexy 8 alluring, charming, enticing, tempting 9 beguiling, disarming 10 attractive, bewitching, come-hither, enchanting, voluptuous 11 captivating, provocative

seductress 4 vamp 5 siren 7 charmer, Jezebel, Lorelei, mantrap 9 temptress 11 adventuress, enchantress **French:** 7 cocotte 11 femme fatale

sedulous 6 dogged 8 diligent, thorough 9 assiduous, steadfast 10 determined, persistent 11 industrious, painstaking, persevering 13 conscientious, indefatigable

sedulousness 4 zeal 8 industry, tenacity 9 assiduity, diligence 11 persistence 12 perseverance

see 3 dig, eye, spy, woo 4 date, espy, know, meet, mind, spot, view 5 court, grasp, sight, visit, watch 6 attend, behold, descry, escort, fathom, notice, regard, survey 7 consult, discern, glimpse, observe, picture, realize, receive, undergo, witness 8 conceive, consider, discover, envision, meditate, perceive, register, ruminate 9 accompany, apprehend, ascertain, determine, encounter, entertain, interview, recognize, visualize 10 appreciate, comprehend, experience, understand 11 contemplate, distinguish **Latin:** 4 vide

see above **Latin:** 9 vide supra

see after **Latin:** 8 vide post

see as above, see as stated above **Latin:** 11 vide ut supra

see before **Latin:** 8 vide ante

see below **Latin:** 9 vide infra

seed 3 pit, sow 4 germ 5 basis, grain, heirs, issue, ovule, plant, stone 6 embryo, origin, source 7 progeny 8 children 9 beginning, offspring, posterity 11 descendants

seedy 4 worn 5 dingy, faded, lousy, mangy, ratty, spent, tacky 6 scuffy, shabby 7 haggard, sickish, squalid 8 slovenly 10 threadbare 11 debilitated

see eye to eye 5 agree 6 concur 11 be of one mind

see fit 5 deign 6 choose, please

see further **Latin:** 8 vide post

seek 3 try 4 hunt 5 court, essay, trace 6 demand, invite, pursue 7 attempt, examine, explore, inspect, request, solicit, venture 8 endeavor 9 undertake 10 scrutinize 11 investigate

seek out 4 find 6 pursue 7 embrace, look for, solicit

seek proof 4 test 6 try out 7 analyze, examine 8 research 10 experiment 11 investigate

seem 4 look 6 appear

seeming 7 evident, obvious, surface 8 apparent, presumed, putative, supposed 10 ostensible 11 superficial

seemly 3 due 5 right 6 decent, polite, proper 7 correct, fitting, prudent, refined 8 becoming, decorous, suitable, tasteful, well-bred 9 befitting, courteous 10 acceptable, felicitous 11 appropriate 12 conventional **French:** 11 comme il faut

seep 4 drip, leak, ooze, soak 7 diffuse, dribble, suffuse, trickle 8 permeate 9 penetrate

seepage 4 ooze 5 flour, issue 7 leakage, outflow 9 discharge, dribbling, secretion, trickling

seer 4 sage 5 augur 6 medium, oracle 7 diviner, prophet, psychic 8 conjurer, sorcerer 9 sorceress, stargazer 10 astrologer, soothsayer 11 clair-

voyant, necromancer
13 fortuneteller
14 prognosticator

seesaw 5 waver **6** teeter **9** alternate, fluctuate, up-and-down, vacillate **12** teeter-totter

seethe 4 boil, brew, cook, fume, rage, rant, rave, roil, stew **5** churn, storm **6** blow up, bubble, simmer **7** bluster, smolder

seething 3 mad **7** boiling **8** agitated, bubbling, frenzied **10** distraught

see through 3 get **6** detect, effect, finish **7** achieve, execute, perform **8** carry out, complete, conclude **9** catch onto, figure out, penetrate **10** comprehend, understand

Segal, Erich
author of: 9 Love Story **12** Oliver's Story **16** Man Woman and Child

Segal, George
born: 9 New York NY
roles: 11 Blume in Love, Where's Poppa? **13** A Touch of Class **18** Fun with Dick and Jane **25** Who's Afraid of Virginia Woolf?

segment 3 leg **4** part **5** cut up, piece, stage **6** cleave **7** disjoin, portion, section, split up **8** disunite, division, separate **9** increment **11** installment

segmented 5 cut up **7** split up **9** sectioned, separated

segregate 6 cut off, detach, divide **7** divorce, isolate, seclude, sort out **8** disunite, insulate, separate **9** sequester **10** disconnect, quarantine

segue
music: 21 continue without a break

seine 3 net **4** drag, fish **5** trawl **7** dragnet

seism 5 quake, shock **6** tremor **8** temblor, upheaval **10** earthquake

seize 3 bag, nab **4** grab, read **5** catch, glean, grasp, pinch, pluck, usurp **6** arrest, clutch, collar, gather, snatch **7** capture, embrace, impound, possess, utilize **8** arrogate **9** apprehend, overpower, overwhelm **10** commandeer, comprehend, confiscate, understand **11** appropriate

seize the day
Latin: 9 carpe diem

seizure 3 fit **5** onset, spell, throe **6** access, arrest, attack, crisis, stroke, taking **7** capture,

episode **8** grasping, paroxysm **9** abduction, snatching **10** convulsion, kidnapping, possession, usurpation, visitation **11** impressment **12** apprehension, confiscation **13** appropriation, commandeering

Sejanus
author: 9 Ben Jonson

Sekhmet
origin: 8 Egyptian
goddess of: 4 evil

Selden, Mr
character in: 15 The House of Mirth
author: 7 Wharton

seldom 6 rarely **8** scarcely **10** uncommonly **12** infrequently, occasionally, sporadically

select 3 tap **4** A-one, pick, posh **5** elect, elite, fancy **6** choice, choose, chosen, opt for, picked, prefer **8** four-star, superior, top-notch **9** exclusive, first-rate, preferred **10** first-class, privileged

selection 4 pick **5** range **6** choice, medley, option **7** program, variety **8** choosing, decision **9** potpourri **10** collection, miscellany, preference

selective 5 fussy, picky **6** choosy **7** careful, finicky **8** cautious **10** discerning, fastidious, meticulous, particular **14** discriminating

Selemnus
vocation: 8 shepherd
loved: 6 Argyra
changed into: 5 river
changed by: 9 Aphrodite

Selene
goddess of: 4 moon
father: 8 Hyperion
mother: 5 Theia
brother: 6 Helios
sister: 3 Eos
loved: 8 Endymion
daughter: 5 Herse **6** Pandia
corresponds to: 5 Diana **7** Artemis

self 3 ego **6** person, psyche **8** identity **10** individual **11** homogeneity, personality
inner: 5 anima **6** animus
Universal: 5 Atman

self-abnegation 7 modesty **8** humility **10** diffidence **11** bashfulness

self-absorbed 4 vain **8** egoistic **9** egotistic **10** egocentric **11** egotistical **12** narcissistic

self-absorption 6 egoism, vanity **7** conceit **11** egocentrism, selfishness **16** self-centeredness

self-admiration 6 vanity **7** conceit, egotism **8** smugness **9** immodesty, vainglory

self-assertive 4 bold **7** dynamic **8** forceful **9** ambitious, confident **10** aggressive

self-assuming 4 vain **8** arrogant, egoistic **9** conceited **10** egotistical **11** egotistical

self-assurance 6 aplomb **9** brashness **12** cocksureness
French: 9 sangfroid

self-assured 6 brash, cocky **8** cocksure **9** confident

self-centered 4 vain **8** egoistic, immodest **9** conceited, egotistic **10** egocentric **11** egotistical, swellheaded **12** narcissistic

self-centeredness 6 egoism, vanity **7** conceit **10** narcissism **11** egocentrism

self-composure 5 poise **6** aplomb **8** calmness **10** equanimity

self-confidence 5 nerve, pluck **6** mettle, spirit **8** boldness, gameness **9** cockiness **10** resolution **12** cocksureness

self-conscious 7 awkward **8** affected **9** chagrined, ill at ease, unnatural **11** discomposed, embarrassed **12** disconcerted

self-consciousness 7 modesty, reserve, shyness **8** timidity **9** abashment, hesitancy, reticence **10** constraint, demureness, diffidence **11** bashfulness, fearfulness **12** apprehension, sheepishness

self-control 5 poise **6** aplomb **8** firmness, patience, sobriety **9** composure, soberness, soundness, stability, willpower **10** temperance **11** forbearance **14** cool-headedness, unexcitability **15** levelheadedness **16** imperturbability
French: 9 sangfroid **11** savoir faire

self-critical 6 humble, modest **9** diffident **13** perfectionist

self-criticism 7 modesty **8** humility **10** diffidence **13** perfectionism

self-deception 7 fantasy **8** delusion, illusion **13** hallucination

self-declared 5 sworn **6** avowed **8** admitted **9** confessed, professed **12** acknowledged

self-denial 8 eschewal **10** abnegation, abstention, abstinence, continence

11 forbearance 12 renunciation 14 abstemiousness

self-deprecation
also: 16 self-depreciation
7 modesty 8 humility, meekness 10 humbleness

self-doubt 11 uncertainty

self-effacement 7 modesty,
shyness 8 humility, meekness
10 diffidence 11 bashfulness

self-esteem 5 pride
10 confidence

self-evident 5 plain 6 patent
7 glaring, obvious 8 apparent,
distinct, explicit, manifest,
palpable 10 unarguable, undeniable 11 unambiguous, unequivocal 12 unmistakable
16 incontrovertible

self-explanatory 5 clear, lucid, plain 7 obvious 8 manifest 12 intelligible
15 straightforward

self-governing 4 free 9 sovereign 10 autonomous
11 independent

self-government 8 autonomy,
home rule 11 sovereignty
12 independence

self-gratifying 11 intemperate

self-importance 6 egoism,
vanity 8 smugness 9 arro-
gance, immodesty, pomposity,
vainglory 11 egocentrism

self-important 4 smug, vain
7 pompous 8 egoistic, immodest 10 egocentric 11 egotistical 12 vainglorious

self-indulgence 12 extravagance, incontinence,
intemperance

self-indulgent 9 libertine,
sybaritic 10 hedonistic, voluptuous 11 extravagant, incontinent, intemperate

selfish 4 mean 5 tight, venal
6 greedy, stingy 7 miserly
8 covetous, egoistic grasping,
grudging 9 egotistic, illiberal,
mercenary, rapacious 10 avaricious, egocentric, ungenerous 11 egotistical
12 parsimonious, uncharitable

self-love 6 egoism, vanity
7 conceit, egotism 9 vainglory
10 narcissism 11 complacency,
egocentrism, haughtiness
13 conceitedness
15 swellheadedness
French: 11 amour propre

self-possessed 4 calm, cool
6 poised 7 assured, courtly, refined 8 balanced, composed,
polished, resolute 9 collected,
confident 12 aristocratic
13 distinguished

self-possession 5 poise
6 aplomb 7 dignity 8 calmness,
coolness 9 composure 10 confidence, equanimity, steadiness 16 imperturbability
French: 9 sangfroid

self-praise 6 vanity 7 conceit,
egotism 8 bragging, smugness
9 arrogance, immodesty, vainglory 12 boastfulness
Italian: 11 braggadocio

self-propelling 9 automatic

self-questioning 10 uneasiness 13 soul-searching

self-reliance 8 sureness 9 assurance 12 independence

Self-Reliance
author: 17 Ralph Waldo
Emerson

self-reliant 5 hardy 6 plucky
7 assured 8 resolute, spirited
10 mettlesome 11 indepen-
dent 12 enterprising

self-reproachful 8 contrite
9 regretful 10 apologetic,
remorseful

self-respecting 5 proud 7 upright 8 decorous 9 dignified,
honorable 10 upstanding
11 circumspect
13 distinguished

self-restraint 9 willpower
10 continence
11 forbearance

self-righteous 4 smug 5 pious
7 pompous 9 insincere, pietistic 10 complacent, moralizing
11 pharisaical, pretentious
12 hypocritical, mealy-
mouthed 13 sanctimonious
14 holier-than-thou

self-sacrificing 6 heroic 7 gallant 9 unselfish 10 altruistic,
martyrlike

self-satisfaction 5 pride
6 vanity 8 smugness
11 complacency

self-satisfied 4 smug, vain
8 cocksure, priggish 9 overproud 10 complacent 11 egotistical 12 narcissistic,
vainglorious 13 overconfident

self-secure 4 smug 7 content
9 contented 10 complacent

self-seeking 6 greedy
8 covetous

self-styled
French: 9 soi-disant

self-willed 8 obdurate, stubborn 9 obstinate, pigheaded
10 headstrong, refractory
11 intractable 12 ungovernable, unmanageable

sell 4 dump, hawk, vend 6 barter, betray, deal in, enlist,

handle, market, peddle, unload 7 deceive, trade in, win
over 8 convince, dispense

Selleck, Tom
roles: 8 Lassiter, Magnum PI
12 Thomas Magnum
15 High Road to China
16 Three Men and A
Baby

seller 6 dealer, jobber, monger,
trader, vendor 7 peddler
8 merchant, retailer, salesman
9 middleman, salesgirl, sales-
lady, tradesman 10 sales-
woman, shopkeeper,
wholesaler 11 salesperson,
storekeeper

Sellers, Peter
real name: 19 Richard Henry
Sellers
born: 7 England 8 Southsea
wife: 11 Britt Ekland
roles: 10 Being There 12 Casino Royale 13 Dr Strangelove, Murder by Death 14 A
Shot in the Dark, The Pink
Panther 16 What's New Pussycat? 17 Inspector Clou-
seau 18 The Mouse that
Roared 21 The World of
Henry Orient

Selli
priests of: 4 Zeus

sell out 6 betray 11 double-
cross

semblance 3 air 4 cast, copy,
look, show 5 image 6 aspect
7 bearing, replica 8 likeness,
pretense 9 duplicate, facsimile
10 simulacrum 11 counterpart
12 reproduction
14 representation
French: 4 mien

Semele
also: 6 Thyone
father: 6 Cadmus
mother: 8 Harmonia
loved by: 4 Zeus
son: 8 Dionysus
sister: 3 Ino 5 Agave
7 Autonoe

seminal 7 primary 8 creative,
fruitful, germinal, original
9 formative 10 generative, productive 11 germinative,
originating

Seminole
language family:
9 Muskogean
tribe: 8 Cow Creek,
Mikasaki
location: 6 Mexico 7 Florida,
Georgia 10 Everglades
leader: 7 Osceola, Wild Cat
10 Coacoochie

Semiramis
queen of: 7 Assyria
husband: 5 Ninus
founder of: 7 Babylon

Semitic
   language family: 11 Afro-Asiatic **13** Hamito-Semitic
   eastern branch: 8 Akkadian, Assyrian **10** Babylonian
   western branch: 4 Geez **5** Tigre **6** Arabic, Gurage, Harari, Hebrew, Minean, Sabean, Syriac **7** Amharic, Aramaic, Argobba, Moabite **8** Ethiopic, Tigrinya, Ugaritic **9** Canaanite **10** Himyaritic, Phoenician, Qatabanian
   southwest branch: 6 Minean, Sabean **7** Amharic **10** Himyaritic, Qatabanian **11** North Arabic **19** South Arabic-Ethiopic

Semo Sancus *see* **6** Sancus

senatus consultum 17 Roman senate decree

send 4 cast, emit, head, hurl, lead, show, toss **5** drive, fling, guide, refer, relay, shoot, throw **6** convey, direct, launch, propel **7** conduct, deliver, forward, give off, project **8** dispatch, transmit **9** broadcast, cause to go, discharge **11** disseminate

send away 4 oust, rout, shoo **5** chase, evict

send forth 4 emit, gush **5** erupt, expel, issue, let go **7** dismiss, release **8** disgorge, dispatch **9** discharge

send off 4 post **7** forward **8** dispatch, disperse, transmit

send out 4 beam, emit **8** dispatch, transmit **9** discharge

send packing 3 axe, can **4** fire, oust, rout, sack, shoo **5** evict **6** bounce **7** cast out, dismiss

send to Coventry 3 cut **5** eject, expel **6** banish, ignore **7** cast out, exclude **9** ostracize

Seneca
   language family: 9 Iroquoian
   location: 7 New York **15** Canandaigua Lake
   leader: 9 John Abeel, John O'Bail **11** Cornplanter
   member: 19 League of the Iroquois

Senegal *see box*

senile 6 doting, infirm **7** foolish **8** decrepit **9** doddering, senescent **13** superannuated

senior, Senior 4 head, over **5** above, chief, doyen, elder, older **6** better **7** veteran **8** superior

seniority 6 tenure **9** longevity **10** precedence
   French: 4 pere

Senegal
   capital/largest city: 5 Dakar
   others: 5 Bakel, Matam, Thies **7** Bignona, Kaolack, Kaollak **8** Diourbel, Kedougou, Linguere, Rufisque **10** Saint-Louis, Ziguinchor **11** Richard-Toll, Tambacounda
   division: 7 Sudanic **8** Sahelian **9** Casamance
      empire: **4** Mali **5** Jolof **6** Tekrur
   monetary unit: 5 franc **7** centime
   island: 5 Goree
   lake: 6 Guiers
   mountain: 6 Gounou
   highest point: 12 Fouta Djallon
   river: 4 Sine **6** Faleme, Gambia, Saloum **7** Senegal **9** Casamance
   sea: 8 Atlantic
   physical feature:
      desert: **5** Ferlo
      peninsula: **9** Cape Verde
   people: 4 Lebu, Peul, Soce **5** Diola, Dyola, Foula, Laobe, Peulh, Serer, Wolof **6** Fulani, Serere **7** Bambara, Malinke, Tukuler, Tukulor **8** Mandingo
   leader: 7 Senghor
   language: 5 Wolof **6** French
   religion: 5 Islam **7** animism **13** Roman Catholic
   feature:
      musical instrument: **4** kora
      tree: **6** acacia, baobab **7** juniper, oil palm **10** raffia palm

---

senor 2 Mr **3** don **5** title **6** mister **8** Spaniard

senora 3 Mrs **4** lady, wife **5** madam, woman **8** mistress

senorita 4 lass, miss
   abbreviation: 4 srta

senorita: 6 wrasse
   genus: 8 Oxyjulis
   species: 11 californica

sensation 3 hit **4** stir, to-do **6** thrill, uproar **7** feeling, scandal **9** agitation, awareness, commotion, detection **10** impression, perception

sensational 5 cheap, lurid **6** superb **8** dramatic, exciting, galvanic, shocking, striking **9** emotional, excellent, thrilling **10** electrical, scandalous **11** exaggerated, exceptional, extravagant, outstanding, spectacular **12** meretricious **13** extraordinary **14** heartthrobbing

sensationalism 7 scandal **9** luridness, melodrama **13** grandstanding **15** blood and thunder **16** yellow journalism

sense 3 see, use **4** aura, espy, feel, good, mind, note **5** grasp, guess, point, sight, smell, taste, touch, value, worth **6** descry, detect, divine, reason, regard, take in, wisdom **7** benefit, discern, faculty, feeling, hearing, meaning, purpose, realize, suspect **8** efficacy, function, judgment, perceive, sagacity **9** apprehend, awareness, intuition, recognize **10** atmosphere, comprehend, definition, denotation, impression, understand **11** connotation, premonition, realization, recognition **12** appreciation, intelligence, perspicacity, practicality, presentiment **13** consciousness, signification, understanding **14** reasonableness

Sense and Sensibility
   author: 10 Jane Austen
   character: 10 Lucy Steele **13** Edward Ferrars, Robert Ferrars **14** Colonel Brandon, John Willoughby **16** Sir John Middleton
      Dashwood family: **4** John **5** Fanny **6** Elinor **8** Marianne

senseless 4 dumb, idle, numb **5** crazy, inane, nutty, silly **6** stupid, unwise **7** aimless, foolish, stunned, useless, witless **8** comatose, deadened **9** brainless, foolhardy, illogical, insensate, pointless **10** groundless, ill-advised, insensible, irrational, ridiculous **11** harebrained, meaningless, purposeless, unconscious **12** unreasonable **13** irresponsible

sense of duty 15 moral obligation **21** sense of responsibility

sensibilities 8 feelings, sore spot, thin skin **12** Achilles' heel **14** susceptibility

sensibility 7 feeling **10** perception **11** temperament **14** responsiveness

sensible 4 just, sage, sane, wise **5** aware, plain, sound **7** evident, knowing, logical, obvious, prudent, visible **8** apparent, apprised, credible, discreet, informed, palpable, possible, rational, tangible **9** cognitive, cognizant, conscious, judicious, plausible, sagacious **10** detectable, discerning, farsighted, noticeable, perceiving, perceptive, reasonable, responsive, thoughtful **11** discernible, enlightened, intelligent, perceptible, susceptible **13** perspicacious **14** discriminating

sensitive 4 fine, keen, sore **5** acute, exact **6** tender, touchy **7** painful, precise **8** accurate, delicate, faithful, sentient **10** perceptive, responsive **11** susceptible, thin-skinned **14** impressionable

sensitiveness 8 delicacy **10** touchiness

sensual 4 lewd, sexy **6** carnal, earthy, erotic **7** fleshly, lustful **9** lecherous **10** hedonistic, licentious, voluptuous

sensualist 8 hedonist, sybarite **9** libertine **10** voluptuary

sensuous 9 delicious, exquisite **10** delightful

sententious 7 orotund, pompous, preachy, stilted **8** didactic, pedantic **9** grandiose, high-flown, pietistic **10** judgmental, moralistic **13** sanctimonious

sentient 5 aware **7** alert to, alive to, awake to, mindful **8** sensible **9** conscious

sentiment, sentiments 4 idea **5** heart **6** notion **7** emotion, feeling, opinion, romance, thought **8** attitude **9** nostalgia, viewpoint **10** tenderness **11** romanticism **12** emotionalism **15** softheartedness

sentimental 5 mushy, weepy **7** maudlin, mawkish, tearful **8** pathetic, romantic **9** emotional, nostalgic **10** lachrymose **12** melodramatic, romanticized

Sentimental Education, A author: **15** Gustave Flaubert character: **6** Arnoux **9** Dambreuse, Rosanette **11** Des Lauriers, Louise Roque **14** Frederic Moreau

sentimentalism 4 corn, mush **5** slush **6** bathos, pathos

8 schmaltz **9** mushiness, soppiness **10** maudlinism, slushiness **11** mawkishness

sentimentality 4 mush **5** heart **6** bathos, pathos **10** sloppiness **11** mawkishness, temperament **12** emotionalism Yiddish: **6** kitsch

Sentimental Journey, A author: **14** Laurence Sterne character: **5** Maria **6** Yorick **7** La Fleur

sentinel 4 ward **5** guard, scout, watch **6** patrol, picket, ranger **7** lookout **8** guardian, watchman **9** guardsman

sentry 5 guard, watch **7** lookout, vedette, vidette **8** sentinel, watchman greeting: **4** halt

Seoul capital of: **10** South Korea

separate 3 cut **4** cull, fork, part, sift **5** break, crack, sever, split **6** bisect, detach, divide, ramify, remove, single, spread, sunder **7** crumble, disjoin, diverge, diverse, divorce, isolate, radiate **8** detached, discrete, distinct, disunite **9** bifurcate, break away, come apart, different, disunited, partition, segregate, subdivide **10** autonomous, disconnect, dissimilar, divaricate, individual **11** distinguish, independent

separated 6 cut off **7** severed **8** detached **10** disengaged **12** disconnected, disentangled

separate from 5 apart, leave

separately 5 apart **6** singly **7** asunder **9** severally **12** individually

Separate Tables director: **11** Delbert Mann based on play by: **15** Terence Rattigan cast: **10** David Niven **11** Deborah Kerr, Wendy Hiller **12** Rita Hayworth **13** Burt Lancaster Oscar for: **5** actor (Niven) **17** supporting actress (Hiller)

separation 3 gap **4** fork **5** break, space, split **6** breach, divide, schism **7** divider, divorce, good-bye, opening, parting, removal, sorting **8** boundary, distance, disunion, division, farewell, interval **9** branching, isolation, partition, severance **10** detachment, divergence **11** bifurcation, disjunction, segregation **12** estrangement **13** disconnection, disengagement **14** disassociation

Sepharvite god 10 Anammelech **11** Adrammelech

Sepharvites residents of: **6** Sippar

Sepher Torah 16 scroll of the Torah literally: **9** book of law

---

September characteristic: **11** harvest moon event: **14** aurora borealis, Northern lights **15** autumnal equinox flower: **5** aster **12** morning glory French: **9** Septembre gem: **8** sapphire **12** star sapphire German: **9** September holiday: **8** Labor Day (1st Monday) **9** Yom Kippur **10** Michaelmas (29) **12** Rosh Hashanah **15** Grandparents' Day Italian: **9** Settembre number of days: **6** thirty origin of name: **6** septum (Latin meaning seven) place in year: *Gregorian:* **5** ninth *Roman:* **7** seventh Spanish: **10** Septiembre Zodiac sign: **5** Libra, Virgo

---

septentrional 6 arctic **8** northern **11** hyperborean

Septuagint abbreviation: **3** LXX author: **10** the Seventy

sepulcher 4 tomb **5** crypt, grave, vault **7** ossuary **8** cenotaph **9** mausoleum, reliquary **10** necropolis

sepulchral 6 hollow **7** charnel **8** funereal, mournful, tomblike **10** lugubrious

sequel 3 end **6** finish, result, upshot **7** outcome, product **8** addendum, epilogue, followup, offshoot **9** aftermath, corollary, outgrowth **10** conclusion, postscript **11** consequence, culmination **12** continuation French: **10** denouement

sequence 3 run **4** flow **5** chain, cycle, order, round, train **6** course, parade, series, string **7** routine **8** schedule **9** cavalcade **10** procession, succession **11** arrangement, progression **14** successiveness **15** consecutiveness

sequester 6 banish, lock up, retire 7 confine, isolate, seclude 8 separate, withdraw 9 segregate 10 quarantine

sequestered 8 closeted, confined, isolated, secluded 9 insulated, sheltered, withdrawn 10 cloistered 11 dissociated

sequin 4 coin, disk 5 ducat 7 spangle 8 ornament French: 9 paillette

seraglio 3 oda 5 harem, serai 6 zenana 9 gynaeceum

Seraiah son: 4 Ezra

serape 4 cape 5 shawl 6 mantle, poncho

seraph 5 angel

seraphic 7 angelic 8 beatific, ethereal, heavenly 9 celestial

Seraphim 6 angels

Serapis origin: 5 Greek 8 Egyptian form: 5 deity combination of: 4 Apis, Hapi 6 Osiris

Serbia see Yugoslavia

sere 3 dry 4 arid 6 barren 7 parched, wizened 8 droughty, scorched, withered 9 shriveled, unwatered, waterless 10 dehydrated, desiccated 12 dehumidified, moistureless

serene 4 calm, cool, fair 5 clear, quiet, still 6 bright, limpid, placid, poised, sedate, smooth 7 halcyon 8 composed, peaceful, pellucid, tranquil 9 dignified, unruffled 10 nonchalant, unobscured, untroubled 11 undisturbed, unexcitable, unperturbed 13 unimpassioned

serenity 7 dignity 8 calmness, coolness, quietude 9 composure, placidity 10 equanimity, quiescence 11 complacence, nonchalance, tranquility 12 peacefulness, tranquillity 13 collectedness French: 9 sangfroid

serf 6 cotter, thrall, vassal 7 bondman, peasant, villein

serfdom 4 yoke 6 thrall 7 bondage, slavery 9 servitude, thralldom, vassalage 11 enslavement, subjugation

Sergeant York director: 11 Howard Hawks cast: 10 Gary Cooper, Joan Leslie 12 George Tobias 13 Walter Brennan Oscar for: 5 actor (Cooper)

Sergestus origin: 6 Trojan companion to: 6 Aeneas

serial 7 regular 9 continued, piecemeal, recurring 10 continuous, sequential, successive 11 consecutive, incremental

series 3 set 5 chain, cycle, group, order 6 course, number, parade, string 8 sequence 10 procession, succession 11 progression

serious 3 bad, sad 4 grim 5 grave, heavy, sober, staid 6 rueful, sedate, severe, solemn, somber 7 crucial, decided, earnest, fateful, harmful, pensive, sincere, weighty 8 alarming, critical, dejected, downcast, frowning, perilous, resolute, resolved 9 crippling, dangerous, important, momentous, saturnine 10 determined, portentous, purposeful, thoughtful 13 consequential 14 incapacitating

seriousness 7 gravity 8 severity 9 sincerity, soberness, solemnity 10 importance 11 earnestness

sermon 6 homily, rebuke, tirade 7 lecture, reproof 8 diatribe, harangue 9 preaching 10 admonition, preachment 11 exhortation

serpent, Serpent 3 asp 5 cheat, devil, rogue, Satan, snake, viper 7 reptile, traitor 8 deceiver 9 trickster constellation of: 7 Serpens

Serpent Holder constellation of: 9 Ophiuchus

serpentine 4 mazy 6 spiral, zigzag 7 coiling, crooked, devious, sinuous, snaking, winding 8 flexuous, tortuous, twisting 10 circuitous, convoluted, meandering, roundabout, undulating 12 labyrinthine

Serpico director: 11 Sidney Lumet based on story by: 9 Peter Maas cast: 8 Al Pacino 9 Jack Kehoe 12 John Randolph setting: 11 New York City

serrate 5 notch 6 jagged, pinked, ridged 7 dentate, grooved, notched, toothed 10 sawtoothed

serration 5 notch, ridge, teeth, tooth 8 notching, sawtooth

servant 3 man 4 cook, girl, help, maid 5 valet 6 butler, flunky, helper, lackey, menial, minion, slavey 7 footman 8 domestic, employee, facto-

tum, henchman, hired man, retainer, scullion 9 attendant, chauffeur, hired girl, hired help, man Friday, underling 10 girl Friday 11 housekeeper

serve 2 do 3 act, aid 4 help, pass, suit, tend, work 5 avail, spend, treat 6 assist, attend, be used, do duty, oblige, supply, wait on 7 content, deliver, further, perform, present, promote, satisfy, suffice, work for 8 carry out, complete, function, hand over, minister 9 officiate 11 fill the bill

service, services 3 aid, use 4 help, mend, rite 5 avail, labor 6 adjust, agency, bureau, effort, employ, profit, repair, ritual, system 7 benefit, support, utility, waiting 8 ceremony, facility, maintain, military 9 advantage, provision, treatment 10 assistance, attendance, ceremonial, department, employment, observance, usefulness 11 celebration, convenience, maintenance 12 ministration 13 accommodation

serviceable 5 tough 6 rugged, strong, sturdy, usable, useful 7 durable, lasting 8 workable 9 effective, operative, practical 10 functional 11 utilitarian

serviceman 6 marine, sailor 7 soldier 9 repairman

servile 4 oily 6 abject, humble, menial 7 fawning, in bonds, slavish 8 cringing, scraping, toadying, unctuous 9 groveling, truckling 10 obsequious, submissive 11 bootlicking, subservient, sycophantic

serving 6 acting 7 dishful, helping, portion, waiting 8 plateful 9 assisting, attending, sufficing 11 ministering

serving counter 3 bar 6 buffet 9 sideboard

servitude 5 bonds 6 chains 7 bondage, fetters, serfdom, slavery 8 shackles 9 thralldom, vassalage 10 oppression 11 enslavement, subjugation 12 enthrallment, imprisonment

Servius Tullius also: 7 Tullius king of: 4 Rome daughter: 6 Tullia son-in-law: 7 Tarquin killed by: 6 Tullia 7 Tarquin

sesame also called: 10 benne seeds botanical name: 14 Sesamum indicum fairy tale: 10 "open sesame" 25 Ali Baba and the Forty Thieves

high in: 7 protein
former/mythical use: 3 oil
8 medicine **10** opens locks
11 lighting oil **16** discovers
secrets **21** discovers secret
places
use: 5 bread **6** salads
10 casseroles
use like: 8 nutmeats
11 chopped nuts

Sesame Street
character: 4 Bert, Elmo **5** Ernie, Herry, Oscar **6** Snuffy
7 Barkley, Big Bird, Mup-
pets **8** the Count **12** Telly
Monster **13** Cookie Monster **15** Mr Snuffleupagus

Sesostris
king of: 5 Egypt

session 4 bout, term **5** round,
synod **6** course, period
7 meeting, quarter, sitting
8 assembly, conclave, semester **10** conference, convention

set *see box*

Set
also: 4 Seth
origin: 8 Egyptian
form: 6 animal
personifies: 6 desert
brother: 6 Osiris
killed: 6 Osiris

set about 5 begin **6** assume
9 undertake **10** surrounded

set against 8 alienate,
estrange

set apart 5 allot **6** detach, divide **7** earmark, isolate **8** allocate, separate **9** apportion,
segregate **11** appropriate

set aside 4 kill **5** allot, annul
6 abjure, cancel, repeal, revoke **7** abandon, abolish, call
off, destroy, discard, earmark,
nullify, put away, rescind, retract, reverse **8** abrogate, allo-

cate, override, overturn
9 designate, repudiate **10** invalidate **11** discontinue

set at ease 5 cheer **6** please
7 appease, comfort, content,
gratify

set at liberty 4 free **5** let go
6 parole **7** manumit, release,
unchain **8** liberate, unfetter
9 unshackle **10** emancipate

setback 4 flop, loss, snag
5 hitch, slump **6** defeat, mishap, rebuff **7** failure, relapse,
reverse, undoing **8** reversal
9 adversity, mischance, worsening **10** misfortune, regression **13** retrogression
14 disappointment

set down 6 record **7** deposit

set forth 2 go **5** be off, leave
6 assert, avouch, depart **7** advance **8** advocate, propound
10 sally forth

set free 5 let go, loose, untie
6 acquit, loosen, pardon, parole, unbind, uncage, unlock
7 deliver, release **8** liberate,
unfetter **9** discharge, disengage, extricate
10 emancipate

Seth *see* **3** Set

Seth
means: 12 compensation
father: 4 Adam
mother: 3 Eve
son: 4 Enos

set in 5 arise, ensue, occur
6 arrive

set in motion 5 begin, start
6 launch **8** initiate **9** instigate,
originate **10** inaugurate

set in order 4 rank, sort
5 align **6** line up **7** arrange,
marshal **8** classify, organize
9 methodize **11** systematize

set of beliefs 5 credo, creed,
dogma, ethos **6** ethnic, tenets
8 doctrine **10** philosophy, principles **11** convictions

set off 6 depart **7** explode, go
forth **8** detonate, start out
10 sally forth

set on fire 4 burn **5** light
6 ignite, kindle

set out 4 pose **5** array, begin,
be off, place, range **6** deploy,
embark, intend **7** arrange, display **9** undertake

set right 7 correct **8** disabuse

set store by 5 prize, value
6 esteem **7** respect **8** treasure

set straight 5 edify **6** advise,
inform **7** educate **8** disabuse
9 enlighten

settee 4 seat, sofa **5** bench

setting 5 scene **6** fixing, locale **7** jelling **8** aligning, ambiance, locating, location,
mounting **9** adjusting, arranging, decreeing, hardening, or-
daining **10** congealing,
regulating, thickening **11** arrangement, determining, environment, prescribing,
solidifying **12** establishing,
surroundings
French: 6 milieu **11** mise-
en-scene

setting sun
god of: 5 Janus

settle 3 fix, pay, sag **4** calm,
drop, land, sink **5** agree, allay,
clear, droop, light, lodge,
perch, quiet **6** alight, choose,
decide, locate, move to, pacify, people, soothe **7** arrange,
clarify, clear up, compose, inhabit, rectify, resolve, satisfy,
sit down, situate **8** colonize,
make good, populate, take
root **9** determine, discharge,
establish, reconcile
11 precipitate

settled 4 sure **7** certain,
decided

settlement 3 sum **4** camp,
post **6** amount, colony, hamlet **7** bequest, outpost, payment, village **8** clearing,
peopling **9** clearance, discharge **10** adjustment, coloniz-
ing, encampment, resolution
11 acquittance, arrangement,
liquidation **12** amortization,
colonization, compensation,
satisfaction **14** reconciliation

settler 7 pioneer **8** colonist,
squatter **9** colonizer, immigrant **11** homesteader
12 frontiersman

settle upon 6 bestow **7** consign **8** bequeath

---

set 3 cut, fit, fix, gel, kit, lay, put, sic **4** club, drop, firm,
line, make, plop, post, rate, sink, stud, suit **5** adapt, align,
array, banal, bunch, crowd, embed, fixed, group, imbed, order, place, plunk, ready, rigid, scene, stale, stiff, stock, style,
trite, usual **6** adjust, assess, assign, attach, common, confer,
create, decree, frozen, harden, line up, locale, locate, ordain,
outfit, studio **7** arrange, bearing, complex, congeal, decided,
faction, install, jellify, machine, prepare, profile, regular, release, routine, scenery, service, setting, situate, station,
thicken, unleash **8** arranged, assembly, backdrop, carriage,
definite, estimate, everyday, familiar, firmness, habitual,
hardened, location, ornament, position, prepared, regulate,
rigidity, solidify, stubborn **9** apparatus, calibrate, customary,
determine, establish, hackneyed, immovable, obstinate, prescribe, represent, steadfast **10** accustomed, assortment, collection, inflexible **11** anticipated, commonplace, consolidate,
established, prearranged **12** conventional
French: 6 clique **7** coterie

settlings 4 lees **5** dregs **7** deposit, grounds, remains, residue **8** leavings

set-to 4 spat **5** brush, clash, run-in **6** battle, fracas **7** dispute, quarrel, scuffle **8** argument, skirmish, squabble **10** engagement, falling out **12** disagreement **13** confrontation
French: **11** contretemps

setup 4 plan **6** scheme, system **8** practice **9** apparatus **11** arrangement **12** organization

set up 3 rig **5** erect, found **7** arrange, install **9** construct, establish, institute **10** inaugurate, prearrange

set upon 3 mug **5** beset, fly at **6** assail, attack **7** besiege, lunge at **9** pitch into

Seurat, Georges Pierre
born: **5** Paris **6** France
artwork: **9** The Chahut, The Circus, The Models, The Parade, The Uproar **10** The Bathers **12** Le Grand Jatte, The Yoked Cart **19** Une Baignade Asnieres **23** A Bathing Scene at Asnieres, The Bec du Hoc at Grandchamp **40** Sunday Afternoon on the Island of La Grand Jatte

Seuss, Dr
real name: **19** Theodore Seuss Geisel
author of: **12** If I Ran the Zoo **14** The Cat in the Hat **15** Green Eggs and Ham, Horton Hears a Who, If I Ran the Circus **19** Horton Hatches the Egg **23** Mister Brown Can Moo Can You? **26** Thidwick The Big-Hearted Moose, How the Grinch Stole Christmas

Seve
nickname of: **20** Severiano Ballesteros

Seven Against Thebes
author: **9** Aeschylus
character: **6** Ismene **8** Antigone, Eteocles **9** Polynices **11** Theban Women
seven heroes: **6** Tydeus **8** Adrastus, Capaneus **9** Polynices **10** Amphiaraus, Hippomedon **13** Parthenopaeus

Seven Beauties
director: **14** Lina Wertmuller
cast: **11** Fernando Rey **13** Shirley Stoler **17** Giancarlo Giannini

Seven Brides for Seven Brothers
director: **12** Stanley Donen
cast: **9** Tammy Rall **10** How-

ard Keel, Jane Powell **11** Julie Newmar (Newmeyer), Russ Tamblyn **12** Jeff Richards **14** Virginia Gibson
score: **11** Saul Chaplin **12** Johnny Mercer
choreography: **11** Michael Kidd

Seven Pillars of Wisdom
author: **10** T E Lawrence

Seven Samurai
director: **13** Akira Kurosawa
cast: **11** Yoshio Inaba **13** Toshiro Mifune **14** Takashi Shimura
remade as: **19** The Magnificent Seven

seven seas 6 Arctic, Indian **9** Antarctic **12** North Pacific, South Pacific **13** North Atlantic, South Atlantic

Seven Sisters colleges
5 Smith **6** Vassar **7** Barnard **8** Bryn Mawr **9** Radcliffe, Wellesley **12** Mount Holyoke

Seventeen
author: **15** Booth Tarkington
character: **7** Genesis **9** Miss Pratt, Mrs Baxter **10** Jane Baxter, May Parcher **21** William Sylvanus Baxter

Seventh Seal, The
director: **13** Ingmar Bergman
cast: **9** Nils Poppe **11** Max von Sydow **13** Bibi Andersson **17** Gunnar Bjornstrand

77 Sunset Strip
character: **6** J R Hale, Kookie (Gerald Lloyd Kookson III), Roscoe **7** Suzanne **11** Jeff Spencer, Rex Randolph **12** Stuart Bailey
cast: **9** Edd Byrnes **10** Louis Quinn, Roger Smith **11** Richard Long, Robert Logan **14** Jacqueline Beer **16** Efrem Zimbalist Jr
Kookie's sayings: **10** a dark seven **12** the ginchiest **13** piling up the Z's **14** lend me your comb **15** play like a pigeon **17** headache grapplers **22** keep the eyeballs rolling

seven wonders of the world 8 pyramids (Egypt) **12** Olympian Zeus (sculpted by Phidias) **15** Temple of Artemis (at Ephesus) **16** Colossus of Rhodes **22** Lighthouse at Alexandria **23** hanging gardens of Babylon (of Semiramis) **24** Mausoleum at Halicarnassus

Seven Year Itch, The
director: **11** Billy Wilder
cast: **8** Tom Ewell **10** Sonny Tufts **11** Evelyn Keyes, Vic-

tor Moore **13** Marilyn Monroe
setting: **11** New York City

sever 3 saw **4** part, rend, rive, tear **5** slice, split **6** bisect, cleave, cut off, lop off **7** disjoin, rupture, split up **8** amputate, break off, cut in two, dissolve, disunite, separate, truncate **9** dismember, terminate **10** disconnect **11** discontinue

several 3 own **4** a few, some **6** divers, single, sundry **7** certain, diverse, express, private, special **8** assorted, distinct, peculiar, personal, separate, specific **9** different, exclusive **10** individual, particular, respective **11** distinctive, independent

severe 4 cold, dour, grim, wild **5** cruel, grave, harsh, plain, rough, sober, stern, stiff **6** biting, bitter, brutal, chaste, fierce, fuming, raging, savage, sedate, simple, somber, strict, taxing **7** austere, cutting, drastic, extreme, furious, intense, painful, serious, uniform, violent **8** piercing, rigorous, ruthless, stinging, vigorous **9** dangerous, demanding, difficult, draconian, merciless, saturnine, turbulent, unadorned, unsparing **10** forbidding, restrained, tumultuous **11** distressing, undecorated, unrelenting **12** conservative

severed 6 cut off **8** detached **9** uncoupled, unhitched **10** unfastened **11** unconnected **12** disconnected

Severini, Gino
born: **5** Italy **7** Cortona
artwork: **9** Harlequin **15** The Armored Train **25** Dancer Sea and Vase of Flowers **32** Dynamic Hieroglyph of the Bal Tabarin

severity 5 rigor **7** cruelty **8** acrimony, violence **9** austerity, gruffness, harshness, sternness **10** asceticism, difficulty, strictness, stringency **11** seriousness **12** grievousness

Seville
former name: **8** Hispalis
landmark: **7** Alcazar, Giralda
plain: **9** Andalusia
river: **12** Guadalquivir
ruler: **5** Moors **6** Romans **7** Vandals **8** Abbasids, Almohads, Iberians **9** Visigoths **10** Almoravids
Spanish: **7** Sevilla

sew 3 hem **4** mend, seam,

tack **5** unite **6** fasten, ground, stitch, suture **10** run aground
loosely: 5 baste

sewage 5 waste **6** efflux, refuse **8** effluent **9** effluence

Seward, Dr
character in: 7 Dracula
author: 6 Stoker

sewing machine
invented by: 4 Howe

sex 4 Eros, love **6** coitus, gender, libido **7** coition **8** maleness **10** copulation, femaleness, femininity, generation, lovemaking **11** masculinity, procreation **12** reproduction

Sexton, Anne
author of: 15 All My Pretty Ones **22** To Bedlam and Part Way Back **23** The Awful Rowing Toward God

sexual 6 coital, erotic **7** amatory, genital, marital, sensual **8** conjugal, intimate, venereal **10** copulatory, generative, libidinous **11** procreative **12** reproductive

sexually stimulating 4 sexy **6** erotic, risque **9** salacious **10** suggestive **12** pornographic

sexy 4 lewd **5** bawdy **6** erotic **8** prurient **9** seductive **10** come-hither, coquettish, suggestive, voluptuous **11** flirtatious, provocative

---

Seychelles
capital/largest city:
8 Victoria
monetary unit: 4 cent
5 rupee
island: 4 Mahe **7** Aldabra, La Digue, Praslin **8** Farquhar **9** Desroches **10** Silhouette
highest point: 16 Morne Seychellois
sea: 6 Indian
people: 5 Asian **6** Creole, French, Indian **7** African, Chinese
leader: 4 Rene
7 Mancham
language: 6 Creole, French **7** English
religion: 8 Anglican
13 Roman Catholic

---

sforzando
music: 12 sudden accent

Shabbas 7 Sabbath

shabby 3 low **4** mean, poor,
torn, worn **5** cheap, dirty, mangy, raggy, ratty, seedy, sorry, tatty, tight **6** frayed, meager, ragged, sordid, unfair **7** ignoble, rundown, scruffy **8** beggarly, decaying, inferior, slovenly, unworthy, wretched **9** illiberal, miserable, neglected **10** ramshackle, threadbare, tumbledown, ungenerous **11** dilapidated **12** contemptible, deteriorated, dishonorable, impoverished

shabby bar 4 dive **5** joint **7** gin mill **9** honky-tonk

shack 3 hut **5** cabin **6** lean-to, shanty

shackle 3 bar, tie **4** balk, bind, cuff, curb, foil, rein **5** block, bonds, chain, check, cramp, cuffs, deter, irons, limit, stall **6** chains, fetter, hamper, hinder, hobble, hogtie, impede, pinion, retard, secure, tether, thwart **7** inhibit, manacle, prevent **8** encumber, handcuff, restrict **9** forestall, frustrate, hamstring, handcuffs **12** circumscribe

shackled 7 chained, in irons **8** in chains, manacled **10** handcuffed

shadchan, schatchen
10 matchmaker **14** marriage broker

Shaddai 3 God

shade 3 bit, dim, hue, jot **4** atom, cast, hint, hood, iota, tint, tone, veil, whit **5** blind, color, drape, tinge, touch, trace **6** awning, canopy, darken, screen, shadow, shield **7** curtain, modicum, shadows, shutter **8** darkness, particle, semidark **9** scintilla **10** suggestion
French: 7 soupcon
form: 6 spirit
location: 5 Hades

shadow, shadows 3 bit, dog **4** blot, hint, tail **5** cloud, ghost, hound, shade, smear, stain, stalk, taint, tinge, touch, trace, track, trail **6** blight, follow, pursue, smirch, smudge, threat **7** blemish, specter, whisper **8** penumbra **10** reflection, silhouette, suggestion

Shadow of a Doubt
director: 15 Alfred Hitchcock
cast: 10 Hume Cronyn **12** Joseph Cotten, Teresa Wright **14** Macdonald Carey **16** Patricia Collinge
remade as: 16 Step Down to Terror

Shadow of the Moon
author: 6 M M Kaye

Shadows on the Rock
author: 11 Willa Cather

shadowy 3 dim **5** shady **6** gloomy, unreal **7** obscure **8** illusory **9** tenebrous **10** indistinct **13** insubstantial

Shadrach
former name: 8 Hananiah
friend: 6 Daniel
companion: 7 Meshach **8** Abednego

shady 5 fishy **7** crooked, devious, dubious, shadowy **9** dishonest, unethical **10** suspicious **11** underhanded **12** disreputable, questionable **13** untrustworthy

shady dealings 5 fraud, graft **7** bribery **10** corruption, dishonesty

shaft 3 cut, pit, ray **4** barb, beam, dart, duct, flue, gibe, hilt, stem, vent, well **5** abyss, arrow, chasm, gleam, lance, patch, pylon, quill, shank, spear, spire, stalk, tower, trunk **6** cavity, column, funnel, handle, insult, pillar, streak, stream **7** affront, chimney, conduit, minaret, obelisk, spindle, steeple **8** brickbat, monolith, pilaster **9** aspersion **10** excavation

shaggy 5 bushy, downy, fuzzy, hairy, nappy, piled, wooly **6** tufted, woolly **7** bearded, hirsute, shagged, unshorn **9** whiskered **11** bewhiskered

shah 4 king **5** ruler **7** emperor, monarch **8** autocrat **9** sovereign

Shahaptian
tribe: 6 Numipu **8** Nez Perce

Shahn, Ben
born: 6 Kaunas **9** Lithuania
artwork: 5 Epoch **8** Handball **12** Seurat's Lunch, The Physicist **16** Pacific Landscape **18** Willis Avenue Bridge **28** The Passion of Sacco and Vanzetti

shake 3 jar, jog, mix **4** jerk, jolt, move, stir, stun, sway, wave **5** elude, quake, swing, touch **6** affect, bounce, jiggle, joggle, jostle, jounce, quaver, quiver, rattle, ruffle, shimmy, shiver, slough, totter, twitch, wobble **7** agitate, disturb, flicker, flutter, perturb, quaking, shudder, stagger, startle, tremble, unnerve, vibrate **8** brandish, disquiet, distress, flourish, frighten, throw off, unsettle, unstring **9** quivering, shivering, trembling **10** discompose, flickering, fluttering

shakedown 6 extort, payoff, search, tryout **7** testing **8** thorough **9** blackmail, extortion, hush money

Shakespeare, William *see* box

shakeup 5 purge **7** cleanup **8** turnover **10** clean sweep **11** realignment **13** rearrangement, redisposition, restructuring **14** redistribution, reorganization

shake up 3 mix **4** stir **5** churn **7** agitate, disturb

shakiness 6 tremor **10** insecurity **11** instability, uncertainty **12** unsteadiness

shaky 4 weak **5** frail, jumpy **6** flimsy, unsafe, unsure, wobbly **7** dubious, fidgety, fragile, halting, jittery, nervous, teetery **8** hesitant, insecure, unstable, unsteady, wavering **9** faltering, hazardous, quivering, teetering, tottering, trembling, tremulous, uncertain, undecided **10** inconstant, irresolute, precarious, unreliable, unresolved **11** vacillating **12** undependable

shallow 5 shoal **6** frothy, slight **7** surface, trivial **8** knee-deep, skin-deep, trifling **9** frivolous **11** meaningless, superficial, unimportant **13** insubstantial **15** inconsequential

shalom 5 peace

shalom aleichem 10 peace to you

sham 3 act **4** copy, fake **5** bogus, false, feign, fraud, phony, put on, trick **6** affect, assume, forged **7** feigned, forgery, imitate, pretend **8** pretense, simulate, spurious **9** imitation, pretended, simulated, synthetic **10** artificial, fraudulent **11** counterfeit, make-believe

Shamash
origin: **8** Akkadian
god of: **3** sun

shamble, shambles 4 limp **5** hitch, lurch, stall **6** hobble **7** shuffle **8** butchery **14** slaughterhouse

shame 5 guilt, odium **6** humble, stigma **7** chagrin, mortify, remorse, scandal **8** contempt, disgrace, dishonor, ignominy **9** disrepute, embarrass, humiliate **10** debasement, disrespect **11** degradation, humiliation, self-disgust **12** unworthiness **13** embarrassment, mortification **14** disappointment

shamed be the one who thinks evil of it
Latin: **20** honi soit qui mal y pense

shamefaced 5 sorry **7** abashed, crushed, humbled, put-down **8** blushing, sheepish **9** chagrined, disgraced, mortified **10** humiliated, remorseful **11** embarrassed

shameful 3 low **4** base, mean, vile **6** odious **7** heinous, ignoble **8** shocking, unworthy **9** dastardly, degrading **10** deplorable, despicable, inglorious, iniquitous, outrageous, villainous **11** disgraceful, ignominious, opprobrious **12** contemptible, dishonorable **13** reprehensible

shameless 4 pert **5** brash, saucy **6** brazen, wanton **7** forward, immoral **8** degraded, flagrant, immodest, impudent, indecent **9** abandoned, audacious, barefaced, boldfaced, dissolute, unabashed **10** indecorous, unblushing, unreserved **11** disgraceful **12** dishonorable

shamelessness 4 gall **5** brass, cheek **8** audacity **10** brazenness, effrontery **11** forwardness, presumption

Shamgar 11 Hebrew judge

shamus 7 gumshoe **9** detective **10** private eye **12** investigator

Shane
director: **13** George Stevens
cast: **8** Alan Ladd **9** Van Heflin **10** Jean Arthur **11** Jack Palance **12** Elisha Cook Jr **13** Edgar Buchanan **14** Brandon de Wilde

Shanghai
area: **23** International Settlement
landmark: **13** Long Hua Temple **17** People's Opera House **28** Shanghai Industrial Exhibition
river: **6** Wusung **7** Huang-P'u, Yangtze

Shangri-La *see* **5** Nepal

shanty 3 hut **5** cabin, hovel, shack **6** lean-to

shape 4 form, make, mold, trim **5** array, build, frame, guide, model, order **6** create, fettle, figure, health **7** contour, develop, fashion, outline, profile **8** physique **9** condition, construct, determine **10** silhouette **12** conformation **13** configuration

shapeless 5 baggy **8** formless **9** amorphous, irregular

shapely 3 fit **4** neat, trim **6** comely, gainly **11** symmetrical

shaper 9 architect, innovator **10** instigator, prime mover

Shapley, Howard
field: **9** astronomy
studied: **6** galaxy

Shapwailutan
tribe: **5** Modoc **11** Kiowa Apache

Shardik
author: **12** Richard Adams

share 3 cut **4** dole, part **5** allot, cut up, quota, split **6** ration **7** deal out, divvy up, mete out, percent, portion **8** allocate **9** allotment, allowance, apportion **10** percentage **13** apportionment

shared 5 joint **6** common, public **7** general **8** communal **10** collective

---

Shakespeare, William
also: **10** bard of Avon **12** immortal bard
author of: **6** Hamlet, Henry V **7** Henry IV, Henry VI, Macbeth, Othello **8** King John, King Lear, Pericles (Prince of Tyre) **9** Cymbeline, Henry VIII, Richard II **10** Coriolanus, Richard III, The Tempest **11** As You Like It **12** Julius Caesar, Twelfth Night **13** Rape of Lucrece, Timon of Athens **14** Romeo and Juliet, The Winter's Tale, Venus and Adonis **15** Titus Andronicus **16** Love's Labour's Lost **17** Measure for Measure, The Comedy of Errors **18** Antony and Cleopatra, Troilus and Cressida **19** Much Ado About Nothing, The Merchant of Venice, The Taming of the Shrew **20** All's Well That Ends Well **21** A Midsummer Night's Dream **22** The Merry Wives of Windsor **23** The Two Gentlemen of Verona
birthplace: **15** Stratford-on-Avon
theater: **4** Swan **5** Globe
wife: **12** Anne Hathaway

share one's sorrow 7 condole **10** sympathize
11 commiserate

Sharif, Omar
real name: **15** Michael
Shalhoub
born: **5** Egypt **10** Alexandria
roles: **3** Che **9** Dr Zhivago,
Funny Girl, Funny Lady
11 Genghis Khan **12** Nick
Arnstein **16** Lawrence of
Arabia
expert on: **6** bridge

shark 3 ace **4** fish **5** cheat
6 expert, usurer, wizard
8 predator **9** trickster
12 extortionist

sharp *see* **box**

Sharp, Becky
character in: **10** Vanity Fair
author: **9** Thackeray

sharp-cornered 6 jagged
7 angular

sharp dresser 3 fop **4** dude
5 dandy **12** Beau Brummell,
clotheshorse, fashion plate

sharpen 4 edge, hone, whet
5 grind, strop

sharply pointed 4 keen
5 acute **6** spiked **7** tapered
8 piercing **10** rapierlike
11 needle-nosed

sharpness 3 nip, wit **4** edge,
tang **6** acuity, acumen **7** acidity, insight **8** acerbity, acridity,
acrimony, keenness, pungency,
saliency, tartness **9** acuteness,
alertness, quickness **10** caus-
ticity, craftiness
12 perspicacity

sharp pain 4 pang, stab
5 cramp **6** twinge

sharpshooter
French: **10** tirailleur

sharp-sighted 5 acute
6 shrewd **8** piercing **9** far-
seeing **10** discerning, perceptive **11** penetrating
13 perspicacious

sharp-witted 4 keen **5** acute,
alert, canny, quick, smart
6 astute, brainy, clever

Shatner, William
born: **6** Canada **8** Montreal
roles: **8** Star Trek, T J
Hooker **17** Captain James T
Kirk

shatter 4 rive, ruin **5** break,
burst, crack, crash, crush,
quash, smash, split, spoil, upset, wreck **6** squash, sunder,
topple **7** crumble, destroy, explode, scuttle **8** demolish, fracture, overturn, splinter
9 devastate, pulverize

shattered 6 broken, dashed
7 crushed, smashed **8** crumbled, decrepit **9** flustered
10 demolished, fragmented,
splintered, tumbledown
11 crestfallen, demoralized
13 disillusioned, disintegrated

shave 3 cut, lop, mow **4** clip,
crop, dock, pare, skin, snip,
trim **5** brush, graze, prune,
shear **6** barber, cut off, fleece,
glance, scrape **7** scissor

Shaw, George Bernard
author of: **7** Candida **9** Pygmalion, Saint Joan **12** Major
Barbara **13** Arms and the
Man **14** Man and Super-
man **15** Heartbreak House
16 Back to Methuselah
17 The Devil's Disciple, The
Doctor's Dilemma **18** Caesar
and Cleopatra **19** Androcles
and the Lion **20** Mrs Warren's Profession
member of: **13** Fabian
Society

Shaw, Irwin
author of: **12** Top of the
Hill **13** The Young Lions
14 Beggarman Thief, Rich
Man Poor Man

Shaw, Robert
born: **7** England
12 Westhoughton
wife: **7** Mary Ure
roles: **4** Jaws **7** The Deep
8 The Sting **12** Swashbuckler **13** The Caretakers **17** A
Man for All Seasons
20 Force Ten from Navarone **28** The Taking of Pelham One-Two-Three
author of: **14** The Hiding
Place **21** The Man in the
Glass Booth

Shawabti
origin: **8** Egyptian
form: **8** figurine
where used: **6** burial

shawl 4 wrap **5** scarf **6** mantle
7 paisley **10** fascinator
Mexican: **6** serape
Spanish: **8** mantilla

Shawnee
language family: **9** Algonkian **10** Algonquian
location: **4** Ohio **6** Kansas
8 Missouri, Oklahoma
9 Tennessee **12** Pennsylvania **13** South Carolina
leader: **8** Tecumseh
11 Tenskwatawa
related to: **8** Delaware

She
author: **13** H Rider Haggard

shear 3 cut, lop **4** clip, crop,
snip, trim **5** prune, shave
6 fleece, remove **7** deprive, relieve, scissor

Shearer, Norma
real name: **17** Edith Norma
Shearer
born: **6** Canada **8** Montreal
husband: **14** Irving Thalberg
roles: **8** The Women **9** A
Free Soul **11** The Divorcee
(Oscar) **14** Romeo and Juliet, Their Own Desire
15 Marie Antoinette **26** The
Barretts of Wimpole Street

shears 5 clips, trims **6** prunes
7 pruners **8** clippers, scissors,
trimmers

sheath 3 pod **4** case, coat,
skin **6** casing, jacket **7** capsule,
coating, wrapper **8** covering,
envelope, membrane, scabbard,
slipcase, wrapping **9** container
10 receptacle

sheathing 6 casing, siding
8 covering

Sheba
father: **6** Bichri, Joktan, Raa-
mah **7** Jokshan

---

sharp 3 sly **4** acid, curt, fine, foxy, high, keen, sour, tart,
wily **5** acrid, acute, alert, angry, awake, blunt, clear, cruel,
edged, gruff, harsh, nippy, piked, quick, rapid, salty, sheer,
spiny, steep **6** abrupt, artful, astute, barbed, biting, bitter,
clever, crafty, crusty, fierce, keenly, marked, pointy, severe,
shrewd, shrill, strong, sudden, thorny, tricky, unkind
7 acutely, alertly, angular, bearish, bristly, brusque, caustic,
closely, crabbed, cunning, cutting, drastic, exactly, extreme,
galling, intense, nipping, piquant, pointed, prickly, quickly,
raucous, toothed, violent **8** abruptly, distinct, on the dot,
piercing, promptly, scathing, serrated, spiteful, stinging, strident, suddenly, venomous, vertical, vigilant, vinegary **9** conniving, deceptive, excessive, on the nose, precisely,
rancorous, unethical, vitriolic **10** contriving, discerning, immoderate, inordinate, perceptive, punctually **11** attentively,
calculating, on the button, penetrating, precipitous **12** unprincipled, unscrupulous **13** precipitously
French: **5** juste
Spanish: **7** en punto

grandfather: 4 Cush **7** Keturah
people of: 7 Sabeans

Shebat 19 eleventh Hebrew month

she carved it
Latin: 8 sculpsit

shed 3 hut **4** cast, doff, drop, emit, molt **5** exude, hovel, shack, spill, strew, throw **6** lean-to, shanty, shower, slough, spread **7** cast off, discard, let fall, let flow, radiate, scatter **8** disperse, lose hair, toolshed **9** broadcast, discharge, tool house **10** distribute **11** disseminate, outbuilding

she died
Latin: 5 obiit

shed light on 7 clarify, explain **9** elucidate, explicate, make clear, make plain **10** illuminate

She Done Him Wrong
director: 13 Lowell Sherman
cast: 7 Mae West (Diamond Lil) **9** Cary Grant, Noah Beery **13** Gilbert Roland

shed tears 3 cry, sob **4** bawl, weep **6** boohoo **7** blubber

Sheehy, Gail
author of: 8 Passages **14** The Pathfinders

Sheeler, Charles
born: 14 Philadelphia PA
artwork: 9 Landscape, Upper Deck **11** Incantation **12** City Interior, Rolling Power **15** Bucks County Barn, River Rouge Plant **31** American Landscape Nineteen Thirty

sheen 4 glow **5** glaze, gleam, glint, gloss, shine **6** luster, patina, polish **7** burnish, glister, glitter, shimmer **8** radiance **9** shininess **10** brightness, brilliance, effulgence, glossiness, luminosity, refulgence **12** luminousness, resplendence

Sheen, Martin
real name: 12 Ramon Estevez
born: 8 Dayton OH
son: 12 Charlie Sheen **13** Emilio Estevez
roles: 8 Badlands **12** The Believers **13** Apocalypse Now **14** Catch Twenty-two **18** The Subject Was Roses **27** The Execution of Private Slovik

Sheena, Queen of the Jungle
creator: 8 SR Powell **13** W Morgan Thomas
character: 3 Bob **4** Chim

she engraved it
Latin: 8 sculpsit

sheep
breed: 5 Iraqi **6** Hirrik, Merino, Panama, Romney, Somali **7** Cheviot, Karakul, Lincoln, Suffolk, Targhee **8** Columbia, Cotswold, Tatarian **9** Montadale, Romeldale, Southdown **10** Corriedale, Dorset Down, Dorset Horn, Shropshire, Sikkim Bera **11** Rambouillet **13** Hampshire Down **15** Border Leicester
female: 3 ewe
family: 7 Bovidae
genus: 4 Ovis
group of: 5 drove, flock **6** cosset
meat: 4 lamb **6** mutton
oil from: 7 lanolin
wild: 5 urial **6** argali **7** bighorn, mouflon
young: 4 lamb **7** lambkin **8** yearling

sheepish 3 shy **4** meek **5** timid **6** docile, guilty, humble **7** abashed, ashamed, bashful, fearful, hangdog, passive, servile **8** blushing, obedient, obeisant, timorous, yielding **9** chagrined, chastened, diffident, mortified, shrinking, tractable **10** shamefaced, submissive **11** embarrassed, subservient, unassertive, unresisting

sheepishness 7 chagrin **8** docility, meekness **10** diffidence **11** bashfulness **12** tractability **13** embarrassment **14** submissiveness **15** unassertiveness

Sheep Well, The
also: 13 Fuente Ovejuna
author: 10 Lope de Vega

sheer 4 fine, pure, thin **5** bluff, filmy, gauzy, plumb, sharp, steep, total, utter **6** abrupt **7** perfect, unmixed **8** absolute, complete, gossamer, vertical **9** out and out, unalloyed, unbounded, unlimited **10** consummate, diaphanous **11** precipitous, transparent, unmitigated, unqualified **12** unrestrained **13** perpendicular, unadulterated, unconditional

sheet 3 top **4** coat, film, leaf, pane, slab **5** layer, panel, piece, plate **6** sheath, square **7** blanket, coating, overlay **8** bed sheet, covering, membrane **9** rectangle

shegetz 12 non-Jewish boy, non-Jewish man

Sheldon, Sidney
author of: 9 Bloodline **12** Rage of Angels, The Na-

ked Face **15** If Tomorrow Comes **20** A Stranger in the Mirror **22** The Other Side of Midnight

shelf 4 bank, prop, reef, slab **5** ledge, shoal **6** mantel, mantle **7** bedrock, bracket, stratum **9** supporter **11** mantelpiece, mantlepiece

shell 3 pod **4** bomb, case, hulk, hull, husk, shot **5** pound, round, shuck **6** bullet, fire on, pepper, rocket **7** barrage, bombard, grenade, missile **8** carapace, skeleton **9** cartridge, framework **10** projectile

shellac 4 beat, drub, lick, whip **7** clobber, lacquer, trounce, varnish

Shelley, Mary Wollstonecraft
father: 13 William Godwin
husband: 18 Percy Bysshe Shelley
author of: 12 Frankenstein

Shelley, Percy Bysshe
author of: 7 Adonais, Alastor **8** Queen Mab, The Cenci **10** To a Skylark **16** A Defence of Poetry, Ode to the West Wind **17** Prometheus Unbound

shellfish 4 clam, crab **5** prawn **6** cockle, mussel, oyster, shrimp **7** abalone, lobster, mollusk, scallop **8** barnacle, crawfish, crayfish **9** trunkfish **10** crustacean **13** softshell crab
spawn: 4 spat

shell out 3 pay **6** expend **8** allocate, disburse, dispense **10** contribute

shelter 5 cover, guard, haven, house, lodge **6** asylum, defend, harbor, refuge, safety, shield, take in **7** care for, housing, lodging, protect **8** quarters, security **9** safeguard, sanctuary **10** protection

Sheltered Life
author: 12 Ellen Glasgow

shelve 5 defer, table **6** put off **7** suspend **8** lay aside, postpone, put aside, put on ice, set aside **10** pigeonhole

Shem
father: 4 Noah
brother: 3 Ham **7** Japheth
son: 8 Arphazed
descendant of: 6 Semite

shenanigans 5 sport **6** antics, capers, hijinx, pranks, stunts, tricks **8** deviltry, mischief, nonsense **9** highjinks, horseplay, silliness **10** buffoonery, tomfoolery **11** roguishness **12** monkeyshines, sportiveness **14** monkey business **15** mischievousness

she painted it
Latin: **6** pinxit

shepherd 4 herd, lead, show, tend **5** guard, guide, pilot **6** direct, escort, herder, keeper, patron, shield **7** protect, shelter **8** champion, defender, guardian, herdsman, provider **9** custodian, protector, safeguard **10** benefactor

Shepherdess and the Sweep, The
author: **21** Hans Christian Andersen

shepherds
god of: **3** Pan **6** Tammuz

sherbet 3 ade, ice **6** sorbet **7** dessert

Shere Khan
character in: **14** The Jungle Books
author: **7** Kipling

Sheridan, Ann
real name: **16** Clara Lou Sheridan
nickname: **9** Oomph Girl
born: **8** Denton TX
husband: **10** Scott McKay **11** George Brent **12** Edward Norris
roles: **8** King's Row **11** Silver River **12** Nora Prentiss **16** Wings for the Eagle **20** Angels with Dirty Faces

Sheridan, Philip H
served in: **8** Civil War **10** Indian Wars
side: **5** Union
commander of: **19** Army of the Shenandoah
rank: **22** general in chief of US army
battle: **9** Five Forks **10** Cedar Creek, Winchester **11** Chattanooga, Chickamauga, Fisher's Hill **12** Sayler's Creek **18** Wilderness Campaign

Sheridan, Richard Brinsley
author of: **9** The Critic, The Duenna, The Rivals **18** A Trip to Scarborough **19** The School for Scandal

sheriff 7 officer **9** constable

Sheriff of Nottingham
character in: **9** Robin Hood

Sherman, William Tecumseh
nickname: **4** Cump
served in: **8** Civil War **10** Mexican War
side: **5** Union
battle: **6** Shiloh **7** Atlanta, Bull Run **8** Savannah **9** Vicksburg **11** Chattanooga **15** Kenesaw Mountain
fought against: **8** Johnston

rank: **20** general in chief of army
famous for: **13** march to the sea (Georgia)
established: **29** Command and General Staff College
saying: **9** War is hell

sherry
type: **4** wine **6** brandy
origin: **5** Spain
varieties: **4** fino (dry) **7** amoroso (sweet), oloroso (medium dry)
drink: **6** Adonis, Bamboo **9** Andalusia
with gin: **11** Renaissance
with vermouth: **6** Brazil

Sherwood, Robert E
author: **13** Idiot's Delight **15** Reunion in Vienna **18** The Petrified Forest **19** Roosevelt and Hopkins, There Shall Be No Night **20** Abe Lincoln in Illinois
screenplay: **22** The Best Years of Our Lives

she sculptured it
Latin: **8** sculpsit

she speaks
Latin: **8** loquitur

She Stoops to Conquer
author: **15** Oliver Goldsmith
character: **6** Marlow **8** Hastings **10** Sir Charles **11** Tony Lumpkin **12** Mr Hardcastle **13** Mrs Hardcastle **14** Kate Hardcastle **16** Constance Neville

she wrote (it)
Latin: **8** scripsit

shibah, shivah 14 mourning period
literally: **9** seven days

shibboleth 6 byword, saying, slogan **8** apothegm **9** catchword

Shibboleth 17 Gileadite password

shield 4 keep, star **5** aegis, badge, cover, guard, house, shade **6** buffer, button, emblem, ensign, fender, harbor, screen, secure **7** buckler, defense, protect, shelter **8** insignia, keep safe, preserve **9** medallion, protecter, protector, safeguard **10** escutcheon, protection

Shield (of Sobieski)
constellation of: **6** Scutum

shielded 6 hidden **7** guarded **9** concealed, protected, sheltered

Shields, Brooke
real name: **20** Christa Brooke Shields
born: **9** New York NY

roles: **10** Pretty Baby **11** Endless Love **13** The Blue Lagoon

shift 2 go **4** move, slip, vary, veer **5** hitch, stint **6** change, swerve, switch **7** chemise, turning, veering **8** exchange, straight, transfer **9** deviation, transpose, variation **10** alteration, assignment, reposition **11** alternating, fluctuation, interchange **12** modification
French: **8** camisole

shiftless 3 lax **4** idle, lazy **8** careless, inactive, indolent, slothful **10** ne'er-do-well **13** lackadaisical **14** good-fornothing **15** unconscientious

shifty 4 foxy, wily **6** crafty, sneaky, tricky **7** cunning, evasive **8** scheming, slippery **9** conniving, deceitful, dishonest **10** contriving, unreliable **11** maneuvering, treacherous **13** untrustworthy

Shikasta
author: **12** Doris Lessing

shiksa 13 non-Jewish girl **14** non-Jewish woman

shillelagh 4 club **5** stick **6** cudgel **9** truncheon

shilly-shally 5 stall, waver **6** dawdle, dither, falter, seesaw **8** hesitate **9** fluctuate, hem and haw, oscillate, vacillate

shilly-shallying 8 dawdling, wavering **9** uncertain, undecided **10** indecision, indecisive, irresolute **11** vacillation

Shimazaki Toson
author of: **5** Hakai **20** The Broken Commandment

shimmer 4 beam, glow **5** blink, dance, flash, gleam, quake, shine, waver **6** quiver, shiver **7** flicker, flutter, glisten, sparkle, tremble, twinkle, vibrate **8** blinking **9** coruscate **11** scintillate **12** phosphoresce

shindig 3 hop **4** ball, bash, prom **5** dance, party **6** affair, shindy **7** blowout, revelry **9** barn dance, festivity, record hop **10** masked ball, the dansant
French: **4** fete, gala **6** soiree **9** bal masque **10** bal costume

shine 3 wax **4** beam, buff, glow **5** blink, flash, glare, gleam, glint, gloss, light, rub up, sheen **6** dazzle, luster, polish, waxing **7** buffing, burnish, flicker, glimmer, glisten, glister, glitter, radiate, shimmer, sparkle, twinkle **8** brighten, radiance **9** coruscate, irradiate,

polishing 10 brightness, brilliance, burnishing, luminosity **11** scintillate **12** illumination, luminousness **13** incandescence

shininess 5 gleam, glint, gloss, sheen **6** luster, polish **7** shimmer

shining 5 aglow **6** glossy **7** glowing, radiant **8** gleaming, luminous, lustrous **9** brilliant, effulgent **11** illustrious **12** incandescent

Shining, The
author: **11** Stephen King

shiny 6 bright, glossy **7** glaring, glowing, radiant **8** gleaming, luminous, lustrous, polished **9** brilliant, burnished, effulgent, sparkling **10** glistening, glittering, shimmering **12** incandescent **13** scintillating

ship 4 crew, send **5** craft, liner, route, tramp, yacht **6** packet, tanker, vessel **7** carrier, cruiser, forward, steamer **8** dispatch **9** destroyer, freighter, steamship, transport **10** ocean liner

Ship of Fools
author: **19** Katherine Anne Porter
director: **13** Stanley Kramer
cast: **9** Jose Greco, Lee Marvin **10** Jose Ferrer **11** George Segal, Oscar Werner, Vivien Leigh **14** Simone Signoret **15** Elizabeth Ashley

shipshape 4 neat, snug, taut, tidy, trip, trim **5** tight **6** spruce **7** orderly

Shirer, William L
author of: **28** The Collapse of the Third Republic **29** The Rise and Fall of the Third Reich

shirk 4 duck, shun **5** avoid, dodge, elude, evade **6** escape, eschew, ignore **7** goof off, neglect **8** malinger, sidestep **9** goldbrick

shirker 5 piker **6** dodger, evader, loafer, rotter, truant **7** deserter, quitter, slacker **9** goldbrick **10** backslider, malingerer

Shirley Temple
ingredient: **9** ginger ale, grenadine
also called: **9** Roy Rogers

shirr 5 crimp, smock **6** gather, pucker **8** bake eggs

shirt 3 top **4** sark **5** frock, waist **6** blouse, bodice **10** underwaist

shirty 5 angry, irked, testy, vexed **7** annoyed **9** irritated **11** disgruntled

Shittimwood 12 Biblical tree

shiver 5 quake, shake **6** quaver, shimmy **7** shudder, tremble

shivers 3 bit **5** piece, shard **6** sliver **8** fragment

shivery 3 icy, raw **4** cold, cool **5** brisk, chill, crisp, nippy **6** arctic, biting, bitter, chilly, frigid, frosty, wintry **7** quaking, trembly **8** chilling **9** quivering **11** penetrating

shoal 3 bar **4** bank, flat **5** crowd, shelf **6** school **7** sand bar, shallow **8** sand bank

shock 3 jar, mat, mop **4** blow, bush, cock, crop, daze, jolt, mane, mass, pile, rick, rock, stun, turn **5** scare, shake, sheaf, stack, start, upset **6** appall, bundle, dismay, impact, offend, revolt, thatch, trauma **7** astound, disgust, disturb, horrify, outrage, perturb, stagger, startle, stupefy **8** astonish, bowl over, disquiet, distress, paralyze, surprise, unsettle **9** collision, overwhelm **10** concussion, discompose, disconcert **11** disturbance **13** consternation

shocking 4 foul **5** awful **6** grisly, horrid, odious **7** ghastly, hideous, jarring, jolting **8** gruesome, horrible, indecent, terrible, wretched **9** abhorrent, appalling, frightful, monstrous, offensive, repellent, repugnant, revolting, startling, upsetting **10** abominable, astounding, detestable, disgusting, disturbing, horrifying, outrageous, perturbing, scandalous, staggering, stupefying, surprising, unsettling **11** astonishing, disgraceful, disquieting **12** insufferable, overwhelming **13** disconcerting, reprehensible

shoddy 3 low **4** base, mean, poor **5** dirty, nasty, tacky **6** shabby, sloppy, stingy **7** lowdown, miserly **8** careless, inferior, slipshod **9** haphazard, negligent, niggardly **10** second-rate, ungenerous **11** inefficient **12** contemptible **13** inconsiderate, reprehensible

shoe
French: **9** chaussure

shoemaker 7 cobbler **9** bootmaker

Shoemaker's Holiday, The
author: **12** Thomas Dekker

Shoes of the Fisherman, The
author: **11** Morris L West

Shogun
author: **12** James Clavell

Sholokhov, Mikhail
author of: **19** And Quiet Flows the Don **21** The Virgin Soul Upturned

shoo 3 out **4** away, oust, rout, scat **5** be off, chase, leave, scram **6** beat it, be gone, depart, get out, go away **7** cast out, get lost, vamoose

shoot 3 bud, fly, hit **4** bolt, cast, dart, dash, drop, fell, fire, hurl, jump, kill, leap, nick, pelt, plug, race, rain, rush, stem, tear, toss, twig, wing **5** eject, fling, go off, hurry, shell, sling, speed, spray, sprig, spurt, sweep, throw, waste **6** charge, launch, let fly, pepper, propel, riddle, shower, spring, sprout **7** bombard, explode, pick off, tendril **8** catapult, detonate, open fire **9** discharge

Shootist, The
director: **9** Don Siegal
cast: **9** John Wayne, Ron Howard **10** Hugh O'Brien **11** Harry Morgan, Sheree North **12** James Stewart, Lauren Bacall, Richard Boone **13** John Carradine **15** Scatman Crothers

Shoot the Piano Player
director: **16** Francois Truffaut
cast: **11** Marie Dubois **12** Nicole Berger **14** Michele Mercier **15** Charles Aznavour
setting: **5** Paris

shoot up 4 rise, soar **6** rocket

shop 3 buy **4** hunt, look, mart, mill **5** plant, store, works **6** browse, market, studio **7** factory **8** emporium, purchase, workshop **9** patronize **10** windowshop **13** establishment
French: **7** atelier **8** boutique

shopkeeper 6 dealer, monger, trader, vendor **8** merchant, purveyor, retailer **9** tradesman

shopworn 5 banal, corny, faded, stale, tired, trite, vapid **6** jejune **10** threadbare

shore 4 bank, hold, land, prop **5** beach, brace, brink, coast **6** hold up, margin, strand **7** bolster, bulwark, seaside, support, sustain **8** buttress, mainstay, seaboard, seacoast, underpin **9** reinforce, riverbank, waterside **10** strengthen
Latin: **10** terra firma

shorebird 3 auk **4** rail, sora **5** snipe, stilt, wader **6** avocet, curlew, plover, puffin **7** lapwing **8** woodcock **9** guillemot, sandpiper **13** oyster catcher

shore up 4 prop **5** brace
6 prop up **7** bolster, support
8 buttress **9** reinforce

short 3 low **4** curt, lean, slim,
thin **5** brief, cross, elfin, fleet,
gruff, hasty, pygmy, quick,
runty, scant, sharp, small,
squat, terse, testy, tight
6 abrupt, bantam, little, meager, scanty, scarce, skimpy,
slight, sparse, stubby
7 brusque, compact, concise,
cursory, lacking, limited, not
long, not tall, slender, stunted,
summary, wanting **8** abridged,
abruptly, dwarfish, fleeting,
impolite, snappish, succinct,
suddenly, unawares **9** condensed, curtailed, deficient,
impatient, momentary, niggardly, pint-sized, truncated
10 by surprise, diminutive,
short-lived **11** abbreviated, ill-
tempered, Lilliputian, pocket-
sized **12** insufficient **13** precipitously **14** without warning

shortage 4 lack, want
6 dearth **7** deficit **8** leanness,
scarcity, sparsity **9** shortfall
10 deficiency, inadequacy,
scantiness, sparseness
13 insufficiency

shortcoming 4 flaw **5** fault
6 defect, foible **7** blemish, failing, failure, frailty **8** drawback, handicap, weakness
10 deficiency, inadequacy
12 imperfection

shorten 3 cut **4** clip, pare,
trim **5** prune, shave, shear
6 lessen, reduce **7** abridge, curtail, cut down **8** condense,
contract, cut short, decrease,
diminish **10** abbreviate

shortening 3 fat, oil **4** lard,
oleo **6** butter, digest **7** cutting,
summary **8** abstract, synopsis,
trimming **9** hemming up, mar-
garine, reduction **11** abridgement, compression,
contraction, curtailment
12 abbreviation, condensation

short form 6 digest, precis
7 summary **8** abstract, synopsis **11** abridgement, contraction **12** abbreviation,
condensation

**Short Happy Life of Francis
Macomber, The**
author: **15** Ernest Hemingway

short journey 5 jaunt **6** outing **7** day trip **9** excursion

short-lived 5 brief **7** passing
8 fleeting **9** ephemeral, momentary, temporary, transient
10 evanescent, transitory,
unenduring **11** impermanent
24 here today and gone
tomorrow

shortly 4 anon, soon **7** by and
by **8** directly, in a trice,
promptly **9** forthwith, presently **10** before long
11 immediately

short narrative 5 essay,
story **6** sketch **8** anecdote
10 short story

shortsighted 4 rash **6** myopic
7 foolish **8** careless, heedless,
purblind, reckless, weak-eyed
9 amblyopic, imprudent **10** ill-
advised, incautious, unthinking **11** improvident, injudicious, nearsighted,
thoughtless **12** undiscerning
13 uncircumspect

short-tempered 4 curt **5** cross,
huffy, sharp, testy **6** abrupt,
cranky, crusty, grumpy, shirty,
touchy **7** bearish, grouchy,
peevish, waspish **8** choleric,
snappish **9** irascible, irritable,
splenetic **10** ill-humored, out
of sorts, short-fused **11** hot-
tempered, ill-tempered
12 cantankerous

Shosha
author: **19** Isaac Bashevis
Singer

Shoshone (Snake)
language family:
10 Shoshonean
location: **4** Utah **5** Idaho
6 Nevada **7** Wyoming
translator: **9** Sacagawea

Shoshonean
tribe: **4** Hopi, Moki **5** Snake
6 Hopitu, Paiute **7** Bannock
8 Comanche, Shoshoni

**Shostakovich, Dmitri
(Dimitri)**
born: **6** Russia **12** St
Petersburg
composer of: **7** The Nose
9 Leningrad (symphony No
7) **11** May the First **12** The
Golden Age **17** Katerina Is-
mailova **19** Lady Macbeth of
Mzensk

shot 2 go **3** hit, try **4** dose,
move, play, toss **5** balls, blast,
crack, drive, essay, guess,
salvo, slugs, throw **6** beat-up,
archer, bowman, chance, report, ruined, shabby, stroke,
volley **7** attempt, bullets, gun-
fire, shooter, surmise, worn-
out **8** decrepit, marksman, rifleman **9** discharge, explosion,
fusillade, injection **10** ammunition, conjecture, detonation
11 dilapidated, projectiles
12 falling apart, sharpshooter

shot in the arm 4 lift
5 boost **6** uplift **8** stimulus
13 encouragement

shot in the dark 5 guess
6 notion, theory **9** guesswork,

suspicion **10** assumption, conjecture, hypothesis

shoulder 3 rim **4** bank, bear,
brow, bump, edge, push, side,
take **5** brink, carry, crest, elbow, lunge, shove, skirt,
verge **6** assume, border, jostle,
margin, take on, thrust, uphold **7** scapula, support, sustain **8** clavicle **9** undertake

shoulder blade 7 scapula
8 omoplate **9** bladebone

shout 3 cry **4** bawl, call, hoot,
howl, roar, yell, yelp **5** burst,
cheer, hollo, whoop **6** bellow,
chorus, clamor, cry out, holler, hurrah, huzzah, outcry,
scream, shriek **7** call out, exclaim, screech, thunder **8** outburst **9** hue and cry
10 hullabaloo

shout down 3 boo **4** hiss
6 hoot at, revile **7** catcall, condemn **8** denounce, drown
out

shove 4 bump, butt, jolt, prod,
push **5** boost, crowd, drive, elbow, force, impel, nudge
6 joggle, jostle, propel, thrust
8 shoulder

show *see* **box**

Showboat
author: **10** Edna Ferber

showcase 7 cabinet, counter,
display, exhibit, vitrine

showdown 3 war **6** battle, climax, combat, crisis **7** face-off
8 clashing, conflict **9** collision,
encounter **13** confrontation

shower 3 wet **4** fall, pour,
rain, rush **5** flood, salvo,
spray, surge **6** deluge, lavish,
splash, stream, volley, wealth
7 barrage, bombard, drizzle,
torrent **8** downpour, plethora,
sprinkle **9** profusion **10** cloudburst, inundation
11 bombardment

showiness 7 glitter **8** splendor
9 jazziness **10** flashiness **11** ostentation **14** grandiloquence

Show-me State
nickname of: **8** Missouri

show-off 6 egoist **7** boaster,
egotist, windbag **8** braggart,
fanfaron, flaunter, strutter
9 extrovert, swaggerer
11 braggadocio **13** cock of the
walk, exhibitionist **14** life of
the party

showpiece 3 gem **5** jewel,
pearl, pride, prize **6** rarity,
wonder **7** classic, paragon
8 treasure **10** masterwork
11 chef d'oeuvre, masterpiece,
prizewinner **17** piece de
resistance

show 4 bare, bill, fair, give, lead, mark, play, pomp, pose, sham, sign 5 argue, coach, drama, endow, favor, front, grant, guide, movie, opera, prove, teach, token, tutor, usher 6 appear, attest, ballet, bestow, comedy, direct, effect, evince, expose, hint at, impart, inform, lavish, reveal, school, tender, unveil 7 bear out, bespeak, certify, conduct, confirm, display, exhibit, explain, lay bare, musical, picture, pretext, proffer, program, suggest, uncover 8 ceremony, delusion, disclose, dispense, evidence, illusion, indicate, instruct, intimate, manifest, operetta, point out, pretense, vaunting 9 establish, make clear, make known, represent, spectacle 10 appearance, disclosure, distribute, exhibition, exposition, expression, impression, indication, pretension, production, revelation 11 affectation, attestation, corroborate, counterfeit, demonstrate, performance, testimonial 12 bring to light, substantiate 13 demonstration, entertainment, manifestation, motion picture

show up 4 come 5 outdo 6 appear, arrive, attend, crop up, expose, loom up, reveal, turn up 9 be present 11 come to light, make a fool of 12 come into view 13 become visible

showy 4 loud 5 gaudy, vivid 6 flashy, florid, garish, ornate 7 pompous 8 colorful, gorgeous, imposing, splendid, striking 9 brilliant 11 magnificent, pretentious 12 ostentatious

Shqyptare, Shqiprija, Shqiperi see 7 Albania

shred 3 bit, ion, jot, rag 4 atom, band, hair, iota, spot, whit 5 grain, piece, scrap, speck, strip, trace 6 morsel, ribbon, sliver, tatter 7 snippet 8 fragment, molecule, particle 9 scintilla

shrew 3 hag, nag 5 harpy, scold, vixen, yenta 6 kvetch, virago 7 she-wolf 8 battle-ax, fishwife, harridan, spitfire 9 termagant, Xanthippe

shrewd 3 sly 4 foxy, keen, wily, wise 5 acute, cagey, canny, quick, sharp, slick, smart 6 artful, astute, clever, crafty, shifty, smooth, tricky 7 careful, cunning, knowing, probing, prudent 8 cautious, piercing, scheming, sensible, slippery 9 designing, farseeing, sagacious 10 contriving, discerning, farsighted, perceptive 11 calculating, circumspect, intelligent, penetrating, quick-witted, self-serving, sharp-witted 12 disingenuous 13 Machiavellian, perspicacious

shrewdness 6 acumen 7 cunning, slyness 8 foxiness, keenness, wiliness 9 acuteness, cageyness, sharpness, slickness, smartness 10 artfulness, astuteness, cleverness, craftiness, smoothness, trickiness 11 carefulness, discernment 12 slipperiness 16 disingenuousness

shriek 3 cry 4 call, hoot, howl, peal, yell, yelp 5 shout, whoop 6 cry out, holler, outcry, scream, squawk, squeak, squeal 7 screech

shrift 7 penance 9 atonement, expiation 10 confession

shrill 4 high, loud 6 piping 7 blaring, raucous 8 piercing, strident 9 clamorous 10 screeching 11 high-pitched, penetrating

shrine 5 altar 6 chapel, church, temple 7 sanctum 8 monument 9 sanctuary

shrink 3 ebb, shy 4 balk, duck, wane 5 cower, demur, dry up, quail, stick, wince 6 blench, bridle, cringe, flinch, lessen, pucker, recoil, reduce, refuse, retire 7 curtail, decline, deflate, dwindle, retreat, shorten, shrivel, shudder 8 compress, condense, contract, decrease, diminish, draw back, hang back, make less, withdraw 9 constrict 11 make smaller 12 draw together 13 become smaller

shrink from 4 hate, shun 5 abhor, evade 6 balk at, detest, eschew, loathe, resist 7 despise 8 recoil at 9 abominate, shudder at 12 be revolted by 13 find repulsive

shrinking 3 shy 5 timid 6 ebbing, waning 7 bashful 8 reticent, retiring, timorous 9 declining, dwindling 10 decreasing, shriveling 11 contraction, diminishing

shrive 6 pardon 7 absolve, forgive

shrivel 5 dry up, parch, wizen 6 pucker, scorch, shrink, wither 7 wrinkle

Shropshire Lad, A
author: 9 A E Housman

shroud 4 hide, pall, veil, wrap 5 cloak, cloud, cover, sheet 6 clothe, mantle, screen, swathe 7 blanket, conceal, envelop 8 covering 9 cerecloth, cerements 11 burial cloth 12 graveclothes, winding sheet

shrub 4 bush 5 brush 8 beverage 10 fruit drink

shrubbery 4 bush 5 brush 6 bushes, shrubs 9 brushwood 10 underbrush 11 undergrowth

Shuara see 6 Jivaro

shuck 4 husk, peel, shed 5 chaff, shell, strip

shudder 4 jerk, pang 5 quake, shake, spasm, throb 6 quaver, quiver, shimmy, shiver, tremor, twitch 7 flutter, tremble 8 paroxysm 9 pulsation, trembling 10 convulsion

shudder at 4 hate 5 abhor 6 detest, loathe 8 recoil at 9 abominate, can't stand 10 recoil from, shrink from

shuffle 3 mix 4 drag, gimp, limp, step 5 scuff, slide 6 clumsy, jumble, scrape 7 shamble 8 scramble 9 rearrange 10 disarrange 11 interchange

shul, schul 9 synagogue

shun 5 avoid, dodge, elude, evade, forgo 6 eschew, forego, ignore, refuse, reject 7 boycott, disdain 10 circumvent, fight shy of, shrink from 11 keep clear of, shy away from 12 have no part of, keep away. from, steer clear of, turn away from

shut 3 box 4 cage, coop, draw, fold, lock, snap 5 clasp, close, drawn, latch 6 closed, closet, corral, draw to, fasten, intern, locked, lock in, secure 7 confine, drawn to, enclose, fence in, impound, latched, secured 8 cloister, closed up, fastened, imprison 9 barricade, constrain 11 incarcerate

shut down 4 halt, stop 5 cease 7 suspend 9 close down, interrupt 11 discontinue

Shute, Nevil
author of: 10 On the Beach

shut in 4 cage 5 caged, pen in 6 coop up, encage, lock up 7 confine, encaged, en-

close 8 confined, cooped up, enclosed, locked up, restrain, restrict 10 restrained, restricted

shut one's eyes to 5 allow 6 ignore, wink at 8 overlook 9 connive in, disregard 11 pay no heed to 14 turn one's back on

shut out 3 bar 5 debar 6 defeat 7 exclude 8 obstruct, prohibit

shutter 5 blind, close, shade 6 screen 7 curtain

shut the door on 3 ban, bar 6 forbid, refuse, reject 7 exclude, keep out, shut out 8 prohibit

shut up 4 cage, coop, hush, lock, pent 5 close, pen in 6 immure 7 be quiet, confine, silence 8 imprison 11 incarcerate

shy 4 balk, meek, wary 5 chary, cower, dodge, leery, minus, scant, short, timid, under, wince 6 blench, demure, flinch, in need, modest, shrink, swerve 7 anxious, bashful, careful, fearful, lacking, needing, nervous, wanting 8 cautious, draw back, jump back, reserved, reticent, skittish, timorous 9 deficient, diffident, shrinking, tremulous 10 suspicious 11 distrustful 12 apprehensive 13 self-conscious

shy away from 4 duck, shun 5 avoid, dodge, spurn 6 balk at, refuse, reject 10 shrink from 12 steer clear of

Shylock
  character in: 19 The Merchant of Venice
  author: 11 Shakespeare

shyness 8 meekness, timidity 9 reticence 10 diffidence, insecurity 11 bashfulness 12 sheepishness, timorousness 14 self-effacement 15 unassertiveness

shyster 5 rogue 6 lawyer 8 attorney 10 mouthpiece 11 pettifogger 15 ambulance chaser

si 3 yes

Siam *see* 8 Thailand

Sibelius, Jean
  born: 7 Finland 10 Tavastehus
  composer of: 6 En Saga 7 Karelia, Legends, Tapiola, The Band 8 Kalevala 9 Finlandia 10 The Tempest 12 The Oceanides, Voces Intimae 14 Ride and Sunrise

Siberia, Siber 8 disfavor 10 punishment 14 undesirability
  city: 4 Omsk 5 Chita, Tomsk 6 Kurgan 7 Irkutsk, Yakutsk
  conqueror: 9 Timafeyev 11 Genghis Khan
  continent: 4 Asia
  gulf: 2 Ob
  inhabitant: 4 Yaku 5 Sagai, Tatar 6 Tartar 7 Yukagir 8 prisoner 17 political prisoner
  mountain range: 4 Ural 5 Altai, Altay
  river: 2 Ob 3 Ket, Ili, Taz 4 Amga, Amur, Lena, Onon 5 Ishim, Tobol 6 Olekma
  sea: 4 Kara 6 Laptev 7 Okhotsk

sibyl 4 seer 5 augur 6 oracle 7 diviner 9 predictor, sorcer-

ess 10 forecaster, prophetess, soothsayer 13 fortune teller 14 prognosticator

Sibyls
  form: 10 prophetess
  inspired by: 5 deity 6 Apollo
  names: 6 Libyan 7 Cumaean 10 Erythraean
  prophecies: 14 Sibylline Books

sic 2 so 4 thus

Sicilian Vespers, The
  also: 20 Les Vepres Siciliennes
  opera by: 5 Verdi
  character: 5 Elena 6 Arrigo 7 Procida 8 Monforte

Sicily *see box*

sick 3 ill 4 weak 5 frail, tired, weary 6 ailing, infirm, laid up, poorly, queasy, sickly, uneasy,

---

Sicily
  other name: 7 Sicilia 9 Trinacria, Triquetra
  capital/largest city: 7 Palermo
  others: 3 Aci 4 Enna, Noto 6 Ragusa 7 Augusta, Catania, Marsala, Messina, Trapani 8 Syracuse 10 Montelepre
  division: 4 Enna 6 Ragusa 7 Catania, Messina, Palermo, Trapani 8 Siracusa, Syracuse 9 Agrigento 13 Caltanissetta
  government: 13 region of Italy
  measure: 5 salma 7 caffiso
  monetary unit: 5 litra, oncia, uncia 6 carlin 7 carline, oncetta
  island: 5 Egadi 6 Lipari, Ustica 7 Pelagie 11 Pantelleria
  lake: 7 Pergusa 8 Camarina
  mountain: 4 Erei, Moro, Sori 5 Atlas, Erici, Hybla, Iblei, Ibrei 7 Nebrodi, Vulcano 9 Apennines, Le Madonie, Stromboli 10 Peloritani
  highest point: 4 Etna 5 Aetna
  river: 4 Acis 5 Salso, Torto 6 Belice, Simeto 7 Mazzaro, Platani
  sea: 6 Ionian 10 Tyrrhenian 13 Mediterranean
  physical feature:
    cape: 4 Boeo, Faro 7 Lilibeo, Passaro, Passero, Pelorus
    gulf: 4 Noto 7 Catania
    strait: 7 Messina
    wind: 7 sirocco
  people: 5 Elymi, Sican, Sicel 6 Sicani, Siculi
    author: 9 Lampedusa 10 Pirandello
    composer: 7 Bellini
    king: 4 Eryx 5 Bomba, Henry, Peter, Roger 7 Charles, Cocalus, Leontes 9 Ferdinand, Frederick
    ruler: 4 Rome 5 Arabs, Goths, Spain 6 Greeks 7 Germans, Normans, Vandals, Vikings 8 Carthage, Saracens 9 Aragonese, Byzantium, Egyptians, Phoenicia 15 Holy Roman Empire
  language: 7 Italian
  religion: 13 Roman Catholic
  place:
    cathedral: 8 Monreale
    resort: 4 Enna 8 Taormina
    ruins: 14 Villa Imperiale 15 Temple of Concord 18 Valley of the Temples
  feature:
    brigands: 5 Mafia
    evening stroll: 11 passeggiata

unwell **7** crushed, grieved, invalid, unsound **8** delicate, stricken, troubled, wretched **9** afflicted, bored with, disturbed, miserable, nauseated, perturbed, suffering, unhealthy **10** disquieted, distressed, indisposed **11** discomposed, heartbroken **15** under the weather

sicken 5 repel, shock, upset **6** offend, revolt **7** disgust, horrify, make ill, repulse **8** nauseate **14** turn the stomach

sickening 4 foul, vile **5** nasty **7** noisome **8** horrible, unsavory **9** abhorrent, loathsome, offensive, repellent, repugnant, repulsive, revolting **10** disgusting, nauseating **11** distasteful

sickly 3 ill, wan **4** drab, flat, lame, pale, sick, weak **5** ashen, faint, frail, silly **6** ailing, feeble, flimsy, guilty, infirm, leaden, peaked, poorly, sneaky, torpid, unwell **7** insipid, invalid, unsound **8** delicate, smirking **9** afflicted, apathetic, bloodless, simpering, unhealthy **10** cadaverous, lackluster, namby-pamby, snickering, spiritless, uninspired, wishy-washy **11** ineffective **12** unconvincing **13** selfconscious

sickness 6 malady, nausea **7** ailment, disease, illness **8** debility, disorder, vomiting **9** complaint, frailness, ill health, infirmity **10** affliction, disability, invalidism, poor health, queasiness **11** unsoundness **12** qualmishness **13** indisposition

sic passim 12 so throughout

sic semper tyrannis 19 thus always to tyrants
   motto of: 8 Virginia

sic transit gloria mundi 33 thus passes away the glory of this world

Siddhartha
   author: 12 Hermann Hesse
   story of: 6 Buddha

siddur 16 Jewish prayer book
   literally: 5 order

side 3 hem, rim **4** area, body, brim, edge, half, hand, part, sect, team, view **5** angle, bound, cause, facet, flank, group, house, light, limit, minor, party, phase, skirt, slant, stand, stock **6** allied, aspect, behalf, belief, border, circle, clique, fringe, lesser, margin, region, sector, strain **7** askance, coterie, faction, lateral, lineage, oblique, opinion,

postern, quarter, related, section, segment, surface **8** alliance, attitude, boundary, division, indirect, marginal, position, skirting **9** accessory, bloodline, coalition, on one side, perimeter, periphery, secondary, territory, viewpoint **10** collateral, contingent, federation, incidental, standpoint, subsidiary **11** affiliation, association, unimportant **13** insignificant

Side
   origin: 5 Irish
   form: 7 fairies
   owner: 14 Tuatha De Danann

sideboard 6 buffet **8** credenza

side by side 7 abreast **8** abutting, together **9** adjoining **11** cheek by jowl, in proximity
   Latin: 9 pari passu

Side Effects
   author: 10 Woody Allen

sidekick 3 pal **4** aide **5** buddy **6** deputy, friend **9** assistant **10** lieutenant

sideline 5 bench, hobby **8** boundary **9** avocation **14** put out of action

sidestep 4 duck **5** avert, avoid, dodge, elude, evade, skirt **6** bypass, escape **10** circumvent, fight shy of **12** steer clear of

sidestepping 7 dodging, ducking, eluding, evasion **8** skirting **9** avoidance **13** circumvention

sidewalk 4 curb **8** footpath, pavement **9** promenade

sideways, sideway 6 aslant **7** askance, lateral, oblique **8** crabwise, edgeways, edgewise, sidelong, sideward, sidewise **9** cross wise, laterally, obliquely, to the side **11** from one side

side with 5 agree **7** stand by, stick by, support **8** champion **12** take one's part

sidle 4 cant, edge, skew, veer **10** lateralize

Sidney, Sir Philip
   author of: 7 Arcadia **15** Defence of Poesie, Defence of Poetry **18** Apologie for Poetrie, Astrophel and Stella

Sidney, Sylvia
   real name: 11 Sophia Kosow
   born: 7 Bronx NY
   husband: 11 Luther Adler **12** Bennett A Cerf
   roles: 4 Fury **7** Dead End **11** Street Scene **13** Les Mise-

rables **15** Madame Butterfly **17** An American Tragedy **24** Summer Wishes Winter Dreams

Sidrophel
   character in: 8 Hudibras
   author: 6 Butler

siecle 3 age **6** period **7** century

Siegel, Jerry
   creator/artist of: 8 Superman

Siegfried
   origin: 8 Germanic
   mentioned in: 14 Nibelungenlied
   father: 7 Sigmund
   mother: 9 Sieglinde
   wife: 9 Kriemhild
   killed by: 5 Hagen
   same as: 6 Sigurd
   killed: 6 Fafnir
   won for Gunther: 10 Brunnhilde
   stole: 9 Tarnkappe

Sieg Heil 13 hail to victory
   salute used by: 5 Nazis

Sieglinde
   origin: 8 Germanic
   mentioned in: 14 Nibelungenlied
   husband: 7 Sigmund
   son: 9 Siegfried

Sienkiewicz, Henryk
   author of: 8 Quo Vadis?

Sierra Leone *see box, p. 892*

siesta 3 nap **4** rest **5** break, sleep **6** cat nap, snooze **10** forty winks

sieve 4 sift **6** filter, riddle, screen, sorter, strain **7** tattler **8** colander, strainer **9** separator **12** blabbermouth

sift 4 sort **5** drift, probe, study **6** filter, review, screen, search, winnow **7** analyze, inspect, scatter, sort out **8** separate **10** scrutinize **11** distinguish, investigate **12** discriminate

Siggeir
   origin: 12 Scandinavian
   king of: 5 Goths
   wife: 5 Signy
   causes death of: 7 Volsung

sigh 3 sob **4** hiss, long, moan, pine, weep **5** brood, groan, mourn, whine, yearn **6** grieve, lament, sorrow

sight 3 ken, see, spy **4** bead, espy, gaze, spot, view **5** image, scene, vista **6** behold, seeing, survey, vision **7** display, exhibit, eyeshot, glimpse, observe, pageant, scenery, viewing **8** eyesight, perceive, prospect, scrutiny **9** peepsight,

Sierra Leone
  name means: 12 lion mountain
  other name: 9 Gold Coast **10** Grain Coast, Ivory Coast
  capital/largest city: 8 Freetown
  others: 2 Bo **5** Hepel, Kissi, Lungi, Pepel **6** Bonthe, Kenema, Makeni, Shenge, Sulima
  school: 6 Njaia U **9** Fourah Bay
  measure: 4 load **6** kettle
  monetary unit: 4 cent **5** leone
  island: 4 York **6** Banana, Turtle **7** Sherbro
  mountain: 4 Loma **10** Tingi Hills
  highest point: 9 Bintimani
  river: 3 Moa **4** Jong, Mano, Meli, Ribi, Sewa, Taia **5** Bagbe, Mongo, Morro, Rokel **6** Mabole, Rokkel, Scarcy, Waanje **13** Great Scarcies **14** Little Scarcies
  sea: 8 Atlantic
  physical feature:
    bay: **5** Yawri **7** Sherbro
    cape: **8** Shilling **11** Sierra Leone
    peninsula: **7** Turners **11** Sierra Leone
    wind: **9** harmattan
  people: 3 Vai **4** Kono, Loko, Susu **5** Bulom, Kissi, Limba, Mende, Mendi, Temne **6** Creole, Fulani, Syrian **7** Gallina, Koranko, Kuranko, Sherbro, Yalunka **8** Lebanese, Mandingo
    explorer: **6** Cintra
    leader: **6** Margai **7** Stevens
  language: 4 Krio **5** Limba, Mende, Mendi, Temne **6** Creole **7** English
  religion: 5 Islam **7** animism **12** Christianity
  place:
    wharf: **10** King Jimmys
  feature:
    cloth: **5** garra
    clothing: **5** lappa **6** caftan
    secret society: **4** poro
  food:
    dish: **4** fufu **7** cassava
    sauce: **7** palaver

sighthole, spectacle **10** appearance, visibility

sighted 3 saw **4** seen **6** seeing **8** not blind, observed

sightless 5 blind **8** unseeing **9** unsighted

sightly 4 fair **6** lovely, pretty **8** handsome, pleasing **9** appealing, beautiful **10** attractive

Sigmund
  origin: 8 Germanic **12** Scandinavian
  mentioned in: 8 Volsunga **14** Nibelungenlied
  king of: 11 Netherlands
  father: 7 Volsung
  mother: 4 Liod, Ljod **5** Hliod
  wife: 7 Hiordis, Hjordis **8** Borghild **9** Sieglinde
  sister: 5 Signy
  lover: 5 Signy
  son: 6 Sigurd **9** Siegfried, Sinfiotli

sign 3 nod **4** clue, hint, mark, note, omen, wave **5** badge, brand, index, stamp, token, trait **6** emblem, ensign, figure, herald, motion, signal, symbol **7** earmark, endorse, feature, gesture, go-ahead, placard, portent, presage, symptom, warning **8** evidence, forecast, inscribe, neon sign, road sign, signpost **9** autograph, billboard, guidepost, harbinger, indicator, nameplate, trademark **10** indication, intimation, prognostic, suggestion, underwrite **11** forewarning **13** manifestation **14** characteristic

signal 3 cue, nod **4** sign **6** beckon, famous, motion, unique **7** command, eminent, gesture, guiding, honored, notable, warning **8** high sign, password, pointing, renowned, singular, striking **9** arresting, directing, direction, important, indicator, memorable, momentous, prominent, watchword **10** commanding, impressive, indicating, indication, noteworthy, one-of-a-kind, remarkable **11** conspicuous, distinctive, exceptional, illustrious, outstanding, significant **12** considerable **13** consequential, distinguished, extraordinary, unforgettable

significance 3 aim **4** note **5** drift, force, merit, sense, value, worth **6** import, intent, moment, object, virtue, weight **7** concern, gravity, meaning, portent, purpose **8** eminence, interest, priority **9** authority, direction, influence, intention, relevance **10** excellence, importance, notability, prominence **11** consequence, distinction, implication

significant 4 main **5** chief, grave, great, major, prime, vital **6** cogent, signal **7** eminent, knowing, notable, serious, telling, weighty **8** critical, distinct, eloquent, eventful, material, pregnant, symbolic **9** important, momentous, paramount, principal, prominent **10** emblematic, expressive, indicative, meaningful, noteworthy, portentous, remarkable, suggestive **11** exceptional, influential, outstanding, substantial, symptomatic **12** considerable **13** consequential, demonstrative **14** representative

signify 4 mean, omen, show, tell **5** argue, augur, imply **6** convey, denote, evince, herald, hint at, import, reveal, typify **7** bespeak, betoken, connote, declare, exhibit, express, portend, predict, presage, promise, suggest **8** announce, disclose, evidence, forebode, foretell, indicate, intimate, manifest, proclaim, set forth, stand for **9** be a sign of, designate, represent, symbolize **10** foreshadow **11** communicate, demonstrate

signing up 7 joining **9** enlisting, enrolling **10** enlistment, enrollment **11** registering **12** registration **13** matriculating, matriculation

Sign of Four, The
  author: 19 Sir Arthur Conan Doyle
  character: 11 Mary Morstan **12** Dr John Watson **13** Jonathan Small **14** Sherlock Holmes, Thaddeus Sholto

Signoret, Simone
  real name: 32 Simone-Henriette-Charlotte Kaminker
  born: 7 Germany **9** Wiesbaden
  husband: 11 Yves Montand **12** Yves Allegret

roles: 10 Madame Rosa **11** Ship of Fools **12** Room at the Top (Oscar) **14** Is Paris Burning?
autobiography: 27 Nostalgia Isn't What It Used to Be

sign up 4 join **6** enlist, enroll, join up **8** register **9** volunteer **11** matriculate

Signy
origin: 12 Scandinavian
mentioned in: 8 Volsunga
father: 7 Volsung
brother: 7 Sigmund
son: 9 Sinfiotli
husband: 7 Siggeir

Sigrdrifa
also: 18 Brynhildr Sigrdrifa
origin: 9 Icelandic
mentioned in: 9 Elder Edda
member of: 9 Valkyries
disobeyed: 4 Odin **5** Othin
sleeps in circle of: 4 fire
awakened by: 6 Sigurd

Sigurd
origin: 12 Scandinavian
mentioned in: 8 Volsunga
father: 7 Sigmund
mother: 7 Hiordis, Hjordis
wife: 6 Gudrun, Kudrun **7** Guthrun
killed: 6 Fafnir
acquired treasure of: 8 Andavari
won for Gunnar: 8 Brynhild

Sigyn
origin: 12 Scandinavian
husband: 4 Loki

Sikes, Bill
character in: 11 Oliver Twist
author: 7 Dickens

Sikkim *see box*

Sikorsky, Igor
nationality: 7 Russian **8** American
invented: 10 helicopter

Silas Marner
author: 11 George Eliot
character: 5 Eppie **11** Dunstan Cass, Godfrey Cass **13** Aaron Winthrop, Nancy Lammeter

silence 3 gag **4** calm, curb, halt, hush, kill, rout, stop **5** allay, check, crush, peace, quash, quell, quiet, still **6** banish, deaden, defeat, muffle, muzzle, repose, squash, stifle, subdue **7** conquer, nullify, put down, quieten, repress, reserve, squelch **8** choke off, dumbness, muteness, overcome, serenity, suppress, vanquish **9** lay to rest, placidity, quietness, reticence, stillness, tongue-tie **10** extinguish, placidness, put an end to, strike dumb **11** taciturnity, tranquility **12** tranquillity **13** noise-

Sikkim
capital/largest city: 7 Gangtok
others: 6 Dikchu, Lachen, Namchi, Rangpo, Rumtek **7** Lachung **9** Chungtang
government: 12 state of India
mountain: 7 Dongkya, Donkhya **9** Himalayas, Singalili **10** Darjeeling **12** Kanchenjunga
river: 5 Tista **6** Ranjit **9** Lachen Chu **10** Lachung Chu
physical feature:
   mountain pass: **6** Natu La **7** Jelep La
   storm: **7** monsoon
people: 4 Rong **5** Bhote **6** Bhotia, Bhutia, Indian, Lepcha **7** Tibetan **8** Nepalese **9** Mongoloid
   king: **7** chogyal
religion: 5 Hindu **7** Lamaism **15** Tibetan Buddhism

lessness, secretiveness, soundlessness **14** speechlessness **16** closemouthedness **19** uncommunicativeness

silent 3 mum **4** calm, dumb, idle, mute **5** inert, muted, quiet, still, tacit **6** covert, hidden, hushed, placid, serene, unsaid **7** dormant, implied, muffled **8** discreet, implicit, inactive, inferred, lifeless, peaceful, reserved, reticent, taciturn, tranquil, unspoken, wordless **9** concealed, intimated, noiseless, quiescent, secretive, soundless, suggested, unsounded, unwritten **10** insinuated, mysterious, speechless, tongue-tied, undeclared, understood, unrevealed, unstirring, untalked-of **11** close-lipped, tight-lipped, unexpressed, unmentioned, unpublished, untalkative, unvocalized **12** closemouthed, unpronounced **15** uncommunicative

Silent Spring
author: 13 Rachel L Carson

Silenus
god of: 6 forest
oldest: 5 satyr
father: 3 Pan **6** Hermes
foster father of: 8 Dionysus
teacher of: 8 Dionysus
companion of: 8 Dionysus
sons: 6 Sileni

silicon
chemical symbol: 2 Si

silk
fabric: 4 crin **5** crepe, ninon, satin, surah, tulle **6** faille, pongee, sendal, tussah **7** chiffon, foulard, organza, raw silk, taffeta **8** organzie, paduasoy **10** peau de soie **12** crepe de chine
lining: 7 sarsnet **8** sarcenet
measure: 6 denier
raw silk: 5 grege **6** greige **8** marabout
source: 6 cocoon **9** silkworms
waste: 4 noil **5** floss
watered: 5 moire
yarn/thread: 4 tram **5** floss

silk-stocking 6 uptown **8** highborn, highbred, wellborn **9** patrician **10** upperclass **11** blue-blooded **12** aristocratic

Silk Stockings
director: 15 Rouben Mamoulian
cast: 10 Janis Paige, Peter Lorre **11** Cyd Charisse, Fred Astaire
setting: 5 Paris
score: 10 Cole Porter
remake of: 9 Ninotchka

silky 4 fine, soft **6** satiny, smooth **11** fine-grained

silliness 5 folly **6** drivel, idiocy **7** inanity **9** absurdity, asininity, frivolity **10** buffoonery, tomfoolery **11** foolishness **13** pointlessness **14** playing the fool, ridiculousness

Sillitoe, Alan
author of: 10 Her Victory **29** Saturday Night and Sunday Morning **36** The Loneliness of the Long-Distance Runner

silly 3 mad **4** dumb **5** crazy, giddy, inane **6** absurd, frothy, insane, stupid, unwary, unwise **7** aimless, asinine, fatuous, foolish, idiotic, shallow, witless **8** childish, farcical **9** brainless, foolhardy, frivolous, laughable, ludicrous, pointless, senseless **10** illadvised, irrational, ridiculous **11** empty-headed, harebrained, meaningless, nonsensical, purposeless **12** muddleheaded, preposterous, simpleminded, unreasonable **13** inappropriate, irresponsible, muddlebrained, rattlebrained **14** featherbrained **15** inconsequential

Silmarillion, The
author: 10 J R R Tolkien

Silone, Ignazio
real name: 17 Secondo Tranquilli
author of: 9 Fontamara **12** Bread and Wine **26** The Story of a Humble Christian

Silvanus
also: **8** Sylvanus
god of: **5** herds, house,
woods **12** farm boundary
16 uncultivated land

silver 5 coins, plate **6** argent,
change **7** jewelry **8** argentum,
platinum **9** argentine
10 silverware
chemical symbol: **2** Ag

Silver, Long John
character in: **14** Treasure
Island
author: **9** Stevenson

Silver, Mattie
character in: **10** Ethan
Frome
author: **7** Wharton

Silvers, Phil
real name: **17** Philip
Silversmith
born: **10** Brooklyn NY
roles: **9** Top Banana **13** Ser-
geant Bilko **15** High Button
Shoes **22** A Guide for the
Married Man **37** A Funny
Thing Happened on the
Way to the Forum
autobiography: **14** The Laugh
Is on Me

Silvius
father: **6** Aeneas

s'il vous plait 6 please **11** if
you please

Simenon, Georges
author of: **8** The Train
12 Act of Passion **14** The
Little Saint **15** Maigret's
Memoirs **28** The Strange
Case of Peter the Lett
character: **21** Inspector Jules
Maigret

Simeon
father: **5** Jacob
mother: **4** Leah
brother: **3** Dan, Gad **4** Levi
5 Asher, Judah **6** Joseph,
Reuben **7** Zebulun **8** Benjamin, Issachar, Naphtali
sister: **5** Dinah
canticle: **12** nunc dimittis
descendant of: **9** Simeonite

similar 4 akin, like, twin
5 close **6** allied **7** cognate,
kindred **8** agreeing, matching,
parallel **9** analogous, duplicate **10** comparable, equivalent, resembling
11 approximate, correlative,
much the same, nearly alike
13 correspondent,
corresponding

similarity 7 harmony, kinship,
oneness **8** affinity, likeness,
nearness, sameness **9** agreement, closeness, congruity,
semblance **10** congruence, similitude **11** concordance, conformance, equivalence,

parallelism, reciprocity, resemblance **13** comparability
14 conformability,
correspondence

similarly 4 thus **5** alike
7 equally **8** likewise **11** furthermore, identically
15 correspondingly

similitude 7 analogy **8** likeness,
sameness **10** similarity **11** parallelism, resemblance

simmer 4 boil, burn, foam,
fume, stew **5** chafe, smart
6 bubble, burble, gurgle,
seethe, sizzle

simmer down 7 cool off
8 calm down **14** collect oneself, compose oneself

Simmons, Jean
born: **6** London **7** England
husband: **13** Richard Brooks
14 Stewart Granger
roles: **4** Trio **6** Hamlet **7** Desiree, Ophelia, The Robe
9 Spartacus, Young Bess
11 Elmer Gantry **12** Guys
and Dolls **14** The Happy
Ending **17** Great Expectations **19** Androcles and the
Lion

Simois
god of: **5** river

Simoisius
killed by: **14** Telamonian
Ajax

Simon
also known as: **5** Peter
son: **13** Judas Iscariot
disciple of: **5** Jesus

Simon, Neil
author of: **10** Chapter Two,
Plaza Suite **11** Biloxi Blues
12 The Odd Couple **15** The
Sunshine Boys **16** Come
Blow Your Horn **17** Barefoot
in the Park **21** Last of the
Red Hot Lovers **25** The Prisoner of Second Avenue

Simon & Simon
character: **7** AJ Simon **9** Rick
Simon **12** Cecilia Simon
13 Downtown Brown
cast: **7** Tim Reid **10** Mary
Carver **13** Gerald McRaney,
Jameson Parker
setting: **8** San Diego

Simon Boccanegra
opera by: **5** Verdi
setting: **5** Genoa
character: **5** Maria, Paolo
6 Andrea, Fiesco, Pietro
14 Amelia Grimaldi, Gabriele Adorno

Simonov, Konstantin
author of: **13** Days and
Nights

simpatico 7 likable **9** agreeable, congenial, gemutlich

simper 5 smirk **6** giggle, tee-
hee, titter **7** snicker, snigger

simple 4 bare, dull, dumb,
easy, open, slow, soft, true
5 basic, blunt, dense, frank,
green, homey, naive, naked,
plain, quiet, sheer, stark,
thick **6** callow, candid, common, direct, honest, modest,
obtuse, rustic, stupid **7** artless,
foolish, natural, sincere **8** absolute, innocent, not fancy,
ordinary, peaceful, straight,
workaday **9** downright, elemental, guileless, ingenuous,
out-and-out, unadorned, unfeigned, untrimmed, un-
worldly **10** elementary,
manageable, not complex, unaffected, uninvolved **11** commonplace, fundamental, plain-
spoken, rudimentary,
thick-witted, undecorated, unvarnished **12** not difficult, not
elaborate, uncompounded
13 inexperienced, uncomplicated, unembellished, unpretentious **15** straightforward,
unsophisticated

simple house 3 cot, hut
5 shack **6** chalet **7** cottage
8 bungalow

simpleminded 4 dull, dumb,
slow **5** dense, silly, thick
6 stupid **7** asinine, fatuous,
foolish, idiotic, moronic, witless **8** retarded **9** brainless,
dim-witted, imbecilic **10** dull-
witted, half-witted **11** empty-
headed, harebrained, lamebrained **12** feeble-minded

simpleton 3 ass, oaf **4** dolt,
dope, fool, hick, jerk, rube
5 booby, dummy, dunce,
goose, idiot, ninny, stupe
6 donkey, rustic **7** dullard,
jackass **8** dumbbell, imbecile,
numskull **9** blockhead, greenhorn, ignoramus, numbskull
10 nincompoop

simplicity 6 candor, purity
7 clarity, honesty, naivete
8 easiness, openness, serenity
9 austerity, clearness, innocence, plainness, restraint, sincerity **10** directness
11 artlessness, cleanliness, naturalness, obviousness
12 truthfulness **13** guilelessness, unworldliness
19 straightforwardness

simply 7 clearly, lucidly,
plainly, starkly **8** directly,
modestly **9** naturally **10** explicitly **11** ingenuously **12** in-
telligibly, unaffectedly
15 uncomplicatedly, unpretentiously **17** straightforwardly

Simpson, O J (Orenthal James)
　nickname: **5** Juice
　sport: **8** football
　position: **11** running back
　team: **10** USC Trojans **12** Buffalo Bills **23** San Francisco Forty-Niners

simulate 3 act, ape **4** copy, fake, play, pose, sham **5** feign, mimic, put on **6** affect, assume, invent **7** imitate, play-act, pretend **9** dissemble, fabricate **11** counterfeit, make believe

simulated 4 fake, sham **5** phony **6** forged **7** manmade, pretend **9** imitation, synthetic **10** artificial, fabricated **11** counterfeit, make-believe

simultaneous 6 coeval **10** coexistent, coexisting, coincident, concurrent, synchronal, synchronic **11** concomitant, synchronous **12** accompanying, contemporary **15** contemporaneous

sin 3 err **4** evil, fall, slip, vice **5** crime, error, lapse, shame, stray, wrong **6** breach, do evil, offend **7** do wrong, misdeed, offense, scandal **8** disgrace, evil deed, iniquity, trespass, villainy **9** violation **10** infraction, transgress, wrongdoing **13** transgression

Sin
　origin: **8** Akkadian
　god of: **4** moon

Sinaiticus 16 Greek uncial codex

Sinatra, Frank
　real name: **20** Francis Albert Sinatra
　nickname: **8** The Voice **11** Old Blue Eyes
　born: **9** Hoboken NJ
　wife: **9** Mia Farrow **10** Ava Gardner
　daughter: **12** Nancy Sinatra
　son: **14** Frank Sinatra Jr
　leader of: **7** Rat Pack
　roles: **8** Tony Rome **12** Angelo Maggio, Guys and Dolls, The Detective **14** The Joker Is Wild **17** The First Deadly Sin **18** From Here to Eternity **22** The Man with the Golden Arm

Sinbad the Sailor
　character in: **27** Arabian Nights' Entertainments

since 2 as **3** ago, for, yet **4** ergo, from **5** after, hence, later **6** thence, whence **7** because, whereas **8** in as much **9** therefore **10** afterwards **11** accordingly, considering **12** subsequently

　archaic: **4** sith
　prefix: **3** cis
　Scottish: **4** syne

sincere 4 real **5** frank **6** candid, honest **7** artless, earnest, genuine, natural, serious **8** truthful **9** authentic, guileless, heartfelt, ingenuous, unfeigned **10** forthright, unaffected **11** in good faith, undeceitful **12** wholehearted **15** straightforward

sincerely 5 truly **6** really **8** honestly **9** earnestly, genuinely, seriously **10** truthfully **14** wholeheartedly

sincerity 6 candor **7** honesty, probity **8** openness **9** frankness, good faith **11** artlessness, earnestness, genuineness, seriousness **12** truthfulness **13** guilelessness, ingenuousness **14** forthrightness, unaffectedness **16** wholeheartedness **19** straightforwardness

Sinclair, Upton
　author of: **9** The Jungle, World's End **12** Dragon's Teeth
　character: **9** Lanny Budd

Sindhi
　language family: **12** Indo-European
　branch: **11** Indo-Iranian
　group: **5** Indic
　spoken in: **13** Northern India

sine die 17 without fixing a day (for future action or a future meeting)
　literally: **13** without the day

sine prole 14 without progeny **16** without offspring

sine qua non 15 without which not **18** something essential **22** indispensable condition

sinew, sinews 4 grit, thew **5** fiber, nerve, power, vigor **6** muscle, tendon **7** stamina **8** ligament, strength, virility, vitality **10** resilience, strengthen

sinewy 4 wiry **5** beefy, nervy, thewy, tough **6** brawny, robust, strong **7** fibrose, stringy **8** muscular, powerful, vigorous

Sinfiotli
　origin: **12** Scandinavian
　mentioned in: **8** Volsunga
　mother: **5** Signy
　father: **7** Sigmund

sinful 3 bad **4** evil, vile **5** wrong **6** errant, unholy, wicked **7** corrupt, heinous, immoral, impious, ungodly, wayward **8** criminal, depraved, shameful **9** miscreant **10** de-

generate, despicable, iniquitous, profligate, villainous **11** disgraceful, irreligious, unrighteous

sing 3 hum **4** lilt, pipe **5** carol, chant, chirp, croon, trill, tweet **6** intone, warble **7** chirrup, whistle **8** melodize

Sing Along with Mitch
　regulars: **10** Diana Trask **11** Mitch Miller **12** Leslie Uggams, Louise O'Brien, Sandy Stewart **13** Gloria Lambert, Sing Along Gang, Sing Along Kids

Singapore *see box, p. 896*

singe 4 burn, char, sear **5** brand **6** scorch

singer 4 alto, bard, bass, diva, lark **5** tenor **7** crooner, soprano **8** baritone, minstrel, songbird, songster, vocalist **9** chanteuse, chantress, contralto **10** songstress, troubadour **11** nightingale **12** countertenor, mezzosoprano

singer, female
　French: **9** chanteuse

Singer, Isaac Bashevis
　author of: **6** Shosha **7** Old Love **8** The Manor **9** The Estate **13** Gimpel the Fool **15** The Family Moskat **16** In My Father's Court **24** The Spinoza of Market Street

singer, professional
　French, Italian: **10** cantatrice

singing group 4 trio **5** choir **6** chorus **7** quartet **8** glee club **13** choral society **17** barbershop quartet

Singin' in the Rain
　director: **9** Gene Kelly **12** Stanley Donen
　cast: **9** Gene Kelly, Jean Hagen **11** Cyd Charisse **13** Donald O'Connor **14** Debbie Reynolds
　song: **11** Make 'em Laugh

single 3 one **4** lone, sole **5** unwed **6** maiden **7** only one **8** bachelor, singular, solitary, spinster, wifeless **9** unmarried **10** individual, spouseless **11** husbandless

single file 8 one by one **10** Indian file, one at a time **13** in a single line **16** one behind another

single-handedly 5 alone **7** unaided **9** by oneself, on one's own **10** unassisted **11** without help

single-minded 4 firm **6** dogged **7** devoted, intense,

Singapore
  other name: **8** Singa Pur
  name means: **13** city of the lion
  capital/largest city: **9** Singapore
  others: **4** Tuas **6** Changi, Jurong **7** Nee Soon **9** Paya Lebar, Woodlands **10** Bukit Timah, Queenstown **12** Bukit Panjang **15** Toa Payoh New Town
    medieval town: **7** Temasek
  school: **7** Nanyang **8** National **9** Singapore
  monetary unit: **4** cent **6** dollar
  island: **4** Ubin **5** Brani, Bukum, Pesek **7** Semakau **8** Merlimau, Southern **10** Ayer Chawan, Ayer Merbau **11** Blakang Mati, Tekong Besar **12** Tekong Kechil
  mountain: **6** Mandai **7** Panjang
  highest point: **10** Bukit Timah
  river: **6** Jurong, Sungei **7** Kallang, Seletar **9** Singapore
  sea: **6** Indian **10** South China
  physical feature:
    harbor: **6** Keppel **9** Serangoon
    strait: **6** Johore, Pandan **8** Sembilan **9** Singapore
  people: **5** Malay **6** Indian **7** Chinese **9** Malaysian, Pakistani, Sri Lankan
    founder: **7** Raffles
    leader: **10** Lee Kwan Yew
  language: **5** Malay, Tamil **7** Chinese, English **8** Mandarin
  religion: **4** Sikh **5** Hindu, Islam **6** Taoism **8** Buddhism **12** Christianity, Confucianism
  place:
    amusement park: **8** New World **10** Great World, Happy World
    aquarium: **8** Van Kleef
    cathedral: **9** St Andrews
    gardens: **7** Botanic
    hall: **16** Victoria Memorial
    industrial park: **6** Jurong
    mosque: **6** Sultan
    park: **6** Farber **7** Merlion **12** Raffles Place
    street: **16** Raffles Boulevard
    temple: **17** One Thousand Lights
  feature:
    boat: **4** junk **6** sampan
    clothing: **4** sari

staunch, zealous **8** resolved, tireless, untiring **9** dedicated, steadfast, tenacious **10** determined, inflexible, persistent, relentless, unswerving, unwavering **11** persevering, unflinching

singleness 12 bachelorhood, spinsterhood **14** unmarried state **17** single blessedness

single out 4 pick, take **6** choose, opt for, select **7** call out, extract, fix upon, pick out **8** decide on, set apart, settle on **11** distinguish

sing the praises of 4 hail, laud, tout **5** boost, cheer, exalt, extol, honor **6** praise **7** acclaim, applaud, approve, commend **8** eulogize **9** celebrate **10** compliment

singular 3 odd **4** rare **5** queer **6** choice, quaint, select, unique **7** bizarre, curious, strange, unusual **8** aberrant, abnormal, atypical, freakish, peculiar, peerless, superior, uncommon, unwonted **9** anomalous, different, eccentric, fantastic, marvelous, matchless, unequaled, unnatural, wonderful **10** noteworthy, outlandish, prodigious, remarkable, surpassing, unfamiliar **11** exceptional, uncustomary **12** unparalleled **13** extraordinary, unaccountable, unprecedented **14** unconventional **16** out-of-the-ordinary

Sinhalese
  language family: **12** Indo-European
  branch: **11** Indo-Iranian
  group: **5** Indic
  spoken in: **6** Ceylon **8** Sri Lanka

sinister 4 dark, dire, evil, foul, rank, vile **5** black **6** cursed, malign, wicked **7** adverse, fearful, hellish, ominous, unlucky **8** accursed, alarming, damnable, devilish, infernal, menacing, rascally **9** dismaying, insidious, malignant **10** despicable, detestable, diabolical, disturbing, malevolent, perfidious, villainous **11** disquieting, frightening, threatening, treacherous, unfavorable, unpromising **12** blackhearted, inauspicious, unpropitious **13** Machiavellian, reprehensible

sink 3 dig, dip, ebb, lay, sag, set **4** bore, bowl, bury, drop, fall, seep, slip, soak, tilt, wane **5** basin, drill, drive, droop, drown, gouge, lower, slant, slope, slump, stoop, yield **6** engulf, go down, lessen, plunge, reduce, shrink, worsen **7** decline, descend, give way, go to pot, go under, put down, regress, subside, succumb **8** diminish, excavate, languish, lavatory, scoop out, submerge, submerse, washbowl **9** hollow out, wash basin **10** degenerate, depreciate, go downhill, retrogress **11** deteriorate, go to the dogs

sinless 4 good, holy, pure **6** chaste **7** upright **8** innocent, spotless, virtuous **9** reputable, righteous

sinner 8 apostate, evildoer, offender **9** miscreant, misfeasor, reprobate, wrongdoer **10** backslider, malefactor, malfeasant, recidivist, trespasser **12** transgressor

Sinnis *see* **5** Sinis

Sinoeis *see* **3** Pan

Sinon
  pretended to be: **13** Greek deserter
  told Trojans of: **11** Trojan Horse

Sino-Tibetan
  language branch: **7** Sinitic **12** Tibeto-Burman
  includes: **4** Naga **5** Karen **7** Burmese, Chinese **8** Kuki-Chin, Mandarin

Sins, Seven 4 envy, lust **5** anger, pride, sloth **8** gluttony **12** covetousness

sinuosity 10 slinkiness **11** convolution, sinuousness **12** tortuousness

sinuous 6 curved, folded, volute, zigzag **7** bending, coiling, curving, twisted, winding **8** indirect, mazelike, rambling, tortuous, twisting **9** wandering **10** circuitous, convoluted, meandering, roundabout, serpentine, undulating **12** labyrinthine

sinuousness 9 sinuosity
10 slinkiness **11** convolution
12 tortuousness

Sinus
also: 6 Sinnis
vocation: 6 robber
daughter: 8 Perigune
killed by: 7 Theseus
epithet: 12 Pityocamptes

Siouan
tribe: 4 Crow, Iowa **5** Ioway,
Omaha, C age, Sioux **6** Dakota, Mandan **7** Hidatsa
8 Minitari, Wazhazhe
10 Assiniboin, Gros Ventre
11 Assiniboine

Sioux *see* **6** Dakota

Sioux State
nickname of: 11 North
Dakota

sip 3 lap, nip, sup **4** dram,
drop **5** drink, savor, taste
6 sample **7** soupcon, swallow
10 thimbleful

siphon 4 tube **5** drain **7** draw
off

siphonaptera
class: 8 hexapoda
phylum: 10 arthropoda
group: 4 flea

Sippar residents
11 Sepharvites

Siqueiros, David Alfaro
born: 6 Mexico **9** Chihuahua
artwork: 12 New Democracy
13 Echo of a Scream
14 Trial of Fascism **15** Ascent of Culture, Burial of a
Worker **16** Towards the Cosmos **17** Death to the Invader **18** Polyforum
Siqueiros **22** March of Humanity on Earth
24 Cuauhtemoc Against the
Myth

sir
French: 8 monsieur

sire 4 king, lord **5** beget,
breed **6** create, father **7** creator **9** originate **10** originator,
progenitor

siren, Siren 4 horn, vamp
5 alarm, nymph, witch **6** sexpot **7** charmer, whistle **8** deceiver, sea nymph
9 temptress **10** seductress
11 enchantress **13** warning
signal **15** bewitching woman
French: 11 femme fatale
form: 5 nymph
location: 3 sea
lured sailors by: 7 singing

**Sir Gawain and the Green
Knight**
author: 7 unknown
character: 10 King Arthur

22 Sir Bernlak de
Hautdesert
horse: 9 Gringalet

Sirian Experiments, The
author: 12 Doris Lessing

Sisera
commander for: 5 Jabin
defeated by: 5 Barak

sissified 6 prissy **7** unmanly
8 womanish **10** effeminate

sissy 6 coward **8** weakling
9 fraidy-cat **10** scaredy-cat

sister 3 nun, kin, sib **5** nurse
6 female **7** sibling **8** feminist,
relation, relative
nautically: 6 secure
10 strengthen
society: 8 sorority

Sister Carrie
author: 15 Theodore Dreiser
character: 11 G W Hurstwood **12** Carrie Meeber
13 Charles Drouet

Sister Woman
character in: 16 Cat on a
Hot Tin Roof
author: 8 Williams

Sisyphean 4 hard **5** tough
6 uphill **7** arduous, onerous
8 toilsome **9** demanding, difficult, strenuous, wearisome
10 exhausting

Sisyphus
king of: 7 Corinth
father: 6 Aeolus
mother: 7 Enarete
brother: 9 Salmoneus
wife: 6 Merope
son: 5 Almus **7** Glaucus
8 Ornytion **10** Thersander
founded: 6 Ephyra **7** Corinth
rolled: 5 stone

sit 3 lie **4** loll, meet, mind,
rest, rule, stay **5** abide, chair,
nurse, perch, reign, roost,
squat, stand, teach, watch
6 attend, endure, gather, govern, linger, remain, reside, settle, sprawl **7** baby-sit, care for,
convene, preside **8** assemble,
be placed, be seated, chaperon **9** have a seat, officiate
10 deliberate **11** be in session

site 4 area, post, spot, zone
5 field, locus, place, point,
scene **6** ground, locale, region,
sector **7** section, setting, station **8** district, locality, location, position, province
9 territory **11** whereabouts

sit in judgment 5 judge **6** decide, settle **7** adjudge, mediate **9** arbitrate, reconcile
10 adjudicate **12** bring to
terms

situ 5 place

situate 3 put, set **4** post

5 build, house, lodge, place,
plant, stand **6** billet, locate,
settle **7** install, station **8** ensconce, position **9** construct,
establish

situation 3 fix, job **4** case,
duty, post, role, seat, site,
spot, work **5** berth, place,
state **6** locale, office, plight,
status **7** dilemma, posture, station **8** capacity, function, locality, location, position,
quandary **9** condition **10** assignment, livelihood **11** predicament **13** circumstances
14 state of affairs

sit upon 5 brood, cover,
hatch **8** incubate

Sivan 16 third Hebrew month

**Six Characters in Search
of an Author**
author: 15 Luigi Pirandello

six cubits 4 reed

Six Million Dollar Man
character: 11 Dr Rudy Wells,
(Col) Steve Austin **12** Oscar
Goldman
cast: 9 Lee Majors **13** Martin
E Brooks **15** Alan Oppenheimer, Richard Anderson
spinoff: 11 Bionic Woman

Sixty Minutes
correspondent: 9 Dan
Rather **10** Andy Rooney
11 Diane Sawyer, Mike Wallace, Morley Safer **13** Harry
Reasoner

sizable 5 ample, broad, large,
roomy **7** immense **8** spacious
9 capacious, good-sized

size 3 sum **4** area, bulk, mass,
sort **5** array, grade, group,
scope, total **6** amount, extent,
spread, volume **7** arrange, bigness, content, expanse,
stretch **8** capacity, classify,
quantity, totality **9** aggregate,
amplitude, greatness, largeness, magnitude **10** dimensions **11** measurement,
proportions

sizzle 3 fry **4** hiss, spit
7 crackle, frizzle, hissing, sputter **8** splutter **10** sputtering

skate 3 nag, ray **4** skid, skim,
slip **5** blade, coast, glide,
horse, slide **6** rotter
female: 4 maid
genus: 4 Raja
mark: 4 cusp

skein 4 coil, hank, reel, yarn
5 twist **6** tangle, thread **9** filaments, twistings
members: 4 fowl **5** ducks,
flock, geese **6** flyers

skeletal 4 bony, thin **5** gaunt

6 wasted **9** emaciated
10 cadaverous

skeleton 4 hulk **5** bones,
frame, shell **9** framework
purpose: 7 support **8** protects **9** framework

Skelton, Red
real name: 21 Richard Bernard Skelton
born: 11 Vincennes IN
roles: 7 I Dood It **8** Ship
Ahoy **12** Panama Hattie
16 Neptune's Daughter
17 The Fuller Brush Man
18 Clem Kadiddlehopper,
Whistling in the Dark
20 Freddie the Freeloader

skeptic, sceptic 7 atheist,
doubter, scoffer **8** agnostic
10 questioner, unbeliever
14 doubting Thomas

skeptical, sceptical 6 unsure
7 cynical, dubious **8** doubtful,
doubting, scoffing **9** uncertain
11 incredulous, questioning,
unbelieving, unconvinced
12 disbelieving
13 hypercritical

skepticism 5 doubt **7** dubiety
8 distrust, mistrust, unbelief
9 disbelief, suspicion **11** agnosticism, incredulity
12 doubtfulness
13 faithlessness

sketch 3 map **4** draw, plot,
skit **5** chart, draft, graph,
scene **6** depict, digest, precis,
satire **7** drawing, lampoon,
mark out, outline, picture,
portray, summary, takeoff
8 abstract, rough out, synopsis,
vignette **9** blueprint, burlesque,
delineate, short play, summarize **11** preliminary
16 characterization

Sketch Book, The
author: 16 Washington Irving

sketchy 4 bare, hazy **5** brief,
crude, light, rough, short,
vague **6** meager, skimpy,
slight **7** cursory, outline, shallow, slender **9** essential,
rough-hewn, unrefined **10** incomplete, undetailed, unfinished, unpolished
11 preliminary, preparatory,
provisional, superficial

skewed 5 slued **6** veered,
warped **7** oblique, sheered,
slanted, swerved, twisted
9 distorted

skewer 3 pin, rod **4** spit, stab
5 truss **6** pierce, skiver **7** impale **9** brochette **10** run
through

skid 3 ski **4** drag, dray, skim,
skip, sled, slip **5** coast, glide,
skate, slide **6** runner, sledge

7 skitter **8** glissade, platform,
sideslip

Skidbladnir
origin: 12 Scandinavian
ship of: 4 Frey **5** Freyr
feature: 11 collapsible

Skidegatta
tribe: 5 Haida

**Skidmore, Owings, and
Merrill**
partners: 13 John Merrill Sr,
Louis Skidmore **15** Nathaniel
Owings
architects of: 10 Lever House
(NYC) **11** AEC town site
(Oak Ridge TN) **13** Banque
Lambert (Brussels) **16** John
Hancock Tower (Chicago)
17 Terrace Plaza Hotel (Cin-
cinnati), US Air Force Acad-
emy (CO) **18** Mauna Kea
Beach Hotel (Kamuela HI)
19 Istanbul Hilton Hotel
(Turkey) **23** Beinecke Rare
Book Library (Yale)
26 Chase Manhattan Bank
Building (NYC) **33** American
Republic Insurance Building
(Des Moines IA)
world's tallest building:
10 Sears Tower (Chicago)

skiff 4 boat **6** dinghy **7** rowboat

skiing
athlete: 9 Phil Mahre **11** Bill
Johnson, Cindy Nelson
13 Gustavo Thoeni, Robert
Cochran **14** Marilyn Cochran, Martha Rockwell
15 Debbie Armstrong, Inge-
mar Stenmark, Jean Claude
Killy **16** Michael Gallagher
17 Barbara Ann Cochran
20 Annemarie Proell Moser

Skikne, Larushka Misch
real name of: 14 Laurence
Harvey

skill 4 gift **5** craft, knack
6 acumen, talent **7** ability,
cunning, faculty, knowhow,
mastery, prowess **8** artistry, capacity, deftness, facility
9 adeptness, dexterity, expertise, handiness, ingenuity
10 adroitness, cleverness, competence, experience, expertness **11** proficiency
12 skillfulness **13** inventiveness

skilled 6 adroit, expert
7 trained **8** skillful **9** competent, masterful, practiced
10 proficient **12** accomplished

skilled worker 7 artisan
9 craftsman **10** technician
15 master craftsman

skillful 3 apt **4** able, deft, keen
5 adept, handy, sharp, slick
6 adroit, clever, expert, facile,
gifted **7** capable, cunning,
skilled, trained, veteran

8 masterly, talented **9** competent, dexterous, ingenious,
masterful, practiced, qualified
10 proficient, well-versed
11 experienced **12** accomplished, professional

skim 3 fly **4** flip, ream, sail,
scan, scud, skid, skip **5** coast,
float, glide, skate, sweep
6 bounce, scrape **7** dip into
8 glissade **10** glance over
11 leaf through, move lightly
12 thumb through

skimp 5 pinch, stint **6** scrimp,
slight **8** be frugal, be stingy,
hold back, withhold **9** economize **11** cut expenses, scrape
along

Skimpole, Harold
character in: 10 Bleak House
author: 7 Dickens

skimpy 5 close, scant, small,
spare, tight **6** frugal, meager,
modest, scanty, slight, sparse,
stingy **7** miserly, scrimpy,
sparing, wanting **8** exiguous,
grudging, smallish, stinting
9 illiberal, niggardly, penurious, scrimping **10** inadequate, incomplete, too thrifty
11 close fisted, tightfisted
12 insufficient, parsimonious
13 pennypinching
14 inconsiderable

skin 3 fur, pod **4** bark, case,
coat, flay, hide, hull, husk,
peel, pelt, rind, shell, abrade,
casing, fleece, jacket, scrape,
sheath, lay bare, epidermis,
complexion, integument, body
covering, outer coating
outer layer: 9 epidermis
contains: 4 fat **4** hair, pore,
root **5** nerve **6** vessel **8** oil
gland **10** sweat gland
body's largest: 5 organ
sense of: 4 cold, heat, pain
5 touch **8** pressure, tickling

skinflint 5 miser **7** hoarder,
niggard, scrooge **8** tightwad
10 pinchpenny **12** penny
pincher

Skinner, Cornelia Otis
author of: 23 The Pleasure of
His Company (with Samuel
Taylor) **24** Our Hearts Were
Young and Gay (with Emily
Kimbrough)

skinny 4 lank, lean, thin,
wiry **5** gaunt, gawky, lanky,
spare **6** slight **7** angular,
scraggy, scrawny, slender,
spindly **8** gangling, rawboned,
shrunken, skeletal **9** emaciated

Skin of Our Teeth, The
author: 14 Thornton Wilder

skip 3 bob, cut, hop **4** flee, flit,
jump, leap, miss, omit, romp,
shun, trip **5** bound, caper,

dodge, elude, evade 6 bounce,
escape, eschew, gambol, ignore, prance, spring 7 abscond, make off, neglect
8 leap over, leave out, overlook, pass over 9 disappear,
disregard, do without, play
hooky, skedaddle 10 fly the
coop 12 be absent from

skirmish 4 fray, tilt 5 brush,
clash, joust, run-in, scrap, set-
to 6 action, affray, battle, fracas, tussle 7 scuffle 8 struggle
9 encounter, firefight, scrimmage 10 engagement

skirmisher
   French: 10 tirailleur

Skirnir
   origin: 12 Scandinavian
   servant of: 4 Frey 5 Freyr

Skirophoria see 11 Scirophoria

skirt 3 hem, rim 4 edge, gird,
kilt, maxi, mini, ring, shun
5 avoid, evade, flank, hem in,
verge 6 border, bounds, circle,
dirndl, fringe, girdle, margin
7 enclose, envelop 8 boundary,
encircle, go around, lie along
9 crinoline, outer area, perimeter, periphery 10 circumvent,
fight shy of 12 circumscribe,
detour around

skittish 3 shy 4 wary 5 chary,
jumpy, leery, shaky, timid
6 fitful, unsure 7 bashful, fearful, fidgety, flighty, guarded,
jittery, nervous, restive 8 cautious, restless, unstable, unsteady, volatile 9 demurring,
excitable, impulsive, mercurial,
reluctant 10 suspicious
11 distrustful

skittles
   equipment: 4 pins 6 cheese
   also called: 5 closh 6 cloddy
      8 roly-poly 10 Dutch bowls
   tabletop version: 15 Enfield
      skittles

Skrymir
   also: 10 Utgardloki
   origin: 12 Scandinavian
   form: 5 giant
   took to Jotunheim: 4 Loki,
      Thor 7 Thialfi

Skuld 4 Norn
   origin: 12 Scandinavian
   form: 5 dwarf
   personifies: 6 future
   developed from: 5 Urdar
   companions: 3 Urd
      8 Verdandi

skulduggery, skullduggery
   7 knavery 8 trickery 9 chicanery, deception 10 dirty trick
   12 pettifoggery

skulk 4 hide, lurk 5 cower,
creep, prowl, slink, sneak
9 pussyfoot

skull
   contains: 5 brain

Skull place 7 Calvary
   8 Golgotha

sky 5 space 9 firmament 10 atmosphere, outer space, the
heavens 12 arch of heaven
   goddess of: 3 Fri, Nut
      5 Frigg, Frija 6 Frigga

sky blue 5 azure 8 cerulean,
pale blue 9 clear blue, light
blue

Sky King
   character: 5 Penny 7 Clipper
   cast: 10 Kirby Grant 11 Ron
      Haggerty 13 Gloria Winters
   ranch: 11 Flying Crown
   plane: 8 Songbird

skylarking 5 sport 6 antics
7 hijinks, romping
10 frolicking

skypilot 5 padre, rabbi 6 cleric,
parson, priest 8 chaplain, minister 9 clergyman

skyward 2 up 6 upward 8 to
the sky 10 heavenward 12 to
the heavens

slab 3 wad 4 hunk, slat
5 block, board, chunk, plank,
slice, wedge 10 thick slice

slack 3 lax 4 dull, easy, free,
lazy, limp, slow, soft 5 baggy,
loose, quiet, relax 6 easily,
flabby, freely, limply, loosen,
pliant, remiss, slowly, untied
7 flaccid, let up on, loosely,
not busy, not firm, not taut,
offhand, relaxed, slacken
8 careless, dilatory, flexible,
heedless, inactive, indolent,
listless, not tight, slapdash,
slipshod, slothful, sluggish
9 leisurely, lethargic, negligent, slow-paced, unmindful,
untighten 10 neglectful, nonchalant, permissive, slow-
moving, sluggishly, unexacting, unfastened, unthinking
11 inattentive, indifferent,
thoughtless, unconcerned,
undemanding

slacken 4 curb, ease, flag, free,
slow 5 abate, check, let go, let
up, limit, loose, relax, slack
6 arrest, go limp, lessen,
loosen, reduce, retard, soften,
temper, weaken 7 dwindle, inhibit, release 8 decrease, diminish, keep back, mitigate,
moderate, restrain, slow down,
taper off 9 untighten

slacker 5 idler 6 dodger, loafer,
truant 7 dallier, dawdler, goof-
off, laggard, quitter, shirker
9 do-nothing, goldbrick
10 malingerer 14 good-for-
nothing, procrastinator

slag 5 dross 6 cinder, scoria
8 clinkers

slake 4 calm, cool, curb, ease,
hush, sate 5 allay, quell, quiet,
still 6 modify, quench, soothe,
subdue, temper 7 appease, assuage, compose, gratify, mollify, relieve, satiate, satisfy
8 decrease, mitigate, moderate 9 alleviate 11 tranquilize
14 take the edge off

slake off 4 wane 5 abate
6 lessen, reduce, weaken
7 decline, subside 8 diminish,
fade away, slack off

slam 3 hit 4 bang, bump, slap
5 crash, smack, smash, throw

slammer 3 jug, pen 4 jail, stir
5 clink 6 cooler, lockup,
prison 8 big house, hoosegow
9 calaboose, jailhouse
12 penitentiary

Slammin' Sammy
   nickname of: 8 Sam Snead

slander 4 soil 5 libel, smear,
sully 6 defame, malign, revile,
vilify 7 calumny 8 besmirch
9 falsehood 10 defamation, distortion 12 vilification 14 false
statement 17 misrepresentation

Slaney, Mary see 10 Mary
Decker

slang 4 cant, jive 5 argot, idiom, lingo 6 jargon 7 dialect

slant 4 bias, lean, list, rake,
tilt, view 5 angle, color, pitch,
slope 7 distort, incline, leaning 8 attitude 9 prejudice,
viewpoint

slanted 4 awry 6 biased, tilted
7 colored, crooked, leaning,
pitched, sloping 8 inclined
9 on an angle, on the bias
10 prejudiced

slanting 4 bias 5 alean, atilt
7 oblique, sloping 8 diagonal,
glancing, inclined 10 distorting

slap 3 cut, hit 4 blow, clap,
cuff, snub, swat 5 smack,
whack 6 insult, rebuff, strike,
wallop 9 rejection

slapdash 6 casual, sloppy
8 careless, slipshod, slovenly
9 haphazard

Slapsie Maxie
   nickname of: 15 Maxie
      Rosenbloom

slash 3 cut, rip 4 drop, gash,
mark, pare, rend, rent, slit,
tear 5 lower, slice 6 reduce,
stroke 8 decrease, lacerate,
lowering 9 reduction
10 laceration

slate 4 list 6 ballot, tablet,
ticket 10 blackboard,
chalkboard

slattern 4 drab, slob, slut
5 bitch, frump 6 harlot,
sloven 7 trollop

slatternly 6 frowsy, frumpy,
sloppy, untidy 7 unkempt
8 slipshod, slovenly

slaughter 4 kill, slay 6 pogrom 7 butcher, destroy, killing, wipe out 8 decimate,
massacre 9 bloodbath 10 annihilate, butchering, mass murder 11 exterminate

Slaughterhouse Five
author: 12 Kurt Vonnegut
character: 12 Billy Pilgrim
setting: 7 Dresden

Slav 4 Pole, Serb, Sorb, Wend
5 Croat, Czech 6 Bulgar, Slovak 7 Russian, Serbian, Slovene, Sorbian 8 Bohemian,
Croatian, Moravian 9 Bulgarian, Ruthenian, Slavonian,
Slovadian, Ukrainian

slave 4 prey, serf, toil 6 addict,
drudge, menial, thrall, toiler,
vassal, victim 7 chattel, plodder 8 bondsman 9 workhorse
11 bond servant

slaver 5 drool 6 drivel
7 slobber

slavery 4 toil 5 grind, labor,
sweat 6 strain 7 bondage, serfdom, travail 8 drudgery, struggle 9 captivity, treadmill,
vassalage 11 enslavement, impressment, subjugation
12 enthrallment

Slavic
language family: 12 Indo-
European
group: 11 Balto-Slavic
subgroup: 12 Old Bulgarian
13 Eastern Slavic, Western
Slavic 14 Southern Slavic
15 Old Church Slavic

slavish 5 exact 6 strict 7 literal,
servile 9 imitative, slavelike
10 derivative, obsequious, submissive, unoriginal 11 subservient 13 unimaginative

slay 4 do in, kill 6 murder
7 destroy, execute 8 massacre
9 slaughter 10 annihilate

slayer 6 hit man, killer
7 butcher 8 assassin, murderer 11 executioner
12 exterminator

slaying 6 murder 7 killing
8 homicide 9 execution

sleazy 5 cheap, tacky 6 flimsy,
shabby, shoddy, trashy, vulgar 7 schlock 13 insubstantial

sleek 4 oily 5 shiny, silky,
slick, suave 6 glossy, satiny,
smooth 7 fawning, velvety
8 lustrous, unctuous
12 ingratiating

sleep 3 nap 4 doze, rest
5 death, peace 6 repose,
snooze 7 slumber
god of: 6 Hypnos, Hypnus,
Somnus

sleeping 6 asleep, dozing
7 dormant, napping, resting
8 snoozing 9 quiescent, somnolent 11 hibernating 19 in the
arms of Morpheus

Sleeping Beauty, The
composer: 11 Tchaikovsky

sleeping car (railroad)
invented by: 7 Pullman

sleeping infants
goddess of: 6 Cunina

sleeping place 3 bed, cot
4 bunk 5 berth 6 pallet 7 bedroom 9 dormitory
10 bedchamber

sleepless 5 alert 7 wakeful
8 restless, watchful 9 insomniac, wide awake
11 industrious

sleeplessness 8 insomnia
9 alertness, attention
11 wakefulness
12 restlessness

sleep lightly 3 nap, nod
4 doze 6 catnap, snooze
15 catch forty winks

sleepy 4 dull 5 quiet, tired,
weary 6 drowsy 8 fatigued, inactive 9 exhausted

sleigh 4 dray, sled 6 cutter,
sledge, troika 8 transport

Sleipnir
origin: 12 Scandinavian
horse of: 4 Odin 5 Othin
legs: 5 eight

slender 4 lean, poor, slim,
thin, weak 5 faint, scant,
small, spare 6 feeble, little,
meager, narrow, remote,
skinny, slight 7 willowy
8 delicate

Slender
character in: 22 The Merry
Wives of Windsor
author: 11 Shakespeare

Sleuth
director: 17 Joseph L
Mankiewicz
based on play by: 14 An-
thony Shaffer
cast: 12 Michael Caine
15 Laurence Olivier

slew 3 lot, ton 4 gang, heap,
load, lots, peck, pile, raft
5 batch, did in 6 killed 8 murdered 12 assassinated

Slezak, Walter
born: 6 Vienna 7 Austria
father: 9 Leo Slezak
roles: 5 Fanny 8 Lifeboat
11 Dr Coppelius

slice 3 cut 4 pare 5 carve,
piece, sever, shave 6 cut off,
divide 7 portion, section, segment, whittle 8 separate
9 dismember

slick 3 sly 4 coat, film, foxy,
oily, scum, waxy, wily
5 sharp, shiny, sleek 6 clever,
glassy, glossy, greasy, satiny,
smooth, tricky 7 coating, cunning 8 slippery 10 make
glossy 11 fast-talking
13 smooth-talking

slicker 8 raincoat 9 sou'wester
10 mackintosh, waterproof

slide 4 fall, pass, ramp, skid,
slip, veer 5 chute, coast, glide,
lapse, slope 7 slither 8 sideslip 11 diapositive
12 transparency

slide by 4 go by 5 lapse
6 elapse, roll by, slip by
7 glide by 8 slip away

slight 3 cut 4 lean, slap, slim,
snub, thin, tiny 5 frail, small,
spare 6 insult, little, modest,
rebuff 7 fragile, limited, slender 8 moderate 10 incivility,
negligible, restricted 11 unimportant 13 imperceptible, inappreciable, infinitesimal

slight amount 3 bit 4 dash,
drop 5 pinch, touch, trace
6 little 7 smidgen, smidgin,
soupcon 8 smidgeon 9 little
bit 10 smattering

slightly 6 feebly, rarely 8 meagerly, scantily, scarcely, somewhat 10 negligibly
13 superficially
15 insignificantly

slim 4 lean, thin 5 faint, small
6 meager, remote, skinny,
slight, svelte 7 distant, slender,
thready, willowy 10 negligible

slime 3 mud 4 mire, muck,
ooze 6 sludge

slimy 4 foul, vile 5 gummy,
mucky, nasty 6 creepy, putrid,
sticky 7 viscous 9 glutinous,
loathsome, obnoxious, offensive, repulsive

sling 3 net 4 cast 5 fling,
throw 9 slingshot 10 arm
support

Slingin' Sammy
nickname of: 10 Sammy
Baugh

slingshot 5 sling 8 catapult

slink 4 slip 5 creep, prowl,
skulk, sneak, steal 6 tiptoe

slip 3 put 4 dock, drop, fail,
fall, leak, pass, sink, skid
5 berth, error, glide, lapse,
scrap, shoot, shred, slide,
sneak, sprig, steal, strip 6 es-

cape, sprout, ticket, worsen **7** blunder, chemise, cutting, decline, faux pas, receipt, sapling, voucher **9** petticoat, stripling, youngling, youngster **10** be revealed, get clear of, imprudence, underdress **12** indiscretion

slip away 4 go by **5** lapse **6** elapse, escape **7** run away, slide by **8** creep off **9** tiptoe off

slip by 4 go by, pass **5** lapse **6** elapse, pass by, roll by **7** glide by, slide by

slip of the tongue, a
　Latin: **13** lapsus linguae

slipper 4 mule, shoe **5** scuff **6** sandal

slippery 4 foxy, oily, waxy, wily **5** slick, soapy **6** crafty, glassy, greasy, shifty, smooth, sneaky, tricky **7** devious **9** deceitful **10** contriving, unreliable **11** treacherous **13** untrustworthy

slipshod 3 lax **5** loose, messy **6** casual, sloppy, untidy **7** offhand **8** careless, slovenly **11** thoughtless

slip-up 4 flub, goof **5** botch, error, gaffe, lapse **6** boo-boo, bungle, foul-up, mess-up, miscue **7** blooper, blunder, clinker, faux pas, mistake, screw-up **9** oversight

slit 3 cut **4** gash **5** crack, slash **7** crevice, fissure **8** incision

slither 5 glide, slide **25** move with a side-to-side motion

sliver 5 crumb, shred, slice, snick **6** morsel **8** splinter

slivovitz
　type: **6** brandy **7** liqueur
　origin: **10** Yugoslavia
　flavor: **4** plum

slob 6 sloven **8** slattern

slobber 4 slop **5** drool **6** drivel, slaver **7** dribble, sputter **8** salivate, splutter

sloe gin
　type: **7** liqueur
　flavor: **9** sloe berry **15** blackthorn berry
　drink: **11** Sloe Gin Fizz
　with bourbon: **9** Black Hawk
　with rum: **11** Shark's Tooth
　with vermouth: **10** Blackthorn

slogan 5 motto **6** byword **9** battle cry, catchword, watchword

sloop 4 boat, brig, ship **5** smack **8** sailboat, schooner

slop 3 mud **4** mire, muck, ooze **5** filth, slosh, slush, spill, swash, swill, waste **6** refuse, sludge, splash **7** garbage, spatter **8** splatter

slope 3 tip **4** bank, bend, lean, tilt **5** angle, pitch, slant **7** descent, incline **9** downgrade **11** inclination

sloping 5 alean, steep **6** aslant **7** leaning, oblique, tilting **8** diagonal, inclined, on a slant, slanting **9** slantways **11** declivitous

sloppiness 5 chaos, mix-up, upset **6** jumble **7** clutter **8** disarray, disorder, shambles **9** messiness **10** disharmony, untidiness **12** dishevelment **14** disarrangement **15** disorganization

sloppy 3 wet **5** dirty, messy, muddy **6** marshy, sloshy, slushy, sodden, soiled, swampy, untidy, watery **7** unclean **10** disorderly

sloppy person 4 slob **6** sloven

slosh 3 lap **4** drop, mire, stir **5** slush, spill, swash **6** splash **8** flounder

slot 3 gap **4** slit **5** crack, niche, notch
　machine: **14** one-armed bandit

sloth 6 phlegm, torpor **7** languor **8** idleness, laziness, lethargy **9** indolence, lassitude, torpidity **12** listlessness, sluggishness **13** do-nothingness, shiftlessness

slothful 3 lax **4** idle, lazy **5** inert **6** drowsy, otiose, supine, torpid **8** indolent, listless, sluggish **9** do-nothing, lethargic, negligent, shiftless **10** sluggardly **11** unambitious

slouch 4 bend **5** droop, hunch, idler, slump, stoop **6** loafer **7** laggard, shirker, slacker **8** sluggard **9** goldbrick, lazybones

Slovakia
　formerly part of:
　　14 Czechoslovakia
　capital/largest city:
　　10 Bratislava
　others: **6** Kosice
　head of state: **9** president
　government: **8** republic
　monetary unit: **5** crown **6** koruna
　mountain: **7** Sudetes **8** Low Tatra **9** High Tatra, Slovak Ore **10** Carpathian, Nizke Tatry **11** Visoke Tatry **15** White Carpathian

　river: **2** Uh **3** Vah **4** Hron **5** Nitra, Slana **6** Danube, Hornad, Ondava, Poprad **7** Laborec **8** Latorica
　people: **5** Czech **6** Slavik, Slovak **9** Hungarian
　language: **6** Slavik, Slovak
　religion: **9** Christian **13** Roman Catholic

Slovenia
　capital/largest city: **9** Ljubljana
　others: **5** Celje, Koper, Kranj **7** Maribor
　head of state: **9** president
　government: **8** republic
　monetary unit: **5** tolar
　river: **4** Sava **5** Drava
　sea: **8** Adriatic
　people: **8** Slovenes
　language: **7** Slovene
　religion: **13** Roman Catholic

slovenly 5 dirty, dowdy, messy **6** frowzy, sloppy, untidy **7** unclean, unkempt **8** careless, slapdash, slipshod **10** disorderly, slatternly **11** indifferent, unconcerned

slow 3 dim, off **4** curb, dull, dumb, flag, late, long **5** brake, check, dense, heavy, loath, quiet **6** averse, boring, falter, hinder, hold up, impede, obtuse, retard, stupid, torpid **7** belated, delayed, laggard, lumpish, not busy, overdue, tedious, unhasty **8** backward, cautious, dawdling, dilatory, dragging, drawn out, extended, hesitant, inactive, obstruct, sluggish, tarrying **9** dim-witted, leisurely, lingering, ponderous, prolonged, reluctant, snail-like, unhurried **10** behind time, decelerate, deliberate, dull-witted, indisposed, protracted, unexciting, unpunctual **11** disinclined, halfhearted, reduce speed **12** impercipient, lose momentum, tortoiselike, unperceptive

slowdown 4 curb, flag **5** brake, delay, letup, slump **6** ease-up, falter, hinder, impede, lessen, retard, slow-up **7** decline, falloff, letdown, setback, slowing, subside **8** diminish, downturn, flagging **9** grind down **10** decelerate, slackening, stagnation **11** reduce speed, retardation **12** deceleration

slow-moving 4 poky **5** pokey **6** idling **8** crawling, creeping, dawdling, sluggish **9** leisurely, snaillike **10** turtlelike **12** tortoiselike
　creature: **4** slug **5** loris, sloth, snail **6** turtle **8** tortoise

slowness 6 tedium **8** dullness **9** torpidity **10** snail's pace **12** backwardness, sluggishness

slow-paced 4 easy **7** gradual, laggard **8** sluggish **9** leisurely, lethargic, unhurried **10** deliberate

slowpoke 4 slug **5** idler, snail **7** dallier, dawdler, laggard, lie-abed, plodder **8** lingerer, slug-abed, tortoise **9** saunterer, straggler **11** foot-dragger

slow to learn 4 dull **5** dense, inapt **6** stupid **8** retarded **10** slow-witted

slow up 4 stem **5** delay **6** detain, hinder, impede, re-tard **8** slow down

slow-witted 4 dull **5** dense **7** doltish, idiotic, moronic **8** backward, retarded **9** imbecilic

sludge 3 mud **4** mire, muck, ooze, slop **5** dregs, slime, slush **8** sediment

slug 3 bat, hit **4** bash, belt, sock **5** baste, clout, pound, punch, smite, thump, whack, whale **6** batter, strike, wallop **7** clobber **8** lambaste

sluggard 4 lazy **5** drone, idler, sloth, snail **6** loafer, truant, turtle **7** dawdler, laggard **8** loiterer, slothful, slowpoke, tortoise **9** do-nothing, lazybones **11** couch potato **12** lounge lizard **13** stick-in-the-mud

sluggish 4 lazy, slow **5** inert **6** torpid **7** languid **8** inactive, indolent, lifeless, listless, slothful **9** leisurely, lethargic, soporific, unhurried **10** phlegmatic, protracted, spiritless

sluggishness 6 torpor **7** inertia **8** lethargy, slowness **9** lassitude **10** inactivity **12** listlessness

slum
    Portuguese: **6** favela

slumber 3 nap **4** doze **5** sleep **6** snooze **8** vegetate **9** hibernate **10** be inactive, lie dormant

slump 3 dip, sag **4** drop, fall, slip **5** droop, lapse **6** plunge, slouch, tumble **7** decline, give way, reverse, setback **8** collapse

slur 3 cut, dig **4** mark, skip, spot **5** smear, stain, sully, taint **6** defame, ignore, insult, malign, mumble, mutter, slight **7** affront, blacken, blemish, let pass **8** mumbling, overlook, pass over **9** disregard, gloss over, muttering **11** run together

slush 4 slop **6** bathos **9** soppiness **11** mawkishness, melting snow **14** sentimentalism, sentimentality

slushiness 5 slush **10** sponginess **11** mawkishness **14** sentimentalism, sentimentality

slut 4 doxy, jade **5** bimbo, frump, hussy, tramp, wench, whore **6** floozy, harlot, sloven, wanton **7** jezebel, trollop **8** slattern, strumpet **10** prostitute

sly 4 foxy, wily **6** artful, covert, crafty, secret, shrewd, sneaky, tricky **7** cunning, furtive, playful, private **8** stealthy **9** conniving **11** dissembling, mischievous **12** confidential

Slye, Leonard
    real name of: **9** Roy Rogers

slyness 5 craft **7** cunning, stealth **8** archness, foxiness, subtlety, wiliness **10** artfulness, craftiness, shrewdness, trickiness **11** furtiveness

smack 3 bit, hit, rap **4** blow, buss, clap, cuff, dash, hint, kiss, slap **5** savor, smell, smite, spank, taste, tinge, touch, trace, whack **6** buffet, flavor **7** suggest

small 4 mean, tiny, weak **5** faint, minor, petty, scant **6** feeble, lesser, little, meager, modest, narrow, petite, slight **7** bigoted, fragile, ignoble, trivial **8** not great, trifling **10** diminutive, provincial, undersized **11** of no account, opinionated, superficial, unimportant **13** insignificant

small details
    Latin: **8** minutiae

smaller 4 less **5** lower **6** lesser, tinier **7** dinkier, littler, pettier, reduced, shorter **8** inferior

smallest 5 least **6** lowest **7** tiniest **8** dinkiest, pettiest, shortest **9** slightest

small intestine
    part of: **15** digestive system
    lined with: **5** villi

small-minded 4 mean **5** petty **6** narrow **7** bigoted **9** parochial **10** prejudiced **12** mean-spirited

smallness 8 meanness, tininess **9** pettiness **10** meagerness, triviality **12** dwarfishness **14** insignificance **18** inconsequentiality

small piece 3 bit, dab **4** chip, drop, snip **5** crumb, grain, piece, pinch, scrap, shred, speck **6** dollop, morsel **7** granule, smidgen, smidgin **8** fragment, particle, smidgeon

small quantity 3 bit, dab, few **5** touch **7** smidgen, smidgin, soupcon **8** smidgeon **9** little bit

small round window
    French: **11** oeil-de-boeuf

small spot 3 dab, dot **5** fleck, speck

small talk 6 banter, gossip **7** chatter, prattle **8** chitchat, idle talk, repartee **9** bavardage, prattling **12** tittle-tattle

smart 4 ache, burn, chic, hurt, keen, neat, trim **5** brash, brisk, quick, sassy, sharp, sting, wince, witty **6** astute, blench, brainy, bright, clever, flinch, modish, shrewd, suffer **7** elegant, stylish **8** feel pain, vigorous **9** be painful, energetic **10** smart-aleck **11** fashionable, intelligent

smart aleck 6 smarty **7** showoff, windbag, wiseass, wise guy **8** blowhard, braggart, saucebox, wiseacre **9** know-it-all **11** smarty-pants **12** grandstander **13** exhibitionist

smarten up 7 dress up, improve **8** beautify, spruce up

smartness 6 acumen, wisdom **8** keenness, sagacity **9** acuteness **10** astuteness, cleverness, perception, shrewdness **12** intelligence, perspicacity

smash 3 hit **4** bang, bash, beat, blow **5** break, clout, crack, crash, crush **6** batter, strike, winner **7** clobber, crack-up, destroy, shatter, success, triumph **8** accident, demolish, splinter **9** collision, sensation **12** disintegrate

smash against 4 beat, lash **5** crash, pound, smite **6** batter, buffet **7** break on

smashed 5 drunk **6** soused, wasted, zapped, zonked **7** crashed, crushed **8** squashed **9** plastered, shattered **10** inebriated **11** intoxicated **17** under the influence **20** three sheets to the wind

smashing 5 great, super **6** superb **8** fabulous, terrific **9** fantastic, marvelous, wonderful **10** stupendous **11** magnificent, sensational **13** extraordinary

smashup 5 crash, wreck **7** crackup **8** accident **9** collision **12** fender bender

smattering 3 bit, dab **4** dash, drop **5** scrap **7** smidgen, smidgin, snippet **8** smidgeon **10** sprinkling

smear 3 mar, rub **4** blur, coat, daub, soil **5** cover, lay on, libel, stain **6** blotch, injure, malign, smirch, smudge, spread, streak **7** blacken, blemish, degrade, slander, splotch, tar-

nish **8** besmirch, besmudge
9 denigrate **10** accusation,
obliterate

smell 4 feel, nose, odor, reek
5 aroma, fetor, scent, sense,
sniff, stink **6** detect, stench
7 bouquet, perfume, suspect
8 perceive **9** emanation, fragrance, get wind of

smelly 4 rank **5** fetid **6** putrid
7 noisome, odorous, reeking
8 stinking **10** malodorous

Smerdyakov
character in: **20** The Brothers
Karamazov
author: **10** Dostoevsky

Smetana, Bedrich
born: **7** Bohemia **8** Litomysl
11 Leitomischl
14 Czechoslovakia
composer of: **7** Ma Vlast
9 My Country **10** From My
Life **11** Czech Dances
12 The Two Widows **16** The
Bartered Bride

**smidgen, smidgin, smid-
geon 3** bit, dab **4** mite, snip
5 crumb, pinch, scrap, shred,
speck, trace **6** dollop, morsel

Smike
character in: **16** Nicholas
Nickleby
author: **7** Dickens

smile 4 beam, grin **5** favor,
shine, smirk **6** simper

Smiles of a Summer Night
director: **13** Ingmar Bergman
cast: **11** Eva Dahlbeck
13 Ulla Jacobsson **15** Margit
Carlquist **16** Harriet
Andersson
remade as: **17** A Little Night
Music

Smiley's People
author: **11** John Le Carre

Smintheus
epithet of: **6** Apollo

smirch 4 blot, mark, soil, spot
5 dirty, smear, stain, sully,
taint **6** blotch, damage,
smudge, stigma **7** begrime,
blacken, blemish, slander, tarnish **8** besmirch, besmudge,
dishonor **9** discredit

smirk 4 grin, leer **5** sneer
6 simper **7** grimace

Smirke, Sir Robert
architect of: **12** King's College (U of London) **13** British Museum (London)
19 Covent Garden Theater
(London)
style: **12** Greek Revival

smite 3 hit **4** swat **5** knock,
smack, whack **6** enamor,
strike, wallop **7** clobber

Smith, Adam
author of: **18** The Wealth of
Nations

Smith, Al
creator/artist of: **11** Mutt
and Jeff

Smith, Betty
author of: **20** A Tree Grows
in Brooklyn

Smith, Charles Aaron
nickname: **5** Bubba
sport: **8** football
team: **14** Baltimore Colts

Smith, David
born: **8** Decatur IN
artwork: **3** Zig **4** Cubi **6** Ocu-
lus **8** Agricola, Main View,
Sentinel, Star Cage **9** Australia, Royal Bird, Tank Totem **10** The Banquet
12 Detroit Queen **15** Lectern
Sentinel **17** Medals for Dishonor **20** Hudson River
Landscape **23** Song of an
Irish Blacksmith

Smith, Gladys Mary
real name of: **12** Mary
Pickford

Smith, Harriet
character in: **4** Emma
author: **6** Austen

Smith, Lillian
author: **12** Strange Fruit

Smith, Maggie
born: **6** Ilford **7** England
husband: **14** Robert Stephens
roles: **7** Othello **15** California
Suite, The Pumpkin Eater
17 Travels with My Aunt
24 The Prime of Miss Jean
Brodie (Oscar)

Smith, Winston
character in: **18** Nineteen
Eighty-Four
author: **6** Orwell

smithereen 3 bit **4** atom
5 crumb, shard **8** fragment,
particle **9** scintilla

Smithson, James
field: **9** chemistry
nationality: **7** British
discovered: **11** smithsonite
13 zinc carbonite
funded: **22** Smithsonian
Institution

smitten 8 enamored **9** bewitched **10** enraptured,
infatuated

smoke 4 draw, fume, pipe,
puff, reek, suck **5** cigar,
fumes **6** billow, inhale **7** light
up, smolder **9** cigarette, have
a drag

Smoke
author: **12** Ivan Turgenev
character: **5** Irina **7** Potugin
13 Tanya Shestoff **16** Gen-

eral Ratmiroff, Grigory Litvi-
noff **18** Kapitolina Shestoff

smoke screen 4 ruse **5** cover,
dodge, front **6** screen **9** deception **10** camouflage, subterfuge

smoky 5 dingy, grimy, sooty
6 fuming, smudgy **7** reeking
10 smoldering

smolder 4 burn, fume, rage
5 smoke **6** seethe

Smollett, Tobias George
author of: **14** (The Expedition
of) Humphry Clinker, Roderick Random **15** Peregrine
Pickle

smooch 3 pet **4** buss, kiss,
neck **5** smack, spoon **7** make
out

smooth 4 calm, ease, easy,
even, flat, glib, help, mild,
open, pave **5** allay, level, silky,
sleek, suave **6** facile, mellow,
placid, polish, refine, serene,
soften, soothe, steady **7** appease, assuage, flatten, mollify,
orderly, perfect, prepare, velvety **8** civilize, composed,
make even, mitigate, peaceful,
pleasant **9** collected, cultivate,
easygoing, make level **10** facilitate, flattering, harmonious,
methodical, uneventful
11 well-ordered **12** ingratiating **13** self-possessed, well-
regulated

smoothness 8 evenness, fineness, flatness **9** silkiness,
sleekness

smooth the feathers 4 calm
6 pacify, soothe **7** appease, assuage, mollify, placate
10 conciliate

smooth-tongued 4 glib
5 suave **6** fluent **8** unctuous
10 flattering **11** fast-talking
12 hypocritical, ingratiating

smother 4 hide, mask, wrap
5 choke, quash, snuff
6 deaden, quench, shower
7 conceal **8** keep down, strangle, suppress, surround
9 choke back, envelop in, suffocate **10** asphyxiate,
extinguish

**Smothers Brothers Comedy
Hour, The**
regulars: **10** Don Novello, Pat
Paulsen **11** Bob Einstein,
Leigh French, Steve Martin,
Tom Smothers **12** Betty
Aberlin, Dick Smothers,
John Hartford, Nino Sen-
porty, Spencer Quinn
13 Mason Williams **14** Jennifer Warren, Sally Struthers **16** Anita Kerr Singers
17 Jimmy Joyce Singers
18 Louis DaPron Dancers

19 Marty Paich Orchestra
20 Denny Vaughn Orchestra, Ron Poindexter Dancers **21** Nelson Riddle Orchestra

smudge 4 blot, mark, soil, spot **5** dirty, smear, stain **6** smutch

smudgy 5 dirty, messy **6** filthy, grubby, smeary **7** sullied **8** befouled, unwashed **9** besmeared

smug 8 superior, virtuous **10** complacent **13** self-righteous, self-satisfied

smuggle 5 sneak **15** export illegally, import illegally

smuggled goods 10 contraband **14** illegal exports, illegal imports **18** prohibited articles

smuggler 6 runner **9** gunrunner, rumrunner **10** bootlegger **13** contrabandist

smugness 7 egotism **9** immodesty **11** superiority **12** virtuousness **16** self-satisfaction **17** self-righteousness

smut 4 dirt, porn, soot **5** filth, grime **6** smudge **9** obscenity, scatology **11** pornography

smutty 4 lewd **5** dirty, grimy, sooty **6** filthy, soiled, vulgar **7** obscene **8** indecent **12** pornographic

Smyrna see **6** Myrrha

Smythe, Reginald
creator/artist of: **8** Andy Capp

snack 3 eat, tea **4** bite, nosh **5** munch **6** nibble, tidbit **7** take tea **8** lap lunch, munchies, nibblies, pick-me-up, snackies **9** collation, crunchies, elevenses **10** finger food, light lunch **11** casse-croute, coffee break, light repast, refreshment

snag 3 bar, rip **4** grab, stub, tear **5** block, catch, hitch, stump **7** barrier **8** obstacle **9** hindrance **10** difficulty, impediment, projection, protrusion **11** encumbrance, obstruction **14** stumbling block

Snagsby
character in: **10** Bleak House
author: **7** Dickens

snail
French: **8** escargot

snake see **box**

Snake see **8** Shoshoni

snake, poisonous 9 Coactrice

Snake, the
nickname of: **10** Ken Stabler

snake 5 sneak, viper **7** reptile, serpent, traitor **8** ophidian **9** reptilian
combining form: **4** ophi **5** ophio, ophis **6** herpes **7** herpeto
expert: **13** herpetologist
fear of: **13** herpetophobia
genus: **7** Ophidia
kind: **3** asp, boa, sea **4** file, habu, wart, whip **5** aboma, adder, cobra, coral, krait, mamba, tiger, viper **6** bongar, elapid, garter, gopher, python, taipan **7** rattler, sunbeam **8** anaconda, cerastes, moccasin, pit viper, ringhals **9** boomslang, colubrina, mole viper, puff adder **10** black mamba, bushmaster, copperhead, fer-de-lance, sidewinder **11** cottonmouth, diamond back, Gaboon viper, rattlesnake **12** slender blind **13** elephant-trunk, water moccasin **14** boa constrictor
shedding: **7** ecdysis **8** moulting
skin: **6** exuvia
snake killer: **8** mongoose

Snake Pit, The
author: **12** Sigrid Undset

snap 3 nip, pop **4** bark, bite, grab, lock, yelp **5** break, catch, cinch, clasp, click, close, crack, growl, hasty, latch, quick, snarl, spell **6** breeze, period, secure, snatch, sudden **8** careless, fastener, fracture **9** impulsive **11** thoughtless

snapdragon 11 Antirrhinum
varieties: **4** wild **5** dwarf **6** common, garden, lesser **7** spurred **8** withered

snappish 4 edgy **5** cross, huffy, surly, testy **6** crabby, cranky, shirty, touchy **7** grouchy, huffish, peevish, waspish **8** captious, petulant **9** irascible, irritable, querulous **10** ill-humored, ill-natured, out of sorts **11** hot-tempered **12** cantankerous **13** quick-tempered, short-tempered

snappy 4 fast, tony **5** hasty, quick, rapid, ritzy, sharp, smart, swank, swift, swish **6** classy, dapper, jaunty, speedy, spiffy **7** stylish **12** lickety-split

snare 3 net **4** bait, hook, lure, ruse, trap **5** catch, decoy, noose, seize, trick **6** entrap **7** capture, ensnare, pitfall **9** deception **12** entanglement

snarl 3 mat **4** bark, clog, kink, knot, mess, snap **5** chaos, growl, ravel, twist **6** hinder, impede, jumble, muddle, tangle **7** confuse, lash out **8** disorder, entangle **9** confusior

snatch 3 bit, nab **4** grab, part, pull, take **5** catch, grasp, piece, pluck, seize, wrest **7** snippet **8** fragment

Snead, Sam
nickname: **12** Slammin' Sammy
sport: **4** golf
won: **7** Masters

sneak 3 sly **4** slip **5** creep, knave, rogue, scamp, steal **6** lurker, rascal, secret, spirit **7** bounder, furtive, skulker, slinker, smuggle **8** scalawag, surprise **9** miscreant, scoundrel, secretive, underhand **11** rapscallion **13** surreptitious

sneak attack 4 raid **6** ambush **7** assault **9** ambuscade, incursion

sneak off 5 elope **6** decamp **7** abscond **9** steal away

sneaky 3 sly **4** mean **7** devious, furtive, vicious **9** malicious, secretive, underhand **10** traitorous **11** treacherous

sneer 4 jeer, leer, mock **5** scoff, scorn, smirk **6** deride, rebuff **7** disdain **8** belittle, ridicule

sneer at 5 knock, scorn **6** deride, malign **7** disdain, put down, run down **8** pooh-pooh **16** cast aspersions on

Sneerwell, Lady
character in: **19** The School for Scandal
author: **8** Sheridan

snicker 5 snort **6** cackle, giggle, simper, titter **7** snigger

snide 5 nasty **7** mocking **8** scoffing **9** malicious, sarcastic **11** insinuating **12** contemptuous

Snider, Edwin
nickname: **4** Duke
sport: **8** baseball
position: **7** fielder
team: **15** Brooklyn Dodgers

sniff 4 jeer, mock, odor **5** aroma, scoff, smell, snort, snuff, whiff **6** snivel **7** disdain, sniffle, snuffle **9** disparage

snip 3 bit, bob, cut, lop **4** brat, clip, crop, punk, snap, trim

5 clack, click, piece, prune, scrap, shear, twerp **6** sample, shrimp, swatch **7** cutting **8** fragment

snippy 4 curt, rude **5** sassy, saucy, short **6** cheeky, snotty **7** brusque **8** flippant, impudent, insolent, snippety **11** ill-mannered, impertinent, smart-alecky

snivel 3 cry **5** sniff, whine **6** boohoo **7** sniffle **8** complain

sniveler 6 coward, whiner **7** crybaby **10** complainer

snob 7 elitist **13** social climber

snobbish 4 vain **6** snooty, snotty **7** haughty, high-hat, stuck-up **8** arrogant, superior **10** disdainful **11** overbearing, patronizing, pretentious **13** condescending

Snodgrass
    character in: 14 Pickwick Papers
    author: 7 Dickens

snoop 3 pry **7** meddler, Paul Pry **8** busybody **10** Nosy Parker **12** eavesdropper

snoopy, Snoopy 4 nosy **6** beagle, prying **7** curious **8** meddling **10** meddlesome **11** inquisitive
    brother: 5 Spike
    creator: 6 Schulz
    friend: 9 Woodstock
    master: 12 Charlie Brown

snooze 3 nap **4** doze **5** sleep **6** cat nap, drowse, siesta **7** slumber **10** forty winks

Snopes family
    characters in: 9 The Hamlet
    members: 2 Ab **4** Flem, Mink **5** Isaac
    author: 8 Faulkner

snort 4 blow, gasp, huff, jeer, pant, puff, rage **5** blast, grunt, scoff, sneer, storm

snout 3 neb **4** beak, bill, nose **5** snoot, spout **6** muzzle, nozzle **9** proboscis

Snow, C P (Charles Percy Snow, Lord Snow)
    author of: 9 The New Men **10** Last Things, The Masters **14** A Coat of Varnish **16** Corridors of Power **20** Strangers and Brothers

Snow-Bound
    author: 21 John Greenleaf Whittier

snowfall 4 firn, neve **6** flurry **8** blizzard
    Scottish: 6 onding

Snow Leopard, The
    author: 16 Peter Matthiessen

Snow Queen, The
    author: 21 Hans Christian Andersen

Snows of Kilimanjaro, The
    author: 15 Ernest Hemingway

snow-white 4 pure **5** snowy **9** lily-white, pure white **11** white as snow

Snow White
    author: 15 Donald Barthelme

snowy 4 pure **5** white **7** nievous **8** pristine, spotless **9** blizzardy

snub 3 cut **5** blunt, check, scorn, short **6** ignore, rebuff, slight, stubby **7** disdain **9** retrousse **11** repudiation **12** cold shoulder **16** turn up one's nose at **19** give the cold shoulder

snuff 5 scent, smell, sniff, whiff **7** sniffle, snuffle

snuff out 5 crush **8** suppress **10** extinguish, put an end to

snug 4 cozy, neat, safe **5** close, tight **6** secure **7** compact **8** tranquil **9** sheltered, skintight **11** comfortable **12** close-fitting, tight-fitting **13** well-organized

snuggle 3 hug **4** nest **6** cuddle, curl up, enfold, nestle, nuzzle

Snyder, Peggy Lou
    real name of: 21 Harriet Hilliard Nelson

so
    Latin: 3 sic

soak 3 wet **4** seep **5** bathe, enter, steep **6** absorb, drench, sink in, take in, take up **7** immerse, pervade **8** permeate, saturate **9** penetrate

soaked 5 soggy **6** sodden, soused **7** sopping **8** drenched **9** saturated **11** waterlogged, wringing wet

soak up 4 blot **6** absorb, take up **8** sponge up

soak up warmth 4 bask **11** warm oneself **12** toast oneself

Soames Forsyte
    character in: 14 The Forsyte Saga
    author: 10 Galsworthy

Soap
    character: 5 Major **6** Benson **9** Billy Tate **10** Eunice Tate **11** Chester Tate, Corrine Tate, Danny Dallas, Jessica Tate, Jodie Dallas **12** Burt Campbell **18** Mary Dallas Campbell
    cast: 7 Ted Wass **9** Jimmy Baio **11** Diana Canova

12 Billy Crystal, Cathryn Damon, Jennifer Salt, Robert Mandan **14** Arthur Peterson **15** Richard Mulligan, Robert Guillaume **16** Katherine Helmond

soar 3 fly **4** rise, wing **5** climb, float, glide, mount, tower **8** take wing

soave
    music: 6 gentle

sob 3 cry **4** howl, wail, weep **6** lament, plaint, snivel **7** blubber, whimper

so be it 4 amen **7** let it be **9** let it be so

sober 3 dry, sad **4** cool, drab, dull, grim, sane **5** grave, sound, staid **6** dreary, sedate, solemn, somber, steady **7** joyless, prudent, serious, subdued **8** moderate, not drunk, rational **9** judicious, realistic, sorrowful, temperate **10** abstemious **11** levelheaded **13** dispassionate

So Big
    author: 10 Edna Ferber

sobriety 10 abstention, abstinence, continence, temperance **13** nonindulgence **14** abstemiousness

sobriquet 7 epithet, pet name **8** nickname **11** appellation

so-called
    French: 9 soi-disant

soccer
    athlete: 4 Pele **11** Johan Cruyff
    players/team: 6 eleven
    position: 6 goalie **7** forward **8** fullback, halfback **10** goalkeeper
    championship: 8 World Cup **11** European Cup, National Cup **13** Cup Winner's Cup
    violation: 5 hands **7** hacking, offside **11** obstructing
    gaining control of ball: 4 trap

sociable 6 social **7** affable, cordial **8** friendly, gracious, outgoing **9** agreeable, congenial, convivial **10** gregarious, neighborly **11** extroverted **13** companionable

social 2 in **5** smart **7** stylish **8** friendly, pleasant, sociable **9** agreeable **10** gregarious, neighborly **11** cooperative, fashionable **14** interdependent

Social Contract, The
    author: 19 Jean-Jacques Rousseau

social order
    goddess of: 4 Hour **5** Horae

society 4 body, club **5** elite, group **6** circle, gentry, league **7** mankind **8** alliance, humanity, nobility **9** community, humankind **10** blue bloods **11** aristocracy, association, high society, social order **12** organization **14** the four hundred **16** the general public

sociologist
American: 4 Mead, Park, Ward **5** Coser, Gerth, Mills, Small, Wirth **6** Bendix, Cooley, Merton, Speier, Sumner, Thomas **7** Parsons, Sorokin **8** Eberhard **10** Lazarsfeld
British: 4 Webb **8** Hobhouse, Mannheim **12** Carr-Saunders
Danish: 6 Geiger
French: 4 Aron **5** Comte **8** Durkheim, Gurvitch **9** Friedmann
German: 5 Konig, Weber, Wiese **6** Simmel **8** Habermas, Luckmann **10** Dahrendorf, Horkheimer
Hungarian: 6 Lukacs **8** Mannheim
Israeli: 5 Buber **10** Eisenstadt
Norwegian: 6 Aubert **7** Galtung
Swedish: 8 Carlsson

sociopathic 9 alienated **10** antisocial, rebellious

sock 3 box, hit, sox **4** belt, blow, slap **5** punch, smack, smash **6** strike, wallop **7** clobber **8** knee sock **9** ankle sock **13** short stocking

sod 4 soil, turf **5** divot, earth, grass, sward **10** greensward

soda 3 pop **4** base, cola **5** tonic **6** bicarb, sodium **7** barilla, seltzer **8** beverage, root beer **9** ginger ale, soft drink **11** bicarbonate **12** sarsaparilla
ash: 6 alkali
in faro: 9 first card
maker: 4 jerk

sodden 4 dull **5** heavy, lumpy, mushy, pasty, soggy, soppy **6** doughy, soaked **7** sopping **8** besotted, drenched, dripping, listless **9** saturated **10** wet through **14** expressionless

Soddy, Frederick
field: 9 chemistry
nationality: 7 British
discovered: 8 isotopes
worked with: 13 William Ramsay **16** Ernest Rutherford
awarded: 10 Nobel Prize

sodium
chemical symbol: 2 Na

Sodom
destroyed with: 5 Admah **6** Zeboim **8** Gomorrah

sofa 5 couch, divan **6** canape, lounge, settee **8** love seat **9** davenport **12** chesterfield

Sofia
Roman name: 12 Ulpia Serdica
Byzantine name: 9 Triaditsa
capital of: 8 Bulgaria
landmark: 13 Buyuk Dzhamiya **16** Saint Sofia Church **17** Saint George Church **24** Alexander Nevsky Cathedral **32** Cyril and Methodius National Library

soft 4 easy, kind, mild, pale, weak **5** downy, faint, furry, muted, quiet, silky, sleek **6** feeble, gentle, hushed, pliant, satiny, shaded, silken, smooth, supple, tender **7** lenient, not hard, pitying, pliable, restful, subdued, velvety **8** delicate, not sharp, shadowed, tolerant, tranquil, twilight **9** malleable, not strong **10** harmonious **11** sentimental, sympathetic **12** easily molded, low intensity **13** compassionate, pleasantly low **16** easily penetrated **19** having a breathy sound **21** requiring little effort **25** incapable of great endurance

soften 5 lower **6** lessen, subdue, temper **7** cushion, mollify **8** make soft, mitigate, moderate, palliate, tone down, turn down **10** ameliorate, make softer

softhearted 4 kind, soft, warm **6** benign, gentle, humane, kindly, tender **8** generous **9** forgiving, indulgent **10** benevolent **11** considerate, kindhearted, sympathetic, warmhearted **13** compassionate, tenderhearted

softly 6 easily, gently, mildly, weakly **7** quietly

softness 8 mildness **9** downiness, silkiness **10** fluffiness, gentleness, smoothness, tenderness **11** tranquility **12** tranquillity

soft soap 7 blarney **8** cajolery, flattery **10** persuasion

sogginess 7 wetness **8** dampness **9** mushiness **10** soddenness

soggy 5 heavy, mushy, pasty, soppy **6** doughy, soaked, sodden **7** sopping **8** drenched, dripping **9** saturated

Sogliardo
character in: 22 Every Man out of His Humour
author: 6 Jonson

Soglow, Otto
creator/artist of: 13 The Little King

Sohrab and Rustum
author: 13 Matthew Arnold

soi-disant 8 so-called **9** pretended **10** self-styled **18** calling oneself thus

soigne, soignee 4 chic, neat, tidy **5** sleek, smart **6** classy, modish **7** elegant **11** wellgroomed

soil 4 dirt, foul, land, loam, ruin, soot, spot **5** dirty, earth, grime, humus, muddy, smear, stain, sully **6** debase, defile, ground, region, smudge **7** blacken, country, tarnish **8** disgrace

soiled 5 dirty, grimy, messy **6** filthy, grubby, smudgy **7** muddied, sullied, unclean **8** begrimed, unwashed **9** besmeared

soiree 4 ball, prom **5** dance, party **9** cotillion, promenade

sojourn 4 stay **5** abide, pause, visit **6** stay at **7** holiday, layover **8** stay over, stopover, vacation

sojourner 6 lodger, tenant **7** pilgrim, tourist, visitor **8** traveler **9** transient, weekender **10** daytripper, vacationer

Sol
origin: 5 Roman
form: 3 god
personifies: 3 sun
corresponds to: 6 Helios **7** Mithras **8** Hyperion

sola, solus 5 alone **9** by oneself

solace 4 calm **5** cheer **6** soothe **7** assuage, comfort, console **8** reassure **10** help in need **11** consolation, reassurance **18** relief in affliction

solder 4 fuse, join, weld **5** braze, stick

soldier 2 GI **3** PFC **5** major **6** worker, zealot **7** colonel, general, private, servant, trooper, veteran, warrior **8** follower, partisan, sergeant **10** lieutenant, serviceman **11** enlisted man, military man **14** militant leader **16** brigadier general

Soldier of Orange
director: 13 Paul Verhoeven

based on novel by: 13 Erik Hazelhoff
cast: 10 Peter Faber **11** Derek De Lint, Eddy Habbema, Rutger Hauer **12** Jeroen Krabbe **15** Susan Penhaligon
setting: 14 The Netherlands

Soldier's Embrace, A
author: 14 Nadine Gordimer

soldiery 4 army **6** legion, troops **7** legions, militia **8** military, soldiers **11** fighting men

sole 4 lone, only **6** single **8** solitary **9** exclusive

solely 5 merely, purely, singly **8** uniquely **11** exclusively **14** single-handedly

solemn 4 dark, drab, grim, holy **5** grave, sober, staid **6** formal, gloomy, sacred, sedate, somber **7** earnest, serious, sincere **8** absolute **9** dignified, religious, spiritual, steadfast **10** ceremonial, depressing, determined **11** ceremonious **12** awe-inspiring

solemnity 3 awe **7** dignity **8** ceremony **9** formality, reverence **11** seriousness **12** circumstance

solemnize 4 mark **5** honor **6** hallow **7** observe **9** celebrate **10** consecrate **11** commemorate

solicit 3 ask **4** seek **5** plead **7** entreat, request **9** appeal for, importune

solicitation 6 appeal **7** request **8** entreaty **11** importuning

solicitor 6 beggar, lawyer **7** counsel **8** salesman **10** supplicant

solicitous 4 avid, keen **5** eager **6** ardent, intent **7** anxious, intense, longing, mindful, zealous **8** desirous **9** attentive, concerned, regardful **10** thoughtful **12** enthusiastic

solicitude 4 care, zeal **5** worry **7** anxiety, avidity, concern **9** attention **10** enthusiasm, inquietude, uneasiness **11** disquietude, fearfulness, overconcern **12** apprehension

solid 4 firm, hard, pure, real **5** dense, massy, sober, sound, tough **6** rugged, stable, steady, strong, sturdy **7** durable, genuine, lasting, unmixed **8** complete, concrete, constant, rational, reliable, sensible, tangible, thorough, unbroken **9** not hollow, unalloyed, unanimous, undivided, wellbuilt **10** continuous, dependable, solidified **11** impermeable,

levelheaded, substantial, trustworthy **12** impenetrable **13** uninterrupted **15** wellconstructed

solidarity 5 union, unity **7** harmony **9** closeness **11** cooperation, unification

solidify 3 fix, gel, set **4** cake, jell **6** cement, harden **7** congeal, stiffen, thicken **9** coagulate **11** crystallize **12** agglomerate

soliloquy 9 monologue **10** solo speech

Solinus
character in: 17 The Comedy of Errors
author: 11 Shakespeare

solitariness 8 solitude **9** aloneness, seclusion **13** reclusiveness

solitary 4 lone **6** hidden, lonely, remote, single **8** desolate, isolated, lonesome, secluded **9** concealed **10** cloistered **11** out-of-theway, uninhabited **13** companionless

solitude 9 aloneness, isolation, seclusion, wasteland **10** desolation, loneliness, remoteness, wilderness

solo 5 alone **8** solitary **9** by oneself **10** unattended **12** singlehanded **13** unaccompanied
operatic: 4 aria

solo dance
ballet: 7 pas seul

Solomon
father: 5 David
mother: 9 Bathsheba
wife: 6 Naamah
son: 8 Rehoboam
brother: 5 Amnon **7** Absalom, Chileab **8** Adonijah
sister: 5 Tamar
visitor: 5 Sheba
wrote: 8 Proverbs **12** Ecclesiastes **13** Song of Solomon
built: 6 temple

Solomon Islands *see box*

so long
Spanish: 12 hasta la vista

solution 3 key **5** blend **6** answer, cipher **7** mixture, solving **8** emulsion **9** resolving **10** resolution, suspension, unraveling **11** explanation

solve 7 resolve, unravel, work out **8** decipher, unriddle, untangle **9** figure out **10** find the key **13** find the answer

solvent 7 diluent, soluble **9** dilutable **10** dissoluble, dissolvent **11** dissolvable **16** financially sound

Solymi
origin: 9 Asia Minor
occupation: 8 warriors

Solzhenitsyn, Aleksandr
author of: 13 The Cancer Ward **14** The First Circle **19** The Gulag Archipelago **22** August Nineteen-Fourteen **31** One Day in the Life of Ivan Denisovich

Somalia *see box, p. 908*

Solomon Islands
capital/largest city: 7 Honiara
others: 4 Auki, Bina, Gizo, Luti **5** Kieta, Munda **6** Tulagi **7** Yandina **8** Kira Kira **9** Tangarare **10** Sasamungga
head of state: 14 British monarch **15** governor-general
member of: 14 Spearhead Group
monetary unit: 4 cent **6** dollar
island: 4 Buka, Gizo, Savo **5** Ndeni, Ulawa **6** Tulagi **7** Malaita, Rennell, Solomon, Vangunu **8** Choiseul, Sikaiana, Vanikoro **9** Santa Cruz **10** New Georgia, Ontong Java **11** Guadalcanal, Santa Isabel **12** Bougainville, San Cristobal
mountain: 5 Balbi
highest point: 11 Popomanasiu
ocean: 7 Pacific
physical feature:
  gulf: **4** Huon, Kula
  sound: **10** New Georgia
  strait: **13** Indispensable
people: 7 Chinese **8** European **10** Melanesian, Polynesian
  explorer: **14** Mendana de Neyra
  leader: **8** Mamaloni **9** Kenilorea
language: 7 English **13** Pidgin English **16** Melanesian pidgin
religion: 8 Anglican **13** Roman Catholic

Somalia
 other name: 4 Punt **10** Somaliland **12** Horn of Africa
 capital/largest city: 9 Mogadishu **10** Mogadiscio
 others: 5 Burao, Merca **6** Mereka, Galkayu, Kismayu **8** Belet Uen, Hargeisa **9** Chisimaio
 division: 6 Hawiya **9** Mijirtein **10** Midjertein
  colonial: 17 British Somaliland, Italian Somaliland
 measure: 3 top **4** caba **5** chela, darat, tabla **6** cubito **8** parsalah
 monetary unit: 4 besa **6** somalo **8** shilling **9** centesimi
 weight: 8 parsalah
 mountain: 5 Guban **11** Migiurtinia, Ogo Highland
 highest point: 7 Surud Ad
 river: 4 Juba **5** Daror, Nogal **9** Nugaaleed **11** Webi Shebeli **13** Webi Shabeelle
 sea: 6 Indian
 physical feature:
  bay: 5 Negro
  cape: 9 Guardafui
  desert: 4 Aror
  gulf: 4 Aden
  plateau: 3 Ogo **4** Haud
 people: 3 Sab **4** Asha **5** Galla **6** Hawiya, Isbaak, Somali **7** Danakil, Hamitic, Marehan, Samaale, Shuhali **8** Rahanwin
  leader: 9 Siad Barre **12** Ali Shermarke
 language: 6 Arabic, Somali **7** English, Italian
 religion: 5 Islam
 feature:
  boat: 4 dhow
  cloth: 7 banadir
  clothing: 4 futa, toga **6** sarong
  tree: 6 acacia, baobab **7** incense

Somaliland *see* **7** Somalia

somber 4 dark, drab, gray, grim **5** grave, sober **6** dreary, gloomy, solemn **7** serious **8** funereal, mournful, toneless **9** cheerless **10** depressing, melancholy

Sombrero Fallout
 author: 16 Richard Brautigan

Some Like It Hot
 director: 11 Billy Wilder
 cast: 9 Joe E Brown, Pat O'Brien **10** George Raft, Jack Lemmon, Tony Curtis **13** Marilyn Monroe

Somers Islands *see* **7** Bermuda

something essential
 Latin: 10 sine qua non

something for something
 Latin: 10 quid pro quo

Something Happened
 author: 12 Joseph Heller

sometime 4 late, once **5** later **6** former **7** quondam **8** formerly, previous **9** erstwhile **10** occasional

sometimes 7 at times **10** now and then, on occasion **12** occasionally, once in a while

somewhat 6 fairly, kind of, partly, sort of **8** passably **9** tolerably **10** moderately, more or less, reasonably **13** approximately

somnolent 4 dozy, dull **5** dopey **6** drowsy, groggy, sleepy, torpid **7** languid, nodding, out of it, yawning **8** hypnotic, sluggish **9** halfawake, lethargic, sopoforic **10** half-asleep, slumberous **11** heavy-lidded **13** semiconscious

Somnus
 origin: 5 Roman
 god of: 5 sleep
 mother: 3 Nyx
 brother: 4 Mors
 corresponds to: 6 Hypnos, Hypnus

son
 French: 4 fils

song 4 call, poem, tune **5** ditty, lyric, verse **6** ballad, melody, number, piping
 French: 7 chanson

songbird 4 chat, lark, wren

5 robin, veery, vireo **6** canary, singer, thrush **7** warbler **11** nightingale

Song of Bernadette, The
 author: 11 Franz Werfel
 character: 13 Dean Peyramale **18** Sister Marie Therese **19** Bernadette Soubirous
 director: 9 Henry King
 cast: 8 Lee J Cobb **12** Vincent Price, William Eythe **13** Jennifer Jones **15** Charles Bickford
 Oscar for: 7 actress (Jones)

Song of Hiawatha *see* **8** Hiawatha

Song of Roland, The *see* **15** Chanson de Roland

Song of Solomon
 author: 12 Toni Morrison

Song of Solomon
 bride: 9 Shulamite

Song of Songs, The
 author: 16 Hermann Sudermann

Song of the Lark, The
 author: 11 Willa Cather

Songs of Experience
 author: 12 William Blake

Songs of Innocence
 author: 12 William Blake

Sonnets from the Portuguese
 author: 24 Elizabeth Barrett Browning

Sonnets to Orpheus
 author: 16 Rainer Maria Rilke

Sonny
 nickname of: 13 Charles Liston

Son of the Morning
 author: 15 Joyce Carol Oates

sonorous 4 deep, rich **6** florid **7** ringing, vibrant **8** eloquent, resonant **9** full-toned, grandiose **10** flamboyant, impressive, resounding **13** reverberating

Sons and Lovers
 author: 10 D H Lawrence
 character: 10 Clara Dawes **11** Baxter Dawes **13** Miriam Leivers
  Morel family: 4 Paul **5** Annie **6** Arthur, Walter **7** William **8** Gertrude

Sons of thunder 4 John **5** James
 also: 9 Boanerges

soon 4 anon **6** pronto **7** betimes, by and by, early on, ere long, quickly, shortly **8** directly **9** any minute, forthwith, instantly, presently, right away **10** before long **12** without delay **14** in a little while

sooner 6 before, in time **7** earlier **9** before now, in advance **10** beforehand **11** ahead of time

sooner or later 6 one day **7** finally, someday **8** in the end, sometime **10** eventually, ultimately **17** in the course of time, sometime or another

Sooner State
nickname of: **8** Oklahoma

soot 4 dirt, smut **5** crock, grime **6** carbon, smudge, smutch **7** residue **9** lampblack

soothe 4 calm, ease **6** lessen, pacify **7** appease, comfort, console, mollify, placate, relieve **8** mitigate, moderate **9** alleviate **11** tranquilize

soothing 4 mild **7** calming, healing, salving **9** appeasing, consoling, emollient, pacifying, placating **10** comforting, mitigating **13** tranquilizing

soothsayer 4 seer **5** sibyl **7** diviner, prophet **10** forecaster **13** fortune-teller

soothsaying 6 augury **8** divining, prophecy **10** divination, predicting, prediction **11** foretelling, prophesying

sooty 4 inky **5** black, dingy, dirty, grimy **6** smudgy, smutty **9** coal-black

sop 3 dip, tip, wet **4** dunk, soak **5** bribe **6** absorb, drench, payoff, payola, take up **8** gratuity, saturate **9** baksheesh, become wet, hush money

Sophie's Choice
author: **13** William Styron

Sophisms
author: **9** Aristotle

sophisticate 8 civilize **11** cosmopolite, disillusion, make worldly **12** cosmopolitan

sophisticated 6 subtle **7** complex, studied, worldly **8** advanced, cultured, highbrow, mannered, precious, seasoned **9** difficult **10** artificial, cultivated **11** complicated, experienced, worldly-wise **12** cosmopolitan, intellectual

sophistry 6 deceit **7** fallacy **8** subtlety **9** casuistry, chicanery, deception **10** distortion **12** speciousness

Sophocles
author of: **4** Ajax **7** Electra, Oedipus **8** Antigone **10** Oedipus Rex, Trachiniae

11 Philoctetes **16** Oedipus at Colonus **18** The Trachinian Women

sophomoric 6 callow **7** foolish, puerile **8** childish, immature, juvenile **9** infantile **10** adolescent **12** schoolboyish

soporific 4 lazy **5** balmy, heavy **6** drowsy, sleepy **8** hypnotic, sedative, sluggish **9** lethargic, somnolent **10** slumberous **11** somniferous **12** sleep-inducer **13** sleep-inducing

soppiness 4 corn, mush **5** slush **6** bathos **7** wetness **9** mushiness **10** slushiness **11** mawkishness **14** sentimentalism, sentimentality

sopping 3 wet **5** soggy, soppy **6** soaked, sodden **8** drenched, dripping **9** saturated **10** bedraggled, soaking wet

sorcerer 5 witch **6** shaman, wizard **7** warlock **8** magician **11** medicine man

sorceress 5 siren, witch **11** enchantress

sorcery 8 witchery, wizardry **9** shamanism **10** black magic, necromancy, witchcraft **11** enchantment

Sordello
author: **14** Robert Browning

sordid 3 low **4** base, rank, vile **5** dirty, gross **6** filthy, putrid, rotten, vulgar, wicked **7** corrupt, ignoble, squalid, unclean **8** degraded, depraved **9** debauched **12** disreputable

Sordido
character in: **22** Every Man out of His Humour
author: **6** Jonson

sordino, con
music: **11** with the mute

sore 4 hurt **5** acute, angry, great, harsh, irked, sharp, upset, wound **6** aching, pained, severe, tender **7** bruised, extreme, grieved, hurting, painful **8** agonized, critical, grievous, smarting, sore spot, wounding **9** agonizing, desperate, indignant, irritated, sensitive **10** distressed, unbearable **11** distressing **12** inflammation

So Red the Rose
author: **10** Stark Young

Sorel, Julien
character in: **17** The Red and the Black
author: **8** Stendhal

sorely 5 badly **7** greatly **8** se-

verely **9** extremely **10** critically **11** desperately

soreness 4 ache, pain **10** discomfort, irritation, tenderness

sorrel 3 bay **4** herb, roan, weed **5** brown, plant, Rumex **8** chestnut **12** reddish-brown
varieties: **3** red **4** dock, tree, wood **5** lady's, sheep **6** common, French, garden, Indian **7** redwood **8** Jamaican, mountain **10** violet wood **12** European wood

Sorrel, Hetty
character in: **8** Adam Bede
author: **5** Eliot

sorrow 3 woe **4** loss, weep **5** be sad, mourn, trial **6** grieve, lament **7** despair, sadness, travail, trouble **8** disaster, hardship **10** affliction, bad fortune, misfortune **11** catastrophe, unhappiness
French: **9** tristesse

sorrowful 3 sad **6** woeful **7** unhappy **8** affected, grieving, mournful **9** lamenting

Sorrows of Young Werther, The
author: **6** Goethe
character: **6** Albert **9** Charlotte (Lotte)

sorry 3 sad **6** woeful **7** grieved, pitiful, unhappy **8** contrite, pathetic, pitiable, wretched **9** miserable, regretful, repentant, sorrowful **10** deplorable, melancholy, remorseful, ridiculous **11** crestfallen **13** brokenhearted

sort 4 kind, list, make, sift, type **5** brand, class, grade, group, index, order **6** divide, person **7** arrange, catalog, species, variety **8** classify, organize, separate, take from **9** segregate **10** categorize, individual **11** systematize **14** classification

sortie 4 rush **5** onset **6** attack, charge **7** assault **8** storming **9** onslaught

sortilege 6 augury **7** auspice, sorcery **10** divination, witchcraft

sorting 8 dividing, grouping **9** arranging **10** organizing **11** classifying **12** categorizing

so-so 4 blah, fair **5** ho-hum **6** casual, modest **7** average, humdrum **8** adequate, bearable, mediocre, middling, ordinary, passable **9** tolerable **10** second-rate **11** commonplace, indifferent **12** run-of-the-mill **13** unexceptional **15** undistinguished

Sospita
epithet of: 4 Juno

sot 4 lush, soak **5** drunk, rummy, souse, toper **8** drunkard, rumhound **9** alcoholic, inebriate **11** dipsomaniac

Soter
epithet of: 4 Zeus
means: 6 savior

Sothern, Ann
real name: 13 Harriette Lake
born: 12 Valley City ND
husband: 10 Roger Pryor
14 Robert Sterling
roles: 6 Maisie 8 Cry Havoc
10 Lady Be Good 16 Private
Secretary 19 A Letter to
Three Wives

so throughout
Latin: 9 sic passim

sotto voce
music: 11 in a low voice
13 in an undertone, under
the voice

sought 6 hunted **7** pursued, quested **9** attempted, looked for **10** endeavored

soul 5 being, force **6** person, spirit **7** essence **8** creature, vitality **9** inner core **10** embodiment, individual, vital force **11** inspiration **12** quintessence

soul-searching 10 discontent, insecurity, uneasiness **15** dissatisfaction, self-questioning

soul-stirring 7 rousing **8** electric, exciting, stirring **9** inspiring, thrilling **11** galvanizing

sound 3 fit **4** deep, firm, good, seem, tone, wise **5** drift, hardy, noise, range, sober, solid, tenor, utter, voice **6** intact, robust, severe, signal, stable, strong, sturdy **7** durable, earshot, healthy, lasting, perfect, solvent **8** announce, rational, reliable, sensible, thorough, unmarred **9** come off as, competent, enunciate, pronounce, undamaged, wellbuilt **10** articulate, dependable, make a noise, reasonable, suggestion, untroubled **11** implication, penetrating, responsible, substantial **13** thoroughgoing **15** hearing distance, well-constructed

Sound and the Fury, The
author: 15 William Faulkner
character: 6 Dilsey 17 Sydney
Herbert Head
Compson family: 5 Jason
7 Candace (Caddy), Quentin 8 Benjamin (Benjy)

Sounder
director: 10 Martin Ritt
cast: 8 Taj Mahal 10 Kevin
Hooks 11 Cicely Tyson

12 Paul Winfield 13 Carmen
Mathews
sequel: 13 Sounder Part II

sound measure 7 decibel

sound mind in a sound body
Latin: 21 mens sana in corpore sano

soundness of mind 6 reason, sanity **9** normality **12** mental health

Sound of Music, The
director: 10 Robert Wise
cast: 9 Peggy Wood 12 Julie
Andrews (Maria Von
Trapp) 13 Eleanor Parker
18 Christopher Plummer
setting: 7 Austria
score: 21 Rodgers and
Hammerstein
Oscar for: 7 picture
8 director
song: 5 Maria 6 Do-Re-Mi
9 Edelweiss 16 My Favorite
Things

sound out 3 ask **8** approach
15 make a proposal to, make overtures to, put out feelers to

soup
French: 6 potage

soupcon 3 bit, dab, jot, tad **4** clue, dash, drop, hint **5** pinch, shade, taint, taste, tinge, touch, trace, whiff **6** little, trifle **7** smidgen, smidgin, vestige **8** smidgeon **9** little bit, suspicion **10** smattering, sprinkling, suggestion **12** slight amount

Soupy Sales
character: 9 White Fang
10 Black Tooth 13 Herman
the Flea, Hippy the Hippo,
Pookie the Lion, Willie the
Worm 14 Marilyn Monwolf

sour 3 bad **4** acid, dour, keen, tart, turn **5** nasty, sharp, spoil, surly, tangy, testy **6** crabby, cranky, curdle, rancid, sullen, turned **7** acerbic, bilious, crabbed, curdled, ferment, grouchy, peevish, spoiled, turn off, uncivil, waspish **8** alienate, choleric, embitter, jaundice, petulant, unsavory, vinegary **9** acidulous, clabbered, fermented, irritable, jaundiced, of-

South Africa
capital: 8 Cape Town, Pretoria 12 Bloemfontein
largest city: 12 Johannesburg
others: 3 Aus 4 Mara, Stad 6 Benoni, Bononi, Braker, Durban, Garies, Severn, Soweto, Umtata, Untata 7 Brakpan, Kokstad 8 Kaapstad, Mafeking, Modjadji 9 Germiston, Kimberley 10 East London, Oudtshoorn 11 Krugersdorp, Vereeniging 13 Port Elizabeth 16 Pietermaritzburg
school: 5 Natal 8 Capetown 13 Witwatersrand 15 Orange Free State
division: 5 Natal 8 Backveld 9 Transvaal 10 Basutoland 12 Cape Province 14 Cape of Good Hope 15 Orange Free State
independent homelands: 5 Venda 6 Ciskei 8 Transkei 10 bantustans 14 Bophuthatswana
goverment:
legislature: 4 Raad
measure: 4 vara
monetary unit: 4 cent, pond, rand 5 pound 6 florin 7 daalder 9 krugerand
mountain: 3 Aux, Kop 5 Table 7 Kathkin 9 Stormberg 10 Devil's Peak, Sneeuwberg 11 Drakensberg 12 Giant's Castle 13 Witwatersrand 14 Mont-aux-Sources 15 Great Escarpment
highest point: 8 Injasuti
river: 3 Hex 4 Vaal 5 Nosob 6 Modder, Molopo, Orange, Tugela 7 Caledon, Kurumam, Limpopo 8 Olifants 9 Crocodile, Great Fish
ocean: 6 Indian 8 Atlantic
physical feature:
bay: 5 Algoa, False, Table 6 Mossel, Walvis 7 Walfish 8 Richard's, Saldanha 11 Saint Helena
cape: 7 Agulhas 8 Good Hope
current: 8 Benguela
desert: 5 Namib 8 Kalahari
plateau: 6 Karroo
region: 8 Highveld, Zululand 9 Kaffraria 11 Great Karroo 12 Little Karroo

fensive, prejudice, repugnant
10 astringent, ill-dispose, ill-
humored, unpleasant **11** bad-
tempered, distasteful, ill-
tempered **12** disagreeable

sourball 4 crab **5** crank,
grump **6** grouch **9** hard candy
10 curmudgeon

source 4 font, head, root **5** basis, cause, fount **6** author, father, origin, rising, spring
8 begetter, fountain **9** authority, beginning, headwater
10 antecedent, derivation,
foundation, prime mover,
wellspring

source and origin
Latin: **11** fons et origo

Sourdough State
nickname of: **6** Alaska

sourness 7 acidity, vinegar
8 acerbity, acrimony, ill humor, pungency, tartness **9** acridness, greenness
10 bitterness

sourpuss 4 bear, crab **5** crank,
grump **6** griper, grouch
7 grouser, killjoy **8** grumbler,
sorehead **10** bellyacher, complainer, crosspatch, curmudgeon, spoilsport

Sousa, John Philip
born: **12** Washington DC
composer of: **9** El Capitan
14 Washington Post **25** The
Stars and Stripes Forever

souse 3 dip, sot **4** duck, dunk,
lush, soak **5** douse, drunk,
rummy, steep, toper **6** barfly,
boozer, drench, pickle **7** immerse, tippler **8** drunkard, inundate, marinate, saturate,
submerge **9** alcoholic, inebriate **11** dipsomaniac

soused 5 drunk **6** dunked, potted, zapped, zonked **7** pickled,
sloshed, smashed **8** immersed
9 plastered **10** inebriated
11 intoxicated **17** under the
influence **20** three sheets to
the wind

South Africa *see box*

South America *see box*

South Carolina *see box, p.*
912

South Dakota *see box, p.*
913

southeast wind
associated with: **5** Eurus
9 Volturnus

South America
bird: **5** macaw **7** seriema,
tinamou **8** caracara
cape: **4** Horn
country: **4** Peru **5** Chile
6 Brazil, Guyana **7** Bolivia, Ecuador, Surinam,
Uruguay **8** Colombia,
Paraguay **9** Argentina,
Venezuela **12** French
Guiana
desert: **7** Atacama
explorer: **16** Francisco
Pizarro **18** Pedro Al-
vares Cabral
hero: **12** Simon Bolivar
15 Jose de San Martin
16 Bernardo O'Higgins
18 Antonio Jose de
Sucre
highest mountain:
9 Aconcagua
islands: **8** Falkland
9 Galapagos
lake: **8** Titicaca
9 Maracaibo
mountain range:
5 Andes
native: **2** Ge **3** Ona
4 Inca **5** Carib, Mayan
7 Quechua
10 Araucanian
plain: **5** llano, pampa
region: **9** Patagonia
river: **3** Apa **5** Plata
6 Amazon **7** Orinoco

South Africa (*continued*)
people: **3** San **4** Boer, Yosa, Zulu **5** Asian, Bantu, Namas,
Nguni, Pondo, Sotho, Swazi, Tembu, Venda, Xhosa **6** Damara, Kaffir **7** African, British, Bushmen, English, Swahili **8** Bechuana, Coloured, Khoikhoi **9** Afrikaner,
Hottentot
author: **5** Paton **7** Luthuli **8** Gordimer
civil rights advocate: **6** Gandhi
explorer: **8** Riebeeck
leader: **4** Biko, Tutu **5** Botha, Malan, Smuts, Tomba
6 Kruger, Rhodes **7** de Klerk, Hertzog, Mandela, Vor-
ster **8** Verwoerd **9** Buthelezi, Pretorius
language: **4** Taal, Zulu **5** Bantu, Hindi, Nguni, Sotho,
Swazi, Tamil, Venda, Xhosa **6** Telegu, Thonga **7** English,
Khoisan, Ndebele, Sesotho **8** Bujarati, Fanakalo
9 Afrikaans
religion: **5** Hindu, Islam **7** animism, Judaism **8** Anglican
9 Methodist **12** Episcopalian, Presbyterian **13** Dutch Reformed, Roman Catholic
place:
Cecil Rhodes' estate: **11** Groote Shuur
game reserve: **5** Mkuze **6** Kruger **8** Hluhluwe
monument: **11** Voortrekker
feature:
bird: **4** taha
bride price: **6** lobolo
flower: **5** coral **6** clivia, protea **7** cowslip, fuchsia **9** phy-
gelius **10** lachenalia
organization: **3** ANC **7** Inkatha **23** African National
Congress
segregation: **9** apartheid
tree: **7** assagai **9** jacaranda
food:
corn: **6** mealie
drink: **9** sundowner
meat: **7** biltong **8** sosaties **9** boerewors

Southern Comfort
type: **7** liqueur
origin: **10** New Orleans
flavor: **5** peach
base: **7** bourbon
drink: **13** Scarlett O'Hara
15 Plantation Punch
with bourbon: **14** Blended
Comfort

Southern Cross
constellation of: **4** Crux

Southern Crown
constellation of: **15** Corona
Australis

Southerner, The
director: **10** Jean Renoir
cast: **10** Betty Field **11** Beulah Bondi **12** Zachary Scott
13 Bunny Sunshine

Southern Fish
constellation of: **15** Piscis
Austrinus

Southern Fly
constellation of: **5** Musca

Southern Rhodesia *see*
8 Zimbabwe

Southern Slavic
language family: **12** Indo-
European

South Carolina
abbreviation: **2** SC
nickname: **7** Calinky **8** Palmetto
capital/largest city: **8** Columbia
others: **5** Aiken, Greer, Union **6** Belton, Camden, Cheraw, Conway, Dillon, Seneca, Sumter **7** Bamberg, Laurens, Manning **8** Beaufort, Florence, Newberry, Rock Hill, Walhalla **9** Greenwood **10** Charleston, Greenville, Orangeburg **11** Spartanburg
college: **5** Allen, Coker **6** Furman, Lander **7** Claffin, Clemson, Erskine, Wofford **8** Benedict, Bob Jones, Columbia, Winthrop **13** Francis Marion **15** Citadel Military
explorer: **6** Ayllon, Ribaut
feature:
 beach: **6** Myrtle
 dam: **6** Saluda
 fort: **6** Sumter
 gardens: **7** Cypress
tribe: **5** Pedee, Sewee **6** Cusabo, Santee, Waxhaw, Yamasi **7** Catawba, Shawnee, Sugeree, Wateree **8** Congaree
people: **11** James Byrnes **12** Althea Gibson, John C Calhoun **13** Bernard Baruch, Francis Marion **14** Dizzy Gillespie
island: **3** Sea **6** Parris **10** Hilton Head
lake: **6** Marion, Murray **7** Catawba, Wateree **8** Hartwell, Moultrie **9** Clark Hill
land rank: **8** fortieth
mountain: **5** Kings **6** Little **9** Blue Ridge, Sassafras
physical feature:
 bay: **8** Carolina
 plateau: **8** Piedmont
president: **13** Andrew Jackson
river: **5** Broad **6** Edisto, Pee Dee, Saluda, Santee **7** Ashepoo **8** Savannah
state admission: **6** eighth
state bird: **12** Carolina wren
state flower: **13** yellow jasmine **17** Carolina jessamine
state motto: **18** While I Breathe I Hope **26** Prepared in Mind and Resources
state song: **8** Carolina
state tree: **8** palmetto

group: **11** Balto-Slavic
branch: **6** Slavic
language: **7** Slovene **9** Bulgarian **10** Macedonian **13** Serbo-Croatian

Southern Triangle
constellation of: **18** Triangulum Australe

South Korea *see* **5** Korea

South Vietnam *see* **7** Vietnam

South West Africa *see* **7** Namibia

south wind
associated with: **5** Notus

South Wind
author: **13** Norman Douglas

South Yemen *see* **5** Yemen

souvenir 4 scar **5** relic, token **6** emblem, memory, trophy **7** memento **8** keepsake, reminder **11** remembrance

sovereign 4 czar, free, king, lord, main, tsar **5** chief, major, prime, queen, regal, royal **6** kingly, potent, prince, ruling, utmost **7** emperor, highest, leading, monarch, queenly, supreme **8** absolute, autocrat, dominant, foremost, imperial, overlord, powerful, princely, reigning **9** chieftain, governing, paramount, potentate, prepotent, principal, uppermost **10** autonomous, self-ruling **11** all-powerful, crowned head, independent, monarchical **12** supreme ruler **13** self-directing, self-governing

sovereignty 4 sway **5** crown, power **6** throne **7** command, control, freedom, primacy, scepter **8** autonomy, dominion, home rule, kingship, lordship, self-rule **9** authority, supremacy **10** ascendancy **11** paramountcy **12** independence, jurisdiction, predominance **14** self-government **17** self-determination

Soviet Union *see* **6** Russia

sow 4 cast, seed **5** lodge, plant, set in, strew **6** inject, spread **7** implant, instill, scatter **8** disperse, sprinkle **9** broadcast, establish, introduce **11** disseminate

space 3 gap, sky **4** area, part, rank, room, seat, span, spot, term, time **5** berth, blank, break, chasm, ether, field, order, place, range, reach, scope, sweep, swing, width **6** hiatus, lacuna, line up, margin, period, set out, spread **7** arrange, breadth, compass, expanse, mark out, the void **8** distance, duration, infinity, interval, latitude, omission, organize, schedule, separate **9** amplitude, emptiness, keep apart, territory **10** distribute, interspace, interstice, outer space, separation, the heavens **11** nothingness, reservation, the universe **12** interruption, the firmament **13** accommodation

Space
author: **13** James Michener

spacecraft 4 ship **6** rocket **7** orbiter, shuttle **9** satellite **10** rocketship

space flight
US mission: **6** Apollo, Gemini, Skylab **7** Mercury
US rocket: **5** Atlas, Titan **6** Saturn **8** Redstone
US space shuttle: **8** Columbia **9** Discovery **10** Challenger
Soviet mission: **5** Soyuz **6** Salyut, Vostok **7** Voskhod
Soviet astronaut:
 first man in space:
  11 Yuri Gagarin
 first woman in space:
  19 Valentina Tereshkova
 first space walk by:
  13 Aleksei Leonov
American astronaut: **9** John Glenn, John Young **11** Alan Shepard, Edward White, Edwin Aldrin, Frank Borman, James Lovell **12** Roger Chaffee, Wally (Walter) Schirra **13** Charles Conrad, L Gordon Cooper, Virgil Grissom **14** Scott Carpenter, Thomas Stafford
 first man on moon:
  13 Neil Armstrong
 Challenger seven: **12** Michael Smith, Ronald McNair **13** Francis Scobee, Gregory Jarvis, Judith Resnick **14** Ellison Onizuka **16** Christa McAuliffe

Spacek, Sissy
real name: **19** Mary Elizabeth Spacek
born: **9** Quitman TX

South Dakota
abbreviation: 2 SD **4** S Dak
nickname: 6 Coyote **8** Blizzard, Sunshine
capital: 6 Pierre
largest city: 10 Sioux Falls
others: 4 Lead, Leap **5** Huron **6** Custer, Eureka, Lemmon, Miller, Winner **7** Sturgis, Webster, Yankton **8** Aberdeen, Deadwood, Sisseton **9** Brookings, Rapid City **10** Vermillion
college: 5 Huron **7** Yankton **9** Augustana **10** Mount Marty, Sioux Falls **14** Dakota Wesleyan
explorer: 8 Varennes **13** Lewis and Clark
feature: 8 Deadwood
  battlefield: **11** Wounded Knee
  dam: **4** Oahe
  mine: **9** Homestake
  monument: **13** Mount Rushmore
  national park: **8** Badlands, Wind Cave
tribe: 5 Brule, Sioux **6** Dakota, Sutaio **8** Cheyenne
people: 10 Crazy Horse **11** Sitting Bull **14** George McGovern, Hubert Humphrey
lake: 4 Oahe **5** Sharp **8** Big Stone, Traverse **11** Francis Case **13** Lewis and Clark
land rank: 9 sixteenth
mountain: 4 Bear **5** Sheep, Table **6** Crook's, Moreau
  highest point: **6** Harney
  hills: **5** Black **7** Prairie
physical feature:
  butte: **7** Thunder **9** Deer's Ears **10** Castle Rock
  cave: **5** Jewel
river: 3 Bad **5** Grand, James, White **6** Moreau **8** Big Sioux, Cheyenne, Missouri **10** Vermillion
state admission: 8 fortieth **11** thirty-ninth (with North Dakota)
state bird: 18 ring-necked pheasant
state flower: 12 pasqueflower
state animal: 6 coyote
state motto: 21 Under God the People Rule
state song: 15 Hail South Dakota
state tree: 11 white spruce **16** Black Hills spruce

roles: 6 Carrie **7** Missing **8** Badlands, The River **10** Raggedy Man **16** Crimes of the Heart **18** Coal Miner's Daughter (Oscar)

spacious 4 vast, wide **5** ample, broad, large, roomy **7** immense, sizable **8** enormous **9** capacious, expansive, extensive, uncrowded **10** commodious

spaciousness 9 amplitude, largeness, roominess **13** capaciousness **14** commodiousness

Spade, Sam
character in: 16 The Maltese Falcon
author: 7 Hammett

Spain *see box, p. 914*

span 4 arch, area, last, term, wing **5** cover, cross, range, reach, scope, spell, sweep, vault **6** bridge, endure, extent, length, period **7** archway, breadth, measure, stretch, survive, trestle **8** distance, duration, interval **9** extension, reach over, territory **10** bridge over, dimensions **11** proportions, reach across, stretch over **12** extend across

spangle 4 star **5** bedew **6** sequin **7** glisten, glitter, shimmer, twinkle **9** bugle bead, coruscate, paillette

spaniel
dog breed: 5 field **6** cocker, Sussex **7** clumber, Tibetan **10** Irish water **13** American water, English cocker, Welsh springer **15** English springer

Spanish (language, person)
7 espanol

Spanish Guinea *see* **16** Equatorial Guinea

Spanish Sahara *see* **13** Western Sahara

Spanish Tragedy, The
author: 9 Thomas Kyd
character: 7 Horatio, Lorenzo, Villupo **9** Alexandro, Balthazar, Hieronimo **10** Bel-Imperia **16** Ghost of Don Andrea

spank 3 hit, tan **4** beat, belt, blow, cane, flog, hide, lick, slap, whip, whop **5** birch, strap, whale **6** paddle, strike, switch, thrash, wallop **8** paddling **10** flagellate

spanking 4 very **5** brisk, fresh **7** beating **8** paddling, whipping **9** extremely, thrashing **10** punishment **12** chastisement

spanking new 5 fresh **6** unused **8** brand new **9** untouched

spar 4 boom, mast, pole **5** argue, fight, sprit **6** bicker **7** dispute, quarrel, wrangle **8** crossbar **10** crosspiece

spare 3 odd **4** bony, cede, free, give, keep, lank, lean, save, thin **5** amass, extra, forgo, gaunt, grant, guard, hoard, lanky, lay up, limit, pinch, rangy, scant, stint, weedy **6** acquit, afford, defend, donate, excess, exempt, forego, let off, meager, not use, pardon, scanty, shield, skimpy, skinny, slight, unused **7** forgive, haggard, husband, let go of, protect, release, relieve, reserve, scraggy, scrawny, shelter, skimp on, slender, surplus **8** conserve, hold back, leftover, liberate, part with, reprieve, set aside, skeletal, withhold **9** auxiliary, emaciated, exonerate, fleshless, safeguard, show mercy **10** additional, extraneous, relinquish, substitute, unconsumed **11** economize on, have mercy on, superfluous, unnecessary, use frugally **12** be merciful to, dispense with, supplemental **13** supernumerary, supplementary

spared 5 freed **6** exempt, immune **7** excused **8** absolved, excepted, relieved

sparing 4 near **5** close, scant **6** frugal, meager, saving, scanty, stingy **7** careful, miserly, thrifty **8** grudging, stinting **9** niggardly, penurious **10** economical, ungenerous **11** closefisted, tightfisted **12** parsimonious

spark 3 bit, jot **4** atom, beam, fire, iota, life **5** brand, ember, flash, gleam, pique, trace **6** arouse, excite, incite, spirit **7** flicker, glimmer, glitter, inspire, provoke, sparkle **8** vitality **9** animation, instigate, stimulate **10** get-up-and-go

Spain
other name: 6 Iberia 8 Hispania
capital/largest city: 6 Madrid
others: 4 Adra, Aspe, Baza, Elda, Horo, Irun, Jaen, Leon, Noya, Olot, Reus, Rota, Sama,
Vigo 5 Baena, Bejar, Cadiz, Cieza, Cueta, Ecija, Eibar, Elche, Gades, Gadir, Gijon, Ibiza,
Jerez, Jodar, Liego, Lorca, Oliva, Palma, Palos, Ronda, Siero, Ubeda, Xeres, Yecla, Zafra
6 Abdera, Aviles, Azuaga, Bilbao, Burgos, Coruna, Duenca, Gandia, Gerona, Getafe, Guadix,
Hellin, Huelva, Huesca, Lerida, Lucena, Malaga, Mataro, Merida, Murcia, Orense,
Oviedo, Termel, Toledo, Utrera, Zamora 7 Almeria, Badajos, Cordoba, Daimiel, Granada,
Jumilla, Linares, Logrono, Manresa, Segovia, Sevilla, Seville, Tarrasa, Vitoria 8 Alicante, Bad-
alona, Figueras, Pamplona, Sabadell, Santiago, Torrente, Valencia, Zaragoza 9 Barcelona, Las
Palmas, Saragossa
school: 6 Ciudad, Madrid
division: 4 Jaen, Leon, Lugo 5 Alava, Avila, Cadiz, Soria 6 Basque, Burgos, Coruna, Cuenca,
Gerona, Huelva, Huesca, Lerida, Madrid, Malaga, Murcia, Orense, Oviedo, Teruel, Toledo,
Zamora 7 Almeria, Caceres, Cordoba, Granada, Logrono, Navarra, Segovia, Sevilla, Vizcaya,
Zadajoz 8 Albacete, Alicante, Baleares, Palencia, Valencia, Zaragoza 9 Catalonia
    kingdom: 4 Leon 6 Aragon 7 Castile, Galicia, Granada, Navarre 8 Asturias 9 al-Andalus, Cat-
alonia 12 Spanish March
government: 8 monarchy
    legislature: 6 Cortes
head of state: 4 king
measure: 3 pie 4 codo, dedo, paso, vara 5 braza, cahiz, carga, legua, medio, palmo, sesma
6 cordel, cuarta, fanega, racion, yugada 7 azumbre, celemin, estadel, pulgada 8 fanegada
monetary unit: 3 cob 4 duro, peso 5 dobla 6 cuarto, dinero, escudo 7 alfonso, centimo, pistole 8 doubloon
weight: 4 onza 5 frail, libra, marco, tomin 6 arroba, dinero, dracma 7 arienzo, quilate, quintal 8 tonelada
island: 5 Ceuta, Ibiza, Iviza, Palma 6 Canary, Gomera, Hierro 7 Alboran, Majorca, Melilla, Minorca 8 Balearic, Mallorca, Tagomago, Tenerife 9 Lanzarote 13 Fuerteventura
lake: 4 lago 8 Albufera
mountain: 4 Gata 5 Aneto, Rouch 6 Cuenca, Estats, Europa, Gredos, Magina, Morena, Nethou,
Nevada, Teleno, Toledo 7 Alcaraz, Banuelo, Catalan, Cerredo, Demanda, Iberian, La Sagra,
Moncayo, Perdido 8 Almanzor, Asturias, Galician, Maladeta, Monegros, Montseny, Penalara,
Pyrenees 10 Albarracin, Cantabrian, Guadarrama, Torrecilla
highest point: 5 Teide 8 Mulhacen
river: 3 Sil, Ter 4 Cega, Ebro, Esla, Lima, Mino, Muga, Tajo, Ulla 5 Adaja, Cinca, Douro,
Duero, Genil, Jalon, Jucar, Navia, Odiel, Riaza, Segie, Tagus, Tinto, Turia 6 Alagon, Aragon,
Eresma, Huerva, Jarama, Orbigo, Segura, Torote 7 Almeria, Almonte, Arlanza, Barbate, Ca-
briel, Gallego, Henares, Mijares, Perales 8 Duration, Guadiana 12 Guadalquivir
sea: 8 Atlantic, Balearic 13 Mediterranean
physical feature:
    bay: 5 Bahia 6 Biscay
    cape: 9 Trafalgar
    gulf: 5 Cadiz 8 San Jorge, Valencia
    peninsula: 7 Iberian
    plateau: 6 meseta
    strait: 9 Gibraltar
people: 5 Diego, Gente, Latin 6 Basque, Espana 7 Catalan, Espanol, Iberian 8 Galician, Gallegos, Maragato
    architect: 5 Gaudi
    artist: 4 Dali, Goya, Gris, Miro 6 Ribera 7 El Greco, Murillo, Picasso 8 Zurbaran
    9 Velazquez

Spark, Muriel
    author of: 11 Memento
    Mori 14 The Driver's Seat,
    The Only Problem 17 The
    Mandelbaum Gate, Territo-
    rial Rights 19 Loitering with
    Intent 21 A Far Cry from
    Kensington 24 The Prime of
    Miss Jean Brodie

sparkle 3 pep, pop, vim
4 dash, elan, fizz, foam, glow,
life 5 be gay, brand, cheer,
ember, flash, froth, gleam,
glint, light, shine, verve
6 bubble, dazzle, fizzle, gaiety,

spirit 7 be witty, flicker, glimmer, glisten, glitter, jollity, rejoice, shimmer, twinkle
8 radiance, vitality, vivacity
9 alertness, animation, briskness, coruscate, quickness
10 be cheerful, brilliance,
ebullience, effervesce, effulgence, exuberance, liveliness,
luminosity 11 be vivacious,
scintillate 12 cheerfulness, exhilaration, luminousness 13 effervescence, scintillation

sparkling 5 fizzy 6 bubbly
7 fizzing, twinkly 8 bubbling,

dazzling, glittery 9 twinkling
10 glistening, glittering
11 coruscating 12 effervescent
13 scintillating

Sparky Lyle
    nickname of: 16 Albert Wal-
ter Lyle

sparse 3 few 4 thin 5 scant,
spare 6 meager, scanty, scarce,
skimpy, spotty, strewn 7 diffuse 8 exiguous, sporadic
9 dispersed, scattered, spaced-
out, uncrowded 10 infrequent
16 few and far between

author: **4** Cela, Vega **5** Barea, Cueva, Rojas **6** Aleman, Alonso, Azorin, Baroja, Castro, En-
cina, Felipe, Ibanez, Miguel **7** Alarcon, Becquer, Cernuda, Ercilla, Gongora, Guillen, Jimenez, Machado, Unamuno **8** Montalvo, Zorrilla **9** Benavente, Cervantes, Goytisola
10 Aleixandre, Espronceda, Lope de Vega, Pardo Bazan **11** Garcia Lorca **12** Lopez de Ay-
ala **13** Tirso de Molina **17** Calderon de la Barca
composer: **7** Albeniz **8** Granados, Victoria **13** Manuel de Falla
converted Moslem: **7** morisco
dynasty: **7** Almohad, Umayyad **9** Almoravid
explorer: **6** Balboa, Cortes **7** Pizarro **8** Columbus
Jesuit founder: **14** Ignatius Loyola
king: **6** Pelayo, Philip, Ramiro, Sancho, Witiza **7** Alfonso, Charles **8** al-Mansur, Reccared,
Roderick **9** Ferdinand, Leovigild **10** Juan Carlos **11** Abd al-Rahman, Reccosvinth
leader: **4** Prim **5** Godoy **6** Franco **7** Canovas **11** Calvo Sotelo **13** Primo de Rivera **14** Suarez-
Gonzalez
queen: **8** Isabella **16** Elizabeth Farnese
ruler: **4** Rome **5** Celts, Moors **6** Greece **7** Almeria, Vandals **8** Carthage **9** Phoenicia,
Visigoths
scholar: **8** Averroes
warrior: **14** El Cid Campeador
language: **6** Basque **7** Catalan, Spanish **8** Balearic, Galician **9** Castilian, Valencian
religion: **7** Judaism **10** Protestant **13** Roman Catholic
place:
  aqueduct: **7** Segovia
  bridge: **7** Cordoba
  castle: **7** Alcazar **12** Santa Barbara
  cathedral bell tower: **7** Giralda
  center of Madrid: **12** Puerto del Sol
  church/cathedral: **4** Leon **6** Burgos, Gerona, Toledo **7** Seville **9** Barcelona, San Isidro
  10 Santa Maria **14** Sagrada Familia
  fountain: **6** Cibele
  library: **8** Columbus
  minaret: **7** Seville
  mosque: **11** Great Mosque **19** Santo Cristo de la Cruz
  museum: **5** Prado **15** Museo de Pinturas
  palace: **7** Granada, Naranco **8** Alhambra, Escorial **9** Real Mayor
  park: **6** Retiro
  resort: **8** Marbella **10** Costa Brava **12** Torremolinos
  shrine: **32** Saint James at Santiago de Compostela
  street: **7** Ramblas **13** Paseo del Prado **16** Plaza de la Cibeles **19** Paseo de la
  Castellana
  synagogue: **10** El Transito
  theater: **6** Merida
  wall paintings/caves: **8** Altamira
possession: **5** Ceuta **6** Melill
feature:
  bar: **6** tascas
  dance: **5** tango **8** fandango, flamenco
  estate: **10** latifundia
  matador's suit: **12** traje de luces
  political party: **7** Falange
food:
  dish: **6** cocido, paella **8** zarzuela
  soup: **8** gazpacho

---

sparseness 7 paucity **8** sparsity, thinness **10** meagerness,
scantiness

Sparsit, Mrs
  character in: 9 Hard Times
  author: 7 Dickens

Spartacus
  director: 14 Stanley Kubrick
  cast: 8 Nina Foch **9** John
  Gavin **10** Tony Curtis
  11 Jean Simmons, Kirk
  Douglas **12** Peter Ustinov
  15 Charles Laughton, Laurence Olivier

  setting: 4 Rome
  score: 9 Alex North

spartan 4 hard **5** plain, stark,
stern, stiff **6** frugal, severe,
simple, strict **7** ascetic, austere **8** exacting, rigorous
9 stringent **10** abstemious,
inexorable, inflexible, restrained, restricted **11** disciplined, self-denying **15** self-
disciplined

Sparti
  occupation: 8 warriors

spasm 3 fit, tic **4** grip, jerk,

pang **5** burst, cramp, crick,
flash, onset, spell, spurt, start,
storm, throe **6** access, attack,
frenzy, twitch **7** seizure, shudder, tempest **8** eruption, paroxysm **9** explosion **10** convulsion

spasmodic 6 fitful **7** erratic,
flighty **8** fleeting, periodic,
sporadic **9** desultory, irregular,
mercurial, transient **10** capricious, inconstant, occasional
12 intermittent
13 discontinuous

spat 4 tiff **5** argue, fight, scrap,

set-to 6 bicker, differ **7** contend, dispute, dissent, quarrel, wrangle **8** disagree, squabble **10** difference **11** altercation **12** disagreement **16** misunderstanding

spatter 4 slop, soil, spot **5** fleck, plash, spray, spurt, stain, swash **6** mottle, shower, splash **7** speckle, stipple **8** splatter, sprinkle

spawn 4 eggs, seed, teem **5** beget, breed, brood, fruit, yield **7** lay eggs, produce, product **8** engender, generate, multiply **9** offspring, propagate, reproduce **10** bring forth, give rise to **11** deposit eggs, give birth to, proliferate

speak 3 air, say **4** call, chat, deal, talk, tell **5** imply, orate, refer, shout, sound, state, treat, voice **6** advise, confer, convey, cry out, dilate, impart, mumble, murmur, mutter, preach, recite, relate, remark, report, reveal **7** bespeak, comment, consult, declaim, declare, discuss, divulge, expound, express, lecture, mention, suggest, whisper **8** announce, converse, disclose, harangue, indicate, proclaim, vocalize **9** discourse, enunciate, expatiate, hold forth, make known, pronounce, sermonize **10** articulate **11** communicate, give a speech

speakeasy 3 bar **6** saloon, tavern **7** gin mill **14** cocktail lounge

speaker 5 voice **6** orator, reader, talker **7** reciter **8** advocate, lecturer, preacher **9** declaimer, spokesman **10** discourser, monologist, mouthpiece, sermonizer **11** rhetorician, speechmaker, spokeswoman **13** valedictorian

speak highly of 4 laud **5** exalt, extol **6** praise **7** commend **8** eulogize **10** compliment **16** sing the praises of

speak ill of 4 slur **5** curse, knock, libel **6** defame, insult, malign, vilify **7** slander **8** badmouth **9** criticize, denigrate, discredit, disparage **13** find fault with **14** inveigh against

speak loudly 3 cry **4** bawl, call, hail, roar, yell **5** shout **6** bellow, clamor, cry out, halloo, holler **7** call out, speak up

speak of 7 mention, refer to **8** allude to **9** talk about, touch upon

speak to 6 talk to **7** address, lecture

speak together 3 gab, jaw, rap **4** chat, chin, talk **6** confer **7** chatter, palaver **8** chitchat, converse **10** chew the fat, chew the rag **11** communicate, confabulate

speak well of 4 laud **5** boost, extol **6** praise **7** acclaim, approve, commend, flatter, root for **8** eulogize **9** sweet talk **10** compliment, stick up for **13** speak highly of **16** sing the praises of **17** put in a good word for

spear 4 bolt, dart, gaff, gore, pike, spit, stab **5** lance, prick, shaft, spike, stick **6** impale, pierce **7** harpoon, javelin **8** puncture, transfix **9** penetrate **10** run through

spearhead 4 iron, lead **5** begin, found, start **6** launch, leader **7** creator, develop, founder, pioneer **8** begetter, conceive, initiate **9** establish, initiator, institute, originate, spokesman **10** inaugurate, instituter, prime mover **11** establisher, inaugurator, spokeswoman **12** avant-gardist

special 4 fast, good, rare **5** close, great, novel **6** ardent, proper, select, signal, unique **7** bargain, certain, devoted, endemic, feature, staunch, typical, unusual **8** distinct, especial, intimate, peculiar, personal, sale item, singular, specific, uncommon **9** headliner, high point, highlight, important, momentous, specialty, steadfast **10** attraction, individual, noteworthy, particular, remarkable **11** distinctive, exceptional, outstanding, specialized **12** extravaganza **13** distinguished, extraordinary **14** representative, unconventional **16** out of the ordinary **17** piece de resistance

specialist 4 buff **5** adept, maven **6** expert, master **9** authority **10** past master **11** connoisseur

specialization 5 focus, forte, major **6** metier **8** province **10** speciality **13** concentration

specialize 5 adapt, focus, major **6** pursue **10** narrow down **11** concentrate

specialty 4 bent, mark, turn **5** badge, focus, forte, hobby, major, stamp **6** genius, talent **7** earmark, faculty, feature, pursuit, special **8** aptitude **9** endowment, trademark **10** competence, profession **11** claim to fame, distinction

species 4 form, kind, make,

sort, type **5** breed, class, genre, group, order **6** kidney, nature, stripe **7** variety **8** category, division **11** designation, subdivision **14** classification

specific 5 exact, fixed **6** minute, stated, unique **7** bounded, certain, endemic, limited, pointed, precise, special, typical **8** clear-cut, concrete, confined, definite, detailed, especial, peculiar, personal, relevant, singular, tied-down **9** intrinsic, pertinent, specified **10** individual, particular, pinned-down, restricted **11** categorical, determinate, distinctive, unequivocal **13** circumscribed **14** characteristic

specification 6 detail **7** clarity **9** condition, precision, substance **11** enumeration, itemization, requirement, stipulation **12** concreteness **13** particularity, qualification **17** particularization

specifics 4 cure, fact, item **5** datum **6** detail, physic **10** medication, particular **12** circumstance

specify 4 cite, name **5** order **6** adduce, define, denote, detail **7** call for, focus on, itemize **8** describe, indicate, set forth **9** designate, enumerate, stipulate **13** particularize

specimen 4 case, type **5** model **6** sample **7** example **8** exemplar, instance **9** prototype **14** representative **15** exemplification

specious 5 false **6** faulty, tricky, untrue **7** dubious, invalid, unsound **8** slippery, spurious **9** casuistic, deceptive, illogical, incorrect, unfounded **10** fallacious, inaccurate, misleading **11** sophistical **12** questionable **15** unsubstantiated

speck 3 bit, dot, jot, pin **4** drop, hair, iota, mark, mite, mote, spot, whit **5** fleck, grain, pinch, trace **6** shadow, trifle **7** glimmer, modicum, speckle **8** farthing, flyspeck, particle **9** scintilla

speckled 4 pied **6** dotted **7** flecked, spotted, studded **8** freckled, peppered **9** sprinkled

spectacle 5 scene, sight **6** marvel, parade, rarity, wonder **7** display, exhibit, pageant **9** curiosity, rare sight **10** exhibition, exposition, phenomenon, production **12** extravaganza, presentation **13** demonstration

spectacles 6 lenses, shades **7** glasses **8** bifocals, pince-nez **10** eyeglasses

spectacular 4 gala, rich **5** grand, showy **6** daring **7** jeweled, opulent, stately **8** dramatic, fabulous, glorious, gorgeous, splendid, striking **9** daredevil, elaborate, marvelous, spectacle, sumptuous, thrilling **10** astounding, bespangled, eye-filling, impressive, theatrical **11** ceremonious, hair-raising, magnificent, sensational **12** extravaganza, overwhelming **16** ostentatious show **19** elaborate production

spectator 3 fan **5** house **6** viewer **7** gallery, witness **8** audience, beholder, kibitzer, observer, onlooker **9** bystander, sightseer **10** aficionado, eyewitness **11** afficionado, theatergoer **12** rubbernecker

Spectator, The
    author: **13** Joseph Addison, Richard Steele

specter 5 demon, ghost, ghoul, shade, spook **6** spirit, sprite, vision, wraith **7** banshee, fantasy, phantom **8** phantasm, presence, revenant **9** hobgoblin **10** apparition

spectral 4 airy **5** eerie, weird **6** creepy, spooky, unreal **7** ghastly, ghostly, phantom, shadowy, uncanny **8** ethereal, gossamer, vaporous **9** unearthly **10** chimerical, phantasmal, wraithlike **11** incorporeal **12** otherworldly, supernatural **13** insubstantial

speculate 4 muse **5** brood, dream, fancy, guess, study, think, wager **6** chance, gamble, hazard, ponder, reason, wonder **7** imagine, reflect, suppose, surmise, venture **8** cogitate, consider, meditate, ruminate, theorize **10** conjecture, deliberate, excogitate, play a hunch **11** contemplate, hypothesize, take a chance **13** play the market

speculation 4 risk **7** venture **8** gambling **9** guesswork **10** conjecture, estimation **11** supposition

speculative 4 iffy **5** dicey, risky **6** chancy **8** academic **11** conjectural, theoretical **12** experimental, hypothetical **13** suppositional

speculator 7 gambler, plunger **8** investor, operator, theorist **10** adventurer, arbitrager **11** arbitrageur

speech 4 talk **5** idiom, lingo,

slang, voice **6** appeal, gossip, homily, jargon, sermon, tirade, tongue **7** address, chatter, comment, dialect, diction, lecture, oration, palaver, prattle, remarks, talking **8** chitchat, colloquy, converse, dialogue, diatribe, harangue, language, parlance, rhetoric, speaking **9** discourse, elocution, monologue, soliloquy, statement, utterance **10** discussion, expression, recitation, salutation **11** declamation, declaration, enunciation, exhortation, observation, valedictory **12** articulation, conversation, dissertation, vocalization **13** colloquialism, confabulation, pronouncement, pronunciation, verbalization

speechless 3 mum **4** dumb, mute **6** silent **7** aphonic **8** wordless **9** stupefied **10** tongue-tied

speed 3 aid, hie, run, zip **4** dart, dash, help, race, rate, rush, tear, zoom **5** boost, favor, gun it, haste, hurry, impel, speed, tempo **6** assist, barrel, gallop, hasten, hurtle, hustle, pick up, plunge, propel, scurry, step up **7** advance, further, hurry up, promote, quicken, tear off **8** alacrity, celerity, dispatch, expedite, hightail, make time, momentum, rapidity, step on it, velocity **9** bowl along, briskness, fleetness, give a lift, hastiness, make haste, move along, quickness, rapidness, swiftness **10** accelerate, expedition, get a move on, go hell-bent, lose no time, promptness, spurt ahead **11** push forward **12** acceleration **13** burn up the road

speedily 4 fast **5** apace, quick **6** pronto **7** hastily, rapidly, swiftly **8** in no time, promptly **9** post haste, right away, summarily **11** on the double **12** lickety-split

speed up 4 rush **5** hurry **6** hasten, step up **7** hop to it, quicken **8** expedite, multiply, step on it **9** encourage, intensify **10** accelerate, facilitate, get a move on **12** step on the gas

speedy 4 fast **5** brisk, early, fleet, hasty, quick, rapid, ready, swift **6** abrupt, lively, sudden **7** express, hurried, running, summary **8** headlong **9** quick-fire, rapid-fire **10** not delayed **11** precipitate

Spelaites
    epithet of: **6** Hermes
    means: **9** of the cave

spell 2 go **3** bit, hex **4** bout, free, lull, mean, omen, snap, term, time, tour, turn, wave **5** augur, break, charm, hitch, imply, magic, pause, round, stint, trick, while **6** allure, course, denote, herald, hoodoo, make up, period, recess, tenure, typify, voodoo **7** bespeak, betoken, connote, glamour, portend, presage, promise, purport, rapture, release, relieve, respite, signify, sorcery, stretch, suggest **8** amount to, cover for, duration, forebode, forecast, foretell, indicate, interval, stand for, witchery **9** form a word, influence, interlude, represent, symbolize **10** assignment, invocation, mumbo jumbo, open-sesame **11** abracadabra, bewitchment, enchantment, fascination, incantation, pinchhit for, take over for **12** magic formula

spellbind 5 charm **7** bewitch, enchant **8** enthrall, entrance, intrigue, transfix **9** enrapture, fascinate, hypnotize, mesmerize, transport

spellbound 4 rapt **5** agape **7** charmed **8** wordless **9** awestruck, bewitched, enchanted, entranced, possessed **10** breathless, dumbstruck, enraptured, enthralled, fascinated, hypnotized, mesmerized, speechless, tongue-tied, transfixed **11** openmouthed, transported

Spellbound
    director: **15** Alfred Hitchcock
    cast: **9** John Emery **11** Gregory Peck, Leo G Carroll **13** Ingrid Bergman **14** Michael Chekhov
    score: **11** Miklos Rosza
    Oscar for: **5** score
    dream sequences by: **12** Salvador Dali

spell out 6 define, detail **7** clarify, clear up, explain, expound, specify **8** describe **9** delineate, designate, elucidate, explicate, interpret, make plain **10** illustrate

Spemann, Hans
    field: **7** zoology
    nationality: **6** German
    worked in: **20** embryonic development
    awarded: **10** Nobel Prize

Spencer, Sir Stanley
    born: **7** Cookham, England **9** Berkshire
    artwork: **22** Resurrection of Soldiers, The Resurrection Cookham **31** Christ Preaching at Cookham Regatta **43** Double Nude Portrait—

the Artist and his Second Wife

spend 3 pay, use 4 dole, fill, give, pass 5 drain, empty, use up, waste 6 devote, employ, expend, invest, occupy, outlay, pay out, take up 7 burn out, consume, deplete, destroy, exhaust, fork out, scatter, wear out 8 allocate, disburse, dispense, shell out, squander 9 dissipate, while away 10 impoverish

spendable 9 available 10 expendable 13 discretionary

spend foolishly 5 waste 8 misspend, squander 9 dissipate, throw away 11 fritter away

spendthrift 6 lavish, waster 7 wastrel 8 prodigal, spend-all, wasteful 10 big spender, profligate, squanderer 11 extravagant, improvident 12 overgenerous

Spengler, Oswald
  author of: 19 The Decline of the West

Spenlow, Dora
  character in: 16 David Copperfield
  author: 7 Dickens

Spenser, Edmund
  author of: 8 Amoretti 12 Epithalamion 15 The Faerie Queene 22 The Shephearde's Calendar

spent 4 beat, done, weak 5 faint, weary 6 bushed, done in, used up 7 laid low, wearied, worn out 8 drooping, fatigued, tired out 9 enfeebled, exhausted, fagged out, played out, powerless, prostrate 11 debilitated, ready to drop 12 strengthless 14 on one's last legs

Sperry, Elmer Ambrose
  invented: 11 gyrocompass 22 airplane automatic pilot

spew 5 eject, expel, heave, vomit 6 cast up 7 spit out 8 disgorge, throw out 11 regurgitate

spew up 4 spew 5 eject, expel, spout, vomit 6 cast up 7 cough up, throw up 8 disgorge 11 regurgitate

sphere 3 orb 4 area, ball, beat, pale 5 globe, orbit, range, realm, scope 6 domain 7 compass, globule 8 province, spheroid 9 bailiwick, round body, territory 10 experience

spherical 5 orbic, round 6 global, rotund 7 globate, glo-

bose, orbical 8 globular 9 orbicular 11 globe-shaped
  nearly: 8 obrotund

spheroid 3 orb 4 ball 5 globe 6 sphere 7 globule

spherule 4 ball, bead, drop 6 pellet 7 droplet, globule

Sphinx
  form: 7 monster
  bust of: 5 woman
  body of: 4 lion
  father: 6 Typhon 7 Orthrus
  mother: 7 Echidna 8 Chimaera
  proposed: 7 riddles
  location: 6 Thebes
  answered by: 7 Oedipus

spice 3 zip 4 herb, kick, snap, tang, zest 5 savor 6 accent, flavor, relish, stacte 7 pizzazz 8 piquancy, pungency 9 condiment, flavoring, seasoning 10 excitement

spicule 4 barb 5 point, spine 7 prickle

spicy 3 hot 4 keen, racy 5 acute, bawdy, fiery, nippy, pithy, salty, sharp, tangy, witty, zippy 6 clever, ribald, risque, snappy, strong 7 gingery, peppery, piquant, pungent 8 aromatic, improper, incisive, indecent, off-color, piercing, redolent, spirited 9 sparkling, trenchant 10 indelicate, scandalous, suggestive 11 provocative 12 questionable 13 scintillating

spider
  black widow marking: 9 hourglass
  class: 9 Arachnida
  combining form: 6 arachn 7 arachno
  family: 7 Attidae 9 Drassidae 10 Citigradae, Pisauridae
  famous: 9 Charlotte
  fear of: 13 arachnophobia
  kind: 4 crab, wolf 5 taint 7 jumping 8 trap-door 9 orb weaver, solpugida, tarantula 10 black widow 13 daddy longlegs
  mythology: 7 Arachne
  nest: 5 nidus
  order: 7 Araneae
  part: 4 claw, coxa 5 femur, tibia 6 tarsus 7 abdomen, mammula, patella, pedicel, scopula 9 chelicera, protarsis, spinneret 10 pedipalpus, trochanter 11 calamistrum 13 cephalothorax
  study of: 10 araneology 11 arachnology
  young: 11 spiderlings

Spielberg, Steven
  director of: 4 Jaws 14 The Color Purple 19 Raiders of the Lost Ark 21 ET The Ex-

tra Terrestrial (in his adventures on earth) 29 Close Encounters of the Third Kind

spike 3 peg, pin 4 barb, nail, spur, tine 5 briar, point, prong, rivet, spine, stake, thorn 6 needle, skewer 7 bramble, bristle, hobnail 8 spikelet

spill 3 run 4 blab, drip, drop, dump, fall, flow, shed, slop, tell, toss 5 slosh, throw, waste 6 reveal, splash 7 let flow, pour out 8 disclose, overflow, overturn

Spillane, Mickey
  real name: 13 Frank Morrison
  author of: 8 I the Jury 12 Kiss Me Deadly 14 The Girl Hunters 15 The Death Dealers
  character: 10 Mike Hammer

spin 4 roll, tell, turn 5 swirl, twirl, wheel, whirl 6 gyrate, invent, relate, render, rotate, unfold 7 concoct, narrate, recount, revolve 8 rotation, spinning 9 fabricate, pirouette

spinach 3 rot 4 bull, bunk 5 hokum, hooey, stuff 6 bunkum, hot air, humbug 7 baloney, blather, hogwash, potherb 8 claptrap, nonsense, tommyrot 9 poppycock, vegetable 10 applesauce 11 foolishness 16 stuff and nonsense

spinach 16 Spinacia oleracea
  varieties: 4 wild 5 Cuban 6 Indian 7 Malabar 8 mountain 10 New Zealand 11 round-seeded 13 prickly-seeded

spinal column 4 back 5 spine 8 backbone

spindly 4 puny 5 frail, leggy 6 skinny 7 scraggy 8 skeletal

spine 4 barb, horn, spur 5 briar, point, prong, quill, spike, thorn 6 needle 7 bramble, bristle, prickle 8 backbone 9 vertebrae 12 spinal column

spinel
  source: 5 Burma, Mogok
  color: 3 red 5 mauve

spineless 4 weak 5 timid 7 fearful 8 cowardly, cowering, cringing, timorous, wavering 10 indecisive, irresolute, spiritless, weak-willed 11 lily-livered, vacillating 12 fainthearted 13 pusillanimous 14 chickenhearted

spinelessness 8 timidity, weakness 9 cowardice 10 indecision 11 fearfulness

12 cowardliness, irresolution **13** pusillanimity

spine-tingling 7 rousing **8** exciting **9** thrilling **11** hair-raising, sensational **12** breathtaking, electrifying

spinning jenny
    invented by: 10 Hargreaves

spinoff 5 issue **6** result **7** adjunct, outcome **8** offshoot **9** byproduct, outgrowth **10** descendant, side effect, supplement **11** aftereffect, consequence

spin out 4 skid **7** draw out **8** lengthen **9** attenuate

spinster 6 virgin **7** old maid **14** unmarried woman

spinsterhood 8 celibacy **9** virginity **11** old maidhood

spiral 4 coil, curl, gyre **5** helix, screw, whirl, whorl **6** coiled, curled **7** helical, ringlet, spiroid, whorled, winding **8** curlicue, twisting **9** corkscrew **11** screw-shaped

Spiral Staircase, The
    director: 13 Robert Siodmak
    based on story by: 14 Ethel Lina White (Some Must Watch)
    cast: 9 Kent Smith **11** George Brent **13** Rhonda Fleming **14** Dorothy McGuire, Ethel Barrymore

spire 3 cap, tip **4** apex, cone, peak **5** crest, point, shaft, tower **6** belfry, summit, turret, vertex **7** minaret, obelisk, steeple **8** pinnacle **9** bell tower, campanile

spirit 3 elf **4** mind, soul, urge, will **5** fairy, ghost, ghoul, heart, shade, spook **6** animus, dybbuk, goblin, psyche, sprite, wraith **7** banshee, bugaboo, bugbear, impulse, phantom, resolve, specter **8** phantasm, presence **9** hobgoblin, intellect **10** apparition, motivation, resolution
    German: 5 Geist

spirited 4 bold **5** fiery, nervy **6** frisky, lively, plucky **8** fearless, intrepid **10** courageous, mettlesome

spiritless 4 dull, limp, tame **6** abject **8** cowardly, lifeless, listless **9** apathetic, spineless **10** unanimated, world-weary **11** passionless

spirit of the time
    German: 9 Zeitgeist

spirits 3 aim, vim **4** bond, elan, fire, gist, glow, grit, guts, mood, sand, tone, vein, zeal, zest **5** ardor, drive, hu-mor, pluck, sense, spunk, tenor, valor, verve, vigor **6** daring, effect, elixir, energy, fervor, intent, liquor, mettle, morale, stripe, temper, warmth **7** alcohol, avidity, bravery, courage, essence, extract, feeling, loyalty, meaning, purport, purpose, sparkle **8** attitude, audacity, backbone, boldness, devotion, emotions, feelings, tincture, vitality, vivacity **9** animation, eagerness, fortitude, intention, sentiment, stoutness, substance **10** allegiance, attachment, enterprise, enthusiasm, liveliness **11** disposition, doughtiness, staunchness **12** fearlessness, significance **13** dauntlessness, sprightliness **16** stoutheartedness **17** alcoholic solution

spiritual 4 holy **5** godly, inner, moral, pious **6** divine, mental **7** blessed, churchy, ghostly, phantom, psychic **8** cerebral, hallowed, heavenly, platonic, priestly, spectral, supernal **9** celestial, Christian, innermost, of the soul, religious, unearthly, unfleshly, unworldly **10** devotional, immaterial, intangible, sacrosanct, sanctified **11** consecrated, incorporeal **12** metaphysical, otherworldly, supernatural **13** insubstantial, psychological **14** ecclesiastical

spirituality 5 piety **8** devotion, holiness **9** godliness, reverence **10** devoutness

spirituous 4 hard **6** strong **9** alcoholic, distilled **12** intoxicating

spit 3 bar, pop, rod **4** foam, hiss, reef, spew **5** atoll, drool, eject, fling, froth, shoal, throw **6** saliva, shower, shriek, skewer, slaver, sputum **7** dribble, scatter, slobber, spatter, spittle, sputter **8** headland, sandbank, turnspit **9** brochette, peninsula **10** promontory **11** expectorate

spite 3 irk, vex **4** gall, hate, hurt, pain **5** annoy, odium, sting, venom, wound **6** animus, enmity, grudge, harass, hatred, injure, malice, misuse, nettle, put out, rancor **7** ill will, mortify, provoke **8** bad blood, ill-treat, irritate, loathing, meanness **9** animosity, antipathy, hostility, humiliate, malignity, nastiness, vengeance **10** bitterness, resentment **11** detestation, malevolence **12** vengefulness **13** maliciousness, slap in the face **14** revengefulness, vindictiveness

spiteful 4 evil **5** nasty **6** bitter, malign, wicked **7** caustic, envious, hateful, hostile, vicious **8** grudging, vengeful, venomous **9** malicious, merciless, rancorous, resentful, sarcastic, splenetic **10** ill-natured, malevolent, vindictive **11** acrimonious, unforgiving **12** antagonistic

spitting image (the) 4 copy, mate, twin **6** double **9** duplicate **15** perfect likeness

splash 3 ado, hit **4** cast, dash, daub, soil, stir, toss, wash **5** bathe, break, fling, plash, slosh, smack, smear, stain, strew, surge, swash **6** batter, blazon, buffet, effect, impact, paddle, plunge, shower, spread, streak, strike, uproar, wallow, welter **7** bestrew, scatter, spatter, splotch **8** besmirch, discolor, disperse, splatter, sprinkle **9** bespatter, broadcast, commotion, sensation **10** spattering **11** splattering

splashy 5 jazzy, showy **6** flashy **10** glittering **11** spectacular **12** ostentatious

splatter 4 dash **6** splash **7** spatter

splay 4 awry **5** askew, broad **6** aslant, clumsy, extend, tilted, warped **7** awkward, crooked, fanlike, slanted, sloping, turn out **8** inclined, slanting **9** distorted, fan-shaped, irregular, outspread, spread out **10** stretch out

spleen 4 bile, gall **5** anger, spite, venom **6** animus, enmity, hatred, malice, rancor **7** ill will **8** acrimony, ill humor, vexation **9** animosity, bad temper, hostility **10** bitterness, resentment **11** malevolence, peevishness **12** irritability, spitefulness

splendid 4 fine, high, rare, rich **5** grand, lofty, noble, regal, royal **6** august, costly, ornate, superb **7** elegant, eminent, exalted, stately **8** dazzling, elevated, flashing, gleaming, glorious, gorgeous, imposing, majestic, palatial, peerless, terrific **9** admirable, beautiful, brilliant, effulgent, estimable, excellent, marvelous, sumptuous, wonderful **10** glittering, preeminent, remarkable, surpassing **11** exceptional, illustrious, magnificent, outstanding, resplendent, splendorous **12** transcendent **13** distinguished, splendiferous

Splendid Splinter
  nickname of: 11 Ted
   Williams

splendor 4 fire, pomp 5 gleam,
  glory, light, sheen, shine
  6 beauty, dazzle, luster, renown 7 burnish, glitter
  8 grandeur, nobility, opulence,
  radiance 9 intensity, sublimity 10 augustness, brilliance,
  effulgence, irradiance, luminosity 11 preeminence, stateliness 12 gorgeousness,
  luminousness, magnificence,
  resplendence 13 incandescence

Splendor in the Grass
  director: 9 Elia Kazan
  based on story by: 11 William Inge
  cast: 9 Pat Hingle 11 Natalie
   Wood 12 Sean Garrison,
   Warren Beatty 14 Audrey
   Christie

splenetic 5 cross, nasty, surly,
  testy 6 cranky, malign 7 bilious, hostile, peevish 8 choleric, spiteful, venomous
  9 irascible, rancorous 11 acrimonious, ill-tempered 12 cantankerous, disagreeable

splice 3 wed 4 join, knit
  5 graft, merge, plait, unite
  7 connect 8 dovetail 9 interlace 10 intertwine, interweave 12 interconnect

splinter 4 chip 5 smash, split
  6 needle, shiver, sliver 7 break
  up, crumble, explode, shatter
  8 fly apart, fracture, fragment
  9 pulverize 12 disintegrate

split 3 hew 4 deal, dole, dual,
  mete, part, rent, rift, rive,
  snap, tear, torn 5 allot, break,
  burst, cleft, crack, halve,
  mixed, riven, sever, share
  6 bisect, breach, broken,
  cleave, differ, divide, ripped,
  schism, shiver, sunder, varied
  7 be riven, cracked, diverge,
  divided, divorce, divvy up, fissure, give way, opening, portion, quarrel, rupture, severed,
  twofold 8 alienate, allocate,
  cleavage, disagree, dispense,
  disperse, dissever, disunion,
  disunite, division, fracture,
  ruptured, splinter 9 apportion,
  fractured, parcel out, partition,
  segmented, segregate, separated, set at odds, subdivide,
  undecided 10 alienation, ambivalent, break apart, difference, dissension, dissevered,
  distribute, divergence, falling
  out, separation, splintered
  11 come between, part company, tear asunder 12 disagreement, estrangement

split off 7 deviate, diverge
  8 separate 9 draw apart

split the difference 5 agree
  6 settle 9 make a deal
  10 compromise 11 come to
  terms, meet halfway 14 strike
  a bargain

splitting off 9 diverging
  10 separating 12 drawing
  apart

splitting up 8 dividing 9 di-
  vorcing 10 breaking up, separating 11 subdividing
  12 partitioning

splotch 4 blot, daub, mark,
  spot 5 smear, stain 6 blotch,
  smudge 13 discoloration

splurge 5 binge, spree
  6 bender 8 live it up 10 indulgence, showing off
  12 showy display 13 be extravagant, shoot the works
  14 indulge oneself, self-
  indulgence 22 throw caution
  to the winds

splutter 4 hiss, spew, spit
  5 burst, spray 6 gibber, jabber,
  mumble, seethe 7 bluster,
  slobber, spatter, sputter, stammer, stumble, stutter 9 hem
  and haw 11 expectorate

Spodius
  epithet of: 6 Apollo
  means: 10 god of ashes

spodumene
  variety: 7 kunzite

spoil 3 mar, rot 4 baby, flaw,
  harm, mold, ruin, sour, turn
  5 addle, botch, decay, go bad,
  humor, taint 6 blight, bungle,
  coddle, damage, deface, foul
  up, impair, injure, mess up,
  mildew, muddle, pamper
  7 blemish, destroy, disrupt,
  putrefy 8 mutilate 9 decompose, disfigure 11 deteriorate,
  mollycoddle, overgratify,
  overindulge

spoiled 3 bad, off 6 putrid, rotten, ruined 7 coddled, corrupt,
  decayed, gone bad, went bad
  8 indulged, overripe, pampered 9 putrefied 10 decomposed, frustrated
  12 deteriorated 15 rotten to
  the core

spoiler 6 vandal 8 underdog
  9 deflector

Spoilers, The
  author: 8 Rex Beach

spoils 4 haul, loot, swag, take
  5 booty 6 bounty, prizes,
  quarry 7 plunder, profits
  8 benefits, comforts, pickings
  9 amenities, patronage 11 per-
  quisites 12 acquisitions

spoilsport 4 drag 10 wet blanket 11 party-pooper

spoken 4 oral, said 5 parol
  6 verbal, voiced 7 uttered
  9 expressed 10 pronounced
  11 articulated

spokesman 5 agent, PR man,
  proxy 6 backer, deputy
  7 speaker 8 delegate, promoter 9 middleman, proponent, supporter, surrogate
  10 mouthpiece, negotiator,
  press agent 11 protagonist

sponge 3 bum, dry, mop, rub
  4 blot, swab, wash 5 cadge,
  clean, leech, mooch, towel
  6 borrow, live on 7 cleanse,
  moisten 8 freeload, impose on,
  scrounge 9 panhandle

sponger 5 leech 6 cadger,
  sponge 7 moocher 8 barnacle,
  borrower, deadbeat
  9 scrounger 10 freeloader
  11 bloodsucker

sponsor 4 back 5 angel, set
  up 6 backer, patron, uphold
  7 finance, promote, support
  8 advocate, champion, defender, financer, guardian,
  partisan, promoter, start out,
  upholder, vouch for, warranty 9 guarantee, financier,
  guarantor, proponent, protecter, protector, supporter
  10 advertiser, stand up for,
  underwrite

sponsorship 5 aegis 7 support
  8 advocacy, auspices 9 patronage 12 championship

spontaneity 7 freedom 11 impetuosity, naturalness 12 unconstraint 13 impulsiveness,
  offhandedness
  18 extemporaneousness

spontaneous 4 free 5 ad lib
  7 natural, offhand, willing
  8 unbidden 9 automatic, extempore, impetuous, im-
  promptu, impulsive,
  ingenuous, unplanned, unstudied, voluntary 10 unguitous,
  improvised, off the cuff, unprompted 11 independent, instinctive, uncontrived
  12 unhesitating 13 unconstrained 14 extemporaneous,
  unpremeditated

spoof 3 kid 4 joke, josh, twit
  6 parody, satire, sendup
  7 joshing, kidding, lampoon,
  mockery, ribbing, takeoff
  8 satirize, travesty 9 burlesque,
  take off on 10 caricature

spook 5 alarm, bogey, ghost,
  haunt, scare, shade 6 goblin,
  shadow, spirit 7 disturb, phantom, specter, startle, terrify,
  unnerve 8 disquiet, frighten,
  unsettle 9 hobgoblin, terrorize
  10 apparition, intimidate

spooky 5 eerie, jumpy, scary,
  weird 6 creepy 7 ghostly,

nervous 8 skittish
10 mysterious

sporadic 3 few 4 rare, thin
6 fitful, meager, random,
scarce, sparse, spotty 8 isolated, periodic, uncommon
9 haphazard, irregular, scattered, spasmodic 10 infrequent, now and then,
occasional 11 fragmentary
12 intermittent, widely
spaced 13 discontinuous
16 few and far between

sport 3 fun, toy 4 bear, butt,
game, goat, jest, joke, lark,
play, romp, trip 5 abuse, caper, carry, chaff, dally, frisk,
hobby, mirth, revel 6 antics,
cavort, frolic, gaiety, gambol,
misuse, monkey, take in, trifle 7 buffoon, contest, display,
disport, exhibit, gambler, jesting, jollity, kidding, mockery,
rollick, show off, skylark
8 badinage, derision, fair
game, flourish, hilarity, illtreat, raillery, ridicule, scoffing, trifling 9 amusement, athletics, daredevil, diversion,
festivity, joviality, make
merry, play games, scapegoat
10 persiflage, pleasantry, recreation, relaxation, skylarking
11 competition, distraction,
merrymaking 12 depreciation
13 entertainment, laughingstock 14 divertissement

sporting house 4 stew
5 house 6 bagnio, bordel
7 brothel 8 bordello, cathouse
10 bawdy house, fancy house,
whorehouse 14 house of ill
fame 16 house of ill repute
19 house of prostitution

sportive 6 blithe, frisky
7 playful 8 animated
10 frolicsome

sportsman 6 hunter
9 fisherman

Sportsman's Notebook, A
author: 12 Ivan Turgenev

sporty 6 casual, flashy, jaunty
8 informal

spot 3 dot, fix, see, spy 4 area,
bind, blot, daub, espy, flaw,
mark, part, seat, site, slur,
soil 5 brand, fleck, grime, locus, patch, place, point,
smear, space, speck, stain,
sully, taint, tract 6 blotch, defect, detect, locale, locate,
plight, region, sector, smirch,
smudge, splash, stigma
7 blemish, dilemma, discern,
light on, pick out, quarter,
section, spatter, speckle,
splotch, station 8 discolor, discover, disgrace, district, flyspeck, locality, location,
position, premises, reproach,

sprinkle 9 aspersion, discredit,
recognize, situation, territory
10 difficulty, imputation
11 predicament 12 bad situation, neighborhood
13 discoloration

spotless 4 pure 5 clean,
snowy 7 perfect, shining
8 flawless, gleaming, pristine,
unflawed, unmarred, unsoiled
9 faultless, stainless, unspotted,
unstained, unsullied, untainted 10 immaculate, impeccable 11 unblemished,
untarnished 14 irreproachable
15 unexceptionable

spotted 3 saw 6 dotted, espied,
soiled 7 dappled, located, mottled, stained 8 detected, speckled 9 blemished, discerned,
spattered 10 discovered
13 caught sight of

spotty 6 fitful, pimply, random, uneven 7 blotchy, dappled, erratic, flecked, mottled,
spotted 8 episodic, freckled,
splotchy, sporadic, unsteady,
variable, wavering 9 broken
out, desultory, irregular, spasmodic, uncertain 10 capricious, inconstant, unreliable,
variegated 11 full of spots
12 disorganized, intermittent,
undependable, unmethodical,
unsystematic

spouse 4 mate, wife 7 consort,
husband, partner 8 helpmate
10 better half

spout 3 jet, lip 4 beak, flow,
go on, gush, nose, pipe, rant,
spew, tube, vent, well 5 eject,
erupt, expel, exude, issue,
mouth, shoot, snout, spray,
spurt, surge, vomit 6 nozzle,
outlet, sluice, squirt, stream,
trough 7 bluster, carry on,
channel, conduit, pour out
8 disgorge, fountain, harangue 9 discharge, hold
forth 10 waterspout 11 pontificate 12 emit forcibly 14 speak
pompously

sprawl 4 flop, lean, loll, wind
5 slump 6 branch, extend,
lounge, slouch 7 gush out,
meander, recline 8 languish,
reach out, straggle 9 spread
out 10 stretch out 11 spreadeagle

spray 4 coat, mist, posy, twig
5 bough, burst, shoot, sprig,
treat, vapor 6 dampen, nozzle,
shower, splash, switch, volley
7 atomize, barrage, blossom,
bouquet, drizzle, moisten,
nosegay, scatter, spatter,
sprayer, syringe 8 atomizer,
disperse, droplets, moisture,
sprinkle 9 discharge, fusillade,
sprinkler, vaporizer

spread 3 air, lay 4 area, cast,
coat, open, pave, shed, span,
vent 5 apply, bruit, cloak,
cover, feast, field, issue, range,
reach, scope, smear, spray,
story, strew, sweep, table,
tract, width 6 bedaub, be
shed, blazon, extend, extent,
herald, length, notice, repeat,
report, unfold, unfurl, unroll
7 account, advance, article,
banquet, besmear, bestrew,
breadth, circuit, compass, declare, diffuse, divulge, expanse,
overlay, overrun, pervade,
plaster, publish, radiate, scatter, spatter, stretch, suffuse,
trumpet, untwine, write-up
8 announce, coverage, disperse, distance, increase, permeate, proclaim, sprinkle
9 broadcast, circulate, diffusion, expansion, extension,
make known, penetrate, pervasion, propagate, publicize,
radiation, spreading, suffusion,
ventilate 10 dispersion, distribute, make public, permeation,
promulgate, stretch out
11 communicate, disseminate,
noise abroad, proliferate
13 amplification, dissemination, proliferation

spread out 5 broad, widen
6 expand, extend 7 broaden,
diffuse, enlarge, radiate,
stretch 8 expanded, extended,
open wide 9 dispersed, outspread, scattered 10 distribute,
unhampered 11 unconfirmed
12 unrestricted
14 unconcentrated

spree 4 bout, orgy, toot
5 binge, drunk, fling, revel
6 bender 7 carouse, debauch,
revelry, splurge, wassail 8 carousal 9 bacchanal
10 saturnalia

sprightliness 8 buoyancy,
spryness, vivacity 9 animation,
briskness 10 breeziness, liveliness 16 lightheartedness

sprightly 3 gay 4 keen, spry
5 agile, alive, brisk, jolly,
merry 6 active, blithe, breezy,
cheery, jaunty, jovial, lively,
nimble 7 buoyant, chipper,
dashing, dynamic, playful
8 animated, cheerful, spirited,
sportive 9 energetic, vivacious
10 blithesome, frolicsome
12 lighthearted

spring 3 hop, jet, pop, spa
4 come, dart, flow, gush,
jump, kick, leap, loom, pool,
pour, rise, rush, stem, well
5 arise, baths, begin, bound,
caper, ensue, fount, issue,
lunge, shoot, spout, spurt,
start, surge, vault 6 appear,
bounce, derive, gambol, recoil,

reflex, result, sprout, stream
7 burgeon, crop out, descend, emanate, proceed, release, shoot up, start up, stretch, trigger **8** buoyancy, commence, fountain, mushroom **9** come forth, entrechat, germinate, originate, saltation, waterhole **10** break forth, burst forth, elasticity, resiliency **11** flexibility
  goddess of: 4 Hebe **5** Venus

spring back 6 bounce, recoil **7** rebound **8** ricochet

spring flowers
  goddess of: 6 Thallo

Springhaven
  author: 11 R D Blackmore

springlike 4 mild, soft, warm **5** balmy

springs
  god of: 4 Fons **6** Palici
  goddess of: 4 Idun **5** Idura, Ithun **6** Ithunn

spring up 4 grow, rise **5** arise, occur, pop up **6** crop up, emerge, happen, sprout **9** originate **10** burst forth

springy 6 bouncy, spongy, supple **7** elastic **9** resilient **10** rebounding

sprinkle 4 dash, dust, rain **5** spray, strew, water **6** powder, shower, splash, spread, squirt **7** bestrew, diffuse, drizzle, moisten, scatter, spatter **8** splatter

sprinkling 4 dash, drop, hint **5** pinch, touch **7** droplet, minimum, modicum, soupcon **8** sprinkle **10** smattering

sprint 3 run **4** dart, dash, kick, race, rush, tear, whiz **5** burst, shoot, spurt, whisk **7** scamper

sprit 3 bar **4** spar **8** crossbar **10** crosspiece

sprite 3 elf **5** fairy, pixie **10** leprechaun

sprout 3 bud, wax **4** grow **5** bloom, shoot, sprig **6** come up, flower, spread, thrive **7** blossom, burgeon **8** multiply, offshoot, put forth, spring up **9** germinate, outgrowth

spruce 4 chic, neat, tidy, trim **5** kempt, natty, sharp, smart **6** dapper **7** conifer, elegant **9** evergreen, shipshape **11** well-groomed **12** spick-and-span
  French: 6 soigne

spruce 5 Picea
  varieties: 3 bog, cat, red **4** blue **5** black, Hondo, Sitka, snake, white, Yeddo **6** double, Norway **7** Alberta,

big-cone, Finnish, hemlock **8** Colorado, Sakhalin, Siberian **9** Himalayan, tiger-tail **10** Black Hills **12** Colorado blue, Japanese bush

spry 4 deft, hale **5** agile, brisk, quick **6** active, frisky, hearty, jaunty, lively, nimble, supple **7** buoyant, chipper, playful **8** animated, spirited, sportive, vigorous **9** energetic, sprightly, vivacious **11** lightfooted

spunk 4 fire, grit, guts, salt, sand **5** heart, nerve, pluck **6** daring, ginger, mettle, pepper, spirit **7** bravery, courage **8** backbone, boldness, gumption **10** feistiness

spur 3 arm, leg **4** fork, goad, prod, whet, whip, wing **5** prick **6** branch, feeder, fillip, hasten, motive, siding **7** impetus, impulse **8** excitant, stimulus **9** boot spike, encourage, incentive, stimulant, stimulate, tributary **10** incitement, inducement **11** instigation, provocation, stimulation **13** encouragement

spurge 9 Euphorbia **11** Pachysandra
  varieties: 5 caper, leafy, melon **6** ipecac, myrtle, tramp's **7** cypress, mottled, seaside, slipper **8** fiddler's, Japanese **9** Allegheny, flowering **10** Indian tree

spurious 4 fake, mock, sham **5** bogus, false, phony **6** faulty, forged, hollow **7** feigned, unsound **8** specious **9** imitation, simulated **10** fallacious, fraudulent, not genuine **11** counterfeit, make-believe, unauthentic **12** illegitimate

spurn 4 mock, snub **5** flout, repel, scorn **6** rebuff, refuse, reject, slight **7** condemn, decline, disdain, dismiss, repulse, scoff at, sneer at **8** turn down **9** cast aside, disparage, repudiate **12** coldshoulder, look down upon **16** turn up one's nose at

spur-of-the-moment 5 ad-lib **7** offhand **9** extempore, impromptu **10** improvised, unprepared **11** extemporary, spontaneous, unrehearsed **14** extemporaneous, unpremeditated

spurt 3 jet **4** dart, dash, emit, flow, gush, gust, rush, tear, whiz **5** burst, flash, issue, lunge, scoot, shoot, speed, spout, spray, surge **6** access, spring, sprint, squirt, stream **7** pour out **8** disgorge, ejection, eruption, fountain, outbreak, outburst **9** discharge,

explosion, spring out **10** outpouring

spy 3 pry, see **4** find, peep, spot, view **5** scout, sight, snoop **6** behold, descry, detect, notice, shadow **7** discern, glimpse, make out, observe **8** discover, informer, Mata Hari, perceive, saboteur **9** keep watch, operative, recognize **11** reconnoiter, secret agent **12** catch sight of **13** undercover man, watch secretly **14** espionage agent, fifth columnist **16** agent provocateur **17** intelligence agent

Spy 5 Caleb

Spy, The
  author: 19 James Fenimore Cooper

Spy Who Came In from the Cold, The
  director: 10 Martin Ritt
  based on novel by: 11 John LeCarre
  cast: 11 Claire Bloom, Oskar Werner **12** Peter Van Eyck **13** Richard Burton

Spy Who Loved Me, The
  author: 10 Ian Fleming
  director: 12 Lewis Gilbert
  cast: 10 Bernard Lee (M), Roger Moore (James Bond) **11** Barbara Bach, Curt Jurgens (Stromberg), Richard Kiel (Jaws)

squabble 3 row, war **4** spat, tiff **5** argue, brawl, clash, fight, run-in, scrap, set-to, words **6** battle, bicker, differ **7** contend, contest, dispute, quarrel, wrangle **8** argument **9** have words, lock horns **10** bandy words, contention, difference, dissension **11** altercation, controversy **12** disagreement

squadron 5 fleet **6** armada **8** flotilla **9** naval unit **10** escadrille **11** cavalry unit **12** military unit

squalid 4 foul, mean **5** dirty, nasty **6** abject, filthy, horrid, rotten, shabby, sloppy, sordid **7** decayed, reeking, run-down, unclean **8** battered, degraded, slovenly, wretched **9** miserable **10** broken-down, disheveled, ramshackle, slatternly, tumbledown **11** dilapidated **12** deteriorated

squalidness 4 dirt **5** filth **7** squalor **8** foulness, meanness, vileness **9** dirtiness **10** sordidness **11** degradation, uncleanriess

squalor 4 dirt **5** filth **6** misery **7** neglect, poverty **8** foulness, meanness, ugliness **9** dinginess, dirtiness, nastiness, seediness **10** abjectness, grubbiness, sordidness **11** squalidness, uncleanness **12** wretchedness **13** uncleanliness

squander 4 blow **5** spend, waste **6** lavish, misuse **7** consume, deplete, exhaust **8** misspend **9** dissipate, throw away **10** run through **11** fritter away **14** spend like water

squanderer 6 waster **7** wastrel **8** prodigal **10** dissipater, profligate **11** spendthrift

squandering 7 wasting **8** prodigal, wasteful **9** imprudent **10** profligate **11** dissipating, extravagant, improvident, spendthrift **12** overspending, throwing away **14** frittering away **17** spending like water

square 3 box, fit **4** even, fogy, heal, hick, jerk, jibe, just, mend, park, prig **5** agree, align, blend, block, close, equal, green, match, place, plane, plaza, prude, tally **6** accord, adjust, candid, circus, cohere, common, concur, even up, fall in, honest, pay off, settle, smooth **7** arrange, balance, clear up, compose, conform, even out, flatten, mediate, patch up, rectify, resolve **8** block out, cornball, make even, quadrate, set right, settle up, truthful **9** arbitrate, discharge, equitable, harmonize, liquidate, make level, reconcile **10** clodhopper, correspond, quadrangle, straighten **11** marketplace **12** apple knocker, conservative **13** quadrilateral, stick-in-the-mud **15** straightforward
  type: **1** T **3** try
    11 combination

Square
  character in: **8** Tom Jones
  author: **8** Fielding

Square
  constellation of: **5** Norma

square centimeter
  abbreviation: **4** sq cm

square decimeter
  abbreviation: **4** sq dm

square dekameter
  abbreviation: **5** sq dam

square foot
  abbreviation: **4** sq ft

square hectometer
  abbreviation: **4** sq hm

square inch
  abbreviation: **4** sq in

square kilometer
  abbreviation: **4** sq km

square meter
  abbreviation: **3** sq m

square mile
  abbreviation: **4** sq mi

square millimeter
  abbreviation: **4** sq mm

square rod
  abbreviation: **4** sq rd

square yard
  abbreviation: **4** sq yd

squash 3 jam **4** cram, mash, pulp **5** crowd, crush, level, quash, quell, smash, upset **6** dispel, squish **7** compact, destroy, flatten, put down, ram down, repress, squeeze, squelch, trample **8** compress, suppress **9** dissipate, overthrow, prostrate, undermine **10** annihilate, obliterate **11** concentrate

squash 9 Cucurbita
  varieties: **4** bush **5** acorn **6** autumn, banana, summer, turban, winter **7** Hubbard, scallop **8** pattypan, zucchini **9** cocozelle, crookneck **12** Boston marrow **13** sweet dumpling **15** Canada crookneck, summer crookneck, winter crookneck

squat 5 cower, dumpy, dwell, kneel, pudgy **6** chunky, cringe, crouch, encamp, hunker, lie low, locate, move in, shrink, square, stocky, stubby, stumpy **8** thickset

squawk 5 blare, croak, gripe **6** scream, squall **7** grumble, protest, screech **8** complain

squeak 3 cry **4** peep, yelp **5** cheep, chirp, creak, grate **6** shriek, shrill, squeal **7** screech

squeal 3 cry **4** bawl, blab, fink, peep, sing, wail, yell, yelp **5** cheep, whine **6** inform, scream, shriek, shrill, squeak **7** screech

squealer 3 pig, rat **4** fink **6** canary, piglet, snitch **7** stoolie, tattler, traitor **8** informer **10** tattletale **11** stool pigeon **12** blabbermouth

squeamish 3 coy **4** prim, sick **5** fussy **6** demure, modest, proper, queasy **7** finical, finicky, mincing, prudish, sickish **8** delicate, nauseous, priggish, qualmish **9** finicking **10** fastidious **11** puritanical, straitlaced **13** sanctimonious

Squeers, Wackford
  character in: **16** Nicholas Nickleby
  author: **7** Dickens

squeeze 3 hug, jam, pry, ram

4 butt, cram, edge, grip, hold, pack, push **5** clasp, cramp, crowd, drive, elbow, grasp, press, shove, stuff, wedge, wrest, wring **6** clutch, coerce, compel, defile, elicit, extort, jostle, thrust, wrench **7** compact, draw out, embrace, extract, passage, pull out, tear out **8** compress, crowding, crushing, force out, pinching, press out, pressure, shoulder, withdraw **9** extricate, narrowing, stricture **10** bottleneck **11** compression, concentrate, consolidate **12** constriction

squelch 4 hush **5** abort, crush, quash, quell, quiet, smash **6** retort, squash **7** put down, riposte, silence **8** silencer, suppress

squire 4 date, take **5** court **6** attend, escort **7** consort, gallant, planter **8** cavalier, chaperon **9** accompany, attendant, boyfriend, chauffeur, companion, landowner **14** lord of the manor **16** country gentleman

Squire
  character in: **18** The Canterbury Tales
  author: **7** Chaucer

squirm 4 bend, jerk, toss, turn **5** pitch, shift, smart, sweat, twist, wince **6** blench, fidget, flinch, shrink, twitch, wiggle, writhe **7** agonize, contort, wriggle **8** flounder

squirt 3 jet **4** dash, gush, punk, runt **5** piker, shoot, spout, spray, spurt **6** shower, splash, stream **7** spatter **8** sprinkle **9** discharge, pipsqueak **10** besprinkle

Sri Lanka *see box, p. 924*

SS-GB
  author: **11** Len Deighton

SS troops, chief of
  12 Reichsfuhrer

stab 2 go **3** cut, jab, try **4** ache, bite, gash, gore, hurt, pain, pang, pass, shot, spit **5** essay, gouge, knife, lance, lunge, prick, qualm, slash, spear, spike, stick, sting, trial, wound **6** cleave, dagger, effort, impale, pierce, shiver, stroke, thrill, thrust, twinge **7** attempt, bayonet **8** endeavor, lacerate, transfix **10** laceration, run through

stability 5 poise **6** aplomb, fixity **7** balance **8** evenness, firmness, security, solidity **9** constancy, fixedness, solidness, soundness **10** continuity, durability, permanence, stableness, steadiness, sturdiness **11** abidingness, equilibrium,

Sri Lanka
other name: **6** Ceylon **8** Serendib **9** Taprobane
capital/largest city: **7** Colombo
  ancient capital: **11** Polonnaruwa **12** Anuradhapura
others: **3** Uva **5** Galle, Kandy **6** Jaffna, Mannar, Matale, Matara **7** Badulla, Kegalle, Negombo **8** Kalutara, Mankulem, Moratuwa, Puttalam **9** Ratnapura **10** Batticaloa, Mullaitivu **11** Ambalangoda, Trincomalee
division: **8** Dambulla, Sri Lanka **9** Taprobane
measure: **4** para, seer **5** parah **6** amunam, parrah
monetary unit: **4** cent **5** rupee
island: **5** Delft **6** Mannar **8** Sri Lanka
mountain: **5** Pedro **7** Sri Pada **9** Adam's Peak
highest point: **14** Pidurutalagala
river: **4** Kala **6** Deduru, Gal Ova **8** Aruvi Aru **9** Deburu Ova **11** Kelani Ganga **13** Mahaweli Ganga
sea: **6** Indian
physical feature:
  bay: **6** Bengal **8** Koddiyar
  falls: **8** Lazapana
  gulf: **6** Mannar
  peninsula: **6** Jaffna
  plateau: **6** Hatton
  strait: **4** Palk
people: **5** Malay, Tamil, Vedda **6** Veddah, Weddah **7** Burgher, Mahinda, Malabar **8** Eurasian **9** Cingalese, Dravidian, Sinhalese **10** Singhalese
  leader: **11** Jayawardene **12** Bandaranaike
  ruler: **5** Dutch **7** British, Chinese **10** Portuguese
language: **4** Pali **5** Tamil **7** English **9** Sinhalese
religion: **5** Hindu, Islam **8** Buddhism
place:
  fortress: **8** Sigiriya
  gardens: **8** Hakgalle **10** Peradiniya
  national park: **6** Ruhuna **8** Wilpattu
  temple: **5** Tooth **6** Gal Oya **7** Kelanya **8** Runaweli **9** Ruanvelli **10** Dankahlaka **12** Asokharamaya
feature:
  animal: **5** loris **12** wild elephant
  clothing: **4** sari **5** camba **6** sarong **7** cambaya **8** sherwani
  dancer: **7** Kandyan
  drama: **5** kolam **7** nadagam
  festival: **8** Perahera
  shrine: **6** dagoba
  tree: **4** doon, hora, palu, tala **5** domba, ebony **7** talipot **8** halmilla, ironwood **9** satinwood **11** allaeanthus **12** shimohabodhi

reliability **13** steadfastness **14** changelessness **16** unchangeableness

stabilize 7 balance **8** hold firm, make firm **10** hold steady, make steady

stabilizer 7 balance, ballast **8** additive **9** equipoise, gyroscope **10** ballasting **12** airplane part **14** counterbalance

stable 4 barn, byre, even, firm, mews, safe, true **5** fixed, loyal, solid, sound **6** moored, secure, steady, sturdy **7** abiding, durable, staunch, uniform **8** anchored, constant, cowhouse, cowshed, enduring, faithful, reliable, resolute, stalwart **9** immovable, steadfast **10** dependable, persisting, stationary, unchanging, unwavering **11** established, unfaltering **12** indissoluble, unchangeable

Stabler, Ken
nickname: **8** the Snake
sport: **8** football
position: **11** quarterback
team: **13** Houston Oilers **14** Oakland Raiders

staccato
music: **12** disconnected **16** each note separate

stack 4 bank, flue, heap, load, lump, mass, pile, rick **5** amass, batch, bunch, clump, hoard, mound, sheaf **6** bundle, funnel, gather **7** chimney **8** assemble, mountain **9** amassment **10** accumulate **11** aggregation **12** accumulation

Stack, Robert
born: **12** Los Angeles CA
roles: **9** Eliot Ness **13** Name of the Game **15** The Untouchables **16** Written on the Wind **19** The High and the Mighty **24** The Bullfighter and the Lady

Stackpole, Henrietta
character in: **18** The Portrait of a Lady
author: **5** James

Stacte 5 spice

stadium 4 bowl, park **5** arena, field, stade **6** circus **8** ballpark, coliseum **9** palaestra **10** hippodrome **12** amphitheater

Stael, Madame de
author of: **7** Corinne **8** Delphine **9** On Germany **35** The Influence of Literature upon Society

staff 3 bat, man, rod **4** cane, crew, help, pole, team, tend, wand, work **5** cadre, force, group, stave, stick **6** crutch, cudgel, manage **7** retinue, scepter, service, support **8** advisors, bludgeon, flagpole **9** billy club, employees, flagstaff, personnel **10** alpenstock, assistants, shillelagh **12** walking stick

staff member 4 aide **6** worker **8** employee

stage 3 act **4** dais, play, spot, step **5** arena, drama, grade, level, phase, put on, sight, stump **6** acting, locale, period, podium, pulpit **7** perform, present, produce, rostrum, setting, show biz, soapbox, theater **8** bearings, locality, location, position, scaffold **9** dramatize, the boards

Stagecoach
director: **8** John Ford
cast: **9** John Wayne **10** Andy Devine **11** Louise Platt **12** Claire Trevor **13** John Carradine **14** George Bancroft, Thomas Mitchell
Oscar for: **15** supporting actor (Mitchell)

stagecraft 5 drama **7** theater **9** theatrics **10** dramaturgy **11** thespianism **12** dramatic arts

Stage Door
author: **10** Edna Ferber **14** George S Kaufman
director: **13** Gregory La Cava
cast: **11** Andrea Leeds, Gail Patrick **12** Ginger Rogers **13** Adolphe Menjou **16** Katharine Hepburn

stage setting
French: 11 mise en scene

stagger 3 jar 4 jolt, reel, stun, sway 5 amaze, lurch, shake, shock, waver 6 hobble, totter, wobble 7 astound, blunder, nonplus, overlap, shamble, startle, stumble, stupefy 8 astonish, bewilder, bowl over, confound, flounder, unsettle 9 alternate, dumbfound, give a turn, overwhelm, spread out 10 disconcert, knock silly, strike dumb 11 cause to reel, cause to sway, consternate, flabbergast, take in turns 12 make unsteady 15 throw off balance

staggering 7 amazing 8 shocking, stunning 9 startling 10 astounding 11 astonishing 12 breathtaking

stagnant 4 dead, dull, foul, lazy, slow 5 close, inert, quiet, slimy, stale, still 6 filthy, leaden, putrid, static, supine, torpid 7 dormant, dronish, languid, tainted 8 inactive, lifeless, listless, polluted, sluggish, standing 9 lethargic, ponderous, putrefied, quiescent 10 monotonous, motionless, not flowing, not running, stationary, unstirring, vegetative 13 uncirculating

stagnate 7 go to pot, lie idle, putrefy 8 go to seed, lie still, vegetate 10 stand still 11 cease to flow, deteriorate, stop growing 14 become inactive, become polluted, become sluggish

stagy 5 phony 8 affected, mannered 9 unnatural 10 artificial, factitious, theatrical

staid 5 grave, quiet, sober, stiff 6 decent, demure, proper, sedate, seemly, solemn, somber 7 earnest, prudish, serious, settled, subdued 8 decorous, priggish, reserved 9 dignified 10 complacent 15 undemonstrative

stain 3 dye, mar 4 blot, daub, flaw, foul, mark, ruin, slur, soil, spot, tint 5 brand, color, dirty, grime, libel, patch, shame, smear, speck, spoil, sully, taint 6 befoul, blotch, debase, defile, impair, malign, smirch, smudge, stigma, vilify 7 blacken, blemish, pigment, slander, splotch, subvert, tarnish 8 besmirch, coloring, discolor, disgrace, dishonor, dyestuff, tincture 9 denigrate, discredit, disparage, undermine 10 imputation, stigmatize 13 discoloration

stainless 5 clean, moral

6 chaste, decent 8 spotless, unsoiled 9 exemplary, unspotted, unsullied, untainted 11 unblemished

Stairway to Heaven
director: 13 Michael Powell 17 Emeric Pressburger cast: 9 Kim Hunter 10 David Niven 12 Roger Livesey 13 Raymond Massey original title: 21 A Matter of Life and Death

stake 3 bar, bet, peg, pot, rod 4 ante, back, grab, haul, lash, loot, moor, pale, pawn, pile, play, pole, post, prop, risk, stay, take 5 booty, brace, hitch, kitty, prize, purse, share, spike, stand, stick, treat, wager 6 chance, column, define, fasten, fetter, hazard, hold up, marker, picket, pillar, reward, secure, spoils, tether 7 delimit, finance, jackpot, mark off, mark out, outline, peg down, returns, sponsor, support, trammel, venture 8 interest, make fast, pickings, standard, winnings 9 delineate, demarcate, speculate, subsidize 10 investment, jeopardize, underwrite 11 involvement, speculation

Stalag 17
director: 11 Billy Wilder cast: 9 Don Taylor 11 Peter Graves 12 Neville Brand 13 Harvey Lembeck, Otto Preminger, Richard Erdman, Robert Strauss, William Holden Oscar for: 5 actor (Holden)

stale 4 dull, flat 5 banal, close, fusty, musty, trite, vapid 6 common 7 humdrum, insipid, prosaic, tedious, worn-out 8 mediocre, not fresh, ordinary, stagnant, unvaried 9 hackneyed, savorless, tasteless 10 monotonous, pedestrian, threadbare 11 commonplace 13 unimaginative, uninteresting

stalemate 3 tie 4 draw, halt 7 dead end, impasse 8 blockage, cul-de-sac, dead heat, deadlock, standoff 10 standstill

stalk 4 hunt, lurk, stem 5 haunt, march, prowl, shaft, spire, stamp, steal, stomp, strut, track, tramp, trunk 6 column, menance, stride 7 pedicel, pervade, swagger 8 hang over, threaten 9 creep up on, go through, sneak up on

stall 3 box, pen 4 cell, coop, halt, shed, shop, stop 5 block, booth, check, delay, kiosk, stand 6 arcade, arrest, hobble,

impede, pull up, put off 7 bed down, confine, cubicle, disable, trammel 8 obstruct, paralyze, postpone 9 be evasive, interrupt, stop short, temporize 10 equivocate 11 compartment, play for time, stop running 12 incapacitate 13 orchestra seat

Stallone, Sylvester
born: 9 New York NY nickname: 3 Sly roles: 4 FIST 5 Rambo, Rocky 9 John Rambo 10 First Blood, Rhinestone 11 Rocky Balboa 18 The Lords of Flatbush

stalwart 4 bold, firm, hale 5 beefy, brave, hardy, hefty, husky, manly, sound 6 brawny, gritty, heroic, mighty, plucky, robust, rugged, spunky, stable, strong, sturdy 7 gallant, staunch, valiant 8 constant, intrepid, muscular, powerful, resolute, valorous, vigorous 9 steadfast, strapping, unbending, undaunted 10 able-bodied, courageous, persistent, unflagging, unshakable, unswerving, unwavering, unyielding 11 indomitable, lionhearted, undeviating, unfaltering, unflinching, unshrinking 12 intransigent, stouthearted, strong-willed 14 uncompromising

stamina 4 pith 5 vigor 6 energy 8 vitality 9 endurance, hardiness, stoutness 10 ruggedness, sturdiness 12 perseverance, staying power

stammer 6 falter, fumble, mumble 7 sputter, stumble, stutter 8 splutter 9 hem and haw

stamp
collecting: 9 philately first: 10 Penny Black issued by: 12 Great Britain inscribed with: 8 One Penny picture of: 13 Queen Victoria first-day hand stamper: 6 cachet hole measurer: 16 perforation gauge mounting paper: 5 hinge not perforated: 11 imperforate paper design: 9 watermark rolls: 4 coil tear holes: 12 perforations tear slit: 8 roulette unseparated group: 5 block used mark: 8 postmark 12 cancellation value suspended: 11 demonetized

stamp, stamp out 2 OK
3 die, tag **4** cast, kind, make, mark, mint, mold, seal, sort, type **5** brand, breed, clump, crush, erase, genre, label, march, order, print, pound, punch, quash, smash, stalk, stomp, strut, thump, tramp **6** banish, betray, emblem, expose, matrix, nature, put out, reveal, rub out, signet, step on, strain, stride, trudge **7** abolish, blot out, display, engrave, exhibit, impress, imprint, put down, squelch, trample, variety, voucher **8** get rid of, hallmark, identify, inscribe, intaglio, manifest, suppress, typecast **9** character, eliminate, engraving, eradicate, personify, signature, trademark **10** annihilate, do away with, extinguish, imprimatur, stigmatize, validation **11** attestation, certificate, demonstrate, distinguish, endorsement, exterminate, **12** characterize, official mark, ratification **13** certification **14** authentication, characteristic, identification

stampede 4 bolt, dash, flee, race, rout, rush **5** chaos, flood, panic **6** engulf **7** overrun, retreat, scatter **8** inundate **10** take flight **11** crowd around, pandemonium **12** beat a retreat
     French: 12 sauve qui peut

stanchion 4 post, prop, stay **5** brace, strut **7** support, upright

stand 2 be **3** put, set **4** draw, face, hold, last, move, rank, rear, rest, rise, stay, step, take, tent **5** abide, argue, booth, brook, erect, exist, get up, hoist, honor, kiosk, mount, place, put up, raise, shift, stall, treat **6** bear up, effort, endure, obtain, pay for, policy, remain, remove, stance, suffer, uphold **7** carry on, commend, counter, defense, endorse, finance, hold out, opinion, persist, posture, prevail, provide, stick up, stomach, support, survive, sustain, undergo, weather **8** advocate, be placed, champion, continue, pavilion, position, sanction, submit to, tolerate **9** be located, be present, be upright, persevere, put up with, sentiment, undertake, viewpoint **10** resistance, set upright **11** be permanent, countenance, disposition, point of view **13** remain in force, take a position

Stand, The
     author: 11 Stephen King

standard 3 leg **4** base, flag, foot, jack, post **5** basic, canon, guide, ideal, stock, usual **6** banner, column, common, ensign, normal, pillar **7** measure, pennant, regular, support, typical, upright **8** accepted, ordinary, streamer **9** criterion, customary, guideline, principle, prototype, stanchion, universal, yardstick **10** foundation, touchstone **11** requirement **13** specification

stand behind 4 back **7** endorse, support **8** champion, vouch for **9** recommend

standby 6 backup **9** alternate, available **10** substitute, understudy **11** old reliable **12** tried-and-true

stand by 4 keep **5** cling **6** adhere, be true, defend, hold to, keep to **7** be loyal, stick by **8** cleave to, maintain **10** be constant, be faithful, stick up for

stand fast 4 hold **6** resist **8** stand pat

stand for 4 bear **5** abide, favor, stand **6** embody **7** signify **8** advocate, submit to, tolerate **9** personify, put up with, represent, symbolize

stand-in 3 sub **5** agent, proxy **6** backup, deputy, double, fill-in, second **9** alternate, assistant, surrogate **10** substitute, understudy **11** pinch hitter, replacement

standing 3 age **4** life, rank, term, time **5** erect, fixed, grade, inert, order, place, still **6** at rest, static, status, tenure **7** dormant, footing, lasting, station, upended, upright **8** duration, inactive, position, stagnant, vertical **9** immovable, permanent, perpetual, quiescent, renewable **10** continuing, importance, motionless, reputation, stationary, unstirring **11** continuance **13** perpendicular

standoff 7 impasse **8** deadlock

standoffish 4 cool **5** aloof **6** formal, remote **7** distant, haughty **8** detached, reserved, solitary, taciturn **9** reclusive, withdrawn **10** antisocial, restrained, unfriendly, unsociable **12** inaccessible, misanthropic, unresponsive **14** unapproachable **15** uncommunicative, uncompanionable

standpoint 4 side **5** angle, slant **6** aspect **9** viewpoint **11** point of view

standstill 3 end **4** halt, stop **5** pause **6** hiatus **7** dead end, impasse **8** abeyance, deadlock, dead stop, full stop **9** breakdown, cessation, stalemate **10** suspension **11** termination **14** discontinuance

stand up for 4 back **5** boost **6** defend **7** further, promote, support **8** advocate, champion

stand up to 4 defy, face **5** brave **6** resist **8** confront **9** challenge

Stant, Charlotte
     character in: 13 The Golden Bowl
     author: 5 James

Stan the Man
     nickname of: 10 Stan Musial

Stanton, Adam
     character in: 14 All the King's Men
     author: 6 Warren

Stanwyck, Barbara
     real name: 11 Ruby Stevens
     born: 10 Brooklyn NY
     husband: 8 Frank Fay
     12 Robert Taylor
     roles: 9 Big Valley, The Colbys **10** Ball of Fire, The Lady Eve **11** Meet John Doe **12** Stella Dallas **15** Double Indemnity **16** Sorry Wrong Number **20** Cattle Queen of Montana **22** Christmas in Connecticut

staple 3 key **4** main **5** basic, chief, major, prime, vital **6** leader **7** feature, primary, product **8** resource, vendible **9** commodity, essential, necessary **11** fundamental, raw material **13** indispensable

Stapleton, Jean
     real name: 12 Jeanne Murray
     born: 9 New York NY
     roles: 7 Dingbat **11** Edith Bunker **14** All in the Family

Stapleton, Maureen
     born: 6 Troy NY
     roles: 7 Airport **9** Interiors **12** Lonelyhearts **13** The Rose Tattoo **18** A View from the Bridge

star, stars *see box*

Starbuck
     character in: 8 Moby Dick
     author: 8 Melville

starch 5 vigor **6** sizing **8** backbone, gumption **10** stiffening

starched 5 crisp, sized, stiff **7** starchy **9** stiffened

starchy 5 rigid, stiff **6** formal, proper **7** correct **10** meticulous

star, stars 3 god, sun, VIP 4 diva, fate, hero, idol, lead, lion, name 5 comet, excel, giant, great, omens, shine 6 bigwig, do well, galaxy, meteor, nebula, planet 7 destiny, feature, fortune, goddess, heroine, notable, soloist, starlet, succeed, top draw 8 asteroid, cynosure, eminence, immortal, luminary, mainstay, Milky Way, portents, showcase, stand out, virtuoso 9 celebrity, headliner, meteoroid, principal, satellite, top banana 10 prima donna 11 All-American, drawing card, play the lead, protagonist 12 famous person, gain approval, heavenly body 13 celestial body, constellation 14 main attraction, predestination, prima ballerina
   brightest: 6 Sirius
   brightness measure: 9 magnitude 10 luminosity
   color: 3 red 4 blue 5 black, white 6 orange, yellow
   distance measure: 6 parsec 9 light year
   double star: 6 binary
   exploding star: 4 nova 9 supernova
   French: 6 etoile
   name: 4 Mira, Ross, Vega, Wolf 5 Cygni, Deneb, Rigel, Spica 6 Altair, Luyten, Pollux 7 Antares, Canopus, Capella, Lalande, Polaris, Procyon, Regulus, Tau Ceti 8 Achernar, Arcturus, Barnard's, Lacaille, Pleiades 9 Aldebaran, Fomalhaut 10 Beta Crucis, Betelgeuse 11 Delta Cephei, Epsilon Indi, Groombridge 12 Beta Centauri 14 Epsilon Eridani
   nearest: 13 Alpha Centauri
   position/motion: 7 azimuth 8 parallax 11 declination
   type: 5 dwarf, giant 6 pulsar 7 cluster, neutron 8 variable 9 black hole, collapsed

stare 3 eye 4 gape, gawk, gaze, ogle, peep, peer 5 glare, lower, watch 6 gaping, glower, goggle, ogling, regard 7 staring 8 once-over, scrutiny 9 fixed look 10 inspection, rubberneck

stare at 3 eye 4 ogle 5 watch 6 behold, gaze at, look at, regard 7 inspect, observe 10 scrutinize 11 contemplate

Star Is Born, A
   director:
     1937 version: 14 William Wellman
     1954 version: 11 George Cukor
     1976 version: 12 Frank Pierson
   cast:
     1937 version: 11 Janet Gaynor 13 Adolphe Menjou, Frederic March
     1954 version: 10 Jack Carson, James Mason 11 Judy Garland 15 Charles Bickford
     1976 version: 9 Gary Busey 11 Oliver Clark 15 Barbra Streisand 17 Kris Kristofferson
   Oscar for:
     1937 version: 5 story
   song:
     1954 version: 17 The Man That Got Away

stark 4 bare, bold, cold, grim, pure 5 bleak, blunt, clean, empty, fully, gross, harsh, naked, plain, plumb, quite, sheer, total, utter 6 arrant, barren, chaste, patent, severe, simple, vacant, wholly 7 austere, evident, forlorn, glaring, obvious, staring, utterly 8 absolute, complete, deserted, desolate, entirely, flagrant, forsaken, outright, palpable 9 abandoned, downright, out-and-out, unadorned, unalloyed, veritable 10 absolutely, altogether, completely, consummate 11 conspicuous, unmitigated 12 unmistakable

Stark, Johannes
   field: 7 physics
   nationality: 6 German
   described: 11 Stark Effect 14 dispersed light
   awarded: 10 Nobel Prize

Stark, Willie
   character in: 14 All the King's Men
   author: 6 Warren

starlet 7 actress, ingenue 9 bit player, pinup girl

Starsky and Hutch
   character: 5 Hutch (Ken Hutchinson) 7 (Dave) Starsky 9 Huggy Bear 11 (Capt) Harold Dobey
   cast: 9 David Soul 13 Antonio Fargas 14 Bernie Hamilton 17 Paul Michael Glaser
   car: 10 Ford Torino

start 3 aid, shy 4 dawn, drop, edge, form, gush, jerk, jolt, jump, lead, leap, odds, rush, turn 5 beget, begin, birth, blink, bound, eject, erupt, evict, flush, forge, found, issue, leave, leg up, onset, rouse, set up, shoot, spasm, spurt, wince 6 blench, broach, chance, create, depart, embark, emerge, fall to, father, flinch, ignite, kindle, launch, origin, outset, pop out, propel, recoil, set off, set out, spring, take up, twitch 7 advance, backing, disturb, genesis, make off, opening, push off, scatter, set sail, support, take off, turn out, usher in 8 advocacy, commence, creation, displace, embark on, engender, generate, get going, initiate, organize, priority, set about, set going, touch off 9 advantage, beginning, establish, fabricate, first step, inception, institute, introduce, originate, propagate, undertake, venture on 10 assistance, break forth, bring about, buckle down, burst forth, give rise to, inaugurate, initiation, plunge into, sally forth, venture out 11 break ground, put in motion, set in action 12 commencement, inauguration, introduction 14 set in operation

starting point 5 onset, start 8 zero hour 9 beginning
   Latin: 12 terminus a quo

startle 3 jar 4 faze 5 alarm, scare, shake, shock, upset 7 perturb, unnerve 8 disquiet, frighten, surprise, unsettle 9 give a turn 10 discompose, disconcert, intimidate

Star Trek
   character: 4 Sulu 5 Uhura 6 Scotty (Engineer Montgomery Scott), (Ensign) Chekov 7 Mr Spock 10 (Captain) James T Kirk, (Yeoman) Janice Rand 12 (Dr) Leonard McCoy 15 (Nurse) Christine Chapel
   cast: 11 George Takei, James Doohan 12 Leonard Nimoy, Majel Barrett, Walter Koenig 13 DeForest Kelly 14 William Shatner 15 Grace Lee Whitney, Nichelle Nichols
   ship: 10 (USS) Enterprise
   aliens: 8 Klingons, Romulans
   Spock's planet: 6 Vulcan
   pet: 7 tribble

starve 3 yen 4 burn, deny, fast, gasp, long, lust, pine 5 crave, raven, yearn 6 aspire, cut off, famish, hunger, refuse, thirst 7 deprive 8 be hungry, go hungry, languish

Star Wars
director: 11 George Lucas
cast: 10 Kenny Baker, Mark Hamill (Luke Skywalker) **12** Alec Guinness, Carrie Fisher (Princess Leia), Harrison Ford (Han Solo), Peter Cushing **14** Anthony Daniels *voice of Darth Vader:* **14** James Earl Jones
score: 12 John Williams
Oscar for: 5 score
sequel: 15 Return of the Jedi **20** The Empire Strikes Back

stasimon 9 choral ode
literally: 8 standing

state 3 put **4** form, land, mind, mode, mood, pass, pomp **5** guise, offer, phase, realm, shape, stage **6** aspect, luxury, morale, nation, people, plight, recite, relate, report, ritual, status **7** comfort, country, declare, explain, expound, express, kingdom, narrate, posture, present, recount, spirits **8** attitude, ceremony, describe, dominion, monarchy, official, position, propound, republic, set forth **9** condition, elucidate, formality, full dress, high style, situation, structure **10** ceremonial, government **11** body politic, frame of mind, predicament, state of mind **12** commonwealth, constitution, governmental, principality **13** circumstances

state abbreviations *see box*

state admittance *see box*

state capitals *see box*

State Fair
author: 9 Phil Stong

state in detail 7 explain, expound **8** describe, spell out **9** explicate **16** give a full account

stateliness 7 dignity, majesty **10** augustness

stately 5 grand, lofty, noble, proud, regal, royal **6** august, formal, lordly **7** awesome, elegant, eminent **8** glorious, imperial, imposing, majestic **9** dignified, grandiose **10** ceremonial, impressive **11** magnificent

statement 3 tab **4** bill **5** check, claim, count, tally **6** avowal, charge, record, remark, report, speech **7** account, comment, invoice, mention, recital **8** relation, sentence **9** assertion, manifesto, reckoning, testimony, utterance, valuation

---

state abbreviations
Alabama: 2 AL **3** Ala
Alaska: 2 AK **4** Alas
Arizona: 2 AZ **4** Ariz
Arkansas: 2 AR **3** Ark
California: 2 CA **3** Cal **5** Calif
Colorado: 2 CO **4** Colo
Connecticut: 2 CT **4** Conn
Delaware: 2 DE **3** Del
Florida: 2 FL **3** Fla
Georgia: 2 GA
Hawaii: 2 HI
Idaho: 2 ID **3** Ida
Illinois: 2 IL **3** Ill
Indiana: 2 IN **3** Ind
Iowa: 2 IA
Kansas: 2 KS **4** Kans
Kentucky: 2 KY
Louisiana: 2 LA
Maine: 2 ME
Maryland: 2 MD
Massachusetts: 2 MA **4** Mass
Michigan: 2 MI **4** Mich
Minnesota: 2 MN **4** Minn
Mississippi: 2 MS **4** Miss
Missouri: 2 MO
Montana: 2 MT
Nebraska: 2 NE **4** Nebr

Nevada: 2 NV **3** Nev
New Hampshire: 2 NH
New Jersey: 2 NJ
New Mexico: 2 NM **4** N Mex
New York: 2 NY
North Carolina: 2 NC **4** N Car
North Dakota: 2 ND **4** N Dak
Ohio: 2 OH
Oklahoma: 2 OK **4** Okla
Oregon: 2 OR **4** Oreg
Pennsylvania: 2 PA **4** Penn **5** Penna
Rhode Island: 2 RI
South Carolina: 2 SC
South Dakota: 2 SD **4** S Dak
Tennessee: 2 TN **4** Tenn
Texas: 2 TX **3** Tex
Utah: 2 UT
Vermont: 2 VT
Virginia: 2 VA
Washington: 2 WA **4** Wash
West Virginia: 2 WV **3** W Va
Wisconsin: 2 WI **3** Wis
Wyoming: 2 WY **3** Wyo

---

10 accounting, allegation, communique, exposition, profession, recitation **11** declaration, delineation, explanation, observation **12** announcement, balance sheet **13** pronouncement, specification

---

state admittance
first: 8 Delaware
second: 12 Pennsylvania
third: 9 New Jersey
fourth: 7 Georgia
fifth: 11 Connecticut
sixth: 13 Massachusetts
seventh: 8 Maryland
eighth: 13 South Carolina
ninth: 12 New Hampshire
tenth: 8 Virginia
eleventh: 7 New York
twelfth: 13 North Carolina
thirteenth: 11 Rhode Island
fourteenth: 7 Vermont
fifteenth: 8 Kentucky
sixteenth: 9 Tennessee
seventeenth: 4 Ohio
eighteenth: 9 Louisiana
nineteenth: 7 Indiana
twentieth: 11 Mississippi
twenty-first: 8 Illinois
twenty-second: 7 Alabama
twenty-third: 5 Maine
twenty-fourth: 8 Missouri
twenty-fifth: 8 Arkansas
twenty-sixth: 8 Michigan

twenty-seventh: 7 Florida
twenty-eighth: 5 Texas
twenty-ninth: 4 Iowa
thirtieth: 9 Wisconsin
thirty-first: 10 California
thirty-second: 9 Minnesota
thirty-third: 6 Oregon
thirty-fourth: 6 Kansas
thirty-fifth: 12 West Virginia
thirty-sixth: 6 Nevada
thirty-seventh: 8 Nebraska
thirty-eighth: 8 Colorado
thirty-ninth/fortieth: 11 North Dakota, South Dakota
forty-first: 7 Montana
forty-second: 10 Washington
forty-third: 5 Idaho
forty-fourth: 7 Wyoming
forty-fifth: 4 Utah
forty-sixth: 8 Oklahoma
forty-seventh: 9 New Mexico
forty-eighth: 7 Arizona
forty-ninth: 6 Alaska
fiftieth: 6 Hawaii

state capitals
Alabama: 10 Montgomery
Alaska: 6 Juneau
Arizona: 7 Phoenix
Arkansas: 10 Little Rock
California: 10 Sacramento
Colorado: 6 Denver
Connecticut: 8 Hartford
Delaware: 5 Dover
Florida: 11 Tallahassee
Georgia: 7 Atlanta
Hawaii: 8 Honolulu
Idaho: 5 Boise
Illinois: 11 Springfield
Indiana: 12 Indianapolis
Iowa: 9 Des Moines
Kansas: 6 Topeka
Kentucky: 9 Frankfort
Louisiana: 10 Baton Rouge
Maine: 7 Augusta
Maryland: 9 Annapolis
Massachusetts: 6 Boston
Michigan: 7 Lansing
Minnesota: 6 St Paul
Mississippi: 7 Jackson
Missouri: 13 Jefferson City
Montana: 6 Helena
Nebraska: 7 Lincoln
Nevada: 10 Carson City

New Hampshire:
7 Concord
New Jersey: 7 Trenton
New Mexico: 7 Santa Fe
New York: 6 Albany
North Carolina: 7 Raleigh
North Dakota: 8 Bismarck
Ohio: 8 Columbus
Oklahoma: 12 Oklahoma City
Oregon: 5 Salem
Pennsylvania:
10 Harrisburg
Rhode Island:
10 Providence
South Carolina:
8 Columbia
South Dakota: 6 Pierre
Tennessee: 9 Nashville
Texas: 6 Austin
Utah: 12 Salt Lake City
Vermont: 10 Montpelier
Virginia: 8 Richmond
Washington: 7 Olympia
West Virginia:
10 Charleston
Wisconsin: 7 Madison
Wyoming: 8 Cheyenne

state of affairs 5 state **6** status **9** condition, situation **13** circumstances

State of the Union
director: **10** Frank Capra
cast: **10** Van Johnson
12 Spencer Tracy
13 Adolphe Menjou **14** Angela Lansbury **16** Katharine Hepburn

stateroom 5 cabin **8** quarters **11** compartment

statesman 8 diplomat **15** political leader

statesmanship 9 diplomacy **19** political leadership

static 5 fixed, inert, still, **8** immobile, inactive, stagnant, unmoving **9** crackling, suspended **10** changeless, motionless, stationary, unchanging **12** interference

station 4 post, rank, site, spot, stop **5** caste, class, depot, grade, level, place **6** assign, degree, locate, sphere, status **7** footing, install **8** ensconce, facility, location, position, prestige, terminal, terminus **9** condition, firehouse, placement **10** dispensary, guardhouse, importance **11** emplacement, whistle-stop **12** headquarters

stationary 4 even, firm **5** fixed, inert **6** intact, moored, stable,

steady **7** riveted, uniform **8** constant, immobile, standing **9** dead-still, immovable, immutable, unchanged, unvarying **10** motionless, stock-still, transfixed **11** not changing, undeviating **12** unchangeable **13** standing still

Statius
author of: **6** Silvae **10** The Thebaid **12** The Achilleid

statue 8 monument **9** sculpture **14** representation

statuesque 5 regal **7** stately **8** majestic **9** dignified

stature 4 rank, size **5** place **6** height, regard **8** eminence, position, prestige, standing, tallness **9** elevation **10** importance, prominence, reputation **11** distinction

status 4 rank **5** caste, class, grade, place, state **6** degree **7** caliber, footing, station **8** eminence, position, prestige, standing **9** condition, situation **10** estimation **11** distinction

statute 3 law **7** precept **9** prescript

statute law
Latin: **10** lex scripta

staunch, stanch 3 dam **4** firm, stem, true **5** check, loyal, solid, sound, stout

6 impede, rugged, steady, strong, sturdy **7** contain, zealous **8** constant, faithful, hold back, obstruct, resolute, stalwart **9** steadfast, well-built **10** watertight **11** substantial

stave off 7 beat off, fend off, keep off, ward off **9** keep at bay

stay 3 aim, guy, rib, rod **4** bunk, curb, foil, halt, live, pole, prop, rest, room, stem, stop **5** abide, block, brace, check, delay, dwell, lodge, quell, shore, stick, tarry, visit **6** endure, keep in, linger, rein in, remain, reside, splint, stifle, thwart **7** carry on, hold out, holiday, last out, persist, sojourn, support, ward off **8** abeyance, buttress, continue, hold back, mainstay, postpone, reprieve, restrain, standard, stopover, suppress, vacation, withhold **9** deferment, frustrate, persevere, staunchion **10** hang around, see through, suspension **12** postponement, reinforcement

stay put 4 stay **6** remain **8** stand pat

St Clare, Eva
character in: **14** Uncle Tom's Cabin
author: **5** Stowe

steadfast 4 keen, rapt **5** fixed **6** direct, intent, steady **8** resolute **9** attentive, obstinate, tenacious, undaunted **10** deep-rooted, deep-seated, inflexible, unchanging, unflagging, unwavering, unyielding **11** indomitable, persevering, unalterable, undeviating, unfaltering, unflinching **12** intransigent, single-minded, unchangeable, undistracted **14** uncompromising

steadfastness 8 tenacity **10** resolution **11** persistence **12** perseverance, resoluteness **13** determination

Steadfast Tin Soldier, The
author: **21** Hans Christian Andersen

steadiness 4 care **5** poise **6** aplomb **8** calmness, coolness, evenness, firmness **9** composure, sangfroid, stability **10** equanimity, resolution **11** carefulness, persistence, self-control, tranquility **12** resoluteness, tranquillity **13** dependability, steadfastness **14** presence of mind, self-possession **16** imperturbability

steady 4 even, firm, sure **5** sober **6** secure, stable **7** balance, careful, devoted, regular,

serious, staunch **8** constant,
faithful, frequent, habitual,
hold fast, reliable, resolute,
unending, untiring **9** ceaseless,
confirmed, dedicated, immovable, incessant, stabilize, steadfast, tenacious, unceasing
10 continuing, continuous,
coolheaded, deliberate, dependable, methodical, persistent,
unflagging, unwavering
11 levelheaded, persevering,
substantial, undeviating, unfaltering, unremitting **12** single-
minded **13** conscientious

steal 3 buy, cop **4** copy, crib,
flit, flow, lift, slip, take
5 creep, drift, filch, glide,
pinch, skulk, slide, slink,
sneak, swipe, usurp **6** borrow,
elapse, escape, extort, filter,
pilfer, pocket, rip off, snatch,
snitch, thieve **7** bargain, defraud, diffuse, good buy, imitate, purloin, swindle
8 abstract, embezzle, good
deal, liberate **10** burglarize,
plagiarize **11** abscond with,
appropriate, make off with
14 misappropriate

steal away 3 fly **4** bolt, flee,
skip **5** elope **6** escape **7** get
away, make off, slip out
8 creep off, slip away, sneak
off **9** break free, tiptoe out
10 break loose, fly the coop
12 make a getaway

stealth 7 secrecy, slyness
10 covertness, sneakiness, subterfuge **11** furtiveness
12 stealthiness **13** secretiveness **15** unobtrusiveness
17 surreptitiousness

stealthy 3 sly **5** shady **6** covert,
shifty, sneaky **7** devious, furtive **8** slippery, sneaking **9** secretive, underhand
11 clandestine, underhanded
12 hugger-mugger
13 surreptitious

steamboat
  invented by: **6** Fulton
  9 Symington

steamed up 5 angry, het up,
irate **6** raging **7** enraged, furious, riled up **8** heated up,
inflamed **10** infuriated **12** mad
as a wet hen **14** hot and
bothered **17** hot under the
collar

steamer 4 boat, clam, ship
5 liner, trunk **10** paddleboat
11 side-wheeler **12** stern-
wheeler **13** paddle-wheeler

steel 4 dirk, foil, gird **5** blade,
brace, knife, nerve, saber,
sword **6** dagger, rapier **7** bayonet, cutlass, fortify, machete
8 falchion, scimitar
10 broadsword

process invented by:
  8 Bessemer

Steele, Sir Richard
  pseudonym: **16** Isaac
  Bickerstaff
  author of: **9** The Tatler (with
  Joseph Addison) **10** The Fu-
  neral **12** The Spectator (with
  Joseph Addison) **13** The
  Lying Lover **16** The Tender
  Husband **18** The Conscious
  Lovers

steely 4 hard **5** stony **6** flinty
9 heartless, unfeeling **10** forbidding **11** cold-hearted

Steen, Jan
  born: **6** Leiden, Leyden
  14 The Netherlands
  artwork: **7** Cabaret **11** The
  Egg Dance **12** Merry Company **14** Garden of the Inn
  15 The Doctor's Visit, The
  Rhetoricians **16** The Morning Toilet **17** The Skittle
  Players **18** The World
  Topsy-Turvy, Young Woman
  Dressing

Steenburgen, Mary
  roles: **10** Cross Creek
  13 Time After Time

steep 4 brew, bury, fill, soak
5 imbue, sharp, sheer, souse
6 abrupt, drench, engulf, infuse, plunge **7** immerse, pervade, suffuse **8** marinate,
saturate, submerge **10** impregnate **11** precipitous

steeple 5 spire, tower **6** belfry
9 campanile

steer 3 aim, lay, run **4** bear,
head, lead, make, sail **5** coach,
guide, pilot **6** direct, govern,
manage **7** conduct, proceed
8 navigate **9** supervise

steer clear of 4 shun **5** avert,
avoid, dodge, evade, forgo,
skirt **6** escape, eschew, forego
8 sidestep **9** keep shy of
11 abstain from, refrain from
16 give a wide berth to

Steerforth
  character in: **16** David
  Copperfield
  author: **7** Dickens

Steffens, Lincoln
  author of: **19** The Shame of
  the Cities

Stegosaurus
  type: **8** dinosaur
  10 ornithopod
  location: **12** North America
  period: **8** Jurassic
  characteristic: **6** plated

Steiger, Rod
  real name: **20** Rodney Stephen Steiger
  born: **13** Westhampton NY
  wife: **11** Claire Bloom

  roles: **8** Waterloo **13** The
  Longest Day, The Pawnbroker, W C Fields and Me
  15 On the Waterfront **19** In
  the Heat of the Night
  (Oscar)

Stein, Clarence S
  architect of: **13** Temple
  Emanu-El (NYC)

Stein, Gertrude
  author of: **10** Three Lives
  13 Tender Buttons **20** The
  Making of Americans
  27 Autobiography of Alice B
  Toklas
  coined phrase: **14** lost
  generation

Steinbeck, John
  author of: **8** The Pearl
  10 Cannery Row, East of
  Eden, The Red Pony **12** Of
  Mice and Men, Tortilla
  Flat **15** In Dubious Battle
  16 The Grapes of Wrath
  18 Travels with Charley
  24 The Winter of Our
  Discontent

Steinmetz, Charles P
  field: **11** engineering
  developed: **2** AC **18** alternating current

Stella, Frank
  born: **8** Malden MA
  artwork: **4** Jill **5** Itata
  14 Jasper's Dilemma
  15 Guadalupe Island

Stella, Joseph
  born: **5** Italy **6** Naples
  artwork: **8** Full Moon (Barbados) **9** Sunflower, The
  Bridge **14** Brooklyn Bridge
  16 Pittsburgh Winter
  18 New York Interpreted
  28 Battle of the Lights Coney Island

Stella Dallas
  director: **9** King Vidor
  cast: **9** John Boles **11** Anne
  Shirley **12** Barbara O'Neil
  15 Barbara Stanwyck

stellar 6 astral, starry **7** leading **8** starring **9** brilliant, celestial, principal **11** outstanding

stem 3 dam **4** buck, cane,
come, curb, grow, halt, rise,
stay, stop **5** arise, block,
check, deter, ensue, issue,
quell, shank, shoot, speak,
spire, stalk, stall, stock, trunk
6 arrest, derive, hinder,
impede, oppose, resist, result,
retard, spring, stanch, thwart
7 counter, pedicel, petiole, prevent, proceed, tendril **8** hold
back, obstruct, peduncle, restrain, surmount **9** leafstalk,
originate, withstand

stem from 5 arise, begin,
start **6** derive **9** originate

stench 4 odor, reek 5 fetor, stink 8 bad smell 9 fetidness

Stendhal (Henri Marie Beyle)
author of: 17 The Red and the Black 18 Memoirs of an Egotist 22 The Charterhouse of Parma

Stengel, Charles Dillon
nickname: 5 Casey
sport: 8 baseball
position: 7 manager
team: 11 New York Mets 14 New York Yankees 15 Brooklyn Dodgers

Stentor
vocation: 6 herald
characteristic: 10 loud-voiced
voice as loud as: 8 fifty men

step 3 act 4 clip, gait, move, pace, rank, rung, span, walk 5 notch, phase, point, riser, stage, stair, strut, track, tramp, tread 6 action, degree, hobble, period, remove, stride 7 footing, measure, process, shamble, shuffle, swagger, trample 8 footfall, foothold, maneuver, purchase 9 footprint, gradation, procedure 10 proceeding

step down 4 quit 5 leave 6 resign, retire

Stephens, James
author of: 7 Deirdre 14 The Crock of Gold 21 The Charwoman's Daughter

Stephenson, George and Robert
nationality: 7 English
developed: 15 steam locomotive

Steppenwolf
author: 12 Hermann Hesse
character: 5 Maria, Pablo 7 Hermine 11 Harry Haller

Steps
author: 13 Jerzy Kosinski

step up 4 spur 6 come up 7 quicken, speed up 8 approach, escalate, expedite, increase 9 intensify 10 accelerate

stereotype 4 type 6 cliche 7 formula 8 typecast 10 categorize, pigeonhole 13 preconception

stereotyped 5 stale, trite 9 hackneyed 11 commonplace 13 unimaginative

sterile 4 bare, pure, vain 5 empty 6 barren, fallow, futile 7 aseptic, useless 8 abortive, bootless, impotent, infecund, sanitary 9 childless, fruitless, infertile, worthless 10 antiseptic, profitless, sterilized, unavailing, unfruitful, uninfected 11 disinfected, ineffective, ineffectual, unrewarding 12 unproductive, unprofitable 13 free from germs 14 uncontaminated

sterilize 6 purify 9 autoclave, disinfect 13 decontaminate

sterling 4 pure, true 5 noble 6 silver, superb, worthy 7 genuine, perfect 8 flawless, superior 9 admirable, estimable, first-rate, honorable 10 invaluable 11 meritorious, superlative

stern 4 cold, grim, hard 5 cruel, grave, harsh, rigid, sharp, stiff 6 brutal, gloomy, severe, somber, strict, unkind 7 austere, serious 8 coercive, despotic, frowning, pitiless, rigorous, ruthless, ungentle 9 reproving, stringent, unfeeling 10 forbidding, implacable, ironfisted, ironhanded, tyrannical, unmerciful 11 admonishing, cold-blooded, reproachful 12 unreasonable 13 unsympathetic 14 unapproachable

Stern (of Argo)
constellation of: 6 Puppis

Sterne, Laurence
author of: 14 Tristram Shandy 19 A Sentimental Journey
character: 9 Uncle Toby 12 Parson Yorick, Walter Shandy

sternum
bone of: 6 breast

Sterope
also: 8 Asterope
member of: 8 Pleiades
son: 8 Oenomaus

Steve Canyon
creator: 12 Milton Caniff
character: 7 Cheetah 9 Madam Lynx 10 Doe Redwood, Miss Mizzou 11 Savannah Gay 13 Copper Calhoun 14 Herself Muldoon 17 Princess Sun Flower
wife: 6 Summer
ward/cousin: 12 Poteet Canyon
Summer's son: 13 Leighton Olson

Stevens, George
director of: 5 Giant (Oscar), Shane 8 Gunga Din 9 Swing Time 13 I Remember Mama, Penny Serenade 14 A Place in the Sun (Oscar), Woman of the Year 16 The Talk of the Town 19 The Diary of Anne Frank

Stevens, Gowan
character in: 9 Sanctuary
author: 8 Faulkner

Stevens, James
author of: 10 Paul Bunyan

Stevens, Ruby
real name of: 15 Barbara Stanwyck

Stevens, Wallace
author of: 7 The Rock 9 Harmonium 13 Sunday Morning 17 Transport to Summer 23 Peter Quince at the Clavier, The Idea of Order at Key West, The Man with the Blue Guitar

Stevenson, Robert
director of: 8 Jane Eyre 10 Back Street 11 Mary Poppins

Stevenson, Robert Louis
author of: 9 Kidnapped 13 The Black Arrow 14 Treasure Island 18 Travels with a Donkey 21 A Child's Garden of Verses, Doctor Jekyll and Mr Hyde, The Master of Ballantrae

St Evremond, Marquis
character in: 16 A Tale of Two Cities
author: 7 Dickens

stew 4 fret, fume, fuss 5 chafe, gripe, steep, tizzy, worry 6 grouse, ragout, seethe, simmer 7 agonize, fluster, flutter, grumble, mixture 10 miscellany

steward 5 agent, proxy 6 deputy, factor, waiter 7 bailiff, manager, trustee 8 executor, overseer 10 controller, supervisor 11 comptroller 13 administrator 14 representative, ship's attendant 15 flight attendant

Stewart, James
born: 9 Indiana PA
roles: 4 Rope 6 Harvey 7 Vertigo 10 Rear Window, Shenandoah 11 Elwood P Dowd 14 Cheyenne Autumn 16 Anatomy of a Murder, Destry Rides Again, The Stratton Story 17 Bell Book and Candle, It's a Wonderful Life 18 It's a Wonderful World, The Spirit of St Louis 19 The Glenn Miller Story 20 The Philadelphia Story (Oscar), You Can't Take It with You 22 The Greatest Show on Earth 23 Mr Smith Goes to Washington

Stewart, Mary
real name: 22 Florence Rainbow Stewart
author of: 11 Crystal Cave 14 The Hollow Hills 15 The Moon-Spinners 16 My Brother Michael, The Ga-

briel Hounds **18** Airs Above
the Ground, The Last
Enchantment

St George's
 capital of: **7** Grenada

Sthenelaus
 vocation: **7** warrior
 killed by: **9** Patroclus

Sthenele
 father: **7** Acastus
 son: **9** Patroclus

Sthenelus
 king of: **7** Mycenae
 father: **5** Actor **7** Perseus
 mother: **9** Andromeda
 brother: **6** Mestor **9** Electryon
 son: **10** Eurystheus
 daughter: **6** Medusa
  7 Alcyone
 member of: **7** Epigoni
 companion of: **8** Hercules

Sthenius
 epithet of: **4** Zeus
 means: **6** strong

Stheno
 member of: **7** Gorgons

Stichius
 origin: **8** Athenian
 rank: **7** captain
 killed by: **6** Hector

stick 3 bar, bat, cue, dig, fix,
jab, pin, put, rod, set **4** balk,
bind, cane, club, curb, fuse,
glue, hold, join, last, mire,
nail, pink, poke, pole, seal,
snag, stab, stop, tack, twig,
wand, weld **5** abide, affix, baton, billy, block, catch, check,
fagot, leave, lodge, paste,
place, plant, prick, punch,
shift, snarl, spear, spike, staff,
stall, stake, stand, stave,
stump **6** adhere, attach, boggle, branch, burden, cement,
cudgel, detain, endure, fasten,
hamper, hinder, hog-tie,
impede, insert, pierce, puzzle,
scotch, skewer, stymie, switch,
thrust, thwart **7** confuse, crosier, inhibit, perplex, shackle,
trammel **8** bewilder, bludgeon,
caduceus, continue, obstruct,
puncture **9** checkmate, constrain, perforate, truncheon,
victimize **10** immobilize,
shillelagh

stick fast 4 hold **5** cling,
stick **6** adhere, cleave

stickler 3 bug, nut **5** crank,
poser **6** enigma, purist, puzzle,
riddle, zealot **7** devotee, dilemma, fanatic, mystery,
stumper **8** martinet **10** enthusiast, monomaniac

sticks 4 skis **5** bonds, glues,
twigs **6** pastes, Podunk **7** ad-
heres, boonies, catches, ce-
ments, country **8** kindling

9 backwoods, boondocks, golf
clubs, provinces **10** hicksville,
hinterland **11** countryside,
hinterlands

stick together 4 bind, fuse,
glue, hold, join **5** cling, stick,
unite **6** cement, cohere

stick-to-itiveness 8 tenacity
9 endurance **10** resolution
11 persistence **12** perseverance,
resoluteness **13** determination,
tenaciousness

stickum 3 gum **4** glue **5** paste
6 cement **8** adhesive, mucilage **12** rubber cement

stick up for 5 boost **6** defend
7 root for **11** speak well of
17 put in a good word for

stick with 4 stay **5** abide
6 keep at **7** stand by **9** accompany, persevere

sticky 3 wet **4** damp, dank
5 gluey, gooey, gummy, humid, moist, muggy, pasty,
tacky **6** clammy, clingy,
steamy, sultry, viscid **7** viscous **8** adherent, adhesive,
clinging, cohesive, sticking
9 glutinous, tenacious **10** gelatinous **12** mucilaginous

stiff *see box*

stiff-necked 6 mulish **7** willful **8** contrary, obdurate, stubborn **9** obstinate, pigheaded,
unbending **10** bullheaded, refractory, self-willed, unshakable, unyielding **11** intractable
12 intransigent, pertinacious

stiffness 7 tension **8** firmness,
rigidity **9** aloofness, formality,
tenseness, tightness **10** constraint **11** starchiness

stifle 3 gag **4** curb **5** check,
choke **6** muffle, subdue **7** garrote, inhibit, repress, smother,
squelch, swelter **8** keep back,
restrain, strangle, suppress,
throttle **9** suffocate
10 asphyxiate

stifling 3 hot **6** stuffy **7** airless
10 overheated

stigma 4 blot, flaw, mark,
scar **5** brand, odium, shame,
stain, taint **6** smirch, smudge
7 blemish, tarnish **8** disgrace,
dishonor **11** mark of shame
12 besmirchment

stigmatize 5 brand, smear
6 debase, defame, smirch
7 villify **9** discredit, disparage

still 4 calm, hush **5** inert,
quiet **6** at rest, hushed, pacify,
settle, silent **7** appease, assuage, gratify, put down, repress, silence, turn off
8 immobile, overcome, restrain, suppress, unmoving
9 noiseless, soundless **10** motionless, put an end to, stationary, unstirring

stillness 4 calm, hush **5** quiet
6 repose **7** silence **8** calmness,
inaction, quietude **9** composure **10** immobility, inactivity,
quiescence **11** tranquility
12 tranquillity

Stillness at Appomattox, A
 author: **11** Bruce Catton

stilted 4 cold, prim **5** rigid,
stiff **6** forced, formal, stuffy,
wooden **7** awkward, labored,
pompous, starchy, studied, uptight **8** mannered, priggish,
starched **9** graceless, unnatural **10** artificial **11** ceremonious, constrained

stiff 4 body, cold, cool, firm, grim, hard, high, iron, keen,
prim, sore, taut **5** aloof, awful, brave, brisk, crisp, cruel,
dense, fixed, gusty, harsh, heavy, rigid, sharp, smart, solid,
steep, stern, tense, thick, tight, tough, undue **6** bitter, brutal,
chilly, clumsy, corpse, dogged, forced, formal, raging, severe,
steady, steely, strong, uneasy, viscid, wooden **7** austere, awkward, cadaver, clotted, decided, distant, drastic, extreme,
fearful, intense, jellied, labored, precise, remains, settled,
starchy, stately, staunch, steeled, stilted, uptight, valiant, violent, viscous **8** affected, constant, dead body, exacting, forceful, grievous, mannered, pitiless, pounding, powerful,
resolute, resolved, rigorous, ruthless, spanking, stubborn, ungainly, unlimber, unshaken, vigorous **9** difficult, draconian,
excessive, graceless, inelastic, inelegant, laborious, merciless,
obstinate, resistant, steadfast, stringent, tenacious, unnatural
10 artificial, courageous, determined, exorbitant, formidable,
gelatinous, immoderate, inflexible, inordinate, persistent, solidified, unswerving, unyielding **11** ceremonious, constrained,
extravagant, indomitable, straitlaced, unfaltering, unflinching,
unwarranted **12** strong-willed, unreasonable
14 uncompromising

Stilwell, Joseph W
   nickname: 10 Vinegar Joe
   served in: 3 WWI 4 WWII
   chief of staff for: 13 Chiang
     Kai-shek
   driven out of: 5 Burma

stimulant 5 tonic, upper 6 bracer 8 excitant 9 energizer

stimulate 3 fan 4 spur, stir,
wake 5 alert, rouse 6 arouse,
awaken, excite, incite, prompt,
vivify 7 actuate, animate, inflame, inspire, quicken,
sharpen 8 activate, enkindle,
initiate, inspirit

stimulating 5 tonic 7 piquing
8 arousing, exciting, spurring,
stirring, whetting 9 animating,
provoking 10 energizing, refreshing 11 interesting,
provocative

stimulus 4 goad, spur, whet
5 tonic 6 bracer, fillip, motive
7 impetus 8 excitant 9 activa-
tor, energizer, incentive,
quickener, stimulant 10 incitement, inducement 11 provocation 13 encouragement

sting 3 cut, nip, rub, vex
4 ache, barb, bite, blow, burn,
fire, gall, gnaw, goad, grip,
hurt, itch, lash, move, pain,
prod, rack, rasp, rile, sore,
spur, stab, whip 5 anger,
chafe, cross, egg on, grate,
impel, pinch, pique, prick,
shake, shock, smart, venom,
wince, wound 6 arouse,
awaken, excite, harrow, incite,
insult, kindle, madden, nettle,
offend, pierce, prompt, propel,
stir up, tingle, twinge 7 actuate, agonize, disturb, incense, inflame, prickle,
provoke, quicken, scourge,
stinger, torment, torture 8 irritate, motivate, vexation
9 infuriate, instigate, penetrate 10 affliction, irritation

Sting, The
   director: 13 George Roy Hill
   cast: 10 Paul Newman, Ray
    Walston, Robert Shaw
    13 Eileen Brennan, Robert
    Redford 14 Charles Durning
   score: 11 Scott Joplin
   Oscar for: 7 picture
    8 director

stinginess 6 penury 9 parsimony 11 miserliness 13 niggardliness, penny-pinching
15 tight-fistedness

stinging 4 acid 5 harsh, sharp
6 biting, bitter 7 burning,
caustic, cutting, pungent
8 piercing 9 sarcastic, satirical
10 astringent

stingy 4 lean, mean, thin
5 close, scant, small, tight
6 frugal, meager, modest, paltry, scanty, skimpy, sparse
7 miserly, scrimpy, slender,
sparing 8 piddling, stinting
9 illiberal, niggardly, penurious 10 inadequate, ungenerous 11 closefisted, tightfisted
12 cheeseparing, insufficient,
parsimonious 13 penny-
pinching

stink 4 odor, reek 5 fetor
6 stench 8 bad smell 17 smell
to high heaven

stint 3 job 4 curb, duty, part,
save, task, term, turn 5 check,
chore, limit, quota, shift 6 reduce, scrimp 8 hold back, restrain, restrict, withhold
9 constrain, cut down on,
economize 10 assignment, engagement 12 circumscribe,
pinch pennies

stipend 5 grant, wages 6 income, salary 7 pension 8 fixed
pay 9 allowance, emolument
10 honorarium, recompense
11 scholarship 12 compensation, remuneration

stipulate 4 cite, name 5 agree,
allow, grant, state 6 assure,
insure, pledge 7 promise, provide, specify, warrant 8 indicate, set forth 9 designate,
guarantee

stipulation 4 term 7 proviso
9 condition 10 limitation
11 requirement, restriction

stipulative 7 limited 9 qualified, tentative 10 contingent,
restricted 11 conditional, provisional 16 with reservations

stir 3 act, mix 4 beat, fire,
goad, jolt, move, prod, rush,
spur, to-do, whip 5 blend,
rouse, shake, sough, start
6 arouse, awaken, bustle, commix, excite, flurry, hasten,
hustle, kindle, mingle, mixing,
moving, pother, quiver, rustle,
shiver, tumult, twitch, uproar,
vivify, work up 7 agitate, animate, enflame, flutter, inspire,
provoke, quicken, scamper
8 energize, inspirit, intermix,
mingling, movement, prod-
ding, rustling, scramble, stirring 9 agitation, commingle,
commotion, electrify, stimulate 10 get a move on, step
lively 11 set in motion 12 exert oneself, make an effort

Stiria
   also: 8 Stiritis
   epithet of: 7 Demeter

Stiritis *see* 6 Stiria

stirred up 5 riled, upset
7 aroused, excited, kindled, ruffled 8 agitated, inflamed 9 disturbed 10 stimulated

stirring 5 astir, awake 6 moving 7 rousing 8 electric, exalting, exciting, in motion,
spirited 9 inspiring, thrilling
10 up and about 11 galvanizing, stimulating 12 electrifying

stir up 5 upset 6 arouse,
awaken, excite, kindle, ruffle
7 agitate, disturb 9 call forth,
stimulate 10 antagonize

stir vigorously 3 mix 4 beat,
whip 7 agitate

stitch 3 bit, jot, sew 4 ache,
iota, kink, mend, pain, pang,
seam, tack 5 baste, cramp,
crick, piece, scrap, shoot,
shred 6 suture, tingle, twinge,
twitch 7 article, garment
8 particle 9 embroider
12 charley horse

St John's
   capital of: 17 Antigua and
    Barbuda

St Louis
   baseball team: 9 Cardinals
   football team: 9 Cardinals
   founded by: 13 Pierre
    Laclede
   hockey team: 5 Blues
   landmark: 11 Gateway Arch
   newspaper: 12 Post-Dispatch
   river: 11 Mississippi
   site of: 10 Exposition (1904)
   university: 10 Washington

stock 4 butt, clan, form, fund,
haft, herd, hold, kind, line,
pull, race, root, type 5 array,
basic, birth, blood, breed,
broth, cache, caste, equip,
goods, grasp, hoard, house, offer, shaft, store, tribe, wares
6 cattle, family, fit out, formal, handle, origin, people,
shares, source, staple, strain,
supply 7 appoint, capital, descent, dynasty, furnish, lineage, provide, regular, reserve,
routine 8 accoutre, ancestry,
bouillon, heredity, pedigree,
pro forma, quantity, standard
9 forebears, genealogy, inventory, livestock, ownership, parentage, provision, reservoir,
selection 10 assortment, background, extraction, family
tree, investment 11 merchandise, nationality, progeniture
12 accumulation 13 capital
shares

Stockhausen, Karlheinz
   born: 7 Germany, Modrath
   composer of: 5 Cycle,
    Tempi 6 Groups, Hymnen,
    Mantra, Zyklus 7 Anthems,
    Gruppen, Momente 8 Attun-
    ing, Gold Dust, Kontakte,
    Stimmung 9 Goldstaub, Zeit-
    masze 10 Procession, Prozes-
    sion 12 Kontrapunkte
    13 Klavierstucke 16 From

the Seven Days **17** Aus den Sieben Tagen

Stockholm
nickname: **16** Venice of the North
capital of: **6** Sweden
sea: **6** Baltic
lake: **7** Malaren
section: **8** Norrmalm **9** Sodermalm **11** Gamla Staden
landmark: **7** Skansen **8** City Hall **11** Great Church
site of: **10** Nobel Prize

stockpile **5** cache, hoard, stock, store **10** accumulate

stocky **5** dumpy, husky, pudgy, solid, squat, stout **6** blocky, chunky, stubby, stumpy, sturdy **8** thickset

stodgy **4** dull, flat **5** dated, heavy, lumpy, passe, staid, thick **6** boring, clumsy, dreary, narrow, prolix, stuffy **7** humdrum, pompous, prosaic, serious, starchy, tedious **8** lifeless, pedantic, tiresome **9** laborious, lumbering, wearisome **10** antiquated, inflexible, monotonous **12** indigestible, oldfashioned **13** uninteresting

stoic **4** calm **8** detached, fatalist, quietist, tranquil **9** impassive, unruffled **11** philosophic **13** dispassionate, imperturbable, unimpassioned

stoicism **8** fatalism **9** fortitude **11** impassivity, tranquility **12** tranquillity **16** imperturbability

stole **3** fur **4** cape, robe, took, wrap **5** crept, orary, scarf **6** swiped **7** filched, pinched, sneaked, tiptoed **8** mantilla, pilfered, snatched, vestment **9** embezzled, purloined

stolen **3** hot **5** taken **6** swiped **7** filched, hot **8** pilfered, snatched **9** embezzled, illgotten, purloined

stolid **4** dull **5** dense **6** bovine, obtuse **7** lumpish **8** sluggish **9** apathetic, impassive, lethargic **10** phlegmatic **11** insensitive, unemotional

stolidity **6** apathy **8** lethargy **9** inertness **11** impassivity **12** sluggishness

stomach **3** maw, pot **4** bear, bent, bias, craw, crop, guts, mind, take **5** abide, belly, brook, fancy, humor, stand, taste, tummy **6** desire, endure, hunger, liking, middle, paunch, relish, retain, suffer, temper, thirst **7** abdomen, gizzard, leaning, midriff, swallow **8** affinity, appetite, bear with, keenness, overlook, pass

over, pleasure, potbelly, sympathy, tolerate **9** put up with **10** attraction, midsection, partiality, proclivity, propensity **11** breadbasket, countenance, disposition, inclination **12** predilection

stone **3** gem, nut, pip, pit **4** rock, seed **5** bijou, jewel **6** kernel, pebble **9** brilliant **10** throw rocks

Stone, Edward Durell
architect of: **9** US Embassy **17** Museum of Modern Art **33** Kennedy Center for the Performing Arts

Stone, Irving
author of: **9** The Origin **11** Lust for Life **12** Those Who Love **17** Sailor on Horseback, The President's Lady **19** Adversary in the House **21** The Agony and the Ecstasy

Stone, Oliver
born: **9** New York NY
profession: **6** writer **8** director
films: **3** JFK **7** Platoon **10** Wall Street **14** Heaven and Earth **15** Midnight Express **21** Born on the Fourth of July

stoned to death **5** Achan

stonefly
varieties: **5** giant, green **6** spring, winter **8** perlodid **9** roachlike **11** greenwinged **12** rolled-winged

stoneware **5** china **7** ceramic, pottery **8** crockery

stony **3** icy **4** cold **5** blank, bumpy, chill, rocky, rough, stern **6** coarse, craggy, flinty, frigid, jagged, marble, pebbly, rugged, severe, steely, stolid, uneven **7** austere, callous, granite, lithoid, stoical **8** concrete, deadened, gravelly, hardened, indurate, obdurate, ossified, pitiless, rocklike, soulless, uncaring **9** bloodless, heartless, merciless, petrified, unfeeling, untouched **10** adamantine, forbidding, fossilized, hard-boiled, inexorable, insensible, unaffected, unyielding

stool **5** bench **7** cricket, hassock, ottoman

stool pigeon **3** rat, spy **4** fink **5** decoy, patsy **6** snitch **7** peacher, stoolie, tattler **8** informer, squealer **10** talebearer, tattletale

stoop **3** bow, sag **4** bend, fall, sink **5** deign, droop, porch, slump, steps, yield **6** resort,

slouch, submit **7** concede, descend, succumb **8** doorstep **9** acquiesce **10** condescend **11** entranceway **19** roundshoulderedness

stooped **4** bent **5** bowed **7** deigned, hunched **9** contorted **12** condescended

stop **3** ban, bar, end **4** curb, fill, halt, hold, idle, plug, quit, rest, seal, stay, stem, wait **5** abide, block, brake, break, caulk, cease, check, close, depot, deter, dwell, lapse, lodge, pause, put up, spell, stall, stand, tarry, visit **6** alight, arrest, cut off, desist, draw up, expire, falter, finish, hamper, hiatus, hinder, pull up, recess, rein in, repose, run out, stanch, stop up, thwart **7** close up, halting, layover, occlude, prevent, respite, sojourn, station, suspend **8** abeyance, break off, conclude, cut short, hold back, intermit, interval, leave off, obstruct, pass away, peter out, postpone, preclude, restrain, suppress, surcease, terminal, terminus, wind down **9** cessation, frustrate, interlude, stand fast, terminate **10** desistance, drop anchor, put an end to, standstill, suspension **11** come to a halt, come to an end, destination, discontinue, prohibition, termination **12** intermission, interruption **17** come to a standstill **18** bring to a standstill

stopgap **7** stand-by **9** contrived, emergency, expedient, impromptu, makeshift, temporary, tentative **10** improvised, substitute **11** provisional
Latin: **5** ad hoc **6** pro tem

stop in **4** call **5** visit **6** drop in, look in

stop off **4** call **5** visit **6** drop in, look in, stop by

stoppage **4** halt **5** check, tieup **6** arrest **7** barrier, embargo, staying **8** blockage, checking, clogging, gridlock, obstacle **9** checkmate, hindrance, restraint, stricture **10** disruption, impediment **11** curtailment, obstruction **12** interruption

Stoppard, Tom
author of: **10** Travesties **33** Rosencrantz and Guildenstern Are Dead

stopper **3** lid **4** bung, cock, cork, plug **5** spile

Stopping by Woods on a Snowy Evening
author: **11** Robert Frost

Stop the Music
host: 9 Bert Parks
orchestra: 11 Harry Salter
vocalist: 9 June Valli 11 Jaye
P Morgan, Jimmy Blaine
12 Marion Morgan 13 Betty
Ann Grove, Estelle Loring

stop up 3 jam 4 clog 5 block,
choke 8 obstruct

Storax 12 Biblical tree

store 3 lot 4 fund, hold, host,
keep, mart, pack, pile, save,
shop 5 amass, array, cache,
faith, hoard, lay by, lay in,
lay up, stash, stock, trust,
value, wares 6 credit, esteem,
gather, heap up, legion, market, plenty, regard, riches,
scores, supply, volume,
wealth 7 deposit, effects, husband, put away, reserve, satiety 8 emporium, lay aside,
overflow, plethora, quantity,
reliance, richness, salt away,
sock away, stow away
9 abundance, inventory, multitude, profusion, provision, reservoir, stockpile
10 accumulate, confidence,
cornucopia, dependence, estimation, exuberance, luxuriance 11 copiousness, full
measure, prodigality, supermarket 12 accumulation
13 establishment

storehouse 4 bank, silo 5 depot, vault 7 arsenal, granary
8 elevator, magazine, treasury
9 stockroom, warehouse
10 depository, repository

storied 4 epic 6 fabled 8 fabulous 9 legendary

**Stories and Texts for
Nothing**
author: 13 Samuel Beckett

storm 3 ado, row 4 blow,
fume, fuss, gale, rage, rant,
rave, roar, rush, stir, tear, to-
do 5 burst, furor, snarl, stalk,
stamp, stomp, tramp 6 assail,
attack, charge, clamor, deluge,
flurry, hubbub, pother, ruckus,
squall, strike, tumult, uproar
7 assault, besiege, bluster,
carry on, cyclone, rampage,
tempest, tornado, torrent, turmoil, twister, typhoon 8 blizzard, brouhaha, downpour,
eruption, fall upon, outbreak,
outburst, upheaval 9 agitation,
commotion, explosion, fulminate, hurricane, raise hell
10 cloudburst, hullabaloo
11 blow one's top, disturbance 12 blow one's cool, vent
one's rage

storm and stress
German: 13 Sturm und Drang
name of 18th century:
16 literary movement

storms
goddess of: 11 Tempestates

storm troopers
German: 14 Sturmabteilung

stormy 4 foul, wild 5 rainy,
rough, snowy, windy 6 raging,
rugged 7 howling, roaring,
squally, violent 8 blustery
9 inclement, turbulent
10 blustering 11 tempestuous

story 3 fib, lie 4 news, plot,
tale, word, yarn 5 alibi, fable,
piece 6 excuse, legend, report,
sketch 7 account, article, parable, romance, tidings, version
8 allegory, anecdote, argument, dispatch, news item,
white lie 9 falsehood, narrative, statement, testimony
10 allegation 11 fabrication,
information 13 prevarication

Story of a Bad Boy, The
author: 19 Thomas Bailey
Aldrich

Story of G I Joe, The
director: 14 William
Wellman
cast: 13 Freddie Steele, Robert Mitchum 15 Burgess
Meredith (Ernie Pyle)

**Story of Louis Pasteur,
The**
director: 15 William Dieterle
cast: 8 Paul Muni (Pasteur)
11 Anita Louise 19 Jose-
phine Hutchinson
Oscar for: 5 actor (Muni)

stout 3 big, fat, fit 4 able,
bold, firm, true 5 brave,
bulky, burly, hardy, heavy,
hefty, husky, large, obese,
plump, pudgy, round, solid,
tough, tubby 6 brawny,
chubby, daring, fleshy, heroic,
mighty, plucky, portly, robust,
rotund, rugged, spunky,
steady, stocky, strong, sturdy
7 doughty, gallant, staunch,
valiant 8 athletic, constant, enduring, faithful, fearless, intrepid, leathery, muscular,
resolute, resolved, stalwart,
thickset, untiring, valorous,
vigorous 9 confident, corpulent, dauntless, steadfast, strapping 10 able-bodied,
courageous, determined, inflexible, unshakable, unswerving,
unwavering 11 indomitable,
lionhearted, unfaltering, unflinching, unshrinking

Stout, Rex
author of: 10 Fer-de-Lance
12 Too Many Cooks 16 If
Death Ever Slept
character: 5 Fritz 9 Nero
Wolfe 13 Archie Goodwin

stouthearted 4 bold 5 brave,
gutsy, hardy 6 heroic, plucky,

spunky 7 valiant 8 fearless, intrepid, resolute, spirited, stalwart, unafraid, valorous
9 dauntless, undaunted
10 courageous 11 indomitable,
lionhearted, unblenching,
unflinching

stoutheartedness 4 grit, guts,
sand 5 nerve, pluck, spunk,
valor 6 daring, mettle 7 bravery, courage 8 boldness
12 fearlessness
13 dauntlessness

stoutness
French: 10 embonpoint

stow 3 jam, put, set 4 cram,
load, pack, tuck 5 cache,
crowd, place, stash, store,
stuff, wedge 7 deposit,
squeeze 8 ensconce, salt away

Stowe, Harriet Beecher
author of: 12 Oldtown Folks
14 Uncle Tom's Cabin

Strachey, Lytton
author of: 13 Queen Victoria 17 Elizabeth and Essex,
Eminent Victorians
member of: 15 Bloomsbury
Group

strafe 7 bombard 8 fire upon
10 machine-gun

straggle 4 rove 5 drift, stray
6 sprawl, wander 7 deviate,
meander 8 divagate

straight 4 even, neat, tidy,
true 5 clear, frank, right,
solid, sound 6 candid, direct,
evenly, honest, square, unbent 7 aligned, erectly, in order, orderly, upright
8 accurate, adjusted, arranged,
directly, on a level, reliable,
squarely, truthful, unbroken
9 ceaseless, forthwith, incessant, instantly, not curved,
shipshape, sorted out, sustained, veracious 10 aboveboard, continuous, forthright,
four-square, methodical, persistent, straightly, successive,
unrelieved, unswerving, unwavering 11 consecutive, coordinated, immediately,
trustworthy, undeviating
13 uninterrupted

straighten 4 tidy 5 align 6 adjust, neaten, unbend 7 even
out 8 level out, square up
9 put in line 10 put in order,
stand erect

straightening 7 tidying 9 adjusting, alignment, evening
up, unbending 10 evening
out 11 leveling out 13 putting
in line 14 putting in order

straighten out 6 unbend 7 re-
align 8 redirect 10 discipline

straighten up 4 tidy 5 align,

clean, order 6 neaten, tidy up
7 arrange, stand up 8 organize

straightforward 4 open
5 blunt, frank 6 candid, direct,
honest, square 7 ethical, upright 8 straight 9 guileless,
honorable 10 aboveboard,
creditable, forthright, scrupulous 11 plainspoken,
trustworthy

straightforwardness 6 candor 7 honesty 12 truthfulness
14 forthrightness

straight from the shoulder
4 open 5 frank 6 candid, direct, openly 7 bluntly, frankly,
sincere 8 candidly, directly
9 downright

straightness 7 honesty
8 evenness 10 directness
11 uprightness

strain 3 air, tax, tug 4 kind,
line, pull, sift, song, sort, toil,
tune, type, vein 5 blood,
breed, drain, force, grain,
grind, group, heave, labor,
people, press, sieve, streak,
stock, trait, twist 6 burden,
drudge, effort, extend, family,
filter, genius, injure, injury,
melody, overdo, purify, refine,
screen, sprain, stress, weaken,
winnow, wrench 7 descent,
distend, exhaust, fatigue, lineage, overtax, species, stretch,
tension, tighten, try hard, variety, wear out 8 ancestry,
bear down, elongate, exertion,
hardship, heredity, make taut,
overwork, pressure, protract,
struggle, tendency 9 draw
tight, make tense, overexert,
parentage 10 buckle down,
derivation, extraction, overburden 11 disposition, huff and
puff, inclination 12 do double
duty, drive oneself, exert oneself 14 predisposition, work
like a horse, work like a slave

strained 5 tense 6 touchy
8 volatile 9 explosive
10 precarious

strait 7 channel, narrows,
passage

straitened 5 broke, needy
6 hard-up 7 pinched 8 bankrupt, indigent, strapped,
wiped-out 9 destitute, penniless, penurious 10 distressed,
pauperized, restricted 11 embarrassed 12 impoverished
15 poverty-stricken

Strait Is the Gate
author: 9 Andre Gide

straitlaced 4 prim 5 rigid,
stiff 6 formal, narrow, proper,
severe, strict 7 austere, prudish, uptight 8 reserved 9 inhibited 11 puritanical

14 overscrupulous
15 undemonstrative

straits 3 fix 4 hole 6 pickle,
plight 8 distress 9 extremity
10 difficulty 11 predicament
13 embarrassment

strand 4 bank, cord, lock,
rope 5 beach, braid, coast, fiber, leave, shore, tress, twist
6 desert, ground, maroon,
string, thread 8 filament, necklace, seacoast, seashore
9 component, go aground, riv-
erside, shipwreck 10 ingredient, run aground 15 leave
high and dry, leave in the
lurch

stranded 5 stuck 6 ashore
7 aground, beached
8 grounded 9 foundered
11 shipwrecked 14 left high
and dry, left in the lurch

strange 3 new, odd 4 lost
5 alien, queer 6 uneasy, unused 7 awkward, bizarre, curious, erratic, foreign,
unknown, unusual 8 aberrant,
abnormal, freakish, peculiar,
singular, uncommon 9 alienated, anomalous, eccentric, estranged, fantastic, ill at ease,
irregular, unnatural 10 bewildered, farfetched, out of place,
outlandish, unexplored, unfamiliar 11 discomposed, disoriented, out-of-the-way
12 unaccustomed, undiscovered, unhabituated 13 extraordinary, unaccountable,
uncomfortable
14 unconventional

Strange Fruit
author: 12 Lillian Smith

Strange Interlude
author: 12 Eugene O'Neill

strangeness 7 anomaly, oddness 9 queerness 10 aberration 11 abnormality,
peculiarity 12 eccentricity, idiosyncrasy, irregularity, unconformity 13 nonconformity

stranger 5 alien 8 newcomer,
outsider 9 auslander, foreigner,
immigrant, outlander

Stranger, The
author: 11 Albert Camus

Strangers on a Train
director: 15 Alfred Hitchcock
cast: 9 Ruth Roman 11 Leo
G Carroll, Marion Lorne
12 Robert Walker 13 Farley
Granger 17 Patricia
Hitchcock
remade as: 20 Once You
Kiss a Stranger

strange to say
Latin: 13 mirabile dictu

strangle 3 gag 4 stop 5 burke,

check, choke, crush, quell
6 muzzle, stifle 7 garrote, put
down, repress, smother,
squelch 8 choke off, snuff out,
suppress, throttle 9 suffocate
10 asphyxiate, extinguish

strangulate 8 choke off, compress, strangle 9 constrict

strap 3 tie 4 band, beat, belt,
bind, cord, flog, lash, whip
5 flail, leash, thong, truss
6 tether, thrash 7 scourge

strapped 8 bankrupt, wiped
out 9 insolvent, penniless
12 impoverished, without
funds

strapping 5 burly, hardy,
husky, stout 6 brawny, robust,
strong, sturdy 8 muscular,
powerful, stalwart

stratagem 4 game, plan, plot,
ploy, ruse, wile 5 bluff,
dodge, feint, trick 6 deceit, device, scheme, tactic 8 artifice,
intrigue, maneuver, trickery
9 deception 10 subterfuge
11 contrivance, machination

strategic 3 key 4 wary 5 vital
6 clever 7 careful, crucial, cunning, guarded, planned, politic, prudent, turning
8 cautious, critical, decisive,
military, tactical, vigilant
9 important, momentous, principal 10 calculated, deliberate,
diplomatic 11 significant
13 consequential,
precautionary

strategy 4 game 5 craft, wiles
6 policy, scheme 7 cunning,
devices, tactics 8 artifice, art
of war, game plan, plotting
9 war policy 10 artfulness,
craftiness 11 grand design,
machination, maneuvering
12 military plan 15 military
science

stratosphere 3 sky 5 ozone
7 heavens 8 upper air 12 high
altitude 14 wild blue yonder

stratum 4 band, belt, seam,
zone 5 layer

Strauss, Johann (the Elder)
composer of: 13 Radetzky
March

**Strauss, Johann (the
Younger)**
composer of: 6 The Bat
13 Die Fledermaus, The
Gipsy Baron 16 Der
Zigeunerbaron
waltz: 12 Emperor Waltz
13 The Blue Danube
23 Tales from the Vienna
Woods

Strauss, Joseph
composer of: 17 Music of

the Spheres **27** The Village Swallows in Austria

Strauss, Richard
 born: **6** Munich **7** Germany
 composer of: **6** Salome
 7 Don Juan, Elektra **8** Arabella **9** Capriccio **10** Don Quixote **14** Ein Heldenleben **15** Ariadne auf Naxos **16** Der Rosenkavalier, Domestic Symphony, Till Eulenspiegel **19** Die Frau ohne Schatten **20** Die Aegyptische Helena, Thus Spake Zarathustra **21** Also Sprach Zarathustra **23** Death and Transfiguration

Stravinsky, Igor Feodorovich
 born: **6** Russia
 11 Oranienbaum
 composer of: **4** Agon
 6 Threni **7** Orpheus **8** The Flood **9** Card Party, Fireworks **10** Oedipus Rex, Petrouchka, Petruschka, Pulcinella **11** Jeu de Cartes, The Firebird **13** Dumbarton Oaks, Psalm Symphony **14** The Nightingale
 15 Abraham and Isaac, The Rite of Spring **16** Requiem Canticles, The Rake's Progress **18** Le Sacre du Printemps

straw 3 hay **4** tube **5** chaff **7** pipette

strawberry 8 Fragaria
 varieties: **4** mock **5** beach
 6 barren, Dunlap, garden, Indian **7** sow-teat **8** Klondike, Rosacean, Virginia, woodland
 liqueur: **13** creme de fraise

Straw Dogs
 director: **12** Sam Peckinpah
 cast: **9** T P McKenna **11** Susan George **12** Peter Vaughan **13** Dustin Hoffman

straw man 6 effigy **9** scapegoat, scarecrow

stray 4 lost, roam, rove, waif **5** drift **6** random, wander **7** digress, drifter **8** go astray, separate, set apart, straggle, straying, vagabond, wanderer **9** itinerant, misplaced, scattered, straggler **10** lost animal, lost person **11** lose one's way

straying 5 lapse **8** drifting, rambling **9** departure, deviation, wandering **10** abberation, digression, divergence

streak 3 bar, bed, fly **4** band, blot, blur, cast, dart, dash, daub, line, lode, race, rush, seam, tear, vein, whiz, zoom **5** layer, level, plane, smear, speed, strip, touch **6** blotch,

hurtle, smirch, smudge, strain, stripe **7** portion, splotch, stratum

stream 3 jet, run **4** blow, file, flow, flux, gush, pour, race, rill, rush, teem, tide, waft, wave **5** brook, burst, creek, float, flood, issue, river, shoot, spate, spill, spout, spurt, surge **6** abound, branch, course, deluge, extend, feeder, onrush, sluice **7** current, flutter, freshet, rivulet, torrent **8** effusion, fountain, overflow **9** profusion, tributary **11** watercourse

streamer 4 flag **6** banner, burgee **7** pennant

streamlet 3 run **4** rill **5** brook, creek **7** rivulet

streamlined 4 racy **5** clean, sleek **7** compact **8** up-to-date **9** organized **10** futuristic, modernized, simplified **11** aerodynamic

stream of abuse 6 tirade **8** diatribe, harangue **9** contumely, invective **12** vituperation

streams
 goddess of: **7** Juturna

Streep, Meryl
 real name: **16** Mary Louise Streep
 born: **14** Basking Ridge NJ
 roles: **8** Ironweed, Silkwood **11** Out of Africa **13** Falling in Love, Sophie's Choice (Oscar), The Deer Hunter **14** Kramer vs Kramer **25** The French Lieutenant's Woman

street 3 way **4** lane, mews, road **5** alley, block, route **6** avenue **7** highway, roadway, terrace, thruway **8** turnpike **9** boulevard **10** expressway **12** thoroughfare

Streetcar Named Desire, A
 author: **17** Tennessee Williams
 director: **9** Elia Kazan
 cast: **9** Kim Hunter (Stella Dubois Kowalski) **10** Karl Malden **11** Vivien Leigh (Blanche Dubois) **12** Marlon Brando (Stanley Kowalski)
 setting: **10** New Orleans
 score: **9** Alex North
 Oscar for: **7** actress (Leigh) **15** supporting actor (Malden) **17** supporting actress (Hunter)

Streets of San Francisco, The
 character: **9** (Det Lt) Mike Stone **10** (Inspector) Dan Robbins **11** (Inspector) Steve Keller

cast: **10** Karl Malden **12** Richard Hatch **14** Michael Douglas

strega
 type: **7** liqueur
 origin: **5** Italy
 flavor: **6** spices **10** orange peel
 with brandy: **10** Strega Flip

Streisand, Barbra
 real name: **20** Barbara Joan Streisand
 born: **10** Brooklyn NY
 husband: **11** Elliot Gould
 roles: **5** Yentl **9** Funny Girl (Oscar), Funny Lady **10** Fanny Brice, Hello Dolly, What's Up Doc? **11** A Star Is Born **12** The Main Event, The Way We Were

strength 4 beef, grit, kick, pith, sand, size **5** brawn, force, forte, might, pluck, power, sinew, spice, vigor **6** anchor, mettle, number, purity, spirit, succor, virtue **7** bravery, muscles, potency, stamina, support **8** backbone, buttress, efficacy, firmness, mainstay, security, solidity, tenacity, vitality **9** endurance, fortitude, hardiness, intensity, lustiness, puissance, stoutness, toughness, viability **10** robustness, sturdiness, sustenance **13** concentration, effectiveness **16** stoutheartedness
 Latin: **3** vis

strengthen 4 prop **5** brace, renew, steel **6** harden **7** build up, enhance, fortify, improve, restore, shore up, support, sustain **8** buttress **9** reinforce

strength of character 4 grit, guts **5** pluck, spunk **6** mettle **7** resolve **8** backbone **9** fortitude **10** resolution **12** resoluteness **13** steadfastness

Strength of Fields
 author: **11** James Dickey

strenuous 4 hard **5** eager **6** active, ardent, dogged, taxing, uphill **7** arduous, dynamic, earnest, intense, zealous **8** animated, diligent, sedulous, spirited, untiring, vigorous **9** assiduous, difficult, energetic, laborious, punishing **10** exhausting, on one's toes **11** hardworking, industrious, painstaking **12** enterprising **13** indefatigable

stress 4 beat, mark **5** force, value, worth **6** accent, affirm, assert, burden, moment, repeat, strain, weight **7** anxiety, concern, feature, gravity, meaning, sawdust, tension, urgency **8** emphasis, pressure **9** emphasize, necessity, underline **10** accentuate, importance, insist upon, oppression, prominence, underscore **11** consequence, seriousness **12** accentuation, significance **13** consideration

stretch 4 span, term, tire **5** cover, reach, spell, stint, tract, while, widen **6** burden, deepen, expand, extend, period, sprawl, spread, spring, , strain **7** distend, draw out, expanse, fatigue, lie over, overtax, pull out **8** distance, draw taut, duration, elongate, interval, lengthen, overtask, overwork, protract, put forth, reach out, tautness, traverse **9** be elastic, draw tight, make tense, make tight, overexert **10** elasticity, exaggerate, overburden, overcharge, overstrain, push too far, resiliency **11** carry too far **12** be expandable, be extendable **14** push to the limit

stretchable 7 elastic, rubbery **8** flexible **9** resilient

stretching 9 extending, extension **10** drawing out, elongation **11** attenuation, enlargement, lengthening, protraction **12** prolongation **13** amplification

stretching out 8 outreach **9** expansion, extending, extension **10** elongation **11** attenuation, lengthening **12** prolongation

stretch out 6 expand, extend **7** amplify, augment, draw out **8** elongate, lengthen, protract

Strether
character in: **14** The Ambassadors
author: **5** James

strew 3 sow **6** litter **7** scatter **8** disperse **9** broadcast **11** disseminate

stricken 3 ill **4** hurt, sick **7** injured, smitten, wounded **8** blighted, diseased **9** afflicted, taken sick **13** incapacitated

strict 4 nice **5** exact, rigid, stern **6** severe **7** austere, perfect **8** absolute, complete, exacting, rigorous, unerring **9** stringent **10** fastidious, inflexible, meticulous, scrupulous, unyielding **13** authoritarian, conscientious **14** uncompromising

strictly required
French: **9** de rigueur

stride 4 gait, lope, pace, step **5** march, stalk **7** advance, headway **8** long step, prog-

ress **11** advancement, improvement **13** take long steps

strident 5 harsh **6** shrill **7** grating, jarring, rasping, raucous **8** clashing, grinding, jangling, piercing, twanging **9** dissonant **10** discordant, screeching **11** cacophonous, high-pitched

Striebel, John H
creator/artist of: **10** Dixie Dugan

strife 6 unrest **7** discord, trouble, turmoil, warfare **8** conflict, disquiet, fighting, struggle, upheaval, violence **10** contention, convulsion, disharmony, dissension **11** altercation, disturbance

Strife
author: **14** John Galsworthy

strike 3 bat, box, hit, run, tap **4** bang, beat, belt, bump, clap, clip, club, come, cuff, drub, find, flog, lash, make, meet, pelt, ring, slam, slap, slug, sock, toll, whip, wipe **5** chime, clout, erase, flail, knell, knock, light, pound, punch, reach, smash, smite, sound, thump, tie-up, whack, whale **6** affect, arrive, assail, attack, batter, buffet, cancel, chance, charge, cudgel, delete, effect, fold up, hammer, pommel, remove, seem to, thrash, wallop **7** achieve, arrange, assault, boycott, impress, occur to, protest, put away, ram into, run into, scourge, scratch, stumble, unearth, walk out **8** appear to, bump into, come upon, cross out, dawn upon, discover, fall upon, lambaste, pull down, take down **9** burst upon, devastate, eliminate, encounter, eradicate, knock into, take apart **10** come across, flagellate, meet head-on **11** beat against, collide with, dash against **12** labor dispute, work stoppage

strike a bargain 5 agree **6** settle **9** make a deal **10** compromise **11** come to terms, meet halfway **18** split the difference **20** reach an understanding

strike back 7 counter, get even, hit back, pay back, riposte **9** fight back, retaliate **13** counterattack

strike dumb 4 daze, stun **5** amaze, shock **7** astound, stagger, stupefy **8** astonish, dumfound **9** dumbfound, electrify **11** flabbergast

strike noisily 4 bang, beat, clap, slam **5** thump

strike out 6 delete, fan out, set off, set out **7** take out **10** sally forth

strike sharply 3 rap **4** slap **5** crack

striking 6 marked **7** notable **9** prominent **10** astounding, impressive, noteworthy, noticeable, remarkable, surprising **11** conspicuous, outstanding **13** extraordinary

Strindberg, August
author of: **9** Miss Julie, The Father **10** A Dream Play **12** The Creditors **14** The Ghost Sonata **15** The Dance of Death

string 3 row **4** cord, file, line, rope **5** chain, queue, train, twine **6** column, extend, parade, series, spread, strand, thread **7** binding, stretch **8** necklace, sequence **10** procession, succession

stringent 5 close, harsh, spare, stern, stiff, tight **6** cogent, frugal, severe, strict **7** sparing **8** exacting, forceful, rigorous **9** demanding, effectual, unbending **10** inflexible, unyielding **14** uncompromising

strip 3 rob **4** band, flay, loot, peel, raid, sack, skin, slip, tear **5** field, flake, rifle, shave **6** denude, divest, length, ravage, remove, ribbon, stripe, unwrap **7** deprive, despoil, disrobe, draw off, lay bare, measure, plunder, pull off, ransack, uncover, undrape, undress **8** airstrip, desolate, lay waste, spoliate, unclothe **9** steal from **11** disencumber

stripe 3 bar **4** band, line, tape **5** braid, strip, swath **6** ribbon, streak **7** chevron **8** insignia **9** striation

stripling 3 boy, lad **5** minor, youth **8** teenager, young man **9** schoolboy, youngster **10** adolescent

stripped 4 bare, nude **5** naked **6** peeled, unclad **7** denuded, exposed, unrobed **8** disrobed, divested **9** unclothed, uncovered, undressed

strive 3 vie **4** push **5** essay, fight, labor **6** battle, strain **7** contend, try hard **8** endeavor, struggle **9** take pains, undertake **10** do one's best **12** apply oneself, do one's utmost, exert oneself, spare no pains **15** work like a Trojan **18** move heaven and earth **20** leave no stone unturned

striving 4 toil **5** exert, labor **6** effort, strain **7** toiling, travail **8** exertion, struggle **9** straining **10** struggling

stroke 3 bat, hit, pat, pet, tap **4** blow, chop, coup, deed, feat, poke, slap, sock, swat **5** brush, chime, fluke, punch, whack **6** caress, chance, wallop **7** massage, ringing, seizure, tolling **8** accident, apoplexy, flourish, movement, sounding, striking **11** achievement, coincidence, piece of luck, transaction **15** brain hemorrhage

stroll 4 tour, turn, walk **5** amble, mosey **6** ramble, wander **7** meander, saunter **9** poke along, promenade **14** constitutional

stroller 4 pram **5** buggy **6** ambler, walker **7** rambler **8** carriage **9** itinerant, pushchair, saunterer **10** promenader **12** perambulator

strong 3 hot **4** able, bold, deep, keen, tart **5** burly, clear, close, fiery, hardy, nippy, sharp, solid, sound, stout, tangy, tough, vivid **6** ardent, biting, brawny, bright, cogent, fervid, fierce, gritty, hearty, mighty, moving, plucky, potent, robust, savory, severe, sinewy, sturdy **7** buoyant, capable, devoted, earnest, fervent, healthy, intense, piquant, pungent, skilled, violent, zealous **8** animated, athletic, definite, diligent, distinct, emphatic, faithful, forceful, muscular, powerful, puissant, sedulous, spirited, stalwart, tireless, vehement, vigorous **9** assiduous, competent, confirmed, effective, energetic, herculean, resilient, tenacious, undiluted **10** compelling, convincing, courageous, deepseated, persistent, proficient **11** impassioned, persevering, resourceful **12** advantageous, concentrated, highly spiced, high-spirited, unmistakable **13** indefatigable, wellqualified **14** highly flavored, highly seasoned **Spanish: 5** macho

Strong
character in: **7** Erewhon
author: **6** Butler

strong-arm 3 cow **5** bully, force **6** coerce, compel **8** browbeat, threaten **10** intimidate

strong feeling 4 fear, hate, heat, love, zeal **5** anger, ardor **6** fervor, sorrow, warmth **7** despair, emotion, passion, sadness **8** jealousy **9** happiness, vehemence **12** satisfaction

stronghold 4 fort, hold, home, keep **6** bunker, center, locale, refuge **7** bastion, bulwark, citadel, rampart, redoubt **8** fastness, fortress, safehold, stockade **10** battlement, blockhouse **13** fortification

strongly committed 4 true **5** loyal **6** ardent **7** devoted, staunch, zealous **8** adhering, faithful **9** dedicated, steadfast **10** passionate, unwavering

strong point 5 forte **6** anchor **8** mainstay, strength

strong-willed 5 pushy **8** forceful, positive **9** assertive **10** aggressive **11** domineering, selfassured **13** self-assertive

Strophius
king of: **6** Phocis
reared by: **7** Orestes

structural support 3 bar **4** beam, prop, stud **5** brace, joist **6** girder, rafter, timber **7** trestle **12** underpinning

structure 4 form, plan **6** design, makeup **7** arrange, edifice, pattern **8** assemble, building, conceive, organize **9** construct, formation **11** arrangement, composition, put together **12** conformation, construction, organization **13** configuration

struggle 3 vie, war **4** duel, feud, pull, push, spar, tilt **5** argue, brawl, brush, clash, fight, grind, joust, labor, match, scrap, trial **6** action, battle, combat, differ, effort, engage, jostle, oppose, resist, strain, stress, strife, strive, tussle **7** compete, contend, contest, grapple, quarrel, scuffle **8** conflict, endeavor, exertion, long haul, skirmish, work hard **9** encounter, lock horns, take pains **10** engagement **11** altercation, cross swords **15** work like a Trojan **18** move heaven and earth **20** leave no stone unturned

strut 4 sail **6** parade, sashay **7** peacock, swagger **9** promenade

Struthiomimus
type: **8** dinosaur, theropod
known as: **15** ostrich dinosaur
period: **10** Cretaceous
characteristic: **9** toothless

Stryver
character in: **16** A Tale of Two Cities
author: **7** Dickens

Stuart, Gilbert
born: **15** North Kingston RI
artwork: **16** George Washington

Stuart, J E B
served in: **8** Civil War
side: **11** Confederate
commander of: **7** cavalry
battle: **7** Bull Run **8** Antietam **10** Gettysburg **14** Fredericksburg **16** Chancellorsville **18** Peninsular campaign

Stuart Little
author: **7** E B White

stub 3 end **4** bump, butt, dock, tail **5** crush, knock, snuff, stump **6** fag end, scrape **7** receipt, remains, tamp out, voucher **10** extinguish, torn ticket **11** counterfoil

stubble 5 beard **6** stumps **8** bristles, whiskers **9** cut stalks **16** five-o'clock shadow

stubborn 6 dogged, mulish, strong, sturdy **7** willful **8** forceful, obdurate, perverse, resolute **9** concerted, immovable, obstinate, pigheaded, resistant, tenacious, unbending, unmovable **10** bullheaded, headstrong, inflexible, persistent, purposeful, refractory, self-willed, unshakable, unyielding **11** indomitable, intractable, opinionated, uncompliant **12** hard to handle, recalcitrant, ungovernable, wholehearted

stubbornness 10 mulishness, obstinacy, resistance **11** willfulness **13** intransigence, pigheadedness

stubby 5 dumpy, pudgy, squab, squat, tubby **6** chubby, chunky, stocky, stodgy, stumpy **7** squatty **8** thickset

Stubtoe State
nickname of: **7** Montana

stuck 3 dug, put **4** held **5** bound, fixed, fused, glued, mired, poked **6** balked, curbed, jabbed, joined, nailed, pasted, pinned, placed, sealed, spiked, tacked, thrust, welded **7** adhered, affixed, boggled, impeded, planted, pricked, punched, saddled, snarled, speared, stabbed, stalled, stumped, stymied **8** attached, burdened, cemented, fastened, inserted **9** punctured **10** obstructed, perforated **11** immobilized

stuck-up 4 vain **5** cocky **6** snooty, uppish, uppity **7** haughty, high-hat **8** arrogant, snobbish **9** bigheaded, conceited 10 disdainful, ego-centric, hoity-toity 11 over-bearing, swellheaded 13 self-important, self-satisfied

stud 3 dot 4 beam, buck, dude, sire 5 board, rivet 6 button 7 upright 8 fastener, macho man, nailhead

student 4 coed 5 pupil 6 reader 7 analyst, learner, scholar, watcher 8 disciple, ex-aminer, follower, observer, re-viewer 9 collegian, schoolboy, spectator 10 schoolgirl 11 commentator, interpreter, matriculant 13 undergraduate

studied 8 measured 10 calcu-lated, deliberate, purposeful 11 intentional 12 premeditated

studious 6 brainy, intent 7 bookish, earnest, erudite 8 academic, cerebral, diligent, literate, well-read 9 laborious, scholarly 10 determined, pur-poseful, scholastic 11 pains-taking 12 intellectual

Studs Lonigan
  series includes: 11 Judgment Day 12 Young Lonigan 29 The Young Manhood of Studs Lonigan
  author: 13 James T Farrell

study 3 den 4 cram, read 5 grind, probe 6 office, peruse, review, search, studio, survey 7 examine, explore, inquiry, li-brary, observe, reading 8 anal-ysis, consider, learning, pore over, read up on, research, scrutiny 9 delve into, educa-tion 10 glance over, inspec-tion, scrutinize 11 examination, exploration, hit the books, inquire into, in-struction, investigate, read closely, reading room, scholar-ship 13 consideration, investi-gation, school oneself, search through

Study in Scarlet, A
  author: 19 Sir Arthur Conan Doyle
  character: 12 Dr John Wat-son 13 Jefferson Hope, To-bias Gregson 14 Sherlock Holmes 17 Inspector Lestrade

Study of History, A
  author: 14 Arnold J Toynbee

stuff 3 act, bit, jam, pad, wad 4 best, bosh, bunk, cram, fill, gear, heap, load, pack, pile, sate, stow 5 cache, crowd, gorge, hokum, hooey, stash, store, thing, trash, wedge 6 burden, fill up, humbug, matter, staple, tackle, things, thrust, tricks, utmost 7 effects, essence, hogwash, overeat,

rubbish, satiate, spinach, twad-dle 8 darndest, falderal, mate-rial, nonsense 9 component, empty talk, substance 10 bal-derdash, belongings, glutton-ize, ingredient, make a pig of 11 constituent, foolishness, overindulge, performance, pos-sessions, raw material 12 quintessence 13 paraphernalia

stuff-and-nonsense 3 rot 4 bosh, bull, bunk 5 hokum, hooey, trash 6 bunkum, drivel, humbug 7 baloney, hogwash, spinach, twaddle 8 buncombe, claptrap, nonsense, tommyrot 9 poppycock 10 applesauce, balderdash, tomfoolery 11 foolishness 12 fiddlesticks 13 horsefeathers

stuffed 4 full 6 filled, jammed, loaded, packed, rammed, wad-ded 7 crammed, crushed, re-plete 8 overfull, satiated, squeezed 10 sandwiched

stuff in 4 cram, pack 6 de-vour 8 bolt down, compress, gobble up, wolf down

stuffing 5 farce 7 filling, pack-ing, padding, wadding 8 dress-ing 9 forcemeat

stuffy 4 cold, smug 5 close, fusty, heavy, muggy, musty, staid 6 stodgy, sultry 7 airless, pompous 8 reserved, stagnant, stifling 9 clogged-up, congest-ed, high-flown, stopped-up, stuffed-up 10 old-fogyish, op-pressive, sweltering 11 preten-tious, straitlaced, suffocating 12 supercilious, unventilated 13 ill-ventilated, self-satisfied, stale-smelling

stultify 4 balk 6 hinder, impair, impede, thwart 7 cripple, in-hibit, nullify, vitiate 8 sup-press 9 frustrate, hamstring 11 make useless

stumble 3 hit 4 fall, reel, roll, sway, trip 5 botch, lurch, pitch, spill 6 bungle, falter, happen, hash up, hobble, mess up, slip up, sprawl, top-ple, totter 7 blunder, misstep, shamble, stagger 8 flounder 10 take a spill 12 come by chance, make mistakes, pitch forward

stumble upon 4 find 7 learn of 8 come upon, discover 10 chance upon, happen upon 14 find by accident

stumbling block 3 bar, rub 4 snag 5 block, catch, hitch 6 hamper, hurdle 7 barrier, problem 8 drawback, obstacle 9 detriment, hindrance 10 dif-ficulty, impediment 11 ob-

struction 12 complication, interference

stump 3 end 4 butt, foil, stub, thud 5 befog, clomp, clonk, clump, clunk, stamp, stomp, tramp 6 baffle, nubbin, stymie 7 confuse, mystify, nonplus, perplex 8 bewilder, confound, dumfound, footfall, stomping, tramping 9 bam-boozle, dumbfound

stun 4 daze, numb 5 amaze, shock 7 astound, stagger, star-tle, stupefy 8 astonish, dum-found 9 dumbfound 11 flabbergast

stunner 4 doll 5 beaut, Venus 6 beauty, eyeful 8 knockout 9 dreamboat 16 good-looker

stunning 6 dazing, lovely 7 amazing, numbing 8 shock-ing, striking 9 beautiful, exqui-site, startling 10 astounding, staggering, stupefying 11 as-tonishing, dumfounding 12 dumbfounding, electrifying 14 flabbergasting

stunt 3 act 4 curb, feat 5 abort, check, cramp, dwarf, limit, stint, trick 6 impede, number, stifle 7 curtail, delimit 8 re-strain, restrict, suppress

stunted 5 dumpy, runty 6 bantam 7 dwarfed, squatty, wizened 9 pint-sized 13 foreshortened

Stunt Man, The
  director: 11 Richard Rush
  cast: 9 Alex Rocco 11 Peter O'Toole (Eli Cross) 13 Allen Goorwitz, Sharon Farrell 14 Barbara Hershey, Steve Railsback

stupefaction 5 shock 8 numb-ness, surprise 9 amazement 12 astonishment

stupefied 5 dazed 6 amazed 7 shocked, stunned 8 be-numbed 10 dumbstruck, dum-founded 11 dumbfounded 13 flabbergasted, thunderstruck

stupefy 4 daze, stun 5 amaze, shock 7 astound, nonplus, stagger 8 astonish, confound, dumfound, surprise 9 dumbfound, overwhelm 11 flabbergast

stupefying 8 shocking, stun-ning 11 dumfounding 12 dumbfounding, electrifying, overwhelming 14 flabbergasting

stupendous 3 big 4 huge, vast 5 giant, great, jumbo 6 mighty 7 amazing, immense, mammoth, massive, titanic, unusual 8 colossal, enormous, fabulous, gigantic, imposing, stunning, terrific **9** cyclopean, herculean, marvelous, monstrous, very great, very large, wonderful **10** astounding, gargantuan, incredible, monumental, phenomenal, prodigious, remarkable, surprising, tremendous, unexpected **11** astonishing, elephantine **13** extraordinary

stupid 4 dull, dumb **5** dense, inane, inept, silly **6** absurd, oafish, obtuse, simple, unwise **7** aimless, asinine, boorish, doltish, fatuous, foolish, idiotic, moronic, witless **8** backward, childish, heedless, mistaken, reckless, tactless **9** brainless, cretinous, dimwitted, duncelike, foolhardy, illjudged, imbecilic, imprudent, pointless, senseless **10** halfwitted, ill-advised, indiscreet, irrelevant, weak-minded **11** empty-headed, meaningless, nonsensical, purposeless, thoughtless **12** absentminded, muddleheaded, preposterous, simpleminded, slow-learning, unreasonable **13** ill-considered, inappropriate, irresponsible, rattlebrained, unintelligent

stupor 4 daze **5** faint **6** apathy, torpor **7** inertia **8** blackout, lethargy, numbness **9** inertness **10** somnolence **12** stupefaction **13** insensibility

sturdy 4 able, firm **5** brave, burly, gutsy, hardy, heavy, solid, sound, stout, tough **6** daring, dogged, gritty, heroic, mighty, plucky, robust, rugged, secure, sinewy, spunky, strong **7** defiant, doughty, durable, gallant, lasting, valiant **8** enduring, fearless, forceful, intrepid, muscular, powerful, resolute, spirited, stalwart, stubborn, vigorous, well-made **9** dauntless, strapping, unabashed, undaunted, well-built **10** courageous, determined, invincible **11** indomitable, substantial, unshrinking **12** highspirited, stouthearted **15** well-constructed

Sturges, John
director of: **14** The Great Escape **19** The Magnificent Seven

Sturges, Preston
director of: **10** The Lady Eve **16** Sullivan's Travels **17** The Palm Beach Story, Unfaithfully Yours **21** Hail the Conquering Hero **24** The Miracle of Morgan's Creek

Sturmabteilung 13 storm troopers

Sturm und Drang 22 German literary movement (18th century)
literally: **14** storm and stress

stygian 3 dim **4** dark **5** black, murky **6** dreary, gloomy, somber **7** hellish **8** funereal, infernal, starless **9** tenebrous, unlighted

style 3 fad **4** call, elan, kind, mode, name, pomp, rage, sort, type **5** charm, class, craze, favor, flair, grace, model, taste, trend, vogue **6** design, luxury, manner, polish **7** arrange, comfort, fashion, pattern **8** currency, elegance **9** affluence, designate **10** smoothness **11** savoir faire
French: **4** gout

stylish 3 hip, new **4** chic **5** natty, smart, swank **6** dapper, latest, modern, modish, with-it **7** a la mode, elegant, in vogue, voguish **8** up-to-date **9** in fashion **11** fashionable **13** sophisticated, up-to-the-minute

stymie 4 balk **5** block, check, stump **6** baffle, hinder, puzzle, thwart **7** confuse, mystify **8** confound, obstruct **9** frustrate

Stymphalides
origin: **8** Arcadian
form: **5** birds
attribute: **9** dangerous

Stymphalus
king of: **7** Arcadia
killed by: **6** Pelops
form: **4** lake
home of: **12** Stymphalides

Styracosaurus
type: **8** dinosaur **10** ceratopsid
location: **12** North America
period: **10** Cretaceous
characteristic: **6** horned

Styron, William
author of: **12** The Long March **13** Sophie's Choice **17** Lie Down in Darkness **18** Set This House on Fire **25** The Confessions of Nat Turner

Styx
form: **5** river
location: **5** Hades **10** underworld
father: **7** Oceanus
ferryman: **6** Charon

suave 6 silken, smooth, urbane **7** affable, elegant, politic **8** charming, gracious, mannerly, polished, unctuous **9** civilized **10** diplomatic, flattering **12** ingratiating **13** smooth-tongued

sub 5 below, proxy, under

6 backup, deputy, second **7** beneath, standby, stand-in **9** alternate, submarine, surrogate **10** substitute, understudy **11** pinch-hitter

subaltern 4 aide **6** helper **9** assistant **10** lieutenant **11** subordinate

subconscious 3 dim **7** dawning **9** intuitive **10** subliminal **11** instinctive

subdivide 6 divide **7** split up **8** separate **9** partition

subdivision 3 arm **4** wing **6** branch **7** chapter, section **8** offshoot **11** development **12** neighborhood

subdue 3 bow **4** calm, curb, down, drub, ease, foil, mute, rout, trim, whip **5** allay, break, check, crush, floor, quell, salve, smash, still **6** deaden, defeat, master, mellow, muffle, reduce, soften, soothe, temper, thrash **7** appease, assuage, conquer, mollify, oppress, overrun, put down, relieve, slacken, subject, trample **8** mitigate, moderate, overcome, palliate, surmount, tone down, vanquish **9** meliorate, overpower, overwhelm, quiet down, soft-pedal, subjugate **10** ameliorate **11** triumph over **12** tranquillize

subdued 4 dull **5** cowed, muted, quiet **7** abashed, crushed, humbled, muffled, quelled **8** deadened, overcame **10** humiliated, indistinct, lackluster **11** intimidated, overpowered

subduer 6 victor, winner **9** conqueror, overcomer **10** subjugator, vanquisher **11** intimidator

subject 4 bare, case, gist, open, pith, text **5** field, issue, liege, motif, prone, study, theme, topic **6** affair, expose, liable, matter, submit, thesis, vassal **7** bound by, citizen, concern, exposed, lay open **8** business, disposed, follower, obedient, question **9** dependent, subjected, substance **10** answerable, discipline, in danger of, make liable, put through, vulnerable **11** stipulatory, subordinate, subservient, susceptible

subjection 11 subjugation **12** subservience **13** regimentation, subordination

subjective 5 inner **6** biased **7** partial **8** partisan, personal **9** emotional **10** individual, prejudiced **12** nonobjective

subjoin 5 add on, affix, annex **6** append, attach, tack on

subjugate 4 tame **5** crush, quell **6** subdue **7** conquer, put down **8** dominate, suppress, vanquish **10** overmaster

subjugation 6 chains, thrall **7** bondage, slavery **9** dominance, mastering, servitude, thralldom **10** conquering, domination **11** enslavement, vanquishing

subjugator 6 master, victor **7** subduer **9** conqueror, dominator **10** vanquisher **11** slavemaster

sublimate 4 turn **5** exalt, shift **6** divert, purify **7** channel, convert, elevate, ennoble **8** redirect, transfer **9** transform, transmute **12** spiritualize

sublime 4 high **5** grand, great, lofty, noble **6** superb **7** exalted, stately **8** elevated, imposing, majestic, splendid, terrific, very good **9** estimable, excellent, marvelous, wonderful **12** awe-inspiring, praiseworthy

submarine
  invented by: 7 Holland
  even keel: 4 Lake
  torpedo: 8 Bushnell

submerge 4 dive, sink **5** douse, drown, flood, souse **6** deluge, engulf, go down, plunge **7** go under, immerse **8** inundate, pour over, submerse

submerse 5 drown **6** engulf **7** immerse **8** inundate, submerge

submersion 7 sinking **8** drowning **9** immersion **10** inundation **11** submergence

submission 8 giving in, meekness, tameness, yielding **9** handing in, obedience, passivity, surrender, tendering **10** compliance, remittance, submitting **11** passiveness **12** acquiescence, capitulation, presentation, subservience, tractability **13** nonresistance **14** submissiveness

submissive 4 meek, mild **6** docile, humble, pliant **7** dutiful, fawning, passive, servile, slavish **8** crawling, obedient, toadying, yielding **9** compliant, malleable, tractable, truckling **10** obsequious **11** acquiescent, bootlicking, complaisant, deferential, subservient, unassertive **12** capitulating, ingratiating, nonresisting **13** accommodating

submissiveness 8 docility, meekness **9** passivity **10** compliance **11** resignation **12** complaisance, tractability

submit 3 bow **4** bend, cede **5** agree, argue, claim, defer, kneel, offer, stoop, yield **6** accede, assert, commit, comply, give in, give up, resort, tender **7** contend, hold out, present, proffer, propose, succumb, suggest **8** back down, put forth **9** acquiesce, surrender, volunteer **10** capitulate, put forward **12** knuckle under

submit an offer 3 bid **6** tender **7** proffer, propose

submit to 4 bear, take **5** abide, brave, brook, stand **6** endure, suffer **7** stomach, undergo **8** stand for, tolerate **9** put up with

subnormal 3 bad, low **5** seedy, sorry **6** crummy, dismal, shabby, sleazy, subpar **7** abysmal **8** below par, inferior, mediocre, wretched **9** defective, deficient **10** inadequate, second-rate **11** below normal, substandard **12** insufficient

subordinate 4 help **5** lower **6** junior, lackey, lesser, menial, worker **7** servant, subject **8** hireling, inferior **9** ancillary, assistant, attendant, auxiliary, dependent, of low rank, outranked, secondary, subaltern, underling **10** subsidiary **11** subservient

subordination 10 subjection **11** inferiority, subjugation **12** subservience **13** regimentation

suborn 5 bribe **6** buy off, pay off

sub rosa 8 covertly, in secret, on the sly, secretly **9** in private, privately **12** off-the-record **14** confidentially **15** behind-the-scenes **17** behind closed doors

subscribe 4 help, sign **6** assent, chip in, donate **7** consent, endorse, support **8** hold with **9** undersign **10** contribute

subsequent 4 next **7** ensuing **9** following, proximate **10** consequent, succeeding, successive

subsequently 2 so **5** after, later, since **9** afterward, following **10** succeeding **12** consequently

subservient 6 docile, menial **7** fawning, servile, slavish, subject **8** cringing, toadying **9** accessory, ancillary, auxiliary, prostrate, truckling **10** obsequious, subsidiary

11 bootlicking, subordinate, sycophantic **12** contributory, ingratiating

subside 3 ebb, sag **4** calm, drop, ease, sink, wane **5** abate, let up **6** cave in, lessen, recede, settle, shrink **7** descend, dwindle **8** decrease, diminish, level off, melt away, moderate

subsidence 5 letup **6** easing, ebbing, waning **7** calming **9** abatement, dwindling, lessening, recession, shrinking **10** decreasing, inactivity, moderation **12** diminishment

subsidiary 5 extra, lower, minor **6** branch, junior, lesser **7** adjunct **8** addition, division, inferior **9** accessory, affiliate, auxiliary, secondary **10** additional, supplement **11** subordinate **12** supplemental **13** supplementary

subsidy 3 aid **4** gift **5** award, grant **7** backing, support **9** allotment, provision **10** fellowship, grant-in-aid, honorarium, subvention **11** scholarship, sponsorship **13** appropriation, assistantship

subsist 4 live **5** exist **7** survive **9** stay alive **11** feed oneself, support life **12** make ends meet **23** keep body and soul together

subsistence 6 living, upkeep **7** support **8** survival **10** livelihood, sustenance **11** maintenance, nourishment

substance 4 body, core, germ, gist, pith, soul **5** force, heart, means, money, sense, stuff **6** burden, import, intent, marrow, matter, riches, thrust, wealth **7** element, essence, keynote, purport, reality **8** backbone, material, property, solidity **9** actuality, affluence, basic idea, main point **10** ingredient **11** connotation, constituent, corporality **12** corporeality, quintessence **13** corporealness

substandard 3 bad **4** poor **5** awful, lousy **6** crummy, shoddy **8** below par, inferior, terrible **9** imperfect **10** second-rate **11** second-class **12** below average

substantial 3 big **4** firm, full **5** ample, bulky, large, massy, solid, sound **7** massive, sizable **8** abundant **9** plenteous, plentiful **10** monumental **12** considerable

substantiate 5 prove **6** verify **7** confirm, support, sustain

11 corroborate, demonstrate
12 authenticate

substantiated 6 proved,
proven 7 factual 8 verified
9 supported 11 well-founded
12 corroborated, demonstrated,
well-grounded
13 authenticated

substantiation 5 proof 8 evidence 11 affirmation 12 verification 13 corroboration,
demonstration, documentation 14 authentication

substitute 3 act 6 backup,
change, ersatz, fill in, switch
7 standby, stand in, stopgap
8 deputize, exchange, pinch-
hit, make sense take over 9 alternate,
makeshift, surrogate, temporary 10 understudy 11 alternative, pinch hitter, replacement

substitution 5 shift 6 change,
switch 8 exchange, swapping
9 variation 10 alteration
11 replacement

substructure 4 base 6 ground
10 foundation, groundwork
12 underpinning

subsume 5 cover 6 assume, deduce 7 explain, include, involve 8 consider
13 subcategorize

subterfuge 4 ruse, sham, wile
5 blind, dodge, guile, shift,
trick 6 scheme 7 evasion 8 artifice, intrigue, pretense,
scheming 9 casuistry, chicanery, deception, duplicity, imposture, sophistry, stratagem
10 camouflage, sneakiness
11 deviousness, evasiveness,
game-playing, machination,
make-believe, smoke screen

subtle, subtile 3 sly 4 cagy,
deft, fine, foxy, keen, wily
5 light, quick, sharp, slick
6 artful, astute, clever, crafty,
expert, shifty, shrewd, tricky
7 cunning, devious, elusive,
refined 8 delicate, indirect,
masterly, skillful 9 deceptive,
designing, ingenious, underhand 10 discerning 11 understated 13 perspicacious,
sophisticated 14 discriminating

Subtle
character in: 12 The
Alchemist
author: 6 Jonson

subtleties 7 nuances 10 fine
points 11 refinements
12 distinctions

subtract 6 deduct, detach,
lessen, reduce, remove 8 decrease, diminish, take away,
withdraw

subtraction 7 removal 8 de-

crease 9 deduction, lessening,
reduction 10 diminution, taking away, withdrawal
11 diminishing

suburbs 8 environs, vicinity
9 outskirts, periphery,
precincts

sub verbo 12 under the word
15 under the heading

subversion 4 fall, ruin 6 defeat, mutiny 8 disorder, sabotage 9 overthrow, rebellion
10 corruption, disruption
11 destruction

subversive 7 traitor 8 quisling
9 insurgent, seditious 10 incendiary, traitorous, treasonous 11 seditionary
12 collaborator 13 revolutionary 14 fifth columnist 15 insurrectionary
16 collaborationist

subvert 3 mar 4 ruin, undo
5 smash, spoil, upset, wreck
6 defile, poison, ravage 7 despoil, destroy, disrupt, shatter
8 demolish, overturn 9 devastate, overthrow, undermine
11 contaminate

sub voce 21 under the specified word
literally: 13 under the voice

succeed 3 hit, win 5 avail,
catch, click 6 accede, do well,
follow, move up 7 inherit,
prevail, prosper, replace,
triumph 8 make a hit, make
good, supplant, take over
9 bear fruit, strike oil

succeed at 2 do 6 attain
7 execute, fulfill, perform, realize 8 carry out 9 make a go
of 10 accomplish

succeeding 5 later 6 coming,
future 7 ensuing 8 oncoming
9 following, impending, posterior 10 consequent, subsequent, successive

succeed to 6 follow 7 inherit
15 ascend the throne

succes d'estime 15 critical
success

success 3 hit 4 fame 5 smash
7 triumph, victory 8 conquest
9 affluence 10 ascendancy, attainment, prosperity
11 achievement, advancement,
fulfillment, good fortune

successful 4 rich 6 proven
7 perfect, wealthy, well-off
8 achieved, affluent, complete,
fruitful, thriving 9 effective
10 prosperous, triumphant
11 efficacious, flourishing
12 accomplished,
acknowledged

successful completion 7 success, victory, winning 9 execution 10 making good
11 achievement, culmination,
fulfillment, realization 12 consummation 14 accomplishment

succession 3 run 5 chain, cycle, round, train 6 course, series 8 sequence 9 accession
10 assumption, procession,
stepping-up, taking over
11 inheritance, progression

successive 7 ensuing 10 continuous, succeeding
11 consecutive

successor 4 heir 5 donee
7 devisee, heiress, heritor, legatee 8 follower, parcener
9 heritress, joint heir 10 coparcener, substitute 11 beneficiary, replacement,
reversioner 12 heir apparent

succinct 4 neat 5 brief, crisp,
pithy, short, terse, tight 6 direct, gnomic 7 clipped, compact, concise, summary
9 condensed 10 aphoristic, to
the point 12 epigrammatic

succinctness 7 brevity 9 crispness, terseness 11 compactness, conciseness
12 condensation

succor 3 aid 4 help 5 nurse
6 assist, back up, relief, shield,
wait on 7 comfort, nurture,
protect, relieve, support, sustain 8 befriend 10 assistance,
minister to, sustenance, take
care of 11 give a lift to, helping hand, lend a hand to,
maintenance
13 accommodation

succulent 5 juicy 6 fleshy
9 toothsome 10 appetizing

succumb 3 die 5 yield
6 accede, expire, give in, submit 7 defer to, give way, go
under 8 pass away 9 surrender 10 capitulate, comply
with 12 fall victim to

such as
Latin: 2 eg 13 exempli gratia

such is life
French: 9 c'est la vie

sucker 3 sap 4 boob, butt,
dupe, fool, goat, gull, jerk,
mark 5 chump, patsy 6 pigeon, victim 7 cat's-paw, fall
guy 8 easy mark, fair game,
pushover 9 schlemiel, soft
touch 11 sitting duck

Sucker State
nickname of: 8 Illinois

suck up 6 absorb, soak up
7 drink in 8 sponge up
9 swallow up

Sucre
  legal capital of: **7** Bolivia

Sudan *see box*

Sudanese Republic *see*
  4 Mali

sudden 4 rash **5** hasty, quick,
rapid **6** abrupt, speedy **7** instant **9** immediate, impetuous
10 surprising, unexpected, unforeseen **11** precipitate, unlooked-for **13** instantaneous,
unanticipated, unforeseeable

sudden development
  French: **10** coup de main

suddenly 7 quickly **8** abruptly,
in no time **9** all at once, instantly, on the spot **11** in an
instant **12** all of a sudden, un-

expectedly **13** at short notice
14 without warning **20** on the
spur-of-the-moment **21** in the
twinkling of an eye

sudden movement 4 dart,
jolt **5** flash, spurt

sudden noise 3 pop **4** bang,
clap, slam **5** burst, crash **6** report **9** explosion

Sudermann, Hermann
  author of: **5** Honor **8** Dame
  Care **14** The Song of Songs

suds 3 ale **4** beer, brew, foam
5 draft, froth, lager **10** malt
liquor

sue 3 beg **4** pray **5** plead **6** appeal **7** beseech, entreat, im-

plore **8** petition **9** importune
10 supplicate

Sue, Eugene (Marie-Joseph)
  author of: **15** The Wandering
  Jew **19** The Mysteries of
  Paris

suffer 4 ache, bear, hurt, pine
5 stand **6** endure, grieve, lament **7** agonize, despair, drop
off, fall off, stomach, sustain,
undergo **8** bear with, feel
pain, tolerate **9** go through,
put up with, withstand **10** be
impaired **11** deteriorate

suffer for 6 pay for **8** atone
for **9** answer for

suffering 3 woe **4** ache, care,
hurt, pain, pang **5** agony, dolor, grief, throe, trial **6** misery,
sorrow, twinge **7** anguish,
anxiety, torment, torture, travail **8** distress, soreness
9 heartache **10** affliction, discomfort, heavy heart, irritation **11** tribulation

suffice 2 do **4** last, meet, pass
5 avail, get by, serve **6** answer, make do **7** fulfill, qualify, satisfy

sufficiency 6 enough, plenty
7 surfeit **8** adequacy **9** abundance, ampleness, profusion

sufficient 5 ample **6** enough,
plenty **7** copious, minimal
8 abundant, adequate **9** plenteous, plentiful **11** up to the
mark **12** satisfactory

suffocate 3 gag **5** choke
6 quench, stifle **7** garrote,
smother **8** snuff out, strangle,
throttle **10** asphyxiate,
extinguish

suffuse 4 fill, soak **5** cover,
steep **6** infuse **7** diffuse, overrun, pervade **8** overflow, permeate, saturate **9** transfuse
10 impregnate, infiltrate,
overspread

Sugar State
  nickname of: **9** Louisiana

sugary 5 mushy, sweet **6** syrupy **7** cloying, fulsome, gushing, honeyed, mawkish
8 cajoling, unctuous **10** flattering, saccharine

suggest 3 bid **4** move, urge
5 imply, posit **6** advise, hint
at, submit **7** advance, counsel,
propose **8** advocate, indicate,
intimate, propound **9** give a
clue, recommend **16** lead one
to believe

suggested 6 hinted **7** implied,
oblique **8** implicit, indirect,
possible, proposed

suggestion 3 dab, tip **4** dash,
hint, tint **5** grain, shade, taste,

Sudan
  capital/largest city: **8** Khartoum
  others: **3** Waw, Yei **4** Juba **5** Kosti, Meroe, Nyala, Obeid,
    Opari, Segon **6** Atbara, Suakin **7** Aluboyd, Elobeid, Geneina, Kassala, Malakal **8** Elfasher, Omdurman **9** al-
    Ubayyid, Elgeneina, Port Sudan, Wad Medani
  division: **7** Jonglei **9** Upper Nile **12** Bahr el Ghazal
    16 Eastern Equatoria, Western Equatoria
    ancient kingdom: **4** Alwa, Funj, Kush **7** Maqurra
  measure: **2** ud
  monetary unit: **5** pound **8** piastres
  weight: **5** habba
  lake: **2** No **4** Chad, Toad **6** Nasser
  mountain: **4** Nuba **7** Imatong **9** Dongotona **10** Jabal Marra,
    Jebel Marra **18** Ethiopian Highlands
  highest point: **7** Kinyeti
  river: **4** Nile **5** Sobat **6** Atbara **8** Blue Nile **9** White Nile
    10 Bahr el-Arab **11** Bahr el-Jebel **12** Bahr el-Ghazal
  sea: **3** Red
  physical feature:
    desert: **6** Libyan, Nubian
    gum forest: **8** Kordofan
    plain: **6** Gezira
    sandstorm: **6** haboob
    plateau: **8** Kordufan
    swamp: **4** Sudd
  people: **3** Bor, Dor, Fur **4** Arab, Bari, Beri, Bobo, Daza,
    Egba, Fula, Golo, Nuba, Nuer, Poul, Sere **5** Anuak,
    Bongo, Dinka, Fulah, Hausa, Joluo, Junje, Mosgu, Mossi,
    Negro, Tibbu, Volta **6** Acholi, Azande, Gurusi, Hamite,
    Lotuho, Makari, Nilote, Nubian, Senufo, Surhai, Tuareg
    7 Balante, Baqqara, Gubayna, Jaaliin, Nilotes, Shilluk,
    Songhai, Songhay, Songhoi, Sourhai **8** Kababish, Mandingo, Menkiera **9** Sarakille **10** Gurmantshi, Shaiquiyya
    leader: **5** Mahdi **9** al-Nimeiry **10** Mehemet Ali **22** Jaafar
      Mohammed al-Nemery
  language: **2** Ga **3** Efe, Ewe, Ibo, Kru, Vak, Vei **4** Efik,
    Mole, Tshi **6** Arabic, Nubian, Yoruba **7** English **8** Mandango, Mandingo **9** Ta Bedawie
  religion: **5** Islam **7** animism **12** Christianity
  place:
    canal: **7** Jonglei
    dam: **6** Sennar **8** Roseires **10** Jebel Aulia
    temple: **4** Lion
    tomb: **5** Mahdi
  feature:
    boat: **6** murkab
  food: **4** dura **5** dukhn, kisra

tinge, touch, trace **6** advice, urging **7** counsel, feeling, pointer, soupcon **9** prompting, suspicion **10** intimation, sprinkling **11** exhortation **14** recommendation

suggestive 4 lewd, racy **5** bawdy, loose **6** risque, sexual, wanton **8** allusive, improper, indecent, off-color, prurient, unseemly **9** evocative, remindful, seductive, shameless **10** expressive, indelicate, licentious **11** provocative, reminiscent, stimulating

sui generis 6 unique **12** of her own kind, of his own kind, of its own kind **14** of their own kind

sui juris 14 of one's own right **31** capable of managing one's own affairs **36** capable of assuming legal responsibility

suit 3 fit **4** duds, garb, plea, togs **5** befit, court, getup, habit, match **6** appeal, attire, become, beseem, follow, livery, oblige, outfit, please, prayer, wooing **7** apparel, begging, clothes, content, costume, delight, gladden, gratify, raiment, satisfy, uniform **8** clothing, entreaty, jell with, make glad, petition **9** addresses, agree with, conform to, courtship, do one good, overtures, tally with, trappings **10** accord with, attentions, comply with, fall in with, habiliment, lovemaking, square with **11** accommodate, go along with **12** be becoming to, blandishment, correspond to, dovetail with, solicitation, supplication **13** accoutrements, be agreeable to, harmonize with **14** be acceptable to, be convenient to **15** be appropriate to **16** be appropriate for

suitable 3 apt, fit **4** meet **5** right **6** proper, seemly, worthy **7** apropos, fitting, germane **8** adequate, becoming, relevant **9** befitting, congruous, cut out for, pertinent, qualified **10** applicable, seasonable **11** appropriate **12** commensurate

suitcase 3 bag **4** grip **6** valise **7** satchel **8** knapsack, rucksack **9** duffel bag, gladstone, two-suiter **11** portmanteau **12** overnight bag, traveling bag

suite 3 set **4** flat **5** chain, court, group, rooms, round **6** convoy, series **7** company, cortege, retinue **8** servants **9** apartment,

followers, following **10** attendants **11** progression

suited 3 fit **7** adapted, attired, clothed, dressed, good for, matched **8** adjusted, agreeing, becoming **9** agreeable **11** appropriate, harmonizing

suit of armor 4 mail **5** armor **9** chain mail **10** coat of mail

suitor 4 beau, love **5** flame, lover, swain, wooer **6** fellow **7** admirer, gallant **8** young man **9** boyfriend **10** sweetheart

sulfur
chemical symbol: 1 S

sulk 4 crab, fret, fume, mope, pout **5** brood, chafe, frown, grump, scowl **6** glower, grouch **7** grumble **8** be in a pet, be miffed, be put out, be sullen, look glum **9** be in a huff **11** be resentful **12** be out of humor

sulky 6 morose, sullen **7** pouting **8** petulant

sullen 4 blue, dark, glum, grim, sore, sour **5** cross, heavy, moody, sulky, surly **6** crabby, dismal, dreary, gloomy, grumpy, morose, somber, touchy **7** crabbed, doleful, forlorn, grouchy, peevish **8** brooding, desolate, dolorous, funereal, mournful, petulant, scowling **9** cheerless, glowering, resentful, saturnine, splenetic, unamiable **10** depressing, foreboding, ill-humored, ill-natured, melancholy, out of humor, out of sorts, unsociable **11** ill-tempered **13** temperamental
French: 8 farouche

sullied 5 dirty **6** impure, soiled **7** defiled, stained, unclean **9** tarnished

Sullivan, Elizabeth
real name of: 14 Elsa Lanchester

Sullivan, John Florence
real name of: 9 Fred Allen

Sullivan, John L (Lawrence)
nickname: 15 Boston Strong Boy
sport: 6 boxing
class: 11 heavyweight
fought: 12 bareknuckled

Sullivan, Louis H
architect of: 16 Guaranty (now Prudential) Building (Buffalo NY) **18** Auditorium Building (Chicago), Wainwright Building (St Louis MO) **21** Carson Pirie Scott Store (Chicago), Stock Exchange Building (Chicago), Merchants' National Bank (Grinnell, IA), National

Farmers' Bank (Owatonna, MN)
principle: 21 "form follows function"
student: 16 Frank Lloyd Wright

Sullivan, Pat
creator/artist of: 11 Felix the Cat

Sullivan's Travels
director: 14 Preston Sturges
cast: 10 Joel McCrea **12** Veronica Lake **13** Robert Warwick **15** William Demarest

sully 4 ruin, soil, spot **5** dirty, spoil, stain **6** befoul, defame, defile, smudge **7** begrime, besmear, blemish, corrupt, pollute, tarnish **8** disgrace, dishonor **10** adulterate **11** contaminate

Sully, Thomas
born: 7 England **10** Horncastle
artwork: 13 Queen Victoria **23** The Passage of the Delaware **28** Colonel Thomas Handasyd Perkins **29** Washington Crossing the Delaware

sultan 4 king **5** ruler **7** emperor, monarch **9** sovereign

sultana 5 grape **6** raisin **7** empress **11** sultan's wife

sultry 3 hot **4** sexy **5** close, humid, muggy **6** erotic, stuffy, sweaty **7** sensual **8** stifling **10** oppressive, sweltering, voluptuous **11** provocative, suffocating

sum 4 cash, coin, jack **5** bread, bucks, dough, funds, score, tally, whole **6** amount, moolah **7** lettuce, measure **8** currency, entirety, quantity, sum total, totality **9** aggregate, summation **12** entire amount **13** amount of money

sumac 4 Rhus
varieties: 5 dwarf, lemon, scrub, sugar, swamp **6** desert, laurel, poison, smooth, velvet **7** scarlet, shining, tanner's, tobacco, wing-rib **8** fragrant, lemonade, Sicilian, staghorn, Venetian **9** elm-leaved, evergreen, Virginian **11** small-leaved **12** sweet-scented

sum and substance 4 core, crux, gist, guts, meat **5** heart **7** essence **10** brass tacks **11** nitty-gritty

Sumatra
chevrotain: 4 napu
city: 5 Medan **6** Padang **9** Palembang
country: 9 Indonesia

crop: 3 tea **6** coffee, rubber
currency: 6 rupiah
empire: 9 Srivijaya
highest point: 10 Mt Kerintji
inhabitant: 5 Batak, Malay
  11 Minangkabau
mountain range: 7 Barisan
river: 4 Musi, Siak **6** Asahan
squirrel shrew: 4 tana
strait: 5 Sunda **7** Malacca

Sumerian Mythology *see*
  19 Babylonian Mythology

**Summa Catholicae Fidei
Contra Gentiles**
  author: 13 Thomas Aquinas

summa cum laude 17 with
highest praise

Summanus
  origin: 5 Roman
  god of: 13 thunderstorms

summarily 6 at once
7 quickly **8** directly, promptly,
speedily **9** forthwith, on the
spot **11** arbitrarily, immediately, straightway **12** straightaway, with dispatch, without
delay **13** at short notice, precipitately **14** unhesitatingly
20 on the spur of the
moment

summarize 5 sum up **6** digest
7 abridge, outline **8** abstract,
compress, condense **9** capsul-
ize, epitomize, synopsize
10 abbreviate **11** concentrate
12 recapitulate

summary 4 curt **5** brief, hasty,
rapid, short, terse, token
6 apercu, digest, precis, resume, sketch, sudden, survey
7 concise, cursory, epitome,
hurried, rundown **8** abridged,
abstract, analysis, succinct, syllabus, synopsis **9** breakdown,
condensed **10** abridgment, peremptory **11** perfunctory
12 abbreviation, condensation,
short version **13** instantaneous

Summa Theologiae
  author: 13 Thomas Aquinas

summation 5 total **6** review
7 summary **8** addition **9** reckoning **19** concluding
statement

Summer and Smoke
  author: 17 Tennessee
  Williams
  director: 14 Peter Glenville
  cast: 9 Una Merkel **10** Rita
  Moreno **12** Earl Holliman
  13 Geraldine Page **14** Laurence Harvey

summer fruit
  goddess of: 5 Carpo

summerhouse 5 arbor, cabin,
kiosk **6** cabana, gazebo, pagoda **7** cottage

Summerson, Esther
  character in: 10 Bleak House
  author: 7 Dickens

Summertime
  director: 9 David Lean
  based on story by: 14 Arthur Laurents (The Time of
  the Cuckoo)
  cast: 10 Isa Miranda **13** Darren McGavin, Rossano
  Brazzi **16** Katharine
  Hepburn
  setting: 6 Venice

summery 3 hot **4** warm
5 balmy, close, humid, muggy,
sunny **6** stuffy, sultry, torrid,
vernal **8** aestival, roasting, stifling, sunshiny **9** scorching,
temperate **10** oppressive,
summerlike

summit 3 tip, top **4** acme,
apex, peak **5** crest, crown
6 apogee, climax, height, vertex, zenith **8** pinnacle **11** culmination **12** highest point
13 crowning point

summon 4 call **5** rouse
6 beckon, call on, draw on,
gather, invoke, muster, strain
7 call for, call out, command,
send for **8** activate, subpoena
9 call forth **12** call together
14 call into action, serve with
a writ

summons 4 call **8** citation,
subpoena **12** notification

summon up 4 stir **5** evoke
6 arouse, excite **7** collect, marshal, provoke **8** assemble **9** call
forth, stimulate

summum bonum 9 chief
good **11** highest good

sumptuous 4 dear, posh, rich
5 grand, plush, regal **6** costly,
deluxe, lavish, superb **7** elegant **8** splendid **9** elaborate,
expensive, luxurious **10** exorbitant, munificent **11** extravagant, magnificent, spectacular

sumptuousness 4 luxe **6** luxury **8** elegance, grandeur, richness, splendor
12 magnificence **13** expensive-
ness, luxuriousness

sum total 6 amount **8** totality
9 aggregate **11** final result

sum up 3 add **5** tally, total, tot
up **6** reckon **7** compute, count
up **9** calculate, enumerate,
summarize

sun
  god of: 2 Ra, Re **3** Sol, Utu
  5 Horus **6** Apollo, Helios
  7 Shamesh **8** Hyperion

Sun Also Rises, The
  author: 15 Ernest Hemingway

character: 10 Bill Gorton,
Jake Barnes, Robert Cohn
11 Pedro Romero **15** Lady
Brett Ashley, Michael (Mike)
Campbell

sunbathe 3 tan **4** bask **12** soak
up the sun **13** catch some
rays

Sunday
  means: 11 day of the sun
  heavenly body: 3 sun
  day of: 4 rest **7** worship
  8 blue laws
  observance: 16 Christian
  Sabbath
  French: 8 dimanche
  Italian: 8 domenica
  Spanish: 7 domingo
  German: 7 sonntag

Sunday best 6 finery **8** glad
rags **11** fine clothes **16** best
bib and tucker

Sunday Morning
  author: 14 Wallace Stevens

sunder 4 rend, rive **5** crack,
sever **6** cleave, divide **8** separate **9** tear apart **10** break in
two **11** break in half

sundown 4 dusk **6** sunset
7 evening **8** eventide, twilight
9 nightfall

Sundowners, The
  director: 13 Fred Zinnemann
  cast: 11 Deborah Kerr, Dina
  Merrill, Glynis Johns **12** Peter Ustinov **13** Robert
  Mitchum
  setting: 9 Australia

sundry 4 many **5** mixed **6** divers, motley, myriad, varied
7 diverse, several, various
8 assorted, manifold, numerous **9** different **10** dissimilar
12 multifarious **13** heterogeneous, miscellaneous

sun-filled 4 fair **5** clear, sunny
6 bright, cheery **8** cheerful
9 cloudless

sunfish 5 dwarf, perch, pigmy,
sunny **6** redear **7** lepomis,
longear, teleost **8** bluegill, sailboat **9** blackband **10** Sacramento **11** bluespotted,
centrarchid, pumpkinseed,
yellowbelly

sunflower 10 Helianthus
12 Balsamorhiza
  varieties: 4 ashy **5** giant,
  showy, stiff, swamp **6** common, desert, Oregon **7** dark-
  eye, Mexican **8** thin-leaf
  10 Maximilian **12** cucumber-
  leaf

Sunflower State
  nickname of: 6 Kansas

sunless 4 dark, dull, gray,

hazy **5** bleak, foggy, misty, murky, rainy **6** cloudy, dismal, dreary, gloomy, leaden, somber **8** overcast **9** cheerless **10** depressing

sunny 4 fair, fine **5** clear, happy, jolly, merry **6** blithe, breezy, bright, cheery, genial, jovial, joyful, joyous, sunlit **7** affable, amiable, buoyant, shining, smiling **8** cheerful, sunshiny **9** brilliant, cloudless, sparkling, unclouded **10** optimistic **12** lighthearted

sunrise 4 dawn **5** sunup **6** aurora **7** dawning **8** cockcrow, daybreak, daylight **10** break of day, crepuscule, newborn day **15** dawn's early light **16** rosy-fingered dawn

sunset 4 dusk **7** sundown **8** blue hour, eventide, gloaming, twilight **9** nightfall **10** close of day, crepuscule

Sunset Boulevard
director: **11** Billy Wilder
cast: **8** Jack Webb **9** Fred Clark **11** Hedda Hopper **12** Buster Keaton **13** Cecil B DeMille, Gloria Swanson (Norma Desmond), William Holden **16** Erich von Stroheim

Sunset State
nickname of: **6** Oregon

sunshade 3 hat **5** visor **6** awning **7** parasol, roundel **8** sombrero, umbrella **9** sunscreen

Sunshine State
nickname of: **7** Florida **9** New Mexico

sunstone
species: **8** feldspar

suntan 3 tan **5** brown **6** bronze **7** sunburn

suo jure 14 in one's own right

suo loco 14 in one's own place **19** in one's rightful place

Suomen Tasavalta *see* **7** Finland

Suomi *see* **7** Finland

sup 3 eat, sip **4** dine, feed **5** drink, feast, supra **6** absorb, supper, supply **7** consume **8** superior **10** supplement **11** superlative **13** supplementary

Supai *see* **9** Havasupai

super 4 A-one, fine **5** grand, great, prime, prize, swell **6** grade-A, superb, tip-top **7** capital **8** peerless, superior, terrific, top-notch **9** excellent, fantastic, first-rate, marvelous,

matchless, non pareil, superfine, wonderful **10** first-class, tremendous, unexcelled, world-class **11** outstanding, superlative **12** incomparable **13** extraordinary

superabound 4 teem **5** swarm **6** thrive **7** burgeon **8** be rich in, flourish, overflow

superabundance 4 glut, riot **5** flood, spate **6** deluge, excess, plenty **7** surfeit, surplus **8** overdose, overflow, pleonasm, plethora **9** avalanche **10** inundation, oversupply, redundance **11** superfluity **12** extravagance **13** overabundance **14** more than enough
French: 19 embarras de richesses

superabundant 4 lush **6** lavish **7** copious, profuse, teeming **8** swarming, thriving **9** exuberant, luxuriant **10** burgeoning **11** flourishing, overflowing

superb 4 A-one, rare, rich **5** elect, grand, regal **6** choice, costly, deluxe, golden, lordly, select, tip-top **7** elegant, stately **8** gorgeous, imposing, laudable, majestic, peerless, precious, princely, splendid, top-notch, very fine **9** admirable, excellent, expensive, exquisite, first-rate, luxurious, marvelous, matchless, priceless, sumptuous, top-drawer **10** first-class **11** crackerjack, magnificent **12** breathtaking, praiseworthy **15** of the first water

Super Bowl *see box, p. 948*

supercilious 5 proud **6** lordly, snooty, uppity **7** haughty, pompous, stuck-up **8** arrogant, prideful, snobbish **10** disdainful **11** egotistical, magisterial, overbearing, patronizing **12** vainglorious **13** condescending, high-and-mighty, self-important

superciliousness 4 airs **7** hauteur **8** snobbery **9** arrogance, pomposity **10** lordliness, snootiness **11** haughtiness **12** snobbishness **14** disdainfulness

superficial 4 slim **5** faint, outer, silly, trite **6** flimsy, hollow, myopic, slight **7** cursory, minimal, nodding, partial, passing, shallow, summary, surface **8** exterior, mindless, skin-deep **9** desultory, frivolous **10** incomplete **11** empty-headed, perfunctory **12** lacking depth, narrow-minded, on the surface, shortsighted

superficiality 6 myopia **9** frivolity **11** cursoriness, shallowness **13** desultoriness **16** narrow-mindedness, shortsightedness

superfine 4 A-one **6** choice, grade-A, superb, tip-top **8** superior, top-notch **9** excellent, extra fine, first-rate **10** first-class **11** outstanding, overrefined, superlative **13** extraordinary

superfluity 3 fat **5** extra, frill **6** excess, luxury **7** greater, surfeit, surplus **8** overflow, overmuch, plethora **11** gingerbread **12** extravagance **13** embellishment **14** superabundance

superfluous 5 extra, spare **6** excess **7** surplus **8** needless **9** excessive, redundant **10** extraneous, gratuitous, pleonastic **11** inessential, unnecessary **12** nonessential, overgenerous **13** superabundant, supernumerary **14** supererogatory

superhuman 4 epic **5** great **6** divine, heroic **7** godlike, supreme **8** superior **9** herculean, unearthly **10** miraculous, omnipotent **12** otherworldly, supermundane, supernatural, supranatural, transcendent **13** preternatural

Superi
origin: **5** Roman
collective name for: **4** gods

superintend 3 run **4** boss **6** direct, govern, manage **7** oversee **9** supervise, watch over **10** administer **12** administrate, have charge of

superintendence 6 charge **7** bossing, running **9** direction, governing **10** leadership, management, overseeing **12** jurisdiction **14** administration

superintendent 4 boss, head **5** chief **6** warden **7** foreman, headman, manager, proctor, steward **8** director, guardian, overseer **9** custodian **10** supervisor

superior 4 boss, fine **5** chief **6** better, choice, deluxe, leader, lordly, senior **7** greater, haughty, notable **8** arrogant, foremost, higher-up, peerless, snobbish **9** commander, excellent, first-rate, imperious, matchless, nonpareil, unrivaled **10** inimitable, noteworthy, preeminent, supervisor **11** exceptional, illustrious, patronizing **12** incomparable, more advanced, vainglorious

Super Bowl

1967:
  winner: **15** Green Bay Packers
  loser: **16** Kansas City Chiefs
  site: **8** Coliseum **10** Los Angeles
1968:
  winner: **15** Green Bay Packers
  loser: **14** Oakland Raiders
  site: **5** Miami **10** Orange Bowl
1969:
  winner: **11** New York Jets
  loser: **14** Baltimore Colts
  site: **5** Miami **10** Orange Bowl
1970:
  winner: **16** Kansas City Chiefs
  loser: **16** Minnesota Vikings
  site: **10** New Orleans **13** Tulane Stadium
1971:
  winner: **14** Baltimore Colts
  loser: **13** Dallas Cowboys
  site: **5** Miami **10** Orange Bowl
1972:
  winner: **13** Dallas Cowboys
  loser: **13** Miami Dolphins
  site: **10** New Orleans **13** Tulane Stadium
1973:
  winner: **13** Miami Dolphins
  loser: **18** Washington Redskins
  site: **8** Coliseum **10** Los Angeles
1974:
  winner: **13** Miami Dolphins
  loser: **16** Minnesota Vikings
  site: **7** Houston **11** Rice Stadium
1975:
  winner: **18** Pittsburgh Steelers
  loser: **16** Minnesota Vikings
  site: **10** New Orleans **13** Tulane Stadium
1976:
  winner: **18** Pittsburgh Steelers
  loser: **13** Dallas Cowboys
  site: **5** Miami **10** Orange Bowl
1977:
  winner: **14** Oakland Raiders
  loser: **16** Minnesota Vikings
  site: **8** Pasadena, Rose Bowl
1978:
  winner: **13** Dallas Cowboys
  loser: **13** Denver Broncos
  site: **9** Superdome **10** New Orleans
1979:
  winner: **18** Pittsburgh Steelers
  loser: **13** Dallas Cowboys
  site: **5** Miami **10** Orange Bowl
1980:
  winner: **18** Pittsburgh Steelers
  loser: **14** Los Angeles Rams
  site: **8** Pasadena, Rose Bowl
1981:
  winner: **14** Oakland Raiders
  loser: **18** Philadelphia Eagles
  site: **9** Superdome **10** New Orleans
1982:
  winner: **23** San Francisco Forty-Niners
  loser: **17** Cincinnati Bengals
  site: **7** Pontiac **10** Silverdome
1983:
  winner: **18** Washington Redskins
  loser: **13** Miami Dolphins
  site: **8** Pasadena, Rose Bowl
1984:
  winner: **17** Los Angeles Raiders
  loser: **18** Washington Redskins
  site: **12** Tampa Stadium
1985:
  winner: **23** San Francisco Forty-Niners
  loser: **13** Miami Dolphins
  site: **8** Palo Alto **15** Stanford Stadium
1986:
  winner: **12** Chicago Bears
  loser: **18** New England Patriots
  site: **9** Superdome **10** New Orleans
1987:
  winner: **13** New York Giants
  loser: **13** Denver Broncos
  site: **8** Pasadena, Rose Bowl
1988:
  winner: **18** Washington Redskins
  loser: **13** Denver Broncos
  site: **8** San Diego **17** Jack Murphy Stadium
1989:
  winner: **23** San Francisco Forty-Niners
  loser: **17** Cincinnati Bengals
  site: **5** Miami **16** Joe Robbie Stadium
1990:
  winner: **23** San Francisco Forty-Niners
  loser: **13** Denver Broncos
  site: **9** Superdome **10** New Orleans
1991:
  winner: **13** New York Giants
  loser: **12** Buffalo Bills
  site: **5** Tampa **12** Tampa Stadium
1992:
  winner: **18** Washington Redskins
  loser: **12** Buffalo Bills
  site: **9** Metrodome **11** Minneapolis
1993:
  winner: **13** Dallas Cowboys
  loser: **12** Buffalo Bills
  site: **8** Pasadena, Rose Bowl
1994:
  winner: **13** Dallas Cowboys
  loser: **12** Buffalo Bills
  site: **7** Atlanta **11** Georgia Dome
1995:
  winner: **23** San Francisco Forty-Niners
  loser: **16** San Diego Chargers
  site: **5** Miami **16** Joe Robbie Stadium
1996:
  winner: **13** Dallas Cowboys
  loser: **18** Pittsburgh Steelers
  site: **5** Tempe **7** Arizona **15** Sun Devil Stadium

13 condescending, distinguished, high-and-mighty
French: 13 par excellence

superlative 4 best **5** crack, prime **6** expert **7** supreme **8** foremost, greatest, peerless, superior **9** exquisite, first-rate, matchless, nonpareil, paramount, unequaled, unmatched, unrivaled **10** consummate, preeminent, surpassing **11** magnificent, unsurpassed **12** incomparable, transcendent, unparalleled **15** of the first water **17** of the highest order

superman
German: 10 Ubermensch

Superman
creator: 11 Jerry Siegel
character: 4 Lara **5** Jor-el, Kal-el **8** Eben Kent, Lois Lane, Sy Horton **9** Clark Kent **10** Jimmy Olsen, Martha Kent, Perry White
place: 7 Krypton **10** Metropolis, Smallville
nickname: 10 Man of Steel

supernatural 6 mystic, occult **7** psychic **9** spiritual, unearthly **10** miraculous, paranormal

superpatriotism 8 jingoism **10** chauvinism **11** nationalism

supersede 7 discard, replace, succeed **8** displace, set aside, supplant

supervise 4 boss, head **5** guide **6** direct, govern, handle, manage, survey **7** conduct, control, oversee **8** regulate **9** look after, watch over **10** administer

supervision 6 orders **7** control **8** guidance **9** direction **10** governance, government, management, regulation **12** surveillance **15** superintendence

supervisor 4 boss, head **5** chief **7** foreman, manager, steward **8** director, overseer **9** commander **13** administrator **14** superintendent

supper club 4 cafe **6** bistro **7** cabaret **9** nightclub, night spot

supplant 6 depose **7** replace **8** displace **9** supersede **14** take the place of

supple 5 lithe **6** limber, pliant **7** elastic, lissome, plastic, pliable **8** amenable, bendable, flexible, graceful, yielding **9** adaptable, compliant, malleable, tractable **10** submissive

supplement 5 add to, annex, extra, rider **6** extend, insert **7** adjunct, augment, codicil, section **8** addendum, addition,

appendix, increase **9** added part, corollary, extension **10** attachment, complement, postscript **12** augmentation

supplementary 5 added, extra **6** backup **7** added on, reserve **8** appended, attached, expanded, extended **9** ancillary, auxiliary, enlarging, secondary **10** additional, amplifying, augmenting **11** subordinate

suppliant 5 asker **6** beggar, cadger, seeker, suitor **7** almsman **8** claimant **9** almswoman, appellant, beseecher, entreater, mendicant **10** petitioner, supplicant **11** supplicator

supplicate 3 ask, beg **4** pray **5** plead **6** ask for **7** entreat **8** appeal to, call upon, petition

supplication 3 cry **4** plea, suit **6** appeal, orison, prayer **7** bumming, cadging, request **8** entreaty, mooching, petition **10** invocation **11** application, beseechment, imploration, imprecation, panhandling

supplies 4 gear **5** goods, items **8** material **9** equipment, foodstuff, trappings **10** provisions

supply 4 fund, give **5** cache, equip, grant, quota, stock, store, yield **6** bestow, outfit, render **7** deal out, deliver, furnish, present, provide, reserve **9** providing, provision, reservoir **10** allocation, come up with, contribute, furnishing

support 3 aid **4** base, bear, help, hold, keep, lift, pile, post, prop, stay **5** abide, boost, brace, brook, carry, favor, means, shore, stand **6** assist, back up, bear up, clinch, column, defend, endure, foster, hold up, pay for, pillar, ratify, second, succor, suffer, uphold, upkeep, verify **7** backing, bear out, bolster, comfort, confirm, defense, endorse, espouse, finance, further, keeping, nurture, shore up, sustain, warrant **8** abutment, accredit, advocacy, advocate, buttress, champion, espousal, maintain, pedestal, pilaster, sanction, strength, tolerate, vouch for **9** establish, guarantee, patronage, patronize, promotion, put up with, reinforce, stanchion, subsidize **10** assistance, livelihood, provide for, stand up for, stick up for, strengthen, sustenance, underwrite

supportable 9 endurable **10** defensible, verifiable **11** sustainable **12** demonstrable, maintainable

supporter 4 ally **6** backer, helper, patron **8** adherent, advocate, champion, defender, disciple, follower, partisan, upholder **10** benefactor, wellwisher **11** sympathizer

supposable 8 credible **9** thinkable **10** believable, imaginable **11** conceivable, perceivable

suppose 5 fancy, guess, judge, posit **6** assume, divine, gather, reckon **7** believe, imagine, presume, surmise, suspect **8** conceive, consider **9** predicate **11** hypothesize **14** take for granted

supposed 5 given **7** alleged, assumed **8** probable, putative **9** imaginary **11** conjectural, speculative, theoretical **12** hypothetical

supposition 4 idea, view **5** given, guess **6** belief, notion, theory, thesis **7** opinion, surmise **9** guesswork, postulate, suspicion **10** assumption, conjecture, hypothesis **11** predication, presumption, proposition, speculation

suppress 4 bury, curb, hide **5** check, crush, quash, quell, still **6** keep in, muffle, quench, squash, stifle, subdue **7** conceal, control, cover up, inhibit, put down, repress, silence, smother, squelch **8** hold back, keep back, overcome, restrain, restrict, snuff out, withhold **9** overpower **10** extinguish, keep secret, put an end to

suppressant 4 curb **5** brake **7** control **9** restraint

supremacy 5 power **7** mastery, primacy **10** ascendancy, domination, precedence **11** omnipotence, paramountcy, preeminence, sovereignty, superiority **13** transcendency

supreme 4 tops **5** chief, first, prime **6** ruling **7** extreme, highest, leading, perfect, topmost **8** absolute, dominant, foremost, peerless **9** matchless, nonpareil, paramount, principal, sovereign, unequaled, unlimited, unmatched, unrivaled, uppermost **10** commanding, consummate, unexcelled **11** allpowerful, superlative, unqualified, unsurpassed

Supreme Court
Chief Justices: 3 Jay (John) **4** Taft (William Howard) **5** Chase (Salmon), Stone (Harlan Fiske), Taney (Roger Brooke), Waite (Morrison), White (Edward) **6** Burger (Warren), Fuller (Melville), Hughes (Charles Evans),

Vinson (Frederick), Warren (Earl) **8** Marshall (John), Rutledge (John) **9** Ellsworth (Oliver), Rehnquist (William)
Associate Justices: 5 Black (Hugo), Story (Joseph), White (Byron) **6** Breyer (Stephen), Fortas (Abe), Holmes (Oliver Wendell), Powell (Lewis), Scalia (Antonin), Souter (David), Thomas (Clarence) **7** Brennan (William), Cardozo (Benjamin), Douglas (William O), Kennedy (Anthony), O'Connor (Sandra Day), Stevens (John), Stewart (Potter) **8** Blackmun (Harry), Brandeis (Louis), Ginsburg (Ruth Bader), Goldberg (Arthur), Marshall (Thurgood) **11** Frankfurter (Felix)
Cases: 15 Marbury v Madison **17** Gideon v Wainwright **18** McCulloch v Maryland **20** Griswold v Connecticut
abortion: **8** Roe v Wade
antitrust: **8** E C Knight **11** Standard Oil **15** Swift and Company **22** American Tobacco Company
civil rights: **9** Bakke Case **15** Plessy v Ferguson **30** Brown v Board of Education of Topeka
Japanese internment: **22** Korematsu v United States **24** Hirabayashi v United States
rights of accused: **15** Miranda v Arizona **17** Escobedo v Illinois
slavery: **13** Dred Scott Case **14** Scott v Sandford

surcease **4** quit, rest, stop **5** abate, cease, pause **7** die away, respite **8** conclude, leave off **11** come to an end, discontinue **17** come to a standstill

surcharge **3** tax **4** levy **6** excise, impost

surcingle **4** band, belt **5** girth **6** girdle **8** cincture

sure **4** fast, firm, true **5** solid, sound **6** stable, steady **7** assured, certain **8** accurate, failsafe, faithful, flawless, positive, reliable, surefire, unerring **9** confident, convinced, unfailing **10** dependable, infallible, undoubting **11** trustworthy **12** never-failing

surely **7** no doubt **8** of course, to be sure **9** assuredly, certainly, doubtless **10** by all means, definitely, for certain, infallibly, positively

sureness **6** surety **9** assurance, certainty, certitude **10** confidence **11** assuredness **12** positiveness **13** self-assurance

---

Suriname
other name: 7 Surinam **11** Dutch Guiana
capital/largest city: 10 Paramaribo
others: 4 Albina **7** Totness **9** Groningen **10** Brokopondo, Onverwacht **13** Nieuw Nickerie **14** Nieuw Amsterdam
measure: 7 ketting
monetary unit: 4 cent **7** guilder
lake: 14 Van Blommestein
mountain: 4 Emma **6** Kayser, Oranje **10** Tumuc-Humac, Wilhelmina **13** Eilerts Il Haan, Van Ach Van Wyck **15** Guiana Highlands
highest point: 10 Julianatop
river: 6 Maroni **7** Surinam **8** Nickerie, Suriname **9** Coppename **10** Courantijn, Courantyne, Tapanahoni
ocean: 8 Atlantic
physical feature:
  falls: **7** Kaiteur
people: 4 Boni, Bush, Trio **5** Djuka, Dutch **6** Creole, Wayana **7** African, Chinese **10** Amerindian, Boschneger, West Indian **11** Asian Indian
  settler: **22** Lord Willoughby of Parham
language: 5 Carib, Dutch, Hindi **6** Arawak **7** English **8** Javanese, Taki-Taki **10** Hindustani **11** Sranan Tongo **12** Sranang Tongo
religion: 5 Hindu, Islam **10** Protestant **13** Roman Catholic
feature:
  canoe: **6** corial
  clothing: **4** sari **5** dhoti **6** kamisa, sarong **10** koto-missie
  hat: **3** fez
  hut: **5** benab
  scarf: **9** selendong
  tree: **4** dali, lana, mora **5** dalli, genip, icica **7** acuyari, quassia **9** bethabara
food:
  drink: **7** paiwari

---

sure thing **4** fact **5** cinch **7** reality, sure bet **9** actuality, certainty **13** inevitability

surety **4** bail, bond **8** sureness **9** certainty, certitude, guarantee **10** confidence **12** positiveness

surface **3** top **4** coat, face, skin **5** crust, shell **6** facade, finish, veneer **7** coating, outside **8** covering, exterior **11** superficies

surfeit **4** cloy, glut, sate **5** gorge, stuff **6** excess **7** satiate, satisfy, surplus **8** overmuch, plethora **9** plenitude, profusion, repletion, satiation **10** oversupply, surplusage

surfeited **4** full **5** sated **6** gorged **7** glutted, replete, stuffed **8** overfull, satiated **9** satisfied

surge **4** rush, wave **5** flood, swell **7** torrent

Suriname *see box*

surliness **8** ill humor, rudeness **9** bad temper **11** discourtesy, grouchiness **12** irascibility

surly **4** rude, sour **5** cross, gruff, harsh, testy **6** abrupt, crusty, grumpy, sullen, touchy **7** bearish, crabbed, grouchy, hostile, peevish, uncivil, waspish **8** choleric, churlish, insolent, petulant, snappish, snarling **9** irascible, splenetic, unamiable **10** ill-humored, ill-natured, unfriendly **11** bad-tempered **12** discourteous

surmise **4** deem, idea **5** guess, infer, judge, opine, posit, think **6** belief, notion **7** believe, imagine, opinion, presume, suppose, suspect, thought **8** conclude, consider, theorize **9** suspicion **10** assumption, conjecture, hypothesis, presuppose **11** hypothesize, presumption, speculation, supposition **13** shot in the dark

surmount **3** top **4** best **5** clear, climb, scale, worst **6** defeat, master **7** conquer, get over **8** overcome, vanquish **11** prevail over, triumph over

surpass **3** top **4** beat, best **5** excel, outdo **6** exceed, outrun

7 eclipse **8** go beyond, outclass, outshine, outstrip, override **9** rise above, transcend **10** overshadow **11** go one better, leave behind, outdistance, triumph over **12** be better than, be superior to

surplus 4 glut **5** extra **6** excess **7** overage, surfeit **8** leftover, overflow, plethora, residual **10** oversupply, surplusage **11** superfluity, superfluous

surprise 4 stun **5** amaze, shock **6** ambush, wonder **7** astound, nonplus, set upon, stagger, startle, stupefy **8** astonish, confound, discover, dumfound, fall upon **9** amazement, bombshell, burst in on, dumbfound, take aback **10** defy belief, pounce upon, revelation, wonderment

surprise attack
  French: 10 coup de main

surrender 4 cede **5** forgo, let go, waive, yield **6** accede, forego, give up, render, submit, vacate **7** abandon, concede, forsake **8** delivery, forgoing, give over, giving up, hand over, part with, renounce, turn over, yielding **9** deliver up, foregoing **10** capitulate, relinquish, submission **11** lay down arms

surreptitious 6 covert, hidden, secret, veiled **7** furtive **8** hush-hush, stealthy **9** concealed, secretive **10** undercover **11** clandestine

surrogate 6 acting, deputy **7** interim, stand-in **9** temporary **10** substitute **11** provisional

surround 4 belt, ring **5** hedge, hem in **6** circle, enfold, engird, girdle, shut in **7** close in, compass, enclose, envelop, fence in, hedge in **8** encircle **9** encompass **12** circumscribe

surrounding area 7 suburbs **8** environs, vicinity **9** outskirts, precincts

surroundings 5 scene **6** milieu **7** habitat, setting **8** ambience, environs **10** atmosphere, conditions **11** environment **13** circumstances
  French: 11 mise en scene

Surt
  origin: 12 Scandinavian
  ruler of: 10 Muspelheim

surveillance 5 vigil, watch **8** scrutiny, trailing **11** observation **13** eavesdropping

survey 4 plot, poll, scan **5** gauge, graph, plumb, probe, scout, study **6** fathom, review **7** canvass, delimit, examine, inspect, measure, observe

8 analysis, block out, consider, look over, overview **10** scrutinize **11** contemplate, reconnoiter **12** pass in review **13** investigation

survival 5 relic **6** living **7** atavism, vestige **8** hangover **9** carry-over, throwback **11** subsistence **12** continuation, keeping alive

survive 4 last **5** abide, exist **6** endure, hang on, live on **7** hold out, outlast, outlive, persist, prevail, subsist **8** be extant, continue **9** keep alive **11** live through

surviving 6 extant **7** abiding, lasting **8** enduring, existent, existing, living on **9** hanging on, outliving, to be found **10** continuing, holding out, outlasting, persistent, persisting, subsisting **11** in existence **13** living through

Susanna
  husband: 6 Joakim
  accused of: 8 adultery
  saved by: 6 Daniel

susceptible 4 open **5** prone **7** alive to, subject **8** liable to, sensible **9** sensitive **10** disposed to, responsive, vulnerable **11** conducive to, receptive to, sensitive to, sympathetic

suspect 5 doubt, fancy, guess, judge, opine, posit, think **7** believe, imagine, presume, suppose, surmise **8** distrust, misdoubt, mistrust, question, theorize **9** speculate **10** conjecture **11** hypothesize, wonder about **14** alleged culprit, be suspicious of **19** have one's doubts about

suspend 4 halt, hang, quit, stay, stop **5** cease, check, defer, delay, sling, swing, table **6** append, arrest, dangle, put off, shelve **7** reserve **8** break off, cut short, leave off, postpone, withhold **9** interrupt, stop short **10** put an end to **11** discontinue **12** bring to a stop **18** bring to a standstill

suspenders 6 braces, straps **7** gallows, garters, hangers **8** elastics, galluses **10** supporters

suspense 7 anxiety, tension **8** edginess **9** curiosity **10** indecision **11** expectation, incertitude, uncertainty **12** anticipation **15** indetermination

suspenseful 7 anxious **8** dramatic, exciting **9** climactic, uncertain

suspension 4 stay **5** pause **6** hiatus, recess **7** tabling **8** abey-

ance, deferral **12** postponement **14** discontinuance

suspicion 4 idea **5** guess, hunch **6** notion **7** feeling, surmise **8** distrust, mistrust **10** conjecture, hypothesis **11** supposition

suspicious 4 wary **5** shady **7** dubious, suspect **8** doubtful, doubting, slippery **9** ambiguous **10** untrusting **11** distrustful, incredulous, mistrustful, open to doubt **12** disbelieving, questionable **13** untrustworthy

sustain 4 bear, feed, prop **5** abide, brave, brook, stand **6** bear up, endure, hold up, keep up, suffer, uphold **7** nourish, nurture, prolong, support, undergo **8** maintain, protract, tolerate, underpin **9** keep alive, withstand **10** experience

sustenance 4 food, gear **5** bread, means **6** living **7** aliment, support **9** provender **10** provisions **11** maintenance, nourishment, subsistence
  heaven-sent: 5 manna

sustineo alas 16 I sustain the wings
  motto of: 10 US Air Force

Suva
  capital of: 4 Fiji

svelte 4 fine, lean, neat, slim, thin, trim **5** lithe, spare **7** elegant, lissome, shapely, slender, willowy **8** graceful **9** sylphlike

Svengali
  character in: 6 Trilby
  author: 9 Du Maurier

swab 3 dab, mop **4** daub, lout, wipe **5** clean, cloth, patch, scrub **6** cotton, sponge **7** cleanse **8** specimen
  brand name: 4 Q-tip

swagger 5 strut, sweep **6** parade, sashay, stride **7** saunter **11** swashbuckle

swaggerer 6 gascon **7** boaster, bragger **8** blowhard, braggart, strutter **11** braggadocio

swain 4 beau **6** fellow, suitor **7** admirer, gallant **8** cavalier, young man **9** boyfriend **10** sweetheart

swallow 3 bit, nip, sip **4** down, gulp, swig **5** drink, quaff, swill, taste **6** credit, devour, gobble, guzzle, hold in, imbibe, ingest, tipple **7** believe, fall for, repress **8** gulp down, hold back, keep back, mouthful, suppress, withhold

swallow up 5 drown, eat up, swamp **6** absorb, engulf **7** consume, envelop **8** inundate **9** overwhelm **10** assimilate

swallow words 6 mumble, mutter

swamp 3 bog, fen **4** fill, mire, moor, ooze, quag, sink, slew, slue **5** bayou, beset, flood, marsh, swale **6** deluge, engulf, morass, slough **7** besiege, bottoms, envelop **8** inundate, quagmire, submerge, wash over **9** everglade, marshland, overwhelm, snow under, swallow up

swamped 7 deluged, flooded, glutted, overrun **9** inundated **11** overwhelmed

Swan
constellation of: **6** Cygnus

swan
young: **6** cygnet
group of: **4** bevy

swank 4 airs **5** ritzy **6** la-di-da, snooty, swanky **9** high-class, top-drawer **11** pretensions, pretentious **12** affectations, ostentatious **15** pretentiousness **16** superciliousness

swanky 4 chic, posh, rich **5** fancy, grand, jazzy, plush, ritzy, sharp, showy, smart, swank **6** flashy, snazzy, spiffy, sporty **7** dashing, elegant, splashy, stylish **9** sumptuous **11** fashionable

Swan Lake
composer: **11** Tchaikovsky

Swanson, Gloria
real name: **25** Gloria Josephine Mae Swenson
born: **9** Chicago IL
husband: **12** Wallace Beery
roles: **13** Sadie Thompson, The Trespasser **15** Sunset Boulevard

swap 5 trade **6** barter, dicker, switch **7** bargain **8** exchange **11** give and take

sward 3 sod **4** lawn, rind, skin, turf **5** grass

swarm 4 herd, host, mass, rush, teem **5** cloud, crowd, drove, flock, horde, press, surge **6** abound, legion, myriad, stream, throng **7** cluster, overrun **8** stampede **9** multitude

swarthy 4 dark **5** dusky, swart, tawny **6** brunet **8** brunette **11** dark-skinned **12** brown-colored, brown-skinned, olive-skinned **14** dark-complected **16** dark-complexioned

swashbuckler 9 buccaneer, daredevil **10** adventurer

swashbuckling 4 bold **7** dash-ing **8** boasting **9** audacious, daredevil

swat 3 hit, tap **4** bash, belt, slam, slap, slug, sock **5** clout, knock, smack, smite, whack **6** buffet, strike, thwack, wallop **7** clobber

swathe 4 bind, wrap **5** cloak, cover **6** encase, enfold, enwrap **7** envelop, sheathe, swaddle

sway 4 bend, grip, hold, lead, list, move, reel, rock, roll, rule, spur, vary, wave **5** alter, clout, impel, power, reign, rouse, shift, swing, waver **6** change, domain, incite, induce, prompt, swerve, totter, waving, wobble **7** command, control, dispose, mastery, stagger, swaying **8** hesitate, iron hand, motivate, persuade, swinging, to-and-fro, undulate **9** authority, direction, encourage, fluctuate, influence, oscillate, pendulate, pulsation, stimulate, vacillate **10** domination, government, predispose, suzerainty, undulation **11** fluctuation, oscillation **12** back and forth, dictatorship, jurisdiction, manipulation

Swaziland *see box*

swear 3 vow **4** aver, avow, cuss **5** curse, vouch **6** adjure, assert, attest, pledge **7** certify, promise, warrant **9** blaspheme **10** take an oath, utter oaths **11** bear witness

swear by 7 believe, count on **9** believe in **10** put faith in

sweat 4 ooze, toil **5** exude, worry **6** effort **7** agonize **8** drudgery, hard work, perspire **9** exudation **12** perspiration

sweaty 3 wet **6** clammy, sticky **10** perspiring

Sweden *see box*

Swedish Punch
type: **7** liqueur
origin: **6** Sweden
base: **3** rum
with gin: **5** Biffy
with vermouth: **9** Grand Slam

Sweeney Among the Nightingales
author: **7** T S Eliot

sweep 3 arc, fly **4** dart, dash, race, rush, scud, tear, zoom **5** hurry, spell, swing, swish, swoop, whisk **6** charge, gather, scurry, stroke **7** stretch **8** distance

sweeping 5 broad **7** blanket, radical **9** extensive, out-and-out, wholesale **10** exhaustive, large-scale, widespread **11** far-reaching, wide-ranging **12** all-inclusive **13** comprehensive, thoroughgoing

sweepings 4 dirt, dust **6** refuse

sweep off one's feet 7 enchant **8** bedazzle **9** captivate, overpower, overwhelm

---

Swaziland
capital/largest city: **7** Mbabane
others: **5** Bunya, Hluti, Mpaka, Nsoko, Stegi **6** Gollel, Mhlume **7** Big Bend, Lobamba, Manzini **8** Havelock, Malkerns **9** Geodgegun, Hlatikulu, Mankaiana, Mankayana, Nhlangano, Pigg's Peak, Rocklands
government: **22** constitutional monarchy
head of state: **4** king
monetary unit: **4** rand **9** lilangeni
mountain: **8** Highveld **11** Drakensberg
highest point: **7** Emlembe
river: **5** Usutu **6** Komati, Lomati **8** Mhlatuze, Ngwavuma, Umbeluzi, Umbuluzi
physical feature:
  forest: **5** Usutu
  plateau: **7** Lebombo, Lubombo
people: **5** Asian, Bantu, Swazi **11** Eurafricans
  king: **3** Kbe **5** Nyama **6** Mswati **7** Sobhuza
  prince: **6** Sozisa
language: **5** Ngumi **7** English, Siswati **9** Afrikaans **10** Portuguese
religion: **7** animism **10** Protestant **13** Roman Catholic
feature:
  bride payment: **6** lobolo
  god: **14** Mkhulumngcandi
  ritual dance: **7** Incwala

Sweden

other name: 7 Sverige

capital/largest city: 9 Stockholm

others: 4 Lund, Umea **5** Boden, Boras, Edane, Falun, Gavle, Lulea, Malmo, Pitea, Visby **6** Arvika, Kiruna, Orebro **7** Uppsala **8** Goteborg, Jokkmokk, Vasteras **9** Jonkoping, Linkoping, Sundsvall **10** Eskilstuna, Gottenburg, Norrkoping, Skelleftea **11** Halsingborg

school: 4 Lund **7** Uppsala **8** Goteborg **9** Stockholm

division: 3 Lan **4** Laen **5** Skane **6** Kalmar, Orebro **7** Dalarna, Gotland, Lapland **8** Alvsborg, Blekinge, Elfsborg, Gotaland, Jamtland, Malmohus, Norrland, Svealand

government: 22 constitutional monarchy
   legislature: **7** Riksdag

head of state: 4 king

measure: 3 aln, fot, ref **4** alar, amar, famn, kapp, last, stop **5** carat, foder, kanna, linje, nymil, spann **6** fathom, jumfru **7** oxhuvud, tunland **8** fjarding, koltunna, tunnland

monetary unit: 3 ore **5** krona, krone **7** carolin **8** skilling **9** rigsdaler

weight: 3 ass, lod **4** last, mark, sten **5** carat **6** nylast **7** centner, lispund **8** skalpund, skeppund **9** shippound

island: 5 Oland **7** Gotland

lake: 4 Ster **5** Asnen, Malar, Silja, Vaner **6** Vanern, Vetter, Wenner **7** Hielmar, Malaren, Vattern **8** Dalalven **9** Hjalmaren

mountain: 4 Sarv **5** Ammar **6** Helags, Kjolen, Ovniks, Sarjek **7** Kjollen

highest point: 5 Kebne **10** Kebnekaise

river: 3 Dal **4** Gota, Klar, Lule, Pite, Umea **5** Indal, Kalix, Lulea, Pitea, Ranea, Torne **6** Lainio, Muonio **7** Ljusnan **8** Angerman

sea: 6 Baltic **8** Atlantic

physical feature:
   canal: **4** Gota
   gulf: **7** Bothnia
   sound: **6** Kalmar
   strait: **7** Oresund **8** Kattegat **9** Skagerrak

people: 4 Lapp **5** Norse, Swede **6** Viking
   actress: **9** Liv Ullman **10** Greta Garbo **13** Ingrid Bergman
   astronomer: **7** Celsius **8** Angstrom
   author: **8** Lagerlof **10** Lagerkvist, Strindberg
   diplomat: **12** Hammarskjold
   director: **13** Ingmar Bergman **14** Arne Sucksdorff
   inventor: **5** Nobel
   king: **4** Vosa, Wasa **5** Oscar **6** Gustav **8** Gustavus **10** Carl Gustav **12** Gustav Adolph **13** Charles Gustav **22** Jean Baptiste Bernadotte
   philosopher/scientist: **10** Swedenborg
   queen: **9** Christina
   scientist: **8** Linnaeus

language: 4 Lapp **7** Swedish

religion: 19 Evangelical Lutheran

place:
   castle: **9** Gripsholm
   center of Stockholm: **11** Gamla Staden
   park: **7** Skansen **12** Millesgarden
   theater: **18** Drottningholm Court
   walled city: **5** Visby

food: 11 smorgasbord
   cheese: **7** fontina **8** jarlberg **9** jarlsberg
   dish: **10** kottbullar
   drink: **5** glogg **7** aquavit

---

sweet 4 dear, kind, nice **5** candy, fresh **6** dulcet, mellow, smooth, sugary **7** amiable, cloying, darling, dessert, lovable, nonsalt, not salt, tuneful **8** fragrant, pleasant, pleasing **9** agreeable, melodious, sweetmeat, wholesome **10** attractive, confection, euphonious, saccharine **11** good-natured, mellifluous, silvertoned, sympathetic **12** nonfermented

Sweet Bird of Youth
   director: 13 Richard Brooks
   based on play by: 17 Tennessee Williams
   cast: 8 Ed Begley **10** Paul Newman **13** Geraldine Page, Shirley Knight **17** Madeleine Sherwood
   Oscar for: 15 supporting actor (Begley)

sweetheart 4 beau, dear, love **5** flame, honey, lover, swain **6** fiance, old man, steady, suitor **7** beloved, darling, fiancee, old lady **8** ladylove, mistress, true love **9** boyfriend, inamorata, valentine **10** girlfriend, lady friend **15** gentleman friend
   French: 6 cherie

sweet life
   Italian: 9 dolce vita

Sweet Mama Stringbean
   nickname of: 11 Ethel Waters

sweetmeats 5 candy **6** sweets **7** bonbons **10** sugar candy **11** confections **13** confectionery

sweet-natured 5 sweet **6** benign, gentle, kindly **7** likable, lovable **8** pleasant **13** compassionate

sweetness
   French: 7 douceur

sweet roll 3 bun **6** Danish **7** cruller **8** doughnut **10** coffee cake **11** cinnamon bun

sweets 5 candy **7** goodies **8** desserts **10** sugar candy, sweetmeats **11** confections **13** confectionery

sweet-scented 8 aromatic, fragrant, perfumed, redolent

sweet-smelling 5 spicy **7** scented **8** aromatic, fragrant, perfumed, redolent **9** odiferous

sweet talk 6 cajole, praise **7** blarney, flatter **8** cajolery, flattery, soft soap **10** compliment **11** endearments, loving words **13** blandishments **14** fond utterances

Sweetwater
nickname of: **16** Nathaniel Clifton

sweet words 7 blarney **8** flattery, soft soap **9** sweet talk **12** honeyed words

swell 3 fop, wax **4** A-one, fine, good, grow, okay, puff, rise, wave **5** bloat, bulge, dandy, great, heave, mount, super, surge, throb, widen **6** billow, blow up, comber, expand, extend, fatten, puff up **7** amplify, breaker, burgeon, distend, inflate, stretch, thicken **8** fabulous, heighten, increase, lengthen, splendid, terrific **9** excellent, first-rate, intensify, marvelous, spread out **10** delightful, first-class, tremendous, undulation **11** pleasurable **12** clotheshorse, fashion plate, smart dresser

swell-headed 8 egoistic, puffed up **9** conceited **10** egoistical **11** egotistical **12** vainglorious **13** self-important

swelling 4 bump, lump **5** bulge, swell **8** dilation **9** puffiness **10** distension **11** enlargement **12** protuberance

swell out 5 bloat, bulge **6** billow, expand **7** distend, inflate, puff out

swelter 3 fry **4** boil, cook **5** be hot, broil, sweat **8** languish, perspire

sweltering 3 hot **5** humid, muggy **6** sultry, torrid **7** burning **8** sweating **10** oppressive, perspiring

sweltry 3 hot **4** dank **5** humid, muggy **6** baking, clammy, steamy, sticky, sultry, torrid **7** boiling **8** broiling, roasting, sizzling, stifling **9** scorching **10** blistering **11** suffocating

Swenson, Gloria Josephine Mae
real name of: **13** Gloria Swanson

Swept Away
subtitle: **38** by an unusual destiny in the blue sea of August
director: **14** Lina Wertmuller
cast: **16** Mariangela Melato **17** Giancarlo Giannini

swerve 3 shy, yaw **4** tack, turn, veer **5** avert, dodge, sheer, shift, stray **6** careen, change **7** deviate, digress, diverge **9** turn aside

swift 4 fast **5** brisk, fleet, hasty, quick, rapid **6** abrupt, flying, prompt, speedy **8** headlong **9** immediate **11** expeditious, precipitate

Swift, Jonathan
author of: **11** A Tale of a Tub **15** A Modest Proposal **16** Battle of the Books, Gulliver's Travels
fictional places: **6** Laputa **8** Lilliput **11** Brobdingnag
character: **6** Yahoos **10** Houyhnhnms **14** Lemuel Gulliver

swiftness 5 haste, speed **8** alacrity, celerity, dispatch, rapidity **9** quickness

swill 4 mash, slop, swig **5** quaff, waste **6** guzzle, refuse, scraps, soak up, tipple **7** garbage **8** chugalug, gulp down, leavings

swimming
athlete: **9** Diana Nyad, John Naber, Mark Spitz **10** Dawn Fraser, Kim Linehan, Linda Jezek **11** Claudia Kolb, Debbie Meyer, John Hencken **12** Brian Goodell, Bruce Furniss, Greg Louganis, John Kinsella **13** Jim Montgomery, Kornelia Ender, Michael Burton, Tracy Caulkens **14** Charles Hickcox, Duke Kahanamoku, Esther Williams, Gertrude Ederle **15** Cynthia Woodhead **16** Shirley Babashoff **17** Johnny Weissmuller

Swinburne, Algernon Charles
author of: **16** Hymn to Perserpine **17** Atalanta in Calydon **18** Songs Before Sunrise

swindle 2 do **3** con, gyp **4** bilk, dupe, gull, hoax, rook **5** cheat, cozen, fraud, mulct, steal, trick **6** delude, fleece, racket, rip-off **7** con game, deceive, defraud **8** embezzle, hoodwink **9** bamboozle, defalcate **12** embezzlement **14** confidence game

swindler 3 gyp **5** cheat, crook, faker, fraud **6** con man **7** sharper **8** chiseler, deceiver **9** charlatan, embezzler **10** mountebank **12** rip-off artist

swine 3 cad, cur, rat **4** pigs **5** beast, brute **6** animal
group of: **5** drift **7** sounder

Swineherd, The
author: **21** Hans Christian Andersen

swing 4 drop, hang, loop, move, rein, rock, sway, turn **5** pivot, rally, scope, sweep, whirl **6** dangle, decide, handle, manage, rotate, seesaw, stroke, wangle **7** compass, extract, freedom, inveigh, liberty, license, listing, pull off, rocking, rolling, suspend, swaying **8** maneuver, pitching, undulate **9** determine, influence, oscillate **10** accomplish, manipulate **11** be suspended, oscillation

Swing Time
director: **13** George Stevens
cast: **9** Eric Blore **11** Fred Astaire, Victor Moore **12** Betty Furness, Ginger Rogers **14** Helen Broderick
score: **10** Jerome Kern **13** Dorothy Fields
Oscar for: **4** song
song: **12** A Fine Romance **14** Pick Yourself Up **20** The Way You Look Tonight

swirl 4 bowl, eddy, reel, roll, spin, swim, turn **5** churn, twirl, twist, wheel, whirl **6** gyrate, rotate **7** revolve

Swiss Family Robinson
director: **10** Ken Annakin
cast: **9** John Mills **10** Janet Munro **14** Dorothy McGuire, James MacArthur, Sessue Hayakawa
author: **16** Johann Rudolf Wyss
character: **13** Emily Montrose
Robinson family: **4** Jack **5** Fritz **6** Ernest **7** Francis

switch 3 box, rod, tan **4** cane, jerk, lash, move, whip **5** birch, lever, shift, shunt, stick, swing, trade, whisk **6** button, change, handle **8** exchange **9** sidetrack **11** alternation

Switzerland *see box*

Swiveller, Dick
character in: **19** The Old Curiosity Shop
author: **7** Dickens

swollen 5 puffy **7** bloated, bulging, swelled **8** inflated, puffed-up **9** distended

swoon 5 faint **8** collapse, keel over **13** fall prostrate **17** become unconscious

swoop 4 dive, drop, rush **5** pitch, sweep **6** plunge, pounce, spring **7** descend, plummet **8** nose-dive, swooping **9** sweep down **12** rush headlong

sword 4 epee, foil **5** blade, saber, steel **6** rapier **7** cutlass **8** scimitar **10** broadsword

sybarite 8 hedonist **10** sensualist, voluptuary

sybaritic 4 rich **6** lavish **7** sensual **9** dissolute, epicurean, luxurious **10** dissipated, hedonistic, voluptuous **12** luxuryloving, pleasure-bent **13** self-

Switzerland
   capital: **4** Bern
   largest city: **6** Zurich
   others: **3** Zug **4** Bale, Bern, Biel, Brig, Chur, Nyon, Sion, Thun **5** Basel, Basle, Berne, Coire,
    Surat, Vevey **6** Geneva, Geneve, Glarus, Lugano, Sarnen, Schwyz **7** Altdorf, Fyzabad, Herisau,
    Locarno, Lucerne, Luzerne, Zermatt **8** Lausanne, Montreux, St Moritz **9** Neuchatel, Solo-
    thurn **10** Bellinzona, Interlaken, Winterthur **12** Schaffhausen
   school: **4** Bern **5** Basel **8** Catholic, Lausanne **28** Federal Institute of Technology
   division: **3** Uri, Zug **4** Bern, Chur, Nyon, Vaud **5** Aarau, Basel, Basle, Berne, Sankt, Waadt
    6 Aargau, canton, Gallen, Geneva, Geneve, Glaris, Glarus, Luzern, Obwald, Schwyz, St Gall,
    Tessin, Ticino, Valais, Wallis, Zurich **7** Atldorf, Grisons, Lucerne, Nidwald, Thurgau **8** Fri-
    bourg, Obwalden, St Gallen **9** Appenzell, Neuchatel, Neuenberg, Solothurn **10** Graubunden
    11 Unterwalden **12** Schaffhausen
   measure: **3** imi, pot **4** aune, ·fuss, muid, pied, zoll **5** lieue, linie, maass, pouce, staab, toise
    6 perche, strich **7** klafter, viertel **9** quarteron **10** holzlafter **11** holzklafter
   monetary unit: **5** franc, rappe **6** hallar, rappen **7** centime, duplone **8** baetzner
   weight: **4** fund **5** pfund **7** centner, quintal **12** zugthierlast
   lake: **3** Uri, Zug **4** Biel, Thon, Thun **5** Ageri, Leman, Morat **6** Bienne, Brienz, Geneva, Lugano,
    Sarnen, Wallen, Zurich **7** Hallwil, Lucerne, Lungern **8** Maggiore, Viervald **9** Bielersee, Con-
    stance, Neuchatel, Sarnersee, Thunersee
   mountain: **3** Dom **4** Alps, Jura, Rigi, Rosa, Todi **5** Adula, Blanc, Cenis, Eiger, Genis, Karpf,
    Righi **6** Linard, Pizela, Sentis **7** Bernina, Beverin, Grimsel, Pilatus, Rotondo **8** Balmhorn,
    Jungfrau **9** Weisshorn **10** Diablerets, Matterhorn, St Gotthard, Wetterhorn **11** Burgenstock
    12 Dufourspitze **13** Rheinwaldhorn **14** Finsteraarhorn
    mountain pass: **5** Cenis, Furka, Gemmi **6** Albula, Kinzig, Maloja, Usteri **7** Bernina, Brenner,
     Grimsel, Simplon, Splugen **8** Lotschen **10** St Gotthard
   highest point: **12** Dufourspitze
   river: **2** Po **3** Aar, Inn **4** Aare, Arve, Thur, Toss **5** Broye, Doubs, Linth, Reuss, Rhine, Rhone,
    Saane **6** Limmat, Maggia, Safane, Sarine, Ticino **8** Engadine, Pratigau
   physical feature:
    glacier: **5** Rhone
    plateau: **5** Swiss
   people: **5** Swiss
    artist: **4** Klee
    author: **5** Hesse, Spyri **6** Keller **8** Gotthelf, Rousseau **10** Durrenmatt
    educational reformer: **10** Pestalozzi
    hero: **4** Tell
    psychologist: **4** Jung **6** Piaget
    religious leader: **6** Calvin **7** Zwingli
    scientist: **9** Bernoulli
   language: **5** Ladin **6** French, German **7** Italian **8** Romansch **14** Switzerdeutsch
   religion: **9** Calvinism **10** Protestant **13** Roman Catholic
   place:
    castle: **7** Chillon
    fountain: **7** Jet d'Eau
    playhouse: **6** Zurich
    resort: **5** Arosa, Davos **6** Gstaad **7** Zermatt **8** St Moritz **9** Schwagalp **10** Interlaken
    street: **14** Bahnhofstrasse
    tower: **5** Clock
   feature:
    animal: **4** ibex **7** chamois
    flower: **9** edelweiss
    pageant: **9** Alpenfest
   food:
    cheese: **6** bagnes, sbrinz **7** Gruyere **10** Emmentaler **11** Appenzeller
    dish: **5** rosti **6** fondue **8** raclette **11** grisons beef **14** bundnerfleisch
    drink: **11** cheri-suisse **14** marmot-chocolat

indulgent 14 pleasure-loving
15 pleasure-seeking

Sycamire 12 Biblical tree

sycamore 8 Platanus **18** Acer
pseudoplatanus
  varieties: **7** eastern
  8 Egyptian

Sychaeus
  also: **7** Acerbas
  priest of: **8** Hercules

wife: 4 Dido
  brother-in-law: **9** Pygmalion
  murdered by: **9** Pygmalion

sycophant 4 tool **5** slave,
toady **6** fawner, flunky, jackal,
lackey, puppet, stooge, yes-
man **7** cat's-paw **8** hanger-on,
parasite, truckler **9** flatterer
10 bootlicker **11** lickspittle,
rubber stamp **13** apple-
polisher

Sydney
  bay: **5** Walsh **11** Rushcutter's
  13 Woolloomooloo
  capital of: **13** New South
  Wales
  cove: **4** Farm
  founder: **7** Phillip
  harbor: **7** Darling **11** Port
  Jackson
  island: **4** Goat **6** Garden
  landmark: **10** Opera House
  11 Wynyard Park **13** Har-

bour Bridge **14** Fitzroy Gardens **15** Mitchell Library **16** Australian Museum, Hyde Park Barracks, Saint James Church **18** Rushcutter's Bay Park **21** Royal Botanical Gardens
river: **10** Parramatta
university: **9** Macquarie **13** New South Wales

Syleus
position: **4** king
killed by: **8** Hercules

sylvan **5** bushy, leafy, woody **6** wooded, woodsy **8** arcadian, forested, timbered, woodland **9** luxuriant, overgrown **10** forestlike

Sylvanus *see* **8** Silvanus

Sylvia
character in: **20** Two Gentlemen of Verona
author: **11** Shakespeare

Symaethis
form: **5** nymph
location: **3** sea
mother of: **4** Aeis

symbol **4** mark, sign **5** badge, token **6** emblem, figure, signal **10** indication **14** representation **15** exemplification

symbolize **4** mean **5** imply **6** denote, embody, symbol **7** betoken, connote, express, signify **8** stand for **9** emblemize, exemplify, personify, represent, signalize **10** allegorize **11** emblematize

symmetrical **7** orderly, regular **8** balanced **9** congruent **12** well-balanced **16** well-proportioned

symmetry **4** form **5** order **7** balance, harmony **9** congruity **10** conformity, regularity **11** equilibrium, orderliness, parallelism, shapeliness **15** proportionality

sympathetic **6** benign, humane, kindly **7** feeling, pitying **8** friendly, merciful **9** agreeable, approving, benignant, sensitive **10** benevolent, comforting **11** softhearted, warmhearted **12** sympathizing, well-disposed **13** commiserative, compassionate, tenderhearted, understanding

sympathize **4** back, pity, side **5** agree, favor **7** approve, feel for, go along, support **8** sanction **9** empathize **10** appreciate, be in accord. be sorry for **11** condole with, have pity for, stand behind

sympathy **4** pity **5** amity, favor, grief **6** accord, regard, sorrow **7** concern, concert,

concord, empathy, feeling, harmony, rapport, support **8** advocacy, affinity, approval, sanction **9** agreement, communion, patronage, unanimity **10** compassion, consonance, fellowship, friendship, tenderness **11** well-wishing **12** congeniality, partisanship **13** commiseration, consanguinity, fellow feeling, understanding

Symplegades
form: **5** rocks
location: **8** Bosporus **9** Euxine Sea
characteristic: **8** clashing, dark-blue

symposium **5** forum, synod **6** debate, parley, powwow **7** meeting **8** colloquy, con-

gress **10** conference, discussion, round table **12** deliberation **15** panel discussion

Symposium
author: **5** Plato
character: **7** Agathon **8** Phaedrus, Socrates **9** Pausanias **10** Alcibiades **11** Aristodemus **12** Aristophanes

symptom **4** mark, sign **5** token **6** signal **7** earmark, warning **8** evidence, giveaway **10** indication **15** prognostication

synagogue
Yiddish: **4** shul **5** schul

synchronal **11** concomitant, synchronous **12** contemporary, simultaneous

---

Syria
other name: **4** Aram
capital/largest city: **8** Damascus
others: **4** Hama, Homs, Nawa **5** Busra, Calno, Derra, Emesa, Halab, Hamah, Idlib, Jerud, Raqqa **6** Aleppo, Calneh, Dumeir, Fajami, Tadmor, Ugarit **7** Antioch, Latakia, Palmyra **8** Seleucia **9** Ghabaghib
school: **6** Aleppo, Syrian **11** Arab Academy
measure: **5** makuk **6** garava
monetary unit: **4** lira **5** pound **6** talent **7** piaster
weight: **4** cola **5** artal, ratel **6** talent
lake: **5** Merom **7** Djeboid **8** Tiberias
mountain: **6** Carmel **7** Alawite, Libanus **10** Nusairiyya **11** Anti-Lebanon
highest point: **6** Hermon
river: **3** Asi **6** Balikh, Barada, Jordan, Khabur, Yarmuk **7** Orontes **9** Asi Knabur, Euphrates
sea: **13** Mediterranean
physical feature:
  desert: **5** Hamad **6** Hauran, Syrian
  heights: **5** Golan
people: **4** Arab, Kurd, Turk **5** Alawi, Aptal, Druse, Druze **6** Afshar, Aissor, Aushar, Avshar, Awshar **7** Amorite, Ansarie, Bedouin, Nosaris, Saracen, Shemite **8** Ansarieh, Armenian **9** Ansariyah **10** Circassian **12** Khachaturian
  king: **5** Rezin **6** Faisal, Hazael **8** Benhadad **9** Antiochus
  leader: **10** T E Lawrence **12** Hafiz al-Assad **16** Lawrence of Arabia
  queen: **7** Zenobia
  ruler: **4** Rome **5** Arabs **6** France, Greeks, Persia **7** Mongols **8** Abbasids **9** Mamelukes, Phoenicia, Seleucids **11** Seljuk Turks **12** Ottoman Turks
language: **6** Arabic, French, Syriac **7** Aramaic, English, Kurdish, Turkish **8** Armenian
religion: **5** Druze, Islam **7** Alawite **12** Christianity **13** Greek Orthodox **23** Eastern Rite Christianity
place:
  dam: **5** Tabqa **9** Euphrates
  ruins: **7** Palmyra
  square: **7** Martyrs'
feature:
  animal: **9** dromedary
  clothing: **3** aba **4** abah **7** abayyah **8** kafiyyah
  marketplace: **4** souk
  tent: **8** bayt shar
  village common: **6** maidan

synchronous 10 synchronal
11 concomitant **12** contemporary, simultaneous

syndicalist 5 rebel **9** anarchist, insurgent **13** revolutionary

syndicate 5 group, trust, union **6** cartel, league, merger **7** combine **8** alliance **9** coalition **10** consortium, federation **11** association

Synge, John Millington
author of: **14** Riders to the Sea **19** Deirdre of the Sorrows **20** In the Shadow of the Glen **27** The Playboy of the Western World

synod 4 diet **13** governing body **15** advisory council **21** ecclesiastical council

synonym 8 analogue **10** equivalent **11** another name

synonymous 4 like, same **5** alike, equal **7** coequal **10** equivalent

synopsis 5 brief **6** apercu, digest, precis, resume **7** epitome, outline, rundown, summary

8 abstract, argument
11 abridgement

synopsize 6 digest **7** abridge, outline **8** abstract, condense **9** summarize

Synoptist 12 Gospel writer

synthesize 3 mix **4** fuse **5** blend **7** combine **8** compound **10** amalgamate

synthetic 4 fake, sham **5** phony **6** ersatz **7** man-made **9** unnatural **10** artificial **11** counterfeit **12** manufactured

Syri 16 Greek uncial codex

Syria *see box*

Syrinx
form: **5** nymph
location: **8** mountain
transformed into: **4** reed
transformed by: **3** Pan
made into: **7** panpipe
pipes called: **6** syrinx

system 4 body, unit **5** setup **6** method, scheme, theory

7 program, regimen, routine **8** organism **9** procedure, structure **10** hypothesis **11** arrangement **12** constitution, organization **13** modus operandi **15** mode of operation

systematic 4 neat, tidy **7** ordered, orderly, planned, precise, regular **8** constant **9** organized **10** methodical **12** businesslike, systematized **13** well-organized, well-regulated

systematization 5 order **8** ordering **9** gradation **10** organizing **11** arrangement **12** categorizing, codification, organization **13** methodization **14** categorization, classification

systematize 5 order **7** arrange **8** classify, organize **9** methodize

systematized 7 ordered **8** arranged, codified **9** organized **10** classified, methodized, systematic

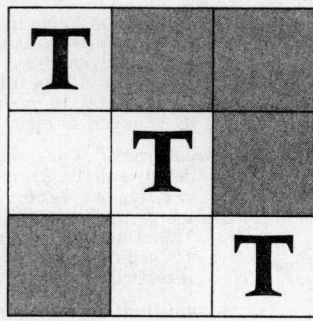

tab 3 lip 4 bill, cost, flap, loop
5 check, price, strip, tally
6 tongue 7 eyehole
10 projection

tabard 4 cape, coat 5 cloak,
tunic

Tabard Inn
   starting point in: 18 The
   Canterbury Tales

tabernacle 6 church, temple
14 house of worship

Tabeth 16 tenth Hebrew
month

Tabitha
   also called: 6 Dorcas
   revived by: 5 Peter
   hometown: 5 Joppa

table 4 fare, list, roll 5 board,
chart, index 6 record, roster,
shelve, spread 7 catalog 8 lay
aside, postpone, put aside, register, schedule, syllabus, synopsis 9 inventory 10 tabulation

Table
   constellation of: 5 Mensa

tableau 4 view 5 scene 7 pageant, picture, setting 8 grouping 9 depiction, spectacle, still
life 11 arrangement, delineation 12 illustration
13 picturization

tableau vivant 13 living
picture

tablespoon
   abbreviation: 4 tbsp

tablet 3 pad 4 leaf 5 bolus,
panel, sheet, wafer 6 pellet,
plaque, troche 7 lozenge,
memo pad, surface 8 flat cake,
thin slab 9 tablature 10 pad of
paper, writing pad

tableware 5 china 6 dishes,
plates 7 cutlery 8 crockery,
utensils 9 chinaware, glassware 10 dinnerware, silverware 14 cups and saucers

taboo, tabu 3 ban 4 no-no

6 banned 8 anathema, out-
lawed, verboten 9 forbidden,
social ban 10 in bad taste,
prohibited, proscribed 11 disapproved, prohibition, unthinkable 12 interdiction,
proscription, religious ban, unacceptable 13 unmentionable

tabulate 4 file, list, rank, rate,
sort 5 chart, grade, group, index, order, range 6 codify
7 arrange, catalog, compute,
diagram, sort out 8 classify,
organize 9 methodize 10 categorize, make a table
11 systematize

tace
   music: 6 silent

tacit 7 assumed, implied 8 implicit, inferred, unspoken, unstated, wordless 10 undeclared,
understood 11 unexpressed
15 taken for granted

taciturn 5 aloof, quiet 6 silent
7 laconic 8 reserved, reticent
9 secretive 11 tight-lipped
12 close-mouthed
15 uncommunicative

tack 3 add, peg, pin, way
4 clap, nail, slap, veer 5 affix,
sheer, shift, spike, thole 6 append, attach, change, fasten,
method, swerve, switch, zigzag 7 go about 8 approach,
tholepin 9 short nail
12 change course 14 course of
action

tackle 3 try 4 gear, lift 5 assay,
begin, crane, hoist, jenny,
throw, tools, winch 6 accept,
assume, attack, take on, take
up 7 attempt, capstan, derrick,
embrace, go about, halyard,
rigging 8 endeavor, engage in,
material, set about, windlass
9 apparatus, enter upon,
equipment, trappings, undertake 10 appliances, embark
upon, implements 11 instruments 12 appointments 13 accoutrements, paraphernalia

tack on 3 add 5 annex 6 adjoin, append, attach 7 stick
on, subjoin 8 fasten to

tacky 5 dowdy, gluey, gooey,
gucky, gummy, messy, ratty,
seedy, tatty 6 grubby, shabby,
shoddy, sloppy, sticky, untidy,
viscid 7 stringy, unkempt, viscous 8 adhesive, frazzled, slipshod, slovenly 10 disordered

tact 7 finesse, suavity 8 delicacy 9 diplomacy, suaveness
10 discretion 11 savoir faire,
sensibility 13 consideration
14 circumspection
   French: 11 savoir-faire

tactful 5 suave 6 polite,
smooth, subtle 7 politic 8 decorous, delicate, discreet, mannerly 9 sensitive
10 diplomatic, thoughtful
11 considerate

tactic 3 way 4 line, plan, tack
6 method, policy, scheme
8 approach 9 stratagem
14 course of action

tactics 9 maneuvers 18 battle
arrangements, military
operations

tactless 4 curt, rude 5 blunt,
brash, rough 6 abrupt, clumsy,
gauche, stupid 7 boorish 8 impolite 9 ham-handed, impolitic,
imprudent, untactful 10 blundering, indelicate, indiscreet
11 insensitive, thoughtless
12 undiplomatic 13 ill-considered, inconsiderate
   French: 6 gauche

tactlessness 8 curtness
9 bluntness, gaucherie
10 abruptness, clumsiness, indelicacy 13 insensitivity,
tastelessness

taedium vitae 5 ennui 12 tedium of life 22 feeling life is
wearisome

Taft, William Howard *see
box*

Taft, William Howard
  presidential rank: 13 twenty-seventh
  party: 10 Republican
  state represented: 2 OH
  defeated: 4 (Eugene Victor) Debs **5** (William Jennings)
    Bryan **6** (Daniel Braxton) Turney, (Eugene Wilder)
    Chafin, (Thomas Edward) Watson, (Thomas Louis) Hisgen
    8 (August) Gillhaus
  vice president: 7 (James Schoolcraft) Sherman
  cabinet:
    state: **4** (Philander Chase) Knox
    treasury: **8** (Franklin) MacVeagh
    war: **7** (Henry Lewis) Stimson **9** (Jacob McGavock)
      Dickinson
    attorney general: **10** (George Woodward) Wickersham
    navy: **5** (George von Lengerke) Meyer
    postmaster general: **9** (Frank Harris) Hitchcock
    interior: **6** (Walter Lowrie) Fisher **9** (Richard Achilles)
      Ballinger
    agriculture: **6** (James) Wilson
    commerce and labor: **5** (Charles) Nagel
  born: 12 Cincinnati OH
  died: 12 Washington DC
  buried: 25 Arlington National Cemetery
  education:
    university: **4** Yale
    law school: **10** Cincinnati
  religion: 9 Unitarian
  interests: 4 golf
  author: 22 Four Aspects of Civic Duty **23** The United States
    and Peace **30** Our Chief Magistrate and His Powers
    33 The Anti-Trust Act and the Supreme Court **65** The
    Presidency: Its Duties Its Powers Its Opportunities and Its
    Limitation
  political career: 18 US Solicitor General
    judge: **19** Federal Circuit Court
    president of: **21** Philippines Commission
    civil governor of: **11** Philippines
    secretary of: **3** War
    US Supreme Court: **12** Chief Justice
  civilian career:
    law professor: **4** Yale
    president: **22** American Bar Association
  notable events of lifetime/term: 19 Postal Savings System
    Act: **10** Webb-Kenyon **11** Mann-Elkinst **12** Payne-Aldrich
    sinking of: **7** Titanic
  father: 8 Alphonso
  mother: 6 Louisa (Maria Torrey)
  siblings: 5 Fanny **11** Henry Waters **12** Horace Dutton
    15 Samuel Davenport
    half-brothers: **11** Peter Rawson **13** Charles Phelps
  wife: 5 Helen (Herron)
    nickname: **6** Nellie
  children: 11 Helen Herron **13** Charles Phelps **14** Robert
    Alphonso
  first lady:
    author: **24** Recollections of Full Years

---

tag 3 add, dog, tab **4** card, heel,
mark, name, slip, stub, tail,
term **5** add on, affix, annex,
hound, label, title, trail **6** append, attach, attend, fasten,
follow, handle, join to,
marker, shadow, tack on,
ticket **7** earmark, moniker,
pendant **8** cognomen, identify,
nickname **9** accompany, appendage, sobriquet

Tahiti
  artist: 7 Gauguin
  author: 9 Stevenson
  capital: 7 Papeete
  formerly: 8 Otaheite
  island group: 7 Society
  isthmus: 7 Taravao
  ocean: 7 Pacific
  volcano: 5 Roniu **7** Orohena
tail 3 dog **4** butt, seat **5** fanny,
stalk, track, trail **6** follow,

shadow **7** back end, rear end
8 buttocks

tail end, tail-end 4 back, butt,
rear, rump, tail **6** caudal **7** hind
end, rear end **8** backside, buttocks, last part **9** posterior

tailor 3 fit, sew **4** make, redo
5 adapt, alter, build, shape
6 change, create, design, devise, modify **7** convert, fashion,
produce **8** clothier, costumer
9 construct, couturier, fabricate,
transform **10** dressmaker,
seamstress

taint 3 mar, rot **4** blot, flaw,
ruin, soil, spot, turn **5** dirty,
fault, go bad, smear, spoil,
stain, sully **6** damage, debase,
defect, defile, smudge, stigma
7 blemish, putrefy, tarnish
8 besmirch **12** imperfection

tainted 5 dirty **6** impure, rotten
7 spoiled, stained, unclean
9 blemished, tarnished
10 besmirched

Taipei
  capital of: 6 Taiwan

Taiwan *see box, p. 960*

Tajikistan
  other name: 12 Tadzhikistan
  capital/largest city:
    8 Dushanbe
  head of state: 9 president
  government: 8 republic
  monetary unit: 5 ruble
  mountain: 13 Communism
    Peak
  people: 5 Tajok, Uzbek
    7 Tadzhik
  language: 7 Tadzhik
  religion: 11 Sunni Muslim

take *see box, p. 961*

take aback 5 amaze **7** astound
8 astonish, surprise
9 overwhelm

take a crack at 3 try **5** essay
6 hazard, tackle, take on **7** attempt, venture **9** have a go at,
undertake **11** make a stab at

take advantage of 3 use
5 avail **7** exploit, utilize
10 profit from

take after 4 copy, echo **6** follow, repeat **7** imitate **8** resemble, simulate **9** duplicate,
reproduce

take apart 7 destroy **8** demolish **9** dismantle, knock down

take a powder 4 blow, exit
5 go out, leave, scram, split
6 cut out, depart, escape
8 withdraw

take away 5 seize **6** lessen, reduce **7** abridge, bear off, curtail, detract **8** carry off,

Taiwan
  name means: 11 terraced bay
  other name: 7 Formosa **11** Ilha Formosa **15** Republic of China
  capital/largest city: 6 Taipei
  others: 4 Suao **5** Shoka, Takao **6** Tainan **7** Chilung, Hualien, Keelong, Keelung, Taoyuan **8** Fengshan, Kaohiung, Taichung **9** Kaohsiung
  school: 7 Soochow, Tunghai **14** National Taiwan
  monetary unit: 4 yuan **6** dollar
  island: 5 Matsu **6** Lan Hsu, Penghu, Quemoy, Taiwan **7** Hungtou, Huoshao **10** Pescadores
  mountain: 5 Tatun **6** Tzukao **7** Taitung **15** Chungyang Shanmo
  highest point: 6 Yu Shan **8** Morrison **10** Sinkao Shan **11** Hsin-Kao Shan
  river: 5 Wuchi **6** Tachia **7** Choshui, Hualien, Tanshui
  sea: 7 Pacific **9** East China **10** Philippine, South China
  physical feature:
    cape: **7** Olwanpi
    channel: **5** Bashi
    gorge: **6** Taroko
    storm: **7** monsoon, typhoon
    strait: **6** Taiwan **7** Formosa
  people: 4 Yami **5** Hakka, Hoklo **7** Chinese, Malayan **9** Fukienese, Taiwanese **10** Indonesian, Polynesian **12** Kwangtungese
    goddess: **5** Matsu
    leader: **7** Koxinga **9** Sun Yat-sen **10** Yen Chia-Kan **13** Chiang Kai-shek **14** Cheng Cheng-Kung, Chiang Ching-kuo
  language: 4 Amon, Amoy **5** Hakka, Kuo Yu **6** Minnan **9** Taiwanese **15** Mandarin Chinese
  religion: 6 Taoism **7** animism **8** Buddhism **12** Christianity, Confucianism
  place:
    museum: **14** National Palace
    square: **12** Presidential
  feature:
    festival: **5** Ghost
    political party: **10** Kuomintang
  food:
    feast: **6** pai-pai

decrease, subtract **9** deprive of **11** make off with

take a whack at 3 try **5** essay **6** hazard, tackle **7** attempt, venture **8** give a try **9** have a go at **10** give a whirl **12** take a crack at

take back 6 abjure, recall, recant, renege **7** disavow, retract, reverse **8** forswear, withdraw

take captive 3 bag **4** snag, take, trap **5** catch, seize, snare **7** capture, ensnare **9** apprehend, lay hold of **12** take prisoner

take care 6 beware, be wary **9** be careful **10** be cautious **17** look before you leap

take care of 4 tend **6** assume **7** nurture **8** attend to, shoulder **10** minister to

take exception 5 demur

6 object, resent **11** look askance

take flight 3 fly **4** flee **6** escape, run off **7** abscond, fly away, run away, run free, take off **9** make a dash **10** fly the coop **12** make a getaway

take for granted 6 assume **10** undervalue

take heed 4 mind **6** beware **7** look out **8** take care, watch out **11** take warning

take hold 4 bite, grab, grip **5** grasp **6** clutch **7** catch on

take in stride 12 not skip a beat **13** be unperturbed

take into custody 3 bag, nab **4** book, bust, hold **5** catch, pinch, seize **6** arrest, collar, detain, secure **7** capture **9** apprehend **12** take prisoner

take into service 4 hire **6** employ, engage, retain, secure, take on

take issue 5 demur **6** differ **8** disagree **12** be at variance, stand opposed

take no notice of 6 ignore **9** disregard **11** pay no heed to **15** fail to recognize **16** pay no attention to **17** fail to acknowledge

take notice
  Latin: 8 nota bene

take notice of 3 see **4** heed, mark, note **6** call on, regard **7** observe **8** call upon **9** recognize **10** get a load of **11** acknowledge **14** pay attention to

take nourishment 3 eat **4** feed **10** break bread **14** take sustenance

takeoff 5 spoof **6** parody, satire **7** lampoon **9** burlesque **10** caricature

take off 4 doff, lift **5** leave **6** decamp, depart, detach, remove **7** lift off, peel off, run away **8** strip off **14** leave the ground

take off guard 5 catch **8** surprise **14** take by surprise

take on 4 bear, hire **6** accept, assume, engage **8** shoulder **9** undertake

take one's breath away 4 daze, stun **5** shock **7** stupefy **8** astonish, dumfound **9** dumbfound, electrify **11** flabbergast **15** make one's eyes pop

take out 4 date **5** court **6** delete, escort, remove **7** extract, isolate **8** abstract, separate, take home, withdraw **9** strike out

take over 4 take **5** seize **6** assume, take on, take up **8** shoulder **10** commandeer, confiscate **11** appropriate, expropriate, gain control

take pains 6 strive **7** attempt, try hard **8** endeavor, go all out **10** do one's best **11** give one's all **12** make an effort **15** knock oneself out **16** give one's best shot

take pleasure in 4 like, love **5** adore, eat up, enjoy, fancy, savor **6** dote on, relish, relish **7** revel in **9** rejoice in **10** appreciate **13** be pleased with, get a kick out of

take possession of 5 claim **10** confiscate **11** appropriate, expropriate

take prisoner 3 bag, nab

4 book, bust **5** catch, pinch, seize **6** arrest, collar **7** capture **9** apprehend **11** take captive **15** take into custody

take sick 3 ail **6** sicken **8** collapse **9** become ill **10** be stricken

take stock of 5 audit, check **6** assess, review, survey **7** examine, inspect **8** look over **9** inventory

take sustenance 3 eat **4** feed **10** break bread **15** take nourishment

take the cake 5 excel **7** beat all, surpass **12** beat the devil, win hands down

take the edge off 6 lessen, pacify, soothe, temper **7** appease, assuage, lighten, mollify **8** tone down

take the first step 5 begin, start **6** launch, set out **8** commence, embark on, initiate **9** undertake **10** inaugurate

take the place of 7 replace **8** displace, supplant **9** supersede

take to be 4 deem, hold **5** count, judge, think **6** assume, regard, view as **7** account, believe **8** consider **10** look upon as

take to heart 4 heed, mind **6** attend **8** consider **9** hearken to **13** give thought to **14** pay attention to

take to one's heels 3 fly **4** flee **6** escape **7** get away, run away **10** fly the coop, make a break, take flight **12** make a getaway **15** head for the hills

take to task 5 chide, scold **6** accuse, berate, charge, rail at, rebuke **7** bawl out, censure, chasten, chew out, reprove, upbraid **8** admonish, chastise, reproach **9** castigate, criticize, dress down, reprimand **10** tongue-lash **11** remonstrate **13** call to account

take turns 5 share **6** rotate **9** alternate

take under one's wing 6 assist, defend **7** protect **8** befriend **9** look after

take unfair advantage of 5 abuse **6** misuse **7** exploit

take up 4 lift **6** absorb, accept, assume, occupy, pick up, resume, soak up, suck up **7** discuss, drink in **8** consider, continue, sponge up, talk over **9** cultivate, swallow up

taking a siesta 6 dozing **7** napping **8** snoozing **10** taking a nap **18** catching forty winks

takings 4 loot **5** booty **6** spoils **7** plunder **8** pickings

Talamancan
tribe: **7** Cabecar

Talaria
form: **7** sandals
owner: **6** Hermes **7** Mercury
characteristic: **6** winged

Talassio
origin: **5** Roman
form: **3** god
invoked at: **8** weddings
corresponds to: **5** Hymen **9** Hymenaeus

tale 3 fib, lie **4** epic, myth, saga, yarn **5** fable, novel, rumor, story **6** legend, report

7 account, fiction, hearsay, recital, romance, scandal, untruth **8** anecdote **9** falsehood, fish story, narration, narrative, tall story **10** short story **11** fabrication, scuttlebutt **12** tittle-tattle **13** falsification, piece of gossip **16** cock-and-bull story

talebearer 6 gossip **7** blabber, reciter, tattler **8** busybody, informer, reporter, telltale **10** newsmonger, tattletale **11** storyteller **12** blabbermouth **13** scandalmonger

talent 4 bent, gift, turn **5** flair, forte, knack, skill **6** genius **7** faculty **8** aptitude, capacity, facility, strength **9** endowment **10** capability **11** proficiency

Talent 14 Biblical weight

talented 4 able **5** adept **6** expert, gifted **7** born for, capable, endowed, skilled **8** artistic, polished **9** brilliant, competent **10** proficient **11** well-endowed **12** accomplished

Tale of a Tub, A
author: **9** Ben Jonson **13** Jonathan Swift

Tale of Genji
author: **19** Lady Murasaki Shikibu

Tale of Two Cities, A
author: **14** Charles Dickens
character: **7** Gaspard, Stryver **9** Dr Manette, Miss Pross **11** Jarvis Lorry, John Barstad **12** Lucie Manette, Sydney Carton **13** Charles Darnay, Jerry Cruncher, Madame Defarge **18** Marquis St Evremonde
director: **10** Jack Conway
cast: **12** Blanche Yurka, Isabel Jewell, Reginald Owen, Ronald Colman (Sydney Carton) **13** Basil Rathbone, Edna May Oliver **14** Elizabeth Allan
setting: **16** French Revolution

Tales Before Midnight
author: **19** Stephen Vincent Benet

Talese, Gay
author of: **14** Honor Thy Father **16** Thy Neighbor's Wife

Tales of a Fourth Grade Nothing
author: **9** Judy Blume

Tales of a Wayside Inn
author: **24** Henry Wadsworth Longfellow

Tales of Hoffmann, The
also: **18** Les Contes d'Hoffmann
opera by: **9** Offenbach

take 3 buy, get, lug, nab, net, see, use **4** bear, bilk, deem, draw, feel, gain, grab, grip, haul, have, heed, hire, hold, know, lead, loot, mark, mind, move, need, obey, read, rent, sack, tote, work **5** bring, brook, carry, catch, cheat, claim, clasp, filch, grasp, gross, guide, infer, lease, seize, stand, steal, use up, usher, usurp **6** accept, assume, attain, clutch, convey, deduce, deduct, demand, derive, divest, employ, endure, escort, fleece, follow, look on, obtain, pilfer, pocket, profit, regard, remove, secure, snatch, suffer **7** acquire, agree to, believe, call for, capture, conduct, consume, deliver, make out, observe, pillage, plunder, purloin, receive, require, respect, stomach, succeed, suppose, undergo **8** accede to, assent to, conceive, conclude, consider, listen to, perceive, proceeds, purchase, shoulder, submit to, subtract, take away, tolerate, transfer **9** ascertain, be ruled by, consent to, deprive of, eliminate, get hold of, interpret, lay hold of, put up with, respond to, transport, undertake **10** commandeer, comply with, comprehend, confiscate, experience, lay hands on, take effect, understand **11** appropriate, begin to work, go along with, necessitate **13** help oneself to **14** avail oneself of, misappropriate

character: 6 Stella **7** Antonia, Olympia **9** Dr Miracle, Giulietta **11** E T A Hoffmann

Tales of Manhattan
author: 16 Louis Auchincloss

talisman 5 charm **6** amulet, fetish **10** lucky piece

Talisman, The
author: 14 Sir Walter Scott
character: 7 Conrade, El Hakim **10** Sir Kenneth **15** Queen Berengaria **19** Theodorick of Engaddi **20** Lady Edith Plantagenet **21** Richard the Lion-Hearted **31** Grand Master of the Knights Templars

talk 3 gab, jaw, rap, say **4** cant, chat, word **5** argot, idiom, lingo, noise, prate, rumor, slang, speak, state, utter **6** babble, bunkum, confab, confer, gossip, hot air, intone, jargon, parley, patois, powwow, preach, report, sermon, speech, take up, tirade **7** address, blarney, blather, chatter, consult, declare, deliver, dialect, discuss, express, hearsay, lecture, oration, palaver, prattle, twaddle **8** chitchat, colloquy, converse, dialogue, harangue, language, proclaim, rattle on, verbiage **9** discourse, enunciate, negotiate, pronounce, tete-a-tete, utterance **10** bandy words, conference, discussion, rap session, recitation, speak about **11** declamation, exhortation, pontificate, scuttlebutt **12** blatherskite, consultation, conversation, tittle-tattle **13** confabulation

talkative 5 gabby, talky, windy, wordy **6** babbly, chatty, prolix **7** gossipy, verbose, voluble **8** effusive **9** garrulous **10** long-winded, loquacious

talk big 4 brag, crow **5** boast, vaunt **13** puff oneself up **15** blow one's own horn **19** pat oneself on the back

talk down to 9 patronize **10** condescend

talker 6 gabber, gossip, magpie, orator **7** babbler, speaker, windbag **8** lecturer, prattler **9** chatterer, converser **10** chatterbox, mouthpiece **11** rumormonger, speechifier, speechmaker **12** blatherskite, spokesperson **13** scandalmonger **17** conversationalist

talk nonsense 6 babble, drivel, ramble

Talk of the Town, The
director: 13 George Stevens

cast: 9 Cary Grant **10** Jean Arthur **12** Ronald Colman **13** Edgar Buchanan, Glenda Farrell

talk out of 4 balk **6** thwart **8** dissuade **10** discourage

talk over 6 confer, review **7** consult, discuss, hash out

talk to 7 address, lecture, speak to **12** converse with

talk together 4 talk **6** confer **7** discuss **8** converse **9** discourse

tall 3 big **4** high **5** lanky, lofty, rangy **6** absurd **7** soaring, stringy **8** elevated, gangling, towering **10** incredible, long-limbed **11** embellished, exaggerated, implausible **12** preposterous, unbelievable **13** hard to believe, hard to swallow

tallow 3 fat, tip **5** taper **6** bougie, candle, cierge **9** rushlight

Tall State
nickname of: 8 Illinois

tall story 3 fib, lie **4** yarn **5** fable **7** fiction, untruth, whopper **9** fairy tale, falsehood, fish story, invention **11** fabrication **16** cock-and-bull story

tally 3 add, sum **4** jibe, list, mark, poll, post **5** agree, count, match, score, sum up, total **6** accord, census, concur, muster, reckon, record, square **7** catalog, compute, conform **8** coincide, mark down, register, scorepad, tabulate **9** calculate, harmonize, reckoning, scorecard **10** correspond **11** enumeration

talon 4 claw, nail, spur

Talos
form: 5 youth **7** monster
made of: 5 brass **6** bronze
made by: 10 Hephaestus
guarded: 5 Crete
destroyed by: 5 Medea
uncle: 8 Daedalus
killed by: 8 Daedalus

Talthybius
occupation: 6 herald
employer: 9 Agamemnon

Tamar
author: 15 Robinson Jeffers

Tamar
father: 5 David **7** Absalom
mother: 6 Maacah
husband: 2 Er **4** Onan **5** Judah, Uriah
brother: 5 Amnon **7** Absalom, Chileab, Solomon **8** Adonijah
son: 5 Zarah **6** Pharez

daughter: 8 Maachiah
father-in-law: 5 Judah

Tamburlaine the Great
author: 18 Christopher Marlowe
character: 6 Cosroe **7** Mycetes, Orcanes **8** Bajazeth **9** Callepine, Techelles, Zenocrate **10** Theridamas, Usumcasane

tame 4 curb, damp, dull, flat, meek, mild, rein **5** break, check, quiet, timid, train **6** boring, bridle, broken, docile, gentle, govern, manage, master, placid, pliant, serene, subdue **7** conquer, control, pliable, prosaic, repress, subdued, tedious **8** amenable, domestic, dominate, lifeless, overcome, regulate, restrain, suppress, timorous, tranquil **9** tractable **10** make docile, submissive, unexciting **11** complaisant, domesticate, unresisting **12** domesticated **13** uninteresting

tameness 8 docility **9** placidity **10** gentleness, insipidity **12** complaisance, tractability **13** domestication **14** submissiveness

Taming of the Shrew, The
author: 18 William Shakespeare
character: 6 Bianca, Gremio, Tranio **8** Baptista, Lucentio **9** Hortensio, Katharina, Petruchio, Vincentio
director: 16 Franco Zeffirelli
cast: 11 Michael York, Natasha Pyne **13** Richard Burton (Petruchio) **14** Michael Hordern **15** Elizabeth Taylor (Katharina), Vernon Dobtcheff
score: 8 Nino Rota

Tammuz
origin: 8 Sumerian
god of: 9 shepherds
Hebrew month: 6 fourth

Tam O'Shanter
author: 11 Robert Burns

Tampa Bay
football team: 7 Bandits **10** Buccaneers

tamper 3 mix **4** muck **6** butt in, fiddle, horn in, meddle, tinker **7** intrude, obtrude **9** interfere, intervene **10** fool around, mess around **12** monkey around

tamper with 5 alter **6** change, doctor **7** falsify

tan 4 roan **5** beige, brown, khaki, sandy, tawny **6** bronze, sorrel, suntan **7** bronzed

8 brownish, cinnamon, sunburnt **9** sunburned, suntanned **10** light brown **11** yellowbrown

Tanah Airkita *see* **9** Indonesia

Tananarive, Antananarivo
capital of: **10** Madagascar

Tanaquil
origin: **5** Roman
form: **5** queen
husband: **7** Tarquin **17** Tarquinius Priscus

Tandy, Jessica
born: **6** London **7** England
husband: **10** Hume Cronyn **11** Jack Hawkins
roles: **8** The Birds **10** The Gin Game **12** Forever Amber **21** A Streetcar Named Desire

tang 3 bit **4** bite, hint, odor, reek **5** aroma, punch, savor, scent, smack, smell, sting, tinge, touch, trace **6** flavor **8** acridity, piquancy, pungency, tartness **9** acridness, sharpness, spiciness **10** suggestion

Tange, Kenzo
architect of: **11** Press Center (Kofu) **16** Shizuoka Building (Tokyo) **19** Olympic Sports Stadia (Tokyo) **24** Kagawa Prefectural Offices (Takamatsu) **30** Imabara Municipal Office Building

tangibility 11 materiality, palpability **12** touchability

tangible 4 real **5** solid **6** actual **7** obvious **8** clear-cut, concrete, manifest, material, palpable, physical, positive **9** corporeal, touchable **10** verifiable **11** indubitable, substantial

tangle 3 fix, net, web **4** knot, maze, mesh, muss **5** ravel, skein, snarl, twist **6** jumble, jungle, ruffle, rumple, tousle **7** impasse, network **8** dishevel, disorder **9** labyrinth **10** disarrange

tangled 6 knotty **7** chaotic, complex, jumbled, mixed-up, snarled **11** complicated, intertwined

Tanguy, Yves
born: **5** Paris **6** France
artwork: **4** Fear **17** Mama Papa is Wounded, Untitled Landscape **18** Rose of the Four Winds **20** Slowly Toward the North **22** Four O'Clock in Summer Hope, Indefinite Divisibility **23** Multiplication of the Arcs **25** Extinction of Useless Lights

tank 3 vat **6** boiler **7** cistern **8** aquarium, fish tank **9** container, reservoir **10** armored car, receptacle **11** storage tank

Tannhauser and the Tournament of Song at Wartburg
opera by: **6** Wagner
also: **41** Tannhauser und der Sangerkrieg auf dem Wartburg
character: **5** Venus **7** Wolfram **9** Elizabeth

Tanoan
tribe: **4** Tuei **5** Kiowa **6** Isleta

tantalize 4 bait **5** charm, taunt, tease, tempt **6** entice, lead on **7** bewitch, provoke, torment **8** intrigue **9** captivate, fascinate, titillate **15** whet the appetite **18** make one's mouth water

tantalizing 7 teasing **8** inviting, tempting **9** appealing, leading on **10** intriguing **11** fascinating

Tantalus
king of: **4** Pisa **7** Phrygia
father: **8** Thyestes
wife: **12** Clytemnestra
son: **6** Pelops
daughter: **5** Niobe
punishment in Hades:
6 hunger, thirst

tantamount 4 like **5** equal **9** analogous **10** comparable, equivalent, on a par with **12** commensurate **13** commensurable

tantrum 3 fit **5** storm **7** flareup, rampage **8** outburst, paroxysm **9** explosion **12** fit of passion **13** burst of temper, conniption fit

Tanystropheous
type: **8** dinosaur
period: **8** Triassic

Tanzania *see box, p. 964*

Tao Te Ching
author: **6** Lao-tzu

Taotieh
origin: **7** Chinese
form: **6** animal

tap 3 pat, rap, use **4** cock, drum, peck, thud **5** spout, touch, valve **6** broach, employ, faucet, hammer, spigot, stroke, uncork, unplug **7** draw off, exploit, utilize **8** draw upon, stopcock **9** put to work, unstopper

taper 3 dip, wax **4** wick **5** light **6** candle, cierge, narrow **8** decrease **9** narrowing **10** diminution **12** come to a point

taper off 4 wane **5** abate **6** weaken **7** slacken, subside **8** decrease, diminish, fade away, slack off

tapestry 3 rug **5** arras, tapis **6** Bruges, fabric, mosaic **7** Gobelin, hanging, montage, weaving **8** Aubusson **12** wallcovering

Tapley, Mark
character in: **16** Martin Chuzzlewit
author: **7** Dickens

Tappertit, Simon
character in: **12** Barnaby Rudge
author: **7** Dickens

Taprobane *see* **8** Sri Lanka

taproom 3 bar, pub **6** lounge, saloon, tavern **8** alehouse **11** bar and grill, public house **14** cocktail lounge

Taranis
god of: **7** thunder

Taras Bulba
author: **12** Nikolai Gogol
character: **5** Ostap **6** Andrii, Yankel **26** Daughter of the Polish Waiwode

Tarascans, Tarascos
location: **6** Mexico **9** Michoacan **14** Central America
leader: **8** Zincicha **9** Tangaxoan, Tariacuri

Tarawa
capital of: **8** Kiribati

Tar Baby
author: **12** Toni Morrison

Tarchetius
king of: **9** Alba Longa

tardy 4 late, slow **5** slack **6** remiss **7** belated, languid, overdue **8** crawling, creeping, dilatory, slowpoke, sluggish **9** leisurely, not on time, reluctant, slow-paced, snail-like **10** behindhand, behind time, unpunctual **14** slow as molasses **15** procrastinating

tare 12 Biblical weed

target 3 aim, end **4** butt, dupe, goal, goat, gull, mark, plan, prey **5** patsy **6** design, intent, object, pigeon, victim **7** purpose **8** ambition **9** intention, objective **13** laughingstock

Targitaus
father: **4** Zeus
first inhabitant of: **7** Scythia

Tar Heel State
nickname of: **13** North Carolina

tariff 3 fee **4** cost, duty, fare, levy, rate, rent **5** price **6** charge, excise, impost **7** expense **8** input tax **9** excise tax, export tax **10** assessment, commission, freightage

Tarkington, Booth
author of: **6** Penrod **9** Seven-

Tanzania
  other name: 12 isle of cloves
  capital/largest city: 11 Dar es Salaam
    new capital: 6 Dodoma
  others: 4 Wete, 5 Kilwa, Lindi, Moshi, Tanga, Ujiji 6 Arusha, Kigoma, Mwadui, Mwanza, Tabora 7 Korogwe, Mtawara 8 Morogoro, Zanzibar 12 Kwasemangube, Zanzibar Town
  division: 8 Zanzibar 17 union of Tanganyika
  monetary unit: 4 cent 8 shilling
  weight: 8 farsalah
  island: 5 Mafia, Pemba 6 Latham 8 Zanzibar
  lake: 5 Eyasi, Nyasa, Rukwa 6 Malawi, Natron, Nyassa 7 Manyara 8 Victoria 10 Tanganyika
  mountain: 4 Kibo, Mero 8 Usambara
  highest point: 11 Kilimanjaro
  river: 4 Lupa, Ruvu, Wami 5 Ruaha 6 Kagera, Luwegu, Mbaesa, Rufiji, Rungwa, Ruvuma 7 Nkululu, Pangani 8 Mbenkuru 11 Mbarangandu
  sea: 6 Indian
  physical feature:
    crater: 10 Ngorongoro
    gorge: 7 Olduvai
    national park: 9 Serengeti
    plains: 9 Serengeti
    steppe: 5 Masai 8 Iwembere
    valley: 9 Great Rift
  people: 2 Ha 4 Arab, Gogo, Goma, Haya, Hehe 5 Asian, Bantu, Masai 6 Arusha, Chagga, Sukuma, Wagogo, Wagoma 7 African, Makonde, Sambara, Sandawe, Shirazi, Swahili, Wabunga, Zongora 8 Nyakyusa, Nyamwezi
    early man: 13 zinjanthropus
    explorer: 6 Da Gama 7 Rebmann 11 Livingstone
    leader: 5 Sayid 6 Karume 7 Nyerere 16 Sultan of Zanzibar
  language: 5 Bantu 6 Arabic 7 English, Khoisan, Nilotic, Swahili 8 Cushitic, Gujarati
  religion: 5 Islam 7 animism 12 Christianity
  feature:
    animal: 6 dik-dik
    cattle barn: 4 byre
    clothing: 4 sari 6 bui bui
    fly: 6 tsetse
    holiday: 8 Saba Saba
    homestead: 8 manyatta
  food:
    dish: 5 ugali

teen 10 Alice Adams 13 Kate Fennigate 14 The Man from Home 17 Monsieur Beaucaire 19 The World Does Not Move 23 The Magnificent Ambersons

Tarleton, Stuart and Brent
  characters in: 15 Gone With the Wind
  author: 8 Mitchell

tarnish 3 dim 4 blot, dull, foul, soil, spot 5 dirty, erode, stain, sully, taint 6 befoul, darken, defame, defile, smirch, vilify 7 blacken, blemish, corrode, degrade, oxidize 8 besmirch, discolor, disgrace, dishonor 9 denigrate, discredit 10 lose luster, stigmatize 17 drag through the mud

tarnished 5 dirty 6 soiled 7 stained, sullied 8 oxidized 10 discolored

Tarnkappe
  origin: 8 Germanic
  mentioned in: 14 Nibelungenlied
  form: 5 cloak
  gives wearer: 8 strength 12 invisibility
  stolen by: 9 Siegfried
  stolen from: 8 Niblungs 9 Nibelungs

tarot
  Italian: 6 naibes 7 attutti 8 tarocchi
  German: 5 tarok
  French: 5 tarau, tarot
  cards/deck: 12 seventy-eight
  division: 11 major arcana, minor arcana 12 lesser arcana 13 greater arcana
  suit: 3 cup 4 coin, wand 5 baton, money, sword 6 cudgel 8 pentacle
  face card: 4 king, page 5 knave, queen, valet 6 knight
  major arcana: 4 Fool, Moon 5 Death 7 Justice 8 Judgment 9 Hanged Man 14 Wheel of Fortune

tarpaulin 4 tarp 6 canvas 9 dropcloth 15 waterproof cover

Tarpeia
  form: 12 vestal virgin
  father: 15 Spurius Tarpeius
  betrayed: 4 Rome
  betrayed to: 7 Sabines
  killed by: 7 Sabines

Tarquin
  king of: 4 Rome
  origin: 8 Etruscan
  also called: 17 Tarquinius Priscus 18 Tarquinius Superbus
  wife: 8 Tanaquil

tarragon
  botanical name: 20 Artemisia dracunculus
  means: 6 dragon 12 little dragon
  Arab: 7 tarkhum
  French: 8 estragon
  origin: 7 Siberia
  used as: 8 purifier
  flavor: 8 licorice
  use: 4 fish 5 salad, sauce 10 mayonnaise 14 Bearnaise sauce

tarry 3 lag 4 bide, rest, stay, wait 5 abide, dally, delay, pause, stall 6 dawdle, linger, put off, remain 7 be tardy 8 hang back, postpone, stave off, take time 9 temporize 10 hang around 13 cool one's heels, procrastinate

tarsal
  bone of: 5 ankle

Tarshish
  father: 5 Javan 6 Bilhan

tart 3 pie 4 acid, sour 5 acerb, acrid, sharp, spicy, tangy 6 acetic, barbed, biting, bitter, crusty 7 caustic, cutting, piquant, pungent, sourish 8 vinegary 10 astringent 11 pastry shell

Tartarean see 8 infernal

Tartarin of Tarascon
  author: 14 Alphonse Daudet

Tartarus
  form: 5 abyss
  below: 5 Hades
  imprisoned: 6 Titans

tartness 7 acidity, sarcasm

8 acerbity **9** sharpness
11 astringency

Tartuffe
author: **7** Moliere
character: **5** Damis, Orgon
6 Dorine, Elmire, Valere
7 Cleante, Mariane **14** Madame Pernelle

Tarzan
author: **18** Edgar Rice
Burroughs
character: **3** Boy **4** Jane
7 Cheetah
Tarzan also called: **15** Lord
of Greystoke, Lord of the
Jungle
comic strip creator: **9** Hal
Foster **12** Burme Hogarth

task 3 job **4** duty, work
5 chore, labor, stint **6** charge,
errand **7** mission **8** business
10 assignment **11** undertaking
14 responsibility

Task, The
author: **13** William Cowper

taskmaster 4 boss **6** despot,
master, tyrant **7** foreman,
headman, manager **8** director,
martinet, overseer, stickler
10 supervisor **11** Simon Legree, slave driver **14** disciplinarian, superintendent

Tasmania
bay: **5** Storm **6** Oyster
capital: **6** Hobart
city: **10** Launceston
country: **9** Australia
formerly: **14** Van Diemen's
Land
island: **4** Echo **6** Sorell
mountain: **4** Ossa **6** Cradle
river: **3** Esk
strait: **4** Bass

Tasso, Torquato
author of: **6** Aminta **7** Rinaldo **18** Jerusalem Delivered

taste 3 bit, nip, sip, try, yen
4 bent, bite, feel, meet, tang,
test, whim **5** crumb, enjoy,
fancy, savor, smack **6** desire,
flavor, hunger, liking, morsel,
relish, sample, thirst **7** craving,
decorum, discern, forkful, insight, leaning, longing, savor
of, smack of, swallow, undergo **8** appetite, delicacy,
fondness, judgment, mouthful,
penchant, piquancy, spoonful,
yearning **9** encounter, hankering, partake of, propriety
10 experience, partiality, propensity, take a sip of **11** correctness, discernment,
disposition, inclination, take a
bite of **12** eat a little of, predilection **14** discrimination,
drink a little of
French: **4** gout

tasteful 7 elegant, refined

8 artistic, becoming, cultured,
esthetic, handsome, suitable
9 beautiful, exquisite **10** attractive, well-chosen

tasteless 3 low **4** flat, mild,
rude, weak **5** bland, cheap,
crass, crude, gaudy, gross,
tacky **6** coarse, common,
flashy, garish, ribald, watery
7 insipid, uncouth **8** improper,
indecent, unseemly **9** inelegant, offensive, unrefined
10 disgusting, flavorless, indecorous, indelicate, uncultured,
unesthetic, unflavored, unsuitable **11** distasteful, insensitive

tastemakers 7 leaders
10 avant-garde, innovators
12 stylesetters, trendsetters

tasty 3 hot **5** spicy, tangy,
yummy **6** savory **7** piquant,
zestful **8** luscious **9** delicious,
flavorful, palatable, toothsome **10** appetizing, delectable,
flavorsome **11** good-tasting,
scrumptious **12** full-flavored,
well-seasoned

Tatar, Mr
character in: **22** The Mystery
of Edwin Drood
author: **7** Dickens

Tatius
also: **5** Titus
co-ruler with: **7** Romulus

Tatler, The
author: **13** Joseph Addison,
Richard Steele

tattered 4 torn **6** broken, ragged, ripped, shabby, shaggy
10 disheveled **11** dilapidated

tatters 4 rags **6** shreds
7 patches

tattle 3 rat **4** blab **5** prate
6 gabble, gossip, snitch,
squeal, tell on **7** blather, chatter, hearsay, prattle, twaddle
8 inform on **9** loose talk
11 mudslinging **12** tittle-tattle
13 tongue-wagging

tattletale 3 rat **4** fink **5** sneak
6 gossip, snitch **7** ratfink,
stoolie, tattler **8** betrayer,
busybody, informer, squealer,
telltale **8** informer **10** newsmonger, talebearer **11** rumormonger, stool pigeon
12 blabbermouth, troublemaker **13** scandalmonger

Tatum, Edward Lawrie
field: **8** genetics
12 biochemistry
discovered: **19** gene
characteristics
awarded: **10** Nobel Prize

taunt 3 guy, rag **4** gibe, jeer,
jive, mock, slur, twit **5** scoff,
sneer, tease **6** deride, harass,
insult, jeer at **7** provoke, rag-

ging, sneer at, snigger, torment **8** chaffing, derision,
ridicule **9** make fun of, poke
fun at, snigger at **10** harassment, make game of, tormenting **11** provocation

Taura
form: **3** cow
attribute: **6** sacred

taurobolium
rite of: **7** baptism

Taurog, Norman
director of: **6** Skippy (Oscar)
8 Boys' Town

Taurus
symbol: **4** bull
planet: **5** Venus
rules: **5** money **9** resources
born: **3** May **5** April

taut 4 neat, snug, tidy, trig,
trim **5** rigid, smart, tense,
tight **6** spruce **7** orderly **8** not
loose, not slack **9** shipshape,
unbending, unrelaxed
10 drawn tight, inflexible, nononsense **11** under strain
12 businesslike **13** well-regulated **15** well-disciplined

tavern 3 bar, pub **4** dive **6** bistro, saloon **7** barroom, gin
mill, taproom **8** alehouse,
drinkery, grogshop **9** beer
joint, brasserie, honky-tonk,
roadhouse **10** restaurant
11 public house **12** watering
hole **14** cocktail lounge
French: **7** auberge
German: **8** Brauhaus

tawdry 4 loud **5** cheap, crass,
gaudy, showy, tacky **6** flashy,
garish, tinsel, vulgar **7** raffish
8 gimcrack **9** inelegant, obtrusive, tasteless **10** flamboyant
11 conspicuous, pretentious
12 meretricious, ostentatious

tawny 3 tan **4** fawn **5** beige,
dusky, olive, sandy **6** bronze
7 swarthy **8** brownish **10** light
brown **14** yellowish-brown

tax 3 sap, try **4** duty, lade,
levy, load, tire, toll **5** drain,
weigh **6** assess, burden,
charge, custom, excise, impost,
saddle, strain, tariff, weight
7 deplete, exhaust, stretch,
wear out **8** exertion, overwork **10** assessment, obligation, overburden
kind: **4** city **5** sales, state
6 county, excise, income,
luxury **8** property **11** inheritance **12** excess profit

Taxi
character: **9** John Burns,
Tony Banta **10** Alex Rieger
11 Elaine Nardo, Latka Gravas **12** Bobby Wheeler,
Louie De Palma
cast: **9** Tony Danza **10** Judd

Hirsch **11** Andy Kaufman, Danny DeVito, Jeff Conaway **12** Marilu Henner **13** Randall Carver
company: 11 Sunshine Cab

taxicab 4 hack **6** jitney **7** droshky, hackney **8** hired car, rickshaw **10** automobile **11** jinrickshaw

Taxi Driver
director: 14 Martin Scorsese
cast: 10 Peter Boyle **11** Jodie Foster **12** Albert Brooks, Harvey Keitel, Robert De Niro **13** Leonard Harris **14** Cybill Shepherd
setting: 11 New York City
score: 15 Bernard Herrmann
script: 12 Paul Schrader

taxonomy
study of: 17 structure contrast **19** structure comparison

Taygete
member of: 8 Pleiades
father: 5 Atlas
son: 10 Lacedaemon

Taylor, Elizabeth
born: 6 London **7** England
husband: 8 Mike Todd **10** John Warner **11** Eddie

Fisher, Nicky Hilton **13** Richard Burton **14** Michael Wilding
roles: 5 Giant **7** Ivanhoe **9** Cleopatra **11** Little Women **12** The Sandpiper **14** A Place in the Sun, National Velvet, Raintree County **16** Butterfield Eight (Oscar), Cat on a Hot Tin Roof, Father of the Bride **18** Suddenly Last Summer **19** The Taming of the Shrew **25** Who's Afraid of Virginia Woolf (Oscar)

Taylor, Robert
real name: 22 Spangler Arlington Brugh
wife: 12 Ursula Thiess **15** Barbara Stanwyck
roles: 7 Camille, Ivanhoe **8** Quo Vadis **11** Billy the Kid **14** Waterloo Bridge **20** Magnificent Obsession

Taylor, Zachary see box

Tchad see **4** Chad

Tchaikovsky, Peter (Piotr Ilyich Chaikovsky)
born: 6 Russia **8** Votkinsk
composer of: 7 Manfred, Mazeppa **8** Iolanthe, Pathetic (symphony No 6), Swan

Lake **9** Joan of Arc **10** Nutcracker **12** Eugene Onegin, Winter Dreams **14** Italian Caprice, Romeo and Juliet, The Enchantress **16** The Queen of Spades **17** Francesca da Rimini, The Sleeping Beauty **22** Eighteen-Twelve Overture

Tchile see **5** Chile

tea 16 Camellia sinensis
varieties: 5 Assam, Bohea, China, green, pekoe, Yerba **6** Ceylon, Oolong, Oswego, Tisane **7** African, Arabian, cambric, crystal, Lapsang, Mexican, redroot, Spanish **8** bergamot, camomile, Earl Grey, Labrador, mountain, Paraguay, Siberian, Souchong, Woodruff **9** gunpowder, lemon balm, New Jersey, sassafras **10** Darjeeling, Philippine **11** Appalachian, Orange Pekoe **14** Irish breakfast **16** English breakfast

teach 5 coach, drill, edify, prime, tutor **6** inform, school **7** educate, implant, prepare **8** exercise, instruct **9** enlighten, inculcate **10** discipline **12** indoctrinate

Teach
character in: 21 The Master of Ballantrae
author: 9 Stevenson

teacher 3 don **5** coach, tutor **6** master, mentor **7** maestro, trainer **8** educator **9** preceptor, professor **10** instructor, schoolmarm **12** schoolmaster **13** schoolteacher **14** schoolmistress

teaching 5 dogma, tenet **6** belief **7** nurture, precept **8** doctrine, pedagogy, training, tutelage, tutoring **9** education, principle, schooling **10** conviction, philosophy **11** inculcation, instructing, instruction, preparation **14** indoctrination

tea dance
French: 10 the dansant

teal
group of: 5 ducks
color: 4 blue **5** green

team 3 rig, set **4** ally, band, crew, five, gang, join, nine, pair, side, unit, yoke **5** force, group, merge, party, squad, staff, unify, unite **6** circle, clique, couple, eleven, league, tandem **7** combine, company, coterie, faction **8** alliance, federate **9** coalition, cooperate **10** amalgamate, federation, sports team, yoked group **11** association, consolidate, get

---

Taylor, Zachary
nickname: 16 Old Rough and Ready
presidential rank: 7 twelfth
party: 4 Whig
state represented: 2 LA
defeated: 4 (Lewis) Cass **8** (Martin) Van Buren
vice president: 8 (Millard) Fillmore
cabinet:
   state: **7** (John Middleton) Clayton
   treasury: **8** (William Morris) Meredith
   war: **8** (George Walker) Crawford
   attorney general: **7** (Reverdy) Johnson
   navy: **7** (William Ballard) Preston
   postmaster general: **8** (Jacob) Collamer
   interior: **5** (Thomas) Ewing
born: 12 Montebello VA **12** Orange County
died: 12 Washington DC
buried: 12 Louisville KY
education: 9 no college **16** privately tutored
religion: 12 Episcopalian
political career: 21 none prior to presidency
civilian career: 7 planter, soldier
military service: 6 US Army **12** major general
   War: **7** Mexican **9** Black Hawk **19** War of Eighteen-Twelve **14** Second Seminole
notable events of lifetime/presidency:
   treaty: **13** Clayton-Bulwer
father: 7 Richard
mother: 5 Sarah (Dabney Strother)
siblings: 6 George **7** Hancock **11** Sarah Bailey **12** Elizabeth Lee, Emily Richard **13** Joseph Pannill **21** William Dabney Strother
wife: 8 Margaret (Mackall Smith)
children: 7 Richard **9** Sarah Knox **10** Ann Mackall **13** Margaret Smith, Mary Elizabeth, Octavia Panill

together, incorporate **12** band together, join together **13** confederation

teammate 4 ally **7** partner **8** co-player, coworker **9** associate, colleague, co-partner **11** confederate **12** collaborator

team spirit 10 group pride, solidarity **13** esprit de corps

team up 4 ally **5** unite **9** cooperate **10** join forces **11** collaborate

tear 3 fly, gap, hie, rip, run **4** bolt, dart, dash, grab, hole, mist, pull, race, rend, rent, rift, rive, rush, scud, slit, snag, swim, whiz, yank **5** abuse, break, crack, fault, pluck, scoot, seize, sever, shoot, shred, speed, split, spurt, sweep, whisk **6** breach, cleave, damage, divide, gallop, hasten, hustle, injury, plunge, ravage, scurry, snatch, sprint, sunder, wrench **7** disrupt, fissure, hard use, opening, rupture, scamper, scuttle **8** disunite, teardrop, scramble, splinter **9** come apart, hotfoot it, pull apart, skedaddle **10** impairment, make tracks **11** destruction **12** pull to pieces

tear down 4 raze **5** level, smash, wreck **7** destroy, flatten **8** demolish **9** dismantle, take apart

tearful 5 teary, weepy **6** crying **7** bawling, crushed, sobbing, wailing, weeping **8** mournful **9** lamenting, sniveling **10** blubbering, lachrymose, whimpering **11** heartbroken **12** inconsolable **13** brokenhearted

tear off 5 sever **6** detach, rip off **7** pull off **8** break off, separate **10** wrench away

Teasdale, Sara author of: **8** Love Song **11** Helen of Troy **13** Dark of the Moon **14** Flame and Shadow, Rivers to the Sea, Strange Victory

tease 3 guy, irk, nag, rag, vex **4** bait, gall, gibe, goad, haze, jeer, josh, mock, pest, rile, twit **5** annoy, chafe, harry, mimic, pique, scoff, sneer, taunt, worry **6** badger, bother, harass, hazing, heckle, hector, mocker, needle, pester, plague, teaser **7** bedevil, chafing, laugh at, needler, provoke, razzing, snigger, taunter, torment, worrier **8** derision, heckling, irritate, needling, ridicule **9** aggravate, make fun of, mimicking, persecute, tantalize, tormentor **10** harassment, tantalizer **11** persecution

teaspoon abbreviation: **3** tsp

Teazle, Sir Peter and Lady characters in: **19** The School for Scandal author: **8** Sheridan

technical 5 trade **10** mechanical, vocational **11** complicated, nonacademic **13** technological

technique 3 art, way **4** form **5** craft, knack, style **6** manner, method, system **7** formula, know-how **8** approach, facility **9** procedure **10** adroitness, expertness, technology **11** proficiency **12** skillfulness

Tecmessa father: **8** Teuthras son: **9** Eurysaces carried off by: **14** Telamonian Ajax

tedious 3 dry **4** drab, dull, long, slow **5** vapid **6** boring, dismal, dreary, jejune, tiring **7** humdrum, insipid, irksome, onerous, prosaic **8** drawn-out, lifeless, tiresome, wearying **9** fatiguing, laborious, wearisome **10** burdensome, exhausting, monotonous, oppressive, unexciting **13** time-consuming, unimaginative, uninteresting

tediousness 5 ennui **7** boredom **8** dullness, monotony

tedium 3 rut **5** ennui **7** boredom **8** drabness, dullness, monotony, sameness **10** dreariness **11** routineness **12** tiresomeness

tedium of life Latin: **12** taedium vitae

teem 4 brim, gush **5** swarm **6** abound **8** be full of, overflow **9** be overrun **15** burst at the seams

teeming 4 full **7** crowded **8** swarming **9** abounding, bounteous **11** overflowing

teeny-weeny 3 wee **4** tiny **5** dwarf **6** little, minute, petite **9** miniature, minuscule **10** diminutive, pocket-size **11** lilliputian, microscopic, pocket-sized

teeter 4 reel, sway **5** lurch, waver **6** seesaw, totter, wobble **7** stagger **8** hesitate **9** vacillate

teetotaler 3 dry **9** abstainer **10** nondrinker **14** prohibitionist

Tegeates father: **6** Lycaon

Tegucigalpa capital of: **8** Honduras

Tegyrius king of: **6** Thrace

Tehani character in: **17** Mutiny on the Bounty authors: **4** Hall **8** Nordhoff

Tehran, Teheran capital of: **4** Iran landmark: **10** Melaat Park **12** Marble Palace, Marmar Palace **14** Azadai Monument, Gulestan Palace, Saadabad Palace **15** Freedom Monument, Hosseineh Mosque, Shahyad Monument **23** Center for Islamic Studies means: **9** warm place mountain: **6** Elburz **8** Demavend ruler: **8** Khomeini **23** Muhammad Reza Shah Pahlavi

te igitur 13 thee therefore

Teiresias *see* **8** Tiresias

Telamon king of: **7** Salamis member of: **9** Argonauts father: **6** Aeacus mother: **6** Endeis brother: **6** Peleus half-brother: **6** Phocus wife: **6** Glauce **7** Eriboea son: **4** Ajax **6** Teucer friend: **8** Hercules

Telchines form: **6** beings characteristic: **9** malicious

Telegonus father: **7** Proteus **8** Odysseus mother: **5** Circe wife: **2** Io **8** Penelope killed: **8** Odysseus killed by: **8** Hercules

telegraph invented by: **5** Morse, Woods **6** Edison **7** Marconi

Telemachus father: **8** Odysseus mother: **8** Penelope son: **7** Latinus

Telemann, Georg Philipp born: **7** Germany **9** Magdeburg composer of: **9** Fantasias **10** Times of Day **12** Don Quichotte **14** Die Tageszeiten, Musique de Table

Telemus vocation: **4** seer father: **7** Eurymus warned: **10** Polyphemus

telepathy 3 ESP **10** sixth sense **11** second sight **12** clairvoyance **19** spirit communication, thought transference **22** extrasensory perception

Telephassa
husband: **6** Agenor

telephone
invented by: **4** Bell

Telephus
king of: **5** Mysia
father: **8** Hercules
mother: **4** Auge

telescope
invented by: **7** Galileo
10 Lippershey
astronomical: **6** Kepler

Telesphorus
god of: **15** illness recovery

telesterion
form: **8** building
purpose: **8** religion
11 celebration

television
invented by: **5** Baird **8** Zworykin **10** Farnsworth

tell 3 ask, bid, own, say, see **4** blab **5** bruit, count, order, speak, spout, state, utter, weigh, write **6** advise, babble, betray, blazon, depict, detail, direct, figure, impart, inform, number, recite, reckon, relate, report, reveal, sketch, unfold **7** apprise, command, compute, confess, declare, discern, divulge, express, find out, mention, narrate, portray, predict, publish, recount, request **8** acquaint, count off, describe, disclose, estimate, forecast, foretell, identify, instruct, perceive, register, set forth **9** apprehend, ascertain, broadcast, calculate, chronicle, enumerate, enunciate, influence, make known, pronounce, recognize **10** take effect **11** communicate, distinguish **12** discriminate **17** breathe a word about

Teller, Edward
field: **7** physics
developed: **8** atom bomb
12 hydrogen bomb

telling 5 solid, valid **6** cogent, potent **7** decided, weighty **8** decisive, definite, forceful, material, positive, powerful, striking **9** effective, effectual, important, momentous, trenchant **10** conclusive, definitive, impressive **11** efficacious, influential, significant **13** consequential

telltale 6 gossip **7** tattler **8** busybody, giveaway, informer, squealer **9** affirming, betraying, divulging, revealing, verifying **10** confirming, disclosing, newsbearer, talebearer, tattletale **11** informative **12** blabber-

mouth, enlightening
13 scandalmonger

Tellus
called: **10** Terra Mater
origin: **5** Roman
goddess of: **5** earth **8** marriage **9** fertility
11 agriculture
corresponds to: **4** Gaea

Telphusa
form: **5** nymph
location: **6** spring
characteristic: **7** cunning

Temenus
father: **8** Pelasgus
12 Aristomachus
brother: **11** Aristodemus, Cresphontes
reared: **4** Hera

temerity 4 gall **5** brass, cheek, nerve **8** audacity, boldness, chutzpah, rashness **9** brashness, freshness, impudence, insolence, pushiness, sauciness **10** brazenness, effrontery **11** forwardness **12** impertinence, indiscretion **13** foolhardiness, intrusiveness

Temin, Howard Martin
field: **8** genetics, oncology
discovered: **20** reverse transcriptase
awarded: **10** Nobel Prize

temper 3 ire **4** bile, calm, fury, gall, mood, rage **5** allay, anger, humor, pique, quiet, still, wrath **6** animus, anneal, choler, dander, harden, pacify, soften, soothe, spleen **7** appease, balance, compose, dudgeon, emotion, ferment, passion, toughen, umbrage **8** acrimony, bad humor, calmness, mitigate, moderate, palliate, vexation **9** annoyance, composure, huffiness **10** irritation, strengthen **11** displeasure, disposition, equilibrium, frame of mind, indignation, peevishness, tranquilize **12** churlishness, irascibility, irritability

temperament 4 bent, cast, mood, soul, tone **5** humor, tenor **6** makeup, nature, spirit, temper **7** leaning, quality **8** tendency **9** character **10** complexion **11** disposition, frame of mind, personality

temperamental 5 fiery, moody **6** fickle **7** erratic, peppery, willful **8** unstable, volatile **9** emotional, excitable, explosive, hotheaded, mercurial, sensitive, turbulent **10** capricious, headstrong, high-strung, hysterical, mettlesome, passionate, unreliable **11** tempestuous, thin-skinned

12 undependable
13 unpredictable

temperance 8 prudence, sobriety **9** restraint **10** abstention, abstinence, discretion, moderation, self-denial **11** forbearance, prohibition, self-control, teetotalism **14** abstemiousness, self-discipline

temperate 4 calm, cool, even, mild, sane, soft, warm **5** balmy, sober, sunny **6** gentle, mellow, sedate, steady **7** clement, patient, sparing **8** composed, moderate, pleasant, rational, tranquil **9** collected, easygoing, unruffled **10** coolheaded, reasonable **11** levelheaded **13** dispassionate, self-possessed, unextravagant, unimpassioned **14** self-controlled, self-restrained

temperature measurement 6 degree, Kelvin **7** Celsius **10** Fahrenheit

tempest 5 chaos, furor, storm **6** hubbub, tumult, uproar **8** brouhaha, outbreak, upheaval **9** agitation, cataclysm, commotion **10** hurly-burly, turbulence **11** disturbance

Tempest, The
author: **18** William Shakespeare
character: **5** Ariel **6** Alonso **7** Antonio, Caliban, Gonzalo, Miranda **8** Prospero **9** Ferdinand, Sebastian

Tempestates
origin: **5** Roman
goddesses of: **6** storms

tempestuous 3 hot **5** fiery **6** raging, stormy **7** excited, frantic, furious, violent **8** agitated, feverish, frenzied **9** emotional, explosive, turbulent, wrought-up **10** hysterical, passionate, tumultuous **11** impassioned, overwrought

Templar, Simon
character in: **8** The Saint
author: **9** Charteris

temple 4 fane, kirk **6** chapel, church, mosque, pagoda, priory, shrine **7** convent **8** basilica, pantheon **9** cathedral, joss house, monastery, sanctuary, synagogue **10** house of God, tabernacle **12** meetinghouse

Temple, Shirley
married name: **18** Shirley Temple Black
born: **13** Santa Monica CA
roles: **5** Heidi **10** Bright Eyes **15** Wee Willie Winkie **16** Little Miss Marker, The Little Colonel, The Littlest Rebel **18** Poor Little Rich

Girl **21** Susannah of the Mounties **23** Rebecca of Sunnybrook Farm

Temple, The
author: **13** George Herbert

Temple Beau, The
author: **13** Henry Fielding

tempo 4 clip, gait, pace, rate, time **5** meter, speed **6** pacing, stride, timing **8** momentum, velocity

tempo giusto
music: **10** strict time

temporal 3 lay **5** civil **6** mortal **7** mundane, passing, profane, secular, worldly **8** day-to-day, fleeting, fugitive **9** ephemeral, temporary, transient **10** evanescent, noneternal **11** impermanent, nonclerical **12** nonspiritual **17** nonecclesiastical

temporary, temporarily 5 brief, fleet **7** interim, passing, stopgap **8** fleeting, fugitive **9** ephemeral, momentary, provisory, transient **10** evanescent, short-lived, transitory **11** impermanent, provisional **13** flash-in-the-pan
Latin: **10** pro tempore

temporary dwelling
French: **10** pied-a-terre

temporize 5 delay, hedge, stall, tarry, waver **8** hang back, maneuver **9** hem and haw, vacillate **10** equivocate **11** play for time **12** drag one's feet, tergiversate **13** procrastinate

tempt 3 try, woo **4** bait, draw, goad, lure, pull, risk **5** charm, decoy, prick, rouse **6** allure, arouse, entice, incite, invite, seduce **7** attract, bewitch, provoke **8** appeal to, intrigue, inveigle **9** captivate, tantalize **12** put to the test **13** take one's fancy **14** fly in the face of **15** whet the appetite

temptation 4 bait, draw, lure, pull, urge **5** charm, snare, spell **8** stimulus, tempting **9** incentive, seduction **10** allurement, attraction, enticement, incitement, inducement **11** captivation, fascination, provocation

tempter 5 Satan **7** enticer, seducer **8** the Devil

temptress 4 vamp **5** Circe, flirt, siren **7** charmer, Delilah, Jezebel, Lorelei, vampire **8** coquette **9** odalisque, sorceress **10** seductress **11** enchantress, femme fatale

tempus fugit 9 time flies

Ten (10)
director: **12** Blake Edwards
cast: **7** Bo Derek **11** Dudley Moore **12** Julie Andrews

tenable 6 viable **8** arguable, rational, sensible, workable **9** excusable **10** condonable, defendable, defensible, vindicable **11** justifiable, warrantable **12** maintainable

tenacious 3 set **4** fast, firm, hard, iron **6** dogged, mulish **7** adamant, staunch **8** clinging, constant, obdurate, resolute, stalwart, stubborn **9** immovable, obstinate, pigheaded, steadfast, unbending **10** determined, inexorable, inflexible, persistent, relentless, unswerving, unwavering, unyielding **11** persevering, undeviating, unfaltering, unremitting **12** intransigent, unchangeable **14** uncompromising

tenaciousness 8 tenacity **9** endurance **10** resolution **11** persistence **12** perseverance, resoluteness **13** determination **16** stick-to-itiveness

tenacity 8 strength **9** toughness **10** resolution **11** persistence **12** cohesiveness, perseverance, resoluteness **13** determination, tenaciousness **16** stick-to-itiveness

tenant 6 lessee, lodger, renter, roomer **7** boarder, denizen, dweller **8** occupant, resident **10** inhabitant **11** householder, leaseholder, paying guest

Tenant of Wildfell Hall, The
author: **10** Anne Bronte

Tenants, The
author: **14** Bernard Malamud

Ten Commandments *see box*

Ten Commandments, The
director: **13** Cecil B DeMille
cast: **8** Nina Foch **9** John Derek **10** Anne Baxter, Debra Paget, Yul Brynner **11** Martha Scott **12** Vincent Price **13** John Carradine, Yvonne De Carlo **14** Charlton Heston (Moses), Judith Anderson **15** Cedric Hardwicke, Edward G Robinson

tend 3 aim **4** bear, head, lead, lean, mind, move **5** be apt, guide, nurse, point, watch **6** extend, foster, manage, wait on **7** care for, nurture **8** attend to, be liable, be likely **9** bid fair to, gravitate, look after, supervise, watch over **10** minister to, predispose, take care of **11** keep an eye on

Ten Commandments
also: **9** Decalogue
given to: **5** Moses
where given: **10** Mount Sinai
inscribed on: **12** stone tablets
first: **32** Thou shalt have no other Gods before me
second: **37** Thou shalt not bow down before graven images
third: **44** Thou shalt not take the name of the Lord thy God in vain
fourth: **34** Remember the Sabbath Day and keep it holy
fifth: **26** Honor thy father and thy mother
sixth: **16** Thou shalt not kill
seventh: **26** Thou shalt not commit adultery
eighth: **17** Thou shalt not steal
ninth: **46** Thou shalt not bear false witness against thy neighbor
tenth: **17** Thou shalt not covet

tendency 3 aim, set **4** bent **5** drift, drive, habit, trend **6** course **7** heading, impulse, leaning, turning **8** penchant **9** direction, proneness, readiness **10** proclivity, propensity **11** disposition, gravitation, inclination **14** predisposition

tender 3 raw **4** fond, give, good, kind, soft, sore, weak **5** frail, green, place, young **6** aching, benign, callow, caring, dainty, extend, feeble, gentle, hand in, loving, prefer, submit, weakly **7** advance, fragile, hold out, painful, present, proffer, propose, suggest, swollen **8** delicate, generous, immature, inflamed, juvenile, merciful, propound, underage, youthful **9** lay before, sensitive, volunteer **10** benevolent, put forward, thoughtful, vulnerable **11** considerate, sentimental, softhearted, sympathetic, warmhearted **12** affectionate **13** compassionate, inexperienced, understanding **14** impressionable **15** unsophisticated

tenderfoot 4 tyro **6** novice, rookie **8** beginner, neophyte **9** fledgling, greenhorn **10** apprentice

tenderhearted 4 mild **6** benign, gentle, humane **8** generous, merciful **10** altruistic, benevolent, responsive, thoughtful **11** considerate, kindhearted, softhearted, sympathetic, warmhearted **13** compassionate, understanding

tenderheartedness 4 pity **5** heart **7** empathy **8** sympathy **10** compassion

tendering 6 giving **8** offering **9** advancing, extending, proposing **10** holding out, preferring, proffering, submitting, suggesting **11** propounding **12** volunteering

Tender Is the Night
   author: 16 F Scott Fitzgerald
   character: 8 Abe North **9** Dick Diver **11** Nicole Diver, Tommy Barban **12** Rosemary Hoyt

tenderness 4 love **6** aching, warmth **7** rawness **8** delicacy, fondness, goodness, humanity, kindness, mildness, smarting, softness, soreness, sympathy **9** affection **10** compassion, gentleness, humaneness, kindliness, lovingness **11** beneficence, benevolence, painfulness, sensitivity **12** mercifulness **14** loving kindness

tendon
   part of: 21 musculoskeletal system

tendril 4 coil, curl **5** crook, shoot, sprig, twist **6** winder **7** climber, ringlet

tenebrous 3 dim **4** dark **5** murky **6** gloomy **7** obscure, shadowy **8** darkened, obscured **13** unilluminated

Tenes
   father: 6 Cycnus
   mother: 7 Proclea
   stepmother: 9 Phylonome
   sister: 8 Hemithea

tenet 4 rule, view **5** canon, credo, creed, dogma, maxim **6** belief, thesis **7** opinion **8** doctrine, ideology, position, teaching **9** principle **10** conviction, persuasion

Tennessee *see box*

tennis
   athlete: 8 Don Budge, Jan Kodes, Rod Laver, Tom Okker **9** Bjorn Borg, Ivan Lendl, Stan Smith **10** Arthur Ashe, Bill Tilden, Jack Kramer, Maria Bueno, Pam Shriver, Roy Emerson, Steffi Graf **11** Alice Marble, Andre Agassi, Edward Dibbs, Ilie Nastase, John McEnroe,

Ken Rosewall, Tracy Austin **12** Althea Gibson, Darren Cahill, Francois Durr, Jimmy Connors, John Newcombe, Mats Wilander, Roscoe Tanner, Virginia Wade **13** Dennis Ralston, Harold Solomon, Manuel Orantes, Manuel Santana, Martin Riessen, Wendy Turnbull **14** Brian Gottfried, Guillermo Vilas, Hana Mandlikova, Pancho Gonzalez, Rosemary Casals **15** Charles Pasarell, Chris Evert Lloyd, Maureen Connolly, Richard

Stockton, Vitas Gerulaitis **17** Donald Schollander, Nancy Richey Gunter **18** Margaret Smith Court, Martina Navratilova **20** Helen Wills Moody Roark **21** Billie Jean Moffitt King, Evonne Goolagong Cawley

Tennyson, Alfred, Lord
   author of: 4 Maud **7** Mariana, Ulysses **10** Enoch Arden, In Memoriam (A A H) **12** Locksley Hall, Morte d'Arthur **16** The Lady of Shalott **18** The Idylls of the

---

Tennessee
   abbreviation: 2 TN **4** Tenn
   nickname: 7 Big Bend **9** Volunteer **11** Old Franklin
   capital: 9 Nashville
   largest city: 7 Memphis
   others: 5 Alcoa, Paris **6** Camden, Sparta **7** Bristol, Dickson, Pulaski **8** Franklin, Gallatin, Oak Ridge **9** Cedar Hill, Cleveland, Inglewood, Kingsport, Knoxville, Lexington **10** Greenbrier, Morristown, Old Hickory **11** Chattanooga, Clarksville, Springfield **12** Fayetteville, Murfreesboro **14** Hendersonville
   college: 4 Fisk, Lane **5** Bryan, Siena **6** Bethel **7** Belmont, Lambuth, Lemoyne **8** Milligan, Tusculum **10** Vanderbilt **12** Southwestern **13** David Lipscomb **14** Meharry Medical **17** Tennessee Wesleyan
   feature: 12 The Hermitage
     dam: **6** Norris, Wilson **7** Douglas
     fort: **5** Henry **8** Donalson, Nashboro
     national park: **6** Shiloh **13** Cumberland Gap **19** Great Smoky Mountains (with North Carolina)
     national parkway: **12** Natchez Trace
     tribe: **7** Shawnee **8** Cherokee **9** Chickasaw
   people: 7 Sequoya **8** John Bell **9** James Agee **10** Grace Moore **11** Bessie Smith, Cordell Hull **12** Davy Crockett **18** Carey Estes Kefauver **23** Alvin Cullum "Sergeant" York **32** Ernest Jennings "Tennessee Ernie" Ford
     explorer: **6** Arthur, De Soto **7** Jolliet, La Salle, Needham **9** Marquette
   lake: 7 Douglas **8** Barkeley, Cherokee, Reelfoot, Watts Bar **10** Center Hill **11** Chickamauga
   land rank: 12 thirty-fourth
   mountain: 5 Guyot **7** Lookout, Smokies **9** Blue Ridge **10** Cumberland, Great Smoky
     highest point: **13** Clingman's Dome
   physical feature:
     basin: **9** Nashville
     highlands: **11** Appalachian
     plain: **7** Coastal
     plateau: **10** Cumberland
   president: 10 James K Polk **13** Andrew Jackson, Andrew Johnson
   river: 3 Elk **4** Duck **5** Caney, Obion, Stone **6** Clinch **7** Hatchie, Holston **8** Hiwassee **9** Tennessee **10** Cumberland **11** French Broad, Mississippi **15** Little Tennessee
   state admission: 9 sixteenth
   state bird: 11 mockingbird
   state flower: 4 flag, iris **6** maypop **13** passion flower
   state motto: 16 America at Its Best **22** Agriculture and Commerce
   state song: 11 My Tennessee **17** The Tennessee Waltz **19** My Homeland Tennessee **26** When It's Iris Time in Tennessee
   state tree: 11 tulip poplar **12** yellow poplar

King **26** The Charge of the Light Brigade

tenor 4 gist **5** drift, sense, trend **6** course, import, intent, nature, object **7** content, essence, meaning, purport, purpose **8** argument, tendency **9** direction, intention, substance **11** connotation, implication **12** significance

tense 4 taut **5** brace, drawn, rigid, shaky, stiff, tight **6** braced, draw up, on edge, uneasy **7** anxious, excited, fearful, fidgety, jittery, nervous, restive, stiffen, uptight **8** agitated, make taut, restless, strained, timorous **9** tighten up, tremulous, wrought-up **10** high-strung, inflexible, unyielding **12** apprehensive

tension 5 dread **6** spring, strain, stress **7** anxiety, pulling, tugging **8** bad vibes, exertion, pressure, rigidity, tautness, traction **9** hostility, misgiving, stiffness, straining, tightness **10** stretching **11** fearfulness, nervousness, restiveness, trepidation **12** apprehension, elastic force, perturbation **13** bad vibrations, combativeness

tent 3 pup **4** care, hard **5** gauze, probe, tepee **6** bigtop, canvas, search, teepee, wigwam **7** shelter **8** pavilion **10** tabernacle

tentacle 3 arm **6** feeler **9** appendage

tentative 4 iffy **5** trial **6** acting **8** not final, proposed **9** ad interim, temporary, undecided, unsettled **10** contingent, indefinite, not settled **11** conditional, probational, provisional, speculative, unconfirmed **12** experimental, probationary **15** subject to change **18** under consideration

tentative procedure 4 test **5** flier, trail **6** feeler, tryout **7** venture **10** experiment **12** trial balloon

tenuous 4 slim, thin, weak **5** frail, shaky **6** flimsy, paltry, slight **7** fragile, shallow, slender **8** delicate, gossamer **9** uncertain **10** indefinite **11** halfhearted, unsupported **12** unconvincing **13** unsubstantial

tenure 4 rule, term, time **5** reign **7** tenancy **9** occupancy, retention **10** incumbency, occupation, permanency, possession **11** entitlement, job security **14** administration

tepee, teepee 4 chum, tent **5** lodge **6** wigwam **7** wickiup

tepid 4 cool, mild **7** languid, warmish **8** lukewarm, moderate **9** apathetic, impassive, temperate **10** nonchalant, phlegmatic **11** halfhearted, indifferent, unemotional **13** lackadaisical **14** unenthusiastic

tequila
  type: 6 spirit
  origin: 6 Mexico
  made from: 5 agave
    6 maguey
  used with: 4 lime, salt
    5 lemon
  drink: 7 Chapala **8** El Diablo
  with creme de cacao:
    8 Toreador
  with kahlua: 9 Brave Bull
  with orange juice: 7 Sunrise
  with Tia Maria: 9 Brave Bull
  with triple sec: 9 Margarita

Terah
  son: 5 Abram, Haran, Nahor

Teraphim
  origin: 6 Hebrew
  form: 4 idol

Ter Borch, Gerard (Terburg)
  born: 6 Zwolle **14** The Netherlands
  artwork: 8 Flea Hunt **10** The Concert **14** Peace of Munster **21** The Parental Admonition

Terbrugghen, Hendrick
  born: 8 Deventer **14** The Netherlands
  artwork: 8 The Flute Player **19** Liberation of St Peter **21** The Calling of St Matthew

terefah, trefah 9 not kosher

Tereus
  prince of: 6 Thrace
  father: 4 Ares
  wife: 6 Procne
  sister-in-law: 9 Philomela
  raped: 9 Philomela
  son: 4 Itys

tergal 4 back **6** dorsal

Terkel, Studs
  author of: 7 Working **9** Hard Times **14** American Dreams

term, terms 3 age, dub, era, tag **4** call, cite, item, name, span, time, word **5** catch, cycle, epoch, idiom, reign, spell, stage, state, style, while **6** clause, course, detail, period, phrase, status, string **7** dynasty, footing, proviso **8** duration, interval, position, standing **9** condition, designate, provision, relations, requisite **10** expression, span of

time **11** appellation, designation, requirement, stipulation **12** characterize, circumstance, prerequisite **14** administration

termagant 3 nag **4** fury **5** scold, shrew, vixen **6** ogress, virago **7** hellcat, hellion, shewolf, tigress **8** battle-ax, fishwife, harridan, spitfire **9** Xanthippe

Termagant
  character in: 21 medieval morality plays

terminal 3 end **4** last **5** depot, fatal, final, stand **6** deadly, lethal, mortal **7** station **8** terminus **10** concluding

terminate 3 end **4** stop **5** cease, close, lapse **6** expire, finish, run out, wind up **8** complete, conclude **11** come to an end, discontinue **12** bring to an end

termination 3 end **4** halt **5** close, finis, lapse **6** ending, finale, finish, windup **7** closing **8** stoppage **9** cessation **10** completion, concluding, conclusion, expiration **15** discontinuation

terminus 3 end **4** stop **5** depot, limit **6** ending **7** extreme, station **8** boundary, last stop, terminal **9** extremity **10** conclusion

Terminus
  origin: 5 Roman
  god of: 9 landmarks
    10 boundaries

terminus ad quem 10 end to which, final limit **11** ending point

terminus a quo 9 beginning **12** end from which **13** starting point

termite
  variety: 6 desert **7** dry wood **8** damp wood **10** powderpost, rotten wood **11** soldierless **12** subterranean

Terms of Endearment
  director: 12 James L Brooks
  based on novel by: 13 Larry McMurtry
  cast: 11 Debra Winger **13** Jack Nicholson **15** Shirley MacLaine
  Oscar for: 7 actress (MacLaine), picture **8** director **15** supporting actor (Nicholson)

Terpsichore
  member of: 5 Muses
  personifies: 7 dancing
    10 choral song

Terra
  goddess of: 5 Earth

Greek: 4 Gaea
mother: 5 Chaos
offspring: 6 Pontus, Titans,
Uranus **7** Erinyes, Oceanus
8 Cyclopes **9** mountains
13 Hecatonchires

terrace 4 roof **5** level, patio,
plane, porch **6** street **7** balcony, plateau **9** esplanade,
promenade **10** embankment

Terraced Bay *see* **6** Taiwan

terra-cotta 4 clay **6** russet
8 brownish **12** reddish-brown
14 brownish-orange

terrain 4 area, zone **5** tract
6 ground, milieu, region **7** setting **8** district **9** territory
10 topography **11** countryside,
environment **12** surroundings

terra incognita 11 unknown
land **14** unexplored land, unknown subject **16** unknown
territory

Terra Mater *see* **6** Tellus

terrapin 3 box **4** emyd, emys
6 slider, turpin, turtle **8** tortoise **11** diamond back
family: 8 Emydidae
female: 6 heifer
male: 4 bull

terrestrial 4 land **6** earth's,
global, ground **7** earthly, mundane, worldly **8** riparian
10 earthbound

terrible 3 bad **4** dire, huge
5 awful, great, harsh, rough,
scary **6** brutal, fierce, horrid,
odious, severe, strong
7 beastly, extreme, fearful,
ghastly, hateful, heinous, hideous, intense **8** alarming,
dreadful, enormous, fearsome,
horrible, shocking, terrific
9 appalling, excessive, harrowing, monstrous, obnoxious, offensive, repulsive, revolting,
upsetting **10** disturbing, formidable, horrifying, immoderate,
inordinate, terrifying, tremendous, unpleasant **11** distasteful,
distressing, frightening, intolerable **12** insufferable
13 objectionable

terrier
dog breed: 3 fox **4** bull,
Skye **5** Cairn, Irish, Welsh
6 border, Boston **7** Norfolk,
Tibetan, wire fox **8** Airedale,
Lakeland, Scottish, Sealyham **9** Kerry Blue **10** Australian, Bedlington,
Manchester **13** Dandie Dinmont **17** soft-coated wheat-
en, Staffordshire bull, West
Highland white **18** miniature schnauzer **21** American
Staffordshire

terrific 3 fab **4** fine, good,

huge 5 awful, great, harsh,
marvy, scary, super **6** bang-up,
fierce, severe, superb **7** extreme, fearful, intense, sen-
sash **8** alarming, dreadful,
enormous, fabulous, fearsome,
smashing, splendid, terrible
9 excellent, excessive, fantastic, harrowing, marvelous,
monstrous, upsetting, wonderful **10** disturbing, horrifying,
immoderate, inordinate, remarkable, stupendous, super-
duper, terrifying, tremendous
11 distressing, exceptional,
frightening, sensational **13** extraordinary **14** out of this
world

terrified 6 afraid, scared
7 alarmed, panicky **9** petrified
10 frightened **11** scared stiff
13 panic-stricken **14** terror-
stricken **17** frightened to death

terrify 3 cow **5** abash, alarm,
daunt, panic, scare, unman,
upset **6** appall, dismay **7** agitate, disturb, horrify, overawe,
petrify **8** disquiet, frighten
10 intimidate **17** make one's
skin crawl **20** make one's
blood run cold **22** make one's
hair stand on end

terrifying 5 awful, dread
7 fearful **8** alarming, dreadful
9 frightful **11** frightening, hair-
raising

territory 4 area, land, pale,
zone **5** clime, realm, state,
tract **6** bounds, colony, domain, empire, limits, locale,
nation, region, sector
7 acreage, kingdom, mandate,
terrain **8** confines, district, dominion, province **9** bailiwick
10 dependency **11** countryside
12 commonwealth, principality, protectorate

terror 3 awe **4** fear **5** alarm,
dread, panic **6** dismay, fright,
horror **7** anxiety **8** affright,
disquiet **9** agitation **11** disquietude, trepidation **12** apprehension, perturbation
13 consternation **16** fear and
trembling

terrorize 3 cow **5** abash, force
6 menace **7** terrify **8** browbeat,
bulldoze, threaten
10 intimidate

terror-stricken 6 afraid,
scared **7** alarmed, panicky
9 horrified, petrified, terrified
11 scared green, scared stiff
13 panic-stricken, scared to
death

Terry and the Pirates
creator: 12 Milton Caniff
character: 7 Pat Ryan **8** Terry
Lee **10** Dragon Lady

terse 4 curt, neat **5** brief, clear,
crisp, pithy, short **6** abrupt
7 clipped, compact, concise, laconic, pointed, summary
8 clearcut, incisive, succinct
9 axiomatic, condensed,
trenchant **10** compressed
11 unambiguous **12** epigrammatic **18** brief and to the
point

terseness 7 brevity **8** curtness
9 crispness **10** abruptness
11 compactness, conciseness
12 succinctness

Tesman family
characters in: 11 Hedda
Gabler
members: 5 Hedda **6** George
7 Juliana
author: 5 Ibsen

Tess (of the D'Urbervilles)
author: 11 Thomas Hardy
director: 13 Roman Polanski
cast: 8 John Bett **10** Peter
Firth, Tom Chadbon
14 Rosemary Martin
15 Nastassia Kinski (Tess)

test 4 exam, quiz **5** check, final, flyer, probe, proof, prove,
trial **6** dry run, feeler, try out,
verify **7** analyze, confirm, examine, midterm **8** analysis,
validate **9** catechism **11** corroborate, examination, investigate, questioning
12 confirmation, substantiate,
verification **13** comprehensive,
corroboration, investigation,
questionnaire

Testament 5 Bible **7** the
Book **10** Scriptures **12** New
Testament, Old Testament

testament 6 legacy **7** bequest
10 settlement

tester 6 canopy **8** examiner
10 questioner

testify 4 show **5** prove, swear
6 affirm, attest, evince **7** declare, signify **8** evidence, indicate, manifest **11** bear witness,
demonstrate **12** give evidence

testimonial 5 medal **6** ribbon,
trophy **7** tribute **8** citation,
memorial, monument **9** affidavit, reference **10** deposition
11 certificate, endorsement
12 commendation
14 recommendation

testimony 5 proof **6** avowal
7 witness **8** averment, evidence **9** affidavit, statement
10 deposition, indication,
profession **11** affirmation, attestation, endorsement
12 confirmation, verification
13 certification, corroboration,
demonstration, documentation,
manifestation
14 acknowledgment

testy 5 cross, moody **6** crabby, cranky, crusty, filthy, grumpy, snappy, sullen, touchy **7** fretful, peevish, waspish **8** captious, caviling, choleric, churlish, perverse, petulant, snappish, snarling **9** fractious, impatient, irascible, irritable, splenetic **10** ill-humored **11** acrimonious, contentious **12** cantankerous, faultfinding, sharp-tongued **13** quick-tempered, temperamental

tete-a-tete 4 chat, talk **6** parley **9** interview **12** conversation **13** confabulation

tether 3 tie **4** cord, rein, rope **5** chain, leash **6** fasten, halter, hobble, secure

Tethys
member of: **6** Titans
father: **6** Uranus
mother: **4** Gaea
husband: **7** Oceanus
mother of: **8** Oceanids **9** river gods
daughters: **13** three thousand
foster child: **4** Hera

Teucer
king of: **4** Troy
father: **7** Telamon **9** Scamander
mother: **5** Idaea **7** Hesione
half-brother: **9** Great Ajax **14** Telemonian Ajax
daughter: **5** Batia
skilled in: **7** archery
founded: **7** Salamis

Teuthis
also: **7** Ornytus
rank: **7** general
wounded: **6** Athena

Teuthras
mentioned in: **5** Iliad
king of: **5** Mysia **7** Phrygia
mother: **8** Leucippe
daughter: **8** Tecmessa
killed: **4** boar
boar sacred to: **7** Artemis
killed by: **6** Hector

Teutonic 5 Dutch **6** German, Gothic, Nordic **7** British, English **8** Germanic **12** Scandinavian
alphabet character: **4** rune
demon: **3** alp
goddess of death: **3** Hel, Ran
goddess of peace: **7** Nerthus
god of peace: **6** Balder
god of thunder: **4** Thor
god of war: **3** Tiu, Tyr
god of wisdom: **4** Odin

Teutonic Mythology *see* **17** Germanic Mythology

Texas *see box*

text 5 motif, theme, topic, verse, words **6** manual, primer, sermon, thesis **7** content, passage, subject, word-

ing **8** argument, sentence, textbook, workbook **9** paragraph, quotation **10** schoolbook **13** subject matter

textile 4 yarn **5** cloth, fiber **6** fabric **8** filament, material **9** yard goods **10** piece goods

texture 3 nap **4** feel, look **5** grain, touch, weave **6** makeup **7** quality, surface **8** fineness **9** character, structure **10** coarseness **11** composition

Tey, Josephine
real name: **19** Elizabeth MacKintosh
author of: **10** Brat Farrar **15** Miss Pym Disposes, The Singing Sands **17** The Daughter of Time **19** A Shilling for Candles
character: **9** Alan Grant

Thackeray, William Makepeace
author of: **9** Pendennis **10** Vanity Fair **11** Barry Lyndon, Henry Esmond, The Newcomes **13** The Virginians

Thaddeus of Arimathea *see* **5** Judas

Thaddeus of Warsaw
author: **10** Jane Porter

Thai-Austronesian
language branch: **9** Thai-Kadai **12** Austronesian
includes: **5** Batak, Malay **6** Fijian, Samoan **7** Tagalog **8** Hawaiian, Javanese **15** Bahasa Indonesia
spoken in: **4** Fiji, Java **5** China, Samoa **6** Hawaii, Taiwan **7** Sumatra **9** Indonesia, Polynesia **10** Madagas-

Texas
abbreviation: **2** TX **3** Tex
nickname: **8** Lone Star
capital: **6** Austin
largest city: **7** Houston
others: **4** Gail, Rice, Vega, Waco **5** Bryan, Marfa, Ozona, Pampa, Tyler, Wiley **6** Baylor, Borger, Dallas, Denton, El Paso, Kileen, Laredo, Odessa, Quanah, Sonora **7** Abilene, Denison, Lubbock **8** Amarillo, Beaumont, Floydada **9** Fort Worth, Galveston **10** San Antonio **13** Corpus Christi
college: **3** SMU, TCU **4** Rice **5** Lamar, Wiley **6** Austin, Baylor **7** St Mary's, Trinity **10** Texas A and M **12** Southwestern **14** Texas Christian **16** Abilene Christian **17** Southern Methodist
feature:
  fort: **5** Alamo
  national park: **7** Big Bend **18** Guadalupe Mountains
  national seashore: **11** Padre Island
  state park: **10** San Jacinto
tribe: **4** Adar, Waco **5** Caddo, Lipan **6** Apache, Biloxi, Jumano, Kichai, Shuman, Tejano **7** Alabama, Hasinai, Tonkawa **8** Comanche, Querecho **9** Coushatta, Karankawa
people: **10** James S Hogg **12** Edward M House, Thomas C Clark **13** John B Connally, Samuel Houston **14** Chester W Nimitz, Mirabeau B Lamar, Samuel T Rayburn, Stephen F Austin, William B Travis **15** John Nance Garner, Thomas T Connally **19** Katherine Anne Porter
  explorer: **4** Vaca **7** La Salle
island: **5** Padre
lake: **6** Falcon, Sabine, Texoma **7** Amistad
river: **3** Red **5** Pecos **6** Brazos, Neches, Nueces, Sabine **7** Trinity **8** Colorado **9** Rio Grande **10** San Jacinto
land rank: **12** second
physical feature:
  bay: **13** Corpus Christi
  port: **7** Houston **9** Galveston **13** Corpus Christi
president: **14** Lyndon B Johnson **17** Dwight D Eisenhower
  Republic of Texas: **10** Sam Houston
state admission: **12** twenty-eighth
state bird: **11** mockingbird
state flower: **10** bluebonnet, yellow rose
state motto: **10** Friendship
state song: **13** Texas Our Texas
state tree: **5** pecan
baseball team: **7** Rangers

Thailand
  name means: 13 land of the free
  other name: 4 Siam 11 Prathet Thai
  capital/largest city: 6 Bankok 7 Bangkok
    old capital: 8 Thonburi 9 Ayutthaya
  others: 4 Ubon 5 Puket 6 Nakhon, Ranong 7 Ayudhya, Ayuthea, Lampang, Lamphur, Lopburi, Rahaeng, Singora, Songkla 8 Khonkaen, Kiangmai, Songkhla, Sukhotai, Thonburi 9 Ayutthaya, Chiangmai, Chiengmai 10 Ratchasima 11 Phitsanulok 14 Ubonratchthani
  kingdom: 5 Funan 6 Khymer 8 Thonburi 9 Ayutthaya, Chiang Mai, Dvaravati, Sukhothai 12 Subarnabhumi
  school: 9 Thammasat 13 Chulalongkorn
  head of state: 4 king
  measure: 2 wa 3 can, ken, niv, rai, sat, sok, wah 4 cohi, keup, niou, tang 5 kwien, leeng, sesti, vouah 6 kabiet, kanahn 7 chaimeu 8 changawn 9 anukabiet
  monetary unit: 2 at 3 att 4 baht 5 cutty, fuang 6 pynung, salung 11 bullet money
  weight: 3 bat, hap, pay, sen, sok 4 baht, haph, kati, klam 5 catty, chang, fuang, picul, pilul, tical 6 fluang, graini, salung, 7 tamlung
  island: 2 Ko 3 Kut, Tao 4 Chan, Rawi 5 Chang, Lanta, Samui, Thalu 6 Libong, Phuket 7 Phangan, Terutao
  lake: 9 Nong Lahan
  mountain: 5 Dawna, Khieo 6 Phanom 8 Dang Raek, Kao Prawa, Maelamun 9 Khao Luang 11 Bilauktaung
  highest point: 8 Inthanon 11 Doi Inthanon
  river: 3 Chi, Mun, Nan, Yom 4 Ping 5 Menam 6 Mekong, Meping 7 Salween 10 Chaophraya
  sea: 7 Andaman
  physical feature:
    gulf: 4 Siam 8 Thailand
    isthmus: 3 Kra
    pass: 12 Three Pagodas
    peninsula: 5 Malay
    plateau: 5 Korat 6 Khorat
  people: 3 Lao, Mon 4 Lawa, Shan, Thai 5 Malay 6 Indian, Khymer 7 Chinese, Siamese 9 Cambodian 10 Vietnamese
    king: 4 Rama 7 Chakkri, Mongkut 10 Chao Phraya 12 Prahjadhipok 13 Chulalongkorn 17 Bhumibol Adulyadej
    leader: 9 Phraruang 12 Kukrit-Pramoj
  language: 3 Lao, Tai 4 Ahom, Shan, Thai 5 Kadai, Malay 7 Bangkok, Chinese, English 9 Krung Thep
  religion: 5 Islam 8 Buddhism 12 Christianity, Confucianism 17 Theravada Buddhism
  place:
    dam: 8 Bhumibol
    palace: 5 Grand
    ruins: 7 Ayuthia 9 Ayutthaya
    street: 7 Yawarai
    temple: 4 Dawn 7 Trimitr 10 Wat Phra Keo 11 Royal Chapel 13 Emerald Buddha
  feature:
    canal: 5 klong
    clothing: 6 panung, sarong 12 saffron robes
    festival: 12 Surin Round Up
    houseboat: 6 sampan
    temple: 3 wat
    tree: 4 teak
  food:
    fruit: 5 camut 6 durian, litchi, pomelo 8 rambutan 10 mangosteen

car 11 Philippines 12 Easter Island

Thailand *see box*

Thais
  author: 13 Anatole France
  character: 8 Athanael
  composer: 8 Massenet

Thalassa
  personifies: 3 sea

thalassic 6 marine 7 aquatic, deep-sea, neritic, oceanic, pelagic

Thales
  field: 11 mathematics
  nationality: 5 Greek
  discovered: 18 geometry principles
  predicted: 11 sun's eclipse

Thalestris
  character in: 16 The Rape of the Lock
  author: 4 Pope

Thalia
  member of: 5 Muses 6 Graces
  personifies: 6 comedy 13 idyllic poetry
  lover: 4 Zeus
  killed by: 5 Erato

Thallo
  member of: 5 Horae
  goddess of: 13 spring flowers

Thamyris
  vocation: 4 poet 8 musician
  father: 9 Philammon
  mother: 7 Argiope
  punished for: 9 arrogance
  punished by: 5 Muses

punishment: 7 maiming **8** blinding

thanatophobia
  fear of: 5 death

Thanatos
  personifies: 5 death

thank 5 bless **12** be grateful to **13** be much obliged **18** express gratitude to

thankful 7 obliged **8** beholden, grateful **10** indebted to **12** appreciative, full of thanks **16** feeling gratitude **22** expressing appreciation

thankfulness 6 thanks **9** gratitude **12** appreciation, gratefulness

thankless 4 vain **7** ingrate, useless **8** bootless, caviling, critical, heedless **9** fruitless, unmindful, unwelcome **10** profitless, ungracious, ungrateful, uninviting, unpleasant, unrewarded, unthankful **11** distasteful, thoughtless, undesirable, unrewarding **12** disagreeable, faultfinding **13** inconsiderate, unappreciated **14** unacknowledged, unappreciative

thanks 5 grace **8** blessing **9** gratitude **11** benediction **12** appreciation, gratefulness

thanks be to God
  Latin: 10 Deo gratias

thanksgiving 6 thanks **8** blessing

Thanksgiving
  started by: 8 Bradford, Pilgrims
  traditional food: 4 corn, yams **6** turkey **10** pumpkin pie **13** sweet potatoes **14** cranberry sauce
  symbol: 9 ear of corn **12** horn of plenty

thank you
  French: 5 merci
  German: 5 danke
  Spanish: 7 gracias
  Italian: 6 grazie
  Japanese: 4 domo

Thank You, Fog
  author: 7 W H Auden

Thank You, Jeeves
  author: 11 P G Wodehouse

thank you very much
  French: 9 merci bien **13** merci beaucoup
  German: 10 danke schon
  Japanese: 11 domo arigato
  Spanish: 13 muchas gracias

That Certain Feeling
  author: 12 Kingsley Amis

Thatcher, Becky
  character in: 9 Tom Sawyer
  author: 5 Twain

Thatcher, Judge
  character in: 15 (The Adventures of) Huckleberry Finn
  author: 5 Twain

That Girl
  character: 8 Ann Marie, Lou Marie **10** Helen Marie, Ruth Bauman **11** Jerry Bauman **12** Don Hollinger, Judy Bessemer **14** Dr Leon Bessemer
  cast: 9 Lew Parker **10** Ted Bessell **11** Alice Borden, Bonnie Scott, Marlo Thomas **12** Bernie Kopell **13** Dabney Coleman **14** Carolyn Daniels, Rosemary DeCamp

that is
  Latin: 2 ie **5** id est

that is to say
  Latin: 3 viz **9** videlicet

that's life
  French: 9 c'est la vie

thaw 4 melt, warm **5** relax **6** soften, unbend, warm up **7** liquefy, melting, thawing **8** dissolve **11** break the ice

Thea
  companion of: 7 Artemis
  ravished by: 6 Aeolus
  changed into: 4 mare
    mare named: **6** Euippe

Theale, Milly
  character in: 17 The Wings of the Dove
  author: 5 James

theater 4 site **5** arena, drama, house, movie, odeum, place, scene, stage **6** cinema, lyceum **7** gallery, setting **8** assembly, audience, coliseum **9** colosseum, music hall, playhouse **10** assemblage, auditorium, movie house, spectators **11** histrionics, lecture hall, theatricals **12** amphitheater, show business

theatrical 4 film **5** hammy, movie, showy, stage, stagy **6** flashy **7** fustian, show-biz, stilted **8** affected, dramatic, mannered, thespian **9** grandiose, unnatural **10** artificial, histrionic **11** exaggerated, extravagant, pretentious, spectacular **12** magniloquent, ostentatious, show-business **13** entertainment, grandiloquent **14** larger-than-life

theatrical trick
  French: 13 coup de theatre

Thebaid
  author: 7 Statius
  character: 4 Atys **5** Creon **6** Ismene, Tydeus **7** Jocasta,

Theseus 8 Antigone, Capaneus, Eteocles, Opheltes, Tiresias **9** Menoeceus, Polynices **10** Amphiaraus, Hippomedon, Melanippus

the bottle 5 booze, drink, sauce **6** liquor **7** alcohol **8** demon rum

the dansant 8 tea dance

thee therefore
  Latin: 8 te igitur

theft 5 fraud **7** larceny, looting, robbery **8** burglary, filching, rustling, stealing, thievery **9** hijacking, pilfering, swindling **10** purloining **11** shoplifting **12** embezzlement
  god of: 6 Hermes **7** Mercury

Theia
  also: 4 Thia
  member of: 6 Titans
  father: 6 Uranus
  mother: 4 Gaea
  brother: 8 Hyperion
  mother of: 8 Cercopes
  son: 6 Helios
  daughter: 3 Eos **6** Selene

the life of the land is maintained by righteousness
  Hawaiian: 52 ua mau ke ea o ka aina i ka pono
  motto of: 6 Hawaii

Them
  author: 15 Joyce Carol Oates

theme 3 air **4** song, text, tune **5** essay, focus, motif, point, topic, tract **6** melody, report, review, strain, thesis **7** keynote, premise, subject **8** argument, critique, question, treatise **9** discourse, leitmotif, monograph **10** commentary **11** composition, proposition **12** dissertation

Themis
  member of: 6 Titans
  father: 6 Uranus
  mother: 4 Gaea
  sister: 6 Phoebe
  consort of: 4 Zeus
  husband: 7 Iapetus
  mother of: 5 Fates, Horae **6** Moerae **7** Seasons
  son: 10 Prometheus
  personifies: 7 justice

Themiste
  father: 8 Laomedon
  mother: 8 Eurydice
  son: 8 Anchises

Then Again, Maybe I Won't
  author: 9 Judy Blume

thence 6 whence **9** from there, therefore **11** accordingly, in due course **13** from that place

the next world 6 Heaven

8 eternity, paradise **12** the hereafter **14** the world to come

the norm 7 the mean, the rule **9** the median **10** the average **14** the common thing

the Occident 7 the West **20** the western hemisphere

Theoclymenus
king of: **5** Egypt
father: **7** Proteus
mother: **8** Psamathe
vocation: **4** seer

theologian *see* **22** philosopher/theologian

theological 4 holy **6** sacred **8** Biblical, dogmatic **9** apostolic, canonical, doctrinal, religious, spiritual **10** scriptural **14** ecclesiastical

theology 5 dogma **8** divinity, doctrine, religion

Theonoe
father: **7** Proteus, Thestor

Theophane
bore: **3** ram
fleece of ram: **6** golden

theoretical 8 abstract, academic, putative **11** conjectural, postulatory, speculative **12** hypothetical, nonpractical **13** suppositional

theorize 5 infer, posit, think **6** assume **7** imagine, presume, propose, suppose, surmise **8** propound **9** formulate, postulate, predicate, speculate **10** conjecture **11** hypothecate, hypothesize

theory 3 law **4** idea, view **5** guess **6** belief, notion, thesis **7** concept, opinion, science, surmise, thought **8** doctrine, ideology, judgment **9** deduction, postulate, principle **10** conclusion, conjecture, hypothesis, persuasion, philosophy **11** presumption, speculation, supposition

therapeutic, therapeutical 7 healing **8** curative, remedial, salutary, sanative **11** restorative **12** ameliorative

Therapne
means: **12** burial ground

therapy 7 healing **9** treatment **14** rehabilitation

thereafter 5 later **9** after that, afterward **10** afterwards, from then on **11** thenceforth **12** subsequently **14** from that time on

therefore 2 so **4** ergo, thus **5** hence **11** accordingly **12** consequently, on that ground **13** for that reason, in

consequence, on that account **14** for which reason

there is no disputing about tastes
Latin: **27** de gustibus non est disputandum

there it is
French: **5** voila

Therese Raquin
author: **9** Emile Zola
character: **7** Camille, Laurent

There Shall Be No Night
author: **15** Robert E Sherwood

thereupon 4 then **6** at once **7** thereon **8** directly, suddenly, upon that **9** forthwith, in a moment, upon which **11** immediately **12** straightaway, without delay

Therimachus
father: **8** Hercules
mother: **6** Megary
killed by: **8** Hercules

Theritas *see* **4** Ares

Thermasia
epithet of: **7** Demeter
means: **6** warmth

thermometer
invented by: **7** Galileo, Reaumur
mercury: **10** Fahrenheit

Thero
nurse of: **4** Ares

theropod
type of: **8** dinosaur
member: **10** Allosaurus, Antrodemus **11** Coelophysis, Gorgosaurus **13** Albertosaurus, Compsognathus, Struthiomimus, Tyrannosaurus

Theroux, Paul
author of: **9** Saint Jack **16** The Mosquito Coast **20** Riding the Iron Rooster **21** The Great Railway Bazaar **23** The Old Patagonian Express

Thersander
member of: **7** Epigoni

Thersilochus
mentioned in: **5** Iliad
killed by: **8** Achilles

Thersites
mentioned in: **5** Iliad
origin: **5** Greek
characteristics: **4** ugly **8** deformed **11** quarrelsome
accused Agamemnon of: **5** greed
accused Achilles of: **9** cowardice
fought in: **9** Trojan War
killed by: **8** Achilles

the same as 4 like **7** equal to **9** a match for **12** comparable to, equivalent to, tanta-

mount to **16** commensurate with

thesaurus 8 synonymy **10** word finder **11** synonymicon **12** word treasury **13** synonym finder **17** synonym dictionary **18** semantic dictionary

Thescelosaurus
type: **8** dinosaur **10** ornithopod
location: **6** Canada **12** United States
period: **10** Cretaceous

These Three
director: **12** William Wyler
based on play by: **14** Lillian Hellman (The Children's Hour)
cast: **10** Alma Kruger, Joel McCrea **11** Merle Oberon **13** Miriam Hopkins **15** Bonita Granville, Catherine Doucet

These Twain
author: **13** Arnold Bennett

Theseus
king of: **6** Athens
father: **6** Aegeus **8** Poseidon
mother: **6** Aethra
wife: **7** Phaedra
consort: **9** Hippolyta
lover: **7** Ariadne
son: **6** Acamas **8** Demophon **10** Hippolytus, Melanippus
helmsman: **10** Nausithous
killed: **5** Sinis **6** Sciron **8** Minotaur **10** Cretan bull, Procrustes

thesis 5 essay, paper, tract **6** notion, theory **7** article, concept, surmise **8** argument, critique, proposal, treatise **9** discourse, monograph, postulate, term paper **10** commentary, conjecture, hypothesis **11** composition, proposition, speculation, supposition **12** disquisition, dissertation

Thesmia
epithet of: **7** Demeter
means: **12** goddess of law

Thesmophorus
epithet of: **7** Demeter
means: **8** lawgiver

Thesophoria
origin: **5** Greek
event: **8** festival

thespian 3 ham **4** star **5** actor, extra **6** co-star, player, walk-on **7** actress, ingenue, trouper **8** juvenile **9** bit-player, guest star, performer, tragedian **10** leading man **11** leading lady, stage player

Thespian Lion
attacked: **6** flocks
flock owner: **10** Amphitryon
killed by: **8** Hercules

Thespius
founded city of: **8** Thespiae
wife: **8** Megamede
daughters: **5** fifty

Thessalus
king of: **8** Thessaly
father: **5** Jason **8** Hercules
mother: **5** Medea **9** Chalciope

the state
Latin: **10** res publica

Thestius
king of: **7** Aetolia
father: **4** Ares
mother: **8** Demonice

Thestor
son: **7** Calchas
daughter: **7** Theonoe
8 Leucippe

Thetis
member of: **7** Nereids
husband: **6** Peleus
sister: **8** Eurynome
son: **8** Achilles

the very words
Latin: **14** ipsissima verba

the world over 10 every
place, everywhere, far and
wide, near and far **11** in all
places

**They Shoot Horses, Don't
They?**
director: **13** Sydney Pollack
cast: **8** Gig Young **9** Bruce
Dern, Jane Fonda **10** Red
Buttons **12** Susannah York
13 Bonnie Bedelia **15** Michael Sarrazin
Oscar for: **15** supporting actor (Young)

They Won't Forget
director: **11** Mervyn LeRoy
cast: **10** Lana Turner, Otto
Kruger **11** Allyn Joslyn,
Claude Rains **12** Elisha Cook
Jr **13** Gloria Dickson

Thia *see* **5** Theia

Thialfi
origin: **12** Scandinavian
servant of: **4** Thor
talent: **8** fastness

Thiasos *see* **7** Thiasus

thiasus
also: **7** thiasos
group worshipping: **11** patron deity
followers of: **8** Dionysus
followers called: **6** satyrs
7 maenads

Thiazi
also: **6** Thjazi
origin: **12** Scandinavian
form: **5** giant
carried away: **4** Iden **6** apples

thick 3 big, fat **4** deep, dull,
dumb, slow, wide **5** broad,
bulky, close, dense, fuzzy,
great, heavy, husky, piled,
solid **6** chummy, heaped,
hoarse, lavish, obtuse, packed,
strong, stupid, viscid, wooden
7 blurred, clotted, compact, copious, crowded, decided, devoted, doltish, extreme,
intense, liberal, muffled, profuse, teeming, throaty, viscous **8** abundant, familiar,
friendly, generous, guttural,
intimate, profound, sisterly,
swarming **9** brotherly, condensed, fatheaded, glutinous,
plenteous, unstinted **10** coagulated, dull-witted, gelatinous,
indistinct, munificent, pronounced, slow-witted **11** inseparable, overflowing
12 concentrated, impenetrable,
inarticulate

thicken 3 set **4** cake, clot, jell
5 muddy **6** darken, deepen,
muddle **7** compact, congeal,
jellify **8** condense **9** coagulate,
intensify **10** gelatinize

thicket 4 bush, wood **5** brake,
brush, copse, grove, scrub
6 bushes, covert, forest,
shrubs **7** bracken **9** shrubbery
10 underbrush **11** undergrowth

thickheaded 4 dull, dumb,
slow **5** blank, dense, dopey,
thick **6** obtuse, stupid **8** ignorant **9** dim-witted, fatheaded
10 boneheaded, dull-witted,
half-witted, slow-witted
11 blockheaded, thick-witted
12 dunderheaded, thickskulled **13** chuckleheaded,
knuckleheaded

thickset 5 bulky, close, dense,
dumpy, husky, solid, squat,
stout, tubby **6** chunky, packed,
stocky, stubby, stumpy,
sturdy **8** close-set, heavyset,
roly-poly

thickskinned 4 hard **5** horny,
tough **6** inured **7** callous
8 callused, hardened **9** unfeeling, unmovable **10** impervious,
insensible **11** insensitive, unconcerned **13** imperturbable,
unsusceptible
14 pachydermatous

thick-skulled 4 dull **5** dense
6 stupid **11** thickheaded
12 dunderheaded

thick-witted 4 dull, slow
5 dense **6** stupid **7** idiotic, moronic **9** dim-witted, imbecilic
11 thickheaded **12** dunderheaded, simple-minded

thief 5 crook **6** bandit, mugger,
robber **7** burglar, filcher, rustler **8** hijacker, pilferer, swindler **9** defrauder, embezzler,
holdup man, larcenist, purloiner, racketeer **10** highwayman,
pickpocket, shoplifter
12 housebreaker, kleptomaniac **13** confidence man, pursesnatcher **14** second-story man

Thief of Bagdad, The
director: **9** Tim Whelan
12 Ludwig Berger **13** Michael Powell
cast: **4** Sabu **9** Rex Ingram
10 John Justin, June Duprez **11** Conrad Veidt

Thieves' Carnival
also: **15** Le Bal des Voleurs
author: **11** Jean Anouilh

thievish 3 sly **6** sneaky **7** furtive **8** stealthy, thieving **9** dishonest, larcenous, secretive,
thieflike **13** light-fingered, surreptitious **14** sticky-fingered

thigh 3 ham, leg **4** hock **5** femur, flank, ilium **6** gammon
pain: **8** meralgia

Thimbu, Thimphu
capital of: **6** Bhutan

thin 4 fine, lank, lean, slim,
weak **5** faint, gaunt, lanky,
prune, runny, scant, sheer,
spare, water **6** dilute, feeble,
narrow, not fat, reduce,
skinny, slight, sparse, watery
7 curtail, diluted, fragile,
scrawny, slender, spindly
8 delicate, diminish, finespun
9 emaciated, water down
10 inadequate, threadlike
11 transparent **12** insufficient
13 unsubstantial

thin-blooded 3 wan **4** pale,
weak **6** anemic, sickly

thing, things 3 act **4** deed,
feat, gear, item **5** event,
gizmo, goods, point **6** action,
affair, aspect, detail, dingus,
entity, gadget, matter, object,
person **7** article, clothes, concern, effects, feature, thought
8 business, clothing, creature,
movables **9** doohickey, equipment, happening, statement
10 belongings, human being,
occurrence, particular, proceeding **11** eventuality, living
being, possessions, thingamabob, thingamajig, transaction
12 circumstance
13 paraphernalia

thing already done
French: **12** fait accompli

thingamajig 5 gizmo **6** doodad,
gadget **11** contraption, contrivance, thingamabob
15 whatchamacallit

thing of no value
Latin: **5** nihil

things done
Latin: **9** res gestae

think 4 deem, mean, plan
5 brood, fancy, guess, judge

6 design, expect, intend, ponder, reason, recall, reckon 7 believe, dwell on, imagine, presume, propose, purpose, reflect, suppose, surmise 8 cogitate, conceive, conclude, contrive, meditate, mull over, remember, ruminate 9 recollect, speculate 10 anticipate, deliberate, have in mind, keep in mind 11 contemplate, use one's mind, use one's wits 13 rack one's brain

thinkable 8 knowable 10 imaginable 11 conceivable, perceivable

think about 4 mull 6 debate, ponder 7 reflect 8 consider, mull over 10 deliberate

think alike 5 agree 11 be of one mind, see eye to eye

thinker 4 sage 6 savant, wizard 7 egghead, scholar 9 intellect 10 mastermind 11 mental giant, philosopher 13 metaphysician

think fit 4 deem 5 deign, stoop 7 consent 10 condescend

think highly of 5 favor, honor, value 6 admire, esteem, revere 7 approve, respect 8 look up to, venerate 10 set store by

think ill of 4 hate 5 decry 6 detest 7 condemn, deplore, despise, dislike 8 object to 9 abominate, disparage, frown upon 10 disapprove 13 look askance at 14 discountenance 15 take exception to 16 find unacceptable, view with disfavor

thinking 4 view 5 smart, stand, study 6 belief, bright 7 concept, surmise, thought 8 cultured, educated, judgment, position, rational, studious 9 brainwork, deduction, inference, reasoning 10 conclusion, cultivated, impression, meditation, meditative, reflection, reflective, rumination, thoughtful 11 intelligent, speculation 12 deliberation 13 consideration, contemplation, contemplative, philosophical, sophisticated, using one's head 15 paying attention

Thinking Reed, The
author: 15 Dame Rebecca West

think over 5 study, weigh 8 cogitate, consider, mull over 11 reflect upon 12 deliberate on

think through 5 weigh 6 ponder 7 analyze 8 appraise, consider, evaluate

think up 5 frame, hatch 6 create, invent 7 concoct, dream up 8 conceive, contrive

think well of 4 like 6 admire 8 look up to 10 appreciate

Thin Man, The
author: 15 Dashiell Hammett
character: 7 Morelli 11 Nick Charles, Nora Charles 13 Arthur Nunheim, Mimi Jorgensen 15 Herbert Macaulay 18 Christian Jorgensen
Wynant family: 5 Clyde 7 Dorothy, Gilbert
director: 11 W S Van Dyke II
cast: 4 Asta 8 Myrna Loy (Nora Charles) 13 William Powell (Nick Charles)
sequel (film): 14 Another Thin Man 15 After the Thin Man 16 Song of the Thin Man 18 The Thin Man Goes Home

Thin Mountain Air, The
author: 10 Paul Horgan

thin out 5 prune 6 dilute, reduce, weaken 7 weed out 9 water down 10 adulterate

thinskinned 5 cross, huffy, sulky, testy 6 grumpy, sullen, touchy 7 crabbed, peevish 8 petulant, snappish 9 irascible, irritable, sensitive, squeamish 11 ill-tempered, quarrelsome, susceptible 12 cantankerous 13 oversensitive 14 hypersensitive

third estate
French: 9 tiers etat

Third Man, The
director: 9 Carol Reed
based on story by: 12 Graham Greene
cast: 10 Alida Valli 11 Orson Welles (Harry Lime) 12 Joseph Cotten, Trevor Howard 16 Wilfrid Hyde-White
setting: 6 Vienna

Third Wave, The
author: 12 Alvin Toffler

thirst 3 yen 4 itch, lust, pant 5 ardor, covet, crave, yearn 6 desire, fervor, hunger, relish 7 craving, passion, stomach 8 appetite, keenness, voracity, yearning 9 hanker for, hankering 11 thirstiness

thirsty 3 dry 4 avid 5 eager 7 parched 9 thirsting

Thirteen O'Clock
author: 19 Stephen Vincent Benet

Thirty-Nine Steps, The (The 39 Steps)
author: 10 John Buchan
director: 15 Alfred Hitchcock

cast: 11 Robert Donat 13 Godfrey Tearle, Lucie Mannheim, Peggy Ashcroft 16 Madeleine Carroll

This Above All
author: 10 Eric Knight

Thisbe
loved: 7 Pyramus
location: 7 Babylon
death by: 7 suicide
death at tomb of: 5 Ninus

this is
Latin: 6 hoc est

This Is Your Life
host: 12 Ralph Edwards
announcer: 9 Bob Warren

Thisoa
form: 5 nymph
tended: 4 Zeus

thistle 7 Cirsium
varieties: 3 Oat 4 Bull, Holy, Milk, Star 5 Glove, Plume, White 6 Canada, Cotton, Golden, Scotch, Silver 7 Blessed, St Mary's 8 Fishbone, Mountain, Plumless 9 Argentine, Thornless 10 Great globe, Small globe 11 Mountain sow 14 Acanthus-leaved

Thjazi see 6 Thiazi

Thoas see 5 Thoon

Thokk
origin: 12 Scandinavian
form: 8 giantess
refused to weep for: 5 Baldr 6 Balder, Baldur
possible disguise of: 4 Loki

Thomas 7 apostle
means: 4 twin
also called: 7 Didymus, Doubter 8 Doubting

Thomas, Ambroise
born: 4 Metz 6 France
composer of: 6 Mignon

Thomas, Danny
real name: 16 Amos Muzyad Jacobs
born: 11 Deerfield MI
daughter: 11 Marlo Thomas
roles: 13 The Jazz Singer 16 Make Room for Daddy 19 I'll See You in My Dreams

Thomas, Dylan
author of: 8 Fern Hill 13 Under Milk Wood 23 A Child's Christmas in Wales

Thomas, George H
nickname: 20 The Rock of Chickamauga
served in: 8 Civil War 10 Mexican War
side: 5 Union
commander of: 19 Army of the Cumberland

battle: 9 Nashville **11** Chattanooga, Chickamauga

Thomas, Marlo
real name: 14 Margaret
Thomas
born: 9 Detroit MI
father: 11 Danny Thomas
husband: 11 Phil Donahue
roles: 8 That Girl

Thomas, W Morgan
creator/artist of: 22 Sheena
Queen of the Jungle

Thomas a Kempis
author of: 20 The Imitation
of Christ

**Thompson, Estelle Merle
O'Brien**
real name of: 11 Merle
Oberon

Thomson, Joseph John
field: 7 physics
nationality: 7 British
discovered: 8 electron
awarded: 10 Nobel Prize

Thomson, Thomas John
born: 6 Canada **9** Claremont
artwork: 9 Spring Ice **11** The
Jack Pine **12** Northern
Lake **13** Northern River

Thomson, Virgil
born: 12 Kansas City MO
composer of: 9 Portraits
16 The Mother of Us All
21 Four Saints in Three
Acts

thong 4 band **5** strap, strip
6 sandal **7** binding

Thoon
also: 5 Thoas
11 Nebrophonus
member of: 8 Gigantes
attacked wall of: 6 Greeks
killed by: 8 Hercules
10 Antilochus

Thor
origin: 12 Scandinavian
god of: 4 rain **7** farming,
thunder
rode: 7 chariot
chariot pulled by: 5 goats
wielded: 6 hammer **7** Miolnir
father: 4 Odin **5** Othin

thorax 5 chest, trunk **6** breast,
cavity **8** forebody

Thoreau, Henry David
author of: 6 Walden (Life in
the Woods) **17** Civil
Disobedience

thorium
chemical symbol: 2 Th

thorn 3 woe **4** bane, barb,
care, gall, spur **5** cross, curse,
spike, spine, sting **6** plague
7 prickle, scourge, torment,
trouble **8** nuisance, vexation
9 annoyance, sore point **10** af-

fliction, bitter pill, infliction,
irritation

thorn 9 Crataegus
varieties: 3 Box **4** Lily, Pear
5 Camel, Hedge, White
6 Christ, Karroo, Mysore,
Sallow, Sickle, Winter
7 Thirsty **8** Cockspur, Egyptian, Kangaroo, Quick-set
9 Jerusalem, Paper-bark
10 Washington **11** Crucifixion **13** Yellow-fruited

Thornbirds, The
author: 17 Colleen
McCullough

Thornburg, Betty June
real name of: 11 Betty
Hutton

Thornfield
house in: 8 Jane Eyre
author: 6 Bronte

Thornhill, Squire
character in: 19 The Vicar of
Wakefield
author: 9 Goldsmith

thorn in the side 4 bane
7 torment **9** annoyance
10 irritation

thorny 4 dire, hard **5** spiny,
tough **6** barbed, spiked, sticky,
trying **7** arduous, brambly,
complex, crucial, irksome,
prickly **8** annoying, critical, involved, ticklish **9** bristling,
dangerous, difficult, vexatious
10 formidable, nettlesome, perplexing **11** complicated,
troublesome

thorough 4 full, pure **5** sheer,
total, utter **6** entire **7** careful,
perfect, uniform **8** absolute,
complete, of a piece **9** downright, out-and-out **10** consistent, definitive, exhaustive,
meticulous **11** painstaking, unmitigated, unqualified **12** all-
embracing, all-inclusive

**thoroughbred, Thorough-
bred 7** unmixed **8** purebred
9 blueblood, pedigreed, racehorse **10** aristocrat **11** full-
blooded, pure-blooded
12 silkstocking

thoroughfare 4 road **6** avenue,
street **7** freeway, highway,
parkway, roadway, thruway
8 main road, turnpike
9 boulevard, concourse
10 expressway, interstate
12 superhighway **13** through
street

thoroughgoing 5 utter **6** arrant **7** extreme **8** outright
9 confirmed, notorious, out-
and-out **11** undisguised,
unmitigated

thoroughly 5 fully **7** totally,
utterly **8** entirely **9** carefully,

downright, out-and-out, perfectly, uniformly **10** absolutely,
completely, throughout **11** in-
clusively **12** consistently, ex-
haustively, meticulously **13** in
all respects **15** from top to
bottom **17** through and
through **18** from beginning to
end

Thorpe, Isabella
character in: 15 Northanger
Abbey
author: 6 Austen

**Thorpe, Jim (James
Francis)**
sport: 8 football **13** track and
field
won: 8 Olympics
named: 11 All-American

Thorvaldsen, Albert Bertel
born: 7 Denmark
10 Copenhagen
artwork: 4 Hope **9** Lord Byron **14** Cupid and Psyche
16 The Lion of Lucerne
22 Cupid and the Three
Graces **24** Jason with the
Golden Fleece

Thoth
origin: 8 Egyptian
god of: 5 magic **6** wisdom
8 learning
scribe of: 4 gods
inventor of: 6 letter
7 numbers
corresponds to: 6 Hermes
head of: 4 ibis **6** baboon

though 3 tho, yet **4** even, that
5 still **6** albeit, even if
7 granted **8** although, granting **9** admitting **12** nevertheless **15** notwithstanding

thought 3 aim, end **4** goal,
idea, plan, view **5** credo,
dogma, fancy, tenet **6** belief,
caring, design, intent, musing,
notion, object, regard,
scheme **7** concept, concern,
opinion, purpose, reverie, surmise **8** doctrine, judgment,
kindness, thinking **9** attention,
intention, objective, sentiment **10** brown study, cogitation, conception, conclusion,
meditation, reflection, rumination **11** expectation, imagination, speculation, supposition
12 anticipation, deliberation
13 consideration, contemplation, introspection
French: 6 pensee

thoughtful 4 kind **6** caring,
loving, musing **7** pensive,
probing, serious, wistful
8 thinking **9** attentive **10** meditative, neighborly, reflective,
solicitous **11** considerate, kindhearted **13** contemplative,
introspective

thoughtfulness 7 probing,

thought 8 kindness, thinking
10 meditation, reflection
11 questioning 13 attentiveness, consideration, contemplation 14 solicitousness
15 kindheartedness

thoughtless 4 dumb, rash,
rude 5 silly 6 stupid, unkind
7 foolish 8 careless, heedless,
impolite, reckless 9 imprudent
10 ill-advised, indiscreet, neglectful, unthinking 11 harebrained, improvident,
inadvertent, inattentive, insensitive 12 absent-minded, unreflecting 13 ill-considered,
inconsiderate, rattlebrained
14 scatterbrained

thoughtlessness 7 neglect
8 rashness, rudeness 9 oversight, unconcern 10 imprudence, negligence, unkindness
11 inattention 12 carelessness,
heedlessness, impoliteness,
recklessness 13 insensitivity
15 inattentiveness
16 absentmindedness

Thousand Clowns, A
director: 7 Fred Coe
based on play by: 11 Herb
Gardner
cast: 11 Barry Gordon 12 Jason Robards, Martin Bal-
sam 13 Barbara Harris
setting: 11 New York City
Oscar for: 15 supporting actor (Balsam)

Thousand Days, A
author: 20 Arthur M Schlesinger Jr

thou too
Latin: 8 tu quoque

thrall 4 serf 5 slave 6 chains
7 bondage, serfdom, servant,
slavery 9 servitude 11 enslavement, subjugation

thralldom 6 chains 7 bondage,
serfdom, slavery 9 servitude
11 enslavement, subjugation

thrash 4 beat, cane, drub, flog,
jerk, lash, maul, toss, whip
5 birch, flail, heave, solve,
spank, strap 6 jiggle, joggle,
plunge, pommel, squirm,
switch, thresh, tumble, wiggle,
writhe 7 flounce, resolve,
scourge, trounce 8 argue out,
lambaste 9 thresh out
10 flagellate

Thrasydemus
also: 11 Thrasymelus
squire of: 8 Sarpedon
killed by: 9 Patroclus

Thrasymedes
father: 6 Nestor
brother: 10 Antilochus

Thrasymelus *see*
11 Thrasydemus

threadbare 4 dull, worn
5 banal, stale, stock, tacky,
trite 6 boring, frayed, jejune,
ragged, shabby 7 cliched,
humdrum, napless, prosaic,
raveled, routine, worn-out
8 bromidic, everyday, pile-
worn 9 hackneyed, well-
known 11 commonplace, stereotyped 12 conventional, overfamiliar 16 the worse for wear

threads 4 duds, togs 6 attire
7 apparel, clothes, strands,
strings 8 clothing, garments
9 filaments

threat 4 omen, risk 5 peril
6 danger, hazard, menace 7 ill
omen, portent, warning
8 jeopardy 10 foreboding
11 commination, premonition
12 intimidation

threaten 3 cow 4 warn 6 impend, menace 7 imperil 8 endanger, forewarn, hang over
9 terrorize 10 be imminent,
intimidate, jeopardize

threatening 4 grim 7 baleful,
ominous, warning 8 alarming,
imminent, menacing, sinister
9 ill-omened, impending
10 forbidding, foreboding
11 approaching, forewarning,
terrorizing 12 inauspicious, intimidating, unpropitious

three
French: 5 trois

Three-Cornered Hat, The
author: 21 Pedro Antonio de
Alarcon

Three Faces of Eve, The
director: 15 Nunnally
Johnson
cast: 8 Lee J Cobb 9 Nancy
Kulp 10 David Wayne
12 Vince Edwards
14 Joanne Woodward
narration by: 13 Alistair
Cooke
Oscar for: 7 actress
(Woodward)

Three Lives
includes: 9 Melanctha 11 The
Good Anna 13 The Gentle
Lena
author: 13 Gertrude Stein

Three Men in a Boat
author: 13 Jerome K Jerome

Three Musketeers, The
author: 14 Alexandre Dumas
(pere)
director: 13 Richard Lester
character: 5 Athos 6 Aramis
7 Porthos 8 Planchet
9 D'Artagnan 12 Lady de
Winter 17 Cardinal Riche-
lieu 18 Constance Bonacieux
cast: 10 Oliver Reed 11 Faye
Dunaway (Milady), Michael
York (D'Artagnan), Raquel

Welch 12 Frank Findlay
14 Charlton Heston, Christopher Lee 16 Geraldine Chaplin 18 Richard Chamberlain
sequel: 17 The Four
Musketeers

Three's Company
character: 5 Larry 9 Janet
Wood 10 Helen Roper
11 Chrissy Snow, Jack Tripper 12 Stanley Roper
cast: 10 John Ritter, Norman
Fell 11 Joyce DeWitt
12 Audra Lindley, Richard
Kline 13 Suzanne Somers

Three Sisters
director: 10 John Sichel
15 Laurence Olivier
author: 12 Anton Chekhov
character: 13 Fyodor Kuli-
gin 14 Baron Tusenbach,
Vassily Solyony 17 Alexandr
Vershinin
Prozorov family: 4 Olga
5 Irina, Masha 6 Andrey
7 Natasha
cast: 9 Alan Bates 11 Derek
Jacobi, Jeanne Watts
13 Joan Plowright, Louise
Purnell 15 Laurence Olivier

Three Soldiers
author: 13 John Dos Passos

threnody 5 dirge, elegy 6 lament 7 requiem

threshold 4 dawn, door, edge,
sill 5 brink, limen, onset,
start, verge 6 portal 7 doorway, gateway, opening, prelude 8 doorsill, entrance
9 beginning, groundsel, inception 10 groundsill 11 en-
tranceway 12 commencement
13 starting point

Thriae
form: 6 nymphs
nursed: 6 Apollo
taught: 6 Hermes

Thriambus
epithet of: 8 Dionysus

thrift 7 economy 8 prudence
9 frugality, husbandry, parsimony 10 moderation 11 spar-
ingness, thriftiness
14 reasonableness 15 closefistedness 16 parsimoniousness

thriftiness 5 tight 6 thrift
7 economy 8 prudence 9 frugality, parsimony 13 penny-
pinching 15 closefistedness,
tightfistedness
16 parsimoniousness

thriftless 6 lavish 8 feckless,
prodigal, wasteful 11 extravagant, improvident

thrifty 6 frugal, saving, stingy
7 sparing 9 niggardly, penny-
wise 10 economical 11 closefisted, economizing, tight-

fisted **12** parsimonious **13** penny-pinching

thrill 4 fire, glow, kick, stir **5** flush, rouse, throb **6** arouse, excite, quiver, tickle, tingle, tremor **7** delight, impress, inspire, tremble **9** adventure, electrify, enrapture, galvanize, stimulate, transport **12** satisfaction

thrilled 4 agog **7** excited **9** delighted, overjoyed **11** transported

thrilling 7 awesome **8** engaging, exciting, riveting, stirring **9** absorbing, exquisite **10** delightful **11** fascinating, pleasurable, provocative, sensational, tantalizing, titillating **12** electrifying

thrip
variety: **6** banded **10** tube tailed **11** heterothrip, merothripid

thrive 3 wax **4** boom **5** bloom, get on **6** fatten **7** burgeon, prosper, succeed **8** flourish, get ahead, grow rich

thriving 4 busy, lush, rank, rich **7** wealthy, well-off **8** blooming, in clover, vigorous, well-to-do **9** flowering, luxuriant **10** blossoming, prospering, prosperous, succeeding, successful **11** flourishing

throat 3 maw **4** craw, gula, neck **5** gorge **6** gullet **7** chamber, jugulum, passage, pharynx
lozenge: **6** pastil
nautical: **3** jaw **4** jaws, nock
part: **6** fauces, larynx, tonsil **7** glottis, trachea
pertaining to: **5** gular
seizing: **4** knot **5** hitch **12** cuckold's knot
swelling: **6** goiter

throaty 3 dry, low **4** base, deep **5** gruff, husky, thick **6** hoarse **7** cracked, grating, rasping **8** croaking, guttural, resonant, sonorous **9** full-toned

throb 4 beat, jerk, pant **5** heave, pulse, shake **6** quiver, tremor, twitch **7** beating, flutter, pulsate, shaking, tremble, vibrate **9** palpitate, pulsation, quivering, throbbing, trembling, vibration **10** fluttering **11** oscillation, palpitation **13** reverberation

throes 5 agony, chaos, pangs **6** ordeal, spasms, tumult **7** anguish, turmoil **8** disorder, paroxysm, upheaval **9** confusion, paroxysms **10** convulsion, disruption

thrombus 4 clot **9** blood clot **11** coagulation

throng 3 jam **4** army, cram, herd, host, mass, mill, pack, rush **5** bunch, crowd, crush, flock, flood, horde, press, surge, swarm **6** deluge, gather, huddle, stream **7** cluster, collect **8** assemble, converge **9** multitude **10** assemblage, congregate

thronged 4 full **6** jammed, mobbed, packed **7** crammed, crowded, flocked, swarmed, teeming **8** swarming **9** congested, jampacked **11** overflowing

throttle 3 gag, gas **4** stop **5** block, burke, check, choke **6** stifle **7** garrote, seal off, shut off, silence, smother **8** choke off, gas pedal, strangle **9** fuel lever, fuel valve **11** strangulate

through, thru 4 done, past **5** ended **6** direct **7** express **8** finished, from A to Z, to the end **9** all the way, completed, concluded **10** terminated **12** long-distance **15** from first to last **18** from beginning to end **20** from one end to the other

through and through 5 total **6** wholly **7** totally, utterly **8** complete **10** completely, thoroughly **15** from top to bottom **18** from beginning to end **20** from one end to the other

through my fault
Latin: **8** mea culpa

throughout 7 all over **10** all the time, everywhere **11** in every part **16** all the way through **18** from beginning to end

Through the Looking Glass
sequel to: **17** Alice in Wonderland
author: **12** Lewis Carroll
character: **4** Gnat, Lion **5** Alice, Dinah **7** Red King, Unicorn **8** Red Queen **9** Red Knight, White King **10** Tweedledee, Tweedledum, White Queen **11** Black Kitten, White Kitten, White Knight **12** Humpty Dumpty

throw 3 lob, pit, put, shy **4** cast, hurl, shot, toss **5** chuck, fling, floor, heave, impel, pitch, place, put in, put on, sling **6** hurtle, launch, let fly, propel, unseat **7** project **8** delivery **9** knock down, put around

throw away 7 cast off, discard **8** get rid of

throw down 5 let go **8** drop hard, hurl down, toss down **9** fling down

throw into disorder 5 upset **7** agitate, disrupt **10** disarrange

throw off 4 emit, gush **5** exude **7** abandon, cast off, mislead **8** get rid of, shake off, shrug off **9** cast aside, discharge, give forth, pour forth

throw off the scent 7 confuse, mislead **8** confound **19** throw out a red herring

throw out 4 beam, emit, oust **5** eject, evict, expel, exude **6** banish, bounce, remove **7** discard, dismiss, toss out **8** get rid of, jettison **9** cast aside, throw away

throw overboard 4 dump **7** cast off, discard **8** jettison, toss over

throw suspicion upon 11 cast doubt on **17** bring into question

throw up 4 barf, spew **5** eject, expel, spout, vomit **6** cast up, spew up **7** cough up **8** disgorge **9** discharge **11** regurgitate

thrust 3 jab, jam, ram **4** butt, pass, poke, prod, push, raid, stab **5** boost, drive, foray, force, impel, lunge, press, sally, shove, swipe **6** attack, charge, pierce, plunge, propel, sortie, strike, stroke **7** assault, impetus, impulse, riposte **8** momentum **9** incursion **10** aggression

thrust aside 4 dump **6** shelve **7** discard **8** get rid of, throw off, throw out **9** cast aside, dispose of, throw away

thrust at 6 assail, attack **7** lunge at **8** strike at

thrust out 4 spew, spit **5** eject, expel, vomit **6** extend, propel **7** protrude

Thrym
origin: **12** Scandinavian
form: **5** giant
killed by: **4** Thor
demanded return of: **5** Freia, Freya

Thucydides
author of: **28** History of the Peloponnesian War

thud 4 bang **5** clunk, knock, smack, thump

thug 4 hood **6** bandit, gunman, hit man, killer, mugger, robber **7** hoodlum, mobster, ruffian **8** assassin, gangster, murderer **9** cutthroat

thumb 5 hitch **6** finger, handle **9** hitchhike **10** catch a ride, hitch a ride **11** flip through, leaf through

Thumbelina
author: 21 Hans Christian Andersen

thumbnail 5 brief, short 7 compact, concise

thump 3 hit, jab, rap 4 bang, beat, clip, cuff, poke, slam, slap, swat, thud 5 clout, clunk, knock, pound, punch, smack, whack 6 batter, bounce, buffet, pommel, strike, thwack 8 collapse, lambaste

thunder 4 boom, clap, echo, peal, roar, roll 5 crack, crash 6 rumble 7 explode, resound 8 rumbling 9 discharge, explosion 11 reverberate, thunderbolt, thunderclap
god of: 4 Thor 5 Donar 7 Taranis

thunderbolt 4 dart 5 flash, shaft 6 stroke

Thunderstorms, god of 8 Summanus

thunderstruck 4 agog, awed 5 agape 6 aghast, amazed 8 confused, overcome 9 astounded, awestruck, perplexed, surprised 10 astonished, bewildered 11 dumbfounded 13 flabbergasted

Thunder-ten-Tronckh
character in: 7 Candide
author: 8 Voltaire

Thurber, James
author of: 12 The New Yorker 14 Is Sex Necessary (with E B White), The Catbird Seat 16 The Owl in the Attic 18 My Life and Hard Times, The Thurber Carnival 26 The Secret Life of Walter Mitty

Thurber Carnival, The
author: 12 James Thurber

Thurio
character in: 20 Two Gentlemen of Verona
author: 11 Shakespeare

Thursday
French: 5 jeudi
from: 4 Thor
German: 10 donnerstag
heavenly body: 4 Jove 7 Jupiter
Italian: 7 giovedi
Latin: 9 Dies Jovis
observance: 12 Holy Thursday, Thanksgiving 13 Corpus Christi 14 Maundy Thursday 17 Ascension Thursday
Scandinavian: 7 torsdag
Spanish: 6 jueves

Thurso's Landing
author: 15 Robinson Jeffers

thus 2 so 4 ergo 5 hence 6 like so 8 like this 9 as follows, in this way, therefore, wherefore 11 accordingly 12 consequently, in this manner 13 for this reason
Latin: 3 sic

thus always to tyrants
Latin: 17 sic semper tyrannis
motto of: 8 Virginia

thus passes away the glory of this world
Latin: 21 sic transit gloria mundi

Thus Spake Zarathustra
also: 21 Also Sprach Zarathustra
author: 18 Friedrich Nietzsche

thwack 3 box, hit, rap 4 bang, blow, slam, slap 5 baste, clout, knock, smack, thump, whack 6 buffet, paddle, strike, wallop

Thwackum
character in: 8 Tom Jones
author: 8 Fielding

thwart 3 bar 4 balk, foil, stop 5 check, cross 6 baffle, hinder, oppose 7 inhibit, prevent, ward off 8 obstruct, stave off 9 frustrate 10 contravene

Thyestean banquet
meal of: 10 human flesh

Thyestes
author: 6 Seneca

Thyestes
father: 6 Pelops
mother: 10 Hippodamia
brother: 6 Atreus
half-brother: 10 Chrysippus
sister-in-law: 6 Aerope
son: 9 Aegisthus
daughter: 7 Pelopia

Thyiad see 9 bacchante

Thymbraeus
father: 7 Laocoon

thyme
botanical name: 6 Thymus 9 T vulgaris
varieties: 4 Wild 5 Basil, Lemon, Water 6 Common, Garden, Golden 7 Caraway, Spanish
symbol of: 8 activity
attracts: 4 bees
conjures: 9 fairy folk
use: 4 fish 7 poultry 8 stuffing 10 Creole food 21 New England clam chowder

Thymoetes
king of: 6 Athens
elder of: 7 Trojans

Thyone see 6 Semele

Thyoneus
epithet of: 8 Dionysus
means: 11 son of Thyone

Thyrsis
author: 13 Matthew Arnold

Thyrus
staff of: 8 Dionysus
tipped with: 8 pine cone
twined with: 3 ivy 5 vines

thysanoptera
class: 8 hexapoda
phylum: 10 arthropoda
group: 5 thrip

thysanura
class: 8 hexapoda
phylum: 10 arthropoda
group: 8 firebrat 10 silverfish 11 bristletail

Tia Maria
type: 6 brandy 7 liqueur
origin: 7 Jamaica
flavor: 6 coffee
with rum: 10 Black Maria
with tequila: 9 Brave Bull
with vodka: 12 Black Russian

Tiamat
origin: 8 Akkadian
consort of: 4 Apsu
children: 4 gods

tiara 4 band 5 crown, miter 6 diadem 7 coronet 8 frontlet, ornament 9 headdress

Tiaxcaltec
language family: 5 Nahua
location: 6 Mexico 14 Central America

Tiber
god of: 9 Tiberinus

Tiberinus
origin: 5 Roman
god of: 5 Tiber

Tibet see box

tibia
bone of: 4 shin

tic 6 twitch 12 facial twitch 13 tic douloureux 19 trigeminal neuralgia

tick 3 dot, tap 4 beat, line, list, mark, nick, note 5 blaze, check, clack, click, enter, notch, swing, throb 6 record, slight, stroke 7 scratch, vibrate 8 mark down, register, ticktock 9 checkmark, chronicle, oscillate, pulsation, vibration

ticket 3 tag 4 card, mark, pass, slip, stub 5 label, slate 6 ballot, coupon, marker, roster 7 sticker, voucher 14 list of nominees, traffic summons
type: 4 trip 7 parking, traffic 9 admission

tickle 4 itch 5 amuse, cheer, prick, sting, throb 6 divert, please, regale, stroke, thrill, tingle, twitch 7 delight, enchant, enliven, gladden, gratify, prickle, rejoice 8 enthrall, entrance 9 captivate, fascinate, titillate 12 scratchiness 15 do one's heart good

Tibet
  other name: 3 Bod **4** Bhot **5** Tobet **8** Hsitsang **10** Land of Snow **14** Roof of the World
  capital: 5 Lassa, Lhasa
  city: 3 Noh **5** Karak **6** Chamdo, Gartok **7** Changtu, Totling **8** Gyangtse, Jihkatse, Shigatse **9** Chiangtzu
  government: 23 autonomous region of China
  monetary unit: 5 tanga
  lake: 3 Aru, Bam, Bun, Nam **4** Mema, Tosu **5** Jagok, Tabia **6** Dagtse, Garhur, Kashun, Nam Iso, Seling, Tangra, Yamdok **7** Kyaring, Teriman, Tsaring, Zilling **8** Jiggitai **9** Tengrinor **11** Manasarowar
  mountain: 5 Kamet, Sajum **6** Kailas, Kunlun **7** Bandala **8** Himalaya **9** Karakoram
  highest point: 7 Everest
  river: 3 Nak, Nau, Sak **4** Song **5** Hwang, Indus **6** Mekong, Sutlej, Yellow **7** Hwang Ho, Matsang, Melsang, Salween, Tsangpo, Yangtze **11** Brahmaputra
  physical feature:
    plain: **4** Kham **9** Chang Tang
    valley: **7** Tsangpo
  people: 5 Asian, Balti, Bodpa, Drupa **6** Bhotia, Champa, Drokpa, Khamba, Khambu, Panaka, Sherpa, Tangut **7** Bhotiya, Bhutani, Gyarung, Taghlik, Tibetan **9** Mongoloid
    patron god: **14** Avalokitesvara
    ruler: **4** Yuan **6** Mongol **9** dalai lama **13** Songtsan Gampo
  language: 5 Balti **6** Ladkhi **7** Bhutani, Bodskad **8** Sanskrit **9** Bhutanese
  religion: 5 Bonko **7** Lamaism
  place:
    Indian border: **11** McMahon Line
    palace: **7** Potalaf
    temple: **7** Jokhang **10** Tashi Lumpo **11** Tashi Lhunpo
  feature:
    animal: **3** dzo, yak **5** kiang **7** mastiff **8** musk deer **10** giant panda
    clothing: **5** chuba
    dance: **4** cham **9** achelhamo
    dog: **9** lhasa apso
    leader: **9** dalai lama
    legend: **4** yeti **17** abominable snowman
    monastery: **8** lamasery
    monk: **4** lama
  food:
    dish: **6** tsamba, tsampa
    drink: **5** chang

ticklish 4 hard **5** itchy, tough **6** knotty, thorny, tickly, touchy, tricky **7** awkward, prickly **8** critical, delicate, scratchy, tingling **9** difficult, intricate, sensitive, uncertain **11** complicated

tidal basin 3 bay **5** inlet, sound **6** lagoon **7** estuary **11** arm of the sea

tidbit 3 bit **4** item **5** treat **6** morsel **8** delicacy, mouthful **9** choice bit

tide 4 flow, neap, wave **5** drift, state **7** current **8** movement, tendency, undertow **9** direction **10** ebb and flow, wax and wane **11** rise and fall

tidings 4 news, word **6** advice, notice, report **8** good word **11** declaration, information **12** announcement, intelligence, notification

tidy 4 neat, trig, trim **5** ample, array, clean **6** goodly, neaten, tidy up **7** arrange, careful, clean up, orderly, precise, regular, sizable **8** neaten up, spotless, spruce up **9** organized, regulated, shipshape **10** immaculate, methodical, meticulous, put in order, straighten, systematic **11** substantial **12** businesslike, considerable, straighten up **15** in apple-pie order

tidy up 5 clean **6** neaten **9** freshen up **10** put in order, straighten

tie 3 rod **4** ally, band, beam, belt, bind, bond, cord, draw, duty, join, knot, lash, line, link, rope, sash, yoke **5** brace, cable, cinch, limit, marry, match, truss, unite **6** attach, bow tie, clinch, couple, cravat, engage, fasten, girdle, hamper, hinder, ribbon, secure, string, tether **7** confine, connect, kinship, necktie, support **8** affinity, cincture, dead heat, make a bow, make fast, relation, restrain, restrict, tied vote **9** constrain, crossbeam, fastening **10** allegiance, connection, cummerbund, obligation **11** affiliation, come out even **12** relationship **13** connecting rod **15** divide the honors

Tiepolo, Giovanni Battista (Giambattista)
  born: 5 Italy **6** Venice
  artwork: 10 Kaisersaal (salon) **11** Treppenhaus (staircase) **14** The Crucifixion **16** Ronaldo and Armida **20** Madonna of Mount Carmel **21** The Communion of St Lucia, The Triumph of Aphrodite **24** St Thekla and the Pestilence **28** Apotheosis of Francesco Barbaro **28** The Worship of the Bronze Serpent

tier 3 row **4** bank, file, line, rank, step **5** layer, level, range, story **7** stratum **14** stratification

Tierney, Gene
  born: 10 Brooklyn NY
  husband: 11 Oleg Cassini
  roles: 5 Laura **10** Belle Starr **11** Tobacco Road **13** A Bell for Adano **16** Leave Her to Heaven **18** The Ghost and Mrs Muir

tiers etat 11 third estate
in French politics: 7 commons

tie-up 3 jam **4** snag **5** block, hitch, snarl **6** slow-up **7** failure **8** blockage, gridlock, stoppage **9** breakdown **10** bottleneck, disruption **11** malfunction **13** embouteillage

tie up 3 tie **4** bind, gird, lash, rope **5** hitch, snarl, strap, truss **6** engage, fasten, hinder, impede, occupy, secure, tangle **8** entangle

tiff 4 huff, miff, rage, snit, spat **5** clash, run-in, scrap, tizzy, words **6** hassle **7** dispute, quarrel, rhubarb, wrangle **8** argument, ill humor, squabble **10** difference **11** altercation **12** disagreement **16** misunderstanding

tiger 3 cat 6 cougar, jaguar
7 fighter, wildcat
young: 5 whelp

Tiger Joy
author: 19 Stephen Vincent
Benet

tiger's-eye
species: 6 quartz

Tigger
character in: 13 Winnie-the-
Pooh
author: 5 Milne

tight 4 busy, firm, full, hard,
high, snug, taut 5 blind, close,
dense, drunk, exact, happy,
harsh, lit up, rigid, scant,
solid, stern, stiff, tense, tipsy,
tough 6 firmly, frugal, gorged,
hard-up, jammed, juiced,
loaded, scarce, secure, severe,
skimpy, sloppy, soused,
stewed, stingy, stoned, strict,
trying, zonked 7 austere,
closely, compact, crammed,
crowded, drunken, miserly,
onerous, pickled, pie-eyed,
smashed, solidly, sparing,
stuffed 8 grudging, rigorous,
securely, too small 9 deficient,
difficult, illiberal, jam-packed,
niggardly, penurious, plastered,
skintight, stringent, worrisome 10 burdensome, com-
pressed, glassy-eyed,
impassable, inadequate, inebriated, inflexible, in one's cups,
nip-and-tuck, nose-to-nose, tyrannical, ungenerous, unyielding 11 closefisted, constricted,
dictatorial, impermeable, intoxicated, troublesome,
well-matched 12 close-fitting,
impenetrable, insufficient,
parsimonious 13 closely fitted,
feeling no pain 14 fitting
closely, uncompromising
20 three sheets to the wind

tighten 5 pinch 6 anchor, fasten, narrow, secure 7 squeeze
8 contract, make fast, make
taut 9 constrict 14 take up the
slack

tighten one's belt 4 save
5 skimp, stint 6 scrimp 8 conserve, cut costs 9 economize
11 cut expenses 12 pinch
pennies

tightfisted 5 cheap, mingy,
tight 6 greedy, stingy 7 miserly 9 illiberal, niggardly,
penurious 10 avaricious
11 closefisted 12 cheeseparing,
parsimonious 13 penny-
pinching

tightfistedness 6 penury
9 parsimony 10 stinginess
11 miserliness 13 niggardliness, penny-pinching

tight-fitting 4 snug 5 tight

8 too small 9 skintight
11 constricted 12 constricting
15 like a second skin

tight-laced 4 prim 6 prissy,
stuffy 7 prudish 8 priggish
9 inhibited, repressed, Victorian 11 puritanical, standoffish,
straitlaced 13 self-righteous

tight-lipped 3 mum 4 curt
5 brief, quiet, short, terse
8 discreet, reserved, reticent,
taciturn 10 unsociable 11 untalkative 12 close-mouthed
15 uncommunicative

tightly packed 5 dense
6 jammed 7 compact,
crammed, stuffed 10 com-
pressed 12 concentrated

tightwad 5 miser, piker 7 niggard, Scrooge 9 lickpenny,
skinflint 10 cheapskate, pinchpenny 12 moneygrubber

till 3 sow 4 even, farm, plow,
seed, tray, unto up to 6 before, coffer, drawer, harrow,
plough 7 as far as, develop,
prepare 8 moneybox, treasury
9 cultivate 12 cash register
geological: 5 drift

tillable 6 arable 8 farmable,
plowable 10 cultivable

tillage 7 farming, plowing
11 agriculture, cultivation

Till Eulenspiegel
also: 16 Tyll Eulenspiegel
origin: 8 Germanic
means: 14 practical joker

Tillie the Toiler
creator: 12 Russ Westover
character: 3 Mac 7 Mr Chase

Tilney, Henry
character in: 15 Northanger
Abbey
author: 6 Austen

tilt 3 row, tip 4 cant, lean, list,
rake, spar, tiff 5 brawl, fence,
fight, grade, joust, pitch, slant,
slope 6 affray, battle, combat,
oppose 7 contest, dispute, incline, quarrel 8 argument,
skirmish, squabble 9 encounter 10 tournament
11 altercation

Timaeus
author: 5 Plato

Timandra
father: 9 Tyndareus
mother: 4 Leda
brother: 6 Castor, Pollux
sister: 5 Helen
12 Clytemnestra
husband: 7 Echemus, Phyleus
son: 5 Meges
cursed by: 9 Aphrodite

timber 4 bush, logs, wood
5 copse, trees, woods 6 boards,
forest, lumber 7 thicket

timberland 5 woods 6 forest,
sticks 8 woodland

timbre 4 tone 5 pitch
9 resonance

time, times 3 age, day, eon,
era 4 beat, days, hour, term,
week, year 5 clock, cycle, epoch, event, match, month,
phase, spell, stage, tempo,
while, years 6 adjust, chance,
decade, moment, period,
rhythm, season 7 century, episode, freedom, instant, liberty,
measure, stretch 8 duration,
incident, interval, occasion
10 experience, generation
11 opportunity, synchronize

time flies
Latin: 11 tempus fugit

time-honored 6 common, normal 7 regular, revered 8 accepted, standard 9 customary,
respected, universal

timeless 7 abiding, durable,
endless, eternal, lasting, undying 8 enduring, immortal, infinite, unending 9 boundless,
ceaseless, deathless, immutable, incessant, permanent, perpetual 10 continuous,
persistent 11 everlasting,
never-ending 12 interminable,
unchangeable 13 never-stop-
ping 14 indestructible

timely 6 prompt 8 punctual
9 opportune, well-timed
10 convenient, felicitous, seasonable 12 providential

Time Machine, The
author: 7 H G Wells
character: 4 Eloi 5 Weena
8 Morlocks 12 Time Traveler

Time of Your Life, The
author: 14 William Saroyan
director: 8 H C Potter
cast: 8 Ward Bond 11 James
Cagney, Wayne Morris
12 Jeanne Cagney 13 Wil-
liam Bendix 17 Broderick
Crawford

timepiece 5 clock, watch
8 horologe 11 chronometer

Time Remembered
author: 11 Jean Anouilh

Timerman, Jacobo
author of: 38 Prisoner Without a Name Cell Without a
Number

timesaving 5 quick 6 speedy
9 efficient 11 expeditious

time without end 7 forever
8 eternity, infinity

timeworn 3 old 4 aged, worn
5 dated, hoary, passe, stale,
trite 6 age-old, beat-up, old-
hat, shabby 7 ancient, antique 8 battered, dog-eared,

obsolete, overused **9** hackneyed, out of date, venerable, weathered **10** antiquated **12** antediluvian

timid 3 coy, shy **6** afraid, humble, modest, scared **7** bashful, fearful **8** cowardly, retiring, sheepish, timorous **9** diffident, shrinking, spineless, weak-kneed **10** unassuming **12** apprehensive, fainthearted **13** pusillanimous

timidity 7 modesty, shyness **8** cold feet, humility **9** cowardice, timidness **10** diffidence **11** bashfulness, fearfulness, trepidation **12** sheepishness, timorousness **13** spinelessness **16** faint-heartedness

timidness 7 shyness **8** meekness, timidity **10** diffidence, insecurity **11** bashfulness **12** timorousness **14** submissiveness **15** unassertiveness **16** faintheartedness

Timon of Athens
author: 18 William Shakespeare
character: 6 Lucius **7** Flavius **8** Lucullus **9** Apemantus, Ventidius **10** Alcibiades, Sempronius

Timor
capital: 4 Dili
country: 8 Portugal **9** Indonesia
islands: 5 Sunda **11** Lesser Sunda
strait: 5 Ombai

timorous 3 shy **4** meek **5** timid **6** afraid **7** anxious, bashful, fearful **8** retiring **9** shrinking **10** submissive **12** fainthearted

timorousness 7 shyness **8** cold feet, meekness, timidity **9** cowardice **11** fearfulness, trepidation **16** faintheartedness

Timothy
mother: 6 Eunice
grandmother: 4 Lois
companion: 4 Paul **8** Silvanus

tin
chemical symbol: 2 Sn

tincture 6 elixir **7** essence, extract, spirits **8** solution **11** concentrate

Tinder Box, The
author: 21 Hans Christian Andersen

Tin Drum, The
author: 11 Gunter Grass
director: 17 Volker Schlondorff
character: 14 Oskar Matzerath
cast: 10 Mario Adorf **12** David Bennett (Oskar)

13 Angela Winkler **16** Daniel Olbrychski **17** Katharina Tahlbach
Oscar for: 11 foreign film

tine 3 die, tip **4** barb, lose, tyne **5** point, prong, spike **6** bodkin, branch, perish, skewer **7** destroy, forfeit

tinge 3 dye **4** cast, dash, hint, lace, tint, tone, vein **5** color, imbue, shade, smack, stain, taste, touch, trace **6** flavor, infuse, nuance, season **7** instill, soupcon **9** suspicion

tingle 5 sting, throb **6** thrill, tickle, tremor **7** flutter, prickle **9** prickling, pulsation **11** palpitation

Tinia
origin: 8 Etruscan
chief: 3 god

Tinker, Tailor, Soldier, Spy
author: 11 John Le Carre

Tinker Bell
character in: 8 Peter Pan
author: 6 Barrie

tinkle 4 ding, peal, ping, ring **5** chime, chink, clank, clink, plink **6** jingle **9** ting-a-ling

tin lizzie 3 car **4** auto, heap **5** motor **6** jalopy, wheels **7** flivver, machine, motorcar, vehicle **10** automobile **12** motor vehicle

Tin Man, Tin Woodsman
character in: 13 The Wizard of Oz
author: 4 Baum

tinsel 4 sham, show **5** gloss **6** sequin **7** glitter, spangle **8** pretense **9** gaudiness **10** camouflage, decoration, masquerade **11** affectation, false colors, make-believe, ostentation

tint 3 dye, hue **4** hint, tone, wash **5** color, frost, shade, stain, tinge, touch, trace **6** nuance **7** pigment **8** coloring, tincture **10** suggestion

Tintern Abbey
author: 17 William Wordsworth

tintinnabulate 4 peal, ring, toll **5** chime, clang, knell, sound **6** jingle, tinkle

tintinnabulation 4 gong, peal, ring, toll **5** chime, knell **6** jingle **7** clangor, pealing, ringing **8** clanging, ding-dong, jingling, tinkling **11** peal of bells

Tintoretto, Jacopo
real name: 13 Jacopo Robusti
born: 5 Italy **6** Venice
artwork: 8 Paradise **13** The

Last Supper **14** The Crucifixion **16** The Road to Calvary **17** Bacchus and Ariadne **18** Apotheosis of St Roch, The Flight into Egypt **20** Susannah and the Elders **21** The Temptation of Christ **26** St Mark Frees a Christian Slave **27** The Finding of the Body of St Mark **32** The Miracle of St Mark Rescuing a Slave

tiny 3 wee **5** pygmy, runty, small, teeny **6** bantam, little, midget, minute, petite **8** dwarfish **9** itsy-bitsy, miniature, minuscule, pint-sized **10** diminutive, teeny-weeny, undersized **11** Lilliputian, microscopic, pocket-sized **12** teensy-weensy

Tiny Alice
author: 11 Edward Albee

Tiny Tim
character in: 15 A Christmas Carol
author: 7 Dickens

tip 3 cap, pat, tap, top **4** acme, apex, barb, brow, cant, clue, head, hint, hook, lean, list, peak, rake, tilt **5** crest, crown, pitch, point, prong, slant, slope, spike, upend, upset **6** advice, reward, stroke, summit, tip-off, topple, upturn, vertex, zenith **7** capsize, incline, leaning, lowdown, pointer, sharpen, tilting, tipping, warning **8** gratuity, overturn, pinnacle, slanting **9** baksheesh, lagniappe **10** admonition, inside dope, perquisite, suggestion, turn turtle **11** forewarning **13** word to the wise
French: 7 douceur

tipcart 4 cart **8** dumpcart, pushcart

Tiphys
member of: 9 Argonauts
occupation: 9 steersman

tip off 3 tip **4** warn **5** alert **6** caveat **7** caution, warning **8** forewarn **11** forewarning

tip over 5 upend, upset **7** capsize **8** flip over, keel over, overturn, turn over **10** turn turtle

Tippett, Michael Kemp
born: 6 London **7** England
composer of: 9 King Priam **13** The Knot Garden **15** A Child of Our Time **20** The Midsummer Marriage **22** The Vision of St Augustine **32** Concerto for Double String Orchestra

tipple 5 drink, quaff **6** guzzle, imbibe, liquor **8** beverage

tippler 3 sot 4 lush, soak, wino 5 drunk, rummy, souse, toper 6 bibber, boozer, sponge 7 guzzler, imbiber, swiller, tosspot 8 drunkard 9 alcoholic, inebriate 10 booze hound 11 dipsomaniac

tipsy 4 high 5 awash, blind, drunk, happy, lit-up, stiff, tight 6 juiced, loaded, sloppy, sodden, soused, stewed, stoned 7 drunken, pickled, pie-eyed, smashed 9 inebriate, plastered 10 glassy-eyed, inebriated, in one's cups 11 intoxicated 12 half seas over 13 feeling no pain 20 three sheets to the wind

tip-top 4 A-one 5 elite, super 7 supreme 8 very fine 10 consummate 11 exceptional, superlative 13 extraordinary

tirade 5 curse 6 screed 7 lecture 8 diatribe, harangue, jeremiad, scolding 9 invective, reprimand 11 castigation, fulmination 12 condemnation, denunciation, dressing-down, vilification, vituperation

tirailleur 10 skirmisher 12 sharpshooter

Tirane, Tirana
    capital of: 7 Albania

tire 3 fag, irk 4 bore 5 annoy, weary 6 bother, tucker 7 disgust, exhaust, fatigue, wear out 8 be sick of 10 make sleepy 11 be fed up with 12 lose interest, lose patience

tire
    invented by: 6 Dunlop
        7 Thomson

tired 4 beat 5 all in, weary 6 bushed, drowsy, fagged, pooped, sleepy 7 wearied, worn out 8 dog-tired, fatigued, tuckered 9 enervated, exhausted, played out

tireless 6 steady 7 devoted, staunch 8 constant, faithful, resolute, untiring 9 steadfast, unceasing, unwearied 10 determined, unflagging, unswerving 11 hard-working, industrious, never-tiring, persevering, unfaltering, unremitting 13 indefatigable

Tiresias
    also: 9 Teiresias
    vocation: 7 prophet
    father: 6 Everes
    mother: 8 Chariclo
    grandfather: 6 Udaeus
    home: 6 Thebes
    struck: 5 blind
    character in: 7 Odyssey
        10 Oedipus Rex
    characteristic: 9 blind seer

tiresome 4 drab, dull, hard 6 boring, deadly, dismal, tiring, trying, vexing 7 arduous, fagging, humdrum, irksome, tedious, wearing 8 annoying, wearying 9 difficult, fatiguing, laborious, wearisome 10 bothersome, exhausting, monotonous 13 uninteresting

Tisamenus
    leader of: 9 Boeotians
    father: 7 Orestes
    mother: 8 Hermione
    vocation: 4 seer
    killed by: 10 Heraclidae

Tishri 18 seventh Hebrew month

Tisiphone
    member of: 6 Furies

'Tis Pity She's a Whore
    author: 8 John Ford
    character: 6 Donado, Florio, Putana 7 Soranzo, Vasques 8 Bergetto, Giovanni, Grimaldi 9 Annabella, Hippolita 11 Richardetto 16 Friar Bonaventura

tissue
    kind: 4 bone, skin 5 nerve 6 muscle

titan 5 giant, great, mogul 7 magnate

Titan
    race of: 4 gods
    father: 6 Uranus
    mother: 2 Ge 4 Gaea
    names: 5 Coeus, Crius 6 Cronus 7 Iapetus, Oceanus 8 Hyperion
    sisters: 8 Titaness
        names of sisters: 4 Rhea 5 Theia 6 Phoebe, Tethys, Themis 9 Mnemosyne

Titan, The
    sequel to: 12 The Financier
    author: 15 Theodore Dreiser
    character: 13 Peter Laughlin 15 Berenice Fleming, Stephanie Platow 16 Aileen Cowperwood 23 Frank Algernon Cowperwood

Titan, the *see* 6 Helios

Titaness *see* 5 Titan

Titania
    character in: 21 A Midsummer Night's Dream
    author: 11 Shakespeare

titanic 4 huge, vast 5 giant, great, stout 6 mighty, strong 7 immense, mammoth 8 colossal, enormous, gigantic, whopping 9 herculean, humongous, monstrous 10 gargantuan, monumental, prodigious, stupendous

titanium
    chemical symbol: 2 Ti

Titanomachy
    revolt of: 7 Iapetus

tit for tat 8 exchange 10 quid pro quo 13 an eye for an eye

Tithonus
    father: 8 Laomedon
    brother: 5 Priam
    loved by: 3 Eos
    son: 6 Memnon 8 Emathion

Titian
    real name: 15 Tiziano Vecellio
    born: 5 Italy 13 Pieve di Cadore
    artwork: 5 Pieta 12 The Bacchanal, Tribute Money 13 Noli Me Tangere 15 Diana and Actaeon, The Rape of Europa 16 The Pesaro Madonna, The Venus of Urbino 17 Bacchus and Ariadne, The Death of Actaeon, The Girl in a Fur Wrap, The Three Ages of Man 18 Charles V at Muhlberg, The Adrian Bacchanal, The Young Englishman 19 Francis I Roi de France 20 Sacred and Profane Love 21 Venus and the Lute Player 23 The Madonna of the Cherries 24 Pope Paul III and his Nephews, The Assumption of the Virgin

titillate 5 charm, rouse, tease, tempt 6 allure, arouse, excite, seduce, tickle, turn on 7 attract, provoke 8 entrance 9 captivate, fascinate, stimulate 15 whet the appetite

titillating 8 alluring, exciting, tempting 9 seductive 10 suggestive 11 provocative

title 3 dub 4 deed, name, rank, term 5 claim, crown, grade, label, place, right 6 status, tenure 7 entitle, epithet, station 8 christen, nobility, position 9 condition, designate, ownership 10 legal right, lordly rank, noble birth, possession 11 appellation, designation 12 championship

titled 5 named, noble, regal, royal 6 called, lordly 7 courtly 8 entitled 10 designated 11 blue-blooded 12 aristocratic

Titograd
    capital of: 10 Montenegro

titter 5 chirp, smirk 6 cackle, giggle, simper, teehee 7 chuckle, snicker, snigger

tittle 3 bit, dot, jot 4 atom, iota, mite 5 speck 8 particle

Tittle, Y A (Yelberton Abraham)
    sport: 8 football

position: 11 quarterback
team: 13 New York Giants
14 Baltimore Colts **23** San
Francisco Forty-Niners

titular 7 known as, nominal
8 so-called **10** in name only,
ostensible **11** in title only

Titus
  surname: 6 Justus
  hometown: 7 Corinth
  companion: 4 Paul

Titus *see* **6** Tatius

Titus Andronicus
  author: 18 William
  Shakespeare
  character: 5 Aaron **6** Chiron,
  Marcus, Tamora **7** Alarbus,
  Lavinia **9** Bassianus, Demetrius **10** Saturninus

Tityus
  form: 5 giant
  father: 4 Zeus
  mother: 2 Ge **5** Elara
  home: 6 Euboea
  threatened: 4 Leto
  killed by: 6 Apollo **7** Artemis

tizzy 4 snit **6** dither, swivet
7 dudgeon **8** tailspin
  British: 8 sixpence

Tjaden
  character in: 25 All Quiet on
  the Western Front
  author: 8 Remarque

Tlepolemus
  father: 8 Hercules
  mother: 10 Astyocheia
  wife: 6 Polyxo
  son: 8 Deipylus
  killed by: 8 Sarpedon

Tmolus
  king of: 5 Lydia

to 2 ad, on **3** for **4** into, near,
unto, upon, with **5** about, until **6** at hand, closed, toward
7 against, forward **8** together
10 concerning, included in
11 contained in
  prefix: 2 ac, ad
  Scottish: 3 tae

toad
  group of: 4 knot

toady 4 fawn **6** fawner, flunky,
stooge, yes-man **8** hanger-on,
kowtow to, parasite, truckler
9 flatterer, sycophant **10** bootlicker, curry favor **11** apple-
polish, lickspittle **13** apple-
polisher, backscratcher

To Althea, From Prison
  author: 15 Richard Lovelace

to a man 3 all **8** every one
9 one and all **10** completely
12 to the last man

To a Skylark
  author: 18 Percy Bysshe
  Shelley

toast 3 dry **4** heat, warm
5 brown, grill, honor **6** salute,
warm up **9** celebrate **10** compliment **11** commemorate
12 browned bread, clink
glasses **15** drink one's health

tobacco
  varieties: 4 tree, wild **6** Indian **7** jasmine, Turkish
  9 broadleaf, flowering, Nicotiana **12** long-flowered
  16 Nicotiana rustica, Nicotiana tabacum

Tobacco Road
  author: 15 Erskine Caldwell
  character: 3 Ada **4** Dude
  5 Pearl **6** Bessie **8** Ellie
  May **9** Lov Bensey **12** Jeeter
  Lester

To Be or Not To Be
  director: 13 Ernst Lubitsch
  cast: 9 Jack Benny **11** Robert
  Stack **12** Lionel Atwill
  13 Carole Lombard, Felix
  Bressart
  setting: 6 Poland

Tobias
  father: 5 Tobit
  grandfather: 6 Tobiel
  son: 8 Hycranus

Tobit
  father: 6 Tobiel
  son: 6 Tobias

To Catch a Thief
  director: 15 Alfred Hitchcock
  cast: 9 Cary Grant **10** Grace
  Kelly **12** John Williams
  17 Jessie Royce Landis
  setting: 13 French Riviera

Tocharian
  language family: 12 Indo-
  European
  spoken in: 11 Central Asia

Tocqueville, Alexis de
  author of: 18 Democracy in
  America

tocsin 4 bell **5** alarm **7** warning

today 3 now **7** this day, this
era **8** nowadays, this time **9** in
this era, on this day, this epoch **10** the present **11** in this
epoch, modern times **13** in
modern times, the present
age, the present day **15** in
this day and age

Todd, Richard
  real name: 27 Richard Andrew Palethorpe-Todd
  born: 6 Dublin **7** Ireland
  roles: 13 The Hasty Heart,
  The Longest Day **14** The
  Virgin Queen **15** A Man
  Called Peter

toddle 6 waddle, wobble
14 take short steps, walk
unsteadily

toddler 3 tot **4** babe, baby,

tyke **5** child **6** infant **9** little
one

to-do 3 ado **4** fuss, stir **5** furor,
noise **6** bustle, flurry, hubbub,
hustle, pother, racket, ruckus,
rumpus, tumult, uproar **7** turmoil **8** activity **9** agitation,
commotion **10** excitement,
hullabaloo, hurly-burly
11 disturbance

Toe, The
  nickname of: 8 Lou Groza

to err is human
  Latin: 16 errare humanum est

toff 3 nob **4** beau **5** dandy,
swell **10** young blood

Toffler, Alvin
  author of: 11 Future Shock
  12 The Third Wave

toga 3 aba **4** garb, gown, robe
6 trabea **7** garment
12 outergarment
  virilis: 9 white robe **11** manhood robe

Togo *see box, p. 988*

togs 4 duds **6** attire, outfit
7 apparel, clothes, threads
8 clothing, garments

To Have and Have Not
  director: 11 Howard Hawks
  based on novel by: 15 Ernest Hemingway
  cast: 12 Dolores Moran, Lauren Bacall **13** Walter Brennan **14** Humphrey Bogart
  15 Hoagy Carmichael
  remade as: 13 The Gunrun-
  ners **16** The Breaking Point

To His Coy Mistress
  author: 13 Andrew Marvell

toil 4 grub, moil, work **5** grind,
labor, pains, slave, sweat
6 drudge, effort **7** travail
8 drudgery, exertion, hardship,
hard work, industry, struggle,
work hard **11** application, elbow grease **12** apply oneself,
exert oneself **14** work like a
horse

toiler 4 peon, serf, swot
5 navvy, prole, slave **6** drudge,
flunky, menial, slavey,
worker **7** grubber, laborer, servant, slogger **9** workhorse
10 wage earner **11** galley slave

toilet 2 WC **3** can, loo **4** john
5 privy **7** commode, latrine
8 facility, lavatory, men's
room, outhouse, rest room,
washroom **10** ladies' room
11 convenience, water closet

toilet water 5 scent **7** cologne,
essence, perfume **9** fragrance

toilsome 4 hard **5** tough **6** tiring, uphill **7** arduous, onerous,
tedious **8** wearying **9** difficult,

Togo
 other name: 14 French Togoland
 capital/largest city: 4 Lome
 others: 5 Badon, Kpeme **6** Anecho, Ansoho, Blitta, Klonto, Nuatja, Palime, Sokode **7** Bassari, Dopango, Pagonda **8** Atakpame, Tabligbo **10** Niamtougou
 school: 5 Benin **6** Mawull
 monetary unit: 5 franc **7** centime
 mountain: 4 Togo **7** Atakora, Koronga
 highest point: 7 Baumann
 river: 3 Oti **4** Anie, Haho, Mono, Ogou
 sea: 8 Atlantic
 physical feature:
  bight: 5 Benin
  gulf: 6 Guinea
  plain: 4 Mono
 people: 3 Ana, Ewe, Twi **4** Mina **5** Hausa **6** Akposa, Kabrai **7** Bassari, Cabrais, Kabrais, Ouatchi **8** Konkomba, Kotokoli, Lotokoli
  leader: 7 Eyadema **15** Sylvanus Olympio **16** Nicolas Grunitzky
 language: 3 Ana, Ewe, Twi **4** Mina **5** Hausa **6** French, Kabrai, Kabrie **7** Bassari, Dagomba, Ouatchi **8** Kotokoli, Lotocoli
 religion: 5 Islam **7** animism **12** Christianity

effortful, fatiguing, herculean, laborious, strenuous, wearisome **10** burdensome, exhausting **12** backbreaking

To Jerusalem and Back
 author: 10 Saul Bellow

token 4 mark, sign **5** index, proof **6** jetton, symbol **7** for show, memento, minimal, nodding, nominal, passing **8** evidence, keepsake, reminder, souvenir, symbolic **9** vestigial **10** expression, indication **11** perfunctory, remembrance, superficial, testimonial **13** manifestation

To Kill a Mockingbird
 director: 14 Robert Mulligan
 based on novel by: 9 Harper Lee
 cast: 9 John Megna **10** Mary Badham **11** Gregory Peck **12** Philip Alford
 Oscar for: 5 actor (Peck)

Tokyo
 airport: 6 Haneda
 capital of: 5 Japan
 district: 5 Ginza **6** Keihin **7** Chiyoda **8** Yokohama **10** Marunouchi **18** Tama New Town Project
 former name: 3 Edo
 island: 6 Honshu
 landmark: 8 Ueno Park **11** Meiji Shrine **12** National Diet **14** Imperial Palace, Kitanomaru Park **19** Komazawa Olympic Park
 means: 14 Eastern capital

Tola 11 Hebrew judge

Told in the Dog Watches
 author: 12 Frank T Bullen

tolerable 4 fair, so-so **7** allowed, average **8** abidable, accepted, adequate, bearable, mediocre, middling, ordinary, passable **9** allowable, endurable, innocuous, permitted **10** acceptable, admissible, fairly good, sufferable **11** commonplace, indifferent, permissible **12** run-of-the-mill **14** fair-to-middling

tolerance 7 charity **8** fairness, goodwill, patience, sympathy **9** endurance **10** compassion, sufferance **11** forbearance **13** brotherly love, fair treatment, fellow feeling, power to endure **15** lack of prejudice

tolerant 4 easy, fair, soft **7** lenient, liberal, patient, sparing **8** moderate **9** easygoing, forgiving, indulgent, unbigoted **10** charitable, forbearing, permissive **11** broad-minded, kindhearted, softhearted, sympathetic **12** unprejudiced **13** compassionate, uncomplaining, understanding

tolerate 3 let **4** bear, take **5** abide, admit, allow, brook, stand **6** endure, permit, suffer, wink at **7** indulge, stomach, undergo **8** be easy on, be soft on, sanction, submit to **9** consent to, put up with, recognize, vouchsafe

To Let
 author: 14 John Galsworthy

to life
 Hebrew: 7 lehayim **8** lechayim

Tolkien, J R R
 author of: 9 The Hobbit **12** Silmarillion **17** The Lord of the Rings
 fictional setting: 11 Middle Earth

toll 3 fee, tax **4** duty, levy, loss **6** charge, impost, tariff **7** payment, penalty, tribute, undoing **8** exaction **9** depletion, sacrifice **10** assessment, disruption, extinction **11** destruction **12** annihilation **13** extermination

Tolstoy, Leo
 author of: 11 War and Peace **12** Anna Karenina, Resurrection **17** The Kreutzer Sonata **18** Death of Ivan Ilyitch

Toltec
 tribe: 4 Itza

To Lucasta, Going to the Wars
 author: 15 Richard Lovelace

Tolumnius
 vocation: 5 augur

tom 3 cat **6** tomcat **10** male turkey

tomato 12 Lycopersicon **24** Lycopersicon lycopersicum
 varieties: 4 Husk, Pear, Tree **6** Cherry **7** Currant **10** Gooseberry, Strawberry **11** Mexican husk
 soup: 8 gazpacho
 sauce: 6 catsup **7** ketchup

tomb 5 crypt, grave, vault **8** monument **9** mausoleum, sepulcher **11** burial place **12** resting place **13** burial chamber

tomboy 3 meg **4** girl, romp **5** rowdy **6** female, gamine, hoiden, hoyden, tomrig **8** strumpet

Tom Brown's School Days
 author: 12 Thomas Hughes

tombs
 god of: 6 Anubis

tomcat 3 cat, tom **9** womanizer

To-meri see **5** Egypt

tomfoolery 4 play **6** antics **8** drollery, nonsense **9** high jinks, horseplay, silliness **10** goofing off, skylarking **11** foolishness **12** lollygagging, monkeyshines, prankishness **13** fooling around, messing around, playing around

Tom Jones
   also: 29 The History of Tom Jones Foundling
   author: 13 Henry Fielding
   character: 6 Square **7** Bridget, Western **8** Mrs Honor, Thwackum **9** Mrs Miller, Partridge **11** Black George, Nightingale **12** Master Blifil **13** Lady Bellaston, Sophia Western **15** Squire Allworthy
   director: 14 Tony Richardson
   cast: 11 Joyce Redman **12** Albert Finney, Diane Cilento, Hugh Griffith, Susannah York **14** Dame Edith Evans
   score: 11 John Addison
   Oscar for: 5 score **7** picture **9** direction **10** screenplay

Tomlin, Lily
   real name: 14 Mary Jean Tomlin
   born: 9 Detroit MI
   roles: 7 Laugh-In **8** Edith Ann **9** Ernestine, Nashville **11** The Late Show **14** Moment By Moment **27** The Incredible Shrinking Woman

Tomlinson, Mary
   real name of: 12 Marjorie Main

tommyrot 3 rot **4** bosh, bull, bunk, crap, tosh **5** bilge, hokum, hooey, trash **6** bunkum, drivel, humbug **7** baloney, hogwash, spinach, rubbish, twaddle **8** buncombe, claptrap, folderol, malarkey, nonsense **9** poppycock **10** applesauce, balderdash, tomfoolery **11** foolishness **12** bullfeathers, fiddle-faddle **13** horsefeathers **16** stuff-and-nonsense

tomorrow 9 the future, the morrow **11** in the future **12** in days to come **16** the day after today **17** the next generation
   Spanish: 6 manana

Tompkins, Yewell
   real name of: 8 Tom Ewell

Tom Sawyer
   author: 9 Mark Twain
   character: 8 Huck (Huckleberry) Finn, Injun Joe **9** Aunt Polly, Joe Harper **10** Muff Potter **13** Becky Thatcher

Tom Thumb the Great
   author: 13 Henry Fielding

ton
   abbreviation: 1 t

tone 3 hue **4** cast, lilt, mood, note, tint **5** color, pitch, shade, sound, style, tenor, tinge **6** accent, chroma, firm up, manner, soften, spirit, stress, subdue, temper **7** cadence, quality **8** attitude, harmonic, make firm, moderate, modulate, overtone, tonality **10** inflection, intonation, make supple, modulation

Tone, Franchot
   real name: 27 Stanislas Pascal Franchot Tone
   born: 14 Niagara Falls NY
   wife: 11 Jean Wallace **12** Joan Crawford **13** Barbara Payton **15** Dolores Dorn-Heft
   roles: 10 Uncle Vanya **11** Phantom Lady **13** Three Comrades **16** Advise and Consent **17** Five Graves to Cairo, Mutiny on the Bounty **23** The Lives of a Bengal Lancer

tone up 7 make fit, shape up **9** condition **10** put in shape

Tonga *see box*

tongue 3 lap **4** flap, lick, spit **5** point, shaft **6** lingua, patois, speech **7** dialect, lingula **8** language **10** promontory, vernacular, vocabulary **13** organ of speech, power of speech, style of speech
   tastes: 4 salt, sour **5** sweet **6** bitter

tongue-lash 5 scold **6** berate, rail at, rebuke **7** bawl out, chew out, reprove, upbraid **8** reproach **9** castigate, reprimand **10** take to task

tongue-lashing 6 rebuke **7** censure, chiding, reproof **8** reproach, scolding **9** reprimand **10** bawling-out, chewing-out, upbraiding **11** castigation, reprobation **12** dressing-down, remonstrance

tonic 6 bracer, pickup **7** keynote **8** pick-me-up **9** analeptic, refresher, stimulant **10** invigorant **11** restorative

tonne
   abbreviation: 1 t

Tono-Bungay
   author: 7 H G Wells

tonsure 3 cut **4** trim **8** bald spot **11** shaven patch

too
   French: 4 trop

tool *see box, p. 990*

too little 4 lack **6** dearth, scanty, scarce **7** paucity **8** scarcity, shortage **9** deficient, not enough, scantness **10** deficiency, inadequacy, inadequate **12** insufficient **13** insufficiency

Tonga
   other name: 15 Friendly Islands
   capital/largest city: 9 Nukualofa
   others: 3 Mua, Pea **6** Neiafu **7** Haakame, Kolonga, Kolovai **8** Fuaamotu
   division: 5 Vavau **6** Haapai **9** Tongatapu
   government: 8 monarchy
   head of state: 4 king
   monetary unit: 6 paanga, seniti
   island: 3 Eua, Kao, Ono **4** Kotu **5** Tofua, Vavau **6** Haapai, Lifuke, Nomuka **7** Otu Tolu **9** Tongatapu
   highest point: 3 Kao
   sea: 7 Pacific
   people: 10 Polynesian
   explorer: **4** Cook **5** Bligh **6** Tasman
   king: **11** George Tupou **14** Taufaahau Tupou
   missionary: **12** Shirley Baker
   queen: **6** Salote
   language: 6 Tongan **7** English
   religion: 9 Methodist **12** Christianity **25** Wesleyan Free Church of Tonga
   feature:
   fabric: **4** tapa
   spiritual king: **8** tui tonga

too many
   French: 6 de trop

too much 4 glut **5** flood **6** excess **7** profuse, surfeit, surplus **8** fullness, overflow, plethora **9** avalanche, excessive, profusion, repletion **10** inundation, oversupply **12** overabundant **13** overabundance **14** superabundance
   French: 4 trop

Toonerville Folks
   creator: 11 Fontaine Fox
   character: 7 skipper **13** Aunt Eppie Hogg **15** Little Scorpions, Powerful Katrina, Suitcase Simpson **20** Mickey Himself McGuire **22** Terrible Tempered Mr Bang
   rode on: 7 trolley

to one side 4 over **5** aloof, apart, aside **6** aslant **14** on the sidelines

to one's liking 7 fitting **8** pleasant, pleasing, suitable **9** agreeable **10** acceptable,

tool 4 dupe, pawn **5** agent, means **6** device, medium, puppet, stooge **7** cat's-paw, machine, utensil, vehicle **8** hireling **9** apparatus, appliance, implement, mechanism **10** instrument **11** contrivance, wherewithal **12** intermediary **15** instrumentality

  carpenter's: 3 adz, awl, bit, peg, saw **4** adze, nail, rasp, vise **5** auger, brace, edger, gouge, knife, lathe, plane, ruler, screw **6** bodkin, chisel, gimlet, hammer, pliers, router, sander **7** bradawl, scraper **9** hand drill, try square **11** screwdriver

  cutting/shaping: 2 ax **3** adz, axe, saw **4** adze, burr, file, froe, frow, rasp **5** burin, croze, gouge, knife, plane, razor, shave, wedge **6** chisel, sander, shears, trepan **7** hatchet, scraper **8** scissors

  drilling/boring: 3 awl, bit, zax **4** pick **5** chuck, drill **6** gimlet, wimble **7** bradawl **11** countersink

  farmer's: 2 ax **3** axe, hoe **4** plow, rake **5** spade **6** cradle, harrow, pickax, plough, scythe, seeder, shovel, sickle, tiller, trowel **7** hayfork **9** plowshare **10** cultivator

  gripping/turning: 6 pliers, wrench **11** screwdriver

  holding: 4 vise **5** clamp

  measuring: 4 rule **5** gauge, level **6** square **7** caliper **8** dividers **10** micrometer

  mechanic's: 3 awl, zax **4** burr, file, vise **5** bevel, lathe **6** bodkin, pliers **7** bradawl, crowbar **8** calipers **9** jackscrew **11** screwdriver **12** monkey wrench

  pounding/striking: 4 maul **5** punch, wedge **6** hammer, mallet

gratifying **11** appropriate, to one's taste **12** satisfactory

toot 4 blow, honk **5** binge, blare, blast, spree **6** bender **7** trumpet **8** wingding

tooth 3 cog, nib **4** barb, cusp, fang, spur, tang, tine, tusk **5** molar, point, spike, thorn **6** canine, cuspid **7** grinder, incisor **8** bicuspid, sprocket **9** serration

toothed 6 fanged, tusked **7** dentate, notched, serrate, virgate

toothsome 6 savory **8** luscious **9** delicious, palatable **10** appetizing

Toots
  character in: 12 Dombey and Son
  author: 7 Dickens

top 3 cap, lid, van **4** acme, apex, best, brow, cork, fore, head, lead, peak **5** chief, cover, crest, crown, excel, front, noted, outdo, upper **6** better, exceed, famous, summit, tiptop, vertex, zenith **7** eclipse, eminent, highest, notable, put over, stopper, surpass, topmost **8** complete, foremost, greatest, outshine, outstrip, pinnacle, renowned **9** paramount, principal, put a top on, transcend, uppermost, upper part **10** celebrated, first place, overshadow, preeminent

topaz
  color: 4 blue **5** brown **6** yellow
  source: 5 Japan **6** Brazil, Mexico, Saxony **13** Ural Mountains **18** Cairngorm Mountains
  month: 8 November

Topaze
  author: 12 Marcel Pagnol

topaz quartz
  species: 6 quartz
  color: 4 blue, pink **5** brown, green **6** sherry

toper 3 sot **4** lush, soak **5** drunk **6** boozer **7** tippler **8** drunkard **9** alcoholic **11** dispomaniac

Top Hat
  director: 12 Mark Sandrich
  cast: 9 Eric Blore **11** Fred Astaire **12** Ginger Rogers **14** Helen Broderick **19** Edward Everett Horton
  score: 12 Irving Berlin
  song: 12 Cheek to Cheek **22** Top Hat White Tie and Tails

topic 4 text **5** theme **6** thesis **7** keynote, subject

topical 5 local **6** timely **7** current, limited **9** localized, parochial **10** particular, restricted **12** contemporary

Topkapi
  director: 11 Jules Dassin
  cast: 12 Peter Ustinov, Rob-

ert Morley **14** Melina Mercouri **16** Maximilian Schell
  setting: 8 Istanbul
  Oscar for: 15 supporting actor (Ustinov)

topknot 4 comb, tuft **5** crest **9** cockscomb, headdress, headpiece

topmost 3 top **4** head **5** chief **7** highest, leading, supreme **8** foremost **9** paramount, principal, uppermost **10** preeminent

topnotch 3 ace **4** best **5** prime **6** choice, finest, tip-top **7** supreme **8** superior, very fine **9** excellent, first-rate, nonpareil, unequaled, unrivaled **10** preeminent **11** outstanding, unsurpassed **12** incomparable, unparalleled

top of the head 4 dome, pate **5** crown **6** noggin, noodle

Topper
  director: 13 Norman Z McLeod
  based on novel by: 11 Thorne Smith
  cast: 9 Cary Grant **11** Alan Mowbray, Billie Burke, Hedda Hopper, Roland Young **16** Constance Bennett
  sequel: 13 Topper Returns **16** Topper Takes a Trip

topple 4 fall **5** crush, quash, quell, smash, upset **6** defeat, sprawl, tumble **7** abolish, shatter, tip over **8** fall over, overcome, overturn, turn over, vanquish **9** bring down, overpower, overthrow **12** pitch forward

tops 4 aces, A-one, fine **5** great, prime, super, swell **6** choice, grade-A, superb, tiptop **7** capital **8** peerless, sterling, superior, terrific, topnotch **9** excellent, first-rate, marvelous, matchless, superfine, wonderful **10** first-class, inimitable, out-of-sight, tremendous **11** outstanding, superlative **12** incomparable **13** extraordinary

top-secret 5 privy **7** private **8** eyes-only, hush-hush **12** confidential

topsoil 4 dirt, loam **5** earth

Topsy
  character in: 14 Uncle Tom's Cabin
  author: 5 Stowe

topsy-turvy 5 messy **6** untidy **7** chaotic **8** confused, inverted, reversed **9** confusing, inside out **10** disorderly, upside down **11** disarranged, wrong side up **12** disorganized

Torah 10 law of Moses

torch 5 brand **7** cresset **8** arsonist, flambeau **9** firebrand **9** set fire to **10** flashlight

torment 3 nag, vex **4** bane, pain, rack **5** agony, annoy, curse, worry **6** harass, harrow, misery, pester, plague **7** afflict, agonize, anguish, despair, scourge, torture, trouble **8** distress, irritate **9** annoyance, persecute, suffering **10** irritation

tormenter 5 bully, tease **6** despot, tyrant **7** coercer **9** oppressor **10** browbeater **11** intimidator

tormenting 7 painful, racking **9** agonizing, torturous **10** unbearable **11** unendurable **12** excruciating, insufferable

torn 4 rent, slit **5** split **6** ragged, ripped **8** ruptured, shredded **9** unraveled

tornado 4 wind **5** storm **6** funnel, squall, vortex **7** cyclone, twister, typhoon **8** outburst **9** hurricane, whirlwind, windstorm **10** waterspout **12** thunderstorm
  belt: 7 Midwest
  cloud: 4 tuba

torn apart 4 rent **6** ripped **7** asunder **8** in pieces, in shreds, shredded

toro 4 bull

Toronto
  baseball team: 8 Blue Jays
  bay: 6 Humber
  football team:
    9 Argonauts
  former name: 4 York
  harbor: 5 Inner
  hockey team: 10 Maple Leafs
  lake: 7 Ontario
  landmark: 7 CN Tower **12** Ontario Place, O'Keefe Centre **13** Dufferin Grove **14** Dominion Centre **15** Roy Thompson Hall **16** Maple Leaf Stadium, St Lawrence Centre **17** Commerce Court West **18** Royal Ontario Museum **20** Nathan Phillips Square
    park: **7** Chorley, Stanley, Trinity **8** Winthrow **9** Cedarvale **12** Center Island **16** Winston Churchill
  street: 5 Yonge
  university: 4 York

Torosaurus
  type: 8 dinosaur **10** ceratopsid

torpedo 4 sink **5** wreck **7** destroy, missile, scuttle **9** explosive **10** projectile

torpedo (marine)
  invented by: 6 Fulton

torpid 4 dull, lazy **5** inert **6** drowsy, sleepy **7** dormant, languid, passive **8** inactive, indolent, listless, sluggish **9** apathetic, lethargic, somnolent **10** half asleep, languorous, slow-moving, spiritless **12** slow-thinking **13** lackadaisical

torpor, torpidity 6 apathy **7** inertia, languor **8** dullness, laziness, lethargy **9** indolence, lassitude **10** drowsiness, inactivity, sleepiness, somnolence **11** languidness, passiveness **12** listlessness, sluggishness

torrent 4 gush, rain, rush **5** burst, flood, salvo **6** deluge, rapids, stream, volley **7** barrage, cascade, Niagara **8** cataract, downpour, effusion, eruption, outburst **9** discharge, heavy rain, rapid flow, waterfall **10** cloudburst, outpouring, white water

Torrey, John
  field: 6 botany
  developed: 16 botanical library

Torricelli, Evangelista
  nationality: 7 Italian
  discovered concept leading to development of:
    9 barometer

torrid 3 hot **4** sexy **5** fiery **6** ardent, erotic, fervid, heated, sexual, sultry **7** amorous, boiling, burning, excited, fervent, intense, lustful **8** broiling, desirous, parching, sizzling, spirited, tropical, vehement **9** hot and dry, scorching **10** passionate, sweltering **11** hot and heavy, impassioned

torte 4 cake **7** dessert **9** layer cake

tortilla 7 tostada **8** corncake **11** Mexican cake
  griddle: 5 comal

Tortilla Flat
  author: 13 John Steinbeck

tortuous 4 bent **5** snaky **6** spiral, zigzag **7** crooked, devious, sinuous, turning, winding, wriggly **8** indirect, involved, twisting, wrongful **9** ambiguous **10** circuitous, convoluted, meandering, roundabout, serpentine **11** complicated **12** full of curves, hard to follow, labyrinthine

tortuousness 9 sinuosity **11** indirection, sinuousness **12** convolutions **14** circuitousness

torture 4 pain, rack **5** abuse, agony, prick, smite, trial, wring **6** harrow, ordeal **7** anguish, cruelty, torment **8** distress, maltreat, mistreat **9** brutality, suffering **10** infliction, punishment **11** tribulation **12** put to the rack

torturous 5 cruel **7** galling, irksome, painful, racking **8** annoying **9** agonizing, anguished, harrowing, miserable, tormented, torturing **10** anguishing, distressed, tormenting, unpleasant **11** distressful, distressing **12** disagreeable, excruciating

tory 8 loyalist, royalist **12** conservative

Tosca
  opera by: 7 Puccini
  character: 7 Scarpia **9** Angelotti **16** Mario Cavaradossi

To Sir With Love
  director: 12 James Clavell
  cast: 4 Lulu **10** Judy Geeson **11** Suzy Kendall **13** Sidney Poitier **16** Christian Roberts
  setting: 6 London

toss 3 lob **4** cast, flip, hurl, jerk, rock, roll, sway **5** churn, fling, heave, pitch, shake, sling, throw **6** joggle, let fly, propel, tumble, wiggle, writhe **7** agitate, flounce, wriggle **8** flourish, undulate **9** oscillate

toss about 4 roil **5** bandy **6** jostle, jounce

toss back and forth 5 bandy **8** exchange

total 3 add, sum **4** full **5** add up, gross, sheer, solid, sum up, utter, whole **6** entire, figure, reckon, tote up **7** add up to, compute, perfect, total up **8** absolute, combined, complete, entirety, figure up, integral, outright, sum total, sweeping, thorough, totality **9** aggregate, calculate, downright, out-and-out, unlimited, wholesale **10** full amount, undisputed, unmodified **11** unqualified, whole amount **13** comprehensive, unconditional

totaling 8 addition, coming to **9** reckoning **10** adding up to

totalitarian 7 fascist **8** despotic **9** fascistic, tyrannous **10** autocratic, tyrannical **11** dictatorial **12** undemocratic **16** unrepresentative

totally 7 solidly, utterly **8** entirely **9** downright, out-and-out, perfectly **10** absolutely, completely, thoroughly, throughout **15** unconditionally **18** from beginning to end **20** without qualification

tote 3 lug **4** bear, cart, drag, haul, move, pack, pull **5** carry, fetch **6** convey **7** schlepp **9** transport

to the city and the world
Latin: **10** urbi et orbi
form of address used on: **10** papal bulls

to the four winds 7 all over **10** everywhere, far and wide **26** to the four corners of the world

to the letter 5 exact, right **7** correct, precise **8** accurate, explicit, specific **9** on the nose

To the Lighthouse
author: **13** Virginia Woolf
character: **4** Prue **5** James **7** Camilla **8** Mr Ramsey **9** Mr Tansley, Mrs Ramsey **11** Lily Briscoe **12** Mr Carmichael

To the North
author: **14** Elizabeth Bowen

to the point 6 direct **7** apropos, germane **8** explicit, relevant **9** pertinent **12** to the purpose

to the rear 3 aft **4** back **5** abaft **6** astern, behind **8** backward, rearward **9** backwards, sternward **10** to the stern **14** toward the stern

to the stern 6 astern, behind **8** rearward **9** sternward **10** to the stern

to the word
Latin: **8** ad verbum

to this extent
Latin: **8** quoad hoc

Toto
dog in: **13** The Wizard of Oz
author: **4** Baum

totter 4 reel, rock, sway **5** lurch, shake, waver **6** falter, teeter, waddle, wobble **7** shuffle, stagger, stumble **9** oscillate, vacillate

tottering 5 shaky **6** wobbly **7** rickety, shaking **8** insecure, topheavy, unstable, unsteady, wobbling **9** doddering, quivering, trembling **10** ramshackle, staggering

Toucan
constellation of: **6** Tucana

touch *see box*

touched 3 mad **4** daft, felt, nuts **5** crazy, moved, nutty **6** insane, joined **7** abutted, cracked, handled **8** demented, deranged, unhinged **10** unbalanced **12** mad as a hatter **13** off one's rocker, out of one's head **14** off one's trolley **15** mad as a March hare

Touchett, Ralph
character in: **18** The Portrait of a Lady
author: **5** James

touching 5 sad **6** moving, tender **7** pitiful **8** dramatic, pathetic, poignant, stirring **9** affecting, emotional, heartfelt, saddening, sorrowful **11** distressing, sentimental **12** heartrending **13** heartbreaking

touch me not
Latin: **13** noli me tangere

Touch of Evil
director: **11** Orson Welles
cast: **10** Janet Leigh, Ray Collins **11** Joanna Moore,

Orson Welles, Zsa Zsa Gabor **12** Akim Tamiroff, Dennis Weaver **13** Joseph Calleia **14** Charlton Heston *cameo:* **15** Marlene Dietrich **19** Mercedes McCambridge

touch off 5 shoot **6** set off **7** explode, fire off, trigger **8** activate, detonate **9** discharge

touch on 4 pose **6** broach, submit **7** advance, bring up, mention, propose, suggest **9** introduce

touchstone 4 norm, rule **5** basis, gauge, guide, model, proof **7** example, measure, pattern **8** standard **9** benchmark, criterion, guideline, precedent, principle, yardstick

Touchstone
character in: **11** As You Like It
author: **11** Shakespeare

touch upon 7 apply to, concern, mention, refer to **8** allude to, bear upon, relate to **9** appertain

touchy 5 cross, huffy, surly, testy **6** bitter, crabby, grumpy **7** awkward, fragile, grouchy, peevish, waspish **8** captious, critical, delicate, petulant, snappish, ticklish **9** concerned, difficult, irascible, irritable, querulous, resentful, sensitive **10** precarious **11** thinskinned **12** cantankerous **13** quicktempered

tough 4 cold, firm, hard, hood, lout, mean, punk, wily **5** bully, cagey, canny, cruel, hardy, rigid, rough, rowdy, solid, stern **6** brutal, crafty, dogged, knotty, mulish, rugged, savage, strict, strong, sturdy, thorny, trying **7** adamant, arduous, callous, complex, durable, hoodlum, inhuman, irksome, lasting, onerous, ruffian, vicious **8** baffling, barbaric, enduring, exacting, grievous, hooligan, involved, leathery, obdurate, perverse, pitiless, puzzling, ruthless, stubborn, ticklish, toilsome **9** barbarian, confusing, difficult, enigmatic, heartless, heavy-duty, intricate, laborious, obstinate, pigheaded, resistant, roughneck, strenuous, unbending, unfeeling **10** bullheaded, delinquent, exhausting, formidable, hardheaded, inflexible, perplexing, unyielding **11** bewildering, calculating, cold-blooded, complicated, hardhearted, hard-to-solve, infrangible, insensitive,

---

touch 3 art, bit, paw, pet, rub, use **4** abut, cite, dash, feel, fire, form, gift, hand, hint, join, meet, melt, move, note, stir, sway, tint, work **5** equal, flair, match, pinch, rival, rouse, skill, smack, speck, style, taste, thumb, tinge, trace, unite **6** adjoin, affect, arouse, border, broach, caress, excite, finger, finish, fondle, handle, hint at, manner, method, pawing, polish, sadden, soften, strike, stroke, thrill **7** concern, consume, contact, feeling, finesse, impress, inflame, inspire, mastery, mention, quality, refer to, soupcon, surface, texture, utilize **8** allude to, artistry, bear upon, come near, come up to, converge, deal with, deftness, fineness, fondling, handling, inspirit, resort to, thumbing **9** awareness, direction, electrify, fingering, influence, palpation, pertain to, suspicion, technique **10** adroitness, intimation, manipulate, perception, sprinkling, suggestion, virtuosity **11** be in contact, compare with, familiarity, guiding hand, realization **12** acquaintance, manipulation **13** communication, comprehension, understanding

troublesome **12** bloodthirsty, impenetrable **13** unsympathetic **14** uncompromising

toughen 4 firm **5** inure, steel **6** firm up, harden, season, temper **7** fortify, stiffen **8** accustom **9** acclimate, habituate **10** discipline, strengthen **11** acclimatize

Toulouse-Lautrec, Henri Marie Raymond de
born: **4** Albi **6** France **8** Albigois
artwork: **7** Friends **13** The Inspection **16** At the Moulin Rouge **24** Au Salon de la Rue des Moulins **27** Jane Avril at the Jardin de Paris **29** Cirque Fernando The Equestrienne **29** In the Parlor at the Rue des Moulins **29** The English Girl at Le Star Le Havre **30** La Goulue Entering the Moulin Rouge

toupee 3 rug, wig **6** carpet, peruke **7** periwig **9** hairpiece

tour 4 trek, trip **5** jaunt, visit **6** junket, safari, travel, voyage **7** inspect, journey **8** sightsee **9** excursion, itinerary

tourist 7 pilgrim, tripper, voyager **8** traveler, vagabond, wanderer, wayfarer **9** journeyer, sightseer **10** rubberneck **12** excursionist, globetrotter

tourmaline
color: **3** red **4** blue, pink **5** green

tournament 4 game **5** event, match **7** contest, rivalry, tourney **11** competition

Tourneur, Cyril
author of: **19** The Revenger's Tragedy

tourney 4 game **5** event, match **7** contest, rivalry **10** tournament **11** competition

tousled 5 messy **6** mussed, untidy **7** rumpled, tangled, unkempt **8** mussed-up, uncombed **10** disheveled, disordered

tout 4 plug, push **5** boost, exalt, extol, vaunt **6** praise, talk up **7** acclaim, commend, glorify, promote, tipster **8** ballyhoo, eulogize, give a tip **9** advertise, brag about, celebrate, publicize, recommend **10** aggrandize, noise about

tout a fait 8 entirely
literally: **12** wholly to fact

tout a l'heure 7 just now **8** very soon **9** presently **14** just a moment ago
literally: **15** wholly to the hour

tout de suite 6 at once **11** immediately
literally: **19** wholly consecutively

tout ensemble 11 all together

tout le monde 8 everyone **9** everybody **13** the whole world

tovarich 7 comrade

tow 3 lug **4** drag, draw, haul, lift, pull **5** hoist, trail

toward the end
Latin: **5** ad fin

toward the front 5 ahead **6** before **7** forward **9** to the fore **13** in the vanguard **14** in the forefront

toward the rear 4 back **6** astern **8** backward, rearward **9** sternward

toward the stern 6 astern **8** rearward **9** sternward **10** to the stern

tower 4 keep, loom, rock, soar **5** mount, outdo, spire, surge **6** ascend, belfry, castle, column, exceed, pillar, refuge, turret **7** bulwark, eclipse, minaret, obelisk, overtop, shoot up, steeple, surpass **8** mainstay, outclass, outshine, overhang, rise high **9** bell tower, rise above, transcend **10** foundation, overshadow, skyscraper, stronghold, wellspring **12** fountainhead

towering 4 high, tall **5** lofty **6** alpine **7** soaring, sublime, supreme **8** dominant, foremost, mounting, peerless, snowclad, superior **9** ascending, matchless, paramount, principal, unequaled, unmatched, unrivaled **10** cloud-swept, preeminent, surpassing, unexcelled **11** cloud-capped, overhanging **12** incomparable, second to none, transcendent, unparalleled **13** extraordinary

Tower of London, The
author: **24** William Harrison Ainsworth

tower over 5 dwarf **7** surpass **8** dominate **9** rise above

town 4 burg, city **6** hamlet, parish **7** borough, village **9** citizenry, residents **10** settlement **11** inhabitants, townspeople **12** municipality

Town, The
author: **13** Conrad Richter

Townes, Charles Hard
field: **7** physics
invented: **5** maser
awarded: **10** Nobel Prize

town hall
German: **7** Rathaus

town house 8 row house **10** pied-a-terre **13** city residence

township 4 town **7** village **11** subdivision **12** municipality

Toxeus
father: **6** Oeneus
mother: **7** Althaea
killed by: **6** Oeneus

toxic 5 fatal **6** deadly, lethal, mortal **7** noxious **8** poisoned, venomous **9** poisonous, unhealthy **10** pernicious

toxin 4 bane **5** venom **6** poison **8** pathogen

toy 4 play, tiny **5** dally, pygmy, sport **6** bantam, bauble, fiddle, gadget, gewgaw, little, midget, trifle **7** dwarfed, for play, stunted, trinket **8** gimcrack **9** miniature, plaything, small-size **10** diminutive, small-scale **11** Lilliputian

Toy Bulldog
nickname of: **12** Mickey Walker

Toynbee, Arnold
author of: **15** A Study of History

to your health
French: **11** a votre sante

toy with 8 play with **9** flirt with **10** trifle with **16** amuse oneself with

trace 3 bit, jot, map **4** draw, drop, find, hint, hunt, iota, mark, seek, sign **5** dig up, relic, shade, tinge, token, touch, track, trail **6** depict, flavor, trifle **7** diagram, hunt for, look for, mark out, nose out, outline, remains, uncover, unearth, vestige **8** describe, discover, draw over, evidence **9** delineate, ferret out, footprint, light upon, little bit, search for, suspicion, track down **10** come across, indication, suggestion **11** small amount

trace to 6 credit **7** ascribe **8** charge to **9** attribute

Trachiniae
author: **9** Sophocles
characters: **4** Iole **6** Hyllus, Nessus **8** Deianira, Heracles

track 3 way **4** mark, path, rail, sign, tack **5** dirty, route, scent, spoor, trace, trail **6** course, follow **9** footprint, guide rail

track and field *see box,* **p. 994**

tract 3 lot **4** area, plot, zone **5** essay **6** parcel, region **7** booklet, expanse, leaflet,

track and field
athlete: **7** Jim Ryun, Ray Ewry **8** Al Oerter, Lee Evans, Zola Budd **9** Bob Beamon, Carl Lewis, Henry Rono, Jim Thorpe **10** Ben Johnson, Bob Mathias, Bob Seagren, Edwin Moses, Grete Waitz, James Hines, Jesse Owens, John Carlos, Lasse Viren, Mac Wilkins, Paavo Nurmi, Peter Snell, Steve Ovett, Wyomia Tyus **11** Bill Rodgers, Bruce Jenner, Marty Liouri, David Wottle, Dick Fosbury, Doug Padilla, Emil Zatopek, Joni Huntley, Ralph Boston, Randy Matson, Tommie Smith **12** Dwight Stones, Frank Shorter, Harvey Glance, Jay Silvester, Kathy Hammond, Maren Seidler, Rafer Johnson, Sebastian Coe, Willie B White, Wilma Rudolph **13** Allan Feurbach, Arnie Robinson, Janice Merrill, Kathy McMillan, Kipchoge Keino, Rodney Milburn, Ronny Ray Smith, Rosalyn Bryant, William Toomey **14** Alberto Salazar, Francie Larrieu, Roger Bannister **15** Martha Rae Watson, Renaldo Nehemiah, Willie Davenport **16** Madeleine Manning, Mary Decker Slaney, Richard Wohlhuter, Steve Prefontaine **17** Alberto Juantoreno **18** Jackie Joyner-Kersee, Stephanie Hightower **21** Babe Didrikson Zaharias **22** Florence Griffith-Joyner

quarter, stretch **8** brochure, district, pamphlet, treatise **9** monograph, territory **12** disquisition

tractable 4 tame **6** docile **8** amenable, obedient, yielding **9** compliant, teachable, trainable **10** governable, manageable, submissive **12** controllable, easy to manage **13** easy to control

tractate 8 treatise **9** discourse, monograph **12** disquisition, dissertation

Tracy, Spencer
born: **11** Milwaukee WI
costar: **16** Katharine Hepburn
roles: **7** Desk Set **8** Adam's Rib, Boys' Town (Oscar) **10** Pat and Mike **12** San Francisco, Tortilla Flat **13** The Last Hurrah **14** Cass Timberlane, Inherit the Wind, Woman of the Year **15** State of the Union **16** Father of the Bride, Keeper of the Flame **17** Bad Day at Black Rock **18** Captains Courageous (Oscar), The Old Man and the Sea **19** Judgment at Nuremberg **23** Guess Who's Coming to Dinner

Traddles
character in: **16** David Copperfield
author: **7** Dickens

trade 3 buy **4** deal, line, shop, swap **5** craft **6** barter, buyers **7** calling, patrons, pursuit **8** business, commerce, exchange, shoppers, vocation **9** clientele, customers, patronize **10** buy and sell, do busi-

ness, employment, handicraft, line of work, occupation, profession **12** transactions **13** merchandising **16** business dealings, buying and selling

trade commodity 5 goods, wares

trademark 6 emblem **7** feature **8** property **9** specialty **11** peculiarity **14** characteristic

trade off 4 swap **5** trade **6** barter **8** exchange

trader 6 dealer, monger, seller **7** drummer **8** merchant, retailer **10** shopkeeper, trafficker, wholesaler **11** salesperson, storekeeper **12** merchandiser, tradesperson **14** businessperson

tradesman 6 dealer, seller **8** merchant, retailer **9** craftsman **10** shopkeeper **11** storekeeper

Trade Wind
author: **6** M M Kaye

tradition 4 lore, myth, saga, tale **5** habit, usage **6** custom, legend **8** folklore, practice **10** convention **12** superstition

traditional 3 old **5** fixed, usual **7** typical **8** habitual, historic **9** ancestral, customary **10** accustomed, inveterate **11** established **12** acknowledged, conventional

traduce 5 abuse, libel, smear, sully **6** defame, malign, vilify **7** run down, slander **8** backbite, bad-mouth, besmirch **9** deprecate, disparage **10** calumniate

traffic 4 cars, deal **5** buses, ships, trade **6** barter, doings,

planes, riders, trains, trucks **7** bootleg, contact, freight, smuggle **8** business, commerce, dealings, exchange, tourists, voyagers **9** commuters, relations, smuggling, travelers **10** buy and sell, enterprise, passengers **11** bootlegging, intercourse, pedestrians, proceedings **12** transactions, vacationists **13** excursionists

tragedy 3 woe **4** blow **5** grief **6** misery, sorrow **7** anguish, setback **8** accident, calamity, disaster, reversal, sad thing **9** heartache **10** affliction, heartbreak **11** catastrophe

tragic 3 sad **4** dire **5** awful, fatal **6** deadly, dreary, woeful **7** piteous, pitiful, ruinous, serious, unhappy **8** dramatic, dreadful, grievous, horrible, mournful, pathetic, pitiable, shocking, terrible **9** appalling, frightful **10** calamitous, deplorable, disastrous, lamentable **11** destructive, devastating, unfortunate **12** catastrophic **13** heartbreaking

trail 3 dog, tow, way **4** drag, draw, fall, flow, hunt, mark, path, poke, sign, tail **5** float, hound, scent, spoor, trace, track **6** be down, course, dangle, dawdle, follow, lessen, shrink, stream **7** dwindle, pathway, subside **8** decrease, diminish, footpath, grow weak, hand down, peter out, taper off **9** drag along, grow faint, grow small, lag behind **10** bridle path, drag behind, footprints, move slowly **11** beaten track **14** bring up the rear

trailblazers 7 leaders **8** pioneers **10** avant-garde, innovators **11** forerunners, originators, tastemakers **12** trendsetters

train 2 el **3** aim, set **4** line **5** break, chain, drill, focus, level, point, queue, sight, teach, trail, tutor **6** column, direct, escort, school, series, subway **7** caravan, cortege, educate, prepare, retinue **8** elevated, exercise, instruct, practice, rehearse, sequence **9** afterpart, appendage, entourage, followers **10** attendants, discipline, get in shape, procession, succession **11** bring to bear, domesticate, progression **12** continuation

Train, The
director: **17** John Frankenheimer
cast: **10** Albert Remy **11** Michel Simon **12** Jeanne

Moreau, Paul Scofield
13 Burt Lancaster

trained 4 able 6 expert, master 7 capable, skilled
8 schooled, seasoned 9 competent, qualified 11 experienced
12 accomplished

trainee 4 boot 5 cadet
6 rookie 7 private, rookie, student 9 greenhorn
10 apprentice

trainer 5 coach, tutor
7 teacher 16 athletic director

training 5 drill 8 coaching, drilling, practice, teaching
9 education, schooling 10 discipline 11 preparation 14 apprenticeship, indoctrination

traipse 3 gad 4 roam, walk
5 range, tramp, tread 6 stroll, trapes, wander 7 meander, saunter 8 gadabout 9 gallivant

trait 4 mark 5 quirk 7 earmark, feature, quality 8 hallmark
9 attribute, mannerism 11 peculiarity 12 idiosyncracy
14 characteristic

traitor 3 rat 5 Judas, rebel
6 ratter 7 ratfink, serpent
8 apostate, betrayer, deceiver, deserter, mutineer, quisling, renegade, turncoat 9 hypocrite 11 false friend 12 double-dealer 13 double-crosser, revolutionary 14 fifth columnist
15 snake in the grass 20 wolf in sheep's clothing

traitorous 5 false 7 corrupt
8 disloyal, renegade 9 betraying, faithless 10 perfidious, treasonous, unfaithful
11 treacherous

tramp 3 bum 4 hike, hobo, roam, rove, slog, trek, walk
5 march, prowl, stamp, stomp
6 ramble, trudge, wander
7 floater, meander, traipse, trample, vagrant 8 derelict
9 gallivant, itinerant 10 panhandler 11 perambulate, peregrinate 15 knight-of-the-road

trample 5 crush, stamp, stomp 6 squash 7 flatten, run over 14 grind under foot
15 step heavily upon

trance 4 coma, daze 5 dream, spell 6 stupor, vision 7 reverie 8 daydream, hypnosis
9 pipe dream 10 absorption, brown study 11 abstraction
12 sleepwalking 13 concentration, preoccupation, woolgathering

tranquil 4 calm, cool, mild
5 quiet, still 6 gentle, placid, serene 7 halcyon, restful
8 composed, peaceful 9 unexcited, unruffled 11 undis-

turbed, unperturbed
13 self-possessed

tranquility 4 calm, hush
5 peace, quiet 6 repose 7 concord, harmony 8 quietude, serenity 9 composure, placidity, stillness 11 restfulness
12 peacefulness

tranquilize 4 calm, drug, lull
5 allay, quiet, relax, still 6 becalm, pacify, sedate, settle, soothe 7 appease, assuage
9 alleviate

·transact 2 do 5 exact 6 handle, manage, settle 7 achieve, carry on, conduct, execute, perform
8 carry out, exercise 9 discharge 10 accomplish, take care of 12 carry through

transaction 4 deal 6 affair
7 bargain, dealing, venture
8 exchange 9 operation 10 enterprise, settlement 11 negotiation 15 business dealing, piece of business

transcend 5 excel, outdo 6 exceed 7 eclipse, outrank, surpass 8 go beyond, outrival, outshine, outstrip, overleap, overstep, surmount 9 rise above 10 overshadow
11 outdistance

transcendence 5 merit 8 eminence 9 exceeding, greatness
10 exaltation, excellence, surpassing 11 distinction, preeminence, superiority

transcendental 5 great
6 mental 7 supreme, unusual
8 elevated, peerless, superior, uncommon 9 exceeding, intuitive, matchless, spiritual, unequaled, unrivaled
10 surpassing 11 unsurpassed
12 incomparable, metaphysical 13 extraordinary

transfer 4 cede, deed, move, send 5 bring, carry, shift
6 change, convey, moving, remove 7 consign, deeding, removal, sending 8 bringing, carrying, hand over, make over, relegate, relocate, shifting, shipment, transmit, turn over 9 conveying, transport
10 delivering, relegation, relocating, relocation 11 consignment, transmittal
12 transporting
14 transportation

transferable 8 catching
10 contagious, infectious
12 communicable 13 transmissible, transmittable

transferal 8 delivery, transfer
10 giving over 11 handing over, transmittal
12 transmission

transference 5 shift 6 change
7 passage, removal 9 transport 11 transmittal 12 dislodgement, displacement, transmission 13 transmittance

transfiguration 10 conversion
13 metamorphosis, transmutation 14 transformation

transfigure 6 change 9 transform 12 metamorphose

transfix 3 pin 4 hold, stab, stun 5 rivet, spear, spike, stick 6 absorb, impale, pierce, skewer 7 astound, bewitch, enchant, engross, fix fast, terrify 8 astonish, hold rapt, intrigue 9 captivate, fascinate, hypnotize, mesmerize, penetrate, spellbind 10 run through

transform 4 turn 5 alter
6 change, recast, remold
7 convert, remodel 8 make over 9 refurbish, transmute
11 reconstruct, transfigure
12 metamorphose, transmogrify

transformation 6 change 9 restyling 10 alteration, conversion, remodeling
13 metamorphosis, transmutation 15 transfiguration

transgress 3 err, sin 4 slip
5 break, cross, fault, lapse, wrong 6 exceed, impose, offend 7 digress, infract, violate
8 infringe, trespass

transgression 3 sin 5 crime, error, lapse, wrong 6 breach
7 misdeed, offense 8 evil deed, iniquity, trespass 9 violation
10 immorality, infraction, wrongdoing 11 lawbreaking
12 encroachment, infringement, overstepping
13 contravention

transgressor 5 felon 6 sinner
7 culprit 8 criminal, evildoer, offender, violator 9 miscreant, wrongdoer 10 lawbreaker, malefactor, trespasser

transience 7 brevity 11 evanescence 12 ephemerality, impermanence

transient 5 brief 7 passing
8 fleeting, soon past, temporal 9 ephemeral, momentary, short-term, temporary
10 evanescent, perishable, short-lived, transitory, unenduring 11 impermanent
14 passing through 24 here today and gone tomorrow

transistor
invented by: 7 Bardeen
8 Brattain, Shockley

transition 4 jump, leap
6 change 7 passage, passing
8 shifting 9 gradation, varia-

tion **10** alteration, changeover, conversion, graduation **11** progression **13** transmutation **14** transformation

transitory 5 brief **7** passing **8** fleeting, fugitive **9** ephemeral, temporary, transient **10** evanescent, not lasting, short-lived, unenduring **11** impermanent **24** here today and gone tomorrow

translate 4 turn **5** alter, apply **6** change, decode, recast, render, reword **7** clarify, convert, explain **8** decipher, rephrase, simplify, spell out **9** elucidate, interpret, make clear, transform, transmute **10** paraphrase

translucence 7 clarity **8** lucidity **10** luminosity **12** transparency **16** semi-transparency

translucent 8 pellucid **10** semiopaque, translucid **15** semitransparent

transmissible 8 catching **10** contagious, infectious **12** communicable, transferable **13** transmittable

transmission 4 note **7** message, passage, passing, sending **8** delivery, dispatch, transfer **9** broadcast **10** conveyance, forwarding, remittance **11** handing over, transmittal **12** transference, transferring **13** communication **14** transportation

transmit 4 send, ship **5** carry, issue, relay, remit **6** convey, pass on, spread **7** deliver, forward **8** dispatch, televise, transfer **9** broadcast **11** communicate, disseminate

transmittable 8 catching **10** contagious, infectious **12** communicable, transferable

transmittal 7 sending **8** delivery, transfer **10** giving over, transferal **11** handing over **12** transmission

transmutation 6 change **10** conversion **13** metamorphosis **14** transformation **15** transfiguration

transmute 5 alter **6** change **7** convert **9** transform **12** metamorphose

transparency 6 purity **7** clarity **8** lucidity **9** clearness, sheerness **11** obviousness **14** diaphanousness

transparent 4 thin **5** clear, gauzy, lucid, plain, sheer **6** glassy, limpid, patent **7** evident, obvious, visible **8** apparent, clear-cut, distinct, explicit, manifest, palpable, peekaboo,

pellucid **10** diaphanous, seethrough **11** perceptible, self-evident, translucent, unambiguous, unequivocal **12** crystal-clear, unmistakable

transpire 5 arise, occur **6** appear, befall, chance, crop up, evolve, happen, turn up **7** come out, leak out **9** be met with, eventuate, take place **10** be revealed, come to pass, make public **11** become known, be disclosed, come to light, show its face

transplant 5 graft, repot, shift **7** replant **8** displace, relocate, resettle, transfer **9** transport, transpose

transport 3 bus, lug **4** bear, cart, lift, move, send, ship, take, tote **5** bring, carry, charm, fetch, train, truck **6** convey, moving, remove, thrill **7** bearing, bewitch, carting, delight, deliver, enchant, freight, removal, sending, vehicle **8** airplane, carrying, delivery, dispatch, enthrall, entrance, shipment, shipping, transfer, transmit, trucking **9** captivate, cargo ship, carry away, conveying, electrify, enrapture, freighter, overpower **10** cargo plane, conveyance **12** freight train

transportation 7 cartage, haulage, portage, removal, transit **8** delivery, dispatch, movement, shipment **9** transport **10** conveyance, transferal **12** transference, transmission **13** transmittance

transported 5 moved **6** lifted **7** charmed **8** ecstatic, thrilled, uplifted **9** bewitched, entranced **10** captivated, enthralled **11** carried away, electrified **13** beside oneself

transverse 5 cross **6** across **7** athwart, oblique, transom **8** crossbar, crossing, diagonal, traverse **9** crosswise **10** crosspiece, horizontal

transversely 9 crossways, crosswise, laterally

trap 3 net, pit **4** lure, ploy, ruse, seal, stop, wile **5** catch, feint, snare, trick **6** ambush, device, enmesh, entrap, lock in **7** ensnare, pitfall, springe **8** artifice, entangle, hold back, hunt down, maneuver **9** booby trap, stratagem **11** machination **16** compartmentalize

trappings 4 garb, gear **5** array, dress **6** attire, outfit, things **7** apparel, clothes, costume, effects, raiment, vesture **8** adjuncts, clothing, fittings

9 ornaments, trimmings **10** adornments, habiliment, investment **11** decorations **13** accoutrements, paraphernalia **14** embellishments

trash 3 rot **4** bums, crap, junk, scum **5** dregs, dross, tripe, waste **6** debris, drivel, idlers, litter, refuse, rubble, tramps **7** garbage, hogwash, loafers, residue, rubbish, twaddle **8** castoffs, leavings, nonsense, riffraff **9** poppycock, sweepings **10** balderdash **11** foolishness, ne'er-do-wells, odds and ends **15** good-for-nothings, unsavory element

trashy 4 vile **5** cheap, inane, junky, tacky **6** flashy, flimsy **7** rubbish, trivial, useless **8** riffraff, trumpery, wasteful **9** worthless **13** insignificant

trauma 4 hurt **5** shock, wound **6** injury, stress

travail 4 pain, toil **5** labor, worry **6** strain, stress **7** anguish **8** delivery, distress, drudgery, exertion, hard work, hardship **9** suffering **10** birth pains, childbirth, labor pains **11** parturition **12** accouchement

travel 2 go **4** be on, move, roam, rove, sail, tour, trek, wend **5** cross, drive, range, visit **6** cruise, junket, voyage, wander **7** journey, proceed **8** pass over, progress, sightsee, traverse **9** globetrot, hitchhike, take a trip **11** pass through, press onward

traveler 5 gypsy, nomad, rover **7** drummer, migrant, pilgrim, tourist, trekker, tripper, voyager **8** vagabond, wanderer, wayfarer **9** itinerant, journeyer, sightseer **10** vacationer **12** excursionist, globetrotter

Traveller Without Luggage author: **11** Jean Anouilh

Travels with a Donkey author: **20** Robert Louis Stevenson donkey: **9** Modestine

Travels with My Aunt author: **12** Graham Greene

travel through 2 do **5** cover, cross, visit **8** traverse **9** negotiate **11** pass through

traverse 4 span **5** cross **6** bridge, travel **8** go across, move over, overpass **9** cross over, cut across, intersect, move along, negotiate, reach over **10** extend over, run through, travel over **11** move through, pass through, reach across

travesty 4 sham **5** farce, spoof **6** parody, satire **7** lampoon, mockery, takeoff **8** disgrace **9** burlesque **10** caricature, distortion, perversion **17** misrepresentation

Traviata, La
also: 9 The Misled **23** The Woman Who Was Led Astray
opera by: 5 Verdi
based on a story by: 14 Alexandre Dumas (fils)
called: 7 Camille **17** La Dame aux Camelias
character: 8 Violetta **14** Alfredo Germont

Travolta, John
born: 11 Englewood NJ
roles: 6 Carrie, Grease **10** Tony Manero **11** Urban Cowboy **12** Staying Alive **14** Moment By Moment **15** Vinnie Barbarino **17** Welcome Back Kotter **18** Saturday Night Fever

trawl 3 net **4** drag, fish, haul, line **5** seine, troll **6** dredge **7** dragnet

Treacher, Arthur
real name: 11 Arthur Veary
born: 7 England **8** Brighton
roles: 11 Mary Poppins **14** National Velvet, Thank You Jeeves **16** David Copperfield **20** Magnificent Obsession

treacherous 5 false, risky **6** tricky, unsafe, untrue **7** devious **8** disloyal, perilous, two-faced **9** dangerous, deceitful, deceptive, faithless, hazardous **10** misleading, perfidious, precarious, traitorous, treasonous, unfaithful **12** falsehearted **13** untrustworthy

treachery 5 guile **6** deceit **7** perfidy, treason **8** apostasy, betrayal, trickery **9** deception, duplicity, falseness **10** disloyalty, infidelity **11** double cross **13** breach of faith, deceitfulness, double-dealing, faithlessness **15** underhandedness **17** untrustworthiness

tread 4 gait, hike, pace, roam, rove, step, walk **5** prowl, range, stamp, stomp, tramp **6** step on, stride, stroll, trudge, walk on **7** trample **8** footfall, footstep

treason 6 mutiny, revolt **7** perfidy **8** apostasy, betrayal, sedition **9** duplicity, rebellion, treachery **10** conspiracy, disloyalty, insurgence, revolution, subversion **12** insurrection

treasonable 9 faithless, seditious **10** perfidious, subversive, traitorous **11** treacherous

treasure 3 gem **4** gold **5** hoard, jewel, prize, store, value **6** esteem, jewels, regard, revere, riches, silver **7** cherish, deposit, paragon **8** bank upon, dote upon, gold mine, hold dear **11** pride and joy **14** apple of one's eye **17** pearl of great price

treasure chest 3 box **4** case **5** chest, trunk **6** coffer

treasured 4 dear **5** loved **6** adored, valued **7** beloved **8** precious **9** cherished

Treasure Island
author: 20 Robert Louis Stevenson
character: 7 Ben Gunn **8** Smollett **9** Dr Livesey **10** Jim Hawkins **14** Long John Silver **15** Squire Trelawney
director:
 1934 version: 13 Victor Fleming
 1950 version: 11 Byron Haskin
based on novel by: 20 Robert Louis Stevenson
cast:
 1934 version: 10 Lewis Stone **12** Jackie Cooper (Jim Hawkins), Wallace Beery (Long John Silver) **15** Lionel Barrymore
 1950 version: 11 Basil Sydney **12** Robert Newton (Long John Silver) **13** Bobby Driscoll (Jim Hawkins) **16** Walter Fitzgerald

Treasure of the Sierra Madre, The
director: 10 John Huston
cast: 7 Tim Holt **12** Bruce Bennett, Walter Huston **13** Alfonso Bedoya, Barton MacLane **14** Humphrey Bogart
Oscar for: 8 director **10** screenplay **15** supporting actor (Huston)

treasurer 6 banker, bursar, purser, teller **7** auditor, cashier **9** financier **10** accountant, bookkeeper, cash-keeper, controller **16** financial officer **17** minister of finance **22** secretary of the treasury **24** Chancellor of the Exchequer

Treasure State
nickname of: 7 Montana

treasury 4 bank, safe, till **5** funds, purse, vault **6** coffer **8** money box **9** anthology, exchequer, strongbox, thesaurus **10** collection, compendium, depository, repository, storehouse **11** bank account, compilation

treasury note 4 bill **8** bank note **9** greenback **12** currency note **17** silver certificate

treat 3 joy **4** blow, coat, give **5** apply, cover, favor, grant, imbue, stand **6** attend, divert, doctor, handle, manage, remedy, spring, thrill **7** comfort, delight, discuss, patch up, take out **8** consider, deal with, look upon, medicate, pleasure, relate to **9** act toward, small gift, try to cure, try to heal **10** impregnate, minister to, speak about, write about **12** prescribe for, satisfaction **13** gratification

treat as inferior 7 disdain **9** patronize **12** condescend to **18** look down one's nose at **19** discriminate against

treatise 4 text **5** essay, study, tract **6** manual, memoir, report, thesis **8** textbook, tractate **9** discourse, monograph **12** dissertation

treatment 3 way **4** cure **6** course, remedy **7** conduct, process, regimen, therapy **8** antidote, approach, handling, treating **9** doctoring, operation, procedure **10** management, medication **11** application, medical care **12** manipulation

treaty 4 deal, pact **6** accord **7** bargain, compact, entente **8** covenant **9** concordat **13** understanding **15** formal agreement **22** international agreement

tree 3 ash, elm, fir, oak **4** bush, palm, pine, wood **5** beech, birch, chase, maple, plane, plant, scrub, staff, stake, stick **6** corner, cudgel, redbud, spruce, timber, willow **7** gallows, lineage, live oak, sapling **8** ancestry, chestnut, hardwood, mahogany, pedigree, seedling **9** ailanthus, evergreen **10** cottonwood, eucalyptus

Tree Grows in Brooklyn, A
author: 10 Betty Smith
character:
 Nolan family: 5 Katie **6** Neeley **7** Francie, Johnnie
director: 9 Elia Kazan
cast: 9 James Dunn **10** Lloyd Nolan **12** Joan Blondell **14** Dorothy McGuire, Peggy Ann Garner
Oscar for: 7 special (Garner) **15** supporting actor (Dunn)

treeless 4 bald, bare **6** barren **7** denuded **8** unwooded **10** unforested

Treeplanters State
nickname of: 8 Nebraska

trek 4 hike, plod, roam, rove, sail, slog, trip 5 jaunt, march, range, tramp 6 junket, outing, travel, trudge, voyage, wander 7 journey, odyssey, passage 8 traverse 9 excursion, migration 10 expedition, pilgrimage 11 peregrinate 13 peregrination

trellis 5 arbor, bower, cross, frame, grill, trail 6 gazebo, screen 7 lattice, network, pergola 8 espalier 10 interweave 11 summerhouse

tremble 5 quail, quake, shake, waver 6 quaver, quiver, shiver 7 flutter, pulsate, shudder 9 palpitate

trembling 5 shaky 7 quaking, shaking 8 unsteady 9 doddering, quavering, quivering, shivering 10 shuddering 11 palpitating

tremblor 5 quake, seism, shock 6 tremor 8 upheaval 10 earthquake

tremendous 4 fine, huge, vast 5 giant, great, major 7 amazing, awesome, immense, mammoth, sizable, titanic, unusual 8 colossal, enormous, fabulous, gigantic, terrific, towering, uncommon 9 excellent, fantastic, first-rate, humongous, important, marvelous, monstrous, wonderful 10 formidable, gargantuan, incredible, noteworthy, stupendous 11 elephantine, exceptional 12 considerable 13 consequential, extraordinary

tremolo
music: 9 trembling, vibrating 30 rapid reiteration of a single pitch

tremor 3 jar 4 jolt 5 quake, shake, shock, spasm, throb, waver 6 quiver, shiver 7 flutter, shaking, shudder, tremble 8 paroxysm 9 pulsation, quavering, quivering, shivering, trembling, vibration 10 convulsion 11 palpitation

tremulous 5 jumpy, shaky, timid 6 wobbly 7 aquiver, excited, fearful, jittery, keyed-up, nervous, panicky, quaking 8 aflutter, agitated, atremble, hesitant, restless, wavering, worked-up 9 faltering, impatient, quivering, trembling, uncertain 10 irresolute, stimulated 13 on tenterhooks, panic-stricken

trench 3 cut, rut 4 scar 5 canal, ditch, drain, fosse, slash, slice 6 dugout, furrow, gutter, trough 7 channel,

wrinkle 8 aqueduct 9 earthwork 10 depression

trenchant 4 acid, keen, tart 5 crisp 6 bitter 7 acerbic, caustic, concise, mordant, probing 8 clear-cut, distinct, incisive, scathing 9 sarcastic, scorching 10 razor-sharp 11 acrimonious, penetrating, well-defined

trend 4 bent, flow, mode 5 drift, style 7 fashion, impulse, leaning 8 movement, tendency 9 direction 10 proclivity, propensity 11 inclination

trendsetters 7 leaders 8 trendies, vanguard 10 avant-garde, innovators 11 pacesetters, tastemakers 12 advance guard, stylesetters, trailblazers

trendy 2 in 4 chic, tony 5 swank 6 modern, modish, with-it 7 current, faddish, popular, stylish, voguish 8 up-to-date 10 all the rage 11 fashionable 13 up-to-the-minute

Trenor, Gus and Judy
characters in: 15 The House of Mirth
author: 7 Wharton

Trent, Little Nell
character in: 19 The Old Curiosity Shop
author: 7 Dickens

trepidation 4 fear 5 alarm, dread, panic, worry 7 anxiety, jitters 8 cold feet, disquiet 10 uneasiness 11 butterflies, disquietude, jitteriness, nervousness 12 apprehension 13 consternation

trespass 3 sin 5 error, wrong 6 invade 7 impinge, intrude, misdeed, offense 8 encroach, infringe, iniquity, invasion 9 evildoing, intrusion, violation 10 immorality, infraction, misconduct, wrongdoing 11 delinquency, misbehavior 12 encroachment, infringement, overstepping 13 transgression, unlawful entry, wrongful entry

tress 4 curl, hair, lock, mane 5 braid, plait 6 strand 7 ringlet, wimpler 8 spitcurl

trestle 4 beam 5 board, brace, frame, table 6 timber 9 framework

trial 2 go 3 try, woe 4 care, pain, shot, test 5 agony, essay, flyer, whirl, worry 6 burden, effort, misery, ordeal, trying, tryout 7 anguish, attempt, bad luck, hearing, testing, test run, torment, trouble, ven-

ture 8 accident, distress, endeavor, hardship, vexation 9 adversity, court case, heartache, suffering 10 affliction, litigation, misfortune 11 cross to bear 12 misadventure, wretchedness

Trial, The
author: 10 Franz Kafka
character: 4 Leni 7 Joseph K 9 Titorelli 11 The Advocate

trial and error 10 experiment 13 investigation 15 experimentation 20 process of elimination

Triassic period
dinosaur from: 11 Coelophysis, Mandasuchus 12 Melanosaurus, Pisanosaurus, Plateosaurus 13 Tanystropheus 17 Heterodontosaurus

tribe see 11 ethnic group

Tribes of Israel see 6 Israel

tribulation 3 woe 4 care, pain 5 agony, grief, trial, worry 6 misery, ordeal, sorrow 7 anguish, bad luck, torment, trouble 8 distress, hardship, vexation 9 adversity, heartache, suffering 10 affliction, ill fortune, misfortune 11 unhappiness 12 wretchedness

Tribulation Wholesome
character in: 12 The Alchemist
author: 6 Jonson

tribunal 3 bar 5 bench, court, forum 6 judges 9 authority, judiciary 10 ruling body 11 judge's bench, judge's chair 14 seat of judgment

tributary 6 branch, feeder, source, stream 7 helping, subject 8 affluent 9 ancillary, auxiliary, confluent, secondary 10 subjugated, subsidiary 11 subordinate 12 contributing, contributory

tribute 3 tax 4 duty, levy, toll 5 bribe, honor, kudos 6 esteem, eulogy, excise, impost, payoff, praise, ransom 7 payment, respect 8 accolade, encomium, memorial 9 extolling, gratitude, laudation, panegyric 10 assessment, blood money, compliment, settlement 11 recognition, testimonial 12 commendation, pound of flesh 13 consideration, peace offering 14 acknowledgment

trice 3 sec 4 jiff, wink 5 blink, flash, jiffy, shake 6 minute, moment, second 7 instant 9 coup d'oeil, twinkling 11 split second

trichophobia
fear of: **4** hair

trichoptera
class: **8** hexapoda
phylum: **10** arthropoda
group: **3** fly **6** caddis

trick 3 art, gag **4** bait, dupe, feat, gift, gull, have, hoax, joke, ploy, ruse, trap, wile **5** antic, blind, bluff, caper, cheat, dodge, feint, fraud, knack, prank, put-on, skill, stunt **6** deceit, device, number, outfox, outwit, resort, secret, take in **7** deceive, gimmick, know-how, mislead, swindle **8** artifice, deftness, flimflam, hoodwink, maneuver **9** bamboozle, chicanery, deception, dexterity, imposture, sophistry, stratagem, technique **10** adroitness, hocus-pocus, manipulate, subterfuge **11** contrivance, machination, outmaneuver **13** practical joke, sleight of hand **16** prestidigitation

trickery 5 guile **6** bunkum, deceit **8** artifice, flimflam, pretense, quackery, wiliness **9** chicanery, deception, duplicity, imposture, rascality, stratagem **10** artfulness, craftiness, hocus-pocus, shiftiness **11** crookedness, deviousness **12** charlatanism, skullduggery, slipperiness **13** deceitfulness

trickiness 6 deceit **7** cunning, slyness **8** trickery **9** duplicity **10** craftiness **15** underhandedness

trickle 4 drip, leak, ooze, seep **5** exude **7** dribble, seepage **9** percolate

trickster 5 cheat, joker **6** dodger, rascal **8** deceiver, impostor, sleeveen **9** prankster

tricky 3 sly **4** foxy, wily **5** risky **6** artful, crafty, shifty, unsafe **7** cunning, devious **8** rascally, slippery, unstable **9** dangerous, deceptive, difficult, hazardous **10** touch-and-go, unreliable **11** complicated, underhanded **12** hard to handle, undependable **13** temperamental, unpredictable

trident
form: **5** spear
number of prongs: **5** three

trifle 3 bit, dab, jot, nip, toy **4** dash, drop, idle, iota, mite, play **5** crumb, dally, pinch, scrap, speck, tinge, touch, trace **6** bauble, dawdle, gewgaw, linger, little, morsel, sliver **7** modicum, nothing, trinket **8** fragment, gimcrack, kill time **9** bagatelle, play-

thing, waste time **10** dillydally, knickknack, sprinkling, triviality **11** deal lightly, small matter **12** amuse oneself, treat lightly **13** small quantity

trifler 5 flirt, idler **6** coquet **7** dabbler, dallier **8** coquette **10** dilettante

trifling 4 puny **5** petty, small, sorry, token **6** paltry, slight **7** nominal, trivial **8** beggarly, niggling, nugatory, picayune, piddling **9** worthless **10** negligible **11** unimportant **13** beneath notice, inappreciable, insignificant **14** inconsiderable **15** inconsequential

trifling circumstances
Latin: **8** minutiae

trifling matter
French: **10** peu de chose

trigger 5 shoot **6** set off **7** fire off **8** activate, detonate, touch off **9** discharge

trikerion 11 candelabrum, candlestick **12** candleholder

Trilby
author: **15** George du Maurier
character: **5** Gecko, Sandy, Taffy **8** Svengali **12** Little Billee **14** Trilby O'Ferrall

trill
music: **7** shaking, tremolo **9** quavering

trim 3 cut, fit, lop **4** clip, crop, deck, form, lean, pare, slim, thin **5** adorn, array, lithe, prune, shape, shave, shear, shift, sleek, state **6** adjust, bedeck, border, change, fettle, kilter, limber, paring, piping, supple, svelte **7** arrange, balance, bedizen, compact, cutting, fitness, furbish, garnish, lissome, pruning, shapely, slender, willowy **8** athletic, beautify, clipping, cropping, decorate, equalize, ornament, shearing, trick out, trimming **9** adornment, condition, embellish, embroider, shipshape **10** decoration, distribute **11** streamlined **13** embellishment, ornamentation

Trim, Corporal
character in: **14** Tristram Shandy
author: **6** Sterne

trimming 4 trim **5** frill **7** cutting, pruning, slicing **8** clipping **9** adornment **10** decoration, shortening, truncation **11** abridgement, contraction, curtailment **12** abbreviation **13** embellishment

Trinacria see **6** Sicily

Trinidad and Tobago see box, p. 1000

Trinity
author: **8** Leon Uris

trinket 3 toy **5** bijou, charm, jewel **6** bauble, gewgaw, notion, trifle **8** gimcrack, ornament **9** bagatelle, plaything **10** knickknack

trip 3 bob, err **4** flip, flub, fool, muff, pull, skip, slip, tour, trek, undo **5** caper, catch, dance, fluff, foray, jaunt, outdo, throw, upset **6** bungle, cruise, frolic, gambol, junket, outfox, outing, prance, safari, set off, slip up, voyage **7** blunder, commute, confuse, flounce, journey, misstep, release, scamper, stumble **8** activate, fall over, flounder, hoodwink, throw off **9** excursion **10** disconcert, expedition, pilgrimage **11** step lightly

Triple Crown 7 Belmont **9** Preakness **13** Kentucky Derby
winner: **5** Omaha **7** Assault **8** Affirmed, Citation **9** Sir Barton, Whirlaway **10** Count Fleet, Gallant Fox, War Admiral **11** Seattle Slew, Secretariat

Triple Sec see **9** Cointreau

Tripoli
capital of: **5** Libya

Triptolemos, Triptolemus
favorite of: **7** Demeter
inventor of: **4** plow **5** wheel
patron of: **11** agriculture

Triquetra see **6** Sicily

triskaidekaphobia
fear of: **14** number thirteen

Trismegistus see **5** Thoth

Tristan and Isolde
also: **16** Tristan und Isolde
opera by: **6** Wagner
character: **5** Melot **8** Brangane, Kurwenal **18** King Mark of Cornwall

triste 3 sad **10** melancholy

tristesse 6 sorrow **7** sadness **10** melancholy

Tristram
author: **22** Edwin Arlington Robinson
character in: **16** Arthurian romance

Tristram Shandy
author: **14** Laurence Sterne
character: **6** Dr Slop **8** Mr Yorick **10** Toby Shandy **11** Widow Wadman **12** Corporal Trim, Walter Shandy

trite 5 banal, silly, stale **6** common **7** cliched, hum-

Trinidad and Tobago
  capital/largest city: 11 Port of Spain
  others: 4 Debe, Toco 5 Arima 6 Canaan, Coryal, Labrea
    7 San Juan, Siparia 8 Rio Claro, Tunapuna 10 Roxbor-
    ough 11 San Fernando, Scarborough 12 Princess Town,
    Sangre Grande 14 Charlotteville
  school: 6 Fatima 7 St Mary's 11 Queen's Royal
  head of state: 14 British monarch 15 governor general
  monetary unit: 4 cent 6 dollar
  island: 12 Chacachacare, Little Tobago 14 Bird of Paradise
  lake: 5 Pitch
  mountain:
    hills: 7 Trinity 10 Montserrat 12 Three Sisters
  highest point: 5 Aripo
  river: 6 Caroni 7 Ortoire 8 Oropuche, Trinidad
  sea: 8 Atlantic 9 Caribbean
  physical feature:
    bay: 5 Cocos, Guapo 6 Matura, Mayaro
    channel: 12 Dragon's Mouth 13 Serpent's Mouth
    gulf: 5 Paria
    point: 5 Radix 6 Arenal, Galera 7 Chupara, Galeota
      8 Columbus
  people: 5 Irish 6 French, Syrian 7 African, Chinese,
    English, Spanish 8 European, Lebanese 10 East Indian,
    Portuguese, Venezuelan 11 Asian Indian 13 Latin
    American
    explorer: 8 Columbus
    leader: 8 Williams
  language: 6 French 7 Chinese, English, Spanish 10 Portu-
    guese 12 French Patois
  religion: 5 Hindu, Islam 8 Anglican 10 Protestant
    12 Christianity 13 Roman Catholic
  place:
    asphalt lake: 9 Pitch Lake
    mansions: 16 Magnificent Seven
    park: 18 Queen's Park Savannah
  feature:
    bird: 7 oilbird 8 cocorico
    clothing: 4 sari 5 dhoti
    dance: 6 Dragon, Shango
    festival: 6 Hosein, Lights
    fish: 5 guppy
    music: 7 calypso, goombay
    tree: 4 mora
  food:
    drink: 16 Angostura Bitters

drum, routine, shallow, worn-
out 8 bromidic, everyday,
ordinary, overdone, shopworn
9 frivolous, hackneyed 10 pedestrian, threadbare 11 commonplace, oft-repeated,
stereotyped, unimportant
12 run-of-the-mill
13 platitudinous

Tritogeneia *see* 6 Athena

Triton
  god of: 3 sea
  father: 8 Poseidon
  mother: 10 Amphitrite
  shape: 6 merman
  trumpet: 10 conch-shell

triumph 3 hit, win 4 best,
coup 5 smash 6 subdue 7 conquer, mastery, prevail, succeed, success, surpass, victory
8 conquest, overcome, smash

hit, vanquish 9 overwhelm
10 ascendancy, attainment,
gain the day 11 achievement,
superiority 12 come out on
top, take the prize 14 accomplishment, get the better of

triumphal 5 proud 6 joyous
8 exultant 9 ascendant, rewarding 10 fulfilling, gratifying, successful, triumphant,
victorious 11 spectacular

triumphant 6 elated, joyful
7 winning 8 exultant, jubilant
9 rejoicing 10 conquering,
first-place, successful, victorious 11 celebrating
12 prizewinning

Triumph of Death, The
  author: 17 Gabriele
    D'Annunzio

trivia
  Latin: 8 minutiae

trivial 4 idle, puny, slim
5 banal, petty, small, trite
6 common, flimsy, little, meager, paltry, slight, two-bit
7 foolish 8 beggarly, everyday,
niggling, nugatory, ordinary,
picayune, piddling, trifling
9 rinky-dink, worthless 10 incidental, pedestrian 11 commonplace, meaningless,
unessential, unimportant
13 inappreciable, insignificant,
of little value 14 inconsiderable 15 inconsequential

triviality 5 frill 6 trifle 9 frivolity 10 paltriness 12 nonessential, unimportance
14 insignificance
18 inconsequentiality

troglodyte 5 brute 6 hermit
9 barbarian 11 cave dweller

Troilus
  father: 5 Priam
  mother: 6 Hecuba

Troilus and Cressida
  author: 18 William
    Shakespeare
  character: 4 Ajax 5 Priam
    6 Hector 7 Ulysses
    8 Achilles, Diomedes, Panda-
    rus 9 Agamemnon

Troilus and Criseyde
  author: 15 Geoffrey Chaucer
  character: 8 Diomedes,
    Pandarus

trois 5 three

Trojan Horse
  made of: 4 wood
  made by: 7 Epeiosk
  contained: 8 Odysseus,
    warriors

Trojans, The
  also: 10 Les Troyens
  opera by: 7 Berlioz
  part one: 14 La Prise de
    Troie 16 The Capture of
    Troy
  part two: 19 Les Troyens a
    Carthage 20 The Trojans in
    Carthage
  character: 4 Dido 6 Aeneas,
    Hector

Trojan War
  length: 8 ten years
  combatants: 6 Greeks
    7 Trojans
  cause: 5 Helen, Paris 14 Ap-
    ple of Discord

Trojan Women, The
  author: 9 Euripides
  character: 5 Helen 6 Hecuba
    8 Astyanax, Menelaus, Odys-
    seus, Polyxena 9 Agamem-
    non, Cassandra
    10 Andromache, Talthybius
    11 Neoptolemus

troll 3 imp 4 ogre 5 dwarf, gnome 6 goblin
  origin: 12 Scandinavian
  form: 12 supernatural
  inhabits: 10 subterrain

trollop 4 doxy, slut 5 bitch, doxie, frump, hussy, trull, whore 6 floozy, harlot, wanton 7 baggage 8 slattern, strumpet 10 prostitute

Trollope, Anthony
  author of: 9 Orley Farm, The Warden 15 The Way We Live Now 16 Barchester Towers, Framley Parsonage
  character: 11 Phineas Finn

troop, troops 4 army, band, file, gang, herd, step, unit 5 bunch, crowd, crush, drove, flock, horde, march, press, swarm, tramp 6 parade, stride, throng, trudge 7 cavalry, company, militia 8 infantry, soldiers, soldiery, troopers 9 aggregate, gathering 10 armed force, assemblage 11 cavalry unit, fighting men, police force 12 congregation 13 military force

trop 3 too 7 too many, too much

Tropaean
  epithet of: 4 Zeus
  means: 14 giver of victory

Trophonius
  vocation: 7 builder
  father: 7 Erginus
  brother: 8 Agamedes
  god of: 5 earth
  killed: 8 Agamedes
  became: 6 oracle
    oracle called: 14 Zeus Trophonius

trophy 4 palm 5 award, booty, honor, kudos, medal, prize, relic, spoil 6 wreath 7 laurels,

memento 8 citation, souvenir 9 loving cup 10 blue ribbon 11 testimonial

tropical 5 muggy 6 sultry, torrid 8 stifling 10 sweltering 11 hot and humid

troppo, non
  music: 10 not too much

Tros
  king of: 4 Troy
  father: 12 Erichthonius
  mother: 8 Astyoche
  wife: 10 Callirrhoe
  son: 4 Ilus 8 Ganymede 9 Assaracus

trot 3 jog 9 go briskly 11 step quickly, walk smartly

troth 8 fidelity 9 betrothal 10 affiancing, engagement 12 faithfulness

Trotwood, Betsey
  character in: 16 David Copperfield
  author: 7 Dickens

trouble *see box*

troubled 5 upset 7 worried 8 bothered, careworn 9 disturbed, perturbed 10 distressed 12 heavyhearted

troublemaker 6 gossip 7 inciter 8 agitator, fomenter, provoker 9 miscreant 10 incendiary, instigator 11 rumormonger, scaremonger 12 rabble-rouser 13 mischief-maker, scandalmonger 16 agent provocateur

troublesome 4 hard 5 heavy, pesky, tough 6 cursed, knotty, taxing, thorny, tiring, trying, vexing 7 arduous, irksome, onerous, tedious 8 annoying, tiresome, unwieldy 9 demanding, difficult, fatiguing, harassing, herculean, laborious,

wearisome, worrisome 10 bothersome, burdensome, cumbersome, disturbing, irritating, oppressive, tormenting, unpleasant 11 disobedient, distressing 12 disagreeable, exasperating, inconvenient, uncontrolled 13 undisciplined

troublesomeness 5 trial 10 difficulty 11 arduousness 13 inconvenience, laboriousness, vexatiousness, worrisomeness 14 bothersomeness

Trouble with Harry, The
  director: 15 Alfred Hitchcock
  cast: 11 Edmund Gwenn 12 John Forsythe 14 Mildred Dunnock, Mildred Natwick 15 Shirley MacLaine

troubling 6 vexing 8 worrying 9 worrisome 10 bothersome, disturbing, unsettling

trough 4 duct, moat, race, tray 5 canal, ditch, flume, gorge, gully 6 furrow, hollow, ravine, trench 7 channel 8 aqueduct 10 depression

trounce 4 beat, drub, lick, trim, whip 5 cream, skunk 6 humble 7 clobber 8 vanquish 9 overpower, overwhelm 10 take care of 11 carry the day 14 get the better of

troupe 4 band, cast 5 group, troop 6 actors 7 company, players 10 performers 11 road company

trouper 5 actor 7 actress 8 thespian 9 performer 13 touring player 15 repertory player

trousers 5 jeans, pants 6 chinos, slacks 7 drawers 8 breeches, britches, jodhpurs, knickers, overalls 9 dungarees 10 pantaloons 11 bellbottoms 12 pedal pushers 14 knickerbockers

Trovatore, Il
  also: 13 The Troubadour
  opera by: 5 Verdi
  character: 7 Azucena, Leonora, Manrico 11 Count di Luna

Troy
  abducted queen: 5 Helen
  archaeologist: 6 Blegen 8 Dorpfeld 10 Schliemann
  defender: 5 Eneas 6 Aeneas
  Greek name: 5 Ilion
  hero: 6 Hector
  king: 5 Priam
  Latin name: 5 Ilium
  modern name: 9 Hissarlik
  mountain: 3 Ida
  neighboring city: 6 Albany 10 Watervliet

---

trouble 3 fix, row, vex, woe 4 blow, care, fuss, heed, mess, pain, pass, snag, work 5 agony, annoy, grief, harry, labor, pains, pinch, think, trial, upset, worry 6 affect, attend, badger, bother, burden, crisis, defect, dismay, effort, grieve, harass, misery, ordeal, pester, pickle, plague, pother, put out, scrape, sorrow, strain, strait, stress, strife, unrest 7 afflict, agitate, ailment, attempt, concern, depress, dilemma, discord, disturb, ferment, ill wind, oppress, perturb, reverse, setback, torment 8 disaster, disorder, disquiet, distress, disunity, exertion, hardship, hot water, quandary, rainy day, struggle, take time, unsettle, vexation 9 adversity, agitation, annoyance, attention, breakdown, challenge, commotion, deep water, hard times, suffering 10 affliction, convulsion, difficulty, disability, discommode, discompose, disconcert, discontent, dissension, irritation, make uneasy, misfortune, opposition 11 competition, disturbance, embroilment, instability, malfunction, predicament, tribulation 12 entanglement, exert oneself 13 inconvenience, make the effort 14 discontentment 15 dissatisfaction

river: 6 Hudson
state: 7 Alabama, New York **8** Michigan
story: 5 Iliad **7** Odyssey
surrounding region: 5 Troad, Troas

Troy, Sergeant
character in: 22 Far From the Madding Crowd
author: 5 Hardy

truancy 3 cut **7** absence **11** absenteeism, nonpresence **12** playing hooky **13** nonappearance, nonattendance **14** cutting classes, skipping school

truant 4 gone **5** idler **6** absent, dodger, evader, loafer, no show **7** drifter, goof-off, missing, not here, shirker, slacker, vagrant **8** absentee, deserter, layabout **9** goldbrick **10** delinquent, malingerer, nonpresent, not present **11** boondoggler, hooky-player **12** nonattendant, playing hooky

truce 4 halt, lull, rest, stay, stop **5** break, pause **7** respite **9** armistice, cease-fire **12** interruption **14** breathing spell, discontinuance **23** suspension of hostilities

Trucial Oman, Trucial States *see* **18** United Arab Emirates

truck 3 rig, van **5** lorry **15** eighteen-wheeler
type: 5 panel **6** pickup **7** trailer **8** delivery

truckle 3 bow **4** fawn **5** court, defer, yield **6** grovel, pander, submit **7** flatter **8** bootlick, butter up, suck up to **9** shine up to **10** curry favor, take orders **11** apple-polish, fall all over **12** knuckle under **17** ingratiate oneself

truculence 8 defiance, ill humor **9** hostility, ill temper, pugnacity, surliness **10** fierceness **11** bellicosity **12** belligerence, churlishness **14** aggressiveness

truculent 4 rude, sour **5** cross, nasty, sulky, surly **6** fierce, touchy **7** defiant, hostile, peevish **8** churlish, insolent, petulant, snappish, snarling **9** bellicose **10** aggressive, ill-humored, ill-natured, pugnacious, ungracious **11** bad-tempered, belligerent, ill-tempered

Trudeau, Garry
creator/artist of: 10 Doonesbury

trudge 4 drag, limp, plod

5 clump, march, tramp **6** hobble, lumber **7** shamble

true 4 even, firm, full, just, pure, real **5** exact, legal, loyal, right, usual, valid **6** actual, lawful, normal, proper, steady, strict, trusty **7** correct, devoted, factual, genuine, literal, precise, regular, staunch, typical **8** absolute, accurate, bona fide, constant, faithful, official, positive, reliable, rightful, true-blue, truthful **9** authentic, simon-pure, steadfast **10** dependable, legitimate, unswerving, unwavering **11** trustworthy **14** unquestionable

true being 4 core, soul **6** nature, psyche, spirit **7** essence

True Grit
director: 13 Henry Hathaway
based on novel by: 13 Charles Portis
cast: 8 Kim Darby **9** John Wayne **11** Jeremy Slate **12** Glen Campbell, Robert Duvall **14** Strother Martin
Oscar for: 5 actor (Wayne)

Truffaut, Francois
director of: 11 Day for Night, Jules and Jim **19** Shoot the Piano Player, The Four Hundred Blows

truism 3 saw **5** adage, axiom **6** cliche, dictum, saying **9** platitude

truly 6 indeed, in fact, really, surely, verily **7** exactly, in truth, no doubt **8** actually, honestly, to be sure **9** assuredly, certainly, correctly, factually, genuinely, literally, precisely, sincerely **10** absolutely, accurately, definitely, faithfully, positively, truthfully, upon my word **11** beyond doubt, in actuality, indubitably, so help me God **12** indisputably **13** incontestably, unequivocally **14** beyond question, unquestionably **15** all kidding aside, without question

Truman, Harry S *see box*

Trumbull, John
born: 9 Lebanon CT
artwork: 21 The Battle of Bunker Hill **26** The Resignation of Washington **28** The Declaration of Independence **29** The Surrender of General Burgoyne **32** The Capture of the Hessians at Trenton **38** The Surrender of Lord Cornwallis at Yorktown **46** The Death of General Montgomery in the Attack of Quebec, The

Death of General Warren at the Battle of Bunker Hill

trumpery 5 showy, trash **6** deceit, trashy, trivia **7** rubbish, twaddle, useless **8** frippery, nonsense, trifling **9** deception, worthless **11** nonsensical

trumpet 4 honk, horn **5** blare, bugle **6** cornet **7** clarion **8** proclaim **10** hearing aid

Trumpet of the Swan, The
author: 7 E B White

trump up 4 fake **6** invent, make up **7** concoct, falsify **9** fabricate

truncate 3 bob, lop, nip **4** clip, crop, dock, snub, trim **5** prune **7** abridge, curtail, shorten **8** amputate, condense, cut short **10** abbreviate

truncheon 3 bat **4** club **5** baton, billy, stick **6** cudgel **8** bludgeon **9** billyclub

trunker 3 box, die **4** body, bole, dado, line, main **5** chief, pants, shaft, snout, stock, torso **6** coffer, engine, locker, shut up, thorax **7** baggage, close in

Truscott-Jones, Reginald
real name of: 10 Ray Milland

truss 3 tie **4** beam, bind, prop, stay **5** brace, hitch, shore, strap, tie up **6** bind up, fasten, girder, pinion, secure **7** confine, support **8** make fast **9** constrict, framework, stanchion **12** underpinning

trust 4 care, duty, hope **5** faith, hands **6** accept, assume, belief, charge, credit, expect, look to, rely on **7** believe, count on, custody, keeping, presume, swear by **8** credence, feel sure, reliance, sureness **9** certainty, certitude, count upon **10** anticipate, confidence, conviction, depend upon, obligation, protection **11** assuredness, contemplate, have faith in, safekeeping, subscribe to, take on faith, take stock in **12** guardianship **14** give credence to, responsibility, take for granted

trusted 6 trusty **9** reliable **9** unfailing **10** dependable **11** trustworthy

trustee 8 guardian **9** caretaker, custodian, protector

trusteeship 4 care **6** charge **7** custody **10** protection **11** safekeeping **12** guardianship

trusting 8 gullible, trustful

Truman, Harry S
nickname: **15** Give Em Hell Harry
presidential rank: **11** thirty-third
party: **10** Democratic
state represented: **8** Missouri
succeeded upon death of: **9** Roosevelt
defeated: **5** (Farrell) Dobbs, (Thomas Edmund) Dewey
  6 (Claude A) Watson, (Norman) Thomas **7** (Henry Agard)
  Wallace **8** (Edward A) Teichert, (James Strom) Thurmond
vice president: **7** (Alben William) Barkley
cabinet:
  state: **6** (James Francis) Byrnes **7** (Dean Gooderham)
    Acheson **8** (George Catlett) Marshall **10** (Edward Reilly)
    Stettinius (Jr)
  treasury: **6** (Frederick Moore) Vinson, (John Wesley)
    Snyder **10** (Henry) Morgenthau (Jr)
  war: **6** (Kenneth Claiborne) Royall **7** (Henry Lewis) Stim-
    son **9** (Robert Porter) Patterson
  defense: **6** (Robert Abercrombie) Lovett **7** (Louis Arthur)
    Johnson **8** (George Catlett) Marshall **9** (James Vincent)
    Forrestal
  attorney general: **5** (Thomas Campbell) Clark **6** (Francis)
    Biddle **7** (James Howard) McGrath **9** (James Patrick)
    McGranery
  navy: **9** (James Vincent) Forrestal
  postmaster general: **6** (Frank Comerford) Walker
    8 (Robert Emmet) Hannegan **9** (Jesse Monroe)
    Donaldson
  interior: **4** (Julius Albert) Krug **5** (Harold LeClaire) Ickes
    7 (Oscar Littleton) Chapman
  agriculture: **7** (Charles Franklin) Brannan, (Claude Ray-
    mond) Wickard **8** (Clinton Presba) Anderson
  commerce: **6** (Charles) Sawyer **7** (Henry Agard) Wallace
    8 (William Averell) Harriman
  labor: **5** (Maurice Joseph) Tobin **7** (Frances), Perkins
    (Wilson) **13** (Lewis Baxter) Schwellenbach
born: **2** MO **5** Lamar **8** Missouri
died: **2** MO **8** Missouri **10** Kansas City
buried: **2** MO **8** Missouri **12** Independence
education:
  law school: **21** Kansas City School of Law (did not
    graduate)
religion: **7** Baptist
interests: **5** piano **7** history
vacation spot: **2** FL **7** Florida, Key West
author: **14** Year of Decision **19** Years of Trial and Hope
political career: **8** US Senate **13** Vice President
  presiding judge of: **13** Jackson County
civilian career: **6** farmer
  owned: **9** men's store **12** haberdashery
military service: **5** major **9** World War I **15** MO National
  Guard **18** Army Reserve colonel
notable events of lifetime/term: **4** NATO **5** V-E Day
  8 Fair Deal **9** Korean War **17** iron-curtain speech **20** assassination attempt **31** North Atlantic Treaty Organization
  act: **11** Taft-Hartley **12** Bretton-Woods
  airlift to: **6** Berlin
  conference: **7** Potsdam
  dropping of first: **5** A-bomb **8** atom bomb
  plan: **8** Marshall **9** Point Four
  signing of: **9** UN charter
  Treaty of: **12** Rio de Janeiro
  trial of: **9** Alger Hiss
father: **12** John Anderson
mother: **6** Martha (Ellen Young)
siblings: **8** Mary Jane **10** John Vivian
wife: **9** Elizabeth (Virginia Wallace)
  nickname: **4** Bess
children: **12** Mary Margaret

9 believing, credulous
12 unsuspicious

trustworthy 4 true **5** loyal
6 honest **7** ethical, trusted, upright **8** faithful, reliable, true-
blue **9** honorable, steadfast
10 aboveboard, dependable,
scrupulous **11** responsible
12 tried and true **13** incorruptible, unimpeachable **14** high-
principled

trusty 7 trusted **8** reliable
9 unfailing **10** dependable
11 trustworthy

trusty companion 3 pal
5 buddy, crony **6** friend **8** intimate, sidekick **9** confidant
10 bosom buddy, confidante

truth 3 law **4** fact **5** facts
6 verity **7** reality **8** accuracy,
fidelity, trueness, veracity
9 actuality, exactness, integrity **11** reliability **12** authenticity, faithfulness,
truthfulness **15** proven principle, trustworthiness
  Russian: 6 Pravda
  also name of: 9 newspaper
  god of: 7 Mithras

truth conquers all things
  Latin: 18 vincit omnia veritas

truthful 4 open, true **5** exact,
frank **6** candid, honest **7** artless, correct, factual, precise,
sincere **8** accurate, faithful, reliable **9** authentic, guileless,
veracious **10** aboveboard, meticulous, scrupulous **11** trustworthy, undeceitful,
unvarnished **13** unadulterated
15 straightforward

truthfulness 6 candor **7** honesty **8** veracity

Truth or Consequences
  host: **10** Jack Bailey, Steve
  Dunne **12** Ralph Edwards

try 2 go **3** aim, use **4** risk,
seek, shot, test, turn **5** crack,
essay, fling, prove, trial,
whack **6** effort, sample, strain,
strive, tackle **7** adjudge, attempt, venture **8** endeavor
9 have a go at, partake of,
undertake **10** adjudicate, deliberate, put to a test **11** opportunity **12** have a fling at,
make an effort, take a crack
at

Trygon
  nurse of: **9** Asclepius

trying 4 hard **5** pesky, tough
6 taxing, vexing **7** arduous,
irksome, onerous, tedious
8 tiresome **9** difficult, fatiguing, harrowing, wearisome
10 bothersome, burdensome,
exhausting, irritating **11** aggravating, distressing, troublesome **12** exasperating

tryout 4 test **5** trial **7** hearing **8** audition **10** experiment

try out 3 fry **6** render **7** compete **8** audition **9** give a test **11** performance

tryst 4 date **7** meeting, vis-a-vis **9** tete-a-tete **10** engagement, rendezvous **11** appointment, assignation

try the patience of 5 annoy **7** provoke **8** irritate **10** exasperate

try to equal 5 rival **7** compete, emulate

Tuatha De Danann 4 gods **origin: 5** Irish **mother: 4** Danu

tub 3 keg, kit, pot, tun, vat **4** bath, boat, butt, cask, ship, tank, tram, wash **5** barge, bathe, fatso, fatty, keeve, tramp **6** barrel, bucket, firkin, ore car, vessel **7** cistern, tankard **8** cauldron, slow boat **9** container, freighter

Tubalcain father: 6 Lamech **mother: 6** Zillah **half-brother: 5** Jabal, Jubal **progenitor of: 12** metalworkers

tube 4 duct, hose, pipe **7** conduit **8** cylinder

tuber 3 anu, yam **4** beet, bulb, corm, eddo, root, taro **5** jalop, shoot **6** potato, turnip **8** rutabaga, swelling **11** enlargement

Tuchman, Barbara W author of: 14 A Distant Mirror, The First Salute **15** The Guns of August, The March of Folly **17** Practicing History

tuck 3 put **4** cram **5** pleat, shove, stick, stuff **6** enwrap, gather, insert, pucker, roll up, ruffle, shroud, swathe, thrust **7** crinkle, swaddle

tucker 3 fag **4** bush, poop, tire **5** weary **7** exhaust, fatigue

tuckered out 5 all in, tired, weary **6** bushed, done in, pooped **8** fatigued **9** exhausted, fagged out

Tudor, Antony choreographer of: 11 Lilac Garden **12** Pillar of Fire

tuebor 11 I will defend

Tuei see **6** Isleta

Tuesday from: 3 Tiw **heavenly body: 4** Mars **French: 5** mardi **Italian: 7** martedi

Spanish: 6 martes **German: 8** dienstag

tuft 4 wisp **5** batch, brush, bunch, clump, crest, plume, sheaf **6** bundle, tassel **7** cluster, topknot

tug 3 lug, tow **4** drag, draw, haul, jerk, pull, yank **6** wrench **7** wrestle

tulip 6 Tulipa **varieties: 4** lady, star **5** globe **7** Turkish **9** butterfly, guinea-hen, waterlily **10** Sierra star **11** golden globe, purple globe **16** common late garden **17** common early garden

Tulkinghorn character in: 10 Bleak House **author: 7** Dickens

Tullia father: 14 Servius Tullius **husband: 7** Tarquin

Tullius see **14** Servius Tullius

Tulsa football team: 7 Outlaws

tumble 3 mix **4** dive, drop, fall, flip, roll, toss **5** whirl **6** bounce, jumble, plunge, stir up, topple **7** descend, shuffle, stumble **9** cartwheel **10** somersault

tumbledown 5 shaky **7** rickety, run-down **8** decaying, decrepit, unstable **9** crumbling, tottering **10** broken-down, jerry-built, ramshackle **11** dilapidated, falling-down **14** disintegrating

tumbler 3 cog, dog **5** drier, glass, lever **6** goblet, vessel **7** acrobat, athlete, gymnast, juggler **12** somersaulter

tumbrel 4 cart **5** wagon **7** tip-cart **8** dumpcart

tumbril French: 7 fourgon

tumid 5 puffy **6** turgid **7** bloated, bulging, dilated, pompous, swollen **8** enlarged, expanded, inflated **9** bombastic, distended, edematous, tumescent **11** protuberant **12** magniloquent **13** grandiloquent

tummy 3 gut **5** belly **6** paunch, tum-tum **7** abdomen, midriff, stomach **9** bay window **11** breadbasket

tumor 3 wen **4** cyst, lump, wart **5** pride **6** cancer, growth **7** bombast, sarcoma **8** hematoma, neoplasm, swelling, tubercle **9** carcinoma, papilloma, pomposity **11** tumefaction

tumult 3 ado, din **6** bedlam, bustle, clamor, hubbub, racket, uproar **7** turmoil **8** disorder, upheaval **9** agitation, commotion, confusion **10** excitement, hullabaloo **11** disturbance, pandemonium

tumultuous 4 loud **5** noisy, rough, rowdy **6** stormy, unruly **7** chaotic, furious, lawless, raucous, riotous, violent **8** agitated, confused **9** clamorous, disturbed, turbulent **10** boisterous, disorderly, uproarious **11** tempestuous

tun 3 keg, tub, vat **4** butt, cast, drum **6** barrel **8** hogshead

tune 3 air **4** aria, line, song, step **5** adjust, ditty, motif, pitch, theme **6** accord, adjust, melody, number, strain, unison **7** concert, concord, harmony **9** agreement **10** conformity

tuneful 6 catchy, dulcet **7** lyrical, musical **9** melodious

tungsten chemical symbol: 1 W

Tungusic language family: 6 Altaic **includes: 6** Manchu

tunic 4 robe **5** cloak **6** jacket, mantle, poncho, tabard **7** garment, surcoat

Tunica tribe: 10 Chitimacha

Tunis capital of: 7 Tunisia

Tunisia see **box**

Tunney, Gene real name: 17 James Joseph Tunney **nickname: 14** Fighting Marine **sport: 6** boxing **class: 11** heavyweight

Tuonela also: 6 Manala **origin: 7** Finnish **name of: 10** afterworld **form: 6** island **lacked: 3** sun **4** moon

Tupman character in: 14 Pickwick Papers **author: 7** Dickens

tu quoque 7 thou too

Turandot opera by: 7 Puccini **character: 3** Liu **4** Pang, Ping, Pong **5** Calaf, Timur **8** Turandot (Princess of China)

turbid 5 muddy, murky **6** cloudy, opaque, roiled **7** clouded, unclear **8** agitated

Tunisia
  other name: 8 Carthage 9 Ifriqiyah
  capital/largest city: 5 Tunis
  others: 4 Beja, Sfax, Susa 5 Gabes, Gofsa 6 Djerba, Mateur, Nabeul, Remada, Sousse, Tozeur 7 Bizerte, Kairwan 8 Carthage, Jendouba, Kairouan, Monastir, Tebourba, Zaghouan 9 Grombalia 10 Ferryville
  empire: 8 Carthage 13 Barbary States
  school: 5 Tunis 16 Pasteur Institute
  measure: 3 saa 4 saah 5 cafiz 6 mettar 8 milerole
  monetary unit: 5 dinar 6 dollar 7 millime
  weight: 3 saa 4 rotl 5 artal, ratel, uckia
  island: 6 Djerba, Galite
  lake: 6 Achkel, Djerid 7 Bizerte
  mountain: 5 Atlas 6 Mrhila 7 Tebessa 8 High Tell, Zaghouan 12 Northern Tell 17 Dorsale Tunisienne
  highest point: 6 Chambi
  river: 8 Medjerda, Mellegue
  sea: 13 Mediterranean
  physical feature:
    cape: 3 Bon 5 Blanc 8 Rasaddar
    desert: 6 Sahara
    gulf: 5 Gabes, Tunis 8 Hammamet
    oasis: 5 Gabes, Gafsa, Nefta 6 Djerba, Tozeur 9 El Oudiane 13 El Hamma Djerid
    plains: 5 Sahel
    salt lake: 11 Chott Djerid, Shatt Djerid
    valley: 8 Medjerda
    wind: 5 chile 6 chilli 7 sirocco
  people: 3 Jew 4 Arab 6 Berber
    artist: 5 Gorgi, Turki
    dynasty: 6 Hafsid 7 Fatimid 8 Aghlabid, Almohade 10 Husseinite
    leader: 6 Ben Ali 9 Bourguiba
  language: 6 Arabic, Berber, French
  religion: 5 Islam 7 Judaism 12 Christianity
  place:
    center of Tunis: 13 Place d'Afrique
    mosque: 5 Great 7 Zitouna
    museum: 5 Bardo, Kouba 6 Sousse
    palace: 14 Dar Ben Abdallah
    ruins: 8 Carthage
    street: 14 Habib Bourguiba
  feature:
    cap: 7 chechia
    clothing: 5 jebba 7 safasri 9 babbouche
    market: 4 souk
  food:
    dish: 7 mesfouf 8 couscous
    drink: 4 iban 5 legmi
    fruit: 12 deglet en nour

9 disturbed, stirred up, unsettled

turbulence 4 fury 6 frenzy, hubbub, tumult, unrest, uproar 7 ferment, rioting, torrent, turmoil 8 disorder, violence 9 agitation, commotion 10 excitement, unruliness 11 disturbance

turbulent 5 rowdy 6 fierce, raging, stormy, unruly 7 chaotic, furious, riotous, violent 8 agitated, restless 9 clamorous, disturbed 10 blustering, boisterous, disorderly, tumultuous, uproarious

11 tempestuous

tureen 4 bowl, dish 9 casserole, container 10 receptacle

turf 3 sod 4 area, peat, plot, soil 5 divot, grass, haunt, sward, track 7 verdure 9 racetrack, territory 10 greensward

Turgenev, Ivan
  author of: 5 Smoke 9 First Love 10 Virgin Soil 14 Fathers and Sons 18 A Month in the Country 19 A Sportsman's Notebook, A Sportsman's Sketches, The Torrents of Spring

turgid 5 puffy, showy 6 florid, ornate 7 flowery, pompous,

swollen 8 inflated, puffed up 9 bombastic, grandiose, overblown 10 hyperbolic

Turkey *see box, p. 1006*

Turkic
  language family: 6 Altaic
    group: 5 Kazak, Nogai, Uigur, Uzbek, Yakut 7 Chuvash, Kirghiz 8 Turkoman 10 Karakalpak 11 Azerbaijani 14 Osmanli Turkish

Turkmenistan
  capital/largest city: 9 Ashkhabad
  head of state: 9 president
  government: 8 republic
  monetary unit: 5 ruble
  river: 8 Amu Darya
  sea: 7 Caspian
  physical feature: 13 Kara Kum Desert
  people: 7 Turkmen 10 Turkmenian
  language: 6 Turkic 10 West Turkic
  religion: 11 Sunni Muslim
  feature: 9 Altyn Depe

turmeric
  botanical name: 12 Curcuma longa
  also called: 7 tumeric 13 Crocus indicus, Indian saffron
  family: 6 ginger
  color: 6 yellow
  used as: 3 dye 6 amulet 8 cosmetic, medicine
  origin: 4 Asia 9 Caribbean, East India
  charm against: 5 ghost 10 tree spirit

turmoil 4 mess 5 chaos 6 tumult, uproar 7 ferment 8 disorder 9 agitation, commotion, confusion 10 convulsion 11 disturbance, pandemonium
  French: 14 bouleversement

turn 2 do, go 3 act, arc, lie, put 4 bend, coil, come, deed, flex, hang, look, loop, make, rest, ride, roll, send, shot, sour, spin, time, veer, walk, wing 5 alter, apply, crack, curve, drive, eject, fling, hinge, pivot, round, scare, shift, shock, spell, spoil, start, stint, swing, throw, twist, whack, wheel, whirl 6 action, become, chance, change, curdle, depend, direct, effort, fright, gyrate, invert, period, reside, rotate, sprain, stroll, swerve, swivel, wrench, zigzag 7 acidify, attempt, convert, deliver, execute, ferment, perform, reverse, revolve, service, winding 8 gyration, overturn, roll over, rotation, surprise 9 cause to go, deviation, discharge, transform 10 accomplish, alteration, revolution

Turkey
capital: **6** Angora, Ankara
largest city: **8** Istanbul
others: **4** Enos, Troy, Urfa **5** Adana, Bursa, Izmir, Konya, Maras, Siirt, Sivas **6** Aintab, Edessa,
Edirne, Elaziz, Marash, Samsun, Smyrna **7** Antakya, Antioch, Erzurum, Kayseri, Mersin, Scutari, Trabzon, Uskudar **8** Stamboul **9** Byzantium, Eskisehir, Gaziantep **10** Adrianople
14 Constantinople
school: **6** Aegean, Ankara **8** Istanbul
division: **4** Pera, Sert **5** Siirt, Troad **6** Angora, Eyalet, Thrace **7** Anadolu, Beyoglu, Cilicia **8** Anatolia **9** Asia Minor, Kurdistan
measure: **3** dra, oka, pik **4** draa, khat, kile, zira **5** berri, kileh, zirai **6** arshin, chinik, fortin,
halebi **7** nocktat
monetary unit: **4** lira, para **5** akcha, asper, kurus, pound, rebia **6** akcheh, zequin **7** aetilik,
beshlik, piaster **8** medjidie
weight: **3** oka, oke **4** aqui, dram, rotl **5** artal, cheke, kerat, obolu, ratel **6** batman, dirhem,
kantar, maunch, miskal **7** drachma, quintal, yusdrum
island: **6** Cyprus, Kibris
lake: **3** Tuz, Van **7** Egridir **8** Beysehir
mountain: **2** Ak **3** Ala **4** Alai, Dagh, Kara **5** Hasan, Hinis, Honaz, Murat, Murit **6** Ala Dag,
Bingol, Bolgar, Pontic, Suphan, Taurus **7** Aladagh, Erciyas **8** Karacali **10** Kackar Dagi
highest point: **6** Ararat
river: **4** Aras, Kura **5** Araks, Dicle, Firat, Gediz, Goksu, Halys, Irmak, Kizil, Mesta, Murat,
Sarus **6** Araxes, Ceyhan, Seihun, Seyhan, Seylan, Tigris **7** Kurucay, Muradsu, Orontes, Sak-
arya **8** Granicus, Macestus, Maeander, Menderes **9** Euphrates **13** Buyukmenderes
sea: **4** Aral **5** Black **6** Aegean **7** Marmara **13** Mediterranean
physical feature:
cape: **4** Baba, Ince **5** Bafra **6** Anamur, Helles, Hinzir **7** Karatas, Kerempe
gulf: **3** Cos **5** Izmir **7** Antalya
inlet: **10** Golden Horn
peninsula: **9** Anatolian, Gallipoli
plateau: **9** Anatolian
strait: **8** Bosporus **9** Bosphorus **11** Dardanelles
people: **4** Arab, Kurd, Turk **6** Seljuk
king: **8** Mausolus
leader: **5** Inonu, Osman **6** Ecevit **7** Demirel **8** Menderes, Suleiman **12** Kemal Ataturk
poet: **5** Homer
language: **6** Arabic **7** Kurdish, Turkish
religion: **5** Islam **7** Judaism **12** Christianity **13** Greek Orthodox, Roman Catholic
place:
bridge: **6** Galata
dam: **9** Gokcekaya
mosque: **4** Blue, Yeni **8** Selimiye **11** Hagia Sophia, Sultan Ahmed
ruins: **4** Troy **7** Ephesus **8** Pergamum
tomb: **12** Kemal Ataturk
feature:
cap: **3** fez **6** calpac **7** calpack
clothing: **6** caftan, dolman, jelick **7** yashrak **8** charshaf, maharmah, shakseer
goat hair: **6** mohair
grill: **6** mangal
harem: **5** serai **8** seraglio
musical instrument: **5** canum, kanum **6** canoon, johnie, kussir, zither **8** crescent, jingling
pipe: **10** meerschaum
food:
dish: **5** halva, pilaw **10** doner kebab, shish kebab
drink: **4** boza, raki **5** airan, pasha, rakee **6** mastic
pastry: **7** baklava
turkey: **4** hind

turn a deaf ear to 6 ignore,
slight **9** disregard

turn aside 5 avert **6** divert
7 deflect, deviate **8** turn away

turn away 5 avert **6** give up
8 alienate, estrange, send
away **9** turn aside **12** turn
one's back

turnback 4 fold, quit, tack
5 repel **6** defect, desert, return,
revert **7** forsake, regress, relapse, repulse, retrace, retreat,
reverse **9** backslide

turncoat 5 Judas **6** bolter
7 traitor **8** apostate, betrayer,
defector, deserter, quisling,
renegade **12** double-dealer

turn down 5 spurn **6** refuse,
reject **14** lower the volume,
refuse to accept

**Turner, Joseph Mallord
William**
born: **6** London **7** England
artwork: **12** The Shipwreck,
The Slave Ship, Tintern Ab-
bey **17** Dawn After the
Wreck **20** Dido Building
Carthage **22** Venice S Gior-
gio Maggiore **24** The Sun of
Venice Going to Sea **25** The
Thames near Walton Bridge,
Ulysses Deriding Polyphe-

mus **30** Burning of the Houses of Parliament **32** Snowstorm Hannibal Crossing the Alps **32** The Falls of the Rhine at Schaffhausen **34** The Bay of Baiae with Apollo and the Sibyl **37** Fighting Temeraire Tugged to her Last Berth **47** The Parting of Hero and Leander from the Greek of Musaeus **50** The Shipwreck Fishing Boats Endeavoring to Rescue the Crew

Turner, Kathleen
  roles: **8** Body Heat **12** Prizzi's Honor **17** Romancing the Stone, The Jewel of the Nile **18** Peggy Sue Got Married

Turner, Lana
  real name: **29** Julia Jean Mildred Frances Turner
  nickname: **11** Sweater Girl
  born: **9** Wallace ID
  discovered at: **16** Schwab's Drugstore
  husband: **9** Artie Shaw, Lex Barker **10** Bob Topping **12** Stephen Crane
  roles: **7** Madame X **11** Peyton Place **15** By Love Possessed, Imitation of Life **26** The Postman Always Rings Twice

turning 4 bend **5** curve **7** bending, curving, winding **8** pivoting, rotating, spinning, twisting, whirling **9** revolving, swiveling

turnip 12 Brassica rapa
  group: **8** Rapifera
  varieties: **6** Indian **7** Italian, Swedish **8** seven-top

turn off 4 bore, exit **5** douse, leave, repel **6** revolt, sicken **7** disgust, repulse **8** alienate, turn away **9** switch off **10** deactivate

turn of phrase 5 idiom **8** locution, phrasing **10** expression **11** phraseology

Turn of the Screw, The
  author: **10** Henry James
  character: **5** Flora, Miles **7** Mr Quint **8** Mrs Grose **10** Miss Jessel **12** The Governess

turn on 5 start, tempt **6** allure, attack, entice, excite **7** actuate, attract **8** activate, energize, interest, switch on

turn one's stomach 6 revolt, sicken **7** disgust **8** nauseate

turnout 5 crowd **6** output, throng **8** assembly, audience **9** gathering **10** assemblage, production

turn out 4 garb, oust **5** array, dress, eject, end up, evict, exile, expel **6** appear, attend, attire, banish, clothe, evolve, fit out, invest, rig out, show up, unfold **7** cast out, come out, costume, develop, kick out **8** drive out, send away **9** switch off **11** come to light

turn over 4 flip **5** upset **6** bestow, rotate **7** deliver **8** flip-flop, give over, hand over, overturn **9** surrender **10** relinquish, somersault

turn pale 4 fade **6** blanch, whiten **7** lighten

turn tail 4 flee **7** retreat, run away **8** back away **12** beat a retreat

turn to account 7 exploit, utilize **8** profit by, put to use **9** make use of **12** capitalize on

turn topsy turvy 5 upset **7** capsize, confuse, tip over **8** flip-flop, overturn, put askew **10** disarrange, turn turtle **11** disorganize

turn turtle 5 upset **7** capsize, tip over **8** flip over, keel over, overturn, turn over **14** turn upside down

turn up 4 come **6** appear, arrive, crop up, drop in, emerge, loom up, show up **7** develop, surface **11** come to light

Turnus
  father: **6** Daunus
  mother: **7** Venilia
  sister: **7** Juturna
  sought to win: **7** Lavinia
  killed by: **6** Aeneas

Turpentine State
  nickname of: **13** North Carolina

turpitude 4 evil, vice **8** baseness, lewdness, vileness **9** depravity **10** corruption, debauchery, defilement, degeneracy, immorality, perversion, sinfulness, wickedness, wrongdoing **13** dissoluteness **14** licentiousness

turquoise 4 aqua **5** stone **7** mineral, sky-blue **10** aquamarine **12** greenish-blue, Prussian-blue
  source: **12** United States

turret 5 tower **6** belfry, cupola, garret, gazebo, louver, terret **7** minaret, rotator, steeple **8** gunhouse, gunmount **9** belvedere, pepperbox **10** watchtower
  tool: **5** lathe

turtle 3 box **4** musk, wood **6** slider **7** painted, reptile,

snapper, spotted **8** slowpoke, terrapin, tortoise **10** turtledove **11** leatherback
  dorsal shell: **8** carapace
  nautical: **5** upset **6** pocket **7** capsize **8** overturn
  order: **8** Chelonia
  ventral shell: **8** plastron
  young: **7** turtlet

Turveydrop
  character in: **10** Bleak House
  author: **7** Dickens

tussle 4 fray **5** brawl, fight, melee, scrap, set-to **6** battle, fracas **7** grapple, scuffle, wrestle **8** conflict, struggle **10** donnybrook, free-for-all **11** altercation

tussock 4 hair, tuft **5** brush, bunch, clump, grass, sedge **7** bulrush, cluster, thicket **8** feathers

tutelage 8 coaching, guidance, teaching, training, tutoring **9** direction, education, schooling **10** discipline **11** inculcation, instruction, supervision, trusteeship **12** guardianship **14** indoctrination

tutor 4 guru **5** coach, drill, teach **6** master, mentor, school **7** prepare, teacher **8** instruct **10** instructor **11** give lessons

tutorial 5 class **8** didactic, edifying **11** educational, instructive **12** prescriptive

tutti
  music: **3** all **18** all players together, all singers together

---

Tuvalu
  other name: **13** Ellice Islands, Lagoon Islands
  capital: **8** Funafuti
  head of state: **14** British monarch **15** governor general
  monetary unit: **4** cent **6** dollar
  island: **3** Nui **6** Niutao **7** Nanumea, Vaitupu **8** Funafuti **9** Nanumanga, Niulakita, Nukufetau **10** Nukulaelae
  highest point: **5** Nuwak
  sea: **7** Pacific
  people: **6** Samoan **10** Polynesian
    leader: **5** Lauti
  language: **6** Samoan **7** English **8** Tuvaluan **10** Polynesian
  religion: **10** Protestant **12** Tuvalu Church

Tuvim, Judith
real name of: **12** Judy Holliday

twaddle 3 rot **4** bosh, bunk **5** trash, tripe **6** babble, drivel, gabble, jabber, piffle **7** chatter, prattle, rubbish **8** claptrap, idle talk, nonsense, tommyrot **9** jabbering, silly talk **10** balderdash **16** stuff-and-nonsense

Twain, Mark
real name: **13** Samuel Clemens
author of: **9** Tom Sawyer **10** Roughing It **12** A Tramp Abroad, The Gilded Age **15** (Adventures of) Huckleberry Finn **18** The Innocents Abroad **20** Life on the Mississippi **21** The Mysterious Stranger, The Prince and the Pauper **29** The Man That Corrupted Hadleyburg **36** A Connecticut Yankee in King Arthur's Court **41** The Celebrated Jumping Frog of Calaveras County

twang 9 resonance, vibration **10** nasal sound **13** reverberation

Tweedledee
character in: **22** Through the Looking Glass
author: **7** Carroll

Tweedledum
character in: **22** Through the Looking Glass
author: **7** Carroll

tweet 4 peep **5** cheep, chirp **7** chirrup, chitter, twitter

Twelfth-Night
author: **18** William Shakespeare
character: **5** Feste, Maria, Viola (Cesario) **6** Olivia, Orsino **7** Antonio **8** Malvolio **9** Sebastian **12** Sir Toby Belch **18** Sir Andrew Aguecheek

Twelve Angry Men
director: **11** Sidney Lumet
cast: **8** Ed Begley, Lee J Cobb **10** E G Marshall, Henry Fonda, Jack Warden **11** Jack Klugman, John Fiedler **12** Martin Balsam

Twelve O'Clock High
director: **9** Henry King
cast: **10** Dean Jagger **11** Gary Merrill, Gregory Peck, Hugh Marlowe **15** Millard Mitchell
Oscar for: **15** supporting actor (Jagger)

Twentieth Century
director: **11** Howard Hawks
based on play by: **8** Ben Hecht **16** Charles MacArthur
cast: **11** Roscoe Karns **13** Carole Lombard, John Barrymore **14** Walter Connolly

Twentieth Century, The
narrator: **14** Walter Cronkite

twenty-one see **9** blackjack

Twenty Questions
host: **10** Bill Slater, Jay Jackson
panelist: **11** Herb Polesie **12** Bobby McGuire **13** Johnnie McPhee **14** Dickie Harrison, Florence Rinard **15** Fred Van De Venter

Twenty Thousand Leagues Under the Sea
author: **10** Jules Verne
character: **7** Conseil, Ned Land **11** Captain Nemo **22** Professor Pierre Aronnax
submarine: **8** Nautilus

Twenty Years After
author: **14** Alexandre Dumas (pere)

Twice-Told Tales
author: **18** Nathaniel Hawthorne

Twightwee see **5** Miami

twilight 3 ebb, eve **4** dusk **6** sunset **7** decline, evening, sundown **8** eventide, gloaming, moonrise **9** half-light, last phase, nightfall **14** edge of darkness

Twilight of the Gods
8 Ragnorak
German:
15 Gotterdammerung

Twilight Zone, The
host: **10** Rod Serling

twin 4 dual, like **5** alike **6** double, paired **7** matched, twofold **9** duplicate, identical

Twin 6 Thomas

twine 4 coil, cord, rope, wind **5** braid, cable, plait, twist, weave **6** string, thread **7** binding, entwine **9** interlace **10** intertwine

twinge 4 pain, pang, stab **5** cramp, spasm, throb **6** stitch, tingle, twitch

twinkle 4 glow **5** blaze, flare, flash, gleam, shine **7** flicker, glimmer, glisten, shimmer, sparkle **11** scintillate

Twinkleton, Miss
character in: **22** The Mystery of Edwin Drood
author: **7** Dickens

Twins
constellation of: **6** Gemini

twirl 4 spin **5** pivot, twine, wheel, whirl **6** gyrate, rotate **7** revolve **9** pirouette

twist 3 arc, way **4** bend, coil, curl, idea, kink, knot, pull, roll, spin, turn, veer, wind, wrap, yank **5** curve, pivot, ravel, slant, snake, swing, twine, whirl, wrest **6** change, method, notion, rotate, spiral, sprain, swerve, swivel, system, tangle, wrench, zigzag **7** contort, distort, entwine, meander **8** approach, rotation, surprise **9** corkscrew, interlace, treatment **10** intertwine, involution **11** convolution, development

twisted 4 bent **6** warped **7** crooked, gnarled **8** deformed **9** contorted, distorted, misshapen

twisting 7 crooked, curving, turning **9** contorted, revolving, spiraling, swiveling

twist out of shape 4 warp **6** deform **7** contort, distort

twitch 3 tic **4** jerk **5** shake, spasm, throb **6** quaver, quiver, squirm, tremor, wiggle, writhe **7** tremble **8** paroxysm **10** convulsion

twitter 4 fuss, peep, stew **5** cheep, chirp, tizzy, tweet, whirl **6** bustle, flurry, pother, uproar, warble **7** chatter, chirrup, ferment, fluster, flutter **8** chirping **10** turbulence **11** chirrupping

two-faced 5 false **7** devious **8** slippery **9** deceitful, deceptive, dishonest, insincere **10** perfidious **11** dissembling, double-faced, duplicitous, forktongued, treacherous, underhanded **12** dishonorable, disingenuous, falsehearted, hypocritical **13** double-dealing, untrustworthy

twofold 4 dual **6** double **7** two-part

Two Gentlemen of Verona, The
author: **18** William Shakespeare
character: **5** Julia **6** Silvia, Thurio **7** Proteus **9** Valentine **11** Duke of Milan

Two Lands, The see **5** Egypt

two of a kind 4 pair **5** twins **6** couple **7** doublet

two-part 4 dual, twin **6** double, paired **9** bipartite

twosome 3 duo **4** pair **5** brace **6** couple

2001: A Space Odyssey
author: **13** Arthur C Clarke
director: **14** Stanley Kubrick
character: **4** Dave **5** Steve
computer: **3** HAL

cast: 3 HAL 10 Keir Dullea 12 Gary Lockwood 16 William Sylvester
song: 20 Thus Spake Zarathustra (Richard Strauss)
sequel: 24 Two Thousand Ten: Odyssey Two

two-time 6 betray 10 be disloyal 11 double-cross 12 be unfaithful 13 be treacherous, play false with 14 break faith with

two-timing 5 false 6 tricky 7 perfidy 8 bad faith, betrayal, disloyal, trickery 9 deceiving, deception, duplicity, falseness, treachery 10 disloyalty, perfidious 11 double-cross, duplicitous, treacherous 13 breach of faith, double-dealing, faithlessness 14 double-crossing

two-wheeler 4 bike 5 cycle 7 bicycle

Two Years Before the Mast
author: 18 Richard Henry Dana Jr

Tybalt
character in: 14 Romeo and Juliet
author: 11 Shakespeare

Tyche
origin: 5 Greek
goddess of: 7 fortune
corresponds to: 7 Fortuna

tycoon 4 boss 5 mogul, nabob 6 big gun, bigwig 7 big shot, magnate 8 big wheel 9 potentate 12 entrepreneur 13 industrialist 17 captain of industry

Tydeus
father: 6 Oeneus
mother: 8 Periboea
uncle: 5 Melas 6 Agrius 9 Alcathous
son: 8 Diomedes

tyke 3 kid, tad, tot 5 child 6 shaver, squirt, wee one 9 little one

Tyler, John see box

Tyll Eulenspiegel see 16 Till Eulenspiegel

Tyndall, John
field: 7 physics
nationality: 5 Irish
studied diffusion of: 5 light

Tyndareus
wife: 4 Leda
daughter: 6 Phoebe 8 Philonoe, Timandra 12 Clytemnestra

Tyndaridae see 15 Castor and Pollux

type 4 font, kind, race, sort 5 brand, class, genus, group, model, order, print 6 design,

---

Tyler, John
presidential rank: 5 tenth
party: 4 Whig 20 Democratic-Republican
state represented: 2 VA 8 Virginia
defeated: 5 no-one
succeeded upon death of: 8 Harrison
vice president: 4 none
cabinet:
state: 6 (Abel Parker) Upshur 7 (Daniel) Webster, (John C) Calhoun
treasury: 4 (George Mortimer) Bibb 5 (Thomas) Ewing 7 (John Canfield) Spencer, (Walter) Forward
war: 4 (John) Bell 7 (John Canfield) Spencer, (William) Wilkins
attorney general: 6 (Hugh Swinton) Legare, (John) Nelson 10 (John Jordan) Crittenden
navy: 5 (John Young) Mason 6 (Abel Parker) Upshur, (George Edmund) Badger, (Thomas Walker) Gilmer
postmaster general: 7 (Francis) Granger 9 (Charles Anderson) Wickliffe
born: 2 VA 8 Greenway, Virginia 17 Charles City County
died/buried: 2 VA 8 Richmond, Virginia
education: 14 William and Mary
religion: 12 Episcopalian
vacation spot: 2 VA 7 Hampton 8 Virginia
political career: 8 US Senate 12 State Council 13 vice president 24 US House of Representatives
delegate to: 13 State Assembly
governor of: 8 Virginia
civilian career: 6 farmer, lawyer
military service: 19 War of Eighteen Twelve
notable events of lifetime/term:
act: 6 Tariff (of 1842)
annexation of: 5 Texas
treaty: 16 Webster-Ashburton
father: 4 John
mother: 4 Mary (Marott Armistead)
siblings: 7 William 8 Wat Henry 10 Maria Henry 12 Anne Contesse 14 Christina Booth 15 Martha Jefferson 18 Elizabeth Armistead
wife: 5 Julia (Gardiner) 7 Letitia (Christian)
children: 4 John, Mary 5 Alice, Julia, Pearl 6 Robert 7 Lachlan, Letitia 8 Tazewell 9 Elizabeth 12 Anne Contesse, Lyon Gardiner 13 David Gardiner, John Alexander 16 Robert FitzWalter

---

family, phylum, sample 7 pattern, species, variety 8 category, division, specimen, typeface 9 archetype, prototype 10 typography

type, movable
invented by: 9 Gutenberg

Typee
author: 14 Herman Melville
character: 3 Tom (Melville) 4 Toby 6 Marnoo, Mehevi 7 Fayaway 8 Kory-Kory

typewriter
invented by: 5 Soule 6 Sholes 7 Glidden

Typhoeus
form: 7 monster
father: 8 Tartarus
mother: 2 Ge
number of heads: 10 one hundred

Typhon
form: 7 monster
father: 8 Typhoeus
son: 5 Ladon

typhoon 4 gale, gust, wind 5 storm 7 cyclone, tempest, tornado, twister 9 hurricane, whirlwind

Typhoon
author: 12 Joseph Conrad

typical 5 model, stock, usual 6 normal 7 average, regular 8 ordinary, orthodox, standard 9 exemplary, in keeping 10 individual, prototypal, true to type 11 distinctive, in character 12 conventional, to be expected 14 characteristic, representative

typify 5 sum up 6 embody 7 betoken, connote, pass for 8 instance, stand for 9 epitomize, exemplify, incarnate, personify, represent **10** illustrate **12** characterize

typography measure 2 em, en **4** pica **5** point

Tyr
origin: **12** Scandinavian
god of: **7** victory
father: **4** Odin **5** Othin
mother: **3** Fri **5** Frigg, Frija **6** Frigga
killed by: **4** Garm

tyrannical 7 fascist **8** despotic **9** imperious **10** oppressive **11** dictatorial, domineering **13** authoritarian

tyrannize 7 oppress **8** domineer, overlord **10** slave drive

tyrannized 9 exploited, oppressed **11** downtrodden, subservient **12** harshly ruled

Tyrannosaurus
type: **8** dinosaur, theropod
location: **7** Montana **12** North America
period: **10** Cretaceous

tyrannous 8 despotic **9** imperi-

ous **10** iron-handed, oppressive, repressive, tyrannical

tyranny 7 cruelty, fascism **8** coercion, iron fist, iron hand, iron rule, severity **9** despotism, harshness **10** domination, oppression, repression **11** persecution **12** dictatorship **13** reign of terror **15** totalitarianism

tyrant 5 bully **6** despot **8** dictator, martinet **10** persecutor, taskmaster **11** cruel master, slave driver

Tyre
king of: **5** Hiram

tyro 6 intern, novice, rookie **7** learner, recruit, trainee **8** beginner, initiate, neophyte, newcomer **9** greenhorn **10** apprentice, tenderfoot

Tyro
father: **9** Salmoneus
loved by: **8** Cretheus, Poseidon
son: **5** Aeson **6** Neleus, Pelias
grandson: **5** Jason **6** Nestor

Tyrrheus
occupation: **8** shepherd

Tyson, Cicely
born: **9** New York NY
roles: **5** Roots **7** Sounder **33** The Autobiography of Miss Jane Pittman

Tyson, Mike
original name: **7** Michael
nickname: **8** Iron Mike
born: **2** NY **8** Brooklyn **17** Bedford-Stuyvesant
wife: **11** Robin Givens
manager: **9** Cus D'Amato **10** Bill Cayton **11** Jimmy Jacobs
trainer: **12** Angelo Dundee
promoter: **7** Don King
boxing title: **3** IBF, WBA, WBC **11** heavyweight
defeated: **6** Holmes, Spinks, Thomas, Tillis, Tucker **7** Berbick
defeated by: **7** Douglas (Buster)
convicted of: **4** rape

tzimmes 4 fuss **6** uproar **10** hullabaloo
literally: **4** stew **9** mixed dish

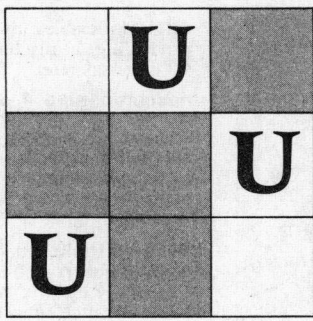

Ubangi-Shari *see* **22** Central African Republic

Ubermensch 8 superman

ubiquitous 7 allover **9** pervading, pervasive, prevalent, universal, worldwide **10** everywhere, widespread **11** everpresent, omnipresent **12** all-pervading

ubiquitously 10 everywhere **11** extensively

ubi supra 19 where mentioned above

Ucalegon
  counselor to: **5** Priam

Uccello, Paolo
  real name: **11** Paolo di Dono
  born: **5** Italy **8** Florence
  artwork: **8** The Flood **12** The Night Hunt **15** Sir John Hawkwood **18** The Rout (Battle) of San Romano **20** St George and the Dragon

Udaeus
  member of: **6** Sparti
  grandson: **8** Tiresias

Udall, Nicholas
  author of: **19** Ralph Roister Doister

Uganda *see* box, p. 1012

ugliness 8 ill-favor **9** grossness **10** homeliness **11** hideousness, monstrosity **12** unseemliness **13** frightfulness, grotesqueness, monstrousness, repulsiveness, unsightliness **14** unpleasantness **16** unattractiveness

ugly 4 foul, mean, vile **5** nasty **6** homely, horrid, odious **7** hideous, hostile, ominous **8** dreadful, horrible, menacing, unseemly **9** abhorrent, dangerous, difficult, frightful, grotesque, monstrous, obnoxious, offensive, repellent, repugnant, repulsive, sickening, unsightly **10** abominable, disgusting

ugly as sin 7 hideous **9** frightful, grotesque, monstrous, repulsive

Ugly Duckling, The
  author: **21** Hans Christian Andersen

ukase 4 fiat **5** edict, order **6** decree, dictum, ruling **7** command, mandate, statute **9** directive, manifesto, ordinance **10** injunction **12** proclamation **13** pronouncement

Ukraine
  capital/largest city: **4** Kiev
  others: **4** Lviv (Lvov), **6** Odessa **7** Donetsk, Kharkov, Lugansk (Voroshilovgrad) **8** Mariupol (Zhdanov) **9** Krivoi Rog, Zaporozhe **14** Dnepropetrovsk
  head of state: **9** president
  government: **8** republic
  monetary unit: **6** grivna **10** karbovanet
  mountain: **7** Crimean **10** Carpathian
  river: **3** Bug **6** Donets **7** Dnieper
  sea: **5** Black
  people: **7** Russian **9** Ukrainian
  language: **9** Ukrainian
  religion: **17** Ukrainian Catholic, Ukrainian Orthodox
  feature: **25** Askaniya Nova Nature Reserve

Ulan Bator
  capital of: **8** Mongolia

ulcer 4 sore **6** canker

Uller
  also: **4** Ullr
  origin: **8** Teutonic
  god of: **12** winter sports
  stepfather: **4** Thor

Ullmann, Liv
  born: **5** Japan, Tokyo
  nationality: **9** Norwegian
  roles: **7** Persona **10** Face to Face **11** Forty Carats, Lost Horizon **12** The Emigrants **16** Cries and Whispers **19** Scenes from a Marriage

Ullr *see* **5** Uller

Ulman, Douglas Elton
  real name of: **16** Douglas Fairbanks

ulna
  bone of: **8** lower arm

ulterior 6 covert, hidden, secret **7** selfish **9** concealed **10** undivulged, unrevealed **11** self-serving, undisclosed, unexpressed **13** opportunistic

ultimate 3 end **4** acme, apex, last, peak **5** final **6** height, utmost **7** extreme, maximum, supreme **8** crowning, eventual, greatest, terminal **9** at the peak, high point, last straw, long-range, resulting **10** conclusive, definitive
  French: **7** dernier

ultramodern 8 advanced, brand-new **10** avant-garde, newfangled **13** in the vanguard, up-to-the-minute

Ulysses
  author: **10** James Joyce
  character: **10** Molly Bloom **12** Blazes Boylan, Buck Mulligan, Leopold Bloom **14** Stephen Dedalus

Ulysses *see* **8** Odysseus

umber 5 brown **7** pigment **9** dark-brown **14** yellowish-brown

umbrage 5 pique, shade **6** leaves, shadow **7** foliage, offense, outrage **10** resentment

Umbrellas of Cherbourg, The
  director: **11** Jacques Demy
  cast: **10** Anne Vernon **15** Nino Castelnuovo

Uganda
  capital/largest city: 7 Kampala
  others: 4 Arua, Gulu, Lira 5 Atiak, Jinja, Mbale, Mengo
  6 Kasese, Kiboga, Kitgum, Masaka, Moroto, Pajule, So-
  roti, Tororo 7 Entebbe, Kachung, Kilembe, Mbarara,
  Mombasa 8 Kyenjojo 11 Port Masindi
  school: 8 Makerere
  division: 4 Toro 6 Ankole, Busoga 7 Buganda, Bunyoro
  monetary unit: 4 cent 8 shilling
  island: 4 Sese
  lake: 5 Kioga, Kyoga 6 Albert, Edward, George 8 Victoria
  mountain: 4 Oboa 5 Elgon 7 Virunga 9 Mufumbiro, Ruwenzori 18 Mountains of the Moon
  highest point: 10 Margherita
  river: 4 Aswa, Kafu 5 Pager 7 Katonga 9 White Nile
  10 Albert Nile 12 Victoria Nile
  physical feature:
    falls: 5 Owens 8 Kabalega 9 Murchison
    plateau: 6 Ankole 11 East African
    valley: 9 Great Rift
  people: 4 Alur, Gisu, Soga, Teso 5 Ateso, Bantu, Chiga,
  Ganda, Langi, Lango, Nkole, Pygmy 6 Acholi, Ankole,
  Bagisu, Bakiga, Basoga, Batoro 7 Baganda, Banyoro, Bunyoro, Hamitic, Lugbara, Nilotic, Sudanic 9 Nyoro-Toro
  10 Banyankole, Karamojong
    explorer: 5 Baker, Speke 7 Stanley
    king: 6 Mutesa, Mwanga 8 Kabarega
    leader: 5 Obote 6 Mutesa 7 Omukama 11 Idi Amin Dada
  language: 5 Ateso, Ganda 7 English, Luganda, Swahili
  religion: 5 Islam 7 animism 8 Anglican 10 Protestant
  13 Roman Catholic
  place:
    airport: 7 Entebbe
    dam: 10 Owens Falls
    national park: 6 Kidepo 14 Murchison Falls, Queen
    Elizabeth
  feature:
    clothing: 7 busuuti
    council of chiefs: 6 lukiko
    dance group: 17 Heart Beat of Africa
    king: 6 kabaka
  food:
    drink: 6 waragi

16 Catharine Deneuve
  score: 13 Michel Legrand

Umbrian
  language family: 12 Indo-
  European
  branch: 6 Italic

umpire 5 judge 7 arbiter, mediate, referee 8 mediator, moderate 9 arbitrate, go-between,
moderator 10 adjudicate, arbitrator, negotiator 11 adjudicator, intercessor

Una
  character in: 15 The Faerie
  Queene
  author: 7 Spenser

unabbreviated 5 uncut 8 complete, undocked, unpruned
9 uncropped, unreduced, un-
snipped, untrimmed 10 un-
abridged 11 uncondensed,
uncurtailed, unshortened
12 uncompressed,
unexpurgated

unable 5 unfit 6 cannot
8 helpless, impotent 9 incapable 10 inadequate, une-
quipped 11 incompetent,
unqualified
  to tell pitch: 8 tone deaf

unabridged 5 uncut 6 entire,
intact 8 complete 10 full-
length 11 uncondensed

unacceptable 8 below par, improper, unseemly, unworthy
9 deficient, out of line, unwelcome 10 disallowed, inadequate, unsuitable
11 displeasing, intolerable
12 inadmissible, not allowable,
not up to snuff 13 insupportable 14 unsatisfactory 15 not
up to standard

unacceptableness 8 disfavor,
disgrace, ignominy
18 unsatisfactoriness

unaccommodating 4 rude
8 churlish 9 difficult, unhelp-

ful 10 inflexible, intolerant,
unyielding 11 disobliging
13 inconsiderate

unaccompanied 4 lone, solo
5 alone, apart 6 single, singly
8 isolated, lonesome, separate,
solitary 9 a cappella, by oneself 10 unattended, unes-
corted 12 all by oneself
13 companionless

unaccountable 3 odd 4 free
5 clear, queer, weird 6 exempt,
immune 7 bizarre, curious, excused, strange, unusual 8 baffling, innocent, peculiar
9 blameless, not liable,
unheard-of 10 inculpable, intriguing, mysterious, surprising 11 astonishing,
unexplained 12 inexplicable,
unfathomable 13 extraordinary, not answerable 14 not
responsible
16 incomprehensible

unaccustomed 3 new, odd
4 rare, wild 5 green, new to,
novel, queer 6 quaint, unique,
unused 7 amazing, bizarre, curious, foreign, not used,
strange, ungiven, untried, unusual 8 original, peculiar, singular, uncommon 9 fantastic,
startling, unheard-of 10 remarkable, surprising, unfamiliar, unversed in
11 astonishing, out-of-the-way,
unpracticed 12 unacquainted,
unhabituated, unimaginable
13 extraordinary, inexperienced 14 unfamiliar with
16 out of the ordinary

unacknowledged 9 anonymous 10 unanswered 11 disregarded 12 unidentified,
unrecognized

unadorned 4 bald, bare 5 naked, plain, stark 6 simple
7 austere 11 undecorated
12 unornamented 13 unem-
bellished 15 straightforward

unadulterated 4 pure, true
5 clear, uncut 7 genuine 9 unalloyed, untainted
14 untampered-with

unadventurous 5 chary,
timid 7 careful 8 cautious, hesitant 11 circumspect

unadvisable 5 silly 6 stupid,
unwise 8 unseemly 9 imprudent 11 inadvisable, inexpedient, injudicious, undesirable
15 disadvantageous

unaesthetic 9 tasteless 10 inartistic 11 insensitive
16 undiscriminating

unaffected 4 open 5 frank, naive, plain 6 candid, direct,
honest, simple 7 genuine, natural, sincere, unmoved 8 in-

nocent **9** childlike, guileless, ingenuous, unfeeling, unstirred, untouched, unworldly, wholesome **10** impervious, unbothered, unreserved **11** indifferent, insensitive, openhearted, plain-spoken, unconcerned, undesigning, undisturbed **12** unresponsive **13** unsympathetic **15** straightforward, unsophisticated

unaffectedness 4 ease **11** naturalness **12** unconstraint

unafraid 4 bold **5** brave **6** daring, heroic, plucky **7** valiant **8** fearless, intrepid, stalwart, valorous **9** audacious, daredevil, dauntless **10** courageous **11** indomitable, lionhearted, venturesome **12** stouthearted **13** adventuresome

unaggressive 3 shy **4** meek **5** timid **7** passive **8** peaceful, timorous **9** peaceable, shrinking **11** unambitious **14** unenterprising

unagitated 4 calm **6** gentle, placid, serene **8** composed, tranquil **9** collected, unexcited, unruffled **10** untroubled **11** undisturbed, unperturbed **13** self-possessed

unalloyed 4 pure **7** unmixed **11** unqualified **13** unadulterated

unalterable 5 fixed, rigid **6** stable **8** constant **9** immutable, indelible, obstinate, permanent, perennial **10** inflexible, persistent **11** irrevocable **12** indissoluble, unchangeable **13** irretrievable

unambitious 4 easy, lazy **6** humble, modest, simple **8** slothful **10** unaspiring **12** unaggressive **14** unenterprising

unamiable 4 sour **5** cross, surly, testy **6** sullen **7** grouchy, hostile, peevish **8** churlish **9** irascible **10** ill-humored, unfriendly, unpleasant, unsociable **11** bad-tempered, uncongenial **12** disagreeable

unamorous 4 cold, cool **6** frigid **8** unloving **11** passionless

unanimated 4 dull, flat, limp **5** inert, vapid **7** insipid **8** lifeless **10** insentient **11** unconscious

unanimity 6 accord **7** concord, harmony **8** agreement, consensus **11** concordance, concurrence **17** meeting of the minds

unanimous 6 allied, united

9 accordant, consonant, of one mind **10** harmonious, likeminded

unannounced 6 secret, sudden **8** surprise, withheld **10** suppressed, unheralded **11** undisclosed, unlooked for, unpublished **12** unadvertised **13** unanticipated

unanticipated 6 sudden **8** surprise **10** unexpected, unforeseen, unheralded **11** unannounced, unlooked-for, unpredicted

unappealing 10 disgusting, uninviting, unpleasant **11** displeasing **12** disagreeable, unappetizing, unattractive

unappetizing 6 horrid **7** insipid **10** bad-tasting, disgusting, uninviting **11** unpalatable **12** disagreeable

unapproachable 4 cold, cool **5** aloof **6** remote, unique **7** austere, awesome, distant, supreme **8** foremost, peerless, superior **9** matchless, nonpareil, unequaled, unrivaled **10** forbidding, inimitable, preeminent **11** beyond reach, stand-offish, unreachable **12** inaccessible, incomparable, intimidating, second to none, unattainable, unparalleled **13** beyond compare

unasked 6 wanton **8** unbidden, unsought, unwanted **9** uninvited, unwelcome **10** gratuitous **11** uncalled-for, undesirable, unrequested, unsolicited

unassertive 3 shy **5** timid **6** humble, modest **7** bashful **8** sheepish **9** diffident, shrinking

unassertiveness 7 modesty, shyness **8** docility, timidity **9** timidness **10** diffidence, humbleness **11** bashfulness **12** sheepishness

unassuming 5 muted, plain **6** homely, modest, simple **7** natural **9** easygoing **11** unassertive, unobtrusive **13** unpretentious **14** unostentatious

unattached 5 apart, split **6** single **8** detached, separate **9** separated **11** unconnected **12** disconnected

unattractive 4 dull, ugly **5** plain **6** homely **8** frumpish **11** unappealing, undesirable **12** unappetizing

unauthentic 4 fake, mock, sham **5** bogus, false, phony **6** untrue **7** dubious **8** doubtful **9** imitation, synthetic

10 fraudulent **11** counterfeit **12** questionable

unauthenticated 8 disputed **10** apocryphal, unverified **15** unsubstantiated

unauthorized 6 banned, covert **7** furtive **8** outlawed, unlawful **9** concealed, unallowed, underhand **10** prohibited, unapproved, unofficial **11** clandestine, uncertified, unpermitted, unwarranted **12** unaccredited, unsanctioned **13** under-the-table

unavailable 5 taken **6** scarce **7** lacking, married **9** not at hand **10** nonpresent **11** nonexistent

unavailing 4 idle, vain, weak **5** empty, inept **6** futile, no good **7** invalid, useless **8** bootless, impotent **9** fruitless, worthless **11** ineffective, ineffectual **12** unproductive, unsuccessful

unavoidable 4 sure **5** fated, fixed **7** certain **9** necessary, requisite **10** compulsory, imperative, inevitable, obligatory **11** inescapable **13** unpreventable **14** uncontrollable

unaware 8 heedless, ignorant, unwarned **9** in the dark, unalerted, unknowing, unmindful **10** unapprised **11** incognizant, unconscious **12** off one's guard, unacquainted, unsuspecting **13** unenlightened

unawares 8 abruptly, by chance, suddenly **9** by mistake **10** by accident, by surprise, mistakenly **11** unknowingly, unwittingly **12** accidentally, out of nowhere, unexpectedly, unthinkingly **13** inadvertently, involuntarily, unconsciously **14** without warning **15** unintentionally **16** like a thunderbolt **20** like a bolt from the blue, like a thief in the night

unbalanced 3 mad **4** daft, loco **5** batty, nutty, wacky **6** crazed, uneven, warped **7** bonkers, cracked, leaning, unequal, unglued, unsound **8** demented, deranged, lopsided, unhinged, unpoised, unstable, unsteady **9** disturbed, illogical, psychotic, unsettled **10** irrational, unadjusted **11** not all there **12** psychopathic

unbearable 11 intolerable, unendurable, unthinkable **12** inadmissible, insufferable, unacceptable **13** insupportable

unbecoming 4 ugly 6 homely, vulgar 8 improper, unfitted, unseemly, unsuited 9 offensive, tasteless, unsightly 10 indecorous, unsuitable 11 unappealing, unbefitting 12 unattractive 13 inappropriate

unbelief 5 doubt 7 dubiety 9 disbelief 10 skepticism 11 incredulity 12 doubtfulness

unbelievable 5 false 6 absurd, insane 7 amazing, asinine, idiotic 10 astounding, farfetched, incredible, irrational, remarkable, ridiculous 11 astonishing 12 preposterous, unimaginable, unreasonable 13 hard to swallow

unbeliever 7 atheist, heathen infidel, skeptic 8 apostate 10 godless one 11 disbeliever, nonbeliever

unbelieving 7 dubious 8 doubting 9 quizzical, skeptical 10 suspicious 11 distrustful, incredulous, questioning, unconvinced 12 disbelieving, nonbelieving

unbend 5 relax 6 relent, unflex 10 straighten 12 straighten up 13 straighten out

unbending 4 firm 5 rigid, stiff, tough 6 severe, strict 8 stubborn 9 obstinate 10 inflexible, stone-faced, unyielding 11 hard as nails 14 uncompromising

unbent 5 erect 7 relaxed, unbowed, upright, yielded 8 relented, straight, uncurved, unflexed 9 unstooped 12 straightened

unbiased 4 fair, just 7 liberal, neutral 8 detached, tolerant 9 impartial, unbigoted 10 fair-minded, open-minded, undogmatic 11 broad-minded 12 uninfluenced, unprejudiced 13 disinterested, dispassionate

unbigoted 8 tolerant, unbiased 10 open-minded 11 broad-minded 12 unprejudiced

unbind 4 free, undo 5 loose, untie 6 detach, loosen, ungird 7 deliver, release, undress 8 let loose, unfasten

unblamable 5 clear 8 innocent 9 blameless, guiltless, not guilty 10 inculpable, not at fault 14 not responsible

unblemished 4 pure 7 perfect 8 flawless, spotless, unmarred, unsoiled 9 unsullied 10 immaculate, unvitiated 11 white as snow 13 unadulterated

14 uncontaminated 15 clean as a whistle

unblock 4 free, open 5 unbar, unjam 6 unclog, unstop

unborn 5 fetal, later 6 coming, future, to come 7 in utero 9 embryonic 10 subsequent, succeeding 11 prospective

unbosom oneself 7 confess, confide, lay bare 15 unburden oneself

unbound 4 free 5 freed, loose 6 loosed, untied 8 detached, let loose, loosened, released 10 unconfined, unfastened 12 unrestrained

unbounded 8 absolute 9 boundless, unbridled, unlimited 12 uncontrolled, unrestrained, unrestricted 13 unconditional, unconstrained

unbreakable 5 tough 6 strong

unbroken 5 whole 6 entire, intact 7 endless 8 complete 9 ceaseless, continual, incessant, uncracked, undivided, unsmashed 10 continuous, sequential, successive, unruptured 11 consecutive, progressive, unremitting, unshattered 12 undiminished 13 uninterrupted

unbuckle 4 undo 6 loosen 7 release, unhitch, unstrap 8 uncouple, unfasten

unburden 4 free 6 reveal 7 confess, confide, relieve, unbosom 8 disclose 9 disburden 10 unencumber 11 disencumber 15 get off one's chest 18 get out of one's system

unbusinesslike 6 casual, sloppy 8 informal 11 impractical, inefficient

uncalculated 9 unplanned 10 accidental, unintended 11 inadvertent 14 unpremeditated

uncalled-for 6 wanton 7 unasked 8 needless, unneeded, unsought, unwanted 9 redundant, uninvited 10 gratuitous, unprompted 11 unjustified, unnecessary, unsolicited 12 nonessential 14 supererogatory

uncanny 5 eerie, weird 6 spooky 7 curious, strange 8 inspired 9 fantastic, intuitive, marvelous, unearthly, unheard-of, unnatural 10 incredible, mysterious, prodigious, remarkable, unexampled 11 astonishing, exceptional 12 unbelievable, unimaginable 13 extraordinary, uncomfortable

uncanonical 12 unauthorized, unscriptural

Uncas
character in: 20 The Last of the Mohicans
author: 6 Cooper

unceasing 7 endless, eternal 8 constant 9 continual, incessant, perpetual, sustained 10 continuous, persistent, without end

uncelebrated 6 unsung 7 obscure, unknown 9 anonymous 14 uncommemorated

unceremonious 4 curt, rude 5 hasty, rough 6 abrupt 7 brusque 8 informal 11 precipitate

uncertain 4 hazy 6 fitful, unsure 7 dubious, erratic, not sure, obscure, unclear 8 doubtful, hesitant, nebulous, not fixed, variable, wavering 9 debatable, undecided, unsettled 10 disputable, indefinite, indistinct, in question, irresolute, unresolved, up in the air 11 conjectural, fluctuating, not definite, speculative, unconfirmed, vacillating 12 not confident, questionable, undetermined 13 indeterminate, unpredictable

uncertainty 4 odds, risk 5 doubt 6 chance, gamble 8 quandary 9 ambiguity, confusion, hesitancy, vagueness 10 hesitation, indecision, perplexity, unsureness 11 ambivalence, vacillation 12 equivocation, irresolution, shilly-shally 14 indefiniteness

unchain 4 free 7 release, set free 8 liberate, unfetter 9 unshackle

unchangeable 5 rigid 6 stable 7 uniform 8 stubborn 9 immutable, obstinate, permanent 10 inflexible, invariable 11 unalterable 12 intransigent

unchanging 4 fast, firm 5 fixed 6 stable, static 7 abiding, durable, lasting 8 constant 9 immutable, permanent, steadfast 10 monotonous 11 everlasting 12 indissoluble

unchaperoned 10 unattended, unescorted 12 unsupervised 13 unaccompanied

uncharacteristic 8 atypical 12 out of keeping 16 unrepresentative

uncharitable 5 tight 6 stingy, unkind 7 miserly 9 illiberal, niggardly, unfeeling 10 unfriendly, ungenerous, ungracious 11 closefisted, insensitive, tightfisted 12 par-

simonious **13** unsympathetic
15 uncompassionate

unchaste 4 lewd **5** loose
6 erotic, impure **7** corrupt, immoral **8** immodest **9** abandoned, debauched
10 dishonored

unchecked 4 free **5** loose
6 unruly **7** liberal, rampant
8 reinless, unreined **9** out of hand, unbridled, unmuzzled
10 unhindered **12** out of control, unrestrained,
unsuppressed

uncivil 4 curt, rude **5** blunt,
surly **6** abrupt, gauche **7** boorish, brusque **8** impolite **10** ungracious **11** ill-mannered
12 disagreeable, discourteous

uncivilized 4 rude **6** savage,
vulgar **7** boorish, brutish, illbred, uncouth, untamed
8 barbaric, churlish **9** barbarous, obnoxious, ungenteel
10 uncultured, unpolished
12 uncultivated

unclad 4 bare, nude **5** naked
7 exposed, unrobed **8** disrobed,
in the raw, starkers, stripped
9 in the nude, unclothed, uncovered, undressed **10** starknaked **15** in the altogether

unclean 4 evil, foul, tref, vile
5 dirty, dusty, grimy, messy,
muddy, sooty **6** filthy, impure,
soiled **7** defiled, immoral, obscene, smutted, stained **8** polluted, unchaste **9** blemished
10 besmirched

unclear 3 dim **4** hazy **5** blear,
faint, foggy, fuzzy, misty,
vague **6** bleary, cloudy, vapory **7** clouded, obscure, shadowy **8** shrouded, vaporous
9 ambiguous, uncertain **10** indefinite, indistinct

Uncle Remus
author: **18** Joel Chandler
Harris

Uncle Tom's Cabin
author: **19** Harriet Beecher
Stowe
character: **5** Eliza, Topsy
10 Eva St Clare **11** Simon
Legree

Uncle Vanya
author: **12** Anton Chekhov
character: **6** Marina **12** Mihail Astrov **13** Ivan Voynitsky (Uncle Vanya) **14** Marya
Voynitsky **15** Sonya Andreyevna **16** Yelena Andreyevna **19** Alexandr Serebryakov

unclose 4 open **6** reveal, unclog, unfold, unshut, unstop,
unwrap **7** unblock
poetic: **3** ope

unclothed 4 bare, nude **5** na-

ked **6** unclad **7** exposed, unrobed **8** stripped **9** in the
nude, uncovered, undressed

unclouded 5 clear, light,
sunny **6** bright, serene
10 unobscured

uncollected 4 owed **5** owing,
upset **6** shaken **8** agitated,
troubled **9** disturbed, perturbed **11** discomposed,
outstanding

uncolored 4 bald, bare, true
5 plain, stark **6** simple **9** unadorned **11** unvarnished
12 unelaborated **13** unembellished **15** straightforward

uncombed 5 messy **6** blowsy,
frowzy, matted, mussed, untidy **7** ruffled, rumpled,
snarled, tangled, tousled, unkempt **11** disarranged

uncomfortable 4 edgy **5** tense,
upset **6** on edge, uneasy
7 awkward, keyed up, nervous, painful **8** confused,
strained, troubled **9** ill at ease
10 bothersome, disquieted, irritating, out of place **11** discomfited, discomposed,
distressful **13** on tenterhooks

uncommitted 9 unpledged
11 undedicated

uncommon 4 rare **5** novel
6 scarce, unique **7** bizarre, curious, notable, supreme, unusual **8** peculiar, peerless,
superior **9** matchless, unmatched **10** infrequent, remarkable, unexcelled,
unfamiliar **11** exceptional, outstanding, superlative **12** incomparable, unparalleled
13 extraordinary **14** unconventional **15** once in a lifetime **16** few and far between

uncommunicative 3 mum,
shy **4** dumb, mute **5** quiet
6 silent **8** reserved, reticent,
retiring, taciturn **9** secretive,
withdrawn **10** speechless,
tongue-tied, unsociable **11** untalkative **12** close-mouthed,
inexpressive

uncomplicated 4 easy **5** clear,
plain **6** simple **10** uninvolved

uncomplimentary 8 critical,
derisive, negative **9** insulting
10 unadmiring **11** disparaging
12 disapproving, unflattering

uncompromising 4 firm
5 rigid, stiff **6** strict **8** exacting,
hardline, obdurate **9** immovable, unbending, unvarying
10 inexorable, inflexible, scrupulous, unyielding
11 unrelenting

unconcealed 4 bald, bare,
open **5** overt **6** in view **7** ex-

posed, in sight, obvious, visible **8** apparent, manifest,
revealed **9** uncovered **11** discernible, perceivable, perceptible **12** in plain sight, out in
the open

unconcentrated 4 weak **7** diffuse, diluted, thinned **9** dispersed, scattered, spread out
11 watered down

unconcern 10 dispassion
11 insouciance, nonchalance
12 indifference

unconcerned 4 cold **5** aloof
6 serene **7** distant, unaware,
unmoved **8** composed, uncaring **9** apathetic, oblivious, unfeeling, unmindful
10 impervious, nonchalant,
uninvolved, untroubled **11** indifferent, insensitive, passionless, unperturbed
12 unresponsive
13 unsympathetic

unconditional 5 utter **6** entire
8 absolute, complete, outright
9 downright, unlimited
10 conclusive **11** categorical,
unqualified **12** unrestricted
13 thoroughgoing

Unconditional Surrender
author: **11** Evelyn Waugh

unconfident 3 shy **5** timid
7 bashful **8** reticent, retiring,
timorous **9** diffident, shrinking,
uncertain

unconfirmed 7 dubious **8** unproved **10** unapproved, unverified **11** unvalidated
12 questionable **14** uncorroborated **15** unsubstantiated

unconformity 7 anomaly **9** deviation **10** aberration, divergence **11** abnormality,
peculiarity **12** eccentricity, idiosyncrasy, irregularity
13 nonconformity

uncongenial 9 ill-suited, unamiable **10** dissimilar,
unfriendly, unpleasant **12** disagreeable, incompatible
13 unsympathetic

unconnected 7 severed **8** detached, discrete, separate
9 uncoupled, unhitched, unrelated **12** disconnected

unconquerable 6 innate **9** ingrained **10** inveterate, invincible, unbeatable
12 impenetrable, invulnerable,
undefeatable **14** insurmountable, unvanquishable

unconscionable 7 extreme
9 excessive **10** immoderate, inordinate, outrageous **11** inexcusable, unjustified,
unwarranted **12** indefensible,
preposterous, unforgivable, un-

pardonable, unreasonable
13 unjustifiable

unconscious 3 out **6** latent
7 in a coma, out cold **8** comatose, in a faint **9** insensate, senseless, unknowing, unmindful **10** suppressed, unrealized **11** incognizant **12** unsuspecting **14** dead to the world

unconstitutional 7 illegal
8 unlawful **12** unauthorized

unconstrained 4 bold, easy
7 natural, relaxed **8** unforced
9 abandoned **10** unaffected
11 spontaneous, uninhibited
French: **6** degage

unconstraint 4 ease **7** abandon **8** boldness, free will, openness **9** frankness **11** naturalness, spontaneity

uncontrollable 6 unruly
7 wayward **12** ungovernable, unmanageable

uncontrolled 4 free, wild
8 absolute **9** abandoned, unlimited **10** ungoverned
12 unrestrained

unconventional 3 odd **4** rare
5 crazy, kinky, nutty, queer, wacky, weird **6** far-out, quaint, unique **7** bizarre, curious, offbeat, strange, unusual **8** aberrant, atypical, bohemian, freakish, original, peculiar, singular, uncommon **9** different, eccentric, fantastic, irregular **10** newfangled, outlandish, unorthodox **11** exceptional
12 unaccustomed **13** extraordinary, idiosyncratic, nonconforming, nonconformist
15 individualistic

unconvinced 7 dubious
8 doubtful **9** skeptical, uncertain, unsettled

unconvincing 5 false, fishy
7 dubious, suspect **10** suspicious **11** implausible **12** questionable, unbelievable

uncooked
French: **9** au naturel

uncooperative 6 ornery **7** selfish **8** perverse, stubborn **9** difficult, unhelpful, unwilling
11 intractable **12** intransigent

uncoordinated 4 clumsy
7 awkward **8** ungainly
9 graceless

uncouple 4 undo **6** detach, loosen, unhook **7** release, unhitch **8** unbuckle

uncoupled 8 detached, loosened **9** separated, unhitched
10 disengaged **11** unconnected **12** disconnected

uncourageous 5 timid **8** cow-

ardly, timorous **9** dastardly, shrinking **13** pusillanimous

uncourtly 7 ill-bred, uncivil, uncouth **9** ungallant **10** illbehaved, ungracious, unmannerly **11** uncourteous **12** discourteous **13** ungentlemanly

uncouth 4 rude **5** crass, crude, gross, rough **6** callow, coarse
7 boorish, brutish, ill-bred, loutish, uncivil **8** barbaric, churlish, impolite **9** unrefined
10 indelicate, uncultured, unmannerly **11** ill-mannered, uncivilized **12** uncultivated

uncover 4 bare, undo **5** dig up, strip **6** denude, dig out, expose, reveal, unmask, unveil, unwrap **7** disrobe, lay bare, uncloak, undrape, undress, unearth **8** disclose, unclothe
9 make known, unsheathe
11 make visible **12** bring to light

uncovered 4 bare **5** bared, dug up, naked **7** exposed, noticed
8 detected, revealed **9** disclosed, made known **10** discovered **13** brought to view
14 brought to light

uncovering 8 exposure **9** divulging, unmasking **10** disclosure, divulgence, laying open, revelation **15** bringing to light **20** bringing out in the open

uncritical 4 dull, dumb **6** casual, obtuse, stupid **7** inexact, offhand, shallow **8** careless, ignorant, slipshod **9** imprecise, untutored **10** inaccurate, uneducated, unschooled, unthinking **11** perfunctory, superficial
12 unreflecting
16 undiscriminating

unctuous 4 oily, smug
6 smarmy **7** fawning, honeyed, servile **8** slippery, too suave
9 pietistic, too smooth **10** flattering, obsequious **11** sycophantic **12** honey-tongued, ingratiating **13** sanctimonious, self-righteous

uncultivated 3 raw **4** wild
7 uncouth **8** unfarmed, unplowed, untilled **9** unrefined
10 unimproved
11 undeveloped

uncultivated land
god of: **8** Silvanus, Sylvanus

uncultured 5 crass **6** coarse, common, vulgar **7** low-bred
9 inelegant, unrefined **10** unpolished **12** uncultivated

uncustomary 4 rare **6** unique
7 amazing, unusual **8** singular, uncommon, unwonted
9 unheard-of **10** incredible, un-

expected **11** astonishing, exceptional **12** unaccustomed, unbelievable **13** extraordinary, unanticipated

undaunted 5 brave **6** gritty, heroic, plucky **7** unfazed, valiant **8** fearless, intrepid, resolute, stalwart, valorous **9** not put off **10** courageous, undismayed **11** indomitable, unflinching, unperturbed, unshrinking **12** stouthearted
13 undiscouraged

undeceive 8 disabuse **10** disenchant **11** disenthrall, disillusion **12** open one's eyes
13 break the spell **15** burst one's bubble **19** bring one down to earth **20** shatter one's illusions

undecided 4 open **5** vague
6 unsure **7** dubious, pending
8 not final, wavering **9** tentative, uncertain, unsettled
10 indecisive, indefinite, in abeyance, in a dilemma, irresolute, of two minds, openminded, unresolved, up in the air **11** fluctuating, vacillating
12 undetermined, unformulated **16** hemming and hawing **17** blowing hot and cold
20 going around in circles

undecorated 4 bare **5** blank, plain, stark **6** simple **7** austere **9** unadorned
13 unembellished

undedicated 11 indifferent, uncommitted

undefiled 4 pure **5** clean
6 chaste, intact, virgin **7** natural **8** innocent, spotless
9 stainless, unsullied
10 unpolluted

undemanding 4 easy **6** lowkey, simple **7** patient, relaxed
9 easygoing **10** submissive
12 easy to please, laissez-faire
14 live-and-let-live

undemonstrative 3 shy
4 cold **5** aloof **7** distant, stoical **8** reserved **9** impassive
11 unemotional **12** inexpressive, unresponsive **14** selfcontrolled

undeniable 4 sure **6** patent, proven **7** certain, obvious
8 decisive, manifest **10** conclusive **11** established, indubitable, irrefutable **12** beyond a doubt, demonstrable, indisputable **13** incontestable **14** unquestionable
16 incontrovertible

undeniably 6 surely **9** certainly **10** decisively, definitely
11 irrefutably **12** conclusively, demonstrably, indisputably
13 incontestably **14** beyond

question, unquestionably
16 incontrovertibly

undependable 6 fickle **7** erratic, flighty **8** unstable, variable, wavering **10** capricious, changeable, inconstant, unreliable **13** irresponsible, unpredictable, untrustworthy

under 3 sub **5** below, lower, neath, short **7** beneath **8** inferior, less than **9** because of **11** subordinate

undercover 3 sly **6** covert, hidden, secret **7** furtive, sub rosa **8** hush-hush, stealthy **9** concealed, disguised, incognito **10** unrevealed **11** clandestine, undisclosed **12** confidential
French: **8** a couvert

undercurrent 4 aura, hint, mood **5** sense, tinge, vibes **7** quality, riptide **8** undertow **9** undertone **10** atmosphere, intimation, suggestion, vibrations **12** crosscurrent

undercut 9 discredit, undermine, undersell **10** compromise

underestimate 7 dismiss, put down **8** belittle, minimize, misjudge **9** deprecate, discredit, disparage, disregard, sell short, underrate, undersell **10** depreciate, undervalue **11** detract from **12** miscalculate

undergarment 3 bra **4** BVDs, slip **5** pants, shift, teddy **6** corset, girdle, shorts **7** chemise, panties **8** bloomers, camisole, knickers, lingerie, skivvies **9** brassiere, petticoat, union suit **12** jockey shorts

undergo 5 brave, stand **6** endure, suffer **7** sustain, weather **8** submit to **9** encounter, go through, withstand **10** experience

undergraduate 4 coed, soph **5** frosh, plebe **6** junior, senior **7** scholar, student **8** freshman **9** sophomore, undegreed **10** degreeless, nondegreed **13** underclassman, upperclassman

underground 6 buried, covert, secret **7** sub-rosa **10** undercover **11** belowground, clandestine **12** subterranean **13** surreptitious **15** below the surface

underground chamber 4 tomb **5** crypt, vault **6** cellar **8** catacomb **9** sepulcher

underhand, underhanded 6 covert, crafty, sneaky, tricky **7** corrupt, crooked, cunning, devious, evasive, furtive,

illegal **8** sneaking, stealthy **9** conniving, dishonest, unethical **10** fraudulent **12** unprincipled, unscrupulous **13** surreptitious

underhandedness 5 guile **6** deceit **7** slyness **8** trickery **9** chicanery, deception, duplicity **10** sneakiness, trickiness **13** secretiveness

underline 6 accent, stress **7** dwell on, point up **9** emphasize, press home **10** accentuate, underscore **15** bring into relief

underling 4 serf **6** flunky, lackey, menial, minion, thrall, vassal **7** servant, subject **8** employee, hireling, inferior **9** attendant, hired hand **11** subordinate

underlying 5 basic **6** covert **7** beneath, radical **8** implicit **9** elemental, essential **10** subtending **11** fundamental

undermine 4 foil, ruin **5** erode **6** injure, riddle, scotch, thwart, weaken **7** cripple, destroy, subvert, torpedo **8** sabotage **9** eat away at, frustrate, hamstring **10** neutralize **11** burrow under, tunnel under

underneath 5 below, lower **6** bottom, hidden **9** disguised, subject to **14** misrepresented

undernourished 8 starving, underfed **12** malnourished

under obligation 5 bound **6** liable **7** obliged **8** beholden, indebted **9** obligated **10** answerable, in one's debt **11** accountable, responsible

underpart 4 sole **5** belly, tails **6** bottom **9** lower side, underside

underpin 4 bear **7** bolster, support **10** strengthen **12** substantiate

underpinning 4 base **5** basic **6** ground **7** support **9** essential **10** foundation, groundwork **11** fundamental **12** substructure

underplay 8 play down **11** deemphasize

underprivileged 4 poor **5** needy **6** in need **7** hapless, unlucky **8** badly-off, deprived, ill-fated, indigent **9** destitute, penniless, penurious **10** illstarred, pauperized **11** handicapped, unfortunate **12** impoverished **13** disadvantaged **22** in adverse circumstances

underrate 6 slight **8** belittle, derogate, minimize **9** deni-

grate, deprecate, disparage **10** depreciate, undervalue **13** underestimate

underscore 4 mark **6** accent, deepen, play up, stress **7** feature, point up **8** heighten **9** emphasize, intensify, press home, underline **10** accentuate **15** draw attention to

underscoring 6 stress **8** emphasis **11** underlining

underside 4 back, sole **5** belly, tails **6** bottom **7** reverse **9** lower side, underpart

undersized 4 tiny **5** elfin, short, small **6** little, petite, slight **7** stunted **8** dwarfish **10** diminutive **11** lilliputian

underskirt 4 slip **7** pannier **9** crinoline, hoopskirt, petticoat

understand 3 dig, get, see **4** hear, know, read, take **5** grasp, learn **6** absorb, accept, assume, can see, fathom, gather, take it **7** be aware, discern, make out, presume, realize **8** conclude, perceive **9** apprehend, interpret, recognize **10** appreciate, comprehend, take to mean **14** sympathize with, take for granted

understandable 8 apparent **12** recognizable, unmistakable **14** comprehensible

understanding 4 pact **5** grasp **7** empathy, insight, knowing **8** sympathy, tolerant **9** agreement, awareness, intuition, knowledge, sensitive **10** cognizance, compassion, compromise, discerning, perception, perceptive, responsive **11** concordance, sensitivity, sympathetic **12** appreciation, appreciative, apprehension **13** compassionate, comprehension **17** meeting of the minds

understate 8 minimize **11** deemphasize

understated 9 minimized **10** restrained **12** conservative, deemphasized

understatement 7 litotes **10** minimizing **20** conservative estimate

understudy 3 sub **6** backup, double, fill-in, relief **7** standby, stand-in **9** alternate, surrogate **10** substitute **11** pinch hitter, replacement

undertake 3 try **5** begin, essay, start **6** assume, strive, tackle, take on **7** attempt **8** commence, embark on, endeavor, set about, shoulder **9** agree to do, enter upon **11** promise to do **13** get involved in

undertaking 3 job **4** task **6** effort **7** concern, project, pursuit, venture **8** endeavor **10** commitment, enterprise

Under the Greenwood Tree
author: **11** Thomas Hardy

under the influence 5 drunk **6** sodden, soused, wasted, zapped, zonked **7** smashed **8** besotted **9** plastered **10** inebriated **11** intoxicated **20** three sheets to the wind

under the weather 3 bad, ill **4** sick **6** ailing, sickly, unwell **9** unhealthy **10** indisposed

undertone 4 aura, hint, mood **5** scent, sense, tinge, trace **6** flavor, mumble, murmur, nuance **7** feeling, inkling, low tone, quality, whisper **8** coloring **10** atmosphere, intimation, suggestion **11** connotation, implication **12** subdued voice, undercurrent

undervalue 6 slight **8** belittle, derogate **9** discredit, disparage, underrate **10** depreciate **13** underestimate

underwear 3 bra **4** BVDs, slip **5** pants, teddy **6** briefs, corset, girdle, shorts **7** chemise, panties **8** bloomers, camisole, knickers, lingerie, skivvies **9** brassiere, petticoat, union suit **12** jockey shorts, smallclothes **14** unmentionables

underweight 4 bony, lank **5** gaunt, lanky **6** skinny **7** scrawny, spindly **8** skeletal, underfed **9** emaciated **12** skin-and-bones **13** hollow-cheeked **14** spindle-shanked, undernourished

underworld 4 Hell **5** Hades, limbo **6** the mob **8** mobsters, the Mafia **9** criminals, gangsters, purgatory **10** Cosa Nostra **11** shades below **12** the syndicate **13** bottomless pit, nether regions **14** organized crime **15** criminal element, infernal regions **16** abode of the damned
  god of: **3** Dis **5** Hades, Orcus, Pluto **8** Dis Pater

under wraps 6 hidden, secret **9** concealed **10** suppressed, under cover

underwrite 3 aid **4** back **7** approve, endorse, finance, sponsor, support, warrant **8** invest in, sanction, validate **9** guarantee, subsidize **11** countersign

underwriter 5 angel **6** backer, patron **7** sponsor **8** investor **9** financier, guarantor

undeserving 3 bad **8** inferior, unworthy

undesirable 5 unfit **8** disliked, improper, unbidden, unsavory, unseemly, unwanted, unworthy **9** offensive, unpopular **10** unbecoming, uninviting, unsuitable, unwelcomed **11** distasteful, unbefitting, unwished-for **12** disagreeable, inadmissible, unacceptable, unattractive **13** inappropriate, objectionable **14** unsatisfactory

undetectable 12 unnoticeable, unobservable **13** imperceptible, unsubstantial

undetermined 6 chance **7** unfixed, unknown **8** unproved, unproven **9** uncertain, undecided **10** indefinite, irresolute **13** indeterminate, unascertained

undeveloped 3 raw **5** crude, green **6** callow, unripe **8** immature, inchoate, unformed **9** embryonic, half-baked **10** unfinished **11** rudimentary, unexploited **12** uncultivated

undignified 3 low **7** boorish **8** improper, shameful, unseemly, unworthy **9** degrading, inelegant, tasteless, unrefined **10** beneath one, indecorous, indelicate, in bad taste, unbecoming, unladylike, unsuitable **11** unbefitting **13** discreditable, inappropriate, ungentlemanly **18** beneath one's dignity
  Latin: **8** infra dig **15** infra dignitatem

undiluted 4 neat, pure **5** sheer **7** unmixed **8** straight **11** unfortified **12** full-strength **13** unadulterated

Undine
form: **6** spirit
location: **5** water
sex: **6** female

undiscerning 11 insensitive **12** unperceptive **14** indiscriminate

undisciplined 4 wild **6** fickle, fitful **7** erratic, wayward, willful **8** unsteady, untaught **9** mercurial, untrained, untutored **10** capricious, changeable, inconstant, uneducated, unfinished, unreliable, unschooled **11** unpracticed **12** obstreperous, uncontrolled, undependable, unrestrained **13** unpredictable

undisclosed 6 hidden, secret **7** private **9** concealed **10** unrevealed **12** confidential

undisguised 4 open **5** clear, utter **7** evident, obvious **8** com-

plete, distinct, manifest, unhidden **9** out-and-out **10** plain as day, pronounced, unreserved **11** unconcealed **12** unmistakable, wholehearted **13** thoroughgoing **24** plain as the nose on one's face

undismayed 7 uncowed **8** unafraid, unscared **9** confident, unabashed, unalarmed, undaunted **12** unfrightened **13** undiscouraged, unintimidated

undisputed 4 sure **7** certain, granted **8** accepted **9** undoubted **10** conclusive, undeniable **11** beyond doubt, indubitable, irrefutable, past dispute, uncontested **12** acknowledged, indisputable, unchallenged, unquestioned **13** a matter of fact, incontestable **14** beyond question, freely admitted, unquestionable **15** without question **16** incontrovertible

undistinguished 5 plain, usual **6** common **7** prosaic **8** everyday, mediocre, ordinary **10** pedestrian, unexciting **11** commonplace **12** run-of-the-mill, unremarkable **13** unexceptional **18** nothing to rave about

undistracted 4 calm **6** serene, stolid **7** unfazed **9** impassive, unruffled **10** untroubled **11** undisturbed

undisturbed 4 calm, cool **5** quiet **6** placid, serene, steady **7** equable, unmoved **8** composed, peaceful, tranquil **9** collected, inviolate, unexcited, unruffled, untouched **10** of solitude, unagitated, unbothered, untroubled **11** left in order, unperturbed **13** imperturbable, self-possessed, uninterrupted

undivided 5 solid, whole **6** entire, united **7** unified, unsplit **8** complete **9** of one mind, unanimous **10** not divided, unstinting **12** wholehearted

undo 3 end **4** free, open, ruin, void **5** annul, erase, loose, quash, untie **6** cancel, defeat, loosen, offset, repair, unbind, unfold, unhook, unknot, unlace, unlock, unwrap **7** destroy, nullify, rectify, reverse, subvert, unchain, unravel, wipe out **8** demolish, overturn, unbutton, unfasten **9** disengage, eliminate, make up for, undermine **10** counteract, invalidate, neutralize **11** disentangle **13** compensate for **14** counterbalance

undogmatic 7 liberal **8** flexible, tolerant **10** open-minded **11** broad-minded

undoing 4 doom, jinx, ruin **5** upset **6** defeat **7** erasure, nemesis **8** collapse, downfall, negation, reversal, weakness **9** annulment, breakdown, overthrow, ruination, thwarting, wiping out **11** cause of ruin, destruction **12** Achilles' heel, cancellation, invalidation **13** counteraction, nullification **14** neutralization

undomesticated 4 wild **5** feral **6** ferine, savage **7** untamed **8** barbaric **9** barbarous **11** uncivilized

undone 6 ruined **9** come apart, destroyed **10** incomplete, unfastened **12** not completed

undoubted 4 sure **5** utter **7** certain **8** absolute, complete, definite, positive **11** indubitable, unequivocal **12** indisputable **13** unimpeachable **14** unquestionable

undoubtedly 6 surely **7** no doubt **9** assuredly, certainly, decidedly, doubtless **10** absolutely, definitely, positively, undeniably **11** indubitably **12** beyond a doubt, unmistakably, without doubt **13** unequivocally **14** beyond question, unquestionably **15** without question

undress 5 strip **6** nudity **7** disrobe, uncover, undrape **8** disarray, unclothe **9** nakedness **10** dishabille **18** take off one's clothes

undressed 4 bare, nude **5** naked **6** unclad **7** denuded, exposed, unrobed **8** disrobed, stripped, undraped **9** unclothed, uncovered

Undset, Sigrid
   author of: 6 The Axe
   20 Kristin Lavransdatter, The Master of Hestviken

undue 6 unmeet **8** impolite, improper, needless, overmuch, too great, unseemly, unworthy **9** excessive, tasteless **10** ill-advised, indiscreet, in bad taste, inordinate, not fitting, unbecoming, unsuitable **11** superfluous, uncalled-for, unjustified, unnecessary, unwarranted **13** inappropriate, objectionable

undulate 4 coil **5** slink, weave **9** fluctuate **11** rise and fall

undulating 4 wavy **5** bumpy **6** uneven

undulation 7 coiling **8** slinking,

twisting **10** contortion **11** convolution **16** rising and falling

undutiful 6 remiss **8** disloyal **11** disobedient

undying 6 steady **7** abiding, endless, eternal, lasting **8** constant, enduring, immortal, unending, unfading, untiring **9** continual, deathless, incessant, perennial, permanent, perpetual, unceasing **10** continuing **11** everlasting, never-ending, unfaltering, unrelenting, unremitting **12** imperishable, never-failing, undiminished **13** uninterrupted **14** indestructible

unearth 4 find, show **5** dig up **6** dig out, exhume, expose, reveal **7** display, divulge, exhibit, root out, uncover **8** disclose, discover, disinter, dredge up, excavate **9** disentomb, ferret out **10** come across, come up with **12** bring to light

unearthly 5 awful, eerie, weird **6** absurd **7** extreme, ghostly, phantom, strange, uncanny, ungodly, unusual **8** abnormal, ethereal, spectral, terrible **10** horrendous, unpleasant **11** disembodied, incorporeal, unspeakable **12** disagreeable, extramundane, supernatural **13** extraordinary, preternatural

unease 5 worry **7** tension **8** disquiet **9** misgiving **10** discomfort, uneasiness **11** disquietude **12** apprehension

uneasiness 5 dread **6** dismay **7** anxiety **9** agitation, misgiving **10** discomfort, foreboding **11** disquietude, distraction, nervousness **12** apprehension, discomfiture, discomposure, perturbation **16** apprehensiveness

uneasy 4 edgy **5** nervy, tense, upset **6** on edge, queasy, unsure **7** awkward, irksome, nervous, uptight, worried **8** strained, troubled, worrying **9** disturbed, ill at ease, perturbed, upsetting **10** bothersome, disquieted, disturbing, unpleasant **11** constrained, disquieting **12** apprehensive **13** uncomfortable

uneatable 8 inedible **11** not fit to eat

uneconomical 4 dear **6** costly **8** wasteful **9** expensive **10** exorbitant, high-priced, immoderate, overpriced **11** extravagant **12** unreasonable

uneducated 8 ignorant, untaught **9** unlearned, untrained,

untutored **10** illiterate, uncultured, unlettered, unschooled **12** uncultivated, uninstructed **13** unenlightened

unelaborated 4 bald, bare **5** plain, stark **6** simple **9** essential, unadorned, uncolored **11** fundamental, unvarnished **13** unembellished **15** straightforward

unembellished 4 bald, bare **5** naked, plain, stark **7** austere **9** unadorned **11** undecorated **12** unornamented

unemotional 4 cold, cool **6** formal, remote **7** distant **8** lukewarm, reserved **9** apathetic, impassive, unfeeling **11** indifferent, passionless, unconcerned **12** unresponsive **15** undemonstrative

unemployed 4 axed, idle **5** fired **6** canned, sacked, unused **7** bounced, jobless, laid-off **8** workless **9** at leisure, at liberty, booted-out, dismissed, on the dole, on welfare, out of a job, out of work **10** discharged, unoccupied **11** pink-slipped

unencumbered 4 free **6** vacant **7** unladen **8** expedite **10** unburdened, unhindered **13** unhandicapped

unending 6 steady **7** endless, eternal, lasting **8** constant, enduring **9** continual, incessant, perennial, permanent, perpetual, unceasing **10** continuous, unwavering **11** everlasting, never-ending, unremitting **12** undiminished **13** uninterrupted

unendurable 7 racking **9** agonizing, torturous **10** tormenting, unbearable **11** intolerable **12** excruciating, insufferable

unenlightened 8 ignorant **9** in the dark, unlearned **10** uneducated, uninformed **11** uninitiated **12** uninstructed

unenterprising 4 lazy **11** unambitious **12** unaggressive

unenthusiastic 8 lukewarm **10** unspirited **11** halfhearted, indifferent **13** unimpassioned

unequal 6 biased, uneven, unfair, unjust, unlike **7** bigoted, partial **9** different, disparate, unmatched **10** dissimilar, not uniform, prejudiced **11** inequitable

unequaled 7 supreme **8** peerless **9** matchless, paramount, unmatched, unrivaled **10** consummate, unexcelled **11** ne plus ultra, unsurpassed **12** incomparable, second to none,

unapproached, unparalleled
13 beyond compare **16** beyond comparison

unequivocable 4 bald **5** utter **8** outright **9** out-and-out **11** categorical, unqualified

unequivocal 5 clear, final **7** certain **8** absolute, clear-cut, decisive, definite, emphatic **11** unambiguous **12** indisputable **13** incontestable **16** incontrovertible

unequivocally 7 clearly **9** certainly, downright **10** completely, decisively, definitely, thoroughly **12** emphatically, indisputably, unmistakably **13** incontestably **14** unquestionably, wholeheartedly **16** incontrovertibly

unerring 4 sure **7** certain, precise **8** constant, faithful, reliable **9** faultless, unfailing **10** infallible, unchanging

unessential 8 nonvital **9** accessory, extrinsic **10** disposable, expendable **11** dispensable, superfluous, unimportant, unnecessary **12** nonessential

unethical 5 dirty, shady, wrong **6** shoddy, unfair **7** devious **8** unworthy **9** dishonest, underhand **10** unladylike **12** dishonorable, disreputable, questionable, unprincipled **13** ungentlemanly **14** unconscionable

uneven 4 awry, bent **5** bumpy, lumpy, rough **6** angled, coarse, craggy, curved, jagged, tilted, unfair, unjust, unlike **7** crooked, not flat, slanted, sloping, unequal **8** lopsided, not level, not plumb, one-sided, unsmooth **9** different, disparate **10** dissimilar, ill-matched, unbalanced

unevenness 7 oddness **9** bumpiness, lumpiness, roughness **10** jaggedness, ruggedness **11** crookedness **12** irregularity **14** changeableness

uneventful 4 dull **5** quiet, usual **6** boring **7** average, humdrum, prosaic, routine, tedious **8** ordinary, standard, tiresome **10** monotonous **11** commonplace **12** conventional **13** insignificant, unexceptional, uninteresting

unexcelled 7 supreme **8** flawless, peerless, superior, unbeaten **9** faultless, matchless, unequaled, unmatched, unrivaled **10** consummate **11** unsurpassed **12** incomparable, second to none, transcendent,

unapproached, unparalleled
13 beyond compare

unexceptional 5 usual **6** normal **7** mundane, typical **8** ordinary, standard **9** customary **12** conventional, run of the mill

unexcited 4 calm, cool **6** placid, serene **7** unmoved **8** composed, detached **9** collected, unruffled **11** undisturbed, unemotional **13** dispassionate, unimpassioned

unexciting 4 dull, flat **5** vapid **6** boring **7** insipid **10** lackluster

unexpected 6 sudden **9** startling, unplanned **10** accidental, surprising, undesigned, unforeseen, unintended **11** astonishing, unlooked-for, unpredicted **12** out of the blue **13** unanticipated, unintentional

unextinguished 5 alive **10** unquenched **12** still burning

unfaded 5 fresh **6** bright **8** undimmed **10** unwithered

unfailing 4 true **5** loyal **6** steady **7** endless **8** constant, enduring, faithful, reliable **9** continual **10** continuous, dependable, infallible, unchanging, unwavering **12** neverfailing **13** inexhaustible

unfair 4 foul **5** dirty **6** biased, unjust **7** corrupt, crooked, partial, unequal **8** not right, one-sided, partisan **9** dishonest, underhand, unethical **10** not cricket, prejudiced **11** inequitable **12** dishonorable, unprincipled, unreasonable, unscrupulous **14** unconscionable

unfaithful 5 false **6** faulty, untrue **7** inexact **8** disloyal, unchaste **9** deceitful, distorted, erroneous, faithless, imperfect **10** adulterous, inaccurate, inconstant, perfidious **11** not accurate, treacherous **12** falsehearted **13** untrustworthy

Unfaithfully Yours
    director: 14 Preston Sturges
    cast: 10 Rudy Vallee **11** Rex Harrison **12** Edgar Kennedy, Linda Darnell **15** Barbara Lawrence

unfaithfulness 7 falsity, perfidy **9** falseness, treachery **10** disloyalty, fickleness, infidelity **11** inconstancy **13** faithlessness **14** perfidiousness

unfaltering 4 firm, sure **6** steady **8** enduring, resolute **9** obstinate, steadfast, unfail-

ing **10** dependable, persistent, unflagging, unswerving, unwavering **11** persevering, undeviating **12** never-failing, wholehearted

unfamiliar 3 new **5** novel **6** exotic, unique **7** curious, foreign, strange, unknown, unusual **9** different **10** ignorant of, unversed in **11** a stranger to, little known, out-of-the-way, unexposed to, uninitiated, unskilled in **12** not well-known, unacquainted, unconversant **13** not acquainted, unpracticed in **14** unaccustomed to **15** inexperienced in, uninformed about **18** unenlightened about

unfamiliarity 9 ignorance **11** strangeness **12** inexperience **15** lack of knowledge

unfashionable 5 dated, dowdy, passe **6** frumpy, old-hat **8** outmoded **9** out-of-date, unstylish **12** old-fashioned

unfasten 4 undo **5** unpin, untie **6** detach, unbind, unbolt, unhook, unlace, unlash, unlink, unlock **7** unclose, unhitch, unlatch, unstick **8** unbutton, uncouple

unfastened 5 apart, undid **6** undone, untied **7** severed, unlaced, unstuck **8** detached, unhooked **9** unbuckled, uncoupled, unhitched **11** unconnected **12** disconnected

unfathomable 4 deep, vast **6** arcane, remote, subtle **7** complex, extreme, obscure **8** abstract, abstruse, esoteric, profound, puzzling **9** enigmatic **10** bottomless, perplexing **16** hard to understand, incomprehensible

unfavorable 3 bad **4** poor **7** adverse, unhappy **8** unsuited, untimely **9** ill-suited **10** ill-favored, regretable **11** inopportune, regrettable, unfortunate, unpromising **12** inauspicious, inconvenient, infelicitous, unpropitious, unseasonable **15** disadvantageous

unfeasible 10 impossible, infeasible, unsuitable, unworkable **11** impractical **12** unachievable **13** impracticable

unfeeling 4 cold **5** cruel **9** heartless **11** hardhearted, insensitive **13** unsympathetic

unfeigned 4 real, true **7** genuine, sincere **10** unaffected

unfetter 4 free **7** release, set free, unchain **8** liberate **9** unshackle

unfilled 4 open **5** blank, empty **6** hollow, vacant **7** drained **9** available **10** unoccupied

unfinished 5 crude, rough **6** undone **7** lacking, sketchy, wanting **8** immature **9** deficient, imperfect, unnatural, unpainted, unrefined, unstained **10** incomplete, unexecuted, unpolished **11** uncompleted, unfulfilled, unlacquered, unvarnished

unfit 4 sick, weak **5** frail **6** infirm, not fit, sickly **7** not up to, unequal, unready, unsound, useless **8** delicate, disabled, unsuited **9** incapable, not suited, unhealthy, unskilled, untrained **10** inadequate, ineligible, not equal to, unequipped, unprepared, unsuitable **11** debilitated, ill-equipped, incompetent, ineffective, inefficient, not designed, unqualified **12** ill-contrived, not cut out for **13** inappropriate, incapacitated

unflagging 4 firm **5** fixed **6** steady **7** staunch **8** constant, enduring, resolute, tireless, unshaken, untiring **9** steadfast, tenacious, undaunted **10** determined, persistent, relentless, undrooping, unswerving, unwavering, unyielding **11** indomitable, persevering, undeviating, unfaltering, unremitting **13** indefatigable **14** uncompromising

unflappable 4 calm, cool **6** placid, serene **8** composed **9** collected **10** cool-headed **11** unexcitable **13** imperturbable, self-possessed

unflinching 4 firm, game **6** gritty, plucky, steady, strong **7** staunch **8** fearless, resolute, stalwart, unshaken **9** steadfast, tenacious, unabashed, undaunted **10** persistent, unswerving, unwavering, unyielding **11** indomitable, unfaltering, unshrinking **12** unhesitating

unfold 4 bare, show, tell **6** open up, reveal, unfurl, unroll, unveil, unwrap **7** divulge, explain, expound, lay open, open out, present, recount, uncover **8** describe, disclose, set forth **9** elucidate, explicate, make known, spread out **10** stretch out

unfolding 4 rise **5** birth, start **9** beginning, evolution, inception, unfurling **10** revelation **11** development

unforced 4 easy **5** frank **6** candid, casual **7** natural, relaxed

8 informal **9** easygoing **10** unaffected **13** unconstrained

unforeseen 6 abrupt, sudden **8** surprise **9** unplanned **10** accidental, surprising, unexpected, unintended **11** unlooked-for, unpredicted **12** out of the blue **13** unanticipated

unforeseen danger 7 pitfall **8** exigency **9** emergency **11** contingency

unforgettable 7 notable **8** eventful, exciting **9** important, memorable, thrilling **10** noteworthy **11** significant

unfortunate 5 sorry **6** cursed, jinxed, woeful **7** hapless, unblest, unhappy, unlucky **8** ill-fated, ill-timed, luckless, untimely, wretched **10** disastrous, ill-advised, ill-starred **11** inopportune, regrettable, unfavorable **12** inauspicious, infelicitous, unpropitious, unprosperous, unsuccessful

unfounded 4 idle **5** false **6** untrue **8** baseless, spurious **9** erroneous **10** fabricated, groundless

unfrequented 5 empty **6** lonely **7** remote, uncouth **8** isolated, solitary **9** unvisited **11** out-of-the-way **16** off the beaten path

unfriendly 4 cold **5** aloof **6** at odds, chilly **7** distant, haughty, hostile, warlike **8** inimical, snobbish **9** on the outs, reclusive, withdrawn **10** ungracious, unsociable **11** belligerent, contentious, quarrelsome, uncongenial **12** antagonistic, disagreeable, disputatious, inhospitable **13** at loggerheads, at sword's point, unsympathetic

unfruitful 4 vain **6** barren, fallow, futile **7** useless, worn-out **8** infecund **9** fruitless **10** unavailing **11** purposeless, unrewarding **12** impoverished, unproductive, unprofitable **14** unremunerative

unfulfilled 8 thwarted **10** frustrated, unrealized **11** unsatisfied
  French: **6** manque

unfurl 4 open **6** expand, spread, unfold, unroll **7** develop, roll out **8** shake out **9** spread out

ungainly 5 stiff **6** clumsy, klutzy **7** awkward **9** lumbering, maladroit **10** ungraceful **13** uncoordinated

ungallant 4 rude **7** boorish, uncivil, uncouth **8** impolite **9** uncourtly **10** ill-behaved, un-

gracious, unmannerly **11** ill-mannered, uncourteous **12** discourteous **13** ungentlemanly

ungenerous 4 mean, near **5** close, cruel, petty, small, venal **6** greedy, shabby, sordid, stingy **7** miserly, selfish, sparing **8** churlish, covetous, cowardly, grudging **9** illiberal, mercenary, niggardly, penurious, rapacious **10** avaricious **11** small-minded **12** narrow-minded, parsimonious, uncharitable

ungifted 8 mediocre **9** unskilled **10** amateurish, unskillful, untalented **14** unaccomplished

unglue 6 unseal **7** peel off, unstick **9** pull apart

ungodly 4 base, vile **5** awful **6** rotten, sinful, wicked **7** corrupt, ghastly, godless, heinous, immoral, impious **8** depraved, dreadful, terrible **9** dissolute **10** degenerate, horrendous, iniquitous, outrageous, villainous **11** blasphemous **12** dishonorable, unreasonable

ungovernable 6 unruly **7** defiant, froward, naughty, wayward **8** contrary, mutinous, perverse, stubborn **9** fractious, obstinate **10** disorderly, rebellious, refractory **11** disobedient, intractable **12** noncompliant, recalcitrant, unmanageable, unsubmissive

ungraceful 5 inept **6** clumsy **7** awkward **9** inelegant

ungracious 4 rude **5** bluff, blunt, gruff, harsh, short **6** abrupt, coarse, crusty, vulgar **7** boorish, brusque, loutish, uncivil, uncouth **8** churlish, grudging, impolite **9** uncourtly, ungallant **10** ill-behaved, unladylike, unmannerly **11** bad-mannered, ill-mannered, impertinent, uncourteous **12** disagreeable, discourteous, inhospitable **13** disrespectful, ungentlemanly

unguarded 6 unwary **8** careless, tactless, too frank **9** imprudent, unmindful, unwatched **10** incautious, indiscreet, undefended **11** defenseless, unpatrolled, unprotected **12** undiplomatic, unrestrained **13** ill-considered, uncircumspect

unguent 4 balm **5** cream, salve **6** lotion **8** ointment **9** emollient

ungulate 2 ox **3** cow, gnu, hog, pig, yak **4** boar, calf, deer, goat, ibex **5** camel, daman, horse, llama, tapir **6** hoofed, vicuna **7** buffalo, caribou, giraffe, peccary **8** antelope, elephant, hooflike, ruminant **9** dromedary **10** hartebeest, rhinoceros, wildebeest **12** hippopotamus

unhampered 4 free **8** expedite **9** unimpeded **10** unconfined **12** unencumbered, unrestrained, unrestricted

unhandy 5 inept **6** clumsy, gauche, klutzy **7** awkward **8** bumbling, fumbling, inexpert, unwieldy **9** all thumbs, ham-handed, maladroit, unskilled **10** cumbersome, unskillful **11** inefficient **12** inconvenient, unmanageable **14** butterfingered

unhappiness 3 woe **5** grief **6** misery, sorrow **7** anguish, sadness **8** distress **9** heartache

unhappy 3 bad, sad **4** blue, poor **5** inapt, sorry **6** gloomy, somber, unwise **7** adverse, awkward, doleful, foolish, forlorn, hapless, joyless, unlucky **8** dejected, downcast, luckless, unseemly **9** depressed, imprudent, long-faced, sorrowful, woebegone **10** despondent, dispirited, ill-advised, melancholy, unbecoming, unsuitable **11** crestfallen, injudicious, regrettable, unbefitting, unfortunate **12** heavyhearted, infelicitous, unsuccessful **13** inappropriate **14** down in the mouth

unharmed 5 whole **6** unhurt **9** uninjured, unscathed, untouched **10** in one piece, unaffected **14** with a whole skin

unhealthy 3 bad **4** sick, weak **6** ailing, feeble, infirm, morbid, poorly, sickly, unwell **7** harmful, hurtful, invalid, not well, noxious, unsound **8** depraved, diseased, negative, perilous **9** dangerous, degrading, hazardous **10** corrupting, indisposed, morally bad **11** destructive, detrimental, undesirable, unhealthful, unwholesome **12** demoralizing, in poor health, insalubrious **13** contaminating

unheard-of 3 odd **4** rare **6** unique **7** amazing, curious, unknown, unusual **8** freakish, original, singular, uncommon **9** irregular, matchless **10** incredible, outlandish, outrageous, phenomenal, unexpected **11** exceptional **12** incomparable, preposterous, unbelievable, unparalleled, un-

reasonable **13** extraordinary, inconceivable, unprecedented

unheated 3 icy **4** cold **6** chilly, drafty, frosty **7** ice-cold **8** unwarmed

unheeding 7 ignored **8** mindless **12** disregarding

unhelpful 7 of no use, useless **8** in the way **9** hindering **11** disobliging **13** inconsiderate, uncooperative

unheralded 6 unsung **10** unexpected, unforeseen **11** unacclaimed, unannounced, unlooked-for **12** unproclaimed, unpublicized, unrecognized **13** unanticipated

unhesitating 5 eager, quick, ready **6** direct, prompt **9** immediate **10** unreserved **11** unflinching **12** wholehearted, without delay **13** instantaneous **18** without reservation

unhinge 6 detach **7** disrupt **8** separate, unsettle **9** disengage, dislocate, disorient, unbalance **10** disconnect **13** disarticulate

unhitch 6 detach **8** separate, uncouple, unfasten **9** disengage **10** disconnect

unhitched 8 detached **9** uncoupled **10** unfastened **12** disconnected

unholy 4 base, evil, vile **5** awful **6** rotten, sinful, wicked **7** corrupt, heinous, immoral, ungodly **8** depraved, dreadful, shocking **9** dishonest **10** horrendous, iniquitous, outrageous, villainous **12** dishonorable, unreasonable

Unholy Loves
    author: **15** Joyce Carol Oates

unhurried 4 easy, slow **7** gradual **9** leisurely **10** deliberate, slow-moving

unicorn
    form: **5** horse
    feature: **4** horn
    symbolizes: **6** purity
        8 chastity
    constellation of: **9** Monoceros

unidentified 5 vague **7** unknown, unnamed **8** nameless **9** anonymous, unlabeled **11** unspecified **12** undesignated, unrecognized

unification 5 union, unity **6** fusion, merger **7** uniting **8** alliance, junction **9** coalition, combining **11** coalescence, combination, confederacy **12** amalgamation **13** confederation, consolidating, consolidation, incorporation

uniform 4 even, garb **5** alike, array, at one, dress, equal, habit **6** attire, in line, in step, livery **7** apparel, costume, regalia, regular, similar, the same **8** agreeing, constant, in accord, of a piece, unvaried, vestment **9** consonant, identical, of one mind, unaltered, unvarying **10** conforming, consistent, harmonious, unchanging **11** regimentals, undeviating

uniformity 8 equality, monotony, sameness **10** consonance **11** consistency, equivalency, homogeneity **15** standardization

unify 3 wed **4** ally, fuse, join **5** blend, merge, unite **6** couple, link up **7** combine **8** coalesce, federate **10** amalgamate **11** confederate, consolidate, form into one, incorporate **12** lump together **13** bring together

unilluminated 3 dim **4** dark **5** murky, unlit **6** gloomy **7** obscure **8** darkened **9** lightless, unlighted

unimaginable 10 incredible **12** unbelievable **13** inconceivable **16** incomprehensible

unimaginative 4 dull **5** stale, stock, trite, usual, vapid **6** dreary **7** cliched, humdrum, prosaic, routine, tedious **8** everyday, mediocre, ordinary **9** hackneyed **10** pedestrian, uncreative, unexciting, uninspired, unoriginal, unromantic **11** commonplace, predictable **12** run-of-the-mill, unremarkable **13** uninteresting

unimpaired 4 good **5** clear, sound **6** intact, unhurt **8** unbroken, unharmed **9** uninjured, unscathed, unspoiled **10** undeformed

unimpassioned 4 calm, cool **6** placid, serene, stolid **7** unmoved **8** detached, unloving **9** apathetic, impassive, objective, unexcited **11** indifferent, unemotional **13** dispassionate

unimpeachable 4 pure **5** clean, solid **7** perfect **8** reliable, spotless, unmarred **9** blameless, faultless, inviolate, stainless, undefiled, untainted **10** immaculate, impeccable, inculpable, infallible **11** trustworthy, unblemished **12** unassailable **13** above reproach, totally honest **14** beyond question, irreproachable, unquestionable **15** beyond criticism, unchallengeable

unimportant 5 minor **6** lesser,

meager, paltry, slight **7** trivial **8** inferior, mediocre, not vital, nugatory, piddling, trifling **10** immaterial, irrelevant, low-ranking, negligible, of no moment, second-rate **11** subordinate **12** nonessential, not important **13** insignificant **14** inconsiderable **15** inconsequential, of no consequence

uninformed 6 unread **7** unaware **8** ignorant **9** in the dark, not with it, unadvised, unknowing, unlearned **10** uneducated, unschooled **12** unconversant, uninstructed **13** unenlightened

uninhabited 5 empty **6** vacant **8** deserted, forsaken **9** abandoned, unlived in, unpeopled, unsettled **10** unoccupied, untenanted **11** unpopulated

uninhibited 4 fast, free, open, rash **6** frank **6** candid, daring, madcap, not shy, unwary **8** careless, heedless, immodest, reckless, uncurbed, unreined **9** abandoned, impetuous, impulsive, outspoken, unbridled, unchecked, unguarded, unimpeded, unstopped **10** capricious, flamboyant, forthright, headstrong, incautious, indiscreet, unhampered, unhindered, unreserved **11** instinctive, plainspoken, spontaneous **12** free-spirited, uncontrolled, unobstructed, unrestrained, unrestricted **13** unconstrained **15** straightforward, unself-conscious

uninjured 5 whole **6** intact, unhurt **8** unharmed **9** unscathed, untouched **10** in one piece **14** with a whole skin

uninspired 4 dull **5** stale, stock, trite, vapid **7** cliched, humdrum, prosaic, unmoved **8** ordinary **9** hackneyed, unexcited, unstirred, untouched **10** pedestrian, unaffected, unexciting, unoriginal **11** commonplace, indifferent, predictable, unemotional, unimpressed **12** run-of-the-mill, uninfluenced, unstimulated **13** unimaginative, uninteresting

uninspiring 4 dull **5** bland, stale **6** boring **7** insipid, prosaic **10** lackluster **13** uninteresting

uninstructive 6 barren **9** unhelpful **10** unedifying **12** unproductive **13** uninformative

unintelligent 4 dull, dumb, slow **5** blank, dense, dopey, thick **6** obtuse, stupid **7** asinine, doltish, idiotic, moronic **8** retarded **9** cretinous, dim-

witted, imbecilic **10** dull-witted, half-witted, slow-witted **11** blockheaded, thickheaded **12** simpleminded

unintelligible 8 baffling, puzzling **9** confusing, illegible, insoluble **10** incoherent, perplexing **11** meaningless **12** impenetrable, inarticulate, unfathomable **14** undecipherable **16** incomprehensible

unintentional 9 unplanned, unwitting **10** accidental, fortuitous, undesigned, unintended, unthinking **11** inadvertent, involuntary, unconscious **14** unpremeditated

uninterested 5 aloof, blase **6** remote **8** heedless, listless, uncaring **9** apathetic, incurious, unmindful **10** above it all, uninvolved **11** indifferent, unconcerned **13** unimpressible

uninteresting 3 dry **4** drab, dull **5** trite, vapid **6** boring, dreary, jejune **7** humdrum, insipid, prosaic, tedious **8** lifeless, ordinary, tiresome, unmoving **9** colorless, wearisome **10** monotonous, pedestrian, uneventful **11** uninspiring **12** unsatisfying **13** insignificant

uninterrupted 8 unbroken **9** ceaseless, continual, incessant **10** continuous **11** unremitting

uninviting 8 annoying **9** offensive **10** unalluring, unpleasant, untempting **11** displeasing, distasteful, unappealing, undesirable, unwelcoming **12** disagreeable, unappetizing, unattractive

uninvolved 4 easy **5** clear **6** simple **7** neutral, obvious, outside **8** detached **9** impartial **10** unaffected **13** disinterested, dispassionate, uncomplicated

union 5 blend, guild, unity **6** fusion, league, merger **7** amalgam, joining, mixture, oneness, uniting, wedding **8** alliance, marriage, unifying **9** synthesis **10** federation, fraternity **11** affiliation, association, combination, corporation, partnership, unification **12** amalgamation **13** confederation, consolidation
  type: **5** craft, labor, trade

unique 8 by itself, peerless, singular **9** matchless, nonpareil, unequaled, unmatched, unrivaled **10** inimitable, one of a kind, surpassing, unexampled, unexcelled **11** distinctive, unsurpassed **12** incomparable, unapproached, unparalleled

unit 4 part **5** group, whole **6** entity, member **7** element, measure, package, section, segment **8** category, division, quantity **9** component **10** detachment **11** constituent, measurement **12** denomination

Unitas, Johnny
  nickname: 7 Johnny U
  sport: 8 football
  position: 11 quarterback
  team: 14 Baltimore Colts

unite 4 ally, fuse, join, pool **5** blend, merge, unify **6** couple **7** combine **8** coalesce, federate, lock arms, organize **10** amalgamate, homogenize, join forces **11** confederate, consolidate, incorporate **12** join together, lump together **13** stand together

united 3 one **5** fused **6** allied, joined, merged, pooled **7** blended, coupled, leagued, unified **8** combined **9** federated, of one mind, unanimous **10** collective **11** amalgamated, in agreement **12** consolidated, incorporated **14** joined together, lumped together

---

United Arab Emirates
  other name: 11 Pirate Coast, Trucial Oman **13** Trucial States
  capital/largest city: 8 Abu Dhabi
  others: 5 Ajman, Dubai, Kalba, Tarif **6** Sharja **7** Fujaira **11** Ras al Khaima **12** Umm al Qaiwain
  division: 5 Ajman, Dibai, Dubai **6** Sharja **7** Fujaira, Sharjah **8** Abu Dhabi, Fujairah **11** Ras al Khaima, Umm al Qaiwan **12** Ral al Khaimah, Umm al-Qaiwain
  monetary unit: 3 fil **6** dirham
  highest point: 5 Hafit
  physical feature:
    desert: **10** Rub al Khali
    gulf: **4** Oman **7** Persian
    oasis: **7** Buraimi **9** Al Buraymi
    peninsula: **7** Arabian
  people: 4 Arab **6** Indian **7** African, Iranian **9** Pakistani **10** South Asian
  leader: **22** Zaid Bin Sultan al-Nahayan
  language: 5 Farsi **6** Arabic **7** English, Persian
  religion: 5 Islam
  war: 4 Gulf **11** Desert Storm

United Kingdom *see*
7 England

United States *see box*

unity 5 peace, union **6** accord,
entity, fusion, league, merger
7 concord, harmony, joining,
oneness, rapport **8** alliance,
goodwill **9** synthesis, unanimity, wholeness **10** federation,
fellowship, friendship **11** affiliation, association, cooperation,
partnership, unification
12 amalgamation, amicableness **13** compatibility, confederation, consolidation,
understanding **14** like-
mindedness

universal 7 general **9** worldwide **10** ubiquitous, widespread **11** omnipresent
12 affecting all, all-embracing,
all-inclusive **13** international

Universal creator
Egyptian: **4** Ptah

universality 8 currency
10 prevalence **12** predominance **17** comprehensiveness

universe
god of: **6** Amen Ra, Amon
Ra

university 6 campus, school
7 academy, college
11 institution
British: **6** Oxford **9** Cambridge
Cambridge: **7** Harvard
former: **9** alma mater
French: **8** Sorbonne
Hanover: **9** Dartmouth
lecturer: **9** prelector
New Haven: **4** Yale
New Jersey: **9** Princeton
New York: **8** Columbia
Providence: **5** Brown
session: **4** term **7** seminar
8 semester
Wit: **4** Lyly, Nash **5** Peele
6 Greene

unjust 6 biased, unfair,
warped **7** partial **8** one-sided,
partisan, wrongful **9** unmer-
ited **10** prejudiced, unbalanced,
undeserved **11** inequitable, unjustified, unwarranted

unjustifiable 11 inexcusable
12 indefensible

unjustly 7 falsely, wrongly
8 unfairly **10** wrongfully
11 dishonestly, faithlessly, in-
equitably **12** undeservedly

unkempt 5 messy **6** sloppy, untidy **7** rumpled, tousled
8 mussed-up, slovenly, uncombed **9** ungroomed **10** disheveled, disordered
11 disarranged

unkind 4 mean **5** nasty **7** abusive **8** uncaring **9** malicious,
unfeeling **10** unfriendly, un-

generous, ungracious **11** insensitive, thoughtless
12 inhospitable, uncharitable
13 inconsiderate,
unsympathetic

unknot 5 untie **7** unsnarl **8** untangle **11** disentangle

unknowable 12 inaccessible
13 inconceivable

unknown 7 obscure, unnamed
8 nameless **9** anonymous,
unheard-of **10** unrenowned
12 uncelebrated, undesignated,
undetermined, undiscovered,
unidentified

Unknown authors
author of: **4** Edda (elder)
7 Beowulf **8** Everyman, King
Horn, Stasimon **10** Cinderella **11** Poema del Cid
12 Panchatantra, Vercelli
Book, Volsunga Saga
14 Gesta Romanorum, Sibylline Books **15** Chanson de
Roland, The Forty Thieves,
The Song of Roland
16 Grettir the Strong **17** The
Nibelungenlied **20** Aucassin
and Nicolette, Robin Hood's
Adventures **23** The Dream
of the Red Chamber, The
Thousand and One Nights
26 Sir Gawain and the
Green Knight **29** Collection
of Ten Thousand Leaves
29 The Arabian Nights'
Entertainment

unladylike 4 rude **6** coarse,
common, vulgar **7** ill-bred, uncouth **8** impolite **10** unmannerly **12** discourteous

unlawful 7 illegal, illegit, illicit,
lawless **8** criminal **9** forbidden
10 prohibited, unlicensed, unofficial **12** unauthorized
13 against the law
16 unconstitutional

unlawful act 5 crime **6** felony **10** wrongdoing **11** lawbreaking, malfeasance,
misdemeanor

unleash 4 free **5** let go **7** release, set free **8** let loose, liberate **12** give free rein

unlettered 8 ignorant, untaught **9** unlearned, untutored
10 illiterate, uneducated, unschooled **11** unscholarly

unlighted 3 dim **4** dark
5 murky, unlit **6** gloomy
7 stygian, sunless **8** moonless
9 lightless **13** unilluminated

unlikable, unlikeable 7 hateful **9** offensive, unlovable
10 hard to like, unloveable,
unpleasant **11** displeasing, unappealing **12** disagreeable

unlike 7 diverse, unalike, un-

equal **9** different, disparate
10 dissimilar

unlikelihood 12 doubtfulness,
unlikeliness **13** improbability

unlikely 8 hopeless **10** improbable **11** unpromising **12** questionable, unbelievable,
unpropitious **19** scarcely
conceivable

unlikeness 8 contrast, variance **9** disparity, variation
10 difference, divergence
13 dissimilarity, dissimilitude

unlimited 4 huge, vast **5** total
7 endless, immense **8** absolute,
complete, infinite **9** boundless,
limitless, unbounded, un-
checked **11** unqualified **12** immeasurable, totalitarian,
uncontrolled, unrestrained, unrestricted **13** comprehensive,
inexhaustible, unconstrained
15 all-encompassing

unload 4 dump **7** off-load **8** get
rid of, unburden **9** dispose of
10 unencumber

unlooked for 6 sudden **7** unasked **8** surprise **10** unexpected, unforeseen,
unheralded **11** unannounced,
uncalled for, unpredicted, unsolicited **13** serendipitous,
unanticipated

unlovable, unloveable
7 hateful **9** unlikable **10** hard
to like, unlikeable, unpleas-
ant **11** displeasing, unappealing **12** disagreeable

unloving 4 cold, cool **6** frigid
11 indifferent, passionless
13 unimpassioned

unlucky 6 cursed, jinxed
7 hapless, unhappy **8** ill-fated,
luckless, untoward **9** ill-
omened **10** ill-starred **11** star-
crossed, unfortunate **12** inauspicious, misfortunate

unman 7 unnerve **8** castrate
10 discourage, emasculate

unmanageable 5 balky, bulky
6 mulish, unruly **7** awkward,
unhandy, wayward, willful
8 ungainly, unwieldy **9** fractious, pigheaded **10** cumbersome, rebellious, refractory
11 disobedient, intractable,
troublesome **12** incorrigible
14 uncontrollable

unmanly 5 timid **6** yellow
8 cowardly, sissyish, womanish **9** sissified, weak-kneed
10 effeminate **11** lily-livered,
unmasculine, weakhearted
12 fainthearted **13** pusillanimous **14** chickenhearted

unmannerly 5 crude, gross,
surly **6** coarse **7** boorish, ill-

United States
capital: 12 Washington DC
largest city: 11 New York City
others: 4 Nome **5** Miami **6** Boston, Dallas, El Paso **7** Chicago, Detroit, Houston, Memphis, Phoenix, San Jose, Seattle **8** Columbus, Honolulu, San Diego **9** Anchorage, Baltimore, Cleveland, Milwaukee **10** Los Angeles, New Orleans, San Antonio **12** Indianapolis, Jacksonville, Philadelphia, Salt Lake City, San Francisco
school: 3 MIT **4** Penn, Yale **5** Brown **6** Baylor, Drexel, Vassar **7** Amherst, Colgate, Cornell, Fordham, Harvard, Oberlin **8** Bryn Mawr, Columbia, Stanford, Wesleyan **9** Dartmouth, Princeton, Radcliffe **10** Bennington **12** Johns Hopkins, Mount Holyoke
division: 4 Iowa, Ohio, Utah **5** Idaho, Maine, Texas **6** Alaska, Hawaii, Kansas, Nevada, Oregon **7** Alabama, Arizona, Florida, Georgia, Indiana, Montana, New York, Vermont, Wyoming **8** Arkansas, Colorado, Delaware, Illinois, Kentucky, Maryland, Michigan, Missouri, Nebraska, Oklahoma, Virginia **9** Louisiana, Minnesota, New Jersey, New Mexico, Tennessee, Wisconsin **10** California, Puerto Rico, Washington **11** Connecticut, Mississippi, North Dakota, Rhode Island, South Dakota **12** New Hampshire, Pennsylvania, West Virginia **13** Massachusetts, North Carolina, South Carolina **18** District of Columbia
island: 4 Guam, Long, Maui, Oahu **5** Block, Ellis, Kauai, Lanai, Umnak **6** Hawaii, Kodiak, Niihau, Unimak, Virgin **7** Baranof, Key West, Long Key, Molokai, Nunivak, Sanibel **8** Aleutian, Hawaiian, Key Largo, Shumagin, Unalaska **9** Atka Amlia, Canal Zone, Chichagof, Kahoolawe, Nantucket, Snipe Keys **10** Islamorada, Oyster Keys, Puerto Rico, St Lawrence **11** Longboat Key **12** Santa Barbara **13** American Samoa, Marquesas Keys, Prince of Wales, Santa Catalina, Summerland Key **15** Martha's Vineyard **16** Cantout Enderbury **26** Trust Territory of the Pacific
lake: 4 Erie, Mead **5** Huron, Tahoe **6** Cayuga, Finger, George, Itasca, Oneida, Seneca **7** Iliamma, Ontario **8** Michigan, Superior **9** Champlain, Great Salt, Salton Sea, Teshekpuk, Winnebago **10** Okeechobee **11** Yellowstone **13** Pontchartrain, Wallenpaupack, Winnipesaukee **14** Lake of the Woods
mountain: 4 Hood **5** Coast, Green, Kenai, Ozark, Rocky, White **6** Alaska, Brooks, DeLong, Elbert, Helena, Mesabi, Pocono, Shasta **7** Cascade, Chugach, Foraker, Harvard, Kilauea, Massive, Olympic, Olympus, Rainier, St Elias, Whitney **8** Catskill, Davidson, Endicott, Katahdin, Mauna Loa, Mitchell, Ouachita, St Helens, Wrangell **9** Allegheny, Blue Ridge, Kuskokwim, North Peak, Pikes Peak **10** Black Hills, Blanca Peak, Grand Teton, Washington, Williamson **11** Appalachian, Santa Monica **12** Sierra Nevada **14** Berkshire Hills
highest point: 6 Denali **8** McKinley
river: 3 New, Red **4** Gila, Iowa, Milk, Ohio, Rock **5** Black, Cedar, Coosa, Flint, Grand, Green, James, Neuse, Osage, Pearl, Pecos, Snake, White, Yukon **6** Brazos, Hudson, Neches, Neosho, Nueces, Owybee, Pee Dee, Platte, Powder, Sabine, Salmon, Wabash **7** Alabama, Big Horn, John Day, Klamath, Potomac, Roanoke, San Juan, St Johns, Trinity **8** Arkansas, Big Black, Canadian, Cheyenne, Cimarron, Colorado, Columbia, Delaware, Humboldt, Illinois, Kentucky, Kootenay, Missouri, Niabrana, Ouachita, Savannah **9** Allegheny, Deschutes, Des Moines, Minnesota, Rio Grande, Smoky Hill, St Francis, Tennessee, Tombigbee, Wisconsin **10** Cumberland, Republican, Sacramento, San Joaquin, St Lawrence, Tallapoosa **11** Connecticut, Mississippi, North Platte, South Platte, Susquehanna, Yellowstone **12** Tallahatchie **14** Little Colorado, Little Missouri
sea: 6 Arctic, Bering **7** Pacific **8** Atlantic, Beaufort
physical feature:
  bay: **5** Tampa **7** Bristol, Prudhoe **8** Biscayne, Monterey **9** Apalachee **10** Chesapeake **12** San Francisco
  desert: **4** Gila **6** Mojave **7** Painted **8** Colorado, Vizcaino **9** Black Rock **11** Death Valley
  falls: **7** Niagara
  gulf: **6** Alaska, Mexico **10** California
  plain: **5** Great
  plateau: **8** Colorado, Piedmont **10** Cumberland **11** Appalachian
  strait: **6** Bering **7** Florida
people:
  architect: **4** Root **5** Davis **6** Upjohn, Wright **7** Burnham, Downing, Furness, Gilbert, Gropius, Latrobe **8** Bogardus, Holabird, Sullivan **9** Bullfinch, Jefferson **10** Richardson **14** Mies van der Rohe
  artist: **5** Henri, Homer, Leutz, Moses, Peale, Wyeth **6** Copley, Durand, Millet, Rothko, Stuart **7** Audubon, Cassatt, O'Keeffe, Pollock, Sargent **8** Whistler
  author: **3** Poe **4** Grey, Inge, Loos, Luce, West, Wouk **5** Aiken, Albee, Beach, Benet, Crane, Eliot, Frost, Guest, Harte, Hecht, James, Lewis, Oates, Odets, O'Hara, Paine, Pound, Stowe, Twain, Vidal, Welty, Wolfe, Wylie **6** Bellow, Bierce, Bryant, Cabell, Capote, Cather, Cooper, Cullen, Ferber, Holmes, Hughes, Irving, Kilmer, Lanier, London, Lowell, Mather, Millay, Miller, Norris, O'Neill, Porter, Styron, Updike, Wilder **7** Angelou, Baldwin, Clemens, Costain, Dreiser, Emerson, Gallico, Hammett, Hellman, Howells, Jeffers, Kerouac, Lardner, Malamud, Nabokov, Roethke, Stevens, Thoreau, Webster, Wharton, Whitman **8** Anderson, Bradbury, Caldwell, Cummings, Faulkner, Macleish, McCarthy, Melville, Michener, Mitchell, Morrison, Rawlings, Robinson, Sandburg, Schwartz, Sherwood, Sinclair, Teasdale, Whit-

(continued)

United States (*continued*)
tier, Williams **9** Burroughs, Dickinson, Dos Passos, Hawthorne, Hemingway, McCullers, Steinbeck **10** Fitzgerald, Longfellow, Tarkington
composer: **4** Ives, Kern **5** Cohan, Loewe, Sousa **6** Berlin, Foster, Joplin, Lerner, Porter **7** Copland, Gilbert, Rodgers **8** Gershwin, Sullivan **9** Bernstein **11** Hammerstein
explorer: **4** Byrd, Pike **5** Boone, Cabot, Clark, Lewis, Perry **6** Hudson, Joliet **7** Jolliet **8** Columbus **9** Marquette **10** Eric the Red
leader: **3** Jay **4** Clay, King, Penn **5** Bryan, Davis, Henry, Paine **6** Revere, Sumner **7** Stevens, Webster **8** Franklin, Humphrey **9** Goldwater
military leader: **3** Lee **4** Pike **5** Clark, Gates, Grant, Meade, Tyler **6** Austin, Custer, Marion, Patton **7** Bradley, Houston, Jackson, Sherman **8** Marshall, Pershing **9** MacArthur, Roosevelt, Stillwell **10** Eisenhower, Vandenburg, Washington **11** Schwarzkopf
president: **4** Bush, Ford, Polk, Taft **5** Adams, Grant, Hayes, Nixon, Tyler **6** Arthur, Carter, Hoover, Monroe, Pierce, Reagan, Taylor, Truman, Wilson **7** Clinton, Harding, Jackson, Johnson, Kennedy, Lincoln, Madison **8** Buchanan, Coolidge, Fillmore, Garfield, Hamilton, Harrison, McKinley, Van Buren **9** Cleveland, Jefferson, Roosevelt **10** Eisenhower, Washington
sculptor: **4** Rush **6** Calder, French, Rogers **7** Borglum **9** Greenough, Remington **12** Saint-Gaudens
language: **7** English, Spanish
religion: **5** Amish **6** Mormon **7** Baptist, Judaism, Shakers **8** Lutheran **9** Methodist **10** Protestant **11** Pentacostal **12** Episcopalian, Presbyterian **13** Roman Catholic **14** Church of Christ, Congregational **15** Eastern Orthodox, Latter Day Saints **19** Seventh Day Adventist
place:
national park: **4** Zion **5** Platt **6** Acadia **7** Big Bend, Glacier, Olympic, Redwood, Sequoia **8** Wind Cave, Yosemite **9** Haleakala, Mesa Verde, Multnomah **10** Crater Lake, Everglades, Grand Teton, Hot Springs, Isle Royale, Shenandoah **11** Bryce Canyon, Canyonlands, Grand Canyon, Kings Canyon, Mammoth Cave, Yellowstone **12** Mount Rainier **13** Mount McKinley, Virgin Islands **14** Lassen Volcanic, Rocky Mountains **15** Carlsbad Caverns, Petrified Forest **19** Great Smoky Mountains
possession: **4** Guam **10** Puerto Rico **13** American Samoa, Virgin Islands **14** Mariana Islands **15** Caroline Islands, Marshall Islands
feature:
colony: **7** Roanoke **8** Plymouth **9** Jamestown **11** Rhode Island **12** New Amsterdam, New Hampshire **14** New Netherlands **16** Massachusetts Bay
festival: **9** Mardi Gras
national symbol: **9** bald eagle
tree: **7** redwood, sequoia

---

bred, loutish, uncivil, uncouth **8** impolite **10** ungracious, unladylike **11** ill-mannered **12** badly behaved, discourteous **13** ungentlemanly

unmarked 5 clean, clear **9** undamaged, undefaced, unnoticed **10** unobserved **11** unblemished **15** undistinguished

unmarried 4 free **5** unwed **6** maiden, single **7** old maid, widowed **8** bachelor, divorced, spinster, unwedded, virginal, wifeless **9** available, fancy free **10** spouseless, unattached **11** husbandless **21** footloose and fancy-free

unmarried girl
French: **10** jeune fille
German: **8** fraulein
Spanish: **8** senorita

Unmarried Woman, An
director: **12** Paul Mazursky
cast: **9** Alan Bates **11** Cliff Gorman **13** Jill Clayburgh, Michael Murphy

unmask 4 bare, show **6** betray, expose, reveal, unveil **7** lay open, uncover **8** disclose, discover **12** bring to light

unmasking 6 baring **8** betrayal, exposure **9** discovery, unveiling **10** disclosure, laying open, revelation, uncovering **15** bringing to light

unmatched 6 unlike **7** diverse, supreme, unequal **8** peerless, variable **9** differing, disparate, matchless, unequaled **10** dissimilar **12** second to none, unparalleled **13** beyond compare

unmerciful 4 cold, evil **5** cruel, harsh **6** brutal, severe, unkind **7** brutish, extreme, inhuman **8** inhumane, pitiless, ruthless **9** excessive, heartless, inclement, merciless, unfeeling, unpitying, unsparing **10** malevolent, relentless **11** hardhearted **14** unconscionable

unmindful 3 lax **6** remiss **7** unaware **8** careless, derelict, heedless **9** forgetful, negligent,

oblivious, unheeding **11** thoughtless, unconscious

unmistakable 5 clear, plain **6** patent **7** evident, glaring, obvious **8** apparent, distinct, manifest, palpable **9** prominent **10** pronounced, undeniable **11** conspicuous, unequivocal **12** indisputable **14** unquestionable

unmistakably 7 clearly, plainly **8** palpably, patently **9** certainly, decidedly, downright, evidently, glaringly, obviously **10** definitely, distinctly, manifestly, positively, thoroughly, undeniably **11** prominently **12** indisputably **13** conspicuously, unequivocally **14** unquestionably **17** beyond all question

unmitigated 6 arrant **8** absolute, unabated, unbroken **9** downright, out-and-out **10** persistent, unrelieved **11** unqualified **12** unalleviated **13** uninterrupted

unmixed 4 neat, pure **5** sheer **6** simple **8** straight **9** unalloyed, unblended, undiluted, unmingled **13** unadulterated

unmoved 4 calm, cold, firm **5** aloof **6** dogged **7** devoted, staunch **8** resolute, resolved, uncaring, unshaken **9** dedicated, obstinate, steadfast, unfeeling, unpitying, unstirred, untouched **10** determined, inflexible, not shifted, persistent, relentless, unaffected, unswerving, unwavering **11** indifferent, unconcerned, undeviating, undisturbed, unfaltering **12** stonyhearted, uninterested, unresponsive **14** uncompromising

unmoving 4 dead, dull **5** fixed, inert, still **6** boring, serene **8** immobile **9** powerless **10** motionless, stationary **11** emotionless **13** at a standstill

unnamed 8 nameless, unsigned **9** anonymous, incognito **10** innominate, uncredited, unreported, unrevealed **11** undisclosed, unspecified **12** pseudonymous, undesignated, undiscovered, unidentified **14** unacknowledged

unnatural 4 fake **5** phony, put-on **6** forced **7** assumed, stilted, studied, unusual **8** aberrant, abnormal, affected, freakish, mannered, peculiar **9** anomalous, contrived **10** artificial, theatrical **13** self-conscious

unnecessary 5 extra **6** excess **7** surplus **8** needless, overmuch **9** auxiliary, excessive **10** expendable, gratuitous, unrequired **11** dispensable, superfluous, uncalled-for, unessential **13** supplementary

unnerve 5 daunt, scare, upset **7** agitate, unhinge **8** frighten, unsettle **10** intimidate

unnerving 5 scary **8** daunting **9** upsetting **10** enervating, unsettling **11** frightening

unnoticeable -3 dim **5** faint **6** hidden **7** obscure **9** concealed **10** indistinct, unassuming, unemphatic, unobserved **11** unobtrusive **12** undetectable **13** imperceptible, inconspicuous, insignificant, undiscernible **14** unostentatious

unnoticed 6 unfelt, unseen **7** unheard, unnoted **8** unheeded, untasted **10** not smelled, overlooked, unobserved **11** disregarded, unperceived **12** undiscovered

unobservant 4 dull **5** blind

8 unseeing **9** unmindful **11** incognizant

unobstructed 4 fair, free, open **5** clear **8** apparent **9** unimpeded **10** unhampered, unhindered **11** unprevented

unobtainable 9 hard to get **10** impossible, out of reach, out of touch **11** unavailable, unreachable **12** improcurable, inaccessible

unobtrusive 3 shy **6** humble, modest **7** bashful **8** reserved, reticent, retiring **9** diffident **10** unassuming **11** unassertive **13** inconspicuous, unpretentious **14** unostentatious

unoccupied 4 idle **5** empty **6** vacant **8** unfilled **9** abandoned, unengaged **10** untenanted **11** uninhabited

unofficial 8 informal **12** unauthorized

unorganized 5 loose **6** casual, random **7** aimless, chaotic **8** confused **9** haphazard, orderless, unordered **10** disjointed, unarranged, undirected **11** harum-scarum **12** unclassified, unsystematic **13** helter-skelter **14** unsystematized

unornamented 4 bald, bare **5** blank, naked, plain, stark **6** simple **7** austere **9** unadorned **11** undecorated **13** unembellished

unorthodox 7 erratic **9** eccentric, irregular **14** unconventional

unostentatious 3 shy **5** plain, quiet **6** humble, modest, simple **9** unadorned, unaffected **10** unassuming **11** constrained **13** inconspicuous, unpretentious **14** unpresumptuous

unpaid 3 due **4** owed **5** owing **9** in arrears **11** outstanding

unpaid debt 5 debit **7** arrears **9** liability **10** balance due, obligation **12** indebtedness

unpalatable 5 nasty **8** inedible, unsavory **9** repellent, repulsive **10** bad-tasting, unpleasant **11** displeasing, distasteful **12** disagreeable, unappetizing **13** hard to swallow

unparalleled 4 best, rare **5** alone, crack, elect **6** unique **8** gilt-edge, peerless, singular **9** matchless, superfine, unequaled, unmatched, unrivaled **10** crackajack, inimitable, unimitated **11** unsurpassed **12** unapproached **13** unprecedented **15** of the first water

unperceptive 5 blind **9** unfeeling **11** insensitive, unobservant **12** imperceptive, impercipient **13** unsympathetic

unperturbed 4 calm, cool **6** poised **8** composed, tranquil **9** collected, unexcited, unruffled **10** coolheaded, nonchalant, unagitated, undismayed, untroubled **11** levelheaded, undisturbed **13** unimpassioned

unplanned 9 impromptu **10** accidental, fortuitous, improvised, unexpected, unforeseen **11** spontaneous **12** uncalculated **13** unintentional **14** extemporaneous, unpremeditated **15** spur-of-the-moment

unpleasant 5 nasty, pesky **7** irksome, noisome **8** annoying, churlish **9** obnoxious, offensive, repugnant, repulsive, unlikable, vexatious **10** ill-humored, ill-natured **11** displeasing, distasteful **12** disagreeable, unattractive **13** objectionable

unpleasantness 8 ugliness **9** ill nature, nastiness **12** churlishness **13** obnoxiousness, offensiveness, repulsiveness **15** distastefulness **16** disagreeableness, unattractiveness

unpointed 4 dull **5** blunt **6** dulled **11** unsharpened

unpolished 3 raw **5** gawky, inept, rough **6** cloudy, clumsy **7** amateur, awkward, unwaxed **8** inexpert, unbuffed, unglazed, unshined **9** inelegant, unrefined, unskilled **10** uncultured, unfinished, unskillful **11** unburnished, unpracticed **12** uncultivated **13** inexperienced **14** unaccomplished **15** unsophisticated

unpopular 7 snubbed **8** disliked, rebuffed, rejected, slighted, unwanted **9** disdained, neglected, unwelcome **10** unaccepted **11** disapproved, undesirable **12** looked down on, unacceptable

unpopulated 5 rural **9** backwoods, unpeopled, unsettled

unprecedented 5 novel **6** unique **9** unheard-of **10** unexampled **11** exceptional **12** unparalleled **13** extraordinary **15** hitherto unknown

unpredictable 6 fitful **7** erratic **8** fanciful, unstable, variable **9** arbitrary, eccentric, impulsive, mercurial, uncertain, whimsical **10** capricious, changeable, inconstant

unprejudiced 4 fair, just 8 unbiased, unswayed 9 impartial, objective, unbigoted 10 evenhanded, fair-minded, open-minded, undogmatic 11 broadminded 12 uninfluenced 13 disinterested

unpremeditated 5 ad-lib 9 impetuous, impromptu, impulsive, unplanned 10 accidental, improvised, unintended 11 involuntary, spontaneous 12 uncalculated, unthought-out 13 unintentional 14 extemporaneous 15 spur-of-the-moment

unprepared 5 ad-lib 7 offhand, unready 8 off guard 9 extempore, impromptu 10 flat-footed, improvised 11 spontaneous, unrehearsed 14 extemporaneous 15 spur-of-the-moment

unprepossessing 4 grim 5 seedy 10 ill-favored, ill-looking 12 unattractive

unpressed 5 baggy 6 mussed, sloppy 7 creased, rumpled 8 unironed, wrinkled 9 shapeless, uncreased

unpretentious 5 plain 6 homely, humble, modest, simple 10 unassuming, unimposing 11 unelaborate, unobtrusive 14 unostentatious

unprincipled 6 amoral 12 unscrupulous 14 conscienceless, unconscionable

unproductive 4 poor 6 barren 7 sterile, useless 8 bootless 9 infertile 10 unfruitful, unyielding 11 ineffective, ineffectual, inefficient 12 unprofitable

unprofessional 6 shoddy, sloppy 7 amateur 8 bungling, careless 9 negligent, unethical 10 amateurish 11 incompetent, inefficient, unpracticed 12 unprincipled 13 inexperienced, undisciplined, unworkmanlike 14 unbusinesslike

unprofitable 4 vain 7 useless 8 bootless 11 ineffective, ineffectual

unprogressive 7 diehard 8 backward, standpat, stubborn 9 benighted, right-wing 11 reactionary, reactionist 12 conservative 17 ultraconservative

unprolific 6 barren 7 sterile 9 infertile, unfertile 10 nonbearing 12 unproductive

unpromising 5 bleak 9 ill-omened 10 forbidding 11 unfavorable 12 inauspicious, unpropitious

unpropitious 7 adverse 8 contrary 9 unfitting 10 unsuitable 11 unfavorable 12 antagonistic, inauspicious, infelicitous

unprotected 4 open 5 naked 6 unsafe 7 exposed, unarmed 8 helpless, insecure, perilous 9 dangerous, hazardous, unguarded 10 undefended, vulnerable 11 defenseless

unproven 7 in doubt 8 arguable, doubtful 10 indefinite, in question, up in the air 11 open to doubt, unconfirmed 12 experimental, inconclusive, questionable 13 unestablished 14 open to question

unpunctual 4 late 5 tardy 7 belated 10 behindhand, behindtime

unqualified 5 total, unfit, utter 8 absolute, complete, inexpert, positive, thorough, unsuited 9 downright, out-and-out, unskilled, untrained 10 consummate, undisputed, uneducated, unprepared, unschooled 11 ill-equipped, incompetent 13 inexperienced, unconditional

unquenched 8 unslaked 11 unsatisfied 14 unextinguished

unquestionable 4 sure 5 clear, plain 6 proven 7 certain, evident, obvious, perfect 8 definite, flawless 9 blameless, errorless, faultless 10 impeccable, undeniable 11 beyond doubt, irrefutable, self-evident, unequivocal 12 indisputable, uncensurable 13 uncontestable, unimpeachable 14 irreproachable

unquestionably 6 surely 7 totally 9 certainly, doubtless 10 absolutely, completely, definitely, positively, unarguably 12 conclusively, indisputably, without doubt 13 unequivocally

unravel 4 undo 5 feaze, solve 6 unfold, unfurl, unknit 7 clear up, resolve 8 decipher, separate, untangle 9 pull apart 10 disinvolve 11 disentangle

unreachable 10 impossible, out of touch 11 out of the way, unavailable, unrealistic 12 inaccessible, unobtainable 14 unapproachable

unreal 4 airy 5 dream 6 dreamy 7 ghostly, not real, phantom, shadowy 8 ethereal, illusive, illusory, imagined, spectral 9 dreamlike, fantastic,

imaginary, legendary 10 chimerical, fictitious, idealistic, intangible 11 nonexistent 13 insubstantial 16 phantasmagorical

unrealistic 4 wild 5 crazy, silly 6 absurd 7 asinine, foolish 8 crackpot, delusory, fanciful 9 illogical 10 idealistic, improbable, infeasible, starry-eyed 11 impractical 12 unreasonable

unrealized 8 thwarted 10 frustrated, incomplete 11 nonexistent, unfulfilled, unsatisfied 14 unaccomplished

unreasonable 5 undue 6 absurd, biased, mulish, unfair 7 bigoted 8 obdurate, stubborn, too great 9 excessive, fanatical, illogical, obstinate, pig-headed, senseless, unbending 10 bullheaded, exorbitant, far-fetched, headstrong, immoderate, inflexible, inordinate, irrational, prejudiced, unyielding 11 extravagant, intractable, nonsensical, opinionated, uncalled-for, unwarranted 12 closed-minded, preposterous, ungovernable, unmanageable 13 unjustifiable

unreasoning 8 careless, heedless 9 impulsive 10 irrational, unthinking 11 thoughtless 13 unintelligent

unrecognizable 9 disguised, incognito 10 in disguise 11 camouflaged 14 unidentifiable

unrecognized 6 unsung 7 cryptic, unknown 9 incognito, unnoticed

unrefined 3 raw 5 crude, rough 6 coarse, vulgar 7 boorish, low-bred 9 inelegant

unrehearsed 7 offhand 8 informal 9 extempore, impromptu, impulsive, unplanned, unstudied 10 improvised, off-the-cuff, unprepared 11 extemporary, spontaneous 14 extemporaneous, unpremeditated 15 improvisational, spur-of-the-moment 19 off the top of one's head

unrelated 6 not kin, unlike 7 foreign 8 unallied 10 dissimilar, extraneous, irrelevant, non-germane 11 unconnected 12 inapplicable, incompatible, unassociated 13 inappropriate

unrelenting 5 rigid 6 steady 7 adamant, endless 8 constant, unabated, unbroken 9 ceaseless, incessant, tenacious, unbending 10 implacable, inexorable, inflexible, relentless, unrelieved, unswerving, unwavering, unyielding **11** undeviating, unremitting **14** uncompromising

unreliable 4 fake **5** false, phony **6** fickle **8** fallible, mistaken, unstable **9** deceitful, erroneous, uncertain **10** capricious, changeable, inaccurate, inconstant **12** questionable, undependable **13** irresponsible, untrustworthy

unremarkable 5 usual **6** common **7** average **8** everyday, mediocre, ordinary **11** commonplace **12** unimpressive, unsurprising **13** insignificant, unexceptional **15** undistinguished

unremitting 6 dogged **8** constant, tireless, untiring **9** ceaseless, continual, incessant, unceasing **10** continuous, persistent **11** persevering

unrepentant 7 callous **8** hardened, obdurate, unatoned **9** unashamed **10** uncontrite, unexpiated **11** remorseless **12** incorrigible, unregenerate

unrepressed 4 free, open **7** liberal **8** effusive, outgoing **9** expansive, exuberant **11** extroverted, uninhibited **12** unrestrained

unreserved 4 full, open **5** frank **6** entire **11** unqualified **12** wholehearted

unresolved 4 moot **5** vague **7** pending **8** doubtful, unsolved **9** tentative, uncertain, undecided, unsettled **10** disputable, unanswered **11** contestable, speculative **12** questionable, undetermined **13** problematical, unascertained

unresponsive 4 cold, cool, dull, limp **5** inert **6** frigid **7** passive **8** lifeless **9** apathetic, unfeeling **11** cold-blooded, inattentive, indifferent, unemotional **12** dispassionate, unsympathetic

unresponsiveness 6 apathy **7** inertia **9** lassitude, passivity **11** inattention, passiveness **12** indifference

unrest 5 chaos **6** tumult **7** anarchy, discord, ferment, protest, turmoil **8** disorder, disquiet, upheaval **9** agitation, rebellion **10** discontent, turbulence **12** restlessness **15** dissatisfaction

unrestrained 8 uncurbed **9** abandoned, boundless, excessive, unbridled, unchecked, unlimited **10** immoderate, in-

ordinate, unfettered, ungoverned, unhampered, unhindered, unreserved **11** extravagant, intemperate, uninhibited, unrepressed **12** uncontrolled, unrestricted, unsuppressed **13** irrepressible

unrestraint 6 excess **7** abandon **9** uncontrol **10** unruliness **12** extravagance, immoderation, recklessness **13** excessiveness, impulsiveness

unrestricted 8 absolute, complete **9** out-and-out, unbounded, unlimited **11** unqualified **12** unrestrained **13** unconditional

unrigid 3 lax **4** easy, limp, soft **5** loose **6** giving, limber, mobile, pliant, supple **7** elastic, lenient, plastic, pliable **8** flexible, informal, merciful, tolerant, yielding **9** indulgent, malleable **11** conformable

unrigorous 4 easy **5** loose, slack **6** casual, sloppy **7** inexact **8** careless, slapdash **9** imprecise

unripe 5 green **8** immature **10** unseasoned **11** undeveloped **14** underdeveloped

unrivaled 8 superior, topnotch **9** unequaled **10** undisputed **11** unsurpassed

unroll 6 reveal, uncoil, unfold, unfurl, unwind **7** display, lay open, play out **9** spread out

unruffled 4 calm, cool, even, mild **5** quiet, still **6** placid, serene, smooth **8** composed, tranquil **9** collected **10** coolheaded, nonchalant, unagitated, untroubled **11** undisturbed, unperturbed **13** self-possessed

unruly 4 wild **5** rowdy **7** restive, wayward, willful **8** contrary, perverse **9** fractious, unbridled **10** boisterous, disorderly, headstrong, refractory **11** disobedient, intractable **12** obstreperous, ungovernable, unmanageable **13** undisciplined **14** uncontrollable

unsafe 5 risky **7** exposed **8** insecure, perilous **9** dangerous, hazardous, unguarded **10** undefended, unreliable, vulnerable **11** defenseless, treacherous, unprotected **13** untrustworthy

unsatisfactory 4 poor **5** inept, unfit **8** below par, inferior, unworthy **9** deficient **10** inadequate, ineligible, unsuitable **12** inadmissible, unacceptable **13** inappropriate

unsavory 3 bad **4** flat, foul **5** nasty **7** insipid, tainted

9 tasteless **10** bad-tasting, nauseating, unpleasant **11** distasteful, unpalatable **12** disagreeable, unappetizing

unscathed 5 sound, whole **6** entire, intact, unhurt **7** perfect **8** unharmed **9** uninjured, untouched **10** unimpaired **11** unscratched **13** all in one piece

unscholarly 8 ignorant **9** unlearned **10** illiterate, uneducated, uninformed **11** illinformed **13** unintelligent

unschooled 3 raw **5** green **6** callow **8** ignorant, untaught **9** unlearned **10** illiterate, uneducated, uninformed, unlettered, unseasoned **11** uninitiated **13** inexperienced

unscrupulous 5 sharp **6** amoral **7** crooked, devious, immoral **9** unethical **12** dishonorable, unprincipled

unseasonable 6 too hot **7** too cold, too warm **8** abnormal, untimely

unseasoned 3 raw **5** bland, green, plain **6** callow **7** untried **8** immature **13** inexperienced

unseeing 5 blind **7** unaware **9** oblivious, sightless **11** unobservant

unseemly 4 rude **5** crude, gross **6** coarse, vulgar **7** boorish, loutish **8** churlish, improper, indecent, unworthy **9** incorrect, offensive, tasteless **10** indecorous, indelicate, out of place, unbecoming, unladylike, unsuitable **11** distasteful, ill-mannered, unbefitting, undignified **12** discourteous, disreputable **13** discreditable, inappropriate, reprehensible, ungentlemanly

unselfconscious 7 artless **10** unaffected **13** unpretentious

unselfish 7 liberal **8** generous, handsome, princely, selfless **10** altruistic, benevolent, bighearted, charitable, openhanded **11** considerate, magnanimous, magnificent **12** humanitarian **13** philanthropic **15** self-sacrificing

unserviceable 7 useless **8** unusable

unsettle 5 upset **6** bother, rattle, ruffle **7** agitate, confuse, disturb, fluster, perturb, trouble, unhinge **8** bewilder, confound, disorder **9** unbalance **10** disconcert **13** throw off guard

unsettled 5 fazed **7** anxious, nervous, ruffled **8** agitated, confused, doubtful **9** disturbed, nonplused, perturbed, undecided **10** disquieted, distracted, nonplussed, up in the air **11** discomfited **12** disconcerted **16** at sixes and sevens

unshackle 4 free **7** release, set free, unchain **8** liberate, unfetter

unshakable 4 fast **6** stable **7** abiding, staunch **8** constant, enduring **9** dauntless, permanent, steadfast, unruffled **10** changeless, inflexible, unsinkable, unwavering **11** levelheaded, unflappable **13** imperturbable

unshaken 4 calm, cool **6** poised, serene, stable **7** staunch, unmoved **8** composed, constant, resolved **9** steadfast, tenacious, undaunted, unexcited, unruffled **10** controlled, determined, inflexible, relentless, unaffected, unswerving, untroubled, unwavering **11** levelheaded, undeviating, undisturbed, unemotional, unfaltering, unflinching, unperturbed **13** selfpossessed **14** uncompromising

unshapely 5 baggy **9** amorphous, shapeless

unshaven 5 hairy **7** bearded, bristly, hirsute, stubbly, unkempt **9** whiskered **11** bewhiskered

unsheathe 4 bare **6** expose **7** pull out **8** withdraw

unsightly 4 ugly **6** horrid, odious **7** hideous **9** obnoxious, offensive, repellent, repulsive, revolting, sickening **11** distasteful **12** unattractive

unsigned 9 anonymous **13** bearing no name

unskilled 5 green, inept **7** untried **9** untrained **10** amateurish, apprentice **11** incompetent, unqualified **13** inexperienced

unskillful 5 inept **6** clumsy, unable **7** awkward **8** inexpert **9** incapable, maladroit, untrained **10** amateurish **11** incompetent, ineffective, unpracticed **13** inexperienced

unsmiling 3 sad **4** glum, grim **5** grave **6** dismal **7** austere, joyless, serious **9** cheerless, grim-faced

unsociable 7 haughty **9** withdrawn **10** antisocial, unfriendly, ungracious **11** introverted **14** unapproachable

unsoiled 4 pure **5** clean, fresh, white **6** chaste **8** innocent, pristine, spotless **9** unstained, unsullied **10** immaculate **11** unblemished, untarnished

unsolicited 4 free **8** unforced, unsought, unwanted **9** undesired, uninvited, unwelcome, voluntary **10** gratuitous, unasked for **11** spontaneous, unnecessary, unrequested, unwished for, volunteered

unsophisticated 4 open **5** green, naive **6** candid **7** artless, natural **8** homespun, innocent, trusting **9** ingenuous, unstudied, unworldly **10** unaffected, unassuming **11** uncontrived **13** undissembling, unpretentious **15** straightforward

unsound 3 mad, off **4** weak **5** risky, shaky, unfit, wrong **6** absurd, ailing, faulty, feeble, flawed, infirm, insane, marred, sickly, unsafe **7** foolish, invalid, rickety, tottery **8** confused, crippled, decrepit, deranged, diseased, drooping, impaired, insecure, not solid, not valid, perilous, specious, spurious, unhinged, unstable, unsteady **9** blemished, dangerous, defective, erroneous, hazardous, illogical, imperfect, incorrect, senseless, uncertain, unfounded, unhealthy, unsettled, untenable **10** disordered, fallacious, groundless, irrational, precarious, unbalanced, unreliable **11** languishing, mentally ill **12** in poor health **13** off one's rocker, unsubstantial

unsoundness 7 frailty **8** delicacy, weakness **9** fragility, frailness, shakiness **11** decrepitude, derangement, instability **12** unsteadiness

unsparing 4 full **6** giving, lavish **7** copious, liberal, profuse **8** abundant, generous **9** bountiful, plenteous, plentiful, unlimited **10** big-hearted, munificent, ungrudging, unstinting **11** extravagant, magnanimous, unqualified **13** unconditional

unspeakable 4 huge, vast **5** awful, great **6** odious **7** fearful, immense **8** enormous, shocking **9** abhorrent, frightful, loathsome, monstrous, repellent, repulsive, revolting, sickening, unheard-of **10** abominable, disgusting, incredible, nauseating, prodigious **11** astonishing, unutterable **12** overwhelming, unimaginable **13** extraordi-

nary, inconceivable, inexpressible, undescribable

unspecified 5 vague **7** general, unnamed **9** undefined, unsettled **10** indefinite **11** unannounced, unindicated, unmentioned **12** undesignated, undetermined, unpublicized, unstipulated

unspoiled 4 open **7** artless, natural, perfect **8** pristine, spotless, trusting, unharmed, unmarred **9** preserved, undamaged, unscarred, unspotted, unstudied, unworldly **10** unaffected, unassuming, unimpaired, unpampered **11** unblemished, uncorrupted **13** unpretentious **15** unselfconscious, unsophisticated

unspoken 5 tacit **6** silent **7** implied **8** implicit **9** ineffable, not voiced, unuttered **10** understood **11** unexpressed

unspotted 5 clean **8** spotless, unsoiled **9** undefiled, unstained, unsullied **11** unblemished

unstable 4 weak **5** frail, shaky, tippy **6** fickle, fitful, flimsy, wobbly **7** erratic, fragile, rickety **8** changing, insecure, shifting, unsteady, volatile **9** emotional, mercurial, tottering **10** capricious, changeable, fly-by-night, irrational **11** fluctuating, vacillating **12** inconsistent **13** irresponsible, unpredictable, unsubstantial

unstained 5 clean **8** spotless **9** unspotted, unsullied, untainted **11** unblemished, uncorrupted

unsteady 6 fickle, wobbly **7** rickety **8** doubtful, unstable **10** unreliable **12** questionable, undependable **13** untrustworthy

unstinting 11 unqualified **12** enthusiastic, unrestrained, wholehearted

unstooped 5 erect **6** unbent **7** upright **8** straight, vertical

unstudied 4 glib **6** casual **7** artless, natural **8** informal, unforced, unversed **9** guileless, unuttered **10** unaffected **11** spontaneous **12** uncalculated

unsubmissive 6 unruly **7** defiant, froward, naughty, wayward **8** contrary, mutinous, perverse, stubborn **9** fractious, insurgent, obstinate, seditious, undutiful **10** disorderly, rebellious, refractory, unyielding **11** disobedient, intractable **12** noncompliant, recalcitrant,

ungovernable, unmanageable
13 insubordinate

unsubstantial 4 airy, weak
5 filmy **6** feeble, flimsy **7** unsound **8** ethereal, fanciful, illusory **9** idealized, imaginary
10 jerrybuilt **11** lightweight
12 undetectable **13** imperceptible **17** indistinguishable

unsubstantiated 8 disputed
10 unverified
15 unauthenticated

unsuccessful 4 poor, vain
6 foiled, futile, hard up **7** baffled, hapless, unlucky, useless
8 abortive, badly off, luckless, strapped, thwarted **9** fruitless, moneyless, penniless **10** illstarred, profitless, unavailing, unfruitful **11** ineffectual, unfortunate **12** unproductive, unprofitable, unprosperous
14 unremunerative

unsuitability 9 unfitness, wrongness **11** impropriety, uselessness **12** unseemliness
13 inconsistency **15** incompatibility, unacceptability
17 inappropriateness

unsuitable 5 inapt, unfit **7** unhappy, useless **8** improper, unseemly **9** unfitting, worthless
10 inadequate, indecorous, out of place, unbecoming, unsuitable **11** incongruous, unbefitting **12** inadmissible, incompatible, inconsistent, infelicitous, out of keeping, unacceptable **13** inappropriate

unsuited 5 inapt, wrong **9** unfitting **10** out of place
13 inappropriate

unsullied 5 clean **8** spotless, unsoiled **9** undefiled, uninjured, untainted **10** unpolluted **11** unblackened, unblemished, uncorrupted, untarnished **14** uncontaminated

unsupportable 6 faulty **9** unfounded, untenable
12 indefensible

unsure 3 shy **5** timid **7** bashful **8** hesitant, insecure, reserved **9** unassured, uncertain, undecided **11** in a quandary, unconfident, unconvinced
12 self-doubting **15** selfdistrustful

unsurpassed 4 best **7** highest, supreme **8** greatest, peerless, superior **9** matchless, nonpareil, paramount, unequaled, unmatched, unrivaled **10** consummate, unexcelled **11** exceptional **12** incomparable, transcendent, unparalleled

unsuspecting 5 naive **6** unwary **7** unaware **8** gullible, off

guard, trusting **9** believing, credulous **12** overtrustful, unsuspicious **13** overcredulous

unsuspicious 5 naive **8** gullible, trustful, trusting **9** credulous **12** unsuspecting
13 unquestioning

unswerving 4 firm **6** steady, strong **7** devoted, staunch
8 faithful, resolute, resolved, unshaken, untiring **9** dedicated, steadfast, undaunted
10 determined, inflexible, unflagging, unwavering, unyielding **11** undeviating, unfaltering, unflinching, unremitting **12** single-minded
14 uncompromising

unsympathetic 7 callous
8 pitiless, uncaring **9** heartless, repellent, repugnant, unfeeling, unlikable **10** hard-boiled, unlikeable, unmerciful, unpleasant **11** coldhearted, displeasing, hardhearted, indifferent, uncongenial
12 antipathetic, unattractive
15 uncompassionate

unsystematic 6 sloppy **7** chaotic, jumbled, muddled **8** confused **9** haphazard, unplanned
10 disordered, disorderly
12 disorganized, unmethodical

untainted 4 pure **5** clear **9** unsullied **11** uncorrupted
13 unadulterated

untalented 5 inept **8** mediocre, ungifted **9** unskilled **10** amateurish, unskillful
14 unaccomplished

untamed 4 wild **5** feral **6** savage **9** unsubdued **11** uncivilized **12** uncultivated

untangle 5 solve **7** clear up, unravel, unsnarl, untwist
9 extricate **11** disentangle
13 straighten out

untarnished 6 bright **7** perfect, shining **8** flawless, polished, spotless, unsoiled **9** faultless, undefiled, unstained, unsullied, untainted **10** immaculate, impeccable, undisputed, unoxidized **11** unblackened, unblemished **12** unbesmirched **13** unimpeachable

untaught 6 unread **7** natural
8 ignorant **9** untutored **10** illiterate, uneducated, unlettered, unschooled
11 spontaneous
12 uninstructed

untenable 4 weak **6** faulty, flawed **7** invalid, unsound
8 baseless, specious, spurious
9 debatable, erroneous, illogical **10** fallacious, groundless, unreliable **11** contestable

12 indefensible, questionable
13 insupportable, unjustifiable, unsustainable
14 unmaintainable

unthinkable 11 unwarranted
12 unimaginable **13** inconceivable, insupportable, unjustifiable **16** incomprehensible, out of the question

unthinking 7 witless **8** careless, heedless, mindless, tactless
9 imprudent, negligent, senseless **11** inadvertent, insensitive, thoughtless **12** undiplomatic
13 inconsiderate, uncircumspect

untidiness 5 chaos, mix-up, upset **6** jumble **7** clutter **8** disarray, disorder, scramble, shambles **9** confusion, messiness **10** sloppiness **12** dishevelment **14** disarrangement
15 disorganization

untidy 5 dowdy, messy
6 frowsy, mussed, sloppy
7 chaotic, rumpled, tousled, unkempt **8** careless, confused, littered, mussed up, slipshod, slovenly **9** cluttered **10** bedraggled, disarrayed, disheveled, disorderly, slatternly, topsy-turvy **12** unmethodical
13 helter-skelter

untie 4 free, undo **5** loose
6 loosen, unbind, unlace
7 unchain, unstrap **8** make free, unfasten **11** disentangle

untilled 6 fallow **8** unplowed
12 uncultivated

until we meet again
French: **5** adieu **8** au revoir
German: **14** auf Wiedersehen
Hawaiian: **5** aloha
Italian: **4** ciao **5** addio
11 arrivederci
Japanese: **8** sayonara
Spanish: **5** adios

untimely 5 inapt **7** unhappy
8 ill-timed, mistimed, unseemly **9** imprudent, premature, unfitting **10** ill-advised, malapropos, out of place, unbecoming, unexpected, unsuitable **11** inopportune, unbefitting, unfortunate **12** inconvenient, infelicitous
13 inappropriate

untiring 5 fresh **6** steady **7** devoted, earnest, patient, staunch, zealous **8** constant, diligent, resolute, sedulous, tireless **9** assiduous, dedicated, steadfast, tenacious, unceasing, unwearied **10** determined, persistent, relentless, unflagging
11 never tiring, persevering, unfaltering, unremitting
12 wholehearted
13 indefatigable

untold **6** myriad, secret, unsaid **7** endless, private, unknown **8** hushed up, infinite, numerous, unspoken, withheld **9** concealed, countless, limitless, unbounded, uncounted, unrelated **10** numberless, suppressed, unnumbered, unreported, unrevealed **11** innumerable, undisclosed, unexpressed, unpublished **12** immeasurable, incalculable, undetermined

Untouchables, The
　character: **7** Rossman **9** Eliot Ness, Lee Hobson **10** Cam Allison, Frank Nitti **11** Enrico Rossi **14** Martin Flaherty **18** William Youngfellow
　cast: **10** Jerry Paris **11** Bruce Gordon, Paul Picerni, Robert Stack, Steve London **13** Abel Fernandez, Anthony George, Nick Georgiade
　narrator: **14** Walter Winchell

untouched **3** new **4** pure **5** alone **6** intact, virgin **8** pristine, unharmed **9** uninjured **10** unaffected, unmolested

untoward **5** amiss **6** unruly **7** adverse **8** contrary **9** difficult **11** unfavorable **12** inauspicious, unpropitious

untrainable **6** unruly **11** intractable, unteachable **12** ungovernable

untrained **3** raw **5** green **7** untried **9** unskilled **11** unqualified **13** inexperienced

untried **3** raw **5** green **6** callow **8** immature, untested **10** unseasoned **13** inexperienced

untroubled **4** calm **6** placid, serene **7** halcyon, relaxed **8** carefree, careless, peaceful, tranquil **9** easygoing, unworried **10** unbothered **11** free-and-easy, undisturbed, unperturbed **12** happy-go-lucky, lighthearted

untrue **4** fake, sham **5** false **6** made up **7** not true **8** disloyal, spurious, unchaste **9** dishonest, erroneous, faithless, falsified, incorrect, unfounded **10** adulterous, fallacious, fictitious, fraudulent, groundless, inaccurate, inconstant, perfidious, unfaithful, untruthful **11** promiscuous, treacherous **12** meretricious **13** double-dealing

untrustworthy **5** false **6** fickle, shifty, untrue **7** corrupt, crooked, devious **8** disloyal, fallible, slippery, two-faced **9** corrupted, deceitful, dishon-

est, faithless, insincere, uncertain, unethical **10** capricious, inconstant, perfidious, unfaithful, unreliable, untruthful **11** treacherous **12** dishonorable, disreputable, questionable, undependable, unprincipled, unscrupulous **13** irresponsible **15** unauthenticated

untruth **3** fib, lie **4** hoax, tale, yarn **5** fable, story **6** canard, humbug **8** flimflam **9** deception, falsehood, fish story, invention **11** fabrication **12** equivocation **13** falsification, prevarication **16** cock-and-bull story **17** misrepresentation

untruthful **5** false, lying **8** specious, spurious **9** deceptive, dishonest **10** fraudulent, mendacious

untutored **5** naive **6** native, unread **8** ignorant, untaught **10** illiterate, uneducated, unlettered, unschooled **12** uninstructed **15** unsophisticated

untypical **3** odd **4** rare **5** alien **7** bizarre, deviant, strange, unusual **8** aberrant, abnormal, atypical, uncommon **9** anomalous, irregular, unnatural **10** unfamiliar **16** unrepresentative

unused **3** new **7** strange, untried **8** left over, not given, pristine, unopened **9** remaining, untouched **10** unemployed **12** unaccustomed, unacquainted, unhabituated

unusual **4** rare **5** novel **6** unique **7** curious, offbeat, strange **8** atypical, peculiar, singular, uncommon **9** unequaled, unheard-of, unmatched, untypical **10** noteworthy, one of a kind, phenomenal, remarkable, surprising, unfamiliar **11** exceptional **12** incomparable, unparalleled **13** extraordinary, unprecedented **16** out of the ordinary

unvaried **4** even **5** fixed **6** steady **7** regular, uniform **8** all alike, constant **9** identical, unchanged **10** all the same, invariable, monotonous, unchanging **11** homogeneous, unalterable, undeviating

unvarnished **3** raw **4** bald, bare **5** blunt, crude, frank, naked, plain, stark **6** candid, direct, honest, simple **7** sincere **8** straight **9** unadorned, uncolored **10** unfinished **11** fundamental, undisguised **13** unembellished **15** straightforward **23** straight-from-the-shoulder

unvarying **4** even **6** steady **7** regular, uniform **8** constant **10** unwavering

unveil **4** bare **6** reveal **7** divulge, publish, uncloak, uncover **8** announce, disclose **9** broadcast, make known, unsheathe **12** bring to light

unveiled **5** bared **8** divulged, laid bare, revealed **9** announced, broadcast, disclosed, made known, published, uncovered **14** brought to light

unveiling **4** show **5** array **7** display, exhibit, showing **10** exhibition, exposition **13** demonstration

unverified **7** alleged, rumored **8** disputed **15** unauthenticated, unsubstantiated

unwarranted **7** illegal **8** culpable, unlawful **9** arbitrary, unfounded **10** censurable, groundless, unapproved **11** inexcusable, uncalled-for, unjustified **12** indefensible, unauthorized, unreasonable, unsanctioned

unwary **4** rash **5** hasty **7** unalert **8** careless, headlong, heedless, reckless **9** imprudent, unguarded **10** incautious, indiscreet, unwatchful **11** precipitate **12** disregardful **13** uncircumspect

unwashed **4** foul **5** dirty, grimy, muddy **6** filthy, grubby, smudgy, soiled **7** unclean **8** begrimed

unwasteful **6** frugal **7** thrifty **9** effective, effectual, efficient **10** productive

unwavering **4** firm **6** steady, strong **7** staunch **8** faithful, resolute, unshaken, untiring **9** dedicated, steadfast, tenacious **10** determined, persistent, unflagging, unswerving **11** persevering, undeviating, unfaltering, unflinching, unremitting **12** single-minded **14** uncompromising

unwelcome **7** outcast **8** excluded, rejected, unwanted **9** thankless, uninvited, unpopular **10** uncared for, unpleasant, unrequired **11** displeasing, distasteful, undesirable, unessential, unnecessary, unwished for **12** disagreeable, unacceptable

unwell **3** ill, low **4** sick **5** frail **6** ailing, infirm, laid up, poorly, queasy, sickly **7** rundown **8** delicate, qualmish **10** indisposed **11** off one's feed **15** under the weather

unwholesome **3** bad **4** evil,

foul **5** toxic **6** deadly, filthy,
sinful, wicked **7** baneful,
harmful, hurtful, immoral,
noxious, ruinous **8** depraved,
venomous **9** corrupted, dangerous, degrading, poisonous, polluting, unhealthy
10 corrupting, pernicious
11 deleterious, detrimental,
undesirable, unhealthful
12 demoralizing, dishonorable,
insalubrious, unnourishing
13 contaminating

unwieldy 5 bulky, heavy
6 clumsy **7** awkward, weighty
8 not handy **10** burdensome,
cumbersome **12** hard to handle, incommodious, inconvenient **13** uncomfortable

unwilled 6 reflex **9** automatic
11 involuntary, unconscious
12 uncontrolled
13 nonvolitional

unwilling 5 loath **6** averse
7 against, opposed **9** demurring, reluctant, resistant
10 dissenting, indisposed, un-
desirous **11** disinclined **12** not
in the mood, recalcitrant
14 unenthusiastic

unwillingness 8 aversion
10 opposition, reluctance, resistance **13** indisposition
14 disinclination

unwise 4 dumb **5** crazy, silly
6 stupid **7** foolish, unsound
8 reckless **9** foolhardy, imprudent, senseless **10** ill-advised
11 improvident, inadvisable,
injudicious **12** shortsighted,
unreasonable **13** irresponsible,
unintelligent

unwitting 7 unaware, unmeant **9** unknowing, unplanned **10** accidental,
undesigned, unexpected, unthinking **11** inadvertent, involuntary **12** unconsenting
13 unintentional
14 unpremeditated

unwonted 4 rare **7** unusual
8 atypical, uncommon **10** infrequent, remarkable, unexpected, unfamiliar
11 exceptional **12** unaccustomed **13** extraordinary

unworkmanlike 6 clumsy,
sloppy **11** inefficient

unworldly 4 holy, pure
5 godly, green, moral, naive,
pious **6** callow, devout, divine,
sacred, solemn **7** ethical
8 ethereal, heavenly, innocent,
trusting **9** aesthetic, celestial,
religious, spiritual, unearthly
10 idealistic, immaterial, provincial **12** intellectual, metaphysical, overtrusting
13 inexperienced, philosophi-

cal **14** transcendental
15 unsophisticated

unworried 4 calm **6** serene
7 relaxed **8** carefree, composed, peaceful, tranquil
9 easygoing, unruffled
10 untroubled

unworthy 5 unfit **7** ignoble
8 improper, shameful, unseemly **9** degrading, unethical
10 unbecoming, unsuitable
11 unbefitting **12** dishonorable,
disreputable, unacceptable
13 discreditable, inappropriate,
objectionable

unwrap 4 open **6** loosen, unbind **7** uncover

unwrinkled 4 even, flat
6 ironed, smooth **7** unlined
8 smoothed **9** uncreased,
unrumpled

unwritten 4 oral **5** tacit, vocal
7 assumed, implied **8** implicit,
inferred, unstated **9** customary **10** spoken only, understood, unrecorded
11 traditional, unexpressed
12 unformulated, unregistered
13 by word of mouth

unwritten law
    Latin: **13** lex non scripta

unyielding 4 firm, hard **5** rigid,
stiff, stony, tough **6** wooden
8 resolute, rocklike, stubborn
9 obstinate, steadfast, unbending, unpliable **10** determined,
inexorable, inflexible, persistent, unswerving, unwavering
11 undeviating
14 uncompromising

up 4 atop, lift, over, rear
5 about, above, aloft, along,
aside, astir, at bat, built, close,
equal, erect, raise **6** apiece, ascend, higher, lifted **7** abreast,
batting, forward, promote,
skyward, through **8** advanced,
cheerful, increase, out of bed,
overhead, standing, together,
windward **9** northward **10** optimistic **11** constructed

up and about 5 afoot, astir
6 active, mobile, roused
7 walking **8** out of bed
10 ambulatory, on one's feet

up-and-down 6 fitful, seesaw,
uneven **7** bobbing **8** jouncing,
wavering **11** alternating, fluctuating, vacillating

upbraid 5 scold **6** berate, rebuke, revile **7** bawl out, censure, chew out, reprove
8 admonish, chastise, denounce, reproach **9** castigate,
dress down, reprimand
10 tongue-lash

upbringing 7 rearing **8** breeding, training **10** background

upcoming 6 coming, nearby
7 looming, nearing, pending
8 imminent **9** impending, momentary **11** approaching,
drawing nigh, forthcoming, in
the offing, prospective

update 5 amend, emend, renew **6** recast, revamp, revise,
rework **7** restore, touch up,
upgrade **8** overhaul, renovate
9 refurbish **10** rejuvenate, reorganize, streamline

up for grabs 4 open
9 available

upgrade 5 raise, slope **6** ascent,
better **7** advance, dignify, elevate, incline, inflate, promote
8 gradient

upheaval 5 flood, quake
6 blowup, tumult **7** turmoil
8 disorder, upthrust **9** cataclysm, explosion, tidal wave
10 disruption, earthquake, revolution **11** catastrophe,
disturbance

uphill 4 hard **5** tough **6** rising,
taxing, tiring, upward **7** arduous, onerous **8** toilsome,
wearying **9** ascending, difficult,
fatiguing, strenuous, wearisome **10** burdensome, enervating, exhausting
12 backbreaking

uphill work 8 struggle, tough
job **10** difficulty, rough going
11 arduousness **12** hard sledding **13** laboriousness

uphold 4 bear, prop **5** brace,
carry, raise, shore **6** defend,
hold up, prop up **7** approve,
bolster, confirm, elevate, endorse, protect, shore up, support, sustain **8** advocate,
buttress, champion, maintain,
preserve, underpin **9** encourage **10** stand up for, under-
brace **11** acknowledge,
corroborate

upholder 7 devotee **8** adherent,
advocate, defender, partisan
9 supporter

up in the clouds 6 elated,
joyful, joyous **8** ecstatic, euphoric **9** exuberant, rapturous
11 on cloud nine **15** in seventh heaven

Upis
    goddess of: **10** childbirth

Upjohn, Richard
    architect of: **13** Trinity
        Church (NYC)
    style: **13** Gothic Revival

upkeep 4 keep **6** living **7** support **8** expenses, overhead
10 management, sustenance
11 maintenance, subsistence
12 conservation, preservation

upland 4 high, rise 5 ridge
6 height 7 plateau 8 eminence,
highland 9 elevation, high
place, high point 10 prominence

uplift 5 edify, raise 6 better, refine 7 advance, bracing, elevate, improve, inspire, lifting,
shoring, support, upgrade
8 civilize, propping 9 cultivate,
elevation 10 betterment, bol-
stering, enrichment, refinement 11 advancement,
buttressing, cultivation, edification, enhancement, improvement 12 underpinning

uplifting 9 elevating, elevation,
improving, inspiring 11 improvement 12 enlightening
13 enlightenment, inspirational

upon 2 at, on 4 atop 5 about
6 toward 7 against, thereon
9 by means of, thereupon
10 after which, thereafter

upper 3 top 4 high 5 major
6 higher, inland 7 eminent,
greater, topmost 8 elevated,
northern, superior 9 important

upper-case letter 7 capital
9 majuscule 13 capital letter

upper class 5 elite 6 gentry,
uptown 7 (high) society
8 highborn, highbred, wellborn 9 beau monde, haut
monde, high-class, patrician,
top drawer 10 upper crust

11 aristocracy, blue-blooded
12 aristocratic, silk-stocking
14 creme de la creme, to the
manor born 15 to the manner
born

upper crust 5 elite 6 gentry
7 (high) society 9 beau monde,
haut monde, top drawer
10 upper class 11 aristocracy
14 creme de la creme

upper hand 4 edge, sway
5 power 7 command, control,
mastery 8 whip hand 9 advantage, authority, supremacy
10 domination
12 predominance

upper house 6 Senate
12 House of Lords

uppermost, upmost 3 top
4 main 5 chief, first, major,
prime 7 highest, leading, primary, supreme, topmost
8 crowning, dominant, foremost, greatest, loftiest 9 essential, paramount, principal
10 preeminent 11 predomi-
nant 12 transcendent 13 most
important

Upper Volta *see box*

upright 3 rib 4 fair, good, just,
pale, pier, pile, pole, post,
prop 5 erect, moral, shaft,
stake, strut 6 column, honest,
picket, pillar 7 ethical, support, upended 8 reliable, stan-

dard, vertical 9 honorable,
righteous, stanchion 10 aboveboard, high-minded, principled, standing-up, upstanding
11 trustworthy 12 on the up-
and-up 13 perpendicular

uprightness 5 honor 7 dignity,
honesty 8 morality 9 integrity
13 righteousness
15 trustworthiness

uprising 4 riot 6 mutiny, revolt 8 outbreak 9 rebellion
10 insurgence, revolution
12 insurrection

uproar 3 ado 4 stir, to-do 5 furor 6 clamor, tumult 7 turmoil 9 agitation, commotion
11 disturbance, pandemonium
16 state of confusion

uproarious 4 loud, wild
5 noisy 6 raging, stormy 7 furious, intense, riotous 9 clamorous, hilarious, turbulent,
very funny 10 boisterous, disorderly, hysterical, tumultuous 11 tempestuous
13 sidesplitting

uproot 6 banish 7 abolish, cast
out, destroy, root out, wipe
out 8 dislodge, displace, force
out 9 eliminate, extirpate
10 annihilate, do away with
11 exterminate

upset 3 ire, irk, mad, vex
4 beat 5 anger, annoy, crush,
irked, messy, mix up, pique,
quash, smash, upend, vexed,
worry 6 bother, cancel,
change, defeat, enrage, grieve,
invert, jumble, muddle,
mussed, rattle, thrash, untidy
7 agitate, angered, annoyed,
capsize, chaotic, confuse, conquer, disturb, enraged, fluster,
furious, grieved, incense, jumbled, mixed-up, perturb, reverse, tip over, trouble,
trounce, unnerve, upended,
worried 8 agitated, bothered,
capsized, confused, demolish,
disorder, distress, incensed, inverted, overcome, overturn,
slovenly, troubled, turn over,
unnerved, upturned, vanquish
9 discomfit, disturbed, infuriate, overpower, overthrow,
overwhelm, perturbed 10 discompose, disconcert, disheveled, disordered, disorderly,
disquieted, distressed, hysterical, overturned, tipped over,
topple over, topsy-turvy,
turned over, upside-down
11 disarranged, disorganize,
overwrought, wrong side up
12 disorganized 13 make miserable 14 turn topsy-turvy

upsetting
  French: 14 bouleversement

upshot 3 end 6 effect, payoff,

Upper Volta
  other name: 11 Burkina Faso (Fasso)
  capital/largest city: 11 Ouagadougou
  others: 4 Kaya 7 Banfora 9 Koudougou 10 Ouahigouya
  division: 7 Yatenga 9 Tenkodogo 11 Fada Ngourma
  monetary unit: 5 franc 7 centime
  mountain: 4 Tema
  highest point: 8 Nakourou 10 Tenakourou, Tenekourou
  river: 5 Komoe 6 Mekrou, Sourou 8 Pendjari, Red Volta
    10 Black Volta, White Volta
  physical feature:
    plateau: 5 Sahel 7 Sikasso, Voltaic
    wind: 9 harmattan
  people: 4 Bobo, Lobi, Samo 5 Bella, Bissa, Dyula, Fulbe,
    Hausa, Mande, Marka, Mossi, Puehl 6 Fulani, Senufo,
    Tuareg 7 Grunshi, Voltaic, Yatenga 8 Mandingo 9 Gour-
    ounsi 15 Bunsansi Gambaga
    French governor: 7 Hesling
    god: 4 Wuro 5 Tenga
    king: 4 Naba 5 Mogho
    leader: 5 Oubri, Zerbo 7 Yameogo 8 Lamizana 9 Mogho
    Naba
  language: 4 Bobo, Lobi, More, Samo 5 Dyula, Mande,
    Mossi 6 French
  religion: 5 Islam 7 animism 12 Christianity
  place:
    game reserve: 11 Arlyand Pama
  feature:
    animal: 5 hyena 6 duiker, jackal 7 gazelle, warthog
      10 hartebeest
    tree: 4 shea 6 acacia, baobab, karite, locust

result, sequel 7 outcome 8 off-shoot 9 aftermath, outgrowth 10 conclusion 11 aftereffect, consequence, culmination eventuality 16 final development

upside down 7 chaotic 8 reversed 10 disorderly 11 topsy turvey 12 bottomside up 16 at sixes and sevens

upstairs 2 up 11 above stairs, second floor

upstanding 4 good, tall, true 5 erect, moral, on end 6 honest 7 ethical, upright 8 straight, truthful, vertical, virtuous 9 honorable, righteous 11 trustworthy 13 incorruptible, perpendicular

upstart 4 snip, snob, snub 6 nobody 7 bounder, parvenu 8 mushroom 9 conceited, newly-rich 10 adventurer 12 nouveau riche 13 self-assertive

upsurge 4 gain, push, rise 5 spurt 6 pickup, thrust, upturn 7 advance, upswing 8 increase 11 improvement

upswing 4 rise 6 pickup 7 upsurge 11 improvement, upward trend

uptight 5 tense 7 anxious, fearful, nervous, worried, wound up 8 insecure, neurotic, troubled 9 unbending 10 unyielding 12 apprehensive

up-to-date 2 in 3 new 5 today 6 modern, modish, timely, trendy, with-it 7 current, stylish 9 in fashion 12 contemporary 13 up-to-the-minute
French: 9 au courant

upturn 4 gain, push 6 thrust 7 advance, upsurge 8 increase 9 expansion 11 improvement

upward 4 high, more 5 above, aloft 7 skyward 9 ascending, uppermost

upward movement 4 rise 5 climb 6 ascent, rising, upturn 7 scaling, takeoff 8 climbing, mounting 9 ascension

upward trend 4 rise 5 boost 6 pickup 7 advance, upsurge, upswing 8 increase 11 improvement

Uralic
  language branch: 7 Samoyed 10 Finno-Ugric

Urania
  also: 9 Aphrodite
  member of: 5 Muses
  personifies: 9 astronomy

uranium
  chemical symbol: 1 U

Uranus
  mother: 4 Gaea
  wife: 4 Gaea
  father of: 6 Giants, Titans 8 Cyclopes 10 Titanesses 13 Hecatonchires
  castrated by: 6 Cronos, Cronus, Kronos

Uranus
  position: 7 seventh
  satellite: 5 Ariel 6 Oberon 7 Miranda, Titania, Umbriel
  color: 9 blue-green
  characteristic: 5 rings

Urartu see 7 Armenia

urban 4 city, town 5 civic 8 citified 9 municipal 11 worldly-wise 12 cosmopolitan, metropolitan 13 sophisticated

urban area 4 city 9 inner city 10 metropolis 11 megalopolis 16 metropolitan area

urbane 5 civil, suave 6 polite, smooth 7 courtly, elegant, gallant, genteel, politic, refined, tactful 8 debonair, gracious, mannerly, polished, well-bred 9 civilized, courteous 10 chivalrous, cultivated, diplomatic 11 gentlemanly 12 cosmopolitan, well-mannered 13 sophisticated

urchin 3 boy, imp, lad 4 brat, waif 5 gamin, stray, whelp, youth 6 gamine, laddie 8 young pup 9 stripling, young punk, youngster 10 young rogue, young tough 11 guttersnipe

Urd 4 Norn
  origin: 12 Scandinavian
  form: 8 giantess
  personifies: 4 past
  developed from: 5 Urdar
  companion: 5 Skuld 8 Verdandi

Urdar 12 original Norn
  origin: 12 Scandinavian
  form: 8 giantess
  children: 3 Urd 5 Skuld 8 Verdandi

Urey, Harold Clayton
  field: 9 chemistry
  isolated: 9 deuterium
  awarded: 10 Nobel prize

urge 3 yen 4 back, coax, goad, itch, poke, prod, push, spur, sway, wish 5 drive, egg on, fancy, force, press, prick, speed 6 advise, desire, exhort, hasten, hunger, motive, reason, thirst 7 beseech, counsel, craving, dictate, entreat, implore, impulse, longing, passion, push for, quicken,

request, solicit, suggest 8 advocate, appeal to, argue for, champion, convince, persuade, petition, pressure, stimulus, yearning 9 hankering, importune, incentive, plead with, prescribe, prompting, recommend 10 accelerate, inducement, motivation, supplicate 11 prevail upon, provocation

urgency 4 need, urge, want 5 press 6 stress 8 exigency, pressure 9 necessity 10 importance, insistence 11 persistence 14 imperativeness 15 importunateness

urgent 5 grave 6 ardent 7 crucial, earnest, fervent, intense, serious, weighty, zealous 8 critical, pleading, pressing, required, spirited 9 demanding, essential, heartfelt, important, insistent, momentous, necessary 10 beseeching, compelling, compulsory, imperative, obligatory, passionate 12 wholehearted 13 indispensable

urge on 4 push 5 boost 7 cheer on, pull for, root for

urging 7 bidding, counsel, goading 8 egging on 9 prompting 11 exhortation

Uriah
  father: 7 Shemiah
  wife: 9 Bathsheba
  served: 5 David

urinary system
  component: 6 kidney, ureter 7 bladder, urethra
  rids body of: 5 salts, waste, water 8 minerals

Uris, Leon
  author of: 5 Topaz 6 Exodus 7 Trinity 9 Battle Cry 10 Armageddon

urn 3 jar, pig 4 ewer, kist, tomb, vase 5 grave, steen 6 teapot 7 samovar 9 coffeepot
  botanical: 7 capsule 11 sporebearer
  in keno: 5 goose

Urn Burial
  author: 15 Sir Thomas Browne

Uruguay *see box, p. 1036*

USA
  author: 13 John Dos Passos
  character: 10 Ben Compton, Mary French 11 Joe Williams 12 Margo Dowling 13 Fainy McCreary (Mac), Janey Williams 14 J Ward Morehouse 15 Charley Anderson, Eleanor Stoddard, Eveline Hutchins 18 Anne Elizabeth Trent 22 Richard Ellsworth Savage

Uruguay
  other name: **10** Purple Land
  capital/largest city: **10** Montevideo
  others: **4** Fray, Melo **5** Minas, Rocha, Salto **6** Bentos, Rivera **7** Artigas, Colonia, Dolores, Durazno, Florida, San Jose **8** Mercedes, Paysandu, Trinidad **9** Maldonado **10** Las Piedras, Santa Lucia, Tacarembo **12** Treinta y Tres **13** San Jose de Mayo
  measure: **4** vara **6** cuadra, suerte
  monetary unit: **4** peso **9** centesimo, centisimo
  weight: **7** quintal
  island: **5** Lobos
  lake: **5** Merin, Mirim **18** Embalse del Rio Negro
  mountain: **6** Animas **10** Grand Hills **14** Cuchilla Grande
  highest point: **15** Mirador Nacional
  river: **4** Malo **5** Mirim, Negro, Plata **6** Parana, Ulimar **7** Cuareim, Queguay, Uruguay **8** Yaguaron **9** Cebollati **10** Tacarembo
  sea: **8** Atlantic
  physical feature:
    estuary: **5** Plata
  people: **4** Yaro **5** Swiss **6** Indian **7** Italian, mestizo, Russian, Spanish **8** Charruas
    artist: **6** Figari
    author: **4** Rodo **5** Reyes **6** Onetti **7** Sanchez **9** San Martin **10** Ibarbourou
    leader: **5** Oribe **6** Rivera **7** Artigas **9** Lavelleja **10** Borda-berry **14** Batlle y Ordonez
  language: **7** Italian, Spanish
  religion: **13** Roman Catholic
  place:
    resort: **12** Punta del Este
    square: **13** Independencia
  feature:
    animal: **4** puma **6** jaguar **8** capybara **9** armadillo
    bird: **4** rhea **5** nandu **7** hornero, ostrich
    cattle ranch: **8** estancia
    cowboy: **6** gaucho
    dance: **5** tango **7** milonga
    festival: **8** Carnival **13** Semana Criolla
    lasso: **10** boleadoras
    metal straw: **8** bombilla
    music: **9** candomble
    musical drama: **7** tablado
    ruling class: **10** Patriciado
  food:
    barbecue: **5** asado
    dish: **7** puchero **9** churrasco **13** asado con cuero
    drink: **4** mate

usable 5 handy **6** useful **9** adaptable **10** functional **11** serviceable

usage 3 use **4** care, mode **5** habit **6** custom, manner, method, system **7** control **8** good form, habitude, handling, practice **9** etiquette, operation, tradition, treatment **10** convention, employment, management **12** manipulation

use 3 aid, ply, sap **4** good, help, work **5** apply, avail, drain, exert, spend, treat, usage, value, waste, wield, worth **6** devour, employ, expend, handle, profit **7** benefit, consume, deplete, exhaust, exploit, operate, service, utilize **8** deal with, exercise, function, handling, profit by, put to use, resort to, squander **9** act toward, advantage, dissipate, enjoyment, make use of, operation, swallow up, throw away **10** employment, manipulate, run through, usefulness **11** application, convenience, fritter away, utilization **12** behave toward, capitalize on **13** make the most of **14** serviceability

used 3 old **5** eaten, spent **7** applied, treated **8** actuated, consumed, depleted, employed, occupied, operated, utilized **9** customary, exercised, exhausted, exploited, practiced **10** accustomed, habituated, secondhand **11** implemented, manipulated

used up 4 beat, shot **5** all in, spent **6** wasted **7** worn out **8** depleted, tired out **9** exhausted

useful 5 handy **7** helpful **8** valuable **9** effective, practical, rewarding **10** beneficial, convenient, functional, profitable, time-saving, worthwhile **11** serviceable, utilitarian **12** advantageous

usefulness 5 avail, value, worth **6** profit **7** benefit, purpose, utility **9** advantage **11** convenience, helpfulness, suitability **12** adaptability, practicality **13** effectiveness **14** serviceability

useless 4 vain **6** futile **7** of no use **8** bootless, unusable **9** fruitless, unhelpful, worthless **10** inadequate, profitless, unavailing **11** incompetent, ineffectual, inefficient **12** unproductive **13** impracticable, inefficacious, nonfunctional, unserviceable

uselessness 6 vanity **8** futility, idleness **9** inutility **10** inefficacy **13** fruitlessness, worthlessness

Uses of Enchantment, The
  author: **15** Bruno Bettelheim

use sparingly 4 save **5** hoard, stint **6** scrimp **7** cut back, dole out **8** conserve, not waste, preserve

use to advantage 7 exploit **8** profit by **12** capitalize on **13** turn to account

use up 5 drain, spend **6** expend, finish **7** consume, deplete, exhaust **9** dissipate **10** run through

Ushant
  author: **11** Conrad Aiken

usher 4 lead, show **5** guide, steer **6** attend, convoy, direct, escort, herald, launch, leader, porter, ring in, squire **7** conduct, precede, preface **8** announce, director, proclaim **9** conductor, introduce **10** doorkeeper, gatekeeper, inaugurate

Usnach
  also: **6** Usnech
  origin: **5** Irish
  daughter: **6** Naoise

Usnech *see* **6** Usnach

USSR *see* **6** Russia

Ustinov, Peter
  born: **6** London **7** England

roles: 7 Topkapi 8 Quo Vadis? 9 Billy Budd, Spartacus 12 We're No Angels

usual 5 stock, trite 6 common, normal, wonted 7 popular, regular, routine, typical 8 expected, familiar, habitual, ordinary, orthodox, standard 9 customary, hackneyed 10 accustomed, prescribed, threadbare 11 commonplace, established, oft-repeated, traditional 12 conventional, run-of-the-mill 15 well-established

usurp 4 grab 5 steal 7 preempt 8 arrogate 10 commandeer 11 appropriate 12 encroach upon, infringe upon

usurpation 6 taking 7 seizure 8 grabbing, stealing 10 arrogation, preemption 13 appropriation

Utah *see box*

utensils 4 gear 5 tools 6 outfit, silver, tackle 8 flatware 9 apparatus 10 implements, silverware 11 instruments 13 paraphernalia

Utgard
origin: 12 Scandinavian
realm of: 7 Skrymir 10 Utgardloki
location: 9 Gatunheim

Utgardloki *see* 7 Skrymir

utilitarian 5 handy 6 usable, useful 8 sensible, valuable, workable 9 effective, efficient, practical, pragmatic 10 beneficial, convenient, functional, profitable 11 serviceable 12 advantageous

utility 3 aid, gas, use 4 help 5 avail, extra 6 backup 7 benefit, reserve, service 8 function 9 accessory, advantage, alternate, auxiliary, secondary,

surrogate, telephone 10 additional, substitute, usefulness 11 convenience, electricity 12 availability, supplemental 13 public service 14 serviceability

utilization 3 use 10 employment 11 application 12 exploitation

utilize 3 use 6 employ 7 exploit 8 profit by, put to use, resort to 9 make use of 12 capitalize on 13 bring into play, make the most of, turn to account 14 avail oneself of, have recourse to, put into service 15 take advantage of

utmost, uttermost 4 acme, best, main, peak, tops 5 chief, first, major, prime 6 tiptop, zenith 7 capital, highest, leading, maximum, primary, supreme, the most 8 cardinal, foremost, greatest, last word, ultimate 9 paramount, principal, sovereign 10 preeminent 11 predominant

Uto-Aztecan (Nahuatl)
tribe: 4 Pima 5 Aatam, Aztec, Nahua 6 Mexica, Papago 8 Pima Alto

utopia 4 Eden 6 heaven 7 Erewhon 8 paradise 9 ideal life, Shangri-la 12 perfect bliss, perfect place 13 seventh heaven

utopian 9 visionary 10 idealistic, unfeasible, unworkable 11 unrealistic 12 otherworldly, unattainable, unrealizable 13 impracticable, insubstantial, unfulfillable

Utrillo, Maurice
born: 5 Paris 6 France
mother: 14 Suzanne Valadon
artwork: 16 The Church at Deuil, The Church of Blevy 17 Church at St Hilaire 19 La Petite Communiante 22 Sacre Coeur de Montmartre

ut supra 7 as above

utter 3 say 4 emit, pure, talk, tell, yell 5 sheer, shout, speak, state, total, voice 6 entire, mutter, reveal 7 declare, deliver, divulge, exclaim, express, perfect, whisper 8 absolute, complete, disclose, outright, proclaim, thorough, vocalize 9 downright, enunciate, out-and-out, pronounce, unchecked 10 articulate, unmodified, unrelieved 11 categorical, unequivocal, unmitigated, unqualified

utterance 4 talk, word 6 an-

Utah
abbreviation: 2 UT
nickname: 6 Mormon 7 Beehive
capital/largest city: 12 Salt Lake City
others: 3 Roy 4 Moab, Orem 5 Delta, Heber, Kanab, Logan, Magna, Manti, Nepli, Ogden, Price, Provo 6 Beaver, Eureka, Kearns, Layton, Murray, Tooele, Vernal 7 Bingham 8 American 9 Bountiful 11 Brigham City
college: 5 Weber 11 Westminster 12 Brigham Young
feature:
  bridge: 7 Rainbow
  dam: 6 Hoover 10 Glen Canyon
  gorge: 7 Flaming
  national historic site: 11 Golden Spike
  national monument: 8 Dinosaur 14 Natural Bridges
  national park: 4 Zion 6 Arches 11 Bryce Canyon, Canyonlands, Capital Reef
  reef: 7 Capital
tribe: 3 Ute 5 Piute, Uinta(h), Yampa 6 Navajo, Paiute 7 Gosiute 8 Paviotso, Shoshoni
people: 7 Mormons 10 Maude Adams 11 Karl G Maeser 12 Brigham Young 13 John M Browning 15 Latter-Day Saints 16 George Sutherland 19 Daniel Cowan Jackling
  explorer: 9 Dominguez, Escalante
lake: 4 Mead, Swan, Utah 6 Powell, Sevier 9 Great Salt
land rank: 8 eleventh
mountain: 4 Lena, Lion, Waas 5 Cedar, Henry, Hogup, Peale, Rocky, Trail, Uinta 6 Frisco, Navajo, Swasey, Wahwah 7 Granite, Griffin, Hawkins, Pennell, Terrace, Wasatch 8 Linnaeus 9 Confusion
  highest point: 9 Kings Peak
physical feature:
  basin: 5 Great
  canyon: 4 Echo
  desert: 6 Sevier
  plateau: 7 Wasatch 8 Colorado, Tavaputs
river: 4 Bear 5 Grand, Green, Weber 6 Jordan, Sevier, Virgin 7 San Juan 8 Colorado
state admission: 10 forty-fifth
state bird: 7 seagull
state flower: 8 sego lily
state motto: 8 Industry
state song: 14 Utah We Love Thee
state tree: 10 blue spruce

swer, remark, speech **7** opinion
9 discourse, statement **10** expression **11** declaration, exclamation **12** articulation,
proclamation, vocalization
13 pronouncement,
verbalization

utterly 4 just **5** fully **6** wholly
7 totally **8** entirely, outright
9 downright, extremely, perfectly **10** absolutely, completely, thoroughly **14** to the
nth degree

uttermost 6 utmost **7** extreme,
maximum, supreme **9** outermost, sovereign **12** extreme
limit

Utu
origin: **8** Sumerian
god of: **3** sun

Uzbekistan
capital/largest city: **8** Tashkent
others: **9** Samarkand
head of state: **9** president
government: **8** republic
monetary unit: **5** ruble

river: **8** Amu Darya, Syr
Darya
sea: **4** Aral
people: **5** Uzbek
language: **5** Uzbek
religion: **5** Islam **11** Sunni
Muslim

Uzziah
also: **7** Azariah
king of: **5** Judah
father: **7** Amaziah
son: **6** Jotham **7** Jehoram
8 Jonathan

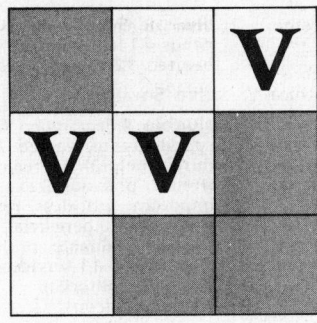

vacancy 3 gap **4** hole, void **5** abode, place **6** breach, cavity, hollow **7** crevice, fissure, housing, lodging, opening **9** emptiness, situation **10** empty space, vacantness **11** room for rent **12** house for rent

vacant 4 dull, free, idle, open **5** aloof, blank, blase, clear, empty, vapid **6** unused, wooden **7** deadpan, for rent, leisure, vacuous **8** deserted, detached, for lease, forsaken, not in use, unfilled **9** abandoned, apathetic, incurious, oblivious, poker-face, unengaged **10** tenantless, unemployed, unoccupied, untenanted **11** indifferent, unconcerned, unfurnished, uninhabited **12** unencumbered **14** expressionless **15** uncomprehending

vacate 4 quit **5** empty, leave **6** give up, resign **8** abdicate, evacuate, hand over **9** surrender **10** depart from, relinquish

vacate the throne 4 cede, flee, quit **5** yield **6** give up, resign, retire **7** abandon **8** abdicate **10** relinquish

vacation 4 rest **5** leave, R and R **6** recess **7** holiday **8** furlough, holidays **10** sabbatical **12** intermission **13** take a vacation **14** leave of absence **17** rest-and-recreation
　French: 8 vacances

vacillate 4 reel, rock, roll, sway, toss **5** pitch, shift, waver **6** falter, teeter, totter, wobble **7** flutter, vibrate **8** hesitate **9** fluctuate, hem and haw, oscillate **11** shilly-shally **14** blow hot and cold

vacillating 7 swaying **8** wavering **9** diffident, uncertain, vibrating **10** hesitating, irresolute, on the fence **11** fluctuating, uncertainty

12 irresolution **15** shilly-shallying

vacillation 7 swaying **8** wavering **9** faltering, vibration **10** indecision **11** fluctuation, uncertainty **12** irresolution **15** shilly-shallying

Vacuna
　origin: 6 Sabine
　goddess of: 11 agriculture

vacuous 4 dull, idle, void **5** blank, empty, inane, silly **6** stupid, vacant **7** fatuous, foolish **8** indolent, unfilled **9** senseless **11** empty-headed, purposeless

Vaduz
　capital of: 13 Liechtenstein

vae victis 18 woe to the vanquished

vagabond 4 hobo **5** gypsy, nomad, rover, tramp **6** roamer, roving **7** drifter, floater, migrant, nomadic, rambler, roaming, vagrant **8** bohemian, carefree, homeless, rambling, wanderer, wayfarer **9** footloose, itinerant, transient, traveling, wandering, wayfaring **10** journeying **11** beachcomber

Vagabond Lover
　nickname of: 10 Rudy Vallee

vagary 4 kink, whim **5** fancy, humor, quirk **6** notion, oddity, whimsy **7** caprice, fantasy, impulse **8** crotchet, daydream **10** brainstorm, erraticism **11** peculiarity **12** eccentricity, idiosyncrasy, passing fancy

vagrant 3 bum **4** hobo **5** nomad, rover, tramp **6** beggar, loafer, roamer, roving **7** floater, migrant, nomadic, roaming **8** homeless, rambling, vagabond, wanderer **9** itinerant, transient, wandering **10** panhandler **11** peripatetic **15** knight-of-the-road

vague 4 hazy **5** fuzzy, loose

6 casual, random, unsure **7** general, unclear **8** confused, nebulous **9** imprecise, uncertain, unsettled **10** ill-defined, indefinite, inexplicit, undetailed, unspecific **11** not definite, unspecified **12** undetermined

vaguely 5 dimly **6** hazily **7** loosely **8** dreamily, slightly, vacantly **9** obscurely, sketchily **10** nebulously **11** ambiguously **12** indistinctly

vagueness 8 haziness **9** ambiguity, confusion, fuzziness **11** uncertainty **13** lack of clarity **14** indefiniteness

vain 4 idle **5** cocky, proud, silly **6** futile **7** foolish, pompous, stuck-up, useless **8** arrogant, boastful, bootless, dandyish, egoistic, nugatory, puffed-up, trifling **9** conceited, egotistic, fruitless, pointless, worthless **10** disdainful, profitless, swaggering, unavailing **11** egotistical, ineffective, ineffectual, superficial, timewasting **12** self-admiring, supercilious, unprofitable, unsuccessful, vainglorious **13** self-important, self-satisfied

Vainamoinen
　origin: 7 Finnish
　hero of: 8 Kalevala
　form: 8 magician
　opposes: 5 Louhi
　　11 Joukahainen

vainglorious 5 cocky **7** haughty, pompous, stuck-up **8** affected, arrogant, boastful, bragging, insolent **9** conceited **10** egoistical, pretentious, swaggering **11** egotistical, swell-headed **12** narcissistic, supercilious **13** full of oneself, self-important

vainglory 6 vanity **7** conceit, swagger **9** cockiness **10** pretension **11** braggadocio

14 self-importance 16 over-bearing pride

vale 6 good-by 8 farewell

valedictory 4 last 5 final 7 parting 8 farewell, terminal, ultimate 9 departing 10 conclusive 11 leavetaking 14 farewell speech 19 commencement address

Valentine
character in: 20 Two Gentlemen of Verona
author: 11 Shakespeare

Valentino, Rudolph
real name: 16 Rodolfo (Alfonzo Raffaele Pierre Philibert) Guglielmi
born: 5 Italy 12 Castellaneta
wife: 9 Jean Acker 14 Natasha Rambova
roles: 8 The Sheik 12 Blood and Sand 16 The Son of the Sheik 17 Monsieur Beaucaire 30 The Four Horsemen of the Apocalypse

valerian 9 Valeriana
varieties: 3 red 5 Greek 6 common 7 African 8 American 11 long-spurred

Valery, Paul
author of: 7 Cahiers, Charmes 12 The Young Fate 13 Le Jeune Parque 16 Sketch of a Serpent 20 The Graveyard by the Sea

Valhalla
origin: 8 Teutonic
hall of: 4 Odin 5 Othin

valiant 4 bold 5 brave, noble 6 daring, heroic 7 gallant 8 fearless, intrepid, knightly, resolute, stalwart, unafraid, valorous 9 audacious, dauntless, undaunted 10 chivalrous, courageous 11 lionhearted, unflinching 12 bold-spirited, great-hearted, stouthearted

valid 4 good 5 legal, licit, sound 6 lawful, proper, strong 7 fitting, genuine, logical, weighty 8 accurate, decisive, forceful, official, powerful, suitable, truthful 9 authentic, effective, legalized, realistic 10 acceptable, applicable, compelling, convincing, legitimate 11 substantial, well-founded 12 well-grounded 13 authoritative, being in effect 14 constitutional, legally binding

validate 5 enact, prove, stamp 6 ratify, verify 7 certify, confirm, sustain, warrant, witness 8 legalize, sanction 9 authorize, make legal, make valid 10 make lawful 11 corroborate, countersign 12 au-

thenticate, make official, substantiate

validation 8 sanction 12 confirmation, legalization, ratification 13 authorization, certification

validity 5 force, logic, power, right 6 weight 7 grounds, potency 8 accuracy, legality, strength 9 authority, soundness, substance 10 legal force, legitimacy, properness 11 suitability 12 authenticity, truthfulness 13 acceptability, applicability, effectiveness 14 conclusiveness, convincingness

valise 3 bag 4 grip 7 handbag, luggage, satchel 8 suitcase 9 briefcase, Gladstone 11 portmanteau

Valjean, Jean
character in: 13 Les Miserables
author: 4 Hugo

Valkyrie
origin: 8 Teutonic
home: 8 Valhalla
attendant of: 4 Odin 5 Othin
queen: 8 Brunhild, Brynhild 10 Brunnhilde

Vallee, Rudy
real name: 17 Hubert Prior Vallee
nickname: 16 The Vagabond Lover
born: 13 Island Point VT
played: 9 saxophone
wife: 9 Jane Greer
roles: 16 The Vagabond Lover 17 The Palm Beach Story, Unfaithfully Yours 41 How to Succeed in Business Without Really Trying

Valletta
capital of: 5 Malta

valley 3 cut, dip, gap 4 dale, dell, glen, vale 5 basin, chasm, glade, gorge, gulch, gully 6 bottom, canyon, divide, hollow, ravine 8 water gap

Valley Forge
author: 15 Maxwell Anderson

Valley of Horses, The
author: 9 Jean M Auel

Valley of the Dolls
author: 16 Jacqueline Susann

valor 4 grit, guts 5 nerve, pluck, spunk 6 daring, mettle 7 bravery, courage, heroism 8 boldness, chivalry 9 fortitude, gallantry 11 intrepidity 12 fearlessness 13 dauntlessness

valorous 4 bold 5 brave, gutsy 6 heroic, plucky 7 valiant 8 fearless, intrepid, stalwart,

unafraid 9 dauntless 10 courageous 11 indomitable, lionhearted 12 stouthearted

valse 5 waltz

valuable 4 dear, good 6 costly, prized, useful, valued 7 admired, helpful 8 esteemed, fruitful, precious 9 expensive, important, priceless, respected, treasured 10 beneficial, high-priced, invaluable, profitable, worthwhile 11 serviceable, significant, utilitarian 12 advantageous

valuation 9 appraisal 10 assessment, evaluation 14 estimated value

value, values 3 use 4 cost, help, rate 5 assay, count, judge, merit, price, prize, rules, weigh, worth 6 admire, amount, assess, charge, esteem, ideals, profit, reckon, revere, size up 7 beliefs, benefit, cherish, compute, customs, respect, service, utility 8 appraise, evaluate, prestige, treasure 9 advantage, appraisal, greatness, moral code, practices, standards 10 admiration, appreciate, assessment, estimation, excellence, importance, set store by, usefulness 11 conventions, market price, superiority 12 code of ethics, institutions, significance

valued 6 prized 7 revered 8 esteemed 9 cherished, respected, treasured 11 appreciated 14 highly regarded

valueless 7 trivial, useless 9 worthless 11 of no account, unimportant 13 insignificant 14 good for nothing 15 inconsequential

vamoose 3 out 4 away, scat, shoo 5 be off, leave, scram 6 beat it, begone, depart, get out, go away 7 get lost

vamp 5 siren 9 temptress 10 seductress 11 enchantress, femme fatale 12 introduction

Vamp
nickname of: 9 Theda Bara

vampire 3 bat 7 Dracula 11 bloodsucker

van 4 cart, dray, head 5 lorry, scout, truck, wagon 6 camper, picket 7 trailer 8 sentinel, vanguard 9 first line, forefront, front rank 10 avant-garde, large truck 12 advance guard, covered truck 13 front of an army 16 foremost division
french: 7 fourgon

Van, Bobby
real name: 10 Robert King
born: 9 New York NY

roles: 10 Kiss Me Kate, On Your Toes **11** No No Nanette **12** It's Only Money, The Ladies' Man **13** Small Town Girl **23** The Affairs of Dobie Gillis

van Alen, William
architect of: **16** Chrysler Building (NYC)

Van Allen, James Alfred
field: **7** physics
invented: **18** radio proximity fuse
discovered: **22** Van Allen radiation belts

Van Buren, Martin *see box*

Vance, Vivian
real name: **11** Vivian Jones
born: **12** Cherryvale KS
roles: **9** I Love Lucy **10** Ethel Mertz

Vancouver
hockey team: **7** Canucks

vandal 6 looter, raider **7** ravag-

er, wrecker **8** marauder, pillager, saboteur **9** barbarian, despoiler, destroyer, plunderer **10** demolisher

vandalism 6 damage **10** defacement **11** destruction **17** malicious mischief

vandalize 3 mar **5** trash, wreck **6** damage, deface **7** despoil, destroy

Vanderlyn, John
born: **10** Kingston NY
artwork: **14** Ariadne on Naxos **20** The Death of Jane McCrea **28** Marius Amid the Ruins of Carthage **31** Ariadne Asleep on the Island of Naxos

Van Dyck, Sir Anthony
born: **7** Antwerp **8** Flanders
artwork: **8** Charles I (in Hunting Dress) **11** Iconography **18** Madonna of the Rosary **19** Blessed Herman Joseph, Cardinal Bentiro-

glio **20** Ecstasy of St Augustine **21** Marchesa Elena Grimaldi

Van Dyke, Dick
born: **12** West Plains MO
roles: **11** Mary Poppins **12** Bye Bye Birdie **15** Dick Van Dyke Show

Vane, Sutton
author of: **12** Outward Bound

Vanessa
author: **11** Hugh Walpole

Van Gogh, Vincent
born: **12** GrootZundert **14** The Netherlands
artwork: **10** Pere Tanguy **11** Cafe at Night, L'Arlesienne **13** The Olive Grove **14** The Starry Night **15** The Potato Eaters **16** The Bridge at Arles **18** Portrait of Dr Gachet, The Chair and the Pipe **22** Cornfield with Cypresses

vanguard 3 van **7** leaders **8** forerank **9** first line, forefront, front line, front rank, spearhead **10** avant-garde, innovators, leadership, modernists **11** pacesetters, tastemakers **12** advance guard, trailblazers, trendsetters

Van Helsing, Dr
character in: **7** Dracula
author: **6** Stoker

Vanir
origin: **12** Scandinavian
race: **4** gods
conflicting with: **4** Asar **5** Aesir

vanish 3 die, end **5** cease **6** die out, expire, perish **7** die away **8** dissolve, fade away, melt away, pass away **9** disappear, evaporate, terminate **13** dematerialize **15** become invisible

vanished 4 dead, gone, lost **7** defunct, died out, extinct **11** disappeared

vanishing 8 dying out **10** extinction, fading away **11** passing away **12** disappearing **13** disappearance **15** dematerializing

vanitas vanitatum 16 vanity of vanities

vanity 4 sham **5** folly, pride **6** mirage **7** compact, conceit, egotism, falsity, inanity **8** delusion, futility, idleness, selflove **9** emptiness, powder box, vainglory, vanity bag **10** hollowness, narcissism, self-praise, vanity case **11** makeup table, mirror table, self-conceit, uselessness **13** dressing table, fruitlessness, worthlessness

---

Van Buren, Martin
nicknames: **9** The Red Fox **17** The Little Magician **18** The Careful Dutchman
presidential rank: **6** eighth
party: **8** Democrat
state represented: **7** New York
defeated: **5** (Hugh Lawson) White **6** (William Person) Mangum **7** (Daniel) Webster **8** (William Henry) Harrison
vice president: **7** (Richard Mentor) Johnson
cabinet:
  state: **7** (John) Forsyth
  treasury: **8** (Levi) Woodbury
  war: **8** (Joel Roberts) Poinsett
  attorney general: **6** (Benjamin Franklin) Butler, (Felix) Grundy, (Henry Dilworth) Gilpin
  navy: **8** (James Kirke) Paulding **9** (Mahlon) Dickerson
  postmaster general: **5** (John Milton) Niles **7** (Amos) Kendall
born/died/buried: **12** Kinderhook NY
education:
  Academy: **10** Kinderhook
  college: **4** none
  studied: **3** law
religion: **13** Dutch Reformed
vacation:
  toured: **6** Europe (1853-1855)
author: **64** Inquiry into the Origin and Course of Political Parties in the United States
political career: **8** US Senate **11** state Senate **13** vice president **20** state Attorney General
  governor of: **7** New York
  secretary of: **5** State
  minister: **12** Great Britain
civilian career: lawyer
notable events of lifetime/term: **5** Panic (of 1837)
  treaty: **16** Webster-Ashburton
  war: **9** Aroostook
father: **7** Abraham
mother: **5** Maria (Hoes Van Alen)
siblings: **6** Derike, Hannah **7** Abraham **8** Lawrence
wife: **6** Hannah (Hoes)
children: **4** John **6** Martin **7** Abraham **13** Smith Thompson

14 self-admiration, superficiality

Vanity Fair
   author: 25 William Makepeace Thackeray
   character: 10 Becky Sharp **11** Miss Crawley **12** Amelia Sedley, Joseph (Jos) Sedley **13** George Osborne, Rawdon Crawley **14** Sir Pitt Crawley **20** Captain William Dobbin

vanity of vanities
   Latin: 16 vanitas vanitatum

vanquish 4 beat, best, drub, lick, rout **5** crush **6** defeat, master, subdue, thrash **7** conquer **8** overcome **9** overpower, overthrow, overwhelm, subjugate **11** triumph over

vanquisher 6 master, victor, winner **7** subduer **8** champion **9** conqueror **10** subjugator

vanquishment 6 defeat **7** mastery, triumph, victory, winning **8** conquest **10** conquering, overcoming

Van Slyke, Helen
   author of: 10 No Love Lost **15** A Necessary Woman, The Heart Listens **18** Always Is Not Forever

Van Tassel, Katrina
   character in: 23 The Legend of Sleepy Hollow
   author: 6 Irving

Vanuatu *see box*

vapid 4 dull, flat, lame, tame **5** bland, empty, stale **7** insipid **8** lifeless **9** colorless, pointless **10** flavorless, wishywashy **11** meaningless, uninspiring **12** unsatisfying **13** characterless

vapor 3 dew, fog **4** haze, mist, smog **5** fumes, smoke, steam **6** miasma **8** moisture

vaporize 5 dry up **7** distill **8** condense, melt away **9** dissipate, evaporate

Varden, Gabriel/Dolly
   character in: 12 Barnaby Rudge
   author: 7 Dickens

Vargas Llosa, Mario
   author of: 13 The Green House **16** The Time of the Hero **26** Conversation in the Cathedral **27** Aunt Julia and the Scriptwriter **34** Captain Pantoja and the Special Service

variable 6 fickle, fitful, uneven, unlike **7** diverse, mutable **8** changing, shifting, unstable, wavering **9** alterable, different, spasmodic, unsettled **10** capri-

---

Vanuatu
   other name: 11 New Hebrides
   capital/largest city: 4 Vila
   others: 5 Santo **6** Forari **10** Luganville
   school: 7 Malapoa
   monetary unit: 5 franc **7** centime
   island: 3 Api, Epi **4** Aoba, Gaua, Malo, Tana, Vate **5** Banks, Efate, Maewo, Santo, Tanna **6** Ambrym, Mabrim, Torres **8** Aneityum, Malekula **9** Erromanga, Pentecost, Vanua Lava **13** Espiritu Santo
   mountain: 6 Lopevi
   highest point: 11 Tabwemasana
   sea: 7 Pacific
   people: 8 European **10** Melanesian, Polynesian **11** Micronesian
      explorer: **4** Cook **7** Queiros
      leader: **4** Lini
   language: 6 French **7** Bislama, English **16** Melanesian Pidgin
   religion: 7 animism **8** Anglican, John Frum **10** Protestant **12** Presbyterian **13** Roman Catholic
   feature:
      cult: **5** cargo

---

cious, changeable, inconstant, indefinite **11** fluctuating

variance 4 odds **6** change **7** dispute, quarrel **9** deviation, disparity **10** contention, difference, dissension, divergence, unlikeness **11** discrepancy, incongruity **12** disagreement, modification **13** dissimilarity, inconsistency

variant 7 altered, derived, takeoff **8** modified **9** departure, different, divergent, variation **10** alteration **11** transformed **12** modification **14** transformation

variation 6 change **7** variant, variety **8** mutation, variance **9** departure, deviation, diversity **10** aberration, alteration, difference, divergency, innovation **11** discrepancy **12** disagreement, modification **13** metamorphosis **14** transformation

varicolored 6 calico, motley, tartan **7** dappled, flecked, marbled, mottled, piebald **9** multi-

---

hued **10** iridescent, opalescent, variegated **11** rainbowlike, technicolor **12** multicolored, parti-colored **13** polychromatic

varied 5 mixed **6** motley, sundry **7** diverse, various **8** assorted **9** different **10** variegated **11** diversified **13** heterogeneous, miscellaneous

variegated 4 pied **6** motley **7** checked, dappled, mottled, piebald **9** checkered **12** particolored

variety 4 hash, kind, race, sort, type **5** brand, breed, class, genre, genus, group, stock, tribe **6** change, family, jumble, medley, motley, strain **7** melange, mixture, species **8** category, division, pastiche **9** diversity, patchwork, variation **10** assortment, collection, difference, hodgepodge, innovation, miscellany, subspecies **11** subdivision **12** denomination, multiplicity, unconformity **13** dissimilarity, heterogeneity, nonuniformity **14** classification, omniumgatherum **15** diversification

various 3 few **4** many, some **5** other **6** divers, myriad, sundry, varied **7** diverse, several **8** assorted, manifold, numerous **9** countless, different **10** dissimilar **11** innumerable **12** multifarious **13** miscellaneous, multitudinous

varlet 3 cur **6** rascal, wretch **7** villain **9** scoundrel **10** blackguard

Varner, Will
   character in: 9 The Hamlet
   author: 8 Faulkner

varnish 4 gilt **5** adorn, cover, gloss, stain **6** excuse, soften **7** conceal, lacquer **8** disguise, mitigate **9** embellish, gloss over **10** smooth over

vary 4 veer **5** alter, shift **6** change, depart, differ, modify **7** deviate, dissent, diverge **8** be unlike, contrast, disagree **9** alternate, disaccord, diversify, fluctuate

vase 3 jar, jug, pot, urn **5** crock, diota **8** canister **9** container **10** jardiniere

Vashti
   husband: 9 Ahasuerus
   replaced by: 6 Esther

vassal 4 serf **5** helot, liege, slave **6** tenant, thrall **7** bondman, servant, subject, villein **8** retainer **9** bondslave, bondwoman, dependent **11** subordinate

vassalage 4 yoke **7** bondage, serfdom, slavery **9** servitude **11** enslavement

vast 4 huge, wide **5** great, jumbo **7** endless, immense, titanic, very big **8** colossal, enormous, far-flung, gigantic, infinite, spacious **9** boundless, capacious, extensive, limitless, monstrous, unbounded, unlimited, very large **10** monumental, prodigious, stupendous, tremendous, voluminous, widespread **11** far-reaching, measureless, significant, substantial **12** immeasurable, interminable

vastness 7 bigness **8** enormity, hugeness **9** immensity, largeness **12** enormousness

Vathek
　author: **15** William Beckford

Vaticanus 16 Greek uncial codex

Vaughan Williams, Ralph
　born: **7** Britain **10** Down Ampney
　composer of: **3** Job **8** The Wasps **9** Flos Campi **10** Antarctica (symphony No 7), **11** Old King Cole **12** A Sea Symphony **13** Hugh the Drover, On Wenlock Edge, Sir John in Love; Songs of Travel **14** Riders to the Sea, The House of Life, The Sons of Light **15** A London Symphony, The Poisoned Kiss **16** The Lark Ascending **17** A Pastoral Symphony **18** Five Tudor Portraits, Sinfonia Antarctica **19** The Pilgrim's Progress **22** Toward the Unknown Region

Vaughn, Robert
　born: **9** New York NY
　roles: **7** Bullitt **12** Napoleon Solo **15** The Man from UNCLE **19** The Magnificent Seven **22** The Young Philadelphians

vault 4 arch, dome, jump, leap, safe, tomb **5** bound, clear, crypt **6** arcade, cupola, hurdle, spring **7** ossuary **8** catacomb, jump over, leapfrog, leap over, wall safe **9** mausoleum, polevault, sepulcher, strongbox **10** arched roof, spring over, strongroom **13** arched ceiling, burial chamber

vaunt 5 strut **6** brag of, flaunt **7** exult in, show off, swagger **9** crow about, gasconade, gloat over **10** boast about

vaunted 7 exalted, praised **11** gloated over, overpraised **12** boasted about

Veary, Arthur
　real name of: **14** Arthur Treacher

veer 3 yaw **4** jibe, tack, turn **5** curve, dodge, drift, shift, wheel **6** swerve, zigzag **7** go about **9** come round, turn aside **15** change direction

Vegas
　character: **5** Angie **6** Binzer **8** Beatrice, Dan Tanna **10** Bernie Roth **11** (Sgt) Bella Archer
　cast: **10** Tony Curtis **11** Judy Landers, Robert Urich **12** Naomi Stevens, Phyllis Davis **13** Bart Braverman

vegetable 3 pea **4** bean, beet, corn **6** carrot, greens, legume, squash, turnip **7** cabbage, lettuce, parsnip, produce, spinach **8** broccoli, eggplant, lima bean, rutabaga, zucchini **10** string bean **11** cauliflower

vegetarian 5 vegan **8** meatless **9** herbivore **11** herbivorous

vegetation 5 flora, grass, sloth, weeds **6** leaves, plants, torpor **7** foliage, herbage, languor, loafing, verdure **8** dormancy, idleness, lethargy **9** flowerage, indolence, plant life, shrubbery **10** inactivity **11** hibernation, languidness, rustication **12** sluggishness
　god of: **6** Dumuzi

vehemence 4 heat, zeal **5** ardor **6** fervor, warmth **7** passion **9** intensity

vehement 3 hot **4** wild **5** eager, fiery, rabid **6** ardent, fervid, fierce, heated, stormy **7** earnest, excited, fanatic, fervent, furious, intense, violent, zealous **8** agitated, forceful, frenzied, vigorous **9** emotional, fanatical, hotheaded **10** passionate **11** impassioned, tempestuous **12** enthusiastic

vehemently 5 hotly **6** wildly **7** eagerly **8** ardently, fiercely, strongly **9** earnestly, excitedly, fervently, furiously, intensely, violently, zealously **10** vigorously **11** emotionally, fanatically **12** passionately **13** tempestuously **16** enthusiastically

vehicle 3 bus, car **4** tool **5** agent, means, organ, plane, train, truck **6** agency, device, medium **7** bicycle **9** mechanism **10** automobile, conveyance, instrument, motorcycle, rocket ship **12** intermediary **14** transportation

veil 3 dim **4** hide, mask **5** cloak, cloud, cover **6** enwrap, mantle, screen, shroud **7** blanket, conceal, curtain, envelop, obscure **8** covering **10** camouflage

veiled 3 dim **5** murky **6** draped, hidden **7** muffled **8** obscured, shrouded **9** concealed, covered up, disguised, enveloped, enwrapped **11** camouflaged

veiling 3 net **4** mesh **8** cloaking, covering **9** obscurity **10** concealing

vein 3 rib, web **4** bent, hint, line, lode, mark, mood, seam, tone **5** fleck, layer, stria, style, touch **6** furrow, manner, marble, nature, strain, streak, stripe, temper, thread **7** stratum **8** tendency **9** capillary, character **10** complexion, propensity **11** blood vessel, disposition, inclination, temperament **12** predilection **14** predisposition

Veiovis
　god of: **4** dead

Velazquez (Velasquez), Diego Rodriguez de Silvay
　born: **5** Spain **7** Seville
　artwork: **8** Philip IV **10** Las Meninas **13** Luis de Gongora, Pope Innocent X, Venus and Cupid **14** Cardinal Borgia **17** Don Gaspar de Guzman, Isabella of Bourbon **18** Adoration of the Magi, The Tapestry Weavers **19** The Infanta Margarita, The Surrender of Breda **20** Infanta Maria Theresia **21** An Old Woman Cooking Eggs **22** Portrait of a Court Jester, Portrait of Juan de Pareja **23** The Immaculate Conception **30** Prince Balthasar Carlos at the Hunt

veloce
　music: **4** fast

velocity 4 pace **5** haste, speed **8** alacrity, celerity, rapidity **9** fleetness, quickness, swiftness **10** expedition, speediness

venal 5 shady **6** greedy **7** corrupt, crooked, selfish **8** bribable, covetous, grasping **9** dishonest, mercenary, rapacious **10** avaricious **11** corruptible **12** unprincipled, unscrupulous **13** moneygrubbing

venality 7 avarice **10** corruption **11** bribe-taking **13** mercenariness, money-grubbing

vend 4 hawk, sell **5** trade **6** barter, deal in, market, peddle, retail **7** auction, trade in **8** huckster **11** merchandise

Vendetta, La
　author: **14** Honore de Balzac

vendor, vender 6 dealer, hawker, monger, seller, trader 7 peddler 8 huckster, merchant, purveyor, retailer, salesman, supplier 9 trades- man 10 wholesaler 12 mer- chandiser 13 street peddler

veneer 4 coat, mask, show 5 front, layer 6 casing, facade, facing, jacket, sheath 7 coat- ing, overlay, wrapper 8 cover- ing, envelope, pretense 10 outer layer

venerable 3 old 4 aged 5 hoary 6 august 7 admired, ancient, elderly, honored, re- vered 8 esteemed 9 respected, venerated 11 patriarchal, white-haired

venerate 5 adore, extol, honor 6 admire, esteem, hal- low, revere 7 cherish, glorify, idolize, respect, worship 8 look up to 9 reverence 11 pay homage to

venerated 4 holy 5 loved 6 adored, sacred 7 honored, revered 8 hallowed 9 re- spected 10 reverenced, wor- shipped 12 paid homage to

veneration 3 awe 5 honor 6 esteem, homage, wonder 7 respect, worship 8 devotion 9 adoration, adulation, rever- ence 10 admiration, exalta- tion 11 idolization 13 glorification

venereal 6 carnal, sexual 7 genital

Venezuela *see box*

vengeance 7 revenge 8 aveng- ing, reprisal, requital 11 ma- levolence, retaliation, retribution 12 ruthlessness 13 an eye for an eye, implac- ability 14 revengefulness, vin- dictiveness 15 a tooth for a tooth

veni, vidi, vici 19 I came I saw I conquered
    author: 12 Julius Caesar

venial 5 minor 6 slight 7 triv- ial 9 allowable, excusable 10 defensible, forgivable, not serious, pardonable 11 justifia- ble, unimportant, warrantable

Venice *see box*

Venn, Diggory
    character in: 17 Return of the Native
    author: 5 Hardy

venom 3 ire 4 gall, hate 5 an- ger, spite, toxin, virus 6 choler, enmity, grudge, hatred, malice, poison, rancor, spleen 7 ill will 8 acrimony, savagery 9 animosity, barbar-

Venezuela
    name means: 12 little Venice
    capital/largest city: 7 Caracas
    others: 4 Aroa, Coro 6 Atures, Cumana, Merida 7 Barinas, Barines, Cabello, Guaware, Maracay, Maturin 8 Asuncion, Carupano, La Guaira, La Gyayra, Tacupita, Valencia 9 Barcelona, Maracaibo, Tacarigua 12 Barquisimeto, Puerto La Cruz, San Cristobal 13 Cuidad Bolivar, Puerto Cabello 18 Santo Tome de Guayana
    division: 4 Lara 5 Apure, Sucre, Zulia 6 Aragua, Falcon, Merida 7 Barinas, Bolivar, Cojedes, Guarico, Monagas, Tachira, Yaracuy 8 Carabobo, Trujillo
    measure: 5 galon 6 fanega 7 estadel
    monetary unit: 4 peso 5 medio 6 fuerte 7 bolivar, cen- timo 8 morocota 10 venezolano
    weight: 3 bag 5 libra
    island: 4 Aves 7 Cubagua, Tortuga 9 La Orchila, Los Roques, Margarita 11 Los Hermanos 12 La Blanquilla
    lake: 9 Maracaibo, Tacarigua
    mountain: 3 Pao 4 Pava, Yair 5 Andes, Duida, Icutu 6 Concha, Cuneva, Merida, Parima, Sierra, Yumari 7 Imutaca, Masaiti, Roraima 8 Gurupira 9 Pacaraima 10 Auyan-Tepui 11 Turimiquire 18 Cordillera del Norte
    highest point: 7 Bolivar
    river: 3 Oro, Pao 4 Meta 5 Apure, Caura, Negro, Suata, Tigre, Unare, Zulia 6 Amazon, Arauca, Caroni, Cuyuni 7 Guanare, Guanipa, Guarico, Orinoco, Oritueo, Paragua, Suapure, Vichada, Yuruari 8 Guaviare, Manapire, Ventu- ari 9 Cuchivero 10 Casiquiare, Portuguesa
    sea: 8 Atlantic 9 Caribbean
    physical feature:
        falls: 5 Angel
        gulf: 5 Paria 6 Triste 9 Venezuela
        highlands: 6 Guiana 7 Guayana, Segovia
        plains: 6 Llanos
    people: 4 Bare, Pume 5 Bello, Carib, pardo, zambo 6 Ara- wak, Creole, Timote 7 Charoya, Guahibo, Kaliana, mes- tizo, mulatto, Otomaca, Timotex 8 Caquetio, Guarauno, Matilone 11 Maquiritare
        artist: 7 Marisol
        author: 5 Bello 8 Gallegos 13 Diaz-Rodriguez
        explorer: 8 Columbus
        god: 5 Tsuma
        leader: 4 Paez 5 Gomez, Leoni 6 Castro 7 Bolivar, Mi- randa 10 Betancourt 12 Guzman Blanco 14 Herrera Campins
    language: 4 Pume 7 Spanish
    religion: 5 Islam 7 Judaism 10 Protestant 13 Roman Catholic
    feature:
        animal: 4 puma 5 sloth 6 jaguar, ocelot 7 manatee, pec- cary 8 anteater, capybara 9 armadillo
        cowboy: 7 llanero
        dance: 6 joropo 16 diablos danzantes
        folk entertainment: 10 burriquita
        musical instrument: 6 cuatro 7 maracas
        street performance: 8 parranda
    food:
        black beans: 8 caraotas
        bread: 5 arepa
        dish: 7 hallaca 8 cachapos, pabellon
        soup/stew: 8 sancocho

Venice
  art exhibition:
    8 Biennale
  artist: 7 Bellini, Codussi
    8 Fabriano, Longhena,
    Mantegna, Palladio,
    Scamozzi, Veronese
    9 Canaletto, Carpaccio,
    Giorgione, Sansovino
    10 Tintoretto
  capital of: 6 Veneto
    15 Venezia province
  church: 18 San Giorgio
    Maggiore, Santa Maria
    dei Frari 19 Santi Gio-
    vanni e Paolo
  Italian: 7 Venezia
  landmark: 6 Ca' d'Oro
    9 Campanile 10 Grand
    Canal 11 Doge's Palace
    13 Bridge of Sighs
    15 Libreria Vecchia
    16 Palazzo Rezzonico,
    Saint Mark's Church
    20 Accademia di Belle
    Arti 21 Palazzo dei Pro-
    curatori 22 Scuola
    Grande di San Rocco
    23 Palazzo Vendramin-
    Calergi
  port: 8 Marghera
  resort: 9 Lido Beach
  sea: 8 Adriatic
  small canal: 3 rii
  tomb: 5 Titan
  traveler: 9 Marco Polo

ity, brutality, hostility 10 bitterness, resentment
11 malevolence 12 spitefulness 13 maliciousness,
rancorousness

venomous 5 cruel, fatal, toxic
6 bitter, brutal, deadly, lethal,
malign, savage 7 abusive,
caustic, hostile, noxious, vicious 8 spiteful, virulent
9 malicious, malignant, poisonous, rancorous, resentful
10 malevolent 11 ill-disposed
12 bloodthirsty

vent 3 air, tap 4 bare, drip,
emit, gush, hole, ooze,
pipe 5 exude, spout, utter,
voice 6 effuse, escape, faucet,
let out, outlet, reveal, spigot
7 air hole, chimney, debouch,
declare, divulge, express, opening, orifice, release 8 aperture,
disclose, exposure, venthole
9 discharge, let escape, pour
forth, utterance 10 disclosure,
expression, revelation, smokestack, ventilator 11 communicate, declaration

ventilate 3 air, sow 5 voice
6 aerate, air out, report, review, spread 7 analyze, de-

clare, discuss, dissent, divulge,
examine, express 9 broadcast,
circulate, comment on, criticize, oxygenate, publicize, talk
about 10 bandy about 11 disseminate, noise abroad

ventilator 3 fan 4 flue 7 aera-
tor 10 exhaust fan, smokestack 14 air conditioner

venture 2 go 3 bet, try 4 dare,
risk 5 flyer, offer, wager
6 chance, gamble, hazard,
plunge, submit, tender, travel
7 advance, attempt, hold out,
presume, proffer, project 8 endeavor, make bold 9 adventure, risk going, strive for,
undertake, volunteer 10 enterprise, put forward, take a
flyer 11 speculation, uncertainty, undertaking

**venturesome, adventure-
some** 4 bold, rash 5 risky
6 daring, tricky, unsafe, unsure 7 dubious 8 doubtful, insecure, perilous, reckless,
ticklish 9 ambitious, audacious,
dangerous, daredevil, energetic, foolhardy, hazardous,
impetuous, impulsive, uncertain 10 aggressive, precarious
11 adventurous, speculative
12 enterprising, questionable

venturesomeness 6 daring
8 audacity, boldness 9 derring-
do 11 impetuosity
12 recklessness

Venus
  origin: 5 Roman 7 Italian
  goddess of: 6 spring
    7 gardens
  son: 6 Aeneas
  grandson: 5 Iulus
  epithet: 7 Erycina 8 Gene-
    trix 10 Erticordia
  corresponds to: 9 Aphrodite

Venus and Adonis
  author: 18 William
    Shakespeare

veracious 4 true 6 honest
7 sincere 8 accurate, faithful,
truthful 10 scrupulous
11 punctilious

veracity 5 truth 6 candor, verity 7 honesty, probity 8 accuracy, openness 9 exactness,
frankness, integrity, sincerity
10 exactitude 11 correctness
12 truthfulness 13 guilelessness, ingenuousness
14 verisimilitude

Vera-Ellen
  real name: 13 Vera-Ellen
    Rohe
  born: 12 Cincinnati OH
  roles: 9 On the Town
    14 White Christmas

veranda
  Hawaiian: 5 lanai

verbal 4 oral, said 5 vocal
6 spoken, voiced 7 in words,
of verbs, of words, uttered
9 expressed, unwritten

verbal exchange 6 dialog
8 dialogue 10 discussion
12 conversation

verbalize 5 speak, utter, voice
7 express 10 articulate 12 put
into words

verbal thrust 3 dig 4 gibe,
jeer 5 taunt 13 cutting remark

verbatim 5 exact 7 exactly, literal, precise 8 accurate, faithful 9 literally, literatim,
precisely 10 accurately, faithfully 11 to the letter, word for
word 15 chapter and verse,
letter for letter
  Latin: 14 ipsissima verba

verbatim et literatim 21 in
exactly the same words
29 word for word and letter
for letter

verbena
  varieties: 4 moss, rose, sand
    5 clump, lemon, shrub 7 red
    sand 8 pink sand 9 beach
    sand 10 desert sand, Mojave
    sand, yellow sand 12 com-
    mon garden

verbiage 9 logorrhea, loquacity, prolixity, verbosity, wordiness 10 volubility
11 verboseness 12 effusiveness 14 circumlocution, grandiloquence, long-windedness

verbose 5 gabby, wordy 6 prolix 7 voluble 8 effusive 9 garrulous, talkative
10 longwinded, loquacious
13 grandiloquent
14 circumlocutory

verbosity 9 diffusion, prolixity,
talkiness, wordiness 11 diffuseness 13 talkativeness
14 long-windedness

verboten 9 forbidden
10 prohibited

Verdandi 4 Norn
  origin: 12 Scandinavian
  form: 3 elf
  personifies: 7 present
  developed from: 5 Urdar
  companions: 3 Urd 5 Skuld

verdant 4 lush 5 green, leafy,
shady, turfy 6 grassy 7 mea-
dowy 8 blooming, thriving
9 luxuriant 10 burgeoning,
springlike 11 flourishing

Verdi, Giuseppe
  born: 5 Italy 7 Busseto
  composer of: 4 Aida
    6 Otello 7 Macbeth, Na-
    bucco, Othello 8 Falstaff
    9 Don Carlos, Il Corsaro,
    Rigoletto, The Misled 10 La

Traviata **11** Il Trovatore
13 The Troubadour
14 Manzoni Requiem **15** Simon Boccanegra

verdict 6 answer, decree, ruling **7** finding, opinion **8** decision, judgment, sentence **9** valuation **10** assessment, estimation **11** arbitrament, arbitration **12** adjudication **13** determination

Vere, Captain
character in: **9** Billy Budd
author: **8** Melville

Vereen, Ben
born: **7** Miami FL
roles: **5** Roots **6** Pippin **13** Chicken George **20** Jesus Christ Superstar

verge 3 end, hem, lip, rim **4** brim, edge **5** bound, brink, ledge, limit, skirt **6** be near, border, flange, fringe, margin **7** confine, extreme **8** approach, boundary, frontier, terminus **9** threshold **11** approximate **12** be on the brink

verge upon 4 abut **5** flank **6** adjoin, border **8** be next to **10** neighbor on

Vergil, Virgil
author of: **6** Aeneid **8** Bucolics, Eclogues, Georgics

verification 5 proof **7** support **9** guarantee **10** validation **12** confirmation **13** accreditation, certification, corroboration, documentation **14** authentication, substantiation

verify 5 prove **7** certify, confirm, support, sustain, witness **8** accredit, attest to, document, validate, vouch for **9** establish, guarantee, testify to **11** corroborate **12** authenticate, substantiate

verily 4 amen **5** truly **6** really **9** certainly, yes indeed **10** positively

veritable 4 real, true **5** utter, valid **6** actual **7** genuine, literal **8** absolute, bona fide, complete, positive, true-blue **9** authentic **13** incontestable, unimpeachable **14** unquestionable **17** through-and-through

Verlaine, Paul
author of: **6** Wisdom **7** Sagesse **8** Langueur **17** Songs Without Words **19** Romances sans Paroles

Vermeer, Jan
born: **5** Delft **7** Holland
artwork: **11** View of Delft **12** The Lace Maker, The Procuress **13** Drinking Scene **14** A Street in Delft,

The Head of a Girl **15** Allegory of Faith, Girl with a Red Hat **16** The Artist's Studio **18** Girl Reading a Letter, Girl with a Wine-glass **19** A Girl Asleep at a Table, A Painter in his Studio **20** A Woman Weighing Pearls **22** Maidservant Pouring Milk **23** Young Woman with a Water Jug **24** A Soldier and a Laughing Girl **31** Christ in the House of Mary and Martha

vermilion 3 red **7** scarlet **8** cinnabar **9** bright red **15** mercuric sulfide

vermin 4 ants, lice, mice, owls, rats **5** crows, fleas, foxes, pests **6** snakes, wolves **7** bedbugs, coyotes, roaches, spiders, weasels **8** termites, varmints **9** water bugs **10** centipedes, silverfish **11** birds of prey **18** pestiferous insects

Vermont *see box*

vermouth
type: **4** wine **6** brandy **8** aperitif
origin: **5** Italy **6** France

varieties: 3 dry **5** sweet
drink: 9 Boomerang **11** Bittersweet
with bourbon: **9** Allegheny
with brandy: **3** BVD
with Dubonnet: **3** BVD
gin: **5** Bijou, Bronx, Tango **6** Caruso **7** Bermuda, Caberet, Martini **10** Bloodhound
with rum: **6** Bolero **8** Apple Pie **10** Black Devil **11** Shark's Tooth
with rye: **8** Brooklyn **9** Algonquin
with scotch: **8** Affinity **10** Bobby Burns
with sherry: **6** Bamboo, Brazil
with sloe gin: **10** Blackthorn
with vodka: **8** Kangaroo **9** Corkscrew
with whiskey: **9** Manhattan

vernacular 4 cant **5** idiom, lingo, slang **6** jargon, patois **7** dialect **8** parlance, shoptalk **9** the vulgar **12** common speech, native tongue **13** natural speech **14** informal speech, native language

vernal 3 new **5** fresh, green

Vermont
abbreviation: **2** VT
nickname: **13** Green Mountain **20** Four-Season Recreation
capital: **10** Montpelier
largest city: **10** Burlington
others: **5** Barre, Stowe **7** Grafton, Newfane, Newport, Rutland **8** St Albans, Winooski **9** Bountiful, Vergennes **10** Bennington **11** Brattleboro
college: **7** Goddard, Norwich, Trinity, Windham **8** Marlboro **10** Bennington, Middlebury, St Michaels
feature:
covered bridge: **5** Scott
house: **15** Old Constitution
monument: **6** Battle
people: **9** John Deere, John Dewey **10** Ethan Allen **12** Brigham Young **13** Warren R Austin **15** Stephen A Douglas
lake: **7** Caspian, Dunmore, Seymour **8** Bomoseen **9** Champlain **10** Willoughby **12** Memphremagog
land rank: **10** forty-third
mountain: **5** Green, White **7** Bromley, Hogback, Taconic **8** Prospect, Stratton
highest point: **9** Mansfield
physical feature:
uplands: **10** New England
valley: **9** Champlain
president: **14** Calvin Coolidge, Chester A Arthur
river: **4** West **5** Otter, White **7** Saxtons **8** Lamoille, Nulhegan, Winooski **10** Missisquoi **11** Connecticut
state admission: **10** fourteenth
state bird: **12** hermit thrush
state animal: **11** Morgan horse
state flower: **9** red clover
state motto: **15** Freedom and Unity
state song: **11** Hail Vermont
state tree: **10** sugar maple

6 spring 8 youthful
10 springlike

Verne, Jules
author of: 19 Five Weeks in
a Balloon 21 From the
Earth to the Moon
26 Around the World in
Eighty Days 32 Twenty
Thousand Leagues Under
the Sea
character: 11 Captain Nemo,
Phineas Fogg
12 Passepartout

Veronese, Paolo (Cagliari)
born: 5 Italy 6 Verona
artwork: 12 Book of Esther
13 The Last Supper 14 Supper at Emmaus 15 The Rape
of Europa, Triumph of Venice 17 Mary with the Saints,
The Finding of Moses, The
Marriage at Cana, Wisdom
and Strength 19 Martyrdom
of St George, The Choice of
Hercules 21 Esther before
Ahasuerus 22 Feast at the
House of Simon 24 Mars
and Venus United in Love,
The Feast in the House of
Levi, The Temptation of St
Anthony 31 Jesus and the
Centurion of Capernaum
32 The Family of Darius before Alexander

Verrocchio, Andrea del
real name: 31 Andrea di
Michele di Francesco Cione
born: 5 Italy 8 Florence
artwork: 5 David 15 Boy
with a Dolphin 17 Christ
and St Thomas 18 The Bap-
tism of Christ 19 Bartolommeo Colleoni 23 Christ and
Doubting Thomas 25 Be-
heading of John the Baptist

versatile 3 apt 4 able 5 handy
6 adroit, clever, expert, gifted
7 protean 8 talented 9 adaptable, all-around, ingenious,
many-sided 10 proficient
11 many-skilled, resourceful
12 accomplished, multifaceted

verse 4 poem 5 meter, rhyme,
stave 6 jingle, poetry, stanza
7 measure, strophe

versed 4 able 5 adept 6 expert,
taught 7 erudite, learned,
skilled, tutored 8 lettered,
schooled, skillful, well-read
9 competent, practiced, scholarly 10 at home with, in-
structed, proficient
11 enlightened, experienced
12 accomplished, familiar
with, well-informed 14 acquainted with, conversant
with

versifier 4 bard 6 rhymer,
writer 8 minstrel, poetizer,
poetling, rhymster 9 poetaster,

rhymester 10 rhymesmith,
troubadour, versemaker, verse-
smith 11 versemonger
12 balladmonger

version 4 side 5 story 6 report
7 account 9 depiction, rendering 10 adaptation, paraphrase,
re-creation 11 description, restatement, translation
14 interpretation

vers libre 9 free verse

vertebral column
bone of: 5 spine 8 backbone

vertex 3 cap, tip 4 apex, peak
5 crown 6 summit, zenith
8 pinnacle 12 highest point
13 crowning point

vertical 5 plumb, sheer 7 upright 12 ninety-degree
13 perpendicular

vertiginous 5 dizzy, giddy,
shaky 6 whirly 7 reeling
11 lightheaded

vertigo 7 reeling 8 fainting
9 dizziness, giddiness 12 unsteadiness 15 lightheadedness

Vertigo
director: 15 Alfred Hitchcock
cast: 8 Kim Novak 12 James
Stewart 16 Barbara Bel
Geddes
setting: 12 San Francisco
score: 15 Bernard Herrmann

Vertumnus
also: 9 Vortumnus
origin: 5 Roman
god of: 5 fruit 7 gardens, seasons 8 orchards
wife: 6 Pomona

verve 3 vim, zip 4 dash, elan,
fire, zeal 5 ardor, drive, force,
gusto, punch, vigor 6 energy,
fervor, relish, spirit, warmth
7 abandon, feeling, passion,
rapture, sparkle 8 vitality, vivacity 9 animation, eagerness,
vehemence 10 enthusiasm,
liveliness

Verver, Maggie
character in: 13 The Golden
Bowl
author: 5 James

very 4 bare, mere, most, much,
pure 5 exact, extra, plain,
quite, sheer, truly 6 deeply,
highly, hugely, mighty, really,
simple, vastly 7 awfully, exactly, fitting, greatly, notably,
perfect, precise, totally 8 actually, entirely, markedly, specific, suitable, terribly
9 assuredly, certainly, decidedly, eminently, essential, extremely, immensely, intensely,
necessary, obviously, perfectly,
precisely, unusually, veritably
10 abnormally, absolutely,
abundantly, completely, defi-

nitely, especially, particular,
profoundly, remarkably, strikingly, thoroughly, uncom-
monly, undeniably
11 appropriate, exceedingly,
excessively 12 emphatically,
surpassingly, tremendously
13 exceptionally, significantly
14 unquestionably

very best
French: 14 creme de la
creme

Very Easy Death, A
author: 16 Simone de
Beauvoir

very great 4 huge 6 severe
7 extreme, intense, mammoth,
titanic 8 colossal, enormous,
gigantic 9 excessive, monstrous 10 gargantuan, immoderate, inordinate, prodigious
11 magnificent, spectacular
14 Brobdingnagian

very nearly 6 almost 7 close
to 9 just about 10 more or
less, not far from
13 approximately

very old 4 aged 6 primal 7 ancient, antique, archaic 8 primeval 10 antiquated,
primordial 11 prehistoric
12 antediluvian

very soon
French: 11 tout a l'heure

vessel 3 cup, jar, jug, keg,
mug, pot, tub, vat 4 boat,
bowl, butt, cask, dish, duct,
scow, ship, tube, vase, vein
5 barge, craft, crock, flask,
glass, liner, plate, yacht 6 artery, barrel, beaker, carafe,
flagon, goblet, packet, tanker,
whaler 7 caldron, collier,
cruiser, platter, tankard, trawler, tugboat, tumbler, utensil
8 decanter, paquebot, sailboat
9 capillary, container, ferry-
boat, freighter, houseboat,
steamboat, steamship 10 ocean
liner, receptacle

vest 3 rig 4 garb, robe 5 array,
drape, dress 6 attire, clothe,
enwrap, fit out, jacket, jerkin
7 apparel, deck out, doublet,
envelop 8 accouter 9 waistcoat

Vesta
origin: 5 Roman
goddess of: 6 hearth
festival: 8 Vestalia
corresponds to: 4 Caca
6 Hestia

vestal 4 pure 6 chaste, maiden,
simple, virgin 8 maidenly, virginal, virtuous 9 pure woman,
undefiled, unmarried, un-
worldly 10 immaculate
15 unsophisticated

vested 5 fixed 7 settled 8 abso-

lute, complete **9** permanent
10 guaranteed **11** established,
inalienable **12** indisputable
14 unquestionable

vestibule 4 hall **5** entry, foyer,
lobby **6** lounge **7** hallway, passage **8** anteroom, corridor
10 passageway **11** antechamber, entrance way, waiting
room **12** entrance hall

vestige 4 sign **5** relic, token,
trace **6** record **7** memento,
remnant **8** evidence, souvenir

vestments 4 garb, gear
5 dress **6** livery, outfit **7** apparel, clothes, costume, rai-
ment, regalia, uniform
8 clothing **9** trappings
13 accoutrements

vesture 4 robe **5** robes **7** apparel, clothes, garment, raiment **8** clothing, garments
9 vestments

vetch 5 Vicia
varieties: **3** cow **4** bard, bird,
milk **5** crown, hairy, Sitka
6 bitter, common, kidney,
purple, smooth, spring,
tufted, winter **8** Narbonne
9 horseshoe, Hungarian,
woolly-pod **12** large Russian

veteran 3 vet **6** expert, master
7 old hand **8** old-timer, seasoned **9** ex-soldier **10** campaigner, old soldier, war
veteran **11** experienced **12** ex-
serviceman **13** long-practiced

veto 4 deny, void **6** denial, enjoin, forbid, negate, reject
7 nullify, prevent, refusal
8 disallow, prohibit, turn
down **9** rejection **10** prevention **11** disallowing, prohibition **12** disallowance **16** turn
thumbs down on

vex 3 bug, irk **4** fret, gall, miff,
pain, rile **5** anger, annoy;
chafe, harry, pique, upset,
worry **6** badger, bother, grieve,
harass, hassle, nettle, pester,
plague, ruffle **7** chagrin, disturb, provoke, torment, trouble **8** distress, irritate
9 displease **10** exasperate
18 ruffle one's feathers

vexation 5 pique, trial **6** hassle **7** torment **8** headache, nuisance **9** annoyance
10 affliction, harassment, irritation **11** aggravation **13** pain
in the neck

vexatious 5 pesky **6** thorny,
vexing **8** annoying, nettling
9 badgering, harassing, hector-
ing, provoking, troubling, worrisome **10** bothersome,
irritating **11** disquieting, pestiferous, troublesome

vexed 5 irked, riled, testy
6 galled, miffed, piqued **7** annoyed, nettled, peevish **8** provoked **9** irritated
11 disgruntled, exasperated

viable 6 usable **8** feasible,
workable **9** adaptable, practical **10** applicable
11 practicable

viaduct 4 ramp, span
8 overpass

vial 5 ampul, flask, phial
7 ampoule

via media 10 a middle way

viands 4 cate, diet, eats, fare,
food **7** cuisine, edibles, vittles
8 victuals **9** provender
10 foodstuffs, provisions

vibrancy 4 fire **5** ardor **7** elation **8** vitality, vivacity **9** animation **10** enthusiasm **11** high
spirits

vibrant 4 deep, loud **5** alive,
eager, vital, vivid **6** ardent,
bright, florid, lively **7** fervent,
glowing, intense, orotund,
pealing, pulsing, radiant, ringing **8** animated, bell-like, colorful, forceful, luminous,
lustrous, resonant, sonorous,
spirited, vehement **9** brilliant,
deep-toned, energetic, quivering, thrilling, throbbing, vibrating, vivacious
10 fluttering, glittering, resounding, shimmering **11** full
of vigor, resplendent, reverberant **12** electrifying,
enthusiastic

vibrate 4 beat, sway **5** quake,
swing, throb, waver **6** quaver,
quiver, ripple, wobble **7** flutter, pulsate, tremble **8** undulate **9** oscillate, palpitate,
pendulate **11** reverberate

vibration 5 quake **6** quiver,
tremor **7** quaking **9** quivering,
throbbing, trembling

vicar 6 cleric, parson, pastor
8 preacher **9** churchman, clergyman **12** ecclesiastic

vicarious 6 mental **7** by proxy
8 imagined, indirect **9** imaginary, surrogate **10** empathetic,
fantasized, secondhand **11** at
one remove, sympathetic

Vicar of Wakefield, The
author: **15** Oliver Goldsmith
character: **6** George, Olivia,
Sophia **7** Deborah **10** Dr
Primrose, Mr Burchill
14 Arabella Wilmot
15 Squire Thornhill **19** Sir
William Thornhill

vice 4 flaw **5** fault **6** defect
7 blemish, failing, frailty **8** iniquity, weakness **9** depravity,

weak point **10** corruption, debauchery, degeneracy, profligacy, wantonness, wickedness
11 shortcoming **12** imperfection **14** licentiousness

vice president
resigned: **10** Spiro Agnew
12 John C Calhoun
accused of treason: **9** Aaron
Burr **17** John C
Breckinridge
youngest elected: **17** John C
Breckinridge
elected by Senate: **14** Richard Johnson
elected but did not serve:
11 William King
rejected nomination:
11 Frank Lowden, Silas
Wright
lived longest: **15** John Nance
Garner
succeeded to presidency:
9 John Tyler **10** Gerald
Ford **12** Harry S Truman
13 Andrew Johnson **14** Calvin Coolidge, Chester A Arthur, Lyndon B Johnson
15 Millard Fillmore
17 Theodore Roosevelt

vice versa 9 in reverse
10 conversely **12** contrariwise
16 the other way round **18** in
the opposite order

vicinity 4 area **6** region **8** environs, locality, vicinage **9** adjoining, precincts, proximity
11 environment, propinquity
12 neighborhood, surroundings

vicious 3 bad **4** base, evil, foul,
mean, vile, wild **5** awful,
cruel, gross, nasty, surly
6 brutal, fierce, horrid, savage,
sullen, wicked **7** hateful, heinous, hellish, immoral, inhuman, untamed, violent
8 churlish, depraved, fiendish,
libelous, shocking, spiteful,
terrible, venomous **9** abhorrent, atrocious, barbarous,
dangerous, ferocious, invidious, malicious, monstrous, nefarious, offensive, predatory,
rancorous **10** abominable,
defamatory, diabolical, ill-
humored, ill-natured, malevolent, pernicious, slanderous,
villainous, vindictive **11** acrimonious, ill-tempered, treacherous **12** bloodthirsty

viciousness 4 evil **6** malice
7 cruelty **8** ferocity, savagery,
villainy, violence **9** barbarity,
brutality, ill nature **10** fierceness, wickedness
11 heinousness

vicissitude 6 change **8** mutation **9** variation **10** difficulty,
mutability, succession
11 fluctuation

Vicomte of Bragelonne, The
   author: 14 Alexandre Dumas (pere)

victim 4 butt, dead, dupe, gull, mark, pawn, prey, tool **5** patsy **6** pigeon, quarry, sucker, target **7** injured, wounded **8** casualty, fatality, innocent **9** scapegoat

victimize 3 con **4** dupe, gull, hoax **5** bully, cheat, cozen **6** betray, delude **7** deceive, defraud **8** hoodwink **9** bamboozle

victor 6 winner **8** champion, medalist **9** conqueror **10** vanquisher **11** prizewinner

Victoria
   capital of: 8 Hong Kong **10** Seychelles

Victoria
   origin: 5 Roman
   goddess of: 7 victory
   corresponds to: 4 Nike

Victorian 4 prim, smug **6** narrow, proper, stuffy **7** insular, prudish **8** priggish **9** pietistic **10** tight-laced **11** puritanical, straitlaced **12** conventional, hypocritical **13** sanctimonious

victorious 7 winning **8** champion **10** conquering, successful, triumphant **11** vanquishing **12** championship, prizewinning

Victor Victoria
   director: 12 Blake Edwards
   cast: 10 Alex Karras **11** James Garner **12** Julie Andrews **13** Robert Preston **14** John Rhys-Davies **15** Lesley Ann Warren
   setting: 5 Paris

victory 7 laurels, success, the palm, triumph **8** conquest, the prize **9** supremacy **10** ascendancy **11** superiority
   god of: 3 Tyr
   goddess of: 4 Nike **8** Victoria

Victory
   author: 12 Joseph Conrad
   character: 4 Lena, Wang **5** Jonas, Pedro **8** Davidson **9** Axel Heyst, Schomberg **13** Martin Ricardo

victuals 4 chow, diet, eats, fare, feed, food, grub, meat **5** meals **6** fodder, forage, repast, stores, viands **7** cooking, cuisine, edibles, rations, vittles **8** supplies **9** groceries, provender **10** foodstuffs, provisions **11** comestibles, nourishment, refreshment

Vidal, Gore
   author of: 4 Burr **5** Kalki **6** Julian **8** Creation **16** Myra Breckinridge **18** Eighteen

Seventy-Six, The Judgment of Paris **19** Visit to a Small Planet

Vidar
   origin: 12 Scandinavian
   father: 4 Odin **5** Othin
   killed: 6 Fenrir, Fenris

vide 3 see

vide ante 9 see before

vide infra 8 see below

videlicet 6 namely **11** that is to say
   abbreviation: 3 viz

vide post 8 see after **10** see further

vide supra 8 see above

vide ut supra 10 see as above **16** see as stated above

Vidor, King
   director of: 8 The Crowd **12** Stella Dallas, The Big Parade **16** Northwest Passage

vie 4 life **5** fight **6** strive **7** compete, contend, contest **8** be a rival, struggle, tilt with **9** challenge

Vienna
   airport: 9 Schwechat
   area: 11 Innere Stadt
   capital of: 7 Austria
   early name: 4 Wena **9** Vindobono
   German: 4 Wein
   landmark: 7 Hofburg **10** Stadtsoper **13** Saint Stephen's **15** Albertina Museum, Belvedere Palace **16** Historical Museum, Schonbrunn Palace
   river: 6 Danube
   ruler: 8 Hapsburg
   street: 11 Ringstrasse

Vientiane, Viengchan
   capital of: 4 Laos

vi et armis 20 with force and with arms

Vietnam *see box, p. 1050*

view 3 eye, ken, see **4** gaze, look, note, peek, peep, scan **5** judge, scene, sight, study, vista, watch **6** behold, belief, gaze at, glance, look at, notion, regard, survey, take in, theory, vision **7** diorama, examine, explore, feeling, glimpse, inspect, observe, opinion, outlook, picture, scenery, thought, witness **8** attitude, consider, glance at, judgment, panorama, perceive, pore over, prospect **9** landscape, sentiment, spectacle **10** conception, conviction, scrutinize, think about **11** contemplate, perspective

view as 4 deem, hold **5** count,

judge, think **6** regard **7** account, believe **8** consider, take to be **10** look upon as

viewpoint 4 bias, side **5** angle, slant **6** aspect, belief **7** feeling, opinion **8** attitude, position **9** sentiment **10** conviction, standpoint **11** orientation, perspective **12** vantage point **16** frame of reference

view with disfavor 7 condemn, dislike **8** object to **9** frown upon **10** disapprove, think ill of **13** look askance at, regard as wrong **14** discountenance **15** take exception to

view with horror 5 abhor **6** eschew **8** sicken at **9** abominate, shudder at **10** recoil from, shrink from

vif
   music: 6 lively

vigilance 4 care, heed **7** caution, concern **8** prudence **9** alertness, attention **10** precaution **11** carefulness, forethought, guardedness, heedfulness **12** cautiousness, watchfulness **14** circumspection

vigilant 4 wary **5** alert, chary **7** careful, guarded, heedful, on guard, prudent **8** cautious, watchful **9** attentive, observant, wide-awake **10** on one's toes, on the alert **11** circumspect, on one's guard **12** on the lookout, on the qui vive

vigor 3 pep, vim, zip **4** dash, elan, fire, zeal **5** ardor, drive, force, might, power, verve **6** energy, fervor, spirit **7** passion, stamina **8** haleness, strength, vitality, vivacity **9** animation, hardiness, intensity, vehemence **10** enthusiasm, liveliness, robustness **11** earnestness **12** forcefulness

vigorous 4 bold, hale **5** hardy, lusty, vital **6** active, ardent, brawny, lively, mighty, robust, strong, sturdy, virile **7** dynamic, intense, vibrant **8** forceful, muscular, powerful, spirited **9** assertive, energetic **10** aggressive

vigorously 4 hard **7** briskly, lustily **8** actively, cogently, forcibly, robustly, strongly, sturdily **9** with force **10** forcefully, powerfully **11** strenuously **13** energetically

Vigrid
   origin: 12 Scandinavian
   final battlefield of: 4 gods

Viking, viking 4 Dane **6** pirate **7** mariner **8** Norseman,

Vietnam
   other name: 5 Annam 15 French Indochina
   capital: 5 Hanoi 6 Saigon
   largest city: 6 Saigon 13 Ho Chi Minh City
   others: 3 Hue, Ron 4 Ngai, Vinh 5 Dalat, Hoa Da, Hoian
      6 Annhon, Cholon, Danang, Hongay 7 Bacninh, Cam
      Ranh, Caobang, Donghoi, Hoabinh, Namdinh, Quinhon,
      Songoan, Tayninh, Viettri, Vinhloi 8 Binhdinh, Haiphong,
      Nhatrang, Panthiet, Phan Rang, Quangtri, Quangyen,
      Thanhhoa, Vinhlong 9 Haiphoang, Longxuyen
      11 Dienbienphu
   school: 3 Hue 5 Hanoi 9 Ho Chi Minh
   division: 5 Annam, North, South 6 Tonkin 11 Cochin
      China
   measure: 4 gang, phan, thon
   monetary unit: 2 xu 4 dong 7 piaster
   weight: 3 can, yet 4 uyen
   mountain: 6 Badinh, Badink 7 Nindhoa, Ninhhoa 8 Fansi-
      pan, Knontran, Ngoolinh, Ngoolink, Tchepone, Tclepore
      18 Annamese Cordillera
   highest point: 8 Fan Si Pan
   river: 2 Bo, Ca, Da, Lo, Ma 3 Chu, Gam, Koi, Red
      4 Chay 5 Nhiha 6 Mekong 7 Dongnai
   sea: 10 South China
   physical feature:
      delta: 6 Mekong 8 Red River
      gulf: 4 Siam 6 Tonkin 7 Tonking 8 Thailand
      peninsula: 11 Indochinese
   people: 3 Hoa, Man, Meo, Tai, Tay 4 Cham, Kinh, Nung,
      Thai 5 Khmer, Malay, Muong 7 Chinese 8 Annamese,
      Annamite 9 Cambodian 10 montagnard, Vietnamese
      leader: 5 Le Loi 8 Le Duc Tho 9 Ho Chi Minh 11 Ngo
         Dinh Diem, Pham Van Doug 14 Nguyen Van Thieu
   language: 3 Yue 4 Cham 5 Khmer, Rhade 6 French
      7 Chinese, English 9 Cantonese 10 Vietnamese
   religion: 6 Cao Dai, Hoa Hao, Taoism 7 animism 8 Bud-
      dhism 12 Christianity, Confucianism 13 Roman Catholic
   place:
      ruins: 10 Nguyen tomb
   feature:
      army: 4 ARVN 5 COSVN 8 Communsi, Viet Cong, Viet
         Minh
      clothing: 5 ao dai
      new year: 3 Tet

Northman, searover 9 plunderer 12 Scandinavian
boat: 8 long ship
burial: 9 ship grave
chieftain: 4 jarl
exploration: 5 Italy, Spain
   6 France, Russia 7 England,
   Germany, Iceland, Ireland,
   Vinland 9 Greenland
famous: 4 Eric 8 Eirikson, Ericsson 10 Eric the Red
   11 Leif Ericson
governing council: 4 Ting
   5 Thing 8 Folkmoot
legend: 4 Edda, saga
origin: 6 Norway, Sweden
   7 Denmark, Finland
warrior: 7 beserk 9 berserker
writing: 4 rune

Vila
   capital of: 7 Vanuatu

vile 3 bad, low 4 base, evil,
   foul, lewd, mean, ugly 5 awful, gross, nasty 6 coarse,
filthy, odious, sinful, smutty,
sordid, vulgar, wicked
7 beastly, hateful, heinous, ignoble, immoral, obscene, vicious 8 depraved, shameful,
shocking, wretched 9 abhorrent, degrading, execrable, invidious, loathsome, nefarious,
obnoxious, offensive, perverted, repellent, repugnant,
repulsive, revolting, salacious
10 abominable, degenerate,
despicable, detestable, disgusting, iniquitous, unpleasant,
villainous 11 disgraceful, foul-
mouthed, humiliating 12 contemptible 13 objectionable

Vile Bodies
   author: 11 Evelyn Waugh

vileness 4 evil 8 foulness, iniquity, villainy 9 depravity, nastiness 10 immorality,
   odiousness 11 degradation,
   heinousness, viciousness

12 wretchedness 13 offen-
siveness

Vili
   origin: 12 Scandinavian
   brother: 4 Odin 5 Othin

vilification 5 libel 7 calumny,
   slander 10 defamation
   13 disparagement

vilifier 5 scold 6 carper, critic
   7 reviler 9 backbiter

vilify 5 abuse 6 defame, revile
   7 slander 8 bad-mouth, dishonor 9 criticize, disparage
   14 inveigh against

vilifying 7 abusive 8 libelous
   9 malignant 10 calumnious,
   defamatory, slanderous

villa, Villa 5 aldea, dacha
   6 castle, Pancho 7 chateau,
   mansion 9 residence 13 country estate

village 4 burg 6 hamlet, suburb 8 hick town 9 small
   town 11 whistlestop
   12 municipality

Village, A
   author: 10 Sholem Asch

villain 3 cad, cur, rat 5 knave,
   louse, rogue 6 rascal, rotter,
   varlet 7 caitiff, stinker 8 evildoer, scalawag 9 miscreant,
   scoundrel 10 blackguard, malefactor 11 rapscallion 12 transgressor, wicked person
   15 snake in the grass

villainous 4 base, evil, foul,
   vile 6 wicked 7 caddish, heinous 8 horrible, infamous
   9 monstrous, nefarious
   10 abominable, despicable, detestable, maleficent 12 black-
   guardly 13 reprehensible

villainy 4 evil 8 vileness 9 depravity, rascality 10 wickedness 11 viciousness,
   maleficence

Villa-Lobos, Heitor
   born: 6 Brazil 12 Rio de
      Janeiro
   composer of: 6 Choros
      20 Bachianas Brasileiras

Villefort
   character in: 21 The Count
      of Monte Cristo
   author: 5 Dumas (pere)

villein 4 carl, esne, serf 5 ceorl,
   churl, slave 6 drudge 7 bondman, peasant 9 bondwoman

Villette
   author: 15 Charlotte Bronte

Villon, Francois
   author of: 9 The Legacy
      16 Le grand testament, Le
      petit testament
   quote: 25 Mais ou sont les

neiges d'antan **31** But where are the snows of yesteryear

Villuppo
  character in: **17** The Spanish Tragedy
  author: **3** Kyd

vim 2 go **3** pep, zip **4** dash, fire, snap, zeal **5** ardor, drive, force, might, power, punch, verve, vigor **6** energy, fervor, spirit **7** passion, potency **8** strength, vitality, vivacity **9** animation, intensity, vehemence **10** enthusiasm, liveliness

vin 4 wine

Vincentio
  character in: **17** Measure for Measure
  author: **11** Shakespeare

vincit omnia veritas 16 truth conquers all **22** truth conquers all things

vindicate 4 free **5** clear **6** acquit, assert, defend, excuse, uphold **7** absolve, bear out, bolster, justify, support **8** advocate, champion, maintain **9** discharge, exculpate, exonerate **11** corroborate **12** substantiate

vindication 6 excuse **7** apology, defense **11** explanation **13** justification

vindictive 6 bitter, malign **8** avenging, punitive, spiteful, vengeful **9** malicious **10** malevolent, revengeful **11** retaliative, retaliatory, unforgiving

vinegarish 4 acid, sour, tart **5** harsh **6** acidic, biting **7** acerbic, pungent **9** acidulous **10** astringent

vin ordinaire 12 ordinary wine **20** inexpensive table wine

vintage 3 era, old **4** aged, date, fine, rare **5** epoch, great, prime, prize **6** choice, period **7** ancient, antique **8** sterling, superior **9** excellent, out-of-date, wonderful **11** outstanding **12** old-fashioned

Viola (Cesario)
  character in: **12** Twelfth Night
  author: **11** Shakespeare

violate 4 rape **5** abuse, break **6** defile, invade, ravish **7** disobey, outrage, profane **8** dishonor, infringe, trespass **9** blaspheme, desecrate, disregard, trample on **10** contravene, transgress **12** encroach upon

violation 5 abuse **6** breach **8** trespass **9** sacrilege **10** defile-

ment, infraction **11** desecration, dishonoring **12** encroachment, infringement **13** contravention, nonobservance, transgression

violence 4 fury, rage **5** force, might, power **6** impact **7** outrage **8** ferocity, savagery, severity **9** brutality, intensity, onslaught **10** bestiality, fierceness **11** desecration, profanation **13** ferociousness, physical force **16** bloodthirstiness

violent 3 hot **4** wild **5** cruel, fiery **6** brutal, fierce, insane, raging, savage, severe, strong, unruly **7** berserk, furious, intense, rampant **8** maniacal, vehement **9** explosive, ferocious, hotheaded, murderous, unbridled **10** passionate **11** full of force, intractable, tempestuous **12** ungovernable **14** uncontrollable

Violent Bear It Away, The
  author: **15** Flannery O'Connor

Violent Land, The
  author: **10** Jorge Amado

violet 5 Viola
  varieties: **3** dog, red **4** bush, pale, pine, rock, tree, wood **5** coast, cream, dame's, false, flame, green, marsh, pansy, sweet, water **6** Alaska, alpine, Canada, garden, German, horned, plains, stream **7** African, English, Mexican, Olympic, Persian, redwood, scarlet, striped, two-eyed **8** bird-foot, crowfoot, dog-tooth, florist's, hook-spur, Labrador, larkspur, Missouri, trailing **9** early blue, evergreen, ivyleaved, marsh blue, sagebrush, tall white **10** Australian, great basin, Philippine, sweet white, western dog, woolly blue, yellow wood **11** Alpine marsh, American dog, arrow-leaved, Confederate, downy yellow, early yellow, lance-leaved, longspurred, northern bog, strapleaved **12** eastern water, great-spurred, kidney-leaved, northern blue, smooth yellow **13** common African, Halberd-leaved, northern downy, northern white, purple prairie, southern coast, white dog-tooth, yellow prairie **14** primrose-leaved, triangle-leaved **16** California golden, large-leaved white **17** round-leaved yellow, western sweet white **18** western round-leaved

violin family
  instruments: **3** kit **5** cello, re-

bec, viola **7** baryton **8** bass viol, lyra viol, violetta **10** hurdy-gurdy **11** viola d'amore, violoncello **12** tromba marina, viola pomposa **13** lira da braccio **14** violino piccolo **15** hardanger fiddle

viper
  group of: **4** nest

Viper's Tangle, The
  author: **15** Francois Mauriac

virago 3 nag **4** fury **5** harpy, scold, shrew, vixen **6** dragon, gorgon **7** she-wolf **8** battle-ax, fishwife, harridan **9** termagant, Xanthippe

Virbius
  origin: **5** Roman
  god of: **6** forest **7** hunting

Virchow, Rudolf
  field: **8** medicine **9** pathology
  nationality: **6** German
  completed formulation of:
    10 cell theory

Virgil *see* **8** Vergil

virgin 4 girl, lass, maid, pure **6** chaste, damsel, maiden, unused **7** unmixed **8** pristine **9** unalloyed, undefiled, unsullied, untouched **10** unpolluted **13** unadulterated **14** uncontaminated
  constellation of: **5** Virgo

Virgin *see* **4** Mary

Virginia *see box, p. 1052*

Virginian, The
  author: **10** Owen Wister
  character: **5** Betsy, Randy, Steve **6** Shorty **7** Trampas **9** Molly Wood **10** Judge (Henry) Garth
  cast: **8** Lee J Cobb **10** Gary Clarke, James Drury, Pippa Scott, Randy Boone **11** Doug McClure **12** Roberta Shore
  setting: **11** Shiloh Ranch **16** Wyoming Territory

Virginians, The
  author: **25** William Makepeace Thackeray

Virgin Mary
  ingredient: **11** tomato juice

Virgin Soil
  author: **12** Ivan Turgenev

Virgo
  symbol: **6** virgin
  planet: **7** Mercury
  rules: **7** service
  born: **6** August **9** September

virile 4 bold **5** brave, hardy, husky, lusty, manly **6** brawny, heroic, manful, mighty, potent, robust, strong **7** valiant **8** fearless, forceful, muscular, powerful, resolute, stalwart, vigorous **9** audacious, mascu-

Virginia
abbreviation: 2 VA
nickname: 11 Old Dominion
capital: 8 Richmond
largest city: 7 Norfolk
others: 5 Galax, Luray, Salem 6 Marion 7 Bedford, Bristol, Emporia, Fairfax, Pulaski, Roanoke 8 Danville, Hopewell, Manassas, Staunton, St Albans, Tazewell, Yorktown 9 Arlington, Lexington, Lynchburg 10 Alexandria, Appomattox, Petersburg, Portsmouth, Waynesboro, Winchester 11 Newport News 12 Hampton Roads, Martinsville, Williamsburg 13 Virginia Beach 14 Fredericksburg 15 Charlottesville
college: 3 Lee 7 Hampton, Madison, Radford 8 Longwood, Richmond 10 Washington 11 Mary Baldwin, Old Dominion 13 Randolph Macon 14 Averett Hollins, Mary Washington, William and Mary
feature:
  battle site: 7 Bull Run 8 Fair Oaks, Manassas, Richmond, Yorktown 10 Petersburg, Seven Pines, Wilderness 12 Spotsylvania 14 Fredericksburg 16 Chancellorsville
  dam: 4 Kerr
  historical site: 10 Monticello 11 Mount Vernon 12 Williamsburg 13 Stratford Hall
  national monument: 26 George Washington Birthplace
  national park: 10 Shenandoah 26 Colonial National Historical
tribe: 6 Saponi, Tutelo 7 Monacan 8 Manahoac, Meherrin, Nottaway, Pamunkey, Powhatan 9 Matchotic 10 Appomuttoc
people: 9 Henry Clay, John Rolfe, John Smith 10 Robert E Lee, Walter Reed 11 George Mason 12 John Marshall, Patrick Henry 13 Samuel Houston 14 Cyrus McCormick 15 Meriwether Lewis 17 Booker T Washington, Richard Evelyn Bird 18 Light-Horse Harry (Henry) Lee
lake: 4 Kerr 5 Smith
land rank: 11 thirty-sixth
mountain: 5 Cedar 6 Clinch, Elliot 8 Baldknob 9 Allegheny, Blueridge
  highest point: 6 Rogers
physical feature:
  bay: 10 Chesapeake
  bridge: 7 Natural
  caverns: 5 Luray
  port: 7 Norfolk 8 Richmond 10 Portsmouth 11 Newport News
  tunnel: 7 Natural
  valley: 10 Shenandoah
president: 9 John Tyler 11 James Monroe 12 James Madison 13 Woodrow Wilson, Zachary Taylor 15 Thomas Jefferson 16 George Washington 20 William Henry Harrison
river: 3 Dan 4 York 5 James 7 Potomac, Rapidan, Roanoke 10 Appomattox, Shenandoah 12 Rappahannock
state admission: 5 tenth
state bird: 8 cardinal
state flower: 16 flowering dogwood
state motto: 17 Thus Ever To Tyrants
state song: 24 Carry Me Back to Old Virginia
state tree: 7 dogwood

line, masterful, strapping, undaunted 10 courageous 12 stouthearted

virtual 5 tacit 7 implied 8 implicit, indirect 9 essential, practical 11 substantial

virtually 8 in effect 9 in essence 11 essentially, in substance, practically

virtue 5 honor, value 6 purity, reward 7 benefit, decency, honesty, modesty, probity 8 chastity, goodness, morality, strength 9 advantage, good

13 substantially 14 for the most part 23 for all practical purposes, to all intents and purposes

point, innocence, integrity, principle, rectitude, virginity 11 strong point, uprightness

virtuosity 7 mastery 8 artistry, wizardry 14 accomplishment

virtuoso 4 whiz 6 expert, genius, master, wizard 7 artiste, prodigy 10 master hand

virtuous 4 good, just, pure 5 moral 6 chaste, decent, modest 7 ethical, upright 8 innocent, laudable, virginal 9 continent, exemplary, honorable, righteous, unsullied 11 commendable, meritorious 12 praiseworthy 14 high-principled

virtuous person
  Hebrew: 6 zaddik

Virtus
  personifies: 7 courage

virtute et armis 15 by virtue and arms
  motto of: 11 Mississippi

virulent 5 toxic 6 bitter, deadly, lethal, malign 7 harmful, hostile, hurtful, noxious, vicious 8 spiteful, venomous 9 injurious, malicious, poisonous, rancorous, resentful, unhealthy 10 malevolent, pernicious 11 acrimonious, deleterious

virus 3 bug 4 germ 7 microbe 13 microorganism

vis 5 force, power 8 strength

visage 3 air 4 face, look, mien 5 image 6 aspect 7 profile 8 demeanor, features 9 semblance 10 appearance 11 countenance, physiognomy

vis-a-vis 8 eye to eye, together 9 in company, privately, tete-a-tete 10 face-to-face, side by side 11 as opposed to 12 in contrast to 14 as compared with, confidentially 19 as distinguished from

viscera 4 guts 6 bowels 7 innards, insides 8 entrails 10 intestines

visceral 3 gut 5 crude 6 earthy 11 instinctive

viscous 5 gluey, gooey, gummy, slimy, tacky, thick 6 sticky, syrupy, viscid 9 glutinous

visibility 7 ceiling, clarity, horizon 10 definition, prominence 11 range of view 12 distinctness 14 perceptibility 15 conspicuousness, discernibleness

visible 4 open 5 clear, plain 6 in view, marked, patent

7 blatant, evident, glaring, in focus, in sight, obvious, pointed, salient, seeable **8** apparent, distinct, manifest, palpable, revealed **9** prominent **10** noticeable, observable, pronounced **11** conspicuous, discernible, inescapable, perceivable, perceptible, well-defined **12** unmistakable

vision 4 idea **5** dream, fancy, ghost, sight **6** notion **7** concept, fantasy, phantom, specter **8** daydream, eyesight, illusion **9** foresight **10** apparition, conception, perception, revelation **11** discernment, imagination **15** materialization

visionary 4 seer **6** dreamy, unreal, zealot **7** dreamer, fanatic, fancied, utopian **8** delusive, fanciful, idealist, illusory, romantic, theorist **9** imaginary, unfounded **10** chimerical, daydreamer, idealistic, starry-eyed **11** imaginative, impractical **13** insubstantial

Vision of Judgement, The
    author: **9** Lord Byron

visit 4 call, stay **5** haunt, smite **6** affect, assail, attack, befall, call on, punish **7** afflict, assault, go to see, sojourn **8** drop in on, frequent, happen to, look in on, stay with **9** sojourn at **10** be a guest of

Visit, The
    author: **19** Friedrich Durrenmatt

visitant 5 alien **7** arrival, visitor

visitor 5 guest **6** caller **7** company, tourist, tripper, voyager **8** traveler **9** journeyer, sightseer, sojourner, transient **10** house guest, vacationer

vista 4 view **5** scene **6** vision **7** outlook, picture, scenery **8** panorama, prospect **9** landscape **11** perspective

visual 5 optic **6** ocular **7** optical, seeable, visible **9** for the eye **10** noticeable, observable, ophthalmic **11** perceptible

visualize 5 fancy, image **7** dream of, foresee, imagine, picture **8** envision **10** conceive of, daydream of **16** see in the mind's eye

vital 4 life, live **5** alive, basic, chief, quick **6** lively, living, urgent, viable **7** animate, crucial, dynamic, primary, serious, vibrant **8** animated, cardinal, critical, existing, forceful, foremost, material, pressing, spirited, vigorous **9** breathing, energetic, essential, important, necessary, par-

amount, requisite, vivifying **11** fundamental, significant **13** indispensable

vitality 3 pep, vim, zip **4** zeal, zest **5** verve, vigor **6** energy **8** dynamism, strength, vivacity **9** animation, life force **10** ebullience, enthusiasm, exuberance, liveliness **13** animal spirits

vitalize 6 excite, vivify **7** animate, quicken **8** activate, energize **9** stimulate **10** invigorate, strengthen **11** bring to life

vital part 9 essential, necessity, requisite **10** key element, sine qua non **11** requirement

Vital Parts
    author: **12** Thomas Berger

vital principle 5 blood **6** source **9** lifeblood **10** sine qua non

vitals 5 belly **6** bowels **10** intestines **11** vital organs **14** liver and lights

Vita Nuova
    author: **14** Dante Alighieri

vitiate 3 mar **4** thin, undo, void **5** spoil, taint **6** blight, cancel, debase, defile, dilute, impair, infect, injure, poison, weaken **7** abolish, corrupt, pervert, pollute **8** sabotage **9** discredit, undermine **10** adulterate, depreciate, invalidate, make faulty, obliterate **11** contaminate

vitriolic 4 acid **5** acerb, nasty, sharp **6** biting **7** abusive, acerbic, caustic, cutting **8** sardonic, scathing **9** sarcastic, satirical, withering **11** acrimonious **13** hypercritical

vituperate 5 abuse **6** carp at, defame, malign, rail at, rebuke, revile, vilify **7** censure **9** castigate **10** speak ill of **14** inveigh against

vituperation 5 abuse, blame, scorn **6** insult, rebuke, tirade **7** censure, obloquy, slander **8** acrimony, scolding **9** invective **10** defamation, revilement, scurrility **11** castigation, deprecation **12** calumniation, denunciation, faultfinding, vilification **13** tongue-lashing

vituperative 5 harsh **7** abusive **8** scornful **9** insulting, maligning, vilifying **10** censorious, defamatory, scurrilous, slanderous **11** acrimonious, deprecatory

vivace
    music: **5** quick **9** vivacious

vivacious 3 gay **5** jolly, merry, sunny, vital **6** active, bright,

bubbly, cheery, genial, lively **7** buoyant **8** animated, bubbling, cheerful, spirited **9** convivial, ebullient, sparkling, sprightly **10** frolicsome, full of life **12** effervescent, lighthearted

vivacity 3 zip **4** dash, elan **5** gaity, verve, vigor **6** energy, spirit **8** buoyancy, vitality **9** animation **10** ebullience, liveliness **13** effervescence

Vivaldi, Antonio
    born: **5** Italy **6** Venice
    composer of: **10** Gloria Mass **14** L'Estro Armonico, The Four Seasons **16** Judith Triumphant **17** Juditha Triumphans, Le Quattro Stagioni **19** Harmonic Inspiration

Viva Zapata!
    director: **9** Elia Kazan
    cast: **10** Jean Peters **12** Anthony Quinn, Marlon Brando
    Oscar for: **15** supporting actor (Quinn)
    script: **13** John Steinbeck

vive 8 long live (whomever)

vive valeque 15 live and keep well

Vivian
    also: **16** The Lady of the Lake
    character in: **16** Arthurian romance
    lover: **6** Merlin

Vivian Grey
    author: **16** Benjamin Disraeli

vivid 3 gay **4** deep, loud, rich **5** clear, shiny, showy **6** bright, florid, garish, lively, moving, strong **7** glowing, graphic, intense, radiant, shining **8** colorful, definite, distinct, dramatic, emphatic, forceful, lifelike, luminous, lustrous, powerful, stirring, striking, true-life, vigorous **9** brilliant, effulgent, energetic, marvelous, memorable, pictorial, realistic **10** astounding, expressive, impressive, remarkable **11** astonishing, conspicuous, descriptive, inescapable, luminescent, picturesque, resplendent **12** unmistakable **13** extraordinary

vividness 9 intensity **10** brightness, brilliance

vivified 7 revived **8** animated, awakened **9** enlivened, quickened, vitalized **11** invigorated

vivify 6 revive, wake up **7** animate, enliven, quicken **8** vitalize **10** invigorate

vixen 4 fury **5** scold, shrew, witch **6** virago **8** fishwife, harridan, spitfire **9** female fox, termagant

Vladimir
  character in: 15 Waiting for Godot
  author: 7 Beckett

Vlaminck, Maurice de
  born: 5 Paris **6** France
  artwork: 8 Red Trees, The Storm **15** Hamlet in the Snow, Winter Landscape **17** The Bridge at Chatou **18** Picnic in the Country, Street at Marly-le-Roi **21** Landscape with Red Trees

vocabulary 4 cant **5** argot, idiom, lingo, slang, style **6** jargon, patois, speech, tongue **7** dialect, lexicon **8** language, phrasing **9** word stock **10** vernacular **11** phraseology, terminology

vocal 4 open, oral, sung **5** blunt, frank, lyric **6** candid, choral, direct, spoken, voiced **7** uttered, voluble **8** operatic **9** outspoken, vocalized **10** forthright, of the voice **11** articulated, plainspoken

vocalize 3 air, say **4** vent **5** speak, utter **7** express **9** ventilate **10** articulate **12** put into words

vocation 3 job **4** line, post, role, task **5** berth, field, stint, trade **6** career, estate, metier **7** calling, pursuit, station **8** business, lifework **9** situation **10** assignment, employment, line of work, occupation, profession

vocational 3 job **5** trade **6** career **9** technical **11** specialized **12** occupational

vociferate 4 howl, yell, yelp **5** shout, shout **6** bellow, clamor, cry out, holler, shriek, squeal **7** bluster, call out, exclaim, screech **9** ejaculate **11** make a racket **12** raise a rumpus

vociferation 3 cry **4** howl, yell, yelp **5** noise, shout **6** bellow, clamor, outcry, shriek, squeal, uproar **7** screech **11** ejaculation, exclamation

vociferous 4 loud **5** noisy, vocal **6** shrill **7** blatant **8** piercing, shouting, strident, vehement **9** clamorous, outspoken **10** boisterous, loud-voiced, uproarious **11** importunate

vodka
  origin: 6 Poland, Russia
  drink: 10 Moscow Mule
  with amaretto: 9 Godmother
  with bouillon: 8 Bullshot
  with cider: 15 Brewster Special

with Cognac: 7 Cossack
with cranberry juice: 10 Cape Codder
with creme de cacao: 7 Barbara **9** Ninotchka **11** Russian Bear **12** Velvet Hammer, White Russian
with curacao: 8 Aqueduct
with Galliano: 16 Harvey Wallbanger
with gin: 15 Russian Cocktail
with kahlua or Tia Maria: 12 Black Russian
with kirsch: 12 Volga Boatman
with orange juice: 11 screwdriver
with tomato juice: 10 Bloody Mary
with vermouth: 8 Kangaroo **9** Corkscrew

Vogt, Carl Henry
  real name of: 12 Louis Calhern

vogue 3 fad **4** mode, rage **5** craze, style, trend **6** custom **7** fashion **8** currency, practice, the thing **10** acceptance, popularity **11** the last word **12** popular favor **14** the latest thing **15** prevailing taste

voguish 4 chic **5** smart **6** modish **7** faddish, stylish **11** fashionable

voice 3 air, say **4** alto, bass, part, role, tone, vent, vote, will, wish **5** speak, state, tenor, utter **6** choice, desire, option, reveal, singer, speech **7** declare, divulge, express, opinion, singers, soprano **8** announce, baritone, delivery, disclose, proclaim, vocalize **9** contralto, enunciate, pronounce, ventilate **10** articulate, intonation, modulation, preference, vocal sound **11** communicate **12** articulation, mezzo-soprano **13** participation, power of speech

voiceless 3 mum **4** deaf, mute, surd **6** silent **7** anaudia, aphonic, spirate

voice of the people
  Latin: 9 vox populi

void 4 bare, emit, free, null, pass **5** annul, blank, clear, drain, eject, empty, purge **6** barren, cancel, devoid, recant, repeal, revoke, vacant, vacuum **7** abolish, drained, emptied, exhaust, invalid, lacking, nullify, pour out, rescind, reverse, vacuity, wanting **8** depleted, evacuate, nugatory, renounce, throw out **9** destitute, discharge, emptiness, exhausted, repudiate **10** empty space, invalidate, not in force **11** countermand, inoperative

voidance 7 voiding **8** ejection, emission **9** discharge, expulsion

Voight, Jon
  born: 9 Yonkers NY
  roles: 7 Joe Buck **8** The Champ **10** Coming Home (Oscar) **11** Deliverance **13** The Odessa File **14** Catch Twenty-Two, Midnight Cowboy

voila 3 see **4** look **9** there it is

volatile 4 rash, wild **5** brash, giddy, moody **6** fickle, fitful **7** erratic, flighty, gaseous **8** eruptive, reckless, unstable, unsteady, vaporous, variable **9** explosive, frivolous, mercurial, spasmodic, unsettled **10** capricious, changeable, evaporable, inconstant, irresolute, vaporizing **12** undependable **13** temperamental, unpredictable

volition 4 will **6** choice, option **8** choosing, decision, free will **10** discretion, resolution **13** determination

volley 5 burst, salvo **6** shower **7** barrage **8** outbreak, outburst **9** broadside, discharge, fusillade **10** outpouring

Volpone (The Fox)
  author: 9 Ben Jonson
  character: 5 Celia, Mosca **7** Bonario, Corvino, Voltore **9** Corbaccio, Peregrine **18** Lady Politic Would-Be, Lord Politic Would-Be

Volsung
  origin: 12 Scandinavian
  mentioned in: 8 Volsunga
  grandfather: 4 Odin **5** Othin
  son: 7 Sigmund
  daughter: 5 Signy

Volsunga
  origin: 9 Icelandic **12** Scandinavian
  form: 4 saga
  time: 17 thirteenth century
  subject: 8 Volsungs

Volta, Alessandro, Count
  nationality: 7 Italian
  invented: 15 electric battery
  discovered: 10 methane gas

Voltaic
  also: 3 Gur
  language family: 16 Niger-Kordofanian
  group: 10 Niger-Congo
  includes: 5 Mossi

Voltaire, Francois
  real name: 19 Francois Marie Arouet
  author of: 5 Zadig, Zaire **6** Alzire, Merope **7** Candide, L'Ingenu, Mahomet **11** The Henriade **16** The Maid of

Orleans **23** Philosophical Dictionary
member of: 11 Philosophes

Volturnus
origin: 5 Roman
personifies: 4 wind **8** east wind **13** southeast wind

voluble 4 glib **5** wordy **6** chatty, fluent **7** twining **8** effusive, flippant, rotating, twisting **9** garrulous, talkative **10** loquacious

volume 4 book, bulk, heap, mass, size, tome **5** folio, sound, tract **6** amount, extent, quarto **7** measure **8** capacity, loudness, quantity, treatise, vastness **9** abundance, aggregate, magnitude, monograph **10** dimensions

voluminous 5 ample, large **7** copious, massive, sizable **8** abundant **9** extensive

Volund *see* **7** Wayland

voluntary 6 willed **8** free-will, intended, optional, unforced **10** deliberate **11** intentional, volunteered **13** discretionary, noncompulsory

volunteer 5 offer **6** extend, tender, unpaid **7** advance, present, proffer, recruit **8** enlistee **9** voluntary **10** put forward **11** step forward **12** unpaid worker **13** charity worker

Volunteer State
nickname of: 9 Tennessee

Voluptas
origin: 5 Roman
goddess of: 8 pleasure

voluptuary 4 rake, roue **7** epicure, gourmet, seducer **8** gourmand, hedonist, sybarite **9** bon vivant, debauchee, high liver, libertine, womanizer **10** gastronome, sensualist **14** pleasure seeker

voluptuous 4 soft **6** carnal, erotic, sexual, smooth, wanton **7** fleshly, lustful, sensual **8** sensuous **9** debauched, dissolute, luxurious, sybaritic **10** dissipated, hedonistic, lascivious, licentious, profligate **13** self-indulgent **14** pleasure-loving **15** pleasure-seeking

vomit 4 barf, emit, puke **5** eject, expel, heave, retch **7** bring up, throw up, upchuck **8** disgorge **9** discharge, spew forth **10** belch forth **11** regurgitate **15** toss one's cookies

Vonnegut, Kurt, Jr
author of: 8 Jailbird **9** Slapstick **10** Cat's Cradle, Palm

Sunday **11** Player Piano **18** Slaughterhouse Five **20** Breakfast of Champions **22** Happy Birthday Wanda June

Von Sternberg, Josef
director of: 12 The Blue Angel

Von Sydow, Max
real name: 18 Carl Adolph von Sydow
born: 4 Lund **6** Sweden
roles: 12 The Emigrants **14** The Seventh Seal **15** The Virgin Spring **16** Wild Strawberries **24** The Greatest Story Ever Told

voracious 6 greedy **7** hoggish **8** edacious, ravenous **10** gluttonous, insatiable, omnivorous

Voragine, Jacobus de
author of: 12 Legenda Aurea (Golden Legend)

vortex 4 eddy **7** cyclone, twister **9** maelstrom, whirlpool, whirlwind

votary 3 fan **4** buff **6** zealot **7** admirer, devotee, fanatic, habitue **8** adherent, champion, disciple, follower, partisan **10** aficionado, enthusiast **11** afficionado

vote 3 say **4** poll **5** voice **6** ballot, choice, option, ticket **8** approval, decision, election, judgment, suffrage **9** franchise, selection **10** plebiscite, preference, referendum **11** cast a ballot **13** determination

vouch 4 back **6** affirm, attest, back up, uphold, verify **7** certify, confirm, endorse, support, sustain, swear to, warrant, witness **8** attest to, maintain **9** guarantee **11** corroborate **12** authenticate

voucher 4 chip, chit **5** check, proof **6** surety, ticket **7** receipt, warrant **8** warranty **9** affidavit, debenture **10** credential **11** certificate **12** verification **14** authentication

vouchsafe 4 give **5** allow, deign, favor, grant **6** bestow, convey, tender **7** concede **10** condescend

vow 4 oath, word **5** swear, troth, vouch **6** affirm, assert, assure, parole, pledge, plight, stress **7** declare, promise, resolve **8** contract **9** emphasize **11** word of honor **13** solemn promise

vox populi 14 popular opinion **16** voice of the people

voyage 4 sail **6** cruise **7** passage **8** crossing, navigate **9** ocean trip **10** sea journey

Voyage of the Beagle, The
author: 13 Charles Darwin

voyager 5 rover **7** cruiser, pilgrim, rambler, tourist **8** traveler, wayfarer **9** jet-setter, journeyer, sightseer **10** adventurer **12** excursionist, globetrotter, peregrinator **13** world traveler

Voyage to the Bottom of the Sea
character: 6 Doctor **8** Kowalsky, Stu Riley, (Cdr/Capt) Lee Crane **9** Patterson **10** (Lt Cdr) Chip Morton **11** (Chief Petty Officer) Curley Jones **12** Chief Sharkey **14** (Adm) Harriman Nelson
cast: 9 Allan Hunt, Del Monroe **10** Henry Kulky, Paul Trinka **11** Richard Bull, Terry Becker **12** David Hedison **13** Robert Dowdell **15** Richard Basehart
submarine: 7 Seaview
explorer: 7 Sea Crab
mini-sub: 10 Flying Fish

Vronsky, Count Alexei
character in: 12 Anna Karenina
author: 7 Tolstoy

Vulcan
origin: 5 Roman
god of: 4 fire **12** metalworking
epithet: 8 Mulciber
corresponds to: 10 Hephaestus, Hephaistos

vulgar 3 low **4** base, rude **5** crude, dirty, gross, rough **6** coarse, common, filthy, ribald, risque, smutty **7** boorish, ill-bred, lowbrow, obscene, uncouth **8** impolite, indecent, off-color, ordinary, plebeian **9** offensive, tasteless, unrefined **10** suggestive **11** ill-mannered, proletarian **12** pornographic, uncultivated

vulgarian 3 oaf **4** boor, lout **5** brute, yahoo **7** Babbitt **9** ignoramus **10** philistine **16** anti-intellectual

vulgarity 8 bad taste, rudeness **9** crudeness, grossness, indecency, indecorum, obscenity **10** coarseness, ill manners, indelicacy, smuttiness **11** boorishness, pornography **12** impoliteness **13** tastelessness

vulnerable 4 weak **7** exposed **8** helpless, insecure **9** sensitive, unguarded **10** easily hurt, undefended **11** defenseless, susceptible, thin-skinned, unprotected

Vye, Eustacia
character in: 17 Return of the Native
author: 5 Hardy

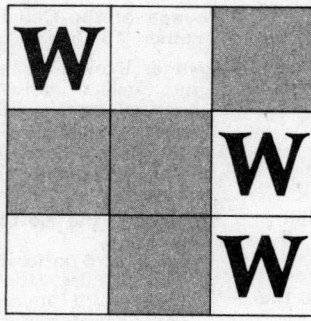

wacky, whacky 3 odd **4** nuts **5** crazy, kooky **6** cuckoo, insane, kookie **7** cracked, foolish, touched **9** eccentric, senseless **10** irrational **12** crackbrained

wad 3 bat, pad **4** cram, head, heap, lump, mass, tuft **5** money, stuff **6** bundle, riches, stop up **7** fortune **8** bankroll, plumbago

waddle 3 wag **4** sway **6** hobble, toddle, totter, wobble

wade 4 ford, plod, plow, toil, trek **5** labor **6** drudge, trudge **9** walk in mud **11** walk in water

wafer 4 chip **5** candy, flake **6** cookie **7** cracker **15** unleavened bread

waft 4 blow, puff **5** drift, float

wag 3 bob, wit **4** card, move, stir, wave **5** clown, droll, flick, joker, shake **6** jester, jiggle, switch, twitch, waggle, wiggle, wigwag **7** buffoon, farceur, flicker, flutter **8** comedian, humorist, jokester **9** oscillate **11** wisecracker **14** life of the party

wage 3 fee, pay **6** income, salary **7** carry on, conduct, payment, revenue, stipend **8** earnings, engage in, maintain, practice **9** emolument, undertake **10** recompense **12** compensation, remuneration

wage earner 6 worker **8** employee **9** job holder **12** hourly worker

wager 3 bet, pot **4** ante, pool, risk **5** fancy, guess, stake **6** assume, gamble, hazard **7** imagine, jackpot, presume, suppose, surmise, venture **8** make a bet, theorize **9** speculate **10** conjecture, take a flyer **11** speculation, try one's luck

12 tempt fortune **15** hazard an opinion

wages 3 bet, fee, pay **4** gage, hire **6** fights, reward, return, salary **7** engages, payment, stipend **8** conducts, earnings **9** emolument **10** prosecutes, recompense **12** remuneration

wage war 5 fight **6** combat **7** contend, make war **8** do battle **12** march against

waggery 5 chaff **6** banter, riding **7** joshing, kidding, ragging, ribbing **8** chaffing, drollery, raillery, twitting French: **8** badinage

waggish 5 droll, funny **7** comical, puckish **8** humorous

waggle 4 wave **5** wield **8** brandish

Wagner, Honus
  real name: **15** John Peter Wagner
  nickname: **14** Flying Dutchman
  sport: **8** baseball
  position: **9** shortstop
  team: **17** Pittsburgh Pirates

Wagner, Richard
  born: **7** Germany, Leipzig
  composer of: **5** Faust **6** Rienzi **7** Die Feen **8** Parsifal **9** Lohengrin **10** Tannhauser, The Fairies **14** Siegfried Idyll **16** The Mastersingers, Tristan and Isolde, Wesendonck Lieder **17** The Flying Dutchman **20** Der Ring des Nibelungen, The Ring of the Nibelungs **27** Die Meistersinger von Nurnberg
    the Ring Cycle Part 1: **12** Das Rheingold, The Rhine Gold
    the Ring Cycle Part 2: **10** Die Walkure **11** The Valkyrie
    the Ring Cycle Part 3: **9** Siegfried

    the Ring Cycle Part 4: **15** Gotterdammerung **17** Twilight of the Gods

Wagner, Robert
  born: **9** Detroit MI
  wife: **11** Natalie Wood
  roles: **6** Switch **10** Hart to Hart **13** It Takes a Thief, Prince Valiant, The Longest Day **24** All the Fine Young Cannibals

wagon 3 car, van **4** cart, dray, tram, wain **5** coach, lorry, tonga, truck **7** caisson **10** automobile, battleship
  covered: **15** prairie schooner
  maker: **10** wainwright
  police: **10** Black Maria
  Russian: **6** telega
  sideless: **6** rolley
  track: **3** rut

Wagon Train
  character: **9** Bill Hawks **11** Barnaby West, Cooper Smith, Duke Shannon **14** Charlie Wooster, Major Seth Adams **15** Christopher Hale, Flint McCullough
  cast: **8** Ward Bond **11** Scott Miller, Terry Wilson **12** Frank McGrath, John McIntire, Michael Burns, Robert Fuller, Robert Horton

waif 5 gamin, stray **6** gamine, urchin **7** mudlark **9** foundling **10** ragamuffin, street arab **11** guttersnipe **13** homeless child **14** tatterdemalion

wail 3 cry **4** bawl, howl, keen, moan, roar, weep, yell **5** groan, shout, whine **6** bellow, bemoan, bewail, cry out, lament, outcry, plaint **7** keening, moaning, wailing **9** caterwaul **10** rend the air **11** lamentation

waist 3 top **5** shirt **6** blouse, bodice, middle **7** midriff **9** midregion, waistband, waistline **10** middle part, midsection, shirtwaist

waistband 4 belt, sash
5 cinch 6 girdle

waistcoat 4 vest 5 benjy
6 jacket, jerkin, veskit, vestee,
weskit 7 singlet
French: gilet

wait 4 halt, stay, stop 5 dally,
delay, pause, tarry 6 linger,
put off 7 suspend 8 postpone,
stopover 9 deferment 10 suspension 11 continuance
12 postponement

wait for 6 expect 10 anticipate

Waiting for Godot
author: 13 Samuel Beckett
character: 8 Estragon,
Vladimir

wait on 5 serve 6 assist, attend

waive 4 stay 5 defer, forgo, let
go, table, yield 6 give up, not
use, put off, shelve 7 forbear,
lay over 8 disclaim, forswear,
postpone, renounce
9 surrender

waiver 9 dismissal 10 abdication, disclaimer 11 abandonment 12 renunciation
14 relinquishment

Wakashan
tribe: 6 Nootka 8 Kwakiutl,
Puyallup

wake 4 fire, path, stir, wash
5 rally, rouse, trail, train,
vigil 6 arouse, course, excite,
kindle, revive 7 enliven, provoke, quicken 8 backwash
9 galvanize, stimulate
11 resuscitate

wakeful 4 wary 5 alert, astir
7 careful, heedful 8 cautious,
restless, vigilant, watchful
9 insomniac, observant, sleepless 10 unsleeping
11 circumspect

wake up 4 rise 5 arise 6 vivify 7 animate, enliven 8 vitalize 9 stimulate

Walcott, Joe
real name: 18 Arnold Ray-
mond Cream
nickname: 9 Jersey Joe
sport: 6 boxing
class: 11 heavyweight

**Walden, or Life in the
Woods**
author: 17 Henry David
Thoreau

Wales *see box*

wander aimlessly 5 amble,
stray 6 ramble, stroll 7 meander, saunter

Wanderer, The
author: 13 Alain Fournier

wandering 5 lapse 8 rambling,
straying 9 deviation 10 aber-

Wales
other name: 5 Cymru 7 Cambria
capital: 7 Cardiff
cities: 4 Rhyl, Ross 5 Flint, Towyn 6 Amlwch, Bangor,
Brecon, Sidney 7 Cwmbran, Herford, Newport, Rhondda,
Swansea 8 Aberdare, Caerleon, Holyhead, Pembroke
9 Fishguard, Glamorgan 10 Caernarvon, Caerphilly, Carmarthen 11 Aberystwyth 12 Milford Haven 13 Kidder-
minster, Merthyr-Tydfil
division: 5 Clwyd, Dyfed, Flint, Gwent, Powys 6 Radnor
7 Denbigh, Gwynedd 8 Anglesey, Cardigan, Monmouth,
Pembroke 9 Brecknoch, Glamorgan, Merioneth 10 Caernarvon, Carmarthen, Montgomery
government: 29 constituent part of Great Britain
measure: 5 cover 7 cantred, crannoc, listred
island: 4 Mona 5 Caldy 8 Anglesey, Holyhead
lake: 4 Bala 6 Vyrnwy
mountain: 6 Berwyn 8 Cambrian 9 Prescelly 13 Brecon
Beacons
highest point: 7 Snowdon
river: 3 Dee, Usk, Wye 4 Alun, Taff, Tawe, Teme, Towy
5 Clwyd, Conwy, Dovey, Neath, Teifi 6 Conway, Severn,
Vyrnwy
sea: 5 Irish 8 Atlantic
physical feature:
 bay: 7 Swansea 8 Cardigan, Tremadoc, Tremadog
 channel: 7 Bristol 9 St George's
 hills: 7 Malvern
 peninsula: 5 Lleyn
 strait: 5 Menai
 valley: 7 Rhondda
people: 4 Celt, Kelt 5 Cymry, Kymry, Welsh 7 Brython,
Silures, Taffies 8 Awabokal, Cambrian 9 Siluridan
 actor: 6 Burton 8 Williams
 artist: 4 John
 author: 3 Map 5 Jones, Lewis, Mapes, Parry 6 Machan,
Thrale 9 Llewellyn 11 Dylan Thomas 14 Dafydd ap
Gwylym
 god: 3 Deu, Dew 4 Bran, Gwyn 5 Dylan 7 Gwydion
 leader: 5 Bevan 6 Rhodri 8 Hywel Dwa 11 Cadwallader
12 Bishop Morgan 13 Owen Glendower 16 David Lloyd
George 18 Llewelyn ap Gruffydd
language: 5 Welsh 6 Celtic, Cymric, Keltic, Kymric 7 Cymraeg, English
religion: 8 Anglican 9 Methodist 10 Protestant
12 Presbyterian
place:
 bridge: 6 Severn
 castle: 6 Conway 7 Harlech 9 Beaumaris 10 Caernarvon,
Caerphilly 11 Aberystwyth
feature:
 festival: 10 Eisteddfod
 stories: 10 Mabinogion
food:
 dish: 8 flummery

---

ration, digressive, discursive,
maundering, meandering,
roundabout 11 abnormality
12 idiosyncrasy 13 nonconformity 14 circumlocutory

Wandering Jew, The
author: 9 Eugene Sue

Wanderings
author: 10 Chaim Potok

wane 3 ebb 4 fade, sink
5 abate, droop, waste 6 ebbing, fading, lessen, weaken,

wither 7 abating, decline,
dwindle, subside 8 decrease,
diminish, fade away 9 dwindling, lessening, recession,
subsiding, weakening,
withering

wangle 4 worm 5 trick
6 jockey, scheme 7 finagle,
wheedle 8 engineer, intrigue,
maneuver 9 machinate
10 manipulate

wanness 6 pallor 8 grayness,
paleness 9 ashenness 10 sal-

lowness, sickliness
13 colorlessness

want 4 hunt, lack, need, seek, wish 5 covet, crave, fancy 6 dearth, demand, desire, hunger, penury 7 be needy, craving, hope for, long for, paucity, pine for, poverty, require, wish for 8 scarcity, shortage, yearn for, yearning 9 indigence, necessity, pauperism, privation, requisite 10 deficiency, insolvency 11 destitution, requirement 13 impecuniosity, insufficiency, pennilessness 14 impoverishment

Wanted: Dead or Alive
character: 11 Josh Randall
cast: 12 Steve McQueen
job: 12 bounty hunter
gun: 8 Mare's Leg

wanting 5 short 6 absent 7 lacking, missing 9 defective, deficient, imperfect 10 inadequate 11 substandard 12 insufficient

wanton 4 bawd, fast, jade, lewd, rake, roue, slut, tart 5 gross, hussy, loose, satyr, whore 6 chippy, harlot, lecher 7 bestial, immoral, lustful, obscene, seducer, trollop, willful 8 careless, heedless, mindless, needless, strumpet, sybarite, unchaste 9 abandoned, adulterer, concubine, debauched, debauchee, dissolute, lecherous, libertine, malicious, senseless, womanizer 10 deliberate, fornicator, groundless, licentious, malevolent, profligate, prostitute, sensualist, unprovoked, voluptuary 11 fornicatrix, promiscuous, unjustified, whoremaster 13 inconsiderate, irresponsible

wapiti 3 elk 4 deer 11 American elk
female: 3 cow
literally: 9 white rump
male: 4 bull
species: 16 Cervus canadensis

Wapshot Chronicle
author: 11 John Cheever

war 5 clash, fight 6 attack, battle, combat, invade 7 contend 8 conflict, fighting, struggle 10 opposition 11 hostilities
god of: 4 Ares, Odin 5 Othin 8 Quirinus
goddess of: 4 Enyo 6 Athena, Athene, Inanna, Ishtar, Pallas, Saitis 7 Bellona, Mylitta 11 Tritogeneia 12 Pallas Athena 18 Alalcomenean Athena

War and Peace
author: 10 Leo Tolstoy

character: 7 Kutuzov 8 Napoleon 13 Natasha Rostov, Nikolay Rostov, Pierre Bezuhov 14 Anatole Kuragin 15 Andrey Bolkonsky 19 Ellen Kuragin Bezuhov 22 Princess Marya Bolkonsky

War and Remembrance
author: 10 Herman Wouk

warble 4 lump, purl, sing 5 carol, larva, trill, tumor, yodel 6 growth, quaver, ripple 7 twitter, vibrate, whistle

war cry 6 slogan 8 Geronimo

ward 4 zone 5 avert, block, repel 6 charge, thwart 7 beat off, fend off, prevent, quarter 8 pavilion, precinct, stave off, turn away 9 dependent, forestall
French: 7 protege

warden 5 guard 6 keeper, ranger, sentry 7 curator, manager 8 guardian, watchman 9 protector 14 superintendent

Warden, The
author: 15 Anthony Trollope

ward off 5 avert 7 prevent

wardrobe 4 togs 5 chest 6 attire, closet, outfit 7 apparel, clothes 8 clothing, garments 10 cedar chest 12 clothespress
French: 6 bureau 7 armoire, commode 10 chiffonier 11 habillement

wares 4 line 5 stock 7 staples 8 supplies 9 inventory 11 commodities, merchandise

warfare 5 fight 6 battle, combat 8 conflict, fighting 11 hostilities

Warhol, Andy
born: 14 Philadelphia PA
artwork: 9 Brillo Box, Liz Taylor 13 Marilyn Monroe 16 Campbell's Soup Can 20 Green Coca-Cola Bottles

wariness 7 caution 9 alertness, suspicion, vigilance 11 carefulness, guardedness, heedfulness 12 watchfulness 14 circumspection

warlike 7 hostile, martial, valiant 8 inimical, militant, military 9 bellicose, combative 10 unfriendly 11 belligerent, contentious, threatening
Indian: 8 Arapahoe

warlike attitude 9 hostility, pugnacity 11 bellicosity 12 belligerence, belligerency 13 combativeness 14 aggressiveness

warm 3 hot 4 cook, heat, kind, melt, thaw 5 cheer, happy,

sunny, tepid, vivid 6 bright, heated, heat up, joyful, joyous, kindly, lively, loving, simmer, tender 7 affable, cordial, earnest, fervent, glowing, intense 8 animated, cheerful, friendly, gracious, outgoing, pleasant, spirited, vehement, vigorous 9 brilliant 10 passionate 11 kindhearted, sympathetic 12 affectionate, enthusiastic 13 compassionate, tenderhearted

warmhearted 4 kind 6 genial, kindly, loving 7 cordial 10 solicitous 11 sympathetic 12 affectionate 13 compassionate

warm-hued 3 red 4 rosy 5 ruddy, vivid 6 golden, orange, yellow 7 crimson, roseate, scarlet 8 blushing

warmish 5 tepid 7 cooling

warm oneself 4 bask 12 soak up warmth, toast oneself

warmth 3 joy 4 fire, heat, zeal 5 ardor, cheer, verve, vigor 6 fervor, spirit 7 hotness, passion 8 kindness, sympathy 9 animation, happiness, intensity, vehemence 10 affability, compassion, cordiality, enthusiasm, excitement, joyfulness, kindliness, liveliness, lovingness, tenderness 11 earnestness 12 cheerfulness, friendliness, graciousness 15 kindheartedness 17 tenderheartedness

warn 5 alert 6 advise, inform, notify, signal 7 apprise, caution, counsel 8 admonish

warning 4 hint, omen, sign 5 alarm, token 6 advice, notice, signal 7 portent, presage 8 apprisal 9 foretoken 10 intimation 12 notification

War of the Worlds, The
author: 7 H G Wells
invasion by: 8 Martians

war of words 7 dispute, quarrel 8 argument 11 altercation, controversy 12 disagreement

warp 4 bend, bent, bias 5 quirk, twist 6 debase, deform, infect 7 contort, corrupt, distort, leaning, mislead, pervert 8 misguide, misshape, tendency 9 prejudice, proneness 10 contortion, distortion, partiality, proclivity, propensity 11 deformation, disposition, inclination 14 predisposition

warrant 3 vow 4 aver, avow 5 swear 6 affirm, assert, assure, attest, permit, pledge 7 certify, declare, justify, license, promise 9 authorize,

guarantee 10 asseverate, permission **13** authorization

warranty 6 pledge **9** agreement **11** certificate

Warren, Robert Penn
  author of: 5 Flood **7** Audubon **8** Promises **10** Now and Then **12** Incarnations **14** All the King's Men **18** World Enough and Time
  member of: 12 the Fugitives

warring 7 hostile **8** battling, clashing, fighting, opposing **9** combatant **10** contending **11** belligerent, conflicting, contentious

warrior 7 fighter, soldier, veteran **9** combatant, man-at-arms **10** campaigner **11** legionnaire

Warsaw
  area: 11 Stare Miasto
  capital of: 6 Poland

landmark: 14 Kazimierzowski **25** Palace of Culture and Science
Polish: 8 Warszawa
river: 7 Vistula
square: 5 Rynek

warship 5 Maine, U-boat **6** corvet **7** Alabama, cruiser, frigate, gunboat, Monitor **8** Bismarck, corvette, Graf Spee, ironclad, man-of-war **9** destroyer, ironsides, Merrimack, submarine **11** dreadnought, torpedo boat **12** Constitution, Old Ironsides **13** Constellation **15** aircraft carrier **16** superdreadnought
  fleet: 6 armada
  part: 6 turret
  plating: 5 armor

wary 5 alert **7** careful, guarded, heedful, mindful, prudent, wakeful **8** cautious, discreet, vigilant, watchful **10** suspicious **11** circumspect

War Within and Without
  author: 19 Anne Morrow Lindbergh

wash 3 mop, rub, wet **4** bath, lave, soak, swab, wipe **5** bathe, clean, float, flood, rinse, scour, scrub **6** drench, shower, sponge **7** cleanse, immerse, launder, laundry, moisten, mopping, shampoo **8** ablution, cleaning, inundate, irrigate, lavation, scouring **9** cleansing **10** laundering

washbasin 3 tub **4** bowl **5** laver **6** lavabo **8** lavatory

washed out 4 drab, dull, pale **5** dingy, faded, white **6** dreary, grayed **8** bleached **9** colorless

washed up, washed-up 4 lost, shot **6** bathed, broken, ruined, undone **7** done for, preened, through **8** bankrupt, done with, fatigued, finished,

---

Washington
  abbreviation: 2 WA **4** Wash
  nickname: 7 Chinook **9** Evergreen
  capital: 7 Olympia
  largest city: 7 Seattle
  others: 4 Omak **5** Pasco **6** Renton, Tacoma, Yakima **7** Ephrata, Everett, Hoquiam, Othello, Pullman, Spokane **8** Aberdeen, Bellevue, Longview, Puyallup, Richland **9** Anacortes, Bremerton, Kennewick, Vancouver, Wenatchee **10** Bellingham, Burlington, Walla Walla **11** Port Angeles
  college: 7 Gonzaga, Seattle, Whitman **9** Evergreen, Whitworth **10** Puget Sound **14** Seattle Pacific **15** Pacific Lutheran
  feature:
    dam: **10** Bonneville **11** Grand Coulee
    fort: **5** Lewis
    national park: **7** Olympic **12** Mount Rainier **13** North Cascades
  tribe: 3 Hoh **5** Lummi, Makah, Twana **6** Cayuse, Samish, Skagit, Yakima **7** Chinook, Clallam, Clatsop, Cowlitz, Dwamish, Nooksak, Palouse, Quaitso, Sanpoil, Spokane, Squaxon, Tulalip **8** Chehalis, Chimakum, Colville, Nespelim, Nez Perce, Okanagon, Pishquow, Puyallup, Quileute, Quinault, Sahaptin, Salishan, Sinkiuse **9** Nisqually, Quinaielt, Semiahmoo, Skokomish, Swinomish **10** Senijextee, Shoalwater **11** Shahaptaine
  people: 7 Seattle **10** Bing Crosby **11** Hank Ketcham **12** Elisha P Ferry **13** Marcus Whitman **15** William O Douglas **19** Isaac Ingalls Stevens
    explorer: **4** Cook, Gray **6** Heceta **9** Vancouver **13** Lewis and Clark
  lake: 4 Soap **5** Moses, Union **6** Chelan, Ozette **7** Cle Elum, Cushman, Kachess **8** Crescent, Quinault **9** Keechelus, Wenatchee **10** Washington
  land rank: twentieth
  mountain: 4 Blue, Jack, Tunk **5** Adams, Baker, Lemei, Logan, Moses, Sloan **6** Kettle, Quartz, Simcoe, Stuart **7** Shuksan **8** Cascades, Olympics, St Helens **11** Kettle River
    highest point: **7** Rainier
  physical feature:
    falls: **10** Snoqualmie
    port: **6** Tacoma **7** Everett, Seattle **10** Bellingham
    sound: **5** Puget **7** Rosario
  river: 5 Snake, White **6** Yakima **7** Spokane **8** Columbia, Quinault **9** Snohomish **10** Snoqualmie **11** Pend Oreille
  state admission: 11 forty-second
  state bird: 15 willow goldfinch
  state fish: 14 steelhead trout
  state flower: 17 coast rhododendron **19** western rhododendron
  state motto: 7 By and By (Alki)
  state song: 16 Washington My Home
  state tree: 14 western hemlock

scrubbed **9** played out, showered

washing 6 laving **7** bathing, laundry, purging, rinsing, soaking **8** cleaning, scouring **9** ablutions, drenching, scrubbing, showering **10** laundering, shampooing

Washington (state) *see box, p. 1059*

Washington, George *see box*

Washington DC *see box*

Washington Square
author: **10** Henry James

wash one's hands of
4 deny, quit **6** give up **7** abandon, decline, disavow, forsake **8** abnegate, cast away, disclaim, forswear, renounce **9** repudiate **10** relinquish

washout 6 fiasco, fizzle **7** failure, letdown **8** disaster **14** disappointment

wash out 4 fade, fail **6** bleach **7** deplete, fatigue **8** enervate, enfeeble **10** debilitate, devitalize

wasp
variety: **5** paper **6** cuckoo, ensign, hornet, potter, spider **12** yellow jacket

waspish 5 huffy, testy **6** crabby, cranky, ornery, shirty **7** bearish, fretful, peevish, pettish **8** petulant, snappish **9** crotchety, fractious, irascible, irritable, querulous **12** cantankerous

Wasps, The
author: **12** Aristophanes
character: **10** Bdelycleon, Philocleon
dog: **5** Labes

wassail 5 drink, punch, revel, toast **6** liquor, tipple **7** carouse, revelry **8** beverage, carousal

waste 3 die, ebb, rob **4** fade, loot, melt, rape, raze, ruin,

sack, sink, void, wane **5** abate, crush, decay, drain, dregs, droop, empty, offal, smash, spoil, strip, trash, wreck **6** barren, burn up, debris, devour, litter, misuse, ravage, razing, refuse, scraps, steppe, tundra, weaken, wither **7** crumble, decline, deplete, despoil, destroy, dwindle, exhaust, garbage, looting, pillage, plunder, rubbish, shatter, subside **8** badlands, decrease, demolish, diminish, leavings, misapply, misspend, needless, prey upon, remnants, squander, wrecking **9** devastate, disappear, dissipate, emptiness, evaporate, excrement, leftovers, misemploy, ruination, sweepings **10** demolition, plundering, remainders, wilderness **11** destruction, devastation, dissipation, expenditure, fritter away, prodigality, squandering **12** despoliation, extravagance **14** misapplication

waste away 4 fail, rust **7** corrode, decline, eat into

wasted 5 spent **6** used-up **7** ravaged **9** emaciated, exhausted **12** unproductive

wasteful 8 prodigal **9** unthrifty **10** thriftless **11** extravagant, improvident, spendthrift, squandering **12** uneconomical

wastefulness 10 imprudence, lavishness **11** prodigality, squandering **12** extravagance, improvidence

wasteland 6 desert

Waste Land, The
author: **7** T S Eliot

waste time 5 dally **6** dawdle, loiter **10** dillydally

watch 3 eye, see **4** heed, look, mark, mind, note, ogle, save, tend **5** alert, guard, scout, stare **6** attend, be wary, gaze at, guards, look at, look on, notice, patrol, peep at, peer at, picket, regard, sentry, survey, tend to **7** be chary, care for, examine, lookout, observe, oversee, protect, stare at **8** pore over, preserve, sentinel, sentries, take heed **9** attention, patrolman, vigilance **10** observance, scrutinize **11** contemplate, observation, superintend, supervision **15** superintendence

watch fire 6 beacon
kinds: **4** bale **6** signal

watchful 4 wary **5** alert, aware, canny, chary **6** shrewd **7** careful, guarded,

---

Washington, George
nickname: **18** Father of His Country
presidential rank: **5** first
party: **10** Federalist
state represented: **2** VA
elected: **11** unanimously
vice president: **5** (John) Adams
cabinet:
  state: **9** (Thomas) Jefferson
  treasury: **8** (Alexander) Hamilton
  war: **4** (Henry) Knox **7** (James) McHenry **9** (Timothy) Pickering
  attorney general: **3** (Charles) Lee **8** (Edmund Jennings) Randolph, (William) Bradford
born: **2** VA **9** Wakefield **18** Westmoreland County
died/buried: **11** Mount Vernon
religion: **12** Episcopalian
interests: **7** fishing, hunting, theater **17** scientific farming
vacation: **11** Mount Vernon
author: **33** The Journal of Major George Washington
political career: **9** president **16** House of Burgesses **24** First Continental Congress **25** Second Continental Congress
  signed: **12** Constitution
civilian career: **6** farmer **8** surveyor
military service:
  war: **13** Revolutionary **15** French and Indian
notable events of lifetime/term: **18** American Revolution
  crossed: **13** Delaware River
  rebellion: **7** Whiskey
  winter at: **11** Valley Forge
father: **9** Augustine
mother: **4** Mary (Ball)
siblings: **5** Betty **6** Samuel **7** Charles, Mildred **13** John Augustine
  half-brother: **6** Butler **8** Lawrence **9** Augustine
  half-sister: **4** Jane
wife: **6** Martha (Dandridge Custis)
children:
  stepchildren: **15** John Parke Custis **17** Martha Parke Custis

Washington DC
  airport: **6** Dulles **8** National
  basketball team: **7** Bullets
  capital of: **12** United States
  designed by: **7** L'Enfant
  football team: **8** Redskins
  landmark: **4** Mall **7** Capitol, Ellipse **8** Pentagon **10** White House **11** National Zoo **12** Ford's Theatre, Franklin Park, Supreme Court **13** Lafayette Park, Rock Creek Park **14** Farragut Square, Reflecting Pool, Watergate Hotel **15** Lincoln Memorial, McPherson Square **16** National Archives **17** Jefferson Memorial, Library of Congress, National Arboretum **18** Washington Monument **21** Frederick Douglass Home, Robert F Kennedy Stadium **22** Smithsonian Institution **23** National Sculpture Garden **25** Arlington National Cemetery **33** Kennedy Center for the Performing Arts
  museum: **5** Freer **7** Renwick **8** Corcoran **9** Hirshhorn **10** African Art **11** Smithsonian **13** Dumbarton Oaks **15** National Gallery **17** Folger Shakespeare **18** Phillips Collection **23** National Portrait Gallery
  river: **7** Potomac **9** Rock Creek
  street/avenue: **4** Ohio **7** New York, Potomac **12** Constitution, Independence, Pennsylvania **13** Massachusetts
  university: **6** Howard **8** American, Catholic **10** Georgetown **11** George Mason **16** George Washington

heedful, mindful, prudent **8** cautious, open-eyed, vigilant **9** attentive, observant **11** circumspect

watchfulness 4 care, heed **9** attention, diligence, vigilance **13** attentiveness

watchman 5 guard, scout **6** patrol, picket, sentry **7** lookout **8** sentinel **9** patrolman

Watch on the Rhine
  director: **13** Herman Shumlin
  based on play by: **14** Lillian Hellman
  cast: **9** Paul Lukas **10** Bette Davis **19** Geraldine Fitzgerald
  Oscar for: **5** actor (Lukas)

watch over 5 guard **6** attend **7** oversee, protect **11** superintend

watchtower 6 beacon, pharos, signal **7** seamark **8** landmark **10** lighthouse

watchword 5 motto **6** byword, slogan

water 3 cut, dip, sea, wet **4** damp, lake, pond, pool, soak, tear, thin **5** douse, flood, H two O, ocean, river, souse **6** dampen, deluge, dilute, drench, lagoon, splash, stream **7** immerse, moisten **8** inundate, irrigate, sprinkle, submerge **10** adulterate
  goddess of: **4** Enki

Water Carrier (Water Bearer)
  constellation of: **8** Aquarius

watercolor
  French: **9** aquarelle

watercourse 5 canal, river **6** strait **7** channel, conduit, narrows, passage **8** aqueduct

water down 3 cut **6** censor, dilute, weaken **7** thin out **9** expurgate **10** adulterate

watered down 4 weak **6** dilute **7** diluted **8** weakened **11** adulterated

waterfall 7 cascade, Niagara **8** cataract

waterfront 4 dock, mole, pier, quay **5** basin, jetty, levee, wharf **6** marina **7** landing

waterless 3 dry **4** arid, sere **6** barren **7** parched, thirsty **10** desertlike

Waterloo Bridge
  director: **11** Mervyn LeRoy
  cast: **11** Vivien Leigh **12** Lucile Watson, Robert Taylor **13** Virginia Field
  remade as: **4** Gaby

Water Monster (Sea Serpent)
  constellation of: **5** Hydra

water of life
  Latin: **9** aqua vitae

Waters, Ethel
  nickname: **19** Sweet Mama Stringbean

born: **9** Chester PA
  roles: **5** Pinky **6** Beulah **21** The Member of the Wedding

Watership Down
  author: **12** Richard Adams

Water Snake
  constellation of: **6** Hydrus

watertight 9 nonporous **10** impervious **11** impermeable

waterway 5 canal, inlet, river, route **6** gutter, strait, strake, stream **7** channel

Water Wonderland
  nickname of: **8** Michigan

watery 3 wet **4** damp, thin, weak **5** fluid, moist, teary **6** liquid, rheumy **7** aqueous, diluted, tearful, tearing **11** adulterated

Watling, Belle
  character in: **15** Gone With the Wind
  author: **8** Mitchell

Watt, James
  nationality: **8** Scottish
  developed: **11** steam engine **12** piston engine

Watteau, Jean Antoine
  born: **6** France **12** Valenciennes
  artwork: **6** Gilles **8** Mezzetin **9** La Finette **10** La Toilette **12** Joys of Living, L'indifferent **13** La Gamme d'Amour **16** Company in the Park, La Lecon de Musique **18** Enseigne de Gersaint, Gersaint's Signboard, La Comedie Francaise, La Concert de Famille **20** Le Dejeuner en plein air, L'assemblee dans un parc **21** Harlequin and Columbine **23** Embarquement pour Cythere, Italian and French Theater, Jupiter Surprises Antiope, Les Amusements Champetres **24** Conversation in the Open Air, The Embarkation for Cythera

wattle 6 Acacia
  varieties: **5** black, broom, cedar, glory, green, hairy, oven's, Sally, swamp **6** frosty, golden, mudgee, orange, silver, sticky **7** bramble, buffalo, coastal, prickly, weeping, Wyalong **8** blueleaf, cinnamon, graceful, screw-pod, sunshine **9** redleaved **10** golden-rain, needle-bush **11** Cootamundra, Mount Morgan, Wallangarra **12** Sydney golden **14** Peppermint-tree **16** Queensland silver

Watts, Sir George Frederic
born: 6 London 7 England
artwork: 4 Hope 14 Physical
Energy 17 Paolo and Fran-
cesca 19 Anastasio
degl'Onesti 45 Caractacus
Led in Triumph Through
the Streets of Rome
54 Alfred Inciting his Sub-
jects to Prevent the Landing
of the Danes

Waugh, Evelyn
author of: 9 Men at Arms
10 Vile Bodies 11 The Loved
One 13 Black Mischief, Edmund Campion 14 A Hand-
ful of Dust, Decline and
Fall 15 A Little Learning
19 Brideshead Revisited
20 Officers and Gentlemen
22 Unconditional
Surrender

wave 4 coil, curl, file, flap,
line, rank, rise, roll, rush,
sway, tier 5 curve, flood,
pulse, shake, surge, swell,
swing, train, twirl, wield
6 billow, column, comber, deluge, motion, quiver, ripple,
roller, signal, spiral, string
7 breaker, flutter, gesture, pulsate, tremble, vibrate, winding 8 brandish, flourish,
increase, undulate, whitecap
9 advancing, oscillate, pulsation, vibration 10 salutation,
undulation 11 gesticulate,
heightening 13 gesticulation

wave at 4 hail 6 signal
7 gesture

wave on 6 beckon, signal
7 gesture 11 gesticulate

waver 4 flap, reel, sway, vary
5 pause, shake, swing, weave
6 careen, change, falter,
quiver, totter, wobble 7 flutter,
stagger, tremble 8 hesitate, undulate 9 fluctuate, vacillate
10 dillydally 12 shilly-shally

wavering 8 hesitant, waffling
9 undecided 10 hesitating, indecisive, irresolute
11 vacillating

Waverley
author: 14 Sir Walter Scott
character: 12 Flora MacIvor
14 Donald Bean Lean, Ed-
ward Waverley 15 Rose
Bradwardine 16 Baron Bradwardine 17 Evan Dhu
MacCombich 24 Fergus
MacIvor Vich Ian Vohr
25 Prince Charles Edward
Stuart

wavy 5 curly 6 coiled, curved
7 rolling, sinuous, winding
8 mazelike, rippling, tortuous
10 meandering, serpentine,
undulating 11 curvilinear
12 labyrinthine

wax 4 grow 5 swell, widen
6 become, blow up, dilate, expand, extend, thrive 7 balloon,
develop, enlarge, fill out, inflate, puff out 8 increase

way 3 far, off 4 area, form,
lane, pass, path, road, room,
wont 5 habit, means, route,
space, trail, usage 6 course,
custom, far off, manner,
method, nature, region, system 7 conduct, passage, pathway, process 8 behavior,
distance, practice, remotely,
vicinity 9 direction, procedure,
technique 12 neighborhood

wayfarer 8 traveler, wanderer
9 sojourner

Wayfaring Stranger
nickname of: 8 Burl Ives

way in 4 door, gate 5 entry
6 access, portal 7 doorway,
gateway, ingress 8 approach,
entrance

Wayland
also: 6 Volund 7 Wieland
origin: 8 European
king of: 5 elves

waylay 4 lure 5 decoy 6 ambush, assail, attack, entrap
7 assault, ensnare, set upon
8 inveigle

Wayne, Anthony
nickname: 10 Mad Anthony
served in: 10 Indian Wars
16 Revolutionary War
captured: 10 Stony Point
battle: 10 Brandywine, Ger-
mantown 13 Fallen Timbers

Wayne, David
real name: 13 Wayne
McMeekan
born: 14 Traverse City MI
roles: 6 Sakini 8 Adam's Rib
12 The Front Page 13 Mis-
ter Roberts, Tonight We
Sing 15 Huckleberry Finn
16 Portrait of Jennie 26 The
Teahouse of the August
Moon

Wayne, John
real name: 21 Marion Mi-
chael Morrison
nickname: 4 Duke
born: 11 Winterset IA
roles: 5 Hondo 6 Chisum
8 Ringo Kid, Rio Bravo, The
Alamo, True Grit (Oscar)
9 McLintock, Rio Grande
10 Stagecoach 11 The Quiet
Man, The Shootist 12 The
Searchers 14 Rooster Cog-
burn, The Green Berets
16 How the West Was
Won 17 The Sands of Iwo
Jima 27 The Man Who
Shot Liberty Valance

Way of All Flesh, The
author: 12 Samuel Butler

character: 9 Mr Overton
Pontifex family: 5 Ellen
6 Althea, Ernest, George
8 Theobald 9 Christina

Way of the World, The
author: 15 William Congreve
character: 6 Foible 7 Fainall,
Witwoud 8 Mirabell, Wait-
well 10 Mrs Fainall, Mrs
Marwood 12 Lady Wishfort,
Mrs Millamant 17 Sir Wil-
full Witwoud

way of thinking 7 beliefs
9 principle 10 conviction
11 persuasions

way out 4 exit 6 egress, escape, outlet

Ways of Escape
author: 12 Graham Greene

wayward 5 balky 6 fickle, fitful, mulish, unruly 7 erratic,
restive, willful 8 contrary, perverse, stubborn, variable
9 mercurial, obstinate, whimsical 10 capricious, changeable,
headstrong, inconstant, rebellious, refractory, self-willed
11 disobedient, fluctuating, intractable, troublesome 12 inconsistent, incorrigible,
recalcitrant, undependable, ungovernable, unmanageable
13 insubordinate

Wazhazhe *see* 5 Osage

weak 4 lame, poor, puny, soft,
thin 5 faint, frail, shaky,
spent 6 feeble, flimsy, unsafe,
wasted, watery 7 brittle, diluted, exposed, fragile, insipid,
lacking, unmanly 8 cowardly,
delicate, helpless, timorous,
unsteady, wide open 9 breakable, enervated, exhausted,
frangible, powerless, spineless,
tasteless, unguarded, untenable 10 assailable, effeminate,
irresolute, namby-pamby, vulnerable, wishy-washy 11 adulterated, debilitated, defenseless,
ineffective, ineffectual, inefficient, unprotected, unsupported 12 unconvincing
13 inefficacious, unsubstantial,
untrustworthy
14 unsatisfactory

weaken 3 sap 4 fade, fail, flag,
thin, wane 5 abate, droop,
lower, unman, waste 6 dilute,
expose, impair, lessen, soften
7 cripple, dwindle, exhaust,
thin out 8 diminish, enervate,
mitigate, moderate 9 undermine 10 devitalize, emasculate

weakened 5 frail 6 dilute,
faulty, flawed, watery 7 diluted 8 delicate, disabled 9 enfeebled 10 undermined
11 adulterated, debilitated, watered down

weakling 4 twit, wimp
5 mouse, sissy **6** coward
7 chicken, milksop **9** cream
puff, jellyfish **10** namby-
pamby, pantywaist **11** milquetoast, mollycoddle

weak-minded 4 daft, dull
7 foolish **8** backward, mindless **10** irresolute **11** addle-
headed, vacillating **12** feeble-
minded, muddleheaded,
thick-skulled

weakness 4 bent, bias **5** fault
6 defect, hunger, thirst **7** failing, frailty, leaning, passion
8 appetite, debility, fondness,
lameness, penchant, tendency
9 prejudice, proneness, shakiness **10** deficiency, feebleness,
flimsiness, proclivity, propensity **11** inclination **12** debilitation, imperfection,
unsteadiness **13** vulnerability
14 susceptibility **15** ineffectiveness **16** unconvincingness, un-
substantiality
17 untrustworthiness

weak point 4 flaw **5** break,
crack, fault **6** defect **10** deficiency **11** shortcoming

weak position 8 handicap
12 disadvantage

weak-willed 8 hesitant, wavering **10** hesitating, indecisive,
irresolute

wealth 4 fund, mine **5** goods,
means, money, store **6** assets,
bounty, estate, luxury, mammon, riches **7** capital, fortune
8 chattels, fullness, opulence,
property, richness **9** abundance, affluence, amplitude,
plenitude, profusion, re-
sources **10** easy street, prosperity **11** copiousness
12 independence
13 luxuriousness

wealthy 4 rich **5** flush
6 loaded **7** moneyed, well-off
8 affluent, well-to-do **9** well-
fixed **10** prosperous, well-
heeled

weapon 3 arm **5** guard,
means **6** attack, resort **7** bulwark, defense, measure, offense **8** armament, resource,
security **9** offensive, safeguard
10 protection
14 countermeasure

weaponry 4 arms, guns **8** armament, materiel, ordnance

wear 3 don, tax, use **4** duds,
fray, last, tire, togs, wrap
5 drain, erode, put on, shred,
weary **6** abrade, attire, damage, endure, injury, shroud,
slip on, swathe **7** apparel,
clothes, corrode, dress in, eat
away, exhaust, fatigue, frazzle,

rub away, service, swaddle,
utility **8** clothing, costumes,
garments, overwork, wash
away **9** disrepair **10** employment, overburden **11** application, consumption, utilization
12 dilapidation **13** deterioration **14** disintegration

wear away 4 rust **5** erase,
erode **7** corrode, eat into

weariness
French: **5** ennui

wearing apparel 4 duds, garb,
rags, togs, wear **5** dress **6** attire, finery **7** clothes, costume,
raiment, regalia, threads
8 clothing, ensemble, garments, wardrobe
French: **11** habillement

wearing away 7 erosion
8 abrasion, friction, grinding,
scraping **9** corrosion

wearing down 6 tiring
7 eroding, erosion **8** abrasion,
friction, grinding, scraping
10 overcoming

wearisome 4 dull **6** boring,
dreary, tiring, trying **7** arduous, irksome, tedious **8** annoying, tiresome, toilsome
9 fatiguing, laborious, vexatious **10** bothersome, burdensome, exhausting, irritating,
monotonous, oppressive

wear out 4 tire **7** exhaust, fatigue **8** enervate, enfeeble
10 debilitate

weary 3 fag **4** beat, dull, tire
5 all in, blase, bored, fed up,
jaded, spent, tired **6** boring,
bushed, done in, drowsy,
pooped, sleepy, tiring, tucker
7 annoyed, drained, exhaust,
fatigue, humdrum, overtax,
play out, routine, tedious, tire
out, worn-out **8** dog tired, fatigued, overwork, tiresome
9 disgusted, exhausted, fatiguing, impatient, soporific,
wearisome **10** dispirited, exhausting, monotonous, overburden **11** somniferous
12 discontented, dissatisfied

weather 3 dry, tan **4** face,
rust **5** brave, clime, stand
6 bleach, season **7** climate, oxidize, toughen **8** confront,
windward **9** withstand
11 temperature
god of: **4** Jove **7** Jupiter

weave 4 fuse, join, knit, lace,
link, loom, meld, wind
5 blend, braid, curve, plait,
snake, twist, unify, unite
6 mingle, writhe, zigzag
7 combine, entwine, meander,
texture **9** interlace **10** crisscross, intertwine
11 incorporate

Weaver, Earl
nickname: **15** Earl of
Baltimore
sport: **8** baseball
position: **7** manager
team: **16** Baltimore Orioles

Weaver, Dennis
born: **8** Joplin MO
roles: **7** Chester, McCloud
8 Gunsmoke **9** Gentle Ben
13 Kentucky Jones

Weaver, Sigourney
born: **12** Los Angeles CA
roles: **5** Alien **6** Aliens
10 Eyewitness **12** Ghostbusters **17** Gorillas in the Mist
26 The Year of Living
Dangerously

Weavers, The
author: **16** Gerhart
Hauptmann

web 3 net **4** maze, mesh, trap
5 snare **6** screen, tangle, tissue **7** complex, netting, network **8** gossamer **9** labyrinth,
screening

Web and the Rock, The
author: **11** Thomas Wolfe
character: **10** Esther Jack
12 George Webber

Webb, Jack
born: **13** Santa Monica CA
wife: **11** Julie London
roles: **6** The Men **7** Dragnet
9 Joe Friday **15** Sunset
Boulevard

Webber, George
character in: **16** The Web
and the Rock **18** You Can't
Go Home Again
author: **5** Wolfe

Webb family
characters in: **7** Our Town
member: **5** Emily, Wally
author: **6** Wilder

**Weber, Karl Maria Fried-
rich Ernst von**
born: **6** Lubeck **7** Germany
composer of: **6** Oberon
9 Euryanthe **13** Der Freischutz **20** Invitation to the
Dance

Weber, Max
born: **6** Russia **9** Bialystok
artwork: **11** The Geranium
17 Chinese Restaurant
18 Adoration of the Moon

Webfoot State
nickname of: **6** Oregon

Webster
character: **6** George **7** Webster **9** Katherine
cast: **10** Alex Karras, Susan
Clark **13** Emmanuel Lewis

Webster, John
author of: **13** The White

Devil **17** The Duchess of Malfi

we cannot
Latin: **11** non possumus

we command
Latin: **8** mandamus

wed 3 tie **4** bind, fuse, link, mate, meld **5** blend, hitch, marry, merge, unify, unite, weave **6** attach, commit, couple, devote, pledge, splice **7** combine, espouse, make one, win over **8** dedicate **11** incorporate

wedded 4 tied **5** bound, fused **6** joined, linked, melded, merged, united **7** blended, devoted, marital, married, pledged, unified **9** committed, connected **12** incorporated

wedding 8 marriage, nuptials

---

wedding anniversaries
first: **5** clock, paper
second: **5** china **6** cotton
third: **5** glass **7** crystal, leather
fourth: **4** silk **5** linen **20** electrical appliances
fifth: **4** wood **10** silverware
sixth: **4** iron, wood
seventh: **4** wool **6** copper **8** desk sets **16** pen and pencil sets
eighth: **4** lace **6** bronze, linens
ninth: **5** china **7** leather, pottery
tenth: **3** tin **8** aluminum **14** diamond jewelry
eleventh: **5** steel **11** accessories **14** fashion jewelry
twelfth: **4** silk **6** pearls **11** colored gems
thirteenth: **4** furs, lace **8** textiles
fourteenth: **5** ivory **11** gold jewelry
fifteenth: **7** crystal, watches
twentieth: **5** china **8** platinum
twenty-fifth: **6** silver **21** sterling silver jubilee
thirtieth: **5** pearl **7** diamond
thirty-fifth: **4** jade **5** coral
fortieth: **4** ruby
forty-fifth: **8** sapphire
fiftieth: **4** gold **13** golden jubilee
fifty-fifth: **7** emerald
sixtieth: **7** diamond

---

weddings
god of: **8** Talassio

wedge 3 jam, ram **4** cram, pack, rend, rive **5** chock, chunk, crowd, force, press, split, stuff **6** cleave **7** squeeze

wedlock 8 marriage **9** matrimony

Wednesday
Dutch: **8** woensdag
French: **8** mercredi
German: **8** mittwoch
heavenly body: **7** Mercury
Italian: **9** mercoledi
name comes from: **4** Odin **5** Woden
observance: **12** Ash Wednesday
Spanish: **9** miercoles
Swedish: **6** onsdag

wee 4 tiny **5** dwarf, scant, teeny **6** little, minute, petite, scanty **9** itty-bitty, miniature, minuscule **10** diminutive, teeny-weeny, undersized **11** Lilliputian, microscopic

weed 3 bur, hoe, nag, pot **4** burr, butt, cull, dock, hemp, rake **5** cigar, joint, vetch **6** darnel, harrow, pull up, root up, uproot **7** tobacco **8** nuisance, plantain, purslane, toadflax **9** cigarette, crabgrass, cultivate, dandelion, eliminate, extirpate, marijuana **12** mourning band

weed out 6 banish **7** abolish, discard **8** get rid of, throw out **9** eliminate

Weena
character in: **14** The Time Machine
author: **5** Wells

weeny 3 wee **4** tiny **5** frank, small, teeny **6** hotdog, little, teensy, wiener **11** frankfurter

weep 3 cry, orp, sob **4** bawl, bend, drip, leak, lerm, ooze, shed, tear, wail **5** exude, mourn **6** bewail, boohoo, lament, shower **7** blubber, lapwing, whimper **8** sweating **9** exudation
genus: **8** Vanellus

weep over 5 mourn **6** bemoan, bewail, lament

weevil
variety: **4** boll, rice

Wegener, Alfred L
field: **10** geophysics **11** meteorology
nationality: **6** German
theory of: **16** continental drift

Wegg
character in: **15** Our Mutual Friend
author: **7** Dickens

weigh 4 lift **5** count, hoist, raise, scale **6** burden, charge, ponder, regard **7** balance, compare, measure **8** consider, encumber, evaluate, ruminate **11** contemplate **12** counterbalance

weigh anchor 4 sail **7** cast off, set sail, ship out

weigh down 4 load **6** anchor, burden **7** oppress **8** encumber, obligate, overload

weight 3 tax **4** heft, load, mass **5** value **6** burden, import, saddle, strain, stress **7** ballast, concern, oppress, tonnage, urgency **8** emphasis, encumber, poundage, pressure **9** heaviness, influence, magnitude **10** importance **11** consequence **12** significance **13** consideration, ponderousness

weight, unit of *see box*

weightlessness 8 buoyancy **9** lightness **11** zero gravity

weighty 5 grave, heavy, hefty, vital **6** solemn, taxing, trying, urgent **7** arduous, crucial, earnest, massive, onerous, serious **8** critical, crushing, cumbrous, pressing **9** difficult, essential, important, ponderous **10** burdensome, cumbersome, oppressive **11** significant, substantial, troublesome **12** considerable **13** consequential

Weill, Kurt
born: **6** Dessau **7** Germany
composer of: **8** Happy End **13** Lady in the Dark **15** Down in the Valley **18** The Lindbergh Flight, The Threepenny Opera **19** Die Dreigroschenoper **31** Rise and Fall of the City of Mahagonny **32** Aufstieg und Fall der Stadt Mahagonny

Weir, Peter
director of: **7** Witness **9** Gallipoli **11** The Last Wave **26** The Year of Living Dangerously

weird 3 odd **4** wild **5** crazy, eerie, kooky, nutty, queer **6** farout, mystic, spooky **7** bizarre, curious, ghostly, magical, strange, unusual **8** abnormal, freakish, peculiar **9** eccentric, grotesque, irregular, unearthly, unnatural **10** mysterious, outlandish, phantasmal, unortho-

1065

weight, unit of
  of Afghanistan: 3 pau, paw, ser, sir
  of Algeria: 4 rotl
  of Argentina: 4 last **5** grano, libra **7** quintal **8** tonelada
  of Austria: 4 marc, saum, unze **5** denat, karch, pfund, stein **7** centner, pfennig **8** vierling **9** quantchen
  of Belgium: 4 last **5** carat, livre, pound **6** charge **7** chariot **9** esterling
  of Bolivia: 5 libra, marco
  of Borneo: 4 para **6** chapah
  of Brazil: 3 bag **4** onca, onza **5** libra **6** arroba, oitava **7** arratel, quilate, quintal **8** tonelada
  of Bulgaria: 3 oka, oke **5** tovar
  of Cambodia: 4 mace, tael
  of Chile: 5 grano, libra **7** quintal
  of China: 3 fan, fen, hao, kin, ssu, tan, yin **4** chee, chin, dong, shih, tael, tsin **5** catty, chien, picul, tchin, tsien **6** kungli **7** haikwan, kungfen, kungssu, kungtun **8** kungchin **9** candareen **10** kupingtael
  of Colombia: 3 bag **4** saco **5** carga, libra **7** quilate, quintal
  of Costa Rica: 3 bag **4** caja **5** libra
  of Cuba: 5 libra **6** tercio
  of Ecuador: 5 libra
  of Egypt: 3 kat, ket, oka, oke **4** dera, heml, khar, okia, rotl **5** artal, artel, deben, kerat, minae, minas, okieh, pound, ratel, uckia **6** hamlah, kantar **7** drachma, quintal
  of El Salvador: 3 bag **4** caja **5** libra
  of England: 3 bag, kip, tod, ton **4** keel, last, mast, maun **5** barge, fagot, grain, maund, pound, score, stand, stone, truss **6** bushel, cental, fangot, firkin, fother, fotmal, pocket **7** quarter, quintal, sarpler
  of Estonia: 4 lood, nael, puud
  of Ethiopia: 3 pek **4** kasm, natr, oket, rotl **5** alada, artal, mocha, neter, ratel, wakea **6** wogiet **8** farasula **9** mutagalla
  of France: 3 sol **4** gros, kilo, marc, once **5** carat, livre, pound, tonne, uckia **6** gramme, passir **7** tonneau **8** esterlin **9** esterling
  of Greece: 3 mna, oka, oke **4** mina, obol **5** litra, livre, maneh, pound **6** diobol, dramme, kantar, obolos, obolus, stater, talent **7** chalcon, chalque, drachma **8** diobolon, talanton
  of Guatemala: 4 caja **5** libra
  of Guinea: 4 akey, piso, uzan **5** benda, seron **6** quinto **8** aguirage
  of Hungary: 7 vamfont **8** vammazsa
  of Iceland: 4 pund **5** pound, tunna **6** smjors
  of India: 3 mod, pai, ser, vis **4** dhan, drum, hoen, kona, myat, pala, pank, pice, raik, ruay, tael, tali, tank, tola, wang, yava **5** adpad, bahar, hubba, masha, maund, tical **6** abucco, karsha **8** mangelin
  of Indonesia: 5 catty, ounce, thail **6** soekoe
  of Iran: 3 ser **4** dram, dung, rotl, sang, seer **5** abbas, artel, maund, pinar, ratel **6** dirhem, gandum, karwar, miscal, nakhod, nimman **7** abbassi **8** tcheirek
  of Italy: 5 carat, libra, oncia, pound **6** carato, denaro, libbra, ottava
  of Japan: 2 mo **3** fun, kin, kon, rin, shi **4** kati, kwan, niyo **5** carat, catty, momme, picul **6** kwamme **8** hiyakkin
  of Java: 4 amat, pond, tali **5** pound **6** soekel
  of Korea: 3 won
  of Latvia: 9 liespfund
  of Libya: 3 pik, saa **4** kele **5** teman, uckia **6** gorraf, misura **7** mattaro, termino **8** kharouba
  of Malaysia: 4 chee, mace, tael, wang **7** tampang
  of Mexico: 3 bag **4** onza **5** carga, libra, marco **6** adarme, arroba, ochava, tercio **7** quintal
  of Mongolia: 3 lan
  of Morocco: 4 rotl **5** artal, artel, gerbe, ratel **6** dirhem, kintar **7** quintal
  of Myanmar: 2 ta **3** can, mat, moo, pai, vis **4** binh, dong, kyat, ruay, viss **5** bahar, behar, candy, tical, ticul **6** abucco **7** peiktha
  of the Netherlands: 3 ons **4** last, lood, pond **5** bahar, grein **6** korrel **7** wichtje **8** esterlin
  of Nicaragua: 3 bag **4** caha, caja **8** tonelada
  of Norway: 3 lod **4** mark, pund **9** skaalpund **10** bismerpund
  of Pakistan: 4 seer, tola **5** maund
  of Paraguay: 7 quintal
  of Peru: 5 libra **7** quintal
  of the Philippines: 5 catty, fardo, picul, punto **6** lachsa **7** quilate **8** chinanta
  of Poland: 3 lut **4** funt **5** uncya **6** kamian **7** centner, skrupul
  of Portugal: 4 grao, onca, once **5** libra, marco **6** arroba, oitava **7** arratel, quintal **9** excropulo
  of Russia: 3 lof, lot **4** dola, funt, lana, last, loof, loth, once, pood, poud **5** dolia
  of Saudi Arabia: 3 oke
  of Scotland: 4 boll, drop **5** trone **6** bushel
  of Somalia: 8 parsalah
  of Spain: 4 onza **5** frail, grano, libra, marco, tomin **6** adarme, arroba, dinero, dracma, ochava **7** arienzo, quilate, quintal **8** caracter, tonelada

(*continued*)

weight, unit of (*continued*)
  of Sudan: 5 habba
  of Sweden: 3 ass, lod, ort **4** last, mark, sten **5** carat **6** nylast **7** centner, lispund **8** skalpund, skeppund **9** shippound
  of Switzerland: 4 fund **5** pfund **7** centner, quintal **12** zugthierlast
  of Syria: 4 cola, rotl **5** artal, artel, ratel **6** talent
  of Tanzania: 8 farsalah
  of Thailand: 3 bat, hap, pai, pay, sen, sok **4** baht, haph, kati, klam, klom **5** catty, chang, coyan, fuang, picul, pilul, tical **6** fluang, graini, salung, sompay **7** tamlung
  of Tunisia: 3 saa **4** rotl **5** artal, artel, ratel, uckia **6** kantar
  of Turkey: 3 oka, oke **4** aqui, dram, kile, rotl **5** artal, artel, cheke, kerat, obolu, ratel **6** batman, dirhem, kantar, maunch, miskal **7** drachma, quintal, yusdrum
  of Uruguay: 7 quintal
  of Venezuela: 3 bag **5** libra
  of Vietnam: 3 can, yet **4** uyen
  of Yugoslavia: 3 oka **5** dramm, tovar, wagon **7** satlijk

dox **12** supernatural **14** unconventional

weirdo 3 nut **4** kook **5** flake, freak **6** looney **7** lunatic, oddball **8** crackpot, original **9** character, eccentric, screwball **10** one-of-a-kind

Weird sisters 5 Fates, Norns

Weisenfreund, Muni
  real name of: 8 Paul Muni

Weismuller, Johnny
  real name: 20 Peter John Weissmuller
  born: 9 Windbar PA
  Olympic sport: 8 swimming
  Olympic gold medals: 4 five
  wife: 9 Lupe Velez
  roles: 6 Tarzan **9** Jungle Jim

Weiss, Peter
  author of: 10 Marat/Sade **14** Vanishing Point

welcome 4 meet **5** admit, greet **6** at home, salute, wanted **7** embrace, receive, usher in, winning **8** accepted, admitted, charming, engaging, enticing, greeting, inviting, pleasant, pleasing **9** agreeable, entertain, reception **10** delightful, gratifying, salutation **11** comfortable

Weld, Tuesday
  real name: 12 Susan Ker Weld
  born: 9 New York NY
  husband: 11 Dudley Moore
  roles: 12 I Walk the Line **14** Play It as It Lays **16** The Cincinnati Kid, Wild in the Country **19** Looking for Mr Goodbar

welfare 4 good **6** health, profit, relief **7** benefit, success, the dole **9** advantage, happiness

well *see box*

well-adjusted 6 normal, secure **8** sensible

Welland, May
  character in: 17 The Age of Innocence
  author: 7 Wharton

well-behaved 6 polite, sedate **8** decorous

well-being 4 ease, good, luck, weal **6** health, profit **7** benefit, comfort, fortune, success, welfare **8** felicity, good luck **9** advantage, affluence, happiness **10** prosperity

wellborn 8 highbred **9** patrician **10** upper-class **12** aristocratic, silk-stocking

Wellbred
  character in: 19 Every Man in His Humour
  author: 6 Jonson

well-bred 5 civil, suave **6** polite, urbane **7** elegant, gallant, genteel, refined **8** cultured, ladylike, mannerly, polished **9** civilized, courteous **10** cultivated **11** gentlemanly **13** sophisticated

well-chosen 3 apt **4** fine

5 prize **6** choice, seemly, select **7** apropos, correct, fitting, special **8** superior **9** excellent **11** appropriate

well-considered 7 careful, prudent **8** cautious **10** thoughtful **11** circumspect

well-coordinated 6 smooth **8** graceful **9** dexterous **10** effortless

well-defined 5 clear, plain **8** clear-cut, definite, distinct, palpable **10** pronounced

well-dressed 4 chic **5** natty, smart **6** dapper **11** fashionable

well-educated 7 erudite, learned **8** cultured, literate **9** scholarly **10** cultivated **13** knowledgeable

Weller, Sam
  character in: 14 Pickwick Papers
  author: 7 Dickens

Welles, Orson
  real name: 17 George Orson Welles

well 3 jet, run **4** flow, fund, good, gush, hale, mine, ooze, pool, pour, rise **5** amply, fount, fully, issue, lucky, right, shaft, sound, spout, spurt, store, surge **6** easily, fairly, hearty, justly, kindly, nicely, proper, robust, source, spring, stream, strong, warmly **7** chipper, fitting, healthy, readily, rightly **8** famously, fountain, laudably, properly, suitably, very much, vigorous **9** agreeably, capitally, carefully, correctly, favorable, favorably, fortunate, promising, quite well **10** abundantly, acceptably, adequately, auspicious, completely, familiarly, felicitous, intimately, personally, prosperous, splendidly, successful, thoroughly **11** approvingly, commendably **12** advantageous, auspiciously, considerably, propitiously, satisfactory, successfully, sufficiently **13** substantially **14** advantageously, satisfactorily **15** sympathetically **16** enthusiastically
    hole drilled in ground for: **3** gas, oil **5** water

born: 9 Kenosha WI
wife: 9 Paola Mori **12** Rita Hayworth
formed: 14 Mercury Theatre
radio show: 14 War of the Worlds
roles: 8 Jane Eyre **11** Citizen Kane, The Third Man, Touch of Evil
director of: 7 Macbeth, Othello **8** Falstaff **11** Citizen Kane, The Stranger, Touch of Evil **23** The Magnificent Ambersons

well-favored 4 fair **5** bonny **6** comely, pretty **7** sightly, winsome **8** fetching, handsome **9** beautiful **10** attractive **11** good looking

well-fed 5 hefty, plump, stout **6** portly, rotund **9** corpulent

well-fixed 4 rich **7** moneyed, wealthy **8** affluent **10** prosperous

well-founded 7 factual **9** supported **12** corroborated **13** substantiated

well-groomed 4 neat, tidy **5** natty **6** spruce **10** impeccable

well-grounded 5 valid **7** factual **8** reliable **9** supported **10** undeniable, undisputed, unshakable **11** irrefutable **12** corroborated, indisputable **13** incontestable, substantiated **16** incontrovertible

well-heeled 4 rich **7** moneyed, wealthy **8** affluent **10** in the chips, in the money, prosperous

Wellington
  capital of: 10 New Zealand

Wellington, Duke of
  also: 15 Arthur Wellesley
  nickname: 6 Hookey **12** The Great Duke
  nationality: 7 British
  served in: 5 India **14** Napoleonic Wars
  battle: 6 Assaye **7** Vitoria **8** Talavera, Waterloo **9** Salamanca
  served as: 13 prime minister
  memoirs: 20 Wellington Dispatches

well-kept 4 heat, neat, tidy **7** orderly **9** organized **10** systematic **11** disciplined, uncluttered

well-known 4 open **5** famed, noted **6** common, famous **7** big-time, eminent, evident, leading, obvious, popular **8** familiar, infamous, renowned **9** important, notorious, prominent **10** celebrated, scandalous, understood **11** established, illustrious, outstanding

well-lighted 5 lit up **6** ablaze, bright **11** illuminated

well-made 4 fine **7** perfect **8** executed, flawless **9** faultless **11** beautifully

Wellman, William
  director of: 5 Wings **9** Beau Geste **11** A Star Is Born **13** Nothing Sacred **15** The Story of GI Joe **16** The Ox-Bow Incident

well-mannered 6 polite **7** genteel, refined **8** cultured, decorous, ladylike, polished **9** courteous, dignified **10** cultivated **11** gentlemanly

well-matched 5 close **10** nip-and-tuck

well-off 4 rich **5** flush **6** loaded **7** moneyed, wealthy **8** affluent **10** prosperous **11** comfortable

well-padded 5 plump, stout **6** chubby, fleshy, portly, rotund **9** corpulent

well-proportioned 7 classic, elegant, shapely **8** graceful **11** symmetrical

well-read 7 erudite, learned **8** cultured, literate **9** scholarly **10** cultivated

well-reasoned 4 wise **10** perceptive, thoughtful **11** intelligent

well-rehearsed 6 smooth **7** planned **8** prepared **9** practiced

Wells, H G (Herbert George)
  author of: 5 Kipps **10** Tono-Bungay **11** Ann Veronica **14** The Time Machine **15** The Invisible Man **16** Outline of History **17** Love and Mr Lewisham, The War of the Worlds **19** The History of Mr Polly **22** The Shape of Things to Come **23** Mr Britling Sees It Through

Wells, Julia Elizabeth
  real name of: 12 Julie Andrews

wellspring 4 font **6** origin, source **9** beginning **10** birthplace **12** fountainhead

well-stocked 4 full **11** overflowing

well-suited 6 proper **7** correct, fitting **8** suitable **9** congenial, congruous **10** compatible, harmonious **11** appropriate

well-to-do 4 rich **7** moneyed, wealthy **8** affluent **10** in the chips, in the money, prosperous

well up 4 boil, rise **6** bubble **7** surface

well-ventilated 4 airy **5** windy **6** breezy, drafty

well-versed 7 knowing **9** qualified **10** conversant **11** experienced **13** knowledgeable
  French: 9 au courant

well-wisher 6 friend **8** advocate, champion **9** supported

Welsh Mythology
  goddess: 3 Don
  goddess of fire / fertility / agriculture / household / wisdom: 6 Brigit
  king: 4 Bran, Llud, Ludd, Nudd
  magician: 5 Lloyd
  paradise: 5 Annwn **6** Annfwn
  prince: 5 Pwyll **7** Kilwich
  princess: 5 Olwen
  romantic tales: 10 Mabinogian

welt 4 bump, lump, mark, wale, weal **6** bruise, streak, stripe **8** swelling **9** contusion

Weltanschauung 25 manner of looking at the world

Weltansicht 9 world view

welter 4 heap, mass, mess, pile, roll, toss **5** heave, storm **6** bustle, grovel, hubbub, jumble, racket, tumult, wallow, writhe **7** tempest, turmoil **9** commotion, confusion **10** hodgepodge, turbulence

Welter, Blanca Rosa
  real name of: 14 Linda Christian

Weltschmerz 6 sorrow **9** world pain **20** sentimental pessimism

Welty, Eudora
  author of: 12 Delta Wedding, Golden Apples **13** Losing Battles **14** The Ponder Heart **15** A Sweet Devouring **19** The Robber Bridegroom **20** The Optimist's Daughter

wench 4 doxy, girl, lass, maid, slut **5** whore **6** damsel, lassie, maiden **8** strumpet **10** prostitute

wend 4 make **5** hie to

went 3 ran **4** flew, left **5** faded, got on **6** flew by, lapsed, passed **7** elapsed, sallied **8** departed, filed off, passed by, took wing, vanished **9** proceeded, took leave **10** shuffled on, took flight **11** disappeared, forged ahead **12** sallied forth **13** pressed onward

Wentworth, Captain Frederick
character in: 10 Persuasion
author: 6 Austen

Werfel, Franz
author of: 9 Mirror Man
19 Forty Days of Musa
Dagh, The Song of
Bernadette

Werle, Gregers
character in: 11 The Wild
Duck
author: 5 Ibsen

Werner, Oskar
real name: 24 Oskar Josef
Bschliessmayer
born: 6 Vienna 7 Austria
roles: 11 Jules and Jim, Ship
of Fools 17 Voyage of the
Damned 22 Fahrenheit Four
Fifty One, The Shoes of the
Fisherman 26 The Spy Who
Came in from the Cold

Wertmuller, Lina
director of: 9 Swept Away
(by an unusual destiny in
the blue sea of August)
13 Seven Beauties

Wescott, Glenway
author of: 14 The Grand-
mother, The Pilgrim Hawk
16 The Apple of the Eye
17 Apartment in Athens

Wessex
fictional place created by:
5 Hardy

West, Benjamin
born: 13 Springfield PA
artwork: 17 Death on a Pale
Horse 19 Death of General
Wolfe 22 Saul and the
Witch of Endor

West, Dame Rebecca
real name: 28 Cicily Isabel
Fairfield Andrews
author of: 8 The Judge
11 Harriet Hume 13 Birds
Fall Down 15 The Thinking
Reed 19 The Strange Necessity 20 The Fountain Over-
flows 21 The Return of the
Soldier 22 Black Lamb and
Grey Falcon

West, Jessamyn
author of: 11 Leafy Rivers
13 A Matter of Time
18 Except for Me and Thee
21 The Friendly Persuasion
22 The Massacre at Fall
Creek

West, Mae
born: 10 Brooklyn NY
roles: 3 Sex 8 Sextette 9 I'm
No Angel 10 Diamond Lil
13 Klondike Annie 14 Go
West Young Man 15 Night
After Night, She Done Him
Wrong 16 Myra Breckin-

ridge 17 My Little
Chickadee
autobiography: 28 Goodness
Had Nothing To Do With It
quote: 18 Beulah peel me a
grape 22 Come up and see
me sometime

West, Morris L
author of: 7 Proteus 9 Harlequin 13 The Salamander
14 The Clowns of God
15 The Tower of Babel
17 The Devil's Advocate
22 The Shoes of the
Fisherman

West, Nathanael
author of: 12 A Cool Mil-
lion 16 Miss Lonelyhearts
17 The Day of the Locust

Westcott, Edward Noyes
author of: 10 David Harum

Westenra, Lucy
character in: 7 Dracula
author: 6 Stoker

Western, Sophia
character in: 8 Tom Jones
author: 8 Fielding

Western Sahara *see box*

Western Samoa *see box*

Western Star
author: 19 Stephen Vincent
Benet

Western Sahara
other name: 13 Spanish
Sahara
capital: 6 Al Aiun 7 El
Aaiun
city: 3 Zug 5 Daora,
Smara 6 Aargub,
Dakhla, Tichla 9 As-
queimat, Bir Gandus
10 Bir Enzaran
12 Guelta Zemmur
government: 33 disputed
territory claimed by
Morocco
river: 7 Uad Atui 8 Uad
Assag 13 Saguia el
Hamra
sea: 8 Atlantic
physical feature:
cape: 6 Barbas
7 Bojador
desert: 6 Sahara
wind: 5 leste 6 gibleh
people: 4 Arab 6 Berber
language: 16 Hassaniyya
Arabic
religion: 5 Islam
feature:
political group:
14 Polisario Front

Western Samoa
other name: 17 Naviga-
tor's Islands
capital/largest city:
4 Apia
others: 6 Safotu, Sataua
7 Faleolo, Palauli, Pou-
tasi, Tuasivi 8 Faga-
malo, Falelima,
Lufilufi 9 Falealupo,
Mulifanua 10 Sama-
laeulu, Satupaitea
monetary unit: 4 sene,
tala
island: 5 Upolu 6 Mano-
no, Savaii 7 Apolima
mountain: 4 Fito, Vaea
highest point: 13 Mauga
Silisili
sea: 7 Pacific
physical feature:
bay: 4 Asau, Salu
6 Safata 7 Lafanga,
Matautu 8 Fangaloa,
Salealua 9 Saluofata
strait: 7 Apolima
people: 6 Samoan
10 Melanesian,
Polynesian
author: 20 Robert
Louis Stevenson (Tus-
itala, Teller of Tales)
explorer: 6 Wilkes
9 Roggeveen
12 Bougainville
language: 6 Samoan
7 English
religion: 9 Methodist
10 Protestant 13 Roman
Catholic
14 Congregational
place:
observatory: 4 Apia
tomb: 9 Stevenson
feature:
chief: 5 matai
clothing: 5 pareu
8 lavalava, puletasi
dance: 4 siva
daughter of chief:
5 taupo
house: 4 fale
food:
dish: 8 palusami
drink: 3 ava

Westhus, Haie
character in: 25 All Quiet on
the Western Front
author: 8 Remarque

West Indies *see box*

Westinghouse, George
nationality: 8 American
invented: 8 air brake 12 railroad frog 20 railroad signal
system

West Indies
11 archipelago
Associated States:
  7 Antigua, Grenada, St
  Lucia 8 Anguilla, Dom-
  inica 12 St Kitts-Nevis
bird: 4 tody 6 mucaro
channel: 7 Jamaica 9 Old
  Bahama
component: 4 Cuba
  5 Haiti 6 Tobago 7 Ba-
  hamas, Jamaica 8 Bar-
  bados, Trinidad
  10 Hispaniola, Puerto
  Rico 13 Virgin Islands
  14 Leeward Islands,
  Lesser Antilles
  15 Greater Antilles,
  Windward Islands
  17 Dominican Republic
crop: 6 coffee
  9 sugarcane
fish: 4 pega 5 pelon
formerly: 10 federation
fruit: 5 papaw 6 paw-
  paw 7 genipap
islands: 5 Turks 6 Caicos,
  Cayman, Virgin 7 Ba-
  hamas, Leeward
  8 Windward
kale: 7 malanga
lizard: 6 arbalo
music: 7 calypso
passage: 4 Mona
  8 Windward
rodent: 5 hutia
sea: 9 Caribbean
shark: 4 gata
sorcery: 3 obi 5 obeah
tree: 5 genip 6 aralie
tribesman: 5 Carib 6 Arawak 7 Ciboney
vessel: 6 droger, drogher
volcano: 5 Pelee

Westlake, Donald E
author of: 8 Bank Shot
  10 The Hot Rock 13 Dancing Aztecs 15 Brothers
  Keepers
  as Richard Stark: 9 The
  Hunter 10 The Seventh
  as Tucker Coe: 19 Murder
  Among Children

Westover, Russ
creator/artist of: 15 Tillie
  the Toiler

West Side Story
director: 10 Robert Wise
  13 Jerome Robbins
cast: 10 Rita Moreno
  11 Natalie Wood, Russ Tamblyn 13 Richard Beymer
  14 George Chakiris
score: 15 Stephen Sondheim
  16 Leonard Bernstein

Oscar for: 7 picture 8 director 15 supporting actor
  (Chakiris) 17 supporting actress (Moreno)

West Virginia *see box*

Westward Ho!
author: 15 Charles Kingsley

west wind
associated with: 8 Favonius,
  Zephyrus

wet 3 dip 4 damp, dank, rain,
  soak 5 humid, moist, rainy,
  soggy, steep, storm, water
  6 clammy, dampen, drench,
  liquid, shower, soaked, sodden, splash, stormy, watery
  7 immerse, moisten, showery,
  soaking, sopping, squishy, wetness 8 dampened, dampness,
  dankness, drenched, dripping,
  inundate, irrigate, moisture,
  sprinkle, submerge 9 exudation, liquified, moistness, rain-
  storm 10 clamminess
  11 waterlogged 12 condensation 13 precipitation

---

wet blanket 4 drag 6 damper
  10 spoilsport 11 party-pooper

wet down 5 spray 6 dampen
  7 moisten 8 sprinkle

wettish 4 damp 5 moist
  6 clammy

**we who are about to die
salute thee**
  Latin: 19 morituri te
  salutamus
  said by: 15 Roman gladiators
  said to: 13 Roman emperors

whack 2 go 3 box, hit, rap,
  try 4 bang, belt, blow, cuff,
  slam, slap, slug, sock, stab,
  turn 5 baste, clout, crack,
  knock, pound, punch, smack,
  smite, thump, trial 6 strike,
  wallop 7 attempt, venture
  8 endeavor

whale 4 beat, cane, drub, flog,
  orca, whip 6 baleen, thrash
  9 bastinado
  constellation of: 5 Cetus
  group of: 3 gam, pod

West Virginia
abbreviation: 2 WV 3 W Va
nickname: 8 Mountain 9 Panhandle
capital: 10 Charleston
largest city: 10 Huntington
others: 5 Logan 6 Elkins, Keyser, Ripley, Vienna, Weston
  7 Beckley, Grafton, Spencer, Weirton 8 Fairmont, Wheeling 10 Clarksburg 11 Moundsville, Parkersburg
college: 5 Salem 7 Bethany, Concord 8 Marshall, Wheeling 9 Bluefield 10 Charleston 14 Davis and Elkins
  16 Alderson Broaddus 20 West Virginia Wesleyan
feature:
  historical site: 12 Harper's Ferry
  national road: 10 Cumberland
tribe: 7 Moneton
people: 9 Pearl Buck 14 Arthur I Boreman 19 Walter
  Philip Reuther 24 Thomas "Stonewall" Jackson
  explorer: 12 Morgan Morgan
island: 14 Blennerhassett
lake: 4 Lynn
land rank: 10 forty-first
mountain:
  highest point: 10 Spruce Knob
physical feature:
  cavern: 6 Seneca
  plateau: 9 Allegheny
  rock: 6 Seneca
  spring: 8 Berkeley 12 White Sulphur
river: 3 Elk 4 Ohio 6 Gauley 7 Kanawha, Potomac, Tug
  Fork 8 Big Sandy, Guyandot 11 Monongahela
state admission: 11 Thirty-fifth
state bird: 8 cardinal
state fish: 10 brook trout
state flower: 11 great laurel 15 big rhododendron
  17 great rhododendron
state motto: 25 Mountaineers Are Always Free
state song: 17 West Virginia Hills 20 This Is My West
  Virginia 27 West Virginia My Home Sweet Home
state tree: 10 sugar maple

whammy 3 hex 4 jinx 5 curse 7 evil eye 9 evil spell

wharf 3 key 4 dock, pier, quai, quay, slip 5 jetty 6 marina 7 landing 10 breakwater

Wharton, Edith
author of: 10 Ethan Frome, The Old Maid 15 The House of Mirth 17 The Age of Innocence 21 The Custom of the Country

Whatever Happened to Baby Jane?
director: 13 Robert Aldrich
cast: 10 Bette Davis 11 Victor Buono 12 Joan Crawford 15 Marjorie Bennett

What Every Woman Knows
author: 12 James M Barrie
character: 9 John Shand 15 Charles Venables 18 Comtesse de la Briere, Lady Sybil Tenterden
Wylie family: 5 Alick, David, James 6 Maggie

what it takes 5 skill 7 ability, mastery 9 expertise 10 capability, competence, expertness 11 proficiency 13 the right stuff

What Mrs McGillicuddy Saw!
author: 14 Agatha Christie

What Price Glory?
author: 15 Maxwell Anderson

What's Happening!!
character: 5 Rerun 6 Dwayne 7 Shirley 9 Dee Thomas, (Mama) Mrs Thomas 11 Roger (Raj) Thomas
cast: 9 Fred Berry, Mabel King 12 Ernest Thomas 13 Haywood Nelson 15 Danielle Spencer, Shirley Hemphill

What's My Line?
host: 8 John Daly
panelist: 8 Hal Block 9 Fred Allen 10 Steve Allen 11 Bennett Cerf 13 Arlene Francis 15 Louis Untermeyer 16 Dorothy Kilgallen

wheat 8 Triticum
varieties: 4 club, rice 5 durum, dwarf, India, river 6 Alaska, common, German, Polish, starch 7 English, poulard 8 hedgehog 10 one-grained, two-grained 13 Mediterranean
product: 4 bran 5 bread, flour, pasta 6 cereal 8 macaroni 9 spaghetti

Wheat State
nickname of: 6 Kansas

wheedle 4 coax, lure 5 charm 6 cajole, entice, induce 7 beguile, flatter 8 butter up, inveigle, persuade, soft soap

wheel 4 disk, drum, hoop, ring, roll, spin 5 pivot, round, swirl, twirl, whirl 6 caster, circle, gilgal, gyrate, roller, rotate, swivel 7 revolve 9 pirouette

Wheel of Fortune
host: 8 Pat Sajak
assistant: 10 Vanna White

wheels 3 car 4 auto, heap 5 motor 6 jalopy 7 flivver, vehicle 8 motorcar 9 tin lizzie 10 automobile

wheeze 4 gasp, hiss, pant, puff 7 panting, whistle

whelp 3 boy, cub, kid, lad, pup 4 brat 5 child, puppy, youth 6 urchin 9 stripling, youngster 14 whippersnapper

whence 9 from where 10 antecedent 14 from what source

Where Eagles Dare
director: 12 Brian G Hutton
based on novel by: 15 Alistair MacLean
cast: 7 Mary Ure 12 Robert Beatty 13 Clint Eastwood, Patrick Wymark, Richard Burton 14 Michael Hordern

wherefore 2 so 3 why 7 because 13 for what reason

where I may stand
Greek: 6 pou sto

where mentioned above
Latin: 8 ubi supra

whereupon 8 upon what 10 after which 14 upon which point

wherewithal 4 cash 5 funds, means 6 assets 7 capital 9 financing, resources

whet 4 edge, hone, stir 5 grind, pique, strop, tempt 6 allure, arouse, awaken, entice, excite, induce, kindle 7 animate, provoke, quicken, sharpen 9 stimulate 11 put an edge on

whether willing or not
Latin: 12 nolens volens

which see
Latin: 2 qv 8 quod vide

which was to be demonstrated
Latin: 3 QED 21 quod erat demonstrandum

which was to be done
Latin: 17 quod erat faciendum

which was to be shown
Latin: 3 QED 21 quod erat demonstrandum

whiff 4 hint, odor, puff 5 aroma, draft, scent, smell, sniff, trace 6 breath, breeze, zephyr 7 bouquet
French: 7 soupcon

Whig Party
president belonging to: 5 Tyler 6 Taylor 8 Fillmore, Harrison

while 2 as 3 yet 4 idle, till, time, when 5 until 6 during, effort, whilst 7 filling, interim, trouble, whereas 8 although, occasion

whim 4 urge 5 fancy, quirk 6 notion, vagary 7 caprice, conceit, impulse 8 crotchet 11 inspiration 12 eccentricity

whimper 3 sob 4 pule 5 whine 6 snivel 7 blubber, sniffle, sobbing 9 cry softly, sniveling 11 sob brokenly 16 whine plaintively

whimsical 5 droll 6 fickle, fitful, quaint 7 amusing, erratic, waggish 8 fanciful, notional, quixotic 9 eccentric 10 capricious, changeable, chimerical 12 inconsistent

whimsy, whimsey 4 bent, wish 5 fancy, humor, prank, quirk 6 notion, vagary 7 caprice, fantasy 8 escapade, drollery 11 make-believe

whine 3 cry, sob 4 fret, mewl, moan, wail 6 grouse, murmur, mutter, snivel 7 grumble, whimper 8 complain 9 complaint 11 gripe meekly 12 plaintive cry 14 cry plaintively

whip 3 rod 4 beat, cane, drub, flap, flog, jerk, jolt, lash, lick, maul, rout 5 birch, flick, spank, strap, thong, whisk 6 rattan, snatch, switch 7 cowhide, rawhide, scourge, trounce 8 birch rod, vanquish 9 horsewhip, toss about 10 blacksnake, flagellate 13 cat-o'-nine-tails, defeat soundly, move violently 14 beat decisively, beat into a froth

Whip 8 scorpion

whip hand 4 sway 5 power 7 control, mastery 9 advantage, authority, dominance, supremacy, upper hand 10 ascendancy, domination

whipped 5 caned, waled 6 beaten, darted, flayed, frothy, lashed, roused 7 flogged, frothed, incited, revived, spanked, subdued, swished, whisked 8 defeated, overlaid, punished, scourged,

switched **9** chastised
10 vanquished

whir 3 hum **4** buzz, purr
5 drone **7** whisper

whirl 2 go **3** try **4** reel, spin,
stab, turn **5** crack, fling, pivot,
swirl, trial, twirl, whack,
wheel **6** circle, dither, flurry,
gyrate, rotate **7** attempt, revolve, turning **8** circling, gyration, pivoting, rotation,
spinning, swirling, twirling,
wheeling **9** feel dizzy, feel
giddy, turning **8** circling, gyra-
giddy, pirouette, revolving,
turn round **10** dizzy round,
rapid round, revolution
12 merry-go-round **17** state of
excitement **18** dizzying
succession

whirlpool 4 eddy **5** swirl,
whirl **6** vortex **9** maelstrom
15 whirling current

whirlwind 4 rash **5** hasty,
quick, rapid, short, swift **7** cyclone, tornado, twister
8 headlong **9** breakneck, impetuous, impulsive
10 waterspout

whirly 5 dizzy, giddy, shaky
7 reeling **8** spinning
11 vertiginous

whisk 3 fly, zip **4** beat, bolt,
dart, dash, race, rush, tear,
whip, whiz **5** bound, brush,
flick, hurry, scoot, shoot,
speed, spurt, sweep **6** hasten,
scurry, spring, sprint
  type: **4** wire **6** French
  8 omelette

whiskbroom 5 brush

whiskered 5 bushy, hairy
6 shaggy **7** bearded, bristly,
hirsute **8** unshaven **11** bewhiskered, mustachioed

whiskers 5 beard **7** stubble
8 bristles

whiskey, whisky 3 gin, rum,
rye **4** corn, shot **5** booze,
hooch, Irish, juice, vodka **6** liquor, red eye, rotgut, Scotch
7 alcohol, aquavit, blended,
bourbon, spirits **8** eau-de-vie
9 aquavitae, firewater, moonshine, unblended **10** sneaky
pete, usquebaugh **11** mountain
dew **14** John Barleycorn,
white lightning
  type: 3 rye **6** Scotch
  7 bourbon
  drink: 8 hot toddy **14** Klondike Cooler
  with beer: 11 Boilermaker
  with Benedictine: 10 Frisco
  Sour
  with Cointreau: 16 Canadian
  Cocktail
  with vermouth: 9 Manhattan

whisper 3 hum **4** blab, buzz,

hint, purr, sigh, tell **5** blurt,
bruit, drone, rumor **6** gossip,
murmur, mutter, reveal, rustle **7** breathe, confide, divulge,
inkling **8** disclose, innuendo,
intimate **9** undertone **10** suggestion **11** insinuation

whist
  derived from: 8 triomphe
  descendant: 6 bridge
  number of players: 4 four
  six tricks: 4 book

Whistle
  author: 10 James Jones

**Whistler, James Abbott
McNeill**
  born: 8 Lowell MA
  artwork: 6 Etudes **9** Harmo-
  nies, Nocturnes **10** Rosa
  Corder **12** Arrangements,
  The White Girl **13** Thomas
  Carlyle **15** Cicely Alexander,
  Wapping-on-Thames
  24 Venetian Palaces Noc-
  turnes **28** Arrangement in
  Grey and Black No 1 (The
  Artist's Mother) **29** Chelsea
  Nocturne in Blue and
  Green **31** Princess of the
  Land of the Porcelain
  35 Falling Rocket Nocturne
  in Black and Gold **37** Cre-
  morne Lights Nocturne in
  Blue and Silver

whistle-stop 5 stump **8** campaign **11** electioneer

whit 3 dab, dot, jot **4** chip,
dash, drop, iota, mite, snip
5 crumb, grain, pinch, speck
6 morsel, tittle, trifle **7** modicum, smidgen **8** fragment, particle, splinter **9** scintilla

white 3 wan **4** ashy, fair, gray,
pale, pure **5** ashen, blond,
clean, filmy, hoary, ivory,
milky, pasty, pearl, smoky,
snowy **6** benign, chalky,
chaste, cloudy, frosty, leaden,
pallid, pearly, sallow, silver
7 ghostly, silvery **8** blanched,
bleached, grizzled, harmless,
innocent, spotless, virtuous
9 alabaster, bloodless, Caucasian, colorless, stainless, undefiled, unspotted, unstained,
unsullied **10** cadaverous, immaculate **11** translucent, unblemished, unmalicious

White, E B (Elwyn Brooks)
  author of: 11 One Man's
  Meat **12** Stuart Little
  13 Charlotte's Web **14** Is
  Sex Necessary? (with James
  Thurber) **19** The Trumpet of
  the Swan
  column: 13 Talk of the
  Town

White, Stanford *see* **17** Mead
McKim and White

**White, T H (Terence
Hanbury)**
  author of: 15 The Book of
  Merlyn **16** The Ill-Made
  Knight **17** The Witch in the
  Wood **18** The Candle in the
  Wind, The Sword in the
  Stone **20** The Once and Fu-
  ture King

White Album
  author: 10 Joan Didion

White Company, The
  author: 19 Sir Arthur Conan
  Doyle

White Heat
  director: 10 Raoul Walsh
  cast: 11 James Cagney
  12 Edmond O'Brien, Virginia Mayo **16** Margaret
  Wycherly

White-Jacket
  author: 14 Herman Melville

whiten 4 pale **5** clean, frost
6 blanch, bleach, silver
7 lighten

whiteness 6 pallor **7** wanness
8 paleness **9** snowiness **10** sallowness **13** colorlessness

White Nights
  director: 14 Taylor Hackford
  cast: 12 Gregory Hines
  18 Mikhail Baryshnikov
  choreographer: 10 Twyla
  Tharp

White Rabbit
  character in: 28 Alice's Adventures in Wonderland
  author: 7 Carroll

whitewash 6 excuse **7** absolve,
cover up, justify **8** downplay,
minimize, play down **9** calci-
mine, exonerate, vindicate
  paint made by mixing:
  12 lime and water

Whitewater
  author: 10 Paul Horgan

whitish 4 buff, pale **6** chalky,
creamy **7** grayish

Whitman, Bert
  creator/artist of: 14 The
  Green Hornet

Whitman, Walt
  author of: 12 Song of Myself **13** Leaves of Grass
  18 Oh Captain My Captain
  33 When Lilacs Last in the
  Dooryard Bloom'd

Whitmore, James
  born: 13 White Plains NY
  roles: 4 Them **5** Bully
  8 Oklahoma **9** Battlecry
  10 Will Rogers **11** Black
  Like Me **12** Battleground,
  Harry S Truman, Tora Tora
  Tora **15** Command Decision,
  Give 'em Hell Harry **19** The
  Next Voice You Hear

Whitney, Eli
nationality: **8** American
invented: **9** cotton gin
pioneered use of: **14** mass
production

Whittier, John Greenleaf
author of: **9** Snow-Bound
10 Maud Muller **14** The
Barefoot Boy **16** Barbara
Frietchie

whittle 3 cut **4** clip, pare
5 carve, shave, slash **7** curtail,
shorten **8** decrease

whiz 3 fly, hum, zip **4** bolt,
buzz, dart, dash, hiss, race,
rush, scud, tear, whir, zoom
5 adept, drone, scoot, shark,
shoot, speed, spurt, sweep,
swish, whine, whisk **6** expert,
genius, hasten, master, scurry,
sizzle, sprint, wizard **7** prodigy,
scuttle, whistle **11** crackerjack

who goes there?
French: **7** qui vive

who knows?
Spanish: **9** quien sabe

whole 4 body, bulk, full, hale,
unit, well **5** sound, total, uncut **6** entire, intact, robust,
system **7** essence, healthy, perfect **8** complete, ensemble, entirety, totality, unbroken,
unharmed, vigorous **9** aggregate, undivided, uninjured
10 assemblage, unabridged
12 completeness, quintessence,
undiminished

wholehearted 4 true **7** earnest, serious, sincere, zealous
8 complete, emphatic **9** unfeigned **10** unreserved, unstinting **12** enthusiastic

wholesome 4 hale, nice, pure,
well **5** clean, fresh, hardy,
moral, sound **6** decent, honest,
worthy **7** chipper, dutiful, ethical, healthy, upright **8** blooming, hygienic, innocent,
sanitary, vigorous, virtuous
9 exemplary, healthful, honorable, uplifting **10** nourishing,
nutritious, principled **11** meritorious, responsible **12** invigorating **13** strengthening

whole world, the
French: **11** tout le monde

wholly 5 fully, quite **7** totally,
utterly **8** as a whole, entirely
9 perfectly **10** altogether, completely, thoroughly
Latin: **6** in toto

whoop 3 cry **4** hoot, howl,
roar, yell **5** cheer, hollo,
shout **6** bellow, cry out, holler, hurrah, outcry, scream,
shriek **7** screech **9** hue and cry

whopper 3 fib, lie **6** big one
7 fiction **9** falsehood, fish

story, tall story **16** cock-and-
bull story

whopping 4 huge **5** giant,
large **8** thumping, whacking,
whapping **10** incredible
13 extraordinary

whore 3 pro **4** bawd, doxy,
jade, slut, tart **5** hussy, tramp
6 chippy, harlot, hooker,
prosty, wanton **7** demirep,
hustler, trollop **8** call girl, mistress, strumpet **9** concubine
10 prostitute **12** streetwalker
French: **9** courtesan
12 demimondaine

whorl 4 coil, curl, roll **5** helix
6 circle, spiral **9** corkscrew
11 convolution

**Who's Afraid of Virginia
Woolf?**
author: **11** Edward Albee
director: **11** Mike Nichols
cast: **11** George Segal, Sandy
Dennis **13** Richard Burton
15 Elizabeth Taylor
Oscar for: **7** actress (Taylor)
17 supporting actress
(Dennis)

Who Said That?
host: **8** John Daly **11** Robert
Trout **13** Walter Kiernan
panelist: **9** Bill Henry **12** Bob
Considine, H V Kaltenborn,
June Lockhart **14** John Mason Brown, Morey Amster-
dam **17** John Cameron
Swayze

Who's on First?
author: **17** William F Buckley
Jr

wicked 3 bad, low **4** base, evil,
foul, vile **5** acute, awful, gross,
rowdy **6** cursed, fierce, impish,
raging, severe, sinful **7** corrupt, extreme, fearful, galling,
heinous, hellish, immoral, intense, knavish, naughty, painful, rampant, Satanic, serious,
vicious **8** depraved, devilish,
dreadful, fiendish, infamous,
rascally, shameful **9** atrocious,
malicious, monstrous, nefarious **10** abominable, bothersome, degenerate, iniquitous,
malevolent, scandalous, villainous **11** disgraceful, mischievous, troublesome
12 blackhearted, dishonorable,
incorrigible **13** reprehensible

wickedness 4 evil **6** infamy
8 baseness, foulness, iniquity,
vileness **9** depravity, malignity **10** immorality, sinfulness
11 malevolence **13** maliciousness, nefariousness

Wicked Witch of the West
character in: **13** The Wizard
of Oz
author: **4** Baum

Wickfield, Agnes
character in: **16** David
Copperfield
author: **7** Dickens

Wickford Point
author: **13** John P Marquand

Wickham, Mr
character in: **17** Pride and
Prejudice
author: **6** Austen

wide 4 vast **5** ample, broad,
fully, great, large, roomy **7** dilated, immense **8** expanded,
extended, spacious **9** boundless, capacious, distended, extensive, outspread
10 commodious, completely

wide-awake 2 up **5** alert,
aware, quick **8** vigilant, watchful **9** attentive, insomniac, observant, sleepless

widely 3 far **5** broad **6** abroad
7 broadly, greatly, largely
10 by and large, far and near
11 extensively

widely known 6 common
7 popular **8** familiar **9** universal, worldwide

widen 6 expand, extend,
spread **7** broaden, enlarge,
stretch

widened 7 swelled, swollen
8 enlarged, expanded, extended **9** broadened, distended,
stretched

wide open 4 ajar, vast
5 agape **6** gaping **7** exposed,
yawning **8** extended, unfenced **9** cavernous, expansive,
outspread, unbounded **12** outstretched, unobstructed

wide open spaces 7 boonies,
country **9** boondocks **11** countryside, hinterlands

wide-ranging 5 broad **7** immense **8** sweeping **9** extensive,
universal, unlimited **10** exhaustive **11** diversified, far-
reaching **12** encyclopedic
13 comprehensive

Wide Sargasso Sea
author: **8** Jean Rhys

widespread 5 broad **9** extensive, outspread, pervasive,
worldwide **10** nationwide
11 far-reaching

Widmark, Richard
born: **9** Sunrise MN
roles: **4** Coma **7** Madigan
8 The Alamo **11** Kiss of
Death **12** The Long Ships
16 Halls of Montezuma,
How the West Was Won
19 Judgment at Nuremberg

Widow Douglas
character in: 15 (The Adventures of) Huckleberry Finn
author: 5 Twain

wie geht's 9 how are you?

Wieland
author: 20 Charles Brockden Brown

wield 3 ply, use 4 wave 5 apply, exert, swing 6 employ, handle, manage 7 display, utilize 8 brandish, exercise, flourish 10 manipulate

wife 3 rib 4 mate 5 bride, squaw, woman 6 missus, spouse 7 consort, old lady 8 helpmate, helpmeet 9 companion
French: 5 femme
German: 4 frau

Wife of Bath
character in: 18 The Canterbury Tales
author: 7 Chaucer

Wifey
author: 9 Judy Blume

wig 3 rug 4 fall 6 carpet, peruke, switch, topper, toupee, wiglet 7 periwig 9 hairpiece

Wiggin, Kate Douglas
author of: 23 Rebecca of Sunnybrook Farm

wiggle 3 wag 4 jerk 5 shake, twist 6 quiver, squirm, twitch, writhe 7 flutter 8 writhing 9 squirming

wigwam, Wigwam 3 hut 4 tent, tipi 5 hogan, lodge, tepee 6 teepee 7 weekwam, wickiup 11 Tammany Hall

Wilcox family
characters in: 10 Howard's End
members: 4 Paul, Ruth 5 Henry 7 Charles
author: 7 Forster

wild, wilds, the wild 3 mad 4 bush, rash 5 bleak, feral, giddy, madly, nutty, rabid, rough, waste 6 choppy, crazed, fierce, insane, madcap, raging, raving, rugged, savage, unruly, wooded 7 berserk, bizarre, flighty, frantic, furious, howling, lawless, natural, untamed, violent 8 barbaric, blustery, demented, desolate, fanciful, forested, frenzied, insanely, maniacal, reckless, unbroken, unhinged 9 abandoned, fanatical, fantastic, ferocious, furiously, illogical, lawlessly, naturally, overgrown, primitive, rampantly, screwball, turbulent, violently, wasteland 10 disorderly, maniacally, uninformed 11 harebrained, impractical, tempestuous,

uncivilized, uninhabited 12 uncultivated, ungovernable, unrestrained 13 rattlebrained, undisciplined 14 undomesticated

wild animal 5 beast, brute

Wild Ass's Skin
author: 14 Honore de Balzac

Wild Bunch, The
director: 12 Sam Peckinpah
cast: 10 Ben Johnson, Robert Ryan 11 Warren Oates 12 Edmond O'Brien 13 William Holden 14 Ernest Borgnine

wildcat 3 cat 4 lynx 6 ocelot

Wild Duck, The
author: 11 Henrik Ibsen
character: 5 Werle 8 Old Ekdal 9 Gina Ekdal 12 Gregers Werle, Hjalmar Ekdal 13 Hedvig Relling

Wilde, Cornel
real name: 19 Cornelius Louis Wilde
born: 9 New York NY
wife: 11 Jean Wallace
roles: 9 Maracaibo 11 Omar Khayyam 12 Forever Amber, The Naked Prey 15 A Song to Remember 21 A Thousand and One Nights 22 The Greatest Show on Earth

Wilde, Oscar
author of: 6 Salome 17 The Critic as Artist 18 Lady Windermere's Fan 22 The Ballad of Reading Gaol, The Picture of Dorian Gray 27 The Importance of Being Earnest

Wilder, Billy
director of: 11 One Two Three 12 The Apartment (Oscar) 13 Some Like It Hot 14 The Lost Weekend (Oscar) 15 Double Indemnity, Stalag Seventeen, Sunset Boulevard 16 The Seven Year Itch 18 Love in the Afternoon 24 Witness for the Prosecution

Wilder, Gene
real name: 14 Jerry Silberman
born: 11 Milwaukee WI
roles: 12 Silver Streak, The Producers 14 Blazing Saddles, Bonnie and Clyde 17 Young Frankenstein 22 The World's Greatest Lover 27 Start the Revolution Without Me 43 The Adventures of Sherlock Holmes' Smarter Brother

Wilder, Laura Ingalls
author of: 26 The Little House on the Prairie

Wilder, Thornton
author of: 7 Our Town 9 The Cabala 13 The Matchmaker 14 The Ides of March 16 The Woman of Andros 17 The Skin of Our Teeth 20 Heaven's My Destination 21 The Bridge of San Luis Rey

wilderness 4 bush 5 waste 6 barren, desert, forest, plains, tundra 7 barrens 8 badlands, wasteland 9 mountains

Wildeve, Damon
character in: 17 Return of the Native
author: 5 Hardy

Wild Is the River
author: 14 Louis Bromfield

Wild Kingdom
host/narrator: 9 Jim Fowler, Stan Brock 13 Marlin Perkins

Wild One, The
director: 12 Laslo Benedek
cast: 9 Lee Marvin 10 Mary Murphy 12 Marlon Brando

Wild Strawberries
director: 13 Ingmar Bergman
cast: 12 Ingrid Thulin 13 Bibi Andersson 14 Victor Sjostrom 17 Gunnar Bjornstrand

Wild Wild West
character: 10 James T West 13 Artemus Gordon
cast: 10 Ross Martin 12 Robert Conrad
traveled by: 5 train

wile, wiles 4 coax, lure, ploy, ruse, trap 5 charm, guile 6 cajole, entice, gambit, seduce 7 cunning 8 artifice, maneuver, persuade, subtlety, trickery 9 chicanery, expedient, stratagem 10 artfulness, craftiness, subterfuge 11 contrivance, machination

Wilfer, Bella
character in: 15 Our Mutual Friend
author: 7 Dickens

Wilhelm, Kate
author of: 10 City of Cain, Fault Lines 11 The Planners 14 The Infinity Box 16 The Clewiston Test 19 More Bitter than Death 26 Where Late the Sweet Birds Sang

Wilhelm Meister
author: 6 Goethe

Wilhelm Tell
also: 11 William Tell
author: 17 Johann von Schiller

wiliness 5 guile 7 cunning, slyness **8** artifice, foxiness, scheming, trickery **10** artfulness, craftiness **11** machination

Wilkes family
   characters in: **15** Gone With the Wind
   members: **4** John **5** Honey, India **6** Ashley **15** Melanie Hamilton
   author: **8** Mitchell

will 4 want, wish **5** endow **6** bestow, confer, desire **7** craving, feeling, longing, resolve, wish for **8** attitude, bequeath, pleasure, yearning **9** hankering, testament **10** conviction, preference, resolution **11** disposition, inclination **12** resoluteness **13** determination

Willard, Frank
   creator/artist of: **11** Moon Mullins

Willet, John
   character in: **12** Barnaby Rudge
   author: **7** Dickens

willful 6 mulish, unruly **7** planned, studied **8** designed, intended, obdurate, perverse, stubborn **9** obstinate, pigheaded **10** bullheaded, deliberate, determined, headstrong, inflexible, persistent, purposeful, unyielding **11** intentional, intractable **12** contemplated, premeditated, ungovernable **13** undisciplined **14** uncompromising

Williams, Esther
   nickname: **13** Mermaid Tycoon **14** Queen of the Surf **17** Hollywood's Mermaid
   born: **12** Los Angeles CA
   husband: **13** Fernando Lamas
   roles: **13** Bathing Beauty **15** Jupiter's Darling, Ziegfeld Follies **16** Dangerous When Wet, Neptune's Daughter **20** Million Dollar Mermaid

Williams, Janey
   character in: **3** USA
   author: **9** Dos Passos

Williams, Myrna
   real name of: **8** Myrna Loy

Williams, Robin
   born: **9** Chicago IL
   roles: **6** Popeye **12** Mork and Mindy **18** Good Morning Vietnam **23** The World According to Garp

Williams, Ted
   nickname: **6** the Kid **16** Splendid Splinter
   sport: **8** baseball
   position: **8** outfield
   team: **12** Boston Red Sox

Williams, Tennessee
   author of: **10** Camino Real **13** The Rose Tattoo **14** Summer and Smoke **16** Cat on a Hot Tin Roof, Night of the Iguana, Sweet Bird of Youth **17** Orpheus Descending, The Glass Menagerie **18** Small Craft Warnings, Suddenly Last Summer **21** A Streetcar Named Desire **24** The Roman Spring of Mrs Stone

Williams, William Carlos
   author of: **7** Tempers **8** Paterson **9** White Mule **11** Al Que Quiere **20** Pictures from Brueghel

William Tell
   also: **13** Guillaume Tell
   opera by: **7** Rossini
   character: **6** Arnold **7** Gessler

William the Conqueror
   also: **17** William of Normandy **21** William I King of England
   fought against: **8** Harold II
   battle: **8** Hastings
   succeeded by: **6** Henry I **9** William II

Willie and Joe
   creator: **11** Bill Mauldin

willing 4 game **5** ready **7** content **8** amenable **9** agreeable, compliant, not averse **10** responsive

willingly 4 gain, lief, soon **6** freely, gladly, liefly **7** eagerly, happily, readily **8** by choice **10** cheerfully, graciously **11** voluntarily **12** with pleasure

willingness 4 zeal **8** alacrity **9** eagerness, readiness **10** enthusiasm **11** inclination

Willoughby, John
   character in: **19** Sense and Sensibility
   author: **6** Austen

willow 5 Salix
   varieties: **3** bay, red **4** bush, goat, gray, seep **5** black, crack, false, Niobe, Pekin, pussy, silky, water, white **6** Arctic, arroyo, basket, desert, golden, laurel, puzzle, woolly, yellow **7** brittle, prairie, sandbar, scouler, shining, weeping **8** creeping, florist's, polished, Virginia **9** bay-leaved, bearberry, flowering, sprouting **10** cricket-bat, dragon-claw, large pussy, small pussy **11** green-scaled, heart-leaved, peach-leaved, Port Jackson **13** halberd-leaved **16** Wisconsin weeping

willowy 5 lithe **6** limber,

pliant, supple, svelte **7** lissome **8** flexible **9** sylphlike

Wills, Chill
   born: **12** Seagoville TX
   group: **26** Chill Wills and the Avalon Boys
   voice of: **21** Francis the Talking Mule
   roles: **5** Giant **8** The Alamo **10** Way Out West **11** The Yearling **15** Meet Me in St Louis

Wills, Garry
   author of: **14** Nixon Agonistes, Reagan's America **16** Inventing America

Will Scarlet
   character in: **9** Robin Hood

willy-nilly 8 perforce **10** helplessly, inevitably **11** inescapably, unavoidably **12** compulsively, irresistibly **14** uncontrollably
   Latin: **12** nolens volens

Wilmer
   character in: **16** The Maltese Falcon
   author: **7** Hammett

Wilson, Edmund
   author of: **11** Axel's Castle **19** To the Finland Station

Wilson, Myrtle
   character in: **14** The Great Gatsby
   author: **10** Fitzgerald

Wilson, Sloan
   author of: **26** The Man in the Gray Flannel Suit

Wilson, Woodrow *see box*

wilt 3 die, ebb, sag **4** fade, flag, sink, wane **5** droop **6** recede, weaken, wither **7** decline, dwindle, shrivel, subside **8** decrease, diminish, languish **10** degenerate **11** deteriorate

Wilt the Stilt
   nickname of: **15** Wilt Chamberlain

wily 3 sly **4** foxy **5** alert, sharp **6** artful, crafty, shifty, shrewd, tricky **7** crooked, cunning, devious **8** guileful, scheming **9** deceitful, deceptive, designing, underhand **10** intriguing **11** calculating, treacherous

win 3 bag, get, net **4** earn, gain, sway **6** attain, induce, master, obtain, pick up, secure **7** achieve, acquire, collect, conquer, convert, prevail, procure, realize, receive, success, triumph, victory **8** conquest, convince, overcome, persuade, vanquish **9** influence **10** accomplish

win acceptance 9 establish **10** ingratiate

Wilson, Woodrow
  name at birth: **19** Thomas Woodrow Wilson
  nickname: **5** Tommy
  presidential rank: **12** twenty-eighth
  party: **10** Democratic
  state represented: **2** NJ
  defeated: **4** (Eugene Victor) Debs, (William Howard) Taft **5** (James Franklin) Hanly **6** (Allen
    Louis) Benson, (Arthur Edward) Reimer, (Charles Evans) Hughes, (Eugene Wilder) Chafin
    9 (Theodore) Roosevelt
  vice president: **8** (Thomas Riley) Marshall
  cabinet:
    state: **5** (Bainbridge) Colby, (William Jennings) Bryan **7** (Robert) Lansing
    treasury: **5** (Carter) Glass **6** (William Gibbs) McAdoo **7** (David Franklin) Houston
    war: **5** (Newton Diehl) Baker **8** (Lindley Miller) Garrison
    attorney general: **6** (Alexander Mitchell) Palmer **7** (Thomas Watt) Gregory **10** (James Clark)
      McReynolds
    navy: **7** (Josephus) Daniels
    postmaster general: **8** (Albert Sidney) Burleson
    interior: **4** (Franklin Knight) Lane **5** (John Barton) Payne
    agriculture: **7** (David Franklin) Houston **8** (Edwin Thomas) Meredith
    commerce: **8** (William Cox) Redfield **9** (Joshua Willis) Alexander
    labor: **6** (William Bauchop) Wilson
  born: **2** VA **8** Staunton
  died/buried: **2** DC **10** Washington
  education:
    college: **8** Davidson **18** College of New Jersey (later known as Princeton U)
    law School: **20** University of Virginia
    university: **12** Johns Hopkins
  religion: **12** Presbyterian
  author: **8** The State **16** George Washington **18** Division and Reunion **27** A History of the
    American People **28** More Literature and Other Essays **34** An Old Master and Other Political
    Essays **41** President Wilson's Case for the League of Nations **47** Congressional Government:
    A Study in American Politics
  political career:
    governor of: **9** New Jersey
  civilian career: **6** lawyer
    professor of history: **15** Bryn Mawr College **18** Wesleyan University
    professor of jurisprudence: **9** Princeton
    president of: **9** Princeton
  notable events of lifetime/term: **14** Fourteen Points **15** League of Nations
    Act: **7** Adamson **8** Sedition **9** Espionage **10** Child Labor **11** Liberty Loan, Panama Canal
      14 Federal Reserve **15** Federal Farm Loan **16** Clayton Antitrust, Selective Service **22** Fed-
      eral Trade Commission
    conference: **3** ABC **10** Paris Peace
    18th Amendment: **11** Prohibition
    program: **10** New Freedom
    sinking of: **9** Lusitania
    Treaty: **10** Versailles
    won: **15** Nobel Peace Prize
  quote: **34** The world must be made safe for democracy
  father: **13** Joseph Ruggles
  mother: **5** Janet (Woodrow)
  siblings: **13** Joseph Ruggles **14** Annie Josephson **16** Marion Williamson
  wife: **5** Edith (Bolling Galt), Ellen (Louise Axson)
  children: **13** Jessie Woodrow **15** Eleanor Randolph, Margaret Woodrow

wince 5 cower, quail **6** cringe, flinch, recoil, shrink **7** grimace, shudder **8** cowering, cringing, draw back, quailing **9** shrinking

wind 3 air, lap **4** bend, blow, clue, coil, curl, fold, gale, gust, hint, loop, news, puff, roll **5** blast, bluff, curve, draft, scent, smell, snake, twine, twirl, twist, whiff **6** breath, breeze, hot air, ramble, report, wander, zephyr, zigzag **7** bluster, bombast, cyclone, entwine, inkling, meander, sinuate, tempest, tidings, tornado, twaddle, twister, typhoon, whisper **8** boasting, idle talk **9** aerophone, hurricane, knowledge, whirlwind **10** intimation, suggestion **11** braggadocio, fanfaronade, information **12** intelligence
  god of: **5** Eurus, Niord, Njord, Notus **6** Aquilo, Auster, Boreas **8** Favonius, Zephyrus
  father: **8** Astraeus
  mother: **3** Eos

windfall 7 bonanza

Windhoek
  capital of: **7** Namibia

Wind in the Willows, The
  author: **14** Kenneth Grahame
  character: **4** Mole, Toad **6** Badger **8** Water Rat

windless 4 calm 5 still 8 stifling

window 3 bay 5 oriel 6 dormer 7 opening, orifice, transom 8 aperture, casement, porthole, skylight

Winds of War, The
author: 10 Herman Wouk

windstorm 4 gale 6 squall 7 cyclone, tempest, tornado, twister, typhoon 9 hurricane, whirlwind

windswept 4 bare 5 bleak 6 barren 8 desolate 13 weatherbeaten

windup 3 end 5 close 6 ending, finish 10 completion, conclusion, expiration 11 termination

wind up 3 end 4 halt, stop 5 cease, close 6 finish, settle 8 complete, conclude 9 terminate

windy 5 blowy, empty, gabby, gusty, wordy 6 breezy 7 verbose 8 blustery, rambling 9 bombastic, garrulous, talkative 10 loquacious, meandering, rhetorical 13 grandiloquent

wine
French: 3 vin
Italian: 4 vino
god of: 7 Bacchus
goddess of: 6 Libera

wine-colored 6 claret 8 burgundy, cardinal

winemaking
god of: 9 Aristaeus

Winesburg, Ohio
author: 16 Sherwood Anderson

wing 3 ala, fly, set 4 band, clip, flap, knot, nick, soar, zoom 5 annex, graze, group 6 circle, clique, pennon, pinion 7 adjunct, aileron, coterie, faction, section, segment 8 addition, coulisse 9 appendage, extension 10 fraternity

Winged Horse
constellation of: 7 Pegasus

Winger, Debra
husband: 13 Timothy Hutton
roles: 10 Black Widow, Cannery Row 11 Urban Cowboy 17 Terms of Endearment 22 An Officer and a Gentleman

Wingert, Dick
creator/artist of: 6 Hubert

Wingfield family
characters in: 17 The Glass Menagerie

member: 3 Tom 5 Laura 6 Amanda
author: 8 Williams

Wings
director: 15 William A Wellman
cast: 8 Clara Bow 10 Gary Cooper 12 Richard Arlen 18 Charles Buddy Rogers
Oscar for: 7 picture

Wings of the Dove, The
author: 10 Henry James
character: 8 Kate Croy, Lord Mark 9 Mrs Lowder 11 Milly Theale 12 Mrs Stringham 13 Merton Densher, Sir Luke Strett

wink at 6 ignore 7 condone, let pass 8 overlook 9 disregard

Winkle
character in: 14 Pickwick Papers
author: 7 Dickens

winner 5 champ 6 master, victor 8 champion 9 conqueror 10 vanquisher

Winnie-the-Pooh
author: 7 A A Milne
character: 3 Owl 5 Kanga 6 Eeyore, Piglet, Rabbit, Tiger 7 Baby Roo 16 Christopher Robin

winning 7 amiable 8 charming, engaging, pleasing 9 appealing, beguiling, disarming 10 attractive, bewitching, entrancing 11 captivating 12 ingratiating, irresistible

Winnipeg
hockey team: 3 Jets

win over 4 beat, best 5 charm 6 defeat, seduce 7 convert 8 overcome, vanquish 9 captivate, overpower

winsome 5 sweet 6 comely 7 amiable, likable, lovable 8 charming, cheerful, engaging, pleasing 9 agreeable, appealing, endearing 10 attractive, bewitching, delightful

Winter, Lady de
character in: 18 The Three Musketeers
author: 5 Dumas (pere)

Winter, Maxim de
character in: 7 Rebecca
author: 9 Du Maurier

Winterbourne
character in: 11 Daisy Miller
author: 5 James

Winter of Our Discontent, The
author: 13 John Steinbeck

Winters, Shelley
real name: 14 Shirley Schrift
born: 9 St Louis IL
husband: 13 Tony Franciosa 15 Vittorio Gassman
roles: 11 A Double Life 12 A Patch of Blue 14 A Place in the Sun 16 A House Is Not a Home 19 The Diary of Anne Frank 20 The Poseidon Adventure

Winterset
author: 15 Maxwell Anderson

winter sports
god of: 4 Ullr 5 Uller

Winter's Tale, The
author: 18 William Shakespeare
character: 7 Camillo, Leontes, Paulina 8 Florizel, Hermione 9 Autolycus, Polixenes

Winter Wonderland
nickname of: 8 Michigan

wintry 3 icy, raw 4 cold 5 bleak, chilly, harsh, polar, snowy, stark 6 arctic, chilly, dreary, frigid, frosty, frozen, gloomy, stormy 7 glacial 8 Siberian 9 cheerless

wipe 3 dry, mop, rub 4 swab 5 apply, brush, clean, erase, rub on, scour, scrub, swipe, towel 6 banish, remove, rub off, sponge, stroke

wiped out 5 broke 6 failed, ruined 8 bankrupt, indigent, strapped 9 destitute, insolvent, penniless 12 impoverished

wipe out 4 ruin 5 erase 7 abolish, destroy, eclipse 8 bankrupt 9 devastate, eliminate, eradicate, extirpate, liquidate 10 annihilate, obliterate 11 exterminate

wiping out 7 erasing 9 eclipsing, expunging 10 abolishing, destroying 11 eliminating, eradicating 12 annihilating, obliterating

wire 5 cable 8 filament, telegram 9 cablegram, telegraph

wiry 4 lean 5 agile, kinky, lanky, spare, stiff 6 limber, pliant, sinewy 7 brittle

Wisconsin *see box*

wisdom 6 brains 8 sagacity 9 teachings 10 philosophy, principles, profundity 11 discernment, penetration 12 apperception, intelligence 13 comprehension, judiciousness, understanding
god of: 2 Ea 4 Enki, Odin 5 Othin, Thoth
goddess of: 6 Athena, Athene, Brigit, Pallas, Saitis

Wisconsin
  abbreviation: 2 WI 3 Wis
  nickname: 6 Badger
  capital: 7 Madison
  largest city: 9 Milwaukee
  others: 5 Ripon 6 Antigo, Beloit, Cudahy, Neenag, Racine,
    Wausau 7 Ashland, Baraboo, Bloomer, Kenosha, Men-
    asha, Oshkosh, Portage, Shawano 8 Appleton, Boscobel,
    Green Bay, Lacrosse, Superior, Waukesha 9 Eau Claire,
    Fond du Lac, Sheboygan, Shorewood, Wauwatosa, West
    Allis 10 Brookfield, Janesville 12 Steven's Point
  college: 5 Ripon 6 Beloit 7 Alverno, Carroll, Viterbo
    8 Carthage, Lawrence 9 Marquette, Northland
  feature:
      fort: 6 Howard 8 Crawford 9 Winnebago
      national lakeshore: 14 Apostle Islands
  tribe: 3 Fox, Sac 4 Sauk 5 Huron 6 Oneida, Ottawa
    8 Chippewa, Kickapoo 9 Winnebago 10 Potawatomi
  people: 11 Orson Welles 12 Fredric March, Harry Houdini,
    Spencer Tracy 13 Hamlin Garland 14 Joseph McCarthy,
    Georgia O'Keeffe, Thornton Wilder 16 Frank Lloyd
    Wright 17 Robert M LaFollette
      explorer: 6 Joliet 7 Allouez, Nicolet 8 Radisson 9 Mar-
      quette 12 Groseilliers
  island: 8 Madeline
  lake: 6 Geneva, Poygan 7 Kenosha, Mendota, Wissota
    8 Michigan, Superior 9 Winnebago
  land rank: 11 twenty-sixth
  mountain: 7 Baraboo 9 Sugarbush 10 Blue Mounds
      highest point: 9 Timm's Hill
  physical feature:
      glacial hills: 13 Kettle Moraine
      rock formations: 8 The Dells
  river: 3 Fox 4 Wolf 7 St Croix 8 Chippewa 9 Black Rock,
    Wisconsin 11 Mississippi
  state admission: 9 thirtieth
  state bird: 5 robin
  state fish: 11 muskellunge
  state flower: 5 pansy 6 violet 10 wood violet
  state motto: 7 Forward
  state song: 11 On Wisconsin
  state tree: 10 sugar maple

7 Minerva 11 Tritogeneia
12 Pallas Athena 18 Alalcomenean Athena

wise 3 way 4 sage 6 manner
7 knowing, respect, sapient
8 profound 9 judicious, sagacious 10 discerning, perceptive 11 intelligent
13 knowledgeable, perspicacious, understanding

Wise, Robert
  director of: 11 I Want to
  Live 13 West Side Story
  (with Jerome Robbins, Oscar) 15 The Sound of Music
  (Oscar)

wiseacre 4 fool, sage 5 idiot
7 tomfool 9 know-it-all, simpleton 10 smart aleck

Wise Blood
  author: 15 Flannery
  O'Connor

wisecrack 4 jest, joke, quip

5 flash, sally 8 cut jokes
9 witticism 11 smart saying

Wise men *see* 4 Magi

wise up 5 edify 6 advise, inform 7 apprise 9 enlighten,
make aware

wish 3 yen 4 hope, long, love,
pine, want, whim, will
5 crave, yearn 6 aspire, desire,
hunger, thirst 7 command,
craving, leaning, longing, request 8 ambition, appetite,
fondness, penchant, yearning
10 aspiration, partiality 11 inclination 12 predilection

wishes 11 compliments 13 felicitations 15 congratulations

wish for 4 want 5 covet,
crave 6 desire

Wishfort, Lady
  character in: 16 The Way of
  the World
  author: 8 Congreve

wishful 4 avid 5 eager 6 keen
on, pining 7 anxious, craving,
hopeful, longing, wanting,
wistful 8 aspiring, bent upon,
desirous, fanciful, yearning
9 ambitious, expectant

wish well 10 felicitate
12 congratulate

wishy-washy 4 dull, weak
5 inane, vapid, wimpy 6 jejune 7 insipid 8 wavering
10 indecisive, irresolute 11 ineffective, ineffectual, vacillating 12 equivocating,
noncommittal 14 tergiversat-
ing 15 shilly-shallying

wisp 4 lock, tuft 5 bunch,
shred, torch, twist 6 bundle,
rumple 8 fragment 10 whisk
broom 11 ignis fatuus
13 friar's lantern

wispy 4 thin 5 frail 6 slight
8 fleeting, nebulous

wistaria, wisteria
  varieties: 4 pink, wild 5 silky,
  water 7 Chinese 8 Japanese
  9 Rhodesian

Wister, Owen
  author of: 12 The Virginian

wistful 3 sad 6 musing, pining
7 craving, doleful, forlorn,
longing, pensive 8 desirous,
mournful, yearning 9 hankering, sorrowful, woebegone
10 meditative, melancholy, reflective 12 disconsolate
13 contemplative, introspective

wit 3 wag 4 gags 5 comic, humor, joker, jokes, quips,
sense 6 acumen, banter,
brains, jester, joking, levity,
wisdom 7 cunning, funster,
gagster, insight, punster, sparkle, waggery 8 comedian, drollery, humorist, jokester,
judgment, raillery, sagacity,
satirist, vivacity 9 funniness,
intellect 10 astuteness, brightness, cleverness, jocularity,
perception, shrewdness, witticisms 11 discernment, penetration, wisecracker
12 intelligence, perspicacity
13 comprehension, epigram-
matist, sagaciousness,
understanding
  French: 8 badinage 9 bel-esprit 10 persiflage

witch 3 hag 4 fury 5 crone,
scold, shrew, vixen 6 ogress,
virago 7 seeress 8 battle-ax,
harridan 9 sorceress, temptress,
termagant 10 prophetess
11 enchantress
  French: 6 beldam

witchcraft 6 hoodoo, voodoo
7 sorcery 8 black art, witchery,
wizardry 9 diabolism, fetish-
ism, voodooism 10 black

magic, divination, necro-
mancy **11** conjuration,
enchantment

with
French: **4** avec, chez

with a grain of salt
Latin: **13** cum grano salis

with a lawsuit pending
Latin: **12** pendente lite

with authority
Latin: **10** ex cathedra

withdraw 2 go **5** leave, split
6 depart, go away, recall, recant, remove, retire **7** extract,
rescind, retract, retreat, take
off, vamoose **9** disappear,
unsheathe

withdrawal 4 exit **6** egress
7 leaving, retreat **9** departure
10 retirement, retraction
14 discontinuance

withdrawn 3 shy **5** quiet **8** reserved, retiring, unsocial **9** reclusive **10** unfriendly
11 introverted
15 uncommunicative

wither 4 fade, wilt **5** abash,
blast, droop, dry up, shame
7 cut down, mortify, shrivel
9 dehydrate, desiccate,
humiliate

withered 3 dry **4** arid, sere
5 dried, faded **6** shrunk,
wilted **7** decayed, dried up,
drooped, stunned, wizened
9 petrified, shriveled
10 languished

withering 6 biting **7** caustic
8 scathing **9** shrinkage, shrinking, wrinkling **10** shriveling
11 contracting, contraction,
devastating

with few words
Latin: **12** paucis verbis

with force and with arms
Latin: **9** vi et armis

with great praise
Latin: **13** magna cum laude

withheld 4 kept **7** checked, for-
bore, refused, starved **8** kept
back **9** boycotted, refrained

with highest praise
Latin: **13** summa cum laude

withhold 4 hide, keep **6** hush
up, retain **7** conceal, cover
up **8** suppress

withhold from 4 deny **6** refuse

within 2 on **4** into **5** inner
6 during, inside **7** indoors
8 inwardly
  combining form: **3** eso
  4 endo
  prefix: **5** intra

within an inch of 4 near
6 all but, almost, nearly

with-it 7 current **8** up-to-date
French: **9** au courant

**with one's own two
hands 7** oneself, unaided
10 unassisted

without 4 save **5** minus **6** beyond, except, unless **7** lacking,
nowhere, outside, wanting
8 exterior, external, free from,
outdoors **9** excepting
10 externally
  appointment: **7** sine die
  care: **8** sine cure
  charge: **4** free **6** gratis **8** sine
    cure
  combining form: **4** ecto
  doubt: **9** sine dubio
  feet: **4** apod **6** apodal
  French: **4** sans
  horns: **7** acerous
  Latin: **4** sine
  law: **8** anarchic
  light: **7** aphotic
  life: **5** amort **9** inanimate
  luster: **3** mat **5** matte
  offspring: **9** sine prole
  prefix: **2** in
  roads: **7** invious
  saddles: **8** asellate, bareback
  subcalyx leaves: **9** bractless
  teeth: **5** morne **8** edentate
  this: **7** sine hoc
  tongue, teeth, or claws:
    5 morne
  which not: **10** sine qua non
  wings: **7** apteral **8** apterous

without a doubt 6 surely **8** of
course **9** certainly **10** absolutely, positively **11** indubitably **12** indisputably
14 unquestionably

without basis 7 unsound
9 unfounded **10** groundless,
ungrounded **11** unjustified, unsupported **15** unsubstantiated

without care
French: **9** sans souci

without charge 4 free
10 gratuitous, on the house
13 complimentary
Latin: **6** gratis

without doubt
French: **9** sans doute

without end 7 endless, eternal, forever **8** immortal, infinite, timeless, unending
9 ceaseless, continual, endlessly, eternally, perpetual
10 immortally, infinitely, time-
lessly, unendingly **11** ceaselessly, continually, everlasting,
never-ending **13** everlastingly
14 lasting forever

without equal
French: **10** sans pareil

without error 4 true **5** exact,
right **7** correct, perfect, precise, sinless **8** accurate, truthful, unerring **9** faultless
10 infallible

without exception 5 never
6 always, wholly **8** entirely
10 absolutely, completely, invariably, positively

**without fear and without
reproach**
French: **22** sans peur et sans
reproche

Without Feathers
author: **10** Woody Allen

without funds 5 broke **6** ruined **8** bankrupt, indigent,
strapped, wiped out **9** destitute, flat broke, insolvent,
penniless **10** stone broke
12 impoverished

without light 3 dim **4** dark
5 black, dusky, murky, shady
6 opaque **7** obscure, shadowy,
stygian, sunless

without limit
Latin: **11** ad infinitum

without limitation 6 wholly
7 totally, utterly **8** entirely
9 endlessly **10** absolutely, completely, definitely, positively,
thoroughly **11** boundlessly
13 unequivocally
15 unconditionally
French: **12** carte blanche

without notice 5 ad-lib **9** impromptu **10** improvised **11** extemporary **14** extemporaneous
Latin: **9** extempore

**without offspring, without
progeny**
Latin: **9** sine prole

without the day
Latin: **7** sine die

without which not
Latin: **10** sine qua non

with praise
Latin: **8** cum laude

withstand 4 bear, defy
5 brave **6** endure, resist, suffer **7** weather **8** confront, cope
with, tolerate

witless 3 mad **5** crazy **6** insane, stupid **7** fatuous, foolish,
unaware **9** slaphappy

witness 3 see **4** mark, note,
sign, view **5** proof **6** attend,
behold, look on, notice, verify **7** bear out, certify, confirm, endorse, initial, observe
8 attester, attest to, beholder,
deponent, document, evidence,
looker-on, observer, onlooker,
perceive, validate, vouch for
9 establish, spectator, testifier,
testimony **10** validation

11 corroborate, countersign
12 authenticate, confirmation, substantiate, verification
13 corroboration, documentation **14** authentication, substantiation

Witness for the Prosecution
   director: 11 Billy Wilder
   based on play by: 14 Agatha Christie
   cast: 11 Tyrone Power
     14 Elsa Lanchester
     15 Charles Laughton, Marlene Dietrich

wits 4 mind **6** sanity **9** composure **14** coolheadedness

witticism 4 jest, joke, quip
5 sally **7** epigram
   French: 6 bon mot **10** jeu d'esprit

witty 5 comic, droll, funny
6 bright, clever, jocose
7 amusing, jocular, waggish
8 humorous, mirthful **9** brilliant, sparkling, whimsical
11 quick-witted **13** scintillating

witty saying 4 jest, quip
6 bon mot **7** epigram **9** witticism **13** clever comment

Witwoud, Sir Wilfull
   character in: 16 The Way of the World
   author: 8 Congreve

wizard 4 sage, seer, whiz
5 adept, shark **6** expert, genius, oracle **7** diviner, prodigy, wise man **8** conjurer, magician, sorcerer, virtuoso **9** enchanter **10** soothsayer
11 clairvoyant, necromancer

Wizard of Id, The
   creator: 10 Johnny Hart
     11 Brant Parker
   character: 4 King **5** Spook
     6 jester, Rodney, Tyrant

Wizard of Oz, The
   director: 13 Victor Fleming
   author: 10 L Frank Baum
   cast: 4 Toto **8** Bert Lahr
     (Cowardly Lion) **9** Jack
     Haley (Tin Woodsman), Ray
     Bolger (Scarecrow) **11** Billie
     Burke (Good Witch of the
     North), Frank Morgan (wizard), Judy Garland (Dorothy) **13** Clara Blandick
     15 Charley Grapewin
     16 Margaret Hamilton
     (Wicked Witch of the West),
     The Singer Midgets
     (Munchkins)
   score: 9 E Y Harburg
     11 Harold Arlen
   remade as: 6 The Wiz
   place: 6 Kansas **8** Land of
     Oz **11** Emerald City
   Dorothy wore: 8 red shoes

wizened 3 dry **5** dried **7** dried

up **8** shrunken, withered, wrinkled **9** shriveled

WKRP in Cincinnati
   character: 10 Andy Travis,
     Herb Tarlek, Les Nessman
     12 Venus Flytrap **13** Arthur
     Carlson, Dr Johnny Fever
     14 Bailey Quarters **15** Jennifer Marlowe
   cast: 7 Tim Reid **9** Gary
     Sandy **10** Gordon Jump
     11 Frank Bonner, Jan
     Smithers **12** Loni Anderson
     14 Howard Hesseman, Richard Sanders

wobble 4 reel, sway **5** quake,
shake, waver **6** shimmy, teeter, totter **7** quaking, shaking,
stagger, swaying **8** wavering
9 shimmying, teetering, tottering **12** unsteadiness

wobbly, Wobbly 5 loose,
shaky **7** doubtful **8** hesitant, insecure, unstable, unsteady,
wavering **9** quavering, trembling **11** vacillating
   union: 17 Industrial Workers

Wodehouse, P G (Pelham Grenville)
   author of: 8 Full Moon
     14 Thank You Jeeves
     15 The Mating Season
   character: 6 Jeeves **13** Bertie
     Wooster

Woden
   origin: 10 Anglo-Saxon
   chief of: 4 gods

woe 5 agony, gloom, grief,
trial, worry **6** misery, sorrow
7 anguish, anxiety, despair,
torment, torture, trouble **8** calamity, distress **9** adversity, dejection, heartache, suffering
10 affliction, depression, melancholy, misfortune **11** tribulation **12** wretchedness

woebegone 3 sad **4** glum
6 gloomy **7** doleful, forlorn
8 dejected, funereal, mournful,
tortured, troubled, wretched
9 agonizing, anguished, miserable, sorrowful, suffering
10 distressed

woeful 3 bad, sad **5** awful,
cruel **6** tragic **7** doleful, painful, unhappy **8** crushing,
dreadful, grievous, hopeless,
horrible, terrible, unlikely,
wretched **9** agonizing, appalling, miserable, sorrowful
10 calamitous, deplorable, depressing, disastrous, lamentable **11** distressing,
unpromising **12** catastrophic,
heartrending **13** disheartening,
heartbreaking

woe to the vanquished
   Latin: 9 vae victis

Wofford, Chloe Anthony
   real name of: 12 Toni
     Morrison

Wojtyla, Karol
   real name of: 14 Pope John
     Paul II **18** Archbishop of
     Krakow

wolf 4 bolt, gulp **5** scarf **6** devour, gobble **7** consume
   constellation of: 5 Lupus
   group of: 4 pack

Wolf, The
   author: 11 Frank Norris

Wolfe, Thomas
   author of: 14 The Hills Beyond **16** The Web and the
     Rock **17** Look Homeward
     Angel, Of Time and the
     River **18** You Can't Go
     Home Again
   character: 10 Eugene Gant
     12 George Webber

Wolfe, Tom
   author of: 11 Radical Chic
     13 The Right Stuff **14** The
     Painted Word **16** The Pump
     House Gang **21** From Bauhaus to Our House **23** The
     Bonfire of the Vanities
     24 Mau-mauing the Flak
     Catchers **26** The Electric
     Kool-Aid Acid Test
     43 The Kandy Kolored
     Tangerine Flake Streamline
     Baby

Wollstonecraft, Mary
   husband: 13 William Godwin
   daughter: 25 Mary Wollstonecraft Shelley
   author of: 30 A Vindication
     of the Rights of Women

Wolverine State
   nickname of: 8 Michigan

woman 4 girl, lady, maid,
wife **5** flame, lover **6** damsel,
maiden, matron **7** beloved,
darling, dowager, females, fiancee, sweetie **8** ladylove, mistress **9** charwoman,
concubine **10** girlfriend, handmaiden, sweetheart, sweetie
pie **11** chambermaid, housekeeper, maidservant
   French: 5 femme **8** paramour
   Latin: 9 inamorata

Woman, first
   Scandinavian: 5 Embla

Woman in White, A
   author: 13 Wilkie Collins

womanish 7 unmanly **8** feminine, ladylike **9** sissified
10 effeminate

womanlike 8 feminine
10 effeminate

womanly 8 feminine, matronly

Woman of Substance, A
author: 21 Barbara Taylor Bradford

Woman of the Year
director: 13 George Stevens
cast: 10 Fay Bainter 12 Reginald Owen, Spencer Tracy 16 Katharine Hepburn

Woman's Life, A
author: 15 Guy de Maupassant

Women, The
director: 11 George Cukor
based on play by: 15 Clare Boothe Luce
cast: 11 Hedda Hopper 12 Joan Crawford, Joan Fontaine, Marjorie Main, Norma Shearer 15 Paulette Goddard, Rosalind Russell
remade as: 14 The Opposite Sex

Women at Point Sur, The
author: 15 Robinson Jeffers

Women in Love
director: 10 Ken Russell
based on novel by: 10 DH Lawrence
character: 11 Gerald Crich 12 Rupert Birkin 14 Gudrun Brangwen, Ursula Brangwen
cast: 9 Alan Bates 10 Oliver Reed 11 Eleanor Bron 12 Jennie Linden 13 Glenda Jackson
Oscar for: 7 actress (Jackson)

wonder 3 awe 4 gape 5 sight, stare 6 marvel, ponder, rarity 7 miracle 8 cogitate, meditate, question 9 amazement, spectacle, speculate 10 conjecture, phenomenon 11 fascination 12 astonishment, stupefaction

wonder child
German: 10 wunderkind

wonderful 4 fine, good 5 great, super 6 divine, superb, tiptop, unique 7 amazing, capital 8 fabulous, singular, smashing, striking, terrific 9 admirable, excellent, fantastic, marvelous 10 astounding, incredible, miraculous, phenomenal, staggering, surprising 11 astonishing, crackerjack, fascinating, magnificent, sensational, spectacular 13 extraordinary

Wonderland State
nickname of: 5 Maine

wonderstruck 4 agog 6 amazed 8 thrilled 9 astounded, stupefied 10 astonished, enthralled, spellbound 11 dumbfounded 13 flabbergasted

Wonder Woman
character: 9 (Corp) Etta Candy 11 Diana Prince, Joe

Atkinson, (Maj) Steve Trevor 13 Gen Blankenship
cast: 11 Lynda Carter 12 Lyle Waggoner 13 Beatrice Colen, Normann Burton 14 Richard Eastham

wont 3 apt, use 4 used, vain 5 habit, haunt, usage 6 custom, desire 8 accustom, inclined, practice 10 accustomed

wonted 3 apt 5 prone 6 likely 7 given to 10 accustomed, habituated

woo 3 sue 5 chase, court 6 cajole, pursue 7 address, entreat, solicit 8 petition 9 importune

wood 3 log 4 bush 5 brake, brush, copse, grove 6 boards, forest, lumber, planks, siding, timber 7 thicket 8 firewood, kindling 9 clapboard, wallboard 10 timberland

Wood, Grant
born: 9 Anamosa IA
artwork: 12 Spring in Town 13 Stone City Iowa 14 American Gothic 15 Woman with Plants 16 Parson Weems' Fable 18 Dinner for Threshers, John B Turner Pioneer 21 Daughters of Revolution

Wood, John, Sr
architect of: 6 Circus (Bath)

Wood, Natalie
real name: 13 Natasha Gurdin
born: 14 San Francisco CA
husband: 12 Robert Wagner
roles: 5 Gypsy 10 Brainstorm 12 The Great Race, The Searchers 13 West Side Story 17 Inside Daisy Clover 18 Rebel Without a Cause, Splendor in the Grass 19 Sex and the Single Girl 23 This Property Is Condemned 25 Love with the Proper Stranger 27 Miracle on Thirty-fourth Street

wooded 5 treed 8 forested

wooden 4 dull 5 frame, rigid, stiff 6 clumsy, vacant 7 awkward, deadpan 8 lifeless, ungainly 9 impassive, unbending 10 inflexible, ungraceful 11 unemotional 14 expressionless

Woodhouse, Emma
character in: 4 Emma
author: 6 Austen

woodland 5 copse, grove, treed 6 forest 7 coppice, thicket 8 forested

wood of life
Latin: 11 lignum vitae

woods
god of: 8 Silvanus, Sylvanus

Woods, Sara
real name: 13 Sara Bowen-Judd
author of: 11 Done to Death 12 My Life Is Done 13 Yet She Must Die 15 A Show of Violence, Knives Have Edges 16 And Shame the Devil 17 The Third Encounter, Trusted Like the Fox 18 Bloody Instructions
character: 15 Anthony Maitland

Woodstock
also called: 11 The Cavalier
author: 14 Sir Walter Scott

Woodstock
director: 15 Michael Wadleigh
cast: 6 The Who 7 Santana 8 Joan Baez 9 Joe Cocker 12 Richie Havens 13 John Sebastian, Ten Years After 17 Jefferson Airplane 19 Crosby Stills and Nash 20 Country Joe and the Fish, Sly and the Family Stone
Oscar for: 11 documentary

Woodward, Bob
author of: 4 Veil 19 All the President's Men (with Carl Bernstein)

Woodward, Joanne
born: 13 Thomasville GA
husband: 10 Paul Newman
roles: 12 A Fine Madness, Rachel Rachel 15 Three Faces of Eve (Oscar) 16 The Long Hot Summer 43 The Effect of Gamma Rays on Man-in-the-Moon Marigolds

woodwind instrument
4 oboe 5 flute 7 bassoon, piccolo 8 clarinet 9 bass flute 10 cor anglais 12 bass clarinet 13 double bassoon

wooer 4 beau, love 5 flame, lover, swain 6 adorer, suitor 7 admirer, courter 8 paramour 10 sweetheart

wool
fabric: 4 felt 5 crepe, llama, serge, tweed, twill 6 alpaca, angora, boucle, covert, faille, melton, vicuna, woolen 7 challis, doeskin, Donegal, worsted 8 cashmere, homespun, shetland 9 Astrakhan, camelhair, gabardine, sharkskin 10 hopsacking 11 Harris tweed, herringbone

Woolf, Virginia
author of: 7 Orlando 8 The Waves, The Years 10 Jacob's Room 11 Mrs Dalloway

14 A Room of One's Own
15 To the Lighthouse
member of: 15 Bloomsbury
Group

wool-gather 8 daydream,
muse idly

woolly, wooly 5 downy, furry,
fuzzy, hairy, sheep, vague
6 fleecy, lanate, lanose
7 blurred, muddled, unclear
8 confused, floccose, peronate
10 flocculent, indistinct
12 disorganized

woozy 4 hazy **5** dizzy, faint,
foggy, fuzzy, giddy, shaky
6 punchy **7** muddled **9** befuddled **11** light-headed

word, words 3 vow **4** chat,
dirt, news, poop, term **5** edict,
order, rumor, set-to, voice
6 advice, avowal, decree, gossip, letter, notice, phrase,
pledge, remark, report, ruling,
signal **7** command, comment,
dictate, dispute, explain, express, hearsay, lowdown, mandate, message, promise,
quarrel, summons, tidings
8 argument, audience, bulletin,
chitchat, colloquy, decision,
describe, dialogue, dispatch,
locution, telegram **9** assertion,
assurance, bickering, direction,
discourse, interview, sobriquet,
ultimatum, utterance, wrangling **10** articulate, communique, conference, contention,
discussion, expression **11** altercation, appellation, declaration, designation, information,
scuttlebutt **12** consultation, intelligence, tittle-tattle **13** communication, pronouncement
French: 9 tete-a-tete

**word for word and letter
for letter**
Latin: 19 verbatim et
literatim

wordiness 9 diffusion, prolixity, verbosity **11** diffuseness,
profuseness

wording 8 language, phrasing
11 phraseology

wordless 4 dumb, mute
5 tacit **6** silent **8** implicit, taciturn **10** speechless
11 unexpressed

word of honor 3 vow **4** oath
6 pledge **9** assurance

word play 6 banter **7** jesting,
kidding
French: 8 badinage, repartee

Words, The
author: 14 Jean-Paul Sartre

Wordsworth, William
author of: 7 Michael **9** Ode
to Duty **10** The Prelude
12 Tintern Abbey **14** Lyrical

Ballads (with Coleridge)
16 The Ruined Cottage
24 Intimations of Immortality **25** Resolution and
Independence
home: 11 Dove Cottage

wordy 5 windy **6** prolix, turgid **7** fustian, gushing, verbose **8** effusive, mumbling
9 bombastic, garrulous, redundant, talkative **10** discursive,
loquacious, rhetorical, roundabout **12** tautological
13 grandiloquent

work, works 2 do, go
3 act, job, run, win
4 book, deed, duty, feat,
form, gain, line, make,
mill, mold, move, shop,
song, task, toil, yard **5** beget, cause, chore, craft, enact, labor, opera, piece,
plant, shape, slave, solve,
sweat, trade **6** drudge, effect, effort, office, output
7 achieve, calling, drawing,
execute, exploit, factory,
fashion, foundry, innards,
insides, operate, perform,
produce, product, pursuit,
succeed, trouble **8** building,
business, concerto, con-
tents, creation, drudgery,
endeavor, engender, exer-
tion, function, industry,
maneuver, painting, prog-
ress, symphony, transmit,
vocation **9** originate, sculpture, structure **10** assignment, employment,
enterprise, manipulate, occupation, production,
profession **11** achievement,
composition, performance,
transaction
Latin: 4 opus
French: 6 metier

work, artistic or literary
French: 6 oeuvre

workaday 5 plain **6** common
7 humdrum, prosaic, routine
8 ordinary **10** unexciting
11 commonplace

work at 3 try **5** essay **6** tackle
7 attempt **8** endeavor

workbench 5 board, table
7 counter

work conquers all
Latin: 16 labor omnia vincit
motto of: 8 Oklahoma

worker 4 doer, hand **5** grind
6 drudge, toiler **7** artisan, hustler, laborer, plodder

8 achiever, employee, producer **9** craftsman, performer
11 breadwinner, eager beaver,
proletarian

work for 6 assist **7** support
8 champion

working 3 job **4** duty, toil
5 labor, tasks **6** action, chores,
fluent, usable, useful **8** business, drudgery, employed, exertion, industry, laboring
9 effective, operation, operative, practical **10** employment,
occupation, profession **11** as-
signments, functioning,
performance

Working
author: 11 Studs Terkel

working-class 5 labor **8** plebeian **10** blue-collar
11 proletarian

working class 9 commoners,
common man **11** blue collars,
proletariat
Greek: 9 hoi polloi

workmanlike 5 adept **8** skillful **9** efficient **10** productive

workmanship 5 skill **9** hand-
craft, handiwork, technique
10 handicraft **11** manufacture
12 construction

work out 5 solve, train **6** figure, reckon **7** compute, resolve **8** exercise, practice
9 ascertain, calculate,
determine

Works and Days
author: 6 Hesiod

work saver 9 appliance
11 convenience

work-saving 4 easy **6** simple
9 efficient

worktable 4 desk **5** bench,
board, table **7** counter

work together 5 unite **7** pitch
in, share in **8** take part **9** cooperate **11** collaborate,
participate

work toward 3 try **4** seek
6 aim for **7** attempt **8** aspire
to, endeavor, reach for

work up 4 goad, urge **5** upset
6 excite **7** agitate, ferment,
provoke

work with 5 coach, drill,
teach, train **6** assist **8** exercise,
instruct **9** cooperate
11 collaborate

world 3 age, era, orb **4** gobs,
lots, star **5** class, Earth, epoch,
globe, group, heaps, realm,
times **6** domain, nature, oodles, people, period, planet,
sphere, system **7** mankind, society **8** creation, division, du-

ration, everyone, humanity, industry, universe **9** everybody, humankind, macrocosm **10** profession
Latin: 6 cosmos
Russian: 3 mir

World According to Garp, The
author: 10 John Irving
director: 13 George Roy Hill
cast: 10 Glenn Close, Hume Cronyn **11** John Lithgow **12** Jessica Tandy, Mary Beth Hurt **13** Robin Williams

World Enough and Time
author: 16 Robert Penn Warren

worldly 5 blase **6** astute, shrewd, urbane **7** callous, earthly, fleshly, knowing, mundane, profane, secular **8** material, physical, temporal **9** corporeal, mercenary **11** experienced, terrestrial **12** cosmopolitan **13** sophisticated

world pain
German: 11 Weltschmerz

world view
German: 11 Weltansicht

world-weary 5 blase, bored, jaded **9** unexcited

worldwide 4 rife **6** global **8** catholic, ecumenic, globular, planetal, sweeping **9** universal

worm 4 edge, inch **5** crawl, creep, steal **6** writhe **7** wriggle **9** penetrate **10** infiltrate
kinds: 4 inch, tape **5** angle, earth

worn 4 weak **5** dingy, drawn, faded, seedy, spent, tired, weary **6** frayed, shabby, wasted **7** abraded, haggard, pinched, rickety, wearied **8** battered, decrepit, dog-tired, drooping, fatigued **9** enfeebled, exhausted **10** threadbare, tumbledown **11** debilitated, dilapidated

worn-out 4 dead, shot **5** spent, tired **6** beat-up, effete, shabby, used-up **7** run-down **9** exhausted **10** threadbare **11** dilapidated **12** deteriorated

worn thin 9 motheaten **10** threadbare **11** dilapidated

worried 6 afraid, scared **7** anxious, fearful **9** concerned **10** distressed **12** apprehensive

worrisome 5 fussy, pesty **6** trying, uneasy, vexing **7** anxious, fretful, irksome **8** annoying **10** bothersome, despairing, disturbing, irritating, tormenting **11** aggravating, troublesome **12** apprehensive

worry 3 vex, woe **4** care, fret, stew **5** agony, beset, dread, grief, harry, upset **6** badger, bother, dismay, harass, hector, misery, pester, plague **7** agitate, agonize, anguish, anxiety, bugaboo, concern, despair, disturb, perturb, problem, torment, trouble **8** distress, vexation **9** misgiving, persecute **10** difficulty, uneasiness **12** apprehension **13** consternation

worsen 4 fail, slip **5** erode, lapse, slide **7** decline **10** degenerate, retrogress **11** deteriorate **12** disintegrate

worsening 7 setback **9** inflaming **10** increasing, regressing, regression **11** aggravating, heightening **12** exacerbating, intensifying **13** retrogressing, retrogression

worship 5 adore, exalt, extol **6** admire, esteem, praise, pray to, revere **7** adulate, glorify, idolize, lionize **8** dote upon, venerate **9** adoration, reverence **10** exaltation, veneration **11** devotionals

worshipful 5 pious **6** devout **8** reverent

worshiping 7 adoring **8** exalting **9** adoration, adulation, adulating, idolizing, reverence **10** exaltation, glorifying, magnifying, venerating, veneration **11** idolization **13** glorification, magnification

worst 3 bad **4** beat, best, rout **5** floor, outdo **6** defeat, lowest, outwit **7** conquer, poorest, triumph **8** inferior, overcome, vanquish **9** discomfit **10** overmaster, unpleasant

worth 3 use **4** cost, good **5** merit, price, value **6** assets, estate, wealth **7** benefit, effects, utility **8** holdings **9** appraisal, resources, valuation **10** importance, usefulness **11** consequence, possessions

worth having 8 valuable **9** desirable

Worthing, Jack
character in: 27 The Importance of Being Earnest
author: 5 Wilde

worthless 6 futile, paltry **7** trivial, useless **8** bootless, piddling, unusable **9** fruitless, meritless, pointless **10** unavailing **11** ineffectual, undeserving, unimportant **12** meretricious, unproductive **13** insignificant **14** good-for-nothing

worthless objects 4 junk

5 trash **7** garbage, rubbish **8** discards **11** odds and ends

worthwhile 4 good **6** usable, useful **8** valuable **9** rewarding **10** beneficial, profitable

worthy 3 fit, VIP **4** good, name **5** moral, noble **6** bigwig, decent, honest, leader, proper **7** big shot, ethical, fitting, notable, upright **8** big wheel, great man, immortal, laudable, luminary, official, reliable, suitable, virtuous **9** admirable, befitting, deserving, dignitary, estimable, excellent, honorable, personage, reputable **10** creditable **11** appropriate, commendable, meritorious, respectable

worthy of imitation 5 model **9** emulative, exemplary

Wotan
origin: 8 Germanic
chief of: 4 gods
corresponds to: 4 Odin **5** Othin

Wouk, Herman
author of: 13 The Winds of War **14** The Caine Mutiny **17** War and Remembrance **19** Marjorie Morningstar
character: 12 Captain Queeg

wound 3 cut **4** gash, harm, hurt, pain, slit, tear **5** slash, sting **6** bruise, damage, grieve, injure, injury, lesion, offend, pierce, trauma **7** anguish, mortify, torment **8** distress, lacerate, vexation **9** contusion **10** affliction, irritation, laceration **11** provocation

wounded 3 cut **4** hurt **6** mauled **7** damaged, injured, pierced, stabbed **8** impaired, ruptured, stricken **11** traumatized

wrack 4 kelp, ruin **5** ruins, trash **6** clouds, refuse **7** destroy, seaweed, torment **8** downfall, eelgrass, wreckage **9** cloud rack **11** destruction, storm clouds

wraith 5 ghost, shade, spook **6** spirit **7** phantom, specter **8** phantasm **10** apparition **15** materialization
Irish: 7 banshee
German: 12 doppelganger
French: 8 revenant

wrangle 4 tiff **5** argue, brawl **6** bicker **7** dispute, quarrel **8** squabble

wrangling 6 strife **7** arguing, discord **8** clashing, friction **9** bickering **10** contention **11** quarrelling

wrap 4 bind, cape, coat, fold, gird, hide, mask, veil, wind

5 cloak, cover, scarf, shawl, stole **6** bundle, clothe, encase, enfold, girdle, jacket, mantle, shroud, swathe **7** conceal, enclose, envelop, sweater **8** surround

wrapper, wrapping paper
4 case **6** casing, jacket, sheath **8** covering, envelope, slipcase **9** container

wrapping 6 caping, hiding **7** veiling **8** cerement, bundling, swathing **9** embracing, packaging, shrouding **10** engrossing, enswathing, enveloping **11** enshrouding, surrounding

wrap up 3 end **4** pack **6** finish, wind up **7** engross, envelop, involve, package **8** bundle up, complete, conclude **9** polish off **11** dress warmly

wrath 3 ire **4** bile, fury, gall, rage **5** anger **6** animus, choler, rancor, spleen **8** vexation **9** animosity, hostility **10** irritation, resentment **11** displeasure, indignation **13** irritableness

wrathful 3 mad **5** angry, irate **6** bitter, raging **7** furious **8** incensed, virulent

wreak 4 vent, work **5** visit **7** execute, indulge, inflict, unleash

wreak vengeance 6 avenge **7** get even, revenge **9** retaliate

wreath 5 crown **6** diadem, laurel **7** chaplet, coronet, festoon, garland
    Hawaiian: 3 lei

wreathe 4 bend, coil, wind **5** curve, twist **7** entwine, envelop **8** encircle **10** intertwine, interweave

wreck 3 end **4** mess, raze, ruin **5** break, crash, death, level, ruins, smash, total, upset **6** finish, ravage, wretch **7** breakup, crack-up, destroy, shatter, undoing **8** demolish, derelict **9** devastate, overthrow **10** disruption **11** destruction, devastation, dissolution **12** annihilation

wreckage 4 ruin **5** ruins **6** jetsam **7** flotsam, remains **8** shambles **11** destruction

Wren, P C
    author of: 9 Beau Geste

wrench 3 rip **4** jerk, pull, tear, warp **5** force, twist, wrest, wring **6** sprain, strain **7** distort, pervert **12** misrepresent
    type: 6 monkey, socket **7** spanner

wrest 3 get, rip **4** earn, gain, grab, jerk, make, pull, take,

tear **5** force, glean, twist, wring **6** attain, obtain, secure, wrench **7** achieve, extract, squeeze

wrestle 4 toil **5** labor **6** battle, strive, tussle **7** contend, grapple, scuffle **8** struggle **10** struggling

wrestling
    athlete: 8 Dan Gable

wretch 3 cur, pig, rat **4** hobo, waif, worm **5** knave, louse, rogue, swine, tramp **6** misfit, rascal, rotter, varlet **7** castoff, outcast, stinker, villain **8** derelict, scalawag, sufferer, vagabond **9** scoundrel **10** blackguard **11** unfortunate

wretched 3 low **4** base, mean, vile **5** awful, lousy, sorry **6** abject, gloomy, rotten, shabby, sleazy **7** crushed, doleful, forlorn, hapless, pitiful, scruffy, unhappy, worried **8** dejected, downcast, dreadful, hopeless, inferior, pathetic, pitiable, terrible **9** cheerless, depressed, miserable, niggardly, sorrowful, woebegone, worthless **10** abominable, despairing, despicable, despondent, melancholy **11** crestfallen, unfortunate **12** contemptible, disconsolate, disheartened, inconsolable **13** brokenhearted

wretchedness 4 pain **6** misery, sorrow **7** despair, torment, trouble **8** distress, hardship **9** adversity **10** affliction, melancholy, misfortune **11** unhappiness **12** hopelessness

wriggle 5 twist **6** squirm, wangle, writhe **7** meander

Wright, Archibald Lee
    real name of: 11 Archie Moore

Wright, Frank Lloyd
    architect of: 8 Taliesin (Spring Green WI) **10** Robie House (Chicago) **11** Martin House (Buffalo NY), Unity Church (Oak Park IL) **12** Fallingwater (Kaufmann House Bear Run PA), Taliesin West (near Phoenix AZ) **13** Imperial Hotel (Tokyo) **16** Guggenheim Museum (NYC) **22** Marin County Civic Center (CA) **35** Larkin Company Administration Building (Buffalo NY) **45** S C Johnson and Son Wax Company Administration Center (Racine WI)
    style: 6 Modern **7** Organic, Prairie

Wright, Orville and Wilbur
    invented: 8 airplane

first plane: 6 Flyer I **9** Kitty Hawk

Wright, Richard
    author of: 8 Black Boy **9** Native Son **17** Uncle Tom's Children

wring 4 hurt, pain, rend, stab **5** choke, force, press, twist, wrest **6** coerce, grieve, pierce, sadden, wrench **7** agonize, extract, squeeze, torture **8** compress, distress

wrinkle 4 fold, idea **5** crimp, fancy, pleat, slant, trick **6** crease, device, furrow, gather, notion, pucker, rimple, rumple **7** crumple, gimmick **9** crow's-feet, viewpoint **11** corrugation

wrinkled 3 old **4** aged **5** lined **6** folded, ridged, rucked, rugate, rugose, rugous, seamed **7** creased, crimped, rimpled, rippled, ruckled, rumpled **8** crimpled, furrowed, puckered **9** shriveled

writ 10 court order **11** sealed order **14** mandatory order

write 3 pen **4** copy, show **5** draft **6** author, draw up, record, scrawl **7** compose, dash off, jot down, make out, produce, set down, turn out **8** inscribe, scribble **10** transcribe

write down 3 jot **4** note, post **5** enter **6** record

write in full 5 add to **6** expand, extend, pad out **7** amplify, augment, stretch **9** expatiate

write out 6 expand, extend **7** amplify, enlarge, stretch **8** lengthen

writer 4 hack, poet **6** author, critic, penman, scribe **7** copyist **8** essayist, novelist, reporter, reviewer, scrawler **9** columnist, dramatist, scribbler **10** journalist, librettist, playwright, songwriter **11** penny-a-liner **12** calligrapher, newspaperman **13** correspondent **14** newspaperwoman
    French: 11 litterateur

write to 7 address **8** send word **9** drop a line, send a card, send a note **10** correspond **11** send a letter

write-up 4 item **5** piece, story **7** article

write up 5 cover **6** report

writhe 4 jerk **5** flail **6** squirm, thrash, thresh, wiggle **7** contort, wriggle

writing 4 book, play, poem,

tome, work **5** diary, essay, novel, print, story **6** column, letter, report, script, volume **7** article, copying, journal, penning **8** critique, document, drafting, libretto, longhand **9** authoring, composing, editorial, recording **10** inscribing, manuscript, penmanship **11** calligraphy, composition, publication **12** transcribing **Latin: 4** opus

writings
  Hebrew: 7 Ketubim

written agreement 6 treaty **7** compact **8** contract

written law
  Latin: 10 lex scripta

written-out form 9 extension **12** augmentation **13** amplification

wrong 3 bad, sin **4** awry, bilk, evil, harm, hurt, ruin, vice **5** abuse, amiss, cheat, crime, false, inapt, kaput, unfit **6** faulty, fleece, injure, injury, ruined, sinful, unfair, unjust, untrue, wicked **7** crooked, defraud, illegal, illicit, immoral, inexact, inverse, misdeed, offense, reverse, swindle, unhappy, unsound **8** criminal, dishonor, evil deed, ill-treat, immodest, improper, iniquity, maltreat, mistaken, mistreat, opposite, trespass, unlawful, unseemly, villain **9** dishonest, erroneous, felonious, illogical, incorrect, injustice, unethical, unfitting **10** dishonesty, fallacious, illegality, immorality, inaccurate, indecorous, indelicate, iniquitous, malapropos, mistakenly, sinfulness, unbecoming, unfairness, unsuitable, wickedness, wrongdoing **11** blameworthy, erroneously, incongruous, incorrectly, inexcusable, unbefitting, undesirable, unwarranted **12** dishonorable, inaccurately, infelicitous, unlawfulness **13** inappropriate, reprehensible, transgression, unjustifiable **15** unrighteousness

wrongdoer 5 crook, felon, knave, rogue **6** rascal, sinner **7** culprit, misdoer, villain **8** evildoer, offender **9** miscreant, scoundrel **10** blackguard, delinquent, lawbreaker, malefactor, trespasser **11** perpetrator **12** transgressor

wrongdoing 3 sin **4** evil, vice **5** crime **8** misdeeds **10** misconduct **11** delinquency, malfeasance, misbehavior

wrongful 3 bad **6** unfair, unjust **7** illegal **8** criminal, un-lawful **10** iniquitous, inequitable **12** illegitimate
  act: 4 tort
  dispossession: 6 ouster

wrongheaded 3 wry **8** perverse, stubborn **9** misguided

wrong side out 9 backwards **10** topsy-turvy

wrought 4 made **6** beaten, formed, worked **7** crafted **8** hammered **9** fashioned **11** constructed, handcrafted

wrought-up 7 excited **8** agitated **9** emotional **10** hysterical

wry 3 dry **5** askew, droll **6** bitter, ironic, warped **7** amusing, caustic, crooked, cynical, satiric, twisted **8** perverse, sardonic **9** contorted, distorted, sarcastic

Wunderkind 11 wonder child **12** child prodigy

Wurster, William
  architect of: 13 Cowell College (UC Berkeley) **17** Ghirardelli Square (San Francisco CA)

Wuthering Heights
  character: 9 Ellen Dean **10** Heathcliff, Mr Lockwood **11** Edgar Linton **14** Isabella Linton **15** Catherine Linton, Frances Earnshaw, Hareton Earnshaw, Hindley Earnshaw **16** Linton Heathcliff **17** Catherine Earnshaw
  director: 12 William Wyler
  author: 11 Emily Bronte
  cast: 10 David Niven **11** Donald Crisp, Flora Robson, Leo G Carroll, Merle Oberon (Cathy) **15** Laurence Olivier (Heathcliff) **19** Geraldine Fitzgerald

Wyatt, James
  architect of: 8 Pantheon

Wyoming
  abbreviation: 2 WY **3** Wyo
  nickname: 8 Equality
  capital: 8 Cheyenne
  largest city: 6 Casper
  others: 4 Cody, Lusk **7** Bighorn, Buffalo, Laramie, Rawlins, Worland **8** Gillette, Greybull, Kemmerer, Riverton, Sheridan, Sundance **11** Rock Springs
  feature:
    center: 11 Buffalo Bill
    dam: 8 Shoshone
    fort: 7 Laramie
    historical preserve: 11 Fort Bridger
    national grassland: 11 Tunder Basin
    national monument: 11 Devil's Tower, Fossil Butte
    national park: 10 Grand Teton **11** Yellowstone
    reservoir: 12 Flaming Gorge
  tribe: 4 Crow **5** Kiowa, Sioux **7** Arapaho, Bannock **8** Cheyenne
  people: 11 Buffalo Bill **14** Jackson Pollock **16** Nellie Tayloe Ross **18** Francis Emroy Warren
    explorer: 6 Colter, Stuart **7** Bridger **10** Bonneville
  lake: 7 Jackson **11** Yellowstone
  land rank: 5 ninth
  mountain: 3 Elk **5** Cloud, Moran **6** Absaro, Hoback, Tetons **7** Bighorn, Fremont, Laramie, Rockies **8** Atlantic, Sheridan **9** Wind River **10** Black Hills **11** Rattlesnake
    highest point: 11 Gannett Peak
  physical feature: 11 Jackson Hole
    basin: 7 Wyoming
    cave: 8 Shoshone
    hot springs: 11 Thermopolis
    plains: 5 Great
  river: 4 Bear, Wind **5** Green, Snake **6** Platte, Powder, Tongue **7** Bighorn **8** Cheyenne, Shoshone **10** Sweetwater **11** Yellowstone **12** Belle Fourche
  state admission: 11 forty-fourth
  state bird: 17 western meadowlark
  state flower: 10 painted cup **16** Indian paintbrush
  state motto: 11 Equal Rights
  state song: 7 Wyoming
  state tree: 10 cottonwood

(London) **9** Lee Priory
(Kent) **10** Stoke Poges
(Buckinghamshire) **13** Font-
hill Abbey (Wiltshire)
14 Dodington House (Gloucestershire) **15** Heveningham
Hall (Suffolk) **16** Sandleford
Priory (Berkshire)
style: 13 Gothic Revival

Wyatt, Jane
  born: 9 Campgaw NJ
  roles: 9 Boomerang **11** Lost
  Horizon **15** Father Knows
  Best **17** Great Expectations
  19 Gentleman's Agreement
  21 None But the Lonely
  Heart

**Wyatt Earp, The Life and
Legend of**
  character: 10 Morgan Earp,
  Virgil Earp **11** Ben Thompson, Doc Holliday **12** Bat
  Masterson, Bill Thompson
  13 Old Man Clanton
  cast: 9 Hal Baylor **10** Denver
  Pyle, Dirk London, Hugh
  O'Brien **12** John Anderson
  13 Douglas Fowley **14** Trev-
  or Bardette **20** Mason Alan
  Dinehart III

setting: 8 OK Corral **9** Dodge
City, Ellsworth, Tombstone
Wyatt's pistols: 15 Buntline
Special

Wyeth, Andrew Newell
  born: 2 PA **10** Chadds Ford
  father: 7 N C Wyeth
  artwork: 9 Grape Wine, River
  Cove **12** Nick and Jamie
  14 Christina Olson, Distant
  Thunder **15** Christina's
  World **22** Winter Nineteen
  Forty-six

Wyler, William
  director of: 6 Ben Hur (Oscar) **7** Jezebel **9** Dodsworth,
  Funny Girl, The Letter
  10 Mrs Miniver (Oscar), The
  Heiress, These Three **12** Roman Holiday **14** The Little
  Foxes **15** Counsellor-at-Law
  16 Wuthering Heights
  18 Friendly Persuasion
  22 The Best Years of Our
  Lives (Oscar)

Wylie, Philip
  author of: 13 Opus Twenty-
  one **19** A Generation of
  Vipers

Wyman, Jane
  real name: 14 Sarah Jane
  Fulks
  born: 10 St Joseph MO
  husband: 12 Ronald Reagan
  daughter: 13 Maureen
  Reagan
  son: 13 Michael Reagan
  roles: 5 So Big **9** Pollyanna
  11 Falcon Crest, The Blue
  Veil, The Yearling
  13 Johnny Belinda (Oscar)
  14 Angela Channing, The
  Lost Weekend **17** The Glass
  Menagerie **20** Magnificent
  Obsession

Wyndham, John
  real name: 16 John Beynon
  Harris
  author of: 14 The Kraken
  Wakes **15** Consider Her
  Ways **17** The Midwich
  Cuckoos, Trouble with Li-
  chen **19** The Day of the
  Triffids

Wyoming *see box*

Wyss, Johann Rudolf
  author of: 22 The Swiss
  Family Robinson
  adaptation of: **14** Robinson Crusoe

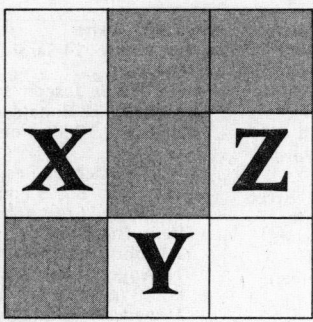

Xanthippe, Xantippe 3 hag
4 fury 5 scold, shrew, vixen
6 dragon, virago 7 scolder
8 spitfire 9 termagant
husband: 8 Socrates

Xanthus and Balius
horses of: 8 Achilles
trait: 8 immortal

Xenia
epithet of: 6 Athena
means: 10 hospitable

Xenoclea
form: 9 priestess

xenon
chemical symbol: 2 Xe

xenophobia
fear of: 9 strangers

Xerxes *see* 9 Ahasuerus

x-ray 9 radiogram 10 radio-
graph 13 roentgenogram
14 roentgenograph

X-ray tube
invented by: 8 Coolidge

Xuthus
father: 6 Hellen
mother: 6 Orscis
wife: 6 Creusa
son: 3 Ion 7 Achaeus

yacht 4 boat, race, sail, ship,
yawl 5 ketch, sloop 6 cruise,
cutter 7 catboat 8 schooner
race: 11 America's Cup

yachting
athlete: 9 Ted Turner
11 Lowell North

yahoo 4 lout 5 brute, yokel
7 lowbrow 9 barbarian, ignoramus, vulgarian

Yahoos
fictional people in: 16 Gulliver's Travels
author: 5 Swift

Yahweh 3 God 4 Lord 5 Jahve,
Jahwe, Yahve 6 Author, I am
I am, Jahveh 7 Creator, Eternal, Jehovah 8 Absolute, Almighty, Infinite
component: 2 he 3 yod, vav
pronunciation: 6 Adonai, Elohim 9 forbidden
transliteration: 4 YHVH

Yale, Linus, Jr
invented: 12 cylinder lock
27 dial-operated combination
lock

yam 9 Dioscorea 14 Ipomoea
batatas
varieties: 4 wild 5 Negro, water, white 6 Attoto, potato,
yellow 7 Chinese 11 sweet
potato

Yamasaki, Minoru
architect of: 14 St Louis Airport (MO) 16 World Trade

Center (NYC) 21 Woodrow
Wilson Building (Princeton
NJ)

yammer 3 cry 4 carp, harp,
howl, wail, yell 5 whine
7 grumble, whimper
8 complain

yank 3 tug 4 jerk, pull 5 pluck,
wrest 6 snatch, wrench 7 draw
out, extract, pull out

Yankee, Yank 2 GI 5 teddy
6 gringo 8 American, doughboy 10 Northerner
Spanish: 6 yanqui

Yankee Doodle Dandy
director: 13 Michael Curtiz
cast: 10 Joan Leslie
11 James Cagney (George M
Cohan) 12 Irene Manning,
Walter Huston
Oscar for: 5 actor (Cagney)

yanqui 6 Yankee 9 US citizen

Yaounde
capital of: 8 Cameroon

yap 3 yip 4 blab, gush, rave,
talk, yawp, yelp 5 scold
6 babble, gabble, gossip, jabber, rave on, tattle 7 blather,
chatter, lecture, palaver, prattle 8 complain, converse

Yaqui
language family: 6 Cahita
location: 6 Mexico, Sonora
7 Arizona

yard 4 lawn 5 close, court

6 garden 7 confine, grounds,
pasture 8 compound 9 enclosure, three feet
abbreviation: 2 yd

yardbird 3 con 5 felon 7 convict 8 prisoner

yard goods 5 cloth 6 fabric
8 material, textiles

Yard of Sun
author: 14 Christopher Fry

yardstick 4 rule 7 measure
8 standard 9 criterion

Yaren District
capital of: 5 Nauru

yarn 4 tale 5 story 7 account
8 anecdote 9 adventure, narrative 10 experience

Yastrzemski, Carl
nickname: 3 Yaz
sport: 8 baseball
team: 12 Boston Red Sox

Yates, Peter
director of: 7 Bullitt
12 Breaking Away

yawn 3 gap 4 bore, gape
5 chasm 8 open wide, oscitate

yawp 4 roar, yelp 5 noise
6 clamor, squawk, yammer

Yaz
nickname of: 15 Carl
Yastrzemski

Yazoo
author: 12 Willie Morris

1086

year, years 3 age, era 4 time 5 cycle, epoch 6 period
abbreviation: 2 yr

Yearling, The
director: 13 Clarence Brown
author: 22 Marjorie Kinnan Rawlings
cast: 9 Jane Wyman 10 Chill Wills 11 Gregory Peck 14 Claude Jarman Jr
character: 9 Ora Baxter 10 Jody Baxter 11 Oliver Hutto, Penny Baxter 12 Grandma Hutto 14 Twink Weatherby 19 Fodder-Wing Forrester

Year of Living Dangerously, The
director: 9 Peter Weir
cast: 9 Linda Hunt (Billy Kwan), Mel Gibson 15 Sigourney Weaver
setting: 7 Jakarta
Oscar for: 17 supporting actress (Hunt)

year of wonders
Latin: 14 annus mirabilis

yearn 4 ache, long, pine, sigh, want, wish 5 crave 6 hanker, hunger, thirst 8 languish

yearning 3 yen 4 ache, want, wish 5 fancy 6 desire, hunger, thirst 7 craving, longing, passion 9 hankering 10 aspiration 11 inclination

Yeats, William Butler
author of: 7 A Vision 8 The Tower 9 Last Poems 14 Leda and the Swan 15 The Winding Stair 18 Sailing to Byzantium 19 Among School Children, The Wild Swans at Coole 21 Easter Nineteen Sixteen 22 The Lake Isle of Innisfree 29 An Irish Airman Foresees His Death

yegg 6 bomber 9 cracksman 11 safecracker

yell 3 boo, cry 4 bawl, hoot, howl, roar, yowl 5 cheer, hollo, shout, whoop 6 bellow, clamor, cry out, holler, hurrah, huzzah, outcry, scream, shriek, squall, squeal 7 screech

yellow 4 gold 5 blond, lemon, ocher 6 afraid, canary, craven, flaxen 7 chicken, fearful, saffron 8 cowardly, timorous 10 frightened 12 apprehensive, fainthearted 13 pusillanimous 14 chickenhearted

yellow-belly 6 coward 7 caitiff, chicken, dastard 8 poltroon

Yellowhammer State
nickname of: 7 Alabama

yellowish 4 buff 5 blond, cream 6 blonde, creamy, flaxen

Yemen, North
other name: 4 Sana
capital/largest city: 4 Sana 5 Sanaa
others: 4 Moka, Taiz 5 Dahhi, Damar, Jibla, Mocha, Mukha, Taizz, Umram 7 Hodeida, Hudayda
monetary unit: 4 fils, rial 5 riyal
island: 5 Zugar 6 Hanish
highest point: 6 Shuayb
river: 5 Abrad, Zabid 6 al-Jawf, Surdud
sea: 3 Red
physical feature:
    desert: 10 Rub al Khali
    gulf: 4 Aden
    lowlands: 6 Tihama
    peninsula: 7 Arabian
    strait: 11 Bab el Mandeb
people: 4 Arab 5 Zaidi 6 Shafai, Yemeni 8 Yemenite
    leader: 16 Ali Abdallah Saleh 19 Abd al-Aziz Abd al-Ghani
language: 6 Arabic
religion: 5 Islam
place:
    ruins: 5 Marib
feature:
    dagger: 7 jambiya
    king: 4 imam
    kingdom: 4 Saba 5 Sheba 11 Arabia Felix
    tree: 3 fig 5 carob, mango, myrrh
food:
    coffee: 5 mocha

Yemen, South
capital: 4 Aden 14 Madinat al-Shaab
largest city: 4 Aden
others: 5 Ahwar, Shihr, Tarim 6 Balhaf, Damqut, Seiyun, Shabwa, Shibam, Zamakh 7 Mukalla
monetary unit: 4 fils 5 dinar
island: 5 Perim 7 Kamaran, Socotra
mountain: 7 Djehaff
highest point: 6 Thamir
river: 4 Bana 6 Tibban 7 Masilah 9 Hadramaut
sea: 6 Indian 7 Arabian
physical feature:
    desert: 10 Rub al Khali 12 Empty Quarter
    gulf: 4 Aden
    peninsula: 7 Arabian
    valley: 9 Hadramawt
people: 4 Arab
language: 6 Arabic
religion: 5 Islam
feature:
    animal: 4 ibex, oryx
    clothing: 4 futa

Yellow Kid, The
creator: 10 R F Outcault
trademark: 10 nightshirt
place: 5 slums 11 Hogan's Alley
coined term: 16 yellow journalism
first: 10 comic strip

yelp 3 yap, yip 4 bark, howl 5 shout 6 clamor, holler, scream, shriek, squeal 7 screech

Yemen, North *see box*

Yemen, South *see box*

yen 4 ache, long, pine, sigh, want, wish 5 crave, fancy, yearn 6 aching, desire, hanker, hunger, relish, thirst 7 craving, longing, passion 8 appetite, languish, yearning 9 hankering 10 aspiration 11 inclination

---

yenta 3 hen 6 gossip 8 busybody 12 blabbermouth

Yentl
director: 15 Barbra Streisand
based on story by: 19 Isaac Bashevis Singer
cast: 13 Mandy Patinkin 15 Barbra Streisand

Yeobright, Thomasin and Clym
characters in: 17 Return of the Native
author: 5 Hardy

yeoman 4 chap, exon 5 churl, clerk, swain 6 farmer, fellow 7 granger, plowman, servant 8 graycoat, retainer 9 beefeater 10 freeholder 12 petty officer

Yerby, Frank
author of: 8 Fair Oaks 10 Health Card 11 Griffin's Way 12 Pride's Castle 16 The Foxes of Harrow 21 Hail the Conquering Hero

yes 3 aye, yea 4 amen, okay, true 5 truly 6 assent, indeed, it is so, just so, really, so be it, surely, verily 7 consent, exactly, granted, no doubt 8 approval, of course, to be sure 9 agreement, assuredly, certainly, doubtless, precisely 10 acceptance, positively 11 af-

firmation, undoubtedly **12** acquiescence, emphatically **13** affirmatively, authorization
French: 3 oui
German: 2 ja
Spanish: 2 si

yesterday 7 the past **10** bygone days, days of yore, olden times, time gone by **11** former times **13** the recent past **14** the good old days **17** the day before today **22** on the day preceding today

yet 3 but **4** also, even, then, up to **5** again, still, while, until **6** no less, though **7** besides, earlier, even now, further, however, thus far **8** although, hitherto, moreover **9** presently **10** eventually, ultimately **12** nevertheless **15** notwithstanding

yew 5 Taxus
varieties: 4 plum **5** Irish **6** golden **7** Chinese, English, Florida, Western **8** American, Japanese, Southern **11** Chinese plum, Plumfruited **12** Japanese plum, Prince Albert **14** Harrington plum

Yggdrasil
also: 9 Iggdrasil
origin: 12 Scandinavian
kind of tree: 12 evergreen ash
roots: 5 three
binds: 6 Asgard **7** Midgard **8** Niflheim **10** Mithgarthr

yield 3 pay, sag **4** bear, crop, earn, gain, give **5** beget, break, burst, defer, droop, forgo, grant, spawn, split, waive **6** accede, cave in, give in, give up, kowtow, render, return, submit, supply **7** bow down, concede, forbear, furnish, give way, harvest, payment, premium, produce, product, provide, revenue, succumb, truckle **8** collapse, cry uncle, earnings, generate, interest, proceeds, renounce **9** acquiesce, gleanings, procreate, surrender **10** capitulate, relinquish

yielding 3 lax **4** soft **6** ceding, spongy **7** sagging **8** flexible, obedient **9** compliant **11** complaisant **13** accommodating

Yigdal 22 Jewish liturgical prayer
literally: 12 becomes great

Yizkor 33 Jewish service to commemorate the dead
literally: 9 be mindful

Ymir
origin: 12 Scandinavian
progenitor of: 6 giants

earth made from: 5 flesh
water made from: 5 blood
heavens made from: 5 skull

yogi 5 Hindu **6** mystic **7** ascetic

Yogi Bear
creator: 12 Hanna-Barbera
character: 6 BooBoo
setting: 14 Jellystone Park

yoke 3 tax **4** bond, join, link, load, pair, span, team **5** brace, clasp, hitch, trial, unite **6** attach, burden, collar, couple, fasten, strain, weight **7** bondage, coupler, harness, serfdom, slavery **8** distress, pressure, troubles **9** servitude, thralldom, vassalage **10** oppression **11** enslavement, tribulation

yokel 4 clod, hick, rube **7** bumpkin, hayseed, peasant, plowboy **10** clodhopper, provincial

yolk 6 yellow

yonder 3 yon **5** there **6** far-off **7** faraway, farther, thither

Yorick
skull in: 6 Hamlet
author: 11 Shakespeare

Yorick, Mr
character in: 14 Tristram Shandy
author: 6 Sterne

York, Michael
born: 6 Fulmer **7** England
roles: 6 Tybalt **7** Cabaret **11** Lost Horizon **14** Four Musketeers, Romeo and Juliet, The Forsyte Saga **15** Three Musketeers **19** The Island of Dr Moreau **24** The Last Remake of Beau Geste

York, Susannah
real name: 23 Susannah Yolande Fletcher
born: 6 London **7** England
roles: 5 Freud **6** Images **8** Jane Eyre, Tom Jones **12** The Awakening
author of: 18 In Search of Unicorns

Yossarian
character in: 14 Catch-Twenty-two
author: 6 Heller

You Asked for It
host: 8 Art Baker **9** Jack Smith

You Bet Your Life
host: 11 Groucho Marx
announcer: 14 George Fenneman

You Can't Go Home Again
author: 11 Thomas Wolfe
character: 10 Esther Jack **11** Lloyd McHarg **12** George Webber **13** Else von Kohler **14** Foxhall Edwards

You Can't Take It With You
author: 8 Moss Hart **14** George S Kaufman
director: 10 Frank Capra
cast: 10 Jean Arthur, Mischa Auer **12** Edward Arnold, James Stewart **15** Lionel Barrymore
Oscar for: 7 picture **8** director

young 3 cub, pup **4** baby, kids **5** child, issue, minor, whelp **6** boyish, callow, junior, kitten, youths **7** budding, girlish, growing, progeny, puerile, teenage **8** childish, children, immature, juvenile, underage, youthful **9** beardless, infantile, juveniles, offspring, teenagers **10** adolescent, descendant, sophomoric, youngsters **11** adolescents, undeveloped **13** inexperienced
god of: 7 Angus Og
goddess of: 4 Hebe

Young, Chic
creator/artist of: 7 Blondie

Young, Denton True
nickname: 2 Cy **7** Cyclone
sport: 8 baseball
position: 7 pitcher
team: 12 Boston Braves, Boston Red Sox **16** Cleveland Indians, St Louis Cardinals

Young, Loretta
real name: 13 Gretchen Young
husband: 12 Grant Withers
roles: 13 Cause for Alarm **14** The Bishop's Wife **15** Come to the Stable **18** The Farmer's Daughter (Oscar) **20** Rachel and the Stranger

Young, Robert
born: 9 Chicago IL
roles: 10 Relentless **11** H M Pulham Esq **13** Marcus Welby M D **15** Father Knows Best **16** Strange Interlude

Young Adventure
author: 19 Stephen Vincent Benet

Young Frankenstein
director: 9 Mel Brooks
cast: 8 Teri Garr **10** Gene Wilder, Peter Boyle **11** Gene Hackman **12** Madeline Kahn, Marty Feldman **14** Cloris Leachman
score: 10 John Morris

young girl
French: 10 jeune fille

young lady
German: 8 fraulein

Young Lonigan
author: 13 James T Farrell

Young Manhood of Studs Lonigan
author: 13 James T Farrell

youngster 3 boy, kid, tot 4 baby, girl 5 child, minor, youth 7 progeny 8 juvenile, teenager 9 fledgling, offspring 10 adolescent

young Turks 6 rebels 8 radi-cals, upstarts 9 activists 10 insurgents 15 revolutionaries

young woman
French: 10 demoiselle

you're welcome
German: 5 bitte

Your Show of Shows
regular: 9 Bill Hayes, Jerry Ross, Sid Caesar 10 Carl Reiner 11 Imogene Coca 12 Howard Morris, Nellie Fisher 13 James Starbuck, Robert Merrill 16 Marguerite Piazza

youth 3 boy, kid, lad 4 kids 5 bloom, child, minor, prime, teens 6 heyday 7 boyhood 8 children, girlhood, juvenile, minority, teenager 9 child-

---

Yugoslavia
other name: 8 Dalmatia 34 Kingdom of the Serbs Croats and Slovenes
capital/largest city: 7 Beograd 8 Belgrade
others: 3 Nis 4 Pola, Pula, Savo, Zara 5 Agram, Bosna, Budva, Fiume, Kotor, Pirot, Rieka, Rtanj, Senta, Split, Tuzla, Uskub, Zadar 6 Bitola, Bitolj, Ca Haro, Maglaj, Morava, Mostar, Osijek, Prilep, Ragusa, Rijeka, Skopje, Trogir, Visoko, Zagreb 7 Cetinje, Laibach, Maribor, Novisad, Skoplje, Spalato 8 Monastir, Pristina, Sarajevo, Subotica, Titograd 9 Banja Luka, Dubrovnik, Ljubljana, Podgorica, Smederevo
division/former division: 6 Bosnia, Serbia 7 Croatia 8 Crna Gora, Slovenia 9 Macedonia, Vojvodina, Voyvodina 10 Montenegro 11 Hercegovina, Herzegovina 14 Kosovo-Metohija
measure: 3 oka, rif 4 akov, ralo 5 donum, khvat, lanaz, plaze, stopa 6 motyka, ralico 9 danoranja
monetary unit: 4 para 5 dinar
weight: 3 oka 5 dramm, tovar, wagon 7 satlijk
island: 3 Rab 4 Arbe, Brac, Cres, Hvar, Pago 5 Mljet, Solta, Susac, Susak 7 Korcula
lake: 4 Bled 5 Ohrid 6 Prespa 7 Ochrida, Scutari
mountain: 5 Karst 6 Balkan 7 Rhodope 8 Crna Gora, Durmitor 9 Sar-Pindus 10 Karawanken
    Alps: 6 Carnic, Julian 7 Dinaric 9 Slovenian 16 Northern Albanian
highest point: 7 Triglav
river: 3 Una 4 Drim, Drin, Ibar, Krka, Kupa, Sava, Tisa 5 Anube, Bosna, Cazma, Drava, Drina, Raska, Tamis, Timok, Tisza, Vrbas 6 Danube, Morava, Vardar, Velika 7 Neretva 9 Vojvodina
sea: 8 Adriatic
physical feature:
    bay: 5 Kotor
    cave: 8 Postojna
    channel: 7 Narento
    gulf: 5 Kotor 7 Kvarner, Trieste
    hot springs: 16 Krapinske Toplice
    peninsula: 6 Balkan 7 Istrian
people: 4 Serb, Slav 5 Croat 7 Slovene 8 Albanian 10 Macedonian 11 Montenegrin
    author: 6 Andric, Djilas, Krleza 7 Dedijer
    leader: 4 Tito 5 Dusan, Pasic 6 Djilas 7 Nemanja 9 Milosevic, Obrenovic 13 Mikhailovitch
    ruler: 5 Peter 9 Hapsburgs 12 Ottoman Turks
    sculptor: 9 Mestrovic
language: 7 Bosnian, Slovene 8 Albanian, Croatian 9 Hungarian, Slovenian 10 Macedonian 11 Montenegrin 13 Herzegovinian, Serbo-Croatian
    alphabet: 5 Latin 8 Cyrillic
religion: 5 Islam 13 Roman Catholic 15 Eastern Orthodox, Serbian Orthodox
place:
    amphitheater: 4 Pula
    bridge: 9 Stari Most
    fortress: 10 Kalemegdan
    monastery: 8 Sopocani
    mosque: 6 Begova 15 Bajrakli Dzamija
    ruins: 14 Hadrian's Palace
    square: 8 Republic
feature:
    coffee house: 7 kafanas
    fields: 5 polje
    military governor: 7 vojvodi
    musical instrument: 5 gusla
    poems: 5 pesme
    slippers: 6 opanki
food:
    dessert: 4 pita
    drink: 5 rakia 6 rakija 7 maraska 9 slivovitz 10 sljivovice 13 Turkish coffee
    meat: 7 shaslik 9 cevapcici 10 culbastija
    soup: 6 corbas

hood, fledgling, juveniles, schoolboy, stripling, teenagers, youngster **10** adolescent, pubescence, youngsters **11** adolescence, adolescents

youthful 5 fresh, young **6** boyish, callow **7** girlish, puerile, teenage **8** childish, immature, juvenile **10** adolescent, sophomoric **12** enthusiastic, lighthearted **13** inexperienced

yowl 3 bay, cry **4** bawl, roar, wail, yelp **5** shout, whine **6** bellow, holler, scream, shriek, squeal **7** screech **9** caterwaul

yucca
    varieties: **4** blue **6** banana

Zachariah
    father: **4** Babi, Elam **9** Barachias
    wife: **9** Elizabeth
    son: **3** Abi **14** John the Baptist
    succeeded: **8** Jeroboam
    visitor: **7** Gabriel

zaddik 14 virtuous person **15** righteous person

Zadkine, Ossip
    born: **6** Russia **8** Smolensk
    artwork: **4** Stag **6** Christ **7** Orpheus **9** Musicians **10** The Prophet **13** Woman with a Fan **14** Mother and Child **16** The Destroyed City

Zadok
    father: **5** Baana, Immer **6** Ahitub
    son: **7** Shallum
    daughter: **7** Jerusha
    served: **5** David

zaftig 5 buxom, plump **6** bosomy

Zagreus
    form: **5** child, deity
    father: **4** Zeus
    mother: **6** Semele **10** Persephone

Zaire *see box*

Zambia *see box*

zany 3 nut **4** wild **5** balmy, batty, booby, buffo, clown, comic, crazy, cutup, daffy, dizzy, goofy, inane, nutty, silly, wacky **6** jester, nitwit, screwy, weirdo **7** buffoon, half-wit, lunatic **8** bonehead, clownish, imbecile, lunkhead, numskull **9** blockhead, eccentric, harlequin, ludicrous, pantaloon, simpleton, slapstick **10** nincompoop, noodlehead, outlandish **11** nonsensical person
    French: **7** farceur

9 San Angelo, spineless **11** twisted-leaf

Yugoslavia *see box, p. 1089*

Yuit *see* **6** Eskimo

Yukon Territory
    border: **6** Alaska **15** British Columbia, Selwyn Mountains **18** Mackenzie Mountains
    capital: **10** Whitehorse
    country: **6** Canada
    event: **8** gold rush (1897)
    Indian: **4** Dene **6** Eskimo **7** Kutchin **8** Loucheux **9** Athabasca
    lake: **6** Kluane **9** Great Bear

Zapotec
    language family: **5** Otomi **6** mixtec
    location: **6** Mexico, Oaxaca

mineral: 4 gold **6** silver
mountain: 3 Joy **5** Logan **6** Harper **7** Kennedy **8** Campbell
region: 8 Klondike
river: 5 Pelly **9** Porcupine
sea: 8 Beaufort
town: 4 Elsa, Faro, Mayo, Snag **5** Rocky **6** Dawson **8** Franklin, Wernecke **9** Mackenzie

yule 4 Noel **9** Christmas

Yule, Joe, Jr
    real name of: **12** Mickey Rooney

Yuman
    tribe: **6** Mohave, Mojave **8** Hualapai

zapped 5 drunk **6** killed, soused, wasted, zonked **7** smashed **9** destroyed, plastered **10** inebriated

Zaire
    other name: **5** Congo **12** Belgian Congo **13** Congo-Kinshasa **17** Congo-Leopoldville
    capital/largest city: **8** Kinshasa
    others: **4** Baya, Boma, Lebo **5** Aketi, Ilebo **6** Banana, Kamina, Kasaji, Kikwit, Matadi, Sandoa **7** Butembo, Kananga, Kolwezi **8** Bakwanga, Yangambi **9** Kisangani **10** Lubumbashi, Luluabourg, Mutshatsha **12** Port-Francqui, Stanleyville **14** Elisabethville
    school: **5** Zaire **8** Lovanium
    division: **4** Kivu **5** Kasai, Shaba **7** Equator, Katanga **8** Oriental
    monetary unit: **5** zaire **6** makuta
    lake: **4** Kivu **5** Mweru, Tumba **6** Albert, Edward, Upemba **9** Mai-Ndombe **10** Tanganyika
    mountain: **7** Crystal, Mitumba, Virunga **9** Ruwenzori **10** Nyaragongo **18** Mountains of the Moon
    highest point: **10** Margherita
    river: **4** Ruki, Uele **5** Congo, Dengu, Ibina, Kasai, Lindi, Zaire **6** Likati, Lomami, Lukuga, Ubangi **7** Aruwimi, Lualaba, Lulonga
    sea: **8** Atlantic
    physical feature:
        falls: **4** Kivu **6** Tshopo **7** Stanley
        forest: **5** Ituri
        valley: **9** Great Rift
    people: **4** Kuba, Luba, Yaka **5** Bantu, Bashi, Bemba, Kongo, Lulue, Lunda, Mongo, Pygmy **6** Azande, Baluba, Watusi **7** Bakongo, Nilotes, Tshokwe **8** European, Mangbetu, Sudanese
        explorer: **3** Cao **7** Stanley
        leader: **6** Mobutu (Sese Seko) **7** Lumumba, Tshombe **8** Kasavubu
        ruler: **7** Belgium, Leopold
    language: **5** Bantu **6** French **7** Chiluba, Kikongo, Lingala, Swahili **8** Sudanese, Tshiluba
    religion: **5** Islam **7** animism, Kimbang **10** Protestant **13** Roman Catholic
    place:
        dam: **4** Inga **9** Le Marinee **10** Del Commune
        national park: **6** Albert, Upemba **7** Garamba
    feature:
        animal: **5** hyena, okapi **7** giraffe, gorilla **10** rhinoceros
        fish: **11** electric eel

Zambia
  other name: 16 Northern Rhodesia
  capital/largest city: 6 Lusaka
  others: 4 Kafu 5 Choma, Isoka, Kabwe, Kitwe, Mansa,
    Mbala, Mongu, Mpika, Mumba, Ndola 6 Mwenda 7 Chi-
    pata, Luapula, Mankoya 8 Balovale, Chingola, Luanshya,
    Mazabuka, Mufulira, Mulobezi 11 Livingstone
  division: 7 Puapula 10 Copperbelt 11 Barotseland
  monetary unit: 5 ngwee 6 kwacha
  lake: 5 Mweru 6 Kariba 9 Bangweulu 10 Tanganyika
  mountain: 8 Muchinga
  highest point: 12 Mafinga Hills
  river: 5 Congo, Kafue 7 Luangwa, Luapula, Zambezi
    8 Chambezi 9 Chambeshi
  physical feature:
    cave: 5 Nsalu 14 Chifabwa Stream
    falls: 7 Kalambo 8 Victoria
    gorge: 6 Kariba
    plateau: 7 Zambian
    swamp: 7 Lukanga 9 Bangweulu 12 Mweru Wantipa
    valley: 8 Chambezi 9 Great Rift
  people: 4 Lozi 5 Bantu, Bemba, Ngoni, Tonga
    developer: 6 Rhodes
    explorer: 11 Livingstone
    hero: 11 Chitimukulu
    leader: 6 Kaunda
  language: 4 Lozi 5 Bemba, Lunda, Tonga 6 Luvale,
    Nyanja 7 English 9 Afrikaans
  religion: 5 Hindu, Islam 7 animism 10 Protestant 13 Ro-
    man Catholic
  place:
    botanical garden: 10 Munda Wanga
    dam: 5 Kafue 6 Kariba
    game reserve: 6 Valley
    library: 20 Hammerskjold Memorial
    museum: 11 Livingstone
    national park: 5 Kafue, Sumbu 12 South Luangwa
  feature:
    canoe: 10 nalikwanda
    king: 7 litunga
    king's aide: 5 sungu, twite 8 inabanza
    taxi: 6 zamcab

11 annihilated, intoxicated

zeal 4 fire, zest 5 ardor, gusto, verve, vigor 6 fervor, relish 7 passion 8 devotion, industry 9 animation, eagerness, intensity, vehemence 10 enthusiasm, fanaticism, fierceness, intentness 11 earnestness

zealot 3 fan, nut 4 buff 5 bigot, crank 6 pusher 7 devotee, fanatic, hustler 8 believer, champion, crackpot, go-getter, live wire, partisan 9 extremist 10 enthusiast

zealous 5 eager, rabid 6 ardent, fervid, fierce, gung ho, raging, raving 7 devoted, earnest, fanatic, fervent, intense 8 animated, vehement, vigorous 10 passionate 11 impassioned, industrious 12 enthusiastic

Zebedee
  wife: 6 Salome
  son: 4 John 5 James

Zeboim
  destroyed with: 5 Admah, Sodom 8 Gomorrah

Zebulun
  father: 5 Jacob
  mother: 4 Leah
  brother: 3 Dan, Gad 4 Levi 5 Asher, Judah 6 Joseph, Reuben, Simeon 8 Benjamin, Issachar, Naphtali
  sister: 5 Dinah
  descendant of: 10 Zebulunite

Zechariah
  father: 5 Bebai, Hosah 6 Jehiel, Pashur 7 Isshiah 8 Jehoiada, Jonathan 9 Berechiah 11 Jeberechiah, Meshelemiah
  grandfather: 4 Iddo
  mother: 6 Merari
  son: 8 Jahaziel
  daughter: 6 Abijah

Zeffirelli, Franco
  director of: 14 Romeo and Juliet 19 The Taming of the
    Shrew 20 Brother Sun Sister Moon

Zeitgeist 18 the spirit of the time

Zelos
  origin: 5 Greek
  personifies: 4 zeal 9 emulation
  father: 11 Titan Palles
  mother: 4 Styx
  brother: 3 Bia 6 Cratus
  sister: 4 Nike

Zemeckis, Robert
  director of: 15 Back to the Future 17 Romancing the Stone

zenith 4 acme, apex, best, peak 6 apogee, climax, summit, vertex 7 maximum 8 pinnacle 11 culmination

Zenobia (Zeena)
  character in: 10 Ethan Frome
  author: 7 Wharton

Zephaniah
  father: 8 Masseiah
  son: 3 Hen 6 Josiah
  succeeded: 8 Jehoiada
  deathplace: 6 Riblah

zephyr 8 west wind 9 puff of air 10 gentle wind 11 breath of air, light breeze

Zephyrus
  personifies: 8 west wind
  father: 8 Astraeus
  mother: 3 Eos
  loved: 10 Hyacinthus
  son: 6 Balius 7 Xanthus

Zeppelin, Ferdinand Graf von
  nationality: 6 German
  invented: 9 dirigible 21 rigid dirigible airship
  famous ship: 10 Hindenberg

Zernbbabel
  father: 7 Pedaiah 9 Shealtiel

zero 2 no 3 nil, zip 5 aught, nadir, zilch 6 cipher, naught 7 nothing 8 goose egg 11 nonexistent, nothingness

zero hour 5 onset, start 7 liftoff 9 beginning 12 commencement

zest 3 joy, zip 4 salt, tang, zeal, zing 5 gusto, savor, spice, taste, verve 6 flavor, relish, thrill 7 delight, passion 8 appetite, piquancy, pleasure 9 eagerness, flavoring, seasoning 10 enthusiasm, excitement 12 exhilaration, satisfaction

zestful 6 active, lively 7 dynamic, vibrant 8 animated, spirited, vigorous 9 vivacious 12 invigorating

zesty 5 spicy, tangy 7 piquant 9 flavorful

Zetes
  origin: 5 Greek
  member of: 9 Argonauts
  father: 6 Boreas
  mother: 8 Orithyia
  twin brother: 6 Calais

Zethus
  father: 4 Zeus
  mother: 7 Antiope
  wife: 5 Thebe
  twin brother: 7 Amphion

Zeus *see box*

zigzag 4 awry, tack 6 angles, forked, jagged 7 chevron, crankle, crooked, notched, sinuous, stagger 8 crotched, serrated, sideling, traverse 9 bifurcate 10 circuitous, deflection

Zillah
  husband: 6 Lamech
  son: 9 Jubal-cain, Tubul-cain

Zilpah
  slave of: 4 Leah
  concubine of: 5 Jacob
  son: 3 Gad 5 Asher

Zimbabwe *see box*

Zimbalist, Efrem, Jr
  born: 9 New York NY
  father: 14 Efrem Zimbalist
  mother: 9 Alma Gluck
  daughter: 18 Stephanie Zimbalist
  roles: 3 FBI 13 Wait Until Dark 15 By Love Possessed 16 The Chapman Report 62 Seventy-seven Sunset Strip

Zimmerman, Ethel Agnes
  real name of: 11 Ethel Merman

zinc
  chemical symbol: 2 Zn

zing 3 pep, vim, zap, zip 4 dash, snap, tang, whiz, zest 5 gusto, speed, vigor, whine 6 energy, spirit 7 liven up 8 satirize, vitality 9 animation, criticize 10 enthusiasm, liveliness

zingara, zingaro 5 gypsy

Zinnemann, Fred
  director of: 5 Julia 8 High Noon, Oklahoma 9 The Search 12 The Nun's Story 13 The Sundowners 17 A Man for All Seasons (Oscar) 18 From Here to Eternity (Oscar)

Zion 6 utopia 9 city of God 11 City of David 13 ancient Israel
  hill in: 9 Jerusalem
  built on the hill: 6 Temple

Zeus
  also: 7 Cenaean 9 Atabyriam, Ithomatas 10 Anchesmius 11 Panomphaeus 12 Cithaeronian
  birthplace: 5 Crete
  brother: 5 Hades 8 Poseidon
  corresponds to: 4 Amen, Amon, Jove 5 Ammon 6 Amen Ra, Amon Ra 7 Jupiter
  daughter: 4 Hebe 6 Athene 10 Eileithyia, Persephone
  epithet: 5 Areus, Arius, Sotor 6 Aqueus, Nemean, Philus 7 Alastor, Apemius, Ctesius, Lycaeus, Polieus, Stenius 8 Agoraeus, Aphesius, Apomyius, Catharius, Chthonius, Coccygius, Hecaleius, Lecheates, Mechaneus 10 Cataebates, Coryphaeus, Homagyrius, Laphystius, Meilichius 11 Eleutherius 12 Panhellenius
  father: 6 Cronus
  form: 5 deity
  god of: 7 heavens
  lover: 4 Leto 7 Demeter
  mother: 4 Rhea
  position: 7 supreme
  sister: 4 Hera 6 Hestia 7 Demeter
  son: 4 Ares 6 Apollo, Hermes
  wife: 4 Hera 5 Metis

Zimbabwe
  other name: 8 Rhodesia 16 Southern Rhodesia
  capital/largest city: 6 Harare 9 Salisbury
  others: 5 Gwelo, Gweru 6 Kariba, KweKwe, Mutare, QueQue, Umtali 7 Gatooma, Rusambo, Selukwe, Shabani 8 Bulawayo, Zimbabwe 10 Beitbridge
  monetary unit: 4 cent 6 dollar
  lake: 4 Kyle 6 Kariba
  mountain: 5 Vumba 6 Manica 7 Inyanga 11 Chimanimani, Matopo Hills
  highest point: 9 Inyangani
  river: 4 Sabi, Save 5 Lundi 6 Shashi 7 Limpopo, Umniati, Zambezi
  physical feature:
    falls: 8 Victoria
    grassland: 4 veld
    plateau: 8 Highveld 11 Mashonaland
  people: 3 Ila 4 Sena 5 Asian, Bantu, Bemba, Sotho, Tongo, White 6 Indian 7 Barotse, Chinese, English, Mashoma, Mashona, Ndebele 8 Coloured, Japanese, Matabele 9 Afrikaner 10 Balokwakwa
    developer: 6 Rhodes
    explorer: 11 Livingstone
    king: 9 Lobengula, Mzilikaze
    leader: 5 Nkomo 6 Mugabe 7 Sithole 8 Muzorewa 9 Ian D Smith
  language: 3 Ila 5 Bantu, Shona 7 English, Ndebele
  religion: 7 animism 8 Anglican 12 Christianity, Presbyterian 13 Dutch Reformed, Roman Catholic
  place:
    dam: 6 Kariba
    national park: 6 Hwange, Wankie 7 Matopos 9 Inyangani 13 Victoria Falls
    ruins: 5 Khami 6 Temple 8 Zimbabwe 9 Acropolis 13 Valley of Ruins
  feature:
    cattle pen: 5 kraal
    game: 5 tsoro 7 mandani
    hut: 4 kaia
    kingdom: 5 Rozwi 10 Monomotapa
    tree: 4 teak 6 baobab, mopani

zip 3 fly, nil, pep, run, vim
4 buzz, dart, dash, hiss, life, nada, rush, zero, zest **5** aught, close, drive, force, gusto, hurry, power, punch, speed, verve, vigor, whine, zilch **6** cipher, energy, impact, naught, spirit, streak **7** nothing, whistle **8** goose egg, strength, vitality, vivacity **9** animation, intensity **10** enthusiasm, exuberance, liveliness **13** effervescence

zipper
invented by: **6** Judson

Zipporah
father: **5** Reuel **6** Jethro
husband: **5** Moses
son: **7** Eliezer, Gershom

zircon
source: **5** Burma **6** Ceylon **8** Cambodia, Sri Lanka **9** Kampuchea

zirconium
chemical symbol: **2** Zr

zodiac 4 belt, zone **5** stars **7** circuit
fire sign: **3** Leo **5** Aries **11** Sagittarius
earth sign: **5** Virgo **6** Taurus **9** Capricorn
air sign: **5** Libra **6** Gemini **8** Aquarius
water: **6** Cancer, Pisces **7** Scorpio

division: **4** sign **5** decan **6** trigon
number of houses: **6** twelve
falling between two signs: **4** cusp

Zoimo, Vincent Edward
real name of: **12** Vince Edwards

Zola, Emile
author of: **4** Nana **7** The Soil **8** Germinal **10** L'Assommoir **11** The Downfall, The Dram Shop **13** Therese Raquin **14** The Human Animal **20** The Experimental Novel

zone 4 area, belt, ward **5** tract **6** region, sector **7** quarter, section, terrain **8** district, locality, location, precinct **9** territory

zonked 5 drunk **6** soused, wasted, zapped **7** smashed **9** plastered **10** inebriated **11** intoxicated

zoo 8 vivarium **9** menagerie

zoom 3 fly, zip **4** buzz, race, rise, soar **5** climb, flash, shoot, speed **6** ascend, rocket, streak **7** advance, take off **9** skyrocket

zoophobia
fear of: **7** animals

Zophar
friend: **3** Job **5** Elihu **6** Bildad **7** Eliphaz

Zorba the Greek
director: **17** Michael Cacoyannis
based on the story by: **11** Kazantzakis
cast: **9** Alan Bates **11** Irene Pappas, Lila Kedrova **12** Anthony Quinn
score: **16** Mikis Theodorakis
Oscar for: **17** supporting actress (Kedrova)

Zosteria
epithet of: **6** Athena
means: **20** one who girds with armor

zucchini 5 gourd **6** squash **12** summer squash

Zuck, Alexandra
real name of: **9** Sandra Dee

Zuckerman Unbound
author: **10** Philip Roth

Zurich
festival: **12** Sechselanten
landmark: **8** Rietberg **9** Kunsthaus **15** CG Jung Institute **17** Centre Le Corbusier, Fraumunster Kirche **21** Grossmunster Cathedral
religious figure: **7** Zwingli **9** Bullinger
river: **6** Limmat
Roman name: **7** Turicum

Zweig, Arnold
author of: **7** Claudia **24** The Case of Sergeant Grischa